lonely planet

Europe

on a shoestring

THIS EDITION WRITTEN AND RESEARCHED BY

Tom Masters

Carolyn Bain, James Bainbridge, Mark Baker, Oliver Berry, Greg Bloom, Kerry Christiani, Chris Deliso, Marc Di Duca, Peter Dragicevich, Mark Elliott, Steve Fallon, Duncan Garwood, Anthony Ham, Anna Kaminski, Craig McLachlan, Anja Mutić, Brandon Presser, Tim Richards, Andrea Schulte-Peevers, Tamara Sheward, Regis St Louis, Andy Symington, Ryan Ver Berkmoes, Luke Waterson, Nicola Williams, Neil Wilson

PLAN YOUR TRIP

Welcome to Europe **6**
Europe Map **8**
24 Top Experiences **10**
Need to Know **22**
If You Like... .... **24**
Month by Month **27**
Itineraries **32**

BERNKASTEL-KUES (P482), GERMANY

BRIGITTE MERZ/GETTY IMAGES ©

MEDITERRANEAN COAST (P1170), TURKEY

MICHAEL MARQUAND/GETTY IMAGES ©

ON THE ROAD

ALBANIA **42**
Tirana **45**
Shkodra 48
Kruja 49
Berat 49
Saranda 50
Gjirokastra 51

AUSTRIA **54**
Vienna **58**
Krems an der Donau 67
Melk 68
Linz 68
Graz 69
Klagenfurt 71
Salzburg **72**
Hallstatt 77
Innsbruck 78
Kitzbühel 81
Lienz 81
Vorarlberg **82**

BELARUS **89**
Minsk **92**
Brest **96**

BELGIUM & LUXEMBOURG **100**
Brussels **104**
Antwerp 112
Ghent 117
Bruges 119
Ypres 123
Wallonia **124**
Luxembourg **126**

BOSNIA & HERCEGOVINA **136**
Sarajevo **139**
Mostar 145

BRITAIN **153**
London **155**
Windsor & Eton 183
Canterbury 184
Dover 185
Brighton & Hove 186
Salisbury 187
Stonehenge 188
Bath 188
Bristol 191
Newquay 194
St Ives 195
Penzance 196
Oxford 197
Stratford-upon-Avon 199
Peak District National Park 200
Cambridge 201
York 202
Newcastle-upon-Tyne ... 206
Manchester 208
Chester 211
Liverpool 211
Lake District National Park 213
Cardiff 215
Snowdonia National Park 217
Edinburgh 218
Glasgow 223
Loch Lomond 228
Stirling 228
Inverness 230
Glen Coe 231
Fort William 231
Isle of Skye 232

BULGARIA **243**
Sofia **246**
Plovdiv 253
Veliko Târnovo 255

Contents

Varna ... 257
Burgas ... 261

CROATIA ... 266
Zagreb ... 270
Pula ... 276
Split ... 278
Hvar Island ... 281
Korčula Island ... 283
Dubrovnik ... 284

CZECH REPUBLIC ... 294
Prague ... 297
Karlštejn ... 307
Kutná Hora ... 308
Karlovy Vary ... 308
Plzeň ... 310
Český Krumlov ... 311
Brno ... 312

ESTONIA ... 319
Tallinn ... 322
Lahemaa National Park ... 330
Tartu ... 331
Pärnu ... 334

FRANCE ... 338
Paris ... 342
Lille ... 365
Calais ... 366
Rouen ... 368
Bayeux ... 369
Quimper ... 371
St-Malo ... 372
Reims ... 374
Épernay ... 375
Strasbourg ... 376
Metz ... 378
Blois ... 379
Tours ... 380
Amboise ... 382
Dijon ... 383
Beaune ... 384
Lyon ... 385
Chamonix ... 390
Sarlat-La-Canéda ... 392
Bordeaux ... 393
Biarritz ... 395
Nîmes ... 396
Toulouse ... 398
Marseille ... 400
Aix-en-Provence ... 403
Avignon ... 404
Nice ... 407
Cannes ... 410
St-Tropez ... 411
Monaco ... 413
Ajaccio ... 414
Bastia ... 415
Bonifacio ... 416

GERMANY ... 427
Berlin ... 429
Potsdam ... 445
Dresden ... 447
Leipzig ... 449
Weimar ... 451
Erfurt ... 452
Munich ... 454
Bavarian Alps ... 460
Rothenburg ob der Tauber ... 463
Würzburg ... 463
Nuremberg ... 464
Bamberg ... 466
Regensburg ... 467
Stuttgart ... 468
Heidelberg ... 469
Black Forest ... 471
Freiburg im Breisgau ... 472
Constance ... 474
Frankfurt-am-Main ... 475
Moselle Valley ... 481
Trier ... 482
Cologne ... 483
Düsseldorf ... 486
Aachen ... 487
Hanover ... 488
Bremen ... 490
Hamburg ... 491
Lübeck ... 496

GREECE ... 505
Athens ... 507
The Peloponnese ... 515
Meteora ... 519
Thessaloniki ... 520
Ioannina ... 522
Mykonos ... 523
Paros ... 525
Naxos ... 526
Ios ... 528
Santorini (Thira) ... 528
Crete ... 530
Dodecanese ... 535
Samos ... 538
Lesvos (Mytilini) ... 539
Skiathos ... 540
Corfu ... 541

HUNGARY ... 552
Budapest ... 554
Sopron ... 566
Lake Balaton ... 567
Pécs ... 569
Szeged ... 570
Eger ... 571

IRELAND ... 578
Dublin ... 581

ON THE ROAD

Kilkenny 589
Cork 591
Killarney 594
Ring of Kerry 595
Galway 596
Aran Islands 598
Sligo 600
Belfast 602
Derry 609

ITALY 617
Rome 620
Genoa 643
Cinque Terre 645
Turin 646
Milan 647
Verona 650
Padua 652
Venice 653
Bologna 662
Ravenna 664
Florence 666
Pisa 673
Siena 675
Lucca 676
Perugia 677
Assisi 679
Naples 680
Capri 686
Sorrento 687
Amalfi Coast 688
Matera 689
Lecce 691
Sicily 692
Sardinia 698

KOSOVO 710
Pristina 712
Peja (Peć) 713
Prizren 714

LATVIA 716
Rīga 719
Liepāja 727
Sigulda 728

LITHUANIA 732
Vilnius 734
Trakai 742
Kaunas 743
Klaipėda 745
Curonian Spit 745

MACEDONIA 750
Skopje 752
Ohrid 757
Bitola 760

MOLDOVA 765
Chişinău 768
Tiraspol 773

MONTENEGRO 777
Morinj 780
Kotor 780
Budva 781
Sveti Stefan 782
Ulcinj 783
Cetinje 783
Lake Skadar National Park 784
Durmitor National Park 784

THE NETHERLANDS . . . 788
Amsterdam 791
Haarlem 798
Leiden 799
Den Haag 800
Delft 801
Rotterdam 802
Utrecht 806
Maastricht 808

POLAND 815
Warsaw 818
Kraków 824
Lublin 832
Zamość 834
Zakopane 835
Wrocław 836
Poznań 839
Gdańsk 841
Toruń 845
Great Masurian Lakes 847

PORTUGAL 852
Lisbon 855
Sintra 864
Cascais 865
Faro 866
Tavira 867
Lagos 868
Sagres 869
Évora 869
Peniche 870
Nazaré 872
Tomar 872
Coimbra 873
Luso & the Buçaco Forest 874
Serra da Estrela 874
Porto 875
Viana do Castelo 879
Braga 880
Parque Nacional da Peneda-Gerês 881

ROMANIA 887
Bucharest 889

Contents

Braşov 896
Sighişoara 898
Sibiu 900
Cluj-Napoca 901
Timişoara..............903

RUSSIA............911
Moscow 914
St Petersburg 922
Kaliningrad 929

SCANDINAVIA.....939
Denmark 942
Copenhagen 942
Zealand 948
Odense.................950
Jutland.................951
Sweden...............953
Stockholm..............953
Uppsala 959
Göteborg 960
Norrland...............963
Norway...............964
Oslo....................964
Bergen & the Western Fjords 968
Finland 975
Helsinki 975
Turku 979
Tampere...............980
Lakeland 982
Lapland 983

SERBIA........... 991
Belgrade.............994
Novi Sad 1000
Subotica 1001

SLOVAKIA 1005
Bratislava.............1008
Tatra Mountains 1014
Levoča 1017
Slovenský Raj & Around............... 1017
Košice................1019
Bardejov............. 1021

SLOVENIA 1026
Ljubljana 1028
Lake Bled.............1034
Lake Bohinj 1037
Postojna & Škocjan Caves 1039
Koper 1039
Piran.................1040

SPAIN...........1045
Madrid 1047
Salamanca............1063
Segovia...............1065
Toledo................1067
Barcelona 1068
Tarragona.............1082
Aragón 1083
Santiago de Compostela..........1088
Valencia 1090
Mallorca..............1093
Ibiza 1095
Seville................1097
Córdoba 1102
Granada..............1104
Málaga 1107
Tarifa................1109
Cáceres 1110

SWITZERLAND....1121
Geneva 1123
Lausanne.............1129
Gruyères 1131
Zermatt 1131
Bern 1133
Lucerne 1134
Interlaken 1135
Jungfrau Region....... 1136
Zürich.............. 1138
Basel.................1142
Lugano 1143
St Moritz 1144

TURKEY 1151
İstanbul 1153
Gallipoli (Gelibolu) Peninsula.............1164
Çanakkale 1164
İzmir 1166
Selçuk...............1166
Kuşadası 1168
Bodrum 1168
Marmaris.............1169
Fethiye 1170
Kaş 1172
Olympos & Çıralı 1173
Antalya..............1173
Ankara 1174
Konya 1176
Göreme 1177

UKRAINE 1187
Kyiv................ 1189
Lviv................ 1195

SURVIVAL GUIDE

Directory A–Z 1202
Transport...........1215
Language...........1225
Index...............1237
Map Legend......... 1259

welcome to Europe

Where to Begin?

Overwhelming it can be, confusing for sure – just perusing a map of the crowded Old World will reveal cities, mountain ranges, seas and even countries you may never have even heard of. But the good news is that whatever you decide to do here, you'll leave blown away by the sights, sounds, tastes and other sensations you'll experience: there simply is no way to tour Europe and not be awestruck.

First timers might try a sprinkling of the classics (Britain, Ireland, France, Switzerland, Germany, Spain) and spice it up with a dash of something classical (Italy, Greece, Turkey), while those who have covered the essentials might try lesser-explored destinations (the Balkans, Scandinavia, Portugal or Poland, for example). Those wanting to explore Europe's extremes can head to challenging Russia, fabulous Albania or surprising Romania – there's literally no end to the options.

Endless Variety

Europe's almost unmanageable wealth of attractions is its single biggest draw. Among its astonishing cultural heritage you'll find everything from the birthplace of democracy in Athens, the Renaissance art of Florence, the graceful canals of Venice and the Napoleonic splendour of Paris, to less obvious attractions such as the Moorish palaces of Andalucía, the remains

Europe is a patchwork of more than 40 compulsively individualistic countries and is a dazzling and spectacular place to explore. Jump in almost anywhere and join the party.

(left) Amsterdam's Canal Belt (p791), the Netherlands
(below) Geirangerfjorden (p971), Norway

of one of the Seven Wonders of the World in Turkey, and the majesty of a second Venice in Russia's former capital, St Petersburg.

You'll also find glorious scenery (try the Scottish Highlands, the Swiss Alps or Norway's fjords), world-leading architecture, art, design, fashion and music (see London, Berlin, Paris, Antwerp and Copenhagen) and some of the best nightlife in the world (as well as London, Berlin and Paris, don't miss Moscow, Belgrade, Budapest and Madrid).

Smashing Stereotypes

A trip around Europe's patchwork of nations will inevitably make you rethink what you thought you knew about the place. As with any form of travel, surprises await: nationalities about which you know little beyond lazy clichés will become familiar friends, both complex and contradictory; you will feel the chill on your spine when you see that iconic work of art in the flesh or find yourself standing right where *that* happened. You will at least once find yourself on a beach, up a mountain, at a cafe or in a club thinking 'these people know how to live'.

Yes, Europe has and offers it all. So don't delay – get planning your own European odyssey as soon as you can. With so many extraordinary destinations offering incredible things to see and do, your only problem will be where to begin...

› Europe

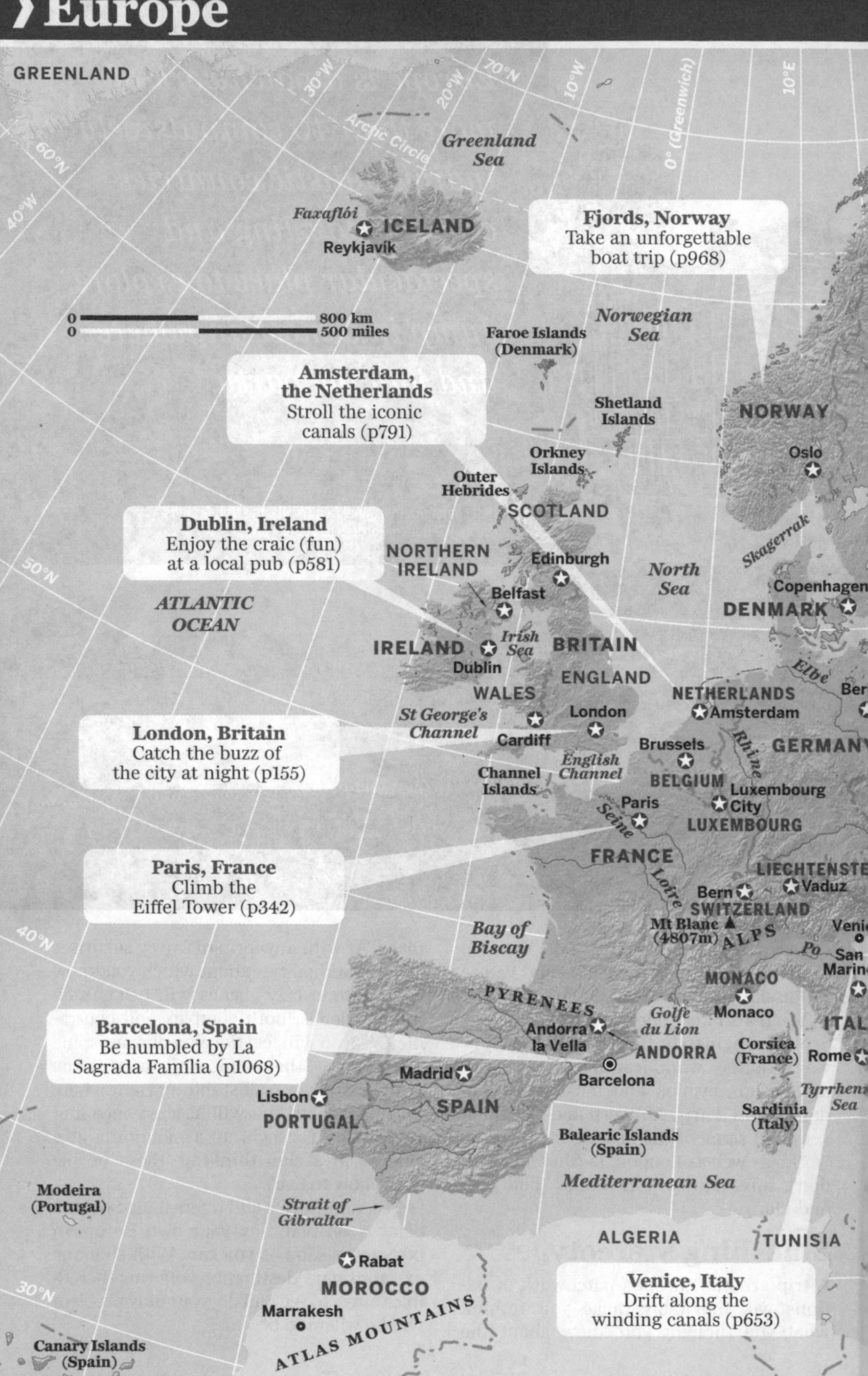

GREENLAND
Greenland Sea
Arctic Circle
Faxaflói
ICELAND
Reykjavík
Fjords, Norway
Take an unforgettable boat trip (p968)
0 800 km
0 500 miles
Norwegian Sea
Faroe Islands (Denmark)
Amsterdam, the Netherlands
Stroll the iconic canals (p791)
Shetland Islands
NORWAY
Oslo
Orkney Islands
Outer Hebrides
SCOTLAND
Dublin, Ireland
Enjoy the craic (fun) at a local pub (p581)
NORTHERN IRELAND
Edinburgh
North Sea
Skagerrak
Copenhagen
DENMARK
ATLANTIC OCEAN
Belfast
IRELAND
Dublin
Irish Sea
BRITAIN
ENGLAND
WALES
Elbe
NETHERLANDS
Amsterdam
St George's Channel
London
Cardiff
London, Britain
Catch the buzz of the city at night (p155)
Brussels
Rhine
GERMANY
English Channel
Channel Islands
BELGIUM
Luxembourg City
Paris
Seine
LUXEMBOURG
Paris, France
Climb the Eiffel Tower (p342)
FRANCE
Loire
Bern
Vaduz
SWITZERLAND
Bay of Biscay
Mt Blanc (4807m)
ALPS
Po
San Marino
MONACO
Monaco
PYRENEES
Andorra la Vella
ANDORRA
Golfe du Lion
Barcelona, Spain
Be humbled by La Sagrada Família (p1068)
Barcelona
Corsica (France)
Rome
Madrid
Lisbon
SPAIN
PORTUGAL
Sardinia (Italy)
Balearic Islands (Spain)
Mediterranean Sea
Modeira (Portugal)
Strait of Gibraltar
ALGERIA
TUNISIA
Rabat
MOROCCO
Venice, Italy
Drift along the winding canals (p653)
Marrakesh
ATLAS MOUNTAINS
Canary Islands (Spain)

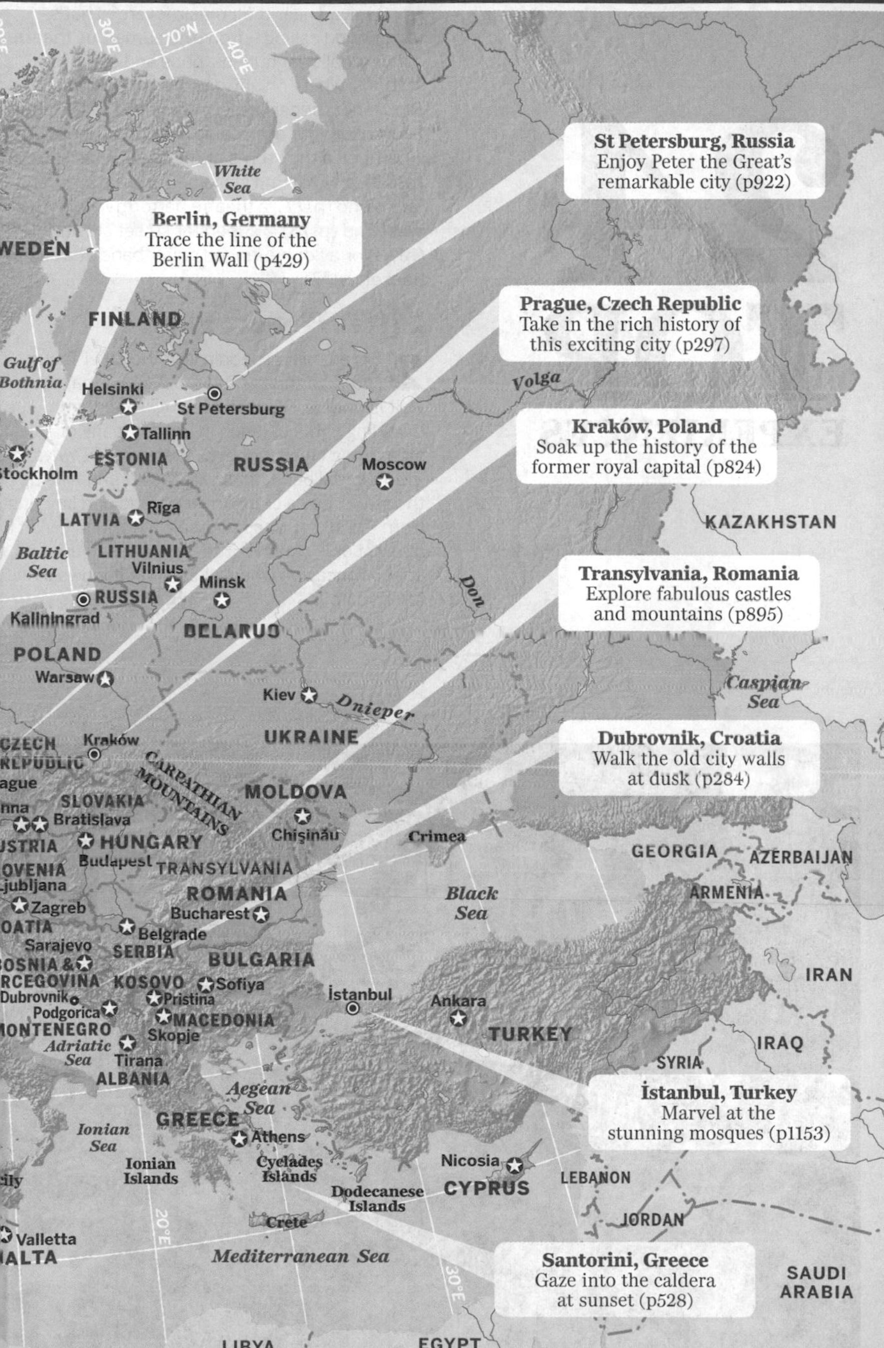
St Petersburg, Russia
Enjoy Peter the Great's remarkable city (p922)
Berlin, Germany
Trace the line of the Berlin Wall (p429)
Prague, Czech Republic
Take in the rich history of this exciting city (p297)
Kraków, Poland
Soak up the history of the former royal capital (p824)
Transylvania, Romania
Explore fabulous castles and mountains (p895)
Dubrovnik, Croatia
Walk the old city walls at dusk (p284)
İstanbul, Turkey
Marvel at the stunning mosques (p1153)
Santorini, Greece
Gaze into the caldera at sunset (p528)
70°N
30°E
40°E
20°E
White Sea
FINLAND
Gulf of Bothnia
Helsinki
St Petersburg
Tallinn
ESTONIA
Stockholm
RUSSIA
Moscow
Volga
KAZAKHSTAN
Rīga
LATVIA
LITHUANIA
Vilnius
Minsk
Baltic Sea
RUSSIA
Kaliningrad
BELARUS
Don
POLAND
Warsaw
Kiev
Dnieper
Caspian Sea
Kraków
UKRAINE
CARPATHIAN MOUNTAINS
MOLDOVA
SLOVAKIA
Bratislava
HUNGARY
Chişinău
Crimea
GEORGIA
AZERBAIJAN
Budapest
TRANSYLVANIA
ROMANIA
ARMENIA
Zagreb
Bucharest
Black Sea
Belgrade
Sarajevo
SERBIA
BULGARIA
KOSOVO
Sofiya
Pristina
İstanbul
Ankara
IRAN
Dubrovnik
Podgorica
MACEDONIA
TURKEY
Skopje
Adriatic Sea
Tirana
ALBANIA
IRAQ
SYRIA
Aegean Sea
GREECE
Ionian Sea
Athens
Ionian Islands
Cyclades Islands
Nicosia
CYPRUS
LEBANON
Dodecanese Islands
Crete
JORDAN
Valletta
Mediterranean Sea
SAUDI ARABIA
LIBYA
EGYPT

24 TOP EXPERIENCES

London's Nightlife, Britain

1 Can you hear that, music lovers? That's London calling – from the numerous theatres, concert halls, nightclubs, pubs and even tube stations, where on any given night hundreds, if not thousands, of performers are taking to the stage. Search for your own iconic London experience, whether it's the Proms at the Royal Albert Hall (p180), an East End singalong around a clunky pub piano (p177), a theatre performance in the West End (p178), a superstar DJ set at Fabric (p178) or a floppy-fringed guitar band at a Hoxton boozer (p177).

Eiffel Tower, France

2 Seven million people visit the Eiffel Tower (p342) annually and most agree that each visit is unique. From an evening ascent amid twinkling lights to lunch in the company of a staggering city panorama, there are 101 ways to 'do' it. Pedal beneath it, skip the lift and hike up the stairs, buy a crêpe from a stand or a key ring from the street, snap yourself in front of it, visit it at night or – our favourite – experience the odd special occasion when all 324m of it glows a different colour.

1

DIVERSE IMAGES/UIG/GETTY IMAGES ©

O. LOUIS MAZZATENTA/GETTY IMAGES ©

RUTH EASTHAM & MAX PAOLI/GETTY IMAGES ©

Venice, Italy

3 There's something magical about Venice on a sunny winter's day. With far fewer tourists around and the light sharp and clear, it's the perfect time to lap up the city's unique and magical atmosphere. Ditch your map and wander Dorsoduro's shadowy backlines (p653) while imagining secret assignations and whispered conspiracies at every turn. Then visit two of Venice's top galleries, the Gallerie dell'Accademia (p654) and the Collezione Peggy Guggenheim (p655), which houses works by many of the giants of 20th-century art.

Remembering the Berlin Wall, Germany

4 Even after more than 20 years, the disbelief that the Berlin Wall (p434) really cut through this city doesn't sink in. But the best way to examine its role in Berlin is to make your way – on foot or by bike – along the Berlin Wall Trail (p429). Passing the Brandenburg Gate, analysing graffiti at the East Side Gallery (p438) or learning about its history at the Documentation Centre: the path brings it all into context. It's heartbreaking and hopeful and sombre, but integral in trying to understand Germany's capital.

Above right: East Side Gallery

Santorini, Greece

5 On first view, startling Santorini (p528) grabs your attention and doesn't let it go. The submerged caldera, surrounded by lava-layered cliffs topped by villages that look like a sprinkling of icing sugar, is one of nature's great wonders, and is best experienced by a walk along the clifftops from the main town of Fira to the northern village of Oia. The precariousness and impermanence of the place is breathtaking. Recover from your efforts with an ice-cold Mythos beer in Oia as you wait for the town's famed picture-perfect sunset.

5

CHRIS HEPBURN/GETTY IMAGES ©

St Petersburg, Russia

6 Marvel at how many masterpieces there are in the Hermitage (p922); window shop and people watch along Nevsky Prospekt (p923); glide down canals past the grand facades of palaces and golden-domed churches; enjoy a ballet at the beautiful Mariinsky Theatre (p928); have a banquet fit for a tsar then dance till dawn at a dive bar in a crumbling ruin – Russia's imperial capital is a visual stunner and hedonist's delight, best visited at the height of summer when the White Nights see the city party around the clock. Right: St Petersburg's St Isaac's Cathedral (p923)

6

HOLGER LEUE/GETTY IMAGES ©

Fjords, Norway

7 The drama of Norway's fjords is difficult to overstate. They cut deep into the country's interior, adding texture and depth to northwestern Scandinavia. Rock walls plunge from high meadows into water-filled canyons shadowed by pretty villages. Sognefjorden (p971), more than 200km long, and Hardangerfjorden are Norway's most extensive fjord networks, but the quiet, precipitous beauty of Nærøyfjorden (part of Sognefjorden), Lysefjorden (p970) and – the king of fjords – Geirangerfjorden (p971) are prime candidates for Scandinavia's most beautiful corner. Below: Geirangerfjorden

Kraków, Poland

8 Poland's former royal capital never disappoints. It's hard to pinpoint why it's so special, but there's a satisfying aura of history radiating from the sloping stone buttresses of the medieval buildings in the Old Town (p825) that makes its streets seem, well, just right. Add the extremes of a spectacular castle and the low-key oh-so-cool bar scene within the tiny worn buildings of the Kazimierz back streets (p830), and it's a city you'll want to seriously get to know. Below: Cafe in Kazimierz

7

8

9
CHRISTOPHER GROENHOUT/GETTY IMAGES ©

10
FRANCESCO IACOBELLI/GETTY IMAGES ©

11
DEA/C.SAPPA/GETTY IMAGES ©

Dubrovnik's Old City Walls, Croatia

9 Get up close and personal with the city by walking Dubrovnik's spectacular city walls (p284), as history is unfurled from the battlements. No visit is complete without a leisurely walk along these ramparts, the finest in the world and Dubrovnik's main claim to fame. Built between the 13th and 16th centuries, they are still remarkably intact today and the vistas over the terracotta rooftops and the Adriatic Sea are sublime, especially at dusk when the sundown makes the hues dramatic and the panoramas unforgettable.

Prague, Czech Republic

10 Prague's big attractions – Prague Castle (p297) and Old Town Sq (p297) are highlights of the Czech capital, but for a more insightful look at life two decades after the Velvet Revolution, head to local neighbourhoods around the centre. Working class Žižkov and energetic Smíchov are crammed with pubs, while elegant tree-lined Vinohrady features a diverse menu of cosmopolitan restaurants. Prague showcases many forms of art, from iconic works from the last century to more recent but equally challenging pieces. Above left: Old Town Sq

Transylvania, Romania

11 The southern swipe of the Carpathian Mountains in Transylvania is packed with opportunities. There's cycling in the Bucegi Mountains (p900), day and multiday hikes in the Făgăraş Mountains, and skiing in Sinaia. The area also features the vampiric Bran Castle (p899), the ruins of the 13th-century Râşnov Fortress (p899) and Peleş Castle. Above right: Bran Castle

12

GORDON ESLER/GETTY IMAGES ©

13

Budapest, Hungary

12 Hungary's capital (p554) has cleaned up its act in recent years. Gone are those old Soviet-era cars that used to spew their choking blue haze over the flat landscape of Pest. Now, the hills on the Buda side of the city are gleaming and Pest itself is teeming with energy and life. It's no stretch to say that these days Budapest combines the beauty of Prague and the buzz of Berlin into something that's uniquely Hungarian. Above left: Budapest's Széchenyi Baths (p557)

Barcelona's La Sagrada Família, Spain

13 One of Spain's top sights, La Sagrada Família (p1072), the Modernista brainchild of Antoni Gaudí, remains a work in progress more than 80 years after its creator's death. Fanciful and profound, inspired by nature and barely restrained by a Gothic style, Barcelona's quirky temple soars skyward with an almost playful majesty. The improbable angles and departures from architectural convention will have you shaking your head in disbelief, and the detail of the decorative flourishes on the Passion and Nativity facades are worth studying.

Dublin, Ireland

14 Ireland's capital city can boast all the attractions and distractions of a major international metropolis, but manages to retain the friendliness, intimacy and atmosphere of a small town. Whether wandering the leafy Georgian terraces of St Stephen's Green (p581) or getting up close and personal with the past at Kilmainham Gaol (p584), you're never far from a friendly pub where the beer is grand and the craic (fun) is flowing. And, of course, there's the chance to sink a pint of the black stuff at that fountainhead of froth, the Guinness Storehouse (p581). Above right: Dublin's Temple Bar district (p587)

14

JOHN HARPER/GETTY IMAGES ©

Bay of Kotor, Montenegro

15 There's a sense of secrecy and mystery to the Bay of Kotor (p780). Grey mountain walls rise steeply from steely blue waters, getting higher and higher as you progress through their folds to the hidden reaches of the inner bay. Here, ancient stone settlements hug the shoreline, with Kotor's ancient alleyways concealed in its innermost reaches behind hefty stone walls. Talk about drama! But you wouldn't expect anything else of the Balkans, where life is exuberantly Mediterranean and lived full of passion on these ancient streets.

15

GREG HAHN/GETTY IMAGES ©

Imperial Vienna, Austria

16 Imagine what you could do with unlimited riches and Austria's top architects at your hands for 640 years. The result is the Vienna of the Habsburgs. The graceful Hofburg (p58) whisks you back to the age of empires as you marvel at the treasury's imperial crowns, the equine ballet of the Spanische Hofreitschule (p66) and Empress Elisabeth's chandelier-lit apartments (p58). The palace is rivalled in grandeur only by Schloss Schönbrunn (p59) and the baroque Schloss Belvedere (p59), both set in exquisite landscaped gardens. Below: Hofburg

Granada's Alhambra, Spain

17 The palace complex of the Alhambra (p1104) is close to architectural perfection. It is perhaps the most refined example of Islamic art in the world, not to mention the most enduring symbol of 800 years of Moorish rule. From afar, the Alhambra's red fortress towers dominate the Granada skyline, set against a backdrop of the Sierra Nevada's snow-capped peaks. Up close, the Alhambra's perfectly proportioned Generalife gardens complement the exquisite detail of the Palacio Nazariés. This is Spain's most beautiful monument.

16

17

WILL SALTER/GETTY IMAGES ©

JEAN-PHILIPPE TOURNUT/GETTY IMAGES ©

SYLVAIN SONNET/GETTY IMAGES ©

Amsterdam's Canals, The Netherlands

18 To say Amsterdammers love the water is an understatement. Sure, the city made its first fortune in maritime trade, but that's ancient history. Today, you can stroll next to the canals and check out some of the city's 3300 houseboats, or, better, go for a ride (p791). From boat level you'll get to see a whole new set of architectural details, like the ornaments that bedeck the bridges. And when you pass the canalside cafe terraces, you can just look up and wave.

Overnight Train, Eastern Europe

19 With the windows down, the wind rushing through your hair and the scenery racing past, there are few modes of transport more pleasurable than the overnight sleeper train (p1224), the best way to get about in eastern Europe. Whether you're in *platzkart* with Bulgarian peasants drinking and playing cards while discussing life under communism or enjoying the more private *kupe*, this is an essential experience and a great way to avoid paying for a hotel.

Ancient Rome, Italy

20 Rome's famous seven hills (actually, there are nine) offer some superb vantage points. A favourite is the Palatino (p620), a gorgeous green expanse of evocative ruins, towering umbrella pines and unforgettable views over the Roman Forum (p620). This is where it all began, where Romulus supposedly founded the city and where the ancient Roman emperors lived in unimaginable luxury. Nowadays, it's a truly haunting spot; as you walk the gravel paths you can almost sense the ghosts in the air.

Above right: Roman Forum

Ancient Greece

21 From the magnificence of Athens' Acropolis (p507) to the monastery-crowned rock spires of Meteora (p519), Greece offers some of Europe's most impressive historical sights. Top temples include oracular Delphi (p519), perched above the sparkling Gulf of Corinth, and Olympia (p518), home to the first Olympic Games. The theatre of Epidavros (p517) sits alongside the mystical Sanctuary of Asclepius (p517), an ancient healing centre. Olive and orange groves surround the vast ruins of Mystras (p517), the one-time capital of the Byzantine Empire. Above: Acropolis

Mostar, Bosnia & Hercegovina

22 If the 1993 bombardment of Mostar's iconic 16th-century stone bridge, Stari Most (p145), underlined the heartbreaking pointlessness of Yugoslavia's brutal civil war, its painstaking reconstruction is symbolic of a peaceful new era. Parts of Mostar (p145) are still dotted with shockingly bombed-out buildings, but its charming Ottoman quarter has been convincingly rebuilt and is once again a delightful patchwork of stone mosques, souvenir peddlers and inviting cafes. Above: Stari Most

SALVATOR BARKI/GETTY IMAGES ©

FAREMAGNUM/GETTY IMAGES ©

İstanbul, Turkey

23 Straddling Europe and Asia, İstanbul's history includes stints as the capital of the Byzantine and Ottoman Empires. The historical highlights cluster in Sultanahmet – the Aya Sofya (p1153), Blue Mosque (p1158), Topkapı Palace (p1158) and Grand Bazaar (p1158). After marvelling at their ancient domes and glittering interiors, it's time to experience this huge metropolis' vibrant contemporary life. Cross the Galata Bridge, passing ferries and fish kebap stands, to Beyoğlu (p1159), where the nightlife thrives from chic rooftop bars to rowdy taverns. Above: Whirling dervishes in İstanbul

Lisbon's Alfama, Portugal

24 The Alfama (p855), with its labyrinthine alleyways, hidden courtyards and curving, shadow-filled lanes, is a magical place to lose all sense of direction and delve into the soul of the city. On the journey, you'll pass breadbox-sized grocers, brilliantly tiled buildings and cosy taverns filled with easygoing chatter, the scent of chargrilled sardines and the mournful rhythms of fado drifting in the breeze. Then you round a bend and catch sight of steeply pitched rooftops leading down to the glittering Tejo and you know you're hooked...

need to know

Trains

» Europe's train network is fast and efficient but rarely a bargain unless you book well in advance or use a rail pass wisely.

Buses

» Usually taken for short trips in more remote areas, though long-distance buses can be very cheap.

When to Go?

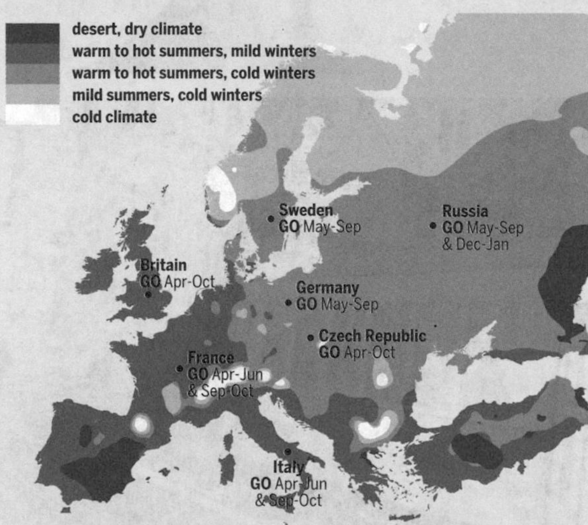

High Season (Jun–Aug)

» Everybody comes to Europe and all of Europe hits the road

» Hotel prices and temperatures are their highest

» Expect all the major attractions to be nightmarishly busy

Shoulder Season (Apr–May & Sep–Oct)

» Crowds and prices drop

» Temperatures are comfortable but it can still be hot in southern Europe

» Overall these are the best months to travel in Europe

Low Season (Nov–Mar)

» Outside ski resorts, hotels drop their prices or close down

» The weather can be cold and days short, especially in northern Europe

» Some places, such as resort towns, are like ghost towns

Set Your Budget

Budget less than €60

» Dorm beds: €10–€20

» Grocery stores and markets are great value for self-catering

» Walk around cities and take overnight trains to save costs

Midrange €60–€200

» Double room in a small hotel: €50–€100

» Stay at small hotels and eat in restaurants at lunchtime

» Meals in good restaurants: around €20 per person

Top end more than €200

» Stay at iconic hotels: starting at €150

» Car hire: starting at around €30 per day

» Enjoy the duty-free refund from an afternoon's stylish shopping

Cars

» You can hire a car or drive your own through Europe. Roads are excellent but petrol is expensive.

Ferries

» Main ferry routes connect Britain and Ireland with mainland Europe; Scandinavia to the Baltic countries and Germany; and Italy to the Balkans and Greece.

Bicycles

» Western Europe is best set up for cyclists, but the two-wheeler is a great way to get around just about anywhere.

Planes

» Cheap airfares take you from one end of the continent to the other.

Websites

» **Lonely Planet** (www.lonelyplanet.com/thorntree) Ask other travellers questions

» **Deutsche Bahn** (www.bahn.de) The best online train timetable for Europe

» **Flycheapo** (www.flycheapo.com) Find out which low-cost airlines fly where

» **Couchsurfing** (www.couchsurfing.org) Find a free bed and make friends in any European country

» **Tourist Office Directory** (www.towd.com) Links to every tourist office on the continent

Money

The main currencies are listed below:

» **Euro (€)** Austria, Belgium, Estonia, Finland, France, Germany, Greece, Ireland, Italy, Kosovo, Luxembourg, Montenegro, Netherlands, Portugal, Slovakia, Slovenia, Spain

» **Pound (£)** Britain, Northern Ireland

» **Swiss franc (Sfr)** Switzerland

Visas

» Citizens of Australia, Canada, New Zealand and the USA don't need visas for visits of less than 90 days to all EU countries.

» EU citizens can stay indefinitely in other member countries. The Schengen Agreement means there are no passport controls at borders between most EU members.

» Citizens of Australia, Canada, the EU, New Zealand and the US need a visa to visit Belarus and Russia. Citizens of Australia and New Zealand need a visa to visit Moldova and Ukraine.

Arriving in Europe

» **Schipol Airport, Amsterdam** Trains to the centre (20min)

» **Heathrow Airport, London** Trains (15min) and tube (1hr) to the centre

» **Aéroport Roissy Charles de Gaulle, Paris** Many buses (1hr) and trains (30min) to the centre

» **Frankfurt Airport, Frankfurt** Trains (15min) to the centre

» **Leonardo da Vinci Airport, Rome** Buses (1hr) and trains (30min) to the centre

What to Take

» **Flip-flops (thongs)** For overnight train rides, in hostel bathrooms and for the beach.

» **Hiking boots** For Europe's fantastic walks.

» **Ear plugs** Helpful anywhere, but especially in hostels.

» **Anti-mosquito plugs** Useful in summer, particularly in the Baltic and Scandinavia.

» **European plug adaptors** Essential if you're coming from outside Europe.

» **An unlocked mobile phone** For picking up a local SIM card for making cheap calls.

» **Smart clothes** So you look the part when breaking the budget.

if you like...

Castles & Palaces

All corners of Europe have these amazing historical repositories, from ancient bunkers impervious to attack to later showpieces designed to astound rather than to defend.

Leeds Castle, Britain The 'loveliest castle in the world' is no empty PR rhetoric – this absolute stunner set on an island in the middle of a large lake in Kent is perhaps Europe's ultimate medieval castle (p185)

Versailles, France The vast formal palace against which all others are measured includes the Hall of Mirrors and Marie Antoinette's refuge (p364)

Neuschwanstein, Germany So what if it's not even 200 years old? Neuschwanstein, in the heart of the Bavarian Alps, is everybody's (including Disney's) castle fantasy (p462)

Winter Palace, Russia The name alone evokes the brutality of the Russian Revolution, but the golden-green baroque reality is unmatched anywhere for sheer tsarist splendour (p922)

Beaches

Between the Mediterranean, Aegean, Adriatic, Ionian, Baltic and Black Seas, not to mention the pristine lakes and rivers across the region, definitely plan on being able to take it easy on a beautiful stretch of sand during your trip.

Cyclades, Greece The names Mykonos, Paros and Naxos all conjure up images of perfect golden beaches and the reality is sure not to disappoint (p523)

Drymades beach, Albania The stuff of legend among backpackers, this white-sand beach on Albania's fast-disappearing undeveloped coastline remains the one to head for (p50)

Menorca, Spain Beaches so beautiful you think they may merely be dreams are tucked away in little coves all around the most beautiful and sandiest of the Balearic Islands (p1094)

Black Sea coast, Bulgaria Bulgaria boasts the best beaches on the Black Sea, but we recommend avoiding the big resort towns and heading instead to smaller Sozopol (p257)

Spectacular Scenery

Criss-crossed by mountain ranges, gentle rolling hills and thick forest, and with hiking of all levels never far away, walkers and mountain lovers will be spoilt rotten in Europe, where the scenery never fails to captivate even the most seasoned explorers.

The Alps, Switzerland There's no competition for the most stunning landscape in Europe – even its neighbours wouldn't dare suggest that theirs could rival that of beautiful Switzerland (p1136)

Scottish Highlands, Britain Almost certainly the most scenic part of Britain, the wonderful Scottish Highlands are packed full of mountains, misty lochs and spectacular stretches of coastline to explore (p228)

Fjords, Norway It's tough to do Norway on a budget, but that shouldn't put you off: even a short trip along its impossibly beautiful coastline is an unmissable European highlight (p968)

Cappadocia, Turkey In the centre of Turkey, Anatolia's mountain-fringed plains give way to a land of otherwordly rock formations and underground cities – definitely one of the region's strangest landscapes (p1177)

BUENA VISTA IMAGES/GETTY IMAGES ©

» Pizza (p684) in Naples, Italy

Nightlife

Whether it's dancing to cutting-edge international DJs on the dance floors of superclubs in Berlin and London or altogether more traditional live music in Dublin's pubs, Paris' taverns or Barcelona's jazz clubs, you won't be left wanting.

Berlin, Germany There's nothing quite like arriving at superclub Berghain as the sun comes up, and dancing until sundown in Europe's most serious party city (p443)

London, Britain Whether it's a quiet session down at the local pub or a full-blown night on the tiles of east London, you can be sure to have a good time in the hedonistic bars and clubs of London town (p177)

Moscow, Russia Once famed for its 'face control' (strict door policies), Moscow is now becoming an essential stop on the clubber's world map with a slew of new democratically run bars and clubs (p920)

Budapest, Hungary Romkertek, Budapest's so-called 'ruin gardens' – essentially pop-up clubs in abandoned buildings – have put the Hungarian capital's nightlife on par with that of Berlin or London. Come here yourself to see why (p562)

Great Food

With dozens of rich and varied cuisines, you could eat some of the best meals of your life on a trip across Europe. Sadly, you'll often need to pay handsomely for the pleasure, but here are some superb experiences to splurge on.

Copenhagen, Denmark Yes, Denmark's sophisticated capital is *the* place to sample Europe's most sought-after menu, at Noma, which San Pellegrino and Michelin agree is among the world's best (p946)

London, Britain British cuisine may have been the butt of international jokes for decades, but its culinary revolution continues to produce new and delightful eating options. Or try Europe's best range of Indian food in the East End (p176)

Pizza in Naples, Italy The peasant dish that ate the world – or the other way around – is still the best in the city of its birth: accept no imitations! (p684)

San Sebastián, Spain Spain's Basque powerhouse boasts an impressive array of Michelin-starred restaurants (p1085)

Lyon, France Forget Paris, the French gastronomic capital is Lyon, a city that runs on pork and will have gourmands swooning (p389)

Outdoor Fun

With its wide-open spaces, innovative tourism industries and endless variety of landscape, Europe literally is your playground.

Bovec and Bled, Slovenia The unrivalled capital of extreme sports in eastern Europe is tiny Slovenia, where you can do everything from canyoning to hydrospeeding at Bovec and Bled (p1035)

Cycling the Loire Valley, France There's a gorgeous chateau around every bend in the river in this beautiful valley (p380)

Skiing year-round, Austria Experience Olympic-sized skiing in Innsbruck, the Austrian Alpine city ringed by famous pistes; if you're passing through in August, head to the glaciers for downhill action (p81)

Rafting and kayaking, Bosnia & Hercegovina Fast-flowing rivers provide world-class rafting and kayaking, especially in the Vrbas Canyons between Jajce and Banja Luka (p148)

Cycling, the Netherlands There is nowhere better to cycle than along the shimmering canals of joyously flat and cycle-friendly Holland (p813)

» St Petersburg's State Hermitage Museum (p922), Russia

Art Collections

Itself a kind of warehouse of art history, featuring works from ancient Greek statues to contemporary pieces that defy description, Europe's great art galleries – or even artfully great cities – are reason enough for a trip.

The Louvre, France It's not really France's museum, it's the world's; treasures from Europe and all over the planet in exhaustive quantity will simply dazzle you. Better yet, it's free the first Sunday of each month and for some age groups (p346)

Florence, Italy It starts with the Duomo, continues through the Uffizi Gallery and crosses the Ponte Vecchio – the entire Renaissance embodied in one city (p666)

State Hermitage Museum, Russia Housed in the Winter Palace, this is quite simply one of the world's greatest art collections, stuffed full of treasures from Egyptian mummies to a superb cache of Picassos. Free to students and on the first Thursday of the month (p922)

Van Gogh Museum, the Netherlands Despite his troubled life and struggles with poverty and madness, Van Gogh's superb creations are gloriously easy to enjoy at this Amsterdam museum (p792)

Music

Classical music of royalty, soulful songs of the masses, pop culture that changed the world: these are just some of the ways you can join in Europe's love of music.

Vienna's Staatsoper, Austria The premier venue in a city synonymous with opera and classical music. Wait – isn't that Mozart I hear? (p65)

Berlin, Germany Everything from the world's most acclaimed techno venue to the Berlin Philharmonic under the baton of Sir Simon Rattle can be seen in Germany's music-obsessed capital. (p443)

Irish music, Ireland The Irish love their music and it takes little – sometimes just a pint of beer – to get them singing. The West Coast hums with music pubs, especially in Galway (p612)

Fado, Portugal The Portuguese love the melancholic and nostalgic songs of fado; hear it in Lisbon's Alfama district (p855)

Cafes & Bars

Whether it's a coffee savoured for an hour or a drink with a roomful of new friends, you'll find plenty of places for liquid joy.

Vienna's coffee houses, Austria Unchanged in decades and redolent with the air of refinement; pause for a cup served just so (p65)

Irish pubs, Ireland Come and join the warm and gregarious crowds of locals in any pub in Ireland for a true cultural experience (p587)

Paris's cafe society, France What's more clichéd? The practised curtness of the Parisian waiter or the studied boredom of the customer? Both are, probably, and we wouldn't miss the show for anything (p355)

Amsterdam's tiny havens, the Netherlands The Dutch call them 'brown cafes' for the stains on the walls from legions of smokers, but they should just call them cosy, for the warm and friendly atmosphere (p795)

month by month

Top Events

1 **Carnevale**, February

2 **Glastonbury Festival**, June

3 **Roskilde Festival**, June

4 **Edinburgh International Festival**, August

5 **Oktoberfest**, September

January

While it's cold in Europe, January is a great time to experience the region's winter-wonderland appearance under blankets of snow. Most towns are relatively tourist free and hotel prices are rock bottom.

Kiruna Snöfestivalen, Sweden

The last weekend in January sees this Lapland snow festival (www.kirunalapland.se), based around a snow-sculpting competition that draws artists from all over Europe. There's also a husky dog competition and a handicrafts fair.

Küstendorf Film & Music Festival, Serbia

Created and curated by Serbian director Emir Kusturica, this international indie-fest (wwww.kustendorf-filmandmusicfestival.org) in the town of Drvengrad, near Zlatibor in Serbia, eschews traditional red-carpet glitz for oddball inclusions vying for the 'Golden Egg' prize.

Great-Value Skiing, Eastern Europe

Head to Eastern Europe's ski slopes for wallet-friendly prices. After the first week of January most hotels offer their lowest rates, making skiing affordable to all. Bosnia and Bulgaria are your best bets.

Empty Streets, Czech Republic

Wander Prague's Old Town unencumbered by groups of tourists. You'll have lesser-known sights and cities across the region almost to yourself during the quietest time of year.

February

Carnival in all its manic glory sweeps the Catholic regions. Cold temperatures are forgotten amid masquerades, street festivals and general bacchanalia. Expect to be kissed by a stranger.

Carnaval, Netherlands

Pre-Lent is celebrated with greater vigour in Maastricht than anywhere else in northern Europe. While the rest of the Netherlands hopes the canals will freeze for ice skating, this Dutch corner cuts loose with a celebration that would have done its former Roman residents proud.

Carnevale, Italy

In the period before Ash Wednesday, Venice goes mad for masks. Costume balls, many with traditions centuries old, enliven the social calendar in this storied old city. Even those without a coveted invite are swept up in the pageantry.

Carnival, Croatia

For colourful costumes and nonstop revelry head to Rijeka, where Carnival is the pinnacle of the year's calendar. Zadar and Samobor host Carnival celebrations too, with street dancing, concerts and masked balls.

Karneval/ Fasching, Germany

Germany doesn't leave the pre-Lent season solely to its neighbours. Karneval is celebrated with abandon in the traditional Catholic regions including Bavaria, along the Rhine and particularly vibrantly in Cologne. It's the wild bookend to Oktoberfest in Munich.

March

Spring arrives in southern Europe, while further north the rest of the continent continues to freeze, though days are often bright.

St Patrick's Day, Ireland

Parades and celebrations are held on 17 March in Irish towns big and small to honour the beloved patron saint of Ireland. While elsewhere the day is a commercialised romp of green beer, in his home country it's time for a parade and celebrations with friends and family.

Budapest Spring Festival, Hungary

This two-week festival in late March is one of Europe's top classical music events (www.springfestival.hu). Concerts are held in a number of beautiful venues, including stunning churches, the opera house and the national theatre.

April

Spring arrives with a burst of colour, from the glorious bulb fields of Holland to the blooming orchards of Spain. On the most southern beaches it's time to shake the sand out of the umbrellas.

Semana Santa, Spain

There are parades of penitents and holy icons in Spain, notably in Seville, during Easter week. Thousands of members of religious brotherhoods parade in trad garb before thousands of spectators. Look for the pointed *capirotes* (hoods).

Settimana Santa, Italy

Italy celebrates Holy Week with processions and passion plays. By Holy Thursday Rome is thronged with the faithful and even nonbelievers are swept up in the emotion and piety of hundreds of thousands thronging the Vatican and St Peter's Basilica.

Greek Easter, Greece

The most important festival in the Greek Orthodox calendar has an emphasis on the Resurrection, so it's a celebratory event. The most significant part is midnight on Easter Saturday, when candles are lit and fireworks and a procession hit the streets.

Feria de Abril, Spain

Hoods off! A week-long party in Seville in late April counterbalances the religious peak of Easter. The beautiful old squares of this gorgeous city come alive during the long, warm nights for which the nation is known.

Koningsdag (King's Day), the Netherlands

The nationwide celebration on 27 April is especially fervent in Amsterdam, awash with orange costumes and fake afros, beer, dope, leather boys, temporary roller coasters, clogs and general craziness.

May

May is usually sunny and warm and full of things to do – an excellent time to visit. It's not too hot or too crowded, though you can still expect the big destinations to feel busy.

Beer Festival, Czech Republic

An event dear to many travellers' hearts, this Prague beer festival (www.ceskypivnifestival.cz) offers lots of food, music and – most importantly – around 70 beers from around the country from mid- to late May.

Brussels Jazz Marathon, Belgium

Around-the-clock jazz performances hit Brussels during the second-last weekend in May (www.brusselsjazzmarathon.be). The saxophone is the instrument of choice for this international-flavoured city's most joyous celebration.

Queima das Fitas, Portugal

Coimbra's annual highlight is this boozy week of fado music and revelry that begins on the first Thursday in May, when students celebrate the end of the academic year.

June

The huge summer travel season hasn't started yet, but the sun has broken through the clouds and the weather is gorgeous, from the hot shores in the south to the cool climes of the north.

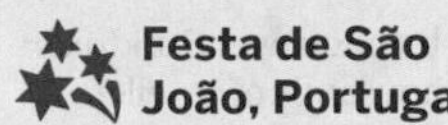

Festa de São João, Portugal

Elaborate processions, live music on Porto's plazas and merrymaking all across Portugal's second city. Squeaky plastic hammers (for sale everywhere) come out for the unusual custom of whacking one another. Everyone is fair game – expect no mercy.

White Nights in Northern Europe

By mid-June the Baltic sun only just sinks behind the horizon at night, leaving the sky a grey-white colour and encouraging locals to forget their routines and party hard. The best place to join the fun is St Petersburg, Russia, where balls, classical-music concerts and other summer events keep spirits high.

Glastonbury Festival, Britain

The town's youthful summer vibe peaks for this long weekend of music, theatre and New Age shenanigans (www.glastonburyfestivals.co.uk). It's one of England's favourite outdoor events and more than 100,000 turn up to writhe around in the grassy fields (or deep mud) at Pilton's Worthy Farm.

Roskilde Festival, Denmark

Northern Europe's largest music festival (www.roskilde-festival.dk) rocks Roskilde for four consecutive days each summer. It takes place in late June to early July but advance ticket sales are on offer in December and the festival usually sells out.

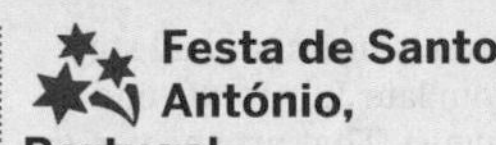

Festa de Santo António, Portugal

Feasting, drinking and dancing in Lisbon's Alfama in honour of St Anthony (12 to 13 June) caps off the even-grander three-week Festas de Lisboa, which features processions and dozens of street parties.

Hellenic Festival, Greece

The ancient theatre at Epidavros and the Theatre of Herodes Atticus are the headline venues of Athens' annual cultural shindig (www.greekfestival.gr). The festival, which runs from mid-June to August, features music, dance, theatre and much more besides.

Christopher Street Day, Berlin

The annual pan-European celebration of Gay Pride happens on a summer weekend, usually in late June but at times as late as August.

July

Visitors have arrived from around the world and outdoor cafes, beer gardens and beach clubs are hopping. Expect beautiful – even steamy – weather anywhere you go.

Il Palio, Italy

Siena's great annual event is the Palio (2 July and 16 August), a pageant culminating in a bareback horse race round Il Campo. The city is divided into 17 *contrade* (districts), of which 10 compete for the *palio* (silk banner), with emotions exploding.

Montreux Jazz Festival, Switzerland

It's not all that jazz as big-name rock acts also hit town for this famous festival (www.montreuxjazz.com) during the first two weeks of July. Glitterati from across the globe gather for a top-end celebration of top-flight music on the shores of Lake Geneva.

Sanfermines (Running of the Bulls), Spain

The Fiesta de San Fermín (Sanfermines) is the week-long nonstop festival and party in Pamplona with the daily *encierro* (running of the bulls) as its centrepiece. Anything can happen, but it rarely ends well for the bull. The antibullfighting event, the Running of the Nudes, takes place two days earlier.

Bastille Day, France

Fireworks, balls, processions, and – of course – good food and wine, for France's national day on 14 July, celebrated in every French town and city. Go to the heart of town and get caught up in this patriotic festival.

EXIT Festival, Serbia

Eastern Europe's most talked about music festival (www.exitfest.org) takes place within the walls of the Petrodvaradin Fortress in Serbia's second city, Novi Sad. Book early as it attracts music lovers from all over the continent with big international acts headlining.

De Gentse Feesten, Belgium

Ghent is transformed into a 10-day party of music and theatre (www.gentsefeesten.be), a highlight of which is a vast techno celebration called 10 Days Off. This underappreciated gem of the Low Country is high on fine bars serving countless kinds of beer.

Medieval Festival of the Arts, Romania

The beautiful Romanian city of Sighişoara hosts open-air concerts, parades and ceremonies, all glorifying medieval Transylvania and taking the town back to its fascinating 12th-century origins.

Bažant Pohoda, Slovakia

Slovakia's largest music festival (www.pohodafestival.sk) represents all genres of music from rock to orchestral over eight different stages. It's firmly established as one of Europe's biggest and best summer music festivals.

August

Everybody's going someplace as half of Europe shuts down to enjoy the traditional month of holiday with the other half. If it's near the beach, from Germany's Baltic to Spain's Balearics, it's mobbed, and the temperatures are hot, hot, hot!

Salzburg Festival, Austria

Austria's most renowned classical-music festival (www.salzburgfestival.at) attracts international stars from late July to the end of August. That urbane person sitting by you having a glass of wine who looks like a famous cellist probably is.

Zürich Street Parade, Switzerland

In Switzerland, it's Zürich's turn to let its hair down with an enormous techno parade (www.street-parade.ch). All thoughts of numbered accounts are forgotten as bankers, and everybody else in this otherwise staid burg, party to orgasmic, deep-base thump, thump, thump.

Notting Hill Carnival, Britain

This is Europe's largest – and London's most vibrant – outdoor carnival, where London's Caribbean community shows the city how to party. Food, frolic and fun are just a part of this vast multicultural two-day celebration.

Edinburgh International Festival, Britain

Three weeks of innovative drama, comedy, dance, music and more (www.eif.co.uk). Two weeks overlap with the celebrated Fringe Festival (www.edfringe.com), which draws innovative acts from around the globe. Expect cutting-edge productions that defy description.

Trumpeting Insanity, Serbia

Guca's Dragačevo Trumpet Assembly (www.guca.rs) is one of the most exciting and bizarre events in all of Eastern Europe. Hundreds of thousands of revellers descend on the small Serbian town to damage their eardrums, livers and sanity in a cacophonous day of revelry.

Terraneo Festival, Croatia

Croatia's newest festival (www.terraneofestival.com) has quickly become a summer highlight. This big five-day dance party, located in an old army barracks in Šibenik, draws in Croatian hipsters for its amazing line-up of international and local performers.

Sziget Music Festival, Hungary

A week-long, great-value world-music festival (www.sziget.hu) held all over Budapest. Sziget features bands from around the world playing at more than 60 venues.

September

It's cooling off in every sense, from the northern countries to the romance started on a dance floor in Ibiza. Maybe the best time to visit: the weather's still good and the crowds have thinned.

Venice International Film Festival, Italy

The Mostra del Cinema di Venezia (www.labiennale.org) is Italy's top film fest and one of the world's top indie film fests. The judging here is seen as an early indication of what to look for at the next year's Oscars.

Oktoberfest, Germany

Germany's legendary beer-swilling party (www.oktoberfest.de) starts mid-September in Munich and lasts a week into October. Millions descend for beer and carousing that has no equal. If you didn't plan ahead, you'll have to sleep in Austria.

Dvořák Autumn, Czech Republic

This festival of classical music (www.kso.kso.cz) honours the work of the Czech Republic's favourite composer, Anton Dvořák. The event is held over three weeks in the spa town of Karlovy Vary.

Festes de la Mercè, Spain

Barcelona knows how to party until dawn and it outdoes itself for the Festes de la Mercè (around 24 September). The city's biggest celebration has four days of concerts, dancing, *castellers* (human-castle builders), fireworks and *correfocs* – a parade of fireworks-spitting dragons and devils.

October

Another good month to visit – almost everything is still open, while prices and visitor numbers are way down. Weather can be unpredictable, though, and even cold in northern Europe.

Festival at Queen's, Ireland

Belfast hosts the second-largest arts festival (www.belfastfestival.com) in the UK for three weeks in late October/early November in and around Queen's University. It's a time for the city to shed its gritty legacy, and celebrate the intellectual and the creative without excessive hype.

Wine Festival, Moldova

Wine-enriched folkloric performances in Moldova draw oenophiles and anyone wanting to profit from the 10-day visa-free regime Moldova introduces during the festival.

November

Leaves have fallen and snow is about to in much of Europe. Even in the temperate zones around the Med it can get chilly, rainy and blustery. Most seasonal attractions have closed for the year.

Guy Fawkes Night, Britain

Bonfires and fireworks erupt across Britain on 5 November, recalling the foiling of a plot to blow up the Houses of Parliament in the 1600s. Go to high ground in London to see glowing explosions erupt everywhere.

December

December is a magical time to visit Europe. Christmas decorations brighten the dark streets and, despite the cold across much of the region, prices remain surprisingly low provided you avoid Christmas and New Year's Eve.

Christmas Markets, Germany & Austria

Christkindlmarkts are held across Germany and Austria. The most famous are in Nuremberg and Vienna, but every town has one. Warm your hands through your mittens holding a hot mug of mulled wine and find that special (or kitsch) present.

Natale, Italy

Italian churches set up intricate cribs or *presepi* (nativity scenes) in the lead-up to Christmas. Some are quite famous, most are works of art, and many date back hundreds of years and are venerated for their spiritual ties.

Christmas, Eastern Europe

Christmas is celebrated in different ways in Eastern Europe: most countries celebrate on Christmas Eve (24 December), with an evening meal and midnight Mass. In Russia, Ukraine and Belarus, Christmas falls in January, as per the Gregorian calendar.

Itineraries

First-Time Europe

Six Weeks

Italy, Switzerland, Germany, the Netherlands, France and Britain are the absolute essentials for any first-time visitor to Europe – all are crammed with world-famous sights, cultural icons and unforgettable experiences.

1

RUBBERBALL/ALAN BAILEY/GETTY IMAGES ©

» Begin in **Rome** and spend several days in this incredible city.

» Go north to heartbreakingly beautiful **Florence** and then revel in timeless **Venice**.

» Carry on to majestic Switzerland. Spend a day in **Zürich**, visit lovely **Lucerne** and then see the amazing Swiss Alps by taking the train to the **Jungfrau** region.

» Head to **Munich** for Oktoberfest if you're there in September.

» Hit **Berlin** at the weekend to check out Europe's most hedonistic city; see the remains of the Wall and dance your nights (and days) away.

» Next is **Amsterdam**, perfect for a couple of days' exploration, Rembrandt and canal wandering.

» Hop on the train to **Paris**. Spend several days here visiting the Louvre, Versailles and the Eiffel Tower.

» Take the Eurostar to **London** – see the wealth of great sights and enjoy the city's superb eating, drinking and clubbing.

» Travel west to historic **Oxford** and **Bath**. Savour incredible Stonehenge along the way and then swing north to **Liverpool**.

» End your journey with several days in Scotland – check out magical **Edinburgh**, happening **Glasgow** and have a walk in the **Highlands**.

Clockwise from top left

1 Florence (p666), Italy **2** The Great Court (architects: Foster + Partners) at London's British Museum (p161), England **3** Train to Jungfraujoch (p1137), Switzerland

2

WALTER BIBIKOW/GETTY IMAGES ©

3

JORG GREUEL/GETTY IMAGES ©

Mediterranean Europe

Four Weeks

Think Europe doesn't do beaches? Think again – it does, but with lashings of culture on the side, as you'll find during this romp along its southern shores, starting in Madrid and ending in Turkey.

» Fly into **Madrid**. Head directly for the Mediterranean by taking a train to **Barcelona** and soak up the seaside ambience of Gaudí's city.

» Head along the Côte d'Azur via **Nice** and spend time exploring **Monaco** and the beautiful villages of **Provence**.

» From Nice, take the train to historic **Rome**. Continue south to energetic **Naples**, peer into ill-fated **Pompeii** and explore the stunning Amalfi Coast.

» Cross Italy to Bari, from where you head across the Adriatic by ferry to the Croatian pearl of **Dubrovnik**.

» Bus south through Montenegro and Albania – two of Europe's least-known but most-breathtaking gems – and then head to the beautiful Greek island of **Corfu**.

» From **Patra**, do a loop of the Peloponnese: catch a bus to Byzantine pin-up city **Mystras**, ancient heavyweight **Mycenae** and then venerable **Athens**.

» Go south to Piraeus for an island-hopping expedition to **Mykonos**, **Paros** and volcanic **Santorini**.

» Continue to island-hop until you've had your fill, then set sail for **Turkey** from Samos or Lesvos.

» Visit ancient **Ephesus**. Next, bus north along the Aegean coast to the ruins of Troy and **Çanakkale** and to throbbing, beautiful and chaotic **İstanbul**.

Clockwise from top left

1 Casino de Monte Carlo (p413), Monaco **2** İstanbul's Grand Bazaar (p1158), Turkey **3** Corfu (p541), Greece **4** Pompeii (p685), Italy

2

3

From London to the Sun

Four Weeks

Combining the best of both worlds, this itinerary begins with cultural show-stoppers London and Paris and ends up soaking up the sun in Spain and Portugal, themselves not exactly culturally barren.

GUIZIOU FRANCK/GETTY IMAGES ©

» Enjoy **London** for several days of museums, galleries, world-class shopping and clubbing, then head to **Bath** by train before returning to London.

» Take the Eurostar to romantic **Paris** and make side trips to the **D-Day Beaches** and **Mont St-Michel**.

» Rail south to **Barcelona**, possibly stopping at **Limoges** for the **Dordogne Valley** en route. From Barcelona, it's possible to make a longish round trip to the **Balearic Islands** and **Valencia**.

» Zip up to the Basque seaside resort of **San Sebastián** and the Museo Guggenheim in happening **Bilbao**.

» Next make a beeline for energetic **Madrid**, making day trips to Moorish **Toledo** and enchanting **Segovia**.

» Then board a bus to the Alhambra – the Islamic fortress of **Granada** – and see the stunning Mezquita of **Córdoba**, before dancing the flamenco in **Seville**.

» Get the bus to **Lisbon** and relax and eat custard tarts in Portugal's breezy capital. Sidestep to **Sintra**.

» North lies **Porto** and the **Parque Nacional da Peneda-Gerês**, with lots of hiking opportunities.

» The southern **Algarve** is touristy, but the train journey along the coast is beautiful.

Above
1 Flamenco dancer in Seville (p1097), Spain **2** Seine river in Paris (p342), France

Scandinavian Highlights

Three Weeks

This is a three-week hop around the classic sights of Scandinavia, though you can easily spend far longer in these fascinating countries. Extra time allows more detailed exploration and side-trips to quieter places.

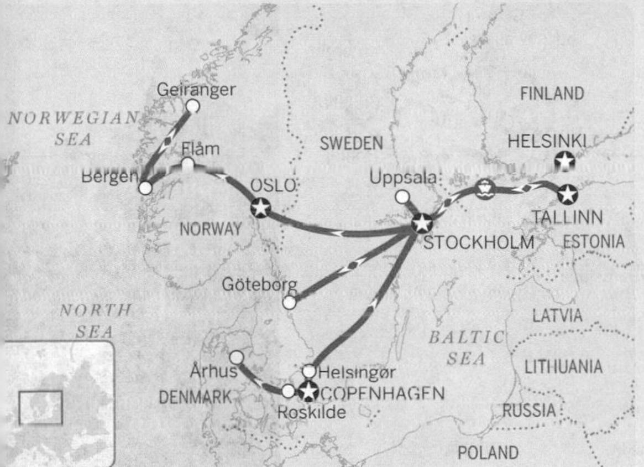

» Start in funky and fashionable **Copenhagen**, admiring the waterfront and museums and enjoying the world-class eating options (book ahead!).

» Take a day trip to the cathedral and Viking boat museum at **Roskilde** and Hamlet's' castle at **Helsingør**. Alternatively, make a trip to **Århus** – don't miss the ARoS art museum.

» Next, take the train to **Stockholm** and admire the stately, watery centre of town. Side-trip to **Uppsala**, Sweden's spiritual heart, or creative and happening **Göteborg**, the country's second city, to soak up its bonhomie.

» A ferry trip from Stockholm could take you to quirky **Helsinki**, a great base for exploring the natural wonders of Finland, or to picturesque **Tallinn**, the charming Estonian capital.

» An overnight train from Stockholm takes you to **Oslo**, where you can check out much of Munch's work in a stunning setting.

» From Oslo, a long but very scenic day includes the 'Norway in a Nutshell' rail trip to **Flåm** and a combination boat/bus journey along the Sognefjord to **Bergen**, Norway's prettiest city.

» From Bergen take a side-trip to the mighty **Geirangerfjord**, one of Scandinavia's most spectacular sights.

Above
1 Uppsala's domkyrka (p959), Sweden **2** Bergen's Bryggen district (p968), Norway

The Alps to the Iberian Peninsula

One to Two Months

If you can't get enough of gorgeous towns on the shores of brilliant-blue lakes surrounded by soaring peaks, then this itinerary is bound to please. Abundant opportunities to hike or ski are available.

» Start with a couple of days on the Danube in elegant **Vienna** before dropping in to lovely **Bled** and perhaps to nearby **Bohinj** in Slovenia.

» Head back to Austria for a couple of days exploring the beautiful **Salzkammergut** region.

» Detour to Bavaria's fairy-tale **Neuschwanstein Castle** in Germany. By now you'll be ready to sample some beers in nearby **Munich**.

» Head into Switzerland for a few days in the unbeatable **Swiss Alps**. Visit lovely **Lucerne** and take the train to the top of Jungfrau. Enjoy sophisticated **Zürich** or head to the charming and frequently overlooked Swiss capital, **Bern**.

» Head across to Italy to check out the sawtooth peaks of the **Dolomites**.

» Make your way to **Chamonix** in France – a great base to explore around Mont Blanc. Then it's time for some coffee, wine and sun along the Côte d'Azur travelling via **Monaco** and **Nice**.

» Spain's two most exciting cities, **Barcelona** and **Madrid** beckon. Head south from here to see the beautiful Alhambra in **Granada** and the stunning Mezquita of **Córdoba**.

» End your journey in fabulous **Lisbon**, Portugal's fascinating capital.

Clockwise from top left

1 The Dolomites (p665), Italy **2** Lake Bled (p1034), Slovenia **3** Tapas bar in Madrid (p1058), Spain **4** Schloss Neuschwanstein (p462), Germany

2

SEAN CAFFREY/GETTY IMAGES ©

3

DIEGO LEZAMA/GETTY IMAGES ©

Eastern Europe Today

Four Weeks

Forget the stereotypes of the grim and grey 'Eastern Bloc' of the early 1990s – this half of Europe is one of the most dynamic and fast-changing places in the world: come and explore it yourself.

WALTER BIBIKOW/GETTY IMAGES ©

» Pick a flight to **Berlin**, now a veritable music, art and nightlife mecca.

» Next travel to vibrant **Warsaw** and beautiful **Kraków**, Poland's amazingly preserved royal capital.

» Take in the Old Town in Lithuania's capital **Vilnius**, wander the streets of gorgeous art nouveau **Rīga** and party in technophile **Tallinn**.

» Head into Russia and split your time between imperial **St Petersburg** and modern-day supercity **Moscow**.

» Swing into the past by taking a train to **Minsk** in Belarus to see how things were under communism.

» Continue into Ukraine and spend a few days in its bustling Soviet capital **Kyiv**, then contrast it with more traditional **Lviv**.

» Entering Romania, you should make a beeline for **Transylvania**. Sharpen your fangs at 'Dracula's' castle in **Bran** and enjoy the gorgeous old towns nearby.

» Romania's capital **Bucharest** is next, where urban renewal of the communist kind awaits.

» A train zips you through the mountains to Bulgaria's loveliest town, **Veliko Târnovo**. Travel on to the relaxed capital **Sofia** and then by train to Serbia's vibrant capital, **Belgrade**.

Above

1 Restaurants in Berlin's Friedrichshain district (p442), Germany **2** St Petersburg's Church of the Saviour on Spilled Blood (p923), Russia

On the Road

1 **Estonia** p319
2 **Latvia** p716
3 **Lithuania** p732
4 **Russia** p911
5 **The Netherlands** p788
6 **Belgium & Luxembourg** p100
7 **Switzerland** p1121
8 **Czech Republic** p294
9 **Slovakia** p1005
10 **Austria** p54
11 **Hungary** p552
12 **Slovenia** p1026
13 **Croatia** p266
14 **Bosnia & Hercegovina** p136
15 **Serbia** p991
16 **Montenegro** p777
17 **Kosovo** p710
18 **Albania** p42
19 **Macedonia** p750
20 **Moldova** p765

Albania

Includes »

Tirana ... 45
Northern Albania ... 48
Shkodra ... 48
Theth & Valbonë ... 49
Central Albania ... 49
Kruja ... 49
Berat ... 49
Southern Coast ... 50
Drymades ... 50
Saranda ... 50
Butrint ... 51
Eastern Albania ... 51
Gjirokastra ... 51
Understand Albania ... 52
Survival Guide ... 52

Best Places to Eat

» Kujtimi (p51)
» Era (p46)
» Tradita G&T (p48)
» Oda (p47)

Best Places to Stay

» Tradita G&T (p48)
» Kotoni B&B (p51)
» Brilant Antik (p45)

Why Go?

Albania has natural beauty in such abundance that you might wonder why it's taken 20 years for the country to take off as a tourist destination, since the end of a particularly brutal strain of communism in 1991. So backward was Albania when it emerged, blinking into the bright light of freedom, that it needed two decades just to catch up with the rest of eastern Europe. Now that it arguably has done so, Albania offers a remarkable array of unique attractions, largely due to this very isolation: ancient mountain codes of behaviours, forgotten archaeological sites and villages where time seems to have stood still are all on the menu. With its stunning mountain scenery, a thriving capital in Tirana and beaches to rival any elsewhere in the Mediterranean, Albania has become the sleeper hit of the Balkans. But hurry, as word is well and truly out.

When to Go?

Tirana

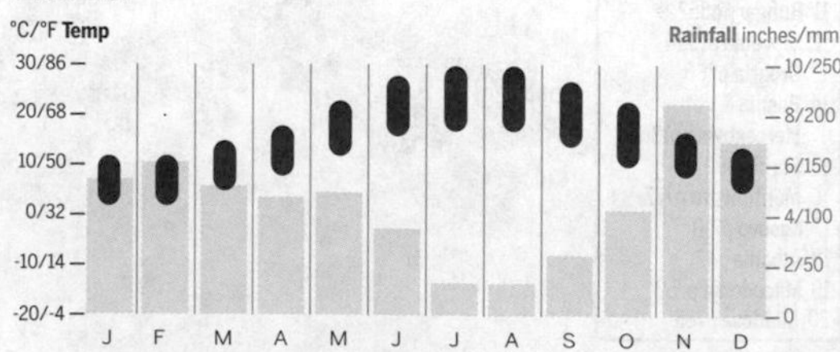

Jun Enjoy the perfect Mediterranean climate and deserted beaches.

Aug Albania's beaches may be packed, but this is a great time to explore the mountains.

Dec See features and shorts at the Tirana Film Festival, while the intrepid can snowshoe to Theth.

Connections

Albania has good connections in all directions: daily buses go to Kosovo, Montenegro, Macedonia and Greece. The southern seaport of Saranda is a short ferry trip from Greece's Corfu, while in summer ferries also connect Himara and Vlora to Corfu. Durrës has regular ferries to Italy. Travellers heading south from Croatia can pass through Montenegro to Shkodra (via Ulcinj), and loop through Albania before heading into Macedonia via Pogradec, or Kosovo via the Lake Koman Ferry or new superfast Albania–Kosovo highway. There are, however, no international train routes from Albania.

ITINERARIES

One Week

Spend a day in busy Tirana, checking out the various museums as well as the Blloku bars and nightclubs. On day two, make the two-hour trip to the Ottoman-era town of Berat. Spend a few nights in Berat, before continuing down the coast for a couple of days on the beach in Drymades. Loop around for one last night in charming Gjirokastra before returning to Tirana.

Two Weeks

Follow the first week itinerary and then head north into Albanian's incredible 'Accursed Mountains'. Start in Shkodra, from where you can get transport to Koman for the stunning morning ferry ride to Fierzë. Continue the same day to the charming mountain village of Valbonë for a couple of nights, before trekking to Theth and spending your last couple of nights in the beautiful Theth National Park.

Essential Food & Drink

» **Byrek** Pastry with cheese or meat.

» **Fergesë** Baked peppers, egg and cheese, and occasionally meat.

» **Midhje** Wild or farmed mussels, often served fried.

» **Paçë koke** Sheep's head soup, usually served for breakfast.

» **Qofta** Flat or cylindrical minced-meat rissoles.

» **Sufllaqë** Doner kebab.

» **Tavë** Meat baked with cheese and egg.

» **Konjak** Local brandy.

» **Raki** Popular spirit made from grapes.

» **Raki mani** Spirit made from mulberries.

AT A GLANCE

» **Currency** Lekë

» **Language** Albanian

» **Money** ATMs in most towns

» **Visas** Most visitors don't need one – a 90-day stamp is issued at the border

Fast Facts

» **Area** 28,748 sq km

» **Capital** Tirana

» **Country code** ☎355

» **Emergency** Ambulance ☎127, fire ☎128, police ☎129

Exchange Rates

Australia	A$1	114.59 lekë
Canada	C$1	107.95 lekë
Euro Zone	€1	140.19 lekë
Japan	¥100	116.24 lekë
New Zealand	NZ$1	91.85 lekë
UK	UK£1	165.99 lekë
USA	US$1	109.70 lekë

Set Your Budget

» **Budget hotel** €10–15 per person

» **Two-course meal** €8

» **Museum entrance** €1–3

» **Local beer** €1.50

» **City transport ticket** 30 lekë

Resources

» **Albania-Hotel** (www.albania-hotel.com)

» **Balkanology** (www.balkanology.com/albania)

» **Journey to Valbona** (www.journeytovalbona.com)

Albania Highlights

1. Catch the **Lake Koman Ferry** (p48) through stunning mountain scenery, then continue to **Valbonë** (p49) and trek the 'Accursed Mountains'
2. Explore the Unesco World Heritage–listed museum towns of dramatic **Berat** (p49), the so-called 'city of a thousand windows'
3. Catch some sun at **Drymades** (p50), just one of the many beaches on the south's dramatic Ionian Coast
4. Travel back in time to the ruins of **Butrint** (p51), hidden in the depths of a forest in a serene lakeside setting
5. Feast your eyes on the wild colour schemes and experience the hip Blloku cafe culture in **Tirana** (p45)
6. Take a trip into the traditional Southern Albanian mountain town of **Gjirokastra** (p51), with its spectacular Ottoman-era mansions and impressive hilltop fortress

TIRANA

☎04 / POP 764,000

Lively, colourful Tirana is the beating heart of Albania, where this tiny nation's hopes and dreams coalesce into a vibrant whirl of traffic, brash consumerism and unfettered fun. Having undergone a transformation of extraordinary proportions since it awoke from its communist slumber in the early 1990s, Tirana is now unrecognisable, with its buildings painted in primary colours, and public squares and pedestrianised streets a pleasure to wander. Loud, crazy, colourful and dusty – Tirana is never dull.

Sights

NORTH OF THE RIVER

Sheshi Skënderbej SQUARE

(Skanderbeg Sq) Skanderbeg Sq is the best place to start witnessing Tirana's daily goings-on. Until it was pulled down by an angry mob in 1991, a 10m-high bronze statue of Enver Hoxha stood here, watching over a mainly car-free square. Now only the **equestrian statue of Skanderbeg** remains, deaf to the cacophony of screeching horns as cars four lanes deep try to shove their way through the battlefield below.

TOP CHOICE **National History Museum** MUSEUM

(Muzeu Historik Kombëtar; Sheshi Skënderbej; adult/student 200/60 lekë; ⊙10am-5pm Tue-Sat, to 2pm Sun) The largest museum in Albania holds most of the country's archaeological treasures and a replica of Skanderbeg's massive sword. The mosaic mural entitled *Albania* adorning the museum's facade shows Albanians victorious and proud from Illyrian times through to WWII. The collection is almost entirely signed in English and takes you chronologically from ancient Illyria to the postcommunist era.

National Art Gallery GALLERY

(Galeria Kombëtare e Arteve; www.gka.al; Blvd Dëshmorët e Kombit; admission 200 lekë; ⊙10am-6pm Mon-Sat) Tracing the relatively brief history of Albanian painting from the early 19th century to the present day, this beautiful space also has temporary exhibits that are worth a look.

SOUTH OF THE RIVER

Pyramid NOTABLE BUILDING

(Blvd Dëshmorët e Kombit) Designed by Enver Hoxha's daughter and son-in-law and completed in 1988, this monstrously unattractive building was formerly the Enver Hoxha Museum, and more recently a convention centre and nightclub. Today, covered in grafitti and surrounded by the encampments of Tirana's homeless, its once white marble walls are now crumbling, but no decision on whether to demolish or restore it appears to have yet been reached.

Congress Building NOTABLE BUILDING

(Blvd Dëshmorët e Kombit) Another creation of the former dictator's daughter and son-in-law is the square Congress Building, just a little down the boulevard from the Pyramid. Follow Rr Ismail Qemali two streets north of the Congress Building and enter the once totally forbidden but now totally trendy Blloku area. This former Communist Party elite hang-out was opened to the general public for the first time in 1991. Security still guards the **former residence of Enver Hoxha** (cnr Rr Dëshmorët e 4 Shkurtit & Rr Ismail Qemali).

Sleeping

TOP CHOICE **Brilant Antik** HOTEL €€

(☎2251 166; www.hotelbrilant.com; Rr Jeronim de Rada 79; s/d €50/60; ❄📶) This charming house-cum-hotel has plenty of character, a central location and welcoming English-speaking staff to ease you into Tirana life. Rooms are spacious, decently furnished with the odd antique, and breakfast downstairs is a veritable feast each morning.

TOP CHOICE **Tirana Backpacker Hostel** HOSTEL €

(☎068-4682 353, 068-3133 451; www.tiranahostel.com; Rr Myslym Shyri, Vila 7, behind Alpet petrol station; dm €13, d €40, without bathroom €28; ❄📶) Albania's first ever hostel now boasts very smart new premises in the centre of town, and at first glance looks more like a fancy restaurant than a hostel. There are three six-bed dorms, all with their own facilities, and several comfortable doubles, including one with a great balcony. All rooms are equipped with air-con, but you'll need to pay €3 extra per room per night to turn it on. The place is very social, with a busy bar/restaurant downstairs and plenty of atmosphere.

Hostel Albania HOSTEL €

(☎067-2783 798; www.hostel-albania.com; Rr Beqir Luga 56; dm €11-12, d €30; @📶) This hostel has small four- and six-person dorms, though the basement's 14-bed dorm (€11) is the coolest spot in summer; dividers hide the fact that there are so many bunks down

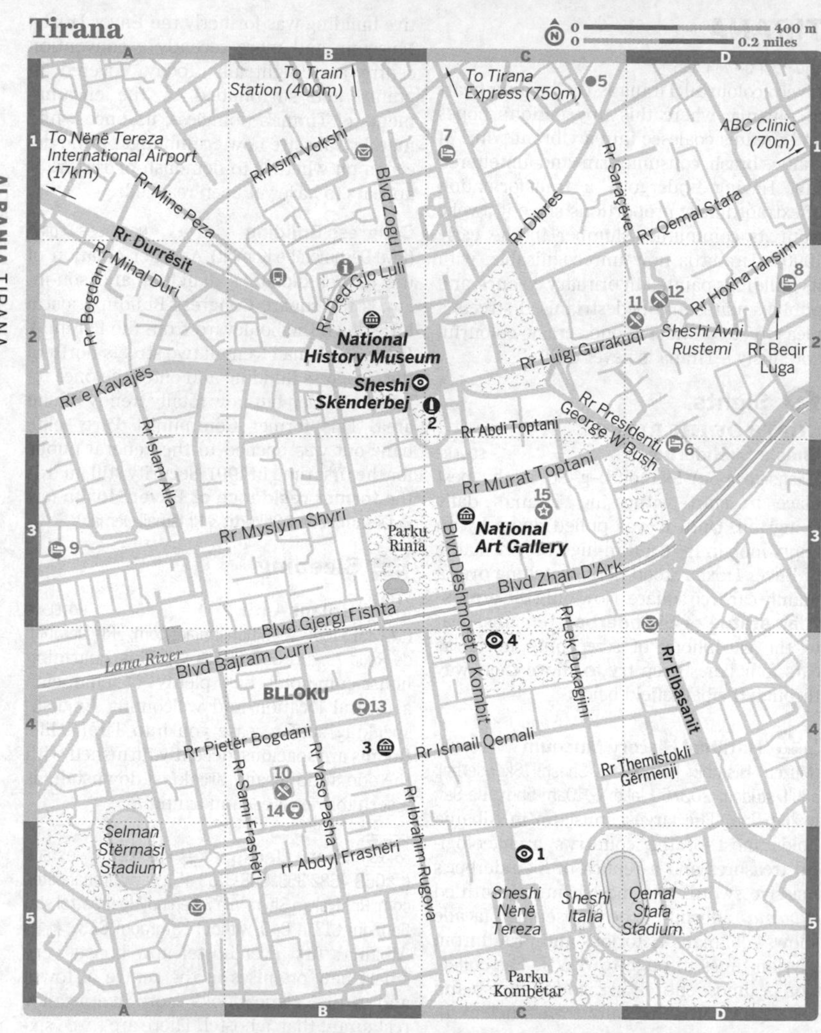

there. Zen space is in the outdoor shoes-off oriental lounge, and a filling breakfast with filter coffee is included. The artist owners provide great information about the local art scene and the location is central.

Freddy's Hostel HOTEL €€

(☎068-2035 261, 2266 077; www.freddyshostel.com; Rr Bardhok Biba 75; dm €12, r €32-56; ❄📶) Freddy's is run by a friendly family whose knowledge of the city is second to none. The clean, basic bunk-free rooms have lockers and come in different configurations. Breakfast isn't included with the cheapest dorm places, but the central location is hard to beat. The owners can also arrange long-term apartment rentals.

Eating

TOP CHOICE Era ALBANIAN, ITALIAN €€

(☎2266 662; www.era.al; Rr Ismail Qemali; mains 300-700 lekë; ⏱11am-midnight; 🖉) This local institution serves traditional Albanian and Italian fare in the heart of Blloku. The inventive menu includes oven-baked veal and eggs, stuffed eggplant, pizza, and pilau with chicken and pine nuts. Be warned: it's sometimes

Tirana

Top Sights

- National Art Gallery C3
- National History Museum B2
- Sheshi Skënderbej B2

Sights

1 Congress Building C5
2 Equestrian Statue of Skanderbeg C2
3 Former Residence of Enver Hoxha B4
4 Pyramid C4

Activities, Courses & Tours

5 Outdoor Albania C1

Sleeping

6 Brilant Antik D3
7 Freddy's Hostel C1
8 Hostel Albania D2
9 Tirana Backpacker Hostel A3

Eating

10 Era B4
11 Oda D2
12 Stephen Centre D2

Drinking

13 Charl's B4
14 Radio B4

Entertainment

15 Folic C3

quite hard to get a seat as it's fearsomely popular, so you may have to wait. Delivery and takeaway are both available.

TOP CHOICE **Oda** ALBANIAN €€
(Rr Luigj Gurakuqi; mains 350-550 lekë; ⊙noon-11pm) Bright flashing lights will guide you to this endearing little restaurant down a lane, where you can choose from two brightly lit dining rooms or an atmospheric terrace. The place is stuffed full of traditional Albanian arts and crafts, and while its popularity with travellers means you won't feel like you've discovered a truly authentic slice of the country, the delicious menu and pleasant atmosphere make it well worth a visit.

Stephen Centre CAFE €€
(Rr Hoxha Tahsim 1; mains 400-700 lekë; ⊙8am-8pm Mon-Sat; 📶) If you like your fries thin, your wi-fi free and the spirit Christian, here's the cafe for you. A veritable institution in Tirana, the Stephen Centre also offers accommodation upstairs in single-bed configurations (single/double €35/50).

Drinking

Most of Tirana's nightspots are concentrated in the Blloku neighbourhood, and most will have you partying on to the wee hours.

Radio BAR
(Rr Ismail Qemali 29/1) Set back from the street is this very cool yet understated and friendly bar. Check out the owner's collection of antique Albania-made radios while sipping cocktails with groovy locals.

Charl's BAR
(Rr Pjetër Bogdani 36) Charl's is a consistently popular bar with Tirana's students because of its ever-varying live music on the weekends, and disco/dance crowd-pleasers the rest of the time. The relaxed vibe is enhanced by the bar's open-air garden.

Entertainment

TOP CHOICE **Tirana Express** GALLERY, CONCERT VENUE
(www.tiranaekspres.wordpress.com; Rr Karl Gega) This fantastic nonprofit arts project has converted a warehouse behind Tirana's semiderelict train station into an arts space that hosts revolving temporary exhibits, concerts, installations and other events that appeal to Tirana's arty, alternative crowd.

Folie CLUB
(Rr Murat Toptani) This is where the big-name DJs come to play, and though the crowd can be a little more concerned with being seen than actually enjoying themselves, it's a great outdoor venue for a loud night out.

Information

Tirana Tourist Information Centre (☎2223 313; www.tirana.gov.al; Rr Ded Gjo Luli; ⊙9am-5pm Mon-Fri, to 2pm Sat) Friendly staff make getting information easy at this government-run initiative just off Skanderbeg Sq.

Getting There & Around

AIR The modern **Nënë Tereza International Airport** (Mother Teresa Airport; ☎2381 800; www.tirana-airport.com.al) is at Rinas, 17km northwest of Tirana. The Rinas Express airport bus operates an hourly (8am to 7pm) service from Rr Mine Peza on the western side of the National History Museum for 250 lekë one way.

BUS There is no official bus station in Tirana, though there's a makeshift bus station beside the train station where some buses drop passengers off. Confusingly, other buses and *furgons* (shared minibuses) depart from ever-changing places in and around the city, so check locally for the latest departure points. You can almost guarantee that taxi drivers will be in the know; however, you may have to dissuade them from taking you the whole way.

TRAIN The rundown train station is at the northern end of Blvd Zogu I. Trains are dirt cheap and run to Durrës, Shkodra, Vlora and Pogradec. Check timetables at the station the day before travelling.

NORTHERN ALBANIA

Shkodra

☎022 / POP 95,000

Shkodra (Shkodër), the traditional centre of the Gheg cultural region, is one of the oldest cities in Europe. The ancient Rozafa Fortress has stunning views over the nearby lake, while a concerted effort to renovate the buildings in the Old Town has made wandering through Shkodra a treat for the eyes.

Sights

Rozafa Fortress CASTLE

(admission 200 lekë; ⏲8am-10pm) The Rozafa Fortress was founded by the Illyrians in antiquity and rebuilt much later by the Venetians and then the Turks. The fortress derives its name from a woman named Rozafa, who was allegedly walled into the ramparts as an offering to the gods so that the construction would stand. Municipal buses (30 lekë) stop near the turn-off to the castle, and it's a short walk up from there.

Marubi Permanent Photo Exhibition GALLERY

(Rr Muhamet Gjollesha; admission 100 lekë; ⏲8am-4pm Mon-Fri) Hidden behind a block of shops and flats, the Marubi Permanent Photo Exhibition has fantastic photography by the Marubi 'dynasty', Albania's first and foremost photographers. The exhibition shows fascinating portraits, places and events.

Sleeping

TOP CHOICE **Tradita G&T** BOUTIQUE HOTEL €€

(☎068-2086 056, 2240 537; www.traditagt.com; Rr Edith Durham; s/d/tr €35/50/55; P 📶) The best choice in town, this innovative, well-managed guesthouse is a delight. Housed in a painstakingly restored 17th-century mansion that once belonged to a famous Shkodran writer, the Tradita heaves with Albanian arts and crafts and has traditional yet very comfortable rooms with terracotta-roofed bathrooms and locally woven bed linen. A homemade, home-grown breakfast awaits guests in the morning and the restaurant serves excellent fish dishes in an ethnographic museum atmosphere.

Hotel Kaduku HOTEL €€

(HK; ☎42 216, 069-2551 230; www.hotel-kaduku.com; Sheshi 5 Heronjtë; s/d/tr/ste €23/32/48/50; ❄📶) This popular, modern hotel is behind Raiffeisen Bank on the roundabout near Hotel Rozafa. It's clean and friendly.

Getting There & Away

There are hourly *furgons* and buses to and from Tirana (300 lekë, two hours, 6am to 4pm). Catch the 7am bus to Lake Koman (800 lekë, two hours) in time for the wonderful ferry trip along the lake to Fierzë near Kosovo. *Furgons* depart for Theth daily at 7am (700 lekë).

DON'T MISS

THE LAKE KOMAN FERRY

One of Albania's undisputed highlights is this superb three-hour ferry ride through Lake Koman, connecting the towns of Koman and Fierzë. Lake Koman was created in 1978 when the River Drin was dammed, with the result that you can cruise through spectacular mountain scenery where many incredibly hardy peasants still live as they have for centuries, tucked away in tiny mountain villages.

The ferry is not set up for tourism, which makes the entire trip feel like a great adventure. Normally there are two daily ferries in the summer months: a passenger ferry that leaves Koman at 9am and a car ferry that leaves Koman at 10am. However, the car ferry didn't run in 2012 due to declining demand, and so it's likely that in future only the passenger ferry will run. Check www.journeytovalbona.com for the latest information. The passenger ferry (500 lekë per person) arrives in Fierzë at around 1pm and is met by *furgons* that will take you to either Bajram Curri (200 lekë) or to Valbonë (400 lekë).

Theth & Valbonë

These small villages deep in the 'Accursed Mountains' are a magnet for those seeking beauty, isolation, mystery and adventure. From Theth, three circular hikes are very clearly marked out with red and white markers. It's possible to hike in the region without a guide, but they're helpful and charge between 3000 and 4000 lekë per day. Official guides charge €50.

The main hike is from Theth to Valbonë (or vice versa) and takes roughly six to seven hours. It takes around three hours to trek from Theth's centre (742m) to Valbonë pass (1812m), then a further two hours to the houses of Rragam and 1½ hours along a riverbed to near Bajram Curri. It's a spectacular walk and many visitors' highlight of Albania. If possible, combine it with the Koman Ferry for the ultimate Albanian mountain experience, though you're far better doing the circuit anticlockwise (ie going from Valbonë to Theth) if you choose to include the ferry.

CENTRAL ALBANIA

Kruja

☎0511 / POP 20,000

Kruja is Skanderbeg's town. Yes, Albania's hero was born here, and although it was over 500 years ago, there's still a great deal of pride in the fact that he and his forces defended Kruja from the Ottomans until his death.

From the road below, Kruja's houses appear to sit in the lap of a mountain. An ancient castle juts out to one side, and the massive Skanderbeg Museum juts out of the castle itself. Kruja's sights can be covered in a few hours, making this an ideal town to visit en route to Tirana's airport.

Sights

National Ethnographic Museum MUSEUM

(admission 300 lekë; ⏲9am-1pm & 4-7pm Tue-Sun) This traditional home in the castle complex below the Skanderbeg Museum is one of the best in the country. The English-speaking guide's detailed explanations are excellent; offer a tip if you can.

Skanderbeg Museum MUSEUM

(admission 200 lekë; ⏲9am-1pm & 4-7pm Tue-Sun) Designed by Enver Hoxha's daughter and son-in-law, this museum opened in 1982, and its spacious seven-level interior displays replicas of armour and paintings depicting Skanderbeg's struggle against the Ottomans.

Bazaar MARKET

This Ottoman-style bazaar is the country's best place for souvenir shopping and has WWII medical kits, antique gems and quality traditional ware, including beautifully embroidered tablecloths, copper coffee pots and plates.

Getting There & Away

Kruja is 32km from Tirana. Make sure your *furgon* from Tirana (150 lekë, 30 minutes) is going to Kruja, not just Fush Kruja, the modern town below.

Berat

☎032 / POP 71,000

A highlight of any trip to Albania is a visit to beautiful Berat. Its most striking feature is the collection of white Ottoman houses climbing up the hill to its castle, earning it the title of 'town of a thousand windows' and helping it join Gjirokastra on the list of Unesco World Heritage sites in 2008. Berat today is now a big centre for tourism in Albania, though it has managed to retain its easygoing charm and friendly atmosphere.

Sights

TOP CHOICE **Kalasa** CASTLE

(admission 100 lekë, audioguide 500 lekë; ⏲24hr) The neighbourhood inside the castle's walls still lives and breathes and is great for wandering. The highest point is occupied by the Inner Fortress, where ruined stairs lead to a Tolkienesque water reservoir. Views are spectacular in all directions.

TOP CHOICE **Onufri Museum** GALLERY

(admission 200 lekë; ⏲9am-1pm & 4-7pm May-Sep, 9am-4pm Oct-Apr, closed Mon) The **Church of the Dormition of St Mary** (Kisha Fjetja e Shën Mërisë) is the site of the Onufri Museum, where spectacular 16th-century artworks are displayed on the ground level along with a beautifully gilded iconostasis.

Sleeping & Eating

TOP CHOICE **Berat Backpackers** HOSTEL €

(☎069-3064 429, 069-474 8060; www.beratbackpackers.com; Gorica; tent/dm/r €7/12/28; ⏲Apr-Nov; @🛜) Albania's best hostel is the brainchild of Englishman Scott; he's transformed a traditional house in the Gorica quarter into a vine-clad hostel with a basement bar, alfresco drinking area and a cheery, relaxed atmosphere. There's a shaded camping area on the terrace, cheap laundry available, two airy dorms with original ceilings, and one excellent-value double room that shares the bathroom facilities with the dorms.

White House ITALIAN €€
(Rr Santa Lucia; mains 200-1000 lekë; ⏲8am-11pm) On the main road that runs north of the river, this smart place has a superb roof terrace with sweeping views over Berat, and serves up a mean pizza to boot. There's also a classier dining room downstairs with air-conditioning, perfect for a blowout meal.

Getting There & Away

Buses and *furgons* run between Tirana and Berat (400/500 lekë, 2½ hours) half-hourly until 3pm.

SOUTHERN COAST

Drymades

As you zigzag down the mountain from the Llogaraja Pass National Park, the white crescent-shape beaches and azure waters lure you from below. To get to one of the best beaches, turn right just after the beginning of the walk down to Dhërmi beach and you'll be on the sealed road that twists through olive groves. After a 20-minute walk you'll be on its rocky white beach.

Sleeping & Eating

TOP CHOICE **Sea Turtle** CAMPGROUND €
(☎069-4016 057; per person incl half-board from 1000 lekë; ⏲Jun-Sep) This great little set-up is run by two brothers. Each summer they turn the family orange orchard into a vibrant tent city, and the price includes the tent (with mattresses, sheets and pillows), breakfast and a family-cooked dinner (served up in true camp style). Hot showers are under the shade of old fig trees.

Saranda

☎0852 / POP 37,700

Saranda, the capital of the Albanian riviera, has grown rapidly in the past decade; skeletal high-rises crowd around its horseshoe shape and hundreds more are being built in the outlying region. The mesmerising ancient archaeological site of Butrint and the hypnotic Blue Eye Spring are the best reasons to visit.

Sights

Castle of Lëkurësit CASTLE
This former castle is now a restaurant with superb views over Saranda and Butrint lagoon, especially at sunset. A taxi there costs about 1000 lekë return; arrange a time for the driver to pick you up, or it's a 15-minute walk up from the Saranda–Tirana road.

Blue Eye Spring SPRING
(Syri i Kaltër; per person/car 50/200 lekë) Twenty-two kilometres east of Saranda, the Blue Eye Spring is a hypnotic pool of deep blue water surrounded by electric blue edges like the iris of an eye. Bring your swimming gear and a towel, as it's a great spot for a dive into the cold water on a summer's day. If you don't mind a 2km walk, any bus travelling between Saranda and Gjirokastra can drop you off at the spring's turn-off.

Sleeping & Eating

SR Backpackers HOSTEL €
(☎069-4345 426; www.backpackerssr.hostel.com; Rr Mitat Hoxha 10; dm €11; @📶) The hostel with the most central location in Saranda, this is also the cheapest option. Housed in an apartment and hosted by the gregarious English-speaking Tomi, the 14 beds here are spread over three dorms, each with its own balcony.

Hairy Lemon HOSTEL €
(☎069-3559 317; www.hairylemonhostel.com; cnr Mitat Hoxha & E Arberit; dm €12; 📶) With a prime 8th-floor location, a clean beach at its base and a friendly, helpful atmosphere, this Irish-run backpacker hostel is a good place to chill out. Follow the port road for around 10 minutes and continue when it becomes dirt; it's the orange-and-yellow apartment block on your right.

Tani SEAFOOD €€
(mains 250-550 lekë) This portside seafood restaurant is run by chef Tani, who prides himself on serving dishes he's invented himself. The oven-baked filled mussels are a cheesy delight, and it's in a cool vine-draped location.

Information

ZIT information centre (Rr Skënderbeu; ⏲8am-4pm Mon-Fri, 9am-2pm & 4-9pm Sat &

Sun Oct-Jun, 8.30am-2pm & 4-10pm Jul-Sep) Saranda's ZIT information centre is the most established in Albania and provides information about transport and local sights. The newer, bigger tourist information centre on the promenade sells travel guides, souvenirs, Ismail Kadare novels and maps.

Getting There & Away

BUS The main bus station is uphill from the ruins on Rr Vangjel Pando. Municipal buses go to Butrint via Ksamil on the hour from 7am to 5pm (100 lekë, 30 minutes), leaving from the roundabout near the port and opposite ZIT. Buses to Tirana (1300 lekë, eight hours) via Gjirokastra (350 lekë) leave at 5am, 6.30am, 8.30am, 9.30am, 10.30am, 2pm and 10pm.

FERRY Finikas (260 57, 067-2022 004; www.finikas-lines.com; Rr Mithat Hoxha) at the port sells ferry tickets for Corfu with a daily departure at 10.30am (€19, 45 minutes). A slower boat departs daily at 4.30pm (€19, 90 minutes).

Butrint

The ancient ruins of **Butrint** (www.butrint.org; admission 700 lekë; 8am-dusk), 18km south of Saranda, are renowned for their size, beauty and tranquillity. They're in a fantastic natural setting and are part of a 29-sq-km national park. Set aside at least two hours to explore this fascinating place.

The municipal bus from Saranda to Butrint costs 100 lekë and leaves hourly from 7am to 5pm.

EASTERN ALBANIA

Gjirokastra

084 / POP 43,000

Defined by its castle, roads paved with chunky limestone and shale, imposing slate-roofed houses and views out to the Drina Valley, Gjirokastra is an intriguing hillside town with its 600 'monumental' houses that attract visitors. Some of these magnificent houses, a blend of Ottoman and local architectural influence, have caved in on themselves, and Unesco funding is being spent to maintain them.

Sights

Gjirokastra Castle CASTLE

(admission 200 lekë; 8am-8pm) The town's moody castle hosts an eerie collection of armoury and has been the site of a fortress here since the 12th century, although much of what can be seen today dates to the early 19th century.

TOP CHOICE **Zekate House** HISTORIC BUILDING

(admission 200 lekë; 9am-6pm) This incredible three-storey house dates from 1811 and has twin towers and a double-arched facade. It's fascinating to nose around the almost totally unchanged interiors of an Ottoman-era home, especially the upstairs galleries, whichare the most impressive.

Sleeping

Kotoni B&B B&B €

(263 526, 069-2366 846; www.kotonihouse.com; Rr Bashkim Kokona 8; s/d from €20/25; P ❄ ✦) Hosts Haxhi and Vita will look after you in true Albanian style here: they love Gjirokastra and are happy to pass on information, as well as pack picnics for guests' day trips. The 220-year-old rooms are small, but the astonishing views and friendly cats sweeten the deal. Laundry is available, and fishing trips and hikes can be arranged.

Hotel Sopoti HOSTEL €

(069-399 8922; Sheshi Çerçiz Topulli; per person 1000 lekë) The shared bathrooms here are extremely basic, but if you can get past that, this budget place is a steal. It boasts a great location in the heart of the Old Town, as well as clean rooms.

Eating

TOP CHOICE **Kujtimi** ALBANIAN €

(mains 200-600 lekë; 11am-11pm) On the left-hand side of the path to Fantazia Restaurant is this wonderfully laid-back outdoor restaurant, run by the Dumi family. The terrace here is the perfect place to absorb the charms of the Old Town and on a typical night it's bustling with locals.

Information

Information Centre (8am-4pm Mon-Fri, 9am-2pm & 4-9pm Sat & Sun Oct-Jun, 8.30am-2pm & 4-10pm Jul-Sep) Opposite Çajupi Hotel behind the statue of the partisans.

Getting There & Away

Buses pass through the new town on their way to Tirana and Saranda, and *furgons* also go to Saranda (300 lekë, one hour). Buses to Tirana (1200 lekë, 7 hours) leave on the hour from 5am – the last one passes through after 11pm.

UNDERSTAND ALBANIA

History

The Illyrians, ancestors of the Albanians, occupied the western Balkans during the 2nd millennium BC. The Greeks arrived in the 7th century BC, and the Romans took control by 167 BC.

Under the Romans, Illyria enjoyed peace and prosperity. The main trade route between Rome and Constantinople ran from the port at Durrës. When the Roman Empire was divided in AD 395, Illyria fell within the Byzantine Empire.

In 1344 Albania was annexed by Serbia, but after the defeat of Serbia by the Turks in 1389 the region was open to Ottoman attack. The national hero Skanderbeg (Gjergj Kastrioti) led Albanian resistance to the Turks from his castle at Kruja. After Skanderbeg's death, the Ottomans took control of the country in 1479. Ottoman rule lasted 400 years.

Uprisings in the late 19th century culminated in a proclamation of independence in 1912. During WWI Albania was occupied in succession by the armies of Greece, Serbia, France, Italy and Austria-Hungary. In 1920 a republican government helped to stabilise the country, but in 1924 it was overthrown by the interior minister, Ahmed Bey Zogu, who declared himself King Zogu I in 1928. His close collaboration with Italy backfired in April 1939 when Mussolini invaded. On 8 November 1941 the Albanian Communist Party was founded, with Enver Hoxha as first secretary. The communists led the resistance against the Italians and, after 1943, against the Germans.

In September 1948 Albania allied itself with Stalin's USSR until 1960, when it reoriented itself towards the People's Republic of China. From 1966 to 1967 Albania experienced a Chinese-style cultural revolution; agriculture was collectivised and organised religion banned. It was a dark time for many Albanians. With the death of Mao Zedong in 1976, Albania's unique relationship with China also came to an end, and the country was left isolated and without allies. The economy was devastated and food shortages became more common.

Hoxha died in April 1985 and his associate Ramiz Alia took over the leadership. In June 1990, inspired by the changes that were occurring elsewhere in eastern Europe, around 4500 Albanians took refuge in Western embassies in Tirana and were granted political asylum in Italy. The March 1992 elections ended 47 years of communist rule and parliament elected Sali Berisha president. Albania quickly switched from a tightly controlled communist regime to a rambunctious free-market free-for-all. In 1996 70% of Albanians lost their savings when private pyramid-investment schemes collapsed. Riots ensued, elections were called, and the victorious Socialist Party under Fatos Nano was able to restore some degree of security.

The general election of 2005 saw a return of Berisha's Democratic Party to government, and in 2009 they narrowly won again.

Albania managed to avoid being caught in the crippling economic crisis that struck many countries in 2008 and economic growth has continued. Despite this, infrastructure deficiencies still plague the country. Albania joined NATO in 2009, and may well become an official EU membership candidate in 2013, if elections to be held then are deemed fair.

There are still many challenges facing contemporary Albania, but the country's outlook has never before looked so optimistic.

People

Albania's population is made up of approximately 95% Albanians, 3% Greeks and 2% 'other' – comprising Vlachs, Roma, Serbs, Macedonians and Bulgarians. The majority of young people speak some English, but speaking a few words of Albanian (or Italian, and, on the south coast, Greek) will be useful. Like most Balkan people, Albanians shake their heads sideways to say yes *(po)* and usually nod and 'tsk' to say no (*jo* – pronounced 'yo'). Albanians familiar with foreigners often take on the nod-for-yes way, which increases confusion.

SURVIVAL GUIDE

Directory A–Z

Accommodation

The following price categories for the cost of a double room in high season are used in the listings in this chapter.

€ less than €30

€€ €30 to €80

€€€ more than €80

Activities

Hiking and adventure sports are gaining popularity in Albania, and **Outdoor Albania** (☎2227 121; www.outdooralbania.com; Rr Sami Frasheri, Pallati Metropol) is an excellent organisation at the forefront of the industry. Smaller operatives are starting up: **Albania Rafting** (☎2006 621; www.albrafting.com) runs rafting tours of the Osumi River and canyons in Berat. Hiking in the Alps, particularly around Theth and Valbonë, is popular (with and without guides), as is mountain biking around the country.

Business Hours

Banks 9am to 3.30pm Monday to Friday

Cafes & Bars 8am to midnight

Offices 8am to 5pm Monday to Friday

Restaurants 8am to midnight

Shops 8am to 7pm; siesta time can be any time between noon and 4pm

Food

The following price categories for the cost of a main course are used in the listings in this chapter.

€ less than 200 lekë

€€ 200 lekë to 500 lekë

€€€ more than 500 lekë

Money

The lekë is the official currency, though the euro is widely accepted; you'll get a better rate in general if you use lekë. ATMs (found in most of Albania's towns, bar remote villages) usually offer to dispense cash in either currency. Albanian lekë can't be exchanged outside the country, so exchange them or spend them before you leave.

Public Holidays

New Year's Day 1 January

Summer Day 16 March

Nevruz 23 March

Catholic Easter March or April

Orthodox Easter March or April

May Day 1 May

Mother Teresa Day 19 October

Independence Day 28 November

Liberation Day 29 November

Christmas Day 25 December

Visas

Visas are not required for citizens of EU countries or nationals of Australia, Canada, New Zealand, Japan, South Korea, Norway, South Africa or the USA. Passports are stamped for a 90-day stay.

Women Travellers

Albania is a safe country for women travellers, but outside Tirana it is mainly men who go out and sit in bars and cafes in the evenings. You may tire of being asked why you're travelling alone.

Getting There & Away

Air

Nënë Tereza International Airport (Mother Teresa Airport; ☎2381 800; www.tirana-airport.com.al) is 17km northwest of Tirana and is a modern, well-run terminal. There are no domestic flights within Albania.

Land

From Tirana, regular buses head to Pristina, Kosovo; to Struga, Tetovo and Skopje in Macedonia; to Budva and Ulcinj in Montenegro; and to Athens and Thessaloniki in Greece. *Furgons* and buses leave Shkodra for Montenegro, and buses head to Kosovo from Durrës. Buses travel to Greece from Albanian towns on the southern coast and buses to Italy leave from Vlora.

Sea

Two or three ferries per day ply the route between Saranda and Corfu, in Greece, and there are plenty of ferry companies making the journey to Italy from Vlora and Durrës, as well as additional ferries from Vlora to Corfu.

Getting Around

Cycling in Albania is tough but certainly feasible. Expect lousy road conditions including open drains, some abysmal driving from fellow road users and roads that barely qualify for the title.

The first bus/*furgon* departure is often at 5am and things slow down around lunchtime. There are many buses catering for the crowds along the coast in July and August. Fares are low, and you either pay the conductor on board or when you hop off.

Austria

Includes »

Vienna ... 58
Krems an der Donau ... 67
Melk ... 68
Linz ... 68
Graz ... 69
Klagenfurt ... 71
Salzburg ... 72
Hallstatt ... 77
Innsbruck ... 78
Kitzbühel ... 81
Lienz ... 81
Hohe Tauern National Park ... 82
Understand Austria ... 83
Survival Guide ... 84

Best Places to Eat

» Mill (p64)
» Chez Nico (p80)
» Bärenwirt (p76)
» Der Steirer (p70)
» Restaurant Maria Loretto (p71)

Best Places to Stay

» my MOjO vie (p63)
» Haus Ballwein (p73)
» Nepomuks (p80)
» Snowbunny's Hostel (p81)
» Pension Sarstein (p78)

Why Go?

For such a small country, Austria has made it big. This is, after all, the land where Mozart was born, Strauss taught the world to waltz and Julie Andrews grabbed the spotlight with her twirling entrance in *The Sound of Music*. This is where the Habsburgs built their 600-year empire, and where past glories still shine in the resplendent baroque palaces and chandelier-lit coffee houses of Vienna, Innsbruck and Salzburg. This is a perfectionist of a country, and whatever it does – mountains, classical music, new media, castles, cake, you name it – it does exceedingly well.

Beyond its grandiose cities, Austria's allure lies outdoors. And whether you're schussing down the legendary slopes of Kitzbühel, climbing high in the Alps of Tirol or pedalling along the banks of the sprightly Danube, you'll find the kind of inspiring landscapes that no well-orchestrated symphony, camera lens or singing nun could ever quite do justice.

When to Go

Vienna

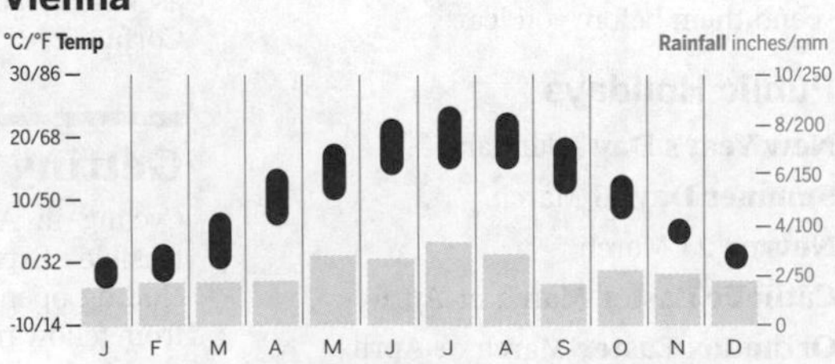

Jul–Aug Alpine hiking in Tirol, lake swimming in Salzkammergut and lots of summer festivals.

Sep–Oct New wine in vineyards near Vienna, golden forest strolls and few crowds.

Dec–Jan Christmas markets, skiing in the Alps and Vienna waltzing into the New Year.

Connections

Bang in the heart of Europe, Austria has speedy connections to its eight neighbouring countries. Trains from Vienna run to many eastern European destinations, including Bratislava, Budapest, Prague and Warsaw; there are also connections south to Italy via Klagenfurt and north to Berlin. Salzburg is within sight of the Bavarian border, and there are many trains Munich-bound and beyond from the baroque city. Innsbruck is on the main rail line from Vienna to Switzerland, and two routes also lead to Munich. Look out for the fast, comfortable RailJet services to Germany and Switzerland.

ITINERARIES

Two Days

Spend this entire time in Vienna, making sure to visit the Habsburg palaces and Stephansdom before cosying up in a *Kaffeehäus* (coffee house). At night, check out the pumping bar scene.

One Week

Spend two days in Vienna, plus another day exploring the Wachau wine region, a day each in Salzburg and Innsbruck, one day exploring the Salzkammergut lakes, and finally one day in St Anton am Arlberg or Kitzbühel hiking or skiing (depending on the season).

Essential Food & Drink

» **Make it meaty** Go for a classic Wiener schnitzel, *Tafelspitz* (boiled beef with horseradish sauce) or *Schweinebraten* (pork roast). The humble wurst (sausage) comes in various guises.

» **On the side** Lashings of potatoes, either fried (*Pommes*), roasted (*Bratkartoffeln*), in a salad (*Erdapfelsalat*) or boiled in their skins (*Quellmänner*); plus *Knödel* (dumplings) and *Nudeln* (flat egg noodles).

» **Kaffee und Kuchen** Coffee and cake is Austria's sweetest tradition. Must-tries: flaky apple strudel, rich, chocolatey *Sacher Torte* and *Kaiserschmarrn* (sweet pancakes with raisins).

» **Wine at the source** Jovial locals gather in rustic *Heurigen* (wine taverns) in the wine-producing east, identified by an evergreen branch above the door. Sip crisp Grüner Veltliner whites and spicy Blaufränkisch wines.

» **Cheese fest** Dig into gooey *Käsnudeln* (cheese noodles) in Carinthia, *Kaspressknodel* (fried cheese dumplings) in Tirol and *Käsekrainer* (cheesy sausages) in Vienna. The hilly Bregenzerwald is studded with dairies.

AT A GLANCE

» **Currency** Euro (€)

» **Language** German

» **Money** ATMs widely available; banks open Monday to Friday

» **Visas** Schengen rules apply

Fast Facts

» **Area** 83,871 sq km

» **Capital** Vienna

» **Country code** ☎43

» **Emergency** ☎112

Exchange Rates

Australia	A$1	€0.82
Canada	C$1	€0.77
Japan	¥100	€0.83
New Zealand	NZ$1	€0.65
UK	UK£1	€1.18
USA	US$1	€0.78

Set Your Budget

» **Budget hotel room** €50

» **Two-course meal** €15

» **Museum entrance** €8

» **Beer** €3

» **City transport ticket** €2

Resources

» **ÖAV** (www.alpenverein.at)

» **ÖBB** (www.oebb.at)

» **Österreich Werbung** (www.austria.info)

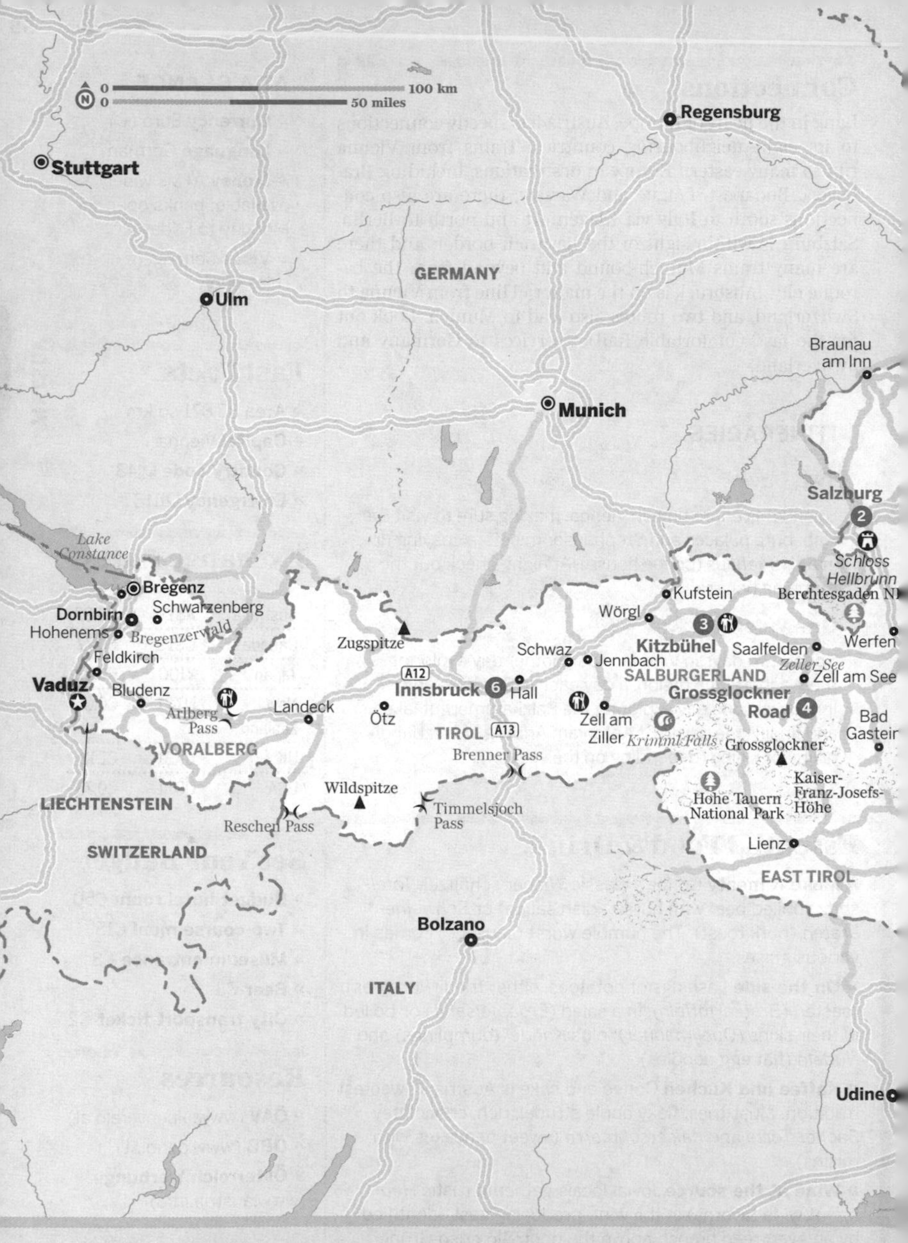

Austria Highlights

1. Discover the opulent Habsburg palaces, coffee houses and cutting-edge galleries of **Vienna** (p58)
2. Survey the baroque cityscape of **Salzburg** (p72) from the giddy height of 900-year-old Festung Hohensalzburg
3. Send your spirits soaring from peak to peak hiking and skiing in **Kitzbühel** (p81)
4. Buckle up for a rollercoaster ride of Alps and glaciers on the **Grossglockner Road** (p82), one of Austria's greatest drives

5 Dive into the crystal clear lakes of **Salzkammergut** (p77), Austria's summer playground

6 Whiz up to the Tyrolean Alps in Zaha Hadid's space-age funicular from picture-perfect **Innsbruck** (p78)

7 Explore the romantic Wachau and technology trailblazer Linz in the **Danube Valley** (p67)

VIENNA

☎01 / POP 1.72 MILLION

Few cities in the world waltz so effortlessly between the present and the past like Vienna. Its splendid historical face is easily recognised: grand imperial palaces and bombastic baroque interiors, revered opera houses and magnificent squares.

But Vienna is also one of Europe's most dynamic urban spaces. A stone's throw from Hofburg (the Imperial Palace), the MuseumsQuartier houses some of the world's most provocative contemporary art behind a striking basalt facade. In the Innere Stadt (Inner City), up-to-the-minute design stores sidle up to old-world confectioners, and Austro-Asian fusion restaurants stand alongside traditional *Beisl* (small taverns). In this Vienna, it's OK to mention poetry slam and Stephansdom in one breath.

Throw in the mass of green space within the confines of the city limits and the 'blue' Danube cutting a path east of the historical centre, and this is a capital that is distinctly Austrian.

Sights

Heading into the Innere Stadt will take you to a different age. Designated a Unesco World Heritage site, the heart of the city is blessed with a plethora of architectural wonders that hint at Vienna's long and colourful history.

FREE Hofburg PALACE

(Imperial Palace; www.hofburg-wien.at; Michaelerkuppel, 01; 1A, 2A Michaelerplatz, M Herrengasse, 1, 2, D, 71, 46, 49 Burgring) Nothing symbolises the culture and heritage of Austria more than its Hofburg, home base of the Habsburgs from 1273 to 1918. The **Kaiserappartements** (Imperial Apartments; www.hofburg-wien.at; Michaelerkuppel, 01; adult/child with audioguide €10.50/6.50, with guided tour €13/7.50; 9am-5.30pm; M Herrengasse), once occupied by Franz Josef I and Empress Elisabeth, are extraordinary for their chandelier-lit opulence.

Included in the entry price, the **Sisi Museum** is devoted to the life of Austria's beauty-obsessed Empress Elisabeth, nicknamed 'Sisi'. The **Kaiserliche Schatzkammer** (Imperial Treasury; www.kaiserliche-schatzkammer.at; Schweizerhof, 01; adult/under 19yr €12/free; 9am-5.30pm Wed-Mon) holds all manner of wonders including the 10th-century Imperial Crown, a 2860-carat Columbian emerald and even a thorn from Christ's crown.

Stephansdom CHURCH

(www.stephanskirche.at; Stephansplatz, 01; side aisle free, main nave adult/child €3.50/free; cathedral, catacombs & towers with audioguide adult plus child €16; 6am-10pm Mon-Sat, 7am-10pm Sun, main nave & Domschatz audio tours 9-11.30am & 1-5.30pm Mon-Sat, 1-5.30pm Sun; M Stephansplatz) Rising high and mighty above Vienna with its dazzling mosaic tiled roof is Stephansdom, or Steffl (little Stephen) as the Viennese call it. The cathedral was built on the site of a 12th-century church but its most distinctive features are Gothic. Only limited areas can be visited without a ticket. Entry is free for worshippers.

A magnificent 16th-century Gothic stone pulpit and baroque high altar take centre stage inside. Negotiating 343 steps brings you to a viewing platform for a stunning panorama of Vienna from the 136.7m-high **Südturm** (adult/child €3.50/1; 9am-5.30pm). You can also explore the cathedral's **Katakomben** (tours adult/child €5/2.50; 10-11.30am & 1.30-4.30pm Mon-Sat, 1.30-4.30pm Sun), housing the remains of plague victims, and urns containing some of the organs of Habsburg rulers.

Albertina GALLERY

(www.albertina.at; Albertinaplatz 3, 01; adult/child €11/free; 10am-6pm Thu-Tue, 10am-9pm Wed; M Karlsplatz, Stephansplatz, D, 1, 2, 71 Kärntner Ring/Oper) Simply reading the highlights should have any art fan lining up for entry into this gallery. Among its enormous collection (1.5 million prints and 50,000 drawings) are 70 Rembrandts, 145 Dürers (including the famous *Hare*) and 43 Raphaels, as well as works by da Vinci, Michelangelo, Rubens, Cézanne, Picasso, Klimt and Kokoschka.

MORE FOR YOUR MONEY

The **Wien-Karte** (Vienna Card; €19.90) gives you 72 hours of unlimited travel plus discounts at selected museums, attractions, cafes and shops. It's available from hotels and ticket offices.

The City of Vienna runs some 20 **municipal museums** (www.museum.vienna.at), which are included in a free booklet available at the Rathaus. Permanent exhibitions in all are free on the first Sunday of the month.

Schloss Schönbrunn PALACE, MUSEUM
(www.schoenbrunn.at; Schönbrunner Schlossstrasse 47, 13; Imperial Tour with audioguide adult/child €10.50/7.50, gardens admission free, maze adult/child €3.50/2.20; ⊙8.30am-5.30pm, gardens 6am-dusk, maze 9am-6pm) The Habsburgs' overwhelmingly opulent summer palace is now a Unesco World Heritage site. Of the palace's 1441 rooms, 40 are open to the public; the Imperial Tour takes you into 26 of these. Fountains dance in the French-style formal gardens.

The gardens harbour the world's oldest zoo, the **Tiergarten** (www.zoovienna.at; adult/child €15/7; ⊙9am 6.30pm), founded in 1752; a 630m-long hedge **maze**; and the **Gloriette**, whose roof offers a wonderful view over the palace grounds and beyond. Take U4 to Schönbrunn.

Kaisergruft CHURCH
(Imperial Burial Vault; www.kaisergruft.at; Neuer Markt, 01; adult/child €5/2; ⊙10am-6pm; MStephansplatz, Karlsplatz, D, 1, 2, 71 Kärntner Ring/Oper) Beneath the Kapuzinerkirche (Church of the Capuchin Friars), the high-peaked Kaisergruft is the final resting place of most of the Habsburg elite, including Empress Elisabeth.

Kunsthistorisches Museum MUSEUM
(Museum of Fine Arts; www.khm.at; Maria Theresien-Platz, 01; adult/under 19yr €14/free; ⊙10am-6pm Tue-Sun, to 9pm Thu; MMuseumsquartier, Volkstheater) When it comes to classical works of art, nothing comes close to the Kunsthistorisches Museum. It houses a huge range of art amassed by the Habsburgs and includes works by Rubens, Van Dyck, Holbein and Caravaggio.

MuseumsQuartier MUSEUM COMPLEX
(Museum Quarter; www.mqw.at; Museumsplatz, 07; combined ticket €25; ⊙information & ticket centre 10am-7pm; MMuseumsquartier) Occupying the former imperial stables, this remarkable ensemble of museums, cafes, restaurants and bars is one of the world's most ambitious cultural spaces.

The highpoint is undoubtedly the **Leopold Museum** (www.leopoldmuseum.org; Museumsplatz 1, 07; adult/child/family €12/7/25; ⊙10am-6pm Wed-Mon, to 9pm Thu, free guided tour 3pm Sun; MMuseumsquartier, Volkstheater), which showcases the world's largest collection of Egon Schiele paintings, alongside some fine Klimts and Kokoschkas.

The dark basalt **MUMOK** (Museum of Modern Art; www.mumok.at; Museumsplatz 1, 07; adult/child €10/free; ⊙2-7pm Mon, 10am-7pm Tue-Sun, to 9pm Thu, free guided tour 2pm Sat & Sun, 7pm Thu; MMuseumsquartier, Volkstheater, 49 Volkstheater) contains Vienna's premier collection of 20th-century art.

Schloss Belvedere PALACE, GALLERY
(www.belvedere.at; combined ticket adult/child €16/free; D) Belvedere is a masterpiece of total art and one of the world's finest baroque palaces, designed by Johann Lukas von Hildebrandt (1668–1745).

The first of the palace's two main buildings is the **Oberes Belvedere** (Upper Belvedere; 03, Prinz-Eugen-Strasse 27; adult/child €11/free; ⊙10am-6pm; D), showcasing Gustav Klimt's *The Kiss* (1908), which perfectly embodies Viennese art nouveau, accompanied by other late-19th- to early-20th-century Austrian works.

The lavishly baroque **Unteres Belvedere** (Lower Belvedere; Rennweg 6, 03; adult/child €11/free; ⊙10am-6pm Thu-Tue, to 9pm Wed; D) shelters state apartments such as the richly frescoed Marmorsaal (Marble Hall). The buildings sit at opposite ends of a manicured garden.

Prater PARK
(www.wiener-prater.at; MPraterstern) This large park encompasses meadows, woodlands, an amusement park and one of the city's icons, the **Riesenrad** (www.wienerriesenrad.com; Prater 90, 02; adult/child €9/4; ⊙9am-11.45pm, shorter hrs in winter). Built in 1897, this 65m-high Ferris wheel of *The Third Man* fame affords far-reaching views of Vienna. Take U1 to Praterstern.

Secession LANDMARK, GALLERY
(www.secession.at; Friedrichstrasse 12, 01; adult/child €8.50/5, audioguide €3; ⊙10am-6pm Tue-Sun; MKarlsplatz) This popular art nouveau 'temple of art', with an intricately woven gilt dome, contains the 34m-long *Beethoven Frieze* by Klimt.

Haus der Musik MUSEUM
(513-48 50; www.hdm.at; Seilerstätte 30, 01; adult/child €12/5.50, with Mozarthaus €17/7; ⊙10am-10pm; MKarlsplatz, D, 1, 2 Kärntner Ring/Oper) A fun, interactive museum that journeys through music; best of all is the room where you can virtually conduct the Vienna Philharmonic.

Pestsäule MEMORIAL
(Plague Column; Graben, 01) Graben is dominated by the knobbly outline of this memorial, designed by Fischer von Erlach in 1693

Central Vienna

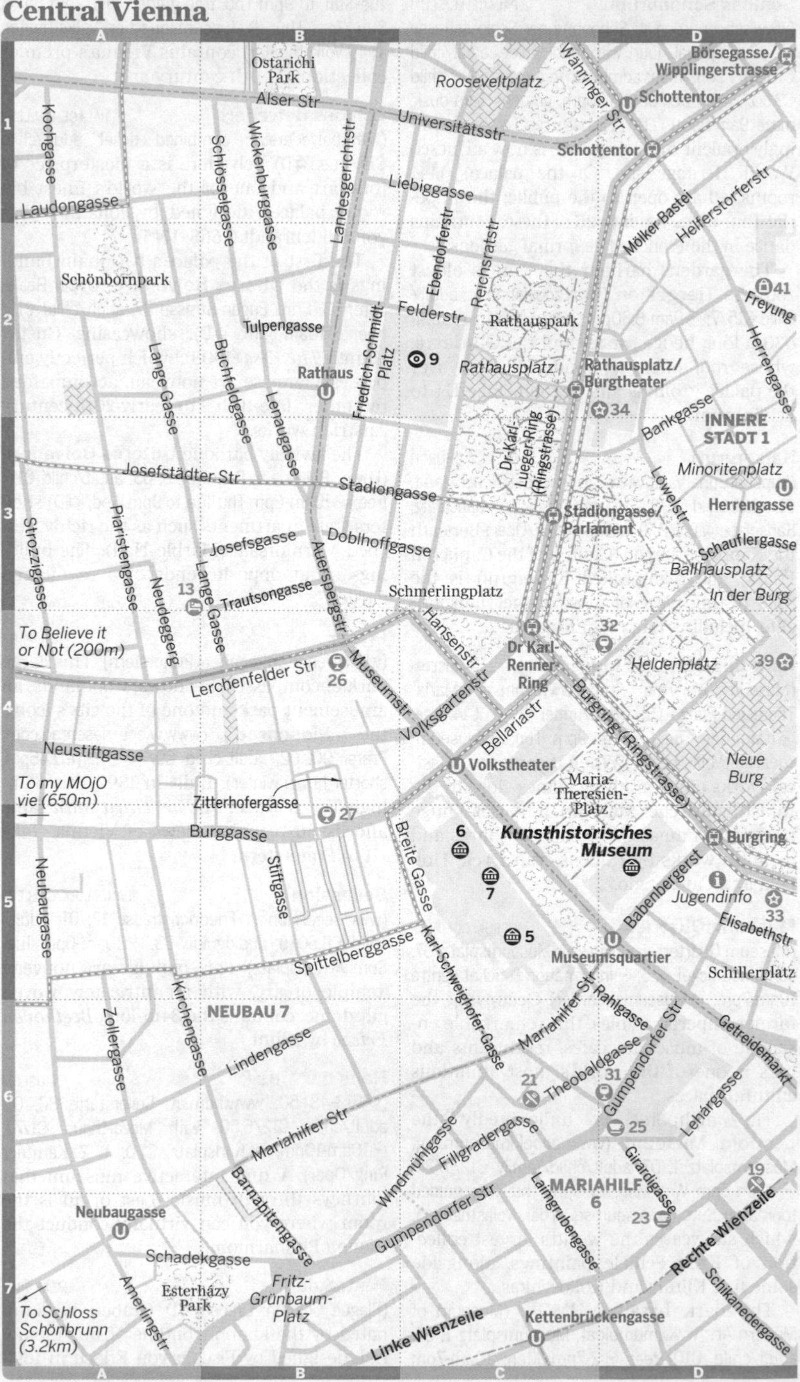

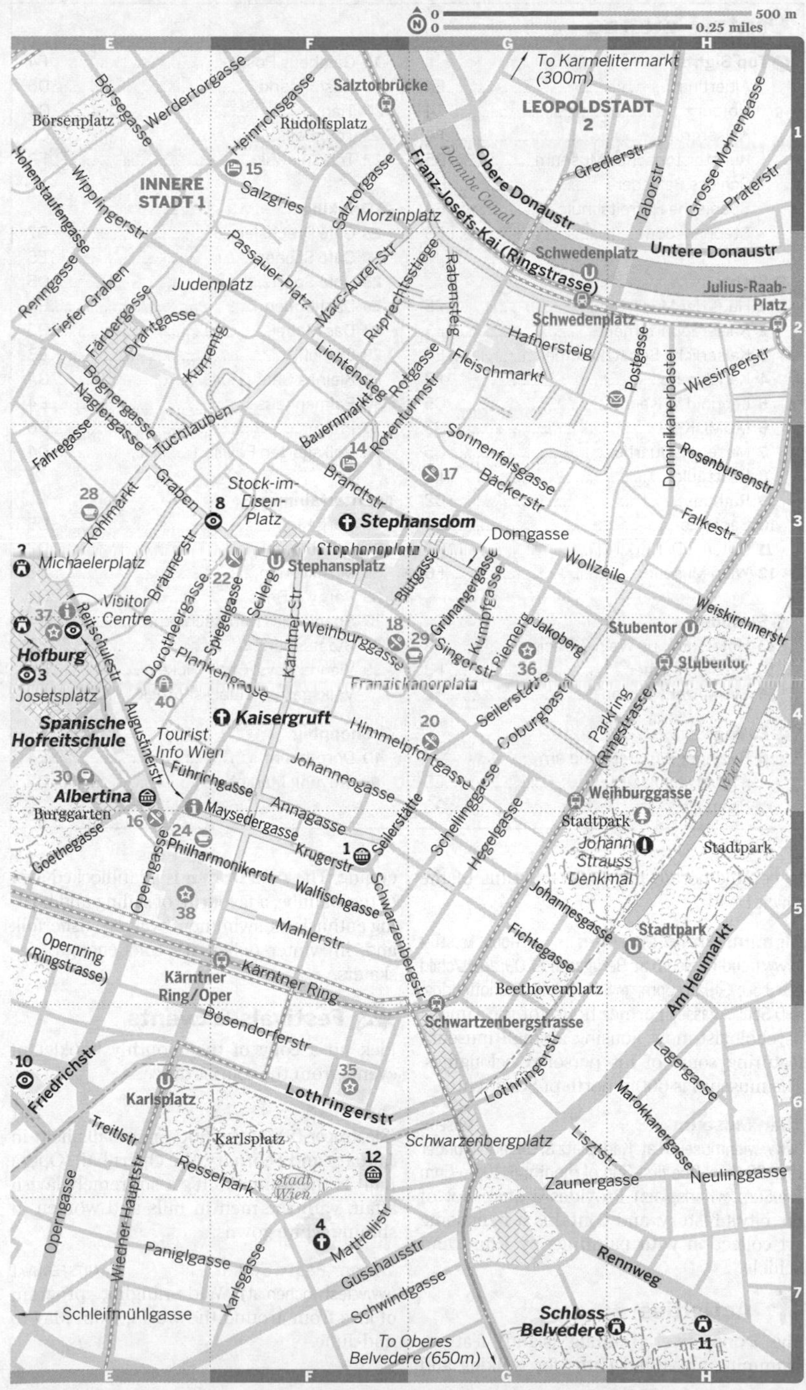

0 500 m
0 0.25 miles
To Karmelitermarkt (300m)
LEOPOLDSTADT 2
INNERE STADT 1
Salztorbrücke
Rudolfsplatz
Börsenplatz
Börsegasse
Werdertorgasse
Heinrichsgasse
Hohenstaufengasse
Wipplingerstr
Salzgries
Salztorgasse
Morzinplatz
Danube Canal
Obere Donaustr
Franz-Josefs-Kai (Ringstrasse)
Gredlerstr
Taborstr
Grosse Mohrengasse
Praterstr
Untere Donaustr
Schwedenplatz
Julius-Raab-Platz
Renngasse
Tiefer Graben
Judenplatz
Passauer Platz
Marc-Aurel-Str
Ruprechtsstiege
Rabensteig
Färbergasse
Drahtgasse
Kurrentg
Lichtensteg
Rotgasse
Fleischmarkt
Hafnersteig
Postgasse
Dominikanerbastei
Wiesingerstr
Bognergasse
Naglergasse
Tuchlauben
Bauernmarkt
Rotenturmstr
Sonnenfelsgasse
Rosenbursenstr
Fahregasse
Kohlmarkt
Graben
Stock-im-Eisen-Platz
Brandstr
Bäckerstr
Falkestr
Stephansdom
Domgasse
Stephansplatz
Michaelerplatz
Bräunerstr
Seilerg
Kärntner Str
Blutgasse
Grünangergasse
Kumpfgasse
Wollzeile
Weiskirchnerstr
Visitor Centre
Reitschulestr
Dorotheergasse
Spiegelgasse
Weihburggasse
Singerstr
Piemerg
Jakoberg
Stubentor
Hofburg
Josefsplatz
Plankengasse
Franziskanerplatz
Seilerstätte
Coburgbastei
Parkring (Ringstrasse)
Spanische Hofreitschule
Kaisergruft
Augustinerstr
Tourist Info Wien
Himmelpfortgasse
Führichgasse
Johannesgasse
Schellinggasse
Albertina
Burggarten
Maysedergasse
Annagasse
Weihburggasse
Stadtpark
Johann Strauss Denkmal
Goethegasse
Operngasse
Philharmonikerstr
Krugerstr
Seilerstätte
Hegelgasse
Walfischgasse
Schwarzenbergstr
Johannesgasse
Mahlerstr
Fichtegasse
Am Heumarkt
Opernring (Ringstrasse)
Kärntner Ring
Kärntner Ring/Oper
Beethovenplatz
Bösendorferstr
Schwartzenbergstrasse
Lagergasse
Friedrichstr
Karlsplatz
Lothringerstr
Marokkanergasse
Treitlstr
Schwarzenbergplatz
Lisztstr
Resselpark
Stadt Wien
Zaunergasse
Neulinggasse
Operngasse
Wiedner Hauptstr
Paniglgasse
Mattiellistr
Gusshausstr
Rennweg
Karlsgasse
Schwindgasse
Schleifmühlgasse
Schloss Belvedere
To Oberes Belvedere (650m)
AUSTRIA VIENNA

Central Vienna

Top Sights

Albertina ... E4
Hofburg ... E4
Kaisergruft ... F4
Kunsthistorisches Museum ... D5
Schloss Belvedere ... H7
Spanische Hofreitschule ... E4
Stephansdom ... F3

Sights

1 Haus der Musik ... F5
2 Kaiserappartements ... E3
3 Kaiserliche Schatzkammer ... E4
4 Karlskirche ... F7
5 Leopold Museum ... C5
6 MUMOK ... C5
7 MuseumsQuartier ... C5
8 Pestsäule ... F3
9 Rathaus ... C2
10 Secession ... E6
11 Unteres Belvedere ... H7
12 Wien Museum ... F6

Sleeping

13 Hotel Rathaus Wein & Design ... A3
14 Pension Sacher ... F3
15 Schweizer Pension ... F1

Eating

16 Bitzinger Würstelstand am Albertinaplatz ... E5
17 Figlmüller ... G3
18 Gasthaus Pöschl ... F4
19 Naschmarkt ... D6
20 Tian ... G4
21 Tongues ... C6
22 Trzesniewski ... F3

Drinking

23 Café Drechsler ... D7
24 Café Sacher ... E5
25 Café Sperl ... D6
26 Dachboden ... B4
27 Das Möbel ... B5
28 Demel ... E3
29 Kleines Café ... G4
30 Palmenhaus ... E4
31 Phil ... D6
32 Volksgarten Pavillon ... D4

Entertainment

33 Burg Kino ... D5
34 Burgtheater ... D2
35 Musikverein ... F6
36 Porgy & Bess ... G4
37 Spanische Hofreitschule ... E4
38 Staatsoper ... E5
39 Vienna Boys' Choir Tickets ... D4
Volksgarten ClubDiskothek ... (see 32)

Shopping

40 Dorotheum ... E4
41 Freyung Market ... D2

to commemorate the 75,000 victims of the Black Death.

Sigmund Freud Museum HOUSE MUSEUM
(www.freud-museum.at; Berggasse 19, 09; adult/child €8/3.50; 9am-6pm; Schottentor, Schottenring, D Schlickgasse) Former house of the famous psychologist, now housing a small museum featuring some of his personal belongings. The museum is 600m north of Schottentor.

Wien Museum MUSEUM
(www.wienmuseum.at; Karlsplatz 8, 04; adult/under 19yr €8/free, free first Sun of month; 10am-6pm Tue-Sun; Karlsplatz) Provides a snapshot of the city's history, and contains a handsome art collection with paintings by Klimt and Schiele.

Activities

The **Donauinsel** (Danube Island) features swimming areas and paths for walking and cycling. The **Alte Donau** is a landlocked arm of the Danube, a favourite of sailing and boating enthusiasts, swimmers, walkers, fisherfolk and, in winter (when it's cold enough), ice skaters.

Festivals & Events

Pick up a copy of the monthly booklet of events from the tourist office.

Opernball BALL
(Staatsoper, 01) Of the 300 or so balls held in January and February, the Opernball (Opera Ball) is the ultimate. It's a supremely lavish affair, with the men in tails and women in shining white gowns.

Wiener Festwochen ARTS FESTIVAL
(www.festwochen.at) Wide-ranging program of arts from around the world, from May to mid-June.

Donauinselfest MUSIC FESTIVAL
(https://donauinselfest.at) Free three-day festival of rock, pop, hardcore, folk and country music on the Donauinsel in June.

Musikfilm Festival FILM FESTIVAL
(Rathausplatz, 01) Screenings of operas, operettas and concerts outside the Rathaus in July and August.

Viennale Film Festival FILM FESTIVAL
(☎0152-65 947; www.viennale.at) The country's biggest and best film festival, featuring fringe and independent films from around the world in October.

Christkindlmärkt CHRISTMAS MARKET
(www.christkindlmarkt.at) Vienna's much-loved Christmas market season runs from mid-November to Christmas Eve.

Sleeping

my MOjO vie HOSTEL €
(☎0676-551 11 55; http://mymojovie.at; Kaiserstrasse 77, 07; dm/d/tr/q €26/58/84/108; @; MBurggasse) An old-fashioned cage lift rattles up to these incredible backpacker digs. Everything you could wish for is here: design-focused dorms, a kitchen with free supplies, netbooks for surfing, books for browsing, even musical instruments for your own jam session. Tram 5 stops close by.

Pension Sacher PENSION €€
(☎0533-32 38; www.pension-sacher.at; 01, Rothenturmstrasse 1; apt €90-136;) Filled with chintzy knick-knacks, florals and solid wood furnishings, these super-central, spacious apartments are lovingly kept by the Sacher family of chocolate cake fame. The views of Stephansdom are phenomenal.

Believe It Or Not HOSTEL €
(☎0676-550 00 55; www.believe-it-or-not-vienna.at; Myrthengasse 10, 07; dm €25-30; @; MVolkstheater) It may look nondescript, but you really won't believe what a cosy, homely hostel this is. We love the dorms with mezzanine-style beds, laid-back lounge, kitchen with free basics, and laptops for guest use.

Pension Kraml PENSION €
(☎0587-85 88; www.pensionkraml.at; Brauergasse 5, 06; s €35, d €56-76, tr €78-87, q €120; @; MZieglergasse) A quiet and cosy family-run pension, where old-school politeness and comfort are paramount. Rooms are large (if a little dated).

Hotel Rathaus Wein & Design BOUTIQUE HOTEL €€
(☎0400-11 22; www.hotel-rathaus-wien.at; Lange Gasse 13, 08; s/d/tr €150/210/240; @; MRathaus, Volkstheater) Each of the open-plan, minimalist-chic rooms at this boutique hotel is dedicated to an Austrian winemaker. The chandelier-lit wine bar zooms in on a different winery every month.

Schweizer Pension PENSION €
(☎0533-81 56; www.schweizerpension.com; Heinrichsgasse 2, 01, s €56-75, d €75-98; MSchottentor, 1 Salztorbrücke) This small, family-run pension is a superb deal, with homely touches and eco credentials. Book in advance, though, as it has only 11 rooms and is popular among those on squeezed budgets.

Boutiquehotel Stadthalle HOTEL €€
(☎0982-42 72, www.hotelstadthalle.at; Hackengasse 20, 15; s €78-138, d €118-198; ; MSchweglerstrasse) Vienna's most sustainable hotel has a lavender-clad rooftop, organic breakfasts and rooms that blend modern with polished antiques. Arrive by bike or train for a 10% discount. The hotel is 650m northwest of Westbahnhof.

Eating

Self-caterers can stock up at central Hofer, Billa and Spar supermarkets. Some have delis that make sandwiches to order.

SPIN OF THE RING

One of the best deals in Vienna is a self-guided tour on tram 1 or 2 of the monumental Ringstrasse boulevard encircling much of the Innere Stadt. For the price of a single ticket you'll take in the neo-Gothic **Rathaus** (City Hall; ☎525 50; www.wien.gv.at; Rathausplatz 1, 01; guided tours 1pm Mon, Wed & Fri; MRathaus, 1, 2, D Rathaus), the Greek Revival–style parliament, the 19th-century **Burgtheater** (National Theatre; ☎514 44 4440; www.burgtheater.at; Universitätsring 2, 01; box office 9am-5pm Mon-Fri; MRathaus, 1, 2, D Rathausplatz) and the baroque **Karlskirche** (St Charles' Church; www.karlskirche.at; Karlsplatz; adult/child €8/4, audioguide €2; 9am-5.30pm Mon-Sat, 11.30am-5.30pm Sun; MKarlsplatz), among other sights.

Würstelstande (sausage stands) are great for a cheap bite on the run.

Mill AUSTRIAN €€

(0966-40 73; www.mill32.at; Millergasse 32, 06; mains €8-17.50; 11.30am-3pm & 5pm-midnight Mon-Fri, 11am-4pm Sun; Westbahnhof) This art-slung bistro, with a hidden courtyard for summer days, creates an inviting backdrop for spot-on seasonal food like chanterelle cannelloni and Styrian chicken salad drizzled with pumpkin seed oil. The two-course lunch is a snip at €6.90. Mill is 400m south of the U3 Westbahnhof station on Mariahilfer Strasse.

Tian VEGETARIAN €€

(0890-46 65; www.tian-vienna.com; Himmelpfortgasse 23, 01; 3-course lunch €12.50-16, 3-6-course evening menu €39-69, mains €18; noon-4pm, 6pm-midnight Mon-Fri, from 9am Sat; ; Stephansplatz, 2 Weihburggasse) Vaulted charm meets urban attitude at this sleek lounge-style restaurant which takes vegetarian cuisine to delicious heights. Lunch menus offer the best value; you can also enjoy a drink at the cocktail bar.

Gasthaus Pöschl AUSTRIAN €€

(0513-52 88; 01, Weihburggasse 17; mains €9-18; lunch & dinner) Close to pretty Franziskanerplatz, this small, wood-panelled *Beisl* brims with Viennese warmth and bonhomie. Austrian classics like *Tafelspitz* (boiled beef) and schnitzel are cooked to a T.

DON'T MISS

FOOD MARKET FINDS

The sprawling **Naschmarkt** (Linke & Rechte Wienzeile, 06; 6am-7.30pm Mon-Fri, to 6pm Sat; Karlsplatz, Kettenbrückengasse) is the place to *nasch* (snack) in Vienna. Stalls are piled high with meats, fruits, vegetables, cheeses, olives, spices and wine. There are also plenty of cafes dishing up good-value lunches, along with delis and takeaway stands.

Freyung Market (Freyung, 01; 9am-6pm Fri & Sat; Herrengasse, Schottentor) sells farm-fresh produce, as does the bustling **Karmelitermarkt** (Karmelitermarkt, 02; 6am-7.30pm Mon-Fri, 6am-5pm Sat; Taborstrasse, 2 Karmeliterplatz). Head to the Saturday farmers market at the latter for brunch at one of the excellent deli-cafes.

Tongues DELI €

(www.tongues.at; Theobaldgasse 16, 06; lunch mains €3.60; 11am-8pm Mon-Fri, 11am-6pm Sat; ; Museumsquartier) DJs can sometimes be found on the decks at this record shop and deli. Pop in for a healthy lunch or some locally sourced cheese, salami, honey and wood-oven bread.

Trzesniewski SANDWICHES €

(Dorotheergasse 1, 01; bread & spread €1.10, glass of wine €2.10; 8.30am-7.30pm Mon-Fri, 9am-5pm Sat; Stephansplatz) Possibly Austria's finest open-sandwich shop, with delectably thick spreads, from tuna with egg to Swedish herring. Plan on sampling a few; two bites and they're gone.

Figlmüller BISTRO PUB €€

(0512-61 77; www.figlmueller.at; 01, Wollzeile 5; mains €12.90-22.90; 11am-10.30pm, kitchen closes 9.30pm; ; Stephansplatz) This famous *Beisl* has been sizzling up some of the biggest (and best) schnitzels in town since 1905. Sure, the rural decor is contrived, but it doesn't get more Viennese than this.

Bitzinger Würstelstand am Albertinaplatz SAUSAGE STAND €

(Albertinaplatz, 01; sausages €3.70-4.10; 9.30-5am, drinks from 8am; Kärntner Ring/Oper) Located behind the Staatsoper, this is one of Vienna's best sausage stands.

Drinking

Pulsating bars cluster north and south of the Naschmarkt, around Spittelberg and along the Gürtel (mainly around the U6 stops of Josefstädter Strasse and Nussdorfer Strasse).

Vienna's *Heurigen*, or wine taverns, cluster in the wine-growing suburbs to the north, southwest, west and northwest of the city. Opening times are approximately from 4pm to 11pm, and wine costs around €3 per *Viertel* (250mL).

Palmenhaus BAR, CAFE

(www.palmenhaus.at; Burggarten, 01; 10am-2am; 1, 2, D, 71 Burgring) Housed in a beautifully restored Jugendstil palm house, the Palmenhaus has a relaxed vibe. In summer, tables spill out onto the terrace overlooking the Burggarten, and DJs spin here on Friday nights.

Phil BAR, CAFE

(www.phil.info; Gumpendorfer Strasse 10-12, 06; 5pm-1am Mon, 9am-1am Tue-Sun; Museumsquartier, Kettenbrückengasse) A retro bar, book

DON'T MISS

COFFEE HOUSE CULTURE

Vienna's legendary *Kaffeehäuser* (coffee houses) are wonderful places for people-watching, daydreaming, chatting and browsing the news. Most serve light meals alongside mouth-watering cakes and tortes. Expect to pay around €8 for a coffee with a slice of cake. Here are five favourites:

Café Sperl (www.cafesperl.at; Gumpendorfer Strasse 11, 06; 7am-11pm Mon-Sat, 11am-8pm Sun; ; M Museumsquartier, Kettenbrückengasse) Gorgeous Jugendstil fittings, grand dimensions, cosy booths and an unhurried air. The must-try is *Sperl Torte* – an almond and chocolate cream dream.

Kleines Café (Franziskanerplatz 3, 01; 10am-2am Mon-Sat, 1pm-2am Sun; M Stubentor, 2 Weihburggasse) Tiny bohemian cafe with wonderful summer seating on Franziskanerplatz.

Café Sacher (Philharmonikerstrasse 4, 01; 8am-midnight) This opulent coffee house is celebrated for its *Sacher Torte* (€4.90), a rich chocolate cake with apricot jam once favoured by Emperor Franz Josef.

Demel (Kohlmarkt 14, 01; 9am-7pm; 1A, 2A Michaelerplatz, M Herrengasse, Stephansplatz) An elegant, regal cafe near the Hofburg. Demel's speciality is the *Anna Torte*, a chocolate and nougat calorie-bomb.

Café Drechsler (www.cafedrechsler.at; Linke Wienzeile 22; open 23hr, closed 2-3am; ; M Kettenbrückengasse) Sir Terence Conran revamped this stylish yet distinctly Viennese cafe. Its goulash is legendary, as are the DJ tunes.

and record store, Phil attracts a bohemian crowd happy to squat on kitsch furniture your grandma used to own. The vibe is as relaxed as can be.

Volksgarten Pavillon BAR
(www.volksgarten-pavillon.at; Burgring 1, 01; 11am-2am Apr–mid-Sep; ; M Volkstheater, 1, 2, D, 71 Dr-Karl-Renner-Ring) A lovely 1950s-style pavilion with views of Heldenplatz and an ever-popular garden.

Das Möbel BAR, CAFE
(http://dasmoebel.at; Burggasse 10, 07; 10am-midnight; ; M Volkstheater) This bar near the MuseumsQuartier is remarkable for its funky decor and furniture – cube stools, assorted moulded lamps – and everything is up for sale.

Dachboden BAR
(http://25hours-hotels.com; 25hours Hotel, Lerchenfelder Strasse 1-3, 07; 2pm-1am Tue-Sat, to 10pm Sun; ; M Volkstheater) The terrace with knockout views of Vienna is the big deal at this arty attic bar, with low cushion seating and the occasional DJ night.

TOP CHOICE **Strandbar Herrmann** BAR
(www.strandbarherrmann.at; Herrmannpark, 03; 10am-2am Apr-early Oct; ; M Schwedenplatz, Hintere Zollamtsstrasse) You'd swear you're by the sea at this hopping canalside beach bar, with beach chairs, sand and hordes of Viennese livin' it up on hot summer evenings.

☆ Entertainment

Vienna is, and probably will be till the end of time, the European capital of opera and classical music. The line-up of music events is never-ending and even the city's buskers are often classically trained musicians.

Box offices generally open from Monday to Saturday and sell cheap (€3 to €6) standing-room tickets around an hour before performances.

For up-to-date listings, visit www.falter.at (in German).

Staatsoper OPERA
(0514-447 880; www.wiener-staatsoper.at; Opernring 2, 01; M Karlsplatz, 1, 2, D Oper) Performances at Vienna's premier opera and classical music venue are lavish, formal affairs, where people dress up.

Musikverein CONCERT VENUE
(0505-81 90; www.musikverein.at; Bösendorferstrasse 12, 01; M Karlsplatz) The opulent Musikverein, home to the Vienna Philharmonic Orchestra, is celebrated for its acoustics.

Pratersauna CLUB
(www.pratersauna.tv; Waldsteingartenstrasse 135, 02; club 9pm-6am Wed-Sun, pool 1-9pm Fri & Sat

Jun-Sep; Ⓜ Messe-Prater) Pool, cafe, bistro and club converge in a former sauna. Sweat it up on the dance floor, with DJs playing mostly techno and electro. Take U2 to Messe-Prater and walk south 600m.

Porgy & Bess JAZZ
(☎0512-88 11; www.porgy.at; Riemergasse 11, 01; €18 most nights; ⊙concerts from 7pm or 8pm; Ⓜ Stubentor, 🚋2) Presents a top-drawer line-up of modern jazz acts, and DJs fill spots on weekends.

Volksgarten ClubDiskothek CLUB
(www.volksgarten.at; Burgring 1, 01; admission from €6; ⊙10pm-4am or later Tue & Thu-Sat; Ⓜ Museumsquartier, Volkstheater, 🚋1, 2, D, 71 Dr-Karl-Renner-Ring) This club attracts a well-dressed crowd, keen to strut their stuff and scan for talent from the long bar. The quality sound system pumps out an array of music styles.

Burg Kino CINEMA
(☎0587-84 06; www.burgkino.at; Opernring 19, 01; Ⓜ Museumsquartier, 🚋1, 2, D) English films; has regular screenings of *The Third Man*.

Shopping

In the alley-woven Innere Stadt, go to Kohlmarkt for designer chic, Herrengasse for antiques and Kärntnerstrasse for high-street brands. Tune into Vienna's creative pulse in the idiosyncratic boutiques and concept stores in Neubau, especially along Kirchengasse and Lindengasse.

Stop by and simply browse at the **Dorotheum** (www.dorotheum.com; Dorotheergasse 17, 01; ⊙10am-6pm Mon-Fri, 9am-5pm Sat; Ⓜ Stephansplatz), one of Europe's largest auction houses – it's as entertaining as visiting many of Vienna's museums.

IMPERIAL ENTERTAINMENT

The world-famous **Vienna Boys' Choir** (www.wsk.at) performs on Sunday at 9.15am (September to June) in the Burgkapelle (Royal Chapel) in the Hofburg. **Tickets** (☎0533-99 27; www.hofburgkapelle.at; Schweizerhof, 01; Sunday in Burgkapelle €5-29) should be booked around six weeks in advance. The group also performs regularly in the Musikverein.

Another throwback to the Habsburg glory days is the **Spanische Hofreitschule,** (Spanish Riding School; ☎0533-90 31; www.srs.at; Michaelerplatz 1, 01; ⊙performances 11am Sat & Sun mid-Feb–Jun & late Aug-Dec) where Lipizzaner stallions gracefully perform equine ballet to classical music. For **Morning Training** (adult/child/family €14/7/28; ⊙10am-noon Tue-Fri Feb-Jun & mid-Aug–Dec) sessions, same-day tickets are available at the **visitor centre** (⊙9am-4pm Tue-Sun) on Michaelerplatz.

Information

Many cafes and bars offer free wi-fi for their customers. Free public hotspots include Rathausplatz, Naschmarkt and Prater.

Airport Information Office (⊙6am-11pm) Located in the arrivals hall.

Allgemeines Krankenhaus (☎404 000; www.akhwien.at; Währinger Gürtel 18-20, 09) Hospital with a 24-hour casualty ward.

Jugendinfo (Vienna Youth Information; ☎4000-84 100; www.jugendinfowien.at; Babenbergerstrasse 1, 01; ⊙2-7pm Mon-Wed, 1-6pm Thu-Sat) Offers various reduced-price tickets for 13 to 26 year olds.

Lonely Planet (www.lonelyplanet.com/austria/vienna)

Main Post Office (Fleischmarkt 19, 01; ⊙7am-10pm Mon-Fri, 9am-10pm Sat & Sun)

Police Station (☎31 310; 01, Schottenring 7-9)

Tourist Info Wien (☎245 55; www.wien.info; Albertinaplatz, 01; ⊙9am-7pm; 📶; Ⓜ Stephansplatz, 🚋1, 2, D, 71 Kärntner Ring/Oper) Vienna's main tourist office, with a ticket agency, hotel booking service, free maps and every brochure you could ever wish for.

Getting There & Away

Air

For details on flying to Vienna, see p86.

Boat

Fast hydrofoils travel eastwards to Bratislava (one way €19 to €33, 1¼ hours) daily from April to October. From May to September, they also travel twice weekly to Budapest (one way/return €109/125, 5½ hours). Bookings can be made through **DDSG Blue Danube** (☎58 880; www.ddsg-blue-danube.at; Handelskai 265).

Bus

Vienna currently has no central bus station. National Bundesbuses arrive and depart from several different locations, depending on the destination. Bus lines serving Vienna include **Eurolines** (☎0798-29 00; www.eurolines.com; Erdbergstrasse 200; ⊙6.30am-9pm).

Car & Motorcycle

The Gürtel is an outer ring road that joins up with the A22 on the north bank of the Danube and the A23 southeast of town. All the main road routes intersect with this system, including the A1 from Linz and Salzburg, and the A2 from Graz.

Train

Vienna is one of central Europe's main rail hubs. **Österreichische Bundesbahn** (Austrian Federal Railway, ÖBB; www.oebb.at) is the main operator. There are direct services and connections to many European cities. Sample destinations include Budapest (€37.40, 2½ to three hours), Munich (€88, four to five hours), Paris (€88, 11½ to 15 hours), Prague (€64.40, 4½ hours) and Venice (€63 to €99, seven to 11 hours). Vienna's main station is the Hauptbahnhof, formerly the Südbahnhof. Following a massive construction project, it became partially operational in December 2012 and is set for completion in 2015. In the meantime, some long-distance trains are being rerouted among the rest of Vienna's train stations, including the Westbahnhof and Wien Meidling. Further train stations include Franz-Josefs-Bahnhof (which handles trains to/from the Danube Valley), Wien Mitte and Wien Nord.

Getting Around

Bicycle

Vienna's city bike scheme is called **Vienna City Bike** (www.citybikewien.at; 1st hr free, 2nd/3rd hr €1/2, per hr thereafter €4), with more than 60 bicycle stands across the city. A credit card is required to rent bikes – just swipe your card in the machine and follow the instructions (in a number of languages).

Public Transport

Vienna's unified public transport network encompasses trains, trams, buses, and underground (U-Bahn) and suburban (S-Bahn) trains. Free maps and information pamphlets are available from **Wiener Linien** (☎0790-91 00; www.wienerlinien.at).

All tickets must be validated at the entrance to U-Bahn stations and on buses and trams (except for weekly and monthly tickets). Singles cost €2 from ticket machines, or €2.20 on board.

A 24-hour ticket costs €6.70, a 48-hour ticket €11.70 and a 72-hour ticket €14.50. Weekly tickets (valid Monday to Sunday) cost €15.

GETTING INTO TOWN

The fastest transport into the centre is **City Airport Train** (CAT; www.cityairporttrain.com; return adult/child under 15 yrs €19/free; ⏲5.36am-11.06pm from airport), which runs every 30 minutes and takes 16 minutes between the airport and Wien Mitte; book online for a €2 discount. The S-Bahn (S7) does the same journey (single €4) but in 25 minutes.

THE DANUBE VALLEY

The stretch of Danube between Krems and Melk, known locally as the Wachau, is arguably the loveliest along the entire length of the mighty river. Both banks are dotted with ruined castles and medieval towns, and lined with terraced vineyards. Further upstream is the industrial city of Linz, Austria's avant-garde art and new technology trailblazer.

Krems an der Donau

☎02732 / POP 24,110

Sitting on the northern bank of the Danube against a backdrop of terraced vineyards, Krems marks the beginning of the Wachau. It has an attractive cobbled centre, some good restaurants and the gallery-dotted Kunstmeile (Art Mile).

Sights & Activities

Kunsthalle GALLERY

(www.kunsthalle.at; Franz-Zeller-Platz 3; adult/concessions €10/9; ⏲10am-6pm) The flagship of Krems' **Kunstmeile** (www.kunstmeile-krems.at), the Kunsthalle has a program of small but excellent changing exhibitions.

Sleeping

Arte Hotel Krems HOTEL €€

(☎71 123; www.arte-hotel.at; Dr-Karl-Dorrek-Strasse 23; s €85-105, d €128-162; P 📶) This comfortable new art hotel close to the university has large, well-styled rooms in bright colours and with open-plan bathrooms.

Hotel Unter den Linden HOTEL €€

(☎82 115; www.udl.at; Schillerstrasse 5; s €50, d €74-98) This big, yellow, family-run hotel has knowledgeable and helpful owners, bright comfortable rooms and a convenient location in Krems itself.

Information

Krems Tourismus (☎82 676; www.krems.info; Utzstrasse 1; ⏲9am-6pm Mon-Fri) Has excellent city walk and vineyard maps, and stocks a *Heurigen* calendar.

ON YOUR BIKE

Many towns in the Danube Valley are part of a bike hire network called **Next-bike** (☎to pick up or return a bike 02742-229 901; www.nextbike.at; per hour/24 hours €1/8). After registering using a credit card (either by calling the hotline or on the website), a refunded €1 is deducted and you can begin renting bicycles.

Getting There & Away

Frequent daily trains connect Krems with Vienna's Franz-Josefs-Bahnhof (€15.20, one hour) and Melk (€11.90, 1¼ hours).

Melk

☎02752 / POP 5257

With its sparkling and majestic abbey-fortress, Melk is a highlight of any visit to the Danube Valley. Many visitors cycle here for the day – wearily pushing their bikes through the cobblestone streets.

Sights

Stift Melk ABBEY

(Benedictine Abbey of Melk; ☎5550; www.stift-melk.at; Abt Berthold Dietmayr Strasse 1; adult/child €9.50/5, with guided tour €11.50/7; 9am-5.30pm May-Sep, tours at 11am & 2pm only Oct-Apr) Rising like a vision on a hill overlooking the town, twin-spired Stift Melk is Austria's most famous abbey, home to Benedictine monks since the 11th century and redesigned in the 18th century by mastermind Jakob Prandtauer.

It's an elaborate example of baroque architecture, most often lauded for its imposing marble hall and beautiful library, but is just as unforgettable for the curved terrace connecting these two rooms.

From around November to March, the monastery can only be visited by guided tour (11am and 2pm daily). Always phone ahead to ensure you get an English-language tour.

Sleeping & Eating

Restaurants and cafes with alfresco seating line the Rathausplatz.

Hotel Restaurant zur Post HOTEL €€

(☎523 45; www.post-melk.at; Linzer Strasse 1; s €62-74, d €102-117, tr €125-145, q €150; P@) This bright hotel in the heart of town has large, comfortable rooms. There's a sauna, free bike use for guests and a decent restaurant serving Austrian classics.

Information

The centrally located **tourist office** (☎51 160; www.niederoesterreich.at/melk; Kremser Strasse 5; 9.30am-6pm Mon-Sat, 9.30am-4pm Sun) has maps and plenty of useful information.

Getting There & Away

Boats leave from the canal by Pionierstrasse, 400m north of the abbey. There are hourly trains to Vienna (€17.10, 1¼ hours).

Linz

☎0732 / POP 191,107

In Linz beginnt's (It begins in Linz) goes the Austrian saying, and it's spot on. The technology trailblazer and European Capital of Culture 2009 is blessed with a leading-edge cyber centre and world-class contemporary-art gallery.

Sights & Activities

Ars Electronica Center MUSEUM

(www.aec.at; Ars Electronica Strasse 1; adult/child €8/5; 9am-5pm Wed-Fri, to 9pm Thu, 10am-6pm Sat & Sun) This cutting-edge, shipshape museum zooms in on tomorrow's technology, science and digital media. In themed labs you can interact with robots, animate digital objects and (virtually) travel to outer space.

Lentos GALLERY

(www.lentos.at; Ernst-Koref-Promenade 1; adult/child €6.50/4.50; 10am-6pm Wed-Mon, to 9pm Thu) Across the Danube and also strikingly illuminated by night, this rectangular glass-and-steel gallery guards one of Austria's finest modern art collections.

Neuer Dom CHURCH

(New Cathedral; Herrenstrasse 26; 7.30am-7pm Mon-Sat, 8am-7pm Sun) This neo-Gothic giant of a cathedral was designed in the mid-19th century by Vinzenz Statz of Cologne Dom fame.

Pöstlingbergbahn VIEWPOINT

(adult/child €5.60/2.80; 6am-10.30pm Mon-Sat, 7.30am-10.30pm Sun) This gondola features in the *Guinness Book of Records* as the world's steepest mountain railway – quite some feat for such a low-lying city!

Sleeping & Eating

Hotel am Domplatz HOTEL €€
(☎77 30 00; www.hotelamdomplatz.at; Stifterstrasse 4; s €125-145, d €154-184; P❄@📶) Sidling up to the Neuer Dom, this glass-and-concrete design hotel reveals light, streamlined interiors. Wind down with a view at the rooftop spa.

k.u.k. Hofbäckerei CAFE €
(Pfarrgasse 17; coffee & cake €3-6; ⏲6.30am-6pm Mon-Fri, 7am-12.30pm Sat) The empire lives on at this gloriously stuck-in-time cafe. Here Fritz Rath bakes *the* best *Linzer Torte* in town – rich, spicy and with lattice pastry that crumbles just so.

Cubus FUSION €€
(Ars-Electronica-Strasse 1; mains €10.50-23.50; ⏲9am-1am Mon-Sat, 9am-6pm Sun; 📶) On the 3rd floor of the Ars Electronica Center, this glass cube has stellar Danube views. The menu is strictly fusion and the two-course lunch a snip at €7.20.

Information

Hotspot Linz (www.hotspotlinz.at) Free wi-fi at 120 hotspots in the city, including Ars Electronica Center and Lentos.

Tourist Information Linz (☎7070 2009; www.linz.at; Hauptplatz 1; ⏲9am-7pm Mon-Sat, 10am-7pm Sun, shorter hours winter) Free city maps and room reservation service.

Getting There & Around

AIR Ryanair flies to the **Blue Danube Airport** (www.linz-airport.at), 13km southwest of Linz. An hourly shuttle bus (€2.70, 20 minutes) links the airport to the main train station.

PUBLIC TRANSPORT Single bus and tram tickets cost €2, and day passes €4.

TRAIN Linz is halfway between Salzburg and Vienna on the main road and rail routes. Trains to Salzburg (€23.70, 1¼ hours) and Vienna (€34.30, 1½ hours) leave approximately twice hourly.

THE SOUTH

Austria's two main southern states, Styria (Steiermark) and Carinthia (Kärnten), often feel worlds apart from the rest of the country, both in climate and attitude. Styria is a blissful amalgamation of genteel architecture, rolling green hills, vine-covered slopes and soaring mountains. Its capital, Graz, is one of Austria's most attractive cities.

A fashion-conscious crowd heads to sun-drenched Carinthia in summer. Sidling up to Italy, the region exudes an atmosphere that's as close to Mediterranean as this staunch country gets.

Graz

☎0316 / POP 265,318

Austria's second-largest city is probably its most relaxed and, after Vienna, its liveliest for after-hours pursuits. It has bristling green parkland, red rooftops and a small, fast-flowing river gushing through its centre. Architecturally, it has Renaissance courtyards and provincial baroque palaces complemented by innovative modern designs.

The surrounding countryside, a mixture of vineyards, mountains, forested hills and thermal springs, is within easy striking distance.

Sights & Activities

Graz is a city easily enjoyed by simply wandering aimlessly. Admission to all of the major museums with a 24-hour ticket costs €11/4 for adults/children.

Neue Galerie Graz Joanneumsviertel GALLERY
(www.museum-joanneum.at; Joanneumsviertel; adult/child €8/3; ⏲10am-5pm Tue-Sun; 📶; 🚊1, 3, 4, 5, 6, 7 Hauptplatz) The crowning glory of this Styria-wide ensemble of museums and palaces is the new **Joanneumsviertel** (www.joanneumsviertel.at; Kalchberggasse ; ⏲visitor centre 10am-5pm) cultural quarter, seamlessly bringing together baroque and contemporary architecture. The biggest draw is **Neue Galerie Graz** (Joanneumsviertel, Kalchberggasse; adult/child €8/3; ⏲10am-5pm Tue-Sun), with an outstanding collection of 19th and 20th century art, placing the emphasis on Austrian masters from Klimt to Otto Wagner.

Kunsthaus Graz GALLERY
(www.kunsthausgraz.at; Lendkai 1; adult/child €8/3; ⏲10am-5pm Tue-Sun; 🚊1, 3, 6, 7 Südtiroler Platz) Designed by British architects Peter Cook

LINZ CARD

The Linz Card, giving entry to major sights and unlimited use of public transport, costs €15/25 for one/three days.

HUNDERTWASSER SPA

East Styria is famed for its thermal springs. Fans of Friedensreich Hundertwasser's playful architectural style won't want to miss the surreal **Rogner-Bad Blumau** (☎03383-51 00; www.blumau.com; adult/child €40/22; ⏲9am-11pm), 50km east of Graz. The spa has all the characteristics of his art, including uneven floors, grass on the roof, colourful ceramics and golden spires. Overnight accommodation includes entry to the spa. Call ahead to book treatments from sound meditation to invigorating Styrian elderberry wraps.

and Colin Fournier, this world-class contemporary art space looks something like a space-age sea slug. Exhibitions change every three to four months.

Schloss Eggenberg PALACE
(Eggenberger Allee 90; adult/child €8/3; ⏲palace tours 10am-4pm Tue-Sun Palm Sunday-Oct; 🚊1 Schloss Eggenberg) A blend of gothic, Renaissance and baroque styles, this beautiful Unesco World Heritage palace can be reached by tram 1 from Hauptplatz. Admission includes a guided tour (on the hour except at 1pm), taking in 24 astrology and mythology themed *Prunkräume* (state rooms).

FREE **Murinsel** BRIDGE
(🚌4, 5 Schlossplatz/Murinsel, 🚊1, 3, 6, 7 Südtiroler Platz) This artificial island-cum-bridge in the Mur River is an open seashell of glass, concrete and steel by New York artist Vito Acconci. It houses a trendy cafe-bar in aqua blue and a small stage.

FREE **Schlossberg** VIEWPOINT
(glass lift 1hr ticket €1.90; 🚌4, 5 Schlossplatz/Murinsel for lift) The wooded slopes of Schlossberg (473m) can be reached on foot, with the funicular **Schlossbergbahn** (Castle Hill Railway; 1hr ticket adult/child €2/1) from Kaiser-Franz-Josef-Kai, or by **Glass Lift** from Schlossbergplatz. Napoleon was hard-pressed to raze this fortress, but raze it he did. Today the medieval **Uhrturm** (Clock Tower) is the legacy.

Landeszeughaus MUSEUM
(www.museum-joanneum.at; Herrengasse 16; adult/child €8/3; ⏲10am-5pm Mon & Wed-Sun; 🚊1, 3, 4, 5, 6, 7 Hauptplatz) A must-see for fans of armour and weapons, housing an astounding array of 30,000 gleaming exhibits.

FREE **Burg** CASTLE, PARK
(Hofgasse; 🚌30 Schauspielhaus, 🚊1, 3, 4, 5, 6, 7 Hauptplatz) At the far end of Graz' 15th-century castle is an ingenious **double staircase** (1499). Adjoining it is the **Stadtpark**, the city's largest green space.

Sleeping

Hotel zum Dom HOTEL €€
(☎82 48 00; www.domhotel.co.at; Bürgergasse 14; s €84-99, d €124-219, ste €194-239; P❄📶) Hotel zum Dom's individually furnished rooms come with power showers or whirlpools, and one suite even has a terrace whirlpool.

Hotel Daniel HOTEL €
(☎711 080; www.hoteldaniel.com; Europaplatz 1; r €59-79, breakfast per person €9; P❄@) The Daniel is a design hotel with minimalist-style rooms. You can rent a Vespa (€15 per day) and there's a 24-hour espresso bar.

Gasthof-Pension zur Steirer-Stub'n GUESTHOUSE €
(☎71 68 55; www.pension-graz.at; Lendplatz 8; s/d €43/86, apt €120 180; P📶) A bright and breezy guesthouse where many of the good-sized rooms have patios overlooking Lendplatz.

Eating

Aside from the following listings, there are plenty of cheap eats near Universität Graz, particularly on Halbärthgasse, Zinzendorfgasse and Harrachgasse.

Stock up for a picnic at the **farmers markets** (⏲6am-noon, closed Sun) on Kaiser-Josef-Platz and Lendplatz. For **fast-food stands**, head for Hauptplatz and Jakominiplatz.

Der Steirer BEISL €€
(☎703 654; www.dersteirer.at; Belgiergasse 1; mains €10-19.50, tapas €2, lunch menu €7.90; ⏲11am-midnight; 🍴; 🚊1, 3, 6, 7 Südtiroler Platz) This Styrian neo-*Beisl* and wine bar has a small but excellent selection of local dishes. The goulash with fried polenta is easily one of the best in the country.

Landhauskeller AUSTRIAN €€
(☎83 02 76; Schmiedgasse 9; mains €10.50-28.50; ⏲11.30am-midnight Mon-Sat; 🚊1, 3 ,4, 5, 6, 7 Hauptplatz) What started as a spit-and-sawdust pub in the 16th century evolved into an

atmospheric, medieval-style restaurant serving specialities like its four different sorts of *Tafelspitz* (prime broiled beef).

Drinking & Entertainment

The bar scene in Graz is split between three main areas: around the university; adjacent to the Kunsthaus; and on Mehlplatz and Prokopigasse (dubbed the 'Bermuda Triangle').

Kulturhauskeller BAR, CLUB
(www.kulturhauskeller.at; Elisabethstrasse 30; ⌚9pm-5am Tue-Sat; 🚋7 Lichtenfelsgasse) Next to Orange, the Kulturhauskeller is a cavernous cellar bar that heaves with raunchy students on weekends.

Orange BAR, CLUB
(www.cbo.at; Elisabethstrasse 30; ⌚8am-3am; 🚋7 Lichtenfelsgasse) A student crowd flocks to this modern cafe, bar and club, with a patio for summer evenings. DJs spin regularly here.

Information

Graz Tourismus (☎80 75; www.graztourismus.at; Herrengasse 16; ⌚10am-6pm; 📶; 🚋1, 3, 4, 5, 6, 7 Hauptplatz) Graz' main tourist office, with loads of free information on the city. Inside the train station is an information stand and terminal, and a free hotline to the tourist office.

Getting There & Away

AIR Ryanair (www.ryanair.com)has regular flights from London Stansted to Graz airport (p86), 10km south of the centre, while **Air Berlin** (www.airberlin.com) connects the city with Berlin.

BICYCLE Bicycle rental is available from **Bicycle** (☎688 645; Körösistrasse 5; per 24hr €15; ⌚7am-1pm & 2-6pm Mon-Fri).

PUBLIC TRANSPORT Single tickets (€2) for buses, trams and the Schlossbergbahn are valid for one hour, but you're usually better off buying a 24-hour pass (€4.50).

TRAIN Trains to Vienna depart hourly (€37, 2½ hours), and six daily go to Salzburg (€48.60, four hours). International train connections from Graz include Ljubljana (€37.60, 3½ hours) and Budapest (€64, 5½ hours).

Klagenfurt

☎0463 / POP 94,796

With its captivating location on Wörthersee and more Renaissance than baroque beauty, Klagenfurt has a distinct Mediterranean feel. Carinthia's capital makes a handy base for exploring Wörthersee's lakeside villages and elegant medieval towns to the north.

Sights & Activities

Boating and swimming are usually possible from May to September.

TOP CHOICE **Wörthersee** LAKE
Owing to its thermal springs, the Wörthersee is one of the region's warmer lakes (an average 21°C in summer) and is great for swimming, lakeshore frolicking and water sports. The 40km **cycle path** circumnavigating the lake is one of Austria's best. In summer the tourist office cooperates with a hire company for bicycles (per 24 hours €10).

Europapark PARK
Europapark's green expanse and *Strandbad* (beach) on the shores of the Wörthersee are especially good for kids. The park's biggest draw is **Minimundus** (www.minimundus.at; Villacher Strasse 241; adult/child €13/8; ⌚9am-btwn 6pm & 8pm Mar-Oct), a 'miniature world' with 150 replicas of the world's architectural icons, downsized to a scale of 1:25. To get there, take bus 10 or 20 from Heiligengeistplatz.

Sleeping & Eating

When you check into accommodation in Klagenfurt, ask for a *Gästekarte* (guest card), entitling you to discounts.

Hotel Geyer HOTEL €€
(☎578 86; www.hotelgeyer.com; Priesterhausgasse 5; s €70-88, d €102-135, q €155-170; P@📶) Colourful fabrics, paintings and objets d'art lend a personal feel to this central pick. There is a little spa area for relaxing moments and breakfast is served on the patio in summer.

Restaurant Maria Loretto AUSTRIAN €€
(☎24 465; Lorettoweg 54; mains €15-25; ⌚lunch & dinner) A wonderful restaurant situated on a headland above Wörthersee near the *Strandbad*, serving fresh lake fish and dishes prepared with home-grown herbs. Reserve for an outside table.

FREE TOURS

Free guided tours depart from Klagenfurt's tourist office at 10am every Friday and Saturday during July and August.

Information

Tourist Office (☎53 722 23; www.info.klagenfurt.at; Neuer Platz 1, Rathaus; ⊙8am-6pm Mon-Fri, 10am-5pm Sat, 10am-3pm Sun) Books accommodation and sells Kärnten cards (www.kaerntencard.at, adult/child €36/15.50), which give free entry to 100 sights in the region over a one-week period.

Getting There & Around

AIR Klagenfurt's **airport** (www.klagenfurt-airport.com; Flughafenstrasse 60-66) is served by Ryanair from London Stansted and **TUIfly** (www.tuifly.com) from major German cities.

BUS Bus drivers sell single tickets (€2) and 24-hour passes (€4.40). Bus 42 shuttles between the Hauptbahnhof and the airport.

TRAIN Two hourly direct trains run from Klagenfurt to Vienna (€50, 3¾ hours) and Salzburg (€38.70, three hours). Trains to Graz depart every two to three hours (€38.70, 2¾ hours). Trains to western Austria, Italy, Slovenia and Germany go via Villach (€7.80, 30 to 40 minutes, two to four per hour).

SALZBURG

☎0662 / POP 149,528

The joke 'If it's baroque, don't fix it' is a perfect maxim for Salzburg; the tranquil Old Town burrowed below steep hills looks much as it did when Mozart lived here 250 years ago.

A Unesco World Heritage site, Salzburg's overwhelmingly baroque Old Town (Altstadt) is entrancing both at ground level and from Hohensalzburg fortress high above. Across the fast-flowing Salzach River rests Schloss Mirabell, surrounded by gorgeous manicured gardens.

If this doesn't whet your appetite, then bypass the grandeur and head straight for kitsch-country by joining a tour of *The Sound of Music* film locations.

Sights

Old Town — HISTORIC AREA

Presiding over stately Residenzplatz is the **Residenz** (www.residenzgalerie.at; Residenzplatz 1; adult/child €9/3; ⊙10am-5pm), once home to the powerful prince-archbishops and worth visiting for its opulently frescoed state rooms and gallery of Old Master paintings.

The overwhelmingly baroque **Dom** (Cathedral; Domplatz; ⊙8am-7pm Mon-Sat, from 1pm Sun), slightly south, has bronze doors symbolising faith, hope and charity, and the **Dommuseum** (adult/concession €5/1.50; ⊙10am-5pm Mon-Sat, 11am-6pm Sun May-Oct), a treasure-trove of ecclesiastical art.

From here, head west along Franziskanergasse and turn left into a courtyard for **Stiftskirche St Peter** (St Peter's Abbey Church; St Peter Bezirk 1-2; ⊙church 8.30am-noon & 2.30-6.30pm, cemetery 6.30am-7pm), an abbey church founded around 700. Among the lovingly tended graves in the grounds you'll find the **Katakomben** (adult/student €1.50/1; ⊙10.30am-5pm Tue-Sun). The **Stift Nonnberg** (Nonnberg Convent; Nonnberggasse 2; ⊙7am-dusk), where *The Sound of Music* first finds Maria, is back east of Festung Hohensalzburg.

Festung Hohensalzburg — FORT

(www.salzburg-burgen.at; Mönchsberg 34; adult/child/family €7.80/4.40/17.70, with Festungsbahn funicular €11/6.30/25.50; ⊙9am-7pm) Salzburg's most visible icon is this mighty clifftop fortress. Built in 1077, it was home to many prince-archbishops who ruled Salzburg from 798. Inside are the impressively ornate staterooms, torture chambers and two museums.

It takes 15 minutes to walk up the hill to the fortress, or you can catch the **Festungsbahn funicular** (Festungsgasse 4).

Salzburg Museum — MUSEUM

(www.salzburgmuseum.at; Mozartplatz 1; adult/child/family €7/3/14; ⊙9am-5pm Tue-Sun, to 8pm Thu) Housed in the baroque Neue Residenz palace, this flagship museum presents a romp through Salzburg past and present. Ornate rooms showcase everything from medieval sacred art to prince-archbishop portraits.

Schloss Mirabell — PALACE

(Mirabellplatz 4; ⊙palace 8am-4pm Mon, Wed & Thu, 1-4pm Tue & Fri, gardens dawn-dusk) Prince-Archbishop Wolf Dietrich built this splendid palace in 1606 for his mistress Salome Alt. Its lavish baroque interior, replete with stucco, marble and frescos, is free to visit. For stellar fortress views, stroll the fountain-dotted **gardens**. *The Sound of Music* fans will of course recognise the Pegasus statue, the gnomes and the steps where the mini von Trapps practised 'Do-Re-Mi'.

Mozarts Geburtshaus — MUSEUM

(Mozart's Birthplace; www.mozarteum.at; Getreidegasse 9; adult/child/family €10/3.50/21; ⊙9am-5.30pm) Mozart was born in this bright-yellow town house in 1756 and spent the first 17 years of his life here.

Mozart-Wohnhaus MUSEUM
(Mozart's Residence; www.mozarteum.at; Makartplatz 8; adult/child/family €10/3.50/21, incl Mozarts Geburtshaus €17/5/36; 9am-5.30pm) Mozart's one-time residence showcases family portraits, documents and instruments. There's a film and music archive downstairs.

Museum der Moderne GALLERY
(www.museumdermoderne.at; Mönchsberg 32; adult/child €8/6; 10am-6pm Tue-Sun, to 8pm Wed) Straddling Mönchsberg's cliffs, this contemporary gallery shows first-rate exhibitions of 20th- and 21st-century art. There's a free guided tour at 6.30pm every Wednesday.

Tours

If you would rather go it alone, the tourist office has four-hour iTour audioguides (€9), which take in big-hitters like the Residenz, Mirabellgarten and Mozartplatz.

Fräulein Maria's Bicycle Tours BICYCLE TOURS
(www.mariasbicycletours.com; Mirabellplatz 4; adult/child €26/18; 9.30am & 4.30pm May-Sep) Wannabe Marias on bicycles. No booking required; just turn up at the Mirabellplatz meeting point.

Segway Tours SEGWAY TOURS
(www.segway-salzburg.at; Wolf-Dietrich Strasse 3; city/Sound of Music tour €33/65; tours 9am, noon, 3pm & 5pm Mar-Oct) These guided Segway tours take in the sights by zippy battery-powered scooter.

Bob's Special Tours COACH TOURS
(84 95 11; www.bobstours.com; Rudolfskai 38; office 10am-3pm Mon-Fri, noon-2pm Sat & Sun) Minibus tours to *The Sound of Music* locations and the Bavarian Alps. Reservations essential.

Salzburg Schiffsfahrt RIVER CRUISES
(www.salzburghighlights.at; Makartsteg; adult/child €14/7; Apr-Oct) Hour-long cruises depart from Makartsteg bridge.

Festivals & Events

Austria's most renowned classical music festival, the **Salzburg Festival** (www.salzburgerfestspiele.at) attracts international stars from late July to late August. Book online well in advance if you want cheap tickets.

Sleeping

Haus Ballwein GUESTHOUSE €
(82 40 29; www.haus-ballwein.at; Moosstrasse 69a; s €35-45, d €58-68, apt €100-115; P) With its bright, pine-filled rooms, mountain views, free bike hire and garden patrolled by duck duo Rosalee and Clementine, this farmhouse guesthouse is big on charm. It's a 10-minute trundle from the Old Town on bus 21.

SALZBURG CARD

The money-saving **Salzburg Card** (1-/2-/3-day card €26/35/41) gets you entry to all of the major sights, a free river cruise, unlimited use of public transport (including cable cars) plus numerous discounts on tours and events. The card is €3 cheaper in the low season.

Arte Vida GUESTHOUSE €€
(87 31 85; www.artevida.at; Dreifaltigkeitsgasse 9; s €55-140, d €80-152;) Arte Vida has the boho-chic feel of a Marrakesh *riad*, with its lantern-lit salon, communal kitchen and individually designed rooms. Your affable host Reinhold arranges yoga sessions in the quiet garden, and outdoor activities.

YOHO Salzburg HOSTEL €
(879 649; www.yoho.at; Paracelsusstrasse 9; dm €19-23, d €65-75; @) Comfy bunks, free wi-fi, plenty of cheap beer – what more could a backpacker ask for? Except, perhaps, *The Sound of Music* screened daily (yes, *every* day). The friendly crew can arrange tours, adventure sports and bike hire.

Hotel Am Dom BOUTIQUE HOTEL €€
(84 27 65; www.hotelamdom.at; Goldgasse 17; s €90-160, d €130-280;) Antique meets boutique at this Old Town hotel, where the original vaults and beams of the 800-year-old building contrast with razor-sharp design features.

Stadtalm HOSTEL €
(84 17 29; www.diestadtalm.com; Mönchsberg 19C; dm €19) This turreted hostel plopped on top of Mönchsberg takes in the entire Salzburg panorama, from the city's spires and fortress to Kapuzinerberg.

Haus Steiner GUESTHOUSE €
(83 00 31; www.haussteiner.com; Moosstrasse 156; s/d/tr €34/56/78; P) Kind-natured Rosemarie runs a tight ship at this chalet-style guesthouse. The petite, wood-clad rooms have balconies with mood-lifting mountain views. The Old Town is a 15-minute ride away on bus 21.

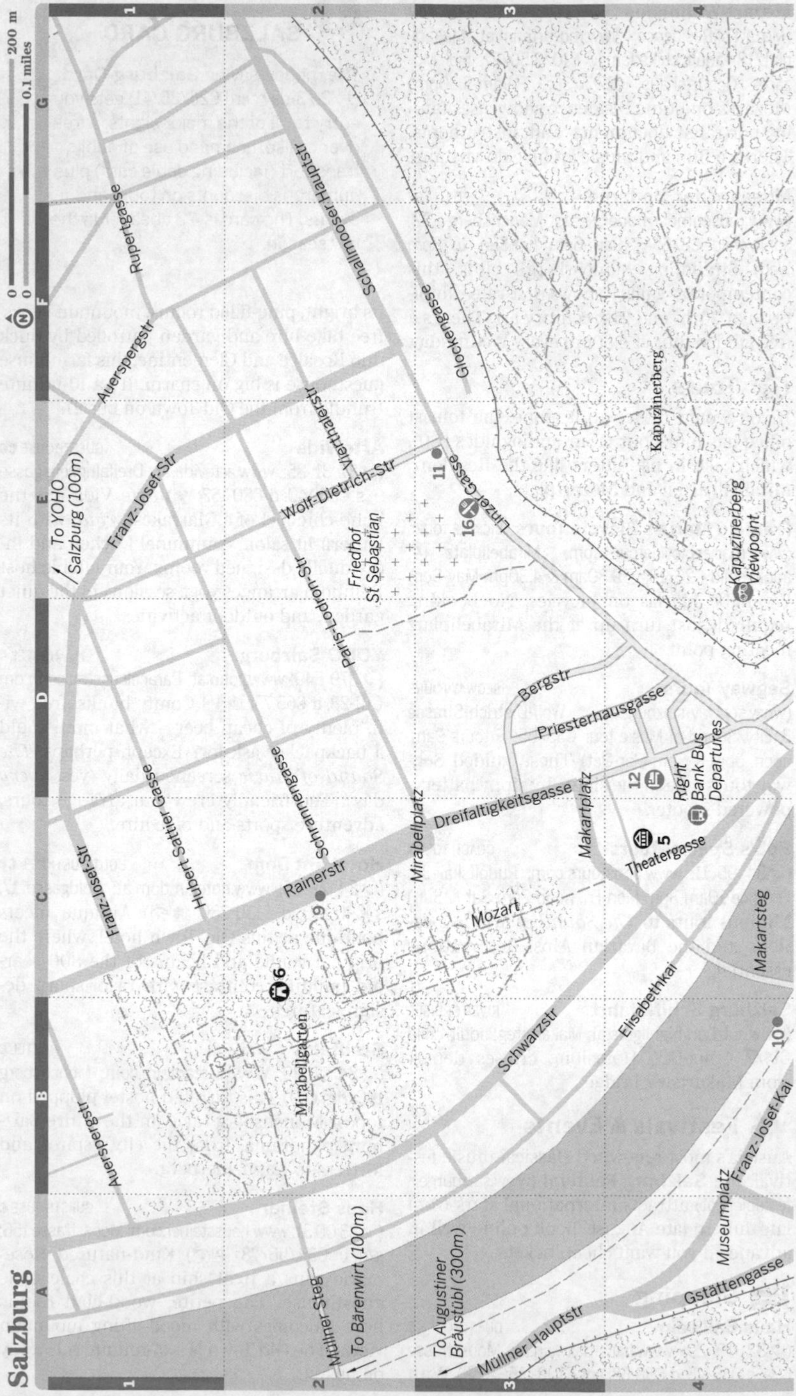

Salzburg

0 200 m
0 0.1 miles

A B C D E F G
1 2 3 4

Franz-Josef-Str
Auerspergstr
Rupertgasse
Hubert Sattler Gasse
Schrannengasse
Paris-Lodron-Str
Wolf-Dietrich-Str
Vierthalerstr
Schallmooser Hauptstr
Glockengasse
Linzer Gasse
Friedhof St Sebastian
To YOHO Salzburg (100m)
Rainerstr
9
6
Mirabellgarten
Mirabellplatz
Dreifaltigkeitsgasse
Mozart
Makartplatz
Theatergasse
5
12
Right Bank Bus Departures
Priesterhausgasse
Bergstr
11
16
Kapuzinerberg
Kapuzinerberg Viewpoint
Schwarzstr
Elisabethkai
Makartsteg
10
Müllner-Steg
To Bärenwirt (100m)
To Augustiner Bräustübl (300m)
Müllner Hauptstr
Gstättengasse
Museumplatz
Franz-Josef-Kai

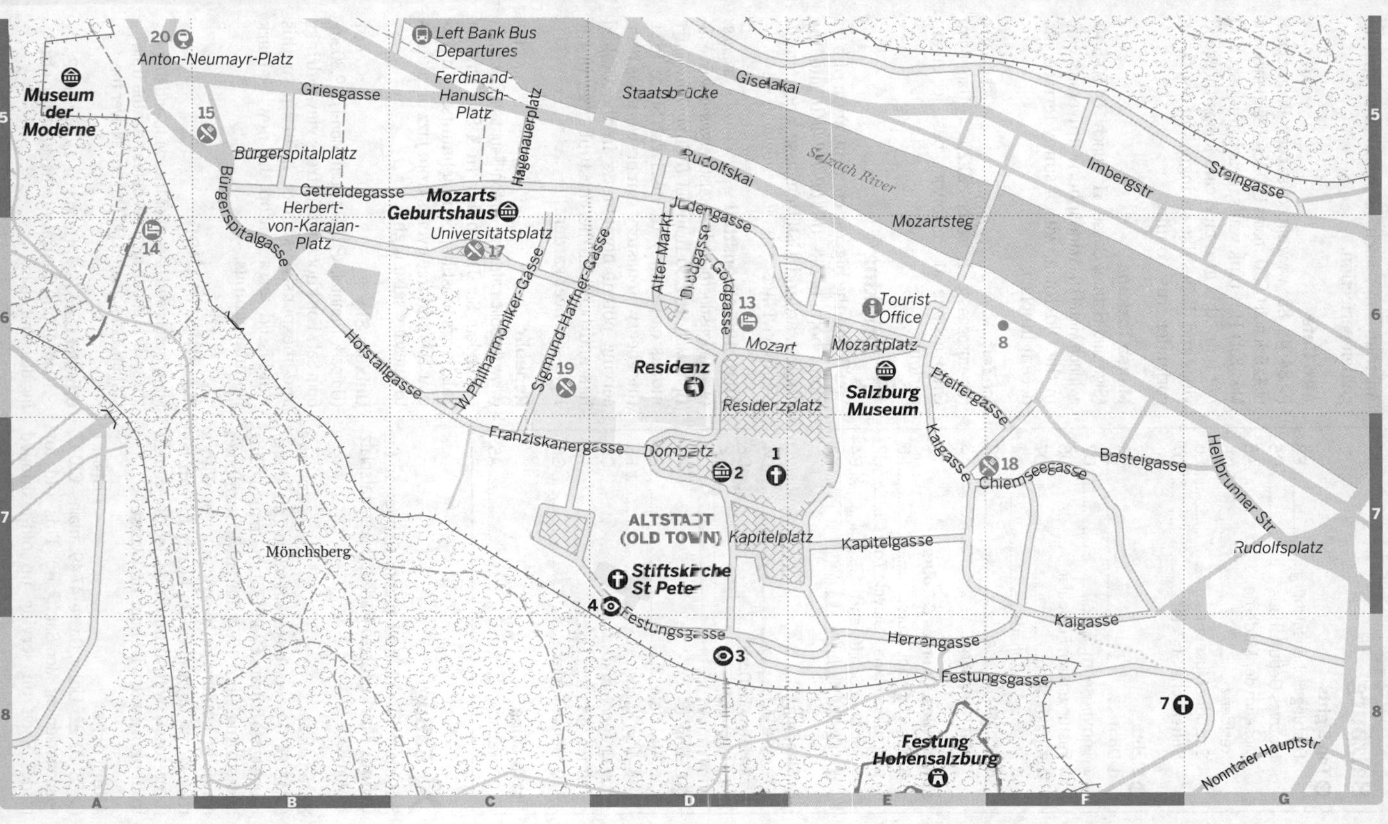

5
6
7
8
A
B
C
D
E
F
G
20
Anton-Neumayr-Platz
Left Bank Bus Departures
Museum der Moderne
15
Griesgasse
Ferdinand-Hanusch-Platz
Staatsbrücke
Giselakai
Bürgerspitalplatz
Hagenauerplatz
Rudolfskai
Salzach River
Imbergstr
Steingasse
Bürgerspitalgasse
Getreidegasse
Mozarts Geburtshaus
Herbert-von-Karajan-Platz
Universitätsplatz
17
14
Judengasse
Mozartsteg
Alter Markt
Brodgasse
Goldgasse
13
Tourist Office
Sigmund-Haffner-Gasse
W Philharmoniker-Gasse
Hofstallgasse
19
Residenz
Mozart
Mozartplatz
8
Salzburg Museum
Residenzplatz
Pfeifergasse
Franziskanergasse
Domplatz
2
1
Kaigasse
18
Chiemseegasse
Basteigasse
Hellbrunner Str
ALTSTADT (OLD TOWN)
Kapitelplatz
Kapitelgasse
Rudolfsplatz
Mönchsberg
Stiftskirche St Peter
4
Festungsgasse
3
Herrengasse
Kaigasse
Festungsgasse
7
Festung Hohensalzburg
Nonntaler Hauptstr

Salzburg

Top Sights

	Festung Hohensalzburg	E8
	Mozarts Geburtshaus	C5
	Museum der Moderne	A5
	Residenz	D6
	Salzburg Museum	E6
	Stiftskirche St Peter	D7
	Sights	
1	Dom	D7
2	Dommuseum	D7
3	Festungsbahn Funicular	D8
4	Katakomben	D7
5	Mozart-Wohnhaus	C4
6	Schloss Mirabell	C2
7	Stift Nonnberg	F8
	Activities, Courses & Tours	
8	Bob's Special Tours	F6
9	Fräulein Maria's Bicycle Tours	C2
10	Salzburg Schiffsfahrt	B4
11	Segway Tours	E3
	Sleeping	
12	Arte Vida	D4
13	Hotel Am Dom	D6
14	Stadtalm	A6
	Eating	
15	Afro Café	B5
16	Alter Fuchs	E3
17	Grüner Markt	C6
18	IceZeit	F7
19	Mensa Toskana	C6
	Drinking	
20	Republic	A5

Eating

Self-caterers can find picnic fixings at the **Grüner Markt** (Green Market; Universitätsplatz; Mon-Sat).

Bärenwirt AUSTRIAN €

(42 24 04; www.baerenwirt-salzburg.at; Müllner Hauptstrasse 8; mains €9-18; 11am-11pm) Sizzling and stirring since 1663, Bärenwirt combines a woody, hunting-lodge-style interior with a river-facing terrace. Go for hearty *Bierbraten* (beer roast) with dumplings, locally caught trout or organic wild boar bratwurst.

Alter Fuchs AUSTRIAN €

(88 20 22; Linzer Gasse 47-49; mains €10-17; noon-midnight Mon-Sat;) This old fox prides itself on serving up old-fashioned Austrian fare, such as schnitzels fried to golden perfection.

Afro Café AFRICAN €

(84 48 88; www.afrocoffee.com; Bürgerspitalplatz 5; lunch €6.70, mains €10-15; 9am-midnight Mon-Sat) Hot-pink walls, beach-junk art and *big* hair...this afro-chic cafe keeps the good vibes and dishes like springbok in a sesame-coriander crust coming.

Mensa Toskana CAFE €

(Sigmund-Haffner-Gasse 11; lunch €4.50-5.40; lunch Mon-Fri) Atmospheric university cafe in the Old Town, with a sunny terrace and decent lunches.

IceZeit ICE CREAM €

(Chiemseegasse 1; scoop €1.20; 11am-8pm) Grab a cone at Salzburg's best ice-cream parlour.

Drinking

You'll find the biggest concentration of bars along both banks of the Salzach and the hippest around Gstättengasse and Anton-Neumayr-Platz.

Augustiner Bräustübl BREWERY

(www.augustinerbier.at; Augustinergasse 4-6; 3-11pm Mon-Fri, 2.30-11pm Sat & Sun) Who says monks can't enjoy themselves? Since 1621, this cheery monastery-run brewery has been serving potent homebrews in the vaulted hall and beneath the chestnut trees in the 1000-seat beer garden.

Republic BAR

(www.republic-cafe.at; Anton-Neumayr-Platz 2; 8am-1am Sun-Thu, to 4am Fri & Sat) One of Salzburg's most happening haunts, with regular DJs and free events from jazz breakfasts to Tuesday salsa nights.

Unikum Sky CAFE

(Unipark Nonntal; 10am-7pm Mon-Fri, 9.30am-6pm Sat) For knockout fortress views, drinks and inexpensive snacks, head up to this sun-kissed terrace atop the new Unipark Nonntal campus.

Information

Many hotels and bars offer free wi-fi, and there are several cheap internet cafes near the train station. *Bankomaten* (ATMs) are all over the place.

City Net Café (Gstättengasse 11; per hr €2; 10am-10pm) Central internet cafe also offering discount calls.

Tourist Office (☎889-87 330; www.salzburg.info; Mozartplatz 5; ⊙9am-6pm or 6.30pm, closed Sun Sep-Mar) Plenty of information about the city and its surrounds. There's a ticket booking agency in the same building.

Getting There & Away

AIR Low-cost airlines including **Ryanair** (www.ryanair.com) and **easyJet** (www.easyjet.com) serve **Salzburg airport** (www.salzburg-airport.com), 5.5km west of the city centre.

BUS Buses depart from just outside the Hauptbahnhof on Südtiroler Platz. For bus timetables and fares, see www.svv-info.at and www.postbus.at.

TRAIN Salzburg's Hauptbahnhof is undergoing extensive renovation until 2014.

Fast trains leave hourly for Vienna (€49.90, three hours) via Linz (€23.70, 1¼ hours). There is a two-hourly express service to Klagenfurt (€38.70, three hours). The quickest way to Innsbruck (€41.30, two hours) is by the 'corridor' train through Germany via Kufstein; trains depart at least every two hours.

Getting Around

TO/FROM THE AIRPORT Bus 2 runs from the Hauptbahnhof (€2.30, 19 minutes) to the airport.

BICYCLE **Top Bike** (www.topbike.at; Staatsbrücke; ⊙10am-5pm) rents bikes for around €15 per day (half price for kids). The Salzburg Card yields a 20% discount.

BUS Bus drivers sell single (€2.30) and 24-hour (€5.20) tickets. Weekly tickets (€13.60) can be purchased from machines and *Tabak* shops.

AROUND SALZBURG

Schloss Hellbrunn

A prince-archbishop with a wicked sense of humour, Markus Sittikus built Italianate **Schloss Hellbrunn** (www.hellbrunn.at; Fürstenweg 37; adult/concession/family €9.50/6.50/24; ⊙9am-5.30pm, to 9pm Jul & Aug; 👪) as a 17th-century summer palace and an escape from his Residenz functions.

The ingenious trick fountains and water-powered figures are the big draw. When the tour guides set them off, expect to get wet! Admission includes entry to the baroque palace. The rest of the sculpture-dotted gardens are free to visit. Look out for *The Sound of Music* pavilion of 'Sixteen Going on Seventeen' fame.

Bus 25 runs to Hellbrunn, 4.5km south of Salzburg, every 20 minutes from Rudolfskai in the Old Town.

Werfen

☎06468 / POP 2999

More than 1000m above Werfen in the Tennengebirge mountains is **Eisriesenwelt** (www.eisriesenwelt.at; adult/concession €9/8, with cable car €20/18; ⊙9am-3.30pm May-Oct; 👪). Billed as the world's largest accessible ice caves, this glittering ice empire is a once-seen-never-forgotten experience. Wrap up warm for subzero temperatures. Well below the caves is **Burg Hohenwerfen** (adult/concession/family €14/12/33; ⊙9am-5pm Apr-Oct; 👪), a formidable clifftop fortress dating from 1077.

Both the ice caves and fortress can be visited as a day trip from Salzburg if you start early (tour the caves first and be at the castle by 3.15pm for the falconry show); otherwise consult the **tourist office** (☎53 88; www.werfen.at; Markt 24; ⊙9am-12.30pm & 1-6pm Mon-Fri year-round, 2-4pm Sat May-Sep) for accommodation options.

Werfen is 45km south of Salzburg on the A10/E55 motorway. Trains run frequently to Salzburg (€10, 40 minutes). In summer, minibuses (single/return €3.10/6.10) run every 25 minutes between Eisriesenstrasse in Werfen and the car park, a 20-minute walk from the cable car to Eisriesenwelt.

SALZKAMMERGUT

A wonderland of glassy lakes and craggy peaks, Austria's Lake District is a long-time favourite holiday destination. The peaceful lakes attract visitors in droves, who come to boat, fish, swim or just laze on the shore.

Bad Ischl is the region's transport hub, but Hallstatt is its true jewel. For info visit **Salzkammergut Touristik** (☎0613 224 000; www.salzkammergut.co.at; Götzstrasse 12; ⊙9am-7pm, closed Sun Oct-Mar). The Salzkammergut Card (€4.90, available May to October) provides up to 30% discounts on sights, ferries, cable cars and some buses.

Hallstatt

☎06134 / POP 794

With pastel-hued homes, swans and towering mountains on either side of a glassy green lake, Hallstatt looks like some kind of

WORTH A TRIP

OBERTRAUN

Near Hallstatt, Obertraun has the intriguing **Dachstein Rieseneishöhle** (www.dachstein-salzkammergut.com; cable car return plus one cave adult/child €27/15, all-inclusive ticket adult/child €39/23). The caves are millions of years old and extend into the mountain for almost 80km in places.

From Obertraun it's also possible to catch a cable car to **Krippenstein** (return adult/child €23/14; closed mid-Oct–Nov & Easter–mid-May), where you'll find the freaky **5 Fingers viewing platform**, which protrudes over a sheer cliff face – not for sufferers of vertigo.

greeting card for tranquillity. Now a Unesco World Heritage site, Hallstatt was settled 4500 years ago and over 2000 graves have been discovered in the area, most of them dating from 1000 to 500 BC.

Sights & Activities

Salzbergwerk SALT MINE
(funicular return plus tour adult/child €24/12, tour only €12/6; 9.30am-4.30pm, closed early Nov–late Apr) Hallstatt's trophy sight is the Salzbergwerk, where the fully preserved body of a prehistoric miner was found in 1734 (today he is known as the 'Man in Salt'). A tour revolves around his fate, with an underground railway and miners' slides to an illuminated subterranean salt lake.

Beinhaus CHURCH
(Bone House; Kirchenweg 40; admission €1.50; 10am-6pm, closed Nov-Apr) Don't miss the macabre yet beautiful Beinhaus behind Hallstatt's parish church, which contains rows of stacked skulls. The old Celtic pagan custom of mass burial has been practised here since 1600 (mainly due to a lack of graveyard space).

Hallstätter See LAKE
(boat hire per hr from €11) If you don't fancy a chilly dip in the crystal-clear waters, hire a rowboat, kayak or pedalo for a spin of the lake.

Sleeping & Eating

Pension Sarstein GUESTHOUSE €
(8217; Gosaumühlstrasse 83; d €55-70, apt €65-100;) The affable Fischer family take pride in their little guesthouse, a few minutes' walk along the lakefront from central Hallstatt. The cosily old-fashioned rooms have balconies with dreamy lake and mountain views.

Gasthof Simony AUSTRIAN €€
(206 46; www.gasthof-simony.at; Wolfengasse 105; mains €9-17; lunch Thu-Sun, dinner Thu-Tue) What a view! With a garden right on the lakeshore, this is a prime setting for a panoramic lunch or dinner. Try classics like smoked trout with horseradish, goulash, strudel and the like.

Information

Tourist Office (82 08; www.dachstein-salzkammergut.at; Seestrasse 169; 9am-6pm Mon-Fri, 9am-4pm Sat & Sun, closed Sat & Sun Sep-Jun) Turn left from the ferry to reach the office. It stocks the free leisure map of lakeside towns, as well as hiking and cycling trail maps.

Getting There & Away

BOAT The last ferry connection leaves Hallstatt train station at 6.50pm (€2.40, 10 minutes). Ferry excursions do the circuit Hallstatt Lahn via Hallstatt Markt, Obersee, Untersee and Steeg return (€10, 90 minutes) three times daily from July to early September.

BUS Eight to 10 buses connect Hallstatt (Lahn) town with Obertraun (€2.20, eight minutes) daily.

TRAIN Hallstatt train station is across the lake. The boat service from there to the village coincides with train arrivals. About a dozen trains daily connect Hallstatt and Bad Ischl (€3.80, 22 minutes).

TIROL

With converging mountain ranges behind lofty pastures and tranquil meadows, Tirol (also Tyrol) captures a quintessential Alpine panoramic view. Occupying a central position is Innsbruck, the region's jewel, while in the northeast and southwest are superb ski resorts. In the southeast, separated somewhat from the main state since part of South Tirol was ceded to Italy at the end of WWI, lies the protected natural landscape of the Hohe Tauern National Park, an Alpine wonderland of 3000m peaks, including the country's highest, the Grossglockner (3798m).

Innsbruck

0512 / POP 121,329

Tirol's capital is a sight to behold. The mountains are so close that within 25 minutes it's possible to travel from the heart of the city to over 2000m above sea level. Summer and winter outdoor activities abound, and it's understandable why some visitors only take a peek at Innsbruck proper before heading for the hills. But to do so is a shame, for Innsbruck has its own share of gems, including an authentic medieval Altstadt (Old Town), inventive architecture and vibrant student-driven nightlife.

Sights

Goldenes Dachl & Museum MUSEUM
(Golden Roof; Herzog-Friedrich-Strasse 15; adult/child €4/2; ⏲10am-5pm, closed Mon Oct-Apr) Innsbruck's golden wonder is this Gothic oriel, built for Emperor Maximilian I in 1500 and glittering with 2657 fire-gilt copper tiles. An audioguide whizzes you through the history in the museum.

Hofkirche CHURCH
(www.tiroler-landesmuseum.at; Universitätstrasse; adult/child €5/4, combined Volkskunstmuseum ticket adult/child €10/6; ⏲9am-5pm Mon-Sat, 12.30-5pm Sun) The 16th-century Hofkirche is one of Europe's finest royal court churches. Top billing goes to the empty **sarcophagus** of Emperor Maximilian I (1459–1519), a masterpiece of German Renaissance sculpture, guarded by 28 giant bronze figures.

Next door the **Volkskunstmuseum** (Folk Art Museum; www.tiroler-landesmuseum.at; Universitätstrasse; combined Hofkirche ticket adult/child €10/6; ⏲9am-5pm) houses Tyrolean folk art, from handcarved sleighs to Christmas cribs.

Hofburg PALACE
(Imperial Palace; www.hofburg-innsbruck.at; Rennweg 1; adult/child €8/free, Hofgarten admission free; ⏲palace 9am-5pm, garden 6am-dusk) Empress Maria Theresia gave this Habsburg palace a total baroque makeover in the 16th century. The highlight of the state apartments is the lavishly frescoed **Riesensaal** (Giant's Hall).

Tucked behind the palace is the **Hofgarten**, an attractive garden for a botanical stroll.

Bergisel SKI JUMP
(www.bergisel.info; adult/child €9/4; ⏲9am-6pm) This glass-and-steel ski jump was designed by much-lauded Iraqi architect Zaha Hadid. It's 455 steps or a two-minute funicular ride to the 50m-high **viewing platform**, with a breathtaking panorama of the Nordkette range, Inn Valley and Innsbruck. Tram 1 trundles from central Innsbruck to Bergisel.

Schloss Ambras CASTLE
(www.khm.at/ambras; Schlossstrasse 20; adult/child €10/free; ⏲10am-5pm) A grand fortress turned Renaissance palace. Don't miss the dazzling armour collection and the gallery's Velázquez and Van Dyck originals. It's free to visit the expansive **gardens**. Take bus 4134 from the Hauptbahnhof.

Activities

Anyone who loves playing in the great outdoors will be itching to head up into the Alps in Innsbruck.

Nordkettenbahnen FUNICULAR
(www.nordkette.com; one way/return to Hungerburg €4/6.80, Seegrube €14.60/23.40, Hafelekar €16.20/27; ⏲Hungerburgbahn 7am-7.15pm Mon-Fri, 8am-7.15pm Sat, Seegrubenbahn 8.30am-5.30pm, Hafelekarbahn 9am-5pm) Zaha Hadid's space-age funicular runs every 15 minutes, whizzing you from the Congress Centre to the slopes in no time. Walking trails head off in all directions from **Hungerburg** and **Seegrube**.

The 2334m summit of **Hafelekar** affords tremendous views over Innsbruck to the snow-capped giants of the Austrian Alps, including 3798m Grossglockner.

Inntour ADVENTURE SPORTS
(☎214 466; www.inntour.com; Leopoldstrasse 4; ⏲9am-6.30pm Mon-Fri, to 5pm Sat) A one-stop adrenalin shop, taking you canyoning (€75), tandem paragliding (€95), white-water rafting (€45) and bungee jumping (€140) from the 192m Europabrücke.

Olympia SkiWorld Innsbruck SKIING
This massive ski arena spans nine surrounding resorts and 300km of slopes. The most central place to pound powder is the **Nordkette/Seegrube**. A three-/seven-day OlympiaWorld Ski Pass covering all areas costs €117/218.

CITY SAVERS

The **Innsbruck Card** gives one visit to Innsbruck's main sights and attractions, a return journey on seven cable cars, unlimited use of public transport including the Sightseer bus, and five-hour bike rental. It's available at the tourist office and costs €31/39/45 for 24/48/72 hours.

DON'T MISS

FREE GUIDED HIKES

From late May to October, Innsbruck Information arranges daily **guided hikes**, from sunrise walks to half-day mountain jaunts. The hikes are free with a **Club Innsbruck Card**, which you receive automatically when you stay overnight in Innsbruck. Pop into the tourist office to register and browse the program.

Sleeping

The tourist office has lists of private rooms costing between €20 and €40 per person.

TOP CHOICE **Nepomuks** HOSTEL €
(☎584 118; www.nepomuks.at; Kiebachgasse 16; dm €23-25, d €56;) Could this be backpacker heaven? Nepomuks sure comes close, with its Altstadt location, well-stocked kitchen and high-ceilinged dorms with homely touches like CD players. The delicious breakfast in attached Café Munding, with homemade pastries, jam and fresh-roasted coffee, gets your day off to a grand start.

Hotel Weisses Kreuz HISTORIC HOTEL €€
(☎594 79; www.weisseskreuz.at; Herzog-Friedrich-Strasse 31; s €38-78, d €78-142; P@) Beneath the Altstadt's arcades, this atmospheric 500-year-old pile has played host to famous guests including a 13-year-old Mozart. With its wood-panelled parlours and twisting staircase, the hotel oozes history with every creaking beam. Rooms are supremely comfortable, staff charming and breakfast is a lavish spread.

Pension Paula GUESTHOUSE €
(☎292 262; www.pensionpaula.at; Weiherburggasse 15; s/d €41/65; P) Nestled in the hills above Innsbruck and with great city views, this family-run pension has super-clean, homely rooms (most with balcony). It's 1km north of the Altstadt, near the Alpenzoo.

Weisses Rössl GUESTHOUSE €€
(☎583 057; www.roessl.at; Kiebachgasse 8; s €70-110, d €100-160; P@) An antique rocking horse greets you at this late 16th-century guesthouse, with vaulted interiors and bright, spacious rooms. Host Mr Plank is a keen hunter and the restaurant (mains €10 to €26) has a meaty menu.

Eating

Find Tyrolean picnic goodies under one roof at the **Markthalle** (www.markthalle-innsbruck.at; Innrain; 7am-6.30pm Mon-Fri, to 1pm Sat).

Chez Nico VEGETARIAN €€
(☎0650-451 06 24; www.chez-nico.at; Maria-Theresien-Strasse 49; lunch €12.50, 6-course menu €51; lunch & dinner Tue-Fri, dinner Sat;) Take a petit bistro and a creative Parisian chef with a passion for herbs, *et voilà*, you get Chez Nico. Nicolas Curtil (Nico) cooks seasonal vegetarian delights like porcini-sage ravioli and baked figs with rose sorbet at this intimate bistro.

Mamma Mia PIZZERIA €
(☎562 902; Kiebachgasse 2; mains €7-9; lunch & dinner) No-frills Italian bistro with a great buzz, huge pizzas and a shady terrace.

Madhuban INDIAN €
(☎589 157; www.madhuban.at; Templstrasse 2; mains €7-12; lunch & dinner Mon-Fri, dinner Sat & Sun) If you've had your fill of schnitzel and strudel, Madhuban does a spot-on curry. The two-course lunch is a snip at €7.50.

Cafe Munding CAFE €
(www.munding.at; Kiebachgasse 16; cake €2-4; 8am-8pm) Scrumptious fruit tortes, cheesecakes, chocolate cake and home-roasted coffee.

Drinking

Moustache BAR
(www.cafe-moustache.at; Herzog-Otto-Strasse 8; 11am-2am Tue-Sun) Playing spot-the-moustache (Einstein, Charlie Chaplin and co) is the preferred pastime at this retro bar, with a terrace on Domplatz and Club Aftershave in the basement.

Hofgarten Café BAR
(Rennweg 6a; 11am-2am Tue-Thu, to 4am Fri-Sun) DJs spin at this tree-shaded beer garden and star-studded pavilion, with a happening line-up of events.

360° BAR
(Rathaus Galerien; 10am-1am Mon-Sat) Drink in 360-degree views of the city and Alps from the balcony skirting the circular bar.

Information

Bubble Point (Innstrasse 11; 7.30am-10.30pm Mon-Fri, 7.30am-10pm Sat & Sun) A laundry with high-speed internet for €2 per hour.

Innsbruck Information (☎535 60; www.innsbruck.info; Burggraben 3; 9am-6pm)

Main tourist office with truckloads of info on the city and surrounds. Sells ski passes, public-transport tickets and city maps (€1), and will book accommodation.

Getting There & Away

AIR EasyJet flies to Innsbruck Airport (p86), 4km west of the city centre.

CAR & MOTORCYCLE Heading south by car through the Brenner Pass to Italy, you'll hit the A13 toll road (€8). Toll-free Hwy 182 follows the same route, although it is less scenic.

TRAIN Fast trains depart at least every two hours for Bregenz (€34.40, 2½ hours), Salzburg (€41.30, two hours), Kitzbühel (€19.20, 1½ hours) and Munich (€39.60, two hours). There are several daily services to Lienz (€19.20 to €35.20, 3¼ to 4½ hours).

Getting Around

Single tickets on buses and trams cost €1.90 (from the driver; valid upon issue). A 24-hour ticket is €4.30. Bus F runs between the airport and Maria-Theresien-Strasse.

Kitzbühel

☎05356 / POP 8450

Kitzbühel began life in the 16th century as a silver- and copper-mining town, and today preserves a charming medieval centre despite its other persona – as a fashionable and prosperous winter resort. It's renowned for the white-knuckled Hahnenkamm downhill ski race in January and the excellence of its slopes.

Activities

Skiing SKIING

In winter there's first-rate intermediate skiing and freeriding on 170km of well-groomed slopes. A one-day AllStarCard ski pass covering Kitzbühel and the surrounding region costs €46.50.

Hiking HIKING

Dozens of summer hiking trails thread through the Kitzbühel Alps; the tourist office gives walking maps and runs free guided hikes for guests staying in town. The Flex-Ticket covering all cable cars costs €43.50/36 with/without bus for three out of seven days.

Sleeping & Eating

Rates leap by up to 50% in the high winter season.

For self-caterers, there's a **Spar supermarket** (Bichlstrasse 22) and **Metzgerei Huber** (Bichlstrasse 14; snacks €3.50-7; ⏰8am-6pm Mon-Fri, 8am-12.30pm Sat) for carnivorous snacks.

Snowbunny's Hostel HOSTEL €

(☎067-6794 0233; www.snowbunnys.co.uk; Bichlstrasse 30; dm €25-40, d €74-100; @📶) Friendly, laid-back hostel, a bunny-hop from the slopes. Breakfast is DIY-style in the kitchen, and there's a TV lounge, ski storage and shop for backpacker staples (Vegemite, Jägermeister etc).

Huberbräu Stüberl AUSTRIAN €€

(☎656 77; Vorderstadt 18; mains €7-13) This vaulted tavern serves hearty portions of Austrian classics, such as schnitzel and liver dumplings, cooked to perfection.

Information

The **tourist office** (☎66 660; www.kitzbuehel.com; Hinterstadt 18; ⏰8.30am-6pm Mon-Fri, 9am-6pm Sat, 10am-noon & 4-6pm Sun) has loads of info in English and a 24-hour accommodation board.

Getting There & Away

Trains run frequently from Kitzbühel to Innsbruck (€19.20, 1¾ hours) and Salzburg (€28, 2½ hours). For Kufstein (€10, one hour), change at Wörgl.

It's quicker and cheaper to reach Lienz by bus (€14.70, two hours, twice daily) than train.

Lienz

☎04852 / POP 11,816

With the jagged Dolomites crowding its southern skyline, the capital of East Tirol is a scenic staging point for travels through the Hohe Tauern National Park.

Sights & Activities

Schloss Bruck CASTLE

(Schlossberg 1; adult/child €7.50/2.50; ⏰10am-6pm mid-May–late Oct) Lienz' biggest crowd-puller is its medieval fortress, displaying everything from Tyrolean costumes to emotive paintings by famous local son Albin Egger-Lienz.

Aguntum ARCHAEOLOGICAL SITE

(www.aguntum.info; Stribach 97; adult/child €6/4; ⏰9.30am-5pm, closed Nov-Apr) For an insight into Lienz' Roman past, visit the Aguntum archaeological site.

Skiing SKIING

A €36 day pass covers skiing on the nearby **Zettersfeld** and **Hochstein** peaks. However, the area is more renowned for its 100km of cross-country trails.

Sleeping & Eating

The tourist office can point you in the direction of good-value guesthouses and camping grounds.

Hotel Haidenhof HOTEL €€

(☎624 40; www.haidenhof.at; Grafendorferstrasse 12; s €89-101, d €140-186; P) High above Lienz, this country retreat has a dress-circle view of the Dolomites. Home-grown produce features in the restaurant (mains €16.50 to €26).

Kirchenwirt AUSTRIAN €€

(☎625 00; www.kirchenwirt-lienz.at; Pfarrgasse 7; mains €9-18; 9am-midnight) Dine under the vaults or on the streamside terrace on local dishes like East Tyrolean milk-fed lamb.

Information

The **tourist office** (☎0502-124 00; www.lienzerdolomiten.info; Europaplatz 1; 8am-6pm Mon-Fri, 9am-noon & 4-6pm Sat)will find rooms free of charge.

Getting There & Away

There are several daily services to Innsbruck (€19.20 to €35.20, 3¼ to 4½ hours). Trains run every two hours to Salzburg (€37, 3½ hours). To head south by car, you must first divert west or east along Hwy 100.

WORTH A TRIP

KRIMML FALLS

The thunderous, three-tier **Krimml Falls** (www.wasserfaelle-krimml.at; adult/child €2.50/0.50, free Dec-Apr; ticket office 8am-6pm mid-Apr–late Oct) is Europe's highest waterfall at 380m, and one of Austria's most unforgettable sights. The pretty Alpine village of Krimml has a handful of places to sleep and eat – contact the **tourist office** (☎72 39; www.krimml.at; Oberkrimml 37; 8am-noon & 2-6pm Mon-Fri, 8.30-10.30am & 4.30-6pm Sat) for more information.

Krimml is on Hwy 168 (which becomes Hwy 165). Buses run year-round from Krimml to Zell am See (€9.90, 1¼ hours, hourly), with frequent onward train connections to Salzburg (€21.50, 1½ hours).

Hohe Tauern National Park

Straddling Tirol, Salzburg and Carinthia, this national park is the largest in the Alps; a 1786-sq-km wilderness of 3000m peaks, Alpine meadows and waterfalls. At its heart lies **Grossglockner** (3798m), Austria's highest mountain, which towers over the 8km-long Pasterze Glacier, best seen from the outlook at **Kaiser-Franz-Josefs-Höhe** (2369m).

The 48km **Grossglockner Road** (www.grossglockner.at; Hwy 107; car/motorcycle €32/22; May-early Nov) from Bruck in Salzburgerland to Heiligenblut in Carinthia is one of Europe's greatest Alpine drives. A feat of 1930s engineering, the road swings giddily around 36 switchbacks, passing jewel-coloured lakes, forested slopes and wondrous glaciers.

The major village on the Grossglockner Road is **Heiligenblut**, famous for its 15th-century pilgrimage church. Here the **tourist office** (☎04824-27 00; www.heiligenblut.at; Hof 4; 9am-6pm) can advise on guided ranger hikes, mountain hiking and skiing. The village also has a spick-and-span **Jugendherberge** (☎22 59; www.oejhv.or.at; Hof 36; dm/s/d €20.50/28.50/49; P@).

Bus 5002 runs frequently between Lienz and Heiligenblut on weekdays (€15.80, one hour), less frequently at weekends.

VORARLBERG

Vorarlberg has always been a little different. Cut off from the rest of Austria by the snow-capped Arlberg massif, this westerly region has often associated itself more with nearby Switzerland than distant Vienna, and also provides a convenient gateway to Germany and Liechtenstein.

The capital, **Bregenz**, sits prettily on the shores of Lake Constance and holds the **Bregenzer Festspiele** (Bregenz Festival; ☎40 76; www.bregenzerfestspiele.com) in July/August, when opera is performed on a floating stage on the lake.

The real action here, though, is in the Arlberg region, shared by Vorarlberg and neighbouring Tirol. Some of the country's best downhill and off-piste skiing – not to mention après-ski partying – is in **St Anton**

am Arlberg, where the first ski club in the Alps was founded in 1901. The centrally located **tourist office** (☎22 690; www.stantonamarlberg.com; Dorfstrasse 8; ⏰8am-6pm Mon-Fri, 9am-6pm Sat, 9am-noon & 3-6pm Sun) has maps, and information on accommodation and activities.

A ski pass covering the whole Arlberg region and valid for all 85 ski lifts costs €47/257 for one/seven days in the high season.

Accommodation is mainly in small B&Bs. Many budget places (rates from €30 per person) are booked months in advance.

St Anton is on the main railway route between Bregenz (€19.20, 1½ hours) and Innsbruck (€21.50, 1¼ hours). It's close to the eastern entrance of the Arlberg Tunnel, the toll road connecting Vorarlberg and Tirol (€8.50).

WORTH A TRIP

BREGENZERWALD

Only a few kilometres southeast of Bregenz, the forest-cloaked slopes, velvet-green pastures and limestone peaks of the Bregenzerwald unfold. In summer it's a glorious place to spend a few days hiking the hills and filling up on homemade cheeses in Alpine dairies. Winter brings plenty of snow, and the area is noted for its downhill and cross-country skiing. The **Bregenzerwald tourist office** (☎05512-23 65; www.bregenzerwald.at; Impulszentrum 1135, Egg; ⏰9am-5pm Mon-Fri, 8am-1pm Sat) has information on the region.

UNDERSTAND AUSTRIA

History

Austria has been a galvanic force in shaping Europe's history. This landlocked little country was once the epicentre of the mighty Habsburg empire and, in the 20th century, a pivotal player in the outbreak of WWI.

Civilisation & Empire

Like so many European countries, Austria has experienced invasions and struggles since time immemorial. There are traces of human occupation since the ice age, but it was the Celts who made the first substantial mark on Austria around 450 BC. The Romans followed 400 years later, and in turn were followed by Bavarians and, in 1278, the House of Habsburg, which took control of the country by defeating the head of the Bavarian royalty.

The Habsburg Monarchy

For six centuries the Habsburgs used strategic marriages to maintain their hold over a territory that encompassed much of central and eastern Europe and, for a period, even Germany.

The 16th and 17th centuries saw the Ottoman threat reach the gates of Vienna, and in 1805 Napoleon defeated Austria at Austerlitz. Austrian Chancellor Metternich cleverly reconsolidated Austria's power in 1815 after Waterloo, but the loss of the 1866 Austro-Prussian War, and creation of the Austro-Hungarian empire in 1867, diminished the Habsburg's influence in Europe.

However, these setbacks pale beside Archduke Franz Ferdinand's assassination by Slavic separatists in Sarajevo on 28 June 1914. When his uncle, the Austro-Hungarian emperor Franz Josef, declared war on Serbia in response, the ensuing 'Great War' (WWI) would prove the Habsburgs' downfall.

WWII & Postwar Austria

During the 1930s the Nazis began to influence Austrian politics, and by 1938 the recession-hit country was ripe for picking. Invading German troops met little resistance and Hitler was greeted on Heldenplatz as a hero by 200,000 Viennese.

Austria was heavily bombed during WWII, but the country recovered well, largely through the Marshall Plan and sound political and economic decisions (excluding its foray with the far-right Freedom Party and its controversial leader, Jörg Haider, in the 1990s). Austria has maintained a neutral stance since 1955, been home to a number of international organisations, including the UN, since 1979, and joined the EU in 1995.

Arts

What other country can match the musical heritage of Austria? Europe's best composers were drawn to Vienna by the Habsburgs' generous patronage during the 18th and 19th centuries. The era most strongly associated with Austrian music is *Wiener Klassik* (Vienna Classic), which dates back to the mid- and late 18th century and has

BAROQUE HEYDAY

Thanks to the Habsburg monarchy and its obsession with pomp and splendour, Austria is packed with high-calibre architecture, which reached giddy heights of opulence during the baroque era of the late 17th and early 18th century. Among the highlights are the Karlskirche (Vienna), Dom (Salzburg), Hofburg (Innsbruck), Schloss Schönbrunn (Vienna) and Stift Melk (Melk).

defined the way we perceive classical music today.

Joseph Haydn (1732–1809) is considered to be the first of the great composers of the *Wiener Klassik* era, followed by Salzburg Wunderkind Wolfgang Amadeus Mozart (1756–91). Beethoven's musical genius reached its zenith in Vienna. *Lieder* (song) master Franz Schubert (1797–1828) was the last of the heavyweight *Wiener Klassik* composers. The Viennese waltz originated in Vienna and was perfected by Johann Strauss Jr (1825–99).

In 1897, 19 progressive artists broke away from the conservative artistic establishment and formed the Vienna Secession (*Sezession*) movement, synonymous with art nouveau. Vienna turned out such talents as the painter Gustav Klimt (1862–1918); Schloss Belvedere showcases one of his finest works, *The Kiss*. Vienna-born architect Otto Wagner (1841–1918) ushered in a new, functional direction around the turn of the 20th century and gave the capital a metro system replete with attractive art nouveau stations.

Food & Drink

Staples & Specialities

Austria is famous for its Wiener schnitzel, goulash and desserts like *Sacher Torte* (Sacher cake) and *Kaiserschmarrn* (sweet pancakes with raisins). Certainly, these classics are not to be missed, but the Austrian table offers other regional and seasonal delights, such as Waldviertel game and poppy dishes, Mostviertel cider, Wachau *Marillen* (apricots), and Styrian *Almochsen* (meadow beef) and pumpkin oil. Upper Austria is *Knödel* (dumpling) country. Try freshwater fish in Carinthia, *Heumilchkäse* (hay milk cheese) from Vorarlberg and Tirol's hearty *Gröstl* (a fry-up from leftover potatoes, pork and onions) on your travels, too.

Throw in excellent red wines from Burgenland and quality whites and reds from Lower Austria, Styria and elsewhere, and you have the makings of an exciting and unexpected culinary experience.

Where to Eat & Drink

Solid Austrian fare is on the menu in Vienna's homely, good-value inns called *Beisl* (from the Yiddish word for 'little houses'). Besides cake, most coffee houses serve light or classic dishes like goulash. For cheap food, try *Mensen* (university canteens). Another money-saving trick is to make lunch the main meal of the day, as many Austrians do; most restaurants provide a good-value *Tagesteller* or *Tagesmenü* (fixed-price menu). Or assemble your own picnic at local farmers markets.

SURVIVAL GUIDE

Directory A–Z

Accommodation

From simple mountain huts to five-star hotels fit for kings – you'll find the lot in Austria. Tourist offices invariably keep lists and details, and some arrange bookings for free or for a nominal fee. Some useful points:

» Book ahead for the high seasons: July and August and December to April (in ski resorts).

» Some hostels and some rock-bottom digs have an *Etagendusche* (communal shower).

» In mountain resorts, high-season prices can be up to double the prices charged in the low season (May to June and October to November).

» Some resorts issue a *Gästekarte* (guest card) when you stay overnight, offering discounts on things such as cable cars and admission.

Some useful websites include the following:

Austrian Hotelreservation (www.austrian-hotelreservation.at)

Austrian National Tourist Office (www.austria.info)

Booking.com (www.booking.com)

Hostelling International (HI; www.hihostels.com)

Hostelworld (www.hostelworld.com)

PRICE RANGES

For a standard double with bathroom in the high season.

€ less than €80

€€ €80 to €200

€€€ more than €200

ACCOMMODATION TYPES

Hostels In Austria over 100 hostels *(Jugendherberge)* are affiliated with Hostelling International (HI). Facilities are often excellent. Four- to six-bed dorms with shower/toilet are the norm, though some places also have doubles and family rooms. See www.oejhv.or.at or www.oejhw.at for details.

Private Rooms *Privatzimmer* (private rooms) are cheap (often about €50 per double). On top of this, you will find *Bauernhof* (farmhouses) in rural areas, and some *Öko-Bauernhöfe* (organic farms).

Alpine Huts There are over 530 of these huts in the Austrian Alps; most are maintained by the **Österreichischer Alpenverein** (ÖAV, Austrian Alpine Club; www.alpenverein.at). Bed prices for nonmembers are around €26 to €44 in a dorm; OAV members pay half-price.

Rental Accommodation *Ferienwohnungen* (self-catering apartments) are ubiquitous in Austrian mountain resorts. Contact a local tourist office for lists and prices.

Camping Austria has over 400 camping grounds, many well equipped and scenically located. Prices can be as low as €4 per person or small tent, and as high as €10. Many close in winter, so phone ahead to check. Search by region at www.camping-club.at (in German).

Activities

Austria is a wonderland for outdoorsy types, with much of the west given over to towering Alpine peaks. Opportunities for hiking and mountaineering are boundless in Tirol, Salzburgerland and the Hohe Tauern National Park, all of which have extensive Alpine hut networks (see www.alpenverein.at). Names like St Anton, Kitzbühel and Mayrhofen fire the imagination of serious skiers, but you may find cheaper accommodation and lift passes in little-known resorts; visit www.austria.info for the lowdown.

Business Hours

Banks 8am to 3pm Monday to Friday, to 5.30pm Thursday

Clubs 10pm to late

Post offices 8am to noon and 2pm to 6pm Monday to Friday, 8am to noon Saturday

Pubs 6pm to 1am

Cafes 7.30am to 8pm; hours vary widely

Restaurants Noon to 3pm and 7pm to 11pm

Shops 9am to 6.30pm Monday to Friday, 9am to 5pm Saturday

Supermarkets 9am to 8pm Monday to Saturday

Discount Cards

Student & Youth Cards International Student Identity Cards (ISIC) and European Youth Card (Euro<26; check www.euro26.org for discounts) will get you discounts at most museums, galleries and theatres. Admission is generally a little higher than the price for children.

Discount Rail Cards See p88.

Embassies & Consulates

The following are all located in Vienna. For a complete listing of embassies and consulates, look in the Austrian telephone book under *Botschaften* (embassies) or *Konsulate* (consulates).

Australian Embassy (☎506 740; www.australian-embassy.at; Mattiellistrasse 2-4, Vienna)

Canadian Embassy (☎0531-383 000; www.canadainternational.gc.ca; Laurenzerberg 2, Vienna)

THROUGH THE GRAPEVINE

In the winegrowing regions, rustic *Heurigen* (wine taverns) sell their wine directly from their own premises and food is available buffet-style. They open on a roster so pick up the local *Heurigen* calendar from the tourist offices. Some of the best can be found on the 830km **Weinstrasse Niederösterreich** (www.weinstrassen.at; Lower Austria Wine Rd), which wends through eight wine-producing regions in Lower Austria.

New Zealand Embassy (☎0505-30 21; www.nzembassy.com/austria; Mattiellistrasse 2-4, Vienna)

UK Embassy (☎716 130; http://ukinaustria.fco.gov.uk; Jaurèsgasse 12, Vienna)

US Embassy (☎313 390; http://austria.usembassy.gov; Boltzmanngasse 16, Vienna)

Food

Price ranges in this chapter are for a two-course meal excluding drinks:

€ less than €15

€€ €15 to €30

€€€ more than €30

Money

Austria's currency is the euro. An approximate 10% tip is expected in restaurants. Pay it directly to the server; don't leave it on the table.

Public Holidays

New Year's Day (Neujahr) 1 January

Epiphany (Heilige Drei Könige) 6 January

Easter Monday (Ostermontag) March/April

Labour Day (Tag der Arbeit) 1 May

Whit Monday (Pfingstmontag) Sixth Monday after Easter

Ascension Day (Christi Himmelfahrt) Sixth Thursday after Easter

Corpus Christi (Fronleichnam) Second Thursday after Whitsunday

Assumption (Maria Himmelfahrt) 15 August

National Day (Nationalfeiertag) 26 October

All Saints' Day (Allerheiligen) 1 November

Immaculate Conception (Mariä Empfängnis) 8 December

Christmas Day (Christfest) 25 December

St Stephen's Day (Stephanitag) 26 December

Telephone

» Austrian telephone numbers consist of an area code followed by the local number.

» The country code is ☎43 and the international access code is ☎00.

» The mobile network works on GSM 1800 and is compatible with GSM 900 phones. Phone shops sell prepaid SIM cards for about €10.

» Phone-cards in different denominations are sold at post offices and *Tabak* (tobacconist) shops. Call centres are widespread in cities, and many internet cafes are geared for Skype calls.

Tourist Information

Tourist offices, which are dispersed far and wide in Austria, tend to adjust their hours from one year to the next, so business hours may have changed slightly by the time you arrive.

The **Austrian National Tourist Office** (www.austria.info) has a number of overseas offices. There is a comprehensive listing on the ANTO website.

Visas

Schengen visa rules apply. See p1212 for further details. The Austrian Foreign Ministry website www.bmeia.gv.at lists embassies.

Getting There & Away

Air

Among the low-cost airlines, Ryanair and Air Berlin fly to Graz, Innsbruck, Klagenfurt, Linz, Salzburg and Vienna (Ryanair to Bratislava for Vienna).

Following are the key international airports in Austria (and neighbouring Slovakia):

Airport Bratislava (☎421 2 3303 33 53; www.airportbratislava.sk) Serves Bratislava and has good transport connections to Vienna. Used by Ryanair.

Blue Danube Airport (☎0722-16 00; www.flughafen-linz.at) Outside Linz.

Graz Airport (☎29 020; www.flughafen-graz.at)

Innsbruck Airport (☎0512-22 525; www.innsbruck-airport.com)

Klagenfurt Airport (☎0463-41 500; www.klagenfurt-airport.com)

Salzburg Airport (☎0662-85 800; www.salzburg-airport.com)

Vienna Airport (☎01-7007 22 233; www.viennaairport.com)

Land

BUS

Buses depart from Austria for as far afield as England, the Baltic countries, the Netherlands, Germany and Switzerland. But most significantly, they provide access to eastern European cities small and large – from the likes of Sofia and Warsaw, to Banja Luka, Mostar and Sarajevo.

Services operated by **Eurolines** (www.eurolines.at) leave from Vienna and from several regional cities.

CAR & MOTORCYCLE

There are numerous entry points into Austria by road from Germany, the Czech Republic, Slovakia, Hungary, Slovenia, Italy and Switzerland. All border-crossing points are open 24 hours.

Standard European insurance and paperwork rules apply (see p87 for more details).

TRAIN

Austria has excellent rail connections. The main services in and out of the country from the west normally pass through Bregenz, Innsbruck or Salzburg en route to Vienna. Trains to eastern Europe leave from Vienna. Express services to Italy go via Innsbruck or Villach; trains to Slovenia are routed through Graz.

For online timetables and tickets, visit the Austrian National Railways website **ÖBB** (☎05 17 17; www.oebb.at). SparSchiene (discounted tickets) are often available when you book online in advance and can cost as little as a third of the standard train fare.

River & Lake

Hydrofoils run to Bratislava and Budapest from Vienna; slower boats cruise the Danube between the capital and Passau. The **Danube Tourist Commission** (www.danube-river.org) has a country-by-country list of operators and agents who can book tours.

Getting Around

Air

The national carrier **Austrian Airlines** (www.austrian.com) and its joint flight operator Tyrolean offer several flights daily between Vienna and Graz, Innsbruck, Klagenfurt, Linz and Salzburg.

Bicycle

» All cities have at least one bike shop that doubles as a rental centre; expect to pay around €10 to €15 per day.

» Most tourist boards have brochures on cycling facilities and plenty of designated cycling routes within their region.

» You can take bicycles on any train with a bicycle symbol at the top of its timetable. A day ticket costs €5 for regional, €10 for national (InterCity) and €12 for international trains.

Boat

Services along the Danube are generally slow, scenic excursions rather than functional means of transport.

Bus

Postbus services usually depart from outside train stations. In remote regions, there are fewer services on Saturday and often none on Sunday. For information, visit www.postbus.at.

Car & Motorcycle

A *Vignette* (toll sticker) is imposed on all motorways, charges for cars/motorbikes are €8.30/4.80 for 10 days and €24.20/12.10 for two months. *Vignette* can be purchased at border crossings, petrol stations and *Tabak* shops. There are additional tolls (usually €2.50 to €10) for some mountain tunnels.

Speed limits are 50km/h in built-up areas, 130km/h on motorways and 100km/h on other roads.

Multinational car-hire firms Avis, Budget, Europcar and Hertz all have offices in major cities. The minimum age for hiring small cars is 19 years, or 25 years for larger, 'prestige' cars. Customers must have held a driving licence for at least a year. Many contracts forbid customers to take cars outside Austria, particularly into eastern Europe.

Crash helmets are compulsory for motorcyclists.

Train

Austria has a clean, efficient rail system, and if you use a discount card it's very inexpensive.

» Disabled passengers can use the 24-hour ☎051 717 customer number for special travel assistance; do this at least 24 hours ahead of travel (48 hours ahead for international services). Staff at stations will help with boarding and alighting.

» Fares quoted here are for 2nd-class tickets.

» ÖBB (☎051 717; www.oebb.at) is the main operator, supplemented with a handful of private lines. Tickets and timetables are available online.

» It's worth seeking out RailJet train services connecting Vienna, Graz, Villach, Salzburg, Innsbruck, Linz and Klagenfurt, as they travel up to 200km/h.

» Reservations in 2nd class within Austria cost €3.50 for most express services; recommended for travel on weekends.

RAIL PASSES

Depending on the amount of travelling you intend to do in Austria, rail passes can be a good deal.

Eurail Austria Pass This handy pass is available to non-EU residents; prices start at €123 for three days' unlimited 2nd-class travel within one month, and youths under 26 receive substantial discounts. See the website at www.eurail.com for all options.

Interrail Passes are for European residents and include One Country Pass Austria (three/four/six/eight days €181/205/267/311). Youths under 26 receive substantial discounts. See www.interrail-net.com for all options.

Vorteilscard Reduces fares by at least 45% and is valid for a year, but not on buses. Bring a photo and your passport or ID. It costs adult/under 26 years €100/20.

Belarus

Includes »

Minsk 92
Brest 96
Understand Belarus 97
Survival Guide 98

Best Places to Eat

» Strawnya Talaka (p94)
» Jules Verne (p97)
» Stolle (p94)

Best Sights

» Brest Fortress (p96)
» Belarusian State Art Museum (p93)
» Museum of the Great Patriotic War (p92)
» National Library of Belarus (p93)

Why Go?

Eastern Europe's outcast, Belarus (Беларусь) lies at the edge of the region and seems determined to avoid integration with the rest of the continent at all costs. Taking its lead from the Soviet Union rather than the European Union, this little-visited dictatorship may seem like a strange choice for travellers, but its isolation is at the heart of its appeal.

While the rest of eastern Europe has charged headlong into capitalism, Belarus allows the chance to visit a Europe with minimal advertising and no litter or graffiti. Outside the monumental Stalinist capital of Minsk, Belarus offers a simple yet pleasing landscape of cornflower fields, thick forests and picturesque villages. The country also offers two excellent national parks Belavezhskaya Pushcha and Pripyatsky), and is home to Europe's largest mammal, the *zoobr* (or European bison). While travellers will always be subject to curiosity, they'll also be on the receiving end of warm hospitality and genuine welcome.

When to Go

Minsk

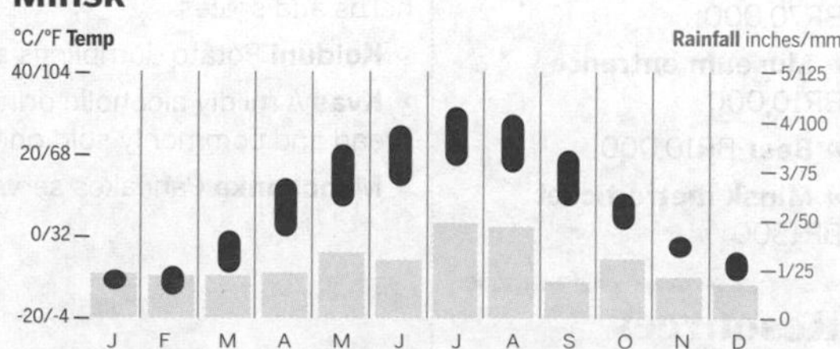

Jun–Aug Don't worry about high season: come to escape the crowds elsewhere.

Mid-Jul A fine time to enjoy a Belarusian festival or two.

May International Workers' Day still sees parades and much festivity all over Belarus.

AT A GLANCE

» **Currency** Belarusian rouble (BR)

» **Language** Belarusian, Russian

» **Money** ATMs taking international cards are widely available

» **Visas** Needed by almost everybody

Fast Facts

» **Area** 207,600 sq km

» **Capital** Minsk

» **Country code** ☎375

» **Emergency** Ambulance ☎03, fire ☎01, police ☎02

Exchange Rates

Australia	A$1	BR9065
Canada	C$1	BR8525
Euro Zone	€1	BR11,072
Japan	¥100	BR9178
New Zealand	NZ$1	BR7253
UK	UK£1	BR13,122
USA	US$1	BR8677

Set Your Budget

» **Budget hotel room** €20

» **Two-course meal** BR70,000

» **Museum entrance** BR10,000

» **Beer** BR10,000

» **Minsk metro ticket** BR1800

Resources

» **Belarus Embassy in the UK** (www.uk.mfa.gov.by)

» **Belarus Tourism** (eng.belarustourism.by)

Connections

Belarus has good overland links to all neighbouring countries. Daily trains from Minsk serve Moscow and St Petersburg in Russia, Vilnius in Lithuania, Warsaw in Poland (via Terespol) and Kyiv in Ukraine. Bus services, which tend to be less comfortable, connect Minsk to Moscow, St Petersburg, Kyiv, Warsaw and Vilnius; Vitsebsk to Moscow and St Petersburg; and Brest to Terespol in Poland.

ITINERARIES

Three Days

Spend two days getting to know Minsk – its Stalinist architecture belies a lively and friendly city – before taking a day trip to to the medieval castle at Mir and the ancient Belarusian town of Nyasvish to get a feel for the charming Belarusian countryside.

One Week

Begin with two nights in funky and fun Brest, where the fascinating Brest Fortress awaits exploration, then take a train to quirky Minsk for a few nights, allowing yourself time for a day trip to Mir and Nyasvish before continuing on to Russia by train.

Essential Food & Drink

» **Belavezhskaya** A bitter herbal alcoholic drink.

» **Draniki** Potato pancakes, usually served with sour cream *(smetana)*.

» **Kletsky** Dumplings stuffed with mushrooms, cheese or potato.

» **Khaladnik** A local variation on cold borsch, a soup made from beetroot and garnished with sour cream, chopped up hard-boiled eggs, and potatoes.

» **Kindziuk** A pig-stomach sausage filled with minced pork, herbs and spices.

» **Kolduni** Potato dumplings stuffed with meat.

» **Kvas** A mildly alcoholic drink made from black or rye bread and commonly sold on the streets in Belarus.

» **Manchanka** Pancakes served with a meaty gravy.

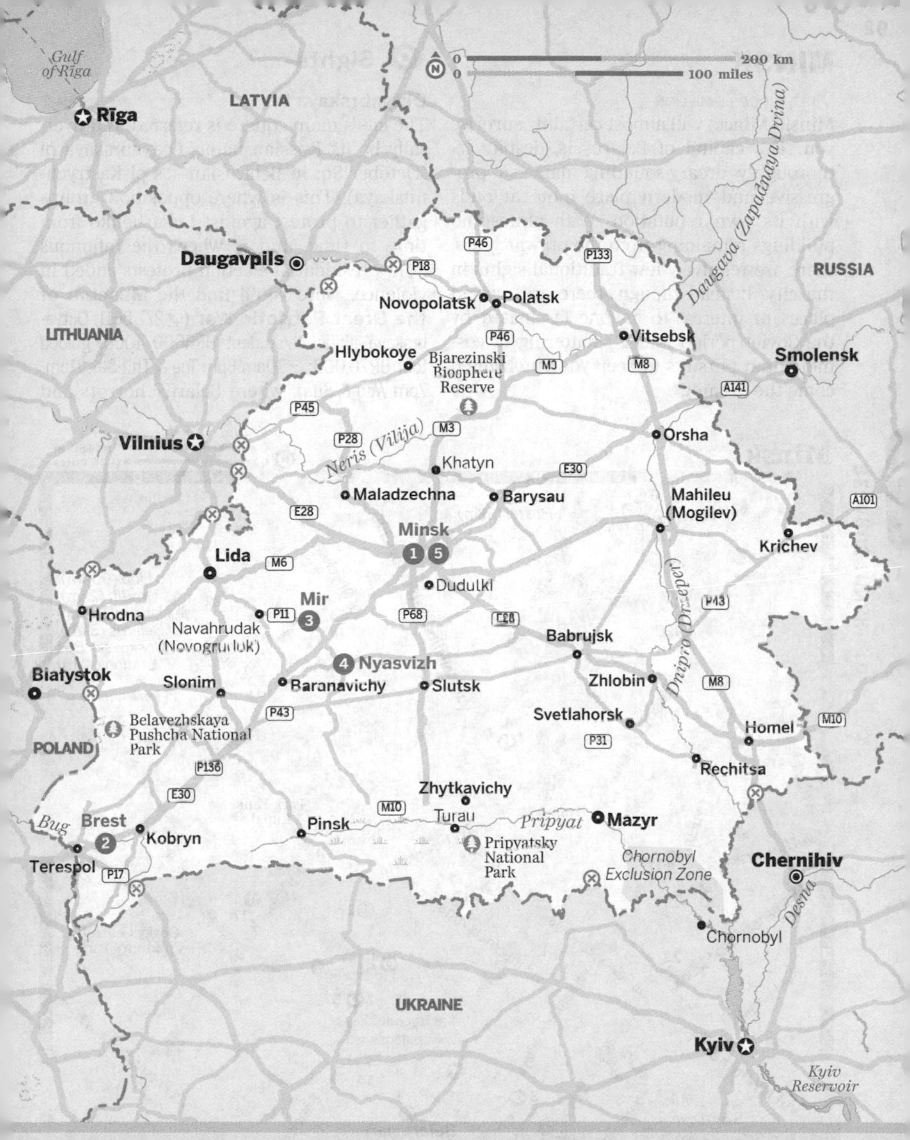

Belarus Highlights

1. Get under the skin of **Minsk** (p92), the showpiece of Stalinist architecture and a friendly, accessible city

2. Stroll through the mellow pedestrian streets of cosmopolitan Brest to the epic WWII memorial that is **Brest Fortress** (p96)

3. See the fairy-tale 16th-century castle at **Mir** (p96), which presides over the tranquil town of the same name

4. Explore one of the few historical complexes to have survived WWII at **Nyasvizh**, (p96) amid beautiful lakes and the picturesque Radziwill Palace Fortress

5. Discover centuries of heritage at the fascinating and newly extended **Belarusian State Art Museum** (p93)

MINSK

☎017 / POP 1.9 MILLION

Minsk (Минск) will almost certainly surprise you. The capital of Belarus is, despite its thoroughly dreary-sounding name, a progressive and modern place quite at odds with its own reputation. With almost no buildings remaining from the prewar years, there are relatively few traditional sights in the city. Instead though, there are myriad places of interest to anyone fascinated by the Soviet period and a smattering of cosmopolitan pursuits to keep you entertained come the evening.

Sights

Oktyabrskaya Pl SQUARE

The city's main square is referred to universally by its Russian name, Oktyabrskaya pl (October Sq; in Belarusian, it's pl Kastrychnitskaya). This is where opposition groups gather to protest against Lukashenko from time to time, and is where the infamous 2010 presidential election protests ended in violence. Here you'll find the **Museum of the Great Patriotic War** (☎277 5611; Oktyabrskaya pl; adult/student BR6000/4000, guided tour BR20,000; ⏲10am-6pm Tue & Thu-Sat, 11am-7pm Wed & Sun), where Belarus' horrors and

Minsk

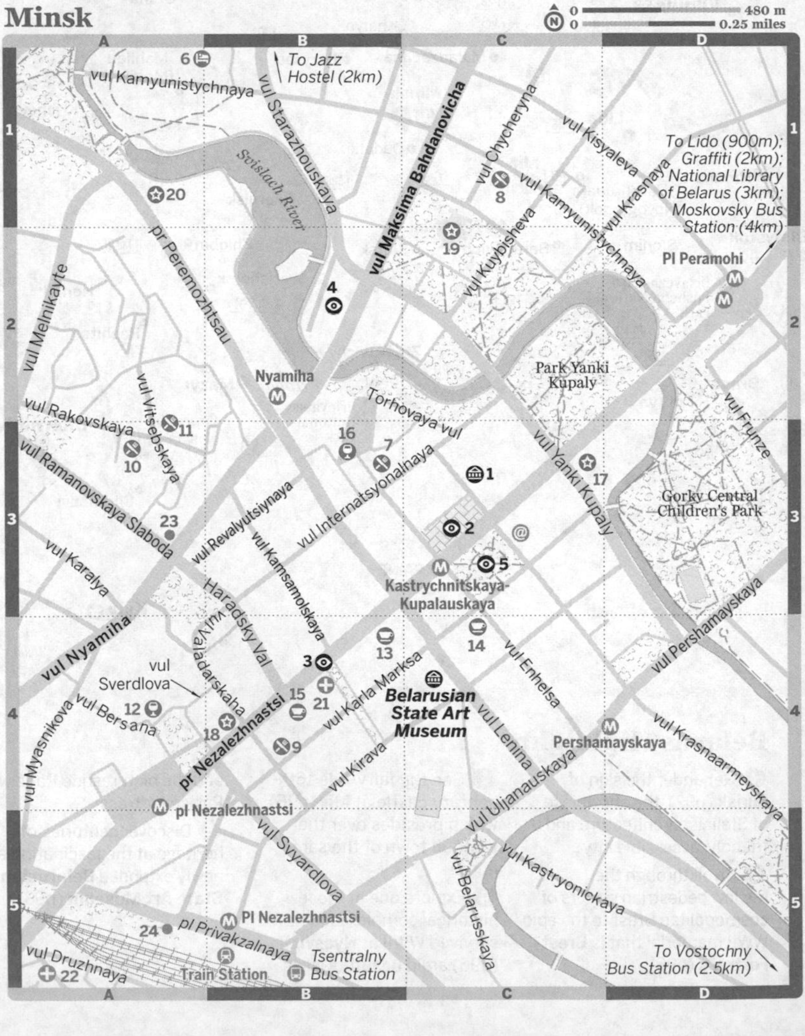

heroism during WWII are exhibited in photographs, huge dioramas and other media. A new building next door to house the museum is due to be completed in 2014, after which the old museum building is slated to become a luxury hotel.

TOP CHOICE **Belarusian State Art Museum** MUSEUM
(vul Lenina 20; admission BR20,000; ⏲11am-7pm Wed-Mon; Ⓜ Kupalawskaja/Kastrychnitskaja) This excellent state museum has been renovated and now includes a light-bathed extension out the back that features local art from the 1940s to the 1970s. There's also an impressive collection of icons, some great realist depictions of late 19th-century life in the Russian Empire, and several works by Nikolai Ge, Ilya Repin, Isaak Levitan, Isaak Brodsky, Mikhail Nesterov and Konstantin Makovsky.

National Library of Belarus LIBRARY
(☎293 2853; old.nlb.by/en; pr Nezalezhnastsi 116; viewing platform admission BR3000; ⏲10am-9pm Mon-Fri, 10am-6pm Sat & Sun, closed Sun Jun-Aug, viewing platform 1-9pm Tue-Fri, 10am-6pm Sat & Sun; Ⓜ Vostok) For a taste of post-Soviet Belarus, head north of the centre to the new National Library of Belarus, a ghastly piece of Lukashenko-approved hubris. The building is a giant rhombicuboctahedron (look it up!) that is lit at night and contains more than two million records as well as art galleries and a **viewing platform** on the 22nd floor.

Pr Nezalezhnastsi AVENUE
Making up the bustling heart of Minsk, including the Soviet-era GUM department store, is pr Nezalezhnasti (Independence Av). An entire block at No 17 is occupied by the still active **KGB headquarters**.

Tsentralny Skver SQUARE
Facing Oktyabrskaya pl is Tsentralny Skver (Central Sq), a small park on the site of a 19th-century marketplace. Beyond this is the lifeless-looking, seriously guarded **Presidential Administrative Building**, from where Alexander Lukashenko rules.

Traetskae Pradmestse OLD TOWN
In lieu of any real remaining Old Town is Traetskae Pradmestse, a pleasant – if tiny – re-creation of Minsk's prewar buildings on a pretty bend of the river north of the centre. At the end of a little footbridge nearby is the evocative Afghan war memorial, **Island of Courage and Sorrow**, more commonly called the Island of Tears by locals. It commemorates the Belarusian soldiers who perished in the war between the Soviet Union and Afghanistan (1979–89).

Minsk

Top Sights
Belarusian State Art Museum C4

Sights
1 Museum of the Great Patriotic War C3
2 Oktyabrskaya pl C3
3 Pr Nezalezhnastsi B4
4 Traetskae Pradmestse B2
5 Tsentralny Skver C3

Sleeping
6 Hotel Belarus A1

Eating
7 Byblos B3
8 Gurman C1
9 Pizza Tempo B4
10 Stolle A3
11 Strawnya Talaka A3

Drinking
12 Drozhzhi United A4
13 London B4
My English Granny .... (see 14)
14 News Café C4
15 Stary Mensk B4
16 U Ratushi B3

Entertainment
17 Belarusian State Circus C3
18 Central Ticket Office B4
19 National Academic Opera & Ballet Theatre C2
20 Overtime A1

Information
21 24-hour Pharmacy B4
22 EcoMedservices A5

Transport
23 Belavia A3
24 International Train Ticket Office A5

Sleeping

Minsk's accommodation scene is generally limited to fusty old Soviet hotels or overpriced business accommodation. A much better option is to rent an apartment. Try **Belarus Rent** (www.belarusrent.com) and **Belarus Apartment** (www.belarusapartment.com). Rates range from €40 to €100 per night.

40 Let Pobedy HOTEL €
(☎294 7963; vul Azgura 3; s/d from €18/25; wi-fi) This slightly out-of-the-way yet central place offers decent, good-value rooms and friendly service. The hotel has made a good effort to modernise itself (even if it is with cheap furnishings) and all the bathrooms have been redone. It's a 10-minute walk from Pl Peramohi metro station.

Hotel Belarus HOTEL €
(☎209 7337, 209 7537; www.hotel-belarus.com; vul Starazhouskaya 15; s/d incl breakfast from €16/20; wi-fi, pool) Set in parkland amid plenty of open space a 15-minute amble from the city centre, this Soviet-era place has undergone little change since it was built, although a swimming pool with a waterslide sets it apart from other hotels of this standard. There's an enormous number of room categories, but at the lowest prices, it's an ok deal.

Jazz Hostel HOSTEL €
(☎03 3361 633; hostel.jazz@gmail.com; vul Mazyrskaya 37A; dm per person €10) Yes, there's finally a hostel in Minsk, and yes it's miles from anywhere and highly weird. What else did you expect? This large house has 43 beds spread over its two floors, a large kitchen and even some double rooms for more privacy. The whole place is not really set up for foreigners and there isn't much English spoken, but excursions and visa registration can be arranged. It's definitely an experience, as is getting here: take tram 4 from outside the main train station and get off at the Vozera stop.

Eating

Minsk has a decent eating scene and plenty of choice – don't believe the hype about food in Belarus; in the capital, at least, you'll eat well. However, decent budget options are thin on the ground, and you'll usually need to pay more than you normally might for a good meal.

Stolle PIE SHOP €
(www.stolle.by; vul Rakovskaya 23; mains BR50,000-80,000, pies BR15,000; ⏲9am-11pm; menu) This St Petersburg institution has finally hit Minsk and very welcome it is too, with its delicious freshly baked sweet and savoury pies. The most central location of the three now open has a very pleasant upstairs dining room, as well as a takeaway counter downstairs. There's also a full non-pie menu serving up traditional Russian and Belarusian cuisine.

Strawnya Talaka TRADITIONAL €€
(☎203 2794; vul Rakovskaya 18; mains BR35,000-195,000; ⏲10am-6am; menu) This relaxed and cosy basement place is the best restaurant in Minsk for an authentic local meal, and also has handy long opening hours. Try the hare in bilberry sauce, the mushroom soup served in a loaf of bread or just a bowl of their fantastic beer snacks and the fabulous *draniki* (potato pancakes). Staff are dressed in traditional peasant garb and the enormous wooden menus are fully pictorial and hilariously translated.

Pizza Tempo PIZZA €€
(☎292 1111; www.pizzatempo.by; vul Karla Marksa 9; mains BR16,000-100,000; ⏲9am-11pm; menu) This chain of seven pizzerias is spread across the city, with each restaurant stylishly decorated and enjoying a relaxed vibe. Citywide delivery is available and the pizza is the best we've found in Minsk.

Gurman RUSSIAN €
(☎290 6774; vul Kamyunistychnaya 7; mains BR10,000-60,000; ⏲8am-11pm) This Minsk institution specialises in many varieties of delicious, freshly made *pelmeni* (Russian-style ravioli) and also offers a wide selection of pastas, curries and other international cuisine. The light and airy premises and friendly staff make this well worth the wander from the metro. It's worth booking a table for dinner.

Byblos LEBANESE €€
(vul Internatsyanalnaya 21; mains BR20,000-85,000; ⏲noon-midnight, until 2am Fri-Sat; wi-fi, menu) What this Lebanese-style place lacks in authenticity it makes up for in value, quick service and an English menu. Great for an easy lunch; the kebabs and hummus are decent enough, given that you're in Belarus, and there's great people-watching from the enclosed terrace. There's wi-fi available until 5pm.

Lido CANTEEN €
(pr Nezalezhnastsi 49/1; mains BR5000-20,000; ⏲8am-11pm Mon-Fri, 11am-11pm Sat & Sun; menu)

This excellent place is a real lifesaver for a quick and filling meal. The large cafeteria has a huge array of food on display, so it's easy for non-Russian speakers: just point at what you want. Lunchtime is always packed, but it's usually easy to find a seat among the curious faux-medieval village decor.

Drinking

Bars & Nightclubs

Drozhzhi United PUB
(vul Sverdlova 2; 9am-2am) Centrally located, Minsk's Irish pub is instantly recognisable to anyone who has ever been an expat, anywhere. There's good food, Guinness on tap and a friendly atmosphere though.

U Ratushi PUB
(vul Gertsena 1, Pl Svabody; 10am-2am) This multilevel pub-style restaurant, right across from the *ratusha* (town hall), is packed with a raucous, fun-loving crowd on weekends (there is often a small cover charge for live bands). Come early at the weekend to get a seat.

Graffiti BAR
(www.graffiti.by; pr Kalinina 16; cover BR20,000-40,000; 11am-11pm, to 2am Fri & Sat) For something contemporary and underground, Graffiti offers nightly concerts from local bands and big weekend parties popular with an alternative and anti-Luka crowd. It's a 10-minute walk from the Park Chelyuskintsev metro station: head up vul Tolbukhina, turn right onto vul Knorina and then left onto vul Belinskogo. Graffiti can be found in the unlikely looking industrial building on the corner.

Overtime CLUB
(pr Peremozhtsau 4; cover free-BR50,000; 6pm-6am) Currently the hippest place in town despite its premises being better suited for use as a venue for a high-school disco, this club attracts a chic and monied crowd of local glitzy gals and their muscly boyfriends. Dress up to get in – face control can be tough.

Cafes

The best cafes in Minsk include the sleek **News Café** (vul Karla Marksa 34; 8am-midnight; wi-fi), where free wi-fi (until 7pm), good coffee and full meals make for a great hang-out, and the bizarre **My English Granny** (vul Karla Marksa 36; 9am-11pm; wi-fi) next door, a cafe that has pulled off the incredible feat of making kitschy Victoriana look trendy, where you'll get a lovely pot of tea and some good cakes, as well as meals and a great breakfast selection. Two other slightly more bohemian options are sister cafes **Stary Mensk** (pr Nezalezhnastsi 14; 10am-11pm) and **London** (pr Nezalezhnastsi 18; 10am-midnight; wi-fi), which both serve hot drinks and are favoured by Minsk's intellectual crowd.

Entertainment

A pleasant hangover from Soviet times is that performing arts are of very good quality and tickets are cheap.

To buy advance tickets or to find out what's on, head to the **central ticket office** (pr Nezalezhnastsi 13; 9am-7pm). There are more places for tickets in the underpass at the junction of pr Nezalezhnastsi and vul Lenina in the centre. Same-day tickets are often available only from the performance venues.

Don't miss the highly respected **National Academic Opera & Ballet Theatre** (234 8074; pl Parizhskoy Kamunni 1; ticket office 9am-1pm & 2-6pm Mon-Fri), where there are several different operas performed each month; performances take place at 7pm on Thursday, Saturday and Sunday. The **Belarusian State Circus** (226 1008; pr Nezalezhnastsi 32) reopened in 2011 following a full refit and is now a modern and well-appointed venue.

Information

24-hour Pharmacy (pr Nezalezhnastsi 16)

EcoMedservices (207 7474; www.ems.by; vul Tolstoho 4; 8am-9pm) Just south of the train station.

Soyuz Online (2nd fl, vul Krasnaarmeyskaya 3; 24hr) Large internet cafe in the centre of town. Food and drinks available. Go up the steps to the Dom Ofitserov and enter the far door near the tank monument.

Getting There & Away

Air

International flights entering and departing Belarus do so at the **Minsk-2 international airport** (279 1300; www.airport.by), about 40km east of Minsk. Some flights to the former Soviet Union depart from the smaller **Minsk-1 airport** (006; vul Chkalova 38), only a few kilometres south of the city centre.

Bus

Tsentralny Bus Station (227 0473; vul Bobruyskaya 6) The main bus station is next to the train station in the centre of Minsk. Buses to Mir (Novgrorodok), Brest, Hrodna and Nyasvizh depart from here.

Moskovsky Bus Station (☎219 3622; vul Filimonava 63) Near Maskouskaya metro station, about 4km east of the city.

Vostochny Bus Station (☎247 4984; vul Vaneeva 34) To get here from the train station (or metro Pl Lenina), take bus 8 or trolley 20 or 30 and get off at Avtovokzal Vostochny.

Train

The busy and modern **Minsk train station** (☎105, 225 7000; Privakzalnaya pl; ⏱24hr) is pretty easy to deal with. Very basic food and complex **left-luggage services** (lockers BR1000, luggage room BR2000; ⏱24hr) are available here, as well as an internet cafe on the 3rd floor, ATMs and exchange facilities. Buy domestic and CIS (Commonwealth of Independent States) tickets here.

Domestic Train Ticket Office (☎225 6271; pr Nezalezhnastsi 18; ⏱9am-8pm Mon-Fri, 9am-7pm Sat & Sun) Tickets for domestic and CIS destinations.

International Train Ticket Office (☎213 1719; vul Bobruyskaya 4; ⏱24hrs) Advance tickets for non-CIS destinations; located to the right of the train station.

Getting Around

To/From the Airport

From Minsk-2 airport, a 40-minute taxi ride into town should cost anywhere from €30, depending on your bargaining skills. There are buses and *marshrutky* (shared minibuses; BR10,000, 90 minutes, hourly) that bring you to the city centre, though you can get out at the first metro station (Uruchye) to get elsewhere in the city. From Minsk-1 airport, take bus 100 to the centre; it goes along pr Nezalezhnastsi.

Public Transport

Minsk's metro is simple: just two lines with one transfer point at the Kastrychnitskaya-Kupalauskaya interchange on pr Nezalezhnastsi. A third line is under construction, but at present the system isn't hugely useful to travellers. It's open daily from dawn until just after midnight. One token *(zheton)* costs BR1800. Buses, trams, trolleybuses also cost BR1800 per ride. Many locals don't bother to buy tickets, as even the fines are miniscule.

AROUND MINSK

Heading out of Minsk into the gently appealing Belarusian countryside is a great way to get to know the country. There are several places that can easily be visited on a day trip from the capital.

The magical old buildings of **Nyasvizh** make it a great place to get in touch with Belarus' past. This green and attractive town 120km southwest of Minsk is also one of the oldest in the country, dating from the 13th century. While here visit the **Farny Polish Roman Catholic Church** and walk the causeway to the beautiful 16th-century **Radziwill Palace Fortress** – the town's main sight. From Minsk's Vostochny Bus Station there are two daily buses to and from Nyasvizh (BR34,000, 2½ hours).

The charming small town of **Mir**, 85km southwest of Minsk, is dominated by the impossibly romantic 16th-century **Mir Castle** (☎23 035; admission BR25,000; ⏱10am-5pm). It was once owned by the powerful Radziwill princes and has been under Unesco protection since 1994. The town of Mir itself is a delightful backwater.

From Minsk's Vostochny and Tsentralny Bus Stations, there are hourly buses to Navahrudak (Novogrudok in Russian) that stop in Mir (BR28,000 to BR34,000, 2½ hours).

BREST

☎0162 / POP 312,000

The prosperous and cosmopolitan border town of Brest (Брэст) looks far more to the neighbouring EU than to Minsk. It has plenty of charm and has performed a massive DIY job on itself over the past few years. The city's main sight is the Brest Fortress, a moving WWII memorial.

Sights

FREE **Brest Fortress** MUSEUM COMPLEX

(Brestskaya krepost; pr Masherava) Very little remains of Brest Fortress. Certainly don't come here expecting a medieval turreted affair – this is a Soviet WWII memorial to the devastating battle that resulted when German troops advanced into the Soviet Union in the early days of Operation Barbarossa in 1941. The large complex occupies a beautiful spot at the confluence of the Buh and Mukhavets Rivers, a 20-minute walk from the town centre or a short hop on the hourly 17 bus from outside the Hotel Intourist.

Of the several museums here, head to the **Defence of Brest Fortress Museum** (adult/student BR10,000/5000; ⏱9am-6pm), where extensive exhibits demonstrate the plight of the defenders.

Museum of Confiscated Art MUSEUM
(vul Lenina 39; admission BR10,000; ⏲10am-5.30pm Tue-Sun) Here you'll find an extraordinary display of icons, paintings, jewellery and other valuables that were seized from smugglers trying to get them across the border to Poland during the 1990s.

Sleeping

Hotel Molodyozhnaya HOTEL €€
(☎216 376; vul Kamsamolskaya 6; s/d €20/32; 📶) This small and very centrally located place is a short walk from the station. The rooms are comfortable and clean, all have private facilities and the welcome is almost warm.

Hotel Buh HOTEL €
(☎236 417; vul Lenina 2; s/d €20/33, without bathroom €15/22; 📶) The cheapest and oldest of Brest's hotels is also the best choice for some character – the brightly painted Stalin-era foyer is a highlight and service is friendly. The renovated rooms with private bathrooms are often booked up in advance though, leaving the older facility-free rooms as the only option.

Eating

Pizzeria PIZZA €
(vul Pushkinskaya 20; pizzas BR20,000-60,000) It's not well signed, but you can pretty much follow your nose into the building through a garish bakery and then down the stairs. Surprisingly good thin-crust pizzas are made to order and consumed in this basement place, while dubbed Mexican soap operas entertain the diners.

Information

24-hour Pharmacy (vul Hoholya 32)

Cyber Brest (3rd fl, vul Kamsamolskaya 36; per hr BR10,000; ⏲9am-midnight) Internet access at your choice of 50 computers; follow the footprints to the top floor.

Getting There & Around

BUS The **bus station** (☎004, 114; vul Mitskevicha) is in the centre of town and has both left-luggage lockers and an internet cafe. There are five daily buses to Minsk (BR58,000 to BR70,000, five hours).

TRAIN The **train station** (☎005) has on-site customs. Trains leave for Minsk (BR35,000/65,000 platzkart/kupe – third-/second-class – four hours) several times daily. The city is a short walk from the train station: mount a steep flight of steps from the platform and once you're up, go right on the overpass.

SPLURGE

It's almost a miracle that a great restaurant such as **Jules Verne** (vul Hoholya 29; mains BR40,000-150,000; ⏲noon-midnight) exists in Brest. Decked out like a gentleman's club and with a travel theme, this dark, atmospheric joint manages to be refined without being stuffy. It serves up cracking dishes – from mouthwatering curries and a range of French cooking, to sumptuous desserts and the best coffee in town. Don't miss it.

UNDERSTAND BELARUS

History

Belarus has an unhappy history. In the 1930s, under Stalin, hundreds of thousands of people were executed in purges here. The savage Nazi occupation during WWII was ended in 1944 by the Red Army, with massive destruction on both sides. At least 25% of the Belarusian population died between 1939 and 1945, most in Nazi concentration camps. The 1986 nuclear accident at Chornobyl, just over the border in Ukraine, left about a quarter of the country seriously contaminated, and its effects are still felt today. On 25 August 1991 Belarus declared independence from the USSR.

Since 1994, Belarus has been governed by Alexander Lukashenko, whose autocratic presidential style and poor human rights record has led to Belarus' almost total international isolation. Despite regular elections, there's little democracy to be found in Belarus, where Lukashenko's party always gets enormous majorities despite the low standard of living in the country as a whole.

In December 2010 Lukashenko again won a highly implausible 79% of the vote and protestors on the main square in Minsk were violently dispersed. The protests left more than 600 people in jail, including several of the opposition candidates, many of whom were allegedly beaten while the main opposition leader was reported as being forcibly abducted from the hospital where he was being treated. However, despite criticism from all sides, including once-loyal Russia, Lukashenko remains as entrenched in power as ever.

People

There are approximately 9.4 million people in Belarus, of which 81.2% are Belarusian, 11.4% Russian, 4% Polish and 2.4% Ukrainian. Prior to WWII, 10% of the national population was Jewish. They now make up less than 1% of the country's population.

Generally speaking, Belarusians are quiet, polite and reserved people. Because they tend to be shy, they seem less approachable than Russians and Ukrainians, but they are just as friendly and generous (often more so) once introductions are made.

Environment

Belarus is, for the most part, completely flat, with marshes and swamps in the south and lakes in the north. The 1986 disaster at Chornobyl in neighbouring Ukraine has been the defining event for the Belarusian environment, although the dangers of exposure to radiation for travellers are almost nonexistent; ironically, the exclusion zone has proved a boon for nature thanks to the absence of human habitation.

SURVIVAL GUIDE

Directory A–Z

Accommodation

While budget and midrange accommodation standards in Belarus tend to be lower than in western Europe, they are still generally acceptable and often better than in Russia or Ukraine. Belarus is not cheap by eastern European standards and good budget sleeping and eating options are sorely lacking.

Our price ranges are for a double room with private bathroom unless otherwise indicated, but do not include breakfast. The standard (though not universal) practice for hotels due to the rapid fluctuation of exchange rates is to quote prices in euros and then charge for them in BYR at the day's exchange rates.

€ less than €25

€€ €25 to €60

€€€ more than €60

Business Hours

Banks 9am to 5pm Monday to Friday

Office hours 9am to 6pm Monday to Friday

Shops 9am or 10am to 9pm Mon to Sat, to 6pm Sun if open at all

Some businesses will close for lunch, which is usually for an hour and occurs any time between noon and 2pm. Restaurants and bars usually open between 10am and midday and close between 10pm and midnight.

Embassies & Consulates

There is no representation for Canada, Australia or New Zealand in Belarus.

Russian Embassy Minsk (☎017-222 4985; vul Novolvilenskaya 1a); Brest (☎016-223 7842; vul Pushkinskaya 10)

UK Embassy (☎017-229 8200; www.ukinbelarus.fco.gov.uk; vul Karla Marksa 37)

US Embassy (☎017-210 1283; http://minsk.usembassy.gov; vul Staravilenskaya 46)

Festivals & Events

The night of 6 July is **Kupalye**, a celebration with pagan roots when young girls gather flowers and throw them into a river as a method of fortune-telling, while everyone else sits by lake or riverside fires drinking beer.

Food

Price ranges are based on the average cost of a main course.

€ less than BR50,000

€€ BR50,000 to BR100,000

€€€ more than BR100,000

Money

The Belarusian rouble (BR) is the national currency and the money's wide spectrum of bill denominations is overwhelming to the newcomer. Ensure you change any remaining roubles before leaving Belarus, as it's almost impossible to exchange the currency outside the country. ATMs and currency-exchange offices are not hard to find in Belarusian cities.

Public Holidays

New Year's Day 1 January

Orthodox Christmas 7 January

International Women's Day 8 March

Constitution Day 15 March

Catholic & Orthodox Easter March/April

Unity of Peoples of Russia and Belarus Day 2 April

International Labour Day (May Day) 1 May

Victory Day 9 May

Independence Day 3 July

Dzyady (Day of the Dead) 2 November

Catholic Christmas 25 December

Visas

Nearly all visitors require a visa and arranging one before you arrive is usually essential. Visas on arrival are only issued at the Minsk-2 international airport, but they are expensive and are just as much hassle. Visa costs vary depending on the embassy you apply at and your citizenship. Transit visas cost around €65; single-entry visas cost about €90. Tourist visas are issued if you have an invitation from an accredited Belarusian travel agency or a hotel reservation voucher. Single-entry and double-entry visas are valid for 30 days. If you won't be in the country for more than 48 hours, you can apply for a transit visa, for which no invite is necessary. You simply have to show a train or air ticket to prove your need to transit through Belarus. If you are staying in Belarus for more than five working days, you must have your visa officially registered. Hotels do this automatically and the service is included in the room price.

Getting There & Away

Once you have your visa in your passport, the process of entering Belarus is relatively simple. Ensure you fill out one of the white migration cards in duplicate before presenting your passport to the immigration officer.

Air

Belarus' national airline is **Belavia** (☎017-220 2555; www.belavia.by; vul Nyamiha 14, Minsk), which has flights to London, Paris, Frankfurt, Berlin, Vienna, Rome, Milan, Barcelona, İstanbul, Tel Aviv, Warsaw, Prague, Rīga and many Russian cities, including Moscow and St Petersburg.

Land

Bus travel is a common and fast way to enter the country, with services including the four-hour trip between Vilnius (Lithuania) and Minsk, and the seven-hour trip between Minsk and Białystok (Poland). Services also run to Białystok (Poland) from Brest.

From Minsk there are train services to Russia, Lithuania and Poland, plus connections to the rest of Europe via Brest.

Getting Around

Bus services cover much of the country and are generally a reliable, if crowded, means of transportation. You can always buy tickets on the day, usually before you board, at the bus-station ticket desk. As in Russia, normal bus services are supplemented by *marshrutka* (shared minibus) routes. Train is a popular and scenic way to travel between the major towns of Belarus, though the bus network is far more extensive and prices are similar.

Belgium & Luxembourg

Includes »

Brussels 104
Leuven 112
Mechelen 112
Antwerp 112
Ghent 117
Bruges 119
Ypres 123
Liège 124
Luxembourg City 126
Northern Luxembourg 130
Echternach 131
Moselle Valley 131
Understand Belgium & Luxembourg 131
Survival Guide 133

Best Places to Eat

» De Stove (p121)
» Salon des Lumières (p124)
» L'Ogenblik (p109)
» In 't Nieuwe Museum (p122)

Best Places to Stay

» Hôtel Le Dixseptième (p109)
» Hôtel Simoncini (p127)
» Auberge Aal Veinen (p130)
» B&B Dieltiens (p121)

Why Go?

Stereotypes of comic books, chips and sublime chocolates are just the start in eccentric little Belgium: its self-deprecating people have quietly spent centuries producing some of Europe's finest art and architecture. Bilingual Brussels is the dynamic yet personable EU capital, but also sports what's arguably the world's most beautiful city square. Flat, Dutch-speaking Flanders has many other alluring medieval cities, all easily linked by regular train hops. In hilly, French-speaking Wallonia, the attractions are contrastingly rural – castle villages, outdoor activities and extensive cave systems. Independent Luxembourg, the EU's richest country, is compact and hilly with its own wealth of castle villages, while its capital city is famed for banking but also sports a fairy-tale Unesco-listed historic Old Town. And from the brilliant beers of Belgium to the sparkling wines of Luxembourg's Moselle Valley, there's plenty to lubricate some of Europe's best dining. Welcome to the good life.

When to Go

Brussels

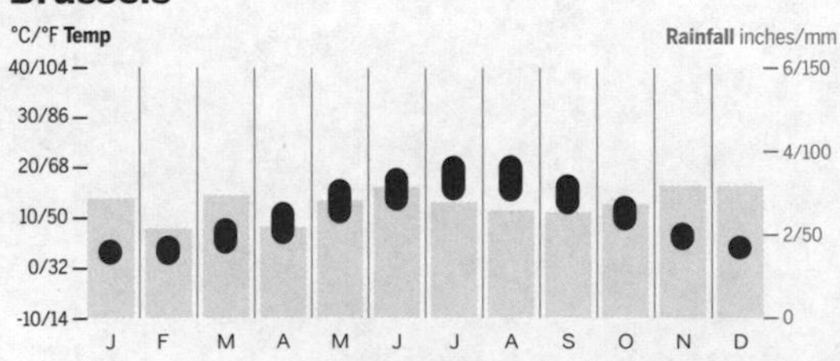

Pre-Easter weekends Belgium hosts many of Europe's weirdest carnivals, not just at Mardi Gras.

Feb–Mar Both countries symbolically burn the spirit of winter on the first weekend after Carnival.

Jul–Aug Countless festivals, hotels packed at the coast but cheaper in Brussels and Luxembourg City.

Connections

Amsterdam, Paris, Cologne and London are all under 2½ hours from Brussels by high-speed train. Liège, Luxembourg City and Antwerp are also on high-speed international routes. Go via Tournai to reach France by train if you want to avoid such lines and their compulsory reservations. Budget airlines offer cheap deals to numerous European destinations particularly from Charleroi (an hour south of Brussels).

ITINERARIES

Four Days

Just long enough to get a first taste of Belgium's four finest 'art cities': Bruges, Ghent, Brussels and Antwerp, all easy jump-offs or short excursions while you're train-hopping between Paris and Amsterdam. Bruges is the fairy-tale 'Venice of the north', Ghent has similar canalside charms without the tourist hordes, and Brussels' incomparable Grand Place is worth jumping off any train for, even if you have only a few hours to spare. Cosmopolitan Antwerp goes one further, adding in fashion and diamonds. If you're overnighting make sure to hit Brussels on a weekend and Bruges on a weekday to get the best deals on accommodation.

Ten Days

Add an extra night in each of the above and consider stops in Mechelen and Lier, practising your French in Mons and Tournai on the 'back route' to France or in Luxembourg en route to Koblenz, Germany.

Essential Food & Drink

» **Chicons au gratin** Endive rolled in ham and cooked in cheese/béchamel sauce.

» **Filet Américain** A blob of raw minced beef, typically topped with equally raw egg yolk.

» **Mosselen/moules** Steaming cauldrons of in-the-shell mussels, typically cooked in white wine and served with a mountain of *frites* (chips).

» **Paling in 't groen** Eel in a sorrel or spinach sauce.

» **Stoemp** Mashed veg-and-potato dish.

» **Vlaamse stoverij/carbonade flamande** Semisweet beer-based meat casserole.

» **Waterzooi** A cream-based chicken or fish stew.

» **Judd mat gaardebounen** Luxembourg's national dish; smoked pork-neck in a cream-based sauce with chunks of potato and broad beans.

» **Kniddelen** 'Dumplings'; often gnocchi-style balls served in various sauces, but the term can also refer to meatballs, which are known as ballekes/bouletten in Belgium.

AT A GLANCE

» **Currency** Euro (€)

» **Languages** Dutch, French, German, Lëtzebuergesch

» **Money** ATMs common; credit cards widely accepted

» **Visas** Schengen rules apply

Fast Facts

» **Area** 30,278 sq km (Belgium), 2586 sq km (Luxembourg)

» **Capitals** Brussels (Belgium), Luxembourg City (Luxembourg)

» **Country code** ☎32 (Belgium), ☎352 (Luxembourg)

» **Emergency** ☎112

Exchange Rates

Australia	A$1	€0.82
Canada	C$1	€0.77
Japan	¥100	€0.83
New Zealand	NZ$1	€0.65
UK	UK£1	€1.18
USA	US$1	€0.78

Set Your Budget

» **Budget hotel room** under €60

» **Two-course meal** from €10

» **Museum entrance** €5–10

» **Beer** €2

» **City transport ticket** €1.20–2

Resources

» **Belgium** (www.belgium.be)

» **Luxembourg** (www.ont.lu)

Belgium & Luxembourg Highlights

1. Come on weekdays off-season to appreciate the picture-perfect canal scenes of medieval **Bruges** (p119), without the tourist overload
2. Be wooed by underappreciated **Ghent** (p117), one of Europe's greatest all-round discoveries
3. Savour the 'world's most beautiful square', then seek out the remarkable cafes, chocolate shops and art nouveau survivors in **Brussels** (p104)
4. Follow fashion to hip yet historic **Antwerp** (p112)
5. Spend the weekend in Unesco-listed **Luxembourg City** (p126) then head out to the grand duchy's evocative castle villages.
6. Ponder the heartbreaking futility of WWI in Flanders' fields around meticulously rebuilt **Ypres** (p123)
7. Explore the caves and castles of rural Wallonia around **Rochefort** (p125)

0 30 km
0 20 miles
NETHERLANDS
Tilburg
Roosendaal
Eindhoven
Venlo
Turnhout
Antwerp
Antwerp Airport
Herentals
Mol
Neerpelt
Roermond
Lier
Mechelen
Diest
National Park Hoge Kempen
Genk
Hasselt
Bokrijk Openluchtmuseum
GERMANY
Brussels Airport
Leuven
Brussels
Maastricht
Waterloo
Louvain-la-Neuve
Braine l'Alleud
Ottignies
Liège Airport
Liège
Verviers
Hautes Fagnes-Eifel Nature Park
Nivelles
Jehay
Huy
Remouchamps
BELGIUM
Hautes Fagnes
Herzogenhugel
Hautes Fagnes Nature Reserve
Charleroi Airport
Namur
Modave
Coo
Stavelot
Charleroi
Durbuy
Barvaux
Wallonia
Godinne
Hotton
Dinant
Marloie
Rochefort
Jemelle
La Roche-en-Ardenne
Houyet
Lavaux-Ste-Anne
Han-sur-Lesse
Champlon
Clervaux
GERMANY
Chimay
Couvin
Bastogne
Wiltz
Libramont
ARDENNES
Parc Naturel de la Haute Sûre
Vianden
Diekirch
Ettelbrück
Rochehaut
LUXEMBOURG
Echternach
Bouillon
Gutland
Mersch
Bourglinster
Charleville-Mezières
Luxembourg City
Findel Airport
Arlon
Orval
Virton
Rodange
Dudelange

BRUSSELS

POP 1.12 MILLION

Like the country it represents, Brussels (Bruxelles, Brussel) is a surreal, multilayered place pulling several disparate identities into one enigmatic core. It subtly seduces with great art, tempting chocolate shops and classic cafes. Meanwhile a confusing architectural smorgasbord pits awesome art nouveau and 17th-century masterpieces against shabby suburbanism and the glass-faced anonymity of the EU area. Note that Brussels is officially bilingual, so all names – from streets to train stations – have both Dutch and French versions, but for simplicity we use only the French versions in this chapter.

Sights

The **BrusselsCard** (www.brusselscard.be; 24/48/72hr €24/34/40) allows free visits to over 30 Brussels-area museums and free transport but you'll need to be a hyperactive museum fan to save much money. On the first Wednesday afternoon of each month many museums are free.

CENTRAL BRUSSELS

Grand Place SQUARE

(MGare Centrale) Topping any Brussels itinerary, this magnificent central square is ringed by elegant guildhalls. They were rebuilt shortly after 1695 when the originals were bombarded by French forces. One older survivor is the splendidly spired Gothic-style **Hôtel de Ville** (city hall) – ironic, as that was the main French target.

Opened in 1847, the nearby **Galeries St-Hubert** (www.galeries-saint-hubert.com; off Rue du Marché aux Herbes; MGare Centrale) were Europe's first covered shopping arcades. Directly south of there, **Rue des Bouchers** is a narrow, colourful dazzle of close-packed seafood eateries. The scene is undoubtedly photogenic but beware of scams if you eat here.

Manneken Pis MONUMENT

(Cnr Rue de l'Étuve & Rue du Chêne; MGare Centrale) A perversely perfect national symbol for surreal Belgium, the Mannekin Pis is a diminutive statue of a little boy cheerfully taking a leak into a fountain pool. Sexual equality is ensured by his lesser known squatting sister, the **Jeanneke Pis** (www.jeannekepisofficial.be; Impasse de la Fidélité; MGare Centrale).

Musées Royaux des Beaux-Arts ART MUSEUM

(02-508 32 11; www.fine-arts-museum.be; Rue de la Régence 3; adult/student/BrusselsCard €8/5/free, €13 combined with Magritte Museum; 10am-5pm Tue-Sun; MGare Centrale, Parc) Belgium's national gallery has a superb collection ranging from 15th-century Flemish Primitives via the fleshy religious canvases of Rubens to a top quality selection of 20th-century works. Next door the **Magritte Museum** (www.musee-magritte-museum.be; Place Royale; adult/under 26yr/BrusselsCard €8/2/free; 10am-5pm Tue-Sun; MGare Centrale, Parc)

COMIC-STRIP CULTURE

In Belgium, comic strips (*bande dessinée*) are revered as the 'ninth art'. Over 40 cartoon murals enliven Brussels buildings, most mapped on www.brusselscomics.com/en/route_bd.cfm. Some favourites include the following:

Tibet & Duchâteau (Rue du Bon Secours 9)

Josephine Baker Mural (Rue des Capucins 9)

Tintin (Rue de l'Étuve)

Peeping Policeman (Rue Haute)

Cubitus (Rue de Flandre)

Serious comic fans might also enjoy Brussels' comprehensive **Centre Belge de la Bande Dessinée** (02-219 19 80; www.comicscenter.net; Rue des Sables 20; adult/concession €8/6; 10am-6pm Tue-Sun; MRogier) in a distinctive Horta-designed art nouveau building. Comic shops include **Brüsel** (www.brusel.com; Blvd Anspach 100; 10.30am-6.30pm Mon-Sat, noon-6.30pm Sun) and **Multi-BD** (www.multibd.com; Blvd Anspach 122-124; 10.30am-7pm Mon-Sat, 12.30-6.30pm Sun). There's even a cartoon-based cafe-restaurant, **Le Village de la Bande Dessinée** (02-523 13 23; comicscafe.be; Place du Grand Sablon 8; snacks from €6), complete with Tintin statue and original Hergé sketches.

traces the stylistic development of Belgium's foremost surrealist artist

MIM MUSEUM

(Musée des Instruments de Musique; ☎02-545 01 30; www.mim.fgov.be; Rue Montagne de la Cour 2; adult/concession €5/4; ⏰9.30am-5pm Tue-Fri, 10am-5pm Sat & Sun; Ⓜ Gare Centrale, Parc) An incredible collection of musical instruments 'play' themselves in your headphones when you stand on the automated floor panels in front of them. Much of the museum's appeal is the 1899 art nouveau Old England building in which it's housed, along with the panoramic rooftop cafe and terrace on top.

Palais de Justice LAW COURTS

(Ⓜ Louise, 🚇92, 94) When constructed in 1883, this gigantic domed law court was Europe's biggest building. Outside there's a panoramic viewpoint looking across rooftops towards the distant Atomium and **Koekelberg Basilica**, one of the world's biggest churches. A glass **elevator** (admission free; ⏰7.30am-11.45pm) leads down into the quirky **Marolles quarter**.

BEYOND THE CENTRE

Musée Horta MUSEUM

(☎02-543 04 90; www.hortamuseum.be; Rue Américaine 25; adult/child €7/3.50; ⏰2-5.30pm Tue-Sun; Ⓜ Horta, 🚇91, 92) Superstar architect Victor Horta's 1898 house-museum makes a fine introduction to Brussels' art nouveau heritage. It's in the Ixelles district, 2.5km south of centre, along with several other architectural masterpieces of the same era. For more info, see www.brusselsartnouveau.be.

Cantillon Brewery BREWERY

(Musée Bruxellois de la Gueuze; ☎02-521 49 28; www.cantillon.be; Rue Gheude 56; admission €6; ⏰9am-5pm Mon-Fri, 10am-5pm Sat; Ⓜ Clemenceau) This fascinating traditional brewery produces Brussels' unique, if startlingly tart, lambic beers, created through the miracle of spontaneous fermentation. From Bruxelles-Midi station walk 800m north via Pl Bara and Rue Limnander.

Cinquantenaire ARCHITECTURE

(Ⓜ Mérode) Designed to celebrate Belgium's 50th anniversary in 1880, Brussels' version of the Arc de Triomphe was only finally completed in 1905, 25 years late. It is flanked by three impressive museums: the **Musées Royaux d'Art et d'Histoire** (☎02-741 72 11; www.kmkg-mrah.be; Parc du Cinquantenaire 10; adult/child/BrusselsCard €5/free/free; ⏰9.30am-5pm Tue-Fri, 10am-5pm Sat & Sun; Ⓜ Mérode), a **military museum** (Royal Museum of the Armed Forces and of Military History; ☎02-737 78 11; www.klm-mra.be; Parc du Cinquantenaire 3; admission/audioguide free/€3; ⏰9am-noon & 1-4.45pm Tue-Sun; Ⓜ Mérode), and **Autoworld** (www.autoworld.be; adult/BrusselsCard €9/free; ⏰10am-6pm Apr-Sep, to 5pm Oct-Mar; Ⓜ Mérode).

USE IT

Use-It (☎02-218 39 06; www.use-it.be; Galerie Ravenstein 17; ⏰10am-6pm Mon-Sat; 📶; Ⓜ Ste-Catherine), a meeting place for young travellers, has free coffee and tea, sofas, internet and an invaluable list of live-music events. Its free city tour (Mondays, 2pm) emphasises social history and nightlife over conventional sights. It creates superb free info map-guides not only for Brussels but also Antwerp, Bruges, Ghent, Leuven and Mechelen.

Atomium MONUMENT, MUSEUM

(www.atomium.be; Sq de l'Atomium; adult/BrusselsCard €11/9; ⏰10am-7pm May-Sep, to 6pm Oct-Apr; 🅿; Ⓜ Heysel, 🚇51) This space-age leftover from the 1958 World Fair consists of nine house-sized metallic balls linked by steel tube-columns containing escalators and lifts. Like an alien schoolchild's chemistry set, this represents an iron crystal lattice enlarged 165 billion times.

Waterloo Battlefield BATTLE SITE

(www.waterloo1815.be) A day trip from Brussels, Waterloo battlefield (20km south) is where the course of European history changed in June 1815 with the final defeat of Napoleon. Today the rolling fields are marked by a striking cone of grassy hill topped with a great bronze lion. You can climb the lion (adult/child €6/4) via entry through the visitor centre, which offers a range of battle-related activities. TEC bus W from Bruxelles-Midi gets you within 800m. Don't use Waterloo train station, which is 5km further away.

Sleeping

Many business hotels drop their rates dramatically at weekends and in summer. Double rooms with September midweek rates of €240 might cost as little as €69 in August – so why use a hostel? Brussels has

Central Brussels

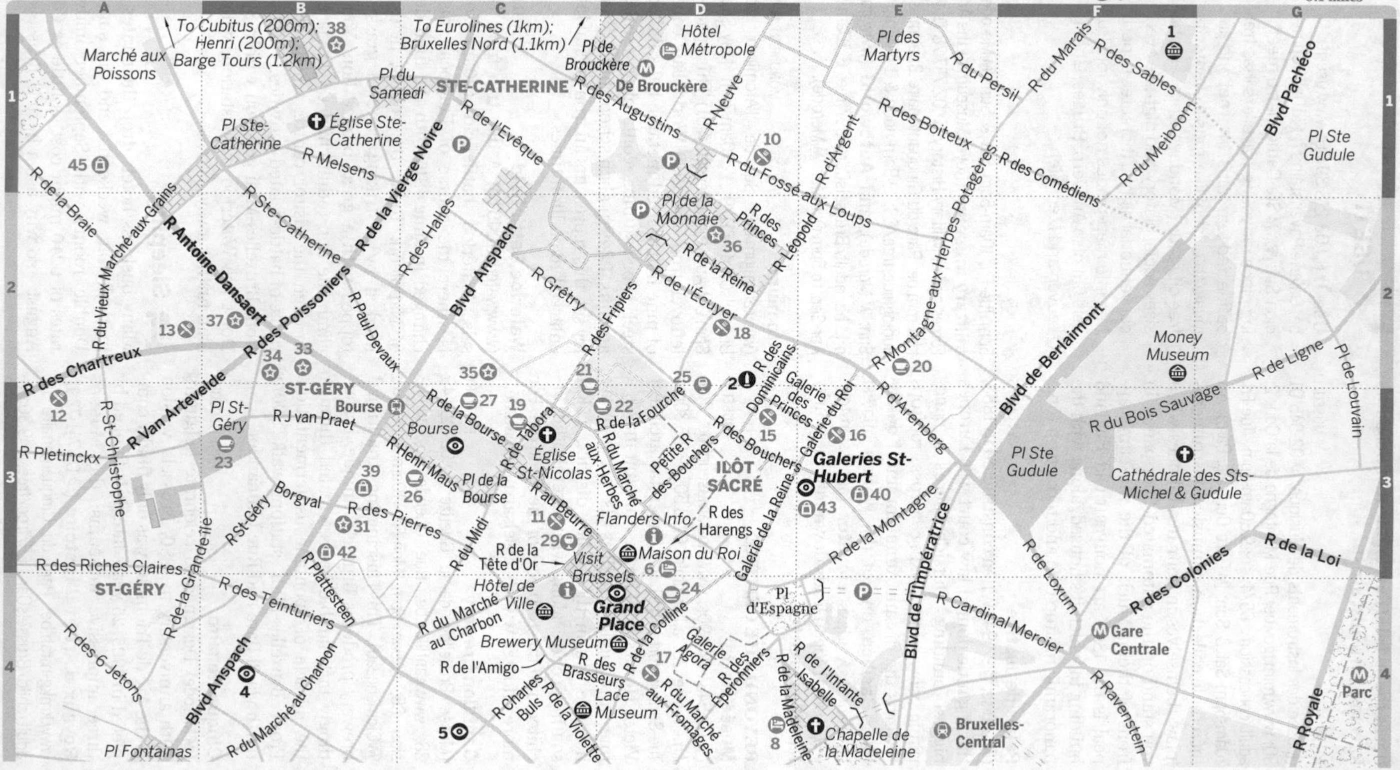

0 — 200 m
0 — 0.1 miles

A B C D E F G
1 2 3 4

To Cubitus (200m); Henri (200m); Barge Tours (1.2km)
38
Marché aux Poissons
To Eurolines (1km); Bruxelles Nord (1.1km)
Pl de Brouckère
Hôtel Métropole
De Brouckère
Pl des Martyrs
R du Persil
R du Marais
R des Sables
1
Blvd Pachéco
Pl Ste Gudule
Pl du Samedi
STE-CATHERINE
R des Augustins
R Neuve
R des Boiteux
R du Meiboom
Pl Ste-Catherine
Église Ste-Catherine
R de l'Evêque
R Melsens
45
R de la Vierge Noire
10
R du Fossé aux Loups
R d'Argent
R des Comédiens
R de la Braie
R Antoine Dansaert
R du Vieux Marché aux Grains
R Ste-Catherine
R des Halles
Blvd Anspach
Pl de la Monnaie
36
R des Princes
R Léopold
R Montagne aux Herbes Potagères
R de la Reine
R Grétry
R de l'Écuyer
18
R des Poissoniers
R Paul Devaux
R des Fripiers
13
37
34
33
R des Chartreux
35
21
25
2
R des Dominicains
Galerie des Princes
Galerie du Roi
20
R d'Arenberg
Blvd de Berlaimont
Money Museum
R de Ligne
Pl de Louvain
12
R Van Artevelde
ST-GÉRY
Pl St-Géry
R J van Praet
Bourse
27
19
22
R de la Fourche
15
16
R du Bois Sauvage
R St-Christophe
R Pletinckx
23
R de la Bourse
R de Tabora
Église St-Nicolas
R du Marché aux Herbes
Petite R des Bouchers
R des Bouchers
Galeries St-Hubert
Pl Ste Gudule
Cathédrale des Sts-Michel & Gudule
39
R Henri Maus
26
Pl de la Bourse
ILÔT SACRÉ
40
43
Borgval
R St-Géry
R des Pierres
31
11
R au Beurre
29
Flanders Info
R des Harengs
Galerie de la Reine
R de la Montagne
Blvd de l'Impératrice
R de Loxum
R de la Loi
R des Colonies
R de la Grande Île
42
R du Midi
R de la Tête d'Or
Visit Brussels
Maison du Roi
6
R des Riches Claires
R Plattesteen
Hôtel de Ville
Grand Place
24
Pl d'Espagne
R Cardinal Mercier
ST-GÉRY
R des Teinturiers
R du Marché au Charbon
R de la Colline
Galerie Agora
Gare Centrale
Brewery Museum
R des Éperonniers
R de l'Infante Isabelle
R des 6 Jetons
Blvd Anspach
4
R de l'Amigo
R des Brasseurs
17
R de la Madeleine
R Ravenstein
Parc
R du Marché au Charbon
R Charles Buls
R de la Violette
Lace Museum
R du Marché aux Fromages
8
Chapelle de la Madeleine
Bruxelles-Central
R Royale
5
Pl Fontainas

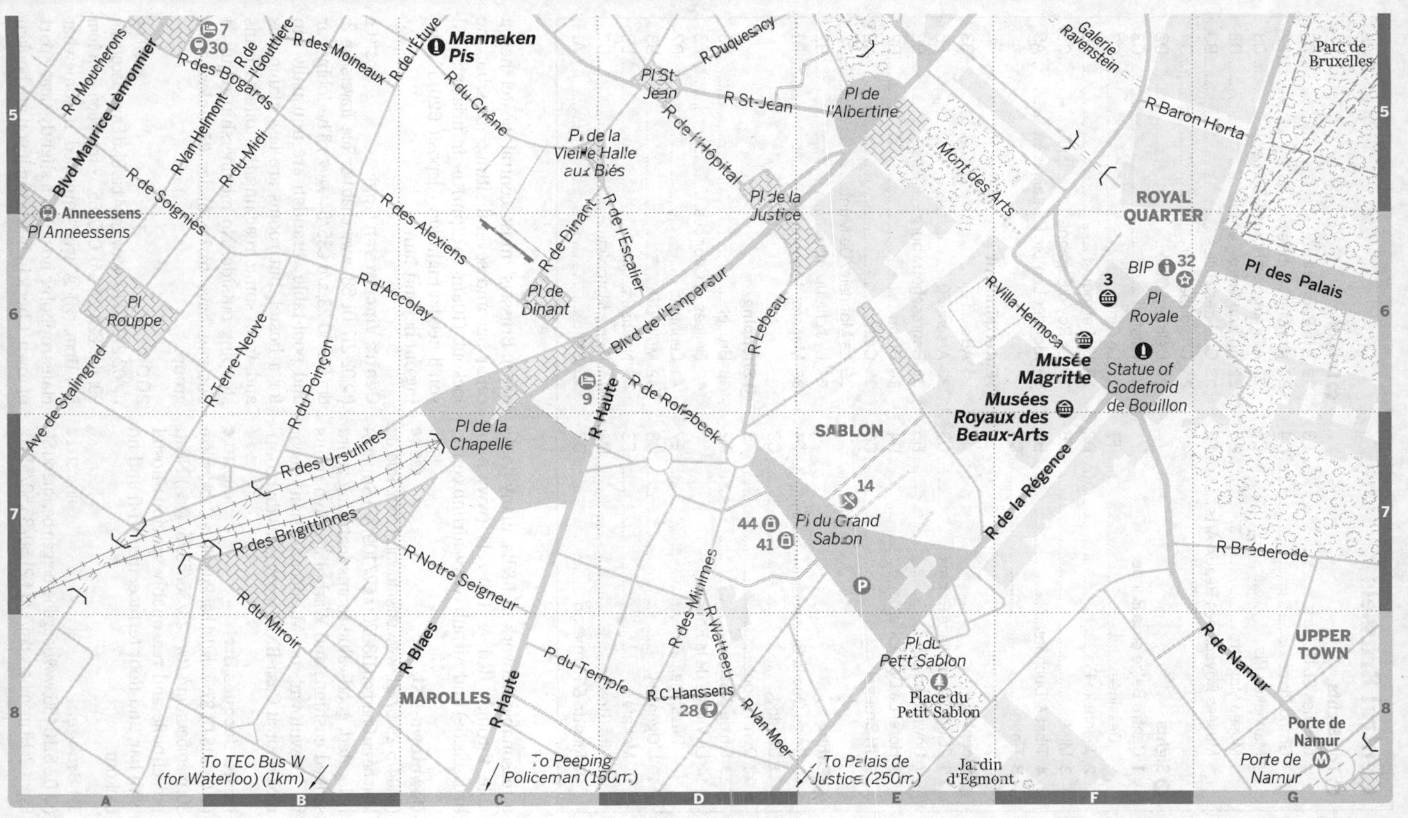
R d Moucherons
Blvd Maurice Lemonnier
7
30
R des Bogards
R de l'Gouttière
R des Moineaux
R de l'Etuve
Manneken Pis
R du Chêne
R Van Helmont
R du Midi
R de Soignies
Anneessens
Pl Anneessens
Pl Rouppe
Ave de Stalingrad
R Terre-Neuve
R du Poinçon
R des Alexiens
R d'Accolay
Pl de la Vieille Halle aux Blés
R de Dinant
R de l'Escalier
Pl de Dinant
Pl St Jean
R Duquesnoy
R St-Jean
R de l'Hôpital
Pl de la Justice
Pl de l'Albertine
Mont des Arts
Galerie Ravenstein
R Baron Horta
Parc de Bruxelles
ROYAL QUARTER
BIP
32
3
Pl des Palais
Pl Royale
R Villa Hermosa
Musée Magritte
Statue of Godefroid de Bouillon
Musées Royaux des Beaux-Arts
Blvd de l'Empereur
R Lebeau
9
R Haute
R de Ruysbroeck
Pl de la Chapelle
SABLON
R des Ursulines
R des Brigittinnes
R Notre Seigneur
R du Miroir
14
44
41
Pl du Grand Sablon
R de la Régence
R Bréderode
R des Minimes
R Watteeu
R Blaes
R Haute
MAROLLES
P du Temple
R C Hanssens
28
R Van Moer
Pl du Petit Sablon
Place du Petit Sablon
R de Namur
UPPER TOWN
Porte de Namur
Porte de Namur
To TEC Bus W (for Waterloo) (1km)
To Peeping Policeman (150m)
To Palais de Justice (250m)
Jardin d'Egmont

Central Brussels

Top Sights
- Galeries St-Hubert ... E3
- Grand Place ... D4
- Manneken Pis ... C5
- Musée Magritte ... F6
- Musées Royaux des Beaux-Arts ... F6

Sights
- 1 Centre Belge de la Bande Dessinée ... F1
- 2 Jeanneke Pis ... D2
- 3 MIM ... F6
- 4 Tibet & Duchâteau ... B4
- 5 Tintin ... C4

Sleeping
- 6 2Go4 Grand Place Rooms ... D3
- 7 Downtown-BXL ... B5
- 8 Hôtel Le Dixseptième ... D4
- 9 JH Bruegel ... C6

Eating
- 10 Belga Queen Brussels ... D1
- 11 Dandoy ... C3
- 12 Den Teepot ... A3
- 13 Fin de Siècle ... A2
- 14 Le Village de la Bande Dessinée ... E7
- 15 L'Ogenblik ... D3
- 16 Mokafé ... E3
- 17 Pita Street ... D4
- 18 Ricotta & Parmesan ... D2

Drinking
- 19 À la Bécasse ... C3
- 20 À la Mort Subite ... E2
- 21 A l'Image de Nostre-Dame ... C3
- 22 Au Bon Vieux Temps ... D3
- 23 Café des Halles ... B3
- 24 Chaloupe d'Or ... D4
- 25 Délirium Café ... D2
- 26 Falstaff ... C3
- 27 Le Cirio ... C3
- 28 Le Perroquet ... D8
- 29 Le Roy d'Espagne ... C3
- 30 Moeder Lambic Fontainas ... A5

Entertainment
- 31 AB ... B3
- 32 Arsène50 ... F6
- 33 Beursschouwburg ... B2
- 34 Bizon ... B2
- 35 Celtica ... C2
- 36 La Monnaie/De Munt ... D2
- 37 L'Archiduc ... B2
- 38 Madame Moustache ... B1

Shopping
- 39 Brüsel ... B3
- 40 Délices et Caprices ... E3
- 41 Leonidas ... D7
- 42 Multi-BD ... B3
- 43 Neuhaus ... E3
- 44 Pierre Marcolini ... D7
- 45 Stijl ... A1

a reasonable network of B&Bs, many bookable through Bed & Brussels (www.bnb-brussels.be) and Airbnb (www.airbnb.com).

Downtown-BXL B&B €€
(☎0475 29 07 21; www.downtownbxl.com; Rue du Marché au Charbon 118-120; r €77-109; wi-fi) Superbly located, good-value rooms featuring zebra striped cushions and Warhol Marilyn prints in 'Downtown', or Moroccan-Asian decor next door at Casa-BXL (www.lacasabxl.com).

Hostel Jacques Brel HI HOSTEL €
(☎02-218 01 87; www.laj.be; Rue de la Sablonnière 30; members dm/s/tw €23/36/53.75; @ wi-fi) Neat, presentable and reasonably spacious hostel with bar, 2nd-floor terrace, free wi-fi and no lockout.

JH Bruegel HI HOSTEL €
(☎02-511 04 36; www.jeugdherbergen.be; Rue du St-Esprit 2; HI members dm/s/d €21.50/35.50/51.50; @ wi-fi) Brussels' most central hostel has a cellar bar and several sitting areas but the lockout (10am to 2pm) is infuriating and you'll need a night key (deposit €20) if staying out beyond 1am.

Centre Vincent van Gogh HOSTEL €
(☎02-217 01 58; www.chab.be; Rue Traversière 8; dm €19.50-23, s/d €35/54; @ wi-fi) The lobby bar and pool-table verandah are unusually hip for a hostel, but rooms are less glamorous and, from some, reaching the toilets means stepping outside. No membership required but you have to be under 35 unless in a group.

2GO4 HOSTEL €
(☎02-219 30 19; www.2go4.be; Blvd Émile Jacqmain 99; dm €24-27, s/d €50/65; ⏲reception 7am-1pm & 4-11pm; wi-fi) A well-equipped if somewhat claustrophobic hostel in a slightly sleazy part of town. Check in here even if you are booked

into its other accommodation, the fabulously central **Grand Place Rooms** (Rue des Harengs; d €59-70, tr €90-105), which feature low ceilings and hefty beams. There's an age limit of 45 for dorm rooms.

Eating

Henri FUSION €€
(☎02-218 00 08; www.restohenri.be; Rue de Flandre 113; mains €15-20; ⏲noon-2pm Tue-Fri & 6pm-10pm Tue-Sat; Ⓜ Ste-Catherine) Henri concocts tangy fusion dishes. There's an astute wine list and well-briefed staff.

Fin de Siècle BELGIAN €
(Rue des Chartreux 9; mains €11.25-20; ⏲bar 4.30pm-1am, kitchen 6pm-12.30am) No sign on the door, no reservations possible – just join the student-aged throng awaiting a table for giant portions of unsophisticated home cooking chosen from a blackboard menu.

Belga Queen Brussels BELGIAN €€
(☎02-217 21 87; www.belgaqueen.be; Rue du Fossé aux Loups 32; mains €16-25, weekday lunch €16; ⏲noon-2.30pm & 7pm-midnight) Belgian cuisine is given a chic, modern twist within a magnificent if reverberant 19th-century bank building with classical stained-glass ceilings and marble columns.

Ricotta & Parmesan ITALIAN €
(www.ricottaparmesan.com; Rue de l'Écuyer 31; mains €9-15; ⏲noon-2.30pm & 6.30pm-11pm Mon-Sat) Excellent-value Italian food enjoyed in a pair of antique buildings decorated with olive-oil bottles and antique cooking implements, some fancifully framed.

Pita Street KEBABS €
(Rue du Marché aux Fromages; ⏲11am-3am) Falafels and döner kebab snacks from €3 in a bustling pedestrian street just behind the Grand Place.

Den Teepot VEGAN €
(Rue des Chartreux 66; ⏲noon-2pm Mon-Sat; 🖉) Macrobiotic, vegie lunch place located above a mustard-yellow organic grocery.

Mokafé WAFFLES €
(☎02-511 78 70; Galerie du Roi; waffles from €3; ⏲7.30am-11.30pm; Ⓜ De Brouckère) Locals get their waffles in this old-fashioned cafe in the Galeries-St Hubert.

L'Horloge du Sud AFRICAN €
(www.horlogedusud.be; Rue du Trône 141; mains from €12; Ⓜ Porte de Namur) Matonge, the city's Congolese district, is a great area to sample African food of various types, and L'Horloge du Sud is a fine place to get started.

Dandoy BISCUITS €
(☎02-511 03 26; www.maisondandoy.com; Rue au Beurre 31; ⏲9.30am-7pm Mon-Sat, 10.30am-7pm Sun; Ⓜ Bourse) Atmospheric 1829 biscuit-maker's shop full of antique wooden moulds for giant *speculoos* (gingerbreads).

Drinking

Cafe culture is one of Brussels' greatest attractions. On the Grand Place itself, 300-year-old gems like **Le Roy d'Espagne** (www.roydespagne.be; Grand Place 1) and **Chaloupe d'Or** (Grand Place 24) are magnificent but predictably pricey.

Le Perroquet CAFE
(Rue Watteeu 31; light meals €6.50-11; ⏲noon-1am; Ⓜ Porte de Namur) This authentically preserved art nouveau cafe with stained glass, marble tables and timber panelling is comparatively inexpensive for a drink or an imaginatively filled pitta snack.

Moeder Lambic Fontainas BEER HALL
(www.moederlambic.eu; Place Fontainas 8; ⏲11am-1am Mon-Thu & Sun, to 2am Fri & Sat; 🚇 Annessens, Bourse) Dozens of artisanal draft beers served in a setting that's unusually contemporary and upbeat for a beer specialist.

SPLURGE

A hushed magnificence greets you in this alluring **Hôtel Le Dixseptième** (☎02-502 57 44; www.ledixseptieme.be; Rue de la Madeleine 25; s/d/ste from €180/200/270, weekend from €100/100/200; ❄📶), partly occupying the former 17th-century residence of the Spanish ambassador. Spacious executive suites come with four-poster beds.

The archetypal bistro-restaurant **L'Ogenblik** (☎02-511 61 51; www.ogenblik.be; Galerie des Princes 1; mains €23-28, lunch €11; ⏲noon-2.30pm & 7pm-midnight) looks casual with its lace curtains, marble-topped tables and cheeky waiters but the classic French dishes and fish specialities show a deft culinary expertise.

DON'T MISS

BOURSE CAFES

Many of Brussels's most iconic cafes are within stumbling distance of the Bourse. Don't miss century-old **Falstaff** (www.lefalstaff.be; Rue Henri Maus 17; ⌚10am-1am; Bourse) with its festival of stained glass ceilings, or **Le Cirio** (Rue de la Bourse 18; ⌚10am-midnight), a sumptuous yet affordable 1866 marvel full of polished brasswork serving great-value pub meals. Three more classics are hidden up shoulder-wide alleys: the medieval yet unpretentious **A l'Image de Nostre-Dame** (off Rue du Marché aux Herbes 5; ⌚noon-midnight Mon-Fri, 3pm-1am Sat, 4-10.30pm Sun); the 1695 Rubenseque **Au Bon Vieux Temps** (Impasse Saint Michel; ⌚11am-midnight), which sometimes stocks ultra-rare Westvleteren beers (€10!); and lambic specialist **À la Bécasse** (www.alabecasse.com; Rue de Tabora 11; ⌚11am-midnight, to 1am Fri & Sat ; MGare Centrale), with its vaguely Puritanical rows of wooden tables.

If those classics seem a little staid for your taste, head a block west of the Bourse to Place Saint-Géry where a whole series of characterful but youthfully fashion-conscious cafes surround the **Café des Halles** (www.cafedeshalles.be), an 1881 market hall that's now part bar, part exhibition hall, and hosts a free weekend nightclub in its cellars. Great options for sipping a quiet coffee by day or being buffeted by music at night.

Délirium Café PUB
(www.deliriumcafe.be; Impasse de la Fidélité 4A; ⌚10am-4am Mon-Sat, to 2am Sun) The main bar has barrel tables, beer-tray ceilings and over 2000 world beers. The tap house has 25 more on draft. And associated bars (from 8pm) serve hundreds of *jenevers* (Dutch gin), vodkas and absinthes. No wonder it's lively. Live music after 10pm.

À la Mort Subite CAFE
(☎02-513 13 18; www.alamortsubite.com; Rue Montagne aux Herbes Potagères 7; ⌚11am-1am Mon-Sat, noon-midnight Sun; MGare Centrale) An absolute classic, unchanged since 1928, with lined-up wooden tables, arched mirror panels and entertainingly brusque service.

☆ Entertainment

AB LIVE MUSIC
(Ancienne Belgique; ☎02-548 24 00; www.ab-concerts.be; Blvd Anspach 110; Bourse) Venue for mid-level local and international rock bands.

La Monnaie/De Munt OPERA HOUSE
(www.demunt.be; Pl de la Monnaie; MDe Brouckère) Opera, theatre and dance.

Beursschouwburg LIVE MUSIC
(☎02-513 82 90; www.beursschouwburg.be; Rue Auguste Orts 22; ⌚exhibition area 10am-6pm Mon-Sat, cafe 7.30pm-late Thu-Sun; Bourse) Diverse mix of contemporary music including rock, jazz, rap and disco. The cafe approximates to a free nightclub late on weekend nights.

L'Archiduc JAZZ
(☎02-512 06 52; www.archiduc.net; Rue Antoine Dansaert 6; beer/wine/cocktails €2.70/3.60/8; ⌚4pm-late) Ring the doorbell to enter a packed parcel of jazz.

FREE **Bizon** BLUES
(☎02-502 46 99; www.cafebizon.com; Rue du Pont de la Carpe 7; admission free; ⌚6pm-late) Happening little grunge bar in St-Géry featuring home-grown live blues.

Celtica BAR
(www.celticpubs.com/celtica; Rue De Marche Aux Poulets 55; MBourse) Lairy, loud, central and cheap – just €1 for a beer, early evening. Later there's boozy dancing with different musical styles on different floors.

Madame Moustache CLUB
(www.madamemoustache.be; Quai au Bois à Brûler 5-7; ⌚9pm-4am Tue-Sun ; MSte-Catherine) Cute Ste-Catherine club with a retro, burlesque feel. It hosts funk all-nighters, swing nights and DJ sets.

Shopping

Tourist-oriented shops selling chocolate, beer, lace and Atomium baubles stretch between the Grand Place and Manneken Pis. For better **chocolate shops** in calmer, grander settings, peruse the resplendent **Galeries St-Hubert** or the upmarket Sablon area. Place du Jeu-de-Balle has a daily **flea market** (⌚6am-2pm). Antwerp more than Brussels is Belgium's fashion capital but Rue Antoine Dansaert has several cutting edge boutiques including **Stijl** (www.stijl.be; Rue Antoine Dansaert 74).

Supermarkets sell a range of **Belgian beers** relatively cheaply but for wider selections and the relevant glasses, try **Beermania** (www.beermania.be; Chaussée de Wavre 174; ⌚11am-9pm Mon-Sat) or the very personal little **Délices et Caprices** (www.the-belgian-beer-tasting-shop.be; Rue des Bouchers 68; ⌚2-8pm Thu-Mon).

Information

ATMs are widespread. Exchange agency rates are usually best around the Bourse.

As well as the following there are info counters at Brussels Airport and Bruxelles-Midi station.

Flanders Info (☎02-504 03 90; www.visitflanders.com; Rue du Marché aux Herbes 61; ⌚9am-6pm Mon-Sat, 10am-5pm Sun; 📶) For Flanders-specific information, obviously. Free wi-fi.

Lonely Planet (www.lonelyplanet.com/belgium/brussels)

Visit Brussels (☎02-513 89 40; visitbrussels.be; Hôtel de Ville; ⌚9am-6pm; Ⓜ Bourse) Stacks of city-specific information. A less crowded second branch (☎02-548 04 58; www.biponline.be; Rue Royale 2-4; ⌚10am-6pm) at Rue Royale 2 has an Arsène50 (☎02-512 57 45; www.arsene50.be; Rue Royale 2; ⌚12.30-5.30pm Tue-Sat) desk providing discounts for cultural events.

Getting There & Away

BUS International bus service **Eurolines** (☎02-274 13 50; www.eurolines.be; Rue du Progrès 80; ⌚5.45am-8.45pm; 🚉 Gare du Nord) has buses departing from Bruxelles-Nord train station.

TRAIN Brussels has two major stations. All main domestic trains from Brussels stop at both stations as do some Amsterdam services. Eurostar, TGV and Thalys high-speed trains stop only at Bruxelles-Midi (Brussel-Zuid). That's not in the best part of town so, on arrival, jump straight onto any local service for the four-minute hop to more conveniently central Bruxelles-Central.

Consult www.belgianrail.be for timetable information.

Getting Around

To/From the Airports

BRUSSELS AIRPORT

TAXI Fares start around €35. Very bad idea in rush-hour traffic.

TRAIN Four per hour (5.30am to 11.50pm), €7.60. Takes 20 minutes to Bruxelles-Central, 24 minutes to Bruxelles-Midi.

CHARLEROI ('BRUSSELS-SOUTH') AIRPORT

BUS Direct services operated by **L'Elan** (www.voyages-lelan.be) run half-hourly to Bruxelles-Midi station (single/return €13/22); last services to/from the airport are 8.30pm/11.45pm. Should take one hour, but allow far more time at rush hour.

TRAIN TEC bus A (€3, 18 minutes) links at least hourly from Charleroi Airport to Charleroi-Sud station, a 50-minute train ride from Brussels. Combined bus-and-rail tickets cost €12 maximum to anywhere in Belgium.

Bicycle

Brussels Bike Tours (☎0484 89 89 36; www.brusselsbiketours.com; tour incl bicycle rental adult/student €22/25; ⌚10am Feb-Nov, 10am & 3pm Apr-Sep) start from the Grand Place taking 3½ hours including stops for beer and *frites*.

FietsPunt/PointVelo (www.recyclo.org; per 1/3 days €7.50/15; ⌚7am-7pm Mon-Fri) rents longer term: it's on the left as you leave Bruxelles-Central station by the Madeleine exit.

Villo! (☎078-05 11 10; http://en.villo.be; subscription day/week €1.60/7.50) has 180 automated pick-up/drop-off short-term rental stands. Credit card required, read the online instructions carefully.

Public Transport

STIB/MIVB (www.stib.be) tickets are sold at metro stations, newsagents and on buses and trams. Single-/five-/10-journey tickets valid one hour from validation cost €1.80/7.50/12 including transfers. Unlimited one/two/three-day passes cost €6/10/13. Airport buses are excluded.

INTERNATIONAL BUSES FROM BRUSSELS

DESTINATION	STANDARD PRICE (€)	SUPER-PROMO PRICE (€)	DURATION (HR)	FREQUENCY
Amsterdam	20	9	3½-4½	up to 9 daily
Frankfurt	46	23	6	2 daily
London	51	9	6 (day), 8½ (night)	2 daily
Paris	34	19	4	10 daily

FLANDERS

Excellent free info-maps of each major city are given away by youth hostels or available to download from www.use-it.be.

Leuven

Home to the vast **Stella Artois brewery** (www.breweryvisits.com; Vuurkruisenlaan), lively, self-confident Leuven (Louvain in French; www.leuven.be) is Flanders' oldest university town. Its greatest attraction is a flamboyant 15th-century **Stadhuis** (Grote Markt 9; tour €2; ⊙tour 3pm) lavished with exterior statuary. Other architectural attractions are patchy due to heavy damage sustained in 20th-century wars, but the iconic university library has been rebuilt. Twice. Muntstraat is a loveable medieval alley full of restaurants and Oude Markt is a very lively square of wall-to-wall bars that hum till the wee hours. Homely **Leuven City Hostel** (☎016 84 30 33; www.leuvencityhostel.com; Ravenstraat 37; dm/d €22/52; ⊙reception 4-8pm; @📶) and stylish B&B **Casa Bollicine** (☎0497 83 97 17; www.casabollicine.be; Parijsstraat 7; s/d €120/150; 📶) are good, relatively central accommodation choices. Directly behind the station, around 1km east, the **HI Hostel** (☎016 63 90 62; www.leuven-hostel.com; Martelarenlaan 11a; dm/d €24/56, youth €22/51, HI members save €3; 🚭@📶) and **Ibis Budget hotel** (☎016 47 98 80; Martelarenlaan 10; r €49-71; 📶) make good choices for those wanting to sleep near Brussels Airport, a mere 16 minutes away by train.

Mechelen

Belgium's religious capital, Mechelen (Malines in French) has a cathedral featuring a 97m, 15th-century tower that soars above a particularly memorable central market square. There are other splendid churches on Keizerstraat, where the courthouse and theatre were both once royal palaces in the days when the Low Countries were effectively run from Mechelen. Other top sights include a brilliant Toy Museum and the Schepenhuis gallery tower on Ijzerenleen, a street of fine baroque facades leading towards the main station passing close to Vismarkt, the compact bar-cafe zone. If the modern **HI Hostel** (☎015 27 85 39; www.mechelen-hostel.com; Zandpoortvest 70; dm/s/d €24.50/39.20/57.40, youth €19.20/33.10/47.60, HI members save €3; ⊙check-in 5-10pm; P📶) is full, **Muske Pitter** (☎015 43 63 03; www.muskepitter.be; Hanswijkstraat 70; s/d €47/64) has fair value, unpretentious rooms above a simple tavern.

WORTH A TRIP

BRUSSELS TO ANTWERP

Direct Brussels–Antwerp trains take just over half an hour. But if you're not in a hurry consider stopping en route at a trio of historic cities, none more than a minor diversion by train: Leuven (30 minutes) then Mechelen (22 minutes) then Lier (15 minutes). In each town the station is around 15 minutes' walk from the centre. All have imaginative accommodation if you're too charmed to move on; Mechelen and Leuven have hostels.

Lier

Ringed by a circular waterway, compact Lier has a delightful *begijnhof* (founded 1258), a fanciful **clocktower** (www.zimmertoren.be) and a small but excellent art gallery. On the market square the *stadhuis* (city hall) has an elfin-spired 1369 belfry and hosts the **tourist office** (www.toerismelier.be; Grote Markt 57) in its basement.

Antwerp

POP 511, 700

Cosmopolitan, confident and full of contrasts, Antwerp (Antwerpen in Dutch, Anvers in French) was one of northern Europe's foremost cities in the 17th century when it also was home to Pieter Paul Rubens, diplomat, philosopher and northern Europe's greatest baroque artist. Today it once again revels in fame and fortune, attracting art lovers and mode moguls, club queens and diamond dealers.

Sights

CITY CENTRE

Brabo Fountain STATUE

(Grote Markt) In voluptuous baroque style, the **Brabo Fountain** graphically depicts Antwerp's hand-throwing toponymic legend. It forms a centrepiece of the city's medieval heart, the classic, triangular **Grote Markt** (market square). This beautiful pedestrianised space is flanked on two sides by very photogenic **guildhalls** and dominated by an impressive Italo-Flemish Renaissance-style **stadhuis** (town hall), completed in 1565.

Onze-Lieve-Vrouwekathedraal CATHEDRAL
(www.dekathedraal.be; Handschoenmarkt; adult/concession €5/3; ⌚10am-5pm Mon-Fri, to 3pm Sat, to 4pm Sun) Wherever you wander in Antwerp, this Gothic cathedral's gracious, 123m-high spire has a habit of popping unexpectedly into view. The sight rarely fails to jolt a gasp of awe. Inside, the cathedral's collection of art masterpieces is currently augmented by priceless items from the temporarily closed KMSKA collection.

Museum Plantin-Moretus HISTORIC BUILDING
(www.museumplantinmoretus.be; Vrijdag Markt 22; adult/child €8/1; ⌚10am-5pm Tue-Sun) Once home to the world's first industrial printing works, this impressive medieval courtyard mansion preserves a library (from 1640), historic bookshop, a roomful of antique printing presses and a priceless collection of manuscripts, paintings and tapestries.

Rubenshuis MUSEUM
(www.rubenshuis.be; Wapper 9-11; adult/child €8/1, audioguide €2; ⌚10am-5pm Tue-Sun) Once the home and studio of celebrated painter Pieter Paul Rubens, this architecturally indulgent baroque mansion was rescued from ruins in 1937. It displays a splendid art collection.

Het Steen CASTLE
(Steenplein) On a riverside knoll, Het Steen is a dinky but photogenic castle from AD 1200 occupying the site of Antwerp's original Gallo-Roman settlement. Outside is a humorous statue of **Lange Wapper**, a tall folkloric 'peeping Tom' figure showing off his codpiece to two diminutive onlookers.

Fashion District AREA
Style museum, **MoMu** (www.momu.be; Nationalestraat 28; adult/concession €8/6; ⌚10am-6pm Tue-Sun) is the epicentre of Antwerp's world-class 'fashion district' where boutique lovers will swoon at the incredible choice of designer outlets, notably along Schuttershofstraat, Huidevettersstraat and Nationalestraat. Kammenstraat focuses more on street wear.

TOP CHOICE **Antwerpen-Centraal** TRAIN STATION
With its neo-Gothic facade, vast main hall and splendidly proportioned dome, the 1905 Antwerpen-Centraal train station is one of the city's premier landmarks. Right outside is famous **Antwerp zoo** (www.zooantwerpen.be) and the surprisingly unglamorous **Diamond Quarter** (Hoveniersstraat, Schapstraat) where an astounding 80% of the world's uncut diamonds are traded.

ANTWERP MONEYSAVERS

Website www.antwerpforfree.be lists a daily calendar of free concerts and events. Most major city-run museums are free on the last Wednesday of each month. At other times a 48-hour Antwerp Card (€28) will usually save you money if you visit at least four of the city's splendid museums.

MEIR

If walking from the main train station to Groenplaats, revel in the grand, statue-draped architecture of pedestrianised Meir and Leystraat. The gilt-overloaded **Stadsfeestzaal** (www.stadsfeestzaal.com; Meir 76; ⌚9.30am-7pm Mon-Sat) is one of the world's most indulgently decorated shopping malls. Watch top-quality chocolates being made behind **Chocolate Line** (www.thechocolateline.be; ⌚10.30am-6.30pm), a shop that fills a mural-lined room of the 1745 **Paleis op de Meir** (www.paleisopdemeir.be; Meir 50; tour €8; ⌚tour 2pm Tue-Sat).

'T ZUID

Around 1km south of the fashion district, 't Zuid is a conspicuously prosperous area dotted with century-old architecture, hip bars, fine restaurants and museums. The classic centrepiece art gallery, **KMSKA** (www.kmska.be; Leopold De Waelplaats), is closed for renovation until 2017, but there's still **MHKA** (☎03-238 59 60; www.muhka.be; Leuvenstraat 32; adult/child €8/1; ⌚11am-6pm Tue-Sun, to 9pm Thu) for contemporary art and **FoMu** (FotoMuseum; ☎03-242 93 00; www.fotomuseum.be; Waalsekaai 47; adult/child €7/1; ⌚10am-5pm Tue-Sun) for photography.

Sleeping

Over 40 B&Bs can be sorted by price or map location on www.bedandbreakfast-antwerp.com, but relatively few are central.

Hotel O HOTEL €€
(☎03-500 89 50; www.hotelhotelo.com; Handschoenmarkt 3; r €89-129) In an unbeatable location staring right at the cathedral frontage,

Antwerp

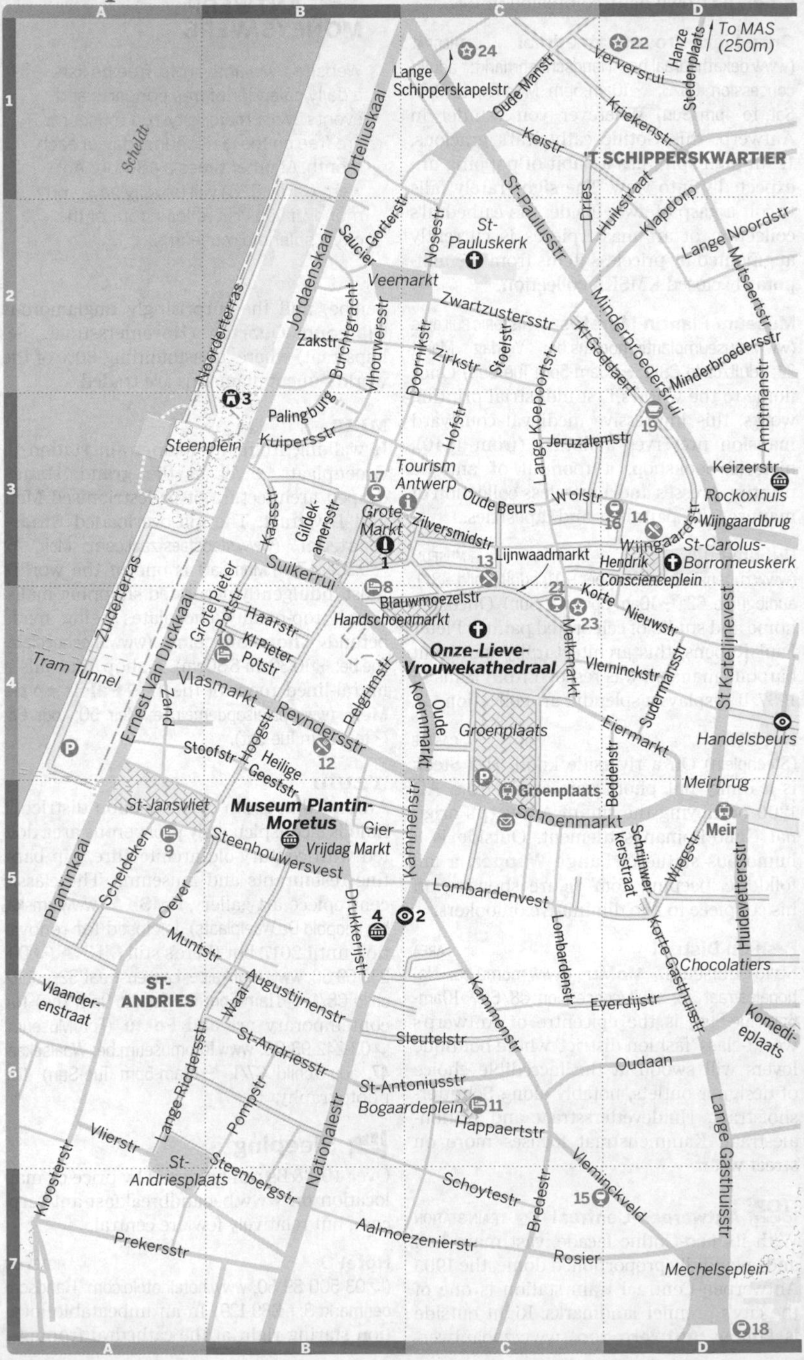

A B C D

To MAS (250m)
24
22
Lange Schipperskapelstr
Oude Manstr
Verversrui
Hanze Stedenplaats
Kriekenstr
Keistr
'T SCHIPPERSKWARTIER
Scheldt
Orteliuskaai
St-Paulusstr
Dries
Huikstraat
Klapdorp
Lange Noordstr
Gorterstr
Saucier
Jordaenskaai
Nosestr
St-Pauluskerk
Mutsaertstr
Veemarkt
Zwartzustersstr
Minderbroedersrui
Kl Goddaert
Noorderterras
Zakstr
Burchtgracht
Vlhouwersstr
Doornikstr
Zirkstr
Stoelstr
Minderbroedersstr
Amtmanstr
3
Palingburg
Hofstr
Lange Koepoortstr
19
Kuipersstr
Jeruzalemstr
Steenplein
Tourism Antwerp
Keizerstr
17
Grote Markt
Gildekamersstr
Kaasstr
Oude Beurs
Wolstr
Rockoxhuis
16
14
Wijngaardstr
Wijngaardbrug
Zilversmidstr
Suikerrui
1
13
Lijnwaadmarkt
Hendrik Conscienceplein
St-Carolus-Borromeuskerk
Zuiderterras
Grote Pieter Potstr
8
Blauwmoezelstr
21
Korte Nieuwstr
23
Haarstr
Handschoenmarkt
Ernest Van Dijckkaai
10
Kl Pieter Potstr
Onze-Lieve-Vrouwekathedraal
Melkmarkt
Tram Tunnel
Vleminckstr
Zand
Vlasmarkt
Reyndersstr
Pelgrimstr
Oude Koornmarkt
Groenplaats
Sudermanstr
St Katelijnevest
Eiermarkt
Handelsbeurs
Stoofstr
Hoogstr
Heilige Geeststr
12
Beddenstr
Meirbrug
Groenplaats
St-Jansvliet
Museum Plantin-Moretus
Gier
Schoenmarkt
Meir
9
Scheldeken
Steenhouwersvest
Vrijdag Markt
Schrijnwerkersstraat
Wiegstr
Kammenstr
Plantinkaai
Oever
Lombardenvest
4
2
Drukkerijstr
Lombardenstr
Korte Gasthuisstr
Huidevettersstr
Muntstr
Chocolatiers
Vlaanderenstraat
ST-ANDRIES
Augustijnenstr
Waai
Kammenstr
Everdijstr
Komedieplaats
St-Andriesstr
Sleutelstr
Oudaan
Lange Riddersstr
Nationalestr
St-Antoniusstr
Pompstr
Bogaardeplein
11
Happaertstr
Vlierstr
St-Andriesplaats
Steenbergstr
Vleminckveld
Schoytestr
Bredestr
Lange Gasthuisstr
Kloosterstr
15
Aalmoezenierstr
Prekersstr
Rosier
Mechelseplein
18

Antwerp

Top Sights

	Museum Plantin-Moretus	B5
	Onze-Lieve-Vrouwekathedraal	C4

Sights

1	Brabo Fountain	B3
	Chocolate Line	(see 5)
2	Fashion District	C5
3	Het Steen	B3
4	MoMu	B5
5	Palois op de Meir	E5
6	Rubenshuis	E5
7	Stadsfeestzaal	F5

Sleeping

8	Hotel O	B4
9	Hotel Scheldezicht	A5
10	Katshuis	B4
11	Pulcinella	C6

Eating

12	De Groote Witte Arend	B4
13	Kathedraalcafe	C3
14	't Brantyser	D3

Drinking

15	Bierhuis Kulminator	C7
16	De Kat	D3
17	Den Engel	B3
18	Korsåkov	D7
19	Normo	D3
20	Oud Arsenaal	E6
21	Pelikaan	C4

Entertainment

22	Café d'Anvers	D1
23	De Muze	C4
24	Red & Blue	C1

the O has an intriguing little foyer of 1950s radios and big low-wattage lamp-bulbs. All-black interior decor is relieved in midsized rooms by giant Rubens prints spilling over onto the ceilings. Some rooms are very small.

Hotel Rubenshof HOTEL **€€**
(☎03-237 07 89; www.rubenshof.be; Amerikalei 115-117; s/d €55/76, without bathroom €33/52; 🚇12) Rooms range from tired through floral to neatly renovated, but the big selling points here are the modest prices and fabulous art nouveau breakfast room.

Hotel Scheldezicht HOTEL **€**
(☎03-231 66 02; www.hotelscheldezicht.be; St-Jansvliet 12; s/d with shared bathroom from €50/70;

⌚reception 7am-10pm; 📶) This sweetly old-fashioned hotel has irregular floors and most rooms share toilets, but many are spacious, the decor has been recently spruced up, and the location is delightful on a small, central tree-lined square.

Pulcinella HOSTEL €
(☎03-234 03 14; www.vjh.be/antwerpen.htm; Bogaardeplein 1; dm/d €26/59, members save €3; @📶) This giant, tailor-made HI Hostel is hard to beat for its Fashion District location and brand new facilities.

ABhostel HOSTEL €
(☎0473 57 01 66; www.abhostel.com; Kattenberg 110; dm/d €21/50; ⌚reception noon-3pm & 6-8pm; 📶) This adorable family-run hostel has lots of little added extras to make it comfy. Its inner-suburban setting is 20-minutes' walk east of Antwerpen-Centraal station, past inexpensive shops, ethnic restaurants and African wig shops. Take bus 31 to the de Roma stop.

Katshuis HOTEL €
(☎0476 20 69 47; www.katshuis.be; Grote Pieter Potstraat 18 & 19; r €45-120) In this pair of quiet, Old Town houses, stairs are steep and rooms vary considerably, but while none are overly polished, they're great value for the location. Phone to arrange arrivals.

Eating

For cheap, central snacks, stroll Hoogstraat, near the cathedral. For cosy if pricier options look in parallel Pelgrimstraat (with its 'secret' medieval alley, Vlaaikeusgang) or the picturesque lanes leading to Rubens' wonderful St-Carolus-Borromeuskerk. There are many more excellent options in 't Zuid, north and west of KMSKA.

De Groote Witte Arend BELGIAN €€
(☎03-233 50 33; www.degrootewittearend.be; Reyndersstraat 18; mains €13-22; ⌚10.30am-midnight, kitchen 11.30am-3pm & 5-10pm; 📶) Retaining the Tuscan stone arcade of a 15th–17th century convent building, this relaxed central gem combines the joys of a good beer bar with the satisfaction of well-cooked, sensibly priced Flemish home cuisine.

't Brantyser EUROPEAN €
(☎03-233 18 33; www.brantyser.be; Hendrik Conscienceplein 7; snacks €6-12.50, mains €16.50-26.50; ⌚11.15am-10pm) This well-pitched tourist-oriented restaurant serves generous portions at an enviable terrace location, surveying one of old Antwerp's most appealing pedestrian squares.

Kathedraalcafe BELGIAN €€
(www.kathedraalcafe.be; Torfbrug 10; mains €14-24.50, sandwiches €8.50; ⌚noon-11pm) This ivy-clad medieval masterpiece has an astounding interior decked with angels, saints, pulpits and several deliciously sacrilegious visual jokes.

Aahaar INDIAN, VEGAN €
(www.aahaar.com; Lange Herentalsestraat 23; buffet €9; ⌚noon-3pm & 5.30-9.30pm Mon-Fri, 1-9.30pm Sat & Sun; 🌿) Inexpensive, 100% vegetarian Jain-Indian buffets. From Antwerpen-Centraal walk a block west along De Keyserlei then a block south on Appelmansstraat.

Drinking

To sound like a local, stride into a pub and ask for a *bolleke*. Don't worry, that means a 'little bowl' (ie glass) of De Koninck, the city's favourite ale. Cheap places to try it include classic cafes **Oud Arsenaal** (Pijpelincxstraat 4; ⌚10am-10pm Wed-Fri, 7.30am-7.30pm Sat & Sun), **De Kat** (Wolstraat 22) and the livelier **Pelikaan** (www.facebook.com/cafepelikaan; Melkmarkt 14; ⌚8.30am-3am). Mechelseplein bars including **Korsåkov** (Mechelseplein 21; snacks €3.50-5.50, Primus/Chouffe €2/2.50; ⌚10am-4am) open till very late as do countless other great options around KMSKA in the Zuid area.

Den Engel PUB
(www.cafedenengel.be; Grote Markt 5; ⌚9am-2am) Historic guildhall pub with cathedral views from the terrace.

Bierhuis Kulminator BEER PUB
(Vleminckveld 32; ⌚4pm-midnight Tue-Sat, 8pm-midnight Mon) Classic beer-pub boasting 700 mostly Belgian brews, including rare 'vintage' bottles.

Normo CAFE
(www.normocoffee.com; Minderbroedersrui 30; coffees €2-3.50, muffins €2; ⌚10am-7pm Mon-Fri, to 6pm Sat) Coffee as art, student vibe.

Entertainment

For listings consult www.weekup.be/antwerpen/week; www.zva.be in summer; and www.gratisinantwerpen.be for free events.

Café Local CLUB
(www.cafelocal.be; Waalsekaai 25; cover €7-15; ⌚10pm-late Wed-Sun; 🚊4) Popular, friendly 't Zuid nightclub.

De Muze JAZZ
(☎03-226 01 26; jazzmuze.be; Melkmarkt 15; ⊙noon-4am) Very appealing triple-level cafe with an Escher-like interior hosting great live jazz from 10pm Monday to Saturday (but not Wednesday or Thursday in summer).

Café d'Anvers DISCO, CLUB
(www.cafe-d-anvers.com; Verversrui 15; €10; ⊙11pm-7.30am Thu-Sat; 7) Lurid scarlet interiors reflect the red-light-district setting.

Red & Blue CLUB
(www.redandblue.be; Lange Schipperskapelstraat 11; ⊙11pm-7am Thu-Sat; 7) Great dance venue with decent sized yet still intimate dance floor, most famous for its Saturday gay night.

Information

Tourism Antwerp (☎03-232 01 03; www.visitantwerpen.be; Grote Markt 13; ⊙9am-5.45pm Mon-Sat, to 4.45pm Sun & holidays) Central tourist office with a branch on level zero of Antwerpen-Centraal train station.

Getting There & Away

BUS International **Eurolines** (☎03-233 86 62; www.eurolines.com; Van Stralenstraat 8; ⊙9am-5.45pm Mon-Fri, to 3.15pm Sat) buses depart from points near Franklin Rooseveltplaats. Many regional buses (eg to Lier) and **Ecolines** (www.ecolines.net; Paardenmarkt 65, ticket agent Euro-Maror) services for eastern Europe depart from near Antwerpen-Berchem train station, 2km southeast of Antwerpen-Centraal.

TRAIN Regular services to Bruges (€14.25, 75 minutes), Brussels (€6.90, 35-49 minutes) and Ghent (€9, 46 minutes). High speed service to Amsterdam.

Getting Around

Franklin Rooseveltplaats and Koningin Astridplein are hubs for the integrated network of **De Lijn** (www.delijn.be) buses and trams (some running underground metro-style).

Ghent

POP 248,200

Known as Gent in Dutch and Gand in French, Ghent is like a grittier Bruges without the crush of tourists. Nonetheless it sports photogenic canals, medieval towers, great cafes and some of Belgium's most inspired museums. Always a lively student city, Ghent goes crazy in mid-July during the 10-day **Gentse Feesten** (www.gentsefeesten.be; ⊙Jul).

Sights

Most major sights are strolling distance from Korenmarkt, the westernmost of three interlinked squares that form the heart of Ghent's historic core.

Grasbrug VIEWPOINT
To admire Ghent's towers and gables at their most photogenic, stand just west of the little Grasbrug bridge at dusk. **Canalboat trips** depart from four points nearby.

St-Baafskathedraal CHURCH
(www.users.skynet.be/sintbaafskathedraal-gent; St-Baafsplein; ⊙8.30am-6pm Apr-Oct, to 5pm Nov-Mar) Massive without majesty, this vast cathedral is an essential stop for fans of Flemish Primitive art who flock to see Jan van Eyck's world-famous 1432 masterpiece the **Adoration of the Mystic Lamb** (Het Lam Gods; http://vaneyck.kikirpa.be; St-Baafskathedraal; adult/child €4/1.50, audioguide €1; ⊙9.30am-4.45pm Mon-Sat, 1-4.30pm Sun, closes 4pm Nov-Mar), though some panels are currently absent for restoration. See what it should look like for free in the photo-replica in side-chapel 30.

Belfort BELFRY
(Botermarkt; adult/concession €5/3.75; ⊙10am-5.30pm) Climbing Ghent's 14th-century belfry affords spectacular views of the city

SEE MORE OF GHENT

The good value **Museumpass** (www.visitgent.be; 3-day ticket €20) provides three days' free city transport and entrance to all the sights reviewed (except boat tours) plus much more including the dynamic industrial museum, **MIAT** (Museum voor Industriële Archeologie en Textiel; www.miat.gent.be; Minnemeers 9; adult/child €5/1; ⊙10am-6pm Tue-Sun), the interesting **Design Museum** (www.designmuseumgent.be; J Breydelstraat 5; adult/child €5/free; ⊙10am-6pm Tue-Sun), and the interactive new city museum **STAM** (www.stamgent.be; Bijloke Complex; adult/concession €6/4.50; ⊙10am-6pm Tue-Sun; 4). In Citadelpark near Gent-St-Pieters station, excellent art galleries **MSK** (Museum voor Schone Kunsten; ☎09-240 07 00; www.mskgent.be; Citadelpark; adult/child €5/1; ⊙10am-6pm) and **SMAK** (www.smak.be; Citadelpark; adult/child €6/free, 10am-1pm Sun free; ⊙10am-6pm Tue-Sun; 5) are also included.

Gravensteen CASTLE
(St-Veerleplein; adult/child €8/4; ⏲10am-6pm Apr-Oct, 9am-5pm Nov-Mar) Now lovingly restored, this quintessential 12th-century castle actually spent the 19th century recycled as a factory. An imaginative video story-tour compensates for a relative lack of period furnishings.

Werregarensteeg STREET
(www.ghentizm.be) Graffiti is positively encouraged as an artform in this tiny central alley.

Museum Dr Guislain MUSEUM
(www.museumdrguislain.be; Jozef Guislainstraat 43; adult/child €6/1; ⏲9am-5pm Tue-Fri, 1-5pm Sat & Sun; 1) An enthralling mental-health museum hidden away in an 1857 neo-Gothic lunatic asylum. Tram 1 stops outside.

Sleeping

Ghent offers innovative accommodation in all budget ranges. Websites www.gent-accommodations.be and www.bedandbreakfast-gent.be help you judge availability in the city's numerous appealing B&Bs.

Hostel 47 HOSTEL €€
(0478 71 28 27; www.hostel47.com; Blekerijstraat 47-51; dm €26.50-29.50, d €71;) Inviting hostel in a revamped high-ceilinged historic house offers virginal white walls, spacious bunk-rooms and designer fittings. Calm, no bar.

Uppelink HOSTEL €€
(09-279 44 77; www.hosteluppelink.com; Sint-Michielsplein 21; dm €27.50-37.50 d without bathroom €71) Brand new hostel with unbeatable views of Ghent's main towers from cheaper dorms.

Hotel Flandria HOTEL €€
(09-223 06 26; www.hotelflandria-gent.be; Barrestraat 3; s/d €60/70, without bathroom €45/55; @) Map-plastered walls beckon you into this helpfully central hotel. Rooms are mostly cramped and simple, some better appointed than others. Good beds.

Eating

Enchanting **Patershol** (www.patershol.be) is a web of twisting cobbled lanes with old-world houses that are now interspersed with small restaurants. Others jostle for summer terrace space on Graslei's gorgeous canalside terrace. There's fast food around Korenmarkt and great value Turkish options along Sleepstraat. Numerous vegetarian and organic choices feature on the tourist office's free Veggieplan Gent guide map. Thursday is Veggieday.

Panda VEGETARIAN €
(09-225 07 86; Oudburg 38; mains €16.50-20.50, lunch €13-22.50; ⏲noon-2pm & 6.15-8.45pm Mon-Sat;) Excellent vegie food set to classical music and served on pressed linen tablecloths at the back of an organic grocery shop.

't Oud Clooster TAVERN €
(09-233 78 02; Zwartezusterstraat 5; mains €9-17; ⏲6pm-late Mon-Sat, kitchen till midnight) Candle-lit cherubs and Madonnas watch over you in this double level 'pratcafe' serving well-priced cafe food.

Pizza Gülhan TURKISH €
(Sleepstraat 70; pide €4-6.50, grills €9-13.50, beer/cava/tea €1.80/3.20/1.25; ⏲11.30am-midnight Wed-Mon) Fill up for around €5 with groaning plate-loads of excellent, garnished fresh pide.

Amadeus RIBS €
(09-225 13 85; www.amadeusspareribrestaurant.be; Plotersgracht 8/10; mains €13.75-19; ⏲6.30-11pm) All-you-can-eat spare ribs at four atmospheric Ghent addresses.

Drinking & Entertainment

Try **Hot Club de Gand** (www.hotclubdegand.be; Schuddevisstraatje; ⏲3pm-late) for live acoustic music, **Hotsy Totsy** (www.hotsytotsy.be; Hoogstraat 1; ⏲6pm-1am Mon-Fri, 8pm-2am Sat & Sun) for jazz buzz, **Rococo** (Corduwaniersstraat 5; ⏲from 10pm) for candle-lit conversation, **Het Waterhuis aan de Bierkant** (www.waterhuisaandebierkant.be; Groentenmarkt 12; ⏲11am-1am) for beer choice, **Pink Flamingo's** (www.pinkflamingos.be; Onderstraat 55; ⏲noon-midnight Mon-Wed, noon-3am Thu-Sat, 2pm-midnight Sun) for retro-kitsch and **Charlatan** (www.charlatan.be; Vlasmarkt 9; ⏲7pm-late Tue-Sun during term) for raucous partying.

Information

Ghent Tourist Office (09-266 56 60; www.visitgent.be; Oude Vismijn, St-Veerleplein 5; ⏲9.30am-6.30pm mid-Mar–mid-Oct, to 4.30pm winter) Very helpful for free maps and accommodation bookings.

Getting There & Away

BUS Some longer distance buses depart from **Gent-Zuid bus station** (Woodrow Wilsonplein).

others from various points around Gent-St-Pieters train station.

TRAIN **Gent-Dampoort**, 1km west of the old city, is the handiest station but only some trains stop here, including three hourly runs to Antwerp (€8.50, fast/slow 42/64 minutes) and an hourly Bruges service (€6.20, 36 minutes).

Gent-St-Pieters, 2.5km south of centre, is the main station for Brussels (€9, 36 minutes, twice hourly). From here there are five hourly hops to Bruges (fast/slow 24/42 minutes).

Getting Around

BICYCLE HIRE **Max Mobiel** (www.max mobiel.be; Vokselslaan 27; per day/week/month €9/25/30) is two minutes' walk south of Gent-St-Pieters station. Branch kiosk at Gent-Dampoort station.

BUS & TRAM One-hour/all-day tickets cost €1.20/5 if purchased ahead of time from ticket machines or De Lijn offices beside **Gent-St-Pieters** (7am 1.30pm & 2-7pm Mon-Fri) or in the **centre** (www.delijn.be; Cataloniestraat 4; 10.15am-5pm Mon-Sat). Handy tram 1 runs from Gent-St-Pieters to and through the centre passing walkably close to most major sites.

Bruges

POP 117,000

Cobblestone lanes, dreamy canals, soaring spires and whitewashed old almshouses combine to make central Bruges (Brugge in Dutch) one of Europe's most picture-perfect historic cities. The only problem is that everyone knows.

Sights

A **Bruges City Card** (www.bruggecitycard.be; 48/72 hours €35/€40) gets you into numerous museums and scores you a free **canal boat tour** (adult/child €7.60/3.40; 10am-6pm Mar–mid-Nov) and discounts on bicycle rental. But the real joy of Bruges is simply wandering alongside the canals, soaking up the atmosphere. To avoid the worst crowds, explore east of pretty Jan van Eyckplein.

Markt SQUARE

The heart of ancient Bruges, the old market square is lined with pavement cafes beneath step-gabled facades. Magnificent neo-Gothic buildings include the Post Office and new multimedia **Historium** (www.historium.be; Markt 1; adult/child €11/5.50; 10am-9pm), but the square's dominating feature is the 84m, 13th-century **Belfort** (Belfry; adult/child €8/5; 9.30am-5pm, last tickets 4.15pm). Climbing its 366 steps can get claustrophobic.

Burg SQUARE

Bruges' 1420 **Stadhuis** (City Hall; Burg 12) is smothered in statuettes and contains a breathtaking **Gotishe Zaal** (Gothic Hall; Burg; adult/concession €4/3; 9.30am-5pm). The easily missed **Basilica of the Holy Blood** next door is so named for a phial supposedly containing a few drops of Christ's blood that was brought here after the 12th-century Crusades. It's still venerated daily (usually 2pm).

Groeningemuseum ART GALLERY

(www.brugge.be; Dijver 12; adult/concession €8/6; 9.30am-5pm Tue-Sun) Bruges' most celebrated art gallery packs 11 rooms with an astonishingly rich collection, from Flemish Primitive works to surrealist canvases by Magritte and Delvaux.

Museum St-Janshospitaal MUSEUM

(Memlingmuseum; Mariastraat 38; adult/child €8/free; 9.30am-5pm Tue-Sun) This restored 12th-century hospital-chapel displays nightmarish historical medical implements but also six masterpieces by 15th-century artist Hans Memling.

FREE **Begijnhof** BEGIJNHOF

(6.30am-6.30pm) One of Bruges' quaintest spots, the walled Begijnhof is an area of hushed calm an 800m walk south of the Markt, close to the romantic **Minnewater** (Lake of Love).

Choco-Story MUSEUM

(www.choco-story.be; Wijnzakstraat 2, on Sint-Jansplein; adult/child €7/4; 10am-5pm) This

WHAT'S A BEGIJNHOF?

Usually enclosed around a central garden, a *begijnhof* (*béguinage* in French) is a pretty cluster of historic houses originally built to house lay sisters. The idea originated in the 12th-century when many such women were left widowed by their crusader-knight husbands. Today 14 of Flanders' historic *begijnhoven* have been declared Unesco World Heritage sites with great examples at **Diest**, **Lier**, **Turnhout**, **Kortrijk** and **Bruges**; the latter also has dozens of smaller *godshuizen* (almshouses).

Bruges

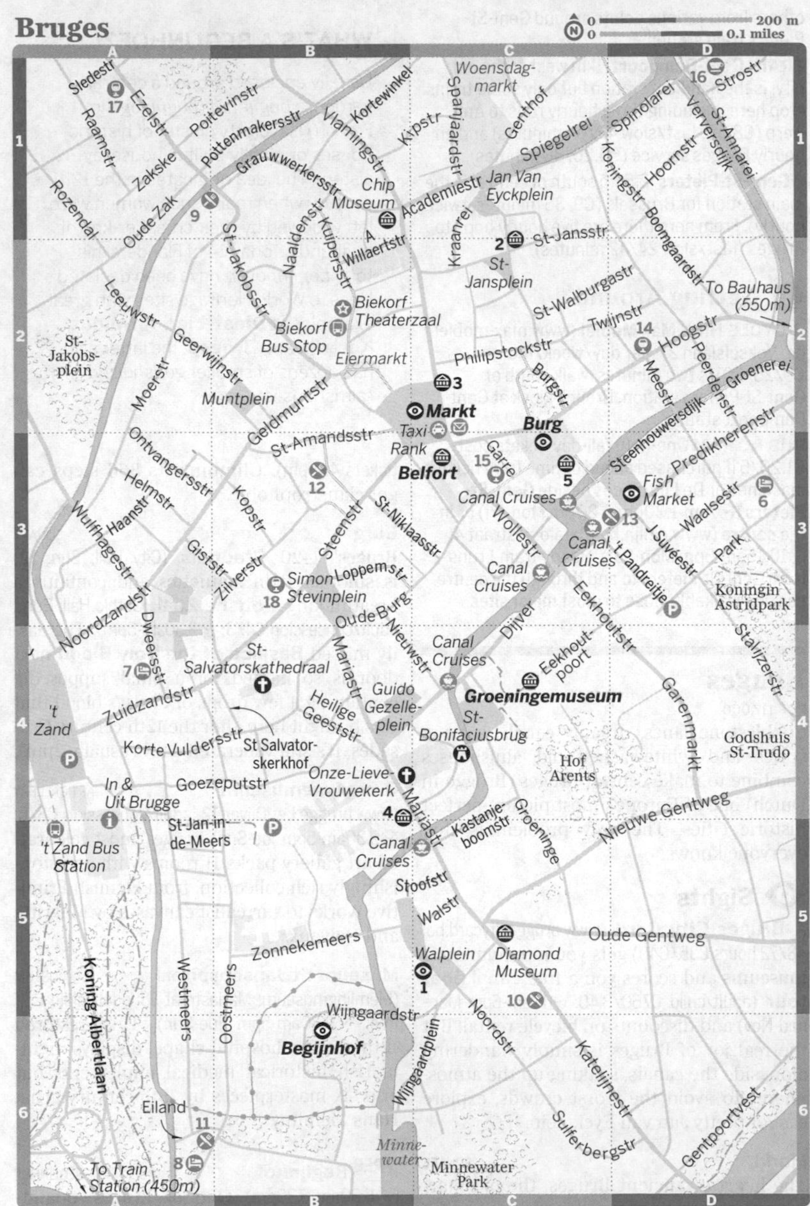

highly absorbing chocolate museum traces the cocoa bean back to its role as an Aztec currency, shows videos on cocoa production, and provides a sample praline that's made as you watch (last demonstration 4.45pm).

Brouwerij De Halve Maan BREWERY
(☎050 33 26 97; www.halvemaan.be; Walplein 26; ⊙10.30am-6pm, closed 2 weeks mid-Jan) Founded in 1856, this family brewhouse offers 45-minute multilingual **guided visits** (tours €6.50; ⊙11am-4pm Apr-Sep, 11am & 3pm

Bruges

Top Sights

- Begijnhof B6
- Belfort C3
- Burg C3
- Groeningemuseum C4
- Markt C2

Sights

- 1 Brouwerij De Halve Maan C5
- 2 Choco-Story C2
- Gotische Zaal .... (see 5)
- 3 Historium C2
- 4 Museum St-Janshospitaal B4
- 5 Stadhuis C3

Sleeping

- 6 B&B Dieltiens D3
- 7 Passage Bruges A4
- 8 't Keizershof A6

Eating

- 9 De Bottelier A1
- 10 De Bron C5
- 11 De Stoepa A6
- 12 De Stove B3
- 13 Est Wijnbar D3

Drinking

- 14 Charlie Rockets D2
- 15 De Garre C3
- 16 Herberg Vlissinghe D1
- 17 Snuffel Hostel A1
- 18 't Brugs Beertje B3

Oct-Mar), include a tasting of its excellent *Brugse Zot* beer.

Damme VILLAGE

Historic, quaint if often tourist-jammed, the inland port-village of Damme makes a popular summer excursion by bicycle or canal paddle steamer. It's 5km along the tree-lined canal from Bruges' Noorweegse Kaai.

Sleeping

Although there are well over 250 hotels and B&Bs, accommodation can still prove oppressively overbooked from Easter to September, over Christmas and especially at weekends, when two-night minimum stays are commonly required. In the lowest seasons (early November, late January), midrange options sometimes give big last-minute discounts. An all-night touch-screen computer outside the main tourist office displays hotel availability and contact information. Website www.brugge.be has a booking engine.

B&B Dieltiens B&B €€

(☎050 33 42 94; www.bedandbreakfastbruges.be; Waalsestraat 40; s €60-80, d €70-90) Old and new art fills this lovingly restored classical mansion, which remains an appealingly real home run by charming musician hosts. Superbly central yet quiet.

Tine's Guesthouse GUESTHOUSE €€

(☎050 34 50 18; www.tinesguesthouse.com; Zwaluwenstraat 11; s/d €60/70; P) Superfriendly B&B 1.5km northwest of the belfry, with games to play, free bike rental and free station pick-up/drop off.

't Keizershof HOTEL €

(☎050 33 87 28; www.hotelkeizershof.be; Oostermeers 126; s €25-44, d €45; P) Remarkably tasteful and well kept for this price, the seven rooms with shared bathrooms are above a breakfast room that retains the atmosphere of a former brasserie-cafe. Free parking.

Bauhaus HOSTEL €

(☎050 34 10 93; www.bauhaus.be, Langestraat 145; hostel dm/tw €16/50, hotel s/d €16/50, 2-4 person apt per weekend from €240; @) Almost a backpacker 'village', Bauhaus incorporates a bustling hostel, apartments, a nightclub, internet cafe, bike rental and laundrette. The bar-restaurant (Sacré Coeur) is excellent except when you're trying to sleep above it. 'Pod beds' are little more than a bunk with a curtain. Bus 6 or 16 from the train station.

Passage Bruges HOSTEL €

(☎050 34 02 32; www.passagebruges.com; Dweersstraat 26-28; dm €16, d €67, without bathroom €52) This recently renovated hostel has dorms above an invitingly old-fashioned cafe-restaurant. The next door building houses spartan but large and well-priced hotel rooms.

Ibis Budget HOTEL €

(☎050-40 51 20; Marie Popelinplantsoen 4, Bruges Station; r €46-70;) This new, 184-room hotel has retro fittings that are unexpectedly hip for a budget chain. Reception is attended 24 hours. Wi-fi extra.

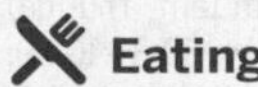

Eating

De Stove GASTRONOMIC €€

(☎050 33 78 35; www.restaurantdestove.be; Kleine St-Amandsstraat 4; mains €19-33, menu without/

with wine €48/64; noon-1.30pm Sat & Sun, 7-9pm Fri-Tue) Calm one-room family restaurant with a reliable yet inventive monthly changing menu that often favours fresh fish.

In 't Nieuwe Museum BROWN CAFE **€€**
(050 33 12 22; Hooistraat 42; mains €16-22; noon-2pm & 6-10pm Thu-Tue, closed lunch Sat) Great value lunches (€7 to €12.50) and dinners of succulent meat, cooked at a 17th-century open fireplace, supplement vegie burgers, eel dishes and creamy *vispannetje* (fish casserole).

De Bottelier MEDITERRANEAN **€€**
(050 33 18 60; www.debottelier.com; St-Jakobsstraat 63; pasta/veg dishes from €9/13.50, mains from €16; lunch & dinner Tue-Fri, dinner Sat) Decorated with hats and old clocks, this adorable little restaurant sits above a wine shop overlooking a delightful handkerchief of canalside garden.

De Stoepa BISTRO **€€**
(050 33 04 54; www.stoepa.be; Oostmeers 124; noon-2pm & 6pm-midnight Tues-Sat, noon-3pm & 6pm-11pm Sun) Upmarket bistro-style food served in a peaceful residential area with oriental statues, terracotta-coloured walls and wooden floors. Leafy terrace garden.

Est Wijnbar TAPAS **€**
(050 33 38 39; www.wijnbarest.be; Braambergstraat 7; mains €9.50-12.50, tapas €3.50-9.50; 4pm-midnight Wed-Sun;) In a 1637 building, this attractive little wine bar is especially convivial on Sunday's acoustic music nights. Raclette, pasta, snacks and salads dominate the menu.

De Bron VEGETARIAN **€**
(050 33 45 26; Katelijnestraat 82; 11.45am-2pm Mon-Fri;) Neat, tidy, glass-roofed place for vegetarian soups and lunch-of-the-day. Vegan options on request.

Drinking

Hostels Bauhaus, Passage Bruges, **Charlie Rockets** (050 33 06 60; www.charlie-rockets.com; Hoogstraat 19; 8am-4am) and **Snuffel** (www.snuffel.be) all have congenial backpacker-oriented pubs, most serving decent yet inexpensive food. Beer-specialist cafes include **'t Brugs Beertje** (www.brugs-beertje.be; Kemelstraat 5; 4pm-1am Thu-Tue) and alley-hidden **De Garre** (050 34 10 29; www.degarre.be; Garre 1; noon-midnight). which serves its own fabulous 11% Garre house brew. Old-world classic **Herberg Vlissinghe** (050 34 37 37; www.cafevlissinghe.be; Blekerstraat 2; 11am-10pm Wed-Sat, to 7pm Sun) dates from 1515. Eiermarkt, just north of Markt, has many plain but lively bars, with DJs and seemingly endless happy hours.

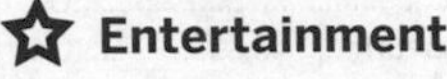

Entertainment

Cactus Muziekcentrum LIVE MUSIC
(050 33 20 14; www.cactusmusic.be; Magdalenastraat 27) Venue for contemporary and world music, both live and DJ.

Information

The **tourist office** (050 44 46 46; www.brugge.be; 't Zand 34; 10am-6pm Mon-Sun) is situated at street level of the big, red Concertgebouw concert hall with a branch at the train station. Standard city maps cost €0.50, comprehensive guide pamphlets €2. Excellent *Use-It* guide-maps (www.use-it.be) are free if you ask for one.

Bruggecentraal (www.bruggecentraal.be) has events listings.

Getting There & Away

Bruges' train station is about 1.5km south of the Markt, a lovely walk via the Begijnhof. Services include the following:

Antwerp (€14.25, 75 minutes, twice hourly)

Brussels (€14, one hour, twice hourly)

Ghent (€6.20, fast/slow 24/42 minutes, five hourly) Two continue to more central Gent-Dampoort.

Ypres (Ieper in Dutch), take a train to Roeselare (€4.50, fast/slow 22/33 minutes), then bus 94 or 95: both buses pass key WWI sites en route.

Eurolines (www.eurolines.eu) runs buses from Bruges to London (€48 standard/€9 super-promo, 4¼ hours, four weekly, daily in holidays). Bookings are essential.

Getting Around

Bicycle

B-Bike (0499 70 50 99; Zand Parking 26; per hr/day €4/12; 10am-7pm Apr-Oct)

Quasimundo (050 33 07 75; www.quasimundo.eu; adult/student €25/23; approx Mar–Oct) Guided bicycle tours around Bruges (2½ hours, morning) or via Damme to the Dutch border (four hours, afternoons). Bike rental included. Book ahead.

Rijwielhandel Erik Popelier (050 34 32 62; www.fietsenpopelier.be; Mariastraat 26; per hr/half-/full day €4/8/12, tandem per hr/half-/full day €10/17/25; 10am-6pm) Good bicycles for adults and kids; helmets for hire, free map, no deposit.

Bus

To get from the train station to Markt, take any bus marked 'Centrum'. For the way back, buses stop at Biekorf, just northwest of Markt on Kuiperstraat.

Around Bruges

Quasimodo (☎050 37 04 70; www.quasimodo.be) has minibus **Triple Treat tours** (under/over 26yr €45/55; ⏲9am Mon, Wed & Fri Feb–mid-Dec) visiting a selection of castles plus the fascinating **WWII coastal defences** near Ostend. Its **Flanders Fields tours** (under/over 26yr €45/55; ⏲9am Tue-Sun Apr-Oct) visit Ypres Salient.

Ypres

POP 35,500

During WWI (1914–18), historic Ypres (pronounced *eepr*, Ieper in Dutch) was bombarded into oblivion while futile battles raged between trench networks in the surrounding poppy fields. Today, many medieval buildings have been meticulously rebuilt and the battlefields in Ypres' rolling agricultural hinterland (called the Ypres Salient) are a moving reminder of the horrors of war, with their seemingly endless graveyards and memorials.

Sights

CENTRAL YPRES

Grote Markt SQUARE

Dominating this very photogenic central square is the brilliantly rebuilt 13th-century **Lakenhallen**, a vast Gothic edifice that originally served as the cloth market. It sports a 70m-high belfry, reminiscent of London's Big Ben, and hosts the gripping **In Flanders Fields** (www.inflandersfields.be; Lakenhalle, Grote Markt 34; adult/child €8/1; ⏲10am-6pm Apr–mid-Nov, 10am-5pm Tue-Sun mid-Nov–Mar), a highly recommended multimedia WWI museum honouring ordinary people's experiences of wartime horrors. The ticket allows free entry to three other minor city museums.

Menin Gate MEMORIAL

(Menenpoort) A block east of Grote Markt, this huge stone gateway straddles the main road at the city moat. It's inscribed with the names of 54,896 'lost' British and other Commonwealth WWI troops whose bodies were never found.

Last Post CEREMONY

(www.lastpost.be; ⏲8pm daily) At 8pm, traffic through the Menin Gate is halted while buglers sound the *Last Post* in remembrance of the WWI dead, a moving tradition started in 1928. Every evening the scene is different, possibly accompanied by pipers, troops of cadets or maybe a military band.

YPRES SALIENT

Many WWI sites are in rural locations that are awkward to reach without a car or tour bus. But the following are all within 600m of Ypres–Roeselare bus routes 94 and 95 (once or twice hourly weekdays, five daily weekends), so could be visited en route between Ypres and Bruges.

Memorial Museum Passchendaele 1917 MUSEUM

(www.passchendaele.be; Ieperstraat 5; admission €5; ⏲10am-6pm Feb-Nov; 🚌94) In central **Zonnebeke village** (www.zonnebeke.be), a lake-fronted Normandy chalet-style mansion (built 1922) now hosts an impressive WWI museum. It charts local battle progressions with plenty of multilingual commentaries but the highlight is a well executed 'trench experience'.

FREE **Tyne Cot** CEMETERY

(⏲24hr, visitor centre 9am-6pm Feb-Nov; 🚌94) With 11,956 graves, this is the world's biggest British Commonwealth war cemetery. A huge semicircular wall commemorates another 34,857 lost-in-action soldiers whose names wouldn't fit on Ypres' Menin Gate. Bus 94 stops 600m away.

FREE **Deutscher Soldatenfriedhof** CEMETERY

The area's main German WWI cemetery is smaller than Tyne Cot but arguably more memorable. Each granite grave slab marks up to ten bodies and four eerie silhouette statues survey the site. It's beyond the northern edge of Langemark (bus 95).

Tours

Two WWI specialist bookshops towards Menin Gate offer twice-daily, half-day guided minibus tours of selected war sites:

Over the Top BOOKSHOP, TOURS

(☎0472 34 87 47; www.overthetoptours.be; Meensestraat 41; ⏲9am-12.30pm, 1.30-5.30pm & 7.30-8.30pm)

British Grenadier BOOKSHOP, TOURS
(☎057 21 46 57; www.salienttours.be; Meensestraat 5; ⏲9.30am-1pm, 2-6pm & 7.30-8.30pm)

Sleeping & Eating

The nearest youth hostel is located in Kortrijk, 30 minutes away by train.

B&B Ter Thuyne B&B €€
(☎057 36 00 42; www.terthuyne.be; Gustave de Stuersstraat 19; d €85; @) Three comfortable rooms that are luminously bright and scrupulously clean but not overly fashion conscious.

Hotel Regina HOTEL €€
(☎057 21 88 88; www.hotelregina.be; Grote Markt 45; s/d from €70/85; ☁) Location, location, location. You can forgive the sometimes dated decor to be right on the central square overlooking the Lakenhalle. Friendly staff, decent food.

De Ruyffelaer FLEMISH €€
(☎057 36 60 06; www.deruyffelaer.be; Gustave de Stuersstraat 9; mains €13-19, menus €24-33; ⏲11.30am-3.30pm Sun, 5.30-9.30pm Thu-Sun) Traditional local dishes served in an adorable, wood-panelled interior with old checkerboard floors and a *brocante* decor, including dried flowers, old radios and antique biscuit tins.

Information

The well-equipped **tourist office** (☎057 23 92 20; www.ieper.be; Grote Markt 34; ⏲9am-6pm) is within the Lakenhallen.

Getting There & Around

BICYCLE Rent bicycles from **Hotel Ambrosia** (☎057 36 63 66; www.ambrosiahotel.be; D'Hondtstraat 54; standard/electric bike per day €12/35; ⏲7.30am-7pm).

BUS Services pick up passengers in Grote Markt's northeast corner (check the direction carefully!). For Bruges take Roeselare-bound routes 94 or 95 then change to train.

TRAIN Services run hourly to Ghent (€11, one hour) and Brussels (€16.75, 1¾ hours) via Kortrijk (€5, 30 minutes), where you could change for Bruges or Antwerp.

WALLONIA

Parlez-vous français? You'll need to in hilly Wallonia, Belgium's French-speaking southern half. Wallonia's cities do have their charms, though none quite manage to outshine the many Flemish 'art cities'. Wallonia's foremost attractions are mostly rural – outdoor activities, fabulous caves and ancient rural castles. This is where you'll really appreciate having your own wheels for easier access.

Tournai

POP 69,400

Pleasant Tournai (Doornik in Dutch) is Wallonia's oldest city. Though battered by WWII bombs, the very photogenic **Grand Place** has since been convincingly rebuilt and the skyline is dominated by five iconic spires of the Romanesque **Cathédrale Notre Dame** (Pl de l'Évêché; admission free; ⏲9.30am-noon & 2-6pm Apr-Oct, to 5pm Nov-Mar). It's a Unesco World Heritage site, as is the 72m-high **belfry** (adult/concession €2/1; ⏲9.30am-12.15pm & 2-4.15pm Tue-Sun). Several enjoyable museums (free first Sunday of each month) are clustered near the HI Hostel **Auberge de Jeunesse** (☎069 21 61 36; www.laj.be; Rue St-Martin 64; dm/s/d €23/36.50/54.75, HI members save €3; ⏲check-in 5-10pm), 400m southwest. The train station, 1km northeast of the centre, has connections to Brussels (€12.25, fast/slow 61/73 minutes), Mons (€6.90, fast/slow 23/43 minutes) and Lille-Flandres (€6.50, 25 minutes) in France.

Mons

POP 93,100

Historic Mons (Bergen in Dutch) is being smartened up for its role as European City of Culture in 2015 when its new gallery (www.bam.mons.be) plans to host a major Van Gogh exhibition. Till then, highlights include the 80m baroque belfry (Beffroi), the over-sized 15th-century church of **Ste-Waudru** (www.waudru.be; Place du Chapitre; ⏲9am-6pm) and the attractive Grand Place. This great square comes to life on Trinity Sunday when the festivities of the Ducasse (www.ducassedemons), reach a raucous culmination with a George versus the dragon battle. The **Hôtel St James** (☎065 72 48 24; www.hotelstjames.be; Place de Flandre 8; r €73-83; P☁) offers good value accommodation, and for an unforgettable dinner in 17th-century style don't miss the **Salon des Lumières** (☎0474 29 25 84; www.salondeslumieres.com; Rue du Mirroir 23; mains €16.50-20; ⏲7-10pm Wed-Sun, from 6pm winter).

Liège

POP 195,600

Beneath its brutally disfigured, post-industrial surface, sprawling Liège (Luik in Dutch) is a living architectural onion

WORTH A TRIP

ON THE ROAD IN WALLONIA

By public transport you'll spend longer reaching most of the Wallonia's rural sites than actually enjoying them. But by car, combining a handful of destinations can make for a very enjoyable day out. For in-depth coverage, see Lonely Planet's *Belgium & Luxembourg*.

Kayaking & Outdoor Activities

Durbuy (www.durbuyinfo.be) The 'world's smallest town' is quaint if touristy and is well set up for all manner of sporting fun. Plenty of hotels.

La Roche-en-Ardenne (www.ardenne-aventures.be) Water sports and mountain biking from a charmingly compact town nestled around a medieval castle ruin.

Coo (www.coo-adventure.com) The hamlet's famous 15m 'waterfall' is underwhelming but outdoor options are numerous and there's a family amusement park (www.plopsa.be). Accommodation is limited in Coo but is more plentiful in nearby Stavelot.

Caves

Belgium's publicly accessible cave systems each have their own character. Visits take over an hour with set departure times that vary seasonally (check websites). There's no 'escape' once you've started so don't forget appropriate footwear, warm clothes and a pre-emptive bathroom stop.

Han-sur-Lesse (www.grotte-de-han.be) Belgium's foremost stalactite-rich caves are accessed by a little train ride then guided walk. Gets very busy in summer.

Rochefort (www.valdelesse.be) The Grotte de Lorette, remarkable for its depth more than its stalagmites, is walking distance from attractive Rochefort, famous for its Trappist beers and offering a good choice of accommodation.

Hotton (www.grottesdehotton.com) Great grottoes and a jaw-dropping vertical subterranean chasm, yet relatively uncommercial.

Remouchamps (www.grottes.be) Lacks the drama of the three 'greats' above, but you get to ride an underground river in a boat.

Castles

Wallonia's capital **Namur** (www.namurtourisme.be) is dominated by a massive, sober, fortified **citadel** (www.citadelle.namur.be; admission free), but the region has many more romantic castles including the following:

Château de Jehay (www.chateaujehay.be; adult/student €5/2.50, audioguide €1; ⌚2-6pm Tue-Fri, 11am-6pm Sat & Sun Apr-Sep) A gingerbread fantasy (dating from 1550) of alternating brick and stone layers rising from a tree-ringed moat. The interior is under reconstruction.

Château de Modave (www.modave-castle.be; adult/child €7.50/free; ⌚10am-5pm Tue-Sun Apr–mid-Nov) Palatial chateau with 20 majestically furnished rooms and 17th-century stucco ceilings.

Château de Lavaux-Sainte-Anne (www.chateau-lavaux.com; adult/child €7/5; ⌚9am-5.30pm Wed-Sun, last entry 4.15pm) Partly furnished moated fortress (dating from 1450) visible west of the E411 motorway as you pass junction 22a, just 10km from Han-sur-Lesse.

Château de Bouillon (☎061 46 42 02; www.bouillon-initiative.be; Rue du Château; adult/child €6.50/4.50; ⌚10am-7pm Jul & Aug, to 5pm Mar-Jun & Sep-Nov, short hours in winter; P 👪) Attractive small town dominated by a central crusader castle ruin that once belonged to the 'Belgian' conqueror of Jerusalem. While there, do drive or kayak the lovely Semois Valley overlooked by panoramic viewpoints at **Rochehaut** and **Tombeau du Géant**.

concealing layer upon layer of history. Fine churches abound, as befits a city that spent 800 years as the capital of an independent principality run by bishops. Proudly free-spirited citizens are disarmingly friendly and no Belgian city bubbles with more joie de vivre.

The somewhat grimy historic zone has several excellent museums. The **Grand Curtius** (www.grandcurtiusliege.be; Féronstrée 136; adult/child €9/free; ⏲10am-6pm Wed-Mon) presents a millenium's development of decorative arts. Art gallery **Musée de l'Art Wallon** (Rue St-Georges; adult/child €5/free; ⏲1-6pm Tue-Sat, 11am-6pm Sun) is richly endowed, if architecturally hideous.

Love it or loathe it, Liège is quirky and oddly compulsive especially during its chaotic August 15th festival, held just across the river in the self-declared 'republic' of Outremeuse where there's a handy **HI Hostel** (☎04-344 56 89; www.laj.be; Rue Georges Simenon 2; dm/s/d €23/36.50/54.75, HI members save €3; @). The most appealing central accommodation options is the cosy little **Hôtel Hors Château** (☎04-250 60 68; www.hors-chateau.be; Rue Hors Château 62; s/d/ste €78/95/125; wifi). For real Liègois food dine at **Amon Nanesse** (www.maisondupeket.be; Rue de l'Epée 4; meals €10.50-18.50; ⏲10am-2am, kitchen noon-2.30pm & 6-10.30pm).

Liège's great archtectural masterpiece is its 21st-century Guillermins train station, shaped vaguely like a giant concrete manta-ray. That's on the Brussels–Frankfurt mainline, though Liège-Palais station is far more central.

LUXEMBOURG

Ruled by its own monarchy, the Grand Duchy of Luxembourg is famed for its bank but visually it's mostly an undulating series of pretty wooded hills dotted with castle villages. These are made accessible from the attractive capital city by excellent roads and a very well organised single-price public transport system.

Luxembourg City

POP 100,000

World Heritage–listed Luxembourg City sits high on a promontory overlooking the deep-cut valleys of the Pétrusse and Alzette Rivers. These gorges were the key to the city's defence from AD 963 when Count Sigefroi (or Siegfried) of Ardennes built a castle here. Luxembourg eventually grew to become one of Europe's strongest fortresses, earning the nickname 'Gibraltar of the North'. In 1867 the majority of the fortifications were removed as part of a treaty to reduce tensions between France and Germany, though a remarkable mass of bastion remnants and tunnels survive, providing visitors with spectacular viewpoints overlooking the interesting old quarters of Clausen, Pfaffenthal and the Grund.

Sights

OLD TOWN

Within the compact, mostly pedestrianised Old Town all sights are walking distance from each other. Access to the appealing Grund area is easiest using a public elevator on Plateau du St-Esprit.

TOP CHOICE Chemin de la Corniche PROMENADE

Hailed as 'Europe's most beautiful balcony', this pedestrian view-promenade winds along the course of the former 17th-century city ramparts. Cut into the rock beneath, the mildly intriguing **Bock Casemates** (Montée de Clausen; adult/child €3/2.50; ⏲10am-5pm Mar-Oct) are a honeycomb of damp 18th-century subterranean rock-cut passages.

Royal Palace PALACE

(17 Rue du Marché-aux-Herbes; with guided tour only €7; ⏲guided tours 4pm, Mon-Sat mid-Jul & Aug) Photogenic with little pointy turrets, this much-extended palace (1573) now houses the Grand Duke's office with parliament using its 1859 annex. In mid-summer, gently humorous 45-minute guided tours get you inside. Pre-book tours via the tourist office.

TOP CHOICE Musée d'Histoire de la Ville de Luxembourg MUSEUM

(www.mhvl.lu; 14 Rue du St-Esprit; adult/LC €5/free; ⏲10am-6pm Tue-Sun, to 8pm Thu) This remarkably engrossing and interactive city history museum hides within a series of 17th-century houses.

MNHA MUSEUM

(Musée National d'Histoire et d'Art; www.mnha.lu; Marché-aux-Poissons; adult/LC €5/free; ⏲10am-6pm Tue-Sun, to 8pm Thu) Startlingly modern for its Old Town setting, this unusual museum offers a fascinating if uneven coverage of art and history.

Cathédrale Notre Dame CHURCH
(Blvd Roosevelt; ⏲10am-noon & 2-5.30pm) The cathedral has elongated black spires and a crypt containing the graves of Luxembourg's royalty.

FREE **Spuerkeess** MUSEUM, ARCHITECTURE
(www.spuerkeess.lu; 1 Place de Metz) In a dramatic, century-old, castle-style building, Spuerkeess, the state savings bank, hosts an intriguing **Bank Museum** (⏲9am-5.30pm Mon-Fri).

KIRCHBERG

Luxembourg's shiny glass business district and Eurocrat 'ghetto' is across the Pont Grande-Duchesse Charlotte, the city's giant, iconic red bridge.

TOP CHOICE **Mudam** ART MUSEUM
(www.mudam.lu; 3 Parc Dräi Eechelen; adult/LC €5/free; ⏲11am-8pm Wed-Fri, to 6pm Sat-Mon) Ground-breaking exhibitions of modern, installation and experiential art in a 2006 architectural icon. It's 2km from the centre by buses 1, 13 or 16 to 'Philharmonie'. On foot climb a long stairway from near the Youth Hostel via Fort Obergrünwald.

Sleeping

Luxembourg City's accommodation scene is heavy with business options but online rates are slashed at weekends and in summer.

Hôtel Simoncini HOTEL €€
(☎22 28 44; www.hotelsimoncini.lu; 6 Rue Notre Dame; s/d midweek from €140/165, weekend €115/125; @☏) A delightful contemporary option in the city centre, the Simoncini's foyer is a modern art gallery and the smart, bright rooms have slight touches of retro-cool.

Hôtel Vauban HOTEL €€
(☎22 04 93; www.hotelvauban.lu; 10 Place Guillaume II; s/d €95/130) The location is fabulously central and the 16 rooms were pleasantly spruced up in 2011, though smaller singles are rather claustrophobic.

Auberge de Jeunesse HOSTEL €
(☎22 68 89; luxembourg@youthhostels.lu; 2 Rue du Fort Olizy; dm/s/d €20.75/32.75/51.25, HI members €17.75/29.75/45.50; P⊖❄@☏; 🚌9) This state-of-the-art HI hostel has very comfortably appointed, sex-segregated dorms, ample relaxing space, and views towards an arc of the old city. If full, there are other hostels within an hour's bus ride at Bourglinster, Larochette and Remerschen.

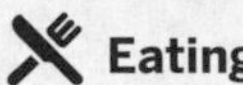

Eating

Tree-shaded Place d'Armes overflows with terrace seating in summer and covers all bases from fast food to ritzy resto. Cheaper terraced places can be found on or near unexotic Place de Paris while for intimate and more original dining options, hunt out the alleys and passages collectively nicknamed Ilôt Gourmand, directly behind the palace.

Am Tiirmschen LUXEMBOURGISH €€
(☎26 27 07 33; www.amtiirmschen.lu; 32 Rue de l'Eau; mains €10-25; ⏲noon-2.30pm Mon-Fri, 7-10.30pm Tue-Sat) This is a great place to sample typical Luxembourg dishes, but it also serves good fish and French options in case your companions don't fancy *kniddelen* (dumplings) or smoked pork. Decor comprises a semi-successful mix of old and pseudo-old beams.

Anabanana VEGAN €
(www.anabanana.lu; 117 Rue de la Tour Jacob; sandwich/lunch/dinner €5/12/19; ⏲noon-2pm Tue-Fri, 7-9.45pm Tue-Sat; ⊘) Quaint, colourful little vegan-fusion restaurant with a fixed dinner choice that changes daily. Juice €4.50, no alcohol.

Bosso ALSACE, GERMAN €
(www.bosso.lu; 7 Bisserwée; mains €8.50-16; ⏲5pm-midnight Mon-Thu, 11am-midnight Fri-Sun) Good value tourist-centric restaurant with a hidden courtyard garden and a speciality of *flammeküeche*, wafer-thin Alsatian 'pizzas' made with sour cream instead tomato sauce.

Á la Soupe SOUP €
(www.alasoupe.net; Rue Chimay; breakfast €3.50-7, soup €4.50-6.50; ⏲7.30am-7.30pm Mon-Sat) Central soup station.

Exki ORGANIC, FAST FOOD €
(www.exki.lu; 72 Grand Rue; snacks & light meals €4-7; ⏲7am-7pm Mon-Fri, 8am-6.30pm Sat; ☏) Modern self-service cafe offering wholesome

LUXEMBOURG CARD

The brilliant value **Luxembourg Card** (www.ont.lu/en/luxembourg-card; 1-/2-/3-day adult €11/19/27, family €22/38/54), marked LC in reviews, allows free admission to most of the Grand Duchy's main attractions and unlimited use of public transport nationwide. You can buy it from tourist offices, museums or certain hotels.

Luxembourg City

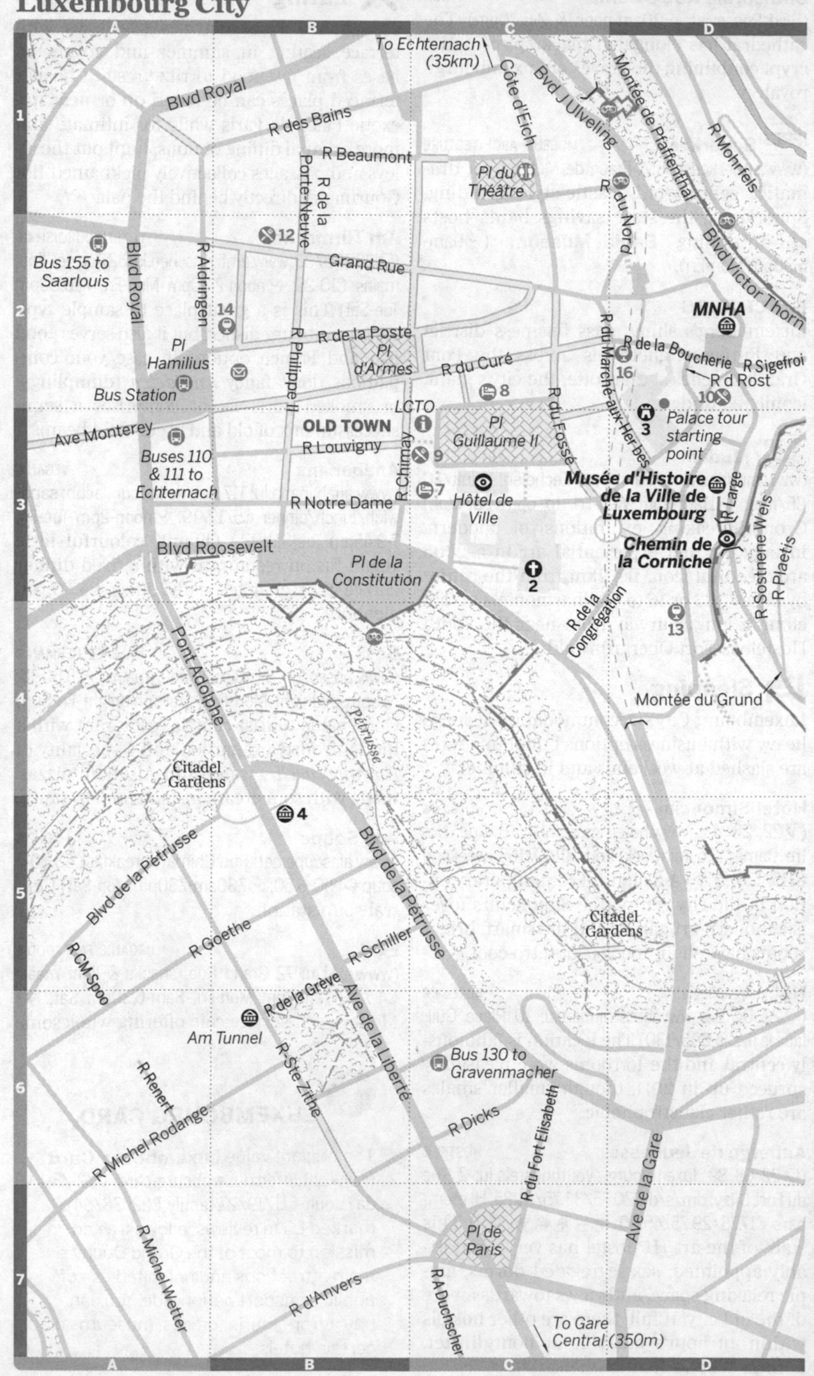

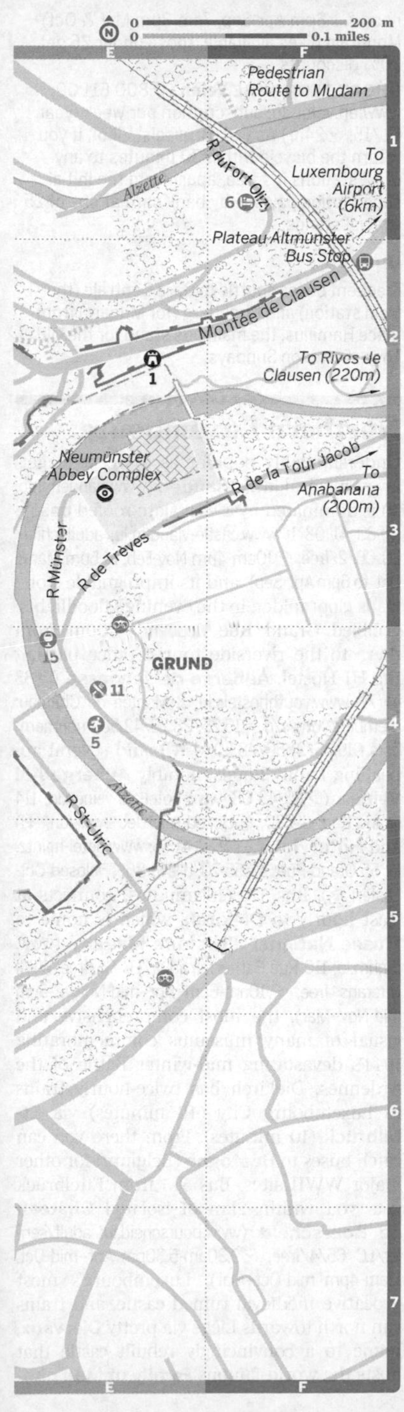

Luxembourg City

Top Sights

Chemin de la Corniche	D3
MNHA	D2
Musée d'Histoire de la Ville de Luxembourg	D3

Sights

1 Bock Casemates	E2
2 Cathédrale Notre Dame	C3
3 Royal Palace	D3
4 Spuerkeess	B5

Activities, Courses & Tours

5 Vélo en Ville	E4

Sleeping

6 Auberge de Jeunesse	F1
7 Hôtel Simoncini	C3
8 Hôtel Vauban	C2

Eating

9 Á la Soupe	C3
10 Am Tiirmchen	D2
11 Bosso	E4
12 Exki	B2

Drinking

13 D:qliq	D4
14 L'Interview	B2
15 Liquid Café	E4
16 Urban Bar	D2

organic food and free wi-fi. Before 11am coffee costs €1.

Drinking & Entertainment

Nearly a dozen themed bar-restaurant clubs in the **Rives de Clausen** (www.rivesdeclausen.com) form the city's liveliest youth scene. Fun central area cafe-bars include **Urban Bar** (www.urban.lu/urbancity.html; 2 Rue de la Boucherie; ⌚noon-late, kitchen 1-6pm), **L'Interview** (Rue Aldringen; ⌚7.30am-1am), **D:qliq** (www.dqliq.com; 17 Rue du St-Esprit; ⌚5pm-1am Tue-Thu, 6pm-3am Fri & Sat) and **Liquid Café** (www.liquid.lu; 17 Rue Münster; ⌚5pm-1am Mon-Fri, 8pm-1am Sat & Sun). Ethereal all-white **Atmosphere** (1 Rue Joseph Heintz; ⌚Tue 10pm-1am, Fri & Sat to 6am) is the most appealing of several nightspots along/near the entirely unpromising-looking Rue de Hollerich, 500m west of Gare Centrale. Another 200m further west, factory-like **Den Atelier** (☎49 54 66; www.atelier.lu; 56 Rue de Hollerich) hosts a fine range of alternative music gigs. Smoking is allowed in Luxembourg's pubs.

Information

Bibliothèque Municipale (3 Rue Génistre; ⏲10am-7pm Tue-Fri, to 6pm Sat) Sign up (with ID) for one hour's free internet. No printing.

Cyber (3 Rue du Curé; per 10min/hr €1/3.90; ⏲9am-10pm Mon-Fri, 2-8pm Sat) Internet with printing possible, upstairs above Brasserie Curé.

LCTO (☎22 28 09; www.lcto.lu; Place Guillaume II; ⏲9am-6pm Mon-Sat, 10am-6pm Sun) Free city maps, walking-tour pamphlets and event guides.

Getting There & Away

Bus

Useful international connections from beside the train station include **Bitburg** (bus 401, 1¼ hours) and **Trier** (bus 118, one hour).

Train

Gare Centrale, 1km south of the old city, has trains to the following destinations:

Brussels (€36.25, three hours)

Diekirch (30 minutes) Hourly via Ettelbrück.

Liège (from €35, 2½ hours) Every two hours via Clervaux (one hour) and Coo (1¾ hours).

Paris (from €56, 145 minutes) By TGV.

Trier (€9-16, 50 minutes) Hourly, several continuing to Koblenz (€34, 130 minutes).

There are **left-luggage lockers** (Gare Centrale; per day €2-4; ⏲6am-9.30pm) at the far north end of platform 3; inaccessible at night.

Getting Around

To/From Luxembourg Airport

Luxembourg Airport (www.lux-airport.lu) is 6km east of Place d'Armes, 20 minutes by bus 16.

Bicycle

LONG-TERM HIRE **Vélo en Ville** (☎47 96 23 83; 8 Bisserwée; per half-day/full day/weekend/week €12.50/20/37.50/75; ⏲10am-noon & 1-8pm Apr-Sep, 7am-3pm Mar & Oct) Mountain bikes available, those under 26 get 20% discounts.

SHORT-TERM HIRE **Velóh** (☎800 611 00; www.en.veloh.lu; subscription per week/year €1/15; ⏲24hr) As with Brussels' Villo!, if you return the bicycle within 30 minutes to any of 72 stations it's free, apart from the initial subscription payable by bank card at one of 25 special stands.

Bus

Frequent buses shuttle to Gare Centrale (the train station) and Kirchberg (for Mudam) from Place Hamilius, the main bus stand for the Old Town. Fewer on Sundays.

LUXEMBOURG'S SIMPLIFIED TRANSPORT SYSTEM

Using bus, train or any combination, travel between any two points in the entire country (except border stations) costs €2/4 for two hours/one day. Buy tickets aboard buses, at train stations or in post offices.

See www.autobus.lu and www.cfl.lu for timetables.

Northern Luxembourg

Understandably popular as a weekend getaway, magical little **Vianden** (www.vianden-info.lu) is dominated by a vast slate-roofed **castle** (☎83 41 08 1; www.castle-vianden.lu; adult/child/LC €6/2/free; ⏲10am-4pm Nov-Feb, to 5pm Mar & Oct, to 6pm Apr-Sep), and its impregnable stone walls glow golden in the evening's floodlights. Cobbled Grand Rue descends 700m from there to the riverside tourist office passing the HI Hostel, **Auberge de Jeunesse** (☎83 41 77; www.youthhostels.lu; 3 Montée du Château; members dm/s/d €16.25/28.25/42.50, nonmembers €19.25/31.50/48.50; 🚭📶), and several appealing family hotels, notably **Auberge Aal Veinen** (☎83 43 68; www.hotel-aal-veinen.lu; 114 Grand Rue; d €80; ⏲closed mid-Dec–mid-Jan; 📶) and **Hôtel Heintz** (☎83 41 55; www.hotel-heintz.lu; 55 Grand Rue; s €55-70, d €61-86; ⏲closed Oct-Easter; 📶). Bus 570 (18 minutes) connects at least hourly to **Diekirch**, which is home to **Musée National d'Histoire Militaire** (www.mnhm.lu; 110 Rue Bamertal; adult/LC €5/free, WWII veterans free; ⏲10am-6pm Apr–mid-Nov, 2-6pm mid-Nov–Mar), the most comprehensive and visual of many museums commemorating 1944's devastating mid-winter Battle of the Ardennes. Diekirch has twice-hourly trains to Luxembourg City (40 minutes) via **Ettelbrück** (10 minutes). From there you can catch buses to **Bastogne** (Belgium) for other major WWII sites. Bus 545 from Ettelbrück gets you within 2km of isolated **Château de Bourscheid** (www.bourscheid.lu; adult/senior/LC €5/4/free; ⏲9.30am-5.30pm Apr–mid-Oct, 11am-4pm mid-Oct–Mar), Luxembourg's most evocative medieval ruined castle, and trains run north towards Liège via pretty **Clervaux**, home to a convincingly rebuilt castle that hosts the world-famous **Family of Man pho-**

tography exhibition (www.steichencollections.lu), due to re-open in summer 2013. Bus 663 (32 minutes) departs Luxembourg City for Vianden at at 8.30am, 10am, 2pm and 5pm.

Echternach

POP 5600

Echternach is home to sparse Roman excavations and Luxembourg's most important religious building, a sombre neo-Romanesque basilica rebuilt after merciless WWII bombing. The town makes a useful base for hiking the well-signposted Müllerthal Trails (www.mullerthal-trail.lu) through shoulder-wide microgorges. Trail E1 (11.7km) starts from Echternach bus station, reached via pedestrianised, cafe-lined Rue de la Gare from the attractive main square. Mountain bikes (half-/full day €8/15) can be rented from Echternach's modern **HI hostel** (Auberge de Jeunesse; 72 01 58; echternach@youthhostels.lu; dm/s €18.25/29, nonmembers €21.25/32; reception 8am-10am & 5-10pm;), set in a lakeside country park 2km south of town. Head 800m southwest to the fire station (bus stop Centre de Secours on route 110 Luxembourg City–Echternach). Then walk 1.2km southeast in the direction of Rodenhof (Roudenhaff). Bus 111 (55 minutes, hourly) takes an alternative route to Luxembourg City via Berdorf.

Moselle Valley

Smothering the Moselle River's steeply rising banks are the neatly clipped vineyards that produce Luxembourg's balanced rieslings, fruity rivaners and excellent crémants (sparkling *méthode traditionelle* wines). Taste a selection at the grand **Caves Bernard-Massard** (75 05 45 1; www.bernard-massard.lu; 8 Rue du Pont; tour adult/child/LC from €4/2.50/free; 9.30am-6pm Apr-Oct) in central **Grevenmacher** where frequent 20-minute **winery tours** (adult/child from €4/2.50) are multilingual and spiced with humour. The Enner der Bréck bus stop outside is on bus routes 130 from Rue Heine in Luxembourg City (55 minutes, once or twice hourly). **Rentabike Miselerland bicycles** (www.visitmoselle.lu/rentabike-miselerland; per day €7, LC free) can be rented from Grevenmacher's Butterfly Garden, allowing you to cycle along the riverside route via several other wineries. Return the bicycle at Remich bus station where bus 175 returns to Luxembourg City.

UNDERSTAND BELGIUM & LUXEMBOURG

History

Bruges, Ghent and Ypres boomed in the 13th and 14th centuries as northern Europe's foremost cloth-trading cities. Craftspeople established powerful guilds that built elaborate guildhouses around fine market squares, typically adorned with a belfry symbolizing civic freedoms.

When Protestantism swept across Europe in the 16th century, the Low Countries (present-day Belgium, the Netherlands and Luxembourg) embraced it, much to the chagrin of their ruler, the fanatically Catholic Philip II of Spain. The result, from 1568, was a war that lasted 80 years and in the end roughly laid the region's present-day borders. Holland and its allied provinces victoriously expelled the Spaniards, while Belgium and Luxembourg stayed under their Catholic rule.

For the next 200 years Belgium remained a battlefield for successive foreign powers. After the Spaniards came the Austrians, and, in turn, the French. After Napoleon was trounced in 1815 at Waterloo near Brussels, the Dutch took over for 15 years. In 1830, the Catholic Belgians split from protestant Holland and finally formed their own kingdom, taking half of Luxembourg with them. The other half remained under the Dutch crown till an odd quirk of succession in 1890 resulted in Luxembourg's previously nominal independence becoming an actual reality.

From the late 19th century, Belgium rapidly grew wealthy, both through industrialisation and through King Léopold II's profiting from the Congo, which was brutal even by the colonial standards of that era.

When WWI kicked off in 1914 Belgium was officially neutral, but the Germans invaded anyway. Western Flanders became a blood-soaked killing field and whole towns, including historic Ypres, were bombarded into the mud. Incredibly Ypres' ancient heart has since been meticulously rebuilt, and tours of the Ypres Salient offer poignant WWI reminders.

During WWII, Belgium was taken over within three weeks of a surprise German attack in May 1940 and, during Nazi occupation, most of the Jewish population was deported to death camps. After an initial 1944 liberation, both Luxembourg and eastern

Belgium suffered a second devastation during Hitler's last-gasp counter-attack in the Ardennes. Despite the wars, for much of the 20th century Wallonia's mining, glassware, steel and other heavy industries made Belgium one of Europe's strongest economies. But since the 1970s, the old economic balance has reversed, with a serious post-industrial decline affecting much of Wallonia, while formerly agricultural Flanders has boomed with new higher-tech industries. A parallel series of political changes has increasingly emphasised the north–south linguistic divide. With ever less communication between the regions, forming a national consensus has proved ever more difficult in recent years. After the 2010 elections Belgium proved unable to agree a new government coalition for well over a year, a deadlock only eventually broken with the institution of constitutional reforms that took the country one stage closer to separation. But the risk of Flanders rapidly declaring unilateral independence is probably overstated since nobody quite knows what would then become of Brussels. And it would all be very expensive.

Meanwhile postwar Luxembourg's governments diversified the economy such that the little country rode out a depression in the iron and steel industries during the 1970s to become a noted financial centre and tax haven. Luxembourg also became home to several key EU institutions. Today the country has the highest per capita GDP in the EU and its Grand Ducal family's considerable popularity was on display in 2012 for the wedding of the heir apparent.

People

Belgium's population is predominantly split north–south by language: in Flanders (Vlaanderen) the Flemish dialect of Dutch is spoken, in Wallonia (La Wallonie) a Belgian variant of French. Brussels is officially bilingual but, in day-to-day reality, spoken French (and English) predominates there. Luxembourg has its own language, Lëtzebuergesch, in which *moien* is the standard greeting. But most Luxembourgers also speak French and German. Religiously, both countries follow a low-key form of tolerant Roman Catholicism, often as a badge of social status more than as spiritual dogma. The vast majority of Belgium's roughly 600,000 Muslims are of immigrant background. The small Jewish community is most visible in Antwerp's diamond district.

Arts

In the late Middle Ages, the secularisation of painting was led by sophisticated artists known quite misleadingly as the Flemish 'Primitives'. Notable figures Jan van Eyck and Hans Memling were later followed by Brussels' Breugel/Breughel family who created some of the 16th century's most memorable art, from peasant scenes to terrifying Bosch-like allegories of hell and damnation. Styles changed radically with the 17th-century Counter-Reformation when the Catholic God's mystical power was emphasised by baroque altarpieces and giant paintings full of angelic awe. That era's foremost artist was Antwerp-based Pieter Paul Rubens. In the 19th and early 20th centuries, Victor Horta and other architects put Belgium at the forefront of the sinuously beautiful art nouveau movement. Belgian art greats of the era include expressionist pioneer James Ensor, fauvist Rik Wouters, symbolist Fernand Khnopff and surrealist René Magritte. Among Belgium's best-known contemporary artists are Panamarenko, Luc Tuymans and Jan Fabre, famous for covering a ceiling in Brussels' Palais Royal with 1.4 million iridescent beetle wing-cases.

Belgium owes its independence to an 1830 revolution that started improbably with an opera: anti-Dutch demonstrations, stoked by crowds, stirred into a patriotic fervor after watching Auber's *Muette de Portici* at La Monnae in Brussels.

Jazz owes much to Dinant-born Adolphe Sax who invented the saxophone. In late May, the Brussels Jazz Marathon (www.brusselsjazzmarathon.be) is one of the capital's most joyous free festivals.

Contemporary names in Belgian music include Arid, Ghinzu, Puggy and dEUS (alternative-rock), Soulwax/2manyDJs (electro/mash-up), Axelle Red (pop-chanson) and Hooverphonic (trip-hop).

Food & Drink

Dining is a treat in Belgium and Luxembourg, where meals are often described as being French in quality, German in quantity. See p101 for local specialities.

To save money, order restaurants' weekday lunch deals (*dagmenu/menu du jour*), eat in cafes or frequent Asian places where the rice is generally included in meal prices. A *belegd broodje/sandwich garni* (filled half-baguette) makes a great, inexpensive snack. Belgian cafes almost always serve alcohol as well as coffee and are convivial places to sample the nation's amazing range of beers. Although tap water is always drinkable, in restaurants it's never served. Buy the bottled stuff – or beer, which could be cheaper.

Belgium's famous lagers (eg Stella Artois) and white beers (Hoegaarden) are now global brands. But what has connoisseurs really drooling are the robust, rich 'abbey' beers (which were originally brewed in monasteries), and the 'Trappist beers' (that still are). Chimay, Rochefort, Westmalle and Orval are the best known. But for beer maniacs the one that really counts is ultrarare Westvleteren 12°.

Belgian chocolates are world-beaters. Although maligned by some Belgian choco snobs, ubiquitous **Leonidas** (www.leonidas.com; per kg €24.30) has a price quality ratio that's hard to beat. You'll pay around double at **Galler** (www.galler.com), **Chocolate Line** (www.thechocolateline.be) and **Neuhaus** (☎02-512 63 59; www.neuhaus.be; Galerie de la Reine 25, Brussels; chocolate per kg €52; ⊙10am-8pm Mon-Sat, 10am-7pm Sun; ; Ⓜ Gare Centrale), creator of Belgium's original pralines, or roughly three times at exclusive **Pierre Marcolini** (☎02-512 43 14; www.marcolini.be; Rue des Minimes 1, Brussels; per kg €70; ⊙10am-7pm Sun-Thu, to 6pm Fri & Sat; Ⓜ Porte de Namur).

SURVIVAL GUIDE

Directory A–Z

Accommodation

Tourist offices often provide free assistance for accommodation booking.

PRICE RANGES

Our sleeping reviews refer to double rooms with a private bathroom, except in hostels or where otherwise specified. The rates quoted are for high season, which is May to September in Bruges and Ypres, but September to June in business cities.

€ less than €60

€€ €60 to €150

€€€ more €150

Note that top-end business establishments in Brussels and Luxembourg City often cut prices radically at weekends and in summer.

ACCOMODATION TYPES

B&Bs Rooms rented in local homes *(gastenkamers/chambres d'hôtes)* can be cheap and cheerful but some offer standards equivalent to a boutique hotel (up to €160 double). Discounts of around €10 per room are common if you stay at least a second night.

Holiday houses *(gîtes)* Are easily rented in Wallonia (www.gitesdewallonie.be) and Luxembourg (www.gites.lu), but minimum stays apply and there's a hefty 'cleaning fee' on top of quoted rates.

Short-term apartments Bookable through sites including www.airbnb.com and www.wimdu.com.

Hostels Typically charge around €20 to €26 for dormitory beds, somewhat less in Bruges. HI hostels (*jeugdherbergen* in Dutch, *auberges de jeunesse* in French) affiliated with **Hostelling International** (www.youthhostels.be), charge €3 less for members, and some take off €2 for under-26-year-olds. Prices usually include sheets and a basic breakfast. Always read the conditions.

Camping Opportunities are plentiful. For extensive listings see www.campingbelgique.be (Wallonia), www.camping.be (Flanders) and www.camping.lu (Luxembourg).

Activities

In mostly flat **Flanders** (www.fietsroute.org), **bicycles** are a popular means of everyday travel and many roads have dedicated cycle lanes. In **Wallonia** (www.ravel.wallonie.be), the hilly terrain favours mountain bikes (VTT).

Canoeing and **kayaking** are best in the Ardennes region, but don't expect rapids of any magnitude.

Local tourist offices have copious information about footpaths and sell regional **hiking** maps.

Business Hours

Opening hours given in the text are for high season. Many tourism-based businesses reduce their hours off season.

Banks 9am to 3.30pm Monday to Friday, Saturday mornings too in Luxembourg

Brasseries 11am to midnight

Clubs 11pm to 6am Friday to Sunday

Pubs & cafes to 1am or later

Restaurants 11.30am to 2.30pm and 6.30 to 10.30pm

Shops 10am to 6pm Monday to Saturday, some close for lunch; limited opening Sunday in Belgium

Supermarkets 9am to 8pm Monday to Saturday, some open Sundays

Embassies & Consulates

Embassies are listed at www.diplomatie.belgium.be/en and www.mae.lu. The following are located in Brussels:

Australian Embassy (02-286 05 00; www.belgium.embassy.gov.au; Rue Guimard 6-8)

Canadian Embassy (02-741 06 11; bru@international.gc.ca; Ave de Tervueren 2)

New Zealand Embassy (02-512 10 40; www.nzembassy.com/belgium; Ave des Nerviens, 9-31, Level 7)

UK Embassy (02-287 63 55; http://ukinbelgium.fco.gov.uk/en; Ave d'Auderghem 10)

US Embassy (02-811 40 00; http://belgium.usembassy.gov; Blvd du Régent 27)

Food

Restaurant price ranges for average main courses are as follows:

€ less than €15

€€ €15 to €25

€€€ more than €25

Money

» Banks usually offer better exchange rates than exchange bureaux (*wisselkantoren* in Dutch, *bureaux de change* in French), though often only for their banking clients, especially in Luxembourg.

» ATMs are widespread, but often hidden within bank buildings.

» Tipping is not expected in restaurants or cabs: service and VAT are always included.

Public Holidays

School holidays are July and August (slightly later in Luxembourg), one week in early November; two weeks at Christmas; one week around Carnival; two weeks at Easter; one week in May (Ascension).

Public holidays are as follows:

New Year's Day 1 January

Easter Monday March/April

Labour Day 1 May

Ascension Day Fortieth day after Easter

Whit Monday Seventh Monday after Easter

National Day (Luxembourg) 23 June

Flemish Community Festival 11 July (Flanders only)

National Day (Belgium) 21 July

Assumption 15 August

Francophone Community Festival 27 September (Wallonia only)

All Saints' Day 1 November

Armistice Day 11 November (Belgium only)

German-Speaking Community Festival 15 November (eastern cantons only)

Christmas Day 25 December

Telephone

» Dial full numbers: there's no optional area code.

» The international telephone code is 1234 for Belgium and 12410 for Luxembourg.

» Useful websites include www.whitepages.be (Belgium) and www.editus.lu/ed/en (Luxembourg).

Visas

Schengen visa rules apply.

Getting There & Away

Air

Brussels airport (www.brusselsairport.be) is Belgium's main long-haul gateway. Budget airlines **Ryanair** (www.ryanair.com), **JetAirFly** (www.jetairfly.com) and **WizzAir** (www.wizzair.com) use the misleadingly named **Brussels-South Charleroi Airport** (07-125 12 11; www.charleroi-airport.com), which is 55km south of Brussels, 6km north of the ragged, post-industrial city of Charleroi. Luxembourg's **airport** (www.lux-airport.lu) has various European connections including **easyJet** (www.easyjet.com) budget flights to London Gatwick.

Land

BUS

Ecolines (www.ecolines.net; Paardenmarkt 65, Brussels, ticket agent Euro-Maror) and **Eurobus**

(☎02-527 50 12; www.eurobus.pl) operate from Brussels and Antwerp to various destinations in eastern Europe.

Eurolines (www.eurolines.eu) is a Europe-wide network. Prebookings are compulsory but, although nine Belgian cities are served, only Brussels, Antwerp, Ghent and Liège have ticket offices.

Useful local cross-border buses include De Panne–Dunkerque and Luxembourg City–Trier.

CAR & MOTORCYCLE

» Border crossings are not usually controlled.

» Diesel is cheaper than unleaded. Both are cheaper in Luxembourg than almost anywhere else in western Europe.

» **EuroStop** (www.eurostop.be; €4 per 100km) matches paying hitchhikers with drivers for long-distance international rides.

» As in France, give way to the right.

» Motorways are toll free, with a speed limit of 120/130km/h in Belgium/Luxembourg.

TRAIN

There are excellent train links with neighbouring countries. For comprehensive timetables and international bookings, see www.belgianrail.be or www.cfl.lu. Railcards are valid on standard services but there are surcharges for high-speed lines including **Eurostar** (www.eurostar.com) to London and Lille, **Thalys** (www.thalys.com) to Amsterdam and Paris, and **Fyra** (www.fyra.com) to Amsterdam. **ICE** (www.db.de) runs high-speed trains Brussels–Liège–Aachen–Cologne–Frankfurt (3¼ hours) while **TGV** (www.sncf.com) links to numerous French destinations, albeit bypassing central Paris. To avoid high-speed surcharges, useful 'ordinary' cross-border services include Liège–Aachen, Tournai–Lille, Antwerp–Rosendaal (for Amsterdam) and Luxembourg–Trier.

Sea

There are two direct Belgium–UK ferry services:

Ostend–Ramsgate With **TransEuropa Ferries** (www.transeuropaferries.com; motorbike €30-57, car €59-106); cars/motorbikes but no pedestrians, 4½ hours, three times daily.

Zeebrugge–Hull With **P&O** (www.poferries.com); pedestrians from UK£106 one-way plus £6.75 for the connecting bus to Bruges train station. Fourteen hours overnight.

Getting Around

For Luxembourg see p130.

Bicycle

Cycling is a great way to get around in flat Flanders, less so in chaotic Brussels or undulating Wallonia. The Belgian countryside is riddled with cycling routes and most tourist offices sell helpful regional cycling maps.

» Bike hire is available in or near most major train stations. Short-hop hire schemes are available in Brussels, Antwerp and Luxembourg City.

» Bikes on the train are free in Luxembourg. In Belgium it costs €5 one-way (or €8 all day) on top of the rail fare. A few busy city-centre train stations don't allow bicycle transportation.

Bus & Tram

Regional buses are well coordinated with Belgium's rail network, but in rural regions you can still find that relatively short distances can involve long waits. In Brussels and Antwerp, trams that run underground are called '*premetro*'. Bus companies:

De Lijn (www.delijn.be) In Flanders.

STIB (www.stib.be) In Brussels.

TEC (www.infotec.be) In Wallonia.

Car & Motorcycle

Motorways are toll free. Speed limits are 50km/h in most towns (30km/h near schools), 70km/h to 90km/h on intertown roads, and 120/130km/h on motorways in Belgium/Luxembourg. The maximum legal blood-alcohol limit is 0.05%. Car hire is available at airports and major train stations, but is usually cheaper from city-centre offices.

Taxi

Taxis must usually be prebooked but there are ranks near main stations. Tips and taxes are always included in metered fares.

Train

NMBS/SNCB (Belgian Railways; ☎02-528 28 28; www.b-rail.be) trains are nonsmoking. B-Excursions are good-value one-day excursion fares including return rail ticket plus selected entry fees. Weekend return tickets valid from 7pm Friday to Sunday night cost just 20% more than a single but on weekdays a return costs twice the single price.

Bosnia & Hercegovina

Includes »

Sarajevo......................... 139
Hercegovina......................145
Mostar..............................145
Eastern Bosnia & Hercegovina......................148
Central & Western Bosnia..............................148
Understand Bosnia & Hercegovina..................149
Survival Guide.............. 150

Best Places to Eat

» Bridge-view restaurants, Mostar (p147)

» Riverside restaurants on the Una (p149)

Best Places to Stay

» Muslibegović House (p148)

» Hotel Platani (p148)

» Želenkovac (p149)

» Kostelski Buk (p149)

Why Go?

This craggily beautiful land retains some lingering scars from the heartbreaking civil war of the 1990s. But today's visitors will more likely remember Bosnia and Hercegovina (BiH) for its deep, unassuming human warmth and for the intriguing East-meets-West atmosphere born of fascinatingly blended Ottoman and Austro-Hungarian histories.

Major drawcards are the reincarnated antique centres of Sarajevo and Mostar, where rebuilt historical buildings counterpoint fashionable bars and wi-fi–equipped cafes. Elsewhere Socialist-era architectural monstrosities are surprisingly rare blots on predominantly rural landscapes. Many Bosnian towns are lovably small, wrapped around medieval castles and surrounded by mountain ridges or cascading river canyons. Few places in Europe offer better rafting or such accessible, inexpensive skiing.

When to Go

Sarajevo

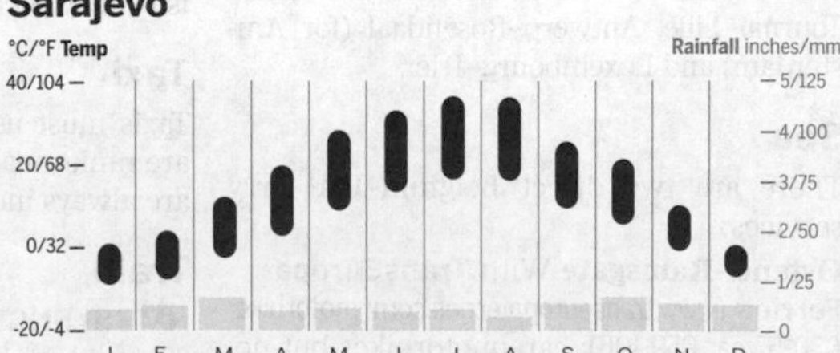

Apr–Jun Beat the heat in Hercegovina; flowers bloom in Bosnia; peak-flowing rivers.

Summer Accommodation fills up in Mostar and Sarajevo. Calmer rivers in July suit rafting beginners.

Mid-Jan–mid-Sep Skiing gets cheaper after the New Year holidays.

Connections

Regular buses link major BiH cities to Vienna and to various Croatian and Serbian destinations. There's also a handy, little-publicised Trebinje–Dubrovnik service. Non-sleeper trains link Sarajevo to Zagreb, Belgrade and Budapest – the only direct overland link to Hungary.

ITINERARIES

Six Days

Arriving from Dubrovnik (coastal Croatia), roam Mostar's Old Town and join a day tour visiting Počitelj, Blagaj and the Kravice waterfalls. After two days in Sarajevo head for Jajce then bus down to Split (Croatia). Or visit Višegrad en route to Mokra Gora and Belgrade (Serbia).

Two Weeks

As above, but add Trebinje, spend some days skiing or cycling at Bjelašnica around Sarajevo, visit the controversial Visoko pyramid and old-town Travnik en route to Jajce, and consider adding white water rafting in the Una Valley around Bihać.

Essential Food & Drink

» **Ćevapi (Ćevapčići)** Minced meat formed into cylindrical pellets and served in fresh bread with melting *kajmak* (thick semi-soured cream).

» **Pljeskavica** Patty-shaped Ćevapi.

» **Burek** Bosnian *burek* are cylindrical lengths of filo-pastry filled with minced meat, often wound into spirals. *Buređici* is the same served with kajmak and garlic, *sirnica* is filled instead with cheese, *krompiruša* with potato and *zeljanica* with spinach. Collectively these pies are called *pita*.

» **Sarma** Small dolma-parcels of rice and minced meat wrapped in a cabbage or other green leaf.

» **Bosanski Lonac** Slow-cooked meat-and-veg hotpot.

» **Uštipci** Bready fried dough-balls often eaten with sour cream, cheese or jam.

» **Sogan Dolma** Slow-roasted onions filled with minced meat.

» **Klepe** Small ravioli-like triangles served in a butter-pepper drizzle with grated raw garlic.

» **Hurmastica** Syrup-soaked sponge fingers.

» **Tufahija** Whole stewed apple with walnut-filling and topped with whipped cream.

» **Ražnijići** Shish kebab (ie meat barbequed on skewers).

» **Pastrmka** Trout.

» **Rakija** Fruit brandy or grappa.

» **Ligne** Squid.

AT A GLANCE

» **Currency** Convertible mark (KM, BAM)

» **Languages** Bosnian, Croatian, Serbian

» **Visas** Not required for most visitors

Fast Facts

» **Area** 51,129 sq km

» **Capital** Sarajevo

» **Country code** ☎387

» **Emergency** Ambulance ☎124, fire ☎123, police ☎122

Exchange Rates

Australia	A$1	1.59KM
Canada	C$1	1.51KM
Euro Zone	€1	1.96KM
Japan	¥100	1.62KM
New Zealand	NZ$1	1.28KM
UK	UK£1	2.32KM
USA	US$1	1.53KM

Set Your Budget

» **Budget hotel room** 70KM

» **Two-course meal** 18KM

» **Museum entrance** 1–5KM

» **Beer** 2–4KM

» **City bus ticket** 1.80KM

Resources

» **BiH Tourism** (www.bhtourism.ba)

» **Bosnian Institute** (www.bosnia.org.uk)

» **Office of the High Representative** (www.ohr.int)

Bosnia & Hercegovina Highlights

1. Nose about Mostar's atmospheric Old Town and admire the rebuilt **Stari Most** (p145)
2. Raft down one of BiH's fast-flowing rivers – whether from **Foča** (p148), **Bihać** (p149) or **Banja Luka** (p148)
3. Ski the 1984 Olympic pistes at **Jahorina** or **Bjelašnica** (p141) or explore the wild uplands behind them
4. Potter around the timeless pedestrian lanes of **Sarajevo** (p139) and sample its fashionable cafes and eclectic nightlife
5. Gaze through willow fronds at the Unesco-listed 16th-century bridge in **Višegrad** (p148) that inspired a Nobel Prize–winning novel
6. Wine and dine in historic little **Trebinje** (p148) and wander the low-key, stone-flagged Old Town
7. Tune in to the mystical energy of **Visoko** (p148), asking yourself if you are really climbing the world's biggest pyramid

SARAJEVO

☎033 / 436,000

The nation's vibrant capital is folded into steep contours polka-dotted with red-roofed homes, church towers and endless minarets. Distinctive Ottoman-era bazaars along cobblestone lanes date from the city's 16th-century glory days as a Turkic silk-trading entrepôt. After 1878 the Austro-Hungarians added grand central-European buildings. In 1984 Sarajevo hosted the Winter Olympics but just eight years later the city endured an appalling three-year siege. Over 10,500 Sarajevans died and six centuries of heritage was pounded into rubble by Bosnian-Serb shelling.

In the southern suburbs some buildings remain bullet-pocked but in the centre, major reconstruction means that today's visitor will be hard-pressed to notice any signs of the conflict in what is now an enticing, low-key city brimming with a very personal warmth and charm.

Sights & Activities

OLD SARAJEVO

Baščaršija is old Sarajevo's delightful warren of marble flagged pedestrian lanes and open courtyards, fanning out from the distinctive 1891 **Sebilj Drinking Fountain** (Pigeon Sq).

Cafes, souvenir shops, mosques, copper workshops and charming little restaurants surround Ottoman-era architectural gems, including the imposing **Gazi-Husrevbey Mosque** (www.vakuf-gazi.ba; Sarači 18; admission 2KM; ⏲9am-noon, 2.30-3.30pm & 5-6.15pm May-Sep, closed Ramadan), the **Dugi Bezistan covered bazaar** (www.vakuf-gazi.ba; ⏲8am-8pm Mon-Fri, 9am-2pm Sat) and the 1551 **Bursa Bezistan** (www.muzejsarajeva.ba; Abadžiluk 10; admission 3KM; ⏲10am-6pm Mon-Fri, 10am-3pm Sat). Originally a silk-trading bazaar, the latter now houses a small museum of city history, a theme continued into the Austro-Hungarian era by the **Sarajevo 1878–1918** (Zelenih Beretki 2; admission 2KM; ⏲10am-6pm Mon-Fri, 10am-3pm Sat) museum. WWI was triggered directly outside, in 1914, by the assassination of Austro-Hungarian crown prince Franz Ferdinand who was returning from the grand Moorish-styled **City Hall**. Later becoming the national library, the City Hall was devastated by Serb shelling during the 1990s siege and is now under reconstruction.

Despite the awful 20th-century events, Sarajevo's history is traditionally one of religious tolerance. Emblematic of this, you'll find within a couple of blocks several mosques, a **synagogue/Jewish Museum** (Muzej Jevreja BiH; Mula Mustafe Bašeskije 40; admission 2KM; ⏲10am-6pm Mon-Fri, 10am-1pm Sun), the artfully floodlit 1872 **Orthodox Cathedral** (Saborna Crkva Presvete Bogordice; Trg Oslobođenja) and the **Catholic Cathedral** (Katedrala Srca Isusova; Trg Fra Grge Martića 2; ⏲9am-4pm) where Pope John Paul II served Mass in 1997.

BJELAVE & VRATNIK

The once-vast Vratnik Citadel was built in the 1720s and reinforced in 1816. Not much remains but it is worth climbing up to the grassy-topped **Yellow Bastion** (Žuta Tabija; Jekovac bb) for panoramas (minibus 55 gets you reasonably close) then walking back down via the **Izetbegović Museum** (www.muzejalijaizetbegovica.ba; Ploča bb; admission 2KM; ⏲10am-6pm Mon-Fri, 10am-3pm Sat), commemorating BiH's first president in a pair of historic towers above the movingly overcrowded Kovači cemetery. Don't miss the 18th-century **Svrzo House** (Svrzina Kuća; ☎535264; Glođina 8; admission 3KM; ⏲10am-6pm Mon-Fri, 10am-3pm Sat) museum, an oasis of white-washed walls, cobbled courtyards and partly vine-draped dark timbers, brilliantly restored and appropriately furnished helping visitors imagine Sarajevo life in eras past.

NOVO SARAJEVO

Palatial, wide-ranging but sadly closed due to a funding crisis, the **National Museum** (Zemaljski Muzej Bosne-i-Hercegovine; www.zemaljskimuzej.ba; Zmaja od Bosne 3; ⏲temporarily closed) houses the 'world's most valuable book' and a wealth of archaeological gems. Next door, the small but engrossing **History Museum** (Zmaja od Bosne 5; admission 4KM; ⏲9am-7pm Mon-Fri, 10am-2pm Sat & Sun) 'non-ideologically' charts the course of the 1990s conflict with affectingly personal exhibits. Tucked behind is an amusingly tongue-in-cheek Tito-themed cafe . From the town centre take tram 3 and hop off just beyond the startling pudding-and-custard-coloured Holiday Inn, which was wartime home to besieged international journalists in the early 1990s.

ILIDŽA & BUTMIR

Way out in Butmir, the unmissable **Tunnel Museum** (Tunel Spasa; tunelspasa.ba; Tuneli bb 1; admission 5KM; ⏲9.15am-5pm,

Central Sarajevo

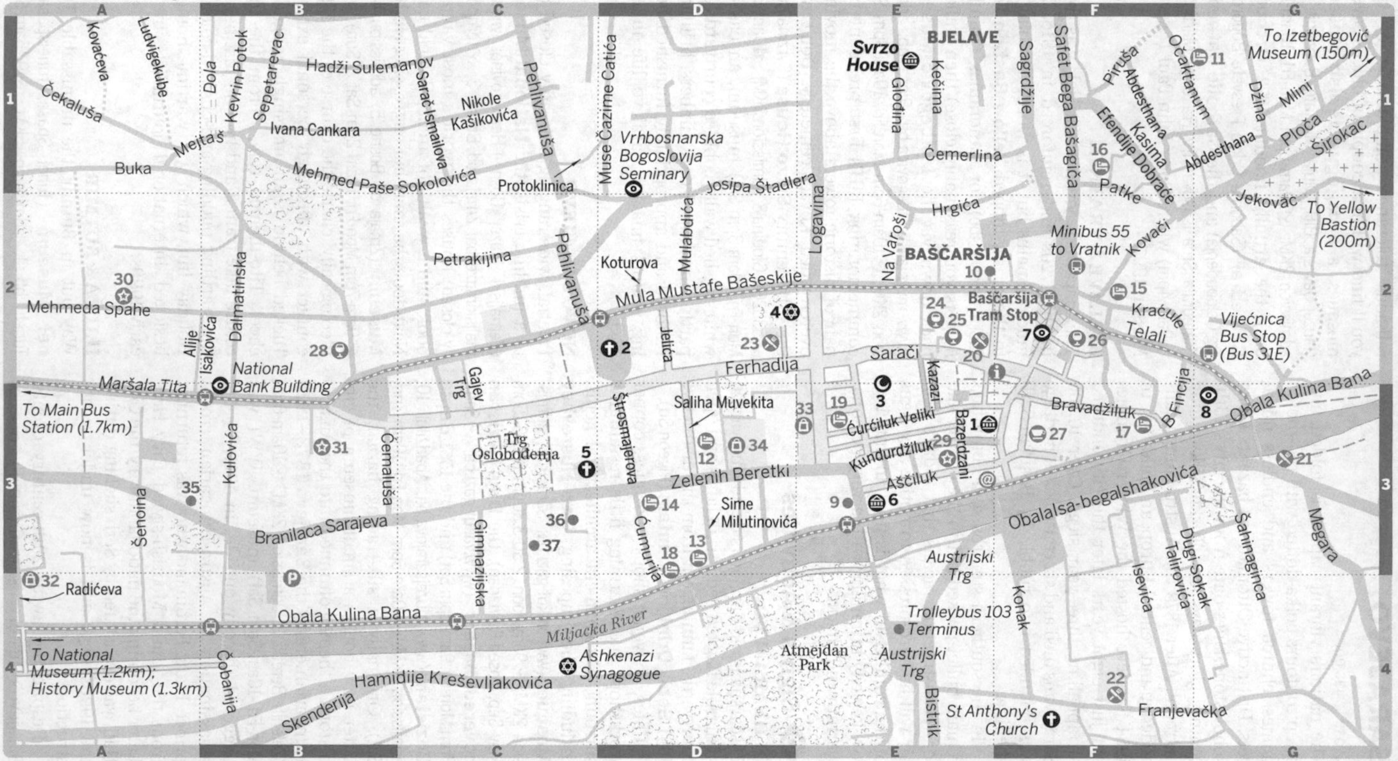

0 — 200 m
0 — 0.1 miles

BJELAVE
BAŠČARŠIJA
Svrzo House
To Izetbegović Museum (150m)
To Yellow Bastion (200m)
To Main Bus Station (1.7km)
To National Museum (1.2km); History Museum (1.3km)
Vrhbosnanska Bogoslovija Seminary
National Bank Building
Baščaršija Tram Stop
Minibus 55 to Vratnik
Vijećnica Bus Stop (Bus 31E)
Trolleybus 103 Terminus
Ashkenazi Synagogue
St Anthony's Church
Atmejdan Park
Trg Oslobođenja
Gajev Trg
Austrijski Trg
Miljacka River
Kovaćeva
Ludvigekube
Čekaluša
Dola
Kevrin Potok
Sepetarevac
Mejtaš
Buka
Hadži Sulemanov
Ivana Cankara
Sarač Ismailova
Nikole Kašikovića
Pehlivanuša
Muse Ćazime Ćatića
Mehmed Paše Sokolovića
Protoklinica
Josipa Štadlera
Petrakijina
Koturova
Mulabdića
Logavina
Mula Mustafe Bašeskije
Jelića
Mehmeda Spahe
Alije Isakovića
Dalmatinska
Maršala Tita
Ferhadija
Sarači
Kazazi
Na Varoši
Hrgića
Ćemerlina
Glođina
Kečima
Sagrdžije
Safet Bega Bašagića
Piruša
Abdesthana
Kasima Efendije Dobrače
Očaktanum
Džina
Mlini
Ploča
Širokac
Jekovac
Patke
Kovači
Kraćule
Telali
Bravadžiluk
B Fincija
Obala Kulina Bana
Čurčiluk Veliki
Bazerdzani
Kundurdžiluk
Aščiluk
Saliha Muvekita
Štrosmajerova
Zelenih Beretki
Sime Milutinovića
Ćumurija
Obalalsa-begalshakovića
Branilaca Sarajeva
Čemaluša
Kulovića
Šenoina
Radićeva
Gimnazijska
Čobanija
Hamidije Kreševljakovića
Skenderija
Konak
Bistrik
Isevića
Dugi Sokak
Talirovića
Šahinaginca
Megara
Franjevačka

1 2 3 4 5 6 7 8 9 10 11 12 13 14 15 16 17 19 20 21 22 23 24 25 26 27 28 29 30 31 32 33 34 35 36 37

A B C D E F G

Central Sarajevo

Top Sights
Svrzo House ... E1

Sights
1 Bursa Bezistan ... E3
2 Catholic Cathedral ... D2
3 Gazi-Husrevbey Mosque ... E3
4 Jewish Museum ... D2
5 Orthodox Cathedral ... C3
6 Sarajevo 1878–1918 ... E3
7 Sebilj Drinking Fountain ... F2
8 Vijećnica ... G3

Activities, Courses & Tours
9 Insider ... E3
10 Sarajevo Funky Tours ... E2

Sleeping
11 Ćiro ... G1
12 HCC Sarajevo Hostel ... D3
13 Hostel Old City ... D3
14 Hotel Central ... D3
15 Hotel Kovači ... F2
16 Hotel Safir ... F1
17 Pansion Divan ... F3
18 Travellers Home ... D3
19 Villa Wien ... E3

Eating
20 Dveri ... E2
21 Inat Kuća ... G3
22 Pivnica HS ... F4
23 Vegehana ... D2

Drinking
24 Barhana ... E2
25 Caffe Divan ... E2
26 Dibek ... F2
27 Kuća Sevdaha ... F3
28 Zlatna Ribica ... B2

Entertainment
29 Hacienda ... E3
30 Sloga ... A2
31 Underground ... B3

Shopping
32 BuyBook ... A4
33 Dugi Bezistan ... E3
34 Šahinpašić ... D3

Transport
35 BH Airlines ... A3
36 Gir ... C3
37 JAT ... C3

last entry 4.30pm) gives visitors a glimpse of the make-shift 1m-wide tunnel hand-dug beneath Sarajevo's airport during the 1992–95 siege. Without the food and armaments that passed through it, the besieged city would probably have capitulated. A 20-minute video helps conjure up the wartime tunnel experience. City tours are the easiest way to get here. Alternatively take tram 3 to Ilidža (35 minutes, 11km from Baščaršija), then take Kotorac-bound bus 32 (10 minutes, twice hourly, 3km) to the last stop, walk across the bridge, turn immediately left and walk 500m down Tuneli.

There's superb-value skiing at two 1984 Winter Olympic centres, both around 30km from Sarajevo. **Jahorina** (www.oc-jahorina.com; ski pass per day/week 33/160KM, ski-set rentals per day 25-40KM) has a wide selection of hotels and several ski lifts. Much smaller **Bjelašnica** (www.bjelasnica.ba; ski pass per day/night/week 27/15/180KM) doubles as a great summer getaway with a web of appealing highland villages accessible by road and cycle-track; bicycle rental is available from the recommended **Hotel Han** (☎584150; www.hotelhan.ba; s/d summer 56.50/95KM, d mid-Dec–Mar 155-185KM; 📶).

Tours

Insider TOUR
(☎061 190591; www.sarajevoinsider.com; Zelenih Beretki 30; ⏲9am-6pm Mon-Fri, 9.30am-2pm Sat & Sun) Wide range of tours in and beyond Sarajevo. Popular daily offerings include the two-hour Tunnel Tour (€15, 2pm) and excellent three-hour 'Times of Misfortune' (€27, 11am), visiting sites related to the 1990s conflict.

Sarajevo Funky Tours TOUR
(☎062 910546; www.sarajevofunkytours.com; Besarina Čikma 5) A similar range of tours to Insider.

Sarajevo Free Tour WALKING TOUR
Impressive 90-minute city walking tour starting at 3pm from the tourist office or 4.30pm from Insider. Runs most days in summer. Tips appropriate.

Green Visions ECOTOUR
(☎717290; www.greenvisions.ba; opposite Radnička 66; ⏲9am-5pm Mon-Fri) Ecotourism specialist offering a range of mountain and village hiking trips.

Festivals & Events

Baščaršijske Noći ARTS
(Baščaršija Nights; www.bascarsijskenoci.ba) Wide-ranging arts fest lasting all July.

Jazz Festival MUSIC
(www.jazzfest.ba) Local and international jazz in early November.

Sleeping

Accommodation agencies on the north side of Mula Mustafe Bašeskije at Baščaršija tram stop offer cheap, if generally unimpressive, dorms and a wide range of homestay beds dotted widely across town.

TOP CHOICE **Villa Wien** GUESTHOUSE €€
(Ćurčiluk Veliki 3; s/d 143/186KM; ❄📶) Six well equipped rooms decorated in opulent pseudo–belle époque style are hidden away above the Wiener Café. Check in at **Hotel Art** (☎232855; www.hotelart.ba; Ferhadija 30a), on the other side of the covered bazaar.

TOP CHOICE **Hostel Old City** HOSTEL €
(☎555355; www.hosteloldcity.ba; Sime Milutinovića 1; dm €15; ❄@📶) One floor of a regal 1908 townhouse has been given a very impressive makeover in keeping with its heritage. The lounge has Latin Bridge balcony views.

Hotel Kovači HOTEL €€
(☎573700; www.hotelkovaci.com; Kovači 12; s/d/tr/apt €50/70/90/100; ❄📶) This wonderfully central family hotel blends a chic, understated modernism with the basic design of a traditional Ottoman house with overhanging *(doksat)* windows.

SPLURGE

The grand Austro-Hungarian facade of **Hotel Central** (☎561800; www.hotelcentral.ba; Cumurija 8; s/d/ste 200/240/300KM; ❄📶🏊) hides 15 huge, fashionably appointed guest rooms leading off corridors painted lugubriously deep purple. The excellent gym complex includes saunas and big indoor pool.

Ćiro GUESTHOUSE €
(☎440068; www.guesthouseciro.com.ba; Očaktanum 16; s/d/tr/apt without bathroom 35/60/80/120KM) Six well-appointed if oddly coloured rooms in a converted, relatively new family home.

HCC Sarajevo Hostel HOSTEL €
(☎062 993330; www.hcc.ba; 3rd fl, Saliha Muvekita 2; dm €12-16, s €20-25, d €28-35; ❄@📶) Sociable hostel with a stylishly decorated kitchen/dining area and a bright lounge/lobby with DVDs to watch and a guitar to strum.

Pansion Divan PENSION €
(☎061420254; www.facebook.com/pansion.divan-sarajevo; Brandžiluk 38; s €20-30, tw €30-35; 📶) Ten neat, en suite rooms above an Ali Baba's cave of a restaurant. No reception or common room; wi-fi in five rooms.

Hotel Safir HOTEL €€
(☎475040; www.hotelsafir.ba; Jagodića 3; s/d €50/72; ❄📶) Eight good-value rooms with conical basins and beam-me-up-Scotty shower booths. Six have kitchenette.

Travellers Home HOSTEL €
(☎70 242 400; www.myhostel.ba; Ćumurija 4, 1st fl; dm 25-38KM, d 62-92KM; ⏲24hr; 📶) Well-furnished, high-ceilinged house-hostel with outstandingly helpful, informative staff and a central yet peaceful location.

Eating

For inexpensive snack meals look along Bradžiluk or Kundurdžiluk; try Bosna for *burek*, Hadžić, Mrkva or Željo for *ćevapi*.

Dveri EUROPEAN €€
(☎537020; www.dveri.co.ba; Prote Bakovića 12; meals 11-18KM; ⏲8am-11pm; 📶📋) This tourist-friendly 'country cottage' eatery is densely hung with loops of garlic, corn cobs and gingham-curtained 'windows'.

Biban BOSNIAN €€
(☎232026; Hošin Brijeg 95a; mains 7-16KM; ⏲10am-10pm Mon-Fri, 10am-9pm Sun; 📋) Worth the 5KM taxi ride for splendidly panoramic city views enjoyed over simple but fairly priced local food. Minibus 56 from Latin Bridge passes nearby.

Pivnica HS INTERNATIONAL €€
(sarajevska-pivara.ba/restaurant; Franjevačka 15; pasta 8-10KM, mains 13-25KM; ⏲10am-1am; 📋) This expansive, reverberant hall decorated in Las Vegas vaudeville style serves satisfying, well-presented meals and Sara-

jevskaya's full range of tap beers - brewed next door.

Inat Kuća BOSNIAN €€
(Spite House; ☎447867; www.inatkuca.ba; Velika Alifakovac 1; mains 12-20KM, snacks 10KM; ⏰10am-10pm; 📋) This Sarajevo institution occupies a classic Ottoman-era house that's a veritable museum piece with antique decor and a great little riverside terrace.

Vegehana VEGETARIAN €
(www.vegehana.ba/; Ferhadija 39; mains 5-10KM; ⏰10am-9pm Mon-Fri, noon-9pm Sat; 🌿📋) Sarajevo's first fully vegetarian, organic eatery.

Drinking & Entertainment

The cafe choice is joyfully overwhelming, especially as summer warms up and tables overflow onto many old-town streets. Two gaggles of Old City bar-cafes get lively late at night: one set is near HCC (p142), the other around **Hacienda** (Bazerdzani 3; ⏰10am-very late).

TOP CHOICE **Zlatna Ribica** BAR
(Kaptol 5; ⏰10am-2am) This marvelously Gothic cafe-bar is loaded with eccentricities including a uniquely stocked toilet that will have you laughing out loud.

Caffe Divan CAFE
(Morića Han, Saraći 77; ⏰8am-midnight) Relax in wicker chairs beneath the wooden beams of a gorgeous, historic caravanserai courtyard. No alcohol.

Dibek BAR
(Laledžina 3; ⏰8am-11pm) DJ-led *nargile*-bar on a quaint Old Town square. Water pipe 5KM.

Barhana BAR
(Đugalina 8; beer/rakija 2/3KM, mains 6-20KM; ⏰10am-midnight) Sample a selection of flavoured local shots in a hidden courtyard behind the equally enticing Babylon bar.

Kuća Sevdaha CAFE
(www.artkucasevdaha.ba/en/; Halači 5; ⏰9am-11pm) Sip Bosnian coffee, juniper sherbet or rose water, sitting in a glassed-in historic museum courtyard listening to the lilting wails of *sevdah* (traditional Bosnian music).

Underground LIVE MUSIC
(www.underground.ba; Maršala Tita 56; ⏰7pm-5am) Especially at weekends talented bands give classic rock songs a romping rework in this basement venue. Free entry, tap beers 2.50KM.

Sloga CLUB
(www.cinemas.ba; Seljo, Mehmeda Spahe 20; ⏰8pm-3am) Cavernous, blood-red club-disco-dancehall catering to an excitable, predominantly student crowd.

Shopping

Baščaršija's pedestrian lanes are full of jewellery stalls and wooden-shuttered souvenir shops flogging slippers, Bosnian flags, carpets, archetypal copperware and wooden spoons, though if you're heading to Mostar, you might find prices better there.

Bookshops **BuyBook** (☎716450; www.buybook.ba; Radićeva 4; ⏰9am-8pm Mon-Fri, 10am-6pm Sat) and **Šahinpašić** (☎667210; www.btcsahinpasic.com; Vladislava Skarića 8; ⏰9am-9pm Mon-Sat) stock guidebooks, magazines and English-language books on ex-Yugoslavia.

Information

ATMs can be found outside the main bus station, inside the airport and sprinkled all over the city. There are exchanges at the airport **post counter** (⏰9am-5pm Mon-Fri), in many banks along Ferhadija and at the **Postbank** (⏰8am-4pm Mon-Fri) branch hidden around the west side of the train station building. At weekends try the Hotel Europe.

City.Ba (www.city.ba/en) Reviews of clubs, pubs, restaurants and more.

Internet Caffe Baščaršija (Aščiluk bb; per hr 2KM; ⏰8am-midnight)

Lonely Planet (www.lonelyplanet.com/bosnia-and-hercegovina/sarajevo)

Sarajevo Navigator Useful free maps and monthly guide pamphlets. Widely available.

Sonar (www.sonar.ba) Listings and information.

Tourist Office (www.sarajevo-tourism.com; Sarači 58; ⏰9am-8pm Mon-Fri, 10am-6pm Sat-Sun)

Getting There & Away

Bus

Sarajevo's **main bus station** (☎213100; Put Života 8) primarily serves locations in the Federation, Croatia and Western Europe. Most services to the Republik Srpska (RS) and Serbia leave from **Lukovica (East Sarajevo) bus station** (☎057-317377; Nikole Tesle bb). The latter lies way out in the suburb of Dobrijna, 400m beyond the western terminus stop of trolleybus 103 and bus 31E. To some destinations, buses leave from both stations.

BUSES FROM SARAJEVO

DESTINATION	DEPARTURE POINT	PRICE (KM)	DURATION	FREQUENCY
Banja Luka	Main bus station	32.90	5hr	5am, 7.45am, 9.15am, 2.30pm, 3.30pm, 4.30pm, 6.30pm
Banja Luka	East Sarajevo bus station	31	5hr	9.30am, 11.30am
Belgrade (Serbia)	Main bus station	47	7½hr	6am
Belgrade (Serbia)	East Sarajevo bus station	40-55	8-11hr	8am, 9.45am, 12.30pm, 3pm, 10pm
Bihać	Main bus station	42	6½hr	7.30am, 1.30pm, 10pm
Dubrovnik (Croatia)	Main bus station	47	7hr	7.15am, 10am, plus 2.30pm, 10.15pm insummer
Foča	East Sarajevo bus station	9	1½hr	11.15am, 6.15pm & Trebinje, Podgorica & Herceg Novi services
Herceg Novi	East Sarajevo bus station	46	7½hr	9am plus summer specials
Jajce	Main bus station, East Sarajevo bus station	23.50	3½hr	take Banja Luka buses
Ljubljana (Slovenia)	Main bus station	92	8½hr	8.40pm Tue, Fri, Sun
Mostar	Main bus station	18	2½hr	15 daily, 6.50am-7.55pm
Munich (Germany)	Main bus station	140	19hr	8am
Niš	East Sarajevo bus station	46	11hr	8.40am, 6pm
Novi Pazar	Main bus station	32	7-8hr	3pm, 9pm, 10pm
Pale	East Sarajevo bus station	3.50	40min	14 daily Mon-Fri, but only 6 Sat & Sun
Pale	Main bus station	5.70	25min	7am, 10am, 2pm
Podgorica (Montenegro)	East Sarajevo bus station	36	6hr	8.15am, 2pm, 8pm, 10.30pm
Split (Croatia), via Mostar	Main bus station	53.50	7½hr	10am, 9pm, plus 7am in summer
Split (Croatia), via Livno	Main bus station	53.50	7¼hr	6am via Livno
Travnik	Main bus station	17	2hr	9 daily
Trebinje	East Sarajevo bus station	26	5hr	7.45am, 1pm, 4.05pm (via Sutjeska National Park)
Tuzla	Main bus station	21	3¼hr	9 daily
Visoko	Main bus station	6.30	50min	at least hourly by Kakanj bus
Vienna (Austria)	Main bus station	100	14½hr	11.15am
Zagreb (Croatia)	Main bus station	54	9½hr	6.30am, 12.30pm, 10pm
Zagreb (Croatia)	Main bus station	54	8½hr	9.30am via Bosanski Brod

Train

From the **train station** (☎033-655330; Put Života 2) useful services include the following:

Belgrade (51.20KM, eight hours) Departs 11.49am.

Budapest (1st/2nd class 122.40KM, 11¼ hours) Via Osijek (Croatia, 55.40KM). Departs 6.55am, returning from Budapest-Keleti at 9.56am.

Mostar (9.90KM, 2¼ hours) Departs 7.05am, 8.05am and 6.18pm.

Zagreb (74.30KM, 9¼ hours) Departs 10.54am and 9.27pm..

Getting Around

To/From the Airport

Sarajevo's tiny if modern international **airport** (☎234841; www.sarajevo-airport.ba; Kurta Schorka 36; closed 11pm-5am) is about 12km southwest of Baščaršija. That's around 16KM by metered taxi. Trolleybus 103 and bus 31E pick up around 700m from the terminal. To find the stop turn right out of the airport, then take the first left. Shimmy right-left-right past Hotel Octagon, then turn third right at the Panda car wash (Brače Mulića 17). The stop is across the main road before the Mercator Hypermarket.

Bicycle Rental

Gir (☎350523; www.gir.ba; Zelenih Berekti 14a; city bike per hr/day/5-days 3/15/25KM, mountain bike 4/20/35KM; 10am-6pm) This cycle shop is 'hidden' within the commercial passageway that leads to Club Jež.

Public Transport

Bus, tram and trolleybus tickets cost 1.60/1.80KM from kiosks/drivers. Validate them in the on-board machines. For timetables click on 'Redove Vožnje' on www.gras.co.ba, then select mode of transport.

Tram 1 connects the main bus/train stations to Baščaršija every 15 minutes. More frequent tram 3 runs from Ilidža (6am to 11.45pm), following the north bank past the Holiday Inn then looping anticlockwise around Baščaršija.

Taxi

Taxis from the central ranks (Latin Bridge, Hotel Kovači, etc) often want to fix a set fee. For reliable on-the-metre fares (2KM plus about 1KM per kilometre) call **Paja Taxis** (☎412555) .

HERCEGOVINA

Mostar

☎036 / POP 111,600

Set in a deep valley flanked by arid mountains, Mostar's splendidly rebuilt Ottoman-era core forms one of Eastern Europe's most photogenic scenes. Be aware that between November and April many tourist facilities go into wholesale hibernation.

Sights

Stari Most BRIDGE

Arcing majestically between the rugged cliff-banks of the Neretva River, the world-famous 16th-century Stari Most (Old Bridge) is the indisputable visual focus that gives Mostar Old Town its special magic. Infamously destroyed in the 1990s, but since meticulously reconstructed, it is now a powerful and very beautiful symbol of BiH's reconciliation. In summer Mostar's **bridge mdivers** plunge 21m off the parapet into the icy waters below...at least once enough photo money has been collected from watching tourists.

Bišćevića Ćošak HOUSE

(Turkish House; Bišćevića 13; admission 4KM; 8.00am-8.30pm mid-Apr–Oct, closed winter except by tour) Bišćevića Ćošak is a slightly ramshackle 350-year-old Ottoman-Bosnian house with a colourfully furnished interior sporting a selection of traditional metal-work and carved wooden furniture.

Former Front Line WAR DAMAGE

Back in 1992–95, Croats and Bosniaks shelled each other almost incessantly across an intercommunal 'front line' that roughly followed the Bulevar. Twenty years later Mostar still retains a scattering of shell-peppered building ruins including the stumpy shell of the once splendid **Hotel Neretva** (Trg Musala) and the triangular nine-storey skeleton that was formerly **Ljubljanska Banka** (Kralja Zvonimira bb). At least four different places screen DVDs showing original footage of the town's destruction and reconstruction. Showings are free at the historic **Old Hamam** (beside Tabhana; 10am-4pm May-Oct).

Tours

Some homestays and hostels including Majdas (p147), Nina (p147) and **Miran's** (☎062 115333; www.hostelmiran-mostar.com; Pere Lažetića 13) offer great-value full-day trips driving to a selection of key rural sites around Mostar for around 70KM per person. These include the picturesque village of **Blagaj**, the Catholic pilgrimage town of **Međugorje**, the photogenic part-ruined Turkish-era citadel of **Počitelj** and the splendid **Kravice waterfalls**, Hercegovina's 25m mini-Niagara.

Mostar

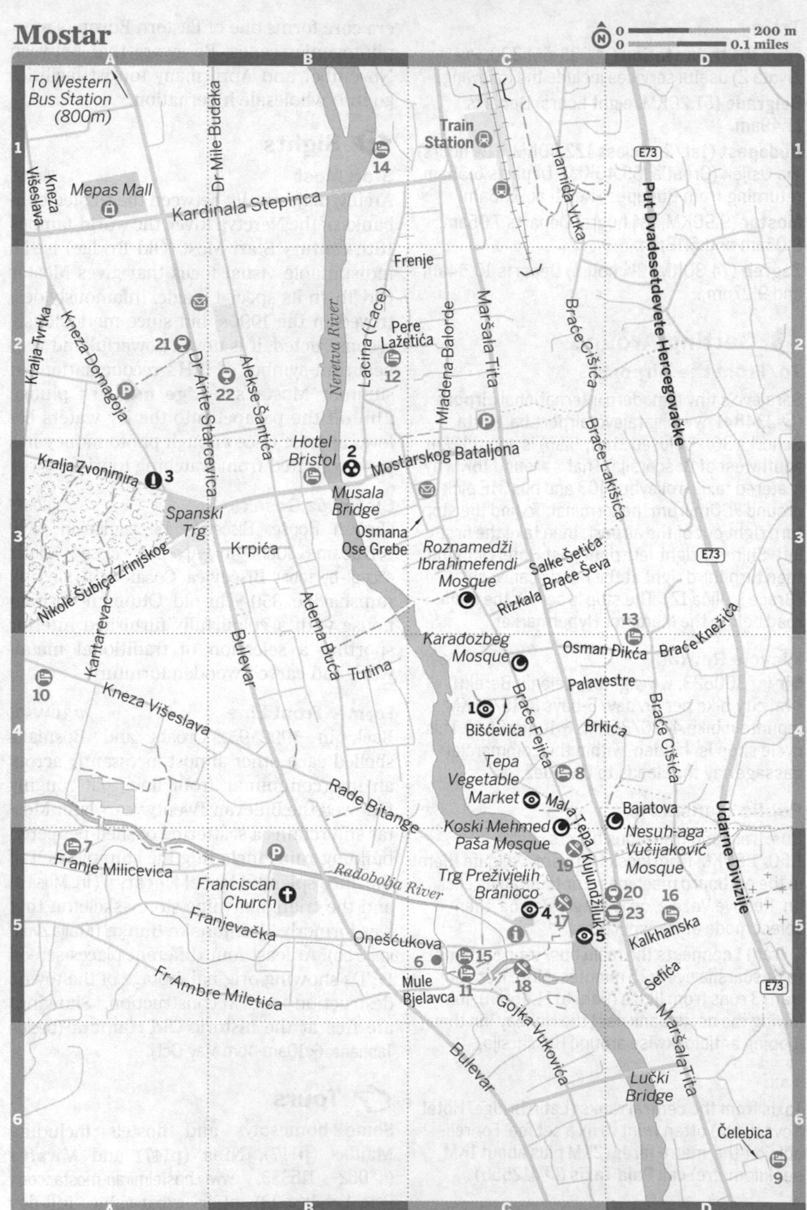

Sleeping

Most budget options are in people's homes without reception or full-time staff, so calling ahead can prove wise.

Kriva Ćuprija MILLHOUSE €€
(☎550953; www.motel-mostar.ba; r 70-130KM, apt 100-180KM; ❄📶) Impeccably clean, if not necessarily large, above a mill-house restaurant that's soothed by the sounds of gushing

Mostar

Sights

1 Biščevića Ćošak C4
2 Hotel Neretva ruins B3
3 Ljubljanska Banka A3
4 Old Hamam C5
5 Stari Most C5

Activities, Courses & Tours

6 Tourist Info BH C5

Sleeping

7 Hostel Majdas A5
8 Hostel Miturno C4
9 Hostel Nina D6
10 Hostel Nina Annex A4
11 Kriva Ćuprija C5
12 Miran's Hostel & Tours B2
13 Muslibegović House D4
14 Pansion Aldi B1
15 Pansion Oscar C5
16 Shangri-La D5

Eating

17 Babilon C5
18 Hindin Han C5
19 Urban Grill C5

Drinking

20 Ali Baba D5
21 Club Calamus A2
22 OKC Abrašević B2
23 Terasa D5

streams. It's behind the famous little 'Crooked Bridge', a miniature version of Stari Most.

Shangri-La B&B €
(☎551819; www.shangrila.com.ba; Kalhanska 10; d €49-59; P❄📶) Quiet yet central, a pseudo-19th-century facade hides B&B rooms that are contemporary and better appointed than those of many Mostar hotels.

Hostel Majdas HOUSE-HOSTEL €
(☎061 382940, 062 265324; www.hostelmajdas.com; 1st fl, Franje Milicevica 39; dm/d without bathroom €12/27; ⊙closed Oct-Mar; ❄@📶) Although located 600m west of the centre in a very ordinary apartment block, the family's warmth, sharp wit and great-value regional tours have made Majdas a cult house-hostel.

Hostel Nina HOSTEL €
(☎061 382743; www.hostelnina.ba; Čelebica 18; dm/d without bathroom €11/22; ❄@) Popular homestay-hostel run by an obliging English-speaking lady whose husband, a war survivor and former bridge jumper, runs regional tours that often end up over bargain beers at his bar in the Tabhana. Sometimes when the main hostel has been full, guests have been relocated to an **annex** that lacks much charm and is far less central.

Pansion Oscar PENSION €
(☎061 823649, 580237; Oneščukova 33; s/d €30/40/45, s/d/tr/q without bathroom €20/30/50/60; ❄📶) Nine rooms in a pair of family homes above a summer-only cocktail/shisha garden-bar slap bang in the historic centre. Standards vary, with the best options in the eaves of the newer back house.

Hostel Miturno HOSTEL €
(☎552408; www.hostel-miturno.ba; Braće Felića 67; dm/d €10/20; ⊙closed Jan & Feb; 🚭❄📶) Youthful, party-loving mini-hostel above a main-street shop.

Pansion Aldi HOSTEL €
(☎552185, 061 273457; www.pansion-aldi.com; Laćina 69a; dm €10; P❄@📶) Slightly austere but handy for the bus station and with a river-facing terrace-garden.

Eating

Along Mala Tepa/Braće Fejića are groceries, a vegetable market and several inexpensive places for Bosnian snacks.

Babilon BALKAN €€
(Tabhana; mains 8-20KM; 📋) Cafes and restaurants with divine terrace views of the river and Stari Most are unapologetically tourist-oriented, but their meal prices are only a *maraka* or two more than any ordinary dive. Unlike most, the Babilon remains open in winter, but in summer Bella Vista and Teatr next door have similarly splendid views.

Hindin Han BALKAN €€
(Jusovina bb; mains 7-20KM; ⊙11am-11pm; 📶📋) Hindin Han is a rebuilt historic building with several layers of summer terrace perched pleasantly above a side stream. Try the stuffed squid.

Urban Grill BOSNIAN €
(Mala Tepa 26; mains 5-17KM; ⊙8am-11pm Mon-Sat, 9am-11pm Sun) A brightly modern take on Bosnian-rustic with Stari Most views from its 'secret' lower terrace.

SPLURGE

In summer, tourists pay to visit the historic Ottoman **Muslibegović House** (☎551379; www.muslibegovichouse.com; Osman Đikća 41; s/d/ste €60/90/105; ❄📶) but it's simultaneously a charming boutique hotel with elements of traditional Bosnian, Turkish or even Moroccan design.

Drinking & Entertainment

Ali Baba BAR
(Kujundžiluk; ⏲24hr Jun-Sep, 7am-7pm Oct, closed winter) Unique bar-club that burrows off Kujundžiluk into the cliff-face.

OKC Abrašević BAR
(☎561107; www.okcabrasevic.org; Alekse Šantića 25) Hidden and understatedly intellectual this smoky bar attracts an alternative crowd and has occasional gigs.

Terasa CAFE
(Maršala Tita bb; ⏲weather dependent) This spectacular open-air perch-terrace surveys Stari Most from a little roof-garden.

Club Calamus COCKTAIL BAR
(Integra Bldg, 5th fl, Dr Ante Starčevića bb; ⏲10am-2am) DJs spin trancy beats after 10pm in this top-floor cocktail bar.

Shopping

There are cute, stone-roofed shop-houses along Kujundžiluk that sell colourful, inexpensive souvenirs.

Information

While no longer officially sanctioned, some Mostar businesses still accept euros and Croatian kuna. Main commercial street Braće Fejića has banks, ATMs and an internet cafe. Useful websites include **Grad Mostar** (www.turizam.mostar.ba), the **Hercegovina Tourist Board** (www.hercegovina.ba) and **Visit Mostar** (www.visitmostar.org).

Tourist Information Centre (☎397350; Trg Preživjelih Branioco; ⏲9am-9pm Jun-Sep, closed Oct-May) See also **Tourist Info BH** (☎061 564146, 561127; www.tourist-infobh.com; Oneščukova 39; ⏲8am-10.30pm May-Sep, 10am-8pm Oct-Apr).

Getting There & Away

BUS From the **main bus station** (☎552025; Trg Ivana Krndelja) services include Dubrovnik (32KM, three to four hours, three daily), Herceg Novi (71KM, 4½ hours, 7am), Sarajevo (20KM, 2½ hours, 10 daily), Split (33KM, 4½, four each morning) and Trebinje (21KM, three hours, three daily). Yellow **Mostar Bus** (☎552250; www.mostarbus.ba/linije.asp) services to Blagaj additionally pick up passengers at Lučki Most stop.

TRAIN Trains to Sarajevo (9.90KM, 2¼ hours) depart at 8.02am, 2.10pm and 6.43pm daily.

EASTERN BOSNIA & HERCEGOVINA

Appealing **Trebinje** (www.trebinjeturizam.com) is the most attractive town in the RS. It has a modest, walled **Old Town** (Stari Grad), distinctive 1574 **Arslanagić Bridge** (Perovića Most) and two eye-catching hilltop **Orthodox churches**. On a lovely, tree-shaded central square, **Hotel Platani** (www.hotel-platani-trebinje.com; Trg Svobode; s/d/tr Platani-1 63/85/100KM, Platani-2 72/104/128KM; ❄📶) consists of two nearby stone buildings both with distinctly Gallic-looking glass/wrought-iron overhangs. Choose Platini-2 for its stylish contemporary rooms, virginal white sheets, Klimt-esque art and excellent restaurant. A bus to Dubrovnik (10KM, 45 minutes, Monday to Saturday) leaves Trebinje at 10am, returning at 1.30pm. Three daily buses link to Podgorica in Montenegro via Nikšič (33KM, 3½ hours). Buses to Sarajevo (24KM, four hours at 5am, 7.30am and 11am) and to Belgrade (52KM, 11 hours at 8am and 9.45pm) travel via the glorious **Sutjeska National Park** (www.npsutjeska.srbinje.net) and war-battered **Foča**, a centre for world-class rafting organised through Foča's extreme-sports outfit **Encijan** (☎058-211220, 058-211150; www.pkencijan.com; Kraljapetra-I 1; ⏲9am-5pm Mon-Sat). Belgrade buses continue via **Višegrad** (www.visegradturizam.com), home to the 1571 'Bridge on the Drina', immortalised by Nobel Prize-winning author Ivo Andrić. A new Andrić-themed historical park is under construction in Višegrad town centre, surrounding river gorges are magnificent and a narrow-gauge tourist railway links to Mokra Gora, Serbia, on summer weekends.

CENTRAL & WESTERN BOSNIA

Between Sarajevo and Zagreb lies a series of mildly interesting historic towns, plus green wooded hills, rocky crags and river canyons.

The apparently unremarkable leather-tanning town of **Visoko** draws throngs of visitors, both sceptics and believers in the 'spiritual power' of Visočica Hill which, according to archaeologist Semir Osmanagic's bold theory, might be the **World's Greatest Pyramid** (Piramida Sunca; www.piramidasunca.ba). Associated ancient tunnels can be visited.

In **Travnik** (www.tzsbk.com), 1¼ hours further west, Plava Voda restaurants attractively line a gushing stream at the foot of the fortress ruins of **Stari Grad** (☎518140; adult/student 2/1.50KM; ⏲8am-8pm Apr-Oct, by appointment Nov-Mar). The central **Motel Aba** (☎511462; www.aba.ba; Šumeća 166a; s 35-40KM, d/tr/q 50/70/80KM; ⓦ) is a remarkable budget bargain.

Jajce (http://jajcetourism.com) has a compact, picturesque old town topped by a powerful fortress ruin where Bosnia's medieval kings were once crowned. Viewed from the Banja Luka road, the scene is photogenically fronted by a signature waterfall. Accommodation choices include the simple **Jajce Youth Hostel** (☎063 262168; www.jajce-youth-hostel.com; S Tomaševića 11; dm/d/tr 8/20/24KM; Ⓟ@ⓦ), the cute and central **Hotel Stari Grad** (☎654006; www.jajcetours.com; Svetog Luke 3; s/d 57/84KM, apt 82-154KM; ❄ⓦ) and the **Plaža Motel** (☎647200; www.motel-plaza.com; M5 (Bihać highway) km91; s/d/tr/q 40/70/99/120KM, pizza 7-11KM, mains 9-14KM) 5km west. That's beside picture-perfect lake **Plivsko Jezero**, 1km from a wonderfully quaint collection of miniature watermills.

Hidden down a forest lane 7km south of Podbrdo is the inspiringly arty 'eco-village' of **Želenkovac** (☎030-278649; www.zelenko-vac.org; John Lenon Sq; bed per person 10-25KM). North of Jajce the main Zagreb road passes through canyon valleys. To descend them by raft, visit **Kanjon Rafting Centre** (☎065 882085; www.guidelinebl.com; Karanovac; ⏲Apr-Oct) at Karanovac 8km east of **Banja Luka**, the fun-loving but architecturally challenged Republika Srpska capital.

UNDERSTAND BOSNIA & HERCEGOVINA

History

Ancient Illyrians, followed by Romans from AD 9 and Slavs from the late 6th century, were Bosnia's early arrivals. The medieval Bosnian kingdom had its own rather mysterious Christian church and reached several cultural zeniths between 1180 and 1463. It was later absorbed by the Turkish Ottoman Empire and Islam became the predominant religion of Bosnia's elite, though much of the peasantry remained Christian.

After 1878 predominantly Catholic Austria Hungary controlled BiH, alienating Muslim

WORTH A TRIP

UNA RIVER VALLEY

Either side of regional transport hub Bihać, in western BiH, the beautiful emerald-green Una Valley is popular for climbing, canyoning, kayaking and a full grade-range of white-water rafting (€25 to €55, six person minimum). Most adventure-sports outfits are rurally based with their own campsite and provide transfers from Bihać. Choices include:

Una Kiro Rafting (☎037-361110; www.una-kiro-rafting.com) Multi-sports centre with extensive if over-manicured facilities at the southeast edge of greater Bihać.

Bjeli Una Rafting (☎037-380222, 061 138853; www.una-rafting.ba; Klokot) At Klokot west of Bihać.

Una-Aqua (☎061 604313; www.una-aqua.com; Račić) At Račić, across the river from the appealing seasonal restaurant-guesthouse **Neron Turistički Centar** (☎061 142585; www.neronraft.com; Lohovo; per person without/with bathroom 25/30KM; ⏲May-Sep).

Further southeast the lonely but dramatic **Štrbački Buk** (5KM; ⏲8am-7pm May-Oct) waterfalls are the centrepiece of the new Una National Park.

There are lovely waterside restaurants near Otoka Bosanska, at Bosanska Krupa and at **Kostelski Buk** (☎037-302340; www.kostelski-buk.com; M14, Kostela; s/d €40/59, superior €44/70.50; Ⓟ❄ⓦ) which is also one the region's best value hotels, 9km from Bihać, towards Banja Luka.

Bosniaks and Orthodox Serbs. In 1914 a Bosnian Serb assassinated Austria-Hungary's imperial heir, Franz Ferdinand, in Sarajevo ultimately igniting WWI, which killed an astonishing 15% of the Bosnian population. Postwar BiH joined proto-Yugoslavia and in WWII its mountains were the scene of numerous battles between Nazi occupiers and Tito's communist Partizans.

In 1991 BiH's Croats and Bosniaks united to declare independence from Serb-dominated Yugoslavia. In reply Bosnian-Serb nationalists started seizing territory and 'cleansing' Muslims from the north and east. By 1992 a three-way war was raging between Serbs, Croats and Bosniaks. Atrocities were committed by all sides. Most infamously, Croats senselessly destroyed Mostar's Stari Most, while Bosnian Serbs besieged Sarajevo for three years and slaughtered over 7000 Srebrenica Muslims.

Eventually NATO air strikes forced the Bosnian Serbs into 1995 peace talks. The resulting Dayton Accords recognised two decentralised 'entities' within BiH: the Federation of Bosnia and Hercegovina (Muslims and Croats, capital Sarajevo), and Republika Srpska (RS: Serbs, capital Banja Luka). Today these entities retain their own administrations, but 'borders' between them have become virtually invisible. Massive aid has helped rebuild the country's visible scars, but psychological wounds will long remain.

People

The population of BiH is composed of around 48% Bosniaks (Bosnian Muslims), now living mostly in central BiH, 37% Serbs (Orthodox Christians) to the north and east in the Republika Srpska, and Croats (Catholics, 14%) mainly in the south and west. Despite some differences in vocabulary, all three communities speak effectively the same language, though Bosniaks call it 'Bosanski', Croats 'Hrvatski' and Serbs 'Српски' using Cyrillic script.

Useful phrases: *zdravo* (hello), *molim* (please), *hvala* (thanks), *koliko to košta?* (how much does it cost?).

Arts

BiH excels in crafts from *kilims* (woollen flat-weaves) to copperware to *stećci* (archetypal medieval stone grave-carvings). Traditional Bosnian music, *sevdah*, typically uses wailing heart-wrenching vocals to recount tales of unhappy amours. Works by BiH's Nobel Prize-winning author Ivo Andrić – (1892–1975) include classic epics *The Bridge on the Drina* (set in Višegrad) and *Bosnian Chronicle* (set in Travnik).

Environment

BiH is predominantly mountainous. The mostly arid south (Hercegovina) dips one tiny toe of land into the Adriatic Sea at Neum then rises swiftly into bare limestone uplands carved with deep canyons. The mostly arid central mountain core has some 30 peaks over 1700m. Towards the Montenegrin border landscapes become increasingly forested with dramatic alpine valleys. Further north peaks subside into rolling bucolic hills, flattening out altogether in the far north.

SURVIVAL GUIDE

Directory A–Z

Accommodation

Sarajevo and Mostar's no-frills house-hotels are mostly glorified homestays. In midsummer occupancy and prices rise noticeably but touts helpfully appear at Mostar and Sarajevo stations. In the provinces decent-value motels and pansions are usually less expensive and sometimes better than hotels.

Our price ranges for a double room:

€ less than 80KM

€€ 80KM to 190KM

€€€ more than 190KM

Activities

Hiking and mountain biking Many upland areas and national parks have mine-safe, marked trails.

Rafting Reaches terrifyingly difficult class V in April/May but is more suitable for beginners in summer. Top spots are around Foča, Bihać and Banja Luka.

Skiing Inexpensive yet high quality around Sarajevo.

Business Hours

Office hours 8am to 4pm Monday to Friday

Banks 8am to 6pm Monday to Friday, 8.30am to 1.30pm Saturday

Shops 8am to 6pm daily

Restaurants 11.30am to 10.30pm, often later in summer. Restaurant closing time depends on customer demand more than fixed schedules.

Embassies & Consulates

You can find a list of foreign embassies and consulates in Sarajevo on www.bosnia.org.uk/bosnia/viewtype.cfm?typeID=229.

Food

Average costs for restaurant main courses:

€ less than 10KM

€€ 10KM to 25KM

€€€ more than 25KM.

Money

» ATMs are ubiquitous and accept Visa and MasterCard.

» Bosnia's convertible mark (KM or BAM) is pronounced *kai-em* or *maraka* and divided into 100 fenig. It's tied to the euro at approximately €1=1.96KM. Though no longer officially sanctioned, many businesses still unblinkingly accept euros, for minor purchases using a slightly customer-favourable 1:2 rate. Exchanging euros is markedly better than changing other currencies as there's no rate-split.

» Exchange of travellers cheques usually requires the original purchase receipt.

Post

BiH fascinates philatelists by having three parallel postal organisations, each issuing their own stamps: **BH Pošta** (www.posta.ba) (Federation), **Pošte Srpske** (www.postesrpske.com) (RS) and **HP Post** (www.post.ba) (Croat areas, western Mostar).

Public Holidays

NATIONWIDE HOLIDAYS

New Year's Day 1 January

Independence Day 1 March

May Day 1 May

National Statehood Day 25 November

FEDERATION ONLY

Kurban Bajram (Islamic Feast of Sacrifice)

Ramazanski Bajram (end of Ramadan)

Western Easter March/April

Western Christmas 25 December

RS ONLY

Orthodox Easter April/May

Orthodox Christmas 6 January

Safe Travel

Landmines and unexploded ordnance still affect 2.8% of BiH's area. There were six mine-deaths in 2010. **BHMAC** (www.bhmac.org) clears more every year but total clearance isn't envisaged before 2019. Stick to asphalt/concrete surfaces or well-worn paths in affected areas, avoiding war-damaged buildings.

Visas

Stays of under 90 days require no visa for citizens of most Europeans countries and Australia, Brunei, Canada, Japan, Malaysia, New Zealand, Singapore, South Korea, Turkey and the USA. Other nationals should consult www.mfa.ba.

Getting There & Away

Air

All BiH flights use Sarajevo airport. Alternatively fly to Dubrovnik, Split or Zagreb (Croatia) and connect overland.

AIRLINES

Adria (www.adria.si) Ljubljana

Austrian (www.austrian.com) Vienna.

BH Airlines (☎033-550125, 768335; www.bhairlines.ba; Branilaca Sarajeva 15; ⊙9am-5pm Mon-Fri, 9am-2pm Sat) Copenhagen, İstanbul and Zürich via Banja Luka.

Croatia Airlines (www.croatiaairlines.com) Zagreb.

Germanwings (www.germanwings.com) Köln-Bonn.

JAT (www.jat.com) Belgrade.

Lufthansa (www.lufthansa.com) Munich.

Norwegian (www.norwegian.no) Twice weekly to Stockholm and Oslo.

Turkish Airlines (www.thy.com) İstanbul.

Land

BUS

Buses to Zagreb and/or Split (Croatia) run at least daily from most towns in the

Federation. Serbia and/or Montenegro buses serve many RS towns. Several weekly Vienna and Germany services run from bigger BiH cities.

TRAIN

The modest international network links Sarajevo to Belgrade, Zagreb (via Banja Luka), Budapest (via Osijek, Croatia) and to Ploče (coastal Croatia via Mostar).

Getting Around

Bus

» Frequency drops drastically at weekends, especially Sundays.

» The fare is around 7KM per hour travelled. Return tickets are often cheaper than two singles but limited to one specific company.

» You usually pay 2KM per stowed bag.

There are 'Garderob' left-luggage offices at some bus stations.

Car

Wheels are almost essential to reach BiH's ski areas and remotest villages. Call ☎1282 for roadside assistance.

» Speed limits are sometimes absurdly slow and are rigorously enforced.

» Headlights must stay on when driving.

» Rental prices drop from October to April. You can find good deals with www.hyundai.ba including full insurance, CDW and open jaws possible (Mostar, Sarajevo, Sarajevo airport) at no extra cost.

Train

Trains are generally slower than buses but around 30% cheaper. **RS Railways** (www.zrs-rs.com/red_voznje.php) has online timetables.

Britain

Includes »

London 155
Brighton & Hove.......... 186
Bath 188
Oxford..........................197
Cambridge.................. 201
York.............................202
Manchester 208
Liverpool....................... 211
Lake District National Park 213
Cardiff............................215
Edinburgh.................... 218
Glasgow....................... 223
Understand Britain 233
Survival Guide............. 236

Best Places to Eat

» Laughing Gravy (p176)
» Porthminster Beach Café (p195)
» The Broad Chare (p207)
» Sam's Chop House (p210)
» Ubiquitous Chip (p227)

Best Places to Stay

» Hoxton Hotel (p175)
» Kipps Brighton (p186)
» Manchester YHA (p209)
» Smart City Hostel (p219)
» Clachaig Inn (p231)

Why Go?

Few places cram so much history, heritage and scenery into such a compact space as Britain. Twelve hours is all you'll need to travel from tip-to-tip, but you could spend a lifetime exploring – from the ancient relics of Stonehenge and Hadrian's Wall, to the great medieval cathedrals of Westminster and Canterbury and the magnificent country houses of Chatsworth and Castle Howard.

In fact, Britain isn't really one country at all, but three. While they haven't always been easy bedfellows, the contrast between Britain's nations makes this a rewarding place to visit. With a wealth of glorious coastline, rolling countryside, stately cities, world-class museums and national parks to explore, Britain really is one of Europe's most unmissable destinations. And despite what you may have heard, it doesn't rain *all* the time – but even so, a brolly and a raincoat will certainly come in handy...

When to Go

London

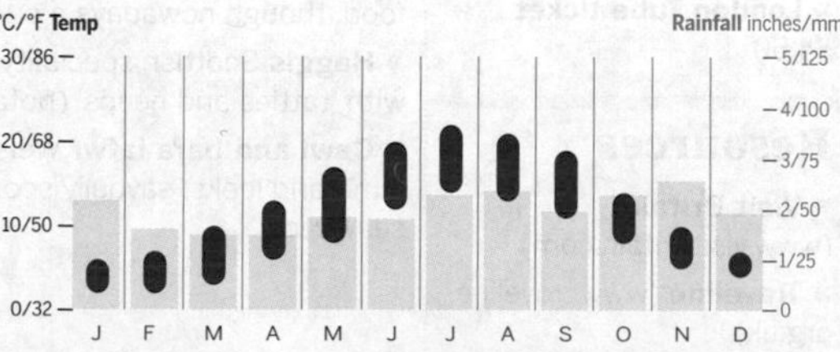

Easter–May Fewer crowds, especially in popular spots such as Bath, York and Edinburgh.

Jun–Aug The weather is at its best but the coast and national parks are busy.

Mid-Sep–Oct Prices drop and the weather is often surprisingly good.

AT A GLANCE

» **Currency** Pound sterling (£)

» **Languages** English, Welsh, Scottish Gaelic

» **Money** Change bureaus and ATMs widely available

» **Visas** Schengen rules do not apply

Fast Facts

» **Area** 88,500 sq miles

» **Capital** London

» **Country code** ☎44

» **Emergency** ☎999

Exchange Rates

Australia	A$1	UK £0.68
Canada	C$1	UK £0.64
Euro Zone	€1	UK £0.84
Japan	¥100	UK £0.70
New Zealand	NZ$1	UK £0.55
USA	US$1	UK £0.65

Set Your Budget

» **Budget hotel room** £60–80

» **Two-course meal** £10–15

» **Pint of beer** £3–4

» **London Tube ticket** £4.50

Resources

» **Visit Britain** (www.visitbritain.com)

» **Traveline** (www.traveline.org.uk)

Connections

The quickest way to Europe from Britain is via the Channel Tunnel, which has direct Eurostar rail services from London to Paris and Brussels. Ferries sail from southern England to French ports in a couple of hours; other routes connect eastern England to the Netherlands, Germany and northern Spain, and Ireland from southwest Scotland and Wales.

ITINERARIES

One Week

With just seven days, you're pretty much limited to sights in England. Start in London, then branch out to Canterbury and Brighton, or Salisbury and Stonehenge (or all four). Sample the delights of historic Bath, tootle up to Oxford and Stratford-upon-Avon, then head east to Cambridge before returning to London.

Two Weeks

Start in London, then head west to Salisbury for a trip to Stonehenge and nearby Avebury. Enjoy more history in beautiful Bath. Head over to Cardiff for a taste of Wales, then cruise across the classic English countryside of the Cotswolds to reach Oxford. Not far away is Stratford-upon-Avon, for everything Shakespeare. Strike out north via Manchester and the Lake District to Scotland's capital Edinburgh, detour via Glencoe and Loch Lomond to the UK's highest mountain, Ben Nevis, before recrossing the border to York, then Cambridge and back to London.

Essential Food & Drink

» **Roast beef with Yorkshire pudding** Iconic English dish: beef with baked-batter pudding.

» **Bangers and mash** Another icon: sausages and mashed potato.

» **Fish and chips** Once the nation's most popular takeaway food, though nowadays a curry is favourite.

» **Haggis** Scottish speciality of sheep-offal pudding served with 'tatties and neeps' (potatoes and turnips).

» **Cawl and bara lafwr** Welsh treats: a broth made with lamb and leeks; savoury scones made with oatmeal and seaweed.

LONDON

POP 7.51 MILLION

London has enough history, vitality and cultural drive to keep you occupied for weeks. And fresh from its stint as host for the Queen's Golden Jubilee celebrations and the 2012 Olympics, it's riding the crest of a creative wave, so there's never been a better time to visit this most cosmopolitan of cities.

The downside of this renaissance is increasing cost: London is Europe's most expensive city for visitors, whatever their budget. But with some careful planning and a bit of common sense, you can find great bargains and freebies among the popular attractions. And don't forget that many of London's greatest assets – its wonderful parks, bridges, squares and boulevards, not to mention many of its landmark museums – come completely free.

History

London first came into being as a Celtic village near a ford across the River Thames, but the city only really took off after the Roman invasion in AD 43. The Romans enclosed their Londinium in walls that still find refrain in the shape of the City of London today. Then came the Saxons, and the town (called Lundenwic) prospered.

London grew in global importance during the medieval period, surviving devastating challenges including the 1665 Plague and 1666 Great Fire. Many of its great landmarks such as St Paul's Cathedral were built at this time by visionary architect Christopher Wren.

By the early 1700s Georgian London had become one of Europe's largest and richest cities, and during the Victorian era London really hit its stride, fuelled by vast mercantile wealth and a huge global empire.

The ravages of the Great War were followed by the economic troubles of the 1920s and 1930s, but it was WWII that wrought the greatest damage: huge swathes of the city were reduced to rubble during a series of devastating bombings known as the Blitz.

During the 1960s, Swinging London became the world's undisputed cultural capital, with an explosion of innovative new art, music, writing, theatre and fashion. The 1970s proved even more turbulent, with widespread unrest and economic discontent, while the 1980s was marked by an economic boom in London's financial district (known as the City), which brought a forest of new skyscrapers to the city's skyline.

In 2000 London got its first elected Mayor, left-wing Ken Livingstone, who served for two terms and oversaw the city's bid for the 2012 Olympics; as well as dealing with the grim aftermath of the 7/7 bombings in

continued on p160

London

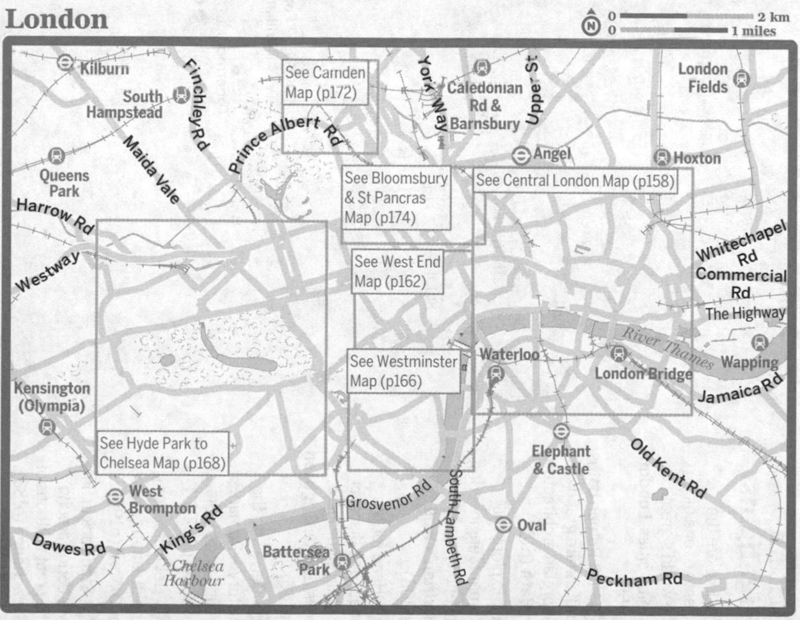

Britain Highlights

1 Explore the streets of one of the world's greatest capital cities, **London** (p155)

2 Visit Roman baths and admire grand Georgian architecture in **Bath** (p188)

3 Explore the Romans' engineering ingenuity along **Hadrian's Wall** (p208)

4 Head for the coast and discover Britain's quirkiest seaside city, **Brighton** (p186)

5 Delve into the history – Roman, Viking and medieval – of **York** (p202)

6 Get lost among the dreaming spires of **Oxford** (p197)

7 Step back in time wandering around the great trilithons of **Stonehenge** (p188)

8 Join the party in Scotland's festival city, **Edinburgh** (p218)

9 Head north to experience the epic grandeur of the **Scottish Highlands** (p229)

10 Marvel at the mountainous scenery of Wales' **Snowdonia National Park** (p217)

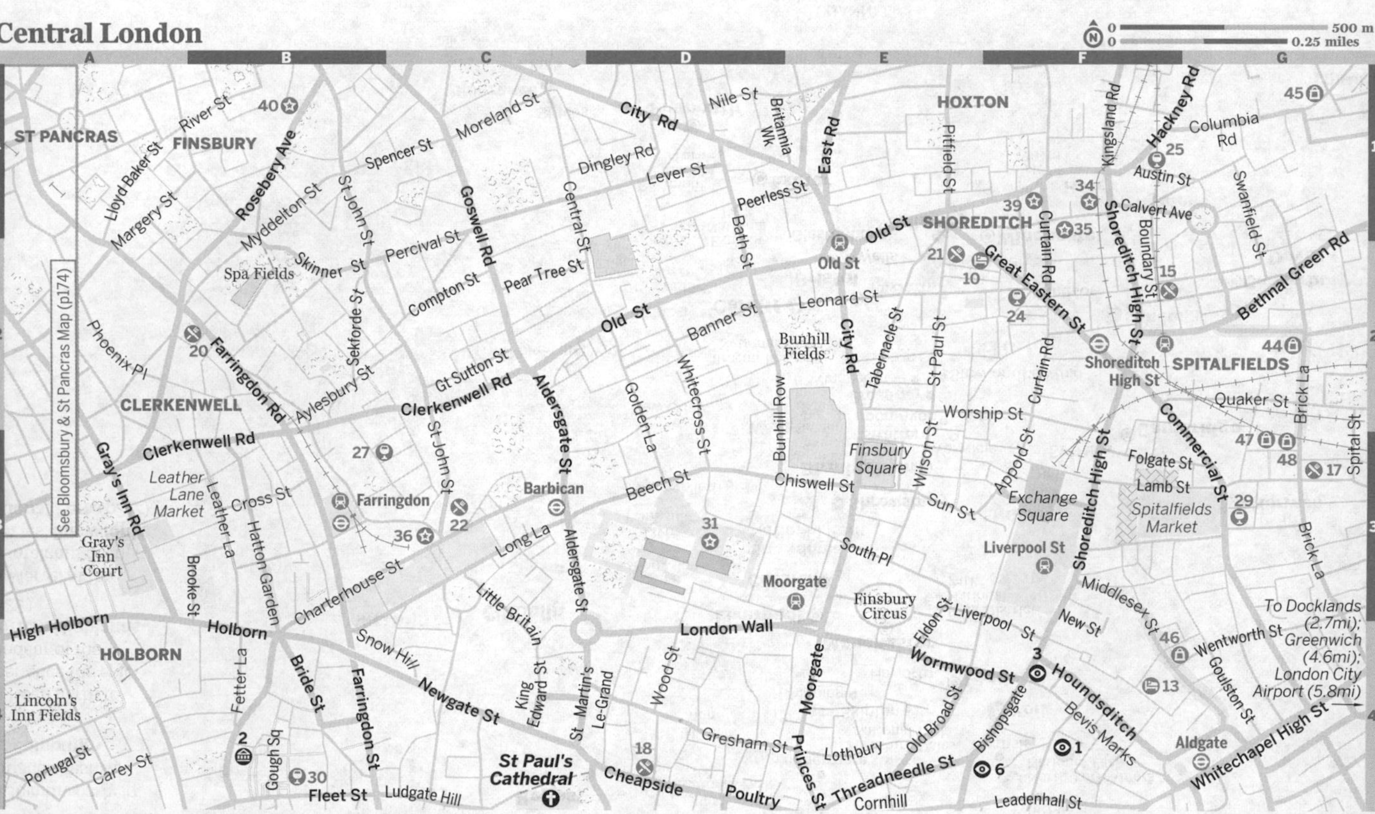
Central London
500 m
0.25 miles
See Bloomsbury & St Pancras Map (p174)
ST PANCRAS
FINSBURY
CLERKENWELL
HOLBORN
HOXTON
SHOREDITCH
SPITALFIELDS
River St
Lloyd Baker St
Margery St
Rosebery Ave
Myddelton St
Spa Fields
Skinner St
Phoenix Pl
Farringdon Rd
CLERKENWELL
Clerkenwell Rd
Gray's Inn Rd
Leather Lane Market
Leather La
Cross St
Hatton Garden
Gray's Inn Court
Brooke St
High Holborn
Holborn
Lincoln's Inn Fields
Fetter La
Bride St
Portugal St
Carey St
Gough Sq
Fleet St
Ludgate Hill
Farringdon St
Spencer St
St John St
Percival St
Sekforde St
Aylesbury St
Compton St
Moreland St
Goswell Rd
Pear Tree St
Gt Sutton St
Clerkenwell Rd
St John St
Farringdon
Charterhouse St
Snow Hill
Newgate St
St Paul's Cathedral
Aldersgate St
Barbican
Long La
Little Britain
King Edward St
St Martin's Le-Grand
Cheapside
City Rd
Nile St
Britannia Wk
East Rd
Dingley Rd
Lever St
Central St
Peerless St
Bath St
Old St
Old St
Leonard St
Banner St
Golden La
Whitecross St
Beech St
Bunhill Fields
Bunhill Row
City Rd
Tabernacle St
Finsbury Square
Chiswell St
South Pl
Moorgate
Finsbury Circus
London Wall
Wood St
Gresham St
Moorgate
Princes St
Poultry
Lothbury
Threadneedle St
Cornhill
HOXTON
Pitfield St
St Paul St
Wilson St
Sun St
Worship St
Curtain Rd
Great Eastern St
Appold St
Exchange Square
Liverpool St
Eldon St
Liverpool St
Wormwood St
Old Broad St
Bishopsgate
Houndsditch
Bevis Marks
Leadenhall St
Kingsland Rd
Hackney Rd
Columbia Rd
Austin St
Calvert Ave
Boundary St
Shoreditch High St
Swanfield St
Bethnal Green Rd
Shoreditch High St
Brick La
Quaker St
Commercial St
Spital St
Folgate St
Lamb St
Spitalfields Market
Shoreditch High St
Middlesex St
New St
Wentworth St
Goulston St
Aldgate
Whitechapel High St
To Docklands (2.7mi); Greenwich (4.6mi); London City Airport (5.8mi)

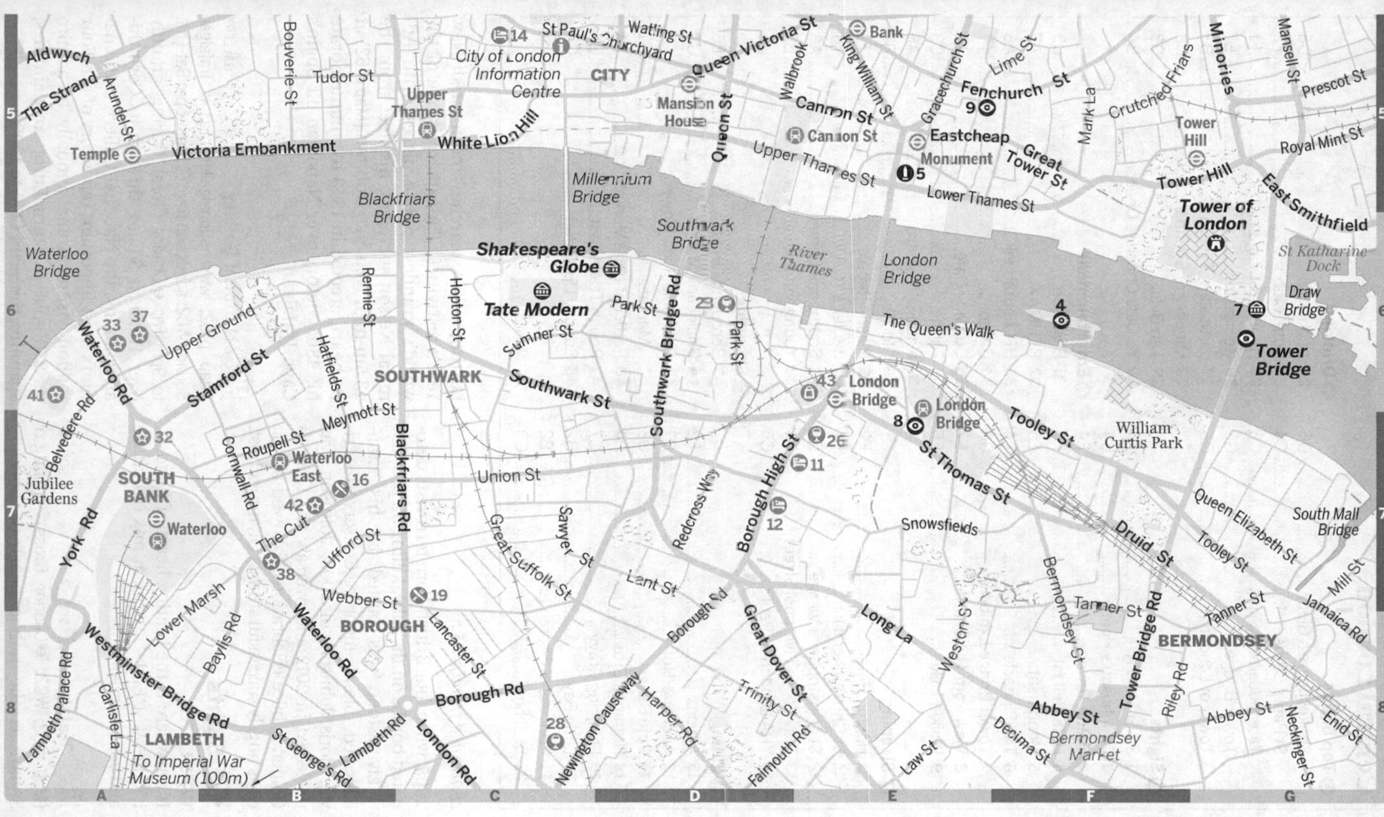

Aldwych
The Strand
Arundel St
Bouverie St
Tudor St
Upper Thames St
White Lion Hill
Temple
Victoria Embankment
St Paul's Churchyard
Watling St
City of London Information Centre
CITY
Queen Victoria St
Mansion House
Queen St
Walbrook
Bank
King William St
Cannon St
Upper Thames St
Gracechurch St
Fenchurch St
Lime St
Eastcheap
Monument
Great Tower St
Lower Thames St
Mark La
Crutched Friars
Minories
Mansell St
Prescot St
Tower Hill
Royal Mint St
East Smithfield
Tower of London
St Katharine Dock
Draw Bridge
Tower Bridge
Waterloo Bridge
Blackfriars Bridge
Millennium Bridge
Southwark Bridge
River Thames
London Bridge
Shakespeare's Globe
Tate Modern
Park St
Sumner St
Hopton St
Rennie St
Upper Ground
Stamford St
Hatfields St
SOUTHWARK
Southwark St
Southwark Bridge Rd
The Queen's Walk
Tooley St
William Curtis Park
Waterloo Rd
Belvedere Rd
Meymott St
Roupell St
Waterloo East
Cornwall Rd
Blackfriars Rd
Union St
Redcross Way
Borough High St
St Thomas St
SOUTH BANK
Jubilee Gardens
Waterloo
York Rd
The Cut
Ufford St
Great Suffolk St
Sawyer St
Lant St
Snowsfields
Druid St
Queen Elizabeth St
South Mall Bridge
Tooley St
Mill St
Jamaica Rd
Lower Marsh
Baylis Rd
Webber St
BOROUGH
Lancaster St
Borough Rd
Great Dover St
Long La
Weston St
Bermondsey St
Tanner St
Tower Bridge Rd
BERMONDSEY
Westminster Bridge Rd
Lambeth Palace Rd
Carlisle La
LAMBETH
To Imperial War Museum (100m)
St George's Rd
Lambeth Rd
London Rd
Newington Causeway
Harper Rd
Trinity St
Falmouth Rd
Law St
Abbey St
Decima St
Bermondsey Market
Riley Rd
Neckinger St
Enid St

Central London

Top Sights

Shakespeare's Globe D6
St Paul's Cathedral C4
Tate Modern C6
Tower Bridge G6
Tower of London G6

Sights

1 30 St Mary Axe F4
2 Dr Johnson's House B4
3 Heron Tower F4
4 HMS Belfast F6
5 Monument E5
6 The Pinnacle F4
7 Tower Bridge Exhibition G6
8 View from The Shard E7
9 Walkie Talkie E5

Sleeping

10 Hoxton Hotel E2
11 St Christopher's Inn E7
12 St Christopher's Village D7
13 Travelodge Liverpool Street F4
14 YHA London St Paul's C5

Eating

15 Albion F2
16 Anchor & Hope B7
17 Cafe Bangla G3
18 Hummus Bros D4
19 Laughing Gravy C7
20 Little Bay B2
21 Princess of Shoreditch E2
22 St John C3

Drinking

23 Anchor D6
24 Book Club F2
25 George & Dragon F1
26 George Inn E7
27 Jerusalem Tavern B3
28 Ministry of Sound C8
29 Ten Bells G3
30 Ye Olde Cheshire Cheese B4

Entertainment

31 Barbican D3
32 BFI IMAX A7
33 BFI Southbank A6
34 Cargo F1
35 Comedy Café F1
36 Fabric C3
37 National Theatre A6
38 Old Vic B7
39 Plastic People F1
40 Sadler's Wells B1
41 Southbank Centre A6
42 Young Vic B7

Shopping

43 Borough Market E6
44 Brick Lane Market G2
45 Columbia Road Flower Market G1
46 Petticoat Lane Market F4
47 Rough Trade East G3
48 Sunday UpMarket G3

continued from p155

2005, when four British-born terrorists detonated bombs on the tube, killing 52 people.

Livingstone was ousted by his Eton-educated, blonde-mopped Conservative rival, Boris Johnson, in 2008. Johnson was re-elected in 2012 and oversaw the Queen's Golden Jubilee celebrations, followed by the city's hugely successful stint as Olympics host.

Sights

WEST END

If anywhere is the beating heart of London, it's the West End – a strident mix of culture and consumerism.

TOP CHOICE **Trafalgar Square** SQUARE

(Map p162; WC2; Charing Cross) Trafalgar Square is the public heart of London, hosting rallies, marches and feverish New Year's festivities. The square is one of the world's grandest public places, with Admiral Nelson surveying his fleet from the 43.5m-high **Nelson's Column** (Map p162) at its heart, erected in 1843 to commemorate his 1805 victory over Napoleon off Spain's Cape Trafalgar.

TOP CHOICE **National Gallery** GALLERY

(Map p162; www.nationalgallery.org.uk; Trafalgar Square, WC2; admission free; 10am-6pm Sat-Thu, to 9pm Fri; Charing Cross) Gazing grandly over Trafalgar Square through its Corinthian columns, the National Gallery is the nation's most important repository of art. Four million visitors come annually to admire its 2300-plus western European paintings, spanning the years 1250 to 1900.

FREE **National Portrait Gallery** GALLERY
(Map p162; www.npg.org.uk; St Martin's Pl, WC2; ⏲10am-6pm Sat-Wed, to 9pm Thu & Fri; ⊖Charing Cross or Leicester Sq) The fascinating National Portrait Gallery is like stepping into a picture book of English history. Founded in 1856, the permanent collection (around 11,000 works) starts with the Tudors on the 2nd floor and descends to contemporary figures (from pop stars to scientists), including Marc Quinn's *Self*, a frozen self-portrait of the artist's head cast in blood and recreated every five years.

Piccadilly Circus SQUARE
(Map p162; ⊖Piccadilly Circus) Despite the crowds and traffic, Piccadilly Circus has become a postcard for the city, buzzing with the liveliness that makes it exciting to be in London. At its centre is the famous aluminium statue, **Anteros** (Map p162), twin brother of Eros.

Covent Garden Piazza SQUARE
(Map p162; www.coventgardenlondonuk.com/-/covent-garden-piazza; ⊖Covent Garden) London's first planned square, Covent Garden Piazza, now hosts bands of tourists shopping in quaint old arcades and ringing street entertainers and buskers.

WESTMINSTER, ST JAMES'S & PIMLICO

Westminster has been the centre of political power for a millennium, and the area's many landmarks combine to form an awesome display of strength, gravitas and historical import.

TOP CHOICE **Westminster Abbey** CHURCH
(Map p166; ☎7222 5152; www.westminster-abbey.org; 20 Dean's Yard, SW1; adult/child £18/8, verger tours £3; ⏲9.30am-4.30pm Mon, Tue, Thu & Fri, to 7pm Wed, to 2.30pm Sat; ⊖Westminster) Westminster Abbey has never been a cathedral (the seat of a bishop). It's what is called a 'royal peculiar' and is administered directly by the Crown. Every monarch since William the Conqueror has been crowned here, with the exception of a couple of unlucky Eds who were murdered (Edward V) or abdicated (Edward VIII) before the magic moment. Look out for the **Coronation Chair**.

Apart from the royal graves, many famous commoners are interred here, especially in **Poets' Corner**, where you'll find the resting places of Chaucer, Dickens, Hardy, Tennyson, Dr Johnson and Kipling as well as memorials to some other greats (Shakespeare, Austen, Brontë etc).

Verger-led tours are held several times a day (except Sundays) and are limited to 25 people per tour; call ahead to secure your place.

Westminster Cathedral CHURCH
(Map p166; www.westminstercathedral.org.uk; Victoria St, SW1; ⏲7am-7pm; 📶; ⊖Victoria) Not to be confused with the eponymous abbey, the neo-Byzantine Westminster Cathedral dates from 1895 and is the headquarters of Britain's Roman Catholic church. The distinctive 83m red-brick and white-stone **tower** (adult £5) offers splendid views of London.

FREE **Houses of Parliament** HISTORIC BUILDING
(Map p166; www.parliament.uk; Parliament Sq, SW1; ⊖Westminster) Photos just don't do justice to the ornate stonework and golden filigree of Charles Barry and Augustus Pugin's neo-Gothic masterpiece (1840), the seat of power for the British parliament. The palace's most famous feature is its clock tower, aka **Big Ben** (Map p166). Ben is actually the 13-tonne bell, named after Benjamin Hall, who was

DON'T MISS

BRITISH MUSEUM

The vast **British Museum** (Map p162; ☎7323 8000; www.britishmuseum.org; Great Russell St, WC1; admission free; ⏲10am-5.30pm Sat-Thu, to 8.30pm Fri; ⊖Russell Sq) isn't just the nation's largest museum, it's one of the oldest and finest anywhere in the world. Among the must-see antiquities are the **Rosetta Stone**, the key to deciphering Egyptian hieroglyphics, discovered in 1799; the controversial **Parthenon Sculptures**, stripped from the walls of the Parthenon in Athens by Lord Elgin (the British ambassador to the Ottoman Empire); and the Anglo-Saxon **Sutton Hoo relics**. The **Great Court** was restored and augmented by Norman Foster in 2000 and now has a spectacular glass-and-steel roof.

You'll need multiple visits to savour even the highlights here; happily there are 15 half-hour free **Eye Opener tours** between 11am and 3.45pm daily, focusing on different parts of the collection.

West End

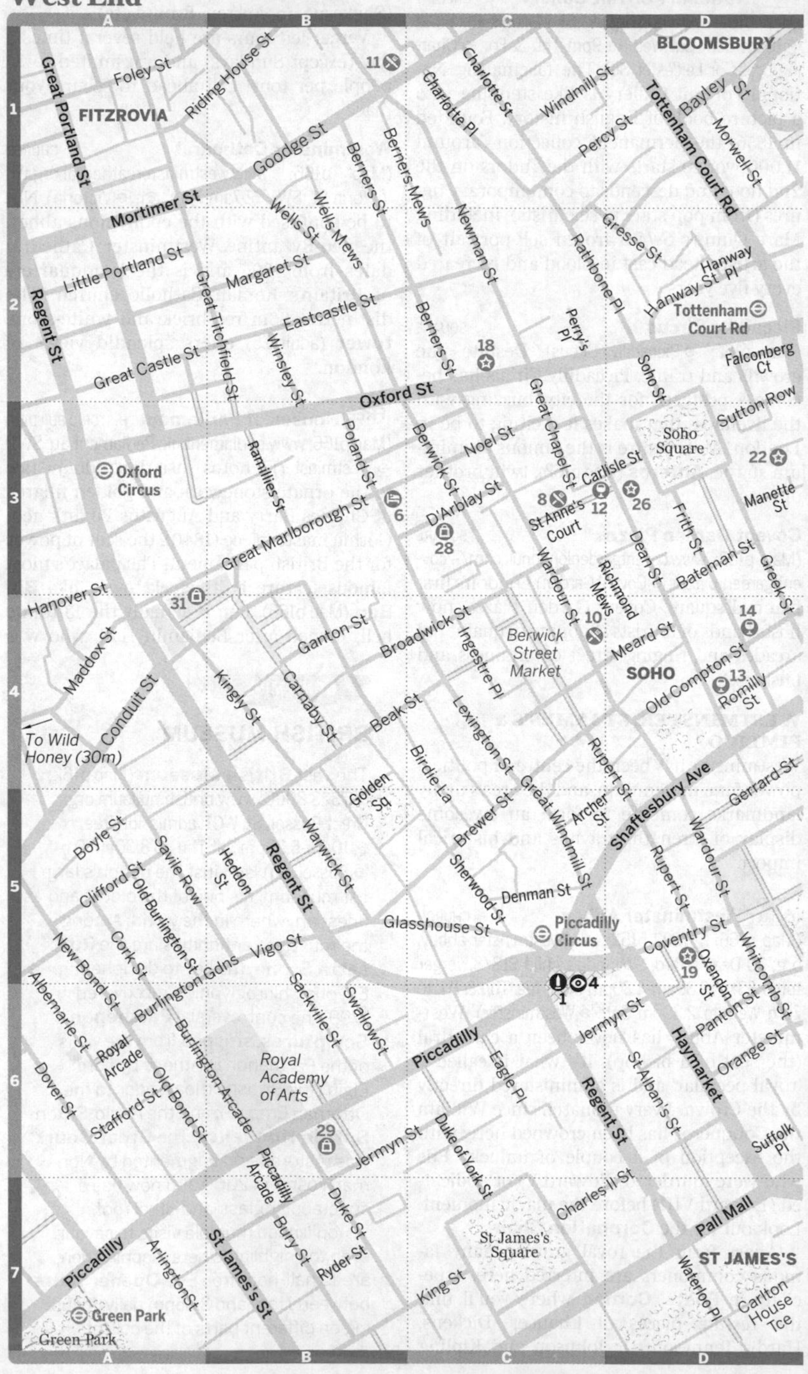

A
B
C
D
1
2
3
4
5
6
7
BLOOMSBURY
FITZROVIA
SOHO
ST JAMES'S
Great Portland St
Foley St
Riding House St
Charlotte St
Charlotte Pl
Windmill St
Tottenham Court Rd
Bayley St
Morwell St
Percy St
Goodge St
Berners St
Berners Mews
Newman St
Mortimer St
Wells St
Wells Mews
Gresse St
Rathbone Pl
Little Portland St
Margaret St
Great Titchfield St
Hanway St
Hanway Pl
Regent St
Eastcastle St
Winsley St
Perry's Pl
Tottenham Court Rd
Great Castle St
Oxford St
Soho St
Falconberg Ct
Sutton Row
Great Chapel St
Soho Square
Oxford Circus
Ramillies St
Poland St
Berwick St
Noel St
Carlisle St
D'Arblay St
St Anne's Court
Frith St
Manette St
Great Marlborough St
Dean St
Wardour St
Richmond Mews
Bateman St
Greek St
Hanover St
Ganton St
Broadwick St
Ingestre Pl
Berwick Street Market
Meard St
Maddox St
Kingly St
Carnaby St
Beak St
Lexington St
Old Compton St
Romilly St
Conduit St
To Wild Honey (30m)
Birdie La
Rupert St
Shaftesbury Ave
Gerrard St
Golden Sq
Great Windmill St
Archer St
Brewer St
Boyle St
Savile Row
Heddon St
Warwick St
Clifford St
Old Burlington St
Sherwood St
Denman St
Cork St
Glasshouse St
Piccadilly Circus
Coventry St
Whitcomb St
New Bond St
Vigo St
Burlington Gdns
Sackville St
Swallow St
Oxendon St
Panton St
Albemarle St
Royal Arcade
Burlington Arcade
Piccadilly
Eagle Pl
Jermyn St
Haymarket
Orange St
Dover St
Stafford St
Old Bond St
Royal Academy of Arts
St Alban's St
Duke of York St
Suffolk Pl
Piccadilly Arcade
Charles II St
Pall Mall
Duke St
Bury St
Ryder St
St James's Square
Arlington St
St James's St
King St
Waterloo Pl
Carlton House Tce
Green Park
1
4
6
8
10
11
12
13
14
18
19
22
26
28
29
31

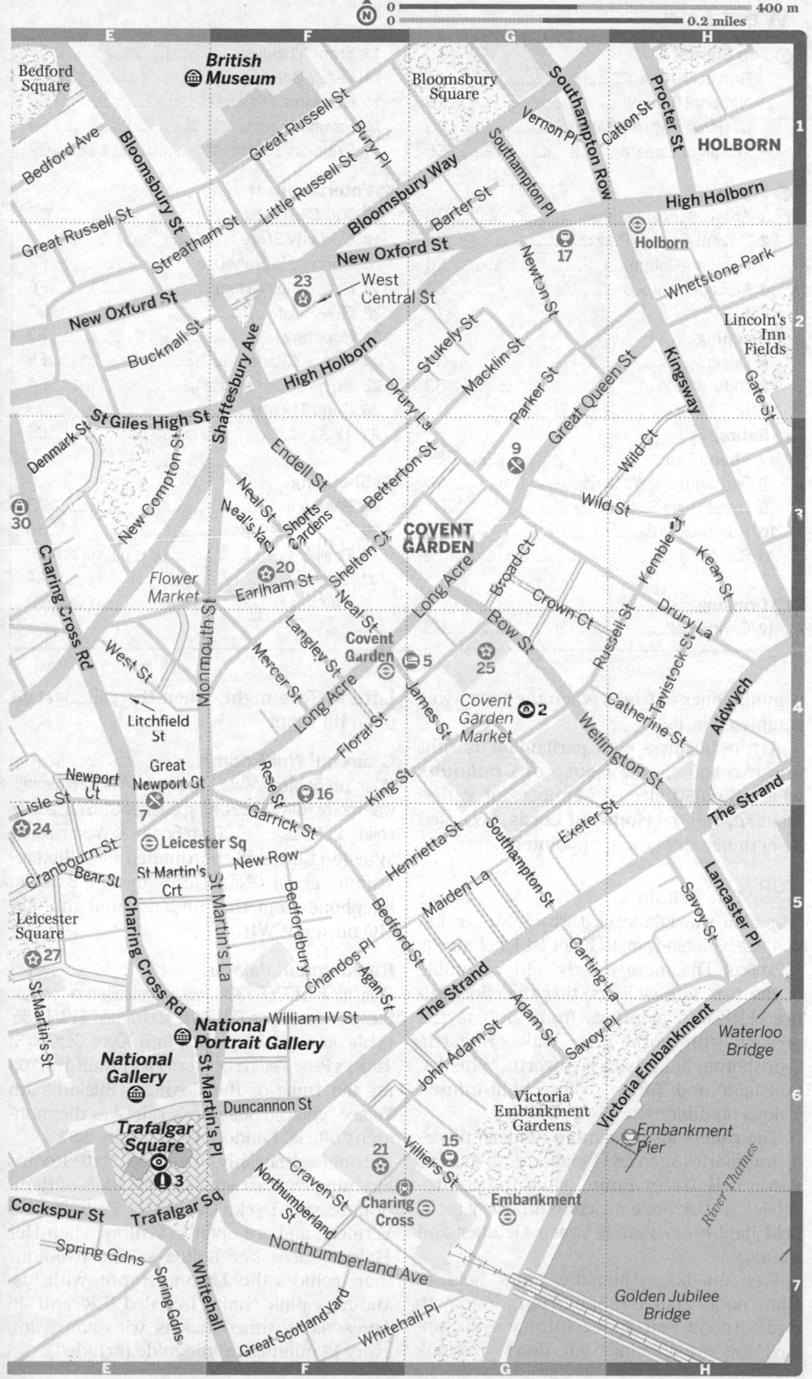

0 400 m
0 0.2 miles
E
F
G
H
1
2
3
4
5
6
7
British Museum
Bedford Square
Bloomsbury Square
HOLBORN
Bedford Ave
Bloomsbury St
Great Russell St
Bury Pl
Little Russell St
Bloomsbury Way
Southampton Row
Vernon Pl
Southampton Pl
Catton St
Procter St
High Holborn
Barter St
Streatham St
New Oxford St
Holborn
17
23
West Central St
Whetstone Park
Newton St
Lincoln's Inn Fields
Bucknall St
Shaftesbury Ave
Stukely St
Macklin St
Great Queen St
Kingsway
Gate St
St Giles High St
Denmark St
Drury La
Parker St
Endell St
9
Wild Ct
New Compton St
Betterton St
Wild St
Neal St
Neal's Yd
Shorts Gardens
COVENT GARDEN
30
Charing Cross Rd
Shelton St
Long Acre
Broad Ct
Kemble St
Kean St
20
Flower Market
Earlham St
Monmouth St
Crown Ct
Neal St
Langley St
Bow St
Russell St
Drury La
Covent Garden
5
25
Tavistock St
West St
Mercer St
James St
Covent Garden Market
2
Catherine St
Aldwych
Litchfield St
Floral St
Wellington St
Great Newport St
Newport Ct
Rose St
16
King St
The Strand
Lisle St
7
Garrick St
Exeter St
24
Leicester Sq
Henrietta St
Southampton St
Cranbourn St
New Row
Bear St
St Martin's Ct
St Martin's La
Bedfordbury
Maiden La
Savoy St
Lancaster Pl
Leicester Square
Bedford St
27
Charing Cross Rd
Chandos Pl
Carting La
Agar St
The Strand
Waterloo Bridge
St Martin's St
William IV St
Adam St
National Portrait Gallery
John Adam St
Savoy Pl
Victoria Embankment
National Gallery
St Martin's Pl
Duncannon St
Victoria Embankment Gardens
Trafalgar Square
Embankment Pier
21
15
Craven St
Villiers St
River Thames
3
Northumberland St
Charing Cross
Embankment
Cockspur St
Trafalgar Sq
Spring Gdns
Northumberland Ave
Spring Gdns
Whitehall
Golden Jubilee Bridge
Great Scotland Yard
Whitehall Pl

West End

Top Sights

British Museum ... E1
National Gallery ... E6
National Portrait Gallery ... E6
Trafalgar Square ... E6

Sights

1 Anteros (Eros) statue ... C5
2 Covent Garden Piazza ... G4
3 Nelson's Column ... E6
4 Piccadilly Circus ... C5

Sleeping

5 Oasis ... G4
6 Oxford St YHA ... B3

Eating

7 Abeno Too ... E4
8 Fernandez & Wells Espresso Bar ... C3
9 Great Queen Street ... G3
10 Hummus Bros ... C4
11 Salt Yard ... B1

Drinking

12 Candy Bar ... C3
13 French House ... D4
14 G-A-Y Bar ... D4
15 Gordon's Wine Bar ... G6
16 Lamb & Flag ... F4
17 Princess Louise ... G2

Entertainment

18 100 Club ... C2
19 Comedy Store ... D5
20 Donmar Warehouse ... F3
21 G-A-Y Club@Heaven ... F6
22 G-A-Y Late ... D3
23 Popstarz ... F2
24 Prince Charles ... E5
25 Royal Opera House ... G4
26 Soho Theatre ... D3
27 Tkts ... E5

Shopping

28 BM Soho ... C3
29 Fortnum & Mason ... B6
30 Foyle's ... E3
31 Liberty ... A4
Ray's Jazz ... (see 30)

commissioner of works when the tower was completed in 1858.

At the business end, parliament is split into two houses: the **House of Commons** where the 650 elected Members of Parliament sit, and the **House of Lords**, occupied by both hereditary and appointed peers.

TOP CHOICE Tate Britain GALLERY

(Map p166; www.tate.org.uk; Millbank, SW1; admission free; 10am-6pm, to 10pm 1st Fri of month; Pimlico) The more elderly and venerable of the two Tate siblings, this riverside edifice celebrates paintings from 1500 to the present, with works from Blake, Hogarth, Gainsborough, Barbara Hepworth, Whistler, Constable and Turner, whose light-infused visions dominate the **Clore Gallery**.

The gallery also has more modern pieces by luminaries such as Lucian Freud, Francis Bacon and Tracey Emin, while the controversial Turner Prize for contemporary art is held here every year between October and January.

Free one-hour thematic tours held at 11am, noon, 2pm and 3pm from Monday to Friday (noon and 3pm Saturday and Sunday) are eye-opening, but don't overlook **Late at Tate night**, when the gallery stays open till 10pm.

Churchill War Rooms MUSEUM

(Map p166; http://www.iwm.org.uk/visits/churchill-war-rooms; Clive Steps, King Charles St, SW1; adult/child £17/free; 9.30am-6pm; Westminster) Winston Churchill coordinated the Allied resistance against Nazi Germany on a Bakelite telephone from this underground military HQ during WWII.

Buckingham Palace PALACE

(Map p166; 7766 7300; www.royalcollection.org.uk; Buckingham Palace Rd, SW1; adult/child £19/10.85; late Jul-Aug 9.30am-7pm, to 6.30pm Sep; St James's Park, Victoria or Green Park) Built in 1703 for the Duke of Buckingham, Buckingham Palace replaced St James's Palace as the monarch's official London residence in 1837.

Nineteen lavishly furnished State Rooms are hung with artworks by the likes of Rembrandt, van Dyck, Canaletto, Poussin and Vermeer, and are open to visitors when Her Majesty takes her holidays. The two-hour tour includes the **Throne Room**, with his-and-hers pink chairs initialed 'ER' and 'P'. Access is by timed tickets with admission every 15 minutes (audioguide included).

The **Changing of the Guard** is held at 11.30am daily May to July (on alternate days, weather permitting, for the rest of the year).

THE CITY

For centuries, the City (note the capital C) *was* London. Its boundaries have changed little from the Roman walls built in this area two millennia ago, and today it's London's central business district (also known as the 'square mile').

TOP CHOICE St Paul's Cathedral CHURCH
(Map p158; www.stpauls.co.uk; St Paul's Churchyard EC4; adult/child £15/6; ⏲8.30am-4.30pm Mon-Sat, last entry at 4pm; ⊖St Paul's) Dominating the City, St Paul's Cathedral was built by 'London's architect' Christopher Wren between 1675 and 1710. Beneath the iconic dome, attractions include the **Whispering Gallery** – if you talk close to the wall it carries your words around to the opposite side – and the **Golden Gallery** at the very top, for an unforgettable view of London.

TOP CHOICE Tower of London CASTLE
(Map p158; ☎0844 482 7777; www.hrp.org.uk/toweroflondon; Tower Hill EC3, EC3; adult/child £21.45/10.75, audioguide £4/3; ⏲9am-5.30pm Tue-Sat, from 10am Sun & Mon, until 4.30pm Nov-Feb; ⊖Tower Hill) A former royal residence, treasury, mint and arsenal, the Tower of London is one of London's three World Heritage sites, not to mention one of the city's absolutely unmissable sights. Highlights include the central **White Tower** and the famous **Crown Jewels**. Also keep an eye out for the Tower's ravens, which legend says could cause the White Tower to collapse should they leave (their wings are clipped in case they get any ideas).

Hour-long tours with the tower's Beefeaters (Yeoman Warders) leave every 30 minutes near the main entrance. Book online for cheaper rates for the Tower.

Tower Bridge BRIDGE
(Map p158; ⊖Tower Hill) London was still a thriving port in 1894 when Tower Bridge was built. It was designed to be raised to allow ships to pass, but electricity has now taken over from the original steam engines. A lift leads up from the northern tower to the overpriced **Tower Bridge Exhibition** (Map p158; www.towerbridge.org.uk; adult/child £8/3.40; ⏲10am-6pm Apr-Sep, 9.30am-5.30pm Oct-Mar, last admission 30min before closing; ⊖Tower Hill), where the story of its building is recounted within the upper walkway.

Dr Johnson's House MUSEUM
(Map p158; www.drjohnsonshouse.org; 17 Gough Sq EC4, EC4; adult/child £4.50/1.50, audioguide £2; ⏲11am-5.30pm Mon-Sat May-Sep, to 5pm Mon-Sat Oct-Apr; ⊖Chancery Lane) The Georgian house where Samuel Johnson and his assistants compiled the first English dictionary (between 1748 and 1759) is full of prints and portraits of friends and intimates, including the good doctor's Jamaican servant to whom he bequeathed this grand residence.

Monument TOWER
(Map p158; www.themonument.info; Fish Street Hill EC3, EC4; adult/child £3/1; ⏲9.30am-5.30pm; ⊖Monument) Designed by Wren to commemorate the Great Fire, the towering Monument is 60.6m high, the exact distance from its base to the bakery on Pudding Lane where the blaze began. Corkscrew your way up the 311 tight spiral steps (claustrophobes beware) for some of London's best wraparound views.

SOUTH BANK

Londoners once crossed the river to the area controlled by the licentious Bishops of Southwark for all manner of bawdy frolicking frowned upon in the City. It's a much more seemly area now, but the frisson of theatre and entertainment remains.

FREE Tate Modern MUSEUM
(Map p158; www.tate.org.uk; Queen's Walk, SE1; ⏲10am-6pm Sun-Thu, to 10pm Fri & Sat; 📶; ⊖Southwark) One of London's most popular attractions, this outstanding modern and contemporary art gallery is housed in the creatively revamped **Bankside Power Station** south of the Millennium Bridge. An extension is under construction, aiming for a 2016 completion date.

The multimedia guides (£3.50) are worthwhile and there are free 45-minute guided tours of the collection's highlights (Level 3

MAPS

No Londoner would be without a pocket-sized *London A–Z* map-book – you can buy them at newsstands and shops everywhere. For getting around the London Underground system ('the tube'), maps are free at underground stations.

Westminster

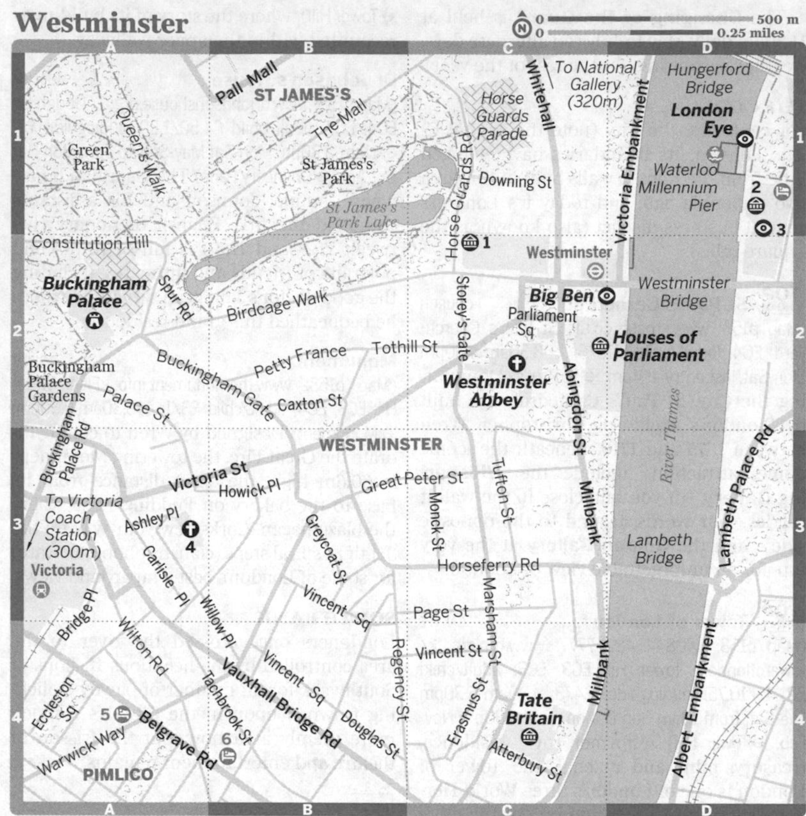

Westminster

Top Sights

Big Ben	C2
Buckingham Palace	A2
Houses of Parliament	C2
London Eye	D1
Tate Britain	C4
Westminster Abbey	C2

Sights

1 Churchill War Rooms	C2
2 London Dungeon	D1
3 Sea Life	D1
4 Westminster Cathedral	A3

Sleeping

5 easyHotel	A4
6 Luna Simone Hotel	B4
7 Premier Inn London County Hall	D1

at 11am and noon; Level 5 at 2pm and 3pm). Note the late-night opening hours on Friday and Saturday.

TOP CHOICE Shakespeare's Globe HISTORIC BUILDING
(Map p158; www.shakespearesglobe.com; 21 New Globe Walk SE1, SE1; adult/child £13.50/8; 9am-5.30pm; London Bridge) Completed in 1997, this authentic reconstruction recreates the original London theatre where many of Shakespeare's plays were performed. Admission includes the **exhibition hall** and **guided tour** of the theatre (departing every 15 to 30 minutes).

Plays are still performed here from April to October. As in Elizabethan times, 'groundlings' can watch in all-weather conditions (£5; seats £15 to £39) for the best views.

TOP CHOICE London Eye VIEWPOINT
(Map p166; 0871 781 3000; www.londoneye.com; adult/child £19.20/12.30; 10am-8pm; Waterloo)

This 135m-tall, slow-moving Ferris-wheel-like attraction is the tallest in the western hemisphere. Passengers ride in enclosed egg-shaped pods; the wheel takes 30 minutes to rotate completely, offering 25-mile views on clear days. Save money and shorten queues by buying tickets online, or cough up an extra £10 to show off your fast-track swagger.

FREE Imperial War Museum MUSEUM

(www.iwm.org.uk; Lambeth Rd, SE1; ⏲10am-6pm; ⊖Lambeth North) Fronted by a pair of intimidating 15in naval guns that could lob a 1938lb shell over 16 miles, this riveting war museum is housed in what was once Bethlehem Royal Hospital, known as Bedlam.

HMS Belfast SHIP

(Map p158; http://hmsbelfast.iwm.org.uk; Queen's Walk, SE1; adult/child £14.50/free; ⏲10am-5pm; ⊖London Bridge) White Ensign flapping on the Thames breeze, HMS *Belfast* is a magnet for naval-gazers. This large, light cruiser served in WWII, helping sink the German battleship *Scharnhorst* and shelling the Normandy coast on D-Day.

London Dungeon HISTORIC BUILDING

(Map p166; www.thedungeons.com/london; 28-34 Tooley St, SE1; adult/child £24.60/19.20; ⏲10am-5pm, extended hours during holidays; ⊖Westminster or Waterloo) The London Dungeon is all spooky music, ghostly boat rides, macabre hangman's drop-rides, fake blood and actors dressed up as torturers and gory criminals (including Jack the Ripper and Sweeney Todd).

Sea Life AQUARIUM

(Map p166; ☎0871 663 1678; www.sealife.co.uk/london; County Hall, SE1; adult/child £18/13; ⏲10am-6pm; 📶; ⊖Waterloo) One of the largest aquariums in Europe, Sea Life has all sorts of aquatic creatures organised into different zones (coral cave, rainforest, River Thames), culminating with the shark walkway. Check the website for shark-feeding times and book online for a 10% discount.

CHELSEA, KENSINGTON & KNIGHTSBRIDGE

It's called the Royal Borough of Kensington and Chelsea, and residents are certainly paid royally, earning the highest incomes in the UK (shops and restaurants will presume you do too).

FREE Natural History Museum MUSEUM

(Map p168; www.nhm.ac.uk; Cromwell Rd, SW7; ⏲10am-5.50pm; ⊖South Kensington) A sure-fire hit with kids of all ages, this splendid museum is crammed with fascinating archaeological discoveries, starting with the giant **Diplodocus** skeleton that greets you in the main hall.

FREE Victoria & Albert Museum MUSEUM

(V&A; Map p168; www.vam.ac.uk; Cromwell Rd, SW7; ⏲10am-5.45pm Sat-Thu, to 10pm Fri; ⊖South Kensington) Part of Prince Albert's legacy to Londoners in the wake of the Great Exhibition of 1851, this gargantuan museum houses the world's greatest collection of decorative arts, including the sumptuous **China Collection** and **Japan Gallery** (Rooms 44 and 47e, Level 1), the astonishing **Cast Courts** (Room 46a, Level 1) and the stunning **Jewellery Gallery** (Rooms 91–93, Level 3). You'll need to plan as the museum is epic, but it's open late on Friday evenings, with less crowds.

FREE Science Museum MUSEUM

(Map p168; www.sciencemuseum.org.uk; Exhibition Rd, SW7; ⏲10am-6pm; ⊖South Kensington) With seven floors of interactive and educational exhibits, this scientifically spellbinding museum will mesmerise even the most

LONDON'S NEW SKYSCRAPERS

The Olympic effect saw a sudden scramble for high-altitude towers in London. Most famous is **The Shard** (Map p158; www.the-shard.com; The Shard, 32 London Bridge St; adult/child £29.95/23.95; ⏲9am-10pm; ⊖London Bridge), rising over London Bridge like a vast glass splinter. The City of London's tallest building, the straight-edged **Heron Tower** (Map p158; 110 Bishopsgate EC2; ⊖Aldgate or Bank) was completed just up the road from **30 St Mary Axe** (The Gherkin; Map p158; www.30stmaryaxe.co.uk; 30 St Mary Axe EC3, EC3; ⊖Aldgate) in 2011. Aiming for a 2014 completion date, the top-heavy **Walkie Talkie** (20 Fenchuch St; Map p158; 20 Fenchurch St EC3, EC3) will be topped with a vast sky garden boasting magnificent views over town. Further construction on the concrete stub of the radical looking **Pinnacle** (Helter Skelter; Map p158; 22-24 Bishopgate; ⊖Aldgate or Bank) – nicknamed the Helter Skelter due to its cork-screwing top – was on hold at the the time of writing.

Hyde Park to Chelsea

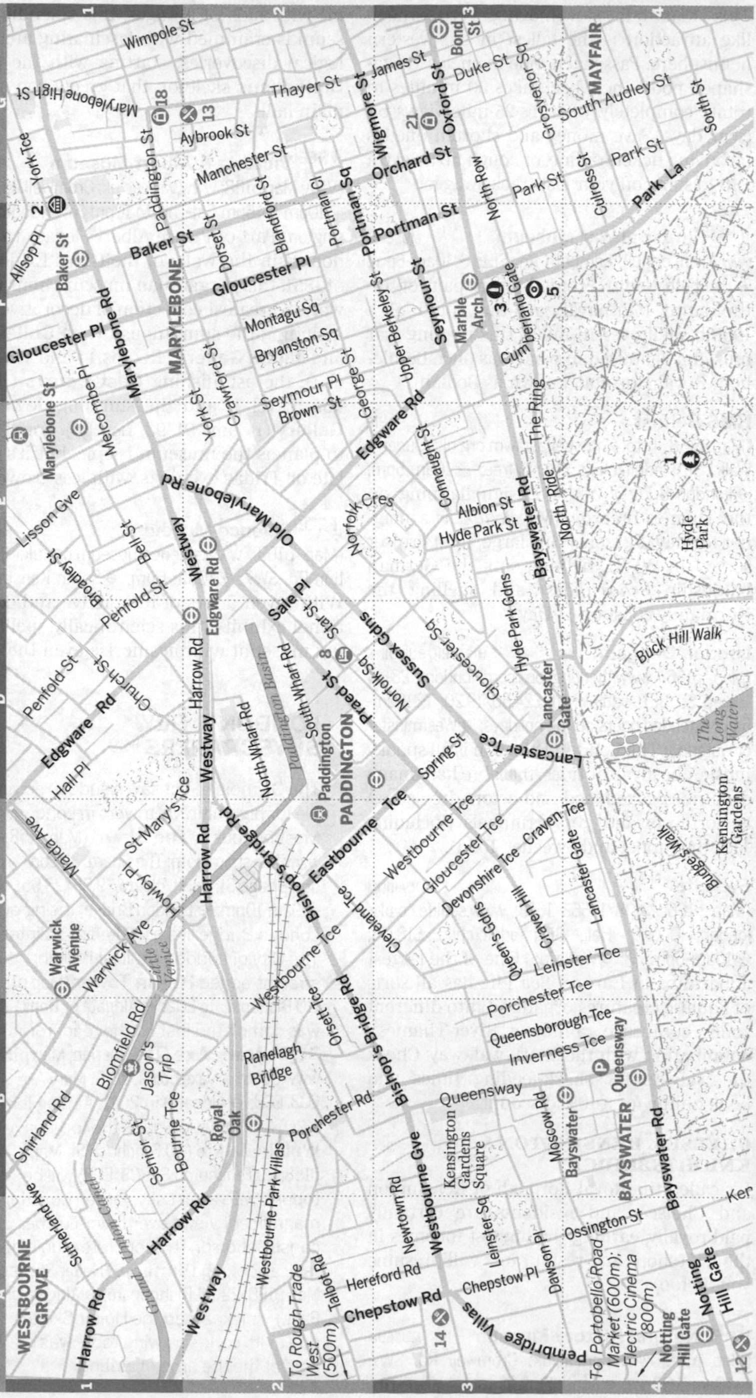

0 500 m
0 0.25 miles

A B C D E F G
1 2 3 4

WESTBOURNE GROVE
Sutherland Ave
Shirland Rd
Harrow Rd
Grand Union Canal
Senior St
Bourne Tce
Blomfield Rd
Jason's Trip
Warwick Avenue
Maida Ave
Warwick Ave
Little Venice
Howley Pl
St Mary's Tce
Westway
Royal Oak
Westbourne Park Villas
Ranelagh Bridge
Westbourne Tce
Harrow Rd
Westway
Edgware Rd
Hall Pl
Penfold St
Church St
Broadley St
Lisson Gve
Penfold St
Bell St
Marylebone St
Melcombe Pl
Gloucester Pl
Allsop Pl
Baker St
2
York Tce
Marylebone High St
Wimpole St
Marylebone Rd
Baker St
Paddington St
18
MARYLEBONE
13
Aybrook St
Harrow Rd
Westway
Edgware Rd
York St
Crawford St
Dorset St
Manchester St
Gloucester Pl
North Wharf Rd
Paddington Basin
South Wharf Rd
Sale Pl
Old Marylebone Rd
Seymour Pl
Brown St
Bryanston Sq
Montagu Sq
Blandford St
Thayer St
To Rough Trade West (500m)
Talbot Rd
Chepstow Rd
Hereford Rd
Porchester Rd
Orsett Tce
Bishop's Bridge Rd
Eastbourne Tce
Paddington
PADDINGTON
Praed St
8
Star St
Norfolk Cres
Edgware Rd
George St
Portman Cl
Portman Sq
Wigmore St
James St
Newtown Rd
Westbourne Gve
Bishop's Bridge Rd
Cleveland Tce
Norfolk Sq
Sussex Gdns
Upper Berkeley St
Orchard St
Portman St
21
Seymour St
Oxford St
Bond St
14
Kensington Gardens Square
Queensway
Westbourne Tce
Gloucester Tce
Spring St
Gloucester Sq
Connaught St
Marble Arch
Pembridge Villas
Chepstow Pl
Leinster Sq
Queen's Gdns
Devonshire Tce
Craven Hill
Craven Tce
Lancaster Tce
Hyde Park Gdns
Hyde Park St
Albion St
3
Cumberland Gate
North Row
Duke St
Dawson Pl
Moscow Rd
Bayswater
Inverness Tce
Queensborough Tce
Porchester Tce
Leinster Tce
Lancaster Gate
Lancaster Gate
Bayswater Rd
The Ring
5
Park St
Grosvenor Sq
North Ride
Culross St
South Audley St
MAYFAIR
To Portobello Road Market (600m); Electric Cinema (800m)
Ossington St
BAYSWATER
Queensway
Notting Hill Gate
Bayswater Rd
Notting Hill Gate
Budge's Walk
Buck Hill Walk
1
Hyde Park
Park La
Park St
South St
12
Ker
Kensington Gardens
The Long Water

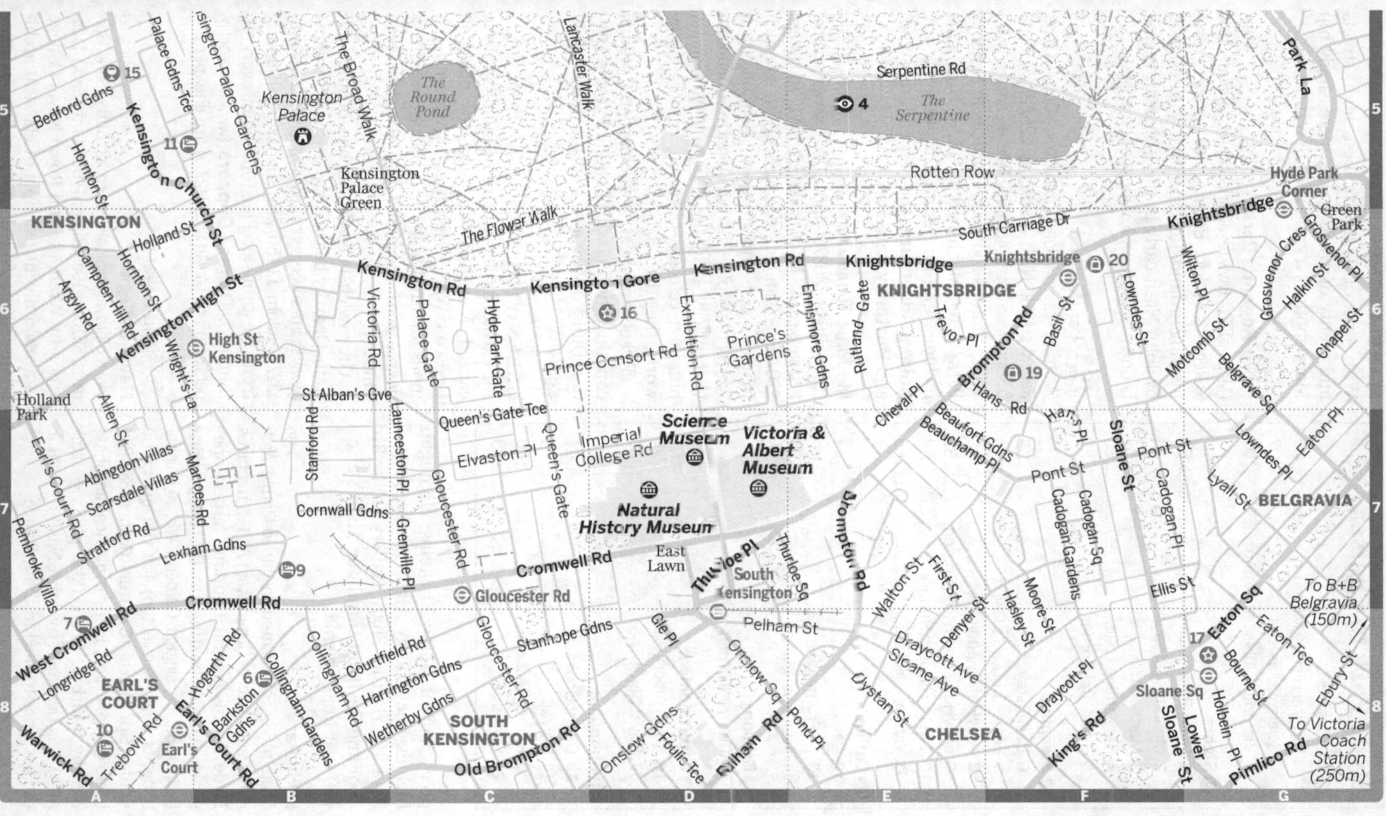

Palace Gdns Tce
Kensington Palace Gardens
The Broad Walk
The Round Pond
Lancaster Walk
Serpentine Rd
The Serpentine
Park La
Bedford Gdns
Kensington Church St
Kensington Palace
Hornton St
Kensington Palace Green
Rotten Row
Hyde Park Corner
Green Park
KENSINGTON
Holland St
The Flower Walk
South Carriage Dr
Knightsbridge
Grosvenor Cres
Grosvenor Pl
Campden Hill Rd
Hornton St
Kensington Rd
Kensington Gore
Kensington Rd
Knightsbridge
Knightsbridge
Lowndes St
Wilton Pl
Halkin St
Argyll Rd
Kensington High St
Victoria Rd
Palace Gate
Hyde Park Gate
Exhibition Rd
Ennismore Gdns
Rutland Gate
KNIGHTSBRIDGE
Trevor Pl
Brompton Rd
Basil St
Motcomb St
Chapel St
Wright's La
High St Kensington
Prince Consort Rd
Prince's Gardens
Belgrave Sq
Holland Park
Allen St
St Alban's Gve
Stanford Rd
Launceston Pl
Queen's Gate Tce
Cheval Pl
Hans Rd
Beaufort Gdns
Beauchamp Pl
Hans Pl
Sloane St
Lowndes Pl
Eaton Pl
Earl's Court Rd
Abingdon Villas
Scarsdale Villas
Marloes Rd
Elvaston Pl
Queen's Gate
Imperial College Rd
Science Museum
Victoria & Albert Museum
Pont St
Pont St
Cadogan Pl
Lyall St
BELGRAVIA
Pembroke Villas
Stratford Rd
Cornwall Gdns
Grenville Pl
Gloucester Rd
Natural History Museum
Brompton Rd
Cadogan Gardens
Cadogan Sq
Lexham Gdns
Cromwell Rd
East Lawn
Thurloe Pl
Thurloe Sq
South Kensington
Walton St
First St
Moore St
Hasley St
Ellis St
Eaton Sq
To B+B Belgravia (150m)
Cromwell Rd
Gloucester Rd
Pelham St
Denyer St
West Cromwell Rd
Hogarth Rd
Collingham Rd
Courtfield Rd
Stanhope Gdns
Gle Pl
Draycott Ave
Sloane Ave
Eaton Tce
Bourne St
Ebury St
Longridge Rd
EARL'S COURT
Barkston Gdns
Collingham Gardens
Harrington Gdns
Gloucester Rd
Onslow Sq
Oystan St
Draycott Pl
Sloane Sq
Holbein Pl
Wetherby Gdns
SOUTH KENSINGTON
Onslow Gdns
Foulis Tce
Pond Pl
CHELSEA
King's Rd
Sloane St
Lower
To Victoria Coach Station (250m)
Warwick Rd
Trebovir Rd
Earl's Court
Earl's Court Rd
Old Brompton Rd
Fulham Rd
Pimlico Rd

Hyde Park to Chelsea

Top Sights

Natural History Museum....................D7
Science Museum..............................D7
Victoria & Albert Museum.................D7

Sights

1 Hyde Park.......................................E4
2 Madame Tussauds...........................F1
3 Marble Arch.....................................F3
4 Serpentine Lake..............................E5
5 Speakers' Corner.............................F3

Sleeping

6 Base2stay..B8
7 easyHotel Earl's Court......................A8
8 easyHotel Paddington.......................D2
9 easyHotel South Kensington.............B7
10 Twenty Nevern Square....................A8
11 Vicarage Hotel................................A5

Eating

12 Geales...A4
13 La Fromagerie..................................G2
14 Taquería..A3

Drinking

15 Churchill Arms.................................A5

Entertainment

16 Royal Albert Hall..............................D6
17 Royal Court Theatre.........................G8

Shopping

18 Daunt Books....................................G1
19 Harrods...F6
20 Harvey Nichols.................................F6
21 Selfridges.......................................G3

precocious of young Einsteins. Highlights include the Energy Hall on the ground floor, the riveting Flight Gallery on the 3rd floor and the flight simulator. There's also a 450-seat Imax cinema.

Hyde Park PARK
(Map p168; 5.30am-midnight; Marble Arch, Hyde Park Corner or Queensway) At 145 hectares, Hyde Park is central London's largest open space. There's boating on the **Serpentine** (Map p168; Kensington Gardens, W8; Knightsbridge or South Kensington) for the energetic, while **Speakers' Corner** (Map p168; Park Lane; Marble Arch) is for oratorical acrobats. Nearby **Marble Arch** (Map p168; Marble Arch) was designed by John Nash in 1828 as the entrance to Buckingham Palace.

MARYLEBONE

With one of London's best high streets and plenty of green space, increasingly hip Marylebone is a great area to wander.

TOP CHOICE **Regent's Park** PARK
(Map p172; www.royalparks.org.uk; 5am-dusk; Regent's Park or Baker St) A former royal hunting ground, Regent's Park was designed by John Nash early in the 19th century and is one of London's loveliest open spaces.

TOP CHOICE **London Zoo** ZOO
(Map p172; www.londonzoo.co.uk; Outer Circle, Regent's Park, NW1; adult/child £25/19; 10am-5.30pm Mar-Oct, to 4pm Nov-Feb; Camden Town) These famous zoological gardens in Regent's Park were established in 1828. Highlights include **Penguin Beach**, **Gorilla Kingdom**, **Animal Adventure** (the new childrens' zoo) and **Butterfly Paradise**.

Madame Tussauds MUSEUM
(Map p168; 0870 400 3000; www.madame-tussauds.co.uk; Marylebone Rd, NW1; adult/child £30/26; 9am-7pm; Baker St) With so much fabulous free stuff to do in London, it's a wonder people still join lengthy queues to visit pricey Madame Tussauds waxworks, but in a celebrity-obsessed, camera-happy world, they do.

Tickets are cheaper when ordered online; combined tickets with London Eye and London Dungeon are also available (adult/child £65/48).

GREENWICH

An extraordinary cluster of buildings have earned 'Maritime Greenwich' its place on Unesco's World Heritage list. It's also famous for straddling the hemispheres; this is degree zero, the home of Greenwich Mean Time.

Greenwich is easily reached on the DLR train. Or go by boat: **Thames River Services** (www.thamesriverservices.co.uk; adult/child one-way £12/6, return £15.50/7.75) depart half-hourly from Westminster Pier (one hour, every 40 minutes). **Thames Clippers** (www.thamesclippers.com; adult/child £5.30/2.65) are cheaper.

FREE **Old Royal Naval College** HISTORIC BUILDING
(www.oldroyalnavalcollege.org; 2 Cutty Sark Gardens, SE10; 10am-5pm; DLR Cutty Sark) Designed by Wren, the Old Royal Naval College is a magnificent example of classical architecture. Yeomen-led tours of the complex

leave at 2pm daily, taking in areas not otherwise open to the public (£6, 90 minutes).

FREE **National Maritime Museum** MUSEUM
(http://www.rmg.co.uk/national-maritime-museum/; Romney Rd, SE10; 10am-5pm; DLR Cutty Sark) With its newly opened Sammy Ofer Wing, the National Maritime Museum houses a splendid collection of nautical paraphernalia recounting Britain's brine-soaked seafaring history.

WEST LONDON

Kew Gardens GARDENS
(www.kew.org.uk; Kew Rd; adult/child £16/free, Kew Explorer adult/child £4/2; 9.30am-6.30pm Apr-Aug, earlier closing Sep-Mar; Kew Bridge, Kew Gardens, boat Kew Pier) In 1759 botanists began rummaging around the world for specimens they could plant in the 3-hectare plot known as the Royal Botanic Gardens. They never stopped collecting, and the gardens, which have bloomed to 120 hectares, harbour the most comprehensive botanical collection on earth. The gardens are now a Unesco World Heritage site.

The gardens are easily reached by tube, but a more scenic option is the **Westminster Passenger Services Association** (020-7930 2062; www.wpsa.co.uk; adult/child return to Kew Gardens £18/9), which runs several daily boats from April to October, departing from Westminster Pier (return adult/child £18/9, 90 minutes).

Hampton Court Palace PALACE
(www.hrp.org.uk/HamptonCourtPalace; adult/child £17.60/8.80; 10am-6pm Apr-Oct, to 4.30pm Nov-Mar; Hampton Court, boat Hampton Court Palace) Built by Cardinal Thomas Wolsey in 1514 but coaxed from him by Henry VIII, Hampton Court Palace is England's largest and grandest Tudor structure. It's easily reached by train from Waterloo. Alternatively, the riverboats that head from Westminster to Kew continue here (return adult/child £22.50/11.25, three hours).

Tours

One of the best ways to orientate yourself when you first arrive in London is with a 24-hour hop-on/hop-off pass for the double-decker bus tours. The buses loop around interconnecting routes throughout the day, providing a commentary as they go, and the price includes a river cruise and three walking tours. You'll save a couple of pounds by booking online.

Original Tour BUS TOUR
(www.theoriginaltour.com; adult/child/family £26/13/91; every 20min 8.30am-5.30pm)

Big Bus Tours BUS TOUR
(www.bigbustours.com; adult/child £29/12/70; every 20min 8.30am-6pm Apr-Sept, to 5pm Oct & Mar, to 4.30pm Nov-Feb) Informative commentaries in eight languages. The ticket includes a free river cruise with City Cruise and four thematic walking tours (Royal London, Harry Potter film locations, the Beatles, and the Ghosts by Gaslight).

Festivals & Events

University Boat Race BOAT RACE
(www.theboatrace.org) A posh-boy grudge match held annually since 1829 between the rowing crews of Oxford and Cambridge Universities (late March).

London Marathon RUNNING RACE
(www.london-marathon.co.uk) Up to half a million spectators watch the whippet-thin champions and bizarrely clad amateurs take to the streets in late April.

Trooping the Colour ROYAL PARADE
This ceremonial procession of troops celebrates the Queen's official birthday in June.

Meltdown Festival MUSIC
(www.southbankcentre.co.uk) A musician-curated program of concerts, talks and films in late June.

LONDON'S OLYMPIC LEGACY

From 2008, a huge, once-contaminated and largely neglected swathe of industrial East London was ambitiously regenerated and transformed into London's **Olympic Park** (http://noordinarypark.co.uk; Stratford) for the 2012 Games.

Alongside the iconic sporting venues, the Queen Elizabeth Olympic Park also incorporates wetlands, woodlands, meadows and other wildlife habitats. The twisted, abstract tangle of metal overlooking everything is the **ArcelorMittal Orbit**, aka the 'Hubble Bubble Pipe', a 115m-high observation tower that opened during the games.

Panoramic views of the Olympic Park can also be had from the **View Tube** (www.theviewtube.co.uk; Greenway; 9am-5pm; DLR Pudding Mill Lane) on the Greenway, next to the park.

Camden

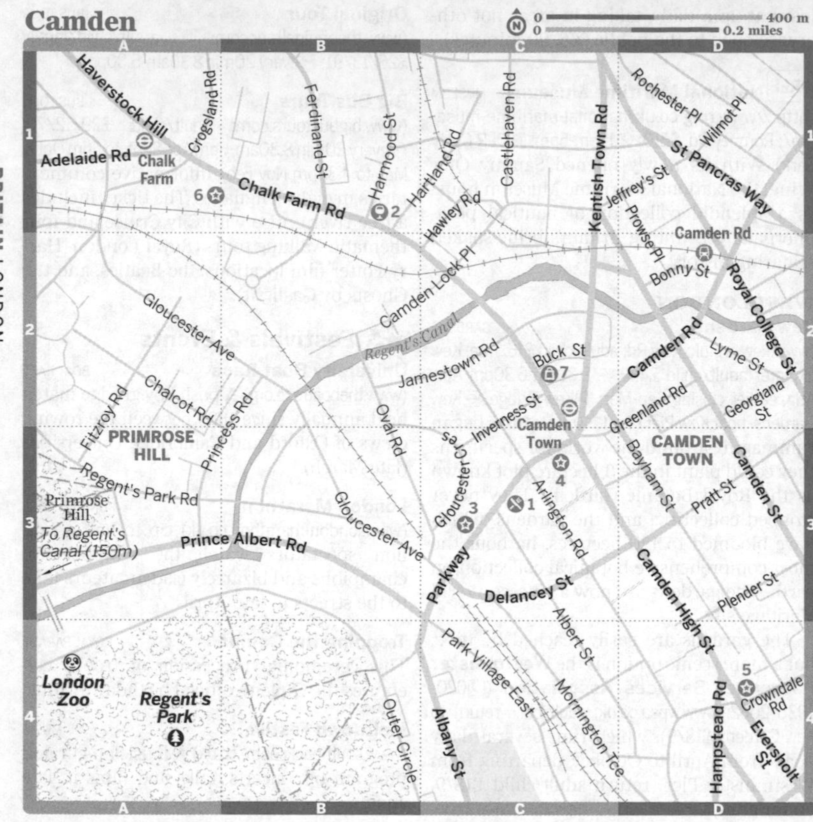

Wimbledon Lawn Tennis Championships TENNIS
(www.wimbledon.com) The world's most splendid tennis event takes place in late June.

Pride GAY & LESBIAN
(www.pridelondon.org) The big event on the gay and lesbian calendar, a technicolour street parade heads through the West End in late June or early July, culminating in a concert in Trafalgar Square.

Notting Hill Carnival STREET PARADES
(www.thenottinghillcarnival.com) Held over two days in August, this is London's most vibrant outdoor carnival.

Sleeping

When it comes to accommodation, London is one of the most expensive places in the world. 'Budget' is pretty much anything below £90 per night for a double; double rooms ranging between £90 and £180 per night are considered midrange; more expensive options fall into the top-end category. Public transport is good, so you don't need to be sleeping at Buckingham Palace to be at the heart of things.

WEST END & WESTMINSTER

Like in Monopoly, land on a Mayfair hotel and you may have to sell your house, or at least remortgage.

B+B Belgravia B&B ££
(020-7259 8570; www.bb-belgravia.com; 64-66 Ebury St, SW1; d/apt from £84/225, studio £89-140; @; Victoria) This lovely place marries contemporary chic with Georgian elegance. Studio rooms with compact kitchens are along the road at No 82.

Oxford St YHA HOSTEL £
(Map p162; 7734 1618; www.yha.org.uk; 14 Noel St, W1; dm/tw from £18/46; @; Oxford Circus) Bog-standard YHA hostel, with tidy rooms

Camden

Top Sights

London Zoo....A4
Regent's Park....A4

Eating

1 Market....C3

Drinking

2 Lock Tavern....B1

Entertainment

3 Dublin Castle....C3
4 Jazz Café....C3
5 KOKO....D4
6 Roundhouse....A1

Shopping

7 Camden Market....C2

and the usual facilities (kitchen, TV room, laundry), but with a terrific (albeit noisy) location and views over London's rooftops from some rooms.

Luna Simone Hotel B&B ££
(Map p166; ☎020-7834 5897; www.lunasimonehotel.com; 47-49 Belgrave Rd, SW1; s £70-75, d £95-120; @; ⊖Pimlico) Rooms are quite compact, but clean and calming at this central, welcoming hotel; the ones at the back are quieter.

THE CITY

Travelodge Liverpool Street HOTEL ££
(Map p158; ☎0871 984 6190; 1 Harrow Pl, E1; ⊖Aldgate) This branch of the budget hotel chain charges £75 to £105, and offers the usual generic facilities.

YHA London St Paul's HOSTEL £
(Map p158; ☎7236 4965; www.yha.org.uk; 36 Carter Lane , EC4; dm £17-25, d £40-50; @; ⊖St Paul 's) This 208-bed heritage hostel stands in the shadow of St Paul's Cathedral. There's a licensed cafeteria but no kitchen (plus a lot of stairs and no lift).

SOUTH BANK

Immediately south of the river is good if you want to immerse yourself in workaday London and still be central.

Premier Inn London County Hall HOTEL ££
(Map p166; ☎0871 527 8648; www.premierinn.com; County Hall, Belvedere Rd; r £112-160; ; ⊖Waterloo) Location, location, location is what this chain hotel is all about, with a choice position within a landmark historic building and a few steps from the London Eye, Westminster and Big Ben.

St Christopher's Village HOSTEL £
(Map p158; ☎020-7939 9710; www.st-christophers.co.uk; 163 Borough High St, SE1; dm/r from £14/62; @; ⊖London Bridge) The Village – a huge, up-for-it party hostel, with a club hopping till 4am at weekends and a roof terrace bar – is the main hub of three locations on the same street. **St Christopher's Inn** (Map p158; 121 Borough High St , SE1) is above a very nice pub, while **Oasis** (Map p162; 59-61 Borough High St, SE1) is women-only.

CHELSEA, KENSINGTON & KNIGHTSBRIDGE

These classy zones offer easy access to the museums and big-name fashion stores. It's all a bit sweetie-darling, along with the prices.

Vicarage Hotel B&B ££
(Map p168; ☎020-7229 4030; www.londonvicaragehotel.com; 10 Vicarage Gate, W8; s/d £110/138, without bathroom £65/110; @; ⊖High St Kensington or Notting Hill Gate) On the corner with Palace Gardens Tce (with its astonishing cherry trees in spring), this place is all about location (between Notting Hill Gate and Kensington High St) and value for money.

BLOOMSBURY & ST PANCRAS

One step from the West End and crammed with Georgian townhouse conversions, are these more affordable neighbourhoods.

TOP CHOICE **Clink78** HOSTEL £
(Map p174; ☎020-7183 9400; www.clinkhostels.com; 78 King's Cross Rd, WC1; dm/r from £9/40; @; ⊖King's Cross St Pancras) If anyone can think of a more right-on London place to stay than the courthouse where The Clash went on trial, please let us know. You can watch TV from the witness box or sleep in the converted cells or purpose-built rooms.

WANT MORE?

For in-depth information, reviews and recommendations at your fingertips, head to the Apple App Store to purchase Lonely Planet's *London City Guide* iPhone app.

Alternatively, head to **Lonely Planet** (www.lonelyplanet.com/england/london) for planning advice, author recommendations, traveller reviews and insider tips.

Bloomsbury & St Pancras

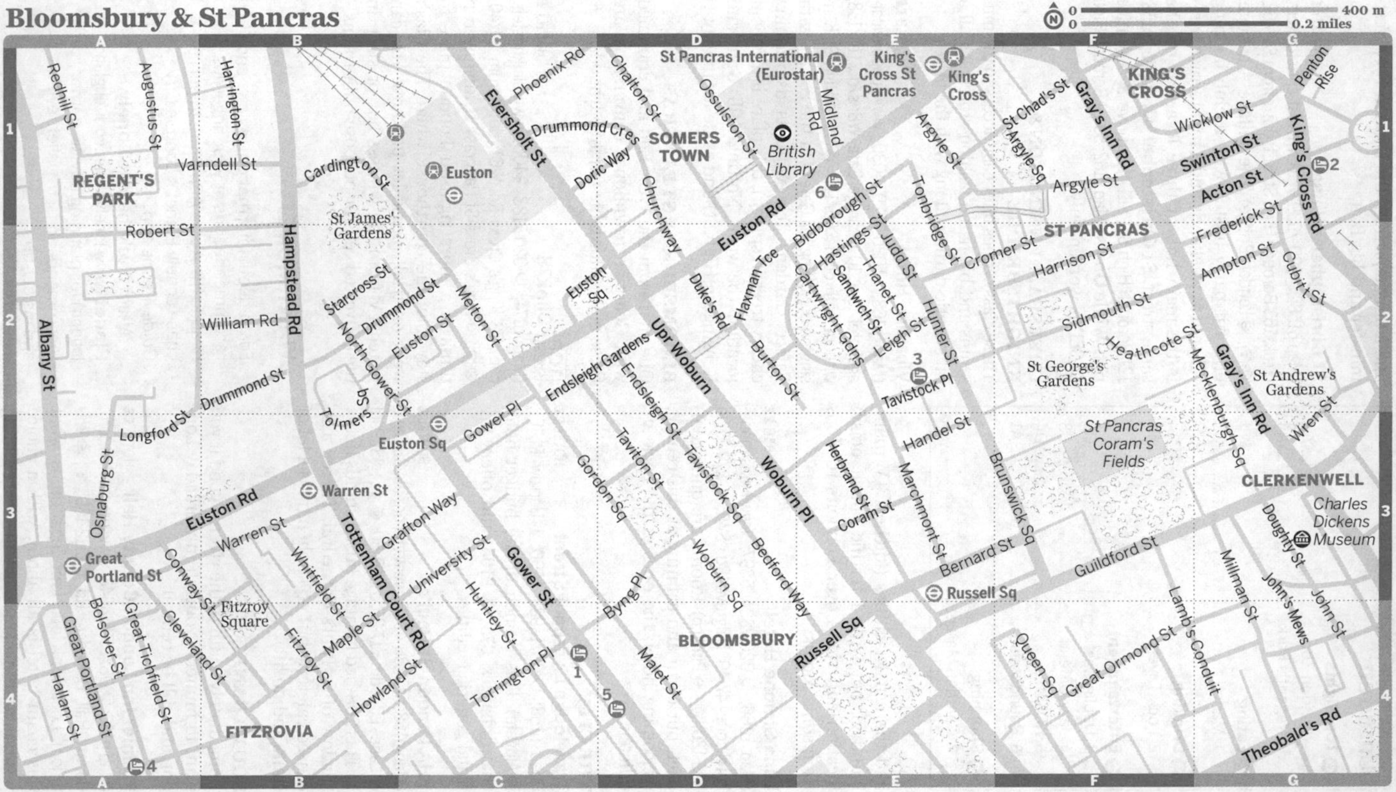

0 400 m
0 0.2 miles

Redhill St
Augustus St
Harrington St
Varndell St
REGENT'S PARK
Robert St
Albany St
William Rd
Drummond St
Longford St
Osnaburg St
Great Portland St
Bolsover St
Great Portland St
Great Tichfield St
Hallam St
Conway St
Cleveland St
Fitzroy Square
FITZROVIA
4
Hampstead Rd
Cardington St
Euston
St James' Gardens
Starcross St
Drummond St
North Gower St
Euston St
Tolmers Sq
Euston Sq
Warren St
Euston Rd
Warren St
Whitfield St
Fitzroy St
Maple St
Howland St
Tottenham Court Rd
Grafton Way
University St
Huntley St
Melton St
Gower Pl
Eversholt St
Phoenix Rd
Drummond Cres
Doric Way
Chalton St
SOMERS TOWN
Churchway
Euston Sq
Endsleigh Gardens
Endsleigh St
Gordon Sq
Tavinton St
Gower St
Torrington Pl
1
5
Byng Pl
Malet St
Upr Woburn
Ossulston St
St Pancras International (Eurostar)
British Library
Midland Rd
6
Euston Rd
Duke's Rd
Flaxman Tce
Burton St
Tavistock Sq
Woburn Sq
Woburn Pl
Bedford Way
BLOOMSBURY
Russell Sq
King's Cross St Pancras
King's Cross
Bidborough St
Hastings St
Cartwright Gdns
Sandwich St
Thanet St
Judd St
Leigh St
Hunter St
Tonbridge St
3
Tavistock Pl
Handel St
Herbrand St
Coram St
Marchmont St
Bernard St
Russell Sq
Argyle St
St Chad's St
Argyle Sq
Argyle St
Cromer St
ST PANCRAS
Harrison St
Sidmouth St
Heathcote St
St George's Gardens
Brunswick Sq
St Pancras Coram's Fields
Guildford St
Queen Sq
Great Ormond St
Gray's Inn Rd
KING'S CROSS
Wicklow St
Swinton St
Acton St
Frederick St
Ampton St
Mecklenburgh Sq
Gray's Inn Rd
St Andrew's Gardens
Wren St
CLERKENWELL
Charles Dickens Museum
Doughty St
Millman St
Lamb's Conduit
John's Mews
John St
Theobald's Rd
King's Cross Rd
2
Cubitt St
Penton Rise

Bloomsbury & St Pancras

Sleeping

1 Arosfa Hotel C4
2 Clink78 ..... G1
3 Generator E2
4 London Central YHA A4
5 Ridgemount Hotel D4
6 YHA London St Pancras E1

Arosfa Hotel B&B ££
(Map p174; ☎7636 2115; www.arosfalondon.com; 83 Gower St, WC1; s/d/tr/q £72/107/130/160; ⊖Goodge St) While the decor of the immaculately presented rooms is more unnoticeable, Arosfa's guest lounge is blinged up with chandeliers and clear plastic chairs.

Ridgemount Hotel B&B £
(Map p174; ☎7636 1141; www.ridgemounthotel.co.uk; 65-67 Gower St, WC1; s/d/tr/q £67/98/123/136, without bathroom £52/78/102/124; @; ⊖Goodge St) About half of this hotel's 30 utilitarian rooms have bathrooms; there are a number of triples and quadruples that will be useful for groups of friends and families.

London Central YHA HOSTEL £
(Map p174; ☎0845 371 9154; www.yha.org.uk; 104-108 Bolsover St, W1; dm £21-32, q from £70; @; ⊖Great Portland St) One of London's new breed of YHA hostels, most of the four- to six-bed rooms have en suites. There's a flash cafe-bar attached to reception and a wheelchair-accessible kitchen downstairs.

YHA London St Pancras HOSTEL £
(Map p174; ☎020-7388 9998; www.yha.org.uk; 79 Euston Rd, NW1; dm/r from £20/61; @; ⊖King's Cross St Pancras) Recent renovations have made this 185-bed hostel a dependable central London choice – despite the busy road. Rooms range from private doubles to six-bed dorms; most have bathrooms. There's a bar and cafe but no kitchen.

Generator HOSTEL £
(Map p174; ☎7388 7666; www.generatorhostels.com/London; 37 Tavistock Pl, WC1; dm/r from £12/50; @; ⊖Russell Sq) This former police barracks has 820 beds; a bar that stays open until 2am; safe-deposit boxes; and a large eating area (but no kitchen). Come to party.

EARL'S COURT & FULHAM

Earl's Court is lively, cosmopolitan and so popular with travelling antipodeans that it's been nicknamed Kangaroo Valley.

Barclay House B&B ££
(☎020-7384 3390; www.barclayhouselondon.com; 21 Barclay Rd, SW6; r £110-125; @; ⊖Fulham Broadway) A proper homestay B&B with a handful of rooms with en suite in a charming Victorian townhouse. Its popularity means there's a four-night minimum stay requirement.

Twenty Nevern Square HOTEL ££
(Map p168; ☎020-7565 9555; www.20nevernsquare.com; 20 Nevern Sq, SW5; r from £115; ; ⊖Earl's Court) An Ottoman theme runs through this Victorian townhouse hotel, where a mix of wooden furniture, luxurious fabrics and natural light helps maximise space, even in the excellent-value cheaper rooms.

Base2stay HOTEL ££
(Map p168; ☎020-7244 2255; www.base2stay.com; 25 Courtfield Gardens, SW5; s/d from £93/99; @; ⊖Earl's Court) With comfort, smart decor, power showers, flat-screen TVs with internet access, artfully concealed kitchenettes, neat rooms and a sustainable credo, this boutique establishment feels like a four-star hotel without the wallet-emptying price tag.

easyHotel HOTEL £
(www.easyhotel.com; r from £45) Earl's Court (Map p168; 44 West Cromwell Rd, SW5; ⊖Earl's Court); Paddington (Map p168; 10 Norfolk Pl, W2; ⊖Paddington); South Kensington (Map p168; 14 Lexham Gardens, W8; ⊖Gloucester Rd); Victoria (Map p166; 36 Belgrave Rd, SW1; ⊖Victoria) Run along the same principles as its sibling business easyJet, this no-frills chain has tiny rooms with even tinier bathrooms.

HOXTON, SHOREDITCH & EAST END

Hoxton Hotel HOTEL ££
(Map p158; ☎020-7550 1000; www.hoxtonhotels.com; 81 Great Eastern St, EC2; d & tw £59-199; @; ⊖Old St) A revolutionary pricing structure means that while all the rooms are identical, the hotel aims at constantly full occupancy. Book a couple of months ahead and you can nab £49 to £69 deals.

AIRPORTS

Yotel HOTEL £
(☎020-7100 1100; www.yotel.com; s/d £69/85, or per 4hr £29/45 then per additional hour £8; @) Gatwick (South Terminal); Heathrow (Terminal 4) The best news for early morning flyers since coffee-vending machines, Yotel's tiny 'cabins' offer pint-sized luxury: comfy beds, soft lights, internet-connected TVs, monsoon showers and fluffy towels.

Eating

Dining out in London has become so fashionable that you can hardly open a menu without banging into a celebrity chef, while the range and quality of eating options has increased massively over the last few decades.

WEST END

Between them, Mayfair, Soho and Covent Garden are the gastronomic heart of London, with stacks of restaurants and cuisines at a wide range of budgets.

Great Queen Street BRITISH ££
(Map p162; ☎7242 0622; 32 Great Queen St, WC2; mains £12-16; ⊙lunch daily, dinner till 10.30 Mon-Sat; ⊖Holborn) The claret-coloured walls and mismatched wooden chairs convey cosiness and tie-loosening informality, but the daily changing seasonal menu is still the very best of British, and booking is a must.

Abeno Too JAPANESE £
(Map p162; www.abeno.co.uk; 17-18 Great Newport St, WC2; mains £8-13; ⊖Leicester Sq) This restaurant specialises in *soba* (noodles) and *okonomi-yaki* (Japanese-style pancakes), which are cooked in front of you on a hotplate.

Fernandez & Wells Espresso Bar CAFE £
(Map p162; ☎020-7494 4242; 16a St Anne's Crt, W1; ⊖Oxford Circus) A wonderful Soho mini-chain. The Cafe and the Espresso Bar both do sandwiches and incredibly good coffee.

Hummus Bros CAFE £
(www.hbros.co.uk; mains £4-8;) Soho (Map p162; 88 Wardour St, W1; ⊖Piccadilly Circus); Holborn (37-63 Southampton Row, W1; ; ⊖Holborn); Cheapside (Map p158; 128 Cheapside, EC2; ⊖St Paul's) Don't come here if you're chickpea-challenged, because this informal place is hummus heaven.

Salt Yard TAPAS ££
(Map p162; ☎020-7637 0657; www.saltyard.co.uk; 54 Goodge St, W1; tapas £4-8; ⊖Goodge St) Named after the place where cold meats are cured, this softly lit joint serves delicious Spanish and Italian tapas.

SOUTH BANK

For a feed with a local feel, head to Borough Market or Bermondsey St.

Laughing Gravy BRITISH ££
(Map p158; ☎020-7998 1707; www.thelaughinggravy.co.uk; 154 Blackfriars Rd, SE1; mains £8.50-17.50; ⊙11am-late Mon-Fri, 5.30pm-late Sat, noon-6pm Sun; ⊖Southwark) This restaurant is a Southwark gem, with a sure-fire menu combining locally sourced food and culinary talent, plus splendid roasts on Sunday and attentive service all round.

Anchor & Hope PUB ££
(Map p158; 36 The Cut, SE1; mains £12-20; ⊙noon-2.30pm Tue-Sat, 6-10.30pm Mon-Sat, 2pm lunch Sun; ⊖Southwark) The hope is that you'll get a table without waiting hours because you can't book at this quintessential gastropub, except for Sunday lunch at 2pm.

NOTTING HILL, BAYSWATER & PADDINGTON

Taquería MEXICAN £
(Map p168; www.taqueria.co.uk; 139-143 Westbourne Grove; tacos from £4.10; ⊙noon-11pm Mon-Thu, noon-11.30pm Fri, 10am-11.30pm Sat, noon-10.30pm Sun; ; ⊖Notting Hill Gate) You won't find fresher, limper (they're not supposed to be crispy!) tacos anywhere in London because they're made on the premises.

Geales SEAFOOD ££
(Map p168; ☎7727 7528; www.geales.com; 2 Farmer St, W8; 2/3-course lunch £11.95/14.95, mains £10.95-22.95; ⊙closed lunch Mon; ⊖Notting Hill Gate) Since 1939 Geales has enjoyed fame for its succulent fish and chips.

MARYLEBONE

La Fromagerie CAFE ££
(Map p168; www.lafromagerie.co.uk; 2-6 Moxon St, W1; mains £7-16.50; ⊙8am-7.30pm Mon-Fri, 9am-7pm Sat, 10am-6pm Sun; ⊖Baker St) This deli-cafe has bowls of delectable salads, antipasto, peppers and beans scattered about the long communal table.

CLERKENWELL & FARRINGDON

Clerkenwell's hidden gems are well worth digging for; Exmouth Market is a good place to start.

St John BRITISH ££
(Map p158; ☎020-7251 0848; www.stjohnrestaurant.com; 26 St John St, EC1; mains £17-23; ⊖Farringdon) Nose-to-tail offerings such as chitterlings and ox tongue at this modern London classic.

Little Bay EUROPEAN £
(Map p158; ☎020-7278 1234; www.little-bay.co.uk; 171 Farringdon Rd, EC1; mains before/after 7pm £6.45/8.45; ⊖Farringdon) Weird but fun bistro: expect a crushed-velvet ceiling, elaborately painted bar and hearty, good-value food.

CAMDEN TOWN

Camden's great for cheap eats, while neighbouring Chalk Farm and Primrose Hill are salted with gastropubs and upmarket restaurants.

TOP CHOICE **Market** MODERN BRITISH ££

(Map p172; ☎020-7267 9700; www.marketrestaurant.co.uk; 43 Parkway, NW1; 2-course lunch £10, mains £10-14; ⏰noon-2.30 & 6-10.30pm Mon-Sat, 1-3.30pm Sun; ⊖Camden Town) This fabulous restaurant is an ode to great, simple British food with a hint of European thrown in.

HOXTON, SHOREDITCH & SPITALFIELDS

From the hit-and-miss Bangladeshi restaurants of Brick Lane to the Vietnamese strip on Kingsland Rd, the East End's cuisine is as multicultural as its residents.

Albion BRITISH £

(Map p158; www.albioncaff.co.uk; 2-4 Boundary St, E2; mains £9-13; ⏰8am-11pm; 📶; ⊖Old St) This self consciously retro 'caff' serves up top-quality bangers and mash, steak-and-kidney pies, devilled kidneys and, of course, fish and chips.

Sông Quê VIETNAMESE £

(www.songque.co.uk; 134 Kingsland Rd, E2; mains £6-9; ⊖Hoxton) Arrive after 7.30pm and you can expect to queue: this humble eatery is one of the best Vietnamese restaurants in London, and you'll be shunted out shortly after your last bite.

Princess of Shoreditch PUB ££

(Map p158; ☎020 7729 9270; www.theprincessofshoreditch.com; 76 Paul St; mains £10-18.50; 📶; ⊖Old St) The Princess can get busy thanks to its excellent gastropub menu, fine wine list, choice ales and good-looking interior.

Cafe Bangla BANGLADESHI £

(Map p158; 128 Brick Lane, E1; mains £5-15; ⊖Liverpoool St) Among the hordes of practically interchangeable curry houses on Brick Lane, this one stands out for quality.

Drinking

As long as there's been a city, Londoners have loved to drink – and, as history shows, often immoderately.

WEST END

Gordon's Wine Bar BAR

(Map p162; www.gordonswinebar.com; 47 Villiers St, WC2; ⏰11am-11pm Mon-Sat, noon-10pm Sun; ⊖Embankment) What's not to love about this cavernous, candlelit wine cellar that's practically unchanged for the last 120 years? Get here before the office crowd (generally around 6pm) or forget about getting a table.

French House BAR

(Map p162; http://frenchhousesoho.com; 49 Dean St, W1; ⏰noon-11pm Mon-Sat, to 10.30pm Sun; ⊖Leicester Sq) French House is Soho's legendary boho boozer with a history to match: Dylan Thomas, Peter O'Toole and Francis Bacon all frequently ended up on the wooden floors.

Princess Louise PUB

(Map p162; 208 High Holborn, WC1; ⏰11.30am-11pm Mon-Fri, noon-11pm Sat, to 10.30pm Sun; ⊖Holborn) This late-19th-century Victorian boozer is arguably London's most beautiful pub.

Lamb & Flag PUB

(Map p162; lambandflagcoventgarden.co.uk; 33 Rose St, WC2; ⏰11am-11pm Mon-Sat, noon-10.30pm Sun; ⊖Covent Garden) Everyone's Covent Garden 'find', this historic pub is often as jammed with punters as it is packed with history. Built in 1623 and formerly called the 'Bucket of Blood', inside it's all brass fittings and creaky wooden floors.

THE CITY & EAST END

Book Club BAR

(Map p158; ☎020-7684 8618; www.wearetbc.com; 100 Leonard St; ⏰8am-midnight Mon-Wed, 8am-2am Thu & Fri, 10am-2am Sat & Sun; 📶; ⊖Old St) One-time Victorian warehouse in Shoreditch that hosts cultural events and DJ nights to complement the drinking, ping-pong and pool-playing.

Jerusalem Tavern PUB

(Map p158; www.stpetersbrewery.co.uk; 55 Britton St, EC1; 📶; ⊖Farringdon) This tiny 1720 coffee shop-turned-inn (named after the Priory of St John of Jerusalem) serves St Peter's fantastic beers and ales, brewed in North Suffolk.

Ten Bells PUB

(Map p158; cnr Commercial & Fournier Sts, E1; ⊖Liverpool St) Landmark Victorian is famous for being one of Jack the Ripper's pick-up joints.

Ye Olde Cheshire Cheese PUB

(Map p158; Wine Office Crt, 145 Fleet St EC4, EC4; ⏰11am-11pm Mon-Fri, from noon Sat; ⊖Chancery Lane) Rebuilt six years after the Great Fire, this hoary pub was popular with Dr Johnson, Thackeray, Dickens and the visiting Mark Twain.

SOUTH BANK

George Inn PUB

(Map p158; www.nationaltrust.org.uk/main/w-georgeinn; 77 Borough High St SE1, SE1; ⏲11am-11pm; ⊖London Bridge) This glorious old boozer is London's last surviving galleried coaching inn, dating from 1676 and now a National Trust property.

Anchor PUB

(Map p158; 34 Park St, SE1; ⏲11am-11pm Sun-Wed, to midnight Thu-Sat; ⊖London Bridge) This 18th-century riverside boozer replaced the 1615 original where Samuel Pepys witnessed the Great Fire.

NOTTING HILL, BAYSWATER & PADDINGTON

Churchill Arms PUB

(Map p168; www.churchillarmskensington.co.uk; 119 Kensington Church St; ⏲11am-11pm Mon-Wed, 11am-midnight Thu-Sat, noon-10.30pm Sun; 📶; ⊖Notting Hill Gate) Adorned with a gob-smacking array of flower baskets and Union Jacks, this magnificent old boozer on Kensington Church St is a London classic.

CAMDEN TOWN

Lock Tavern PUB

(Map p172; www.lock-tavern.co.uk; 35 Chalk Farm Rd, NW1; ⏲noon-midnight Mon-Thu, to 1am Fri & Sat, to 11pm Sun; ⊖Chalk Farm) The archetypal Camden pub, the Lock has both a rooftop terrace and a beer garden.

☆ Entertainment

Theatre

London is a world capital for theatre and there's a lot more than mammoth musicals to tempt you into the West End. On performance days, you can buy half-price tickets for West End productions (cash only) from the official agency **tkts** (Map p162; www.tkts.co.uk; Leicester Sq, WC2; ⏲10am-7pm Mon-Sat, noon-4pm Sun; ⊖Leicester Sq). The booth is the one with the clock tower; beware of touts selling dodgy tickets. For more, see www.officiallondontheatre.co.uk or www.theatremonkey.com.

Royal Court Theatre THEATRE

(Map p168; ☎020-7565 5000; www.royalcourttheatre.com; Sloane Sq, SW1; ⊖Sloane Sq) Progressive theatre and champion of new talent.

National Theatre THEATRE

(Map p158; ☎020-7452 3000; www.nationaltheatre.org.uk; South Bank, SE1; ⊖Waterloo) Cheaper tickets for classics and new plays from some of the world's best companies.

Royal Shakespeare Company THEATRE

(RSC; ☎0844 800 1110; www.rsc.org.uk) Productions of the Bard's classics and other quality stuff.

Old Vic THEATRE

(Map p158; ☎0844 871 7628; www.oldvictheatre.com; The Cut, SE1; ⊖Waterloo) Kevin Spacey continues his run as artistic director (and occasional performer) at this venue, which features classic, highbrow drama.

Donmar Warehouse THEATRE

(Map p162; ☎0844 871 7624; www.donmarwarehouse.com; 41 Earlham St, WC2; ⊖Covent Garden) A not-for-profit company that has forged itself a West End reputation.

Young Vic THEATRE

(Map p158; ☎020-7922 2922; www.youngvic.org; 66 The Cut, SE1; ⊖Waterloo) One of the capital's most respected theatre troupes – bold, brave and talented – the Young Vic stages winning performances.

Nightclubs

Clubland is no longer confined to the West End, with megaclubs scattered throughout the city wherever there's a venue big enough, cheap enough or quirky enough to hold them. The big nights are Friday and Saturday. Admission prices vary widely; it's often cheaper to arrive early or prebook tickets.

Fabric CLUB

(Map p158; www.fabriclondon.com; 77a Charterhouse St, EC1; admission £8-18; ⏲10pm-6am Fri, 11pm-8am Sat, 11pm-6am Sun; ⊖Farringdon) Consistently rated by DJs as one of the world's greatest, Fabric has three dance floors that occupy a converted meat coldstore opposite the Smithfield meat market.

Plastic People CLUB

(Map p158; www.plasticpeople.co.uk; 147-149 Curtain Rd, EC2; admission £5-10; ⏲10pm-3.30am Fri & Sat, to 2am Sun; ⊖Old St) Taking the directive 'underground club' literally, Plastic People provides a low-ceilinged subterranean den of dubsteppy, wonky, funky, no-frills fun times.

Ministry of Sound CLUB

(Map p158; www.ministryofsound.com; 103 Gaunt St, SE1; admission £16-25; ⏲11pm-6.30am Fri & Sat; ⊖Elephant & Castle) Where the global brand started; it's London's most famous club and still packs in a diverse crew with big local and international names.

GAY & LESBIAN LONDON

The West End, particularly Soho, is the visible centre of gay and lesbian London, with numerous venues clustered around Old Compton St – but many other areas have their own mini-scenes.

To find out what's going on pick up the free press from a venue (Pink Paper, Boyz, QX). The gay section of *Time Out* is useful, as are www.gaydarnation.com (for men) and www.gingerbeer.co.uk (for women). Some venues to get you started are listed here:

Candy Bar (Map p162; www.ku-bar.co.uk; 4 Carlisle St, W1; 3pm-3am Mon & Wed-Fri, from 1pm Sat, 1-9.30pm Sun; Tottenham Court Rd) Long-running lesbian hang-out.

G-A-Y (www.g-a-y.co.uk) G-A-Y Bar (Map p162; 30 Old Compton St, W1; Leicester Sq); G-A-Y Late (Map p162; 5 Goslett Yard, WC2; 11pm-3am; Tottenham Court Road); G-A-Y Club@Heaven (Map p162; The Arches, Villiers St, WC2; 11pm-4am Thu-Sat; Charing Cross) G-A-Y now operates bars and club nights at one of gaydom's most internationally famous venues, Heaven.

George & Dragon (Map p158; 2 Hackney Rd , E2; Old Street) Appealing corner pub where the crowd is often as eclectically furnished as the venue.

Popstarz (Map p162; www.popstarz.org; The Den, 18 West Central St, WC1; 10pm-4am Fri; Tottenham Court Rd) This grand dame of gay indie has been revitalised by a recent transfer to the heart of the West End. It's popular with a studenty, friendly, mixed crowd. There are three rooms of great indie pop.

Royal Vauxhall Tavern (RVT; www.rvt.org.uk; 372 Kennington Lane, SE11; admission free-£9; Vauxhall) Much-loved pub with crazy cabaret and drag acts.

Cargo CLUB
(Map p158; www.cargo-london.com; 83 Rivington St, EC2; admission free-£16; Old St) Cargo is one of London's most eclectic clubs. Under its brick railway arches you'll find a dance-floor room, bar and outside terrace.

Live Music

KOKO CONCERT VENUE
(Map p172; www.koko.uk.com; 1a Camden High St, NW1; 7-11pm Sun-Thu, to 4am Fri & Sat; Mornington Cres) Occupying the grand Camden Palace theatre, KOKO hosts live bands most nights and the regular Club NME (New Musical Express; £5) on Friday.

O2 Academy Brixton LIVE MUSIC
(www.o2academybrixton.co.uk; 211 Stockwell Rd, SW9; Brixton) This Grade II–listed art-deco venue hosts big-name acts in a relatively intimate setting (5000 capacity).

Jazz Café LIVE MUSIC
(Map p172; www.mamacolive.com/thejazzcafe; 5 Parkway, NW1; gigs from £8, club nights £5; 7pm-2am; Camden Town) Jazz is just one part of the picture at this intimate club that stages a full roster of rock, pop, hip hop and dance, including famous names.

100 Club LIVE MUSIC
(Map p162; 7636 0933; www.the100club.co.uk; 100 Oxford St, W1; admission £8-15; Oxford Circus or Tottenham Court Rd) Has hosted live music for 70 years; this legendary London venue once showcased the Rolling Stones and was at the centre of the punk revolution.

Roundhouse LIVE MUSIC
(Map p172; www.roundhouse.org.uk; Chalk Farm Rd, NW1; Chalk Farm) Built in 1847 as a railway shed, Camden's Roundhouse has been an iconic concert venue since the 1960s (capacity 3300), hosting the likes of the Stones, Led Zeppelin and The Clash.

Dublin Castle LIVE MUSIC
(Map p172; 020-7485 1773; www.thedublincastle.com; 94 Parkway, NW1; Camden Town) There's live punk or alternative music most nights in this pub's back room (cover usually £6).

Comedy

Comedy Store COMEDY
(Map p162; 0844 871 7699; www.thecomedystore.co.uk; 1A Oxendon St, SW1; admission £15-22.50; Piccadilly Circus) One of London's first comedy clubs, featuring the capital's most famous improvisers, the Comedy Store Players, on Wednesdays (8pm) and Sundays (7.30pm).

Comedy Café COMEDY
(Map p158; 020-7739 5706; www.comedycafe.co.uk; 68 Rivington St, EC2; admission free-£15; Wed-Sat; Old St) This major venue can be

a little too try-hard and wacky, but it's worth seeing the Wednesday night try-out spots.

Soho Theatre COMEDY
(Map p162; ☎7478 0100; www.sohotheatre.com; 21 Dean St, W1; ⊖Tottenham Court Rd) This is where grown-up comedians graduate to once crowds start paying attention.

Cinemas

Electric Cinema CINEMA
(☎020-7908 9696; www.electriccinema.co.uk; 191 Portobello Rd, W11; tickets £8-18; ⊖Ladbroke Grove) The UK's oldest cinema, updated with leather armchairs, footstools, tables in the auditorium and an excellent brasserie next door.

BFI Southbank CINEMA
(Map p158; ☎020-7928 3232; www.bfi.org.uk; Belvedere Rd, SE1; tickets £9; ⊙11am-11pm; ⊖Waterloo) The city's famous temple to film screens some 2000 flicks a year, from old classics to foreign arthouse.

BFI IMAX CINEMA
(Map p158; ☎020-7199 6000; www.bfi.org.uk/imax; Waterloo Rd; tickets £9-16; ⊖Waterloo) Watch 3-D movies on the UK's biggest screen: 20m high (nearly five double-decker buses) and 26m wide.

Prince Charles CINEMA
(Map p162; www.princecharlescinema.com; 7 Leicester Pl, WC2; ⊖Leicester Sq) Dodge eye-watering West End ticket prices at this brilliant budget cinema off Leicester Sq, which also hosts mini-festivals and late-night singalongs.

Classical Music, Opera & Dance

Royal Albert Hall CONCERT HALL
(Map p168; ☎020-7589 8212; www.royalalberthall.com; Kensington Gore, SW7; ⊖South Kensington) This landmark elliptical Victorian arena – classically based on a Roman amphitheatre – is best known as the venue for the annual classical music festival, the Proms.

Barbican PERFORMING ARTS
(Map p158; ☎0845 121 6823; www.barbican.org.uk; Silk St EC2, EC2; ⊖Barbican) Home to the London Symphony Orchestra, this famously hulking complex (named after a Roman fortification) has a rich program of film, music, theatre, art and dance including concerts.

Southbank Centre CONCERT HALL
(Map p158; ☎020-7960 4200; www.southbankcentre.co.uk; Belvedere Rd, SE1; ⊖Waterloo) Home to the **London Philharmonic Orchestra** (www.lpo.co.uk), **Sinfonietta** (www.londonsinfonietta.org.uk) and the **Philharmonia Orchestra** (www.philharmonia.co.uk), among others.

Royal Opera House OPERA
(Map p162; ☎7304 4000; www.roh.org.uk; Bow St, WC2; tickets £7-175; ⊖Covent Garden) Covent Garden is synonymous with opera thanks to this world-famous venue, which is also the home of the Royal Ballet, Britain's premier classical ballet company. Backstage tours take place three times a day on weekdays and four times on Saturdays (£10.50; book ahead).

Sadler's Wells DANCE
(Map p158; ☎0844 412 4300; www.sadlerswells.com; Rosebery Ave, EC1; tickets £10-49; ⊖Angel) A glittering modern venue that was, in fact, first established in the 17th century, Sadler's Wells has been given much credit for bringing modern dance to the mainstream.

Shopping

Department Stores

London's famous department stores are an attraction in themselves, even if you're not interested in buying.

Selfridges DEPARTMENT STORE
(Map p168; www.selfridges.com; 400 Oxford St, W1; ⊙9.30am-8pm Mon-Wed, to 9pm Thu-Sat, 11.30am-6.15pm Sun; ⊖Bond St) The funkiest of London's one-stop shops bursts with fashion labels, an unparalleled food hall and Europe's largest cosmetics department.

Fortnum & Mason DEPARTMENT STORE
(Map p162; www.fortnumandmason.com; 181 Piccadilly, W1; ⊙10am-8pm Mon-Sat, 11.30am-6pm Sun; ⊖Piccadilly Circus) A byword for quality and service from a bygone era. The old-world basement food hall is where Britain's elite come for their pantry provisions.

Liberty DEPARTMENT STORE
(Map p162; www.liberty.co.uk; Great Marlborough St, W1; ⊙10am-8pm Mon-Sat, noon-6pm Sun; ⊖Oxford Circus) An irresistible blend of contemporary styles and indulgent pampering in a mock-Tudor fantasyland of carved dark wood.

Harrods DEPARTMENT STORE
(Map p168; www.harrods.com; 87 Brompton Rd, SW1; ⊙10am-8m Mon-Sat, 11.30am-6pm Sun; ⊖Knightsbridge) Garish, stylish, kitsch, yet perennially popular department store.

Harvey Nichols DEPARTMENT STORE
(Map p168; www.harveynichols.com; 109-125 Knightsbridge, SW1; ⊙10am-8pm Mon-Sat, 11.30am-6pm

ROLL OUT THE BARROW

London has more than 350 markets selling everything from antiques and curios to flowers and fish. Some, such as Camden and Portobello Road, are full of tourists, while others exist just for the locals.

Columbia Road Flower Market (Map p158; Columbia Rd, E2; ⏲8am-3pm Sun; ⊖Old St) The best place for East End barrow-boy banter ('We got flowers cheap enough for ya muvver-in-law's grave'). Unmissable.

Borough Market (Map p158; Southwark St; ⊖London Bridge) A farmers market sometimes called London's Larder.

Camden Market (Map p172; Camden High St, NW1; ⏲10am-6pm; ⊖Camden Town or Chalk Farm) Actually a series of markets spread along Camden High St; the Lock and Stables markets are the place for punk fashion, cheap food, bongs and hippy-dippy stuff.

Portobello Road Market (www.portobellomarket.org; Portobello Rd, W10; ⏲8am-6.30pm Mon-Sat, to 1pm Thu; ⊖Notting Hill Gate or Ladbroke Grove) One of London's most famous (and crowded) street markets; new and vintage clothes, antiques and food.

Broadway Market (www.broadwaymarket.co.uk; London Fields; ⏲9am-5pm Sat; ⊖Bethnal Green) Graze from the organic food stalls or choose a cooked meal.

Brixton Market (www.brixtonmarket.net; Electric Ave & Granville Arcade; ⏲8am-6pm Mon-Sat, 8am-3pm Wed; ⊖Brixton) Immortalised in the Eddie Grant song, Electric Ave is a cosmopolitan treat that mixes everything from reggae music to exotic spices.

Sunday UpMarket (Map p158; www.sundayupmarket.co.uk; The Old Truman Brewery, Brick Lane, E1; ⏲10am-5pm Sun; ⊖Liverpool St) Handmade handbags, jewellery, new and vintage clothes and shoes.

Brick Lane Market (Map p158; www.visitbricklane.org; Brick Lane, E1; ⏲8am-2pm Sun; ⊖Liverpool St) A sprawling East End bazaar featuring everything from fruit to paintings and bric-a-brac.

Petticoat Lane Market (Map p158; Wentworth St & Middlesex St, E1; ⏲9am-2pm Sun-Fri; ⊖Aldgate) A cherished East End institution overflowing with cheap consumer durables and jumble sale ware.

Sun; ⊖Knightsbridge) London's temple of high fashion, jewellery and perfume.

Music

As befitting a global music capital, London has a wide range of music stores.

Ray's Jazz MUSIC
(Map p162; www.foyles.co.uk; 113-119 Charing Cross Rd, WC2; ⏲9.30am-9pm Mon-Sat, 11.30am-6pm Sun; ⊖Tottenham Court Rd) Where aficionados find those elusive back catalogues from their favourite jazz and blues artists.

BM Soho MUSIC
(Map p162; www.bm-soho.com; 25 D'Arblay St, W1; ⊖Oxford Circus) Your best bet for dance – if they haven't got what you're after, they'll know who has.

Rough Trade MUSIC
(www.roughtrade.com) East (Map p158; www.roughtrade.com; Dray Walk, Old Truman Brewery, 91 Brick Lane, E1; ⏲8am-8pm Mon-Fri, 11am-7pm Sat & Sun; ⊖Liverpool St); West (www.roughtrade.com; 130 Talbot Rd, W11; ⏲10am-6.30pm Mon-Sat, 11am-5pm Sun; ⊖Ladbroke Grove) The best place to come for anything of an indie or alternative bent.

Bookshops

Foyle's BOOKS
(Map p162; www.foyles.co.uk; 113-119 Charing Cross Rd WC2, WC2; ⏲9.30am-9pm Mon-Sat, 11.30am-6pm Sun; ⊖Tottenham Court Rd) London's most legendary bookshop.

Daunt Books BOOKS
(Map p168; www.dauntbooks.co.uk; 83 Marylebone High St, W1; ⏲9am-7.30pm Mon-Sat, 11am-6pm Sun; ⊖Baker St) Famous travel bookshop, with guidebooks, travel literature, fiction and reference books, all sorted by country.

ℹ Information

City of London Information Centre (www.visitthecity.co.uk; St Paul's Churchyard EC4,

EC4; 9.30am-5.30pm Mon-Sat, 10am-4pm Sun; St Paul's) Tourist information, fast-track tickets to City attractions and guided walks (adult/child £6/4).

Getting There & Away

Bus & Coach

The London terminus for long-distance buses (called 'coaches' in Britain) is **Victoria Coach Station.** (164 Buckingham Palace Rd SW1, SW1; Victoria)

Train

Most of London's main-line rail terminals are linked by the Circle line on the tube.

Charing Cross Canterbury

Euston Manchester, Liverpool, Carlisle, Glasgow

King's Cross Cambridge, Hull, York, Newcastle, Scotland

Liverpool Street Stansted airport (Express), Cambridge

London Bridge Gatwick airport, Brighton

Marylebone Birmingham

Paddington Heathrow airport (Express), Oxford, Bath, Bristol, Exeter, Plymouth, Cardiff

St Pancras Gatwick and Luton airports, Brighton, Nottingham, Sheffield, Leicester, Leeds, Paris Eurostar

Victoria Gatwick airport (Express), Brighton, Canterbury

Waterloo Windsor, Winchester, Exeter, Plymouth

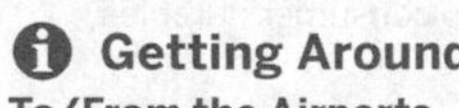

Getting Around

To/From the Airports

GATWICK

Main-line trains run every 15 minutes between Gatwick's South Terminal and Victoria (from £12, 37 minutes), hourly at night, or to/from St Pancras (from £12, 66 minutes) via London Bridge, City Thameslink, Blackfriars and Farringdon.

Gatwick Express (www.gatwickexpress.com) trains run to/from Victoria every 15 minutes from 5am to 11.45pm (one way/return £16/26, 30 minutes, first/last train 3.30am/12.32am).

The **EasyBus** (www.easybus.co.uk) minibus service between Gatwick and Earl's Court (every 30 minutes from 4.25am to 1am, about 1¼ hours) costs from £2 to £10, depending on when you book. You're charged extra if you have more than one carry-on and one check-in bag.

HEATHROW

The cheapest option from Heathrow is to take the underground (tube). The Piccadilly line is accessible from every terminal (£5.30, one hour to central London, departing from Heathrow every five minutes from around 5am to 11.30pm).

Faster, and much more expensive, is the **Heathrow Express** (www.heathrowexpress.com) train to Paddington station (one way/return £18/34, 15 minutes, every 15 minutes 5.12am to 11.48pm). You can purchase tickets on board (£5 extra), from self-service machines (cash and credit cards accepted) at both stations, or online.

LONDON CITY

The Docklands Light Railway (DLR) connects London City Airport to the tube network, taking 22 minutes to reach Bank station (£4.30). A black taxi costs around £25 to/from central London.

LUTON

There are regular National Rail services from St Pancras (£13, 29 to 39 minutes) to Luton Airport Parkway station, where a shuttle bus (£1.50) will get you to the airport within 10 minutes. EasyBus minibuses head from Victoria, Earl's Court and Baker St to Luton (from £2, walk-on £10, allow 1½ hours, every 30 minutes). A taxi costs around £65.

OYSTER CARD

The best-value way to get around London is with an **Oyster Card**, a reuseable travel card which covers most of the city's public transport system. The card itself costs £5 (refundable when you leave).

London is divided into six travel zones; most sights are in Zones 1 and 2. A weekly/monthly season ticket covering all tube, bus and rail services within these zones currently costs £29/112. All you need to do is touch your card to the sensors on the station turnstiles or at the front of the bus.

Alternatively, you can load the card with credit, and have fares deducted each time you use a train or bus. Fares are much cheaper compared to standard paper tickets (a Zone 1 tube journey on an Oyster Card is £2.10, compared to £4.50 for a paper ticket).

Oyster Cards can be bought at any London tube or train station, as well as some newsagents, garages and off-licences. Alternatively you can buy Oyster Cards in advance online from the **Transport for London** (http://visitorshop.tfl.gov.uk).

STANSTED

The **Stansted Express** (☎0845 850 0150; www.stanstedexpress.com) connects with Liverpool Street station (one way/return £21.50/29.50, 46 minutes, every 15 minutes 6am to 12.30am).

EasyBus (www.easybus.co.uk) also has services between Stansted and Baker St (from £2, £10 walk-on, 1¼ hours, every 20 minutes). The Airbus A6 links with Victoria Coach Station (£11, allow 1¾ hours, at least every 30 minutes).

National Express (www.nationalexpress.com) also runs buses to Stansted from Liverpool Street station (one way £9, 80 minutes, every 30 minutes).

Bicycle

Central London is mostly flat, relatively compact and the traffic moves slowly – all of which make it surprisingly good for cyclists. It can get terribly congested though, so you'll need to keep your wits about you – and lock your bike (including both wheels) securely.

Bikes can be hired from numerous self-service docking stations through London's **Cycle Hire** (www.tfl.gov.uk; 1st 30min free, then 1/2/3/6/24hr £1/6/15/35/50) scheme.

Boat

Thames Clippers (www.thamesclippers.com) runs regular commuter services between Embankment, Waterloo, Blackfriars, Bankside, London Bridge, Tower, Canary Wharf, Greenwich, North Greenwich and Woolwich piers (adult/child £5.30/2.65) from 7am to midnight (from 9.30am weekends).

London Waterbus Company (☎020-7482 2660; www.londonwaterbus.com; one-way/return £7.20/10.30) and **Jason's Trip** (Map p168; www.jasons.co.uk; opposite 42 Blomfield Rd, W9; one-way/return £8/9) both run canal boat journeys between Camden Lock and Little Venice; see websites for times.

There are also boats to Kew Gardens and Hampton Court Palace.

Bus

Buses run regularly during the day, while less frequent night buses (prefixed with the letter 'N') wheel into action when the tube stops. Single-journey bus tickets (valid for two hours) cost £2.30 (£1.35 on Oyster, capped at £4.20 per day); a weekly pass is £18.80. Buses stop on request, so clearly signal the driver with an outstretched arm.

Car

Don't. London was recently rated western Europe's second-most congested city (congratulations Brussels). In addition, you'll pay £8 per day simply to drive into central London from 7am to 6pm on a weekday. If you're hiring a car to continue your trip around Britain, take the tube or train to a major airport and pick it up from there.

Taxi

London's famous black cabs are available for hire when the yellow light above the windscreen is lit. Fares are metered, with flag fall of £2.20 and the additional rate dependent on time of day, distance travelled and taxi speed. A 1-mile trip will cost between £5.20 and £8.40.

Minicabs are a cheaper alternative to black cabs and quote trip fares in advance. Only use drivers from proper agencies; licensed minicabs aren't allowed to tout for business or pick you up off the street without a booking.

Underground & DLR

'The tube', as it's universally known, extends its subterranean tentacles throughout London and into the surrounding counties, with services running every few minutes from roughly 5.30am to 12.30am (7am to 11.30pm Sunday).

Lines are colour-coded (Red for the Central Line, yellow for the Circle Line, black for the Northern Line and so on). It helps to know the direction you're travelling in (ie northbound or southbound, eastbound or westbound) as well as the terminus of the line you're travelling on. If you get confused, don't worry, as copies of the tube's famous map are posted everywhere, showing how the 14 different routes intersect. Be warned, however – the distances between stations on the tube map aren't remotely to scale.

The Docklands Light Railway (DLR) links the City to Docklands, Greenwich and London City Airport.

AROUND LONDON

'When you're tired of London, you're tired of life', opined 18th-century Londoner Samuel Johnson. But he wasn't living in an age when too many days on the tube can leave you exhausted and grouchy. Luckily, the capital is surprisingly close to some excellent day escapes. Brighton and Oxford are well-known day-trip haunts, while Windsor and Eton are two gems that are an easy train ride from the capital.

Windsor & Eton

POP 31,000

Dominated by the massive bulk and heavy influence of Windsor Castle, these twin towns have a rather surreal atmosphere, with the morning pomp and ceremony of the changing of the guards in Windsor and the sight of school boys dressed in formal tailcoats wandering the streets of Eton.

Sights

Windsor Castle CASTLE

(www.royalcollection.org.uk; adult/child £17.75/10.60, when State Apartments closed £9.70/6.45; 9.45am-5.15pm Mar-Oct, 9.45am-4.15pm Nov-Feb; 701 or 702 from Victoria coach station, Windsor Central or Windsor Riverside) The largest and oldest occupied fortress in the world, Windsor Castle is a majestic vision of battlements and towers used for state occasions and is the Queen's weekend retreat. You can enter large sections of the castle complex, now fully restored after a devastating fire in 1992. Highlights include Queen Mary's giant doll's house, and St George's Chapel containing the tombs of several monarchs, including Henry VIII.

While you're here, don't miss a picnic in the groomed grounds of Windsor Great Park, and the chance to watch the ceremonial **Changing of the Guard** (11am Mon-Sat Apr-Jul, alternate days Aug-Mar).

Eton College NOTABLE BUILDING

(www.etoncollege.com; adult/child £.7.50/6.50, extended tour £11; guided tours 2pm & 3.15pm daily school holidays, Wed, Fri, Sat & Sun term time) Founded in 1440, England's oldest and most prestigious public school, Eton College, has been educating the great and good of English society for over five centuries. All the boys are boarders and must wear formal tailcoats, waistcoats and white collars to lessons (though the top hats went out in 1948); fencing, shooting, polo and beagling all feature on the curriculum.

Tours take in the **chapel**, the **cloisters**, the **lower school**, with names etched into its ancient desks by bored students, and the **school yard**, with a memorial to Etonians who died in the two world wars. You may recognise some of the buildings, as *Chariots of Fire, The Madness of King George, Mrs Brown* and *Shakespeare in Love* are just some of the movies that have been filmed here.

Tickets must be purchased in advance at the tourist office.

Information

Royal Windsor Information Centre (www.windsor.gov.uk; Old Booking Hall, Windsor Royal Shopping Arcade; 9.30am-5pm Mon-Sat, 10am-4pm Sun)

Getting There & Away

Trains from Windsor Central station on Thames St go to London Paddington (27 to 43 minutes). Trains from Windsor Riverside station go to London Waterloo (56 minutes). Services run half-hourly from both stations and tickets cost £9.40.

SOUTHEAST ENGLAND

Rolling chalk downs, venerable Victorian resorts, seaside towns – the southeast makes for a bracing change from London's traffic-clogged streets and a great day trip from the capital. England's stateliest cathedral, in Canterbury, the mighty Dover Castle and the laid-back charm of Brighton are all within easy reach. For general information, see www.visitsoutheastengland.com.

Canterbury

POP 43,432

This World Heritage city has been a Christian pilgrimage site for several centuries thanks to the majestic **Canterbury Cathedral** (www.canterbury-cathedral.org; adult/child £8/7, tour adult/child £5/3, audio tour adult/child £3.50/2.50; 9am-5pm Mon-Sat, 12.30-2.30pm Sun), the mothership for the Church of England and one of the nation's great Gothic landmarks. The spot in the northwest transept where Archbishop Thomas Becket met his grisly end has been drawing pilgrims for more than 800 years and is marked by a flickering candle and striking modern altar.

Sleeping

Arthouse B&B B&B ££

(01227-453032; www.arthousebandb.com; 24 London Rd; r £60-65;) A night at Canterbury's newest and most laid-back digs, housed in a 19th-century fire station, are a bit like kipping over at a really cool art student's pad.

Kipp's Independent Hostel HOSTEL £

(01227-786121; www.kipps-hostel.com; 40 Nunnery Fields; dm/s/d £16/22/36;) Occupying a red-brick townhouse less than a mile from the city centre, these superb backpackers' digs enjoy a homely atmosphere and clean, though cramped, dorms.

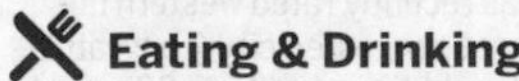

Eating & Drinking

Boho INTERNATIONAL £

(43 St Peter's St; snacks £3-10; 9am-6pm Mon-Sat, 10am-5pm Sun) Tuck into humungous

burgers, full-monty breakfasts and imaginative, owner-cooked international mains. No bookings, so be prepared to queue.

Tiny Tim's Tearoom CAFE £
(☎01227-450793; 34 St Margaret's St; mains £7-9; ⏲9.30am-5pm Tue-Sat, 10.30am-4pm Sun) Swish 1930s English tearoom offering hungry shoppers big breakfasts bursting with Kentish ingredients and tiers of cakes, crumpets and scones plastered in clotted cream.

Goods Shed MARKET ££
(☎01227-459153; Station Rd West; mains £12-20; ⏲market 9am-7pm Tue-Sat, 10am 4pm Sun, restaurant breakfast, lunch & dinner Tue-Sat, lunch Sun) Farmers market, food hall and fabulous restaurant all rolled into one.

Information

Tourist Office (☎01227-378100; www.canterbury.co.uk; 18 High St; ⏲9am-5pm Mon-Wed, Fri & Sat, to 7pm Thu, 10am-5pm Sun) Recently moved to the Royal Museum & Art Gallery on High St; staff can help book accommodation, excursions and theatre tickets.

Getting There & Away

There are two train stations: Canterbury East for London Victoria and Dover; and Canterbury West for London's Charing Cross and St Pancras stations. Connections include Dover Priory (£7.50, 25 minutes, every 30 minutes), London St Pancras (£31.80, one hour, hourly) and London Victoria/Charing Cross (£26.80, 1¾ hours, two to three hourly).

Dover

POP 39,078

Dover's shabby town centre is a sad introduction to Britain for travellers arriving by boat, but the town has a couple of stellar attractions to redeem it.

Sights

Dover Castle CASTLE
(EH; www.english-heritage.org.uk; adult/child £16.50/9.90; ⏲10am-6pm Apr-Jul & Sep, from 9.30am Aug, to 5pm Oct, 10am-4pm Sat & Sun Nov-Mar; P) This most impressive of English castles was built to bolster the country's weakest point at this, the shortest sea-crossing to mainland Europe. The robust 12th-century **Great Tower** is filled with interactive exhibits, but the biggest draw here is the network of claustrophobic secret wartime tunnels.

The new 50-minute guided tour (every 20 minutes) tells the story of one of Britain's most famous WWII operations: the evacuation of thousands of troops from Dunkirk, codenamed Operation Dynamo.

White Cliffs of Dover LANDMARK
Immortalised in song, film and literature, these iconic cliffs are embedded in the national consciousness. The cliffs rise to 100m high and extend on either side of Dover, but the best bit is the 6-mile stretch that starts about 2 miles east of town, properly known as the Langdon Cliffs.

The area is managed by the National Trust and there's a small information office, marking the start of a bracing 2-mile walk to the **South Foreland Lighthouse** (NT; www.nationaltrust.org.uk; adult/child £4/2; ⏲guided tours 11am-5.30pm Fri-Mon mid-Mar–Oct)

Information

Tourist Office (☎01304-205108; www.whitecliffscountry.org.uk; Market Sq; ⏲9.30am-5pm Mon-Sat year-round, 10am 3pm Sun Apr-Sep) Located in Dover Museum, this friendly office can book accommodation and ferries for a small fee.

Getting There & Away

BUS & COACH Services include bus 15 to Canterbury (45 minutes, twice hourly) and coach 077 to London Victoria (£13.50, 2¾ hours, 19 daily).

TRAIN Services include London Charing Cross (£21.10, two hours, twice hourly) and the high-speed service to London St Pancras (£36.20, one hour, hourly).

WORTH A TRIP

LEEDS CASTLE

Leeds Castle (www.leeds-castle.com; adult/child £19.75/12.50; ⏲10am-6pm Apr-Sep, to 5pm Oct-Mar) is one of the most visited attractions in Britain. It's not in Leeds, despite the rather confusing name – it's actually just east of Maidstone. This impressive structure balancing on two islands amid a large lake has been transformed from fortress to lavish palace over the centuries, and the vast estate is ideal for peaceful walks.

Trains run from London Victoria to Bearsted (£19.60, one hour) where you catch a special shuttle coach to the castle (£5 return, daily March to October, weekends only in winter).

Getting Around

The ferry companies run regular shuttle buses between the docks and the train station (five minutes) as they're a long walk apart.

Taxis offering 24-hour services include **Heritage** (☎01304-204420) and **Star Taxis** (☎01304-228822).

Brighton & Hove

POP 247, 817

Brighton is Britain's most colourful and outrageous seaside city. It's also home to Britain's biggest gay community, and has a fantastic cultural and clubbing scene to boot. Brighton rocks all year round, but really comes to life during the summer months.

Sights

Royal Pavilion PALACE
(www.royalpavilion.org.uk; Royal Pavilion Gardens; adult/child £10.50/5.90; ⌚9.30am-5.45pm Apr-Sep, 10am-5.15pm Oct-Mar) The city's must-see attraction is the Royal Pavilion, the glittering party pad and palace of Prince George, who later became King George IV. It's one of the most opulent buildings in England, and certainly the finest example of 19th-century Chinoiserie anywhere in Europe.

Brighton Pier AMUSEMENT PARK
(www.brightonpier.co.uk; Madeira Dr) This grand old centenarian pier is the place to experience Brighton's tackier side, from fairground rides to dingy amusement arcades. Look west and you'll see the sad remains of the once-grand **West Pier** (www.westpier.co.uk).

FREE **Brighton Museum & Art Gallery** MUSEUM
(www.brighton-hove-museums.org.uk; Royal Pavilion Gardens; ⌚10am-5pm Tue-Sun) Set in the Royal Pavilion's renovated stable block, this museum and art gallery has a glittering collection of 20th-century art and design, including a crimson Salvador Dalí sofa modelled on Mae West's lips.

The Lanes NEIGHBOURHOOD
Brighton's original fishing-village heart is the Lanes, a cobblestone web of 17th-century cottages housing a gentrified cornucopia of independent shops, pubs and one-of-a-kind eateries. The adjacent **North Laine** has a funkier vibe with streets of multicoloured shops, secondhand record stores and vegetarian cafes for local hipsters.

Sleeping

Despite a glut of hotels in Brighton, prices are high, especially at weekends. Brighton's hostels are a varied bunch. Several cater to stag and hen nights; others are more homely. Choose wisely!

TOP CHOICE **Kipps Brighton** HOSTEL £
(☎01273-604182; www.kipps-brighton.com; 76 Grand Pde; dm/d from £15/40; @📶) Owners of Canterbury's award-winning hostel have created equally commendable budget digs here in Brighton. There's a real cafe vibe around reception and facilities include a communal kitchen.

Baggies Backpackers HOSTEL £
(☎01273-733740; www.baggiesbackpackers.com; 33 Oriental Pl; dm/d £13/35; 📶) A warm atmosphere, worn-in charm and clean, snug dorms have made this hostel an institution. Only takes phone bookings. Cash only.

Snooze HOTEL ££
(☎01273-605797; www.snoozebrighton.com; 25 St George's Tce; s/d from £55/65; @📶) This eccentric Kemptown pad is fond of retro styling. You'll find it just off St James' St about 500m east of New Steine.

Seadragon Backpackers HOSTEL £
(☎01273-711854; www.seadragonbackpackers.co.uk; 36 Waterloo St; dm/tw from £15/50; 📶) Perched on the edge of Hove, but just a short bus ride from Churchill Sq, this no-frills, uncluttered and well-equipped hostel lacks vibe but is ideal for budget nomads.

Eating

Iydea VEGETARIAN £
(www.iydea.co.uk; 17 Kensington Gardens; mains £5.50-7; ⌚9am-5.30pm Mon-Sat, from 9.30am Sun; 📶🥕) The food at this new vegetarian cafe is a treat. All of the daily changing menus of curries, lasagnes, falafel, enchiladas and quiches can be eaten in or taken away.

JB's American Diner BISTRO £
(31 King's Rd; burgers £7, mains £6.50-12) A hefty slab of authentic Americana teleported to the Brighton seafront, complete with shiny leather booths, 1950s soundtrack and colossal burgers, fries and milkshakes.

Foodilic BUFFET £
(www.foodilic.com; 60 North St; buffet £6.45; ⌚8am-9.30pm Mon-Sat, to 6pm Sun; 📶) As good for breakfast (£2) as a late dinner, but it's the eat-till-you-burst buffet of scrumptious,

healthy fare that packs this funky place all day long.

Piccolo's ITALIAN £
(56 Ship St; mains £5-7.50) Cheap, tasty pizza and pasta served in a frantic, friendly restaurant – just what everyone expects from an Italian eatery.

Drinking & Entertainment

Brighton has cafes, clubs, pubs and bars to fulfil every whim. For pointers, visit www.drinkinbrighton.co.uk.

Dorset PUB
(www.thedorset.co.uk; 28 North Rd;) Laid-back Brighton institution that throws open its doors and windows in fine weather and spills tables onto the pavement.

Evening Star PUB
(www.eveningstarbrighton.co.uk; 55-56 Surrey St; noon-11pm Sun-Thu, 11.30am-midnight Fri & Sat) This cosy, unpretentious pub is a beer drinker's nirvana, with a wonderful selection of award-winning real ales, Belgian beers, organic lagers and seasonal brews.

Coalition BAR
(171-181 Kings Rd Arches) On a summer's day, there's nowhere better to sit and watch the world go by than at this popular beach bar, diner and club.

Concorde 2 CLUB
(www.concorde2.co.uk; Madeira Dr) Brighton's best known and best-loved club is a disarmingly unpretentious den, where DJ Fatboy Slim pioneered the Big Beat Boutique and still occasionally graces the decks.

Audio CLUB
(www.audiobrighton.com; 10 Marine Pde) Some of the city's top club nights can be found at this ear-numbing venue where the music is top priority, attracting a young, up-for-it crowd.

Information

Tourist Office (01273-290337; www.visitbrighton.com; Royal Pavilion Shop; 9.30am-5.30pm) Superbly run office with an accommodation booking service (£1.50), train and bus ticketing and a highly recommended (free) greeter scheme.

Getting There & Away

All London-bound services pass through Gatwick Airport (£9.50, 30 to 40 minutes, up to five hourly). Services include Eastbourne (£9.50, 30 to 40 minutes, half-hourly), London St Pancras (£15.40, 1¼ hours, half-hourly) and London Victoria (£16, 50 minutes, three hourly).

GAY & LESBIAN BRIGHTON

For more than a century, Brighton has been a gay haven. With more than 25,000 gay men and around 15,000 lesbians living here, it is the most vibrant queer community in the country outside London. Kemptown (aka Camptown), on and off St James' St, is where it's all at. The old Brunswick Town area of Hove is a quieter alternative.

For up-to date information on gay Brighton, check out www.gay.brighton.co.uk and www.realbrighton.com, or pick up the free monthly magazine *Gscene* (www.gscene.com) from the tourist office.

SOUTHWEST ENGLAND

England's southwest is simply spectacular. Here the past is ever present – prepare for close encounters with iconic stone circles, Iron Age hillforts and Roman baths.

Then there are three wildlife-rich national parks, fossil-studded shores, England's best surf spots and a coastline flecked with exquisite bays and tranquil sweeps of sandy beach.

For general information, see www.visitsouthwest.com.

Salisbury

POP 43,335

Centred on a majestic cathedral topped by the tallest spire in England, the gracious city of Salisbury has been an important provincial city for more than 1000 years.

Sights

Salisbury Cathedral CHURCH
(01722-555120; www.salisburycathedral.org.uk; requested donation adult/child £5/3; 7.15am-6.15pm) England is endowed with countless stunning churches, but few can match the sheer spectacle of Salisbury Cathedral. Built between 1220 and 1258, the structure bears all the hallmarks of the early English Gothic style. The 90-minute **tower tours** (01722-555156; adult/child £8.50/6.50; 11am-2.30pm Apr-Sep, 1 per day Mon-Sat Nov-Mar) climb 332

vertigo-inducing steps up the spire for jaw-dropping views. Bookings are required.

Sleeping & Eating

Salisbury YHA HOSTEL £
(☎0845-371 9537; www.yha.org.uk; Milford Hill; dm £18; P@) A real gem: neat rooms in a rambling, listed Victorian building. Choose from doubles or dorms; a cafe-bar, laundry and dappled gardens add to the appeal.

Spire House B&B ££
(☎01722-339213; www.salisbury-bedandbreakfast.com; 84 Exeter St; s £65-75, d £80, f £95-100; P) Comfy rooms have four-poster beds, Georgian-themed wallpaper and, at the front, cracking cathedral views.

Pheasant PUB ££
(☎01722-322866; www.restaurant-salisbury.com; 19 Salt Lane; mains £7-15; ⏲food noon-9.30pm) This chilled-out gastropub does the basics well; try the pheasant stuffed with bacon and leeks, and the gooey, crumbly Eton mess. To drink? Perhaps a pint of Pigswill (honestly – it's a local ale).

Information

Tourist Office (☎01722-334956; www.visitwiltshire.co.uk/salisbury; Fish Row, Market Sq; ⏲9.30am-6pm Mon-Sat, 10am-4pm Sun Jun-Sep, 9.30am-5pm Mon-Sat Oct-Apr)

Getting There & Away

BUS National Express services include Bath (£11, 1¼ hours, one daily), Bristol (£10, 2¼ hours, daily) and London (£10, three hours, three daily) via Heathrow. Tour buses leave Salisbury for Stonehenge regularly.

TRAIN Trains run half-hourly from London Waterloo (£35, 1½ hours). Hourly connections include Bath (£9, one hour), Bristol (£11, 1¼ hours) and Exeter (£30, two hours).

DON'T MISS

AVEBURY

While the tour buses usually head straight to Stonehenge, prehistoric purists make for **Avebury Stone Circle**. Though it lacks the dramatic trilithons ('gateways') of its sister site across the plain, Avebury is the largest stone circle in the world and a more rewarding place to visit simply because you can get closer to the giant boulders.

A large section of Avebury village is actually inside the circle, meaning you can sleep, or at least have lunch and a pint, inside the mystic ring.

To get here, bus 5/6/96 runs from Salisbury (1¾ hours, hourly Monday to Saturday, five on Sunday).

Stonehenge

This compelling ring of monolithic stones has been attracting a steady stream of pilgrims, poets and philosophers for the last 5000 years and is easily Britain's most iconic archaeological site.

The landscape around **Stonehenge** (EH; ☎0870-333 1181; www.english-heritage.org.uk; adult/child £6.90/3.50; ⏲9am-7pm) is undergoing a long-overdue revamp, which should dramatically improve the experience of those visiting when it's completed. But even before the changes, and despite the huge numbers of tourists who traipse around the perimeter, Stonehenge still manages to be a mystical, ethereal place – a haunting echo from Britain's forgotten past, and a reminder of the people who once walked the many ceremonial avenues across Salisbury Plain.

Even more intriguingly, it's still one of Britain's great archaeological mysteries: despite countless theories about what the site was used for, ranging from a sacrificial centre to a celestial timepiece, in truth, no one knows for sure what drove prehistoric Britons to expend so much time and effort on its construction.

Admission to Stonehenge is free for both EH and NT members.

Getting There & Around

BUS No regular buses go to the site. The **Stonehenge Tour** (☎01722-336855; www.thestonehengetour.info; return adult/child £11/5) leaves Salisbury's railway and bus stations half-hourly in June and August, and hourly between September and May.

TAXI Taxis charge £40 to go to Stonehenge from Salisbury, wait for an hour and come back.

Bath

POP 90,144

Britain is littered with beautiful cities, but precious few can hold a candle to Bath. Founded on top of a network of natural hot springs, Bath's heyday was during the 18th century, when local entrepreneur Ralph Allen and the father-and-son architects John Wood the Elder and Younger, turned this sleepy backwater into the toast of Georgian society, and constructed fabulous landmarks such as the Circus and Royal Crescent.

Sights

TOP CHOICE **Roman Baths** HISTORIC SITE
(www.romanbaths.co.uk; Abbey Churchyard; adult/child/family £12.75/8.50/36; ⌚9am-10pm July & Aug, 9am-6pm Mar-Jun, Sep & Oct, 9.30am-5.30pm Nov-Feb) Ever since the Romans arrived in Bath, life in the city has revolved around the three geothermal springs that bubble up near the abbey. The Romans constructed a glorious complex of bathhouses above these thermal waters to take advantage of their natural temperature, which emerge at a constant 46°C.

The baths get unbelievably busy; you can usually avoid the worst crowds by buying tickets online, visiting early on a midweek morning, and by avoiding July and August.

Royal Crescent STREET
Bath's grandest street is the Royal Crescent, a semicircular terrace of majestic townhouses overlooking the green sweep of Royal Victoria Park. For a glimpse into the splendour and razzle-dazzle of Georgian life, head for **No 1 Royal Crescent** (www.bath-preservation-trust.org.uk; adult/child £6.50/2.50; ⌚10.30am-5pm Tue-Sun late Feb–mid-Dec), which has been restored using only 18th-century materials.

TOP CHOICE **Bath Abbey** CHURCH
(www.bathabbey.org; requested donation £2.50; ⌚9.30am-6pm Mon, 9am-6pm Tue-Sat, 1-2.30pm & 4.30-5.30pm Sun) Looming above the centre of the city, Bath's huge abbey church was built between 1499 and 1616, making it the last great medieval church raised in England.

FREE **Holburne Museum** GALLERY
(www.holburne.org; Great Pulteney St; temporary exhibitions incur fee; ⌚10am-5pm) Fresh from a three-year refit, this art museum houses an impressive roll call of works by artists including Turner, Stubbs, William Hoare and Thomas Gainsborough.

TOP CHOICE **Assembly Rooms** HISTORIC BUILDING
(NT; www.nationaltrust.org.uk/bath-assembly-rooms; 19 Bennett St; adult/child £2/free; ⌚10.30am-6pm) Opened in 1771, the city's glorious Assembly Rooms were where fashionable Bath socialites once gathered to waltz, play cards and listen to the latest chamber music. You're free to wander around the rooms, as long as they haven't been reserved for a special function; all are lit by their original 18th-century chandeliers.

Fashion Museum MUSEUM
(www.fashionmuseum.co.uk; Assembly Rooms, Bennett St; adult/child £7.75/5.75; ⌚10.30am-5pm) In the basement of the Assembly Rooms, this museum contains a wonderful collection of costumes worn from the 16th to late 20th centuries.

Jane Austen Centre MUSEUM
(www.janeausten.co.uk; 40 Gay St; adult/child £7.45/4.25; ⌚9.45am-5.30pm) Though Jane Austen only lived in Bath for five years from 1801 to 1806, she remained a regular visitor. This museum houses a small collection of memorabilia relating to the writer's time in Bath, and costumed guides bring the era to life.

STONE CIRCLE ACCESS VISITS

Visitors to Stonehenge normally have to stay outside the stone circle itself. But on **Stone Circle Access Visits** (☎01722-343830; www.english-heritage.org.uk; adult/child £14.50/7.50) you get to wander round the core of the site, getting up-close views of the iconic bluestones and trilithons. The walks take place in the evening or early morning, so the quieter atmosphere and the slanting sunlight add to the effect. Each visit only takes 26 people; to secure a place book at least two months in advance.

DON'T MISS

THE THERMAE BATH SPA

Larking about in the Roman Baths might be off the agenda, but you can still sample the city's curative waters at the ultra-modern **Thermae Bath Spa** (☎0844-888 0844; www.thermaebathspa.com; Bath St; ⌚9am-9.30pm, last entry 7pm). The New Royal Bath ticket includes steam rooms, waterfall showers and the open-air rooftop pool, where you can swim in the thermal waters with a backdrop of Bath's stunning cityscape.

Bath

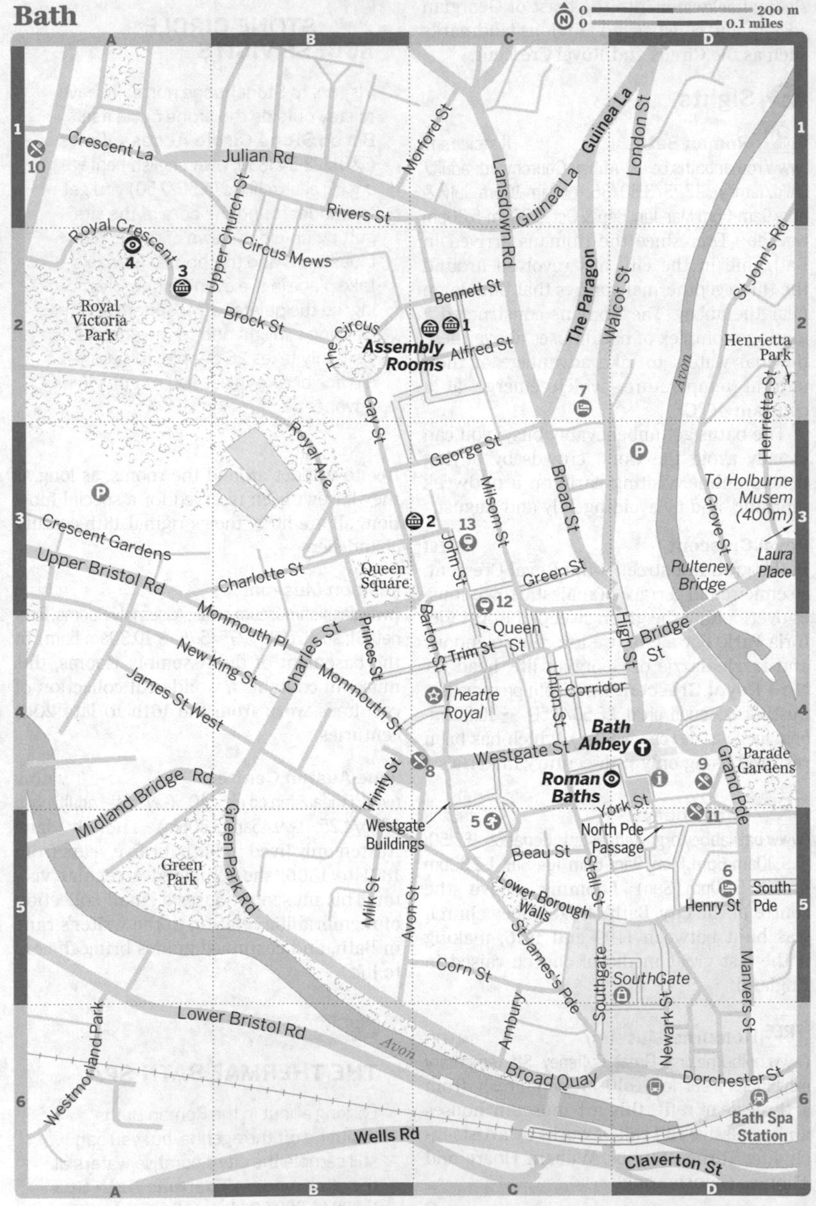

Sleeping

Henry B&B ££

(☎01225-424052; www.thehenry.com; 6 Henry St; d £80-120, f £145-165) This tall, slim townhouse offers a good choice of clean, uncluttered rooms finished in crisp whites and smooth beiges. Two-night minimum stay at weekends.

Bath YHA HOSTEL £

(www.yha.org.uk; Bathwick Hill; dm £20.40, d from £59; P@) Lodged inside an Italianate man-

Bath

Top Sights

	Assembly Rooms	C2
	Bath Abbey	D4
	Roman Baths	D4

Sights

1	Fashion Museum	C2
2	Jane Austen Centre	C3
3	No 1 Royal Crescent	A2
4	Royal Crescent	A2

Activities, Courses & Tours

5	Thermae Bath Spa	C5

Sleeping

6	Henry	D5
7	YMCA	C2

Eating

8	Boston Tea Party	C4
9	Café Retro	D4
10	Marlborough Tavern	A1
11	Sally Lunn's	D5

Drinking

12	Raven	C3
13	Salamander	C3

sion and a more modern annexe, a steep climb (or a short hop on bus 18) from the city centre, this hostel offers decent rooms, spacious kitchens and lovely grounds.

YMCA HOSTEL £
(☎01225-325900; www.bathymca.co.uk; International House, Broad St Pl; dm £20-22, s £31-35, d & tw £54-60; @) Institutional, yes, but bright, clean and bang in the centre – it even has a health suite and cafe.

Appletree Guest House B&B ££
(☎01225-337642; www.appletreeguesthouse.co.uk; 7 Pulteney Gardens; s £55-66, d £85-110, f £135-149;) It's tiny, but this welcoming B&B is worth recommending for the sunny disposition of its husband-and-wife owners, Lynsay and Les.

Eating & Drinking

Marlborough Tavern PUB ££
(☎01225-423731; www.marlborough-tavern.com; 35 Marlborough Buildings; mains £12-17) Half cosy boozer, half contemporary bistro, with big wooden tables, deep seats, and a crackling fire on winter nights.

Café Retro CAFE £
(18 York St; mains £5-11; breakfast, lunch & dinner Tue-Sat, breakfast & lunch Mon) The paint job's scruffy, the crockery's ancient and none of the furniture matches, but that's all part of the charm at this old-school cafe. Takeaway available from Retro to Go next door.

Boston Tea Party CAFE
(19 Kingsmead Sq; mains from £4; 7.30am-7pm Mon-Sat, from 8.30am Sun) The city's original lunch stop is still jamming in the punters with its zingy citrus drinks, fruit smoothies and gourmet wraps, soups and sandwiches.

Sally Lunn's CAFE £
(4 North Pde Passage; lunch mains £5-6, dinner mains from £8) This fabulously frilly tearoom occupies one of Bath's oldest houses, and makes the perfect venue for classic cream tea and the trademark Sally Lunn's Bun.

Raven PUB
(Queen St) This traditional pub commands a devoted following for its well-kept real ales and trad atmosphere, complete with beer mats, bar and brass trinkets.

Salamander PUB
(3 John St) Run by local brewer Bath Ales, this modern pub offers a range of bespoke ales.

Information

Bath Visitor Centre (www.visitbath.co.uk; Abbey Churchyard; 9.30am-5pm Mon-Sat, 10am-4pm Sun) Sells the Bath City Card (£3), which is valid for three weeks and offers discounts at many local shops, restaurants and attractions.

Getting There & Away

BUS Bath's **bus and coach station** (Dorchester St; 9am-5pm Mon-Sat) is near the train station. National Express coaches run directly to London (£20.70, 3½ hours, eight to 10 daily) via Heathrow (£20.70, 2¾ hours).

TRAIN Bath Spa station is at the end of Manvers St. Many services connect through Bristol (£9.90, 20 minutes, two or three per hour), especially to the north of England. Direct services include Cardiff Central (£18, one hour, hourly), Exeter (£27.50, 1¼ hours, hourly), London Paddington/London Waterloo (£39, 1½ hours, half-hourly) and Salisbury (£15.70, one hour, hourly).

Bristol

POP 393,300

Bristol might just be Britain's most overlooked city. While most visitors speed past en route to Bath without giving the southwest's biggest metropolis so much as a second glance, they're missing out on one of Britain's quirkiest and coolest cities.

Sights

TOP CHOICE **SS Great Britain** SHIP

(www.ssgreatbritain.org; Great Western Dock, Gas Ferry Rd; adult/child/family £12.50/6.25/33.50; ⊙10am-5.30pm Apr-Oct) Bristol's pride and joy is the mighty steamship SS *Great Britain*, designed by the genius engineer Isambard Kingdom Brunel in 1843. Built from iron and driven by a revolutionary screw propeller, this massive vessel was one of the largest and most technologically advanced steamships ever built. A painstaking 30-year restoration program has since brought it back to stunning life.

FREE **M Shed** MUSEUM

(www.mshed.org; Princes Wharf; ⊙10am-5pm Tue-Fri, 10am-6pm Sat & Sun) It's taken four years and £27 million to build, but Bristol's brand-new museum is finally open – and it's really rather brilliant. The 3000-odd exhibits are divided into three sections (People, Place and Life), and provide a panoramic overview of Bristol's history.

Clifton Village NEIGHBOURHOOD

During the 18th and 19th centuries, wealthy Bristol merchants transformed the former spa resort of Clifton into an elegant hilltop suburb packed with impressive Georgian mansions. Some of the finest examples can be seen along **Cornwallis Crescent** and **Royal York Crescent**.

Clifton Suspension Bridge BRIDGE

(www.cliftonbridge.org.uk) Clifton's most famous (and photographed) landmark is a Brunel masterpiece, the 76m-high Clifton Suspension Bridge, which spans the Avon Gorge from Clifton over to Leigh Woods in northern Somerset. It's free to walk or cycle across the bridge; car drivers pay a 50p toll.

At-Bristol MUSEUM

(www.at-bristol.org.uk; Anchor Rd; adult/child/family £12.50/8/35.50; ⊙10am-5pm Mon-Fri, to 6pm Sat & Sun) Bristol's interactive science museum has several zones spanning space, technology and the human brain. In the Curiosity Zone you get to walk through a tornado, spin on a human gyroscope and strum the strings of a virtual harp.

Arnolfini GALLERY

(www.arnolfini.org.uk; 16 Narrow Quay; ⊙10am-6pm Tue-Sun) The city's avant-garde art gallery occupies a hulking red-brick warehouse by the river, and remains the top venue in town for modern art. There are also occasional exhibitions of dance, film and photography.

Sleeping

Bristol YHA HOSTEL ££

(bristol@yha.org.uk; 14 Narrow Quay; dm/s/d £22/37/74; @) Few hostels can boast a position as good as this one, right beside the river in a red-brick warehouse. Facilities include kitchens, cycle store, games room and the excellent Grainshed coffee lounge.

Brooks Guest House B&B ££

(☎0117-930 0066; www.brooksguesthousebristol.com; Exchange Ave; d £70-99; wi-fi) Bristol has been crying out for a smart, modern B&B near the city centre for years – and at long last it has one, and in a fantastic spot right next door to St Nick's market too.

Premier Inn, King St HOTEL ££

(☎0871 527 8158; www.premiertravelinn.com; King St; r £59-89; ❄ wi-fi) Yes, we realise this is a Premier Inn, but stop being snobby and just appreciate the cheap rates and riverside spot.

Future Inn Cabot Circus HOTEL ££

(☎0845 094 5588; www.futureinns.co.uk/bristol-hotels; Bond St South; d £59-99; P wi-fi) This hotel

> **WORTH A TRIP**
>
> ### GLASTONBURY
>
> A long-time bohemian haven and still a favourite hang-out for mystics and counter-cultural types, Glastonbury is best-known for its massive music **festival** (www.glastonburyfestivals.co.uk), held (nearly) every year on Michael Eavis' farm in nearby Pilton.
>
> The town owes much of its spirtual notoriety thanks to nearby **Glastonbury Tor** (NT; www.nationaltrust.org.uk), a grassy hump about a mile from town, topped by the ruins of St Michael's Church. According to local legend, the tor is said to be the mythical Isle of Avalon, King Arthur's last resting place. It's also allegedly one of the world's great spiritual nodes, marking the meeting point of many mystical lines of power known as ley-lines.
>
> There is no train station in Glastonbury, but bus 376/377 runs to Wells (30 minutes, hourly Monday to Saturday, seven on Sundays) and Bristol (1¼ hours).

TRANSPORT FROM BRISTOL

Bus

DESTINATION	PRICE (£)	DURATION (HR)	FREQUENCY
Birmingham	21.30	2	6-8 daily
Cardiff	8.70	1¼	every 2hr
Exeter	15	2	4 daily
London	21	2½	hourly

Train

DESTINATION	PRICE (£)	DURATION (HR)	FREQUENCY
Birmingham	47	1½	hourly
Edinburgh	136.50	6½	hourly
Exeter	25	1	hourly
Glasgow	136.50	6½	hourly
London Paddington	39	1¾	hourly
Penzance	42	5½	hourly
Truro	42	5	hourly

mini-chain is modern and businessy, but the rooms are clean in beige, white and pine, and the rates are fantastic this close to the centre.

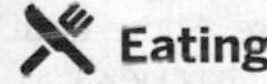

Eating

Thali Café INDIAN £

(☎0117-974 3793; www.thethalicafe.co.uk; 1 Regent St; meals £7.95-10.50) This mini-chain of Indian canteens now has four outlets, including this one in Clifton. It specialises in fresh, authentic *thalis* (multicourse Indian meals).

Pieminister BAKERY £

(24 Stokes Croft; pies around £4.50; ⏲10am-7pm Sat, 11am-4pm Sun) Bristol's best-loved pie shop is on Stokes Croft, but there's another outlet in St Nick's market.

Clifton Sausage PUB ££

(☎0117-973 1192; www.cliftonsausage.co.uk; 7-9 Portland St; sausage & mash £9.95, other mains £14-18) At least six different bangers grace the menu at this gastropub, from Gloucester Old Spot to Beef and Spitfire Ale (there's always a vegie version, too).

St Nicholas Market MARKET

(Corn St; ⏲9.30am-5pm Mon-Sat) The city's lively street market has a bevy of food stalls selling everything from artisan bread to cheese toasties.

Drinking

Apple THEME BAR

(Welsh Back) Cider lovers won't want to miss this converted barge on Welsh Back, which offers over 40 varieties, including raspberry and strawberry, and six different perries (pear ciders).

Grain Barge PUB

(www.grainbarge.com; Mardyke Wharf, Hotwell Rd) Built in 1936, overhauled in 2007, this barge near SS *Great Britain* is owned by the city's microbrewery, the Bristol Beer Factory.

Entertainment

Bristol's nightclub scene moves fast, so check the latest listings at **Venue** (www.venue.co.uk).

Thekla CLUB

(www.thekla.co.uk; The Grove) Bristol's venerable club-boat has nights for all moods: electro-punk, indie, disco and new wave, plus regular live gigs.

Colston Hall LIVE MUSIC

(www.colstonhall.org; Colston St) Bristol's historic concert hall tends to attract the best bands and big-name comedy acts.

Information

Bristol Tourist Information Centre (☎0333-321 0101; www.visitbristol.co.uk; E-Shed, 1 Canons Rd; ⏲10am-6pm)

Getting There & Away

BUS Bristol has excellent bus and coach connections with National Express. Useful local buses include express bus X39/339 to Bath (50 minutes, several per hour) and bus 376 to Wells (one hour, half-hourly Monday to Saturday, hourly on Sunday), with onward connections to Glastonbury (1¼ hours).

TRAIN Bristol is an important train hub.

Exeter

TRANSPORT HUB

Well heeled and comfortable, Exeter exudes evidence of its centuries-old role as the spiritual and administrative heart of Devon. The city's most outstanding landmark is its glorious Gothic **cathedral** (01392-285983; www.exeter-cathedral.org.uk; The Close; adult/child £6/free; 9am-4.45pm Mon-Sat), but if you have time its busy city centre is worth exploring. If not, it still serves as a useful gateway for the rest of Devon and Cornwall.

The centrally located **Globe Backpackers** (01392-215521; www.exeterbackpackers.co.uk; 71 Holloway St; dm/d £17.50/43;) is the best option for budget travellers.

Getting There & Away

BUS On Sundays between June and mid-September bus 82, the Transmoor Link, makes five trips from Exeter to Plymouth via Moretonhampstead, Postbridge, Princetown and Yelverton. For Plymouth (£6.50, 1¼ hours, two-hourly Monday to Saturday, three on Sunday), catch bus X38.

TRAIN Main-line and branch-line trains run from Exeter St David's and Exeter Central stations. Destinations include Bristol (£15, 1¼ hours, half-hourly), London Paddington (£35, 2½ hours, half-hourly) and Penzance (£15, three hours, hourly).

Dartmoor National Park

Dartmoor is a compelling landscape, very different from the rest of Devon. Exposed granite hills (called 'tors') crest the horizon, linked by swathes of moorland. Naturally, the charms of Dartmoor include superb walking and cycling, rustic pubs and country-house hotels – perfect boltholes when the mist rolls in.

Dartmoor's villages range from brooding Princetown and picturesque Widecombe-in-the-Moor to genteel Chagford. There are a number of excellent hostels to base yourself in, including **Bellever YHA** (0845 371 9622; www.yha.org.uk; d/dm £35/18;) and **Bracken Tor YHA** (0844 293 0555; www.yha.org.uk; Saxongate; d/dm £25/20;).

Useful bus routes for getting to the moor include bus 83/84/86 from Plymouth to Tavistock, via Yelverton (hourly) and bus X9 from Okehampton to Exeter (hourly, Monday to Saturday)

For more info, see www.dartmoor.co.uk.

Newquay

POP 19,423

Bright, breezy and unashamedly brash, Newquay in Cornwall is the undisputed capital of British surfing. All summer, a nonstop parade of beach-lovers and boozed-up clubbers creates a drink-till-dawn party atmosphere that's more Costa del Sol than Cornwall.

If you've come to catch the waves, the best-known beach is **Fistral** – the venue for the annual Boardmasters surfing festival. Below town are **Great Western** and **Towan**; a little further up the coast you'll find **Tolcarne**, **Lusty Glaze**, **Porth** and **Watergate Bay**. All these beaches are good for swimming and supervised by lifeguards in summer.

Sleeping

Newquay Townhouse B&B £
(01637-620009; www.newquaytownhouse.co.uk; 6 Tower Rd; d £50-70;) Near the town centre, with bright rooms livened up with stripy cushions and wicker furniture. Some have window seats, but only one has bay views.

Eating & Drinking

Beach Hut BISTRO ££
(01637-860877; Watergate Bay; mains £9.75-19.95; breakfast, lunch & dinner) This bistro by the sand has a beachy feel, and the menu is simple surf 'n' turf: sticky pork ribs, 'extreme' burgers and a different fish every day.

Café Irie CAFE £
(01637-859200; www.cafeirie.co.uk; 38 Fore St; lunch £3-8; 10am-5pm Mon-Sat) A surfer's favourite in the centre of Newquay, perfect for hot chocolate, sticky cakes and jacket spuds before hitting the waves.

Chy BAR
(www.thekoola.com/the-chy-bar; 12 Beach Rd) Chrome, wood and leather dominate this cafe-bar overlooking Towan Beach. The action continues till late at the Koola nightclub downstairs.

Information

Tourist Office (01637-854020; www.newquay.co.uk; Marcus Hill; 9.30am-5.30pm Mon-Sat, to 12.30pm Sun)

Getting There & Away

BUS The 585/586 is the fastest service to Truro (50 minutes, twice hourly Monday to Saturday).

TRAIN There are trains every couple of hours on the branch line between Newquay and Par (£4.30, 45 minutes) on the main London–Penzance line.

St Ives

POP 9870

Once a busy pilchard harbour, St Ives later became the centre of Cornwall's arts scene in the 1920s and 1930s, and the town's cobbled streets are crammed with quirky galleries, cafes and restaurants.

Nearby, receding tides reveal 3 miles of golden beach at **Gwithian** and **Godrevy Towans**, both popular spots for kiteboarders and surfers.

Sights

Tate St Ives GALLERY

(01736-796226; www.tate.org.uk/stives; Porthmeor Beach; adult/child £7/4.50, joint ticket with Barbara Hepworth Museum £10/7; 10am-5pm Mar-Oct, to 4pm Tue-Sun Nov-Feb) This far-westerly outpost of the Tate focuses mainly on the work of the artists of the so-called 'St Ives School'. Key works by Terry Frost, Patrick Heron, Naum Gabo, Ben Nicholson and Barbara Hepworth are all on show, as well as the naive paintings of fisherman-turned-artist Alfred Wallis. On the top floor there's a stylish cafe-bar which has a great panorama across St Ives.

A joint ticket with the Barbara Hepworth Museum costs adult/child £10/5.50.

Barbara Hepworth Museum MUSEUM

(01736-796226; Barnoon Hill; adult/child £6/4, joint ticket with Barbara Hepworth Museum £10/7; 10am-5pm Mar-Oct, 10am-4pm Tue-Sun Nov-Feb) Barbara Hepworth (1903–75) was one of the leading abstract sculptors of the 20th century, and a key figure in the St Ives art scene. Her studio on Barnoon Hill has remained almost untouched since her death, and the adjoining garden contains several of her most notable sculptures.

Sleeping

Little Leaf Guest House B&B ££

(01736-795427; www.littleleafguesthouse.co.uk; Park Ave; r £85-120;) This five-room B&B is on a hill uphill from town. Rooms are sweet and simple, finished in creamy colours and pine furniture.

DON'T MISS

EDEN PROJECT

If any one thing is emblematic of Cornwall's regeneration, it's the **Eden Project** (01726-811911; www.edenproject.com; adult/child £23.50/10.50; 10am-6pm Apr-Oct, to 4.30pm Nov-Mar). Ten years ago the site was an exhausted clay pit; a symbol of the county's industrial decline. Now it's home to the largest plant-filled greenhouses on the planet – a monumental education project about the natural world. Tropical, temperate and desert environments have been recreated inside the massive biomes, so a single visit carries you from the steaming rainforests of South America to the dry deserts of northern Africa.

Treliska B&B ££

(01736-797678; www.treliska.com; 3 Bedford Rd; d £65-85;) The smooth decor at this B&B is attractive – chrome taps, wooden furniture, cool sinks – but it's the position that sells it, just steps from the town centre.

Eating & Drinking

Porthminster Beach Café BISTRO ££

(01736-795352; www.porthminstercafe.co.uk; Porthminster Beach; lunch £10.50-16.50, dinner £10-22; 9am-10pm) For a seaside lunch there's nowhere better than this designer beach cafe, with its gorgeous suntrap terrace and Mediterranean-influenced menu.

Blas Burgerworks BURGERS ££

(01736-797-272; www.blasburgerworks.co.uk; The Warren; burgers £5-10; noon-10pm;) Imaginative burger-joint with an ecofriendly, fair trade, homemade manifesto.

The Hub CAFE, BAR

(www.hub-stives.co.uk; The Wharf) The open-plan Hub is the heart of St Ives' (limited) nightlife: frothy lattes by day, cocktails after dark, concertina doors onto the harbour.

Sloop Inn PUB

(The Wharf) A classic fishermen's boozer, complete with tankards behind the bar and a comprehensive selection of Cornish ales.

Information

St Ives Tourist Office (01736-796297; www.stivestic.co.uk; Street-an-Pol; 9am-5.30pm

Mon-Fri, 9am-5pm Sat, 10am-4pm Sun) Inside the Guildhall.

Getting There & Away

BUS The quickest bus to Penzance is bus 17 (30 minutes, twice hourly Monday to Saturday, hourly on Sunday). In summer the open-top bus 300 takes the scenic route via Zennor, Land's End and St Just.

TRAIN The gorgeous branch line from St Ives is worth taking just for the coastal views: trains terminate at St Erth (£3, 14 minutes, half-hourly), on the Penzance–London Paddington main line.

Penzance

POP 21,168

The historic harbour town of Penzance is a hotchpotch of winding streets, old shopping arcades and a grand seafront promenade. It feels more authentic than prettified St Ives, and makes an excellent base for exploring the rest of west Cornwall.

Sights

TOP CHOICE St Michael's Mount MONASTERY

(NT; ☎01736-710507; www.stmichaelsmount.co.uk; castle & gardens adult/child £9.60/4.80; ⏰house 10.30am-5.30pm Sun-Fri late Mar-Oct, gardens Mon-Fri Apr-Jun, Thu & Fri Jul-Sep) Looming from the waters of Mount's Bay is the unmistakeable silhouette of St Michael's Mount, a dreamy abbey set on a rocky island that's connected to the small seaside town of Marazion by a cobbled causeway. You can catch a ferry (adult/child £2/1) at high tide from Marazion, about 3 miles from Penzance. At low tide you can walk across on the causeway, just as the monks and pilgrims did centuries ago.

The 513 bus runs three times daily from Penzance.

Sleeping

TOP CHOICE Artist Residence Penzance B&B ££

(☎01736-365664; www.arthotelcornwall.co.uk; Chapel St; d £80-120; 📶) This deliciously different new hotel on Chapel St is like sleeping inside an art gallery. All the rooms have their own bespoke design courtesy of a local artist.

Penzance YHA HOSTEL £

(☎0845-371 9653; penzance@yha.org.uk; Castle Horneck, Alverton; dm from £14; P@) Penzance's YHA is inside an 18th-century house on the edge of town, with a cafe, laundry and four- to 10-bed dorms. It's a 15-minute walk from the front; buses 5 and 6 stop nearby.

Eating & Drinking

Bakehouse MEDITERRANEAN ££

(☎01736-331331; www.bakehouserestaurant.co.uk; Chapel St; mains £10-19.50; ⏰6.15-10pm Mon-Sat) This attractive double-floored diner is tucked down an alley off Chapel St.

Archie Brown's CAFE £

(☎01736-362828; Bread St; mains £4-10; ⏰9am-5pm Mon-Sat) Archie Brown's is perched above a health shop, and serves quiches, salads and home-baked cakes with a wholefood ethos.

Turk's Head PUB

(Chapel St) They pull a fine pint of ale at Penzance's oldest boozer.

Getting There & Away

BUS Take buses 17/17A/17B to St Ives (30 minutes, half-hourly Monday to Saturday, hourly on Sunday) and bus X18 to Truro (one hour, three or four daily Monday to Saturday).

TRAIN Penzance is the last stop on the line from London Paddington. Trains run roughly hourly. Services include Exeter (£39.50, three hours), London Paddington (£56, hourly, 5½ hours), St Ives (£3.80, 30 minutes) and Truro (£9.50, 30 minutes).

Land's End

Just 9 miles from Penzance, Land's End is the most westerly point of mainland England, where cliffs plunge dramatically into the pounding Atlantic surf. Unfortunately, the **Legendary Land's End** (www.landsend-landmark.co.uk; adult/child £10/7; ⏰10am-5pm Mar-Oct) theme park hasn't done much to enhance the view. Take our advice: skip the tacky multimedia shows and opt for an exhilarating clifftop stroll instead.

Bus 1/1A travels from Penzance (one hour, eight daily, five on Saturday) to Land's End; half the buses go via Sennen, the other half via Treen and Porthcurno.

CENTRAL ENGLAND

The geographic heartland of England is a mix of wildly differing scenes, with historic towns including Oxford and Stratford-upon-Avon, flower-decked villages in the Cotswolds, and rejuvenated former industrial cities such as Birmingham.

Oxford

POP 134,300

Oxford is a privileged place, one of the world's most famous university towns. The city is a wonderful place to ramble: the oldest of its 39 separate colleges date back almost 750 years, and little has changed inside the hallowed walls since then (with the notable exception of female admissions, which only began in 1878).

Sights

Not all Oxford's colleges are open to the public. Check www.ox.ac.uk/colleges for full details.

Christ Church College NOTABLE BUILDING
(www.chch.ox.ac.uk; St Aldate's; adult/child £8/6.50; ⏲9am-5pm Mon-Sat, 2-5pm Sun) The largest and grandest of all of Oxford's colleges; also the most popular thanks to the magnificent buildings and its latter-day fame as a location used in the Harry Potter films

Magdalen College NOTABLE BUILDING
(www.magd.ox.ac.uk; High St; adult/child £5/4; ⏲noon-7pm) Set amid lawns, woodlands, river walks and deer park, Magdalen (*mawdlen*), founded in 1458, is one of the wealthiest and most beautiful of Oxford's colleges.

Merton College NOTABLE BUILDING
(www.merton.ox.ac.uk; Merton St; admission £2, guided tour £2; ⏲2-5pm Mon-Fri, 10am-5pm Sat & Sun, guided tour 45min) Founded in 1264, Merton is the oldest college and was the first to adopt collegiate planning, bringing scholars and tutors together into a formal community and providing a planned residence for them.

Bodleian Library LIBRARY
(www.bodley.ox.ac.uk; Broad St; Divinity School adult/child £1/free, audioguide £2.50, library tours £7, 30min tours £5, extended tour £13; ⏲9am-5pm Mon-Fri, to 4.30pm Sat, 11am-5pm Sun, library tours 10.30am, 11.30am, 1pm & 2pm Mon-Sat, 11.30am, 2pm & 3pm Sun) Oxford's Bodleian Library is one of the oldest public libraries in the world. It currently holds over 11 million items, 117 miles of shelving and has seating space for up to 2500 readers. Most of the rest of the library is closed to visitors, but **library tours** allow access to the medieval Duke Humfrey's library.

Radcliffe Camera LIBRARY
(Radcliffe Sq; extended tours £13) This spectacular circular library/reading room was built between 1737 and 1749 in grand Palladian style, and has Britain's third-largest dome. Tours from the Bodleian Library take place on Wednesdays and Saturdays at 9.15am and most Sundays at 11.15am and 1.15pm, and last about an hour and a half.

FREE **Ashmolean Museum** MUSEUM
(www.ashmolean.org; Beaumont St; ⏲10am-6pm Tue-Sun) This is Britain's oldest public museum. Its collections span the world and include everything from Egyptian mummies to rare porcelain, tapestries and European art (including works by Raphael and Michelangelo). The recent makeover has added interactive features, a giant atrium and a beautiful rooftop restaurant.

Oxford Covered Market MARKET
(www.oxford-covered-market.co.uk, Market St; ⏲9am-5.30pm) A haven of traditional butchers, fishmongers, cobblers, barbers, delis, little eateries and independent shops, this lively market makes a good spot for lunch.

DON'T MISS

BLENHEIM PALACE

One of the country's greatest stately homes, **Blenheim Palace** (www.blenheimpalace.com; adult/child £20/10; ⏲10.30am-5.30pm mid-Feb–Oct) is a monumental baroque fantasy designed by Sir John Vanbrugh and Nicholas Hawksmoor between 1705 and 1722. Now a Unesco World Heritage Site, it's home to the 11th Duke of Marlborough. Highlights include the **Great Hall**, a vast space topped by 20m-high ceilings adorned with images of the first duke in battle; the opulent **Saloon**, the most important public room; the three **state rooms** with their plush decor and priceless china cabinets; and the magnificent 55m **Long Library**. You can also visit the **Churchill Exhibition**, dedicated to the life, work and writings of Sir Winston, who was born at Blenheim in 1874.

Blenheim Place is near the town of Woodstock, a few miles northwest of Oxford. To get there, Stagecoach bus S3 runs every half-hour (hourly on Sunday) from George St in Oxford.

Sleeping

Oxford YHA HOSTEL £
(☎0845-371 9131; www.yha.org.uk; 2a Botley Rd; dm/d from £23/50; @📶) Oxford's best budget option, with simple but comfortable four- and six-bed en suite dorms, private rooms and loads of facilities, including a restaurant, library, garden, laundry and a choice of lounges (though internet is not free).

Oxford Rooms STUDENT ROOMS ££
(www.oxfordrooms.co.uk; s/d from £50/90; @) During university holidays, you can sleep inside the hallowed college grounds. Most rooms are functional singles with basic furnishings and shared bathrooms, though there are some en suite, twin and family rooms available.

Central Backpackers HOSTEL £
(☎01865-242288; www.centralbackpackers.co.uk; 13 Park End St; dm £19-22; @📶) A friendly budget option right in the centre of town, this small hostel has basic, bright and simple rooms that sleep four to 12 people, a rooftop terrace and a small lounge with satellite TV – all in a right-on-top-of-a-nightclub location.

Burlington House B&B ££
(☎01865-513513; www.burlington-house.co.uk; 374 Banbury Rd, Summertown; s/d from £66/92; P@📶) Twelve big, bright, elegant rooms with brightly patterned wallpaper and splashes of colour are available at this Victorian merchant house.

WORTH A TRIP

THE COTSWOLDS

A rural landscape, filled with glorious honey-coloured villages, old mansions, thatched cottages and atmospheric churches – welcome to the Cotswolds. This is prime tourist territory, however, and the most popular villages can be besieged by traffic in summer.

A handy gateway town is **Moreton-in-Marsh**: a bus service runs to/from Cheltenham (seven times daily, one hour, Monday to Saturday) via Stow-on-the-Wold (15 minutes), with two Sunday services from May to September; there are trains roughly every two hours to/from London Paddington (£26.90, one hour 40 minutes) via Oxford (£7.90, 40 minutes).

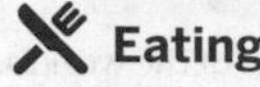

Eating

Door 74 MODERN BRITISH ££
(☎203374; www.door74.co.uk; 74 Cowley Rd; mains £10-14; ⏰noon-11pm Tue-Sat, 11am-4pm Sun) This cosy little place woos its fans with a rich mix of British and Mediterranean flavours and friendly service.

Atomic Burger AMERICAN £
(www.atomicburger.co.uk; 96 Cowley Rd; mains £5.25-11; ⏰closed breakfast Mon-Fri) Try the inventive Messy Jessie, Dead Elvis, the barbeque ribs and nachos and curly fries, all washed down with mega shakes.

Café Coco MEDITERRANEAN £
(www.cafe-coco.co.uk; 23 Cowley Rd; mains £6-10.50) This Cowley Rd institution is a hip hang-out, with classic posters on the walls and a bald plaster-cast clown in an ice bath. The food combines Mediterranean mains with waffles and pecan pie, and most people come for the atmosphere.

Drinking

Turf Tavern PUB
(4-5 Bath Pl; ⏰11am-11pm) Hidden away down a narrow alleyway, this tiny medieval pub is one of the town's best loved and bills itself as 'an education in intoxication'.

Bear PUB
(6 Alfred St) Arguably the oldest pub in Oxford (there's been a pub on this site since 1242).

Eagle & Child PUB
(49 St Giles) Affectionately known as the 'Bird & Baby', this atmospheric place, dating from 1650, was once the favourite haunt of Tolkien and CS Lewis.

Information

Tourist Office (☎01865-252200; www.visitoxfordandoxfordshire.com; 15-16 Broad St; ⏰9.30am-5pm Mon-Sat, 10am-3.30pm Sun, closes 30 mins later in winter)

Getting There & Away

BUS Oxford's main bus/coach station is at Gloucester Green. Services to London (£18 return) run up to every 15 minutes, day and night, and take about 90 minutes. There are also regular buses to/from Heathrow and Gatwick airports.

TRAIN Oxford's train station has half-hourly services to London Paddington (£23, one hour) and roughly hourly trains to Birmingham (£16, 1¼ hours). Hourly services also run to Bath (£16, 1¼ hours) and Bristol (£22, one to two hours), but require a change at Didcot Parkway.

Birmingham

TRANSPORT HUB

Once a byword for bad town planning, England's second-largest city – known to locals as 'Brum' – is finally shaking off its industrial decline and looks better than it has done in decades, helped in no small part by the revitalised Bullring centre. Still, it's short on sights, and mainly useful as a transport hub for reaching Scotland and England's other northern cities.

Sleeping

Birmingham Central Backpackers HOSTEL £
(☎0121-643 0033; www.birminghamcentralbackpackers.com; 58 Coventry St; dm from £13; @) Birmingham's purple and turquoise backpacker hostel is handy for the bus station and offers multicoloured dorms and funky Japanese-style pods.

Getting There & Away

BUS Most intercity buses run from the **Birmingham Coach Station** (Digbeth High St), but the X20 to Stratford-upon-Avon (1¼ hours, hourly Monday to Friday, every two hours at weekends) leaves from Moor St.

National Express (☎08718 81 81 81; www.nationalexpress.com) runs coaches to London (£15.70, 2¾ hours, every 30 minutes), Manchester (£12.60, 2½ hours, 12 daily) and Oxford (£11.60, 1½ to two hours, five daily).

TRAIN Most long-distance trains leave from New St station, including services to London Euston (£40.90, 1½ hours, half-hourly) and Manchester (£30.50, 1¾ hours, every 15 minutes).

Stratford-upon-Avon

POP 22,187

William Shakespeare was born in Stratford in 1564 and died here in 1616. The five houses linked to his life form the centrepiece of a tourist attraction that verges on a cult of personality. Experiences range from the tacky (Bard-themed tearooms) to the humbling (Shakespeare's modest grave in Holy Trinity Church) and the sublime (a play by the world-famous Royal Shakespeare Company).

Sights & Activities

Shakespeare Houses MUSEUM
(☎01789-204016; www.shakespeare.org.uk; all 5 properties adult/child £21.50/13.50, 3 in town £14/9; ⏰9am-5pm Apr-Oct, hours vary Nov-Mar) Five of the most important buildings associated with Shakespeare, all run by the Shakespeare Birthplace Trust, contain museums that form the core of the visitor experience at Stratford. You can buy individual tickets, but it's more cost-effective to buy a combination ticket, either covering the three houses in town, or all five properties. Expect long queues throughout the summer.

Holy Trinity Church CHURCH
(☎01789-266316; www.stratford-upon-avon.org; Old Town; church free, Shakespeare's grave adult/child £1.50/50p; ⏰8.30am-6pm Mon-Sat, 12.30-5pm Sun Apr-Sep, shorter hours Oct-Mar) The final resting place of the Bard is said to be the most visited parish church in England.

Sleeping

White Sails GUESTHOUSE ££
(☎01789-264326; www.white-sails.co.uk; 85 Evesham Rd; r from £95) Plush fabrics, framed prints, brass bedsteads and shabby-chic tables and lamps set the scene at this gorgeous, intimate guesthouse.

Stratford-upon-Avon YHA HOSTEL £
(☎0845 371 9661; www.yha.org.uk; Hemmingford House, Alveston; dm from £16; P@) Set in a large, 200-year-old mansion 1.5 miles east of the town centre along Tiddington Rd, this superior hostel attracts travellers of all ages. There's a canteen, bar and kitchen, and buses 18 and 18a run here from Bridge St.

ROYAL SHAKESPEARE COMPANY

You just can't come to Stratford without seeing one of the Bard's plays performed by the **Royal Shakespeare Company** (RSC; ☎0844 800 1110; www.rsc.org.uk; Waterside; tickets £8-38), especially since the multimillion pound redevelopment of its two main theatres, the Royal Shakespeare Theatre and Swan Theatre on Waterside.

There are often special deals for under-25-year-olds, students and seniors, and a few tickets are held back for sale on the day of performance.

Eating & Drinking

Sheep St is clustered with eating options, mostly aimed at theatregoers (look out for good-value pretheatre menus).

Edward Moon's MODERN BRITISH ££
(☎01789-267069; www.edwardmoon.com; 9 Chapel St; mains £10-15) Named after a famous travelling chef who cooked up the flavours of home for the British colonial service, this snug and just-refurbished eatery serves delicious, hearty English dishes, many livened up with herbs and spices from the East.

Dirty Duck PUB
(Waterside) Officially called the 'Black Swan', this enchanting riverside alehouse is a favourite thespian watering hole, boasting a roll call of former regulars (Olivier, Attenborough etc) that reads like a *Who's Who* of actors.

Windmill Inn PUB
(Church St) Ale was flowing here at the same time as rhyming couplets gushed from Shakespeare's quill – this pub with low ceilings has been around a while.

Information

Tourist Office (☎01789-264293; www.shakespeare-country.co.uk; 62 Henley St; ⊙10am-5pm, to 4pm winter)

Getting There & Away

BUS National Express coaches and other bus companies run from Stratford's Riverside bus station (behind the Stratford Leisure Centre on Bridgeway). Destinations include Birmingham (£8.80, one hour, twice daily), London Victoria (£17.60, three to four hours, five daily) and Oxford (£11.20, one hour, twice daily). Bus 16 runs to Warwick (40 minutes, hourly).

TRAIN From Stratford train station, London Midland runs to Birmingham (£6.80, one hour, hourly), and Chiltern Railways runs to London Marylebone (£25, 2¼ hours, four daily).

Warwick

POP 25,434

Regularly name-checked by Shakespeare, Warwick is a treasure house of medieval architecture, dominated by the soaring turrets of **Warwick Castle** (☎0870 442 2000; www.warwick-castle.co.uk; castle adult/child £19.95/11.95, castle & dungeon £27.45/19.45; ⊙10am-6pm Apr-Sep, to 5pm Oct-Mar; Ⓟ), founded in 1068 by William the Conqueror, and later the ancestral home of the earls of Warwick. It's now been transformed into a major tourist attraction by the owners of Madame Tussauds, with kid-centred activities and waxworks populating the private apartments.

Stagecoach bus 16 goes to Stratford-upon-Avon (40 minutes, hourly). Trains run to Birmingham (£7.40, 45 minutes, every half-hour), Stratford-upon-Avon (£5.20, 30 minutes, hourly) and London (£30, 1¾ hours, every 20 minutes).

Peak District National Park

Squeezed between the industrial Midlands to the south and the cities of Manchester and Sheffield to the west and east, the surprisingly rural **Peak District** (☎01629-816200; www.peakdistrict.gov.uk) is one of the finest areas in England for walking, cycling and other outdoor activities. Don't be misled by the name; there are few peaks, but plenty of wild moors, rolling farmland and deep valleys – plus hardy villages, prehistoric sites and limestone caves.

The park's best-known attraction is **Chatsworth House** (☎01246-582204; www.chatsworth.org; house & gardens adult/child £15/9, gardens only £10/6, playground £5, park free; ⊙11am-5.30pm mid-Mar–late Dec, closed late Dec–mid-Mar), occupied by the earls and dukes of Devonshire for centuries. Packed with priceless paintings and period furniture, the house also has 25 sq miles of grounds and ornamental gardens, some landscaped by Lancelot 'Capability' Brown.

The towns of Buxton to the west or Matlock to the east are good gateways, or you can stay right in the centre at Edale, Bakewell or Castleton.

Getting There & Around

National Express coaches run from London Victoria to Manchester and Buxton, from where you can switch to a local bus. Derby, south of the park, is another good gateway, easily reached by coach and train, and from there trains run to Matlock. Trains also run between Sheffield and Manchester via Edale and several other Peak villages.

The hourly **Transpeak** (www.transpeak.co.uk) service cuts across the Peak District from Nottingham and Derby to Manchester, via Matlock, Bakewell and Buxton.

EASTERN ENGLAND

The vast flatland of Eastern England (or East Anglia, as it's usually called) is a mix of lush farms, melancholy fens, big skies and the bucolic scenery that once inspired Constable and Gainsborough.

Cambridge

POP 119,100

Drowning in exquisite architecture, steeped in history and tradition, and renowned for its quirky rituals, Cambridge is a university town extraordinaire. The tightly packed core of ancient colleges, the picturesque riversides and the leafy green meadows that seem to surround the city give it a far more tranquil appeal than rival Oxford.

Sights

Cambridge University comprises 31 colleges, though not all are open to the public. Opening hours given are only a rough guide, so contact the colleges or the tourist office for information.

Trinity College NOTABLE BUILDING
(www.trin.cam.ac.uk; Trinity St; adult/child £1.50/1; ⏲10.30am-4.30pm) The largest of Cambridge's colleges is entered via an impressive gateway. Don't miss the statue of the founder, Henry VIII; his right hand grips not a sceptre but a table leg, put there by student pranksters and never replaced.

King's College Chapel CHURCH
(www.kings.cam.ac.uk/chapel; King's Pde; adult/child £7.50/free, Evensong free; ⏲9.45am-4.30pm Mon, from 9.30am Tue-Sun, Evensong 5.30pm Mon-Sat, 10.30am & 3.30pm Sun, term time only) This college chapel is one of the most extraordinary examples of Gothic architecture in England. The vast 80m-long **fan-vaulted canopy** is the largest expanse of fan vaulting in the world.

The Backs PARK
Behind the grandiose facades of the city's central colleges are the Backs, a swathe of green spaces that offer unparalleled views. Several bridges cross the river, including the fanciful **Bridge of Sighs**, built in 1831, and the **Mathematical Bridge**, built in 1749.

Fitzwilliam Museum MUSEUM
(www.fitzmuseum.cam.ac.uk; Trumpington St; admission by donation, guided tour £5; ⏲10am-5pm Tue-Sat, noon-5pm Sun) This museum is filled with priceless treasures from ancient Egyptian sarcophagi to Greek and Roman art, Chinese ceramics to English glass, as well as some dazzling illuminated manuscripts. You can join a one-hour guided tour of the museum on Saturdays at 2.30pm.

Corpus Christi College NOTABLE BUILDING
(www.corpus.cam.ac.uk; King's Pde; admission £2.50; ⏲10am-4.30pm) Entry to this illustrious college is via the so-called **New Court**, which dates back a mere 200 years. On the corner of Bene't St you'll find the college's new **Corpus Clock**. The clock is only accurate once every five minutes. At other times it slows or stops and then speeds up, which, according to its creator, JC Taylor, reflects life's irregularity.

Sleeping

Benson House B&B ££
(☎01223-311594; www.bensonhouse.co.uk; 24 Huntingdon Rd; d from £90; P) Just a 15-minute walk from the city centre, the rooms at this B&B range from monochrome minimalism to muted classical elegance. To get here follow Castle St north of the city centre into Huntingdon Rd.

Cambridge Rooms COLLEGE ROOMS ££
(www.cambridgerooms.co.uk; s/d from £41/78) If you wish to experience life inside the hallowed college grounds, you can stay in a student room in one of several colleges. There's a good choice of rooms during university holidays.

Cambridge YHA HOSTEL £
(☎0845 371 9728; www.yha.org.uk; 97 Tenison Rd; dm/tw £19/45; @) Busy, popular hostel with compact dorms and good facilities near the train station.

Eating

Oak Bistro MODERN BRITISH ££
(☎01223-323361; www.theoakbistro.co.uk; 6 Lensfield Rd; mains £12-20, 2-/3-course set lunch £12/15; ⏲Mon-Sat) This great local favourite serves up simple, classic dishes with modern flair. Reservations are essential even for lunch.

Hakka CHINESE ££
(☎01223-568988; www.hak-ka.co.uk; 24 Milton Rd; mains £7.50-11.50; ⏲closed lunch;) Chef Daniel's mother has taught him the secrets of Hakka cooking and once you've tasted his signature salt and chilli chicken, you'll be inclined to give her a hug and a kiss.

Chop House TRADITIONAL BRITISH ££
(www.cambscuisine.com/cambridge-chop-house; 1 Kings Pde; mains £9.50-24) If you're craving sausage and mash, a sizzling steak, suet pudding, fish pie or potted ham, look no further. Sister restaurant **St John's Chop**

TRANSPORT FROM CAMBRIDGE

Bus

DESTINATION	PRICE (£)	DURATION	FREQUENCY
Gatwick	37	3½-4hr	
Heathrow	31	2½-3hr	
Oxford	11	3¼-3½hr	2 hourly
Stansted	13	50min	

Train

DESTINATION	PRICE (£)	DURATION	FREQUENCY
Birmingham New Street	30	3hr	hourly
Ely	14	15min	3 hourly
Ely	19	50min-1¼hr	

House (www.cambscuisine.com/st-johns-chop-house; 21-24 Northampton St) has the same menu.

Stickybeaks CAFE £
(www.stickybeakscafe.co.uk; 42 Hobson St; mains £3-7; ⊙8am-5.30pm Mon-Fri, 9am-5.30pm Sat, 10am-5pm Sun; ✎) Nibble cakes or tuck into imaginative salads (couscous with pomegranate, puy lentils with goat's cheese) at this popular new cafe.

Drinking

Eagle PUB
(Bene't St) Cambridge's most famous pub has loosened the tongues and pickled the grey cells of many an illustrious academic.

Maypole PUB
(www.maypolefreehouse.co.uk; 20a Portugal Pl) This friendly, popular pub has hit a winning formula: serve a good selection of real ales, throw in some great cocktails, and host a successful beer festival in 2012 (set to become an annual event).

Entertainment

Corn Exchange THEATRE
(www.cornex.co.uk; Wheeler St) The city's main centre for arts and entertainment, attracting the top names from pop and rock to ballet.

Information

Tourist Office (☎0871-266 8006; www.visitcambridge.org; Old Library, Wheeler St; ⊙10am-5.30pm Mon-Fri, to 5pm Sat, 11am-3pm Sun)

Getting There & Away

BUS From Parkside there are regular **National Express** (www.nationalexpress.com) buses.

TRAIN The train station is off Station Rd, which is off Hills Rd.

NORTHEAST ENGLAND

By turns wild and pretty, rural and urban, modern and historic, northeast England contains the large and varied counties of Yorkshire and Northumberland. For general information, see www.yorkshirevisitor.com and www.visitnortheastengland.com.

York

POP 181,100

Nowhere in northern England says 'medieval' quite like York, a city of extraordinary historical wealth that has lost little of its preindustrial lustre. Its spider's web of narrow streets is enclosed by a magnificent circuit of 13th-century walls and the city's rich heritage is woven into virtually every brick and beam.

Sights

TOP CHOICE York Minster CHURCH
(www.yorkminster.org; Deangate; adult/child £9/free, combined ticket incl tower £14/3.50; ⊙9am-5.30pm Mon-Sat Apr-Oct, 9.30am-5.30pm Mon-Sat Nov-Mar, noon-5.30pm Sun year-round) Not content with being Yorkshire's most important historic building, the awe-inspiring

York Minster is also the largest medieval cathedral in all of Northern Europe. Seat of the archbishop of York, primate of England, it is second in importance only to Canterbury, home of the primate of *all* England. Built mainly between 1220 and 1480, it encompasses all the major stages of Gothic architecture, with highlights including the west front, octagonal chapter house, the towers, and the fabulous stained-glass windows.

Jorvik Viking Centre MUSEUM
(www.jorvik-viking-centre.co.uk; Coppergate; adult/child £9.25/6.25; ⏲10am-5pm Apr-Oct, to 4pm Nov-Mar) This is a smells-and-all reconstruction of the Viking settlement that was unearthed here during excavations in the late 1970s, brought to you courtesy of a 'time-car' monorail that transports you through 9th-century Jorvik (the Viking name for York). You can cut time spent waiting in the queue by booking your tickets online and choosing the time you want to visit – it costs £1 extra.

FREE **City Walls** ARCHAEOLOGICAL SITE
(⏲8am-dusk) If the weather's good, don't miss the chance to walk the city walls, which follow the line of the original Roman walls. The full circuit is 4.5 miles (allow 1½ to two hours); if you're pushed for time, the short stretch from Bootham Bar to Monk Bar is worth doing for the views of the minster.

FREE **National Railway Museum** MUSEUM
(www.nrm.org.uk; Leeman Rd; ⏲10am-6pm) York's National Railway Museum is the biggest in the world, with more than 100 locomotives. Highlights for trainspotters include a replica of George Stephenson's *Rocket* (1829), the world's first 'modern' steam locomotive and the world-famous *Flying Scotsman*, the first steam engine to break the 100mph barrier.

Yorkshire Museum MUSEUM
(www.yorkshiremuseum.org.uk; Museum St; adult/child £7.50/free; ⏲10am-5pm) Most of York's Roman archaeology is hidden beneath the medieval city, so the recently revamped displays in the Yorkshire Museum are invaluable for an idea of what the Roman city was like.

Shambles STREET
(www.yorkshambles.com) The narrow, cobbled lane known as the Shambles, lined with 15th-century Tudor buildings that overhang so far they seem to meet above your head, is the most visited street in Europe. It takes its name from the Saxon word *shamel*, meaning 'slaughterhouse' – in 1862 there were 26 butcher shops on this one street.

TOP CHOICE **Clifford's Tower** CASTLE
(EH; www.english-heritage.org.uk; Tower St; adult/child £4/2.40; ⏲10am-6pm Apr-Sep, to 5pm Oct) There's precious little left of York Castle except for this evocative stone tower. There's not much to see inside but the views over the city are excellent.

Tours

Ghost Hunt of York WALKING TOUR
(www.ghosthunt.co.uk; adult/child £5/3; ⏲tours 7.30pm) Award-winning and highly entertaining 75-minute tour laced with authentic ghost stories. Begins at the Shambles, whatever the weather (they never cancel).

Yorkwalk WALKING TOUR
(www.yorkwalk.co.uk; adult/child £5.50/3.50; ⏲tours 10.30am & 2.15pm Feb-Nov) Two-hour themed walks, including Roman York, and the inevitable graveyard, coffin and plague tour. Walks depart from Museum Gardens Gate on Museum St.

FREE **Association of Voluntary Guides** WALKING TOUR
(http://avgyork.co.uk; ⏲tours 10.15am & 2.15pm Apr-Oct, also 6.45pm Jun-Aug, 10.15am Nov-Mar) Two-hour walking tours of the city starting from Exhibition Sq in front of York City Art Gallery.

Sleeping

Beds are tough to find midsummer, even with the inflated prices of the high season.

YORK PASS

If you plan on visiting a lot of sights, you can save yourself some money by using a **York Pass** (www.yorkpass.com; 1/2/3 days adult £34/48/58, child £18/22/26). It grants you free access to more than 70 pay-to-visit sights in Yorkshire, including all the major attractions in York. Available at York Visitor Centre, or you can buy online.

York

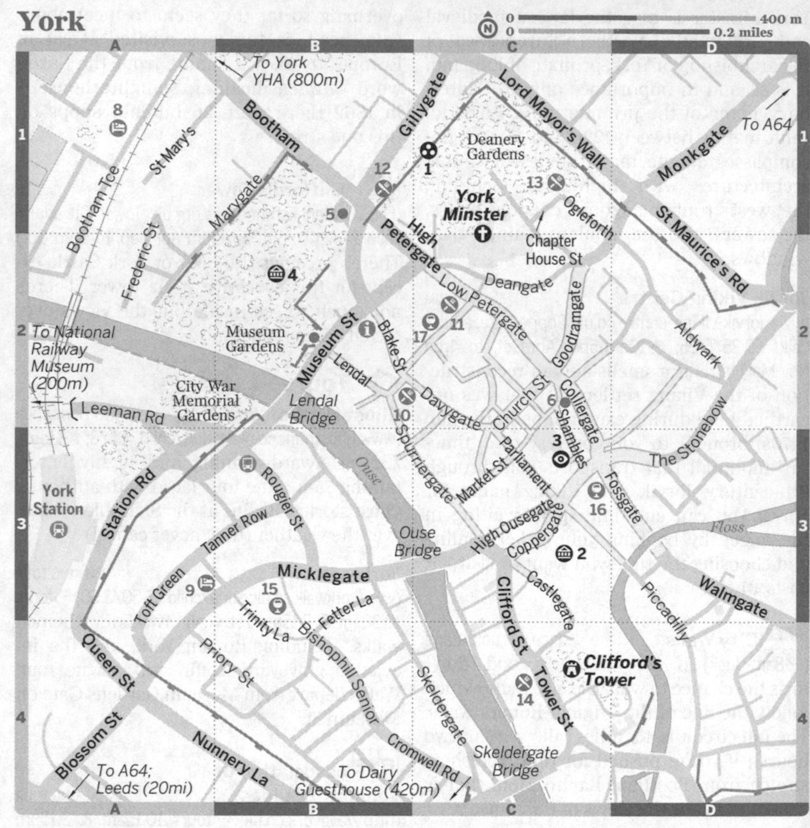

Abbeyfields B&B ££

(☎01904-636471; www.abbeyfields.co.uk; 19 Bootham Tce; s/d from £49/79; 📶) Expect a warm welcome and thoughtfully arranged bedrooms here, with chairs and bedside lamps for comfortable reading.

Dairy Guesthouse B&B ££

(☎01904-639367; www.dairyguesthouse.co.uk; 3 Scarcroft Rd; s/d from £55/75; 📶) A lovely Victorian home that has retained many of its original features, including pine doors, stained glass and cast-iron fireplaces. Minimum two-night stay at weekends.

York YHA HOSTEL £

(☎0845 371 9051; www.yha.org.uk; 42 Water End, Clifton; dm £18-23; P@📶) Originally the Rowntree (Quaker confectioners) mansion, this handsome Victorian house makes a spacious and child-friendly youth hostel, with most of the rooms being four-bed dorms. It's about a mile northwest of the city centre; take bus 2 from Station Ave or Museum St.

Ace Hotel HOSTEL £

(☎01904-627720; www.acehotelyork.co.uk; 88-90 Micklegate; dm £18-30, tw £68; @📶) Housed in a Grade I Georgian building, this is a large and well-equipped hostel that is popular with school groups and stag and hen parties – don't come for peace and quiet!

Eating

Cafe No 8 BISTRO £

(☎01904-653074; www.cafeno8.co.uk; 8 Gillygate; mains £7-10, 2-course lunch £14; ⏰11am-10pm Mon-Fri, 10am-10pm Sat & Sun; 📶👪) A cool little bistro with modern artwork mimicking the Edwardian stained glass at the front. Booking recommended.

York

Top Sights

Clifford's Tower C4
York Minster C1

Sights

1 City Walls C1
2 Jorvik Viking Centre C3
3 Shambles C3
4 Yorkshire Museum B2

Activities, Courses & Tours

5 Association of Voluntary Guides B1
6 Ghost Hunt of York C2
7 Yorkwalk B2

Sleeping

8 Abbeyfields A1
9 Ace Hotel A3

Eating

10 Bettys B2
11 Bettys Stonegate C2
12 Cafe No 8 .... B1
13 Grays Court 01
14 Olive Tree C4

Drinking

15 Ackhorne B3
16 Blue Bell C3
17 Ye Olde Starre C2

Grays Court CAFE ££
(www.grayscourtyork.com; Chapter House St; mains £6-10; ⏲lunch) Enjoy gourmet coffee and cake in the sunny garden, or indulge in a light lunch in the historic setting of the oak-panelled Jacobean gallery.

Bettys CAFE ££
(www.bettys.co.uk; St Helen's Sq; mains £6-13, afternoon tea £18; ⏲9am-9pm; 👪) Afternoon tea, old-school style, with white-aproned waitresses, linen tablecloths and a teapot collection ranged along the walls. Betty's younger sister, **Bettys Stonegate** (www.bettys.co.uk; 46 Stonegate; mains £6-13; ⏲10am-5.30pm Sun-Fri, 9am-5.30pm Sat; 👪), is more demure and less crowded, and just as good.

Olive Tree MEDITERRANEAN ££
(☎01904-624433; www.theolivetreeyork.co.uk; 10 Tower St; mains £10-17; ⏲lunch & dinner) Local produce gets a Mediterranean makeover at this bright and breezy bistro with a view across the street to Clifford's Tower. The lunchtime and early evening menu offers two courses for £13.

Drinking

With only a couple of exceptions, the best drinking holes in town are the older, traditional pubs.

Blue Bell PUB
(53 Fossgate) This is what a real English pub looks like – a tiny, wood-panelled room with a smouldering fireplace, decor (and beer and smoke stains) dating from c 1798, and Timothy Taylor and Black Sheep ales on tap.

Ye Olde Starre PUB
(40 Stonegate) Licensed since 1644, this is York's oldest pub – a warren of small rooms and a small beer garden, with a half-dozen real ales on tap.

Ackhorne PUB
(9 St Martin's Lane) Tucked away off beery, sloppy Micklegate, this locals' inn is as comfortable as old slippers – some of the old guys here look like they've merged with the furniture.

Information

York Visitor Centre (☎01904-550099; www.visityork.org; 1 Museum St; ⏲9am-6pm Mon-Sat, 10am-5pm Sun Apr-Sep, shorter hours Oct-Mar)

Getting There & Away

BUS For timetable information call **Traveline Yorkshire** (☎0871 200 2233; www.yorkshiretravel.net). All local and regional buses stop on Rougier St, about 200m northeast of the train station.

There are **National Express** (☎08717 81 81 78; www.nationalexpress.com) coaches to London (£28, 5½ hours, four daily), Birmingham (£28, 3¼ hours, one daily) and Newcastle (£15, 2¾ hours, four daily).

TRAIN York is a major railway hub with frequent direct services to Birmingham (£45, 2¼ hours), Newcastle (£15, one hour), Leeds (£11, 30 minutes), London's King's Cross (£80, two hours), Manchester (£15, 1½ hours) and Scarborough (£10, 50 minutes). There are also trains to Cambridge (£60, 2¾ hours), changing at Peterborough.

Castle Howard

Stately homes may be two a penny in England, but you'll have to try hard to find one as breathtakingly stately as **Castle Howard** (www.castlehoward.co.uk; adult/child house &

THE SETTLE–CARLISLE RAILWAY

The 72-mile **Settle–Carlisle Railway** (www.settle-carlisle.co.uk), built between 1869 and 1875, was one of the greatest engineering projects of the Victorian era and today offers one of England's most scenic railway journeys, travelling over a breathtaking assortment of hills, valleys, tunnels, embankments and viaducts – including the famous 400m-long Ribblehead Viaduct.

The journey from Leeds to Carlisle takes just under three hours. Various hop-on-hop-off passes are available; see the website.

grounds £13/7.50, grounds only £8.50/6; ⌚house 11am-4.30pm Apr-Oct, grounds 10am-5.30pm Mar-Oct & 1st 3 weeks Dec, 10am-4pm Nov-Feb), a work of theatrical grandeur and audacity, and one of the world's most beautiful buildings. It's instantly recognisable from its starring role in the 1980s TV series *Brideshead Revisited* and more recently in the 2008 film of the same name. It's 15 miles northeast of York. By public transport, Yorkshire Coastliner bus 840 (40 minutes from York, one daily) links Leeds, York, Castle Howard and Whitby.

Yorkshire Dales National Park

The **Yorkshire Dales** (☎752748; www.yorkshiredales.org.uk; Colvend, Hebden Road, Yorkshire Dales National Park Authority; 🚌from Skipton or Richmond, 🚆from Skipton or Carlisle) – named from the Old Norse word *dalr*, meaning 'valleys' – is the central jewel in the necklace of three national parks strung across the neck of northern England, with the dramatic fells of the Lake District to the west and the brooding heaths of the North Yorkshire Moors to the east.

Characterised by rolling valleys such as Wensleydale and Ribblesdale, the Dales have been protected as a national park since the 1950s, assuring their status as a walkers' and cyclists' paradise. The website is a useful resource.

Horton-in-Ribblesdale, Grassington, Richmond, Settle and Skipton all make good bases, and there are several good YHA hostels, including in **Malham** (☎0845 371 9529; www.yha.org.uk; dm £19.50; Ⓟ) and **Hawes** (☎0845 371 9120; www.yha.org.uk; Lancaster Tce; dm £19.50; Ⓟ).

Newcastle-upon-Tyne

POP 189,863

Once synonymous with postindustrial decline, today's Newcastle is reborn and brimming with confidence. All of a sudden, this unfailingly friendly city, with its Geordie accent thicker than molasses, has kick-started a brand-new arts and entertainment scene, while riotous nightlife remains an established tradition.

Sights

CITY CENTRE

FREE **Great North Museum** MUSEUM
(www.greatnorthmuseum.org; Barras Bridge; ⌚10am-5pm Mon-Sat, 1-5pm Sun) This outstanding museum is a fascinating jumble of dinosaurs, Roman altar stones, Egyptian mummies, Samurai warriors and some impressive taxidermy, all presented in an engaging and easily digestible way.

Life Science Centre MUSEUM
(www.life.org.uk; Times Sq; adult/child £9.95/6.95; ⌚10am-6pm Mon-Sat, 11am-6pm Sun) This excellent science village is one of the more interesting attractions in town. Through a series of hands-on exhibits and the latest technology you can discover the incredible secrets of life. The highlight is the Motion Ride, a motion simulator that lets you 'feel' what it's like to experience things such as bungee jumping and other extreme sports (the 3-D film changes every year).

FREE **Discovery Museum** MUSEUM
(www.twmuseums.org.uk; Blandford Sq; ⌚10am-5pm Mon-Sat, 2-5pm Sun) Tyneside's rich history is uncovered through a fascinating series of exhibits at this unmissable museum.

GATESHEAD

As you cross the Tyne to its southern side you've technically left Newcastle and entered the town of Gateshead.

FREE **BALTIC – Centre for Contemporary Art** MUSEUM
(www.balticmill.com; Gateshead Quays; ⌚10am-6pm Wed-Mon, from 10.30am Tue) Once a huge,

dirty, yellow grain store overlooking the Tyne, BALTIC is now a huge, dirty, yellow art gallery to rival London's Tate Modern. The constantly rotating shows feature the work and installations of some of contemporary art's biggest show-stoppers. There's also a viewing box for a fine Tyne vista.

Sleeping

CITY CENTRE

Backpackers Newcastle HOSTEL £
(0191-340 7334; www.backpackersnewcastle.com; 262 Westgate Rd; dm from £17.95;) This clean, well-run budget flophouse has just 26 beds, lending it a bit more of a backpacker vibe than its competitors in the city.

Sleeperz HOTEL ££
(0191-261 6171; www.sleeperz.com; 15 Westgate St; r from £67) A good location makes this new hotel a good choice for revellers, who won't care that the tidy rooms are on the smallish side.

Albatross Backpackers In! HOSTEL £
(0191-233 1330; www.albatrossnewcastle.com; 51 Grainger St; dm/d from £17.50/49;) Clean, fully equipped hostel with decent-sized dorms and a self-catering kitchen. There's even a small car park.

JESMOND

Newcastle YHA HOSTEL £
(0845 371 9335; www.yha.org.uk; 107 Jesmond Rd; dm from £18.50) This nice, rambling place has small dorms that are generally full, so book in advance. It's close to the Jesmond Metro stop.

Eating

The Broad Chare PUB ££
(0191-211 2144; www.thebroadchare.co.uk; 25 Broad Chare; mains £11; lunch & dinner Mon-Sat, lunch Sun) Classic English pub grub – the grilled pork chop with black pudding and cider sauce is divine – and superb cask ales.

Scrumpy Willow & the Singing Kettle ORGANIC ££
(0191-221 2323; www.scrumpywillowandthesingingkettle.co.uk; 89 Clayton St; mains £5-11; Mon-Sat, lunch Sun;) Voted one of the UK's top organic eateries by *Guardian* readers, this incredibly popular place bursts at the seams at mealtimes.

Pizzeria Francesca PIZZERIA ££
(134 Manor House Rd; pizzas & pastas £5, other mains £7-15; Mon-Sat) One of the northeast's best pizza and pasta joints, this chaotic, friendly place is how all Italian restaurants should be. Get in line and wait because you can't book in advance.

Drinking

It's no secret that Geordies like a good night out, epitomised by the cheap and colourful cocktails of the Bigg Market. The Ouseburn area attracts a mellower crowd; the western end of Neville St has a decent mix of great bars and is home to the best of the gay scene.

TRANSPORT FROM NEWCASTLE-UPON TYNE

Bus

DESTINATION	COMPANY	PRICE (£)	DURATION (HR)	FREQUENCY
Edinburgh	National Express	17.50	3	2 daily
London	National Express/ Megabus	12-35	7	9 daily
Manchester	National Express	21	5	5 daily

Train

DESTINATION	PRICE (£)	DURATION	FREQUENCY
Berwick	23.50	45min	hourly
Carlisle	14.40	1½hr	hourly
London King's Cross	116.20	3hr	half-hourly
York	33.50	1hr	every 20min

BRIDGING THE TYNE

Newcastle is famous for its bridges. Most prestigious of all is the **Tyne Bridge**, built by the same company as the Sydney Harbour Bridge. The quaint little **Swing Bridge** pivots in the middle to let ships through. The **High Level Bridge**, designed by Robert Stephenson, was the world's first combined road and railway bridge (1849). The most recent addition is the **Millennium Bridge** (2002), which lifts like an eyelid to let ships pass.

Centurion Bar BAR
(Central Station) Voted Newcastle's best bar in 2008, the former 1st-class waiting room at Central Station is ideal for a pre-club drink in style or a pre-train brew on the hop.

Blackie Boy PUB
(11 Groat Market) Locals grumble that this darkened boozer, one of the city's original taverns, has become too upmarket, but it's still a popular place to drink even if the decor has gone all weird.

Cumberland Arms PUB
(off Byker Bank, Ouseburn) Sitting on a hill at the top of the Ouseburn, this 19th-century bar has a sensational selection of ales and ciders as well as a range of Northumberland meads.

Information

Tourist Offices (www.visitnewcastlegateshead.com) Main branch (☎0191-277 8000; www.visitnewcastlegateshead.com; Central Arcade, Market St; ⊙9.30am-5.30pm Mon-Sat, 10am-4pm Sun); Guildhall (☎0191-277 8000; www.visitnewcastlegateshead.com; Guildhall; ⊙10am-5pm Mon-Fri, 9am-5pm Sat, 9am-4pm Sun); Sage Gateshead (☎0191-478 4222; www.visitnewcastlegateshead.com; Sage Gateshead; ⊙10am-5pm).

Getting There & Away

BUS Local and regional buses leave from Haymarket or Eldon Sq bus stations. National Express buses arrive and depart from the coach station on St James Blvd.

TRAIN Newcastle is on the main rail line between London and Edinburgh and is the starting point of the scenic Tyne Valley Line west to Carlisle.

Hadrian's Wall

Built in AD 122 to mark the edge of the Roman Empire, this 73-mile coast-to-coast barrier across England aimed to protect Roman-occupied Britain from the unruly Pictish tribes to the north, in the area we know now as Scotland.

Although some parts of the wall have virtually disappeared, other stretches are still in fairly good repair, and several of the original forts that once guarded the wall are still standing, including the ones at **Chesters** (EH; ☎01434-681379; Chollerford; adult/child £4.80/2.40; ⊙10am-6pm Apr-Sep) near Chollerford, **Vindolanda** (www.vindolanda.com; adult/child £6.25/3.75, with Roman Army Museum £9.50/5.25; ⊙10am-6pm Apr-Sep, to 5pm Feb, Mar & Oct) near Bardon Mill and **Housesteads** (EH; adult/child £6/3.60; ⊙10am-6pm Apr-Sep), between Bardon Mill and Haltwhistle.

For general information, see www.hadrianswall.org.

Getting There & Away

The Newcastle–Carlisle train line runs parallel to the wall a mile or two to the south, with stations at Hexham, Haydon Bridge, Bardon Mill, Haltwhistle and Brampton. There are hourly buses between Carlisle and Newcastle, via most of the same towns.

From June to September the hail-and-ride Hadrian's Wall Bus (number AD 122 – geddit?) shuttles between all the major sites, towns and villages along the way.

NORTHWEST ENGLAND

A place of two halves, Northwest England offers two very contrasting experiences: culture, music and big nights out in the world-famous cities of Manchester and Liverpool; and peace, quiet, fresh air and high peaks in the mountainous Lake District. So pack your dancing shoes and your hiking boots, and come on over.

Manchester

POP 394,270

Even accounting for northern bluster, the uncrowned capital of the north is well deserving of the title of 'England's second city'. While history and heritage make the city interesting, its distractions of pure pleasure make Manchester fun: you can dine, drink and dance yourself into happy oblivion in the swirl of hedonism that is one of Manchester's most cherished characteristics.

Sights

CITY CENTRE

FREE Museum of Science & Industry MUSEUM
(MOSI; ☎0161-832 2244; www.msim.org.uk; Liverpool Rd; charges vary for special exhibitions; ⏰10am-5pm) If there's anything you want to know about the Industrial (and post-Industrial) Revolution and Manchester's key role in it, you'll find the answers among the Museum of Science & Industry's collection of steam engines and locomotives, factory machinery from the mills, and the excellent exhibition telling the story of Manchester from the sewers up.

FREE People's History Museum MUSEUM
(☎0161-838 9190; www.phm.org.uk; Left Bank, Bridge St; ⏰10am-5pm) The story of Britain's 200-year march to democracy is told in all its pain and pathos at this superb museum, housed in a refurbished Edwardian pumping station.

National Football Museum MUSEUM
(☎0161-605 8200; www.nationalfootballmuseum.com; Corporation St, Urbis, Cathedral Gardens; ⏰10am-5pm Mon-Sat, 11am-5pm Sun) It's the world's most popular game and Manchester is home to both the world's most popular and the world's richest teams, so it makes sense that a museum dedicated to the global charms of football should find its home here.

FREE Manchester Art Gallery GALLERY
(☎0161-235 8888; www.manchestergalleries.org; Mosley St; ⏰10am-5pm Tue-Sun) A superb collection of British art and a hefty number of European masters are on display at the city's top gallery.

SALFORD QUAYS

It's a cinch to get to Salford Quays from the Manchester city centre via Metrolink (£2). For the Imperial War Museum North and the Lowry, look for the Harbour City stop; get off at Old Trafford for the eponymous stadium.

FREE Imperial War Museum North MUSEUM
(☎0161-836 4000; www.iwm.org.uk/north; Trafford Wharf Rd; ⏰10am-5pm) Daniel Libeskind's visually stunning Imperial War Museum North covers the main conflicts of the 20th century through a broad selection of displays and powerful films. Take the Metrolink to Harbour City or MediaCityUK.

The Lowry ARTS CENTRE
(☎0161-876 2020; www.thelowry.com; Pier 8, Salford Quays; ⏰11am-8pm Tue-Fri, 10am-8pm Sat, 11am-6pm Sun & Mon) Looking more like a shiny steel ship than an arts centre, the Lowry is home to more than 300 paintings and drawings by northern England's favourite artist, LS Lowry (1887–1976), famous for his humanistic depictions of industrial landscapes and northern towns.

Old Trafford STADIUM
(☎0870 442 1994; www.manutd.com; Sir Matt Busby Way; ⏰9.30am-5pm) Home of the world's most football famous club, the Old Trafford stadium is both a theatre and a temple for its millions of fans worldwide. The **tour** (adult/child £12.50/8.50; ⏰every 10min except match days 9.40am-4.30pm) includes a seat in the stands, a peek at the players' lounge and a walk down the tunnel to the pitch-side dugout. The **museum** (adult/child £9/7; ⏰9.30am-5pm) has a comprehensive history of the club.

Sleeping

TOP CHOICE Manchester YHA HOSTEL £
(☎0845 371 9647; www.yha.org.uk; Potato Wharf; dm incl breakfast from £16; P@☜)

ANGEL OF THE NORTH

This extraordinary, gigantic statue of a winged human figure looms over the main A1 highway about 5 miles south of Newcastle. At 20m high, 200 tonnes and with a wingspan wider than a Boeing 767, it's Antony Gormley's best-known sculpture and – thanks to all those passing cars – the most viewed piece of public art in the country.

You can walk right up to the base of the statue, and feel absolutely dwarfed. Buses 21 and 22 from Eldon Sq will take you there.

This purpose-built canalside hostel in the Castlefield area is one of the best in the country. It's a top-class option with four- and six-bed dorms, all with bathroom, as well as three doubles and a host of good facilities.

Hatters HOSTEL £
(☎0161-236 9500; www.hattersgroup.com; 50 Newton St; dm/s/d/tr from £15.50/28/52/65; P@☎) The old-style lift and porcelain sinks are the only leftovers of this former milliner's factory, now one of the best hostels in town.

Eating

Manchester has something for every palate and every budget. To dine like an in-the-know Mancunian, go to suburbs such as Didsbury, about 5 miles south of the city centre (take bus 43 or 143 from Oxford St).

The Oast House INTERNATIONAL ££
(☎0161-829 3830; www.theoasthouse.uk.com; Crown Sq, Spinningfields; mains £9-15) Tim Bacon's exciting new BBQ restaurant serves grilled delights including burgers, kebabs, steaks and rotisserie chickens.

Sam's Chop House BRITISH £
(☎0161-834 3210; www.samschophouse.co.uk; Back Pool Fold, Chapel Walks, off Cross St; mains £6-8) Arguably the city's top gastropub, Sam's is a Victorian classic that serves dishes straight out of a Dickens novel. The owners also run **Mr Thomas' Chop House** (52 Cross St; mains £10).

Richmond Tea Rooms CAFE £
(☎0161-237 9667; www.richmondtearooms.com; Richmond St; mains £5-8) Sandwiches, salads, rarebits and quiches are the mainstay at this retro tearoom.

Mark Addy MODERN BRITISH ££
(☎0161-832 4080; www.markaddy.co.uk; Stanley St; mains £8.90-12.50; ⊙lunch & dinner Wed-Fri, dinner Sat) Another contender for best pub grub in town. It recently opened a riverside deck.

Drinking

Bluu BAR
(☎0161-839 7740; www.bluu.co.uk; Smithfield Market Buildings, Thomas St; ⊙noon-midnight Sun-Mon, to 1am Tue-Thu, to 2am Fri & Sat) Our favourite of the Northern Quarter's collection of great bars.

Britons Protection PUB
(☎0161-236 5895; 50 Great Bridgewater St) Whisky – 200 different kinds of it – is the beverage of choice at this liver-threatening, proper English pub that also does Tudor-style meals (£8).

Lass O'Gowrie PUB
(☎0161-273 6932; 36 Charles St) A Victorian classic, off Princess St, that brews its own beer in the basement. It also does good-value bar meals (£6).

Odd BAR
(☎0161-833 0070; www.oddbar.co.uk; 30-32 Thomas St; ⊙11am-11pm Mon-Sat, to 10.30pm Sun) With its oddball furnishings, wacky tunes and anti-establishment customers, this is the perfect antidote to generic modern bars.

Entertainment

Sankey's CLUB
(☎0161-950 4201; www.sankeys.info; Radium St, Ancoats; admission free-£12; ⊙10pm-3am Thu & Fri, to 4am Sat) If you're a fan of techno, electro or any kind of nonmainstream house music, then a pilgrimage to Manchester's best nightclub should on no account be missed.

Fac251 CLUB
(☎0161-272 7251; www.factorymanchester.com; 112-118 Princess St; admission £1-6; ⊙9.30pm-3am Mon-Sat) Fac251, in Tony Wilson's former Factory Records HQ, stands on its own two feet as one of the best venues in town.

Information

Tourist Office (www.visitmanchester.com; Piccadilly Plaza, Portland St; guided tours £6/5 per adult/child daily; ⊙10am-5.15pm Mon-Sat, 10am-4.30pm Sun)

Getting There & Away

BUS National Express (☎08717 81 81 81; www.nationalexpress.com) serves most major cities almost hourly from Chorlton St coach station in the city centre. Destinations include Leeds (£8.40, one hour, hourly), Liverpool (£6.80, 1¼ hours, hourly) and London (£25, 3¾ hours, hourly).

TRAIN Manchester Piccadilly is the main station. Services include Liverpool Lime St (£11, 45 minutes, half-hourly), London Euston (£73.20, three hours, seven daily) and Newcastle (£54.20, three hours, six daily).

Chester

Marvellous Chester is one of English history's greatest gifts to the contemporary visitor. Its red-sandstone wall, which today gift-wraps a tidy collection of Tudor and Victorian buildings, was built during Roman times. The town was then called Castra Devana, and was the largest Roman fortress in Britain.

Sights

FREE City Walls LANDMARK

A good way to get a sense of Chester's unique character is to walk the 2-mile circuit along the walls that surround the historic centre, originally built by the Romans around AD 70 and substantially enhanced over the following centuries.

The Rows ARCHITECTURE

A series of two-level galleried arcades line Chester's four main streets. The architecture is a handsome mix of Victorian and Tudor (original and mock).

Chester Cathedral CHURCH

(☎01244-324756; www.chestercathedral.com; 12 Abbey Sq; adult/child £6/2.50; ⏰9am 5pm Mon-Sat, 1-4pm Sun) Originally a Benedictine abbey, Chester's cathedral was given a substantial Victorian facelift, but the 12th-century cloister and its surrounding buildings are essentially unaltered.

Sleeping

Chester Townhouse B&R ££

(☎01244-350021; www.chestertownhouse.co.uk; 23 King St; s/d £45/75; P) Five beautifully decorated rooms in a handsome 17th-century house within the city walls make Chester Townhouse a terrific option.

Chester Backpackers HOSTEL £

(☎01244-400185; www.chesterbackpackers.co.uk; 67 Boughton; dm from £15.50; wi-fi) Comfortable dorm rooms with nice pine beds in a typically Tudor white-and-black building.

Eating

Old Harker's Arms PUB ££

(☎01244-344525; www.harkersarms-chester.co.uk; 1 Russell St; mains £9-14; ⏰lunch & dinner) An old-style boozer with a gourmet kitchen, this is the perfect place to tuck into Cumberland sausages or a pint of local ale such as Cheshire Cat.

Getting There & Away

BUS National Express (☎08717 81 81 81; www.nationalexpress.com) coaches stop on Vicar's Lane, just opposite the tourist office. Destinations include Liverpool (£7.90, one hour, four daily), London (£23, 5½ hours, three daily) and Manchester (£7.40, 1¼ hours, three daily).

TRAIN The train station is about a mile from the city centre. City-Rail Link buses are free for people with rail tickets. Destinations include Liverpool (£6.20, 45 minutes, hourly), London Euston (£73.20, 2½ hours, hourly) and Manchester (£11 30, one hour, hourly).

Liverpool

POP 469,020

Few English cities are as shackled by reputation as Liverpool, and none has worked so hard to outgrow the cliches that for so long have been used to define it. A hardscrabble town with a reputation for wit and an obsessive love of football, Liverpool also has an impressive cultural heritage: its collection of museums and galleries is easily among the best in the country. And then, of course, there's the Beatles...

Sights

CITY CENTRE

FREE World Museum MUSEUM

(☎0151-478 4399; www.liverpoolmuseums.org.uk/wml; William Brown St; ⏰10am-5pm) Natural history, science and technology are the themes of this sprawling museum, whose exhibits range from birds of prey to space exploration.

FREE Walker Art Gallery GALLERY

(☎0151-478 4199; www.liverpoolmuseums.org.uk/walker; William Brown St; ⏰10am-5pm) The city's foremost gallery is the national gallery for northern England, housing an outstanding collection of art from the 14th to the 21st centuries.

FREE St George's Hall CULTURAL CENTRE

(☎0151-707 2391; www.stgeorgesliverpool.co.uk; William Brown St; ⏰10am-5pm Tue-Sat, 1-5pm Sun) Arguably Liverpool's most impressive building is the Grade I–listed St George's Hall, a magnificent example of neoclassical architecture, completed in 1854. **Tours** (☎0151-225 6909; adult £3.50; ⏰2pm Wed, 11am & 2pm Sat & Sun) of the hall are run in conjunction with the tourist office.

Liverpool Cathedral CHURCH

(☎0151-709 6271; www.liverpoolcathedral.org.uk; Upper Duke St; visitor centre & tower admission £5; ⏲8am-6pm) Liverpool's Anglican cathedral is Britain's largest church. The visitor centre features the **Great Space**, a 10-minute movie about the history of the cathedral, and access to the cathedral's 101m tower.

ALBERT DOCK

Liverpool's biggest tourist attraction is **Albert Dock** (☎0151-708 8854; www.albertdock.com; admission free), the city's former port and now a Unesco World Heritage site. It's also home to the city's famous trio of buildings known as the 'Three Graces': the **Port of Liverpool Building**, the **Cunard Building** and the **Royal Liver Building**.

FREE **International Slavery Museum** MUSEUM

(☎0151-478 4499; www.liverpoolmuseums.org.uk/ism; Albert Dock; ⏲10am-5pm) The extraordinary International Slavery Museum reveals slavery's unimaginable horrors – including Liverpool's own role in the triangular slave trade.

Beatles Story MUSEUM

(☎0151-709 1963; www.beatlesstory.com; Albert Dock; adult/student/child £12.95/9/7, incl Elvis & Us £15.95/12/7; ⏲9am-7pm, last admission 5pm) Liverpool's most popular museum won't illuminate any dark, juicy corners in the turbulent history of the world's most famous foursome – there's ne'er a mention of internal discord, drugs or Yoko Ono – but there's plenty of genuine memorabilia to keep a Beatles fan happy. Particularly impressive is the full-size replica of the Cavern Club (which was actually tiny) and the Abbey Rd studio where the lads recorded their first singles.

FREE **Tate Liverpool** MUSEUM

(☎0151-702 7400; www.tate.org.uk/liverpool; Albert Dock; special exhibitions adult/child from £5/4; ⏲10am-5.50pm Jun-Aug, 10am-5.50pm Tue-Sun Sep-May) Touted as the home of modern art in the north, this gallery features a substantial checklist of 20th-century artists across its four floors, as well as touring exhibitions from the mothership on London's Bankside.

Sleeping

CITY CENTRE

Hotel Indigo HOTEL ££

(☎0151-559 0111; www.hotelindigoliverpool.co.uk; 10 Chapel St; r from £65; @📶) It's labelled as a boutique hotel, but the 151-room Indigo is just too big and part of a franchise, so the feel is more corporate swish than bespoke boutique.

International Inn HOSTEL £

(☎0151-709 8135; www.internationalinn.co. uk; 4 South Hunter St; dm/d from £15/36; 📶) A superb converted warehouse in the middle of uniland: heated rooms with tidy wooden beds and bunks accommodate from two to 10 people. Facilities include a lounge, baggage storage, laundry and 24-hour front desk.

AROUND ALBERT DOCK

Liverpool YHA HOSTEL £

(☎0845 371 9527; www.yha.org.uk; 25 Tabley St; dm from £16; P📶) It may have the look of an eastern European apartment complex, but this award-winning hostel, adorned with plenty of Beatles memorabilia, is one of the most comfortable you'll find anywhere in the country.

Eating

Monro PUB ££

(☎0151-707 9933; www.themonro.com; 92 Duke St; 2-course lunch £11.95, dinner mains £14-20; ⏲lunch & dinner) Tough to find pub grub this good elsewhere, unless you go to its sister pub, the **James Monro** (☎0151-236 9700; www.thejamesmonro.com; 69 Tithebarn St; ⏲lunch & dinner Tue-Sun).

Italian Club ITALIAN £

(☎0151-708 5508; www.theitalianclubliverpool.co.uk; 85 Bold St; mains £6-11; ⏲10am-7pm Mon-Sat) The kind of Italian food relatives visiting from the home country would be glad to tuck into. For seafood, try **Italian Club Fish** (☎0151-707 2110; 128 Bold St; mains £8-14; ⏲Tue-Sun) just down the street.

Drinking

Philharmonic PUB

(36 Hope St; ⏲to 11.30pm) This extraordinary bar was designed by the shipwrights who built the *Lusitania*. The marble men's toilets are the only heritage-listed lav in the country.

Magnet BAR

(www.magnetliverpool.co.uk; 39 Hardman St) Red leather booths, plenty of velvet and a suitably seedy New York–dive atmosphere where Iggy Pop or Tom Waits would feel right at home.

Rigby's PUB

(21 Dale St) A traditional boozer that serves 'real ale' (ie a traditional brew with no ex-

TRANSPORT FROM LIVERPOOL

Bus

DESTINATION	PRICE (£)	DURATION (HR)	FREQUENCY
Birmingham	13.80	2¾	5 daily
London	28	5-6	6 daily
Manchester	6.80	1¼	hourly
Newcastle	24.50	6½	3 daily

Train

DESTINATION	PRICE (£)	DURATION
Chester	6.20	45min
London Euston	73.20	3¼hr
Manchester	11	45min

traneous carbon dioxide), Rigby's looks, feels and smells like an old-school pub.

Entertainment

Most of the city's clubs and late-night bars are concentrated in the area of Ropewalks.

Masque CLUB
(☎0151-707 6171; www.chibuku.com; 90 Seel St; admission £4-11; ⊙Mon-Sat) This converted theatre is home to our favourite club in town. The fortnightly Saturday Chibuku is one of the best club nights in all of England.

Nation CLUB
(☎0151-709 1693; 40 Slater St, Wolstenholme Sq; admission £4-13) It looks like an air-raid shelter, but it's the big-name DJs dropping the bombs at the city's premier dance club, formerly the home of Cream.

Academy LIVE MUSIC
(☎0151-794 6868; Liverpool University, 11-13 Hotham St) Good spot to see midsize bands on tour.

Cavern Club LIVE MUSIC
(☎0151-236 1965; www.cavernclub.org; 8-10 Mathew St) It's a reconstruction, and not even on the same spot, but the 'world's most famous club' is still a great spot to see local bands.

Information

Most of Liverpool's tourist business is done online, including an **accommodation hotline** (☎0845 601 1125; ⊙9am-5.30pm Mon-Fri, 10am-4pm Sat). There is a small tourist office in Albert Dock.

Getting There & Away

BUS The **National Express Coach Station** (www.nationalexpress.com; Norton St) is 300m north of Lime St station. There are services to/from most major towns.

TRAIN Liverpool's main station is Lime St. It has hourly services to almost everywhere.

Lake District National Park

A dramatic landscape of ridges, lakes and peaks, including England's tallest mountain, Scafell Pike (978m), the Lake District is a beautiful corner of Britain. The awe-inspiring geography here shaped the literary personae of some of Britain's best-known poets, including William Wordsworth.

Often called simply the Lakes, the national park and surrounding area attract around 15 million visitors annually. But if you avoid summer weekends, and especially if you do a bit of hiking, it's easy enough to miss the crush.

There's a host of B&Bs and country-house hotels in the Lakes, plus over 20 YHA hostels, many of which can be linked by foot.

Information

Brockhole National Park Visitor Centre (☎015394-46601; www.lake-district.gov.uk; ⊙10am-5pm Easter-Oct) Three miles north of Windermere on the A591, this is the Lake District's flagship visitor centre, and also has a teashop, adventure playground and gardens.

Getting There & Away

BUS

There's one daily National Express coach from London (£30, eight hours) via Lancaster and Kendal. Local buses include the following:

555/556 Lakeslink (half-hourly Monday to Saturday, hourly at weekends) Windermere, Brockhole Visitor Centre (seven minutes), Ambleside (15 minutes), Grasmere (30 minutes) and Keswick (one hour).

505 Coniston Rambler (eight daily Monday to Saturday, six on Sunday) Windermere to Coniston (50 minutes).

599 Lakes Rider (three times hourly Monday to Saturday, hourly on Sunday in summer) Open-top bus between Bowness, Dove Cottage and Grasmere.

TRAIN

Windermere is the only town accessible by train. It's on the branch line to Kendal (£4.20, 15 minutes) and Oxenholme (£4.90, 20 minutes), which has connections north and south, including Edinburgh (£55, 2½ hours), Glasgow (£43.40, 2¾ hours) and London Euston (£92.10, 3¼ hours). The train to Manchester Piccadilly (£32.40, 1½ to two hours) runs via Lancaster (£12.60, 45 minutes).

WINDERMERE & BOWNESS

POP 8432

Windermere – the lake and the town of the same name – has been a centre for Lakeland tourism since the first steam trains arrived in 1847. The station is still there, making this an excellent gateway.

DON'T MISS

HILL TOP

The button-cute farmhouse of **Hill Top** (NT; ☎015394-36269; www.nationaltrust.org.uk/hill-top; adult/child £8/4; ⏲10am-5pm Sat-Thu mid-Feb–Oct, shorter hours outside summer) is a must for Beatrix Potter buffs: it was her first house in the Lake District, and is also where she wrote and illustrated several of her famous tales.

The cottage is in Near Sawrey, 2 miles from Hawkshead and Ferry House. The **Cross Lakes Experience** (http://www.lakedistrict.gov.uk/visiting/planningyourvisit/travelandtransport/crosslakes; ⏲Mar-Oct) stops en route from Ferry House to Hawkshead.

Windermere Lake Cruises (☎015395-31188; www.windermere-lakecruises.co.uk) offers scheduled boat trips across the lake from the lakeside settlement of Bowness-on-Windermere.

Sleeping

Windermere YHA HOSTEL £
(☎0845-371 9352; www.yha.org.uk/hostel/windermere; Bridge Lane; dm £19.65; ⏲reception 7.30-11.30am & 1-11pm; P @) This sprawling period house is the closest YHA to Windermere. The rooms are modern, and facilities include a well-stocked shop, canteen and gear-drying room. Buses stop at Troutbeck Bridge, a mile-long walk uphill to the hostel.

Archway B&B £
(☎015394-45613; www.the-archway.com; 13 College Rd; d £50-55) A no-nonsense, old-fashioned, great-value B&B, worth a mention for its fell views, knock-down rates and absurdly generous breakfast.

Lake District Backpackers Lodge HOSTEL £
(☎015394-46374; www.lakedistrictbackpackers.co.uk; High St; dm £15; @) Windermere's indie hostel is handy for the station, but it's cramped and showing its age. Dorms and kitchen are small, but rates include bed linen and breakfast.

AMBLESIDE

POP 3382

Windermere and Bowness are tourist towns, but Ambleside is 100% for walkers and other outdoor types – with plenty of gear shops and the start point of several classic hikes.

Sleeping

Lakes Lodge B&B ££
(☎015394-33240; www.lakeslodge.co.uk; Lake Rd; r £79-129; P 📶) This modish minihotel offers a touch more luxury than Ambleside's other guesthouses. Some rooms are in an annexe next to the main building.

Ambleside YHA HOSTEL £
(☎0845 371 9620; ambleside@yha.org.uk; Windermere Rd; dm/d £23/40; P 📶) One of the YHA's flagship Lake District hostels, this huge lakeside house organises activity holidays (everything from kayaking to ghyll-scrambling). Great facilities (kitchen, bike rental, boat jetty and bar) mean it's heavily subscribed, so book well ahead.

Ambleside Backpackers HOSTEL £
(☎015394-32340; www.englishlakesbackpackers.co.uk; Old Lake Rd; dm £16; P@) Cottage hostel a short walk south from Ambleside's centre.

GRASMERE

Grasmere is a gorgeous little Lakeland village, all the more famous because of its links with Britain's leading Romantic poet, William Wordsworth.

Literary pilgrims come to **Dove Cottage** (☎015394-35544; www.wordsworth.org.uk; adult/child £7.50/4.50; ⊙9.30am-5.30pm), his former home, where highlights include some fine portraits of the man himself, a cabinet containing his spectacles, and a set of scales used by his pal Thomas de Quincey to weigh out opium. At **St Oswald's Church** you'll see a memorial to the poet, and in the churchyard you'll find his grave.

To cure any sombre thoughts, head for **Sarah Nelson's Gingerbread Shop** (www.grasmeregingerbread.co.uk; Church Stile; 12 pieces of gingerbread £4.95; ⊙9.15am-5.30pm Mon-Sat, 12.30-5pm Sun) and stock up on Grasmere's famous confectionery.

KESWICK

POP 5257

The main town of the north Lakes, Keswick sits beside lovely Derwent Water, a silvery curve studded by wooded islands and criss-crossed by puttering cruise boats, operated by the **Keswick Launch** (☎01768/-72263; www.keswick-launch.co.uk; round-the-lake ticket adult/child £9.25/4.50).

Sleeping

TOP CHOICE **Howe Keld** B&B ££
(☎017687-72417; www.howekeld.co.uk; 5-7 The Heads; s £55-58, d £90-130;) This Gold-standard B&B pulls out all the stops – goose-down duvets, slate-floored bathrooms, chic colours and furniture made by a local carpenter.

Oakthwaite House B&B ££
(☎017687-72398; www.oakthwaite-keswick.co.uk; 35 Helvellyn St; d £66-80) One of the top choices in the B&B-heavy neighbourhood round Helvellyn St. There are just four rooms (so not too crowded), all with power showers, white linen and soothingly neutral tones.

Keswick YHA HOSTEL £
(☎0845-371 9746; keswick@yha.org.uk; Station Rd; dm £23.40; @) Keswick's YHA is a beauty, lodged inside a converted woollen mill by the clattering River Rothay. Dorms are cosy, there's an excellent cafe and some rooms even have balconies over Fitz Park.

WALES

Lying to the west of England, the nation of Wales is a separate country within the state of Great Britain. It's a nation with Celtic roots, its own language and a rich historic legacy. While some areas in the south are undeniably scarred by coal mining and heavy industry, overall Wales boasts a landscape of wild mountains, rolling hills, rich farmland and some of the most beautiful beaches in all of Britain.

Cardiff

POP 324,800

The capital of Wales since only 1955, Cardiff has embraced its new role with vigour, emerging as one of Britain's leading urban centres in the 21st century.

Sights

CENTRAL CARDIFF

TOP CHOICE **Cardiff Castle** CASTLE
(www.cardiffcastle.com; Castle St; adult/child £11/8.50, incl guided tour £14/11; ⊙9am-5pm) The grafting of Victorian mock-Gothic extravagance onto Cardiff's most important historical relics makes Cardiff Castle the city's leading attraction. A 50-minute guided tour takes you through the interiors of this flamboyant fantasy world.

Millennium Stadium STADIUM
(☎029-2082 2228; www.millenniumstadium.com; Westgate St; tours adult/child £8.50/5) This spectacular stadium squats like a stranded spaceship in the heart of the city – and in this rugby-mad nation somehow gets away with it.

CARDIFF BAY

The redeveloped waterfront of Cardiff Bay is about 2 miles from the city centre, lined with bars, restaurants and shops – and a collection of stunning buildings.

Doctor Who Experience EXHIBITION
(☎0844 801 2279; www.doctorwhoexperience.com; Porth Teigr; adult/child £15/11; ⊙10am-5pm (last admission 3.30pm) Wed-Mon, daily school holidays) The reinvented *Doctor Who*, produced by BBC Wales, has brought Cardiff to the attention

of sci-fi fans worldwide. This exhibition houses props and costumes alongside video clips from the episodes they feature in. Fans can pick up a locations guide (30p) from the nerdalicious shop.

FREE **Wales Millennium Centre** ARTS CENTRE
(029-2063 6464; www.wmc.org.uk; Bute Pl; guided tour adult/child £5.50/4.50; 11am & 2.30pm) This architectural masterpiece of slate and bronze is the premier arts complex of Wales.

FREE **Senedd (National Assembly Building)** NOTABLE BUILDING
(0845 010 5500; www.assemblywales.org; 9.30am-4.30pm Mon-Fri, 10.30am-4.30pm Sat & Sun) Designed by Lord Richard Rogers (the architect behind London's Lloyd's Building and Paris' Pompidou Centre), the Senedd houses Wales' National Assembly.

Sleeping

NosDa HOSTEL £
(029-2037 8866; www.nosda.co.uk; 53-59 Despenser St; dm/s/tw from £21/32/46; P@) You won't find a better budget bed closer to the city centre than at this stylishly refurbished hostel right across the river from the Millennium Stadium.

TOP CHOICE **River House Backpackers** HOSTEL £
(029-2039 9810; www.riverhousebackpackers.com; 59 Fitzhamon Embankment; dm/r from £18/35; @) Professionally run by a young brother-and-sister team, the River House has a well-equipped kitchen, a small garden and a TV lounge. Free breakfast (cereal and toast) and pizza nights are a nice touch.

HAY-ON-WYE

This pretty little town on the banks of the River Wye, just inside the Welsh border, has become famous as one of Wales' literary landmarks thanks to its bevy of secondhand bookshops and the famous **Hay Festival** (01497-822629; www.hayfestival.com) – dubbed 'the Woodstock of the mind' by Bill Clinton. The 10-day festival is held in late May, when accommodation is almost impossible to find unless you've booked in advance.

Eating

TOP CHOICE **Riverside Market** MARKET £
(www.riversidemarket.org.uk; Fitzhamon Embankment; 10am-2pm Sun;) This riverside market has stalls heaving with cooked meals, cakes, cheese, organic meat, charcuterie, apple juice and real ale.

Restaurant Minuet ITALIAN £
(www.restaurantminuet.co.uk; 42 Castle Arcade; mains £4-11; 11am-4.30pm Mon-Sat;) It may look like a greasy spoon from the outside, but this unassuming eatery produces excellent cheap and cheerful Italian food.

Goat Major PUB £
(www.sabrain.com/goatmajor; 33 High St; pies £7.50; food noon-6pm Mon-Sat, noon-4pm Sun) A solidly traditional pub with armchairs, a fireplace and lip-smacking Brains Dark real ale on tap.

Zerodegrees ITALIAN ££
(www.zerodegrees.co.uk; 27 Westgate St; mains £8-16; noon-midnight Mon-Sat, noon-11pm Sun;) Within a big factory-like space this microbrewery and restaurant combines all-day food with superb artisan-crafted beers.

Drinking & Entertainment

TOP CHOICE **Gwdihw** BAR
(www.gwdihw.co.uk; 6 Guildford Cres; 3pm-midnight Sun-Wed, noon-2pm Thu-Sat) The last word in Cardiff hipsterdom, this cute little bar has an eclectic lineup of entertainment (ukelele jams; comedy nights; cake and craft markets; lots of live music, including micro-festivals that spill over into the car park).

Clwb Ifor Bach LIVE MUSIC
(029-2023 2199; www.clwb.net; 11 Womanby St) Truly an independent music great, *Y Clwb* has given many a Welsh band their break since the early 1980s.

Information

Cardiff Tourist Office (029-2087 3573; www.visitcardiff.com; Old Library, The Hayes; 9.30am-5.30pm Mon-Sat, 10am-4pm Sun)

Getting There & Away

BUS National Express travels to London (£11, 3½ hours). Other destinations include Birmingham (£11, three hours), Bristol (£9, 1¼ hours), Chepstow (£5.40, 45 minutes) and Monmouth (£11, 1¼ hours).

The First Greyhound service travels regularly between Cardiff and Swansea (peak/off-peak £7/5 return, one hour).

TRAIN **Arriva Trains Wales** (www.arrivatrainswales.co.uk) operates all train services in Wales. Direct services from Cardiff include London Paddington (£39, 2¼ hours), Swansea (£7.70, 50 minutes), Fishguard Harbour (£22, three hours), Abergavenny (£12, 40 minutes) and Bangor (£75, 4¼ hours).

Pembrokeshire Coast National Park

Established in 1952, **Pembrokeshire Coast National Park** (Parc Cenedlaethol Arfordir Sir Benfro; www.pembrokeshirecoast.org.uk) takes in almost the entire coast and its offshore islands, as well as the Preseli Hills in the north and the inland waters of the Cleddau rivers near Milford Haven. Pembrokeshire's sea cliffs and islands support huge breeding populations of seabirds, while seals, dolphins, porpoises and whales are frequently spotted in coastal waters.

There are three national park information centres – in Tenby, St Davids and Newport – or you can contact the **Pembrokeshire Coast National Park Authority** (www.pcnpa.org.uk) for further info.

Snowdonia National Park

Snowdonia National Park (Parc Cenedlaethol Eryri; www.eryri-npa.gov.uk) was founded in 1951 (making it Wales' first national park). Around 350,000 people travel to the national park to climb, walk or take the train to the summit of Mt Snowdon, Wales' highest mountain.

BETWYS-Y-COED

If you're looking for a base with an Alpine feel from which to explore Snowdonia National Park, the bustling little stone village of Betws-y-Coed (bet-us-ee-koyd) stands out as a natural option.

Sleeping & Eating

Tŷ Gwyn Hotel HISTORIC HOTEL ££
(01690-710383; www.tygwynhotel.co.uk; r £56-130; P wi-fi) This former coaching inn has been welcoming guests since 1636. The menu focuses on hearty, meaty mains (£13 to £18). It's located on the A5, just across Waterloo Bridge.

Betws-y-Coed YHA HOSTEL, CAMPGROUND £
(01690-710796; www.swallowfallshotel.co.uk; Holyhead Rd, Swallow Falls; dm/tw £17/40, site per adult/child £7/3; P wi-fi) A functional hostel that's part of a bustling traveller hub with camping and a pub.

Information

National Park Information Centre (01690-710426; www.eryri-npa.gov.uk; Royal Oak Stables; 9.30am-4.30pm)

Getting There & Away

BUS Snowdon Sherpa buses S2 and S6 stop outside the train station, with services to Swallow Falls (five minutes), Capel Curig (10 minutes), Pen-y-Pass (20 minutes) and Llanberis (30 minutes).

TRAIN Betws-y-Coed is on the **Conwy Valley Line** (www.conwyvalleyrailway.co.uk), with six daily services (three on Sunday) to Llandudno (£5.60, 52 minutes) and Blaenau Ffestiniog (£4.50, 27 minutes).

CAPEL CURIG

Tiny Capel Curig, 5 miles west of Betws-y-Coed, is one of Snowdonia's oldest hill stations, and has long been a magnet for walkers, climbers and other outdoor junkies. At the western edge of the village, the **Plas y Brenin Nation Mountain Centre** (01690-720214; www.pyb.co.uk; A4086) offers an array of residential courses including rock climbing, mountaineering, kayaking and canoeing. Taster days run throughout the school holidays with an introduction to two activities for £35.

The superb five star **Plas Curig Hostel** (01690-720225; www.snowdoniahostel.co.uk; A5; dm/d from £23/50; P wi-fi), opened in 2011, offers great views across to the Snowdon Horseshoe.

Snowdon Sherpa buses S2 and S6 stop here.

SNOWDON

No Snowdonia experience is complete without coming face-to-face with Snowdon (1085m). On a clear day the views stretch to Ireland and the Isle of Man. Even on a gloomy day you could find yourself above the clouds. At the top is the striking **Hafod Eryri** visitor centre, opened in 2009 by Prince Charles.

Six paths of varying length and difficulty lead to the summit, all taking around six hours return, or you can cheat and catch the **Snowdon Mountain Railway** (0844 493 8120; www.snowdonrailway.co.uk; return diesel

WORTH A TRIP

CONWY CASTLE

On the north coast of Wales, the historic town of Conwy is utterly dominated by the Unesco-designated cultural treasure of **Conwy Castle** (Cadw; adult/child £4.80/4.30; ⏲9.30am-6pm Jul & Aug, 9.30am-5pm Mar-Jun, Sep & Oct, 10am-4pm Mon-Sat, 11am-4pm Sun Nov-Feb), the most stunning of all Edward I's Welsh fortresses. Built between 1277 and 1307 on a rocky outcrop, it has commanding views across the estuary and Snowdonia National Park.

adult/child £27/18, steam £35/25; ⏲9am-5pm mid-Mar–Oct), opened in 1896 and still the UK's only public rack-and-pinion railway.

However you get to the summit, take warm, waterproof clothing, wear sturdy footwear and check the weather forecast before setting out.

Sleeping & Eating

Snowdon Ranger Youth Hostel HOSTEL £
(☎0845 371 9659; www.yha.org.uk; dm/q £18/72; P) On the A4085, 5 miles north of Beddgelert, at the trailhead for the Snowdon Ranger Path, this former inn is full of character.

Bryn Gwynant YHA HOSTEL £
(☎0845 371 9108; www.yha.org.uk; Nantgwynant; dm/tw £22/50; ⏲Mar-Oct; P) Victorian mansion overlooking the lake, 4 miles east of Beddgelert.

Getting There & Away

The Welsh Highland Railway stops at the trailhead of the Rhyd Ddu path, and there is a request stop (Snowdon Ranger Halt) where you can alight for the Snowdon Ranger path.

Snowdon Sherpa buses (£1 on buses S1, S2, S6, adult/child day ticket £4/2) stop at all of the trailheads.

SOUTHERN SCOTLAND

Scotland's two largest cities have been rivals for as long as anyone cares to remember: for many years, visitors tended to favour the capital and overlook Glasgow, but recently Scotland's second city has enjoyed a cultural and architectural renaissance. Rather than weighing up which of the two cities to see, try to fit both into your itinerary.

Edinburgh

POP 440,000

Edinburgh is a city that begs to be explored. From the vaults and *wynds* (lanes) that riddle the Old Town to the urban villages of Stockbridge and Cramond, it's filled with quirky come-hither nooks that tempt you to walk just a little bit further.

Sights

Edinburgh's city centre is divided into two parts – Old Town and New Town – split by Princess Street Gardens.

OLD TOWN

TOP CHOICE **Edinburgh Castle** CASTLE
(www.edinburghcastle.gov.uk; adult/child incl audioguide £16/9.60; ⏲9.30am-6pm Apr-Sep, to 5pm Oct-Mar, last admission 45min before closing) Dominating the skyline like a city in the clouds, this historic hilltop fortress should be the first stop for any visitor. It's a mix of architectural styles, representing centuries of use. Highlights include **St Margaret's Chapel** (the oldest building in Edinburgh) and the **Royal Palace** (including the Stone of Destiny and the Scottish Crown Jewels).

If you're pushed for time, the other key sights not to miss are the views from Argyle Battery, the One O'Clock Gun, the Great Hall, and the Prisons of War.

Real Mary King's Close HISTORIC BUILDING
(☎0845 070 6244; www.realmarykingsclose.com; 2 Warriston's Close, High St; adult/child £12.95/7.45; ⏲10am-9pm Apr-Oct, to 11pm Aug, 10am-5pm Sun-Thu, to 9pm Fri & Sat Nov-Mar) This medieval Old Town alley survived untouched for 250 years, and now gives visitors a fascinating insight into 16th- and 17th-century daily life. Costumed characters give tours through a 16th-century townhouse and the plague-stricken home of a 17th-century gravedigger. Advance booking recommended.

Camera Obscura CAMERA OBSCURA
(www.camera-obscura.co.uk; Castlehill; adult/child £10.95/7.95; ⏲9.30am-9pm Jul & Aug, 9.30am-7pm Apr-Jun & Sep-Oct, 10am-6pm Nov-Mar) Edinburgh's camera obscura is a curious 19th-century device – in constant use since 1853 – that uses lenses and mirrors to throw a live image of the city onto a large horizontal screen. Stairs lead up through various displays to the **Outlook Tower**, which offers great views over the city.

FREE **Scottish Parliament Building** NOTABLE BUILDING

(☎0131-348 5200; www.scottish.parliament.uk; ⏰9am-6.30pm Tue-Thu, 10am-5.30pm Mon & Fri in session, 10am-6pm Mon-Fri in recess Apr-Oct, 10am-4pm in recess Nov-Mar; 📶) The Scottish parliament building, built on the site of a former brewery close to the Palace of Holyroodhouse, was officially opened by HM the Queen in October 2005.

TOP CHOICE **Palace of Holyroodhouse** PALACE

(www.royalcollection.org.uk; adult/child £11/6.65; ⏰9.30am-6pm Apr-Oct, to 4.30pm Nov-Mar; 📶) This palace is the royal family's official residence in Scotland, but is more famous as the 16th-century home of the ill-fated Mary, Queen of Scots. The palace is closed to the public when the royal family is visiting and during state functions (usually in mid-May, and mid-June to early July; check the website for exact dates).

Holyrood Park PARK

The former hunting ground of Scottish monarchs, this park covers 263 hectares of varied landscape, including crags, moorland and a loch. The highest point is the 251m summit of **Arthur's Seat**, the deeply eroded remnant of a long extinct volcano.

FREE **Scottish National Gallery** GALLERY

(www.nationalgalleries.org; The Mound; fee for special exhibitions; ⏰10am-5pm Fri-Wed, to 7pm Thu; 📶) Designed by William Playfair, this imposing classical building houses an important collection of European art from the Renaissance to post-Impressionism.

Royal Yacht Britannia SHIP

(www.royalyachtbritannia.co.uk; Ocean Terminal; adult/child £11.75/7.50; ⏰9.30am-4.30pm Jul-Sep, to 4pm Apr-Jun & Oct, 10am-3.30pm Nov-Mar, last admission 90min before closing; 📶) One of Scotland's biggest tourist attractions is the former Royal Yacht *Britannia*. It was the British royal family's floating home during their foreign travels from the time of its launch in 1953 until it was decommissioned in 1997, and is now moored permanently in front of Ocean Terminal. Britannia was joined in 2010 by the 1930s racing yacht *Bloodhound*, which was owned by the Queen in the 1960s.

The Majestic Tour bus runs from Waverley Bridge to *Britannia* during opening times. Alternatively, take Lothian Bus 11, 22 or 35 to Ocean Terminal.

Sleeping

OLD TOWN

TOP CHOICE **Smart City Hostel** HOSTEL £

(☎0870 892 3000; www.smartcityhostels.com; 50 Blackfriars St; dm from £22, tr £107; @📶) A big (620 beds), bright, modern hostel that feels more like a hotel. Lockers in every room, a huge bar and a central location just off the Royal Mile make this a favourite place to stay for the young, party-mad crowd.

Castle Rock Hostel HOSTEL £

(☎0131-225 9666; www.scotlands-top-hostels.com; 15 Johnston Tce; dm/d £22/50; @📶) With its bright, spacious, single-sex dorms, superb views and central location, the 200-bed Castle Rock has lots to recommend it.

Budget Backpackers HOSTEL £

(☎0131-226 6351; www.budgetbackpackers.com; 9 Cowgate; dm from £16, tw £54; @) This fun spot piles on the extras, with bike storage, pool tables, laundry and a colourful chill-out lounge.

NEW TOWN & AROUND

Dene Guest House B&B ££

(☎0131-556 2700; www.deneguesthouse.com; 7 Eyre Pl; per person £25-50) The Dene is a friendly and informal place, set in a charming Georgian townhouse. The inexpensive single rooms make it ideal for solo travellers.

West End Hostel HOSTEL £

(☎0131-202 6107; www.hosteledinburgh.co.uk; 3 Clifton Tce; dm £18-22; 📶) This relatively new hostel is still clean and bright, with six- to 16-bed dorms (including female-only ones). Handy for train travellers (Edinburgh Haymarket station is across the road).

FESTIVAL CITY

Edinburgh boasts a frenzy of festivals throughout the year, including the world-famous **Edinburgh Festival Fringe** (☎0131-226 0026; www.edfringe.com; 180 High St), held over 3½ weeks in August, the last two weeks overlapping with the first two weeks of the **Edinburgh International Festival** (☎0131-473 2099; www.eif.co.uk).

See www.edinburghfestivals.co.uk for more.

Central Edinburgh

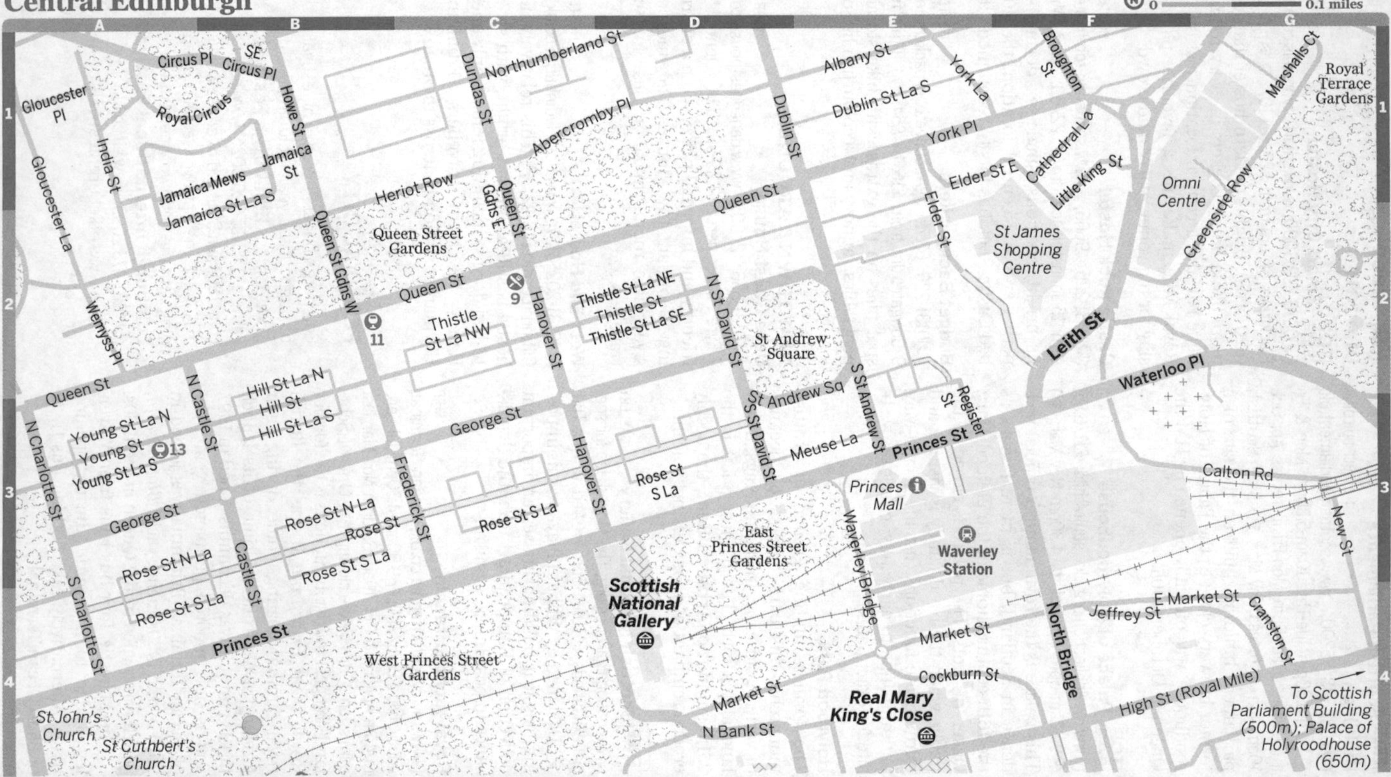

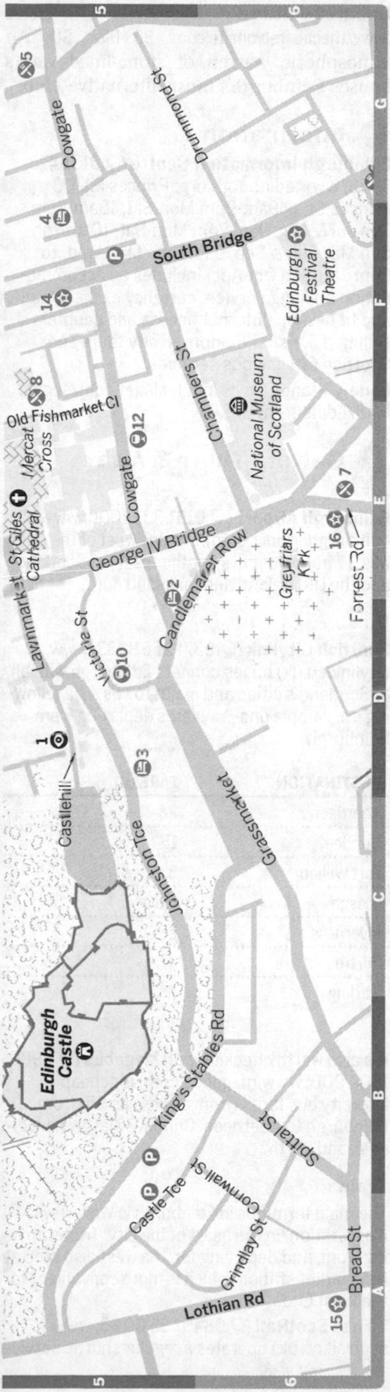

Central Edinburgh

Top Sights

	Edinburgh Castle	B5
	Real Mary King's Close	E4
	Scottish National Gallery	D4

Sights

1	Camera Obscura	D5

Sleeping

2	Budget Backpackers	E5
3	Castle Rock Hostel	D5
4	Smart City Hostel	F5

Eating

5	David Bann	G5
6	Mosque Kitchen	G6
7	Mums	E6
8	Passepartout	F5
9	The Dogs	C2

Drinking

10	Bow Bar	D5
11	Bramble	B2
12	BrewDog	E5
13	Oxford Bar	A3

Entertainment

14	Cabaret Voltaire	F5
15	Henry's Cellar	A6
16	Sandy Bell's	E6

Eating

OLD TOWN

Passepartout INTERNATIONAL £

(☎0131-629 0252; 7 Old Fishmarket Close; platters for 2 £12-13) Hidden down a steep cobbled alley off the Royal Mile, this French-owned, Indian-inspired bistro offers an eclectic menu of dishes – from lobster with mussels to chickpea curry to kebabs – served as sharing platters for two.

Mums CAFE £

(www.monstermashcafe.co.uk; 4a Forrest Rd; mains £6-9; ⊙9am-10pm Mon-Sat, 10am-10pm Sun) This nostalgia-fuelled cafe serves up classic British comfort food – bacon and eggs, bangers and mash, and shepherd's pie.

David Bann VEGETARIAN ££

(☎0131-556 5888; www.davidbann.com; 56-58 St Mary's St; mains £9-13; ⊙noon-10pm Mon-Fri, 11am-10pm Sat & Sun; ✎) If you want to convince a carnivorous friend that cuisine à la veg can be as tasty and inventive as a meat-muncher's menu, take them here.

Mosque Kitchen INDIAN £
(www.mosquekitchen.com; 31 Nicolson Sq; mains £3-6; ⌚11.30am-12.50pm & 1.50-11pm; ✎) Sophisticated it ain't – expect shared tables and disposable plates – but this is the place to go for cheap, authentic and delicious homemade curries. No alcohol.

NEW TOWN

TOP CHOICE **The Dogs** BRITISH ££
(☎0131-220 1208; www.thedogsonline.co.uk; 110 Hanover St; mains £9-13; ⌚noon-4pm & 5-10pm) This bistro-style place uses cheaper cuts of meat and less-well-known, more-sustainable species of fish to create its hearty dishes.

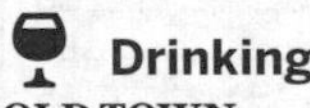

Drinking

OLD TOWN

Bow Bar PUB
(80 West Bow) One of the city's best traditional-style pubs (it's not as old as it looks), serving a range of excellent real ales and a vast selection of malt whiskies.

BrewDog BAR
(www.brewdog.com; 143 Cowgate; 📶) A new bar from Scotland's self-styled 'punk brewery', BrewDog stands out among the grimy, sticky-floored dives that line the Cowgate.

Oxford Bar PUB
(www.oxfordbar.co.uk; 8 Young St) 'The Ox' has been immortalised by Ian Rankin, author of the Inspector Rebus novels, whose fictional detective is a regular here.

Bramble COCKTAIL BAR
(www.bramblebar.co.uk; 16a Queen St) Bramble is an unmarked cellar bar where a maze of stone and brick hideaways conceals what is arguably the city's best cocktail bar.

☆ Entertainment

The comprehensive source for what's on is *The List* (www.list.co.uk).

Henry's Cellar LIVE MUSIC
(www.musicglue.com/theraft; 8a Morrison St) Henry's has something going on most nights of the week, from rock and indie to 'Balkan-inspired folk'. Open till 3am at weekends.

Sandy Bell's TRADITIONAL MUSIC
(25 Forrest Rd) This unassuming pub is a stalwart of the traditional music scene (the founder's wife sang with The Corries).

Cabaret Voltaire CLUB
(www.thecabaretvoltaire.com; 36 Blair St) An atmospheric warren of stone-lined vaults houses Edinburgh's most 'alternative' club.

ℹ Information

Edinburgh Information Centre (☎0131-473 3868; www.edinburgh.org; Princes Mall, 3 Princes St; ⌚9am-9pm Mon-Sat, 10am-8pm Sun Jul & Aug, 9am-7pm Mon-Sat, 10am-7pm Sun May-Jun & Sep, 9am-5pm Mon-Wed, to 6pm Thu-Sun Oct-Apr) Includes an accommodation booking service, currency exchange, gift and bookshop, internet access and counters selling tickets for Edinburgh city tours and Scottish Citylink bus services.

Lonely Planet (www.lonelyplanet.com/scotland/edinburgh)

ℹ Getting There & Away

Air

Edinburgh Airport (☎0131-333 1000; www.edinburghairport.com), 8 miles west of the city, has numerous flights to other parts of Scotland and the UK, Ireland and mainland Europe.

Bus

Scottish Citylink (☎0871 266 3333; www.citylink.co.uk) buses connect Edinburgh with all of Scotland's cities and major towns. The following are sample one-way fares departing from Edinburgh.

DESTINATION	FARE (£)
Aberdeen	28
Dundee	15
Fort William	33
Glasgow	6.80
Inverness	28
Portree	47
Stirling	7.50

It's also worth checking with **Megabus** (☎0900 160 0900; www.megabus.com) for cheap intercity bus fares (from as little as £5) from Edinburgh to Aberdeen, Dundee, Glasgow, Inverness and Perth.

Train

The main terminus in Edinburgh is Waverley train station, in the heart of the city. Trains arriving from, and departing for, the west also stop at Haymarket station, which is more convenient for the West End.

First ScotRail (☎08457 55 00 33; www.scotrail.co.uk) operates a regular shuttle service between Edinburgh and Glasgow (£12.90, 50 minutes, every 15 minutes), and frequent daily services to all Scottish cities, including Aberdeen (£45, 2½ hours), Dundee (£23, 1¼ hours) and Inverness (£40, 3½ hours).

Glasgow

POP 634,680

Displaying a disarming blend of sophistication and earthiness, Scotland's biggest city has evolved over the last couple of decades to become one of Britain's most intriguing metropolises. Its Victorian architectural legacy is now swamped with stylish bars, top-notch restaurants, and a hedonistic club culture that will bring out your nocturnal instincts.

Sights

CITY CENTRE

Glasgow's main square in the city centre is grand **George Square**, built in the Victorian era to show off the city's wealth, and dignified by statues of notable Scots, including Robert Burns, James Watt, John Moore and Sir Walter Scott.

TOP CHOICE **Glasgow School of Art** HISTORIC BUILDING

(☎0141-353 4526; www.gsa.ac.uk/tours; 167 Renfrew St; adult/child/family £8.75/7/24; ⏲9.30am-6.30pm Apr-Sep, 10.30am-5pm Oct-Mar) Mackintosh's greatest building, the Glasgow School of Art, is strikingly austere, with simple colour combinations (often just black and cream) and the uncomfortable-looking high-backed chairs for which Mackintosh is famous. The 1907 library is a masterpiece.

Excellent hour-long guided tours (roughly hourly in summer; 11am, 1pm and 3pm in winter) run by architecture students leave from here; this is the only way (apart from enrolling) you can visit the building's interior.

FREE **Willow Tearooms** HISTORIC BUILDING

(www.willowtearooms.co.uk; 217 Sauchiehall St; ⏲9am-5pm Mon-Sat, 11am-5pm Sun) Admirers of the great Mackintosh will love the Willow Tearooms, an authentic reconstruction of tearooms Mackintosh designed and furnished in the early 20th century for restaurateur Kate Cranston. Reconstruction took two years and the Willow reopened as a tearoom in 1980 (having been closed since 1926).

EAST END

TOP CHOICE **Glasgow Cathedral** CHURCH

(HS; www.historic-scotland.gov.uk; Cathedral Sq; ⏲9.30am-5.30pm Mon-Sat, 1-5pm Sun Apr-Sep, closes 4.30pm Oct-Mar) Glasgow Cathedral is a shining example of Gothic architecture, and, unlike nearly all Scotland's cathedrals, survived the turmoil of the Reformation mobs almost intact. Most of the current building dates from the 15th century.

THE CLYDE

Once a thriving shipbuilding area, the Clyde sank into dereliction during the postwar era, but is being rejuvenated.

Glasgow Science Centre MUSEUM

(☎0141-420 5000; www.gsc.org.uk; 50 Pacific Quay; Science Mall adult/child £9.95/7.95, IMAX, tower or planetarium £2.50; ⏲10am-5pm Wed-Sun) Scotland's flagship millennium project, this superb museum consists of an egg-shaped titanium-covered IMAX theatre (phone for current screenings) and an interactive Science Mall. There's also a rotating observation tower, 127m high. To get here take bus 24 from Renfield St or bus 89 or 90 from Union St. It closes earlier in winter.

FREE **Riverside Museum** MUSEUM

(www.glasgowmuseums.com; 100 Pointhouse Pl; ⏲10am-5pm Mon-Thu & Sat, 11am-5pm Fri & Sun; 📶) The latest development along the

> **THE GENIUS OF CHARLES RENNIE MACKINTOSH**
>
> Charles Rennie Mackintosh (1868–1928) is to Glasgow what Gaudí is to Barcelona. A designer, architect and master of the art nouveau style, his quirky, linear and geometric designs are seen all over Glasgow.
>
> Many of the buildings are open to the public. If you're a fan, the **Mackintosh Trail ticket** (£16), available at the tourist office or any Mackintosh building, gives you a day's free admission to all his creations plus unlimited bus and subway travel.

Glasgow

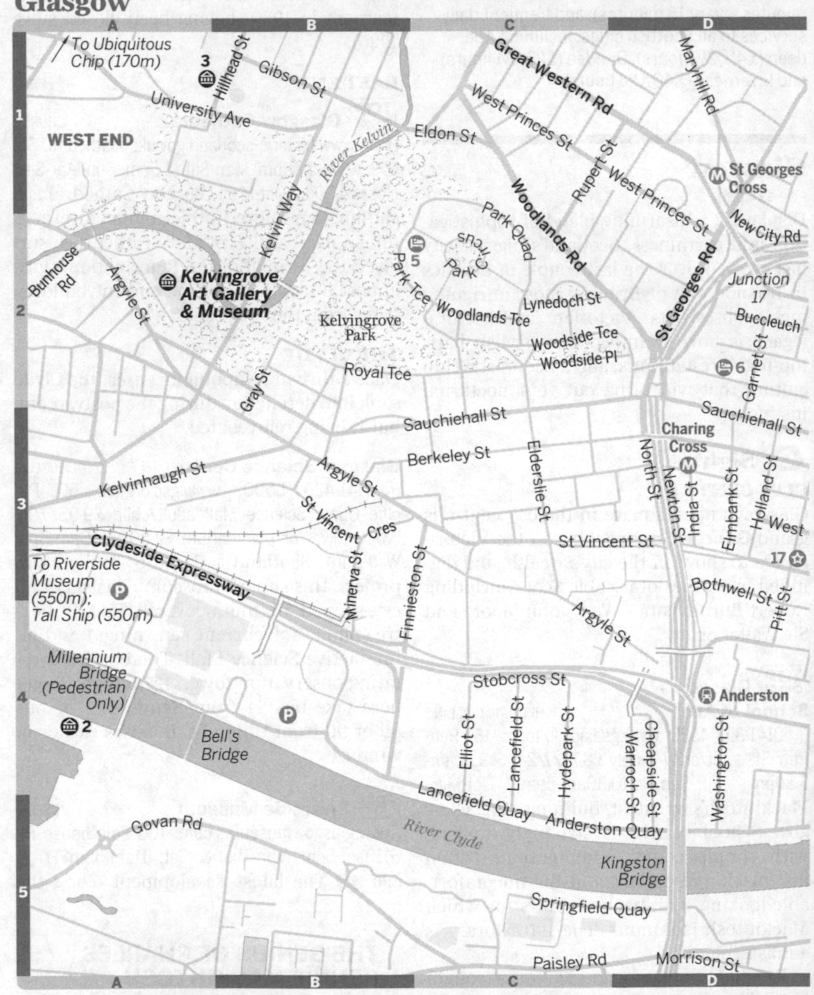

Clyde is this visually impressive new transport museum. Inside, you'll find an excellent series of cars made in Scotland, plus assorted railway locos, trams, bikes and model Clyde-built ships. The magnificent **Tall Ship Glenlee** (www.thetallship.com; adult/child £5/3; ⏲10am-5pm Mar-Oct, till 4pm Nov-Feb), a beautiful three-master launched in 1896, is berthed alongside the museum.

The Riverside is west of the centre at Glasgow Harbour; you can reach it on bus 100 from the north side of George Sq, or via the Clyde Clippers boat service.

WEST END

With its expectant buzz, trendy bars and nonchalant swagger, the West End is as close as Glasgow gets to bohemian. To get here from the centre, buses 9, 16 and 23 run towards Kelvingrove; 8, 11, and 16 to the university.

TOP CHOICE **Kelvingrove Art Gallery & Museum** MUSEUM

(www.glasgowmuseums.com; Argyle St; admission free; ⏲10am-5pm Mon-Thu & Sat, 11am-5pm Fri & Sun) A magnificent stone building, this grand Victorian cathedral of culture has

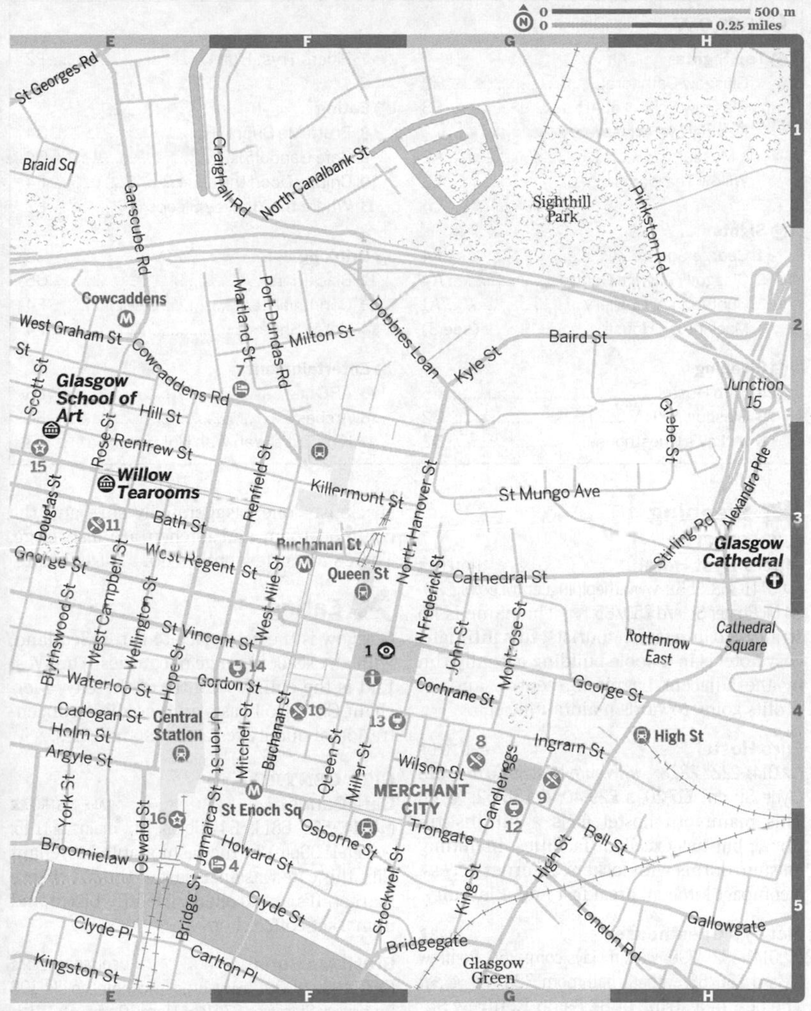

been revamped into a fascinating and unusual museum, with a bewildering variety of exhibits. You'll find fine art alongside stuffed animals, and Micronesian shark-tooth swords alongside a Spitfire plane.

There are free hour-long guided tours beginning at 11am and 2.30pm. Bus 17, among many others, runs here from Renfield St.

FREE Hunterian Art Gallery GALLERY
(www.hunterian.gla.ac.uk; 82 Hillhead St; ⏲10am-5pm Tue-Sat, 11am-4pm Sun) Across the road from the Hunterian Museum, the bold tones of the Scottish Colourists (Samuel Peploe, Francis Cadell, JD Fergusson and Leslie Hunter) are well represented in this gallery, which also forms part of Hunter's bequest to the university.

Mackintosh House HISTORIC BUILDING
(www.hunterian.gla.ac.uk; 82 Hillhead St; adult/concession £5/3; ⏲10am-5pm Tue-Sat, 11am-4pm Sun) Attached to the Hunterian Art Gallery, this is a reconstruction of the first home that Charles Rennie Mackintosh bought with his wife, noted artist Mary Macdonald.

Glasgow

Top Sights

- Glasgow Cathedral ... H3
- Glasgow School of Art ... E3
- Kelvingrove Art Gallery & Museum ... A2
- Willow Tearooms ... E3

Sights

1. George Square ... F4
2. Glasgow Science Centre ... A4
3. Hunterian Art Gallery ... A1
   Mackintosh House ... (see 3)

Sleeping

4. Euro Hostel ... F5
5. Glasgow SYHA ... C2
6. McLay's Guesthouse ... D2
7. Pipers Tryst Hotel ... F2

Eating

8. Brutti Ma Buoni ... G4
9. Café Gandolfi ... G4
10. Chippy Doon the Lane ... F4
11. Where the Monkey Sleeps ... E3

Drinking

12. Blackfriars ... G5
13. Corinthian ... F4
14. Horse Shoe ... F4

Entertainment

15. ABC ... E3
16. Arches ... E5
17. King Tut's Wah Wah Hut ... D3

Sleeping

CITY CENTRE

Pipers Tryst Hotel HOTEL ££

(0141-353 5551; www.thepipingcentre.co.uk; 30-34 McPhater St; s/d £50/65;) The name is no strategy to lure tartan tourists; this intimate, cosy hotel is in a noble building actually run by the adjacent bagpiping centre, and all profits going towards maintaining it.

Euro Hostel HOSTEL £

(0141-222 2828; www.euro-hostels.co.uk; 318 Clyde St; dm £17-20, s £29-40, d £36-52;) This mammoth hostel feels a bit institutional, but has excellent facilities, including en suite dorms with lockers, internet access, a compact kitchen, breakfast and a laundry.

McLay's Guesthouse B&B £

(0141-332 4796; www.mclays.com; 260 Renfrew St; s/d £36/56, without bathroom £28/48;) The best of a string of B&Bs on Renfrew St.

WEST END

Glasgow SYHA HOSTEL £

(0141-332 3004; www.syha.org.uk; 8 Park Tce; dm/tw £23/62;) Perched on a hill overlooking Kelvingrove Park in a charming townhouse, this place is one of Scotland's best official hostels. Dorms are mostly four to six beds with padlock lockers and all have their own en suite – very posh.

Bunkum Backpackers HOSTEL £

(0141-581 4481; www.bunkumglasgow.co.uk; 26 Hillhead St; dm/tw £14/36; P) Bunkum Backpackers occupies a noble old Victorian terrace on a quiet street. The dorms are spacious – one exaggeratedly so – and the common room and kitchen are also large. There's no curfew but it's not a party hostel.

Eating

Glasgow is the best place to eat in Scotland, with an excellent range of eateries. The West End is the culinary centre of the city; Merchant City also boasts an incredible concentration of quality restaurants and cafes.

CITY CENTRE

Café Gandolfi CAFE, BISTRO ££

(0141-552 6813; 64 Albion St; mains £11-15; 9am-11.30pm) In the fashionable Merchant City, this cafe was once part of the old cheese market. It's an excellent, friendly bistro and upmarket coffee shop.

Brutti Ma Buoni MEDITERRANEAN £

(0141-552 0001; www.brunswickhotel.co.uk; 106 Brunswick St; mains £7-11; 11am-10pm;) With dishes such as 'ugly but good' pizza and 'angry or peaceful' prawns, Brutti's menu draws a smile for its quirkiness and its prices.

Chippy Doon the Lane FISH & CHIPS £

(www.thechippyglasgow.com; McCormick Lane, 84 Buchanan St; meals £6-11; noon-9.30pm) Don't be put off by its location in a down-at-heel alleyway off the shopping precinct: this is a cut above your average chip shop.

Where the Monkey Sleeps CAFE £

(www.monkeysleeps.com; 182 West Regent St; dishes £4-7; 7am-5pm Mon-Fri) A perfect escape from the ubiquitous coffee chains. Laid-back and a little hippy, the bagels and paninis – with names like Burn the Witch or Meathammer – are highlights, as are the 'nuclear' beans, dripping with cayenne and Tabasco.

WEST END

TOP CHOICE **Ubiquitous Chip** SCOTTISH £££
(☎0141-334 5007; www.ubiquitouschip.co.uk; 12 Ashton Lane; 2-/3-course dinner £35/40, brasserie mains lunch £7-12, dinner £12-15) The original champion of Scottish produce, the Ubiquitous Chip has won lots of awards for its unparalleled Scottish cuisine.

Heart Buchanan CAFE £
(www.heartbuchanan.co.uk; 380 Byres Rd; light meals £6-10; ⏲9am-4pm Mon-Sat, 10am-6pm Sun) Enjoy Glasgow's best breakfasts, a refreshing juice or milkshake, and regularly changing lunch options.

Drinking

Horse Shoe PUB
(www.horseshoebar.co.uk; 17 Drury St) This legendary city pub and popular meeting place dates from the late 19th century and is largely unchanged.

Corinthian BAR
(www.thecorinthianclub.co.uk; 191 Ingram St; 📶) Originally a bank and later Glasgow's High Court, this regal building's main bar has to be seen to be believed.

Blackfriars PUB
(www.blackfriarsglasgow.com; 36 Bell St) Merchant City's most relaxed and atmospheric pub, Blackfriars' friendly staff and chilled-out house make it special.

☆ Entertainment

Arches CLUB
(www.thearches.co.uk; 253 Argyle St) The Godfather of Glaswegian clubs, based around hundreds of arches slammed together, and a must for funk and hip-hop freaks.

King Tut's Wah Wah Hut LIVE MUSIC
(☎0141-221 5279; www.kingtuts.co.uk; 272a St Vincent St) One of the city's premier live-music pub venues, the excellent King Tut's Wah Wah Hut hosts bands every night of the week. Oasis was signed after playing here.

ABC CLUB
(O2 ABC; www.o2abcglasgow.co.uk; 300 Sauchiehall St) Both nightclub and venue, this star of Sauchiehall has two large concert spaces and several attractive bars.

ℹ Information

Glasgow Information Centre (☎0141-204 4400; www.seeglasgow.com; 11 George Sq;

TRANSPORT FROM GLASGOW

Bus

DESTINATION	PRICE (£)	DURATION	FREQUENCY
Aberdeen	28.80	2½-3hr	hourly
Edinburgh	6.80	1¼hr	every 15min
Fort William	22	3hr	7 daily
Inverness	27.50	3½hr	8 daily
Stirling	7.30	45min	at least hourly

Train

DESTINATION	PRICE (£)	DURATION	FREQUENCY
Aberdeen	45.20	2½hr	hourly
Dundee	25.30	1½hr	hourly
Edinburgh	12.90	50min	every 15min
Fort William	26.30	3¾hr	4-5 daily
Inverness	79	3½hr	10 daily Mon-Sat, 4 Sun
Oban	21.60	3hr	3-4 daily

⏲9am-5pm Mon-Sat) Excellent tourist office; makes local and national accommodation bookings (£4).

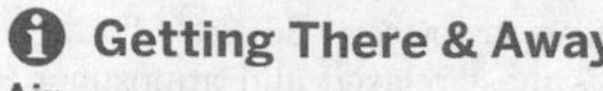

Getting There & Away

Air

Ten miles west of the city, **Glasgow International Airport** (GLA; www.glasgowairport.com) handles domestic traffic and international flights. **Glasgow Prestwick Airport** (PIK; www.glasgowprestwick.com), 30 miles southwest of Glasgow, is used by budget airlines, with many connections to Britain and Europe.

Bus

All long-distance buses arrive at and depart from **Buchanan bus station** (☎0141-333 3708; www.spt.co.uk; Killermont St), which has pricey lockers, ATMs and a cafe with wi-fi.

Scottish Citylink (☎0871 266 3333; www.citylink.co.uk) has buses to most major towns in Scotland.

Train

As a general rule, Glasgow Central station serves southern Scotland, England and Wales, and Queen St station serves the north and east. Buses run between the two stations every 10 minutes.

Scotrail (☎08457 55 00 33; www.scotrail.co.uk) runs Scottish trains. Destinations include Edinburgh (£12.90, 50 minutes, every 15 minutes), Oban (£21.60, three hours, three to four daily), Fort William (£26.30, 3¾ hours, four to five daily), Dundee (£25.30, 1½ hours, hourly), Aberdeen (£45.20, 2½ hours, hourly) and Inverness (£79, 3½ hours, 10 daily, four on Sunday).

CENTRAL SCOTLAND

Central Scotland is less a geographical region and more a catch-all term for everything between the Glasgow–Edinburgh conurbation and the mountains of the northwestern Highlands. Anything you ever dreamed about Scotland you can find here: lochs, hills, castles, whisky distilleries and some truly beautiful islands.

Loch Lomond

The 'bonnie banks' and 'bonnie braes' of Loch Lomond have long been Glasgow's rural retreat, and today the loch's popularity shows no sign of decreasing. The main tourist focus is on the loch's western shore, along the A82. The eastern shore, followed by the West Highland Way long-distance footpath, is a little quieter. The region's importance was recognised when it became the heart of **Loch Lomond & the Trossachs National Park** (www.lochlomond-trossachs.org) – Scotland's first national park, created in 2002.

The main centre for boat trips is Balloch, where **Sweeney's Cruises** (☎01389-752376; www.sweeneyscruises.com; Balloch Rd, Balloch) offers a range of trips including a one-hour cruise to Inchmurrin and back (adult/child £8.50/5, departs hourly).

Sleeping & Eating

Loch Lomond Youth Hostel HOSTEL £
(SYHA; ☎01389-850226; Arden; dm £18; ⏲Mar-Oct; P@≋) Forget about roughing it, this is one of the most impressive hostels in the country – an imposing 19th-century country house set in beautiful grounds overlooking the loch. It's 2 miles north of Balloch and very popular, so book in advance in summer.

TOP CHOICE **Drover's Inn** PUB ££
(☎01301-704234; www.thedroversinn.co.uk; bar meals £7-12; ⏲lunch & dinner) This is one *howff* (drinking den) you shouldn't miss – a low-ceilinged place with smoke-blackened stone, bare wooden floors spotted with candle wax, barmen in kilts, and walls festooned with moth-eaten stags' heads and stuffed birds.

Getting There & Away

BUS First Glasgow (☎0141-423 6600; www.firstglasgow.com) buses 204 and 215 run from Argyle St in central Glasgow to Balloch and Loch Lomond shores (1½ hours, at least two per hour). **Scottish Citylink** (www.citylink.co.uk) coaches from Glasgow to Oban and Fort William stop at Luss (£8.20, 55 minutes, six daily), Tarbet (£8.20, 65 minutes) and Ardlui (£14.30, 1¼ hours).

TRAIN Take the Glasgow to Balloch train (£4.70, 45 minutes, every 30 minutes) or the Glasgow to Ardlui (£14, 1½ hours, three or four daily), which continues on to Oban and Fort William.

Stirling

POP 32,673

With an utterly impregnable position atop a mighty wooded crag (the plug of an extinct volcano), Stirling's beautifully preserved Old Town is a treasure-trove of noble buildings and cobbled streets winding up to the

TRANSPORT FROM STIRLING

Bus

DESTINATION	PRICE (£)	DURATION	FREQUENCY
Dundee	13	1½hr	hourly
Edinburgh	7.50	1hr	hourly
Glasgow	7	40min	hourly

Train

DESTINATION	PRICE (£)	DURATION	FREQUENCY
Aberdeen	43.30	2¼hr	hourly weekdays, every 2hr Sun
Dundee	17.70	1hr	hourly weekdays, every 2hr Sun
Edinburgh	7.70	55min	2 hourly Mon-Sat, hourly Sun
Glasgow	8	40min	2 hourly Mon-Sat, hourly Sun

ramparts of its dominant castle, which offer views for miles around.

Sights

Stirling Castle CASTLE

(HS; www.historic-scotland.gov.uk; adult/child £13/6.50; ⏲9.30am-6pm Apr-Sep, to 5pm Oct-Mar) Hold Stirling and you control Scotland, or so the saying goes. This impressive fortress has played a pivotal role in Scotland's fortunes down the centuries, and it's every bit as dramatic as Edinburgh Castle. It also draws a similar number of visitors, so it's advisable to visit in the afternoon; many tourists come on day trips, so you may have the castle to yourself by about 4pm.

National Wallace Monument MONUMENT

(www.nationalwallacemonument.com; adult/child £8.25/5.25; ⏲10am-5pm Apr-Jun, Sep & Oct, to 6pm Jul & Aug, 10.30am-4pm Nov-Mar) Towering over Scotland's narrow waist, this nationalist memorial commemorates the bid for Scottish independence depicted in the film *Braveheart*. Buses 62 and 63 run from Murray Pl in Stirling to the tourist office, otherwise it's a half-hour walk from central Stirling.

Sleeping

Willy Wallace Backpackers Hostel HOSTEL £

(☎01786-446773; www.willywallacehostel.com; 77 Murray Pl; dm/tw £16/36; @ 📶) This central hostel is friendly, roomy and sociable. The colourful, spacious dormitories are clean and light, there's free tea and coffee, a good kitchen and a laissez-faire atmosphere.

Stirling SYHA HOSTEL £

(☎01786-473442; www.syha.org.uk; St John St; dm/tw £18.75/48; P @ 📶) Right in the Old Town, this hostel has an unbeatable location and great facilities. Though its facade is that of a former church, the interior is modern and efficient. The dorms are compact but comfortable, with lockers and en suite bathrooms.

Information

Tourist Office (☎01786-475019; stirling@visitscotland.com; 41 Dumbarton Rd; ⏲10am-5pm Mon-Sat, plus Sun Jun–mid-Sep)

Getting There & Away

BUS The **bus station** (☎01786-446474) is on Goosecroft Rd. **Citylink** (☎0871 266 33 33; www.citylink.co.uk) offers a number of services to/from Stirling.

TRAIN **First ScotRail** (www.scotrail.co.uk) has services to/from a number of destinations.

NORTHERN & WESTERN SCOTLAND

This area is a long way north, and takes effort to reach, but it is by far the best bit of Scotland, and one of the best bits of the whole of Britain too. Some folks (well, those who love mountains and wild places) would even say that it's one of the finest parts of the whole of Europe.

It's easy to underestimate the scale of this part of Scotland, so give yourself extra time to explore. See www.visithighlands.com for transport and accommodation advice.

Inverness

POP 55,000

Inverness, the primary city and shopping centre of the Highlands, has a great location astride the River Ness at the northern end of the Great Glen. In summer it overflows with visitors intent on monster hunting at nearby Loch Ness, but it's worth a visit in its own right for a stroll along the picturesque River Ness, a cruise on Loch Ness, and a meal in one of the city's excellent restaurants.

Sleeping

Ardconnel House B&B ££
(01463-240455; www.ardconnel-inverness.co.uk; 21 Ardconnel St; r per person £35-40; wi-fi) The six-room Ardconnel is one of our favourites – a terraced Victorian house with comfortable en suite rooms, and a breakfast menu that includes Vegemite for homesick antipodeans.

Bazpackers Backpackers Hotel HOSTEL £
(01463-717663; www.bazpackershostel.co.uk; 4 Culduthel Rd; dm/tw £17/44; @ wi-fi) This may be Inverness' smallest hostel (30 beds), but it's hugely popular.

Inverness Millburn SYHA HOSTEL £
(SYHA; 01463-231771; www.syha.org.uk; Victoria Dr; dm £18; Apr-Dec; P @ wi-fi) Inverness' modern 166-bed hostel is 10 minutes' walk northeast of the city centre. With its comfy beds and flashy stainless-steel kitchen, some reckon it's the best hostel in the country. Booking advised.

Eating & Drinking

Mustard Seed BISTRO ££
(01463-220220; www.mustardseedrestaurant.co.uk; 16 Fraser St; mains £11-16) The menu at this bright and bustling bistro changes weekly, but focuses on Scottish and French cuisine with a modern twist. And a two-course lunch for £7 is hard to beat.

Clachnaharry Inn PUB
(01463-239806; www.clachnaharryinn.co.uk; 17-19 High St) Just over a mile northwest of the city centre, on the bank of the Caledonian Canal just off the A862, this is a delightful old coaching inn (with beer garden out back) serving an excellent range of real ales and good pub grub.

Information

Inverness tourist office (01463-252401; www.visithighlands.com; Castle Wynd; internet

TRANSPORT FROM INVERNESS

Bus

DESTINATION	PRICE (£)	DURATION (HR)	FREQUENCY
Aberdeen	9	3¾	hourly
Edinburgh	28	3½-4½	hourly
Fort William	12	2	5 daily
Glasgow	28	3½-4½	hourly
London	45	13	1 direct daily
Portree	23	3½	4 daily

Train

DESTINATION	PRICE (£)	DURATION (HR)	FREQUENCY
Aberdeen	28	2¼	8 daily
Edinburgh	40	3½	8 daily
Glasgow	40	3½	8 daily
London	100	8	1 daily direct

access per 20min £1; ⌚9am-6pm Mon-Sat, 9.30am-5pm Sun Jul & Aug, 9am-5pm Mon-Sat, 10am-4pm Sun Jun, Sep & Oct, 9am-5pm Mon-Sat Apr & May)

Getting There & Away

BUS Services depart from **Inverness bus station** (Margaret St). Some London services require a change at Glasgow. Operated by **National Express** (☎08717 81 81 78; www.gobycoach.com).

TRAIN One of Britain's great scenic train journeys is the Kyle of Lochalsh (£13, 2½ hours, four daily Monday to Saturday, two Sunday).

Some London services require a change at Edinburgh.

Loch Ness

Deep, dark and narrow, Loch Ness stretches for 23 miles between Inverness and Fort Augustus. Its bitterly cold waters have been extensively explored in search of the elusive Loch Ness monster, but most visitors see her only in cardboard cut-out form at the monster exhibitions. The village of **Drumnadrochit** is a hotbed of beastie fever, with two monster exhibitions battling it out for the tourist dollar.

The **Loch Ness Exhibition Centre** (☎01456-450573; www.lochness.com; adult/child £6.95/4.95; ⌚9am 6pm Jul & Aug, to 5.30pm Jun, 9.30am-5pm Easter-May & Sep-Oct, 10am-3.30pm Nov-Easter) is the better of the two Nessie-themed attractions, with a scientific approach that allows you to weigh the evidence for yourself.

Scottish Citylink and Stagecoach buses from Inverness to Fort William run along the shores of Loch Ness (six to eight daily, five on Sunday); those headed for Skye turn off at Invermoriston. There are bus stops at Drumnadrochit (£6.20, 30 minutes) and Urquhart Castle (£6.60, 35 minutes).

Glen Coe

Scotland's most famous glen is also one of the grandest and, in bad weather, the grimmest. The southern side is dominated by three massive, brooding spurs, known as the **Three Sisters**, while the northern side is enclosed by the continuous steep wall of the knife-edged **Aonach Eagach** ridge.

The little village of Glencoe stands on the south shore of Loch Leven at the western end of the glen.

Sleeping & Eating

TOP CHOICE **Clachaig Inn** HOTEL ££

(☎01855-811252; www.clachaig.com; s/d from £70/92; P 📶) The Clachaig has long been a favourite haunt of hill walkers and climbers. As well as comfortable en suite accommodation, there's a smart, wood-panelled lounge-bar with lots of sofas and armchairs, mountaineering photos, and climbing magazines to leaf through. It's 2 miles southeast of Glencoe village.

Glencoe Independent Hostel HOSTEL £

(☎01855-811906; www.glencoehostel.co.uk; dm £13-16.50, bunkhouse £11.50-13.50; P @ 📶) This handily located hostel, just 10 minutes' walk from the Clachaig Inn and 1.5 miles south east of Glencoe village, is set in an old farmhouse with six- and eight-bed dorms, and a bunkhouse with another 16 bed spaces in communal, Alpine-style bunks.

Getting There & Away

Scottish Citylink (☎0871 266 3333; www.citylink.co.uk) buses run between Fort William and Glencoe (£7.50, 30 minutes, eight daily) and from Glencoe to Glasgow (£20, 2½ hours, eight daily).

Stagecoach (www.stagecoachbus.com) bus 44 links Glencoe village with Fort William (35 minutes, hourly Monday to Saturday, three on Sunday) and Kinlochleven (25 minutes).

Fort William

POP 9910

Basking on the shores of Loch Linnhe amid magnificent mountain scenery, 'Fort Bill' has carved out a reputation as 'Outdoor Capital of the UK' (www.outdoorcapital.co.uk), and its easy access by rail and bus makes it a good launch pad for Highland exploration.

Sleeping &Eating

Grange B&B ££

(☎01397-705516; www.grangefortwilliam.com; Grange Rd; r per person £58-63; P) An exceptional 19th-century villa set in its own landscaped grounds, the Grange is crammed with antiques and fitted with log fires, chaise longues and Victorian roll-top baths. It's 500m southwest of the town centre.

Fort William Backpackers HOSTEL £

(☎01397-700711; www.scotlands-top-hostels.com; Alma Rd; dm/tw £18/47; P @ 📶) A 10-minute

CLIMBING BEN NEVIS

Looming over Fort William is Ben Nevis (1344m). As the highest peak in the British Isles, it attracts thousands of people who would not normally go anywhere near the summit of a Scottish mountain. Many get to the top with no trouble, but every year a surprisingly large number people have to be rescued.

Even if you're climbing 'the Ben' on a fine summer's day, an ascent should not be undertaken lightly. You will need proper walking boots (the path is rough and stony, and there may be wet snowfields on the summit), warm clothing, waterproofs, a map and compass, and plenty of food and water. And don't forget to check the weather forecast (see www.bennevisweather.co.uk). In thick cloud, visibility at the summit can be 10m or less; in such conditions, the only safe way off the mountain requires careful use of a map and compass to avoid walking over 700m cliffs.

walk from the bus and train stations, this lively and welcoming hostel is set in a grand Victorian villa, perched on a hillside with great views over Loch Linnhe.

Grog & Gruel PUB
(☎01397-705078; www.grogandgruel.co.uk; 66 High St; ⏰bar meals noon-9pm) The Grog & Gruel is a traditional-style, wood-panelled pub with an excellent range of cask ales from regional Scottish and English microbreweries.

Information

Fort William tourist office (☎01397-703781; www.visithighlands.com; 15 High St; internet per 20min £1; ⏰9am-6pm Mon-Sat, 10am-5pm Sun Apr-Sep, limited hours Oct-Mar)

Getting There & Away

BUS Scottish Citylink (www.citylink.co.uk) buses link Fort William with other major towns and cities.

For Edinburgh (£33, 4½ hours) there is one daily direct; seven change at Glasgow; others go via Glencoe and Crianlarich. Other services include Glasgow (£22, three hours, eight daily), Inverness (£12, two hours, five daily), Oban (£9.40, 1½ hours, three daily) and Portree (£28.60, three hours, four daily).

TRAIN The spectacular West Highland line runs from Glasgow to Mallaig via Fort William. The overnight *Caledonian Sleeper* service connects Fort William and London Euston (£103 sharing a twin-berth cabin, 13 hours).

Isle of Skye

POP 9900

The Isle of Skye is the biggest of Scotland's islands, a 50-mile-long smorgasbord of velvet moors, jagged mountains, sparkling lochs and towering sea cliffs. It takes its name from the old Norse *sky-a,* meaning 'cloud island', a Viking reference to the often mist-enshrouded Cuillin Hills. The stunning scenery is the main attraction, but there are plenty of cosy pubs to retire to when the mist closes in.

Sleeping

Portree, the island's capital, has the largest selection of accommodation, eating places and other services.

Ben Tianavaig B&B B&B ££
(☎01478-612152; www.ben-tianavaig.co.uk; 5 Bosville Tce; r £70-80; P Wi-Fi) A warm welcome awaits from the Irish-Welsh couple who runs this appealing B&B bang in the centre of town.

Bayfield Backpackers HOSTEL £
(☎01478-612231; www.skyehostel.co.uk; Bayfield; dm £17; @ Wi-Fi) Clean, central and modern, this hostel provides the best backpacker accommodation in town. The owner really makes you feel welcome, and is a fount of advice on what to do and where to go in Skye.

Bayview House B&B £
(☎01478-613340; www.bayviewhouse.co.uk; Bayfield; r per person from £20; P Wi-Fi) This is a modern house with spartan but sparklingly clean rooms, some with sea and mountain views, and bathrooms with power showers.

Eating & Drinking

Café Arriba CAFE £
(☎01478-611830; www.cafearriba.co.uk; Quay Brae; mains £4-8; ⏰7am-10pm May-Sep, 8am-5.30pm Oct-Apr; ✎) Arriba is a funky little cafe, brightly decked out in primary colours and offering delicious flatbread melts (bacon, leek and cheese is our favourite) and vegie grub.

Getting There & Away

Boat

The Isle of Skye became permanently tethered to the Scottish mainland when the Skye Bridge opened in 1995, but a number of ferries still serve the island.

CalMac (www.calmac.co.uk; per person/car £4.35/22.60) operates the Mallaig to Armadale ferry. It's very popular in July and August, so book ahead if you're travelling by car.

Skye Ferry (www.skyeferry.co.uk; car with up to 4 passengers £14) runs a tiny vessel (six cars only) on the short Glenelg to Kylerhea crossing. The ferry operates from 10am to 6pm daily from Easter to October only, till 7pm June to August.

Bus

Services include the following:

Glasgow to Portree (£40, seven hours, four daily)

Glasgow to Uig (£40, 7½ hours, two daily) Via Crianlarich, Fort William and Kyle of Lochalsh.

Inverness to Portree (£23, 3½ hours, three daily)

John O'Groats & Around

Best known as the endpoint of the epic 874-mile trek from Land's End in Cornwall, **John O'Groats** is really nothing more than a car park surrounded by tourist shops, and offers little to the visitor beyond a means to get across to Orkney. Even the famous pub has been shut for a while now (although there are a couple of cafes).

Two miles east, **Duncansby Head** provides a more solemn end-of-Britain moment with a small lighthouse and 60m cliffs sheltering nesting fulmars.

The most northerly point on the British mainland is actually at **Dunnet Head**, 8 miles east of Thurso, which offers inspiring views of the Orkney Islands.

Public transport is limited, although **Stagecoach** (www.stagecoachbus.com) runs buses between John O'Groats and Wick (40 minutes, two to three daily). There are also three to eight services Monday to Saturday to/from Thurso.

UNDERSTAND BRITAIN

History

Celts & Romans

Britain's earliest settlers were bands of nomadic hunter-gatherers, but it was the Neolithic people who left the most obvious mark in the shape of burial mounds and passage graves, as well as stone circles such as those at Avebury and Stonehenge in southern England. In their wake came the Celts, whose bronze- and iron-smelting skills transformed the British landscape and created a distinct new culture.

The Romans arrived on the island they called Britannia in AD 43, and stayed for the next 350 years. Their legacy still remains in the shape of villas, forts and bathhouses, best seen in Bath, and the great northern barrier of Hadrian's Wall.

The Dark Ages

The Romans abandoned Britain in AD 410, heralding the period now known as the Dark Ages. During this era, southern and central Britain was colonised by Anglo-Saxon settlers and the land was divided into several kingdoms dominated by Wessex (southern England), Mercia (central England) and Northumbria (northern England and southern Scotland).

While the tribal kingdoms of Britain ebbed and flowed, marauding bands of Nordic Vikings occupied much of Scotland, and eastern and northern England, where York became their capital.

After leading great victories against the Vikings, King Alfred was hailed as king of the English – the first time the Anglo-Saxons regarded themselves as a truly united people. His son, Athelstan, was crowned the first King of England in 927.

Medieval Britain

In 1066, the Norman duke, William of Normandy (aka the Conqueror) invaded Britain and won a decisive victory at the Battle of Hastings, when the English King Harold was killed by an arrow in the eye.

The centuries after the Norman invasion saw England racked with intrigue as the monarchy and church vied for power, a struggle epitomised in 1170 when King Henry II had 'turbulent priest' Thomas Becket murdered in Canterbury Cathedral.

Edward I came to the English throne in 1272 and led a bloody invasion of Wales that lasted through much of the 1270s, ending with the defeat of Welsh Prince Llewellyn. There were no more Welsh kings, and just to make it clear who was boss, Edward made his eldest son Prince of Wales – a tradition that continues to this day.

Edward had less luck in Scotland. In 1297, at the Battle of Stirling Bridge, the English were defeated by a Scots army under the leadership of the rebel William Wallace. The Scottish struggle for independence continued under Robert the Bruce, who scored another decisive victory against Edward II at the Battle of Bannockburn in 1314.

Great Dynasties

By 1485 King Henry VII had been crowned, the first of the Tudor dynasty. His son, Henry VIII, struggled to father a male heir – hence the famous six wives. His decision to divorce his first wife, Catherine of Aragon, led to a split with the Catholic Church, beginning a pivotal division between Catholics and Protestants that still exists in some areas of Britain.

In 1536 Henry ordered the 'dissolution' of many abbeys and monasteries, and the romantic ruins of some of these – including Whitby Abbey and Glastonbury Abbey – can still be visited. At the same time, Henry signed the Acts of Union (1536–43), uniting England and Wales for the first time.

When Henry VIII died, he was succeeded by his son Edward VI, then by daughter Mary I, but their reigns were short. So, unexpectedly, a third child, Elizabeth, came to the throne.

During her 45-year reign, Elizabeth I (sometimes called 'The Virgin Queen') oversaw a great cultural and economic renaissance in England, with seafarers such as Walter Raleigh and Francis Drake founding colonies across the New World, and playwrights including William Shakespeare and Christopher Marlowe reinventing the English stage. She also masterminded the defeat of the Spanish Armada, when King Philip II sought to invade England in a botched attempt to reconvert it to Catholicism.

Britain United

Despite a bountiful reign, Elizabeth failed to provide an heir. She was succeeded by her closest relative, the Scottish (and Protestant) King James. He became James I of England and VI of Scotland, the first king of both nations, and the first monarch of the Stuart dynasty.

A century later, in 1707, the Act of Union was passed, bringing England, Wales and Scotland under one unified parliament for the first time in history.

The Industrial Age

By the 19th century, Britain had become the crucible of the Industrial Revolution. The towns of the English Midlands became the first industrial cities, and millions of former country-dwellers migrated in search of work. By the time Queen Victoria took the throne in 1837, Britain's factories dominated world trade and Britain's fleets dominated the oceans.

The rest of the 19th century was seen as Britain's Golden Age – and saw the construction of some of the nation's finest stations, museums and public buildings.

The Modern Era

Most of Britain's 20th century was a period of conflict and decline. Two world wars brought the nation almost to its knees, although many still recall the 1940 Battle of Britain, when the country resisted a three-month air attack from Germany, as its finest hour.

In the 1950s and '60s, the once-great manufacturing industries started to falter, and the 1970s and '80s saw them pretty much die completely. By the 1990s, though, Britain had bounced back and entered the new millennium with one of the world's strongest economies and a cultural scene dubbed (briefly) 'Cool Britannia'.

In the general election of 1997, after nearly 18 years of Conservative rule, 'New' Labour swept to power under Tony Blair. Under the Labour government, Wales and Scotland were granted their own devolved parliaments for the first time in almost 300 years.

In 2010, a record 14 years of Labour government came to an end, and a new coalition between the Conservative and Liberal-Democrat parties took over, with David Cameron as the prime minister. Facing one of the deepest recessions in a century, the Con-Lib coalition has embarked on a program of severe cuts in an effort to solve its financial problems.

While events such as the 2012 London Olympics lifted the nation's spirits, the road out of recession has been rocky. Even more important is Scotland's decision to hold a referendum on independence in 2014, a long-held dream for the Scottish National Party (SNP) and its leader, Alex Salmond. Controversially, only residents of Scotland will have the right to vote in what will be one of the most momentous events in British history since the Act of Union in 1707.

People

Britain's population is 58 million (England around 50 million, Wales around three million and Scotland around five million), making it one of the world's most densely populated regions.

Several big towns and cities in Britain – particularly London, Glasgow, Birmingham and Manchester – have large ethnic-minority communities, mainly from Britain's former colonies in the Caribbean, India, Pakistan and parts of Africa.

In the 2001 national census, around 35 million people in Britain stated their religion as Christian, the majority of which are 'C of E' (Church of England; England's main Protestant church). The most recent census also recorded around 1.5 million Muslims (about 3%), Hindus (1%), Sikhs (0.7%), Jews (0.5%) and Buddhists (0.3%).

Language

The dominant language of Britain is English. Welsh is a Celtic language, entirely different from English; it almost died out in the 1960s, but today about 600,000 people (20% of the population) speak Welsh as a first language, and many more as a strong second tongue.

In Scotland, Gaelic – another Celtic language – is spoken by about 80,000 people, mainly in the Highlands and Islands, while Lallans (or Lowland Scots) is closer to English.

Arts

Literature

Britain's landscape is a literary one. Two of the great figures you'll encounter are William Shakespeare – whose hometown of Stratford-upon-Avon is a must for literary buffs – and Charles Dickens, who set many of his tales in the grimy streets of London's East End. More recent literary heavyweights include Edinburgh-based JK Rowling, author of the Harry Potter stories, and Philip Pullman, whose His Dark Materials trilogy was set among Oxford's dreaming spires.

Britain's most prestigious literary award, the Man Booker Prize, is held in October. Leading contemporary novelists include Martin Amis, Zadie Smith, Ian McEwan, Will Self, Sarah Waters, David Mitchell, Salman Rushdie and Hilary Mantel, along with their more populist counterparts such as Nick Hornby, David Nicholls and Sebastian Faulks.

Cinema & TV

Britain's home-grown film industry ebbs and flows, with most of its contemporary worldwide hits – including *Shakespeare in Love* and *Bend It Like Beckham* – occupying the heart-warming side of film narrative. Mike Leigh and Ken Loach are two of Britain's most successful directors, known for their naturalistic style.

Comedy is another great British export: recent successes include Ricky Gervais and Stephen Merchant (creators of *The Office* and *Extras*) and Edgar Wright, Nick Frost and Simon Pegg (who made *Shaun of the Dead* and *Hot Fuzz*).

Britain's national broadcaster is the BBC, which operates several TV and radio channels, none of which are allowed to include adverts. Their commercial rivals include ITV, C4 and C5, as well as satellite-only Sky, all of which are funded mainly by advertising.

Music

Britain might no longer have an empire, but it still leads the world when it comes to music. The scene is as fast-moving and varied as ever, divided into a host of different genres. Alongside the stalwarts of rock, indie and electronica such as Blur, Coldplay, PJ Harvey and Muse, there's been an increasing interest in British folk in recent years, spearheaded by the all-conquering Mumford & Sons, whose album *Babel* became one of the fastest-selling in music history.

Acts such as Dizzee Rascal, Tinie Tempah and Plan B have heralded a new wave of British hip-hop, grime and garage artists, while singer-songwriters including Adele and the late Amy Winehouse have helped promote a new style of British soul and R&B. For the latest new acts, the prestigious Mercury Prize (www.mercuryprize.com) held in November is usually a good guide.

Britain also hosts a huge number of outdoor festivals, including the world-famous Glastonbury Festival of Performing Arts, held (most) years in rural Somerset.

Sport

If you want to take a shortcut into the heart of British culture, watch the British at play. Scotland, Wales and England all field their own football (soccer) and rugby sides, and little love is lost when the sides meet in international competitions. Sometimes, however, Britain comes together in support of the national team, as clearly displayed during the 2012 Olympics and Paralympics, when a glowing sense of collective pride (briefly) superseded national loyalties.

Key events in the British sporting calendar include the Wimbledon Lawn Tennis Championships (held in June/July), the FA Cup (the main football cup; held at the end of July), horse races including the Grand National (usually in April) and Royal Ascot (June), and the Six Nations rugby tournament (February/March), contested between England, Scotland, Wales, Ireland, France and Italy.

Environment

The island of Britain consists of three nations: England in the south and centre, Scotland to the north and Wales to the west. Northern Ireland is a part of the United Kingdom, while the southern half of Ireland is its own independent state.

Measuring around 600 miles (around 1000km) north to south, and half that at its widest point, Britain is roughly the same size as New Zealand and half the size of France. Though relatively small, Britain's landscape is surprisingly varied, ranging from the flatlands of eastern England to the craggy peaks of Snowdonia and Scotland.

Britain's 15 national parks cover around 10% of the country. For more details, see www.nationalparks.gov.uk.

Food & Drink

Britain's traditional meals include roast beef, fish and chips, bangers and mash, and steak and kidney pie, many of which have been given a modern twist by Britain's celeb chefs.

Another speciality is the fry-up breakfast (also known as 'the full English') containing bacon, sausage, egg, beans, mushrooms, toast and more. In Scotland you may be offered haggis or black pudding, and oatcakes instead of toast.

Alongside the home-grown favourites, most Brits have also embraced many ethnic cuisines, with Chinese and Indian restaurants now as common as traditional chippies, and cities such as Glasgow, Birmingham and Manchester vying to be the nation's curry capital.

SURVIVAL GUIDE

Directory A–Z

Accommodation

Accommodation in Britain is as varied as the sights you will visit. The big cities tend to be more expensive, with London in a class of its own.

» Rates drop in low season (October to April), and rocket during high season (July to September).

» Breakfast is usually included at B&Bs and hotels, but may be an extra at hostels and top-end hotels.

» Rates are often quoted per person, rather than per room, and include a private bathroom unless otherwise stated.

» Smoking is banned in all hotels, B&Bs and other accommodation.

» In summer, popular spots (York, Canterbury, Bath etc) get very crowded, so booking ahead is essential.

» Accommodation can be difficult to find during holidays (especially around Easter and New Year) and major events (such as the Edinburgh Fringe Festival).

» Local TICs often provide an accommodation booking service for a small fee.

PRICE RANGES

Our reviews refer to double rooms with a private bathroom, except in hostels or where otherwise specified. Quoted rates are for a double room in high season.

£ less than £60 (£90 in London)

££ £60 to £130 (£90 to £180 in London)

£££ more than £130 (£180 in London)

CAMPING

The opportunities for camping in Britain range from farmers' fields with a tap and a basic toilet, costing from £3 per person per night, to smarter affairs with hot showers and many other facilities, charging up to £10. You usually need your own kit.

HOSTELS

Britain has two national hostelling organisations: **Youth Hostels Association** (YHA; www.yha.org.uk), covering England and Wales, and **Scottish Youth Hostels Associa-**

tion (SYHA; ☎0845-293 7373; www.syha.org.uk). Dorm beds range from £10 to £20 per night. Larger hostels with more facilities are £15 to £20. London's YHAs cost from £25. Advance bookings and payments with credit card are usually possible.

You don't have to be a member of the YHA/SYHA (or another Hostelling International organisation) to stay, but most hostels charge extra if you're not a member (£3 at YHA hostels; £1 at SYHA hostels). Annual YHA membership costs £16; annual SYHA membership costs £10.

There's a growing array of independent hostels and backpackers across Britain, varying widely in quality, facilities and price (typically from £10 to £25 per night). Some are quiet and cosy, while others are for serious party travellers.

The print and online **Independent Hostel Guide** (www.independenthostelguide.co.uk) is the best listing. North of the English border, an excellent site is www.hostel-scotland.co.uk.

HOTELS

British hotels vary widely in style and quality, from farmhouse conversions to luxury country houses and stylish boutique hotels. At the bargain end, you might find rooms from £50 per night; move up the scale and you could pay £100 to £150 per night or more.

Hotel chains can be a good option for accommodation on a budget, especially in larger cities. They're often a bit short on character, but rates are generally cheap and they're often in great central locations.

Etap Hotels (www.etaphotel.com)

Premier Inn (www.premierinn.com)

Travelodge (☎0871 984 8484; www.travelodge.co.uk; r from £70)

B&BS & GUESTHOUSES

The B&B ('bed and breakfast') is a great British institution. Prices start at around £30 per person for an en suite room, up to £60 or more for special places.

» B&B prices are usually quoted per person, based on two people sharing.

» Single rooms are harder to find and attract a 20% to 50% premium.

» If you haven't booked, most towns have a main drag of B&Bs; look out for 'Vacancies' signs.

» Many B&Bs require a minimum two nights at weekends and during busy periods.

PRACTICALITIES

Newspapers & Magazines Leading tabloids include the *Sun* and *Mirror;* quality papers (from right to left, politically) include the *Telegraph, Times, Independent* and *Guardian*.

Weights & Measures Britain uses both metric and imperial measures. For example, petrol is sold by the litre but beer by the pint; mountain heights are in metres but road distances are in miles.

DVD PAL format, Region 2.

PUBS & INNS

As well as selling drinks, many pubs and inns offer lodging, particularly in country areas. For bed and breakfast, you'll pay around £20 per person for a basic room, around £35 for something better. An advantage for solo tourists is that pubs often have single rooms.

UNIVERSITY ACCOMMODATION

Many universities offer student accommodation to visitors during vacations. Prices range from £15 to £30 per person. A handy portal is www.universityrooms.co.uk.

Activities

Britain is a great destination for outdoor enthusiasts. Walking and cycling are the most popular activities – you can do them on a whim, and they're the perfect way to open up some beautiful corners of the country.

CYCLING

Compact Britain is an excellent destination to explore by bike. Popular regions to tour include southwest England, the Yorkshire Dales, Derbyshire's Peak District, Mid-Wales and the Scottish Borders. Bike hire outlets are widespread; rates range from £10 per day to £60 per week.

The 10,000-mile **National Cycle Network** (www.nationalcyclenetwork.org.uk) is a web of quiet roads and traffic-free tracks that pass through busy cities and remote rural areas.

Sustrans (www.sustrans.org.uk) is another useful organisation, and publishes a wide range of maps, guides and planning tools.

SURFING

Surfing in Britain isn't for the faint-hearted: temperatures in summer rarely get much above 13°C, and can be just a few degrees above freezing in winter. But with a decent wetsuit you'll be able to discover some of Europe's best breaks, especially around south-west Wales, Cornwall and Devon. For info, see www.britsurf.co.uk.

WALKING & HIKING

Hiking is a hugely popular pastime in Britain, especially in scenic areas such as Snowdonia, the Lake District, the Yorkshire Dales and the Scottish Highlands. Various long-distance routes cross the countryside, including the **Coast to Coast** (www.thecoasttocoastwalk.info), the **Cotswold Way** (www.nationaltrail.co.uk/cotswold), the **West Highland Way** (☎01389-722600; www.west-highland-way.co.uk) and the **South West Coast Path** (www.southwestcoastpath.com).

The **Ramblers Association** (☎020-7339 8500; www.ramblers.org.uk) is the country's leading walkers' organisation.

Business Hours

Standard opening hours:

Banks 9.30am to 5pm Monday to Friday; larger branches also open Saturday morning

Post offices 9.30am to 5pm Monday to Saturday

Pubs 11am to 11pm Monday to Saturday, to 10.30pm Sunday; some stay open later, especially on weekends

Restaurants lunch 11am to 3pm, dinner 6pm to 10pm; hours vary widely

Shops 9am to 5pm Monday to Saturday, 10am to 4pm Sunday

Customs & Regulations

The UK has a two-tier customs system:

Duty-free from outside the EU Includes 200 cigarettes or equivalent in cigars, 4L of wine, 1L of spirits, 60cc of perfume, and other goods worth up to £390.

Tax and duty paid within the EU Guidelines are 800 cigarettes, 200 cigars, 10L of spirits, 90L of wine and 110L of beer.

SCOTTISH POUNDS

Scotland issues its own currency (including a £1 note), interchangeable with the money used in the rest of the UK. However, you'll find shops more readily accept Scottish money in the north of England than in the south. Banks will always change Scottish pounds.

Food

The prices we quote are for a main meal unless otherwise indicated. The symbols used in each review indicate the following prices:

£ less than £9

££ £9 to £18

£££ more than £18

Gay & Lesbian Travellers

Most major cities – especially London, Brighton, Manchester and Glasgow – have gay and lesbian scenes. Useful resources include the following:

Diva (www.divamag.co.uk)

Gay Times (www.gaytimes.co.uk)

Pink Paper (www.pinkpaper.com)

Heritage Organisations

Many of the UK's castles, gardens and stately homes are owned by national heritage organisations. If you're a member, you get free admission, free parking, information handbooks and so on.

English Heritage (EH; www.english-heritage.org.uk) annual membership costs £47. An Overseas Visitors Pass allows free entry to most sites for seven/14 days for £23/27. In Wales and Scotland the equivalent organisations are **Cadw** (www.cadw.wales.gov.uk) and **Historic Scotland** (HS; www.historic-scotland.gov.uk).

National Trust (NT; www.nationaltrust.org.uk) annual membership costs £53 (with discounts for under-26s). A Touring Pass allows free entry to NT properties for one/two weeks (£23/28 per person). The **National Trust for Scotland** (NTS; www.nts.org.uk) is similar.

Money

» ATMs, often called 'cash machines', are easy to find in most towns and cities.

» Most banks and some post offices offer currency exchange.

» Smaller businesses may charge a fee for credit cards, and some take cash or cheque only. Nearly everywhere uses a 'Chip and PIN' system (instead of signing).

» The currency of Britain is the pound sterling (£). Paper money ('notes') comes in £5, £10, £20 and £50 denominations, although some shops don't accept £50 notes.

» In Britain, you're not obliged to tip. A 10% tip is fine for restaurants, cafes, taxi drivers and pub meals; if you order drinks and food at the bar, there's no need to tip.

» Travellers cheques are rarely used.

Public Holidays

In many areas of Britain, bank holidays are just for the banks – many businesses and visitor attractions stay open.

New Year's Day 1 January

Easter March/April (Good Friday to Easter Monday inclusive)

May Day First Monday in May

Spring Bank Holiday Last Monday in May

Summer Bank Holiday Last Monday in August

Christmas Day 25 December

Boxing Day 26 December

Safe Travel

Britain is a safe country, but crime does occur, especially in London and other cities. When travelling by tube, tram or urban train at night, choose a carriage containing other people.

Unlicensed minicabs operate in large cities and are usually worth avoiding. Use a metered taxi or phone a reputable minicab company and get an up-front quote for the fare.

Telephone

AREA CODES

Area codes and individual numbers have been listed together, separated by a hyphen. Other codes include ☎0500 or ☎0800 for free calls, ☎0845 for local rates, ☎087 for national rates and ☎089 or ☎09 for premium rates. Mobile phones start with ☎07 and calling them is more expensive than calling a landline.

Dial ☎100 for an operator and ☎155 for an international operator as well as reverse-charge (collect) calls.

To call outside the UK, dial ☎00, then the country code (☎1 for USA, ☎61 for Australia etc), the area code (you usually drop the initial zero) and the number.

For directory enquiries, a host of agencies compete for your business and charge from 10p to 40p; numbers include ☎118 192, ☎118 118, ☎118 500 and ☎118 811.

MOBILE PHONES

Phones from most other countries operate in England, but attract roaming charges. Local SIM cards cost from £10; SIM and basic handset around £30.

PUBLIC PAYPHONES

The famous red telephone boxes are a dying breed now. You'll mainly see two types of public payphones in Britain: one takes money (and doesn't give change), while the other uses prepaid phonecards and credit cards. Some phones accept both coins and cards. The minimum call price is currently 50p.

SCHOOL HOLIDAYS

Roads get busy and hotel prices go up during school holidays.

Easter Holiday Week before and week after Easter.

Summer Holiday Third week of July to first week of September.

Christmas Holiday Mid-December to first week of January.

There are also three weeklong 'half-term' school holidays – usually late February (or early March), late May and late October. These vary between Scotland, England and Wales.

Time

» In winter (late October to late March) Britain is on GMT/UTC 0.

» In summer (late March to late October) Britain uses daylight saving so the time is GMT/UTC +1.

» In summer, if it's noon in London, it's 9pm in Melbourne, Australia and 7am in New York, USA.

Visas

European Economic Area (EEA) nationals don't need a visa to visit (or work in) Britain. Citizens of Australia, Canada, New Zealand, South Africa and the USA can visit for up to six months (three months for some nationalities), but are prohibited from working. For more info see www.ukvisas.gov.uk or www.ukba.homeoffice.gov.uk.

Getting There & Away

Air

LONDON AIRPORTS

London is served by five airports; Heathrow and Gatwick are the busiest.

London Heathrow (www.heathrowairport.com)

London Gatwick (www.gatwickairport.com)

London City Airport (www.londoncityairport.com)

Luton (www.london-luton.co.uk) Some 35 miles north of central London, well-known as a holiday-flight airport.

Stansted (www.stanstedairport.com) About 35 miles northeast of central London, mainly handling charter and budget European flights.

REGIONAL AIRPORTS

Bristol Airport (www.bristolairport.co.uk)

Cardiff Airport (www.tbicardiffairport.com)

Edinburgh Airport (www.edinburghairport.com)

Glasgow Airport (www.glasgowairport.com)

Liverpool Airport (www.liverpooljohnlennonairport.com)

Manchester Airport (www.manchesterairport.co.uk)

Newcastle Airport (www.newcastleairport.com)

Land

BUS & COACH

The international network **Eurolines** (www.eurolines.com) connects a huge number of European destinations.

Services to/from Britain are operated by **National Express** (www.nationalexpress.com).

TRAIN

Eurostar (www.eurostar.com) high-speed passenger services shuttle at least 10 times daily between London and Paris (2½ hours) or Brussels (two hours) via the Channel Tunnel. The normal single fare between London and Paris or Brussels is around £150, but if you buy in advance, deals drop to around £90 return or less.

Vehicles use the **Eurotunnel** (www.eurotunnel.com) at Folkestone in England or Calais in France. The trains run four times an hour from 6am to 10pm, then hourly. The journey takes 35 minutes. The one-way cost for a car and passengers is around £90 to £150 depending on the time of day (less busy times are cheaper); promotional fares bring it nearer to £50.

Travelling between Ireland and Britain, the main train–ferry–train route is Dublin to London, via Dun Laoghaire and Holyhead. Ferries also run between Rosslare and Fishguard or Pembroke (Wales), with train connections on either side.

Sea

The main ferry routes between Britain and mainland Europe include Dover to Calais or Boulogne (France), Harwich to Hook of Holland (Netherlands), Hull to Zeebrugge (Belgium) or Rotterdam (Netherlands), Rosyth to Zeebrugge, Portsmouth to Santander or Bilbao (Spain), and Newcastle to Bergen (Norway) or Gothenberg (Sweden). Routes to/from Ireland include Holyhead to Dun Laoghaire.

Competition from the Eurotunnel and budget airlines means ferry operators discount heavily at certain times of year. The short cross-channel routes such as Dover to Calais or Boulogne can be as low as £20 for a car plus up to five passengers, although around £50 is more likely. If you're a foot passenger, or cycling, crossings can start from as little as £10 each way.

Broker sites covering all routes and options include www.ferrybooker.com and www.directferries.co.uk.

Brittany Ferries (www.brittany-ferries.com)

DFDS Seaways (www.dfds.co.uk)

Irish Ferries (www.irishferries.com)

P&O Ferries (www.poferries.com)

Stena Line (www.stenaline.com)

Getting Around

For getting around Britain, your first main choice is going by car or public transport. Having your own car makes the best use of time and helps reach remote places, but rental, fuel costs and parking can be expensive – so public transport is often the better way to go.

Cheapest but slowest are long-distance buses (called coaches in Britain). Trains are faster but much more expensive.

Air

Britain's domestic air companies include **British Airways** (www.britishairways.com), **easyJet** (www.easyjet.com) and **Ryanair** (www.ryanair.com). On most shorter routes (eg London to Newcastle, or Manchester to Bristol), it's often faster to take the train once airport downtime is factored in.

Bus

Long-distance buses (coaches) nearly always offer the cheapest way to get around. Many towns have separate bus and coach stations; make sure you're in the right place!

National Express (www.nationalexpress.com) is England's main coach operator. North of the border, **Scottish Citylink** (☎08705 505050; www.citylink.co.uk) is the leading coach company. Tickets are cheaper if you book in advance and travel at quieter times. As a rough guide, a 200-mile trip (eg London to York) will cost around £15 to £20 booked a few days in advance.

Also offering cheap fares (if you're lucky, from £1!) is **Megabus** (www.megabus.com), which serves about 30 destinations in Britain.

If the train doesn't get you all the way to your destination, a **PlusBus** supplement (usually around £2) validates your train ticket for onwards travel by bus.

BUS PASSES

National Express offers discount passes to full-time students and under-26s, called **Young Persons Coachcards**. They cost £10 and give 30% off standard adult fares. Also available are coachcards for people over 60, families and disabled travellers.

For touring the country, National Express offers **Brit Xplorer** passes, allowing unlimited travel for seven days (£79), 14 days (£139) and 28 days (£219).

Car & Motorcycle

Most overseas driving licences are valid in Britain for up to 12 months from the date of entry.

RENTAL

Car rental is expensive in Britain; you'll pay from around £120 per week for the smallest model, or £250 per week for a medium-sized car (including insurance and unlimited mileage). All the major players including Avis, Hertz and Budget operate here.

Using a rental-broker site such as **UK Car Hire** (www.ukcarhire.net) or **Auto Europe** (www.auto-europe.co.uk) can also help find bargains.

It's illegal to drive a car or motorbike in Britain without (at least) third-party insurance. This will be included with all rental cars.

TRAVELINE

Traveline (☎0871 200 2233; www.traveline.org.uk) is a very useful information service covering bus, coach, taxi and train services nationwide.

ROAD RULES

The *Highway Code*, available in bookshops (or at www.direct.gov.uk/en/TravelAndTransport/Highwaycode), contains everything you need to know about Britain's road rules. The main ones to remember:

» Always drive on the left
» Give way to your right at junctions and roundabouts
» Always use the left-hand lane on motorways and dual carriageways, unless overtaking (passing)
» Wear seat belts in cars and crash helmets on motorcycles
» Don't use a mobile phone while driving
» Don't drink and drive; the maximum blood-alcohol level allowed is 80mg/100mL
» Yellow lines (single or double) along the edge of the road indicate parking restrictions, red lines mean no stopping whatsoever
» Speed limits are 30mph in built-up areas, 60mph on main roads, and 70mph on motorways and dual carriageways

Train

Around 20 companies operate train services in Britain, including **First Great Western** (www.firstgreatwestern.co.uk), which runs from London to Bristol; **Crosscountry** (☎0844 811 0124; www.crosscountrytrains.co.uk), which runs services all the way from Glasgow to Penzance; and **Virgin Trains** (www.virgintrains.co.uk), which runs the 'west coast' route from London to Birmingham and Glasgow.

National Rail Enquiries (☎08457 48 49 50; www.nationalrail.co.uk) provides booking and timetable information for Britain's entire rail network.

CLASSES

Rail travel has two classes: 1st and standard. Travelling 1st class costs around 50% more than standard. At weekends some train operators offer 'upgrades' for an extra £10 to £15 on top of your standard-class fare.

COSTS & RESERVATIONS

The earlier you book, the cheaper it gets. You can also save if you travel 'off-peak' (ie the days and times that aren't busy). If you buy online, you can have the ticket posted (UK addresses only), or collect it from station machines on the day of travel.

There are three main fare types:

Anytime Buy anytime, travel anytime – usually the most expensive option.

Off-peak Buy anytime, travel off-peak.

Advance Buy in advance, travel only on specific trains (usually the cheapest option).

TRAIN PASSES

If you're staying in Britain for a while, passes known as railcards (www.railcard.co.uk) are available:

16–25 Railcard For those aged 16 to 25, or a full-time UK student.

Senior Railcard For anyone over 60.

Family & Friends Railcard Covers up to four adults and four children travelling together.

Railcards cost around £28 (valid for one year, available from major stations or online) and allow a 33% discount on most train fares, except those already heavily discounted. With the Family card, adults get 33% and children 60% discounts, so the fee is easily repaid in a couple of journeys.

REGIONAL PASSES

Various local train passes are available covering specific areas and lines – ask at a local train station to get an idea of what's available.

NATIONAL PASSES

BritRail (www.britrail.com) passes are available for visitors from overseas. They must be bought in your country of origin (not in Britain) from a specialist travel agency. They're available in three different versions (England only; all Britain; UK and Ireland) and for periods from four to 30 days. Eurail cards are not accepted in Britain, and InterRail cards are only valid if bought in another mainland European country.

Bulgaria

Includes »

Sofia 246
Southern Bulgaria 252
Rila Monastery 252
Plovdiv 253
Central Bulgaria 255
Veliko Târnovo 255
Black Sea Coast 257
Varna 257
North Coast 260
Nesebâr 261
Burgas 261
South Coast 262
Understand Bulgaria 262
Survival Guide 263

Best Places to Eat

» Manastirska Magernitsa (p247)
» Puldin Restaurant (p254)
» Dom na Arkitekta (p259)
» Han Hadji Nikoli (p256)

Best Places to Stay

» Hotel Niky (p247)
» Residence Oborishte (p247)
» Hotel Renaissance (p253)
» Hotel Bolyarski (p256)

Why Go?

Bulgaria (България) may be best known for its long, sandy Black Sea beaches, but there's much more to see. Bulgaria boasts no fewer than seven mountain ranges and varied landscapes ideal for hiking, cycling, climbing and wildlife-watching. The country has some of Europe's most modern ski resorts as well. You'll find churches and monasteries full of vibrant icons, picturesque villages of timber-framed houses and cobbled lanes, and dramatic reminders of the country's ancient heritage, from Thracian tombs and Roman ruins to medieval fortresses, Ottoman mosques and communist monuments slowly crumbling away into history. Bulgaria's cities, too, reward visitors, with treasure-filled museums and galleries, and parks sprinkled with cafes and restaurants. Getting around is easy and still remarkably cheap so brush up on your Cyrillic, buy a bus ticket and get ready to explore.

When to Go

Sofia

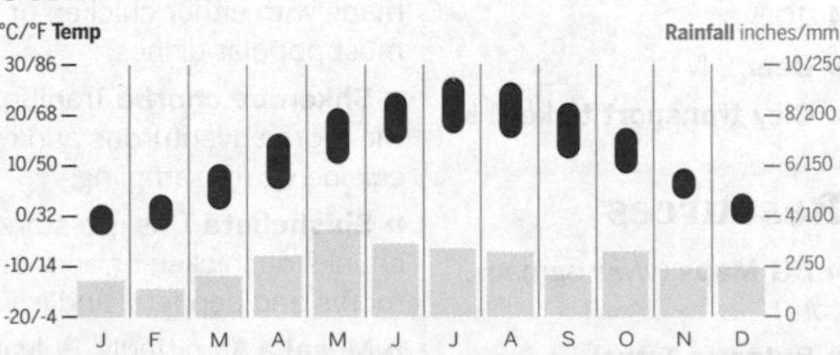

Jan This is a great time to go skiing in Bansko or down Mt Vitosha

Mar–May Fine spring weather welcomes folk and festivals across the country

Jun–Sep Spend lazy days on the Black Sea beaches and nights at Bulgaria's best clubs

AT A GLANCE

» **Currency** Lev (lv)

» **Language** Bulgarian

» **Money** ATMs everywhere

» **Visas** Not required for citizens of the EU, USA, Canada, Australia and New Zealand

Fast Facts

» **Area** 110,910 sq km

» **Capital** Sofia

» **Country code** ☎359

» **Emergency** ☎112

Exchange Rates

Australia	A$1	1.60 lv
Canada	C$1	1.51 lv
Euro Zone	€1	1.96 lv
Japan	¥100	1.63 lv
New Zealand	NZ$1	1.28 lv
UK	UK£1	2.32 lv
USA	US$1	1.53 lv

Set Your Budget

» **Budget hotel room** 50 lv

» **Two-course meal** 10 lv

» **Museum entrance** 4–10 lv

» **Beer** 2 lv

» **City transport ticket** 1 lv

Resources

» **BG Maps** (www.bgmaps.com)

» **Bulgaria Travel** (www.bulgariatravel.com)

» **Beach Bulgaria** (www.beachbulgaria.com)

Connections

Although Sofia has international bus and train connections, it's not necessary to backtrack to the capital if you're heading to Bucharest or İstanbul. From central Veliko Târnovo, for example, there are daily trains both ways – and much of the country offers overnight buses to İstanbul. Heading to Greece or Belgrade by train means going through Sofia.

ITINERARIES

One Week

Start off with a full day in Sofia, visiting the Archaeological Museum and other sights, then take the bus to Veliko Târnovo for a few days of sightseeing and hiking. For the rest of the week, head to Varna for some sea and sand. More adventurous travellers may want to head further south along the coast to prettier resorts closer to the Turkish border.

Two Weeks

After several days in Sofia, catch a bus to Plovdiv and wander the cobbled lanes of the Old Town. From there, make for the coast, staying in Varna and ancient Sozopol. Finish in majestic Veliko Târnovo.

Essential Food & Drink

» **Banitsa** Flaky cheese pasty, often served fresh and hot.

» **Kebabche** Thin, grilled pork sausage.

» **Tarator** On a hot day there's nothing better than this delicious chilled cucumber and yoghurt soup.

» **Beer** Zagorka, Kamenitza and Shumensko are popular nationwide brands.

» **Wine** They've been producing wine here since Thracian times.

» **Kavarma** This 'claypot meal', or meat stew, is normally made with either chicken or pork and is one of the country's most popular dishes.

» **Shkembe chorba** Traditional stomach soup is one of the more adventurous and offbeat highlights of Bulgarian cuisine worth sampling.

» **Shishcheta** This is a standard shish kebab, consisting of chunks of chicken or pork on wooden skewers with mushrooms and peppers, and is widely available.

» **Musaka** Admittedly, Bulgarian moussaka bears more than a passing resemblance to its Greek cousin but it's a delicious staple of cheap cafeteria meals.

Bulgaria Highlights

1 Enjoy the country's best museums and clubs in **Sofia** (p246)

2 Explore the luminous religious treasures of the **Rila Monastery** (p252)

3 Relax along the Black Sea at **Sozopol** (p262)

4 Experience the beaches and nightlife of **Varna** (p257), the most cosmopolitan city on the Black Sea

5 Gallery hop and sip coffee in **Plovdiv** (p253), Sofia's cultural rival

6 Visit the medieval stronghold of **Veliko Târnovo** (p255)

SOFIA

02 / POP 1.3 MILLION

Bulgaria's capital and biggest city, Sofia (София) is at the very heart of the nation's political and cultural life. It's no grand metropolis, true, and it's usually bypassed by tourists heading to the coast or ski resorts, but they're missing something special. The old east-meets-west feel is still here, with a scattering of onion-domed churches, Ottoman mosques and stubborn Red Army monuments. Vast, leafy parks and manicured gardens offer welcome respite from the busy city streets, and the ski slopes and hiking trails of mighty Mt Vitosha are right on the doorstep. With many of Bulgaria's finest museums and art galleries to explore and plenty of excellent bars, restaurants and entertainment venues, Sofia might have you sticking around for longer than you imagined.

Sights

PLOSHTAD ALEKSANDER NEVSKI

FREE **Aleksander Nevski Church** CHURCH
(pl Aleksander Nevski; 7am-7pm) One of *the* symbols of Sofia, this massive church was built between 1882 and 1912 in memory of the 200,000 Russian soldiers who died fighting for Bulgaria's independence during the Russo-Turkish War (1877–78).

Aleksander Nevski Crypt GALLERY
(Museum of Icons; pl Aleksander Nevski; adult/student 6/3 lv; 10am-6pm Tue-Sun; 1) To the left of the church's main entrance, a door leads down to the crypt, which now houses Bulgaria's biggest and best collection of icons, stretching back to the 5th century.

Sveta Sofia Church CHURCH
(ul Parizh; 7am-7pm summer, to 6pm winter; 9) Sveta Sofia Church is the capital's oldest and gave the city its name. Inside the much restored red-brick church, you can see evidence of its earlier incarnations through glass panels in the floor. Outside are the Tomb of the Unknown Soldier and an eternal flame, and the grave of Ivan Vazov, Bulgaria's most revered writer.

SOFIA CITY GARDEN & AROUND

TOP CHOICE **Archaeological Museum** MUSEUM
(www.naim.bg; pl Nezavisimost; adult/student 10/2 lv; 10am-6pm May-Oct, to 5pm Tue-Sun Nov-Apr; 10) Housed in a former mosque built in 1496, this museum displays a wealth of Thracian, Roman and medieval artefacts. Highlights include a mosaic floor from the Sveta Sofia Church, the 4th-century-BC Thracian gold burial mask, and a magnificent bronze head, thought to represent a Thracian king.

Royal Palace PALACE
(ul Tsar Osvoboditel; 20) Originally built for the Ottoman police force, it was here that Bulgaria's national hero, Vasil Levski, was tried and tortured before his execution in 1873. After the liberation, the building was remodelled in 1887 as the home of Prince Alexander Battenberg and became the official residence of the royal family. It houses the National Art Gallery and Ethnographical Museum.

Ethnographical Museum MUSEUM
(pl Battenberg, Royal Palace; adult/student 3/1 lv; 10am-4pm Tue-Sun; 20) Displays on regional costumes, crafts and folklore are spread over two floors, and many of the rooms, with their marble fireplaces, mirrors and ornate plasterwork, are worth pausing over themselves.

PLOSHTAD SVETA NEDELYA & AROUND

TOP CHOICE **Sveta Nedelya Cathedral** CHURCH
(pl Sveta Nedelya; MSerdika) Completed in 1863, this magnificent domed church is one of the city's major landmarks, noted for its rich, Byzantine-style murals. It was blown up by communists on 16 April 1925 in an attempt to assassinate Tsar Boris III.

Sveta Petka Samardzhiiska Church CHURCH
(bul Maria Luisa; MSerdika) Closed due to surrounding excavations at the time of research, this tiny church was built during the early years of Ottoman rule (late 14th century), which explains its sunken profile and inconspicuous exterior. Inside it has 16th-century murals and it's rumoured that Bulgarian national hero Vasil Levski is buried here.

MT VITOSHA & BOYANA

At the southern edge of town, Mt Vitosha is popular for hiking and skiing at a cheaper rate than at the ski resorts (about 30 lv for a lift ticket). The mountain is part of the 227-sq-km **Vitosha Nature Park** (www.park-vitosha.org), the oldest of its kind in Bulgaria (created in 1934). The highest point is Mt Cherni Vrâh (Black Peak; 2290m), the fourth-highest peak in Bulgaria.

Chairlifts, starting around 3km from the village of **Dragalevtsi**, run all year up to Goli Vrâh (1837m). Another option is the six-person gondola at Simeonovo, which runs from Friday to Sunday only.

A trip out here could be combined with the residential suburb of **Boyana**, home to the **National Historical Museum** (www.historymuseum.org; bul Vitoshko Lale 16; adult/student 10/1 lv, combined ticket with Boyana Church 12 lv, guide 20 lv; ⌚9.30am-6pm Tue-Sun Apr-Oct, 9am-5.30pm Nov-Mar), displaying Thracian artefacts, 19th-century weapons and costumes, though there are many reproductions.

More rewarding is the Unesco-listed **Boyana Church** (www.boyanachurch.org; ul Boyansko Ezero 3; adult/student 10/1 lv, combined ticket with National Historical Museum 12 lv, guide 10 lv; ⌚9.30am-5.30pm Apr-Oct, 9am-5pm Nov-Mar; 64, minibus 21), 1.5km south of the museum, built between the 11th and 19th centuries. Its interior is adorned with colourful murals painted in 1259. They are considered among the most important examples of medieval Bulgarian art.

Minibus 21 runs to Boyana from the city centre (pick it up on bul Vasil Levski). It will drop you right outside the gates of the museum and also connects the museum with Boyana Church. You can also take bus 64 from **Hladilnika terminal** (ul Srebârna). A taxi (about 8 lv one way) from the city centre is probably the easiest option; for the museum, ask for the 'Residentsia Boyana'.

Sleeping

Accommodation in Sofia tends to be more expensive than anywhere else in Bulgaria. Good-quality budget hotels are a rarity, and cheaper places that do exist are often either squalid dives or in awkward-to-reach locations; hostels are a better deal.

TOP CHOICE **Hotel Niky** HOTEL €€
(☎953 0110; www.hotel-niky.com; ul Neofit Rilski 16; r/ste from 80/120 lv; P; 1) Offering excellent value and a good central location, Niky has comfortable rooms and gleaming bathrooms, while the smart suites come with kitchenettes. Advance reservations are recommended.

Canapé Connection HOSTEL €
(☎441 6373; www.canapeconnection.com; ul William Gladstone 12a; dm/s/d from 20/46/60 lv; @; 1) Run by three young travellers, Canapé is a homey place with eight- and four-bed dorms featuring smart wooden bunks and wooden floors, as well as private rooms. Homemade *banitsa*, pancakes and croissants are on the breakfast menu.

Hostel Gulliver HOSTEL €
(☎987 5210; www.gulliver1947-bg.com; bul Dondukov 48; dm/s/d 18/38/48 lv; ; 20) Just a couple of blocks north of pl Aleksander Nevski, Gulliver is a clean and brightly furnished place with a couple of five-bed dorms and three doubles. All rooms have TVs and fridges.

Hostel Mostel HOSTEL €
(☎0889 223 296; www.hostelmostel.com; bul Makedoniya 2; dm/s/d from 20/50/60 lv; P; 6, 9, 12) Popular Mostel occupies a renovated 19th-century house, and has six- and eight-bed dorms, either with shared or private bathrooms, as well as a single and a couple of doubles. Guests have use of a kitchen and cosy lounge.

Eating

If you're on a budget, there are plenty of kiosks where you can buy fast food such as *banitsa* and *palachinki* (pancakes). Self-caterers will find an abundance of fresh fruit and veg at the Ladies' Market (p251) and the stalls along ul Graf Ignatiev (outside the Sveti Sedmochislenitsi Church).

TOP CHOICE **Manastirska Magernitsa** DULGARIAN €
(☎980 3883; www.magernitsa.com; ul Han Asparuh 67; mains 5-10 lv; ⌚11am-2am;) This traditional *mehana* (tavern) is among the best places to sample authentic cuisine. The enormous menu features recipes collected from monasteries across the country, with dishes such as 'drunken rabbit' stewed in wine as well as salads, fish, pork and game.

SPLURGE

A salmon-pink 1930s-era home with its own bistro, the **Residence Oborishte** (☎0885 006 810; www.residence-oborishte.com; ul Oborishte 63; s/d/ste from 180/200/220 lv; ; 9, 72) has nine rooms and sumptuous suites with cherry-wood flooring, antique-style furnishings and lots of space. The penthouse (260 lv) has a view over the Aleksander Nevski Church. Prices drop by 20% at weekends.

Sofia

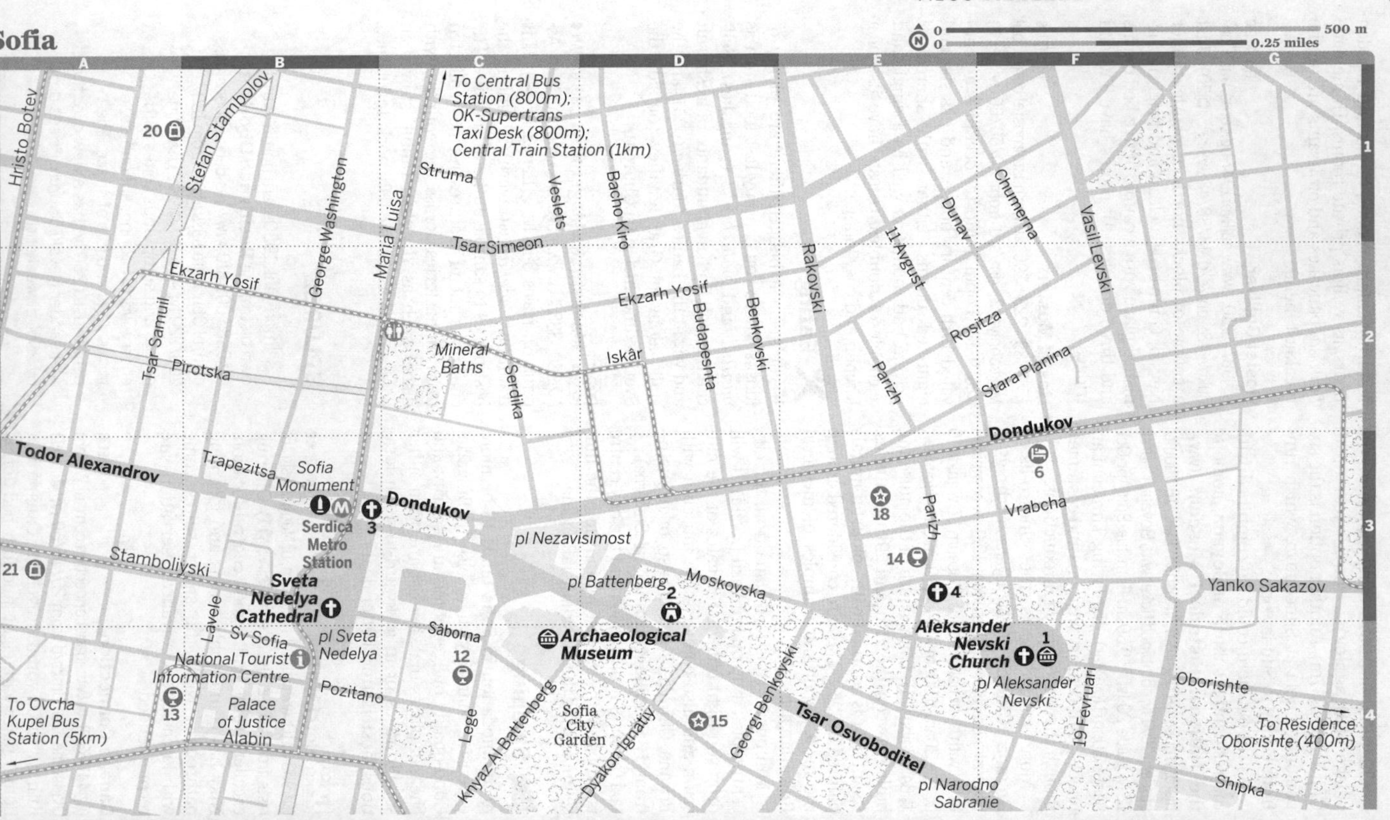
0 500 m
0 0.25 miles
To Central Bus Station (800m); OK-Supertrans Taxi Desk (800m); Central Train Station (1km)
Hristo Botev
Stefan Stambolov
20
Struma
Veslets
Bacho Kiro
Tsar Simeon
George Washington
Maria Luisa
Ekzarh Yosif
Tsar Samuil
Pirotska
Mineral Baths
Serdika
Iskâr
Budapeshta
Benkovski
Rakovski
11 Avgust
Dunav
Chumerna
Vasil Levski
Rositza
Stara Planina
Parizh
Dondukov
6
Todor Alexandrov
Trapezitsa
Sofia Monument
Serdica Metro Station
3
18
Vrabcha
pl Nezavisimost
14
21
Stamboliyski
Sveta Nedelya Cathedral
pl Battenberg
2
Moskovska
4
Yanko Sakazov
Lavele
Sv Sofia
pl Sveta Nedelya
Sâborna
Archaeological Museum
Aleksander Nevski Church
1
12
National Tourist Information Centre
Pozitano
pl Aleksander Nevski
Oborishte
19 Fevruari
To Ovcha Kupel Bus Station (5km)
13
Palace of Justice
Alabin
Lege
Knyaz Al Battenberg
Sofia City Garden
Dyakon Ignatiy
15
Georgi Benkovski
Tsar Osvoboditel
pl Narodno Sabranie
To Residence Oborishte (400m)
Shipka

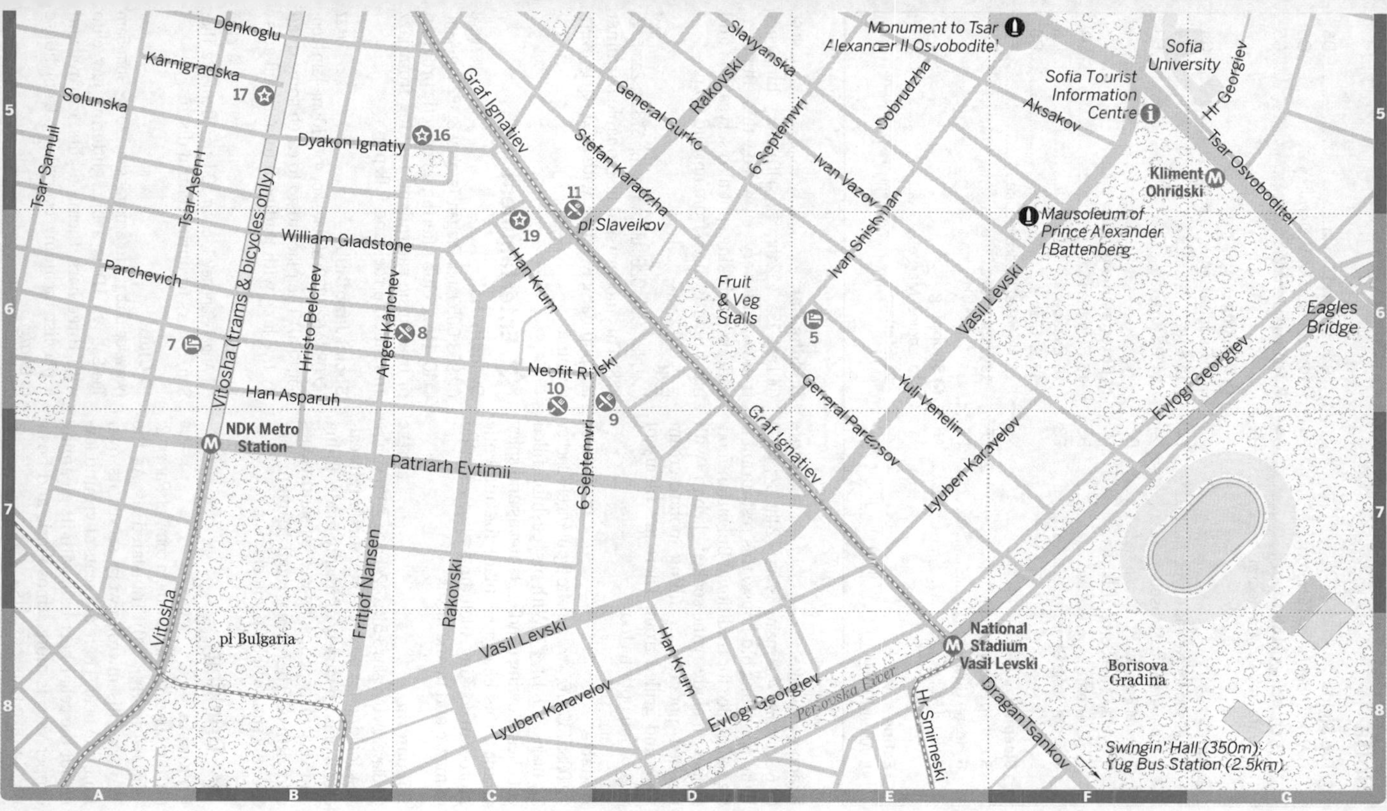
Denkoglu
Kârnigradska
Solunska
Tsar Samuil
Tsar Asen I
Dyakon Ignatiy
Graf Ignatiev
Slavyanska
Rakovski
General Gurko
6 Septemvri
Dobrudzha
Monument to Tsar Alexander II Osvoboditel
Sofia University
Hr Georgiev
Sofia Tourist Information Centre
Aksakov
Tsar Osvoboditel
Kliment Ohridski
Mausoleum of Prince Alexander I Battenberg
Stefan Karadzha
pl Slaveikov
Ivan Vazov
Ivan Shishman
William Gladstone
Parchevich
Vitosha (trams & bicycles only)
Hristo Belchev
Angel Kânchev
Han Krum
Fruit & Veg Stalls
Vasil Levski
Eagles Bridge
Neofit Rilski
Han Asparuh
General Parensov
Yuli Venelin
Evlogi Georgiev
NDK Metro Station
Patriarh Evtimii
6 Septemvri
Lyuben Karavelov
Vitosha
pl Bulgaria
Fritjof Nansen
Rakovski
Vasil Levski
Han Krum
Lyuben Karavelov
Evlogi Georgiev
Perlovska River
National Stadium Vasil Levski
Hr Smirneski
Dragan Tsankov
Borisova Gradina
Swingin' Hall (350m); Yug Bus Station (2.5km)
A
B
C
D
E
F
G
5
6
7
8

Sofia

Top Sights
- Aleksander Nevski Church ... F4
- Archaeological Museum ... C4
- Sveta Nedelya Cathedral ... B3

Sights
- 1 Aleksander Nevski Crypt ... F4
- Ethnographical Museum ... (see 2)
- 2 Royal Palace ... D3
- 3 Sveta Petka Samardzhiiska Church ... B3
- 4 Sveta Sofia Church ... E3

Sleeping
- 5 Canapé Connection ... E6
- 6 Hostel Gulliver ... F3
- 7 Hotel Niky ... A6

Eating
- 8 Annette ... C6
- 9 Krâchme Divaka ... D6
- 10 Manastirska Magernitsa ... C6
- 11 Soupateria ... C5

Drinking
- 12 Buddha Bar ... C4
- 13 Exit ... A4
- 14 Pri Kmeta ... E3

Entertainment
- 15 Bulgaria Hall ... D4
- 16 Escape ... C5
- 17 ID Club ... B5
- 18 National Opera House ... E3
- 19 Social Jazz Club ... C6

Shopping
- 20 Ladies' Market ... A1
- 21 Stenata ... A3

Krâchme Divaka BULGARIAN €
(ul 6 Septemvri 41a; mains 3-7 lv; 24hr; ; 10) In an appealing old house, this restaurant is a good choice for traditional Bulgarian food. Dishes include wine-soaked kebab with mashed potatoes, a filling potato-cream soup and grilled trout. There are plenty of vegetarian options too.

Annette MOROCCAN €€
(0885 139 676; www.annette.bg; ul Angel Kânchev 27; mains 8-18 lv;) With its cushion-filled couches, glowing candles, lanterns and spicy aromas, this is a great place for authentic Moroccan cooking, including a big selection of mezze and tagine meals.

Soupateria BUFFET €
(pl Slaveikov 6; mains 3-5 lv; 24hr;) If you're just looking for a quick bite, this bright cafeteria offers a variety of freshly made, filling and very tasty soups, as well as sandwiches and drinks. There's no English menu, but friendly staff will help you choose.

Drinking

Pri Kmeta PUB
(At the Mayor's; www.prikmeta.com; ul Parizh 2; noon-4am; ; 20) Translated as At the Mayor's, this microbrewery serves its own Kmetsko beer. There are seats at ground level, but the cellar beer hall, with its gleaming copper vats, is more atmospheric and hosts regular live music events.

Buddha Bar LOUNGE
(ul Lege 15a; 24hr; ; 10) Very hip, very trendy and very crowded, this Buddha-bedecked drinking spot also serves food and has a nightly disco from around 9pm.

Exit GAY
(0887 965 026; ul Lavele 16; 8am-2am; ; 8) This modern and fashionable bar/diner is a popular gay venue, with a DJ party every evening.

Entertainment

Swingin' Hall LIVE MUSIC
(963 0059; bul Dragan Tsankov 8; 9pm-4am; 10) Huge club offering an eclectic program of live music each night, ranging from jazz and blues to rock and folk pop.

Social Jazz Club JAZZ
(0884 622 220; pl Slaveikov 4; 10pm-4am Mon-Sat; 10) The place to go to catch some quality live jazz, with leading international acts.

Escape CLUB
(ul Angel Kânchev 1; cover 10 lv; 10pm-late Thu-Sun) Sofia's favourite central disco.

ID Club GAY
(www.idclub.bg; ul Kârnigradska 19b; 9pm-5am Tue-Sat;) ID is a big, glittering gay club with three bars, theme nights, cabaret and a playlist including everything from house to *chalga*.

Performing Arts

National Opera House OPERA
(☎987 1366; www.operasofia.com; bul Dondukov 30, entrance on ul Vrabcha; ⊙ticket office 9am-2pm & 2.30 7pm Mon-Fri, 11am-7pm Sat, 11am-4pm Sun; 🚌9, 🚊20) Opened in 1953, this monumental edifice is the venue for grand opera and ballet performances, as well as concerts.

National Palace of Culture CONCERT VENUE
(NDK; ☎916 6368; www.ndk.bg; pl Bulgaria; ⊙ticket office 9am-7pm; 📶; Ⓜ NDK) The NDK (as it's usually called) has 15 halls and is the country's largest cultural complex. It maintains a regular program of events throughout the year, ranging from film screenings and trade shows to big-name international music acts.

Bulgaria Hall CLASSICAL MUSIC
(☎987 7656; ul Aksakov 1; ⊙ticket office 9am-6pm; 🚌9) The home of the excellent Sofia Philharmonic Orchestra.

Shopping

Bul Vitosha is Sofia's main shopping street, mostly featuring international brand-name boutiques interspersed with restaurants.

Ladies' Market MARKET
(ul Stefan Stambolov; ⊙dawn-dusk; 🚊20) Stretching several blocks between ul Ekzarh Yosif and bul Slivnitsa, this is Sofia's biggest fresh-produce market. Fruit and vegetables, cheap clothes, shoes, car parts, kitchen utensils and pretty much anything else you can think of can be bought here.

Stenata OUTDOOR EQUIPMENT
(☎980 5491; www.stenata.com; ul Bratia Miladinovi 5; ⊙10am-8pm Mon-Fri, 10am-6pm Sat, 11am-6pm Sun; 🚊4) The best place in town to buy hiking, climbing and camping equipment, including backpacks, tents and sleeping bags.

Information

National Tourist Information Centre (☎987 9778; www.bulgariatravel.org; ul Sveta Sofia; ⊙9am-5pm Mon-Fri; 🚊5)
Neomed Pharmacy (☎951 5539; bul General Totleben 2b; ⊙24hr; 🚊4)
Pirogov Hospital (www.pirogov.bg; bul General Totleben 21; 🚊4)
Sofia Tourist Information Centre (☎491 8345; Sofia University underpass; ⊙8am-8pm Mon-Fri, 10am-6pm Sat & Sun; Ⓜ Kliment Ohridski)
Unicredit Bulbank (cnr ul Lavele & ul Todor Alexandrov)

Getting There & Away

Air

Sofia airport (☎937 2211; www.sofia-airport.bg; off bul Brussels; minibus 30) is located 12km east of the city centre. The only domestic flights within Bulgaria are between Sofia and the Black Sea. **Bulgaria Air** (☎402 0405; www.air.bg; bul Dondukov 13; ⊙8.30am-5pm Mon-Fri; 🚊20) flies daily to Varna, with two or three daily flights between July and September. Bulgaria Air also flies between the capital and Burgas.

Minibus 30 shuttles between the airport and pl Nezavisimost for a flat fare of 1.50 lv. Less convenient are bus 84 from Terminal 1 and bus 284 from Terminal 2, both of which take a slow and meandering route before depositing you opposite Sofia University. A taxi from the airport to the city centre should cost no more than 15 lv.

Bus

Sofia's **Central Bus Station** (Tsentralna Avtogara; www.centralnaavtogara.bg; bul Maria Luisa 100; ⊙24hr; 🚊7) is 100m south of the train station, with numerous stands (serving some international destinations) in the Traffic Market in between. There are dozens of counters for individual private companies, as well as an information desk and an **OK-Supertrans taxi desk** (⊙6am-10pm).

Train

The **central train station** (bul Maria Luisa; 🚊1, 7) is a massive, rather cheerless concrete hive, built in the 'Brutalist' style in the 1970s. Destinations for all services are listed on timetables in Cyrillic, but departures and arrivals are listed in English on a large computer screen on the ground floor. Other facilities include a post office, left-luggage office, cafes, a supermarket and accommodation agencies.

Same-day tickets are sold at counters on the ground floor, while advance tickets are sold in the gloomy basement, accessed via an unsigned flight of stairs. Counters are open 24 hours, but normally only a few are staffed and queues are long, so don't turn up at the last moment to purchase your ticket.

Getting Around

Car & Motorcycle

Frequent public transport, cheap taxis and horrendous traffic all provide little or no incentive to drive a private or rented car around Sofia. If you wish to explore further afield, though, a car comes in handy.

Avis (☎945 9224; www.avis.bg; Sofia airport, terminal 2; ⊙9am-9pm)
Hertz (☎439 0222; www.hertz.bg; bul Nikola

TRANSPORT FROM SOFIA

Bus

DESTINATION	COST (LV)	DURATION (HR)	FREQUENCY
Bansko	16	3	5-6 daily
Burgas	30	7	6-10 daily
Nesebâr	37	7	5-10 daily
Plovdiv	14	2	several hourly
Ruse	29	5	hourly
Varna	33	7	every 30-45min
Veliko Târnovo	22	4	hourly

Train

DESTINATION	COST (LV)	DURATION (HR)	FREQUENCY
Burgas	29	7	6 daily
Gorna Oryahovitsa (near Veliko Târnovo)	21	4½	8 daily
Plovdiv	14	2½	9 daily
Ruse	23	6	3 daily
Varna	37	7-8	6 daily

Vaptsarov 53; 9am-5.30pm Mon-Fri, 10am-2pm Sat; 88)

Sixt (945 9276; www.tsrentacar.com; Sofia airport, terminal 2; 8am-11pm)

Public Transport

Public transport – including trams, buses, minibuses, trolleybuses and the underground metro – runs from 5.30am to 11pm every day.

A ticket on any bus, tram or trolleybus within Sofia costs 1 lv, and many of these are now fitted with on-board ticket machines. You can also buy tickets from kiosks at stops along the route.

If you plan to use public transport frequently, buy a one day/five day/one month transit card (4/15/50 lv), valid for all trams, buses and trolleybuses (but not the metro). All tickets must be validated by inserting them in the small machine on-board; once punched, tickets are nontransferable. Inspectors will issue on-the-spot fines (10 lv) if you don't have a ticket.

Taxi

By law, taxis must use meters, but those that wait around the airport, luxury hotels and within 100m of pl Sveta Nedelya will often try to negotiate an unmetered fare – which, of course, will be considerably more. **OK-Supertrans** (973 2121; www.oktaxi.net) and **Yellow Taxi** (911 19) are reliable operators that you order in advance by phone.

SOUTHERN BULGARIA

Many of Bulgaria's most popular hiking trails and ski runs are in the mountainous southwest. The **Rila Mountains** (www.rilanationalpark.org) are south of Sofia, the **Pirin Mountains** (www.pirin-np.com) are further south towards the Greek border and the **Rodopi Mountains** are just east and south of Plovdiv.

Check www.bulgariaski.com for ski information on the three main resorts: **Borovets**, **Bansko** and **Pamporovo**.

Rila Monastery

Рилски Манастир

Many Bulgarians say you haven't really been to Bulgaria without paying your respects to the Unesco-protected **Rila Monastery** (6am-9pm), 120km south of Sofia. Built in 927, and heavily restored in 1469, the monastery helped keep Bulgarian culture and language alive during Ottoman rule. Set in a forested valley offering excellent hikes, it's famed for its mural-filled Nativity Church, dating from the 1830s.

If you have time, hike up the **Tomb of St Ivan**. The 15-minute hike begins along the road 3.7km east behind the monastery.

There are hotels and camping grounds nearby. You can also sleep in at the **Rila Monastery's Rooms** (0896 872 010; www.rilamonastery.pmg-blg.com; r 30-60 lv).

From Sofia's **Ovcha Kupel** (955 5362; bul Tsar Boris III, Zapad; 5) bus station, one daily morning bus (17 lv, 2½ hours) goes to the monastery, returning in the afternoon. The monastery also gets five daily buses from Rila village (4 lv), making the latter a better transport hub.

Plovdiv Пловдив

032 / POP 338,184

With its art galleries, winding cobbled streets and bohemian cafes, Plovdiv (*Plovdiv*) equals Sofia in things cultural and is a determined rival in nightlife as well. Being a smaller and less stressful city, Plovdiv is also great for walking. As a major university town, Plovdiv has a lively, exuberant spirit and great nightlife.

Sights

Most of Plovdiv's main sights are in or around the Old Town, largely restored to its mid-19th-century appearance and marked by winding cobblestone streets. It's literally packed with atmospheric house museums and art galleries, and has eminent artists still living and working within its tranquil confines.

Roman Amphitheatre HISTORIC SITE
(ul Hemus; 3 lv; 8am-6pm) Plovdiv's magnificent 2nd-century-AD amphitheatre, built by Emperor Trajan was only uncovered during a freak landslide in 1972. It once held about 6000 spectators. Now largely restored, it again hosts large-scale special events and concerts.

Roman Stadium HISTORIC STADIUM
While the once huge Roman Stadium is mostly hidden under the pedestrian mall, in 2012 the subterranean southern back end was further renovated, with stairways from different sides now allowing entrance into the gleaming rows up close.

Ethnographical Museum MUSEUM
(625 654; ul Dr Chomakov 2; adult/student 5/1 lv; 9am-noon & 2-5.30pm Tue-Thu, Sat & Sun, 2-5.30pm Fri) This intriguing museum houses 40,000 exhibits, including folk costumes and musical instruments, jewellery and traditional crafts such as weaving, metalworking, winemaking and beekeeping.

Church of Sveti Konstantin & Elena CHURCH
(ul Sâborna 24; 8am-7pm) This is Plovdiv's oldest church, built over a late Roman church. It's dedicated to Constantine the Great, the 4th-century emperor who made Orthodox Christianity the state religion, and his mother, Sveta Helena. The current church, however, dates to 1832.

Dzhumaya Mosque MOSQUE
(pl Dzhumaya; 6am-11pm) The largely renovated Dzhumaya Mosque, one of the Balkans' oldest, dates from the mid-15th century. With a 23m-high minaret, it was the largest of Plovdiv's more than 50 Ottoman-era mosques.

Sleeping

Campers have the **Complex 4th Kilometre** (951 360; campsites per person 3 lv, bungalows 28-38 lv; year-round;) and the **9th Kilometre Complex** (632 992; www.leipzig.bg; bul Pazardzhikoshose; campsites per person 3 lv, tents 3 lv, bungalows 20 lv, r renovated/unrenovated 32/25 lv; year-round;). The former is a shady, loud place about 4km west on the old Sofia Hwy and includes a restaurant-bar and water park. Take bus 4, 18 or 44 west along bul Bulgaria, or bus 222 from the train station to its terminus and walk another 200m. The latter camping ground, owned by Plovdiv's Hotel Leipzig, is snazzier, with a restaurant and 24-hour bar. Take a taxi (12 lv).

TOP CHOICE **Hotel Renaissance** BOUTIQUE HOTEL €€
(266 966; www.renaissance-bg.com; pl Vâzhrazhdane 1; s/d incl breakfast from 115/145 lv;) This lovely boutique hotel between the Old Town and the main shopping streets aims to recreate a National Revival–era home. Each room is unique, with handsome wood floors. Some boast period furniture.

Hikers Hostel HOSTEL €
(0896 764 854; www.hikers-hostel.org; ul Sâborna 53; incl breakfast tent/dm/s/d without bathroom 12/20/43/48 lv;) The ideal place for independent travellers to chill in Plovdiv's Old Town, Hikers has comfy couches, outside tables, and sleeping choices ranging from tents and dorms to lofts and private rooms. There's free wi-fi, a computer, lockers for luggage, and a laundry service (5 lv).

Plovdiv Guest House HOSTEL €
(☎622 432; www.plovdivguest.com; ul Sâborna 20; dm/s/d/q €9/25/30/45; ❄@📶) Another backpacker option on Sâborna, this offers clean and bright dorms with 10, eight and four beds, and there's one spacious attic double. Dorms feature their own self-contained and modern bathroom/shower.

Hotel Leipzig HOTEL €€
(☎654 000; www.leipzig.bg; bul Ruski 70; s/d/apt from 82/100/124 lv; P❄📶) This sharply renovated old fixture has over 60 appealing modern rooms and apartments designed with eclectic, colourful decor uncommon in a place that doubles as a business hotel and wedding-banquet venue.

Hotel Elite HOTEL €€
(☎624 537; ul Rayko Daskalov 53; d/ste 60/100 lv; ❄) The modern and reasonably priced hotel is on the corner of bul 6 Septemvri, just west of the Kapana bar district. Rooms are insulated from road noise, and it's clean and comfortable.

Eating

Malâk Bunardzhik BULGARIAN €
(☎446 140; ul Volga 1; mains 5-10 lv; 📶) Quality Bulgarian cuisine is served at this popular place with garden dining and live music most nights.

Dayana BARBECUE €
(☎623 027; ul Dondukov Korsakov 3; mains 5-9 lv; ⏲9am-late; 📶) This big place off the pedestrian mall, popular with locals and foreigners alike, has a huge (and colourful) menu strong on grilled meats.

Restaurant Renaissance INTERNATIONAL €€
(pl Vâzhrazhdane 1; mains 9-17 lv; ⏲10am-10:30pm Tue-Sun) Cooks up a wide range of inventive appetisers, plus grills, risottos and fresh fish from the Aegean.

SPLURGE

The magical **Puldin Restaurant** (☎631 720; ul Knyaz Tseretelev 8; mains 8-15 lv; ⏲9am-midnight; 📶) is one of Plovdiv's most atmospheric restaurants. In one dining room, the famous whirling dervishes of the Ottoman Empire once whirled themselves into ecstatic exhaustion, while in the cellar hall Byzantine-era walls and Roman artefacts dominate.

Dreams CAFE €
(☎627 142; pl Stambolov; sandwiches around 2 lv; ⏲9am-11pm; 📶) This excellent and popular cafe on pl Stambolov is the perfect place to relax. You can sit before the giant, gushing fountain on a balmy summer's day. In addition to coffee and other drinks, there's a nice (and inexpensive) selection of sandwiches.

Drinking & Entertainment

Several good places occupy the district called Kapana, meaning 'the trap', referring to its tight streets (north of pl Dzhumaya, between ul Rayko Daskalov to the west and bul Tsar Boris Obedinitel to the east).

TOP CHOICE **Naylona** BAR
(☎0889 496 750; ul Giorgi Benkovski 8, Kapana; ⏲noon-4am; 📶) They say the owners of this Kapana dive bar purposely didn't fix the roof so that the rain would trickle in; whatever the story, this damp, bare-bones place usually playing classic (and other) rock remains the unwashed, long-haired antithesis of Plovdiv style.

Art Bar Maria Luiza BAR
(bul Maria Luiza 15; ⏲8am-4am; 📶) Too pretty to be just a dive bar, the Maria Luisa has dedicated owners who keep adapting the decor to suit their whims.

Petnoto CLUB
(☎0898 542 787; ul Ioakim Gruev 36, Kapana; ⏲8am-6am; 📶) The pinstriped Petnoto combines a bar, small restaurant and a music stage where Bulgarian bands and DJs perform.

Information

Exchange offices line ul Knyaz Aleksandâr and ul Ivan Vazov. ATMs are widespread, including around pl Dzhumaya and ul Knyaz Aleksandâr, though not in the Old Town's upper reaches.

Internet Café Speed (2nd fl, bul Maria Luiza 1)

Patrick Penov Personal Trips & Tours (☎0887 364 711; www.guide-bg.com) Licensed tour guide Svetlomir 'Patrick' Penov has two decades of experience leading individual and small-group tours all over Bulgaria, covering everything from gastronomy and wine to churches and culture.

Tourist Information Centre (tic@plovdiv.bg; pl Tsentralen 1; ⏲9am-7pm) This helpful centre by the post office provides maps, finds local accommodation and more.

Getting There & Away

Bus

Yug bus station (☎626 937), diagonally opposite the train station, sends frequent buses to Sofia (9 lv, two hours) every half-hour or hour, plus a few daily buses to Varna (22 lv, seven hours) and Burgas (19 lv, four hours).

More than 1km north of the river, **Sever bus station** (☎953 011) has four daily buses to Veliko Târnovo (20 lv, 4½ hours). Get there by minibus 4 from ul Tsar Boris III Obedinitel.

Etap (☎632 082; Yug bus station) sells bus tickets to İstanbul (40 lv), Athens (140 lv) and more.

Train

Daily direct services from the **train station** (bul Hristo Botev) include to Burgas (14.60 lv, six hours, six daily) and Sofia (7 lv to 9 lv, 2½ hours, frequently).

Plovdiv's train station is well organised, though the staff don't generally speak English. Computer screens at the station entrance and in the underpass leading to the platforms list recent arrivals and upcoming departures. The luggage storage office (2 lv per bag for 24 hours) is always open.

CENTRAL BULGARIA

Bulgaria is bisected by the long **Stara Planina** mountain range, the local name for the Balkans. Some appealing towns line the south side of the range – such as **Kazanlâk**, handy for visiting the tombs in the 'Valley of Thracian Kings', and the lovely museum-village of **Koprivshtitsa**, famed for its National Revival houses. Most visitors head to Central Bulgaria's main hub, the medieval capital of Veliko Târnovo.

Veliko Târnovo

Велико Търново

☎062 / POP 68,735

The evocative capital of the medieval Bulgarian tsars, sublime Veliko Târnovo is dramatically set amid an amphitheatre of forested hills, divided by the ribboning Yantra River. Commanding pride of place is the magisterial Tsarevets Fortress, citadel of the Second Bulgarian Empire. It's complemented by scores of churches and other ruins, many still being unearthed. As the site of Bulgaria's most prestigious university, Veliko Târnovo also boasts a revved-up nightlife that many larger towns would envy.

Sights

As well as the legendary Tsarevets Fortress, there are a handful of museums, plus a few Byzantine-influenced churches open for (fee-paying) visits in the **Asenova quarter** below Tsarevets Hill. For great views of the gorge, walk along cobbled **ul Gurko**, Veliko Târnovo's oldest street.

Tsarevets Fortress FORTRESS

(adult/student 6/2 lv, scenic elevator 2 lv; ⊙8am-7pm Apr-Sep, 9am-5pm Oct-Mar) About 1km east of the centre, this huge citadel and former seat of the medieval tsars sprawls over a vast and commanding site. Today you can see the remains of more than 400 houses, 18 churches, the royal palace, execution rock and several towers. Watch your step though, as there are lots of holes, broken steps and unfenced drops.

Veliko Târnovo Archaeological Museum MUSEUM

(ul Ivan Vazov; adult/student 6/2 lv; ⊙9am-6pm Tue-Sun) Housed in a grand old building with a colonnaded terrace and courtyard full of Roman sculptures, the archaeological museum contains Roman artefacts from Nikopolis-ad-Istrum, and more Roman pottery and statues from elsewhere.

Sarafkina Kâshta MUSEUM

(ul General Gurko 88; adult/student 6/2 lv; ⊙9am-6pm Mon-Fri) Built in 1861 by a rich Turkish merchant, this fine five-storey National Revival–style house museum displays antique ceramics, metalwork, woodcarvings and jewellery.

Museum of National Revival & Constituent Assembly MUSEUM

(ul Ivan Vazov; adult/student 6/2 lv; ⊙9am-6pm Wed-Mon) This museum, in a former Turkish town hall built in 1872, was where Bulgaria's first National Assembly was held to write the country's first constitution in 1879. The ground floor contains costumes, books and photos about Veliko Târnovo's history. The former assembly hall upstairs displays portraits of local personalities. The basement has classic Old Town photos and valuable icons.

Forty Martyrs Church CHURCH

(ul Mitropolska; adult/student 5/1 lv; ⊙9am-5.30pm) The Forty Martyrs Church, in the old Asenova quarter, was built in 1230 to celebrate Tsar Asen II's victory over the Byzantines. It was used as a royal mausoleum, and then as a mosque by the Turks.

SPLURGE

One of the town's best hotels, the **Hotel Bolyarski** (☎613 200; www.bolyarski.com; ul Stefan Stambolov 53a; s/d incl breakfast from 80/130 lv; P❄☎≋) has a phenomenal location on the bluff on ul Stambolov, with magical views of the town and river from its long cafe patio and rooms, and close proximity to all the local restaurants and bars. Its modern, well-kept rooms are pitched at business travellers.

Without doubt the **Han Hadji Nikoli** (☎651 291; www.hanhadjinikoli.com; ul GS Rakovski 19; mains 25-30 lv; ☎) is Veliko Târnovo's finest restaurant. Start with escargots bourguignon, move on to roast chicken with cranberry-and-rose-wine sauce, and finish with chocolate mousse flecked with raspberries and Cointreau.

Activities

Numerous local operators offer **hiking**, **mountain biking**, **horse riding** and **caving**; ask the Tourist Information Centre for hiking maps and contacts. The centre also offers the useful *Climbing Guide*, for serious rock climbers.

One great hike is to the hilltop village of **Arbanasi**, 4km northeast (about a 90-minute walk). The 16th-century **Nativity Church** (Arbanasi; adult/student 6/2 lv), 200m west of the bus stop, is worth a look. It's unremarkable outside but the interior is covered with fabulous murals. The hike begins across a small bridge behind the Tsaravets (go around to the left side); you can also catch the bus up.

Sleeping

The Tourist Information Centre finds private rooms (25/35 lv for single/double). For atmosphere, stay near the Samovodska Charshiya Complex in the Varosha district, along the lower (southeastern) end of ul Gurko, or near Tsarevets Fortress.

Hikers Hostel HOSTEL €
(☎0889 691 661; www.hikers-hostel.org; ul Rezevoarska 91; campsites/dm/d incl breakfast 14/20/52 lv; @☎) Târnovo's most laid-back hostel, Hikers has an unassuming location high in Varosha's old quarter (a 10-minute walk from downtown). Charismatic owner Toshe Hristov does free bus/train station pick-ups and also runs trips. The two dorms (one with four beds, the other with 10) are spartan but clean, and there's one double room, a kitchen and two shared bathrooms.

Slavyanska Dusha GUESTHOUSE €
(☎625 182; www.slavianska-dusha.com; ul Nikola Zlatarski 21; s/d/tr/apt from 25/35/45/60 lv; ❄☎) Affordable and clean, this cheery guesthouse is run by a local couple who grow their own veg for the on-site restaurant. The place offers simple but nice rooms decked out in traditional decor.

Hostel Mostel HOSTEL €
(☎0897 859 359; www.hostelmostel.com; ul Iordan Indjeto 10; campsites/dm/s/d incl breakfast 18/20/46/60 lv; @☎) The famous Sofia-based Hostel Mostel has become Târnovo's biggest, with clean, modern dorm rooms and doubles with sparkling bathrooms. It's just 150m from Tsarevets Fortress – good for exploring there, but a long walk from downtown (free bus/train pickup is possible).

Eating & Drinking

Shtastlivetsa BULGARIAN €€
(☎600 656; ul Stefan Stambolov 79; mains 7-14 lv; ⏲11am-1am; ☎) A local institution, the 'Lucky Man' (as the impossible-to-pronounce name means in Bulgarian) has an ideal location overlooking the river's bend and a great menu of inventive meat dishes, baked-pot specials, nourishing pizzas and delicious soups.

Ego Pizza & Grill PIZZA €€
(☎601 804; ul Nezavisimost 17; mains 5-12 lv; ⏲9am-midnight; ☎) Târnovo's best pizza, Ego has a new location overlooking the river's bend. It's a spacious restaurant with outdoor and indoor seating with excellent views. Service can be hit-or-miss.

Dada Bar BAR
(ul Velcho Dzhamdzhiyata 12; ⏲10pm-4am) This funky place has a subterranean bar and outdoor enclosed courtyard beyond. Good prices, good music, and it gets busy after midnight.

Tequila Bar BAR
(ul Stefan Stambolov 30; ⏲noon-3am) Overlooking the main street and near the Samovodska Charshiya Compex, Tequila Bar is a festively painted student bar with good cocktails and cheap beer.

★ Entertainment

Konstantin Kisimov Dramatic Theatre THEATRE
(☎623 526; ul Vasil Levski) This theatre has regular performances from the international pantheon and Bulgarian plays. Ask the Tourist Information Centre what's on.

Melon Live Music Club CLUB
(☎0895 424 427; bul Nezavistnost 21; ⏲6pm-4am) This great spot for live music (ranging from rock to R&B and Latin jazz) is tucked halfway up the main street.

ℹ Information

Hospital Stefan Cherkezov (☎626 841; ul Nish 1)

I-Net Internet Centre (off ul Hristo Botev; per hour 1.50 lv)

Tourist Information Centre (☎622 148; www.velikoturnovo.info; ul Hristo Botev 5; ⏲9am-6pm Mon-Fri, Mon-Sat summer)

ℹ Getting There & Away

Bus

Two (noncentral) bus stations serve Veliko Târnovo. **Pâtnicheski Prevozi bus station** (Zapad Bus Station; ☎640 908; ul Nikola Gabrovski 74), about 4km from the centre, is the main intercity one. From here, buses serve Kazanlâk (9 lv, 2½ hours, five daily), Burgas (18 lv, four hours, four daily) and Plovdiv (19 lv, four hours, four daily).

The more central **Yug bus station** (☎620 014; ul Hristo Botev) has daily buses to Sofia (21 lv, four hours), Varna (19 lv, four hours) and Burgas (23 lv, 3½ hours).

Etap Adress (☎630 564; ul Ivailo 2, Hotel Etâr) has hourly buses to Sofia (22 lv, 3½ hours) and Varna (18 lv, four hours).

Train

The small **Veliko Târnovo train station** (☎620 065) has three daily trains to Plovdiv (21 lv, five hours). Trains also serve Burgas (21 lv, five hours, three daily), Varna (20 lv, five hours, three daily) and Sofia (21 lv, 4½ hours, six daily). Many of these require a change at the **Gorna Oryakhovitsa train station** (☎826 118), about 10km from town.

BLACK SEA COAST

Every summer, hordes of international package tourists head to bland, overdeveloped resorts such as Sunny Beach (Slânchev Bryag) and Golden Sands (Zlatni Pyasâtsi). Neither is very user-friendly for independent travellers and there are far more interesting places to enjoy the Bulgarian seaside. Varna in the north is a lively, beachfront city, but the best stretches of sand are found to the south.

Varna Варна

☎052 / POP 335,000

Bulgaria's third city and maritime capital, Varna is the most interesting and cosmopolitan town on the Black Sea coast. A combination of port city, naval base and seaside resort, it's an appealing place to while away a few days. Varna is packed with history yet thoroughly modern, and has an enormous park to amble round and a lengthy beach to lounge on. In the city centre you'll find Bulgaria's largest Roman baths complex and its finest archaeological museum, as well as a lively cultural and restaurant scene.

Sights & Activities

The main activity here is **swimming** and the Varna **city beach** is 8km long. The south beach (with its pool complex, water slides and cafes) has a popular stretch while the central beach has thinner sand patches and is dominated by clubs. Beyond to the north is a rocky area lined with restaurants and further north there are some wider and more attractive areas of sand as well as an outdoor **thermal pool** with year-round hot water where locals take a daily dip. Just in from the beach is **Primorski Park**, a vast expanse of greenery dotted with statues, open-air cafes and popcorn vendors.

TOP CHOICE **Archaeological Museum** MUSEUM
(ul Maria Luisa 41; adult/student 10/2 lv; ⏲10am-5pm Tue-Sun Apr-Sep, Tue-Sat Oct-Mar; 🚌3, 9, 109) Exhibits at this vast museum, the best of its kind in Bulgaria, include 6500-year-old bangles, necklaces and earrings said to be

> **SPLURGE**
>
> The **Grand Hotel London** (☎664 100; www.londonhotel.bg; ul Musala 3; s/d Mon-Thu from 170/210 lv, Fri-Sun from 150/190 lv; P ⊖ ❄) is indeed Varna's grandest hotel. The five-star establishment originally opened in 1912. Rooms are spacious and elegantly furnished, if a little chintzy, and the restaurant is especially good.

Varna

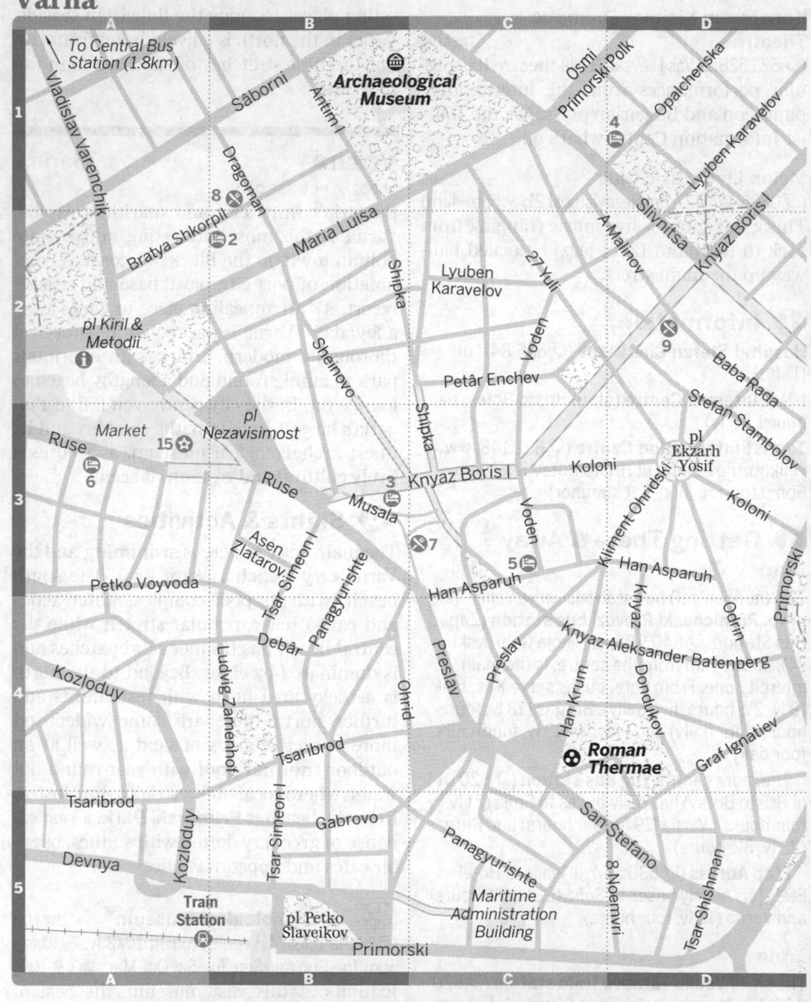

the oldest worked gold found anywhere in the world. It also has Roman surgical implements, Hellenistic tombstones and touching oddities such as a marble plaque that lists in Greek the names of the city's school graduates for AD 221.

TOP CHOICE Roman Thermae RUINS

(cnr ul Han Krum & ul San Stefano; adult/student 4/2 lv; ⏲10am-5pm Tue-Sun May-Oct, Tue-Sat Nov-Apr) The well-preserved ruins of Varna's 2nd-century-AD Roman Thermae are the largest in Bulgaria, although only a small part of the original complex still stands.

Sleeping

Private rooms are plentiful in Varna, and pensioners with spare rooms often wait around the train station to greet new arrivals.

Flag Hostel HOSTEL €

(☎0897 408 115; www.varnahostel.com; ul Bratya Shkorpil 13a; dm incl breakfast 22 lv; P⊖📶; 🚌3, 9) The Flag is a long-established, sociable place with a young, international party atmosphere. It has three dorms with single beds (no bunks) and breakfast is included. Free pick-ups from the bus and train stations are offered.

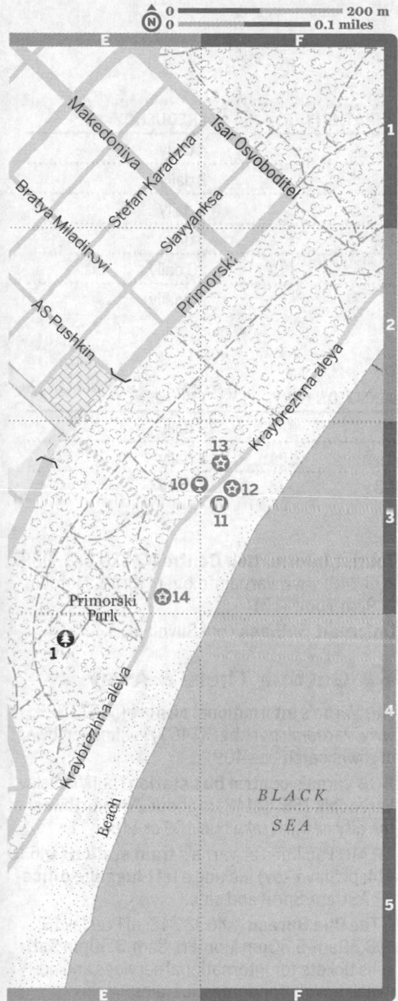

Varna

Top Sights

Archaeological Museum B1
Roman Thermae C4

Sights

1 Primorski Park E4

Sleeping

2 Flag Hostel B2
3 Grand Hotel London B3
4 Hotel Astra D1
5 Hotel Hi C3
6 Yo Ho Hostel A3

Eating

7 Dom na Arkitekta C3
8 Tanasi B1
9 Trops Kâshta D2

Drinking

10 Pench's Cocktails E3
11 Punta Cana F3

Entertainment

12 4aspik F3
13 Copacabana F3
14 Exit E3
15 Varna Opera House A3

Yo Ho Hostel HOSTEL €
(☎0886 382 905; www.yohohostel.com; ul Ruse 23; dm/s/d incl breakfast from 14/30/40 lv; @; 🚌109) Shiver your timbers at this pirate-themed place found just down the street from the Varna Opera House. It has four- and 11-bed dorm rooms, two doubles and one single room. Free breakfast and pick-ups are offered, and staff also organise camping and rafting trips.

Hotel Astra HOTEL €€
(☎630 524; www.hotelastravarna.com; ul Opalchenska 9; s/d 50/60 lv; ❄📶; 🚌9) A real bargain by Varna standards, this central, family-run hotel has 10 spacious and comfortable rooms, all with terraces, and basic but good-sized bathrooms.

Hotel Hi HOTEL €€
(☎657 777; www.hotel-hi.com; ul Han Asparuh 11; s/d 80/112 lv; P❄📶) In a quiet neighbourhood south of the main thoroughfare, Hi is a friendly place featuring stylish, cosy rooms – some very small – with TVs and minibars.

Eating

Dom na Arkitekta BULGARIAN €
(ul Musala 10; mains 4-10 lv) 'The Architect's House' is a fine old wooden National Revival–style building with a leafy courtyard popular with local cats. Grills, steaks and salads are on the menu, plus more traditional 'delicacies' such as chicken gizzards with onions.

Trops Kâshta CAFETERIA €
(bul Knyaz Boris I 48; dishes 3-5 lv; ✎) This branch of the dependable nationwide self-service canteen chain is the ideal place for cheap, simple food such as sausage and beans, chicken chops and moussaka. There's no menu; just point at whatever takes your fancy.

TRANSPORT FROM VARNA

Bus

DESTINATION	PRICE (LV)	DURATION (HR)	FREQUENCY
Burgas	14	2	4 daily
İstanbul (Turkey)	60	10	2 daily
Plovdiv	27	6	2 daily
Ruse	15	4	5 daily
Sofia	32	7	20 daily
Veliko Târnovo	18	4	20 daily

Train

DESTINATION	PRICE (LV)	DURATION (HR)	FREQUENCY
Plovdiv	24.20	7	3 daily
Ruse	12.20	4	2 daily
Sofia	23.60	7-8	7 daily

Tanasi GREEK €€
(☎601 138; ul Bratya Shkorpil 16; mains 5-15 lv; 9) This welcoming Greek restaurant has fresh white linen indoors, plus less formal outdoor seating. It also offers an excellent-value three-course set lunch for 5 lv.

Drinking

Varna's trendiest bars are found along the beach on Kraybrezhna aleya, although many have only a brief existence in the summer sunshine. Popular hang-outs to sip seafront margaritas include **Pench's Cocktails** (Kraybrezhna aleya) and **Punta Cana** (Kraybrezhna aleya; 6am-4am).

Entertainment

Exit (10pm-6am), **4aspik** (☎0885 800 297; 10pm-4am), specialising in Bulgarian folk-pop, and **Copacabana** (10pm-5am), with a fondness for '70s and '80s music, are just a few of the many summertime clubs along Kraybrezhna aleya.

Varna Opera House OPERA
(☎650 555; www.operavarna.bg; pl Nezavisimost 1; ticket office 11am-1pm & 2-7pm Mon-Fri, 11am-6pm Sat) Bulgaria's second-most important opera house (after Sofia) hosts performances by the Varna Opera and Philharmonic Orchestra all year except July and August.

Information

Internet Doom (ul 27 Yuli 13; per hour 1.60 lv; 24hr)

Tourist Information Centre (☎820 689, 0887 703 242; www.varnainfo.bg; pl Kiril & Metodii; 9am-7pm; 3)

Unicredit Bulbank (bul Slivnitsa)

Getting There & Away

AIR Varna's international **airport** (☎573 323; www.varna-airport.bg; 409) is 8km northwest of town; catch bus 409.

BUS Varna's **central bus station** (bul Vladislav Varenchik 158; 148) is about 2km northwest of the city centre (take bus 409 or 148).

TRAIN Facilities at Varna's **train station** (☎630 414; pl Slaveikov) include a **left-luggage office** (7.30am-8pm) and cafe.

The **Rila Bureau** (☎632 348; ul Preslav 13; 8.30am-5.30pm Mon-Fri, 8am-3.30pm Sat) sells tickets for international services and advance tickets for domestic trains.

North Coast

As well as pricier package resorts north of Varna such as **Sveti Konstantin** and **Golden Sands**, **Balchik** is a possible day trip. There's not much of a beach – most of the far-north coast is rocky – but the **Summer Palace of Queen Marie and Botanical Gardens** (Dvorets; 10 lv; 8am-8pm May–mid-Oct, 8.30am-6.30pm mid-Oct–Apr), the eccentric former holiday home of the Queen of Romania, is worth a look. The **Hotel Helios** (☎76 970; www.heliosbg.com; d/apt 94/134 lv; P❄@≈♿) is a modern, resort-style hotel and all rooms have balconies, many with superb sea views.

Nesebâr Несебър

0554 / POP 10,300

Around 40km northeast of Burgas, historic but very commercialised Nesebâr occupies a small rocky isthmus on the south end of a wide bay, facing the megaresort of Sunny Beach, with its 8km-long beach.

Nesebâr was settled by Greek colonists in 512 BC and named Messembria, but today it's more famous for its (mostly ruined) medieval churches, including the vast shell of the 6th-century **Sveta Sofia Church** (Old Metropolitan Church; ul Mitropolitska; dawn-dusk). The **Archaeological Museum** (www.ancient-nessebar.org; ul Mesembria 2; adult/child 5/3 lv; 9am-8pm Mon-Fri, 9.30am-1.30pm & 2-7pm Sat & Sun Jul & Aug) has an interesting collection of local Greek and Roman finds.

At the north end of town, **Hotel Tony** (42 403, 0889 268 004; ul Kraybrezhna 20; r from 40 lv; Jun-Sep;) is a family-run hotel with balconies facing Sunny Beach.

Nesebâr is well connected to coastal destinations by public transport, and the town's bus station is on the small square just outside the city walls. From the bus station, there are buses to nearby Sunny Beach (1 lv, 10 minutes, every 15 minutes), Burgas (6 lv, 40 minutes, every 30 minutes), Varna (15 lv, two hours, seven daily) and Sofia (30 lv, seven hours, several daily).

Burgas Бургас

056 / POP 229,000

For most visitors, the port city of Burgas (sometimes written as 'Bourgas') is no more than a transit point for the more obviously appealing resorts and historic towns further up and down the coast. If you do decide to stop over, you'll find a lively, well-kept city with a neat, pedestrianised centre, a long, uncrowded beach and some interesting museums. A clutch of reasonably priced hotels, as well as some decent restaurants, makes it a practical base for exploring the southern coast.

Sleeping

Burgas Hostel HOSTEL €

(825 854; hostelburgas@gmail.com; ul Slavyanska 14; dm incl breakfast 20 lv; @; 12) The only hostel in town didn't bother with a fancy name. It sports five- and eight-bed dorms, plus a small lounge and kitchen.

Hotel Bulair HOTEL €

(844 389; www.hotelbulair.com; ul Bulair 7; r 55 lv; P; 12) In a converted townhouse on a busy road, the 14-room Bulair is very handy for the bus and train stations.

Fotinov Guest House HOTEL €€

(0878 974 703; www.hotelfotinov.com; ul Konstantin Fotinov 22; s/d 72/82 lv;) Conveniently located right in the city centre, with a selection of brightly coloured rooms, featuring fridges, kettles and cable TV. The multilingual staff are friendly and helpful, and there's even a small sauna.

TRANSPORT FROM BURGAS

Bus

DESTINATION	PRICE (LV)	DURATION	FREQUENCY
Nesebâr	6	40min	every 30-40min
Plovdiv	17	4hr	several daily
Sofia	30	7-8hr	several daily
Sozopol	4.50	40min	every 30min
Varna	14	2hr	every 30-40min

Train

DESTINATION	PRICE (LV)	DURATION (HR)	FREQUENCY
Plovdiv	19	5-6	7 daily
Sofia	23.10	7-8	6 daily

Getting There & Away

AIR Bulgaria Air links **Burgas Airport** (☎870 248; www.bourgas-airport.com; 15), 10km northeast of town, with Sofia three times every day (April to October).

BUS **Yug bus station** (cnr ul Aleksandrovska & ul Bulair), outside the train station at the southern end of ul Aleksandrovska, is where most travellers arrive or leave. There are regular buses to coastal destinations. Departures are less frequent outside summer.

TRAIN The historic **train station** (ul Ivan Vazov) was built in 1902. Through the ticket windows (8am to 6pm) on the right, you can buy advance tickets for domestic and international services, while same-day tickets can be bought at the windows (24 hours) on the left. The **left-luggage office** (train station; 6am-10.45pm) is outside the station.

International tickets are available at the **Rila Bureau** (8am-5.30pm Mon-Thu, to 4pm Fri, to 3.30pm Sat) inside the station.

South Coast

The finest sandy beaches dot the coast south from Sozopol to the Turkish border, though some come with less-appealing modern beach resorts. It helps to have wheels, but you can reach many rewarding spots by bus, too.

SOZOPOL СОЗОПОЛ

☎0550 / POP 5000

A curling peninsula of cobbled streets, sandy beaches and ancient Greek heritage, Sozopol is a favourite Bulgarian summer destination. There are two good beaches in town, and a small **Archaeological Museum** (ul Han Krum 2; 4 lv; 9am-6pm, closed Sat & Sun winter).

Sasha Khristov's Private Rooms (☎23 434; ul Venets 17; s/d 20/30 lv) occupies a family home in the Old Town at the end of Sozopol peninsula. It comprises good-sized rooms and a large apartment. Book ahead in summer. The New Town has plenty of hotels with doubles for 40 lv to 50 lv.

There are cheap fish restaurants along harbour-front ul Kraybrezhna in the Old Town. One of the best restaurants if you want to splurge is **Panorama** (ul Morski Skali 21; mains 8-20 lv) with a fantastic view towards Sveti Ivan Island and fresh fish on the menu.

The small public **bus station** (ul Han Krum) is south of the Old Town walls. Buses leave for Burgas (4.50 lv, 40 minutes) about every 30 minutes between 6am and 9pm in summer, and about once an hour in the low season.

UNDERSTAND BULGARIA

History

Thracians moved into the area of modern Bulgaria in around 5000 BC and Greeks founded cities on the Black Sea coast from the 7th century BC on. By AD 100 Bulgaria was part of the Roman Empire.

The first Slavs migrated here from the north in the 5th century AD and the first Bulgarian state was formed in 681.

The Byzantine Empire conquered Bulgaria in 1014. Bulgaria gained independence from Constantinople in 1185 and this second kingdom, based in Veliko Târnovo, lasted until the Ottoman takeover in 1396.

During the 18th and 19th centuries, many 'awakeners' are credited with reviving Bulgarian culture. By the 1860s several revolutionaries (including Bulgarian national hero Vasil Levski), organised *cheti* (rebel) bands for the unsuccessful April Uprising of 1876. With Russia stepping in, the Turks were defeated in 1878, and Bulgaria regained its independence.

Hoping to annex Macedonia, Bulgaria aligned with fascist Germany in WWII, but after the war, Bulgaria embraced communism wholeheartedly (even proposing in 1973 to join the USSR).

Since 1989, Bulgaria has stumbled slightly as a new democracy. It joined NATO in 2004 and the EU in 2007, but low wages, organised crime and corruption are sources of continual complaint and anguish. This anguish came to a head in 2013, when the government of Prime Minister Boyko Borisov was forced to resign in the face of economic stagnation and rising energy prices.

People

The population of Bulgaria is about 7.3 million, and continues to shrink – it has been estimated that 1.4 million people have left the country over the last 20 years. Bulgarians and Slavs constitute roughly 85% of the population, with the largest minorities being Turks (9%) and Roma (4.5%).

There are around 200,000 Pomaks – Muslims of Slavic origin – in the villages of the Rodopi Mountains, although many consider themselves to be ethnic Turks and others claim to be descended from ancient Balkan tribes converted by Arab missionaries a thousand years ago, but nobody knows for sure.

Arts

Bulgaria has an impressive musical tradition, stretching back more than a thousand years. Bulgarian ecclesiastical music is powerfully evocative, especially Orthodox chants and choral music.

One very popular form of modern music is *chalga*, a vaguely Oriental-sounding, warbling folk-pop, often with a scantily clad female vocalist. It's considered pretty low-brow and many Bulgarians will visibly cringe at the mention of it. However, the success of *chalga* clubs suggests many Bulgarians *do* quite like it, even if they'd rather not admit it.

Bulgaria's most treasured art graces the walls of medieval monasteries and churches, such as Boyana Church (p247) near Sofia, Arbanasi's Nativity Church (p256), and the paintings by Zahari Zograf (1810–53) at Rila Monastery (p252).

Bulgaria's 19th-century National Revival saw many town makeovers, with traditionally styled *kâshta* buildings with whitewashed walls and wood-carved ceilings.

Environment

Bulgaria lies in the heart of the Balkan Peninsula, stretching 502km from the Serbian border to the 378km-long Black Sea coast.

The Stara Planina range stretches across central Bulgaria. In the southwest are three higher ranges – the Rila Mountains (home to Mt Musala, Bulgaria's highest point at 2925m), Pirin Mountains and Rodopi Mountains.

Bulgaria has some 56,000 kinds of living creatures, including bears, wild goats and deer. It maintains three national parks (Rila, Pirin and Central Balkans) and 10 nature parks.

SURVIVAL GUIDE

Directory A–Z

Accommodation

Sofia, Plovdiv, Veliko Tărnovo, Varna and Burgas all have hostels, with beds from 18 lv.

Private homestays are another cheap option in summer, available from bus- and train-station touts, accommodation agencies or by posted *'staipod naem'* (rooms for rent) signs. Rates are 10 lv to 25 lv per person.

Average rates for budget hotels (which usually have private bathrooms, TVs and air-con) are around 40 lv for a single and 50 lv for a double.

Camping for most Bulgarians means an area with side-by-side basic bungalows and a couple of spots to pitch a tent. Up in the mountains there are many *hizhas* (mountain huts) of varying conditions.

Price ranges in this chapter are based on the cost of a double room with bathroom:

€ less than 50 lv

€€ 50 lv to 80 lv

€€€ more than 80 lv

Activities

All kinds of outdoor activities are catered for in Bulgaria, with hiking, biking, mountaineering, rock-climbing, diving and skiing being just some of the sports available. Water sports are popular on the Black Sea coast, although these tend to be confined to the big package-holiday resorts. Windsurfing, paragliding, scuba diving and a host of other water activities can be arranged during summer.

Cycling Bulgaria (www.cycling.bg) Multiday mountain-bike tours.

Hiking in Bulgaria (www.bghike.com) Guided hiking trips.

Neophron (www.birdwatchingbulgaria.net) Runs 10- to 14-day guided birdwatching trips across the country, which can be combined with botany and bearwatching tours.

Business Hours

Banks 9am to 4pm Monday to Friday

Post offices 8am to 6pm Monday to Friday

Restaurants 11am to 11pm daily

Shops 9am to 6pm daily

Discount Cards

Most museums offer discounts of up to 75% for students with valid ID, and some travel agents offer discounted air fares.

Food

Price ranges in this chapter are based on the cost of a main course:

€ less than 10 lv

€€ 10 lv to 20 lv

€€€ more than 20 lv

Gay & Lesbian Travellers

Homosexuality is legal in Bulgaria, though opinion polls suggest a majority of Bulgarians have a negative opinion of it. Attitudes among younger people are slowly changing and there are a few gay clubs and bars in Sofia and other major cities. Useful websites include **Bulgayria** (www.gay.bg) and **Gay Bulgaria Ultimate Gay Guide** (www.gay-bulgaria.info).

Money

The local currency is the lev (plural: leva), comprised of 100 stotinki. It is abbreviated as lv. The lev is a stable currency. For major purchases such as organised tours, air fares, car rental and midrange and top-end hotels, prices are often quoted in euros, though payment is usually made in leva.

Banknotes come in denominations of two, five, 10, 20, 50 and 100 leva. Coins come in one, two, five, 10, 20 and 50 stotinki and one lev.

ATMs and foreign-exchange offices are found in major towns. Credit cards are usually accepted in hotels, restaurants and shops in big cities, towns and tourist resorts, but acceptance is less widespread in rural areas.

Public Holidays

New Year's Day 1 January

Liberation Day (National Day) 3 March

Orthodox Easter Sunday and Monday April/May

St George's Day 6 May

Cyrillic Alphabet Day 24 May

Unification Day (National Day) 6 September

Bulgarian Independence Day 22 September

National Revival Day 1 November

Christmas 25 and 26 December

Safe Travel

Pickpocketing or beach grab-and-runs can happen in summer, particularly on Varna's beach. There are plenty of rogue taxi drivers waiting to rip off foreigners; always use a reputable firm, and, if possible, ask your hotel to call your cab.

Telephone

To call Bulgaria from abroad, dial the international access code, add ☎359 (the country code for Bulgaria), the area code (minus the first zero) and then the number.

Mobile phones use the GSM 900/1800 network, the standard throughout Europe as well as in Australia and New Zealand, but not compatible with most mobile phones in North America or Japan. One possibility is to bring or buy an unlocked handset operating on this GSM band and purchase a local SIM card. Mobile telephone numbers can be identified by the prefixes ☎087, ☎088 or ☎089.

Getting There & Away

Air

Most international visitors enter and leave Bulgaria via **Sofia Airport** (☎937 2211; www.sofia-airport.bg; off bul Brussels; minibus 30), and there are frequent flights to the capital from other European cities. The Bulgarian national carrier is **Bulgaria Air** (www.air.bg). It operates flights to destinations across Europe and the Middle East as well as domestic routes to the Black Sea coast.

Other airlines flying to Bulgaria include the following:

Aeroflot (☎943 4489; www.aeroflot.ru)

Air Berlin (www.airberlin.com)

Air France (☎939 7010; www.airfrance.com)

Alitalia (☎981 6702; www.alitalia.it)

British Airways (☎954 7000; www.britishairways.com)

easyJet (www.easyjet.com)

Lufthansa Airlines (☎930 4242; www.lufthansa.com)

Wizz Air (☎960 3888; www.wizzair.com)

Bus

Most international buses arrive in Sofia. You will have to get off the bus at the border and walk through customs to present your passport. When travelling out of Bulgaria by bus, the cost of entry visas for the countries concerned are not included in the prices of the bus tickets.

Car & Motorcycle

In order to drive on Bulgarian roads, you need to purchase a vignette, sold at all border crossings into Bulgaria, petrol stations and post offices. For a car, this costs 10/25 lv for one week/month.

Your home driving licence is valid in Bulgaria for short-term stays. Petrol stations and car-repair shops are common around border crossing areas and along main roads.

Train

There are a number of international trains from Bulgaria, including services to Romania, Greece and Turkey. Sofia is the hub, although trains stop at other towns. The daily *TransBalkan*, running between Budapest and Thessaloniki, stops at Ruse, Gorna Oryakhovitsa (near Veliko Târnovo) and Sofia. The *Balkan Express* normally goes daily between Belgrade and İstanbul, with stops in Sofia and Plovdiv. The *Bulgaria Express* to Bucharest leaves from Sofia.

Tickets for international trains can be bought at any government-run **Rila Bureau** (www.bdz-rila.com; ⏲closed most Sun) or at ticket offices (most open daily) at larger stations with international connections.

Getting Around

Air

The only scheduled domestic flights within Bulgaria are between Sofia and Varna and Sofia and Burgas. Both routes are operated by **Bulgaria Air** (www.air.bg).

Bus

Buses link all cities and major towns and connect villages with the nearest transport hub. There are several private companies operating frequent buses between the larger towns, while older, often cramped minibuses run on routes between smaller towns.

Biomet (☎02-868 8961; www.biomet.bg) Runs between Sofia and Veliko Târnovo, Varna and Burgas.

Etap-Grup (☎02-813 3100; www.etapgroup.com) Buses between Sofia, Burgas, Varna, Ruse and Veliko Târnovo as well as routes between Sofia and Sozopol, Primorsko and Tsarevo.

Union-Ivkoni (☎02-989 0000; www.union-ivkoni.bg) Links most major towns and many smaller ones.

Car & Motorcycle

Bulgaria's roads are among the most dangerous in Europe and the level of fatalities each year is high. The worst time is the holiday season (July to September), with drink-driving, speeding and poor road conditions contributing to accidents.

The **Union of Bulgarian Motorists** (☎02-935 7935, road assistance 02-980 3308; www.uab.org; pl Positano 3, Sofia) offers 24-hour road assistance and has some helpful basic information on its website.

ROAD RULES

» Drive on the right.

» Drivers and passengers in the front must wear seat belts; motorcyclists must wear helmets.

» The blood-alcohol limit is 0.05%.

» Children under 12 are not allowed to sit in front.

» From November to March, headlights must be on at all times.

SPEED LIMITS

Built-up areas 50km/h

Main roads 90km/h

Motorways 120km/h

Train

Bălgarski Dârzhavni Zheleznitsi – the **Bulgarian State Railways** (BDZh; www.bdz.bg) – boasts an impressive 4278km of track across the country, linking most towns and cities.

Most trains tend to be antiquated and not especially comfortable, and journey times are slower than buses. On the plus side, you'll have more room in a train compartment and the scenery is likely to be more rewarding.

Trains are classified as *ekspresen* (express), *bârz* (fast) or *pâtnicheski* (slow passenger). Unless you absolutely thrive on train travel, use a fast or express train.

Croatia

Includes »

Zagreb 270
Istria 276
Pula 276
Dalmatia 278
Split 278
Hvar Island 281
Korčula Island 283
Dubrovnik 284
Understand Croatia 288
Survival Guide 290

Best Places to Eat

» Vinodol (p274)
» Vodnjanka (p277)
» Konoba Menego (p282)
» Konoba Matejuška (p279)

Best Places to Stay

» Studio Kairos (p271)
» Goli + Bosi (p279)
» Hostel Marinero (p282)
» Fresh Sheets (p286)

Why Go?

Touted as the 'new this' and the 'new that' for years since its re-emergence on the tourism scene, Croatia has become a unique destination that holds its own and then some: this is a country with a glorious 1778km-long coast and a staggering 1244 islands.

The Adriatic coast is a knockout: its sapphire waters draw visitors to remote islands, hidden coves and traditional fishing villages, all while touting the glitzy beach and yacht scene. Istria captivates with its gastronomic delights and wines, and the bars, clubs and festivals of Zagreb and Split remain little-explored gems. Eight national parks showcase primeval beauty with their forests, mountains, rivers, lakes and waterfalls.

Save the best till last with dazzling Dubrovnik in the south – just the right finale. Best of all, Croatia hasn't given in to mass tourism: there are pockets of authentic culture and plenty to discover off the grid.

When to Go

Zagreb

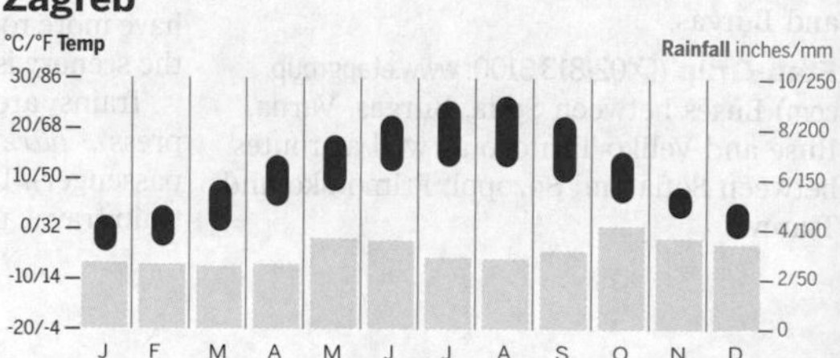

Jul & Aug Lots of sunshine, warm sea and summer festivals; many tourists and highest prices.

Jun Best time to visit: beautiful weather, fewer people, lower prices, the festival season kicks off.

May & Sep Good weather, fewer tourists, full events calendar, great for hiking.

Connections

Croatia is a convenient transport hub for southeastern Europe and the Adriatic. Zagreb is connected by train and/or bus to Venice, Budapest, Belgrade, Ljubljana and Sarajevo. Down south there are easy bus connections from Dubrovnik to Mostar and Sarajevo (Bosnia and Hercegovina; BiH), and to Kotor (Montenegro). There are a number of ferries linking Croatia with Italy, including routes from Dubrovnik to Bari, and Split to Ancona.

ITINERARIES

One Week

Spend a day in dynamic Zagreb, delving into its simmering nightlife, fine restaurants and choice museums, then head down to Split for a day and night at Diocletian's Palace, a living part of this exuberant seafront city. Then hop over to chic Hvar for its beaches and nightlife. Next take it easy down the winding coastal road to magnificent Dubrovnik, for the final two days.

Two Weeks

After two days in Zagreb, head to Istria for a three-day stay, with Pula as your base. Move on down south the Dalmatian coast to Zadar, a real find of a city, perfect for a two-day stay: historic, modern, active and packed with attractions. Then go on south to Split for two days. From here, take ferries to Hvar, spending two days on the island before ending with a three-day sojourn in Dubrovnik.

Essential Food & Drink

» **Ćevapčići** Small spicy sausages of minced beef, lamb or pork.

» **Pljeskavica** An ex-Yugo version of a hamburger.

» **Ražnjići** Small chunks of pork grilled on a skewer.

» **Burek** Pastry stuffed with ground meat, spinach or cheese.

» **Rakija** Strong Croatian brandy comes in different flavours, from plum to honey.

» **Beer** Two top types of Croatian *pivo* (beer) are Zagreb's Ožujsko and Karlovačko from Karlovac.

AT A GLANCE

» **Currency** Kuna (KN)

» **Language** Croatian

» **Money** ATMs available; credit cards accepted in most hotels and many restaurants

» **Visas** None for up to 90 days for most nationalities

Fast Facts

» **Area** 56,538 sq km

» **Capital** Zagreb

» **Country code** ☎385

» **Emergency** Ambulance ☎194, police ☎192

Exchange Rates

Australia	A$1	6.21KN
Canada	C$1	5.85KN
Euro Zone	€1	7.60KN
Japan	¥100	6.30KN
New Zealand	NZ$1	4.97KN
UK	UK£1	8.99KN
USA	US$1	5.94KN

Set Your Budget

» **Budget hotel room** 450KN

» **Two-course meal** 150KN

» **Museum entrance** 10–40KN

» **Beer** 15KN

» **City transport ticket** 10KN

Resources

» **Adriatica.net** (www.adriatica.net)

» **Croatian National Tourist Board** (www.croatia.hr)

Croatia Highlights

1. Gape at the Old Town wall of **Dubrovnik** (p284) which surrounds luminous marble streets and finely ornamented buildings
2. Admire the Venetian architecture and vibrant nightlife of **Hvar Town** (p281)
3. Indulge in the lively and historic delights of Diocletian's Palace in **Split** (p278)
4. Take in the remains of failed romances at the **Museum of Broken Relationships** (p270) in Zagreb
5. Soak up the medieval atmosphere in the walled city of **Korčula** (p283) on the namesake island

0
100 km
0
50 miles
HUNGARY
Čakovec
Goričan
aždin
aždinske
Toplice
Drava
Gola
Koprivnica
Đurđevac
A4
Križevci
Pitomača
Terezino Polje
Pécs
Backi Breg
Bezdan
Bjelovar
Virovitica
E661
Zagreb
Airport
Čazma
Donji
Miholjac
Beli Manastir
Kopački Rit
National Park
Slatina
E70
Daruvar
Kapovac
(790m)
Osijek
Dalj
Bogojevo
Našice
Kutina
Sisak
Petrinja
Pakrac
Slavonska
Požega
Đakoračka
Breznica
E73
Borovo
Vukovar
Novi Sad
Danube
Glina
Novska
Nova
Gradiška
Đakovo
Vinkovci
Bačka
Palanka
Hrvatska
Kostajnica
Slavonski
Brod
E70
Otok
Bosanska
Dubica
Sava
Davor
Županja
Batrovci
Kozara
National
Park
Una
Sava
Brčko
Banja Luka
SERBIA
BOSNIA &
HERCEGOVINA
nin
E71
Sarajevo
Sinj
Trogir
3
Split
Omiš
Imotski
Gorica-
Vinjani
Donji
Supetar
Brela
Šolta
Makarska
Brač
Bol
Piva
E65
2
Stari Grad
Hvar Town
Hvar
Ploče
Metković
Vis
Orebić
Metković-Doljani
Komiža
Korčula
Vela
Luka
5
Town
Korčula
E65
MONTENEGRO
Polače
Pomena
Sobra
Lastovo
Mljet
National
Park
Dubrovnik
1
Ivanica
Cavtat
E65
Podgorica
ALBANIA

ZAGREB

☎01 / POP 792,900

Everyone knows about Croatia's coast and islands, but a mention of the country's capital still draws the confused question: 'Is it worth visiting?' Here is the answer: Zagreb is a great destination, with lots of culture, arts, music, architecture, gastronomy and all the other things that make a quality capital.

Visually, Zagreb is a mixture of straight-laced Austro-Hungarian architecture and rough-around-the-edges socialist structures, its character a sometimes uneasy combination of the two. This mini metropolis is made for strolling the streets, drinking coffee in the permanently full cafes, popping into museums and galleries, and enjoying the theatres, concerts and cinema. It's a year-round outdoor city: in spring and summer everyone scurries to Jarun Lake in the southwest to swim, boat or dance the night away at lakeside discos, while in autumn and winter Zagrebians go skiing at Mt Medvednica, only a tram ride away, or hiking in nearby Samobor.

Sights

As the oldest part of Zagreb, the Upper Town (Gornji Grad) offers landmark buildings and churches from the earlier centuries of Zagreb's history. The Lower Town (Donji Grad) has the city's most interesting art museums and fine examples of 19th- and 20th-century architecture.

UPPER TOWN

TOP CHOICE Museum of Broken Relationships MUSEUM

(http://brokenships.com; Ćirilometodska 2; adult/concession 25/20KN; ⏲9am-10.30pm Jun–mid-Oct, 9am-9pm mid-Oct–May) Explore mementos that remain after a relationship ends at Zagreb's quirkiest museum, displaying donations from around the globe – from a can of love incense from Indiana that 'doesn't work' to an iron from Norway once used to straighten a wedding suit. Check out the store and the cosy cafe.

TOP CHOICE Dolac Market MARKET

(⏲7am-3pm Mon-Fri, to 2pm Sat, to 1pm Sun) Zagreb's colourful Dolac is just north of Trg Josipa Jelačića. Since the 1930s, this buzzing centre of Zagreb's daily activity has drawn in traders from all over Croatia who flog their products here.

Cathedral of the Assumption of the Blessed Virgin Mary CATHEDRAL

(Katedrala Marijina Uznešenja; Kaptol; ⏲10am-5pm Mon-Sat, 1-5pm Sun) Kaptol Square is dominated by the twin neo-Gothic spires of this 1899 cathedral, with an interior containing 13th-century frescos, Renaissance pews and a baroque pulpit.

Lotrščak Tower HISTORICAL BUILDING

(Kula Lotrščak; Strossmayerovo Šetalište 9; adult/concession 10/5KN; ⏲9am-9pm) Climb this medieval tower for a sweeping 360-degree view of the city. The nearby **funicular railway** (ticket 5KN), constructed in 1888, connects the Lower and Upper Towns.

St Mark's Church CHURCH

(Crkva Svetog Marka; Trg Svetog Marka 5; ⏲7.30am-6.30pm) Its colourful tiled roof makes this Gothic church one of Zagreb's most emblematic buildings. Inside are works by Ivan Meštrović, Croatia's most famous modern sculptor.

Croatian Museum of Naïve Art MUSEUM

(Hrvatski Muzej Naivne Umjetnosti; www.hmnu.org; Ćirilometodska 3; adult/concession 20/10KN; ⏲10am-6pm Tue-Fri, to 1pm Sat & Sun) If you like Croatia's naïve art or want a good intro to it, head to this small museum. It houses over 1000 paintings, drawings and some sculpture by the discipline's most important artists.

Meštrović Atelier ARTS CENTRE

(Mletačka 8; adult/concession 30/15KN; ⏲10am-6pm Tue-Fri, to 1pm Sat & Sun) The former home of Croatia's most recognised artist, Ivan Meštrović, now houses an excellent collection of some 100 sculptures, drawings, lithographs and furniture created by the artist.

City Museum MUSEUM

(Muzej Grada Zagreba; www.mgz.hr; Opatička 20; adult/concession 30/20KN; ⏲10am-6pm Tue-Fri, 11am-7pm Sat, 10am-2pm Sun; 👪) Check out the scale model of old Gradec, atmospheric background music and interactive exhibits that fascinate kids. There are summaries in English in each room of the museum, which is in the former Convent of St Clair (1650).

Stone Gate LANDMARK

This eastern gate to medieval Gradec Town is now a shrine. According to legend, a great fire in 1731 destroyed every part of the wooden gate except for the painting of the *Virgin and Child* by an unknown 17th-century artist.

LOWER TOWN

TOP CHOICE Trg Josipa Jelačića SQUARE

Zagreb's main orientation point and its geographic heart has an **equestrian statue** of Jelačić, the famous 19th-century *ban* (viceroy or governor).

TOP CHOICE Museum Mimara MUSEUM

(Muzej Mimara; www.mimara.hr; Rooseveltov trg 5; adult/concession 40/30KN; ⏲10am-7pm Tue-Fri, to 5pm Sat, to 2pm Sun) Housed in a neo-Renaissance palace, this diverse collection includes icons, glassware, sculpture, Oriental art and works by renowned painters such as Rembrandt, Velázquez and Degas.

Art Pavilion ART GALLERY

(Umjetnički Paviljon; www.umjetnicki-paviljon.hr; Trg Kralja Tomislava 22; adult/concession 30/15KN; ⏲11am-7pm Tue-Sat, 10am-1pm Sun Sep–mid-Jul) The yellow Art Pavilion in a stunning 1897 art nouveau building presents changing exhibitions of contemporary art.

OUTSIDE THE CENTRE

Museum of Contemporary Art MUSEUM

(Muzej Suvremene Umjetnosti; www.msu.hr; Avenija Dubrovnik 17; adult/concession 30/15KN, 1st Wed of month free; ⏲11am-6pm Tue-Fri & Sun, to 8pm Sat) Housed in a dazzling new city icon designed by local starchitect Igor Franić, this swanky museum in Novi Zagreb, across the Sava River, puts on solo and thematic group shows by Croatian and international artists. The year-round schedule is packed with film, theatre, concerts and performance art.

Tours

Funky Zagreb GUIDED TOURS

(www.funky-zagreb.com) Personalised tours that range in theme from wine tasting to hiking in Zagreb's surroundings.

Blue Bike Tours BIKE TOUR

(www.zagrebbybike.com) Two-hour tours departing daily. Reserve ahead.

Sleeping

Zagreb's accommodation scene has been undergoing a noticeable change, with many more budget options. If you intend on staying in a private house or apartment, try not to arrive on Sunday because most of the agencies will be closed, unless you've made prior arrangements. Prices for doubles run from about 300KN and studio apartments start at 400KN per night. There's usually a surcharge for staying only one night. Recommended agencies include **Evistas** (☎48 39 554; www.evistas.hr; Augusta Šenoe 28; s/d/apt from 240/290/340KN) and **InZagreb** (☎65 23 201; www.inzagreb.com; Remetinečka 13; apt 490-665KN).

TOP CHOICE Studio Kairos B&B $$

(☎46 40 680; www.studio-kairos.com; Vlaška 92; s 380-440KN, d 560-660KN; ❄📶) This adorable B&B has four well-appointed rooms in a street-level apartment. Rooms are decked out by theme and there's a cosy common space where breakfast is served. The main square (Trg Josipa Jelačića) is a 15-minute stroll away.

Hobo Bear Hostel HOSTEL $

(☎48 46 636; www.hobobearhostel.com; Medulićeva 4; dm 135-175KN, d from 400KN; ❄@📶) Inside a duplex apartment, this sparkling five-dorm hostel has exposed brick walls, hardwood floors, free lockers, a kitchen with free tea and coffee, a common room and book exchange. Take tram 1, 6 or 11 from Jelačića.

TOP CHOICE Funk Lounge Hostel HOSTEL $

(☎55 52 707; www.funkhostel.hr; Rendićeva 28b; dm 135-165KN, d 420KN; @📶) Located steps from Maksimir Park, this new outpost of the original Funk Hostel (southwest of the

FREE THRILLS

Though you'll have to pay to get into most of Zagreb's galleries and museums, there are some gorgeous parks and markets to be enjoyed for nowt – and there's always window shopping!

» Taste bits of food for free at Dolac Market – but don't be too cheeky!

» Smell the herbs at the **Botanical Garden** (Botanički Vrt; Mihanovićeva bb; ⏲9am-2.30pm Mon & Tue, 9am-7pm Wed-Sun Apr-Oct).

» Enjoy the long walks around **Maksimir Park** (www.park-maksimir.hr; Maksimirska bb; ⏲park 9am-dusk, info centre 10am-4pm Tue-Fri, to 6pm Sat & Su).

» See the magnificent **Mirogoj** (⏲6am-8pm Apr-Sep, 7am-6pm Oct-Mar) cemetery.

» Pop inside the ever renovated cathedral.

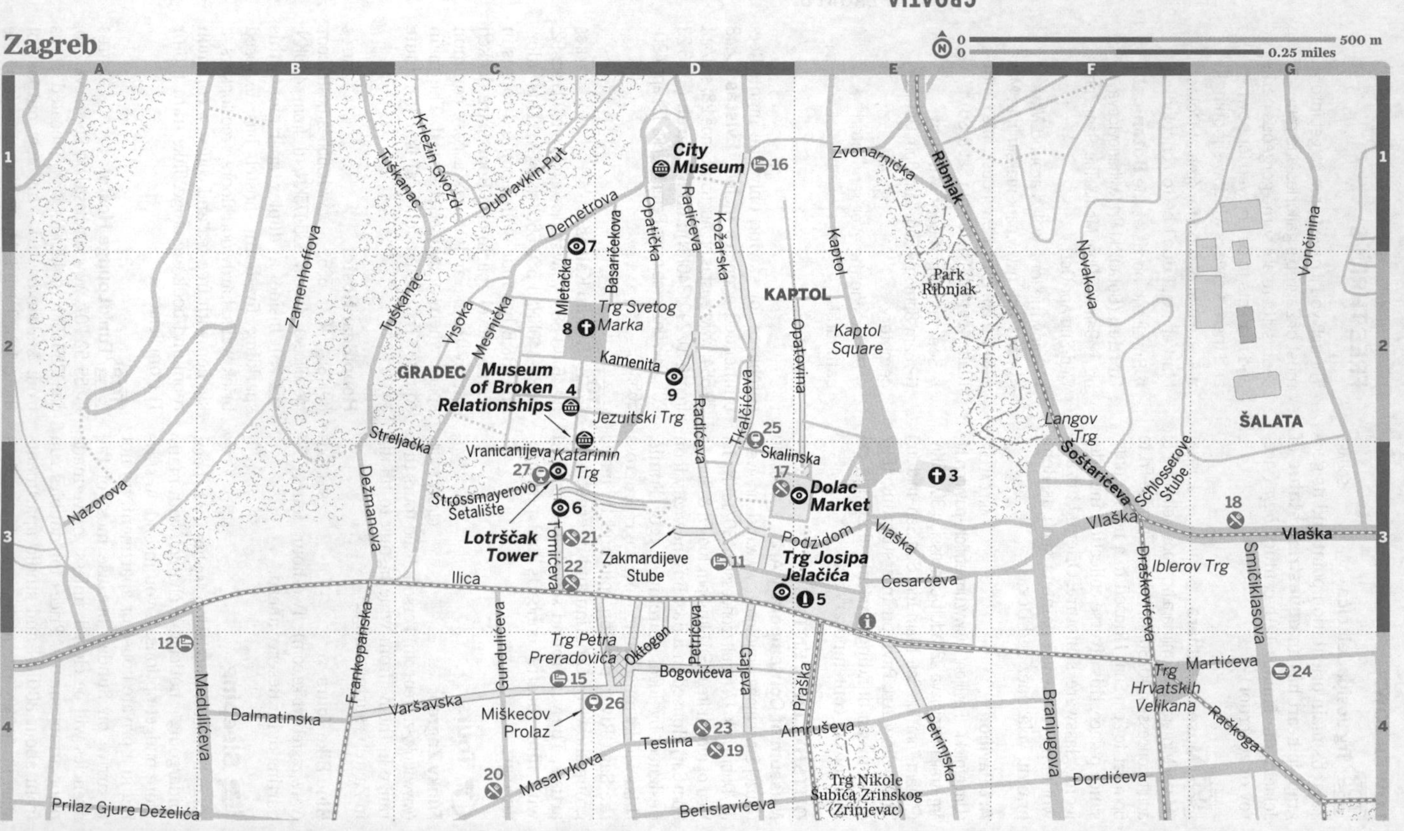
Zagreb
0
0
500 m
0.25 miles
A
B
C
D
E
F
G
1
2
3
4
City Museum
16
Zvonarnička
Ribnjak
Krležin Gvozd
Tuškanac
Dubravkin Put
Demetrova
Opatička
Radićeva
Kožarska
Kaptol
Park Ribnjak
Novakova
Vončinina
Zamenhoffova
Tuškanac
Visoka
Mesnička
Mletačka
Basaričekova
7
Trg Svetog Marka
8
KAPTOL
Opatovina
Kaptol Square
Kamenita
9
GRADEC
Museum of Broken Relationships
4
Jezuitski Trg
Radićeva
Tkalčićeva
25
Skalinska
Langov Trg
ŠALATA
Streljačka
Vranicanijeva
Katarinin Trg
27
Strossmayerovo Šetalište
6
Lotrščak Tower
Tomićeva
21
22
Zakmardijeve Stube
11
17
Dolac Market
3
Šoštarićeva
Schlosserove Stube
18
Vlaška
Vlaška
Vlaška
Podzidom
Trg Josipa Jelačića
5
Cesarčeva
Draškovićeva
Iblerov Trg
Smičiklasova
Nazorova
Dežmanova
Ilica
12
Frankopanska
Gundulićeva
Trg Petra Preradovića
Oktogon
Petrićeva
Gajeva
15
Bogovićeva
Praška
Trg Hrvatskih Velikana
Martićeva
24
Račkoga
Medulićeva
Dalmatinska
Varšavska
Miškecov Prolaz
26
23
Amruševa
Teslina
19
Petrinjska
Branjugova
20
Masarykova
Trg Nikole Šubića Zrinskog (Zrinjevac)
Đorđićeva
Prilaz Gjure Deželića
Berislavićeva

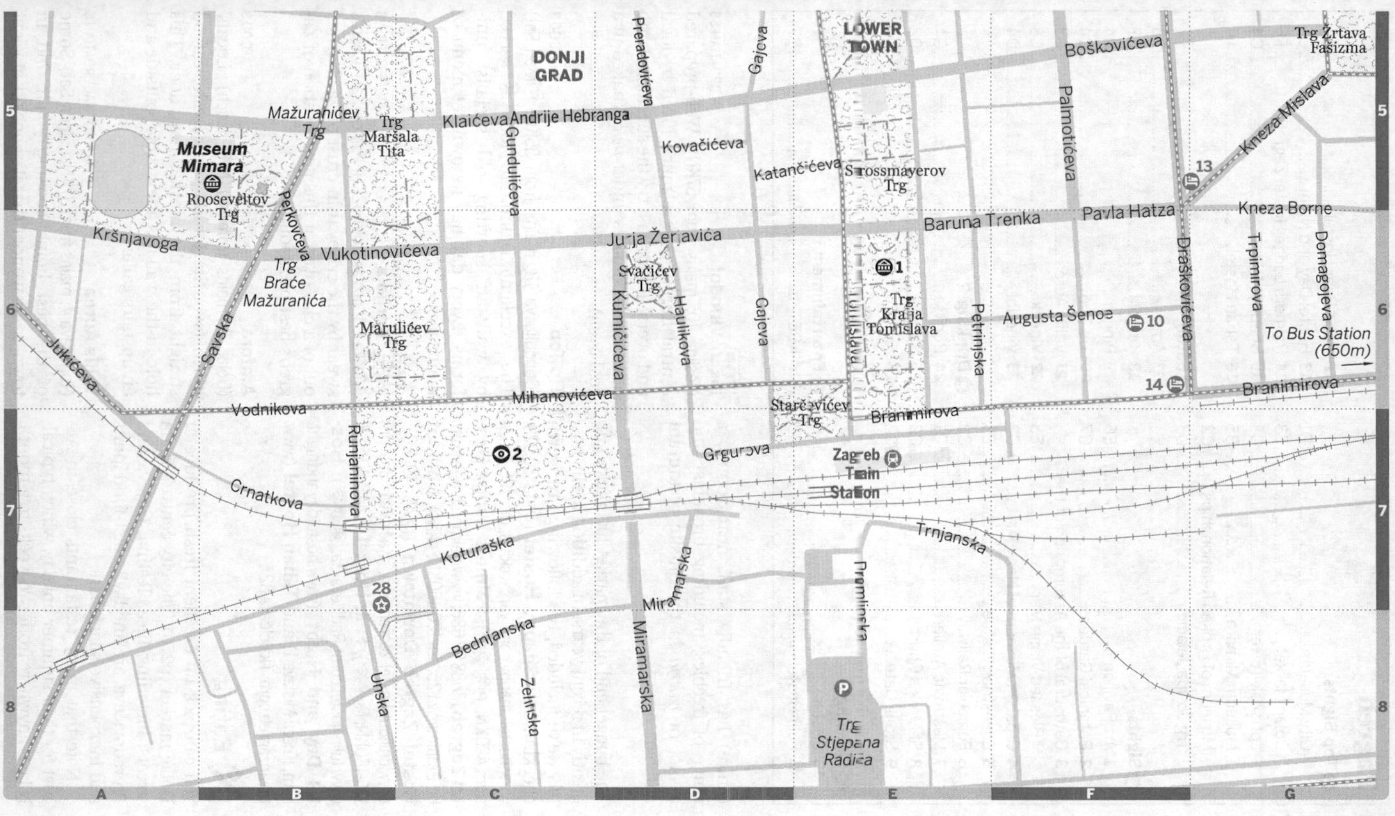
DONJI GRAD
LOWER TOWN
Trg Žrtava Fašizma
Boškovićeva
Preradovićeva
Gajeva
Mažuranićev Trg
Trg Maršala Tita
Klaićeva
Andrije Hebranga
Gundulićeva
Kovačićeva
Katančićeva
Strossmayerov Trg
Palmotićeva
Kneza Mislava
13
Museum Mimara
Rooseveltov Trg
Perkovčeva
Pavla Hatza
Kneza Borne
Baruna Trenka
Kršnjavoga
Vukotinovićeva
Jurja Žerjavića
Draškovićeva
Trpimirova
Domagojeva
Trg Braće Mažuranića
Svačićev Trg
1
Trg Kralja Tomislava
Tomislava
Haulikova
Gajeva
Kumičićeva
Petrinjska
Augusta Šenoe
10
To Bus Station (650m)
Savska
Jukićeva
Marulićev Trg
14
Branimirova
Mihanovićeva
Vodnikova
Starčevićev Trg
Branimirova
Runjaninova
2
Grgurova
Zagreb Train Station
Crnatkova
Trnjanska
Koturaška
Miramarska
28
Dromlinska
Mira
Bednjanska
Miramarska
Unska
Zelinska
Trg Stjepana Radića
P
CROATIA

Zagreb

Top Sights
- City Museum ... D1
- Dolac Market ... E3
- Lotrščak Tower ... C3
- Museum Mimara ... B5
- Museum of Broken Relationships ... C2
- Trg Josipa Jelačića ... D3

Sights
- 1 Art Pavilion ... E6
- 2 Botanical Garden ... C7
- 3 Cathedral of the Assumption of the Blessed Virgin Mary ... E3
- 4 Croatian Museum of Naïve Art ... C2
- 5 Equestrian Statue ... E3
- 6 Funicular Railway ... C3
- 7 Meštrović Atelier ... C1
- 8 St Mark's Church ... C2
- 9 Stone Gate ... D2

Sleeping
- 10 Evistas ... F6
- 11 Fulir Hostel ... D3
- 12 Hobo Bear Hostel ... A4
- 13 Hostel Day and Night ... G5
- 14 Palmers Lodge Hostel Zagreb ... F6
- 15 Shappy Hostel ... C4
- 16 Taban Hostel ... D1

Eating
- 17 Amfora ... D3
- 18 Karijola ... G3
- 19 Pingvin ... D4
- 20 Tip Top ... C4
- 21 Vallis Aurea ... C3
- 22 Vincek ... C3
- 23 Vinodol ... D4

Drinking
- 24 Booksa ... G4
- 25 Cica ... D2
- 26 Kino Europa ... D4
- 27 Stross ... C3

Entertainment
- 28 KSET ... B7

centre) has friendly staff, neat rooms, a range of freebies, including breakfast and a shot of *rakija* in the on-site restaurant and bar.

The budget end of the market has picked up greatly in recent years. In addition to the hostels we've included, the following are worth checking out: **Shappy Hostel** (☎48 30 179; www.hostel-shappy.com; Varšavska 8; dm 128-170, d from 420KN; P❄@☎), **Palmers Lodge Hostel Zagreb** (☎88 92 686; www.palmerslodge.com.hr; Branimirova 25; dm 120-150KN; @☎), **Chillout Hostel Zagreb Downtown** (☎48 49 605; www.chillout-hostel-zagreb.com; Kačićeva 3b; dm 135-180KN; ❄@☎), **Fulir Hostel** (☎48 30 882; www.fulir-hostel.com; Radićeva 3a; ❄@☎), **Hostel Day and Night** (www.hosteldayandnight.com; Kneza Mislava 1) and **Taban Hostel** (www.tabanzagreb.com; Tkalčićeva 82).

Eating

You can pick up excellent fresh produce at Dolac market (p270). The city centre's main streets, including Ilica, Teslina, Gajeva and Preradovićeva, are lined with fast-food joints and inexpensive snack bars.

Note that many restaurants close in August for their summer holiday, which typically lasts anywhere from two weeks to a month.

TOP CHOICE **Vinodol** CROATIAN $$
(Teslina 10; mains from 57KN) Well-prepared central European fare much loved by local and overseas patrons; try the succulent lamb or veal and potatoes under *peka* (baked in a coal oven).

Tip Top SEAFOOD $
(Gundulićeva 18; mains from 55KN; ⊙Mon-Sat) The excellent Dalmatian food is served by waitstaff sporting old socialist uniforms. Every day has its own set menu of mainstays.

TOP CHOICE **Karijola** PIZZERIA $
(Vlaška 63; pizzas from 42KN; ⊙Mon-Sat) Locals swear by the crispy thin-crust pizza churned out of a clay oven at this new location of Zagreb's best pizza joint.

Amfora SEAFOOD $
(Dolac 2; mains from 40KN; ⊙lunch) Locals' lunch favourite for its super-fresh seafood straight from the market next door. This hole-in-the-wall has a few tables outside and an upstairs gallery.

Vallis Aurea TRADITIONAL CROATIAN $
(Tomićeva 4; mains from 37KN; ⊙Mon-Sat) Some of the best home cooking you'll find in town, so no wonder that it's chock-a-block at

lunchtime for its *gableci* (traditional lunches). Right by the lower end of the funicular.

Pingvin SANDWICH SHOP $

(Teslina 7; ⌚9am-4am Mon-Sat, 6pm-2am Sun) This quick-bite institution, around since 1987, offers tasty designer sandwiches and salads which locals savour on a couple of bar stools.

Vincek PASTRIES, CAKES $

(Ilica 18) This institution of a *slastičarna* (pastry shop) serves some of Zagreb's creamiest cakes.

Drinking

In the Upper Town, the chic Tkalčićeva is throbbing with bars and cafes. In the Lower Town, there's bar-lined Bogovićeva and Trg Petra Preradovića (known locally as Cvjetni trg), the most popular spot in the Lower Town for street performers and occasional bands.

One of the nicest ways to see Zagreb is to join in on the *špica* – Saturday-morning pre-lunch coffee drinking on the terraces along Bogovićeva, Preradovićeva and Tkalčićeva.

TOP CHOICE **Cica** BAR

(Tkalčićeva 18) This tiny storefront bar is as underground as it gets on Tkalčićeva. Sample one or – if you dare – all of the 25 kinds of *rakija* that the place is famous for.

Booksa CAFE

(www.booksa.hr; Martićeva 14d; ⌚11am-8pm Tue-Sun; 📶) Bookworms, poets and oddballs all come to chat and drink coffee, browse the library, surf with free wireless and hear readings at this book-themed cafe, located a 10-minute stroll east of the main square.

Stross OUTDOOR BAR

(Strossmayerovo Šetalište; ⌚Jun-Sep) From June to September, a makeshift bar is set up at the leafy Strossmayer promenade in the Upper Town, with cheap drinks, live music most nights and a mixed-bag crowd.

Kino Europa CAFE-BAR

(www.kinoeuropa.hr; Varšavska 3; ⌚Mon-Sat; 📶👪) Zagreb's oldest cinema, from the 1920s, now houses a glass-enclosed cafe, wine bar and *grapperia*, with an outdoor terrace and free wireless.

Entertainment

Club entry ranges from 20KN to 100KN. It doesn't get lively until around midnight.

Tvornica LIVE MUSIC

(www.tvornicakulture.com; Šubićeva 2) Excellent multimedia venue 20 minutes to the east of Trg Josipa Jelačića, showcasing live music performances, from Bosnian *sevdah* (Bosnian blues) to alternative punk rock.

Aquarius CLUB

(www.aquarius.hr; Jarun Lake) Past its heyday but still a fun lakeside club with a series of rooms that opens onto a huge terrace.

Močvara CLUB

(www.mochvara.hr; Trnjanski Nasip bb) In a former factory on the banks of the Sava River, 'Swamp' is one of Zagreb's best venues for the cream of alternative music and attractively dingy charm.

KSET CLUB

(www.kset.org; Unska 3) Zagreb's top music venue, with anyone who's anyone performing here – from ethno to hip-hop sounds.

Medika CLUB

(www.pierottijeva11.org; Pierottijeva 11) This artsy venue in an old pharmaceutical factory calls itself an 'autonomous cultural centre', with a program of concerts, art exhibits and parties.

Information

There are ATMs at the bus and train stations, the airport, and at numerous locations around town. Some banks in the train and bus stations accept travellers cheques.

Several cafes around town offer free wi-fi.

Atlas Travel Agency (☎48 07 300; www.atlas-croatia.com; Zrinjevac 17) Tours around Croatia.

KBC Rebro (☎23 88 888; Kišpatićeva 12; ⌚24hr) East of the city, provides emergency aid.

Lonely Planet (www.lonelyplanet.com/croatia/zagreb)

Main Tourist Office (☎info line 800 53 53, office 48 14 051; www.zagreb-touristinfo.hr; Trg Josipa Jelačića 11; ⌚8.30am-9pm Mon-Fri, 9am-6pm Sat & Sun) Distributes free city maps and leaflets, and sells the Zagreb Card.

Sublink (☎48 19 993; www.sublink.hr; Teslina 12; per hr 15KN; ⌚9am-10pm Mon-Sat, 3-10pm Sun) The city's first cybercafe, still going strong.

Zagreb Card (www.zagrebcard.fivestars.hr; 24/72hr 60/90KN) Provides free travel on all public transport, a 50% discount on museum and gallery entries, plus discounts in some bars and restaurants, and on car rental. The card is sold at the main tourist office and many hostels, hotels, bars and shops.

Getting There & Away

Air

Zagreb Airport (☎45 62 222; www.zagreb-airport.hr) Located 17km southeast of Zagreb, this is Croatia's major airport, offering a range of international and domestic services.

Bus

Zagreb's **bus station** (☎060 313 333; www.akz.hr; Avenija M Držića 4) is 1km east of the train station, there's a **garderoba** (bus station; 1st 4hr 20KN, then per hr 2.50KN; ⏰24hr). Trams 2, 3 and 6 run from the bus station to the train station. Tram 6 goes to Trg Josipa Jelačića.

Frequent domestic departures include Dubrovnik (205KN to 250KN, 9½ to 11 hours, nine to 12 daily), Pula (105KN to 196KN, 3½ to 5½ hours, 17 to 20 daily) and Split (115KN to 205KN, five to 8½ hours, 32 to 34 daily).

International destinations include Belgrade (220KN, six hours, five daily) and Sarajevo (160KN to 210KN, seven to eight hours, four to five daily).

Train

The **train station** (☎060 333 444; www.hznet.hr; Trg Kralja Tomislava 12) is in the southern part of the city; there's a **garderoba** (train station; lockers per 24hr 15KN; ⏰24hr). It's advisable to book train tickets in advance because of limited seating.

Domestic trains head to Split (189KM, five to seven hours, three daily). There are international departures to Belgrade (169KN, 6½ hours, four daily), Ljubljana (130KN, 2½ hours, four daily), Sarajevo (231KN, eight to 9½ hours, two daily) and Vienna (465KN, six to seven hours, two daily).

Getting Around

Zagreb is a fairly easy city to navigate. Traffic is bearable and the tram system efficient.

To/From the Airport

BUS The Croatia Airlines bus to the airport (30KN) leaves from the bus station every half-hour or hour from about 5am to 8pm, and returns from the airport on the same schedule.

TAXI Costs between 110KN and 300KN.

Public Transport

Buy tickets at newspaper kiosks for 12KN. Tickets can be used for transfers within 90 minutes, but only in one direction.

A *dnevna karta* (day ticket), valid on all public transport until 4am the next morning, is available for 40KN at most newspaper kiosks.

Make sure you validate your ticket when you get on the tram by inserting it in the yellow box.

Taxi

For short city rides, **Taxi Cammeo** (☎1212, 060 71 00) is typically the cheapest, as the 15KN start fare includes the first 2km (it's 6KN for every subsequent kilometre).

ISTRIA

☎052

Continental Croatia meets the Adriatic in Istria (Istra to Croats), the heart-shaped 3600-sq-km peninsula just south of Trieste in Italy. While the bucolic interior of rolling hills and fertile plains attracts artsy visitors to its hilltop villages, rural hotels and farmhouse restaurants, the verdant indented coastline is enormously popular with the sun 'n' sea set. Vast hotel complexes line much of the coast and its rocky beaches are not Croatia's best, but the facilities are wide-ranging, the sea is clean and secluded spots are still plentiful.

The coast gets flooded with tourists in summer, but you can still feel alone and undisturbed in 'Green Istria' (the interior), even in mid-August. Add acclaimed gastronomy (starring fresh seafood, prime white truffles, wild asparagus, top-rated olive oils and award-winning wines), sprinkle it with historical charm and you have a little slice of heaven.

Pula

POP 57,800

The wealth of Roman architecture makes the otherwise workaday Pula (ancient Polensium) a standout among Croatia's larger cities. The star of the Roman show is the remarkably well-preserved Roman amphitheatre, which dominates the streetscape and doubles as a venue for summer concerts and festivals.

Historical attractions aside, Pula is a busy commercial city on the sea that has managed to retain a friendly small-town appeal. A short bus ride away, a series of beaches awaits at the resorts that occupy the Verudela Peninsula to the south. Further south along the indented shoreline, the Premantura Peninsula hides a spectacular nature park, the protected cape of Kamenjak.

Sights

THE CITY

Roman Amphitheatre HISTORIC BUILDING

(Arena; Flavijevska bb; adult/concession 40/20KN; ⏰8am-midnight Jul & Aug, around 8am-7pm Sep-Jun) Pula's most imposing sight is this 1st-century amphitheatre, with seating for up to

20,000 spectators, overlooking the harbour northeast of the Old Town. Built entirely from local limestone, the Arena, as it's locally known, was designed to host gladiatorial contests. The **Pula Film Festival** (www.pulafilmfestival.hr) is held here every summer, as are pop and classical concerts.

Temple of Augustus HISTORIC BUILDING
(Forum; adult/concession 20/10KN; ⌚9am-8pm Mon-Fri, to 3pm Sat & Sun Apr-Oct) This Roman temple, erected from 2 BC to AD 14, now houses a small historical museum with captions in English.

THE COAST

The most tourist-packed beaches are undoubtedly those surrounding the hotel complex on the **Verudela Peninsula**, although some locals will dare to be seen at the small turquoise-coloured **Hawaii Beach** near the Hotel Park.

Rt Kamenjak NATURE PARK
(www.kamenjak.hr; pedestrians & cyclists free, per car/scooter 25/20KN; ⌚7am-10pm) For more seclusion, head out to the wild Rt Kamenjak on the Premantura Peninsula, 10km south of town. Take city bus 26 from Pula to Premantura (15KN), then rent a bike to get inside the park.

Sleeping

Any travel agency can give you information and book you into one of the hotels, or you can contact **Arenaturist** (☎529 400; www.arenaturist.hr; Splitska 1a).

Travel agencies in Pula can find you private accommodation, but there is little available in the town centre. Count on paying from 250KN to 490KN for a double room and from 300KN to 535KN for a two-person apartment. You can also browse the list of private accommodation at www.pulainfo.hr.

Hostel Pipištrelo HOSTEL $
(☎393 568; www.hostel-pipistrelo.com; Flaciusova 6; dm/s/d 124/148/296KN; ❄@☎) With its colourful facade, this recent addition to Pula's hostel scene sits right across the harbour. Its quirky thematic rooms were done up by young Pula designers. It is cash only and closed Sundays, so call ahead.

Riviera Guest House HOTEL $$
(☎525 400; www.arenaturist.hr; Splitska 1; s/d 360/590KN; ☎) This once-grand property in a neo-baroque 19th-century building is in dire need of a thorough overhaul. The saving grace: it's in the centre and the front rooms have water views.

Camping Stoja CAMPGROUND $
(☎387 144; www.arenacamps.com; Stoja 37; campsites per person/tent 58/37KN; ⌚Apr-Oct) The closest camping ground to Pula, 3km southwest of the centre, has lots of space on the shady promontory, with a restaurant and a diving centre. Take bus 1 to Stoja.

Eating

For cheap bites, browse around the central market, where you'll find excellent sandwiches at **Garfield** (Narodni Trg 9; sandwiches from 25KN; ⌚9am-3pm Mon-Fri, to 2pm Sat) on the 1st floor.

Vodnjanka ISTRIAN $
(Vitezića 4; mains from 40KN; ⌚closed Sat dinner & Sun winter) Locals swear by the real-deal home cooking at this no-frills spot. It's cheap, casual, cash-only and has a small menu that concentrates on simple Istrian dishes. To get here, walk south on Radićeva to Vitezića.

Drinking & Entertainment

TOP CHOICE **Cabahia** BAR
(Širolina 4) This artsy hideaway in Veruda has a cosy wood-beamed interior, eclectic decor of old objects, dim lighting, South American flair and a great garden terrace out the back. It hosts concerts and gets packed on weekends.

Rojc CULTURAL CENTRE
(www.rojcnet.pula.org; Gajeva 3) For an arty underground experience, check this converted army barracks that now houses a multimedia art centre and studios with occasional concerts, exhibitions and other events.

Information

Active Travel Istra (☎215 497; www.activa-istra.com; Scalierova 1) Excursions around Istria, adventure trips and concert tickets.

Hospital (☎376 548; Zagrebačka 34)

IstrAction (☎383 369; www.istraction.com; Prilaz Monte Cappelletta 3) Offers fun half-day tours to Kamenjak and around Pula's fortifications, as well as full-day excursions around Istria.

Tourist Information Centre (☎212 987; www.pulainfo.hr; Forum 3; ⌚8am-9pm Mon-Fri, 9am-9pm Sat & Sun summer, around 8am-7pm rest of yr) Knowledgeable and friendly staff provide maps, brochures and schedules of events in Pula and around Istria. Pick up *Domus Bonus*, which lists the best-quality private accommodation in Istria.

Getting There & Away

BUS From the Pula **bus station** (☎060 304 091; Šijanska 4), located 500m northeast of the town centre, there are frequent buses heading to Rijeka (97KN, 1½ hours) and Zagreb (190KN, four hours), and less frequent buses to Split (392KN, 10 hours) and Dubrovnik (580KN, 15 hours).

TRAIN There is one direct train daily to Ljubljana (144KN, 4½ hours) and three to Zagreb (140KN, nine hours), but you must board a bus for part of the trip, from Lupoglav to Rijeka.

Getting Around

The city buses of use to visitors are bus 1, which runs to Camping Stoja, and buses 2A and 3A to Verudela. Tickets are sold at *tisak* (news stands) for 6KN, or from the driver for 11KN.

DALMATIA

Roman ruins, spectacular beaches, old fishing ports, medieval architecture and unspoilt offshore islands make a trip to Dalmatia (Dalmacija) unforgettable. Occupying the central 375km of Croatia's Adriatic coast, Dalmatia offers a matchless combination of hedonism and historical discovery. The jagged coast is speckled with lush offshore islands and dotted with historic cities.

Split

☎021 / POP 178,200

The second-largest city in Croatia, Split (Spalato in Italian) is a great place to see Dalmatian life as it's really lived. Always buzzing, this exuberant city has just the right balance of tradition and modernity. Step inside Diocletian's Palace (a Unesco World Heritage site and one of the world's most impressive Roman monuments) and you'll see dozens of bars, restaurants and shops thriving amid the atmospheric old walls. To top it off, Split has a unique setting: the turquoise waters of the Adriatic backed by dramatic coastal mountains.

The Old Town is a vast open-air museum and the information signs at the important sights explain a great deal of Split's history. The seafront promenade, Obala Hrvatskog Narodnog Preporoda, better known as Riva, is the best central reference point.

Sights

DIOCLETIAN'S PALACE

Facing the harbour, **Diocletian's Palace** is one of the most imposing Roman ruins in existence. Don't expect a palace though, nor a museum – this is the living heart of the city, its labyrinthine streets packed with people, bars, shops and restaurants.

It was built as a military fortress, imperial residence and fortified town, with walls reinforced by square corner towers. There are 220 buildings within the palace boundaries, home to about 3000 people.

TOP CHOICE Town Museum MUSEUM

(Muzej Grada Splita; www.mgst.net; Papalićeva 1; adult/concession 10/5KN; ⏲9am-9pm Tue-Fri, to 4pm Sat-Mon Jun-Sep, 10am-5pm Tue-Fri, to 1pm Sat-Mon Oct-May) The three floors of the late-Gothic Papalić Palace showcase a collection of drawings, coats of arms, 17th-century weaponry and fine furniture; captions are in Croatian.

TOP CHOICE Cathedral of St Domnius CATHEDRAL

(Katedrala Svetog Duje; Svetog Duje 5; cathedral/treasury/belfry 15/15/10KN; ⏲8am-7pm Mon-Sat, 12.30-6.30pm Sun Jun-Sep, sporadic hours Oct-May) Split's neo-Romanesque cathedral was built as Diocletian's mausoleum. Its tower rises above the Peristil, a picturesque colonnaded square, which is a great place for a break in the sun. The vestibule at the southern end of Peristil is an open dome above the ground-floor passageway; it is overpoweringly grand and cavernous.

Admission to the cathedral also gets you access to the Temple of Jupiter and its crypt. For 35KN, you can get a ticket that includes access to the cathedral, treasury and belfry.

Temple of Jupiter TEMPLE

(temple/crypt 5/5KN; ⏲8am-7pm Mon-Sat, 12.30-6.30pm Sun May-Sep) Take a look at the headless sphinx in black granite guarding the entrance and, inside, the barrel-vaulted ceiling and a decorative frieze on the walls. You can also pop into the crypt.

OUTSIDE THE PALACE WALLS

Gregorius of Nin MONUMENT

(Grgur Ninski) This 10th-century statue is of the Croatian bishop who fought for the right to use old Croatian in liturgical services. It's said that rubbing his left big toe – now polished to a shine – brings good luck.

Gallery of Fine Arts GALLERY
(Galerija Umjetnina Split; www.galum.hr; Kralja Tomislava 15; adult/concession 20/10KN; ⌚11am-4pm Mon, 11am-7pm Tue-Fri, 11am-3pm Sat May-Sep, 9am-2pm Mon, 9am-5pm Tue-Fri, 9am-1pm Sat Oct-Apr) This gallery housed in a former hospital exhibits nearly 400 works of art spanning almost 700 years.

Bačvice BEACH
The most popular city beach is on the eponymous pebbly inlet, with good swimming, a lively ambience, a great cafe-bar and plenty of water games.

Activities

Marjan WALKING TRAIL
For an afternoon away from the city buzz, head to this hilly nature reserve (178m) with **trails** through fragrant pine forests, scenic **lookouts** and ancient **chapels**.

Sleeping

Hostels have sprouted all around Split in the last couple of years. Private accommodation is still a great option; expect to pay between 300KN and 500KN for a double room; in the cheaper ones you will probably share the bathroom with the proprietor.

Goli + Bosi HOSTEL $$
(☎510 999; www.gollybossy.com; Morpurgova Poljana 2; dm/s/d 245/714/818KN) Split's design hostel is the premier destination for flashpackers, with its sleek futuristic decor, hip vibe and a cool lobby cafe-bar-restaurant.

Villa Varoš GUESTHOUSE $$
(☎483 469; www.villavaros.hr; Miljenka Smoje 1; d/ste 600/900KN; ❄☕) Owned by a New Yorker Croat, Villa Varoš is central, the rooms are simple, bright and airy, and the apartment has a Jacuzzi and a small terrace.

CroParadise Split Hostels HOSTEL $
(☎091 444 4194; www.croparadise.com; Čulića Dvori 29; dm 180KN, d 400-500KN, apt from 500KN; ❄@☕) A great collection of three hostels – Blue, Green and Pink – inside converted apartments in the neighbourhood of Manuš. Five apartments are also available.

Silver Central Hostel HOSTEL $
(☎490 805; www.silvercentralhostel.com; Kralja Tomislava 1; dm 167-190KN; ❄@☕) In an upstairs apartment, this light yellow-coloured boutique hostel has four dorm rooms and a pleasant lounge. It has a two-person apartment nearby and another hostel, **Silver Gate** (☎322 857; www.silvergatehostel.com; Hrvojeva 6; dm per person 167KN), near the food market.

Split Hostel Booze & Snooze HOSTEL $
(☎342 787; www.splithostel.com; Narodni trg 8; dm 200-215KN; ❄@☕) Run by a pair of Aussie Croat women, this party place in the heart of town has four dorms, a terrace, book swap and boat trips. Its newer outpost, **Split Hostel Fiesta Siesta** (Kružićeva 5; dm 200-215KN, d 560KN; ❄@☕) has five dorms and one double above the popular Charlie's Backpacker Bar.

Eating

TOP CHOICE **Figa** INTERNATIONAL $
(Buvinina 1; mains from 50KN) Split's coolest little resto-bar with a funky interior and tables on the stairs outside, Figa serves nice breakfasts, innovative dishes and a wide range of salads, plus live music on some nights.

Konoba Matejuška DALMATIAN $
(Tomića Stine 3; mains from 50KN) Cosy, rustic tavern in an alleyway minutes from the seafront, it specialises in well-prepared seafood that also happens to be well priced.

TOP CHOICE **Villa Spiza** DALMATIAN $
(Kružićeva 3; mains from 40KN; ⌚Mon-Sat) This low-key joint, popular with locals, offers Dalmatian mainstays that change daily – think calamari, risotto, stuffed peppers – at low prices, served at the bar inside, or at a couple of benches outside.

Drinking & Entertainment

Žbirac CAFE
(Bačvice bb) This beachfront cafe is like the locals' open-air living room, a cult hang-out with great sea views, swimming day and night and occasional concerts.

Bifora CAFE-BAR
(Bernardinova 5) A quirky crowd of locals frequents this artsy spot on a lovely little square, much loved for its intimate low-key vibe.

Ghetto Club BAR
(Dosud 10) Split's most bohemian bar, in an intimate courtyard amid flowerbeds, a trickling fountain, great music and a friendly atmosphere.

Fluid CLUB
(Dosud 1) This chic little spot is a jazzy party venue, pretty low-key and cool. Great for people-watching.

Central Split

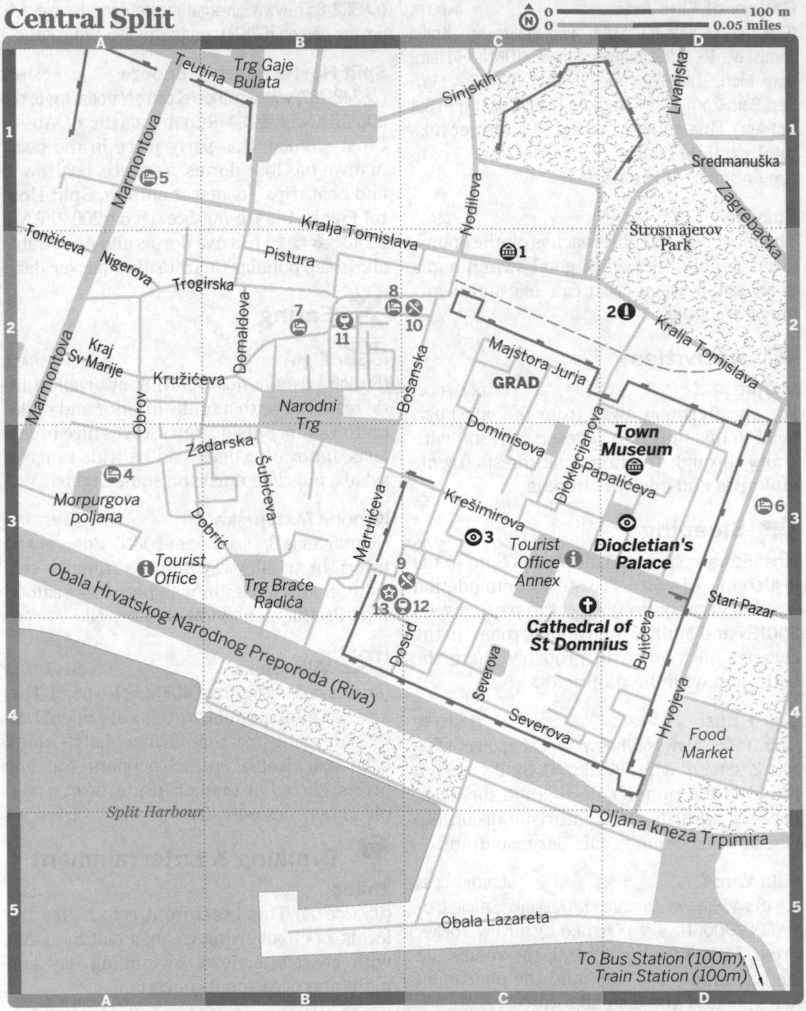

0 — 100 m
0 — 0.05 miles

Teutina
Trg Gaje Bulata
Marmontova
Sinjskih
Livanjska
Sredmanuška
Zagrebačka
Nodilova
Kralja Tomislava
Štrosmajerov Park
Tončićeva
Nigerova
Pistura
Trogirska
Domaldova
Bosanska
Majstora Jurja
Kralja Tomislava
GRAD
Kraj Sv Marije
Kružićeva
Marmontova
Obrov
Narodni Trg
Zadarska
Dominisova
Dioklecijanova
Town Museum
Papalićeva
Šubićeva
Morpurgova poljana
Dobrić
Marulićeva
Krešimirova
Tourist Office Annex
Diocletian's Palace
Tourist Office
Trg Braće Radića
Obala Hrvatskog Narodnog Preporoda (Riva)
Dosud
Cathedral of St Domnius
Bulićeva
Stari Pazar
Severova
Hrvojeva
Food Market
Split Harbour
Poljana kneza Trpimira
Obala Lazareta
To Bus Station (100m); Train Station (100m)

Information

You can change money at travel agencies or the post office. There are ATMs throughout the city.

Backpackers Cafe (☎338 548; Kneza Domagoja bb; internet 30N; ⏰7am-9pm) Sells used books, offers luggage storage and provides information for backpackers.

Croatian Youth Hostel Association (☎396 031; www.hfhs.hr; Domilijina 8; ⏰8am-4pm Mon-Fri) Sells HI cards and has information about youth hostels all over Croatia.

KBC Firule (☎556 111; Spinčićeva 1) Split's hospital.

Turist Biro (☎347 100; www.turistbiro-split.hr; Hrvatskog Narodnog Preporoda 12) Its forte is private accommodation and excursions.

Tourist Office (☎360 066; www.visitsplit.com; Hrvatskog Narodnog Preporoda 9; ⏰8am-9pm Mon-Sat, to 1pm Sun Apr–mid-Oct, 8am-8pm Mon-Fri, to 1pm Sat mid-Oct–Mar) Has info on Split and sells the Split Card (35KN), which offers free and reduced prices to Split attractions and discounts on car rental, restaurants, shops and hotels.

Tourist Office Annex (☎345 606; www.visitsplit.com; Peristil bb; ⏰9am-4pm Mon-Sat, 8am-1pm Sun Apr–mid-Oct, shorter hr rest of yr)

Central Split

Top Sights

Cathedral of St Domnius C3
Diocletian's Palace D3
Town Museum D3

Sights

1 Gallery of Fine Arts C2
2 Gregorius of Nin D2
3 Temple of Jupiter C3

Sleeping

4 Goli + Bosi A3
5 Silver Central Hostel A1
6 Silver Gate D3
7 Split Hostel Booze & Snooze B2
8 Split Hostel Fiesta Siesta B2

Eating

9 Figa C3
10 Villa Spiza C2

Drinking

11 Bifora B2
12 Ghetto Club B3

Entertainment

13 Fluid B3

Getting There & Away

Air

Split airport (www.split-airport.hr) is 20km west of town, just 6km before Trogir. **Croatia Airlines** (☎362 997; www.croatiaairlines.hr; Hrvatskog Narodnog Preporoda 9; ⏰8am-4pm Mon-Fri) operates one-hour flights to Zagreb several times a day and a weekly flight to Dubrovnik (summer only).

A couple of low-cost airlines fly to Split, including **easyJet** (www.easyjet.com), **germanwings** (www.germanwings.com) and **Norwegian** (www.norwegian.com).

Boat

Jadrolinija (☎338 333; www.jadrolinija.hr; Gat Sv Duje bb) handles most of the coastal ferry lines and catamarans that operate between Split and the islands.

There is also a fast passenger boat, the **Krilo** (www.krilo.hr), that goes to Hvar Town (45KN, one hour) daily and on to Korčula (65KN, 2¾ hours).

Car ferries and passenger lines depart from separate docks; the passenger lines leave from Obala Lazareta and car ferries from Gat Sv Duje. You can buy tickets from either the main Jadrolinija office in the large ferry terminal opposite the bus station, or at one of the two stalls near the docks.

Bus

Advance bus tickets with seat reservations are recommended. Most buses leave from the main **bus station** (☎060 327 777; www.ak-split.hr) beside the harbour, which has a **garderoba** (left luggage; 1st hr 5KN, then per hour 1.50KN; ⏰6am-10pm), to the following destinations: Dubrovnik (115KN to 145KN, 4½ hours, 25 daily), Pula (423KN, 10 to 11 hours, three daily) and Zagreb (114KN to 204KN, five to eight hours, 40 daily).

Note that Split–Dubrovnik buses pass briefly through Bosnian territory, so keep your passport handy for border-crossing points.

Train

There are five daily trains between Split **train station** (☎338 525; www.hznet.hr; Kneza Domagoja 9) and Zagreb (189KN, six to eight hours), which is just behind the bus station; two are overnight. There's a **garderoba** (left luggage; per day 15KN; ⏰6am-10pm) at the station.

Hvar Island

☎021 / POP 10,900

Hvar is the number-one carrier of Croatia's superlatives: it's the most luxurious island, the sunniest place in the country and, along with Dubrovnik, the most popular tourist destination. Hvar is also famed for its verdancy and its lilac lavender fields.

The island's hub and busiest destination is Hvar Town. Visitors wander along the main square, explore the sights on the winding stone streets, swim on the numerous beaches or pop off to get into their birthday suits on the Pakleni Islands, but most of all they party at night. There are several good restaurants and a number of top hotels, as well as a couple of hostels.

The interior of the island hides abandoned ancient hamlets, towering peaks and green, largely uncharted landscapes. It's worth exploring on a day trip.

Sights & Activities

St Stephen's Square SQUARE

(Trg Svetog Stjepana) This rectangular square is the town centre. Notice the 1520 **well** at the square's northern end, which has a wrought-iron grill dating from 1780.

Franciscan Monastery & Museum MONASTERY

(admission 25KN; ⏰9am-1pm & 5-7pm Mon-Sat) At the southeastern end of town, this 15th-century Renaissance monastery has a collection of Venetian paintings in the

WORTH A TRIP

PAKLENI ISLANDS

Most visitors to Hvar Town head to the Pakleni Islands (Pakleni Otoci), which got their name, 'Hell's Islands' in Croatian, from Paklina, the resin that once coated boats and ships.

This gorgeous chain of 21 wooded isles has crystal-clean seas, hidden beaches and deserted lagoons. Taxi boats leave regularly during the high season from in front of the Arsenal to the islands of **Jerolim** and **Stipanska** (35KN, 10 to 15 minutes), which are popular naturist islands (although nudity is not mandatory). They continue on to **Ždrilca** and **Mlini** (40KN) and, further out, **Palmižana** (60KN), which has a pebble beach and the **Meneghello Place** (www.palmizana.hr), a beautiful boutique complex of villas and bungalows scattered among lush tropical gardens. Run by the artsy Meneghello family, the estate holds music recitals, and features two excellent restaurants and an art gallery. Also on Palmižana are two top restaurant-cum-hangout spots, Toto and Laganini.

adjoining church and a cloister garden with a cypress tree said to be more than 300 years old.

Fortica FORTRESS
(admission 25KN; ⌚8am-10pm Jun-Sep) On the hill high above town, this Venetian fortress (1551) is worth the climb up to appreciate the sweeping panoramic views. There's a cafe at the top.

Arsenal HISTORIC BUILDING
(Trg Svetog Stjepana; arsenal & theatre 20KN; ⌚9am-9pm) Smack in the middle of town is the imposing Gothic arsenal, and upstairs is the **Renaissance theatre** (Trg Svetog Stjepana; admission 10KN; ⌚9am-9pm) built in 1612 – reported to be the first theatre in Europe open to plebs and aristocrats alike.

Tours

Secret Hvar GUIDED TOURS
(☎717 615; www.secrethvar.com; Trg Svetog Stjepana 4a) Don't miss their great off-road tours to the island's interior, which include lunch in a traditional tavern and a stop on the beach.

Sleeping

Accommodation in Hvar is extremely tight in July and August; try the travel agencies for help. Expect to pay anywhere from 150KN to 300KN per person for a room with a private bathroom in the town centre.

Hostel Marinero HOSTEL $
(☎091 174 1601; Put Sv Marka 7; dm 200-240KN; ❄📶) Location is the highlight at this six-dorm hostel right off the seafront. Dorms are basic but clean, and the restaurant downstairs is a good place to hang out. Be ready for some noise, as the Kiva Bar is right next door.

Hvar Out Hostel HOSTEL $
(☎717 375; hvarouthostel@gmail.com; Burak 23; dm 200-250KN; ❄@📶) By the same owners as Split Hostel Booze & Snooze, this party place, steps from the harbour in the maze of the Old Town, has seven well-equipped dorms, a small shared kitchen and a top-floor terrace

Camping Vira CAMPGROUND $
(☎741 803; www.campingvira.com; campsite per adult/site 60/97KN; ⌚May–mid-Oct; P@📶) This four-star camping ground on a beautiful wooded bay 4km from town is one of the best in Dalmatia. There's a gorgeous beach, a cafe and restaurant, and a volleyball pitch.

Eating

Self-caterers can head to the supermarket next to the bus station, or pick up fresh supplies at the vegetable market next door.

Konoba Menego DALMATIAN $$
(www.menego.hr; Groda bb; mains from 60KN) At this rustic old house, everything is decked out in Hvar antiques and the staff wear traditional outfits. Try the marinated meats, cheeses and vegetables, prepared the old-fashioned Dalmatian way.

Konoba Luviji DALMATIAN $$
(Jurja Novaka 6; mains from 50KN; ⌚dinner) Food brought out of the wood oven at this tavern is simple, unfussy and tasty. Downstairs is the *konoba* where Dalmatian-style tapas are served; the upstairs restaurant has Old Town views.

Nonica PASTRIES, CAKES $
(Burak 23; ⌚8am-2pm & 5-11pm Mon-Sat, 8am-2pm Sun) Savour the best cakes in town, at this tiny storefront cafe right behind the Arsenal. Try the old-fashioned local biscuits such as *rafioli* and *forski koloc*.

Drinking

Falko BEACH BAR
(⌚8am-10pm mid-May–mid-Sep) A 20-minute walk from the town centre, past Hula-Hula and Hotel Amfora, brings you to this adorable hideaway in a pine forest just above the beach. Think low-key artsy vibe, homemade *rakija*, hammocks and a local crowd.

Carpe Diem LOUNGE BAR
(www.carpe-diem-hvar.com; Riva) This swanky harbourfront spot is the mother of Croatia's coastal clubs, with house music spun nightly by resident DJs. The **Carpe Diem Beach** (www.carpe-diem-beach.com) on the island of Stipanska is the hottest place to party.

Hula-Hula BEACH BAR
(www.hulahulahvar.com) *The* spot to catch the sunset to the sound of techno and house music, Hula-Hula is known for its après-beach party (4pm to 9pm).

Kiva Bar BAR
(www.kivabarhvar.com; Fabrika bb) This happening alleyway spot is packed to the rafters most nights, with a DJ spinning old dance, pop and rock classics that really get the crowd going.

Information

Del Primi (☎091 583 7864; www.delprimi-hvar.com; Burak 23) Travel agency specialising in private accommodation. Also rents jet skis.

Francesco (Burak bb; per hr 30KN; ⌚8.30am-midnight) Internet cafe and call centre right behind the post office. Left luggage for 35KN per day and laundry service for 50KN per load.

Hvar Adventure (☎717 813; www.hvar-adventure.com; Obala bb) Adventure activities such as sailing, sea kayaking, cycling, hiking and rock climbing.

Tourist office (☎741 059; www.tzhvar.hr; ⌚8am-2pm & 3-9pm Jul & Aug, shorter hr rest of yr) Right on Trg Svetog Stjepana.

Getting There & Away

The local **Jadrolinija** (☎741 132; www.jadrolinija.hr) car ferry from Split calls at Stari Grad (47KN, two hours) six times a day in summer. Jadrolinija also has three to five catamarans daily to Hvar Town (47KN, one hour). **Krilo** (www.krilo.hr), the fast passenger boat, travels once a day between Split and Hvar Town (45KN, one hour) in summer; it also goes on to Korčula (65KN, 2¾ hours). You can buy tickets at **Pelegrini Tours** (☎742 743; www.pelegrini-hvar.hr; Riva bb).

Getting Around

Buses meet most ferries that dock at Stari Grad and go to Hvar Town (27KN, 20 minutes). There are 10 buses a day between Stari Grad and Hvar Town in summer, but services are reduced on Sunday and in the low season.

A taxi costs from 300KN to 350KN. **Radio Taxi Tihi** (☎098 338 824) is cheaper if there are a number of passengers to fill up the minivan.

Korčula Island

☎020 / POP 16,438

Rich in vineyards and olive trees, Korčula is the largest island in an archipelago of 48, with plenty of opportunities for scenic drives, particularly along the southern coast.

Swimming options abound in the many quiet coves and secluded beaches, while the interior produces some of Croatia's finest wine, especially dessert wines made from the *grk* grape cultivated around Lumbarda.

On a hilly peninsula jutting into the Adriatic sits Korčula Town, a striking walled town of round defensive towers and red-roofed houses. Resembling a miniature Dubrovnik, the gated, walled Old Town is crisscrossed by narrow stone streets designed to protect its inhabitants from winds.

Sights

St Mark's Cathedral CATHEDRAL
(Katedrala Svetog Marka; Statuta 1214; ⌚9am-9pm Jul & Aug, Mass only Sep-Jun) Dominating Trg Svetog Marka (St Mark's Square), the 15th-century Gothic-Renaissance cathedral features two paintings by Tintoretto.

Town Museum MUSEUM
(Gradski Muze; Statuta 1214; admission 25KN; ⌚9am-9pm Jun-Aug, 9am-1pm Mon-Sat Sep-May) The 16th-century Gabriellis Palace opposite the cathedral houses a stone-carving collection, prehistoric objects, and Korčulan traditional dress and art.

Marco Polo Museum MUSEUM
(De Polo; admission 20KN; ⌚9am-7pm Jun-Sep, 10am-4pm May & Oct) It's said that Marco Polo was born in Korčula in 1254; visit what is believed to be his birthplace and climb the steep tower steps for an eagle's-eye vista over the peninsula.

Sleeping & Eating

If you don't fancy staying in any of the big hotels, a more personal option is a guesthouse. Atlas Travel Agency and Marko Polo Tours arrange private rooms (from 250KN in high season).

Villa DePolo APARTMENT, ROOMS $
(☎711 621; tereza.depolo@du.t-com.hr; Svetog Nikole bb; d 350KN; ❄📶) The small, simple but attractive modern rooms (and one apartment) come with comfortable beds; one has a terrace with amazing views. It's a short walk from the Old Town.

Pansion Hajduk PANSION $
(☎711 267; olga.zec@du.t-com.hr; d from 440KN; ❄🏊) It's a couple of kilometres from town on the road to Lumbarda, but you get a warm welcome, air-conditioned rooms with TVs and even a swimming pool.

TOP CHOICE **Konoba Komin** DALMATIAN $
(☎716 508; Don Iva Matijace; mains from 45KN) This family-run *konoba* looks almost medieval, with its *komin* (roaring fire), roasting meat, ancient stone walls and solid wooden tables. Book ahead.

Information

There are several ATMs around town, including one at HVB Splitska Banka. You can also change money at the post office or at any of the travel agencies.

Atlas Travel Agency (☎711 231; atlas-korcula@du.htnet.hr; Plokata 19 Travnja bb) Runs excursions and finds private accommodation.

Kantun Tours (☎715 622; www.kantun-tours.com; Plokata 19 Travnja bb) Private accommodation, lots of excursions, car hire and boat tickets, plus internet access (25KN per hour) and luggage storage.

Tourist office (☎715 701; www.korcula.net; Obala Franje Tuđmana 4; ⏲8am-3pm & 5-8pm Mon-Sat, 9am-1pm Sun Jul & Aug, 8am-2pm Mon-Sat Sep-Jun) On the west harbour; an excellent source of information.

Getting There & Away

There are buses to Dubrovnik (95KN, three hours, one to three daily) and one to Zagreb (245KN, 11 hours). Book ahead in summer.

The island has two major entry ports – Korčula Town and Vela Luka. All the **Jadrolinija** (☎715 410) ferries between Split and Dubrovnik stop in Korčula Town. If you're travelling between Split and Korčula you have several options. There's a daily fast boat, the **Krilo** (www.krilo.hr), which runs from Split to Korčula (65KN, 2¾ hours) all year round, stopping at Hvar en route.

Dubrovnik

☎020 / POP 30,000

No matter whether you are visiting Dubrovnik for the first time or if you're returning to this marvellous city, the sense of awe and beauty when you set eyes on the Stradun (the Old Town's main street) never fades. It's hard to imagine anyone becoming jaded by the marble streets and baroque buildings, or failing to be inspired by a walk along the ancient city walls that protected a civilised, sophisticated republic for five centuries and that now look out onto the endless shimmer of the peaceful Adriatic.

Sights

All the sights are in the Old Town, which is entirely closed to cars. Looming above the city is Mt Srđ, which is connected by cable car to Dubrovnik. Pile Gate is the main entrance to the Old Town; the mains street is Placa (better known as Stradun).

OLD TOWN

TOP CHOICE **City Walls & Forts** CITY WALLS
(Gradske Zidine; adult/concession 70/30KN; ⏲9am-6.30pm Apr-Oct, 10am-3pm Nov-Mar) No visit to Dubrovnik would be complete without a leisurely walk around the spectacular city walls, Dubrovnik's main claim to fame. Built between the 13th and 16th centuries, they are still intact today. The main entrance and ticket office to the walls is by the 1537 **Pile Gate**. You can also enter at the **Ploče Gate** in the east (a wise move at really busy times of day). The walls can only be walked clockwise.

TOP CHOICE **War Photo Limited** PHOTOGRAPHIC GALLERY
(☎326 166; www.warphotoltd.com; Antuninska 6; admission 30KN; ⏲9am-9pm daily Jun-Sep, 9am-3pm Tue-Sat & 9am-1pm Sun May & Oct) This state-of-the-art photographic gallery has beautifully displayed and reproduced exhibitions curated by the gallery owner and former photojournalist Wade Goddard. It closes from November to April.

Franciscan Monastery & Museum MONASTERY
(Muzej Franjevačkog Samostana; Placa 2; adult/concession 30/15KN; ⏲9am-6pm) Inside this

monastery complex is a mid-14th-century **cloister**, the third-oldest functioning **pharmacy** in Europe (in business since 1391) and a small **museum** with a collection of relics, liturgical objects, jewellery and pharmacy items.

Dominican Monastery & Museum MONASTERY
(Muzej Dominikanskog Samostana; off Ulica Svetog Dominika 4; adult/concession 20/10KN; ⏲9am-6pm May-Oct, to 5pm Nov-Apr) This imposing 14th-century structure in the city's north-eastern corner is an architectural highlight, with a forbidding fortress-like exterior that shelters a rich trove of paintings from Dubrovnik's finest 15th- and 16th-century artists.

Rector's Palace PALACE
(Pred Dvorom 3; adult/concession 35/15KN, audioguide 30KN; ⏲9am-6pm May-Oct, to 4pm Nov-Apr) This Gothic-Renaissance Rector's Palace built in the late 15th century houses a museum with artfully restored rooms and historical exhibits.

Cathedral of the Assumption of the Virgin CATHEDRAL
(Stolna Crkva Velike Gospe; Poljana M Držića; ⏲morning & late-afternoon Mass) Completed in 1713 in baroque style, the cathedral is notable for its fine altars and its **treasury** (Riznica; adult/concession 10/5KN; ⏲8am-5.30pm Mon-Sat, 11am-5.30pm Sun May-Oct, 10am-noon & 3-5pm Nov-Apr).

Sponza Palace PALACE
(Placa) The 16th-century Sponza Palace houses the **State Archives** (Državni Arhiv u Dubrovniku; admission 20KN; ⏲8am-3pm Mon-Fri, to 1pm Sat) and the **Memorial Room of the Defenders of Dubrovnik** (⏲10am-10pm Mon-Fri, 8am-1pm Sat), a heartbreaking collection of portraits of young people who perished between 1991 and 1995.

Serbian Orthodox Church & Museum CHURCH, MUSEUM
(Muzej Pravoslavne Crkve; Od Puča 8; adult/concession 10/5KN; ⏲9am-2pm Mon-Sat) This 1877 Orthodox church has a fascinating collection of icons dating from the 15th to 19th century.

Synagogue SYNAGOGUE
(Sinagoga; Žudioska 5; admission 20KN; ⏲10am-8pm Mon-Fri May-Oct, to 3pm Nov-Apr) The oldest Sephardic and second-oldest synagogue in the Balkans, dating back to the 15th century, has a small museum inside.

Orlando Column MONUMENT
(Luža Sq) A popular meeting place that used to be the spot where edicts, festivities and public verdicts were announced.

EAST OF THE OLD TOWN

TOP CHOICE **Cable Car** CABLE CAR
(www.dubrovnikcablecar.com; Petra Krešimira IV; adult/concession 87/50KN; ⏲9am-10pm Tue-Sun May-Oct, shorter hr rest of yr) Dubrovnik's cable car whisks you from just north of the city walls up to Mt Srđ in under four minutes, for a stupendous perspective of the city.

Homeland War Museum MUSEUM
(www.tzdubrovnik.hr; admission 20KN; ⏲8am-6pm Apr-Oct, 9am-4pm Nov-Mar) Learn about Dubrovnik's wartime history at this place inside a Napoleonic Fort, just above where the cable car drops you off.

THE COAST

Banje Beach (outside Ploče Gate) is the most popular city beach. Just southeast is **Sveti Jakov**, a good local beach that doesn't get rowdy and has showers, a bar and a restaurant. Buses 5 and 8 will get you there. **Lapad Bay** brims with hotel beaches that you can use without a problem.

Lokrum Island ISLAND
A better option than the mainland beaches is to take the **ferry** (return 40KN; ⏲last return boat 6pm) that shuttles roughly hourly in summer to lush Lokrum Island, a national park with a rocky nudist beach (marked FKK), a botanical garden, the ruins of a medieval Benedictine monastery and an attractive cafe-restaurant.

Festivals & Events

Dubrovnik Summer Festival CULTURAL
(☎326 100; www.dubrovnik-festival.hr; tickets 50-300KN) A major cultural event over five weeks in July and August, with theatre, music and dance performances at different venues in the Old Town.

Sleeping

Private accommodation is generally the best option in Dubrovnik, which is the most expensive destination in Croatia. Beware the scramble of private owners at the bus station and ferry terminal: some are scamming. Expect to pay from 300KN for a double room, and from 500KN for an apartment in high season.

Dubrovnik

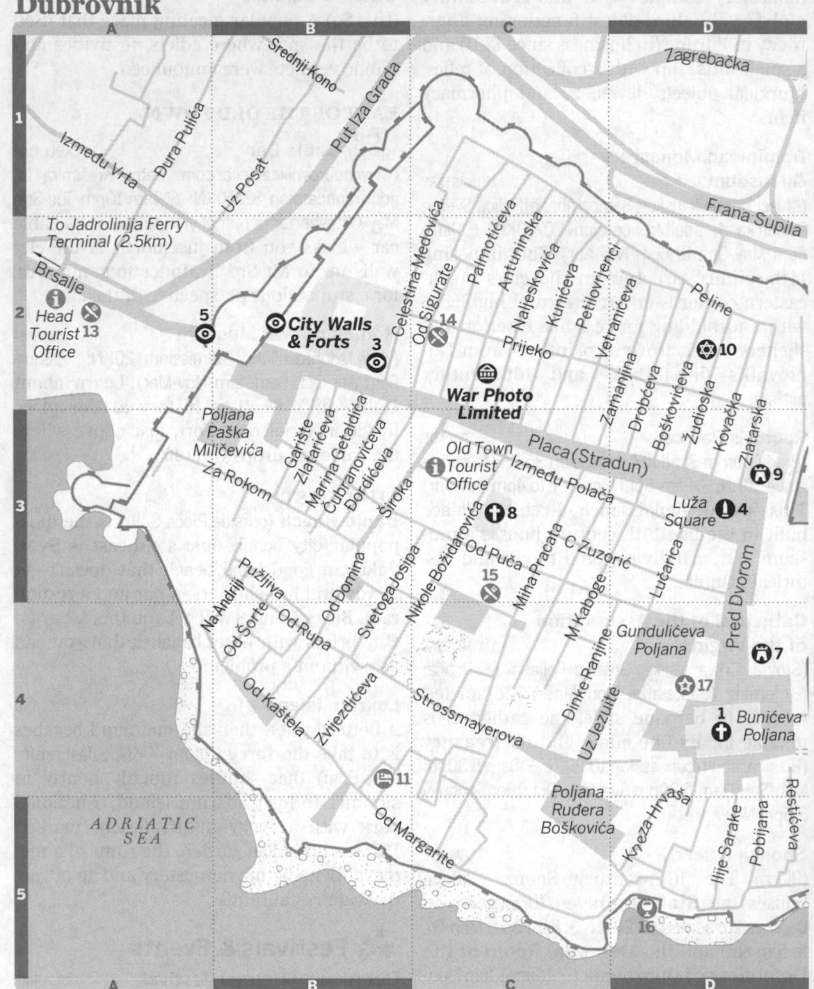

OLD TOWN

TOP CHOICE **Karmen Apartments** APARTMENTS $$

(☎323 433, 098 619 282; www.karmendu.com; Bandureva 1; apt 450-1200KN; ❄📶) Run by an Englishman who has lived in Dubrovnik for decades, these four inviting, homely apartments enjoy a great location a stone's throw from Ploče harbour. All apartments have plenty of character. Book well ahead.

TOP CHOICE **Fresh Sheets** HOSTEL $

(☎091 79 92 086; www.igotfresh.com; Sv Šimuna 15; dm/d 210/554KN; @📶) The only hostel in the Old Town is a warm place right by the city walls, with clean and simple dorms and a double with a sea view. It's run by a hospitable crew who organise imaginative outings, dinners and other fun stuff.

Apartments & Rooms Biličić RENTAL ROOMS $

(☎417 152; www.dubrovnik-online.com/apartments_bilicic; Privežna 2; r/apt 450/870KN; ❄) A highly atmospheric place to stay, reached via some some vertiginous steps from the Old Town. Offers bright, clean and pleasant rooms with a homely touch and TVs (though bathrooms

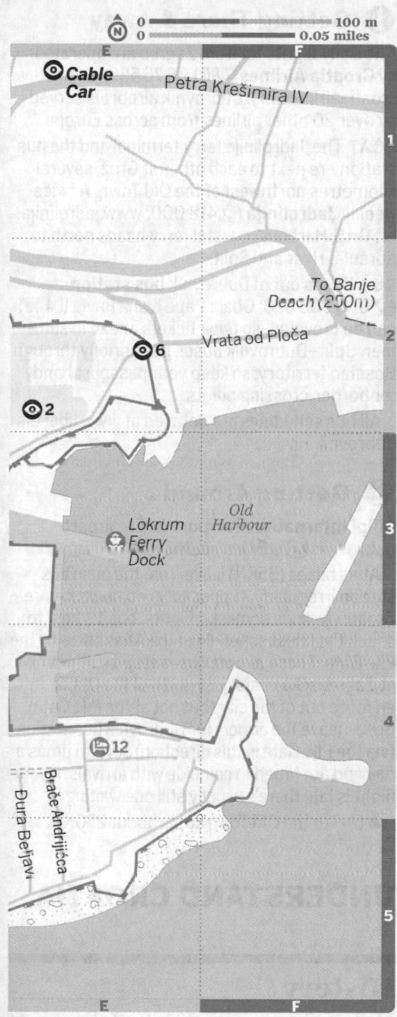

Dubrovnik

Top Sights
- Cable Car F1
- City Walls & Forts B2
- War Photo Limited C2

Sights
1. Cathedral of the Assumption of the Virgin D4
- Cathedral of the Assumption of the Virgin Treasury .... (see 1)
2. Dominican Monastery & Museum E2
3. Franciscan Monastery & Museum B2
- Memorial Room of the Defenders of Dubrovnik .... (see 9)
4. Orlando Column D3
5. Pile Gate A2
6. Ploče Gate E2
7. Rector's Palace D4
8. Serbian Orthodox Church & Museum C3
9. Sponza Palace D3
- State Archives .... (see 9)
10. Synagogue D2

Sleeping
11. Fresh Sheets B4
12. Karmen Apartments E4

Eating
13. Dubravka 1836 .... A2
14. Lucin Kantun C2
15. Taj Mahal C3

Drinking
16. Buža D5

Entertainment
17. Troubadur D4

are not en suite). There's a gorgeous garden and quirky seating.

OUTSIDE THE OLD TOWN

Begović Boarding House PRIVATE ACCOMMODATION $
(☎435 191; www.begovic-boarding-house.com; Primorska 17; dm/r/apt 150/320/385KN; P@) A steep walk uphill from Lapad harbourfront, this welcoming family-run place has smallish but clean pine-trimmed rooms, some opening out onto a communal garden with amazing views. There's free pick-up from the bus or ferry.

Dubrovnik Backpackers Club HOSTEL $
(☎435 375; www.dubackpackers.com; Mostarska 2d; dm 120-170KN; @ᯤ) Run by a very hospitable family, this sociable backpackers has free internet, local calls and tea/coffee, plus a guests' kitchen and a balcony with bay views.

Eating

Lucin Kantun CROATIAN $$
(☎321 003; Od Sigurate bb; mains from 80KN) A modest-looking place with shabby-chic decor and a few pavement tables, this restaurant serves some of the most creative food in Dubrovnik. Virtually everything on

the short mezze-style menu is excellent, although wait times can be long.

Taj Mahal BOSNIAN, INTERNATIONAL $
(www.tajmahaldubrovnik.com; Nikole Gučetićeva 2; mains from 40KN) It's like an Aladdin's cave, with an interior loaded with Ottoman decorations and subdued lighting, and great Bosnian food. There are also three pavement tables.

Dubravka 1836 INTERNATIONAL $
(www.dubravka1836.hr; Brsalje 1; mains from 49KN) This place has arguably Dubrovnik's best dining terrace, with stunning wall and sea views. Though it draws quite a touristy clientele, locals still rate the fresh fish, risotto and salads, pizza and pasta.

Drinking & Entertainment

Buža BAR
(Ilije Sarake) Finding this isolated bar-on-a-cliff feels like a real discovery as you duck and dive around the city walls and finally see the entrance tunnel. It showcases tasteful music and a mellow crowd soaking up the vibes, views and sunshine.

Troubadur LIVE MUSIC
(☎412 154; Bunićeva Poljana 2) Come to this corner bar, a legendary Dubrovnik venue, for live jazz concerts in the summer.

ℹ Information

There are numerous ATMs in town, in Lapad and at the ferry terminal and bus station. Travel agencies and the post office will also exchange cash.

Atlas Travel Agency (www.atlas-croatia.com) Gruž Harbour (☎418 001; Obala Papa Ivana Pavla II 1, Gruž Harbour); Pile Gate (☎442 574; Sv Đurđa 1, Pile Gate) This agency organises excursions within Croatia and to Mostar and Montenegro. Also finds private accommodation.

Lonely Planet (www.lonelyplanet.com/croatia/dubrovnik)

Tourist Office (www.tzdubrovnik.hr; ⊙8am-8pm Jun-Sep, 8am-3pm Mon-Fri & 9am-2pm Sat Oct-May) Head Office (☎020 312 011; Brsalje 5); Gruž Harbour (☎417 983; Obala Stjepana Radića 27); Bus Station (☎417 581; Obala Pape Ivana Pavla II 44a); Lapad (☎437 460; Šetalište Kralja Zvonimira 25) Old Town (☎323 587; Široka 1) Maps, information and the indispensable *Dubrovnik Riviera* guide. The smart new head office that's under construction just west of the Pile Gate should open by the time you read this.

ℹ Getting There & Away

AIR Daily flights to/from Zagreb are operated by **Croatia Airlines** (☎01 66 76 555; www.croatiaairlines.hr). Dubrovnik airport is served by over 20 other airlines from across Europe.

BOAT The Jadrolinija ferry terminal and the bus station are next to each other at Gruž, several kilometres northwest of the Old Town. A twice-weekly **Jadrolinija** (☎418 000; www.jadrolinija.hr; Gruž Harbour) coastal ferry heads north to Korčula, Hvar and Split.

BUS Buses out of Dubrovnik **bus station** (☎060 305 070; Obala Pape Ivana Pavla II 44a) can be crowded, so book tickets ahead in summer. Split–Dubrovnik buses pass briefly through Bosnian territory, so keep your passport handy for border-crossing points.

All bus schedules are detailed at www.libertasdubrovnik.hr.

Getting Around

Čilipi international airport (www.airport-dubrovnik.hr)is 24km southeast of Dubrovnik.

Atlas buses (35KN) leave from the main bus station irregularly, supposedly two hours before Croatia Airlines domestic flights, but it's best to check the latest schedule at the Atlas office by the Pile Gate. These airport buses stop in Dubrovnik at Zagrebačka cesta, just north of the Old Town , en route out of the city (but not at the Pile Gate). Buses leave the airport for Dubrovnik bus station (via the Pile Gate in this direction) several times a day and are timed to coincide with arrivals; if your flight is late there's usually still one waiting.

A taxi to the Old Town costs about 250KN.

UNDERSTAND CROATIA

History

Modern Croatia is on the site of the ancient Roman province of Illyricum. Pula and Split were the two most important Roman towns. Slavs migrated into the region in the 7th century but political disarray tempted the Venetians to attack the coast. They established their first foothold on the coast in the 11th century and remained until Napoleon conquered Venice in 1797. In 1815 the Austro-Hungarian empire took control of Croatia, but with its defeat in WWI, Croatia became part of the Kingdom of Serbs, Croats and Slovenes (Yugoslavia). The Germans invaded in 1941 and tens of thousands of Croats joined the forces of Josip Broz, known as Maršal Tito.

Yugoslavia

After the war, Tito became prime minister of the new Yugoslav Federation. Croatia and Slovenia moved far ahead of the southern republics economically. With Tito's death in 1980, many Croats wanted autonomy. When Slobodan Milošević rose to power in Yugoslavia on a wave of Serbian nationalism, Croatia moved towards independence. Under the leadership of Franjo Tuđman, Croatia declared independence on 25 June 1991.

War & Peace

Heavy fighting broke out in Serbian areas in eastern Croatia and in the Serbian enclave of Krajina (from northeast to east of Zadar). In six months of fighting, 10,000 people died, hundreds of thousands fled and tens of thousands of homes were destroyed.

A series of international peace plans halted the fighting until, in January 1993, the Croatian army suddenly launched an offensive in southern Krajina, recapturing much land. Their hold was consolidated in a new offensive launched on 1 May 1995, which essentially set Croatia's new borders. The Dayton Agreement of December 1995 established borders and finally brought lasting peace to Croatia and a tenuous peace to the rest of the region.

Postwar Politics

Franjo Tuđman became Croatia's first president and led a regime that became increasingly authoritarian. Tuđman succumbed to cancer in 1999 and the 2000 election brought a centre-left coalition to power with Stipe Mesić elected president. He held the presidential throne for 10 years, until January 2010, when Ivo Josipović of the Social Democratic Party of Croatia (SDP) won the presidential election.

Croatian politics took another major turn in the 2011 parliamentary election, when the SDP joined three other centre-left parties to create the so-named Kukuriku coalition, an opposition bloc headed up by Zoran Milanović. Milanović took office as Croatia's prime minister in December 2011.

In January 2012, about 44% of Croats turned up to vote in the referendum on the European Union (EU) accession and supported the joining by a margin of two to one. But attitudes towards the EU accession remain divided, in no small part due to the European debt crisis. The divide aside, Croatia is slated to become the EU's 28th member state, which – on paper at least – will catapult it out of the Balkans and place it firmly in central Europe.

People

According to the most recent census (2011), Croatia has a population of roughly 4.3 million people, a decline from the prewar population of nearly five million. A discouraging economic outlook is largely responsible for a steady decline in Croatia's population, as educated young people leave in search of greater opportunities abroad.

Arts

Croatia's towering literary figure is 20th-century novelist and playwright Miroslav Krleža (1893–1981). His most popular novel is *The Return of Philip Latinovicz* (1932).

Some contemporary writers worth reading include expat writer Dubravka Ugrešić, best known for her *Café Europa – Life After Communism*. Miljenko Jergović's *Sarajevo Marlboro* and *Mama Leone* powerfully conjure up the atmosphere of life in prewar Yugoslavia.

Environment

Croatia is shaped like a boomerang: from the Pannonian plains of Slavonia between the Sava, Drava and Danube Rivers, across hilly central Croatia to the Istrian peninsula, then south through Dalmatia along the rugged Adriatic coast.

Croatia has 1244 offshore islands and islets along the tectonically submerged Adriatic coastline, 50 of them inhabited.

There are eight national parks in the country. These have a total area of 96,135 sq km, of which 74,260 sq km is land and 21,875 sq km is water.

The lack of heavy industry in Croatia has had the happy effect of leaving its forests, coasts, rivers and air generally fresh and unpolluted.

Food & Drink

Croatian food is a savoury smorgasbord of taste, echoing the varied cultures that have influenced the country over the course of its history. You'll find a sharp divide between the Italian-style cuisine along the coast and the flavours of Hungary, Austria and Turkey in the continental parts.

SURVIVAL GUIDE

Directory A–Z

Accommodation

Private accommodation is a lot more affordable and often great value in Croatia. If you don't mind foregoing hotel facilities, it's a great way to go about vacationing in Croatia.

Note that many establishments add a 30% charge for less than three-night stays and include 'residence tax', which is around 7KN per person per day. Prices quoted in this book do not include the residence tax.

PRICE RANGES

The following price categories for the cost of double room with bathroom are used in the listings in this chapter.

€ less than 500KN

€€ 500KN to 900KN

€€€ more than 900KN

CAMPING

Nearly 100 camping grounds are scattered along the Croatian coast. Most operate from mid-April to mid-September. The exact times change from year to year, so it's wise to call in advance if you're arriving at either end of the season.

Nudist camping grounds (marked FKK) are among the best, as their secluded locations ensure peace and quiet. A good site for camping information is www.camping.hr.

HOSTELS

The **Croatian YHA** (☎01-48 29 291; www.hfhs.hr; Savska 5/1, Zagreb) operates youth hostels in Dubrovnik, Zagreb and Pula. Nonmembers pay an additional 10KN per person per day for a stamp on a welcome card; six stamps entitle you to membership. The Croatian YHA can also provide information about private youth hostels in Dubrovnik and Zagreb.

HOTELS

In August, some hotels may demand a surcharge for stays of less than three or four nights, but this is usually waived during the rest of the year, when prices drop steeply.

Breakfast is included in the prices for all hotels.

PRIVATE ROOMS

The best value for money in Croatia is a private room or apartment, often within or attached to a local home – the equivalent of small private guesthouses in other countries.

You'll pay a 30% surcharge for stays of less than four or three nights and sometimes 50% or even 100% more for a one-night stay; it may be waived in the low season. Some will even insist on a seven-night minimum stay in the high season.

Whether you rent from an agency or rent from the owners privately, don't hesitate to bargain, especially for longer stays.

If you land in a room or apartment without a blue *sobe* or *apartmani* sign outside, the proprietor is renting to you illegally (ie, not paying residence tax). They will probably be reluctant to provide their full name or phone number and you'll have absolutely no recourse in case of a problem.

Activities

There are numerous outdoorsy activities in Croatia.

Cycling Croatia has become a popular destination for cycle enthusiasts. See www.bicikl.hr and www.pedala.com.hr.

Diving Most coastal and island resorts have dive shops. For more info see the **Croatian Association of Diving Tourism** (www.croprodive.info), **Croatian Diving Federation** (www.diving-hrs.hr) and **Pro Diving Croatia** (www.diving.hr).

Hiking For information about hiking in Croatia, see the **Croatian Mountaineering Association** (www.plsavez.hr).

Kayaking and rafting Zagreb-based **Huck Finn** (www.huck-finn.hr) is a good contact for sea and river kayaking packages as well as rafting.

Rock climbing and caving For details, contact the Croatian Mountaineering Association or check its speleological department website at www.speleologija.hr.

Business Hours

Hours can vary across the year.

Banks 9am to 7pm Monday to Friday, 8am to 1pm or 9am to 2pm Saturday

Bars and cafes 8am to midnight

Offices 8am to 4pm or 9am to 5pm Monday to Friday, 8am to 1pm or 9am to 2pm Saturday

Restaurants noon to 11pm or midnight, closed Sunday out of peak season

Shops 8am to 8pm Monday to Friday, to 2pm or 3pm Saturday

Embassies & Consulates

The following are all in Zagreb.

Australian Embassy (☎01-48 91 200; Nova Ves 11, Kaptol Centar)

Canadian Embassy (☎01-48 81 200; Prilaz Gjure Deželića 4)

New Zealand Embassy (☎01-46 12 060; Vlaška 50a)

UK Embassy (☎01-60 09 100; I Lučića 4)

US Embassy (☎01-66 12 200; Thomas Jefferson 2)

Food

Prices in this chapter are based on a main course.

€ less than 80KN

€€ 80KN to 150KN

€€€ more than 150KN

Money

CREDIT CARDS

Amex, MasterCard, Visa and Diners Club cards are widely accepted in large hotels, stores and many restaurants, but don't count on cards to pay for private accommodation or meals in small restaurants. You'll find ATMs accepting MasterCard, Maestro, Cirrus, Plus and Visa in most bus and train stations, airports, all major cities and most small towns.

CURRENCY

Croatia uses the kuna (KN). Commonly circulated banknotes come in denominations of 500, 200, 100, 50, 20, 10 and five kuna. Each kuna is divided into 100 lipa. You'll find silver-coloured 50- and 20-lipa coins, and bronze-coloured 10-lipa coins.

Public Holidays

New Year's Day 1 January

Epiphany 6 January

Easter Monday March/April

Labour Day 1 May

Corpus Christi 10 June

Day of Antifascist Resistance 22 June; marks the outbreak of resistance in 1941

Statehood Day 25 June

Homeland Thanksgiving Day 5 August

Feast of the Assumption 15 August

Independence Day 8 October

All Saints' Day 1 November

Christmas 25 and 26 December

Telephone

MOBILE PHONES

If you have an unlocked 3G phone, you can buy a SIM card for about 50KN. You can choose from four network providers: **VIP** (www.vip.hr), **T-Mobile** (www.t-mobile.hr), **Tomato** (www.tomato.com.hr) and **Tele2** (www.tele2.hr).

PHONE CODES

To call Croatia from abroad, dial your international access code, then ☎385 (the country code for Croatia), then the area code (without the initial ☎0) and the local number.

To call from region to region within Croatia, start with the area code (with the initial 0); drop it when dialling within the same code.

Phone numbers with the prefix ☎060 are either free or charged at a premium rate, so watch the small print. Phone numbers that begin with ☎09 are mobile phone numbers.

Tourist Information

Croatian National Tourist Board (www.croatia.hr) is a good source of info.

Visas

Citizens of the EU, USA, Canada, Australia, New Zealand, Israel, Ireland, Singapore and the UK do not need a visa for stays of up to 90 days. South Africans must apply for a 90-day visa in Pretoria. Contact any Croatian embassy, consulate or travel agency abroad for information.

Getting There & Away

Air

There are direct flights to Croatia from a number of European cities; however, there are no nonstop flights from North America to Croatia.

Major airports in Croatia include the following.

Dubrovnik Airport (www.airport-dubrovnik.hr) Nonstop flights from Brussels, Cologne, Frankfurt, Hanover, London (Gatwick and Stansted), Manchester, Munich and Stuttgart.

Pula Airport (www.airport-pula.com) Nonstop flights from London (Gatwick) and Manchester.

Split Airport (www.split-airport.hr) Nonstop flights from Cologne, Frankfurt, London, Munich, Prague and Rome.

Zagreb Airport (www.zagreb-airport.hr) Direct flights from all European capitals, plus Cologne, Hamburg and Stuttgart.

Land

Croatia has border crossings with Hungary, Slovenia, BiH, Serbia and Montenegro.

Buses run to destinations throughout Europe.

From Austria, **Eurolines** (www.eurolines.com) operates buses from Vienna to several destinations in Croatia.

Bus services between Germany and Croatia are good, and fares are cheaper than the train. All buses are handled by **Deutsche Touring GmbH** (www.deutsche-touring.de); there are no Deutsche Touring offices in Croatia, but numerous travel agencies and bus stations sell its tickets.

Sea

Regular boats from the following companies connect Croatia with Italy:

Blue Line (www.blueline-ferries.com)

Commodore Cruises (www.commodore-cruises.hr)

Emilia Romagna Lines (www.emiliaromagnalines.it)

Jadrolinija (www.jadrolinija.hr)

Split Tours (www.splittours.hr)

SNAV (www.snav.com)

Venezia Lines (www.venezialines.com)

Getting Around

Air

Croatia Airlines (☎01-66 76 555; www.croatiaairlines.hr) is the only carrier for flights within Croatia. There are daily flights between Zagreb and Dubrovnik, Pula and Split.

Boat

Jadrolinija (www.jadrolinija.hr) operates an extensive network of car ferries and catamarans along the Adriatic coast. Ferries are a lot more comfortable than buses, though somewhat more expensive.

Services operate year-round, though they are less frequent in winter. Cabins should be booked a week ahead. Deck space is usually available on all sailings.

You must buy tickets in advance at an agency or a Jadrolinija office. Tickets are not sold on board. In summer months, you need to check in two hours in advance if you bring a car.

Bus

Bus services are excellent and relatively inexpensive. There are often a number of different companies handling each route so prices can vary substantially. Luggage stowed in the baggage compartment under the bus costs extra (7KN a piece, including insurance).

At large stations, bus tickets must be purchased at the office, not from drivers. Try to book ahead to be sure of a seat, especially in the summer.

Car & Motorcycle

Croatia's motorway connecting Zagreb with Split is only a few years old and makes some routes much faster.

CAR HIRE

In order to rent a car you must be 21 or over, with a valid driving licence and a valid credit card.

Independent local companies are often much cheaper than the international chains, but the big companies offer one-way rentals.

DRIVING LICENCE

Any valid driving licence is sufficient to drive legally and rent a car; an international driving licence is not necessary.

The **Hrvatski Autoklub** (HAK, Croatian Auto Club; ☎46 40 800; www.hak.hr; Avenija Dubrovnik 44) offers help and advice. For help on the road, you can contact the nationwide **HAK road assistance** (Vučna Služba; ☎987).

Local Transport

The main form of local transport is bus. Buses in major cities such as Dubrovnik and

Split run about once every 20 minutes, less on Sunday. A ride is usually around 10KN, with a small discount if you buy tickets at a *tisak* (newsstand).

Bus transport within the islands is infrequent since most people have their own cars.

Train

Trains are less frequent than buses but more comfortable. For information about schedules, prices and services, contact **Croatian Railways** (Hrvatske Željeznice; ☎060 333 444; www.hznet.hr).

Zagreb is the hub for Croatia's less-than-extensive train system. No trains run along the coast and only a few coastal cities are connected with Zagreb.

Baggage is free on trains; most stations have left-luggage services charging around 15KN a piece per day.

EU residents who hold an InterRail pass can use it in Croatia for free travel, but you're unlikely to take enough trains to justify the cost.

Czech Republic

Includes »

Prague 297
Karlštejn 307
Kutná Hora 308
Bohemia 308
Karlovy Vary 308
Plzeň 310
Český Krumlov 311
Moravia 312
Brno 312
Telč 315
Understand Czech Republic 315
Survival Guide 316

Best Places to Eat

- » Sansho (p304)
- » Moritz (p313)
- » Koishi (p314)
- » Cukrkávalimonáda (p304)

Best Places to Stay

- » Mosaic House (p303)
- » Fusion Hotel (p303)
- » Hostel Mitte (p314)
- » Savic Hotel (p304)

Why Go?

Since the fall of communism in 1989 and the opening of Central and eastern Europe, Prague has evolved into one of Europe's most popular travel destinations. The city offers an intact medieval core that transports you back 500 years. The 14th-century Charles Bridge, traversing two historic neighbourhoods, is one of the continent's most beautiful sights. The city is not just about history. It's a vital urban centre with a rich array of cultural offerings. Outside the capital, castles and palaces abound – including the audacious hilltop chateau at Český Krumlov – which illuminate the stories of powerful families and individuals whose influence was felt throughout Europe.

When to Go

Prague

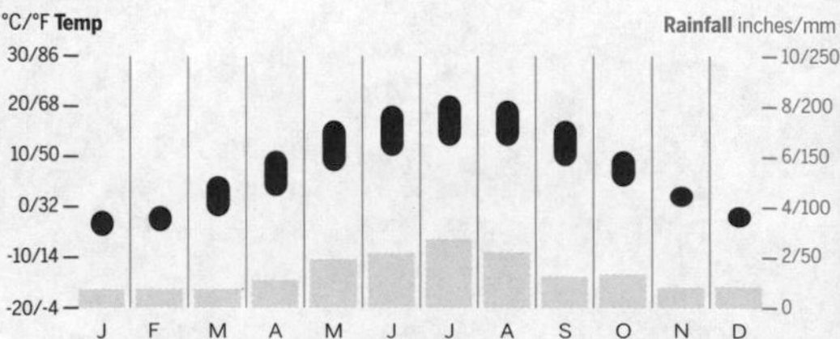

May Prague comes alive with festivals from classical music to fringe arts.

Jul Karlovy Vary shows off its arty side at the sleepy spa town's annual film festival.

Dec Prague's Christmas Market draws visitors from around the world.

Connections

The Czech Republic lies along major European road and rail lines and is a convenient hub for exploring neighbouring countries. Prague has excellent rail connections to Berlin as well as to Kraków, Bratislava, Budapest and Vienna.

ITINERARIES

One Week

Experience Prague's exciting combination of its tumultuous past and energetic present. Top experiences include the grandeur of Prague Castle, Josefov's Jewish Museum, and getting lost amid the bewildering labyrinth of the Old Town. Take an essential day trip to Karlštejn, and then head south to Český Krumlov for a few days of riverside R&R.

Two Weeks

Begin in Prague before heading west for the spa scene at Karlovy Vary. Balance the virtue and vice ledger with a few Bohemian brews in Plzeň before heading south for relaxation and rigour around Český Krumlov. Head east to the Renaissance grandeur of Telč and Brno's cosmopolitan galleries and museums. From the Moravian capital, it's just a skip to stately Olomouc.

Essential Food & Drink

» **Beer** Czechs claim to have the best beer *(pivo)* in the world.

» **Dumplings** Every culture has its starchy side dish; for Czechs it's *knedliky* – big bread dumplings.

» **Pork** Move over beef, pork *(vepřové maso)* is king here.

» **Becherovka** A shot of this sweetish herbal liqueur from Karlovy Vary is a popular way to start (or end) a big meal.

» **Carp** This lowly fish is given pride of place every Christmas at the centre of the family meal.

AT A GLANCE

» **Currency** Crown (Kč)

» **Language** Czech

» **Money** ATMs all over; banks open Monday to Friday

» **Visas** Schengen rules apply; visas not required for most nationalities

Fast Facts

» **Area** 78,864 sq km

» **Capital** Prague

» **Country code** ☎420

» **Emergency** ☎112

Exchange Rates

Australia	A$1	21.06Kč
Canada	C$1	19.84Kč
Euro Zone	€1	25.77Kč
Japan	¥100	21.37Kč
New Zealand	NZ$1	16.88Kč
UK	UK£1	30.51Kč
USA	US$1	20.17Kč

Set Your Budget

» **Budget hotel room** 1500Kč

» **Two-course meal** 300Kč

» **Museum entrance** 150Kč

» **Beer** 40Kč

» **Prague metro-tram ticket** 32Kč

Resources

» **Czech Tourism** (www.czechtourism.com)

» **Prague Welcome** (www.praguewelcome.cz)

Czech Republic Highlights

1. Stroll across the **Charles Bridge** (p301) in the early morning or late evening when the crowds thin out.
2. Enjoy a beer in the open air on a summer evening at Prague's **Letná Beer Garden** (p305).
3. Join the appreciative throngs at Prague's **Astronomical Clock** (p300) at the top of the hour.
4. Repair to **Český Krumlov** (p311) to see the prettiest town in central Europe.
5. Tour the **Pilsner Urquell Brewery** (p310) in Plzeň to see where it all started.
6. Amble through the stately town of **Olomouc** (p313), the most amazing place you've never heard of.

PRAGUE

POP 1.22 MILLION

It's the perfect irony of Prague: you are lured here by the past, but compelled to linger by the present and the future. Fill your days with its illustrious artistic and architectural heritage – from Gothic and Renaissance to art nouveau and cubist. If Prague's seasonal legions of tourists wear you down, that's OK. Just drink a glass of the country's legendary lager, relax and rest reassured that quiet moments still exist: a private dawn on Charles Bridge, a chilled beer in the Letná Beer Garden as you gaze upon the glorious cityscape of Staré Město or getting lost in the intimate lanes of Malá Strana.

Sights

Prague nestles on the Vltava River, separating Hradčany (the Castle district) and Malá Strana (Lesser Quarter) on the west bank, from Staré Město (Old Town) and Nové Město (New Town) on the east.

HRADČANY

TOP CHOICE Prague Castle CASTLE

(Pražský hrad; Map p302; ☎224 372 423; www.hrad.cz; Hradčanské náměstí; grounds free, sights adult/concession full 350/175Kc, reduced 250/125Kc; ⌚grounds 5am-midnight Apr-Oct, 6am-11pm Nov-Mar, gardens 10am-6pm Apr & Oct, to 7pm May & Sep, to 9pm Jul & Aug, closed Nov-Mar, historic buildings 9am-6pm Apr-Oct, to 4pm Nov-Mar; Ⓜ Malostranská, 🚋22) Hradčany (the Castle District in Czech) is home to Prague Castle, the city's most popular tourist attraction. The castle has traditionally been the seat of Czech rulers and today functions as the official residence of the president. Entry to the grounds is free, but to go inside any of the sights, including St Vitus Cathedral, requires a combined-entry ticket.

The castle complex's main attractions include the Old Royal Palace, the **Basilica of St George** (Bazilika Sv Jiří; Map p302; Jiřské náměstí), **Golden Lane** (Zlatá ulička; Map p302;), and St Vitus Cathedral. All four of these sights are included in the lower 'reduced' price admission (which will suffice for most visitors). The more-expensive 'full' admission covers entry to all of the sights in the Castle complex, including smaller galleries and attractions not listed here.

Old Royal Palace

(Starý královský Palác; Map p302) The Old Royal Palace is one of the oldest parts of the castle, dating from 1135. At its heart is the grand **Vladislav Hall** and the **Bohemian Chancellery**, scene of the famous Defenestration of Prague.

St Vitus Cathedral

(Katedrála Sv Víta; Map p302; ☎257 531 622; www.katedralasvatehovita.cz; III nádvoří, Pražský hrad; ⌚9am-6pm Mon-Sat & noon-5pm Sun Apr-Oct, 9am-4pm Mon-Sat & noon-4pm Sun Nov-Mar; Ⓜ Malostranská, 🚋22) St Vitus Cathedral anchors the castle grounds and is visible from around the city. Though it looks ancient, it was only completed in 1929. Its treasures include the baroque silver **tomb of St John of Nepomuk**, the ornate **Chapel of St Wenceslas**, and **art nouveau stained glass** by Alfons Mucha.

Lobkowicz Palace

(Lobkovický Palác; Map p302; ☎233 312 925; www.lobkowicz.cz; Jiřská 3; adult/concession/family 275/200/690Kč; ⌚10.30am-6pm) Also within the castle complex, the 16th-century Lobkowicz Palace houses the 'Princely Collections', which includes priceless paintings, furniture and musical memorabilia. Entry here is not included in the combined ticket for the castle sights.

Šternberg Palace GALLERY

(Šternberský palác; Map p302; ☎233 090 570; www.ngprague.cz; Hradčanské náměstí 15; adult/child 150/80Kč; ⌚10am-6pm Tue-Sun; 🚋22) Just outside the castle's main gate, Šternberg Palace is home to the National Gallery's collection of 14th- to 18th-century European art, including works by Goya and Rembrandt.

STARÉ MĚSTO

The Old Town (Staré Město) is the city's oldest quarter and home to its main market, **Old Town Square** (Staroměstské náměstí; Map p298; Ⓜ Staroměstská), often simply called Staromák. The square has functioned as the centre of the Old Town since the 10th century.

TOP CHOICE Old Town Hall HISTORIC BUILDING

(Staroměstská radnice; Map p298; ☎12444; www.prazskeveze.cz; Staroměstské náměstí 1; guided tour adult/child 105/85Kč; ⌚11am-6pm Mon, 9am-6pm Tue-Sun; Ⓜ Staroměstská) The Old Town Hall, identified by a large clock tower on top, was founded in 1338. It's a hotchpotch of medieval buildings acquired over centuries. The town hall has several historic attractions, and hosts art exhibitions on the ground floor. The **tower** view is the best in town.

Central Prague

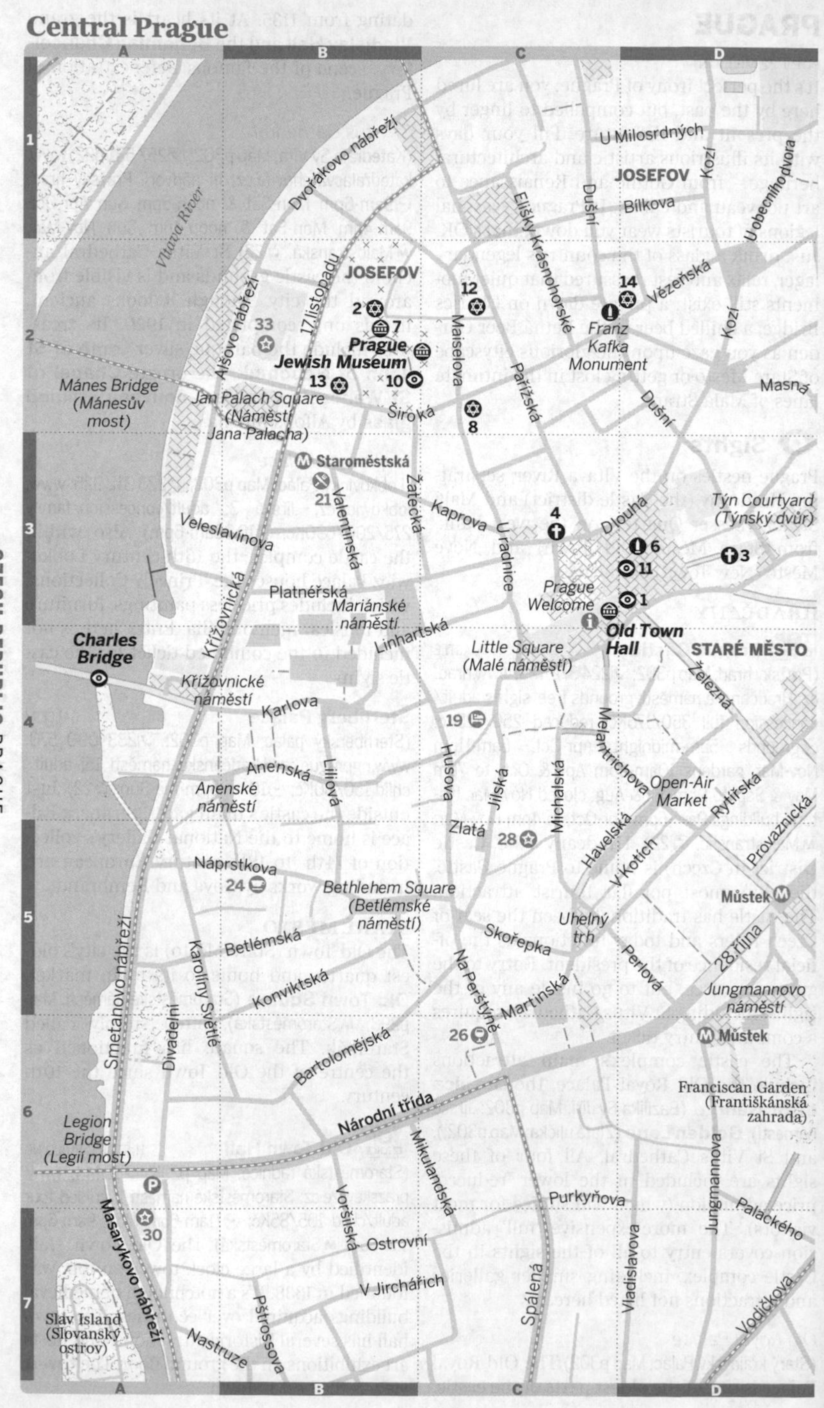

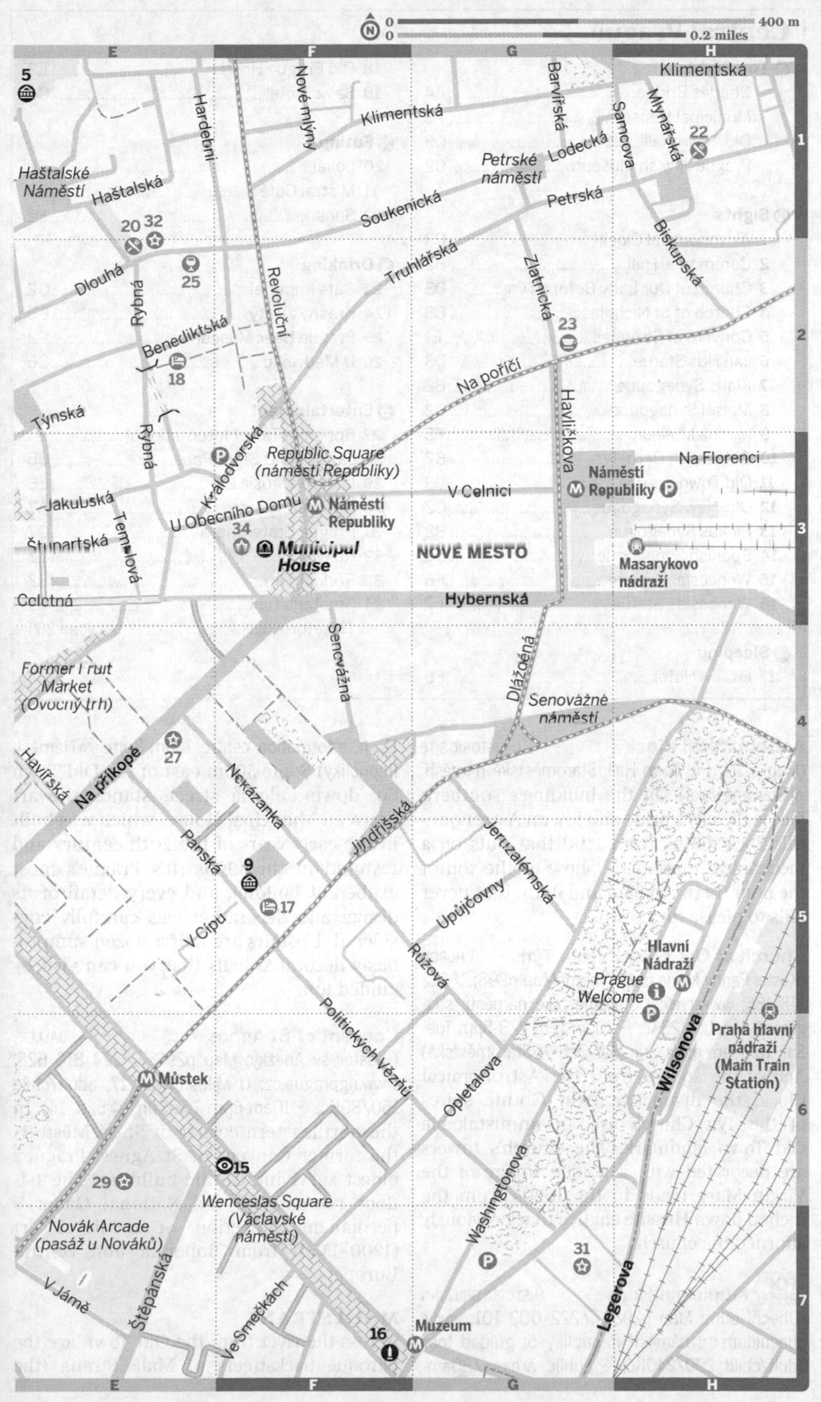
0 400 m
0 0.2 miles
E
F
G
H
1
2
3
4
5
6
7
Klimentská
Nové mlýny
Hardeční
Barvířská
Samcova
Mlynářská
Lodecká
Petrské náměstí
Petrská
Haštalské Náměstí
Haštalská
Soukenická
Biskupská
Truhlářská
Dlouhá
Revoluční
Zlatnická
Rybná
Benediktská
Na poříčí
Havlíčkova
Týnská
Králodvorská
Republic Square (náměstí Republiky)
Na Florenci
Náměstí Republiky
V Celnici
Jakubská
U Obecního Domu
Štupartská
Templová
Municipal House
NOVÉ MESTO
Masarykovo nádraží
Celetná
Hybernská
Sencvážná
Former Fruit Market (Ovocný trh)
Dlážděná
Senovážné náměstí
Havířská
Na příkopě
Nekázanka
Jindřišská
Jeruzalémská
Panská
Upůjčovny
V Cípu
Růžova
Hlavní Nádraží
Prague Welcome
Politických Vězňů
Wilsonova
Praha hlavní nádraží (Main Train Station)
Opletalova
Můstek
Washingtonova
Wenceslas Square (Václavské náměstí)
Novák Arcade (pasáž u Nováků)
V Jámě
Štěpánská
Ve Smečkách
Muzeum
Legerova
5
22
20
32
25
23
18
34
27
9
17
29
15
31
16
CZECH REPUBLIC PRAGUE

Central Prague

Top Sights

Charles Bridge ... A4
Municipal House ... F3
Old Town Hall ... C3
Prague Jewish Museum ... C2

Sights

1 Astronomical Clock ... D3
2 Ceremonial Hall ... B2
3 Church of Our Lady Before Týn ... D3
4 Church of St Nicholas ... C3
5 Convent of St Agnes ... E1
6 Jan Hus Statue ... D3
7 Klaus Synagogue ... B2
8 Maisel Synagogue ... C2
9 Mucha Museum ... F5
10 Old Jewish Cemetery ... B2
11 Old Town Square ... D3
12 Old-New Synagogue ... C2
13 Pinkas Synagogue ... B2
14 Spanish Synagogue ... D2
15 Wenceslas Square ... F6
16 Wenceslas Statue ... F7

Sleeping

17 Fusion Hotel ... F5
18 Old Prague Hostel ... E2
19 Savic Hotel ... C4

Eating

20 Lokál ... E2
21 Mistral Café ... B3
22 Sansho ... H1

Drinking

23 Café Imperial ... G2
24 Krásný ztráty ... B5
25 Prague Beer Museum ... E2
26 U Medvídků ... C6

Entertainment

27 Bohemia Ticket International ... E4
28 Jazz Club U Staré Paní ... C5
29 Lucerna Music Bar ... E6
30 National Theatre ... A7
31 Prague State Opera ... G7
32 Roxy ... E2
33 Rudolfinum ... B2
34 Smetana Hall ... F3
Ticketpro ... (see 29)

Astronomical Clock HISTORIC SITE
(Map p298; Old Town Hall, Staroměstské náměstí; MStaroměstská) On the building's southern face is the city's pride and joy, an Astronomical Clock dating from 1490 that puts on a mechanical marionette show at the top of the hour (between 9am and 9pm) that never fails to please the crowds.

Church of Our Lady Before Týn CHURCH
(Kostel Panny Marie před Týnem; Map p298; 222 318 186; www.tyn.cz; Staroměstské náměstí; suggested donation 25Kč; 10am-1pm & 3-5pm Tue-Sat, 10.30am-noon Sun Mar-Oct; MStaroměstská) Across the square from the Astronomical Clock, the distinctive twin Gothic spires of the Týn Church are an unmistakable Old Town landmark. The church's towers are decorated with a golden image of the Virgin Mary made in the 1620s from the melted down Hussite chalice that previously adorned the church.

TOP CHOICE **Municipal House** HISTORIC BUILDING
(Obecní dům; Map p298; 222 002 101; www.obecnidum.cz; náměstí Republiky 5; guided tour adult/child 290/240Kč; public areas 7.30am-11pm, information centre 10am-8pm; MNáměstí Republiky) Some 500m east of the Old Town Sq, down Celetná street, stands the art nouveau Municipal House, which was built in the early years of the 20th century and restored in the 1990s. It's Prague's most exuberant building and every detail of its design and decoration was carefully considered. Upstairs are half a dozen sumptuously decorated halls that you can visit by guided tour.

Convent of St Agnes GALLERY
(Klášter sv Anežky; Map p298; 224 810 628; www.ngprague.cz; U Milosrdných 17; adult/child 150/80Kč; 10am-6pm Tue-Sun; 5, 8, 14) In the northeastern corner of Staré Město is the former Convent of St Agnes, Prague's oldest surviving Gothic building. The 1st-floor rooms hold the National Gallery's permanent collection of medieval art (1200–1550) from Bohemia and central Europe.

MALÁ STRANA

Across the river from the Old Town are the baroque backstreets of Malá Strana (the

Lesser Quarter), built in the 17th and 18th centuries by victorious Catholic clerics and noblemen on the foundations of their Protestant predecessors' Renaissance palaces.

TOP CHOICE **Charles Bridge** BRIDGE
(Karlův most; Map p298; Malostranské náměstí; 17, 18 to Karlovy lázně) Strolling across the 14th-century Charles Bridge is everybody's favourite Prague activity. In 1357 Charles IV commissioned Peter Parler (the architect of St Vitus Cathedral) to replace an even older bridge, which had been washed away by floods in 1342. The new bridge was completed in 1390, but took Charles' name only in the 19th century. The statues were added starting in the 17th century.

FREE **Church of St Nicholas** CHURCH
(Kostel sv Mikuláše; Map p298; Staroměstské náměstí; noon-4pm Mon, 10am-4pm Tue-Sat, noon-3pm Sun; M Staroměstská) Malá Strana is dominated by the huge green cupola of St Nicholas Church, one of central Europe's finest baroque buildings. It was begun by famed German baroque architect Kristof Dientzenhofer; his son Kilian continued the work and Anselmo Lurago finished the job in 1755.

NOVÉ MĚSTO

Nové Město (New Town) surrounds the Old Town on all sides and was originally laid out in the 14th century. Its main public area is **Wenceslas Square** (Václavské náměstí; Map p298; M Můstek, Muzeum), lined with shops, banks and restaurants, and dominated by a **statue of St Wenceslas** (sv Václav; Map p298; Václavské náměstí; M Muzeum) on horseback.

National Museum MUSEUM
(Národní muzeum; 224 497 111; www.nm.cz; Václavské náměstí 68; closed until 2015; M Muzeum) Looming above the square is the neo-Renaissance hulk of the National Museum, designed in the 1880s by Josef Schulz as an architectural symbol of the Czech National Revival. The museum normally displays rocks, fossils and stuffed animals but it was closed for renovation during our research and not expected to reopen until 2015.

Mucha Museum GALLERY
(Muchovo muzuem; Map p298; 221 451 333; www.mucha.cz; Panská 7; adult/child 180/120Kč; 10am-6pm; M Můstek) Just to the northeast of the square, the fascinating Mucha Museum features the sensuous art nouveau posters, paintings and decorative panels of

PRAGUE'S JEWISH MUSEUM

The **Prague Jewish Museum** (Židovské muzeum Praha; Map p298; 222 317 191; www.jewishmuseum.cz; Reservation Centre, U starého hřbitova 3a; ordinary ticket adult/child 300/200Kč, combined ticket incl entry to Old-New Synagogue 480/320Kč; 9am-6pm Sun-Fri Apr-Oct, to 4.30pm Nov-Mar; M Staroměstská), a collection of four synagogues – the **Maisel** (Maiselova synagóga; Map p298; Maiselova 10), **Pinkas** (Pinkasova synagóga; Map p298; www.jewishmuseum.cz; Široká 3), **Spanish** (Spanélská synagóga; Map p298; Vězeňská 1;) and **Klaus** (Klauzová synagóga; Map p298; U starého hřbitova 1; 17, 18) – the former **Ceremonial Hall** (Obřadní síň; Map p298; 17) and the **Old Jewish Cemetery** (Starý židovský hřbitov; Map p298; Pinkas Synagogue, Široká 3), is one of the city's treasures. The monuments are clustered together in **Josefov**, a small corner of the Old Town that was home to Prague's Jews for some 800 years before an urban renewal project at the start of the 20th century and the Nazi occupation during WWII brought this all to an end.

The monuments cannot be visited separately but require a combined-entry ticket good for all of the sights and available at ticket windows throughout Josefov. A fifth synagogue, the **Old-New Synagogue** (Staronová synagóga; Map p298; www.jewishmuseum.cz; Červená 2; adult/child 200/140Kč; 9am-6pm Sun-Fri Apr-Oct, to 4.30pm Nov-Mar; 17), is still used for religious services, and requires a separate ticket or additional fee.

The museum was first established in 1906 to preserve objects from synagogues that were demolished during the slum clearance at the turn of the 20th century. The collection grew richer as a result of one of the most grotesquely ironic acts of WWII. During the Nazi occupation, the Germans took over management of the museum in order to create a 'museum of an extinct race'. To that end, they brought in objects from destroyed Jewish communities throughout Bohemia and Moravia.

Prague Castle

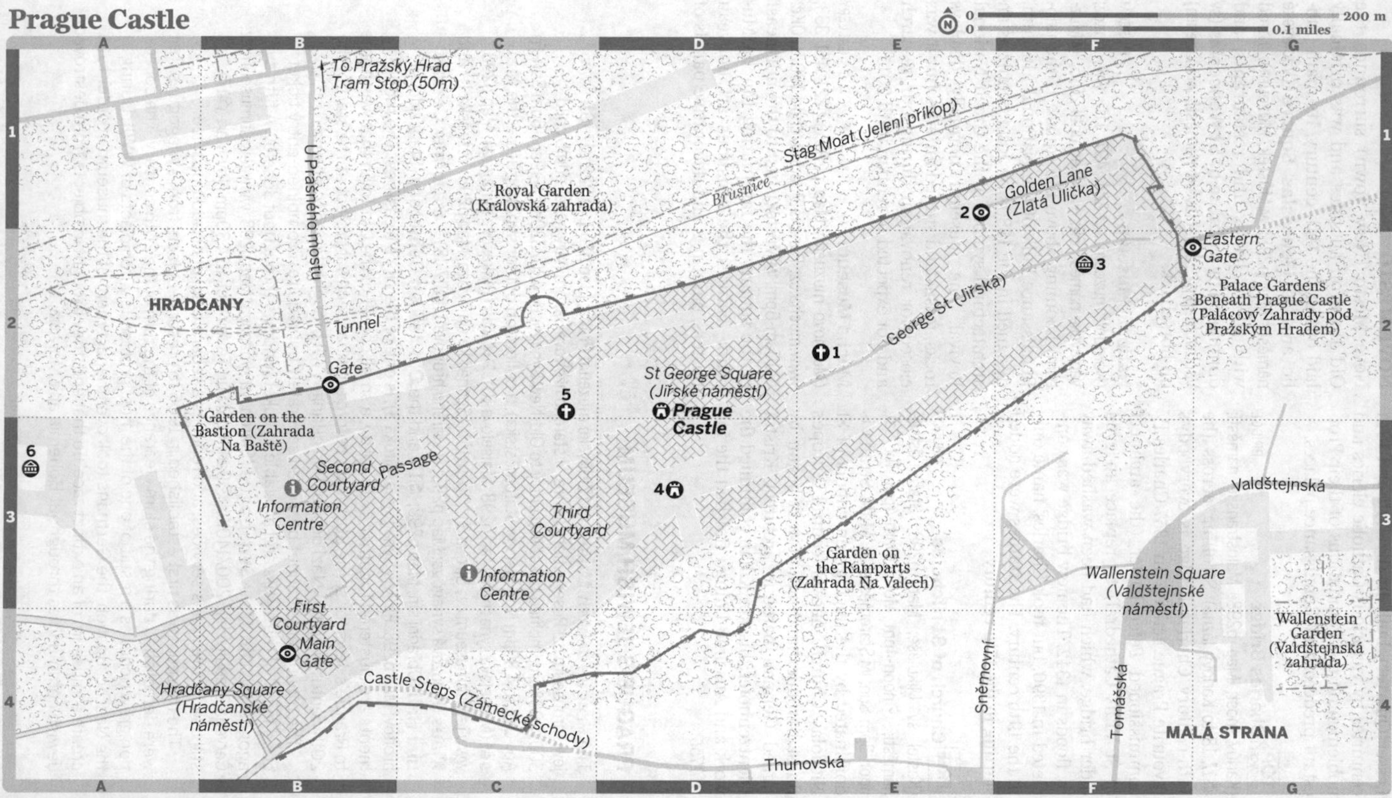

Prague Castle

Top Sights

Prague Castle D2

Sights

1 Basilica of St George E2
2 Golden Lane E1
3 Lobkowicz Palace F2
4 Old Royal Palace D3
5 St Vitus Cathedral C2
6 Šternberg Palace A3

Alfons Mucha (1860–1939). The exhibits include countless artworks showing Mucha's trademark Slavic maidens with flowing hair and piercing blue eyes.

FREE Vyšehrad HISTORIC AREA
(www.praha-vysehrad.cz; ⌚9.30am-6pm Apr-Oct, to 5pm Nov-Mar; Ⓜ Vyšehrad) Take a picnic to Vyšehrad on the southern edge of Nové Město. This ancient hilltop fortress has superb views.

Festivals & Events

Prague Spring CLASSICAL MUSIC
(www.festival.cz) In May, the Czech Republic's biggest annual cultural event, and one of Europe's most important festivals of classical music.

Prague Fringe Festival ARTS
(www.praguefringe.com) Eclectic action in late May and early June.

Christmas Market SEASONAL FESTIVAL
Held during the month of December in the Old Town Sq.

Sleeping

Fusion Hotel HOTEL, HOSTEL €
(Map p298; ☎226 222 800; www.fusionhotels.com; Panská 9; dm/d/tr 400/2000/2600Kč; @ 📶; 🚊3, 9, 14, 24) Billing itself as an 'affordable design hotel', Fusion certainly has style in abundance. From the revolving bar and the funky sofas that litter the public areas, to the individually decorated bedrooms that resemble miniature modern-art galleries – all white walls and black trim with tiny splashes of colour – the place exudes 'cool'.

Czech Inn HOSTEL, HOTEL €
(☎267 267 600; www.czech-inn.com; Francouzská 76, Vinohrady; dm 285-385Kč, s/d 1320/1540Kč, apt from 1650Kč; P ⊖ @ 📶; 🚊4, 22) The Czech Inn calls itself a hostel, but the boutique label wouldn't be out of place. Everything seems sculpted by an industrial designer, from the iron beds to the brushed-steel flooring and minimalist square sinks. The Czech Inn offers a variety of accommodation, from standard hostel dorm rooms to good-value private doubles (with or without attached bathroom) and apartments.

Mosaic House HOTEL, HOSTEL €€
(☎221 595 350; www.mosaichouse.com; Odboru 4; s/d from 1840/2520Kč, dm from 300Kč; ⊖ 📶; Ⓜ Karlovo Náměstí) A blend of four-star hotel and boutique hostel, Mosaic House is a cornucopia of designer detail, from the original 1930s mosaic in the entrance hall to the silver spray-painted tree branches used as clothes-hanging racks. The backpackers dorms are kept separate from the private rooms, but have the same high-quality decor and design.

Old Prague Hostel HOSTEL €
(Map p298; ☎224 829 058; www.oldpraguehostel.com; Benediktská 2; dm from 375Kč, s/d from 1000/1200Kč; ⊖ @ 📶; Ⓜ Náměstí Republiky) Cheerful and welcoming, with colourful homemade murals brightening the walls, this is one of Prague's most sociable hostels, with a good mix of people from backpackers to families. Facilities are good, with lockers in the dorms, luggage storage and 24-hour reception.

Lokál Inn INN €€
(☎257 014 800; www.lokalinn.cz; Míšeňská 12; d/ste from 3475/4475Kč; ⊖ 📶; 🚊12, 20, 22) Polished parquet floors and painted wooden ceilings abound in this 18th-century house designed by Prague's premier baroque architect, Kilian Dientzenhofer. The eight rooms and four suites are elegant and uncluttered, and the rustic, stone-vaulted cellars house a deservedly popular pub and restaurant run by the same folk as Lokál (p304).

Eating

Mistral Café BISTRO €
(Map p298; ☎222 317 737; www.mistralcafe.cz; Valentinská 11; mains 130-250Kč; ⌚9am-11pm Mon-Fri, 10am-11pm Sat & Sun; 📶; Ⓜ Staroměstská) Is this the coolest bistro in the Old Town? Pale stone, bleached birchwood and potted shrubs make for a clean, crisp, modern look, and the clientele of local students and office workers clearly appreciate the competitively priced, well-prepared food. Fish and chips

SPLURGE

From the complimentary glass of wine when you arrive to the comfy king-size beds, the **Savic Hotel** (Map p298; ☎224 248 555; www.savic.eu; Jilská 7; r from 4125Kč; ❄@📶; Ⓜ Můstek) certainly knows how to make you feel welcome. Housed in the former monastery of St Giles, on a back street of the Old Town, the hotel is bursting with character and full of delightful period details including old stone fireplaces, beautiful painted timber ceilings and fragments of frescos.

in crumpled brown paper with lemon and black-pepper mayo – yum!

Cukrkávalimonáda INTERNATIONAL €
(☎257 225 396; www.cukrkavalimonada.com; Lázeňská 7; mains 100-180Kč; ⏰9am-7pm; 🚋12, 20, 22) A cute little cafe-cum-restaurant that combines minimalist modern styling with Renaissance-era painted timber roof-beams, CKL offers fresh pastas, frittatas, ciabattas, salads and pancakes (sweet and savoury) by day and a slightly more sophisticated bistro menu in the evening.

Lokál CZECH €
(Map p298; ☎222 316 265; http://lokal-dlouha.ambi.cz; Dlouhá 33; mains 100-200Kč; ⏰11am-1am Mon-Fri, noon-1am Sat, noon-10pm Sun; 🚭; 🚋5, 8, 14) Who'd have thought it possible? A classic Czech beer hall (albeit with slick modern decor); excellent *tankové pivo* (tanked Pilsner Urquell); a daily changing menu of traditional Bohemian dishes; smiling, efficient, friendly service; and a large no-smoking area.

Kofein SPANISH €€
(☎273 132 145; www.ikofein.cz; Nitranská 9, Vinohrady; tapas plates 55-75Kč; ⏰11am-midnight Mon-Fri, 5pm-midnight Sat & Sun; 📶✏; Ⓜ Jiřího z Poděbrad, 🚋11) One of the hottest restaurants in town is this Spanish-style tapas place not far from the Jiřího z Poděbrad metro station. Descend into a lively space to see a red-faced chef minding the busy grill. Our faves include marinated trout with horseradish and pork-belly confit with celeriac.

U Modré Kachničky CZECH €€€
(☎257 320 308; www.umodrekachnicky.cz; Nebovidská 6; mains 450-600Kč; ⏰noon-4pm & 6.30pm-midnight; 🚋12, 20, 22) A plush 1930s-style hunting lodge hidden away on a quiet side street, 'At the Blue Duckling' is a pleasantly old-fashioned place with quiet, candle-lit nooks perfect for a romantic dinner.

Sansho ASIAN, FUSION €€
(Map p298; ☎222 317 425; www.sansho.cz; Petrská 25; mains 120-300Kč, 6-course dinner 750Kč; ⏰11.30am-10.30pm Tue-Thu, to 11.30pm Fri, 6-11.30pm Sat; 🚭; 🚋3, 8, 24) Friendly and informal best describes the atmosphere at this ground-breaking restaurant where British chef Paul Day champions Czech farmers by sourcing all his meat and vegetables locally. There's no menu – the waiter will explain what dishes are available, depending on market produce – typical dishes include salmon sashimi, pork belly with Asian spices, and 12-hour beef rendang.

Drinking

Czech beers are among the world's best. The most famous brands are Budvar, Plzeňský Prazdroj (Pilsner Urquell) and Prague's own Staropramen. Independent microbreweries and regional Czech beers are also becoming more popular in Prague.

Pivovarský Klub BEER HALL
(☎222 315 777; www.gastroinfo.cz/pivoklub; Křižíkova 17, Karlín; ⏰11am-11.30pm; Ⓜ Florenc) This bar is to beer what the Bodleian Library is to books – wall-to-wall shelves lined with myriad varieties of bottled beer from all over the world, and six guest beers on tap. Perch on a bar stool or head downstairs to the snug cellar and order some of the pub's excellent grub (such as authentic *guláš* with bacon dumplings for 235Kč) to soak up the beer.

U Vystřeleného oka PUB
(☎222 540 465; www.uvoka.cz; U Božích Bojovníků 3, Žižkov; ⏰4.30pm-1am Mon-Sat; 🚋133, 207) You've got to love a pub that has vinyl pads on the wall above the gents' urinals to rest your forehead on. 'The Shot-Out Eye' – the name pays homage to the one-eyed Hussite hero atop the hill behind the pub – is a bohemian (with a small 'b') hostelry with a raucous Friday-night atmosphere where the cheap Pilsner Urquell pulls in a typically heterogeneous crowd.

Prague Beer Museum PUB
(Map p298; ☎732 330 912; www.praguebeermuseum.com; Dlouhá 46; ⏰noon-3am; 🚋5, 8, 14) Although the name seems aimed at the tourist market, this lively and always heaving

pub is very popular with Praguers. There are no fewer than 31 beers on tap (plus an extensive beer menu with tasting notes to guide you).

Letná Beer Garden BEER GARDEN
(Letenský zámeček; ☎233 378 208; www.letensky-zamecek.cz; Letenské sady 341, Bubeneč; ⊙11am-11pm summer only; 🚊1, 8, 15, 25, 26 to Letenské náměstí) No accounting of watering holes would be complete without a nod towards the city's best beer garden, situated at the eastern end of Letná park. Buy a takeaway beer from a small kiosk and grab a picnic table, or sit on a small terrace where you can order beer-by-the-glass and decent pizza.

U Medvídků BEER HALL
(At the Little Bear; Map p298; ☎224 211 916; www.umedvidku.cz; Na Perštýně 7; ⊙beer hall 11.30am-11pm, museum noon-10pm; 📶; Ⓜ Můstek) The most micro of Prague's microbreweries, with a capacity of only 250L, U Medvídků started producing its own beer only in 2005, though its beer hall has been around for years. What it lacks in size, it makes up for in strength – the dark lager produced here is the strongest in the country, with an alcohol content of 11.8%.

Krásný ztráty CAFE
(Map p298; ☎775 755 143; www.krasnyztraty.cz; Náprstkova 10; ⊙9am-1am Mon-Fri, noon-1am Sat & Sun; 📶; 🚊17, 18) This cool cafe doubles as an art gallery and occasional music venue, and is hugely popular with students from nearby Charles University. There are Czech newspapers and books to leaf through, chilled tunes on the sound system, and a menu of gourmet teas and coffees to choose from.

Café Imperial CAFE
(Map p298; ☎246 011 440; www.cafeimperial.cz; Na Poříčí 15; ⊙7am-11pm; Ⓜ Náměstí Republiky) First opened in 1914, and given a complete facelift in 2007, the Imperial is a tour de force of art nouveau tiling – the walls and ceiling are covered in original ceramic tiles, mosaics, sculptured panels and bas-reliefs. The coffee is good, there are cocktails in the evening, and the Czech lunch and dinner offerings are first-rate.

☆ Entertainment

From clubbing to classical music, puppetry to performance art, Prague offers plenty of entertainment. It's an established centre of classical music and jazz. Try the following ticket agencies to see what might be on during your visit and to snag tickets online: **Bohemia Ticket International** (BTI; Map p298; ☎224 215 031; Na příkopě 16, Nové Město; ⊙10am-7pm Mon-Fri, to 5pm Sat, to 3pm Sun) and **Ticketpro** (Map p298; ☎296 333 333; www.ticketpro.cz; Štěpánská 61, Lucerna pasáž; ⊙noon-8.30pm Mon-Fri; Ⓜ Můstek).

Performing Arts

National Theatre OPERA, BALLET
(Národní divadlo; Map p298; ☎224 901 377; www.narodni-divadlo.cz; Národní třída 2; tickets 30-1000Kč; ⊙box offices 10am-6pm; 🚊6, 9, 18, 21, 22) The much-loved National Theatre provides a stage for traditional opera, drama and ballet by the likes of Smetana, Shakespeare and Tchaikovsky, sharing the program with more modern works by composers and playwrights such as Philip Glass and John Osborne. The box office is in the Nový síň building next door.

Prague State Opera OPERA, BALLET
(Státní opera Praha; Map p298; ☎224 901 886; www.opera.cz; Wilsonova 4; opera tickets 100-1150Kč, ballet tickets 100-800Kč; ⊙box office 10am-5.30pm Mon-Fri, 10am-noon & 1-5.30pm Sat & Sun; Ⓜ Muzeum) The impressive neo-rococo home of the Prague State Opera provides a glorious setting for performances of classical, mostly Italian, opera and ballet.

Smetana Hall CLASSICAL MUSIC
(Smetanova síň; Map p298; ☎222 002 101; www.obecnidum.cz; náměstí Republiky 5; tickets 250-600Kč; ⊙box office 10am-6pm; Ⓜ Náměstí Republiky) Smetana Hall is the home venue of the Prague Symphony Orchestra (Symfonický orchestr hlavního města Prahy), and also stages performances of folk dance and music.

WANT MORE?

For in-depth information, reviews and recommendations at your fingertips, head to the Apple App Store to purchase Lonely Planet's *Prague City Guide* and *Czech Phrasebook* iPhone apps.

Alternatively, head to www.lonelyplanet.com/czech-republic/prague for planning advice, author recommendations, traveller reviews and insider tips.

Rudolfinum LIVE MUSIC
(Map p298; ☎227 059 227; www.ceskafilharmonie.cz; náměstí Jana Palacha, Staré Město; ⊙box office 10am-6pm Mon-Fri; MStaroměstska) One of Prague's main venues for classical music concerts is the Dvořák Hall in the neo-Renaissance Ruldolfinum, home to the Czech Philharmonic Orchestra.

Clubs

Cross Club CLUB
(☎736 535 053; www.crossclub.cz; Plynární 23, Holešovice; admission free-150Kč; ⊙cafe noon-2am, club 6pm-4am; ᯤ; MNádraží Holešovice) An industrial club in every sense of the word: the setting in an industrial zone; the thumping music (both DJs and live acts); and the interior, an absolute must-see jumble of gadgets, shafts, cranks and pipes, many of which move and pulsate with light to the music.

Roxy CLUB
(Map p298; ☎224 826 296; www.roxy.cz; Dlouhá 33; admission Fri & Sat free-300Kč; ⊙7pm-midnight Mon-Thu, to 6am Fri & Sat; 🚊5, 8, 14) Set in the ramshackle shell of an art deco cinema, the legendary Roxy is the place to see the country's top DJs and frequent live acts.

Sasazu CLUB
(☎284 097 455; www.sasazu.com; block 25, Holešovice market, Bubenské nábřeží 306, Holešovice; admission 200-1000Kč; ⊙9pm-5am; ᯤ; MVltavská, 🚊1, 3, 5, 25) One of the most popular dance clubs in the city, Sasazu attracts the fashionable elite and hangers-on in equal measure. If you're into big dance floors and long lines (hint: go early), this is your place.

Live Music

Palác Akropolis LIVE MUSIC
(☎296 330 911; www.palacakropolis.cz; Kubelikova 27, Žižkov; admission free-50Kč; ⊙club 7pm-5am; 🚊5, 9, 26 to Lipanska) The Akropolis is a Prague institution, a labyrinthine, sticky-floored shrine to alternative music and drama. Its various performance spaces host a smorgasbord of musical and cultural events, from DJs to string quartets to Macedonian Roma bands to local rock gods to visiting talent – Marianne Faithfull, the Flaming Lips and the Strokes have all played here.

Lucerna Music Bar LIVE MUSIC
(Map p298; ☎224 217 108; www.musicbar.cz; Palác Lucerna, Vodičkova 36; admission 100-500Kč; ⊙8pm-4am; MMůstek, 🚊3, 9, 14, 24) Nostalgia reigns supreme at this atmospheric old theatre, now looking a little dog-eared, with anything from Beatles tribute bands to mainly Czech artists playing jazz, blues, pop, rock and more on midweek nights. But the most popular event is the regular 1980s and '90s video party held every Friday and Saturday night.

JazzDock JAZZ
(☎774 058 838; www.jazzdock.cz; Janáčkovo nábřeží 2, Smíchov; admission 90-150Kč; ⊙4pm-3am; MAnděl, 🚊7, 9, 12, 14) Most of Prague's jazz clubs are smoky cellar affairs. This riverside club is a definite step up, with a clean, modern decor and a decidedly romantic view out over the Vltava. This place draws some of the best local talent and occasional international acts. Go early or book to get a good table.

Jazz Club U Staré Paní JAZZ
(Map p298; ☎602 148 377; www.jazzstarapani.cz; Michalská 9; admission 250Kč; ⊙7pm-1am Wed-Sun, music from 9pm; MMůstek) Located in the basement of the Hotel U Staré Paní, this long-established but recently revamped jazz club caters to all levels of musical appreciation.

Information

The major banks are best for changing cash, but using a debit card in an ATM gives a better rate of exchange. Avoid *směnárna* (private exchange booths), which advertise misleading rates and have exorbitant charges.

Na Homolce Hospital (☎257 271 111; www.homolka.cz; 5th fl, Foreign Pavilion, Roentgenova 2, Motol; 🚌167, MAnděl) The best hospital in Prague, equipped and staffed to Western standards.

Prague Welcome (Map p298; ☎221 714 444; www.praguewelcome.cz; Old Town Hall, Staroměstské náměstí 5; ⊙9am-7pm; MStaroměstská) The city's tourist information office, with branches around town as well as at Prague airport and the **main train station** (Map p298; ☎221 714 444; www.praguewelcome.cz; Wilsonova 8 , Nové Město; ⊙10am-6pm Mon-Sat; MHlavní Nádraží).

Relax Café-Bar (☎224 211 521; www.relaxcafebar.cz; Dlážděná 4; per 15min 20Kč; ⊙8am-10pm Mon-Fri, 2-10pm Sat; ᯤ; MNáměstí Republiky) Internet acess.

Getting There & Away

Please see p317 for details on the main overland and air routes to Prague and the Czech Republic.

Getting Around

To/From the Airport

To get into town from the airport, buy a full-price public transport ticket (32Kč) from the **Prague Public Transport Authority** (DPP; ☎800 191 817; www.dpp.cz) desk in the arrivals hall and take bus 119 (20 minutes, every 10 minutes, 4am to midnight) to the end of metro line A (Dejvická), then continue by metro into the city centre (another 10 to 15 minutes; no new ticket needed).

If you're heading to the southwestern part of the city, take bus 100, which goes to the Zličín metro station (line B).

There's also an **Airport Express** (tickets 50Kč; ⏰5am-10pm) bus that takes 35 minutes and runs every 30 minutes, which runs to Praha hlavní nádraží (main train station), where you can connect to metro line C (buy ticket from driver, luggage goes free).

AAA Radio Taxi (p307) operates a 24-hour taxi service, charging around 500Kč to 700Kč to get to the centre of Prague. You'll find taxi stands outside both arrivals terminals. Drivers usually speak some English and accept credit cards.

Public Transport

Prague's excellent public-transport system combines tram, metro and bus services. It's operated by the Prague Public Transport Authority (DPP), which has information desks at Prague airport (7am to 10pm) and in several metro stations, including Muzeum, Můstek, Anděl and Nádraží Holešovice. The metro operates daily from 5am to midnight.

Tickets valid on all metros, trams and buses are sold from machines at metro stations (coins only), as well as at DPP information offices and many newsstands and kiosks. Tickets can be purchased individually or as discounted day passes valid for one or three days.

A full-price individual ticket costs 32/16Kč per adult/senior aged 65 to 70 and is valid for 90 minutes of unlimited travel. For shorter journeys, buy short-term tickets that are valid for 30 minutes of unlimited travel. These cost 24/12Kč per adult/senior. One-day passes cost 110/55Kč per adult/senior; three-day passes cost 310Kč (no discount for seniors).

Taxi

Taxis are frequent and relatively inexpensive. The official rate for licensed cabs is 40Kč flagfall plus 28Kč per kilometre and 6Kč per minute while waiting. On this basis, any trip within the city centre – say, from Wenceslas Sq to Malá Strana – should cost around 170Kč. A trip to the suburbs, depending on the distance, should run from around 200Kč to 400Kč, and to the airport between 500Kč and 700Kč.

The following companies offer 24-hour service and English-speaking operators:

AAA Radio Taxi (☎222 333 222, 14014; www.aaataxi.cz)

City Taxi (☎257 257 257; www.citytaxi.cz)

AROUND PRAGUE

Karlštejn

Rising above the village of Karlštejn, 30km southwest of Prague, this medieval castle is in such good shape it wouldn't look out of place on Disneyworld's Main St. The crowds come in theme-park proportions as well, but the peaceful surrounding countryside offers views of Karlštejn's stunning exterior that rival anything you'll see on the inside.

Karlštejn Castle (Hrad Karlštejn; ☎311 681 617; www.hradkarlstejn.cz; adult/child Tour 1 270/180Kč, Tour 2 300/200Kč, Tour 3 120/60Kč; ⏰9am-6.30pm Jul & Aug, to 5.30pm Tue-Sun May, Jun & Sep, to 4.30pm Tue-Sun Apr & Oct, reduced hr Nov-Mar) was born of a grand pedigree, starting life in 1348 as a hideaway for the crown jewels and treasury of the Holy Roman Emperor, Charles IV. Run by an appointed burgrave, the castle was surrounded by a network of landowning knight-vassals, who came to the castle's aid whenever enemies moved against it.

Karlštejn again sheltered the Bohemian and the Holy Roman Empire crown jewels during the Hussite Wars of the 15th century, but fell into disrepair as its defences became outmoded. Considerable restoration work in the late 19th century returned the castle to its former glory.

There are three guided tours available: Tour 1 (50 minutes) passes through the Knight's Hall, still daubed with the coats-of-arms and names of the knight-vassals, Charles IV's bedchamber, the Audience Hall and the Jewel House, which includes treasures from the Chapel of the Holy Cross and a replica of the St Wenceslas Crown.

Tour 2 (70 minutes, May to October only) must be booked in advance and takes in the the Marian Tower, with the Church of the Virgin Mary and the Chapel of St Catherine, then moves on the Great Tower for the castle's star attraction, the exquisite Chapel of the Holy Cross.

Tour 3 (40 minutes, May to October only) visits the upper levels of the Great Tower, the highest point of the castle, which provides stunning views over the surrounding countryside.

There are frequent train departures daily from Prague's main station, *hlavní nádraží*. The journey takes 40 minutes and costs around 50Kč.

Kutná Hora

In the 14th century, Kutná Hora, 60km southeast of Prague, rivalled the capital in importance because of the rich deposits of silver ore below the ground. The ore ran out in 1726, leaving the medieval townscape largely unaltered. Now with several fascinating and unusual historical attractions, the Unesco World Heritage–listed town is a popular day trip from Prague.

Interestingly, most visitors come not for the silver splendour but rather to see an eerie monastery, dating from the 19th century, with an interior crafted solely from human bones. Indeed, the remarkable **Sedlec Ossuary** (Kostnice; ☎327 561 143; www.ossuary.eu; Zámecká 127; adult/concession 60/40Kč; ⊙8am-6pm Mon-Sat Apr-Sep, 9am-5pm Mar & Oct, 9am-4pm Nov-Feb), or better 'bone church', features the remains of no fewer than 40,000 people who died over the years from wars and pestilence.

Closer to the centre of Kutná Hora is the town's greatest monument: the Gothic **Cathedral of St Barbara** (Chrám sv Barbora; ☎327 512 115; Barborská; adult/concession 60/40Kč; ⊙10am-4pm Mon, 9am-5.30pm Tue-Sun May-Sep, 10am-4pm daily Oct-Apr). Rivalling Prague's St Vitus in size and magnificence, its soaring nave culminates in elegant, six-petalled ribbed vaulting, and the ambulatory chapels preserve original 15th-century frescos. Other leading attractions include the **Hrádek** (Little Castle) from the 15th century, which now houses the Czech Silver Museum.

Most visitors don't stay the night, but if you decide to linger, try the good-value **Penzión U Kata** (☎327 515 096; www.ukata.cz; Uhelná 596; s/d/tr 500/760/1140Kč; P@📶), a family hotel that's excellent value and just a short stroll from the bus station. For meals, get some froth on your moustache at **Pivnice Dačický** (☎327 512 248; www.dacicky.com; Rakova 8; mains 120-330Kč; ⊙11am-11pm), an old-fashioned, wood-panelled Bohemian beer hall, where you can dine on dumplings and choose from five different draught beers.

Kutná Hora can be reached from Prague by either bus (68Kč, 1¼ hours) or train (101Kč, one hour). The bus station is located on the Old Town's northeastern edge, which is convenient to the central sites, but 3km from the ossuary. Kutná Hora's main train station, by contrast, is just 800m from the ossuary, but 3km from the Old Town.

BOHEMIA

The Czech Republic's western province boasts surprising variety. Český Krumlov, with its riverside setting and dramatic Renaissance castle, is in a class by itself, but lesser-known towns such as Loket exude unexpected charm. Big cities such as Plzeň offer urban attractions, including great museums and restaurants. The spa towns of western Bohemia were world famous in the 19th century and retain old-world lustre.

Karlovy Vary

POP 60,000

Karlovy Vary is the closest the Czech Republic has to a glam resort, but it is still only glam with a small 'g'. While the resort was famous across Europe in the 19th century as a *kurort* (health spa), these days the town attracts mostly day trippers, content to stroll the main colonnade area and sip on allegedly health-restoring sulphuric compounds from ceramic, spouted drinking cups. Despite the spa rep, Karlovy Vary is not entirely welcoming to walk-ins looking for high-end treatments such as exotic massages and peelings; these services are available, but contact the city's Infocentrum (p310) in advance. Good bus services from Prague makes this an easy day trip. Advance hotel bookings are essential in early July, when the town hosts the Karlovy Vary International Film Festival.

Sights

FREE **Hot Spring Colonnade** SPRING
(Vřídelní Kolonáda; www.karlovyvary.cz; Vřídelní Kolonáda; ⊙Pramen Vřídlo 6am-7pm) The Hot Spring Colonnade houses the most impressive of the town's geysers, **Pramen Vřídlo**. The building itself is an an incongruous, mid-'70s structure once dedicated to Soviet cosmonaut Yuri Gagarin. The geyser belches some 15m into the air; people lounge

about inhaling the vapours or sampling the waters from a line of taps in the next room.

Church of SS Peter & Paul CHURCH
(kostel Sv Petra a Pavla; Krále Jiřího; ⌚9am-6pm) The impressive Orthodox Church of SS Peter & Paul, with five polished onion domes and art nouveau exterior murals, was apparently modelled after a similar church near Moscow. One of the church's most prominent decorations is a relief depicting Tsar Peter the Great.

Moser Glass Museum MUSEUM
(Sklářské muzeum Moser; ☎353 416 132; www.moser-glass.com; Kpt Jaroše 19; adult/child museum 80/50Kč, glassworks 120/70Kč, combined ticket 180/100Kč; ⌚9am-5pm, glassworks 9am-2.30pm; 🚌1) The Moser Glass Museum has more than 2000 items on display. Tours of the adjacent **glassworks** and combined tickets are also available. There is a shop here, too, but the prices are not anything special, and there's another shop in town. To get here catch bus 1 from the Tržnice bus station.

Sleeping

Accommodation prices in Karlovy Vary have risen steeply in recent years to be similar to those in Prague, especially in July when the city hosts the international film festival. Indeed, if you're planning a July arrival, make sure to book well in advance. Infocentrum offices can help book rooms.

TOP CHOICE **Hotel Maltézsý Kříž** HOTEL €€
(☎353 169 011; www.maltezskykriz.cz; Stará Louka 50; s/d 1650/2800Kč; @📶) Welcome to Karlovy Vary's best-value midrange hotel. Oriental rugs and wooden floors combine at this spiffy property, with cosy rooms and a more spacious double-storeyed apartment. The bathrooms are decked out in warm, earthy tones.

Hotel Boston HOTEL €
(☎353 362 711; www.boston.cz; Luční vrch 9; s/d 1390/1570Kč; 🚭📶) Tucked away down a quiet lane, this family-owned hotel has relatively spacious rooms decorated in bright colours with updated bathrooms. The flash cafes of Stará Louka are just around the corner.

Hotel Romania HOTEL €€
(☎353 222 822; www.romania.cz; Zahradni 49; s/d 1200/1950Kč; 📶) Don't be put off by the ugly monolith of the Hotel Thermal dominating the views from this good-value, reader-recommended hotel (just squint a little). The spacious rooms are very tidy and the English-speaking staff very helpful.

Carlsbad Plaza HOTEL €€€
(☎353 225 501; www.carlsbadplaza.cz; Mariánskolázeňská 23; s/d 4000/6000Kč ; P🚭❄@📶🏊) Seriously stylish, this relatively new hotel has raised the bar in spa town, with soothingly modern treatment facilities, classy rooms and a vegetarian-friendly Asian restaurant.

WORTH A TRIP

LOKET

Surrounded by a wickedly serpentine loop in the Ohře River, the picturesque village of Loket may as well be on an island. It was apparently Goethe's favourite town and after a lazily subdued stroll around the main square and castle, it may be yours as well. Most people visit Loket as a day trip from Karlovy Vary, but it's also a sleepy place to ease off the travel accelerator for a few days, especially when the day trippers have departed.

Hrad Loket (Loket Castle ; ☎352 684 648; www.hradloket.cz; Hrad; adult/concession with English guide 110/90Kč, with English text 95/75Kč; ⌚9am-4.30pm Apr-Oct, 9am-3.30pm Nov-Mar) is built on the site of a Romanesque fort, of which the only surviving bits are the tall, square tower and fragments of a rotunda. Its present late-Gothic look dates from the late 14th century. From 1788 to 1947 it was used as a prison. Highlights include two rooms filled with the town's lustrous porcelain and views from the castle tower.

There are plenty of cafes and pizzerias that come and go with the season scattered around the main square. The **Hotel Císař Ferdinand** (☎352 327 130; www.hotel-loket.cz; TG Masaryka 136; s/d 1060/1850Kč; P🚭📶🏊) offers clean rooms and an excellent restaurant.

Frequent bus departures link Karlovy Vary to Loket (30Kč, 20 minutes). The bus from Karlovy Vary stops across the bridge from the Old Town.

Eating & Drinking

Hospoda U Švejka CZECH €€
(☎353 232 276; www.svejk-kv.cz; Stará Louka 10; mains 160-370Kč; ⊙11am-11pm; ⊖) A great choice for lunch or dinner, right in the heart of the spa centre. Though the presentation borders on extreme kitsch, the food is actually very good and the atmosphere not unlike a classic Czech pub.

Embassy Restaurant CZECH €€€
(☎353 221 161; www.embassy.cz; Nová Louka 21; mains 200-500Kč) The in-house restaurant of the Embassy Hotel is a destination in its own right. The dining room is richly atmospheric and the food, mostly Czech standards such as roast pork or duck, is top notch. There's an excellent wine list, and in nice weather they sometimes offer outdoor seating.

Café Elefant CAFE
(☎353 223 406; Stará Louka 30; coffee 50Kč) Classy old-school spot for coffee and cake. A tad touristy, but still elegant and refined.

Information

Infocentrum – Dolní nádrazi (☎353 232 838; www.karlovyvary.cz; Západní 2a, Lower bus station; ⊙9am-6pm Mon-Fri, 10am-5pm Sat & Sun) The main tourist information office at the Dolní (Lower) bus station.

Infocentrum – Hot Spring Colonnade (☎773 291 243; www.karlovyvary.cz; Vřídelní kolonáda; ⊙9am-5pm Mon-Fri, 10am-5pm Sat & Sun)

Getting There & Away

Buses are the only practical way of reaching Karlovy Vary from Prague. **Student Agency** (www.studentagency.cz) runs frequent buses to/from Prague Florenc (from 155Kč, 2¼ hours, several daily) departing from the main bus station beside Dolní nádraží train station. Buses to nearby Loket (30Kč, 30 minutes) run throughout the day.

Plzeň

POP 173,000

Plzeň, the regional capital of western Bohemia and the second-biggest city in Bohemia after Prague, is best known as the home of the Pilsner Urquell Brewery, but it has a handful of other interesting sights and enough good restaurants and night-time pursuits to justify an overnight stay. Most of the sights are located near the central square, but the brewery itself is about a 15-minute walk outside the centre. Try to arrive in the morning to tour the nondrinking attractions first, and save the brewery tour and inevitable post-tour beers for the late afternoon (which makes for a more natural progression to dinner, continuing the pub crawl after dark).

Sights

Pilsner Urquell Brewery BREWERY
(Prazdroj; ☎377 062 888; www.prazdroj.cz; U Prazdroje 7; guided tour adult/child 150/80Kč; ⊙8.30am-6pm Apr-Sep, to 5pm Oct-Mar, tours in English 12.45pm, 2.15pm & 4.15pm) Plzeň's most popular attraction is the tour of the Pisner Urquell Brewery, in operation since 1842 and arguably home to the world's best beer. Entry is by guided tour only, with three tours in English available daily. Tour highlights include a trip to the old cellars (dress warmly) and a glass of unpasteurised nectar at the end.

Brewery Museum MUSEUM
(☎377 235 574; www.prazdroj.cz; Veleslavínova 6; adult/child guided tour 120/90Kč, English text 90/60Kč; ⊙10am-6pm Apr-Dec, 10am-5pm Jan-Mar) The Brewery Museum offers an insight into how beer was made (and drunk) in the days before Prazdroj was founded. Highlights include a mock-up of a 19th-century pub, a huge wooden beer tankard from Siberia and a collection of beer mats. All have English captions and there's a good English written guide available.

Underground Plzeň UNDERGROUND
(Plzeňské historické podzemí; ☎377 235 574; www.plzenskepodzemi.cz; Veleslavínova 6; adult/child 90/70Kč; ⊙10am-6pm Apr-Dec, 10am-5pm Feb-Mar, closed Jan; English tour 1pm daily) This extraordinary tour explores the passageways below the old city. The earliest were probably dug in the 14th century, perhaps for beer production or defence; the latest date from the 19th century. Of an estimated 11km that have been excavated, some 500m of tunnels are open to the public. Bring extra clothing (it's a chilly 10°C underground).

Sleeping

Pension Stará Plzeň PENSION €
(☎377 259 901; www.pension-sp.cz; Na Roudné 12; s 600-1000Kč, d 800-1200Kč; P⊖@) The pension 'Old Pilsen' offers light-and-sunny rooms with skylights, wooden floors and comfy beds. The more expensive rooms offer antique-style beds, persian rugs and

exposed, wood-beam ceilings. To get here, walk north on Rooseveltova across the river, then turn right onto Na Roudné and continue for 300m.

U Salzmannů PENSION €
(☎377 235 476; www.usalzmannu.cz, Pražska 8; s & d 950-1350Kč, ste 1500Kč;) This pleasant pension, right in the heart of town, sits above a historic pub. The standard rooms are comfortable but basic; the more luxurious double 'suites' have antique beds and small sitting rooms, as well as kitchenettes. The pub location is convenient if you overdo it; to reach your bed, just climb the stairs.

Pension City PENSION €
(☎377 326 069; www.pensioncityplzen.cz; sady 5 kvetna 52; s/d 1050/1450Kč;) On a quiet street near the river, Pension City has comfortable rooms and friendly, English-speaking staff armed with lots of local information.

Eating

Na Parkánu CZECH €
(☎377 324 485; www.naparkanu.com; Veleslavínova 4; mains 80-180Kč;) Don't overlook this pleasant pub-restaurant, attached to the Brewery Museum. It may look a bit touristy, but the traditional Czech food is top rate, and the beer, naturally, could hardly be better. Try to snag a spot on the summer garden. Don't leave without trying the *nefiltrované pivo* (unfiltered beer).

Aberdeen Angus Steakhouse STEAKHOUSE €€
(☎725 555 631; www.angusfarm.cz; Pražská 23; mains 180-400Kč) For our money, this may be the best steakhouse in all of the Czech Republic. The meats hail from the nearby Angus Farm, where the livestock is raised organically. There are several cuts and sizes on offer; lunch options include a tantalising cheeseburger. The downstairs dining room is cosy; there's also a creekside terrace. Book in advance.

Na Spilce CZECH €
(☎377 062 755; www.naspilce.com; U Prazdroje 7; mains 80-230Kč; ⊙11am-10pm Sun-Thu, 11am-11pm Fri & Sat) This excellent pub and restaurant within the confines of the Pilsner Urquell Brewery feels like a factory canteen. The traditional Czech cooking is above average, and the beer is fresh from tanks next door.

Information

City Information Centre (Informační centrum města Plzně; ☎378 035 330; www.icpilsen.cz; náměstí Republiky 41; ⊙9am-7pm Apr-Sep, to 6pm Oct-Mar) Reserves accommodation, organises guides, sells maps and changes money.

Getting There & Away

From Prague, eight trains (150Kč, 1½ hours) leave daily from the main station, *hlavní nádraží*. The train station is on the eastern side of town, 10 minutes' walk from nám Republiky, the Old Town Sq. From Prague, the bus service to Plzeň (100Kč, one hour) is frequent (hourly), relatively fast and inexpensive.

Český Krumlov

POP 14,050

Outside of Prague, Český Krumlov is arguably the Czech Republic's only other world-class sight and must-see. From a distance, the town looks like any other in the Czech countryside, but once you get closer and see the Renaissance castle towering over the undisturbed 17th-century townscape, you'll feel the appeal; this really is that fairy-tale town the tourist brochures promised. Český Krumlov is best approached as an overnight destination; it's too far for a comfortable day trip from Prague. Consider staying two nights, and spend one of the days hiking or biking in the surrounding woods and fields.

Sights

Český Krumlov Castle CASTLE
(☎380 704 711; www.castle.ckrumlov.cz; Zámek; adult/concession Tour 1 250/160Kč, Tour 2 240/140Kč, Theatre Tour 380/220Kč, tower 50/30Kč; ⊙9am-6pm Tue-Sun Jun-Aug, 9am-5pm Apr, May, Sep & Oct) Český Krumlov's striking Renaissance castle, occuping a promontory high above the town, began life in the 13th century. It acquired its present appearance in the 16th to 18th centuries under the stewardship of the noble Rožmberk and Schwarzenberg families. The interiors are accessible by guided tour only, though you can stroll the grounds and climb the tower on your own.

Egon Schiele Art Centrum MUSEUM
(☎380 704 011; www.schieleartcentrum.cz; Široká 71; adult/concession 120/70Kč; ⊙10am-6pm Tue-Sun) This excellent private gallery houses a small retrospective of the controversial Viennese painter Egon Schiele (1890–1918), who lived in Krumlov in 1911, and raised the ire of townsfolk by hiring young girls as nude models.

Sleeping

Dilettante's Hangout GUESTHOUSE €
(☎728 280 033; www.dilettanteshangout.com; Plesivecke náměstí 93; r 790-990Kč; ⊜) Don't be fooled by the bland exterior. Inside this intimate homestay are three romantic, arty rooms decorated with mementoes of the owner's global wanderings. Each room is unique, but they're all cosy and eclectic. There are kitchenettes for self-catering.

Pension Kapr PENSION €
(☎602 409 360; www.penzionkapr.cz; Rybářská 28; s 1000Kč, d 1200-1800Kč; @ ☏) OK, it may be named after a fish (carp), but this riverside pension, with exposed bricks and 500 years of history, has a quiet location and wonderful views of the Old Town. The lovely rooms, with whitewashed walls and wooden floors, are all named after the owners' children.

Castle Apartments APARTMENT €€
(☎380 725 110; www.zameckaapartma.cz; Latrán 45-47; apt 1800-3800Kč; ⊜ ☏) Three adjoining houses near the castle district have been transformed into comfortable private apartments that offer wooden floors, and modern kitchenettes and bathrooms (no additional charge for the romantic views). Castle Apartments just may be Český Krumlov's best-value accommodation option.

U Malého Vítka HOTEL €€
(☎380 711 925; www.vitekhotel.cz; Radničnì 27; d 1600Kč; P ⊜ ☏) We really like this small hotel in the heart of the Old Town. The room furnishings are of high-quality, hand-crafted wood, and each room is named after a traditional Czech fairy-tale character. The downstairs restaurant and cafe are very good too.

Eating

Laibon VEGETARIAN €€
(☎728 676 654; www.laibon.cz; Parkán 105; mains 90-180Kč; ⊜ ☏ ☑) Candles and vaulted ceilings create a great boho ambience in the best little vegetarian teahouse in Bohemia. Just paging through the menu with seldom-seen words such as guacamole and hummus can start the mouth watering.

Nonna Gina ITALIAN €
(☎380 717 187; Klášteriní 52; pizza 90-155Kč; ⊜) Authentic Italian flavours from the authentic Italian Massaro family feature in this pizzeria down a quiet lane. Grab an outdoor table and pretend you're in Naples.

Hospoda Na Louži CZECH €
(☎380 711 280; www.nalouzi.cz; Kájovská 66; mains 90-170Kč ; ⊜) Nothing's changed in this wood-panelled *pivo* parlour for almost a century. Locals and tourists pack Na Louži for huge meals and tasty dark (and light) beer from the Eggenberg brewery.

Information

Infocentrum (☎380 704 622; www.ckrumlov.info; náměstí Svornosti 1; ⊙9am-7pm Jun-Aug, 9am-6pm Apr, May, Sep & Oct, 9am-5pm Nov-Mar) Transport and accommodation info, maps, internet access (5Kč per five minutes) and audioguides (100Kč per hour). A guide for disabled visitors is available.

Getting There & Away

From Prague (260Kč, 3½ hours), the train journey requires a change in České Budějovice. Buses are usually quicker and cheaper. There's regular train service between České Budějovice and Český Krumlov (32Kč, 45 minutes). From Prague, **Student Agency** (www.studentagency.cz) coaches (195Kč, three hours) leave regularly from the Na Knížecí bus station at Anděl metro station (Line B).

MORAVIA

The Czech Republic's eastern province, Moravia is yin to Bohemia's yang. If Bohemians love beer, Moravians love wine. If Bohemia is towns and cities, Moravia is rolling hills and pretty landscapes. Once you've seen the best of Bohemia, head east for a different side of the Czech Republic. The capital, Brno, has the museums, but the northern city of Olomouc has captivating architecture. The south is dominated by vineyards and, naturally, wine-drinking day-tipplers.

Brno

POP 387,200

Among Czechs, Moravia's capital has a dull rep; a likeable place where not much actually happens. There was even a hit movie a few years back called *Nuda v Brně (Boredom in Brno)*. The reality, though, is different. Tens of thousands of students ensure lively cafe and club scenes that easily rival Prague's. The museums are great too. Brno was one of the leading centres of experimental architecture in the early 20th century, and the Unesco-protected Vila Tugendhat

WORTH A TRIP

OLOMOUC

Olomouc (olla-moats) is one of the Czech Republic's most underrated destinations. There's great nightlife, fuelled by a cosmopolitan student population, and two essential sights worthy of any European city.

Olomouc's Unesco World Heritage–listed **Holy Trinity Column** (Sousoší Nejsvětější trojice; Horní náměstí) was built between 1716 and 1754; the exquisite baroque structure is reminiscent of a Buddhist stupa. The surrounding square is ringed by historic facades and features two of the city's six baroque fountains.

The superb **Archdiocesan Museum** (Arcidiecézni muzeum; ☎585 514 111; www.olmuart.cz; Václavské náměstí 3; adult/concession 50/25Kč, Sun & Wed free; ⊙10am-6pm Tue-Sun) traces the history of Olomouc back 1000 years. The thoughtful layout, with English signage, takes you through the original Romanesque foundations of Olomouc Castle, and highlights the cultural and artistic development of the city during the Gothic and baroque periods.

Stay at **Poet's Corner** (☎777 570 730; www.hostelolomouc.com; Sokolská 1, 3rd fl; dm/tw/tr/q 350/900/1200/1600Kč;), a friendly and well-run hostel. In summer there's a two-night minimum stay. The owners have loads of ideas for interesting day trips.

For a great Czech pub experience, try **Drápal** (☎585 225 818; www.restauracedrapal.cz; Havlíčkova 1; mains 110-150Kč;). The unpasteurised Pilsner Urquell is arguably the best beer in Olomouc. The smallish menu is loaded with Czech classics, such as the ever-popular *Španělský ptáček* (literally 'Spanish bird'), a beef roulade stuffed with smoked sausage, parsley and a hard-boiled egg.

There's also great microbrewery beer and good food at **Moritz** (☎585 205 560; www.hostinec-moritz.cz; Nešverova 2; mains 120-260Kč;). In summer, the beer garden's the only place to be.

Olomouc is on a main train line, with regular service from both Prague (240Kč, three hours) and Brno (100Kč, 1½ hours). The train station is 2km east of the centre. There are around 15 buses daily to/from Brno (92Kč, 1¼ hours); see www.jizdnirady.idnes.cz.

is considered a masterwork of Functionalist design.

Sights

Špilberk Castle CASTLE
(☎542 123 611; www.spilberk.cz; combined entry incl museum adult/concession 200/120Kč; ⊙9am-5pm Tue-Sun Oct-Apr, 9am-5pm daily May & Jun, 10am-6pm daily Jul-Sep) Brno's dramatic hilltop castle is considered the city's most important landmark, and is home to the **Brno City Museum** (muzeum města Brna; ☎542 123 611; www.spilberk.cz; Špilberk Castle). You can also visit the **casemates** (small rooms within the castle walls) and climb the lookout **tower**.

Cathedral of SS Peter & Paul CHURCH, TOWER
(katedrála sv Petra a Pavla; www.katedrala-petrov.cz; Petrov Hill; tower adult/concession 40/30Kč, crypts 20/10Kč; ⊙11am-6pm Mon-Sat, from 11.45am Sun) This 14th-century cathedral atop Petrov Hill was originally built on the site of a pagan temple to Venus and has been reconstructed many times since. The highly decorated 11m-high main altar with figures of SS Peter and Paul was carved by Viennese sculptor Josef Leimer in 1891. You can also climb the **tower** for dramatic views, or visit the **crypts**.

FREE **Old Town Hall** HISTORIC BUILDING
(Stará radnice; Radnická 8; adult/concession tower 30/15Kč; ⊙9am-5pm) Brno's atmospheric Old Town Hall dates from the early 13th century. The tourist office is here, plus oddities including a crocodile hanging from the ceiling (known affectionately as the Brno 'dragon') and a wooden wagon wheel with a unique story. You can also climb the **tower**.

Capuchin Monastery CEMETERY
(Kapucínský klášter; www.kapucini.cz; adult/concession 60/30Kč; ⊙9am-noon & 1pm-4.30pm May-Sep, closed Mon mid-Feb–Apr & Oct–mid-Dec, closed mid-Dec–mid-Feb) One of the city's leading attractions is this ghoulish cellar crypt that holds the mummified remains of several city noblemen from the 18th century. Apparently the dry, well-ventilated crypt has

the natural ability to turn dead bodies into mummies.

Brno Underground UNDERGROUND

(Brněnské podzemí; www.ticbrno.cz; Zelný trh 21; adult/concession 150/75Kč; 9am-6pm Tue-Sun) In 2011, the city opened the first of what will be several opportunities to explore the underground passages of the medieval city. This tour takes around 40 minutes to explore several of the cellars situated 6m to 8m below the Cabbage Market. The cellars were built for two purposes: to store goods and to hide in during wars.

TOP CHOICE **Vila Tugendhat** ARCHITECTURE

(Villa Tugendhat; 515 511 015; www.tugendhat.eu; Černopolni 45; adult/concession 300/180Kč; 10am-6pm Tue-Sun; 3, 5, 11) Brno had a reputation in the 1920s as a centre for modern architecture in the Functionalist and Bauhaus styles. Arguably the finest example is this family villa, designed by modern master Mies van der Rohe in 1930. Entry is by guided tour, booked in advance by phone or over the website.

Sleeping

In February, April, August, September and October, Brno hosts major international trade fairs, and hotel rates increase by 40% to 100%. Book ahead if possible.

TOP CHOICE **Hostel Mitte** HOSTEL €

(734 622 340; www.hostelmitte.com; Panská 22; dm incl breakfast 490Kč, s/d 1000/1100Kč;) Set in the heart of the Old Town, this clean and stylish hostel opened in 2011 and still smells and looks brand new. The rooms are named after famous Moravians (including Milan Kundera) or famous events (Austerlitz) and decorated accordingly.

Hotel Europa HOTEL €€

(545 421 400; www.hotel-europa-brno.cz; třída kpt Jaroše 27; s/d 1375/1625Kč; P) Set in a quiet neighbourhood a 10-minute walk from the centre, this self-proclaimed 'art' hotel (presumably for the wacky futuristic lobby furniture) offers clean and tastefully furnished modern rooms in a historic 19th-century building. The lobby has free wi-fi, while the rooms have cable (ethernet) _connections.

Hotel & Pivnice Pegas HOTEL €€

(542 210 104; www.hotelpegas.cz; Jakubská 4; s/d 2000/2500Kč;) Centrally located, the Pegas has been refurbished to include huge beds, flat-screen TVs and updated bathrooms. Expect a friendly welcome at reception and the lure of the Pegas microbrewery and pub downstairs. The rooms are on the 4th floor, so there is no problem with noise from the bar.

SPLURGE

Sushi lovers have a treat in store in Brno. The restaurant **Koishi** (777 564 744; www.koishi.cz; Údolní 11; mains 395-490Kč; 11am-11pm Mon-Fri, 9am-11pm Sat & Sun;) has earned a reputation for being not just the best sushi spot in the country, but many say the best restaurant in any category thanks to sushi master Tadayoshi Ebina and top seafood chef Petr Fučík. The restaurant is continuing to expand its range, adding more traditional European and Czech cooking, all with an Asian touch.

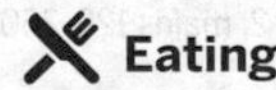

Eating

Spolek CZECH €

(774 814 230; www.spolek.net; Orli 22; mains 60-140Kč; 9am-10pm Mon-Fri, 10am-10pm Sun;) You'll get friendly, unpretentious service at this coolly 'bohemian' (yes, we're in Moravia) haven with interesting salads and soups, and a concise but diverse wine list.

Špaliček CZECH €€

(542 215 526; Zelný trh 12; mains 160-310Kč;) Brno's oldest restaurant sits on the edge of the Cabbage Market. Ignore the irony and dig into huge Moravian meals, partnered with a local Starobrno beer or something from the decent local wine list.

Drinking

U Richarda PUB

(775 027 918; www.uricharda2.cz; Údolní 7) This microbrewery is highly popular with students, who come for the great house-brewed, unpasteurised yeast beers, including a rare cherry-flavoured lager, and good traditional Czech cooking (mains 109Kč to 149Kč).

Avia CAFE

(739 822 215; www.aviacafe.cz; Botanická 1; 11am-10pm;) Popular student cafe-restaurant situated on the ground floor of the Jan Hus Congregational Church, a landmark Functionalist building from 1929.

★ Entertainment

Stará Pekárna LIVE MUSIC

(☎541 210 040; www.starapekarna.cz; Štefánikova 8; ⏰5pm-late Mon-Sat; 🚋1, 6, 7) Old and new music with blues, world beats, DJs and rock. Catch the tram to Pionýrská. Gigs usually kick off at 8pm.

Brno State Philharmonic Orchestra CLASSICAL MUSIC

(☎539 092 811; www.filharmonie-brno.cz; Komenského náměstí 8) City's main venue for classical music. Buy tickets at the **Philharmonic Orchestra Box Office** (Besední ul; ⏰9am-2pm Mon & Wed, 1-6pm Tue, Thu & Fri).

ℹ Information

Tourist information office (☎542 211 090; www.ticbrno.cz; Radnická 8, Old Town Hall; ⏰8am-6pm Mon-Fri, 9am-6pm Sat & Sun) Sells maps and books accommodation. Free internet for up to 15 minutes.

ℹ Getting There & Away

Brno is easily reached from Prague by either bus (165Kč, 2½ hours) or train (210Kč, 2½ hours). Bus service via the local **Student Agency** (☎841 101 101; www.studentagency.cz) is especially good. Express trains run between Brno's train station and Prague's *hlavní nádraží* every couple of hours during the day.

Telč

The Unesco-protected town of Telč, perched on the border between Bohemia and Moravia, possesses one of the country's prettiest and best-preserved historic town squares.

The main attraction is the beauty of the square, **Náměstí Zachariáše z Hradce** (Main Square), itself, which is lined with Renaissance burghers' houses. Most houses were built in the 16th century after a fire levelled the town in 1530. **Telč Chateau** (Zámek; www.zamek-telc.cz; náměstí Zachariáše z Hradce; adult/concession Route A 110/70Kč, Route B 90/60Kč; ⏰9-11.45am & 1-6pm Tue-Sun Apr-Oct), another Renaissance masterpiece, guards the northern end of the square. Entry is by guided tour only.

If you decide to spend the night, **Pension Steidler** (☎721 316 390; www.telc-accommodation.eu; náměstí Zachariáše z Hradce 52; s/d without breakfast 500/800Kč) offers rooms with skylights and wooden floors with a central location.

The town is no gourmet paradise, but **U Marušky** (☎602 432 904; Palackého 28; mains 90-170Kč) is a simple pub that caters to locals and offers decent home-cooked meals (with the added bonus of good Ježek beer on tap).

Around half-a-dozen buses make the run daily from Prague's Florenc bus station (170Kč, 2½ hours), with many connections requiring a change in Jihlava. Regional service is decent, with around five daily buses to Brno (100Kč, two hours). Check www.bus-vlak.cz for times and prices.

UNDERSTAND CZECH REPUBLIC

History

The 'Good King Wenceslas' of Christmas-carol fame was actually a prince, and the land he looked out over was the ancient territory of Bohemia. Beatified as St Wenceslas (svatý Václav in Czech), he remains the country's main patron saint.

The two 'Golden Ages' of Czech history were the rule of Charles IV (r 1346–78), who founded Prague's St Vitus Cathedral, built Charles Bridge and established Charles University, and the reign of Rudolf II (r 1576–1612), who made Prague the capital of the Habsburg empire and drew artists, scholars and scientists to his court.

The tides of war and imperial domination have washed through Bohemia and Moravia for centuries. Events in Czech history have impacted throughout Europe. Two Habsburg councillors were thrown from a Prague Castle window in 1618 (the famous Defenestration of Prague), igniting the Thirty Years War. Hitler's 1938 annexation of the Sudetenland (the western borderlands of Czechoslovakia) triggered the final slide toward WWII.

The 20th century was notable for the 'years of eight'. Czechoslovakia was created after the fall of the Habsburg Empire in 1918 and fell to a communist coup in 1948. The hopeful 'Prague Spring', when censorship was relaxed and political prisoners were released, was crushed by the Soviet invasion of 1968.

The Velvet Revolution – the bloodless overthrow of the communist regime – didn't happen until 1989. It was soon followed by the Velvet Divorce of 1993, when Czechoslovakia split into separate Czech and Slovak republics, the former led by famous playwright and former political prisoner Václav Havel (1936–2011).

The Czech Republic joined the EU on 1 May 2004.

People

The population of the Czech Republic is 10.5 million (2012 estimate); 95% of the population are Czech and 3% are Slovak. Only 150,000 of the three million Sudeten Germans evicted after WWII remain. A significant Roma population (0.3%) is subject to occasional hostility and racism.

Most Czechs profess to be atheist (39.8%) or nominally Roman Catholic (39.2%), but church attendance is low. There are small Protestant (4.6%) and Orthodox (3%) congregations. The Jewish community numbers only a few thousand.

Arts

Famous Czech writers include Franz Kafka (1883–1924; *The Trial, Metamorphosis*), Milan Kundera (b 1929; *The Book of Laughter and Forgetting, The Unbearable Lightness of Being*) and Bohumil Hrabal (1914–97; *I Served The King of England*).

Antonín Dvořák (1841–1904; New World Symphony) is the country's best-known composer, and painter Alfons Mucha (1860–1939) is famous for his art nouveau posters.

The films of Jan Hrebejk (b 1967), *Musíme si pomáhat* (*Divided We Fall*; 2000), *Pupendo* (2003) and *Horem pádem* (*Up and Down*; 2004), all cover different times in the country's tumultuous 20th-century history.

Občan Havel (*Citizen Havel*; 2008) is a fascinating documentary about the late Václav Havel.

Food & Drink

The classic Bohemian dish is *vepřo-knedlo-zelo,* local slang for roast pork, bread dumplings and sauerkraut. Look out for *svíčková na smetaně* (braised beef in a cream sauce) and *kapr na kmíní* (fried or baked carp with caraway seed).

SURVIVAL GUIDE

Directory A–Z

Accommodation

The Czech Republic has a wide variety of accommodation options, ranging from luxurious hotels to simple pensions and campgrounds. In Prague, rates peak in spring and autumn, as well as around the Christmas and Easter holidays. Midsummer is considered 'shoulder season' and rates are about 20% off-peak. Book in advance or over the hotel website to get the cheapest rates.

Prague, Brno and Český Krumlov all have backpacker-oriented hostels. Dorm beds costs around 450Kč in Prague and 350Kč to 450Kč elsewhere. Booking ahead is recommended. The **Czech Youth Hostel Association** (www.czechhostels.com) offers information and booking for Hostelling International (HI) hostels. Another budget option is to take a room in a private house or apartment. In cities, tourist information offices can often help with bookings. In smaller towns and villages, look for signs in house windows saying *'privát'* or, frequently, in German *'Zimmer frei'*.

Campsites are normally open from May to September and charge around 80Kč to 100Kč per person. Camping on public land is prohibited.

PRICE RANGES

In this chapter we've used the following general price indicators (double room in high season):

€ less than 1600Kč

€€ 1600Kč to 3700Kč

€€€ more than 3700Kč

Business Hours

Banks 8.30am to 4.30pm Monday to Friday

Bars 11am to midnight

Museums & Castles Usually closed Monday year-round

Restaurants 11am to 11pm

Shops 8.30am to 6pm Monday to Friday, 8.30am to noon Saturday

Embassies & Consulates

Most embassies and consulates are open at least 9am to noon Monday to Friday. All of the following are in Prague.

Australian Consulate (☎221 729 260; www.dfat.gov.au/missions/countries/cz.html; 6th fl, Klimentská 10, Nové Město; 🚋5, 8, 14, 26) Honorary consulate for emergency assistance only (eg a stolen passport); the nearest Australian embassy is in Vienna.

Canadian Embassy (☎272 101 800; www.canadainternational.gc.ca; Muchova 6, Bubeneč; Ⓜ Hradčanská)

New Zealand Consulate (☎222 514 672; egermayer@nzconsul.cz; Dykova 19, Vinohrady; Ⓜ Jiřího z Poděbrad) Honorary consulate providing emergency assistance only (eg stolen passport); the nearest NZ embassy is in Berlin.

UK Embassy (☎257 402 111; http://ukinczechrepublic.fco.gov.uk; Thunovská 14, Malá Strana; 🚋12, 20, 22)

US Embassy (☎257 022 000; http://czech.prague.usembassy.gov; Tržiště 15, Malá Strana; 🚋12, 20, 22)

Food

In this chapter, the following price indicators apply (for a main meal):

€ less than 200Kč

€€ 200Kč to 500Kč

€€€ more than 500Kč

Gay & Lesbian Travellers

Homosexuality is legal in the Czech Republic, but it's best to be discreet. For online information including links to accommodation and bars see the **Prague Gay Guide** (www.praguc.gayguide.net).

Money

The best places to exchange money are banks or use your credit or debit card to withdraw money as needed from ATMs. Never exchange money on the street and avoid private exchange offices, especially in Prague, as they charge exorbitant commissions.

Keep small change handy for use in public toilets and metro-ticket machines.

Public Holidays

New Year's Day 1 January

Easter Monday March/April

Labour Day 1 May

Liberation Day 8 May

SS Cyril and Methodius Day 5 July

Jan Hus Day 6 July

Czech Statehood Day 28 September

Republic Day 28 October

Freedom and Democracy Day 17 November

Christmas 24 to 26 December

Telephone

All Czech phone numbers have nine digits; dial all nine for any call, local or long distance. Buy phonecards for public telephones from post offices and newsstands from 100Kč.

Mobile-phone coverage (GSM 900/1800) is excellent. If you're from Europe, Australia or New Zealand, your mobile phone should be compatible. Purchase a Czech SIM card from any mobile-phone shop for around 500Kč (including 300Kč of calling credit). Local mobile phone numbers start with ☎601–608 and ☎720–779. The Czech Republic's country code is ☎420.

Visas

The Czech Republic is part of the EU's Schengen area, and citizens of most developed countries can spend up to 90 days in the country in a six-month period without a visa.

Getting There & Away

The Czech Republic is easily reached by air from key European hubs or overland by road or train from neighbouring countries. Flights, tours and rail tickets can be booked online at www.lonelyplanet.com/travel_services.

Air

Nearly all international flights arrive at Prague's **Václav Havel airport** (Letiště Praha; ☎220 111 888; www.prg.aero). Flights to and from destinations outside the EU's Schengen zone use the airport's Terminal 1, which has standard passport and customs checks. Flights within the Schengen zone use Terminal 2 and are treated as domestic flights.

The national carrier **Czech Airlines** (www.czechairlines.com) has a good safety record and is a member of the Skyteam airline alliance.

Land

The Czech Republic has border crossings with Germany, Poland, Slovakia and

Austria. These are all EU member states within the Schengen zone, meaning there are no passport or customs checks.

BUS

The main international terminal is **Florenc bus station** (ÚAN Praha Florenc; ☎900 144 444; www.florenc.cz; Křižíkova 4; ⏲4am-midnight, information counter 6am-9.30pm; Ⓜ Florenc) in Prague. The station is equipped with an information booth, ticket windows, shops and a Burger King restaurant.

Several bus lines run long-haul coach services to and from destinations around Europe. The leaders on the local market are **Student Agency** (☎800 100 300; www.studentagency.cz) and **Eurolines** (www.elines.cz). Both have offices at the bus station.

TRAIN

Praha hlavní nádraží (Main Train Station; ☎840 112 113; www.cd.cz; Wilsonova 8, Nové Město) in Prague is the country's international train gateway, with service to and from Germany, Poland, Slovakia and Austria. Trains to/from the south and east, including from Bratislava, Vienna and Budapest, stop at Brno's main train station.

In Prague, buy international train tickets in advance from **ČD Travel** (☎972 241 861; www.cdtravel.cz; Wilsonova 8), which has an office on the lower level of Praha hlavní nádraží. Credit cards are accepted.

Both InterRail and Eurail passes are valid on the Czech rail network.

Getting Around

Bus

Buses are often faster, cheaper and more convenient than trains. Many bus routes have reduced frequency (or none) at weekends. Buses occasionally leave early so get to the station at least 15 minutes before departure time. Check bus timetables and prices at www.idos.cz.

ČSAD (☎information line 900 144 444) National bus company links cities and smaller towns.

Student Agency (☎800 100 300; www.studentagency.cz) Popular bus company with several destinations, including Prague, Brno, České Budějovice, Český Krumlov, Karlovy Vary and Plzeň.

Car & Motorcycle

For breakdown assistance anywhere in the country, dial ☎1230.

The minimum driving age is 18 and traffic moves on the right. Children under 12 are prohibited from sitting in the front seat.

Drivers are required to keep their headlights on at all times. The legal blood-alcohol limit is zero.

Train

Czech Railways provides efficient train services to almost every part of the country. See www.idos.cz and www.cd.cz for fares and timetables.

Estonia

Includes »

Tallinn 322
Northeastern Estonia .. 330
Lahemaa National Park 330
Southeastern Estonia ... 331
Tartu 331
Western Estonia 334
Pärnu 334
Understand Estonia 335
Survival Guide 336

Best Places to Eat

» F-hoone (p327)
» III Draakon (p328)
» Supelsaksad (p335)
» Must Puudel (p327)
» Olde Hansa (p327)

Best Places to Stay

» Villa Hortensia (p326)
» Toomarahva Turismitalu (p330)
» Tallinn Backpackers (p326)
» Terviseks (p332)

Why Go?

Estonia doesn't have to struggle to find a point of difference: it's completely unique. It shares a similar geography and history with Latvia and Lithuania, but it's culturally very different. Its closest ethnic and linguistic buddy is Finland, yet although they may love to get naked together in the sauna, 50 years of Soviet rule have separated the two. For the past 300 years Estonia's been linked to Russia, but the two states have as much in common as a barn swallow and a bear (their respective national symbols).

In recent decades, and with a new-found confidence, Estonia has crept from under the Soviet blanket and leapt into the arms of Europe. The love affair is mutual: Europe has fallen for the chocolate-box allure of Tallinn and its Unesco-protected Old Town, while travellers seeking something different are tapping into Estonia's captivating blend of eastern European and Nordic appeal.

When to Go

Tallinn

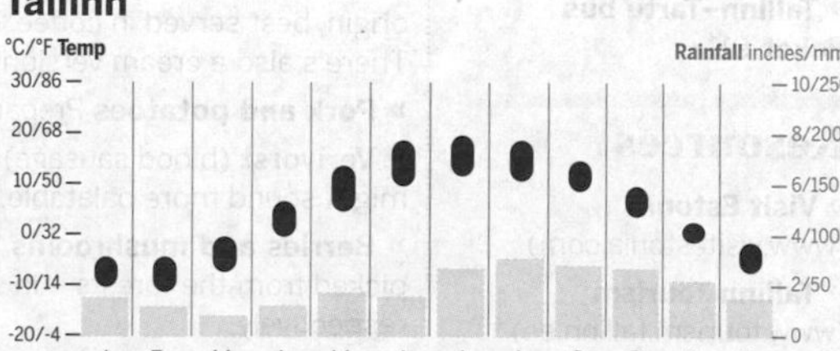

Apr–May See the country shake off winter's gloom.

Jun–Aug White Nights, beach parties and loads of summer festivals.

Dec Christmas markets, mulled wine and long cosy nights.

AT A GLANCE

- **Currency** Euro (€)
- **Language** Estonian
- **Money** ATMs all over
- **Visas** Not required for citizens of the EU, UK, USA, Canada, New Zealand and Australia

Fast Facts

- **Area** 45,226 sq km
- **Capital** Tallinn
- **Country code** ☎372
- **Emergency** Ambulance & fire ☎112, police ☎110

Exchange Rates

Australia	A$1	€0.82
Canada	C$1	€0.77
Japan	¥100	€0.83
New Zealand	NZ$1	€0.65
UK	UK£1	€1.18
USA	US$1	€0.78

Set Your Budget

- **Budget hotel room** €45
- **Two-course meal** €8–15
- **Museum entrance** €3–5
- **Beer** €2–3
- **Tallinn–Tartu bus ticket** €11

Resources

- **Visit Estonia** (www.visitestonia.com)
- **Tallinn Tourism** (www.tourism.tallinn.ee)
- **Estonica** (www.estonica.org)

Connections

Estonia is well connected for visiting its neighbours. It's an easy northern addition to eastern European roaming, as plenty of daily buses connect with Rīga and Vilnius, the Latvian and Lithuanian capitals. There's the option of following the white nights to Scandinavia – Tallinn has daily ferry connections to and from Stockholm and Helsinki. If you're hearing the siren call of Russia, daily trains connect Tallinn with Moscow or St Petersburg, and plenty of buses run to St Petersburg from Tallinn and Tartu.

ITINERARIES

Three Days

Hit Tallinn at a weekend to get in your sightseeing and partying. Get your bearings by heading to Raekoja plats to climb up the town hall tower. Follow this with an in-depth exploration of the Old Town streets down below: museums, shops, churches, courtyards – whatever takes your fancy. That night treat yourself to a medieval feast at Olde Hansa. The following day, do what most tourists don't – step out of Old Town. Explore Kadriorg Park for a first-rate greenery and art fix, and/or consider a cycling tour. Finish with a walk around Kalamaja district and dinner at F-hoone. After the weekend, head northeast to Lahemaa National Park – two (or four) wheels will offer the chance to really explore.

One Week

There'll be time to explore Tallinn more deeply, then Altja in Lahemaa National Park offers a rustic retreat. If the weather's fine, opt for beachside fun in Pärnu; finish with a pub crawl in student-savvy Tartu.

Essential Food & Drink

- **Vana Tallinn** A syrupy, sweet liqueur of indeterminate origin, best served in coffee, over ice or in champagne. There's also a cream version.
- **Pork and potatoes** Prepared a hundred different ways.
- **Verivorst** (blood sausage) Call it black pudding and it might sound more palatable.
- **Berries and mushrooms** Seasonal delights freshly picked from the forests – in summer and autumn, respectively.
- **Coffee and handmade chocolates** In one of Tallinn's cosy cafes.

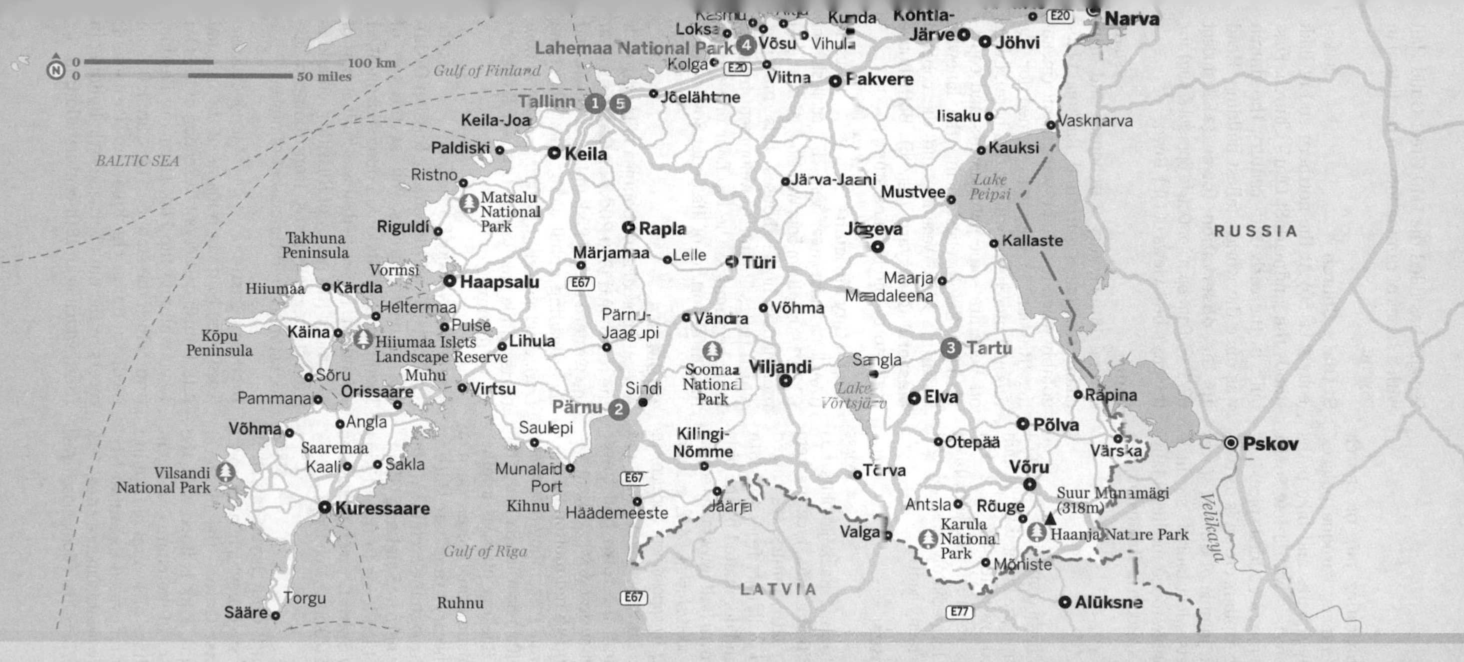

Estonia Highlights

1 Find medieval bliss exploring **Tallinn's Old Town** (p322), then unwind at leafy, lovely Kadriorg Park

2 Get sand in your shorts in **Pärnu** (p334), Estonia's summertime mecca

3 Further your local education among the bars and cafes of **Tartu** (p331), Estonia's second city

4 Cycle between manor houses and discover your own slice of deserted coast in **Lahemaa National Park** (p330)

5 Delve into recent history in **Tallinn's museums** (p322) dedicated to the Soviet era

TALLINN

POP 416,500

Tallinn is an intoxicating mix of church spires, glass skyscrapers, baroque palaces, cafes set on sunny squares and bike paths to beaches and forests – with a few Soviet throwbacks in the mix, for added spice.

The jewel in the capital's crown is its two-tiered Old Town, a jumble of turrets, spires and winding streets. Most tourists see little more than this cobblestoned medieval labyrinth, but Tallinn's modern dimension is a cool surprise.

Sights

The medieval Old Town comprises Toompea (the upper town) and the lower town, which is still surrounded by much of its 2.5km defensive wall. Its centre is Raekoja plats (Town Hall Sq). Immediately east of Old Town is the modern city centre.

LOWER OLD TOWN

Raekoja Plats SQUARE

(Town Hall Sq) Photogenic Raekoja plats has been the heart of Tallinn life since markets began here in the 11th century. It's ringed by pastel-coloured buildings from the 15th to 17th centuries and dominated by the only surviving Gothic **town hall** (www.tallinn.ee/raekoda; Raekoja plats; adult/student €4/2; ⌚10am-4pm Mon-Sat Jul-Aug, by appointment Sep-Jun) in northern Europe, built between 1371 and 1404. You can climb the **town hall tower** (Raekoja plats; adult/student €3/1; ⌚11am-6pm May–mid-Sep) for superb red-rooftop views.

The **Town Council Pharmacy** (Raeapteek; Raekoja plats 11; ⌚10am-6pm Tue-Sat), on the northern side of Raekoja plats, is another ancient Tallinn institution; there's been a pharmacy or apothecary's shop here since at least 1422. Duck through the arch beside the pharmacy into the narrow **Saiakang** (White Bread Passage), which leads to the striking 14th-century **Holy Spirit Church** (Pühavaimu 2; adult/concession €1/0.50; ⌚Mon-Sat).

Pikk STREET

From the Holy Spirit Church you can stroll along Pikk (Long Street), which runs north to the **Great Coast Gate** – the medieval exit to Tallinn's port. Pikk is lined with the 15th-century houses of merchants and gentry, plus the buildings of several old Tallinn guilds. The newly renovated **Estonian History Museum** (www.ajaloomuuseum.ee; Pikk 17; adult/student €5/3; ⌚10am-6pm, closed Wed Sep-Apr) has filled the 1410 Great Guild Hall with a series of ruminations on the Estonian psyche.

St Olaf's Church CHURCH

(entry at Lai 50) At the northern end of Pikk stands the landmark St Olaf's Church. First built in the early 13th century, the church was once the world's tallest building. Head up the **observation tower** (adult/student €2/1; ⌚10am-6pm Apr-Oct, to 8pm Jul & Aug) for the city's best views of Old Town.

Vene STREET

Several 15th-century warehouses and merchant residences surround Raekoja plats, notably when heading towards Vene (meaning 'Russian' in Estonian; named for the Russian merchants who traded here). Lying off Vene are some passageways and courtyards – the loveliest being the laneway, **Katariina käik** (Vene 12), and the cobbled **Masters' Courtyard** (Vene 6). Both house craft stores and artisans' studios.

Tallinn City Museum MUSEUM

(www.linnamuuseum.ee; Vene 17; adult/student €3.20/1.90; ⌚10am-5pm Wed-Mon) A medieval merchant's home houses this museum, which traces Tallinn's development from its early beginnings. The top floor presents an insightful portrait of life under Soviet rule.

TOOMPEA

A regal approach to Toompea hill is through the red-roofed 1380 **Pikk jalg Gate Tower** at the western end of Pikk in Lower Town, and then heading uphill along Pikk jalg (Long Leg). Alternatively, a winding stairway connects Lühike jalg (Short Leg), off Rataskaevu, to Toompea.

Alexander Nevsky Cathedral CHURCH

(Lossi plats) The 19th-century Russian Orthodox cathedral greets you at the top of Toompea in all its onion-domed, icon-filled splendour. The cathedral was built as part of Alexander III's policy of Russification and is sited strategically across from Toompea Castle, Estonia's traditional seat of power.

Toompea Castle HISTORIC BUILDING

(Lossi plats) Nothing remains of the original 1219 Danish castle; only a section of the Old Town wall and the Pikk Hermann Bastion, from which the state flag flies, are left from medieval times. The Riigikogu (Parliament) meets in the pink baroque-style building in front, which is an 18th-century addition.

Kiek in de Kök TOWER, MUSEUM
(☎644 6686; www.linnamuuseum.ee/kok; Komandandi tee; adult/student €4.50/2.60; ⊙10.30am-6pm Tue-Sun) Kiek in de Kök, a formidable cannon tower built around 1475, houses a museum documenting the development of Tallinn's elaborate defences. Its kooky-sounding name is Low German for 'Peep into the Kitchen' – from the upper floors of the tower, medieval voyeurs could see into Old Town kitchens.

Dome Church CHURCH
(Toom-Kooli 6; ⊙9am-5pm) Toompea is named after this sombre and austere Lutheran Dome Church (Toomkirik), founded in 1233. From the church, follow Kohtu to the city's favourite **lookout** over Lower Town.

Museum of Occupations MUSEUM
(www.okupatsioon.ee; Toompea 8; adult/student €4/2; ⊙10am-6pm Tue-Sun) This absorbing museum, just downhill from Toompea, focuses on Estonia's 20th-century occupations (Nazi and Soviet) – and the joy of a happy ending.

CITY CENTRE

TOP CHOICE **Hotel Viru KGB Museum** MUSEUM
(☎680 9300; www.sokoshotels.fi; Viru väljak 4; tour €8; ⊙closed Mon Nov-Mar) When Hotel Viru was built in 1972 it was not only Estonia's first skyscraper, it was the only place for tourists to stay in Tallinn. Having all the foreigners in one place made it easier to keep tabs on them and the locals they had contact with, which is exactly what the KGB did from its 23rd-floor spy base. The hotel offers insightful and entertaining guided tours of the facility; call ahead for times and bookings.

KADRIORG

To reach the lovely wooded **Kadriorg Park**, 2km east of Old Town along Narva mnt, take tram 1 or 3. There are a number of museums here, plus a fine cafe.

Kadriorg Palace PALACE, MUSEUM
(A Weizenbergi 37) Kadriorg Park and its centrepiece, the splendid Kadriorg Palace (1718–36), were designed for Peter the Great's wife Catherine I. The palace is now home to the **Kadriorg Art Museum** (www.ekm.ee; A Weizenbergi 37; adult/student €4.50/2.50; ⊙10am-5pm Tue-Sun May-Sep, 10am-5pm Wed-Sun Oct-Apr), showcasing 17th- and 18th-century foreign art.

FREE THRILLS

» Absorb the medieval magic by wandering Old Town – on your own or on a free tour.

» Admire the bird's-eye views from Toompea viewpoints on Kohtu and off nearby Toom-Kooli.

» Get a breath of fresh air at Kadriorg Park.

» Hit the beach at Pirita or retro-Soviet Stroomi.

» Browse the artisans' studios of Katariina käik and Masters' Courtyard.

Kumu ART MUSEUM
(www.ekm.ee; Weizenbergi 34; adult/student €5.50/3.20; ⊙11am-6pm Tue-Sun May-Sep, 11am-6pm Wed-Sun Oct-Apr) The first-rate, futuristic Kumu (the name is short for *kunstimuuseum*, meaning 'art museum') contains the largest repository of Estonian art as well as constantly changing contemporary exhibits.

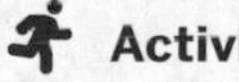

Activities

Waterparks are big business in Estonia; the biggest in Tallinn is the **Kalev Spa Waterpark** (www.kalevspa.ee; Aia 18; 2½hr visit adult/family €10.90/33; ⊙6.45am-9.30pm Mon-Fri, 8am-9.30pm Sat & Sun), just outside Old Town, offering plenty of ways to wrinkle your skin. There's also a gym and day spa there.

The most popular **beaches** are at Pirita (northeast of the centre; bus 1A, 8, 34A and 38) and Stroomi (4km due west of the centre; bus 40).

Tours

Traveller Info Tent WALKING, CYCLING
(☎5837 4800; www.traveller.ee; Niguliste; ⊙9am-9pm mid-May–mid-Sep) Runs entertaining, good-value walking and cycling city tours – including a free, two-hour walking tour of the capital, departing at noon daily. Three-hour bike tours (€13) take in the town's well-known eastern attractions (Kadriorg, Pirita etc), or more offbeat areas to the west. There's also a pub crawl (€16, including drinks) and day trips to Lahemaa National Park (€49). From mid-May to mid-September the tours run from the tent itself; the rest of the year they need to be booked in advance (website or phone). Winter tours are weather dependent.

Tallinn

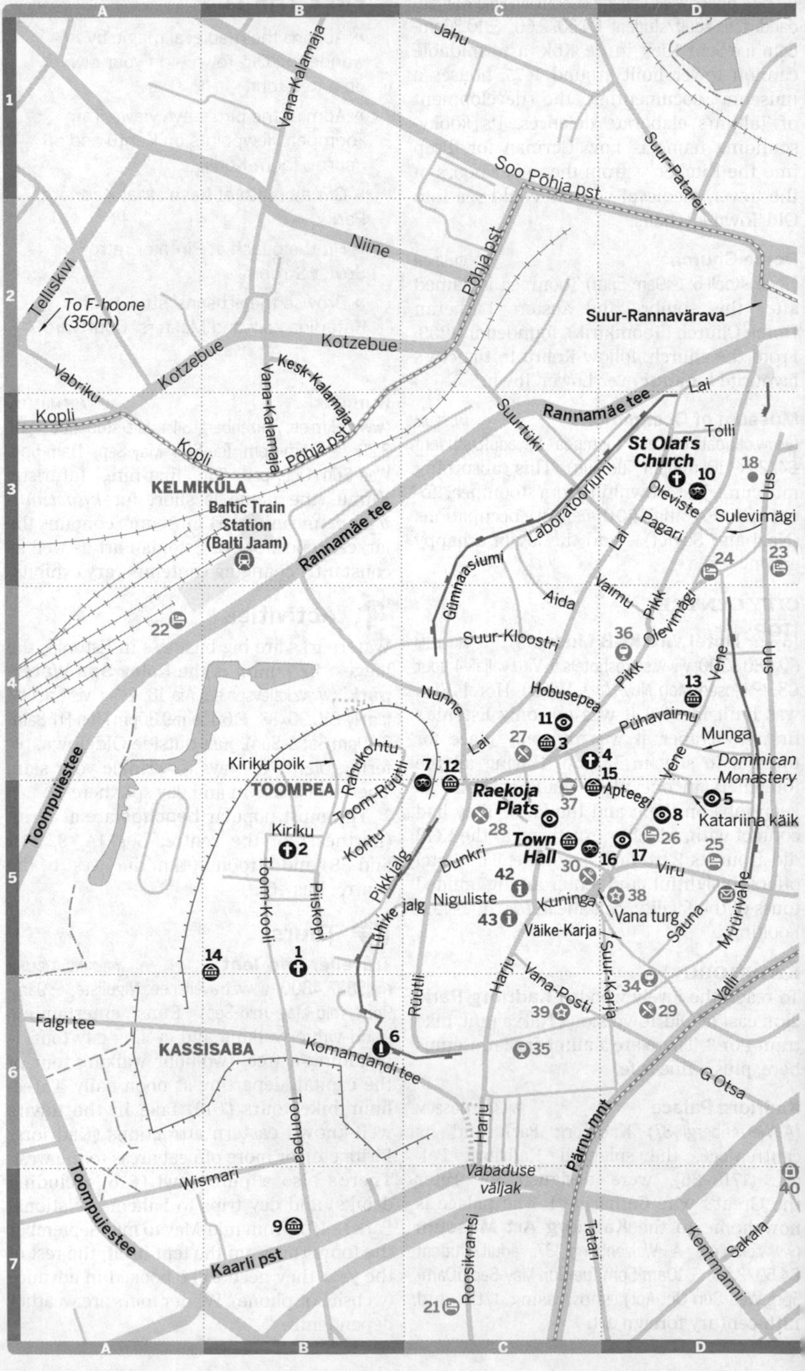

A B C D
1 2 3 4 5 6 7

Jahu
Vana-Kalamaja
Suur-Patarei
Soo
Põhja pst
Niine
Põhja pst
Telliskivi
To F-hoone (350m)
Suur-Rannavärava
Kotzebue
Kotzebue
Kesk-Kalamaja
Vana-Kalamaja
Vabriku
Kopli
Kopli
Põhja pst
Suurtüki
Rannamäe tee
Lai
Tolli
St Olaf's Church
10
18
Uus
Laboratooriumi
Oleviste
Pagari
Sulevimägi
KELMIKÜLA
Baltic Train Station (Balti Jaam)
Rannamäe tee
Gümnaasiumi
Lai
24
23
Vaimu
Aida
Pikk
Olevimägi
22
Suur-Kloostri
36
Uus
Vene
13
Hobusepea
Nunne
Pikk
Pühavaimu
11
27
3
Lai
Munga
Rahukohtu
Kiriku poik
7
12
4
15
Dominican Monastery
TOOMPEA
Toom-Rüütli
37
Apteegi
Vene
5
Raekoja Plats
8
Katariina käik
Kiriku
2
Kohtu
28
Town Hall
26
25
Pikk jalg
Dunkri
30
16
17
Viru
Toom-Kooli
Piiskopi
42
38
Lühike jalg
Niguliste
Kuninga
Vana turg
43
Sauna
Müürivahe
Väike-Karja
1
14
Suur-Karja
Harju
Vana-Posti
34
Valli
39
29
Rüütli
Falgi tee
6
KASSISABA
Komandandi tee
35
G Otsa
Toompuiestee
Toompea
Harju
Pärnu mnt
Wismari
Vabaduse väljak
40
9
Roosikrantsi
Tatari
Kentmanni
Sakala
Toompuiestee
Kaarli pst
21

ESTONIA TALLINN

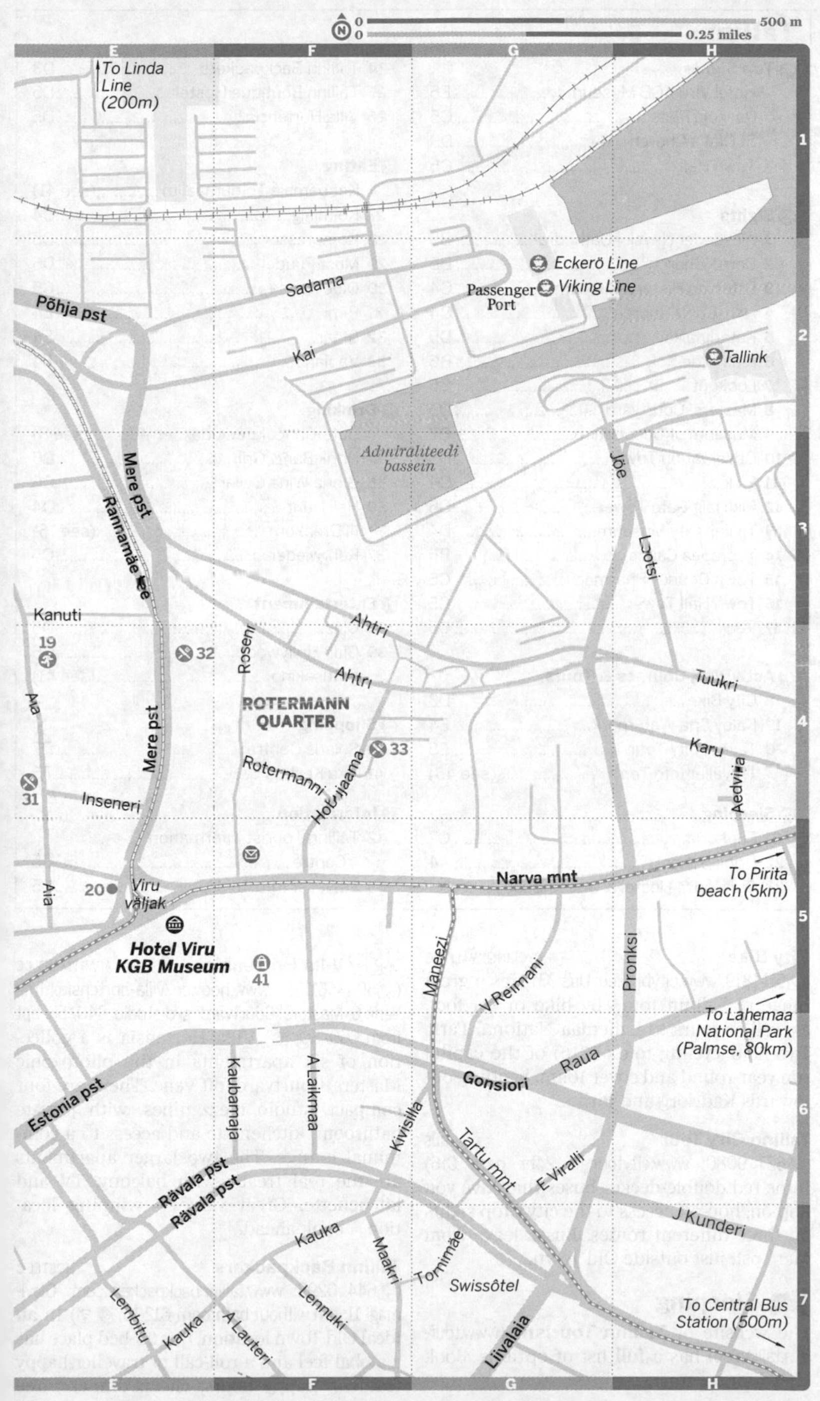

0 500 m
0 0.25 miles
To Linda Line (200m)
Eckerö Line
Viking Line
Passenger Port
Tallink
Sadama
Põhja pst
Kai
Admiraliteedi bassein
Mere pst
Ranniamäe tee
Jõe
Lootsi
Kanuti
19
32
Rotermann
Ahtri
Ahtri
Tuukri
ROTERMANN QUARTER
Aia
Mere pst
33
Karu
Rotermanni
Hobujaama
Aedvilja
31
Inseneri
Narva mnt
To Pirita beach (5km)
Aia
20
Viru väljak
Hotel Viru KGB Museum
41
Maneezi
V Reimani
Pronksi
To Lahemaa National Park (Palmse, 80km)
Estonia pst
Kaubamaja
A Laikmaa
Raua
Gonsiori
Kivisilla
Tartu mnt
E Viralli
Rävala pst
Rävala pst
J Kunderi
Kauka
Maakri
Tornimäe
Swissôtel
To Central Bus Station (500m)
Lembitu
Kauka
A Lauteri
Lennuki
Liivalaia
ESTONIA TALLINN

Tallinn

Top Sights

- Hotel Viru KGB Museum ... E5
- Raekoja Plats ... C5
- St Olaf's Church ... D3
- Town Hall ... C5

Sights

1 Alexander Nevsky Cathedral ... B5
2 Dome Church ... B5
3 Estonian History Museum ... C4
4 Holy Spirit Church ... C4
5 Katariina käik ... D5
6 Kiek in de Kök ... B6
7 Lookout ... C5
8 Masters' Courtyard ... D5
9 Museum of Occupations ... B7
10 Observation Tower ... D3
11 Pikk ... C4
12 Pikk jalg Gate Tower ... C5
13 Tallinn City Museum ... D4
14 Toompea Castle ... B5
15 Town Council Pharmacy ... C5
16 Town Hall Tower ... C5
17 Vene ... D5

Activities, Courses & Tours

18 City Bike ... D3
19 Kalev Spa Waterpark ... E4
20 Tallinn City Tour ... E5
Traveller Info Tent ... (see 43)

Sleeping

21 Euphoria ... C7
22 Hotel Schnelli ... A4
23 Old House Hostel & Guesthouse ... D3
24 Tallinn Backpackers ... D3
25 Tallinn Boutique Hostel ... D5
26 Villa Hortensia ... D5

Eating

Kaubamaja Toidumaailm ... (see 41)
27 Kolmjalg ... C4
28 Kompressor ... C5
29 Must Puudel ... D6
30 Olde Hansa ... C5
31 Rimi ... E4
32 Sfäär ... E4
33 Vapiano ... F4

Drinking

Cafe-Chocolaterie de Pierre ... (see 8)
34 Drink Bar & Grill ... D6
35 Gloria Wine Cellar ... C6
36 Hell Hunt ... D4
III Draakon ... (see 16)
37 Kehrwieder ... C5

Entertainment

38 Clazz ... D5
39 Club Hollywood ... C6
Katusekino ... (see 41)

Shopping

40 Solaris Centre ... D7
41 Viru Keskus ... F5

Information

42 Tallinn Tourist Information Centre ... C5
43 Traveller Info Tent ... C5

City Bike CYCLING, WALKING
(☎511 1819; www.citybike.ee; Uus 33) Has a great range of Tallinn tours by bike or on foot, as well as tours to Lahemaa National Park. Two-hour cycling tours (€16) of the capital run year-round and cover 16km, heading out towards Kadriorg and Pirita.

Tallinn City Tour BUS
(☎627 9080; www.citytour.ee; 24hr pass €16) Runs red double-decker buses that give you hop-on, hop-off access to the city's top sights on three different routes. Buses leave from Mere pst, just outside Old Town.

Sleeping

The website of **Tallinn Tourism** (www.tourism.tallinn.ee) has a full list of options. Book ahead for summer.

TOP CHOICE **Villa Hortensia** APARTMENT €€
(☎504 6113; www.hoov.ee/villa-hortensia.html; Vene 6, Masters' Courtyard; s/d studio €40/55, apt from €60/80; wi-fi) Villa Hortensia is a collection of six apartments in the photogenic Masters' Courtyard, off Vene. There are four compact, studio mezzanines, with private bathroom, kitchenette and access to a communal lounge. The two larger apartments are the real treats, with balcony, TV and kitchenette. Great value + winning location = book ahead.

Tallinn Backpackers HOSTEL €
(☎644 0298; www.tallinnbackpackers.com; Olevimägi 11; dm without bathroom €12-15; @ wi-fi) In an ideal Old Town location, this 26-bed place has a global feel and a roll-call of traveller-happy features: happy hours, cheap dinners, free

wi-fi and internet, lockers, a free sauna and day trips to nearby attractions. Staff organise pub crawls and city tours, and a shuttle bus to Rīga (Latvia). Private rooms are available at the offshoot **Tallinn Boutique Hostel** (☎644 6050; www.tallinnboutiquehostel.com; Viru 5, 3rd fl; s/d without bathroom €25/40; @📶), also known as Viru Backpackers, which has less atmosphere but a central location; one downside is the shortage of shared bathrooms.

Old House Hostel & Guesthouse GUESTHOUSE €
(☎641 1281; www.oldhouse.ee; Uus 22 & Uus 26; dm/s/d without bathroom €15/30/44; P@📶) Although one is called a hostel, these twin establishments feel more like cosy guesthouses, with homey decor (antiques, plants, lamps and bedspreads, with minimal bunks) to appeal to the more mature budgeteer. Dorms and private rooms are available at both (all bathrooms shared); guest kitchen, free wi-fi and parking are quality extras. Management also rents fantastic Old Town apartments at reasonable prices (see website).

Hotel Schnelli HOTEL €€
(☎631 0102; www.gohotels.ee; Toompuiestee 37; r from €55; P@📶) This modern hotel at the train station across the street from Old Town isn't just for train travellers. The block-boring building is home to small but fresh and functional rooms, and offers decent value a short walk from Old Town; rates include buffet breakfast, parking and wi-fi. Green Wing rooms have views to the park opposite and Old Town beyond; cheaper Blue Wing rooms overlook the station.

Euphoria HOSTEL €
(☎5837 3602; www.euphoria.ee; Roosikrantsi 4; dm €11-18, d without bathroom €40; P@📶) So laid-back it's almost horizontal, this backpacker hostel, just south of Old Town, has adopted some very '60s hippie vibes and given them a modern twist. It's a fun place to stay, with a sense of traveller community – especially if you like hookah pipes, bongo drums, jugglers, musos, artists and impromptu late-night jam sessions (pack earplugs if you don't).

Eating

Global cuisines are well represented in Tallinn and prices are low compared with most other European capitals. Many drinking establishments are also an option for food.

OLD TOWN

TOP CHOICE **Must Puudel** CAFE €
(Müürivahe 20; mains under €5) From any angle, the 'Black Poodle' is a near-perfect loungey cafe-bar: mismatched '70s furniture, eclectic soundtrack, courtyard seating, excellent coffee, cooked breakfasts, tasty light meals and long opening hours.

Olde Hansa MEDIEVAL €€
(www.oldehansa.ee; Vana turg 1; mains €13-26) Candlelit Olde Hansa is the place to indulge in a gluttonous feast. And if the medieval music, staff clad in ye-olde garb and aromas of red wine and roast meats sound a bit much, take heart – the chefs have done their research in producing historically authentic fare. It may be pitched heavily at tourists, but even locals rate this place.

Kompressor PANCAKES €
(Rataskaevu 3; pancakes €3.50-4) Under an industrial ceiling you can plug any holes in your stomach with cheap pancakes of the sweet or savoury persuasion. By night, this is a decent detour for a budget drink. It's low on aesthetics but high on value.

OUTSIDE OLD TOWN

TOP CHOICE **F-hoone** INTERNATIONAL €
(Telliskivi 60a; mains €5-8.50) If you suspected there was a cool, casual eatery hidden away somewhere – where in-the-know locals head for quality, cheap feed – you're right. Hidden in an old warehouse complex on the wrong side of the tracks (now used as artist studios, workshops and band rehearsal spaces), this cavernous place embraces industrial chic. We especially love how the budget prices belie an excellent international menu.

Sfäär INTERNATIONAL €€
(www.sfaar.ee; Mere pst 6e; mains €8-18) Chic, multipurpose Sfäär delivers an inventive menu highlighting the best Estonian produce

> **SELF-CATERING**
>
> There's a 24-hour grocery store, **Kolmjalg** (Pikk 11), in Old Town. Good supermarkets include **Rimi** (Aia 7; ⏲8am-10pm), on the outskirts of Old Town, and **Kaubamaja Toidumaailm** (Viru väljak 4; ⏲9am-9pm), in the basement of Viru Keskus shopping centre.

in a warehouse-style setting that's like something out of a Nordic design catalogue.

Vapiano ITALIAN €
(Hobujaama 10; pizza & pasta €5-8) Choose your pasta or salad from the appropriate counter and watch as it's prepared in front of you. If it's pizza you're after, you'll receive a pager to notify you when it's ready. This is 'fast' food done healthy, fresh and cheap in a big, bright setting. There's a second branch inside the Solaris Centre shopping mall.

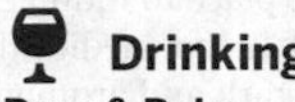

Drinking

Bars & Pubs

Hell Hunt PUB
(www.hellhunt.ee; Pikk 39) See if you can score a few of the comfy armchairs out the back of this trouper of the pub circuit. It boasts an amiable air and reasonable prices for local-brewed beer and cider, plus decent pub grub. Don't let the menacing-sounding name put you off – it means 'Gentle Wolf'.

Drink Bar & Grill PUB
(Väike-Karja 8) You know a bar means business when it calls itself Drink. This place takes its beer (and cider) seriously and offers plenty of beer-friendly accompaniments: traditional pub grub, happy hours, big-screen sports, and comedy and quiz nights.

Gloria Wine Cellar WINE BAR
(www.gloria.ee; Müürivahe 2; ⊙noon-11pm Mon-Sat) This romantic, mazelike cellar has a number of candlelit nooks and crannies where you can secrete yourself with a date and/or a good bottle of shiraz.

Cafes

Kehrwieder CAFE
(www.kohvik.ee; Saiakang 1; ⊙8am-midnight) Sure. Kehrwieder has seating with a view on Raekoja plats, but inside the city's cosiest cafe is where ambience is found in spades – you can stretch out on a couch, read by lamplight and bump your head on the arched ceilings.

III Draakon CAFE
(Raekoja plats; ⊙8am-midnight) There's bucketloads of atmosphere at this lilliputian cafe below the Town Hall, and super-cheap elk soup or oven-hot pies (€1!). The historic setting is amped up: expect costumed wenches with a good line in tourist banter and beer served in ceramic steins.

Cafe-Chocolaterie de Pierre CAFE
(www.pierre.ee; Vene 6, Masters' Courtyard; ⊙10am-11pm) Nestled inside the picturesque Masters' Courtyard, this snug, antique-filled cafe makes you feel like you're hiding away at your granny's place. It's renowned for its handmade chocolates.

☆ Entertainment

TOP CHOICE **Katusekino** OUTDOOR CINEMA
(www.katusekino.ee; Viru väljak, Viru Keskus; ⊙May-Sep) In the warmer months, a fun outdoor cinema is set up on the rooftop of Viru Keskus shopping centre. It screens an eclectic list (cult classics, as well as interesting new releases). Screen times depend on sunset – anything from 9pm (September) to 11pm (July).

Club Hollywood CLUB
(www.club-hollywood.ee; Vana-Posti 8; ⊙11pm-5am Wed-Sat) A multilevel emporium of mayhem, this is the nightclub that draws the largest crowds. Plenty of tourists and Tallinn's young party set mix it up to international and local DJs. Wednesday night is ladies' night (free entry for women), so expect to see loads of guys looking to get lucky.

Clazz LIVE MUSIC
(www.clazz.ee; Vana turg 2) Behind the cheesy name (a contraction of 'classy jazz') is a popular restaurant-bar, featuring live music every night (cover charge varies) and food served into the wee hours.

Shopping

Inside Old Town, dozens of small shops sell Estonian-made handicrafts, linen, leatherbound books, ceramics, jewellery, silverware, stained glass and objects carved from limestone or made from juniper wood. Look for signs for *käsitöö* (handicrafts).

In summer a **souvenir market** is set up weekly (Wednesday) on Raekoja plats.

Viru Keskus SHOPPING MALL
(www.virukeskus.com; Viru väljak) Tallinn's showpiece shopping mall, aka Viru Centre, lies just outside Old Town. It's home to mainstream fashion boutiques and a great bookstore. In summer there's a rooftop cinema. The main terminal for local buses is underneath the complex.

Solaris Centre SHOPPING MALL
(www.solaris.ee; Estonia pst 9) Relative newcomer Solaris hosts a handful of boutiques, an excellent bookstore, popular restaurants, and both mainstream and art-house cinemas.

Information

Discount Cards

Tallinn Card (www.tallinncard.ee; 1-/2-/3-day card €24/32/40) Offers free rides on public transport, admission to museums, free excursions and discounts at restaurants. Buy online, from the tourist information centre or from many hotels.

Internet Access

Tallinn is flooded with free wi-fi, but if you're not packing a laptop you'll find the city light on internet cafes. Most hostels and hotels offer a computer for guest use.

Metro Internet (Viru väljak 4, basement, Viru Keskus; per hr €2.60; ⏲8am-11pm) By the bus terminal under Viru Keskus shopping centre.

Media

Like a Local (www.likealocalguide.com/tallinn) Produces an invaluable map of Tallinn highlighting recommended spots (also for Tartu and Pärnu). The website has great info too.

Lonely Planet (www.lonelyplanet.com/estonia/tallinn)

Tallinn In Your Pocket (www.inyourpocket.com) Full of useful listings. These booklets are on sale at bookshops or can be downloaded free online. Also has booklets covering Tartu and Pärnu.

Medical Services

Apteek 1 (Aia 7; ⏲8.30am-8.30pm Mon-Fri, 9am-8pm Sat, 10am-6pm Sun) One of many well-stocked *apteek* (pharmacies).

East-Tallinn Central Hospital (☎622 7070, emergency department 620 7040; www.itk.ee; Ravi 18) Full range of services plus 24-hour emergency room.

First-Aid Hotline (☎697 1145) English-language advice on treatment, hospitals and pharmacies.

Money

Tavid (Aia 5; ⏲24hr) Reliably good rates. Night-time rates aren't as good as those during business hours.

Post

Central Post Office (Narva mnt 1; ⏲8am-8pm Mon-Fri, 9am-3pm Sat) Entrance beside Nordic Hotel Forum.

Old Town Post Office (Viru 20; ⏲10am-6pm Mon-Fri, 10am-3pm Sat & Sun) Small branch in Old Town. Open weekends in summer.

Tourist Information

Tallinn Tourist Information Centre (www.tourism.tallinn.ee; cnr Kullassepa & Niguliste; ⏲9am-8pm Mon-Fri, to 6pm Sat & Sun mid-Jun–Aug, shorter hours Sep–mid-Jun) A block south of Raekoja plats, with maps and brochures for the capital and further afield. Note that it doesn't offer an accommodation-booking service.

Traveller Info Tent (www.traveller.ee; Niguliste; ⏲9am-9pm mid-May–mid-Sep) Great source of information, set up by young local students in a tent opposite the official tourist info centre. Dispenses lots of local tips and maps, keeps a 'what's on' board, and operates entertaining, well-priced walking and cycling tours.

Travel Agencies

Booking Estonia (☎557 7636; www.apartmentsestonia.com; Kullassepa 9) Agency booking bus and ferry tickets (no commission), and offering accommodation (including apartments in Old Town).

Getting There & Away

Boat

FROM FINLAND

Oodles of daily ferries ply the 85km separating Helsinki and Tallinn (ships take two to 3½ hours, hydrofoils approximately 1½ hours). In high winds or bad weather hydrofoils are often cancelled; they operate only when the sea is free from ice, while larger ferries sail year-round.

All companies provide concessions. Prices are cheaper on weekdays and outside summer. There's lots of competition, so shop around.

Eckerö Line (☎664 6000; www.eckeroline.ee; Terminal A; adult one way from €19; ⏲year-round) Large new vessel that sails once or twice daily in both directions. Journey time is 2½ hours.

Linda Line (☎699 9333; www.lindaliini.ee; Linnahall Terminal; from €31; ⏲late Mar-late Dec) Small, passenger-only hydrofoils up to seven times daily in season. Takes 1½ hours.

GETTING INTO TOWN

From Tallinn's airport, 4km from the centre, take local bus 2 to the city centre; taxis shouldn't charge more than €10 for the same journey. From the bus station (Autobussijaam), walk one block east to Tartu mnt, cross the street and hop on any tram into the centre. The train station is directly across the street, to the northwest, from Old Town and is served by trams 1 and 2, which take you downtown in three or four stops. The main ferry terminals are just 350m from the northeastern edge of Old Town – from these it's best to walk, though local bus 2 also services the port.

Tallink (☎640 9808; www.tallinksilja.com; Terminal D; adult from €19-54; ⊙year-round) Up to seven services daily in each direction. The huge *Baltic Princess* takes 3½ hours; newer high-speed ferries take two hours.

Viking Line (☎666 3966; www.vikingline.com; Terminal A; adult €19-47; ⊙year-round) Operates a giant car ferry, with two departures daily. Takes 2½ hours.

FROM SWEDEN

Tallink sails every night between Tallinn's Terminal D and Stockholm (passage from €39, 16 hours). Book ahead.

Bus

For bus information and advance tickets for Estonian and international destinations, go to the **Central Bus Station** (Autobussijaam; ☎12550; Lastekodu 46), about 2km southeast of Old Town (tram 2 or 4). The website **TPilet** (www.tpilet.ee) has times and prices for all national bus services.

Ecolines (☎606 2217; www.ecolines.net) and **Lux Express** (☎680 0909; www.luxexpress.eu) have offices at the bus station, but you can book online, or **Booking Estonia** (☎557 7636; www.apartmentsestonia.com; Kullassepa 9) in Old Town will issue tickets for no commission.

Ecolines connects Tallinn with several cities in central and eastern Europe. Lux Express has direct services connecting Tallinn with Rīga (Latvia; from €13, 4½ hours, up to eight daily) and Vilnius (Lithuania; from €22, 8½ hours to nine hours, three direct buses daily, plus additional services via Rīga). Lux Express buses leave Tallinn for St Petersburg up to 10 times daily (from €15, six to eight hours). Handily, Lux Express can help arrange Russian visas (see the website); however, due to changing regulations, it's best to arrange Russian visas in your home country. Lux Express offers different travel classes – the most expensive buses have free drinks and wi-fi.

Train

The **Central Train Station** (Balti Jaam; www.baltijaam.ee; Toompuiestee 35) is on the northwestern edge of Old Town, a short walk from Raekoja plats via Nunne, or three stops on tram 1 or 2 heading north from the Mere pst stop.

Train travel is not as popular as bus travel in Estonia, so domestic routes are limited.

There are no rail connections to Rīga (Latvia) or Vilnius (Lithuania), but there are daily services to and from Russia operated by **GO Rail** (☎631 0044; http://tickets.gorail.ee). An overnight train runs between Tallinn and Moscow (€129 in a four-berth compartment, 14½ hours). A daytime service has resumed between Tallinn and St Petersburg (from €22, 6½ hours).

Getting Around

Tallinn has an excellent network of buses, trams and trolleybuses that usually run from 6am to 11pm. The major local bus station is on the basement level of Viru Keskus shopping centre, just east of Old Town. Local public transport timetables are online at www.tallinn.ee.

In an innovative and generous move, public transport became free for Tallinn residents as of January 2013. Visitors still need to pay, using the new e-ticketing system (covers all three modes of local transport). Buy a plastic smartcard to top up with credit, then validate the card at the start of each journey using the orange card-readers. Fares using the e-ticketing system cost €1.10/3/5 for an hour/day/three days. Alternatively, you should still be able to buy a paper ticket *(piletid)* from the driver when you board (€1.60 for a single journey).

As well as offering city cycling and walking tours, City Bike (p326) can help you get around by bike, within Tallinn and around Estonia.

Taxis are plentiful, but it's best to order one by phone: try **Krooni Takso** (☎1212, 638 1212) or **Reval Takso** (☎601 4600).

NORTHEASTERN ESTONIA

Lahemaa National Park

The perfect country retreat from the capital, Lahemaa takes in a stretch of coast indented with peninsulas and bays, plus 475 sq km of forested hinterland. Visitors are looked after with cosy guesthouses, remote seaside camping grounds and a network of pine-scented forest trails.

Lahemaa also features restored manor houses. Park showpiece **Palmse Manor** (www.palmse.ee; adult/concession €4.80/3.20; ⊙10am-6pm or 7pm), next to the visitor centre, was once a wholly self-contained Baltic German estate; the pink-and-white neoclassical **Sagadi Manor** (www.sagadi.ee; adult/concession €2.60/1.30; ⊙10am-6pm May-Sep, by appointment Oct-Apr) was built in 1749. There are also manor houses at **Kolga** and **Vihula** – Vihula's is now part of a picturesque 'country club' featuring activities, a spa, restaurants and pricey accommodation (www.vihulamanor.com).

Sleeping & Eating

TOP CHOICE **Toomarahva Turismitalu** CAMPING, GUESTHOUSE €
(☎505 0850; www.toomarahva.ee; Altja; campsites €10, d €40-60; 📶) A farmstead with

thatch-roofed outhouses and a garden full of flowers and sculptures – this gem offers a taste of rural Estonia in the idyllic fishing village of Altja. There's a yard for camping, a barn full of beds, plus rooms in converted stables. There's also a sauna and bikes for rent. Ülle, the friendly owner, also offers catering. Signage is minimal – it's opposite the yard of the Altja Kõrts.

Sagadi Manor Hotel & Restaurant HOTEL €€
(☎676 7888; www.sagadi.ee; Sagadi; dm €15, s/d from €55/75, restaurant mains €7-15; @📶) With its whitewashed exterior and hanging flower baskets, the hotel on the Sagadi estate offers a cheerful welcome. The complex also has a 31-bed hostel in the old steward's house and a smart restaurant offers quality local flavours.

Altja Kõrts TRADITIONAL ESTONIAN €€
(Altja; mains €5-12; ⏲11am-9pm) Set in an old wooden farmhouse, this uber rustic inn serves delicious home cooking.

Information

Lahemaa National Park visitor centre (☎329 5555; www.lahemaa.ee; ⏲9am-6pm daily mid-Apr–mid-Oct, 9am-5pm Mon-Fri mid-Oct–mid-Apr) is in Palmse, 7km north of Viitna in the park's southeast, next door to Palmse Manor.

Getting There & Away

Hiring a car is one way to reach and explore the park; alternatively, take a tour (p323) from Tallinn. Many operators offer a day exploring the highlights for about €50. City Bike (p326) has accommodation packages that include transfer to the park plus bikes and maps for DIY touring (€93/113 for one/two nights).

Otherwise, for public transport exploration you'll need patience and time. The best starting point for buses to destinations within the park is the town of Rakvere, about halfway between Tallinn and border town Narva.

SOUTHEASTERN ESTONIA

Tartu

POP 102,000

If Tallinn is Estonia's head, Tartu may well be its heart. Small and provincial, Tartu is Estonia's premier university town, with students making up nearly one-fifth of the population. This injects a boisterous vitality into the leafy, historic setting and grants it a surprising sophistication for a city of its size.

Tartu was the cradle of Estonia's 19th-century national revival and it escaped Sovietisation to a greater degree than Tallinn. Today visitors to Estonia's second city can get a more authentic depiction of the rhythm of Estonian life than in its bigger, brasher cousin to the north.

Sights

As the major repository of Estonia's cultural heritage, Tartu has an abundance of first-rate museums. There are plenty more than those listed here (showcasing everything from brewing to sport to postal services to song festivals).

Raekoja plats SQUARE
At the town centre on cafe-filled Raekoja plats is the **town hall** (1782–89), fronted by a fountain and statue of students kissing under an umbrella – the light-hearted symbol of Tartu. At the other end of the square is the wonderfully skew-whiff building housing the **Tartu Art Museum** (www.tartmus.ee; Raekoja plats 18; adult/student €3/1.50; ⏲noon-6pm Wed-Sun).

Tartu University UNIVERSITY
(www.ut.ee; Ülikooli 18) The city's university was founded in 1632 by the Swedish king; the grand neoclassical main university building dates from 1804. It houses the **University Art Museum** (admission €1; ⏲11am-6pm Mon-Fri) and entertaining **Student's Lock-Up** (admission €1; ⏲11am-5pm Mon-Fri), where 19th-century students were held for their misdeeds.

St John's Church CHURCH
(Jaani 5; observation tower adult/child €1.60/1; ⏲10am-6pm Tue-Sat) This magnificent Gothic church features elaborate brickwork and dates back to at least 1323. Climb the 30m-high **observation tower** for panoramas of Tartu.

TOP CHOICE **Toy Museum** MUSEUM
(www.mm.ee; Lutsu 8; adult/child incl Theatre House €4/3; ⏲11am-6pm Wed-Sun) This enchanting museum showcases dolls, model trains, rocking horses, toy soldiers and tons of other desirables dating back a century or so. Down the road is the affiliated **Theatre House** (www.teatrikodu.ee; Lutsu 2; ⏲11am-6pm

Tartu

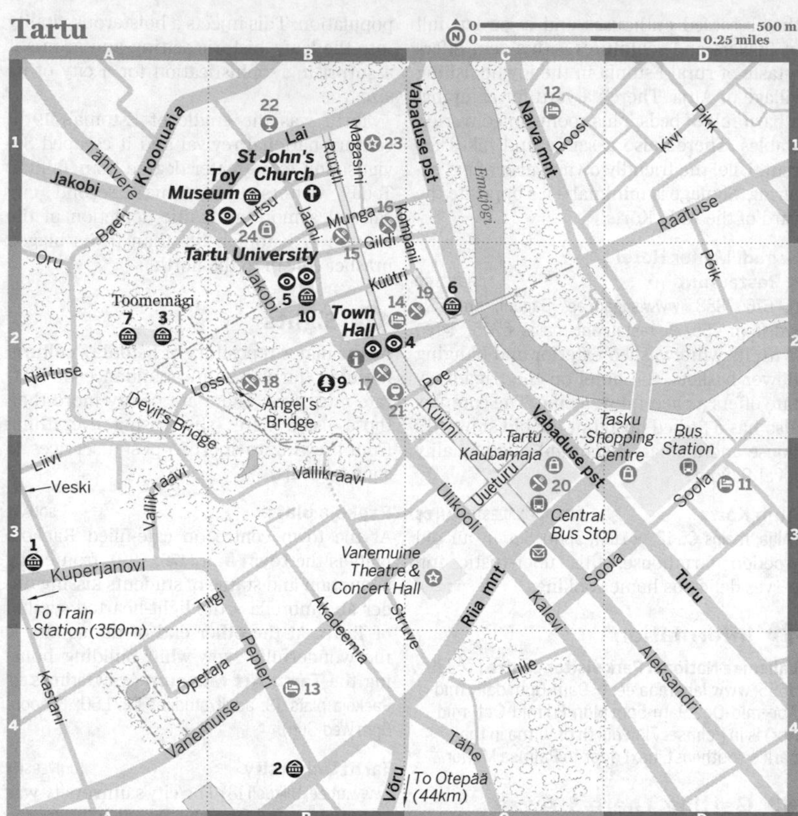

Wed-Sun), a newly restored children's theatre (performances usually in Estonian). In the basement is a petite museum exhibiting theatre puppets of the world. While you're in the neighbourhood, check out the cool crafty studios and workshops of **Antoniuse Gild** (Lutsu 5).

Estonian National Museum MUSEUM
(www.erm.ee; Kuperjanovi 9; all/permanent collections €3/2, admission free Fri; ⏲11am-6pm Tue-Sun) Small, sweet and proud (much like the country itself), this absorbing museum does a fine job tracing the history, life and traditions of the locals. There are ambitious plans to create a new home for the museum at Raadi Manor (on the outskirts of town) by 2015.

KGB Cells Museum MUSEUM
(www.linnamuuseum.tartu.ee; Riia mnt 15b; adult/student €2/1; ⏲11am-4pm Tue-Sat) The former KGB headquarters now houses this sombre and highly worthwhile museum. Chilling in parts, it gives a fascinating rundown of deportations during the Soviet era and life in the Gulag camps. Entrance is on Pepleri.

Toomemägi PARK
(Cathedral Hill) Rising to the west of Raekoja plats is the stroll-worthy Toomemägi, landscaped in the manner of a 19th-century English park. The 13th-century Gothic **Tartu Cathedral** (Toomkirik; Cathedral Hill) at the top was rebuilt in the 15th century, despoiled during the Reformation in 1525 and partly rebuilt in 1804–07 to accommodate the university library, now the **Museum of University History** (museum & tower/museum only €2.60/1.60; ⏲11am-5pm Wed-Sun).

Sleeping

Terviseks HOSTEL €
(☎565 5382; www.terviseksbbb.com; Raekoja plats 10, top fl; dm €15-17, s/d €22/44; @📶) In

Tartu

Top Sights

St John's Church........................B1
Tartu University........................B2
Town Hall........................B2
Toy Museum........................B1

Sights

1 Estonian National Museum........................A3
2 KGB Cells Museum........................B4
3 Museum of University History........................A2
4 Raekoja plats........................B2
5 Student's Lock-Up........................B2
6 Tartu Art Museum........................C2
7 Tartu Cathedral........................A2
8 Theatre House........................B1
9 Toomemägi........................B2
10 University Art Museum........................B2

Sleeping

11 Hotel Tartu........................D3
12 Tartu Student Village Hostels........................C1
13 Tartu Student Village Hostels........................B4
14 Terviseks........................B2

Eating

15 Crepp........................B1
16 La Dolce Vita........................B1
17 Noir........................B2
18 Püssirohukelder........................B2
19 Sõprade Juures........................C2
20 Supermarket........................C3

Drinking

21 Illegaard........................B2
Möku........................(see 15)
22 Zavood........................B1

Entertainment

23 Genialistide Klubi........................B1

Shopping

24 Antoniuse Gild........................B1

a perfect town-square location, this excellent 'backpackers bed & breakfast' (run by a Brit and a Canadian) offers dorms (maximum four beds, no bunks), private rooms, shiny new facilities and lots of switched-on info.

Tartu Student Hostels STUDENT RESIDENCES €
(☎742 7608; www.tartuhostel.eu; s/d €25/40;) Two student residences, Narva and Pepleri, offer outstanding value (but not much by way of character) in prime locations – **Pepleri** (Pepleri 14) is south of the river, **Narva** (Narva mnt 27) opposite parklands north of the city centre. The Narva apartments each have living room, bathroom and kitchenette. Pepleri's standard rooms are smaller (there's no living room), but larger apartments are available (for €50). Advance reservations a must.

Hotel Tartu HOTEL €€
(☎731 4300; www.tartuhotell.ee; Soola 3; hostel s/d/tr €32/44/56, s/d €45/65;) Handily placed across from the bus station and Tasku shopping centre, this hotel houses rooms from the Ikea school of decoration: low-frills and contemporary. The 'hostel' is actually six spotless, older-style hotel rooms (shared bathrooms in the corridor) sleeping three.

Eating & Drinking

The most central **supermarket** (9am-10pm Mon-Sat, 10am-8pm Sun) is in the basement of the Tartu Kaubamaja shopping centre.

La Dolce Vita ITALIAN €€
(Kompanii 10; pizza & pasta €5-10, mains €8-19) Thin-crust pizzas come straight from the wood-burning oven at this cheerful, family-friendly pizzeria. It's the real deal, with a big Italian menu of bruschetta, pizza, pasta, gelati etc and classic casual decor (red-and-white checked tablecloths, Fellini posters: tick).

Noir INTERNATIONAL €€
(Ülikooli 7; mains €7-12) This sexy, black-walled restaurant-cum-vinoteque is a fine place for wining, dining and reclining. It's tucked away in a flower-filled courtyard off Ülikooli, with outdoor tables and a well-priced fusion menu.

Crepp CAFE €
(Rüütli 16; crepes €4; from 11am daily) Locals love this place for its bargain-priced crêpes.

Püssirohukelder PUB €€
(Lossi 28; mains €7-18) Set in a cavernous 18th-century gunpowder cellar under a soaring, 10m-high vaulted ceiling, this is both a boisterous pub and a good choice for meaty meals. There's regular live music too.

STUDENT LIFE IN TARTU

The world over, students gravitate to cheap meals and booze, and in Tartu it's no different. Many of the cafes on Raekoja plats cater to impoverished students with good-value weekday lunches – check out **Sõprade Juures** (Raekoja plats 12), with its soup/dish of the day for €1.85/3.30. In the evening, down cheap beer (a half-litre for about €2) alongside students at dive bars like tiny basement **Möku** (Rüütli 18) and industrial-chic **Zavood** (Lai 30). Other popular drinking spots include **Illegaard** (Ülikooli 5), a laid-back pub where you're likely to encounter foreign students studying in Tartu, and the seriously cool **Genialistide Klubi** (www.genklubi.ee; behind Lai 37, enter from Magasini), an all-purpose, grungy 'subcultural establishment' that manages to simultaneously be a bar, cafe, alternative nightclub, live-music venue, cinema and more.

Information

Tartu Tourist Information Centre (☎744 2111; www.visittartu.com; Raekoja plats, town hall; ⏲9am-6pm Mon-Fri, 10am-5pm Sat & Sun mid-May–mid-Sep, 9am-5pm Mon-Fri, 10am-2pm Sat & Sun mid-Sep–mid-May) Can book accommodation, sell you souvenirs and get you online (free internet access).

Getting There & Away

BUS From the **bus station** (☎12550; Turu 2), daily buses run to and from Tallinn (€11, 2½ to three hours) about every 15 to 30 minutes from 6am to 9pm. At least 10 buses a day run to Pärnu (€10, 2½ to three hours). Four daily Lux Express buses connect Tartu with St Petersburg (from €20, 6½ hours).

TRAIN Four or five daily trains make the journey to and from Tallinn (€6.70, 2½ to three hours).

WESTERN ESTONIA

Pärnu

POP 44,000

Local families, young party-goers and German, Swedish and Finnish holidaymakers join together in a collective prayer for sunny weather while strolling the golden-sand beaches, sprawling parks and picturesque historic centre of Pärnu (*pair*-nu), Estonia's premier seaside resort.

Sights & Activities

Pärnu Beach BEACH

Pärnu's long, wide golden-sand beach – sprinkled with volleyball courts, cafes and tiny changing cubicles – is the city's main drawcard. A curving path stretches along the sand, lined with fountains and park benches perfect for people-watching. Ranna pst, the avenue that runs parallel to the beach, is home to the handsome 1927 neoclassical **Mudaravila** (Ranna pst 1). The legendary mud baths that once operated here have been closed for years, awaiting restoration.

Back from the sand, **Rannapark** holds picnic tables and plenty of fun draws (minigolf, trampolines, playgrounds) and in summer you can rent bikes.

Rüütli STREET

The main thoroughfare of the historic centre is Rüütli, lined with buildings dating back to the 17th century.

Veekeskus WATER PARK

(www.terviseparadiis.ee; Side 14; day ticket adult/concession €18/13; ⏲10am-10pm) At the far end of the beach, Estonia's largest water park beckons with pools, slides and other slippery fun. It's a family-focused draw, especially when bad weather ruins beach plans. It's part of the huge Tervise Paradiis spa hotel complex.

Sleeping

In summer it's worth booking ahead; outside high season you should be able to snare a good deal. Prices listed here are for high season (websites list off-season rates, which can be up to 50% lower).

Hommiku Hostel GUESTHOUSE €€

(☎445 1122; www.hommikuhostel.ee; Hommiku 17; dm/s/d €20/39/58; wi-fi) This modern, year-round option (more like a budget hotel than a hostel) is in a prime in-town position, offering handsome rooms with private bathrooms, TV and kitchenettes.

Konse Motel & Camping CAMPING, GUESTHOUSE €

(☎5343 5092; www.konse.ee; Suur-Jõe 44a; campsites €9-13, plus per person €2, d without/with bathroom €40/52; @ wi-fi) Perched by the river about 1km east of the centre (off Lai), Konse offers campsites and a variety of rooms (all with kitchen access). It's not an especially charming spot (and you're a couple of kilometres from the beach action) but there's a sauna, and bike and rowboat rental. Open year-round.

Eating

The most central supermarket is **Port Artur Toidukaubad** (9am-10pm) inside the Port Artur 2 complex, off Pikk and opposite the bus station.

TOP CHOICE Supelsaksad CAFE €

(cnr Supeluse & Nikolai; mains €6-12) The street of Supeluse is lined with pretty wooden villas and this one houses a colourful all day cafe, looking like it was designed by Barbara Cartland (bright pink and a riot of stripes and prints). The menu holds a mix of wraps, salads and pastas.

Si-si ITALIAN €€

(www.si-si.ee; Supeluse 21; pizza & pasta €5-8, mains €11-18.50) Beachside dining is disappointingly bland, but a walk up Supeluse presents alluring options – including this Italian restaurant-lounge. Inside is smart white-linen dining, outside is a stylishly relaxed terrace.

Mõnus Margarita TEX MEX €€

(Akadeemia 5; mains €4-16) Big, colourful and decidedly upbeat, as all good Tex-Mex places should be.

Drinking & Entertainment

Puhvet A.P.T.E.K. BAR

(www.aptek.ee; Rüütli 40; 7pm-3am Tue-Thu, 7pm-5am Fri & Sat) Drop by the old 1930s pharmacy to admire the clever restoration that has turned it into a smooth late-night haunt. Fabulous decor competes for your attention with DJs and €5 cocktails.

Sweet Rosie PUB

(Munga 2) Revellers jam into the warm, darkwood interior of this fun Irish pub for Guinness, pub grub, occasional live music and general good *craic*.

Sunset Club CLUB

(www.sunset.ee; Ranna pst 3; 11pm-5am or later Fri & Sat Jun-Aug) Pärnu's biggest and most famous summertime nightclub has an outdoor beach terrace and a sleek multifloor interior with plenty of cosy nooks for when the dance floor gets crowded. Imported DJs and bands, plus a young crowd, keep things cranked until the early hours.

Rannakino OUTDOOR CINEMA

(www.rannakino.ee; Ranna pst 3a; tickets €6) From the people behind Tallinn's Katusekino comes this cool summertime cinema, just back from the beach (next to Sunset Club). There's an eclectic mix of cult and classic films, plus a well-stocked bar.

Information

Pärnu Tourist Information Centre (447 3000; www.visitparnu.com; Uus 4; 9am-6pm daily mid-May–mid-Sep, 9am-5pm Mon-Fri, 10am-2pm Sat & Sun mid-Sep–mid May) Pick up maps and brochures, or use the free internet. Staff book accommodation or car hire for a €2 fee. There's information on summertime activities in the region, including guided walks, kayaking, horse riding and watersports.

Getting There & Away

About 25 daily buses connect Pärnu with Tallinn (€8, two hours) and about a dozen services connect Pärnu with Tartu (€10, 2½ to three hours). Tickets for a multitude of other destinations, including Rīga (Latvia) and beyond, are available at the Pärnu **bus station ticket office** (Ringi), across from the bus station. **Lux Express** (www.luxexpress.eu) runs up to seven services daily to Rīga (€8 to €20, 2½ hours).

UNDERSTAND ESTONIA

History

Most of Estonia's history has been one of occupation and domination. The country has been led by Danish, Swedish and Russian rulers and, later, bandied about between European major powers. It has enjoyed only sparse periods of independence, notably in the 20th century, between the world wars and since 1991.

In the 3rd millennium BC Finno-Ugric tribes from the east mixed with the Baltic tribes already there. The Germanic Teutonic Order took control in 1346, placing Estonians under servitude. The country had fallen under Swedish control by 1620, and then became part of the Russian empire after the Great Northern War (1700–21).

During WWI, the Soviet government relinquished Estonia and the country was ruled by benevolent dictator Konstantin Päts, until he was forced to accept Soviet occupation in 1940 following the Molotov-Ribbentrop Pact of 1939 between the USSR and Nazi Germany. During the Soviet occupation,

Estonia was 'accepted' into the USSR after fabricated elections and, within a year, more than 10,000 people in Estonia were killed or deported before the German occupation. Between 1945 and 1949 a further 60,000 Estonians were killed or deported.

Estonia declared independence from the USSR on 20 August 1991. It's now a member of NATO and the EU. The country has come to be seen as *the* post-Soviet economic miracle and in 2011 took the euro as its national currency. Business is recovering after the country was hit hard by the global financial crisis. The new currency highlights Estonia's resolve to look west, catch up with its Nordic neighbours, and to not look back (or east).

People

Estonia's population of 1.3 million is 69% Estonian and 26% Russian. The Russians are concentrated in Tallinn (39% of the city's population) and the industrial cities of the northeast (up to 95% of inhabitants).

Estonians are closely related to the Finns. They are historically a rural people, stereotypically shy and reticent, with a strong emotional connection to their history, folklore and national song tradition.

Environment

Estonia is only slightly bigger than Denmark or Switzerland. At a mere 318m, Suur Munamägi is the highest point in this low-lying country. Swamps, wetlands and forests make up half of Estonia's territory; there are more than 1500 islands along the 3794km-long coastline.

Food & Drink

Traditional Estonian gastronomy mixes Nordic, Russian and German influences, and prizes local and seasonal produce. You can eat amazingly well here, at lower prices than you might expect.

SURVIVAL GUIDE

Directory A–Z

Accommodation

In the budget category you'll find backpackers' lodgings, hostels and basic guesthouses (many with shared bathrooms). A dorm bed generally costs €10 to €15. Midrange options include family-run guesthouses and hotel rooms (private bathroom and breakfast generally included). Top-end accommodation comprises historic hotels and spa resorts.

There are a few *kämpingud* (camping grounds; generally open from mid-May to September) that allow you to pitch a tent, but most consist of permanent wooden huts or cabins, with communal showers and toilets. Farms and homestays offer more than a choice of rooms; in many cases meals, a sauna and activities are available. There's a search engine at Visitestonia.com for all types of accommodation.

The peak tourist season is June to August. If you're visiting during this summer peak you should book well in advance.

The following price indicators apply for a high-season double room:

€ less than €50

€€ €50 to €140

€€€ more than €140

Embassies & Consulates

For up-to-date contact details of Estonian diplomatic organisations, plus foreign embassies in Estonia, check the website of the **Estonian Ministry of Foreign Affairs** (www.vm.ee).

Australian Consulate (☎650 9308; www.sweden.embassy.gov.au; Marja 9) Honorary consulate; embassy in Stockholm.

Canadian Embassy (☎627 3311; www.canada.ee; Toom-Kooli 13, 2nd fl)

French Embassy (☎616 1610; www.ambafrance-ee.org; Toom-Kuninga 20)

German Embassy (☎627 5300; www.tallinn.diplo.de; Toom-Kuninga 11)

Netherlands Embassy (☎680 5500; www.netherlandsembassy.ee; Rahukohtu 4-I)

New Zealand Consulate (☎667 1470; Liivalaia 13) Honorary consulate; embassy in Berlin.

UK Embassy (☎667 4700; http://ukinestonia.fco.gov.uk; Wismari 6)

US Embassy (☎668 8100; http://estonia.usembassy.gov; Kentmanni 20)

Festivals & Events

Estonia has a busy festival calendar celebrating everything from religion to music, art to film, beer to ghosts. Peak festival fun is in summer, with a highlight being midsummer festivities. A list of upcoming major events nationwide can be found at **Culture.ee** (www.culture.ee).

The biggest occasion in Estonia is **Jaanipäev**, a celebration of the pagan midsummer or summer solstice. Celebrations peak on the evening of 23 June and are best experienced far from the city along a stretch of beach, where huge bonfires are lit for all-night parties.

Food

The following price ranges indicate the average cost of a main course:

€ less than €10

€€ €10 to €20

€€€ more than €20

Money

» Estonia joined the eurozone in January 2011, making the euro its official currency.

» Credit cards are widely accepted.

» Tipping in service industries has become the norm, but generally no more than 10% is expected.

Public Holidays

New Year's Day 1 January

Independence Day 24 February

Good Friday March/April

Easter Sunday March/April

May Day 1 May

Whitsunday Seventh Sunday after Easter; May/June

Victory Day (1919; Battle of Võnnu) 23 June

Jaanipäev (St John's Day; Midsummer's Day) 24 June

Day of Restoration of Independence 20 August

Christmas Eve 24 December

Christmas Day 25 December

Boxing Day 26 December

Telephone

There are no area codes in Estonia. All landline numbers have seven digits; mobile numbers have seven or eight digits, beginning with 5.

Post offices, supermarkets and kiosks sell cheap mobile-phone starter kits with prepaid SIM cards (from €5).

Visas

EU citizens can spend unlimited time in Estonia, while citizens of Australia, Canada, Japan, New Zealand, the USA and many other countries can enter visa-free for a maximum 90-day stay over a six month period. Travellers holding a Schengen visa do not need an additional Estonian visa. For information, see the website of the **Estonian Ministry of Foreign Affairs** (www.vm.ee).

Getting There & Away

Buses are the cheapest way of reaching the Baltics. There are international trains between Tallinn and Moscow, and a newly resurrected service connecting Tallinn and St Petersburg. Ferries run to Finland and Sweden from Tallinn. For all transport information for reaching Estonia, see p329.

Getting Around

Bicycle

The flatness and small scale of Estonia make it good cycling territory. Tallinn's **City Bike** (☎511 1819; www.citybike.ee; Uus 33) has good bikes for rent and plenty of useful cycling advice.

Bus

Buses are a good option domestically, as they're more frequent and faster than trains and cover many destinations not serviced by the limited rail network. For detailed bus information and advance tickets, contact Tallinn's **Central Bus Station** (Autobussijaam; ☎12550; Lastekodu 46). The useful website **TPilet** (www.tpilet.ee) has schedules and prices for all national bus services.

Train

Trains are slower and rarer than buses. Regional trains link the capital with Tartu, Viljandi, Narva and Pärnu a couple of times a day; schedules and prices can be found at **Edelaraudtee** (www.edel.ee).

France

Includes »

Paris ... 342
Reims ... 374
Strasbourg ... 376
Tours ... 380
Dijon ... 383
Lyon ... 385
Chamonix ... 390
Bordeaux ... 393
Toulouse ... 398
Marseille ... 400
Avignon ... 404
Nice ... 407
Monaco ... 413
Understand France ... 417
Survival Guide ... 420

Best Places to Eat

» Frenchie (p355)
» Nanashi (p356)
» Candelaria (p356)
» Le Bistrot d'Antoine (p409)
» Le Cheverus Café (p394)

Best Places to Stay

» Hôtel Eldorado (p354)
» Hôtel Lou Cagnard (p412)
» Hôtel Le Boulevardier (p388)
» Hôtel 7e Art (p411)

Why Go?

Few countries provoke such passion as La Belle France. Love it or loathe it, everyone has their own opinion about this Gallic goliath. Snooty, sexy, superior, chic, infuriating, arrogant, officious and inspired in equal measures, the French have long lived according to their own idiosyncratic rules, and if the rest of the world doesn't always see eye to eye with them, well, *tant pis* (too bad) – it's the price you pay for being a culinary trendsetter, artistic pioneer and cultural icon.

If ever there was a country of contradictions, this is it. France is a deeply traditional place: castles, chateaux and ancient churches litter the landscape, while centuries-old principles of rich food, fine wine and joie de vivre underpin everyday life. Yet it is also a country that has one of western Europe's most multicultural make-ups, not to mention a well-deserved reputation for artistic experimentation and architectural invention. Enjoy!

When to Go

Paris

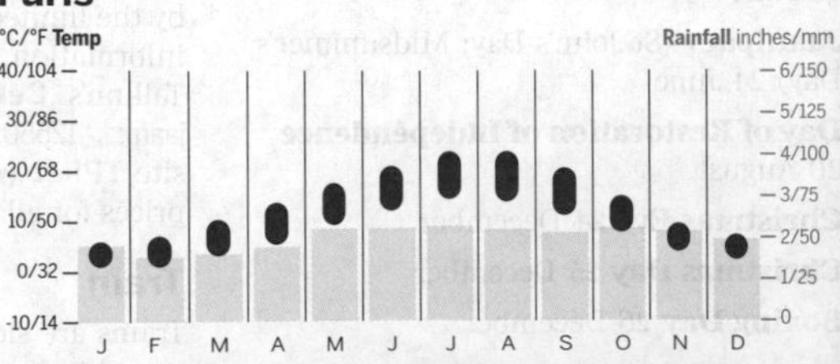

Dec–Mar Hit the French Alps for some serious ski action. Eat truffles.

Apr–Jun France at springtime best, *sans* crowds; June's Fête de la Musique means free concerts.

Sep Cooling temperatures, abundant local produce and the *vendange* (grape harvest).

Connections

High-speed trains link Paris' Gare du Nord with London St Pancras (via the Channel Tunnel/Eurostar rail service) in just over two hours; Gare du Nord is also the point of departure for speedy trains to Brussels, Amsterdam and Cologne. Many more trains make travelling between the French capital and pretty much any city in every neighbouring country a real pleasure. Ferry links from Cherbourg, St-Malo, Calais and other north-coast ports travel to England and Ireland; ferries from Marseille and Nice provide regular links with seaside towns in Corsica, Italy and North Africa.

Regular bus and rail links cross the France–Spain border via the Pyrenees, and the France–Italy border via the Alps and the southern Mediterranean coast.

ITINERARIES

One Week

Start with a few days exploring Paris, taking in the Louvre, Eiffel Tower, Musée d'Orsay, Notre Dame, Montmartre and a boat trip along the Seine. Then head out to Normandy, Monet's gardens at Giverny, and Versailles; or throw yourself into the Renaissance high life at the chateaux in the Loire Valley.

Two Weeks

With Paris and surrounds having taken up much of the first week, concentrate on exploring one or two regions rather than trying to do too much in a whistle-stop dash. High-speed TGV trains zip from Paris to every province: for prehistoric and gastronomic interest, head to the Dordogne; for architectural splendour, you can't top the Loire Valley; for typical French atmosphere, try the hilltop villages of Provence; and for sunshine and seafood, head to the French Riviera on the sparkling Med.

Essential Food & Drink

» **Fondue and raclette** Warming cheese dishes in the French Alps.

» **Oysters and white wine** Everywhere on the Atlantic coast, but especially in Cancale and Bordeaux.

» **Bouillabaisse** Marseille's signature hearty fish stew, eaten with croutons and *rouille* (garlic-and-chilli mayonnaise).

» **Foie gras and truffles** The Dordogne features goose and 'black diamonds' from December to March. Provence is also good for indulging in the aphrodisiacal fungi.

» **Piggy-part cuisine** Lyon is famous for its juicy *andouillette* (pig-intestine sausage), a perfect marriage with a local Côtes du Rhône red.

» **Champagne** Tasting in century-old cellars is an essential part of Champagne's bubbly experience.

AT A GLANCE

» **Currency** Euro (€)

» **Language** French

» **Money** ATMs everywhere

» **Visas** Schengen rules apply

Fast Facts

» **Area** 551,000 sq km

» **Capital** Paris

» **Country code** ☎33

» **Emergency** ☎112

Exchange Rates

Australia	A$1	€0.82
Canada	C$1	€0.77
Japan	¥100	€0.83
New Zealand	NZ$1	€0.65
UK	UK£1	€1.18
USA	US$1	€0.78

Set Your Budget

» **Budget hotel room** €60–80

» **Two-course meal** €15–50

» **Museum entrance** €4–10

» **Glass of wine** €2–5

» **Paris metro ticket** €1.70

Resources

» **Paris by Mouth** (www.parisbymouth.com)

» **Wine Travel Guides** (www.winetravelguides.com)

» **France 24** (www.france24.com)

» **Lost in Cheeseland** (www.lostincheeseland.com)

France Highlights

1. Gorge on the iconic sights and sophistication of Europe's most hopelessly romantic city, **Paris** (p342)
2. Relive the French Renaissance with extraordinary chateaux built by kings and queens in the **Loire Valley** (p379)
3. Do a James Bond and swoosh down slopes in the shadow of Mont Blanc in **Chamonix** (p390)
4. Dodge tides, stroll moonlit sand and immerse yourself in legend at island abbey **Mont St-Michel** (p370)
5. Savour ancient ruins, modern art, markets, lavender and hilltop villages in slow-paced **Provence** (p400)
6. Taste bubbly in ancient *caves* (cellars) in **Reims** (p374) and **Épernay**, (p375), the heart of Champagne
7. Tuck into France's halest, piggy-driven cuisine in a traditional **Lyonnais bouchon** (p389)
8. Soak up the mystery of the world's densest collection of megaliths from the back of a Breton bicycle around **Carnac** (p372)

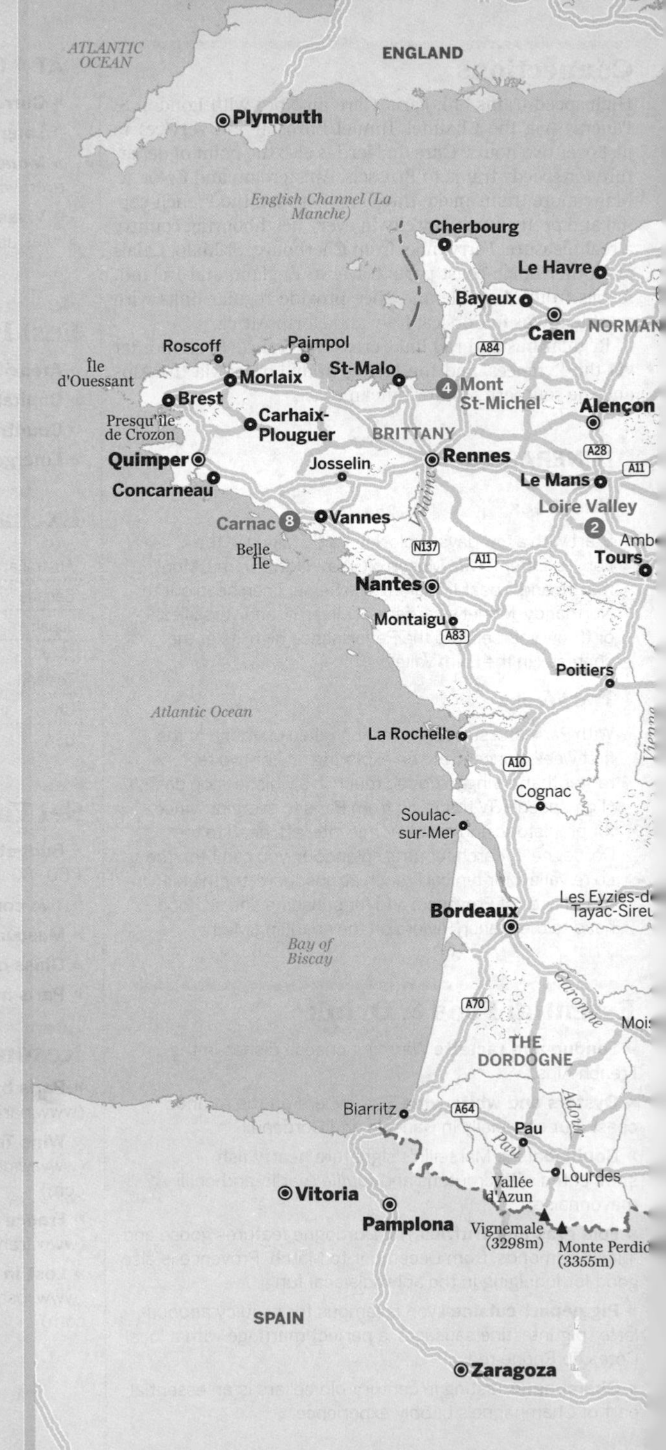

Dunkirk
Calais
Brussels
NETHERLANDS
BELGIUM
Lille
GERMANY
Meuse
Authie
Somme
SOMME
LUXEMBOURG
Mainz
Luxembourg
Oise
Aisne
Reims
Vernon
Marne
Metz
Épernay
Paris
ALSACE
Stuttgart
Strasbourg
Nancy
Dreux
Seine
CHAMPAGNE
Marne
Moselle
Sélestat
Schnellenbuhl
Troyes
LORRAINE
Katzenthal
BURGUNDY
Orléans
Beaugency
Chambord
Auxerre
Saône
Basel
Doubs
AUSTRIA
LA SOLOGNE
Dijon
CÔTE D'OR
Beaune
Arc-et-Senans
Arbois
Métabief Mont d'Or
SWITZERLAND
Le Creusot
JURA
Les Rousses
Lausanne
Lake Geneva
Loire
Cher
Chamonix
Mont Blanc
(4810m)
Lyon
Annecy
Clermont-Ferrand
Rhône
Chambéry
Dordogne
FRENCH ALPS
St-Étienne
Grenoble
ITALY
Puy Mary
(1787m)
Allier
Rhône
Drac
Valence
Sestriere
Vaison la
Romaine
Mt Lozère
(1699m)
Durance
Mt Ventoux
(1912m)
Pont du Gard
Nîmes
Avignon
Les Baux de Provence
Arles
Provence
Monaco
Nice
Ligurian Sea
Montpellier
Cannes
LANGUEDOC
Aix-en-Provence
Marseille
St-Tropez
Golfe
de Beauduc
Perpignan
Île
Rousse
Bastia
Calvi
Monte
Cinto
(2706m)
Puig
Neulós
Mediterranean
Sea
CORSICA
Ajaccio
SPAIN
Bonifacio
Barcelona
ITALY
0
0
200 km
100 miles

PARIS

POP 2.2 MILLION

What can be said about the sexy, sophisticated City of Lights that hasn't already been said a thousand times before? Quite simply, this is one of the world's great metropolises – a trendsetter, market leader and cultural capital for over a thousand years and still going strong. This is the place that gave the world the can-can and the cinematograph, a city that reinvented itself during the Renaissance, bopped to the beat of the jazz age and positively glittered during the belle époque (literally, 'beautiful era').

As you might expect, Paris is strewn with historic architecture, glorious galleries and cultural treasures galore. But the modern-day city is much more than just a museum piece: it's a heady hodgepodge of cultures and ideas – a place to stroll the boulevards, shop till you drop, flop riverside, or simply do as the Parisians do and watch the world buzz by from a streetside cafe. Savour every moment.

Sights

LEFT BANK

Eiffel Tower LANDMARK

(Map p344; ☎01 44 11 23 23; www.tour-eiffel.fr; lift to 3rd fl adult/12-24yr/4-11yr €14/12.50/9.50, lift to 2nd fl €8.50/7/4, stairs to 2nd fl €5/3.50/3; ⏲lifts & stairs 9am-midnight mid-Jun–Aug, lifts 9.30am-11pm, stairs 9.30am-6pm Sep–mid-Jun; Ⓜ Bir Hakeim or RER Champ de Mars-Tour Eiffel) This Paris icon faced massive opposition from the city's artistic and literary elite when it was built for the 1889 Exposition Universelle (World Fair) and it was only spared from being torn down in 1909 because it proved an ideal platform for the transmitting antennas needed for the newfangled science of radio-telegraphy.

Today, the three levels are open to the public (entrance to the 1st level is included in all admission tickets), though the top level will close in heavy wind. Take the lifts (in the east, west and north pillars) or the stairs (in the south pillar) up to the 2nd platform. Highly recommended is the online booking system that allows you to buy your tickets in advance, thus avoiding the monumental queues at the ticket office. Print out your ticket or have it on a smartphone screen that can be read by the scanner at the entrance.

PARIS MUSEUM PASS

If you're visiting more than two or three museums and monuments, buy a **Paris Museum Pass** (www.parismuseumpass.fr; 2/4/6 days €39/54/69), valid for entry to some 38 venues including the Louvre, Centre Pompidou, Musée d'Orsay, Musée Rodin and Château de Versailles. Best up, pass-holders bypass *looong* ticket queues at major attractions. Buy it online, or at participating museums, tourist desks at airports, Fnac outlets and major metro stations.

Musée du Quai Branly MUSEUM

(Map p344; www.quaibranly.fr; 37 quai Branly, 7e; adult/child €8.50/free; ⏲11am-7pm Tue, Wed & Sun, 11am-9pm Thu-Sat; Ⓜ Alma-Marceau or RER Pont de l'Alma) A tribute to the incredible diversity of human culture, this museum presents an overview of indigenous and folk art from around the world. Don't miss the views from the 5th-floor restaurant Les Ombres.

Musée d'Orsay MUSEUM

(Map p344; www.musee-orsay.fr; 62 rue de Lille, 7e; adult/18-25yr/under 18yr €9/6.50/free; ⏲9.30am-6pm Tue, Wed & Fri-Sun, to 9.45pm Thu; Ⓜ Assemblée Nationale or RER Musée d'Orsay) The home of France's national collection from theImpressionist, post-Impressionist and art nouveau movements spanning the 1840s up until 1914 is the glorious former Gare d'Orsay train station – an art nouveau showpiece. Highlights include Manet's *On the Beach* and *Woman with Fans*; Monet's gardens at Giverny; Cézanne's card players and still lifes; Renoir's *Ball at the Moulin de la Galette* and *Girls at the Piano*; Degas' ballerinas; Toulouse-Lautrec's cabaret dancers; and Van Gogh's self-portraits, *Bedroom in Arles* and *Starry Night*.

Jardin du Luxembourg PARK

(Map p348; numerous entrances; ⏲hours vary; Ⓜ St-Sulpice, Rennes or Notre Dame des Champs, or RER Luxembourg) The voyeur's spot to peek on Parisians, this 23-hectare park is where Parisians of all ages flock to jog, practise t'ai chi, gossip with friends, read, romance, play tennis, stroll through terraced gardens and orchards heavy with apples, or chase 1920s sailing boats around the octagonal **Grand Bassin**.

Musée Rodin GARDEN, MUSEUM

(Map p344; www.musee-rodin.fr; 79 rue de Varenne, 7e; adult/under 25yr permanent exhibition €7/5, garden €1/free; ⏲10am-5.45pm Tue-Sun; MVarenne) One of the most relaxing spots in the city with a garden bespeckled with sculptures, this lovely art museum inside 18th-century Hôtel Biron displays vital bronze and marble sculptures by sculptor, painter, sketcher, engraver and collector Auguste Rodin.

Les Catacombes CEMETERY

(Map p344; www.catacombes.paris.fr; 1 av Colonel Henri Roi-Tanguy, 14e; adult/13-26yr/under 13yr €8/4/free; ⏲10am-5pm Tue-Sun; MDenfert Rochereau) Paris' most gruesome and macabre sight is this series of underground tunnels lined with skulls and bones exhumed from the city's overflowing cemeteries. Created in 1810, the Catacombes takes visitors along 2km of subterranean passages with a mind-boggling amount of bones and skulls of millions of Parisians neatly packed along each and every wall.

Musée des Égouts de Paris MUSEUM

(Map p344; place de la Résistance, 7e; adult/child €4.20/3.40; ⏲11am-5pm Sat-Wed May-Sep, 11am-4pm Sat-Wed Oct-Dec & Feb-Apr; MAlma Marceau or RER Pont de l'Alma) Raw sewage flows beneath your feet as you walk through 480m of odoriferous tunnels in this working sewer museum. Enter via a rectangular maintenance hole topped with a kiosk across the street from 93 quai d'Orsay, 7e.

Panthéon MAUSOLEUM

(Map p348; www.monum.fr; place du Panthéon, 5e; adult/under 18yr €8.50/free; ⏲10am-6.30pm Apr-Sep, to 6pm Oct-Mar; MMaubert-Mutualité, Cardinal Lemoine or RER Luxembourg) This domed landmark, completed in 1789, houses the tombs of some of France's greatest thinkers, including Voltaire, Jean-Jacques Rousseau, Louis Braille, and two-time Nobel Prize–winner, Marie Curie (1867–1934).

Église St-Germain des Prés CHURCH

(Map p348; www.eglise-sgp.org; 3 place St-Germain des Prés, 6e; ⏲8am-7pm Mon-Sat, 9am-8pm Sun; MSt-Germain des Prés) Paris' oldest standing church, the Romanesque St Germanus of the Fields, was built in the 11th century on the site of a 6th-century abbey and was the dominant place of worship in Paris until the arrival of Notre Dame.

Église St-Sulpice CHURCH

(Map p348; www.paroisse-saint-sulpice-paris.org; place St-Sulpice, 6e; ⏲7.30am-7.30pm; MSt-Sulpice) Lined inside with 21 side chapels, this striking twin-towered church took six architects 150 years to build. What draws most people is not its Italianate facade with two rows of superimposed columns, its Counter Reformation–influenced neoclassical decor or even the frescos by Delacroix, but its setting for a murderous scene in Dan Brown's *The Da Vinci Code*.

> **FREE PARIS**
>
> Paris' national museums are something of a bargain: admission is reduced for those from 18 to 25 and over 60, and completely free for EU residents under 26 years of age, anyone under 18 years, and everyone on the first Sunday of each month. These include the Louvre, Musée National d'Art Moderne in the Pompidou, Musée du Quai Branly, Musée d'Orsay, Musée Rodin and Cité de l'Architecture et du Patrimoine.
>
> Ditto for the following except they are only free the first Sunday of the month from November to March: Arc de Triomphe, Conciergerie, Panthéon, Ste-Chapelle and the Tours de Notre Dame.

THE ISLANDS

Paris' twin set of islands could not be more different. **Île de la Cité** is bigger, full of sights and very touristy (few people live here). Smaller **Île St-Louis** is residential and quieter, with just enough boutiques and restaurants – and a legendary ice-cream maker – to attract visitors. The area around **Pont St-Louis**, the bridge across to the Île de la Cité, and **Pont Louis Philippe**, the bridge to the Marais, is one of the most romantic spots in Paris.

Cathédrale de Notre Dame de Paris CATHEDRAL

(Map p348; www.cathedraledeparis.com; 6 place du Parvis Notre Dame, 4e; admission free; ⏲7.45am-7pm; MCité) This is the heart of Paris: distances from Paris to every part of metropolitan France are measured from **place du Parvis Notre Dame**, the square in front of this masterpiece of French Gothic architecture. The most visited unticketed site in Paris, Notre Dame is famed for its three spectacular **rose windows** and forest of ornate **flying buttresses**.

The entrance to its famous towers, the **Tours de Notre Dame** (Notre Dame Towers;

Greater Paris

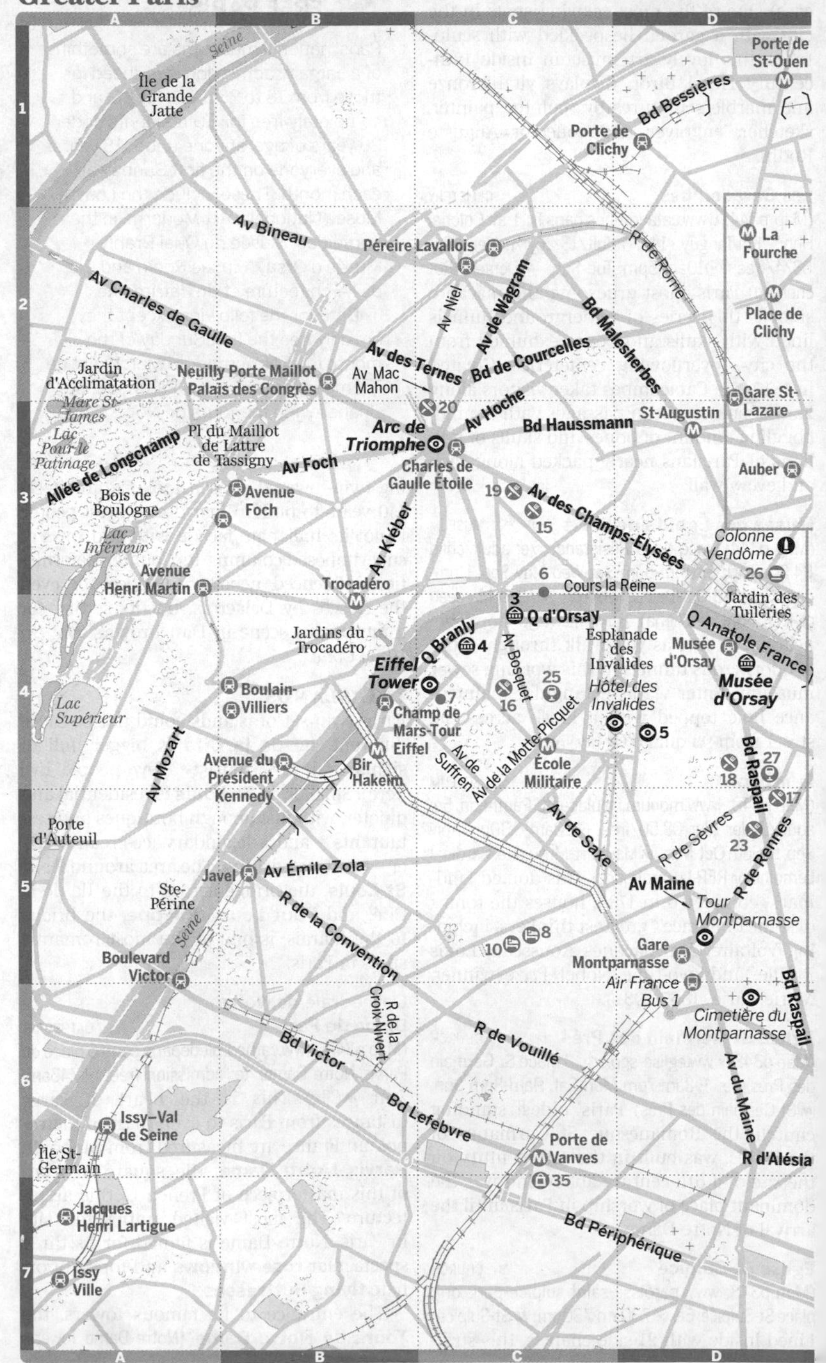

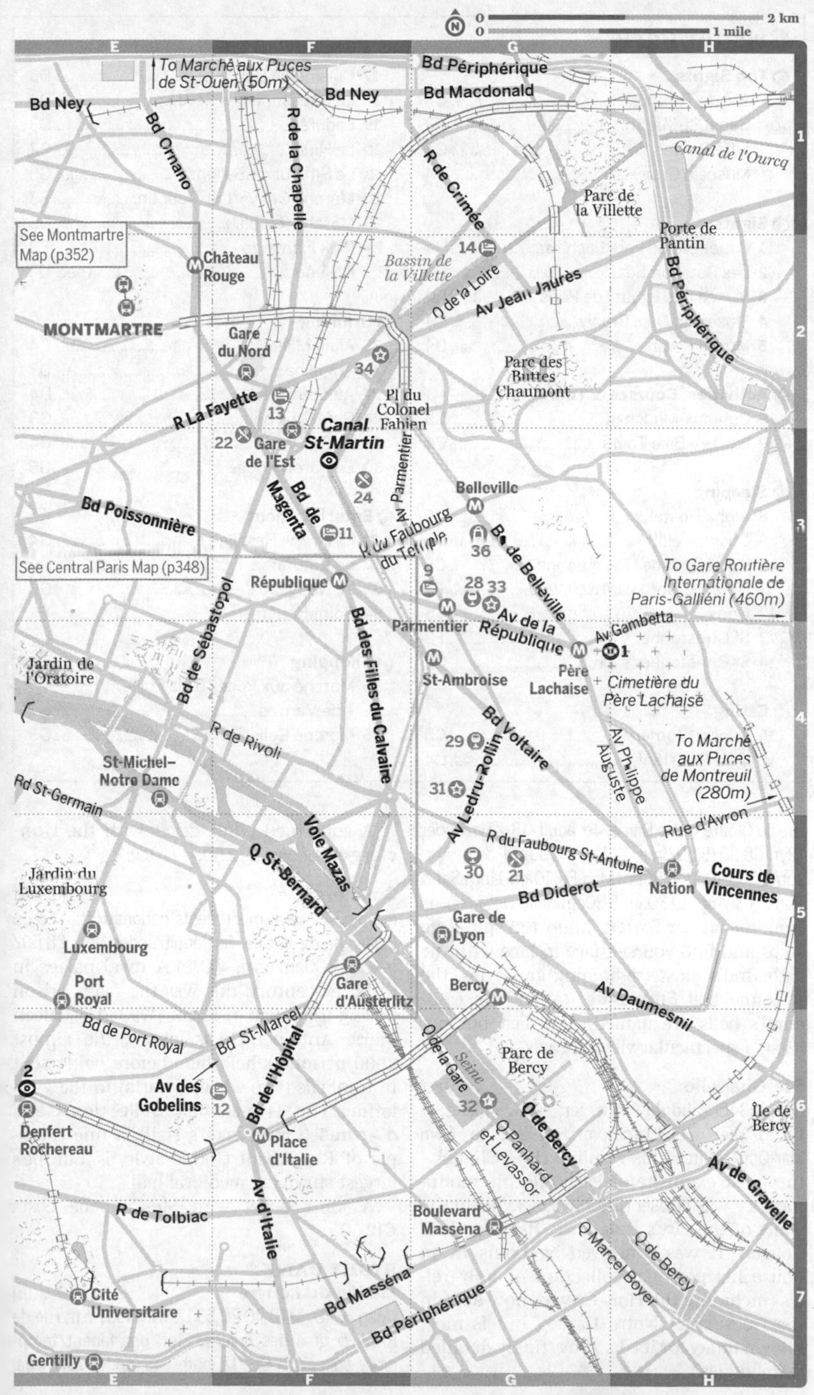

0 2 km
0 1 mile
To Marché aux Puces de St-Ouen (50m)
Bd Périphérique
Bd Ney
Bd Macdonald
Bd Ornano
R de la Chapelle
R de Crimée
Canal de l'Ourcq
Parc de la Villette
See Montmartre Map (p352)
Château Rouge
Bassin de la Villette
Porte de Pantin
Q de la Loire
Av Jean Jaurès
MONTMARTRE
Gare du Nord
Parc des Buttes Chaumont
Pl du Colonel Fabien
R La Fayette
Canal St-Martin
Gare de l'Est
Av Parmentier
Bd de Magenta
Belleville
Bd Poissonnière
R du Faubourg du Temple
Bd de Belleville
See Central Paris Map (p348)
To Gare Routière Internationale de Paris-Galliéni (460m)
République
Bd de Sébastopol
Parmentier
Av de la République
Av Gambetta
Jardin de l'Oratoire
St-Ambroise
Père Lachaise
Cimetière du Père Lachaise
Bd des Filles du Calvaire
R de Rivoli
Bd Voltaire
Av Ledru-Rollin
Av Philippe Auguste
To Marché aux Puces de Montreuil (280m)
St-Michel–Notre Dame
Rd St-Germain
Voie Mazas
Q St-Bernard
R du Faubourg St-Antoine
Rue d'Avron
Jardin du Luxembourg
Nation
Cours de Vincennes
Bd Diderot
Gare de Lyon
Luxembourg
Port Royal
Gare d'Austerlitz
Bercy
Av Daumesnil
Bd de Port Royal
Bd St-Marcel
Bd de l'Hôpital
Q de la Gare
Seine
Parc de Bercy
Av des Gobelins
Q de Bercy
Île de Bercy
Denfert Rochereau
Place d'Italie
Q Panhard et Levassor
Av de Gravelle
Av d'Italie
R de Tolbiac
Boulevard Massèna
Q Marcel Boyer
Q de Bercy
Bd Masséna
Bd Périphérique
Cité Universitaire
Gentilly
FRANCE PARIS

Greater Paris

Top Sights

	Arc de Triomphe	C3
	Canal St-Martin	F3
	Eiffel Tower	C4
	Musée d'Orsay	D4

Sights

1	Cimetière du Père Lachaise	H4
2	Les Catacombes	E6
3	Musée des Égouts de Paris	C4
4	Musée du Quai Branly	C4
5	Musée Rodin	D4

Activities, Courses & Tours

6	Bateaux-Mouches	C3
7	Fat Tire Bike Tours	C4

Sleeping

8	Aloha Hostel	C5
9	Cosmos Hôtel	G3
10	Hôtel Carladez Cambronne	C5
11	Hôtel du Nord – Le Pari Vélo	F3
12	Oops	F6
13	St Christopher's Inn	F2
14	St Christopher's Inn	G2

Eating

15	Aubrac Corner	C3
16	Café Constant	C4
17	Cuisine de Bar	D5
18	La Pâtisserie des Rêves	D4
19	Ladurée	C3
20	Le Hide	C3
21	Le Siffleur de Ballons	G5
22	Marché Couvert St-Quentin	F3
23	Marché Raspail	D5
24	Pink Flamingo	F3
	Poilâne	(see 17)

Drinking

25	Alain Milliat	C4
26	Angelina	D3
27	Au Sauvignon	D4
28	Café Charbon	G3
29	La Fée Verte	G4
30	Le Baron Rouge	G5

Entertainment

31	La Scène Bastille	G4
32	Le Batofar	G6
33	Le Nouveau Casino	G3
34	Point Éphémère	F2

Shopping

35	Marché aux Puces de la Porte de Vanves	C7
36	Marché Belleville	G3

rue du Cloître Notre Dame, 4e; adult/18-25yr/under 18yr €8.50/5.50/free; ⌚10am-6.30pm daily Apr-Jun & Sep, 10am-6.30pm Mon-Fri, 10am-11pm Sat & Sun Jul & Aug, 10.30am-5.30pm daily Oct-Mar), is from the **North Tower**. Climb 422 spiralling steps and find yourself face to face with the cathedral's most frightening gargoyles, the 13-tonne bell **Emmanuel** (all of the cathedral's bells are named) and, last but not least, a spectacular view of Paris.

Ste-Chapelle CHAPEL

(Map p348; 4 bd du Palais, 1er; adult/under 18yr €8.50/free; ⌚9.30am-5pm Nov-Feb, to 6pm Mar-Oct; Ⓜ Cité) This gemlike Holy Chapel – the most exquisite of Paris' Gothic monuments – was consecrated in 1248 within the walls of the city's **Palais de Justice** (Law Courts). It was conceived by Louis IX to house his personal collection of holy relics (including the Holy Crown, now kept in the treasury at Notre Dame), but is most known today for its dazzling, finely detailed stained glass.

A combined adult ticket with the **Conciergerie** costs €12.50.

Conciergerie MONUMENT

(Map p348; www.monuments-nationaux.fr; 2 bd du Palais, Île de la Cité, 1er; adult/under 18yr €8.50/free; ⌚9.30am-6pm; Ⓜ Cité) A royal palace in the 14th century, this was the main prison during the Reign of Terror (1793–94). Queen Marie Antoinette was among the almost 2800 prisoners held here before being sent in tumbrils (two-wheeled carts) to the guillotine. The 14th-century **Salle des Gens d'Armes** (Cavalrymen's Hall), a fine example of Rayonnant Gothic style, is Europe's largest surviving medieval hall.

A joint ticket with Ste-Chapelle costs €12.50.

RIGHT BANK

Musée du Louvre MUSEUM

(Map p348; ☎01 40 20 53 17; www.louvre.fr; rue de Rivoli & quai des Tuileries, 1er; permanent/temporary collection €11/12, both €15, under 18yr free;

(⏰9am-6pm Mon, Thu, Sat & Sun, to 9.45pm Wed & Fri; Ⓜ Palais Royal–Musée du Louvre) The vast Palais du Louvre, overlooking the fashionable Jardin des Tuileries, was constructed as a fortress by Philippe-Auguste in the 13th century and rebuilt in the mid-16th century as a royal residence. The Revolutionary Convention turned it into a national museum in 1793. Its raison d'être: to present Western art from the Middle Ages to about 1848 (at which point the Musée d'Orsay takes over). Late 2012 saw the opening of the new Islamic art galleries in the restored **Cour Visconti**, topped with an elegant, shimmering gold 'flying carpet' roof designed by Italian architects Mario Bellini and Rudy Ricciotti.

Of the some 35,000 paintings and objets d'art displayed, the star attraction is Leonardo da Vinci's *La Joconde,* aka *Mona Lisa* (Room 6, 1st floor, Denon Wing). The most famous works from antiquity include the *Seated Scribe* (Room 22, 1st floor, Sully Wing), *Venus de Milo* (Room 16, ground floor, Sully Wing) and the *Winged Victory of Samothrace* (top of Daru staircase, 1st floor, Denon Wing). From the Renaissance, don't miss Michelangelo's *The Dying Slave* (Room 4, ground floor, Denon Wing) and works by Raphael, Botticelli and Titian (1st floor, Denon Wing).

Arc de Triomphe LANDMARK
(Map p344; www.monuments-nationaux.fr; place Charles de Gaulle; adult/18-25yr €9.50/6; ⏰10am-10.30pm, to 11pm Apr-Sep; Ⓜ Charles de Gaulle–Étoile) If anything rivals the Eiffel Tower as the symbol of Paris, it's this magnificent 1836 monument to Napoleon's 1805 victory at Austerlitz. The intricately sculpted triumphal arch stands sentinel in the centre of **place de l'Étoile**. From the viewing platform on top of the arch (50m up via 284 steps and well worth the climb), you can see the dozen avenues that radiate out from the arch.

Beneath the arch at ground level lies the **Tomb of the Unknown Soldier**, honouring the 1.3 million French soldiers who lost their lives in WWI; an eternal flame is rekindled daily at 6.30pm.

Centre Pompidou MUSEUM
(Map p348; ☎01 44 78 12 33; www.centrepompidou.fr; place Georges Pompidou, 1er; museum, exhibitions & panorama adult/child €13/free; ⏰11am-9pm Wed-Mon; Ⓜ Rambuteau) Paris' premier cultural centre has amazed visitors with its 'inside-out' facade since 1977. France's national collection of art dating from 1905 onward, which includes works by the surrealists and cubists, as well as pop art and contemporary works, fills the **Musée National d'Art Moderne** on its 4th and 5th floors. Sweeping city views thrill on the rooftop terrace; admission is included in museum and exhibition tickets or you can buy a **panorama ticket** (admission €3; ⏰11am-11pm Wed-Mon) just for the roof.

Outside buskers, musicians and mime artists congregate on **place Georges Pompidou** and nearby **place Igor Stravinsky**, known for its fanciful mechanical fountains created by Jean Tinguely and Niki de Saint Phalle.

Basilique du Sacré-Cœur BASILICA
(Map p352; www.sacre-coeur-montmartre.com; place du Parvis du Sacré-Cœur, 18e; Basilica dome admission €5, cash only; ⏰6am-10.30pm, dome 9am-7pm Apr-Sep, to 5.30pm Oct-Mar; Ⓜ Anvers) Crowning the **Butte de Montmartre** (Montmartre Hill), Sacred Heart Basilica was consecrated in 1919. Some 234 spiralling steps lead to its **dome**, which affords one of Paris' most spectacular panoramas.

THE LOUVRE: TICKETS & TOURS

To best navigate the collection, opt for a self-guided **thematic trail** (1½ to three hours; download trail brochures in advance from the website) or a self-paced **multimedia guide** (€5). More-formal, English-language **guided tours** depart from the Hall Napoleon, which also has free English-language maps.

The main entrance and ticket windows are covered by the 21m-high **Grande Pyramide**, a glass pyramid designed by the Chinese-born American architect IM Pei. Avoid the queues outside the pyramid or at the Porte des Lions entrance by entering the Louvre complex via the underground shopping centre **Carrousel du Louvre**, at 99 rue de Rivoli. Buy your tickets in advance – and enter the museum with little or no queue – from the ticket machines inside the latter, by phoning ☎08 92 68 46 94 or ☎01 41 57 32 28, or from *billeteries* (ticket offices) inside Fnac or Virgin Megastores.

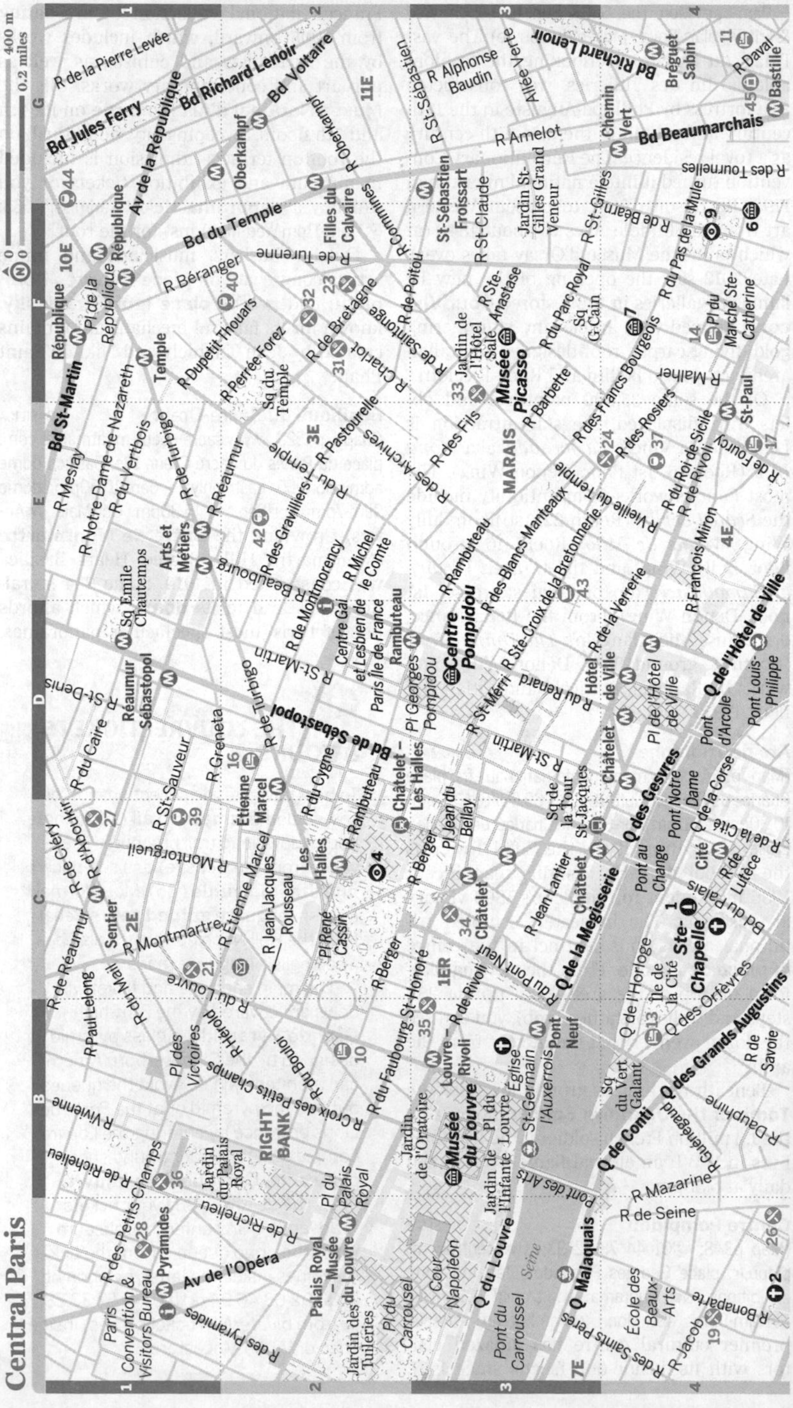

Central Paris

Paris Convention & Visitors Bureau
Pyramides
Av de l'Opéra
R des Pyramides
R des Petits Champs
R de Richelieu
Palais Royal – Musée du Louvre
Jardin des Tuileries
Pl du Carrousel
Cour Napoléon
Q du Louvre
Pont du Carroussel
Seine
Q Malaquais
École des Beaux-Arts
R Jacob
R Bonaparte
R des Saints Pères
7E
R de Seine
R Mazarine
R Guénégaud
R Dauphine
Q de Conti
Pont des Arts
Jardin du Palais Royal
Pl du Palais Royal
RIGHT BANK
Jardin de l'Oratoire
Musée du Louvre
Jardin de l'Infante
Pl du Louvre
Église St-Germain l'Auxerrois
Louvre-Rivoli
R Vivienne
Pl des Victoires
R Croix des Petits Champs
R du Bouloi
R Hérold
R du Mail
R Paul Lelong
R de Réaumur
R du Louvre
R du Faubourg St-Honoré
R de Rivoli
R du Pont Neuf
Pont Neuf
Sq du Vert Galant
Q des Grands Augustins
R de Savoie
Q de l'Horloge
Île de la Cité
Q des Orfèvres
Ste-Chapelle
Bd du Palais
R de Lutèce
Cité
R de la Cité
Q de la Corse
Pont Notre Dame
Pont au Change
Q de la Mégisserie
Châtelet
R Jean Lantier
Sq de la Tour St-Jacques
Pl Jean du Bellay
R Berger
1ER
Pl René Cassin
R Jean-Jacques Rousseau
R Étienne Marcel
R Montmartre
Sentier
2E
R de Cléry
R d'Aboukir
R Montorgueil
R St-Sauveur
R Greneta
Étienne Marcel
Les Halles
R Rambuteau
Châtelet – Les Halles
R du Cygne
Bd de Sébastopol
R du Caire
R St-Denis
Réaumur Sébastopol
Pl Georges Pompidou
Centre Pompidou
R St-Martin
R St-Merri
R du Renard
Hôtel de Ville
Pl de l'Hôtel de Ville
Pont d'Arcole
Pont Louis-Philippe
Q de l'Hôtel de Ville
Q des Gesvres
Rambuteau
Centre Gai et Lesbien de Paris Île de France
R Michel le Comte
R de Montmorency
R de Turbigo
R Beaubourg
Sq Emile Chautemps
Arts et Métiers
R des Gravilliers
R Réaumur
R Notre Dame de Nazareth
R du Vertbois
R Meslay
Bd St-Martin
R du Temple
3E
Sq du Temple
Temple
République
Pl de la République
10E
R Béranger
R Dupetit-Thouars
R Perrée
R Forez
R Pastourelle
R Charlot
R de Bretagne
R de Saintonge
R de Poitou
R des Archives
R des Fils
Jardin de l'Hôtel Salé
Musée Picasso
MARAIS
R Ste-Anastase
R Barbette
R des Francs Bourgeois
R des Rosiers
R Vieille du Temple
R des Blancs Manteaux
R Ste-Croix de la Bretonnerie
R de la Verrerie
R François Miron
4E
R du Roi de Sicile
R de Rivoli
R de Fourcy
St-Paul
R Malher
Pl du Marché Ste-Catherine
R du Pas de la Mule
R de Béarn
R des Tournelles
R St-Gilles
R du Parc Royal
Sq G Cain
Jardin St-Gilles Grand Veneur
R St-Claude
Froissart
St-Sébastien Froissart
R St-Sébastien
R Amelot
Allée Verte
R Alphonse Baudin
Chemin Vert
Bd Beaumarchais
Bréguet Sabin
Bastille
R Daval
Bd Richard Lenoir
11E
R Oberkampf
Oberkampf
R de Turenne
Filles du Calvaire
R Commines
Bd du Temple
Bd Voltaire
Av de la République
Bd Jules Ferry
R de la Pierre Levée

0 400 m
0 0.2 miles

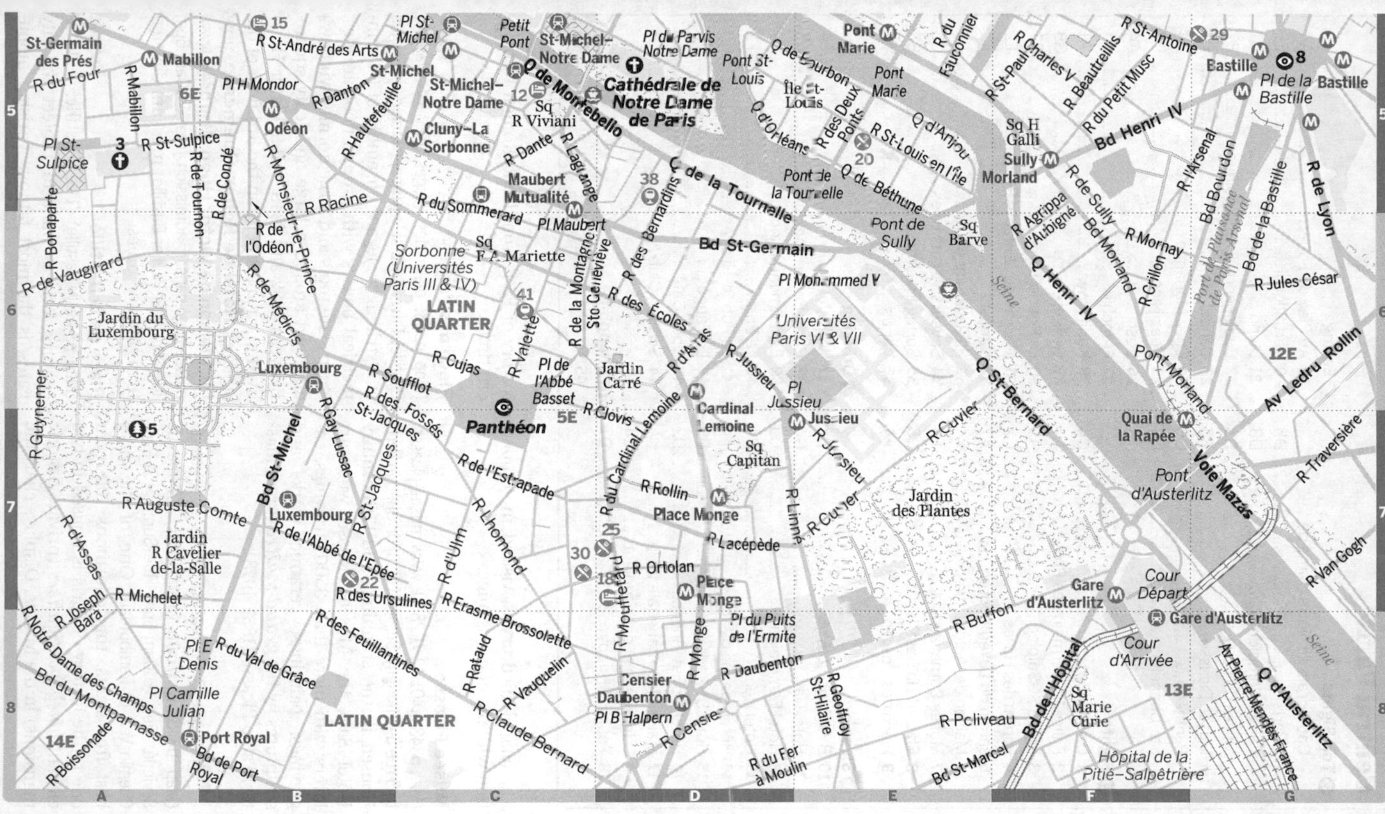
R de Lyon
Pl de la Bastille
Bastille
Bd de la Bastille
R Jules César
Av Ledru Rollin
12E
R Traversière
R Van Gogh
Seine
Q d'Austerlitz
Av Pierre Mendès France
Bd Bourdon
Pont de Plaisance de Paris-Arsenal
R St-Antoine
R de l'Arsenal
Bd Henri IV
R du Petit Musc
R Beautreillis
R Charles V
R St-Paul
R du Fauconnier
R de Sully
Bd Morland
R Mornay
R Crillon
Pont Morland
Voie Mazas
Quai de la Rapée
Pont d'Austerlitz
Cour Départ
Gare d'Austerlitz
Cour d'Arrivée
13E
Hôpital de la Pitié-Salpêtrière
Sq Marie Curie
Bd de l'Hôpital
Sq H Galli
Sully Morland
R Agrippa d'Aubigné
Q Henri IV
Q d'Anjou
R St-Louis en l'Île
Sq Barye
Q St-Bernard
R Cuvier
Jardin des Plantes
R Buffon
R Poliveau
Bd St-Marcel
Pont Marie
Q de Béthune
Pont de Sully
R des Deux Ponts
Q de Bourbon
Île St-Louis
Q d'Orléans
Pont de la Tournelle
Q de la Tournelle
Bd St-Germain
Pl Mohammed V
Universités Paris VI & VII
Jussieu
Pl Jussieu
R Jussieu
R Linné
R Geoffroy St-Hilaire
R Daubenton
Pl du Puits de l'Ermite
R du Fer à Moulin
Pont St-Louis
Pl du Parvis Notre Dame
Cathédrale de Notre Dame de Paris
Q de Montebello
R des Bernardins
Cardinal Lemoine
Sq Capitan
R Lacépède
Place Monge
R Monge
R Censier
Censier Daubenton
Pl B Halpern
St-Michel–Notre Dame
Petit Pont
Sq R Viviani
R Lagrange
Maubert Mutualité
Pl Maubert
R Dante
R des Écoles
R d'Arras
R du Cardinal Lemoine
R Rollin
R Ortolan
R Mouffetard
R de la Montagne Ste Geneviève
Jardin Carré
R Clovis
Pl St-Michel
St-Michel
Cluny–La Sorbonne
R du Sommerard
Sq F L Mariette
Sorbonne (Universités Paris III & IV)
LATIN QUARTER
R Valette
Pl de l'Abbé Basset
5E
Panthéon
R de l'Estrapade
R Lhomond
R Erasme Brossolette
R Vauquelin
R Rataud
R d'Ulm
R Claude Bernard
R Cujas
R Soufflot
R des Fossés St-Jacques
R St-Jacques
R Gay Lussac
R de l'Abbé de l'Épée
R des Ursulines
R des Feuillantines
R Hautefeuille
R St-André des Arts
R Danton
R Racine
R Monsieur-le-Prince
R de l'Odéon
Odéon
Pl H Mondor
R de Médicis
Luxembourg
Bd St-Michel
R du Val de Grâce
Pl E Denis
Pl Camille Julian
Port Royal
Bd de Port Royal
R de Condé
R de Tournon
R St-Sulpice
6E
Mabillon
R Mabillon
Jardin du Luxembourg
R Auguste Comte
Jardin R Cavelier de-la-Salle
R Michelet
R d'Assas
R Joseph Bara
R Notre Dame des Champs
Bd du Montparnasse
14E
R Boissonade
St-Germain des Prés
R du Four
Pl St-Sulpice
R Bonaparte
R de Vaugirard
R Guynemer

Central Paris

Top Sights

Cathédrale de Notre Dame de Paris D5
Centre Pompidou D3
Musée du Louvre B3
Musée Picasso F3
Panthéon C6
Ste-Chapelle C4

Sights

1 Conciergerie C4
2 Église St-Germain des Prés A4
3 Église St-Sulpice A5
4 Forum des Halles C2
5 Jardin du Luxembourg A7
6 Maison de Victor Hugo F4
7 Musée Carnavalet F4
8 Place de la Bastille G5
9 Place des Vosges F4

Sleeping

10 BVJ Paris-Louvre B2
11 Hôtel Daval G4
12 Hôtel Esmeralda C5
13 Hôtel Henri IV B4
14 Hôtel Jeanne d'Arc F4
15 Hôtel St-André des Arts B5
16 Hôtel Tiquetonne D2
17 Maison Internationale de la Jeunesse et des Étudiants E4
18 Young & Happy D7

Eating

19 Au Pied de Fouet A4
20 Berthillon E5
21 Blend C1
22 Boulangerie Bruno Solques B7
23 Candelaria F2
24 Chez Marianne E4
25 Chez Nicos D7
26 Cosi A4
27 Frenchie C1
28 Kunitoraya A1
29 Le Nôtre G5
30 Le Pot de Terre C7
31 Marché aux Enfants Rouges F2
32 Nanashi F2
33 Pink Flamingo F3
34 Saveurs Végét'Halles C3
35 Spring Épicerie B3
36 Verjus B1

Drinking

37 3w Kafé E4
38 Curio Parlor Cocktail Club D5
39 Experimental Cocktail Club C1
40 Le Barav F2
41 Le Pub St-Hilaire C6
42 Le Tango E2
43 Open Café E3
44 Scream Club G1

Shopping

45 Marché Bastille G4

The chapel-lined **crypt**, visited in conjunction with the dome, is huge.

Musée Picasso MUSEUM
(Map p348; 01 42 71 25 21; www.musee-picasso.fr; 5 rue de Thorigny, 3e; MSt-Paul or Chemin Vert) Housed in the stunning, mid-17th-century Hôtel Salé, the Musée Picasso woos art lovers with more than 3500 drawings, engravings, paintings, ceramic works and sculptures by the *grand maître* (great master) Pablo Picasso (1881–1973).

FREE **Musée Carnavalet** MUSEUM
(Map p348; www.carnavalet.paris.fr; 23 rue de Sévigné, 3e; 10am-6pm Tue-Sun; MSt-Paul, Chemin Vert or Rambuteau) One of the city's best free sights, this enormous 100-room ode to the history of Paris is housed in two elegant *hôtels particuliers* (private historic mansions) in the Marais. Displays chart the history of Paris from Gallo-Roman to modern times.

Place des Vosges SQUARE
(Map p348; place des Vosges, 4e; MSt-Paul or Bastille) Paris' oldest square, place des Vosges is a strikingly elegant ensemble of 36 symmetrical houses with ground-floor arcades, steep slate roofs and large dormer windows arranged around a large and leafy square. Between 1832 and 1848 writer Victor Hugo lived in an apartment on the 3rd floor of the square's **Hôtel de Rohan-Guéménée**, now the **Maison de Victor Hugo** (Map p348; www.musee-hugo.paris.fr; admission free; 10am-6pm Tue-Sun; MSt-Paul or Bastille) museum devoted to his life and times.

Place de la Bastille SQUARE
(Map p348; MBastille) The Bastille, a 14th-century fortress built to protect the city gates, is the most famous Parisian monu-

ment that no longer exists. Transformed into a dreaded state prison under Cardinal Richelieu, it was demolished shortly after a mob stormed it on 14 July 1789. First impressions of today's busy traffic circle can be underwhelming. The bronze column topped with the gilded Spirit of Liberty commemorates victims of later revolutions in 1830 and 1848.

Cimetière du Père Lachaise CEMETERY
(Map p344; ☎01 43 70 70 33; www.pere-lachaise.com; 16 rue du Repos & bd de Ménilmontant, 20e; admission free; ⊙8am-6pm Mon-Fri, from 8.30am Sat, from 9am Sun; Ⓜ Père Lachaise or Philippe Auguste) The world's most visited cemetery opened its one-way doors in 1804. Among the 800,000 people buried here are the composer Chopin; the playwright Molière; the poet Apollinaire; writers Balzac, Proust, Gertrude Stein and Colette; the actors Simone Signoret, Sarah Bernhardt and Yves Montand; the painters Pissarro, Seurat, Modigliani and Delacroix; the chanteuse Édith Piaf; the dancer Isadora Duncan, and even those immortal 12th-century lovers, Abélard and Héloïse, whose remains were disinterred and reburied here together in 1817 beneath a neo-Gothic tombstone. Particularly visited graves are those of Oscar Wilde (division 89) and 1960s rock star Jim Morrison (division 6).

Tours

Fat Tire Bike Tours CYCLING
(Map p344; ☎01 56 58 10 54; www.fattirebiketours.com) City bike tours, day and night, plus trips further afield to Versailles, Monet's gardens at Giverny and the Normandy beaches. Reserve in advance.

Bateaux-Mouches BOAT TOUR
(Map p344; ☎01 42 25 96 10; www.bateauxmouches.com; Port de la Conférence, 8e; adult/4-12yr €11/5.50; ⊙Apr-Dec; Ⓜ Alma Marceau) River cruises (70 minutes) with commentary in French and English; set sail from the Right Bank, just east of Pont de l'Alma.

L'Open Tour BUS TOUR
(Map p352; www.pariscityrama.com; 2-day passes adult/child €32/15) Hop-on, hop-off bus tours aboard an open-deck bus.

Paris Walks WALKING TOUR
(www.paris-walks.com; adult/child €12/8) Highly rated by Lonely Planet readers, this long-established company runs thematic tours (fashion, chocolate, the French Revolution).

Festivals & Events

Paris Plages BEACH
(www.paris.fr) 'Paris Beaches' sees three waterfront areas transformed into sand-and-pebble 'beaches', complete with sunbeds, beach umbrellas, atomisers, lounge chairs and palm trees; mid-July to mid-August.

Nuit Blanche EVENT
(www.paris.fr) Museums, bars, clubs and so on don't sleep during Paris' 'White Night' all-nighter; held the first Saturday and Sunday of October.

Sleeping

The Paris Convention & Visitors Bureau can find you a place to stay (no booking fee, but you need a credit card), though queues can be long in high season; it also has information on bed-and-breakfast accommodation. To rent an apartment try **Paris Attitude** (www.parisattitude.com) or **Room Sélection** (www.room-selection.com).

LOUVRE & LES HALLES

The upside of this Right Bank neighbourhood is its central location, excellent transport links and proximity to many major sights and shops. However, the immediate area around the **Forum des Halles** (Map p348; www.forumdeshalles.com; 1 rue Pierre Lescot, 1er; ⊙shops 10am-8pm Mon-Sat; Ⓜ Les Halles or RER Châtelet–Les Halles) may be noisy or inconvenient during construction works (not due for completion till 2016).

Hôtel Tiquetonne HOTEL €
(Map p348; ☎01 42 36 94 58; www.hoteltiquetonne.fr; 6 rue Tiquetonne, 2e; d €65, with shared shower

DON'T MISS

CANAL ST-MARTIN

The shaded towpaths of the tranquil, 4.5km-long **Canal St-Martin** (Map p344; Ⓜ République, Jaurès, Jacques Bonsergent) are a wonderful place for a romantic stroll or a bike ride past nine locks, metal bridges and ordinary Parisian neighbourhoods. The canal's banks have undergone a real urban renaissance, and the southern stretch in particular is an ideal spot for cafe lounging, quayside summer picnics and late-night drinks in hip bistros.

Montmartre

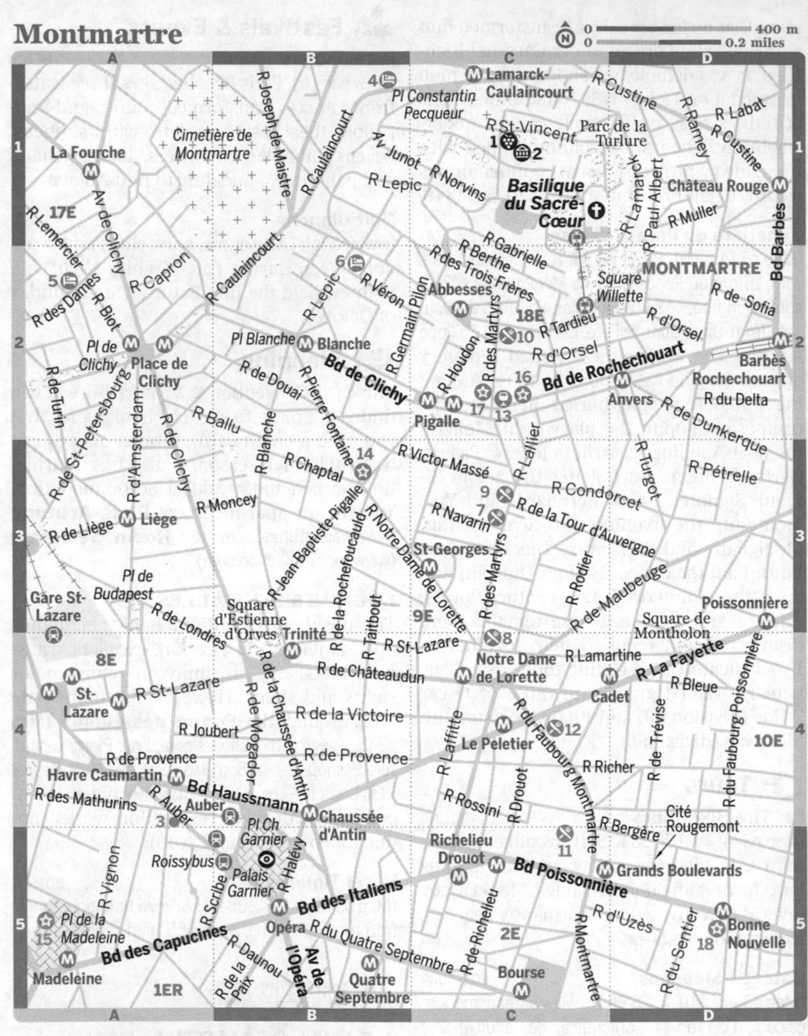

€45; ; Étienne Marcel) What heart-warmingly good value this 45-room vintage cheapie is. This serious, well-tended address in the heart of party land has been in the hotel biz since the 1900s and is much-loved by a loyal clientele of all ages. Rooms straddle seven floors and sport an inoffensive mix of vintage decor – roughly 1930s to 1980s – with brand new bathrooms and parquet flooring in recently renovated rooms. Shared shower *jeton* (tokens) cost €5; ask at reception.

BVJ Paris-Louvre HOSTEL €
(Map p348; 01 53 00 90 90; www.bvjhotel.com; 20 rue Jean-Jacques Rousseau, 1er; dm/d incl breakfast €30/70; @; Louvre Rivoli) This modern, 200-bed hostel has doubles and bunks in single-sex rooms for four to 10 people with showers down the corridor. Guests must be aged 18 to 35. Rooms are accessible from 2.30pm on the day you arrive; no kitchen facilities.

MARAIS & BASTILLE

Buzzing nightlife, hip shopping and an inexhaustible range of eating options ensure the popularity of this trendy Right Bank neighbourhood. Nearby Bastille has fewer tourists, allowing you to better glimpse the daily grind of the 'real' Paris.

Montmartre

Top Sights
Basilique du Sacré-Cœur C1

Sights
1 Clos Montmartre C1
2 Musée de Montmartre C1

Activities, Courses & Tours
3 L'Open Tour A4

Sleeping
4 Hotel Caulaincourt Square B1
5 Hôtel Eldorado A2
6 Plug-Inn Hostel B2

Eating
7 Arnaud Delmontel C3
8 Chez Plume C4
9 Cul de Poule C3
10 Le Miroir C2
11 Le Zinc des Cavistes C5
12 Les Pâtes Vivantes C4

Drinking
13 La Fourmi C2

Entertainment
14 Bus Palladium B3
15 Kiosque Théâtre Madeleine A5
16 La Cigale C2
17 Le Divan du Monde C2
18 Le Rex Club D5

Hôtel Jeanne d'Arc HOTEL €€
(Map p348; ☎01 48 87 62 11; www.hoteljeannedarc.com; 3 rue de Jarente, 4e; s €65, d €81-96, tr €149, q €164; 📶; Ⓜ St-Paul) Book well in advance at this gorgeous address to snag one of its cosy, excellent-value rooms. Games to play, a painted rocking chair for tots in the bijou lounge, knick -nacks everywhere and the most extraordinary mirror in the breakfast room create a real 'family home' air at this 35-room house.

Cosmos Hôtel HOTEL €
(Map p344; ☎01 43 57 25 88; www.cosmos-hotel-paris.com; 35 rue Jean-Pierre Timbaud, 11e; s/d/tr €55/62/78; 📶; Ⓜ République) Cheap, brilliant value and footsteps from the fun and happening bars and music clubs of trendy rue JPT, Cosmos is a shiny star with retro style. It has been around for 30-odd years, but unlike most other hotels in the same price bracket, it's been treated to a thoroughly modern makeover this century. Enjoy.

Maison Internationale de la Jeunesse et des Étudiants HOSTEL €
(MIJE; Map p348; ☎01 42 74 23 45; www.mije.com; 6 rue de Fourcy, 4e; dm incl breakfast €31; Ⓜ St-Paul) The MIJE runs three hostels in attractively renovated 17th- and 18th-century *hôtels particuliers* in the Marais. Rooms are closed from noon to 3pm, and the curfew is 1am. Annual membership is €2.50.

Hôtel Daval HOTEL €
(Map p348; ☎01 47 00 51 23; www.hoteldaval.com; 21 rue Daval, 11e; s/d/tr/q €86/92/112/131; ❄📶; Ⓜ Bastille) This 23-room hotel is a very central option if you're looking for budget accommodation just off place de la Bastille. Rooms and bathrooms are on the small side; to ensure peace and quiet, choose a back room (eg room 13).

THE ISLANDS

Hôtel Henri IV HOTEL €
(Map p348; ☎01 43 54 44 53; www.henri4hotel.fr; 25 place Dauphine, 1er; s/d/tr from €67/72/88; Ⓜ Pont Neuf or Cité) This place, known for its 15 worn and very cheap rooms, has always been a popular choice for its location, location and – above all else – location, right on the tip of the Île de la Cité. It would be impossible to find a hotel more romantically located at such a price in all of Paris – much less the Île de la Cité. What we long expected has happened: under new management, the hotel is cleaning up its act (it now has a website) and refitting its rooms (check out room 4 with its ancient stone wall and wooden floor), and all but one room now has a shower. The views over the square are wonderful. Book well in advance.

LATIN QUARTER

Midrange hotels in this good-value Left Bank neighbourhood are particularly popular with visiting academics, making rooms hardest to find during conferences (March to June and October).

Hôtel Esmeralda HOTEL €
(Map p348; ☎01 43 54 19 20; www.hotel-esmeralda.fr; 4 rue St-Julien le Pauvre, 5e; s €75, d €100-115,

BOHEMIAN SOULS IN MONTMARTRE

No address better captures Montmartre's rebellious, bohemian and artsy past than **Musée de Montmartre** (Map p352; www.museedemontmartre.fr; 12 rue Cortot, 18e; adult/18-25yr/10-17yr €8/6/4; ⊙10am-6pm; Ⓜ Lamarck–Caulaincourt), one-time home to painters Renoir, Utrillo and Raoul Dufy. The 17th-century manor-house museum displays paintings, lithographs and documents and hosts art exhibitions by contemporary artists currently living in Montmartre. It has an excellent bookshop, which also sells bottles of the wine produced from grapes grown in the quartier's very own vineyard, **Clos Montmartre** (Map p352; 18 rue des Saules, 18e).

tr €130, q €150; Ⓜ St-Michel) Tucked away in a quiet street with million-dollar views of Notre Dame (choose room 12!), this no-frills place is about as central to the Latin Quarter as it gets. At these prices, the 19 rooms are no great shakes (the cheapest singles have washbasins only) but they're popular. Book well ahead by phone (no online bookings).

Oops HOSTEL €

(Map p344; ☎01 47 07 47 00; www.oops-paris.com; 50 av des Gobelins, 13e; dm/d €30/70; @; Ⓜ Gobelins) A lurid candyfloss-pink lift scales the six floors of Paris' first 'design hostel', each painted a different colour. Well-sized doubles and modern but locker-less four- to six-bed dorms are all en suite and some have Eiffel Tower views. No kitchen; no credit cards; no alcohol allowed.

Young & Happy HOSTEL €

(Map p348; ☎01 47 07 47 07; www.youngandhappy.fr; 80 rue Mouffetard, 5e; dm €20-33, d €70-90; @; Ⓜ Place Monge) This friendly if frayed Latin Quarter favourite was Paris' first independent hostel. The self-catering kitchen gets a workout from guests trawling rue Mouffetard's markets and food shops; breakfast (included in room rates) is served in the dark stone-vaulted cellar. Beds are in cramped rooms with washbasins, but girls are in luck with an en suite female dorm (€28.95 to €37.95).

ST-GERMAIN, ODÉON & LUXEMBOURG

Staying in St-Germain des Prés (6e) is a delight. But beware – budget places are like gold dust in this chic part of Left Bank Paris.

Hôtel St-André des Arts HOTEL €€

(Map p348; ☎01 43 26 96 16; 66 rue St-André des Arts, 6e; s/d/tr/q incl breakfast €75/95/119/132; ; Ⓜ Odéon) Sitting snug on a lively, restaurant-lined thoroughfare, this 31-room hotel is a veritable bargain in the centre of the action. Rooms are basic, but public areas are evocative of *vieux Paris* (old Paris) with beamed ceilings and stone walls.

GARE DU NORD, GARE DE L'EST & RÉPUBLIQUE

The areas around Gare du Nord and Gare de l'Est are far from the prettiest parts of Paris, but decent-value hotels are a dime a dozen.

Hôtel du Nord – Le Pari Vélo HOTEL €€

(Map p344; ☎01 42 01 66 00; www.hoteldunord-leparivelo.com; 47 rue Albert Thomas, 10e; s/d/q €71/85/110; ; Ⓜ République) Beyond the bric-a-brac charm (and the ever popular dog, Pluto), Hôtel du Nord's other winning attribute is its prized location near place République. Bikes are available to loan for guests.

St Christopher's Inn HOSTEL €

(Map p344; ☎01 40 34 34 40; www.st-christophers.co.uk/paris-hostels; 68-74 quai de la Seine, 19e; dm €22-40, d from €70; @; Ⓜ Riquet or Jaurès) This is one of Paris' best, biggest, and most up-to-date hostels, with a modern design, four types of dorms (six- to 12-bed) and doubles with or without bathrooms. Other perks include a canalside cafe, a bar and a female-only floor. A new **branch** (Map p344; 5 rue de Dunkerque, 10e) has opened across from Gare du Nord.

MONTMARTRE & PIGALLE

What a charmer Montmartre is with its varied accommodation scene embracing everything from boutique to bohemian, hostel to *hôtel particulier*.

TOP CHOICE Hôtel Eldorado HOTEL €

(Map p352; ☎01 45 22 35 21; www.eldoradohotel.fr; 18 rue des Dames, 17e; s €39-65, d €58-85, tr €75-93; ; Ⓜ Place de Clichy) This bohemian place is one of Paris' greatest finds: a welcoming, reasonably well-run place with 23 colourful rooms and a private back garden. Cheaper-category singles have washbasin only.

Plug-Inn Hostel HOSTEL €

(Map p352; ☎01 42 58 42 58; www.plug-inn.fr; 7 rue Aristide Bruant, 18e; dm/d/tr incl breakfast €25/60/90; @📶; Ⓜ Abbesses or Blanche) This 2010 hostel is much loved for its central Montmartre location, its four- to five-person rooms each with shower, its kitchen, and no curfew at night.

Hotel Caulaincourt Square HOSTEL €

(Map p352; ☎01 46 06 46 06; www.caulaincourt.com; 2 square Caulaincourt, 18e; dm €30, s €59-69, d €70-80, tr €97; @📶; Ⓜ Lamarck-Caulaincourt) This hotel with dorm rooms is perched on the backside of Montmartre, beyond the tourist hoopla, in a real Parisian neighbourhood. The rooms are in decent condition, with parquet floors and a funky design, though there is no lift.

MONTPARNASSE

Just east of mammoth train station Gare Montparnasse there are several budget and lower-end midrange places on rue Vandamme and rue de la Gaîté – though the latter street is rife with sex shops and peep shows.

Aloha Hostel HOSTEL €

(Map p344; ☎01 42 73 03 03; www.aloha.fr; 1 rue Borromée, 15e; dm/d per person incl breakfast €28/32; @📶; Ⓜ Volontaires) An aubergine staircase is among the rainbow of colours brightening this laid-back crash pad, with opera music playing in the hybrid reception-lounge, and a stone-walled self-catering kitchen. You'll need a credit card to reserve four- to eight-bed dorms (reservations for doubles aren't guaranteed) but must pay cash on arrival. Rooms are locked from 11am to 5pm; curfew is at 2am.

Hôtel Carladez Cambronne HOTEL €

(Map p344; ☎01 47 34 07 12; www.hotelcarladez.com; 3 place du Général Beuret, 15e; s/d/tr/q €94/97/167/180; 📶; Ⓜ Vaugirard) On a quintessential cafe-clad square, this accommodating hotel rents coffee- and tea-making facilities for you to make yourself at home. Room 11 opens onto a tiny courtyard with a table for two.

Eating

LOUVRE & LES HALLES

Trendy restaurants are on the rise in this central area. Thankfully, the priciest and most popular cook up cheaper, more casual dining as well in adjacent wine bars or takeaway boutiques.

Frenchie BISTRO €€

(Map p348; ☎01 40 39 96 19; www.frenchie-restaurant.com; 5-6 rue du Nil, 2e; menus €34, €38 & €45; ⏲dinner Mon-Fri; Ⓜ Sentier) This bijou bistro with wooden tables and old stone walls serves excellent-value, market-driven dishes with just the right dose of creative flair. But best up is **Frenchie Bar à Vin**, the wine bar it runs across the street. Cheaper and far more casual, the wine bar doesn't require reservations, meaning you can just rock up and devour its thoroughly affordable, tapas-style dishes designed to share between friends.

Kunitoraya JAPANESE €

(Map p348; www.kunitoraya.com; 39 rue Ste-Anne, 1er; mains €12-14; ⏲11.30am-10pm; Ⓜ Pyramides) Grab a stool at the kitchen bar and watch hip young Japanese chefs strut their stuff over steaming bowls of soup, *grands bols de riz* (big bowls of rice) and some of the best udon (handmade Japanese noodles) in town. No credit cards and no reservations.

Blend BURGERS €

(Map p348; www.blendhamburger.com; 44 rue d'Argout, 2e; burgers €10, lunch menus €15 & €17; ⏲lunch & dinner Mon-Sat; Ⓜ Sentier) A burger cannot simply be a burger in gourmet Paris, where burger buffs dissolve into raptures of ecstasy over gourmet burgers at Blend. Think homemade brioche buns and ketchup, hand-cut meat and the most inventive of toppings that transform the humble burger into something really rather special.

Spring Épicerie MODERN FRENCH €

(Map p348; www.springparis.fr; 52 rue de l'Arbre Sec, 1er; soup €12; ⏲noon-8pm Tue-Sat) This tiny wine shop and gourmet grocery, just around the corner from its fine-dining namesake,

> **DON'T MISS**
>
> **THE GOURMET GLACIER**
>
> **Berthillon** (Map p348; 31 rue St-Louis en l'Île, 4e; ice cream from €2; ⏲10am-8pm Wed-Sun; Ⓜ Pont Marie) on Île St-Louis is *the* place to head for Paris' finest ice cream. There are 70 flavours to choose from, ranging from fruity cassis to chocolate, coffee, *marrons glacés* (candied chestnuts), *Agenaise* (Armagnac and prunes), *noisette* (hazelnut) and *nougat au miel* (honey nougat). One scoop just won't be enough...

TOP FIVE PATISSERIES

Ladurée (Map p344; www.laduree.fr; 75 av des Champs-Élysées, 8e; pastries from €1.50; ⌚7.30am-11pm; Ⓜ George V) Paris' most historic and decadent; inventor of the *macaron*.

Le Nôtre (Map p348; www.lenotre.fr; 10 rue St-Antoine, 4e; Ⓜ Bastille) Delectable pastries and chocolate; 10-odd outlets around town.

La Pâtisserie des Rêves (Map p344; www.lapatisseriedesreves.com; 93 rue du Bac, 7e; ⌚10am-8.30pm Tue-Sat, 8.30am-2pm Sun; Ⓜ Rue du Bac) Extraordinary cakes and tarts showcased beneath glass at the chic 'art' gallery of big-name *pâtissier* Philippe Conticini.

Boulangerie Bruno Solques (Map p348; 243 rue St-Jacques, 5e; ⌚6.30am-8pm Mon-Fri; Ⓜ Place Monge or RER Luxembourg) Paris' most inventive *pâtissier*, Bruno Solques, excels at oddly shaped flat tarts and fruit-filled brioches.

Arnaud Delmontel (Map p352; 39 rue des Martyrs, 9e; ⌚7am-8.30pm Wed-Mon; Ⓜ Pigalle) Award-winning baguettes, gorgeous cakes and pastries to die for.

provides a unique chance to scoff a meal-sized bowl of steaming soup, packed with market produce, for a smidgen of the gourmet price. Squat on a bar stool or ask for soup to take away.

Verjus INTERNATIONAL €€€

(Map p348; ☎01 42 97 54 40; www.verjusparis.com; 52 rue de Richelieu, 1er; 4-/6-course tasting menus €55/70, with wine pairings €85/110; ⌚dinner Mon-Fri; Ⓜ Bourse or Palais Royal–Musée du Louvre) Ignore the street-level Verjus restaurant – a hidden and hyped address near Palais Royal – and make a beeline instead to its cellar wine bar, famed in Parisian foodie circles for the best fried buttermilk chicken (€10) in town. Finger-food heaven!

Saveurs Végét'Halles VEGETARIAN €

(Map p348; ☎01 40 41 93 95; www.saveursveget-halles.fr; 41 rue des Bourdonnais, 1er; salads €11.90; ⌚lunch & dinner Mon-Sat; 🌶; Ⓜ Châtelet) This vegan eatery offers quite a few mock-meat dishes like *poulet végétal aux champignons* ('chicken' with mushrooms). No alcohol.

MARAIS & BASTILLE

The Marais is one of Paris' premier dining neighbourhoods; book ahead for weekend dining. Traditional bistros and neo-bistros vie for supremacy in neighbouring Bastille.

TOP CHOICE **Candelaria** TAQUERIA €

(Map p348; www.candelariaparis.com; 52 rue Saintonge; tacos €3, quesadillas & tostadas €3.50; ⌚noon-midnight Thu-Sat, to 11pm Sun-Wed; Ⓜ Filles du Calvaire) You need to know about this clandestine, two-room *taqueria* to find it – it's pure, unadulterated hipness in that brazenly nonchalant manner Paris does so well. Lunch and weekend brunch is served at the bar at the front, or wait for the secret back room to open to scoff real McCoy tacos, quesadillas and tostadas around a shared table. The party can get raucous, and occasional DJ sets, tastings, post-gallery drinks and other happenings only up the cool factor. The Bloody Marys and other more creative cocktails shaken at weekend brunches (noon to 4pm) are addictive. Check its Facebook page or Twitter feed for events.

Nanashi FUSION €

(Map p348; ☎09 60 00 25 59; www.nanashi.fr; 57 rue Charlot, 3e; bento €14-16; ⌚noon-midnight Mon-Fri, to 6pm Sat & Sun; Ⓜ Filles du Calvaire) A fabulous lunch and after-dark address in the Haut Marais, this hip industrial space is ubercool, ultrahealthy and great value. Pick from creative salads, soups and bento boxes, and don't miss the freshly squeezed fruit and veg cocktails – all to eat in or take away. Weekend brunch is €17.

Le Siffleur de Ballons WINE BAR €

(Map p344; www.lesiffleurdeballons.com; 34 rue de Citeaux, 12e; lunch menus €14, mains €7-15; ⌚10.30am-3pm & 5.30-10pm Tue-Sat; Ⓜ Faidherbe Chaligny) This contemporary wine bar clearly has a dash of California in its soul. The wines are French, natural, and paired to perfection with simple but delicious offerings: *tartines* (open-faced sandwiches), soups, lentil salad with truffle oil, cheeses and Iberian charcuterie plates. Look out for the weekly tastings with winemakers.

Chez Marianne JEWISH €€

(Map p348; 2 rue des Hospitalières St-Gervais, 4e; mains €19-24; ⌚noon-midnight; Ⓜ St-Paul) Chez

Marianne translates as elbow-to-elbow eating beneath age-old beams on copious portions of falafel, hummus, purées of aubergine and chickpeas, and 25-odd other *zakouski* (hors d'œuvres; plate of 4/5/6 €12/14/16). Fare is Sephardic and a hole-in-the-wall window sells falafel in pita (€6) to munch on the move.

LATIN QUARTER

From cheap-eat student haunts to chandelier-lit palaces loaded with history, the 5e has something to suit every budget and culinary taste. Rue Mouffetard is famed for its food market and food shops; while its side streets, especially pedestrianised rue du Pot au Fer, cook up fine budget dining.

Chez Nicos CREPERIE €

(Map p348; 44 rue Mouffetard, 5e; crêpes €3.50-6; ⌚10am-2am; Ⓜ Place Monge) The signboard outside crêpe artist Nicos' unassuming little shop chalks up dozens of fillings, but ask by name for his masterpiece 'La Crêpe du Chef', stuffed with aubergines, feta, mozzarella, lettuce, tomatoes and onions. There's a handful of tables inside; otherwise, get it wrapped up in foil and head to a nearby park.

Le Pot de Terre FRENCH €

(Map p348; ☎01 43 31 15 51; www.lepotdeterre.com; 22 rue du Pot de Fer, 5e; lunch/dinner menus from €9/18; ⌚lunch & dinner; Ⓜ Place Monge) This place was built in 1539, and legend has it that d'Artagnan and the Musketeers slaked their thirst here between sword duels. The great-value fare – *tartatouille* (puff-pastry-encased ratatouille), *magret de canard aux framboises* (duck breast in raspberry sauce) – and old-fashioned desserts like chocolate mousse make it worth hunting down on this restaurant-clad street.

ST-GERMAIN, ODÉON & LUXEMBOURG

There's far more to this fabled pocket of Paris than the literary cafes of Sartre or the picnicking turf of Jardin de Luxembourg. Rue St-André des Arts (Ⓜ St-Michel or Ⓜ Odéon) is lined with places to dine lightly or lavishly, as is the stretch between Église St-Sulpice and Église St-Germain des Prés (especially rue des Canettes, rue Princesse and rue Guisarde).

Café Constant NEO-BISTRO €€

(Map p344; www.cafeconstant.com; 139 rue Ste-Dominique, 7e; 2-/3-course menus €16/23; ⌚lunch & dinner Tue-Sun; Ⓜ École Militaire or RER Port de l'Alma) Take a former Michelin-star chef and a simple corner cafe and what do you get? This jam-packed eatery with original mosaic floor, wooden tables and huge queues every meal time.

Cuisine de Bar SANDWICHES €

(Map p344; 8 rue du Cherche Midi, 6e; dishes €7.50-13; ⌚8.30am-7pm Tue-Sat; Ⓜ Sèvres-Babylone) This is not any old sandwich bar, rather an ultrachic spot to lunch between designer boutiques on open sandwiches cut from celebrated **Poilâne** (Map p344; www.poilane.fr; 8 rue du Cherche Midi, 6e; ⌚7.15am-8.15pm Mon-Sat; Ⓜ Sèvres-Babylone) bread and fabulously topped with gourmet goodies such as foie gras, smoked duck, gooey St-Marcellin cheese and Bayonne ham.

Cosi SANDWICHES €

(Map p348; 54 rue de Seine, 6e; sandwich menus €10-15; ⌚noon-11pm; 🚸; Ⓜ Odéon) Paris' most imaginative sandwich maker.

Au Pied de Fouet BISTRO €

(Map p348; ☎01 43 54 87 83; www.aupieddefouet.com; 50 rue St-Benoît, 6e; mains €9-12.50; ⌚Mon-Sat; Ⓜ St-Germain des Prés) Classic bistro dishes such as *entrecôte* (steak), *confit de canard* (duck cooked i its own fat) and *foie de volailles sauté* (pan fried chicken livers) at this busy bistro are astonishingly good value. Round off your meal with a *tarte Tatin* (upside-down caramelised fruit tart), wine-soaked prunes

DON'T MISS

CANAL ST-MARTIN: A PARISIAN-PERFECT PICNIC

Not just another pizza place! *Mais non, chérie!* Once the weather warms up, the **Pink Flamingo** (Map p344; ☎01 42 02 31 70; www.pinkflamingopizza.com; 67 rue Bichat, 10e; pizzas €10.50-16; ⌚lunch Tue-Sun, dinner daily; Ⓜ Jacques Bonsergent) unveils its secret weapon – pink helium balloons that the delivery guy uses to locate you and your canalside picnic spot. Nip into the canalside pizzeria to order Paris' most inventive pizza, grab a balloon, and stroll off along the canal to your perfect picnic spot. There's also a branch in the **Marais** (Map p348; ☎01 42 71 28 20 ; www.pinkflamingopizza.com; 105 rue Vieille du Temple, 3e; pizzas €10.50-16; ⌚noon-3pm & 7-11.30pm; Ⓜ St-Sébastien Froissart).

TOP FIVE FOOD MARKETS

Marché Bastille (Map p348; bd Richard Lenoir; 7am-2.30pm Thu & Sun; M Bastille or Richard Lenoir) Paris' best outdoor food market.

Marché aux Enfants Rouges (Map p348; 39 rue de Bretagne, 3e; 8.30am-1pm & 4-7.30pm Tue-Fri, 4-8pm Sat, 8.30am-2pm Sun; M Filles du Calvaire) The city's oldest food market, in the Marais, with food stalls and communal tables to lunch at.

Marché Belleville (Map p344; bd de Belleville, btwn rue Jean-Pierre Timbaud & rue du Faubourg du Temple, 11e & 20e; 7am-2.30pm Tue & Fri; M Belleville or Couronnes) Fascinating entry into the large, vibrant communities of the eastern neighbourhoods, home to artists, students and immigrants from Africa, Asia and the Middle East.

Marché Couvert St-Quentin (Map p344; 85 bis bd de Magenta, 10e) Iron-and-glass covered market built in 1866; lots of gourmet and upmarket food stalls.

Marché Raspail (Map p344; bd Raspail btwn rue de Rennes & rue du Cherche Midi, 6e; regular market 7am-2.30pm Tue & Fri, organic market 9am-3pm Sun; M Rennes) Much-loved by foodies, particularly on Sunday for its organic produce.

or a bowl of *fromage blanc* (a cross between yoghurt, sour cream and cream cheese).

ÉTOILE & CHAMPS-ÉLYSÉES

The 8e *arrondissement* around the Champs-Élysées is known for its big-name chefs (Alain Ducasse, Pierre Gagnaire, Guy Savoy) and culinary icons (Taillevent), but there are all sorts of under-the-radar restaurants scattered in the backstreets where Parisians who live and work in the area dine. Gourmet food shops, some with attached eateries, garland **place Madeleine**.

Aubrac Corner BURGERS €

(Map p344; www.aubrac-corner.com; 37 rue Marbeuf, 8e; sandwiches from €5, burgers from €9; 7.30am-6.30pm Mon-Sat; M Franklin D Roosevelt) Burgers – served in a hidden wine cellar – come with bowls of fries or *aligot* (mashed potatoes with melted cheese) at this gourmet deli of a famous steakhouse.

Le Hide FRENCH €€

(Map p344; 01 45 74 15 81; www.lehide.fr; 10 rue du Général Lanrezac, 17e; menus from €24; lunch Mon-Fri, dinner Mon-Sat; M Charles de Gaulle–Étoile) This tiny neighbourhood bistro serves scrumptious traditional French fare: snails, baked shoulder of lamb with pumpkin purée or monkfish in lemon butter. Unsurprisingly, this place fills up faster than you can scamper down the steps at the nearby Arc de Triomphe. Reserve in advance.

OPÉRA & GRANDS BOULEVARDS

The neon-lit area around bd Montmartre forms one of the Right Bank's most animated cafe and dining districts.

Les Pâtes Vivantes CHINESE €

(Map p352; 46 rue du Faubourg Montmartre, 9e; noodles €9.50-12; Mon-Sat; M Le Peletier) Feast on *là miàn* (hand-pulled noodles) made to order in the age-old northern Chinese tradition. This place packs in a crowd, so arrive early to stake out a table and watch as the nimble noodle maker works his magic.

Le Zinc des Cavistes BAR, CAFE €

(Map p352; 01 47 70 88 64; 5 rue du Faubourg Montmartre, 9e; lunch menus €16, mains €11-19; 8am-10.30pm; M Grands Boulevards) Don't tell the masses standing dutifully in the Chartier queue that there's a much better restaurant right next door – your formerly friendly waiter will probably run off screaming. A local favourite, Le Zinc des Cavistes is as good for a full-blown meal (duck confit, salads) as it is for sampling new vintages.

Chez Plume ROTISSERIE €

(Map p352; 6 rue des Martyrs, 9e; dishes €4.50-8.50; 10am-3pm Tue-Sun, 5.30-8.30pm Tue-Sat; M Notre Dame de Lorette) This rotisserie specialises in free-range chickens from southwest France, prepared in a variety of fashions: simply roasted, as a crumble, or even in a quiche or sandwich. It's wonderfully casual: add a side or two (potatoes, polenta, seasonal vegies) and pull up a counter seat.

MONTMARTRE & PIGALLE

Neo-bistros, wine bars and world cuisine all feature in this area – pick and choose carefully to avoid tourist traps.

Cul de Poule MODERN FRENCH €€

(Map p352; 01 53 16 13 07; 53 rue des Martyrs, 9e; 2-/3-course menus lunch €15/18, dinner €23/28;

⏲closed Sun lunch; Ⓜ Pigalle) With plastic orange cafeteria seats outside, you probably wouldn't wander into the Cul de Poule by accident. But the light-hearted spirit (yes, there is a mounted chicken's derrière on the wall) is deceiving; this is one of the best and most affordable kitchens in the Pigalle neighbourhood, with excellent neo-bistro fare that emphasises quality ingredients from the French countryside.

Le Miroir BISTRO €€
(Map p352; ☎01 46 06 50 73; 94 rue des Martyrs, 18e; lunch menus €18, dinner menus €25-40; ⏲lunch Tue-Sun, dinner Tue-Sat; Ⓜ Abbesses) This unassuming modern bistro is smack in the middle of the Montmartre tourist trail, yet it remains a local favourite. The lunch special includes a glass of wine, coffee and dessert. Afterwards, pop into its wine shop across the street.

Drinking

The line between bars, cafes and bistros is blurred at best. Sitting at a table costs more than standing at the counter, more on a fancy square than a backstreet, more in the 8e than in the 18e. After 10pm many cafes charge a pricier *tarif de nuit* (night rate).

LOUVRE & LES HALLES

Angelina TEAHOUSE
(Map p344; 226 rue de Rivoli, 1er; ⏲daily; Ⓜ Tuileries) This beautiful, high-ceilinged tearoom has the best, most wonderfully sickening 'African' hot chocolate (€7.20) in Paris.

Experimental Cocktail Club COCKTAIL BAR
(Map p348; www.experimentalcocktailclub.com; 37 rue St-Saveur, 2e; ⏲daily; Ⓜ Réaumur-Sebastopol) Called ECC by trendies, this speakeasy with grey facade and old-beamed ceiling is hip. The cocktail bar – with retro-chic decor by American interior designer Cuoco Black and sister bars in London and New York – is a sophisticated flashback to those *années folles* (crazy years) of prohibition New York. DJs get the space partying until dawn at weekends.

MARAIS & BASTILLE

Le Baron Rouge WINE BAR
(Map p344; 1 rue Théophile Roussel, 12e; ⏲10am-2pm & 5-10pm Mon-Fri, 10am-10pm Sat, 10am-4pm Sun; Ⓜ Ledru-Rollin) Just about the ultimate Parisian wine-bar experience, this place has a dozen barrels of the stuff stacked up against the bottle-lined walls. For a small deposit, fill up one-litre bottles straight from the barrel for under €5.

La Fée Verte BAR
(Map p344; 108 rue de la Roquette, 11e; dishes €10-16; ⏲daily; 📶; Ⓜ Voltaire) Yes, the 'Green Fairy' does specialise in absinthe (served traditionally with spoons and sugar cubes), but this old-fashioned neighbourhood cafe and bar also serves terrific food, including 'Green Fairy' cheeseburgers.

Le Barav WINE BAR
(Map p348; ☎01 48 04 57 59; www.lebarav.fr; 6 rue Charles-François Dupuis, 3e; ⏲Tue-Sat; Ⓜ Temple) This hipster *bar à vin*, on one of the trendiest streets in the Haut Marais, oozes atmosphere and has one of the city's loveliest pavement terraces.

LATIN QUARTER

Curio Parlor Cocktail Club COCKTAIL BAR
(Map p348; www.curioparlor.com; 16 rue des Bernardins, 5e; ⏲7pm-2am Mon-Thu, to 4am Fri-Sun; Ⓜ Maubert-Mutualité) Run by the same switched-on team as the Experimental Cocktail Club, this hybrid bar-club looks to the interwar *années folles* of 1920s Paris, London and New York for inspiration.

Le Pub St-Hilaire PUB
(Map p348; www.pubsainthilaire.com; 2 rue Valette, 5e; ⏲3pm-2am Mon-Thu, 3pm-4am Fri, 4pm-4am Sat, 4pm-midnight Sun; Ⓜ Maubert-Mutualité) 'Buzzing' fails to do justice to the pulsating vibe inside this student-loved pub. Generous happy hours and a trio of pool tables, board games, music on two floors and hearty bar food pack out the place.

BAR-HOPPING STREETS

Prime Parisian drinking spots, perfect for evening meandering to soak up the scene:

Rue Vieille du Temple, 4e Marais cocktail of gay bars and chic cafes.

Rue Oberkampf & **rue Jean-Pierre Timbaud, 11e** Hip bars, bohemian hang-outs and atmospheric cafes.

Rue de Lappe, 11e Lively bars and clubs.

Rue Montmartre, 2e Atmospheric cafes.

Canal St-Martin, 10e Heady summer nights in casual canalside cafes.

Rue Princesse, 6e Student and sports bars.

GAY & LESBIAN PARIS

The Marais (4e), especially the areas around the intersection of rue Ste-Croix de la Bretonnerie and rue des Archives, and eastwards to rue Vieille du Temple, has been Paris' main centre of gay nightlife for some three decades.

The single best source of info on gay and lesbian Paris is the **Centre Gai et Lesbien de Paris** (CGL; Map p348; ☎01 43 57 21 47; www.centrelgbtparis.org; 61-63 rue Beaubourg, 3e; ⏰6-8pm Mon, 3.30-8pm Tue-Thu, 1-8pm Fri & Sat; Ⓜ Rambuteau or Arts et Métiers), with a large library and happening bar.

Top choices are listed below:

Open Café (Map p348; www.opencafe.fr; 17 rue des Archives, 4e; ⏰daily; Ⓜ Hôtel de Ville) This wide, white-seated pavement terrace in the Marais offers prime talent-watching.

Scream Club (Map p348; www.scream-paris.com; 18 rue du Faubourg du Temple, 11e; ⏰daily; Ⓜ Belleville or Goncourt) Saturday night's the night at 'Paris' biggest gay party'.

3w Kafé (Map p348; 8 rue des , 4e; ⏰Tue-Sat; Ⓜ St-Paul) For women.

Le Tango (Map p348; www.boite-a-frissons.fr; 13 rue au Maire, 3e; ⏰Fri-Sun; Ⓜ Arts et Métiers) Historic 1930s dancehall hosting legendary gay tea dances.

ST-GERMAIN, ODÉON & LUXEMBOURG

Au Sauvignon WINE BAR

(Map p344; 80 rue des Saints Pères, 7e; ⏰8.30am-10pm; Ⓜ Sèvres-Babylone) There's no more authentic *bar à vin* than this. Grab a table in the evening sun or head to the quintessential bistro interior, with original zinc bar, tightly packed tables and a hand-painted ceiling celebrating French viticultural tradition.

Alain Milliat JUICE BAR

(Map p344; ☎01 45 55 63 86; www.alain-milliat.com; 159 rue de Grenelle, 7e; ⏰10am-10pm Tue-Sat; Ⓜ La Tour Maubourg) Alain Milliat's fruit juices, all 33 varieties bottled in the south of France, star at his Parisian juice bistro.

MONTMARTRE & PIGALLE

La Fourmi BAR, CAFE

(Map p352; 74 rue des Martyrs, 18e; ⏰8am-1am Mon-Thu, to 3am Fri & Sat, 10am-1am Sun; Ⓜ Pigalle) A Pigalle institution, La Fourmi hits the mark with its high ceilings, long zinc bar and unpretentious vibe. Get up to speed on live music and club nights or sit down for a reasonably priced meal and drinks.

☆ Entertainment

To find out what's on, buy *Pariscope* (€0.40) or *L'Officiel des Spectacles* (€0.50, www.offi.fr, in French) at Parisian news kiosks. *Billeteries* (ticket offices) in **Fnac** (www.fnacspectacles.com) and **Virgin Megastores** (place Raoul Dautry, Gare Montparnasse, 15e; ⏰7am-8.30pm Mon-Thu, to 9pm Fri, 8am-8pm Sat; Ⓜ Montparnasse Bienvenüe) sell tickets.

If you go on the day of a performance, you can snag a half-price ticket (plus €3 commission) for ballet, theatre, opera and other performances at the discount-ticket outlet **Kiosque Théâtre Madeleine** (Map p352; opposite 15 place de la Madeleine, 8e; ⏰12.30-8pm Tue-Sat, to 4pm Sun; Ⓜ Madeleine).

Discounted tickets are avilable on French-language websites www.billetreduc.com, www.ticketac.com and www.webguichet.com.

Live Music

Point Éphémère LIVE MUSIC

(Map p344; www.pointephemere.org; 200 quai de Valmy, 10e; ⏰noon-2am Mon-Sat, noon-10pm Sun; 📶; Ⓜ Louis Blanc) This arts and music venue by the Canal St-Martin attracts an underground crowd for drinks, meals, concerts, dance nights and even art exhibitions.

Le Nouveau Casino LIVE MUSIC

(Map p344; www.nouveaucasino.net; 109 rue Oberkampf, 11e; ⏰Tue-Sun; Ⓜ Parmentier) This club-concert annexe of **Café Charbon** (Map p344; www.lecafecharbon.com; 109 rue Oberkampf, 11e; ⏰daily; 📶; Ⓜ Parmentier) has made a name for itself amid the bars of Oberkampf with its live music concerts and lively weekend club nights. Electro, pop, deep house, rock – the program is eclectic, underground and always up to the minute.

La Cigale LIVE MUSIC

(Map p352; ☎01 49 25 81 75; www.lacigale.fr; 120 bd de Rochechouart, 18e; admission €25-60; Ⓜ Anvers or Pigalle) A historical monument, this music hall dates from 1887 but was redecorated 100 years later by Philippe Starck.

Nightclubs

La Scène Bastille NIGHTCLUB
(Map p344; www.scenebastille.com; 2bis rue des Taillandiers, 11e; ⌚Thu-Sun; MBastille or Ledru-Rollin) The 'Bastille Scene' puts on a mixed bag of concerts but focuses on electro, funk and hip hop.

Le Batofar NIGHTCLUB
(Map p344; www.batofar.org; opposite 11 quai François Mauriac, 13e; ⌚9pm-midnight Mon & Tue, to 4am or later Wed-Sun; MQuai de la Gare or Bibliothèque) This much-loved, red-metal tugboat with rooftop bar and restaurant is known for its edgy, experimental music policy and live performances, mostly electro-oriented but also incorporating hip-hop, new wave, rock, punk or jazz.

Le Divan du Monde LIVE MUSIC
(Map p352; www.divandumonde.com; 75 rue des Martyrs, 18e; ⌚Fri & Sat, open for events Mon-Fri; MPigalle) Inventive, open-minded, cross-cultural venue in Pigalle.

Le Rex Club NIGHTCLUB
(Map p352; www.rexclub.com; 5 bd Poissonnière, 2e; ⌚Wed-Sat; MBonne Nouvelle) Paris' premier house and techno venue.

Bus Palladium NIGHTCLUB
(Map p352; www.lebuspalladium.com; 6 rue Pierre Fontaine, 9e; ⌚11pm-5am Tue, Fri & Sat; MBlanche) Funky DJs and a mixed bag of performances by indie and pop groups.

 Information

Metro stations best avoided late at night include the following: Châtelet-Les Halles and its corridors; Château Rouge in Montmartre; Gare du Nord; Strasbourg St-Denis; Réaumur Sébastopol; and Montparnasse Bienvenüe.

Pickpocketing and thefts from handbags and backpacks is a problem wherever there are crowds (especially of tourists).

American Hospital of Paris (☎01 46 41 25 25; www.american-hospital.org; 63 bd Victor Hugo, Neuilly-sur-Seine; MPont de Levallois)

Hertford British Hospital (☎01 47 59 59 59; www.ihfb.org; 3 rue Barbès, Levallois; MAnatole France)

Hôpital Hôtel Dieu (☎01 42 34 82 34; www.aphp.fr; 1 place du Parvis Notre Dame, 4e; MCité) Government-run public hospital.

Lonely Planet (www.lonelyplanet.com/france/paris)

Paris Convention & Visitors Bureau (Map p348; Office de Tourisme et de Congrès de Paris; ☎08 92 68 30 00; www.parisinfo.com; 25-27 rue des Pyramides, 1er; ⌚9am-7pm Jun-Oct, shorter hours Nov-May; MPyramides)

Pharmacie Les Champs (☎01 45 62 02 41; Galerie des Champs, 84 av des Champs-Élysées, 8e; ⌚24hr; MGeorge V)

 Getting There & Away

Air

Aéroport Roissy Charles de Gaulle (CDG; ☎01 70 36 39 50; www.aeroportsdeparis.fr) Three terminals, 30km northeast of Paris in the suburb of Roissy.

Aéroport d'Orly (ORY; ☎01 70 36 39 50; www.aeroportsdeparis.fr) Aéroport d'Orly is the older, smaller of Paris' two major airports, 19km south of the city.

Aéroport Beauvais (BVA; ☎08 92 68 20 66; www.aeroportbeauvais.com) Used by charter companies and budget airlines, 75km north of Paris.

Bus

Eurolines (☎01 43 54 11 99; www.eurolines.fr; 55 rue St-Jacques, 5e; ⌚9.30am-6.30pm Mon-Fri, 10am-1pm & 2-5pm Sat; MCluny–La Sorbonne)

FREE SHOWS

Paris' eclectic gaggle of clowns, mime artists, living statues, acrobats, roller-bladers, buskers and other street entertainers can be bags of fun and costs substantially less than a theatre ticket (a few coins in the hat is a sweet gesture). Some excellent musicians perform in the long, echo-filled corridors of the metro, a privilege that artists have to audition for. Outside, you can be sure of a good show at:

Place Georges Pompidou, 4e In front of the Centre Pompidou.

Pont St-Louis, 4e Bridge linking Paris' two islands (best enjoyed with Berthillon ice cream in hand).

Pont au Double, 4e Pedestrian bridge linking Notre Dame with the Left Bank.

Place Jean du Bellay, 1er Musicians and fire-eaters near the Fontaine des Innocents.

Parc de la Villette, 19e African drummers at the weekend.

Place du Tertre, 18e Montmartre's original main square wins hands down as Paris' busiest street-artist stage.

DON'T MISS

TOP THREE FLEA MARKETS

Nowhere encapsulates Paris' village atmosphere more than its markets. Not simply places to shop, the city's street markets are social gatherings for the entire neighbourhood. The website www.paris.fr (in French) lists every market by *arrondissement*, including speciality markets such as flower markets and flea markets. Our favourites include the following:

Marché aux Puces de Montreuil (av du Professeur André Lemière, 20e; ⌚8am-7.30pm Sat-Mon; Ⓜ Porte de Montreuil) Known for its secondhand clothing, designer seconds, engravings, jewellery, linen, crockery and old furniture.

Marché aux Puces de St-Ouen (www.marcheauxpuces-saintouen.com; rue des Rosiers, av Michelet, rue Voltaire, rue Paul Bert & rue Jean-Henri Fabre; ⌚9am-6pm Sat, 10am-6pm Sun, 11am-5pm Mon; Ⓜ Porte de Clignancourt) Around since the late 19th century, said to be Europe's largest.

Marché aux Puces de la Porte de Vanves (Map p344; http://pucesdevanves.typepad.com; av Georges Lafenestre & av Marc Sangnier, 14e; ⌚from 7am Sat & Sun; Ⓜ Porte de Vanves) The smallest and – for many – the friendliest.

Gare Routiére Internationale de Paris-Galliéni (☎08 92 89 90 91; 28 av du Général de Gaulle; Ⓜ Galliéni)

Train

Paris has six major train stations. For mainline train information, contact **SNCF** (☎08 91 36 20 20, timetables 08 91 67 68 69; www.sncf.fr).

Gare d'Austerlitz (bd de l'Hôpital, 13e; Ⓜ Gare d'Austerlitz) Trains to/from Spain and Portugal, the Loire Valley and southwestern France.

Gare de l'Est (bd de Strasbourg, 10e; Ⓜ Gare de l'Est) Trains to/from Luxembourg, parts of Switzerland (Basel, Lucerne, Zurich), southern Germany (Frankfurt, Munich) and points further east; regular services to eastern France (Champagne, Alsace and Lorraine).

Gare de Lyon (bd Diderot, 12e; Ⓜ Gare de Lyon) Trains to/from parts of Switzerland (eg Bern, Geneva, Lausanne), Italy and points beyond; domestic services to areas southeast of Paris, including Dijon, Lyon, Provence, the Côte d'Azur and the Alps.

Gare Montparnasse (av du Maine & bd de Vaugirard, 15e; Ⓜ Montparnasse Bienvenüe) Trains to/from Brittany and places en route from Paris (eg Chartres, Angers, Nantes); also to Tours, Nantes, Bordeaux and other destinations in southwestern France.

Gare du Nord (rue de Dunkerque, 10e; Ⓜ Gare du Nord) Terminus of high-speed Thalys trains to/from Amsterdam, Brussels, Cologne and Geneva and Eurostar to London; domestic services to Paris' northern suburbs and northern France.

Gare St-Lazare (rue St-Lazare & rue d'Amsterdam, 8e; Ⓜ St-Lazare) Trains to Normandy.

International train destinations incldue Amsterdam (€89, 3¼ hours), Berlin (€189, 8 hours), Brussels (€69, 1½ hours) and Venice (€100, 11¾ hours).

ℹ Getting Around

To/From the Airports

Getting into town is straightforward and inexpensive thanks to a fleet of public-transport options. Bus drivers sell tickets. Children aged four to 11 years pay half-price on most services.

AÉROPORT ROISSY CHARLES DE GAULLE

RER B (☎32 46; www.ratp.fr; adult €9.10; ⌚5am-11pm) Departs every 10 to 15 minutes, serving Gare du Nord, Châtalet-Les Halles and St-Michel-Notre Dame stations in the city centre. Journey time is approximately 35 minutes.

Air France Bus 2 (☎08 92 35 08 20; www.cars-airfrance.com; adult €15; ⌚6am-11pm) To/from the Arc de Triomphe and Porte Maillot metro station (35 to 50 minutes).

Air France Bus 4 (☎08 92 35 08 20; www.cars-airfrance.com; adult €16.50; ⌚6am-10pm from Roissy Charles de Gaulle, 6am-9.30pm from Paris) Shuttles every 30 minutes to/from Gare de Lyon and Gare Montparnasse (50 to 55 minutes).

Noctilien Buses 140 & 143 (☎32 46; www.noctilien.fr; adult €7.60; ⌚12.30am-5.30am) Hourly night buses to/from Gare de l'Est (140 & 143) and Gare du Nord (143).

RATP Bus 350 (☎32 46; www.ratp.fr; adult €5.10 or 3 metro tickets; ⌚5.30am-11pm) Every 30 minutes to/from Gare de l'Est and Gare du Nord (both one hour).

Roissybus (☎32 46; www.ratp.fr; adult €10; ⏰5.30am-11pm) Every 30 minutes to/from Opéra, 9e (45 minutes).

AÉROPORT D'ORLY

Air France Bus 1 (☎08 92 35 08 20; www.cars-airfrance.com; adult €11.50; ⏰5am-10.20pm from Orly, 6am-11.20pm from Invalides) Shuttle bus to/from Gare Montparnasse (35 minutes), Invalides in the 7e, and the Arc de Triomphe.

Orlybus (☎32 46; www.ratp.fr; adult €6.90; ⏰6am-11.20pm from Orly, 5.35am-11.05pm from Paris) RATP bus every 15 to 20 minutes to/from metro Denfert Rochereau (30 minutes) in the 14e.

Orlyval (☎32 46; www.ratp.fr; adult €10.75; ⏰6am-11pm) Orlyval automatic metro from Orly to Antony station, then RER B to Gare du Nord, Châtelet-Les Halles and St-Michel-Notre Dame RER stations in the city centre.

BETWEEN ORLY & CHARLES DE GAULLE

Air France Shuttle Bus 3 (www.cars-airfrance.com; adult €20; ⏰6am-10.30pm) Every 30 minutes; journey time 30 to 45 minutes.

AÉROPORT BEAUVAIS

Navette Officielle (Official Shuttle Bus; ☎08 92 68 20 64, airport 08 92 68 20 66; adult €15) Links Beauvais airport with metro station Porte de Maillot; journey time 1¼ hours.

Bicycle

Vélib' (www.velib.paris.fr; 1-/7-day subscription €1.70/7, bike hire per 1st/2nd/additional 30min free/€2/4) With this self-service bike scheme, pick up a bike from one roadside Vélib' station and drop it off at another. To get a bike, first purchase a subscription online or at any bike terminal (by credit card with a microchip).

Boat

Batobus (www.batobus.com; 1-/2-/5-day pass €15/18/21; ⏰10am-9.30pm Apr-Aug, to 7pm Sep-Mar) A fleet of glassed-in trimarans dock at eight piers along the Seine; buy tickets at each stop or at tourist offices, and jump on and off as you like.

Public Transport

Paris' public transit system is operated by the **RATP** (www.ratp.fr). The same RATP tickets are valid on the metro, RER, buses, trams and Montmartre funicular. A single ticket/*carnet* of 10 costs €1.70/12.70.

One ticket covers travel between any two metro stations (no return journeys) for 1½ hours; you can transfer between buses and between buses and trams, but not from metro to bus or vice versa. Keep your ticket until you exit the station; ticket inspectors can fine you if you can't produce a valid ticket.

BUS

Buses run from 5.30am to 8.30pm Monday to Saturday, with certain evening lines continuing until midnight or 12.30am, when the hourly **Noctilien** (www.noctilien.fr) night buses kick in.

Short bus rides (ie rides in one or two bus zones) cost one ticket (€1.70, or €1.90 direct from the driver); longer rides require two. Remember to punch single-journey tickets in the *composteur* (ticket machine) next to the driver.

METRO & RER

Paris' underground network consists of the 14-line metro and the RER, a network of suburban train lines. Each metro train is known by the name of its terminus. The last metro train on each line runs sometime between 12.35am and 1.15am (2.15am Friday and Saturday), before starting up again around 5.30am.

TOURIST PASSES

The **Mobilis Card** allows unlimited travel for one day in two to five zones (€6.40 to €14.20) on the metro, the RER, buses, trams and the Montmartre funicular; while the **Paris Visite** pass allows unlimited travel (including to/from airports) plus discounted entry to museums and activities and costs €9.75/15.85/21.60/31.15 for one to three zones for one/two/three/five days.

TRAVEL PASSES

Navigo (www.navigo.fr), like London's Oyster or Hong Kong's Octopus cards, consists of a weekly, monthly or yearly unlimited pass that can be recharged at Navigo machines in most metro stations; swipe the card across the electronic panel to go through turnstiles. Standard Navigo passes, available to anyone with an address in Île de France, are free but take up to three weeks to be issued. Otherwise, pay €5 for a **Nagivo Découverte** (Navigo Discovery) card, issued on the spot. Both require a passport photo and can be recharged for periods of one week or more.

Otherwise, *coupon hebdomadaire* (weekly tickets) cost €19.15 for zones 1 and 2, valid Monday to Sunday.

Taxi

The flag fall is €2.40, plus €0.96 per kilometre within the city limits from 10am and 5pm Monday to Saturday (Tarif A; white light on meter), and €1.21 per kilometre from 5pm to 10am, all day Sunday, and on public holidays (Tarif B; orange light on meter).

Alpha Taxis (☎01 45 85 85 85; www.alphataxis.com)

Taxis Bleus (☎01 49 36 10 10; www.taxis-bleus.com)

Taxis G7 (☎01 41 27 66 99; www.taxisg7.fr)

AROUND PARIS

Versailles

POP 88,900

This leafy suburb, 28km southwest of Paris, is the site of France's grandest and most famous royal residence, **Château de Versailles** (☎01 30 83 78 00; www.chateauversailles.fr; estate-wide access €18, with musical events €25, palace €15; ⏲8am-6pm Tue-Sat, 9am-6pm Sun Apr-Oct, 8.30am-5.30pm Tue-Sat, 9am-5.30pm Sun Nov-Mar), built in the mid-17th century by Louis XIV to reflect his taste for profligate luxury and boundless appetite for grandstanding. Framed by seemingly endless gardens, ponds and fountains, the palace is vast and opulent, climaxing with the **Galerie des Glaces** (Hall of Mirrors), a 75m-long ballroom with 17 huge mirrors on one side and, on the other, an equal number of windows looking out over the gardens and the setting sun.

Getting There & Away

The easiest way to get to/from Versailles is aboard RER line C5 (€4.20, 45 minutes, every 15 minutes) from Paris' Left Bank RER station to Versailles-Rive Gauche, 700m southeast of the chateau.

Chartres

POP 45,600

The magnificent 13th-century **Cathédrale Notre Dame** (www.diocese-chartres.com; place de la Cathédrale; ⏲8.30am-7.30pm daily, to 10pm Tue, Fri & Sun Jun-Aug) of Chartres, crowned by two very different spires – one Gothic, the other Romanesque – rises from rich farmland 88km southwest of Paris and dominates the medieval town. With its astonishing blue stained glass and other treasures, France's best-preserved medieval basilica is a must-see.

The cathedral's west, north and south entrances have superbly ornamented triple portals and its 105m-high **Clocher Vieux** (Old Bell Tower; also called the *Tour Sud* or South Tower) is the tallest Romanesque steeple still standing. Superb views of three-tiered flying buttresses and the 19th-century copper roof, turned green by verdigris, reward the 350-step hike up the 112m-high **Clocher Neuf** (New Bell Tower, also known as the North Tower).

Inside, 172 extraordinary stained-glass windows, mainly from the 13th century, form one of the most important ensembles of medieval stained glass in the world. The three most exquisite – renowned for the depth and intensity of their tones, famously known as 'Chartres blue' – are above the west entrance and below the rose window.

Getting There & Away

Frequent SNCF trains link Paris' Gare Montparnasse (€14.40, 55 to 70 minutes) with Chartres via Versailles-Chantiers (€12.10, 45 minutes to one hour).

LILLE, FLANDERS & THE SOMME

When it comes to culture, cuisine, beer, shopping and dramatic views of land and sea, the friendly Ch'tis (residents of France's

VERSAILLES TOP TIPS

» Don't go on Monday (closed); avoid Tuesday and Sunday (busiest days).

» Ticket and entry queues spiral out of control by noon: arrive early morning.

» Pre-purchase tickets on the chateau's website and head straight to Entrance A.

» Access areas otherwise off limits with a **guided tour** (☎01 30 83 77 88; tours €16; ⏲English-language tours 9.30am & 2pm Tue-Sun) of the Private Apartments of Louis XV and Louis XVI and the Opera House or Royal Chapel. Tour tickets include access to the most famous parts of the palace, such as the Hall of Mirrors and the King's and Queen's State Apartments; prebook online.

» The estate is vast: rent an **electric car** (☎01 39 66 97 66; per hr €30), **bike** (☎01 39 66 97 66; per hr €6.50) or **boat** (☎01 39 66 97 66; per hr €15).

» Be dazzled by 17th-century **Bassin de Neptune** (Neptune's Fountain) dancing during the **Grandes Eaux Musicales** (adult/child €7.50/6.50; ⏲11am-noon & 3.30-5pm Tue, Sat & Sun Apr-Sep) and after-dark **Grandes Eaux Nocturnes** (adult/child €23/19; ⏲9-11.20pm Sat mid-Jun–Aug), magical, summertime water displays set to classical music.

northern tip) and their region compete with the best France has to offer. Highlights include Flemish-style Lille, the cross-Channel shopping centre of Calais, and the moving battlefields and cemeteries of WWI.

Lille

POP 232,200

Lille (Rijsel in Flemish) may be the country's most underrated major city. In recent decades, this once-grimy industrial metropolis has transformed itself – with generous government help – into a glittering and self-confident cultural and commercial hub. Highlights of the city include an attractive Old Town with a strong Flemish accent, three renowned art museums, stylish shopping and a cutting-edge, student-driven nightlife.

Sights

Vieux Lille OLD TOWN

Lille's Old Town is justly proud of its restored 17th- and 18th-century houses. Those along **rue de la Monnaie** house the city's chicest boutiques.

Palais des Beaux Arts MUSEUM

(Fine Arts Museum; www.pba-lille.fr; place de la République; adult/student/child €6.50/4/free; 2-6pm Mon, 10am-6pm Wed-Sun; République Beaux Arts) Lille's world-renowned Fine Arts Museum displays a truly first-rate collection of 15th- to 20th-century paintings, including works by Rubens, Van Dyck and Manet.

Musée d'Art Moderne Lille-Métropole MUSEUM

(03 20 19 68 68; www.musee-lam.fr; 1 allée du Musée; adult/student/child €7/5/free; 10am-6pm Tue-Sun) Colourful, playful and just plain weird works of modern and contemporary art by masters such as Braque, Calder, Léger, Miró, Modigliani and Picasso are the big draw at this renowned, newly renovated museum and sculpture park in the Lille suburb of Villeneuve-d'Ascq, 9km east of Gare Lille-Europe. Take metro line 1 to Pont de Bois, then bus 41 (10 minutes) to Parc Urbain-Musée.

La Piscine Musée d'Art et d'Industrie MUSEUM

(www.roubaix-lapiscine.com; 23 rue de l'Espérance, Roubaix; adult/child €4.50/free; 11am-6pm Tue-Thu, 11am-8pm Fri, 1-6pm Sat & Sun; Gare Jean Lebas) Housed in an art deco municipal swimming pool (built 1927-32), this gallery 12km northeast of Gare Lille-Europe showcases fine arts, applied arts and sculpture in a delightfully watery environment.

Sleeping

Hotel Kanaï HOTEL €

(03 20 57 14 78; www.hotelkanai.com; 10 rue de Bethune; s €47-98, d €65-115; Rihour) In the heart of Lille's pedestrian zone, this newer hotel offers reasonably priced rooms with a clean modern design; all come with coffee makers, attractive tiled bathrooms and cable internet connections. Wi-fi only reaches the lounge and breakfast area.

Auberge de Jeunesse HOSTEL €

(03 20 57 08 94; www.fuaj.org; 12 rue Malpart; dm incl breakfast €21, d €42; Feb–mid-Dec; Mairie de Lille, République Beaux Arts) This central former maternity hospital has 163 beds in rooms for two to eight, kitchen facilities and free parking. A few doubles have en suite showers. Lockout from 11am to 3pm (4pm Friday to Sunday).

Eating

Keep an eye out for *estaminets* (traditional eateries) serving Flemish specialities such as *carbonnade* (beef braised with Flemish beer, spice bread and brown sugar).

TOP CHOICE **Chez la Vieille** FLEMISH €

(03 28 36 40 06; 60 rue de Gand; mains €10-14; dinner Mon, lunch & dinner Tue-Sat) Old-time prints, antiques and fresh hops hanging from the rafters create the cozy ambience of a Flemish village c 1900 at this beloved *estaminet*.

La Source ORGANIC, VEGETARIAN €

(03 20 57 53 07; www.denislasource.com; 13 rue du Plat; menus €9.50-16; 11.30am-2pm Mon-Sat, 7-9pm Fri; République Beaux Arts) This Lille institution serves delicious vegetarian, fowl and fish *plats du jour* (daily special), each accompanied by five hot vegie side dishes. The light, airy ambience and the diners exude health, well-being and cheer.

Marché de Wazemmes MARKET €

(place de la Nouvelle Aventure; 8am-2pm Tue-Thu, 8am-8pm Fri & Sat, 8am-3pm Sun & holidays; Gambetta) Beloved foodie space, 1.7km southwest of the tourist office in Lille's working-class quarter of Wazemmes.

NORTHERN BREWS

French Flanders brews some truly excellent *bière blonde* (lager) and *bière ambrée* (amber beer), with an alcohol content of up to 8.5%. Brands that give the Belgian brewers a run for their money include 3 Monts, Amadeus, Ambre des Flandres, Brasserie des 2 Caps, Ch'ti, Enfants de Gayant, Grain d'Orge, Hellemus, Jenlain, L'Angellus, La Wambrechies, Moulins d'Ascq, Raoul, Septante 5, St-Landelin, Triple Secret des Moines and Vieux Lille.

Drinking

Think two key nightlife zones: Vieux Lille's small, chic bars, and the student-oriented bars around rue Masséna and rue Solférino. In summer, pavement cafe terraces render place de la Théâtre in front of the opera prime beer-sipping terrain.

Meert TEAHOUSE
(www.meert.fr; 27 rue Esquermoise; waffles €3; ⊙9.30am-7.30pm Tue-Sat, 9am-1pm & 3-7pm Sun; Ⓜ Rihour) A delightful spot for morning coffee or mid-afternoon tea, this elegant tearoom dating to 1761, is beloved for its retro decor and its *gaufres* (waffles) filled with sweet Madagascar vanilla paste.

L'Illustration Café BAR, CAFE
(www.bar-lillustration.com; 18 rue Royale; ⊙12.30pm-3am Mon-Sat, 3pm-3am Sun) Adorned with art nouveau woodwork and changing exhibits by local painters, this laid-back bar attracts artists, musicians, budding intellectuals and teachers in the mood to read, exchange weighty ideas...or just shoot the breeze. The mellow soundtrack mixes Western classical with jazz, French *chansons* and African beats.

Information

Tourist Office (☎ from abroad 03 59 57 94 00, in France 08 91 56 20 04; www.lilletourism.com; place Rihour; ⊙9am-6pm Mon-Sat, 10am-noon & 2-5pm Sun & holidays; Ⓜ Rihour)

Getting There & Away

Lille has two train stations: Gare Lille-Flandres for regional services and trains to Paris' Gare du Nord (€42 to €58, one hour, 14 to 18 daily), and ultramodern Gare Lille-Europe for all other trains, including Eurostars to London and TGVs/Eurostars to Brussels-Nord (€18 to €25, 35 minutes, 12 daily).

Eurolines (☎ 08 92 89 90 91; www.eurolines.com; 23 parvis St-Maurice; Ⓜ Gare Lille-Flandres) serves cities such as Brussels (€18, 1½ hours), Amsterdam (€43, five hours) and London (€36, 5½ hours; by day via the Channel Tunnel, at night by ferry). Buses depart from bd de Leeds near Gare Lille-Europe.

Calais

POP 75,200

As Churchill might have put it, 'Never in the field of human tourism have so many travellers passed through a place and so few stopped to visit'. Over 15 million people pass through Calais en route to the cross-Channel ferries, but few explore the town itself – it's worth it, if only to see Rodin's famous sculpture, *The Burghers of Calais*.

Sights

Beffroi de Calais BELL TOWER
(Town Hall Belfry; place du Soldat Inconnu; adult/child €5/3; ⊙10am-noon & 2-5.30pm, closed Mon Oct-Apr) An elevator whisks you to the top of Calais' town hall belfry, a Unesco World Heritage Site, from where you can admire 360-degree views.

Burghers of Calais SCULPTURE
(place du Soldat Inconnu) In front of Calais' Flemish Renaissance-style **town hall** (1911–25) is Rodin's famous statue *Les Bourgeois de Calais* (The Burghers of Calais; 1895), honouring six local citizens who, in 1347, held off the besieging English forces for more than eight months. Edward III was so impressed he ultimately spared the Calaisiens and their six leaders.

Cité Internationale de la Dentelle et de la Mode MUSEUM
(International Centre of Lace & Fashion; ☎ 03 21 00 42 30; www.cite-dentelle.fr; 135 quai du Commerce; adult/child €5/2.50; ⊙10am-6pm Wed-Mon) Enter the intricate world of lace-making, the industry that once made Calais a textile powerhouse, at this informative, cutting-edge exhibition on the history of lace. Situated 500m southeast of the *hôtel de ville* (town hall).

Sleeping & Eating

Restaurants ring place d'Armes and are plentiful just south of there along rue Royale.

Hôtel Meurice HOTEL €€
(☎03 21 34 57 03; www.hotel-meurice.fr; 5-7 rue Edmond Roche; d €92-162; @☎) This veteran downtown hotel with 39 rooms offers plenty of atmosphere, thanks to its grand lobby staircase, antique furnishings and breakfast room with garden views.

Auberge de Jeunesse HOSTEL €
(☎03 21 34 70 20; www.auberge-jeunesse-calais.com; av Maréchal de Lattre de Tassigny; dm/s/tw incl breakfast €21/28/42; ☎; 🚌3, 5, 9) Modern, well equipped and 200m from the beach.

TOP CHOICE **Histoire Ancienne** BISTRO €€
(☎03 21 34 11 20; www.histoire-ancienne.com; 20 rue Royale; lunch menus €15, dinner menus €19-28; ⊙lunch & dinner Tue-Sat, lunch Mon) Specialising in French and regional dishes, some grilled over an open wood fire, this 1930s Paris-style bistro offers excellent value lunch and dinner menus in a classy dining room at the heart of town.

Information

Tourist Office (☎03 21 96 62 40; www.calais-cotedopale.com; 12 bd Georges Clemenceau; ⊙10am-6pm Mon-Sat, to 5pm Sun) .Just across the bridge (north) from the train station.

Getting There & Around

Boat

Each day, over three dozen car ferries from Dover dock at Calais' bustling **car-ferry terminal**, 1.5km northeast of place d'Armes.

P&O Ferries (www.poferries.com; 41 place d'Armes) and **DFDS Seaways** (☎03 28 59 01 01; www.dfdsseaways.co.uk; Ferry Terminal) operate regular trans-Channel services. P&O accepts foot passengers; DFDS accepts passengers with vehicles.

Shuttle buses (€2, roughly hourly from 11am to 6pm) link Gare Calais-Ville (train station) and place d'Armes (stop in front of Café de la Tour) with the car-ferry terminal. Departure times are posted at stops.

Bus

Ligne BCD (☎08 00 62 00 59; www.ligne-bcd.com) links Calais' train station (hours posted) with Dunkirk (€8.20, 50 minutes, six daily Monday to Friday, three Saturday).

Car & Motorcycle

To reach the Channel Tunnel's vehicle-loading area at Coquelles, 6km southwest of the town

DON'T MISS

LOUVRE-LENS

After years of anticipation, Europe's most ballyhooed new art museum has opened its doors. The innovative **Louvre-Lens** (www.louvrelens.fr; 6 rue Charles Lecocq, Lens; Galerie du Temps & Pavillon de Verre free through 2013; ⊙10am-6pm Wed-Mon) showcases hundreds of treasures from Paris' venerable Musée du Louvre in a purpose-built, state-of-the-art exhibition space in the former coal mining town of Lens. The futuristic ensemble of buildings and surrounding parkland was designed to look like five riverboats drifting haphazardly together on the grassed-over site of a former coal mine.

Intended to give museumgoers a completely different experience than its Parisian cousin, the Louvre-Lens is all about making art accessible to everyone, while showing off the Louvre's remarkable holdings in exciting new ways. Visitors are invited behind the scenes to view the museum's storerooms and watch art restoration personnel at work. There is no permanent collection moreover; rather, the central 120m-long exhibition space, **Galerie du Temps**, displays a limited but significant, ever-rotating collection of 200-plus pieces from the original Louvre. The museum's grand opening featured European masterpieces such as Delacroix's *Liberty Leading the People* and Raphael's *Portrait of Baldassare Castiglione* alongside works as diverse as ancient Mesopotamian tablets, Persian glazed tiles, Greek statues, Pompeiian frescos, Roman bronzes, Islamic art from Spain to Syria and 11th-century Italian mosaics.

A second building, the glass-walled **Pavillon de Verre**, displays annually changing themed exhibits (the Renaissance in 2013).

To celebrate Louvre-Lens' grand opening, the main collections will be free of charge through 2013 (temporary exhibits will cost €9). Lens, 18km north of Arras and 40km southwest of Lille, is accessible by TGV trains from Paris' Gare du Nord (€28 to €46, 65 to 70 minutes) and regional trains from Lille (€7.60, 40 minutes) and Arras (€4.20, 15 minutes).

centre, follow the road signs on the A16 to 'Tunnel Sous La Manche' (exit 42).

Train

Calais has two train stations, linked by trains and a *navette* (shuttle bus; €2, free with train ticket).

Gare Calais-Ville (city centre) Serves Amiens (€25.30, 2½ to 3½ hours, six daily), Boulogne (€7.70, 30 minutes, up to 19 daily), Dunkirk (€8.60, 50 minutes, two to six Monday to Saturday) and Lille-Flandres (€17.30, 1¼ hours, eight to 19 daily).

Gare Calais-Fréthun (TGV station 10km southwest of town near Channel Tunnel entrance) Serves Paris' Gare du Nord (€44 to €61, 1¾ hours, three to six daily) and Eurostars to London St Pancras (from €96, one hour, three daily).

NORMANDY

Famous for cows, cider and Camembert, this largely rural region (www.normandie-tourisme.fr) is one of France's most traditional, and most visited, thanks to world-renowned sights such as the Bayeux Tapestry, historic D-Day beaches, Monet's gardens at Giverny and spectacular Mont St-Michel.

Rouen

POP 119,900

With its elegant spires, beautifully restored medieval quarter and soaring Gothic cathedral, the ancient city of Rouen is a Normandy highlight. Devastated several times during the Middle Ages by fire and plague, the city was later badly damaged by WWII bombing raids, but has been meticulously rebuilt over the last six decades. The city makes an ideal base for exploring the northern Normandy coast.

Sights

Église Jeanne d'Arc CHURCH

(place du Vieux Marché; ⏲10am-noon & 2-6pm Apr-Oct) The Old City's main thoroughfare, rue du Gros Horloge, runs from the cathedral west to **place du Vieux Marché**. Dedicated in 1979, the thrillingly bizarre Église Jeanne d'Arc, with its fish-scale exterior, marks the spot where 19-year-old Joan of Arc was burned at the stake in 1431.

Cathédrale Notre Dame CATHEDRAL

(place de la Cathédrale; ⏲2-6pm Mon, 7.30am-7pm Tue-Sat, 8am-6pm Sun) Rouen's stunning Gothic cathedral, with its polished, brilliant-white facade, is the famous subject of a series of paintings by Monet. Its 75m-tall **Tour de Beurre** (Butter Tower) was financed by locals who donated to the cathedral in return for being allowed to eat butter during Lent – or so the story goes.

Musée des Beaux-Arts MUSEUM

(☎02 35 71 28 40; www.rouen-musees.com; esplanade Marcel Duchamp; adult/child €5/free; ⏲10am-6pm Wed-Mon) Rouen's fine-arts museum features canvases by Caravaggio, Rubens, Modigliani, Pissarro, Renoir, Sisley (lots) and (of course) several works by Monet.

Sleeping

La Boulangerie B&B €

(☎06 12 94 53 15; www.laboulangerie.fr; 59 rue St-Nicaise; d €77-92, q €150; P 📶) Tucked into a quiet side street slightly off the historic quarter, this adorable B&B occupying a

DON'T MISS

MONET'S GARDENS

Monet's home for the last 43 years of his life is now the delightful **Maison et Jardins de Claude Monet** (☎02 32 51 28 21; www.fondation-monet.com; adult/child €9/5; ⏲9.30am-5.30pm Apr-Oct), where you can view the Impressionist's pastel-pink house and famous gardens with lily pond, Japanese bridge draped in purple wisteria, and so on. Early to late spring, daffodils, tulips, rhododendrons, wisteria and irises bloom in the flowery gardens, followed by poppies and lilies. By June, nasturtiums, roses and sweet peas are in flower, while September is the month to see dahlias, sunflowers and hollyhocks.

The gardens are in Giverny, 66km southeast of Rouen. Several trains (€10.80, 40 minutes) leave Rouen before noon, with hourly return trains between 5pm and 8pm. From Paris' Gare St-Lazare up to 15 daily trains run to Vernon (€13.30, 50 minutes), 7km west of Giverny, from where **shuttle buses** (€6.50 return, three to six daily April to October) shunt passengers to Giverny.

former bakery offers three pleasingly decorated rooms. The largest 'Levain' room can sleep up to four people. Your charming hosts, Franck and Aminata, are a mine of local information.

Auberge de Jeunesse Robec HOSTEL €
(02 35 08 18 50; www.fuaj.org; 3 rue de la Tour; dm/s/d incl breakfast €22/33/56;) The two- to eight-bed rooms at this modern hostel are comfortable and functional. Sadly, it's some way from the centre of town, off rte de Darnétal – take bus T2 or T3 from Rouen's city centre and get off at the 'Auberge de Jeunesse' stop. Check-in is from 5pm to 10pm only.

Eating

Little eateries crowd the north side of rue Martainville. For ethnic cuisine, head two blocks south to rue des Augustins.

Minute et Mijoté BISTRO €
(58 rue de Fontenelle; mains €20, menus €13-30; lunch & dinner Mon-Sat) The trademark at this smart bistro is freshness and great value for money. There's outdoor seating in summer.

L'Espiguette BISTRO €
(02 35 71 66 27; 25 place St-Amand; mains €13-19, lunch menu €11; lunch & dinner Tue-Sat) No culinary acrobatics here, just pared-down classics such as *joue de bœuf* (ox cheek), beef sirloin and salads. Its fixed-priced menu, with loads of good choices, is a great deal.

Information

Tourist Office (02 32 08 32 40; www.rouentourisme.com; 25 place de la Cathédrale; 9am-7pm Mon-Sat, 9.30am-12.30pm & 2-6pm Sun & holidays)

Getting There & Away

Direct services from Rouen train station, just north of the city centre, include trains to Paris St-Lazare (€21.90, 1¼ hours, at least hourly).

Bayeux

POP 14,400

Bayeux has become famous throughout the English-speaking world thanks to a 68m-long piece of painstakingly embroidered cloth: the 11th-century Bayeux Tapestry, whose 58 scenes vividly tell the story of the Norman invasion of England in 1066. The town is also one of the few in Normandy to have survived WWII practically unscathed, with a centre crammed with 13th- to 18th-century buildings, wooden-framed Norman-style houses, and a spectacular Norman Gothic cathedral.

DON'T MISS

THE CIDER ROAD

Normandy's signposted 40km **Route du Cidre**, about 20km east of Caen, wends its way through the **Pays d'Auge**, a rural area of orchards, pastures, hedgerows, half-timbered farmhouses and stud farms, through picturesque villages such as Cambremer and Beuvron-en-Auge. Along the way, signs reading 'Cru de Cambremer' indicate the way to about 20 small-scale, traditional producers who are happy to show you their facilities and sell you their home-grown cider (€3 a bottle) and Calvados (an apple brandy).

Sights

Bayeux Tapestry TAPESTRY
(02 31 51 25 50; www.tapisserie-bayeux.fr; rue de Nesmond; adult/child incl audioguide €7.80/3.80; 9am-6.30pm mid-Mar–mid-Nov, to 7pm May-Aug, 9.30am-12.30pm & 2-6pm mid-Nov–mid-Mar) The world's most celebrated embroidery recounts the conquest of England from an unashamedly Norman perspective. Fifty-eight scenes fill the central canvas, and religious allegories and illustrations of everyday 11th-century life fill the borders. The final showdown at the Battle of Hastings is depicted in graphic fashion, complete with severed limbs and decapitated heads (along the bottom of scene 52).

Musée Mémorial de la Bataille de Normandie MUSEUM
(Battle of Normandy Memorial Museum; bd Fabien Ware; adult/child €7/3.80; 9.30am-6.30pm May-Sep, 10am-12.30pm & 2-6pm Oct-Apr) Using well-chosen photos, personal accounts, dioramas and wartime objects, this first-rate museum offers an excellent introduction to WWII in Normandy.

Sleeping & Eating

Les Logis du Rempart B&B €
(02 31 92 50 40; www.lecornu.fr; 4 rue Bourbesneur; d €60-80, q €130;) This *maison de famille* (family home) shelters three rooms

oozing old-fashioned cosiness and the hosts run a tasting shop downstairs – the perfect place to stock up on top-quality, homemade Calvados and cider. Breakfast (€6) features organic apple juice and apple jelly.

L'Assiette Normande NORMAN €
(☎02 31 22 04 61; www.lassiettenormande.fr; 1-3 rue des Chanoines; menus €10-35; ⊙lunch Tue-Sat, dinner daily) Crammed at lunchtime and on weekends, this lively eatery beside the cathedral is about uncomplicated food at fair prices, from meat and fish dishes to oysters and mussels. There's an interesting menu with a focus on Bayeux-style pork.

Information

Tourist Office (☎02 31 51 28 28; www.bessin-normandie.com; pont St-Jean; ⊙9.30am-12.30pm & 2-6pm)

Getting There & Away

Trains link Bayeux with Caen (€6.20, 20 minutes, hourly), from where there are connections to Paris' Gare St-Lazare (€33.30, two hours) and Rouen (€24.90, 1½ hours).

D-Day Beaches

Early on 6 June 1944, Allied troops stormed 80km of beaches north of Bayeux, code-named (from west to east) Utah, Omaha, Gold, Juno and Sword. The landings on D-Day – called 'Jour J' in French – ultimately led to the liberation of Europe from Nazi occupation. For context, see www.normandiememoire.com and www.6juin1944.com.

The most brutal fighting on D-Day took place 15km northwest of Bayeux along the stretch of coastline now known as **Omaha Beach**, today a glorious stretch of fine golden sand partly lined with sand dunes and summer homes. **Circuit de la Plage d'Omaha**, trail-marked with a yellow stripe, is a self-guided tour along the beach, surveyed from a bluff above by the huge **Normandy American Cemetery & Memorial** (www.abmc.gov; Colleville-sur-Mer; ⊙9am-5pm). Featured in the opening scenes of Steven Spielberg's *Saving Private Ryan*, this is the largest American cemetery in Europe.

KNOW THE TIDE

Check the *horaire des marées* (tide table) at the tourist office. When the tide is out, you can walk all the way around Mont St-Michel, a distance of about 1km. Stray too far from the Mont and you risk getting stuck in wet sand – from which Norman soldiers are depicted being rescued in one scene of the Bayeux Tapestry – or being overtaken by the incoming tide, providing your next of kin with a great cocktail-party story.

Caen's hi-tech, hugely impressive **Mémorial – Un Musée pour la Paix** (Memorial – A Museum for Peace; ☎02 31 06 06 45; www.memorial-caen.fr; esplanade Général Eisenhower; adult/child €18.80/16.30; ⊙9am-6.30pm, closed Jan & Mon mid-Nov–mid-Dec) uses sound, lighting, film, animation and lots of exhibits to graphically explore and evoke the events of WWII, the D-Day landings and the ensuing Cold War.

Tours

Mémorial MINIBUS TOUR
(www.memorial-caen.fr; adult/child €77/61) Excellent year-round minibus tours (four to five hours). Rates include entry to Mémorial. Book online.

Normandy Sightseeing Tours MINIBUS TOUR
(☎02 31 51 70 52; www.normandywebguide.com) From May to October (and by request the rest of the year), this experienced outfit offers morning tours (adult/child €45/25) of various beaches and cemeteries. These can be combined into an all-day excursion (€90/50).

Mont St-Michel

On a rocky island opposite the coastal town of Pontorson, connected to the mainland by a narrow causeway, the sky-scraping turrets of the abbey of **Mont St-Michel** (☎02 33 89 80 00; www.monuments-nationaux.fr; adult/child incl guided tour €9/free; ⊙9am-7pm, last entry 1hr before closing) provide one of France's iconic sights. The surrounding bay is notorious for its fast-rising tides: at low tide, the Mont is surrounded by bare sand for miles around; at high tide, just six hours later, the bay, causeway and nearby car parks can be submerged.

From the **tourist office** (☎02 33 60 14 30; www.ot-montsaintmichel.com; ⊙9am-12.30pm & 2-6.30pm Mon-Sat, 9am-noon & 2-6pm Sun, no midday closure Jul & Aug) at the base of Mont St-Michel, a cobbled street winds up to the **Église Abbatiale** (Abbey Church), incorporating elements of both Norman and Gothic architecture. Other notable sights include the arched **cloître** (cloister), the barrel-roofed **réfectoire** (dining hall), and the Gothic **Salle des Hôtes** (Guest Hall), dating from 1213. A one-hour tour is included with admission; English tours run hourly in summer, twice daily (11am and 3pm) in winter. In July and August, there are illuminated *nocturnes* (night-time visits) with music from 7pm to 10pm Monday to Saturday.

Bus 6 (☎08 00 15 00 50; www.mobi50.com) links Mont St-Michel with Pontorson (€2.20, 13 minutes), from where there are two to three daily trains to/from Bayeux (€22.30, 1¾ hr) and Cherbourg (€28.10, three hours).

BRITTANY

Brittany is for explorers. Its wild, dramatic coastline, medieval towns, thick forests and the eeriest stone circles this side of Stonehenge make a trip here well worth the detour off the beaten track. This is a land of prehistoric mysticism, proud tradition and culinary wealth, where locals still remain fiercely independent, where Breton culture (and cider) is celebrated, and where Paris feels a very long way away indeed.

Quimper

POP 66,900

Small enough to feel like a village – with its slanted half-timbered houses and narrow cobbled streets – and large enough to buzz as the troubadour of Breton culture, Quimper (pronounced *kam-pair*) is the thriving capital of Finistère (meaning 'land's end'; in Breton Penn ar Bed, meaning 'head of the world').

Sights

Most of Quimper's historic architecture is concentrated in a tight triangle formed by place Médard, rue Kéréon, rue des Gentilhommes and its continuation, rue du Sallé, to place au Beurre.

Cathédrale St-Corentin CHURCH
(place St-Corentin; ⏲8.30am-noon & 1.30-6.30pm Mon-Sat, 8.30am-noon & 2-6.30pm Sun) The cathedral, with its distinctive kink, is said to symbolise Christ's inclined head as he was dying on the cross. Construction began in 1239 but the cathedral's dramatic twin spires weren't added until the 19th century.

Musée Départemental Breton MUSEUM
(☎02 98 95 21 60; 1 rue du Roi Gradlon; adult/child €4/free; ⏲9am-6pm) Beside the cathedral, this superb museum showcases Breton history, furniture, costumes, crafts and archaeology in a former bishop's palace.

Sleeping

Hôtel Manoir des Indes HOTEL €€
(☎02 98 55 48 40; www.manoir-hoteldesindes.com; 1 allée de Prad ar C'hras; s/d from €105/133; P🛜🏊) This stunning hotel conversion, located in an old manor house just a short drive from the centre of Quimper, has been restored with the original world-traveller owner in mind. Decor is minimalist and modern with Asian objets d'art, lots of exposed wood and a couple of elephants outside.

Camping Municipal CAMPGROUND €
(☎02 98 55 61 09; av des Oiseaux; campsites €0.79, person €3.70, car €1.85; ⏲Jun-Oct; 🚌1) This wooded park is 1km west of the Old City and 3km from the train station. From quai

BRETON MUSIC

Celtic culture is synonymous with music and Brittany is no exception. A wealth of indoor and outdoor festivals and concerts feature traditional instruments through to electronica, and everything in between, with some big-name international acts. Keep your finger on the pulse by picking up the free monthly 'zine **Ty Zicos** (www.tyzicos.com) in cafes and bars.

In addition to an array of festivals and events, tune in to the region's top musical trio each year:

Les Vieilles Charrues de Carhaix (www.vieillescharrues.asso.fr) Old-school crooners, electronic beats and much more attract crowds of 300,000-plus to Carhaix in mid-July.

Astropolis (www.astropolis.org) Brest's electronic music fest in early August, with the main event atmospherically set in a castle.

Les Transmusicales de Rennes (www.lestrans.com) Ground-breaking indie bands in Rennes, in early December.

de l'Odet, follow rue Pont l'Abbé northwestwards and continue straight ahead where it veers left. Alternatively, take bus 1 from the train station to the Chaptal stop.

Eating

Crêperie du Quartier CREPERIE €
(☎02 98 64 29 30; 16 rue du Sallé; menus from €6, galettes €5-7.10) In a town where the humble crêpe is king, this cosy stone-lined place is one of the best. Its wide-ranging menu includes a *galette* of the week and, to follow up, you can go for the full monty: a crêpe stuffed with apple, caramel, ice cream, almonds and chantilly. Wash it all down with a tipple from their range of local ciders.

Le Cosy Restaurant REGIONAL CUISINE €
(☎02 98 95 23 65; 2 rue du Sallé; mains €10-14.50; ⏲closed Sun, lunch Mon & dinner Tue) Make your way through the *épicerie* (grocery store) crammed with locally canned sardines, ciders and other Breton specialities to this eclectic dining room where you can tuck into top-quality gratins and *tartines*.

Information

Tourist Office (☎02 98 53 04 05; www.quimper-tourisme.com; place de la Résistance; ⏲9am-7pm Mon-Sat, 10am-12.45pm & 3-5.45pm Sun Jul-Aug, 9.30am-12.30pm & 1.30-6.30pm Mon-Sat, 10am-12.45pm Sun Jun & Sep)

WORTH A TRIP

CULINARY CANCALE

No day trip from St-Malo is tastier than one to **Cancale**, an idyllic Breton fishing port 14km east, famed for its offshore *parcs à huîtres* (oyster beds).

Learn all about oyster farming at the **Ferme Marine** (☎02 99 89 69 99; www.ferme-marine.com; corniche de l'Aurore; adult/child €7/3.70; ⏲guided tours in French 11am,3pm & 5pm Jul-Aug, in English 2pm, in German 4pm), and afterwards lunch on oysters fresh from their beds at the **Marché aux Huîtres** (12 oysters from €3.50, lunch platters €20; ⏲9am-6pm), the local oyster market atmospherically clustered around the Pointe des Crolles lighthouse.

Keolis Emeraude runs buses from St-Malo (€2, 30 minutes) that stop in Cancale at Port de la Houle, next to the pungent fish market.

Getting There & Away

Frequent trains serve Paris' Gare Montparnasse (€70 to €86, 4¾ hours).

Carnac

Pre-dating Stonehenge by about a hundred years, Carnac comprises the world's greatest concentration of megalithic sites. There are more than 3000 of these upright stones scattered across the countryside between **Carnac-Ville** and **Locmariaquer** village, most of which were erected between 5000 BC and 3500 BC. No one's quite sure what purpose these sites served, although theories abound. A sacred site? Phallic fertility cult? Or maybe a celestial calendar? Even more mysterious is the question of their construction – no one really has the foggiest idea how the builders hacked and hauled these vast granite blocks several millennia before the wheel arrived in Brittany, let alone mechanical diggers.

Because of severe erosion, the sites are usually fenced off to allow vegetation to regenerate. **Guided tours** (€6) run in French year-round and in English early July to late August. Sign up at the **Maison des Mégalithes** (☎02 97 52 29 81; rte des Alignements; tours adult/child €6/free; ⏲10am-8pm Jul & Aug, to 5.15pm Sep-Apr, to 7pm May & Jun). Opposite, the largest menhir field – with no fewer than 1099 stones – is the **Alignements du Ménec**, 1km north of Carnac-Ville. From here, the D196 heads northeast for about 1.5km to the **Alignements de Kermario**. Climb the stone observation tower midway along the site to see the alignment from above. Another 500m further on are the **Alignements de Kerlescan**, while the **Tumulus St-Michel**, 400m northeast of the Carnac-Ville tourist office, dates back to at least 5000 BC.

For background, Carnac's **Musée de Préhistoire** (☎02 97 52 22 04; www.museedecarnac.fr; 10 place de la Chapelle, Carnac-Ville; adult/child €5/2.50; ⏲10am-6pm) chronicles life in and around Carnac from the Palaeolithic and Neolithic eras to the Middle Ages.

St-Malo

POP 48,800

The mast-filled port of fortified St-Malo is inextricably tied up with the deep briny blue: the town became a key harbour during the 17th and 18th centuries, functioning as a base for merchant ships and government-sanctioned privateers, and these days it's a busy cross-Channel ferry port and summertime getaway.

Sights

Walking on top of the city's sturdy 17th-century ramparts (1.8km) affords fine views of the old walled city known as **Intra-Muros** ('within the walls'), or Ville Close; access the ramparts from any of the city gates.

Cathédrale St-Vincent CATHEDRAL
(place Jean de Châtillon; 9.30am-6pm) The city's centrepiece was constructed between the 12th and 18th centuries. The battle to liberate St-Malo destroyed around 80% of the Old City during August 1944, and damage to the cathedral was particularly severe.

Fort National RUIN
(www.fortnational.com; adult/child €5/3; Easter, school holidays & Jun–mid-Sep) From the city ramparts, spot the remains of St-Malo's former prison and the rocky islet of **Île du Grand Bé**, where the great St-Malo-born 18th-century writer Chateaubriand is buried. Walk at low tide, but check the tide times with the tourist office.

Musée du Château MUSEUM
(02 99 40 71 57; adult/child €6/3; 10am-noon & 2-6pm Apr-Sep, Tue-Sun Oct-Mar) Within **Château de St-Malo**, built by the dukes of Brittany in the 15th and 16th centuries, this museum looks at the life and history of the city.

Sleeping

Hôtel San Pedro HOTEL €
(02 99 40 88 57; www.sanpedro-hotel.com; 1 rue Ste-Anne; s €58-60, d €69-79; P) Tucked at the back of the Old City, the San Pedro has a cool, crisp, neutral-toned decor with subtle splashes of colour, friendly service and superb sea views. Private parking is €10 per day.

Camping Aleth CAMPGROUND €
(06 78 96 10 62; www.camping-aleth.com; allée Gaston Buy, St-Servan; per 2-person tent €14.40;) Perched on a peninsula, Camping Aleth has panoramic 360-degree views and is close to beaches and some lively bars.

Auberge de Jeunesse Éthic Étapes HOSTEL €
(02 99 40 29 80; www.centrevarangot.com; 37 av du Père Umbricht; dm incl breakfast €21; @; 3) This efficient place has a self-catering kitchen and free sports facilities. Take bus 3 from the train station.

FANCY UN CAFÉ?

The word 'eccentric' must have been coined to describe St-Malo's extraordinary and insanely named **La Cafe du Coin d'en Bas de la Rue du Bout de la Ville d'en Face du Port... La Java** (02 99 56 41 90; www.lajavacafe.com; 3 rue Sante-Barbe). Think part-museum, part-toyshop and the work of art of an ever-so-slightly-twisted mind. Traditional French accordion music plays in the background and the beady eyes of hundreds of dolls and puppets keep watch from shelves and alcoves in the walls. Customers sit on swings, not chairs, and fake elephant tusks reach down out of the lamp shades. Even the opening times are odd: it opens at 8.31am on the dot during the week and 8.33am on weekends. And the drinks? Ah, well, they're actually quite sane – a hundred different kinds of coffee and a quality beer range.

Eating

Le Bistro de Jean BISTRO €
(02 99 40 98 68; 6 rue de la Corne-de-Cerf; mains €15-19, menus from €12; closed Wed & Sat lunch, all day Sun) Want to know where the locals choose to eat inside the walls? Peer through the windows of this lively and authentic bistro and you'll get your answer.

Crêperie Margaux CREPERIE €
(02 99 20 26 02; www.creperie-margaux.com; 3 place du Marché aux Légumes; crepes €2.50-10; daily Jul-Aug, closed Tue & Wed Sep-Jun) Watch the owner of this wonderful little crêperie on violet-filled place du Marché aux Légumes making traditional crêpes by hand (her motto: 'If you're in a hurry, don't come here'). The aromas wafting through the timber-lined dining room and the scads of happy diners prove it's well worth the wait.

Information

Tourist Office (€0.15 per min 08 25 13 52 00; www.saint-malo-tourisme.com; esplanade St-Vincent; 9am-7.30pm Mon-Sat, 10am-6pm Sun) Just outside the walls.

Getting There & Away

Brittany Ferries (www.brittany-ferries.com) sails between St-Malo and Portsmouth; **Condor**

Ferries (www.condorferries.co.uk) runs to/from Poole via Jersey or Guernsey.

TGV train services include trains to/from Rennes (€13.60, one hour) and Paris' Gare Montparnasse (€52 to €64, three hours, up to 10 daily).

CHAMPAGNE

Known in Roman times as Campania, meaning 'plain', the agricultural region of Champagne is synonymous these days with its world-famous bubbly. This multimillion-dollar industry is strictly protected under French law, ensuring that only grapes grown in designated Champagne vineyards can truly lay claim to the hallowed title. The town of Épernay, 30km south of the regional capital of Reims, is the best place to head for *dégustation* (tasting); a self-drive **Champagne Route** wends its way through the region's most celebrated vineyards.

Reims

POP 185,000

Over the course of a millennium (AD 816 to 1825), some 34 sovereigns – among them two dozen kings – began their reigns in Reims' famed cathedral. Meticulously reconstructed after WWI and again following WWII, the city – whose name is pronounced something like 'rance' and is often anglicised as Rheims – is endowed with handsome pedestrian zones, well-tended parks, lively nightlife and a state-of-the-art tramway.

Sights

Cathédrale Notre Dame CATHEDRAL

(www.cathedrale-reims.culture.fr; place du Cardinal Luçon; tower adult/child €7.50/free, incl Palais du Tau €11/free; 7.30am-7.30pm, tower tours hourly 10am-5pm Tue-Sat, 2-5pm Sun Apr-Sep) The single most famous event to take place at this Gothic edifice, a Unesco World Heritage Site, was the coronation of Charles VII, with Joan of Arc at his side, on 17 July 1429.

The finest stained-glass windows are the western facade's 12-petalled **great rose window**, its cobalt-blue neighbour below, and the **rose window** in the north transept (to the left as you walk from the entrance to the high altar), above the Flamboyant Gothic **organ case** (15th and 18th centuries).

Finish your visit by climbing 250 steps up the **cathedral tower** on a one-hour tour. Book at Palais du Tau.

Palais du Tau MUSEUM

(http://palais-tau.monuments-nationaux.fr; 2 place du Cardinal Luçon; adult/child €7.50/free, incl cathedral tower €11/free; 9.30am-6.30pm Tue-Sun) A Unesco World Heritage Site, this former archbishop's residence, constructed in 1690, was where French princes stayed before their coronations. Now a museum, it displays truly exceptional statuary, liturgical objects and tapestries from the cathedral.

Basilique St-Rémi BASILICA

(place du Chanoine Ladame; 8am-nightfall, to 7pm summer) This 121m-long former Benedictine abbey church, a Unesco World Heritage Site, mixes Romanesque elements from the mid-11th century with early Gothic features. The 12th-century-style chandelier has 96 candles, one for each year of the life of St Rémi, whose tomb (in the choir) is marked by a mausoleum from the mid-1600s. The basilica is about 1.5km southeast of the tourist office; take the Citadine 1 or 2 or bus A or F to the St-Rémi stop.

Tours

The bottle-filled cellars (10°C to 12°C – bring a sweater!) of eight Reims-area Champagne houses can be visited by guided tour which ends, *naturellement*, with a tasting session.

Mumm CHAMPAGNE HOUSE

(03 26 49 59 70; www.mumm.com; 34 rue du Champ de Mars; tours €11; tours begin 9am-11am & 2-5pm daily, closed Sun Nov-Feb) The only *maison de champagne* (Champagne house) in central Reims was founded in 1827 and is now the world's third-largest producer (almost eight million bottles a year). Engaging and edifying one-hour tours take you through cellars filled with 25 million bottles of fine bubbly. Phone ahead if possible.

Taittinger CHAMPAGNE CELLAR

(03 26 85 84 33; www.taittinger.com; 9 place St-Niçaise; tours €16; tours begin 9.30-11.50am & 2pm-4.20pm, closed Sat & Sun Dec–mid-Mar)

REIMS CITY CARD

The **Reims City Card** (€16), available at the tourist office, entitles you to the Champagne house visit (including tasting) and two audioguide tours of your choice.

Parts of the cellars here occupy 4th-century Roman stone quarries; other bits were excavated by 13th-century Benedictine monks. Situated 1.5km southeast of Reims centre; take the Citadine 1 or 2 bus to the St-Niçaise or Salines stops.

Sleeping

Chambre d'Hôte Cathédrale B&B €

(☎03 26 91 06 22; 21 place du Chapitre; s/d/tr without bathroom €50/60/75) The cathedral bells are your wake-up call at this sweet and simple B&B. Rooms are immaculate and old-fashioned, with stripy wallpaper, heavy wood furnishings and shared bathrooms.

Centre International de Séjour HOTEL €

(☎03 26 40 52 60; www.cis-reims.com; chaussée Bocquaine; s/d/q €49/60/84, s/d without bathroom €37/46; 📶) Good-value and well-kept (if charmless) digs, with a shared kitchen, lounge and free parking. Situated 200m south of the Comédie tram stop.

Eating & Drinking

Place Drouet d'Erlon is lined with inexpensive restaurants and pub-cafes. More discerning diners head to rue de Mars, adjacent to rue du Temple and place du Forum.

Brasserie Le Boulingrin BRASSERIE €€

(☎03 26 40 96 22; www.boulingrin.fr; 48 rue de Mars; menus €18.50-29; ⏰lunch & dinner Mon-Sat) A genuine, old-time brasserie – the decor and zinc bar date back to 1925 – whose ambience and cuisine make it an enduring favourite. September to June, the culinary focus is *fruits de mer* (seafood).

Café du Palais CAFE

(www.cafedupalais.fr; 14 place Myron-Herrick; ⏰Tue-Sat) Run by the same family since 1930, this art deco cafe is *the* place to sip a glass of Champagne and see and be seen, at least if you're a *bon bourgeois* or a theatre type.

Information

Tourist Office (☎per minute €0.34 08 92 70 13 51; www.reims-tourisme.com; 2 rue Guillaume de Machault; ⏰9am-7pm Mon-Sat, 10am-6pm Sun & holidays)

Getting There & Away

Direct trains link Reims with Épernay (€6.50, 21 to 50 minutes, seven to 18 daily) and Paris' Gare de l'Est (€26 to €34, 12 to 17 daily), half of which are speedy TGVs (45 minutes).

Épernay

POP 25,000

Prosperous Épernay, 25km south of Reims, is the self-proclaimed *capitale du champagne* and home to many of the world's most celebrated Champagne houses. Beneath the town's streets, some 200 million of bottles of Champagne are slowly being aged, just waiting around to be popped open for some fizz-fuelled celebration.

Sights & Activities

Many of Épernay's *maisons de champagne* (Champagne houses) are based along the handsome and eminently strollable **av de Champagne**. Cellar tours end with tasting and a visit to the factory-outlet bubbly shop.

Comtesse Lafond CHAMPAGNE HOUSE

(☎[illegible]; [illegible]; 70 av de Champagne; 3-glass tasting €9, incl cellar tour €14; ⏰10am-noon & 2-5.30pm daily) The whimsically turreted Comtesse Lafond is the most intimate and charming of the av de Champagne *maisons*. Tastings of three Champagnes take place in the elegant salon or in manicured gardens overlooking vine-streaked hills.

Moët & Chandon CHAMPAGNE HOUSE

(☎03 26 51 20 20; www.moet.com; 20 av de Champagne; adult incl 1/2 glasses €16.50/23, 10-18yr €9.50; ⏰tours 9.30-11.30am & 2-4.30pm, closed Sat & Sun mid-Nov–mid-Mar) Flying the Moët, French, European and Russian flags, this prestigious *maison* offers frequent one-hour tours that are among the region's most impressive.

Mercier CHAMPAGNE HOUSE

(☎03 26 51 22 22; www.champagnemercier.fr; 68-70 av de Champagne; adult incl 1/2/3 glasses €11/16/19, 12-17yr €5.50; ⏰tours 9.30-11.30am & 2-4.30pm, closed mid-Dec–mid-Feb) Everything here is flashy, including the 160,000L barrel that took two decades to build (for the Universal Exposition of 1889), the lift that transports you 30m underground, and the laser-guided touring train.

Sleeping

La Villa St-Pierre HOTEL €

(☎03 26 54 40 80; www.villasaintpierre.fr; 14 av Paul Chandon; d €51-61; 📶) In an early-20th-century mansion, this homey place, with 11 simple rooms, retains some of the charm of yesteryear.

Hôtel de la Cloche HOTEL €
(☎03 26 55 15 15; www.hotel-la-cloche.com; 5 place Mendès-France; d €49-59, tr €59-69; 📶) A slightly stiff hotel with 19 rooms decorated in bright, dissonant colours. Some rooms have park or church views.

Eating & Drinking

C Comme CHAMPAGNE BAR €€
(8 rue Gambetta; light meals €7.50-12, 6-glass Champagne tasting €33; ⏱10am-8.30pm Sun-Wed, 10am-11pm Thu, 10am-midnight Fri-Sat) The downstairs cellar has a stash of 300 different varieties of Champagne; sample them (from €5.50 a glass) in the softly lit bar-bistro upstairs. Accompany your tipple with a tasting plate of regional cheese, charcuterie and *rillettes* (pork pâté).

Le Sardaigne PIZZERIA €
(1 place Mendès-France; pizzas €8-12; ⏱lunch & dinner daily) Best pizza in town.

Information

Tourist Office (☎03 26 53 33 00; www.ot-epernay.fr; 7 av de Champagne; ⏱9.30am-12.30pm & 1.30-7pm Mon-Sat, 11am-4pm Sun & holidays)

Getting There & Away

Direct trains link Reims (€6.20, 20 to 36 minutes, 11 to 18 daily) and Paris' Gare de l'Est (€21, 1¼ hours, five to 10 daily).

ALSACE & LORRAINE

Teetering on the tempestuous frontier between France and Germany, the neighbouring regions of Alsace and Lorraine are where the worlds of Gallic and Germanic culture collide. Half-timbered houses, lush vineyards and forest-clad mountains hint at Alsace's Teutonic leanings, while Lorraine is indisputably Francophile.

STRASBOURG SAVER

The **Strasbourg Pass** (adult/child €14/7), a coupon book valid for three consecutive days, includes a visit to one museum, access to the cathedral platform, half a day's bicycle rental and a boat tour, plus hefty discounts on other tours. Admission to all of Strasbourg's museums (www.musees-strasbourg.org) and the cathedral's platform is free on the first Sunday of the month.

Strasbourg

POP 276,100

Strasbourg is the perfect overture to all that is idiosyncratic about Alsace – walking a fine tightrope between France and Germany and between a medieval past and a progressive future, it pulls off its act in inimitable Alsatian style. Roam the Old Town's twisting alleys lined with crooked half-timbered houses à la Grimm, feast in cosy *winstubs* (Alsatian taverns), and marvel at how a city that does Christmas markets and gingerbread so well can also be home to the glittering EU Quarter and France's second-largest student population.

Sights & Activities

Musée de l'Œuvre Notre-Dame ECCLESIASTICAL MUSEUM
(www.musees.strasbourg.org; 3 place du Château; adult/child €6/free; ⏱10am-6pm Tue-Sun, to 8pm Thu; 🚊Langstross) Hollywood gore seems tame compared with the tortures back when Hell really was Hell. Sure to scare you into a life of chastity is *Les Amants Trépassés* (The Deceased Lovers), painted in 1470, showing a grotesque couple being punished for their illicit lust: both of their entrails are being devoured by dragon-headed snakes. Track it down in this fabulous museum, a world-renowned ecclesiastical museum boasting one of Europe's premier collections of Romanesque, Gothic and Renaissance sculptures, 15th-century paintings and stained glass.

Grande Île HISTORIC QUARTER
(🚊Langstross) Strasbourg's Unesco World Heritage–listed Old Town is made for aimless ambling.

Cathédrale Notre-Dame CATHEDRAL
(place de la Cathédrale; adult/child astronomical clock €2/1.50, platform €5/2.50; ⏱7am-7pm, astronomical clock tickets sold from 11.45am, platform 9am-7.15pm; 🚊Langstross) Strasbourg's centrepiece red-sandstone Gothic cathedral is a riot of filigree stonework and flying buttresses, leering gargoyles and lacy spires. The 30m-high Gothic-meets-Renaissance **astronomical clock** strikes solar noon at

12.30pm with a parade of carved wooden figures portraying the different stages of life and Jesus with his apostles.

Musée d'Art Moderne et Contemporain MUSEUM
(MAMCS; ☎03 88 23 31 31; www.musees.strasbourg.eu; place Hans Jean Arp; adult/child €7/3.5; ⏰10am-6pm Tue-Sun) This striking glass-and-steel cube showcases an outstanding collection of fine art, graphic art and photography.

FREE **Cave des Hospices de Strasbourg** WINERY
(www.vins-des-hospices-de-strasbourg.fr; 1 place de l'Hôpital; ⏰8.30am-noon & 1.30-5.30pm Mon-Fri, 9am-12.30pm Sat; 🚊Porte de l'Hôpital) Founded in 1395, this brick-vaulted wine cellar nestled deep in the bowels of Strasbourg's hospital, has first-rate Alsatian wines.

Brasseries Kronenbourg BREWERY
(☎03 88 27 41 59; www.brasseries-kronenbourg.com; 68 rte d'Oberhausbergen; adult/child €6/4.50; ⏰tours 1.30pm Tue-Sat; 🚊Ducs d'Alsace) Brewery tours in Kronenbourg, 2.5km northwest of Strasbourg's Grande Île; reserve in advance.

Tours

Batorama BOAT TOUR
(www.batorama.fr; rue de Rohan; adult/child €9.20/4.80; ⏰tours half-hourly 9.30am-7pm, hourly 8-10pm; 🚊Langstross) Scenic 70-minute boat trips along the storybook canals of Petite France.

Sleeping & Eating

Hôtel Le Colmar HOTEL €
(☎03 88 32 16 89; www.hotel-lecolmar.com; 1 rue du Maire Kuss; r with/without shower €43/38; 🚊Gare Centrale) Sandwiched between Petite France and the train station, this central, no-frills hotel is a bargain. The high-ceilinged rooms are bright, clean and generously proportioned, though some beds are so springy they are borderline trampoline. Corner rooms look out across the river.

Bistrot et Chocolat CAFE €
(www.bistrotetchocolat.net; 8 rue de la Râpe; snacks €5-8, brunch €10-26; ⏰11am-7pm Tue-Fri, 10am-7pm Sat & Sun; ✎; 🚊Langstross) This boho-flavoured bistro is hailed for its solid and liquid organic chocolate (ginger is superb). The terrace is a local hang-out.

La Tinta CAFE €
(36 rue du Bain aux Plantes; brunch & lunch menus €9.90-10.90; ⏰Tue-Sat; 🚊Alt Winmärik) Boho-flavoured literary cafe good for a gourmet salad, fresh pressed juice or tea and cake.

Information

Tourist Office (☎03 88 52 28 28; www.otstrasbourg.fr; 17 place de la Cathédrale; ⏰9am-7pm)

TRAINS FROM STRASBOURG

Domestic Train

DESTINATION	PRICE (€)	DURATION (HR)	FREQUENCY
Lille	115	4	17 daily
Lyon	71	4½	14 daily
Marseille	161	6¾	16 daily
Metz	24.50	2	20 daily
Paris Gare de l'Est	71	2¼	19 daily

International Train

DESTINATION	PRICE (€)	DURATION	FREQUENCY
Basel SNCF (Switzerland)	22	1¼hr	25 daily
Brussels-Nord (Belgium)	74	5¼hr	3 daily
Karlsruhe (Germany)	25	40min	16 daily
Stuttgart (Germany)	47	1¼hr	4 daily
Vienna (Austria)	153	9¾hr	

Getting There & Away

AIR Strasbourg's international **airport** (www.strasbourg.aeroport.fr) is 17km southwest of the city centre (towards Molsheim).

Ryanair links London Stansted with **Karlsruhe/Baden Baden airport** (www.badenairpark.de), 58km northeast of Strasbourg, across the Rhine in Germany.

TRAIN Direct services go to both European and French cities.

Metz

POP 125,000

Straddling the confluence of the Moselle and Seille Rivers, Metz is Lorraine's graceful capital. Its Gothic marvel of a cathedral, Michelin-star-studded dining scene, beautiful yellow-stone Old Town and regal Quartier Impérial (up for Unesco World Heritage status) are a joy to discover, but nothing can beat the city's show-stopping Centre Pompidou-Metz.

Sights

TOP CHOICE **Centre Pompidou-Metz** MUSEUM

(www.centrepompidou-metz.fr; 1 parvis des Droits de l'Homme; adult/child €7/free; ⌚11am-6pm Mon, Wed & Sun, 11am-8pm Thu, Fri & Sat) This architecturally innovative museum, dazzling white and sinuous, is the satellite branch of Paris' Centre Pompidou. Its gallery draws on Europe's largest collection of modern art to stage ambitious temporary exhibitions. The dynamic space also hosts top-drawer cultural events.

Cathédrale St-Étienne CATHEDRAL

(place St-Étienne; audioguide €7, treasury & crypt adult/child €4/2; ⌚8am-6pm, treasury & crypt 9.30am-12.30pm & 1.30-5.30pm Mon-Sat, 1.30-5.30pm Sun) Exquisitely lit by kaleidoscopic curtains of 13th- to 20th-century stained glass, this cathedral is nicknamed 'God's lantern'. Flamboyant **Chagall windows** in startling jewel-coloured shades of ruby, gold, sapphire, topaz and amethyst adorn the ambulatory.

Quartier Impérial HISTORIC QUARTER

The stately boulevards and bourgeois villas of the German Imperial Quarter, including rue Gambetta and av Foch, are the brainchild of Kaiser Wilhelm II. Built to trumpet the triumph of Metz' post-1871 status as part of the Second Reich, the architecture is a whimsical mix of art deco, neo-Romanesque and neo-Renaissance influences.

GO TO MARKET

If only every market were like Metz' grand **Marché Couvert** (Covered Market; place de la Cathédrale; ⌚8am-5.30pm Tue-Sat). Once a bishop's palace, now a temple to fresh local produce, this is the kind of place where you pop in for a baguette and struggle out an hour later with bags overflowing with charcuterie, ripe fruit and five different sorts of *fromage*.

Make a morning of it, stopping for an early, inexpensive lunch and a chat with the market's larger-than-life characters. **Chez Mauricette** (sandwiches €3-5, antipasti plate €5-7) tempts with Lorraine goodies from herby *saucisson* (cured sausage) to local charcuterie and Mirabelle pâté. Its neighbour, **Soupes á Soups** (soups €3.20), ladles out homemade soups, from mussel to creamy mushroom varieties.

Sleeping & Eating

Cécil Hôtel HOTEL €

(☎03 87 66 66 13; www.cecilhotel-metz.com; 14 rue Pasteur; s €60-75, d €72-85; P 📶) Built in 1920, this family-run hotel's smallish rooms are neat, petite and decorated in warm colours. Parking is €9 per day.

Le Bistro des Sommeliers BISTRO €€

(☎03 87 63 40 20; 10 rue Pasteur; mains €16-20; ⌚closed Sat lunch, Sun) This no-nonsense bistro near the station prides itself on its warm ambience and consistently good French cooking. The three-course *prix fixe* (fixed price) menu is a bargain at €15.

La Baraka NORTH AFRICAN €

(☎03 87 36 33 92; 25 place de Chambre; mains €12-16; ⌚closed Wed) Unassuming North African place for tagines, tender lamb and couscous properly infused with saffron.

Information

Tourist Office (☎03 87 55 53 76; http://tourisme.mairie-metz.fr; 2 place d'Armes; ⌚9am-7pm Mon-Sat, 10am-5pm Sun)

Getting There & Away

Train it from Metz' ornate early-20th-century **train station** (pl du Général de Gaulle) to Paris' Gare de l'Est (€61, 80 minutes, 13 daily) and Strasbourg (€24.50, 1¾ hours, 14 daily).

THE LOIRE VALLEY

One step removed from the French capital, the Loire was historically the place where princes, dukes and notable nobles established their country getaways, and the countryside is littered with some of the most extravagant architecture outside Versailles.

Blois

POP 40,100

Blois' historic chateau was the feudal seat of the powerful counts of Blois, and its grand halls, spiral staircases and sweeping courtyards provide a whistle-stop tour through the key periods of French architecture. Sadly for chocoholics, the town's historic chocolate factory, Poulain, is off-limits to visitors.

Sights

Château Royal de Blois CHATEAU
(www.chateaudeblois.fr; place du Château; adult/child €9.50/4; 9am-6.30pm Apr-Sep, reduced hours Oct-Mar) The Royal Chateau of Blois makes an excellent introduction to the chateaux of the Loire Valley, with elements of Gothic (13th century); Flamboyant Gothic (1498–1503), early Renaissance (1515–24) and classical (1630s) architecture in its four grand wings.

Maison de la Magie MUSEUM
(www.maisondelamagie.fr; 1 place du Château; adult/child €8/5; 10am-12.30pm & 2-6.30pm Apr-Aug, 2-6.30pm Sep) Opposite Blois' chateau is the former home of watchmaker, inventor and conjurer Jean Eugène Robert-Houdin (1805–71), after whom the great American magician Harry Houdini is named. Dragons emerge roaring from the windows on the hour, and the museum hosts magic shows and optical trickery.

Sleeping & Eating

Côté Loire HOTEL €
(02 54 78 07 86; www.coteloire.com; 2 place de la Grève; d €57-89;) If it's charm and colours you want, head for the 'Loire Coast'. Its rooms come in cheery checks, bright pastels and the odd bit of exposed brick.

Hôtel Anne de Bretagne HOTEL €
(02 54 78 05 38; www.hotelannedebretagne.com; 31 av du Dr Jean Laigret; s €45-54, d €56-80;) This creeper-covered hotel has friendly staff and a bar full of polished wood and vintage pictures. Modern rooms are finished in flowery wallpaper and stripy bedspreads.

Les Banquettes Rouges FRENCH €€
(02 54 78 74 92; www.lesbanquettesrouges.com; 16 rue des Trois Marchands; menus €17-32; lunch & dinner Tue-Sat) Handwritten slate menus and wholesome food distinguish 'the Red Benches': rabbit with marmalade, duck with lentils, and salmon with apple vinaigrette, all done with a spicy twist.

Information

Tourist Office (02 54 90 41 41; www.blois-chambord.com; 23 place du Château; 9am-7pm)

Getting There & Away

BUS TLC operates buses from Blois' train station (€2) to Chambord (Line 3; 25 to 40 minutes, two Monday to Saturday) and Cheverny (Line 4; 45 minutes, six to eight Monday to Friday, two Saturday, one Sunday).

TRAIN The train station is 600m uphill from the chateau, on av Jean Laigret. International services include Madrid (€153, 12½ hours). Destinations within France include Amboise (€6.60, 20 minutes, 10 daily), Paris' Gares d'Austerlitz and Montparnasse (from €26.70, 1½ to two hours, 26 daily) and Tours (€10.20, 40 minutes, 13 daily).

Around Blois

CHÂTEAU DE CHAMBORD

For full-blown chateau splendour, you can't top **Chambord** (02 54 50 40 00; www.chambord.org; adult/child €11/free, parking €4; 9am-6pm Apr–Sep, 10am-5pm Oct-Mar), constructed from 1519 by François I as a lavish base for hunting game in the Sologne forests, but eventually used for just 42 days during the king's 32-year reign (1515–47).

The chateau's most famous feature is its **double-helix staircase**, attributed by some to Leonardo da Vinci, who lived in Amboise (34km southwest) from 1516 until his death three years later. The Italianate **rooftop terrace**, surrounded by cupolas, domes, chimneys and slate roofs, was where the royal court assembled to watch military exercises and hunting parties returning at the end of the day.

Several times daily there are 1½-hour **guided tours** (€4) in English, and during school holidays **costumed tours** entertain kids.

CHATEAUX TOURS

Hard-core indie travellers might baulk at the idea of a tour, but don't dismiss it out of hand, especially if you don't have your own transport.

Shuttlebus & Minibus

April to August, Blois' tourist office and TLC (www.tlcinfo.net) offer a twice-daily shuttle (€6) from Blois to the chateaux at Chambord, Cheverny and Beauregard.

Many private companies offer a choice of well-organised itineraries, taking in various combinations of Azay-le-Rideau, Villandry, Cheverny, Chambord and Chenonceau (plus wine-tasting tours). Half-day trips cost between €20 and €35; full-day trips range from €45 to €52. Entry to the chateaux isn't included, although you'll likely get a discount on tickets. Reserve via the tourist offices in Tours or Amboise, from where most tours depart.

Bicycle

The Loire Valley is mostly flat, and as such, is excellent cycling country. **Loire à Vélo** (www.loireavelo.fr) maintains 800km of signposted routes. Pick up a guide from tourist offices, or download route maps, audioguides and bike-hire details online.

Détours de Loire (☎02 47 61 22 23; www.locationdevelos.com) Has bike-rental shops in Tours and Blois and can deliver bikes; also allows you to collect/return bikes along the route for a small surcharge. Classic bikes cost €14/59 per day/week; tandems €45 per day.

Les Châteaux à Vélo (☎in Blois 02 54 78 62 52; www.chateauxavelo.com; per day €12-14) Has a bike-rental circuit between Blois, Chambord and Cheverny, 300km of marked trails and can shuttle you by minibus. Free route maps and MP3 guides online.

Chambord is 16km east of Blois, 45km southwest of Orléans and 17km northeast of Cheverny.

CHÂTEAU DE CHEVERNY

Thought by many to be the most perfectly proportioned chateau of all, **Cheverny** (☎02 54 79 96 29; www.chateau-cheverny.fr; adult/child €8.70/5.70; ⏲9.15am-6.45pm Jul & Aug, 9.15am-6.15pm Apr-Jun & Sep, 9.45am-5.30pm Oct, 9.45am-5pm Nov-Mar) has hardly been altered since its construction between 1625 and 1634. Inside is a formal dining room, bridal chamber and children's playroom (complete with Napoleon III–era toys), as well as a guards' room full of pikestaffs, claymores and suits of armour.

Many priceless art works (including the Mona Lisa) were stashed in the chateau's 18th-century Orangerie during WWII.

Near the chateau's gateway, the kennels house pedigreed French pointer/English foxhound hunting dogs still used by the owners of Cheverny; feeding time is the **Soupe des Chiens** (⏲5pm Apr-Sep, 3pm Oct-Mar).

Cheverny is 16km southeast of Blois and 17km southwest of Chambord. For buses to/from Blois see its Getting There & Away section.

CHÂTEAU DE CHAUMONT

Set on a defensible bluff above the Loire River, **Chaumont-sur-Loire** (www.domaine-chaumont.fr; adult/child €10/6, with gardens €15.50/11; ⏲10am-6.30pm Apr-Sep, to 5pm or 6pm Oct-Mar) presents a resolutely medieval face, with its cylindrical corner turrets and sturdy drawbridge. The castle became a short-lived residence for Catherine de Médici following the death of Henry II in 1560, and later passed into the hands of Diane de Poitiers (Henry II's mistress).

The chateau is 17km southwest of Blois and 20km northeast of Amboise. Onzain, a 2.5km walk from Chaumont across the Loire, has trains to Blois (€3.40, 10 minutes, 13 daily) and Tours (€8, 30 minutes, 10 daily).

Tours

POP 138,600

Hovering somewhere between the style of Paris and the conservative sturdiness of central France, Tours is a key staging post for exploring chateaux country. It's a smart, vivacious kind of town, filled with wide 18th-century boulevards, parks and imposing public buildings, and home to a busy university.

Sights

Musée des Beaux-Arts MUSEUM
(18 place François Sicard; adult/child €4/2; ⌚9am-12.45pm & 2-6pm Wed-Mon) Arranged around the courtyard of the archbishop's gorgeous palace, this fine-arts museum exhibits works spanning several centuries, including paintings by Delacroix, Degas and Monet, a rare Rembrandt miniature and a Rubens *Madonna and Child.*

Cathédrale St-Gatien CHURCH
(place de la Cathédrale; ⌚9am-7pm) With its twin towers, flying buttresses, stained glass and gargoyles, this cathedral is a show-stopper. The interior dates from the 13th to 16th centuries, and the domed tops of the two 70m-high towers are Renaissance.

Sleeping

Hôtel Ronsard BOUTIQUE HOTEL €
(☎02 47 05 25 36; www.hotel-ronsard.com; 2 rue Pimbert; s €58-72, d €66-78; ❄@📶) This recently renovated hotel offers comfort and good value. Halls are lined with colourful photographs, while the sleek, modern and immaculate rooms incorporate muted tones of grey with sparkling white linens.

Auberge de Jeunesse du Vieux Tours HOSTEL €
(☎02 47 37 81 58; www.fuaj.org/Tours; 5 rue Bretonneau; s/tw/tr incl breakfast €23/46/69; ⌚reception 8am-noon & 5-11pm; @📶) This friendly, bustling HI hostel attracts a large foreign student and young-worker contingent. Most rooms have only one to three beds; all share communal bathrooms, small kitchens and lounges. Bike rental available.

Eating

In the Old City, place Plumereau, rue du Grand Marché and rue de la Rôtisserie are crammed with cheap eats (quality variable).

Tartines & Co BISTRO €
(6 rue des Fusillés; sandwiches €9-13, ⌚lunch Mon-Sat, dinner Wed-Fri) This snazzy little bistro reinvents the *croque* (toasted sandwich) amidst jazz and friendly chatter. Choose your topping (chicken, roasted veg, beef carpaccio, foie gras with artichokes and honey vinaigrette) and it's served up quick-as-a-flash on toasted artisanal bread.

Le Zinc FRENCH €€
(☎02 47 20 29 00; 27 place du Grand Marché; menus €19.50-24.50; ⌚lunch Tue & Thu-Sat, dinner Thu-Tue) More concerned with market-fresh staples sourced from the nearby Les Halles than with Michelin stars or haute cuisine cachet, this bistro impresses with authentic, attractive country classics.

Information

Tourist Office (☎02 47 70 37 37; www.tours-tourisme.fr; 78-82 rue Bernard Palissy; ⌚8.30am-7pm Mon-Sat, 10am-12.30pm & 2.30-5pm Sun) Sells chateau tickets at a slight reduction.

DON'T MISS

TOP THREE CHATEAUX TRIPS FROM TOURS

Tours is an excellent base for exploring nearby chateaux:

Château de Chenonceau (☎02 47 23 90 07; www.chenonceau.com; adult/child €11/8.50, with audioguide €15/12; ⌚9am-7pm Apr-Sep, reduced hours Oct-Mar) Framed by a glassy moat and sweeping gardens, and topped by turrets and towers, this 16th-century castle is straight out of a fairy tale. Don't miss the yew-tree labyrinth or the 60m-long Grande Gallerie spanning the Cher River.

Château d'Azay-le-Rideau (☎02 47 45 42 04; azay-le-rideau.monuments-nationaux.fr/en; adult/child €8.50/free; ⌚9.30am-6pm Apr-Sep, to 7pm Jul & Aug, 10am-5.15pm Oct-Mar) Built in the 1500s on an island in the Indre River, this romantic, moat-ringed wonder flouts geometric windows, ordered turrets and decorative stonework. Don't miss its famous loggia staircase and summertime *son et lumière* (sound and light show).

Château de Villandry (☎02 47 50 02 09; www.chateauvillandry.com; château & gardens adult/child €9.50/5.50, gardens only €6.50/4; ⌚9am-6pm Apr-Oct, earlier rest of year, closed mid-Nov-Dec) This major Renaissance chateau is more famous for what's outside than in: its gardens are glorious. Don't miss the magnificent floral illustrations of love in the Ornamental Garden, or the potager (kitchen garden).

TRAINS FROM TOURS

DESTINATION	PRICE (€)	DURATION	FREQUENCY
Amboise	5.20	20min	13 daily
Blois	10.20	40min	13 daily
Bordeaux	50	2¾hr	hourly
Chenonceau	6.40	25min	8 daily
Nantes	29	1½hr	hourly
Paris Gare d'Austerlitz	32.90	2-2¾hr	5 daily (slow trains)
Paris Gare Montparnasse	44-82	1¼hr	8 daily (high-speed TGVs)

Getting There & Away

AIR Tours-Val de Loire Airport (www.tours.aeroport.fr), 5km northeast, is linked to Marseille, Londons Stansted, Manchester, Dublin, Southampton and Porto.

BUS Touraine Fil Vert (☎02 47 31 14 00; www.tourainefilvert.com; single ticket €1.80) line C links Tours bus station, next to the train station, with Amboise (40 minutes, 10 daily Monday to Saturday) and Chenonceau (1¼ hours, one daily).

TRAIN Tours' central train station is linked to TGV station St-Pierre-des-Corps, 4km east, by frequent shuttle trains.

Amboise

POP 12,900

The childhood home of Charles VIII and final resting place of Leonardo da Vinci, elegant Amboise, 23km northeast of Tours, is pleasantly perched along the southern bank of the Loire and overlooked by its fortified chateau.

Sights

Château Royal d'Amboise CASTLE
(www.chateau-amboise.com; place Michel Debré; adult/child €10.20/7, with audioguide €14.20/10; ⊙9am-6pm Apr-Oct, earlier closing Nov-Mar) Sprawling across a rocky escarpment above town, this castle served as a weekend getaway from the official royal seat at nearby Blois.

Le Clos Lucé HISTORIC BUILDING
(www.vinci-closluce.com; 2 rue du Clos Lucé; adult/child €13.50/8.50; ⊙9am-7pm Feb-Oct, 10am-6pm Nov-Jan) Leonardo da Vinci took up residence at this grand manor house in 1516 on the invitation of François I. Already 64 by the time he arrived, da Vinci spent his time sketching, tinkering and dreaming up new contraptions, scale models of which are now abundantly displayed throughout the home and its expansive gardens.

Sleeping & Eating

Centre Charles Péguy-Auberge de Jeunesse HOSTEL €
(☎02 47 30 60 90; www.mjcamboise.fr; Île d'Or; per person incl breakfast €19; @🛜) Efficient 72-bed boarding-school-style hostel on Île d'Or, an island in the middle of the Loire. Private rooms cost the same as dorms.

Hôtel Le Blason HOTEL €
(☎02 47 23 22 41; www.leblason.fr; 11 place Richelieu; s €50, d €53-63, q €83; ❄@🛜) Quirky, creaky budget hotel on a quiet square with 25 higgledy-piggledy rooms, wedged in around corridors: most are titchy, flowery and timber-beamed.

La Fourchette FRENCH €
(☎06 11 78 16 98; 9 rue Malebranche; lunch/dinner menus €15/24; ⊙lunch Tue-Sat, dinner Fri & Sat) Tucked into a back alley behind the tourist office, this is Amboise's favourite address for straightforward home cooking. Chef Christine makes you feel like you've been invited in to her house, with daily specials like *travers de porc* (spare ribs), *poulet rôti* (roast chicken) and *blanquette de veau* (veal stew).

Information

Tourist Office (☎02 47 57 09 28; www.amboise-valdeloire.com; ⊙9.30am-6pm Mon-Sat, 10am-1pm & 2-5pm Sun) In a riverside building opposite 7 quai du Général de Gaulle.

Getting There & Around

From the **train station** (bd Gambetta), 1.5km north of the chateau on the opposite side of the Loire, local trains run at least hourly to Tours (€5.20, 20 minutes) and Blois (€6.60, 20 minutes). Four daily express trains also serve Paris' Gare d'Austerlitz (€30.10, 1¾ hours).

BURGUNDY & THE RHÔNE VALLEY

If there's one place in France where you're really going to find out what makes the nation tick, it's Burgundy. Two of the country's enduring passions – food and wine – come together in this gorgeously rural region; if you're a sucker for hearty food and the fruits of the vine, you'll be in seventh heaven.

Dijon

POP 250,000

Dijon is one of France's most appealing cities. Filled with elegant medieval and Renaissance buildings, dashing Dijon is Burgundy's capital, and the spiritual home of French mustard. Its lively Old Town is wonderful for strolling and shopping, interspersed with some snappy drinking and dining.

Sights & Activities

Palais des Ducs et des États de Bourgogne PALACE

(Palace of the Dukes & States of Burgundy; place de la Libération) Once home to Burgundy's powerful dukes, this monumental palace overlooks **place de la Libération**, Old Dijon's central square dating from 1686. The palace's eastern wing houses the outstanding **Musée des Beaux-Arts**, whose entrance is next to the **Tour de Bar**, a squat 14th-century tower that once served as a prison.

Just off the **Cour d'Honneur**, the 46m-high, mid-15th-century **Tour Philippe le Bon** (adult/child €2.30/free; guided tours every 45min 9am-noon & 1.45-5.30pm late Nov-Easter, 1.30-3.30pm Wed, 9am-3.30pm Sat-Sun late Nov–Easter) affords fantastic views over the city. Spot Mont Blanc on a clear day.

FREE **Musée de la Vie Bourguignonne** MUSEUM

(03 80 48 80 90; 17 rue Ste-Anne; 9am-noon & 2-6pm Wed-Mon) This museum explores village and town life in Burgundy in centuries past; a whole street is recreated on the 1st floor.

Sleeping

Hôtel Le Sauvage HOTEL €

(03 80 41 31 21; www.hotellesauvage.com; 64 rue Monge; s €48-59, d €53-64, tr €85; P wi-fi) Set in a 15th-century *relais de poste* (coaching inn) that ranges around a cobbled, vine-shaded courtyard, this little hotel is definitely good value.

Ethic Étapes Dijon HOSTEL €

(Centre De Recontres et de Séjour Internationales; CRISD; 03 80 72 95 20; www.cri-dijon.com; 1 av Champollion; dm/s/d incl breakfast €21/40/52; P @ wi-fi) This institutional but friendly 219-bed hostel, 2.5km northeast of the centre, has modern two- to six-bed rooms with private bathrooms. Take bus line 3 to the Dallas CRI stop.

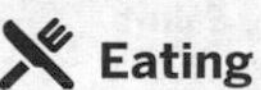

Eating

Eat streets loaded with restaurants include buzzy rue Berbisey, place Émile Zola, rue Amiral Roussin and around the perimeter of the covered market.

DZ'Envies REGIONAL CUISINE €€

(03 80 50 09 26; www.dzenvies.com; 12 rue Odebert; mains €16-20, lunch menus €13-20, dinner menus €29-36; Mon-Sat) This zinging restaurant is a good choice if you're tired of heavy Burgundian classics. At €18, the lunchtime *I love Dijon* (yes) menu is a steal.

Chez Nous BISTRO €

(impasse Quentin; mains €7-8, lunch menus €10-13; lunch noon-2pm Tue-Sat, bar 2pm-1am Mon, 11am-1am Tue-Sat) This quintessentially French *bar du coin* (neighbourhood bar), often crowded, hides down an alleyway near

WORTH A TRIP

MUSEOPARC ALÉSIA

Opened in 2012, the sensational **MuseoParc Alésia** (www.alesia.fr; 1 rte des Trois Ormeaux, Alise-Ste-Reine; 9am-9pm Jul-Aug, 9am-6pm Apr-Jun & Sep, 10am-5pm Oct-Dec & Feb-Mar, closed Jan), near the village of Alise-Ste-Reine in the Pays d'Auxois, is well worth the drive from Dijon (67km). This was the site of what was once Alésia, the camp where Vercingétorix, the chief of the Gaulish coalitions, was defeated by Julius Caesar after a long siege. The defeat marked the end of the Gallic/Celtic heritage in France. You can visit the well-organised interpretative centre as well as the vestiges of the Gallo-Roman city that developed after the battle. Entertaining workshops for kids.

MAD ABOUT MUSTARD

If there is one pilgrimage to be made in **Dijon** it is to **Moutarde Maille** (☎03 80 30 41 02; www.maille.com; 32 rue de la Liberté; ⏰10am-7pm Mon-Sat), the factory boutique of the company that makes Dijon's most famous mustard. The tangy odours of the sharp sauce assault your nostrils instantly upon entry and there are 36 different kinds to buy, including cassis-, truffle- or celery-flavoured; sample three on tap.

Or head to **Moutarderie Fallot** (Mustard Mill; www.fallot.com; 31 rue du Faubourg Bretonnière; adult/child €10/8; ⏰tours 10am & 11.30am Mon-Sat, also afternoons summer, closed Nov–mid-Mar) in neighbouring **Beaune**, where Burgundy's last family-run, stone-ground mustard company offers tours of its facilities and mustard museum. Demonstrations include hand-milling mustard seeds. Reserve ahead at Beaune tourist office.

the covered market. At lunchtime join the flock and go for the fabulous-value *plat du jour* (daily special).

Information

Tourist Office (☎08 92 70 05 58; www.visit-dijon.com; 11 rue des Forges; ⏰9am-6.30pm Mon-Sat, 10am-6pm Sun) Also rents bicycles.

Getting There & Away

BUS Transco (☎03 80 11 29 29; www.mobigo-bourgogne.com) buses stop in front of the train station; tickets sold on board (€1.50). Bus 44 goes to Nuits-St-Georges and Beaune. Bus 43 goes to Abbaye de Cîteaux.

TRAIN Trains leave the **train station** (www.voyages-sncf.com; rue du Dr Remy) for Lyon-Part Dieu (from €22, 1½ hours, 25 daily), Marseille (from €54, 3½ hours by TGV, six direct daily) and Paris' Gare de Lyon (from €49, 1¾ hours by TGV; €42, three hours non-TGV, 25 daily). International destinations include Milan (€80, seven hours).

Côte d'Or

Burgundy's most renowned vintages come from the Côte d'Or (Golden Hillside), a range of hills made of limestone, flint and clay that runs south from Dijon for about 60km. The northern section, the **Côte de Nuits**, stretches from Marsannay-la-Côte south to Corgoloin and produces reds known for their robust, full-bodied character. The southern section, the **Côte de Beaune**, lies between Ladoix-Serrigny and Santenay and produces great reds and whites.

Tourist offices provide brochures. The signposted **Route des Grands Crus** (www.road-of-the-fine-burgundy-wines.com) visits some of the most celebrated Côte de Nuits vineyards; mandatory tasting stops for oenophiles seeking nirvana include 16th-century **Château du Clos de Vougeot** (☎03 80 62 86 09; www.closdevougeot.fr; Vougeot; adult/child €4/3.10; ⏰9am-5.30pm daily), which has excellent guided tours, and **L'Imaginariim** (☎03 80 62 61 40; www.imaginarium-bourgogne.com; av du Jura, Nuits-St-Georges; adult/child €8/5; ⏰2-7pm Mon, 10am-7pm Tue-Sun), an entertaining wine museum, in Nuits-St-Georges.

Wine & Voyages (☎03 80 61 15 15; www.wineandvoyages.com; tours from €53) and **Alter & Go** (☎06 23 37 92 04; www.alterandgo.fr; tours from €70), with an emphasis on history and winemaking methods, run minibus tours in English; reserve online or at the Dijon tourist office.

Beaune

POP 22,720

Beaune (pronounced 'bone'), 44km south of Dijon, is the unofficial capital of the Côte d'Or. This thriving town's raison d'être and the source of its joie de vivre is wine.

Sights & Activities

Beaune's amoeba-shaped Old City is enclosed by **stone ramparts** sheltering wine cellars.

If you'll be taking in a lot of sights and activities, including wine tasting, in the Beaune area, consider picking up the **Pass Pays Beaunois** at Beaune tourist offices. Ticket combos save 5% to 15% depending on the number of sights you plan to visit.

Hôtel-Dieu des Hospices de Beaune HISTORIC BUILDING
(www.hospices-de-beaune.com; rue de l'Hôtel-Dieu; adult/child €7/3; ⏰9am-5.30pm) Built in 1443, this magnificent Gothic hospital (until 1971) is famously topped by stunning turrets and pitched rooftops covered in multicoloured tiles. Interior highlights include the barrel-vaulted **Grande Salle** (look for the dragons and peasant heads up on the roof beams);

an 18th-century **pharmacy** lined with flasks once filled with elixirs and powders; and the multipanelled masterpiece, **The Last Judgement**, by 15th-century Flemish painter Rogier van der Weyden, depicting Judgment Day in glorious technicolour.

Cellar Visits WINE TASTING

Millions of bottles of wine age to perfection in cool dark cellars beneath Beaune's streets; dozens can be visited by guided tour. Our favourites include the candlelit cellars of the former Église des Cordeliers, **Marché aux Vins** (www.marcheauxvins.com; 2 rue Nicolas Rolin; admission €10; 9.30-11.30am & 2-5.30pm, no midday closure Jul-Aug), where 15 wines can be sampled; and **Cellier de la Vieille Grange** (www.bourgogne-cellier.com; 27 bd Georges Clemenceau; 9am-noon & 2-7pm Wed-Sat, by appointment Sun-Tue), where locals flock to buy Burgundy wines *en vrac* (in bulk; bring your own jerrycan or buy a vinibag) for as little as €4.25 per litre for quality AOC wines. Tasting is done direct from barrels using a pipette. **Patriarche Père et Fils** (www.patriarche.com; 5 rue du Collège; audioguide tour €13; 9.30-11.30am & 2-5.30pm), lined with about five million bottles of wine, has Burgundy's largest cellars.

Sleeping & Eating

Café Hôtel-Restaurant de l'Abattoir HOTEL €

(03 80 22 21 46; 19 rue du Faubourg Perpreuil; d €29;) Everything is simple and laid-back at this unfussy hotel five minutes' walk from the centre. The rooms are small but tidy; ask for a renovated one. Accommodation with half board (breakfast and dinner) is available (€39 per person). Note that reception is closed on Sunday. Call ahead.

Koki Food & Shop FUSION, FRENCH €

(03 80 24 06 61; www.kokifoodshop.com; 10 place Félix Ziem; brunch €11-17, menus €15-18; Thu-Tue) If you think the time has come to give your taste buds something new to sing about, this is the place. This upbeat and colourful eatery run by Laurent Peugeot, a Burgundian chef who worked for four years in Japan, gets kudos for its lip-smacking concoctions that arrive via conveyer belt – you pay by the plate (from €4). Set menus are also available.

Information

Tourist Office (03 80 26 21 30; www.beaune-tourisme.fr; 6 bd Perpreuil; 9am-7pm Mon-Sat, 9am-6pm Sun)

Getting There & Away

Bus

Bus 44 links Beaune with Dijon (€1.50, 1½ hours, two to seven daily), stopping at Côte d'Or villages like Vougcot, Nuits-St-Georges and Aloxe-Corton.

Train

Trains run to the following destinations:

Dijon (€7.30, 25 minutes, 40 daily)

Nuits-St-Georges (from €4.50, 10 minutes, 40 daily)

Paris Gare de Lyon (from €41, 2¼ hours by TGV, 3½ hours non-TGV, 20 daily, two direct TGVs daily)

Lyon-Part Dieu (from €30, 1¾ hours, 16 daily)

Lyon

POP 488,000

Gourmets, eat your heart out: Lyon is *the* gastronomic capital of France, with a lavish table of piggy-driven dishes and delicacies to savour. The city has been a commercial, industrial and banking powerhouse for the past 500 years, and is still France's second-largest conurbation, with outstanding art museums, a dynamic nightlife, green parks and a Unesco-listed Old Town.

Sights

VIEUX LYON

Old Lyon, with its cobblestone streets and medieval and Renaissance houses below Fourvière hill, is divided into three quarters: St-Paul at the northern end, St-Jean in the middle and St-Georges in the south. Lovely old buildings languish on **rue du Bœuf**, **rue St-Jean** and **rue des Trois Maries**.

LYON CITY CARD

The **Lyon City Card** (www.lyon-france.com; 1/2/3 days adult €21/31/41, child €12.50/17.50/22.50) covers admission to every Lyon museum and the roof of Basilique Notre Dame de Fourvière, as well as guided city tours, a river excursion (April to October) and discounts on other selected attractions.

The card also includes unlimited travel on buses, trams, the funicular and metro. Buy it online (www.en.lyon-france.com/Lyon-City-Card), from the tourist office, or at some hotels.

Lyon

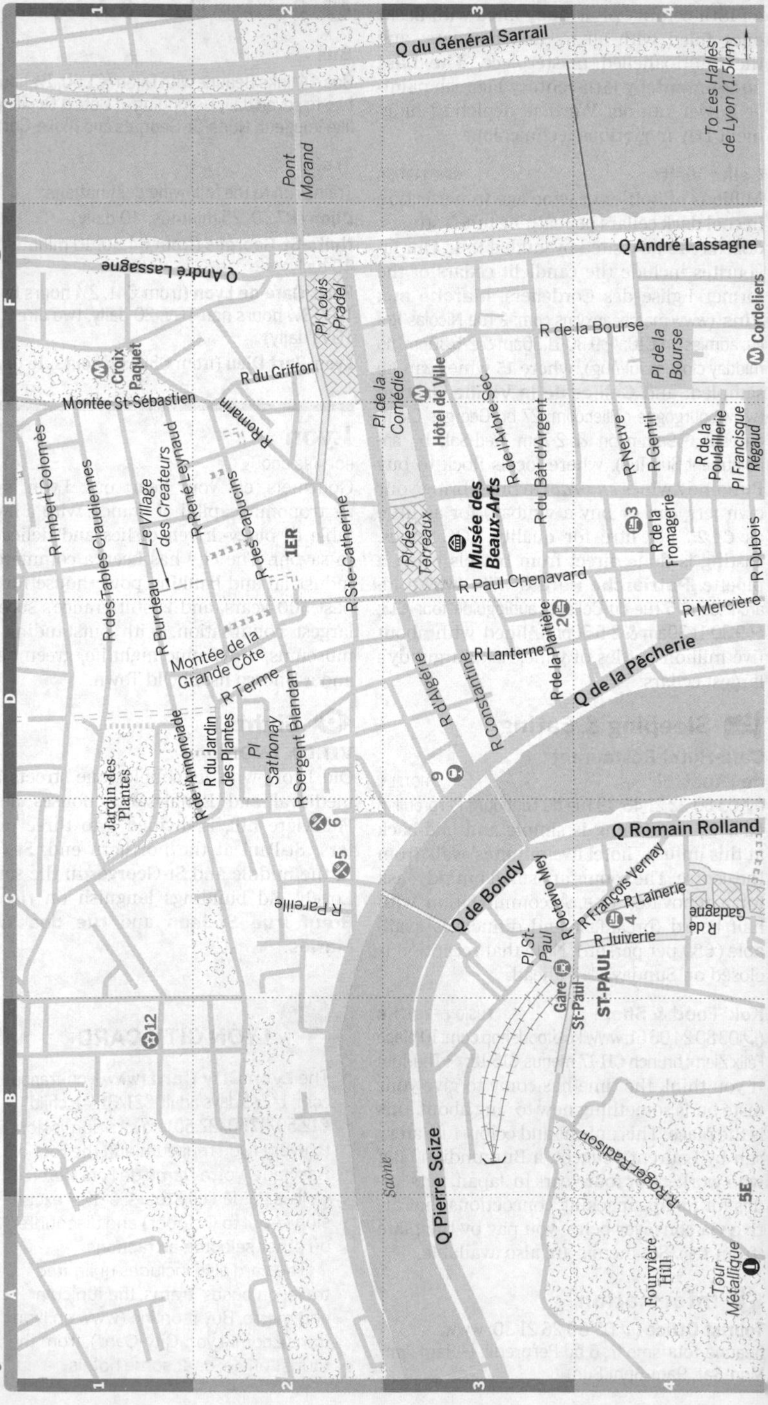

0 200 m
0 0.1 miles

A B C D E F G

Jardin des Plantes
12
R Imbert Colomès
R des Tables Claudiennes
Montée St-Sébastien
Croix Paquet
R Burdeau
Le Village des Createurs
R de l'Annonciade
R du Jardin des Plantes
Montée de la Grande Côte
R René Leynaud
Q André Lassagne
Pl Sathonay
R Terme
R des Capucins
R Romarin
R du Griffon
R Pareille
R Sergent Blandan
1ER
Pont Morand
5
6
Pl Louis Pradel
R Ste-Catherine
Saône
Pl de la Comédie
Pl des Terreaux
Hôtel de Ville
Q Pierre Scize
9
R d'Algérie
Q du Général Sarrail
Q de Bondy
R Constantine
R Lanterne
R Paul Chenavard
Musée des Beaux-Arts
R de l'Arbre Sec
Pl St-Paul
R Octavio Mey
Gare St-Paul
R de la Plaitière
2
R du Bât d'Argent
R de la Bourse
ST-PAUL
R François Vernay
Q de la Pêcherie
R Roger Radison
R Juiverie
4
R Lainerie
Q Romain Rolland
3
R Neuve
Fourvière Hill
R de la Fromagerie
R Gentil
Pl de la Bourse
Q André Lassagne
R de Gadagne
R Mercière
R de la Poulaillerie
Tour Métallique
5E
R Dubois
Pl Francisque Régaud
Cordeliers
To Les Halles de Lyon (1.5km)

1 2 3 4

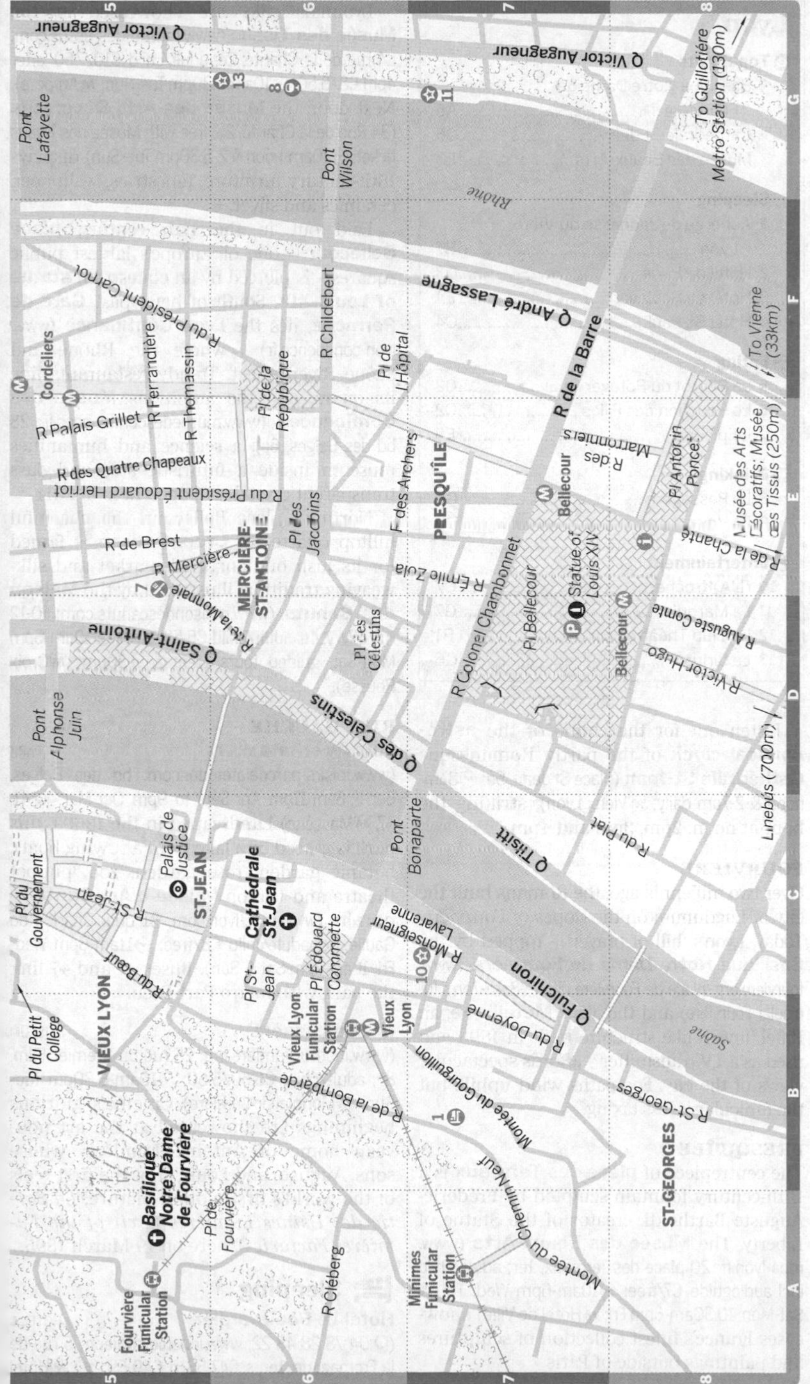
Q Victor Augagneur
Pont Lafayette
Pont Wilson
Rhône
To Guillotière Metro Station (130m)
R du Président Carnot
R Childebert
Q André Lassagne
Cordeliers
R Palais Grillet
R Ferrandière
R Thomassin
Pl de la République
Pl de l'Hôpital
R des Quatre Chapeaux
R du Président Édouard Herriot
R des Archers
PRESQU'ÎLE
R de la Barre
R des Marronniers
Bellecour
Pl Antonin Poncet
To Vienne (33km)
Musée des Arts Décoratifs; Musée des Tissus (250m)
R de Brest
R Mercière
Pl des Jacobins
R de la Chanté
MERCIÈRE-ST-ANTOINE
R de la Monnaie
Q Saint-Antoine
R Émile Zola
Pl des Célestins
R Colonel Chambonnet
Pl Bellecour
Statue of Louis XIV
R Auguste Comte
R Victor Hugo
Pont Alphonse Juin
Q des Célestins
Linebús (700m)
Pl du Gouvernement
Palais de Justice
ST-JEAN
Pont Bonaparte
Q Tilsitt
R du Plat
R St-Jean
Cathédrale St-Jean
R du Bœuf
Pl St-Jean
Pl Édouard Commette
R Monseigneur Lavarenne
Q Fulchiron
VIEUX LYON
Pl du Petit Collège
Vieux Lyon Funicular Station
Vieux Lyon
R du Doyenné
Saône
R de la Bombarde
Montée du Gourguillon
R St-Georges
Basilique Notre Dame de Fourvière
Pl de Fourvière
Chemin Neuf
ST-GEORGES
Montée du Chemin Neuf
Fourvière Funicular Station
R Cléberg
Minimes Funicular Station

Lyon

Top Sights

	Basilique Notre Dame de Fourvière	A5
	Cathédrale St-Jean	C6
	Musée des Beaux-Arts	E3

Sleeping

1	Auberge de Jeunesse du Vieux Lyon	B7
2	Hôtel de Paris	D3
3	Hôtel Le Boulevardier	E4
4	Hôtel St-Paul	C4

Eating

5	Le Bistrot du Potager	C2
6	Le Bouchon des Filles	C2
7	L'Épicerie	E5

Drinking

8	La Passagère	G6
9	Le Voxx	D3

Entertainment

10	(L'A)Kroche	C7
11	La Marquise	G7
12	Le Club Théâtre	B1
13	Le Sirius	G6

Listen out for the chime of the **astronomical clock** of the partly Romanesque **Cathédrale St-Jean** (place St-Jean, 5e; ⏲8am-noon & 2-7pm daily; Ⓜ Vieux Lyon), striking the hour at noon, 2pm, 3pm and 4pm.

FOURVIÈRE

Over two millennia ago, the Romans built the city of Lugdunum on the slopes of Fourvière. Today, Lyon's 'hill of prayer' – topped by the **Basilique Notre Dame de Fourvière** (www.fourviere.org; place de Fourvière, 5e; ⏲8am-7pm; funicular Fourvière) and the **Tour Métallique**, an Eiffel Tower–like structure built in 1893 and used as a TV transmitter – affords spectacular views of the city. Footpaths wind uphill, but the funicular is less taxing.

PRESQU'ÎLE

The centrepiece of **place des Terreaux** is a 19th-century fountain sculpted by Frédéric-Auguste Bartholdi, creator of the Statue of Liberty. The **Musée des Beaux-Arts** (www.mba-lyon.fr; 20 place des Terreaux, 1er; adult/child incl audioguide €7/free; ⏲10am-6pm Wed, Thu & Sat-Mon, 10.30am-6pm Fri; Ⓜ Hôtel de Ville) showcases France's finest collection of sculptures and paintings outside of Paris.

Lyonnais silks are showcased at the **Musée des Tissus** (www.musee-des-tissus.com; 34 rue de la Charité, 2e; adult/child €10/7.50, after 4pm €8/5.50; ⏲10am-5.30pm Tue-Sun; Ⓜ Ampère). Next door, the **Musée des Arts Décoratifs** (34 Rue de la Charité, 2e; free with Musée des Tissus ticket; ⏲10am-noon & 2-5.30pm Tue-Sun) displays 18th-century furniture, tapestries, wallpaper, ceramics and silver.

Laid out in the 17th century, **place Bellecour** – one of Europe's largest public squares – is pierced by an equestrian **statue of Louis XIV**. South of here, past **Gare de Perrache**, lies the **Lyon Confluence** (www.lyon-confluence.fr) , where the Rhône and Saône Rivers meet. Trendy restaurants line its quays, and the ambitious **Musée des Confluences** (www.museedesconfluences.fr; 28 bd des Belges, 6e), a science and humanities museum inside a futuristic steel-and-glass transparent crystal, will open here in 2014.

North of place Bellecour, the charmful hilltop quarter of **Croix Rousse** is famed for its lush outdoor food market and silk-weaving tradition, illustrated by the **Maison des Canuts** (www.maisondescanuts.com; 10-12 rue d'Ivry, 4e; adult/child €6.50/3.50; ⏲10am-6pm Mon-Sat, guided tours 11am & 3.30pm; Ⓜ Croix Rousse).

RIVE GAUCHE

Parc de la Tête d'Or PARK

(www.loisirs-parcdelatetedor.com; bd des Belges, 6e; ⏲6am-11pm Apr-Sep, to 9pm Oct-Mar; 🚌41, 47, Ⓜ Masséna) Landscaped in the 1860s, this park is graced by a lake (rent a rowing boat), botanic garden, rose garden, zoo, puppet theatre and tip-top **Musée d'Art Contemporain** (www.mac-lyon.com; 81 quai Charles de Gaulle, 6e; adult/child €8/free; ⏲11am-6pm Wed-Fri, 10am-7pm Sat & Sun). Buses 41 and 47 link the park with metro Part-Dieu.

Musée Lumière MUSEUM

(www.institut-lumiere.org; 25 rue du Premier Film, 8e; adult/child €6.50/5.50; ⏲10am-6.30pm Tue-Sun; Ⓜ Monplaisir-Lumière) Cinema's glorious beginnings are showcased at the art nouveau home of Antoine Lumière, whose sons, Auguste and Louis, shot the first reels of the world's first motion picture, *La Sortie des Usines Lumières* (*Exit of the Lumières Factories*), here on 19 March 1895.

Sleeping

Hôtel Le Boulevardier HOTEL €

(☎04 78 28 48 22; www.leboulevardier.fr; 5 rue de la Fromagerie, 1er; s €47-56, d €49-59; 📶; Ⓜ Hôtel de Ville, Cordeliers) Quirky touches like old skis and tennis racquets adorn the hallways at this bargain 11-room hotel. It's up a steep spiral staircase above a cool little bistro and jazz club of the same name, which doubles as reception.

Hôtel de Paris HOTEL €€
(☎04 78 28 00 95; www.hoteldeparis-lyon.com; 16 rue de la Platière, 1er; s €52-92, d €64-135; ❄@📶; ⓂHôtel de Ville) This newly remodeled hotel in a 19th century bourgeois building features bright decor and theme rooms with artsy designs. Some have a funky, retro '70s feel.

Hôtel St-Paul HOTEL €
(☎04 78 28 13 29; www.hotelstpaul.fr; 6 rue Lainerie, 5e; d €70-85; @📶; ⓂVieux Lyon, Hôtel de Ville) This 20-room hotel with friendly staff is conveniently located on the edge of Vieux Lyon, and only a five-minute walk across the bridge from the Hôtel de Ville. Aim for one of the brighter street-facing rooms; back rooms off the staircase tend to be claustrophobic.

Auberge de Jeunesse du Vieux Lyon HOSTEL €
(☎04 78 15 05 50; www.fuaj.org/lyon; 41-45 montée du Chemin Neuf, 5e; dm incl breakfast €22; ⏲reception 7am-1pm, 2-8pm & 9pm-1am; @📶; ⓂVieux Lyon) Stunning city views unfold from the terrace of Lyon's only hostel, and from many of the (mostly six-bed) dorms. Bike parking, kitchen and laundry (wash-dry per load €4).

Eating

Lyon's sparkling restaurant line-up embraces all genres: French, fusion, fast and international, as well as traditional Lyonnais *bouchons* (small, friendly bistros serving local city cuisine).

Le Bouchon des Filles REGIONAL CUISINE €€
(☎04 78 30 40 44; 20 rue Sergent Blandan, 1er; menus €25; ⏲dinner daily, lunch Sun; ⓂHôtel de Ville) This contemporary ode to Lyon's legendary culinary *mères* (mothers) is run by an enterprising crew of young women with deep roots in the local *bouchon* scene. The light and fluffy *quenelles* (Lyonnais dumplings) are among the best you'll find in Lyon, and the rustic atmosphere is warm and welcoming.

Le Bistrot du Potager TAPAS €
(☎04 78 29 61 59; www.lebistrotdupotager.com; 3 rue de la Martinière, 1er; tapas €5-12; ⏲lunch & dinner Tue-Sat; ⓂHôtel de Ville) An offshoot of the renowned Potager des Halles restaurant next door; throngs of happy diners linger here over glasses of wine and Provençal duck carpaccio, grilled vegetables with pistou, stuffed artichokes, octopus salad, Tunisian-style chickpeas and platters of cheeses and charcuterie.

L'Épicerie BISTRO €
(☎04 78 37 70 85; 2 rue de la Monnaie, 2e; tartines €3.80-6.30; ⏲noon-midnight; 🖉; ⓂCordeliers) Done out like an early-20th-century grocer's, with distressed cupboards full of china and old boxes and canisters, this place serves thick-sliced *tartines* with toppings like brie, walnut and honey and delicious desserts like pear-chocolate tart. There's a handful of other branches in Lyon and beyond.

Drinking & Entertainment

Cafe terraces on place des Terreaux buzz with all-hours drinkers, as do the British, Irish and other-styled pubs on nearby rue Ste-Catherine, 1er, and rue Lainerie and rue St-Jean, 5e, in Vieux Lyon.

Track new bars and nightclubs with **Le Petit Paumé** (www.petitpaume.com), a savvy city guide penned by local university students.

Floating bars with DJs and live bands rock until around 3am aboard the string of *péniches* (river barges) moored along the

A MARKET LUNCH

Shopping and munching lunch at the market is an unmissable part of the Lyon experience.

Pick up a round of impossibly runny St Marcellin from legendary cheesemonger **Mère Richard**, or a knobbly Jésus de Lyon from pork butcher **Collette Sibilia** at Lyon's famed indoor market **Les Halles de Lyon** (halledelyon.free.fr; 102 cours Lafayette, 3e; ⏲8am-7pm Tue-Sat, to 1pm Sun; ⓂPart-Dieu). Or simply sit down and enjoy a lunch of local produce, lip-smacking *coquillages* (shellfish) included, at one of its stalls.

Alternatively, meander up to the hilltop quarter of **Croix Rousse** and, December to April, indulge in oysters and a glass of white Côtes du Rhône on a cafe pavement terrace – before or after shopping at its huge and glorious morning food market on bd de la Croix Rousse.

Rhône's left bank. Scout out the section of quai Victor Augagneur between Pont Lafayette (Ⓜ Cordeliers or Guichard) and Pont de la Guillotière (Ⓜ Guillotière).

Our favourites are laid-back **Passagère** (21 quai Victor Augagneur, 3e; daily; Ⓜ Place Guichard - Bourse du Travail); party-hard **Le Sirius** (www.lesirius.com; 4 quai Victor Augagneur, 3e; daily; ; Ⓜ Place Guichard - Bourse du Travail); and electro-oriented **La Marquise** (www.marquise.net; 20 quai Victor Augagneur, 3e; Tue-Sun; Ⓜ Place Guichard - Bourse du Travail).

Le Voxx BAR
(1 rue d'Algérie, 1er; 10am-3am daily; Ⓜ Hôtel de Ville) Minimalist but lively riverside bar packed with a real mix of people.

(L'A)Kroche LIVE MUSIC
(www.lakroche.fr; 8 rue Monseigneur Lavarenne, 5e; 11am-1am Tue-Sat, 3-9pm Sun & Mon; Ⓜ Vieux Lyon) Hip concert cafe-bar with DJs spinning electro, soul, funk and disco; bands too.

Ninkasi Gerland LIVE MUSIC
(www.ninkasi.fr; 267 rue Marcel Mérieux, 7e; 10am-late; Ⓜ Stade de Gerland) This microbrewery dishes up DJs, bands and film projections amid a backdrop of fish and chips, build-your-own burgers and other un-French food.

Le Club Théâtre PERFORMING ARTS
(www.thearte.fr; 4 impasse Flesselles, 1er; annual membership fee €2; Ⓜ Croix Rousse) Hip and unique, this hybrid bar-nightclub-cultural centre sits inside Croix Rousse's old neighbourhood wash-house, with the central washbasin doubling as a stage and dance floor.

EAT STREETS

Rue St-Jean, 5e (Ⓜ Vieux Lyon) A surfeit of restaurants jam Vieux Lyon's pedestrian main street.

Cobbled rue Mercière, rue des Marronniers & place Antonin Poncet, 2e (Ⓜ Bellecour) Buzzing streets, chock-a-block with eating options (of widely varying quality) and pavement terraces overflowing in summer.

Rue du Garet & Rue Verdi, 1er (Ⓜ Hôtel de Ville) Twin set of parallel streets snug by Lyon's opera house on the Presqu'île.

Information

Tourist Office (04 72 77 69 69; www.lyon-france.com; place Bellecour, 2e; 9am-6pm; Ⓜ Bellecour)

Getting There & Away

AIR **Lyon-St-Exupéry Airport** (www.lyon.aeroport.fr), 25km east of the city, serves 120 direct destinations across Europe and beyond, including many budget carriers.

BUS In the Perrache complex, **Eurolines** (04 72 56 95 30; www.eurolines.fr; Gare de Perrache) and Spain-oriented **Linebús** (04 72 41 72 27; www.linebus.com; Gare de Perrache) have offices on the bus-station level of the Centre d'Échange (follow the 'Lignes Internationales' signs).

TRAIN Lyon has two main-line train stations with direct TGV services: **Gare de la Part-Dieu** (Ⓜ Part-Dieu), 1.5km east of the Rhône, and **Gare de Perrache** (Ⓜ Perrache).

Getting Around

Tramway **Rhonexpress** (www.rhonexpress.net) links the airport with Part-Dieu train station in under 30 minutes. A single ticket costs €14.

Buses, trams, a four-line metro and two funiculars linking Vieux Lyon to Fourvière are run by **TCL** (www.tcl.fr). Public transport runs from around 5am to midnight. Tickets cost €1.60. Validate tickets on all forms of public transport or risk a fine.

Bikes are available from 200-odd bike stations thanks to **Vélo'v** (www.velov.grandlyon.com; first 30min free, first/subsequent hr €1/2).

THE FRENCH ALPS

Whether it's paragliding among the peaks, hiking the trails or hurtling down a mountainside strapped to a pair of glorified toothpicks, the French Alps is the undisputed centre of adventure sports in France.

Chamonix

POP 9378 / ELEV 1037M

With the pearly white peaks of the Mont Blanc massif as a sensational backdrop, being an icon comes naturally to Chamonix. First 'discovered' by Brits William Windham and Richard Pococke in 1741, this is the mecca of mountaineering. Its knife-edge peaks, plunging slopes and massive glaciers have enthralled generations of adventurers and thrill-seekers ever since. Its après-ski scene is equally pumping.

TRAINS FROM LYON

DESTINATION	PRICE (€)	DURATION (HR)	FREQUENCY
Dijon	from 29	2	at least 7 daily
Lille-Europe	from 90	3	at least 11 daily
Marseille	from 45	1¾	every 30-60min
Paris Gare de Lyon	from 69	2	every 30-60min
Paris Charles de Gaulle Airport	from 69	2	at least 11 daily
Strasbourg	88	3¾	5 daily

Sights

Aiguille du Midi VIEWPOINT

A jagged needle of rock 8km from the hump of Mont Blanc, the Aiguille du Midi (3842m) is one of Chamonix' most distinctive landmarks. If you can handle the height, the 360-degree panorama from the summit is breathtaking.

The vertiginous **Téléphérique de l'Aiguille de Midi** (place de l'Aiguille du Midi; adult/child return to Aiguille du Midi €46/39, Plan de l'Aiguille €26/22; ⏲8.30am-4.30pm) cable car links Chamonix with the Aiguille du Midi. In summer you will need to obtain a boarding card (marked with the number of your departing *and* returning cable car) in addition to a ticket. Bring warm clothes: even in summer, the temperature at the top rarely rises above -10°C.

Late June to early September, continue for a further 30 minutes of mind-blowing scenery in the smaller bubbles of the **Télécabine Panoramic Mont Blanc** (adult/child return from Chamonix €70/59; ⏲8.30am-3.30pm) to Pointe Helbronner (3466m) on the French-Italian border. From here, another cable car descends to the Italian ski resort of Courmayeur.

Mer de Glace GLACIER

The glistening 200m-deep Mer de Glace (Sea of Ice) snakes 7km through mighty rock spires and turrets. The glacier moves up to 90m a year, and has become a popular attraction thanks to the rack-and-pinion railway line opened in 1908. The quaint red mountain train trundles up from **Gare du Montenvers** (35 place de la Mer de Glace; adult/child/family €26/22/79; ⏲10am-4.30pm) in Chamonix to Montenvers (1913m), from where a cable car takes you down to the glacier and cave. Wrap up warm to experience the **Grotte de la Mer de Glace** (⏲late Dec-May & mid-Jun–Sep) ice cave, where frozen tunnels and ice sculptures change colour like mood rings.

Sleeping

Hotel L'Oustalet HOTEL €€

(☎04 50 55 54 99; www.hotel-oustalet.com; 330 rue du Lyret; d/q €148/190; 📶🏊) You'll pray for snow at this Alpine chalet near Aiguille du Midi cable car, just so you can curl up by the fire with a *chocolat chaud* and unwind in the sauna and hot tub. Rooms are snugly decorated in solid pine and open onto balconies with Mont Blanc views.

Le Vert Hôtel HOTEL €€

(☎04 50 53 13 58; www.verthotel.com; 964 rte des Gaillands; s/d/tr/q €80/103/129/151; 📶) Self-proclaimed 'Chamonix' house of sports and creativity', this party house 1km south of town has no-frills rooms, some with microscopically small bathrooms. But what people really come for is the all-happening, ultra-hip bar, a regular venue for top DJs and live music. Minimum four-night stay.

Camping Mer de Glace CAMPGROUND €

(☎04 50 53 44 03; www.chamonix-camping.com; 200 chemin de la Bagna; campsites €23.50; ⏲late Apr-Sep; 📶) Oh, what a beautiful morning! Draw back your tent flap and be dazzled by Mont Blanc and glaciated peaks at this campground, 2km northeast of Chamonix.

Eating

La Petite Kitchen INTERNATIONAL €€

(80 place du Poilu; 2-course lunch menus €12.50, mains €18-28; ⏲lunch & dinner Wed-Mon) The Little Kitchen is just that: a handful of tables for the lucky few who get to indulge in its locally sourced feel-good food – filling English breakfasts, steaks with homemade *frites* (hot chips) and the stickiest of toffee puddings.

Munchie FUSION €€
(☎04 50 53 45 41; www.munchie.eu; 87 rue des Moulins; mains €19-24; ⊙dinner daily) The style of this trendy Swedish-run hang-out is pan-Asian fusion. Sittings go faster than musical chairs, so it's worth a try even if you haven't booked.

Extreme CAFE €
(21 place Balmat; light meals €3.50-8; ⊙9am-9pm; 📶) Fun snack bar where you can grab a wrap and smoothie and log on to the free wi-fi.

Papillon CAFE €
(416 rue Joseph Vallot; light meals €4-8; ⊙9am-8pm Tue-Sat, 11am-5.30pm Sun) Papillon does great homemade curries, chillis, fat-jacket potatoes and deli-style sandwiches.

Drinking & Entertainment

Nightlife rocks. In the centre, riverside rue des Moulins boasts a line-up of après-ski joints serving food as well as booze.

Chambre Neuf BAR
(272 av Michel Croz; ⊙daily; 📶) Cover bands and raucous drinking make 'Room 9' one of Chamonix' liveliest party haunts.

MBC MICROBREWERY
(www.mbchx.com; 350 rte du Bouchet; ⊙4pm-2am daily) This trendy microbrewery run by four Canadians is fab. Be it with its burgers, cheesecake of the week, live music or amazing locally brewed and named beers, MBC delivers.

Elevation 1904 BAR
(259 av Michel Croz; ⊙7am-11pm or later daily) Alpine paraphernalia lines the walls of this merry bet by the train station with an all-day snack shack. The suntrap terrace is just right.

DON'T MISS

A LOFTY LUNCH

Crazy as it sounds for a piste restaurant, you might have to book at **La Crèmerie du Glacier** (☎04 50 54 07 52; www.lacremerieduglacier.fr; 766 chemin de la Glacière; menus €12-22; ⊙lunch & dinner Thu-Tue) to get a chance to bite into its world-famous *croûtes au fromage* (chunky slices of toasted bread topped with melted cheese). Ski to it on the red Pierre à Ric piste in Les Grands Montets.

Information

Tourist Office (☎04 50 53 00 24; www.chamonix.com; 85 place du Triangle de l'Amitié; ⊙8.30am-7pm)

Getting There & Away

BUS From **Chamonix bus station** (www.sat-montblanc.com; place de la Gare), next to the train station, five daily buses run to/from Geneva airport (one-way/return €33/55, 1½ to two hours). Advanced booking only.

TRAIN The Mont Blanc Express narrow-gauge train trundles from St-Gervais-Le Fayet station, 23km west of Chamonix, to Martigny in Switzerland, stopping en route in Les Houches, Chamonix and Argentière. There are nine to 12 return trips daily between Chamonix and St-Gervais (€10, 45 minutes). From St-Gervais-Le Fayet, there are trains to most major French cities.

THE DORDOGNE

Tucked in the country's southwestern corner, the Dordogne fuses history, culture and culinary sophistication in one scenic package. The region is best known for its sturdy *bastides* (fortified towns), clifftop chateaux and spectacular prehistoric cave paintings.

Sarlat-La-Canéda

POP 9940

Part of the fun of Sarlat is getting lost in its twisting, honey-coloured alleyways and backstreets. **Rue Jean-Jacques Rousseau** or **rue Landry** are good starting points, but for the grandest buildings and *hôtels particuliers* explore **rue des Consuls**. Whichever street you take, sooner or later you'll hit the **Cathédrale St-Sacerdos** (place du Peyrou).

Nearby, the former **Église Ste-Marie** (place de la Liberté) houses Sarlat's mouth-watering **Marché Couvert** (covered market) and a state-of-the-art **panoramic lift** (elevator), designed by French architect Jean Nouvel, in its bell tower.

Sleeping & Eating

Hôtel Les Récollets HOTEL €
(☎05 53 31 36 00; www.hotel-recollets-sarlat.com; 4 rue Jean-Jacques Rousseau; d €49-89; ❄📶) Budget rooms with an Old Town location, set around a pretty hidden courtyard.

Le Bistrot REGIONAL CUISINE €€
(☎05 53 28 28 40; place du Peyrou; menus €18.50-28.50; ⊙Mon-Sat) This dinky diner is the best

DON'T MISS

PREHISTORIC PAINTINGS

Fantastic prehistoric caves with some of the world's finest **cave art** is what makes the Vézère Valley so very special. Most of the caves are closed in winter, and get very busy in summer. Visitor numbers are strictly limited, so you'll need to reserve well ahead.

Of the valley's 175 known sites, the most famous include **Grotte de Font de Gaume** (05 53 06 86 00; www.eyzies.monuments-nationaux.fr; adult/child €7.50/free; 9.30am-5.30pm Sun-Fri mid-May–mid-Sep, 9.30am-12.30pm & 2-5.30pm Sun-Fri mid-Sep–mid-May), 1km northeast of Les Eyzies. About 14,000 years ago, prehistoric artists created the gallery of over 230 figures, including bison, reindeer, horses, mammoths, bears and wolves, of which 25 are on permanent display.

About 7km east of Les Eyzies, **Abri du Cap Blanc** (05 53 06 86 00; adult/child €7.50/free; 10am-6pm Sun-Fri mid-May–mid-Sep, 10am-noon & 2-6pm Sun-Fri mid-Sep–mid-May) showcases an unusual sculpture gallery of horses, bison and deer.

Then there is **Grotte de Rouffignac** (05 53 05 41 71; www.grottederouffignac.fr; adult/child €6.50/4.20; 9-11.30am & 2-6pm Jul & Aug, 10-11.30am & 2-5pm Sep-Jun), sometimes known as the 'Cave of 100 Mammoths' because of its painted mammoths. Access to the caves, hidden in woodland 15km north of Les Eyzies, is aboard a trundling electric train.

Star of the show goes hands down to **Grotte de Lascaux** (Lascaux II; 05 53 51 95 03; www.semitour.com; adult/child €8.80/6; 9.30am-6pm), 2km southeast of Montignac, featuring an astonishing menagerie including oxen, deer, horses, reindeer and mammoth, as well as an amazing 5.5m bull, the largest cave drawing ever found. The original cave was closed to the public in 1963 to prevent damage to the paintings, but the most famous sections have been meticulously recreated in a second cave nearby – a massive undertaking that required some 20 artists and took 11 years.

of the bunch on cafe-clad place du Peyrou. Gingham cloths and tiny tables create a cosy bistro feel, and the menu's heavy on Sarlat classics – especially walnuts, *magret de canard* (duck breast) and *pommes sarlardaises* (potatoes cooked in duck fat).

Information

Tourist Office (05 53 31 45 45; www.sarlat-tourisme.com; rue Tourny; 9am-7pm Mon-Sat, 10am-1pm & 2-6pm Sun Jul & Aug, shorter hours Sep-Jun)

Getting There & Away

The **train station** (av de la Gare), 1.3km south of the Old City, serves Périgueux (change at Le Buisson; €14.80, 1¾ hours, three daily) and Les Eyzies (change at Le Buisson; €9.80, 50 minutes to 2½ hours, three daily).

THE ATLANTIC COAST

With quiet country roads winding through vine-striped hills and wild stretches of coastal sands interspersed with misty islands, the Atlantic coast is where France gets back to nature. If you're a surf nut or beach bum, the sandy bays around Biarritz will be right up your alley, while oenophiles can sample the fruits of the vine in the high temple of French winemaking, Bordeaux.

Bordeaux

POP 240,500

The new millennium was a turning point for the city long nicknamed La Belle au Bois Dormant (Sleeping Beauty), when the mayor, ex-prime minister Alain Juppé, roused Bordeaux, pedestrianising its boulevards, restoring its neoclassical architecture, and implementing a hi-tech public-transport system. Today the city is a Unesco World Heritage Site and, with its merry student population and 2.5 million-odd annual tourists, scarcely sleeps at all.

Sights

Cathédrale St-André CATHEDRAL

This Unesco World Heritage Site is almost overshadowed by the gargoyled, 50m-high Gothic belfry, **Tour Pey-Berland** (adult/child €5.50/free; 10am-1.15pm & 2-6pm Jun-Sep, shorter hrs rest of year), topped off in 1863 with a statue of Notre Dame de l'Aquitaine

(Our Lady of Aquitaine). Scaling the tower's 231 narrow steps rewards you with a spectacular panorama of Bordeaux city.

Musée d'Aquitaine MUSEUM
(www.musee-aquitaine-bordeaux.fr; 20 cours Pasteur; permanent collection free, exhibitions adult/student €5/3; ⌚11am-6pm Tue-Sun) Gallo-Roman statues and relics dating back 25,000 years are among the highlights at this impressive museum.

Musée d'Art Contemporain MUSEUM
(www. capc-bordeaux.fr; rue Ferrére, Entrepôt 7; rue Ferrére, Entrepôt 7; adult/student/child €5/3/free; ⌚11am-6pm Tue-Sun) An 1824 warehouse for French colonial produce (coffee, cocoa, peanuts, vanilla and the like) is the dramatic backdrop for cutting-edge modern art here.

Musée des Beaux-Arts MUSEUM
(www.musba-bordeaux.fr; 20 cours d'Albret; permanent collection free, exhibitions adult/student €5/2.50; ⌚11am-6pm Wed-Mon) The evolution of Occidental art from the Renaissance to the mid-20th century.

Sleeping

Hôtel du Théâtre BOUTIQUE HOTEL €
(☎05 56 79 05 26; www.hotel-du-theatre.com; 10 rue Maison-Daurade; s/d from €60/77; @) The owners of this recently renovated hotel, just off the main shopping street, have done up some rooms in an entirely classic style and some in the sun-burst colours of the Mediterranean. Our favourites are full of flashy sequins and glitter, and look like they just got home from the disco.

Auberge de Jeunesse HOSTEL €
(☎05 56 33 00 70; www.auberge-jeunesse-bordeaux.com; 22 cours Barbey; dm incl sheets & breakfast €22.50; ⌚reception closed 11am-2pm;) This ultra-modern building with kitchen reopens after renovation in 2013. From the train station, follow cours de la Marne northwest for 300m and turn left opposite the park; the hostel's about 250m ahead on your left.

Eating

Place du Parlement, rue du Pas St-Georges, rue des Faussets and place de la Victoire are loaded with dining addresses, as is the old waterfront warehouse district around quai des Marques – great for a sunset meal or drink.

Le Cheverus Café BISTRO €
(☎05 56 48 29 73; 81-83 rue du Loup; menus from €11.40; ⌚Mon-Sat) This neighbourhood bistro is friendly, cosy and chaotically busy (be prepared to wait for a table at lunchtime). The food dares to veer slightly away from the bistro standards of steak and chips, and the lunch *menus*, which include wine, are an all-out bargain. Come evening it morphs into something of a tapas bar.

Michels Bistrot BISTRO €
(15 rue du Pas-Saint-Georges; lunch menu €12) In Bordeaux's most bohemian quarter, this buzzing bistro is packed with students and those who wish they were still students. It's renowned for the quality of its beef – whether that be in hamburger form or a more classic steak. It's also a popular early-evening *apero* hang-out.

Information

Main Tourist Office (☎05 56 00 66 00; www.bordeaux-tourisme.com; 12 cours du 30 Juillet; ⌚9am-7.30pm Mon-Sat, 9.30am-6.30pm Sun)

Getting There & Away

AIR Aéroport de Bordeaux (www.bordeaux.aeroport.fr) is in Mérignac, 10km west of the city centre, with domestic and some international services.

TRAIN From Gare St-Jean, 3km from the centre, at least 16 trains daily serve Paris' Gare Montparnasse (€73, three hours).

DON'T MISS

SATURDAY-MORNING OYSTERS

A classic Bordeaux experience is a Saturday morning spent slurping oysters and white wine from one of the seafood stands to be found at **Marché des Capucins** (six oysters & glass of wine €6; ⌚7am-noon). Afterwards, you can peruse the stalls while shopping for the freshest ingredients for a picnic in one of the city's parks. To get there, head south down cours Pasteur and once at place de la Victoire, turn left onto rue Élie Gintrec.

Dune du Pilat

This colossal sand dune (sometimes referred to as the Dune de Pyla because of its location in the resort town of Pyla-sur-Mer), 65km west of Bordeaux, stretches from the mouth of the Bassin d'Arcachon southwards for al-

WORTH A TRIP

ON THE WINE TRAIL

Thirsty? The 1000-sq-km wine-growing area around the city of Bordeaux is, along with Burgundy, France's most important producer of top-quality wines. Whet your palate with Bordeaux tourist office's introductory wine-and-cheese courses (€24).

Serious students of the grape can enrol in a two-hour (€25) or two- to three-day course (€335 to €600) at the **École du Vin** (Wine School; ☎05 56 00 22 66; www.bordeaux.com) inside the **Maison du Vin de Bordeaux** (3 cours du 30 Juillet).

Bordeaux has over 5000 estates where grapes are grown, picked and turned into wine. Smaller chateaux often accept walk-in visitors, but at many places, especially better-known ones, you have to reserve in advance. If you have your own wheels, one of the easiest to visit is **Château Lanessan** (☎05 56 58 94 80; www.lanessan.com; Cussac-Fort-Medoc).

Favourite vine-framed villages brimming with charm and tasting/buying opportunities include medieval **St-Émilion** (www.saint-emilion-tourisme.com), port town **Pauillac** (www.pauillac-medoc.com) and **Listrac-Médoc**. In **Arsac-en-Médoc**, Philippe Raoux's vast glass-and-steel wine centre, **La Winery** (☎05 56 39 04 90; www.lawinery.fr; Rond-point des Vendangeurs, D1), stuns with concerts and contemporary art exhibitions alongside tastings to determine your *signe œnologique* ('wine sign'; booking required).

Many chateaux close during October's *vendange* (grape harvest).

most 3km. Already the largest in Europe, it's spreading eastwards at 4.5m a year – it has swallowed trees, a road junction and even a hotel.

The view from the top – approximately 114m above sea level – is magnificent. To the west you can see the sandy shoals at the mouth of the Bassin d'Arcachon, including the **Banc d'Arguin bird reserve** and Cap Ferrat. Dense dark-green pine forests stretch from the base of the dune eastwards almost as far as the eye can see.

Take care swimming in this area: powerful currents swirl out to sea from the deceptively tranquil *baïnes* (little bays).

Although an easy day trip from Bordeaux, the area around the dune is an enjoyable place to kick back for a while. Most people camp in one of the swag of seasonal campgrounds; see www.bassin-arcachon.com.

Biarritz

POP 26,000

Edge your way south along the coast towards Spain and you arrive in stylish Biarritz, just as ritzy as its name suggests. The resort took off in the mid-19th century (Napoleon III had a rather soft spot for the place) and it still shimmers with architectural treasures from the belle époque and art deco eras. Big waves – some of Europe's best – and a beachy lifestyle are a magnet for Europe's hip surfing set.

Sights & Activities

Beaches BEACHES

Biarritz' raison d'être is its fashionable beaches, particularly central **Grande Plage** and **Plage Miramar**, lined with sunbathing bodies on hot summer days. Stripy 1920s-style beach tents can be hired for €9.50 per day. North of Pointe St-Martin, the adrenalin-pumping surfing beaches of **Anglet** (the final 't' is pronounced) continue northwards for more than 4km. Take bus 10 or 13 from the bottom of av Verdun (just near av Édouard VII).

Cité de l'Océan MUSEUM

(☎05 59 22 75 40; www.citedelocean.com; 1 av de la Plage; adult/child €10.50/7; ⏰10am-10pm) Inside an eye-catching, wave-shaped building south of town, this museum will teach you everything about the ocean and, in between, get you to ride to its depths in a submarine and watch giant squid and sperm whales do battle. A combined ticket with the Musée de la Mer costs €17.50/13 per adult/child.

Musée de la Mer MUSEUM

(☎05 59 22 75 40; www.museedelamer.com; Esplanade du Rocher de la Vierge; adult/child €13/9.50; ⏰9.30am-midnight Jul-Aug, shorter hours Sep-Jun) Housed in a wonderful art deco building, Biarritz' Sea Museum is seething with underwater life from the Bay of Biscay and beyond. Its tanks house sharks and tropical reef fish, but it's the seals that steal the show (feeding times 10.30am and 5pm).

Sleeping

Hôtel Mirano BOUTIQUE HOTEL €€
(05 59 23 11 63; www.hotelmirano.fr; 11 av Pasteur; d €68-130; P) Squiggly purple, orange and black wallpaper and oversize orange perspex light fittings are some of the rad '70s touches at this retro boutique hotel, a 10-minute stroll from the town centre.

Auberge de Jeunesse de Biarritz HOSTEL €
(05 59 41 76 00; www.hihostels.com; 8 rue Chiquito de Cambo; dm incl sheets & breakfast €24.20; reception 8.30-11.30am & 6-9pm, to noon & 10pm May-Sep, closed mid-Dec–early Jan; @) This popular place offers outdoor activities including surfing. From the train station, follow the railway westwards for 800m.

Eating

The area around covered market **Les Halles** (rue des Halles, rue du Centre, rue du Vieux Port) is the hot spot in Biarritz for character-infused tapas bars loaded with tasty treats.

Casa Juan Pedro SEAFOOD €
(05 59 24 00 86; Port des Pêcheurs; mains €7-10) Down by the old port, this cute fishing shack cooks up tuna, sardines and squid with plenty of friendly banter.

Bistrot des Halles BASQUE €€
(05 59 24 21 22; 1 rue du Centre; mains €15-17) One of a cluster of restaurants along rue du Centre that shop for their produce at the nearby covered market, this bustling place is known for its excellent fish and fresh modern French market fare.

Drinking

Great bars stud rue du Port Vieux, place Clemenceau and the central food-market area.

Ventilo Caffé BAR
(rue du Port Vieux; closed Tue Oct-Easter) Dressed up like a boudoir, this fun and funky place continues its domination of the Biarritz bar scene.

Arena Café Bar BAR
(Plage du Port Vieux; 9am-2am daily Apr-Sep, 10am-2am Wed-Sun Oct-Mar) Tucked into a tiny cove, this beachfront hang-out combines a style-conscious restaurant and a fashionista bar with DJs and sunset views.

Information

Tourist Office (05 59 22 37 10; www.biarritz.fr; square d'Ixelles; 9am-7pm)

Getting There & Away

AIR **Biarritz-Anglet-Bayonne Airport** (www.biarritz.aeroport.fr), 3km southeast of Biarritz, is served by several low-cost carriers.

BUS **ATCRB buses** (www.transdev-atcrb.com) runs services down the coast to the Spanish border.

TRAIN Biarritz-La Négresse train station, 3km south of town, is linked to the centre by bus A1.

LANGUEDOC-ROUSSILLON

Languedoc-Roussillon comes in three distinct flavours: Bas-Languedoc (Lower Languedoc), land of bullfighting, rugby and robust red wines, where the region's major sights are found; sunbaked Nîmes with its fine Roman amphitheatre; and fairy-tale Carcassonne, crowned with a ring of witch-hat turrets.

Inland, Haut Languedoc (Upper Languedoc) is a mountainous, sparsely populated terrain made for lovers of the great outdoors; while Roussillon sits to the south, snug against the rugged Pyrenees and frontier to Spanish Catalonia. Meanwhile, Languedoc's traditional centre, Toulouse, was shaved off when regional boundaries were redrawn almost half a century ago, but we've chosen to include it in this section.

Nîmes

POP 146,500

This buzzy city boasts some of France's best-preserved classical buildings, including a famous Roman amphitheatre, although the city is most famous for its sartorial export, *serge de Nîmes* – better known to cowboys, clubbers and couturiers as denim.

Sights

A **Pass Nîmes Romaine** (adult/child €10/7.70), valid for three days, covers all three sights; buy one at the first place you visit.

Les Arènes ROMAN SITE
(www.arenes-nimes.com; place des Arènes; adult/child €7.90/6; 9am-8pm Jul-Aug, earlier closing Sep-Jun) Nîmes' twin-tiered amphitheatre, the best preserved of the Roman Empire, was built around AD 100 to stage gladiatorial contests and public executions – watched by an audience of 24,000 spectators.

Maison Carrée ROMAN SITE
(place de la Maison Carrée; adult/child €4.60/3.80; ⏲10am-8pm Jul-Aug, earlier closing Sep-Jun) This gleaming limestone temple built around AD 5 to honour Emperor Augustus' two adopted sons is not actually square despite its name, meaning 'Square House' – to the Romans, 'square' simply meant a building with right angles.

Carré d'Art MUSEUM
(www.carreartmusee.com; place de la Maison Carrée; permanent collection free, exhibitions adult/child €5/3.70; ⏲10am-6pm Tue-Sun) The striking glass-and-steel art museum facing the Maison Carrée was designed by British architect Sir Norman Foster.

Festivals & Events

Nîmes becomes more Spanish than French during its two *férias* (bullfighting festivals): the five-day **Féria de Pentecôte** (Whitsuntide Festival; ⏲Jun), and the three-day **Féria des Vendanges** (⏲Sep) celebrating the grape harvest. Each is marked by daily *corridas* (bullfights). Buy tickets in situ or online at the **Billeterie des Arènes** (www.arenesde-nimes.com; 2 rue de la Violette).

Sleeping & Eating

Hôtel Amphithéâtre HOTEL €
(☎04 66 67 28 51; www.hoteldelamphitheatre.com; 4 rue des Arènes; s/d €65/85) Tucked away along a narrow backstreet, this tall townhouse hotel run by an ex-pat Cornishman and his wife has chic and stylish rooms; some have balconies overlooking place du Marché.

Auberge de Jeunesse HOSTEL €
(☎04 66 68 03 20; www.hinimes.com; 257 chemin de l'Auberge de Jeunesse, La Cigale; dm/d €15.55/36; ⏲reception 7.30am-1am) It's out in the sticks, 4km from the station, but there's lots in its favour: spacious dorms, family rooms, a sweet garden with camping pitches, and a choice of self-catering kitchen or cafe. Take bus I, direction Alès or Villeverte, to the Stade stop.

L'Imprévu MODERN FRENCH €€
(☎04 66 38 99 59; www.l-imprevu.com; 6 place d'Assas; mains €19.50-27.50; ⏲lunch & dinner) The simple, amber-stoned facade of this fine-dining French bistro looks homey, but the interior is light and contemporary with swirly modern art, an open-plan kitchen and interior courtyard. There's a posh mix of *terre-et-mer* (surf-and-turf) dishes, mainly served à la carte.

Information

Tourist Office (☎04 66 58 38 00; www.ot-nimes.fr; 6 rue Auguste; ⏲8.30am-8pm Mon-Fri, 9am-7pm Sat, 10am-6pm Sun Jul & Aug, shorter hours Sep-Jun)

DON'T MISS

PONT DU GARD

Southern France has some fine Roman sites, but for audacious engineering, nothing can top Unesco World Heritage site **Pont du Gard** (☎04 66 37 50 99; www.pontdugard.fr; car & up to 5 passengers €18, after 8pm €10, cyclists & walkers free; ⏲visitors centre & museum 9am-7pm Jun-Sep, 9am-6pm Mar-May & Sep, 9am-5pm Oct-Feb, parking lots 9am-1am), 21km northeast of Nîmes. This three-tiered aqueduct was once part of a 50km-long system of water channels, built around 19 BC to transport water from Uzès to Nîmes. The scale is huge: 50m high, 275m long and graced with 35 precision-built arches, the bridge was sturdy enough to carry up to 20,000 cu metres of water per day. Each block was carved by hand and transported here from nearby quarries – no mean feat, considering the largest blocks weigh over 5 tonnes.

The **Musée de la Romanité** provides background on the bridge's construction, while kids can try out educational activities in the **Ludo** play area. Nearby, the 1.4km **Mémoires de Garrigue** walking trail winds upstream through typically Mediterranean scrubland, and offers some of the best bridge views.

There are large car parks on both banks of the river, about a 400m walk from the bridge. Parking costs a flat-rate €5.

Crowds can be a real problem in high summer; early evening is usually a great time to visit, especially since parking is free after 7pm and the bridge is stunningly lit after dark.

WORTH A TRIP

LOURDES

If you've ever wondered what a Catholic version of Las Vegas might look like, chances are it'd be pretty close to **Lourdes**, a sprawling town 43km southeast of Pau in the Pyrenees. It has been one of the world's most important pilgrimage sites since 1858, when 14-year-old Bernadette Soubirous (1844–79) saw the Virgin Mary in a series of 18 visions in a rocky grotto. The visions were subsequently confirmed by the Vatican, and Bernadette was beatified in 1933.

Grotte de Massabielle is the most revered site. **Esplanade des Processions**, lined with enormous flickering candles left by previous pilgrims, leads along a river to the grotto's entrance, where people queue to enter the cave or dip in one of the 19 holy **baths**. It's not for wallflowers: once you're behind the curtain, you're expected to strip off before being swaddled in a sheet and plunged backwards into the icy water.

The main 19th-century section of the sanctuaries is divided between the neo-Byzantine **Basilique du Rosaire**, the **crypt** and the spire-topped **Basilique Supérieure** (Upper Basilica). From Palm Sunday to mid-October, nightly torchlight processions start from the Massabielle Grotto at 9pm, while at 5pm there's the **Procession Eucharistique** (Blessed Sacrament Procession) along Esplanade des Processions.

When the crowds of pilgrims gets too much, seek refuge on the rocky 94m-high pinnacle of **Pic du Jer** – the panorama of Lourdes and the Pyrenees is inspiring. Walk three hours along a marked trail or ride six minutes in the century-old **funicular** (www.picdujer.info; bd d'Espagne; adult/child €9.50/8; ⊙9.30am-6pm or 7pm Mar-Nov). The summit is a superb picnic spot.

Lourdes is well connected by train; destinations include Toulouse (€26.80, two hours) and Paris' Gare Montparnasse (€75 to €107, 6½ hours).

Getting There & Away

AIR Ryanair is the only airline to use Nîmes' **airport** (☎04 66 70 49 49; www.nimes-aeroport.fr), 10km southeast of the city on the A54.

BUS The **bus station** (☎04 66 38 59 43; rue Ste-Félicité) is next to the train station. Destinations include Pont du Gard (30 minutes, five to seven daily in summer).

TRAIN More than 12 TGVs daily run to/from Paris' Gare de Lyon (€52 to €99.70, three hours). Local destinations include Arles (€8 to €14, 30 minutes) and Avignon (€9, 30 minutes).

Toulouse

POP 446,200

Elegantly set at the confluence of the Canal du Midi and the Garonne River, this vibrant southern city – nicknamed *la ville rose* (the pink city) after the distinctive hot-pink stone used in many buildings – is one of France's liveliest metropolises. Busy, buzzy and bustling with students, this riverside dame has a history stretching back over 2000 years and has been a hub for the aerospace industry since the 1930s. With a thriving cafe and cultural scene, a wealth of impressive *hôtels particuliers* and an enormously atmospheric old quarter, France's fourth-largest city is one place you'll love to linger.

Sights

TOP CHOICE **Cité de l'Espace** MUSEUM
(☎08 20 37 72 33; www.cite-espace.com/en; av Jean Gonord; adult €19.50-23, child €14-15; ⊙9.30am-5pm or 6pm, to 7pm mid-Jul–Aug, closed Jan) This fantastic space museum on the city's eastern outskirts explores Toulouse's illustrious aeronautical history.

The city's high-flying credentials stretch all the way back to WWI, when it was a hub for pioneering mail flights to Africa and South America. Since WWII, Toulouse has been the centre of France's aerospace industry, developing many important aircraft (including Concorde and the 555-seat Airbus A380), as well as components for many international space programs.

The museum brings this interstellar industry vividly to life through hands-on exhibits including a shuttle simulator, planetarium, 3D cinema and simulated observatory. There are even full-scale replicas of iconic spacecraft including the Mir Space Station and a 53m-high Ariane 5 space rocket. Multilingual audioguides allow you to explore at your own pace, but you'll need a full day to do it justice.

To get there, catch bus 15 from allée Jean Jaurès to the last stop, from where it's a 500m walk. Dodge queues by buying your tickets online or at the tourist office.

Place du Capitole SQUARE

Toulouse's magnificent main square is the city's literal and metaphorical heart, where Toulousiens turn out en masse on sunny evenings to sip a coffee or an early aperitif at a pavement cafe. On the eastern side is the 128m-long facade of the **Capitole**, the city hall, built in the 1750s. To the south is the city's **Vieux Quartier** (Old Quarter), a tangle of lanes and leafy squares brimming with cafes, shops and eateries.

Basilique St-Sernin CHURCH

(place St-Sernin; ⌚8.30am-noon & 2-6pm Mon-Sat, 8.30am-12.30pm & 2-7.30pm Sun) This red-brick basilica is one of France's best-preserved Romanesque structures.

Musée des Augustins MUSEUM

(www.augustins.org; 21 rue de Metz; adult/child €3/free; ⌚10am-6pm, to 9pm Wed) Toulouse's fabulous fine arts museum spans the centuries from the Roman era right through to the early 20th century.

Les Abattoirs MUSEUM

(www.lesabattoirs.org; 76 allées Charles de Fitte; adult/student & child €7/free; ⌚11am-7pm Wed-Sun) As its name suggests, this red-brick structure was once the city's main abattoir – now it's a cutting-edge art gallery.

Airbus Factory AEROPLANES

(☎05 34 39 42 00; www.taxiway.fr) Dedicated plane-spotters can arrange a guided tour of Toulouse's massive JL Lagardère Airbus factory, 10km west in Colomiers. There are three options: the main tour of the A380 production line (adult/child €14.50/11.50), a 'Heritage Tour' of the factory's vintage planes (including Concorde, adult/child €11.50/10), and a 'Panoramic Tour' of the 700-hectare site by minibus (adult/child €10/8.50). Book in advance online or by phone; bring a passport or photo ID.

Tours

Toulouse is a river city, and you couldn't possibly leave without venturing out onto the water. Between March and November, several operators run scenic hour-long boat trips (adult/child €8/5) along the Garonne from quai de la Daurade; in summer, trips also pass through the St-Pierre lock onto the Canal du Midi and Canal de Brienne. Buy tickets on the boat, up to 10 minutes before departure, from **Les Bateaux Toulousains** (www.bateaux-toulousains.com), **Toulouses Croisières** (www.toulouse-croisieres.com) or **L'Occitania** (www.loccitania.fr).

Sleeping

Hôtel St-Sernin BOUTIQUE HOTEL €€

(☎05 61 21 73 08; www.hotelstsernin.com; 2 rue St-Bernard; d from €130; 📶) This swish number

DON'T MISS

CARCASSONNE

Perched on a rocky hilltop and bristling with zig-zag battlements, stout walls and spiky turrets, the fortified city of Carcassonne looks like something out of a children's storybook from afar. It's most people's perfect idea of a medieval castle, and it's undoubtedly an impressive spectacle – not to mention one of the Languedoc's biggest tourist draws.

Unfortunately the medieval magic's more than a tad tarnished by an annual influx of over four million visitors and it can be a tourist hell in high summer.

The Old City, **La Cité**, is dramatically illuminated at night and enclosed by two rampart walls punctuated by 52 stone towers, Europe's largest city fortifications. Successive generations of Gauls, Romans, Visigoths, Moors, Franks and Cathars reinforced the walls, but only the lower sections are original; the rest, including the turrets, were stuck on by the 19th-century architect Viollet-le-Duc.

A drawbridge leads to the old gate of **Porte Narbonnaise** and rue Cros Mayrevieille en route to place Château and the 12th-century **Château Comtal** (adult/child €8.50/free; ⌚10am-6.30pm Apr-Sep). South is **Basilique St-Nazaire** (⌚9-11.45am & 1.45-5pm or 5.30pm), illuminated by delicate medieval rose windows.

Carcassonne is on the main rail line to/from Toulouse (€14, 50 minutes).

opposite the Basilique St-Sernin has been stylishly renovated by a Parisian couple; the best rooms have floor-to-ceiling windows overlooking the basilica.

Hôtel La Chartreuse HOTEL €
(☎05 61 62 93 39; www.chartreusehotel.com; 4bis bd de Bonrepos; s/d/tr €45/51/63) Toulouse's station hotels are definitely on the scruffy side, but this family-run establishment is a welcome surprise: clean, friendly and quiet, with a lovely breakfast room and back garden patio.

Auberge de Jeunesse HOSTEL €
(☎05 34 30 42 80; 2 av Yves Brunaud; dm from €17; ⌚reception 1-10pm; @☜) Built in 2002, Toulouse's main hostel is as functional as they come (military beds, institutional decor), and it's a pretty long walk from the centre. The hostel is about 1km northwest of Gare Matabiau along av Georges Pompidou; take care around the station after dark.

Eating

Bd de Strasbourg, place St-Georges and place du Capitole are perfect spots for alfresco summer dining. Rue Pargaminières is the street for kebabs, burgers and other late-night student grub.

TOP CHOICE **Chez Navarre** REGIONAL CUISINE €€
(☎05 62 26 43 06; 49 Grande Rue Nazareth; menus €13-20; ⌚lunch & dinner Mon-Fri) Fancy rubbing shoulders with the locals? This *table d'hôte* is the place, with honest Gascon cuisine served up beneath a creaky beamed ceiling at communal candlelit tables.

Les Halles Victor Hugo BISTROS €
(place Victor Hugo; menus €10-20; ⌚lunch Tue-Sun) For a quintessentially Toulousien experience, join the punters at the string of tiny restaurants on the 1st floor of the Victor Hugo food market. They're open at lunchtime only, and the food is simple and unfussy, but they're full of character and the menus are brilliant value.

Information

Tourist Office (☎05 61 11 02 22; www.toulouse-tourisme.com; Square Charles de Gaulle; ⌚9am-7pm daily)

Getting There & Away

AIR **Toulouse-Blagnac Airport** (www.toulouse.aeroport.fr), 8km northwest of the centre, has frequent flights to Paris and other large French and European cities. A **Navette Aéroport Flybus** (Airport Shuttle; ☎05 61 41 70 70; www.tisseo.fr) links it with town.

TRAIN **Gare Matabiau** (bd Pierre Sémard), 1km northeast of the centre, is served by frequent TGVs to Bordeaux (€38, two hours) and east to Carcassonne (€15, 45 minutes to one hour).

PROVENCE

Provence conjures up images of rolling lavender fields, blue skies, gorgeous villages, wonderful food and superb wine. It certainly delivers on all those fronts, but it's not just worth visiting for its good looks – dig a little deeper and you'll also discover the multicultural metropolis of Marseille, the artistic haven of Aix-en-Provence and the old Roman city of Arles.

Marseille

POP 858,900

There was a time when Marseille was the butt of French jokes. No more. The *cité phocéenne* has made an unprecedented comeback, undergoing a vast makeover. Marseillais will tell you that the city's rough-and-tumble edginess is part of its charm and that, for all its flaws, it is a very endearing place. They're right: Marseille grows on you with its unique history, bustling markets, millennia-old port and spectacular *corniches* (coastal roads).

Sights

Vieux Port HISTORIC QUARTER
(MVieux Port) Ships have docked for more than 26 centuries at Marseille's colourful Old Port. The main commercial docks were transferred to the Joliette area north of here in the 1840s, but the Old Port still overflows with fishing boats, pleasure yachts and tourists.

Guarding the harbour are **Bas Fort St-Nicolas** and **Fort St-Jean**, founded in the 13th century by the Knights Hospitaller of St John of Jerusalem. The 40,000-sq-m, state-of-the-art museum **Musée des Civilisations de l'Europe et de la Méditerranée** (MuCEM; Museum of European & Mediterranean Civilisations; ☎04 96 13 80 90; www.mucem.org; ⌚1pm-7pm Wed, Thu & Sat) will open inside in 2013.

Basilique Notre Dame de la Garde CHURCH
(Montée de la Bonne Mère; ⏲7am-8pm Apr-Sep, to 7pm Oct-Mar) Everywhere you go in Marseille, you see the opulent, domed 19th-century Romano-Byzantine basilica, privy to dazzling 360-degree panoramas of the city's sea of terracotta roofs below.

The church's bell tower is crowned by a 9.7m-tall gilded statue of the Virgin Mary on a 12m-high pedestal. Walk or take bus 60 from the Vieux Port.

Château d'If ISLAND, CASTLE
(www.if.monuments-nationaux.fr; adult/child €5/free; ⏲9.30am-6.30pm May-Sep daily, to 4.45pm Tue-Sun Oct-Apr) Immortalised in Alexandre Dumas' 1844 novel *Le Comte de Monte Cristo* (The Count of Monte Cristo), this 16th-century fortress-turned-prison sits on an island 3.5km west of the Vieux Port. Political prisoners were incarcerated here, along with hundreds of Protestants, the Revolutionary hero Mirabeau, and the Communards of 1871.

Frioul If Express (www.frioul-if-express.com; 1 quai des Belges) boats leave for Château d'If from the Vieux Port. Over 15 daily departures in summer, fewer in winter (€10 return, 20 minutes).

Le Panier HISTORIC QUARTER
(MVieux Port) From the Vieux Port, hike north up to this fantastic history-woven quarter, dubbed Marseille's Montmartre as much for its sloping streets as its artsy ambience. In Greek Massilia it was the site of the *agora* (marketplace), hence its name, which means 'the basket'. During WWII the quarter was dynamited and afterwards rebuilt. Today it's a mishmash of lanes hiding artisan shops, *ateliers* (workshops) and terraced houses strung with drying washing. Its centerpiece is the fascinating **Centre de la Vieille Charité** (2 rue de la Charité, 2e; adult/student €5/2.50; MJoliette).

La Friche La Belle de Mai CULTURAL CENTRE
(☎04 95 04 95 04; www.lafriche.org; 41 rue Jobin; 🚌49 stop Jobin) This former sugar-refining plant and subsequent tobacco factory is now host to artists' workshops, cinema studios, radio stations, multimedia displays, alfresco installation art, skateboard camps and electro/world-music parties – enter the gregarious 'voice' of contemporary Marseille. Check its program online, view art in the **Galerie de la Friche Belle de Mai** (admission free; ⏲3-7pm Tue-Sat) and dine in its stylishly industrial **Les Grandes Tables de la Friche** (☎04 95 04 95 85; www.lesgrandestables.com; 12 rue François Simon; mains €10; ⏲8.30am-8pm Mon-Fri).

MARSEILLE CITY PASS

Buy a cent-saving **Marseille City Pass** (one-/two-day €22/29) at the tourist office. It covers admission to 15 museums, a city tour, unlimited public-transport travel, boat trips and so on.

FREE **Palais de Longchamp** PALACE, PARK
(Longchamp Palace; bd Philippon; MCinq Avenues–Longchamp, 🚋Longchamp) This colonnaded 1860s palace houses Marseille's oldest museum, the **Musée des Beaux-Arts**, slated to reopen after renovations in 2013. The shaded park is one of central Marseille's few green spaces.

Sleeping

Hôtel Vertigo HOSTEL €
(☎04 91 91 07 11; www.hotelvertigo.fr; 42 rue des Petites Maries; dm/d €25/60; @📶; MGare St-Charles) This snappy boutique hostel kisses dodgy bunks and hospital-like decor goodbye and says 'hello' to vintage posters, designer chrome kitchen and groovy communal spaces. No curfew (or lift, alas).

Mama Shelter DESIGN HOTEL €€
(☎01 43 48 48 48; www.mamashelter.com; 64 rue de la Loubière; d €99-139, q €159, ste €209; ❄📶; MNotre Dame du Monte–Cours Julien) The brainchild of Serge Trigano, son of Gilbert (Club Med creator), this affordable-chic new kid on the block sports design by Philippe Starck.

Eating

The Vieux Port overflows with restaurants, but choose carefully. Head to Cours Julien and its surrounding streets for world cuisine.

Café Populaire BISTRO €
(☎04 91 02 53 96; 10 rue Paradis; mains €14-16; ⏲lunch & dinner Tue-Sat; MEstrangin-Préfecture) Vintage tables and chairs, old books on the shelf and a fine collection of glass soda bottles all add to the retro air of this 1950s-styled jazz *comptoir* (counter).

Le Comptoir Dugommier BISTRO €
(☎04 91 62 21 21; www.comptoirdugommier.fr; 14 bd Dugommier; mains €11-12, 3-course menu with drink €20; ⏲7.30am-3.30pm Mon-Wed, 7.30am-1am Thu & Fri; MNoailles, 🚋Canebière Garibaldi)

WORTH A TRIP

LES CALANQUES

Marseille abuts the wild and spectacular Les Calanques, a protected 20km stretch of high, rocky promontories rising from the bright turquoise sea. Sheer cliffs are occasionally interrupted by idyllic beach-fringed coves, many only possible to reach with kayak. They've been protected since 1975 and became a national park in 2012.

Calanque de Sormiou is the largest rocky inlet, with two seasonal restaurants cooking up fabulous views: **Le Château** (☎04 91 25 08 69; mains €18-24; ⏰Apr–mid-Oct) – the better food – and **Le Lunch** (☎04 91 25 05 37/9; http://wp.resto.fr/lelunch; mains €16-28; ⏰Apr–mid-Oct) – nearer the water; both require advance reservation. By bus, take No 23 from the Rond Point du Prado metro stop to La Cayolle, from where it's a 3km walk (note diners with a table reservation can drive through; otherwise, the road is open to cars weekdays only September to June).

Marseille's tourist office leads guided hikes in Les Calanques and has information on walking trails (shut July and August due to forest-fire risk). For great views from out at sea hop aboard a boat trip to the wine-producing port of **Cassis**, 30km east along the coast, with **Croisières Marseille Calanques**. (www.croisieres-marseille-calanques.com; 74 quai du Port).

Tin molding, wooden floors and vintage signs make a homey escape from the busy street outside. The place gets packed for its down-home French fare.

La Casertane ITALIAN, DELICATESSEN €
(☎04 91 54 98 51; 71 rue Francis Davso; pasta €11-12; ⏰lunch Mon-Sat, deli 9am-3pm Mon, 9am-7.30pm Tue-Sat; Ⓜ Vieux Port) Lunch on a mind-boggling array of Italian deli meats and salads, or choose from daily specials, often involving homemade pasta. Convivial staff and the bustling flow of clientele make for lively meals.

La Part des Anges BISTRO €
(33 rue Sainte; mains €15; ⏰lunch Mon-Sat, dinner daily) No address buzzes with Marseille's hip, buoyant crowd more than this fabulous all-rounder wine bistro, named after the amount of alcohol that evaporates through a barrel during wine or whisky fermentation: the angels' share *(la part des anges)*.

Drinking & Entertainment

Options for a coffee or something stronger abound on both quays at the Vieux Port.

Cafes crowd cours Honoré d'Estienne d'Orves, 1er, a large open square two blocks south of quai de Rive Neuve. Another cluster overlooks place de la Préfecture, at the southern end of rue St-Ferréol, 1er.

La Caravelle BAR
(34 quai du Port; ⏰7am-2am; Ⓜ Vieux Port) Look up or miss this upstairs hideaway with a tiny but treasured portside terrace. Come Fridays to hear live jazz 9pm to midnight.

L'Intermédiaire NIGHTCLUB
(63 place Jean Jaurès; ⏰7pm-2am; Ⓜ Notre Dame du Mont–Cours Julien) This grungy venue with graffitied walls is one of the best for live bands or DJs (usually techno or alternative).

Shopping

The small but enthralling **fish market** (quai des Belges; ⏰8am-1pm; Ⓜ Vieux Port) is a daily fixture at the Vieux Port. **Cours Julien** hosts a Wednesday-morning organic fruit and vegetable marke. **Prado Market** (av du Prado; ⏰8am-1pm; Ⓜ Castellane or Périer) is the place to go for anything and everything other than food.

Information

Petty crimes and muggings are common. Avoid the Belsunce area (southwest of the train station, bounded by La Canebière, cours Belsunce and rue d'Aix, rue Bernard du Bois and bd d'Athènes) at night. Walking La Canebière is annoying, but generally not dangerous; expect to encounter kids peddling hash.

Tourist Office (☎04 91 13 89 00; www.marseille-tourisme.com; 4 La Canebière; ⏰9am-7pm Mon-Sat, 10am-5pm Sun; Ⓜ Vieux Port)

Getting There & Away

AIR Aéroport Marseille-Provence (www.marseille.aeroport.fr), 25km northwest in Marignane, has numerous budget flights to various

European destinations. **Shuttle buses** (☎in Marseille 04 91 50 59 34, airport 04 42 14 31 27; www.lepilote.com) link it with the Marseille train station (€8, 25 minutes, every 20 minutes).

BOAT The **passenger ferry terminal** (www.marseille-port.fr; Ⓜ Joliette) is 250m south of place de la Joliette, 1er. **SNCM** (☎08 91 70 18 01; www.sncm.fr; 61 bd des Dames; Ⓜ Joliette) boats sail to Corsica, Sardinia and North Africa.

TRAIN From Marseille's Gare St-Charles, trains including TGVs go all over France and Europe. Services include Avignon (€24, 35 minutes), Lyon (€50, 1¾ hours), Nice (€35, 2½ hours) and Paris' Gare de Lyon (€103, three hours). International destinations include Geneva (€50, 3½ hours).

Getting Around

Marseille has two metro lines, two tram lines and an extensive bus network, all run by **RTM** (☎04 91 91 92 10; www.rtm.fr; 6 rue des Fabres; ⌚8.30am-6pm Mon-Fri, 9am-12.30pm & 2-5.30pm Sat; Ⓜ Vieux Port), where you can obtain information and transport tickets (€1.50).

Pick up a bike from 100-plus stations across the city with **Le Vélo** (www.levelo-mpm.fr).

Aix-en-Provence

POP 141,900

Aix-en-Provence is to Provence what the Left Bank is to Paris: a pocket of bohemian chic crawling with students. It's hard to believe that 'Aix' (pronounced ex) is just 25km from chaotic, exotic Marseille. The city has been a cultural centre since the Middle Ages (two of the town's most famous sons are painter Paul Cézanne and novelist Émile Zola), but for all its polish, it's still a laid-back Provençal town at heart.

Sights

Cours Mirabeau HISTORIC QUARTER

No avenue better epitomises Provence's most graceful city than fountain-studded cours Mirabeau, sprinkled with elegant Renaissance *hôtels particuliers* and crowned with a summertime roof of leafy plane trees.

Cézanne Sights ART APPRECIATION

To see where local lad Paul Cézanne (1839–1906) ate, drank and painted, follow the **Circuit de Cézanne** (Cézanne Trail), marked by footpath-embedded bronze plaques. The informative English-language guide to the plaques, *Cézanne's Footsteps*, is free at the tourist office. A mobile app, *City of Cézanne in Aix-en-Provence* (€2), is available online.

Cézanne's last studio, **Atelier Paul Cézanne** (www.atelier-cezanne.com; 9 av Paul Cézanne; adult/child €5.50/2; ⌚10am-noon & 2-6pm, closed Sun winter), 1.5km north of the tourist office, has been preserved and recreated (not all the tools and still-life models strewn around the single room were his) as it was at the time of his death. Take bus 1 or 20 to the Atelier Cézanne stop, or walk 1.5km from the centre. A 10-minute walk uphill from the

WORTH A TRIP

VAN GOGH'S ARLES

If the winding streets and colourful houses of Arles seem familiar, it's hardly surprising – Vincent van Gogh lived here for much of his life in a yellow house on place Lamartine, and the town regularly featured in his canvases. His original house was destroyed during WWII, but you can still follow in Vincent's footsteps on the **Van Gogh Trail** (☎04 90 18 41 20; www.arlestourism.com; esplanade Charles de Gaulle), marked out by footpath plaques and a brochure handed out by the **tourist office** (☎04 90 18 41 20; www.tourisme.ville-arles.fr; esplanade Charles de Gaulle; ⌚9am-6.45pm daily Apr-Sep, to 4.45pm Mon-Fri & 12.45pm Sun Oct-Mar), which has another branch at the **train station** (☎04 90 43 33 57; ⌚9am-1.30pm & 2.30-5pm Mon-Fri Apr-Sep).

Two millennia ago, Arles was a major Roman settlement. The town's 20,000-seat amphitheatre and 12,000-seat theatre, known as the **Arénes** (Amphitheatre; rue Henri Vadon) and the **Théâtre Antique** (www.theatre-antique.com; adult/child €8.50/6.50, 2nd child free; ⌚9am-6pm Mar-Oct, 9am-4.30pm Nov-Feb), are nowadays used for cultural events and bullfights.

Telleschi (☎04 42 28 40 22) buses go to/from Aix-en-Provence (€9, 1½ hours) and there are regular trains to/from Nîmes (€7.50, 30 minutes), Marseille (€13.55, 55 minutes) and Avignon (€6.60, 20 minutes).

bus stop is the **Terrain des Peintres** (opposite 62 av Paul Cézanne), a wonderful terraced garden perfect for a picnic, from where Cézanne, among others, painted the Montagne Ste-Victoire.

Visits to both the Cézanne family country manor **Le Jas de Bouffan** (☎04 42 16 10 91; adult/child €5.50/2; ⊙guided tours 10.30am-5.30pm daily summer, less frequent other times; 🚌6 stop Corsy) and **Les Carrières de Bibemus** (Bibémus Quarries; ☎04 42 16 10 91; adult/child €6.60/3.10; ⊙tours 9.45am daily Jun-Sep, 10.30am & 5pm Mon, Wed, Fri & Sun Apr, May & Oct, 3pm Wed & Sat Jan-Mar), the cabin the artist rented in 1895 on the edge of town, must be reserved in advance at the tourist office.

Musée Granet MUSEUM
(www.museegranet-aixenprovence.fr; place St-Jean de Malte; adult/child €4/free; ⊙11am-7pm Tue-Sun) Housed in a 17th-century priory, this exceptional museum covers 16th- to 20th-century Italian, Flemish and French works. Modern art reads like a who's-who: Picasso, Léger, Matisse, Monet, Klee, Van Gogh, Giacometti and, of course, Cézanne.

Sleeping

Hôtel les Quatre Dauphins BOUTIQUE HOTEL €
(☎04 42 38 16 39; www.lesquatredauphins.fr; 54 rue Roux Alphéran; s €55-60, d €70-85; ❄📶) This sweet 13-room hotel is fresh and clean, with excellent new bathrooms. The tall terracotta-tiled staircase (no lift) leads to four attic rooms, with sloped beamed ceilings.

Hôtel Cardinal HOTEL €
(☎04 42 38 32 30; www.hotel-cardinal-aix.com; 24 rue Cardinale; s/d €60/70) Slightly rumpled rooms are quaintly furnished with antiques and tasselled curtains. Six gigantic suites in the annexe up the street, each with a kitchenette and dining room, are ideal for longer stays. Wi-fi costs €5 per 24 hours.

Eating

Aix' sweetest treat is the marzipan-like local speciality, *calisson d'Aix,* a small, diamond-shaped, chewy delicacy made with ground almonds and fruit syrup. The daily **produce market** (place Richelme; ⊙mornings) sells olives, goat's cheese, garlic, lavender, honey, peaches, melons and other sun-kissed products.

Charlotte BISTRO €
(☎04 42 26 77 56; 32 rue des Bernardines; 2-/3-course menus €15.50/19; ⊙lunch & dinner Tue-Sat) It's all very cosy at Charlotte, where everyone knows everyone. French classics like veal escalope and beef steak fill the handwritten menu, and there are always a couple of imaginative *plats du jour*. In summer, everything moves into the garden.

Jacquou Le Croquant BISTRO €
(☎04 42 27 37 19; 2 rue Aumône Vielle; 2-course crêpe menu €16, mains from €10; ⊙lunch & dinner) Slide into this tiny, low-key joint for home-cooked, wholesome basics.

Information

Tourist Office (☎04 42 16 11 61; www.aixenprovencetourism.com; 37 av Giuseppi Verdi; ⊙8.30am-7pm Mon-Sat, 10am-1pm & 2-6pm Sun Oct-Jun, to 8pm Jul-Sep)

Getting There & Away

BUS From Aix' **bus station** (☎08 91 02 40 25, 04 42 91 26 80; av de l'Europe), a 10-minute walk southwest from La Rotonde, routes include Marseille (€5, 25 minutes), Arles (€9.20, 1½ hours) and Avignon (€17.40, 1¼ hours).

Half-hourly shuttle buses go to/from Aix TGV station and Aéroport Marseille-Provence.

TRAIN The only useful train from Aix' tiny **city centre train station** is to/from Marseille (€8, 45 minutes). Aix' TGV station, 15km away, serves most of France; Marseille (€8, 20 daily) is a mere 12 minutes away.

Avignon

POP 92,500

Hooped by 4.3km of superbly preserved stone ramparts, this graceful city is the belle of Provence's ball. Famed for its annual

Avignon

Top Sights

Musée Angladon ... B4
Palais des Papes ... B2
Pont St-Bénézet ... B1

Sleeping

1 Hôtel Boquier ... B5
2 Hôtel Mignon ... A3

Eating

3 Ginette et Marcel ... C5
4 L'Epice and Love ... C5

performing arts festival and fabled bridge, Avignon is an ideal spot from which to step out into the surrounding region. Wrapping around the city, Avignon's defensive ramparts were built between 1359 and 1370, and are punctuated by a series of sturdy *portes* (gates).

Avignon

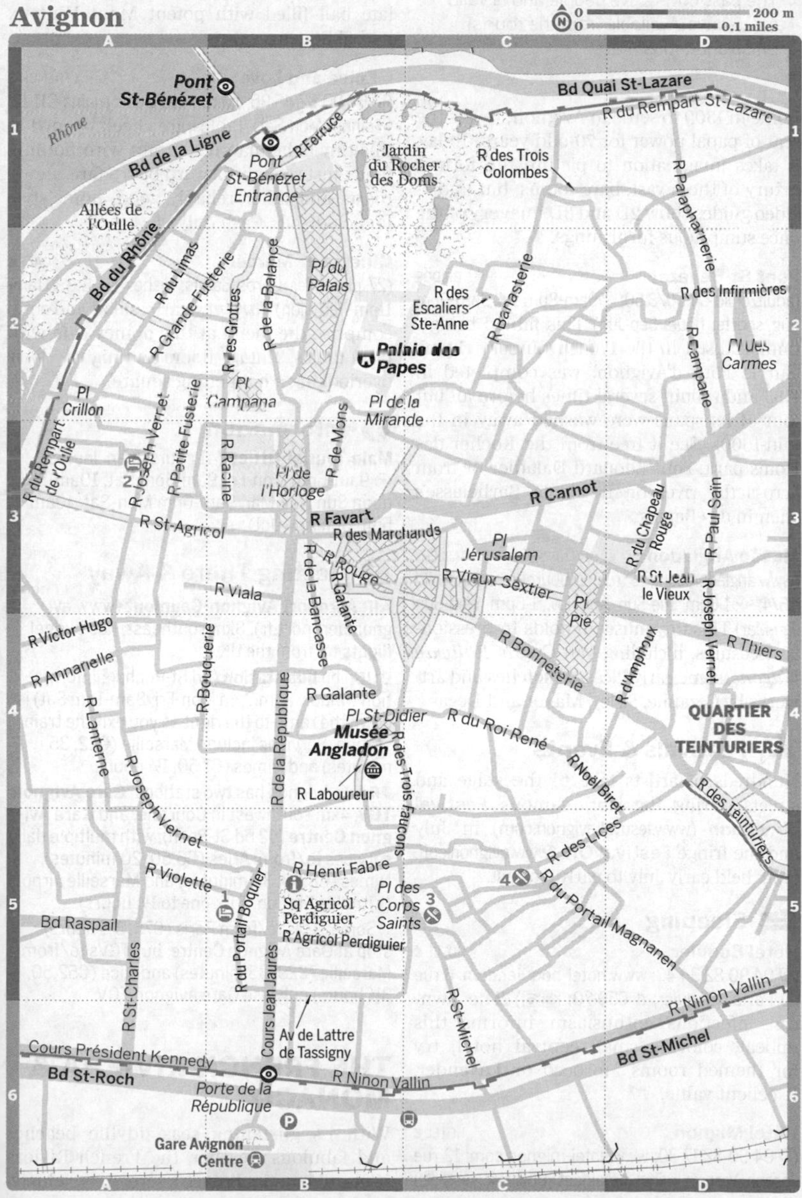

Sights

Palais des Papes PALACE

(Papal Palace; www.palais-des-papes.com; place du Palais; adult/child €6/3; ⏱9am-8pm Jul, 9am-9pm Aug, shorter hours Sep-Jun) This Unesco World Heritage Site, the world's largest Gothic palace, was built when Pope Clement V left

AVIGNON PASSION

Discount card **Avignon Passion** yields discounts of 10% to 50% on city museums, tours and monuments (pay full price at the first site, then receive discounts at each subsequent site). The pass covers five people and is valid for 15 days. Available from the tourist office and tourist sites.

Rome in 1309 to settle in Avignon; it was the seat of papal power for 70-odd years. Today, it takes imagination to picture the former luxury of these vast, bare rooms, but audio-video guides show 2D and 3D imagery of the once sumptuous furnishings.

Pont St-Bénézet BRIDGE
(adult/child €4.50/3.50; 9am-8pm Jul, 9am-9pm Aug, shorter hours Sep-Jun) This fabled bridge, immortalised in the French nursery rhyme 'Sur le Pont d'Avignon', was completed in 1185 and rebuilt several times before all but four of its spans were washed away in the mid-1600s. See it free from the Rocher des Doms park, Pont Édouard Daladier or from across the river on Île de la Barhelasse's chemin des Berges.

Musée Angladon GALLERY
(www.angladon.com; 5 rue Laboureur; adult/child €6/4; 1-6pm Tue-Sun Apr-Nov, 1-6pm Wed-Sun Jan-Mar) This tiny museum holds Impressionist treasures, including Van Gogh's *Railway Wagons,* some early Picasso sketches and artworks by Cézanne, Sisley, Manet and Degas.

Festivals & Events

Hundreds of artists take to the stage and streets during the world-famous **Festival d'Avignon** (www.festival-avignon.com) in July and the fringe **Festival Off** (www.avignonleoff.com), held early July to early August.

Sleeping

Hôtel Boquier HOTEL €
(04 90 82 34 43; www.hotel-boquier.com; 6 rue du Portail Boquier; d €50-70;) The owners' infectious enthusiasm informs this upbeat, colorful, small central hotel; try for themed rooms Morocco or Lavender. Excellent value.

Hôtel Mignon HOTEL €
(04 90 82 17 30; www.hotel-mignon.com; 12 rue Joseph Vernet; r incl breakfast €62-84;) Cute and comfy, with 16 colourful rooms, this good-value hotel within the walled city is tops for no-frills budgeteers. Note: it has tiny bathrooms and steep stairs.

Eating

Place de l'Horloge's touristy cafes have so-so food. *Papaline d'Avignon* is a pink, chocolate ball filled with potent Mont Ventoux herbal liqueur.

L'Epice and Love FRENCH €
(04 90 82 45 96; 30 rue des Lices; mains €11-12; dinner Mon-Sat) Tables are cheek by jowl at this tiny bohemian restaurant with nothing fancy, just straightforward bistro fare, stews, roasts and other reliably good, home-style French dishes. Cash only.

Ginette et Marcel CAFE €
(27 place des Corps Saints; dishes €4-6; 11am-11pm Wed-Mon) *Tartines*, tarts, salad and soup comprise the menu at this homey cafe with farm tables, vintage floors and big windows overlooking a happening square.

Information

Main Tourist Office (41 cours Jean Jaurès; 9am-6pm Mon-Fri, 9am-5pm Sat, 10am-noon Sun Nov-Mar, 9am-6pm Mon-Sat, 10am-5pm Sun Apr-Oct)

Getting There & Away

AIR **Aéroport Avignon-Caumont** (www.avignon.aeroport.fr), 8km southeast, has budget flights to/from the UK.

BUS The **bus station** (bd St-Roch; information window 8am-7pm Mon-Fri, 8am-1pm Sat) is down the ramp to the right as you exit the train station. Services include Marseille (€22, 35 minutes) and Nîmes (€1.50, 1¼ hour).

TRAIN Avignon has two stations. **Gare Avignon TGV**, 4km southwest in Courtine, and **Gare Avignon Centre** (42 bd St-Roch), with multiple daily services to/from: Arles (€6.50, 20 minutes), Nîmes (€8.50, 30 minutes) and Marseille airport (Vitrolles Station, €16, one to 1½ hours).

Some TGVs to/from Paris (€75, 3½ hours) stop at Gare Avignon Centre, but TGVs to/from Marseille (€29, 35 minutes) and Nice (€52.50, 3¼ hours) only use Gare Avignon TGV.

THE FRENCH RIVIERA & MONACO

With its glistening seas, idyllic beaches and fabulous weather, the French Riviera (Côte d'Azur in French) screams exclusivity, extravagance and excess. It has been a favourite getaway for the European jet set since Victorian times and there is nowhere more chichi or glam in France than St-Tropez, Cannes and super-rich, sovereign Monaco.

Nice

POP 344,500

Riviera queen Nice is what good living is all about – shimmering shores, the very best of Mediterranean food, a unique historical heritage, free museums, a charming Old Town, exceptional art and Alpine wilderness within an hour's drive. To get stuck in straight away, make a beeline upon arrival for **Promenade des Anglais**, Nice's curvaceous palm-lined seafront that follows its busy pebble beach for 6km from the city centre to the airport.

Sights & Activities

Vieux Nice HISTORIC QUARTER

(food markets 6am-1.30pm Tue-Sun) Ditch the map and get lost in this mellow-hued rabbit warren of 18th-century passages, alleyways, historic churches and hidden squares. **Cours Saleya**, running parallel to the seafront, remains a joyous, thriving market square with one of France's most vibrant food and flower markets. Rue de la Boucherie and rue Pairolière are excellent for food shopping; a daily fish market fills place St François; and baroque aficionados wil fall head over heels in love with architectural gems such as **Cathédrale Ste-Réparate** and the exuberant **Chapelle de la Miséricorde**.

FREE **MAMAC** MUSEUM

(Musée d'Art Moderne et d'Art Contemporain; www.mamac-nice.org; promenade des Arts; 10am-6pm Tue-Sun) This ode to contemporary art houses some fantastic avant-garde works from the 1960s to the present, including iconic pop art from Roy Lichtenstein and Andy Warhol's 1965 *Campbell's Soup Can*. An awesome panorama of Vieux Nice unfolds from its rooftop garden-gallery.

FREE **Musée Matisse** GALLERY

(www.musee-matisse-nice.org; 164 av des Arènes de Cimiez; 10am-6pm Wed-Mon) About 2km north in the leafy quarter of Cimiez, this museum houses a fascinating assortment of works by Matisse. Its permanent collection is displayed in a red-ochre 17th-century Genoese villa overlooking an olive-tree-studded park. Temporary exhibitions are hosted in the futuristic basement building. The artist is buried in the **Monastère de Cimiez** cemetery, across the park from the museum.

Beaches BEACHES

Nice's beaches are all pebbly; sensitive behinds can opt for a comfy mattress at a private beach (€15 to €20 per day). Of the free public sections of beach, **Plage Publique des Ponchettes**, opposite Vieux Nice, is the most popular.

Art With The Tram TRAM TOUR

(www.tramway-nice.org) As well as Jaume Plensa's glow-in-the-dark *Conversation* on place Masséna, there are 13 more works of art to discover along Nice's tramway, including original sound bites at each stop, the calligraphy of the tram's stops and more visual works. The best way to appreciate this artistic input is to take the tourist office's two-hour **Art dans la Ville** (adult/child €8/3, plus €2 for transport; tours 7pm Fri) guided tour.

Sleeping

Nice Pebbles APARTMENT €€

(04 97 20 27 30; www.nicepebbles.com; 23 rue Gioffredo; 1-/3-bedroom apt from €105/320;) The concept is simple: the quality of a four-star boutique hotel in holiday flats.

Villa St-Exupéry HOSTEL €

(04 93 84 42 83; www.villahostels.com; 22 av Gravier; dm €25-30, s/d €45/90;) Set in a lovely converted monastery in the north of Nice, this is a great place. Chill out in the 24-hour common room housed in the old stained-glass chapel, sip a €1 beer on the barbecue terrace and stock up on travel tips. Breakfast included

Villa staff will pick you up from the nearby Comte de Falicon tram stop or St-Maurice stop for bus 23 (direct from the airport) when you first arrive.

Hôtel Wilson BOUTIQUE HOTEL €

(04 93 85 47 79; www.hotel-wilson-nice.com; 39 rue de l'Hôtel des Postes; s/d €50/55;) Many years of travelling, an experimental nature and exquisite taste have turned Jean-Marie's rambling flat into a compelling place to stay. The 16 rooms have individual, carefully

Nice

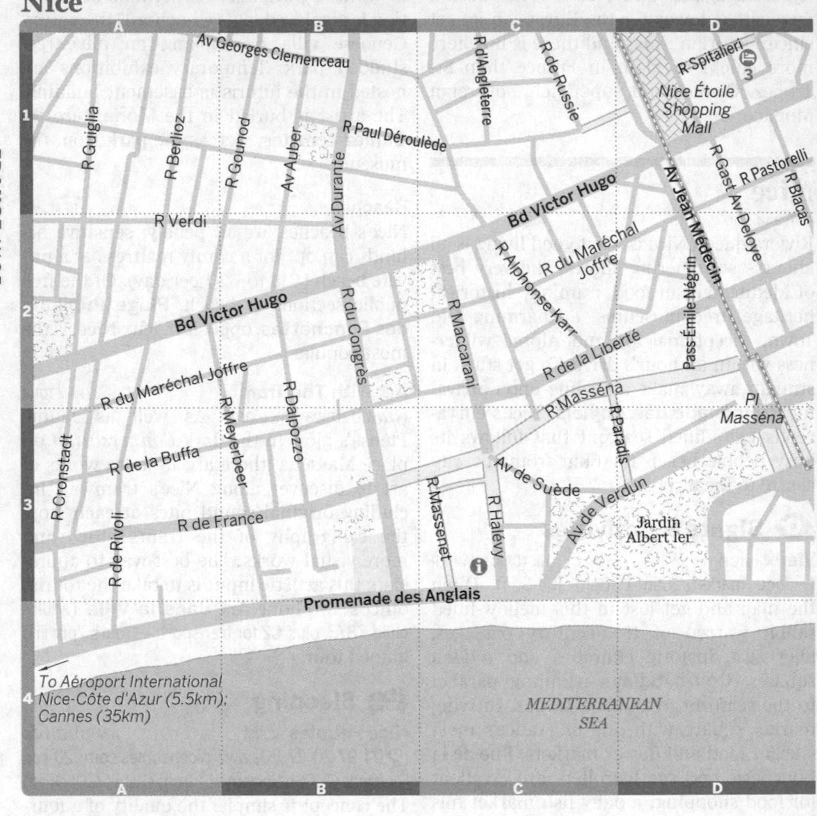

Nice

Top Sights

Vieux Nice F3

Sights

1 MAMAC G1
2 Parc du Château G4

Sleeping

3 Auberge de Jeunesse Les Camélias D1
4 Hôtel Wilson E2
5 Nice Pebbles F1

Eating

6 Fenocchio F3
7 La Merenda E3
8 Le Bistrot d'Antoine F3
9 Le Comptoir du Marché F3
10 Zucca Magica H2

Drinking

11 L'Abat-Jour F3
12 Le Smarties F1
13 Les Distilleries Idéales F3

crafted decor, and share the eclectic dining room.

Auberge de Jeunesse Les Camélias HOSTEL €
(☎04 93 62 15 54; www.fuaj.org; 3 rue Spitaleri; dm incl breakfast €25.80; @📶) This colourful hostel has clean, spacious dorms, a bar, a self-catering kitchen and a laundry. Dorms range from four to eight beds and are single sex. There is a midday lockout (11am to 3pm) but no night curfew. Rates include sheets. It's part of the FUAJ youth hostel

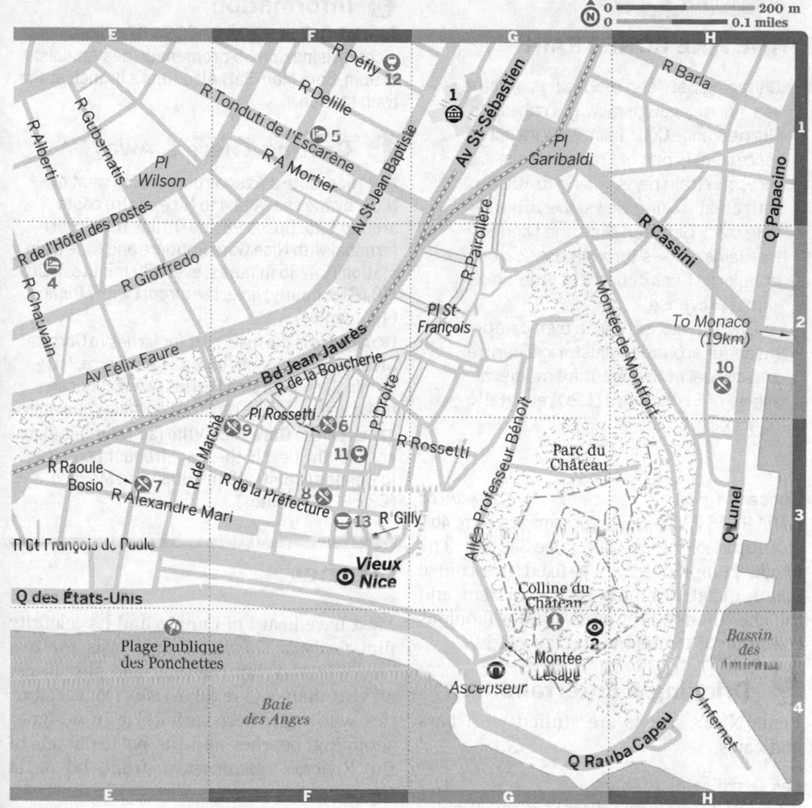

network so you'll need to be a member (€11).

Eating

Niçois nibbles include *socca* (a thin layer of chickpea flour and olive oil batter), *salade Niçoise* and *farcis* (stuffed vegetables). Restaurants in Vieux Nice are a mixed bag, so choose carefully.

Le Bistrot d'Antoine MODERN FRENCH €€
(04 93 85 29 57; 27 rue de la Préfecture; mains €13-18; lunch & dinner Tue-Sat) This brasserie is full every night (booking essential), yet the 'bistro chic' cuisine never wavers, the staff are cool as cucumbers, the atmosphere is reliably jovial and the prices are incredibly good value.

Fenocchio ICE CREAM €
(2 place Rossetti; ice cream from €2; 9am-midnight Feb-Oct) Dither too long over the 70-plus flavours of ice cream and sorbet at this unforgettable *glacier* (ice-cream shop) and you'll never make it to the front of the queue. Eschew predictable favourites and indulge in a new taste sensation: black olive, tomato-basil, avocado, rosemary or lavender.

Le Comptoir du Marché MODERN FRENCH €
(04 93 13 45 01; 8 rue du Marché; mains €13-15; lunch & dinner Tue-Sat) Vintage kitchen decor, recession-proof prices and a creative cuisine that gives a modern twist to French traditional recipes is the secret to the Counter's huge success.

La Merenda NIÇOIS €€
(4 rue Raoul Bosio; mains €12-15; Mon-Fri) Simple, solid Niçois cuisine by former Michelin-starred chef Dominique Le Stanc draws the crowds to this pocket-sized bistro. No credit cards.

WORTH A TRIP

THE PINE CONE TRAIN

Chugging between mountains and the sea, narrow-gauge railway **Train des Pignes** (Pine Cone Train; www.trainprovence.com) is one of France's most picturesque train rides. Rising to 1000m, with breathtaking views, the 151km-long track between Nice and Digne-les-Bains passes through the scarcely populated back country of little-known Haute Provence.

Day-trip suggestion: a picnic and meander around the historical centre and citadel of the beautiful medieval village of **Entrevaux** (€20 return, 1½ hours).

Zucca Magica VEGETARIAN €€
(☎04 93 56 25 27; www.lazuccamagica.com; 4bis quai Papacino; menus €30; ⊙Tue-Sat; ☑) The Magic Pumpkin serves a fixed five-course menu, dictated simply by the market and the chef's fancy. Seating is amid a fabulous collection of pumpkins and fairy lights.

Drinking & Entertainment

Vieux Nice's streets are stuffed with bars and cafes.

Les Distilleries Idéales CAFE
(24 rue de la Préfecture; ⊙9am-12.30am) Whether you're after an espresso on your way to the cours Saleya market or an *apéritif* (complete with cheese and charcuterie platters, €5.20) before trying out one of Nice's fabulous restaurants, Les Distilleries is one of the most atmospheric bars in town.

Le Smarties BAR
(http://nicesmarties.free.fr; 10 rue Défly; ⊙6pm-2am Tue-Sat) We love Smarties' sexy '70s swirly orange style, which draws a hot-looking straight-gay crowd. On weekends, the tiny dance floor fills when DJs spin deep house, electro, techno and occasionally disco; weekdays are mellower. Free tapas with happy hour (nightly 6pm to 9pm).

L'Abat-Jour BAR
(25 rue Benoît Bunico) With its vintage furniture, rotating art exhibitions and alternative music, l'Abat-Jour is all the rage with Nice's young and trendy crowd. The basement has live music or DJ sessions.

ℹ Information

Tourist Office (☎08 92 70 74 07; www.nicetourisme.com; 5 promenade des Anglais; ⊙9am-6pm Mon-Sat) Also runs a branch at the train station.

ℹ Getting There & Away

AIR Nice-Côte d'Azur airport is 6km west of Nice, by the sea. A taxi to Nice centre costs around €25. Buses 98 and 99 link the airport terminal with Nice Gare Routière and Nice train station (€4, 35 minutes, every 20 minutes). Bus 110 (€18, hourly) links the airport with Monaco (40 minutes).

BOAT Nice is the main port for ferries to Corsica. **SNCM** (www.sncm.fr; quai du Commerce, ferry terminal) and **Corsica Ferries** (www.corsicaferries.com; quai Lunel) are the two main companies.

TRAIN From **Gare Nice Ville** (av Thiers), 1.2km north of the beach, there are frequent services to Cannes (€6.40, 40 minutes) and Monaco (€3.60, 20 minutes).

Cannes

POP 74,400

Most have heard of Cannes and its celebrity film festival. The latter only lasts for two weeks in May, but the buzz and glitz linger all year thanks to regular visits from celebrities who come here to indulge in designer shopping, beaches and the palace hotels of the Riviera's glammest seafront, bd de la Croisette.

Sights & Activities

Beaches BEACHES
Cannes is blessed with sandy beaches although much of bd de la Croisette is taken up by private, fee-paying beaches (many open to all). This arrangement leaves only a small strip of free sand near the Palais des Festivals for the bathing hoi polloi; the much bigger **Plage du Midi** (bd Jean Hibert) and **Plage de la Bocca**, west from Vieux Port, are also free.

Le Suquet HISTORIC QUARTER
Cannes' historic quarter, pre-dating the glitz and glam of the town's festival days, retains a quaint village feel with its steep, meandering alleyways. There are wonderful views of the Baie de Cannes from the top of the hill.

Îles de Lérins ISLANDS
Although just 20 minutes away by boat, these tranquil islands feel far from the mad-

ding crowd. **Île Ste-Marguerite**, where the mysterious Man in the Iron Mask was incarcerated during the late 17th century, is known for its bone-white beaches, eucalyptus groves and small marine museum. Tiny **Île St-Honorat** has been a monastery since the 5th century. Boats leave Cannes from quai des Îles on the western side of the harbour.

Sleeping

Hôtel 7e Art BOUTIQUE HOTEL €
(☎04 93 68 66 66; www.7arthotel.com; 23 rue Maréchal Joffre; s €68, d €60-98; ❄📶) Hôtel 7e Art has put boutique style within reach of budgeters. The snappy design of putty-coloured walls, padded headboards and pop art, and perks like iPod docks in every room, far exceed what you'd expect at this price.

Le Romanesque BOUTIQUE HOTEL €€
(☎04 93 68 04 20; 10 rue du Batéguier; s/d/tr €89/109/149; ❄📶) Every room is individually decorated at this eight-room boutique charmer in the heart of the Carré d'Or nightlife district. Gay-friendly. Great service.

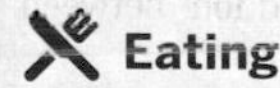

Eating

PhilCat DELICATESSEN €
(La Pantiéro; sandwiches & salads €4-6.50; ⏲8.30am-5pm) Don't be put off by Phillipe and Catherine's unassuming prefab cabin on the Pantiéro: this is Cannes' best lunch house. If you're *really* hungry, try one of their phenomenal *pan bagna* (a moist sandwich bursting with Provençal flavours).

Au Martin Pêcheur PROVENÇAL €€
(4 rue Émile Négrin; 2-course lunch menu €14, mains €17-25; ⏲lunch Tue-Sat, dinner Thu-Sat) This unassuming, family-run restaurant is the place to come for great fish – lunchtime offers the best value. Mother-and-son duo Christel and Maxime prepare traditional and Provençal recipes with whatever the sea has given them that day; there are always a couple of meat options too.

Information

Tourist Office (☎04 92 99 84 22; www.cannes.travel; Palais des Festivals, bd de la Croisette; ⏲9am-7pm)

Getting There & Away

BUS From the **bus station** (place Cornut-Gentille), buses serve Nice (€1, 1½ hours) and Nice airport (€16, 50 minutes, half-hourly).

TRAIN From Cannes train station there are at least hourly services to/from Nice (€6.40, 40 minutes), Antibes (€2.70, 12 minutes), Monaco (€8.70, one hour) and Marseille (€28.40, two hours).

St-Tropez

POP 4990

In the soft autumn or winter light, it's hard to believe the pretty terracotta fishing village of St-Tropez is a stop on the Riviera celebrity circuit. It seems far removed from its glitzy siblings further up the coast, but come spring or summer, it's a different world: the population increases tenfold, prices triple and fun-seekers pile in to party till dawn,

WORTH A TRIP

THE SCENT OF THE CÔTE D'AZUR

Mosey some 20km northwest of Cannes to inhale the sweet smell of lavender, jasmine, mimosa and orange-blossom fields. In **Grasse**, one of France's leading perfume producers, dozens of perfumeries create essences to sell to factories (for aromatically enhanced foodstuffs and soaps) as well as to prestigious couture houses – the highly trained noses of local perfume-makers can identify 3000 scents in a single whiff.

Learn about three millennia of perfume-making at the **Musée International de la Parfumerie** (MIP; www.museesdegrasse.com; 2 bd du Jeu de Ballon; adult/child €3/free; ⏲11am-6pm Wed-Mon) and watch the process first-hand during a guided tour at **Fragonard** (www.fragonard.com; 20 bd Fragonard; ⏲9am-6pm Feb-Oct, 9am-12.30pm & 2-6pm Nov-Jan) perfumery, the easiest to reach by foot. The tourist office has information on other perfumeries and field trips to local flower farms, including the **Domaine de Manon** (☎06 12 18 02 69; www.le-domaine-de-manon.com; 36 chemin du Servan, Plascassier; admission €6). Roses are picked mid-May to mid-June, jasmine July to late October.

strut around the luxury-yacht-packed Vieux Port and enjoy the creature comforts of exclusive A-listers' beaches in the Baie de Pampelonne.

Sights & Activities

Musée de l'Annonciade MUSEUM
(place Grammont; adult/child €6/4; ⌚10am-noon & 2-6pm Wed-Mon Oct & Dec-May, 10am-noon & 3-7pm Wed-Mon Jun-Sep) In a gracefully converted 16th-century chapel, this famous art museum showcases an impressive collection of modern art infused with that legendary Côte d'Azur light.

Plage de Pampelonne BEACH
The golden sands of **Plage de Tahiti**, 4km southeast of town, morph into the 5km-long, celebrity-studded **Plage de Pampelonne**, which sports a line-up of exclusive beach restaurants and clubs in summer.

Citadelle de St-Tropez HISTORIC SITE
(admission €2.50; ⌚10am-6.30pm) Built in 1602 to defend the coast against Spain, the citadel dominates the hillside overlooking St-Tropez to the east. Its dungeons shelter a **Musée Naval**, dedicated to the town's maritime history and the Allied landings in August 1944.

Sleeping & Eating

Multistar camping grounds abound on the road to Plage de Pampelonne. Quai Jean Jaurès at the Vieux Port is littered with restaurants and cafes.

Hôtel Lou Cagnard PENSION €€
(☎04 94 97 04 24; www.hotel-lou-cagnard.com; 18 av Paul Roussel; d €75-156; ⌚Jan-Oct; ❄📶) Book well ahead for this great-value courtyard charmer, shaded by lemon and fig trees. The cheapest rooms have private washbasin and standup-bathtub but share a toilet.

Auberge des Maures PROVENÇAL €€
(☎04 94 97 01 50; 4 rue du Docteur Boutin; mains €31-39; ⌚dinner) The town's oldest restaurant remains the locals' choice for always-good, copious portions of earthy Provençal cooking, like *daube* (a classic stew) or tapenade-stuffed lamb shoulder. Book a table (essential) on the leafy courtyard.

Shopping

One of southern France's busiest and best markets, St-Tropez's **place des Lices market** (⌚mornings Tue & Sat) is a highlight of local life, with colourful stalls groaning under the weight of plump fruit and veg, mounds of olives, local cheeses, chestnut purée and fragrant herbs. Afterwards, meander to the port and duck beneath the stone arch to the bijou **fish market** (⌚mornings Tue-Sun, daily summer), hidden between stone walls on place aux Herbes.

Information

Tourist Office (☎04 94 97 45 21; www.ot-saint-tropez.com; quai Jean Jaurès; ⌚9.30am-8pm Jul & Aug, 9.30am-12.30pm & 2-7pm Apr-Jun & Sep–mid-Oct, 9.30am-12.30pm & 2-6pm mid-Oct–Mar)

TOP FIVE BEACH EATS

Book lunch (well ahead) at the following, open May to September and around €15 to €40 for a main.

Club 55 (www.leclub55.fr; 43 bd Patch, Pampelonne) St-Tropez's oldest-running beach club, this 1950s address was the crew canteen for the filming of *And God Created Woman* with Brigitte Bardot. The rich and famous flock here to be seen, although the food is nothing special.

Nikki Beach (www.nikkibeach.com/sttropez; rte de l'Epi, Epi Plage) Favoured by dance-on-the-bar celebs such as Paris Hilton and Pamela Anderson, the deafening scene ends at midnight.

Aqua Club (☎04 94 79 84 35; www.aqua-club-plage.fr; rte de l'Epi, Pampelonne; mains €22-29; ⌚Jan-Oct) Friendly mixed, gay-straight crowd; the most diverse by far.

Moorea Plage (☎04 94 97 18 17; www.moorea-plage-st-tropez.com; rte des Plages, Tahiti; mains €15-29) Ideal for conversation and backgammon (supplied); tops for steak.

Liberty Plage (☎04 94 79 80 62; www.plageleliberty.com; chemin des Tamaris, Pampelonne; mains €17-19) Clothing optional – eat naked.

Getting There & Away

From the **bus station** (☎04 94 56 25 74; av du Général de Gaulle), buses run by **VarLib** (www.varlib.fr) serve Ramatuelle (€2, 35 minutes) and St-Raphaël train station (€2, 1¼ hours). There are four daily buses to Toulon-Hyères airport (€15, 1½ hours).

Monaco

☎377 / POP 32,400

Your first glimpse of this pocket-sized principality will probably make your heart sink: Monaco's concrete high-rises and astronomic prices come as a shock.

But Monaco is beguiling. The world's second-smallest state (a smidgen bigger than the Vatican), it is as famous for its tax-haven status as for its glittering casino, sports scene (Formula One, world-famous circus festival and tennis open) and a royal family on a par with the British royals for best gossip fodder.

This is a sovereign state but has no border control. It has its own flag (red and white), national holiday (19 November) and telephone country code (☎377), but the official language is French and the country uses the euro even though it is not part of the European Union.

Visit Monaco as a day trip from Nice, a 20-minute train ride away.

Sights & Activities

Casino de Monte Carlo CASINO

(www.casinomontecarlo.com; place du Casino; ⊙European Rooms from noon Sat & Sun, from 2pm Mon-Fri) Living out your James Bond fantasies just doesn't get any better than at Monte Carlo's monumental, richly decorated showpiece, the 1910-built casino. The European Rooms have poker/slot machines, French roulette and *trente et quarante* (a card game), while the Private Rooms offer baccarat, blackjack, craps and American roulette. The jacket-and-tie dress code kicks in after 8pm. Minimum entry age for both rooms is 18; bring photo ID.

Musée Océanographique de Monaco AQUARIUM

(www.oceano.org; av St-Martin; adult/child €13/6.50; ⊙9.30am-7pm) Stuck dramatically to the edge of a cliff since 1910, the world-renowned Musée Océanographique de Monaco, founded by Prince Albert I (1848–1922), is a stunner. Its centrepiece is its **aquarium**, with a 6m-deep **lagoon** where sharks and marine predators are separated from colourful tropical fish by a coral reef.

Pay a visit to the rooftop terrace for sweeping views of Monaco and the Med.

Le Rocher HISTORIC QUARTER

Monaco Ville, also called Le Rocher, thrusts skywards on a pistol-shaped rock. It's this strategic location, overlooking the sea, that became the stronghold of the Grimaldi dynasty. Built as a fortress in the 13th century, the **palace** is now the private residence of the Grimaldis. It is protected by the Carabiniers du Prince; **changing of the guard** takes place daily at 11.55am.

For a glimpse into royal life, you can tour the state apartments inside the **Palais du Prince** (www.palais.mc; adult/child €8/3.50; ⊙10am-6pm Apr-Sep) with an audioguide; rooms are what you would expect of any aristocratic abode – lavish furnishings and expensive 18th- and 19th-century art.

Cathédrale de Monaco CATHEDRAL

(4 rue Colonel) An adoring crowd continually shuffles past Prince Rainier's and Princess Grace's graves, located inside the cathedral choir of the 1875 Romanesque-Byzantine Cathédrale de Monaco.

> **DON'T MISS**
>
> **THE CORNICHES**
>
> Some of the Riviera's most spectacular scenery stretches east between Nice and Monaco. A trio of *corniches* (coastal roads) hugs the cliffs between the two seaside cities, each higher up the hill than the last. The middle *corniche* ends in Monaco; the upper and lower continue to Menton near the France-Italy border.

Eating & Drinking

La Montgolfière FUSION €€

(☎97 98 61 59; www.lamontgolfiere.mc; 16 rue Basse; mains €21-30; ⊙lunch & dinner Mon, Tue, Thu, Fri, Sun, dinner Sat) This tiny fusion wonder is an unlikely find amid the touristy jumble of Monaco's historic quarter. But what a great idea Henri and Fabienne Geraci had to breathe new life into the Rocher. They have spent a lot of time in Malaysia, and Henri's fusion cuisine is outstanding, as is Fabienne's welcome in the pocket-sized dining room.

In winter, Henri cooks *bourride*, a salted cod stew typical of Monaco, every day.

Café Llorca MODERN FRENCH €€
(☎99 99 29 29; www.cafellorca.mc; 10 av Princesse Grace, Grimaldi Forum; mains €15-26; ⊙lunch) This new restaurant is Michelin-starred-chef Alain Llorca's version of a traditional cafe: the menu is classic French fare (pork loin with sautéed potatoes; *daube*, a local beef stew) but elevated to new heights in taste and presentation. In summer, tables are set out on the terrace overlooking the sea.

Brasserie de Monaco MICROBREWERY
(www.brasseriedemonaco.com; 36 rte de la Piscine; ⊙11am-1pm Sun-Thu, 11am-3am Fri & Sat) Tourists and locals rub shoulders at Monaco's only microbrewery, which crafts rich organic ales and lager, and serves tasty (if pricey) antipasti plates. Happy hour is 5pm to 8pm.

Information

Calls between Monaco and France are international calls. Dial ☎00 followed by Monaco's country code (☎377) when calling Monaco from France or elsewhere abroad. To phone France from Monaco, dial ☎00 and France's country code (☎33).

Tourist Office (www.visitmonaco.com; 2a bd des Moulins; ⊙9am-7pm Mon-Sat, 11am-1pm Sun) From mid-June to late September, additional tourist-info kiosks mushroom around the harbour and train station.

Getting There & Away

Monaco's **train station** (av Prince Pierre) has frequent trains to Nice (€3.60, 20 minutes), and east to Menton (€2, 10 minutes) and beyond into Italy.

CORSICA

The rugged island of Corsica (Corse in French) is officially a part of France, but remains fiercely proud of its own culture, history and language. It's one of the Mediterranean's most dramatic islands, with a bevy of beautiful beaches, glitzy ports and a mountainous, maquis-covered interior to explore, as well as a wild, independent spirit all of its own.

Ajaccio

POP 65,000

Ajaccio, Corsica's main metropolis, is all class and seduction. Looming over this elegant port city is the spectre of Corsica's great general: Napoleon Bonaparte was born here in 1769 and the city is dotted with statues and museums relating to the diminutive dictator (starting with the main street in Ajaccio, cours Napoleon).

Sights & Activities

Palais Fesch – Musée des Beaux-Arts MUSEUM
(www.musee-fesch.com; 50-52 rue du Cardinal Fesch; adult/child €8/5; ⊙10.30am-6pm Mon, Wed & Sat, noon-6pm Thu, Fri & Sun year-round, to 8.30pm Fri Jul & Aug) This superb museum established by Napoleon's uncle has France's largest collection of Italian paintings outside the Louvre. Mostly the works of minor or anonymous 14th- to 19th-century artists, there are also canvases by Titian, Fra Bartolomeo, Veronese, Botticelli and Bellini.

Maison Bonaparte MUSEUM
(☎04 95 21 43 89; www.musee-maisonbonaparte.fr; rue St-Charles; adult/child €7/5.50; ⊙10.30am-12.30pm & 1.15-6pm Tue-Sun Apr-Sep, 10am-noon & 2-4.45pm Oct-Mar) Napoleon spent his first nine years in this house, which is now host to various memorabilia of the emperor and his siblings, including a glass medallion containing a lock of his hair. It's closed Monday mornings.

Boat Trips TOURS
Kiosks on the quayside opposite place du Maréchal Foch sell tickets for seasonal boat trips around the Golfe d'Ajaccio and Îles Sanguinaires (€27), and excursions to the **Réserve Naturelle de Scandola** (adult/child €50/35).

Sleeping

TOP CHOICE **Hôtel Kallisté** HOTEL €€
(☎04 95 51 34 45; www.hotel-kalliste-ajaccio.com; 51 cours Napoléon; s/d/tr €77/95/123; P❄@🛜) Exposed brick, neutral tones, terracotta tiles and a funky glass lift conjure a neo-boutique feel at the Kallisté, which occupies a typical 19th-century Ajaccio townhouse. Facilities are fab.

Hôtel Marengo HOTEL €
(☎04 95 21 43 66; www.hotel-marengo.com; 2 rue Marengo; d €65-89, tr €95-115; ⊙Apr-Oct; ❄) For something nearer to the sand, try this charmingly eccentric hotel near the beach. Find it down a cul de sac off bd Madame Mère.

Eating

TOP CHOICE **Le 20123** TRADITIONAL CORSICAN €€
(☎04 95 21 50 05; www.20123.fr; 2 rue du Roi de Rome; menus €34.50; ⊙dinner Tue-Sun) This

one-of-a-kind place started life in the village of Pila Canale (postcode 20123 – get it?), and when the owner upped sticks to Ajaccio he decided to take the old village with him – water pump, washing line, central square et al. The food is 100% authentic, too – everyone feasts on the same four-course *menu*, presented orally and unchanged for 25 years.

Da Mama TRADITIONAL CORSICAN €
(☎04 95 21 39 44; 3 passage de la Ghinghetta; lunch menus €12, dinner menus €17-25; ⊙dinner Mon, lunch & dinner Tue-Sat) Staunchly Corsican cuisine aside, the main draw of this unfussy eatery is its location in the shade of a magnificent rubber tree down a narrow alley.

Information

Tourist Office (www.ajaccio-tourisme.com; 3 bd du Roi Jérôme; ⊙8am-7pm Mon-Sat, 9am-1pm Sun)

Getting There & Away

AIR Bus 8 (€4.50, 20 minutes) links **Aéroport d'Ajaccio-Campo dell'Oro** (☎04 95 23 56 56; www.ajaccio.aeroport.fr), 8km east, with Ajaccio's train and bus stations.

BOAT Boats to/from Toulon, Nice and Marseille depart from Ajaccio's **Terminal Maritime et Routier** (☎04 95 51 21 80; www.2a.cci.fr; quai L'Herminier).

BUS Local bus companies have ticket kiosks inside the ferry terminal building, the arrival/departure point for buses.

TRAIN From the **train station** (place de la Gare), services include Bastia (four hours, three to four daily).

Bastia

POP 44,200

The bustling old port of Bastia has an irresistible magnetism. Allow yourself at least a day to drink in the narrow old-town alleyways of Terra Vecchia, the seething Vieux Port, the dramatic 16th-century citadel perched up high, and the compelling history museum.

Sights & Activities

The 19th-century central square, **place St-Nicholas**, sprawls along the seafront between the ferry port and harbour. Named after the patron saint of sailors – a nod to Corsica's seagoing heritage – the square is lined with plane trees, busy cafes and a **statue of Napoleon Bonaparte**, Corsica's famous son.

A network of narrow lanes leads south towards the neighbourhood of **Terra Vecchia**, a muddle of crumbling apartments and balconied blocks. Further south is the **Vieux Port** (Old Port): the best views of the harbour are from the **Jetée du Dragon** (Dragon Jetty) or from the hillside park of **Jardin Romieu** (Romieu Garden), reached via a twisting staircase from the waterfront. Behind the garden looms Bastia's sunbaked **citadel**, built from the 15th to 17th centuries. Inside, the **Palais des Gouverneurs** (Governers Palace) houses Bastia's top-notch **Musée d'Histoire de Bastia** (☎04 95 31 09 12; www.musee-bastia.com; place du Donjon; admission €5; ⊙10am-7.30pm Tue-Sun Jul–mid-Sep, shorter hours mid-Sep–Jun)

Sleeping & Eating

TOP CHOICE **Hôtel Central** HOTEL €€
(☎04 95 31 71 12; www.centralhotel.fr; 3 rue Miot; s/d €77/90; 📶) From the vintage, black-and-white tiled floor in the entrance to the sweeping staircase and eclectic jumble of plant pots in the minuscule interior courtyard, this family-run address oozes 1940s grace.

Le Lavezzi MODERN FRENCH €€
(☎04 95 31 05 73; 8 rue St-Jean; mains €20-35, lunch menus €19) Le Lavezzi is completely different. Its artsy interior is fabulous and funky, and the real heart stealer is the twin-set of 1st-floor balconies with prime old-port views.

CORSICAN ICE

Wrapping your lips around a rich Corsican ice cream, flavoured with one of the island's distinctive edible products, is an essential part of the Bastia experience. And no address does it better than **Raugi** (2 rue du Chanoine Colombani; 1/2/3 scoops €1.30/2.60/3.90, cups €5-20), an ice-cream house dating to 1937, with its main cafe in town and a waterfront **takeaway parlour** (quai du 1er Bataillon de Choc) at the Old Port. Flavours range from bog-standard raspberry, lemon and so on to Corsican chestnut, mandarin, fig, aromatic *senteur de maquis* (scent of Corsican herbal scrubland) and sweet *myrte* (myrtle). Forget the chocolate flake; top it off with a *canistrelli* (local biscuit) stuck in the top.

Petite Marie REGIONAL CUISINE €
(☎04 95 32 47 83; 2 rue des Zéphyrs; mains €16-19; ⏲dinner Mon-Sat) Everything is home baked at 'Little Marie', a bolt-hole hidden a couple of blocks from the Vieux Port. Do as locals do and kick-start your feast with *friture de rougets* (battered, fried red mullet) followed by grilled crayfish. No credit cards.

Information

Tourist Office (☎04 95 54 20 40; www.bastia-tourisme.com; place St-Nicolas; ⏲8am-6pm Mon-Sat, 8am-noon Sun)

Getting There & Away

AIR **Aéroport Bastia-Poretta** (www.bastia.aeroport.fr), 24km south, is linked by bus (€9, 30 minutes, 10 daily) with the Préfecture building in town.

BOAT **Bastia Port** (www.bastia.port.fr) has two ferry terminals; ferry companies have information offices in the **Southern Ferry Terminal** (www.port-de-bastia.net), usually open for same-day ticket sales a couple of hours before sailings. Ferries sail to/from Marseille, Toulon and Nice (mainland France), and Livorno, Savona, Piombino and Genoa (Italy).

TRAMWAY DE LA BALAGNE

You may well tremble as the *trinighellu* (trembler) – as the **Tramway de la Balagne** (☎04 95 65 00 61, 04 95 60 00 50) is affectionately called – trundles perilously close to the shore along sand-covered tracks between Calvi and Île Rousse. The dinky little train is the easiest way to access the numerous hidden coves and beaches sprinkled along the coast: no traffic jams and an unforgettable trip alongside getaway beaches. The train runs four to eight times daily April to September, calling at 15 stations en route, all by request only. Out of season, regular trains run by **Chemins de Fer de la Corse** (☎04 95 32 80 57; www.train-corse.com) cover the same route. Hop off at an intermediate rocky cove or, for fine golden sand, leave the train at Algajola or Plage de Bodri, the last stop before Île Rousse. It costs €5.40 one-way.

BUS & TRAIN The **bus station** (1 rue du Nouveau Port) is north of place St-Nicolas and bus stops are scattered around town. Many buses depart from in front of Bastia **train station** (av Maréchal Sébastiani), the departure point for daily trains to Ajaccio (€25, 3¾ hours, four daily) via Corte (1¾ hours), and Calvi (three hours, three or four daily) via Île Rousse.

Eurocorse Voyages (☎04 95 31 73 76; www.eurocorse.com; 1 rue Nouveau Port) runs buses to Ajaccio (€21, three hours) via Corte (€11.50, two hours) twice daily, except on Sunday, from Bastia bus station.

Bonifacio

POP 2970

With its glittering harbour, dramatic perch atop creamy white cliffs, and a stout citadel teetering above the cornflower-blue waters of the Bouches de Bonifacio, this dazzling port is an essential stop. Just a short hop from Sardinia, Bonifacio has a distinctly Italianate feel: sun-bleached townhouses, dangling washing lines and murky chapels cram the web of alleyways of the old citadel, while down below on the harbourside, brasseries and boat kiosks tout their wares to the droves of day trippers.

Sights & Activities

Citadel (Haute Ville) HISTORIC NEIGHBOURHOOD
Much of Bonifacio's charm comes from strolling the citadel's shady streets, several spanned by arched aqueducts designed to collect rainwater to fill the communal cistern opposite **Église Ste-Marie Majeure**. From the marina, the paved **steps of montée du Rastello** and **montée St-Roch** bring you up to the citadel's old gateway, complete with an original 16th-century drawbridge. Inside the gateway is the 13th-century **Bastion de l'Étendard** (adult/child €2.50/free; ⏲9am-7pm Mon-Fri, 10am-6pm Sat & Sun Apr-Oct), home to a small history museum. Stroll the ramparts to **place du Marché** and **place de la Manichella** for jaw-dropping views over the Bouches de Bonifacio.

From the citadel, the **Escalier du Roi d'Aragon** (King of Aragon's Stairway; adult/under 12yr €2.50/free; ⏲9am-7pm Mon-Fri, 10am-6pm Sat & Sun Apr-Oct) cuts down the southern cliff-face. Legend says its 187 steep steps were carved in a single night by Aragonese troops during the siege of 1420, only for troops to be rebuffed by retaliating Bonifacio residents at the top. In reality, the steps served as an access path to an underground freshwater well.

Îles Lavezzi ARCHIPELAGO

Paradise! This protected clutch of uninhabited islets were made for those who love nothing better than splashing in tranquil lapis-lazuli waters. The 65-hectare Île Lavezzi, which gives its name to the whole archipelago, is the most accessible of the islands. Savage beauty aside, the island's superb natural pools and scenic stretches of sand beg long-and-lazy sunbathing and swimming sessions. In summer, various companies organise boat trips here; buy tickets at the booths located on Bonifacio's marina and bring your own picnic lunch.

Sleeping & Eating

TOP CHOICE **Domaine de Licetto** HOTEL €€

(☎04 95 73 03 59; www.licetto.com; rte du Phare de Pertusato; s €55-85, d €70-105, q €115-175; ⏰Apr-Oct; P) Tucked in the maquis just a couple of kilometres east of Bonifacio, this motel-style address has seven minimalist rooms sporting stylishly modern bathroms, well-chosen furnishings and a terrace with table and chairs made for lounging. The restaurant on the estate is a feast in traditional dining and, best of all, Bonifacio town is a short idyllic walk away along the clifftop coastal path.

TOP CHOICE **Kissing Pigs** MODERN CORSICAN €

(☎04 95 73 56 09; quai Banda del Ferro; mains €9-15) Soothingly positioned by the harbour, this widely acclaimed restaurant and wine bar serves savoury fare in a seductively cosy interior. It's famed for its cheese and charcuterie platters, and Corsican wine list.

Information

Tourist Office (www.bonifacio.fr; 2 rue Fred Scamaroni; ⏰9am-8pm Jul & Aug, to 7pm May, Jun & Sep, 9am-noon & 2-6pm Oct-Apr)

Getting There & Away

AIR A taxi into town from **Aéroport de Figari** (www.figari.aeroport.fr), 21km north, costs about €40.

BOAT Saremar (www.saremar.it) and **Moby Lines** (www.moby.it) sail between Bonifacio and Santa Teresa di Gallura (on the neighbouring island of Sardinia) in summer.

UNDERSTAND FRANCE

History

France's early history is encapsulated in the Astérix comic books: the Celtic Gauls arrived between 1500 and 500 BC, and were under Roman rule from 52 BC until the 5th century. After the Roman Empire's decline, France was governed by monarchs including Charlemagne (from 800). William the Conqueror extended French rule to England in 1066.

During the Reformation, fighting between Catholics and Protestants brought France close to disintegration. However, that paled beside the seismic events of the 1780s, when the population rose up against Louis XVI and his queen, Marie Antoinette. On 14 July 1789, a Parisian mob stormed the Bastille, unleashing the French Revolution. The vicious Reign of Terror followed; thousands of aristocrats were guillotined, including Louis XVI and his queen in 1793.

A young Corsican general by the name of Napoleon Bonaparte assumed power in 1799 and embarked on European conquest. Initially defeated and exiled to the island of Elba, he staged a short comeback before meeting his final defeat at Waterloo in 1815. The subsequent years were marked by civil strife, with monarchists and revolutionaries vying for power. Napoleon's nephew Louis-Napoleon Bonaparte seized power in 1851, declaring himself Emperor Napoleon III, but he proved no match for his uncle in terms of military prowess: he embroiled France in various catastrophic conflicts, including the Crimean War (1853–56) and the Franco-Prussian War (1870–71).

Central to France's entry into WWI was the desire to regain Alsace and Lorraine, lost to Germany in 1871. This was achieved but at an immense cost: 1.3 million killed and almost one million crippled. The Treaty of Versailles, signed in 1919, demanded punitive reparations from Germany, causing long-lasting bitterness – a fact that was later ruthlessly exploited by an Austrian house painter called Adolf Hitler.

Following the outbreak of WWII, the German blitzkrieg swept west with astonishing speed; by 1940 France had capitulated and the country was divided into an occupied zone in the north and the collaborationist Vichy regime in the south. France had to wait four years for liberation. On 6

June 1944, US, British and Canadian troops stormed the beaches of Normandy and pushed east towards Paris. General Charles de Gaulle, leader of the French government-in-exile, returned to France and established a provisional government.

Political power see-sawed over the next 50 years, a period that saw the end of French colonies in Vietnam and Algeria and the elections of several important French presidents, including Georges Pompidou (president from 1969–74) and François Mitterrand (1981-95), Jacques Chirac (1995–2007) and Nicolas Sarkozy (2007-2012).

France Today

Presidential elections in spring 2012 ushered in France's first socialist president since François Mitterand left office in 1995. The presidential campaign saw incumbent right-wing president Nicolas Sarkozy vie for a second term in office against left-wing candidate François Hollande (b 1954) of the Socialist party. Sarkozy promised to modernise the French economy, reduce the number of immigrants to France, and lower France's budget deficit; but with the electorate tired of the austerity policies of the Conservatives, it was Hollande's ambitious talk of reducing unemployment (at a 12-year high), clearing the country's debts (by 2017), upping tax on corporations and salaries over €1 million per annum, and increasing the minimum salary that proved the more appealing platform. Parliamentary elections a month later sealed Hollande's grip on power with the Socialists winning a comfortable majority in France's 577-seat National Assembly, thus paving the way for Hollande to govern France during Europe's biggest economic crisis in decades.

Culturally, France is savouring a high. Art lovers are bursting with excitement over the reopening in Paris, after months of painstaking renovation, of both the Musée Picasso and the country's most prestigious theatre, the Comédie Française, where Molière trod the boardwalks. At the 2012 Academy Awards, the French-made silent film *The Artist,* starring the quintessentially French-sexy Jean Dujardin, scooped five Oscars to herald the renaissance of French cinema. The grand opening of the striking new Louvre-Lens art museum in northern France on the other hand promises to inject new creativity into the conventional French museum experience.

MULTICULTURAL MUSINGS

No French writer better delves into the mind and politics of France's ethnic population than Faïza Guène (b 1985), writing in a notable 'urban slang' style, born and bred on a ghetto housing estate outside Paris. Her second semi-autobiographical novel, Du Rêve pour les Oeufs (2006), is published in English as Dreams from the Endz (2008). Another French writer to address ethnic issues so engagingly is JMG Le Clézio, born in Nice to a Niçois mother and Mauritian father. He grew up in Nigeria and won the 2008 Nobel Prize in Literature, confirming France's ranking as country with the most literary Nobel Prize winners.

Arts

Literature

The philosophical work of Voltaire (1694–1778) and Jean-Jacques Rousseau dominated the 18th century. A century later, the poems and novels of Victor Hugo – *Les Misérables* and *Notre-Dame de Paris (The Hunchback of Notre-Dame)* among them – became landmarks of French Romanticism.

In 1857, two literary landmarks were published: *Madame Bovary* by Gustave Flaubert (1821–80) and Charles Baudelaire's collection of poems, *Les Fleurs du Mal (The Flowers of Evil).* Émile Zola (1840–1902) meanwhile strove to convert novel-writing from an art to a science in his series *Les Rougon-Macquart.*

Symbolists Paul Verlaine (1844–96) and Stéphane Mallarmé (1842–98) aimed to express mental states through their poetry. Verlaine's poems, with those of Arthur Rimbaud (1854–91), are seen as French literature's first modern poems.

After WWII, the existentialist movement developed around the lively debates of Jean-Paul Sartre (1905–80), Simone de Beauvoir (1908–86) and Albert Camus (1913–60) over coffee and cigarettes in Paris' Left Bank cafes.

Contemporary authors include Françoise Sagan, Pascal Quignard, Anna Gavalda, Emmanuel Carrère and Yasmina Khadra (actually a man, a former colonel in the Algerian army, who adopted his wife's name as a nom de plume).

Marc Levy is France's best-selling writer whose novels have been translated into 42 languages. *L'étrange voyage de Monsieur Daldry* (The Strange Journey of Mr Daldry; 2011) is his latest.

Cinema

Cinematographic pioneers the Lumière brothers shot the world's first-ever motion picture in March 1895 and French film flourished in the following decades. The post-WWII *nouvelle vague* (new wave) film-makers, such as Claude Chabrol, Jean-Luc Godard and François Truffaut, pioneered the advent of modern cinema, using fractured narratives, documentary camerawork and highly personal subjects.

Big-name stars, slick production values and nostalgia were the dominant motifs in the 1980s, as filmmakers switched to costume dramas, comedies and 'heritage movies'. Claude Berri's depiction of prewar Provence in *Jean de Florette* (1986) and Jean-Paul Rappeneau's *Cyrano de Bergerac* (1990) and *Bon Voyage* (2003), set in 1940s Paris – all starring France's best-known actor, Gérard Depardieu – found huge audiences in France and abroad.

Massive international box-office hit *Le Fabuleux Destin de Amélie Poulain* (*Amélie*; 2001) is a feel-good story about a Parisian do-gooder. Or watch *Bienvenue chez les Ch'tis* (2008), another big film of recent years, which debunks grim stereotypes about the industrialised regions of the north of France with high jinks and hilarity.

'New French Extremity' is the tag given to the socially conscious, transgressive films of talented Paris-born, Africa-raised filmmaker Claire Denis. *Chocolat* (1988) and *Matériel Blanc* (*White Material*; 2009), the latter scripted by Parisian novelist Marie NDiaye, both explore the legacy of French colonialism.

No French film has ever wooed the world at large quite like *The Artist* (2011), a silent B&W, French-made romantic comedy set in 1920s Hollywood that scooped five Oscars heralding the renaissance of French film.

Music

French musical luminaries – Charles Gounod (1818–93), César Franck (1822–90) and *Carmen* creator Georges Bizet (1838–75) among them – were a dime a dozen in the 19th century. Claude Debussy (1862–1918) revolutionised classical music with *Prélude à l'Après-Midi d'un Faune* (*Prelude to the Afternoon of a Faun*); while Maurice Ravel (1875–1937) peppered his work, including *Boléro,* with sensuousness and tonal colour.

Jazz was the hot sound of 1920s Paris, with the likes of Sidney Bechet, Kenny Clarke, Bud Powell and Dexter Gordon filling clubs in the capital.

The *chanson française,* a folkish tradition dating from medieval troubadours, was revived in the 1930s by Édith Piaf and Charles Trenet. In the 1950s Paris' Left Bank cabarets nurtured *chansonniers* (cabaret singers) like Léo Ferré, Georges Brassens, Claude Nougaro, Jacques Brel and the much-loved crooner Serge Gainsbourg.

Electronic music (think Daft Punk and Air) has a global following, while French rap was pioneered in the 1990s by MC Solaar and continued by young French rappers such as Disiz La Peste, Monsieur R and IAM. Brittany's Manau trio engagingly fuses hip hop with traditional Celtic sounds.

French pop music has evolved massively since the 1960s *yéyé* (imitative rock) days of Johnny Hallyday. Particularly strong is world music, from Algerian *raï* and other North African music (artists include Natacha Atlas) to Senegalese *mbalax* (Youssou N'Dour) and West Indian zouk (Kassav, Zouk Machine). Musicians who combine many of these elements include Paris-born Manu Chao and Franco-Algerian Rachid Taja.

WORLD-CLASS WORLD MUSIC

No artist has cemented France's reputation in world music more than Paris-born, Franco-Congolese rapper, slam poet and three-time Victoire de la Musique-award winner, Abd al Malik. His albums, *Gibraltar* (2006), *Dante* (2008) and *Château Rouge* (2010) are classics.

Architecture

Southern France is the place to find France's Gallo-Roman legacy, especially at the Pont du Gard (c 19 BC), and the amphitheatres in Nîmes and Arles (c 100 AD).

Several centuries later, architects adopted Gallo-Roman motifs in Romanesque masterpieces such as Poitier's Église Notre Dame la Grande.

Impressive 12th-century Gothic structures include Avignon's pontifical palace, Chartres' cathedral, and of course, Notre Dame in Paris.

Art nouveau (1850–1910) combined iron, brick, glass and ceramics in new ways. See it for yourself at Paris' metro entrances and in the Musée d'Orsay.

Contemporary buildings to look out for include the once-reviled (now much-revered) Centre Pompidou and IM Pei's glass pyramid at the Louvre. In the provinces, notable buildings include Strasbourg's European Parliament, a 1920s art deco swimming pool-turned-art museum in Lille, the stunning new Centre Pompidou in Metz and the Louvre-Lens in the former mining town of Lens.

Painting

Anflowering of artistic talent occurred in 19th- and 20th-century France. The Impressionists, who endeavoured to capture the ever-changing aspects of reflected light, included Edouard Manet, Claude Monet, Edgar Degas, Camille Pisarro, and Pierre-Auguste Renoir. They were followed by the likes of Paul Cézanne (who lived in Aix-en-Provence) and Paul Gauguin, as well as the fauvist Henry Matisse (a resident of Nice on the French Riviera) and cubists including Spanish-born Pablo Picasso and Georges Braque.

Environment

Hexagon-shaped France is the largest country in Europe. Europe's highest peak, Mont Blanc (4810m), crowns the French Alps along France's eastern border, while the rugged Pyrenees define France's 450km-long border with Spain, peaking at 3404m. The country's major river systems include the Garonne, Rhône, Seine, and France's longest river, the Loire.

France has more mammals (around 110) than any other country in Europe, as well as 363 bird species, 30 types of amphibian, 36 varieties of reptile and 72 kinds of fish. Distinctive animals found in the Alps and Pyrenees include the marmot, chamois (mountain antelope), bouquetin (Alpine ibex) and mouflon (wild mountain sheep).

The proportion of protected land is low relative to the country's size: seven national parks (www.parcsnationaux-fr.com) fully protect around 0.8% of the country. Another 13% is protected by 45 regional parks (www.parcs-naturels-regionaux.tm.fr) and a further few per cent by 320 smaller nature reserves (www.reserves-naturelles.org).

SURVIVAL GUIDE

Directory A–Z

Accommodation

Many tourist offices make room reservations, often for a fee of €5; many only do so if you stop by in person. In the French Alps, ski resort tourist offices operate a central reservation service.

Our reviews refer to the cost of a double room with private bathroom, except in hostels or where otherwise specified. Quoted rates are for high season and exclude breakfast unless otherwise noted:

€ less than €80 (€110 in Paris)

€€ €80 to €180 (€110 to €200 in Paris)

€€€ more than €180 (€200 in Paris)

B&BS

For charm, a heartfelt *bienvenue* (welcome) and home cooking, it's hard to beat a *chambre d'hôte* (B&B). Pick up lists at local tourist offices or online:

Bienvenue à la Ferme (www.bienvenue-a-la-ferme.com)

Chambres d'Hôtes France (www.chambres-dhotesfrance.com)

Fleurs de Soleil (www.fleursdesoleil.fr) Selective collection of 550 stylish *maisons d'hôte,* mainly in rural France.

Gîtes de France (www.gites-de-france.com) France's primary umbrella organisation for B&Bs and *gîtes* (self-catering houses and apartments).

Samedi Midi Éditions (www.samedimidi.com) Choose your *chambre d'hôte* by location or theme (romance, golf, design, cooking courses).

CAMPING

Camping has never been more *en vogue.*

» Most camping grounds open March or April to October.

» Euro-economisers should look for good-value but no-frills *campings municipaux* (municipal camping grounds).

» Camping in nondesignated spots *(camping sauvage)* is illegal in France.

Easy-to-navigate websites with campsites searchable by location and facilities include the following:

Camping en France (www.camping.fr)

Camping France (www.campingfrance.com)

Guide du Camping (www.guideducamping.com)

Cabanes de France (www.cabanes-de-france.com) Tree houses.

Gîtes de France (www.gites-de-france.com) Coordinates camping on farms.

Bienvenue à la Ferme (www.bienvenue-a-la-ferme.com) Camping on farms.

HOSTELS

Hostels range from funky to threadbare.

» A dorm bed in an *auberge de jeunesse* (youth hostel) costs about €25 in Paris, and anything from €10.50 to €28 in the provinces; sheets are always included and often breakfast too.

» To prevent outbreaks of bed bugs, sleeping bags are no longer permitted.

» All hostels are nonsmoking.

HOTELS

» French hotels almost never include breakfast in their advertised nightly rates.

» Hotels in France are rated with one to five stars; ratings are based on objective criteria (eg size of entry hall), not service, decor or cleanliness.

» A double room has one double bed (or two singles pushed together); a room with twin beds is more expensive, as is a room with a bathtub instead of shower.

Activities

From glaciers, rivers and canyons in the Alps to porcelain-smooth cycling trails in the Dordogne and Loire Valley – not to mention 3200km of coastline stretching from Italy to Spain and from the Basque country to the Straits of Dover – France's landscapes beg exhilarating outdoor escapes.

» The French countryside is criss-crossed by a staggering 120,000km of *sentiers balisés* (marked walking paths), which pass through every imaginable terrain in every region of the country. No permit is needed to hike.

» The best-known trails are the *sentiers de grande randonnée* (GR), long-distance paths marked by red-and-white-striped track indicators.

» For complete details on regional activities, courses, equipment rental, clubs, companies and organisations, contact local tourist offices.

Business Hours

» French business hours are regulated by a maze of government regulations, including the 35-hour working week.

» The midday break is uncommon in Paris but, in general, gets longer the further south you go.

» French law requires most businesses to close Sunday; exceptions include grocery stores, *boulangeries (bakeries),* florists and businesses catering to the tourist trade.

» In many places shops close on Monday.

» Many service stations open 24 hours a day and stock basic groceries.

» Restaurants generally close one or two days of the week.

» Most (but not all) national museums are closed on Tuesday, while most local museums are closed on Monday, though in summer some open daily. Some museums close for lunch.

We've only listed business hours where they differ from the following standards:

Banks 9am to noon and 2pm to 5pm Monday to Friday or Tuesday to Saturday

Bars 7pm to 1am Monday to Saturday

Cafes 7am or 8am to 10pm or 11pm Monday to Saturday

Nightclubs 10pm to 3am, 4am or 5am Thursday to Saturday

Post offices 8.30am or 9am to 5pm or 6pm Monday to Friday, 8am to noon Saturday

Restaurants Noon to 2.30pm (or 3pm in Paris) and 7pm to 11pm (or midnight in Paris) six days a week

Shops 9am or 10am to 7pm Monday to Saturday (often with lunch break from noon to 1.30pm)

Supermarkets 8.30am to 7pm Monday to Saturday, 8.30am to 12.30pm Sunday

WHICH FLOOR?

In France, as elsewhere in Europe, 'ground floor' refers to the floor at street level; the 1st floor – what would be called the 2nd floor in the US – is the floor above that.

Embassies & Consulates

To find a consulate or an embassy, visit www.embassiesabroad.com.

Australian Embassy (☎01 40 59 33 00; www.france.embassy.gov.au; 4 rue Jean Rey, 15e; Ⓜ Bir Hakeim)

Canadian Embassy (☎01 44 43 29 00; www.amb-canada.fr; 35 av Montaigne, 8e; Ⓜ Franklin D Roosevelt)

New Zealand Embassy (☎01 45 01 43 43; www.nzembassy.com/france; 7ter rue Léonard de Vinci, 16e; Ⓜ Victor Hugo)

UK Embassy (☎01 44 51 31 00; http://ukin-france.fco.gov.uk; 35 rue du Faubourg St Honoré, 8e; Ⓜ Concorde)

US Embassy (☎01 43 12 22 22; http://france.usembassy.gov; 2 av Gabriel, 8e; Ⓜ Concorde)

Food

Price ranges refer to a two-course meal:

€ less than €20

€€ €20 to €40

€€€ more than €40

Gay & Lesbian Travellers

Gay mayors (including Paris' very own Bertrand Delanoë), artists and film directors, camper-than-camp fashion designers…the rainbow flag flies high in France, one of Europe's most liberal countries when it comes to homosexuality.

» Major gay and lesbian organisations are based in Paris.

» Bordeaux, Lille, Lyon, Toulouse and many other towns have active communities.

» Attitudes towards homosexuality tend to be more conservative out of the cities.

» Gay Pride marches are held in major French cities from mid-May to early July.

Online try the following websites:

French Government Tourist Office (www.us.franceguide.com/special-interests/gay-friendly) Information about 'the gay-friendly destination par excellence'.

France Queer Resources Directory (www.france.qrd.org) Gay and lesbian directory.

Language Courses

» The website www.studyabroadlinks.com can help you find specific courses and summer programs, while www.edu france.fr/en has information about university study.

» All manner of French-language courses are available in Paris and provincial towns and cities; many arrange accommodation.

» Prices and courses vary greatly and the content can often be tailored to your specific needs (for a fee).

Some schools you might consider include the following:

Centre Méditerranéen d'Études Françaises (www.monte-carlo.mc/centremed; chemin des Oliviers, Cap d'Ail) Mythical French Riviera school around since 1952.

Eurocentres (www.eurocentres.com) Trio of small, affiliated schools in Amboise, La Rochelle and Paris.

Aix-Marseille Université (www.univ-provence.fr; 29 av Robert Schumann, Aix-en-Provence) A popular choice in Provence; semester-long courses as well as summer classes.

Legal Matters

French police have wide powers of stop-and-search and can demand proof of identity at any time. Foreigners must be able to prove their legal status in France (eg passport, visa, residency permit).

Money

» Credit and debit cards, are accepted almost everywhere in France.

» Some places (eg 24-hour petrol stations and some *autoroute* toll machines) only take credit cards with chips and PINs.

» In Paris and major cities, *bureaux de change* (exchange bureaux) are fast and easy, open longer hours and offer competitive exchange rates.

For lost cards, call your credit card company:

Amex (☎01 47 77 72 00)

Diners Club (☎08 10 31 41 59)

MasterCard (☎08 00 90 13 87)

Visa (Carte Bleue; ☎08 00 90 11 79)

Public Holidays

New Year's Day (Jour de l'An) 1 January

Easter Sunday & Monday (Pâques & lundi de Pâques) March or April

May Day (Fête du Travail) 1 May – traditional parades.

Victoire 1945 8 May – commemorates the Allied victory in Europe that ended WWII.

Ascension Thursday (Ascension) May – celebrated on the 40th day after Easter.

Pentecost/Whit Sunday & Whit Monday (Pentecôte & lundi de Pentecôte) Mid-May to mid-June – celebrated on the seventh Sunday after Easter.

Bastille Day/National Day (Fête Nationale) 14 July – *the* national holiday.

Assumption Day (Assomption) 15 August

All Saints' Day(Toussaint) 1 November

Remembrance Day (L'onze novembre) 11 November – marks the WWI armistice.

Christmas (Noël) 25 December

Telephone

MOBILE PHONES

» French mobile phones numbers begin with ☎06 or ☎07.

» France uses GSM 900/1800, compatible with the rest of Europe and Australia but not with the North American GSM 1900 or the totally different system in Japan (though some North Americans have tri-band phones that work here).

» It's usually cheaper to buy your own French SIM card (€20 to €30) sold at ubiquitous outlets run by France's three mobile phone companies, **Bouygues** (www.bouyguestelecom.fr), France Telecom's **Orange** (www.orange.com) and **SFR** (www.sfr.com).

» Recharge cards are sold at *tabacs* and newsagents; domestic prepaid calls cost about €0.50 per minute.

PHONE CODES

» To call France from abroad, dial your country's international access code, ☎33 (France's country code), and the 10-digit local number *without* the initial ☎0.

» To call internationally from France, dial ☎00 (the international access code), the country code, area code (without the initial zero if there is one) and the local number.

» For France Telecom's *service des renseignements* (directory inquiries), dial ☎11 87 12 or use the online service for free at www.118712.fr. For numbers outside France, dial ☎11 87 00.

» The emergency number is ☎112, which can be dialled from public phones without a phonecard.

Visas

For up-to-date details on visa requirements, visit the **French Foreign Affairs Ministry** (www.diplomatie.gouv.fr).

» EU nationals and citizens of Iceland, Norway and Switzerland need only a passport or national identity card to enter France and stay in the country, even for stays of over 90 days. Citizens of new EU member states may be subject to various limitations on living and working in France.

» Citizens of Australia, the USA, Canada Israel, Hong Kong, Japan, Malaysia, New Zealand, Singapore, South, Korea and many Latin American countries do not need visas to visit France as tourists for up to 90 days. For longer stays of over 90 days, contact your nearest French embassy or consulate.

» Other people wishing to come to France as tourists have to apply for a Schengen Visa.

» Tourist visas cannot be changed into student visas after arrival. However, short-term visas are available for students sitting university-entrance exams in France.

Getting There & Away

Air

International airports include the following:

Paris Charles de Gaulle (www.aeroportsdeparis.fr)

Paris Orly (www.aeroportsdeparis.fr)

Aéroport de Bordeaux (www.bordeaux.aeroport.fr)

Aéroport de Lille (www.lille.aeroport.fr)

Aéroport International Strasbourg (www.strasbourg.aeroport.fr)

Aéroport Lyon-Saint Exupéry (www.lyonaeroports.com)

Aéroport Marseille-Provence (www.marseille.aeroport.fr)

Aéroport Nantes Atlantique (www.nantes.aeroport.fr)

Aéroport Nice Côte d'Azur (http://societe.nice.aeroport.fr)

Aéroport Toulouse-Blagnac (www.toulouse.aeroport.fr)

EuroAirport (Basel-Mulhouse-Freiburg; www.euroairport.com)

Land

BUS

Eurolines (☎in France 08 92 89 90 91; www.eurolines.eu), a grouping of 32 long-haul coach operators (including the UK's National Express), links France with cities all across

Europe and in Morocco and Russia. Discounts are available to people under 26 and over 60. Make advance reservations, especially in July and August.

The standard Paris–London fare is between €45 and €59, but the trip – including a Channel crossing by ferry or the Channel Tunnel – can cost as little as €13 if you book 45 days ahead.

CAR & MOTORCYCLE

A right-hand-drive vehicle brought to France from the UK or Ireland must have deflectors affixed to the headlights to avoid dazzling oncoming traffic.

Departing from the UK, **Eurotunnel Le Shuttle** (www.eurotunnel.com) trains whisk bicycles, motorcycles, cars and coaches in 35 minutes from Folkestone through the Channel Tunnel to Coquelles, 5km southwest of Calais. Shuttles run 24 hours a day, with up to three departures an hour during peak periods. The earlier you book, the less you pay. Fares for a car, including up to nine passengers, start at UK£30.

TRAIN

Rail services – including a dwindling number of overnight services to/from Spain, Italy and Germany – link France with virtually every country in Europe. Book tickets and get train information from **Rail Europe** (www.raileurope.com). In France, ticketing is handled by **SNCF** (☎from abroad +33 8 92 35 35 35, in France 36 35; www.sncf.com); internet bookings are possible but tickets aren't posted outside France.

Sea

Regular ferries travel to France from Italy, the UK, Channel Islands and Ireland. Several ferry companies ply the waters between Corsica and Italy.

Getting Around

Air

France's vaunted high-speed train network has made rail travel between some cities (eg from Paris to Lyon and Marseille) faster and easier than flying.

Air France (www.airfrance.com) and its subsidiaries **Brit Air** (www.britair.fr) and **Régional** (☎36 54; www.regional.com) control the lion's share of France's long-protected domestic airline industry. Good deals can be had if you buy your ticket well in advance (at least 42 days ahead for the very best deals), stay over a Saturday night and don't mind tickets that can't be changed or reimbursed.

FERRIES FROM FRANCE

COMPANY	CONNECTION	WEBSITE
Brittany Ferries	England-Normandy, England-Brittany, Ireland-Brittany	www.brittany-ferries.co.uk www.brittanyferries.ie
Celtic Link Ferries	Ireland-Normandy	www.celticlinkferries.com
Condor Ferries	England-Normandy, England-Brittany, Channel Islands-Brittany	www.condorferries.com
CTN	Tunisia-France	www.ctn.com.tn
Irish Ferries	Ireland-Normandy, Ireland-Brittany	www.irishferries.ie www.shamrock-irlande.com, in French
LD Lines	England-Channel Ports, England-Normandy	www.ldlines.co.uk
Manche Îles Express	Channel Islands-Normandy	www.manche-iles-express.com
Norfolk Line (DFDS Seaways)	England-Channel Ports	www.norfolkline.com
P&O Ferries	England-Channel Ports	www.poferries.com
SNCM	Algeria-France, Sardinia-France, Tunisia-France	www.sncm.fr
Transmanche Ferries	England-Normandy	www.transmancheferries.com

SNCF TRAIN FARES & DISCOUNTS

The Basics

» Full-fare return travel costs twice as much as a one-way fare.

» 1st-class travel, where available, costs 20% to 30% extra.

» Ticket prices for some trains, including most TGVs, are pricier during peak periods.

» The further in advance you reserve, the lower the fares.

» Children under four travel for free (€8.50 to any destination if they need a seat).

» Children aged four to 11 travel for half price.

Discount Tickets

Prem's The SNCF's most heavily discounted, use-or-lose tickets are sold online, by phone and at ticket windows/machines a maximum of 90 days and minimum 14 days before you travel.

Bons Plans A grab-bag of cheap options for different routes/dates, advertised online under the tab 'Dernière Minute' (Last Minute).

iDTGV Cheap tickets on advance-purchase TGV travel between about 30 cities; only sold at www.idtgv.com.

Discount Cards

Reductions of 25% to 60% are available with several discount cards (valid for one year):

Carte 12-25 (www.12-25-sncf.com; €50) For travellers aged 12 to 25 years.

Carte Enfant Plus (www.enfantplus-sncf.com; €71) For one to four adults travelling with a child aged four to 11 years.

Carte Escapades (www.escapades-sncf.com; €76) Discounts on return journeys of at least 200km that include a Saturday night away or only involve travel on a Saturday or Sunday; for 26- to 59-year-olds.

Carte Sénior (www.senior-sncf.com; €57) Over 60 years.

Budget carriers offering flights within France include **easyJet** (www.easyjet.com), **Airlinair** (www.airlinair.com), **Twin Jet** (www.twinjet.net) and **Air Corsica** (www.aircorsica.com).

Bicycle

France is a great place to cycle and French train company SNCF does its best to make travelling with a bicycle easy; see www.velo.sncf.com for full details.

Most French cities and towns have at least one bike shop that rents out mountain bikes (VTTs; around €15 a day), road bikes (VTCs) and cheaper city bikes. You have to leave ID and/or a deposit (often a credit-card slip) that you forfeit if the bike is damaged or stolen. A growing number of cities have automatic bike rental systems.

Bus

You're nearly always better off travelling by train in France if possible, as the SNCF domestic railway system is heavily subsidised by the government and is much more reliable than local bus companies. Nevertheless, buses are widely used for short-distance travel within *départements*, especially in rural areas with relatively few train lines (eg Brittany and Normandy).

Car & Motorcycle

A car gives you exceptional freedom and allows you to visit more-remote parts of France. But it can be expensive and, in cities, parking and traffic are frequently a major headache. Motorcyclists will find France great for touring, with winding roads of good quality and lots of stunning scenery.

» All drivers must carry a national ID card or passport; a valid driving licence (*permis de conduire*; most foreign licences can be used in France for up to a year); car-ownership papers, known as a *carte grise* (grey card); and proof of third-party (liability) insurance.

» Many French motorways *(autoroutes)* are fitted with toll *(péage)* stations that charge a fee based on the distance you've travelled; factor in these costs when driving.

» To hire a car you'll usually need to be over 21 and in possession of a valid driving licence and a credit card. Auto transmissions are very rare in France; you'll need to order one well in advance.

Train

France's superb rail network is operated by the state-owned **SNCF** (www.sncf.com); many rural towns not on the SNCF train network are served by SNCF buses.

» The flagship trains on French railways are the superfast TGVs which reach speeds in excess of 320km/h and can whisk you from Paris to the Côte d'Azur in as little as three hours.

» Before boarding a train, you must validate *(composter)* your ticket by time-stamping it in a *composteur*, one of those yellow posts located on the way to the platform.

RAIL PASSES

The **InterRail One Country Pass** (www.interrailnet.com; 3/4/6/8 days €205/226/288/319, 12–25yr €139/149/190/211), valid in France, entitles residents of Europe who do not live in France to unlimited travel on SNCF trains for three to eight days over a month.

Germany

Includes »

Berlin ... 429
Dresden ... 447
Leipzig ... 449
Munich ... 454
Bavarian Alps ... 460
Nuremberg ... 464
Stuttgart ... 468
Heidelberg ... 469
Black Forest ... 471
Frankfurt-am-Main ... 475
Romantic Rhine ... 479
Cologne ... 483
Hamburg ... 491
Understand Germany ... 497
Survival Guide ... 499

Best Places to Eat

» Fraunhofer (p457)
» Café Schäfer (p472)
» Bratwursthäusle (p465)
» Auerbachs Keller (p450)
» Max und Moritz (p442)

Best Places to Stay

» EastSeven Berlin Hostel (p441)
» Hotel Wedina (p494)
» Wombats City Hostel Munich (p456)
» Casa dei Colori (p452)

Why Go?

Beer or wine? That sums up the German conundrum. One is at the heart of a pilsner-swilling culture, is the very reason for one of the world's great parties (Oktoberfest), and is consumed with pleasure across the land. The other is responsible for gorgeous vine-covered valleys, comes in myriad forms and is enjoyed everywhere, often from cute little green-stemmed glasses.

And the questions about Germany continue. Berlin or Munich? Castle or club? Ski or hike? East or west? BMW or Mercedes? In fact, the answers are simple: both. Why decide? The beauty of Germany is that rather than choosing, you can revel in the contrasts.

Berlin, edgy and vibrant, is a capital in a constant state of reinvention. Munich rules Bavaria, the centre of national traditions. Half-timbered villages bring smiles as you wander their cobblestoned and castle-shadowed lanes. Exploring this country and all its facets keeps visitors happy for weeks.

When to Go

Berlin

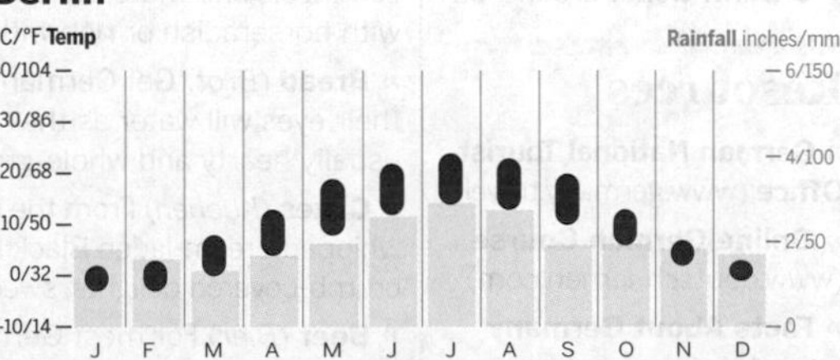

Jun–Aug Warm summers cause Germans to shed their clothes; night never seems to come.

Sep Radiant foliage and often sunny skies invite outdoor pursuits; festivals galore.

Dec It's icy, it's cold, but lines are short and Alpine slopes and twinkly Christmas markets beckon.

AT A GLANCE

» **Currency** Euro (€)

» **Language** German

» **Money** ATMs common, cash preferred for most purchases

» **Visas** Schengen rules apply

Fast Facts

» **Area** 356,866 sq km

» **Capital** Berlin

» **Country code** ☎49

» **Emergency** ☎112

Exchange Rates

Australia	A$1	€0.82
Canada	C$1	€0.77
Japan	¥100	€0.83
New Zealand	NZ$1	€0.65
UK	UK£1	€1.18
USA	US$1	€0.78

Set Your Budget

» **Midrange hotel room** €80–150

» **Two-course meal** €15–25

» **1L of beer** €6–8

» **Bottle of wine** from €4

» **U-Bahn ticket** around €2

Resources

» **German National Tourist Office** (www.germany.travel)

» **Online German Course** (www.deutsch-lernen.com)

» **Facts About Germany** (www.tatsachen-ueber-deutschland.de)

» **Deutschland Online** (www.magazine-deutschland.de).

Connections

At the heart of Europe, Germany has a superb railway network that's well linked to surrounding countries. Freiburg and Stuttgart have services south to Switzerland and Italy, Munich is close to the Czech Republic and Austria (including Salzburg and Innsbruck), Berlin is close to Poland, Hamburg has frequent services to Denmark, Cologne is good for fast trains to the Netherlands and Belgium (including Brussels for the Eurostar to London), and Frankfurt is the base for high-speed trains to Paris, Strasbourg and other parts of France.

ITINERARIES

One Week

Spend three days in and around Berlin, then marvel at Dresden's rebirth and Nuremberg's historical pedigree before wrapping up your journey with a couple of days in Munich.

Two Weeks

Start in Munich for some Bavarian joy followed by an Alpine side trip to the top of Germany – the Zugspitze – aboard a spectacular train-cable-car combo. Admire the sugary confection of Schloss Neuschwanstein before dipping into medieval times along the Romantic Road and being enchanted by Heidelberg. The Romantic Rhine delivers fine wine and ancient castles aplenty. Climb the grand cathedral in charismatic Cologne and finish it all in Berlin.

Essential Food & Drink

» **Sausage** *(Wurst)* More than 1500 types are made countrywide. From sweet, smoky and tiny *Nürnbergers* to crunchy *Thüringers* to that fast-food remedy for the munchies, the sliced and tomato-sauce-drowned *Currywurst*.

» **Mustard** *(Senf)* The perfect accompaniment to sausages, schnitzels and more, German mustards can be hot, laced with horseradish or rich with seeds. Or all three.

» **Bread** *(Brot)* Get Germans talking about bread and often their eyes will water as they describe their favourite type – usually hearty and whole-grained in infinite variations.

» **Cakes** *(Kuchen)* From the confectionery fantasy of the whipped-cream-laden Black Forest cake to apple-laden, crumb-covered delights, sweet tooths never feel ignored.

» **Beer** *(Bier)* For most Germans, intensely hoppy pilsner is the poison of choice, although wheat beer is popular in summer and regional varieties abound such as Kölsch in Cologne and Rauchbier in Bamberg.

» **Wine** *(Wein)* Winning competitions and critics' praises, German wine in the 21st century is leagues removed from that cloyingly sweet stuff of yore. The country's crisp rieslings are the world's best.

BERLIN

030 / POP 3.5 MILLION

You can't escape history in Berlin. You might be distracted by the trendy, gentrified streets, by the cool bars, by the galleries sprouting talent and pushing the envelope, but make no mistake – reminders of the German capital's past assault you while modernity sits around the corner. Norman Foster's Reichstag dome, Peter Eisenman's Holocaust Memorial and the iconic Brandenburg Gate are all contained within a few neighbouring blocks. Potsdamer Platz and its shiny Sony Center hosts Berlin's star-studded film festival each year, on the very site where only 25 years ago you could climb up a viewing platform in the West and peer over the Berlin Wall for a glimpse behind the Iron Curtain.

Renowned for its diversity and tolerance, alternative culture and night-owl stamina, the best thing about Berlin is the way it reinvents itself and isn't shackled by its mind numbing history. And the world knows this – a steady stream of Germans from other parts of the country and a league of global expatriates are flocking here to see what all the fuss is about.

Sights

Key sights like the Reichstag, the Brandenburger Tor, Checkpoint Charlie and Museumsinsel cluster in the historic city centre – Mitte. It also encompasses the mazelike historic Jewish quarter around Hackescher Markt, which now teems with fashionable boutiques, bars and restaurants. North of here, residential Prenzlauer Berg has a lively cafe and restaurant scene, while to the south loom the contemporary high-rises of Potsdamer Platz. Further south, gritty but cool Kreuzberg is party-central, as is socialist-flavoured Friedrichshain east across the Spree River. Western Berlin's hub is Charlottenburg, with great shopping and a swish royal palace.

HISTORIC MITTE

Reichstag HISTORIC BUILDING

(Map p432; www.bundestag.de; Platz der Republik 1; lift ride 8am-midnight, last entry 11pm; 100, S Bundestag, Hauptbahnhof) One of Berlin's most iconic buildings, the Reichstag has been burned, bombed, rebuilt, buttressed by the Berlin Wall, wrapped in fabric and eventually turned into the modern home of Germany's parliament, the Bundestag.

The grand old structure was designed by Paul Wallot in 1894 and given a total post-reunification makeover by Norman Foster. The famous architect preserved only its historical shell while adding the glistening **glass dome**, which can be reached by lift (reservations mandatory; see website for details. At

Berlin

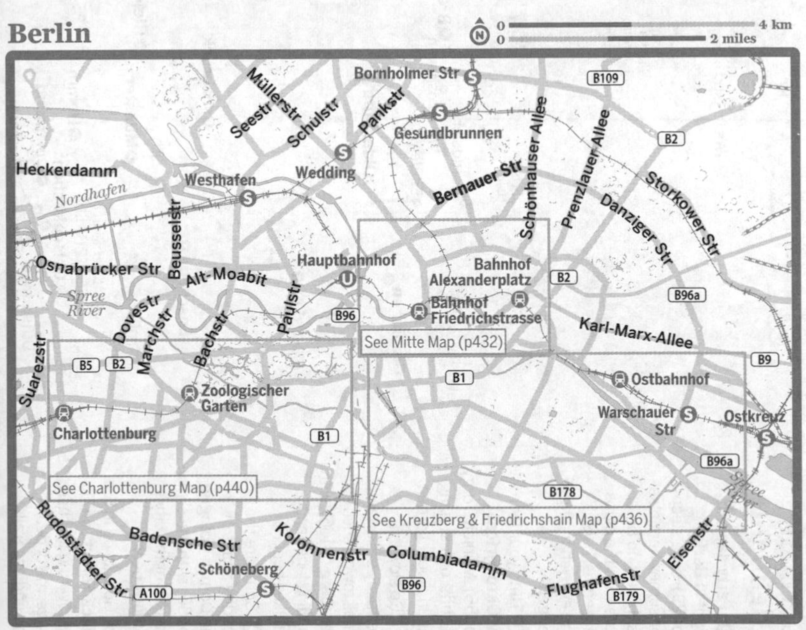

Germany Highlights

1 Party day and night in **Berlin** (p429); save sleep for somewhere else as there's no time here with the clubs, museums, bars and ever-changing zeitgeist

2 Time your journey for **Oktoberfest** (p455), Munich's orgy of suds, or just hang out in a beer garden

3 Go slow in Germany's alluring small towns, such as **Bamberg** (p466), with winding lanes and smoked beer (!)

4 Compare the soaring peaks of the Dom in **Cologne** (p466) with the slinky glasses of the city's famous beer

5 Go cuckoo in the **Black Forest** (p471), discovering its chilly crags, misty peaks and endless trails

6 Get into the swing of **Dresden** (p447), with a creative culture beyond the restorations

7 Cycle around one of the world's great harbours in **Hamburg** (p491), then follow the trail of the Beatles

8 Discover **Regensburg** (p467), Germany's Unesco-recognised ancient gem, with traces of Rome and Tuscany (and great sausages!) around every corner

Mitte

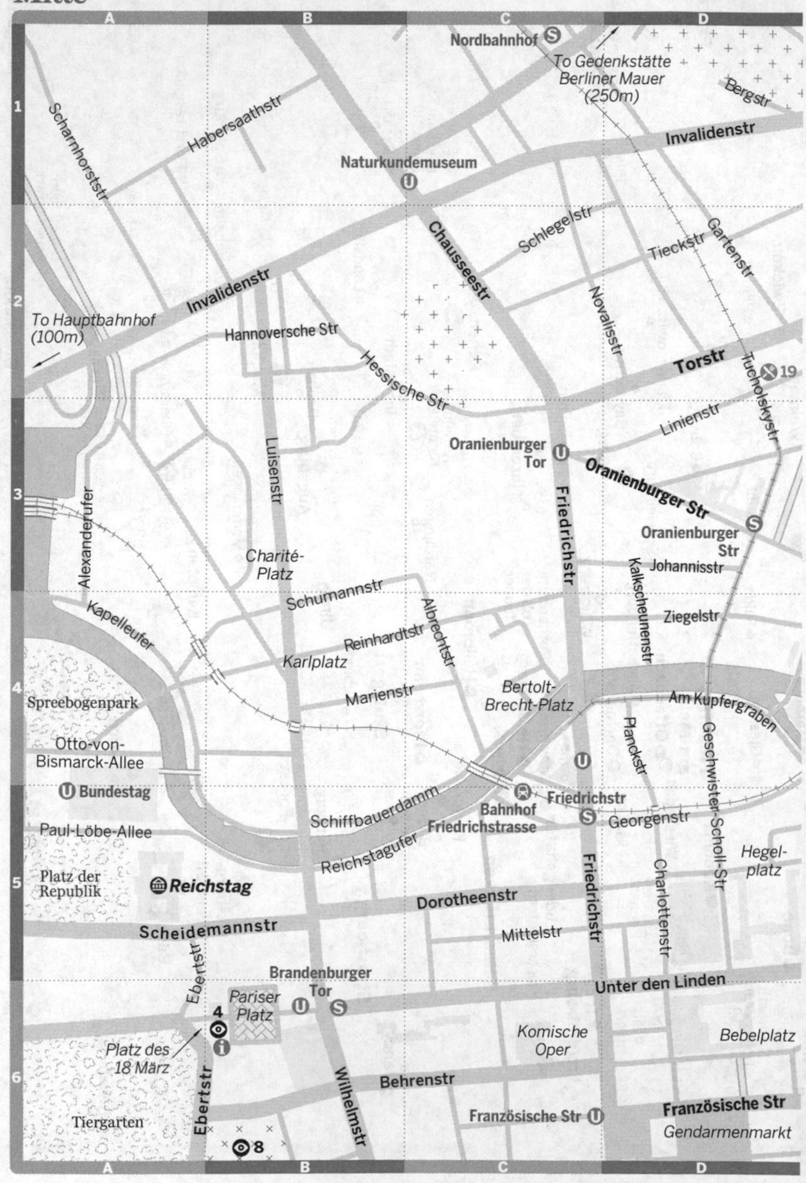

the top, pick up a free auto-activated audioguide and learn about the building, city landmarks and the workings of the parliament while following the ramp spiralling up and around the dome's mirror-clad central funnel.

Brandenburger Tor & Pariser Platz HISTORIC SITE

(Map p432; S Brandenburger Tor, Brandenburger Tor) A symbol of division during the Cold War, the 1791 Brandenburg Gate was modelled after Athens' Acropolis and now epitomises

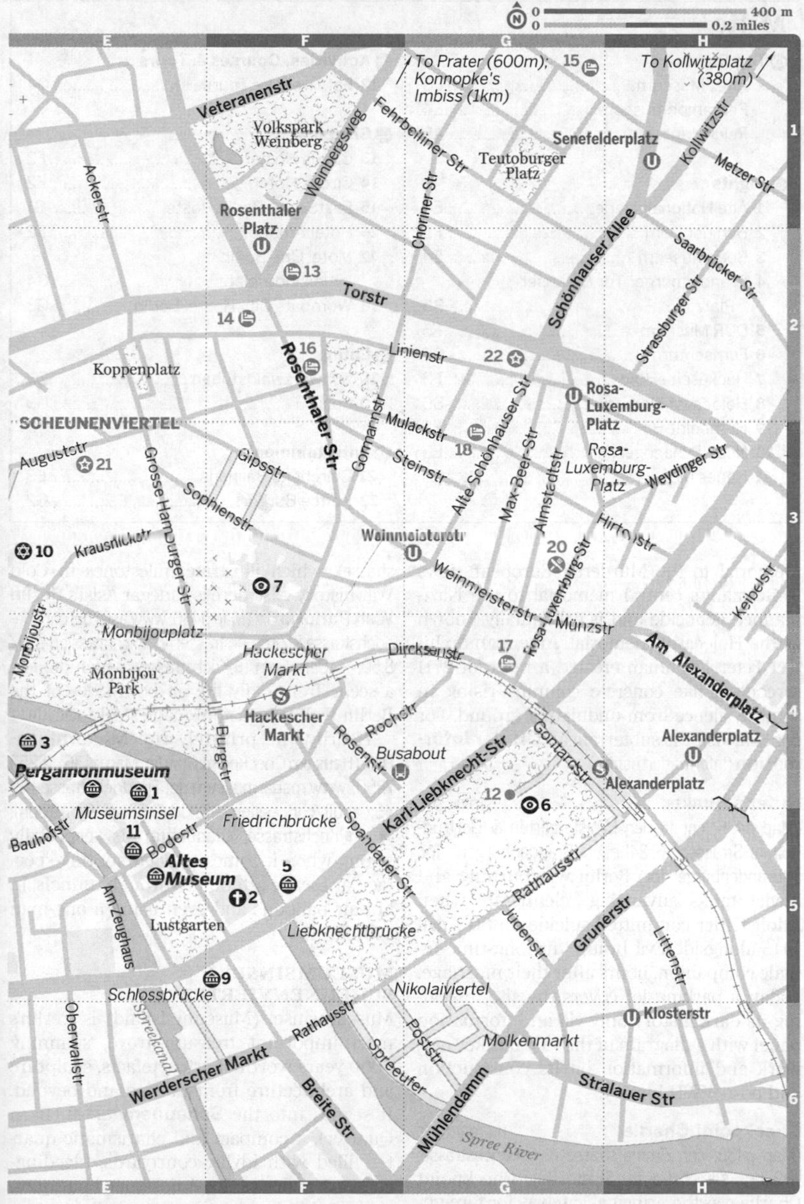

German reunification. It is crowned by the **Quadriga** – representing the winged goddess of victory piloting a horse-drawn chariot. The gate stands sentinel over **Pariser Platz**, a harmoniously proportioned square framed by banks, embassies and the storied Hotel Adlon.

FREE **Holocaust Memorial** MEMORIAL
(Map p432; ☎2639 4336; www.stiftung-denkmal.de; Cora-Berliner-Strasse 1; audioguide €3; ⏲field 24hr, information centre 10am-8pm Tue-Sun, last entry 7.15pm Apr-Sep, 6.15pm Oct-Mar; SBrandenburger Tor, ⓇBrandenburger Tor) The football-field-sized

Mitte

Top Sights

Altes Museum....E5
Pergamonmuseum....E4
Reichstag....A5

Sights

1 Alte Nationalgalerie....E4
2 Berliner Dom....F5
3 Bodemuseum....E4
4 Brandenburger Tor & Pariser Platz....B6
5 DDR Museum....F5
6 Fernsehturm....G4
7 Hackesche Höfe....F3
8 Holocaust Memorial....B6
9 Humboldt-Box....F5
10 Neue Synagoge....E3
11 Neues Museum....E5

Activities, Courses & Tours

12 Fat Tire Bike Tours....G4

Sleeping

13 Circus Hostel....F2
14 Circus Hotel....F2
15 EastSeven Berlin Hostel....G1
16 Hotel Amano....F2
17 Motel One Berlin-Alexanderplatz....G4
18 Wombats City Hostel Berlin....G3

Eating

19 Schwarzwaldstuben....D2
20 Susuru....G3

Entertainment

21 Clärchens Ballhaus....E3
22 Kaffee Burger....G2

Memorial to the Murdered European Jews is Germany's central memorial to the Nazi-planned genocide and is colloquially known as the Holocaust Memorial. American architect Peter Eisenman created a maze of 2711 sarcophagi-like concrete columns rising in sombre silence from undulating ground. For context, visit the subterranean **Ort der Information** (information centre).

Hitler's Bunker HISTORIC SITE
(Map p436; cnr In den Ministergärten & Gertrud-Kolmar-Strasse; 24hr; S Brandenburger Tor, Brandenburger Tor) Berlin was burning and Soviet tanks advancing relentlessly when Adolf Hitler committed suicide on 30 April 1945 alongside Eva Braun, his long-time female companion, hours after their marriage. Today, a parking lot covers the site, revealing its dark history only via an information panel with a diagram of the vast bunker network and information on its construction and post-WWII history.

Checkpoint Charlie HISTORIC SITE
(Map p436; cnr Zimmerstrasse & Friedrichstrasse; 24hr; S Kochstrasse, Stadtmitte) Checkpoint Charlie was the principal gateway for foreigners and diplomats between the two Berlins from 1961 to 1990. This symbol of the Cold War would now be nothing more than a tacky tourist trap were it not for the free **Checkpoint Gallery** and the **BlackBox Kalter Krieg** (Map p436; www.bfgg.de; Friedrichstrasse 47; adult/concession €5/3.50; 10am-6pm; M Kochstrasse), which illustrate milestones in Cold War history. Also here is Yadegar Asisi's **Berlin Wall Panorama** (Map p436; www.asisi.de; cnr Friedrichstrasse & Zimmerstrasse; adult/concession €10/8.50; 10am-6pm; S Kochstrasse), which depicts a scene from daily life on both sides of the Berlin Wall in a custom-made steel rotunda.

Nearby, the privately run **Mauermuseum** (Haus am Checkpoint Charlie; Map p436; 253 7250; www.mauermuseum.de; Friedrichstrasse 43-45; adult/concession €12.50/9.50; 9am-10pm; S Kochstrasse, Stadtmitte) is especially strong when it comes to documenting spectacular escape attempts (through tunnels, in hot-air balloons and even using a one-man submarine).

MUSEUMSINSEL & SCHEUNENVIERTEL

Museumsinsel (Museum Island) is Berlin's most important treasure trove, spanning 6000 years worth of art, artefacts, sculpture and architecture from Europe and beyond. It segues into the **Scheunenviertel** (Barn Quarter), a compact and charismatic quarter filled with idyllic courtyards, bleeding-edge art galleries, local designer boutiques, shabby-chic bars and even a belle époque ballroom. Since reunification, the Scheunenviertel has also reprised its historic role as Berlin's main Jewish quarter.

Museumsinsel MUSEUM
(2090 5577; www.smb.museum; day pass for all museums €14/7; 100, 200, S Hackescher Markt,

Friedrichstrasse) Spread across five grand museums built between 1830 and 1930, the complex takes up the entire northern half of the little Spree Island where Berlin's settlement began in the 13th century, and has been a Unesco World Heritage Site since 1999.

The island's top draw, the **Pergamonmuseum** (Map p432; Am Kupfergraben 5; adult/concession €8/4; ⏲10am-6pm Fri-Wed, to 9pm Thu; 🚌100, 🚆Hackescher Markt, Friedrichstrasse), has monumental architecture from ancient worlds, including the namesake Pergamon Altar and the stunning Babylonian Ishtar Gate.

The first repository to open on the island, the **Altes Museum** (Old Museum; Map p432; Am Lustgarten; adult/concession €8/4; ⏲10am-6pm Fri-Wed, to 8pm Thu; 🚌100, 200, 🚆Friedrichstrasse) opened in 1830 and presents Greek, Etruscan and Roman antiquities. Note the *Praying Boy* bronze sculpture, Roman silver vessels and portraits of Caesar and Cleopatra.

The show-stopper of the Egyptian collection at the **Neues Museum** (New Museum; Map p432; adult/concession €10/5; ⏲10am-6pm Sun-Wed, to 8pm Thu-Sat; 🚌100, 200, 🚆Hackescher Markt) is the 3300-year-old bust of Queen Nefertiti; the equally enthralling Museum of Pre- and Early History has treasure from Troy.

Famous for its European sculpture from the Middle Ages to the 18th century (Riemenschneider, Donatello, Pisano, etc), the **Bodemuseum** (Map p432; Monbijoubrücke; adult/concession €8/4; ⏲10am-6pm Tue, Wed & Fri-Sun, to 10pm Thu; 🚆Hackescher Markt) has a huge coin collection and Byzantine art.

The **Alte Nationalgalerie** (Old National Gallery; Map p432; Bodestrasse 1-3; adult/concession €8/4; ⏲10am-6pm Fri-Wed, to 10pm Thu; 🚌100, 200, 🚆Hackescher Markt) trains the focus on 19th-century European art.

Berliner Dom — CHURCH

(Berlin Cathedral; Map p432; ☎2026 9110; www.berlinerdom.de; Am Lustgarten; adult/concession €7/4; ⏲9am-8pm Mon-Sat, noon-8pm Sun Apr-Sep, to 7pm Oct-Mar; 🚌100, 200, 🚆Hackescher Markt) Pompous yet majestic, the Italian Renaissance-style former royal court church (1905) does triple duty as house of worship, museum and concert hall. Inside it's gilt to the hilt and outfitted with a lavish marble-and-onyx altar, a 7269-pipe Sauer organ and elaborate royal sarcophagi. Climb up the 267 steps to the gallery for glorious city views.

DDR Museum — MUSEUM

(GDR Museum; Map p432; ☎847 123 731; www.ddr-museum.de; Karl-Liebknecht-Strasse 1; adult/concession €6/4; ⏲10am-8pm Sun-Fri, to 10pm Sat; 🚌100, 200, 🚆Hackescher Markt) The touchy-feely GDR Museum does a delightful job at pulling back the iron curtain on an extinct society. You'll learn that kids were put through collective potty training and that nudist holidays were as commonplace as supply shortages and Stasi surveillance.

Humboldt-Box — MUSEUM

(Map p432; ☎018 0503 0707; www.humboldt-box.com; Schlossplatz; adult/concession €4/2.50; ⏲10am-8pm Apr-Oct, to 6pm Nov-Mar; 🚌100, 200, 🚆Alexanderplatz, Hackescher Markt) Come here for a sneak preview of the planned reconstruction of the Berlin City Palace, to be known as Humboldtforum, on Schlossplatz.

BERLIN IN...

One Day

Book ahead for an early time slot on the lift to the **Reichstag** dome, then snap a picture of the **Brandenburger Tor** before stumbling around the **Holocaust Memorial** and admiring the contemporary architecture of **Potsdamer Platz**. Ponder Cold War madness at **Checkpoint Charlie**, then head to **Museumsinsel** to admire Queen Nefertiti and the Pergamon Altar. Finish up with a night of mirth and gaiety around **Hackescher Markt**.

Two Days

Kick off day two coming to grips with what life was like in divided Berlin at the **Gedenkstätte Berliner Mauer**. Intensify the experience at the **DDR Museum** and on a walk along the **East Side Gallery**. Spend the afternoon soaking up the urban spirit of Kreuzberg with its sassy shops and street art, grab dinner along the canal, drinks around Kottbusser Tor and finish up with a night of clubbing at **Watergate** or **Berghain**.

Kreuzberg & Friedrichshain

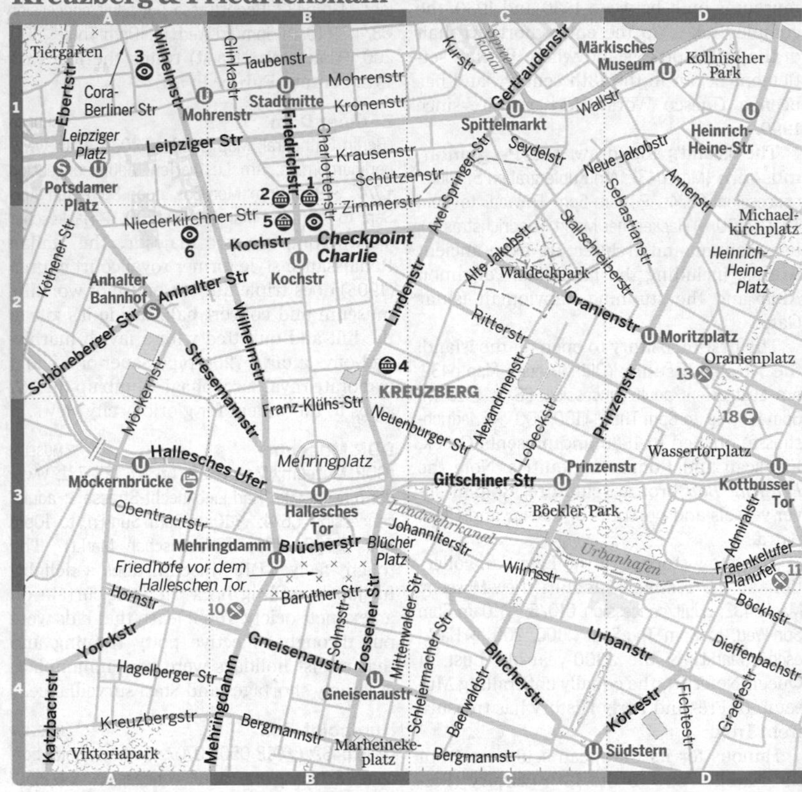

Kreuzberg & Friedrichshain

Top Sights

Checkpoint Charlie B2
East Side Gallery F2

Sights

1 Berlin Wall Panorama B1
2 BlackBox Kalter Krieg B1
3 Hitler's Bunker A1
4 Jüdisches Museum B2
5 Mauermuseum B2
6 Topographie des Terrors A2

Sleeping

7 Grand Hostel A3
8 Michelberger Hotel G2
9 Ostel Hostel F1

Eating

10 Curry 36 .... B4
11 Defne D3
12 Lemon Leaf H1
13 Max und Moritz D2

Drinking

14 Ankerklause E3
15 Freischwimmer G3
16 Hops & Barley H1
17 Madame Claude F3
18 Würgeengel D3

Entertainment

19 Berghain/Panorama Bar F1
20 Club der Visionäre G3
21 Watergate G3

Shopping

22 Türkenmarkt E3

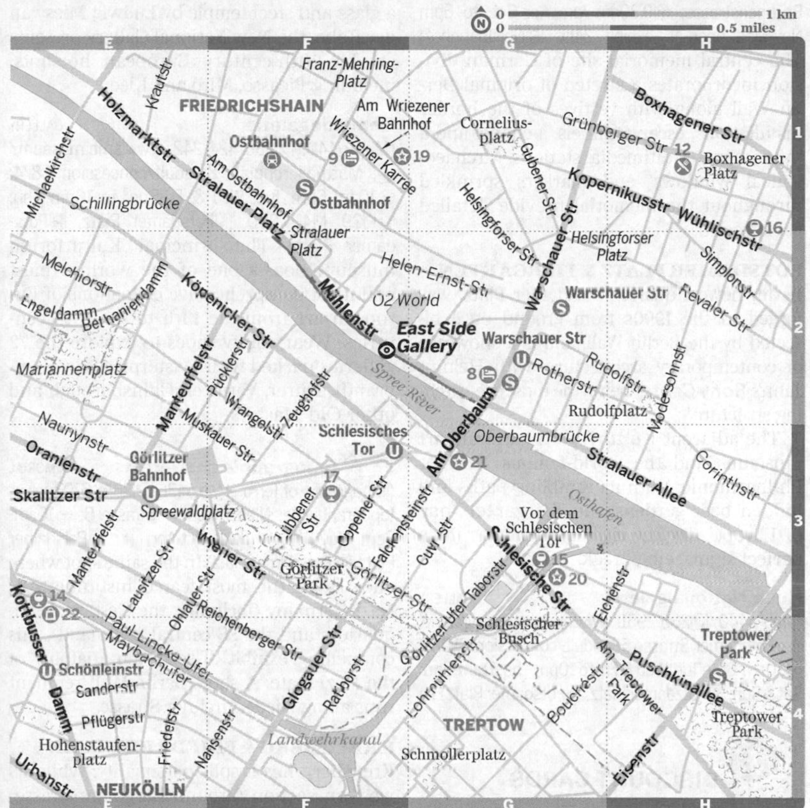

On display is a great city model and teasers from each future resident – the Ethnological Museum, the Museum of Asian Art and a library. Great views from the upstairs cafe terrace.

Fernsehturm LANDMARK

(Map p432; www.tv-turm.de; Panoramastrasse 1a; adult/child €12/7.50, VIP tickets €19.50/11.50; ⏲9am-midnight Mar-Oct, from 10am Nov-Feb; Ⓢ Alexanderplatz, Ⓡ Alexanderplatz) Germany's tallest structure, the needlelike TV Tower has been soaring 368m high since 1969 (including the antenna). Come early to beat the queue for the lift to the panoramic platform at 203m. The cafe makes one revolution in 30 minutes.

FREE **Hackesche Höfe** HISTORIC SITE

(Map p432; ☎2809 8010; www.hackesche-hoefe.com; Rosenthaler Strasse 40/41, Sophienstrasse 6; Ⓣ M1, Ⓡ Hackescher Markt) The Hackesche Höfe is the largest and most famous of the interlinked courtyard complexes in the Scheunenviertel. Take your time pottering around this tangle of cafes, galleries, boutiques and entertainment venues. Court I, festooned with art nouveau tiles, is the prettiest.

Neue Synagoge SYNAGOGUE

(Map p432; ☎8802 8300; www.cjudaicum.de; Oranienburger Strasse 28-30; adult/concession €3/2; ⏲10am-8pm Sun & Mon, to 6pm Tue-Thu, to 5pm Fri; Ⓢ Oranienburger Tor, Ⓡ Oranienburger Strasse) The sparkling gilded dome of the New Synagogue is the most visible symbol of Berlin's revitalised Jewish community. The 1866 original was Germany's largest synagogue but its modern incarnation is more a place of remembrance, called Centrum Judaicum.

FREE **Gedenkstätte Berliner Mauer** MEMORIAL

(☎467 986 666; www.berliner-mauer-gedenkstaette.de; Bernauer Strasse btwn Gartenstrasse &

Brunnenstrasse; ⏲9.30am-7pm Apr-Oct, to 6pm Nov-Mar, open-air exhibit 24hr; Ⓡ Nordbahnhof) The central memorial site of German division incorporates a stretch of original Berlin Wall along with vestiges of the border installations, escape tunnels, a chapel and a monument. Multimedia stations, 'archaeological windows' and markers sprinkled throughout the memorial provide detailed background.

POTSDAMER PLATZ & TIERGARTEN

Berlin newest quarter, Potsdamer Platz, was forged in the 1990s from ground once bisected by the Berlin Wall, and is a showcase of contemporary architecture, with Helmut Jahn's **Sony Center** being the most eye-catching structure.

The adjacent **Kulturforum** harbours art museums and the world-famous Berliner Philharmonie. With its rambling paths and hidden beer gardens, the **Tiergarten**, one of Europe's largest city parks, makes for a perfect sightseeing break.

Neue Nationalgalerie GALLERY

(Map p440; ☎266 2951; www.neue-nationalgalerie.de; Potsdamer Strasse 50; adult/concession €10/5; ⏲10am-6pm Tue, Wed & Fri, to 10pm Thu, 11am-6pm Sat & Sun; Ⓢ Potzdamer Platz, Ⓡ Potsdamer Platz) In a glass and steel temple by Ludwig Mies van der Rohe, the New National Gallery presents art by 20th-century European hotshots, including Picasso, Miró and Klee.

Gemäldegalerie GALLERY

(Map p440; ☎266 424 242; www.smb.museum/gg; Matthäikirchplatz 8; adult/concession €8/4; ⏲10am-6pm Tue, Wed & Fri-Sun, to 10pm Thu; 🚌M29, M41, 200, Ⓢ Potsdamer Platz, Ⓡ Potsdamer Platz) The principal Kulturforum museum boasts one of the world's finest and most comprehensive collections of European art from the 13th to the 18th centuries. Wear comfy shoes to explore the 72 galleries packed with masterpieces by Rembrandt, Dürer, Vermeer, Gainsborough and other Old Masters.

FREE **Topographie des Terrors** MEMORIAL

(Topography of Terror; Map p436; ☎2548 6703; www.topographie.de; Niederkirchner Strasse 8; ⏲10am-8pm May-Sep, to dusk Oct-Apr; 👪; Ⓢ Potsdamer Platz, Ⓡ Potsdamer Platz) In the same spot where once stood the most feared institutions of Nazi Germany (including the Gestapo headquarters and the SS central command), this compelling exhibit dissects the anatomy of the Nazi state. A short Berlin Wall remnant runs along Niederkirchner Strasse.

DISCOUNT CARDS

If you're on a budget, various ticket deals and passes can help you stretch your euros further.

Berlin Museum Pass (www.visitberlin.de; adult/concession €19/9.50) Buys admission to the permanent exhibits of about 60 museums for three consecutive days. Sold at city tourist offices and participating museums.

Berlin Welcome Card (www.visitberlin.de; 48/72hr €17.90/23.90, 48hr incl Potsdam & up to 3 children under 15yr €19.90, 72hr incl Museum Island €34) Unlimited public transport and up to 50% discount to 200 sights, attractions and tours for two, three or five days. Sold at tourist offices, U-Bahn and S-Bahn ticket vending machines and many hotels.

CityTourCard (www.citytourcard.com; 48hr/72hr/5 days €16.90/22.90/29.90) Similar to the Berlin Welcome Card, but a bit cheaper and with fewer discounts.

KREUZBERG & FRIEDRICHSHAIN

Kreuzberg has a split personality: while its western section (around Bergmannstrasse) has an upmarket, genteel air, eastern Kreuzberg (around Kottbusser Tor) is a multicultural mosaic and raucous nightlife hub. You'll find more after-dark action along with some Cold War relics (including Karl-Marx-Allee, East Berlin's showcase socialist boulevard) in student-flavoured Friedrichshain across the Spree.

FREE **East Side Gallery** HISTORIC SITE

(Map p436; www.eastsidegallery-berlin.de; Mühlenstrasse btwn Oberbaumbrücke & Ostbahnhof; ⏲24hr; Ⓢ Warschauer Strasse, Ⓡ Ostbahnhof, Warschauer Strasse) At 1.3km, the East Side Gallery is the longest surviving stretch of Berlin Wall, decorated with some 100 fine murals created by dozens of international artists in 1989.

Jüdisches Museum MUSEUM

(Jewish Museum; Map p436; ☎2599 3300; www.jmberlin.de; Lindenstrasse 9-14; adult/concession €5/2.50; ⏲10am-10pm Mon, to 8pm Tue-Sun, last admission 1hr before closing; Ⓢ Hallesches Tor,

Kochstrasse) The exhibit delineates the trials and triumphs of 2000 years of Jewish history in Germany, but it's Daniel Libeskind's landmark museum building that steals the show. Its zigzag outline symbolises a broken Star of David and represents a 3D metaphor for the tortured history of the Jewish people.

Stasimuseum MUSEUM
(☎553 6854; www.stasimuseum.de; Haus 1, Ruschestrasse 103; adult/concession €5/4; ⊙11am-6pm Mon-Fri, noon-6pm Sat & Sun; SMagdalenenstrasse) At this museum, in the former headquarters of East Germany's much-feared Ministry of State Security, you can marvel at cunningly low-tech surveillance devices (hidden in watering cans, neckties, even rocks), shudder at a claustrophobic prisoner transport van, and tour the obsessively neat offices of Stasi chief Erich Mielke.

Stasi Prison MEMORIAL SITE
(Gedenkstätte Hohenschönhausen; ☎9860 8230; www.stiftung-hsh.de; Genslerstrasse 66; tour adult/concession €5/2.50; ⊙tours hourly 11am-3pm Mon-Fri, 10am-4pm Sat & Sun, English tour 2.30pm daily; 🚊M5 to Freienwalder Strasse) Victims of Stasi persecution often ended up in this grim prison. Tours (some in English, call ahead) reveal the full extent of the terror and cruelty perpetrated upon thousands of suspected regime opponents, many utterly innocent. Take tram M5 from Alexanderplatz to Freienwalder Strasse, then walk 10 minutes along Freienwalder Strasse.

CHARLOTTENBURG

The glittering heart of West Berlin during the Cold War, Charlottenburg has been eclipsed by historic Mitte and other eastern districts since reunification, but is now trying hard to stage a comeback with major redevelopment around Zoo station. Its main artery is the 3.5km-long Kurfürstendamm (Ku'damm for short), Berlin's busiest shopping strip. The main tourist attraction is the nicely restored Charlottenburg palace.

Schloss Charlottenburg PALACE
(☎320 911; www.spsg.de; Spandauer Damm 20-24; day pass adult/concession €15/11; 🚌145, 309, SRichard-Wagner-Platz, Sophie-Charlotte-Platz) The grandest Prussian palace to survive in Berlin consists of the main building and three smaller structures scattered about the sprawling park. Each building charges separate admission; the day pass (*Tageskarte*) is good for one-day admission to every open building.

Charlottenburg palace started out as the summer residence of Sophie Charlotte, wife of King Friedrich I. The couple's baroque living quarters in the palace's oldest section, the **Altes Schloss** (☎320 911; www.spsg.de; Spandauer Damm; adult/concession €12/8; ⊙10am-6pm Tue-Sun Apr-Oct, to 5pm Tue-Sun Nov-Mar; 🚌145, 309, SRichard-Wagner-Platz, Sophie-Charlotte-Platz), are an extravaganza in stucco, brocade and overall opulence, although the private chambers of Frederick the Great in the **Neuer Flügel** (New Wing; ☎320 911; www.spsg.de; Spandauer Damm 20-24; adult/concession incl audioguide €6/5; ⊙10am-6pm Wed-Mon Apr-Oct, to 5pm Wed-Mon Nov-Mar; 🚌M45, 309, SRichard-Wagner-Platz, Sophie-Charlotte-Platz) – designed in flamboyant rococo style – are even more impressive.

Other buildings dotted around the park house 19th-century paintings (**Neuer Pavillon**), fancy porcelain (**Belvedere**) and dead royals (**Mausoleum**).

Kaiser-Wilhelm-Gedächtniskirche CHURCH
(Kaiser Wilhelm Memorial Church; Map p440; ☎218 5023; www.gedaechtniskirche.com; Breitscheidplatz; ⊙9am-7pm; SZoologischer Garten, Kurfürstendamm, 🚉Zoologischer Garten) The bombed-out tower of this landmark church serves as an antiwar memorial, standing quiet and dignified amid the roaring traffic. The adjacent octagonal hall of worship, added in 1961, has amazing midnight-blue glass walls and a giant 'floating' Jesus.

☞ Tours

Most of these English-language walking tours don't require reservations – just show up at any of the meeting points. Since meeting points can change quite suddenly, we have not listed them here. Keep an eye out for flyers at tourist offices or in hotel or hostel lobbies, or contact the companies directly.

ℹ BUS TOUR ON THE CHEAP

Get a crash course in 'Berlinology' by hopping on bus 100 or 200 at Zoologischer Garten or Alexanderplatz and letting the landmarks whoosh by for the price of a standard bus ticket (€2.40, day pass €6.50). Bus 100 goes via the Tiergarten, 200 via Potsdamer Platz. Without traffic and getting off, trips take about 30 minutes.

Charlottenburg

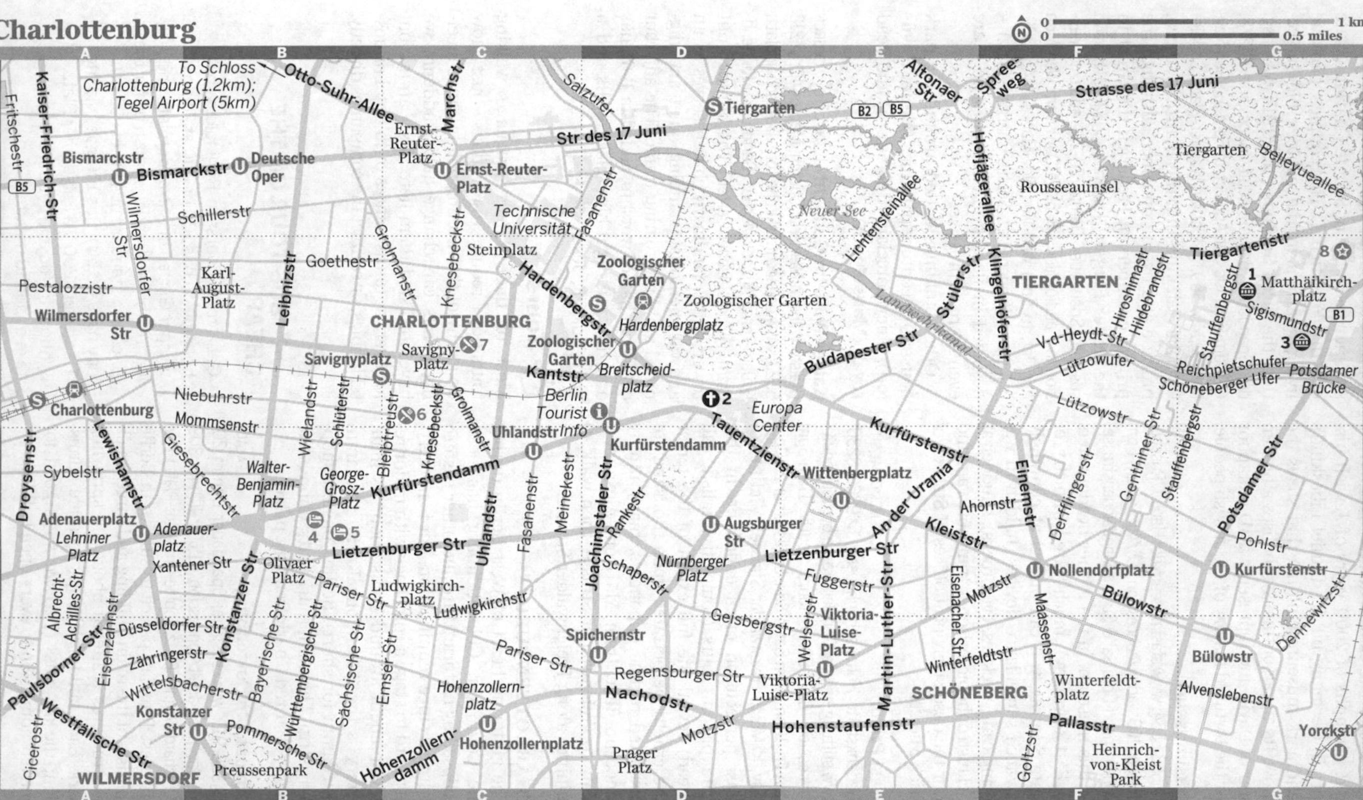

Charlottenburg

Sights

1 Gemäldegalerie G2
2 Kaiser-Wilhelm-Gedächtniskirche D2
3 Neue Nationalgalerie G2

Sleeping

4 Hotel Askanischer Hof B3
5 Hotel Bogota B3

Eating

6 Ali Baba C2
7 Dicke Wirtin C2

Entertainment

8 Berliner Philharmonie G2

Berlin Walks WALKING TOUR
(☎301 9194; www.berlinwalks.de; adult €12-15, concession €9-12) Berlin's longest-running English-language walking-tour company.

New Berlin Tours WALKING TOUR
(www.newberlintours.com; adult €12-15, concession €10-15) The pioneers of the donation-based 'free tour' and the pub crawl.

Fat Tire Bike Tours BICYCLE TOUR
(Map p432; ☎2404 7991; www.fattirebiketours.com/berlin; Panoramastrasse 1a; adult €24, concession €22; S Alexanderplatz, U Alexanderplatz) Explore the city on a guided bike tour.

Sleeping

MITTE & PRENZLAUER BERG

Circus Hostel HOSTEL €
(Map p432; ☎2000 3939; www.circus-hostel.de; Weinbergsweg 1a; dm €23-29, d from €80, with shared bathroom from €64, 2-/4-person apt €95/150; @ 📶; S Rosenthaler Platz) Clean, cheerfully painted rooms, abundant showers and competent, helpful staff are among factors that keep Circus at the top of the hostel heap. Welcome tech touches include laptop-sized in-room lockers with integrated electrical plug.

TOP CHOICE **EastSeven Berlin Hostel** HOSTEL €
(Map p432; ☎9362 2240; www.eastseven.de; Schwedter Strasse 7; dm €17-19, d €50; @ 📶; S Senefelderplatz) Friendly and fun, this small hostel is within strolling distance of hip hangouts and public transport. Cultural and language barriers melt quickly over a barbecue in the garden, dinners in the modern kitchen (with dishwasher!) or chilling in the retro lounge.

Circus Hotel HOTEL €€
(Map p432; ☎2000 3939; www.circus-berlin.de; Rosenthaler Strasse 1; d €80-110; @ 📶; S Rosenthaler Platz) At our favourite budget boutique hotel, none of the mod rooms are alike but all feature upbeat colours, thoughtful design details, sleek oak floors and quality beds. Unexpected perks include a well-stocked library and free iPod, netbook and DVD player rentals. Fabulous breakfast buffet to boot.

Hotel Amano HOTEL €€
(Map p432; ☎809 4150; www.amanogroup.de; Auguststrasse 43; d €80-160; P ❄ @ 📶; S Rosenthaler Platz) This hit with designer-hotel devotees has inviting public areas dressed in brushed-copper walls and cocoa-hued banquettes but rooms are rather twee. Great bar and summer rooftop terrace.

Motel One Berlin-Alexanderplatz HOTEL €
(Map p432; ☎2005 4080; www.motel-one.de; Dircksenstrasse 36; d from €69; P ❄ @ 📶; S Alexanderplatz, U Alexanderplatz) At this fast-growing budget designer chain, smallish rooms come with up-to-the-minute touches (flat-screen TVs, granite counters, massage showerheads, air-con) normally the staples of posher players. Check the website for other Motel One properties around town.

Wombats City Hostel Berlin HOSTEL €
(Map p432; ☎8471 0820; www.wombats-hostels.com; Alte Schönhauser Strasse 2; dm/d €25/70; @ 📶; S Rosa-Luxemburg-Platz) From backpack-sized in-room lockers to individual reading lamps and a guest kitchen with dishwasher, the attention to detail here is impressive. Spacious rooms with bathrooms are as de rigueur as freebie linen and a welcome drink.

KREUZBERG & FRIEDRICHSHAIN

Grand Hostel HOSTEL €
(Map p436; ☎209 5450; www.grandhostel-berlin.de; Tempelhofer Ufer 14; dm €12-15, d €58; @ 📶; S Möckernbrücke) Afternoon tea in the library? Check. Rooms with stucco-ornamented ceilings? Got 'em. Canal views? Yup. OK, the Grand Hostel may be no five-star hotel, but it is one of Berlin's most comfortable and atmospheric hostels, in an 1870s building.

Michelberger Hotel HOTEL €€
(Map p436; ☎2977 8590; www.michelbergerhotel.com; Warschauer Strasse 39; d €80-180; 📶; S Warschauer Strasse, U Warschauer Strasse) Rooms at this creative crash pad don't hide their factory pedigree but are comfortable and come in sizes suitable for lovebirds, families or rock

bands. The bar-reception-lobby often doubles as a party venue.

Ostel Hostel HOSTEL €
(Map p436; ☎2576 8660; www.ostel.eu; Wriezener Karree 5; dm/d/apt from €15/64/80; P@; SOstbahnhof) If you fancy a stay with a *Good Bye, Lenin!* vibe, overnight amid resuscitated socialist charm at this unusual hostel. Rates include linen, towels and wi-fi.

CHARLOTTENBURG

Hotel Askanischer Hof HOTEL €€
(Map p440; ☎881 8033; www.askanischer-hof.de; Kurfürstendamm 53; d €120-180; ; SAdenauerplatz) If you're after character and vintage flair, you'll find heaps of both at this 17-room jewel with a Roaring Twenties pedigree. It's often used for fashion shoots.

Hotel Bogota HOTEL €€
(Map p440; ☎881 5001; www.bogota.de; Schlüterstrasse 45; d €90-150, with shared bathroom €64-77; ; SUhlandstrasse) Bogota has charmed travellers with charisma and vintage flair since 1964. Room sizes and amenities vary greatly, so ask to see a few before settling in.

Eating

Berlin is a snacker's paradise, with Turkish (your best bet), Wurst (sausage), Greek, Italian and Chinese *Imbiss* stalls throughout the city. For a local snack, try a ubiquitous *Currywurst* (slivered sausage drizzled with ketchup and curry powder).

Excellent farmers' markets include those at **Kollwitzplatz** (Kollwitzstrasse; ⏲noon-7pm Thu, 9am-4pm Sat; SSenefelderplatz) in Prenzlauer Berg and the **Türkenmarkt** (Turkish Market; Map p436; www.tuerkenmarkt.de; Maybachufer; ⏲11am-6.30pm Tue & Fri; SSchönleinstrasse, Kottbusser Tor) in Kreuzberg.

MITTE & PRENZLAUER BERG

Oderquelle GERMAN €€
(☎4400 8080; Oderberger Strasse 27; mains €8-16; ⏲dinner; SEberswalder Strasse) It's always fun to pop by this woodsy resto and see what's inspired the chef today. Most likely, it'll be a delicious well-crafted German meal, perhaps with a slight Mediterranean nuance.

Susuru JAPANESE €
(Map p432; www.susuru.de; Rosa-Luxemburg-Strasse 17; mains €6.50-9; ; SRosa-Luxemburg-Platz) Go ye forth and slurp! *Susuru* is Japanese for slurping and, quite frankly, that's the best way to deal with the oodles of noodles at this neatly packaged soup parlour.

Schwarzwaldstuben GERMAN €€
(Map p432; ☎2809 8084; Tucholskystrasse 48; mains €7-14; ROranienburger Strasse) This send-up of the Black Forest complete with plastic pines and baseball-capped Bambi heads serves fabulous 'Maultaschen' (ravioli-like pasta), giant schnitzel and tasty Tannenzäpfle beer.

Lucky Leek VEGAN €€
(☎6640 8710; www.lucky-leek.de; Kollwitzstrasse 46; mains around €12; ⏲dinner Tue & Thu-Sun; ; SSenefelderplatz) At this popular vegan restaurant, quality ingredients, fearless flavour combinations, and enthusiastic staff should make believers of even the most dedicated carnivores.

Konnopke's Imbiss GERMAN €
(Schönhauser Allee 44a; sausages €1.30-1.70; ⏲10am-8pm Mon-Fri, noon-8pm Sat; SEberswalder Strasse) *Currywurst* and other eats from one of the city's cult sausage kitchens.

KREUZBERG & FRIEDRICHSHAIN

Max und Moritz GERMAN €€
(Map p436; ☎6951 5911; www.maxundmoritzberlin.de; Oranienstrasse 162; mains €9-15; ⏲dinner; SMoritzplatz) This ode-to-old-school brewpub has lured hungry diners and drinkers with sudsy home brews and granny-style Berlin fare since 1902.

Defne TURKISH €€
(Map p436; ☎8179 7111; www.defne-restaurant.de; Planufer 92c; mains €7.50-16; ⏲dinner; SKottbusser Tor, Schönleinstrasse) If you thought Turkish cuisine stopped at the doner kebab, canalside Defne will teach you otherwise. The appetiser platter alone elicits intense food cravings (fabulous walnut-chilli paste!).

Curry 36 GERMAN €
(Map p436; www.curry36.de; Mehringdamm 36; snacks €2-6; ⏲9am-4pm Mon-Sat, to 3pm Sun; SMehringdamm) Another top-ranked *Currywurst* purveyor.

Lemon Leaf ASIAN €
(Map p436; ☎2900 9471; Grünberger Strasse 69; mains €5-9; ⏲noon-midnight; ; SFrankfurter Tor) Cheap and cheerful, this place is always swarmed by local loyalists thanks to its light, inventive and fresh Indochina menu and homemade mango lassi.

CHARLOTTENBURG

Ali Baba ITALIAN €
(Map p440; ☎881 1350; www.alibaba-berlin.de; Bleibtreustrasse 45; dishes €3-9; ⏲11am-2am Sun-Thu, to 3am Fri & Sat; RSavignyplatz) Everybody

feels like family at this longstanding port of call, where the thin-crust pizza is delicious, the pasta piping hot and nothing costs more than €9.

Dicke Wirtin GERMAN €€
(Map p440; ☎312 4952; www.dicke-wirtin.de; Carmerstrasse 9; mains €6-15; ⊙noon-1am or later; ⓡSavignyplatz) Old Berlin charm oozes from every nook and cranny of this been-here-forever pub, which pours eight draught beers to go down with such hearty fare as roast pork, fried liver and breaded schnitzel.

Drinking

Kreuzberg and Friedrichshain are currently the edgiest bar-hopping grounds, with swanky Mitte and Charlottenburg being more suited for date nights than late nights.

Madame Claude PUB
(Map p436; Lübbener Strasse 19; ⊙from 7pm; ⓈSchlesisches Tor) Gravity is literally upended at Kreuzberg's David Lynch-ian booze burrow where the furniture dangles from the ceiling and the moulding's on the floor. Bands and DJs provide entertainment, but it rarely fills up before 11pm.

Hops & Barley PUB
(Map p436; ☎2936 7534; Wühlischstrasse 40; ⓈWarschauer Strasse, ⓡWarschauer Strasse) Conversation flows as freely as the unfiltered pilsner, malty *dunkel* (dark), fruity *weizen* (wheat) and potent cider produced right at this congenial Friedrichshain microbrewery in a former butchers shop.

Würgeengel BAR
(Map p436; www.wuergeengel.de; Dresdener Strasse 122; ⊙from 7pm; ⓈKottbusser Tor) For a swish night out, point the compass to this '50s-style Kreuzberg cocktail cave complete with glass ceiling, chandeliers and shiny black tables. Smoking allowed.

Prater BEER GARDEN
(☎448 5688; www.pratergarten.de; Kastanienallee 7-9; ⊙from noon Apr-Sep in good weather; ⓈEberswalder Strasse) Berlin's oldest beer garden (since 1837) has kept much of its traditional charm and is a fantastic place to hang and guzzle a cold one beneath the ancient chestnut trees (self-service).

Ankerklause PUB
(Map p436; ☎693 5649; www.ankerklause.de; Kottbusser Damm 104; ⊙from 4pm Mon, from 10am Tue-Sun; ⓈKottbusser Tor) This nautical kitsch tavern with an ass-kicking jukebox sets sail in an old harbour-master's shack and is great for quaffing and waving to the boats puttering along the canal.

Freischwimmer BEER GARDEN
(Map p436; ☎6107 4309; www.freischwimmer-berlin.de; Vor dem Schlesischen Tor 2a; mains €7-15; ⊙from 4pm Tue-Fri, from 10am Sat & Sun; ⓈSchlesisches Tor) In summertime, few places are more idyllic than this rustic ex-boathouse turned all-day, canal-side chill zone. Snacks and light meals available.

> **WANT MORE?**
>
> For in-depth information, reviews and recommendations at your fingertips, head to the Apple App Store to purchase Lonely Planet's *Berlin City Guide* iPhone app.
>
> Alternatively, head to **Lonely Planet** (www.lonelyplanet.com/germany/berlin) for planning advice, author recommendations, traveller reviews and insider tips.

Entertainment

With no curfew, Berlin is a notoriously late city, where bars stay packed from dusk to dawn and beyond and some clubs don't hit their stride until 6am. For listings consult *Zitty* (www.zitty.de) or *Tip* (www.tip.de).

Berghain/Panorama Bar CLUB
(Map p436; www.berghain.de; Wriezener Bahnhof; ⊙midnight Fri-Mon morning; ⓡOstbahnhof) Only world-class spinmasters heat up this hedonistic bass junkie hellhole inside a labyrinthine ex-power plant. The Berghain floor is gay-leaning and techno-heavy, while smaller Panorama Bar is a more mixed house-electro haunt. Best time: after 5am. Strict door, no cameras.

Kaffee Burger CLUB
(Map p432; ☎2804 6495; www.kaffeeburger.de; Torstrasse 60; ⓈRosa-Luxemburg-Platz) Nothing to do with either coffee or meat patties, this sweaty cult club with lovingly faded Commie-era decor is the famous home of the twice-monthly Russendisko, fun-for-all concerts and eclectic parties.

Clärchens Ballhaus CLUB
(Map p432; ☎282 9295; www.ballhaus.de; Auguststrasse 24; ⊙restaurant 12.30-11.30pm, dancing nightly; ⓣM1, ⓡOranienburger Strasse) Yesteryear

is now at this late, great 19th-century dance hall where groovers and grannies hoof it across the parquet without even a touch of irony. There's different sounds nightly – salsa to swing, tango to disco – and a live band on Saturday.

Club der Visionäre CLUB
(Map p436; ☎6951 8942; www.clubdervisionaere.com; Am Flutgraben 1; ⏲from 2pm Mon-Fri, from noon Sat & Sun; Ⓢ Schlesisches Tor, Ⓤ Treptower Park) It's drinks, pizza and fine electro at this summertime chill and party playground in an old canalside boatshed. Hang out beneath the weeping willows or stake out some turf on the upstairs deck.

Watergate CLUB
(Map p436; ☎6128 0394; www.water-gate.de; Falckensteinstrasse 49a; ⏲from 11pm Fri & Sat; Ⓢ Schlesisches Tor) Top DJs keep electro-hungry hipsters hot and sweaty till way past sunrise at this high-octane riverside club. Long queues, tight door on weekends.

Berliner Philharmonie CLASSICAL MUSIC
(Map p440; ☎2548 8999; www.berliner-philharmoniker.de; Herbert-von-Karajan-Strasse 1; 🚌200, Ⓢ Potsdamer Platz, Ⓤ Potsdamer Platz) This landmark concert hall is the home base of the world-famous Berliner Philharmoniker, currently led by Sir Simon Rattle.

GAY & LESBIAN BERLIN

Berlin's legendary liberalism has spawned one of the world's biggest and most diverse GLBT playgrounds.

The closest that Berlin comes to a 'gay village' is Schöneberg (Motzstrasse and Fuggerstrasse especially, get off U-Bahn station Nollendorfplatz), where the rainbow flag has proudly flown since the 1920s. The crowds skews older and leather. Current hipster central is Kreuzberg, where freewheeling party pens cluster along Mehringdamm and Oranienstrasse. Check Siegessäule (www.siegesaeule.de), the weekly freebie 'bible' to all things gay and lesbian in town, for the latest happenings.

Mann-O-Meter (☎216 8008; www.mann-o-meter.de; Bülowstrasse 106; ⏲5-10pm Tue-Fri, 4-8pm Sat & Sun; Ⓢ Nollendorfplatz) is a one-stop information centre that also operates a hotline to report attacks on gays.

Information

Berlin Tourismus (☎2500 2333; http://visitberlin.de; ⏲call centre 9am-7pm Mon-Fri, 10am-5pm Sat, 10am-2pm Sun) Hauptbahnhof (Europaplatz north exit; ⏲8am-10pm, extended hours Apr-Oct; Ⓤ Hauptbahnhof, Ⓢ Hauptbahnhof); Brandenburger Tor (Map p432; Brandenburger Tor, Pariser Platz; ⏲9.30am-7pm daily; Ⓢ Brandenburger Tor, Ⓤ Brandenburger Tor); Kurfürstendamm (Map p440; Neues Kranzler Eck, Kurfürstendamm 22; ⏲9.30am-8pm Mon-Sat, to 6pm Sun, extended hours Apr-Oct; Ⓢ Kurfürstendamm) Berlin's tourist board operates three walk-in offices and a call centre whose multilingual staff can field general questions and make hotel and ticket bookings.

Getting There & Away

Air

Berlin's new international airport, Berlin Brandenburg Airport has been taking shape about 24km southeast of the city centre since 2006. Construction problems and safety concerns have repeatedly delayed the original 2011 opening; at press time no new date had been announced. In the meantime, international airlines and such discount carriers as Ryanair, easyJet, Air Berlin and Germanwings fly into Berlin's two other airports.

Tegel Airport (TXL; ☎018 0500 0186; www.berlin-airport.de) About 8km northwest of the city centre.

Schönefeld Airport (SXF; ☎018 0500 0186; www.berlin-airport.de) About 22km southeast.

Bus

ZOB (☎3010 0175; www.iob-berlin.de; Masurenallee 4-6; Ⓢ Kaiserdamm, Ⓤ Messe Nord/ICC) Berlin's 'central' bus station is in deepest western Berlin, next to the trade-fair grounds, about 4km west of Zoo Station.

BerlinLinienBus (☎861 9331; www.berlinlinienbus.de) The main operator; buy tickets online or at the ZOB Reisebüro ticket office at the bus station.

Deutsche Touring/Eurolines (☎069-790 3501; www.touring.de) Also has many domestic and international departures.

Busabout (Map p432; www.busabout.com) Backpacker-oriented hop-on, hop-off service stops at the Citystay Hostel in Mitte.

Train

Berlin is well connected by train to other German and European cities, including Prague, Warsaw and Amsterdam. All long-distance trains converge at the **Hauptbahnhof** (www.berlin-hauptbahnhof.de; Europaplatz, Washingtonplatz; Ⓢ Hauptbahnhof, Ⓤ Hauptbahnhof).

The left-luggage office (€5 per piece per 24 hours) is behind the ReiseBank currency

PUBLIC TRANSPORT TICKETS

Berlin's public transport is divided into three tariff zones – AB, BC and ABC. Unless venturing to Potsdam, Sachsenhausen or Schönefeld Airport, you'll only need an AB ticket.

TICKET	AB (€)	BC (€)	ABC (€)
Single	2.40	2.80	3.10
Day pass	6.50	6.80	7
Group day pass (up to 5 people)	15.50	15.80	16
7-day pass	28	28.90	34.60

exchange on the first upper level, opposite the Reisezentrum. Self-service lockers are hidden on the lower level of the parking garage, accessible near the Kaiser's supermarket on the first lower floor.

Getting Around

To/From the Airport

TEGEL

Bus The TXL bus connects Tegel with Alexanderplatz (40 minutes) every 10 minutes. For Kurfürstendamm and Zoo Station, take bus X9 (20 minutes, €2.40).

U-Bahn Tegel is not directly served by the U-Bahn, but both bus 109 and X9 stop at Jakob-Kaiser-Platz (U7), the station closest to the airport. Tickets cost €2.40.

SCHÖNEFELD

Airport-Express Regular Deutsche Bahn regional trains, identified as RE7 and RB14 in timetables, make the 30-minute trip to central Berlin twice hourly.

S-Bahn S9 runs every 20 minutes and is slower but useful if you're headed to Friedrichshain or Prenzlauer Berg. For the Messe (trade-fair grounds), take the S45 to Südkreuz and change to the S41.

Trains stop about 400m from the airport terminals. Free shuttle buses run every 10 minutes; walking takes about five minutes. You need a transport ticket covering zones ABC (€3.10).

Public Transport

One type of ticket is valid on all public transport, including the U-Bahn, buses, trams and ferries run by **BVG** (☎194 49; www.bvg.de), as well as the S-Bahn and regional RE, SE and RB trains operated by **Deutsche Bahn** (www.bahn.de).

Buy tickets from vending machines (English instructions available) in U-Bahn or S-Bahn stations, or aboard trams, from bus drivers and at station offices and news kiosks sporting the yellow BVG logo.

Stamp all tickets, except those bought from bus drivers and aboard trams, before boarding or risk a €40 on-the-spot fine if caught without a validated ticket.

Services operate from 4am until just after midnight on weekdays, with half-hourly *Nachtbus* (night bus) services in between. At weekends, the U-Bahn and S-Bahn run all night long (except the U4 and U55).

Taxi

You can order a **taxi** (☎202 020, 443 311) by phone, flag one down or pick one up at a rank. Flag fall is €3.20, then it's €1.65 per kilometre up to 7km and €1.28 for each kilometre after that. Up to four passengers travel for the price of one. Tip about 10%. There is no surcharge for night trips. Short trips of 2km cost €4 but only if you flag down a cab and request a *Kurzstrecke*.

AROUND BERLIN

Potsdam

☎0331 / POP 150,000

Endowed with ornate palaces and manicured parks, Potsdam was the brainchild of 18th-century Prussian king Friedrich II (Frederick the Great) and the most popular day trip from Berlin. In August 1945 the town made history when the Allies hammered out Germany's postwar fate at the Potsdam Conference.

Sights

Park Sanssouci GARDEN

(dawn-dusk) Unesco-lauded Park Sanssouci is the heart of Potsdam and what everyone comes to see. Its most celebrated palace, **Schloss Sanssouci** (www.spsg.de; adult/concession incl audioguide Apr-Oct €12/8, Nov-Mar €8/5; 10am-6pm Tue-Sun Apr-Oct, to 5pm Nov-Mar; 695, 606), was Frederick the Great's favourite retreat and is a rococo extravaganza inside and out. Admission is by timed ticket; come early or, for guaranteed entry, join the city tour offered by the Potsdam tourist office.

Dominating the park's western end, the vast **Neues Palais** (New Palace; ☎969 4200; Am Neuen Palais; adult/concession €6/5; ⏰10am-6pm Wed-Mon Apr-Oct, to 5pm Nov-Mar; 🚌695 or 605 to Neues Palais, 🚆to Potsdam, Park Sanssouci Bahnhof) was built for representational purposes and only used as a residence by the last German Kaiser, Wilhelm II, until 1918. Ceiling frescos, gilded ornamentation and fanciful wall coverings characterise the interior.

A standout among the park's many other pearls is the **Chinesisches Haus** (Am Grünen Gitter; admission €2; ⏰10am-6pm Tue-Sun May-Oct; 🚌605 to Schloss Charlottenhof, 606 or 695 to Schloss Sanssouci, 🚋91 to Schloss Charlottenhof), a circular pavilion ringed by gilded columns, palm trees and figures of Chinese musicians and animals. It houses a porcelain collection.

Schloss Cecilienhof PALACE
(☎969 4244; www.spsg.de; Im Neuen Garten 11; tours adult/concession €6/5; ⏰10am-6pm Tue-Sun Apr-Oct, to 5pm Nov-Mar; 🚌603) This rustic English-style country palace was completed in 1917 for crown prince Wilhelm and his wife Cecilie but is most famous for hosting the 1945 Potsdam Conference where Stalin, Truman and Churchill (later Atlee) laid the groundwork for Germany's postwar fate. The conference room with its giant round table looks as though the delegates just left.

Altstadt HISTORIC AREA
Potsdam's historic town centre is east of Park Sanssouci. A triumphal arch – the baroque Brandenburger Tor (Brandenburg Gate) – opens up onto pedestrianised **Brandenburger Strasse**, the main shopping drag. Follow it to the pretty **Holländisches Viertel** (Dutch Quarter), a cluster of gabled red-brick houses filled with galleries, boutiques and restaurants.

Tours

Potsdam Sanssouci Tour GUIDED TOUR
(tours with/without Sanssouci Palace €27/16; ⏰Tue-Sun Apr-Oct) The 3½-hour Potsdam Sanssouci Tour, which guarantees admission to Schloss Sanssouci, runs in English and German and leaves at 11.10am from the Hauptbahnhof tourist office.

Schiffahrt in Potsdam BOAT TOUR
(☎275 9210; www.schiffahrt-in-potsdam.de; Lange Brücke 6; ⏰9.45am-7pm Apr-Oct) The most popular boat tour is the palace cruise (*Schlösserrundfahrt*; €13).

Information

Potsdam Tourist Office – Hauptbahnhof (☎2755 8899; www.potsdamtourismus.com; inside the main train station; ⏰9.30am-8pm Mon-Sat, 10am-6pm Sun)

Potsdam Tourist Office – Brandenburger Tor (☎275 580; www.potsdamtourismus.com; Brandenburger Strasse 3; ⏰9.30am-6pm Mon-Sat, to 4pm Sun Apr-Oct, 10am-6pm Mon-Fri, to 4pm Sat & Sun Nov-Mar; 🚆Hauptbahnhof)

Sanssouci Visitors Centre (☎969 4200; www.spsg.de; An der Orangerie 1, at the Historic Windmill; ⏰8.30am-6pm Apr-Oct, to 5pm Nov-Mar)

Getting There & Away

Regional trains leaving from Berlin-Hauptbahnhof and Zoologischer Garten take about 30 minutes to reach Potsdam Hauptbahnhof; some continue on to Potsdam-Charlottenhof and Potsdam-Sanssouci, which are actually closer to the park. The S7 from central Berlin makes the trip in about 40 minutes. You'll need an ABC ticket (€3.10) for either service.

Sachsenhausen Concentration Camp

In 1936 the Nazis opened a *Konzentrationslager* (concentration camp) for men in a disused brewery in Sachsenhausen, 35km north of Berlin. By 1945 about 200,000 prisoners had passed through the gates – cynically labelled, as at Auschwitz in Poland, *Arbeit Macht Frei* (Work Sets You Free). Tens of thousands died from hunger, exhaustion, illness, medical experiments and executions.

After the war the Soviets imprisoned some 60,000 German POWs in what was now Speziallager No 7 (Special Camp No 7); about 12,000 died of malnutrition and disease before it was dissolved in 1950.

Once you get to the **Sachsenhausen Memorial and Museum** (☎03301-200 200; www.stiftung-bg.de; admission free; ⏰8.30am-6pm mid-Mar–mid-Oct, to 4pm mid-Oct–mid-Mar), pick up a leaflet or, better yet, an audioguide at the visitor centre, to get a better grasp of this huge site.

From Berlin take the frequent S1 train to Oranienburg station (€3.10, 45 minutes), from where it's a 2km signposted walk to the camp.

SAXONY

Saxony has everything you could want in a holiday: storybook castles peering down from craggy mountaintops, cobbled marketplaces serenaded by mighty churches, exuberant palaces, nostalgic steam trains and indigenous Sorb folk traditions. Bach, Canaletto, Goethe and Wagner are among those who have shaped the region's cultural landscape.

Dresden and Leipzig grab top billing. The former became synonymous with the devastation of WWII, but has since resurrected its baroque heritage. And it was Leipzig that sparked the 'peaceful revolution' of 1989 that brought down the Berlin Wall and led to the momentous reunification of Germany.

Dresden

☎0351 / POP 512,000

Proof that there is life after death, Dresden has become one of Germany's most visited cities, and for good reason. Restorations have returned its historic core to its 18th-century heyday when it was famous throughout Europe as 'Florence on the Elbe'. Scores of Italian artists, musicians, actors and master craftsmen flocked to the court of Augustus the Strong, bestowing countless masterpieces upon the city.

The devastating bombing raids in 1945 levelled most of these treasures. But Dresden is a survivor and many of the most important landmarks have since been rebuilt, including the elegant Frauenkirche. Today, there's a constantly evolving arts and cultural scene and zinging pub and nightlife quarters, especially in the Outer Neustadt.

Sights

Dresden straddles the Elbe River, with the attraction-studded Altstadt (Old Town) in the south and the Neustadt (New Town) pub and student quarter to the north.

FREE Frauenkirche CHURCH

(www.frauenkirche-dresden.de; Neumarkt; audioguide €2.50; ⊙usually 10am-noon & 1-6pm) One of Dresden's most iconic sites, the 18th-century Frauenkirche has literally risen from the city's ashes. The original graced its skyline for two centuries before collapsing two days after the devastating February 1945 bombing. The East Germans left the rubble as a war memorial, but after reunification a grassroots movement helped raise the funds to rebuild the landmark. It was consecrated in November 2005.

Climb the **dome** (Neumarkt; adult/concession €8/5; ⊙10am-6pm Mon-Sat, 12.30-6pm Sun Mar-Oct, to 4pm Nov-Feb) for sweeping city views and stop by the **Frauenkirche Visitors Centre** (☎6560 6701; Weisse Gasse 8; movie €2; ⊙10am-7pm Mon-Fri, 10am-6pm Sat) to watch an introductory movie or find out about tours, concerts and services.

Residenzschloss PALACE

(☎4914 2000; www.skd.museum; Schlossplatz; adult/concession €10/7.50; ⊙10am-6pm Wed-Mon) Dresden's fortresslike Renaissance city palace shelters four precious collections, including the unmissable **Grünes Gewölbe** (Green Vault), a real-life 'Aladdin's Cave' of precious objects wrought from gold, ivory, silver, diamonds and jewels. There's so much of it, two separate 'treasure chambers' – the Historisches Grünes Gewölbe and the Neues Grünes Gewölbe – are needed to display everything.

Other collections display prints and drawings, coins, armour and Ottoman art.

Tickets are good for all collections *except* for the hugely popular Historisches Grünes Gewölbe, which charges a separate €10 (free under 16). Since only 40% of the timed tickets are sold at the palace for same-day admission, we highly recommend that you get yours in advance – either online or at the office – to avoid disappointment.

Zwinger MUSEUM

(☎4914 2000; www.skd.museum; Theaterplatz 1; adult/concession €10/7.50; ⊙10am-6pm Tue-Sun) This ravishing baroque palace now houses several exhibits, the most important being the **Gemäldegalerie Alte Meister** – a roll call of Old Masters including Botticelli, Titian, Rubens, Vermeer and Dürer. Tickets are also good for the collections of porcelain

DRESDEN-CARD

The Dresden-Card, sold at the tourist offices, provides free public transportation as well as sweeping sightseeing discounts. Various schemes are available, including a one-day version (single/family €10/12.50), a two-day version (€25/46) and a three-day regional version (€48/68).

and of ancient scientific instruments, globes and timepieces.

Semperoper HISTORIC BUILDING

(☎320 7360; www.semperoper-erleben.de; Theaterplatz 2; tour adult/concession €8/4; ⊙varies) One of Germany's most famous opera houses is a stunner inside and out. The original Semperoper burned down a mere three decades after its 1841 inauguration. Buy tour tickets online to skip the queue.

Albertinum GALLERY

(www.skd.museum; enter from Brühlsche Terrasse or Georg-Treu-Platz 2; adult/concession €8/6; ⊙10am-6pm; P) The gorgeously converted Renaissance-era arsenal now houses the **Galerie Neue Meister** (New Masters Gallery), a glorious showcase of paintings from the Romantic period to today (Claude Monet to Gerhard Richter).

Tours

Grosse Stadtrundfahrt BUS TOUR

(☎899 5650; www.stadtrundfahrt.com; day pass adult/concession €20/18; ⊙9.30am-5pm) Narrated hop-on, hop-off tour.

Sleeping

Hostel Mondpalast HOSTEL €

(☎563 4050; www.mondpalast.de; Louisenstrasse 77; dm €14-19.50, d €48-56, linen €2, breakfast €6.50; @) This popular and convivial hostel is smack dab in the Neustadt pub quarter and has dorms decorated with spacey zodiac themes. Kudos for the bike rentals and large kitchen.

Hotel Martha Dresden HOTEL €€

(☎817 60; www.hotel-martha-hospiz.de; Nieritzstrasse 11; d €113-120; 📶) Fifty rooms with big windows, wooden floors and Biedermeier-inspired furnishings combine with an attractive winter garden to make a pleasant place to hang your hat.

Pension am Zwinger PENSION €€

(☎8990 0100; www.pension-zwinger.de; Ostra-Allee 27; d €80-90; P@📶) Self-caterers, families and space-cravers will appreciate these bright, functional but stylish apartment-style rooms with basic kitchens. Check-in is at nearby Maxstrasse 3.

Ibis Budget HOTEL €

(☎8339 3820; www.etaphotel.com; Wilsdruffer Strasse 25; r from €39; ❄@📶) The ship cabin-sized rooms have few frills but the key sights are just a hop, skip and jump away. Inside the Altmarkt-Galerie shopping mall.

Eating & Drinking

The Neustadt has oodles of cafes and restaurants, especially along Königstrasse and

WORTH A TRIP

MEISSEN

Straddling the Elbe around 25km upstream from Dresden, Meissen is the cradle of European porcelain, which was first cooked up in 1710 in its imposing castle, the **Albrechtsburg** (☎352 147 070; www.albrechtsburg-meissen.de; Domplatz 1; adult/concession incl audioguide €8/4; ⊙10am-6pm Mar-Oct, 10am-5pm Nov-Feb). An exhibit on the second floor chronicles how it all began. The highlight of the adjacent **cathedral** (☎452 490; adult/child €4/2; ⊙10am-6pm Mar-Oct, to 4pm Nov-Feb) is an altarpiece by Lucas Cranach the Elder. Both squat atop a ridge overlooking Meissen's cute Altstadt (Old Town).

Since 1863, porcelain production has taken place in a custom-built factory, about 1km south of the Altstadt. Next to it is the **Erlebniswelt Haus Meissen** (☎468 208; www.meissen.com; Talstrasse 9; adult/child €9/4.50; ⊙9am-6pm May-Oct, 9am-5pm Nov-Apr), a popular and unmissable porcelain museum where you can witness the astonishing artistry and craftsmanship that makes Meissen porcelain unique.

For details and further information about the town, stop by the **tourist office** (☎419 40; www.touristinfo-meissen.de; Markt 3; ⊙10am-6pm Mon-Fri, 10am-4pm Sat & Sun Apr-Oct, 10am-5pm Mon-Fri, 10am-3pm Sat Nov, Dec, Feb & Mar).

Half-hourly S1 trains run to Meissen from Dresden's Hauptbahnhof and Neustadt train stations (€5.80, 40 minutes). For the Erlebniswelt, get off at Meissen-Triebischtal. Steam boats operated by **Sächsische Dampfschiffahrt** (☎0331-452 139; www.saechsische-dampfschiffahrt.de; one-way/return €14/19.50; ⊙May-Sep) depart from the Terrassenufer in Dresden. Consider going one way by boat and the other by train.

the streets north of Albertplatz. The latter is also the centre of Dresden's nightlife. Altstadt restaurants are more tourist-geared and pricier.

Raskolnikoff CAFE, BAR €€
(☎804 5706; www.raskolnikoff.de; Böhmische Strasse 34; mains €5-13; ⌚9am-2am) At artsy-boho Raskolnikoff the menu is sorted by compass direction (borscht to fish soup and steak) and the beer is from a local brewer. It also rents eight basic but handsomely done-up rooms (doubles €52 to €70).

PlanWirtschaft INTERNATIONAL €€
(☎801 3187; Louisenstrasse 20; mains €7-14; ⌚9am-1am) The winning formula at this long-time favourite: fresh, local ingredients, an inventive menu and smiley staff. Sit in the woodsy cafe, the romantic garden or the cosy brick cellar.

Cafe Alte Meister INTERNATIONAL €€
(☎481 0426; www.altemeister.net; Theaterplatz 1a; mains €7-15; ⌚10am-1am) If you've worked up an appetite from museum-hopping, retreat to this elegant filling station for coffee and cake or a light lunch.

Grand Café CAKES, SAXON €€
(☎496 2444; www.coselpalais-dresden.de; An der Frauenkirche 12; mains €10-15; ⌚10am-midnight) The gold-trimmed Coselpalais is a stylish refuelling stop after climbing up the Frauenkirche dome.

Information

Dresden Information (☎5016 0160; www.dresden-tourist.de) Hauptbahnhof (Schlossstrasse 23; ⌚10am-7pm Mon-Fri, 10am-6pm Sat, 10am-3pm Sun, reduced hours Jan-Mar); Frauenkirche (Schlossstrasse 23; ⌚10am-7pm Mon-Fri, 10am-6pm Sat, 10am-3pm Sun, reduced hours Jan-Mar)

Getting There & Around

Dresden airport is about 9km north of the city centre and linked by S2 train several times hourly (€2).

There's direct train service to such major cities as Leipzig (€30, 70 minutes) and Berlin (€38, two hours). The S1 train runs to Meissen (€5.80, 40 minutes). Most trains stop at Dresden-Hauptbahnhof and at Dresden-Neustadt north of the river.

Buses and trams are run by **Dresdner Verkehrsbetriebe** (DVB; ☎857 1011). Single tickets cost €2, a day pass €5; both are available from vending machines at stops or aboard trams.

Leipzig

☎0341 / POP 532,000

Bustling Leizpig is an important business and transport centre, a trade-fair mecca, and – aside from Berlin – the most dynamic city in eastern Germany. Relatively low rent and throbbing nightlife are making it an attractive place for students and young professionals.

Leipzig also has some of the finest classical music and opera in the country alongside flourishing art and literary scenes. It was once home to Bach, Wagner and Mendelssohn, as well as Goethe, who set a key scene of *Faust* in the cellar of his favourite watering hole. More recently, Leipzig earned the sobriquet *Stadt der Helden* (City of Heroes) for its leading role in the 1989 democratic revolution.

Sights

Don't rush from sight to sight – wandering around Leipzig is a pleasure in itself, with many of the blocks around the central Markt criss-crossed by historic shopping arcades, including the classic **Mädlerpassage**.

TOP CHOICE **Nikolaikirche** CHURCH
(Church of St Nicholas; www.nikolaikirche-leipzig.de; Nikolaikirchhof 3; ⌚10am-6pm Mon-Sat & during services 9.30am, 11.15am & 5pm Sun) The Church of St Nicholas sports a striking neoclassical interior with palmlike pillars and cream-coloured pews. It played a key role in the nonviolent movement that led to the collapse of East Germany by hosting weekly 'peace prayers' as early as 1982.

FREE **Zeitgeschichtliches Forum** MUSEUM
(Forum of Contemporary History; ☎222 00; www.hdg.de/leipzig; Grimmaische Strasse 6; ⌚9am-6pm Tue-Fri, 10am-6pm Sat & Sun) This fascinating exhibit tells the political history of the GDR from division and dictatorship to fall-of-the-Wall ecstasy and post-*Wende* blues. It's essential viewing for anyone seeking to understand the late country's inner workings.

FREE **Stasi Museum** MUSEUM
(☎961 2443; www.runde-ecke-leipzig.de; Dittrichring 24; ⌚10am-6pm) At the former Leipzig headquarters of the East German secret police (the Stasi), English-language audioguides aid in understanding the displays on propaganda,

preposterous disguises, cunning surveillance devices and other chilling machinations that reveal the GDR's all-out zeal when it came to controlling and repressing its own people.

Bach-Museum Leipzig MUSEUM
(☎913 7202; www.bach-leipzig.de; Thomaskirchhof 16; adult/concession €6/4, under 16yrs free; ⊙10am-6pm Tue-Sun) This updated museum does more than tell you about the life and accomplishments of Johann Sebastian Bach. Learn how to date a Bach manuscript, listen to baroque instruments or listen to his compositions. The **Thomaskirche** (☎222 240; www.thomaskirche.org; Thomaskirchhof 18; tower €2; ⊙church 9am-6pm, tower 1pm, 2pm & 4.30pm Sat, 2pm & 3pm Sun), where he is buried, is steps away.

Sleeping

Motel One HOTEL €
(☎337 4370; www.motel-one.de; Nikolaistrasse 23; d from €69, breakfast €7.50; P ❄ 📶) This budget designer hotel has snug but smartly designed rooms in a five-star location opposite the Nikolaikirche.

Hostel Sleepy Lion HOSTEL €
(☎993 9480; www.hostel-leipzig.de; Jacobstrasse 1; dm/d/apt from €12.50/42/55, linen €2.50, breakfast €3.50; @ 📶) Thumbs up for this clean and cheerfully painted hostel with a super-central location and clued-in staff. Dorms sleep four to 10 and there are private rooms and apartments as well.

arcona Living Bach 14 HOTEL, STUDIOS €€
(☎496 140; http://bach14.arcona.de; Thomaskirchhof 13/14; d from €90) In this musically themed marvel, within earshot of the Thomanerkirche, you'll sleep sweetly in sleek rooms decorated with sound-sculpture lamps and Bach manuscript wallpaper.

Eating

TOP CHOICE **Auerbachs Keller** GERMAN €€€
(☎216 100; www.auerbachs-keller-leipzig.de; Mädlerpassage; mains €14-22) Founded in 1525, cosy Auerbachs Keller is touristy, but the food's actually quite good and the setting is memorable. Goethe's *Faust – Part I* includes a scene here in which Mephistopheles and Faust carouse with students before riding off on a barrell.

Zum Arabischen Coffe Baum CAFE €€
(☎961 0060; www.coffe-baum.de; Kleine Fleischergasse 4; mains €8-16; ⊙11am-midnight) One of Europe's oldest coffeehouses, this rambling outpost has hosted poets, politicians, professors and everyone else since 1720.

Telegraph CAFE €€
(☎149 4990; www.cafe-telegraph.de; Dittrichring 18-20; mains €5-11; ⊙8am-midnight; 📶) Leipzig does cosmopolitan at this high-ceilinged cafe with curved booths, a bilingual menu and a stack of international mags and dailies. Breakfast is served until 3pm.

Gosenschenke 'Ohne Bedenken' BREWPUB €€
(☎566 2360; www.gosenschenke.de; Menckestrasse 5; mains €11-15; ⊙from noon daily Apr-Sep, from 4pm Mon-Fri & noon Sat & Sun Oct-Mar) This historic Leipzig institution, backed by a pretty beer garden, is *the* place to sample *Gose*, a local top-fermented beer often served with a shot of liqueur. The menu has a distinctivly carnivorous bent. Take tram 12 to Fritz-Seger-Strasse.

Drinking & Entertainment

Party activity centres on three main areas: the boisterous Drallewatsch pub strip, the more upmarket theatre district around Gottschedstrasse, and the mix of trendy and alt-vibe joints along Karl-Liebknecht-Strasse (aka 'Südmeile').

Moritzbastei CAFE, BAR
(☎702 590; www.moritzbastei.de; Universitätsstrasse 9; dishes €2-5; ⊙cafe & Schwalbennest from 10am Mon-Fri, noon Sat, 9am Sun, Fuchsbau from 8pm; 📶) This time-honoured warren of historic cellars below the old city fortifications keeps an all-ages crowd happy, posing as a cafe, a wine bar and a cocktail bar. Bands or DJs often take over the space after dark. Summer terrace, too.

Noels Ballroom PUB
(☎303 2007; noels-ballroom.com; Kurt-Eisner-Strasse 43; ⊙5pm-late; 🚊10, 11 to Karl Liebknecht/Kurt-Eisner-Strasse) A high-octane vibe, foamy pints of Guinness and a lovely flower-filled beer garden make Noels one of the best Irish pubs in town.

naTo PUB
(☎391 5539; www.nato-leipzig.de; Karl-Liebknecht-Strasse 46) The mother of Leipzig's alternative-music pub-clubs, with jazz, experimental and indie sounds alongside films and theatre. Great outdoor seating in summer.

Thomanerchor CLASSICAL MUSIC
(☎984 4211; www.thomaskirche.org; Thomaskirchhof 18; tickets €2) This famous boys' choir per-

forms Bach motets and cantatas at 6pm on Friday and 3pm on Saturday and also sings during Sunday services at 9.30am and 6pm at the Thomaskirche. To get in, show up 45 minutes before the concerts begin.

Gewandhausorchester CLASSICAL MUSIC
(☎127 0280; www.gewandhaus.de; Augustusplatz 8; tours €4.50; ⏲tours usually 12.30pm Thu) Once led by Felix Mendelssohn-Bartholdy, the Gewandhaus is one of Europe's finest and oldest civic orchestras (since 1743).

Information

Tourist Office (☎710 4260, room referral 710 4255; www.ltm-leipzig.de; Katharinenstrasse 8; ⏲9.30am-6pm Mon-Fri, to 4pm Sat, to 3pm Sun)

Getting There & Away

Leipzig-Halle airport (LEJ; www.leipzig-halle-airport.de) is about 21km west of Leipzig and linked to town by hourly RE train.

There are frequent long-distance trains to Frankfurt (€75, 3¾ hours), Dresden (€26, 1¼ hours) and Berlin (€45,1¼ hours), among others. Private Interconnex trains also go to Berlin twice daily (€19, 1¼ hours).

Getting Around

Buses and trams are run by **LVB** (☎194 49; www.lvb.de), which operates an information kiosk outside the Hauptbahnhof. Single tickets cost €2.10, day passes €5.

THURINGIA

Thuringia offers outstanding culture in its cities backed by the sprawling expanse of the Thuringian Forest. Top of the pops is Weimar, home to such seminal 18th-century poets and thinkers as Goethe and Schiller and the birthplace of the Bauhaus movement. Eisenach, where Bach was born, is dominated by the famous Wartburg castle, which is closely associated with the reformer Martin Luther, as is Erfurt, the state capital and a lively student town. It was the Nazis who put a dark stain on Thuringia's illustrious legacy when building Buchenwald concentration camp just outside Weimar.

Weimar

☎03643 / POP 65,500

Wandering around Weimar's enchanting old streets, you can sense the presence of such notables as Goethe, Schiller, Bach, Liszt and Nietzsche, who once made their home here. There are plenty of statues, plaques and museums to remind you of their legacy along with parks and gardens to take a break from the intellectual onslaught.

Sights

Goethe Haus & Nationalmuseum MUSEUM
(Frauenplan 1; combined ticket Goethe Haus & museum adult/concession €10.50/8.50, permanent museum exhibition only adult/concession €6.50/5.50; ⏲9am-6pm Tue-Fri & Sun, to 7pm Sat) Johann Wolfgang von Goethe lived in Weimar from 1775 until his death in 1832, the last 50 years in what is now the **Goethe Haus**. His 1st-floor living quarters are reached via an expansive Italian Renaissance staircase featuring sculpture and paintings he brought back from his travel to Italy. His study and the bedroom where he died are both preserved in their original state. Visitors numbers are limited and tickets timed.

The adjacent **museum** provides background on Goethe's life and times.

Herzogin Anna Amalia Bibliothek LIBRARY
(www.klassik-stiftung.de; Platz der Demokratie 1; adult/concession incl audioguide €6.50/5.50; ⏲9.30am-2.30pm Tue-Sun) This magnificent rococo library is crammed with 40,000 tomes once used for research purposes by Goethe, Schiller and other Weimar hot shots. Get your timed ticket in advance or start queuing before the ticket office opens.

Park an der Ilm PARK
This sprawling park, just east of the Altstadt, is as inspiring and romantic now as it was in Goethe's time. **Goethes Gartenhaus** (Goethe's Garden House; Park an der Ilm; adult/concession €4.50/3.50; ⏲10am-6pm Wed-Mon), where the writer lived from 1776 to 1782, is a highlight. A few decades later, the composer Franz Liszt resided – and wrote the *Faust Symphony* – in what is now the **Liszt-Haus** (Liszt House; Marienstrasse 17; adult/concession €4/3; ⏲10am-6pm Tue-Sun Apr-Sep, to 4pm Sat & Sun Oct-Mar).

Bauhaus Museum MUSEUM
(www.das-bauhaus-kommt.de; Theaterplatz; adult/concession €4.50/3.50; ⏲10am-6pm) Considering that Weimar is the birthplace of the influential Bauhaus school, this museum is a rather modest affair. Plans are to move to newer, larger premises.

Sleeping

Labyrinth Hostel HOSTEL €
(☎811 822; www.weimar-hostel.com; Goetheplatz 6; dm €14-21, s/d €35/46, linen €2.50, breakfast €3; @ 📶) Loads of imagination has gone into this professionally run hostel with artist-designed rooms where you sleep in a bed perched on stacks of books. Facilities include a kitchen and rooftop terrace.

TOP CHOICE **Casa dei Colori** PENSION €€
(☎489 640; www.casa-colori.de; Eisfeld 1a; r €84-114; P 📶) This charming pension convincingly imports cheerfully exuberant Mediterranean flair to provincial Thuringia with mostly good-sized rooms dressed in bold colours.

Eating

Residenz-Café INTERNATIONAL €€
(Grüner Markt 4; mains €5-18; ⏲8am-1am; 🖉) Everyone should find something to their taste at the 'Resi', one of Weimar's enduring favourites, no matter what time of day.

ACC GERMAN €
(www.acc-cafe.de; Burgplatz 1; dishes €5-10; ⏲11-1am; 📶) Goethe's first pad upon arriving in Weimar is now an alt-vibe hang-out, where the food and wine are mostly organic and the upstairs gallery delivers a primer on the local art scene.

Estragon HEALTH FOOD €
(Herderplatz 3; soups €3-5.50; ⏲10am-7pm Mon-Sat, noon-6pm Sun) This little soup kitchen turns mostly organic ingredients into delicious flavour combos served in three sizes.

Information

Tourist Office (☎7450; www.weimar.de; Markt 10; ⏲9.30am-7pm Mon-Sat, to 3pm Sun)

Getting There & Away

Weimar's Hauptbahnhof is a 20-minute walk from the centre. Frequent connections include Erfurt (€8, 15 minutes), Eisenach (€14.40, one hour), Leipzig (€22, 1¼ hours), Dresden (€43, 2½ hours) and Berlin-Hauptbahnhof (€54, 2¼ hours).

Around Weimar

The museum and memorial at **Buchenwald concentration camp** (www.buchenwald.de; ⏲9am-6pm Apr-Oct, to 4pm Nov-Mar) are 10km northwest of Weimar. The contrast between the brutality of the former and the humanism of the latter could not be greater.

Between 1937 and 1945, more than one-fifth of the 250,000 people incarcerated here died. After the war, the Soviet victors established Special Camp No 2, in which 7000 so-called anticommunists and ex-Nazis were literally worked to death. Various parts of the camp have been restored and there is an essential **museum** with excellent exhibits.

From Weimar, take bus 6 (direction Buchenwald) from Goetheplatz.

Erfurt

☎0361 / POP 205,000

Thuringia's state capital is a scene-stealing combo of sweeping squares, time-worn alleyways, perky church towers, idyllic river scenery, and vintage inns and taverns. In 1392 rich merchants founded the university whose most famous graduate was Martin Luther, who studied philosophy here before becoming a monk at the local Augustinian monastery in 1505.

Sights

Mariendom CHURCH
(St Mary's Cathedral; Domplatz; ⏲9am-6pm Mon-Sat, 1-6pm Sun) Together with the **Severikirche** (same hours), Erfurt's grand Gothic cathedral dominates the central Domplatz square. It's one of the most richly ornamented medieval churches in Germany and boasts luminous stained-glass windows, elaborate choir stalls and such treasures as a 12th-century human-shaped candelabrum.

Krämerbrücke BRIDGE
This enchanting medieval bridge is flanked by half-timbered shops – it's the only such structure north of the Alps.

Augustinerkloster CHURCH
(Augustinian Monastery; Augustinerstrasse 10, enter on Comthurgasse; tour adult/concession €6/4; ⏲tours hourly 10am-noon & 2-5pm Mon-Sat, 11am & noon Sun) Martin Luther lived at this monastery from 1505 to 1511 and was ordained a priest here in 1507. Tours take you inside the cloister, a recreated Luther cell and an exhibit on the Reformation.

Sleeping

TOP CHOICE **Re_4 Hostel** HOSTEL €
(☎600 0110; www.re4hostel.de; Puschkinstrasse 21; dm €13-16, s/d €26/52, without bathroom

€20/40, linen €2; P@) This cool hostel in a former police station is run by an energetic, clued-in crew – room 13 has a 'chilling' surprise. Take tram 5 from Hauptbahnhof to Pushkinstrasse.

Opera Hostel HOSTEL €
(☎6013 1360; www.opera-hostel.de; Walkmühlstrasse 13; dm €13-18, s/d/tr €45/54/75, without bathroom €37/48/66, linen €2.50; @) Run with smiles and aplomb, this upmarket hostel in a historic building has bright and spacious rooms, many with a sofa for chilling, along with a communal kitchen and lounge-bar. Take bus 51 from Hauptbahnhof to Alte Oper.

Hotel am Kaisersaal HOTEL €€
(☎658 560; www.bachmann-hotels.de; Futterstrasse 8; s/d €89/104; P) Tip-top rooms are appointed with all expected mod cons in this highly rated hotel. Take tram 1 or 5 to Futterstrasse.

Eating

TOP CHOICE **Zwiesel** GERMAN €
(Michaelisstrasse 31; mains €6-9; ⊙6pm-late Mon-Thu, 3pm-late Fri-Sun) This reliable cheapie has 25 mains costing just €5.95 and drinks prices to match.

Zum Goldenen Schwan GERMAN €€
(Michaelisstrasse 9; snacks €3-7, mains €8-17; ⊙11am-1am) This authentic inn serves Thuringian classics, including *Puffbohnenpfanne* (fried broad beans with roast bacon), an Erfurt speciality, and pours an excellent house brew.

Steinhaus GERMAN €
(Allerheiligenstrasse 20-21; mains €4-8; ⊙11am-late, food till midnight) The ceiling beams may be ancient, but the crowd is intergenerational at this rambling gastro pub-cum-beer garden in the historic Engelsburg student centre.

Information

Tourist Office (☎664 00; www.erfurt-tourismus.de; Benediktsplatz 1; ⊙10am-7pm Mon-Fri, to 6pm Sat, to 4pm Sun)

Getting There & Around

Fast trains leave frequently for Berlin (€60, 2½ hours, change in Leipzig), Dresden (€51, 2¼ hours) and Frankfurt-am-Main (€54, 2¼ hours). Regional trains to Weimar (€5, 15 minutes) and Eisenach (€11.10, 45 minutes) depart at least once hourly.

Trams 3, 4 and 6 run from Hauptbahnhof via Anger and Fischmarkt to Domplatz. Single tickets cost €1.80, a day pass €4.20.

WORTH A TRIP

EISENACH

On the edge of the Thuringian forest, Eisenach is the birthplace of Johann Sebastian Bach, but even the town's **museum** (www.bachhaus.de; Frauenplan 21; adult/concession €7.50/4; ⊙10am-6pm) dedicated to the great composer plays second fiddle to the awe-inspiring 11th-century castle perched high above the town.

The **Wartburg** (www.wartburg-eisenach.de; tour adult/concession €9/5, museum & Luther study only €5/4; ⊙tours 8.30am-5pm, in English 1.30pm) hosted medieval minstrel song contests and was the home of Elisabeth, a Hungarian princess later canonised for her charitable deeds. Its most famous resident, however, was Martin Luther, who went into hiding here in 1521 after being excommunicated and placed under papal ban. During this 10-month stay, he translated the New Testament from Greek into German, contributing enormously to the development of the written German language. His modest study is part of the guided tour (also in English).

Arrive before 11am to avoid the worst of the crowds, which can be horrendous between Easter and October.

From April to October, bus 10 runs hourly from 9am to 5pm from the Hauptbahnhof (with stops at Karlsplatz and Mariental) to the Eselstation stop, from where it's a steep 10-minute walk up to the castle. In winter, **shuttle buses** (☎03691-228 822) run on demand.

Regional trains run frequently to Erfurt (€11.10, 45 minutes) and Weimar (€14.40, one hour). The **tourist office** (☎792 30; www.eisenach.de; Markt 24; ⊙10am-6pm Mon-Fri, to 5pm Sat & Sun) can help with finding accommodation.

BAVARIA

From the cloud-shredding Alps to the fertile Danube plain, Bavaria (Bayern) is a place that keeps its clichéd promises. Story-book castles, lazy cows grazing on flower-filled meadows, lederhosen lads lifting frothy steins, walled towns lost in a medieval time warp – you'll find them all.

But there's so much more than the chocolate-box idyll. Learn about Bavaria's state-of-the-art motor industry in Munich, discover its Nazi past in Nuremberg and Berchtesgaden, sip world-class wines in Würzburg or walk in Wagner's footsteps in Bayreuth. Destinations are often described as possessing 'something for everyone', but in Bavaria's case this is no exaggeration.

Munich

089 / POP 1.38 MILLION

If you're looking for Alpine clichés, they're all here, but Munich also has plenty of unexpected cards down its Dirndl. Folklore and age-old traditions exist side by side with sleek BMWs, designer boutiques and high-powered industry. Its museums include world-class collections of artistic masterpieces, and its music and cultural scenes are second only to Berlin's.

Sights

ALTSTADT

Marienplatz SQUARE

(S Marienplatz) The heart and soul of the Altstadt, Marienplatz is anchored by the **Mariensäule** (Mary's Column), built in 1638 to celebrate victory over Swedish forces during the Thirty Years' War.

Its main building is the heavily ornamented neo-Gothic **Neues Rathaus** (New Town Hall) whose highlight is the endearing **Glockenspiel** (carillon) whose 43 bells and 32 figures perform two actual historic events. The top half tells the story of a knight's tournament held in 1568 to celebrate the marriage of Duke Wilhelm V to Renata of Lothringen, while the bottom half portrays the *Schäfflertanz* (coopers' dance). To pinpoint Munich's landmarks without losing your breath, catch the lift up the 85m-tall **tower** (adult/child €2/€1; 9am-7pm Mon-Fri, 10am-7pm Sat & Sun).

NO WAVE GOODBYE

Munich is famous for beer, sausages and surfing. Yep, you read that right. Just go to the southern tip of the English Garden at Prinzregentenstrasse and you'll see scores of people leaning over a bridge to cheer on wetsuit-clad daredevils as they 'hang 10' on an artificially created wave in the Eisbach creek. It's only a single wave, but it's a darn fine one.

St Peterskirche CHURCH

(Church of St Peter; Rindermarkt 1; church admission free, tower adult/child €1.50/1; tower 9am-5.30pm Mon-Fri, from 10am Sat & Sun; S Marienplatz, U Marienplatz) Some 306 steps divide you from wonderful views from the 92m tower of St Peterskirche, Munich's oldest church (1150). Inside, note the Gothic altar, the baroque ceiling fresco and the rococo sculptures.

Viktualienmarkt MARKET

(Mon-Fri & Sat morning; S Marienplatz, U Marienplatz) Quality – and prices – are high at this colourful food and crafts market, many of whose stalls have been run by the same family for generations.

Frauenkirche CHURCH

(Church of Our Lady; Frauenplatz 1; tower €2; 7am-7pm Sat-Wed, to 8.30pm Thu, to 6pm Fri) No other building in central Munich may stand taller than the 99m of this landmark church with its onion-domed twin towers, one of which can be climbed from April to October.

RESIDENZ

The Residenz is a suitably grand palace that reflects the splendour and power of the Bavarian rulers who lived here from 1385 to 1918.

Taking up half the compound is the treasure-packed **Residenzmuseum** (290 671; www.residenz-muenchen.de; adult/child €7/free, combination ticket for the museum, Schatzkammer and Cuvilliés-Theater €13/free; 9am-6pm Apr–mid-Oct, 10am-5pm mid-Oct–Mar). A highlight is **Antiquarium**, a barrel-vaulted hall smothered in frescos and widely regarded as the finest Renaissance interior north of the Alps. Upstairs top billing goes to François Cuvilliés' **Reiche Zimmer** (Rich Rooms), a six-room extravaganza of exuberant rococo, and the **Ahnengallery** (Ancestors Gallery), a roll call of 121 portraits of Bavarian rulers.

The **Schatzkammer der Residenz** (Residence Treasury; adult/concession/under 18yr with parents €7/6/free; 9am-6pm Apr–mid-Oct, 10am-5pm mid-Oct–Mar) displays a veritable banker's bonus worth of jewel-encrusted bling of yesteryear, from golden toothpicks to finely crafted swords, miniatures in ivory to gold entombed cosmetics trunks.

Don't miss the **Cuvilliés-Theater** (adult/child €3.50/free; ⌚2-6pm Mon-Sat, from 9am Sun Apr-Jul & mid-Sep–mid-Oct, 9am-6pm daily Aug–mid-Sep, shorter hours mid-Oct–Mar), named for its architect and one of Europe's finest rococo theatres.

MAXVORSTADT, SCHWABING & ENGLISCHER GARTEN

North of the Altstadt, Maxvorstadt is home to Munich's main university and a cluster of top-drawer art museums. It segues into equally cafe-filled Schwabing which rubs up against the vast **Englischer Garten**, one of Europe's biggest city parks and a favourite playground for locals and visitors alike.

Alte Pinakothek ART MUSEUM
(www.pinakothek.de; Barer Strasse 27; adult/child €7/5, Sun €1, audioguide €4.50; ⌚10am-8pm Tue, to 6pm Wed-Sun; 🚊Pinakotheken, 🚌Pinakotheken) Superb collection of Old Masters, including Cranach, Dürer, Botticelli, Titian and many others.

Neue Pinakothek ART MUSEUM
(www.pinakothek.de; Barer Strasse 29; adult/child €7/5, Sun €1; ⌚10am-6pm Thu-Mon, to 8pm Wed; 🚊Pinakotheken, 🚌Pinakotheken) Contains mostly 19th-century paintings and sculpture, including works by crowd-pleasing impressionists such as Monet, Cézanne and Van Gogh.

Pinakothek der Moderne ART MUSEUM
(www.pinakothek.de; Barer Strasse 40; adult/child €10/7, Sun €1; ⌚10am-6pm Tue, Wed & Fri-Sun, 10am-8pm Thu; 🚊Pinakotheken, 🚌Pinakotheken) The museum unites four collections of modern art, crafts and architecture in one suitably arresting building.

FURTHER AFIELD

Schloss Nymphenburg PALACE
(www.schloss-nymphenburg.de; adult/child €6/5; ⌚9am-6pm Apr–mid-Oct, 10am-4pm mid-Oct–Mar; 🚊Schloss Nymphenburg) About 5km northwest of the Altstadt, ths vast, snowy-white palace and its lavish gardens were the royal family's summer residence. A highlight is the **Schönheitengalerie** (Gallery of Beauties).

BMW Museum MUSEUM
(www.bmw-welt.de; adult/child €12/6; ⌚10am-6pm Tue-Sun) This ode to the auto examines the development of BMW's product line in a stunning building that combines a curvy retro feel with futuristic bridges and huge backlit wall screens.

OKTOBERFEST

Hordes come to Munich for **Oktoberfest** (www.oktoberfest.de), running the 15 days before the first Sunday in October. Reserve accommodation well ahead and go early in the day so you can grab a seat in one of the hangar-sized beer tents spread across the Theresienwiese grounds, about 1km southwest of the Hauptbahnhof. While there is no entrance fee, those €9 1L steins of beer (called *Mass*) add up fast. Although its origins are in the marriage celebrations of Crown Prince Ludwig in 1810, there's nothing regal about this beery bacchanalia now: expect mobs, expect to meet new and drunken friends, expect decorum to vanish as night sets in and you'll have a blast.

Deutsches Museum MUSEUM
(☎217 91; www.deutsches-museum.de; Museumsinsel 1; adult/child €8.50/3; ⌚9am-5pm; 🚊Deutsches Museum) This temple to technology has tons of interactive displays, live demonstrations and experiments, model coal and salt mines and engaging sections on cave paintings, geodesy, microelectronics and astronomy.

☞ Tours

Radius Tours GUIDED TOUR
(☎543 487 7720; www.radiustours.com; opposite track 32, Hauptbahnhof; ⌚8.30am-6pm Apr-Oct, to 2pm Nov-Mar) Home of the two-hour pay-what-you-like Priceless Munich Walk along with themed tours (Third Reich, beer, etc).

Munich Walk Tours WALKING TOUR
(☎2423 1767; www.munichwalktours.de; Arnulfstrasse 2; tours from €12) General and themed tours as well as bicycle rentals (€15 per 24 hours.

Mike's Bike Tours BIKE TOURS
(☎2554 3987; www.mikesbiketours.com; departs Altes Rathaus, Marienplatz; tours from €24) Four- and seven-hour city cycling tours.

City Bus 100 BUS
Ordinary city bus that runs from the Hauptbahnhof to the Ostbahnhof via 21 of the city's museums and galleries.

Central Munich

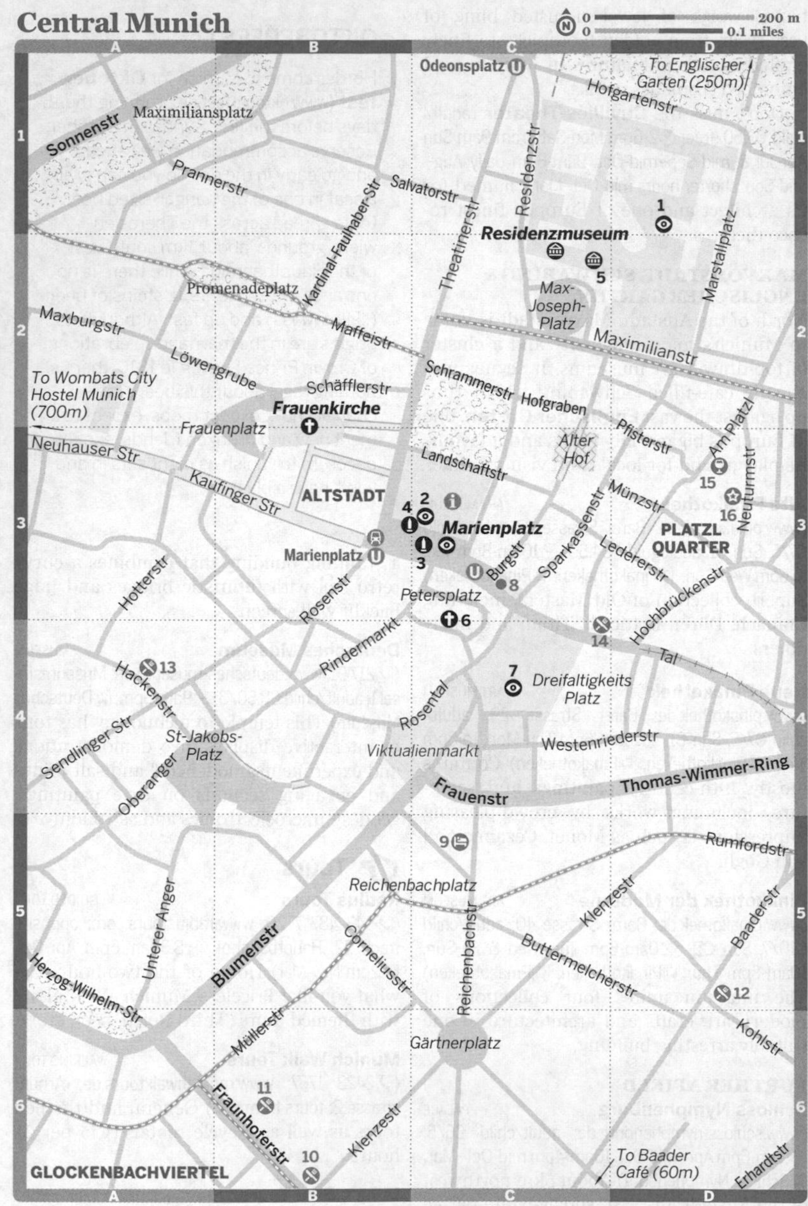

Sleeping

Munich has no shortage of places to stay – except during Oktoberfest or some busy summer periods when you should book well ahead. Many budget and midrange places can be found in the cheerless streets around the train station.

Wombats City Hostel Munich HOSTEL **€**
(5998 9180; www.wombats-hostels.com; Senefelderstrasse 1; dm €12-24, d from €70; ;

Central Munich

Top Sights
Frauenkirche ... B2
Marienplatz ... C3
Residenzmuseum ... C2

Sights
1 Cuviliés-Theater ... D1
2 Glockenspiel ... C3
3 Mariensäule ... C3
4 Neues Rathaus Tower ... B3
5 Schatzkammer der Residenz ... C2
6 St Peterskirche ... C3
7 Viktualienmarkt ... C4

Activities, Courses & Tours
8 Mike's Bike Tours ... C3

Sleeping
9 Hotel am Viktualienmarkt ... C5

Eating
10 Bergwolf ... D6
11 Fraunhofer ... B6
12 Königsquelle ... D5
13 Prinz Myshkin ... A4
14 Weisses Brauhaus ... C4

Drinking
15 Hofbräuhaus ... D3

Entertainment
16 Atomic Café ... D3

Hauptbahnhof, Hauptbahnhof) At this professionally run affair dorms come with attached bathrooms, sturdy lockers and comfy pine bunks. Free welcome drink.

Meininger's HOSTEL, HOTEL €
(5499 8023; www.meininger-hostels.de; Landsbergerstrasse 20; dm/s/d without breakfast from €15/45/80; ; Holzapfelstrasse) About 800m west of the Hauptbahnhof, this hostel-hotel has basic, clean, bright rooms with big dorms divided into two for a bit of privacy.

Hotel Uhland HOTEL €€
(543 350; www.hotel-uhland.de; Uhlandstrasse 1; s/d from €69/87; ; Theresienwiese) An enduring favourite thanks to gracious owners and such thoughtful touches as bike rentals, mix-your-own organic breakfast muesli and free ice cubes.

Hotel Cocoon DESIGN HOTEL €€
(5999 3907; www.hotel-cocoon.de; Lindwurmstrasse 35; s/d €79/99; Sendlinger Tor, Sendlinger Tor) Retro-designer den where rooms are dressed in crisp orange and green and sport glass showers right in the sleeping area. There's a second branch called **Cocoon Stachus** (Adolf-Kolping-Strasse 11).

Hotel am Viktualienmarkt HOTEL €€
(231 1090; www.hotel-am-viktualienmarkt.de; Utzschneiderstrasse 14; d €50-120; ; Marienplatz, Marienplatz) Good-value and centrally located property where modern rooms have wooden floors and framed poster art.

La Maison DESIGN HOTEL €€
(3303 5550; www.hotel-la-maison.com; Occamstrasse 24; s/d from €109/119; ; Münchner Freiheit) Discerningly retro, this sassy number flaunts heated oak floors, jet-black basins and starkly contrasting design throughout. Cool bar on ground level.

Hotel Mariandl HOTEL €€
(552 9100; www.mariandl.com; Goethestrasse 51; s €65-115, d 070-165; Sendlinger Tor, Sendlinger Tor) Rambling neo-Gothic mansion where rooms ooze *Jugendstil* flair and breakfast is served until 4pm.

Tent CAMPGROUND €
(141 4300; www.the-tent.com; In den Kirschen 30; tent bunk/floor space €10.50/7.50, tent pitch from €11; Jun-Nov; Botanischer Garten) A kilometre north of Schloss Nymphenburg, this youth-oriented camping ground has classic tent pitches, as well as a 160-bunk main tent with floor space and foam mats for shoestring nomads.

Eating

Fraunhofer BAVARIAN €€
(Fraunhoferstrasse 9; mains €7-17.50; 4pm-1am; ; Müllerstrasse) With virtually no trace that the last century even happened, this characterful brewpub is one of the city centre's best places to explore the region with a fork.

Prinz Myshkin VEGETARIAN €€
(265 596; www.prinzmyshkin.com; Hackenstrasse 2; mains €10-17; 11am-12.30am; ; Marienplatz, Marienplatz) Munich's premier meat-free dining spot fills out an open-plan, but strangely intimate vaulted dining space in a former brewery with health-conscious eaters.

Wirtshaus in der Au BAVARIAN €€
(448 1400; Lilienstrasse 51; mains €8-19; 5pm-midnight Mon-Fri, from 10am Sat & Sun; Deutsches

Museum) This former brewery with lofty ceiling and fireplace in winter pairs a solid 21st-century vibe with classic Bavarian fare and is famous for its dumplings.

Königsquelle ALPINE €€

(☎220 071; Baaderplatz 2; mains €9-18; ⊙dinner; Isartor, Isartor) At this Munich institution the handwritten, Alpine-inflected menu hopscotches from schnitzel to linguine and goat's cheese to cannelloni.

Weisses Brauhaus BAVARIAN €€

(Tal 7; mains €8-15; S Marienplatz, Marienplatz) This brewpub's *Weisswurst* (veal sausage) sets the standard for the rest to aspire to; sluice down a pair with the unsurpassed Schneider Weissbier.

Bergwolf FAST FOOD €

(Fraunhoferstrasse 17; ⊙noon-2am Mon-Thu, noon-4am Fri & Sat, noon-10pm Sun, closed 3-6pm Sun-Fri; S Fraunhoferstrasse) Popular pit stop with night owl keen on the ultimate hangover prevention: a *Currywurst* (sliced spicy sausage doused in curried ketchup).

Cafe an der Uni CAFE €

(Ludwigstrasse 24; snacks & mains €5-9; ⊙8am-1am Mon-Fri, from 9am Sat & Sun; S Universität) Charismatic any-time-of-day student hang-out great for breakfast, a cuppa Java or a Helles, preferably in the walled-in garden.

Drinking

Apart from the beer halls and gardens, Munich has no shortage of lively pubs. Schwabing and the Glockenbachviertel are good places to follow your ears. Many serve food.

Alter Simpl PUB

(Türkenstrasse 57; ⊙11am-3am Mon-Fri, 11am-4am Sat & Sun; Schellingstrasse) Thomas Mann and Hermann Hesse used to knock 'em back at this well-scuffed and wood-panelled thirst parlour.

Baader Café CAFE

(Baaderstrasse 47; ⊙9.30am-1am; Fraunhoferstrasse) This literary think-and-drink institution lures all sorts, from short skirts to tweed jackets who linger over daytime coffees and night-hour cocktails. Popular Sunday brunch.

Trachtenvogl CAFE, LOUNGE

(Reichenbachstrasse 47; ⊙10am-1am Sun-Thu, to 2am Fri & Sat; Fraunhoferstrasse) At night you'll have to shoehorn your way into this buzzy lair in a converted folklori garment shop. It's favoured by a chatty, boozy crowd of scenesters, artists and students.

Entertainment

Kultfabrik CLUB COMPLEX

(www.kultfabrik.de; Grafingerstrasse 6; Ostbahnhof) This former dumpling factory is party

BEER HALLS & BEER GARDENS

Beer drinking is not just an integral part of Munich's entertainment scene, it's a reason to visit. Beer halls can be vast boozy affairs seating thousands, or much more modest neighbourhood hang-outs. The same goes for beer gardens. What's common is a certain camaraderie among strangers, huge 1L glasses of beer, lots of pretzels and sausages and noisy oompah bands. In beer gardens you are often allowed to bring your own picnic as long as you sit at tables without tablecloths and order something to drink.

Here are our top choices:

Augustiner Bräustuben (Landsberger Strasse 19; ⊙10am-midnight; Holzapfelstrasse) At this authentic beer hall, inside the actual Augustiner brewery, the Bavarian grub here is superb, especially the *Schweinshaxe* (pork knuckles).

Hofbräuhaus (Am Platzl 9; ⊙9am-11.30pm; S Marienplatz, Kammerspiele, Marienplatz) Clichéd but still fun. Wander upstairs for echoes of the past, a small museum and possibly a seat.

Hirschgarten (Hirschgartenallee 1; ⊙11am-11pm; Kriemhildenstrasse, Laim) The Everest of Munich beer gardens can accommodate up to 8000 Augustiner lovers and is a woodsy locale within walking distance of Schloss Nymphenburg.

Chinesischer Turm (Chinese Tower; ☎383 8730; Englischer Garten 3; ⊙10am-11pm; Chinesischer Turm, Tivolistrasse) At Munich's oldest beer garden (open since 1791) beer lovers gather around the wooden pagoda smack dab in the Englischer Garten.

central with more than a dozen venues along with numerous fast-food eateries. Go to **11er** for electro and house, **Titty Twister** for hard rock and **Refugium** for metal. Nostalgic types can become dancing queens at **Noa**, **Rafael** and **Q Club** while rock a billies jive till the wee hours at **Eddy's**.

Jazzclub Unterfahrt im Einstein BLUES, JAZZ
(☎448 2794; www.unterfahrt.de; Einsteinstrasse 42; Ⓢ Max-Weber-Platz) Join a diverse crowd at this long-established, intimate club for acts ranging from old bebop to edgy experimental. Legendary Sunday open jam session.

Atomic Café CLUB
(www.atomic.de; Neuturmstrasse 5; ⊙from 10pm Tue-Sat; 🚋Kammerspiele) This bastion of indie sounds with funky 60s décor is known for bookers with a knack for catching upwardly hopeful bands before their big break.

FC Bayern München SOCCER
(☎6993 1333; www.fcbayern.de; Ⓢ Fröttmaning) Germany's most successful soccer team plays home games at the impressive Allianz Arena, built for the 2006 World Cup. Tickets can be ordered online.

Information

Tourist Office (☎2339 6500; www.muenchen.de) Hauptbahnhof (Bahnhofplatz 2; ⊙9am-8pm Mon-Sat, 10am-6pm Sun) Marienplatz (Marienplatz 8, Neues Rathaus; ⊙10am-7pm Mon-Fri, to 5pm Sat, to 2pm Sun)

City Tour Card (www.citytourcard-muenchen.com; 1/3 days €9.90/19.90) Free public transport and discounts on 50 attractions, tours, eateries and theatres. Available at some hotels, tourist offices, and public transport vending machines.

Getting There & Away

Air

Munich Airport (MUC; www.munich-airport.de) is about 30km northeast of town and linked to the Hauptbahnhof every 20 minutes by S-Bahn (S1 and S8, €10, 40 minutes) and by the Lufthansa Airport Bus (€10.50, 45 minutes, between 5am and 8pm).

Ryanair flies into Memmingen's **Allgäu Airport** (www.allgaeu-airport.de), 125km to the west. Seven buses shuttle daily between here and the Hauptbahnhof (€13, 1¾ hours).

Bus

Sindbad (☎5454 8989; Arnulfstrasse 20) near the Hauptbahnhof sells bus tickets. The **Romantic Road Coach** (☎0171-653 234; 0719-126 268; www.touring-travel.eu) links Munich to the Romantic Road. Buses leave from **Zentraler Omnibusbahnhof** (Central Bus Station, ZOB; Arnulfstrasse 21) at S-Bahn station Hackerbrücke.

Train

All services leave from the Hauptbahnhof, where **Euraide** (www.euraide.de; Desk 1, Reisezentrum, Hauptbahnhof; ⊙10am-7pm Mon-Fri Aug-Apr) is a friendly English-speaking agency that sells train tickets, makes reservations and can create personalised rail tours of Germany and beyond. There's frequent direct service to Nuremberg (€52, 1¼ hours), Würzburg (€67, two hours), Frankfurt (€95, 3¼ hours), Berlin (€121, six hours) and Vienna (€85.80, 4½ hours) as well as twice-daily trains to Prague (€66, six hours).

Getting Around

MVV (www.mvv-muenchen.de) operates a dense network of buses, trams, the U-Bahn and the S-Bahn. For most place of interest you need to buy a ticket for the *Innenraum* (inner zone, €2.50). Day passes are €5.60 for individuals and €10.20 for up to five people travelling together. Stamp your ticket before use or risk a fine of €40 if caught by an inspector.

GAY & LESBIAN MUNICH

In Munich, the rainbow flag flies especially proudly along Müllerstrasse and the adjoining Glockenbachviertel. Keep an eye out for the freebie mags *Our Munich* and *Sergej*, which contain up-to-date listings and news about the community and gay-friendly establishments around town. Another source is www.gaymunich.de, which has a small section in English. For help with lodging, check out www.gaytouristoffice.com.

Around Munich

The first Nazi concentration camp was **Dachau** (Dachau Memorial Site; www.kz-gedenkstaette-dachau.de; Alte Römerstrasse 75; admission free, tours €3; ⊙9am-5pm, tours 11am & 1pm Tue-Sun), built in 1933. More than 200,000 Jews, political prisoners, homosexuals and others deemed 'undesirable' were imprisoned here; more than 30,000 died. For deeper understanding, pick up an audioguide (€3.50), join a 2½-hour tour and watch the English-language documentary at the main museum.

Dachau is about 16km north of Munich. Frm the Hauptbahnhof take the S2 to Dachau station (two-zone ticket, €5, 21 minutes), then catch bus 726 to the camp.

Bavarian Alps

Stretching west from Germany's remote southeastern corner to the Allgäu region near Lake Constance, the Bavarian Alps (Bayerische Alpen) form a stunningly beautiful natural divide along the Austrian border. Ranges further south may be higher, but these mountains shoot up from the foothills so abruptly that the impact is all the more dramatic.

The region is packed with cute villages, sprightly spas and plenty of possibilities for skiing, snowboarding, hiking, canoeing and paragliding. The ski season lasts from about late December until April.

GARMISCH-PARTENKIRCHEN

08821 / POP 26,000

Garmisch-Partenkirchen is blessed with a fabled setting a snowball's throw from Germany's highest peak, the 2964m-high Zugspitze. Garmisch has a cosmopolitan feel, while Partenkirchen retains an old-world Alpine village vibe.

Sights & Activities

Zugspitze MOUNTAIN

(www.zugspitze.de) On good days, views from Germany's rooftop extend into four countries. Skiing and hiking are the main activities here but most people are content to simply make the dramatic trip to the summit aboard a cogwheel train and two steep cablecars. It costs €40/22.50 per adult/child in winter (including ski pass) and €49.50/28 in summer. Trains leave from behind the main station in Garmisch. Beat the crowds by starting early in the day and, if possible, skip weekends altogether.

Partnachklamm GORGE

(www.partnachklamm.eu; adult/child €3/1.50; 9am-5pm Oct-Easter, 8am-6pm Easter-Sep) A loop trail hewn into the rock takes you through this narrow, 700m-gorge whose walls rise up to 80m high. In winter you can walk beneath curtains of icicles and frozen waterfalls.

Sleeping & Eating

Hostel 2962 HOSTEL €

(957 50; www.hostel2962.com; Partnachauenstrasse 3; dm/d from €20/60;) A bed in one of the four-bed dorms in this converted hotel is the cheapest sleep in town.

Bräustüberl GERMAN €€

(2312; Fürstenstrasse 23; mains €6-17) A short walk from the centre, this quintessentially Bavarian tavern is the place to cosy up with some local nosh, served by Dirndl-trussed waitresses.

Information

Tourist Office (180 700; www.gapa.de; Richard-Strauss-Platz 2; 8am-6pm Mon-Sat, 10am-noon Sun)

Getting There & Away

Numerous tour operators run day trips to Garmisch-Partenkirchen from Munich but there's also an hourly direct train service (€19, 80 minutes).

BERCHTESGADEN

08652 / POP 7600

Steeped in myth and legend, Berchtesgaden and the surrounding countryside (the Berchtesgadener Land) is almost preternaturally beautiful. Framed by six formidable mountain ranges and home to Germany's second-highest mountain, the Watzmann (2713m), its dreamy, fir-lined valleys are filled with gurgling streams and peaceful Alpine villages. Alas, Berchtesgaden's history is also indelibly tainted by the Nazi period. The area is easily visited on a day trip from Salzburg.

Sights & Activities

Dokumentation Obersalzberg MUSEUM

(www.obersalzberg.de; Salzbergstrasse 41, Obersalzberg; adult/child €3/free; 9am-5pm daily Apr-Oct, 10am-3pm Tue-Sun Nov-Mar) In 1933 quiet Obersalzberg (3km from the town of Berchtesgaden) became the southern headquarters of Hitler's government, a dark period that's given the full historical treatment at this often compelling exhibit. All facets of Nazi terror are dealt with, including Hitler's near-mythical appeal, his racial politics, the resistance movement, foreign policy and the death camps. Half-hourly bus 838 runs here from Berchtesgaden Hauptbahnhof.

Eagle's Nest HISTORIC SITE

(2969; www.kehlsteinhaus.de; mid-May–Oct) Berchtesgaden's most sinister – yet impressive – draw is Hitler's retreat atop Mt Kehlstein, a sheer-sided peak at Obersalzberg. More than 3000 workers worked feverishly to build this lodge for the Führer's 50th birthday.

Take half-hourly bus 838 from the Hauptbahnhof to the Hotel Intercontinental from where a special **bus** (adult/child €15.50/9) drives you up the mountain (35 minutes). The final stretch to the summit is aboard a snazzy brass-clad lift (elevator). **Eagle's Nest Tours** (☎649 71; www.eagles-nest-tours.com; Königsseer Strasse 2; adult/child €50/35; ⏱1.15pm mid-May–Oct) has four-hour tours in English covering sites related to the Nazi period.

Königssee LAKE

Crossing the serenely picturesque, emerald-green Königssee makes for some unforgettable memories. Framed by steep mountain walls some 5km south of Berchtesgaden, Königssee is Germany's highest lake (603m). Escape the hubbub of the bustling lakeside tourist village by taking an electric **boat** (www.seenschifffahrt.de; return adult/child €13.30/6.70) tour to St Bartholomä, a quaint onion-domed chapel on the western shore.

At some point, the boat will stop while the captain plays a horn towards the Echo Wall – the sound will bounce seven times. Pure magic! The effect only fails during heavy fog. From the dock at St Bartholomä, an easy trail leads to the wondrous **Eiskapelle** in about one hour. Bus 841 runs from the train station to the lakeshore roughly every hour.

Sleeping & Eating

Hotel Bavaria HOTEL €€

(☎660 11; www.hotelbavaria.net; Sunklergässchen 11; r €50-130; P) This family-owned hotel offers a romantic vision of Alpine life with rooms bedecked in frilly curtains, canopied beds, heart-shaped mirrors and knotty wood galore.

Holzkäfer CAFE, BAR €

(☎600 90; Buchenhöhe 40; dishes €4-9; ⏱11am-1am Wed-Mon) This funky log cabin in the Obersalzberg hills is known for its tender pork roasts, dark beer and Franconian wines.

Information

The **tourist office** (www.berchtesgaden.de; Königsseer Strasse 2; ⏱8.30am-6pm Mon-Fri, to 5pm Sat, 9am-3pm Sun Apr–mid-Oct, reduced hours mid-Oct–Mar) is just across the river from the train station.

Getting There & Away

Travelling from Munich by train involves a change at Freilassing (€30.90, three hours, five daily). Bus 840 connects the train stations in Berchesgaden and Salzburg twice hourly (45 minutes).

HITLER'S MOUNTAIN RETREAT

Of all the German towns tainted by the Third Reich, Berchtesgaden has a burden heavier than most. Hitler fell in love with nearby Obersalzberg in the 1920s and bought a small country home, later enlarged into the imposing Berghof.

After seizing power in 1933, the Führer established a part-time headquarters here and brought much of the party brass with him. They bought, or often confiscated, large tracts of land and tore down farmhouses to erect a 7ft-high barbed-wire fence. Obersalzberg was sealed off as the fortified southern headquarters of the NSDAP (National Socialist German Workers' Party).

In the final days of WWII, the Royal Air Force levelled much of Obersalzberg, though the Eagle's Nest, Hitler's mountaintop eyrie, was strangely left unscathed.

Romantic Road

Stretching 400km from the vineyards of Würzburg to the foot of the Alps, the Romantic Road (Romantische Strasse) is by far the most popular of Germany's themed holiday routes. It passes through more than two dozen cities and towns, including Rothenburg ob der Tauber, Dinkelsbühl and Augsburg.

Getting There & Around

Though Frankfurt is the most popular gateway for the Romantic Road, Munich is a good launchpad as well, especially if you decide to take the Romantic Road Coach (p459). From April to October this special service runs one coach daily in each direction between Frankfurt and Füssen (for Neuschwanstein) via Munich; the entire trip takes around 12 hours. There's no charge for breaking the journey and continuing the next day. Note that buses get incredibly crowded in summer.

Tickets are available for the entire route or for short segments. Buy them online or from travel agents, EurAide in Munich or Reisezentrum offices in larger train stations.

FÜSSEN

08362 / POP 14,200

In the foothills of the Alps, Füssen is the gateway to Schloss Neuschwanstein and Hohenschwangau, the two castles associated with King Ludwig II. Should you decide to spend the night, you'll sense a certain Alpine serenity while locals count the change from the day's day-tripper invasion. The **tourist office** (938 50; www.fuessen.de; Kaiser-Maximillian-Platz 1; 9am-5pm Mon-Fri, 10am-2pm Sat, 10am-noon Sun) can help you find lodging.

Sights

Schloss Neuschwanstein CASTLE
(930 830; www.hohenschwangau.de; adult/concession €12/11, with Hohenschwangau €23/21; 8am-5pm Apr-Sep, 9am-3pm Oct-Mar) Appearing through the mountaintops like a misty mirage is the world's most famous castle, and the model for Disney's citadel, fairy-tale Schloss Neuschwanstein.

King Ludwig II planned this castle himself, with the help of a stage designer rather than an architect, and it provides a fascinating glimpse into the king's state of mind. Ludwig foresaw his showpiece palace as a giant stage on which to recreate the world of Germanic mythology in the operatic works of Richard Wagner. At its centre is the lavish **Sängersaal** (Minstrels' Hall), created to feed the king's obsession with Wagner and medieval knights. Other completed sections include Ludwig's bedroom, dominated by a huge Gothic-style bed crowned with intricately carved cathedral-like spires; a gaudy artificial grotto; and the Byzantine **Thronsaal** (Throne Room) with an incredible mosaic floor containing over two million stones. Tours end with a 20-minute **film** on the castle and its creator.

For the postcard view of Neuschwanstein and the plains beyond, walk 10 minutes up to **Marienbrücke** (Mary's Bridge), which spans the spectacular Pöllat Gorge over a waterfall just above the castle.

Schloss Hohenschwangau CASTLE
(930 830; www.hohenschwangau.de; adult/concession €12/11, with Neuschwanstein €23/21; 8am-5.30pm Apr-Sep, 9am-3.30pm Oct-Mar) Ludwig spent his formative years at the sun-yellow Schloss Hohenschwangau. Far less showy than Neuschwanstein, Hohenschwangau has a distinctly lived-in feel and every piece of furniture is original. After his father died, Ludwig's main alteration was having stars, illuminated with hidden oil lamps, painted on the ceiling of his bedroom. Some rooms have frescos from German history and legend.

Museum der Bayerischen Könige MUSEUM
(Museum of the Bavarian Kings; www.museumder-bayerischenkoenige.de; Alpseestrasse 27; adult/concession €8.50/7; 8am-7pm Apr-Sep, 10am-6pm Oct-Mar) This architecturally stunning museum is packed with historical background on Bavaria's first family. The big-window lake views to the Alps are almost as stunning as the royal bling on show, including Ludwig II's famous blue and gold robe.

VISITING THE CASTLES

Both castles must be seen on guided tours (in German or English), which last about 35 minutes each. Timed tickets are only available from the **Ticket Centre** (930 40; www.hohenschwangau.de; Alpenseestrasse 12; tickets 8am-5pm Apr-Sep, 9am-3pm Oct-Mar) at the foot of the castles. In summer, come as early as 8am to ensure you get in that day.

All Munich's tour companies run day excursions (with guaranteed admission) out to the castles.

Sleeping & Eating

Altstadt Hotel zum Hechten HOTEL €€
(916 00; www.hotel-hechten.com; Ritterstrasse 6; s €59-65 d €90-99;) At one of Füssen's oldest hotels, public areas are traditional in style but the bedrooms are mostly airy, light and brightly renovated. One of Füssen's better eateries awaits downstairs.

Franziskaner Stüberl BAVARIAN €€
(371 24; Kemptener Strasse 1; mains €5.50-15; lunch & dinner) This quaint restaurant specialises in *Schweinshaxe* (pork knuckle) and schnitzel, prepared in more varieties than you can shake a haunch at. Noncarnivores go for the scrumptious *Käsespätzle* (rolled cheese noodles) and the huge salads.

Getting There & Away

Trains from/to Munich (€24, two hours) run every two hours. RVO buses 78 and 73 serve the castles from Füssen Bahnhof (€4 return).

The Romantic Road Coach leaves from stop 3 outside Füssen train station at 8am. It arrives in Füssen after 8pm.

Rothenburg ob der Tauber

☎09861 / POP 11,000

In the Middle Ages, Rothenburg's town fathers built strong walls to protect the town from siege. Today those same walls are the reason the town is under siege from tourists. Possibly the most stereotypical of all German walled towns, Rothenburg can't help being so cute.

Sights

Jakobskirche CHURCH

(Klingengasse 1; adult/child €2/0.50; ⏲9am-5pm) Rothenburg's most famous church sports wonderful stained-glass windows, but its real pièce de résistance is the **Heilig Blut Altar** (Sacred Blood Altar) carved with dizzying intricacy by medieval master Tilmann Riemenschneider.

Rathaus HISTORIC BUILDING

(Marktplatz; Rathausturm adult/concession €2/0.50; ⏲tower 9.30am-12.30pm & 1-5pm daily Apr-Oct, noon-3pm daily Dec, shorter hours Sat & Sun Nov & Jan-Mar) The highlight of Rothenburg's Renaissance town hall is the widescreen views of the city and surrounds from the tower's viewing platform (220 steps).

Mittelalterliches Kriminalmuseum MUSEUM

(☎5359; www.kriminalmuseum.rothenburg.de; Burggasse 3-5; adult/child €4.20/2.60; ⏲10am-6pm May-Oct, shorter hours Nov-Apr) Chastity belts, a cage for cheating bakers and a beer-barrel pen for drunks are among the medieval implements of torture and punishment at this gruesomely fascinating museum.

Sleeping & Eating

Altfränkische Weinstube HOTEL €

(☎6404; www.altfraenkische-weinstube-rothenburg.de; Klosterhof 7; r €59-89; 📶) This characterful inn has six atmosphere-laden rooms, most with four-poster or canopied beds, and a restaurant that serves up sound regional dinners.

Zur Höll GERMAN €€

(☎4229; Burggasse 8; mains €6.50-18; ⏲dinner) This medieval slow-food wine tavern has a small regional menu and some excellent wines from nearby Würzburg.

Getting There & Away

There are hourly trains to/from Steinach, a transfer point for service to Würzburg (€12.20, 1¼ hours). The Romantic Road Coach pauses in town for 35 minutes.

> **DRINK AND 'YE SHALL BE FREE**
>
> According to legend, Rothenburg was spared destruction during the Thirty Years' War when the mayor won a challenge by Catholic General Tilly and downed more than 3L of wine at a gulp. This 'Meistertrunk' scene is re-enacted several times daily by the clock figures on the tourist office building and at a festival during Whitsuntide.

Würzburg

☎0931 / POP 133,500

Tucked in among river valleys lined with vineyards, Würzburg beguiles long before you reach the city centre and is renowned for its art, architecture and delicate wines. Its crowning architectural glory is the Residenz, one of the finest baroque structures in Germany and a Unesco World Heritage site.

Sights

Residenz PALACE

(www.residenz-wuerzburg.de; Balthasar-Neumann-Promenade; adult/child €7.50/6.50; ⏲9am-6pm Apr-Oct, 10am-4.30pm Nov-Mar) The undisputed highlight of the former prince-bishops residence is the dazzling **Grand Staircase** designed by Balthasar Neumann and lidded by a humongous Tiepolo fresco that allegorically depicts the four then-known continents (Europe, Africa, America and Asia). Guided tours also take in the **Weisser Saal** (White Hall) with its ice-white stucco and the gilded **Spiegelkabinett** (Mirror Hall). The **Hofgarten** at the back is a beautiful spot to relax.

Festung Marienberg FORTRESS

Panoramic views over the city's red rooftops and vine-covered hills extend from Marienberg Fortress. It has presided over Würzburg since the city's prince-bishops commenced its construction in 1201; they governed from here until 1719.

Their pompous lifestyle is documented at the **Fürstenbaumuseum** (adult/child €4.50/3.50; ⏲9am-6pm Tue-Sun mid-Mar–Oct), which also lays out the entire city history upstairs. Also here is the **Mainfränkisches Museum** (www.mainfraenkisches-museum.de; adult/child €4/2; ⊙10am-5pm Tue-Sun), which boasts a striking collection of Tilman Riemenschneider sculptures.

The fortress is a 30-minute walk up the hill from the 15th-century Alte Mainbrücke via the **Tellsteige trail**, which is part of the 4km-long **Weinwanderweg** (wine hiking trail) through the vineyards around Marienberg.

Sleeping & Eating

Würzburg's many *Weinstuben* (wine taverns) are great for sampling the local vintages.

Babelfish HOSTEL €
(☎304 0430; www.babelfish-hostel.de; Haugerring 2; dm €17-23, s/d €45/70) This uncluttered and spotlessly clean hostel has 74 beds spread over two floors, plus a rooftop terrace and a well-equipped guest kitchen.

Hotel Rebstock HOTEL €€
(☎309 30; www.rebstock.com; Neubaustrasse 7; s/d from €101/120; ❄@☜) In a squarely renovated rococo townhouse, this hotel has 70 unique, stylishly finished rooms, impeccable service and an Altstadt location.

Bürgerspital Weinstube WINE RESTAURANT €€
(☎352 880; Theaterstrasse 19; mains €7-23; ⊙lunch & dinner) The cosy nooks of this labyrinthine medieval place are among Würzburg's most popular eating and drinking spots. Great Franconian wines and regional dishes.

Alte Mainmühle FRANCONIAN €€
(☎167 77; Mainkai 1; mains €7-21; ⊙10am-midnight) At this double-decker terrace suspended above the Main River you can savour modern twists on old Franconian favourites.

Information

Tourist Office (☎372 398; www.wuerzburg.de; Marktplatz; ⊙10am-6pm Mon-Fri, 10am-2pm Sat Apr-Dec, plus 10am-2pm Sun May-Oct, reduced hours Jan-Mar)

Getting There & Away

The Romantic Road Coach stops next to the Hauptbahnhof and at the Residenzplatz. Frequent trains run to Bamberg (€19, one hour), Frankfurt (€33, one hour), Nuremberg (from €19.20, one hour) and Rothenburg ob der Tauber (via Steinach, €12.20, one hour).

Nuremberg

☎0911 / POP 503,000

Nuremberg (Nürnberg) woos visitors with its wonderfully restored medieval Altstadt, its grand castle and, in December, its magical *Christkindlmarkt* (Christmas market). Thriving culinary traditions include sizzling *Nürnberger Bratwürste* (finger-sized sausages) and *Lebkuchen* – large, soft gingerbread cookies, traditionally eaten at Christmas time but available here year-round.

Nuremberg played a major role during the Nazi years and during the war-crimes trials afterwards. It has done an admirable job of confronting this ugly past with museums and exhibits.

Sights

Hauptmarkt SQUARE
This central square hosts a daily farmers market and the famous *Christkindlmarkt*. The church here is the Gothic **Pfarrkirche Unsere Liebe Frau** (Hauptmarkt 14) (aka Frauenkirche); the clock's figures go strolling daily at noon. For good luck touch the golden ring in the wrought-iron gate hemming in the gargoyle-adorned **Schöner Brunnen** (Beautiful Fountain) in the square's centre.

Kaiserburg CASTLE
(www.schloesser.bayern.de; adult/child incl museum €7/6; ⊙9am-6pm Apr-Sep, 10am-4pm Oct-Mar) Construction of Nuremberg's landmark, the vast **Kaiserburg**, began in the 12th century and dragged on for about 400 years. The complex, for centuries the receptacle of the Holy Roman Empire's treasures, consists of three parts: the Kaiserburg and Stadtburg (the Emperor's Palace and City Fortress) and the Burggrafenburg (Count's Residence), which was largely destroyed in 1420.

The **Kaiserburg Museum** chronicles the history of the castle and provides a survey of medieval defence techniques. You can also visit the royal living quarters, the Imperial and Knights' Halls, and the Romanesque **Doppelkapelle** (Twin Chapel).

Enjoy panoramic city views from atop the **Sinwellturm** (Sinwell Tower; 113 steps) or peer into the amazing 48m-deep **Tiefer Brunnen** (Deep Well). The grassy knoll at the southeast corner of the castle gardens (open seasonally) is called Am Ölberg and is a great spot to sit and gaze out over the city's rooftops.

Memorium Nuremberg Trials HISTORIC BUILDING
(☎3217 9372; www.memorium-nuremberg.de; Bärenschanzstrasse 72; adult/concession €5/3; ⏲10am-6pm Wed-Mon) Nazis were tried in 1945 and 1946 for crimes against peace and humanity in Schwurgerichtssaal 600 (Court Room 600) of what is still Nuremberg's regional courthouse. The proceedings became known as the Nuremberg Trials, and were held by the Allies in the city for symbolic reasons.

The initial and most famous trial, conducted by international prosecutors, saw 24 people accused, of whom 19 were convicted and sentenced, many to death by hanging. Hermann Göring, the Reich's field marshall, cheated the hangman by taking a cyanide capsule in his cell hours before his scheduled execution.

In addition to viewing the courtroom (if not in use), a new exhibition provides comprehensive background on the trials. The courthouse is about 2km from the city centre. Take the U1 (direction Bärenschanze) and get off at Sielstrasse.

Reichsparteitagsgelände HISTORIC SITE
(Luitpoldhain) Nuremberg's role during the Third Reich is well known. The Nazis chose this city as their propaganda centre and for mass rallies, which were held at **Luitpoldhain**, a (never completed) sports complex of megalomaniac proportions.

The **Dokumentationszentrum** (☎231 7538; Bayernstrasse 110; adult/concession €5/3; ⏲9am-6pm Mon-Fri, 10am-6pm Sat & Sun) is in the north wing of the unfinished Congress Hall and has absorbing exhibits tracing the rise of Hitler and the Nazis, the Hitler cult, the party rallies and the Nuremberg Trials.

East of here, across an artificial pond, is the **Zeppelinfeld**, fronted by a 350m-long grandstand, where most of the big Nazi parades, rallies and events took place.

Take tram 9 from the Hauptbahnhof to Doku-Zentrum.

Germanisches Nationalmuseum MUSEUM
(www.gnm.de; Kartäusergasse 1; adult/child €6/4; ⏲10am-6pm Tue & Thu-Sun, to 9pm Wed) Spanning prehistory to the early 20th century, the German National Museum is the country's most important museum of German culture. It features paintings and sculptures, an archaeological collection, arms and armour, musical and scientific instruments and toys.

CHRISTMAS MARKETS

Beginning in late November every year, central squares across Germany are transformed into Christmas markets or *Christkindlmärkte* (also known as *Weihnachtsmärkte*). Folks stamp about between the wooden stalls, perusing seasonal trinkets (from hand-carved ornaments to plastic angels) while warming themselves with *Glühwein* (mulled, spiced red wine) and grilled sausages. Locals love 'em and, not surprisingly, the markets are popular with tourists, so bundle up and carouse for hours. Markets in Nuremberg, Dresden, Cologne and Munich are especially famous.

At the museum's entrance is the inspired **Way of Human Rights**, a symbolic row of 29 white concrete pillars (and one oak tree) bearing the 30 articles of the Universal Declaration of Human Rights.

Sleeping

Hotel Elch HOTEL €€
(☎249 2980; www.hotel-elch.com; Irrerstrasse 9; s/d from €75/95; 📶) This 14th-century, half-timbered house is a snug and romantic 12-room gem. Note the multicoloured elk heads throughout (the hotel's name means 'Elk').

Lette'm Sleep HOSTEL €
(☎992 8128; www.backpackers.de; Frauentormauer 42; dm €16-20, r from €50; @📶) This indie hostel near the Hauptbahnhof has colourful dorms, a retro-styled kitchen, a common room for chilling and clued-in staff. Internet, tea and coffee are free.

Eating

Don't leave Nuremberg without trying its famous *Nürnberger Bratwürste*.

Bratwursthäusle GERMAN €€
(http://die-nuernberger-bratwurst.de; Rathausplatz 2; meals €6-14; ⏲closed Sun) Seared over a flaming beech-wood grill, the little links sold at this rustic inn arguably set the standard for grilled sausages across the land.

Hütt'n GERMAN €€
(Bergstrasse 20; mains €5.50-15; ⏲4pm-midnight Mon-Fri, 11am-12.30am Sat, 11am-10.30pm Sun) The specialty at this always-busy local haunt is

Krustenschäufele: roast pork with crackling, dumplings and Sauerkraut salad. Pair it with a tankard of Franconian *Landbier*.

Café am Trödelmarkt CAFE €
(Trödelmarkt 42; dishes €4-8.50; 9am-6pm Mon-Sat, 11am-6pm Sun) This waterfront cafe is especially popular for its continental breakfasts and has fantastic cakes as well as good blackboard lunchtime specials.

Information

Tourist Office (www.tourismus.nuernberg.de) Künstlerhaus (233 60; Königstrasse 93; 9am-7pm Mon-Sat, 10am-4pm Sun); Hauptmarkt (Hauptmarkt 18; 9am-6pm Mon-Sat, 10am-4pm Sun May-Oct)

Getting There & Around

Nuremberg **airport** (NUE; www.airport-nuernberg.de), 5km north of the centre, is served by the U2 from Hauptbahnhof (€2.40, 12 minutes).

Rail connections from Nuremberg include Berlin (€93, five hours), Frankfurt (€51, two hours), Munich (€52, one hour) and Vienna (€94.20, five hours).

The city centre is best explored on foot. Public transport day passes cost €4.80.

Bamberg

0951 / POP 70,000

Off the major tourist routes, Bamberg is revered by those in the know. It boasts a beautifully preserved collection of 17th- and 18th-century buildings, palaces and churches and its own style of beer. No wonder it has been recognised by Unesco as a World Heritage site.

Sights

Bamberger Dom CATHEDRAL
(www.erzbistum-bamberg.de; Domplatz; 8am-6pm Apr-Oct, to 5pm Nov-Mar) The quartet of spires of Bamberg's Dom soars above the cityscape. Its star attraction is the statue of the chivalric knight-king, the **Bamberger Reiter**. Also note the **Lächelnde Engel** (Smiling Angel), who smirkingly hands the martyr's crown to the headless St Denis in the north aisle, and the **marble tomb of Pope Clemens II**, the only papal burial place north of the Alps.

Altes Rathaus HISTORIC BUILDING
(Obere Brücke) Bamberg's frescoed 1462 Old Town Hall perches on an islet between two bridges. The best views are from the small footbridge across the Regnitz River. See if you can spot the cherub's leg sticking out from the fresco on the east side.

Neue Residenz PALACE
(519 390; www.schloesser.bayern.de; Domplatz 8; adult/child €4.50/3.50; 9am-6pm Apr-Sep, 10am-4pm Oct-Mar) Tours of the lavish residence of Bamberg's prince-bishops take in some 40 rooms crammed with furniture and tapestries. It also houses medieval, Renaissance and baroque paintings.

Sleeping

Backpackers Bamberg HOSTEL €
(222 1718; www.backpackersbamberg.de; Heiliggrabstrasse 4; dm €15-18, s/d €27/40;) This well-kept hostel has clean dorms, a guest kitchen and a quiet, family-friendly atmosphere. It's left unstaffed for most of the day so let them know your arrival time.

Hotel Europa HOTEL €€
(309 3020; www.hotel-europa-bamberg.de; Untere Königstrasse 6-8; r €89-119) The Europa is a spick-and-span but unfussy affair above the town's most respected Italian restaurant just outside the Altstadt. Ask for a room at the front with views of the Dom and the red-tiled roofs.

Eating & Drinking

Bamberg's unique style of beer is called *Rauchbier*, which literally means smoked beer. With a bacon flavour at first, it is a smooth brew that goes down easily.

TOP CHOICE **Schlenkerla** GERMAN €€
(Dominikanerstrasse 6; mains €8-15; Wed-Mon) A warren of rooms decked out with antler lamps, this 16th-century restaurant is famous for tasty Franconian specialities and *Rauchbier*, served straight from oak barrels.

Klosterbräu BREWERY €
(522 65; Obere Mühlbrücke 1-3; mains €6-12; 10.30am-11pm Mon-Fri, 10am-11pm Sat, 10am-10pm Sun) This beautiful half-timbered brewery is Bamberg's oldest and a great place for washing down filling slabs of meat and dumplings with an excellent range of ales.

Messerschmidt FRANCONIAN €€
(297 800; Lange Strasse 41; mains €12-25; lunch & dinner) This stylish gourmet eatery in the birth house of aviation engineer Willy Messerschmidt oozes old-world charm, with dark woods, white linens and formal service. Tuck into hearty local fare out on the park-facing terrace or in the attached wine tavern.

Information

Tourist Office (☎297 6200; www.bamberg.info; Geyerswörthstrasse 5; ⌚9.30am-6pm Mon-Fri, to 4pm Sat, to 2.30pm Sun)

Getting There & Away

Bamberg is well connected by train with regular departures to Munich (€59, two to 2½ hours), Nuremberg (from €12, one hour) and Würzburg (€19, one hour).

Regensburg

☎0941 / POP 135,500

On the wide Danube River, Regensburg has relics of historic periods reaching back to the Romans yet doesn't have the tourist mobs you'll find in other equally attractive German cities. Oh well, their loss. At least Unesco noticed. It recognised that Regensburg has the only intact medieval centre in Germany. Amid the half-timbers, Renaissance towers that could be in Tuscany mix with Roman ruins. Meanwhile, some 25,000 students keep things lively.

Sights

Steinerne Brücke BRIDGE

A veritable miracle of engineering for its day, the Stone Bridge was cobbled together between 1135 and 1146 and for centuries remained the only solid crossing along the entire Danube.

Dom St Peter CHURCH

(Domplatz; ⌚6.30am-6pm Apr-Oct, to 5pm Nov-Mar) One of Bavaria's grandest Gothic cathedrals, St Peter's impressive features include kaleidoscopic stained-glass windows and the intricately gilded altar. The **Domschatzmuseum** (adult/child €2/1; ⌚10am-5pm Tue-Sat, noon-5pm Sun) brims with monstrances, tapestries and other church treasures.

Altes Rathaus HISTORIC BUILDING

(Rathausplatz; adult/concession €7.50/4; ⌚English tours 3pm Apr-Oct, 2pm Nov-Mar) Tours of the Altes Rathaus take in the lavishly decorated **Reichssaal** (Imperial Hall), where the Reichstag met for 150 years, and the original **torture chambers**.

Sleeping

Brook Lane Hostel HOSTEL €

(☎696 5521; www.hostel-regensburg.de; Obere Bachgasse 21; dm/s/d/ from €16/40/50, apt per person €55; ⊗☜) Dorms do the minimum required but the apartments and doubles here are applaudable deals. Access to kitchens and washing machines throughout. Enter via the small shop.

Petit Hotel Orphée HOTEL €€

(☎596 020; www.hotel-orphee.de; Wahlenstrasse 1; s €35-125, d €70-135) Behind a humble door in the heart of the city lies a world of genuine charm, unexpected extras and real attention to detail. The wrought-iron beds, original sinks and cosy common rooms create the feel of a lovingly attended home. Another somewhat grander branch of the hotel is located above the **Café Orphée** (☎529 77; Untere Bachgasse 8; mains €7-18; ⌚9am-1am).

Eating & Drinking

Historische Wurstkuchl GERMAN €

(Thundorfer Strasse 3; 6 sausages €7.80; ⌚8am-7pm) The Danube rushes past this little house that's been cooking up traditional finger-size sausages since 1135.

Dicker Mann BAVARIAN €€

(www.dicker-mann.de; Krebsgasse 6; mains €6.50-20; ⌚9am-11pm) Stylish, very traditional and serving all the staples of Bavarian sustenance, the 'Chubby Chappy' is one of the oldest restaurants in town, allegedly dating back to the 14th century. On a balmy eve, be sure to bag a table in the lovely beer garden out back.

Spitalgarten BEER GARDEN

(St Katharinenplatz 1) Overlooking the Danube, this is one of the best places in town for some alfresco quaffing of the house brew (made since 1350).

Information

Tourist Office (www.regensburg.de; Altes Rathaus; ⌚9am-6pm Mon-Fri, to 4pm Sat & Sun)

Getting There & Away

There are frequent trains to Munich (€25.20, 1½ hours) and Nuremberg (€19, one to two hours), among others.

STUTTGART & THE BLACK FOREST

Germany's southwest is taken up by Baden-Württemberg, a prosperous, modern state created in 1951 out of three smaller regions: Baden, Württemberg and Hohenzollern (thank goodness the names stopped at two!). With the exception of cuckoo clocks in the

Black Forest, it runs a distant second in the cliché race to Bavaria. But that's really all the better, as it leaves more for you to discover on your own.

This pretty land of misty hills, shadowy conifers and cute villages rewards exploration. If you want a big and quaint historical town, there's Heidelberg. Baden-Baden is the sybaritic playground for spa-goers, and Freiburg has youthful vibrancy in an intriguing historical package. Finally, Lake Constance is a lovely redoubt bordering Switzerland and has all the pleasures a large body of water can offer.

Stuttgart

0711 / POP 581,000

Hemmed in by vine-covered hills, Stuttgart enjoys a quality of life founded on its fabled car companies – Porsche and Mercedes – which show off their pedigree in two excellent museums. It's also Baden-Württemberg's state capital and the hub of its industries. At the forefront of Germany's economic recovery from the ravages of WWII, Stuttgart started life less auspiciously in 950 as a horse stud farm.

Sights

Mercedes-Benz Museum MUSEUM

(www.museum-mercedes-benz.com; Mercedesstrasse 100; adult/concession €8/4; 9am-6pm Tue-Sun; Neckarpark) A futuristic swirl on the cityscape, the Mercedes-Benz Museum takes a chronological spin through the Mercedes empire. Look out for legends like the 1885 Daimler Riding Car, the world's first gasoline-powered vehicle, and the record-breaking Lightning Benz that hit 228km/h on Daytona Beach in 1909. Free English tour at 11am.

BOHEMIAN BEANS

Stuttgart's most interesting neighbourhood is a short stroll from the centre. The **Bohnenviertel** (Bean District) takes its name from the diet of the poor tanners, dyers and craftsmen who lived here. Today the district's cobbled lanes and gabled houses harbour idiosyncratic galleries, workshops, bookstores, wine taverns, cafes and a red-light district.

Porsche Museum MUSEUM

(www.porsche.com; Porscheplatz 1; adult/concession €8/4; 9am-6pm Tue-Sun; Neuwirtshaus) Like a pearly white spaceship preparing for lift-off, the barrier-free Porsche Museum is every little boy's dream. Groovy audioguides race you through the history of Porsche from its 1948 beginnings. Break to glimpse the 911 GT1 that won Le Mans in 1998.

Neues Schloss HISTORIC BUILDING

(Schlossplatz) Duke Karl Eugen von Württemberg's answer to Versailles was the exuberant three-winged Neues Schloss (New Palace), a baroque-neoclassical royal residence that now houses state government ministries. A bronze statue of Emperor Wilhelm I, looking dashing on his steed, graces nearby **Karlsplatz**.

Schlossgarten GARDEN

Stretching southwest from the Neckar River to the city centre is the Schlossgarten, an extensive strip of parkland divided into three sections (Unterer, Mittlerer and Oberer Garten), complete with ponds, swans, street entertainers and modern sculptures.

Staatsgalerie GALLERY

(www.staatsgalerie-stuttgart.de; Konrad-Adenauer-Strasse 30-32; adult/concession €5.50/4, special exhibitions €10/8, Wed & Sat free; 10am-6pm Tue-Sun, to 8pm Tue & Thu) Alongside big-name exhibitions, this prestigious art museum showcases works by Rembrandt, Picasso, Monet and Dalí as well as 20th-century Pop idols Warhol and Lichtenstein.

Sleeping

Interhostel HOSTEL €

(6648 2797; www.inter-hostel.com; Paulinenstrasse 16; dm/s/d €25/42/64;) A short toddle from Stadtmitte station, this hostel makes backpackers' hearts sing with its free coffee and wi-fi, bright and characterful digs, relaxed lounge and chipper team, plus handy stuff like luggage storage and a guest kitchen.

Abalon Hotel HOTEL €€

(217 10; www.abalon.de; Zimmermannstrasse 7-9; s €74-89, d €89-112;) Affable staff, a top location and wallet-friendly rates make Abalon a great pick. The bright parquet-floored rooms are large and spotless.

Hostel Alex 30 HOSTEL €

(838 8950; www.alex30-hostel.de; Alexanderstrasse 30; dm/s/d/q €24/36/58/100, breakfast

€8; P 📶) Backpackers find a relaxed base in these mellow digs with a bar, sundeck and communal kitchen. The spotless, citrus-bright rooms are light and contemporary.

City Hotel HOTEL €€
(☎210 810; www.cityhotel-stuttgart.de; Uhlandstrasse 18; s €79-89, d €99-115; P 📶) Eschew the anonymity of Stuttgart's cookie-cutter chains for this intimate hotel just off Charlottenplatz. Rooms are light, clean and modern, if slightly lacklustre.

Eating

Stuttgart is a great place to sample Swabian specialities such as *Spätzle* (home-made noodles) and *Maultaschen* (a hearty ravioli in broth). Local wines edge out beer in popularity.

The **food market** (Marktplatz; ⏱7.30am-1pm Tue, Thu & Sat) and the **Markthalle** (Market Hall; Dorotheenstrasse 4; ⏱7am-6.30pm Mon-Fri, 7am-4pm Sat), with their bounty of local produce and gourmet items, are the best features of the otherwise humdrum Marktplatz.

Weinstube Fröhlich SWABIAN €€
(☎242 471; www.weinstube-froehlich.de; Leonhardstrasse 5; mains €12-23; ⏱5.30pm-12.30am) True, it's bang in the heart of the red-light district, but don't be put off. This softly lit, dark wood-panelled restaurant is an atmospheric choice for well-executed Swabian fare and regional wines.

Alte Kanzlei GERMAN €€
(☎294 457; Schillerplatz 5a; mains €10.50-20.50; ⏱daily) Empty tables are gold-dust rare at this convivial, high-ceilinged restaurant. Feast on Swabian favourites like *Spanferkel* (roast suckling pig) and *Flädlesuppe* (pancake soup).

Reiskorn INTERNATIONAL €
(☎664 7633; Torstrasse 27; mains €5.50-12.90; ⏱closed Sun lunch; 🌶) With an easy-going vibe and bamboo-green retro interior, this culinary globetrotter serves everything from tangy Caribbean prawn salad to dim sum.

Drinking & Entertainment

Hans-im-Glück Platz is a hub of bars, while club- and lounge-lined Theodor-Heuss-Strasse is thronged with sashaying hipsters.

Biergarten im Schlossgarten BEER GARDEN
(www.biergarten-schlossgarten.de; ⏱10.30am-1am May-Oct; 📶) Toast summer with beer and pretzels at Stuttgart's best-loved, 2000-seat beer garden in the green heart of the Schlossgarten. Regular live music gets steins a-swinging.

Sky Beach BAR
(www.skybeach.de; Königstrasse 6, top floor Galeria Kaufhof; ⏱noon-12.30am Mon-Sat, 11am-midnight Sun Easter-Sep) When the sun comes out, Stuttgarters live it up at this urban beach, complete with sand, cabana beds, DJs spinning mellow lounge beats and grandstand city views.

Kiste LIVE MUSIC
(www.kiste-stuttgart.de; Hauptstätter Strasse 35; ⏱6pm-1am Mon-Thu, to 2am Fri & Sat) Jam-packed at weekends, this hole-in-the-wall bar is Stuttgart's leading jazz venue, with nightly concerts starting at 9pm or 10pm.

Information

StuttCard (72hr with/without VVS ticket €18/9.70) Free entry to most museums, plus discounts on events, activities and guided tours. Sold at the tourist office and some hotels.

Tourist Office (www.stuttgart-tourist.de; Königstrasse 1a; ⏱9am-8pm Mon-Fri, 9am-6pm Sat, 11am-6pm Sun)

Getting There & Around

Stuttgart International Airport, a major hub for Germanwings, is 13km south of the city and served by S2 and S3 trains from the Hauptbahnhof (€3.50, 30 minutes).

Trains head to all major German cities, including Frankfurt (€59, 1¼ hour), Munich (€54, 2¼ hours) and Nuremberg (€39, 2¼ hours) and many international ones, such as Zürich and Paris.

On public transport, single tickets are €2.10, a day pass €6.10.

Heidelberg

☎06221 / POP 147,000

Germany's oldest and most famous university town is renowned for its baroque Old Town, lively university atmosphere, excellent pubs and evocative half-ruined castle, which draw 3½ million visitors a year. The visitors follow in the footsteps of the late 18th- and early 19th-century romantics, most notably Johann Wolfgang von Goethe. Mark Twain kicked off his European travels in 1878 with a three-month stay in Heidelberg, later recounting his bemused observations in *A Tramp Abroad*.

Sights

Heidelberg's sites cluster in the Altstadt (Old Town) which starts to reveal itself only after a charm-free 15-minute walk east from the main train station. Cut to the chase and go direct to the heart of town with bus 32 to Universitätsplatz or bus 33 to Bergbahn.

Schloss Heidelburg CASTLE
(www.schloss-heidelberg.de; adult/child incl Bergbahn €5/3, audioguide €4; 24hr, ticket required 8am-5.30pm) Sticking up above the Altstadt like a picture-book pop-up, Heidelberg's ruined Schloss is one of the most romantic spots in Germany. Its tumultuous history, lonely beauty and changing moods helped inspire the German Romantic movement two centuries ago. One of its biggest attractions is the **Grosses Fass**, a massive wine barrel capable of holding about 228,000L.

To reach the red-sandstone castle, perched above the Altstadt, either hoof it up the steep, cobbled Burgweg in about 10 minutes, or take the historic funicular called **Bergbahn** (Funicular Railway; www.bergbahn-heidelberg.de; every 10min 9am-about 5pm) from Kornmarkt. Schloss tickets include travel on the Bergbahn.

Studentenkarzer HISTORIC SITE
(Augustinergasse 2; adult/student incl Universitätsmuseum €3/2.50; 10am-6pm Tue-Sun Apr-Sep, 10am-4pm Tue-Sat Oct-Mar) Dominating Universitätsplatz are the 18th-century Alte Universität (Old University) and the Neue Universität (New University). On the back side, the Studentenkarzer, was used as a student jail from 1823 to 1914. Crimes that could get you locked up included public drunkenness, nocturnal singing and duelling.

Heiliggeistkirche CHURCH
(Marktplatz; spire adult/student €2/1; 11am-5pm Mon-Sat, 12.30-5pm Sun & holidays mid-Mar–Oct, 11am-3pm Fri & Sat, 12.30-3pm Sun Nov–mid-Mar) For a bird's-eye view of Heidelberg, climb 208 stairs to the top of the spire.

Philosophenweg TRAIL
Passing through steep fields and orchards on the slopes across the river from the Altstadt, the Philosophers' Way commands panoramic views of the Schloss as it wends its way through the forest to various monuments, towers, ruins, a beer garden and a Nazi-era amphitheatre.

Tours

The tourist office runs English-language **walking tours** (adult/concession €7/5; 10.30am Fri & Sat Apr-Oct) of the Altstadt.

Sleeping

Steffis Hostel HOSTEL €
(778 2772; www.hostelheidelberg.de; Alte Eppelheimer Strasse 50; dm from €18, d without bathroom €52; reception 8am-10pm; P@) In a 19th-century tobacco factory, Steffis offers bright, well-lit rooms, a colourful lounge, a spacious kitchen and an old-time hostel vibe along with such perks as wi-fi, tea and coffee. It's just north of the Hauptbahnhof, above a Lidl supermarket.

Hotel Goldener Hecht HOTEL €€
(166 025; www.hotel-goldener-hecht.de; Steingasse 2; d without breakfast €73-94;) This atmospheric hotel, near the Alte Brücke, has just 13 rooms, six with bridge views; the three corner rooms are bright and gorgeous. It's very central but potentially noisy.

Hotel am Kornmarkt HOTEL €€
(905 830; www.hotelamkornmarkt.de; Kornmarkt 7; s/d from €65/85, without bathroom €40/70;) A block from the Marktplatz, this hotel is a beacon to euro-conscious travellers. The 20 rooms are no-frills but comfortable and spotless; the priciest have Kornmarkt views.

Eating

Schiller's Café CAFE €
(Heiliggeiststrasse 5; cakes €2.50; 10am-8pm Sun-Wed, 10am-midnight Thu-Sat) One of Heidelberg's oldest residential buildings houses this homey cafe which serves over 60 kinds of hot chocolate, homemade cakes, quiche and wines.

KulturBrauerei CAFE €€
(502 980; Leyergasse 6; mains €10.50-26.50; 7am-11pm or later) With its wood-plank floor, black iron chandeliers and time-faded ceiling frescos, this microbrewery is an atmospheric spot to tuck into salad, soup or regional dishes such as *Schäufele* (pork shoulder) with sauerkraut.

Café Burkardt CAFE €
(Untere Strasse 27; cake & snacks €3-8; 9am-11pm Tue-Sat, 9am-6pm Sun) Full of doily-draped tables and dark-wood crannies, this friendly cafe serves salads, German dishes, pasta and some of Heidelberg's scrummiest tarts and cheesecakes.

Drinking & Entertainment

Lots of the action centres on Untere Strasse. Two ancient pubs, **Zum Roten Ochsen** (☎209 77; Hauptstrasse 213) and **Zum Sepp'l** (☎230 85; Hauptstrasse 217), are now filled with tourists.

Kulturhaus Karlstorbahnhof LIVE MUSIC
(☎978 711; www.karlstorbahnhof.de; Am Karlstor 1; ⊙closed Aug) This edgy cultural centre shelters a concert venue, an art-house cinema and the popular **Klub K** (⊙10 or 11pm-5 or 6am Thu-Sat), whose DJs play everything from techno and dubstep to indic rock for a mixed crowd. It's train-track-adjacent 100m east of the Karlstor.

Nachtschicht CLUB
(www.nachtschicht.com; Bergheimerstrasse 147; admission €3-6; ⊙10pm-4am Thu, 8pm-1am Fri, 11pm-5am Sat) Two blocks north of the Hauptbahnhof, this old tobacco factory has morphed into one of Heidelberg's most popular student clubs.

Information

Heidelberg Card (1/2/4 days €11/13/16, 2-day family pass €28) Includes public transport, admission to the Schloss (including the Bergbahn) and discounts at most museums, for bike and boat rental, and for tours. Available at the tourist offices.

Tourist Office (☎584 4444, 194 33; www.heidelberg-marketing.de) Hauptbahnhof (Willy-Brandt-Platz 1; ⊙9am-7pm Mon-Sat, 10am-6pm Sun & holidays Apr-Oct, 9am-6pm Mon-Sat Nov-Mar); Marktplatz (Marktplatz 10; 8am 5pm Mon-Fri, 10am-5pm Sat)

Getting There & Away

There are hourly IC trains to/from Frankfurt (from €16.40, one hour) and Stuttgart (from €21.20, 40 minutes), along with frequent service to the railway hub of Mannheim (€4.90, 19 minutes) with connections throughout Germany.

The fastest way to get to Frankfurt airport (€23, one hour, every hour or two) is to take the eight-seat **Lufthansa Airport Shuttle** (☎06152-976 9099; www.transcontinental-group.com).

Black Forest

The Black Forest (Schwarzwald) gets its name from its dark canopy of evergreens, which evoke mystery and allure in many. Although some parts heave with visitors, a 20-minute walk from even the most crowded spots will put you in quiet countryside interspersed with hulking traditional farmhouses and patrolled by amiable dairy cows. It's not nature wild and remote, but bucolic and picturesque. And, yes, there are many, many places to buy cuckoo clocks (you'll pay at least €150 for a good one).

Getting Around

An hourly train line links Freudenstadt with Offenburg via Alpirsbach, Schiltach and other villages. From Hausach, trains run roughly hourly southeast to Triberg and Constance.

ALPIRSBACH

A small town, Alpirsbach, is worth a stop for its 12th-century Benedictine abbey, **Kloster Alpirsbach** (adult/concession €4/3.30; ⊙10am-5.30pm Mon-Sat, 11am-5.30pm Sun), which conveys the simple, spiritual life in its flat-roofed church, spartan cells and Gothic cloister. The museum has a stash of 16th-century clothing, caricatures (of artistic scholars) and lines (of misbehaving ones).

Just across the old complex you'll find what's kept the monks busy all these years: the **Alpirsbacher Klosterbräu** (☎670; www.alpirsbacher.com; Marktplatz 1; tours €6.90; ⊙2.30pm daily) brewery. Tours include a couple of glasses of the brew.

For more information, stop by the **tourist office** (☎951 6281; www.stadt-alpirsbach.de; Krähenbadstrasse 2; ⊙10am-noon & 2-5pm Mon-Fri, closed Wed afternoon).

Alpirsbach is a stop for the hourly trains linking Schiltach and Freudenstadt.

BLACK FOREST DISCOUNTS

Check into almost any hotel in Baden-Württemberg, pay the nominal *Kurtaxe* (holiday tax) and you automatically receive the money-saving **Gästekarte** (Guest Card), entitling you to free or discounted entry to many attractions and activities plus hefty discounts on everything from bike hire and spas to ski lifts and boat trips. Versions with the **Konus** symbol mean free use of public transport.

Most tourist offices in the Black Forest sell the three-day **Schwarzwald-Card** for admission to around 150 attractions in the Black Forest. Details on both cards are available at www.blackforest-tourism.com.

SCHILTACH

☎07836 / POP 3875

A contender for the prettiest town in the Black Forest is Schiltach, where there is the always-underlying roar of the intersecting Kinzig and Schiltach Rivers. Half-timbered buildings lean at varying angles along the criss-crossing hillside lanes. Centred on a trickling fountain, the sloping, triangular **Marktplatz** is Schiltach at its picture-book best. Don't miss the **Schüttesäge Museum** (Gerbegasse; ⏲11am-5pm daily Apr-Oct, Sat & Sun only Nov-Mar), which illustrates Schiltach's rafting tradition with a reconstructed workshop, a functioning watermill and touchy-feely exhibits for kids.

Nineteen generations of the same family have run the 16th-century inn **Weysses Rössle** (☎387; www.weysses-roessle.de; Schenkenzeller Strasse 42; s/d €52/75; P📶), where countrified rooms feature snazzy bathrooms. The woodsy tavern uses locally sourced, organic fare.

The **tourist office** (www.schiltach.de; Hauptstrasse 5; ⏲10am-5pm Mon-Fri, to 2pm Sat Apr-Oct) can help with accommodation and has a lot of English-language information.

TRIBERG

☎07722 / POP 5000

Heir to the Black Forest cake recipe, nesting ground of the world's biggest cuckoos and spring of Germany's highest waterfall – Triberg is a torrent of Schwarzwald superlatives and attracts gushers of guests.

Niagara they ain't, but Germany's highest **waterfalls** (adult/concession €3.50/3; ⏲Mar-early Nov, 25-30 Dec) do exude their own wild romanticism. The Gutach River feeds the seven-tiered falls, which drop a total of 163m. The trail starts near the tourist office, which also has a small museum.

Triberg is Germany's undisputed cuckoo-clock capital. Two timepieces claim the title of world's largest cuckoo clock, giving rise to the battle of the birds. To the casual observer, the biggest is undeniably the commercially savvy **Eble Uhren-Park** (www.uhren-park.de; Schonachbach 27; admission €2; ⏲9am-6pm Mon-Sat, 10am-6pm Sun), listed in the Guinness World Records, on the B33 between Triberg and Hornberg.

At the other end of town, in Schonach, is its underdog rival, the **1. Weltgrösste Kuckucksuhr** (☎07722-4689; Untertalstrasse 28; adult/concession €1.20/0.60; ⏲9am-6pm May-Oct, 10am-5pm Nov-Apr), nestled inside a snug half-timbered building and complete with gear-driven innards. This giant timepiece – unable to compete in size alone – has taken to calling itself the 'world's first largest cuckoo clock'. It was built in the 1980s.

Above the shop of master woodcarver Gerald Burger is **Kukucksnest** (☎869 487; Wallfahrtstrasse 15; d €58), a beautiful nest he has carved for guests.

The kirsch-scented Black Forest cake at **Café Schäfer** (www.cafe-schaefer-triberg.de; Hauptstrasse 33; cake €3-4; ⏲9am-6pm Mon-Fri, 8am-6pm Sat, 11am-6pm Sun, closed Wed) is the real deal; it has the original recipe to prove it.

The hourly Schwarzwaldbahn train line loops southeast to Constance (€23.30, 1½ hours), and northwest to Offenburg (€11.10, 45 minutes).

Triberg's train station is 1.7km from the centre; take any bus to the Markt.

FOREST FOODIE FAVES

Black Forest specialities include *Schwarzwälder Schinken* (ham), which is smoked and served in a variety of ways. Rivalling those ubiquitous clocks in fame (but not price), *Schwarzwälder Kirschtorte* (Black Forest cake) is a chocolate and cherry concoction. A popular local beer is the crisp pilsener called Rothaus.

Freiburg im Breisgau

0761 / POP 224,200

Sitting plump at the foot of the Black Forest's wooded slopes and vineyards, Freiburg is a sunny, cheerful university town; its medieval Altstadt is a story-book tableau of gabled town houses, cobblestone lanes and cafe-rimmed plazas lorded over by a monumental 13th-century cathedral. Party-loving students spice up the local nightlife. Blessed with 2000 hours of annual sunshine, this is Germany's warmest city.

Sights & Activities

TOP CHOICE **Münster** CATHEDRAL

(Münsterplatz; tower adult/concession €1.50/1; ⏲10am-5pm Mon-Sat, 1-7.30pm Sun, tower 9.30am-5pm Mon-Sat, 1-5pm Sun) Freiburg's 13th-century minster is a red-sandstone pile whose punctured spires and gargoyles flush scarlet in the dusk light. Ascend the tower for an excellent view of the church's intricate construction. Inside, the kaleidoscopic

WORTH A TRIP

SOARING ABOVE THE FOREST

Freiburg seems tiny as you drift up above the city and a tapestry of meadows and forest on the **Schauinslandbahn** (adult/concession return €12/11, one-way €8.50/8; ⏲9am-5pm, to 6pm Jul-Sep) to the 1284m **Schauinsland peak** (www.bergwelt-schauinsland.de). The lift provides a speedy link between Freiburg and the Black Forest highlands.

Up top, enjoy commanding views to the Rhine Valley and Alps from the lookout tower, then hit a trail to capture the scenery from many different angles. You can also bounce downhill on the 8km off-road **scooter track** (www.rollerstrecke.de; €20; ⏲2pm & 5pm Sun May-Jun, Sat & Sun Jul & Sep-Oct, Wed-Sun Aug), one of Europe's longest; it takes around an hour from top to bottom station.

The Schauinslandbahn valley station is about 9km southeast of central Freiburg. Take tram 2 to Günterstal and then bus 21 to Talstation.

stained-glass windows dazzle. The **high altar** features a masterful triptych of the coronation of the Virgin Mary by Hans Baldung.

Rathausplatz SQUARE
(Town Hall Square) Freiburg locals hang out by the fountain in chestnut-shaded Rathausplatz. On its western side (note the red-sandstone) is the step-gabled **Neues Rathaus** (New City Hall; Rathausplatz).

Across the way is the mid-16th-century **Altes Rathaus** (Old City Hall; Universtitatstrasse), a flamboyant, ox-blood red edifice, embellished with gilt swirls and crowned by a clock and a fresco of the twin-headed Habsburg eagle.

Augustinermuseum MUSEUM
(☎201 2531; Salzstrasse 32; adult/child €6/4; ⏲10am-5pm Tue-Sun) This beautiful Augustinian monastery showcases prized medieval, baroque and 19th-century art by such hot shots as Hans Baldung, Matthias Grünewald and Lucas Cranach. There's also lavish medieval stained glass.

Sleeping

Black Forest Hostel HOSTEL €
(☎881 7870; www.blackforest-hostel.de; Kartäuserstrasse 33; dm €14-23, s/d €30/50; @) Funky budget digs with chilled common areas, a shared kitchen, bike rental and spacey stainless-steel showers. It's a five-minute walk from the centre of town.

Hotel Schwarzwälder Hof HOTEL €€
(☎380 30; www.schwarzwaelder-hof.eu; Herrenstrasse 43; s/d/tr €65/99/120; @) This bijou hotel has an unrivalled style-for-euro ratio. A wrought-iron staircase sweeps up to snazzy rooms that are temples to chalk whites and chocolate browns. Some have Altstadt views.

Eating & Drinking

Hausbrauerei Feierling BREWERY €€
(Gerberau 46; mains €6-12; ✎) Starring one of Freiburg's best beer gardens, this brewpub serves vegetarian options and big schnitzels.

Englers Weinkrügle GERMAN €€
(☎383 115; Konviktstrasse 12; mains €9-16; ⏲Tue-Sun) A warm, woody Baden-style *Weinstube* (wine tavern) with wisteria growing out front and regional flavours, including delicious trout, on the menu.

Schlappen PUB
(Löwenstrasse 2; ⏲11am-3am Mon-Sat, 3pm-1am Sun) With its jazz-themed back room and poster-plastered walls, this pub is a favourite. Punters spill onto the terrace in summer.

Information

Tourist office (☎388 1880; www.freiburg.de; Rathausplatz 2-4; ⏲8am-8pm Mon-Fri, 9.30am-5pm Sat, 11am-4pm Sun)

Getting There & Around

Freiburg shares **EuroAirport** (www.euroairport.com) with Basel (Switzerland) and Mulhouse (France). It buzzes with low-cost carriers. From Freiburg it is served hourly by the **Airport Bus** (☎500 500; www.freiburger-reisedienst.de; one-way/return €23/39; ⏲55 minutes).

Fast trains connect Freiburg to Basel (from €16.40, 45 minutes) and Baden-Baden (from €19.20, 45 minutes).

LAKE CONSTANCE

Straddling Germany, Austria and Switzerland, Lake Constance (known locally as Bodensee) is central Europe's third largest lake. Formed by the Rhine Glacier during the last ice age and fed and drained by that same sprightly river today, this whopper of a lake measures 63km long, 14km wide and up to 250m deep. Even if you never make contact with the water, Lake Constance offers a delightful splash of refreshment. Historic towns line its vineyard-dappled periphery, which can be explored by boat or bicycle or on foot.

Getting There & Around

Trains link Lindau and Constance, and buses fill in the gaps to places like Meersburg.

The most enjoyable, albeit slowest, way to get around is by **ferry**. Constance is the main hub, but Meersburg and Friedrichshafen also have plentiful ferry options. The most useful lines, run by **German BSB** (www.bsb-online.com) and **Austrian OBB** (www.bodenseeschifffahrt.at), link Constance with Meersburg (€5.30, 30 minutes), Friedrichshafen (€11.70, 1¾ hours), Lindau (€15.40, three hours) and Bregenz (€16.40, 3½ hours). The websites list timetables.

Euregio Bodensee (www.euregiokarte.com) publishes a free schedule (*Fahrplan*) listing all train, bus and ferry services.

Constance

07531 / POP 84,700

Hugging the Swiss border, Constance (Konstanz) is a feel-good university town with a lively buzz and upbeat bar scene, particularly in the cobbled Altstadt and along the waterfront.

It achieved historical significance in 1414, when the Council of Constance convened to try to heal huge rifts in the Catholic Church. The consequent burning at the stake of the religious reformer Jan Hus as a heretic, and the scattering of his ashes over the lake, did nothing to block the Reformation.

DISCOUNT CARDS

Euregio Bodensee Tageskarte (www.euregiokarte.com) gives you all-day access to land transport around Lake Constance, including areas in Austria and Switzerland. It's sold at train stations and ferry docks and costs €16.50/22/29 for one/two/all zones.

The three-day **Bodensee Erlebniskarte** (adult/child €72/36, not incl ferries €40/21), available at local tourist and ferry offices from early April to mid-October, is good for unlimited travel on almost all boats and mountain cableways on and around Lake Constance (including its Austrian and Swiss shores), as well as free entry to around 180 tourist attractions and museums.

Sights & Activities

TOP CHOICE **Münster** CATHEDRAL

(tower adult/child €2/1; 10am-6pm Mon-Sat, 10am-6pm Sun, tower 10am-5pm Mon-Sat, 12.30pm-5.30pm Sun) Crowned by a filigree spire, Constance's 1000-year-old sandstone cathedral is an architectural potpourri of Romanesque, Gothic, Renaissance and baroque styles. Standouts include the 15th-century **Schnegg**, an ornate spiral staircase, the **ancient crypt** and the sublime **Gothic cloister**. There are great views from the **tower** in good weather.

Mainau GARDEN

(www.mainau.de; adult/concession €16.90/9.50; sunrise-sunset) Jutting out over the Lake Constance and bursting with flowers, the lusciously green islet of Mainau is a 45-hectare Mediterranean garden dreamed up by the Bernadotte family, relatives of the royal house of Sweden. Take bus 4 from Constance's train station or hop aboard a passenger ferry.

Sleeping & Eating

Münsterplatz and Markstätte are peppered with pizzerias and snack bars. Watch out for rip-offs around Stadtgarten.

Hotel Barbarossa HISTORIC HOTEL €€

(128 990; www.barbarossa-hotel.com; Obermarkt 8-12; s €55-75, d €95-130;) This 600-year-old patrician house harbours parquet-floored, individually decorated rooms, which are bright and appealing, if a tad on the small side. The terrace has views over Constance's rooftops and spires.

Münsterhof GERMAN €€

(3638 427; Münsterplatz 3; mains €8.50-17; daily;) Tables set up in front of the Münster, a slick bistro interior and a lunchtime buzz have earned Münsterhof a loyal local following. The two-course €6.90 lunch is a bargain.

Voglhaus CAFE €

(Wessenbergstrasse 8; light meals €2.50-6; 9am-6.30pm Mon-Sat, 11am-6pm Sun;) Locals flock to the 'bird house' for its chilled vibe and contemporary wood-and-stone interior, warmed by an open fire in winter.

Brauhaus Johann Albrecht BREWPUB (Konradigasse 2; ⏲11.30am-1pm) This step-gabled microbrewery is a relaxed haunt for quaffing wheat beer or hoppy lager by the glass or metre, with a terrace for summer imbibing.

Information

Tourist office (☎133 030; www.konstanz-tourismus.de; Bahnhofplatz 43; ⏲9am-6.30pm Mon-Fri, 9am-4pm Sat, 10am-1pm Sun Apr-Oct, 9.30am-6pm Mon-Fri Nov-Mar) Just north of the train station.

Getting There & Away

Constance is Lake Constance's main ferry hub. The town is also the southern terminus of the scenic Schwarzwaldbahn, which trundles hourly through the Black Forest. For northern shore towns, change in Radolfzell.

Meersburg

☎07532 / POP 5630

Tumbling down vine-streaked slopes to Lake Constance and crowned by a perkily turreted medieval castle, Meersburg lives up to all those clichéd knights-in-armour, damsel-in-distress fantasies. Its highlight is the **Altes Schloss** (adult/concession €8.50/6.50; ⏲9am-6.30pm Mar-Oct, 10am-6pm Nov-Feb), an archetypal medieval stronghold, complete with keep, drawbridge, knights' hall and dungeons.

The **tourist office** (☎440 400; www.meersburg.de; Kirchstrasse 4; ⏲9am-12.30pm & 2-6pm Mon-Fri, 10am-3pm Sat, 10am-1pm Sun, shorter hours in winter) is housed in a one-time Dominican monastery.

Meersburg has no train station but is linked eight times daily by express bus 7394 to Constance (€3.25, 40 minutes) and Friedrichshafen (€3.10, 26 minutes).

Lindau

☎08382 / POP 24,800

Cradled in the southern crook of Lake Constance and almost dipping its toes into Austria, Lindau is a good-looking, car-free little town, with a candy-coloured postcard Altstadt, clear-day Alpine views and lakefront cafes. The town's biggest architectural stunner is the 15th-century, step-gabled **Altes Rathaus** (Old Town Hall; Bismarckplatz), a frescoed frenzy of cherubs, merry minstrels and galleons.

Spend at the night at the 18th-century **Hotel Garni-Brugger** (☎934 10; www.hotel-garni-brugger.de; Bei der Heidenmauer 11; s €56-78, d €92-106; @), where bright rooms are done up in floral fabrics and pine, and the owner-family bends over backwards to please. A good bet for regional fare is **Weinstube Frey** (☎947 9676; Maximilianstrasse 15; mains €13-22; ⏲closed Mon), a 500-year-old wine tavern oozing Bavarian charm. For a drink with a cool view, head to Seepromenade.

The **tourist office** (☎260 030; www.lindau.de; Ludwigstrasse 68; ⏲9am-6pm Mon-Fri, 2-6pm Sat & Sun May-Sep, 9am-5pm Mon-Fri Oct-Apr) is opposite the train station.

Lindau is on the B31 and is connected to Munich by the A96. The **Deutsche Alpenstrasse** (German Alpine Route), which winds eastward to Berchtesgaden, begins here. It is also at the eastern terminus of the rail line that goes along the northern lake shore as far as Radolfzell.

FRANKFURT & THE RHINELAND

Rhineland-Palatinate (Rheinland-Pfalz) is deeply riven by rivers, and the names of two – Rhine and Moselle – are synonymous with the wines made from the grapes growing on their hillsides. Created after WWII from parts of the former Rhineland and Rhenish Palatinate regions, its turbulent history goes all the way back to the Romans, as seen in Trier. In recent centuries it was hotly contested by the French and a variety of German states, which produced many of its charismatically crumbling medieval castles.

Frankfurt-am-Main

☎069 / POP 680,000

Unashamedly high-rise, Frankfurt-on-the-Main (pronounced 'mine') is unlike any other German city. Bristling with jagged skyscrapers, 'Mainhattan' is a true capital of finance and business, home base for one of the world's largest stock exchanges and the European Central Bank. It also hosts some of Europe's key trade fairs, including famous book and auto fairs.

Despite its business demeanour, Frankfurt consistently ranks high among Germany's most liveable cities thanks to its rich collection of museums, expansive parks and greenery, a lively student scene and excellent public transport. Take advantage of fine

Frankfurt-am-Main

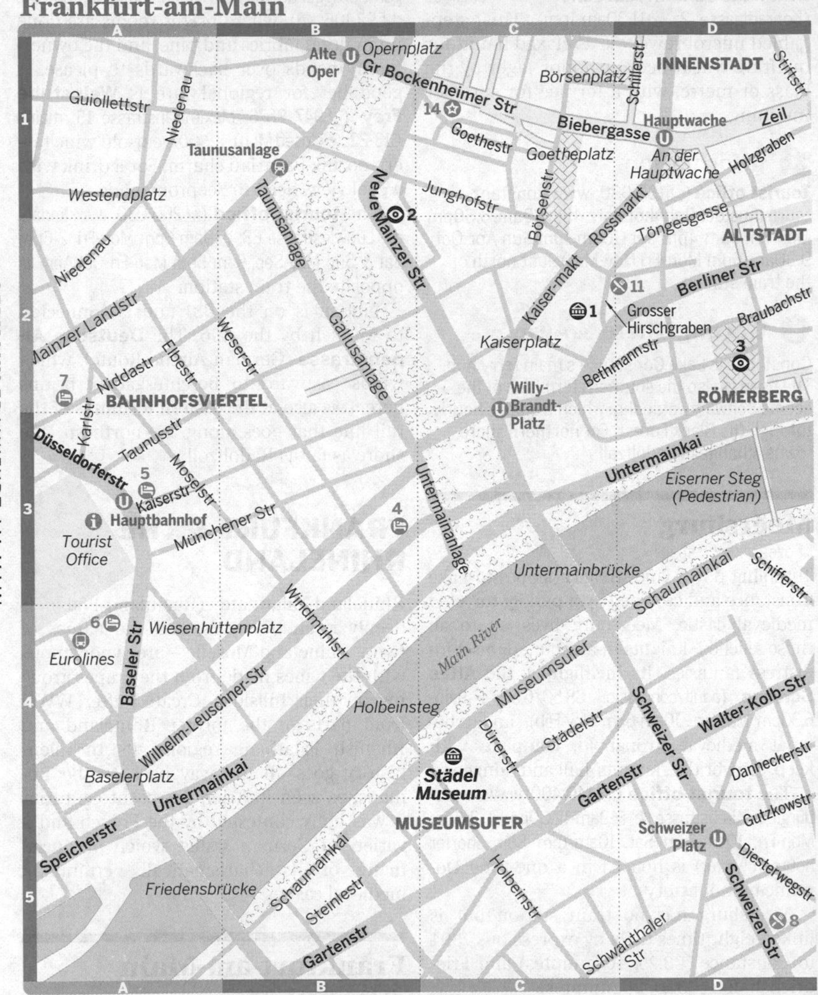

dining and plenty of night-time diversions, from cosy apple-wine taverns to edgy techno clubs.

Sights

Sights are in the city centre, best reached from the Hauptbahnhof via Kaiserstrasse. This leads to Kaiserplatz and another square called An der Hauptwache. From here, stores stretch along in all directions, principally along the Zeil. The area between Hauptwache and the Römerberg contains vestiges of Frankfurt's Altstadt (Old Town).

Römerberg PLAZA

(Dom/Römer) The Römerberg is Frankfurt's old central square. Buildings from the 14th and 15th centuries, reconstructed after WWII, hint at how beautiful the city's medieval core once was. In the northwest corner, the old town hall, or **Römer**, consists of three step-gabled 15th-century houses. In the time of the Holy Roman Empire, it was the site of celebrations during the election and coronation of emperors; today it houses the office of Frankfurt's mayor and the registry office.

Frankfurt-am-Main

Top Sights
Frankfurter Dom E2
Städel Museum C4

Sights
1 Goethe-Haus C2
2 Main Tower B1
3 Römerberg D2

Sleeping
4 Adina Apartment Hotel B3
5 Frankfurt Hostel A3
6 Hotel Excelsior A4
7 Twenty-Five Hours A2

Eating
8 Adolf Wagner D5
9 Bitter & Zart E2
10 Fichte Kränzi F4
11 Karin D2
12 Kleinmarkthalle E1
13 Metropol E2

Entertainment
14 Jazzkeller C1

Frankfurter Dom CATHEDRAL
(Frankfurt Cathedral; www.domkonzerte.de; Domplatz 14; ⌚church 9am-noon & 2.30-8pm) The Frankfurter Dom was where, from 1356 to 1792, the Holy Roman Emperors were elected (and, after 1562, crowned). It's dominated by an elegant 15th-century Gothic **tower**.

Museumsufer Frankfurt MUSEUMS
(www.museumsufer-frankfurt.de; south bank of the Main River, btwn Eiserner Steg and Friedensbrücke) Over a dozen museums line up along a 1.5km stretch along the south bank of the Main River, known as Museumsufer. They include exhibits on applied arts, architecture, archaeology, film and ethnology as well as the **Städel Museum**.

To sample them all, buy a 48-hour **Museumsufer ticket** (www.kultur-frankfurt.de; adult/concession/family €15/8/23). The Museumsuferlinie 46 bus, which leaves from the Hauptbahnhof several times hourly, links most museums.

Städel Museum MUSEUM
(www.staedelmuseum.de; Schaumainkai 63; adult/student/family €12/10/20, child under 12yr free; ⌚10am-5pm Tue & Fri-Sun, to 9pm Wed & Thu; Schweizer Platz) The most outstanding collection along Museumsufer, this world-renowned gallery showcases the talents of key painters from the 14th to the 20th centuries, including Botticelli, Dürer and Rembrandt.

Main Tower VIEWPOINT
(www.maintower.de; Neue Mainzer Strasse 52-58; elevator adult/child/family €5/3.50/13.50; ⌚10am-9pm Sun-Thu, to 11pm Fri & Sat late Mar-late Oct, closes 2hr earlier late Oct-late Mar, cocktail lounge 9pm-midnight or 1am Tue-Sat; Alte Oper) Get your head in the clouds atop the Main Tower, with its open-air viewing platform 200m up. There is also a cocktail bar and restaurant.

Goethe-Haus HISTORIC BUILDING
(www.goethehaus-frankfurt.de; Grosser Hirschgraben 23-25; adult/student/family €7/3/11; ⏲10am-6pm Mon-Sat, 10am-5.30pm Sun; Willy-Brandt-Platz) 'Few people have the imagination for reality' uttered the ever-pithy Johann Wolfgang von Goethe. Read more quotes at the house where he was born in 1749 and which is again furnished in the style of his time.

Sleeping

TOP CHOICE **Frankfurt Hostel** HOSTEL €
(☎247 5130; www.frankfurt-hostel.com; Kaiserstrasse 74, 3rd fl; dm €19-25, s/d from €35/45, during fairs up to €80/100; Frankfurt Hauptbahnhof) This 200-bed hostel is reached via a marble-and-tile lobby and a mirrored lift. Kudos for the chill-out area, guest kitchen and the free spaghetti dinners. Dorms have three to 10 metal bunks and free lockers.

Adina Apartment Hotel HOTEL €€
(☎247 4740; www.adina.eu; Wilhelm-Leuschner-Strasse 6; d without breakfast from €84-135, during fairs up to €377; Willy-Brandt-Platz) Self-caterers and families will appreciate these spacious studios and one- and two-bedroom apartments, all with kitchenettes.

Hotel Excelsior HOTEL €
(☎256 080; www.hotelexcelsior-frankfurt.de; Mannheimer Strasse 7-9; s/d from €61/75, during fairs €199/239; Frankfurt Hauptbahnhof) Behind a light-green facade, this 197-room place offers excellent value and plenty of freebies: a business centre, landline phone calls within Germany, and coffee, tea, fruit and cakes in the lobby.

ALL ABOARD THE EBBELWEI-EXPRSS

The **Ebbelwei-Express** (Apple Wine Express; www.ebbelwei-express.com; adult/child under 14yr €7/3; ⏲half-hourly 1.30-5.30pm Sat, Sun & holidays Apr-Oct & Sat Nov-Mar, approx hourly 1.30-5pm Sun & holidays Nov-Mar) is a historic tram whose 70-minute circuit takes in both banks of the Main between the zoo and the Messe. Jump on at any stop marked with the letters EE – including the Hauptbahnhof and Börneplatz. As you'd expect, the price includes apple wine (*Ebbelwei*) or juice and pretzels.

Twenty-Five Hours BOUTIQUE HOTEL €€
(25h; ☎256 6770; www.25hours-hotels.com; Niddastrasse 58; d without breakfast weekday/weekend from €107/77, during fairs up to €390; Frankfurt Hauptbahnhof) Inspired by Levi's jeans, the 76 themed rooms are styled by decade from the 1940s (calm colours) through the 1980s (tiger-print walls). Guests can jam on the drums and guitars in the Gibson-designed basement music room or admire skyline views from the roof terrace.

Eating & Drinking

The pedestrian strip linking the Alte Oper and the western end of the Zeil is also known as *Fressgass* thanks to its many eateries. Another cluster of places to drink and eat is in Alt-Sachsenhausen on the south bank of the Main River.

Eckhaus GERMAN €€
(☎491 197; Bornheimer Landstrasse 45; mains €8-17.90; ⏲5pm-midnight or 1am; Merianplatz) We love this place with its smoke-stained walls and ancient floorboards. The hallmark *Kartoffelrösti* (shredded potato pancake) has been served here for over 100 years.

TOP CHOICE **Kleinmarkthalle** MARKET €
(Hasengasse 5; ⏲7.30am-6pm Mon-Fri, to 3pm Sat; Dom/Römer) This traditional covered food market has loads of fruit, vegetables and meats as well as hot food.

Karin CAFE €€
(☎295 217; Grosser Hirschgraben 28; mains €8-14; ⏲9am-midnight Mon-Sat, 10am-7pm Sun, 10am-midnight holidays; Willy-Brandt-Platz) This Frankfurt-style cafe serves German and international dishes and nine different breakfasts (until 6pm). Changing exhibits by local artists grace the walls. Cash only.

Bitter & Zart CAFE €
(www.bitterundzart.de; Braubachstrasse 14; ⏲10am-8pm Mon-Sat, 10am-6pm Sun; Dom/Römer) Walk past the chocolate chair then turn left and you're in a delightful shop whose shelves are piled high with the finest chocolates; turn right and order espresso, light meals and breakfast (until noon) or yummy cakes.

Metropol BISTRO €€
(☎288 287; Weckmarkt 13-15; mains €9.50-14.50 ⏲9am-1am or 2am Tue-Sat, 9am-midnight Sun Dom/Römer) Serves dishes from a changing menu that ranges from bistro staples

to inspired. Has a lovely courtyard out the back where children can chill out. Cash only.

Wein-Dünker WINE CELLAR
(www.weinkellerei-duenker.de; Berger Strasse 265; ⏲2pm-1am Mon-Thu, 2pm-3am Fri & Sat, 6pm-midnight Sun; Ⓜ Bornheim Mitte) Descend to this little wine cellar and try some of Germany's finest wines. It only serves snacks, but you can bring your own and picnic atop an upturned barrel.

☆ Entertainment

King Kamehameha CLUB
(☎4800 9610; www.king-kamehameha.de; Hanauer Landstrasse 192; admission Thu €8, Fri & Sat €10; ⏲9pm-4am or later Thu, 10pm-4am or later Fri & Sat) 'KingKa' is legendary, with DJs on weekends and a house band on Thursdays. It's about 2km southeast of the zoo (tram 11).

Jazzkeller JAZZ
(www.jazzkeller.com; Kleine Bockenheimer Strasse 18a; admission €5-25; ⏲8pm-2am Tue-Thu, 10pm-3am Fri, 9pm-2am Sat, 8pm-1am Sun; Ⓜ Alte Oper) A great jazz venue with mood, since 1952. Check out the walls for photos of jazz greats who've played here over the years. On Fridays there's dancing to Latin and funk. In a cellar across from Goethestrasse 27.

ℹ Information

Tourist Office (☎2123 8800; www.frankfurt-tourismus.de) Hauptbahnhof (inside main train station; ⏲8am-9pm Mon-Fri, 9am-6pm Sat & Sun); Römer (Römerberg 27; ⏲9.30am-5.30pm Mon-Fri, 9.30am-4pm Sat, Sun & holidays; Ⓜ Dom/Römer)

ℹ Getting There & Away

Air

Frankfurt Airport (FRA; www.frankfurt-airport.com), 12km southwest of the city centre, is Germany's busiest. Terminals 1 and 2 are linked by a driverless railway, the SkyLine.

The airport has two train stations accessible from Terminal 1. The *Regionalbahnhof* handles regional train and S-Bahn connections, while long-distance trains stop at the *Fernbahnhof*. Coming from Terminal 2, use the yellow shuttle buses (rather than the SkyLine).

To get into town, take S-Bahn lines S8 and S9 from the Regionalbahnhof (€4.10, 15 minutes).

Note that **Frankfurt-Hahn airport** (HHN; www.hahn-airport.de) is 125km west of Frankfurt, near the Moselle Valley.

APPLE-WINE TAVERNS

Apple-wine taverns are Frankfurt's great local tradition. They serve *Ebbelwei* (Frankfurt dialect for *Apfelwein*), an alcoholic apple cider, along with local specialities like *Handkäse mit Musik* (literally, 'hand-cheese with music'). This is a round cheese soaked in oil and vinegar and topped with onions; your bowel supplies the music. Anything with the sensational local sauce made from herbs, *Grüne Sosse*, is a winner.

Some good *Ebbelwei* taverns are in Alt-Sachsenhausen where **Fichtekränzi** (☎612 778; www.fichtekraenzi.de; Wallstrasse 5; mains €7.20-15.50; ⏲5-11pm; 🖉; Ⓜ Lokalbahnhof) and **Adolf Wagner** (☎612 565; www.apfelwein-wagner.com; Schweizer Strasse 71; mains €4.50-13.90; ⏲11am-midnight; 🖉; Ⓜ Südbahnhof) are recommended.

Bus

The Romantic Road Coach (p459) and long-distance buses to many European destinations, operated by **Eurolines** (☎790 3253; www.eurolines.eu; Mannheimer Strasse 15; ⏲7.30am-7.30pm Mon-Fri, 7.30am-2pm Sat, 7.30am-1pm Sun; Ⓜ Frankfurt Hauptbahnhof), leave from the south side of the Hauptbahnhof.

Train

The Hauptbahnhof has train services to pretty much everywhere, including Berlin (€118, four hours) and Munich (€98, 3½ hours).

ℹ Getting Around

Public transportation is handled by **traffiQ** (☎01801-069 960; www.traffiq.de). Single tickets cost €2.50, a day pass is €6.20; both are sold from vending machines at stations.

Romantic Rhine

A trip along the mighty Rhine is justifiably a highlight for most travellers. The section between Koblenz and Mainz is Unesco-protected and called 'Romantic Rhine' for good reason. This is Germany's landscape at its most dramatic – forested hillsides alternate with craggy cliffs and nearly vertical terraced vineyards. Idyllic villages appear around each bend, their neat half-timbered houses and Gothic church steeples seemingly plucked from the world of fairy tales.

High above the river, busy with barge traffic, and the rail lines that run along each bank are the famous medieval castles, some ruined, some restored, all shrouded in mystery.

Spring and autumn are the best times to visit as it's overrun in summer and goes into hibernation in winter. Every river town brims with cute places to stay, eat and drink.

Although Koblenz and Mainz are the best starting points, the Rhine Valley is also accessible from Frankfurt on a very long day trip.

Getting There & Around

Each mode of transport on the Rhine has its own advantages and all are equally enjoyable. Try combining several. The **Köln-Düsseldorfer (KD) Line** (KD; 0221-2088 318; www.k-d.com) runs numerous services daily between Koblenz and Mainz (as well as the less-interesting stretch between Cologne and Koblenz), with boats stopping at riverside towns along the way.

Villages on the Rhine's left bank (eg Bacharach, Oberwesel and Boppard) are served hourly by local trains on the Koblenz–Mainz run. Right-bank villages such as Rüdesheim, Assmannshausen, St Goarshausen and Braubach are linked hourly to Koblenz' Hauptbahnhof and Wiesbaden by the RheingauLinie, operated by Vias.

MAINZ

06131 / POP 199,000

An easy day trip from Frankfurt, Mainz has an attractive Old Town anchored by its massive **Dom** (Marktplatz; 9am-6.30pm Mon-Fri, 9am-4pm Sat, 12.45-6.30pm Sun & holidays, shorter hrs Nov-Feb), which has a blend of Romanesque, Gothic and baroque architecture.

Sampling local wines in a half-timbered Altstadt tavern is as much a part of any Mainz visit as viewing the ethereal Marc Chagall–designed windows in **St-Stephan-Kirche** (Kleine Weissgasse 12; 10am-4.30pm) or the first printed Bible in the **Gutenberg Museum** (www.gutenberg-museum.de; Liebfrauenplatz 5; adult/child €5/3; 9am-5pm Tue-Sat, 11am-5pm Sun), which honours local boy and moveable-type inventor Johannes Gutenberg.

For more information, visit the **tourist office** (286 210; www.touristik-mainz.de; Brückenturm am Rathaus; 9am-6pm Mon-Fri, 10am-4pm Sat, 11am-3pm Sun).

In a 15th-century Carmelite nunnery near the cathedral, **Hotel Hof Ehrenfels** (971 2340; www.hof-ehrenfels.de; Grebenstrasse 5-7; s/d/tr €80/100/120, €10 less Fri-Sun) has Dom views that are hard to beat. For wine and sustenance, sit beneath the soaring Gothic vaults of a medieval hospital at **Heiliggeist** (www.heiliggeist-mainz.de; Mailandsgasse 11; mains €9.80-19.80; 4pm-1am Mon-Fri, 9am-1am or 2am Sat, Sun & holidays).

BACHARACH

06743 / POP 2250

One of the prettiest of the Rhine villages, Bacharach conceals its considerable charms behind a 14th-century wall (you can stroll on top along most of it). Beyond the thick arched gateways awaits a beautiful medieval Old Town graced with half-timbered mansions such as the **Altes Haus**, the **Posthof** and the off-kilter **Alte Münze** along Oberstrasse. All house places to eat, drink and be merry.

The local youth hostel, **DJH Burg Stahleck** (1266; www.jugendherberge.de; Burg Stahleck; dm/d €20.50/52), has a dream location in the hillside medieval castle. Right on the medieval ramparts, the **Rhein Hotel** (1243; www.rhein-hotel-bacharach.de; Langstrasse 50; s €39-65, d €78-130;) has 14 well-lit, soundproofed rooms with original artwork. The restaurant serves regional dishes.

ST GOAR & ST GOARSHAUSEN

06741 / POP 3100

These twin towns face each other across the Rhine. On the left bank, St Goar is lorded over by **Burg Rheinfels** (www.st-goar.de; adult/child €4/2; 9am-6pm mid-Mar–early Nov, 11am-5pm Sat & Sun in good weather early Nov–mid-Mar),

ROMANCING THE RHINE

Nearly every Rhine village has its own charms and is worth at least a quick spin on foot. Just pick one at random and make your own discoveries. Here are a few enticing teasers:

Boppard Roman walls and ruins and cable to Vierseenblick viewpoint (left bank).

Oberwesel Famous for its 3km-long partly walkable medieval town wall punctuated by 16 guard towers (left bank).

Assmannhausen Relatively untouristed village known for its red wines, sweeping views and good hikes (right bank).

Rüdesheim Escape the day-tripper deluged Drosselgasse (alley) to soar above the vineyards to the mighty Niederwalddenkmal monument (right bank).

one of the most impressive castles on the river. Its labyrinthine ruins reflect the greed and ambition of the local count who built the behemoth in 1245 to levy tolls on passing ships.

Across the river, just south of St Goarshausen, is the most fabled spot along the Romantic Rhine, the **Loreley Rock**. This vertical slab of slate owes its fame to a mythical maiden whose siren songs are said to have lured sailors to their death in the river's treacherous currents. Learn more at the multimedia **Loreley Besucherzentrum visitors' centre** (☎599 093; www.loreley-besucherzentrum.de; adult/student €2.50/1.50; ⏰10am-6pm Apr-Oct, 10am-5pm Mar, 11am-4pm Sat & Sun Nov-Feb). The outcrop can be reached by car, by shuttle bus from Goarshausen's Marktplatz (€2.65, hourly 10am to 5pm) and via the 400-step Treppenweg stairway, which begins about 2km upriver from St Goarshausen at the base of the breakwater.

St Goar's **DJH hostel** (☎388; www.djh.de; Bismarckweg 17; dm/s/d €18/30/50) is right below the castle, which also houses the upmarket **Romantik Hotel Schloss Rheinfels** (☎06741-8020; www.schloss-rheinfels.de; d €115-265, cheaper in winter; @📶🏊) and its three restaurants.

KOBLENZ

☎0261 / POP 106,000

Founded the Romans, Koblenz sits at the confluence of the Rhine and Moselle Rivers, a point known as **Deutsches Eck** (German 'Corner') and dominated by a bombastic 19th-century statue of Kaiser Wilhelm I on horseback. On the right Rhine bank high above the Deutsches Eck, **Festung Ehrenbreitstein** (www.diefestungehrenbreitstein.de; adult/child €6/3; ⏰10am-6pm Apr-Oct, to 5pm Nov-Mar) is one one of Europe's mightiest fortresses. Views are great and there's a regional museum inside. It is reached by an 850m-long **Seilbahn** (aerial cable car; www.seilbahn-koblenz.de; adult/6-14yr return €8/4, incl fortress €11.20/5.60, bicycle one-way €3; ⏰10am-6pm or 7pm Apr-Oct, to 5pm Nov-Mar).

The **tourist office** (☎313 04; Bahnhofplatz 17; ⏰9am-6pm Mon-Fri) is outside the Hauptbahnhof. Restaurants and pubs cluster around Münzplatz and Burgstrasse in the Altstadt and along the Rhine.

Several boat companies dock on the Rhine, south of the Deutsches Eck. Koblenz has two train stations, the main Hauptbahnhof on the Rhine's left bank about 1km south of the city centre, and Koblenz-Ehrenbreitstein on the right bank (right below the fortress).

> **DON'T MISS**
>
> **MARKSBURG**
>
> High above the river are the dramatic towers, turrets and crenellations of the 700-year-old **Marksburg** (☎206; www.marksburg.de; adult/student/6-18yr €6/5/4; ⏰10am-5pm mid-Mar–Oct, 11am-4pm Nov–mid-Mar), unusual along the Rhine in that it was never destroyed. The tour takes in the citadel, the Gothic hall and the large kitchen, plus a grisly torture chamber, with its hair-raising assortment of pain-inflicting nasties.

Moselle Valley

Like a vine right before harvest, the Moselle hangs heavy with visitor fruit. Castles and half-timbered towns are built along the sinuous river below steep, rocky cliffs planted with vineyards. It's one of the country's most scenic regions, with a constant succession of views rewarding intrepid hikers who brave the hilly trails. Unlike the Romantic Rhine, it's spanned by plenty of bridges. The region is busiest in May, on summer weekends and during the local wine harvest (mid-September to mid-October).

ℹ Getting There & Around

The most scenic part of the Moselle Valley runs 195km from Trier to Koblenz; it's most practical to begin your Moselle Valley trip from either town.

Trains linking Koblenz with Trier (€19.20, 1½ to two hours, at least hourly) stop at river villages only as far as Bullay. From there, hourly shuttle trains head upriver to Traben-Trarbach. The villages between Traben-Trarbach and Trier, including Bernkastel-Kues, are served by bus 333 run by Moselbahn buses.

Frankfurt-Hahn Airport (p479), served by Ryanair, is 22km east of Traben-Trarbach and 17km east of Bernkastel-Kues and is linked to the railhead of Bullay by shuttle bus (€6.80, 51 minutes).

BEILSTEIN

On the right bank of the Moselle about 50km upriver from Koblenz, Beilstein is a pint-sized village right out of the world of fairy tales. Little more than a cluster of

DON'T MISS

BURG ELTZ

South of Koblenz, at the head of the beautiful Eltz Valley, Burg Eltz is not to be missed. Towering over the surrounding hills, this superb medieval castle has frescos, paintings, furniture and ornately decorated rooms.

Trains link Koblenz and Moselkern (also reachable by boat), where a 35-minute trail to the castle begins at the Ringelsteiner Mühle car park.

houses surrounded by steep vineyards, its historic highlights include the **Marktplatz** and **Burg Metternich**, a hilltop castle reached via a staircase.

The **Zehnthauskeller** (Marktplatz; ⌚11am-evening Tue-Sun) houses a romantically dark, vaulted wine tavern owned by the same family that also runs two local **hotels** (☎1850; www.hotel-lipmann.de).

TRABEN-TRARBACH

Full of fanciful art nouveau villas, the double town of Traben-Trarbach provides respite from the 'romantic half-timbered town' circuit. Pick up a map of the town at the **tourist office** (☎839 80; www.traben-trarbach.de; Am Bahnhof 5, Traben; ⌚10am-5pm Mon-Fri May-Aug, to 6pm Sep & Oct, to 4pm Nov-Apr, 11am-3pm Sat May-Oct; 📶). The ruined medieval **Grevenburg** castle sits high in the craggy hills above Trarbach and is reached via a steep footpath, the Sponheimer Weg, that begins a block north of the bridge.

Weingut Caspari (☎5778; www.weingut-caspari.de; Weiherstrasse 18, Trarbach; mains €6.50-16.90) is a rustic, old-time wine restaurant serving hearty local specialities; it's six short blocks inland from the bridge.

BERNKASTEL-KUES

The twin town of Bernkastel-Kues is at the heart of the middle Moselle region. On the right bank, Bernkastel has a charming **Markt**, a romantic ensemble of half-timbered houses with beautifully decorated gables. On Karlstrasse, the alley to the right as you face the Rathaus, the tiny **Spitzhäuschen** resembles a giant bird's house, its narrow base topped by a much larger, precariously leaning, upper floor.

Get your heart pumping by hoofing it from the Spitzhäuschen up to **Burg Landshut**, a ruined 13th-century castle – framed by vineyards and forests – on a bluff above town; allow 30 minutes. You'll be rewarded with glorious valley views and a cold drink at the **beer garden** (⌚10am-6pm mid-Feb–Nov).

Trier

☎0651 / POP 105,250

Founded by the Romans around 16 BC as Augusta Treverorum, Trier became the capital of Roman Gaul in the 3rd century and the residence of Constantine the Great in the 4th century. To this day, you'll find more – and better preserved – Roman ruins here than anywhere else north of the Alps. Trier's proximity to France can be tasted in its cuisine, while its large student population injects life among the ruins.

Sights

Porta Nigra ROMAN GATE
(adult/student €3/2.10, incl Stadtmuseum Simeonstift €7.20/5.80; ⌚9am-6pm Apr-Sep, to 5pm Mar & Oct, to 4pm Nov-Feb) Trier's chief landmark, the brooding 2nd-century city gate is held together by nothing but gravity and iron rods. Admission is also good for the adjacent **Stadtmuseum Simeonstift** (adult/student €5.50/4, incl Porta Nigra €7.20/5.80; ⌚10am-6pm Tue-Sun), which brings alive two millennia of local history with carefully chosen objects.

Amphitheatre ROMAN SITE
(Olewiger Strasse; adult/child €3/2.10; ⌚9am-6pm Apr-Sep, to 5pm Mar & Oct, to 4pm Nov-Feb) This classic outdoor space once held 20,000 spectators during gladiator tournaments and animal fights – or when Constantine the Great crowned his battlefield victories by feeding his enemies to voracious animals.

Kaiserthermen ROMAN SITE
(Imperial Baths; Palastgarten; adult/student €3/2.10) This vast thermal bathing complex was created by Constantine.

Dom CHURCH
(www.dominformation.de; Liebfrauenstrasse 12; ⌚10am-5pm Mon-Sat, 12.30-5pm Sun, shorter hours Nov-Mar) Built above the palace of Constantine the Great's mother, Helena, this fortress-like cathedral is mostly Romanesque, with some soaring Gothic and eye-popping baroque embellishments.

Konstantin Basilika CHURCH
(www.konstantin-basilika.de; Konstantinplatz; ⌚10am-6pm Apr-Oct, 10am or 11am-noon and 2 or 3pm-4pm Tue-Sat, noon-1pm Sun Nov-Mar) Con-

structed around AD 310 as Constantine's throne hall, the brick-built Konstantin Basilika (Aula Palatina) is now a typically austere Protestant church with mindblowing dimensions.

Karl Marx Haus HISTORIC SITE
(www.fes.de/karl-marx-haus; Brückenstrasse 10; adult/child €3/2; ⏲10am-6pm daily Apr-Oct, 2-5pm Tue-Sun Nov-Mar) The suitably modest birthplace of the author of *Das Kapital* is fast becoming a major pilgrimage stop for the growing numbers of mainland Chinese tourists to Europe.

Sleeping

Hille's Hostel HOSTEL €
(☎710 2785, outside office hrs 0171-329 1247; www.hilles-hostel-trier.de; Gartenfeldstrasse 7; dm from €14, s/d €40/50, breakfast €8; ⏲reception 9am-noon & 4-6pm or later; @📶) This laid-back indie hostel has a piano in the common kitchen and 12 attractive, spacious rooms, most with private bathrooms. Call ahead if arriving outside reception hours, so they'll leave the door code and the key.

Hotel Römischer Kaiser HOTEL €€
(☎977 00; www.friedrich-hotels.de; Porta-Nigra-Platz 6; s/d from €73.50/111; 📶) Built in 1894, this hotel – convenient to the train station and the old centre – offers 43 bright, comfortable rooms with solid wood furnishings, parquet floors and spacious bathrooms.

Eating

Zum Domstein ROMAN €€
(www.domstein.de; Hauptmarkt 5; mains €8.90-18.50, Roman dinner €17-35) A German-style bistro where you can either dine like an ancient Roman or feast on more conventional German and international fare.

Kartoffel Kiste POTATOES €€
(www.kiste-trier.de; Fahrstrasse 13-14; mains €7.20-17; ⏲11am-midnight; 📝) A local favourite, this place specialises in baked, breaded, gratineed, soupified and sauce-engulfed potatoes, as well as schnitzel and steaks.

Information

Tourist Office (☎978 080; www.trier-info.de; just inside Porta Nigra; ⏲9 or 10am-5 or 6pm Mon-Sat, 9 or 10am-1pm or later Sun)

Getting There & Away

Trier has at least hourly train connections to Koblenz (€20.80, 1½ to two hours) and frequent service to Luxembourg (same-day return €10.80, 50 minutes, at least hourly), with onward connections to Paris.

Cologne

☎0221 / POP 1 MILLION

Cologne (Köln) offers lots of attractions, led by its famous cathedral, whose filigree twin spires dominate the skyline. The city's museum landscape is especially strong when it comes to art but also has something in store for fans of chocolate, sports and Roman history. Its people are well known for their joie de vivre and it's easy to have a good time right along with them year-round in the beer halls of the Altstadt (Old Town).

Sights

TOP CHOICE **Kölner Dom** CHURCH
(Cologne Cathedral; ☎1794 0200; www.koelner-dom.de; ⏲6am-10pm May-Oct, to 7.30pm Nov-Apr, south tower 9am-6pm May-Sep, to 5pm Mar-Apr & Oct, to 4pm Nov-Feb) As easy as it is to get church fatigue in Germany, the huge Kölner Dom is one you shouldn't miss. Blackened with age, this gargoyle-festooned Gothic cathedral has a footprint of 12,470 sq metres, with twin spires soaring to 157m. Although its ground stone was laid in 1248, stop-start construction meant it wasn't finished until 1880, as a symbol of Prussia's drive for unification. Just over 60 years later it escaped WWII's heavy bombing largely intact.

Sunshine filtering softly through stained-glass windows and the weak glow of candles are the only illumination in the moody, high-ceilinged interior. Behind the altar lies the cathedral's most precious reliquary, the **Shrine of the Three Magi** (c 1150–1210), which reputedly contains the bones of the Three Wise Men. Brought to Cologne from Milan in the 12th century, it can just be glimpsed through the gates to the inner choir.

To see the shrine properly, you need to take a guided tour. For fine views, embark on the seriously strenuous climb of 509 steps of the Dom's **south tower**, passing the 24-tonne Peter Bell, the world's largest working clanger.

Römisch-Germanisches Museum MUSEUM
(Roman Germanic Museum; ☎2212 2304; www.museenkoeln.de; Roncalliplatz 4; adult/child €8/4; ⏲10am-5pm Tue-Sun) Sculptures and ruins displayed outside are merely the overture to

COLOGNE CARNIVAL

Ushering in Lent in late February or early March, Cologne's **Carnival** (Karneval) rivals Munich's Oktoberfest for exuberance, as people dress in creative costumes and party in the streets. Things kick off the Thursday before the seventh Sunday before Easter, culminate on Monday *(Rosenmontag)*, when there are televised street parades, and end on Ash Wednesday.

a full symphony of Roman artefacts found along the Rhine.

Museum Ludwig MUSEUM
(☎2212 6165; www.museenkoeln.de; Bischofsgartenstrasse 1; adult/child €10/7; ⏲10am-6pm Tue-Sun) This grand art museum gets extra big kudos for its collections of 1960s pop art (Warhol's *Brillo Boxes* are a highlight), German expressionism and Russian avant garde painting, as well as photography.

Kolumba MUSEUM
(☎933 1930; www.kolumba.de; Kolumbastrasse 4; adult/child €5/free; ⏲noon-5pm Wed-Mon, to 7pm Thu) Art, history, architecture and spirituality form a harmonious tapestry in this spectacular collection of religious treasures. Don't miss the 12th-century carved ivory crucifix.

NS Dokumentationszentrum MUSEUM
(☎2212 6332; www.museenkoeln.de; Appellhofplatz 23-25; adult/child €5/2; ⏲10am-6pm Tue-Fri, 11am-6pm Sat & Sun) An exhibit in the basement of the Gestapo (Nazi-era secret police) prison, where scores of people were interrogated, tortured and murdered, documents the history of Cologne during the Third Reich.

Wallraf-Richartz-Museum & Fondation Corboud MUSEUM
(☎2212 1119; www.museenkoeln.de; Obenmarspforten; adult/child €9/6; ⏲10am-6pm Tue-Sun, to 9pm Thu) A famous collection of paintings from the 13th to the 19th centuries, this museum occupies a postmodern cube designed by the late OM Ungers.

Chocolate Museum MUSEUM
(Schokoladen Museum; ☎931 8880; www.schokoladenmuseum.de; Am Schokoladenmuseum 1a; adult/concession €8.50/6; ⏲10am-6pm Tue-Fri, 11am-7pm Sat & Sun) At this high-tech temple to the art of chocolate-making, exhibits on the origin of the 'elixir of the gods', as the Aztecs called it, and the cocoa-growing process are followed by a live-production factory tour and a stop at a chocolate fountain for a sample.

Tours

KD River Cruises BOAT TOUR
(☎258 3011; www.k-d.com; Frankenwerft 35; tour €10; ⏲10.30am-5pm) One of several companies offering one-hour spins taking in the splendid Altstadt panorama.

Sleeping

Station Hostel for Backpackers HOSTEL €
(☎912 5301; www.hostel-cologne.de; Marzellenstrasse 44-56; dm €17-20, s/d from €32/48; @📶) This is a hostel as hostels should be: central, convivial and economical. A lounge gives way to clean, colourful rooms sleeping one to six people. There's lots of free stuff, including linen, internet access, lockers, city maps and guest kitchen.

Meininger City Hostel & Hotel HOSTEL €
(☎355 332 014; www.meininger-hostels.com; Engelbertstrasse 33-35; dm €18-24, s/d from €48/70; @📶) This charming hostel in the Zülpicher Viertel student quarter is loaded with retro appeal coupled with modern rooms featuring lockers, bunkside reading lamps, a small TV and private bathrooms.

Lint Hotel HOTEL €€
(☎920 550; www.lint-hotel.de; Lintgasse 7; s €60-90, d €90-130; 📶) Cute, contemporary and ecoconscious (solar-panelled roof) hotel in the heart of the Altstadt. The 18 rooms have hardwood floors and the breakfast buffet is partly organic.

Cerano Hotel HOTEL €€
(☎925 7300; www.cerano-hotels.de; Elisenstrasse 16; r €60-120; 📶) This unassuming five-storey hotel near the train station is peppered with extra touches: mineral water, juices and more apples than you'd find in an orchard.

Eating

The largest variety and most happening restaurants are in the Zülpicher Viertel and Belgisches Viertel (Belgian Quarter) areas, both in the city centre.

Salon Schmitz MODERN EUROPEAN €
(Aachener Strasse 28; snacks €4-8) No matter whether you prefer sidling up to the long bar or grabbing an ultracomfy sofa in the retro lounge, Schmitz is a perfect pit stop for relaxed chats over coffee, cocktails o

Kölsch. If hunger strikes, pop next door to the affiliated **deli** in a former butcher's shop.

Engelbät EUROPEAN €
(☎246 914; www.engelbaet.de; Engelbertstrasse 7; crepes €3-9; ⊙11am-1am) This cosy restaurant-pub is famous for its habit-forming crêpes, which come as sweet, meat or vegetarian. The sidewalk tables are popular for drinks and there are many other choices nearby.

Bei Oma Kleinmann GERMAN €€
(www.beiomakleinmann.de; Zülpicher Strasse 9; mains €12; ⊙5pm-1am Tue-Sun, kitchen to 11pm) Named for its long-time owner, who was still cooking almost to her last day at age 95 in 2009, this cosy trad restaurant has timeless dishes, including 14 kinds of schnitzel.

Feynsinn INTERNATIONAL €€
(☎240 9210; www.cafe-feynsinn.de; Rathenauplatz 7; mains €7-18) At this well-respected restaurant organic ingredients are woven into sharp-flavoured dishes. The owners raise their own meat. Get a table overlooking the park for a meal or just a drink.

Drinking & Entertainment

As in Munich, beer in Cologne reigns supreme. Local breweries turn out a variety called *Kölsch*, which is relatively light and served in skinny 200mL glasses.

Früh am Dom BEER HALL
(☎258 0394; www.frueh.de; Am Hof 12-14; mains €5-12) This warren of a beer hall near the Dom epitomises Cologne earthiness. It's also known for great breakfasts.

Päffgen BEER HALL
(www.paeffgen-koelsch.de; Friesenstrasse 64-66) Busy, loud and boisterous, Päffgen has been pouring *Kölsch* since 1883 and hasn't lost a step since. In summer you can enjoy the refreshing brew and local specialities beneath starry skies in the beer garden.

Alter Wartesaal CLUB
(☎912 8850; www.wartesaal.de; Johannisstrasse 11; ⊙Thu-Sat) In a former train station waiting hall, this is a stylish bar-disco-restaurant combo. Themed nights range from the erotic KitKatClub to SoulChannel. There are cafe tables out front in the shadow of the Dom where you can take a pause.

Information

Tourist Office (☎2213 0400; www.koelntourismus.de; Unter Fettenhennen 19; ⊙9am-8pm Mon-Sat, 10am-5pm Sun)

Getting There & Away

AIR **Köln Bonn Airport** (CGN; ☎02203-404 001; www.airport-cgn.de) is about 18km southeast of the city centre and connected to the

WORTH A TRIP

BONN

South of Cologne on the Rhine River, Bonn (☎0228, population 312,000) was West Germany's capital from 1949 until 1990. For visitors, the birthplace of Ludwig van Beethoven has plenty in store, not least the great composer's birth house, a string of top-rated museums and a lovely riverside setting.

The **tourist office** (☎775 000; www.bonn.de; Windeckstrasse 1; ⊙10am-6pm Mon-Fri, to 4pm Sat, to 2pm Sun) is a three-minute walk, along Poststrasse, from the Hauptbahnhof, and can fill in the details.

Beethoven fans will want to head straight to the **Beethoven-Haus** (☎981 7525; www.beethoven-haus-bonn.de; Bonngasse 24-26; adult/child €5/4; ⊙10am-6pm Mon-Sat, 11am-6pm Sun Apr-Oct, to 5pm Nov-Mar), where the composer was born in 1770. It contains memorabilia concerning his life and music, including his last piano, with an amplified sounding board to accommodate his deafness.

The **Haus der Geschichte der Bundesrepublik Deutschland** (FRG History Museum; ☎916 50; www.hdg.de; Willy-Brandt-Allee 14; ⊙9am-7pm Tue-Fri, 10am-6pm Sat & Sun) presents Germany's postwar history. It is part of the Museumsmeile, a row of museums in the old government quarter south of the city centre along the B9. It also includes the **Kunstmuseum Bonn** (☎776 260; www.kunstmuseum-bonn.de; Friedrich-Ebert-Allee 2; adult/concession €7/3.50; ⊙11am-6pm Tue & Thu-Sun, to 9pm Wed), which has 20th-century art, especially by August Macke and other Rhenish expressionists.

Bonn is linked to Cologne many times hourly by U-Bahn lines U16 and U18 as well as by regional trains.

Hauptbahnhof by S13 train every 20 minutes (€2.80, 15 minutes).

TRAIN Cologne's Hauptbahnhof sits just a Frisbee toss away from the Dom. Services are fast and frequent in all directions. A sampling: Berlin (€113, 4¼ hours), Frankfurt (€67, 1¼ hours) and Munich (€134, 4½ hours). In addition there are fast trains to Brussels (for connecting to the Eurostar for London or Paris).

Getting Around

Cologne's comprehensive mix of buses, trams, and U-Bahn and S-Bahn trains is operated by **VRS** (☎01803-504 030; www.vrsinfo.de) in cooperation with Bonn's system. Single tickets cost €2.60, day passes are €7.50 (€11.10 for groups of up to five). Buy your tickets from the orange ticket machines at stations and aboard trams; be sure to validate them.

Düsseldorf

☎0211 / POP 589,000

Düsseldorf dazzles with boundary-pushing architecture, zinging nightlife and an art scene to rival many a metropolis. It's a posh and modern city that seems all buttoned-up business at first, yet all it takes is a few hours of bar-hopping around the Altstadt, the historical quarter along the Rhine, to realise that locals have no problem letting their hair down once they slip out of those Boss jackets.

Sights

Marktplatz SQUARE

(Marktplatz) Düsseldorf's historic Marktplatz is framed by the Renaissance **Rathaus** (town hall; 1573) and accented by an equestrian **statue of Jan Wellem**, an art-loving late 17th-century local ruler who's buried nearby in the early-baroque **Andreaskirche** (www.dominikaner-duesseldorf.de; Andreasstrasse 27; ⏲8am-6.30pm).

TOP CHOICE **Kunstsammlung Nordrhein-Westfalen** MUSEUM

(Art Collection of North Rhine Westphalia; www.kunstsammlung.de; combined ticket adult/child €20/5; ⏲10am-6pm Tue-Fri, 11am-6pm Sat & Sun) This modern art collection gives Düsseldorf an edge in the art world. **K20 Grabbeplatz** (☎838 1130; Grabbeplatz 5; adult/child €12/9.50) has fabulous canvases by Paul Klee alongside other big-shots, including Picasso, Matisse, and Düsseldorf's own Joseph Beuys. It is linked by shuttle to the **K21 Ständehaus** (☎838 1630; Ständehausstrasse 1; adult/child €10/2.50), a showcase of cutting-edge paintings, photographs, installations and video art created after 1980. A third gallery, the **Schmela Haus** (Mutter-Ey-Strasse 3), was being redeveloped at research time.

Rheinuferpromenade PROMENADE

(Rhine River Walk) **Burgplatz**, on the northern end of the Altstadt, marks the beginning of the Rhine promenade, whose cafes and benches fill with people in fine weather. The promenade ends in the **Rheinturm** (Stromstrasse 20; adult/child €4/2.50; ⏲10am-11.30pm), which has an observation deck at 168m.

Medienhafen ARCHITECTURE

(Am Handelshafen) South of the Altstadt, the old harbour area has been reborn as the Media Harbour, which is mostly an office quarter but noteworthy for its cutting-edge architecture by celebrated international architects. Frank Gehry's warped **Neuer Zollhof** is especially photogenic. A few cafes and restaurants let you give your feet a rest.

Sleeping

Backpackers-Düsseldorf HOSTEL €

(☎302 0848; www.backpackers-duesseldorf.de; Fürstenwall 180; dm €15-23; @📶) Düsseldorf's adorable indie hostel sleeps 60 in clean four- to 10-bed dorms outfitted with individual backpack-sized lockers. The reception is generally staffed from 8am to 9pm.

Max Hotel Garni HOTEL €€

(☎386 800; www.max-hotelgarni.de; Adersstrasse 65; s/d from €70/85; @📶) Upbeat, contemporary and run with personal flair, this charmer is a Düsseldorf favourite. Rates include coffee, tea, soft drinks and a regional public transport pass. Call ahead to arrange an arrival time.

Eating & Drinking

The local beverage of choice is *Altbier*, a dark and semisweet beer typical of Düsseldorf.

Brauerei im Füchschen GERMAN €€

(☎137 470; www.fuechschen.de; Ratinger Strasse 28; mains €5-15; ⏲9am-1am) Boisterous, packed and drenched with local colour – the 'Little Fox' in the Altstadt is all you expect a Rhenish beer hall to be.

Libanon Express MIDDLE EASTERN €

(Berger Strasse 19-21; mains €3-20) Great kebabs, falafel and other Middle Eastern specialities.

TOP CHOICE **Zum Uerige** BEER HALL

(☎866 990; www.uerige.de; Berger Strasse 1) This cavernous beer hall is a superb place to soak up local colour along with your beer. The suds flow so quickly from giant copper vats that the waiters – called *Köbes* – simply carry huge trays of brew and plonk down a glass whenever they spy an empty.

Information

Tourist Office Altstadt (Marktstrasse/Ecke Rheinstrasse; ⊙10am-6pm); Hauptbahnhof (Immermannstrasse 65b; ⊙9.30am-7pm Mon-Fri, to 5pm Sat)

Getting There & Away

Düsseldorf International Airport (DUS; www.dus-int.de) has three terminals and is served by a wide range of airlines. S-Bahns, regional RE and long-distance trains link it with Düsseldorf Hauptbahnhof, and cities beyond, every few minutes.

Düsseldorf is part of a dense S-Bahn and regional train network in the Rhine-Ruhr region, including Cologne (€12, 30 minutes). ICE/IC train links include Berlin (€107, 4¼ hours), Hamburg (€78, 3¾ hours) and Frankfurt (€78, 1¾ hours).

Getting Around

Rheinbahn (www.rheinbahn.de) operates an extensive network of U-Bahn trains, trams and buses. Most trips within the city cost €2.40. Day passes are €5.70.

Aachen

☎0241 / POP 258,700

A spa town with a hopping student population and tremendous amounts of character, Aachen is most famous for its ancient cathedral. It makes for an excellent day trip from Cologne or Düsseldorf or a worthy overnight stop.

Sights

TOP CHOICE **Aachener Dom** CHURCH

(☎447 090; www.aachendom.de; Münsterplatz; ⊙7am-7pm Apr-Dec, to 6pm Jan-Mar) It's impossible to overstate the significance of Aachen's magnificent cathedral. The burial place of Charlemagne, it's where more than 30 German kings were crowned and where pilgrims have flocked since the 12th century. The **Pfalzkapelle** boasts a colossal brass chandelier that was a gift from Emperor Friedrich Barbarossa during whose reign Charlemagne was canonised in 1165. To accommodate the growing numbers of pilgrims, a fancifully decorated Gothic choir was docked to the chapel in 1414. At the far end is the gilded **shrine of Charlemagne** that has held the emperor's remains since 1215.

Rathaus HISTORIC BUILDING

(Markt; adult/concession €5/3; ⊙10am-6pm) Aachen's mighty Gothic town hall is festooned with 50 life-size statues of German rulers, including 30 German kings that were crowned in town. Inside, highlights are the **Kaisersaal** with its epic 19th-century **frescos** by Alfred Rethel and the replicas of the **imperial insignia**: a crown, orb and sword (the originals are in Vienna).

Sleeping

Hotel Drei Könige HOTEL €€

(☎483 93; www.h3k-aachen.de; Büchel 5; s €90-130, d €120-180, apt €140-240; 📶) The radiant Mediterranean decor is an instant mood enhancer at this family-run favourite with its doesn't get more central location.

DJH Hostel HOSTEL €

(☎711 010; www.aachen.jugendherberge.de; Maria-Theresia-Allee 260; dm/s/d from €26/45/68) Aachen's modernised 180-bed hostel is nicely located in a park overlooking the city. Take bus 2 (direction Preuswald) to the Ronheide stop.

Eating & Drinking

Aachen's students have their own 'Latin Quarter' along Pontstrasse northeast of the Markt.

TOP CHOICE **Leo van den Daele** CAFE €

(www.van-den-daele.de; Büchel 18; treats from €3) Leather-covered walls, tiled stoves and antiques forge the yesteryear flair of this rambling cafe institution. Come for all-day breakfast, a light lunch or divine cakes.

Am Knipp GERMAN €€

(☎331 68; www.amknipp.de; Bergdriesch 3; mains €8-18; ⊙dinner Wed-Mon) Hungry grazers have stopped by this traditional inn since 1698, and you too will have a fine time enjoying hearty German cuisine amid myriad knick-knacks or in the lovely beer garden.

Information

Tourist Office (☎180 2960, 180 2961; www.aachen-tourist.de; Friedrich-Wilhelm-Platz;

⏲9am-6pm Mon-Fri, to 2pm Sat, also 10am-2pm Sun Easter-Dec)

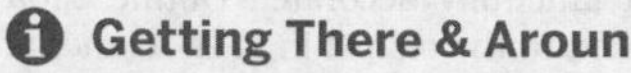

Getting There & Around

Regional trains to Cologne (€16, one hour) run twice hourly, with some proceeding beyond.

Local bus tickets are €1.60; drivers sell tickets.

LOWER SAXONY

Lower Saxony (Niedersachsen) likes to make much of its half-timbered towns such as Hamelin but it is also home to the global headquarters of Volkswagen and the business-minded capital, Hanover.

Hanover

☎0511 / POP 518,000

German comedians like to dismiss Hanover (Hannover in German) as 'the autobahn exit between Göttingen and Walsrode'. However, the capital of Lower Saxony is far livelier than its reputation and boasts acres of greenery in the Versailles-like gardens, Herrenhäuser Gärten, some of the finest in Germany.

Sights & Activities

Neues Rathaus HISTORIC BUILDING
(Trammplatz 2; elevator adult/concession €3/2; ⏲9.30am-6.30pm Mon-Fri, 10am-6.30pm Sat & Sun, elevator closed mid-Nov–Mar) An excellent way to get your bearings in Hanover is to visit the Neues Rathaus (built in 1901–13) and travel 98m to the top in the **curved lift** inside its green dome.

Die Nanas SCULPTURE
(Leibnizufer) Installed beside the Leine River in 1974, the voluptuous and fluorescent-coloured earth-mama sculptures by the late French artist Niki de Saint Phalle are among Hanover's most recognisable, and beloved, landmarks.

TOP CHOICE **Herrenhäuser Gärten** GARDEN
(☎1684 7576; www.herrenhaeuser-gaerten.de; ⏲9am-sunset) The jewel in the crown of the Herrenhäuser Gardens is the **Grosser Garten** (adult/concession incl Berggarten €5/4 Nov–mid-May, €8/5 mid-May–Oct), which is peppered with statues, fountains and the colorfully tiled **Niki de Saint Phalle Grotto**. The **Grosse Fontäne** (Great Fountain; the tallest in Europe) at the park's south end jets water up to 80m high. Popular summer attractions are the **Wasserspiele** (Fountain Display; ⏲11am-noon & 3-5pm Mon-Fri, 11am-noon & 2-5pm Sat & Sun Apr-Oct), water fountains that are synchronised to do some spectacular spurting, and the **Illuminations** (www.hannover.de/herrenhausen; adult/concession €5/3), when the Grosser Garten is lit up for between one and two hours.

The gardens are about 5km outside the city centre and served by tram/U-Bahn 4 or 5 from the Kröpke stop.

Sleeping

City Hotel am Thielenplatz HOTEL €
(☎327 691; www.smartcityhotel.com; Thielenplatz 2; s/d from €59/69, breakfast €9.50; P, wi-fi) This very central 'budget boutique' beauty has a reception and bar (open until 5am) styled with leather seating, black-and-white leaf-patterned wallpaper and lots of wood laminate.

DJH Hostel HOSTEL €
(☎131 7674; www.jugendherberge.de/jh/hannover; Ferdinand-Wilhelm-Fricke-Weg 1; 4-bed dm under/over 27yr from €21.80/25.80, s/d €38.50/57; P @ wi-fi; S3 or 7 to Bahnhof Linden/Fischerhof) This huge, space-lab-like structure houses a modern hostel with breakfast room and terrace bar overlooking the river. It's only a short walk from here to the Maschsee (lake).

Eating & Drinking

TOP CHOICE **Markthalle** MARKET €
(www.hannover-markthalle.de; Kamarschstrasse 49; dishes €3.50-10; ⏲7am-8pm Mon-Wed, to 10pm Thu & Fri, to 4pm Sat; ✎) This huge covered market of food stalls and gourmet delicatessens is fantastic for a quick bite, both carnivorous and vegetarian.

Brauhaus Ernst August PUB
(www.brauhaus.net; Schmiedestrasse 13; ⏲8am-3am Mon-Thu, to 5am Fri & Sat, 9am-3pm Sun) A Hanover institution, this sprawling brewpub makes a refreshing unfiltered pilsner called Hannöversch. A party atmosphere reigns nightly, helped along by a varied roster of live bands and DJs.

Information

Hannover Tourismus (☎information 1234 5111, room reservations 1234 555; www.hannover.de; Ernst-August-Platz 8; ⏲9am-6pm Mon-Fri, to 2pm Sat, also 9am-2pm Sun Apr-Sep)

Getting There & Around

Hanover's **airport** (HAJ; www.hannover-airport.de) has many connections, including on Air Berlin, and is linked to the Hauptbahnhof by S-Bahn (S5, €3, 18 minutes).

Hanover is a major rail hub for European and national services, with frequent ICE trains to/from Hamburg Hauptbahnhof (€43, 1¼ hours), Bremen (€31, one hour), Munich (€125, 4¼ hours), Cologne (€68, 2¾ hours) and Berlin (€65, 1¾ hours), among others.

For public transport, single tickets are €2.30 and day passes €4.50.

Around Hanover

WOLFSBURG

Volkswagen *is* the Lower Saxon town of Wolfsburg – and the huge VW emblem adorning the company's global headquarters (and a factory the size of a small country) won't let you forget it.

The top reason people come here is to experience the theme park called **Autostadt** (Car City; www.autostadt.de; Stadtbrücke; adult/concession €15/12, car tower discovery adult/concession €8/6; ⌚9am-6pm), where exhibitions run the gamut of automotive design and engineering, the history of the Beetle and the marketing of individual marques, including Bentley and Lamborghini.

Nearby, **Phaeno** (www.phaeno.de; Willy-Brandt-Platz 1; adult/child/concession/family €12/7.50/9/26.50; ⌚9am-5pm Tue-Fri, 10am-6pm Sat & Sun, last entry 1hr before closing) is a science centre housed in a sleek piece of futuristic architecture by Zaha Hadid. There's also a great collection of rare and unusual vehicles in the **AutoMuseum** (http://automuseum.volkswagen.de; Dieselstrasse 35; adult/concession/family €6/3/15; ⌚10am-6pm Tue-Sun).

Wolfsburg is about 90km east of Hanover and frequently served by direct train (from €17.50, 30 minutes).

HAMELIN

☎05151 / POP 57,800

According to legend, the Pied Piper *(Der Rattenfänger)* was employed by Hamelin's townsfolk to lure their pesky rodents into the river in the 13th century. When they refused to pay him, however, he picked up his flute again and led their kids away.

However, it is a bedtime story, after all, and everywhere you look along Hamelin's cobbled streets there are – you guessed it – fake rats and happy children.

Sights

Hochzeitshaus HISTORIC BUILDING

(Osterstrasse 2) The Hochzeitshaus (Wedding House, 1610–17) does double duty as city council offices and a police station. The **Rattenfänger Glockenspiel** at the far end of the building chimes daily at 9.35am and 11.35am, while a carousel of Pied Piper figures twirls at 1.05pm, 3.35pm and 5.35pm.

Rattenfängerhaus HISTORIC BUILDING

(Rat Catcher's House; Osterstrasse 28) This is among the finest of the houses built in the ornamental Weser Renaissance style so prevalent throughout the Altstadt. Note the typically steep and richly decorated gable.

Eating

TOP CHOICE **Rattenfängerhaus** GERMAN €€

(Osterstrasse 28; mains €10-23; ⌚11am-10pm) At this tourist-geared but still cute half-timbered tavern, the speciality is 'rats' tails' (pork in reality) flambéed at your table. Schnitzels, herrings, vegie dishes and 'rat killer' herb liquor are also offered.

Information

Tourist Office (☎957 823; www.hameln.de; Diesterallee 1; ⌚9am-6pm Mon-Fri, 9.30am-3pm Sat, 9.30am-1pm Sun) On the eastern edge of the Altstadt (bus stop Bugergarten). Look for the rat symbols cropping up throughout the streets, along with information posts (currently only in German) offering a glimpse into the history of Hamelin and its restored 16th- to 18th-century architecture.

WORTH A TRIP

BERGEN-BELSEN

The Nazi-built concentration camp at **Bergen-Belsen** (www.bergenbelsen.de; Lohheide; ⌚10am-6pm) began its existence in 1940 as a POW camp, but was partly taken over by the SS from April 1943 to hold Jews as hostages in exchange for German POWs held abroad. In all, 70,000 Jews, Soviet soldiers, political hostages and other prisoners died here, most famously Anne Frank.

Bergen-Belsen is about 60km northeast of Hanover but difficult to reach by public transport. If you're driving, take the B3 to the town of Bergen and follow the signs to Belsen.

Getting There & Away

Frequent S-Bahn trains (S5) head to Hamelin from Hanover's Hauptbahnhof (€11.10, 45 minutes).

Bremen

0421 / POP 548,000

It's a shame the donkey, dog, cat and rooster in Grimm's Town Musicians of Bremen never actually made it here – they would have fallen in love with the place. This little city is big on charm, from the fairy-tale character statue to a jaw-dropping art nouveau laneway and impressive town hall. On top of that, the Weser riverside promenade is a relaxing, cafe-lined refuge and the student district along Ostertorsteinweg knows it's got a good thing going.

Sights & Activities

Markt SQUARE

Bremen's Markt is striking, particularly because of its ornate, gabled **Rathaus**. In front stands a 13m-tall medieval statue of the knight **Roland**, Bremen's protector. On the building's western side, you'll find a sculpture of the **Town Musicians of Bremen** (1951). Local artist Gerhard Marcks has cast them in their most famous pose, scaring the robbers who invaded their house, with the rooster atop the cat, perched on the dog, on the shoulders of the donkey.

Dom St Petri CHURCH

(St Petri Cathedral; tower €1; 10am-4.45pm Mon-Fri, to 1.30pm Sat, 2-4.45pm Sun, tower closed Nov-Easter) The 13th-century twin-towered Dom has great ribbed vaults and chapels as well as the intriguing **Bleikeller** (Lead Cellar; adult/child €1.40/1; 10am-5pm Mon-Fri, to 1.45pm Sat, noon-4.45pm Sun Apr-Oct), a cellar where open coffins reveal eight bodies mummified in the incredibly dry air.

Böttcherstrasse STREET

This charming lane is a superb example of expressionist architecture. Enter via an arch festooned with a golden relief, then pop into the **Haus Atlantis** (now the Hilton Hotel) with its glass-walled spiral staircase and the nearby **Kunstsammlungen Böttcherstrasse** (Art Collection Böttcherstrasse; www.pmbm.de; Böttcherstrasse 6-10; combined ticket adult/concession €5/3; 11am-6pm Tue-Sun).

Schnoor NEIGHBOURHOOD

The maze of narrow, winding alleys known as the Schnoorviertel was once the fishermen's quarter and then the red-light district. Now its doll's house–sized cottages house souvenir shops and restaurants.

Beck's Brewery BREWERY

(01805-101 030; www.becks.de/besucherzentrum; Am Deich; tours €10.50; tours 10am, 11.30am, 1pm, 3pm, 4.30pm & 6pm Thu-Sat May-Oct, less frequently Jan-Apr) Two-hour tours of the Beck's brewery must be booked online or by telephone. Take tram 1 or 8 to Am Brill.

Sleeping

Bremer Backpacker Hostel HOSTEL €

(223 8057; www.bremer-backpacker-hostel.de; Emil-Waldmann-Strasse 5-6; dm/s/d €18/29/48; P@) This private hostel is simply furnished but spotless, with a kitchen, communal room and a small courtyard out front for soaking up the sun.

TOP CHOICE **Hotel Bölts am Park** HOTEL €€

(346 110; www.hotel-boelts.de; Slevogtstrasse 23; s/d €65/85; P) This cosy family-run hotel in a leafy neighbourhood has real character, from the wonderfully old-fashioned breakfast hall to its well-proportioned doubles.

Eating & Drinking

The student quarter around Ostertorsteinweg brims with inexpensive restaurants and cafes. The waterfront promenade, Schlachte, is pricier and more mainstream. The Marktplatz has oodles of snack stands.

Piano INTERNATIONAL €

(www.cafepiano-bremen.de; Fehrfeld 64; mains €6.50-11.40; 9am-1am;) Enduringly popular, this bustling cafe place serves pizza, pasta, a few heartier dishes and vegie casseroles to all comers.

TOP CHOICE **Engel Weincafe** BAR, CAFE

(www.engelweincafe-bremen.de; Ostertorsteinweg 31; breakfast €4.90-8.60, Flammkuchen €6.70-9.50, cheeses & meats €4-13.30; 8am-1am Mon-Fri, 10am-1am Sat & Sun;) This double act of cafe and wine bar also does good breakfasts and serves cheeses, cold cuts of meat and platters to accompany the fine wines.

Information

Tourist Office (01805-101 030; www.bremen-tourism.de) Hauptbahnhof (9am-7pm Mon-Fri, 9.30am-6pm Sat & Sun);

Marktplatz (Marktplatz, cnr Obernstrasse/ Liebfraukirchhof; ⊙10am-6.30pm Mon-Sat, to 4pm Sun)

Getting There & Away

Bremen's **airport** (BRE; www.airport-bremen.de) is about 3.5km south of the city and served by tram 6 (€2.35, 15 minutes). Frequent IC trains go to Hamburg (€26, one hour), Hanover (€31, one hour) and Cologne (€63, three hours).

HAMBURG

☎040 / POP 1.8 MILLION

'The gateway to the world' might be a bold claim, but Germany's second-largest city and biggest port has never been shy. Hamburg has engaged in business with the world ever since it joined the Hanseatic League trading bloc back in the Middle Ages, and this 'harbourpolis' is now the nation's premier media hub and among its wealthiest cities. It's also the site of Europe's largest urban-renewal project, the HafenCity, which is efficiently transforming the old docklands into a bold new city quarter.

Hamburg's maritime spirit infuses the entire city; from architecture to menus to the cry of gulls, you always know you're near the water. The city has given rise to vibrant neighbourhoods awash with multicultural eateries, as well as the gloriously seedy Reeperbahn red-light district.

Sights & Activities

Old Town HISTORIC AREA

Hamburg's medieval **Rathaus** (☎428 312 010; tours adult/child €3/0.50; ⊙English-language tours hourly 10.15am-3.15pm Mon-Thu, to 1.15pm Fri, to 5.15pm Sat, to 4.15pm Sun; S Rathausmarkt, Jungfernstieg) is one of Europe's most opulent. North of here, you can wander through the **Alsterarkaden**, the Renaissance-style arcades sheltering shops and cafes alongside a canal or 'fleet'. South of here, in the Merchants' District, is the glorious 1920s **Chile Haus** (cnr Burchardstrasse & Johanniswall; S Mönckebergstrasse/Messberg), a brown-brick architectural jewel shaped like an ocean liner.

Speicherstadt & Harbour HISTORIC AREA

The redbrick **Speicherstadt** archipelago is the world's largest continuous warehouse complex and best appreciated on foot or by taking a boat through its canals.

The Speicherstadt merges into Europe's biggest inner-city urban development, the **HafenCity**. Here, a long-derelict port area of 155 hectares is being redeveloped with restaurants, shops, apartments and offices, all built to very strict sustainability standards. In the next 20 years, it's anticipated that some 40,000 people will work and 12,000 will live here. The main architectural highlight is the stunning concert hall called **Elbphilharmonie** (Elbe Philharmonic Hall; www.elbphilharmonie.de; S Messberg) that is still under construction. For a project overview, head to the **HafenCity InfoCenter** (☎3690 1799; www.hafencity.com; Am Sandtorkai 30; ⊙10am-6pm Tue-Sun; S Messberg).

Reeperbahn NEIGHBOURHOOD

(S Reeperbahn) No discussion of Hamburg is complete without mentioning St Pauli, home of the Reeperbahn, Europe's biggest red-light district with sex shops, peep shows, dim bars and strip clubs lining the streets. Especially notorious is the **Herbertstrasse** (a block-long street lined with brothels that's off-limits to men under 18 and to female visitors of all ages).

Fischmarkt MARKET

(⊙5-10am Sun; Reeperbahn) Here's the perfect excuse to stay up all Saturday night. Every Sunday between 5am and 10am, curious tourists join locals of every age and walk of life at the famous Fischmarkt in St Pauli. The market has been running since 1703, and its undisputed stars are the boisterous *Marktschreier* (market criers) who hawk their wares at full volume. Live bands also entertainingly crank out cover versions of ancient German pop songs in the adjoining *Fischauktionshalle* (Fish Auction Hall). Take bus 112 to Hafentreppe.

Internationales Maritimes Museum MUSEUM

(☎3009 3300; www.internationales-maritimes-museum.de; Koreastrasse 1; adult/concession €12/8.50; ⊙10am-6pm Tue, Wed & Fri-Sun, 10am-8pm Thu; S Messberg) In a vast rehabbed brick shipping warehouse bordering HafenCity, this excellent private collection examines 3000 years of Hamburg's maritime history through displays of model ships, naval paintings, navigation tools and educational exhibits.

Hamburg

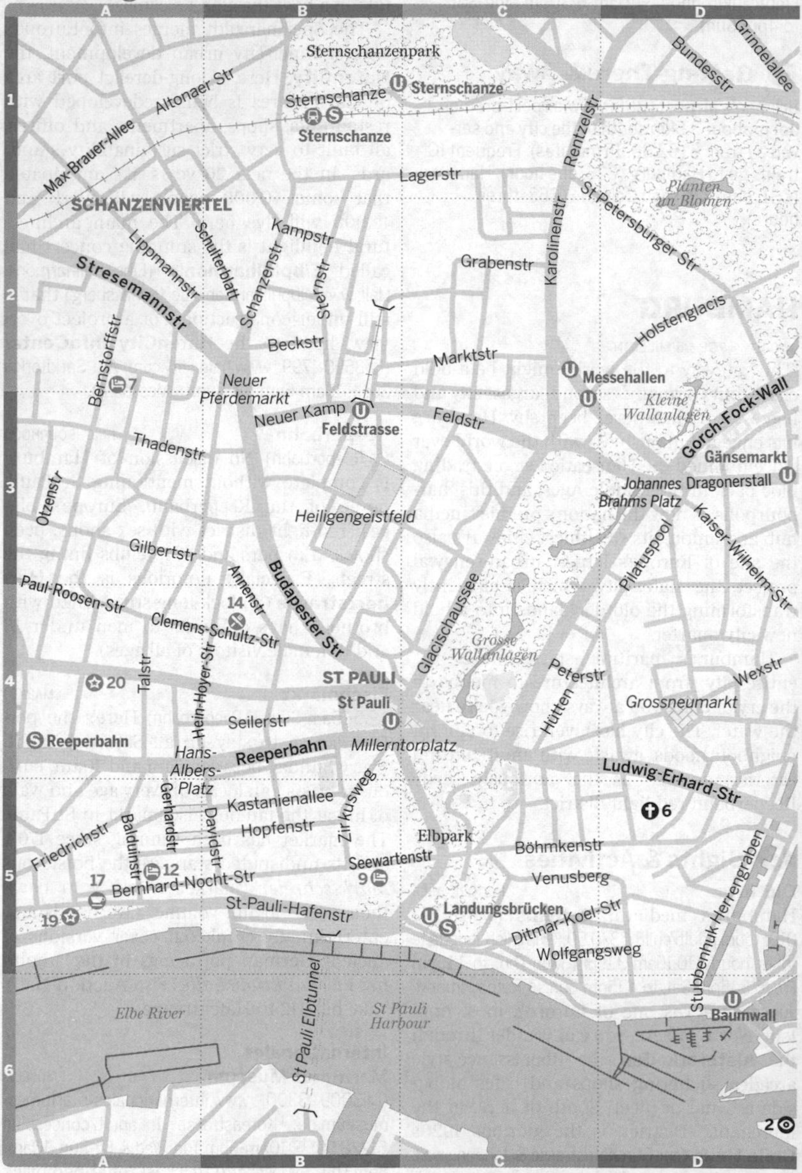

Museum für Völkerkunde MUSEUM
(☎01805-308 888; www.voelkerkundemuseum.com; Rothenbaumchaussee 64; adult/child €7/free; ⏰10am-6pm Tue, Wed & Fri-Sun, to 9pm Thu; Ⓢ Hallerstrasse, Dammtor) The famous ethnology museum is packed with traditional and modern artefacts from Africa, Asia and the South Pacific, including masks, costumes, musical instruments, carved canoes and even a complete Maori meeting hall.

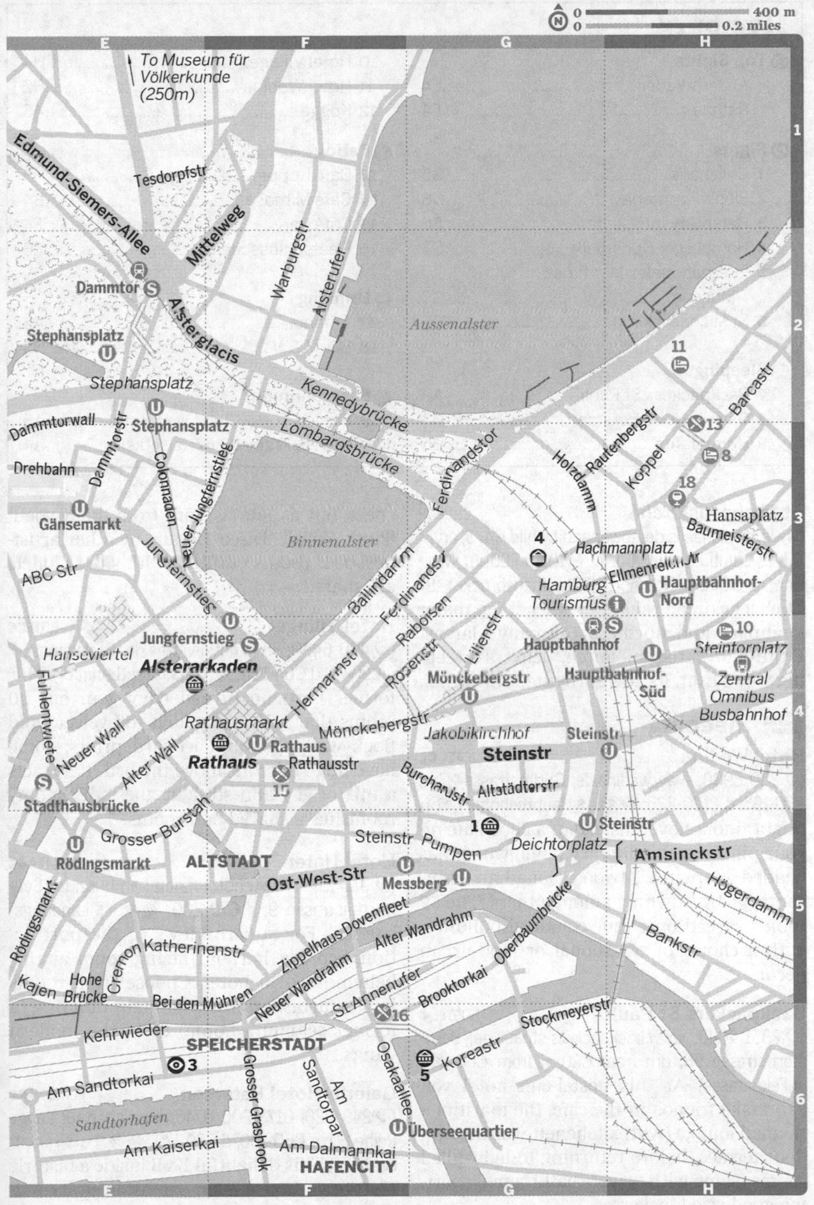

Hamburger Kunsthalle MUSEUM

(☎428 131 200; www.hamburger-kunsthalle.de; Glockengiesserwall; adult/concession €8.50/5; ⏰10am-6pm Tue, Wed & Fri-Sun, to 9pm Thu; 🚇Hauptbahnhof) This renowned art museum houses old masters and 19th-century art in its historic building, and contemporary artists (Baselitz, Richter, Hockney) in a white concrete cube.

Hamburg

Top Sights

	Alsterarkaden	E4
	Rathaus	F4

Sights

1	Chilehaus	G5
2	Elbphilharmonie	D6
3	HafenCity InfoCenter	E6
4	Hamburger Kunsthalle	G3
5	Internationales Maritimes Museum	G6
6	St Michaeliskirche	D5

Sleeping

7	Backpackers St Pauli	A2
8	Galerie-Hotel Petersen	H3
9	Hotel Hafen	B5
10	Hotel Village	H4
11	Hotel Wedina	H2
12	Kogge	A5

Eating

13	Café Koppel	H3
14	Café Mimosa	B4
15	Café Paris	F4
16	Fleetschlösschen	F6

Drinking

17	Amphore	A5
18	Bar M & V	H3

Entertainment

19	Golden Pudel Club Live Music	A5
20	Grosse Freiheit 36/Kaiserkeller	A4

St Michaeliskirche CHURCH
(www.st-michaelis.de; tower adult/child €4/3, crypt €3/2, combo ticket €6/4; 10am-7.30pm May-Oct, to 5.30pm Nov-Apr; Stadthausbrücke) St Michaeliskirche (aka 'Der Michel'), a major landmark and northern Germany's largest Protestant baroque church, delivers sweeping views from its **tower** (by steps or lift).

Sleeping

Hotel Wedina HOTEL €€
(280 8900; www.wedina.de; Gurlittstrasse 23; s €70-195, d €120-225; @; S Hauptbahnhof) You might find a novel instead of a chocolate on your pillow at this literary hotel, which has bedded Margaret Atwood, Jonathan Franzen, and JK Rowling, among others. The 59 rooms spread over four colourful buildings with a choice of traditional or mod-urban decor.

Backpackers St Pauli HOSTEL €
(2351 7043; www.backpackers-stpauli.de; Bernstorffstrasse 98; dm from €20, d from €60; ; S Feldstrasse) At this hostel-cum-hotel you can make friends in the cafe, the maritime-themed lounge (with kitchenette) or the outdoor terrace, before returning to light-filled rooms (some with private bathrooms) sporting good-sized lockers.

Kogge HOTEL €
(312 872; www.kogge-hamburg.de; Bernhard-Nocht-Strasse 59; s €30-35, d €50-60; @; S Landungsbrücken or Reeperbahn) At this rock-and-roll pub deep in noisy, grungy Reeperbahn territory, sleepyhead party-goers can check out as late as 2pm from 'Bollywood', 'Punk Royal', 'Disco Dream' or other artist-designed rooms outfitted with sinks. Toilets are shared.

Hotel Village HOTEL €
(480 6490; www.hotel-village.de; Steindamm 4; s €50-75, d €65-100; @; S Hauptbahnhof) This former bordello turned edgy gem has 20 rooms that mix and match red velvet, gold flock wallpaper and leopard prints; some have huge mirrors above the bed. It attracts a mix of gay and straight guests. Economy rooms have shared bathrooms.

Hotel Hafen HOTEL €€
(311 1370; www.hotel-hafen-hamburg.de; Seewartenstrasse 9; r €70-200; @; S Landungsbrücken) For superb views of the port action, score a harbour-facing room at this behemoth of a hotel. Choose from rooms in a refurbished, historic main building (a former seamen's home) or in the modern wings.

Galerie-Hotel Petersen PENSION €€
(249 826, 0173-200 0746; www.ghsp.eu; Lange Reihe 50; s €60-100, d €70-170; @; S Hauptbahnhof) This delightful B&B inside a historic 1790 town house is an extension of its welcoming artist-owner's personality. Furnishings include a mix of contemporary, antique and art deco styles.

Eating

The **Schanzenviertel** (Feldstrasse or Schanzenstern) swarms with cheap eateries; try

Schulterblatt for Portuguese outlets or Susanenstrasse for Asian and Turkish. St Georg's **Lange Reihe** (U-Bahn to Hauptbahnhof) offers many characterful eating spots to suit every budget. Many fish restaurants around the Landungsbrücken, though, are overrated and touristy.

Fleetschlösschen INTERNATIONAL €€
(Brooktorkai 17; snacks €7-10; ⏲8am-8pm Mon-Fri, 11am-6pm Sat & Sun; Ⓢ Messberg) One of the cutest cafes you ever saw, this former customs post overlooks a Speicherstadt canal and has brilliant outdoor seating areas.

Café Paris FRENCH €€
(www.cafeparis.net; Rathausstrasse 4; mains €10-20; ⏲9am-11.30pm Mon-Fri, from 10am Sat & Sun; Ⓢ Rathaus) Within a spectacularly tiled 1882 butchers' hall and adjoining art deco salon, this elegant yet relaxed brasserie serves classical French cafe fare and a killer breakfast for two.

Café Koppel VEGETARIAN €
(www.cafe-koppel.de; Lange Reihe 66; mains €5-10; ; Ⓢ Hauptbahnhof) Set back from busy Lange Reihe, with a garden in summer, this vegie cafe is a refined oasis.

Café Mimosa CAFE €
(www.cafemimosa.de; Clemens-Schultz-Strasse 87; mains €5-12; Ⓢ St Pauli) Skip the greasy fast-food joints on the nearby Reeperbahn for this gem of a neighbourhood café, and indulge in delicious pastas, salads and home-made cakes in a theatrical space or outside at a pavement table.

Drinking & Entertainment

Good online sources for bars and clubs include www.szene-hamburg.de and www.neu.clubkombinat.de.

Bar M & V BAR
(www.mvbar.de; Lange Reihe 22; ; Ⓤ Hauptbahnhof) The drinks menu is like a designer catalogue at this grand old St Georg bar that's had a beautiful restoration. Settle into one of the wooden booths, smell the freesias and enjoy.

Amphore CAFE
(www.cafe-amphore.de; Hafenstrasse 140; Ⓤ Reeperbahn) Beguiling in its trad beauty, non-fussy Amphore has terrace views out to the Elbe and pavement tables for neighbourhood gawking. An excellent St Pauli spot for a drink.

Strandperle BAR
(www.strandperle-hamburg.de; Schulberg 2; ⏲almost year-round; 🚌112) As the sun sets while huge freighters glide past, the mother of Hamburg's beach bars is the place to be, despite its remote location. From Altona station, take bus 112 west to Neumühlen/Övelgönne.

TOP CHOICE **Hafenklang** CLUB
(www.hafenklang.org; Grosse Elbstrasse 84; Ⓢ Königstrasse) A collective of Hamburg industry insiders present concerts and parties with established and emerging DJs at the decks. Look for the spray-painted name above a blank metal door.

TOP CHOICE **Golden Pudel Club Live Music** LIVE MUSIC
(☎3197 9930; www.pudel.com; St-Pauli-Fischmarkt 27; ⏲from 10pm; Ⓢ St Pauli) In a ramshackle wooden fisherman's hut, this bar-club gets packed to the rafters for its quality electro, hip-hop, R&B and reggae gigs.

Grosse Freiheit 36/Kaiserkeller LIVE MUSIC
(☎3177 7811; Grosse Freiheit 36; Ⓢ Reeperbahn) The Beatles once played in the basement Kaiserkeller at this now-mainstream venue mounting pop and rock concerts. It's the best reason today to detour up the Grosse Freiheit.

Information

Hamburg Tourismus (☎3005 1200; www.hamburg-tourismus.de) Hauptbahnhof Landungsbrücken Airport (Airport Plaza btwn Terminals 1 & 2; ⏲6am-11pm)

Getting There & Away

AIR Hamburg's **airport** (HAM; www.flughafen-hamburg.de) is linked to the city centre by the frequent S1 train (€2.85, 24 minutes).

BUS The **Zentral Omnibus Busbahnhof** (ZOB, Central Bus Station; ☎247 5765; www.zob-hamburg.de; Adenauer Allee 78, Central Bus Station) is southeast of the Hauptbahnhof. **Eurolines** (www.eurolines.com) has buses to Prague (€59) and Warsaw (€50), among many others.

TRAIN Reading timetables, remember that Hamburg has four mainline train stations: the Hauptbahnhof, Dammtor, Altona and Harburg. Frequent trains serve Lübeck (€18.50, 40 minutes), Hanover (€40, 1¼ hours) and Bremen (from €20.80, 55 minutes). Direct ICE trains depart frequently for Berlin-Hauptbahnhof (€68, 2¼ hours), Cologne (€79, four hours), Munich

(€127, six hours), Frankfurt (€106, three hours) and Copenhagen (€78.80, five hours).

Getting Around

HVV (☎194 49; www.hvv.de) operates buses, ferries, and U-Bahn and S-Bahn trains. The city is divided into zones. Ring A covers the city centre, inner suburbs and airport. Single tickets are €2.85, day passes €6.95. Services run around the clock on weekends; between 12.30am and 4am Sunday to Thursday the night bus network takes over, converging on Rathausmarkt.

SCHLESWIG-HOLSTEIN

Lübeck

☎0451 / POP 210,300

Two pointed cylindrical towers of Lübeck's Holstentor city gate greet you upon arrival – if you think they're a tad crooked, you're right. Right behind them, the streets are lined with medieval merchants' homes and spired churches forming the city's so-called 'crown'. It's hardly surprising that this 12th-century gem is on Unesco's World Heritage list.

Sights & Activities

TOP CHOICE Holstentor LANDMARK

Built in 1464, the incredibly photogenic city gate serves as Lübeck's museum as well as its symbol. The six gabled brick buildings east of the Holstentor are the Salzspeicher and once stored the salt so pivotal to Lübeck's Hanseatic trade.

Marienkirche CHURCH

(Schüsselbuden 13; admission €1; ⏲10am-6pm Apr-Sep, to 5pm Oct, to 4pm Tue-Sun Nov-Mar) This 13th-century church is most famous for its shattered bells, left where they fell after a WWII bombing raid. Outside there's a little devil sculpture with an amusing folk tale (in German and English).

Petrikirche CHURCH

(☎397 730; www.st-petri-luebeck.de; Schüsselbuden 13; adult/child €3/2; ⏲9am-9pm Apr-Sep, 10am-7pm Oct-Mar) Panoramic city views unfold from the 50m-high viewing platform reached by lift.

Rathaus HISTORIC BUILDING

(☎122 1005; Breite Strasse 64; adult/concession €3/1.50; ⏲tours 11am, noon & 3pm Mon-Fri) Sometimes described as a 'fairy tale in stone', Lübeck's medieval town hall is widely regarded as one of the most beautiful in Germany.

> **MARZIPAN**
>
> **Niederegger** (☎530 1126; www.niederegger.de; Breite Strasse 89; ⏲9am-7pm Mon-Fri, 9am-6pm Sat, 10am-6pm Sun) is Lübeck's mecca for marzipan, which has been made locally for centuries. The shop's elaborate displays are a feast for the eyes and there's an elegant cafe in back.

Sleeping

Rucksackhotel HOSTEL €

(☎706 892; www.rucksackhotel-luebeck.com; Kanalstrasse 70; dm €15-16, s €28, d €40; P@) This 30-bed hostel has a relaxed atmosphere, good facilities (including a well-equipped kitchen) and colourful decor with the odd tropical touch.

TOP CHOICE Klassik Altstadt Hotel BOUTIQUE HOTEL €€

(☎702 980; www.klassik-altstadt-hotel.de; Fischergrube 52; s €60-100, d €130-160;) Rooms at this elegantly furnished boutique hotel are each dedicated to a famous artist or writer, such as Thomas Mann and Johann Sebastian Bach.

Hotel an der Marienkirche HOTEL €

(☎799 410; www.hotel-an-der-marienkirche.de; Schüsselbuden 4; s €58-78, d €75-95;) This small and bright budget hotel has a super-central location and gets your days started with a healthy breakfast buffet.

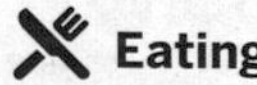

Eating

Brauberger GERMAN €€

(☎702 0606; Alfstrasse 36; mains €9-14; ⏲5pm-midnight Mon-Thu, 5pm-late Fri & Sat) At this brew-up you sit among the kettles while enjoying the sweet, cloudy house brew and one of many excellent schnitzels or other trad fare.

Krützfeld DELI €

(☎728 32; Hüxstrasse 23; snacks from €2; ⏲8am-6pm Tue-Fri, 8am-2pm Sat) This classic deli has been serving all manner of fresh and smoked seafood for decades. Great for picnic supplies.

Information

Lübeck Travemünde Tourismus (☎01805-882 233; www.luebeck-tourismus.de; Holstentorplatz 1; ⏰9.30am-7pm Mon-Fri, 10am-3pm Sat & 10am-2pm Sun Jun-Sep, 9.30am-6pm Mon-Fri &10am-3pm Sat Oct-May)

Getting There & Away

Ryanair and Wizzair serve **Lübeck airport** (LBC; www.flughafen-luebeck.de). There's direct bus service to Hamburg (€10, 55 minutes), while local bus 6 serves Lübeck's Hauptbahnhof and central bus station (€2.70).

Lübeck has hourly trains to Hamburg (€19, 40 minutes).

UNDERSTAND GERMANY

History

Events in Germany have often dominated the European stage, but the country itself is a relatively recent invention: for most of its history Germany has been a patchwork of semi-independent principalities and city-states, occupied first by the Roman Empire, then the Holy Roman Empire and finally the Austrian Habsburgs. Perhaps because of this, many Germans retain a strong regional identity.

The most significant medieval events in Germany were pan-European in nature – Martin Luther brought on the Protestant Reformation with his criticism of the Catholic Church in Wittenberg in 1517, a movement that ultimately sparked the Thirty Years' War (1618–48). Germany became the battlefield of Europe, only regaining stability after the Napoleonic Wars with increasing industrialisation and the rise of the Kingdom of Prussia. In 1866 legendary Prussian 'Iron Chancellor' Otto von Bismarck brought the German states together, largely by force, and a united Germany emerged for the first time in 1871, under Kaiser Wilhelm I.

WWI & the Rise of Hitler

Germany's rapid growth led to mounting tensions with England, Russia and France, contributing to the outbreak of WWI. After Germany's defeat, the Kaiser abdicated and the Weimar Republic was proclaimed, but the new government was hampered by exorbitant reparation payments. Hyperinflation and economic depression bolstered support for extremist groups, including Adolf Hitler's National Socialists (Nazis).

By 1933, the Nazis had manoevered themselves into a position of political dominance. Hitler was appointed chancellor and quickly consolidated absolute power and turned Germany into a one-party dictatorship.

In September 1939 he attacked Poland, provoking war with Britain and France. Behind the scenes, concentration camps exterminated an estimated six million Jews and another one million 'enemies of state'. Germany surrendered in May 1945, soon after Hitler's suicide.

The Two Germanies

After the war, the USA, Britain, France and the Soviet Union divided the country into four occupation zones. In September 1949 the Federal Republic of Germany (FRG) was formed from the three western zones. In response, the communist German Democratic Republic (GDR) was founded in the Soviet zone, with (East) Berlin as its capital. To prevent skilled workers emigrating, the GDR built a wall around West Berlin in 1961, closing its border with the FRG.

For almost 40 years capitalist and socialist Germany coexisted uneasily. In 1989, however, the Peaceful Revolution overtook the reform-shy GDR regime. On 9 November 1989 the Berlin Wall opened, and the two Germanies were reunited on 3 October 1990.

Since German Reunification

In December 1990, Helmut Kohl was elected Germany's postreunification chancellor. Under his leadership East German assets were privatised; state industries were trimmed back, sold or closed; and infrastructure was modernised, all resulting in economic growth of about 10% each year until 1995. The trend slowed dramatically thereafter, however, creating an eastern Germany that consisted of unification winners and losers.

Amid allegations of widespread financial corruption, the Kohl government was replaced with a coalition government of SPD and Alliance 90/The Greens in 1998. This marked the first time an environmentalist party had governed nationally worldwide.

The rise of the Greens and, more recently, the Left has changed the political landscape of Germany dramatically, making absolute majorities by the 'big two' all the more difficult to achieve. In 2005 the CDU/CSU and

SPD formed a grand coalition led by Angela Merkel, the first woman to hold the job of German chancellor.

The election of 2009 confirmed the trend towards smaller partie and a five-party political sytem in Germany. The outcome of national elections in late 2013 will reveal whether this fragmentation has become a permanent feature of German politics.

Germany Today

Germany seems to have weathered the recent financial crisis better than most industrial nations, in large part because it now bears the fruits of decade-old key reforms, especially the liberalisation of its labour laws. The German government launched a slew of proactive measures, such as allowing companies to put workers on shorter shifts without loss of pay and stimulating the economy by providing incentives for Germans to scrap older cars and buy new ones. The beginning of the millennium's second decade has seen the importance of Germany's stable economy grow, as the debt-driven crisis in the Eurozone has spread from Greece to threaten all of southern Europe. Germany is seen to have a key position in propping up the euro, the collapse of which could plunge economies across the globe back into recession. So far, so good.

With a Green Party active in politics since the 1980s, Germany has also played a leading role in environmental and climate protection and is considered a pioneer in the development of renewable energies. In 2011, about 20% of total energy production came from alternative sources. The country has also reduced its greenhouse gas emissions by 24% since 1990, thus exceeding the 21% reduction called for by the 2005 Kyoto Protocol. In 2011, following the nuclear disaster in Fukushima, Japan, Germany became the first industrial nation to completely opt out of nuclear power, immediately shutting down the eight oldest of its 17 reactors, with rest to go off the grid by 2022.

Some 15 million people living in Germany have an immigrant background (foreign born or have at least one immigrant parent), accounting for about 18% of the total population. According to the United Nations, only the USA and Russia absorb a greater number of international migrants. The largest group are people of Turkish descent, a legacy of the post-WWII economic boom when 'guest workers' were recruited to shore up the war-depleted workforce. Many stayed. After reunification, the foreign population soared again as repatriates from the former USSR and refugees from war-ravaged Yugoslavia arrived by the millions. Whether immigration enriches or endangers German culture has been the subject of much recent debate, but the fact is that – thanks to an ageing population and a low birth rate – the country needs newcomers to keep it, and its economy, running.

BEER

Beer is Germany's national beverage and is both excellent and inexpensive. Here's a rundown of the most common beer types:

Pilsner Full beer with pronounced hop flavour and a creamy head.

Weizenbier/Weissbier Fruity and a bit spicy, lovely on a hot day. *Hefeweizen* has a stronger shot of yeast, whereas *Kristallweizen* is clearer with more fizz.

Bockbier Strong, dark beer brewed seasonally (eg *Maibock* in May and *Weihnachtsbock* at Christmas).

Helles Bier Has strong malt aromas and is slightly sweet.

Dunkles Bier Dark and full-bodied.

Arts & Music

Historically Germany has always been strong in the arts, with the legacies of such literary, musical, artistic and architectural greats as Goethe, Johann Sebastian Bach, Karl Friedrich Schinkel and Caspar David Friedrich providing a rich vein of inspiration for modern successors like Günter Grass, Arnold Schönberg, Walter Gropius and Paul Klee. Today, Germany is a hotbed of exciting new architecture, avant garde art and edgy literature.

As the birthplace of Bach, Georg Friedrich Händel, Ludwig van Beethoven, Richard Strauss, Robert Schumann, Johannes Brahms and Richard Wagner, few countries can claim the impressive musical heritage of Germany. Its contributions to contemporary music range from the proto-techno band Kraftwerk to punk icon Nina Hagen, '80s balloon girl Nena, and rock bands from the Scorpions to Die Toten Hosen to Rammstein. Germany has the largest electronic-music scene in the world, based largely in Berlin and Frankfurt.

Food

Germany might not have the culinary pedigree of its neighbours, but its robust, fresh flavours have made it a rising star in Europe's kitchen. Of course, if you crave traditional comfort food, you'll certainly find plenty of places to indulge in pork, potatoes and cabbage. These days, though, 'typical German' fare is lighter, healthier, creative and more likely to come from organic eateries, a UN worth of ethnic restaurants and gourmet kitchens. Vegetarian and even vegan restaurants have been sprouting faster than alfafa, at least in the big cities.

SURVIVAL GUIDE

Directory A–Z

Accommodation

Germany has all types of places to unpack your suitcase, from hostels, camping grounds and family hotels, to chains, business hotels and luxury resorts.

» Reservations are a good idea, especially between June and September. Local tourist offices will often go out of their way to find something in your price range.

» Camping grounds abound. Fees consists of charges per person (between €3 and €10), tent (€6 to €16, depending on size) and car (€3 to €8), plus additional fees for hot showers, resort tax, electricity and sewage disposal.

» **Deutsches Jugendherbergswerk** (DJH; www.jugendherberge.de) coordinates the official Hostelling International (HI) hostels in Germany. Rates in gender-segregated dorms, or in family rooms, range from €13 to €30 per person, including linen and breakfast. People over 27 are charged an extra €3 or €4. Indie hostels are more relaxed and can be found in most large cities.

PRICE RANGES

Unless noted, the following price ranges refer to a double room with private bathroom and breakfast in high season:

€ less than €80

€€ €80 to €150

€€€ more than €150

Business Hours

Banks 9am to 4pm Monday to Friday, extended hours Tuesday or Thursday

Bars 6pm to 1am

Cafes 8am to 8pm

Clubs 10pm to 4am

Post offices 9am to 6pm Monday to Friday, some Saturday mornings

Restaurants 11am to 9pm or 10pm (varies widely, 3pm to 6pm break common in rural areas)

Stores 9.30am to 8pm Monday to Saturday (shorter hours in suburbs and rural areas, possible lunchtime break)

Discount Cards

Tourist offices in many cities sell Welcome Cards entitling visitors to free or reduced admission on museums, sights and tours, plus unlimited local public transportation for the period of their validity (usually 24 or 48 hours). They can be good value if you want to fit a lot in.

Embassies & Consulates

All foreign embassies are in Berlin, but many countries have consular offices in such cities as Frankfurt, Munich, Hamburg and Düsseldorf.

Australian Embassy (☎030-880 0880; www.australian-embassy.de; Wallstrasse 76-79; Ⓤ Märkisches Museum)

Canadian Embassy (☎030-203 120; www.kanada-info.de; Leipziger Platz 17; Ⓢ Potsdamer Platz, Ⓤ Potsdamer Platz)

New Zealand Embassy (☎030-206 210; www.nzembassy.com; Friedrichstrasse 60; Ⓤ Stadtmitte)

UK Embassy (☎030-204 570; www.britischebotschaft.de; Wilhelmstrasse 70; Ⓢ Brandenburger Tor, Ⓤ Brandenburger Tor)

US Embassy (☎030-830 50; www.germany.usembassy.gov; Clayallee 170; Ⓤ Oskar-Helene-Heim)

Food

The following price categories are for the cost of a main course:

€ less than €8

€€ €8 to €15

€€€ more than €15

Gay & Lesbian Travellers

» Germany is a magnet for *schwule* (gay) and *lesbische* (lesbian) travellers, with the rainbow flag flying especially proudly in Berlin and Cologne, and with sizeable communities in Hamburg, Frankfurt and Munich.

» Generally speaking, attitudes towards homosexuality tend to be more conservative in the countryside, among older people and in the eastern states.

Legal Matters

» By law you must carry some form of photo ID (eg passport, national identity card, driving licence).

» Drivers need to carry their driving licence at all times. The permissible blood-alcohol limit is 0.05%; stiff fines and possibly a confiscated licence and even jail time are possible if caught driving over the limit.

» Drinking in public is not illegal, butbe discreet about it.

» Cannabis possession is a criminal offence and punishment may range from a warning to a court appearance.

Money

» Cash is king in Germany, so always carry some with you and plan to pay in cash almost everywhere.

» The easiest and quickest way to obtain cash is by using your debit (bank) card at an ATM (*Geldautomat*) linked to international networks such as Cirrus, Plus, Star and Maestro.

» Credit cards are becoming more widely accepted, but it's best not to assume that you'll be able to use one – enquire first.

» Change currency in foreign-exchange offices (*Wechselstuben*) at airports and train stations, particularly those of the Reisebank.

TIPPING

Restaurant bills always include a service charge *(Bedienung)* but most people add 5% or 10% unless the service was truly abhorrent.

Hotel porters €1 to €1.50 per bag

Room cleaners €1 per night per person

Bartenders 5-10%

Taxi drivers around 10%

Public Holidays

Germany observes eight religious and three secular holidays nationwide. Shops, banks, government offices and post offices are closed on these days. States with predominantly Catholic populations, such as Bavaria and Baden-Württemberg, also celebrate Epiphany (6 January), Corpus Christi (10 days after Pentecost), Assumption Day (15 August) and All Saints' Day (1 November). Reformation Day (31 October) is only observed in eastern Germany.

The following are *gesetzliche Feiertage* (public holidays):

Neujahrstag (New Year's Day) 1 January

Ostern (Easter) Good Friday, Easter Sunday and Easter Monday

Christi Himmelfahrt (Ascension Day) Forty days after Easter

Maifeiertag/Tag der Arbeit (Labour Day) 1 May

Pfingsten (Whit/Pentecost Sunday & Monday) Fifty days after Easter

Tag der Deutschen Einheit (Day of German Unity) 3 October

Weihnachtstag (Christmas Day) 25 December

Zweiter Weihnachtstag (Boxing Day) 26 December

Telephone

German phone numbers consist of an area code followed by the local number, which can be between three and nine digits long. If you're bringing your mobile phone, SIM cards with local numbers and reasonable rates are inexpensive and widely available, eg in supermarket and telecom stores.

Country code ☎49

International access code ☎00

Directory inquiries ☎11837 for an English-speaking operator (charged at €1.99 per minute)

Travellers With Disabilities

Germany is fair at best (but better than much of Europe) for the needs of travellers with disabilities, with access ramps for wheelchairs and/or lifts in some public buildings. Resources include the following:

Deutsche Bahn Mobility Service Centre (☎ext 9 for English 0180-599 663 3512; www.bahn.com; ⏲24hr)

German National Tourist Office (www.germany.travel)

Natko (www.natko.de)

Getting There & Away

Most travellers arrive in Germany by air, or by rail and road connections from neighbouring countries. Flights, tours and rail tickets can be booked online at lonelyplanet.com/bookings.

Air

» Budget carriers, Lufthansa and international airlines serve numerous German airports from across Europe and the rest of the world, with Frankfurt and Munich being the main hubs.

» For details about individual airports, including information about getting to and from them, see the listings within the chapter.

Land

BUS

» Travelling by bus between Germany and the rest of Europe is usually cheaper than by train or plane, but journeys will take a lot longer.

» **Eurolines** (www.eurolines.com) is a consortium of national bus companies operating routes throughout the continent. The German affiliate is **Deutsche Touring** (☎069-790 3501; www.touring.de).

» Children between the ages of four and 12 pay half price, while teens, students and seniors get 10% off regular fares. Tickets can be purchased online and at most train stations throughout Germany.

» Germany is part of the North Loop of backpacker-geared hop-on, hop-off **Busabout** (☎+44 8450 267 514; www.busabout.com) which makes stops in Berlin, Dresden, Munich and Stuttgart.

CAR & MOTORCYCLE

» When bringing your own vehicle to Germany, you need a valid driving licence, car registration and proof of third-party insurance. Foreign cars must display a nationality sticker unless they have official European plates. You also need to carry a warning (hazard) triangle and a first-aid kit.

» To decrease air pollution, many German cities have introduced low-emissions Green Zones that may only be entered by cars displaying an *Umweltplakette* (emissions sticker). To obtain one, check with your local automobile association or order a sticker online trough www.tuev-sued.de or www.tuev-nord.de (English instructions provided). The cost is €6.

TRAIN

» A favourite way to get to Germany from elsewhere in Europe is by train. In Germany ticketing is handled by **Deutsche Bahn** (www.bahn.com). Long-distance trains connecting major German cities with those in other countries are called EuroCity (EC) trains.

» Seat reservations are essential during the peak summer season and around major holidays.

» Germany is also linked by overnight train to many European cities; routes include Amsterdam to Munich, Zurich to Berlin and Paris to Hamburg.

Sea

» Germany's main ferry ports are Kiel, Lübeck and Travemünde in Schleswig-Holstein, and Rostock and Sassnitz (on Rügen Island) in Mecklenburg-Western Pomerania. All have services to Scandinavia and the Baltic states.

» There are no longer any direct ferries between Germany and the UK, but you can go via the Netherlands, Belgium or France and drive or train it from there. For details and tickets, go to www.ferrybooker.com or www.ferrysavers.com.

Getting Around

Germany has an excellent and comprehensive public transport system. Regional bus services fill the gaps in areas not well served by the rail network.

Air

There are lots of domestic flights, many with budget carriers such as **Air Berlin** (www.airberlin.com) and **Germanwings** (www.germanwings.com), as well as **Lufthansa** (www.lufthansa.com). Unless you're flying from one end of the country to the other, say from Berlin or Hamburg to Munich, planes are only marginally quicker than trains once you factor in the check-in and transit times.

Bicycle

» Cycling is allowed on all roads except autobahns (motorways). Helmets are not compulsory (not even for children), but wearing one is a good idea.

» Bicycles may be taken on most trains but require a separate ticket (*Fahrradkarte*). These cost €9 per trip on long-distance trains (IC and EC and City Night Line; €10 for international travel). You need to reserve a space at least one day ahead and leave your bike in the bike compartment (usually at the beginning or end of the train). Bicycles are not allowed on high-speed ICE trains. The fee on local and regional trains (IRE, RB, RE, S-Bahn) is €5 per day and no reservations are needed.

» Bicycle transport is free on some local trains, which are listed in Deutsche Bahn's *Bahn & Bike* brochure (in German; www.bahn.de/bahnundbike). It also notes the almost 250 train stations where you can rent bikes.

» Otherwise, most towns and cities have a private bicycle-hire station, often at or near the train station. Hire costs range from €7 to €20 per day and from €35 to €85 per week, depending on the model of bicycle. A cash security deposit and/or ID are usually required.

Boat

» From April to October, a lovely way to sightsee is by excursion boat plying major lakes and rivers.

» Scheduled boat services also operate along sections of the Rhine, the Elbe and the Danube and on major lakes such as Lake Constance in Baden-Württemberg.

Bus

» In some rural areas buses may be your only option for getting around without your own vehicle. This is especially true of sections of the Bavarian Forest and the Alpine foothills.

» The frequency of bus services varies from 'rarely' to 'constantly'. Commuter-geared routes offer limited or no service in the evenings and at weekends.

» In cities, buses generally converge at the *Busbahnhof* or *Zentraler Omnibus Bahnhof* (ZOB; central bus station), which is often near the Hauptbahnhof (central train station).

» For long-distance travel between German cities, the main operators are **Deutsche Touring** (☎069-790 3501; www.touring.de) and **Berlin Linien Bus** (www.berlinlinienbus.de). Discounts are available for children, students, seniors and groups.

Car & Motorcycle

» Germany's pride and joy is its 11,000km network of autobahns (motorways, freeways). Every 40km to 60km, you'll find elaborate service areas with petrol stations, toilets and restaurants; many are open 24 hours. In between are rest stops (*Rastplätze*) with picnic tables and toilets. Orange emergency call boxes are spaced about 2km apart.

» Autobahns are supplemented by an extensive network of *Bundesstrassen* (secondary 'B' roads, highways) and smaller *Landstrassen* (country roads, 'L'). No tolls are charged on any public roads.

» Cars are impractical in urban areas. Leaving your car in a central *Parkhaus* (car park) can cost €20 per day or more.

» **ADAC** (Allgemeiner Deutscher Automobil-Club; ☎0180-222 2222; www.adac.de) offers roadside assistance to members of its affiliates, including British AA, American AAA and Canadian CAA.

» Visitors do not need an international driving licence to drive in Germany; bring your licence from home.

HIRE

» To hire your own wheels, you'll need to be at least 25 years old and possess a valid driving licence and a major credit card. Some companies lease to drivers between the ages of 21 and 24 for an additional charge (about €12 to €20 per day). Younger people or those without a credit card are usually out of luck.

» For insurance reasons, driving into an eastern European country, such as the Czech Republic or Poland, is usually a no-no.

» All the main international companies maintain branches at airports, major train stations and towns.

» Rental cars with automatic transmission are rare in Germany and will usually need to be booked well in advance.

Local Transport

» Public transport is excellent within big cities and small towns and may include buses, trams (Strassenbahn), S-Bahn (light rail) and U-Bahn (underground/subway trains).

» Tickets cover all forms of transit, and fares are determined by zones or time travelled, sometimes both. Multiticket strips (*Streifenkarte*) and day passes (*Tageskarte*) offer better value than single-ride tickets.
» Tickets must usually be bought from vending machines at the stations or stops. Only buses and some trams let you buy tickets from the driver.
» Normally, tickets must be stamped upon boarding in order to be valid. Inspections are random but getting caught without a valid ticket incurs a fine (usually €40).

Train

» Operated almost entirely by **Deutsche Bahn** (www.bahn.com), the German train system is the finest in Europe and is generally the best way to get around the country.
» Several private operators provide train services on regional routes, such as the Ostdeutsche Eisenbahn in Saxony and the Bayerische Oberlandbahn in Bavaria.
» It's rarely worth buying a 1st-class ticket on German trains; 2nd class is usually quite comfortable. There's more difference between the train classifications – basically the faster a train travels, the plusher (and pricier) it is.
» Most train stations have coin-operated lockers costing from €1 to €4 per 24-hour period. Larger stations have staffed left-luggage offices (*Gepäckaufbewahrung*).
» Seat reservations (€4) for long-distance travel are highly recommended, especially if you're travelling on a Friday or Sunday afternoon, during holiday periods or in summer. Reservations can be made online and at ticket counters as late as 10 minutes before departure.

TICKETS

» Tickets may be bought online at www.bahn.de, using a credit card, at no surcharge. However, you will need to present a printout of your ticket, as well as the credit card used to buy it, to the conductor.
» Larger train stations have a *Reisezentrum* (travel centre), where staff sell tickets (for a small fee) and can help you plan an itinerary (ask for an English-speaking agent).
» Smaller stations may only have a few ticket windows and the smallest ones aren't staffed at all. In this case, you must buy tickets from multilingual vending machines. These are also plentiful at staffed stations and convenient if you don't want to queue at a ticket counter. Both agents and machines accept major credit cards.
» Only conductors on long-distance trains sell tickets on board, at a surcharge; major credit cards are usually accepted. Not having a ticket carries a stiff penalty.

SPECIAL DEALS

Deutsche Bahn offers several permanent rail deals:
» **Schönes-Wochenende-Tickets** (Nice Weekend Ticket; €40 for up to five people travelling together) are good for one day of unlimited 2nd-class travel on regional trains (IRE, RE, RB, S-Bahn), plus local public transport. Available from midnight Saturday or Sunday until 3am the next day.

A PRIMER ON TRAIN TYPES

Here's the low-down on the alphabet soup of trains operated by Deutsche Bahn (DB):

InterCity Express (ICE) Long-distance, high-speed trains that stop at major cities only and run at one- or two-hour intervals.

InterCity (IC), EuroCity (EC) Long-distance trains that are fast but slower than the ICE; also run at one- and two-hour intervals and stop in major cities. EC trains run to major cities in neighbouring countries.

InterRegio-Express (IRE) Regional train connecting cities with few intermediary stops.

City Night Line (CNL) Night trains with sleeper cars and couchettes.

Regional Bahn (RB) Local trains, mostly in rural areas, with frequent stops; the slowest in the system.

Regional Express (RE) Local trains with limited stops that link rural areas with metropolitan centres and the S-Bahn.

S-Bahn Local trains operating within a city and its suburban area.

» The **Quer-durchs-Land-Ticket** (Around Germany Ticket; €42 for the first person and €6 each for up to four additional persons) is a weekday variation of the Schönes-Wochenende-Ticket.

» The **Länder-Ticket** (Regional Ticket) offers one day of unlimited travel on regional trains and local public transport within one of the German states (or, in some cases, also in bordering states). With some variations, tickets are valid for travel Monday to Friday from 9am to 3am the following day and on weekends from midnight until 3am the following day.

» Some passes are priced as a flat rate for up to five people travelling together (eg the Brandenburg-Berlin-Ticket costs €28); other have staggered pricing: the first person buys the main ticket and up to four people may join for a just few euros more per ticket (eg in Bavaria, the first person pays €22, additional tickets cost €4).

» On any of these schemes, children under 15 travel for free if accompanied by their parents or grandparents. See the website for details or check with a *Reisezentrum* if already in Germany.

» Tickets can be purchased online, from vending machines or, for €2 surcharge, from station ticket offices.

GERMAN RAIL PASS

If your permanent residence is outside Europe, including Turkey and Russia, you qualify for the German Rail Pass. Tickets are sold through www.bahn.com, through agents in your home country and on www.raileurope.com.

Greece

Includes »

Athens 507
Patra 515
Thessaloniki 520
Mykonos 523
Paros 525
Naxos 526
Santorini (Thira) 528
Crete 530
Iraklio 531
Rhodes 535
Kos 536
Lesvos (Mytilini) 539
Corfu 541
Understand Greece 542
Survival Guide 546

Best Places to Eat

- » To Meltemi (p536)
- » Michelas (p533)
- » Tzitzikas & Mermingas (p511)
- » Taverna Lava (p530)

Best Places to Stay

- » Stelios Place (p530)
- » Francesco's (p528)
- » Pension Sofi (p527)
- » Hotel Afendoulis (p537)

Why Go?

Don't let headline-grabbing financial woes put you off going to Greece (*Ελλάδα*). The elements that have made Greece one of the most popular destinations on the planet are still all there, and now is as good a time as ever to turn up for some fun in the sun.

That alluring combination of history and hedonism continues to beckon. Within easy reach of magnificent archaeological sites are breathtaking beaches and relaxed tavernas serving everything from ouzo to octopus. Wanderers can island-hop to their heart's content, while party types can enjoy pulsating nightlife in Greece's vibrant modern cities and on islands such as Mykonos, Ios and Santorini. Throw in welcoming locals with an enticing culture and it's easy to see why most visitors head home vowing to come back. Travellers to Greece inevitably end up with a favourite site they long to return to – get out there and find yours.

When to Go

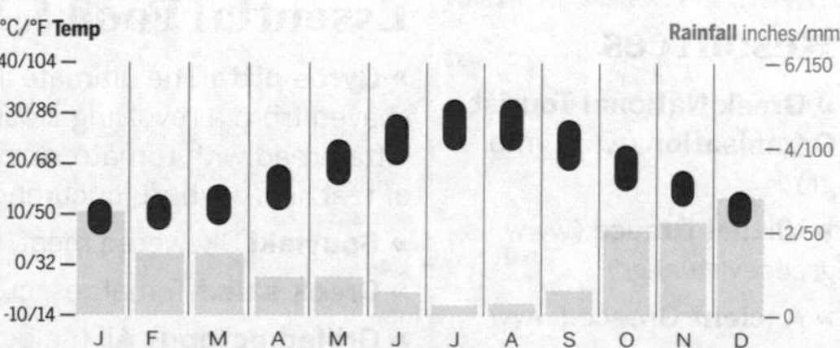

May & Jun Greece opens the shutters in time for Orthodox Easter; the best months to visit.

Jul & Aug Be prepared to battle summer crowds, high prices and soaring temperatures.

Sep & Oct The season winds down; a relaxing and pleasant time to head to Greece.

AT A GLANCE

- **Currency** Euro (€)
- **Language** Greek
- **Money** ATMs all over; banks open Mon-Fri
- **Visas** Schengen rules apply

Fast Facts

- **Area** 131,944 sq km
- **Capital** Athens
- **Country code** ☎30
- **Emergency** ☎112

Exchange Rates

Australia	A$1	€0.82
Canada	C$1	€0.77
Japan	¥100	€0.83
New Zealand	NZ$1	€0.65
UK	UK£1	€1.18
USA	US$1	€0.78

Set Your Budget

- **Budget hotel room** €50
- **Two-course dinner** €20
- **Museum entrance** €5
- **Beer** €2.50
- **Athens metro ticket** €2

Resources

- **Greek National Tourist Organisation** (www.gnto.gr)
- **Virtual Greece** (www.greecevirtual.gr)
- **Ancient Greece** (www.ancientgreece.com)
- **Greek Ferries** (www.openseas.gr)

Connections

For those visiting Greece as part of a trip around Europe, there are various exciting options for reaching onward destinations overland or by sea.

There are regular ferry connections between Greece and the Italian ports of Ancona, Bari, Brindisi and Venice. Similarly, there are ferries operating between the Greek islands of Rhodes, Kos, Samos, Chios and Lesvos and the Aegean coast of Turkey. Island-hopping doesn't have to take you back to Athens.

Overland, it's possible to reach Albania, Bulgaria, Macedonia and Turkey from Greece. If you've got your own wheels, you can drive through border crossings with these four countries. There are train and bus connections with Greece's neighbours, but check ahead as these have been affected by the financial crisis. At the time of writing, no international train services from Greece were running.

ITINERARIES

One Week

Explore Athens' museums and ancient sites on day one before spending a couple of days in the Peloponnese visiting Nafplio, Mycenae and Olympia; ferry to the Cyclades and enjoy Mykonos and spectacular Santorini.

One Month

Give yourself some more time in Athens and the Peloponnese, then visit the Ionian Islands for a few days. Explore the Zagoria Villages before travelling back to Athens via Meteora and Delphi. Take a ferry from Piraeus south to Mykonos, then island-hop via Santorini to Crete. After exploring Crete, take the ferry east to Rhodes, then north to Symi, Kos and Samos. Carry on north to Chios, then head on to Lesvos. Take the ferry back to Piraeus when you're out of time or money.

Essential Food & Drink

- **Gyros pitta** The ultimate in cheap eats. Pork or chicken shaved from a revolving stack of sizzling meat is wrapped in pitta bread with tomato, onion, fried potatoes and lashings of tzatziki (yoghurt, cucumber and garlic). Costs €2 to €3.
- **Souvlaki** Skewered meat, usually pork.
- **Greek salad** Tomatoes, cucumber, onion, feta and olives.
- **Grilled octopus** All the better with a glass of ouzo.
- **Ouzo** Sipped slowly, this legendary Greek aniseed-flavoured tipple turns a cloudy white when ice and water is added.
- **Raki** Cretan firewater produced from grape skins.
- **Greek coffee** A legacy of Ottoman rule, Greek coffee should be tried at least once by all visitors.

ATHENS

POP 3.8 MILLION

Ancient and modern, with equal measures of grunge and grace, bustling Athens (Αθήνα) is a heady mix of history and edginess. Iconic monuments mingle with first-rate museums, lively cafes and alfresco dining, with the result being downright fun. With Greece's financial difficulties Athens has revealed its more restive aspect, but take the time to look beneath the surface and you'll discover a complex metropolis full of vibrant subcultures.

Sights

Acropolis HISTORIC SITE

(Map p512; ☎210 321 0219; http://odysseus.culture.gr; adult/child €12/6; ⏰8am-8pm Mon-Fri, to 3pm

Greece Highlights

1. **Island-hop** (p549) at your own pace under the Aegean sun
2. In **Athens** (p507), trace the ancient to the modern from the Acropolis to booming nightclubs
3. Lose yourself within the medieval walls of **Rhodes Old Town** (p536)
4. Search for the oracle amidst the dazzling ruins of **Delphi** (p519)
5. Stare dumbfounded at the dramatic volcanic caldera of incomparable **Santorini** (p528)
6. Sup **ouzo** (p545) while munching on grilled octopus
7. Climb russet rock pinnacles to the exquisite monasteries of **Meteora** (p519)
8. Hike through Crete's stupendous **Samaria Gorge** (p535)
9. Use quaint **Nafplio** (p516) as a base for exploring the back roads and ruins of the Peloponnese

Central Athens

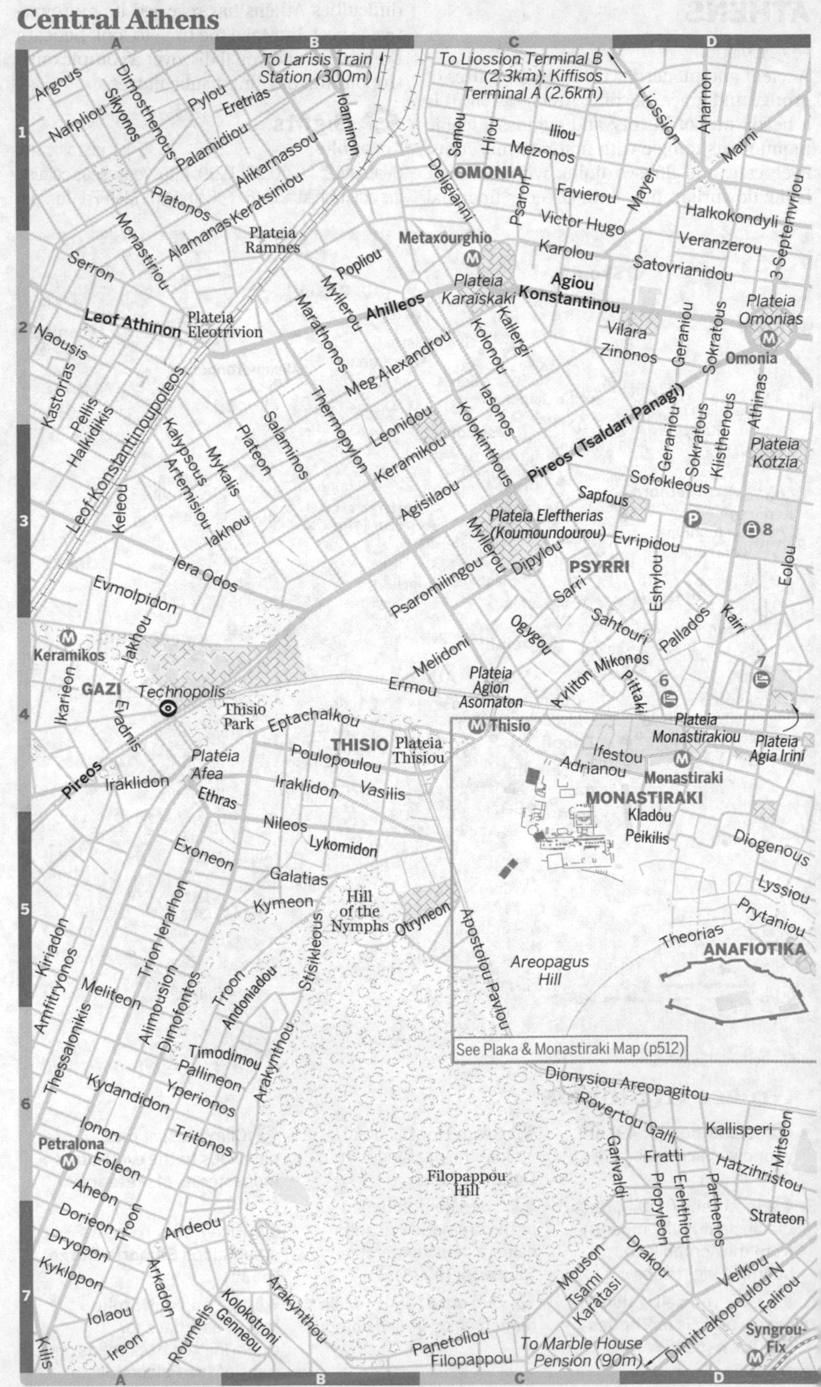

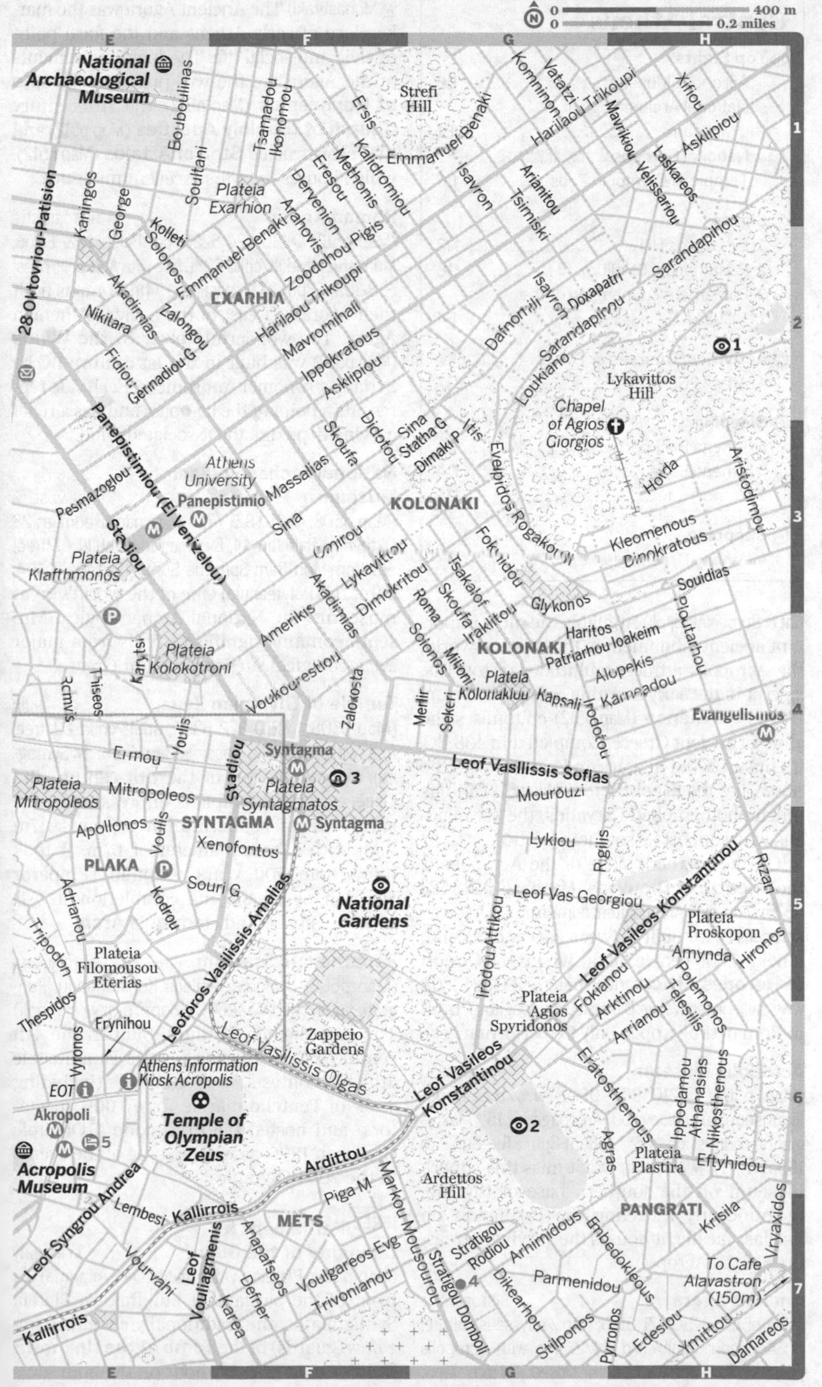
0
400 m
0
0.2 miles
E
F
G
H
1
2
3
4
5
6
7
National Archaeological Museum
Strefi Hill
Plateia Exarhion
EXARHIA
Lykavittos Hill
Chapel of Agios Giorgios
Athens University
Panepistimio
KOLONAKI
Plateia Klafthmonos
Plateia Kolokotroni
Plateia Kolonakiou
Evangelismos
Syntagma
Plateia Syntagmatos
SYNTAGMA
Plateia Mitropoleos
PLAKA
National Gardens
Plateia Filomousou Eterias
Zappeio Gardens
Athens Information Kiosk Acropolis
EOT
Akropoli
Temple of Olympian Zeus
Acropolis Museum
Ardettos Hill
Plateia Agios Spyridonos
Plateia Proskopon
Plateia Plastira
PANGRATI
METS
To Cafe Alavastron (150m)
28 Oktovriou-Patision
Panepistimiou (El Venizelou)
Leof Vasilissis Sofias
Leoforos Vasilissis Amalias
Leof Vasilissis Olgas
Leof Vasileos Konstantinou
Leof Vas Georgiou
Leof Syngrou Andrea
Leof Vouliagmenis
Emmanuel Benaki
Harilaou Trikoupi
Stadiou
Akadimias
Ermou
Mitropoleos
Ardittou
Kallirrois
Markou Mousourou
Irodou Attikou
1
2
3
4
5

Central Athens

Top Sights

Acropolis Museum	E6
National Archaeological Museum	E1
National Gardens	F5
Temple of Olympian Zeus	E6

Sights

1 Lykavittos Hill	H2
2 Panathenaic Stadium	G6
3 Parliament & Changing of the Guard	F4

Activities, Courses & Tours

4 Athens Centre	G7

Sleeping

5 Athens Backpackers	E6
6 Athens Style	D4
7 Tempi Hotel	D4

Shopping

8 Athens Central Market	D3

Sat & Sun; MAkropoli) Arguably the most important ancient monument in the Western world, the Acropolis attracts multitudes of tourists, so visit in the early morning or late afternoon.

The **Parthenon** (Map p512) epitomises the glory of ancient Greece. Completed in 438 BC, it's unsurpassed in grace and harmony. To the north, lies the **Erechtheion** (Map p512) and its much-photographed Caryatids, the six maidens who support its southern portico.

On the southern slope of the Acropolis is the **Theatre of Dionysos** (Map p512; 210 322 4625; Dionysiou Areopagitou; admission €2, free with Acropolis Pass). Built between 340 and 330 BC, it held 17,000 people. To the west is the **Odeon of Herodes Atticus** (Map p512; 210 324 1807; www.hellenicfestival.gr; Dionysiou Areopagitou), built in Roman times (open only for performances).

Acropolis Museum MUSEUM

(Map p508; 210 900 0901; www.theacropolismuseum.gr; Dionysiou Areopagitou 15, Makrygianni; admission €5; 8am-8pm Tue-Sun, to 10pm Fri; ; MAkropoli) Don't miss this superb museum on the southern base of the hill, magnificently reflecting the Parthenon on its glass facade; it houses the surviving treasures of the Acropolis.

Ancient Agora HISTORIC SITE

(Map p512; 210 321 0185; http://odysseus.culture.gr; Adrianou; adult/child €4/2, free with Acropolis pass; 8am-3pm, museum closed 8-11am Mon; MMonastiraki) The Ancient Agora was the marketplace of early Athens and the focal point of civic and social life. The main monuments of the Agora are the well-preserved **Temple of Hephaestus** (Map p512), the 11th-century **Church of the Holy Apostles** (Map p512) and the reconstructed **Stoa of Attalos** (Map p512), which houses the site's excellent **museum**.

Roman Agora HISTORIC SITE

(Map p512; 210 324 5220; cnr Pelopida & Eolou, Monastiraki; adult/child €2/1, free with Acropolis pass; 8.30am-3pm; MMonastiraki) The Romans built their agora just east of the ancient Athenian Agora. The wonderful **Tower of the Winds** (Map p512) was built in the 1st century BC by Syrian astronomer Andronicus. Each side represents a point of the compass and has a relief carving depicting the associated wind.

National Archaeological Museum MUSEUM

(Map p508; 210 821 7717; www.namuseum.gr; 28 Oktovriou-Patision 44, Exarhia; adult/child €7/free; 1-8pm Mon, 8am-3pm Tue-Sun; MViktoria, 2, 4, 5, 9 or 11 to Polytechnio) One of the world's great museums, the National Archaeological Museum contains significant finds from major archaeological sites throughout Greece.

Temple of Olympian Zeus RUIN

(Map p508; 210 922 6330; adult/child €2/free, free with Acropolis pass; 8am-3pm; MSyntagma, Akropoli) Begun in the 6th century BC, Greece's largest temple is impressive for the sheer size of its Corinthian columns: 17m high with a base diameter of 1.7m. It took more than 700 years to build (Emperor Hadrian overseeing its completion in AD 131) and sits behind **Hadrian's Arch**.

Panathenaic Stadium HISTORIC SITE

(Map p508; Leoforos Vasileos Konstantinou, Pangrati; adult/child €3/1.50; 8am-7pm; MAkropoli) The Panathenaic Stadium, built in the 4th century BC as a venue for the Panathenaic athletic contests, was restored (including seats of Pentelic marble for 70,000 spectators) and hosted the first modern Olympic Games in 1896, as well as some of the events in the 2004 Olympics.

FREE **Parliament & Changing of the Guard** CEREMONY

(Map p508; Plateia Syntagmatos; MSyntagma) In front of the parliament building on Plateia Syntagmatos, the traditionally costumed *evzones* (guards) of the **Tomb of the Unknown Soldier** change every hour on the hour.

Lykavittos Hill LANDMARK
(Map p508; Ⓜ Evangelismos) Pine-covered Lykavittos is the highest of the eight hills dotting Athens. Climb to the summit for stunning views of the city, the Attic basin and the islands of Salamis and Aegina (pollution permitting). The main path up starts at the top of Loukianou, or take the **funicular railway** from the top of Ploutarhou.

National Gardens GARDENS
(Map p508; entrances on Leoforos Vasilissis Sofias & Leoforos Vasilissis Amalias, Syntagma; 7am-dusk; Ⓜ Syntagma) A delightful, shady refuge during summer, these gardens contain a large playground, a duck pond and a tranquil cafe.

Festivals

Hellenic Festival PERFORMING ARTS
(www.greekfestival.gr; late May-Oct) Top lineup of local and international music, dance and theatre in venues across Athens and Epidavros' ancient theatre.

Sleeping

Book well ahead for July and August.

TOP CHOICE Athens Backpackers HOSTEL, APARTMENT €
(Map p508; 210 922 4044; www.backpackers.gr; Makri 12, Makrygianni; dm incl breakfast €23-28, 2-/4-/6-person apt €90/120/150; Ⓜ Akropoli) This excellent, popular hostel also has great apartments and boasts a rooftop party bar with Acropolis views, kitchen, daily movies, plus the friendly Aussie management hosts (free!) barbecues. Breakfast and nonalcoholic drinks are included; long-term storage, laundry and airport pick-up available.

Athens Style HOSTEL, APARTMENT €
(Map p508; 210 322 5010; www.athenstyle.com; Agias Theklas 10, Psyrri; dm €20-28, s/d/tr €51/80/96, apt from €90; Ⓜ Monastiraki) This bright, arty hostel, the newest in town, has dorm beds and well-equipped apartments. The cool basement lounge holds art exhibitions, a pool table and home cinema; the rooftop bar has Acropolis views.

Tempi Hotel HOTEL €
(Map p508; 210 321 3175; www.tempihotel.gr; Eolou 29, Monastiraki; d/tr €57/67, s/d without bathroom €35/47; Ⓜ Monastiraki) No-frills rooms may be tiny, but some have balconies overlooking Plateia Agia Irini. A communal kitchen and nearby markets make it ideal for self-caterers.

Marble House Pension PENSION €
(210 923 4058; www.marblehouse.gr; Zini 35a, Koukaki; s/d/tr €35/45/55, d/tr/q without bathroom €40/50/65; Ⓜ Syngrou-Fix) This long-standing Athens favourite is on a quiet cul-de-sac 10 minutes' walk from Plaka. Step through the garden to quiet, spotless rooms. For air-con add €9.

Student & Travellers' Inn HOSTEL €
(Map p512; 210 324 4808; www.studenttravellersinn.com; Kydathineon 16, Plaka; dm €20-22, s/d/tr €45/55/65, without bathroom €30/50/60; Ⓜ Syntagma) The mixed-sex dorms may be spartan and housekeeping a bit lean, but extras (laundry, left luggage) make up for it.

Eating

The fruit and vegetable **market** (Varvakios Agora; Map p508; Athinas , btwn Sofokleous & Evripidou; 7am-3pm Mon-Sat; Ⓜ Monastiraki, Panepistimio, Omonia) is opposite the meat market.

Tzitzikas & Mermingas MEZEDHES €
(Map p512; 210 324 7607; Mitropoleos 12-14, Syntagma; mezedhes €6-11; Ⓜ Syntagma) Greek merchandise lines the walls of this cheery, modern *mezedhopoleio*. The great range of delicious and creative *mezedhes* (appetisers) draws a bustling local crowd.

Thanasis SOUVLAKI €
(Map p512; 210 324 4705; Mitropoleos 69, Monastiraki; gyros €2.50; 8.30am-2.30am; Ⓜ Monastiraki) In the heart of Athens' souvlaki hub, Thanasis is known for its kebabs on pitta with grilled tomato and onions. Live music, grill aromas and crowds give the area an almost permanently festive air.

CHEAPER BY THE HALF-DOZEN

The €12 ticket at the Acropolis (valid for four days) includes entry to the other significant ancient sites: Ancient Agora, Roman Agora, Keramikos, Temple of Olympian Zeus and the Theatre of Dionysos.

Enter the sites free on the first Sunday of the month (except for July, August and September) and on certain holidays. Anyone aged under 19 years or with an EU student card gets in free.

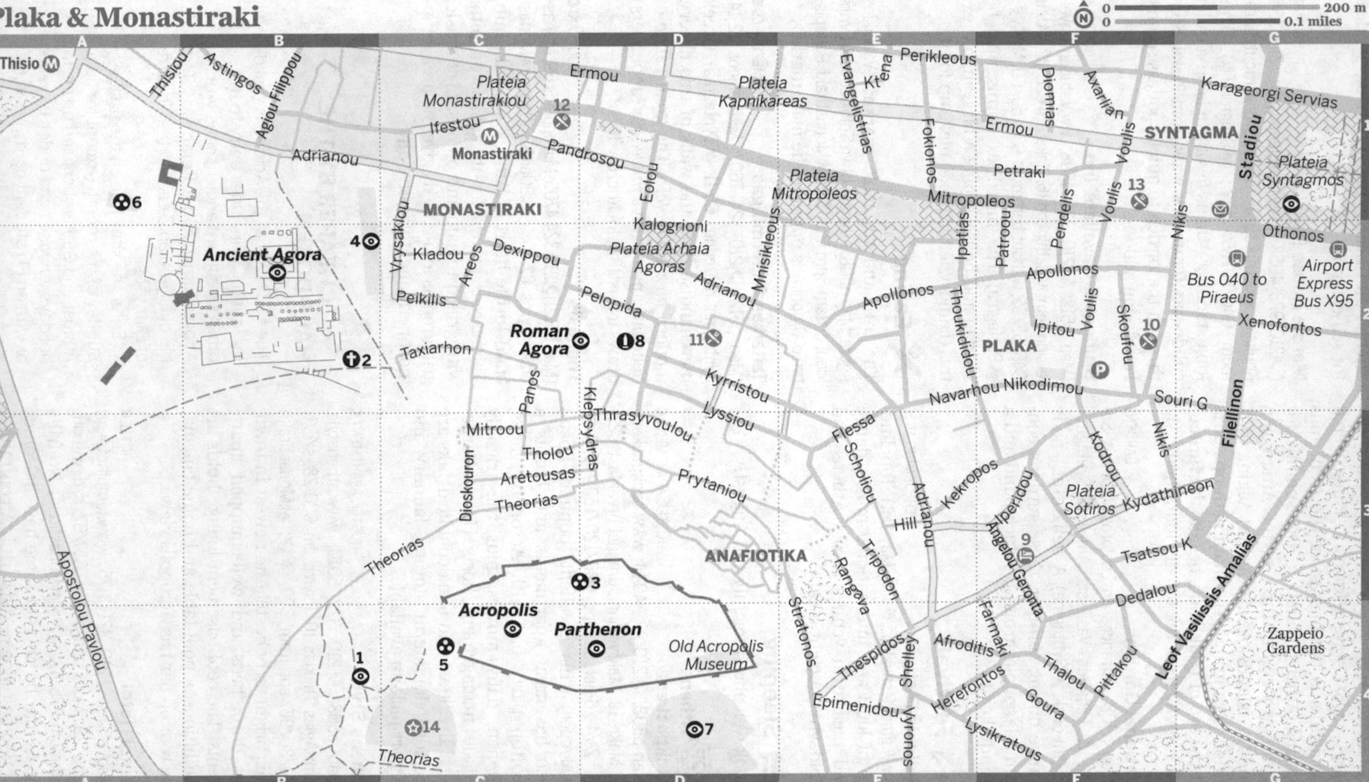
Plaka & Monastiraki
200 m
0.1 miles
Thisio
Thisiou
Astingos
Agiou Filippou
Adrianou
Ancient Agora
Plateia Monastirakiou
Ifestou
Monastiraki
MONASTIRAKI
Ermou
Pandrosou
Eolou
Plateia Kapnikareas
Evangelistrias
Kt ena
Perikleous
Fokionos
Diomias
Axarlian
Voulis
SYNTAGMA
Stadiou
Karageorgi Servias
Plateia Syntagmos
Othonos
Airport Express Bus X95
Bus 040 to Piraeus
Xenofontos
Nikis
Petraki
Mitropoleos
Plateia Mitropoleos
Ipatias
Patroou
Pendelis
Kalogrioni
Plateia Arhaia Agoras
Mnisikleous
Vrysakiou
Kladou
Areos
Dexippou
Peikilis
Pelopida
Apollonos
Thoukididou
Ipitou
Skoufou
PLAKA
Taxiarhon
Roman Agora
Kyrristou
Lyssiou
Navarhou Nikodimou
Souri G
Filellinon
Panos
Klepsydras
Mitroou
Thrasyvoulou
Flessa
Tholou
Aretousas
Theorias
Dioskouron
Prytaniou
Scholiou
Adrianou
Hill
Kekropos
Iperidou
Kodrou
Plateia Sotiros
Kydathineon
ANAFIOTIKA
Rangava
Tripodon
Angelou Geronta
Tsatsou K
Stratonos
Farmaki
Dedalou
Leof Vasilissis Amalias
Apostolou Pavlou
Acropolis
Parthenon
Old Acropolis Museum
Thespidos
Shelley
Afroditis
Thalou
Pittakou
Epimenidou
Vyronos
Herefontos
Goura
Lysikratous
Zappeio Gardens
1 2 3 4 5 6 7 8 9 10 11 12 13 14
A B C D E F G

Plaka & Monastiraki

Top Sights

Acropolis C4
Ancient Agora B2
Parthenon D4
Roman Agora D2

Sights

1 Acropolis Main Entrance B4
2 Church of the Holy Apostles B2
3 Erechtheion D3
4 Stoa of Attalos B2
5 Temple of Athena Nike C4
6 Temple of Hephaestus A1
7 Theatre of Dionysos D4
8 Tower of the Winds D2

Sleeping

9 Student & Travellers' Inn F3

Eating

10 Avocado F2
11 Platanos D2
12 Thanasis C1
13 Tzitzikas & Mermingas F1

Entertainment

14 Odeon of Herodes Atticus C4

Avocado VEGETARIAN €
(Map p512; ☎210 323 7878; www.avocadoathens.com; Nikis 30, Plaka; mains €6.50-9.50; ⊙11am-10pm Mon-Sat, to 7pm Sun; ; MSyntagma) A full array of vegan, gluten-free, and organic treats – a rarity in Greece. Enjoy everything from fresh juices and sandwiches to quinoa with eggplant or mixed veg coconut curry.

Platanos TAVERNA €
(Map p512; ☎210 322 0666; Diogenous 4, Plaka; mains €7-9; ⊙lunch & dinner daily; MMonastiraki) Tasty, home-cooked-style Greek cuisine, including delicious lamb dishes; we love the leafy courtyard.

Drinking & Entertainment

Athenians know how to party. Everyone has their favourite *steki* (hang-out), but expect people to show up after midnight. Head to Gazi (around Voutadon and the Keramikos metro station), Kolonaki (around Ploutarhou and Haritos or Skoufa and Omirou) or Monastiraki (around Plateia Karytsi or Kolokotroni) and explore! Gay bars cluster in Gazi near the railway line on Leoforos Konstantinoupoleos and Megalou Alexandrou. Check out www.athensinfoguide.com, www.gay.gr or a copy of the Greek Gay Guide booklet, available at newspaper kiosks.

For comprehensive events listings, with links to online ticket sales points, try: www.breathtakingathens.gr, www.elculture.gr, www.tickethour.com, www.tickethouse.gr, www.ticketservices.gr. The Kathimerini supplement inside the *International Herald Tribune* contains event listings and a cinema guide.

Information

Dangers & Annoyances

Crime has risen in Athens with the onset of the financial crisis. Though violent street crime remains relatively rare, travellers should be alert on the streets, especially at night, and beware the traps listed here.

» Streets surrounding Omonia have become markedly seedier, with an increase in prostitutes and junkies; avoid the area, especially at night.

» Watch for pickpockets on the metro and at the markets.

» When taking taxis, ask the driver to use the meter or negotiate a price in advance. Ignore stories that the hotel you've chosen is closed or full: they're angling for a commission from another hotel.

» Bar scams are commonplace, particularly in Plaka and Syntagma. Beware the over-friendly!

» With the recent financial reforms in Greece have come strikes in Athens (check http://livingingreece.gr/strikes). Picketers tend to march in Plateia Syntagmatos.

Emergency

Visitor Emergency Assistance (☎112) Toll-free, 24 hours; in English.

Tourist Information

Athens Information Kiosk Acropolis (Map p508; Acropolis; ⊙9am-9pm daily Jun-Aug; MAkropoli)

Athens Information Kiosk Airport (☎210 353 0390; www.breathtakingathens.com; Airport; ⊙8am-8pm daily; MAirport) Maps, transport information and all Athens info.

EOT (Map p508; Greek National Tourist Organisation; ☎210 331 0347, 210 331 0716; www.visitgreece.gr; Dionysiou Areopagitou 18-20, Makrygianni; ⊙8am-8pm Mon-Fri, 10am-4pm Sat & Sun May-Sep, 9am-7pm Mon-Fri Oct-Apr; MAkropoli)

Websites

Official visitor site (www.breathtakingathens.gr)

UNCERTAIN TIMES

» Due to the financial difficulties in Greece, which became especially acute starting in 2010, opening hours, prices and even the existence of some establishments have fluctuated much more than usual.

» At the time of writing the government was running many archaeological sites on their shorter winter hours (closing around 3pm). This could change.

» If in doubt, call ahead.

Getting There & Away

AIR Modern **Eleftherios Venizelos International Airport** (ATH; ☎210 353 0000; www.aia.gr) is 27km east of Athens.

BOAT Most ferries, hydrofoils and high-speed catamarans leave from the massive port at Piraeus. Some depart from smaller ports at Rafina and Lavrio.

BUS Athens has two main intercity **KTEL** (☎14505; www.ktel.org) bus stations, one 5km and one 7km to the north of Omonia. Tourist offices have timetables.

TRAIN Intercity trains to central and northern Greece depart from the central **Larisis train station**, about 1km northwest of Plateia Omonias. For the Peloponnese, take the suburban rail to Kiato and change for other OSE services, or check for available lines at the Larisis station.

Getting Around

To/From the Airport

BUS Tickets cost €5. Twenty-four-hour services include those to Plateia Syntagmatos, Priaeus Port and Terminal A Kifissos Bus Station.

To Plateia Syntagmatos, catch Bus X95 (60 to 90 minutes, every 15 minutes). The Syntagma stop is on Othonos. To get to Piraeus Port, catch Bus X96 (1½ hrs, every 20 minutes) and to get to Terminal A Bus Station, catch Bus X93 (35 minutes, every 30 minutes).

METRO Blue line 3 links the airport to the city centre in around 40 minutes; it operates from Monastiraki from 5.50am to midnight, and from the airport from 5.30am to 11.30pm. Tickets (€8) are valid for all public transport for 90 minutes. The fare for two or more passengers is €14 total.

TAXI Fares vary according to the time of day and level of traffic; expect at least €35 from the airport to the centre and €50 to Piraeus. Both trips can take up to an hour – more in heavy traffic.

Public Transport

The metro, tram and bus system makes getting around central Athens and to Piraeus easy. Athens' road traffic can be horrendous. Get maps and timetables at the tourist offices or **Athens Urban Transport Organisation** (OASA; ☎185; www.oasa.gr; ⌚6.30am-11.30pm Mon-Fri, 7.30am-10.30pm Sat & Sun).

Tickets good for 90 minutes (€1.40), a 24-hour travel pass (€4) and a weekly ticket (€14) are valid for all forms of public transport except for airport services. Buy tickets in metro stations, transport kiosks, or most *periptera* (street kiosks). Validate the ticket in the machine as you board your transport of choice.

BUS & TROLLEYBUS Buses and electric trolleybuses operate every 15 minutes from 5am to midnight.

To get to Piraeus from Syntagma and Filellinon to Akti Xaveriou, catch Bus 040; from the Omonia end of Athinas to Plateia Themistokleous, catch Bus 049.

METRO Trains operate from 5am to midnight (Friday and Saturday to around 2am) every three to 10 minutes. Get timetables at www.ametro.gr.

TRAIN Fast **suburban rail** (☎1110; www.trainose.gr) links Athens with the airport, Piraeus, the outer regions and the northern Peloponnese. It connects to the metro at Larisis, Doukissis Plakentias and Nerantziotissa stations, and goes from the airport to Kiato.

AROUND ATHENS

Piraeus Πειραιάς

TRANSPORT HUB / POP 179,500

The highlights of Greece's main port and ferry hub are the otherworldly rows of ferries, ships and hydrofoils filling its seemingly endless quays. It takes around 40 minutes to get here (10km) from Athens' centre by metro, so there's no reason to stay in shabby Piraeus.

Information

There's free wi-fi around the port.

Getting There & Away

BOAT All ferry companies have online timetables and booths on the quays. EOT (p513) in Athens has a weekly schedule, or check the **Greek Ferries** (www.openseas.gr) online. Schedules are reduced in April, May and October, and are radically cut in winter, especially to smaller islands. When buying tickets, confirm the departure point.

Hellenic Seaways (☎210 419 9000; www.hellenicseaways.gr; cnr Akti Kondyli & Elotikou) operates high-speed hydrofoils and catamarans to the Cyclades from early April to the end of October, and year-round services to the Saronic Gulf Islands. Other high-speed services include **Aegean Speedlines** (☎210 969 0950; www.aegeanspeedlines.gr).

BUS The **X96** Piraeus–Athens Airport Express (€5) leaves from the southwestern corner of Plateia Karaïskaki. **Bus 040** goes to Syntagma in downtown Athens.

METRO The fastest and most convenient link to Athens is the metro (€1.40, 40 minutes, every 10 minutes, 5am to midnight), near the ferries. The station has a left-luggage service (€3 per day).

TRAIN Piraeus has a station for Athens' suburban rail.

THE PELOPONNESE

The Peloponnese (Πελοπόννησος) encompasses a breathtaking array of landscapes, villages and ruins, where much of Greek history has played out.

Patra Πάτρα

POP 168,000

Greece's third-largest city, Patra is the principal ferry port for the Ionian Islands and Italy. Despite its 3000-year history, ancient sites and vibrant social life, few travellers linger here longer than necessary to transfer to their ferries.

Sights

FREE Archaeological Museum of Patras MUSEUM
(☎261 042 0645; cnr Amerikis & Patras-Athens National Rd; ⏰8.30am-3pm Tue-Sun) The country's second-largest museum features objects from prehistoric to Roman times.

FREE Kastro CASTLE
(⏰8.30am-3pm Tue-Sun) The Byzantine castle, originally Roman-built around AD 550, but rebuilt since, has excellent views to the Ionian Islands.

Sleeping

Pension Nikos HOTEL €
(☎261 062 3757; cnr Patreos 3 & Agiou Andreou 121; s/d/tr €30/40/55, s/d without bathroom €25/35; ❄) Marble stairs lead to spotlessly clean rooms smack in the city centre.

Eating & Drinking

Scores of stylish cafes and fast-food eateries lay between Kolokotroni and Ermou. Pedestrianised Trion Navarhon is lined with tavernas.

Kouzina tis Kornilias BISTRO €
(☎261 027 2987; Plateia Kapodistrio 4; mains €8-14; ⏰dinner nightly, also lunch Sat & Sun) Dig in to Turkish braised beef with aubergine puree (€14) and other delicate specialities in this cool bistro tucked in the corner of a quiet square.

Information

Tourist Office (☎261 046 1741; www.infocenterpatras.gr; Agiou Andreou 12-14, between Zaimi & Aratou; ⏰7.30am-9pm; 📶) Friendly multilingual staff with information on transport. A kiosk in central Plateia Trion Symahon operates from 7.30am to 9pm in summer.

Getting There & Away

Boat

Schedules vary; the tourist office provides timetables. Ticket agencies line the waterfront.

Strintzis (☎261 024 0000; www.strintzisferries.gr) routes include Ithaki (€18.60, four hours, one daily) and Kefallonia (€18.20, 2¾ hours, one or two daily).

BUSES FROM PATRA

DESTINATION	PRICE	DURATION	FREQUENCY
Athens via Corinth	€20	3hr	half-hourly
Ioannina	€24	4½hr	2 daily
Kalamata	€23	4hr	2 daily
Kalavryta	€7	2hr	2 daily
Pyrgos (for Olympia)	€10	2hr	10 daily
Thessaloniki	€44	7hr	4 daily

WORTH A TRIP

ANCIENT CORINTH & ACROCORINTH

Seven kilometres southwest of Corinth's modern city, the ruins of **Ancient Corinth** (Αρχαία Κόρινθος; ☎27410 31207; site & museum €6; ⏲8.30am-3pm) and its lovely museum lie at the edge of a small village in the midst of fields sweeping to the sea. It was one of ancient Greece's wealthiest cities, but earthquakes and invasions have left only one Greek monument remaining: the imposing **Temple of Apollo**; the rest of the ruins are Roman. **Acrocorinth** (Ακροκόρινθος; ⏲8am-3pm), the remains of a citadel built on a massive outcrop of limestone, looms majestically over the site.

The great-value digs at **Tasos Taverna & Rooms** (☎27410 31225; s/d/tr €30/45/55; ❄), 200m from the museum, are spotlessly clean and above an excellent eatery serving Greek classics.

Minoan Lines, ANEK Lines and others sail to Igoumenitsa (across from Corfu; €25, seven hours, one daily) and Italy (from €70 to Ancona, from €65 to Venice).

Bus

Most services depart from **KTEL Achaia bus station** (☎261 062 3886; www.ktelachaias.gr; Othonos Amalias 4).

Buses to the Ionian Islands, via the port of Kyllini, leave from the **KTEL Lefkada & Zakynthos bus station** (☎261 022 0993; www.ktelzakynthos.gr; Othonos Amalias 48) or nearby **KTEL Kefallonia bus station** (☎261 027 4938; Othonos Amalias 58).

Nafplio Ναύπλιο

POP 14,000

Elegant Venetian houses and neoclassical mansions dripping with crimson bougainvillea cascade down Nafplio's hillside to the azure sea. Vibrant cafes, shops and restaurants fill winding pedestrian streets. Crenulated Palamidi Fortress perches above it all. What's not to love?

Sights

Palamidi Fortress FORTRESS
(☎27520 28036; admission €4; ⏲8am-7.30pm May–mid-Oct, to 4.30pm mid-Oct–Apr) Enjoy spectacular views of the town and surrounding coast from the magnificent hilltop fortress built by the Venetians between 1711 and 1714.

Archaeological Museum MUSEUM
(☎27520 27502; Plateia Syntagmatos; admission €3; ⏲noon-4pm Mon, 9am-4pm Tue-Sun) Fine exhibits include fire middens from 32,000 BC and bronze armour from near Mycenae (12th to 13th centuries BC).

Peloponnese Folklore Foundation Museum MUSEUM
(☎27520 28379; www.pli.gr; Vas Alexandrou 1; admission €2; ⏲9am-2.30pm) One of Greece's best small museums, with displays of vibrant regional costumes and rotating exhibitions.

Sleeping

The Old Town is *the* place to stay, but it has few budget options. Cheaper spots dot the road to Argos and Tolo.

Pension Dimitris Bekas PENSION €
(☎27520 24594; Efthimiopoulou 26; s/d/tr €25/30/45) The only good, central budget option. Clean, homey rooms (some with shared bathroom) have a top-value location on the slopes of the Akronafplia, and the owner has a killer baseball-cap collection.

Hotel Byron PENSION €
(☎27520 22351; www.byronhotel.gr; Platonos 2; d incl breakfast from €45; ❄) Tucked into two fine Venetian buildings, iron bedsteads, rich carpets and period furniture fill immaculate rooms.

Eating

Nafplio's Old Town streets are loaded with standard tavernas; those on Staïkopoulou or overlooking the port on Bouboulinas get jam-packed on weekends.

TOP CHOICE **Antica Gelateria di Roma** ICE CREAM €
(☎27520 23520; cnr Farmakopoulou & Komninou) The best (yes, best) traditional gelati outside Italy.

To Kentrikon CAFE €
(☎27520 29933; Plateia Syntagmatos; mains €4-10) Relax under the shady trees on this pretty square during extensive breakfasts. Best coffees and teas.

Information

Staikos Tours (☎27520 27950; Bouboulinas 50) Helpful; Avis rental cars; full travel services like occasional day-long boat trips (www.pegasus-cruises.gr) to Spetses, Hydra and Monemvasia.

Getting There & Away

Services from **KTEL Argolis Bus Station** (☎27520 27323; www.ktel-argolidas.gr; Syngrou 8) include Argos (for Peloponnese connections; €1.60, 30 minutes, half-hourly), Athens (via Corinth; €13.10, 2½ hours, hourly), Epidavros (€2.90, 45 minutes, two Mon-Sat) and Mycenae (€2.90, one hour, three daily).

Epidavros Επίδαυρος

Spectacular World Heritage–listed **Epidavros** (☎27530 22009; admission €6; ⏲8am-8pm Apr-Oct, to 5pm Nov-Mar) was the sanctuary of Asclepius, god of medicine. Amid pine-covered hills, the magnificent **theatre** is still a venue during the Hellenic Festival, but don't miss the peaceful **Sanctuary of Asclepius**, an ancient spa and healing centre. Go as a day trip from Nafplio.

Mycenae Μυκήνες

Although settled as early as the 6th millennium BC, **Ancient Mycenae** (☎27510 76585; admission €8; ⏲8am-6pm Mon-Friday, to 3pm Sat & Sun winter), pronounced mih-*kee*-nes, was at its most powerful from 1600 to 1200 BC. Mycenae's grand entrance, the **Lion Gate**, is Europe's oldest monumental sculpture.

Most people visit on day trips from Nafplio. Three buses go daily to Mycenae from Argos (€1.60, 30 minutes) and Nafplio (€2.90, one hour).

Sparta Σπάρτη

POP 14,200

Cheerful, unpretentious modern Sparta (*spar*-tee) is at odds with its ancient Spartan image of discipline and deprivation. Although there's little to see, the town makes a convenient base from which to visit Mystras.

Modern **Hotel Lakonia** (☎27310 28951; www.lakoniahotel.gr; Palaeologou 89; s/d from €40/55;) maintains comfy, welcoming rooms with spotless bathrooms.

Sparta's **KTEL Lakonia bus station** (☎27310 26441; cnr Lykourgou & Thivronos), on the east edge of town, services Athens (€20, 3½ hours, eight daily) via Corinth, Gythio (€4.50, one hour, five daily), Monemvasia (€11, two hours, three daily) and Mystras (€2, 30 minutes, 11 daily).

Mystras Μυστράς

Magical **Mystras** (☎27310 83377; adult/child €5/3; ⏲8.30am-5.30pm Mon-Sat, to 3pm Sun, sometimes longer in summer) was once the effective capital of the Byzantine Empire. Ruins of palaces, monasteries and churches, most of them dating from between 1271 and 1460, nestle at the base of the Taÿgetos Mountains, and are surrounded by verdant olive and orange groves.

Allow half a day to explore the site. While only 7km from Sparta, staying in the village nearby allows you to get there early before it heats up. Enjoy exquisite views and a beautiful swimming pool at **Hotel Byzantion** (☎27310 83309; www.byzantionhotel.gr; s/d/tr €50/70/80;).

Camp at **Castle View** (☎27310 83303; www.castleview.gr; campsites per adult/tent/car €6/4/4, 2-person bungalow €30; ⏲Apr-Oct;), about 1km before Mystras village and set in olive trees. Buses will stop outside if you ask.

Gythio Γύθειο

POP 4490

Gythio (*yee*-thih-o) was once the port of ancient Sparta. Now it's an earthy fishing town on the Lakonian Gulf and gateway to the rugged, much more beautiful Mani Peninsula.

Peaceful **Marathonisi islet**, linked to the mainland by a causeway, is said to be ancient Cranae, where Paris (prince of Troy) and Helen (the wife of Menelaus of Sparta) consummated the love affair that sparked the Trojan War. You'll find the tiny **Museum of Mani History** (☎27330 24484; admission €2; ⏲8am-2.30pm) here in an 18th-century tower.

Sleeping & Eating

The waterfront is packed with fish taverna, like **I Gonia** (Vassilis Pavlou; mains €6-15), and cafes.

Camping Meltemi CAMPGROUND €
(☎27330 23260; www.campingmeltemi.gr; campsites per tent/adult €5.50/6, bungalows €30-60; ⏲Apr-Oct;) Birds chirp in these idyllic silver olive groves, 3km south of Gythio; private beach, swimming pool and summer beauty contests! The Areopoli bus stops here.

Xenia Karlaftis Rooms to Rent PENSION **€**
(☎27330 22719; opposite Marathonisi islet; s/d €25/40) Friendly owner Voula keeps clean (if worn) rooms and offers kitchen access. Several nearby places are of similar quality if you can't get in here.

Getting There & Away

BUS KTEL Lakonia bus station (☎27330 22228; http://ktel-lakonias.gr; cnr Vasileos Georgios & Evrikleos) is on the square near Hotel Aktion. Services include Areopoli (€2.80, 30 minutes, four daily), Athens (€24, 4½ hours, six daily), Geroliminas (€6, 1¼ hours, one daily) and Sparta (€4.50, one hour, four daily).

CAR & BOAT LANE Lines (www.lane.gr) has a weekly ferry to Crete (€23, seven hours) via Kythira (€11, 2½ hours) and Antikythira. Schedules change; check with **Rozakis Travel** (☎27330 22207; rosakigy@otenet.gr; Pavlou 5), which also rents cars.

The Mani Η Μάνη

The Mani occupies the central peninsula of the southern Peloponnese and is divided into two regions: the arid Lakonian (inner) Mani in the south and the verdant Messinian (outer) Mani in the northwest near Kalamata. Explore the winding roads by car.

LAKONIAN MANI

For centuries the Maniots were a law unto themselves, renowned for their fierce independence and their spectacularly murderous internal feuds. To this day, bizarre tower settlements built as refuges during clan wars dot the rocky slopes of Lakonian Mani.

Areopoli (population 775), 30km southwest of Gythio and named after Ares, the god of war, is a warren of cobblestone and ancient towers. Stay in a tastefully decorated 200 year-old tower house at **Londas Pension** (☎27330 51360; www.londas.com; near Church of Taxiarhes; s/d/tr incl breakfast €65/75/103, s/d without bathroom €56/65).

The **bus station** (☎27330 51229) services Athens (€28, four daily) via Gythio (€2.80, 30 minutes), Itilo (for the Messinian Mani, €2, 20 minutes, two daily Monday to Saturday), Gerolimenas (€3.40, 45 minutes, three daily) and the Diros Caves (€1.60, 15 minutes, one daily).

MESSINIAN MANI

Stone hamlets dot aquamarine swimming coves. Silver olive groves climb the foothills to the snow-capped Taÿgetos Mountains. Explore the splendid meandering roads and hiking trails from Itilo to Kalamata.

The people of the enchanting seaside village of **Kardamyli**, 37km south of Kalamata, know how good they've got it. Sir Patrick Leigh Fermor famously wrote about his rambles here in *Mani: Travels in the Southern Peloponnese*. Trekkers come for the magnificent **Vyros Gorge**. Walks are well organised and colour-coded.

Kardamyli has a good choice of small hotels and private rooms for all budgets; book ahead for summer.

Notos Hotel (☎27210 73730; www.notoshotel.gr; studio €110, apt €135-160; P❄) is really a boutique hamlet of individual stone houses with fully equipped kitchens, verandahs and views overlooking the village, the mountains, and the sea.

Olympia Koumounakou Rooms (☎27210 73623; s/d €35/45) is basic but clean and popular with backpackers, who like the communal kitchen and courtyard.

Kardamyli is on the main bus route from Itilo to Kalamata (€4, one hour) and two to four buses stop daily at the central square.

Olympia Ολυμπία

POP 1000

Tucked alongside the Kladeos River, in fertile delta country, the modern town of Olympia supports the extensive ruins of the same name. The first Olympics were staged here in 776 BC, and every four years thereafter until AD 394, when Emperor Theodosius I banned them.

Ancient Olympia (☎26240 22517; adult/child €6/3, site & museum €9/5; ⏰8am-5pm Apr-Oct, 8am-3pm Nov-Mar) is dominated by the immense ruined **Temple of Zeus**, to whom the games were dedicated. Don't miss the statue of **Hermes of Praxiteles**, a classical sculpture masterpiece, at the exceptional **Archaeological Museum** (adult/child €6/3; ⏰1.30-8pm Mon, 8am-8pm Tue-Sun Apr-Oct, to 3pm Nov-Mar).

Sparkling-clean **Pension Posidon** (☎26240 22567; www.pensionposidon.gr; Stefanopoulou 9; s €35, d €40-45, tr €50 inc breakfast; ❄) and quiet, spacious **Hotel Pelops** (☎26240 22543; www.hotelpelops.gr; Varela 2; s/d/tr inc breakfast €40/50/70; ❄@) offer the best value in the centre. Pitch your tent in the leafy grove at **Camping Diana** (☎26240 22314; www.campingdiana.gr; campsites per adult/tent/car €8/6/5;), 250m west of town.

Olympia Municipal Tourist Office (☎26240 22262; Praxitelous Kondyli; ⊙9am-3pm Mon-Fri May-Sep) has transport schedules.

Catch buses at the stop on the north end of town. Northbound buses go via Pyrgos (€2, 30 minutes), where you connect to buses for Athens, Corinth and Patra. Two buses go east from Olympia to Tripoli (€12, 2½ hours) – you must reserve ahead at **KTEL Pyrgos** (☎26210 20600; www.ktelileias.gr). Local trains run daily to Pyrgos (€1, 30 minutes).

CENTRAL GREECE

Central Greece's dramatic landscape of deep gorges, rugged mountains and fertile valleys is home to the magical stone pinnacle-topping monasteries of Meteora and the iconic ruins of ancient Delphi. Established in 1938, **Parnassos National Park** (www.routes.gr), to the north of Delphi, attracts naturalists, hikers (it's part of the E4 European long distance path, www.era-ewv-ferp.com) and skiers.

Delphi Δελφοί

POP 2800

Modern Delphi and its adjoining ruins hang stunningly on the slopes of Mt Parnassos overlooking the shimmering Gulf of Corinth.

The ancient Greeks regarded Delphi as the centre of the world. **Ancient Delphi** (☎22650 82312; www.culture.gr; site or museum €6, combined adult/concession €9/5; ⊙8am-3pm; check, sometimes varies) was built as the Sanctuary of Apollo and is one of Greece's most inspiring archaeological sights.

In the town centre, the welcoming **Hotel Hermes** (☎22650 82318; www.hermeshotel.com.gr; Vasileon Pavlou & Friderikis 27; s/d incl breakfast €40/50; ❄) has spacious rooms sporting balconies with excellent valley views. **Apollon Camping** (☎22650 82762; www.apolloncamping.gr; campsites per person/tent €8.50/4; P@🛜🏊), 2km west of town, has great facilities, including a restaurant, pool and minimarket.

The **bus station** (☎22660 82317) is on modern Delphi's main street, Vasileon Pavlou. Six buses a day go to Athens (€15.50, three hours). Take a bus to Lamia (€9.20, two hours, two daily) or Trikala (€14, 4½ hours, two daily) to transfer for Meteora.

Meteora Μετέωρα

Meteora (meh-*teh*-o-rah) should be a certified Wonder of the World with its magnificent late-14th-century monasteries perched dramatically atop enormous rocky pinnacles. Try not to miss it.

While there were once monasteries on all 24 pinnacles, only six are still occupied: **Megalou Meteorou** (Grand Meteoron; ☎24320 22278; ⊙9am-5pm Wed-Mon Apr-Oct, to 4pm Thu-Mon Nov-Mar), **Varlaam** (☎24320 22277; ⊙9am-4pm Sat-Thu Apr-Oct, to 3pm Sat-Wed Nov-Mar), **Agiou Stefanou** (☎24320 22279; ⊙9am-1.30pm & 3.30-5.30pm Tue-Sun Apr-Oct, 9.30am-1pm & 3-5pm Nov-Mar), **Agias Triados** (Holy Trinity; ☎24320 22220; ⊙9am-5pm Fri-Wed Apr-Oct, 10am-3pm Nov-Mar), **Agiou Nikolaou Anapafsa** (☎24320 22375; ⊙9am-3.30pm Sat-Thu) and **Agias Varvaras Rousanou** (⊙9am-6pm Thu-Tue Apr-Oct, to 4pm Nov-Mar). Admission is €2 for each monastery and strict dress codes apply (no bare shoulders or knees and women must wear skirts; borrow a long skirt at the door if you don't have one). Walk the footpaths between monasteries, drive the back asphalt road, or take the bus (€1.20, 20 minutes) that departs from Kalambaka and Kastraki at 9am, and returns at 1pm.

Meteora's stunning rocks are also a climbing mecca. Licensed mountain guide **Lazaros Botelis** (☎24320 79165, 694 804 3655; meteora.guide@gmail.gr; Kastraki) shows the way.

Sleeping

TOP CHOICE **Doupiani House** PENSION €

(☎24320 75326; www.doupianihouse.com; s/d/tr incl breakfast €40/50/60; P❄@🛜) Gregarious hosts Thanassis and Toula Nakis offer this comfy home from which to explore or simply enjoy the panoramic views. Request a balcony room.

Vrachos Camping CAMPGROUND €

(☎24320 22293; www.campingmeteora.gr; campsites per tent/adult €9/free; 🏊) Great views, excellent facilities and a good taverna; a short stroll from Kastraki.

Getting There & Around

Local buses shuttle between Kalambaka and Kastraki (€1.90). Hourly buses go from Kalambaka's **KTEL bus station** (☎24320 22432; Ikonomou) to the transport hub of Trikala (€2, 30 minutes), from where buses go to Ioannina (€13.10, three hours, two daily) and Athens (€27, 4½ hours, seven daily). From Kalambaka **train station** (☎24320 22451), trains run to Athens (regular/IC €15/25, 5½/4½ hours, both twice daily) and Thessaloniki (€13, four hours, three daily).

NORTHERN GREECE

Northern Greece is graced with magnificent mountains, thick forests, tranquil lakes and archaeological sites. It's easy to get off the beaten track and experience aspects of Greece noticeably different to other mainland areas and the islands.

Thessaloniki Θεσσαλονίκη

POP 342,200

Dodge cherry sellers in the street, smell spices in the air and enjoy waterfront breezes in Thessaloniki (thess-ah-lo-*nee*-kih), also known as Salonica.

Sights & Activites

Check out the seafront **White Tower** (Lefkos Pyrgos; ☎2310 267 832; www.lpth.gr; ⏲8.30am-3pm Tue-Sun) and wander *hammams* (Turkish baths), Ottoman and Roman sites, and churches such as the enormous, 5th-century **Church of Agios Dimitrios** (☎231 027 0008; Agiou Dimitriou 97; ⏲8am-10pm).

The award-winning **Museum of Byzantine Culture** (☎2313 306 400; www.mbp.gr; Leoforos Stratou 2; admission €4; ⏲Tue-Sun 8am-8pm) beautifully displays splendid sculptures, mosaics, icons and other intriguing artefacts. The **Archaeological Museum** (☎231 083 0538; www.amth.gr; Manoli Andronikou 6; admission €6; ⏲8am-3pm) showcases prehistoric, ancient Macedonian, and Hellenistic finds.

Wonderfully seen on foot, Thessaloniki can also be zigzagged by **bus tour** (White Tower; ticket €3; ⏲hourly 8am-9pm Jun-Sep, 9am-

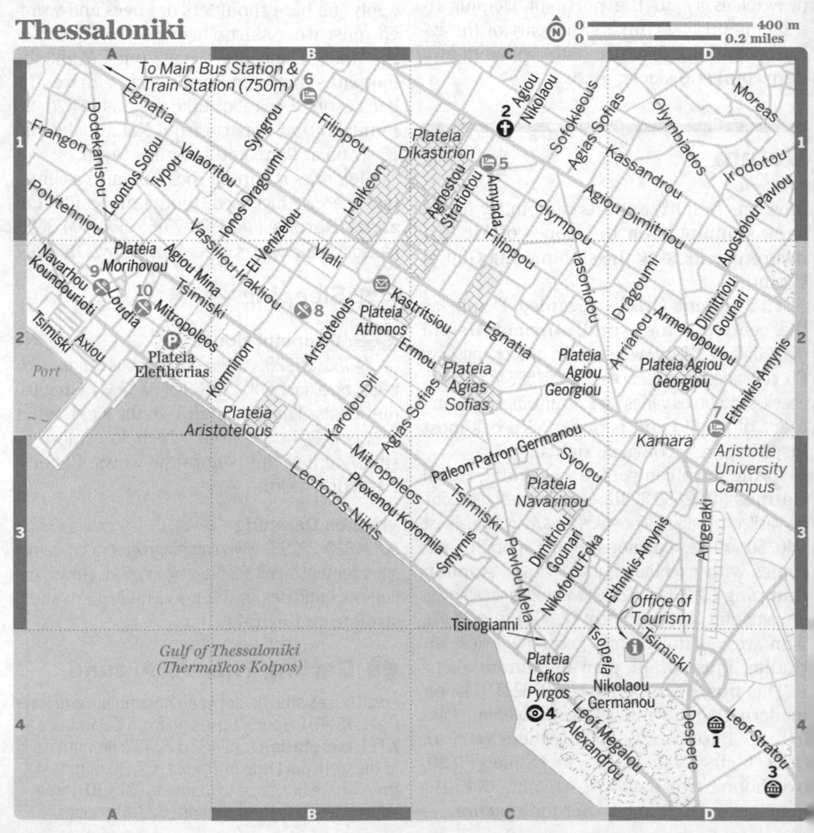

4pm Oct-May) leaving from the White Tower. Get information at the tourist office.

Sleeping

Rent Rooms Thessaloniki HOSTEL €
(231 020 4080; www.rentrooms-thessaloniki.com; Konstantinou Melenikou 9, near Kamara; dm/s/d/tr/q incl breakfast €19/38/49/67/82;) Cheery, clean and modern, with a back-garden cafe looking onto the Rotunda. Communal breakfast/cafe nook and cheap bike hire add to the appeal. Some dorms/rooms have minikitchens, and all have bathrooms. Book ahead.

Hotel Orestias Kastorias HOTEL €
(231 027 6517; www.okhotel.gr; Agnostou Stratiotou 14; s/d/tr €37/46/58; @) A friendly favourite with cosy, clean rooms, renovated in 2011.

Hotel Pella HOTEL €
(231 052 4221; www.pella-hotel.gr; Ionos Dragoumi 63; s/d €30/36;) Quiet and family-run, with spotless rooms.

Eating & Drinking

Tavernas dot Plateia Athonos and cafes pack Leoforos Nikis. Head to **Modiano Market** (Vassiliou Irakliou or Ermo) for fresh fruit and vegetables.

TOP CHOICE **Zythos** TAVERNA €
(Katouni 5; mains €8-12; lunch & dinner) Popular with locals, this excellent taverna with friendly staff serves up delicious standards, interesting regional specialities, good wines by the glass and beers on tap.

TOP CHOICE **Paparouna** MODERN GREEK €
(231 051 0852; www.paparouna.com; Doxis 7 & Pangaiou; mains €8-16; lunch & dinner) This lively restaurant whips up inventive cuisine like chicken with peppermint and honey.

Information

Office of Tourism Directorate (231 022 1100; www.visitgreece.gr; Tsimiski 136; 9am-3pm Mon-Fri)

Getting There & Away

Air

Makedonia Airport (SKG; 231 047 3212; www.thessalonikiairport.com) is 16km southeast of the centre and served by local bus 78 (€0.80, one hour, from 5am to 10pm; www.oasth.gr). Taxis cost €12 (20 minutes).

Olympic Air, Aegean Airlines and **Astra Airlines** (231 048 9392; www.astra-airlines.gr) fly throughout Greece.

Boat

Weekly ferries go to, among others, Limnos (€22, eight hours), Lesvos (€32, 14 hours) and Chios (€35, 19 hours). **Karaharisis Travel & Shipping Agency** (231 051 3005; b_karachari@tincewind_techpath.gr; Navarhou Koundourioti 8; 8am-8.30pm) handles tickets.

Bus

The **main bus station** (231 059 5408; www.ktelmacedonia.gr; Monastiriou 319) services Athens (€42, 6¼ hours, 10 daily), Ioannina (€30, 4¾ hours, six daily) and other destinations. Buses to the Halkidiki Peninsula leave from the **Halkidiki bus terminal** (231 031 6555; www.ktel-chalkidikis.gr; Karakasi 68).

At the time of writing, small bus companies, mostly across from the courthouse (Dikastirion), provided the only services to international destinaions such as Skopje, Sofia and Bucharest. Try **Simeonidis Tours** (231 054 0970; www.simeonidistours.gr; 26 Oktovriou 14). Train company OSE has run buses to Sofia and Tirana but service was in flux at the time of writing. Check at the office on the eastern side of the train station.

Train

The **train station** (231 059 9421; www.trainose.gr; Monastiriou) serves Athens (regular/IC €28/36, 6¾/5½ hours, seven/10 daily) but other lines like Alexandroupolis have been reduced, and all international trains were discontinued at the time of writing. Check schedules at the **train ticket office** (OSE; 231 059 8120; Aristotelous 18) or the station.

Thessaloniki

Sights
1 Archaeological Museum D4
2 Church of Agios Dimitrios C1
3 Museum of Byzantine Culture D4
4 White Tower C4

Sleeping
5 Hotel Orestias Kastorias C1
6 Hotel Pella B1
7 Rent Rooms Thessaloniki D2

Eating
8 Modiano Market B2
9 Paparouna A2
10 Zythos A2

MT OLYMPUS

Just as it did for the ancients, Greece's highest mountain, the cloud-covered Mt Olympus (Ολυμπος Ορος) of the Greek pantheon, fires the visitor's imagination today. The highest of Olympus' eight peaks is **Mytikas** (2917m), popular with trekkers, who use **Litohoro** (elevation 305m), 5km inland from the Athens–Thessaloniki highway, as their base. The main route up takes two days, with a stay overnight at one of the **refuges** (⌚May-Oct). Good protective clothing is essential, even in summer. **EOS** (Alpine Club of Litohoro; ☎23520 82444; eoslitohorou.blogspot.com; Plateia Kentriki, Litohoro; ⌚9am-1pm Mon-Sat, Jun-Sep) has information on treks.

Ioannina Ιωάννινα

POP 64,500

Charming Ioannina (ih-o-*ah*-nih-nah) on the western shore of Lake Pamvotis at the foot of the Pindos Mountains, was a major intellectual centre during Ottoman rule. Today it's a thriving university town with a lively waterfront cafe scene.

Sights

Kastro NEIGHBOURHOOD

The narrow stone streets of the evocative old quarter sit on a small peninsula jutting into the lake. Within its impressive fortifications, **Its Kale**, an inner citadel with lovely grounds and lake views, is home to the splendid **Fetiye Cami** (Victory Mosque), built in 1611, and the gemlike **Byzantine Museum** (☎26510 25989; admission €3; ⌚8am-5pm Tue-Sun).

Lake Pamvotida LAKE

The lake's serene *nisi* (island) shelters four **monasteries** among its trees. Frequent ferries (€2) leave from near Plateia Mavili.

Sleeping

TOP CHOICE **Filyra** BOUTIQUE HOTEL €

(☎26510 83560; http://hotelfilyra.gr; alley off Andronikou Paleologou 18; s/d €45/55; P ❄) Five Old Town self-catering suites fill up fast. The affiliated **Traditional Hotel Dafni** (loustinianou 12; s/d/q €45/65/90) is built into the Kastro's outer walls.

Limnopoula Camping CAMPGROUND €

(☎26510 25265; Kanari 10; campsites per tent/adult €4/8; ⌚Apr-Oct) Tree-lined and splendidly set on the edge of the lake 2km northwest of town.

Eating

Scores of cafes and restaurants line the waterfront.

Taverna To Manteio TAVERNA €

(☎26510 25452; Plateia Georgiou 15; mains €7-8; ⌚lunch & dinner Tue-Sun) Join local families along the flower-filled Its Kale wall for deliciously simple *mezedhes,* salads and grills.

Information

EOT (tourist office; ☎26510 41142; Dodonis 39; ⌚7.30am-2.30pm Mon-Fri)

EOS (Greek Alpine Club; ☎26510 22138; Despotatou Ipirou 2; ⌚7-9pm Mon-Fri)

Getting There & Away

AIR Aegean Airlines (☎26510 64444) and **Olympic Air** (☎26510 26518) fly to Athens. Slow buses ply the 2km road into town.

BUS The **station** (KTEL Ioanninon; ☎26510 25014; www.ktelioannina.gr; Georgiou Papandreou 45) is 300m north of Plateia Dimokratias. Services include Athens (€40, 6½ hours, nine daily), Igoumenitsa (€9.80, 1¼ hours, eight daily), Thessaloniki (€32, 4¾ hours, six daily) and Trikala (€15.50, 2¼ hours, two daily).

Zagorohoria & Vikos Gorge Τα Ζαγορόχωρια & Χαράδρα του Βίκου

Do not miss the spectacular Zagori region, with its deep gorges, abundant wildlife, dense forests and snowcapped mountains. Some 46 charming villages, famous for their grey-slate architecture, and known collectively as the Zagorohoria, are sprinkled across a large expanse of the Pindos Mountains north of Ioannina. Get information on walks from Ioannina's EOT and EOS offices.

Tiny, carless **Dilofo** makes for a peaceful sojourn, especially if you lodge at excellent **Gaia** (☎26530 22570; www.gaia-dilofo.gr; s/d/tr incl breakfast from €60/70/80; ᯤ) or **Arhontiko Dilofo** (☎26530 22455; www.dilofo.com; d incl breakfast from €55; P) and sup on the square at **Sopotseli** (☎26530 22629; mains €5-7).

Delightful **Monodendri**, known for its special pitta bread, is a popular departure point for treks through dramatic 12km-long,

900m-deep **Vikos Gorge**, with its sheer limestone walls. Get cosy at quaint **Archontiko Zarkada** (☎26530 71305; www.monodendri.com; s/d incl breakfast €40/60; P), one of Greece's best-value small hotels.

Exquisite inns with attached tavernas abound in remote (but popular) twin villages **Megalo Papingo** and **Mikro Papingo**. Visit the **WWF Information Centre** (www.wwf.gr; Mikro Papingo; ⌚11am-5.30pm Fri-Wed) to learn about the area.

Infrequent buses run to Ioannina from Dilofo (€3.80, 40 minutes, three weekly), Monodendri (€3.60, one hour, three weekly) and the Papingos (€5.10, two hours, three weekly). It's best to explore by rental car from Ioannina.

Igoumenitsa Ηγουμενίτσα

TRANSPORT HUB / POP 9160

Though tucked beneath verdant hills and lying on the sea, this characterless west-coast port is little more than a ferry hub: it's best to keep moving.

The **bus station** (KTEL Thesprotias; ☎26650 22309; www.ktel-thesprotias.gr; Arhillohou) services Ioannina (€9.80, 2½ hours, nine daily) and Athens (€45, eight hours, five daily).

Several companies operate **ferries to Corfu** (☎26650 99460; person/car €10/40; ⌚hourly) (person/car €10/40, 1½ hours, hourly), and hydrofoils in summer. International ferries go to the Italian ports of Ancona, Bari, Brindisi and Venice. Ticket agencies line the port. Book ahead for car tickets or sleeping cabins.

CYCLADES

The Cyclades (kih-*klah*-dez; Κυκλάδες) are Greek islands to dream about. Named after the rough *kyklos* (circle) they form around the island of Delos, they are rugged outcrops of rock in the azure Aegean, speckled with white cubist buildings and blue-domed Byzantine churches. Throw in sun-blasted golden beaches, more than a dash of hedonism and a fascinating culture, and it's easy to see why many find the Cyclades irresistible.

Mykonos Μύκονος

POP 8000

Sophisticated Mykonos glitters happily under the Aegean sun, shamelessly surviving on tourism. The island has something for everyone, with marvellous beaches, romantic sunsets, chic boutiques, excellent restaurants and bars, and its long-held reputation as a mecca for gay travellers.

Sights & Activities

Mykonos Town NEIGHBOURHOOD

A stroll around Mykonos Town, shuffling through snaking streets with blinding white walls and balconies of flowers is a must for any visitor. This is the centre of the action on the island. **Little Venice**, where the sea laps up to the edge of the restaurants and bars, and Mykonos' famous hilltop row of **windmills** should be included in the spots-to-see list.

Beaches BEACHES

The island's most popular beaches are on the southern coast. **Platys Gialos** has wall-to-wall sun lounges, while nudity is not uncommon at **Paradise Beach**, **Super Paradise**, **Agrari** and gay-friendly **Elia**.

Sleeping

Rooms in Mykonos town fill up quickly in high season; book ahead.

WORTH A TRIP

DELOS

Southwest of Mykonos, the island of **Delos** (Δηλός; sites & museum €5; ⌚8.30am-3pm Tue-Sun) is the Cyclades' archaeological jewel. The opportunity to clamber among the ruins shouldn't be missed.

According to mythology, Delos was the birthplace of Apollo – the god of light, poetry, music, healing and prophecy. The island flourished as an important religious and commercial centre from the 3rd millennium BC, reaching its apex of power in the 5th century BC.

The climb up **Mt Kynthos** (113m), the island's highest point, is a highlight.

Take a sunhat, sunscreen and sturdy footwear. The island's cafeteria sells food and drinks. Staying overnight on Delos is forbidden.

Numerous boat companies offer trips from Mykonos to Delos (€18 return, 30 minutes) between 9am and 1pm. The return boats leave Delos between noon and 3pm. There is also a €5 per person entry fee on arrival at Delos.

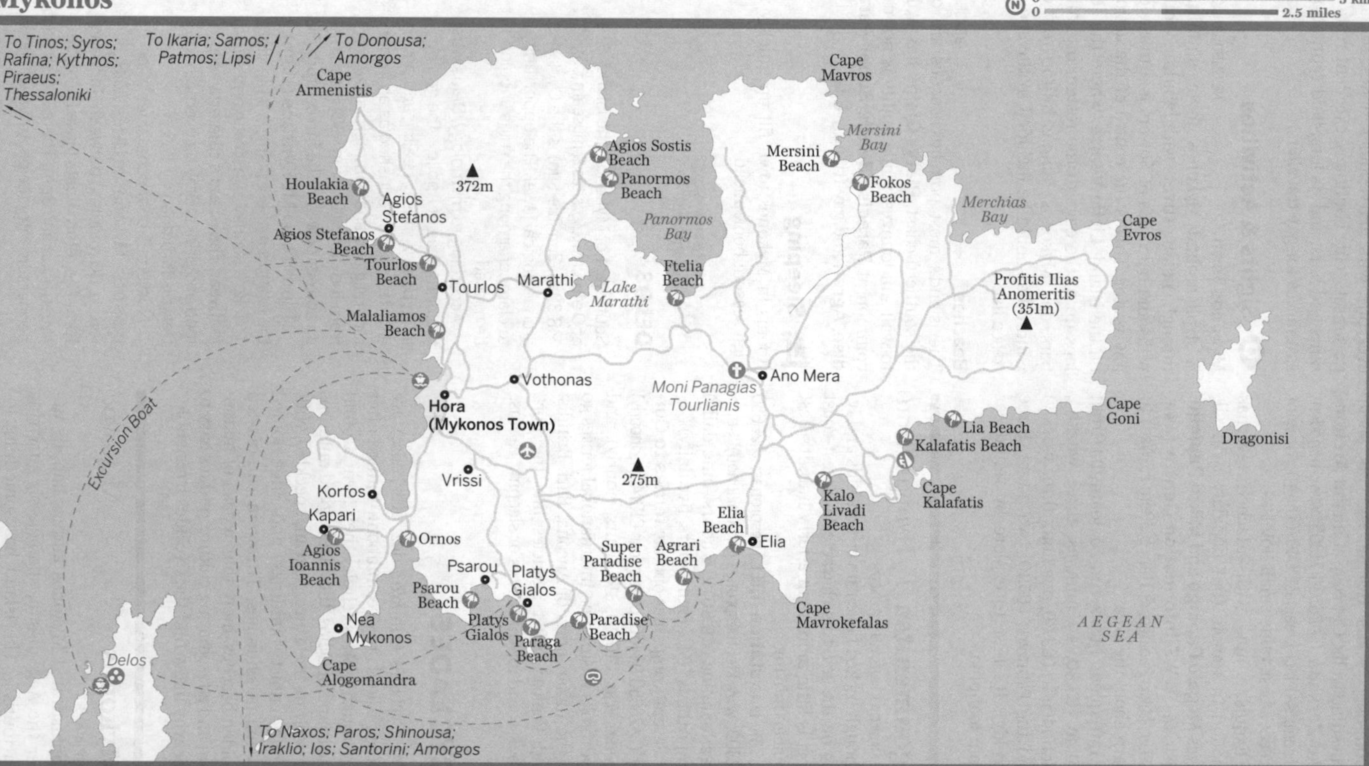

Mykonos
0 5 km
0 2.5 miles
To Tinos; Syros; Rafina; Kythnos; Piraeus; Thessaloniki
To Ikaria; Samos; Patmos; Lipsi
To Donousa; Amorgos
Cape Armenistis
Houlakia Beach
Agios Stefanos
Agios Stefanos Beach
Tourlos Beach
Tourlos
Malaliamos Beach
372m
Agios Sostis Beach
Panormos Beach
Panormos Bay
Marathi
Lake Marathi
Ftelia Beach
Cape Mavros
Mersini Beach
Mersini Bay
Fokos Beach
Merchias Bay
Cape Evros
Profitis Ilias Anomeritis (351m)
Vothonas
Hora (Mykonos Town)
Moni Panagias Tourlianis
Ano Mera
Cape Goni
Lia Beach
Kalafatis Beach
Cape Kalafatis
Dragonisi
Excursion Boat
Vrissi
275m
Korfos
Kapari
Agios Ioannis Beach
Ornos
Psarou
Psarou Beach
Platys Gialos
Platys Gialos
Paraga Beach
Paradise Beach
Super Paradise Beach
Agrari Beach
Elia Beach
Elia
Kalo Livadi Beach
Cape Mavrokefalas
AEGEAN SEA
Nea Mykonos
Cape Alogomandra
Delos
To Naxos; Paros; Shinousa; Iraklio; Ios; Santorini; Amorgos

Mykonos has two camping areas, both on the south coast. Minibuses from both meet the ferries and buses go regularly into town.

Hotel Philippi HOTEL €€
(☎22890 22294; www.philippihotel.com; 25 Kalogera, Mykonos Town; s €60-90, d €75-120; ❄📶) In the heart of the *hora*, Philippi, one of Mykonos' few budget options, has spacious and clean rooms that open onto a railed verandah overlooking a lush garden.

Hotel Lefteris HOTEL €€
(☎22890 23128; www.lefterishotel.gr; 9 Apollonas, Mykonos Town; s/d €99/129, studios €239-279; ❄@) Tucked away just up from Taxi Sq, Lefteris has bright, comfy rooms, and a relaxing sun terrace with superb views over town. A good international meeting place.

Paradise Beach Camping CAMPGROUND €
(☎22890 22852; www.paradisemykonos.com; campsites per tent/person €5/10; @🏊) There are lots of options here on the south coast of the island, including camping, beach cabins and apartments, as well as bars, a swimming pool, games etc. It is skin-to-skin mayhem in summer with a real party atmosphere. The website has it all.

Eating

Cheap eateries are found around Taxi Sq and the southern bus station. Mykonos' top touts are its two resident pelicans, who wander the restaurants looking for handouts, often with visitors following them.

Fato a Mano MEDITERRANEAN €
(Plateia Meletopoulou; mains €8-15) In the middle of the maze, this place is worth taking the effort to find. It serves up tasty Mediterranean and traditional Greek dishes with pride.

Drinking & Entertainment

The waterfront is perfect for sitting with a drink and watching an interesting array of passers-by.

Long feted as a gay travel destination, there are many gay-centric clubs and hangouts.

Cavo Paradiso CLUB
(☎22890 27205; www.cavoparadiso.gr) For those who want to go the whole hog, this place 300m above Paradise Beach picks up around 2am and boasts a pool the shape of Mykonos. A bus transports clubbers from town in summer.

Information

Island Mykonos Travel (☎22890 22232; www.discovergreece.org) On Taxi Sq, where the port road meets the town; helpful for travel information, hotels, transfers and tickets.

Getting There & Around

AIR There are daily flights connecting Mykonos airport (JMK) to Athens, plus a growing number of international flights winging in directly from May to September. The airport is 3km southeast of the town centre; €1.60 by bus from the southern bus station.

BOAT Daily ferries (€32, five hours) and catamarans (€50, three hours) arrive from Piraeus. From Mykonos, there are daily ferries and hydrofoils to most major Cycladic islands and daily services to Crete.

BUS The northern bus station is near the old port. It serves Agios Stefanos, Elia, Kalafatis and Ano Mera. The southern bus station, a 300m walk up from the windmills, serves the airport, Agios Ioannis, Psarou, Platys Gialos and Paradise Beach.

LOCAL BOATS In summer, *caiques* (small fishing boats) from Mykonos Town and Platys Gialos putter to Paradise, Super Paradise, Agrari and Elia Beaches.

Paros Πάρος

POP 13,000

Paros is an attractive, laid-back island with an enticing main town, good swimming beaches and terraced hills that build up to Mt Profitis Ilias (770m). It has long been prosperous, thanks to an abundance of pure white marble (from which the *Venus de Milo* and Napoleon's tomb were sculpted).

Paros' main town and port is **Parikia**, on the west coast.

Sights

Panagia Ekatondapyliani CHURCH
(Parikia; ⊙7.30am-9.30pm) Dating from AD 326 and known for its beautiful ornate interior, this is one of the most impressive churches in the Cyclades. Within the church compound, the **Byzantine Museum** (admission €1.50; ⊙9.30am-2pm & 6-9pm) has an interesting collection of icons and artefacts.

Activities

A great option on Paros is to rent a scooter or car at one of the many outlets in Parikia and cruise around the island. There are sealed roads the whole way, and the opportunity to explore villages such as **Naoussa**, **Marpissa** and **Aliki**, and swim at beaches such

CYCLADIC CONNECTIONS

For planning purposes, it's worth noting that once the season kicks in, a batch of companies run daily catamarans and ferries up and down the Cyclades. You can start from Piraeus (for Athens), Iraklio on Crete, or just about anywhere in between.

One boat heads south daily from Piraeus to Paros, Naxos, Ios and Santorini, returning along the same route. There's also a daily run from Piraeus to Syros, Tinos and Mykonos. Heading north from Iraklio, another catamaran runs to Santorini, Ios, Paros, Mykonos and return.

If it all get a bits much to comprehend (the schedules are constantly changing!), check the online guide **Open Seas** (www.openseas.gr).

as **Logaras**, **Punda** and **Golden Beach**. Naoussa is a cute little fishing village on the northeastern coast that is all geared up to welcome tourists.

Sleeping

Rooms Mike ROOMS €
(☎22840 22856; www.roomsmike.com; Parikia; s/d/tr €25/40/60; ❄📶) A popular and friendly place, Mike's offers good location and local advice. There are options of rooms with shared facilities through to fully self-contained units with kitchens. Mike's sign is easy to spot from the quay, away to the left.

Rooms Rena ROOMS €
(☎22840 22220; www.cycladesnet.gr/rena; Parikia; s/d/tr €35/45/55; ❄📶) The quiet, well-kept rooms here are excellent value. Turn left from the pier then right at the ancient cemetery and follow the signs.

Koula Camping CAMPGROUND €
(☎22840 22801; www.campingkoula.gr; campsites per tent/person €4/8; ⊙Apr-Oct; P📶) A pleasant shaded spot behind the beach at the north end of the waterfront. They have free transfers to and from the port.

Eating & Drinking

Budget eating spots are easy to find near the Windmill roundabout in Parikia. Head along the waterfront to the west of the ferry quay to find a line-up of restaurants and drinking establishments that gaze out at the setting sun.

Happy Green Cows VEGETARIAN €€
(dishes €12-18; ⊙dinner; 🖉) Cheerful service goes with the quirky name of this little eatery at the back of the main square, which is a vegetarian's delight. It's a touch pricey, but worth it for the often saucily named dishes.

Information

There is no tourist office. See the website www.parosweb.com for information.

Santorineos Travel (☎22840 24245; www.traveltoparos.gr) On the waterfront near the Windmill roundabout; good for ticketing, information and luggage storage.

Getting There & Around

AIR Paros' airport (PAS) has daily flight connections with Athens. The airport is 8km south of Parikia; €1.50 by bus.

BOAT Parikia is a major ferry hub with daily connections to Piraeus (€32.50, five hours) and frequent ferries and catamarans to Naxos, Ios, Santorini, Mykonos and Crete. The fast boats generally take half the time but are more expensive, eg a fast boat to Piraeus takes 2½ hours but costs €40.

BUS From Parikia there are frequent bus services to the entire island. A free green bus runs around Parikia at regular intervals from early morning to late at night.

LOCAL BOATS In summer there are excursion boats to Antiparos from Parikia port, or you can catch a bus to Pounta and ferry across.

Naxos Νάξος

POP 12,000

The largest of the Cyclades islands, Naxos could probably survive without tourism – unlike many of its neighbouring islands. Green and fertile, Naxos produces olives, grapes, figs, citrus, corn and potatoes. The island is well worth taking the time to explore with its fascinating main town, excellent beaches, remote villages and striking interior.

Naxos Town, on the west coast, is the island's capital and port.

Sights & Activities

Kastro CASTLE
Behind the waterfront in Naxos Town, narrow alleyways scramble up to the spectacular hilltop 13th-century *kastro*, where the Venetian Catholics lived. The *kastro* looks out over the town, and has a well-stocked **archaeological museum** (admission €3; ⊙8.30am-3pm Tue-Sun).

Temple of Apollo ARCHAEOLOGICAL SITE
From the ferry quay it's a short stroll to the unfinished Temple of Apollo, Naxos' most famous landmark.

Beaches BEACHES
The popular beach of **Agios Georgios** is just a 10-minute walk south from the main waterfront. Beyond it, wonderful sandy beaches stretch as far south as **Pyrgaki Beach**. **Agia Anna Beach**, 6km from town, and **Plaka Beach** are lined with accommodation and packed in summer.

Villages VILLAGES
A hire car or scooter will help reveal Naxos' dramatic and rugged landscape. The **Tragaea** region has tranquil villages, churches atop rocky crags and huge olive groves. **Filoti**, the largest inland settlement, perches on the slopes of **Mt Zeus** (1004m), the highest peak in the Cyclades. The historic village of **Halki**, one-time centre of Naxian commerce, is well worth a visit.

Apollonas is a lovely spot near Naxos' northern tip. There's a **beach**, excellent **taverna**, and the mysterious 10.5m **kouros** (naked male statue), constructed in the 7th century BC, lying abandoned and unfinished in an ancient marble quarry.

Sleeping

Pension Sofi PENSION €€
(☎22850 23077; www.pensionsofi.gr; r €30-90; ⏲year-round; ❄📶) Run by the friendly Koufopoulos family, Pension Sofi is in Naxos Town, while their **Studios Panos** (☎22850 26078; www.studiospanos.com; Agios Georgios Beach; r €30-75; ❄📶) is a 10-minute walk away near Agios Georgios Beach. Guests are met with a glass of family-made wine, and rooms are immaculate with bathroom and kitchen. Rates at both halve out of the high season. Call ahead for port pick-up.

Camping Maragas CAMPGROUND €
(☎22850 42552; www.maragascamping.gr; campsites €9, d €45, studio €70) On Agia Anna Beach to the south of town, this place has all sorts of options, including camping, rooms and studios, and there is a restaurant and minimarket on site.

Eating & Drinking

Naxos Town's waterfront is lined with eating and drinking establishments. South of the waterfront, but only a few minutes' walk away, Main Sq is home to plenty of excellent eateries.

Picasso TEX-MEX €
(www.picassoismexican.com; Agiou Arseniou; dishes €6-18; ⏲all day Jun-Sep, dinner only Oct-May) Definitely the best Mexican fare in Greece... possibly in Europe! Just off Main Sq, Picasso boasts that it serves 'extraordinary Mexican food' and it does. It also offers up exquisite frozen margaritas.

Information

There's no official tourist information office. Try the website www.naxos-greece.net for more information.

Zas Travel (☎22850 23330; www.zastravel.com) Good for boat and air tickets, car rental, internet and luggage storage.

Getting There & Around

AIR Naxos airport (JNX) has daily flight connections with Athens. The airport is 3km south of town; no buses – a taxi costs €15.

BOAT There are daily ferries (€31, five hours) and catamarans (€48, 3¾ hours) from Naxos to Piraeus, and good ferry and hydrofoil connections to most Cycladic islands and Crete.

BUS Buses travel to most villages regularly from the bus terminal in front of the port.

DON'T MISS

KITRON-TASTING IN HALKI

The historic village of Halki, which lies at the heart of the Tragaea region, is a top spot to try *kitron*, a liqueur unique to Naxos. Usually consumed cold after meals, *kitron* is made from the fruit of the citron *(Citrus medica)*. The fruit may be barely edible in its raw state, but when it and its leaves are boiled with pure alcohol, the result is a tasty concoction that has been keeping Naxians happy since the 1870s. While the exact recipe is top secret, visitors can taste it and stock up on supplies at the **Vallindras Distillery** (☎22850 31220; ⏲10am-11pm Jul-Aug, 10am-6pm May-Jun & Sep-Oct) in Halki's main square. There is a **Kitron Museum** (admission free), complimentary **tastings**, and a **shop** selling the distillery's products.

CAR & MOTORCYCLE Having your own wheels is a good option on Naxos. Car and motorcycle rentals are readily available in Naxos Town.

Ios

Ιος

POP 1900

Ios has long held a reputation as 'Party Island'. There are wall-to-wall bars and nightclubs in the village (Hora) that thump all night, and fantastic fun facilities at Milopotas Beach that entertain all day.

Sights & Activities

The village has an intrinsic charm with its labyrinth of white-walled streets, and it's very easy to get lost, even if you haven't had one too many. Milopotas has everything a resort beach could ask for, and parties hard.

Skarkos ARCHAEOLOGICAL SITE

(The Snail; 8.30am-3pm Tue-Sun) An award-winning archaeological triumph for Ios. This Bronze Age settlement crowns a low hill in the plain just to the north of Hora, and its excavations have been opened to the public. There are interpretation boards in Greek and English.

Manganari Beach BEACH

This isolated beach on the south coast is reached by rental vehicle, or by excursion boat or bus in summer. It's a beautiful spot and the drive on Ios' newest sealed road is an experience in itself.

Meltemi Water Sports WATERSPORTS

(22860 91680; www.meltemiwatersports.com) This outfit at Milopotas Beach's far end has everything a beach could possibly provide, including rental windsurfers, sailboats and canoes.

Sleeping

TOP CHOICE **Francesco's** HOSTEL €

(22860 91223; www.francescos.net; s €40-45, d €50-60;) A lively meeting place in the village with superlative views from its terrace bar, legendary Francesco's is convenient for party-going, and rates halve out of high season. The party spirit rules here. Long established and very well run.

Far Out Camping & Beach Club CAMPGROUND €

(22860 91468; www.faroutclub.com; Milopotas; campsites per person €12, bungalows €15-22, studios €100;) Right on Milopotas Beach, this place has tons of options. Facilities include camping, bungalows and hotel rooms, and its pools are open to the public. Details are on the website. It also has rental cars, quad bikes and scooters.

Eating & Drinking

There are numerous places in the village to get cheap eats like gyros. Down at Milopotas Beach, there's a great bakery and stacks of options for during the day. At night, the compact little village erupts with bars.

Ali Baba's THAI €

(Hora; dishes €7-12) This great Ios favourite is the place for tasty Thai dishes. The service is very upbeat and there's a garden courtyard. It's on the same street as the Emporiki bank.

Blue Note BAR

(Hora) A perennial village favourite, where Happy Hour continues all night long!

Information

There's no tourist office. See the website www.iosgreece.com for more information.

Acteon Travel (22860 91343; www.acteon.gr) Has offices in Ormos, the village and Milopotas and is extremely helpful.

Getting There & Around

BOAT Ios has daily ferry (€32.50, seven hours) and catamaran (€55, 3½ hours) connections with Piraeus. Being strategically placed between Mykonos and Santorini, there are frequent catamarans and ferries to the major Cycladic islands and Crete.

BUS There are buses every 15 minutes between the port, the village and Milopotas Beach until early morning. Buses head to Manganari Beach in summer (€3.50 each way).

Santorini (Thira)

Σαντορίνη (Θήρα)

POP 13,500

Stunning Santorini is unique and should not be missed. The startling sight of the submerged caldera almost encircled by sheer lava-layered cliffs – topped off by clifftop towns that look like a dusting of icing sugar – will grab your attention and not let it go.

Sights & Activities

FIRA

Santorini's vibrant main town, with its snaking narrow streets full of shops and restaurants, perches on top of the caldera; the stunning views from here are unparalleled.

AROUND THE ISLAND

At the north of the island, the intriguing village of **Oia** (ee-ah), famed for its postcard sunsets, is less hectic than Fira and a must-visit. Its caldera-facing tavernas are superb spots for brunch. There's a path from Fira to Oia along the top of the caldera that takes three to four hours to walk; otherwise take a taxi or bus.

Excavations in 1967 uncovered the remarkably well-preserved Minoan settlement of **Akrotiri** at the south of the island, with its remains of two- and three-storey buildings. Akrotiri has recently reopened to the public after a seven-year hiatus.

Santorini's black-sand **beaches** of **Perissa** and **Kamari** sizzle – beach mats are essential. Sitting on a mountain between the two are the atmospheric ruins of **Ancient Thira**, first settled in the 9th century BC.

Of the surrounding islets, only **Thirasia** is inhabited. Visitors can clamber around on volcanic lava on **Nea Kameni** then swim into warm springs in the sea at **Palia Kameni**; there are various excursions available to get you there.

Santorini (Thira)

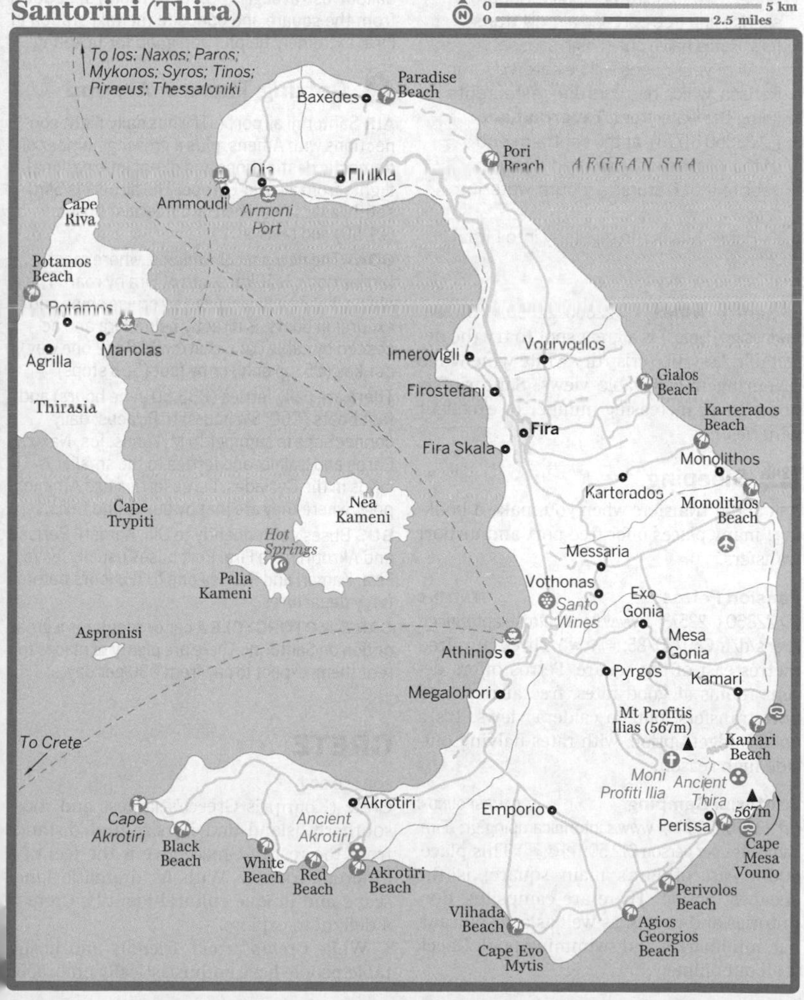

SANTORINI ON A BUDGET

Spectacular Santorini will take your breath away, and if you're on a tight budget, its prices might too. Expect to pay through the nose for caldera views at accommodation and eating establishments in and around Fira.

A budget alternative with the added bonus of a stunning black-sand beach is to head out to Perissa, on the southeast coast, and stay at **Stelios Place** (☎22860 81860; www.steliosplace.com; r €30-120; P❄📶🏊). Stelios is an excellent option one block back from the beach. There's a refreshing pool, very friendly service and free port and airport transfers. Rates halve out of high season.

All of your needs will be catered for in Perissa, which has bars and restaurants lining the waterfront. **Taverna Lava** (☎22860 81776), at the southern end of the waterfront, is an island-wide favourite that features a mouth-watering menu.

Public buses run regularly into Fira.

Santo Wines (☎22860 22596; www.santowines.gr; Pyrgos) is a great spot to try the delectable Assyrtico crisp dry white wine while savouring unbelievable views. Santorini is home to an increasing number of excellent wineries.

Sleeping

Ask about transfers when you make a booking; many places offer free port and airport transfers.

Pension Petros PENSION €
(☎22860 22573; www.hotelpetros-santorini.gr; Fira; s/d/tr €60/70/85; ❄📶🏊) Three hundred metres east of the square, Petros offers decent rooms at good rates, free airport and port transfers, but no caldera views. It's a good budget option, with rates halving outside high season.

Santorini Camping CAMPGROUND €
(☎22860 22944; www.santorinicamping.gr; Fira; campsites per person €12.50; P@🏊) This place, 500m east of Fira's main square, is the cheapest option. There are campsites, dormitories and rooms, as well as a restaurant, bar, minimarket and swimming pool. Check it all out online.

Eating & Drinking

Cheaper eateries are in abundance around the square in Fira. Many of the more popular bars and clubs are clustered along Erythrou Stavrou in Fira.

Many diners head out to Oia, legendary for its superb sunsets, timing their meal with the setting sun, while good-value tavernas line the waterfronts at the beach resorts of Kamari and Perissa.

Information

There is no tourist office. Try the website www.santorini.net for more information.

Dakoutros Travel (☎22860 22958; www.dakoutrostravel.gr; ⌚8.30am-10pm) Just down from the square and opposite the taxi station in Fira; extremely helpful and good for ticketing.

Getting There & Around

AIR Santorini airport (JTR) has daily flight connections with Athens, plus a growing number of domestic destinations and direct international flights from all over Europe. The airport is 5km southeast of Fira; there are frequent buses (€1.50) and taxis (€12).

BOAT The new port of Athinios, where most ferries dock, is 10km south of Fira by road. The old port of Fira Skala, used by cruise ships and excursion boats, is directly below Fira and accessed by cable car (adult/child €4/2 one way), donkey (€5, up only) or by foot (588 steps).

There are daily ferries (€33.50, nine hours) and fast boats (€60, 5¼ hours) to Piraeus; daily connections in summer to Mykonos, Ios, Naxos, Paros and Iraklio; and ferries to the smaller islands in the Cyclades. Large ferries use Athinios port, where they are met by buses and taxis.

BUS Buses go frequently to Oia, Kamari, Perissa and Akrotiri from Fira. Port buses usually leave Fira, Kamari and Perissa one to 1½ hours before ferry departures.

CAR & MOTORCYCLE A car or scooter is a great option on Santorini. There are plenty of places to rent them, expect to pay from €30 per day.

CRETE

POP 550,000

Crete (Κρήτη) is Greece's largest and most southerly island and its size and distance from the rest of Greece give it the feel of a different country. With its dramatic landscape and unique cultural identity, Crete is a delight to explore.

While Crete's proud, friendly and hospitable people have enthusiastically embraced tourism, they continue to fiercely protect their traditions and culture – and it is the people who remain a major part of the island's appeal.

Iraklio Ηράκλειο

POP 138,000

Iraklio (ee-*rah*-klee-oh; often spelt Heraklion), Crete's capital and economic hub, is a bustling modern city and the fifth-largest in Greece. It has a lively city centre, an excellent archaeological museum and is close to Knossos, Crete's major visitor attraction.

Iraklio's harbours face north into the Sea of Crete. Plateia Venizelou, known for its Lion Fountain, is the heart of the city, 400m south of the old harbour up 25 Avgoustou.

Sights & Activities

Archaeological Museum MUSEUM
(odysseus.culture.gr; Xanthoudidou 2; adult/student €4/2; 8.30am-3pm Nov-Mar) The outstanding Minoan collection here is second only to that of the national museum in Athens. The museum was under long-term reconstruction at the time of research, but its key exhibits are beautifully displayed in an annexe.

Koules Venetian Fortress FORTRESS
(admission €2; 8.30am-7pm Tue-Sun May-Oct, to 3pm Nov-Apr) Protecting the old harbour, this impressive fortress is also known as Rocca al Mare, which, like the city walls, was built by the Venetians in the 16th century. It stopped the Turks for 21 years and later became a Turkish prison for Cretan rebels.

City Walls FORTRESS
Iraklio burst out of its city walls long ago, but these massive Venetian fortifications, with seven bastions and four gates, are still very conspicuous, dwarfing the concrete structures of the 20th century.

Morosini Fountain FOUNTAIN
(Plateia Venizelou) Iraklio's much loved 'lion fountain', built in 1628 by the Venetians, spurts water from four lions into eight ornate U-shaped marble troughs.

Cretan Adventures OUTDOORS
(28103 32772; www.cretanadventures.gr; Evans 10, 3rd fl) Cretan Adventures is a well-regarded local company run by Fondas Spinthaikos that can organise hiking tours, mountain biking, and other specialist and extreme activities.

Sleeping

Hotel Mirabello HOTEL €
(28102 85052; www.mirabello-hotel.gr; Theotokopoulou 20; s/d €42/48;) A pleasant, relaxed budget hotel on a quiet street in the centre of town, this place is run by an ex-sea captain who has travelled the world. A good-value option.

Kronos Hotel HOTEL €
(tel, info 28102 82240; www.kronoshotel.gr; Sofokli Venizelou 2; s/d €44/50;) After a thorough makeover, this waterfront hotel has pole-vaulted to the top of the budget hotel category. Ask for one of the rooms with sea views.

Eating & Drinking

There's a congregation of cheap eateries, bars and cafes in the Plateia Venizelou (Morosini Fountain) and El Greco Park area.

Giakoumis Taverna TAVERNA €
Among the tavernas clustered around the 1866 market side streets, this is a favourite. There's a full menu of Cretan specialities and vegetarian options.

Information

Visit www.heraklion-city.gr for more information

Skoutelis Travel (28102 80808; www.skoutelisrentacar.gr; 25 Avgoustou 20) Between Lion Fountain and the old harbour; handles airline and ferry bookings, runs tours and rents cars.

Tourist Office (28102 46299; Xanthoudidou 1; 8.30am-8.30pm Apr-Oct, to 3pm Nov-Mar) Opposite the Archaeological Museum.

DON'T MISS

MARKET ON 1866

Heading inland from Lion Fountain, cross the main street diagonally to the left and you'll be on Odos 1866 (1866 St). This bustling, colourful market street, perfect for people watching, has everything on offer from fruit and vegetables to honey, herbs and succulent olives. Crete is known for its leather goods and this is a good spot to purchase them.

Crete

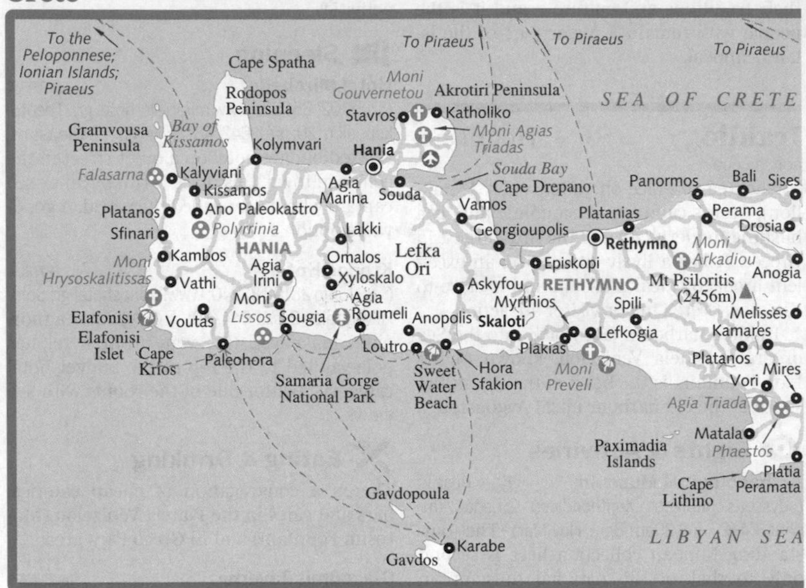

Getting There & Around

AIR Flights depart daily from Iraklio's Nikos Kazantzakis airport (HER) for Athens and there are regular flights to Thessaloniki and Rhodes. International flights buzz in from all over Europe. The airport is 5km east of town. Bus 1 travels between the airport and city centre (€1.20) every 15 minutes from 6am to 11pm.

BOAT Daily ferries service Piraeus (€37, seven hours), and catamarans head daily to Santorini and continue on to other Cycladic islands. Ferries sail east to Rhodes (€28, 12 hours) via Agios Nikolaos, Sitia, Kassos, Karpathos and Halki.

BUS KTEL (www.bus-service-crete-ktel.com) runs the buses on Crete and has useful tourist information inside Bus Station A.

Iraklio has two bus stations. The main **Bus Station A** is just inland from the new harbour and serves eastern Crete (Agios Nikolaos, Ierapetra, Sitia, Malia and the Lasithi Plateau), as well as Hania and Rethymno. **Bus Station B**, 50m beyond the Hania Gate, serves the southern route (Phaestos, Matala and Anogia).

Knossos Κνωσσός

Five kilometres south of Iraklio, **Knossos** (☎28102 31940; admission €6; ⏰8am-7pm Jun-Oct, to 3pm Nov-May) was the capital of Minoan Crete, and is now the island's major tourist attraction.

Knossos (k-nos-*os*) is the most famous of Crete's Minoan sites and is the inspiration for the myth of the Minotaur. According to legend, King Minos of Knossos was given a magnificent white bull to sacrifice to the god Poseidon, but decided to keep it. This enraged Poseidon, who punished the king by causing his wife Pasiphae to fall in love with the animal. The result of this odd union was the Minotaur – half-man and half-bull – who lived in a labyrinth beneath the king's palace, munching on youths and maidens.

In 1900 Arthur Evans uncovered the ruins of Knossos. Although archaeologists tend to disparage Evans' reconstruction, the buildings – incorporating an immense palace, courtyards, private apartments, baths, lively frescos and more – give a fine idea of what a Minoan palace might have looked like.

Buses to Knossos (€1.50, three per hour, 20 minutes) leave from Bus Station A.

Hania Χανιά

POP 54,000

Crete's most romantic, evocative and alluring town, Hania (hahn-*yah*; often spelt Chania) is the former capital and the island's second-largest city. There is a rich mosaic of

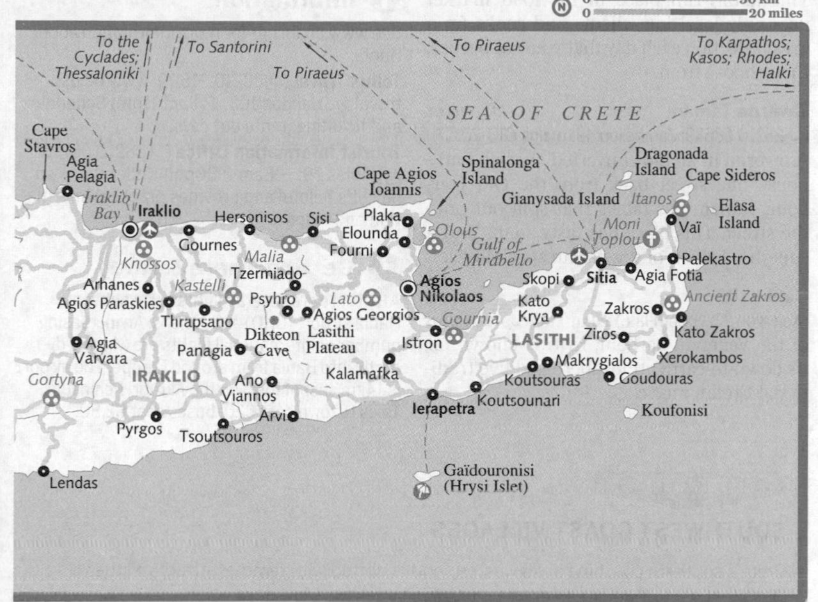

Venetian and Ottoman architecture, particularly in the area of the old harbour, which lures tourists in droves. Modern Hania retains the exoticism of a city caught between East and West, and is an excellent base for exploring nearby idyllic beaches and a spectacular mountainous interior.

Sights & Activities

Old Harbour HISTORIC SITE
From Plateia 1866 in the middle of town, the old harbour is a short walk down Halidon. A stroll around here is a must for any visitor to Hania. It is worth the 1.5km walk around the sea wall to get to the Venetian **lighthouse** at the entrance to the harbour.

Venetian Fortifications FORTRESS
Part of a defensive system built by the Venetians from 1538, Hania's massive fortifications remain impressive. Best preserved is the western wall, running from the Firkas Fortress at the western entrance to the Old Harbour.

Food Market MARKET
Hania's covered food market, in a massive cross-shaped building 400m southeast of the Old Harbour, is definitely worth an inspection.

Sleeping

Pension Lena PENSION €
(☎28210 86860; www.lenachania.gr; Ritsou 5; s/d €35/55; ❄📶) For some real character in where you stay, Lena's pension in an old Turkish building near the mouth of the old harbour is the place to go. Help yourself to one of the appealing rooms if proprietor Lena isn't there – pick from the available ones on the list on the blackboard.

Camping Hania CAMPGROUND €
(☎28210 31138; www.camping-chania.gr; Agii Apostoli; campsites per tent/person €4/7; 🅿🏊) Take the Kalamaki Beach bus from the east corner of Plateia 1866 (every 15 minutes) to get to this camping ground, which is 3km west of town on the beach. There is a restaurant, bar and minimarket.

Eating & Drinking

The entire waterfront of the old harbour is lined with restaurants and tavernas, many of which qualify as tourist traps. Watch out for touts trying to reel you in.

Michelas GREEK €
(☎28210 90026; mains €4-12; ⏲10am-4pm Mon-Sat) Has been serving up authentic Cretan specialities at reasonable prices for 75 years.

This family-run place in the food market uses only local ingredients and cooks up a great selection each day that you can peruse, then choose from.

Taverna Tamam TAVERNA €€
(☎28210 58639; Zambeliou 49; mains €10-20;) A taverna in an old converted Turkish bath-house one street back from the Old Harbour, Tamam has tables that spill out onto the street. This place has tasty soups and a superb selection of vegetarian specialities.

Café Kriti BAR
(Kalergon 22; ⊙8pm-late) Near the eastern end of the Venetian harbour, Kriti is known for its down-to-earth atmosphere and live traditional Cretan music.

Information

See www.chania.gr for more information about Hania.

Tellus Travel (☎28210 91500; www.tellus-travel.gr; Halidon 108; ⊙8am-11pm) Schedules and ticketing; rents out cars.

Tourist Information Office (☎28210 36155; Kydonias 29; ⊙8am-2.30pm) Under the town hall; it's helpful and provides practical information and maps

Getting There & Away

AIR There are several flights a day between Hania airport (CHQ) and Athens. An increasing number of international flights are winging directly into Hania from around Europe. The airport is 14km east of town on the Akrotiri Peninsula. Taxis to town cost €20; buses cost €2.30.

WORTH A TRIP

SOUTHWEST COAST VILLAGES

Crete's southern coastline at its western end is dotted with remote, attractive little villages that are brilliant spots in which to take it easy for a few days.

Heading east from Paleohora are Sougia, Agia Roumeli, Loutro and Hora Sfakion. No road links the coastal resorts, but a daily boat from Paleohora to Sougia (€8.50, one hour), Agia Roumeli (€12.50, 1½ hours), Loutro (€14, 2½ hours) and Hora Sfakion (€16, three hours) connects the villages in summer. The ferry leaves Paleohora at 9.45am and returns along the same route from Hora Sfakion at 1pm. See www.sfakia-crete.com/sfakia-crete/ferries.html for more information.

Sougia At the mouth of the Agia Irini gorge, Sougia (soo-yah) is a laid-back spot with a wide curve of sand-and-pebble beach. It's possible to get here by ferry, by car or on foot. Stay at **Santa Irene Hotel** (☎28230 51342; www.santa-irene.gr; d/tr €55/70;), a smart beachside complex of apartments and studios that has its own cafe and bar.

Agia Roumeli At the mouth of the Samaria Gorge, Agia Roumeli bristles with gorge-walkers from mid-afternoon until the ferry comes to take them away. Take your time to enjoy the village. Right on the waterfront **Paralia Taverna & Rooms** (☎28250 91408; www.taverna-paralia.com; d €30;) offers everything you need – excellent views, tasty Cretan cuisine, cold beer and simple, clean rooms.

Loutro This tiny village is a particularly picturesque spot, curled around the only natural harbour on the southern coast of Crete. With no vehicle access, the only way in is by boat or on foot. **Hotel Porto Loutro** (☎28250 91433; www.hotelportoloutro.com; s/d incl breakfast €50/60;) has tasteful rooms with balconies overlooking the harbour. Take a book and chill out.

Hora Sfakion Renowned in Cretan history for its rebellious streak, Hora Sfakion is an amiable town. It offers a row of seafront tavernas serving fresh seafood, some intriguing and eccentric locals, and an opportunity to see 'the real Crete'. **Hotel Stavris** (☎28250 91220; www.hotel-stavris-chora-sfakion.com; s/d/tr €31/36/41;) has simple rooms and breakfast outside in its courtyard.

Start or finish your Southwest Coast Villages sojourn in Hora Sfakion. There are four buses daily both to and from Hania (€7.60, two hours).

BOAT Daily ferries sail between Piraeus (€35, nine hours) and the port of Souda, 9km southeast of Hania. Frequent buses (€1.65) and taxis (€10) connect town and Souda.

BUS Frequent buses run along Crete's northern coast to Iraklio (€13.80, 2¾ hours, half-hourly); buses run less frequently to Paleohora (€7.60, one hour 50 minutes, four daily), Omalos (€6.90, one hour, three daily) and Hora Sfakion (€7.60, 1½ hours, three daily).

Samaria Gorge

Φαράγγι της Σαμαριάς

The **Samaria Gorge** (☎28250 67179; admission €5; ⊙6am-3pm May–mid-Oct) is one of Europe's most spectacular gorges and a superb hike. Walkers should take rugged footwear, food, drinks and sun protection for this strenuous five- to six-hour trek.

You can do the walk as part of an excursion tour, or independently by taking the Omalos bus from the main bus station in Hania (€6.90, one hour) to the head of the gorge at Xyloskalo (1230m). It's a 16.7km walk out (all downhill) to Agia Roumeli on the coast, from where you take a boat to Hora Sfakion (€10, 1¼ hours) and then a bus back to Hania (€7.60, two hours). You are not allowed to spend the night in the gorge, so you need to complete the walk in a day.

DODECANESE

Strung out along the coast of western Turkey, the 12 main islands of the Dodecanese (Δωδεκάνησα; *dodeca* means 12) have suffered a turbulent past of invasions and occupations that has endowed them with a fascinating diversity.

Conquered successively by the Romans, the Arabs, the Knights of St John, the Turks, the Italians, then liberated from the Germans by British and Greek commandos in 1944, the Dodecanese became part of Greece in 1947. These days, tourists rule.

Rhodes

Ρόδος

POP 98,000

Rhodes (Rodos in Greek) is the largest island in the Dodecanese. According to mythology, the sun god Helios chose Rhodes as his bride and bestowed light, warmth and vegetation upon her. The blessing seems to have paid off, for Rhodes produces more flowers and sunny days than most Greek islands.

THE KNIGHTS OF ST JOHN

Do some island-hopping in the Dodecanese and you'll quickly realise that the Knights of St John left behind a whole lot of castles.

Originally formed as the Knights Hospitaller in Jerusalem in 1080 to provide care for poor and sick pilgrims, the knights relocated to Rhodes (via Cyprus) after the loss of Jerusalem in the First Crusade. They ousted the ruling Genoese in 1309, built a stack of castles in the Dodecanese to protect their new home, then set about irking the neighbours by committing acts of piracy against Ottoman shipping. Sultan Süleyman the Magnificent, not a man you'd want to irk, took offence and set about dislodging the knights from their strongholds. Rhodes finally capitulated in 1523 and the remaining knights relocated to Malta. They set up there as the Sovereign Military Hospitaller of Jerusalem, of Rhodes, and of Malta.

RHODES TOWN

POP 56,000

Rhodes' capital is Rhodes Town, on the northern tip of the island. Its **Old Town**, the largest inhabited medieval town in Europe, is enclosed within massive walls and is a joy to explore. To the north is **New Town**, the commercial centre. The **town beach**, which looks out at Turkey, runs around the peninsula at the northern end of New Town.

The main port, **Commercial Harbour**, is east of the Old Town, and is where the big interisland ferries dock. Northwest of here is **Mandraki Harbour**, lined with excursion boats and smaller ferries, hydrofoils and catamarans.

Sleeping

Mango Rooms ROOMS €

(☎22410 24877; www.mango.gr; Plateia Dorieos 3, Old Town; s/d/tr €44/58/66; ❄@☜) A good-value, friendly one-stop shop near the back of the Old Town, Mango has an outdoor restaurant, bar and internet cafe down below, six well-kept rooms above, and a sun terrace on top. Open year-round.

Hotel International HOTEL €€

(☎22410 24595; www.international-hotel.gr; 12 Kazouli St, New Town; s/d/tr €45/60/75; ❄☜) In New Town, the International is a friendly

DON'T MISS

OLD TOWN

A wander around Rhodes' World Heritage–listed Old Town is a must. It is reputedly the world's finest surviving example of medieval fortification, with 12m-thick walls. Throngs of visitors pack its busier streets, and eating, sleeping and shopping options abound.

The Knights of St John lived in the Knights' Quarter in the northern end of the Old Town. The cobbled **Odos Ippoton** (Avenue of the Knights) is lined with magnificent medieval buildings, the most imposing of which is the **Palace of the Grand Masters** (☎22410 23359; admission €6; ⏰8.30am-3pm Tue-Sun), which was restored (but never used) as a holiday home for Mussolini.

The 15th-century Knight's Hospital now houses the **Archaeological Museum** (☎22410 27657; Plateia Mousiou; admission €3; ⏰8am-4pm Tue-Sun). The splendid building was restored by the Italians and has an impressive collection that includes the ethereal marble statue *Aphrodite of Rhodes*.

The pink-domed **Mosque of Süleyman**, at the top of Sokratous, was built in 1522 to commemorate the Ottoman victory against the knights, then rebuilt in 1808.

family-run operation with immaculately clean and good-value rooms only a few minutes from Rhodes' main town beach. It's a 10-minute stroll to Old Town, and prices drop by a third out of high season.

Hotel Andreas PENSION €€
(☎22410 34156; www.hotelandreas.com; Omirou 28d, Old Town; s/d/tr €45/70/85; ❄@📶) Tasteful Hotel Andreas has individually decorated rooms and terrific views from its terrace. Rates differ by room; check it all out online, and choose your room before you go.

Eating & Drinking

There's food and drink everywhere you look in Rhodes. Outside the city walls are many cheap places in the New Market, at the southern end of Mandraki Harbour.

To Meltemi TAVERNA €
(Kountourioti 8; mains €10-15) At the northern end of Mandraki Harbour, To Meltemi is one place worth heading to. Gaze out on Turkey from this beachside taverna, where the seafood is superb.

Information

Check out www.rodos.gr for more details.

Tourist Information Office (EOT; ☎22410 35226; cnr Makariou & Papagou; ⏰8am-2.45pm Mon-Fri) Has brochures, maps and *Rodos News*, a free English-language newspaper.

Triton Holidays (☎22410 21690; www.tritondmc.gr; Plastira 9, Mandraki) In the New Town. Exceptionally helpful, handling accommodation bookings, ticketing and rental cars. The island-hopping experts, Triton can provide up-to-date guidance in these times of constantly changing flight and boat schedules. Email ahead for advice.

Getting There & Away

AIR

There are plenty of flights daily between Rhodes' **Diagoras airport** (RHO) and Athens, plus less regular flights to Thessaloniki, Iraklio and Samos. International charter flights swarm in summer, plus budget airlines fly in with scheduled flights. The airport is on the west coast, 16km southwest of Rhodes Town; 25 minutes and €2.20 by bus.

BOAT

Rhodes is the main port of the Dodecanese and there is a complex array of departures. There are daily ferries from Rhodes to Piraeus (€59, 13 hours). Most sail via the Dodecanese north of Rhodes, but at least twice a week there is a service via Karpathos, Crete and the Cyclades.

In summer, catamaran services run up and down the Dodecanese daily from Rhodes to Symi, Kos, Kalymnos, Nisyros, Tilos, Patmos and Leros.

TO TURKEY There are boats between Rhodes and Marmaris in Turkey (one-way/return including port taxes €50/75, 50 minutes). Check www.marmarisinfo.com for up-to-date details.

You can also travel between Rhodes and Fethiye, Turkey (one-way/return including port taxes €50/75, 90 minutes). See www.alaturkaturkey.com.

Kos Κως

POP 17,900

Captivating Kos, only 5km from the Turkish peninsula of Bodrum, is popular with history buffs as the birthplace of Hippocrates (460–377 BC), the father of medicine. The island also attracts an entirely different crowd – sun-worshipping beach lovers from northern Europe who flock here during summer.

Sights & Activities

Kos Town has recently developed a number of **bicycle paths** and renting a bike from one of the many places along the waterfront is a great option for getting around town and seeing the sights.

Castle of the Knights CASTLE
(22420 27927; admission €4; 8am-2.30pm Tue-Sun) Built in the 14th century, this impressive castle protected the knights from the encroaching Ottomans, and was originally separated from town by a moat. That moat is now Finikon, a major street.

Asklipieion ARCHAEOLOGICAL SITE
(22420 28763; adult/student €4/3; 8am-7.30pm Tue-Sun) On a pine-clad hill 4km southwest of Kos Town stand the extensive ruins of the renowned healing centre where Hippocrates practised medicine. Groups of doctors come from all over the world to visit.

Ancient Agora RUIN
The ancient agora, with the ruins of the **Shrine of Aphrodite** and **Temple of Hercules**, is just off Plateia Eleftherias. North of the agora is the **Hippocrates Plane Tree**, under which the man himself is said to have taught his pupils.

Sleeping

Hotel Afendoulis HOTEL €
(22420 25321; www.afendoulishotel.com; Evripilou 1; s/d €30/50; Mar-Nov;) In a pleasant, quiet area about 500m south of the ferry quay, this well-kept hotel won't disappoint. Run by charismatic, English-speaking Alexis, this is a great place to relax and enjoy Kos. Port and bus station transfers are complimentary.

Hotel Sonia HOTEL €
(22420 28798; www.hotelsonia.gr; Irodotou 9; s/d/tr €35/50/85;) Recently refurbished, Sonia's place has long been a popular spot to stay in Kos. It has large rooms and a relaxing verandah and garden. They'll pick you up at the port or bus station for free and there are laundry facilities on-site.

Eating

Restaurants line the central waterfront of the old harbour, but you might want to hit the backstreets for value. There are plenty of cheap places to eat on the beach to the north of the harbour.

Information

Visit www.kosinfo.gr for more information.

Exas Travel (22420 28545; www.exas.gr) Near the Archaeological Museum and in the heart of town, to the southwest of the harbour; handles schedules, ticketing and excursions.

Municipal Tourist Office (22420 24460; www.kosinfo.gr; Vasileos Georgiou 1; 8am-2.30pm & 3-10pm Mon-Fri, 9am-2pm Sat May-Oct) On the waterfront directly south of the port; provides maps and accommodation information.

Getting There & Around

Air

There are daily flights to Athens from Kos' Ippokratis airport (KGS), 28km southwest of Kos Town. International charters and scheduled flights wing in throughout the summer from around Europe. Get to/from the airport by bus (€4) or taxi (€30).

Boat

There are frequent ferries from Rhodes to Kos that continue on to Piraeus (€53, 10 hours), as well as ferries heading the opposite way. Daily fast-boat connections head north to Patmos and Samos, and south to Symi and Rhodes.

TO TURKEY In summer boats depart daily for Bodrum in Turkey (€20 return, one hour). Wander the waterfront and take your pick.

Bus

There is a good public bus system on Kos, with the bus station on Kleopatras, near the ruins at the back of town.

Mini-Train

Next to the tourist office is a blue mini-train for Asklipion (€5 return, hourly, Tuesday to Sunday) and a green mini-train that does city tours (€4, 20 minutes).

TALKING TURKEY

Turkey is so close that it looks like you could swim there from many of the Dodecanese and Northeastern Aegean islands. Here are the boat options:

Marmaris or Fethiye From Rhodes (p536)

Bodrum From Kos (p537)

Kuşadasi (near Ephesus) From Samos (p538)

Dikili (near Ayvalık) From Lesvos (p539)

NORTHEASTERN AEGEAN ISLANDS

One of Greece's best-kept secrets, the far-flung Northeastern Aegean Islands (Τα Νησιά του Βορειοανατολικού Αιγαίου) are strewn across the northeastern corner of the Aegean, closer to Turkey than mainland Greece.

Samos Σάμος

POP 32,800

A lush mountainous island only 3km from Turkey, Samos has a glorious history as the legendary birthplace of Hera, wife and sister of god-of-all-gods Zeus. Samos was an important centre of Hellenic culture, and the mathematician Pythagoras and storyteller Aesop are among its sons. The island has beaches that bake in summer, and a hinterland that is superb for hiking.

Getting There & Around

AIR

There are daily flights to Athens from **Samos airport** (SMI), 4km west of Pythagorio, plus less regular flights to Iraklio, Rhodes, Chios and Thessaloniki. Charter flights wing in from Europe in summer.

BOAT

Samos has two main ports: Vathy (Samos Town) in the northeast and Pythagorio on the southeast coast. Those coming from the south by boat generally arrive in Pythagorio. Big ferries use Vathy. Buses between the two take 25 minutes.

A maritime hub, Samos offers daily ferries to Piraeus (€48, 10 hours), plus ferries heading north to Chios and west to the Cyclades. Once the season is up and going, high-speed services head south to Patmos and continue to Kos.

TO TURKEY There are daily ferries to Kuşadasi (for Ephesus) in Turkey (€35/45 one-way/return plus €10 port taxes). Check with ITSA Travel in Vathy for up-to-date details.

BUS

You can get to most of the island's villages and beaches by bus.

CAR & MOTORCYCLE

Rental cars and scooters are readily available around the island (car/scooter from €60/30 per day).

THAT TRIANGLE MAN

You don't need much of an imagination to figure out where the cute little town of Pythagorio got its name! The impressive statue of Pythagoras and his triangle on the town's waterfront should have you recalling his theorem from your high school maths days. If right-angled triangles weren't your thing, buy a T-shirt with the theorem emblazoned on it to remind you.

VATHY (SAMOS TOWN) ΒΑΘΥ ΣΑΜΟΣ

POP 2030

Busy Vathy is an attractive working port town. Most of the action is along Themistokleous Sofouli, the main street that runs along the waterfront. The main square, Plateia Pythagorou, in the middle of the waterfront, is recognisable by its four palm trees and statue of a lion.

ITSA Travel (☎22730 23605; www.itsatravelsamos.gr), opposite the quay, is helpful with travel inquiries, excursions, accommodation and luggage storage. To get to Vathy's bus station, follow the waterfront south and turn left onto Lekati, 250m south of Plateia Pythagorou (just before the police station).

The **Archaeological Museum** (adult/student €3/2, free Sun; ⏰8.30am-3pm Tue-Sun) by the municipal gardens, is first-rate and one of the best in the islands.

Pythagoras Hotel (☎22730 28601; www.pythagorashotel.com; Kallistratou 12; s/d/tr €20/35/45; ⏰Feb-Nov; ❄@📶) is a friendly, great-value place with a convivial atmosphere, run by English-speaking Stelio. There is a restaurant serving tasty home-cooked meals, a bar, satellite TV and internet access on-site. Call ahead for free pick-up on arrival.

PYTHAGORIO ΠΥΘΑΓΟΡΕΙΟ

POP 1300

Pretty Pythagorio, 25 minutes south of Vathy by bus, is where you'll disembark if you've come by boat from Patmos. It is a small, enticing town with a yacht-lined harbour and a holiday atmosphere.

The 1034m-long **Evpalinos Tunnel** (adult/student €4/2; ⏰8am-8pm Tue-Sun), built in the 6th century BC, was dug by political prisoners and used as an aqueduct to bring water from Mt Ampelos (1140m).

Ireon (adult/student €4/2; ⏰8.30am-8pm Tue-Sun), the legendary birthplace of the goddess Hera, is 8km west of Pythagorio. The temple at this World Heritage site was enormous – four times the Parthenon – though only one column remains.

Polyxeni Hotel (☎22730 61590; www.polyxenihotel.com; s/d/tr €40/45/55; ❄📶) is a fun place to stay in the heart of the action. Tavernas and bars line the waterfront.

The cordial **municipal tourist office** (☎22730 61389; deap5@otenet.gr; ⊙8am-9.30pm) is two blocks from the waterfront on the main street, Lykourgou Logotheti. The bus stop is two blocks further inland on the same street.

Lesvos (Mytilini)

Λέσβος (Μυτιλήνη)

POP 93,500

Lesvos, or Mytilini as it is often called, tends to do things in a big way. The third-largest of the Greek islands after Crete and Evia, Lesvos produces half the world's ouzo and is home to over 11 million olive trees.

Lesvos has always been a centre of philosophy and artistic achievement, and to this day is a spawning ground for innovative ideas in the arts and politics. An excellent source of information on the island is www.greeknet.com.

Getting There & Away

AIR

Written up on flight schedules as Mytilene, Lesvos' Odysseas airport (MJT) has daily connections with Athens, plus flights to Thessaloniki, Iraklio and a growing number of domestic destinations. The airport is 8km south of Mytilini town; a taxi costs €9; a bus to town costs €1.50.

BOAT

In summer there are daily fast/slow boats to Piraeus (€37/27, 8/13 hours) via Chios, and boats to Limnos, Thessaloniki and Samos.

TO TURKEY There are regular ferries a week to Dikili port (which serves Ayvalik) and to Fokias (which serves Izmir). Stop by Zoumboulis Tours (p540) for ticketing and schedules.

MYTILINI

ΜΥΤΙΛΗΝΗ

POP 27,300

The capital and main port, Mytilini, is built between two harbours (north and south) with an imposing fortress on the promontory to the east. With a large university campus, Mytilini is a lively place year-round.

Sights & Activities

Teriade Museum MUSEUM
(☎22510 23372; admission €2; ⊙8.30am-2pm & 5-8pm Tue-Sun) Take a local bus 4km south of Mytilini to the village of Varia, where an unexpected treasure awaits: the Teriade Museum, with its astonishing collection of paintings by world-renowned artists like Picasso, Chagall, Miro, Le Corbusier and Matisse.

Fortress FORTRESS
(adult/student €2/1; ⊙8am-2.30pm Tue-Sun) Mytilini's impressive fortress was built in early Byzantine times and enlarged by the Turks. The pine forest surrounding it is a superb place for a stroll or to have a picnic.

Sleeping

Pension Thalia ROOMS €
(☎22510 24640; Kinikiou 1; s/d €25/30) This pension has clean, bright rooms in a large house. It is about a five-minute walk north of the main square, up Ermou, the road that links the south and north harbours. Follow the signs from the corner of Ermou and Adramytiou.

Hotel Sappho HOTEL €€
(☎22510 22888; www.sappho-hotel.gr; Kountourioti 31; s/d/tr €45/60/70; ❄📶) Sappho is an older hotel with the necessary amenities and, fortunately for late-night ferry arrivees, 24-hour reception.

Eating & Drinking

Mytilini's top spots are a road or two back at the northern end of the harbour.

SAPPHO, LESBIANS & LESVOS

Sappho, one of Greece's great ancient poets, was born on Lesvos during the 7th century BC. Most of her work was devoted to love and desire, and the objects of her affection were often female. Because of this, Sappho's name and birthplace have come to be associated with female homosexuality.

These days, Lesvos is visited by many lesbians paying homage to Sappho. The whole island is very gay-friendly, in particular the southwestern beach resort of Skala Eresou, which is built over ancient Eresos, where Sappho was born. The village is well set up to cater to lesbian needs and has a Women Together festival held annually in September. Check out www.sappho-travel.com for details.

There is an excellent statue of Sappho in the main square on the waterfront in Mytilini.

Stou Mihali GREEK €
(☎info 22510 43311; Ikarias 7, Plateia Sapphou; mains €4-10; ⊙9am-9pm) It's getting hard to find a free table at lunch at this tasty and inexpensive place. Everything is good.

Information

See www.lesvos.net for more information.

Tourist Office (EOT; ☎22510 42512; 6 Aristarhou; ⊙9am-1pm Mon-Fri)

Located 50m up Aristarhou inland from the quay; offers brochures and maps, but opening hours are limited.

Zoumboulis Tours (☎22510 37755; Kountourioti 69) On the waterfront, handles flights, boat schedules, ticketing and excursions to Turkey.

Getting Around

Mytilini has two bus stations. For local buses, head along the waterfront to the main square. For long-distance buses, walk 600m from the ferry along the waterfront to El Venizelou and turn right until you reach Agia Irinis park, which is next to the station. There are regular services in summer to Mithymna and Skala Eresou.

MITHYMNA ΜΗΘΥΜΝΑ

POP 1500

The gracious, preserved town of Mithymna (known by locals as Molyvos) is 62km north of Mytilini. Cobbled streets canopied by flowering vines wind up the hill below the impressive castle.

The noble **Genoese castle** (admission €2; ⊙8.30am-7pm Tue-Sun) perches above the town like a crown and affords tremendous views out to Turkey. Pebbly **Mithymna Beach** sits below the town and is good for swimming. Don't forget to stroll down to the harbour.

Eftalou hot springs (public/private bath per person €4/5; ⊙6am-9pm), 4km from town on the beach, is a superb bathhouse complex with a whitewashed dome and steaming, pebbled pool.

Nassos Guest House (☎22530 71432; www.nassosguesthouse.com; Arionis; d & tr €20-35; 📶) is an airy, friendly place with shared facilities and a communal kitchen, in an old Turkish house filled with character. With rapturous views, it's highly recommended. It's the only blue house below the castle.

From the bus stop, walk straight ahead towards the town for 100m to the helpful **municipal tourist office** (www.mithymna.gr), which has good maps.

Buses to Mithymna (€6.90) take 1¾ hours from Mytilini, though a rental car is a good option.

SPORADES

Scattered to the southeast of the Pelion Peninsula, to which they were joined in prehistoric times, the 11 islands that make up the Sporades (Σποράδες) group have mountainous terrain, dense vegetation and are surrounded by scintillatingly clear seas.

The main ports for the Sporades are Volos and Agios Konstantinos on the mainland.

Skiathos Σκιάθος

POP 6150

Lush and green, Skiathos has a beach-resort feel about it. Charter flights bring loads of package tourists, but the island still oozes enjoyment. Skiathos Town and some excellent beaches are on the hospitable south coast.

Sights & Activities

Skiathos has superb beaches, particularly on the south coast. **Koukounaries** is popular with families. A stroll over the headland, **Big Banana Beach** is stunning, but if you want an all-over tan, head a tad further to **Little Banana Beach**, where bathing suits are a rarity.

At the Old Port in Skiathos Town, there are all sorts of offerings in terms of **boat excursions** – trips to nearby beaches (€10), trips around Skiathos Island (€25) and full-day trips that take in Skopelos, Alonnisos and the Marine Park (€35).

Sleeping

Pension Pandora ROOMS €
(☎24270 24357, 694 413 7377; www.skiathosinfo.com/accomm/pension-pandora; r €30-70; P❄📶) Run by the effervescent Georgina, this family-run place is 10 minutes' walk north of the quay and a great budget option. The spotless rooms have TV, kitchens and balconies.

Camping Koukounaries CAMPGROUND €
(☎24270 49250; campsites per tent/person €4/10; P) This place, 30 minutes from town by bus at the southwestern end of the island, is at beautiful Koukounaries Beach. There are good facilities, a minimarket and a taverna.

Eating & Drinking

Skiathos Town is brimming with eateries. There are seafood options around the old harbour, and some excellent places up the stairs from there behind the small church.

TOP CHOICE **Piccolo** ITALIAN €
(☎24270 22780; www.firponet.com/piccolo; mains from €8) This Italian place behind the church up from the Old Harbour does exquisite pizzas and pastas in a lovely setting.

Kentavros BAR
(☎24270 22980) A popular drinking spot just off Plateia Papadiamanti. Expect a mellow ambience and mixture of rock, jazz and blues.

Information

See www.skiathosinfo.com for more information.

Heliotropio Tourism & Travel (☎24270 22430) Opposite the ferry quay; handles ticketing and rents cars and scooters.

Tourist Information Booth (☎24270 23172) At the port, but it opens irregularly.

Getting There & Around

AIR Along with numerous charter flights from northern Europe, in summer there is a daily flight from Athens and one from Thessaloniki. Skiathos airport (JSI) is 2km northeast of Skiathos Town.

BOAT There are frequent daily hydrofoils to/from the mainland ports of Volos (€34, 1¼ hours) and Agios Konstantinos (€36, two hours), as well as cheaper ferries. The hydrofoils head to and from Skopelos (€12, 45 minutes) and Alonnisos (€18, one hour).

BUS Crowded buses ply the south-coast road between Skiathos Town and Koukounaries every 30 minutes between 7.30am and 11pm year-round, stopping at all the beaches along the way.

IONIAN ISLANDS

The idyllic cypress- and fir-covered Ionian Islands (Τα Επτάνησα) stretch down the western coast of Greece from Corfu in the north to Kythira, off the southern tip of the Peloponnese. Mountainous, with dramatic cliff-backed beaches, soft light and turquoise water, they're more Italian in feel, offering a contrasting experience to other Greek islands.

Corfu Κέρκυρα

POP 122,700

Many consider Corfu, or Kerkyra (*ker*-kih-rah) in Greek, to be Greece's most beautiful island – the unfortunate consequence of which is that it's overbuilt and often overrun with crowds.

MOVIES UNDER THE STARS

Greece has such great weather in summer that it not only has a history of open-air theatre, there's also an open-air cinema culture. **Cinema Attikon** (☎24720 22352; ticket €7), on Skiathos Town's main street of Papadiamanti, is a great example. You can catch current English-language movies under the stars, sip a beer and practice speed-reading Greek subtitles at the same time! Films are usually shown in their original language in Greece, not dubbed.

A number of other islands have similar outdoor cinemas.

CORFU TOWN

POP 28,800

Built on a promontory and wedged between two fortresses, Corfu's Old Town is a tangle of narrow walking streets through gorgeous Venetian buildings. Explore the winding alleys and surprising plazas in the early morning or late afternoon to avoid the hordes of day trippers seeking souvenirs.

Sights

Palaio Frourio FORTRESS
(☎26610 48310; adult/concession €4/2; ⊙8am-8pm May-Oct, 8.30am-3pm Nov-Mar) Constructed by the Venetians in the 15th century on the remains of a Byzantine castle and further altered by the British, the Palaio Frourio stands on an eastern promontory; the Neo Frourio (New Fortress) lies to the northwest.

Antivouniotissa Museum MUSEUM
(☎26610 38313; off Arseniou; admission €2; ⊙8am-2.30pm Tue-Sun) Exquisite basilica with an outstanding collection of Byzantine icons and artefacts dating from the 13th to the 17th centuries.

Church of Agios Spiridon CHURCH
(Agios Spiridonos) Richly decorated church displays the remains of St Spiridon.

Sleeping

Accommodation prices fluctuate wildly depending on season; book ahead.

Bella Venezia BOUTIQUE HOTEL €€
(☎26610 46500; www.bellaveneziahotel.com; N Zambeli 4; s/d incl breakfast from €100/120; ⊖❄☎) Impeccable and understated; contemporary rooms are decked out in cream linens and marbles.

Hermes Hotel HOTEL €
(☎26610 39268; www.hermes-hotel.gr; Markora 12; s/d/tr €50/60/75; ❄📶) Completely refurbished, pleasant, well-appointed rooms in the New Town.

Eating & Drinking

Corfu has excellent restaurants. Cafes and bars line the arcaded Liston. Try Corfu Beer.

Chrisomalis TAVERNA €
(☎26610 30342; N Theotoki 6; mains €8-13) In the heart of the Old Town, this ma-and-pa operation dishes out the classics.

Rouvas TAVERNA €
(☎26610 31182; S Desilla 13; mains €5-8; ⏱9am-5pm) Favourite lunch stop for locals.

Information

Tourist Police (☎26610 30265; Samartzi 4, 3rd fl)

Getting There & Around

AIR Ioannis Kapodistrias Airport (CFU; ☎26610 30180) is 3km from Corfu Town. **Olympic Air** (☎801 801 0101) and **Aegean Airlines** (☎26610 27100) fly daily to Athens and a few times a week to Thessaloniki.

easyJet and charters fly internationally in summer. A taxi from the airport to the centre costs around €12. Buses 6 and 10 stop 800m from the airport.

BOAT Ferries go to Igoumenitsa (€10, 1½ hours, hourly). In summer daily ferries and hydrofoils go to Paxi, and international ferries (Italy, Albania) also stop in Patra (€35, six hours).

BUS Daily **buses** (☎26610 28898; www.ktelkerkyras.gr) to Athens (€50, 8½ hours) and Thessaloniki (€45, eight hours) leave from Corfu's **long-distance bus station** (☎26610 28927; Ioannou Theotoki).

Blue buses (€1.10 to €1.50) for villages near Corfu Town leave from Plateia San Rocco. Services to other destinations (around Corfu €1.60 to €4.40) leave from the long-distance terminal.

UNDERSTAND GREECE

History

With its strategic position at the crossroads of Europe and Asia, Greece has endured a long and turbulent history. During the Bronze Age (3000–1200 BC in Greece), the advanced Cycladic, Minoan and Mycenaean civilisations flourished. The Mycenaeans were swept aside in the 12th century BC by the warriorlike Dorians, who introduced Greece to the Iron Age. The next 400 years are often referred to as the Dark Ages, a period about which little is known.

By 800 BC, when Homer's *Odyssey* and *Iliad* were first written down, Greece was undergoing a cultural and military revival with the evolution of the city states, the most powerful of which were Athens and Sparta. The unified Greeks repelled the Persians twice, at Marathon (490 BC) and Salamis (480 BC). Victory over Persia was followed by unparalleled growth and prosperity known as the classical (or Golden) age.

The Golden Age

During this period, Pericles commissioned the Parthenon, Sophocles wrote *Oedipus the King* and Socrates taught young Athenians to think. The Golden Age ended with the Peloponnesian War (431–404 BC), when the militaristic Spartans defeated the Athenians. They failed to notice the expansion of Macedonia under King Philip II, who easily conquered the war-weary city states.

Philip's ambitions were surpassed by those of his son, Alexander the Great, who marched triumphantly into Asia Minor, Egypt, Persia and what are now parts of Afghanistan and India. In 323 BC he met an untimely death at the age of 33, and his generals divided his empire between themselves.

Roman Rule & the Byzantine Empire

Roman incursions into Greece began in 205 BC. By 146 BC Greece and Macedonia had become Roman provinces. After the subdivision of the Roman Empire into eastern and western empires in AD 395, Greece became part of the Eastern (Byzantine) Empire, based at Constantinople.

In the centuries that followed, Venetians, Franks, Normans, Slavs, Persians, Arabs and, finally, Turks, took turns chipping away at the Byzantine Empire.

The Ottoman Empire & Independence

In 1453, when Constantinople fell to the Turks, most of Greece became part of the Ottoman Empire. By the 19th century the Ottoman Empire was in decline. Greek independence was proclaimed on 13 January 1822, only for arguments among the leaders who had been united against the Turks to escalate into civil war. The Turks, with the help of the Egyptians, tried to retake Greece, but the great powers – Britain, France and Russia – intervened in 1827, and Ioannis Kapodistrias was elected the first Greek president.

Kapodistrias was assassinated in 1831 and the European powers stepped in once again, declaring that Greece should become a monarchy. In 1833 Otho of Bavaria was installed as king. His ambition, called the Great Idea, was to unite all the lands of the Greek people to the Greek motherland. In 1862 he was peacefully ousted and the Greeks chose George I, a Danish prince, as king.

During WWI Prime Minister Venizelos allied Greece with France and Britain. King Constantine (George's son), whose wife, Sophia, was the sister of German Emporer Wilhem II, disputed this and left the country.

Smyrna & WWII

After the war Venizelos resurrected the Great Idea. Underestimating the new-found power of Turkey under the leadership of Atatürk (Mustafa Kemal), he sent forces to occupy Smyrna (the present-day Turkish port of İzmir), with its large Greek population. The army was heavily defeated and this led to a brutal population exchange between the two countries in 1923.

In 1930 George II, Constantine's son, was reinstated as king; he appointed the dictator General Metaxas as prime minister. Metaxas' chief claim to fame is his celebrated *ohi* (no) to Mussolini's request to allow Italian troops into Greece in 1940.

Greece fell to Germany in 1941 and resistance movements, polarised into royalist and communist factions, staged a bloody civil war lasting until 1949. This was the trigger for a mass exodus that saw almost one million Greeks head off to countries such as Australia, Canada and the USA.

The Colonels' Coup

Continuing political instability led to the colonels' coup d'état in 1967. The colonels' junta distinguished itself with its appalling brutality, repression and political incompetence. In 1974 it attempted to assassinate Cyprus' leader, Archbishop Makarios, and when he escaped the junta replaced him with the extremist Nikos Samson, prompting Turkey to occupy North Cyprus. The junta had little choice but to hand back power to the people. In November 1974 a plebiscite voted against restoration of the monarchy. Greece became a republic with the right-wing New Democracy (ND) party taking power.

ORIGINAL OLYMPICS

The Olympic tradition emerged around the 11th century BC as a paean to the Greek gods, in the form of contests of athletic feats. By the 8th century BC, attendance had grown to include a wide confederacy of city states; a major event lasting five days at the site of Olympia. A ceremonial truce was enforced for the duration of the games. Crowds of spectators lined the tracks, where competitors vied for victory in athletics, chariot races, wrestling and boxing. Three millennia later, while the scale and scope of the games may have expanded considerably, the basic format has remained essentially unchanged.

The 1980s & 1990s

In 1981 Greece entered the European Community (now the EU) as its 10th, smallest and poorest member. Andreas Papandreou's Panhellenic Socialist Movement (Pasok) won the next election, giving Greece its first socialist government. Pasok, which ruled for most of the next two decades, promised the removal of US air bases and withdrawal from NATO, but delivered only rising unemployment and spiralling debt.

The New Millennium

Greece focused strongly on further integration with Europe and in 2001 admission to the euro club was approved; Greece duly adopted the currency in 2002 and prices have been on the rise ever since.

Greece tilted to the right and in March 2004 elected the ND party led by Costas Karamanlis. This new broom was fortuitous, as the Olympic preparations were running late and suffering budget problems. While the Olympics were successful, Greece is still counting the cost.

During the long hot summer of 2007, forest fires threatened Athens and caused untold damage in the western Peloponnese, Epiros and Evia. Later that year, Karamanlis' government was returned to power for a second term, but amid growing discontent

RECOGNISE THAT TWANG?

Don't be surprised if your hotel receptionist or waiter speaks perfect English with an Australian twang. A growing stream of young second- and third-generation Greeks are repatriating from the USA, Australia, Canada and other reaches of the Greek diaspora. A huge number of Greeks emigrated during their country's tumultuous history and it is said that over five million people of Greek descent live in 140 countries around the world.

that included massive general strikes and riots, was turfed out in elections in October 2009 in favour of Pasok and George Papandreou, son and grandson of former prime ministers.

Financial Mayhem

Textbooks are being written on Greece's 2010 financial crisis. Simply put, Greece almost fell over from years of over-borrowing, over-spending and breaking eurozone rules on deficit management. Financially crippled and looking likely to drag other failing eurozone economies down with it, Greece was on the receiving end of a succession of bail-out packages to help right the ship. Needless to say, austerity measures to help balance the budget were not popular, with citizens angry about cuts in spending, pensions and salaries, along with higher taxes.

Strikes and riots made world news and in May 2012 elections, no party or coalition of parties was able to form a government. New elections were called for June and in what was seen worldwide as a vote that would determine if Greece remained in the eurozone, a coalition of three parties formed a government with New Democracy's Antonis Samaris as prime minister.

Samaris hopes to keep both Greece's creditors and its populace happy, but without doubt, tough times are ahead.

People

Greece's population has topped 11.2 million, with around one-third of the people living in the Greater Athens area and more than two-thirds living in cities – confirming that Greece is now a primarily urban society. Less than 15% live on the islands, the most populous being Crete, Evia and Corfu. Greece has an ageing population and declining birth rate, with big families a thing of the past. Population growth over the last couple of decades is due to a flood of migrants, both legal and illegal.

About 95% of the Greek population belongs to the Greek Orthodox Church. The remainder is split between the Roman Catholic, Protestant, Evangelist, Jewish and Muslim faiths. While older Greeks and those in rural areas tend to be deeply religious, most young people are decidedly more secular.

The Greek year is centred on the saints' days and festivals of the church calendar. Name days (celebrating your namesake saint) are celebrated more than birthdays. Most people are named after a saint, as are boats, suburbs and train stations.

Orthodox Easter is usually at a different time than Easter celebrated by Western churches, though generally in April/May.

Environment

The Land

Greece sits at the southern tip of the Balkan Peninsula. Of its 1400 islands, only 169 are inhabited. Nowhere in Greece is much more than 100km from the sea.

Around 80% of the land is mountainous, with less than a quarter of the country suitable for agriculture.

Greece sits in one of the most seismically active regions in the world – the eastern Mediterranean lies at the meeting point of three continental plates: the Eurasian, African and Arabian. Consequently, Greece has had more than 20,000 earthquakes in the last 40 years, most of them very minor.

National Parks

While facilities in Greek national parks aren't on par with many other countries, all have refuges and some have marked hiking trails. The most visited parks are Mt Parnitha, north of Athens, and the Samaria Gorge on Crete. The others are Vikos-Aoös and Prespa National Parks in Epiros; Mt Olympus on the border of Thessaly and Macedonia; and Parnassos and Iti National Parks in central Greece. There is also a national marine park off the coast of Alonnisos, and another around the Bay of Laganas area off Zakynthos.

Environmental Issues

Greece is belatedly becoming environmentally conscious but, regrettably, it's too late for some regions. Deforestation and soil erosion are problems that go back thousands of years, with olive cultivation and goats being the main culprits. Forest fires are also a major problem.

Food & Drink

Snacks

Greece has a great range of fast-food options. Foremost among them are gyros and souvlaki. The gyros is a giant skewer laden with seasoned meat that grills slowly as it rotates, the meat being steadily trimmed from the outside. Souvlaki are small cubes of meat cooked on a skewer. Both are served wrapped in pitta bread with salad and lashings of tzatziki (a yoghurt, cucumber and garlic dip). Other snacks are pretzel rings, spanakopita (spinach and cheese pie) and *tyropitta* (cheese pie).

Starters

Greece is famous for its appetisers, known as *mezedhes* (literally, 'tastes'; meze for short). Standards include tzatziki, *melitzanosalata* (aubergine dip), taramasalata (fish-roe dip), dolmadhes (stuffed vine leaves; dolmas for short), *fasolia* (beans) and *oktapodi* (octopus). A selection of three or four starters represents a good meal and makes an excellent vegetarian option.

Mains

You'll find moussaka (layers of aubergine and mince, topped with béchamel sauce and baked) on every menu, alongside a number of other taverna staples. They include *moschari* (oven-baked veal and potatoes), *keftedes* (meatballs), *stifado* (meat stew), *pastitsio* (baked dish of macaroni with minced meat and béchamel sauce) and *yemista* (either tomatoes or green peppers stuffed with minced meat and rice).

Kalamaria (fried squid) is the most popular (and cheapest) seafood, while *barbouni* (red mullet) and *sifias* (swordfish) tend to be more expensive than meat dishes.

Fortunately for vegetarians, salad is a mainstay of the Greek diet. The most popular is *horiatiki salata,* normally listed on English-language menus as Greek salad. It's a delicious mixed salad comprising cucumbers, peppers, onions, olives, tomatoes and feta cheese. For the full scoop on Greece's legendary feta cheese, check out www.feta.gr.

Desserts

Most Greek desserts are Turkish in origin and are variations on pastry soaked in honey, such as baklava (thin layers of pastry filled with honey and nuts). Delicious Greek yogurt also makes a great dessert, especially with honey.

Drinks

Bottled mineral water is cheap and available everywhere, as are soft drinks and packaged juices.

Mythos, in its distinctive green bottle, and Alfa, are popular Greek beers.

Greece is traditionally a wine-drinking society. An increasingly good range of wines made from traditional grape varieties is available. Wine enthusiasts should take a look at www.allaboutgreekwine.com. Retsina, wine flavoured with pine-tree resin, is a tasty alternative – though an acquired taste for some. Most tavernas will offer locally made house wines by the carafe.

Metaxa, Greece's dominant brandy, is sweet, while if you are offered some raki, make sure to take a small sip first!

'Greek' coffee should be tried at least once, but don't drink the mudlike grounds at the bottom!

THE ART OF OUZO

Ouzo is Greece's most famous but misunderstood tipple. While it can be drunk as an aperitif, for most Greeks ouzo has come to embody a way of socialising. It is sipped slowly and ritually to clean the palate between tastes. Ouzo is usually served in small bottles or *karafakia* (carafes) with water and a bowl of ice cubes – and is commonly drunk on the rocks, diluted with water (it turns a cloudy white). Mixing it with cola is a foreign abomination!

Made from distilled grapes, ouzo is also distilled with residuals from fruit, grains and potatoes, and flavoured with spices, primarily aniseed, giving it that liquorice flavour.

SURVIVAL GUIDE

Directory A–Z

Accommodation

Prices are for high season (usually July and August); price cateogries are based on double rooms with bathrooms.

€ less than €60

€€ €60 to €150

€€€ more than €150

ACCOMMODATION TYPES

Hotels Classified as deluxe, or A, B, C, D or E class; ratings seldom seem to have much bearing on the price, which is determined more by season and location.

Domatia Greek equivalent of a B&B, minus the breakfast; don't worry about finding them – owners will find you as they greet ferries and buses shouting 'room!'

Youth hostels In most major towns and on some islands; **Greek Youth Hostel Organisation** (☎21075 19530; www.athens-yhostel.com).

Campgrounds Generally open from April to October; standard facilities include hot showers, kitchens, restaurants and minimarkets – and often a swimming pool; **Panhellenic Camping Association** (☎21036 21560; www.panhellenic-camping-union.gr).

> **SEASONAL PRICES**
>
> 'High season' is usually in July and August. If you turn up in the 'middle' or 'shoulder seasons' (May and June; September and October) expect to pay significantly less. During 'low season' (late October to late April) prices can be up to 50% cheaper, but a lot of places, especially on the islands, virtually close their shutters for winter. Websites will usually display these differences in price.
>
> Greek accommodation is subject to strict price controls, and by law a notice must be displayed in every room stating the category of the room and the seasonal price. It's usually on the back of the door. If you think there's something amiss, contact the tourist police.

Mountain refuges Listed in *Greece Mountain Refuges & Ski Centres*, available free of charge at EOT and EOS (Ellinikos Orivatikos Syndesmos, the Greek Alpine Club) offices.

Business Hours

Banks 8am to 2.30pm Monday to Thursday, 8am to 2pm Friday (also 3.30pm to 6.30pm Monday to Friday, 8am to 1.30pm Saturday in citiies)

Cafes 10am to midnight

Post offices 7.30am to 2pm Monday to Friday (in cities 7.30am to 8pm Monday to Friday, 7.30am to 2pm Saturday)

Restaurants 11am to 3pm and 7pm to 1am (although varies greatly)

Supermarkets 8am to 8pm Monday to Friday, 8am to 3pm Saturday

Street kiosks *(periptera)* early to late Monday to Sunday

Embassies & Consulates

The following are all in Athens:

Australian Embassy (☎210 870 4000; www.greece.embassy.gov.au; Ambelokipi, 6th fl, Thon Building, cnr Leoforos Alexandras & Leoforos Kifisias)

Canadian Embassy (☎210 727 3400; www.greece.gc.ca; Genadiou 4)

Japanese Embassy (☎210 670 9900; www.gr.emb-japan.go.jp; Ethnikís Antistáseos 46, Halandri)

New Zealand Embassy (☎210 687 4701; www.nzembassy.com; Kifisias 268, Halandri)

UK Embassy (☎210 723 6211; www.ukingreece.fco.gov.uk; Ploutarhou 1)

US Embassy (☎210 721 2951; http://athens.usembassy.gov; Leoforos Vasilissis Sofias 91)

Food

Price ranges for eating reviews are as follows:

€ less than €15

€€ €15 to €40

€€€ more than €40

Gay & Lesbian Travellers

The church plays a significant role in shaping society's views on issues such as sexuality, and homosexuality is generally frowned upon. It's wise to be discreet and to avoid open displays of togetherness.

That said, Greece is a popular destination for gay travellers. Athens has a busy gay scene that packs up and heads to the islands for summer. Mykonos has long been famous for its bars, beaches and hedonism. A visit to Eresos on Lesvos has become something of a pilgrimage for lesbians.

Internet Access

Greece has embraced the internet. Charges differ wildly (as does the speed of access).

Most midrange and top-end hotels will offer their guests some form of internet connection. Laptop-wielding visitors will often be able to connect to wi-fi at hotels and most internet cafes.

Language Courses

For intensive Greek-language courses check out the **Athens Centre** (Map p508; ☎210 701 2268; www.athenscentre.gr; Arhimidous 48, Mets; Ⓜ Akropoli).

Money

- ATMs are everywhere except the smallest villages.
- While souvenir shops will generally bargain, prices in other shops are normally clearly marked and non-negotiable; accommodation is nearly always negotiable outside peak season, especially for longer stays.
- Cash is king at street kiosks and small shops, and especially in the countryside.
- Banks, post offices and currency-exchange offices are all over the place; exchange all major currencies.
- Credit cards are generally accepted, but may not be on smaller islands or in small villages.
- The service charge is included on the bill in restaurants, but it is the custom to 'round up the bill'; same for taxis.

Post

- *Tahydromia* (post offices) are easily identified by the yellow sign outside.
- Regular postboxes are yellow; red postboxes are for express mail.
- The postal rate for postcards and airmail letters within the EU is €0.60, to other destinations it's €0.80.

Public Holidays

New Year's Day 1 January

Epiphany 6 January

First Sunday in Lent February

Greek Independence Day 25 March

Orthodox Good Friday/Easter Sunday April/May

May Day (Protomagia) 1 May

Feast of the Assumption 15 August

Ohi Day 28 October

Christmas Day 25 December

St Stephen's Day 26 December

Safe Travel

Crime is traditionally low in Greece, but on the rise. Watch out for bar scams and *bombes* (spiked drinks), and be wary of pickpockets on the Athens metro, around Omonia and at the flea market.

Telephone

Maintained by Organismos Tilepikoinonion Ellados, known as OTE (o-*teh*), public phones are everywhere, take all phonecards and are easy to use; pressing the 'i' button brings up the operating instructions in English.

For directory inquiries within Greece, call ☎131 or ☎132; for international directory inquiries, it's ☎161 or ☎162.

MOBILE PHONES

- Mobile phones are a must-have in Greece. If you have a compatible GSM phone from a country with a global roaming agreement with Greece, you will be able to use your phone there.
- There are several mobile service providers in Greece; **CosmOTE** (www.cosmote.gr) has the best coverage. You can purchase a Greek SIM card for around €20.
- The use of a mobile phone while driving in Greece is prohibited.

PHONE CODES

- Telephone codes are part of the 10-digit number within Greece.
- The landline prefix is ☎2 and for mobiles it's ☎6.

PHONECARDS

- All public phones use OTE phonecards, which are sold at OTE offices and street kiosks.
- Phonecards come in €3, €5 and €10 versions; local calls cost €0.30 for three minutes.
- Discount-card schemes are available, offering much better value for money.

Time

There's one time zone throughout Greece, which is two hours ahead of GMT/UTC and three hours ahead on daylight-savings time (from the last Sunday in March to the last Sunday in October).

Toilets

» Public toilets are rare, except at airports and bus and train stations.
» Most places have Western-style toilets.
» Some public toilets may be Asian-style squat toilets.
» Greek plumbing can't handle toilet paper! Anything larger than a postage stamp will cause a blockage. Put your used toilet paper, sanitary napkins and tampons in the small bin provided next to every toilet.

Tourist Information

There is an EOT office or local tourist office In almost every town of consequence and on many of the islands.

Tourist police offices in popular destinations can also provide information; head here if you think you've been ripped off.

Greek National Tourist Organisation (GNTO; www.gnto.gr) Known as EOT within Greece.

Visas

Visitors from most countries don't need a visa for Greece.

Getting There & Away

Air

Most visitors arrive by air, mostly into Athens. There are 17 international airports in Greece; most handle only summer charter flights to the islands.

There's a growing number of direct scheduled services into Greece by European budget airlines.

Greek airlines include the following:

Olympic Air (www.olympicair.com)

Aegean Airlines (www.aegeanair.com)

Land

BORDER CROSSINGS

You can drive or ride through the following border crossings.

From Albania

Kakavia (60km northwest of Ioannina)

Krystallopigi (14km west of Kotas)

Mertziani (17km west of Konitsa)

Sagiada (28km north of Igoumenitsa)

From Bulgaria

Exohi (50km north of Drama)

Ormenio (41km from Serres)

Promahonas (109km northeast of Thessaloniki)

From Macedonia

Doïrani (31km north of Kilkis)

Evzoni (68km north of Thessaloniki)

Niki (16km north of Florina)

From Turkey

Kastanies (139 km northeast of Alexandroupolis)

Kipi (43km east of Alexandroupolis)

BUS

International buses are somewhat in limbo due to Greece's financial problems. The **Hellenic Railways Organisation** (OSE; www.ose.gr) has been operating the following routes, but check the website for the latest:

Albania Athens–Tirana overnight bus (16 hours, daily) via Ioannina and Gjirokastra

Bulgaria Athens–Sofia bus (15 hours, six weekly); Thessaloniki–Sofia (7½ hours, four daily)

Turkey Athens–İstanbul (22 hours, six weekly); stops at Thessaloniki (seven hours) and Alexandroupolis (13 hours).

TRAIN

Both international and domestic train routes have been severely curtailed due to the financial problems. At time of research, no international train routes were running. Be sure to check the current situation well in advance. The following routes may or may not be in operation:

Bulgaria Sofia–Athens (18 hours, daily) via Thessaloniki

Macedonia Thessaloniki–Skopje (five hours, twice daily)

Russia Thessaloniki–Moscow (70 hours, weekly, summer only)

Turkey İstanbul–Thessaloniki (12 hours, daily)

Sea

Check out ferry routes, schedules and services online at www.greekferries.gr.

If you are travelling on a rail pass, check to see if ferry travel between Italy and Greece is included. Some ferries are free, others give a discount. On some routes you will need to make reservations.

FROM ALBANIA

Saranda Petrakis Lines (☎26610 38690; www.ionian-cruises.com) has daily hydrofoils to Corfu (25 minutes).

FROM ITALY

Ancona (20 hours, three daily, summer)

Bari (14½ hours, daily) via Corfu (eight hours) and Kefallonia (14 hours); also to Igoumenitsa (11½ hours, daily)

Brindisi Patra (15 hours, April to early October) via Igoumenitsa

Venice Patra (30 hours, up to 12 weekly, summer) via Corfu (25 hours)

FROM TURKEY

Boat services operate between Turkey's Aegean coast and the Greek Islands:

Marmaris and Fethiye Rhodes (daily in summer, twice weekly in winter)

Bodrum Kos (one hour, daily in summer)

Kuşadasi Samos (daily in summer, weekly in winter; one hour)

Çeşme Chios (one hour, daily in summer)

Ayvalik Lesvos (one hour, four times weekly in summer)

Getting Around

Greece has a comprehensive transport system and is easy to get around.

Air

Domestic air travel has been very price-competitive of late, and it's sometimes cheaper to fly than take the ferry, especially if you book ahead online.

DOMESTIC AIR CARRIERS

Aegean Airlines (www.aegeanair.com) The big competition for Olympic Air offers newer aircraft and similar prices.

Astra Airlines (www.astra-airlines.gr) Based in Thessaloniki; a newcomer flying limited routes.

Athens Airways (☎801 801 4000, 210 669 6600; www.athensairways.com) New kid on the block, but growing steadily.

Olympic Air (www.olympicair.com) Recently privatised; has the most extensive network.

Sky Express (☎281 022 3500; www.skyexpress.gr) Based in Iraklio, Crete; mainly flies routes that the big two don't.

Bicycle

Greece has very hilly terrain and the summer heat can be stifling. In addition, many drivers totally disregard the road rules.

See www.cyclegreece.gr for bicycle tour ideas; bicycles are carried for free on ferries.

Rental bicycles are available at most tourist centres, but these are generally for pedalling around town rather than for serious riding. Prices generally range from €10 to €20 per day.

Boat

FERRY

Ferries come in all shapes and sizes, from state-of-the-art 'superferries' that run on the major routes, to ageing open ferries that operate local services to outlying islands.

Newer high-speed ferries are slashing travel times, but cost much more.

'Classes' on ferries are largely a thing of the past; you have the option of 'deck class', which is the cheapest ticket, or 'cabin class' with air-con cabins and a decent lounge and restaurant.

When buying tickets you will automatically be given deck class.

Tickets can be bought at the last minute at the dock, but in high season, some boats may be full – plan ahead.

ISLAND-HOPPING

For many, the idea of meandering from island to island by boat in the Greek islands is the ultimate dream. It's still a lot of fun, but to some extent not what it used to be. Many of those slow, romantic old ferries you may have seen in the movies have disappeared, replaced by big modern people-movers. If you turn up in high season you might find it just as stressful as rush hour back home.

It's still possible to get away from it all, but it will require some thought – head to smaller islands off the beaten path before high season kicks in. Every island has a boat service of some sort.

Boat operations are highly seasonal and based on the tourist trade, so there's not a lot happening in winter. Services pick up from

Main Ferry Routes

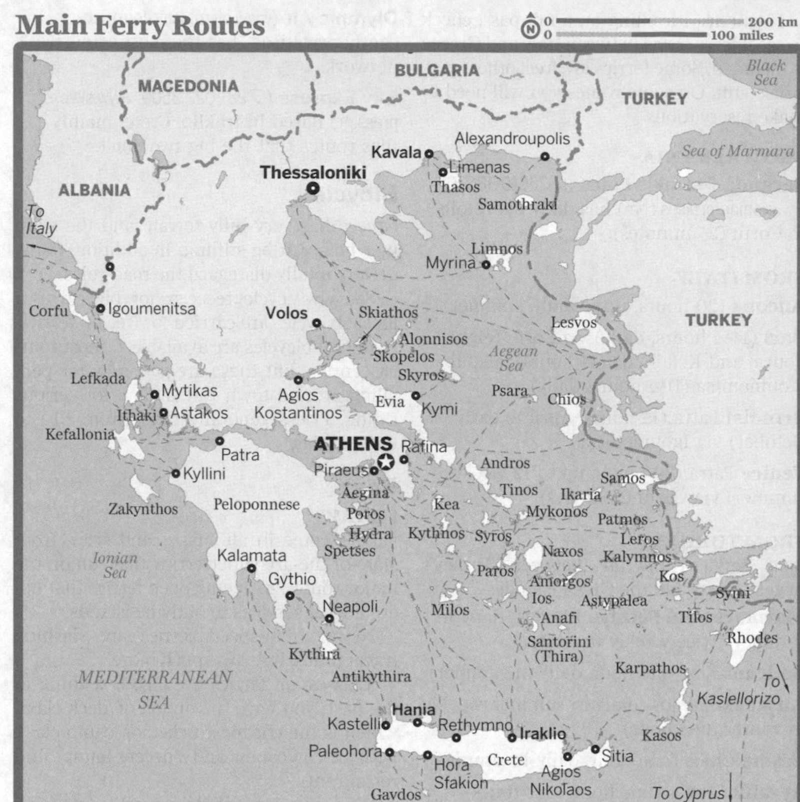

April, and during July and August Greece's seas are a mass of wake and wash.

Summer also brings the *meltemi*, a strong dry northerly wind that can blow for days and cause havoc to ferry schedules.

In any season, changes to schedules can take place at the last minute. Be prepared to be flexible. Boats seldom arrive early, but often arrive late, and some don't come at all. Think of it as part of the fun.

Check out www.openseas.gr for schedules, costs and links to individual boat company websites.

CATAMARAN

High-speed catamarans have become an important part of the island travel scene and are much less prone to cancellation in rough weather.

Catamaran fares are generally more expensive than ferries and about the same as hydrofoils.

HYDROFOIL

A faster alternative to ferries on some routes; they take half the time, but cost twice as much.

Most routes will operate only during the high season.

Tickets for hydrofoils must be bought in advance and they are often sold with seat allocation.

Bus

Long-distance buses are operated by **KTEL** (Koino Tamio Eispraxeon Leoforion; www.bus-service-crete-ktel.com/). Fares are fixed by the government; service routes can be found on the company's website. Buses are comfortable, generally run on time, reasonably priced – eg Athens–Volos (€25, five hours) and Athens–Patra (€17, three hours) – and have frequent services on all major routes. Tickets should be bought at least an hour in advance to ensure a seat. Buses don't have toilets and refreshments, but stop for a break every couple of hours.

Car & Motorcycle

Having your own wheels is a great way to explore areas in Greece that are off the beaten track, but be careful – Greece has the highest road-fatality rate in Europe. The road network has improved dramatically in recent years, but freeway tolls are fairly hefty.

Almost all islands are served by car ferries, but they are expensive; costs vary by the size of the vehicle.

The Greek automobile club, **ELPA** (www.elpa.gr), generally offers reciprocal services to members of other national motoring associations. If your vehicle breaks down, dial ☎104.

EU-registered vehicles are allowed free entry into Greece for six months without road taxes being due; a green card (international third-party insurance) is all that's required.

HIRE

Cars

Available just about anywhere in Greece; you'll get better rates with local companies than with the big multinational outfits. Check the insurance waivers closely; and check how they can assist in case of a breakdown.

High-season weekly rates start at about €280 for the smallest models, dropping to €200 in winter – add tax and extras. Major companies will request a credit-card deposit.

Minimum driving age in Greece is 18, but most car-hire firms require a driver of 21 or over.

Mopeds & Motorcycles

These are available for hire everywhere. Regulations stipulate that you need a valid motorcycle licence stating proficiency for the size of motorcycle you wish to rent – from 50cc upwards.

Mopeds and 50cc motorcycles range from €10 to €25 per day or from €25 per day for a 250cc motorcycle. Outside high season, rates drop considerably.

Check that your travel insurance covers you for injury resulting from motorcycle accidents.

ROAD RULES

» Drive on the right.

» Overtake on the left (not all Greeks do this!).

» Compulsory to wear seatbelts in the front seats, and in the back if they are fitted.

» Drink-driving laws are strict; a blood alcohol content of 0.05% incurs a fine of around €150 and over 0.08% is a criminal offence.

Public Transport

All major towns have local bus systems. Athens is the only city with a metro system.

Taxi

Taxis are widely available and reasonably priced. Yellow city cabs are metered; rates double between midnight and 5am. Grey rural taxis do not have meters; settle on a price before you get in.

Athens taxi drivers are gifted in their ability to somehow make a little bit extra with every fare. If you have a complaint, note the cab number and contact the tourist police. Rural taxi drivers are generally honest, friendly and helpful

Train

Greece's train services were in a precarious state at the time of research. Check the Greek Railways Organisation website (www.ose.gr) for the latest.

Greece has only two main lines: Athens north to Thessaloniki and Alexandroupolis, and Athens to the Peloponnese

There are a number of branch lines, eg Pyrgos–Olympia line and the spectacular Diakofto–Kalavryta mountain railway.

InterRail and Eurail passes are valid; you still need to make a reservation.

In summer make reservations at least two days in advance.

Hungary

Includes »

Budapest ... 554
Szentendre ... 565
Visegrád ... 566
Esztergom ... 566
Western Hungary ... 566
Sopron ... 566
Lake Balaton ... 567
Southern Hungary ... 569
Pécs ... 569
Great Plain ... 570
Szeged ... 570
Northeastern Hungary ... 571
Eger ... 571
Tokaj ... 572
Understand Hungary ... 573
Survival Guide ... 574

Best Places to Eat

- » Múzeum (p562)
- » Margareta (p567)
- » Áfium (p570)
- » Boci Tejivó (p571)

Best Places to Stay

- » KM Saga Guest Residence (p561)
- » Hotel Yacht Club (p568)
- » Nap Hostel (p569)
- » Wieden Panzió (p567)

Why Go?

Hungary is just the place to kick off the 'Eastern' part of your European adventure. A short hop from Vienna, this land of Franz Liszt and Béla Bartók, paprika-lashed dishes and the romantic Danube River continues to enchant visitors. The allure of Budapest, once an imperial city, is obvious at first sight and it also boasts the hottest nightlife in the region. Other cities, too, such as Pécs, the warm heart of the south, and Eger, the wine capital of the north, have much to offer travellers, as does the sprawling countryside, particularly the Great Plain, where cowboys ride and cattle roam. In Hungary you'll find all the excitement, glamour and fun of western Europe – at half the cost.

When to Go

Budapest

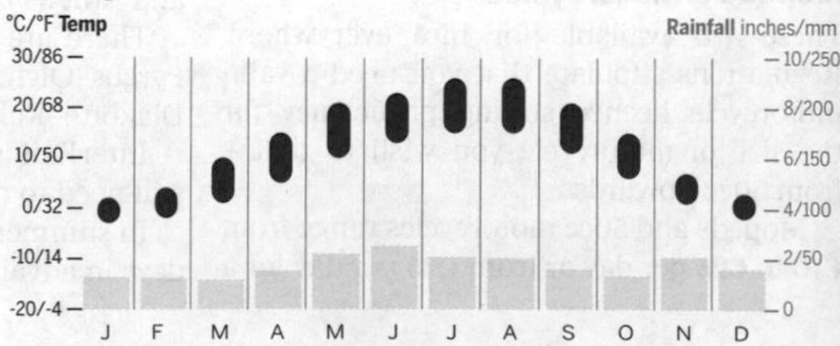

May Spring is in full swing, which means reliable weather and cool temperatures.

Jul & Aug Sunny but very hot, so decamp to the hills or Lake Balaton.

Sep & Oct Sunshine, mild temperatures and grape-harvest festivals.

Connections

Hungary's landlocked status ensures plenty of possibilities for onward travel overland. There are direct train connections from Budapest to major cities in all of Hungary's neighbours. International buses head in all directions and in the warmer months you can take a ferry along the Danube to reach Bratislava in Slovakia or Vienna in Austria.

ITINERARIES

One Week

Spend three days in Budapest, checking out the sights, baths, cafes and *romkertek* (outdoor clubs). On your fourth day take a day trip to a Danube Bend town: see the open-air museum in Szentendre or the cathedral at Esztergom. Day five can be spent getting a morning train to Pécs to see the lovely Turkish remains and many museums. On day six try some local wine in Eger, a baroque town set in wine country.

Two Weeks

In summer make sure you spend time at Lake Balaton. Keszthely is an old town with a great palace as well as a beach and Hévíz has a thermal lake. Try to see something of the Great Plain too: Szeged is a splendid university town and Kecskemét a centre of art nouveau. Finish your trip in Tokaj, home to Hungary's favourite wine.

Essential Food & Drink

» **Gulyás** (goulash) Hungary's signature dish, though here it's more like a soup than a stew and made with beef, onions and tomatoes.

» **Pörkölt** Paprika-infused stew; closer to what we would call goulash.

» **Halászlé** Highly recommended fish soup made from poached freshwater fish, tomatoes, green peppers and paprika.

» **Savanyúság** Literally 'sourness'; anything from mildly sour-sweet cucumbers to almost acidic sauerkraut, eaten with a main course.

» **Wine** Two Hungarian wines are known internationally: the sweet dessert wine Tokaji Aszú and Egri Bikavér (Eger Bull's Blood), a full-bodied red.

» **Pálinka** A strong brandy distilled from all kinds of fruit but especially plums and apricots.

AT A GLANCE

» **Currency** Forint (Ft)

» **Language** Hungarian

» **Money** ATMs abound

» **Visas** None for citizens of the EU, USA, Canada, Australia and New Zealand

Fast Facts

» **Area** 93,030 sq km

» **Capital** Budapest

» **Country code** ☎36

» **Emergency** ☎112

Exchange Rates

Australia	A$1	248Ft
Canada	C$1	234Ft
Euro Zone	€1	303Ft
Japan	¥100	252Ft
New Zealand	NZ$1	199Ft
UK	UK£1	359Ft
USA	US$1	238Ft

Set Your Budget

» **Budget hotel room** 9000Ft (15,000Ft in Budapest)

» **Two-course meal** 3500Ft (4500Ft in Budapest)

» **Museum entrance** 900Ft

» **Beer** 500Ft

» **City transport ticket** 320Ft

Resources

» **Hungarian National Tourist Office** (www.gotohungary.com)

» **Budapest Sun** (www.budapestsun.com)

» **Hungary Museums** (www.museum.hu)

BUDAPEST

☎1 / POP 1.75 MILLION

There's no other Hungarian city like Budapest in terms of size and importance. Home to almost 20% of the national population, Hungary's capital (*főváros*, or 'main city') is the nation's administrative, business and cultural centre.

But it's the beauty of Budapest – both natural and manmade – that makes it stand apart. Straddling a gentle curve in the Danube, the city is flanked by the Buda Hills to the west and the beginnings of the Great Plain to the east. Architecturally it's a gem, with enough baroque, neoclassical, eclectic and art nouveau elements to satisfy anyone.

Hungary Highlights

1. Get lost in Hungary's best nightlife, especially the bars and pubs of **Budapest** (p562)
2. Learn about the bravery of **Eger** (p571) while under Turkish attack, and how the city's Bull's Blood wine got its name
3. Absorb the Mediterranean-like climate and historic architecture of **Pécs** (p569), including its iconic **Mosque Church** (p569)
4. Take a pleasure cruise across **Lake Balaton** (p567) central Europe's largest body of fresh water
5. Ease your aching muscles in the warm waters at the thermal lake in **Hévíz** (p568), and try one of the special treatments on offer
6. Mill about with artists, free thinkers and day trippers at the too-cute-for-words artists' colony **Szentendre** (p565)

In recent years, Budapest has taken on the role of the region's party town. In the warmer months outdoor beer gardens called *romkertek* are heaving with partygoers, and the world-class Sziget Music Festival in August is a major magnet.

Sights & Activities

BUDA

Castle Hill (Várhegy) is arguably Budapest's biggest tourist draw and a first port of call for any visit to the city. Here, you'll find most of Budapest's remaining medieval buildings, the Royal Palace and sweeping views over Pest across the river.

You can walk to Castle Hill up the Király lépcső, the 'Royal Steps' that lead northwest off Clark Ádám tér, or take the Sikló, a funicular railway built in 1870 that ascends from Clark Ádám tér to Szent György tér near the Royal Palace.

Royal Palace PALACE

(Királyi Palota; Map p556; I Szent György tér) The massive former Royal Palace, razed and rebuilt at least a half-dozen times over the past seven centuries, occupies the southern end of Castle Hill. Here you'll find atmospheric medieval streets as well as the **Hungarian National Gallery** (Nemzeti Galéria; Map p556; www.mng.hu; I Szent György tér 6; adult/concession 1200/600Ft; ⌚10am-6pm Tue-Sun; 🚌16, 16/a, 116, 🚋19, 41) and the **Budapest History Museum.** (Budapesti Történeti Múzeum; Map p556; www.btm.hu; I Szent György tér 2; adult/concession 1500/750Ft; ⌚10am-6pm Tue-Sun Mar-Oct, reduced hours Nov-Feb; 🚌16, 16/a, 116, 🚋19, 41)

Matthias Church CHURCH

(Mátyás Templom; Map p556; www.matyas-templom.hu; I Szentháromság tér 2; adult/concession 1000/700Ft; ⌚9am-5pm Mon-Fri, 9am-1pm Sat, 1-5pm Sun) The pointed spire and the colourful tiled roof make neo-Gothic Matthias Church (so named because King Matthias Corvinus held both his weddings here) a Castle Hill landmark. Parts date back some 500 years, but the rest of it was designed by the architect Frigyes Schulek in 1896.

Fishermen's Bastion MONUMENT

(Halászbástya; Map p556; I Szentháromság tér; adult/concession 540/220Ft; ⌚9am-11pm mid-Mar–mid-Oct) Just east of Matthias Church, Fishermen's Bastion is another neo-Gothic folly built as a viewing platform in 1905. In front of it is an ornate equestrian statue of **St Stephen**.

FREE **Citadella** FORT

(Map p556; www.citadella.hu; ⌚24hr) Built by the Habsburgs after the 1848–49 War of Independence to defend the city from further insurrection, the Citadella was obsolete by the time it was ready in 1851 and was never used.

Liberty Monument MONUMENT

(Szabadság szobor; Map p556) The Liberty Monument – a lovely lady with a palm frond proclaiming freedom throughout the city – stands atop Gellért Hill. Some 14m high, she was raised in 1947 in tribute to the Soviet soldiers who died liberating Budapest in 1945.

TOP CHOICE **Memento Park** HISTORIC SITE

(www.mementopark.hu; XXII Balatoni út 16; adult/student 1500/1000Ft; ⌚10am-dusk) Home to almost four dozen statues, busts and plaques of Lenin, Marx and 'heroic' workers that once 'graced' the streets of Budapest, this socialist Disneyland 10km southwest of the city is a mind-blowing place. A direct bus (with park admission adult/child return 4900/3500Ft) departs from in front of the Le Meridien Budapest Hotel on Deák Ferenc tér at 11am year-round, with an extra departure at 3pm in July and August.

TOP CHOICE **Gellért Baths** BATHHOUSE

(Gellért Fürdő; Map p556; ☎466 6166; www.spasbudapest.com; XI Kelenhegyi út, Danubius Hotel Gellért; with/without private changing room 4300/3200Ft ; ⌚6am-8pm) Soaking in the art nouveau Gellért Baths, open to both men and women in separate sections but mixed on Sunday, has been likened to taking a bath in a cathedral. The eight thermal pools range in temperature from 26°C to 38°C.

PEST

TOP CHOICE **Great Synagogue** JEWISH

(Nagy zsinagóga; Map p558; ☎343 6756; www.dohanystreetsynagogue.hu; VII Dohány utca 2-8; adult/student & child 2750/2050Ft; ⌚10am-5.30pm Sun-Thu, to 4pm Fri Apr-Oct, reduced hours Nov-Mar) Northeast of the Astoria metro stop is what remains of the Jewish quarter. The twin-towered, 1859 Great Synagogue contains the **Hungarian Jewish Museum** (Magyar Zsidó Múzeum; Map p558; ☎343 6756; www.zsidomuzeum.hu; VII Dohány utca 2; synagogue & museum adult/student & child 2750/2050Ft; ⌚10am-6pm Sun-Thu, to 4pm Fri Mar-Oct, 10am-4pm Mon-Thu, to 2pm Fri Nov-Feb; Ⓜ M2 Astoria) with a harrowing exhibit on the Holocaust. Call ahead for guided tours.

Buda

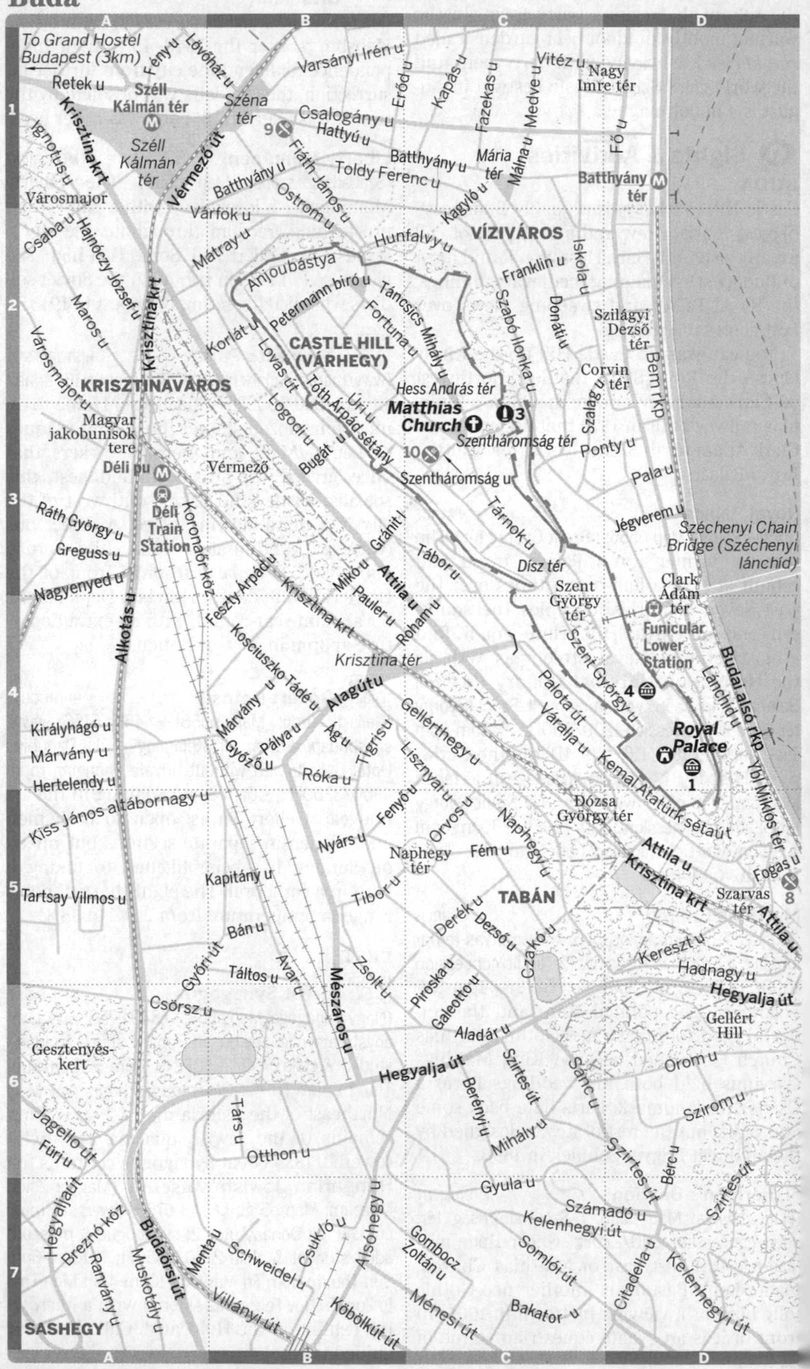
To Grand Hostel Budapest (3km)
Széll Kálmán tér
Széna tér
Városmajor
KRISZTINAVÁROS
CASTLE HILL (VÁRHEGY)
VÍZIVÁROS
Matthias Church
Hess András tér
Szentháromság tér
Batthyány tér
Szilágyi Dezső tér
Corvin tér
Magyar jakobunisok tere
Déli pu
Déli Train Station
Vérmező
Dísz tér
Szent György tér
Clark Ádám tér
Funicular Lower Station
Széchenyi Chain Bridge (Széchenyi lánchíd)
Krisztina tér
Royal Palace
Dózsa György tér
Naphegy tér
TABÁN
Szarvas tér
Gellért Hill
Gesztenyés-kert
SASHEGY
Hegyalja út
Alkotás u
Krisztina krt
Attila u
Budai alsó rkp
Bem rkp
Alagút u
Budaörsi út
Mészáros u
Kelenhegyi út
Szirtes út

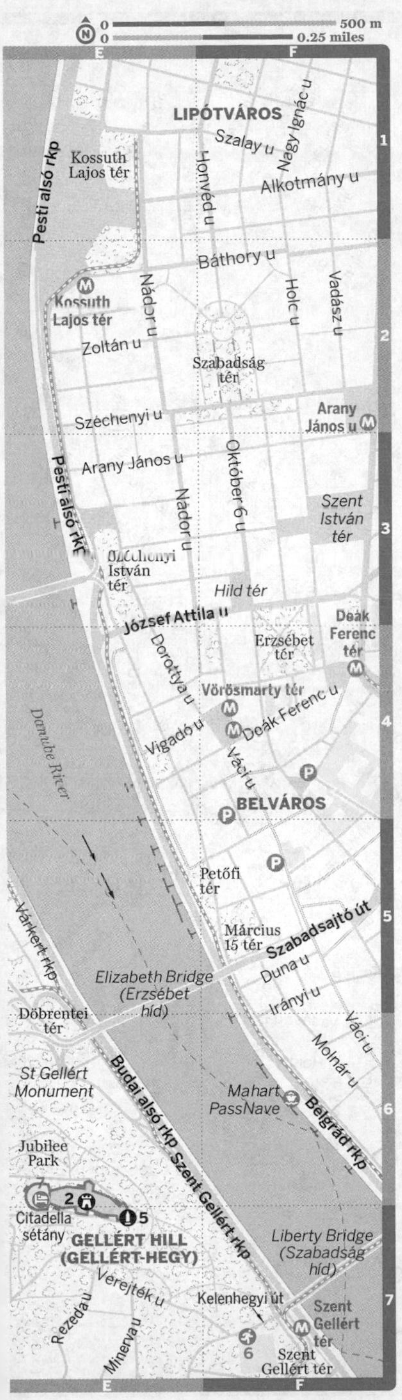

Buda

Top Sights

	Matthias Church	C3
	Royal Palace	D4

Sights

1	Budapest History Museum	D4
2	Citadella	E6
3	Fishermen's Bastion	C3
4	Hungarian National Gallery	D4
5	Liberty Monument	E7

Activities, Courses & Tours

6	Gellért Baths	F7

Sleeping

7	Citadella Hotel	E6

Eating

8	Éden	D5
9	Nagyi Palacsintázója	B1
10	Ruszwurm Cukrászda	C3

Parliament HISTORIC BUILDING
(Országház; Map p558; ☎441 4904; www.parlament.hu; V Kossuth Lajos tér 1-3; adult/concession/EU citizen 3500/1750Ft/free; ⏰8am-4pm Mon-Sat, 8am-2pm Sun) The huge, riverfront Parliament (1902) dominates Kossuth Lajos tér. English-language tours are given at 10am, noon and 2pm.

Hősök tere SQUARE
(Heroes' Sq; Map p558) At the northern end of leafy Andrássy út, this huge public space holds a sprawling monument constructed to honour the millennium, in 1896, of the Magyar conquest of the Carpathian Basin.

Museum of Fine Arts MUSEUM
(Szépművészeti Múzeum; www.mfab.hu; XIV Dózsa György út 41; adult/concession 1800/900Ft, temporary exhibitions 3800/2000Ft; ⏰10am-6pm Tue-Sun) On the northern side of Hősök tere, this gallery houses the city's outstanding collection of foreign artworks. The Old Masters collection includes seven paintings by El Greco.

City Park PARK
(Városliget; Map p558) Pest's green lung, this open space covers almost a square kilometre. It has boating on a small lake in summer and ice-skating in winter. In the park's northern corner is the **Széchenyi Baths** (Széchenyi Fürdő; ☎363 3210; www.spasbudapest.com; XIV Állatkerti út 1; ticket with locker/cabin weekdays 3400/3800Ft; weekends 3550/3950Ft;

Central Pest

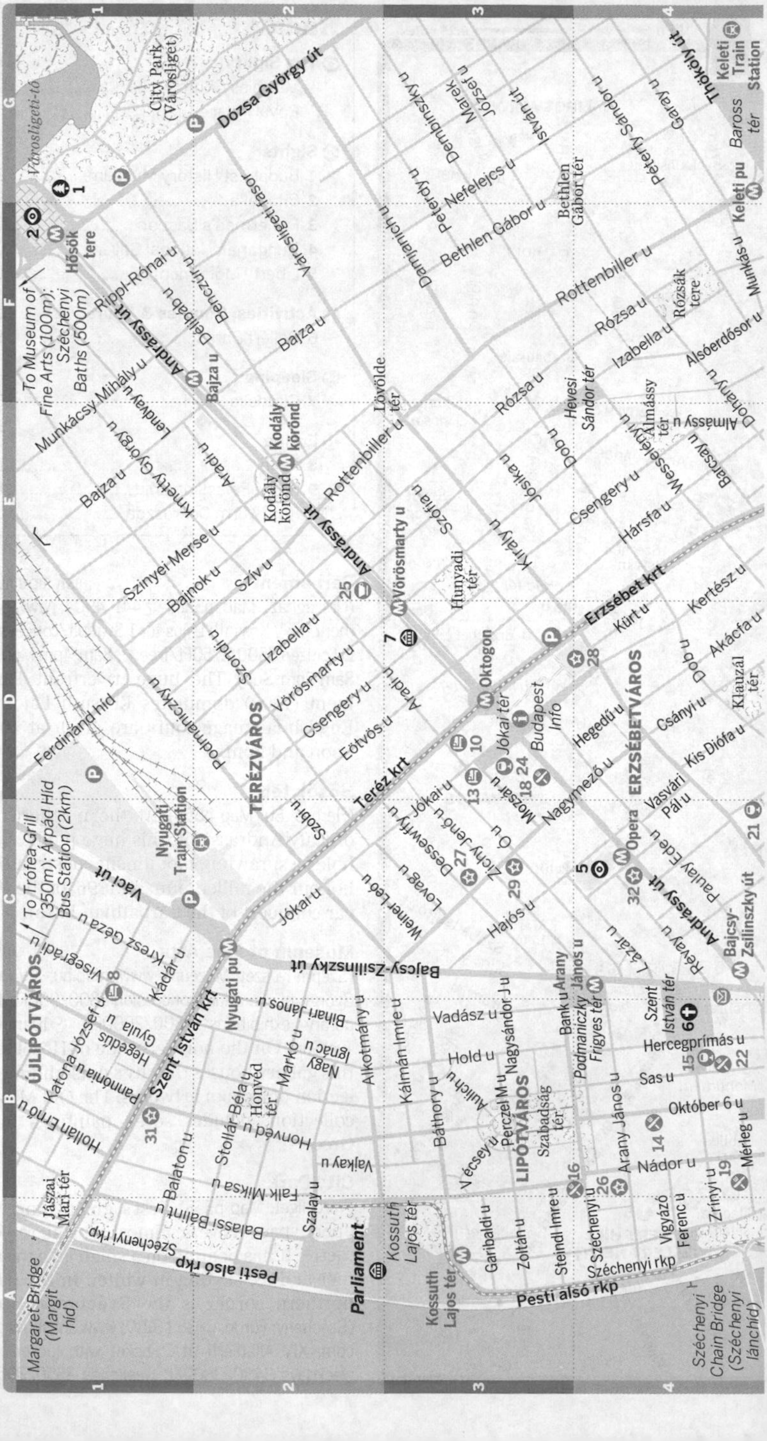

0 — 500 m
0 — 0.25 miles

A B C D E F G
1 2 3 4

Margaret Bridge (Margit híd)
Jászai Mari tér
ÚJLIPÓTVÁROS
To Trófea Grill (350m); Árpád Híd Bus Station (2km)
To Museum of Fine Arts (100m); Széchenyi Baths (500m)
Hősök tere
Városligeti-tó
City Park (Városliget)
Nyugati Train Station
Nyugati pu
TERÉZVÁROS
Kodály körönd
Parliament
Kossuth Lajos tér
Lövölde tér
Vörösmarty u
Hunyadi tér
Oktogon
Jókai tér
Budapest Info
LIPÓTVÁROS
Szabadság tér
Podmaniczky Frigyes tér
Arany János u
Szent István tér
Opera
ERZSÉBETVÁROS
Hevesi Sándor tér
Almássy tér
Bethlen Gábor tér
Rózsák tere
Klauzál tér
Bajcsy-Zsilinszky út
Keleti pu
Baross tér
Keleti Train Station
Széchenyi Chain Bridge (Széchenyi lánchíd)

Pesti alsó rkp
Széchenyi rkp
Hollán Ernő u
Katona József u
Pannónia u
Hegedűs Gyula u
Visegrádi u
Kresz Géza u
Kádár u
Váci út
Szent István krt
Balaton u
Balassi Bálint u
Falk Miksa u
Stollár Béla u
Honvéd u
Honvéd tér
Markó u
Nagy Ignác u
Bihari János u
Szalay u
Vajkay u
Alkotmány u
Kálmán Imre u
Báthory u
Garibaldi u
Vécsey u
Aulich u
Hold u
Vadász u
Perczel M u
Nagysándor J u
Zoltán u
Steindl Imre u
Bank u
Széchenyi u
Nádor u
Sas u
Hercegprímás u
Október 6 u
Vigyázó Ferenc u
Zrínyi u
Mérleg u
Ferdinánd híd
Podmaniczky u
Jókai u
Szobi u
Weiner Leó u
Lovag u
Dessewffy u
Zichy Jenő u
Ó u
Hajós u
Mozsár u
Nagymező u
Lázár u
Révay u
Andrássy út
Paulay Ede u
Vasvári Pál u
Teréz krt
Eötvös u
Csengery u
Vörösmarty u
Izabella u
Szondi u
Aradi u
Hegedű u
Csányi u
Kis Diófa u
Dob u
Erzsébet krt
Kürt u
Akácfa u
Kertész u
Szinyei Merse u
Bajnok u
Szív u
Bajza u
Kmetty György u
Munkácsy Mihály u
Lendvay u
Rippl-Rónai u
Délibáb u
Benczúr u
Rottenbiller u
Király u
Szófia u
Jósika u
Rózsa u
Hársfa u
Wesselényi u
Barcsay u
Almássy u
Dohány u
Alsóerdősor u
Munkás u
Városligeti fasor
Damjanich u
Peterdy u
Bethlen Gábor u
Nefelejcs u
Dembinszky u
Marek József u
István út
Péterfy Sándor u
Garay u
Dózsa György út
Thököly út

1 2 5 6 7 8 10 13 14 15 16 18 19 21 22 24 25 26 27 28 29 31 32

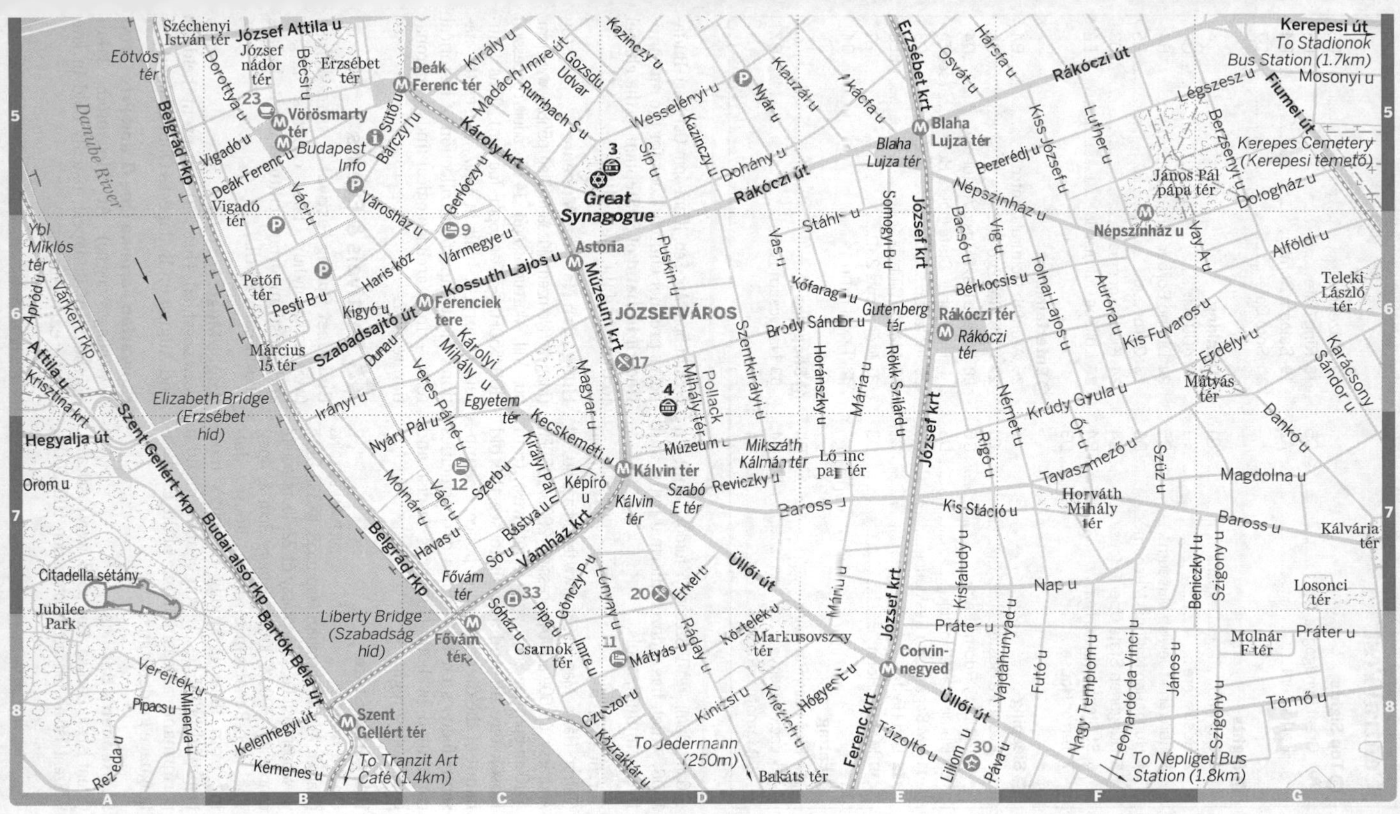

Kerepesi út
To Stadionok Bus Station (1.7km)
Mosonyi u
Fiumei út
Kerepes Cemetery (Kerepesi temető)
Dologház u
Légszesz u
Berzsenyi u
János Pál pápa tér
Alföldi u
Teleki László tér
Karácsony Sándor u
Vay A u
Népszínház u
Dankó u
Erdélyi u
Mátyás tér
Magdolna u
Baross u
Kálvária tér
Losonci tér
Práter u
Molnár F tér
Tömő u
Rákóczi út
Luther u
Auróra u
Kis Fuvaros u
Szűz u
Szigony u
Beniczky I u
János u
Leonardo da Vinci u
To Népliget Bus Station (1.8km)
Kiss József u
Tolnai Lajos u
Krúdy Gyula u
Őr u
Tavaszmező u
Horváth Mihály tér
Nap u
Nagy Templom u
Hársfa u
Pezerédj u
Népszínház u
Víg u
Bérkocsis u
Német u
Futó u
Vajdahunyad u
Osvát u
Blaha Lujza tér
Bacsó u
Rákóczi tér
Rigó u
Kis Stáció u
Kisfaludy u
Práter u
Üllői út
Páva u
Liliom u
30
Erzsébet krt
József krt
Corvin-negyed
Tűzoltó u
Somogyi B u
Gutenberg tér
Rökk Szilárd u
Ferenc krt
Mária u
Stáhly u
Kőfarag u
Bródy Sándor u
Horánszky u
Lőrinc pap tér
Baross u
Mária u
Hőgyes E u
Klauzál u
Nyár u
Vas u
Mikszáth Kálmán tér
Reviczky u
Markusovszky tér
Knézich u
Bakáts tér
Dohány u
Szentkirályi u
Üllői út
Kinizsi u
Kazinczy u
Wesselényi u
Pollack Mihály tér
JÓZSEFVÁROS
Múzeum u
Kálvin tér
Szabó E tér
Erkel u
Ráday u
To Jedermann (250m)
Síp u
Puskin u
3
Great Synagogue
Astoria
4
17
20
Lónyay u
Mátyás u
Gozsdu Udvar
Rumbach S u
Múzeum krt
Magyar u
Kecskeméti u
Képíró u
Gönczy P u
11
Imre u
Czuczor u
Közraktár u
Király u
Madách Imre út
Károly krt
Kossuth Lajos u
Királyi Pál u
Vámház krt
33
Pipa u
Csarnok tér
Deák Ferenc tér
Gerlóczy u
9
Ferenciek tere
Károlyi Mihály u
Egyetem tér
Szerb u
Bástya u
Só u
Sóház u
Fővám tér
Városház u
Vármegye u
Veres Pálné u
12
Váci u
Havas u
Barczy I u
Sütő u
Budapest Info
Haris köz
Kígyó u
Duna u
Nyáry Pál u
Molnár u
Belgrád rkp
Liberty Bridge (Szabadság híd)
Szent Gellért tér
To Tranzit Art Café (1.4km)
Erzsébet tér
József Attila u
Bécsi u
Vörösmarty tér
Petőfi tér
Pesti B u
Szabadsajtó út
Március 15 tér
Irányi u
Kemenes u
Kelenhegyi út
Bartók Béla út
Széchenyi István tér
József nádor tér
23
Dorottya u
Vigadó u
Deák Ferenc u
Vigadó tér
Elizabeth Bridge (Erzsébet híd)
Budai alsó rkp
Eötvös tér
Danube River
Szent Gellért rkp
Minerva u
Verejték u
Pipacs u
Citadella sétány
Jubilee Park
Ybl Miklós tér
Várkert rkp
Apród u
Attila u
Krisztina krt
Hegyalja út
Orom u
Rezeda u

Central Pest

Top Sights
Great Synagogue ... C5
Parliament ... A2

Sights
1 City Park ... G1
2 Hősök tere ... F1
3 Hungarian Jewish Museum ... D5
4 Hungarian National Museum ... D6
5 Hungarian State Opera House ... C4
6 St Stephen's Basilica ... B4
7 Terror House ... D3

Sleeping
8 Aventura Hostel ... C1
9 Gerlóczy Rooms Delux ... C6
10 Home-Made Hostel ... D3
11 KM Saga Guest Residence ... D8
12 Loft Hostel ... C7
13 Medosz Hotel ... D3

Eating
14 Első Pesti Rétesház ... B4
15 LaciPecsenye ... B4
16 Momotaro Ramen ... B4
17 Múzeum ... D6
18 Ring Cafe ... D3
19 Salaam Bombay ... B4
20 Soul Café ... D7

Drinking
21 400 Bar ... C4
22 DiVino Borbár ... B4
23 Gerbeaud ... B5
24 Kiadó Kocsma ... D3
25 Lukács Cukrászda ... E2

Entertainment
26 Aranytíz Cultural Centre ... B4
27 Club AlterEgo ... C3
28 Ferenc Liszt Music Academy ... D4
Hungarian State Opera House ... (see 5)
29 Instant ... C3
30 Mappa Club ... E8
31 Morrison's 2 ... B1
32 Ticket Express ... C4

Shopping
33 Nagycsarnok ... C7

6am-10pm; M1 Széchenyi fürdő), built in 1908, which has a dozen thermal baths and five swimming pools.

Terror House MUSEUM
(Terror Háza; Map p558; www.terrorhaza.hu; VI Andrássy út 60; adult/concession 2000/1000Ft; 10am-6pm Tue-Sun) Walk southwest from Hősök tere on Andrássy út to see the old haunt of the dreaded secret police. The museum focuses on the crimes and atrocities committed by both Hungary's fascist and communist regimes.

Hungarian State Opera House CULTURAL BUILDING
(Magyar Állami Operaház; Map p558; 332 8197; www.operavisit.hu; VI Andrássy út 22; tours adult/concession 3000/2000Ft; tours 3pm & 4pm) The neo-Renaissance opera house, dating from 1884, is among the city's most beautiful buildings. If you cannot attend a performance at least join one of the English-language guided tours.

St Stephen's Basilica CHURCH
(Szent István Bazilika; Map p558; www.basilica.hu; V Szent István tér; adult/concession 500/300Ft; 9am-5pm Apr-Sep, 10am-4pm Oct-Mar) Budapest's premier church. Look for the **mummified right hand** of St Stephen in the chapel to the left of the main altar.

Hungarian National Museum MUSEUM
(Magyar Nemzeti Múzeum; Map p558; www.mnm.hu; VIII Múzeum körút 14-16; adult/concession 1100/550Ft; 10am-6pm Tue-Sun) This museum, purpose-built in 1847, houses the nation's most important collection of historical relics – from archaeological finds to coronation regalia.

Festivals & Events

Budapest Spring Festival PERFORMING ARTS
(www.festivalcity.hu) The capital's largest and most important cultural event; in late March/early April.

Sziget Music Festival MUSIC
(www.sziget.hu) Huge 10-day event held in mid-August on Budapest's Óbuda Island.

Hungarian Formula One Grand Prix SPORT
(www.hungaroring.hu) At Mogyoród, 24km northeast of Budapest, usually held in late July or early August.

Sleeping

BUDA

Back Pack Guesthouse
HOSTEL €

(385 8946; www.backpackbudapest.hu; XI Takács Menyhért utca 33; beds in yurt 3000Ft, dm large/small 3800/4500Ft, d 11,000Ft; P@) A friendly and very laid-back place, though relatively small with just 50 beds. There's a lush garden in the back with a hammock stretched invitingly between trees. Take bus 7 to Tétényi út (from Keleti train station) or tram 18 to Móricz Zsigmond körtér to catch bus 7.

Citadella Hotel
HOSTEL €€

(Map p556; 466 5794; www.citadella.hu; XI Citadella sétány; dm 3200Ft, r 10,500-12,500Ft; @) This hostel in the fortress atop Gellért Hill is pretty threadbare, though the dozen guest rooms are extra large and have their own showers (toilets are on the circular corridor). The dorm room has 14 beds and shared facilities.

Grand Hostel Budapest
HOSTEL €

(www.grandhostel.hu; XII Hüvösvölgyi utca 69; dm 3600-4500Ft s/d from 8400/13,500Ft; P@) 'Grand' might be tooting its own horn a bit, but this colourful hostel does come pretty close, with its cavernlike cocktail bar, tiled rooms, communal barbecues and DJ nights. To get here, take tram 61 to the Kelemen Laszlo utca stop.

Római Camping
CAMPGROUND €

(388 7167; www.romaicamping.hu; III Szentendrei út 189; campsite for 1/2/van/caravan 4720/6000/5665/7220Ft, bungalow for 2/4 people 6000/12,000Ft; year-round; P@) Located in a leafy park north of the city, opposite a huge swimming pool complex, this is the city's largest camping ground. Take the HÉV suburban railway from the Batthyány tér metro station in Buda to the Rómaifürdő station about 900m north of the city.

PEST

Home-Made Hostel
HOSTEL €

(Map p558; 302 2103; www.homemadehostel.com; VI Teréz körút 22; dm/d from 5500/15,000Ft; @) This cosy, extremely welcoming hostel with 20 beds in four rooms has unique decor, with recycled tables hanging upside down from the ceiling, old valises serving as lockers. The old-style kitchen is also a blast from the past.

TOP CHOICE KM Saga Guest Residence
GUESTHOUSE €

(Map p558; 217 1934, 215 6883; www.km-saga.hu; IX Lónyay utca 17, 3rd fl; s €25-63, d €28-80; @) This unique place has five themed rooms, an eclectic mix of 19th-century furnishings and a hospitable, multilingual Hungarian-American owner. It's essentially a gay B&B but everyone is welcome.

Aventura Hostel
HOSTEL €€

(Map p558; 239 0789; www.aventurahostel.com; XIII Visegrádi utca 12, 1st fl; dm/d/apt 4300/15,000/18,800Ft; @) What has got to be the most chilled hostel in Budapest has four themed rooms (India, Japan, Africa and – our favourite – Space) and is run by two affable ladies in Újlipótváros.

Medosz Hotel
HOTEL €

(Map p558; 374 3000; www.medoszhotel.hu; VI Jókai tér 9; s €49-59, d €59-69; P) Well priced for its central location, the Medosz is opposite the restaurants and bars of Liszt Ferenc tér. The 68 rooms are spare but comfortable and many have been renovated.

Loft Hostel
HOSTEL €

(Map p558; 328 0916; www.lofthostel.hu; V Veres Pálné utca 19; dm 4200-5000Ft, d 13,000Ft; @) This hostel may well succeed in its loft-y aspirations to be the hottest backpacker magnet in town.The showers are among the best and it feels like staying at a friend's house. Bike rental and tours available.

Eating

BUDA

Nagyi Palacsintázója
HUNGARIAN €

(Granny's Palacsinta Place; Map p556; www.nagyipali.hu; I Hattyú utca 16; pancakes 160-680Ft;

> **SPLURGE**
>
> Just 15 individually decorated rooms await you at **Gerlóczy Rooms Delux** (Map p558; 501 4000; www.gerloczy.hu; V Gerlóczy utca 1; r €90; @), inside this revamped 1890s building. The rooms themselves are decked out in sombre shades (try to nab one of the two rooms with balconies), but it's details such as the stained glass, art nouveau touches and the original wrought-iron staircase that give the place character. Great cafe-restaurant, too.

⏲24hr; ✎) 'Granny's Palacsinta Place' serves Hungarian pancakes – both the savoury and sweet varieties – round the clock.

Éden VEGETARIAN €
(Map p556; www.edenetterem.hu; I Iskola utca 31; mains 900-1200Ft; ⏲8am-9pm Mon-Thu, 8am-6pm Fri, 11am-7pm Sun; ✎) Located in a town house just below Castle Hill, this self-service place offers solid but healthy vegan and vegetarian fare.

PEST

The **Nagycsarnok** (Great Market; Map p558; IX Vámház körút 1-3; ⏲9am-6pm Mon-Sat) is a vast historic market built of steel and glass. Head here for fruit, vegetables, deli items, fish and meat.

Ring Cafe BURGERS €
(Map p558; ☎331 5790; www.ringcafe.hu; VI Andrássy út 38; burgers 1490-3290Ft; ⏲9am-late Mon-Fri, 10am-1am Sat, 10am-10pm Sun; 📶) Along with the best burgers in town, this place serves imaginative sandwiches, salads and breakfasts. It's no wonder the place is always packed.

Első Pesti Rétesház SWEETS €€
(Map p558; ☎428 0135; www.reteshaz.com; V Október 6 utca 22; mains 2990-5990Ft; ⏲9am-11pm) It may be a bit overdone (think Magyar Disneyland) but the 'First Strudel House of Pest' is just the place to taste Hungarian stretched pastry (360Ft) filled with apple, cheese, poppy seeds or sour cherry.

Momotaro Ramen ASIAN €€
(Map p558; ☎269 3802; www.momotaroramen.com; V Széchenyi utca 16; dumplings 600-1400Ft, noodles 1150-1800Ft, mains 1800-4750Ft; ⏲11am-10.30pm Tue-Sun; ✎) This is a favourite pit stop for noodles and dumplings when *pálinka* (brandy) and other lubricants have been a-flowing the night before.

SPLURGE

Múzeum (Map p558; ☎267 0375; www.muzeumkavehaz.hu; VIII Múzeum körút 12; mains 2800-6700Ft; ⏲6pm-midnight Mon-Sat) is the place to come if you like to dine in old-world style, with a piano softly tinkling in the background. It's a cafe-restaurant that is still going strong after 125 years at the same location near the Hungarian National Museum. The goose-liver dishes are divine and there's a good selection of Hungarian wines.

LaciPecsenye HUNGARIAN €€
(Map p558; ☎333 1717; www.lacipecsenye.eu; V Sas utca 11; mains 2800-4700Ft; ⏲noon-midnight) Inside this minimalist chic bistro, the changing daily mains on black slate are largely for the carnivorous. Try anything with duck liver.

Soul Café INTERNATIONAL €
(Map p558; ☎217 6986; www.soulcafe.hu; IX Ráday utca 11-13; mains 1800-3700Ft) The Soul has inventive Continental dishes, decor and a great terrace on a street heaving with so-so restaurants and cafes.

Trófea Grill BUFFET €€
(☎270 0366; www.trofeagrill.hu; XIII Visegrádi utca 50/a; lunch weekdays/weekends 3899/5499Ft, dinner 5499Ft; ⏲noon-midnight Mon-Fri, 11.30am-midnight Sat, 11.30am-9pm Sun) This is the place to head when you *really* could eat a horse. It's an enormous buffet of more than 100 cold and hot dishes over which diners swarm like bees.

Salaam Bombay INDIAN €€
(Map p558; ☎411 1252; www.salaambombay.hu; V Mérleg utca 6; mains 1490-3900Ft; ⏲noon-3pm & 6-11pm; ✎) If you hanker after a fix of authentic curry or tandoori in a bright, upbeat environment, look no further than this attractive eatery just east of Széchenyi István tér.

Ruszwurm Cukrászda CAFE €
(Map p556; www.ruszwurm.hu; I Szentháromság utca 7; cakes 380-580Ft; ⏲10am-7pm) This is the perfect place for coffee and cakes in the Castle District, though it can get pretty crowded especially in high season.

Drinking

Budapest is loaded with pubs and bars, and there's enough variation to satisfy all tastes. In summer, the preferred drinking venues are the *romkertek*, outdoor spaces for the most part in Pest that double as beer gardens and music clubs.

BUDA

Tranzit Art Café CAFE
(www.tranzitcafe.com; XI Kosztolányi Dezső tér 7; lunch 1200Ft; ⏲9am-11pm Mon-Fri, 10am-10pm Sat & Sun) A disused bus station that now houses a friendly cafe with artwork on walls, hammocks in the green courtyard, and good breakfasts and two-course lunches.

PEST

For coffee in exquisite surroundings, two places are particularly noteworthy. **Gerbeaud** (Map p558; ☎429 9000; www.gerbeaud.hu; V Vörösmarty tér 7; cakes from 750Ft; ⏰9am-9pm; Ⓜ M1 Vörösmarty tér), Budapest's cake-and-coffee-culture king, has been at the same location serving since 1870. Or station yourself at the opulent **Lukács Cukrászda** (Map p558; www.lukacscukraszda.com; VI Andrássy út 70; ⏰9am-7.30pm) for some of the best pastries in town.

DiVino Borbár WINE BAR
(Map p558; ☎06 70 935 3980; www.divinoborbar.hu; V Szent István tér 3; ⏰4pm-midnight Sun-Wed, to 2am Thu-Sat) DiVino is Budapest's most popular wine bar and the crowds spilling out into the square in front of the basilica will immediately tell you that.

400 Bar BAR
(Map p558; www.400bar.hu; VII Kazinczy utca 52; ⏰11am-3am Mon-Wed & Sun, to 5am Thu-Sat) This large cafe-bar with an attractive terrace is in a pedestrian zone in the heart of the city. Great for coffee, cocktails and shooters.

Kiadó Kocsma PUB
(Map p558; VI Jókai tér 3; ⏰10am-1am Mon-Fri, 11am-1am Sat & Sun) The 'Pub for Rent' on two levels is a great place for a swift pint and a quick bite.

☆ Entertainment

Your best source of information in English for what's on in the city is the freebie **Budapest Funzine** (www.budapestfunzine.hu), available at hotels, bars, cinemas and wherever tourists congregate. The monthly freebie **Koncert Kalendárium** has more serious offerings: classical concerts, opera, dance and the like.

You can book almost anything online at www.jegymester.hu and www.kulturinfo.hu. Another useful booking agency is **Ticket Express** (Map p558; ☎303 030 999; www.tex.hu; VI Andrássy út 18; ⏰10am-6.30pm Mon-Fri, to 3pm Sat), the largest ticket office network in the city.

Performing Arts

Hungarian State Opera House OPERA
(Magyar Állami Operaház; Map p558; ☎bookings 814 7225; www.opera.hu; VI Andrássy út 22) Take in a performance while admiring the incredibly rich interior decoration of this sublime building. The ballet company performs here as well.

Ferenc Liszt Music Academy CLASSICAL MUSIC
(Liszt Ferenc Zeneakadémia; Map p558; ☎342 0179; www.zeneakademia.hu; VI Liszt Ferenc tér 8) Budapest's premier venue for classical concerts is not just a place to hear music but to ogle at the wonderful decorative Zsolnay porcelain and frescos as well.

Aranytíz Cultural Centre TRADITIONAL MUSIC
(Aranytíz Művelődési Központ; Map p558; ☎354 3400; www.aranytiz.hu; V Arany János utca 10; ⏰bookings 2-9pm Mon & Wed, 9am-3pm Sat) The wonderful Kalamajka Táncház, one of the best music and dance shows in town, has folk-music programs here from 8.30pm on Saturday.

Nightclubs

Mappa Club CLUB
(Map p558; http://mappaclub.com; IX Lilliom utca 41) An arty crowd and some of the best DJs in town make the scene here a must for visitors as well as locals.

Morrison's 2 CLUB
(Map p558; ☎374 3329; www.morrisons.hu; V Szent István körút 11; ⏰5pm-4am Mon-Sat) Far and away Budapest's biggest party venue, this cellar club attracts a younger crowd with its four dance floors and half-dozen bars. Live bands from 9pm to 11pm in the week.

Instant CLUB
(Map p558; ☎06 30 830 8747; www.instant.co.hu; VI Nagymező utca 38; ⏰1pm-3am) This cavernous space on Pest's most vibrant nightlife strip counts five bars on three levels with underground DJs and dance parties.

Club AlterEgo GAY
(Map p558; www.alteregoclub.hu; VI Dessewffy utca 33; ⏰10pm-6am Fri & Sat) Budapest's premier gay club, with the biggest crowd and the best dance music.

🛍 Shopping

TOP CHOICE **Eceseri Piac** MARKET
(XIX Nagykőrösi út 156; ⏰6am-4pm Mon-Fri, to 3pm Sat, 8am-1pm Sun) One of the biggest flea markets in central Europe; Saturday is said to be the best day. Take the red-numbered express bus 84E, 89E or 94E from the Határ út stop on the M3 metro line and get off at the Fiume utca stop, then follow the crowds.

WANT MORE?

For in-depth information, reviews and recommendations at your fingertips, head to the Apple App Store to purchase Lonely Planet's *Budapest City Guide* iPhone app.

Alternatively, head to www.lonelyplanet.com/hungary/budapest for planning advice, author recommendations, traveller reviews and insider tips.

Information

Discount Cards

Budapest Card (www.budapestinfo.hu; 24/48/72hr card 3900/7900/9900Ft) Access to many museums, unlimited public transport and discounts on tours and other services.

Internet Access

Most hostels and hotels offer wi-fi free of charge. Use of a terminal will cost 200Ft to 400Ft per hour.

Medical Services

FirstMed Centers (24hr emergency hotline 224 9090; www.firstmedcenters.com; I Hattyú utca 14, 5th fl; 8am-8pm Mon-Fri, to 2pm Sat) On call 24/7 for emergencies. Expensive.

SOS Dent (269 6010; www.smilistic.com; VI Király utca 14; 24hr) Round-the-clock dental surgery.

Teréz Gyógyszertár (311 4439; VI Teréz körút 4; 8am-8pm Mon-Fri, to 2pm Sat) Central pharmacy.

Money

There are ATMs everywhere, including in the train and bus stations and at the airport. Moneychangers (particularly those along Váci utca) don't tend to give good rates.

Post

Main Post Office (V Bajcsy-Zsilinsky út 16; 8am-8pm Mon-Fri, to 2pm Sat) A few minutes' walk from central Deák Ferenc tér.

Tourist Information

Budapest Info (Map p558; 438 8080; V Sütő utca 2; 8am-8pm) Also has an **Oktogon branch** (Map p558; VI Liszt Ferenc tér 11; 10am-6pm Mon-Fri; M1 Oktogon, 4, 6) and desks in the arrivals sections of Ferenc Liszt International Airport's Terminals 1, 2A and 2B.

Getting There & Away

Boat

Hydrofoils to Bratislava and Vienna run by **Mahart PassNave** (www.mahartpassnave.hu) from May to late September arrive at and depart from the **International Ferry Pier** (Nemzetközi hajóállomás; 318 1223; V Belgrád rakpart). For details see p576. For information on ferry services to the towns of the Danube Bend, see p565.

Bus

Volánbusz (382 0888; www.volanbusz.hu), the national bus line, has an extensive list of destinations from Budapest. All international buses and some buses to/from western Hungary use **Népliget bus station** (219 8030; IX Üllői út 131). **Stadionok bus station** (220 6227; XIV Hungária körút 48-52) generally serves places to the east of Budapest.

Most buses to the Danube Bend arrive at and leave from the **Árpád híd bus station** (412 2597; XIII Árbóc utca 1, off XIII Róbert Károly körút) though some now leave from the small suburban bus terminal next to **Újpest-Városkapu train station** (XIII Arva utca, off Váci út) on the M3 blue metro line. All stations are on metro lines. If the ticket office is closed, you can buy your ticket on the bus.

Car & Motorcycle

All major international rental firms, including **Avis** (318 4240; www.avis.hu; V Arany János utca 26-28; 7am-6pm Mon-Sat, 8am-6pm Sun), **Budget** (214 0420; www.budget.hu; VII Krisztina körút 41-43, Hotel Mercure Buda; 8am-8pm Mon-Fri, to 6pm Sat & Sun) and **Europcar** (505 4400; www.europcar.hu; V Erzsébet tér 7-8; 8am-6pm Mon & Fri, to 4.30pm Tue-Thu, to noon Sat), have offices in Budapest and at the airport. The best independent rental company with highly competitive rates is **Fox Autorent** (382 9000; www.foxautorent.com; VII Hársfa utca 53-55, Building I, ground floor; 8am-6pm), which also has an office at the airport. Its compact cars cost from €35/170 per day/week.

Train

Hungarian State Railways (MÁV) runs the country's extensive rail network. Contact **MÁV-Start passenger service centre** (512 7921; www.mav-start.hu; V József Attila utca 16; 9am-6pm Mon-Fri) for 24-hour information on domestic train departures and arrivals. Its website has a useful timetable in English for planning routes.

Buy tickets at one of Budapest's three main train stations. Always confirm your departure station when you buy your tickets, since stations can vary depending on the train.

Keleti train station (Eastern Train Station; VIII Kerepesi út 2-4) handles most international trains as well as domestic ones from the north and northeast. For some international destinations (eg Romania), as well as domestic ones to/from the Danube Bend and Great Plain, head for

Nyugati train station (Western Train Station; VI Nyugati tér). For trains bound for Lake Balaton and the south, go to **Déli train station** (Southern Train Station; I Krisztina körút 37). All three stations are on metro lines.

ℹ Getting Around

To/From the Airport

The **Airport Shuttle Minibusz** (☎296 8555; www.airportshuttle.hu; one way/return 3200/5500Ft) ferries passengers in nine-seat vans from the the airport directly to the place you're staying. Tickets are available at a clearly marked desk in the arrivals hall, though you may have to wait while the van fills up.

The cheapest (but slowest) way to get into the city centre is to take city bus 200E (320Ft), which terminates at the Kőbánya-Kispest metro station. From there, take the M3 metro (320Ft) into town.

Public Transport

Public transport is run by **BKV** (Budapest Transport Company; ☎258 4636; www.bkv.hu). The three underground metro lines (M1 yellow, M2 red, M3 blue) meet at Deák tér in Pest; the long-awaited green M4 will open in 2014. The **HÉV** suburban railway runs north from Batthyány tér in Buda. Travel cards are only good on the HÉV within the city limits (south of the Békásmegyer stop).

There's also an extensive network of buses, trams and trolleybuses. Public transport operates from 4.30am until 11.30pm and some 40 night buses run along main roads. Tram 6 on the Big Ring Road now runs around the clock.

A single ticket for all forms of transport is 320Ft (60 minutes of uninterrupted travel on the same metro, bus, trolleybus or tram line *without* transferring/changing); a book of 10 tickets is 2800Ft. A transfer ticket (490Ft) is valid for one trip with one validated transfer within 90 minutes.

The three-day travel card (3850Ft) or the seven-day pass (4600Ft) makes things easier, allowing unlimited travel inside the city limits. Keep your ticket or pass handy; the fine for riding 'black' is 8000Ft on the spot, or 16,000Ft if you pay later at the **BKV office** (☎461 6800; VII Akácfa utca 22; ⏰6am-8pm Mon-Fri, 8am-1.45pm Sat).

Taxi

Taxi drivers overcharging foreigners in Budapest has been a problem since time immemorial. Never get into a taxi that lacks an official yellow licence plate, the logo of the taxi firm and a visible table of fares. Reliable companies include **City Taxi** (☎211 1111; www.citytaxi.hu), **Főtaxi** (☎222 2222; www.fotaxi.hu) and **Rádió Taxi** (☎377 7777; www.radiotaxi.hu).

AROUND BUDAPEST

North of Budapest, the Danube breaks through the Pilis and Börzsöny Hills in a sharp bend before continuing along the Slovak border. The Roman Empire had its northern border here, and medieval kings ruled Hungary from majestic palaces overlooking the river at Esztergom and Visegrád. Szentendre, full of museums and galleries, was once a thriving art colony.

ℹ Getting There & Away

Regular buses serve towns on the west bank of the Danube, but trains only go as far as Szentendre, with a separate line running to Esztergom.

The river itself is a perfect highway during the warmer months. From May to September, a **Mahart PassNave** (www.mahartpassnave.hu) ferry departs Budapest's Vigadó tér at 10am Tuesday to Sunday bound for Szentendre (one way/return 1590/2390Ft, 1½ hours), returning at 5pm; the service runs on Saturday only in April.

Between May and late August there's a ferry from Vigadó tér at 9am, calling at Visegrád (noon; 1790/2690Ft) before carrying on to Esztergom (1.45pm; 1990/2990Ft). It returns from Esztergom/Visegrád at 4.45/5.50pm, reaching Budapest at 8pm. The service is reduced to Saturday only in April and September.

Hydrofoils travel from Budapest to Visegrád (one way/return 2690/3990Ft, one hour) and Esztergom (one way/return 3990/5990Ft, 1½ hours) on Friday, Saturday and Sunday from early May to September; boats leave at 9.30am and return at 5pm from Esztergom and 5.30pm from Visegrád.

Szentendre

☎26 / POP 26,000

Once an artists' colony, now a popular day trip 19km north of Budapest, pretty little Szentendre (*sent*-en-dreh) has narrow, winding streets, a plethora of Serbian churches and host of souvenir and craft shops. The **Tourinform** (☎317 966; www.iranyszentendre.hu; Dumtsa Jenő utca 22; ⏰9.30am-4.30pm Mon-Fri, 10am-2pm Sat & Sun) office hands out maps and info about the town and region.

Just 5km to the northwest is the enormous **Hungarian Open-Air Ethnographical Museum** (Magyar Szabadtéri Néprajzi Múzeum; ☎502 500; www.skanzen.hu; Sztaravodai út; adult/student 1500/750Ft, on festival days 1600/800Ft; ⏰9am-5pm Tue-Sun Apr-Oct, 10am-4pm Sat & Sun Nov–early Dec & Feb-Mar). Walking through reassembled cottages, farms and workshops from around the country will show you what life was – and sometimes still is – like in rural Hungary. Reach it on bus 230 from bay/stop 7 at the bus station next to Szentendre's train station.

The most convenient way to get to Szentendre is to take the HÉV suburban train from Buda's Batthyány tér metro station (630Ft, 40 minutes, every 10 to 20 minutes).

Visegrád

☎26 / POP 1860

The spectacular vista from what remains of the medieval fortress in Visegrád (*vish*-eh-grahd), high on a hill above a curve in the Danube, is what pulls visitors to this sleepy town.

After the Mongol invasions in the 13th century, Hungarian kings built the mighty **Visegrád Citadel** (Visegrádi Fellegvár; ☎598 080; adult/child & student 1400/700Ft; ⏲9am-5pm mid-Mar–Apr & Oct, to 6pm May-Sep, to 4pm Nov-Mar). It's a bit of a climb, but the views are well worth it. The **Royal Palace** (Királyi Palota; ☎597 010; www.visegradmuzeum.hu; Fő utca 29; adult/concession 1100/550Ft; ⏲9am-5pm Tue-Sun) stands on the flood plain at the foot of the hills, closer to the centre of town.

No train line reaches Visegrád, but buses are very frequent (745Ft, 1¼ hours, hourly) to/from Budapest's Újpest-Városkapu train station, Szentendre (465Ft, 45 minutes, every 45 minutes) and Esztergom (560Ft, 45 minutes, hourly).

Esztergom

☎33 / POP 30,850

It's easy to see the attraction of Esztergom – especially from a distance. The city's massive basilica, sitting high above the town and Danube River, is an incredible sight that rises magnificently from its rural setting.

But the significance of this town is even greater than its architectural appeal. The 2nd-century Roman emperor-to-be Marcus Aurelius wrote his famous *Meditations* while he camped here. In the 10th century, Stephen I, founder of the Hungarian state, was born and crowned at the cathedral. From the late 10th to mid-13th centuries Esztergom served as the Hungarian royal seat.

Hungary's largest church is **Esztergom Basilica** (Esztergomi Bazilika; ☎402 354; www.bazilika-esztergom.hu; Szent István tér 1; admission free; ⏲8am-6pm Apr-Sep, to 4pm Oct-Mar). At the southern end of the hill is the extensive **Castle Museum** (Vármúzeum ; ☎415 986; www.mnmvarmuzeuma.hu; Szent István tér 1; adult/concession 1800/900Ft, courtyard only 500/250Ft; ⏲10am-6pm Tue-Sun Apr-Sep, to 4pm Tue-Sun Oct-Mar), with archaeological finds from the 2nd and 3rd centuries.

Frequent buses run to/from Budapest (930Ft, 1½ hours), Visegrád (560Ft, 45 minutes) and Szentendre (930Ft, 1½ hours). Trains depart from Budapest's Nyugati train station (1120Ft, 1½ hours) at least hourly.

WESTERN HUNGARY

A visit to this region is a boon for anyone wishing to see remnants of Hungary's Roman legacy, medieval heritage and baroque splendour. Taking centre stage here is 600-sq-km Lake Balaton, Hungary's inland 'seaside', offering swimming, sailing, sunbathing and fishing during the warmer months.

Sopron

☎99 / POP 60,800

Sopron (*showp*-ron) is an attractive border town with a history that stretches back to Roman times. It has well-preserved ancient ruins and a fetching medieval square, bounded by the original town walls. **Tourinform** (☎517 560; sopron@tourinform.hu; Liszt Ferenc utca 1, Ferenc Liszt Conference & Cultural Centre; ⏲9am-6pm Mon-Fri, to 7pm Sat & Sun mid-Jun–Aug, shorter hours rest of year) offers free internet access and a plethora of tourist information.

Sights & Activities

Fő tér SQUARE

Fő tér is the main square in Sopron; there are several museums, monuments and churches scattered around it, including the massive **Firewatch Tower** (Tűztorony; Fő tér), a 60m-high tower rising above the Old Town's **Fidelity Gate** (Fő tér).

The tower is a true architectural hybrid: the 2m-thick square base, built on a Roman gate, dates from the 12th century; the middle cylindrical and arcaded balcony was built in the 16th century; and the baroque spire was added in 1680.

In the centre of the square is the **Trinity Column** (Szentháromság oszlop; Fő tér), which dates from 1701 and is among the finest ex-

HUNGARY VISEGRÁD

amples of a 'plague pillar' in Hungary. Just off the square, along the town wall, are some small **open-air ruins** (Szabadtéri rom) dating from when Sopron was the Roman outpost Scarbantia.

Sleeping & Eating

Wieden Panzió GUESTHOUSE €€
(☎523 222; www.wieden.hu; Sas tér 13; s/d from 7000/9900Ft; 📶) Sopron's cosiest pension is located in an attractive old town house within easy walking distance of the inner town. Rooms are spacious and bright, and the friendly staff are especially helpful.

Jégverem Fogadó GUESTHOUSE €
(☎510 113; www.jegverem.hu; Jégverem utca 1; s/d 6900/8900Ft; 📶) An excellent and central bet, with five suitelike rooms in an 18th-century ice cellar. Even if you're not staying here, try the terrace restaurant for its enormous portions.

Stubi HUNGARIAN €
(Balfi utca 16; meals 600-1000Ft; ⏰noon-9pm) This is very much a local place for local people. Stick with the Hungarian-style daily specials – *gulyás* (goulash), noodles with crushed poppy seeds and so on.

Getting There & Away

BUS Bus travel to and from Budapest involves lengthy transfers/changes and is not recommended.

TRAIN Trains run to Budapest's Keleti train station (4200Ft, three hours, eight daily) via Győr. Local trains link Sopron with Wiener Neustadt (2800Ft, 40 minutes, 34km, hourly) in Austria, where you change for Vienna.

Lake Balaton

Central Europe's largest expanse of fresh water is Lake Balaton, covering 600 sq km. The main activities here include swimming, sailing and sunbathing, but the lake is also popular with cyclists lured here by more than 200km of marked bike paths that encircle the lake.

KESZTHELY

☎83 / POP 21,000

At the western end of Lake Balaton sits Keszthely (*kest*-hey) with its amazing palace and popular public beaches. The town centre lies about 1km northwest of the lake. Summer activity centres on 'managed' (paid-admission) beaches, waterfront parks and cafes near the ferry pier. The **Tourinform** (☎314 144; keszthely@tourinform.hu; Kossuth Lajos utca 28; ⏰9am-8pm Mon-Fri, to 6pm Sat mid-Jun–mid-Sep, 9am-5pm Mon-Fri, to 12.30pm Sat mid-Sep–mid-Jun) office here has information on the whole Lake Balaton area.

Sights & Activities

TOP CHOICE **Festetics Palace** PALACE
(Festetics Kastély; ☎312 190; www.helikonkastely.hu; Kastély utca 1; Palace & Coach Museum adult/concession 2300/1150Ft; ⏰9am-9pm Jul & Aug, 10am-4pm May, Jun & Sep, reduced hours & closed Mon Oct-Apr) The glimmering white, 100-room Festetics Palace was first built in 1745; the wings were extended out from the original building 150 years later. About a dozen rooms in the baroque south wing have been turned into the **Helikon Palace Museum** (Helikon Kastélymúzeum). Also here is the palace's greatest treasure, the **Helikon Library** (Helikon Könyvtár).

Lakeside Area BEACH
Keszthely's best beaches for swimming or sunbathing are **City Beach** (Városi Strand), which is close to the ferry pier, and reedy **Helikon Beach** (Helikon Strand; adult/child 500/350Ft, 3 days 1050/840Ft; ⏰8am-6pm mid-May mid Sept) further south. There's windsurfing and kitesurfing rental at City Beach in summer. You can take a one-hour **pleasure cruise** (☎312 093; www.balatonihajozas.hu; ferry pier; ⏰adult/concession 1500/650Ft) several times daily from late March to late October.

Sleeping & Eating

Tourinform can help find private rooms to rent (from 3500Ft per person).

Ambient Hostel HOSTEL €
(☎06 30 460 3536; http://keszthely-szallas.fw.hu; Sopron utca 10; dm/d from 3600/7900Ft; @) Only a short walk north of Festetics Palace is this hostel with basic, cheap dorm rooms, each of which comes with its own bathroom. There's also a modern roadside cafe.

TOP CHOICE **Margareta** HUNGARIAN €
(www.margaretaetterem.hu; Bercsényi utca 60; mains 1400-3200Ft; ⏰11am-10pm) Margareta is no beauty, but the wraparound porch and hidden backyard terrace is heaving in the warmer months and the small interior packs them in the rest of the year. Food sticks to the basic-but-hearty Hungarian staples (and your ribs).

WORTH A TRIP

HÉVÍZ

Hévíz (population 4335), just 8km northwest of Keszthely, is the most famous of Hungary's spa towns because of the **Gyógy-tó** (Hevíz Thermal Lake; ☎501 700; www.spaheviz.hu; 3hr/5hr/day 2500/2800/3800Ft; ⏲8am-7pm Jun-Aug, 9am-6pm May & Sep, 9am-5pm Apr & Oct, 9am-4pm Mar & Nov-Feb), Europe's largest 'thermal lake'. A dip into this water-lily-filled lake is essential for anyone visiting the Lake Balaton region.

It's an astonishing sight: a surface of almost 4.5 hectares in the Park Wood, covered for most of the year in pink and white lotuses. The source is a spring spouting from a crater some 40m below ground that disgorges up to 80 million litres of warm water a day, renewing itself every 48 hours or so. The surface temperature averages 33°C and never drops below 22°C in winter, allowing for bathing throughout the year.

A covered bridge leads to the thermal lake's *fin-de-siècle* central pavilion, which contains showers, changing rooms and steps down into the lake.

Buses link Hevíz with Keszthely (250Ft, 15 minutes) almost every half-hour.

Getting There & Away

BUS There are seven buses a day to Budapest (3410Ft, three hours, seven daily).

FERRY From April to September **Balaton Shipping** (www.balatonihajozas.hu) runs ferries to towns on the lake.

TRAIN Keszthely is on a railway branch line linking the lake's southeastern shore with Budapest (3410Ft, four hours, six daily).

SIÓFOK

☎84 / POP 24,350

Siófok (*shee*-oh-fok) is Hungary's unofficial summer capital. In July and August nowhere on the lake parties as hard or stays up as late as this resort town. At other time it's a sleepy lakeside town.

The bus and train stations are in Millennium Park, just off Fő utca, the main drag. **Tourinform** (☎310 117; tourinform@siofokportal.hu; Fő utca 174-176; ⏲8am-7pm Mon-Fri, 10am-7pm Sat & Sun mid-Jun–mid-Sep, 8am-4pm Mon-Fri, 9am-noon Sat mid-Sep–mid-Jun) hands out city maps and can advise on and book rooms in season.

Sights & Activities

FREE Water Tower HISTORICAL BUILDING
(Víztorony; Fő utca 174-176) The wooden water tower, built in 1912, affords an impressive view. It now houses Tourinform.

Nagy Strand BEACH
(Big Beach; adult/concession 1000/500Ft; ⏲8am-7pm) Nagy Strand is centre stage on Petőfi sétány. There are many more managed swimming areas along the lakeshore, which cost about the same.

Sleeping & Eating

Prices quoted here are for high season (July and August). Tourinform can help find a private room starting at about 4000Ft per person.

Hotel Yacht Club BOUTIQUE HOTEL €€
(☎311 161; www.hotel-yachtclub.hu; Vitorlás utca 14; s/d from €55/115; ❄@📶≋) Overlooking the harbour is this excellent little hotel, with cosy rooms and an inviting wellness centre. Bicycles can be rented.

Siófok Város College HOSTEL €
(☎312 244; www.siofokvaroskollegiuma.sulinet.hu; Petőfi sétány 1; dm 2800Ft) Situated close to the action in central Siófok, this college accommodation is hard to beat for price and location.

Roxy INTERNATIONAL €
(Szabadság tér; mains 1300-3000Ft) This pseudo-rustic pub-restaurant on busy Szabadság tér attracts diners with its wide range of international cuisine and surprisingly imaginative Hungarian mains.

Drinking & Entertainment

Renegade BAR
(Petőfi sétány 9) Wild pub near the beach where tabletop dancing and live music are the norm.

Palace CLUB
(www.palace.hu; Deák Ferenc utca 2) Hugely popular club on the Silver Coast, the area to the west of Siofok proper. Accessible by free bus from outside Tourinform between 9pm and 5am daily from mid-May to mid-September.

Getting There & Away

BUS & TRAIN Up to five daily buses and eight trains run to and from Budapest (2200Ft, two hours).

FERRY From April to October **Balaton Shipping** (Balatoni Hajózási Rt; ☎84-310 050; www.balatonihajozas.hu; Krúdy sétány 2, Siófok) passenger ferries run between Siófok and towns along the lake.

SOUTHERN HUNGARY

Southern Hungary is a region of calm; a place to savour life at a slower pace. It's not overly touristed and travelling through the countryside can be like stepping back in time.

Pécs

☎72 / POP 157,700

Blessed with a mild climate, an illustrious past and a number of fine museums and monuments, Pécs (*paich*) is one of the most pleasant and interesting cities to visit in Hungary. Many travellers put it second only to Budapest on their must-see list.

Tourinform (☎213 315; baranya-m@tourinform.hu; Széchenyi tér 9; ⊙9am-5pm Mon-Fri & 10am-3pm Sat & Sun Jun-Aug, closed Sun May, Sep & Oct, closed Sat & Sun Nov-Apr) has heaps of local info available. The train station is a little over 1km south of the centre. The bus station is nearby, a few blocks closer to the centre.

Sights & Activities

TOP CHOICE **Mosque Church** MOSQUE
(Mecset templom; Széchenyi tér; adult/concession 750/500Ft; ⊙10am-4pm mid-Apr–mid-Oct, to noon mid-Oct–mid-Apr, shorter hours Sun) The erstwhile Pasha Gazi Kassim Mosque is now the Inner Town Parish Church (Belvárosi plébánia templom), but it's more commonly referred to as the Mosque Church. It has become the very symbol of Pécs.

Synagogue SYNAGOGUE
(Zsinagóga; Kossuth tér; adult/concession 600/400Ft; ⊙10am-noon & 12.45-5pm Sun-Fri May-Oct) Pécs' beautifully preserved 1869 synagogue is south of Széchenyi tér.

Basilica of St Peter CHURCH
(Szent Péter bazilika; Dóm tér; adult/concession 900/600Ft; ⊙9am-5pm Mon-Sat, 1-5pm Sun) The foundations of this four-towered basilica date from the 11th century and the side chapels are from the 1300s. But most of what you see of the neo-Romanesque structure today is the result of renovations carried out in 1881. Nearby are the 1770 **Bishop's Palace** (Püspöki palota; ☎513 030; Szent István tér 23; adult/child 1900/1000Ft; ⊙tours 2pm, 3pm & 4pm Thu late Jun–mid-Sep) and a 15th-century **barbican** (Barbakán; Esze Tamás utca 2; ⊙garden 7am-8pm May-Sep, 9am-5pm Oct-Apr).

Cella Septichora Visitors Centre RUINS
(Cella Septichora látogatóközpont; www.pecsorokseg.hu; Janus Pannonius utca; adult/concession 1200/600Ft; ⊙10am-6pm Tue-Sun) On the southern side of Dom tér is the Cella Septichora Visitors Centre, which illuminates a series of early Christian burial sites that have been on Unesco's World Heritage list since 2000. The highlight is the so-called **Jug Mausoleum** (Korsós sírkamra; adult/child 300/150Ft; ⊙10am-6pm Tue-Sun), a 4th-century Roman tomb whose name comes from a painting of a large drinking vessel with vines.

TOP CHOICE **Csontváry Museum** MUSEUM
(☎310 544; Janus Pannonius utca 11; adult/child 1500/750Ft; ⊙10am-6pm, closed Mon) This museum exhibits the works of the 19th-century painter Tivadar Kosztka Csontváry (1853–1919), a unique symbolist artist whose tragic life is often compared with that of his contemporary Vincent van Gogh.

Sleeping

In July and August more than a dozen of the city's colleges open up their doors to travellers, and prices average 4000Ft to 6000Ft for a dorm bed; Tourinform has the complete list.

Hotel Főnix HOTEL €€
(☎311 682; www.fonixhotel.hu; Hunyadi János út 2; s/d from 8200/14,000Ft; ❄@🛜) Főnix appears to be a hotel too large for the land it's built on and some of the 16 rooms and suites are not even big enough to swing a, well, phoenix in. Try to bag a room with a balcony; the Mosque Church is just within reach.

Hotel Diána GUESTHOUSE €€
(☎328 594; www.hoteldiana.hu; Tímár utca 4/a; s/d/tr from 11,350/16,350/20,350Ft; ❄@) This very central hotel-cum-guesthouse offers 20 spotless rooms, comfortable kick-off-your-shoes decor and a warm welcome.

Nap Hostel HOSTEL €
(☎950 684; www.naphostel.com; Király utca 23-25; dm/d from 2800/12,350Ft; @🛜) Clean, friendly hostel has dorms and a double room on the 1st floor of a former bank. There's also a large kitchen. Enter from Szent Mór utca.

Eating & Drinking

Áfium BALKAN €

(☎511 434; Irgalmasok utca 2; mains 1500-2200Ft; ⏲11am-1am) With Croatia and Serbia so close, it's a wonder that more restaurants don't offer cuisine from south of the border. Don't miss the bean soup with trotters.

Az Elefánthoz ITALIAN €€

(☎216 055; www.elefantos.hu; Jókai tér 6; mains 2600-4500Ft, pizza 1400-2600Ft) With its welcoming terrace overlooking Jókai tér, and quality Italian dishes, this place is a sure bet for first-rate food in the centre. It has a wood-fired stove for pizzas.

Drinking & Entertainment

Korhely Pub TAVERNA

(☎535 916; Boltív köz 2) This outrageously popular *csapszék* (tavern) with the in-your-face name of 'Drunkard' has peanuts on the table, shells on the floor, a half-dozen beers on tap and a retro feel.

Varázskert CLUB

(Király utca 65; ⏲6pm-3am summer) Big open-air beer garden and late-hours music club at the far end of Király utca.

Getting There & Away

BUS Some five buses a day connect Pécs with Budapest (3010Ft, 4½ hours), eight with Szeged (3010Ft, 4½ hours) and two with Kecskemét (3010Ft, 4½ hours).

TRAIN Pécs is on a main rail line with Budapest's Déli train station (3950Ft, three hours, nine daily). One daily train runs from Pécs to Eszék in Croatia (the town is called Osijek in Croatia; two hours), with continuing service to the Bosnian capital, Sarajevo (nine hours).

WORTH A TRIP

KECSKEMÉT

A worthwhile destination is the small city of Kecskemét (population 107,000), which lies halfway between Budapest and Szeged along the main rail and road arteries. It's a surprisingly green, pedestrian-friendly city with interesting art nouveau architecture. **Tourinform** (☎481 065; www.kecskemet.hu; Kossuth tér 1; ⏲8am-5pm Mon-Fri, 9am-1pm Sat & Sun Jun-Aug, 8am-6pm Mon-Fri Sep-May) is centrally located on the main square. They can advise on sights, places to stay and outings to **Kiskunság National Park** (Kiskunsági Nemzeti Park; www.knp.hu). Kecskemét is served by bus to and from Budapest (1680Ft, 1¼ hours, hourly) and Szeged (1860Ft, two hours, hourly).

GREAT PLAIN

Like the outback for Australians or the Wild West for Americans, the Great Plain (Nagy Alföld) holds a romantic appeal for Hungarians. Many of these notions come as much from the collective imagination, paintings and poetry as they do from history, but there's no arguing the spellbinding potential of big-sky country. The Great Plain is also home to cities of graceful architecture and history, such as Szeged and Kecskemét.

Szeged

☎62 / POP 170,300

Szeged (*seh*-ged) is a bustling border town with a handful of historic sights that line the embankment along the Tisza River and a clutch of sumptuous art nouveau town palaces. Importantly, it's also a big university town, which means lots of culture, lots of partying and an active festival scene that lasts throughout the year.

The train station is south of the city centre on Indóház tér; tram 1 or 2 will take you to the centre. The bus station is west of the centre in Mars tér and within easy walking distance via pedestrian Mikszáth Kálmán utca. **Tourinform** (☎488 690; http://tip.szegedvaros.hu; Dugonics tér 2; ⏲9am-5pm Mon-Fri, to 1pm Sat) is tucked away in a quiet courtyard near the university.

Sights & Activities

Dóm tér SQUARE

'Cathedral Square' contains Szeged's most important buildings and monuments and is the centre of events during the annual **Szeged Open-Air Festival** (☎541 205; www.szegediszabadteri.hu) in summer. Lording above all else is the twin-towered **Votive Church** (Fogadalmi templom; ☎420 157; www.dom.szeged.hu; Dóm tér; admission free; ⏲6.30am-7pm Mon-Sat, from 7.30am Sun), a disproportionate brick monstrosity that was pledged after the 1879 flood but built from 1913 to 1930. Running along three sides of the square is the **National Pantheon** (Nemzeti

Emlékcsarnok; admission free; ⌚24hr), with statues and reliefs of 70 Hungarian notables.

New Synagogue SYNAGOGUE
(Új Zsinagóga; ☎423 849; www.zsinagoga.szeged.hu; Jósika utca 10; adult/concession 400/200Ft; ⌚10am-noon & 1-5pm Apr-Sep, 10am-2pm Oct-Mar, closed Sat) The art nouveau New Synagogue (1903) is the most beautiful Jewish house of worship in Hungary and still in use, though the community has dwindled from 8000 before WWII to about 50 people.

Reök Palace ARCHITECTURE
(Reök Palota; ☎541 205; www.reok.hu; Tisza Lajos körút 56) This mind-blowing green and lilac art nouveau structure (1907) looks like an aquarium decoration. It hosts photography and visual arts exhibitions.

Sleeping & Eating

Familia Panzió GUESTHOUSE €€
(☎441 122; www.familiapanzio.hu; Szentháromság utca 71; s/d/tr from 7000/9500/14,000Ft;) Budget travellers book up this family-run guesthouse with two-dozen contemporary (if nondescript) rooms in a great old building near the train station.

New Szeged Bath & Camping CAMPGROUND €
(Újszegedi partfürdő és kemping; ☎430 843; www.szegedcamping.hu; Középkikötő sor 1-3; campsites per person 990Ft, plus per tent 390Ft, bungalows 8000-11,500Ft; ⌚May-Sep;) The large grassy camping ground with sites for 700 on the Tisza River looks a bit like a public park. Bungalows on stilts are also available. The adjoining spa is open May to September.

Vendéglő A Régi Hídhoz HUNGARIAN €€
(☎420 910; www.regihid.hu; Oskola utca 4; mains 1400-2400Ft) For an authentic meal that won't break the bank, head for 'At the Old Bridge', a traditional Hungarian restaurant with all the favourites and a great terrace just a block in from the river.

Taj Mahal INDIAN €€
(☎452 131; www.tajmahalszeged.hu; Gutenberg utca 12; mains 1540-2290Ft;) This pleasantly genuine Indian-Pakistani restaurant is just metres from the New Synagogue.

Boci Tejivó FAST FOOD €
(☎423 154; www.bocitejivo.hu; Zrínyi utca 2; mains 260-500Ft; ⌚24hr;) This is a very modern take on an old-fashioned idea – the 'milk bar' so popular during socialist times. Order from among the dozens of meatless dishes – especially anything with *túró* (curds).

Entertainment

As a university town Szeged boasts a vast array of bars, clubs and other nightspots. Nightclub programs are listed in the free **Szegedi Est** (www.szegediest.hu) magazine.

Jazz Kocsma LIVE MUSIC
(☎06 70 250 9279; jazzkocsma.blog.hu; Kálmány Lajos 14; ⌚5pm-midnight Mon-Thu, to 2am Fri & Sat) Small, ever-popular music club that gets pretty crowded during the academic year for live music on Friday and Saturday nights.

Getting There & Around

BUS Buses run from Szeged to Pécs (3410Ft, four hours, eight daily) and to the Serbian city of Subotica (1200Ft, 1½ hours, up to four daily).

TRAIN Szeged is on the main rail line to Budapest's Nyugati train station (2420Ft, 2½ hours, hourly); trains also stop halfway along in Kecskemét (2100Ft, one hour).

NORTHEASTERN HUNGARY

This is the home of Hungary's two most famous wines – honey-sweet Tokaj and Eger's famed Bull's Blood – and a region of microclimates conducive to wine production. The chain of wooded hills in the northeast constitutes the foothills of the Carpathian Mountains, which stretch along the Hungarian border with Slovakia.

Eger

☎36 / POP 56,500

Filled with wonderfully preserved baroque buildings, Eger (*egg*-air) is a jewelbox of a town. Learn about the Turkish conquest and defeat at its hilltop castle, climb an original minaret, hear an organ performance at the massive basilica and, best of all, go from cellar to cellar in the Valley of Beautiful Women, tasting the celebrated Bull's Blood wine from the region where it's made. The staff at **Tourinform** (☎517 715; http://mheger.hu; Bajcsy-Zsilinszky utca 9; ⌚9am-6pm Mon-Fri, to 1pm Sat & Sun mid-Jun–mid-Sep, 9am-5pm Mon-Fri, to 1pm Sat mid-Sep–mid-Jun) can supply all the information you need.

The main train station is on Vasút utca, south of the Archbishop's Garden. To reach the city centre, walk north on Deák Ferenc utca and then head along pedestrian Széchenyi István utca. The bus station is west of that street.

Sights & Activities

Eger Castle FORTRESS

(Egri Vár; www.egrivar.hu; Vár köz 1; castle grounds adult/child 800/400Ft, incl museum 1400/700Ft; ⏲exhibits 9am-5pm Tue-Sun Mar-Oct, 10am-4pm Tue-Sun Nov-Feb, castle grounds 8am-8pm May-Aug, to 7pm Apr & Sep, to 6pm Mar & Oct, to 5pm Nov-Feb) The best view of the city can be had by climbing up cobblestone Vár köz from Dózsa György tér to Eger Castle, erected in the 13th century. Models and drawings in the **István Dobó Museum**, housed in the former Bishop's Palace (1470), painlessly explain the history of the castle. Beneath the castle are **casemates** (Kazamata) hewn from solid rock, which can be visited. Other attractions, including the **Panoptikum** (Waxworks; adult/concession 500/350Ft) and a **3D film** (tickets 400-600Ft), cost extra.

Minaret ISLAMIC

(☎06 70 202 4353; Knézich Károly utca; admission 200Ft; ⏲10am-6pm Apr-Oct) This 40m-tall minaret is the only reminder of the Ottoman occupation of Eger. Nonclaustrophobes can brave the 97 narrow spiral steps to the top for awesome views.

Eger Basilica CHURCH

(Egri Bazilika; Pyrker János tér 1; ⏲7.30am-6pm Mon-Sat, from 1pm Sun) The first thing you see as you come into town from the bus or train station is the mustard-coloured, neoclassical basilica, with its gigantic pillars, built in 1836. Try to time your vist for the half-hour **organ concert** (tickets 800Ft; ⏲11.30am Mon-Sat, 12.45pm Sun mid-May–mid-Oct).

TOP CHOICE **Valley of the Beautiful Women** WINE TASTING

(Szépasszony-völgy) Wine tasting is popular in the wine cellars of the evocatively named Valley of the Beautiful Women. This is the place to sample Bull's Blood – one of very few reds produced in Eger – or any of the whites: Leányka, Olaszrizling and Hárslevelű from nearby Debrő. The choice of wine cellars can be a bit daunting so walk around and have a look yourself. But be careful: those 100mL (150Ft) glasses go down pretty fast. The valley is a little over 1km southwest across Rte 25 and off Király utca.

Sleeping

Agria Retur Panzió GUESTHOUSE €

(☎416 650; http://agria.returvendeghaz.hu; Knézich Károly utca 18; s/d 3800/6400Ft; @📶) This charming guesthouse near the Minaret has a cheery communal kitchen/eating area central to four rooms. Out back is a huge garden barbecue at your disposal.

Dobó Vendégház HOTEL €€

(☎421 407; www.vendeghaz.hu; Dobó István utca 19; s/d 9000/13,500Ft; 📶) Tucked away along one of the old town's pedestrian streets just below the castle, this lovely little hotel has seven spick-and-span rooms, some with balconies.

Tulipán Kemping CAMPGROUND €

(☎311 542; www.tulipancamping.com; Szépasszonyvölgy utca 71; campsites per person/tent/caravan 800/900/1600Ft, bungalows d/q 5000/6000Ft) This camping ground is surrounded by vineyards and stumbling distance from the wine cellars of the Valley of the Beautiful Women.

Eating

Palacsintavár CREPERIE €

(Pancake Castle; ☎413 986; www.palacsintavar.hu; Dobó István utca 9, enter from Fazola Henrik utca; mains 1490-1820Ft) Savoury *palacsinták* – 'pancakes', for want of a better word – are served at this eclectic eatery with an abundance of fresh vegetables, and range in taste from Asian to Italian. There's a large choice of sweet ones too.

Szántófer Vendéglő HUNGARIAN €€

(Plough; ☎517 298; www.szantofer.hu; Bródy Sándor utca 3; mains 1700-2400Ft) Choose the 'Plough' for hearty, home-style Hungarian fare and its covered courtyard out back.

Getting There & Away

BUS From Eger buses serve Kecskemét (3130Ft, 4½ hours, three daily) and Szeged (3950Ft, 5¾ hours, two daily). To get to Tokaj by bus, you have to go to Nyíregyháza (2520Ft, three hours, two daily) and catch another bus back.

TRAIN Up to seven direct trains a day head to Budapest's Keleti train station (2830Ft, three hours).

Tokaj

POP 4900

A worthwhile wine destination is the small village of Tokaj, 43km northeast of Eger, which has long been celebrated for its sweet dessert wines. **Tourinform** (950 603; www.tokaj-turizmus.hu; Serház utca 1; 9am-5pm Mon-Sat, 10am-3pm Sun Jun-Aug, 9am-4pm Mon-Fri Sep-May) is just off Rákóczi út and can help with accommodation. Up to 16 trains a day head for Budapest's Keleti station (3950Ft, 2¾ hours).

UNDERSTAND HUNGARY

History

By the 3rd century BC, the Roman Empire had extended its influence far enough to include Pannonia, all of today's Hungary west of the Danube (Transdanubia). By AD 441 the Huns under Attila had ended Roman rule in the area. However, the Huns' empire didn't last long after Attila's death, leaving space for the Avars, Franks and Slavs.

Historians usually date the Magyar (Hungarian) conquest to around 896, when Árpád led an alliance of seven tribes into the region. In the year 1000 Hungary's first king and patron saint, Stephen (István), was crowned, marking the foundation of the Hungarian state.

Medieval Hungary was powerful until 1526, when the Turks invaded and occupied its lands, including Budapest, for more than a century and a half. After the Turks' expulsion from Buda in 1686, the Austrian Habsburgs annexed the lands that had been under Turkish rule. An 1848 revolt for independence led by Transylvanian princes failed, but unrest eventually led to Hungarian autonomy as half of the Austro-Hungarian Empire in 1867.

With Hungary on the losing side during WWI, the 1920 Treaty of Trianon stripped the country of more than two-thirds of its territory. Hungary's ambition to recover its losses drew the nation into WWII on the side of the Axis, led by Germany. When the leadership tried to negotiate a separate peace in 1944, the Germans occupied Hungary and brought the fascist Arrow Cross Party to power. It immediately began deporting hundreds of thousands of Jews to Auschwitz. By early April 1945, Hungary had been defeated by the Soviet army. In 1947 the communists took control of the government.

On 23 October 1956 anti-Soviet student demonstrations prompted Soviet tanks to move into Budapest and by the end of the fighting, several thousand people were dead. Still, Soviet control was not as tight in Hungary as it was in the Slavic satellite states.

Hungary began moving towards full democracy in 1989 and the last Soviet troops left the country in June 1991. Hungary became a member of NATO in 1999 and the EU in 2004. The painful transition to a market economy resulted in declining living standards initially, but the early years of the 21st century saw astonishing economic growth. The 'Great Recession' in 2008 and 2009 pushed Hungary to the brink of bankruptcy.

Economic woes have plagued the nation ever since, but an even bigger concern to many Hungarians is the rise of the far-right Jobbik party, which garnered more than 16% of the vote in the national elections of 2010.

People

Ethnic Magyars make up approximately 92% of Hungary's population of just over 10 million. Non-Magyar minorities include Germans (2.6%), Serbs and other South Slavs (2%), Slovaks (0.8%) and Romanians (0.7%). The number of Roma is officially put at 1.9% of the population – just under 200,000 people – though some sources estimate the figure as high as 4% (800,000 people).

Arts

As you will see from the street names in every Hungarian town and city, the country celebrates and reveres its most influential musician, composer and pianist, Franz (or Ferenc) Liszt (1811–86). Other composers of note include Béla Bartók (1881–1945) and Zoltán Kodály (1882–1967), who made the first systematic study of Hungarian folk music, and both integrated some of their findings into their compositions.

HABITS & CUSTOMS

The Magyar are an especially polite people and their language is filled with courtesies. To toast someone's health before drinking, say *egészégére* (egg-eh-sheg-eh-ray), and to wish them a 'bon appetit' before eating, *jo étvágyat* (*yo* ate-vad-yaht). If you're invited to someone's home, always bring a bunch of flowers or a bottle of good local wine.

READING UP

The Hungarian language and its literature has had a huge influence on the Hungarian psyche. The overall mood in much prose and poetry of the 18th and 19th century is one of *honfibú* – literally 'patriotic sorrow', a longing for something lost. Sándor Petőfi (1823–49) is Hungary's most celebrated poet. The 2002 Nobel Prize winner, Imre Kertész, writes about the Holocaust and its after-effects in the novels *Fatelessness* and *Kaddish for an Unborn Child*.

Roma music, found in restaurants in its schmaltzy 'Gypsy' form, has become fashionable among the young, with bands playing the real thing in trendy bars till the wee hours. Klezmer music (traditional eastern European Jewish music) has also made a comeback onto musicians' playlists.

Favourite painters from the 19th century include realist Mihály Munkácsy (1844–1900), the so-called painter of the *puszta* (plain) and the symbolist Tivadar Kosztka Csontváry (1853–1919). Győző Vásárhelyi (1908–97), who changed his name to Victor Vasarely when he emigrated to Paris, is considered the 'father of op art'. Probably the most successful Hungarian painter in history was the beloved József Rippl-Rónai (1861–1927). The traditional embroidery, weaving and ceramics of the nation's *népművészet* (folk art) walk hand in hand with fine art.

Environment

Hungary occupies the Carpathian Basin to the southwest of the Carpathian Mountains. Water dominates much of the country's geography. The Danube (Duna) River divides the Great Plain (Nagy Alföld) in the east from Transdanubia (Dunántúl) in the west. The Tisza (596km in Hungary) is the country's longest river and historically has been prone to flooding. Hungary has hundreds of small lakes and is riddled with thermal springs. Lake Balaton (596 sq km, 77km long) in the west, is the largest freshwater lake in Europe outside Scandinavia. Hungary's 'mountains' to the north are really hills, with the country's highest peak being Kékes (1014m) in the Mátra range.

SURVIVAL GUIDE

Directory A–Z

Accommodation

Price ranges for doubles, including private bathroom, in Hungary are categorised as follows:

€ less than 9000Ft (15,000Ft in Budapest)

€€ 9000Ft to 16,5000Ft (15,000Ft to 33,500Ft in Budapest)

€€€ more than 16,500Ft (33,500Ft in Budapest)

CAMPING

Hungary's camping grounds are listed in Tourinform's *Camping Hungary* map and brochure; also try the website of the **Hungarian Camping Association** (MKSZ; www.camping.hu).

GUESTHOUSES & HOTELS

Quaint, often family-run *panziók* (pensions, or guesthouses) are abundant and usually less expensive than hotels. Some hotels (*szállók* or *szállodák*) have less expensive room options if you're willing to share the bathroom down the hall.

HOSTELS & STUDENT DORMS

The Hungarian Youth Hostel Association keeps a list of official year-round hostels throughout Hungary. Having an HI card is not required anywhere, but it may get you a 10% discount. From July to August, students throughout Hungary vacate college and university dorms and the administration opens them to travellers. The local Tourinform office can help you find such places.

PRIVATE ROOMS

Renting a private room in a Hungarian home is a good budget option and can be a great opportunity to get up close and personal with the culture. Tourinform offices can usually help with finding these too. Otherwise look for houses with signs reading *szoba kiadó* or *zimmer frei* ('room available' in Hungarian and German respectively).

Activities

CYCLING

Hungary's flat terrain makes it ideal for cycling. Velo-Touring, a large cycling travel agency, has a great selection of seven-night trips in all regions, from a senior-friendly Southern Transdanubia wine tour to a bike ride between spas on the Great Plain. Lake Balaton is circled by a 200km-long cycling track that takes four to five days to complete at a leisurely pace.

HIKING & BIRDWATCHING

Hiking enthusiasts may enjoy the trails around Lake Balaton, the Bükk Hills north of Eger or the plains at Bugac Puszta south of Kecskemét. Birdwatchers should contact Probirder, an information website and guide service.

SPAS

Hungary has more than 100 thermal baths open to the public. Ask **Tourinform** (from abroad 36 1 438 80 80, within Hungary 800 36 000 000; www.tourinform.hu) for the brochure *Hungary: A Garden of Well-Being*. Also try the **Spas in Hungary** (www.spasinhungary.com.) website.

Business Hours

Banks 8am or 9am to 4pm or 5pm Monday to Friday

Museums 9am or 10am to 5pm or 6pm Tuesday to Sunday

Post offices 8am to 6pm Monday to Friday

Restaurants Roughly 11am to midnight

Embassies & Consulates

The following embassies are in Budapest:

Australian Embassy (457 9777; www.hungary.embassy.gov.au; XII Királyhágó tér 8-9, 4th fl; visas 9-11am, general enquiries 8.30-4.30pm Mon-Fri)

Canadian Embassy (392 3360; www.hungary.gc.ca; II Ganz utca 12-14; 8.30-11am & 2-3.30pm Mon-Thu)

French Embassy (374 1100; www.ambafrance-hu.org; VI Lendvay utca 27; 9am-12.30pm Mon-Fri)

Netherlands Embassy (336 6300; www.netherlandsembassy.hu; II Füge utca 5-7; 10am-noon Mon-Fri)

UK Embassy (266 2888; http://ukinhungary.fco.gov.uk/en; V Harmincad utca 6; 9.30am-12.30pm & 2.30-4.30pm Mon-Fri)

US Embassy (475 4400; www.usembassy.hu; V Szabadság tér 12; 8.30am-4.30pm Mon-Fri)

Food

Price ranges for meals in Hungary are broken down as follows:

€ less than 2000Ft (3000Ft in Budapest)

€€ 2000Ft to 3500Ft (3000Ft to 6500Ft in Budapest)

€€€ more than 3500Ft (6500Ft in Budapest)

Money

The Hungarian forint (Ft) comes in coins of five, 10, 20, 50, 100 and 200, and notes are denominated in 500, 1000, 2000, 5000, 10,000 and 20,000. ATMs are everywhere, even in small villages. Tip waiters, hairdressers and taxi drivers approximately 10% of the total.

Post & Telephone

Postcards and small letters mailed within Europe cost 220Ft. To addresses outside Europe, expect to pay 240Ft.

Hungary's country code is 36. To make an outgoing international call, dial 00 first. To dial city-to-city within the country, first dial 06, wait for the second dial tone and then dial the city code and phone number. You must always dial 06 when ringing mobile telephones.

As with the rest of Europe, Hungarian mobile phones operate on the GSM standard. Compatible handsets will connect automatically with local providers, but watch for high roaming fees, particularly for data downloads. A cheaper alternative is to purchase a pay-as-you-go SIM card (available at mobile-phone shops and newsagents), which will give you a temporary local number with which to make calls and send text messages.

Public Holidays

New Year's Day 1 January

1848 Revolution Day 15 March

Easter March/April

International Labour Day 1 May

Whit Monday (Pentecost) May/June

St Stephen's/Constitution Day 20 August

1956 Remembrance/Republic Day 23 October

All Saints' Day 1 November

Christmas Holidays 25 and 26 December

Visas

Citizens of virtually all European countries, as well as Australia, Canada, Israel, Japan,

New Zealand and the USA, do not require visas to visit Hungary for stays of up to 90 days. Check current visa requirements on the Consular Services page of the **Ministry for Foreign Affairs** (http://konzuliszolgalat.kormany.hu/en) website

Getting There & Away

Air

The vast majority of international flights land at **Ferenc Liszt International Airport** (☎296 7000; www.bud.hu), 24km southeast of Budapest. The national carrier, Malév Hungarian Airlines, went into liquidation at the start of 2012.

Budget airlines now serving Hungary include **Air Berlin** (☎06 80 017 110; www.airberlin.com), **easyJet** (www.easyjet.com), **German Wings** (☎1-526 7005; www.germanwings.com), **Ryanair** (www.ryanair.com) and **Wizz Air** (www.wizzair.com).

Land

BUS

Most international buses arrive at the **Népliget bus station** (☎219 8030; IX Üllői út 131) in Budapest and are run by **Eurolines** (www.eurolines.com) in conjunction with its Hungarian affiliate, **Volánbusz** (☎382 0888; www.volanbusz.hu). Useful international routes include buses from Budapest to Vienna in Austria, Bratislava in Slovakia, Subotica in Serbia, Rijeka in Croatia, Prague in the Czech Republic and Sofia in Bulgaria.

CAR & MOTORCYCLE

Third-party insurance is compulsory for driving in Hungary; if your car is registered in the EU, it's assumed you have it. Other motorists must show a Green Card or buy insurance at the border.

TRAIN

Magyar Államvasutak (MÁV; ☎1-371 9449, 06 40 494 949; http://elvira.mav-start.hu/), the Hungarian State Railways, links up with international rail networks in all directions and its schedule is available online.

EuroCity (EC) and Intercity (IC) trains require a seat reservation and payment of a supplement. Most larger train stations in Hungary have left-luggage rooms open from at least 9am to 5pm.

Some direct train connections from Budapest include Austria, Slovakia, Romania, Ukraine (continuing to Russia), Croatia, Serbia, Germany, Slovenia, Czech Republic, Poland, Switzerland, Italy, Bulgaria and Greece.

Sea

Hydrofoils to Bratislava and Vienna run by **Mahart PassNave** (☎484 4000; www.mahartpassnave.hu; V Belgrád rakpart; ⏲8am-6pm Mon-Fri) from May to late September arrive at and depart from the **International Ferry Pier** (Nemzetközi hajóállomás; ☎318 1223; V Belgrád rakpart) in Budapest. Hydrofoils depart the city on Mondays and Wednesdays at 9am, returning from Vienna at the same time on Tuesdays and Thursdays. Adult one way/return fares to Vienna are €99/125. Transporting a bicycle costs €25.

Getting Around

Hungary does not have any scheduled domestic flights.

Bus

Domestic buses, run by the **Volán** (www.volan.eu) association of coach operators, cover an extensive nationwide network. Timetables are posted at all stations. Some footnotes you could come across include *naponta* (daily), *hétköznap* (weekdays), *munkanapokon* (on work days), *munkaszüneti napok kivételével naponta* (daily except holidays) and *szabad és munkaszüneti napokon* (on Saturday and holidays). A few large bus stations have luggage rooms, but these generally close by 6pm.

Car & Motorcycle

In general, you must be at least 21 years old and have had your licence for at least a year to rent a car. There is a 100% ban on alcohol when you are driving and this rule is strictly enforced. Most cities and towns require that you pay for street parking (usually 9am to 6pm workdays) by buying temporary parking passes from machines.

Hitching

Hitching is never entirely safe in any country and we don't recommend it. Travellers who decide to hitch are taking a small but potentially serious risk. Hitchhiking is legal everywhere in Hungary except on motorways.

Local Transport

Public transport is efficient and extensive, with bus and, in many towns, trolleybus services. Budapest and Szeged also have trams, and there's an extensive metro network and suburban commuter railway in Budapest. Purchase tickets at newsstands before travelling and validate them once aboard. Inspectors do check tickets, especially on the metro lines in Budapest.

Train

MÁV (☎1 444 4499; www.mav-start.hu) operates reliable train services on 7600km of tracks. Schedules are available online and computer information kiosks are popping up at rail stations around the country. Second-class domestic train fares range from 155Ft for a journey of less than 5km to 4660Ft for a 300km trip.

IC trains are express trains and are the most comfortable and modern. *Gyorsvonat* (fast trains) take longer and use older cars; *személyvonat* (passenger trains) stop at every village along the way. Seat reservations *(helyjegy)* cost extra and are required on IC and some fast trains; these are indicated on the timetable by an 'R' in a box or a circle (a plain 'R' means seat reservations are available but not required).

In all stations a yellow board indicates departures *(indul)* and a white board is for arrivals *(érkezik)*. Express and fast trains are indicated in red, local trains in black.

Both **InterRail** (www.interrailnet.com) and **Eurail** (www.eurail.com) passes cover Hungary.

Ireland

Includes »

Dublin ... 581
Kilkenny ... 589
Cork ... 591
Killarney ... 594
Ring of Kerry ... 595
The Burren ... 596
Galway ... 596
Aran Islands ... 598
Connemara ... 600
Sligo ... 600
Bundoran ... 601
Northern Ireland ... 601
Belfast ... 602
The Causeway Coast ... 608
Derry ... 609
Understand Ireland ... 611
Survival Guide ... 612

Best Places to Eat

» Farmgate Café (p592)

» Chapter One (p586)

» Ard Bia at Nimmo's (p597)

» Barking Dog (p606)

Best Places to Stay

» Isaacs Hostel (p585)

» Number 31 (p586)

» Garnish House (p591)

» Kinlay House (p591)

Why Go?

Few countries have an image so plagued by cliché.

From shamrocks and shillelaghs to leprechauns and lovable rogues, there's a plethora of platitudes to wade through before you reach the real Ireland.

But it's well worth looking beyond the tourist tat, for the Emerald Isle is one of Europe's gems, a scenic extravaganza of lakes, mountains, sea and sky. From wind-lashed Donegal to picture-postcard County Cork, there are countless opportunities to get outdoors and explore, whether surfing the beach breaks of Bundoran, cycling the coast of Antrim, or hiking the hills of Kerry and Connemara.

There are cultural pleasures too in the land of Joyce and Yeats, U2 and the Undertones. Dublin, Cork and Belfast all have party-on pubs and foot-stomping live-music scenes, while you can enjoy traditional music in the bars of Galway, Doolin and Killarney. So push aside the shamrocks and experience the real Ireland.

When to Go

Dublin

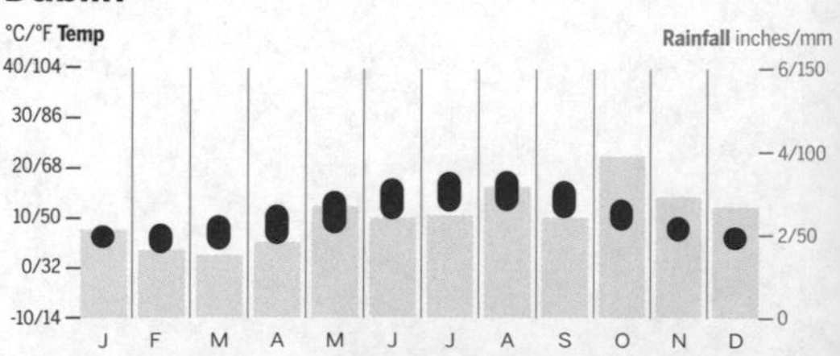

Late Mar Spring has sprung, landscape is greening, St Patrick's Day festivities beckon.

Jun Best chance of dry weather, long summer evenings, Bloomsday in Dublin.

Sep & Oct Summer crowds thin, autumn colours reign, surf's up on the west coast.

Connections

Ireland is just about as far west as you can go in Europe – next stop, North America. But the Emerald Isle can serve as a stepping stone between mainland Europe and the UK. Ferry services run from Roscoff and Cherbourg in northern France to Rosslare (near Wexford) in southeast Ireland, from where you can continue your trip from Dublin to Wales, or from Belfast or Larne to Scotland or the Isle of Man.

ITINERARIES

One Week

Spend a couple of days in Dublin ambling through the excellent national museums, and gorging yourself on Guinness and good company in Temple Bar. Get medieval in Kilkenny before heading on to Cork and discovering why they call it 'The Real Capital'. Meander through lush, idyllic West Cork and take in the friendly spirit and melodious accents of its denizens.

Two Weeks

Follow the one-week itinerary, then make your way from West Cork up to touristy Killarney and the Ring of Kerry on your way to bohemian Galway. Using Galway as your base, explore the alluring Aran Islands and the hills of Connemara. Finally, head north to experience the newly optimistic vibe in fast-changing Belfast.

Essential Food & Drink

» **Champ** Northern Irish dish of mashed potatoes with spring onions (scallions)

» **Colcannon** Potatoes mashed with milk, cabbage and fried onion

» **Farl** Triangular flatbread in Northern Ireland and Donegal

» **Irish stew** Lamb stew with potatoes, onions and thyme

» **Soda bread** Wonderful bread – white or brown, sweet or savoury – made from very soft Irish flour and buttermilk

» **Stout** Dark, almost black beer made with roasted barley; famous brands are Guinness in Dublin, and Murphy's and Beamish & Crawford in Cork

» **Irish whiskey** Around 100 different types are produced by only four distilleries: Jameson, Bushmills, Cooley and recently reopened Kilbeggan.

AT A GLANCE

» **Currency** Euro (€; ROI), pound sterling (£; NI)

» **Languages** English, Irish Gaelic

» **Money** ATMs widespread; credit cards widely accepted

» **Visas** Schengen rules do not apply.

Fast Facts

» **Area** 84,421 sq km

» **Capitals** Dublin (ROI), Belfast (NI)

» **Country code** ☎353 (ROI), ☎44 (NI)

» **Emergency** ☎112

Exchange Rates

Australia	A$1	€0.82/ UK£0.68
Canada	C$1	€0.77/ UK£0.64
Euro Zone	€1	UK£0.84
Japan	¥100	€0.83/ UK£0.70
New Zealand	NZ$1	€0.65/ UK£0.55
UK	UK£1	€1.18
USA	US$1	€0.78/ UK£0.65

Set Your Budget

» **Budget hotel room** €60

» **Two-course meal** €25

» **Pint of beer** €4–6

» **Dublin tram ticket** €2–5

Resources

» **Failte Ireland** (www.discoverireland.ie)

» **Northern Ireland Tourist Board** (www.nitb.com)

IRELAND

Ireland Highlights

❶ Meander through the museums, pubs and literary haunts of **Dublin** (p581), and ask a local, 'Where's the craic?'

❷ Hang out in bohemian **Galway** (p596), with its hip cafes and live-music venues

❸ Hike along the Causeway Coast and clamber across the **Giant's Causeway**

❹ Take a boat trip to the 6th-century monastery perched atop the wild rocky islet of **Skellig Michael** (p595)

❺ Sup a pint of Guinness while tapping your toes to a live music session in one of Dublin's **traditional Irish pubs** (p587)

❻ Cycle through the spectacular lake and mountain scenery of the **Gap of Dunloe** (p594)

❼ Discover the industrial history of the city that built the world's most famous ocean liner in Belfast's **Titanic Quarter** (p602)

❽ Wander the wild, limestone shores of the remote and craggy **Aran Islands** (p598)

DUBLIN

☎01 / POP 1.1 MILLION

Form is temporary, but class is permanent: the good times may have gone, but Dublin still knows how to have a good time. From its music, art and literature to the legendary nightlife that has inspired those same musicians, artists and writers, Dublin has always known how to have fun and does it with deadly seriousness. As you'll soon find out.

There are world-class museums, superb restaurants and the best range of entertainment in the country: from rock music to classical concerts there's almost always something on, and when there's not, there are always a thousand or so pubs to while away an evening in. And should you wish to get away from it all, the city has a handful of seaside towns at its edges that make for wonderful day trips.

Sights

Dublin's finest Georgian architecture, including its famed doorways, is found around **St Stephen's Green** (admission free; ⏲dawn-dusk) and **Merrion Square** just south of Trinity College; both are prime picnic spots when the sun shines.

Trinity College & Book of Kells MUSEUM

(www.bookofkells.ie; College Green; college grounds free, Old Library adult/child €9/free, walking tours per person €10; ⏲9.30am-5pm Mon-Sat year-round, 9.30am-4.30pm Sun May-Sep, noon-4.30pm Sun Oct-Apr, walking tours twice per hour 10.15am-3.40pm Mon-Sat & 10.15am-3pm Sun mid-May–Sep) Ireland's premier university was founded by Queen Elizabeth I in 1592. Its full name is technically the University of Dublin, but **Trinity College** is the institution's sole college. Until 1793 the students were all Protestant, but today most of them are Catholic. Women were first allowed to matriculate in 1903. Student-guided **walking tours** depart from inside the main gate on College St. The tour is an especially good deal since it includes admission to the **Old Library** to see the **Book of Kells**, an elaborately illuminated gospel created by monks on the Scottish isle of Iona around AD 800, and the spectacular **Long Room**, an early-18th-century library lined with marble busts of writers and philosophers.

FREE **National Museum of Ireland – Archaeology** MUSEUM

(www.museum.ie; Kildare St; ⏲10am-5pm Tue-Sat, 2-5pm Sun) Among the highlights of the National Museum's archaeology and history branch are its superb collection of **prehistoric gold objects**; the exquisite 12th-century **Ardagh Chalice**, the world's finest example of Celtic art; and ancient objects recovered from Ireland's bogs, including remarkably well-preserved human bodies. Other exhibits focus on early Christian art, the Viking period, and medieval Ireland.

O'Connell St HISTORIC AREA

Dublin's grandest avenue is dominated by the needle-like **Monument of Light**, better known as 'The Spire', which rises from the spot once occupied by a statue of Admiral Nelson – which disappeared in explosive fashion, thanks to the Irish Republican Army (IRA) in 1966. Soaring 120m into the sky, it is, apparently, the world's tallest sculpture.

Nearby is the 1815 **General Post Office** (www.anpost.ie; O'Connell St; ⏲8am-8pm Mon Sat), an important landmark of the 1916 Easter Rising, when the Irish Volunteers used it as a base for attacks against the British army. After a fierce battle the GPO was burnt out. Upon surrendering, the leaders of the Irish rebellion and 13 others were taken to Kilmainham Gaol and executed.

Guinness Storehouse BREWERY, MUSEUM

(www.guinness-storehouse.com; St James's Gate, South Market St; adult/student/child €16.50/10.50/6.50, Conoisseur Experience €25, discounts apply for online bookings; ⏲9.30am-5pm Sep-Jun, to 7pm Jul-Aug; 🚌21a, 51b, 78, 78a or 123 from Fleet St, 🚋St James's) The Guinness Storehouse sits in

FREE THRILLS

Dublin is not a cheap city, but there are plenty of attractions that won't bust your budget.

» Wander the grounds at Trinity College (p581), Dublin's oldest and most beautiful university.

» Discover the world's finest collection of prehistoric gold artefacts at the National Museum of Archaeology (p581).

» Explore the Chester Beatty Library (p587), with its collection of oriental and religious art.

» Gaze at Irish and European paintings at the National Gallery (p584).

» Laze at St Stephen's Green (p581), the city's most picturesque public park.

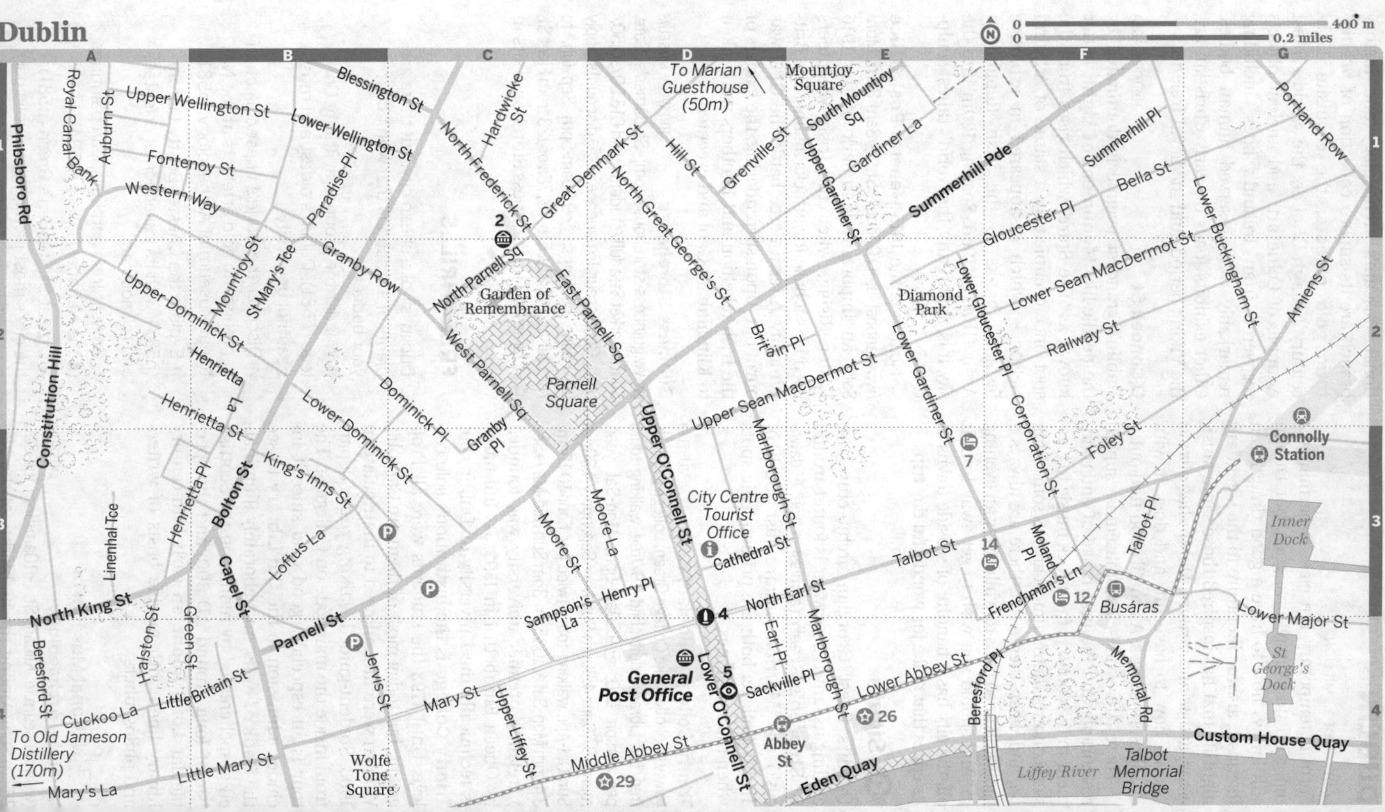
Dublin
0 400 m
0 0.2 miles
Phibsboro Rd
Royal Canal Bank
Auburn St
Upper Wellington St
Lower Wellington St
Blessington St
Fontenoy St
Western Way
Paradise Pl
Mountjoy St
St Mary's Tce
Granby Row
Upper Dominick St
Henrietta La
Henrietta St
Henrietta Pl
Constitution Hill
Linenhal Tce
Bolton St
Capel St
King's Inns St
Lower Dominick St
Dominick Pl
Loftus La
North King St
Beresford St
Halston St
Green St
Little Britain St
Cuckoo La
To Old Jameson Distillery (170m)
Mary's La
Little Mary St
Parnell St
Jervis St
Mary St
Wolfe Tone Square
Upper Liffey St
Middle Abbey St
Hardwicke St
North Frederick St
North Parnell Sq
Garden of Remembrance
East Parnell Sq
West Parnell Sq
Granby Pl
Parnell Square
Great Denmark St
North Great George's St
Hill St
To Marian Guesthouse (50m)
Mountjoy Square
South Mountjoy Sq
Grenville St
Upper Gardiner St
Gardiner La
Summerhill Pde
Summerhill Pl
Bella St
Gloucester Pl
Lower Sean MacDermot St
Lower Buckingham St
Portland Row
Amiens St
Diamond Park
Lower Gloucester Pl
Railway St
Britain Pl
Upper Sean MacDermot St
Lower Gardiner St
Corporation St
Foley St
Connolly Station
Upper O'Connell St
Moore La
Moore St
Henry Pl
Sampson's La
City Centre Tourist Office
Cathedral St
Marlborough St
North Earl St
Talbot St
Moland Pl
Talbot Pl
Frenchman's Ln
Busáras
Lower Major St
Inner Dock
St George's Dock
General Post Office
Lower O'Connell St
Sackville Pl
Earl Pl
Lower Abbey St
Beresford Pl
Memorial Rd
Abbey St
Eden Quay
Custom House Quay
Liffey River
Talbot Memorial Bridge
A
B
C
D
E
F
G
1
2
3
4
2
4
5
7
12
14
26
29

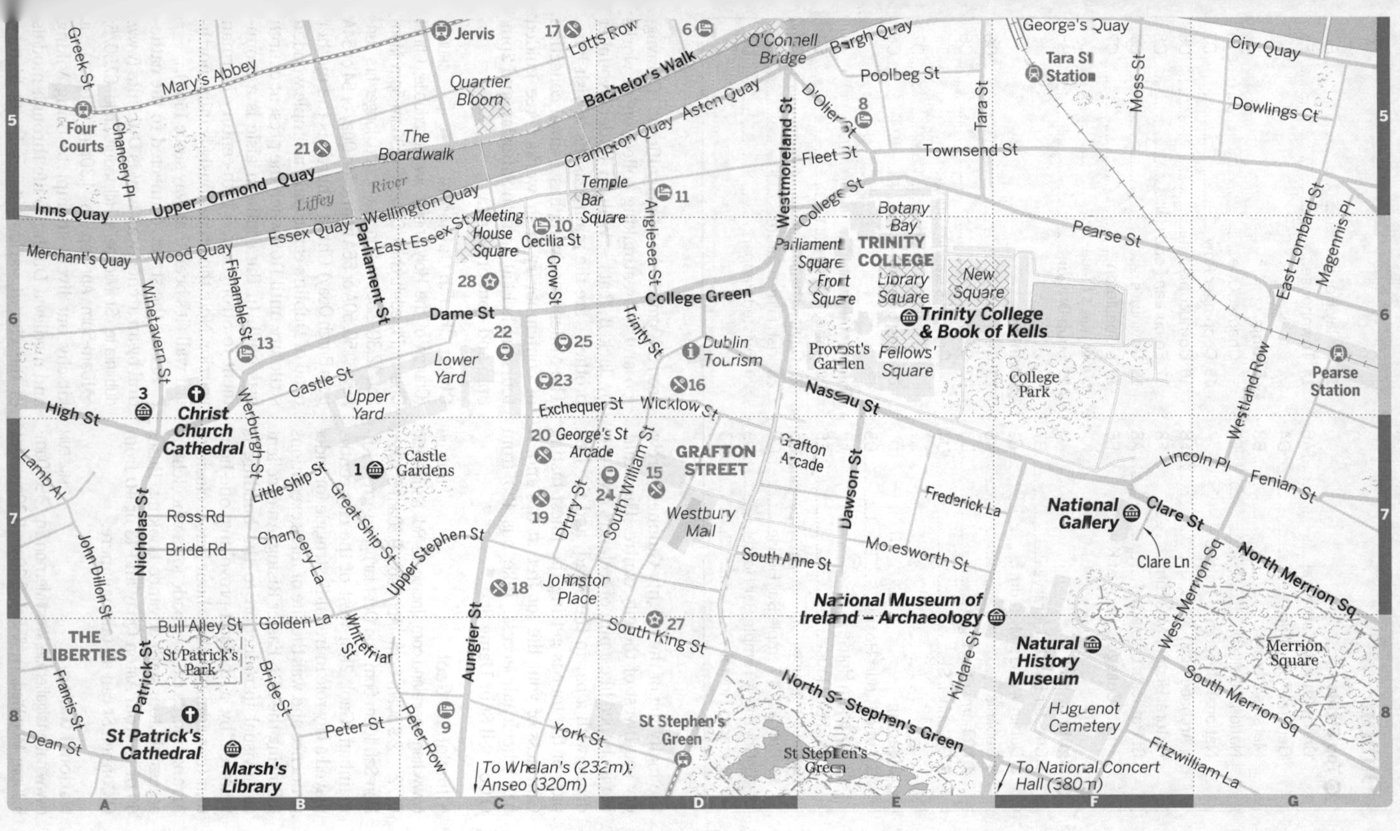

Greek St
Mary's Abbey
Jervis
17
Lotts Row
6
O'Connell Bridge
Burgh Quay
George's Quay
City Quay
Tara St Station
Moss St
Dowlings Ct
Four Courts
Chancery Pl
21
The Boardwalk
Quartier Bloom
Bachelor's Walk
Aston Quay
Crampton Quay
Westmoreland St
D'Olier St
8
Poolbeg St
Tara St
Fleet St
Townsend St
Inns Quay
Upper Ormond Quay
Liffey
River
Wellington Quay
Temple Bar Square
11
College St
Botany Bay
Pearse St
East Lombard St
Magennis Pl
Merchant's Quay
Wood Quay
Essex Quay
East Essex St
Meeting House Square
10
Cecilia St
Anglesea St
Parliament Square
TRINITY COLLEGE
Front Square
Library Square
New Square
Parliament St
28
Crow St
College Green
Winetavern St
Fishamble St
13
Dame St
22
25
Trinity St
Dublin Tourism
Trinity College & Book of Kells
Provost's Garden
Fellows' Square
College Park
Westland Row
Pearse Station
3
Christ Church Cathedral
High St
Castle St
Upper Yard
Lower Yard
23
16
Exchequer St
Wicklow St
Nassau St
20
George's St Arcade
Werburgh St
1
Castle Gardens
GRAFTON STREET
Grafton Arcade
15
24
Lamb Al
Little Ship St
Great Ship St
19
Drury St
South William St
Dawson St
Frederick La
Lincoln Pl
Fenian St
National Gallery
Clare St
Nicholas St
Ross Rd
Bride Rd
Chancery La
Upper Stephen St
Westbury Mall
South Anne St
Molesworth St
Clare Ln
North Merrion Sq
West Merrion Sq
John Dillon St
18
Johnston Place
Aungier St
27
South King St
National Museum of Ireland – Archaeology
Natural History Museum
Merrion Square
THE LIBERTIES
Bull Alley St
Golden La
Whitefriar St
St Patrick's Park
Patrick St
Bride St
Kildare St
South Merrion Sq
Francis St
North St Stephen's Green
Huguenot Cemetery
9
Peter St
Peter Row
York St
St Stephen's Green
Fitzwilliam La
Dean St
St Patrick's Cathedral
Marsh's Library
To Whelan's (232m); Anseo (320m)
To National Concert Hall (380m)
A
B
C
D
E
F
G
5
6
7
8

Dublin

Top Sights

	Christ Church Cathedral	A6
	General Post Office	D4
	Marsh's Library	B8
	National Gallery	F7
	National Museum of Ireland – Archaeology	F8
	Natural History Museum	F8
	St Patrick's Cathedral	A8
	Trinity College & Book of Kells	E6

Sights

1	Chester Beatty Library	B7
2	Dublin Writers Museum	C1
3	Dublinia	A6
4	Monument of Light	D3
5	O'Connell St	D4

Sleeping

6	Abbey Court Hostel	D5
7	Abraham House	E3
8	Ashfield House	E5
9	Avalon House	C8
10	Barnacles Temple Bar House	C6
11	Gogarty's Temple Bar Hostel	D5
12	Isaacs Hostel	F3
13	Kinlay House	B6
14	Townhouse	F3

Eating

	Chapter One	(see 2)
15	Coppinger Row	D7
16	Cornucopia	D6
17	Epicurean Food Hall	C5
18	Govinda's	C7
19	L'Gueuleton	C7
20	Simon's Place	C7
21	Soup Dragon	B5

Drinking

22	George	C6
23	Globe	C6
24	Grogan's Castle Lounge Traditional Pub	D7
25	Stag's Head	C6

Entertainment

26	Abbey Theatre	E4
27	Gaiety Theatre	D8
28	Irish Film Institute	C6
29	Twisted Pepper	D4

the malty fug of the mighty Guinness Brewery southwest of the city centre. The building is shaped like a pint of Ireland's favourite drink, with a bar in the 'head', and the best part of the tour is getting the finest-tasting Guinness of your life for free at the end. It has wheelchair access. Take bus 123 from O'Connell St or Dame St.

Kilmainham Gaol MUSEUM
(www.heritageireland.com; Inchicore Rd; adult/child €6/2; ⏲9.30am-6pm Apr-Sep, 9.30am-5.30pm Mon-Sat, 10am-6pm Sun Oct-Mar) The grey Kilmainham Gaol, 2km west of the city centre, played a key role in Ireland's struggle for independence and was the site of mass executions following the 1916 Easter Rising. An excellent audiovisual introduction to the building is followed by a thought-provoking one-hour tour (last admission one hour before closing). Arrangements can be made for a wheelchair-accessible tour with advance booking. Buses 69 or 79 from Aston Quay and 13 or 40 from O'Connell St can all take you here.

National Gallery MUSEUM
(www.nationalgallery.ie; West Merrion Sq; ⏲9.30am-5.30pm Mon-Wed, Fri & Sat, 9.30am-8.30pm Thu, noon-5.30pm Sun) A magnificent Caravaggio and a breathtaking collection of works by Jack B Yeats – William Butler's younger brother – are the main reasons to visit here. The Millennium wing has a small collection of contemporary Irish works. Free guided tours are held at 3pm on Saturday, and 2pm, 3pm and 4pm on Sunday.

Christ Church Cathedral CHURCH
(Church of the Holy Trinity; www.cccdub.ie; Christ Church Pl; adult/child €6/2; ⏲9.30am-5pm Mon-Sat, 12.30-2.30pm Sun year-round, longer hrs Jun-Aug; 🚌50, 50A or 56A from Aston Quay or 54 or 54A from Burgh Quay) Christ Church is the mother of all of Dublin's cathedrals, a simple wooden structure until 1169 when the present church was built. In the southern aisle is a monument to Strongbow, a 12th-century Norman warrior. Note the precariously leaning northern wall (it's been that way since 1562).

Across the street, connected to the cathedral by an arched walkway, is **Dublinia** (www.dublinia.ie; St Michael's Hill; adult/child €7.50/5; ⏲10am-5pm Apr-Sep, to 4.30pm Oct-Mar), a kitschy but lively attempt to bring Viking and medieval Dublin to life through models of the city at various stages in its history, streetscape tableaux and somewhat old-fashioned interactive displays.

St Patrick's Cathedral CHURCH
(www.stpatrickscathedral.ie; St Patrick's Close; adult/child €5.50/free; ⌚9am-5pm Mon-Sat, 9-10.30am & 12.30-2.30pm Sun year round, longer hours Mar-Oct; 🚌50, 50A or 56A from Aston Quay or 54 or 54A from Burgh Quay) There was a church on the site of St Patrick's Cathedral as early as the 5th century, but the present building dates from 1191. St Patrick's choir was part of the first group to perform Handel's *Messiah* in 1742, and you can hear their successors sing Evensong at 5.45pm most weeknights.

Just around the corner is the antique **Marsh's Library** (www.marshlibrary.ie; St Patrick's Close; adult/child €2.50/free; ⌚9.30am-1pm & 2-5pm Mon & Wed-Fri, 10am-1pm Sat; 🚌50, 50A or 56A from Aston Quay or 54 or 54A from Burgh Quay), the oldest public library in the country, with an atmosphere that has hardly changed since it opened its doors in 1707.

FREE **Natural History Museum** MUSEUM
(www.museum.ie; Merrion St; ⌚10am-5pm Tue-Sat, 2-5pm Sun) Dusty, weird and compelling, this window into Victorian times has barely changed since Scottish explorer Dr David Livingstone opened it in 1857. The creaky-floored interior is crammed with stuffed animals, skeletons, fossils and other specimens from around the world, ranging from West African apes to pickled insects in jars.

Dublin Writers Museum MUSEUM
(www.writersmuseum.com; 18 North Parnell Sq; adult/child €7.50/4.70; ⌚10am-5pm Mon-Sat, 11am-5pm Sun) Celebrates the city's role as a literary centre, with displays on Joyce, Swift, Yeats, Wilde, Beckett and others.

Sleeping

Dublin is *always* bustling, so call ahead or book online, especially on weekends. Don't forget that Dublin Tourism Centres can find and book accommodation for €5, plus a 10% deposit for the first night's stay.

NORTH OF THE LIFFEY

TOP CHOICE **Isaacs Hostel** HOSTEL €
(☎855 6215; www.isaacs.ie; 2-5 Frenchman's Lane; dm/tw from €14/54; @📶) This popular hostel set amid 200-year-old wine vaults has loads of character. The lounge area is where it all happens, from summer BBQs to live music, and the easygoing staff are on hand 24/7 for advice and help.

Generator Hostel HOSTEL €
(☎901 0222; www.generatorhostels.com/en/dublin; Smithfield Sq; dm/tw from €16/70; @📶) This European chain brings its own brand of funky, fun design to Dublin's hostel scene, with bright colours, comfortable dorms (including women-only) and a lively social scene. Good location on a pedestrian mall next to Old Jameson Distillery.

Townhouse Hotel INN €€€
(☎878 8808; www.townhouseofdublin.com; 47-48 Lower Gardiner St; s/d/tr €140/199/219) Elegant but unpretentious, the Georgian Townhouse has beautiful, individually designed bedrooms named after plays by the famous 19th-century playwrights who once lived here (Dion Boucicault and Lafcadio Hearn), and a Japanese garden out back.

Abbey Court Hostel HOSTEL €
(☎878 0700; www.abbey-court.com; 29 Bachelor's Walk; dm/d €18/79) What it lacks in physical charm is made up for in craic (fun) and central location. Many of its residents are long-termers, giving the joint a community feel, and its two large common rooms and fantastic staff make for a convivial atmosphere.

Abraham House HOSTEL €
(☎855 0600; www.abraham-house.ie; 83 Lower Gardiner St; dm incl breakfast €10-18, d incl breakfast €48-60; @📶) Friendly is an understatement at this large and lively hostel; good rates if you book ahead online. It's close to Connolly Station.

SOUTH OF THE LIFFEY

Barnacles HOSTEL €
(☎671 6277; www.barnacles.ie; 19 Lower Temple Lane; dm €19-22; P📶) Plenty bright and immaculately clean, Barnacles' location in the

DUBLIN PASS

If you're planning some heavy-duty sightseeing, you'll save a packet by investing in the **Dublin Pass** (adult/child one-day €35/19, two-day €55/31, three-day €65/39). Not only do you gain free entry to more than 30 attractions but you can skip whatever queue there is by presenting your card; it also includes free transfer to and from the airport on the Aircoach. Available from any of the Dublin Tourism offices.

SPLURGE

Number 31 (☎676 5011; www.number31.ie; 31 Leeson Close; s/d/tr €180/260/300; P wifi), the former dwelling of modernist architect Sam Stephenson (1933–2006), still feels like a 1960s designer pad with sunken sitting room, leather sofas, mirrored bar and floor-to-ceiling windows. A hidden oasis of calm, five minutes' walk from St Stephen's Green.

heart of the Temple Bar district makes it a great place to stay if you don't mind the sound of drunken revellers outside your window; rooms at the back are quieter.

Avalon House HOSTEL €
(☎475 0001; www.avalon-house.ie; 55 Aungier St; dm/s/d from €10/34/54; @ wifi) This grand old Victorian building near St Stephen's Green houses a megahostel with four-, 12- and 20-bed mixed dorms on two levels, offering some privacy. There's a large kitchen, several lounges and a pool room.

Ashfield House HOSTEL €
(☎679 7734; www.ashfieldhouse.ie; 19-20 D'Olier St; dm incl breakfast €9-18, d incl breakfast €48-60; @ wifi) Housed in a converted church a stone's throw from Temple Bar and O'Connell Bridge, this hostel feels more like a small hotel, with a good range of private en suite rooms as well as four-, six- and eight-bed dorms.

Kinlay House HOSTEL €
(☎679 6644; www.kinlaydublin.ie; 2-12 Lord Edward St; dm/d €18/60; wifi) Big, bustling and always up for a party (earplugs available at reception!), this is not a place for shrinking violets.

Gogarty's Temple Bar Hostel HOSTEL €
(☎671 1822; www.gogartys.ie/hostel; 58-59 Fleet St; dm/d €14/50; P wifi) Lively, party-atmosphere hostel right in the middle of Temple Bar action.

Eating

The most concentrated restaurant area is Temple Bar but, apart from a handful of good places, the bulk of eateries offer bland, unimaginative fodder and cheap set menus for tourists. Better food and service can usually be found on either side of Grafton St, while the top-end restaurants are clustered around Merrion Sq and Fitzwilliam Sq. Fast-food chains dominate the northside, though some fine cafes and eateries are finally appearing there too.

NORTH OF THE LIFFEY

Chapter One MODERN IRISH €€€
(☎873 2266; www.chapteronerestaurant.com; 18 North Parnell Sq; 2-course lunch €29, 4-course dinner €65; ⏲12.30-2pm Tue-Fri, 6-11pm Tue-Sat) One of the best restaurants in Dublin, this venerable old trooper in the vaulted basement of the Dublin Writers Museum sets its ambitions no further than modern Irish cuisine, which it has realised so brilliantly that those Michelin lads saw fit to throw one of their sought-after stars its way. Get there between 6pm and 7pm for the three-course Pre-Theatre Special (€36.50).

Soup Dragon TAKEAWAY €
(www.soupdragon.com; 168 Capel St; soups €5-10; ⏲8am-5pm Mon-Fri, 10am-4pm Sat) Eat in or take away one of 12 tasty varieties of homemade soups, including Indian dahl or spicy vegetable gumbo. Bowls come in two different sizes, and prices include fresh bread and a piece of fruit.

Epicurean Food Hall FOOD HALL €
(www.epicureanfoodhall.com; Lower Liffey St; mains €4-12; ⏲8am-8pm Mon-Wed, 8am-9pm Thu-Sat, 11am-7pm Sun) You'll be spoilt for choice in this bustling arcade that houses more than 20 food stalls. The quality can be hit-and-miss, but good choices include Viva Espana (tapas and excellent paella), Burdock's (for fish and chips), El Corte (for coffee) and Istanbul House (for kebabs).

SOUTH OF THE LIFFEY

L'Gueuleton FRENCH €€
(www.lgueuleton.com; 1 Fade St; mains €19-26; ⏲12.30-4pm & 6-10pm Mon-Sat, 1-4pm & 6-9pm Sun) Dubliners just can't get enough of this restaurant's take on French rustic cuisine, which ranges from regulars such as slow-roast pork belly with dauphinoise potatoes, to specials such as braised venison with orange, juniper and roast root vegetables. No reservations – queue for a table, or leave your mobile number and they'll text when a table's ready.

Coppinger Row MEDITERRANEAN €€
(www.coppingerrow.com; Coppinger Row; mains €18-25; ⏲noon-5.30pm & 6-11pm Mon-Sat, 12.30-4pm & 6-9pm Sun) The chefs here add a Mediterranean touch to the best of Irish produce, which can be enjoyed as main courses or

afternoon bar bites. Local crab and crayfish salad comes with basil and lemon, while lamb gets a spiced aubergine and apricot accompaniment.

Simon's Place CAFE €
(George's St Arcade, South Great George's St; sandwiches €5; ⊙9am-5.30pm Mon-Sat) Simon hasn't had to change the menu of sandwiches made with thick-cut bread and wholesome vegetarian soups since he first opened shop two decades ago – and why should he? His grub is as heart-warming and legendary as he is.

Cornucopia VEGETARIAN €
(www.cornucopia.ie; 19 Wicklow St; mains €10-13; ⊙8.30am-9pm Mon & Tue, 8.30am-10.15pm Wed-Sat, noon-9pm Sun; ✎) For those seeking escape from the Irish cholesterol habit, Cornucopia is a popular, mostly vegan cafe turning out scrumptious healthy goodies. There's even a vegetarian breakfast fry-up as an alternative to muesli.

Queen of Tarts CAFE €
(www.queenoftarts.ie; 3-4 Cow's Lane; mains €5-10; ⊙8am-7pm Mon-Fri, 9am-7pm Sat, 10am-6pm Sun) Pocket-sized Queen of Tarts offers a mouth-watering array of savoury tarts and filled focaccias, fruit crumbles, healthy breakfasts and weekend brunch specials.

Govinda's VEGETARIAN €
(www.govindas.ie; 4 Aungier St; mains €7-10; ⊙noon-9pm Mon-Sat; ✎) This place is totally vegetarian, with a wholesome mix of salads and Indian-influenced hot daily specials.

Drinking

Temple Bar, Dublin's 'party district', is almost always packed with raucous stag (bachelor) and hen (bachelorette) parties, scantily clad girls, and loud guys from Ohio wearing Guinness T-shirts. If you're just looking to get smashed and hook up with someone from another country, there's no better place in Ireland. If that's not your style, there's plenty to enjoy beyond Temple Bar. In fact, most of the best old-fashioned pubs are outside the district.

Stag's Head PUB
(1 Dame Ct) Built in 1770, and remodelled in 1895, the Stag's Head is possibly the best traditional pub in Dublin (and therefore the world). You may find yourself philosophising in the ecclesiastical atmosphere, as James Joyce once did. Some of the fitters that worked on this pub probably also worked on churches in the area, so the stained-wood-and-polished-brass similarities are no accident.

Grogan's Castle Lounge PUB
(15 South William St) A city-centre institution, Grogan's has long been a favourite haunt of Dublin's writers and painters, as well as others from the bohemian, alternative set. Drinks are marginally cheaper in the stone-floored public bar than in the lounge.

George GAY BAR
(www.thegeorge.ie; 89 South Great George's St) The mother of Dublin's gay bars is an institution, for years the only place in town where the gay crowd could, well, be gay. There are other places to go, but the George remains the best, if only for tradition's sake. Shirley's legendary Sunday night bingo is as popular as ever.

Dice Bar BAR
(☎674 6710; 79 Queen St) Co-owned by singer Huey from the band Fun Lovin' Criminals, the Dice Bar looks like something you'd find on New York's Lower East Side.

Anseo BAR
(28 Lower Camden St) Unpretentious, unaffected and incredibly popular hipster spot.

Globe BAR
(☎671 1220; www.globe.ie; 11 South Great George's St; 🚌all city-centre) The granddaddy of Dublin's hipster bars.

Entertainment

For events, reviews and club listings, pick up a copy of the fortnightly music review **Hot**

DON'T MISS

CHESTER BEATTY LIBRARY

Bequeathed to the nation by mining engineer Sir Alfred Chester Beatty (1875–1968), the breathtaking collection of the **Chester Beatty Library** (www.cbl.ie; Dublin Castle; ⊙10am-5pm Mon-Fri, 11am-5pm Sat, 1-5pm Sun year-round, closed Mon Oct-Apr, Reference Library by appointment only) includes more than 20,000 manuscripts, rare books, miniature paintings, clay tablets, costumes and other objects of artistic, historical and aesthetic importance. The library runs guided tours at 1pm on Wednesdays and at 3pm and 4pm on Sundays.

Press (www.hotpress.com), or for free cultural events, check out the weekly e-zine **Dublin Event Guide** (www.dublineventguide.com). Friday's *Irish Times* has a pull-out section called 'The Ticket' that has reviews and listings of all things arty.

Twisted Pepper NIGHTCLUB
(☎873 4800; www.bodytonicmusic.com/thetwistedpepper; 54 Middle Abbey St; ⊙bar 4pm-late, cafe 11am-6pm) Dublin's coolest new venue comes in four parts: the basement is where you can hear some of the best DJs in town, the stage is for live acts, the mezzanine is a secluded bar area above the stage and the cafe serves Irish breakfast all day. All run by the Bodytonic crew, one of the most exciting music and production crowds in town.

Whelan's LIVE MUSIC
(☎478 0766; www.whelanslive.com; 25 Wexford St) A Dublin institution, providing a showcase for Irish singer-songwriters and other lo-fi performers.

Abbey Theatre THEATRE
(☎878 7222; www.abbeytheatre.ie; Lower Abbey St) The famous Abbey is Ireland's national theatre, putting on new Irish works as well as revivals of Irish classics. It's scheduled to move to a new location in docklands by 2016.

National Concert Hall LIVE MUSIC
(☎417 0000; www.nch.ie; Earlsfort Tce) Just south of the city centre, Ireland's premier orchestral hall hosts a variety of concerts year-round, including a series of lunchtime concerts from 1.05pm to 2pm on Tuesday from June to August.

Gaiety Theatre THEATRE
(☎677 1717; www.gaietytheatre.com; South King St) This popular theatre – which famously staged the 1971 Eurovision Song Contest – hosts, among other things, a program of classical concerts, operas and musicals.

Irish Film Institute CINEMA
(☎679 5744; www.ifi.ie; 6 Eustace St) The fantastic IFI has two screens showing classic and art-house films. Wheelchair access available.

ℹ Information

All Dublin tourist offices provide walk-in services only – no phone inquiries. For tourist information by phone, call ☎1850 230 330 from within the Republic.

City Centre Tourist Office (14 O'Connell St; ⊙9am-5pm Mon-Sat)

Doctor on Duty (☎453 9333; www.mediserve.ie; ⊙24hr) Request a doctor to come to your accommodation.

Dublin Discover Ireland Centre (www.visitdublin.com; St Andrew's Church, 2 Suffolk St; ⊙9am-5.30pm Mon-Sat, 10.30am-3pm Sun) Offers tourist information for all of Ireland, as well as accommodation bookings, car hire, maps, and tickets for tours, concerts and more. Ask about the **Dublin Pass** (www.dublinpass.ie), which allows you entrance into more than 30 of Dublin's attractions, as well as some tours and other special offers.

Dun Laoghaire Tourist Office (Dun Laoghaire ferry port; ⊙10am-1pm & 2-6pm)

TRANSPORT FROM DUBLIN

Bus

DESTINATION	PRICE (€)	DURATION (HR)	FREQUENCY
Belfast	17	2½	hourly
Cork	14	4½	6 daily
Galway	14	3¾	hourly
Killarney	32	6	5 daily
Rosslare Europort	19.50	3½	4 daily

Train

DESTINATION	PRICE (€)	DURATION (HR)	FREQUENCY
Belfast	35	2¼	up to 8 daily
Cork	60	2¾	hourly
Galway	34	2¾	9 daily

Hickey's Pharmacy (☎873 0427; 55 Lower O'Connell St) Open till 10pm every night.

Lonely Planet (www.lonelyplanet.com/ireland/dublin)

Northern Ireland Tourist Board (NITB; www.discovernorthernireland.com) Has a desk in the Dublin Discover Ireland Centre; same hours.

St James's Hospital (☎410 3000; www.stjames.ie; James's St) Dublin's main 24-hour accident and emergency department.

Well Woman Clinic (☎872 8051; www.well-womancentre.ie; 35 Lower Liffey St; ⏲9.30am-7.30pm Mon, Thu & Fri, 8am-7.30pm Tue & Wed, 10am-4pm Sat) Handles women's health issues and can supply contraception.

Getting There & Away

AIR **Dublin Airport** (☎814 1111; www.dublinair-port.com), about 13km north of the city centre, is Ireland's major international gateway, with direct flights from Europe, North America and Asia. Budget airlines including Ryanair and Flybe land here.

BOAT There are direct ferries from Holyhead in Wales to Dublin Port, 3km northeast of the city centre, and to Dun Laoghaire, 13km southeast. Boats also sail direct to Dublin Port from Liverpool and from Douglas, on the Isle of Man.

BUS **Busáras** (☎01-836 6111; www.buseireann.ie; Store St), Dublin's main bus station, is just north of the Liffey.

The private company **Citylink** (www.citylink.ie) has nonstop services from Dublin airport (picking up in the city centre at Bachelor's Walk, near O'Connell Bridge) to Galway (€16, three hours, hourly).

TRAIN **Connolly station** is north of the Liffey, with trains to Belfast, Derry, Sligo, other points north and Wexford. **Heuston station** is south of the Liffey and west of the city centre, with trains for Cork, Galway, Killarney, Limerick, and most other points to the south and west.

Visit **Iarnród Éireann Travel Centre** (☎1850-366 222; www.irishrail.ie; Connolly Station, Amiens St; ⏲9am-5pm Mon-Fri, to 1pm Sat) for general train information.

Getting Around

Bicycle

Rental rates begin at around €13/70 a day/week; you'll need a €50 to €200 cash deposit and photo ID. **Neill's Wheels** (www.rentabikedublin.com; per day/week €12.50/70) has various outlets, including Kinlay House and Isaacs Hostel.

Public Transport

Various public transport passes are available; one day's unlimited bus travel costs €6.50 (including Airlink); bus and tram costs €7.80; and bus and DART costs €11.75.

BUS **Dublin Bus** (www.dublinbus.ie) local buses cost from €1.40 to €2.65 for a single journey. You must pay the exact fare when boarding; drivers don't give change. The Rambler 1 Day ticket (€6.50) allows one day's unlimited travel on buses including Airlink.

TRAIN **Dublin Area Rapid Transport** (DART; ☎01-836 6222; www.irishrail.ie) provides quick rail access as far north as Howth and south to Bray; Pearse station is handy for central Dublin.

TRAM **Luas** (www.luas.ie; ⏲5.30am-12.30am Mon-Fri, from 6.30am Sat, 7am-11.30pm Sun) runs on two (unconnected) lines: the green line runs from the eastern side of St Stephen's Green southeast to Sandyford, and the red line runs from Tallaght to Connolly station, with stops at Heuston station, the National Museum and Busáras. Single fares range from €1.60 to €2.90 depending on how many zones you travel through.

TAXI Taxis in Dublin are expensive; flag fall costs €4.10, plus €1.03 per kilometre. For taxi service, call **National Radio Cabs** (☎01-677 2222; www.radiocabs.ie).

GETTING INTO DUBLIN

To get to the centre from Busáras, the main bus station, walk west along the river or south to Oliver Plunkett St. Connolly train station, about 1.5km northeast of town, is a little further, but you can easily walk it via MacCurtain St, if you're staying on Wellington Rd. Frequent buses head from the airport (€6, 40 minutes), where there are direct budget flights to major cities all over Europe. Buses run from the Dublin ferry terminal (€3, 25 minutes) to Busáras.

THE SOUTHEAST

Kilkenny

☎056 / POP 26,500

Built from black limestone flecked with fossil seashells, Kilkenny is known as 'the marble city'. Its picturesque huddle of medieval lanes, strung between castle and cathedral along the bank of the Nore River, is one of the southeast's biggest tourist draws – the narrow streets are often clogged with tour coaches. But it's worth braving the crowds to soak up the atmosphere of one of Ireland's creative crucibles – Kilkenny is a centre for arts and crafts, and home to a host of fine restaurants, cafes, pubs and shops.

Sights

Kilkenny Castle HISTORIC BUILDING
(www.kilkennycastle.ie; adult/child €6/2.50, audioguides €5, parkland free; ⌚9.30am-5pm Mar-Sep, 9.30am-4.30pm Oct-Feb, parkland daylight hours) Stronghold of the powerful Butler family, Kilkenny Castle has a history dating back to 1172, when the legendary Strongbow erected a wooden tower on the site, though much of its present look dates from the 19th century. Highlights of the guided tour include the painted roof beams of the Long Gallery, and the collection of Victorian antiques. There's an excellent tearoom in the former castle kitchens, all white marble and gleaming copper.

Craft Centres ARTS CENTRE
The former stables opposite Kilkenny Castle are home to the **National Craft Gallery** (www.nationalcraftgallery.ie; Castle Yard; admission free; ⌚10am-5.30pm Tue-Sat, 11am-5.30pm Sun) and the **Kilkenny Design Centre** (☎056-772 2118; www.kilkennydesign.com; Castle Yard; ⌚10am-7pm), showcases for contemporary Irish crafts. Pick up **Kilkenny Craft Trail** (www.madeinkilkenny.ie) leaflet at the tourist office for a list of local crafts workshops.

St Canice's Cathedral CHURCH
(www.stcanicescathedral.ie; St Canice's Pl; adult/child €4/free, round tower €3/free; ⌚9am-6pm Mon-Sat, 2-6pm Sun Jun-Aug, 10am-1pm & 2-5pm Mon-Sat, 2-5pm Sun Apr-May & Sep, until 4pm other times) Ireland's second-largest cathedral is crammed with medieval monuments and tombs. Outside stands a 30m-tall **round tower** (⌚Apr-Oct), which you can climb – if you're over 12 years of age – for a grand view of the town.

Festivals & Events

Kilkenny is rightly known as the festival capital of Ireland, with several world-class events throughout the year.

Kilkenny Arts Festival ARTS
(www.kilkennyarts.ie) In mid-August the city comes alive with theatre, cinema, music, literature, visual arts, children's events and street spectacles for 10 action-packed days.

Kilkenny Rhythm & Roots MUSIC
(www.kilkennyroots.com; ⌚early May) Over 30 pubs and other venues participate in hosting Ireland's biggest music festival, with an emphasis on country and 'old-timey' American roots music.

Sleeping

Butler House BOUTIQUE HOTEL €€
(☎772 2828; www.butler.ie; 16 Patrick St; s/d from €77/135; P@) You can't stay in Kilkenny Castle, but this historic mansion is surely the next best thing. Once the home of the earls of Ormonde, who built the castle, these days it houses a boutique hotel with aristocratic trappings that include sweeping staircases, marble fireplaces, an art collection and impeccably trimmed gardens.

Celtic House B&B €€
(☎776 2249; www.celtic-house-bandb.com; 18 Michael St; s/d €35/70; P@) Artist Angela Byrne extends one of Ireland's warmest welcomes at her spick-and-span B&B. Some of the bright rooms have views of the castle, and Angela's landscapes adorn many of the walls. Guests return time and again – book ahead.

Kilkenny Tourist Hostel HOSTEL €
(☎776 3541; www.kilkennyhostel.ie; 35 Parliament St; dm/tw €17/42; @) Inside an ivy-covered 1770s Georgian townhouse, this cosy, 60-bed IHH hostel has a sitting room warmed by an open fireplace, and a timber- and lead-light-panelled dining room adjoining the self-catering kitchen. Most pubs are within stumbling distance.

Eating

Cafe Sol MODERN IRISH €€
(☎776 4987; www.restaurantskilkenny.com; William St; mains lunch €11-13, dinner €17-25; ⌚noon-9.30pm Mon-Thu, 11am-10pm Fri & Sat, noon-9pm Sun;) The seasonally changing menu at this funky place lists local sources for most of the produce. The Irish-Mediterranean cuisine, like the bold artwork on the walls, displays unexpected but successful combinations. It's packed by 1pm, so arrive early for lunch. Three-course early-bird menus (€27; 5.30pm to 9.30pm Sunday to Thursday, 5.30pm to 6.45pm Friday and Saturday) are great value.

Gourmet Store SANDWICHES €
(56 High St; sandwiches €3.50; ⌚9am-6pm Mon-Sat) This classy deli is a great place for takeaway sandwiches.

Drinking & Entertainment

Tynan's Bridge House PUB
(St John's Bridge; ⌚11am-late) Looking like it might fall down at any moment, this wonky Georgian pub is the best traditional bar in town.

John Cleere PUB
(22 Parliament St) One of Kilkenny's finest venues for live music, this long bar has blues, jazz and rock, as well as trad music sessions.

Watergate Theatre THEATRE
(www.watergatetheatre.com; Parliament St) Hosts musical and theatrical productions throughout the year.

Information

Tourist Office (www.kilkennytourism.ie; Rose Inn St; ⌚9.15am-5pm Mon-Sat)

Getting There & Away

BUS Buses depart from the train station. Services include Cork (€19, three hours, two daily) and Dublin (€12, 2¼ hours, five daily).

TRAIN **Kilkenny train station** (Dublin Rd) is east of the town centre along John St, next to the MacDonagh Junction shopping mall. Services include Dublin Heuston (€24, 1¾ hours, eight daily) and Galway (€45, four hours, one daily, change at Kildare).

THE SOUTHWEST

Cork

☎021 / POP 120,000

There's a reason the locals call Cork (Corcaigh) 'Ireland's Real Capital' or 'The People's Republic of Cork'; something special is going on here. The city has long been dismissive of Dublin, and with a burgeoning arts, music and restaurant scene, it has a cultural reputation to rival the capital's.

Sights

Crawford Municipal Art Gallery GALLERY
(☎490 7855; www.crawfordartgallery.ie; Emmet Pl; ⌚10am-5pm Mon-Sat, to 8pm Thu) The 18th-century Cork Customs House is blended with 21st-century Dutch design in this intriguing gallery, a must-see for anyone who enjoys art and architecture. Pieces by Irish artists such as Jack Yeats and Cork's own James Barry sit among a fine permanent collection that includes artists from Continental Europe. The gallery has wheelchair access.

English Market MARKET
(Princes St; ⌚9am-5.30pm Mon-Sat) It could just as easily be called the Victorian Market for its ornate vaulted ceilings and columns, but the English Market is a true gem, no matter what you name it. Scores of vendors sell some of the very best meat, fish, cheese and takeaway food in the region. On decent days, take your lunch to nearby Bishop Lucey Park, a popular alfresco eating spot.

Cork City Gaol MUSEUM
(☎430 5022; www.corkcitygaol.com; Convent Ave, Sunday's Well; adult/child €8/4.50; ⌚9.30am-5pm Apr-Oct, 10am-4pm Nov-Mar) Closed down in 1923, this vast 19th-century prison is now a terrific museum about a terrifying subject. Restored cells, mannequins representing prisoners and guards, and a detailed audioguide bring home the horrors of Victorian prison life.

Sleeping

Garnish House B&B €€
(☎427 5111; www.garnish.ie; Western Rd; s/d from €75/88; P 📶) With charming rooms (think flowers and fresh fruit), gourmet breakfasts and hosts who are eager to please, Garnish House is possibly the perfect B&B. From the moment you arrive and are greeted with tea and goodies, until the moment you leave, you will experience nothing short of absolute hospitality.

Brú Bar & Hostel HOSTEL €
(☎455 9667; www.bruhostel.com; 57 MacCurtain St; dm €15-20, d & tr €48-60; @📶) Cork's funkiest hostel also has a popular bar and an internet cafe on the premises. This clean and friendly triple treat can be a rocking good time, especially on the weekends.

Kinlay House HOSTEL €
(☎450 8966; www.kinlayhousecork.ie; Bob & Joan's Walk; dm €15-18, d €48-70; @📶) This labyrinthine hostel is in a bucolic spot near St Anne's Church in Shandon. It has a fun, laid-back atmosphere; services include bureau de change, laundry and luggage storage. Guests can use the next-door gym at a discount.

Sheila's Hostel HOSTEL €
(☎450 5562; www.sheilashostel.ie; 4 Belgrave Pl, off Wellington Rd; dm €16-18, tw €46-52; P@📶) The sauna, cinema room, coffee shop and superfriendly staff make up for the occasionally cramped atmosphere in this always-heaving hostel.

Cork

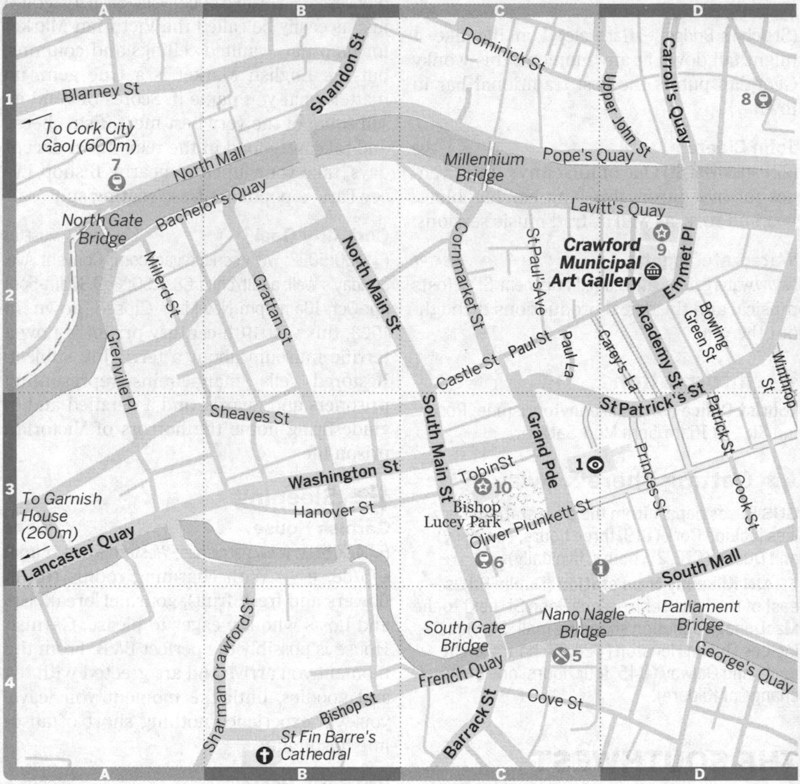

A B C D
1 2 3 4
Blarney St
To Cork City Gaol (600m)
7
North Mall
Bachelor's Quay
North Gate Bridge
Shandon St
Dominick St
Upper John St
Carroll's Quay
8
Millennium Bridge
Pope's Quay
Lavitt's Quay
9
Crawford Municipal Art Gallery
Emmet Pl
Millerd St
Grattan St
North Main St
Cornmarket St
St Paul's Ave
Grenville Pl
Paul St
Paul La
Carey's La
Academy St
Bowling Green St
Winthrop St
Castle St
Sheaves St
St Patrick's St
South Main St
Grand Pde
Patrick St
Washington St
TobinSt
1
10
Princes St
Cook St
To Garnish House (260m)
Hanover St
Bishop Lucey Park
Oliver Plunkett St
Lancaster Quay
6
South Mall
Sharman Crawford St
South Gate Bridge
Nano Nagle Bridge
Parliament Bridge
5
George's Quay
French Quay
Cove St
Bishop St
Barrack St
St Fin Barre's Cathedral

Eating

Market Lane IRISH, INTERNATIONAL €€

(☎427 4710; www.marketlane.ie; 5 Oliver Plunkett St; mains €13-22; ⏲noon-late Mon-Sat, 1-9pm Sun; 📶) It's always hopping at this bright corner bistro with a walk-in policy (no reservations for fewer than six diners, sip a drink at the bar until a table is free). The menu is broad and hearty, changing to reflect what's fresh at the English Market: how about braised ox-cheek stew, or smoked haddock with bacon and cabbage? Lots of wines by the glass.

Farmgate Café CAFE, BISTRO €€

(www.farmgate.ie; Princes St, English Market; mains €6-14; ⏲8.30am-5pm Mon-Sat) An unmissable experience at the heart of the English Market, the Farmgate is perched on a balcony overlooking the market below, the source of all that fresh local produce on your plate. Up the stairs and turn left for table service, right for counter service.

Quay Co-op CAFE €

(☎431 7026; www.quaycoop.com; 24 Sullivan's Quay; mains €9-11; ⏲9am-9pm Mon-Sat; 🥬👪) Flying the flag for alternative Cork, this place offers a range of self-service vegie options, all organic, including big breakfasts and rib-sticking soups and casseroles. It also caters for gluten-, dairy- and wheat-free needs.

Drinking

Cork's pub scene is cracking, easily rivalling Dublin's. Locally brewed Murphy's is the stout of choice here, not Guinness. Check www.corkgigs.com for pubs with live music.

Franciscan Well Brewery PUB

(www.franciscanwellbrewery.com; 14 North Mall; ⏲3-11.30pm Mon-Thu, 3pm-12.30am Fri & Sat, 3-11pm Sun; 📶) The copper vats gleaming behind the bar give the game away: the Fran-

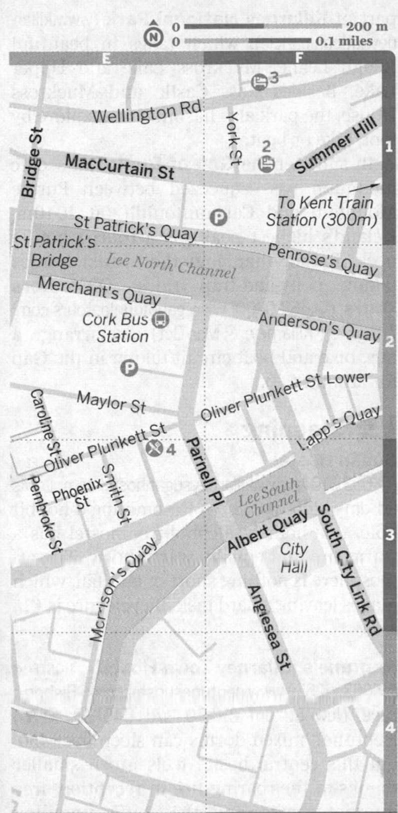

ciscan Well brews its own beer. The best place to enjoy it is in the enormous beer garden at the back.

Sin É PUB

(Coburg St) There are no frills or fuss here – just a comfy, sociable pub, long on atmosphere and short on pretension. There's music most nights, much of it traditional, but with the odd surprise.

An Spailpín Fánac PUB

(South Main St) The 'wandering labourer' hosts trad sessions almost nightly.

☆ Entertainment

Cork's cultural life is generally of a high calibre. To see what's happening grab **WhazOn?** (www.whazon.com), a free monthly booklet available from the tourist office, newsagencies, shops, hostels and B&Bs.

Cork

Top Sights

Crawford Municipal Art Gallery	D2

Sights

1 English Market	C3

Sleeping

2 Brú Bar & Hostel	F1
3 Sheila's Hostel	F1

Eating

Farmgate Café	(see 1)
4 Market Lane	E3
5 Quay Co-op	C4

Drinking

6 An Spailpín Fánac	C3
7 Franciscan Well Brewery	A1
8 Sin É	D1

Entertainment

9 Cork Opera House	D2
10 Triskel Arts Centre	C3

Cork Opera House OPERA

(☎427 0022; www.corkoperahouse.ie; Emmet Pl; ⏲box office 9am-8.30pm, to 5.30pm non-performance nights) Cork's opera house and its Half Moon Theatre stage everything from opera and ballet to drama, comedy and live music. It has wheelchair access.

Triskel Arts Centre ARTS CENTRE

(☎472 2022; www.triskelart.com; Tobin St; tickets around €15) Hosts contemporary art, film, theatre, music and photography.

Information

Cork City Tourist Office (☎425 5100; www.cometocork.com; Grand Pde; ⏲9am-6pm Mon-Sat, 10am-5pm Sun Jul & Aug, 9.15am-5pm Mon-Sat Sep-Jun)

Getting There & Around

BIKE Cycle Scene (☎430 1183; www.cyclescene.ie; 396 Blarney St) has bikes for hire from €15/80 per day/week.

BOAT Brittany Ferries (☎427 7801; www.brittanyferries.ie; 42 Grand Pde) has regular sailings from Cork to Roscoff (France). The ferry terminal is at Ringaskiddy, about 15 minutes by car southeast of the city centre along the N28.

BUS Aircoach (☎01-844 7118; www.aircoach.ie) provides a direct service to Dublin city and airport from St Patrick Quay (€18, four hours, eight daily). **Cork bus station** (cnr Merchants

Quay & Parnell Pl) is east of the city centre. Services include Dublin (€14, 4½ hours, six daily), Kilkenny (€19, three hours, two daily) and Killarney (€18, 1¾ hours, hourly).

TRAIN Cork's **Kent train station** (☎021-450 4777) is across the river. Destinations include Dublin (€60, 2¾ hours, hourly), Galway (€83, five to six hours, seven daily, two or three changes needed) and Killarney (€28, 1½ to two hours, nine daily).

Around Cork

BLARNEY

☎021 / POP 2150

Lying just northwest of Cork, the village of Blarney (An Bhlarna) receives a *gazillion* visitors a year, for one sole reason: **Blarney Castle** (☎438 5252; www.blarneycastle.ie; adult/child €12/5; ⌚9am-7pm Mon-Sat, 9am-6pm Sun Jun-Aug, 9am-6.30pm Mon-Sat, 9am-6pm Sun May & Sep, 9am-6pm Mon-Sat, 9am-5pm Sun Oct-Apr). They come to kiss the castle's legendary **Blarney Stone** and get the 'gift of the gab' (Queen Elizabeth I, exasperated with Lord Blarney's ability to talk endlessly without agreeing to her demands, invented the term 'to talk Blarney' back in the 16th century). The stone is up on the battlements, and bending over backwards to kiss it requires a head for heights, although there's someone there to hold you in position. It also helps if you're not germophobic – there's a greasy mark where millions of lips have been before.

Bus 215 runs from Cork bus station to Blarney (€6.50 return, 30 minutes, every 30 minutes).

Killarney

☎064 / POP 13,500

Killarney is a tourism machine in a sublime landscape of lakes, forests and 1000m peaks. Its manufactured tweeness is renowned, the streets filled with tour-bus visitors shopping for soft-toy shamrocks, and countless placards pointing to trad-music sessions. However, it has many charms beyond its proximity to waterfalls, woodlands, mountains and moors. In a town that's been practising the tourism game for more than 250 years, competition keeps standards high, and visitors on all budgets can expect to find superb restaurants, great pubs and good accommodation.

Sights & Activities

Most of Killarney's attractions are just outside the town. The mountain backdrop is part of **Killarney National Park** (www.killarneynationalpark.ie), which takes in beautiful Lough Leane, Muckross Lake and Upper Lake. Besides Ross Castle and Muckross House, the park also has much to explore by foot, bike or boat.

In summer the **Gap of Dunloe**, a scenic mountain pass squeezed between Purple Mountain and Carrauntouhill (at 1040m, Ireland's highest peak), is a tourist bottleneck. Rather than join the tourist hordes taking pony-and-trap rides, **O'Connors Tours** (☎663 0200; www.gapofdunloetours.com; 7 High St, Killarney; ⌚Mar-Oct) can arrange a bus, bike and boat circuit taking in the Gap for around €30.

Sleeping

Súgán Hostel HOSTEL €
(☎663 3104; www.killarneysuganhostel.com; Lewis Rd; dm €12-15, tw €38; 📶) Resembling a hobbit hole, this homely, alcohol-free hostel has a warm fire and equally warm hosts. The atmosphere is nothing short of familial, which makes leaving a hard task. Bicycle hire is €15 a day.

Neptune's Killarney Town Hostel HOSTEL €
(☎663 5255; www.neptuneshostel.com; Bishop's Lane, New St; dm €16-20, s/d €40/50; @📶) Neptune's mixed dorms can sleep over 150, but this central hostel feels much smaller thanks to the roaring fire in reception, free internet access, and the staff's unfailing helpfulness.

Rathmore House B&B €€
(☎663 2829; www.rathmorehousekillarney.com; Rock Rd; s/d €38/75; ⌚Mar-Nov; P📶) There's a real Irish welcome at this long-established, family-run B&B at the entrance to town.

Killarney Flesk Caravan & Camping Park CAMPGROUND €
(☎663 1704; www.killarneyfleskcamping.com; Muckross Rd; campsites per campervan plus 2 persons €26, hiker €10; ⌚Jun-Sep; P📶) About 1.5km south of the town centre on the N71 to Kenmare, this camping ground has great views of the mountains.

Eating

Smoke House BISTRO €€
(☎662 0801; www.thesmokehouse.ie; High St; mains lunch €7-14, dinner €15-26; ⌚8am-11pm; 🖊) One of Killarney's newest and busiest ventures, this tiled bistro is the first establishment in Ireland to cook with a Josper

(Spanish charcoal oven). Stylish salads include Dingle prawn, and roast fig and feta; its Kerry lamb burger, with mint, tomatoes and pickled onion, is delicious.

Jam CAFE €
(77 High St; mains €5-11; ⏲8am-6pm Mon-Sat;) This funky little cafe is famed for superb and healthy soups, salads and sandwiches, and coffee and cake.

Bricín IRISH €€€
(www.bricin.com; 26 High St; mains €19-26; ⏲dinner Tue Sat) This Celtic deco restaurant doubles as the town museum, with Jonathan Fisher's 18th-century views of the national park taking pride of place. Dishes include Kerry lamb, gourmet nut roast and house speciality *boxty* (potato pancake); the pre-6.30pm menu offers two/three courses for €19/29.

Drinking & Entertainment

Killarney Grand BAR, NIGHTCLUB
(www.killarneygrand.com; Main St) A great place for authentic music (if you can hear it over the boisterous crowd), the Grand has interesting takes on the traditional thing from 9pm. Wednesday night is *ceile* night (9pm to 11pm, €7 admission fee).

O'Connor's PUB
(High St) O'Connor's is a tiny but hugely popular pub that stages a mix of trad music, stand-up comedy, readings and pub theatre.

Courtney's PUB
(www.courtneysbar.com; Plunkett St) With a few fireplaces, barrels used as tables and nearly everything made from wood, Courtney's offers the ultimate Irish pub atmosphere.

Information

Tourist Office (☎663 1633; www.killarney.ie; Beech Rd; ⏲9am-8pm Jun-Aug, 9.15am-5pm Sep-May) Busy but efficient; has free map of national park and details of bus services.

Getting There & Around

BIKE O'Sullivan's (www.killarneyrentabike.com; Beech Rd; per day/week €15/80) rents bikes; opposite the tourist office.

BUS Operating from the train station, Bus Éireann has regular services to Cork (€18, 1¾ hours, hourly), Dublin (€27, six hours, six daily), Galway via Limerick (€24.50, seven hours, six daily) and Rosslare Harbour (€29, seven hours, three daily).

TAXI Taxis can be found at the taxi rank on College St. A cab from the edge of town (eg Flesk campsite) into the town centre costs around €9

TRAIN Travelling by train to Cork (€28, 1½ to two hours, nine daily) or Dublin (€62, six hours, three daily) usually involves changing at Mallow.

Ring of Kerry

☎066

The Ring of Kerry, a 179km circuit around the dramatic coastal scenery of the Iveragh Peninsula, is one of Ireland's premier tourist attractions. Most travellers tackle the ring by bus on guided day trips from Killarney, but you could spend days wandering here.

Sights

The **Ballaghbeama Pass** cuts across the peninsula's central highlands and has spectacular views and little traffic, while the shorter **Ring of Skellig**, at the end of the peninsula, has fine views of the Skellig Rocks and is less touristy. You can forgo roads completely by walking the **Kerry Way**, which winds through the Macgillycuddy's Reeks mountains past Carrauntuohill (1040m), Ireland's highest mountain.

Political hero Daniel O'Connell was born near **Cahirciveen**, one of the ring's larger towns. The excellent **Barracks Heritage Centre** (www.theoldbarracks.com; Bridge St; adult/student €4/2; ⏲10am-5.30pm Mon-Sat, 1-5.30pm Sun May-Sep, other times by arrangement) off Bridge St occupies what was once an intimidating Royal Irish Constabulary (RIC) barracks. Exhibits focus on O'Connell and on the famine's local impact.

South of Cahirciveen the R565 branches west to the 11km-long **Valentia Island**, the jumping-off point for an unforgettable experience: the **Skellig Rocks**, two tiny islands 12km off the coast. The vertiginous climb up uninhabited **Skellig Michael** (www.heritageireland.ie) inspires an awe that monks could have clung to life in the meagre beehive-shaped stone huts that stand on the tiny strip of level land on top. Calm seas permitting, boats run from spring to late summer from Portmagee, just before the bridge to Valentia, to Skellig Michael. The standard fare is around €45 return. Advance booking is essential; there are a dozen boat operators, including **Casey's** (☎947 2437; www.skelligislands.com; Portmagee) and **Sea Quest** (☎947 6214; www.skelligsrock.com).

Sleeping

There are plenty of hostels and B&Bs along the Ring. It's wise to book ahead, though, as some places are closed out of season and others fill up quickly.

TOP CHOICE **Mannix Point Camping & Caravan Park** CAMPGROUND €
(☎947 2806; www.campinginkerry.com; Mannix Point; campsites per person €8.50; ⊙Mar-Oct; 📶) This place regularly wins awards as the best camping ground in Ireland. With a coastal location, sunset views, and a campers' lounge with peat fire, musical instruments and friendly resident cats, it's easy to see why.

Sive Hostel HOSTEL €
(☎947 2717; www.sivehostel.ie; East End, Caherciveen; dm/tw €15/44; 📶) Simple and sweet, this IHH affiliate is a good walking base. There's bike storage, a camping area, and it's close to several good pubs.

Skellig Hostel HOSTEL €
(☎947 9942; www.skellighostel.com; Ballinskelligs; dm/d €15/52; P📶) This modern building is a little characterless, but the rooms, lounge and dining room are comfortable, and it's elevated, with sea views.

Getting Around

Bus Éireann runs a once-daily Ring of Kerry bus service (No 280) from late June to late August. Buses leave Killarney at 11.30am and stop at Killorglin, Glenbeigh, Caherciveen, Waterville, Caherdaniel and Molls Gap, arriving back at Killarney at 4.45pm (€19).

Travel agencies and hostels in Killarney offer daily tours of the Ring for about €20, year-round.

THE WEST COAST

The Burren

The Burren of northern County Clare is a harsh and haunting landscape of bare rock, softened with a sprinkling of rare wildflowers; *Boireann* is Irish for 'Rocky Country', and the name is no exaggeration. The rugged limestone plateau is littered with ancient dolmens, ring forts, round towers, high crosses and a surprisingly diverse range of flora, while rocky foreshores and splendid cliffs line its coast.

A number of bus tours leave Galway every morning for The Burren and the Cliffs of Moher, including **O'Neachtain Tours** (☎091-553 188; www.irelandscenictours.ie). They all cost around €25.

CLIFFS OF MOHER

About 8km south of Doolin are the towering 200m-high Cliffs of Moher, one of Ireland's most famous natural features. In summer the cliffs are overrun with day trippers, so consider staying in Doolin and hiking or biking along The Burren's quiet country lanes, where the views are superb and crowds are never a problem. Either way, be careful along these sheer cliffs, especially in wet or windy weather.

The landscaped **Cliffs of Moher Visitor Centre** (www.cliffsofmoher.ie; adult/child €6/free; ⊙8.30am-7.30pm Jun-Aug, 9am-6pm Mar-May, Sep & Oct, 9am-5pm Nov-Feb) has exhibitions about the cliffs and the environment called the 'Atlantic Edge'.

Galway

☎091 / POP 72,400

Arty and bohemian, Galway (Gaillimh) is legendary around the world for its entertainment scene. Students make up a quarter of the city's population, and brightly painted pubs heave with live music on any given night. Cafes spill out onto cobblestone streets filled with a frenzy of fiddles, banjos, guitars and bodhráns, and jugglers, painters, puppeteers and magicians in outlandish masks enchant passers-by.

Sights & Activities

Little remains of Galway's old city walls apart from the **Spanish Arch**, which is right beside the river. Nearby **Galway City Museum** (www.galwaycitymuseum.ie; Spanish Pde; ⊙10am-5pm Tue-Sat) has exhibits on the city's history from 1800 to 1950, including an iconic Galway Hooker fishing boat, a collection of currachs (boats made from animal hides) and a controversial statue of Galway-born writer and hell-raiser Pádraic O'Conaire (1883–1928), which was previously in Eyre Sq.

Back in the 13th century when the de Burgo family ran the show in Galway, they built the **Hall of the Red Earl** (www.galwaycivictrust.ie; Druid Lane; ⊙9.30am-4.45pm Mon-Fri) as their seat of power. After the 14 tribes took over, the hall fell into ruin and was lost until 1997 when expansion of the city's Custom House uncovered its foundations. Now after a decade of archaeological research, the site is open for exploration. Artefacts and a plethora of fascinating displays give a sense of Galway life some 900 years ago.

Parts of **Lynch's Castle** (cnr Shop & Upper Abbeygate Sts; admission free), now a bank, date back to the 14th century. Lynch, so the story goes, was a mayor of Galway in the 15th century who, when his son was condemned for murder, personally acted as hangman. The stone facade that is the **Lynch Memorial Window** (Market St) marks the spot of the deed.

Festivals

Galway Arts Festival ARTS
(www.galwayartsfestival.ie) Held in July, this is the main event on Galway's calendar

Galway Oyster Festival FOOD, DRINK
(www.galwayoysterfest.com) Going strong for more than 50 years now, this festival draws thousands of visitors in late September.

Sleeping

Kinlay House HOSTEL €
(☎565 244; www.kinlayhouse.ie; Merchants Rd; dm €18-29, tw €58-70; @📶) Easygoing staff, a full range of facilities and a cream-in-the-doughnut location just off Eyre Sq make this a top choice. Spanning two huge, brightly lit floors, the recently revamped interior belies the slightly scruffy exterior. Amenities include two self-catering kitchens and two cosy TV lounges.

TOP CHOICE **Four Seasons B&B** B&B €€
(☎564 078; www.fourseasonsgalway.com; 23 College Rd; s/d from €50/80; P📶) 'If the Ritz is full there's always the Four Seasons.' Of course, this Four Seasons only has seven rooms and the nightly rates will leave you with enough loot for many a pint. One of the best choices on this strip, the Fitzgeralds offer up a large breakfast menu and simple, tidy rooms.

Barnacle's HOSTEL €
(☎568 644; www.barnacles.ie; 10 Quay St; dm €21-27, d €66-70; @📶) Set in a medieval townhouse with a modern extension, Barnacle's is at the heart of the action, surrounded by all the pubs, cafes and restaurants you came to Galway for.

Sleepzone HOSTEL €
(☎566 999; www.sleepzone.ie; Bóthar na mBan; dm €15-25, tw €50-60; @📶) Big, busy backpacker base with bureau de change, pool table and barbecue terrace. Party-goers beware: no alcohol is allowed on the premises.

Eating & Drinking

Griffin's CAFE, BAKERY €
(www.griffinsbakery.com; Shop St; meals €5-8; ⏰8am-6pm Mon-Sat) A local institution since 1876. The small bakery counter is laden with sweet and savoury treats, but the real pleasure lies upstairs in the cafe where you can have fine coffee, tea, sandwiches, hot specials, luscious desserts and much more.

Ard Bia at Nimmo's IRISH €€
(www.ardbia.com; Spanish Arch; mains cafe €6-11, restaurant €19-25; ⏰cafe 10am-3.30pm, restaurant 6-10pm) Tucked behind the Spanish Arch, this informal, cottage-style restaurant with whitewashed interior and mismatched furniture serves some of the finest food in the west of Ireland, from scallops and sea bass to roast Irish lamb. The cafe serves great breakfasts.

Food 4 Thought VEGETARIAN €
(Lower Abbeygate St; mains €6-9; ⏰8am-6pm Mon-Sat, 11.30am-4pm Sun; 🍴🌶) Head to this new-age cafe for organic and vegetarian sandwiches, savoury scones, and wholesome hot dishes such as cashew-nut roast, and moussaka made with textured vegetable protein. Excellent coffee too.

Róisín Dubh PUB
(www.roisindubh.net; Upper Dominick St) A super-pub complete with vast roof terrace, Róisín Dubh is the place to see emerging local indie bands before they hit the big time.

Séhán Ua Neáchtain PUB
(17 Upper Cross St) Painted a bright cornflower blue, this 19th-century pub, known simply as Neáchtain's (*nock*-tans) or Naughtons, has a wraparound string of tables outside, many shaded by a large tree. It's a place where a polyglot mix of locals plop down and let the world pass them by – or stop and join them for a pint.

Information

Tourist Office (www.discoverireland.ie; Forster St; ⏰9am-5.45pm daily Easter-Sep, closed Sun Oct-Easter) In summer there can be a long wait to make accommodation bookings.

Getting There & Around

BIKE On Yer Bike (www.onyourbikecycles.com; 40 Prospect Hill; ⏰9am-5.30pm Mon-Sat) offers bike hire from €10 per day.

BUS Bus Éireann buses depart from outside the train station. **Citylink** (www.citylink.ie) and **GoBus** (www.gobus.ie) use the **coach station** (Bothar St)

Galway City

a block northeast. Citylink has buses to Clifden (€12, 1½ hours, five daily) and Dublin (€10.50, 2½ hours, hourly). Bus Éireann runs a bus to Killarney via Limerick (€24.50, seven hours, six daily).

TRAIN Trains run to and from Dublin (€33.50, three hours, five daily). You can connect with other trains at Athlone.

Aran Islands

The windswept Aran Islands are one of western Ireland's major attractions. As well as their rugged beauty – they are an extension of The Burren's limestone plateau – the

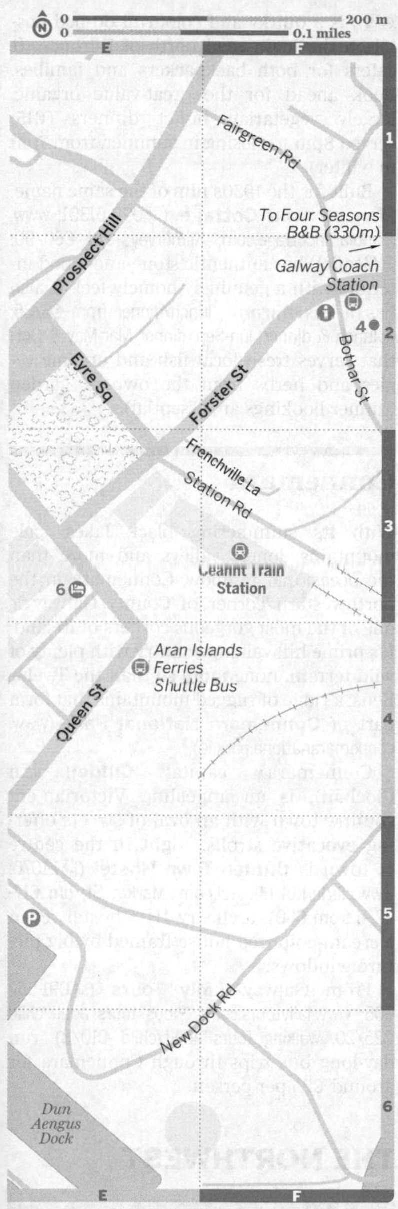

Galway City

Top Sights

Galway City Museum.....C6
Hall of the Red Earl.....C5

Sights

1 Lynch Memorial Window.....C4
2 Lynch's Castle.....C3
3 Spanish Arch.....B6

Activities, Courses & Tours

4 O'Neachtain Tours.....F2

Sleeping

5 Barnacle's.....B5
6 Kinlay House.....E3
7 Sleepzone.....D1

Eating

8 Ard Bia at Nimmo's.....C6
9 Food 4 Thought.....D3
10 Griffin's.....C4

Drinking

11 Róisín Dubh.....A6
12 Séhán Ua Neáchtain.....B5

Irish-speaking islands have some of the country's oldest Christian and pre-Christian ruins.

There are three main islands in the group, all inhabited year-round. Most visitors head for long and narrow (14.5km by a maximum 4km) **Inishmór** (or Inishmore). The land slopes up from the relatively sheltered northern shores of the island and plummets on the southern side into the raging Atlantic. **Inishmaan** and **Inisheer** are much smaller and receive far fewer visitors.

Though seemingly inhospitable, the islands were actually settled much earlier than the mainland, since agriculture was easier to pursue here than in the densely forested Ireland of the pre-Christian era.

The islands can get crowded during holiday times (St Patrick's Day, Easter) and in July and August, when accommodation is at a premium and advance reservations are advised.

The **tourist office** (☎099-61263; Kilronan, Inishmór; ⏰11am-7pm Jun-Sep, 11am-1pm & 2-5pm Mon-Fri, 10am-1pm & 2-5pm Sat & Sun Oct-May) operates year-round at Kilronan, the arrival point and major village of Inishmór. You can leave your luggage and change money here. Around the corner is a Spar supermarket with an ATM (many places do not accept credit cards).

Getting There & Away

AIR

Aer Arann (☎091-593 034; www.aerarann-islands.ie) flights from Connemara regional airport at Minna, near Inverin, 38km west of Galway, cost €45 return. Flights serve Inishmór five times daily on weekdays (two or three daily at weekends) and two or three times daily to the other islands, and take less than 10 minutes. A connecting bus from outside Kinlay House in Galway costs €3 one way.

BOAT

All three islands are served year-round by **Aran Island Ferries** (www.aranislandferries.com; 37-39 Forster St, Galway); the trip takes around 40 minutes (adult/child €25/13 return). The boat leaves from Rossaveal, 37km west of Galway – it's an extra €7/4 return to catch an Island Ferries bus from near Kinlay House in Galway. Buses leave 1½ hours before ferry departure times and are scheduled to meet arriving ferries. If you have a car, you can go straight to Rossaveal and leave it in the car park for free.

From March to November, various companies run ferries from Doolin in County Clare to the islands (around half an hour to Inisheer, and at least 1½ hours to Inishmór). Rates vary as prices are very competitive, with each boat trying to undercut the others. Inisheer should cost about €15 to €25 return. Operators include **Doolin Ferries** (☎065-707 4455; www.doolinferries.com; Doolin, County Clare) and **O'Brien Line** (☎065-707 5555; www.obrienline.com).

INISHMÓR

The 'Big Island', as it's called, has four impressive **stone forts** thought to be 2000 years old. Halfway down the island and about 8km west of the village of Kilronan, semicircular **Dún Aengus** (Dún Aonghasa; www.heritageireland.ie; adult/child €3/1; ⌚9.45am-6pm Apr-Oct, 9.30am-4pm Nov-Mar, closed Mon & Tue Jan-Feb), perched on the edge of the sheer cliffs, is the best known of the four. It's an amazing place, but take great care near the cliff edge as there are no guard rails.

About 1.5km north is **Dún Eoghanachta**, while halfway back to Kilronan is **Dún Eochla**; both are smaller, perfectly circular ring forts. Directly south of Kilronan and dramatically perched on a promontory is **Dún Dúchathair**, surrounded on three sides by cliffs.

Kilronan Hostel (☎099-61255; www.kilronanhostel.com; Kilronan; dm €16-20, tw €45; @📶), perched above Tí Joe Mac's pub, is a friendly hostel just a two-minute walk away from the ferry; staff lend out fishing rods for free and can teach you to play hurling on the beach. **Mainistir House** (☎099-61169; www.aranislandshostel.com; Mainistir; dm/s/d €16/40/50; @📶) is a quirky and colourful 60-bed hostel on the main road north of Kilronan. It caters for both backpackers and families. Book ahead for the great-value organic, largely vegetarian buffet dinners (€15; served 8pm to closing in summer, from 7pm in winter).

Built for the 1930s film of the same name, **Man of Aran Cottage** (☎099-61301; www.manofarancottage.com; Kilmurvey; s/d €60/90; ⌚Mar-Oct) has authentic stone-and-wood interiors with a genuinely homely feel. It also has a **restaurant** (lunch/dinner from €6/35; ⌚lunch & dinner Jun-Sep, dinner Mar-May & Oct) that serves fresh local fish and organic vegies and herbs from the owners' garden (dinner bookings are essential).

Connemara

☎095

With its shimmering black lakes, pale mountains, lonely valleys and more than the occasional rainbow, Connemara in the northwestern corner of County Galway is one of the most gorgeous corners of Ireland. It's prime hillwalking country with plenty of wild terrain, none more so than the Twelve Bens, a ridge of rugged mountains that form part of **Connemara National Park** (www.connemaranationalpark.ie).

Connemara's 'capital', **Clifden** (An Clochán), is an appealing Victorian-era country town with an oval of streets offering evocative strolls. Right in the centre of town is **Clifden Town Hostel** (☎21076; www.clifdentownhostel.com; Market St; dm €17-22, d from €50), a cheery IHH hostel set in a cream-coloured house framed by big picture windows.

From Galway, **Lally Tours** (☎091-562 905; www.lallytours.com; ⌚bus tours adult/child €25/20, walking tours adult/child €10/8) run day-long bus trips through Connemara for around €25 per person.

THE NORTHWEST

Sligo

POP 17,900

William Butler Yeats (1865–1939) was born in Dublin and educated in London, but his poetry is infused with the landscapes, history and folklore of his mother's native Sligo (Sligeach). He returned many times and there are plentiful reminders of his presence in this sweet, sleepy town.

In a pretty setting near Hyde Bridge, the Yeats Building houses the **WB Yeats Exhibition** (www.yeats-sligo.com; Hyde Bridge; ⏲10am-5pm Mon-Fri, tearoom 10am-5pm Mon-Sat), which has a video presentation and valuable draft manuscripts; the €2 exhibition catalogue makes a good souvenir of Sligo. The charming **tearoom** has outdoor tables overlooking the river, and the **tourist office** (☎071-916 1201; O'Connell St; ⏲9am-6pm Mon-Fri, 9am-5pm Sat, 10am-4pm Sun Jun-Aug, 9am-5pm Mon-Fri, 10am-4pm Sat Mar-May & Sep, 9am-5pm Mon-Fri Oct-Feb) is next door.

In the churchyard at Drumcliff, 8km north of Sligo, is the **grave of WB Yeats**. In the 6th century, St Colmcille chose the same location for a monastery – you can still see the stumpy remains of the round tower on the main road nearby. Also in the churchyard is an extraordinary 11th-century **high cross**, carved with intricate biblical scenes. In summer the church shows a 15-minute audiovisual on Yeats and St Colmcille. The island of **Innisfree**, immortalised in Yeats' poem *The Lake Isle of Innisfree*, is in Lough Gill, southeast of Sligo town.

The basic but conveniently located **White House Hostel** (☎071-914 5160; Marklevicz Rd; dm €15; P) is just north of the town centre. For more comfort head to the excellent **Pearse Lodge B&B** (☎071-916 1090; www.pearselodge.com; Pearse Rd; s/d €47/76; P@wifi).

Osta (www.osta.ie; Hyde Bridge, Left Bank; mains €5-10; ⏲8am-7.30pm Mon-Sat, 9am-6pm Sun; wifi) is a superb cafe and wine bar with a prime location overlooking the river and outdoor tables in summer, while **Source** (☎071-914 7605; www.sourcesligo.ie; 1 John St; mains €9-22; ⏲9.30am-9pm Mon-Sat; wifi) is a new cafe-bar-restaurant that champions local suppliers and foodstuffs.

ℹ Getting There & Away

BUS Bus Éireann has services to Derry (€20, 2½ hours, seven daily), Dublin (€18, 3¾ hours, four daily) and Galway (€15, 2¾ hours, seven daily).

TRAIN There are six to eight trains daily to Dublin Connolly station (€34, three hours).

Bundoran

POP 1700

Surfers from all over the world come to Bundoran (Bun Dobhráin) to seek out some of Europe's best beach breaks. Pass by the tacky arcades, fast-food stalls and souvenir shops in the town centre and head for **Tullan Strand**, on the northern edge of town, the focal point of Bundoran's beach scene, or 3km-long **Rossnowlagh Strand**, 5km to the north.

Bundoran Surf Co (☎071-984 1968; www.bundoransurfco.com; Main St) and **Fin McCool** (☎071-985 9020; www.finmccoolsurfschool.com; gear rental per 3hr €29, 2hr lesson incl gear rental €35; ⏲10am-7pm Easter-Oct, 10am-7pm Sat & Sun mid-Mar–Easter & Nov-Christmas) both offer surfing lessons for beginners for €30 to €35 per person. Surf and accommodation packages can also be arranged.

Bundoran is packed with budget accommodation, but music-themed **Homefield Rock Hostel** (☎071-982 9357; www.homefieldbackpackers.com; Bayview Ave; dm/d €20/50; ⏲Apr-Nov, bookings only Dec-Mar; P@wifi) – a 300-year-old building that was once the holiday home of Viscount Enniskillen – is the pick of the bunch.

Main St has no shortage of greasy diners and pubs, but for a better bite head to **Maddens Ould Bridge Bar** (☎071-984 2050; www.maddensbridgebar.com; Main St; mains €10-20), a surfers' hang-out that serves sensational pub grub.

Bus Éireann buses stop on Main St. There are direct daily services to Sligo (€10, 45 minutes), Derry (€18, 1¾ hours), Donegal (€8, 40 minutes) and more.

NORTHERN IRELAND

POP 1.7 MILLION

When you cross from the Republic into Northern Ireland you notice a couple of changes: the accent is different, the road signs are in miles, and the prices are in pounds sterling. But there's no border checkpoint, no guards, not even a sign to mark the crossing point – the two countries are in a customs union, so there's no passport control, no customs declarations. All of a sudden, you're in the UK.

Dragged down for decades by the violence and uncertainty of the Troubles, Northern Ireland today is a nation rejuvenated. The 1998 Good Friday Agreement laid the groundwork for peace and raised hopes for the future, and since then this UK province has seen a huge influx of investment and redevelopment. Belfast has become a happening place with a famously wild nightlife, while Derry is coming into its own as a cool, artistic city, and the stunning Causeway Coast gets more and more visitors each year.

There are still plenty of reminders of the Troubles – notably the 'peace lines' that still divide Belfast – and the passions that have torn Northern Ireland apart over the decades still run deep. But despite occasional setbacks there is an atmosphere of determined optimism.

Belfast

028 / POP 277,000

Once lumped with Beirut, Baghdad and Bosnia as one of the four 'B's for travellers to avoid, Belfast has pulled off a remarkable transformation from bombs-and-bullets pariah to hip-hotels-and-hedonism party town. Despite the economic downturn, the city's skyline is in a constant state of flux as redevelopment continues. The old shipyards are giving way to the luxury waterfront apartments of the Titanic Quarter; and Victoria Sq, Europe's biggest urban regeneration project, has added a massive city-centre shopping mall to a list of tourist attractions that includes Victorian architecture, a glittering waterfront lined with modern art, foot-stomping music in packed-out pubs and the UK's second-biggest arts festival.

The city centre is compact, with the imposing City Hall in Donegall Sq as the central landmark. The principal shopping district is north of the square. North again, around Donegall St and St Anne's Cathedral, is the bohemian Cathedral Quarter.

South of the square, the so-called Golden Mile stretches for 1km along Great Victoria St, Shaftesbury Sq and Botanic Ave to Queen's University and the leafy suburbs of South Belfast; this area has dozens of restaurants and bars and most of the city's budget and midrange accommodation.

Sights

TOP CHOICE Titanic Belfast EXHIBITION

(www.titanicbelfast.com; Queen's Rd; adult/child £13.50/6.75; 9am-7pm Mon-Sat, 10am-7pm Sun Apr-Sep, 10am-5pm daily Oct-Mar) The head of the slipway where the *Titanic* was built is now occupied by the gleaming, angular edifice of Titanic Belfast, an all-singing all-dancing multimedia extravaganza that charts the history of Belfast and the creation of the world's most famous ocean liner.

Cleverly designed exhibits enlivened by historic images, animated projections and soundtracks chart Belfast's rise to turn-of-the-20th-century industrial superpower, followed by a hi-tech ride through a noisy, smells-and-all re-creation of the city's shipyards. You can then explore every detail of the *Titanic*'s construction, from a computer 'fly-through' from keel to bridge, to replicas of the passenger accommodation. Perhaps most poignant are the few flickering images that constitute the only film footage of the ship in existence.

Titanic Quarter HISTORIC SITE

(www.titanicquarter.com) Belfast's **Harland & Wolff shipyards** – whose famous yellow cranes Samson and Goliath dominate the city's eastern skyline – were the birthplace in 1911 of the *Titanic*, the 'unsinkable' ocean liner that struck an iceberg and sank in 1912. The shipyards, now known as the Titanic Quarter, are undergoing a massive redevelopment.

Take a self-guided walking tour of the **Titanic Trail** (pick up a leaflet from the tourist office, or follow the trail on your smartphone at www.ni2012.com/trails). Highlights include the **SS Nomadic** (www.nomadicbelfast.com; Queen's Rd), the only surviving vessel of the White Star Line, and the vast **Thompson Graving Dock** (Queen's Rd, accessed via Thompson Pump House; admission free) where the *Titanic* was fitted out. The neighbouring **Thompson Pump House** (9073 7813; www.titanicsdock.com; guided tour adult/child £7/4; visitor centre 10.30am-4pm, tours hourly noon-3pm) contains exhibits and original film of the building of the great ship, and offers a guided tour into the base of the graving dock.

To get a real feel for the area take to the water on the Lagan Boat Company's excellent **Titanic Tour** (9033 0844; www.laganboatcompany.com; 66 Donegall Quay; adult/child £10/8; departs 12.30pm, 2pm & 3.30pm Apr-Oct).

TOP CHOICE Ulster Museum MUSEUM

(www.nmni.com/um; Stranmillis Rd; admission free; 10am-5pm Tue-Sun;) The Ulster Museum is one of Northern Ireland's must-see attractions. You could spend several hours browsing the beautifully designed displays, but if you're pressed for time don't miss the following: the Armada Room, with artefacts retrieved from the wreck of the Spanish galleon *Girona*; Takabuti, a 2500-year-old Egyptian mummy; the Bann Disc, a superb example of Celtic design dating from the Iron Age; the Malone Hoardof stone axe heads; and the Snapshot of an Ancient Sea Floor, a fossilised portion of a 200-million-year-old seabed.

West Belfast HISTORIC SITE

The Catholic **Falls Rd** and the Protestant **Shankill Rd** have been battlefronts in Belfast's sectarian conflict since the 1970s. Even so, these areas are now quite safe and well worth visiting, if only to see the famous **murals** expressing local political and religious passions, and the infamous **Peace Line** – a 4km-long barrier that divides Catholic and Protestant districts, and which has now been standing longer than the Berlin Wall.

If you don't fancy an organised taxi tour, pick up a **map of the murals** from the Belfast Welcome Centre and explore on foot.

Crown Liquor Saloon HISTORIC BUILDING

(www.crownbar.com; 46 Great Victoria St) There are not too many historical monuments that you can enjoy while savouring a pint of beer, but Belfast's most famous pub is one. It was built by Patrick Flanagan in 1885 and displays Victorian architecture at its most extravagant; the snugs are equipped with bells that were once connected to a board behind the bar, enabling customers to order drinks without leaving their seats.

Ulster Folk & Transport Museums MUSEUM

(www.nmni.com/uftm; Cultra, Holywood; adult/child 1 museum £7/4.50, combined ticket to both museums £8.50/5, ⏲10am-5pm Tue-Sun Mar-Sep, 10am-4pm Tue-Fri & 11am-4pm Sat & Sun Oct-Feb) Farmhouses, forges, churches, mills and a complete village have been reconstructed at the **Folk Museum**, with human and animal extras combining to give a strong impression of Irish life over the past few hundred years. A bridge crosses the A2 highway to the **Transport Museum**, which contains various Ulster-related vehicles, including a prototype of the **De Lorean DMC sports car** (of *Back To The Future* fame), and a display on the *Titanic*. It's 11km northeast of the city centre on the A2 Bangor road near Holywood. From Belfast take Ulsterbus 1 or any Bangor-bound train that stops at Cultra station.

Festivals & Events

Titanic Belfast Festival CULTURE

(www.belfastcity.gov.uk/titanic) A weeklong celebration of the world's most famous ship, and the city that built it, with special exhibitions, tours, lectures and film screenings. First half of April.

Festival at Queen's ARTS

(www.belfastfestival.com) For three weeks in late October/early November, Belfast hosts the second-largest arts festival in the UK, in and around Queen's University.

DON'T MISS

BELFAST CITY TOURS

Many operators, including **Official Black Taxi Tours** (☎9064 2264; www.belfasttours.com) and **Original Belfast Black Taxi Tours** (☎07751 565359; taxitours@live.co.uk) offer taxi tours of West Belfast, with an even-handed account of the Troubles. They run daily for £8 to £10 per person based on a group of three to six sharing (£25 for one or two). Pick-up can be arranged.

There are a number of walking tours available, including the two-hour **Belfast Pub Tour** (☎9268 3665; www.belfastpubtours.com; per person £6; ⏲7pm Thu & 4pm Sat May-Oct), taking in six of the city's historic pubs, beginning at the Crown Dining Rooms, above the Crown Liquor Saloon.

Sleeping

Many B&Bs are concentrated in the pleasant university district of South Belfast, which is well stocked with restaurants and pubs.

Arnie's Backpackers HOSTEL £

(☎9024 2867; www.arniesbackpackers.co.uk; 63 Fitzwilliam St; dm £10-14; @📶) More cosy than cramped, this small-scale hostel has a relaxed, down-home vibe, and Arnie manages to have a kindly disposition, even when faced with an Estonian football fan club who've been drinking vodka for 12 hours straight.

Paddy's Palace Belfast HOSTEL £

(☎9033 3367; www.paddyspalace.com; 68 Lisburn Rd; dm £10-15, d £40-50; P@📶) Paddy's offers clean and comfortable dorms, a big, well-equipped kitchen, a bright and homely common room (though the dorms are a bit gloomy) and friendly staff who are happy to point you to the best local pubs. There's no sign outside, so it's easy to miss – bang on the door on Fitzwilliam St, near the corner of Lisburn Rd.

Kate's B&B B&B ££

(☎9028 2091; katesbb127@hotmail.com; 127 University St; per person £25) Kate's is a homely kind of place, from the window boxes bursting with colourful flowers to the cute dining

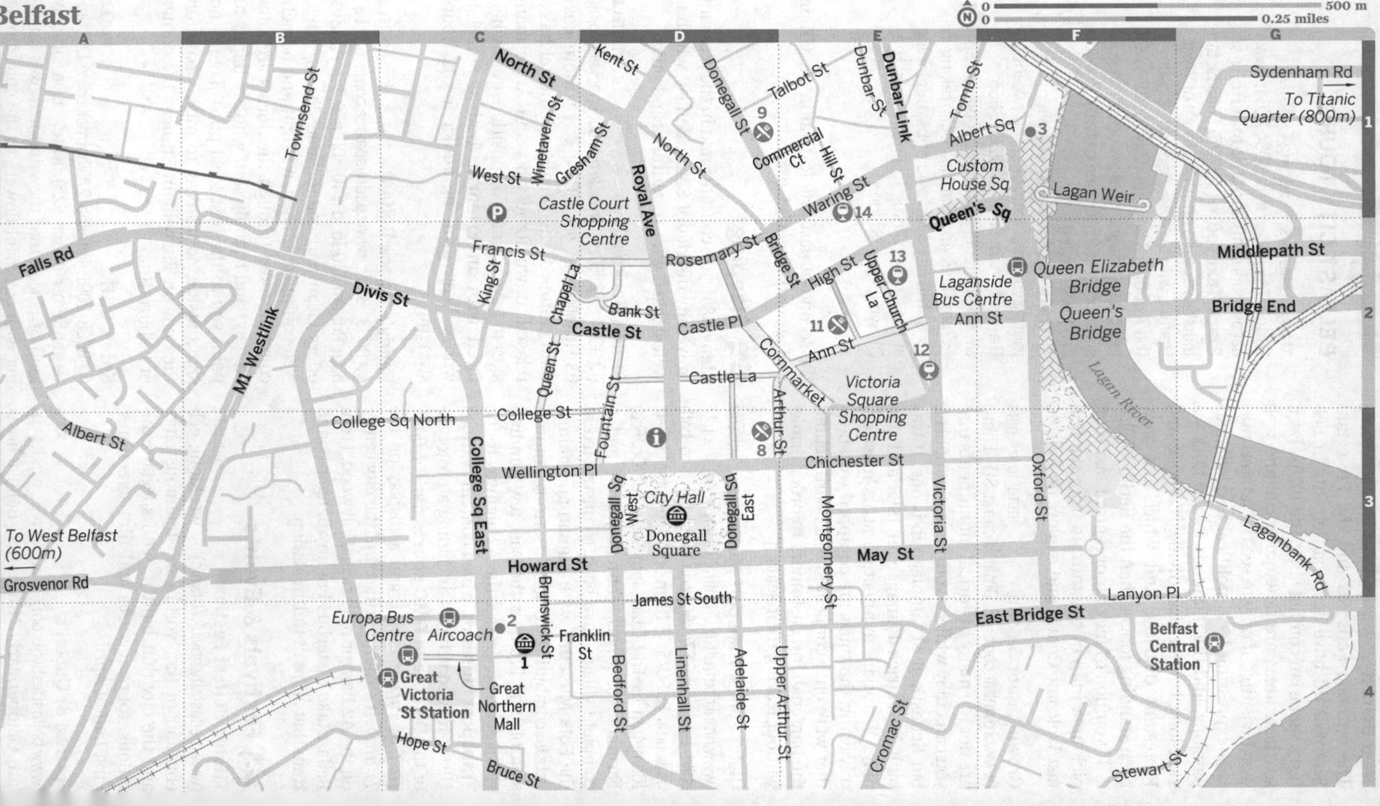
Belfast
0 500 m
0 0.25 miles
Sydenham Rd
To Titanic Quarter (800m)
North St
Kent St
Donegall St
Talbot St
Dunbar St
Dunbar Link
Tomb St
Albert Sq
Custom House Sq
Lagan Weir
Queen's Sq
Commercial Ct
Hill St
Waring St
Winetavern St
Gresham St
West St
Royal Ave
Castle Court Shopping Centre
Francis St
King St
Chapel La
Bank St
Castle St
Castle Pl
Rosemary St
Bridge St
High St
Upper Church La
Laganside Bus Centre
Queen Elizabeth Bridge
Queen's Bridge
Ann St
Middlepath St
Bridge End
Falls Rd
Divis St
M1 Westlink
Townsend St
Albert St
College Sq North
College St
College Sq East
Queen St
Fountain St
Castle La
Cornmarket
Arthur St
Victoria Square Shopping Centre
Lagan River
Wellington Pl
Chichester St
Donegall Sq West
City Hall
Donegall Square
Donegall Sq East
Montgomery St
Victoria St
Oxford St
Laganbank Rd
To West Belfast (600m)
Grosvenor Rd
Howard St
May St
Lanyon Pl
James St South
East Bridge St
Europa Bus Centre
Aircoach
Brunswick St
Franklin St
Bedford St
Linenhall St
Adelaide St
Upper Arthur St
Belfast Central Station
Great Victoria St Station
Great Northern Mall
Hope St
Bruce St
Cromac St
Stewart St

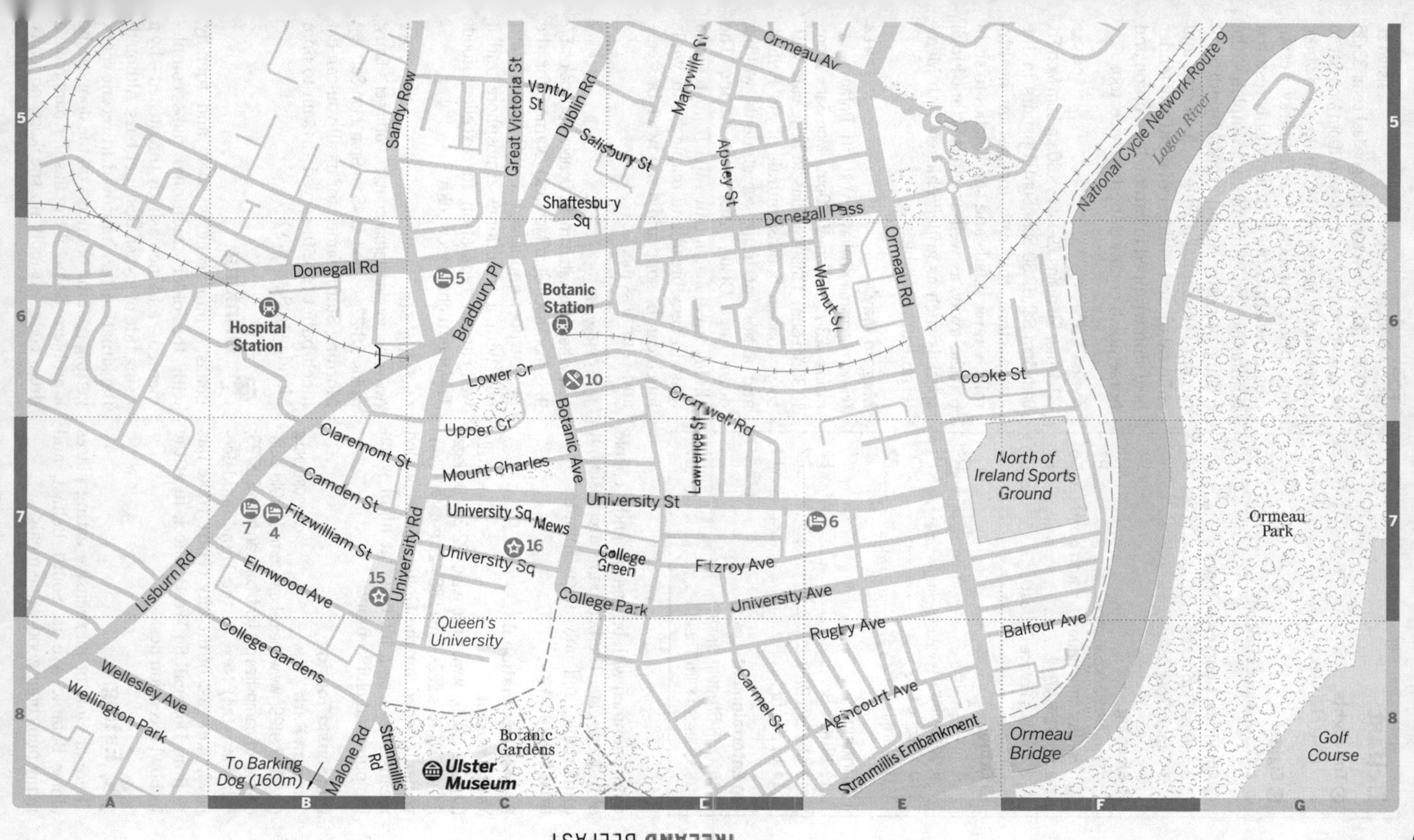

Ormeau Av
Sandy Row
Great Victoria St
Ventry St
Dublin Rd
Maryville St
Salisbury St
Apsley St
National Cycle Network Route 9
Lagan River
Shaftesbury Sq
Donegall Pass
Ormeau Rd
Donegall Rd
5
Bradbury Pl
Botanic Station
Walnut St
Hospital Station
Lower Cr
10
Cooke St
Cromwell Rd
Upper Cr
Botanic Ave
Claremont St
Lawrence St
North of Ireland Sports Ground
Mount Charles
Camden St
University St
7
4
Fitzwilliam St
University Rd
University Sq Mews
6
Ormeau Park
16
University Sq
College Green
Fitzroy Ave
15
Elmwood Ave
Lisburn Rd
College Park
University Ave
Queen's University
Balfour Ave
Rugby Ave
College Gardens
Wellesley Ave
Wellington Park
Carmel St
Agincourt Ave
Botanic Gardens
Stranmillis Embankment
Ormeau Bridge
Golf Course
To Barking Dog (160m)
Malone Rd
Stranmillis Rd
Ulster Museum

Belfast

Top Sights
Ulster Museum C8

Sights
1 Crown Liquor Saloon C4

Activities, Courses & Tours
2 Belfast Pub Tours C4
3 Titanic Tour F1

Sleeping
4 Arnie's Backpackers B7
5 Belfast International Youth Hostel C6
6 Kate's B&B E7
7 Paddy's Palace Belfast B7

Eating
8 Avoca Cafe D3
9 John Hewitt D1
10 Maggie May's C6
11 Morning Star E2

Drinking
12 Bittle's Bar E2
13 Muriel's Bar E2
14 Spaniard E1

Entertainment
15 QUB Student Union B7
16 Queen's Film Theatre C7

room crammed with bric-a-brac and a couple of resident cats. The bedrooms are basic but comfortable, and only a few minutes' walk from Botanic Ave.

Belfast International Youth Hostel HOSTEL £
(☎9031 5435; www.hini.org.uk; 22-32 Donegall Rd; dm £11-16, s £22-32, tw £38-42; P@≋) Conveniently sited on the Golden Mile, which means it can be a bit noisy at night when the pubs and clubs empty.

Dundonald Touring Caravan Park CAMPGROUND £
(☎9080 9129; www.theicebowl.com; 111 Old Dundonald Rd; campsites per tent/caravan from £15/23; ⊙mid-Mar–Oct) Next to the Dundonald Icebowl, 7km east of the city centre (take bus 19 from Donegall Sq West); check in at the Icebowl reception desk.

Eating

There are lots of inexpensive eating places along Botanic Ave in South Belfast, and many pubs offer good-value meals.

TOP CHOICE **Barking Dog** BISTRO ££
(☎9066 1885; www.barkingdogbelfast.com; 33-35 Malone Rd; mains £11-21; ⊙noon-10pm Mon-Sat, to 11pm Fri & Sat, to 9pm Sun) Chunky hardwood, bare brick, candlelight and quirky design create the atmosphere of a stylishly restored farmhouse, and the menu completes the feeling of cosiness and comfort with simple but sensational dishes such as crab and chilli salad, and a burger of meltingly tender beef shin wrapped in caramelised onion and horseradish cream. Superb service, too.

Avoca Cafe CAFE ££
(41 Arthur St; mains £9-14; ⊙9.30am-5pm Mon-Fri, 9am-5pm Sat, 12.30-5pm Sun) Upstairs in the Avoca store, this cafe focuses on healthy rolls, wraps, salads and sandwiches to sit in or take away, as well as offering hot lunch specials such as grilled chicken with Mediterranean vegetables.

Maggie May's CAFE £
(www.maggiemaysbelfast.co.uk; 50 Botanic Ave; mains £3-7; ⊙8am-10.30pm Mon-Sat, 10am-10.30pm Sun) This is a classic little cafe with cosy wooden booths, murals of old Belfast, and a host of hungover students wolfing down huge Ulster fries at lunchtime. The all-day breakfast menu runs from tea and toast to eggy bread and maple syrup, while lunch can be soup and a sandwich or steak-and-Guinness pie.

John Hewitt PUB £
(www.thejohnhewitt.com; 51 Donegall St; mains £7-9; ⊙food noon-3pm Mon-Sat) Named for the Belfast poet and socialist, this is a modern pub with a traditional atmosphere and a well-earned reputation for excellent food. The menu changes weekly.

Morning Star PUB £
(www.themorningstarbar.com; 17 Pottinger's Entry; mains £8-22; ⊙food 11.45am-9pm Mon-Sat; ≋) Morning Star is famed for its all-you-can-eat lunch buffet (£5.50; served 11.45am to 6pm Monday to Saturday).

Drinking

Belfast's pub scene is lively and friendly, with the older traditional pubs complemented – and increasingly threatened – by a rising tide of stylish designer bars. Although the situation has improved in recent years, getting past the bouncers on the door can be a problem. Some of the flashier bars have a dress code – usually no sneakers, no jeans, no baseball caps, and definitely no football colours.

Muriel's Bar BAR

(12-14 Church Lane) Hats meet harlotry (ask who Muriel was) in this snug and welcoming wee bar with retro-chic old sofas and armchairs, heavy fabrics in shades of olive and dark red, gilt-framed mirrors and a cast-iron fireplace. Gin is Muriel's favourite tipple, with a range of exotic brands to mix with your tonic. The food menu is pretty good, too.

Bittle's Bar PUB

(103 Victoria St) A cramped and staunchly traditional bar, Bittle's is a 19th-century triangular red-brick building decorated with paintings of Ireland's literary heroes. Pride of place on the back wall is taken by a large canvas depicting Yeats, Joyce, Behan and Beckett at the bar with glasses of Guinness, and Wilde pulling the pints on the other side.

Spaniard BAR

(www.thespaniardbar.com; 3 Skipper St) Forget 'style': this narrow, crowded bar, which looks as if it's been squeezed into someone's flat, has more atmosphere in one battered sofa than most 'style bars' have in their shiny entirety. Friendly staff, good beer, an eclectic crowd and cool tunes played at a volume that still allows you to talk: bliss.

✩ Entertainment

The Belfast Welcome Centre issues *Whatabout?*, a free monthly guide to Belfast events. Another useful guide is **The Big List** (www.thebiglist.co.uk).

QUB Student Union CLUB

(www.qubsu-ents.com; Queen's Students Union, University Rd) The student union has various bars and music venues hosting club nights, live bands and stand-up comedy.

Queen's Film Theatre CINEMA

(www.queensfilmtheatre.com; 20 University Sq) The QFT is a two-screen art-house cinema, close to the university, and a major venue for the Belfast Film Festival in March.

Lyric Theatre THEATRE

(www.lyrictheatre.co.uk; 55 Ridgeway St) The Lyric, south of the city, stages serious drama; Hollywood star Liam Neeson first trod the boards here. An award-winning new theatre building was opened in 2011.

ℹ Information

Belfast Welcome Centre (☎9024 6609; www.gotobelfast.com; 47 Donegall Pl; ⏲9am-7pm Mon-Sat, 11am-4pm Sun Jun-Sep, 9am-5.30pm Mon-Sat, 11am-4pm Sun Oct-May) Tourist information for all of Ireland, accommodation bookings, left luggage, and internet access for £1 per 20 minutes.

Lonely Planet (www.lonelyplanet.com/ireland/northern-ireland/belfast)

ℹ Getting There & Away

Air

George Best Belfast City Airport (BHD; www.belfastcityairport.com; Airport Rd) Located 6km northeast of the city centre; flights from the UK, Cork and Paris.

Belfast International Airport (BFS; www.belfastairport.com) Located 30km northwest of the city; flights from Galway, UK, Europe and New York.

Boat

Ferries to Belfast from Cairnryan and Liverpool dock at **Victoria Terminal** (West Bank Rd), 5km north of the city centre; exit the M2 motorway at junction 1. Ferries from the Isle of Man arrive at **Albert Quay** (Serkeley Rd), 2km north of the centre.

Other car ferries to and from Scotland dock at Larne, 30km north of Belfast.

Bus

Europa Bus Centre (☎9066 6630; Great Victoria St) Reached via the Great Northern Mall beside the Europa Hotel. Main terminus for buses to Derry (£11, 1¾ hours, twice hourly), Dublin (£14.15, 2½ hours, hourly) and destinations in the west and south of Northern Ireland.

Laganside Bus Centre (☎9066 6630; Oxford St) Near the river. Mainly for buses to County Antrim and eastern County Down.

Aircoach (www.aircoach.ie) Leaves from Glengall St, near the Europa Bus Centre, Belfast, for Dublin airport (£13, 2½ hours, hourly) and Dublin city centre (£14).

BELFAST VISITOR PASS

The **Belfast Visitor Pass** (one/two/three days £6.50/10.50/14) allows unlimited travel on bus and train services in Belfast and around; it can be purchased at airports, main train and bus stations, the Metro kiosk on Donegall Sq, and the Belfast Welcome Centre.

GETTING INTO BELFAST

Belfast's two bus stations – Laganside Bus Centre, near the river, and the bigger Europa Bus Centre, next to Great Victoria St train station – are both central, within five minutes' walk of Donegall Sq. Local trains connect Belfast Central (which, ironically, is not central) with Great Victoria St station via Botanic station. Most local bus services depart from Donegall Sq, near the City Hall, where there's a ticket and information kiosk.

Airport Express 300 buses link Belfast International airport with the Europa Bus Centre every 30 minutes (£7, 30 minutes). A taxi costs about £25.

Train

Belfast has two main train stations: **Great Victoria St** (Great Northern Mall), next to the Europa Bus Centre, and **Belfast Central** (East Bridge St), east of the city centre. If you arrive by train at Central Station, your rail ticket entitles you to a free bus ride into the city centre. A local train also connects with Great Victoria St.

Destinations include Derry (£11, 2¼ hours, seven or eight daily), Dublin (£28, two hours, eight daily Monday to Saturday, five on Sunday) and Larne Harbour (£6.50, one hour, hourly).

Getting Around

BIKE McConvey Cycles (9033 0322; www.rentabikebelfast.com; 183 Ormeau Rd; 9am-6pm Mon-Sat, to 8pm Thu) hires out bikes for £20/80 per day/week. Credit card deposit and photo ID required.

BUS A short trip on a city bus costs £1.40 to £2; a one-day ticket costs £3.50. Most local bus services depart from Donegall Sq, near the City Hall, where there's a ticket kiosk; otherwise, buy a ticket from the driver.

The Causeway Coast

Ireland isn't short of scenic coastlines, but the Causeway Coast between Portstewart and Ballycastle – climaxing in the spectacular rock formations of the Giant's Causeway – and the Antrim Coast between Ballycastle and Belfast, are as magnificent as they come.

From April to September the **Ulsterbus** (028-9066 6630; www.translink.co.uk) Antrim Coaster (bus 252) links Belfast with Coleraine (£11, four hours, two daily Monday to Saturday) via Larne, the Glens of Antrim, Ballycastle, the Giant's Causeway, Bushmills, Portrush and Portstewart; a Sunday service operates from July to September only.

From June to September the Causeway Rambler (bus 402) links Coleraine and Carrick-a-Rede (£5.90, 40 minutes, seven daily) via Bushmills Distillery, the Giant's Causeway, White Park Bay and Ballintoy. The ticket allows unlimited travel in both directions for one day. Bus 172 runs year-round between Ballycastle and Portrush.

There are several hostels along the coast, including the following: **Sheep Island View Hostel** (028-2076 9391; www.sheepislandview.com; 42A Main St; campsites/dm/d £6/15/40; P@), **Ballycastle Backpackers** (028-2076 3612; www.ballycastlebackpackers.net; 4 North St; dm/tw from £15/40; P) and **Mill Rest Youth Hostel** (028-2073 1222; www.hini.org.uk; 49 Main St; dm/tw £18.50/41; closed 11am-2pm Jul & Aug, 11am-5pm Mar-Jun, Sep & Oct; @).

CARRICK-A-REDE ROPE BRIDGE

The 20m-long **rope bridge** (028-2076 9839; http://nationaltrust.org.uk/carrick-a-rede; adult/child £5.60/3.10; 10am-7pm Jun-Aug, to 6pm Mar-May, Sep & Oct, 10.30am-3.30pm Nov & Dec) that connects Carrick-a-Rede Island to the mainland, swaying some 30m above the pounding waves, is a classic test of nerve. The island is the site of a salmon fishery and is a scenic 1.25km walk from the car park. Note that the bridge is closed in high winds.

GIANT'S CAUSEWAY

This spectacular rock formation – Northern Ireland's only Unesco World Heritage site – is one of Ireland's most impressive and atmospheric landscape features. When you first see it you'll understand why the ancients thought it wasn't a natural feature – the vast expanse of regular, closely packed, hexagonal stone columns looks for all the world like the handiwork of giants.

The more prosaic explanation is that the columns are simply contraction cracks caused by a cooling lava flow some 60 million years ago. The phenomenon is explained in the **Giant's Causeway Visitor Experience** (028-2073 1855; www.giantscausewaycentre.com; adult/child £8.50/4.25; 9am-9pm Jul & Aug, to 7pm Apr-Jun & Sep, to 6pm Feb-Mar & Oct, to 7pm Nov-Jan), a spectacular new eco-friendly building half-hidden in a hillside above the sea.

From the centre it's an easy 10- to 15-minute walk downhill to the Causeway itself, but a more interesting approach is to follow the clifftop path northeast for 2km to the **Chimney Tops** headland, then descend the **Shepherd's Steps** to the Causeway. For the less mobile, a minibus shuttles from the visitors centre to the Causeway (£2 return).

If you can, try to visit the Causeway out of season to avoid the crowds, and experience it at its most evocative.

Derry

028 / POP 83,700

Derry or Londonderry? The name you use for Northern Ireland's second-largest city can be a political statement, but today most people just call it Derry, whatever their politics. The 'London' prefix was added in 1613 in recognition of the Corporation of London's role in the 'plantation' of Ulster with Protestant settlers.

In 1968 resentment at the long-running Protestant domination of the city council boiled over into a series of (Catholic-dominated) civil rights marches. In August 1969 fighting between police and local youths in the poor Catholic Bogside district prompted the UK government to send British troops into Derry. In January 1972 'Bloody Sunday' resulted in the deaths of 13 unarmed Catholic civil-rights marchers in Derry at the hands of the British army, an event that marked the beginning of the Troubles in earnest.

Today Derry is as safe to visit as anywhere else in Northern Ireland, while the Bogside and the inner city have been redeveloped. The city's long, dramatic history is still palpable – in the 17th-century city walls, in the captivating Bogside murals – but it's also a laid-back place with a well-founded reputation for musical excellence, from traditional to cutting-edge contemporary, and a lively arts scene that thrives in the city's many innovative venues.

In preparation for Derry's year in the limelight as **UK City of Culture 2013** (www.cityofculture2013.com), the city centre was given a makeover, and an elegant new footbridge – the **Peace Bridge** – was built across the River Foyle.

The centre of old Derry is the walled city on the western bank of the Foyle River. The bus station is just outside the walls at its north end; the modern city centre stretches north from here along Strand Rd. The train station is on the east bank of the Foyle, across Craigavon Bridge, in a district known as the Waterside. The Bogside lies to the west of the walled city.

Sights

FREE City Walls LANDMARK

Built between 1613 and 1618, Derry's city walls were the last to be constructed in Europe, and are the only ones in Ireland to survive almost intact. They're about 8m high, 9m thick and encircle the old city for 1.5km. The walls make for a fantastic walk, and provide a grandstand view of the Bogside (itself worth a closer look on foot) and the **People's Gallery**, a series of murals that decorate the gable ends of houses along Rossville St. Painted between 1997 and 2001 by the Bogside Artists, they commemorate key events in the Troubles, including the Battle of the Bogside, Bloody Sunday, and the 1981 hunger strike.

Tower Museum MUSEUM

(www.derrycity.gov.uk/Museums; Union Hall Pl; adult/child £4.20/2.65; 10am-5pm Tue-Sat, plus 11am-3pm Sun Jul-Sep) O'Doherty's Tower, inside the northern corner of the city walls, is home to the Tower Museum, which traces the story of Derry from the days of St Columb_cille to the present, and has an excellent exhibition telling the story of *La Trinidad Valenciera* – a ship of the Spanish Armada that was wrecked at Kinnagoe Bay in Donegal in 1588.

Museum of Free Derry MUSEUM

(www.museumoffreederry.org; 55-61 Glenfada Park; adult/child £3/2; 9.30am-4.30pm Mon-Fri, plus 1-4pm Sat Apr-Sep, 1-4pm Sun Jul-Sep) Just off Rossville St, this museum chronicles the history of the Bogside, the civil rights movement and the events of Bloody Sunday.

Sleeping

Merchant's House B&B ££

(7126 9691; www.thesaddlershouse.com; 16 Queen St; s £40-60, d £55-70; @) This historic, Georgian-style townhouse has an elegant lounge and dining room with marble fireplaces and antique furniture, TV and coffee-making facilities in all rooms, and homemade marmalade at breakfast; there are even bathrobes in the rooms. Call at Saddler's House first to pick up a key.

Derry City Independent Hostel HOSTEL £

(7128 0542; www.derry-hostel.co.uk; 44 Great James St; dm £12-15, d from £34; @) Run by experienced backpackers and decorated with souvenirs from their travels around the world, this small, friendly hostel is set in a Georgian townhouse, just a short walk northwest of the bus station.

Derry Palace Hostel HOSTEL £
(☎7130 9051; www.paddyspalace.com; Asylum Rd, 1 Woodleigh Tce; dm/tw from £13/36; P@) Part of the Ireland-wide Paddy's Palace chain, this hostel is central, comfortable and as friendly as they come. There's a sunny garden and a good party atmosphere, and the staff regularly organise nights out at local pubs with traditional music.

Eating

Café del Mondo CAFE, IRISH ££
(www.cafedelmondo.org; Craft Village, Shipquay St; mains cafe £5-9, dinner £13-23; 9am-6pm Mon, 9am-11.30pm Tue-Sat, noon-5pm Sun) A bohemian cafe that serves excellent Fairtrade coffee and a range of healthy lunch dishes, including soups, stews and salads, served with homemade bread. The evening menu focuses on local produce, from wild mushroom risotto to Irish steak and seafood.

Encore Brasserie INTERNATIONAL ££
(☎7137 2492; Millennium Forum, Newmarket St; mains lunch £6, dinner £15-18; noon-3pm Mon-Sat, 5-9pm show nights;) Set in the lobby of the city's main cultural venue, the Encore is a stylish little place with friendly, efficient service and a crowd-pleasing menu of perennial favourites, from falafel wraps to steak with pepper sauce.

Café Blooms CAFE £
(www.verbalartscentre.co.uk/fac_cafe.htm; Verbal Arts Centre, Bishop St Within; mains £3-6; 8.30am-5pm Mon-Sat) This cool, literary-themed cafe is situated on top of the city walls, and serves delicious homemade soups, deli sandwiches, panini (a type of Italian sandwich) and excellent cappuccino.

GETTING INTO DERRY

A free shuttle bus connects Derry's Waterside train station with the bus station. From there, follow Foyle St towards the Guildhall and edge along the outside of the town walls towards pedestrianised Waterloo Pl. Bear right down Strand Rd; the hostels and B&Bs all have their check-in points on Great James St, off Strand Rd.

Drinking & Entertainment

Sandino's Cafe LIVE MUSIC
(www.sandinos.com; 1 Water St; live bands £5; 11.30am-1am Mon-Sat, 1pm-midnight Sun) From the posters of Che to the Free Palestine flag, this relaxed cafe-bar exudes a liberal, left-wing vibe. There are live bands on Friday nights, DJ sessions on Saturdays, and occasional jazz, folk or comedy gigs; check the website for what's on.

Peadar O'Donnell's PUB
(http://peadars-gweedorebar.com; 63 Waterloo St) Peadar's goes for traditional music sessions nightly and often in the afternoon on weekends, too.

Playhouse THEATRE
(www.derryplayhouse.co.uk; 5-7 Artillery St; box office 10am-5pm Mon-Fri, Context Gallery 11am-5.30pm Tue-Sat) Housed in beautifully restored former school buildings with an award-winning modern extension at the rear, this community arts centre stages music, dance and theatre performances by local and international performers.

Information

Derry Tourist Information Centre (☎028-7126 7284; www.derryvisitor.com; 44 Foyle St; 9am-5pm Mon-Fri, 10am-5pm Sat, plus 10am-4pm Sun Mar-Oct) Tourist info for all of Northern Ireland and the Republic, as well as Derry. Also internet access (£1 per 20 minutes), currency exchange and accommodation-booking service.

Getting There & Away

Bus

The bus station is just northeast of the city walls, on Foyle St.

Ulsterbus (www.translink.co.uk) service 212, the Maiden City Flyer, is the fastest service between Belfast and Derry (£11, 1¾ hours, every half-hour, fewer on Sunday). Bus 234 goes to Coleraine (£6, one hour, five daily Monday to Friday, two Sunday), where you can connect with the 252 Antrim Coaster service. Bus 274 goes from Derry to Dublin (£18.35, 3½ hours, six daily).

Bus Éireann (www.buseireann.ie) service 64 runs from Derry to Galway (£26, 5½ hours, three daily, two on Sundays) via Donegal and Sligo; another four per day terminate at Sligo.

Lough Swilly Bus Company (www.loughswillybusco.com), with an office upstairs at the

Ulsterbus station, serves County Donegal across the border.

Airporter (☎7126 9996; www.airporter.co.uk; Strand Rd, Quayside Shopping Centre) buses run direct from Derry's Quayside Shopping Centre to Belfast International airport (one way/return £18.50/29.50, 1½ hours) and George Best Belfast City airport (same fare, two hours) every two hours Monday to Friday, five to seven daily at weekends.

Train

Derry's Waterside train station (always referred to as Londonderry in Northern Ireland timetables) lies across the Foyle River from the city centre, but is connected to it by a free Rail Link bus. Trains to Belfast (£11, two hours, five daily) run via Coleraine, where you can change for Portrush (£11, 1½ hours).

UNDERSTAND IRELAND

History

Celtic warriors reached Ireland around 300 BC. Christian monks, including St Patrick, arrived around the 5th century AD, and from the end of the 8th century the rich monasteries were targets of raids by Vikings, who were followed by Anglo-Norman forces in 1169.

Oppression of the Catholic Irish got seriously underway in the 1500s, when Henry VIII and then Elizabeth I attempted to impose a new Protestant church. Land confiscated from Catholic nobles was given to Protestant settlers from Scotland and England, a policy known as 'the Plantation', sowing the seeds of today's divided Ireland.

By the 18th century, Ireland's Catholics held less than 15% of the land and suffered brutal civil restrictions. Irish movements for civil rights alarmed the Protestant gentry, and in 1800 the Act of Union joined Ireland with Britain.

Successive failures of potato crops between 1845 and 1851 brought about the Great Famine – hundreds of thousands starved while the British and Irish ruling classes profited from inflated food prices. About one million people died from disease or starvation, and another million emigrated.

Moves towards Irish home rule were interupted by WWI and a bungled uprising in 1916. Though it is now celebrated as a glorious bid for freedom, the Easter Rising was heavy on rhetoric and light on planning on both sides. After the insurrection was put down, a series of trials and executions (15 in all) transformed the ringleaders into martyrs and roused international support for Irish independence.

In the 1918 election, Irish republicans stood under the banner of Sinn Féin (Ourselves Alone) and won a majority of the Irish seats. Ignoring London's Parliament, the newly elected Sinn Féin deputies declared Ireland independent and formed the Dáil Éireann (Irish Assembly), led by Eamon de Valera.

The resulting Anglo-Irish War (1919–21) pitted Sinn Féin and its military wing, the Irish Republican Army (IRA), against the British. During this period Michael Collins masterminded the IRA's campaign of violence (while serving as finance minister in the new Dáil). After months of negotiations, he and Arthur Griffith led the delegation that signed the Anglo-Irish Treaty in 1921, giving 26 of Ireland's 32 counties their independence; six largely Protestant counties in Ulster chose to remain part of the UK, as the province of Northern Ireland.

To de Valera and many Irish Catholics, the compromise was a betrayal of republican principles and a brief civil war ensued. A new 1937 constitution abolished fealty to Britain and claimed sovereignty over the six counties of Ulster. In 1948 the Irish government declared the country a republic.

In Northern Ireland, the Protestant majority had systematically excluded Catholics from power. In January 1969 civil-rights marchers walking from Belfast to Derry were attacked by a Protestant mob outside Derry. British troops were sent to Derry and Belfast in August to maintain law and order. The peaceful civil-rights movement foundered and an armed independence struggle began, led by the IRA.

Thus the so-called Troubles thundered through the 1970s and 1980s. Passions exploded in 1972 when 13 unarmed Catholics were shot dead by British troops in Derry on 'Bloody Sunday' (30 January), then again in 1981 when 10 IRA prisoners fasted to death.

In August 1994 a 'permanent cessation of violence' by the IRA was announced, to be matched by a Protestant ceasefire two months later. After setbacks, the peace process regained momentum with the May 1997 victory of Britain's Labour Party, and in July 1997, the IRA declared another ceasefire.

In April 1998 all-party talks produced the Good Friday Agreement, which allowed the people of Northern Ireland to decide their future by majority vote, committed its signatories to 'democratic and peaceful means of resolving differences on political issues', and established a new Northern Ireland Assembly.

The new assembly was beset by divisions from the outset – largely over acts of violence and wrangles about how and when the IRA should 'decommission' its weapons – which resulted in no less than four suspensions, the latest from 2002 until 2007. A deal hammered out between the Democratic Unionist Party and Sinn Féin saw the assembly members finally take their seats in Stormont on 8 May 2007.

Today a cautious optimism prevails and, despite economic recession, occasional flare-ups of sectarian violence, and a renewed bombing campaign by republican splinter groups in Northern Ireland in 2010, the vast majority of people north and south of the border are committed to a peaceful future.

People

The total population of Ireland is around six million: 4.3 million in the Republic and 1.7 million in Northern Ireland. Prior to the 1845–51 Great Famine, the population was around eight million; death and emigration reduced it to around six million, and emigration continued at high levels for the next 100 years. It wasn't until the 1960s that the population began to recover.

Thanks to the EU, Ireland has seen a modest influx of immigrants, mostly from eastern Europe, within the past five years.

Religion has played a pivotal role in Irish history. About 90% of residents in the Republic are Roman Catholic, followed by 3% Protestant, 0.5% Muslim and the rest with no professed religious belief. In Northern Ireland, 53% are Protestant and 44% Catholic.

Arts

Literature

The Irish have made an enormous impact on world literature. Important writers include Jonathan Swift, Oscar Wilde, WB Yeats, George Bernard Shaw, James Joyce, Edna O'Brien, Seán O'Casey, Samuel Beckett and Roddy Doyle, whose *Paddy Clarke Ha Ha Ha* won the Booker Prize in 1993. The Ulster-born poet Seamus Heaney was awarded the Nobel Prize for Literature in 1995. Earlier Irish Nobel laureates include Shaw (1925), Yeats (1938) and Beckett (1969). Frank McCourt became a world favourite with his autobiographical *Angela's Ashes* (1996), which won the Pulitzer Prize, and *'Tis* (1999).

Music

Traditional Irish music – played on instruments such as the bodhrán (a flat, goatskin drum), uillean (or 'elbow') pipes, flute and fiddle – is an aspect of Irish culture impossible to miss. Of Irish groups, perhaps the best known are the Chieftains, the Dubliners and the Pogues. Popular Irish singers/musicians who have made it on the international stage include Van Morrison, Thin Lizzy, Sinéad O'Connor, U2, The Cranberries, The Corrs and Damien Rice.

Environment

Ireland is divided into 32 counties: 26 in the Republic and six in Northern Ireland. The island measures 84,421 sq km (about 83% is the Republic) and stretches 486km north to south and 275km east to west. The jagged coastline extends for 5631km. The midlands of Ireland are flat, rich farmland with huge swaths of peat (which is rapidly being depleted for fuel).

Carrauntuohil (1040m) on the Iveragh Peninsula, County Kerry, is the highest mountain on the island. The Shannon River, the longest in Ireland, flows for 259km before emptying into the Atlantic west of Limerick.

Ireland's rivers and lakes are well stocked with fish, and the island is home to some three-dozen mammal species. The Office of Public Works (OPW) maintains six national parks and 76 nature reserves in the Republic; the Department of the Environment owns or leases more than 40 nature reserves in Northern Ireland.

SURVIVAL GUIDE

Directory A–Z

Accommodation

Commercial camping grounds typically charge €10 to €20 for a tent and two people. Unless otherwise indicated, prices quoted for 'campsites' are for a tent, car and two people.

Hostels in Ireland can be booked solid in summer. An Óige (meaning 'youth') and Hostelling International Northern Ireland (HINI) are branches of Hostelling International (HI); An Óige has 26 hostels in the Republic, while HINI has six in the North. Other hostel associations include Independent Holiday Hostels (IHH), a cooperative group with about 120 hostels throughout the island, and the Independent Hostels Owners (IHO) association, which has over 100 members around Ireland.

From June to September a dorm bed at most hostels costs €15 to €20, except for the more expensive hostels in Dublin, Belfast and a few other places.

Typical B&Bs cost around €25 to €45 per person a night (sharing a double room), though more-luxurious B&Bs can cost upwards of €55 per person. Most B&Bs are small, so in summer they quickly fill up.

The following are useful resources:

Fáilte Ireland (Irish Tourist Board; www.discoverireland.ie) Will book accommodation for a 10% room deposit and a fee of €5.

Northern Ireland Tourist Board (NITB; www.discovernorthernireland.com) Books accommodation at no cost but with a 10% deposit upfront.

Gulliver (www.gulliver.ie) Online booking service for both the Republic and Northern Ireland; deposit of 10% and a €5 fee is payable.

An Óige (www.anoige.ie) Hostelling International-associated national organisation with 26 hostels scattered around the Republic.

Hostelling International Northern Ireland (www.hini.org.uk) Northern Irish branch of HI.

Independent Holiday Hostels of Ireland (IHH; www.hostels-ireland.com) Eighty tourist-board approved hostels throughout all of Ireland.

Independent Hostel Owners of Ireland (IHO; www.independenthostelsireland.com) Independent hostelling association.

PRICE RANGES

Prices are listed at high-season rates (low-season rates can be 15% to 20% less), based on two people sharing a double, and include a private bathroom unless otherwise stated. Booking ahead is recommended in peak season (roughly April to October).

In the Republic of Ireland:

€ less than €60

€€ €60 to €150

€€€ more than €150

In Northern Ireland:

£ less than £40

££ £40 to £100

£££ more than £100

Activities

Ireland is great for outdoor activities, and tourist offices have a wide selection of information covering birdwatching (County Donegal and County Wexford), surfing (great along the west coast), scuba diving (West Cork), cycling, fishing, horse riding, sailing, canoeing and many other activities.

Walking is particularly popular, although you must come prepared for wet weather. There are now well over 20 waymarked trails throughout Ireland, one of the most popular being the 132km Wicklow Way.

Business Hours

&Standard business hours are generally the same in both the Republic and Northern Ireland, as below:

Banks 10am to 4pm Monday to Friday, to 5pm Thursday

Offices 9am to 5pm Monday to Friday

Post offices 9am to 5.30pm Monday to Friday and 9am to 12.30pm Saturday in Northern Ireland; 9am to 6pm Monday to Friday and 9am to 1pm Saturday in the Republic. Smaller post offices may close at lunchtime and one day per week.

Pubs 11.30am to 11pm Monday to Saturday and 12.30 to 10pm Sunday in Northern Ireland, pubs with late licences open until 1am Monday to Saturday, and midnight Sunday; 10.30am to 11.30pm Monday to Thursday, 10.30am to 12.30am Friday and Saturday, noon to 11pm Sunday in the Republic. All pubs close Christmas Day and Good Friday.

Restaurants Noon to 10.30pm, many close one day of the week.

Shops 9am to 5.30pm or 6pm Monday to Saturday (to 8pm Thursday and sometimes Friday), noon to 6pm Sunday (in bigger towns); rural shops may close at lunchtime and one day per week.

Food

The following price indicators are used to indicate the cost of a main course at dinner.

In the Republic of Ireland:

€ less than €10

€€ €10 to €20

€€€ more than €20

In Northern Ireland:

£ less than £10

££ £10 to £20

£££ more than £20

Money

The Irish Republic uses the euro (€), while Northern Ireland uses the British pound sterling (£). Banks offer the best exchange rates; exchange bureaux, open longer, have worse rates and higher commissions. Post offices generally have exchange facilities and are open on Saturday morning.

In Northern Ireland several banks issue their own Northern Irish pound notes, which are equivalent to sterling but not readily accepted in mainland Britain. Many hotels, restaurants and shops in Northern Ireland accept euros.

Fancy hotels and restaurants usually add a 10% or 15% service charge onto bills. Simpler places usually don't add a service charge; if you decide to tip, just round up the bill (or add 10% at most). Taxi drivers do not have to be tipped, but if you do, 10% is more than generous.

Public Holidays

Following is a list of the main public holidays in the Republic, Northern Ireland and both:

New Year's Day 1 January

St Patrick's Day 17 March

Easter (Good Friday to Easter Monday inclusive) March/April

May Holiday First Monday in May

Christmas Day 25 December

St Stephen's Day (Boxing Day) 26 December

NORTHERN IRELAND

Spring Bank Holiday Last Monday in May

Orangemen's Day 12 July (following Monday if 12th is at weekend)

August Bank Holiday Last Monday in August

REPUBLIC OF IRELAND

June Holiday First Monday in June

August Holiday First Monday in August

October Holiday Last Monday in October

Telephone

Local telephone calls from a public phone in the Republic cost a minimum of €0.50 for three minutes; in Northern Ireland a local call costs a minimum of £0.30. Some payphones in Northern Ireland accept euro coins. Prepaid phonecards by Eircom or private operators, available in newsagencies and post offices, work from all payphones and dispense with the need for coins.

To call Northern Ireland from the Republic, do not use ☎0044 as for the rest of the UK. Instead, dial ☎048 and then the local number. To dial the Republic from Northern Ireland, however, use the full international code ☎00 353, then the local number.

The mobile (cell) phone network in Ireland runs on the GSM 900/1800 system compatible with the rest of Europe and Australia, but not the USA. Mobile numbers in the Republic begin with ☎085, ☎086 or ☎087. A local pay-as-you-go SIM for your mobile will cost from around €10, but may work out free after the standard phone-credit refund.

Visas

Citizens of the EU, Australia, Canada, New Zealand and the US don't need a visa to visit either the Republic or Northern Ireland. European Union nationals are allowed to stay indefinitely, while other visitors can usually remain for three to six months. United Kingdom nationals born in Britain or Northern Ireland don't need a passport to visit the Republic, but should carry one anyway as identification.

Getting There & Away

Air

There are nonstop flights from Britain, Continental Europe and North America to Dublin, Shannon and Belfast International and nonstop connections from Britain and Europe to Cork. International departure tax is normally included in the price of your ticket.

International airports in Ireland:

Belfast City (☎028-9093 9093; www.belfastcityairport.com)

Belfast International Airport (☎028-9448 4848; www.belfastairport.com)

Dublin Airport (☎01-814 1111; www.dublinairport.com)

Shannon Airport (SNN; ☎061-712 000; www.shannonairport.com)

Sea

There's a wide range of ferry services from Britain and France to Ireland. Prices vary depending on season, time of day, day of the week and length of stay. One-way fares for an adult foot passenger can be as little as £25, but can exceed £75 in summer. For a car plus driver and up to four adult passengers, prices can cost £150 to £300.

Keep an eye out for special deals, discounted return fares and other money savers. And plan ahead – some services are booked up months in advance. **DirectFerries** (www.directferries.co.uk) lists all the available ferry routes and operators.

FERRY OPERATORS

Brittany Ferries (www.brittany-ferries.com) Once weekly April to October.

Celtic Link Ferries (☎040-238 084, in France 02 33 43 23 87; www.celticlinkferries.com) Twice-weekly passenger-only service.

Irish Ferries (www.irishferries.com) Holyhead ferries up to four a day year-round, from France to Rosslare three times a week, mid-February to December.

P&O Irish Sea (www.poirishsea.com) Daily sailings year-round.

Steam Packet (☎1800-805 055, in the UK 0870 222 1333; www.steam-packet.com) Ferries operate daily Easter to September only.

Stena Line (www.stenaline.com)

FERRIES TO IRELAND

From Britain

ROUTE	OPERATOR	DURATION (HR)	ONE-WAY PRICE (£)
Fishguard–Rosslare	Stena Line	3½	29
Pembroke–Rosslare	Irish Ferries	2	29
Holyhead–Dublin	Stena Line, Irish Ferries	3	29
Holyhead–Dublin (fast boat)	Irish Ferries	1¾	34
Holyhead–Dun Laoghaire/ Dublin Port	Stena Line	1½	35
Douglas (Isle of Man)–Dublin	Steam Packet	2¾	45
Douglas (Isle of Man)–Belfast	Steam Packet	2¾	45
Cairnryan–Belfast	Stena Line	3	28
Cairnryan–Belfast (fast boat)	Stena Line	2	28
Cairnryan–Larne (fast boat)	P&O Irish Sea	1	26
Troon–Larne (fast boat)	P&O Irish Sea	2	26

From France

ROUTE	OPERATOR	DURATION (HR)	ONE-WAY PRICE (€)
Roscoff–Rosslare	Irish Ferries	17	64
Cherbourg–Rosslare	Irish Ferries, Celtic Link	20	64
Roscoff–Cork	Brittany Ferries	14	69

DISCOUNTS & PASSES

Eurail Pass Holders get a 50% discount on Irish Ferries crossings to France.

InterRail Pass Holders get a 50% discount on Irish Ferries and Stena Line services.

Britrail Pass Has an option to add on Ireland for an extra fee, including ferry transit.

Getting Around

Travelling around Ireland looks simple, as the distances are short and there's a dense network of roads and railways. But in Ireland, getting from A to B seldom uses a straight line, and public transport can be expensive (particularly trains), infrequent or both. For these reasons having your own transport – either car or bicycle – can be a major advantage.

Bicycle

A bike is useful for exploring in rural areas, but beware of traffic on what are often narrow, potholed roads with no space to get out of the way. Note that there is no 'right to roam' as in the UK, and most off-road cycling is technically illegal without the landowner's permission.

Typical bike hire costs are €20 to €25 per day or around €60 to €100 a week. Bags and other equipment can also be hired.

Bicycles can be transported by bus if there is enough room on board; the charge varies. On trains, the cost is €4 to €8 for a one-way journey, but bikes are not allowed on certain routes, including the Dublin Area Rapid Transit (DART).

Raleigh Rent-a-Bike (www.raleigh.ie) has a network of agencies all over Ireland; like many local bike shops, they offer one-way hire for an extra charge.

Bus

The Republic of Ireland's national bus line, **Bus Éireann** (☎01-836 6111; www.buseireann.ie), operates services all over the Republic and into Northern Ireland. Fares are much cheaper than train fares. Return trips are usually only slightly more expensive than one-way fares, and special deals (eg same-day returns) are often available. Most intercity buses in Northern Ireland are operated by **Ulsterbus** (☎028-9066 6600; www.ulsterbus.co.uk).

DISCOUNTS & PASSES

Bus Éireann offers discounts to ISIC (International Student Identity Cards) holders.

Travel passes for buses in Ireland include:

Open Road Pass (www.buseireann.ie) For bus travel in the Republic. It costs €57 (three days' travel out of six consecutive days), €73 (four out of eight days), €137 (eight out of 16 days) and €249 (15 out of 30 days).

Irish Rover (www.buseireann.ie) Bus travel on Bus Éireann (Republic) and Ulsterbus (Northern Ireland). Pay €88 for three days' travel out of eight consecutive days, €200 (eight out of 15 days) and €295 (15 out of 30 days).

Irish Explorer (www.buseireann.ie) Rail and bus travel in the Republic including DART. It costs €245 for eight days' travel out of 15 consecutive days.

Zone 4 iLink Card (www.translink.co.uk/ilink) Replacement for the Freedom of Northern Ireland pass. Smartcard offering unlimited travel on bus and train in Northern Ireland; one day/one week costs £17/57 plus £1.50 on first purchase (can be topped up).

Car & Motorcycle

People aged under 21 years cannot hire a car; for most hire companies you must be at least 23 and have had a valid driving licence for one year. Some companies will not hire to those aged over 70 or 75. Your own local licence is usually sufficient to hire a car for up to three months.

Train

The Republic of Ireland's railway system, **Iarnród Éireann** (Irish Rail; ☎1850-366 222; www.irishrail.ie), has routes radiating out from Dublin, but there is no direct north–south route along the west coast. Tickets can be twice as expensive as the bus, but travel times may be dramatically reduced. Special fares are often available, and a midweek return ticket sometimes costs just a bit more than the single fare; the flip side is that fares may be significantly higher on Friday and Sunday. **Rail Users Ireland** (www.railusers.ie) is more informative than the official website.

Northern Ireland Railways (NIR; ☎028-9089 9411; www.nirailways.co.uk; Belfast Central Station) has four lines from Belfast, one of which links up with the Republic's rail system.

Italy

Includes »

Rome 620
Genoa 643
Turin 646
Milan 647
Verona 650
Venice 653
Bologna 662
Florence 666
Pisa 673
Siena 675
Naples 680
Sicily 692
Sardinia 698
Understand Italy 701
Survival Guide 704

Best Places to Eat

» Al Gran Sasso (p635)
» Piccolo Napoli (p693)
» Osteria de' Poeti (p663)
» Cucina Casareccia (p691)
» Il Cantuccio (p690)

Best Places to Stay

» Arco del Lauro (p633)
» Pensione Guerrato (p658)
» Academy Hostel (p671)
» Hostel of the Sun (p681)
» Hotel Cairoli (p644)

Why Go?

Italians really do know how to live well. Ever since the Etruscans came, liked what they saw and decided to stay and party, the locals have embraced the finer things in life. Here, family, faith, friendship, food and wine reign supreme, contributing to the famous Italian *dolce vita* (sweet life).

Travellers have been falling under Italy's spell ever since the days of the 18th-century Grand Tour, enticed by its sun-kissed landscape, delectable cuisine and extraordinary art. This is the home of gently rolling Tuscan hills and postcard-perfect coastlines, and the place where simple dishes such as pizza and pasta regularly attain culinary perfection. It's where Michelangelo shocked the establishment with his assertively humanist sculptures and Caravaggio shocked everyone else with his criminal high-jinks and darkly atmospheric paintings.

So make like Julius Caesar. Come and see – you're bound to be conquered.

When to Go

Rome

°C/°F Temp
Rainfall inches/mm
40/104 – 30/86 – 20/68 – 10/50 – 0/32 – -10/14
6/150 – 4/100 – 2/50 – 0
J F M A M J J A S O N D

Apr & May Perfect spring temperatures and blooming wildflowers make hikers happy.

Jun & Jul Summer means beach weather and a packed festival calendar.

Oct Enjoy mild temperatures, autumn cuisine and the *vendemmia* (grape harvest).

AT A GLANCE

- » **Currency** Euro (€)
- » **Language** Italian
- » **Money** ATMs widespread; credit cards widely accepted
- » **Visas** Schengen rules apply

Fast Facts

- » **Area** 301,230 sq km
- » **Population** 60.62 million
- » **Capital** Rome
- » **Country code** ☎39
- » **Emergency** ☎112

Exchange Rates

Australia	A$1	€0.82
Canada	C$1	€0.77
Japan	¥100	€0.83
New Zealand	NZ$1	€0.65
UK	UK£1	€1.18
USA	US$1	€0.78

Set Your Budget

- » **Budget hotel double** €50–110
- » **Two-course dinner** €20 plus (pizza €10–15)
- » **Museum entrance** €6.50–15
- » **Beer** €2.50–5
- » **Intercity train ticket** €12–80

Resources

- » **Delicious Italy** (www.deliciousitaly.com)
- » **Italia** (www.italia.it)
- » **Lonely Planet** (www.lonelyplanet.com/italy)

Connections

Milan and Venice are northern Italy's two main transport hubs. From Milan, trains run to cities across western Europe, including Paris, Geneva and Zürich. Venice is better placed for eastern Europe, with rail connections to Ljubljana, Zagreb and Belgrade, as well as destinations in France, Germany, Austria and Switzerland. You can also pick up summer ferries in Venice for Croatia. Down the east coast, there are ferries from Bari to various Greek ports, as well as to Bar and Dubrovnik. Ferries to Barcelona leave from Genoa, and ferries to Tunis from Genoa and Palermo.

ITINERARIES

One Week

A one-week whistle-stop tour of Italy is enough to take in the country's three most famous cities. After a couple of days exploring Venice's unique canal-scape, head south to Florence, Italy's great Renaissance city. Two days will whet your appetite for the artistic and architectural treasures waiting to be discovered on your final days in Rome.

Two Weeks

After the first week, continue south for some sea and southern passion. Spend a day dodging traffic in Naples, a day investigating the ruins at Pompeii and a day or two admiring the Amalfi Coast. Then backtrack to Naples for a ferry to Palermo and the gastronomic delights of Sicily or to Cagliari and Sardinia's magical beaches.

Essential Food & Drink

- » **Pizza** Two varieties: Roman, with a thin crispy base; and Neapolitan, with a higher, more doughy base. The best are always prepared in a *forno a legna* (wood-fired oven).
- » **Pasta** Comes in hundreds of shapes and sizes; *pasta all'uovo* (egg pasta) is a favourite in the north.
- » **Gelato** Popular ice-cream flavours include *fragola* (strawberry), *nocciola* (hazelnut) and *stracciatella* (milk with chocolate shavings).
- » **Wine** Ranges from big-name reds such as Piedmont's Barolo to light whites from Sardinia and sparkling *prosecco* from the Veneto.
- » **Caffè** Join the locals for a morning cappuccino or post-lunch espresso, both taken standing at a bar.

Italy Highlights

1. Face up to awe-inspiring art and iconic monuments in **Rome** (p620)
2. Cruise past Gothic palaces, domed churches and crumbling piazzas in **Venice** (p653)
3. Explore the Renaissance time capsule of **Florence** (p666)
4. Feast on foodie delights and medieval architecture in hedonistic **Bologna** (p662)
5. Explore ancient rock dwellings in **Matera** (p689)
6. Taste the world's best pizza in **Naples** (p680)
7. Admire art and architecture in **Siena** (p675)
8. Visit regal palaces, magnificent museums and historic cafes in **Turin** (p646)
9. Take in an open-air opera in one of Italy's most romantic cities, **Verona** (p650)
10. Enjoy a bike ride and picnic atop the medieval city walls in **Lucca** (p676)

ROME

POP 2.76 MILLION

Even in this country of exquisite cities, Rome is special. Pulsating, seductive and utterly disarming, the Italian capital is an epic, monumental metropolis that will steal your heart and haunt your soul. They say a lifetime's not enough *(Roma, non basta una vita)*, but even on a short visit you'll be swept off your feet by its artistic and architectural masterpieces, its operatic piazzas, romantic corners and cobbled lanes. Yet while history reverberates all around, modern life is lived to the full – and it's this intoxicating mix of past and present, of style and urban grit that makes Rome such a compelling place.

Sights

Most of Rome's sights are concentrated in the area between Stazione Termini and the Vatican. Halfway between the two, the Pantheon and Piazza Navona lie at the heart of the *centro storico* (historic centre), while to the southeast, the Colosseum lords it over the city's ancient core.

ANCIENT ROME

TOP CHOICE Colosseum AMPHITHEATRE

(Map p626; 06 3996 7700; www.coopculture.it; Piazza del Colosseo; adult/reduced incl Roman Forum & Palatino €12/7.50; 8.30am-1hr before sunset; M Colosseo) Rome's great gladiatorial arena is the most thrilling of Rome's ancient sights. Originally known as the Flavian Amphitheatre, the 50,000-seat stadium was started by Emperor Vespasian in AD 72 and finished by his son Titus in AD 80. It was originally clad in travertine and covered by a huge canvas awning held aloft by 240 masts. Inside, tiered seating encircled the sand-covered arena, itself built over an underground complex (known as the hypogeum) where animals were caged and elaborate stage sets were prepared. Games involved gladiators fighting wild animals or each other, but, contrary to Hollywood folklore, bouts rarely ended in death.

The top tier and hypogeum can be visited on guided tours (€6 or €8 for both), which must be booked in advance, either at www.coopculture.it or by calling 06 399 67 700.

To the west of the Colosseum, the **Arco di Costantino** (Map p626; M Colosseo) was built to celebrate Constantine's victory over rival Maxentius at the battle of Milvian Bridge in AD 312.

TOP CHOICE Palatino RUINS

(Palatine Hill; Map p626; 06 3996 7700; www.coopculture.it; Via di San Gregorio 30; adult/reduced incl Colosseum & Roman Forum €12/7.50; 8.30am-1hr before sunset; M Colosseo) Ancient Rome's most exclusive neighbourhood, the Palatine (Palatino) is where Romulus supposedly founded the city in 753 BC.

Most of the area is covered by the ruins of Emperor Domitian's vast 1st-century palace complex. This served as the main imperial residence for 300 years and is divided into the **Domus Flavia** (Imperial Palace; Map p626), **Domus Augustana** (Emperor's Residence; Map p626) and a **stadio** (Stadium; Map p626).

Among the best-preserved buildings on the Palatine is the **Casa di Livia** (Map p626), home of Augustus' wife Livia, and, in front, Augustus' separate residence, the frescoed **Casa di Augusto** (Map p626; 11am-3.30pm Mon, Wed, Sat & Sun; M Colosseo).

For grandstand views over the Roman Forum, head to the **Orti Farnesiani** (Map p626) in the north of the complex.

Roman Forum RUINS

(Foro Romano; Map p626; 06 3996 7700; www.coopculture.it; Largo della Salara Vecchia; adult/reduced incl Colosseum & Palatino €12/7.50; 8.30am-1hr before sunset; Via dei Fori Imperiali) Now a collection of fascinating, if rather confusing, ruins, the Roman Forum was the social, political and commercial heart of ancient Rome.

As you enter from Largo della Salara Vecchia, ahead to your left is the **Tempio di Antonino e Faustina** (Map p626), built by the senate in AD 141 and transformed into a church in the 8th century. To your right, the **Basilica Aemilia** (Map p626), built in 179 BC, was 100m long with a two-storey porticoed facade lined with shops. Opposite the basilica, over **Via Sacra** (Map p626), the Forum's main drag, stands the **Tempio di Giulio Cesare** (Map p626), erected by Augustus in

COLOSSEUM TICKETS

To avoid queues at the Colosseum, buy your ticket from the Palatine entrance (about 250m away at Via di San Gregorio 30) or at the Roman Forum (Largo della Salara Vecchia). You can also book online at www.coopculture.it (plus booking fee of €1.50).

29 BC on the site where Caesar's body had earlier been cremated.

Head right up Via Sacra to reach the **Curia** (Map p626), the original seat of the Roman senate. Nearby, the **Arco di Settimio Severo** (Map p626) was erected in AD 203 to honour Emperor Septimus Severus' victory over the Parthians. Southwest of the arch, eight granite columns are all that remain of the 5th-century BC **Tempio di Saturno** (Map p626), an important temple that doubled as the state treasury.

To the southeast, the 7th-century **Colonna di Foca** (Column of Phocus; Map p626) stands at the centre of what was once the forum's main square, Piazza del Foro. To your right are the foundations of the **Basilica Giulia** (Map p626), a law court built by Julius Caesar in 55 BC. At the end of the basilica rise three columns, all that's left of the **Tempio di Castore e Polluce** (Map p626), a 489 BC temple dedicated to Castor and Pollux.

Back towards Via Sacra, white statues line the grassy atrium of the **Casa delle Vestali** (Map p626), the once-luxurious home of the Vestal Virgins who kept the sacred flame alight in the adjoining **Tempio di Vesta** (Map p626).

Continuing up Via Sacra, you come to the vast **Basilica di Massenzio** (Basilica di Costantino; Map p626), also known as the Basilica di Costantino, and the 1st-century **Arco di Tito** (Map p626), said to be the inspiration for the Arc de Triomphe in Paris.

TOP CHOICE **Piazza del Campidoglio** PIAZZA
(Map p626; Piazza Venezia) This elegant Michelangelo-designed piazza sits atop the Capitoline Hill (Campidoglio), which, in ancient times, was home to the city's two most important temples: one dedicated to Juno Moneta and the other to Jupiter Capitolinus.

You can reach the piazza from the Roman Forum but a more dramatic approach is via the **Cordonata** (Map p626) staircase. At the top, the piazza is flanked by three *palazzi:* **Palazzo Nuovo** (Map p626) on the left, **Palazzo dei Conservatori** (Map p626) on the right, and, in front, **Palazzo Senatorio** (Map p626), seat of Rome's city government since 1143. In the centre, the bronze **statue of Marcus Aurelius** (Map p626) is a copy; the original is in the Capitoline Museums.

TOP CHOICE **Capitoline Museums** MUSEUM
(Musei Capitolini; Map p626; 06 06 08; www.museicapitolini.org; Piazza del Campidoglio 1; adult/reduced €9.50/7.50; 9am-8pm Tue-Sun, last admission 7pm; Piazza Venezia) Housed in two facing *palazzi* – Palazzo dei Conservatori and Palazzo Nuovo – the Capitoline Museums date to 1471, making them the world's oldest public museums. Their collection of classical art, one of Italy's finest, includes the iconic *Lupa Capitolina* (Capitoline Wolf), a sculpture of Romulus and Remus under a wolf, and the *Galata morente* (Dying Gaul), a moving depiction of a dying Gaul. The 2nd-floor **pinacoteca** (picture gallery) contains paintings by the likes of Titian, Tintoretto, Van Dyck, Rubens and Caravaggio.

ROMA PASS

Definitely worth considering, the **Roma Pass** (www.romapass.it; 3 days €34) provides free admission to two museums or sites (choose from a list of 45), as well as reduced entry to extra sites, unlimited city transport and discounted entry to other exhibitions and events. Valid for three days, it's available online or from tourist information points and participating museums.

Chiesa di Santa Maria in Aracoeli CHURCH
(Map p626; Piazza Santa Maria in Aracoeli; 9am-12.30pm & 2.30-5.30pm; Piazza Venezia) Marking the highest point of the Campidoglio, this 6th-century church sits on the site of the Roman temple to Juno Moneta. According to legend it was here that the Tiburtin Sybil told Augustus of the coming birth of Christ, and the church still has a strong association with the nativity.

FREE **Il Vittoriano** MONUMENT
(Map p626; Piazza Venezia; 9.30am-5.30pm summer, to 4.30pm winter; Piazza Venezia) The massive mountain of white marble, Il Vittoriano (aka the *Altare della Patria;* Altar of the Fatherland), looms over Piazza Venezia. Begun in 1885 to honour Italy's Vittorio Emanuele II, it incorporates the **Tomb of the Unknown Soldier** and the **Museo Centrale del Risorgimento** (Map p626; Via di San Pietro in Carcere; 9.30am-6.30pm), documenting Italian unification. At the back, a **panoramic lift** (Map p626; adult/reduced €7/3.50; 9.30am-6.30pm Mon-Thu, to 7.30pm Fri-Sun) whisks you up to the top for Rome's best 360-degree views.

Rome

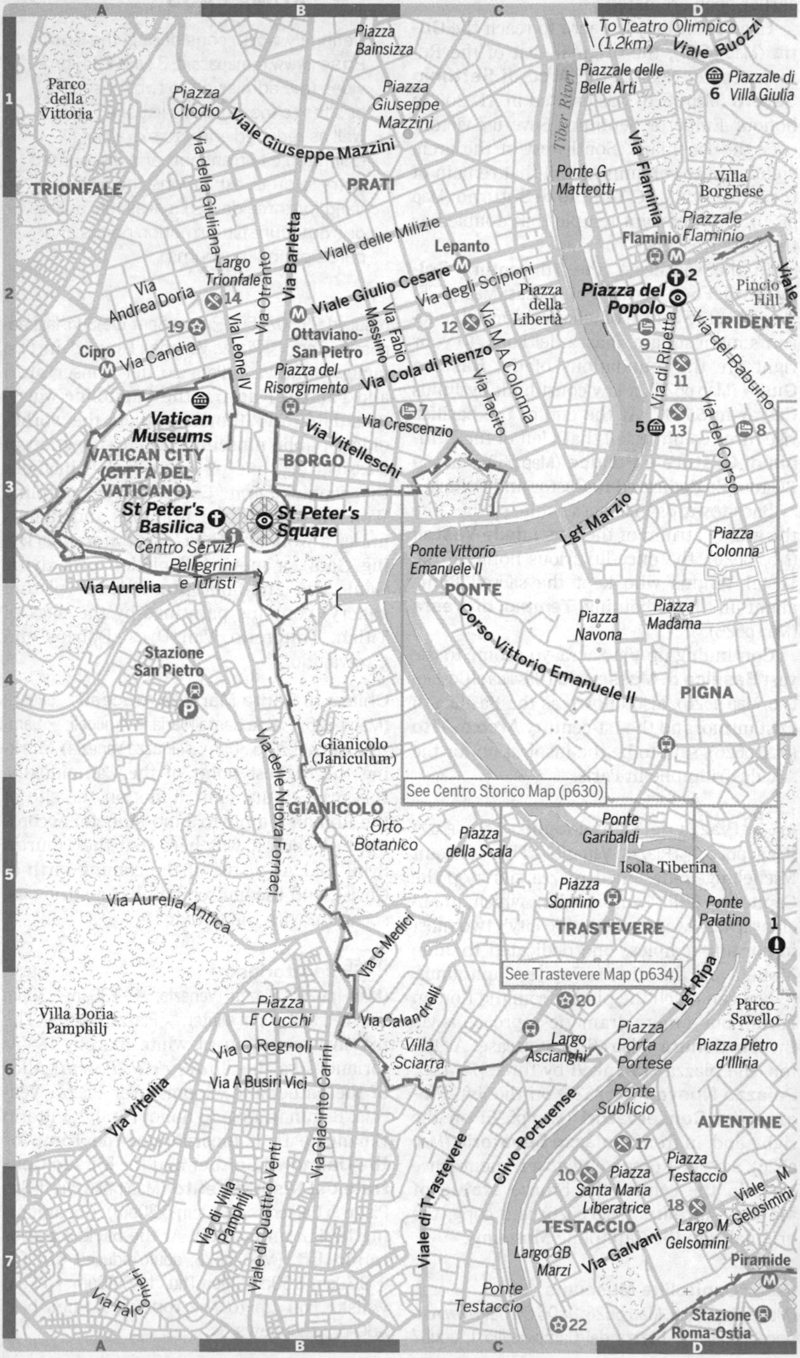

A
B
C
D
1
2
3
4
5
6
7
Parco della Vittoria
Piazza Clodio
Piazza Bainsizza
Piazza Giuseppe Mazzini
To Teatro Olimpico (1.2km)
Viale Buozzi
Piazzale delle Belle Arti
Piazzale di Villa Giulia
6
Viale Giuseppe Mazzini
Via della Giuliana
Tiber River
Via Flaminia
TRIONFALE
PRATI
Ponte G Matteotti
Villa Borghese
Piazzale Flaminio
Flaminio
Viale delle Milizie
Lepanto
Largo Trionfale
Via Otranto
Via Barletta
Viale Giulio Cesare
Via degli Scipioni
Piazza della Libertà
Piazza del Popolo
2
Pincio Hill
Viale
Via Andrea Doria
14
Via Leone IV
Via Fabio Massimo
Ottaviano-San Pietro
12
Via M A Colonna
TRIDENTE
19
Cipro
Via Candia
Piazza del Risorgimento
Via Cola di Rienzo
Via Tacito
9
Via di Ripetta
Via del Babuino
11
Vatican Museums
7
Via Crescenzio
5
13
Via del Corso
8
VATICAN CITY (CITTÀ DEL VATICANO)
Via Vitelleschi
BORGO
St Peter's Basilica
St Peter's Square
Lgt Marzio
Centro Servizi Pellegrini e Turisti
Ponte Vittorio Emanuele II
Piazza Colonna
Via Aurelia
PONTE
Corso Vittorio Emanuele II
Piazza Navona
Piazza Madama
Stazione San Pietro
PIGNA
Via delle Nuova Fornaci
Gianicolo (Janiculum)
See Centro Storico Map (p630)
GIANICOLO
Orto Botanico
Piazza della Scala
Ponte Garibaldi
Isola Tiberina
Piazza Sonnino
Via Aurelia Antica
Ponte Palatino
TRASTEVERE
1
Via G Medici
See Trastevere Map (p634)
Lgt Ripa
20
Piazza F Cucchi
Villa Doria Pamphilj
Via Calandrelli
Parco Savello
Piazza Porta Portese
Largo Ascianghi
Via O Regnoli
Villa Sciarra
Piazza Pietro d'Illiria
Via A Busiri Vici
Via Giacinto Carini
Ponte Sublicio
Via Vitellia
Clivo Portuense
AVENTINE
17
Via di Quattro Venti
Viale di Trastevere
Piazza Testaccio
10
Piazza Santa Maria Liberatrice
Viale M Gelosimini
Via di Villa Pamphilj
18
Largo M Gelsomini
TESTACCIO
Viale di Quattro Venti
Largo GB Marzi
Via Galvani
Piramide
Via Falconieri
Ponte Testaccio
22
Stazione Roma-Ostia

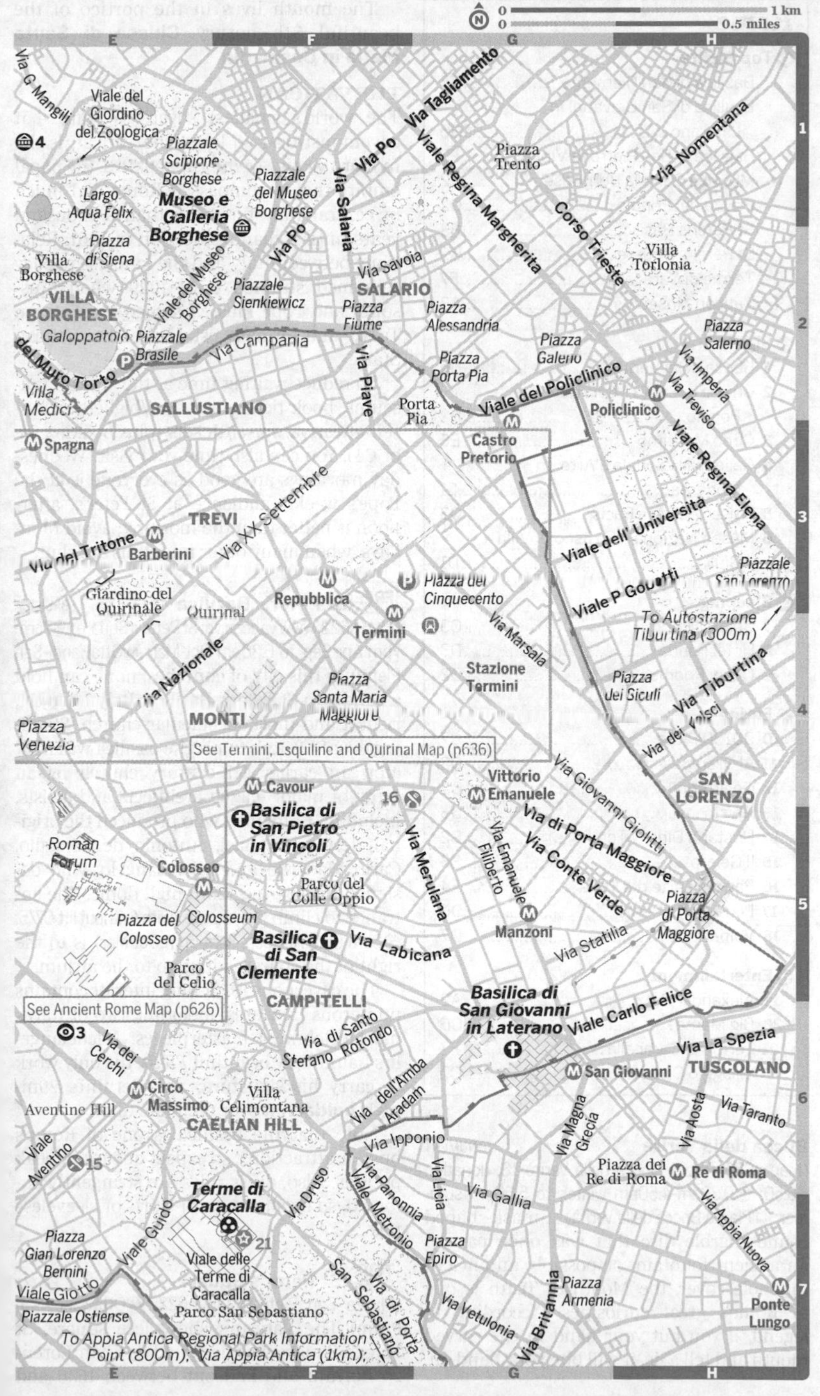

1 km
0.5 miles
Viale del Giordino del Zoologica
Piazzale Scipione Borghese
Largo Aqua Felix
Museo e Galleria Borghese
Piazzale del Museo Borghese
Piazza di Siena
Villa Borghese
VILLA BORGHESE
Galoppatoio
Piazzale Brasile
Viale del Museo Borghese
Piazzale Sienkiewicz
Via Po
Via Salaria
Via Tagliamento
Viale Regina Margherita
Piazza Trento
Via Nomentana
Corso Trieste
Villa Torlonia
Via Savoia
SALARIO
Piazza Fiume
Piazza Alessandria
Via Campania
Via Piave
Piazza Porta Pia
Porta Pia
Piazza Galeno
Piazza Salerno
Via Imperia
Via Treviso
Viale del Policlinico
Policlinico
del Muro Torto
Villa Medici
SALLUSTIANO
Spagna
Castro Pretorio
Viale Regina Elena
TREVI
Via XX Settembre
Via del Tritone
Barberini
Viale dell' Università
Piazzale San Lorenzo
Viale P Gouetti
Giardino del Quirinale
Quirinal
Repubblica
Piazza dei Cinquecento
Termini
To Autostazione Tiburtina (300m)
Via Marsala
Stazione Termini
Via Nazionale
Piazza Santa Maria Maggiore
Piazza dei Siculi
Via Tiburtina
Via dei Volsci
MONTI
Piazza Venezia
See Termini, Esquiline and Quirinal Map (p636)
Cavour
Vittorio Emanuele
Via Giovanni Giolitti
SAN LORENZO
Basilica di San Pietro in Vincoli
Via Merulana
Via di Porta Maggiore
Via Emanuele Filiberto
Via Conte Verde
Roman Forum
Colosseo
Parco del Colle Oppio
Piazza di Porta Maggiore
Piazza del Colosseo
Colosseum
Manzoni
Basilica di San Clemente
Via Labicana
Via Statilia
Parco del Celio
CAMPITELLI
Basilica di San Giovanni in Laterano
Viale Carlo Felice
See Ancient Rome Map (p626)
Via dei Cerchi
Via di Santo Stefano Rotondo
Via La Spezia
TUSCOLANO
San Giovanni
Circo Massimo
Villa Celimontana
Via dell'Amba Aradam
Aventine Hill
CAELIAN HILL
Via Aosta
Via Taranto
Via Magna Grecia
Via Ipponio
Viale Aventino
Piazza dei Re di Roma
Re di Roma
Via Licia
Via Pannonia
Viale Metronio
Via Gallia
Terme di Caracalla
Via Druso
Via Appia Nuova
Piazza Gian Lorenzo Bernini
Viale Guido
Viale delle Terme di Caracalla
Piazza Epiro
Viale Giotto
Via Britannia
Piazza Armenia
Ponte Lungo
Piazzale Ostiense
Parco San Sebastiano
Via di Porta San Sebastiano
Via Vetulonia
To Appia Antica Regional Park Information Point (800m); Via Appia Antica (1km);

Rome

Top Sights

	Basilica di San Clemente	F5
	Basilica di San Giovanni in Laterano	G6
	Basilica di San Pietro in Vincoli	F5
	Museo e Galleria Borghese	F2
	Piazza del Popolo	D2
	St Peter's Basilica	B3
	St Peter's Square	B3
	Terme di Caracalla	F7
	Vatican Museums	A3

Sights

1	Bocca della Verità	D5
2	Chiesa di Santa Maria del Popolo	D2
3	Circo Massimo	E6
4	Galleria Nazionale d'Arte Moderna	E1
5	Museo dell'Ara Pacis	D3
6	Museo Nazionale Etrusco di Villa Giulia	D1

Sleeping

7	Colors Hotel	C3
8	Hotel Panda	D3
9	Okapi Rooms	D2

Eating

10	00100 Pizza	C7
11	Al Gran Sasso	D2
12	Gelarmony	C2
13	'Gusto	D3
14	Hostaria Dino & Tony	B2
15	Il Gelato	E6
16	Panella l'Arte del Pane	F4
17	Pizzeria Da Remo	D6
18	Volpetti Più	D7

Entertainment

19	Alexanderplatz	A2
20	Big Mama	C6
21	Terme di Caracalla	F7
22	Villaggio Globale	C7

Bocca della Verità MONUMENT

(Map p622; Piazza Bocca della Verità 18; donation €0.50; ⌚9.30am-4.50pm winter, to 5.50pm summer; Piazza Bocca della Verità) A mask-shaped round marble disc that was once part of an ancient fountain, or possibly an ancient manhole cover, the Mouth of Truth is one of Rome's great curiosities. According to legend, if you put your hand in the carved mouth and tell a lie, it will bite your hand off.

The mouth lives in the portico of the beautiful 8th-century **Chiesa di Santa Maria in Cosmedin**.

THE VATICAN

The world's smallest sovereign state – it covers just 0.44 sq km – the Vatican is the modern vestige of the Papal States, the papal empire that encompassed Rome and much of central Italy for more than a thousand years until Italian unification in 1861. Relations between Italy and the landless papacy remained strained until 1929 when Mussolini and Pope Pius XI signed the Lateran Treaty and formally established the Vatican State.

To reduce waiting time at the Vatican museums, book tickets at http://biglietteriamusei.vatican.va/musei/tickets (plus booking fee of €4). You can also time your visit: Wednesday mornings are good as everyone is at the Pope's weekly audience at St Peter's; afternoon is better than the morning; avoid Mondays, when many other museums are shut.

FREE **St Peter's Basilica** BASILICA

(Map p622; www.vatican.va; St Peter's Square; ⌚7am-7pm Apr-Sep, to 6.30pm Oct-Mar; M Ottaviano–San Pietro) In this city of churches, none can hold a candle to St Peter's Basilica, Italy's biggest, richest and most spectacular church. Standing over St Peter's tomb, the basilica was built atop an earlier 4th-century church by an army of major -eague architects and artists, including Bramante, who produced the original design, Raphael, Antonio de Sangallo, Carlo Maderno and Michelangelo, who designed the soaring 120m-high dome. The entrance to climb the **dome** (with/without lift €7/5; ⌚8am-6pm Apr-Sep, 8am-5pm Oct-Mar) is to the right of the stairs leading up to the atrium.

The cavernous 187m-long interior contains numerous treasures, including two of Italy's most celebrated masterpieces: Michelangelo's hauntingly beautiful *Pietà,* the only work to carry his signature; and Bernini's 29m-high **baldachin** over the main altar.

Note that the basilica is one of Rome's busiest attractions, so expect queues in peak periods. Also, dress rules are stringently enforced, so no shorts, mini-skirts or sleeveless tops.

TOP CHOICE **St Peter's Square** PIAZZA

(Piazza San Pietro; Map p622; M Ottaviano–San Pietro) The Vatican's showpiece square, St Peter's Square was designed by Gian Lorenzo Bernini and laid out between 1656 and

1667. Seen from above, it resembles a keyhole with two semicircular colonnades, each consisting of four rows of Doric columns, encircling a giant ellipse that straightens out to funnel believers into the basilica. In the centre is a 25m-high obelisk brought to Rome by Caligula from Heliopolis in Egypt.

Each Wednesday at 11am, the Pope addresses his flock at the Vatican (in July and August in Castel Gandolfo near Rome). For details of how to apply for free tickets, see the Vatican website (www.vatican.va/various/prefettura/index_en.html).

TOP CHOICE Vatican Museums MUSEUM

(Musei Vaticani; Map p622; ☎06 6988 4676; http://mv.vatican.va; Viale Vaticano; adult/reduced €16/8, last Sun of month free; ⏰9am-6pm Mon-Sat, last admission 4pm, 9am-2pm last Sun of month, last admission 12.30pm; Ⓜ Ottaviano–San Pietro) Boasting one of the world's great art collections, the Vatican Museums are housed in the Palazzo Apostolico Vaticano, a vast 5.5-hectare complex comprising two palaces and three internal courtyards. You'll never cover it all in one day – there are about 7km of exhibits – so it pays to be selective.

Home to some spectacular classical statuary, the **Museo Pio-Clementino** is one of the museums' must-sees. Highlights include the *Apollo Belvedere* and the 1st-century *Laocoön*, both in the Cortile Ottagono. Further on, the 175m-long **Galleria delle Carte Geografiche** (Map Gallery) features 40 huge topographical maps. Beyond, the magnificent **Stanze di Raffaello** (Raphael Rooms), formerly Pope Julius II's private apartments, were decorated by Raphael from 1508 onwards. They feature a number of remarkable frescos, including his great masterpiece *La Scuola di Atene* (The School of Athens).

From the Raphael Rooms, it's a short walk onto the **Sistine Chapel** (Cappella Sistina), the museum's grand finale. The chapel was originally built in 1484 for Pope Sixtus IV, after whom it is named, but it took on its current look in the early 16th century after Pope Julius II commissioned Michelangelo to decorate it in 1508. Over the next four years, the artist painted the entire 800-sq-metre ceiling with episodes from the book of Genesis. Twenty-two years later he returned at the behest of Pope Clement VII to paint the *Giudizio Universale* (Last Judgement; 1534–41) on the 200-sq-metre west wall. The side walls also feature important frescos by Botticelli, Ghirlandaio, Pinturicchio and Signorelli.

HISTORIC CENTRE

TOP CHOICE Pantheon CHURCH

(Map p630; Piazza della Rotonda; ⏰8.30am-7.30pm Mon-Sat, 9am-6pm Sun; 🚌Largo di Torre Argentina) A striking 2000-year-old temple,

VATICAN MUSEUMS ITINERARY

Follow this three-hour itinerary for the museums' greatest hits.

Cortile della Pigna First stop is this courtyard, named after the huge Augustan-era bronze pine cone in the monumental niche. Cross the courtyard into the long corridor that is the Museo Chiaramonti and head left up the stairs.

Museo Pio Clementino This stunning museum showcases some of the Vatican's finest classical statuary. Follow the flow of people through the Cortile Ottagono and push onto the Sala Croce Greca (Greek Cross Room) from where stairs lead up to the 1st floor of the Belvedere Palace.

Galleria dei Candelabri The Gallery of the Candelabra is the first of three galleries that run the length of the palace. It gets very crowded up here as you're funnelled through the Galleria degli Arazzi (Tapestry Gallery) and onto the striking Galleria delle Carte Geografiche (Map Gallery). At the end of the corridor, carry on through the Sala Sobieski to the Sala di Costantino, the first of the four Raphael Rooms.

Stanze di Raffaello (Raphael Rooms) Anywhere else these magnificent frescoed chambers would be the star attraction but here they're the warm-up for the Sistine Chapel. To get to the Chapel, follow the one-way system past the modern art section and through the chapel's small and surprisingly discreet visitors' entrance.

Sistine Chapel Once in the chapel, head to the far wall to get the best views of the frescos.

Ancient Rome

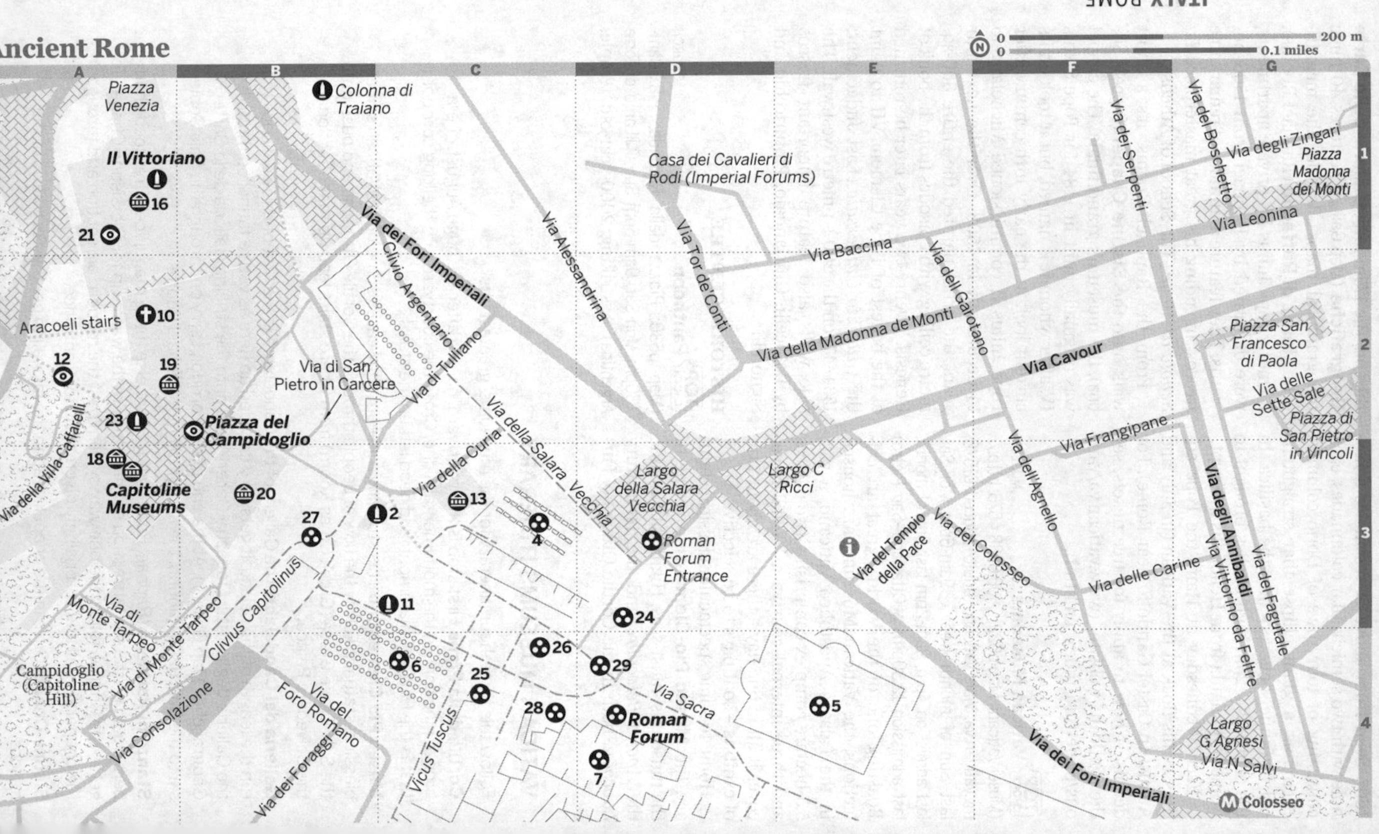

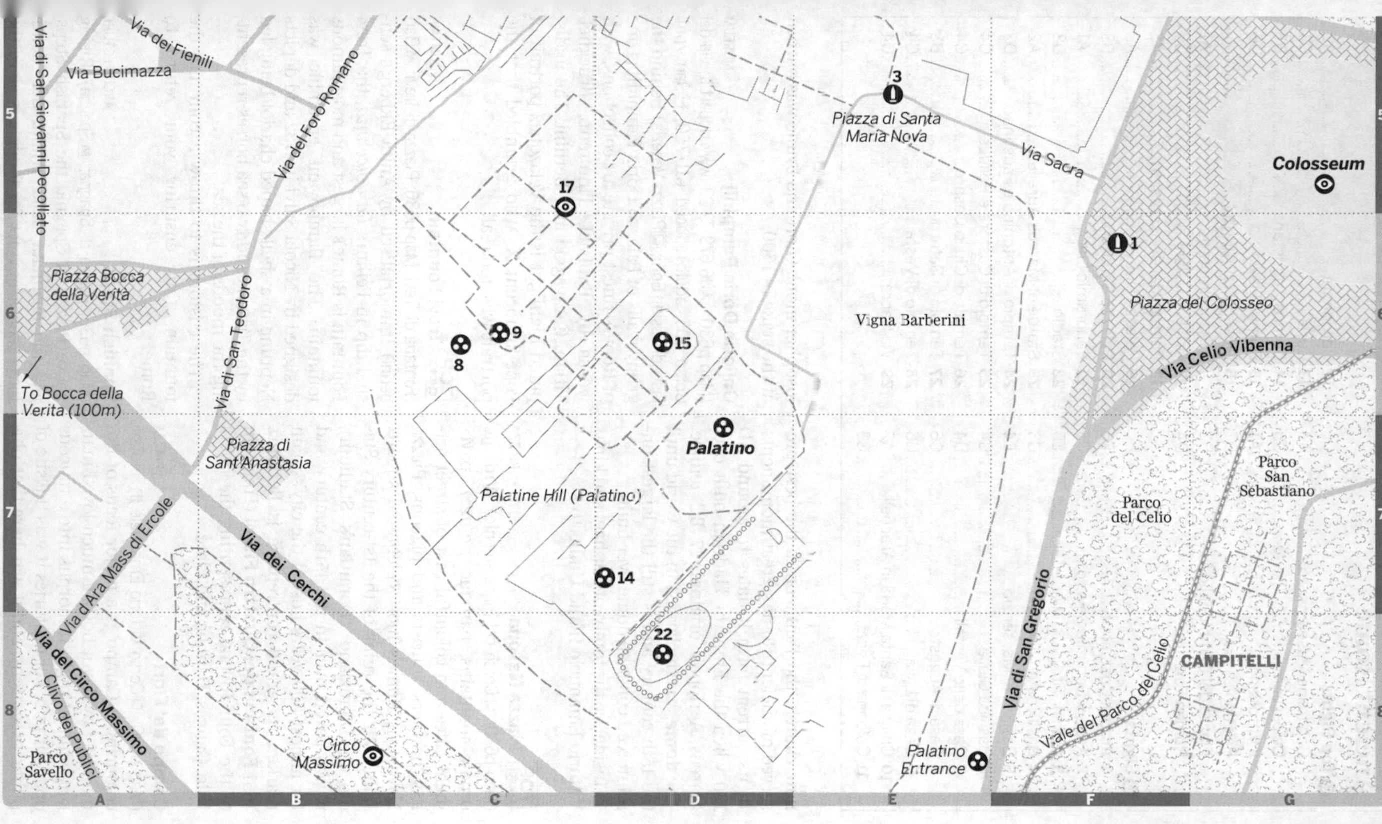
Via di San Giovanni Decollato
Via Bucimazza
Via dei Fienili
Via del Foro Romano
Piazza Bocca della Verità
Via di San Teodoro
To Bocca della Verita (100m)
Piazza di Sant'Anastasia
Via d Ara Mass di Ercole
Via dei Cerchi
Via del Circo Massimo
Clivo dei Publici
Parco Savello
Circo Massimo
17
9
8
15
Palatino
Palatine Hill (Palatino)
14
22
3
Piazza di Santa Maria Nova
Via Sacra
Vigna Barberini
Palatino Entrance
Via di San Gregorio
Colosseum
1
Piazza del Colosseo
Via Celio Vibenna
Parco del Celio
Parco San Sebastiano
CAMPITELLI
Viale del Parco del Celio
A
B
C
D
E
F
G
5
6
7
8

Ancient Rome

Top Sights

Capitoline Museums A3
Colosseum G5
Il Vittoriano A1
Palatino D7
Piazza del Campidoglio B2
Roman Forum D4

Sights

1 Arco di Costantino F6
2 Arco di Settimio Severo C3
3 Arco di Tito E5
4 Basilica Aemilia C3
5 Basilica di Massenzio E4
6 Basilica Giulia C4
7 Casa delle Vestali D4
8 Casa di Augusto C6
9 Casa di Livia C6
10 Chiesa di Santa Maria in Aracoeli A2
11 Colonna di Foca C3
12 Cordonata A2
13 Curia C3
14 Domus Augustana D7
15 Domus Flavia D6
16 Museo Centrale del Risorgimento A1
17 Orti Farnesiani C5
18 Palazzo dei Conservatori A3
19 Palazzo Nuovo A2
20 Palazzo Senatorio B3
21 Panoramic Lift A1
22 Stadio D8
23 Statue of Marcus Aurelius A2
24 Tempio di Antonino e Faustina D3
25 Tempio di Castore e Polluce C4
26 Tempio di Giulio Cesare C4
27 Tempio di Saturno B3
28 Tempio di Vesta C4
29 Via Sacra D4

now church, the Pantheon is the best preserved of ancient Rome's great monuments. In its current form it dates to around AD 120 when the Emperor Hadrian built over Marcus Agrippa's original 27 BC temple. The **dome** was the largest in the world until the 15th century and is still the largest unreinforced concrete dome ever built.

Inside are the tombs of Raphael and kings Vittorio Emanuele II and Umberto I.

TOP CHOICE Piazza Navona PIAZZA

(Map p630; Corso del Rinascimento) With its ornate fountains, baroque *palazzi*, pavement cafes and colourful cast of street artists, hawkers, tourists and pigeons, Piazza Navona is Rome's most celebrated square. Built over the ruins of the 1st-century Stadio di Domiziano (Domitian's Stadium), it was paved over in the 15th century and for almost 300 years hosted the city's main market. Its grand centrepiece is Bernini's 1651 **Fontana dei Quattro Fiumi** (Fountain of the Four Rivers) representing the rivers Nile, Ganges, Danube and Plate.

Campo de' Fiori PIAZZA

(Map p630; Corso Vittorio Emanuele II) Noisy, colourful 'Il Campo' is a major focus of Roman life: by day it hosts a much-loved market, while at night it morphs into a raucous open-air pub. For centuries it was the site of public executions, and it was here that philosopher monk Giordano Bruno was burned at the stake in 1600.

Galleria Doria Pamphilj MUSEUM

(Map p630; 06 679 73 23; www.dopart.it; Via del Corso 305; adult/reduced €11/7.50; 9am-7pm, last admission 6pm; Piazza Venezia) Behind the grimy walls of Palazzo Doria Pamphilj is one of Rome's finest private art collections, with works by Raphael, Tintoretto, Brueghel, Titian, Caravaggio and Bernini. The undisputed highlight is the Velázquez portrait of Pope Innocent X, who grumbled that the portrait was 'too real'.

TOP CHOICE Trevi Fountain FOUNTAIN

(Fontana di Trevi; Map p636; Piazza di Trevi; M Barberini) Immortalised by Anita Ekberg's sensual dip in Fellini's *La dolce vita*, the Trevi Fountain is Rome's largest and most famous fountain. The flamboyant ensemble was designed by Nicola Salvi in 1732 and depicts Neptune in a shell-shaped chariot being led by the Tritons and two sea horses representing the moods of the sea.

The custom is to throw a coin into the fountain, thus ensuring your return to Rome.

Spanish Steps ARCHITECTURE

(Map p636; Piazza di Spagna; M Spagna) Rising above Piazza di Spagna, the Spanish Steps, aka the Scalinata della Trinità dei Monti, have been a magnet for foreigners since the

18th century. The piazza was named after the Spanish embassy to the Holy See, although the staircase, which was built with French money in 1725, leads to the French church, **Chiesa della Trinità dei Monti** (Map p636; Piazza Trinità dei Monti; 6am-8pm Tue-Sun; Spagna).

At the foot of the steps, the fountain of a sinking boat, the **Barcaccia** (1627), is believed to be by Pietro Bernini, father of the more famous Gian Lorenzo. Opposite, **Via dei Condotti** is Rome's top shopping strip.

Piazza del Popolo PIAZZA

(Map p622; Flaminio) This elegant landmark square was laid out in 1538 at what was then Rome's northern entrance. Guarding its southern approach are the almost-twin 17th-century churches of **Santa Maria dei Miracoli** and **Santa Maria in Montesanto**, while on the northern side the art-rich **Chiesa di Santa Maria del Popolo** (Map p622; Piazza del Popolo; 7.30am-noon & 4-7pm; Flaminio) boasts two Caravaggio masterpieces – the *Conversione di San Paolo* (Conversion of St Paul) and the *Crocifissione di San Pietro* (Crucifixion of St Peter) – and other fine works.

Rising above the piazza, the **Pincio Hill** affords great views.

Museo dell'Ara Pacis MUSEUM

(Map p622; 06 06 08; http://en.arapacis.it; Lungotevere in Augusta; adult/reduced €8.50/6.50; 9am-7pm Tue-Sun, last admission 6pm; Flaminio) The first modern construction in Rome's historic centre since WWII, Richard Meier's white pavilion houses the **Ara Pacis Augustae** (Altar of Peace), one of the most important works of ancient Roman sculpture. The vast marble altar was completed in 13 BC as a monument to the peace that Augustus established both at home and abroad.

VILLA BORGHESE

Just north of the historic centre, Villa Borghese is Rome's best-known park. The grounds, which were created in the 17th century by Cardinal Scipione Borghese, are accessible from Piazzale Flaminio, Pincio Hill and the top of Via Vittorio Veneto. Bike hire is available at various points, typically costing €5 per hour.

TOP CHOICE **Museo e Galleria Borghese** MUSEUM

(Map p622; 06 3 28 10; www.galleriaborghese.it; Piazzale del Museo Borghese 5; adult/reduced €9/4.50, plus €2 booking fee and possible exhibition supplement; 9am-7pm Tue-Sun, pre-booking necessary; Via Pinciana) Housing the 'queen of all private art collections', this lavish gallery boasts paintings by Caravaggio, Botticelli and Raphael, as well as spectacular sculptures by Gian Lorenzo Bernini. There are highlights at every turn, but look out for Bernini's *Ratto di Proserpina* (Rape of Persephone) and Antonio Canova's *Venere vincitrice* (Conquering Venus).

MUSEO NAZIONALE ROMANO

Spread over four sites, the **Museo Nazionale Romano** (National Roman Museum) houses one of the world's most important collections of classical art. A combined ticket including each of the sites costs adult €7 (plus possible €3 exhibition supplement), and is valid for three days.

Palazzo Massimo alle Terme (Map p636; 06 3996 7700; www.coopculture.it; Largo di Villa Peretti 1; adult/reduced €7/3.50; 9am-7.45pm Tue-Sun; Termini) A fabulous museum with amazing frescos and wall paintings.

Terme di Diocleziano (Map p636; 06 3996 7700; www.coopculture.it; Viale Enrico de Nicola 78; adult/reduced €7/3.50; 9am-7.30pm Tue-Sun; Termini) Ancient epigraphs and tomb artefacts in the Terme di Diocleziano (Diocletian's Baths), ancient Rome's largest baths complex.

Palazzo Altemps (Map p630; 06 399 67 700; http://archeoroma.beniculturali.it/en/museums/national-roman-museum-palazzo-altemps; Piazza Sant'Apollinare 44; adult/reduced €7/3.50; 9am-7.45pm Tue-Sun; Corso del Rinascimento) Wonderful classical sculpture in an exquisite Renaissance *palazzo*.

Crypta Balbi (Map p630; 06 3996 7700; http://archeoroma.beniculturali.it/en/museums/national-roman-museum-crypta-balbi; Via delle Botteghe Oscure 31; adult/reduced €7/3.50; 9am-7.45pm Tue-Sun ; Via delle Botteghe Oscure) Set atop an ancient Roman theatre, the Teatro di Balbus (13 BC).

Centro Storico

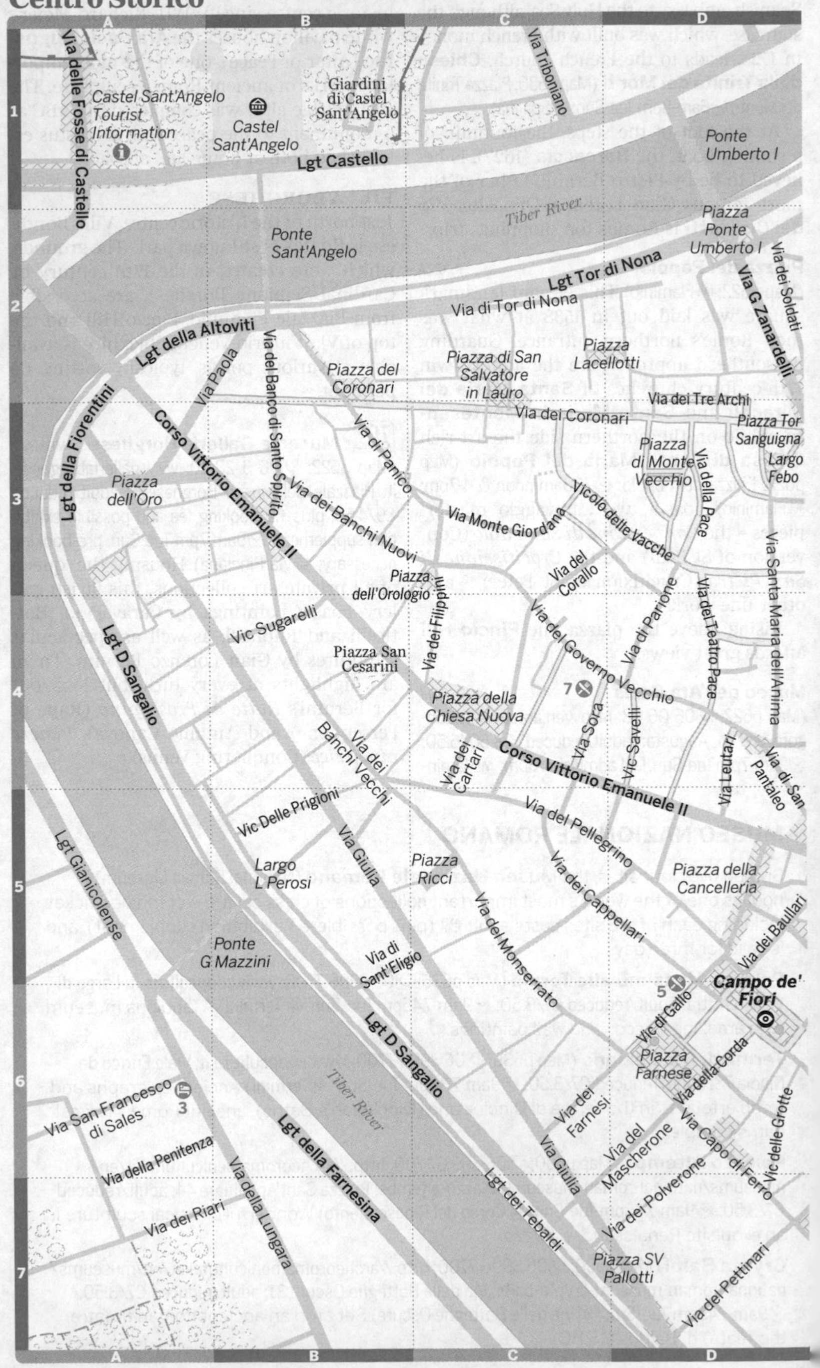

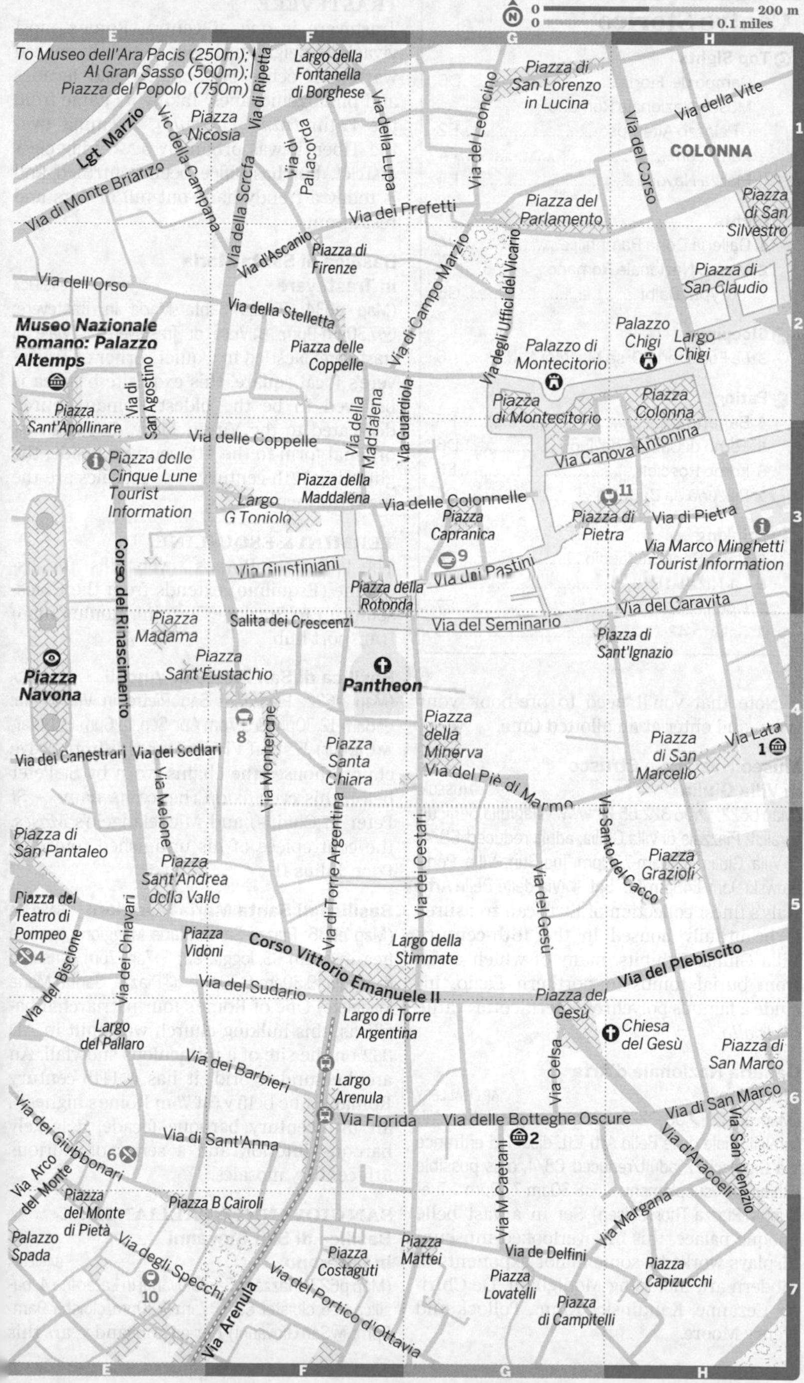

0 200 m
0 0.1 miles
To Museo dell'Ara Pacis (250m); Al Gran Sasso (500m); Piazza del Popolo (750m)
Largo della Fontanella di Borghese
Piazza di San Lorenzo in Lucina
Via della Vite
COLONNA
Piazza Nicosia
Lgt Marzio
Via di Monte Brianzo
Vic della Campana
Via della Scrofa
Via di Ripetta
Via di Palacorda
Via della Lupa
Via del Leoncino
Via del Corso
Via dei Prefetti
Piazza del Parlamento
Piazza di San Silvestro
Via d'Ascanio
Piazza di Firenze
Via di Campo Marzio
Via degli Uffici del Vicario
Piazza di San Claudio
Via dell'Orso
Via della Stelletta
Museo Nazionale Romano: Palazzo Altemps
Piazza delle Coppelle
Palazzo Chigi
Largo Chigi
Palazzo di Montecitorio
Piazza di Montecitorio
Piazza Colonna
Piazza Sant'Apollinare
Via di San Agostino
Via delle Coppelle
Via della Maddalena
Via Guardiola
Via Canova Antonina
Piazza delle Cinque Lune Tourist Information
Piazza della Maddalena
Largo G Toniolo
Via delle Colonnelle
Piazza Capranica
11
Piazza di Pietra
Via di Pietra
Via Marco Minghetti Tourist Information
9
Via Giustiniani
Via dei Pastini
Piazza della Rotonda
Via del Caravita
Corso del Rinascimento
Piazza Madama
Salita dei Crescenzi
Via del Seminario
Piazza di Sant'Ignazio
Piazza Sant'Eustachio
Pantheon
Piazza Navona
8
Piazza della Minerva
Piazza Santa Chiara
Piazza di San Marcello
Via Lata
1
Via dei Canestrari
Via dei Sediari
Via Monterone
Via del Piè di Marmo
Via Santo del Cacco
Via Melone
Via di Torre Argentina
Via dei Cestari
Via del Gesù
Piazza di San Pantaleo
Piazza Sant'Andrea della Valle
Piazza Grazioli
Piazza del Teatro di Pompeo
4
Via del Biscione
Via dei Chiavari
Piazza Vidoni
Corso Vittorio Emanuele II
Largo della Stimmate
Via del Plebiscito
Via del Sudario
Piazza del Gesù
Largo di Torre Argentina
Chiesa del Gesù
Largo del Pallaro
Via dei Barbieri
Piazza di San Marco
Largo Arenula
Via Celsa
Via dei Giubbonari
Via Florida
Via delle Botteghe Oscure
Via di San Marco
2
Via di Sant'Anna
6
Via d'Aracoeli
Via San Venanzio
Via Arco del Monte
Piazza del Monte di Pietà
Piazza B Cairoli
Via M Caetani
Via Margana
Palazzo Spada
Via degli Specchi
Piazza Costaguti
Piazza Mattei
Via de Delfini
Piazza Lovatelli
Piazza Capizucchi
10
Via Arenula
Via del Portico d'Ottavia
Piazza di Campitelli
E
F
G
H
1
2
3
4
5
6
7

Centro Storico

Top Sights

Campo de' Fiori ... D6
Museo Nazionale Romano:
Palazzo Altemps ... E2
Pantheon ... F4
Piazza Navona ... E4

Sights

1 Galleria Doria Pamphilj ... H4
2 Museo Nazionale Romano:
Crypta Balbi ... G6

Sleeping

3 La Foresteria Orsa Maggiore ... A6

Eating

4 Baffetto 2 ... E5
5 Forno di Campo de' Fiori ... D6
6 Forno Roscioli ... E6
7 Pizzeria da Baffetto ... C4

Drinking

8 Caffè Sant'Eustachio ... F4
9 La Tazza d'Oro ... G3
10 Open Baladin ... E7
11 Salotto 42 ... H3

Note that you'll need to pre-book your ticket and enter at an allotted time.

Museo Nazionale Etrusco di Villa Giulia MUSEUM

(Map p622; ☎06 322 65 71; www.villagiulia.beniculturali.it; Piazzale di Villa Giulia; adult/reduced €8/4; ⊙Villa Giulia 8.30am-7.30pm Tue-Sun, Villa Poniatowski 9am-1.45pm Tue-Sat; Via delle Belle Arti) Italy's finest collection of Etruscan treasures is beautifully housed in the 16th-century Villa Giulia. Exhibits, many of which came from burial tombs in northern Lazio, include a famous polychrome terracotta statue of *Apollo*.

Galleria Nazionale d'Arte Moderna ART GALLERY

(Map p622; ☎06 3229 8221; www.gnam.beniculturali.it; Viale delle Belle Arti 131, disabled entrance Via Gramsci 71; adult/reduced €8/4, plus possible exhibition supplement; ⊙8.30am-7.30pm Tue-Sun; Piazza Thorvaldsen) Set in a vast belle époque palace, this oft-overlooked museum displays works by some major exponents of modern art, including Modigliani, De Chirico, Cezanne, Kandinsky, Klimt, Pollock and Henry Moore.

TRASTEVERE

Trastevere is one of central Rome's most vivacious neighbourhoods, a tightly packed warren of ochre *palazzi*, ivy-clad facades and photogenic lanes. Taking its name from the Latin *trans Tiberium*, meaning over the Tiber, it was originally a working-class district, but has since been gentrified and is today a trendy hang-out full of bars and restaurants.

Basilica di Santa Maria in Trastevere BASILICA

(Map p634; Piazza Santa Maria in Trastevere; ⊙7.30am-9pm; Viale di Trastevere, Viale di Trastevere) Nestled in a quiet corner of Trastevere's focal square, this exquisite basilica is believed to be the oldest Roman church dedicated to the Virgin Mary, dating in its original form to the 4th century. Inside, the glittering 12th-century apse mosaics are the main drawcard.

TERMINI & ESQUILINE

The largest of Rome's seven hills, the Esquiline (Esquilino) extends from the Colosseum up to Stazione Termini, Rome's main transport hub.

Basilica di San Pietro in Vincoli BASILICA

(Map p622; Piazza di San Pietro in Vincoli 4a; ⊙8am-12.30pm & 3-7pm Apr-Sep, to 6pm Oct-Mar; MCavour) Just off Via Cavour, this impressive church houses the chains worn by St Peter before his crucifixion (hence its name – St Peter in Chains) and Michelangelo's *Moses*, the centrepiece of his unfinished tomb for Pope Julius II.

Basilica di Santa Maria Maggiore BASILICA

(Map p636; Piazza Santa Maria Maggiore; basilica free, museum €3, loggia €2; ⊙7am-7pm, museum & loggia 9.30am-6.30pm; Piazza Santa Maria Maggiore) One of Rome's four patriarchal basilicas, this hulking church was built in AD 352 on the site of a miraculous snowfall. An architectural hybrid, it has a 14th-century Romanesque belfry (at 75m Rome's highest), an 18th-century baroque facade, a largely baroque interior, and a series of glorious 5th-century mosaics.

SAN GIOVANNI & CAELIAN HILL

Basilica di San Giovanni in Laterano BASILICA

(Map p622; Piazza di San Giovanni in Laterano 4; basilica free, cloister €3; ⊙7am-6.30pm, cloister 9am-6pm; MSan Giovanni) For a thousand years this monumental white cathedral was the most important church in Christendom. Founded by Constantine in AD 324, it was the first Christian basilica built in the city and, until the late 14th century, was the pope's main place of worship. It has been revamped several times, most notably by Borromini in the 17th century, and by Alessandro Galilei, who added the monumental facade in the 1700s.

Basilica di San Clemente BASILICA

(Map p622; www.basilicasanclemente.com; Via di San Giovanni in Laterano; church/excavations free/€5; ⏲9am-12.30pm & 3-6pm Mon-Sat, noon-6pm Sun; ⓂColosseo) Nowhere better illustrates the various stages of Rome's turbulent history than this fascinating, multi-layered church. The ground-level, 12th-century basilica sits atop a 4th-century church, which, in turn, stands over a 2nd-century temple dedicated to the pagan god Mithras and a 1st-century Roman house. Beneath everything are foundations dating from the Roman Republic.

Terme di Caracalla RUINS

(Map p622; ☎06 3996 7700; www.coopculture.it; Viale delle Terme di Caracalla 52; adult/reduced €7/4; ⏲9am-1hr before sunset Tue-Sun, 9am-2pm Mon ; 🚌Viale delle Terme di Caracalla) The vast ruins of the Terme di Caracalla are an awe-inspiring sight. Inaugurated in AD 217, the 10 hectare leisure complex could hold up to 1600 people and included richly decorated pools, gymnasiums, libraries, shops and gardens.

The ruins are now used to stage summer opera.

Sleeping

Rome has plenty of accommodation but rates are universally high. Most of the hostels and budget *pensioni* (guesthouses) are in the area around Stazione Termini – the best on the Via Marsala side.

Always try to book ahead, even if it's just for the first night. You'll find a full list of accommodation options (with prices) at www.060608.it. If you arrive without a booking, there's a **hotel reservation service** (Map p636; ☎06 699 10 00; booking fee €3; ⏲7am-10pm) next to the tourist office at Stazione Termini.

HISTORIC CENTRE & THE VATICAN

Hotel Panda PENSION €

(Map p622; ☎06 678 01 79; www.hotelpanda.it; Via della Croce 35; s €65-80, d €85-108, tr €120-140, q €180; 📶; ⓂSpagna) A great position near the Spanish Steps, small, simply furnished rooms, and honest rates ensure a year-round stream of travellers to this budget stalwart. Cheaper rooms are also available with shared bathrooms. Breakfast, which is optional, costs €5 and is served in a nearby bar.

Okapi Rooms HOTEL €

(Map p622; ☎06 3260 9815; www.okapirooms.it; Via della Penna 57; s €65-80, d €85-120, tr €110-140, q €120-180; ❄📶; ⓂFlaminio) Occupying a tall townhouse near Piazza del Popolo, the Okapi is a bargain low-midrange option. Rooms, spread over six floors, are small and modest with cream walls, terracotta tiled floors and tiny en suite bathrooms. Several also have small terraces.

Colors Hotel HOTEL €

(Map p622; ☎06 687 40 30; www.colorshotel.com; Via Boezio 31; s €35-90, d €45-125; ❄📶; 🚌Via Cola di Rienzo) This is a bright budget hotel with smart, vibrantly coloured rooms on three floors (no lift). There are also cheaper rooms with shared bathrooms and, from June to August, dorms (€12 to €35 per person) for guests under 38.

TRASTEVERE

TOP CHOICE **Arco del Lauro** B&B €€

(Map p634; ☎9am-2pm 06 9784 0350, mobile 346 2443212; www.arcodellauro.it; Via Arco de' Tolomei 27; s €75-125, d €95-145; ❄@📶; 🚌Viale di Trastevere, 🚋Viale di Trastevere) This friendly B&B is in a medieval *palazzo* on a narrow, cobbled street. Its five gleaming doubles sport an understated modern look with white walls, parquet and modern furnishings, while the upstairs quad retains a high wood-beamed ceiling.

Maria-Rosa Guesthouse B&B €

(Map p634; ☎338 770 00 67; www.maria-rosa.it; Via dei Vascellari 55; s €53-73, d €66-86, tr €104-124,

FREE THRILLS

Surprisingly, some of Rome's most famous sights are free:

» Trevi Fountain

» Spanish Steps

» Pantheon

» Bocca della Verità

» All churches, including St Peter's Basilica

» Vatican Museums on the last Sunday of the month.

Trastevere

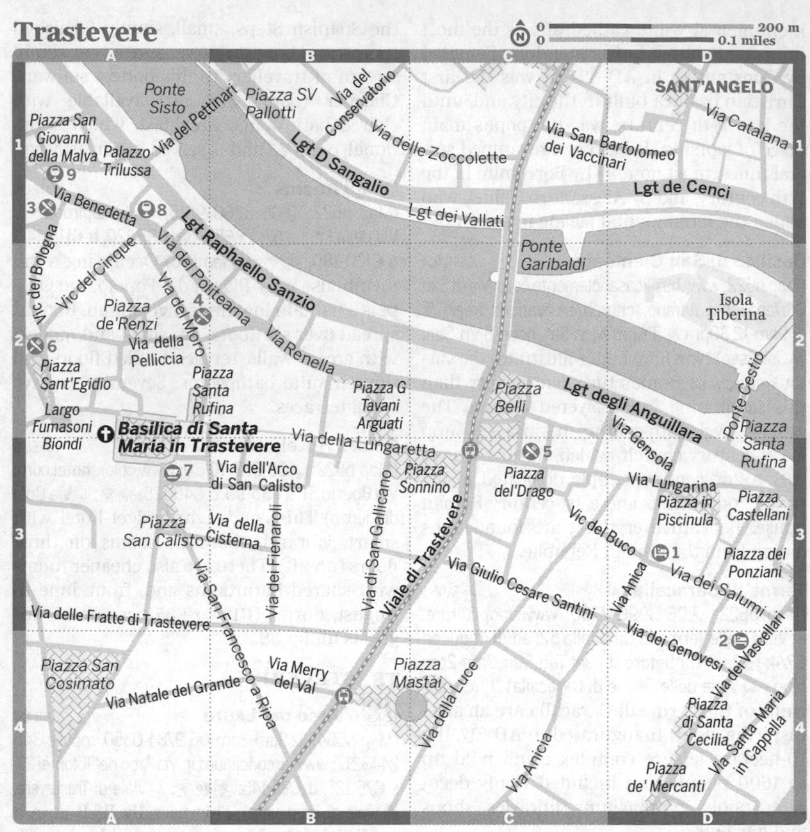

q €122-142; @; Viale di Trastevere, Viale di Trastevere) A delightful B&B on the 3rd floor of a Trastevere townhouse. It's a simple affair with two guest rooms sharing a single bathroom and a small common area, but the sunlight, pot plants and books create a lovely, warm atmosphere. Breakfast not included.

La Foresteria Orsa Maggiore HOSTEL €
(Map p630; 06 689 37 53; www.casainternazionaledelledonne.org; Via San Francesco di Sales 1a, 2nd fl; dm €26-42, s €55-75, d €110-150, without bathroom s €36-55, d €72-100; @; Piazza Trilussa) Housed in a restored 17th-century convent, this well-located women-only hostel has 13 simple, airy rooms set around an attractive internal garden. There's a 3am curfew and minimum two-night stay.

TERMINI & ESQUILINE

TOP CHOICE **Beehive** HOSTEL €
(Map p636; 06 4470 4553; www.the-beehive.com; Via Marghera 8; dm €25-30, s €50-60, d €90-100, without bathroom s €40-50, d €80-90, tr €95-105; ; Termini) More boutique than backpacker, the Beehive is one of the best hostels in town, with vibrant art works, a laid-back lounge and a dedication to ecofriendly practices. Beds are in an eight-person mixed dorm or tastefully decorated private rooms. Breakfast is available at the hostel's vegetarian cafe.

Welrome Hotel HOTEL €
(Map p636; 06 4782 4343; www.welrome.it; Via Calatafimi 15-19; d/tr/q €110/148/187; ; Termini) This is a lovely, low-key budget hotel not far from Termini. Owners Mary and Carlo take great pride in looking after their guests,and their seven, simply decorated rooms provide welcome respite from Rome's relentless streets. No breakfast, but there are kettles and fridges available.

Alessandro Palace Hostel HOSTEL €
(Map p636; 06 446 19 58; www.hostelsalessandro.com; Via Vicenza 42; dm €19-35, d €70-120,

Trastevere

Top Sights

Basilica di Santa Maria in Trastevere....A2

Sleeping

1 Arco del Lauro....D3
2 Maria-Rosa Guesthouse....D4

Eating

3 Dar Poeta....A1
4 Forno la Renella....A2
5 Hostaria dar Buttero....C3
6 Trattoria degli Amici....A2

Drinking

7 Bar San Calisto....A3
8 Freni e Frizioni....A1
9 Ma Che Siete Venuti a Fà....A1

tr €95-120; ; Castro Pretorio) A long-standing favourite in the Termini area, this slick hostel offers spick-and-span hotel-style rooms, as well as dorms sleeping from four to eight. It's managed by an efficient international crew, has 24-hour reception, and serves cut-price beer in the hostel bar.

Eating

Eating out is one of the great joys of visiting Rome and everywhere you go you'll find trattorias, pizzerias, *gelaterie* (ice-cream shops) and restaurants.

The best areas are the historic centre and Trastevere, but there are also excellent choices in San Lorenzo east of Termini and Testaccio. Watch out for overpriced tourist traps around Termini and the Vatican.

HISTORIC CENTRE & THE VATICAN

Hostaria Dino & Tony TRATTORIA €€
(Map p622; 06 397 33 284; Via Leone IV 60; mains €12; Mon-Sat, closed Aug; Ottaviano–San Pietro) An authentic trattoria in the Vatican area. Kick off with the monumental antipasto before plunging into its signature dish, *pasta all' amatriciana* (with guanciale bacon, chilli and tomato sauce). Finish up with a *granita di caffè* (crushed ice coffee served with whipped cream). No credit cards.

HISTORIC CENTRE

TOP CHOICE **Al Gran Sasso** TRATTORIA €
(Map p622; 06 321 48 83; www.trattoriaalgransasso.com; Via di Ripetta 32; meals €25; lunch & dinner Sun-Fri; Flaminio) The perfect lunchtime spot, this is a classic, died-in-the-wool trattoria. It's a relaxed place with a welcoming vibe, garish murals on the walls and tasty country food, including excellent fried antipasti and warming autumnal pastas.

Forno di Campo de' Fiori BAKERY €
(Map p630; Campo de' Fiori 22; pizza slices about €3; 7.30am-2.30pm & 4.45-8pm Mon-Sat; Corso Vittorio Emanuele II) One of Rome's best bakeries, serving bread, panini and delicious straight-from-the-oven *pizza al taglio* (by the slice). Aficionados swear by the *pizza bianca* (white pizza), but the *panini* and *pizza rossa* (with tomato) are just as good.

Pizzeria da Baffetto PIZZERIA €
(Map p630; 06 686 16 17; www.pizzeriabaffetto.it; Via del Governo Vecchio 114; pizzas €6-9; 6.30pm-1am; Corso Vittorio Emanuele II) For the full-on Roman pizza experience, get down to this local institution. Meals are raucous, chaotic and fast, but the thin-crust pizzas are spot on and the vibe is genuine. There's also **Baffetto 2** (Map p630; Piazza del Teatro di Pompeo 18; 6.30pm-12.30am Mon & Wed-Fri, 12.30-3.30pm & 6.30pm-12.30am Sat & Sun; Corso Vittorio Emanuele II) near Campo de' Fiori.

Forno Roscioli PIZZA, BAKERY €
(Map p630; Via dei Chiavari 34; pizza slices from €2, snacks from €1.50; 7.30am-8pm Mon-Fri, 7.30am-2.30pm Sat; Via Arenula) Join the lunchtime crowds at this revered bakery for a slice of *pizza bianca* or a freshly baked pastry. There's also a counter serving hot pastas and vegetable side dishes.

'Gusto RISTORANTE €
(Map p622; 06 322 62 73; Piazza Augusto Imperatore 9; pizzas €7-10; Via del Corso) All exposed brickwork and industrial chic, this '90s-style warehouse operation is a lunchtime favourite, serving everything from thick-crust pizza to cheese platters, salads and overpriced fusion food. At lunch, go for the bargain buffet.

TRASTEVERE

Trattoria degli Amici TRATTORIA €€
(Map p634; 06 580 60 33; www.trattoriadegliamici.org; Piazza Sant'Egidio 6; mains €15; Viale di Trastevere, Viale di Trastevere) Boasting a prime piazza location, this cheerful trattoria is run by a local charity and staffed by volunteers and people with disabilities. Snaffle an outside table and dig into well-prepared Italian classics as you enjoy the neighbourhood vibe.

Termini, Esquiline and Quirinal

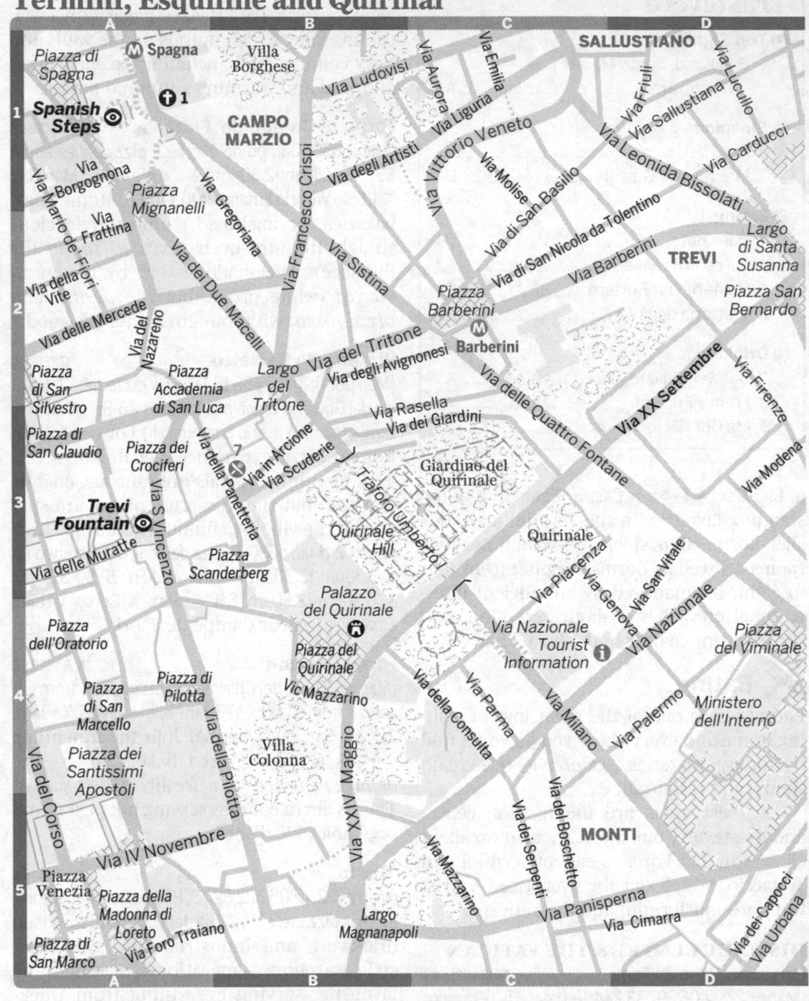

Termini, Esquiline and Quirinal

Top Sights

- Basilica di Santa Maria Maggiore F5
- Museo Nazionale Romano: Palazzo Massimo alle Terme F3
- Museo Nazionale Romano: Terme di Diocleziano F2
- Spanish Steps A1
- Trevi Fountain A3

Sights

1 Chiesa della Trinità dei Monti A1

Sleeping

2 Alessandro Palace Hostel H2
3 Beehive H2
4 Hotel Reservation Service G4
5 Italian Youth Hostel Association F4
6 Welrome Hotel F2

Eating

7 San Crispino B3

Entertainment

8 Teatro dell'Opera di Roma E3

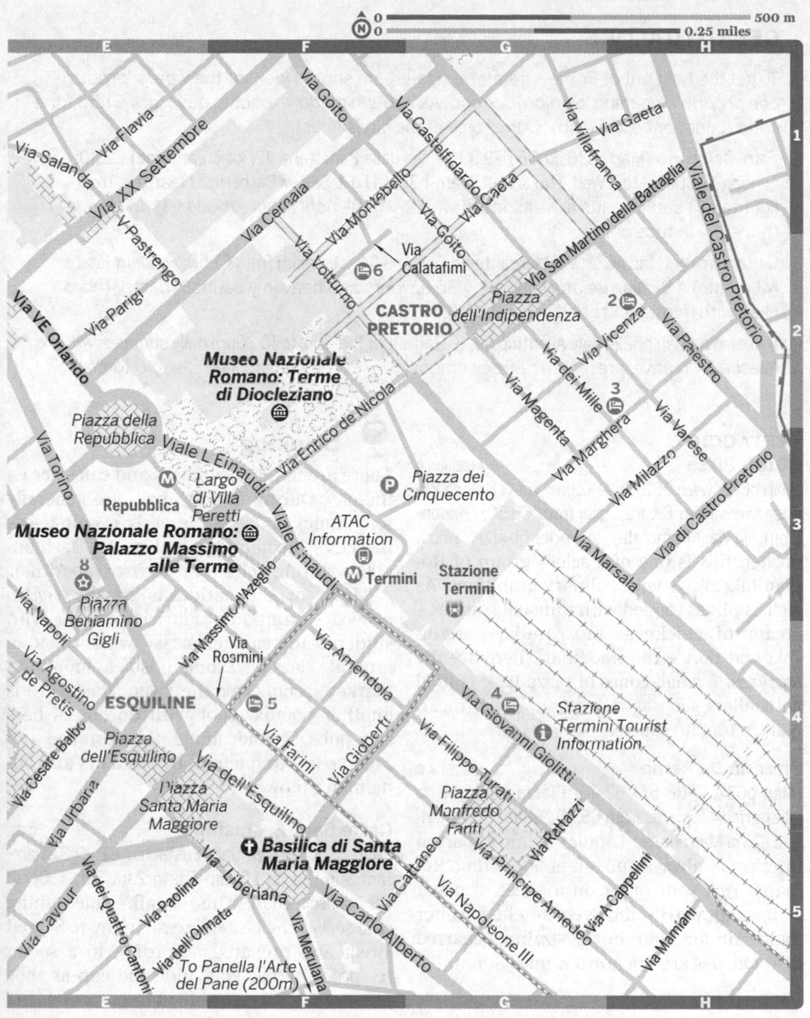

Dar Poeta PIZZERIA €
(Map p634; ☎06 588 05 16; Vicolo del Bologna 46; pizzas from €6; ⊙lunch & dinner; 🚌Piazza Trilussa) Loud and always busy, this much-loved pizzeria guarantees a cheery atmosphere and hearty wood-fired pizzas that fall somewhere between wafer-thin Roman pizzas and the softer, doughier Neapolitan versions.

Forno la Renella BAKERY €
(Map p634; ☎06 581 72 65; Via del Moro 15-16; pizza slices from €2.50; ⊙7am-2am Tue-Sat, to 10pm Sun & Mon; 🚌Piazza Trilussa) The wood-fired ovens at this historic Trastevere bakery produce a delicious daily batch of pizza, bread and biscuits.

Hostaria dar Buttero TRATTORIA €€
(Map p634; ☎06 580 05 17; Via della Lungaretta; mains €13; ⊙Mon-Sat; 🚌Viale di Trastevere, 🚋Viale di Trastevere) On Trastevere's quieter eastern side, this is a typical old-school trattoria. The menu lists all the usual pastas, grilled meats and pizzas (evenings only), but the food is well cooked, the atmosphere is convivial and the prices are honest.

GELATO GALORE

To get the best out of Rome's *gelaterie* (ice-cream shops) look for the words *'produzione proprio'*, meaning 'own production'. As a rough guide, expect to pay from €1.50 for a *cono* (cone) or *coppa* (tub). Our choice of the city's finest:

San Crispino (Map p636; ☎06 679 39 24; Via della Panetteria 42; ice cream from €2.30; ⊙noon-12.30am Mon, Wed, Thu & Sun, 11am-1.30am Fri & Sat; Ⓜ Barberini) Near the Trevi Fountain, it serves natural, seasonal flavours – think *fichi secci* (dried figs) and *miele* (honey) – in tubs only.

Gelarmony (Map p622; Via Marcantonio Colonna 34; ice cream from €1.50; ⊙10am-late; Ⓜ Lepanto) A Sicilian *gelateria* serving 60 flavours and heavenly cannoli (pastry tubes filled with ricotta and candied fruit).

Il Gelato (Map p622; Viale Aventino 59; ⊙11am-9pm Tue-Sun, to 10.30pm daily summer; Ⓜ Circo Massimo) Creative, preservative-free combos from Rome's gelato king Claudio Torcè.

TESTACCIO

00100 Pizza PIZZERIA €

(Map p622; www.00100pizza.com; Via G Branca 88; pizza slices from €3, trapizzini from €3.50; ⊙noon-11pm; 🚌 Via Marmorata) A pocket-size pizza pusher, this is one of a select group of Roman takeaways with culinary ambitions. As well as pizzas topped with unusual combos – cream of chickpea; mozzarella, gorgonzola and port – the trademark here are the *trapizzini,* small cones of pizza base stuffed with fillers such as *polpette al sugo* (meatballs in tomato sauce).

Pizzeria Da Remo PIZZERIA €

(Map p622; ☎06 574 62 70; Piazza Santa Maria Liberatrice 44; pizzas from €5.50; ⊙7pm-1am Mon-Sat; 🚌 Via Marmorata) Popular Remo's spartan interior is always full of noisy young Romans. Tick your order on a sheet of paper slapped down by an overstretched waiter and wait for your huge, sizzling, charred disc. Queues are the norm after 8.30pm.

Volpetti Più CAFETERIA €

(Map p622; Via Volta 8; mains €8; ⊙10.30am-3.30pm & 5.30-9.30pm Mon-Sat; 🚌 Via Marmorata) One of the few places in town where you can sit down and eat well for less than €20, Volpetti Più is a sumptuous *tavola calda* ('hot table') offering an opulent choice of pizza, pasta, soup, meat, vegetables and fried nibbles.

TERMINI & ESQUILINE

Panella l'Arte del Pane BAKERY, CAFE €

(Map p622; ☎06 487 24 35; Via Merulana 54; pizza slices around €3; ⊙noon-midnight Mon-Sat, 10am-4pm Sun Mar-Oct; Ⓜ Vittorio Emanuele) A devilshly tempting bakery-cum-cafe-cum-deli with a sumptuous array of *pizza al taglio, supplì* (fried rice balls), focaccia and fried croquettes.

Drinking

There are hundreds of bars and cafes across the city. During the day, bars are generally for a quick coffee while early evening sees the city's hipsters descend on the fashionable watering holes for *aperitivi* (aperitifs).

Much of the action is in the *centro storico* – Campo de' Fiori is popular with students and can get messy, while the area around Piazza Navona hosts a more upmarket scene. Over the river, Trastevere is another popular spot with dozens of bars and pubs. Further afield, San Lorenzo and Pigneto are frequented by students and bohemian uptowners.

Caffè Sant'Eustachio CAFE

(Map p630; Piazza Sant'Eustachio 82; ⊙8.30am-1am Sun-Thu, to 1.30am Fri, to 2am Sat; 🚌 Corso del Rinascimento) This small, unassuming cafe serves the best espresso in town. Served sweet and prepared according to a secret recipe – the bar staff hide the cup as they prepare it – it's guaranteed to put some zing into your sightseeing.

Open Baladin BAR

(Map p630; www.openbaladinroma.it; Via degli Specchi 6; ⊙noon-2am; 🚌 Via Arenula) This designer bar is a leading light on Rome's burgeoning beer scene. It's a cool, loungey place with more than 40 beers on tap and up to 100 bottled beers, many produced by Italian artisanal breweries.

La Tazza d'Oro CAFE

(Map p630; ☎06 679 27 68; Via degli Orfani 84-86; ⊙7am-8pm Mon-Sat, 10.30am-7.30pm Sun; 🚌 Via del Corso) A busy, burnished coffee house serving superb esspresso and a range of delicious coffee concoctions, including a gorgeous *granita di caffè*.

Salotto 42 BAR
(Map p630; www.salotto42.it; Piazza di Pietra 42; ⊙10am-2am Tue-Sat, to midnight Sun & Mon; 🚌Via del Corso) On a picturesque piazza, this is a hip lounge bar, complete with vintage armchairs, suede sofas and smart, dressed-to-kill drinkers.

Ma Che Siete Venuti a Fà PUB
(Map p634; Via Benedetta 25; ⊙11am-2am; 🚌Piazza Trilussa) This pint-sized pub is a beer-buff's paradise, packing a huge number of artisanal beers into its tiny interior.

Freni e Frizioni BAR
(Map p634; ☎06 5833 4210; www.freniefrizioni.com; Via del Politeama 4-6; ⊙6.30pm-2am; 🚌Piazza Trilussa) Housed in a former garage, this designer-grunge bar draws a spritz-loving crowd that flocks here to slurp on mojitos and fill up at the popular 7pm *aperitivo*.

Bar San Calisto CAFE
(Map p634; ☎06 589 56 78; Piazza San Calisto 3-5; ⊙6am-2am Mon-Sat; 🚌Viale di Trastevere, 🚋Viale di Trastevere) Students, punks, alcoholics, bohemians and card-playing *nonni* (grandpas) congregate at this down-at-heel Trastevere favourite for dirt cheap drinks and its laid-back vibe.

☆ Entertainment

Rome has a thriving cultural scene, with a year-round calendar of concerts, performances and festivals. A useful listings guide is *Trova Roma,* a free insert that comes with *La Repubblica* newspaper every Thursday. Up-coming events are also listed on www.turismoroma.it, www.060608.it and www.auditorium.com.

Classical Music & Opera

Auditorium Parco della Musica CONCERT VENUE
(☎06 8024 1281; www.auditorium.com; Viale Pietro de Coubertin 30; 🚌shuttle bus M from Stazione Termini, 🚋Viale Tiziano) Rome's premier concert venue stages everything from classical music concerts to tango exhibitions, book readings and film screenings. It's also home to Rome's top orchestra, the Orchestra dell'Accademia Nazionale di Santa Cecilia (www.santacecilia.it).

Teatro dell'Opera di Roma OPERA
(Map p636; ☎06 481 70 03; www.operaroma.it; Piazza Beniamino Gigli; ballet €12-80; opera €17-150; ⊙box office 9am-5pm Mon-Sat, 9am-1.30pm Sun; Ⓜ Repubblica) Rome's opera house also hosts the city's ballet company. The opera season runs from December to June, with summer performances staged at the **Terme di Caracalla** (Map p622; Viale delle Terme di Caracalla 52; 🚌Viale delle Terme di Caracalla).

Nightclubs & Live Music

Rome's clubbing scene is centred on Testaccio and the Ostiense area, although you'll also find places in Trastevere and the *centro storico*. Out from the centre, San Lorenzo and Pigneto are happening areas.

You'll need to dress the part for the big clubs, which can be tricky to get into and rarely kick off much before midnight or 1am. Admission is often free but drinks are expensive, typically €10 to €16. Note also that many clubs shut between mid-June and mid-September.

TOP CHOICE Circolo degli Artisti LIVE MUSIC
(☎06 7030 5684; www.circoloartisti.it; Via Casilina Vecchia 42; ⊙7pm-2am Tue-Thu, to 4.30am Fri-Sun; 🚌Ponte Casilino) East of the Pigneto district, this kicking club offers one of Rome's best nights out with live music from Italian and international bands, cracking DJ turns, and a large garden for outdoor beer.

Alexanderplatz JAZZ
(Map p622; ☎06 3974 2171; www.alexanderplatz.it; Via Ostia 9; ⊙concerts 9.45pm Sun-Thu, 10.30pm Fri & Sat; Ⓜ Ottaviano–San Pietro) Rome's top jazz joint attracts international performers and a passionate, knowledgeable crowd. In July and August the club goes alfresco at the under-the-stars Villa Celimontana Jazz Festival.

EAT & DRINK FOR LESS

» Lunch on *pizza al taglio* (by the slice) and ice cream; dine on bar snacks over an *aperitivo* (aperitif).

» Take advantage of the fixed-price lunch menus that some restaurants offer.

» Fill up on the bread they bring when you sit down – you'll pay for it whether you eat it or not.

» Drink standing at the bar rather than sitting at a table.

WORTH A TRIP

VIA APPIA ANTICA

Completed in 190 BC, ancient Rome's *regina viarum* (queen of roads) connected the capital with Brindisi on Italy's Adriatic coast. Nowadays, Via Appia Antica (The Appian Way) is one of Rome's most exclusive addresses, a beautiful cobbled thoroughfare flanked by grassy fields, ancient ruins and towering pine trees. But it has a dark history – Spartacus and 6000 of his slave rebels were crucified here in 71 BC, and it was here that the early Christians buried their dead in underground catacombs.

The two main catacombs are the **Catacombe di San Sebastiano** (☎06 785 03 50; www.catacombe.org; Via Appia Antica 136; adult/reduced €8/5; ⊙10am-5pm Mon-Sat, closed mid-Nov–mid-Dec; 🚌Via Appia Antica), which extends beneath the **Basilica di San Sebastiano**, and the **Catacombe di San Callisto** (☎06 513 01 51; www.catacombe.roma.it; Via Appia Antica 110 & 126; adult/reduced €8/5; ⊙9am-noon & 2-5pm, closed Wed mid-Jan–mid-Feb; 🚌Via Appia Antica), where the remains of thousands of Christians have been unearthed.

To get to Via Appia Antica, take bus 660 from Colli Albani metro station (line A) or bus 118 from Piramide (line B).

For information on the area, stop off at the **Appia Antica Regional Park Information Point** (☎06 513 53 16; www.parcoappiaantica.it; Via Appia Antica 58-60; ⊙9.30am-1.30pm & 2-5.30pm Mon-Sat, to 5pm winter, 9.30am-6.30pm Sun, to 5pm winter).

Big Mama BLUES
(Map p622; ☎06 581 25 51; www.bigmama.it; Vicolo di San Francesco a Ripa 18; ⊙9pm-1.30am, show 10.30pm Thu-Sat, closed Jun-Sep; 🚌Viale di Trastevere, 🚋Viale di Trastevere) To wallow in the Eternal City blues, there's only one place to go – this cramped Trastevere basement. There are weekly residences from well-known Italian musicians and regular blues, jazz, funk, soul and R&B concerts.

Goa NIGHTCLUB
(☎06 574 82 77; www.goaclub.com; Via Libetta 13; ⊙11.30pm-4.30am Thu-Sat ; Ⓜ️Garbatella) Goa is Rome's serious super-club, with international names, a fashion-forward crowd, podium dancers and heavies on the door. Thursday is always a big night with top European DJs.

Villaggio Globale NIGHTCLUB
(Map p622; www.ecn.org/villaggioglobale/joomla; Via Monte del Cocci 22; 🚌Via Marmorata) For a warehouse-party vibe, head to Rome's best-known *centro sociale* (an ex-squat turned cultural centre) in the city's graffiti-sprayed former-slaughterhouse. Live music and DJ sets serve a steady supply of dancehall, reggae, dubstep and drum 'n' bass.

ℹ Information

Dangers & Annoyances

Rome is not a dangerous city but petty theft can be a problem. Watch out for pickpockets around the big tourist sites, at Stazione Termini and on crowded public transport – the 64 Vatican bus is notorious.

Emergency

Main Police Station (Questura; ☎06 4 68 61; http://questure.poliziadistato.it; Via San Vitale 15; ⊙8.30am-11.30pm Mon-Fri)

Internet Access

Free wi-fi is now widely available in hostels, B&Bs and hotels. Some also provide laptops/computers for guests' use.

Internet cafes are fairly thin on the ground, with costs usually between €4 and €6 per hour.

Medical Services

For problems that don't require hospital treatment call the **Guardia Medica Turistica** (☎06 7730 6650; Via Emilio Morosini 30). For emergency treatment, go to the *pronto soccorso* (casualty) section of an *ospedale* (hospital). Pharmacists will serve prescriptions and can provide basic medical advice.

Ospedale Santo Spirito (☎06 6 83 51; Lungotevere in Sassia 1) Near the Vatican; multilingual staff.

Pharmacy (☎06 488 00 19; Piazza Cinquecento 51; ⊙8.30am-7.30pm daily & night service) There's also a pharmacy in Stazione Termini, next to platform 1, open 7.30am to 10pm.

Tourist Information

For phone enquiries, the Comune di Roma runs a multilingual **tourist information line** (☎060608; www.060608.it; ⊙9am-9pm).

There are tourist information points at **Fiumicino** (Terminal 3, International Arrivals; ⊙8am-7.30pm) and **Ciampino** (International Arrivals, baggage reclaim area; ⊙9am-6.30pm) airports, and at the following locations.

Castel Sant'Angelo Tourist Information (Map p630; Piazza Pia; ⏲9.30am-7pm)

Fori Imperiali Tourist Information (Map p626; Via dei Fori Imperiali; ⏲9.30am-7pm; 🚌Via dei Fori Imperiali)

Piazza delle Cinque Lune Tourist Information (Map p630; ⏲9.30am-7pm)

Stazione Termini Tourist Information (Map p636; ⏲8am-8.30pm) In the hall that runs parallel to platform 24.

Via Marco Minghetti Tourist Information (Map p630; ⏲9.30am-7pm)

Via Nazionale Tourist Information (Map p636; ⏲9.30am-7pm)

For information about the Vatican, contact the **Centro Servizi Pellegrini e Turisti** (☎06 6988 1662; St Peter's Square; ⏲8.30am-6pm Mon-Sat).

Websites

060608 (www.060608.it) Provides information on sites, shows, transport etc.

Coop Culture (www.coopculture.it) Information and ticketing for Rome's monuments, museums and galleries.

Lonely Planet (www.lonelyplanet.com/italy/rome)

Turismo Roma (www.turismoroma.it) Rome's official tourist website.

Vatican (www.vatican.va) The Vatican's official website.

Getting There & Away

Air

Rome's main international airport, **Leonardo da Vinci** (☎06 6 59 51; www.adr.it/fiumicino), better known as Fiumicino, is on the coast 30km west of the city. The smaller **Ciampino airport** (☎06 6 59 51; www.adr.it/ciampino), 15km southeast of the centre, is the hub for low-cost carrier **Ryanair** (☎899 552589; www.ryanair.com).

Boat

The nearest port to Rome is at Civitavecchia, about 80km away.

Ferry bookings can be made at the Termini-based **Agenzia 365** (☎06 474 09 23; www.agenzie365.it; ⏲8am-9pm), at travel agents or online at www.traghettionline.net. You can also buy directly at the port.

Half-hourly trains depart from Roma Termini to Civitavecchia (€5 to €14.50, 40 minutes to one hour). On arrival, it's about 700m to the port (to your right) as you exit the station.

The main ferry companies:

Grimaldi Lines (☎081 49 64 44; www.grimaldi-lines.com) To/from Trapani (Sicily), Porto Torres (Sardinia), Barcelona (Spain) and Tunis (Tunisia).

Tirrenia (☎89 21 23; www.tirrenia.it) To/from Arbatax, Cagliari and Olbia (all Sardinia).

Bus

Long-distance national and international buses use the Autostazione Tiburtina in front of Stazione Tiburtina. Take metro line B to Tiburtina.

You can get tickets from the offices next to the bus terminus or at travel agencies. Bus operators:

Interbus (☎091 34 25 25; www.interbus.it) To/from Sicily.

Marozzi (☎080 579 01 11; www.marozzivt.it) To/from Sorrento, Bari, Matera and Lecce.

SENA (☎0861 199 1900; www.sena.it) To/from Siena, Bologna and Milan.

Sulga (☎800 09 96 61; www.sulga.it) To/from Perugia, Assisi and Ravenna.

Car & Motorcycle

Rome is circled by the Grande Raccordo Anulare (GRA), to which all autostradas (motorways) connect, including the main A1 north–south artery (the Autostrada del Sole), and the A12, which runs to Civitavecchia and Fiumicino airport.

Car hire is available at the airport and Stazione Termini.

Near Termini, **Bici & Baci** (☎06 482 84 43; www.bicibaci.com; Via del Viminale 5; ⏲8am-7pm) is one of many agencies renting out scooters. Bank on from €19 per day.

Train

Almost all trains arrive at and depart from Stazione Termini. There are regular connections to other European countries, all major Italian cities, and many smaller towns.

Train information is available from the Customer Service area on the main concourse to the left of the ticket desks. Alternatively, check www.trenitalia.com, or phone the **Trenitalia Call Centre** (☎89 20 21; ⏲24hr).

Left luggage (1st 5hr €5, 6-12hr per hr €0.70, 13hr & over per hr €0.30; ⏲6am-11pm) is on the lower-ground floor under platform 24.

Rome's second train station is Stazione Tiburtina, a short ride away on metro line B. Private **Italo** (☎06 07 08; www.italotreno.it) trains run out of Tiburtina and Ostiense.

Getting Around

To/From the Airports

FIUMICINO

The easiest way to get to/from Fiumicino is by train but there are also bus services. The set taxi fare to the city centre is €48 (valid for up to four people with luggage).

Cotral Bus (www.cotralspa.it; one way €5, if bought on bus €7) Runs to/from Stazione Tiburtina via StazioneTermini. Eight daily departures including night services from the airport at 1.15am, 2.15am, 3.30am and 5am, and from Tiburtina at 12.30am, 1.15am, 2.30am and 3.45am. Journey time is one hour.

FR1 Train (€8) Connects the airport to Trastevere, Ostiense and Tiburtina stations, but not Termini. Departures from the airport every 15 minutes (hourly on Sunday and public holidays) between 5.58am and 11.28pm; from Ostiense between 5.18am and 10.48pm.

Leonardo Express Train (adult/child under 4 €14/free) Runs to/from platform 24 at StazioneTermini. Departures from the airport every 30 minutes between 6.38am and 11.38pm, from Termini between 5.52am and 10.52pm. Journey time is 30 minutes.

SIT Bus (☎06 591 68 26; www.sitbusshuttle.it; Fiumicino one way €6 or €5 online, €4/6 from/to Ciampino) From the airport regular departures between 8.30am and 12.30am to Via Marsala outside Stazione Termini; from Termini between 9.30am and 1.10am. Tickets are available on the bus. Journey time is one hour.

CIAMPINO

The best option is to take one of the regular bus services into the city centre. Alternatively, you can take a bus to Ciampino train station and then pick up a train to Stazione Termini. The set taxi fare to/from the city centre is €30.

Cotral Bus (www.cotralspa.it; one way €3.90) Runs 15 daily services to/from Via Giolitti near Stazione Termini. Also buses to/from Anagnina metro station (€1.20) and Ciampino train station (€1.20).

SIT Bus (www.sitbusshuttle.com; from airport €4, to airport €6) Regular departures from the airport to Via Marsala outside Stazione Termini between 7.45am and 11.15pm, and from Termini between 4.30am and 9.30pm. Get tickets on the bus. Journey time is 45 minutes.

Terravision Bus (www.terravision.eu; one way €4) Twice hourly to/from Via Marsala outside Stazione Termini. From the airport services are between 8.15am and 12.15am; from Via Marsala between 4.30am and 9.20pm. Buy tickets at Terracafé in front of the Via Marsala bus stop. Journey time is 40 minutes.

TICKET TIP

If you have to buy a metro ticket at Termini, get it from one of the newsstands on the concourse in front of the platforms. That way you'll avoid the queues in the metro station.

Public Transport

Rome's public transport system includes buses, trams, metro and a suburban train network.

TICKETS

Tickets are valid for all forms of public transport and come in various forms:

Single (BIT; €1.50) Valid for 100 minutes, during which time you can use as many buses or trams as you like but only go once on the metro.

Daily (BIG; €6) Unlimited travel until midnight of the day of purchase.

Three-day (BTI; €16.50) Unlimited travel for three days.

Weekly (CIS; €24) Unlimited travel for seven days.

Buy tickets at *tabacchi* (tobacconists), newsstands and from vending machines at main bus stops and metro stations. They must be purchased before you start your journey and validated in the machines on buses, at the entrance gates to the metro or at train stations. Ticketless riders risk an on-the-spot €50 fine.

BUS

Buses and trams are run by **ATAC** (☎06 57 003; www.atac.roma.it). The main bus station is in front of Stazione Termini on Piazza dei Cinquecento, where there's an **information booth** (Map p636; ⏰7.30am-8pm). Other important hubs are at Largo di Torre Argentina and Piazza Venezia.

Buses generally run from about 5.30am until midnight, with limited services throughout the night.

METRO

Rome's two main metro lines, A (orange) and B (blue), cross at Termini, the only point at which you can change from one line to the other. There is a third line 'B1', which serves the northern suburbs, but you're unlikely to need it.

Take line A for the Trevi Fountain (Barberini), Spanish Steps (Spagna) and Vatican (Ottaviano-San Pietro); line B for the Colosseum (Colosseo).

Trains run between 5.30am and 11.30pm (to 1.30am on Friday and Saturday).

Taxi

Official licensed taxis are white with the symbol of Rome on the doors. Always go with the metered fare, never an arranged price (the set fares to and from the airports are exceptions). Official rates are posted in taxis.

There are major taxi ranks at the airports, Stazione Termini, Largo di Torre Argentina, Piazza della Repubblica and the Colosseum. You can book a taxi by phoning the Comune di Roma's automated **taxi line** (☎06 06 09) or calling a taxi company direct:

La Capitale (☎06 49 94)
Radio Taxi (☎06 35 70)
Samarcanda (☎06 55 51)

AROUND ROME

Ostia Antica

Ostia Antica, an easy day trip from Rome, is one of Italy's most compelling and under-appreciated archaeological sites. Ancient Rome's main seaport, Ostia was founded in the 4th century BC at the mouth of the Tiber and developed into a major city with a population of around 100,000. Decline came in the 5th century when barbarian invasions and an outbreak of malaria led to its abandonment and slow burial in river silt, thanks to which it has survived so well.

The ruins, the **Scavi Archeologici di Ostia Antica** (☎06 563 52 830; www.ostiantica.info; adult/reduced/EU child €6.50/3.25/free, plus possible exhibition supplement; ⊙8.30am-6pm Tue-Sun Apr-Oct, to 5pm Mar, to 4pm Nov-Feb), are spread out and you'll need a few hours to do them justice. Highlights include the **Terme di Nettuno** (Baths of Neptune) and the steeply stacked **amphitheatre**. Behind the theatre, the **Piazzale delle Corporazioni** (Forum of the Corporations) housed Ostia's merchant guilds and is decorated with well-preserved mosaics.

To get to Ostia Antica take the Ostia Lido train (25 minutes, half-hourly) from Stazione Porta San Paolo next to Piramide metro station. The journey is covered by standard public-transport tickets.

Tivoli

POP 56,530

An ancient resort town and playground for the Renaissance rich, hilltop Tivoli is home to two Unesco-listed sites: Villa Adriana and Villa d'Este.

Information is available at the **tourist information point** (☎0774 31 35 36; Piazzale delle Nazione Unite; ⊙9.30am-5.30pm Tue-Sun) near the bus stop in the historic centre.

Five kilometres from Tivoli proper, **Villa Adriana** (☎06 3996 7900; www.villaadriana.beniculturali.it; adult/reduced €8/4, plus possible exhibition supplement, car park €3; ⊙9am-1hr before sunset; 📶) was Emperor Hadrian's sprawling 1st-century summer residence. One of the largest and most sumptuous villas in the Roman Empire, it was subsequently plundered for building materials, but enough remains to convey its magnificence.

Up in the hilltop centre, the Renaissance **Villa d'Este** (☎0774 331 20 70; www.villadestetivoli.info; Piazza Trento; adult/reduced €8.50/4, plus possible exhibition supplement; ⊙8.30am-1hr before sunset Tue-Sun) was originally a Benedictine convent before Lucrezia Borgia's son, Cardinal Ippolito d'Este, transformed it into a pleasure palace in 1550. More than the villa, it's the elaborate gardens and fountains that are the main attraction.

Tivoli is 30km east of Rome and accessible by Cotral bus (€1.30, 50 minutes, every 10 minutes) from Ponte Mammolo metro station. The fastest route by car is on the Rome–L'Aquila autostrada (A24).

To get to Villa Adriana from Tivoli town centre, take CAT bus 4 or 4X (€1, 10 minutes, half-hourly) from Largo Garibaldi.

NORTHERN ITALY

Italy's well-heeled north is a fascinating area of historical wealth and natural diversity. Bordered by the northern Alps and boasting some of the country's most spectacular coastline, it also encompasses Italy's largest lowland area, the fertile Po valley plain. Of the cities it's Venice that hogs the limelight, but in their own way Turin, Genoa and Bologna offer plenty to the open-minded traveller. Verona is justifiably considered one of Italy's most beautiful cities, while Padua and Ravenna harbour artistic treasures.

Genoa

POP 607,900

One of the Mediterranean's great ports, Genoa (Genova) is an absorbing city of aristocratic *palazzi,* dark, malodorous alleyways, Gothic architecture and industrial sprawl. Its shadowy, sometimes seedy, historic centre, teems with life, and its grand palaces house artistic treasures amassed during its heyday as a powerful maritime republic known as *La Superba* (Christopher Columbus was born here in 1451). The city's main draw is its aquarium, Europe's second largest.

👁 Sights

Most sights are in the *centro storico* and Porto Antico (Old Port) between the city's two main train stations: Stazione Brignole and Stazione Principe.

Piazza de Ferrari PIAZZA
Genoa's main piazza is a good place to start exploring the city. Grandiose and impressive, it's centred on an exuberant fountain and ringed by imposing *palazzi* – **Palazzo della Borsa**, Italy's former stock exchange; **Teatro Carlo Felice**, the city's neoclassical opera house; and the huge **Palazzo Ducale** (www.palazzoducale.genova.it; Piazza Giacomo Matteotti 9; admission depends on exhibition; ⌚exhibitions 9am-9pm), once the seat of the city's rulers but now used to host major art exhibitions.

Musei di Strada Nuova MUSEUM
(www.museidigenova.it; combined ticket adult/concession €8/6; ⌚9am-7pm Tue-Fri, 10am-7pm Sat & Sun) Genoa's main museums are in a series of *palazzi* on Via Garibaldi. The three most important, known collectively as the Musei di Strada Nuova, are housed in **Palazzo Bianco** (Via Garibaldi 11), **Palazzo Rosso** (Via Garibaldi 18) and **Palazzo Doria-Tursi** (Via Garibaldi 9). The first two feature works by Flemish, Dutch, Spanish and Italian masters, while the third displays the personal effects of Genoa's legendary violinist Niccolò Paganini.

Cattedrale di San Lorenzo CHURCH
(Piazza San Lorenzo; ⌚8am-noon & 3-7pm) Genoa's Gothic-Romanesque cathedral is notable for its striking black-and-white-striped facade. It was first consecrated in 1118 but the two bell towers and cupola were added in the 16th century.

Acquario di Genova AQUARIUM
(☎010 2 34 51; www.acquariodigenova.it; Ponte Spinola; adult/child €19/13; ⌚8.30am-10pm daily Jul & Aug, varied hours rest of year) The main attraction in Genoa's **Porto Antico** is Europe's second-largest aquarium. Designed by Italian architect Renzo Piano, it houses 5000 animals in six million litres of water.

Sleeping

TOP CHOICE **Hotel Cairoli** HOTEL €€
(☎010 246 14 54; www.hotelcairoligenova.com; Via Cairoli 14/4; r €60-160; ❄@📶) Colourful, friendly and central, the Cairoli offers individually styled rooms themed on modern artists and bright, welcoming public spaces, including a communal library, chill-out area, internet room and fully equipped gym.

Albergo Carola PENSION €
(☎010 839 13 40; www.pensionecarola.com; 3rd fl, Via Groppallo 4; d €60-90, without bathroom s €23-50, d €40-90; 📶) This is a classic family-run *pensione* with nine simple, well-kept rooms on the 3rd floor of a lovely old building near Stazione Brignole. Rates don't include breakfast.

Ostello Genova HOSTEL €
(☎010 242 24 57; www.ostellogenova.it; Via Costanzi 120; dm €17, s/d €28/50, without bathroom €24/44; ⌚reception 9am-3.30pm & midnight-7am Feb–mid-Dec; P📶) Genoa's hillside hostel is a functional, institutional affair with basic facilities and sweeping city views. HI cards, which are available at check-in, are mandatory. Catch bus 40 from Stazione Brignole or Via Napoli.

Eating

Ligurian specialities include pesto (a sauce of basil, garlic, pine nuts and Parmesan) served with *trofie* (pasta curls), and focaccia (flat bread made with olive oil).

Regina Margherita RISTORANTE €€
(☎010 595 57 53; Piazza della Vittoria 89-103; mains from €15, pizzas from €6) A bright, modern set-up with a two-floor interior and a small outdoor terrace. Though not in a particularly enticing location, it's popular and the food is excellent. Speciality of the house is the wood-fired Neapolitan pizza.

La Cremeria delle Erbe GELATERIA €
(Piazza delle Erbe 15-17; cones from €2; ⌚11am-1am Mon-Thu & Sun, to 2am Fri & Sat) On humming cafe-clad Piazza delle Erbe, this fab *gelateria* is perfectly placed for a quick ice-cream fix. The cream-based flavours are especially good, including a blissful *millefoglie*.

Drinking & Entertainment

Action centres on the *centro storico*, with a number of good bars clustered around Piazza delle Erbe.

Storico Lounge Café CAFE
(Piazza de Ferrari 34/36r; ⌚6am-3am) The daily *aperitivo* (5pm to 10.30pm) draws a mixed crowd to this popular cafe overlooking Piazza de Ferrari. Grab a square-side table and join the locals over a cool, well-mixed cocktail and snacks from the abundant buffet.

Mcafé CAFE
(Piazza Giacomo Matteotti 5; ⌚8am-9.30pm Tue-Fri, 10am-9.30pm Sat & Sun) This swish cafe in the atrium of Palazzo Ducale is good for a morning cappuccino, a quick lunchtime bite or an evening *aperitivo*. Upstairs, a restau

rant serves set lunch menus (€12) on weekdays and brunch (€16) at weekends.

Teatro Carlo Felice THEATRE
(☎010 538 12 24; www.carlofelice.it; Passo Eugenio Montale 4) Genoa's historic four-stage opera house stages a full program of opera, ballet and classical music. Tickets generally start at around €23 for ballet and €25 for opera.

Information

Tourist offices are at the **airport** (☎010 601 52 47; ⊙10am-1pm & 1.30-6.30pm); **De Ferrari** (☎010 860 61 22; www.visitgenoa.it; Largo Pertini 13; ⊙10am-1pm & 3-6pm Mon-Sat); **Via Garibaldi** (☎010 557 29 03; Via Garibaldi 12r; ⊙9am-6.30pm); and **Antico Porto** (010 557 42 00; Piazza Caricamento; ⊙9am-6.30pm summer, to 6pm winter).

Getting There & Around

Air

Genoa's **Cristoforo Colombo airport** (☎010 6 01 51; www.airport.genova.it) is 6km west of the city. To get to/from it, the **Volabus** (€6, 30 minutes, hourly 5.20am to 10.10pm to airport, 6am to 11.30pm from airport) shuttle connects with Stazione Brignole and Stazione Principe. Buy tickets on board or at tourist offices.

Boat

Ferries sail to/from Spain, Sicily, Sardinia, Corsica and Tunisia from the **Terminal Traghetti** (Ferry Terminal; www.porto.genova.it; Via Milano 51), west of the city centre. Ferry companies:

Grandi Navi Veloci (GNV; ☎010 209 45 91; www.gnv.it) To/from Sicily (Palermo; from €58, 20½ hours), Barcelona (€95, 19½ hours) and Tunis (€99, 23½ hours)

Moby Lines (☎199 30 30 40; www.mobylines.it) To/from Sardinia (Olbia; from €80.85, 11 hours).

Tirrenia (☎89 21 23; www.tirrenia.it) To/from Sardinia (Porto Torres; €54, 10 hours), Olbia (€54, 9¾ hours) and Arbatax (€55, 14½ hours).

Bus

Buses to international and regional destinations depart from Piazza della Vittoria, south of Stazione Brignole. Book tickets at **Geotravels** (Piazza della Vittoria 57).

Local buses are run by **AMT** (www.amt.genova.it). Tickets cost €1.50 and are valid for 100 minutes. Bus 20 runs from Via Luigi Cadorna near Stazione Brignole up to Piazza de Ferrari and Via Andrea Doria, stopping near Stazione Principe.

Train

There are direct trains to Turin (€18, two hours, up to 15 daily), Milan (€18.50, 1½ hours, hourly), Pisa (€18, two to three hours, up to 14 daily) and Rome (€44 to €58.50, 4½ to 5½ hours, nine daily).

Regional trains to La Spezia serve the Cinque Terre (€7.30, two hours, hourly).

It generally makes little difference whether you leave from Brignole or Principe.

Cinque Terre

Liguria's eastern Riviera boasts some of Italy's most dramatic coastline, the highlight of which is the Unesco-listed **Parco Nazionale delle Cinque Terre** (Cinque Terre National Park) just north of La Spezia. Running for 18km, this awesome stretch of plunging cliffs and vine-covered hills is named after its five tiny villages: Riomaggiore, Manarola, Corniglia, Vernazza and Monterosso.

It gets very crowded in summer, so try to come in spring or autumn. You can either visit on a day trip from Genoa or La Spezia, or stay overnight in one of the five villages.

Sights & Activities

The Cinque Terre villages are linked by the 9km **Sentiero Azzurro** (Blue Trail; admission with Cinque Terre Card), a magnificent, mildly challenging five-hour trail. To walk it you'll need to buy a **Cinque Terre Card** (adult/child 1 day €5/2.50, 2 days €8/4, family card 1/2 days €12.50/20), available at all park offices, or a **Cinque Terre Treno Card** (adult/child 1 day €10/6, 2 days €19), which also covers unlimited train travel between La Spezia and the five villages.

At the time of research the Sentiero Azzurro was closed for reconstruction work after it sustained severe damage during heavy rainfall in autumn 2011 and a rockfall in September 2012. Check www.parconazionale-5terre.it for the current situation.

The Sentiero Azzurro is just one of a network of footpaths and cycle trails that criss-cross the park; details are available from the park offices. If water sports are more your thing, you can hire snorkelling gear (€10 per day) and kayaks (double per hour €10) at the **Diving Center 5 Terre** (www.5terrediving.com; Via San Giacomo) in Riomaggiore. It also offers a snorkelling boat tour for €20.

Sleeping & Eating

Ostello 5 Terre HOSTEL €
(☎0187 92 00 39; www.hostel5terre.com; Via Riccobaldi 21, Manarola; dm €20-23, d €55-65, q

€88-100; @📶) In Manarola, this is a decent private-run hostel with bright, single-sex dorms and private rooms with en suite bathrooms. Extras include breakfast (€5) and dinner (€10), laundry facilities and a book exchange. Book at least a week ahead in summer.

Marina Piccola SEAFOOD €
(☎0187 76 20 65; www.hotelmarinapiccola.com; Via Lo Scalo 16, Manarola; mains €16, s/d €90/120, half-/full-board per person €90/105; 📶) Dine on fresh-off-the-boat seafood and house speciality *zuppa di datteri* (date soup) at this popular harbour-side restaurant in Manarola. If you want to stay, the adjoining hotel has small, comfortable rooms.

Takeaway FAST FOOD €
(Via Renato Birolli 99, Manarola; fried snacks €7-8) This unmarked takeaway is great for a quick bite on the hoof. For €7 you get a paper cone of piping-hot fried anchovies or calamari.

Information

The most convenient **information office** (☎0187 92 06 33; ⌚8am-7pm) is at Riomaggiore train station. There are also offices in the stations at Manarola, Corniglia, Vernazza, Monterosso and La Spezia (most open 8am to 7pm).

Online information is available at www.parconazionale5terre.it and www.cinqueterre.com.

Getting There & Away

Boat

Between July and September, **Golfo Paradiso** (☎0185 77 20 91; www.golfoparadiso.it) operates excursions from Genoa's Porto Antico to Vernazza and Monterosso (€18 one way, €33 return).

From late March to October, **Consorzio Marittimo Turistico 5 Terre** (☎0187 73 29 87; www.navigazionegolfodeipoeti.it) runs daily ferries between La Spezia and four of the villages (not Corniglia), costing €18 one way. Return trips are covered by a daily ticket (weekdays/weekends €25/27).

Train

From Genoa Principe (€7.30) and Brignole (€6.60) direct trains run to Riomaggiore (1½ to two hours, 18 daily), stopping at each of the Cinque Terre villages.

Between 4.30am and 11.10pm, one to three trains an hour crawl up the coast from La Spezia to Levanto (€3.30, 30 minutes), stopping at all of the villages en route.

Turin

POP 907,600

First-time visitors are often surprised by Turin (Torino). Expecting a bleak, industrial sprawl dominated by Fiat factories, they are instead confronted with a dynamic and attractive city full of regal *palazzi,* historic cafes, baroque piazzas and world-class museums. The city was the seat of the royal Savoy family for centuries, and, between 1861 and 1864, was Italy's first post-unification capital. More recently, it hosted the 2006 Winter Olympics and was European Capital of Design in 2008.

Sights

Mole Antonelliana MUSEUM
(Via Montebello 20) Towering 167m over the city skyline, Turin's signature landmark houses the enjoyable **Museo Nazionale del Cinema** (www.museonazionaledelcinema.org; adult/reduced €9/7, incl panoramic lift €12/9; ⌚9am-8pm Tue-Fri & Sun, to 11pm Sat) and its comprehensive collection of film memorabilia. Don't miss the glass **panoramic lift** (Mole Antonelliana Tower; adult/reduced €6/4, incl museum €12/9; ⌚10am-8pm Tue-Fri & Sun, to 11pm Sat), which whisks you up 85m to the Mole's roof terrace in 59 seconds.

Museo Egizio MUSEUM
(Egyptian Museum; www.museoegizio.org; Via Accademia delle Scienze 6; adult/reduced €8/6; ⌚8.30am-7.30pm Tue-Sun) Opened in 1824, this legendary museum houses the most important collection of Egyptian treasure outside of Cairo. Look out for a statue of Ramesses II that's considered one of the world's most important pieces of Egyptian art.

Piazza Castello PIAZZA
Turin's grandest square is dominated by the part-medieval, part-baroque **Palazzo Madama**, the original seat of the Italian parliament, and the mid-17th-century **Palazzo Reale** (Piazza Castello; adult/reduced €10/5; ⌚8.30am-7.30pm Tue-Sun).

A short walk away, **Piazza San Carlo**, known as Turin's drawing room, is famous for its cafes and twin baroque churches **San Carlo** and **Santa Cristina**.

Cattedrale di San Giovanni Battista CHURCH
(Piazza San Giovanni; ⌚8am-noon & 3-7pm) Turin's 15th-century cathedral houses the famous **Shroud of Turin** *(Sindone)*, supposedly the cloth used to wrap the crucified Christ. A

copy is on permanent display, while the real thing is kept in a vacuum-sealed box and rarely revealed.

Pinacoteca Giovanni e Marella Agnelli GALLERY
(www.pinacoteca-agnelli.it; Via Nizza 230; adult/reduced €4/2.50; ⌚10.30am-7pm Tue-Sun) This Renzo Piano–designed modern art gallery displays masterpieces by Canaletto, Renoir, Manet, Matisse and Picasso in the Lingotto, Fiat's former car factory.

Sleeping

Hotel Montevecchio HOTEL €€
(☎011 562 00 23; www.hotelmontevecchio.com; Via Montevecchio 13; s €40-90, d €55-140; @📶) In a quiet residential area 300m from Stazione Porta Nuova, this two-star offers a friendly welcome and bright, good-sized rooms. Useful extras include a laundry service and wi-fi (€1 for 30 minutes).

Ostello Torino HOSTEL €
(☎011 660 29 39; www.ostellotorino.it; Via Giordano Bruno 191; dm €17, d €50, without bathroom s/d €25/42; @📶) Turin's HI hostel is housed in the ex-Olympic village near Lingotto. It's some way from the centre (take tram 4 from Porta Nuova station), but has clean, airy, private rooms and dorms for between three and six people.

Eating & Drinking

Sample the city's superb gelato at outlets of **Grom** (www.grom.it; Piazza Pietro Paleocapa; ⌚11am-midnight Sun-Thu, to 1am Fri & Sat) at Piazza Paleocapa 1d, Via Accademia delle Scienze 4 and Via Garibaldi 11, or the critically acclaimed newcomer **+ Di Un Gelato** (www.piudiungelato.it; Galleria Subalpina 32, entrance on Piazza Carlo Alberto; small cone or tub €2; ⌚12.30pm-8pm Mon-Fri, to 10pm Sat & Sun).

Early evening is the time to make for one of the city's cafes and enjoy an *aperitivo* (about €8) accompanied by a sumptuous buffet (included in the price). Popular *aperitivo* precincts include Piazza Emanuele Filiberto and Piazza Vittorio Veneto: try **I Tre Galli** (www.3galli.com; Via Sant'Agostino 25; ⌚12.30pm-2.30pm & 6.30pm-midnight Mon-Wed, to 2am Thu-Sat) or **La Drogheria** (www.la-drogheria.it; Piazza Vittorio Veneto 18; ⌚10am-2am).

L'Hamburgheria di Eataly BURGERS €
(Piazza Solferino 16a; burgers from €5.50; ⌚11am-1pm Mon-Thu & Sun, to 1am Sat) Run by the Slow Food–backed Eataly chain, this cool burger bar takes fast food upmarket with a smart brick and steel interior and select menu. Choose your gourmet burger, made from locally sourced Piedmontese beef, and sit back with a bottle of artisanal beer as you wait.

Sfashion PIZZERIA €
(☎011 516 00 85; Via Cesare Battisti 13; pizzas from €5.80, mains from €8.50) Overlooking Piazza Carlo Alberto, Sfashion is the hottest pizza ticket in town. The Neapolitan-style pizzas fly like hot bullets from the ovens of this kooky cafe-cum pizzeria owned by local TV celebrity Piero Chiambretti.

Information

The city's efficient **tourist office** (☎010 53 51 81; www.turismotorino.org) has branches at **Porta Nuova station** (⌚9am-6pm), **Piazza Castello** (⌚9am-7pm) and **Via Giuseppe Verdi** (⌚9am 7pm) near the Mole Antonelliana.

Getting There & Around

In Caselle, 16km northwest of the city centre, **Turin airport** (TRN; www.turin-airport.com) serves flights to/from European and national destinations. **Sadem** (www.sadem.it) runs an airport shuttle (€5.50 or €6 on board, 40 minutes, half-hourly) between the airport and Porta Nuova train station.

Direct trains connect with Milan (€11 to €30, one to two hours, up to 30 daily), Florence (€65, three hours, seven daily), Genoa (€18, two hours, up to 15 daily) and Rome (€90, 4¼ hours, nine daily).

Milan

POP 1.32 MILLION

Few Italian cities polarise opinion like Milan, Italy's financial and fashion capital. Some people love the cosmopolitan, can-do atmosphere, the vibrant cultural scene and sophisticated shopping; others grumble that it's dirty, ugly and expensive. Certainly, it lacks the picture-postcard beauty of many Italian towns, but in among the urban hustle are some truly great sights – Leonardo da Vinci's *Last Supper*, the immense Duomo and La Scala opera house.

Founded by Celtic tribes in the 7th century BC, the city was conquered by the Romans in 222 BC and developed into a major trading centre. From the 13th century it flourished under the rule of two powerful families, the Visconti and Sforza.

Central Milan

Sights

Milan's main attractions are concentrated in the area between Piazza del Duomo and Castello Sforzesco. To get to the piazza from Stazione Centrale, take the yellow MM3 metro line.

TOP CHOICE Duomo CATHEDRAL

(www.duomomilano.it; Piazza del Duomo; roof stairs/lift €7/12; 7am-6.45pm, roof terraces 9am-6pm, baptistry 9.30am-5pm; MDuomo) With a capacity of 40,000 people, this is the world's largest Gothic cathedral and the third-largest church in Europe. Commissioned in 1386 to a florid French-Gothic design and finished nearly 600 years later, it's a fairy-tale ensemble of 3200 statues, 135 spires and 146 stained-glass windows. Climb to the roof for memorable city views with tickets bought at the nearby **Duomo Information Point** (02 720 23 375; www.duomomilano.it; Via dell'Arcivescovado 1; 9am-8.30pm).

TOP CHOICE Teatro alla Scala OPERA HOUSE

(La Scala; www.teatroallascala.org; Via Filodrammatici 2) The elegant **Galleria Vittorio Emanuele II** (Piazza del Duomo; MDuomo) shopping arcade leads from Piazza del Duomo through to Milan's legendary opera house. You can peek inside as part of a visit to the theatre's **Museo Teatrale alla Scala** (La Scala Museum; 02 433 53 521; Largo Ghiringhelli 1; adult/child €6/4; 9am-12.30pm & 1.30-5.30pm) providing there are no performances or rehearsals in progress.

The Last Supper MURAL

(Il Cenacolo Vinciano; 02 928 00 360; www.cenacolovinciano.net; Piazza Santa Maria delle Grazie 2; adult/reduced/EU child €6.50/3.25/free, plus booking fee €1.50; 8.15am-6.45pm Tue-Sun; MCadorna) Milan's most famous tourist attraction, Leonardo da Vinci's mural of *The Last Supper*, is in the Cenacolo Vinciano, the refectory of the **Chiesa d**

Central Milan

Top Sights

Castello Sforzesco	A1
Duomo	C3
Teatro alla Scala	C2

Sights

1 Galleria Vittorio Emanuele II	C3
2 Musei del Castello	A1
3 Museo Teatrale alla Scala	C2
4 Pinacoteca di Brera	C1

Sleeping

5 Hotel Nuovo	D3

Entertainment

6 Box Office	C3
7 Teatro alla Scala	C2

Santa Maria delle Grazie, west of the city centre. To see it you need to book ahead or take a city tour.

TOP CHOICE **Castello Sforzesco** CASTLE
(02 884 63 700; www.milanocastello.it; Piazza Castello; 7am-7pm summer, to 6pm winter; M Cairoli) Originally a Visconti fortress, this immense red-brick castle was later home to the Sforza dynasty that ruled Renaissance Milan. Today, it shelters the **Musei del Castello** (www.milanocastello.it; Piazza Castello 3; adult/EU child €3/free; 9am-5.30pm Tue-Sun), a series of museums dedicated to art, sculpture, archaeology and music.

Pinacoteca di Brera GALLERY
(02 722 63 264; www.brera.beniculturali.it; Via Brera 28; adult/concession/EU child €6/3/free; 8.30am-7.15pm Tue-Sun; M Lanza) This picture gallery houses Milan's most impressive collection of Old Masters, including works by Rembrandt, Goya, van Dyck, Titian, Tintoretto and Caravaggio.

Sleeping

Milan is a business city, which means hotels are expensive and it can be hard to find a room, particularly when trade fairs are on (which is often). Booking is essential.

Zebra Hostel HOSTEL €
(02 367 05 185; www.zebrahostel.it; Viale Regina Margherita 9; dm €24-29;) This vibrant hostel, winner of a 2012 Hostel World 'Hoscar', is cheerfully decorated with excellent communal facilities, a fully equipped kitchen, and clean mixed and single-sex dorms.

Hotel De Albertis HOTEL €€
(02 738 34 09; www.hoteldealbertis.it; Via De Albertis 7; s €50-100, d €50-160;) Out from the centre, this small hotel is a welcoming, family-run affair. There are few frills but rooms are clean and quiet, and breakfast is made with locally sourced organic produce. Take bus 92 from Stazione Centrale or 27 from the Duomo.

Hotel Nuovo HOTEL €€
(02 864 64 444; www.hotelnuovomilano.com; Piazza Beccaria 6; r €60-200;) A budget bastion, the Nuovo offers clean, basic rooms and a winning location not far from the Duomo. Rates don't include breakfast.

Eating & Drinking

Local specialities include *risotto alla milanese* (saffron-infused risotto cooked in bone-marrow stock) and *cotoletta alla milanese* (breaded veal cutlet).

There are hundreds of bars and restaurants in Milan but as a general rule, the area around the Duomo is full of smart business-oriented restaurants, Brera is a fashionable bar haunt and the lively Navigli canal district caters to all tastes.

Piccola Ischia PIZZERIA €
(02 204 76 13; Via Morgagni 7; pizzas €3-8; lunch & dinner Mon, Tue, Thu & Fri, dinner only Sat & Sun) This bustling pizzeria brings a touch of Naples to Milan. Everything from the wood-fired pizza and exuberant decor screams of the sunny south. It's hugely popular so book or expect to queue. Also does takeaway.

Premiata Pizzeria PIZZERIA
(02 894 00 648; Via Alzaia Naviglio Grande 2; pizzas from €8; dinner only) On the canal, in happening Navigli, this is an old-school pizzeria-cum-trattoria serving decent wood-fired pizzas and a full menu of pasta and meat staples such as *cotoletta alla milanese* (breaded veal cutlet).

Rinomata GELATERIA €
(Ripa di Porta Ticinese; ice creams from €2.50) If dining in Navigli, skip dessert and grab an ice cream from this historic hole-in-the-wall *gelateria*.

BQ Navigli BAR
(Birra Artigianale di Qualità; Via Alzaia Naviglio Grande 44; 6pm-2am) This canal-front bar serves a fine selection of local beers ranging from light lagers to dark bitters. Panini and *piadine* (pitta bread-style rolls) provide the solids.

★ Entertainment

The opera season at **Teatro alla Scala** (☎02 8 87 91; www.teatroallascala.org; Piazza della Scala; Ⓜ Duomo) runs from November to July, but you can see theatre, ballet and concerts year-round, with the exception of August. Tickets are available online or from the **box office** (Galleria del Sagrato; ⏲noon-6pm) beneath Piazza del Duomo. Bank on €12 to €187 for opera and €10 to €115 for ballet performances.

For jazz, **Blue Note** (☎02 690 16 888; www.bluenotemilano.com; Via Borsieri 37; tickets €20-35; ⏲Tue-Sun Sep-Jul; ⓂZara, Garibaldi) stages top international and Italian performers.

ℹ Information

There are tourist offices at **Piazza Castello** (☎02 774 04 343; Piazza Castello 1; ⏲9am-6pm Mon-Fri, 9am-1.30pm & 2-6pm Sat, to 5pm Sun) and **Stazione Centrale** (☎02 774 04 318; opposite platform 13, Stazione Centrale; ⏲9am-6pm Mon-Fri, 9am-1.30pm & 2-6pm Sat, to 5pm Sun).

Useful websites include www.visitamilano.it and www.hellomilano.it.

ℹ Getting There & Away

AIR Most international flights fly into **Malpensa airport** (☎02 23 23 23; www.milanomalpensa1.eu/it), about 50km northwest of Milan. Domestic and some European flights use **Linate airport** (☎flight information 02 23 23 23; www.milanolinate.eu/it), about 7km east of the city. Low-cost airlines use **Orio al Serio airport** (☎035 32 63 23; www.sacbo.it), near Bergamo.

TRAIN Regular daily trains depart Stazione Centrale for Venice (€36, 2½ hours), Bologna (€40, one hour), Florence (€50, 1¾ hours), Rome (€86, 3½ hours) and other Italian and European cities.

Most regional trains also stop at Stazione Nord in Piazzale Cadorna.

> **FOOTBALL IN MILAN**
>
> Milan is home to Italy's two most successful *calcio* (football) teams: the Berlusconi-owned AC Milan and Internazionale (Inter). During the season (September to May), the two clubs play on alternate Sundays at the **Stadio Giuseppe Meazza** (Via Piccolomini 5; ⓂLotto), aka the San Siro. Match tickets (from €18) are available from branches of Banca Intesa (AC Milan) and Banca Popolare di Milano (Inter). To get to the stadium on match days, take the free shuttle bus from the Lotto (MM1) metro station.

ℹ Getting Around

To/From the Airport

MALPENSA

Malpensa Shuttle (☎02 585 83 185; www.malpensashuttle.it; adult/child €10/5) Buses run to/from Piazza Luigi di Savoia next to Stazione Centrale every 20 minutes between 4.15am and 12.30pm. Buy tickets at Stazione Centrale or the airport. Journey time is 50 minutes.

Malpensa Bus Express (☎02 805 81 354; www.autostradale.it; adult/child €10/5) To/from Piazza Luigi di Savoia half-hourly between 4am and 12.40am.The trip takes 50 minutes.

Malpensa Express (☎800 50 00 05; www.malpensaexpress.it) Trains depart every 30 minutes to Terminal 1 from Stazione Centrale (adult €10, 45 minutes) and Stazione Nord (adult €11, 40 minutes).

LINATE

ATM (☎800 80 81 81; www.atm-mi.it) Local bus 73 runs from Piazza San Babila every 10 to 15 minutes between 5.30am and 12.30am. Use a regular bus ticket (€1.50).

Starfly (☎02 585 87 237; www.starfly.net; adult €5) Buses to/from Piazza Luigi di Savoia half-hourly between 5.30am and 10.45pm. Journey time is 30 minutes. Buy tickets at newsstands or on board.

ORIO AL SERIO

Autostradale (☎02 720 01 304; www.autostradale.it; adult €5) Half-hourly buses to/from Piazza Luigi di Savoia between 4am and 11.30pm. Journey time is one hour.

Orio Shuttle (☎035 33 07 06; www.orioshuttle.com; adult/child €8/3) Runs half-hourly to/from outside Stazione Centrale (one hour) between 3am and 12.15am.

Bus & Metro

Milan's excellent public transport system is run by ATM. Tickets (€1.50) are valid for one underground ride or up to 90 minutes' travel on city buses and trams. A day ticket costs €4.50. Buy them at metro stations, *tabacchi* and newsstands.

Verona

POP 263,700

Wander Verona's atmospheric streets and you'll understand why Shakespeare set *Romeo and Juliet* here – this is one of Italy's most beautiful and romantic cities.

Known as *piccola Roma* (little Rome) for its importance in ancient times, its heyday came in the 13th and 14th centuries when it was ruled by the Della Scala (aka Scaligeri) family, who built *palazzi* and bridges, sponsored Giotto, Dante and Petrarch, oppressed their subjects and feuded with everyone else.

Sights

Arena di Verona AMPHITHEATRE
(www.arena.it; Piazza Brà; adult/reduced/child €6/4.50/free; 1.30am-7.30pm Mon, 8.30am-7.30pm Tue-Sun, to 4.30pm on performance days) In the corner of Piazza Brà, the 1st-century pink marble Arena is the third-largest Roman amphitheatre in Italy. It can no longer seat 30,000 but it still draws sizeable crowds to its summer opera performances.

Casa di Giulietta MUSEUM
(Juliet's House; 045 803 43 03; Via Cappello 23; adult/reduced €6/4.50; 8.30am-7.30pm Tue-Sun, 1.30-7.30pm Mon) Juliet and her lover Romeo were entirely fictional characters, but that doesn't stop visitors flocking to this 14th-century *palazzo* to act out their romantic fantasies and add their lovelorn words to the graffiti on the arched gateway.

Piazzas PIAZZA
Set over the city's Roman forum, **Piazza delle Erbe** is lined with sumptuous *palazzi* and filled with touristy market stalls. Through the **Arco della Costa**, the quieter **Piazza dei Signori** is flanked by the early Renaissance **Loggia del Consiglio**, aka the Loggia Fra Gioconda, and the **Palazzo del Podestà**, the 14th-century residence of Cangrande I, the most celebrated of the Della Scala rulers. Nearby, the **Arche Scaligere** are the Della Scala family's elaborate Gothic tombs.

Sleeping

High-season prices apply during the opera season and it is absolutely essential to book for this period. If you arrive without a booking, the tourist office has a hotel reservation service.

Appartamenti L'Ospite APARTMENT €€
(045 803 69 94; www.lospite.com; Via XX Settembre 3; apt 1-2 people €35-105, apt 2-4 people €40-180;) Over the river from the *centro storico,* L'Ospite has six self-contained apartments for up to four people. Simple and bright with fully equipped kitchens, and wi-fi. Ideal for small groups.

Villa Francescatti HOSTEL €
(045 59 03 60; www.ostelloverona.it; Salita Fontana del Ferro 15; dm €18-20; 7am-11.30pm) This HI youth hostel is housed in a 16th-century villa on a garden estate a 20-minute walk from central Verona. Dinners cost €9 (reservations required); there are no cooking facilities. Rooms are off-limits 9am to 5pm, but you can use the common rooms. Catch bus 73 (weekdays) or bus 90 (Sunday and holidays) from the train station. There's a strict 11.30pm curfew.

Eating

Boiled meats are a Veronese speciality, as is crisp Soave white wine.

Al Pompiere TRATTORIA €€
(045 803 05 37; www.alpompiere.com; Vicolo Regina d'Ungheria 5; mains €16; Tue-Sat) This handsome trattoria is famed for its vast cheese selection and house-cured *salumi* (cured meat). Make a meal of the starters with wine by the glass, or fill up on robust meaty mains. Reservations recommended.

Café Noir CAFE €
(045 803 05 00; Via Pellicciai 12; mains €7; 7.30am-4pm Mon-Sat) This popular cafe is a favourite with local shoppers who stop by for fresh lunchtime salads, daily pastas and simple risottos. No dinner.

Entertainment

The opera season is held at the **Arena** (045 800 51 51; www.arena.it; Piazza Brà; tickets €23-200; opera season mid-Jun–early Sep). Tickets are available online or at various places across town, including the tourist office; see the website for details.

Shopping

Salumeria G Albertini DELI
(045 803 10 74; www.salumeriaalbertini.it; Corso Sant'Anastasia 39; 8am-2pm & 3-8pm Mon-Sat) Stock up on picnic provisions at this picture-perfect deli laden with fresh bread, prepared pastas, cured meats, local Asiago sheep's cheese and wine.

Information

Information, opera tickets and hotel reservations are available at the central **tourist office** (045 806 86 80; www.tourism.verona.it; Via degli Alpini 9; 9am-7pm Mon-Sat, 10am-4pm

Sun) just off Piazza Brà. There's a second **office** (☎045 861 91 63; Verona-Villafranca airport; ⏰10am-4pm Mon & Tue, to 5pm Wed-Sat) in the airport arrivals hall.

Getting There & Around

The **Aeroporto di Verona** (Valerio Catullo airport; ☎045 809 56 66; www.aeroportidelgarda.it), 12km outside the city, is accessible by bus from the train station (€6, 20 minutes, every 20 minutes between 5.15am and 11.10pm).

From stand A outside the train station, buses 90, 92, 93, 98 and 510 run to Piazza Brà. Tickets cost €1.30 or €1.50 if bought on board.

Direct trains connect with Milan (€11.30 to €19, one hour 20 minutes to two hours, three hourly), Venice (€7.40 to €19, 50 minutes to 2¼ hours, half-hourly) and Bologna (€8.90 to €19, 50 minutes to 1½ hours, 20 daily).

Padua

POP 214,200

The elegant city of Padua (Padova) sees only a fraction of the visitors who pile into nearby Venice. Yet, this handsome medieval city is a fascinating place, with a long and cultured past – Galileo taught astronomy at the city university, Shakespeare set parts of *The Taming of the Shrew* here, and Giotto painted one of Italy's greatest works of art in the city's Cappella degli Scrovegni.

Sights

TOP CHOICE **Cappella degli Scrovegni** CHURCH

(☎049 201 00 20; www.cappelladegliscrovegni.it; Piazza Eremitani 8; adult/reduced €13/8; ⏰9am-7pm Mon, to 10pm Tue-Sun Mar-Oct, 9am-7pm Nov-Dec, by reservation only) Giotto's frescos in the Scrovegni chapel (named after the banker Enrico Scrovegni who originally commissioned it) are one of the defining works of early Renaissance art. Painted between 1303 and 1305, the 38 colourful panels cover the chapel from floor to ceiling, depicting events from the life of Christ and the Virgin Mary.

Visits, which must be booked online or by phone at least 24 hours beforehand, last only 15 minutes and are preceded by a mandatory, 15-minute video introduction.

The picture galleries in the nearby **Musei Civici agli Eremitani** (☎049 8204 5450; Piazza Eremitani 8; adult/reduced €10/8; ⏰9am-7pm Tue-Sun) are home to an impressive collection of paintings and sculptures, including two Giottos.

FREE **Basilica di Sant'Antonio** CHURCH

(Il Santo; www.basilicadelsanto.org; Piazza del Santo; ⏰6.20am-7.45pm Apr-Oct, to 7pm Nov-Mar) Padua's domed basilica is a major pilgrimage site. Thousands come to pay homage to the city's patron saint, St Anthony (1193–1231), whose gaudy tomb is covered with requests and thanks for miracle cures and the recovery of lost objects.

Sleeping

Albergo Verdi HOTEL €

(☎049 836 41 63; www.albergoverdipadova.it; Via Dondi dall'Orologio 7; s €70, d €100; ❄@📶) A modern three-star hotel offering spruce, bright rooms and mod cons such as wi-fi (€2 per three hours) and satellite TV. The guest rooms are not the biggest but it's a friendly place and the central location is handy.

Ostello Città di Padova HOSTEL €

(☎049 875 22 19; www.ostellopadova.it; Via dei Aleardi 30; dm €19-23, d €76; ⏰reception 7.15-9.30am & 3.30-11.30pm; 📶) In the historic centre, Padua's rather drab youth hostel has functional dorms with bunk beds for four to six people. Take bus 8 or 12 or the tram from the train station to Via Cavalletto, then follow on foot.

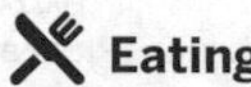

Eating

L'Anfora OSTERIA €€

(☎049 65 66 29; Via dei Soncin 13; meals €25-30; ⏰9am-11pm Mon-Sat) A laid-back *osteria* with bare wooden tables and racked wine bottles, L'Anfora's menu changes daily but the emphasis is on regional, local dishes. It can get pretty busy, particularly on Saturday nights.

Antica Osteria dal Capo OSTERIA €€

(☎049 66 31 05; www.osteriadalcapo.it; Via degli Obizzi 2; mains €10-16; ⏰Tue-Sat) A cosy *osteria* serving earthy Veneto cuisine. Seafood features strongly on the seasonal menu alongside hearty vegetable soups and old-school meat dishes.

Caffè Cavour PASTRIES & CAKES €

(☎049 875 12 24; Piazza Cavour 10; pastries €1.50-4, mains €10-14; ⏰7.30am-8pm Wed-Sun) A landmark in a prime position, this elegant cafe is a good place to people watch over a glass of wine (from €4.50) or indulge your sweet tooth. Pastas and main courses are also available.

Information

There are tourist offices at the **train station** (☎049 875 20 77; www.turismopadova.it; ⊙9.15am-7pm Mon-Sat, 9am-noon Sun), **Galleria Pedrocchi** (☎049 876 79 27; www.turismopadova.it; Vicolo Pedrochhi; ⊙9am-1.30pm & 3-7pm Mon-Sat) and **Piazza del Santo** (☎049 875 30 87; www.turismopadova.it; Piazza del Santo; ⊙10.30am-1.30pm & 3-6pm Tue-Sun).

Getting There & Away

Busitalia (☎049 820 68 44; www.fsbusitalia.it) operates buses from outside the train station for Venice's Marco Polo airport (€8 or €10 on board, one hour, hourly between 6.25am and 8.25pm), stopping off at Venice en route.

Regional trains serve Venice (€3.50, one hour, every 20 minutes), Verona (€5.95, 1½ hours, hourly) and Bologna (€9, 1½ hours, hourly).

Venice

POP 270,900

Arriving in Venice (Venezia) is like stepping into a surreal never-never land. Where most cities have car-choked roads and impenetrable one-way systems, Venice has canals, gondolas and *vaporetti* (small passenger ferries). It's a hauntingly beautiful place and its labyrinthine backstreets exude a unique, almost eerie, atmosphere.

But the beauty comes at a price, both for you (Venice is Italy's most expensive city) and for the city itself: Venice's frequently flooded alleyways simply weren't designed for up to 20 million visitors a year. Surprisingly, though, it's still possible to escape the crowds. Parts of the Cannaregio, Dorsoduro and Castello *sestieri* (districts) rarely see many tourists, and you can lose yourself for hours in the lanes between the Accademia and train station.

History

Venice's origins date to the 5th and 6th centuries when barbarian invasions forced the Veneto's inhabitants to seek refuge on the lagoon's islands. Initially the city was ruled by Byzantines from Ravenna, but in 726 the Venetians went it alone and elected their first *doge* (duke). Over successive centuries, the Venetian Republic grew into a great merchant power, dominating half the Mediterranean and the trade routes to the Levant – it was from Venice that Marco Polo set out for China in 1271. Decline began in the 16th century and in 1797 the city authorities opened the gates to Napoleon, who, in turn, handed the city over to the Austrians. In 1866, Venice was incorporated into the Kingdom of Italy.

Sights

Whet your sightseeing appetite by taking *vaporetto* No 1 along the **Grand Canal** lined with rococo, Gothic, Moorish and Renaissance palaces. Alight at Piazza San Marco, Venice's main square.

TOP CHOICE **Basilica di San Marco** CHURCH

(St Mark's Basilica; Map p656; ☎041 270 83 11; www.basilicasanmarco.it; Piazza San Marco; admission free; ⊙9.45am-4.45pm Mon-Sat, 2-4pm Sun & holidays, baggage storage 9.30am-5.30pm; San Marco) With its spangled spires, Byzantine domes, luminous mosaics and lavish marble work, Venice's signature church is an unforgettable sight. It was first built to house the corpse of St Mark, but the original chapel was destroyed by fire in 932 and a new basilica was built over it in 1094. For the next 500 years it was a work in progress as successive doges added mosaics and embellishments looted from the East.

Inside, behind the main altar, check out the **Pala d'Oro**, a stunning gold altarpiece decorated with priceless jewels.

Outside in the piazza, the basilica's 99m freestanding **campanile** (Bell Tower; Map p656; www.basilicasanmarco.it; Piazza San Marco; admission €8; ⊙9am-9pm Jul-Sep, to 7pm Apr-Jun & Oct, 9.30am-3.45pm Nov-Mar; San Marco) dates from the 10th century, although it collapsed on 14 July 1902 and had to be rebuilt.

Piazza San Marco PIAZZA

(Map p656) Piazza San Marco beautifully encapsulates the splendour of Venice's past and its tourist-fuelled present. Flanked by the arcaded **Procuratie Vecchie** and

NAVIGATING VENICE

Venice is not an easy place to navigate and even with a map you're bound to get lost. The main area of interst lies between Santa Lucia train station (signposted as the *ferrovia*) and Piazza San Marco (St Mark's Square). The path between the two – Venice's main drag – is a good 40- to 50-minute walk.

It also helps to know that the city is divided into six *sestieri* (districts): Cannaregio, Castello, San Marco, Dorsoduro, San Polo and Santa Croce.

Greater Venice

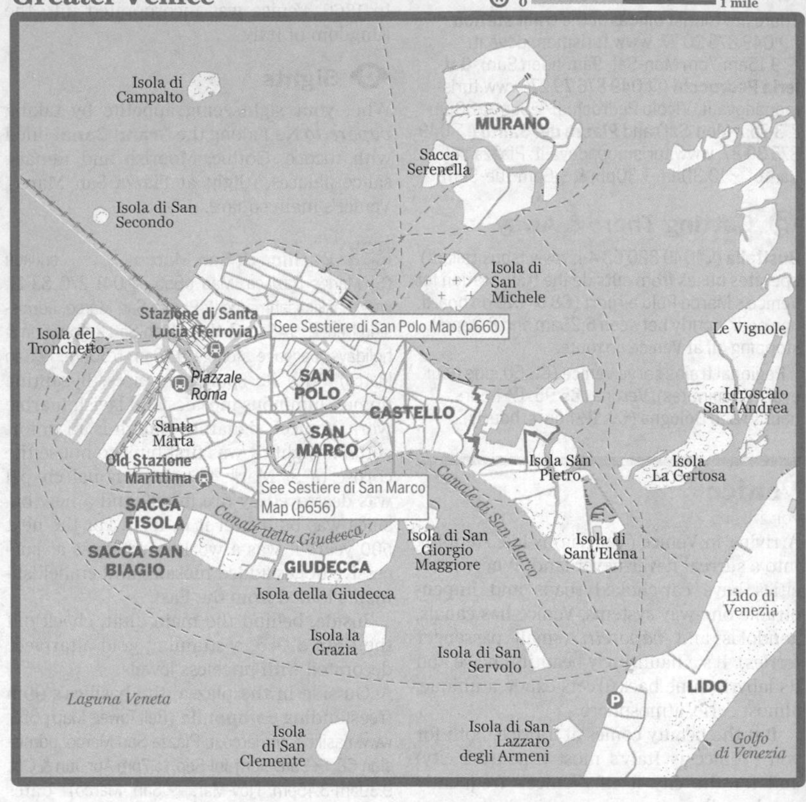

Procuratie Nuove, it's filled for much of the day with tourists, pigeons and policemen. While you're taking it all in, you might see the bronze *mori* (Moors) strike the bell of the 15th-century **Torre dell'Orologio** (Clock Tower; Map p656; ☎041 4273 0892; www.museicivicivenezianі.it; Piazza San Marco; adult/reduced with Museum Pass €12/7; ⊙tours in English 10am & 11am Mon-Wed, 2pm & 3pm Thu-Sun, in Italian noon & 4pm daily, in French 2pm & 3pm Mon-Wed, 10am & 11am Thu-Sun; San Marco).

TOP CHOICE Palazzo Ducale MUSEUM

(Ducal Palace; Map p656; ☎848 08 20 00; www.palazzoducale.visitmuve.it; Piazzetta San Marco 52; adult/reduced/child incl Museo Correr €16/8/free or with Museum Pass; ⊙8.30am-7pm Apr-Oct, to 5.30pm Nov-Mar; San Zaccaria) The official residence of the *doges* from the 9th century and the seat of the Republic's government, Palazzo Ducale also housed Venice's prisons. The *doges'* apartments are suitably lavish, but it's the vast **Sala del Maggiore Consiglio** that really takes the breath away. Measuring 53m by 25m, this echoing hall houses Tintoretto's *Paradiso* (Paradise), one of the world's largest oil paintings.

TOP CHOICE Ponte dei Sospiri BRIDGE

(Map p656) One of Venice's most celebrated sights, the Bridge of Sighs connects Palazzo Ducale to the 16th-century *Priggione Nove* (New Prisons). It's named after the sighs that condemned prisoners – including Giacomo Casanova – emitted en route to the cells.

TOP CHOICE Gallerie dell'Accademia GALLERY

(Map p656; ☎041 520 03 45; www.gallerieaccademia.org; Campo della Carità 1050; adult/reduced/EU child & senior €14/11/free; ⊙8.15am-2pm Mon, to 7.15pm Tue-Sun, last admission 45min before closing; P; Accademia) This grand old gallery traces the development of Venetian art from the 14th to the 18th century with works by Bellini, Titian, Carpaccio, Tintoretto, Giorgione and Veronese.

Collezione Peggy Guggenheim GALLERY
(Map p656; ☎041 240 54 11; www.guggenheim-venice.it; Dorsoduro 701, Palazzo Venier dei Leoni; adult/reduced/child €12/7/free; ⊙10am-6pm Wed-Mon) The spellbinding modern art collection of American heiress Peggy Guggenheim includes canvases by Picasso, Pollock, Braque, Kandinsky, Klee and many more.

Churches CHURCH
As in much of Italy, Venice's churches harbour innumerable treasures; unusually, though, you have to pay to get into many of them. The **Chorus Pass** (☎041 275 04 62; www.chorus-venezia.org; adult/reduced/child €10/7/free) gives admission to 16 of the city's most important churches, which otherwise charge adult/reduced €3/1.50.

Scene of the annual Festa del Redentore, the **Chiesa del Santissimo Redentore** (Church of the Redeemer; Campo del SS Redentore 194; adult/reduced/child €3/1.50/free or with Chorus Pass; ⊙10am-5pm Mon-Sat; Redentore) was built by Palladio on the island of Giudecca to commemorate the end of the Great Plague in 1577.

At the entrance to the Grand Canal, the 17th-century **Chiesa di Santa Maria della Salute** (La Salute; Map p656; ☎041 241 10 18; www.seminariovenezia.it; Campo della Salute 1b; admission free, sacristy adult/reduced €3/1.50; ⊙9am-noon & 3-5.30pm; Salute) contains works by Tintoretto and Titian. Arguably the greatest of Venetian artists, Titian is buried in the **Basilica di Santa Maria Gloriosa dei Frari** (www.basilicadeifrari.it; Campo dei Frari, San Polo; adult/reduced/child €3/1.50/free or with Chorus Pass; ⊙9am-6pm Mon-Sat, 1-6pm Sun), near his celebrated *Assunta* (Assumption; 1518).

The Lido ISLAND
(vehicle ferry from Tronchetto, boat 1, 2, 5.1, 5.2, 6, 8, 10, 14, N) Unless you're on the Lido for the Venice Film Festival, the main reason to visit is to head to the beach. One of the best is **Alberoni**, in the south of the island.

The Lido is accessible by various *vaporetti*, including Nos 1 and 2 from San Zaccaria.

Islands ISLAND
The island of **Murano** is the home of Venetian glass. Tour a factory for a behind-the-scenes look at production or visit the **Museo del Vetro** (Glass Museum; ☎041 73 95 86; www.museovetro.visitmuve.it; Fondamenta Giustinian 8; adult/reduced €8/5.50; ⊙10am-6pm Apr-Oct, to 5pm Nov-Mar; Museo) near the Museo *vaporetto* stop. **Burano**, with its cheery pastel-coloured houses, is renowned for its lace. **Torcello**, the republic's original island settlement, is home to Venice's oldest basilica, the Byzantine **Basilica di Santa Maria Assunta** (Piazza Torcello; adult/reduced €5/4, incl museum €8/6; ⊙10.30am-6pm Mar-Oct, 10am-5pm Nov-Feb; Torcello).

To get to Murano take *vaporetto* 4.1, or 4.2 from San Zaccaria or Fondamente Nove. For Burano take No 12 from Fondamente Nove. Torcello is linked to Burano by *vaporetto* 9.

DISCOUNT CARDS

Venice Card (☎041 24 24; www.venicecard.com; adult/junior €39.90/29.90; ⊙call centre 8am-7.30pm) Valid for seven days, gives free entry to Palazzo Ducale, 10 civic museums, the 16 churches covered by the Chorus Pass, as well as discounts on exhibitions and concerts. Buy it at tourist offices and HelloVenezia booths.

Venice Card San Marco (☎041 24 24; www.venicecard.com; €24.90) Provides free admission to Palazzo Ducale, three civic museums and three Chorus churches, plus discounts on exhibitions and concerts. It's available at tourist offices and HelloVenezia booths.

Rolling Venice Card (☎041 24 24; www.hellovenezia.com; 14-29yr €4) Offers discounts on food, accommodation, shopping, transport and museums. Get it at tourist offices and HelloVenezia booths.

Museum Pass (Musei Civici Pass; ☎041 240 52 11; www.visitmuve.it; adult/reduced €20/14) Valid for single entry to 10 civic museums, or just the four museums around Piazza San Marco (adult/reduced€16/8). Buy it at participating museums or online at www.visitmuve.it or www.veniceconnected.com.

Sestiere di San Marco

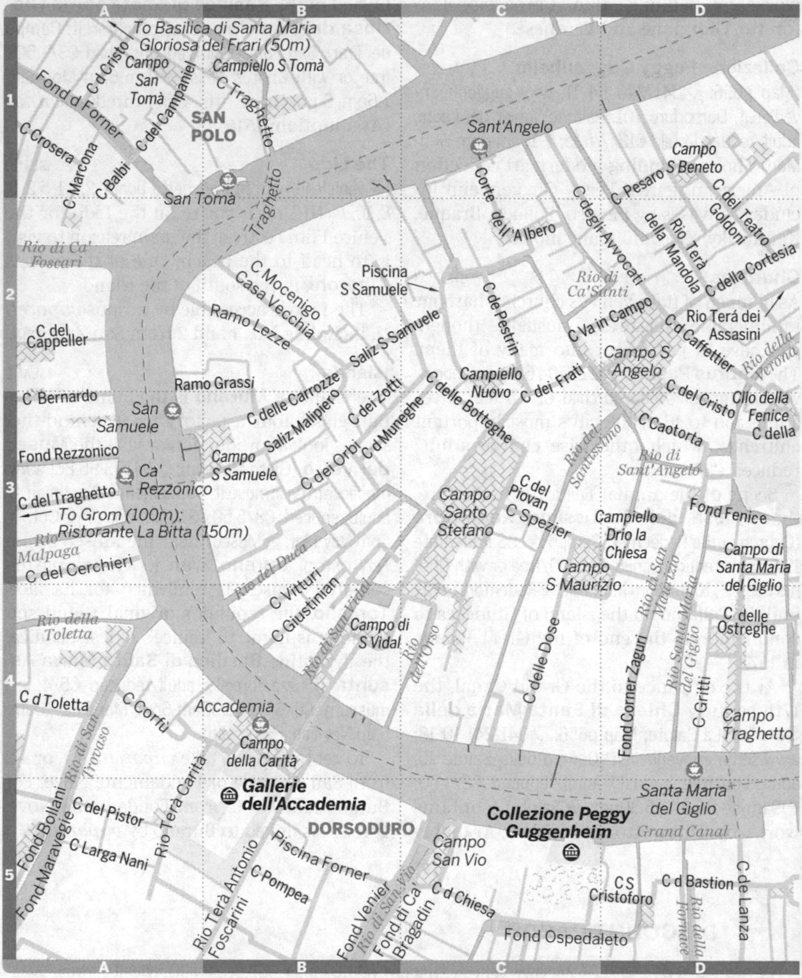

A B C D
1 2 3 4 5
To Basilica di Santa Maria Gloriosa dei Frari (50m)
Campo San Tomà
Campiello S Tomà
C d Cristo
Fond d Forner
C del Campaniel
C Traghetto
SAN POLO
C Crosera
C Marcona
C Balbi
San Tomà
Traghetto
Sant'Angelo
Corte dell'Albero
C degli Avvocati
C Pesaro
Campo S Beneto
C del Teatro Goldoni
Rio Terà della Mandola
C della Cortesia
Rio di Ca' Foscari
C Mocenigo Casa Vecchia
Piscina S Samuele
C de Pestrin
Rio di Ca'Santi
Rio Terá dei Assasini
C del Cappeller
Ramo Lezze
Saliz S Samuele
C Va in Campo
C d Caffettier
Rio della Verona
Campo S Angelo
Ramo Grassi
C Bernardo
San Samuele
C delle Carrozze
Saliz Malipiero
C dei Zotti
C d Muneghe
Campiello Nuovo
C delle Botteghe
C dei Frati
C del Cristo
Cllo della Fenice
C della
C Caotorta
Fond Rezzonico
Campo S Samuele
C dei Orbi
Rio del Santissimo
Rio di Sant'Angelo
Ca' Rezzonico
C del Traghetto
To Grom (100m); Ristorante La Bitta (150m)
Campo Santo Stefano
C del Piovan
C Spezier
Campiello Drio la Chiesa
Fond Fenice
Rio Malpaga
C del Cerchieri
Rio del Duca
Campo S Maurizio
Campo di Santa Maria del Giglio
C Vitturi
C Giustinian
Rio di San Vidal
Campo di S Vidal
Rio dell'Orso
C delle Dose
Rio di San Maurizio
Rio Santa Maria del Giglio
C delle Ostreghe
Rio della Toletta
C d Toletta
C Corfu
Accademia
Campo della Carità
Fond Corner Zaguri
C Gritti
Campo Traghetto
Rio di San Trovaso
Gallerie dell'Accademia
Santa Maria del Giglio
C del Pistor
Rio Terà Carità
Collezione Peggy Guggenheim
DORSODURO
Grand Canal
Fond Bollani
Fond Maravegie
C Larga Nani
Rio Terà Antonio Foscarini
Piscina Forner
C Pompea
Campo San Vio
Fond Venier
Rio di San Vio
Fond di Ca' Bragadin
C d Chiesa
C S Cristoforo
C d Bastion
Rio della Fornace
C de Lanza
Fond Ospedaleto

Activities

Official **gondola** rates start at €80 or €100 from 7pm to 8am (prices per gondola; maximum six people). Additional time is charged in 20-minute increments (day/night €40/50).

Tours

Between April and October, Venice's tourist offices offer a range of tours, including a 35-minute gondola ride (€28 per person); a 40-minute gondola serenade (€40); a 1½-hour city walking tour (€21); and a four-hour trip to Murano, Burano and Torcello (€20).

Festivals & Events

Carnevale CARNIVAL
(www.carnevale.venezia.it) Masked ribaldry takes over town in the two-week run-up to Ash Wednesday.

Palio delle Quattro Antiche Repubbliche Marinare BOAT RACE
(Regatta of the Four Ancient Maritime Republics) Venice, Amalfi, Genoa and Pisa take turns to

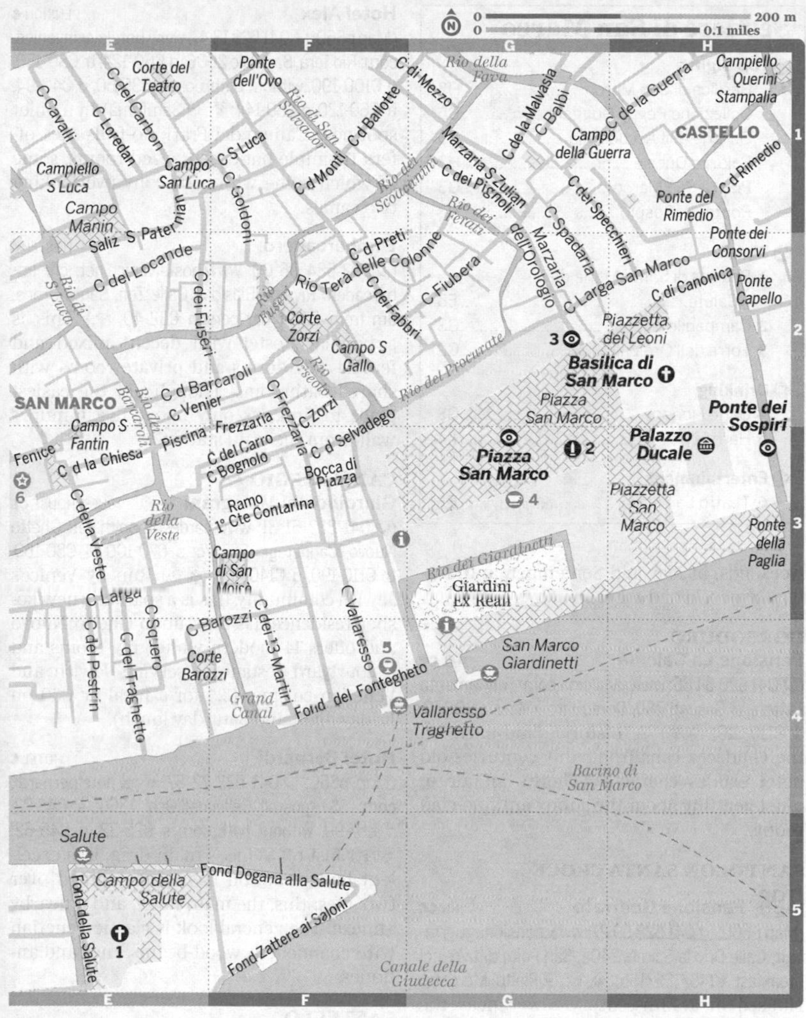

host this historic regatta in early June. It will be in Venice in 2015.

Venice Biennale ART
(www.labiennale.org) An important exhibition of international visual arts. It's held every odd-numbered year from June to November.

Festa del Redentore RELIGIOUS
(Feast of the Redeemer; www.turismovenezia.it) Held on the third weekend in July; celebrations climax with a spectacular fireworks display.

Venice International Film Festival FILM
(Mostra del Cinema di Venezia; www.labiennale.org/en/cinema) Italy's top film fest comes to town in late August or early September at the Lido's Palazzo del Cinema.

Regata Storica BOAT RACE
(www.regatastoricavenezia.it) Costumed parades precede gondola races on the Grand Canal; held on the first Sunday in September.

Sleeping

Venice is Italy's most expensive city. It's always advisable to book ahead, especially at

Sestiere di San Marco

Top Sights

Basilica di San Marco	H2
Collezione Peggy Guggenheim	C5
Gallerie dell'Accademia	B5
Palazzo Ducale	H3
Piazza San Marco	G3
Ponte dei Sospiri	H3

Sights

1 Basilica di Santa Maria della Salute	E5
2 Campanile	G3
3 Torre dell'Orologio	G2

Drinking

4 Caffè Florian	G3
5 Harry's Bar	F4

Entertainment

6 Teatro La Fenice	E3

weekends, in May and September, and during Carnevale and other holidays.

DORSODURO

Pensione La Calcina HOTEL €€

(041 520 64 66; www.lacalcina.com; Fondamenta Zattere ai Gesuati 780, Dorsoduro 780; s €90-170, d €110-310;) A historic landmark on the Giudecca canalfront, this centuries-old hotel exudes character. There's an air of quiet gentility about the sunny antique-clad rooms.

SAN POLO & SANTA CROCE

TOP CHOICE **Pensione Guerrato** INN €€

(Map p660; 041 528 59 27; www.pensioneguerrato.it; Calle Drio la Scimia 240a, San Polo; d/tr/q incl breakfast €145/165/185; ; Rialto Mercato) Housed in a 13th-century tower near the Rialto market, this excellent *pensione* has comfortable, good-sized rooms on several floors (no lift) and friendly, helpful owners. Check the website for low-season offers.

Ca' Angeli BOUTIQUE HOTEL €€

(Map p660; 041 523 24 80; www.caangeli.it; Calle del Traghetto de la Madonnetta 1434, San Polo; d incl breakfast €70-215; ; San Silvestro) An elegant choice overlooking the Grand Canal, Ca' Angeli offers tastefully decorated rooms and suites with canal views. Staff are friendly, the organic breakfast is excellent, and wi-fi is free if you book through the B&B's website.

Hotel Alex PENSION €

(Map p660; 041 523 13 41; www.hotelalexinvenice.com; Rio Terà, San Polo 2606; d €60-124, tr €80-150, q €100-190, without bathroom s €35-60, d €40-94, tr €60-120, q €80-144; ; San Tomà) In a quiet spot near Campo dei Frari, no-frills Alex offers 11 simple but decent-sized rooms, some of which come with a balcony overlooking two canals.

L'Imbarcadero HOSTEL €

(392 584 06 00; www.hostelvenice.net; cnr Imbarcadero Riva de Biasio & Calle Zen, Santa Croce; dm from €27, r per person €32-40;) This is a popular hostel with decent mixed and female-only dorms and private rooms with shared bathrooms. Though not the easiest place to find, it's only about five minutes' walk from the train station,

CANNAREGIO

Giardino dei Melograni GUESTHOUSE €€

(041 822 61 31; www.pardesrimonim.net; Ghetto Nuovo, Cannaregio 2873/c; s €70-100, d €80-160, tr €110-190, q €140-220;) Run by Venice's Jewish community, this is a sparkling new kosher residence. It's on Campo Ghetto Nuovo and offers 14 modern white-grey rooms and a courtyard restaurant serving Jewish and Venetian cuisine (€25 for a meal or €30 on Friday night and Saturday lunch).

Hotel Bernardi HOTEL €

(Map p660; 041 522 72 57; www.hotelbernardi.com; SS Apostoli Calle dell'Oca 4366; s €48-72, d €57-90, without bathroom s €25-32, d €45-62;) Just off Venice's main drag, this excellent budget option has rooms spread over two sites: this, the main hotel, and a nearby annexe. The general look is classic Venetian with chandeliers, wood-beams, rugs and antiques.

CASTELLO

Foresteria Valdese HOSTEL €

(Palazzo Cavagnis; 041 528 67 97; www.foresteriavenezia.it; Castello 5170; dm €30-35, d €70-140, q €95-190; Ospedale, San Zaccaria) One of the cheapest sleeps in the historic centre, this hostel is run by the Waldensian church and housed in a rambling old palace with 18th-century frescos, canal views and a range of rooms.

Eating

Venetian specialities include *risi e bisi* (pea soup thickened with rice) and *sarde in saor* (fried sardines marinated in vinegar and onions).

DORSODURO

Ristorante La Bitta RISTORANTE €€

(041 523 05 31; Calle Lunga San Barnaba 2753a; meals €30-40; dinner Mon-Sat; Ca' Rezzonico) With its woody bottle-lined interior and attractive internal courtyard, this is a lovely place to enjoy rustic dishes from the chalked-up daily menu. Cash only.

Pizza Al Volo PIZZERIA €

(041 522 54 30; Campo Santa Margherita 2944; pizza slices from €2, small pizzas €4.50-7; noon-11.30pm; Ca' Rezzonico) A hole-in-the-wall takeaway great for a quick lunch or late-night filler. Grab a slice – they're cheap and tasty – and munch away on the vibrant square outside.

Grom GELATERIA €

(041 099 17 51; www.grom.it; Campo San Barnaba 2461; gelati €2.50-4; 11am-midnight Sun-Thu, to 1am Fri & Sat; Ca' Rezzonico) A Grom ice cream is a perfect pick-me-up. Flavours are seasonal and made from top international ingredients such as lemons from Sicily and chocolate from South America. There's a second **Grom** (Map p660, Cannaregio 3844, Ca' d'Oro) on the main strip near Ca' d'Oro.

SAN POLO & SANTA CROCE

TOP CHOICE **All'Arco** VENETIAN €

(Map p660; 041 520 56 66; Calle dell'Ochialer 436; cicheti €1.50-4; 8am-3.30pm Mon-Sat, plus 6-9pm Apr-Jun, Sep & Oct, closed Jul & Aug; Rialto-Mercato) Popular with locals from the nearby Rialto market, this authentic neighbourhood *osteria* serves excellent *cicheti* (typical Venetian bar snacks) and a range of good-quality wines by the glass.

Birraria La Corte PIZZERIA, RISTORANTE €€

(Map p660; 041 275 05 70; www.birrarialacorte.it; Campo San Polo 2168; pizzas €8-13, mains €15) Head to this animated eatery for perfectly cooked pizzas, a buzzing atmosphere and square-side seating on Campo San Polo. If you don't fancy pizza there's a full menu of pastas and excellent Italian beers.

Osteria La Zucca MODERN ITALIAN €€

(Map p660; 041 524 15 70; www.lazucca.it; Calle del Tintor 1762, Santa Croce; meals €30-45; 12.30-2.30pm & 7-10.30pm Mon-Sat; ; San Stae) A snug wood-panelled restaurant that serves a range of innovative Mediterranean dishes emphasising fresh, seasonal vegetarian dishes. You can also order classic meat dishes such as duck with green apple.

Ae Oche PIZZERIA €

(Map p660; 041 524 11 61; www.aeoche.com; Calle del Tentor 1552a; pizzas from €5.50, aperitifs from €2.50; noon-2.30pm & 7-10.30pm Mon-Fri, to 11.30pm Sat & Sun; San Stae) Students and budget-minded foodies converge on this bubbly pizzeria for a choice of 70-plus wood-fired pizzas and well-priced ale. Keep things hot with the lip-buzzing *mangiafuoco* (fire-eater) made with spicy salami, Calabrese peppers and Tabasco sauce.

CANNAREGIO

Trattoria da Bepi VENETIAN €€

(Map p660; 041 528 50 31; Cannaregio 4550; mains €10-20; Fri-Wed) One of the better eateries near the touristy main drag, this is a classic old-school trattoria with a few outside tables and a cheerfully cluttered interior. The food is traditional Venetian with an emphasis on seafood, including an excellent *sarde in saor*.

Da Marisa TRATTORIA €€

(041 72 02 11; Fondamenta di San Giobbe 652b; lunch set price €15, dinner €35-40; lunch daily, dinner Tue & Thu-Sat) Search out this modest family-run trattoria for a taste of authentic Venetian home cooking and sunset views over the lagoon. The fixed daily menu is mostly meat but sometimes seafood. Cash only.

Drinking

Cantina Do Spade PUB

(Map p660; 041 521 05 83; www.cantinadospade.it; Calle delle Do Spade 860, San Polo; 10am-3pm & 6-10pm; Rialto) A warm, woody neighbourhood *osteria* great for a relaxed glass of local wine or a double-malt beer. Keep hunger at bay by snacking on *cicheti* (from €1) such as *sarde fritte* (fried sardines) and anchovies.

Al Mercà WINE BAR

(Map p660; 393 992 47 81; Campo Cesare Battisti 213, San Polo; 9.30am-2.30pm & 6-9pm Mon-Sat; Rialto) This hole-in-the-wall bar draws daily crowds for its excellent snacks and keenly priced drinks, including top-notch wines by the glass (from €2).

TOILETS

You'll find public toilets at the train station, Piazzale Roma, Accademia bridge, Campo San Bartolomeo, and by the Giardini ex Reali near Piazza San Marco. To use them you'll need €1.50 in change.

Sestiere di San Polo

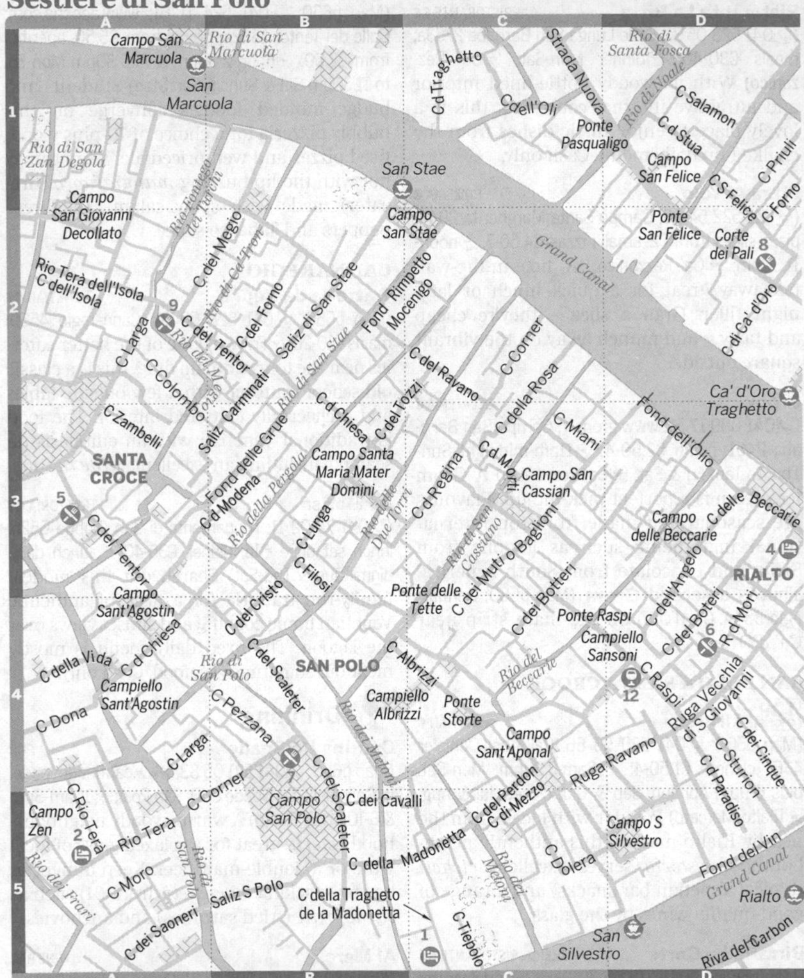

Muro Venezia BAR

(Map p660; www.murovinoecucina.it; Campo Cesare Battisti, San Polo 222; ⏲9am-3pm & 4pm-2am Mon-Sat, 4pm-2am Sun) The centre of a happening nightlife scene in the Rialto market squares, Muro is the watering hole of choice for many young locals. Come at Saturday lunch for a plate of fried fish and glass of Chardonnay for €8.

Il Caffè Rosso CAFE, BAR

(☎041 528 79 98; Campo Santa Margherita 2963; ⏲7am-1am Mon-Sat; ⛴Ca' Rezzonico) The most popular of the bars and cafes on vibrant Campo Santa Margherita. Its sunny piazza seating fills quickly with students drawn by the laid-back buzz and 6pm Spritz cocktails.

Harry's Bar BAR

(Map p656; ☎041 528 57 77; Calle Vallaresso 1323; cocktails €12-22; ⏲10.30am-11pm; ⛴San Marco) Follow in the footsteps of Ernest Hemingway, Charlie Chaplin, Orson Welles and Woody Allen, and try a Bellini (white peach pulp and *prosecco*) at the bar that invented them.

Caffè Florian CAFE

(Map p656; ☎041 520 56 41; www.caffeflorian.com; Piazza San Marco 56/59; drinks €6.50-16; ⏲10am-

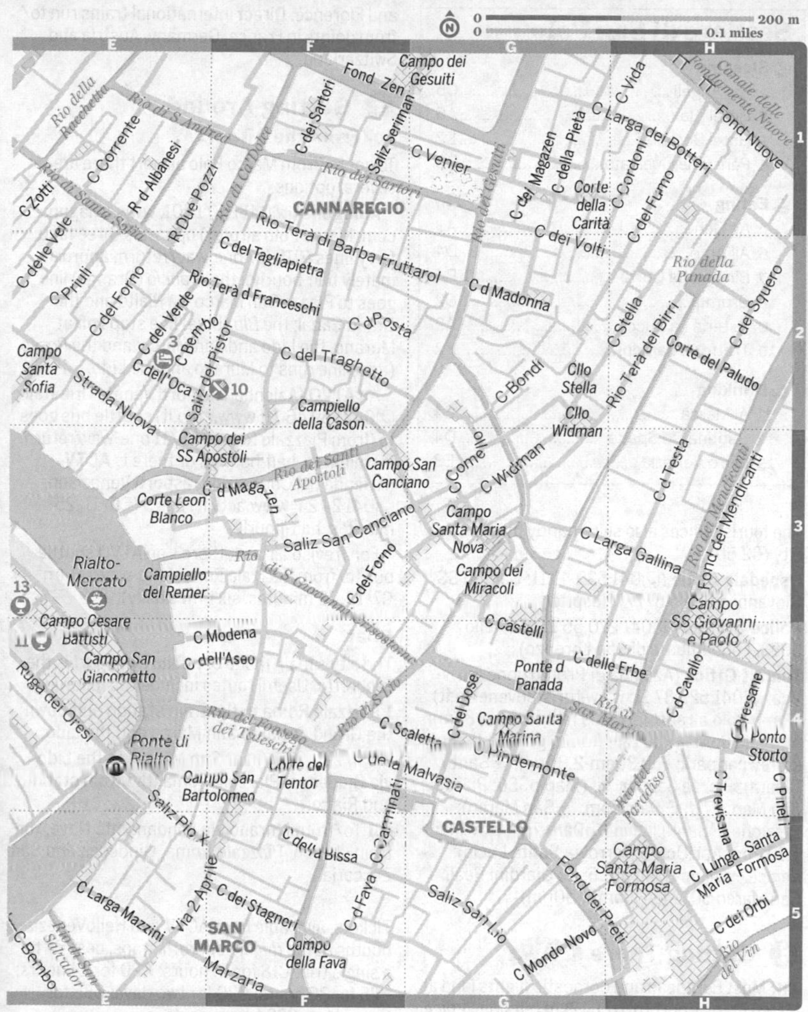

midnight Thu-Tue; San Marco) With its historic pedigree (Byron, Goethe and Rousseau drank here), house orchestra and eye-watering prices (a cappuccino costs €9), Venice's most celebrated cafe is everything you'd expect it be.

☆ Entertainment

Upcoming events are listed in the free *Shows & Events* guide, available at tourist offices, and at www.veneziadavivere.com. Tickets for most events are sold at **HelloVenezia ticket outlets** (☎041 24 24; www.hellovenezia.it) in front of the train station, at Piazzale Roma and near key *vaporetto* stops.

Teatro La Fenice OPERA
(Map p656; ☎041 78 65 11; www.teatrolafenice.it; Campo San Fantin 1965; theatre visits adult/reduced €8.50/6, opera tickets from €40; ⊙tours 9.30am-6pm) One of Italy's top opera houses, La Fenice hosts a year-round program of opera, ballet and classical music. You can also visit on a guided tour between 9.30am and 6pm most days; check www.festfenice.com for details.

ℹ Information

Pick up the free *Shows & Events* guide at tourist offices. It contains comprehensive city listings and up-to-date details of exhibitions and events.

Sestiere di San Polo

Sleeping
1 Ca' Angeli C5
2 Hotel Alex A5
3 Hotel Bernardi E2
4 Pensione Guerrato D3

Eating
5 Ae Oche A3
6 All'Arco D4
7 Birraria La Corte B4
8 Grom D2
9 Osteria La Zucca A2
10 Trattoria da Bepi F2

Drinking
11 Al Mercà E4
12 Cantina Do Spade D4
13 Muro Venezia E3

The tourist offices also sell a handy map of the city (€2.50).

Ospedale Civile (041 529 41 11; Campo SS Giovanni e Paolo 6777) Hospital.

Police Station (041 270 55 11; Castello 5053, Fondamenta di San Lorenzo)

Tourist Office (Azienda di Promozione Turistica; 041 529 87 11; www.turismovenezia.it) Marco Polo airport (arrivals hall; 9am-8pm); Piazzale Roma (Piazzale Roma, ground fl, multistorey car park; 9.30am-2.30pm; Santa Chiara); Piazza San Marco (Map p656; Piazza San Marco 71f; 9am-7pm; San Marco); Stazione di Santa Lucia (9am-7pm Nov-Mar, 1.30-7pm Apr-Oct; Ferrovia Santa Lucia); Venice Pavilion (Map p656; Ex Giardini Reali, San Marco 30124; 9am-2.30pm).

Getting There & Away

AIR Most European and domestic flights land at Marco Polo airport (p707), 12km outside Venice. Ryanair flies to **Treviso airport** (TSF; 0422 31 51 11; www.trevisoairport.it; Via Noalese 63), about 30km away.

BOAT **Venezia Lines** (041 882 11 01; www.venezialines.com) operates high-speed boats to/from several ports in Croatia between mid-April and early October.

BUS **ACTV** (www.actv.it) buses service surrounding areas, including Mestre, Padua and Treviso. Tickets and information are available at the bus station in Piazzale Roma.

TRAIN Venice's Stazione di Santa Lucia is directly linked by regional trains to Padua (€3.50, one hour, every 20 minutes) and Verona (€7.40 to €19, 50 minutes to 2¼ hours, half-hourly) and has fast services to/from Bologna, Milan, Rome and Florence. Direct international trains run to/from points in France, Germany, Austria and Switzerland.

Getting Around

To/From the Airport

To get to/from Marco Polo airport there are several options.

Alilaguna (041 240 17 01; www.alilaguna.com; Marco Polo airport) operates three fast-ferry lines (€15/27 one-way/return, approximately half-hourly): the *Arancio* (Orange) line goes to Piazza San Marco via Rialto and the Grand Canal; the *Blu* (Blue) line stops off at Murano, the Lido and San Marco; and the *Rosso* (Red) line runs to Murano and the Lido.

An **ATVO** (Azienda Trasporti Veneto Orientale; 0421 59 46 71; www.atvo.it) shuttle bus goes to/from Piazzale Roma (€6/11 one-way/return, 20 minutes, half-hourly); or there is **ACTV** (Azienda del Consorzio Trasporti Veneziano; 041 24 24; www.actv.it) bus 5 (€6/11, 25 minutes, half-hourly).

For Treviso airport, there's an ATVO shuttle bus to/from Piazzale Roma (one-way/return €7/13, 70 minutes, six times daily).

Boat

The city's main mode of public transport is the *vaporetto*. Useful routes include the following:

1 Piazzale Roma to the train station and down the Grand Canal to San Marco and the Lido.

2 San Zaccaria (near San Marco) to the Lido via Giudecca, Piazzale Roma, the train station and Rialto.

4.1 To/from Murano via Fondamente Nove, the train station, Piazzale Roma, Giudecca and San Zaccaria.

Tickets, available from ACTV and HelloVenezia booths at the major *vaporetti* stops, cost €7 for a single trip; €18 for 12 hours; €20 for 24 hours; €25 for 36 hours; €30 for two days; €35 for three days; €50 for seven days.

There are significant discounts for holders of the Rolling Venice Card and all tickets are cheaper if you purchase them online at www.veniceconnected.com.

The poor man's gondola, *traghetti* (€2 per crossing), are used to cross the Grand Canal where there's no nearby bridge.

Bologna

POP 380,200

Bologna is one of Italy's great unsung destinations. Its medieval centre is an eye-catching ensemble of red-brick *palazzi*, Renaissance towers and 40km of arcaded porticoes, and there are enough sights to excite without exhausting. A university town since 1088 (Europe's oldest), it is also one of Italy's foremost foodie destinations, home to the eponymous bolognese sauce *(ragù)* as well as *tortellini,* lasagne and *mortadella* (Bologna sausage). Trattorias and restaurants abound and the large student population ensures a high-spirited nightlife.

Sights

Piazza Maggiore PIAZZA

Pedestrianised Piazza Maggiore is Bologna's showpiece square. Marking its southern flank, the Gothic **Basilica di San Petronio** (Piazza Maggiore; 8am-1pm & 3-6pm) is one of the world's largest churches. Work began on it in 1390, but it was never finished and still today the facade is incomplete.

To the west of the basilica, the impressive **Palazzo Comunale** (Town Hall) is home to the city's art collection, the **Collezioni Comunali d'Arte** (051 20 36 29; Palazzo Comunale; adult/reduced/child €5/3/free; 9am-6.30pm Tue-Fri, 10am-6.30pm Sat & Sun).

Adjacent to the square, Piazza del Nettuno is named after the 16th-century **Fontana del Nettuno** (Neptune's Fountain) which depicts an impressively muscled Neptune.

Le Due Torri TOWER

Standing sentinel over Piazza di Porta Ravegnana are Bologna's two leaning towers. You can climb the taller of the two, the 97.6m-high **Torre degli Asinelli** (admission €3; 9am-6pm, to 5pm Oct-May) , but its smaller twin, the 48m-high **Torre Garisenda**, is sensibly out of bounds given its drunken 3.2m tilt.

MAMbo MUSEUM

(Museo d'Arte Moderna di Bologna; www.mambo-bologna-org; Via Don Minzoni 14; adult/reduced/child €6/4/free; noon-6pm Tue, Wed & Fri, to 10pm Thu, to 8pm Sat & Sun) An excellent modern-art museum in a converted bakery. It is also housing **Museo Morandi** (051 20 36 29; www.mambo-bologna.org/museomorandi; Palazzo Comunale; adult/reduced €6/4; 11am-6pm Tue-Fri, 11am-8pm Sat & Sun) and its collection of paintings by Giorgio Morandi while its regular home in the Palazzo Comunale is being renovated.

Sleeping

Try to avoid the busy spring and autumn trade fairs when prices skyrocket and reservations are essential.

Albergo delle Drapperie HOTEL €

(051 22 39 55; www.albergodrapperie.com; Via delle Drapperie 5; s €60-70, d €75-85;) Bed down in the heart of the atmospheric Quadrilatero district at this welcoming three-star. Rooms are attractive with wood-beamed ceilings, wrought-iron beds and the occasional brick arch. Breakfast costs €5 extra and wi-fi €2.

Albergo Panorama PENSION €

(051 22 18 02; www.hotelpanoramabologna.it; Via Livraghi 1, 4th fl; d €65-90, without bathroom s €40-60, d €55-70, tr €70-90, q €90-120;) A budget bolthole within easy walking distance of Piazza Maggiore, this is a cheerful old-school *pensione* with simple, spacious rooms and lovely rooftop views. Note that air con is only in rooms overlooking the street. Cash only.

Ostello Due Torri-San Sisto HOSTEL €

(051 50 18 10; www.ostellodibologna.com; Via Viadagola 5 & 14; dm €18, s/d €26/46, without bathroom €23/42;) Some 6km north of the centre, Bologna's two HI hostels, barely 100m apart, are modern, functional and cheap. Take bus 93 (until 8.20pm) from Via Irnerio, bus 302 (Saturday only) from Piazza dei Martiri or bus 21B (8.40pm to 12.40am) opposite the train station.

Eating

Foodie hot spots include the university district northeast of Via Rizzoli and the Quadrilatero district east of Piazza Maggiore.

Osteria de' Poeti RISTORANTE €€

(www.osteriadepoeti.com; Via de' Poeti 1b; mains €12; closed dinner Mon & Sun) In the wine cellar of a 14th-century *palazzo,* this historic eatery is a bastion of old-style service and classic local cuisine. Take a table by the stone fireplace and enjoy warming regional staples such as *tortellini in brodo di carne* (pasta pockets stuffed with meat in a meat broth).

Trattoria del Rosso TRATTORIA €

(051 23 67 30; www.trattoriadelrosso.com; Via A Righi 30; daily menu €10, mains €7.50-10) The oldest trattoria in town is the perfect place for a cheap lunchtime fill-up. Sit down to filling pastas and honest journeyman's fare, cooked simply and served fast.

La Sorbetteria Castiglione GELATERIA €

(www.lasorbetteria.it; Via Castiglione 44; 8.30am-midnight Tue-Sat, 9am-11.30pm Sun) A walk out of the centre, this much-vaunted *gelateria* produces superb ice cream, as well as *granite* (crushed ice drinks), *frappè* (milkshakes) and smoothies.

Drinking & Entertainment

Bologna's nightlife is one of the most vibrant in the country, with a huge number of bars, cafes and clubs. Thirsty students congregate on and around Piazza Verdi, while the fashionable Quadrilatero district hosts a dressier, more upmarket scene.

Café de Paris BAR
(Piazza del Francia 1c; ⊙7.30am-3am Mon-Sat, 4pm-3am Sun) Modish bar with daily aperitif between 7.30pm and 9.30pm.

La Scuderia BAR, CAFE
(www.lascuderia.bo.it; Piazza Verdi 2; ⊙8am-2.30am; 📶) A popular student hang-out housed in medieval stables. *Aperitivi* and regular live music.

Cantina Bentivoglio JAZZ
(www.cantinabentivoglio.it; Via Mascarella 4b; ⊙8pm-2am) Bologna's top jazz joint is part wine bar (choose from over 500 labels), part restaurant (set-price menu €30) and part concert venue (live music nightly).

Cassero CLUB
(www.cassero.it; Via Don Minzoni 18) Saturday and Wednesday are the big nights at this legendary gay and lesbian (but not only) club, home of Italy's Arcigay organisation.

Information

Tourist Information (www.bolognawelcome.com) Airport (☎051 647 21 13; ⊙9am-7pm Mon-Sat, to 4pm Sun); Piazza Maggiore (☎051 23 96 60; Piazza Maggiore 1/e; ⊙9am-7pm Mon-Sat, 10am-5pm Sun)

Getting There & Around

AIR European and domestic flights serve **Guglielmo Marconi airport** (☎051 647 96 15; www.bologna-airport.it), 6km northwest of the city. From the airport, an Aerobus shuttle (€6, 30 minutes, every 15 to 30 minutes) connects with the train station; tickets can be bought on board.

BUS National and international coaches depart from the bus station on Piazza XX Settembre. However, for most destinations the train is a better bet.

To get to the centre from the train station take bus A, 25 or 30 (€1.20).

TRAIN Bologna is a major rail hub. From the train station on Piazza delle Medaglie d'Oro, fast trains run to Venice (€30, 1½ hours, hourly), Florence (€24 to €36, 40 minutes, half-hourly), Rome (€56 to €81, 2½ hours, half-hourly) and Milan (€32 to €40, one to two hours, hourly).

Ravenna

POP 158,700

Easily accessible from Bologna, and worth a day trip at the very least, the refined town of Ravenna is famous for its early Christian mosaics. These Unesco-listed treasures have been impressing visitors ever since the 13th century when Dante described them in his *Divine Comedy* (much of which was written here).

Sights

Mosaics MOSAICS
Ravenna's mosaics are spread over several sites in and around town, the five main ones being the **Basilica di San Vitale** (Via Fiandrini, entrance on Via San Vitale; ⊙9am-7pm Apr-Sep, to 5.30pm Mar & Oct, 9.30am-5pm Nov-Feb), the **Mausoleo di Galla Placidia** (Via Fiandrini; ⊙9am-7pm Apr-Sep, to 5.30pm Mar & Oct, 9.30am-5pm Nov-Feb), the **Basilica di Sant'Apollinare Nuovo** (Via di Roma; ⊙9am-7pm Apr-Sep, 9.30am-5.30pm Mar & Oct, 10am-5pm Nov-Feb), the **Museo Arcivescovile** (Piazza Arcivescovado; ⊙9am-7pm Apr-Sep, 9.30am-5.30pm Oct & Mar, 10am-5pm Nov-Feb) and the **Battistero Neoniano** (Piazza del Duomo; ⊙9am-7pm Apr-Sep, 9.30am-5.30pm Mar & Oct, 10am-5pm Nov-Feb). These are covered by a single ticket (adult/reduced €9.50/8.50), which is available at any of the five locations. Note also that between March and mid-September there's a €2 booking fee for the Mausoleo.

Five kilometres southeast of town, the apse mosaic of the **Basilica di Sant'Apollinare in Classe** (Via Romea Sud; adult/reduced/child €5/2.50/free; ⊙8.30am-7.30pm Mon-Sat, 1-7.30pm Sun) is a must-see. Take bus 4 (€1.20) from Piazza Caduti per la Libertà.

FREE **Dante's Tomb** MAUSOLEUM
(Via Dante Alighieri 9; ⊙9.30am-6.30pm) Dante Alighieri (1265–1321) spent the last 20 years of his life in Ravenna after he was expelled from his hometown Florence in 1302. As a perpetual act of penance, Florence supplies the oil for the lamp that burns in his tomb.

WORTH A TRIP

THE DOLOMITES

A Unesco Natural Heritage site since 2009, the Dolomites stretch across the northern regions of Trentino-Alto Adige and the Veneto.

Ski resorts abound, offering downhill and cross-country skiing as well as snowboarding and other winter sports. Facilities are generally excellent and accommodation is widely available. Ski passes cover either single resorts or a combination of slopes; the most comprehensive is the **Dolomiti Superski pass** (www.dolomitisuperski.com; 3-/6-day pass €144/254) which covers access to 1220km of runs in 12 valleys.

Popular ski destinations include **Cortina d'Ampezzo**, one of Italy's most fashionable, expensive and well-equipped resorts; **Canazei** in the **Val di Fassa**; and **Ortisei**, **Santa Cristina** and **Selva Gardena** in the **Val Gardena**.

Hiking opportunities run the gamut from gentle strolls to hard-core treks. Recommended areas include the **Alpe di Siusi**, a vast plateau above the Val Gardena; the area around Cortina; and the **Pale di San Martino**, a highland plateau accessible by cable car from **San Martino di Castrozza**.

Tourist offices in individual resorts can provide local advice; for area-wide information contact the offices in **Trento** (☎0461 21 60 00; www.apt.trento.it; Via Manci 2; ⊙9am-7pm) and **Bolzano** (☎0471 30 70 00; www.bolzano-bozen.it; Piazza Walther 8; ⊙9am-7pm Mon-Fri, 9.30am-6pm Sat). The best online resource is www.dolomiti.org.

Most places are accessible by bus, with services run by **Trentino Trasporti** (☎0461 82 10 00; www.ttesercizio.it) in Trento; **SAD** (☎0471 45 01 11; www.sad.it) in Alto Adige; and **Dolomiti Bus** (☎0437 21 71 11; www.dolomitibus.it) in the Veneto. During winter, most resorts also offer 'ski bus' services.

Sleeping & Eating

Ostello Galletti Abbiosi HOSTEL €

(☎0544 3 13 13; www.galletti.ra.it; Via Roma 140; s €50, d €70-140; P❄@☎) More hotel than hostel, this excellent budget option occupies an aristocratic 18th-century *palazzo*. Rooms are spacious, and there's a monumental staircase and handsome internal courtyard.

Ostello Dante HOSTEL €

(☎0544 42 11 64; www.hostelravenna.com; Via Nicolodi 12; dm €16-18, s €26, d €44-48; @☎) Ravenna's bright, colourful HI hostel is in a modern building 1km east of the train station. It closes at 11.30pm but for €1 you can hire a 'night key', allowing you to come and go freely. Take bus 80 from the train station.

La Gardela TRATTORIA €

(☎0544 21 71 47; Via Ponte Marino 3; mains €8-16, fixed-price menu €15-25; ⊙closed Thu) A cheerful, unpretentious eatery that gives you exactly what you want from an Italian trattoria - large helpings of hearty home-cooked food and a jovial, warm atmosphere. Particularly good value is the €15 set menu, ideal for lunch.

Information

Information is available online at www.turismo.ravenna.it and at three tourist offices: the **main office** (☎0544 3 54 04; Via Salara 8; ⊙8.30am-7pm Mon-Sat, 10am-6pm Sun) and branches at **Teodorico** (☎0544 45 15 39; Via delle Industrie 14; ⊙9.30am-12.30pm & 3.30-6.30pm) and **Classe** (☎0544 47 36 61; Via Romea Sud 266, Classe; ⊙9.30am-12.30pm & 3.30-6.30pm).

Getting There & Around

Regional trains run to/from Bologna (€6.80, 1½ hours, 14 daily) and destinations on the east coast.

In town, cycling is popular. The main tourist office runs a free bike-hire service to visitors aged 18 or over (take ID).

TUSCANY

Tuscany is one of those places that well and truly lives up to its hype. The fabled landscape of rolling vine-covered hills dotted with cypress trees and stone villas has long been considered the embodiment of rural chic, and its historically intact cities are home to a significant portfolio of the world's medieval and Renaissance art. Some people never venture beyond Florence, but those who do are inevitably enchanted by their visits to hilltop towns, medieval monasteries and picturesque wine estates.

Florence

POP 371,300

Visitors have rhapsodised about the beauty of Florence (Firenze) for centuries, and once here you'll appreciate why. This Renaissance time capsule is busy year-round but even the enormous and inevitable crowds of tourists fail to diminish its lustre. A list of the city's famous sons reads like a Renaissance who's who – under 'M' alone you'll find Medici, Machiavelli and Michelangelo – and its treasure trove of galleries, museums and churches showcases a magnificent array of Renaissance artworks.

History

Many hold that Florentia was founded by Julius Caesar around 59 BC, but archaeological evidence suggests an earlier village, possibly founded by the Etruscans around 200 BC. Though it was a rich merchant city by the 12th century, Florence's golden age arrived under the auspices of the Medici family between the 14th and 17th centuries; their visionary patronage of writers, artists and thinkers culminated in the Renaissance.

The Medicis were succeeded in the 18th century by the French House of Lorraine, which ruled until 1860, when the city was incorporated into the kingdom of Italy. From 1865 to 1870, Florence was capital of the fledgling kingdom.

During WWII, parts of the city were destroyed by bombing and in 1966 a devastating flood destroyed or damaged many important works of art. In recent decades the city has been undergoing a modern Renaissance spearheaded by the restoration and expansion of the world-famous Uffizi Gallery.

CUT THE QUEUES

To cut queuing time you can book tickets for the Uffizi and Galleria dell'Accademia through **Firenze Musei** (Florence Museums; ☎055 29 48 83; www.firenzemusei.it; ⊙telephone booking line 8.30am-6.30pm Mon-Fri, 8.30am-12.30pm Sat). Note that this entails a booking fee of €4 per museum.

Another option is the **Firenze Card** (www.firenzecard.it; €50). These are valid for 72 hours and allow the holder to bypass both advance booking and queues. Cards can be purchased online, at the tourist offices opposite Stazione Santa Maria Novella and in Via Cavour, and at the Palazzo Pitti, Palazzi Vecchio and Uffizi Gallery (door 2).

Sights & Activities

From the Santa Maria Novella train station, it's a 550m walk along Via de' Panzani and Via de' Cerretani to the Duomo. From Piazza di San Giovanni, next to the Duomo, Via Roma leads down to Piazza della Repubblica and continues as Via Calimala and Via Por Santa Maria to the Ponte Vecchio. Most major sights are within comfortable walking distance of the Duomo.

Piazza del Duomo & Around PIAZZA

Florence's most iconic landmark is the great Gothic **Duomo** (Cattedrale di Santa Maria del Fiore, St Mary of the Flower; www.duomofirenze.it; crypt admission €3; ⊙10am-5pm Mon-Wed & Fri, to 3.30pm Thu, to 4.45pm Sat, to 3.30pm 1st Sat of month, 1.30-4.45pm Sun, Mass in English 5pm Sat, crypt 10am-5pm Mon-Wed & Fri, to 4.45pm Sat) that dominates the city skyline. Officially known as the Cattedrale di Santa Maria del Fiore, it was begun in 1294 and consecrated in 1436. Its most famous feature, the enormous octagonal **Cupola** (Dome; admission €10; ⊙8.30am-6.20pm Mon-Fri, to 5pm Sat), was conceived by Brunelleschi and built after his design won a public competition in 1420.

The interior is decorated with frescos by Vasari and Zuccari, and the stained-glass windows are by Donatello, Paolo Uccello and Lorenzo Ghiberti. The facade is a 19th-century replacement of the unfinished original, pulled down in the 16th century.

Beside the cathedral, the 82m **Campanile** (Bell Tower; www.operaduomo.firenze.it; adult €7; ⊙9am-6pm) was designed by Giotto in 1334 and completed after his death by Andrea Pisano and Francesco Talenti.

The Romanesque **Battistero** (Baptistry; Piazza di San Giovanni; admission €5; ⊙11.15am-7pm Mon-Sat, 8.30am-2pm Sun & 1st Sat of month), one of the oldest buildings in Florence, is famous for its gilded-bronze doors, particularly Lorenzo Ghiberti's *Gate of Paradise*.

Surprisingly overlooked by the crowds, the **Museo dell'Opera di Santa Maria del Fiore** (Cathedral Museum; www.operaduomo.firenze.it; Piazza del Duomo 9; admission €7; ⊙9am-6pm Mon-Sat, 9am-1pm Sun) safeguards treasures that once adorned the Duomo, Battistero and Campanile and is one of the city's most impressive museums.

WORTH A TRIP

SAN GIMIGNANO

This tiny hilltop town deep in the Tuscan countryside is a mecca for day trippers from Florence and Siena. Its nickname is 'The Medieval Manhattan' courtsey of the 14 11th-century towers that soar above its pristine *centro storico* (historic centre).

The **tourist office** (☎0577 94 00 08; www.sangimignano.com; Piazza del Duomo 1; ⏰10am-1pm & 3-7pm Mar-Oct, 10am-1pm & 2-6pm Nov-Feb) is a short walk from Piazza dei Martiri di Montemaggio. Next door, **Palazzo Comunale** (Piazza del Duomo; gallery & tower adult/reduced €5/4; ⏰6.30am-7pm Apr-Sep, 11am-5.30pm Oct-Mar) houses San Gimignano's **Pinacoteca** (art gallery) and tallest tower, the **Torre Grossa**.

For lunch, head to **Dal Bertelli** (Via Capassi 30; panini €3-5, glass of wine €1.50; ⏰1-7pm Mar-early Jan) for a *panino* made with local ingredients.

Regular buses link San Gimignano with Florence (€6.80, 1¼ hours, 14 daily) via Poggibonsi. There are also services to/from Siena (€6, 1¼ hours, hourly).

A combined ticket for the Cupola, the Museo dell'Opera di Santa Maria del Fiore, the Campanile and the Battistero costs €10 and can be purchased at the Museo's ticket desk.

Galleria degli Uffizi MUSEUM

(Uffizi Gallery; www.uffizi.firenze.it; Piazzale degli Uffizi 6; adult/reduced €6.50/3.25, incl temporary exhibition €11/5.50; ⏰8.15am-6.05pm Tue-Sun) Home to the world's greatest collection of Italian Renaissance art, this magnificent gallery occupies the Palazzo degli Uffizi, a 16th-century palace built to house government offices.

The collection, which was bequeathed to the city in 1743 on condition that it never leaves Florence, includes some of Italy's greatest masterpieces: Piero della Francesca's profile portraits of the Duke and Duchess of Urbino, Botticelli's *La nascita di Venere* (Birth of Venus) and *Allegoria della primavera* (Allegory of Spring); Leonardo da Vinci's *Annunciazione* (Annunciation); Michelangelo's *Tondo doni* (Holy Family), as well as works by Giotto, Cimabue, Fra' Angelico, Titian, Raphael and Caravaggio.

Piazza della Signoria PIAZZA

(cnr Via Calimaruzza & Via de' Calzaiuoli) This splendid piazza, hub of city life since the 13th century, is dominated by **Palazzo Vecchio** (☎055 276 82 24; www.palazzovecchio-familymuseum.it; Piazza della Signoria; museum adult/reduced/ €6.50/4.50, tower €6.50, combined ticket €10; ⏰museum 9am-midnight Fri-Wed, 9am-2pm Thu summer, 9am-7pm Fri-Wed, 9am-2pm Thu winter, tower 9am-9pm Fri-Wed, 9am-2pm Thu summer, 10am-5pm Fri-Wed, 10am-2pm Thu winter), the traditional seat of the Florentine government and still the mayor's office today. The best way to visit the *palazzo*, which boasts a series of lavish apartments, is on a guided tour (€2) which you can book at the ticket desk, by telephone or by email.

Also on the square is the **Loggia dei Lanzi**, an open-air showcase of sculpture from the 14th and 16th centuries – look out for Giambologna's dramatic *Ratto delle Sabine* (Rape of the Sabine Women). Other statues in the piazza include a copy of Michelangelo's *David* and Cellini's *Perseo* (Perseus), which shows the Greek hero holding Medusa's severed head.

Museo del Bargello MUSEUM

(☎055 29 48 83; www.polomuseale.firenze.it; Via del Proconsolo 4; adult/reduced €4/2; ⏰8.15am-5pm Tue-Sun & 1st & 3rd Mon of month, to 2pm winter) Home to Italy's most comprehensive collection of Tuscan Renaissance sculpture, the Bargello features Donatello's two versions of *David* plus a number of important early works by Michelangelo.

Palazzo Pitti MUSEUM

(☎055 294 883; www.polomuseale.firenze.it; Piazza Pitti; ticket one adult/EU 18-25/EU child & senior €8.50/4.25/free, ticket two €7/3.50/free, ticket three €11.50/5.75/free; ⏰8.15am-4.30pm Tue-Sun, longer hours high season, closed 1st & last Mon of month) Originally commissioned by the Pitti family, great rivals of the Medici, this vast 15th-century palace was acquired by the Medici in 1549 and became their family residence.

Today it houses four museums, including the **Galleria Palatina** and its collection of works by Raphael, Botticelli, Caravaggio, Filippo Lippi, Titian and Rubens. The other museums are the **Museo degli Argenti**

Florence

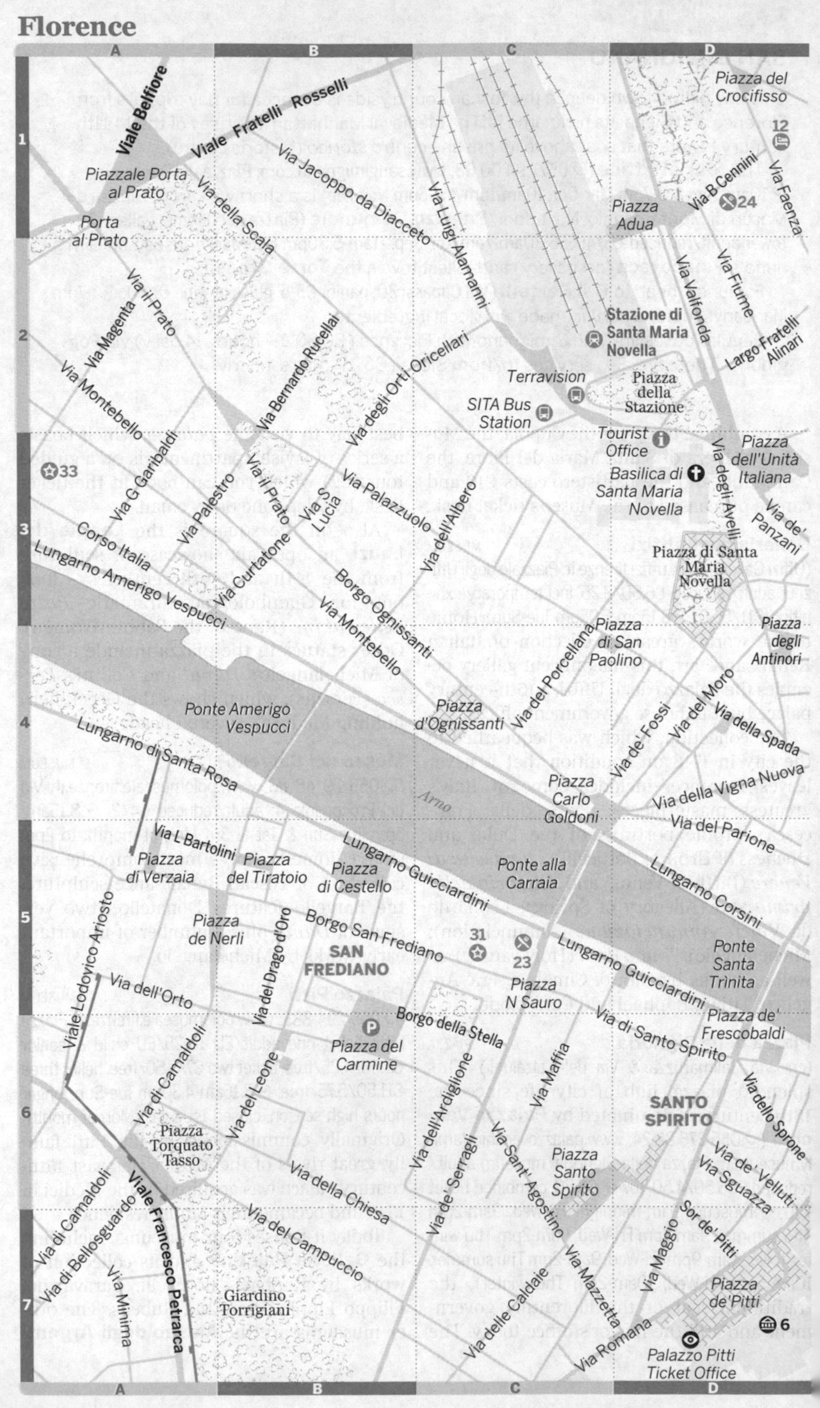

A
B
C
D
1
2
3
4
5
6
7
Viale Belfiore
Viale Fratelli Rosselli
Piazzale Porta al Prato
Porta al Prato
Via della Scala
Via Jacopo da Diacceto
Via Luigi Alamanni
Piazza del Crocifisso
12
Via B Cennini
24
Via Faenza
Piazza Adua
Via Valfonda
Via Fiume
Stazione di Santa Maria Novella
Largo Fratelli Alinari
Terravision
Piazza della Stazione
SITA Bus Station
Tourist Office
Piazza dell'Unità Italiana
Via degli Avelli
Basilica di Santa Maria Novella
Via de' Panzani
Piazza di Santa Maria Novella
Piazza degli Antinori
Via il Prato
Via Magenta
Via Montebello
Via Bernardo Rucellai
Via degli Orti Oricellari
33
Via G Garibaldi
Via Palestro
Via il Prato
Via S Lucia
Via Palazzuolo
Via dell'Albero
Corso Italia
Via Curtatone
Lungarno Amerigo Vespucci
Borgo Ognissanti
Via Montebello
Piazza di San Paolino
Via del Porcellana
Via de' Fossi
Via del Moro
Via della Spada
Piazza d'Ognissanti
Ponte Amerigo Vespucci
Lungarno di Santa Rosa
Arno
Piazza Carlo Goldoni
Via della Vigna Nuova
Via del Parione
Via L Bartolini
Piazza di Verzaia
Piazza del Tiratoio
Piazza di Cestello
Lungarno Guicciardini
Ponte alla Carraia
Lungarno Corsini
Viale Lodovico Ariosto
Piazza de Nerli
Borgo San Frediano
SAN FREDIANO
31
23
Lungarno Guicciardini
Ponte Santa Trìnita
Via dell'Orto
Via del Drago d'Oro
Piazza N Sauro
Borgo della Stella
Via di Santo Spirito
Piazza de' Frescobaldi
Via di Camaldoli
Piazza del Carmine
Via del Leone
Via dell'Ardiglione
Via Maffia
SANTO SPIRITO
Via dello Sprone
Piazza Torquato Tasso
Via della Chiesa
Via de Serragli
Via Sant' Agostino
Piazza Santo Spirito
Via de' Velluti
Via Sguazza
Via di Camaldoli
Viale Francesco Petrarca
Via di Bellosguardo
Via del Campuccio
Sor de' Pitti
Via Minima
Giardino Torrigiani
Via delle Caldaie
Via Mazzetta
Via Maggio
Piazza de'Pitti
6
Via Romana
Palazzo Pitti Ticket Office

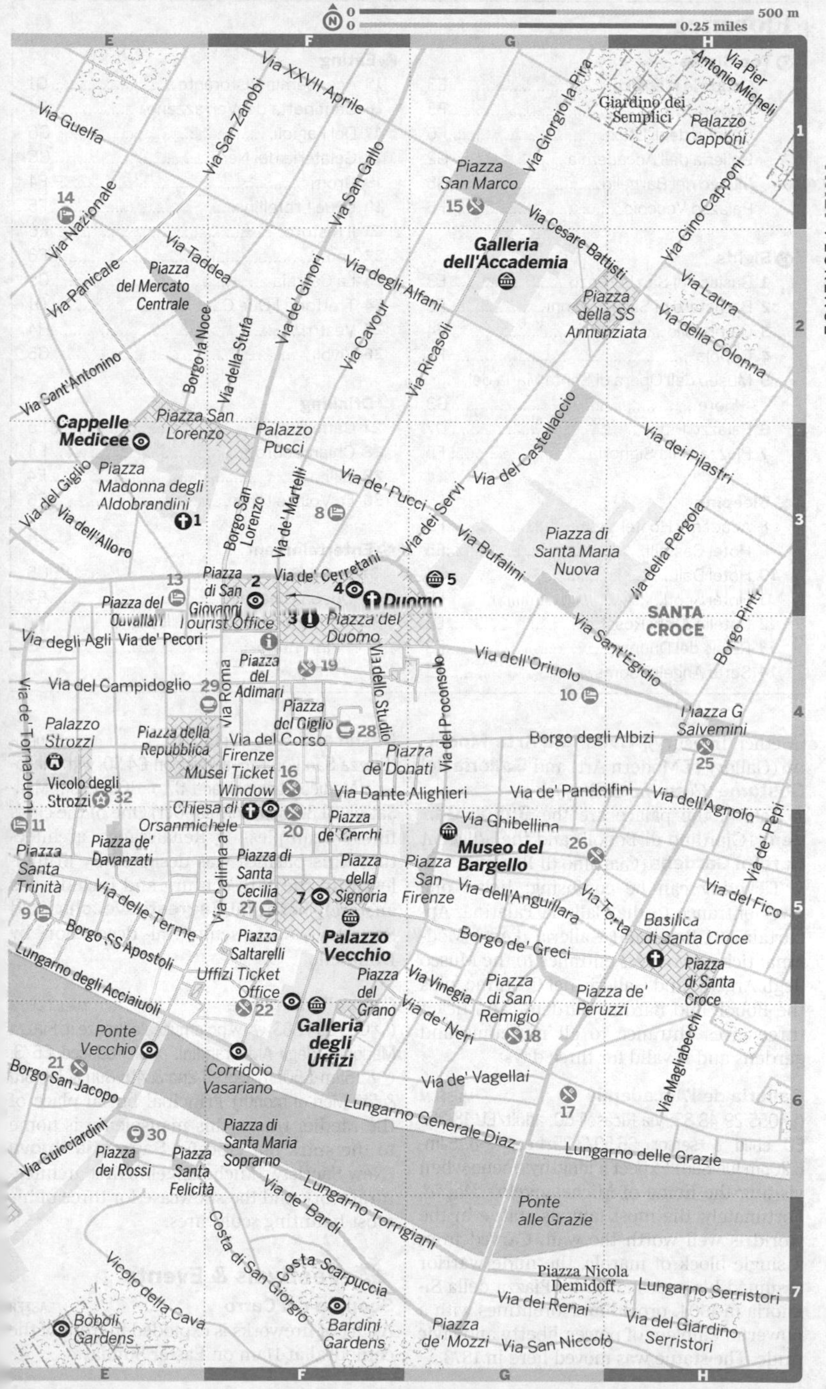
0 500 m
0 0.25 miles
E
F
G
H
Via XXVII Aprile
Via Guelfa
Via San Zanobi
Via San Gallo
Via Nazionale
14
Via Taddea
Piazza del Mercato Centrale
Via Panicale
Via de' Ginori
Via degli Alfani
Via Cavour
Borgo la Noce
Via della Stufa
Via Sant'Antonino
Cappelle Medicee
Piazza San Lorenzo
Palazzo Pucci
Piazza Madonna degli Aldobrandini
Via del Giglio
Via dell'Alloro
Borgo San Lorenzo
Via de' Martelli
Via de' Pucci
Piazza San Marco
15
Galleria dell'Accademia
Via Ricasoli
Via Giorgio la Pira
Via Cesare Battisti
Giardino dei Semplici
Palazzo Capponi
Via Pier Antonio Micheli
Via Gino Capponi
Piazza della SS Annunziata
Via Laura
Via della Colonna
Via del Castellaccio
Via dei Pilastri
Via dei Servi
Via Bufalini
Piazza di Santa Maria Nuova
Via della Pergola
Borgo Pinti
SANTA CROCE
Via Sant'Egidio
Via dell'Oriuolo
10
Piazza G Salvemini
25
Borgo degli Albizi
Via de' Pandolfini
Via dell'Agnolo
Via de' Pepi
26
Via del Fico
Via Ghibellina
Museo del Bargello
Via del Proconsolo
Via dello Studio
Via Dante Alighieri
Piazza de'Donati
Piazza de' Cerchi
Piazza della Signoria
Piazza San Firenze
Via dell'Anguillara
Via Torta
Basilica di Santa Croce
Piazza di Santa Croce
Borgo de' Greci
Piazza di San Remigio
Piazza de' Peruzzi
18
Via Vinegia
Via de' Neri
Via Magliabecchi
Via de' Vagellai
17
Lungarno Generale Diaz
Lungarno delle Grazie
Ponte alle Grazie
Piazza Nicola Demidoff
Lungarno Serristori
Via dei Renai
Via del Giardino Serristori
Piazza de' Mozzi
Via San Niccolò
Costa Scarpuccia
Bardini Gardens
Costa di San Giorgio
Lungarno Torrigiani
Via de' Bardi
Piazza di Santa Maria Soprarno
Piazza Santa Felicità
Piazza dei Rossi
Via Guicciardini
30
Boboli Gardens
Vicolo della Cava
Borgo San Jacopo
21
Ponte Vecchio
Corridoio Vasariano
Galleria degli Uffizi
Uffizi Ticket Office
22
Piazza del Grano
Palazzo Vecchio
Piazza Saltarelli
Lungarno degli Acciaiuoli
Borgo SS Apostoli
Via delle Terme
9
Piazza Santa Trinità
Piazza de' Davanzati
Via Calimala
Piazza di Santa Cecilia
27
7
Chiesa di Orsanmichele
20
16
Musei Ticket Window
Vicolo degli Strozzi
32
11
Palazzo Strozzi
Piazza della Repubblica
Via del Corso
Via Roma
Piazza dei Giglio
28
Piazza del Adimari
19
29
Via del Campidoglio
Via de' Tornabuoni
Via degli Agli
Via de' Pecori
Piazza del Duomo
Duomo
Tourist Office
Piazza di San Giovanni
Piazza del Ouvallali
13
2
3
4
5
Via de' Cerretani
8
1
ITALY FLORENCE
1
2
3
4
5
6
7

Florence

Top Sights

	Cappelle Medicee	E3
	Duomo	F3
	Galleria degli Uffizi	F6
	Galleria dell'Accademia	G2
	Museo del Bargello	G5
	Palazzo Vecchio	F5
	Sights	
1	Basilica di San Lorenzo	E3
2	Battistero di San Giovanni	F3
3	Campanile	F4
4	Cupola	F3
5	Museo dell'Opera di Santa Maria del Fiore	G3
6	Palazzo Pitti	D7
7	Piazza della Signoria	F5
	Sleeping	
8	Academy Hostel	F3
9	Hotel Cestelli	E5
10	Hotel Dalí	G4
11	Hotel Scoti	E5
12	Ostello Archi Rossi	D1
13	Relais del Duomo	E3
14	Sette Angeli Rooms	E1
	Eating	
15	Accademia Ristorante	G1
16	Cantinetta dei Verrazzano	F4
17	Del Fagioli	G6
18	Gelateria dei Neri	G6
19	Grom	F4
20	I Due Fratellini	F5
21	Il Ristoro	E6
22	'Ino	F6
23	La Carraia	C5
24	Trattoria I Due G	D1
25	Vestri	H4
26	Vivoli	G5
	Drinking	
27	Caffè Rivoire	F5
28	Chiaroscuro	F4
29	Gilli	F4
30	Le Volpi e l'Uva	E6
	Entertainment	
31	La Cité	C5
32	Odeon Cinehall	E4
33	Teatro del Maggio Musicale Fiorentino	A3

(Medici Treasury), **Galleria d'Arte Moderna** (Gallery of Modern Art) and **Galleria del Costume** (Costume Gallery).

Behind the palace are the **Boboli Gardens** (Giardino di Boboli) and the adjacent **Bardini Gardens** (Giardino di Bardini).

Ticketing can be confusing: ticket one gives entrance to the Galleria Palatina, Appartamenti Reali and Galleria d'Arte Moderna; ticket two gives entrance to the Museo degli Argenti and Galleria del Costume, plus the Boboli and Bardini Gardens; and ticket three gives entrance to all museums and gardens and is valid for three days.

Galleria dell'Accademia MUSEUM
(☎055 29 48 83; Via Ricasoli 60; adult/EU 18-25/EU child & senior €6.50/3.25/free; ⊙8.15am-6.20pm Tue-Sun) Expect a lengthy queue when visiting the home of Michelangelo's *David*. Fortunately, the most famous statue in the world is well worth the wait. Carved from a single block of marble, the nude warrior assumed his pedestal in the Piazza della Signoria in 1504, providing Florentines with a powerful emblem of power, liberty and civic pride. The statue was moved here in 1873.

Basilica di San Lorenzo CHURCH
(Piazza San Lorenzo; admission €4.50, with Biblioteca Medicea Laurenziana €7; ⊙10am-5pm Mon-Sat, plus 1.30-5pm Sun Mar-Oct) One of the city's finest examples of Renaissance architecture, this basilica was designed by Brunelleschi in the 15th century and includes his austerely beautiful **Sagrestia Vecchia** (Old Sacristry), with sculptural decoration by Donatello.

Cappelle Medicee MAUSOLEUM
(☎055 294 883; www.polomuseale.firenze.it; Piazza Madonna degli Aldobrandini; adult/reduced €6/3; ⊙8.15am-1.50pm, closed 2nd & 4th Sun & 1st, 3rd & 5th Mon of month) Principal burial place of the Medici rulers, this mausoleum is home to the stark but graceful **Sagrestia Nuova** (New Sacristy), Michelangelo's first architectural work and the showcase for three of his most haunting sculptures.

Festivals & Events

Scoppio del Carro EASTER
A cart of fireworks is exploded in front of the cathedral at 11am on Easter Sunday.

Maggio Musicale Fiorentino ARTS
(www.maggiofiorentino.com) Italy's oldest arts festival held from April to June.

Festa di San Giovanni MIDSUMMER
On 24 June Florence celebrates its patron saint, John, with a costumed football match on Piazza di Santa Croce and fireworks over Piazzale Michelangelo.

Sleeping

Although there are hundreds of hotels in Florence, it's still prudent to book ahead. Look out for low-season website deals – prices often drop by up to 50%.

DUOMO & PIAZZA DELLA SIGNORIA

Hotel Dalí HOTEL €
(055 234 07 06; www.hoteldali.com; Via dell'Oriuolo 17; d/tr €85/110, apt from €95, without bathroom s/d €40/70; P@) This overwhelmingly friendly hotel offers 10 light and airy rooms with double-glazed windows, tea- and coffee-making facilities and ceiling fans. No breakfast. Three self-catering apartments sleep between two and six.

Relais del Duomo B&B €
(055 21 01 47; www.relaisdelduomo.it; Piazza dell'Olio 2; s €40-90, d €70-130) Location is the prime selling point of this B&B on a quiet traffic-free street around the corner from the Duomo. The four pastel-coloured rooms are simple but comfortable, and manager Elisabetta is extremely helpful.

Hotel Cestelli PENSION €
(055 21 42 13; www.hotelcestelli.com; Borgo SS Apostoli 25; d €50-100, ste €80-115, without bathroom s €40-60, d €50 80; closed 4 weeks Jan & Feb, 3 weeks Aug) This eight-room hotel on the 1st floor of a 12th-century *palazzo* is wonderfully located. Though dark, rooms are attractively furnished, clean, quiet and cool. No breakfast.

SANTA MARIA NOVELLA

Ostello Archi Rossi HOSTEL €
(055 29 08 04; www.hostelarchirossi.com; Via Faenza 94r; dm €18-27, s €30-60, d €55-80; closed 2 weeks Dec; @) Guests' paintings and graffiti pattern the walls at this ever-busy hostel near Stazione di Santa Maria Novella. Rooms and dorms are simple but very clean, and there's a pleasant garden area. Bonuses include computers in some rooms, free walking tours and dinners in the low season.

Hotel Scoti PENSION €
(055 29 21 28; www.hotelscoti.com; Via de' Tornabuoni 7; s €29-75, d €45-125, tr €75-150;) This *pensione* on Florence's most glamorous shopping strip is a splendid mix of old-fashioned charm and value for money. It offers 16 clean and comfortable rooms and a magnificent frescoed living room. Breakfast costs €5.

SAN LORENZO

TOP CHOICE **Academy Hostel** HOSTEL €
(055 239 86 65; www.academyhostel.eu; Via Ricasoli 9; dm €32-34, s/d €42/86, d without bathroom €76; @) A truly excellent hostel close to the Duomo. Its immaculately maintained dorms sleep between four and six and come with night lights, lockers and one shower and toilet for every four beds. Rates include breakfast.

Johlea & Johanna B&B €€
(055 463 32 92, 055 462 72 96; www.johanna.it; d €60-165; @) This highly regarded operation has two elegant apartments and more than a dozen beautifully decorated and well-equipped en suite B&B rooms. They're housed in five historic residences in the quiet San Marco and San Lorenzo districts.

Sette Angeli Rooms B&B €
(393 949 08 10; www.setteangelirooms.com; Via Nazionale 31; s €45-60, d €85-110, tr €95-135;) Tucked behind the central market on a mainstream shopping street, Seven Angels is a tantalising mix of great value and recent renovation. Its rooms are perfectly comfortable, and guests can pay an extra €10 to use the self-catering kitchen corner.

SAN MINIATO AL MONTE

Campeggio Michelangelo CAMPGROUND €
(055 681 19 77; www.ecvacanze.it; Viale Michelangelo 80; camping adult €9.50-11.70, child 3-11 free-€6.90, car & tent €12.50-15.30; P@) Just off Piazzale Michelangelo, this large and comparatively leafy site has lovely city views. Take bus 13 from Stazione di Santa Maria Novella or walk – steeply uphill!

Eating

Classic Tuscan dishes include *ribollita* (a heavy vegetable soup) and *bistecca alla fiorentina* (Florentine steak served rare). Chianti is the local tipple.

DUOMO & PIAZZA DELLA SIGNORIA

'Ino SANDWICHES €
(Via dei Georgofili 3r-7r; panini €8, tasting platter €12; 11am-8pm Mon-Sat, noon-5pm Sun) Artisan ingredients are sourced locally and utilised creatively at this stylish address near

TOP FIVE GELATERIE

There are plenty of places offering *gelato artiginale* (traditional, usually homemade, ice cream and sorbet). A small cone or tub can cost anywhere from €2 to €3.

La Carraia (Piazza Nazario Sauro 25r; ⌚9am-11pm summer, to 10pm winter) Fantastic *gelateria* next to Ponte Carraia.

Gelateria dei Neri (Via de' Neri 22r; ⌚9am-midnight) Semifreddo-style gelato; known for its Giotto (almond, hazelnut and coconut) flavour.

Gelateria Vivoli (Via dell'Isola delle Stinche 7; tub €2-10; ⌚7.30am-midnight Tue-Sat, 9am-midnight Sun summer, to 9pm winter) Select from the huge choice on offer and scoff it in the pretty piazza opposite.

Grom (www.grom.it; cnr Via del Campanile & Via delle Oche; ⌚10.30am-midnight Apr-Sep, to 11pm Oct-Mar) Delectable flavours and often-organic ingredients.

Vestri (☎055 234 03 74; www.vestri.it; Borgo degli Albizi 11r; ⌚10.30am-8pm Mon-Sat) Specialises in chocolate.

the Uffizi. Create your own combination or pick a house special and scoff on the spot with a glass of wine.

Cantinetta dei Verrazzano BAKERY €
(Via dei Tavolini 18-20; focaccias €3-3.50; ⌚noon-9pm Mon-Sat) Together, a *forno* (baker's oven) and *cantinetta* (small cellar) equal a match made in heaven. Head here for a foccacia straight from the oven and a glass of wine from the Verrazzano estate in Chianti.

I Due Fratellini SANDWICHES €
(www.iduefratellini.com; Via dei Cimatori 38r; panini €3; ⌚9am-8pm Mon-Sat, closed Fri & Sat 2nd half of Jun & all Aug) This hole-in-the-wall has been in business since 1875. Locals flock here to order panini filled to order and eaten standing in the street.

SAN LORENZO

Trattoria I Due G TRATTORIA €€
(☎055 21 86 23; www.trattoriai2g.com; Via B Cennini 6r; mains €10-17; ⌚lunch & dinner Mon-Sat) There isn't a tourist in sight at this old-fashioned trattoria near the train station. Huge servings of tasty salads, pastas and mains tempt every palate, but the favourite is undoubtedly the delicious *pollo fritto* (fried chicken).

SAN MARCO

Accademia Ristorante TRATTORIA €€
(☎055 21 73 43; www.ristoranteaccademia.it; Piazza San Marco 7r; mains €12-22, pizzas €6-18; ⌚lunch & dinner) There aren't too many decent eateries in this area, which is one reason why this family-run restaurant is perennially packed. The friendly staff, cheerful decor and consistently tasty food help, too.

SANTA CROCE

Trattoria Cibrèo TRATTORIA €€
(www.edizioniteatrodelsalecibreofirenze.it; Via dei Macci 122r; meals €30; ⌚lunch & dinner Tue-Sat, closed Aug) The casual dining annexe of Florence's most famous (and considerably more expensive) restaurant is a gem. *Primi* include a justly famous fish soup and *secondi* comprise a small main dish matched with a side of seasonal vegetables. No reservations and no credit cards.

Del Fagioli TRATTORIA €
(☎055 24 42 85; Corso Tintori 47r; mains €8.50-10; ⌚lunch & dinner Mon-Fri, closed Aug) This Slow Food favourite near the Basilica di Santa Croce is the archetypical Tuscan trattoria. It serves well-priced bean dishes, soups and roasted meats to throngs of appreciative local workers and residents. No credit cards.

OLTRANO

Il Ristoro TUSCAN €
(☎055 264 55 69; Borgo San Jacopo 48r; mains €10; ⌚noon-4pm Mon, noon-10pm Tue-Sun) This two-room restaurant with deli counter is a great budget choice. Pick from classics such as *pappa al pomodoro* (tomato and bread soup) or a plate of cold cuts and swoon over views of the Arno swirling beneath your feet.

Drinking

Le Volpi e l'Uva WINE BAR
(www.levolpieluva.com; Piazza dei Rossi 1; crostini €6.50, cheese & meat platter €8; ⌚11am-9pm Mon-Sat) This intimate *enoteca con degustazione* (wine bar with tasting) offers an impressive list of wines by the glass (€4 to €8). To attain true bliss indulge in *crostini*

topped with honeyed speck or *lardo* (pork fat), or a platter of boutique Tuscan cheese and meat.

Caffè Rivoire CAFE
(Piazza della Signoria 4; ⏲Tue-Sun) Rivoire's terrace has the best view in the city. Settle in for a long *aperitivo* or coffee break – it's worth the high prices.

Gilli CAFE, BAR
(www.gilli.it; Piazza della Repubblica 39r; ⏲Wed-Mon) The city's grandest cafe has been serving excellent coffee and delicious cakes since 1733. Claiming a table on the piazza is *molto* expensive – we prefer standing at the spacious Liberty-style bar.

Chiaroscuro CAFE, BAR
(☎055 21 42 47; www.chiaroscuro.it; Via del Corso 36r; ⏲7.30am-9pm Mon-Sat, noon-9pm Sun, closed 1 week mid-Aug) This casual cafe roasts its own beans and serves what may well be the best coffee in Florence. Its *aperitivo* buffet (6pm to 8pm) is justly popular.

☆ Entertainment

Florence's definitive monthly listings guide, *Firenze Spettacolo* (€2), is sold at newsstands and has a small English-language section on the final pages.

Concerts, opera and dance are performed year-round at the **Teatro Comunale** (☎055 28 72 22; www.maggiofiorentino.com; Corso Italia 16), also the venue for events organised by the Maggio Musicale Fiorentino.

English-language films are screened at the **Odeon Cinehall** (☎055 29 50 51; www.cinehall.it; Piazza Strozzi 2; ⏲Oct-Jun).

La Cité LIVE MUSIC
(www.lacitelibreria.info; Borgo San Frediano 20r; ⏲3pm-1am Mon-Thu, 5pm-2am Fri & Sat; 📶) By day it's a popular cafe-bookshop, but by night this intimate space morphs into a vibrant live-music venue: think swing, fusion, jam-session jazz.

ℹ Information

Dr Stephen Kerr: Medical Service (☎055 28 80 55, 335 836 16 82; www.dr-kerr.com; Piazza Mercato Nuovo 1; ⏲3-5pm Mon-Fri, or by appointment) Resident British doctor.

Emergency Doctor (Guardia Medica; ☎north of the Arno 055 233 94 56, south of the Arno 055 21 56 16) For a doctor at night, weekends or on public holidays.

Police Station (Questura; ☎055 4 97 71; http://questure.poliziadistato.it; Via Zara 2; ⏲24hr)

Tourist Office (www.firenzeturismo.it) Via Cavour (☎055 29 08 32; www.firenzeturismo.it; Via Cavour 1r; ⏲8.30am-6.30pm Mon-Sat); airport (☎055 31 58 74; ⏲8.30am-6.30pm); Piazza della Stazione (☎055 21 22 45; www.commune.fi.it; Piazza della Stazione 4; ⏲8.30am-7pm Mon-Sat, to 2pm Sun); Bigallo (☎055 28 84 96; www.comune.fi.it; Loggia del Bigallo, Piazza San Giovanni 1; ⏲9am 7pm Mon-Sat, 9am-2pm Sun)

ℹ Getting There & Away

AIR The main airport serving Florence is Pisa international airport (p707). There's also a small city airport 5km north of Florence, **Florence airport** (www.aeroporto.firenze.it).

BUS The **SITA bus station** (www.sitabus.it; Via Santa Caterina da Siena 17r; ⏲information office 8.30am-12.30pm & 3-6pm Mon-Fri, 8.30am-12.30pm Sat) is just south of the train station. Buses leave for Siena (€7.80, 1¼ hours, every 30 to 60 minutes) and San Gimignano via Poggibonsi (€6.80, 1¼ hours, 14 daily).

TRAIN Florence is well connected by train. There are regular services to/from Pisa (€7.80, one hour, every 30 minutes), Rome (€29, 90 minutes, hourly), Venice (€29 to €45, 2¼ hours, 12 daily) and Milan (€39 to €49, 1¾ hours, hourly).

ℹ Getting Around

To/From the Airport

ATAF (☎800 42 45 00; www.ataf.net) runs a shuttle bus (€5, 25 minutes, half-hourly from 5.30am to 11pm) connecting Florence airport with the SITA bus station.

Terravision (www.terravision.eu) runs a bus service between Pisa (Galileo Galilei) airport and Santa Maria Novella train station (one way/return €6/10, 70 minutes, 12 daily). In Florence, buy your tickets at the Terravision desk inside Deanna Café, opposite the station.

A limited number of trains run from Pisa airport directly to Florence each day (€7.80, one hour); regular services run to Pisa Centrale from where you can change to a Florence train.

Bus

Take bus 12 or 13 from Stazione Santa Maria Novella for Piazzale Michelangelo. Tickets (90 minutes €1.20) are sold at *tabacchi* and newsstands – you can also buy a 90-minute ticket on board (€2).

Pisa

POP 88,300

Most people know Pisa as the home of an architectural project gone terribly wrong, but the Leaning Tower is just one of a number of noteworthy sights in this compact university city.

Pisa's golden age came in the 12th and 13th centuries when it was a maritime power rivalling Genoa and Venice. It was eventually defeated by the Genoese in 1284 and in 1406 it fell to Florence. Under the Medici, the arts and sciences flourished and Galileo Galilei (1564–1642) taught at the university.

Sights & Activities

Piazza dei Miracoli PIAZZA

(Campo dei Miracoli; www.opapisa.it; 10am-5pm Nov-Feb, 9am-6pm Mar, 8am-8pm Apr-Sep, 9am-7pm Oct) The immaculate walled lawns of Piazza dei Miracoli provide the gorgeous setting for Pisa's Romanesque trio of cathedral, baptistry and tower.

The centrepiece is the **Duomo** (Piazza dei Miracoli; adult/reduced €2/1, Nov-Feb free; 10am-8pm Apr-Sep, 10am-7pm Oct, 10am-12.45pm & 2-5pm Nov-Feb, 10am-6pm Mar), whose construction began in 1064. It has a graceful tiered facade and a cavernous interior featuring a carved marble pulpit by Giovanni Pisano.

Construction of the cupcake-like **Battistero** (Piazza dei Miracoli; 8.30am-8pm Apr-Sep, 9am-7pm Oct, 10am-5pm Nov-Feb, 9am-6pm Mar) to the west of the Duomo started in 1153 and was completed under the supervision of Nicola and Giovanni Pisano in 1260. Inside, note Nicola Pisano's beautiful pulpit.

But it's to the campanile, better known as the **Leaning Tower** (Torre Pendente; adult €15, online €17; 8.30am-8pm Apr-May & Sep, 8.30am-11pm Jun-Aug, 9am-7pm Oct, 9.30am-5.30pm Nov & Feb, 10am-4.30pm Dec & Jan, 9am-5.30pm Mar), that all eyes are drawn. Construction began in 1173 but only three of the tower's seven tiers were completed before it started tilting – continuing at a rate of about 1mm per year. By 1990 the lean had reached 5.5 degrees – a tenth of a degree beyond the critical point established by computer models. Stability was finally ensured in 1998 when a combination of biased weighting and soil drilling forced the tower into a safer position. Today it's almost 4.1m off the perpendicular.

Visits to the tower are limited to groups of 40; entry times are staggered and queuing is predictably inevitable. It's wise to book ahead.

To get to the square from the train station it's a straightforward 1.5km walk; follow Viale F Crispi north, cross the Arno, and continue up Via Roma.

PIAZZA DEI MIRACOLI TICKETING

Tickets to the Leaning Tower and Duomo are sold individually, but for the remaining sights combined tickets are available. These cost €5/6/8/10 for one/two/four/five sights.

To ensure your visit to the tower, book tickets online at www.opapisa.it at least 15 days in advance.

Sleeping

Hostel Pisa Tower HOSTEL €

(050 520 24 54, 329 701 73 87; www.hostelpisatower.it; Via Piave 4; dm €18-22, apt €49-69; @) This friendly place near the Piazza dei Miracoli occupies a villa with a rear garden. It's cheerful, clean and comfortable but suffers from a lack of communal kitchen and has only two showers and two toilets for 22 beds. The apartment sleeps two or three and has a small kitchen.

Hostel Pisa HOSTEL

(050 520 18 41; www.hostelpisa.it; Via Corridoni 29; dm €15, d €40, d without bathroom €35; @) Opened in 2011, this hostel is located close to the train station (expect noise) and offers characterless but cheap and clean accommodation. Breakfast costs €5.50 and bike rental (24 hours) costs €10.

Eating

Il Montino PIZZERIA €

(Vicolo del Monte 1; pizza €3-6.50; 10.30am-3pm & 5-10pm Mon-Sat) Students and sophisticates alike adore the *cecina* (chickpea pizza) and *spuma* (sweet, nonalcoholic drink) that are the specialities of this local institution. Order to go or claim one of the outdoor tables.

biOsteria 050 ORGANIC €€

(050 54 31 06; Via San Francesco 36; meals €20-30; lunch Mon-Sun, dinner Tue-Sun;) The chef here uses produce that is strictly local and organic to create his tasty dishes. There are ample choices for vegetarians and coeliac-sufferers, and excellent-value daily lunch specials are chalked on the board outside.

Information

For city information, check www.pisaunicaterra.it or pop into the **tourist office** (050 4 22 91;

www.pisaunicaterra.it; Piazza Vittorio Emanuele II 13, train station; ⌚9am-7pm Mon-Sat, to 4pm Sun) in the city centre.

Getting There & Around

Pisa international airport (p707) is linked to the city centre by train (€1.40, five minutes, 15 daily), or by the **CPT** (www.cpt.pisa.it) LAM Rossa bus (€1.10, 10 minutes, every 10 minutes). Buy bus tickets at the newsstand at the train station or any *tabacchi*.

Terravision buses depart from the airport to Florence (one way/return €6/10, 70 minutes, 12 daily). **Train Spa** (www.trainspa.it) shuttle buses go to Siena via Poggibonsi (€14, one daily).

Regular trains run to Lucca (€3.30, 30 minutes, every 30 to 60 minutes), Florence (€7.80, 1¼ hours, every 30 minutes), Rome (€19 to €44.50, three hours, five daily) and Genoa (€9 to €18, 2½ hours, eight daily).

Siena

POP 54,600

Siena is one of Italy's most enchanting medieval towns. Its walled centre is a beautifully preserved warren of dark lanes punctuated with Gothic *palazzi,* and at its heart Piazza del Campo (Il Campo), the sloping square that is the venue for the city's famous annual horse race, Il Palio.

According to legend, Siena was founded by the sons of Remus. In the Middle Ages its dramatic rise caused political and cultural friction with nearby Florence and the two cities strove to outdo each other with their artistic and architectural achievements. Painters of the Sienese School produced significant works of art, many of which are on show in the city's impressive museums and churches.

Sights

From the train station take bus 8 or 9 (€1.10) to Piazza Gramsci, from where Piazza del Campo is a short, signposted walk away.

From the bus station it's a 10-minute walk up Via La Lizza and Via delle Terme. The centre's main streets – the Banchi di Sopra, Via di Città and Banchi di Sotto – curve around Il Campo.

Piazza del Campo PIAZZA

Il Campo has been Siena's civic and social centre for nearly 600 years. At the foot of the sloping, shell-shaped piazza is **Palazzo Comunale** (aka Palazzo Pubblico), a striking example of Sienese Gothic architecture that is home to the splendid **Museo Civico** (www.comune.siena.it; Palazzo Comunale; adult/EU reduced €8/4.50; ⌚10am-6.15pm mid-Mar–Oct, to 5.15pm Nov–mid-Mar) whose collection includes an important fresco cycle by Ambrogio Lorenzetti.

The museum is on the 1st floor of the *palazzo;* from the ground floor you can access the **Torre del Mangia** (admission €8; ⌚10am-7pm Mar–mid-Oct, to 4pm mid-Oct–Feb), a 102m-high bell tower offering great views over the city. A combined ticket to the museum and tower costs €13.

Duomo CHURCH

(www.operaduomo.siena.it; Piazza del Duomo; admission Mar-Oct €3, Nov-Feb free; ⌚10.30am-7pm Mon-Sat, 1.30-6pm Sun Mar-Oct, 10.30am-5.30pm Mon-Sat, 1.30-5.30pm Sun Nov-Feb) Siena's cathedral is one of Italy's greatest Gothic churches. Begun in 1196, it was opened in 1215, although work continued well into the 13th century. The magnificent facade of white, green and red polychrome marble was finished towards the end of the 14th century and the mosaics were added in the 19th century. Notable features include the carved pulpit by Giovanni and Nicola Pisano, Donatello's bronze of St John the Baptist and the inlaid marble floor.

Battistero di San Giovanni BAPTISTRY

(Piazza San Giovanni; admission €4; ⌚10.30am-7pm Mon-Sat & 1.30-6pm Sun Mar-Oct, 10.30am-5.30pm Mon-Sat & 1.30-5.30pm Sun Nov-Feb) While the baptistry's Gothic facade has remained unfinished, the interior is richly decorated with frescos. The centrepiece is a marble font by Jacopo della Quercia, decorated with bronze panels.

Museo Opera del Duomo MUSEUM

(Piazza del Duomo; admission €7; ⌚10.30am-7pm Mon-Sat & 1.30-6pm Sun Mar-Oct, 10.30am-5.30pm Mon-Sat & 1.30-5.30pm Sun Nov-Feb) This museum is home to a large collection of Sienese painting and sculpture, including works by Duccio di Buoninsegna, the most significant painter of the Sienese School. The ticket also includes access to a panoramic terrace.

Festivals & Events

Siena's great annual event is the **Palio** (⌚2 Jul & 16 Aug), a pageant culminating in a bareback horse race round Il Campo. The city is divided into 17 *contrade* (districts), of which 10 are chosen annually to compete for the *palio* (silk banner).

Sleeping

Booking is essential for August and the Palio.

Hotel Alma Domus HOTEL €
(☎0577 4 41 77; www.hotelalmadomus.it; Via Camporegio 37; s €40-48, d €60-85, tr €80-110; ❄@📶) Owned by the Catholic diocese and still home to six Dominican nuns, this convent is privately operated as a budget hotel. Many of the spotlessly clean rooms have views over to the Duomo. There's a 1am curfew.

Antica Residenza Cicogna B&B €
(☎0577 28 56 13; www.anticaresidenzacicogna.it; Via dei Termini 67; s €70-90, d €85-110, ste €120-150; ❄@📶) A welcoming choice in a recently restored 13th-century building. The seven rooms are clean and well maintained, with comfortable beds, painted ceilings and tiled floors.

Eating & Drinking

Among many traditional Sienese dishes are *panzanella* (summer salad of soaked bread, basil, onion and tomatoes), *pappardelle con la lepre* (ribbon pasta with hare) and panforte (a rich cake of almonds, honey and candied fruit).

Morbidi DELI €
(Via Banchi di Sopra 75; ⏲9am-8pm Mon-Sat,) Local gastronomes shop here, as the range of cheese, cured meats and imported delicacies is the best in Siena. If you are self-catering you can join them, but make sure you also investigate the downstairs lunch **buffet** (€12; ⏲12.30-2.30pm), which offers fantastic value.

Kopa Kabana GELATERIA €
(www.gelateriakopakabana.it; Via dei Rossi 52-55; gelati €1.70-2.30; ⏲11am-midnight mid-Feb–mid-Nov) Come here for fresh gelato made by self-proclaimed ice-cream master, Fabio (we're pleased to concur).

Caffè Fiorella CAFE
(www.torrefazionefiorella.it; Via di Città 13; ⏲7am-8pm Mon-Sat) Squeeze into this tiny space behind the Campo to enjoy Siena's best coffee. In summer, the coffee *granita* with a dollop of cream is a wonderful indulgence.

Information

Tourist Office (☎0577 28 05 51; www.terresiena.it; Piazza del Campo 56; ⏲9am-7pm)

Getting There & Away

Siena is not on a main train line, so it's easier to arrive by bus. From the bus station on Piazza Gramsci, SITA/Siena Mobilità buses run to/from Florence (€7.80, 1½ hours, every 30 to 60 minutes) and San Gimignano (€6, 1¼ hours, hourly), either direct or via Poggibonsi. A Train SPA bus travels to/from Pisa airport (€14, two hours, one daily).

Sena (☎861 199 19 00; www.sena.it) operates services to/from Rome Tiburtina and Fiumicino Airport (€23, 3½/four hours, 11 daily weekdays, fewer on weekends), Milan (€36, 4½ hours, five daily), Perugia (€12, 1½ hours, one daily) and Naples (€32, 6½ hours, one daily). Services to Naples depart from outside the railway station.

Both Train Siena Mobilità and Sena have ticket offices underneath the piazza.

Lucca

POP 85,000

Lucca is a love-at-first-sight type of place. Hidden behind monumental Renaissance walls, its historic centre is chock-full of handsome churches, excellent restaurants and tempting *pasticcerie*. Founded by the Etruscans, it became a city state in the 12th century and stayed that way for 600 years. Most of its streets and monuments date from this period.

Sights & Activities

City Walls FORTIFICATION
Lucca's massive *mura* (walls), built around the old city in the 16th and 17th centuries and defended by 126 cannons, remain in almost perfect condition. Twelve metres high and 4km in length, the ramparts are crowned with a tree-lined footpath that looks down on the old town and out towards the Apuane Alps – it's the perfect spot to stroll, cycle, run and get a feel for Lucchesi life.

Cattedrale di San Martino CATHEDRAL
(Piazza San Martino; sacristy adult/reduced €3/2, with cathedral muusem & Chiesa dei SS Giovanni e Reparata €7/5; ⏲7am-6pm daily summer, to 5pm winter, sacristy 9.30am-4.45pm Mon-Fri, 9.30am-6.45pm Sat, 11.30am-5pm Sun) Lucca's predominantly Romanesque cathedral dates to the start of the 11th century. Highlights include an exquisite facade, constructed in the prevailing Lucca-Pisan style, and, inside, a magnificent *Last Supper* by Tintoretto.

Sleeping & Eating

Ostello San Frediano HOSTEL €
(☎0583 46 99 57; www.ostellolucca.it; Via della Cavallerizza 12; dm/s/d/tr/q €22/45/65/80/105; ⊙mid-Feb–Dec; 📶) Comfort and service levels are high at this HI-affiliated hostel set in a garden. There are 149 beds in private rooms and segregated dorms, a courtyard and a grandiose dining room (breakfast €3 to €5, dinner €11). Wi-fi is free; internet costs €1 per hour.

La Pecora Nera TRATTORIA €
(☎0583 46 97 38; www.lapecoraneralucca.it; Piazza San Francesco 4; pizzas €5-9, mains €8.50-13; ⊙lunch Sat, dinner Wed-Sun) The Slow Food-recommended Black Sheep scores brownie points for social responsibility by using its profits to fund workshops for young people with Down syndrome. It offers a menu of pizzas (dinner only), Tuscan favourites and daily specials.

Amedeo Giusti BAKERY €
(Via Santa Lucia 20; pizzas & filled focaccias per kg €9-16; ⊙7am-1pm & 4-7.30pm Mon-Sat, 4-7.30pm Sun) The best way to enjoy a Lucchese lunch is to picnic on the walls, particularly if you buy delectable provisions from this excellent bakery.

Information

The **Città di Lucca tourist office** (☎0583 58 31 50; www.luccaitinera.it; Piazzale Verdi; ⊙9am-7pm Apr-Oct, to 5pm Nov-Mar) holds luggage (€7.50 per day), offers toilet facilities (€0.50), hires bicyles (€2.50 per hour), operates an internet point (€1 per 30 minutes) and supplies free maps and information.

Getting There & Around

From the bus station on Piazzale Giuseppe Verdi, **VaiBus** (www.vaibus.it) buses run to/from Pisa airport (€3, one hour, hourly Monday to Saturday and every two hours Sunday).

Regional trains run to/from Florence (€7, 1½ hours, every 30 to 90 minutes) and Pisa (€3.30, 30 minutes, every 30 to 60 minutes).

Cicli Bizzarri (☎0583 49 66 82; www.ciclibizzarri.net; Piazza Santa Maria 32; per day €15; ⊙9am-7pm daily summer) and **Biciclette Poli** (☎0583 49 37 87; www.biciclettepoli.com; Piazza Santa Maria 42; per day €15; ⊙9am-7pm daily summer) rent bikes for €3 per hour.

UMBRIA

Dubbed the 'green heart of Italy', this predominantly rural region harbours some of Italy's best-preserved historic *borghi* (villages) and many important artistic, religious and architectural treasures. The regional capital, Perugia, provides a convenient base, with Assisi and Orvieto easy day trips away.

Perugia

POP 168,200

With its hilltop medieval centre and international student population, Perugia is Umbria's largest and most cosmopolitan city, with a buzzing atmosphere that's not always apparent in the region's sleepy hinterland. In July, music fans inundate the city for the prestigious **Umbria Jazz festival** (www.umbriajazz.com) and in the third week of October the **Eurochocolate** (www.eurochocolate.com) festival lures chocoholics from across the globe.

Perugia has a bloody and lively past. In the Middle Ages, the Baglioni and Oddi families fought for control of the city, while later, as a papal satellite, the city fought with its neighbours. All the while art and culture thrived: painter Perugino and Raphael, his student, both worked here.

Sights

Perugia's sights are in the hilltop historic centre, up from the train station at the bottom of the hill and the regional bus station (Piazza dei Partigiani), halfway up. From Piazza Partigiani *scale mobili* (elevators) lead up to Piazza Italia, where local buses terminate. From Piazza Italia, pedestrianised Corso Vannucci runs up to Piazza IV Novembre, the city's focal point.

Piazza IV Novembre PIAZZA
The city's focal square is a popular gathering place for students and tourists. The 14th-century **Cattedrale di San Lorenzo** (Piazza IV Novembre; ⊙7.30am-noon & 4-6.30pm) forms an impressive backdrop and the 13th-century **Fontana Maggiore** (Great Fountain), carved by Nicola and Giovanni Pisano, provides a stolid centrepoint.

TOP CHOICE **Palazzo dei Priori** MUSEUM
Constructed between the 13th and 14th centuries, this *palazzo* houses Perugia's best museums. The highlight is Umbria's foremost art gallery, the **Galleria Nazionale dell'Umbria** (www.gallerianazionaleumbria.it; Corso Vannucci 19; adult/reduced €8/4; ⊙8.30am-7.30pm Tue-Sun), whose collection includes everything from Byzantine art to works by local heroes Pinturicchio and Perugino.

The same building also holds what some consider the most beautiful bank in the world, the **Nobile Collegio del Cambio** (Exchange Hall; Corso Vannucci 25; admission €4.50; ⏲9am-12.30pm & 2.30-5.30pm Mon-Sat, 9am-1pm Sun) with frescos by Perugino.

Courses

The **Università per Stranieri** (☎075 5 74 61; www.unistrapg.it; Piazza Fortebraccio 4) runs hundreds of courses in language, art, history, music and architecture.

Sleeping

Primavera Minihotel GUESTHOUSE €
(☎075 572 16 57; www.primaveraminihotel.it; Via Vincioli 8; s €45-65, d €65-90, tr €95-105; ❄@🛜) On the top floor of a 16th-century *palazzo*, this well-run *pensione* has eight modern rooms that are clean and comfortable (ask for the top-floor room with terrace). Only a few rooms have air-con, and breakfast costs an extra €5 to €8.

Ostello di Perugia HOSTEL €
(☎075 572 28 80; www.ostello.perugia.it; Via Bontempi 13; dm €16, sheet supplement €2; ⏲mid-Jan–mid-Dec) If the 10am to 4pm lockout doesn't scare you off, you're sure to appreciate the sweeping countryside view and wafting sounds of church bells from the hostel's terrace, where guests often gather after making dinner. Enjoy the 16th-century frescoed ceilings and tidy four- to six-person rooms.

Eating & Drinking

Sandri CAFE, PATISSERIE €
(Corso Vannucci 32; ⏲9am-9pm Tue-Sun) Sandri has been serving sweet temptations and the best coffee in town since 1860. Sit at a table on the *corso* or stand at the bar and eye off the decadent cakes, pastries and chocolates on offer.

Civico 25 UMBRIAN €€
(☎075 571 63 76; Via della Viola 25; mains €13.50-14; ⏲dinner Mon-Sat) There's lots to like about this *enoteca* – great jazz on the sound system, friendly staff, delicious food and an excellent range of wines by the glass.

Pizzeria Mediterranea PIZZERIA €
(☎075 572 13 22; Piazza Piccinino 11/12; pizzas €5-12; ⏲daily) Perugians know to come here for the best pizza in town. The wood-fired brick oven cooks margherita and other choices that can be topped with *mozzarella di bufala* (fresh buffalo-milk mozzarella) for a small surcharge.

Information

City maps and printed mini-guides are available at the **tourist office** (☎075 573 64 58; www.perugia.umbria2000.it; Piazza Matteotti 18; ⏲8.30am-6.30pm). For information about what's on in town, buy a copy of *Viva Perugia* (€1) from a local newsstand.

Getting There & Around

From the intercity bus station on Piazza dei Partigiani, **Sulga** (☎800 09 96 61; www.sulga.

WORTH A TRIP

ORVIETO

Strategically located on the main train line between Rome and Florence, this spectacularly sited hilltop town has one major drawcard: its extraordinary Gothic-style **Cattedrale** (☎0763 34 11 67; www.opsm.it; Piazza Duomo; admission €3; ⏲9.30am-7pm Mon-Sat Apr-Oct, 9.30am-1pm & 2.30-5pm Mon-Sat, 2.30-5.30pm Sun Nov-Feb, 1-6.30pm Sun Jun-Sep, to 5.30pm Sun Mar-May & Oct), built over 300 years from 1290. The facade is stunning and the ethereally beautiful interior contains major artworks including Luca Signorelli's *Giudizio Universale* (The Last Judgment) fresco cycle.

The **tourist office** (☎0763 34 17 72; info@iat.orvieto.tr.it; Piazza Duomo 24; ⏲8.15am-1.50pm & 4-7pm Mon-Fri, 10am-1pm & 3-6pm Sat & Sun) is opposite the cathedral.

If you arrive by train, you'll need to take a **cable car** (one way €1, with train ticket €0.80; ⏲every 10min 7.05am-8.25pm Mon-Fri, every 15min 8.15am-8pm Sat & Sun) up to the town centre. Tickets are available from the *tabacchi* at the station.

Trains run to/from Florence (€9 to €20, 1¾ hours, hourly) and Rome (€7.50, 80 minutes, hourly). To get here from Perugia (€7.10, 1¾ hours), change trains at Terontola-Cortona.

it) buses depart for Florence (€10.10, two hours, twice weekly), Rome's Tiburtina bus station (€16, 2½ hours, five daily), Fiumicino airport (€23, 3¾ hours, three daily Monday to Saturday, two Sunday), Naples (€23, 4½ hours, two daily), Assisi (€3.20, 50 minutes, five daily) and Orvieto (€6.90, two hours, once daily). Sena buses go to Siena (€12, 1½ hours, once daily).

Regional trains connect with Rome (€11.20, 2¾ hours, six daily) and Florence (€12.35, two hours, seven daily).

From the train station, take the *minimetrò* (€1.50) to the Pincetto stop just below Piazza Mattootti, or bus G (€1.50, €2 if purchased on bus) to Piazza Italia, bus C to behind the Caltedrale di San Lorenzo or bus R to Via XIV Settembre near Piazza Matteotti.

Assisi

POP 28,200

St Francis was born here in 1182, making this medieval town a major destination for millions of pilgrims. Its major sight is the Basilica di San Francesco, a treasure trove of Renaissance frescos.

Sights

Dress rules are applied rigidly at the main religious sights, so no shorts, miniskirts, low-cut dresses or tops. To book guided tours (in English) of the basilica, telephone or email its **information office** (☎075 819 00 84; www.sanfrancescoassisi.org; ⊙9.15am-noon & 2.15-5.30pm Mon-Sat).

Churches CHURCH

Assisi's headline church, the **Basilica di San Francesco** (☎075 81 90 01; Piazza di San Francesco; ⊙Reliquary Chapel 9am-6pm daily, 1-4.30pm holidays) actually comprises two churches. The **upper church** (⊙8.30am-6.45pm Easter-Oct, to 6pm Nov-Easter), which was built between 1230 and 1253 in the Italian Gothic style, features a huge fresco cycle by Giotto, while the dimly lit **lower church** (⊙6am-6.45pm Easter-Oct, to 6pm Nov-Easter), constructed between 1228 and 1230, harbours a series of colourful frescos by Simone Martini, Cimabue and Pietro Lorenzetti. The crypt where St Francis lies buried is below the church.

The 13th-century **Basilica di Santa Chiara** (☎075 81 22 82; Piazza Santa Chiara; ⊙6.30am-noon & 2-7pm Apr-Oct, to 6pm Nov-Mar) contains the remains of St Clare, friend of St Francis and founder of the Order of Poor Clares.

Sleeping & Eating

You'll need to book ahead during peak times: Easter, August and September, and the Feast of St Francis (3 and 4 October). The tourist office can supply a list of convents and monasteries offering accommodation.

Ostello della Pace HOSTEL €

(☎075 81 67 67; www.assisihostel.com; Via Valecchie 177; dm €17, d €44; ⊙1 Mar-8 Nov & 27 Dec-6 Jan; P@) Student groups, couples appreciating the handful of private rooms, backpackers and pilgrims are all welcome at Assisi's HI hostel. Thrifty travellers will appreciate the dinners (€10.50), hikers will appreciate the boxed lunches (€7) and everyone will appreciate the idyllic setting. You'll find it just off the road coming in from Santa Maria degli Angeli.

Trattoria da Erminio TRATTORIA €

(☎075 81 25 06; www.trattoriadaerminio.it; Via Montecavallo 19; mains €7-11, set menus €16; ⊙lunch & dinner Fri-Wed, closed Feb & 1st half of Jul) Da Erminio is known for its grilled meats, which are prepared on a huge fireplace in the main dining area. In summer, tables on the pretty cobbled street are hot property. You'll find it in the upper town near Piazza Matteotti.

Mangiar di Vino RISTORANTE €€

(☎0758 15 51 32; www.mangiardivino.it; Via Francalancia 2; mains €10-18, pizzas €7-8) This modern *enotoca* serves pastas, simple mains and pizzas. It's a good choice for *aperitivo*, and the two-course *menu del giorno* (menu of the day) is excellent value at only €16.

Information

Tourist Office (☎075 813 86 80; www.assisi.regioneumbria.eu; Piazza del Comune 22; ⊙8am-2pm & 3-6pm Mon-Fri, to 6.30pm in summer, 9.30am-5pm Sat & Sun, later in summer) Supplies maps, brochures and practical information.

Getting There & Away

It is better to travel to Assisi by bus rather than train, as the train station is 4km from Assisi proper, in Santa Maria degli Angeli. Buses arrive at and depart from Piazza Matteotti in the *centro storico*, stopping at Piazza Unita d'Italia below the basilica en route.

Sulga buses connect Assisi with Perugia (€3.20, 50 minutes, five daily), Rome (€18, three hours, one daily) and Florence (€12.50, 2½ hours, twice weekly).

If you arrive by train, a bus (Linea C; €1, half-hourly) runs between Piazza Matteotti and the station. Regional trains run to Perugia (€2.40, 20 minutes, hourly).

SOUTHERN ITALY

A sun-bleached land of spectacular coastlines and rugged landscapes, southern Italy is a robust contrast to the more genteel north. Its beaches, baroque towns and classical ruins exist alongside ugly urban sprawl and scruffy coastal development (sometimes in the space of a few kilometres) and its residents are a raucous lot.

Yet for all its flaws, *il mezzogiorno* (the midday sun, as southern Italy is known) is an essential part of every Italian itinerary, offering charm, culinary masterpieces and architectural treasures galore.

Naples

POP 959,600

Naples (Napoli) is dirty, noisy, dishevelled and totally exhilarating. Founded by Greek colonists, it became a thriving Roman city and was later the Bourbon capital of the Kingdom of the Two Sicilies. In the 18th century it was one of Europe's great cities, something you'll readily believe as you marvel at its profusion of baroque *palazzi*.

The city fronts the waterfront and is divided into *quartieri* (districts). A convenient point of reference is Stazione Centrale, which forms the eastern flank of Piazza Garibaldi, Naples' ugly transport hub. From Piazza Garibaldi, Corso Umberto I skirts the *centro storico*, which is centred on two parallel roads: Via San Biagio dei Librai and its continuation Via Benedetto Croce (together known as Spaccanapoli); and Via dei Tribunali. West of the *centro storico*, Via Toledo, Naples' main shopping strip, leads down to the city's grandest square Piazza del Plebiscito.

Sights

TOP CHOICE Museo Archeologico Nazionale MUSEUM
(☎081 44 01 66; Piazza Museo Nazionale 19; admission €8; 9am-7.30pm Wed-Mon; M Museo, Piazza Cavour) If you visit only one museum in southern Italy, make it this one. Boasting priceless classical sculptures and mosaics and frescos from Pompeii and Herculaneum, its collection is mind-bogglingly impressive.

Highlights include the mighty *Toro Farnese* (Farnese Bull), the muscle-bound *Ercole* (Hercules) and *La battaglia di Alessandro contro Dario* (The Battle of Alexander against Darius), one of many exquisite Pompeii mosaics displayed on the mezzanine floor.

Beyond the mosaics, the **Gabinetto Segreto** (Secret Chamber) contains a small but much-studied collection of ancient erotica.

TOP CHOICE Cappella Sansevero CHAPEL
(☎081 551 84 70; www.museosansevero.it; Via Francesco de Sanctis 19; adult/reduced €7/5; 10am-5.40pm Mon & Wed-Sat, to 1.10pm Sun; M Dante) This chapel sports a sumptuous baroque interior and is home to the *Cristo velato* (Veiled Christ), Giuseppe Sanmartino's incredibly lifelike sculpture of a recumbent dead Christ covered by a veil.

TOP CHOICE Basilica di Santa Chiara BASILICA, CLOISTER
(☎081 797 12 31; www.monasterodisantachiara.eu; Via Benedetto Croce; cloisters adult/reduced €6/4.50; basilica 7.30am-1pm & 4.30-8pm, cloisters 9.30am-5pm Mon-Sat, 10am-2pm Sun; M Dante) This huge basilica is actually a 20th-century recreation of Gagliardo Primario's 14th-century original, which was severely damaged in World War II. The *pièce de résistance*, however, is the basilica's adjoining **Chiostro Maiolicato** (Nuns' Cloister), encrusted with colourful 17th-century majolica tiles and frescos.

Palazzo Reale PALACE, MUSEUM
(Royal Palace; ☎081 40 04 54; Piazza del Plebiscito; adult/reduced/EU under 18 & over 65 €4/3/free; 9am-7pm Thu-Tue) This former residence of the Bourbon and Savoy kings houses a museum showcasing baroque and neoclassical furnishings, statues and paintings. Among the many highlights is the **Teatrino di Corte**, a lavish private theatre built in 1768 to celebrate the marriage of Ferdinand IV and Marie Caroline of Austria.

Certosa e Museo di San Martino MONASTERY, MUSEUM
(☎848 80 02 88; http://cir.campania.beniculturali.it/museosanmartino; Largo San Martino 5; adult/reduced €6/3; 8.30am-7.30pm Thu-Tue, last entry 6.30pm; M Vanvitelli, funicular Montesanto to Morghen) Originally built by Charles of Anjou in 1325, this former Carthisian monastery houses a superb collection of Neapolitan art. Highlights include the main church and

sacristy, the 16th-century Chiostro Grande (Great Cloister) and the Sezione Presepiale, which houses a whimsical collection of rare Neapolitan *presepi* (nativity scenes) carved in the 18th and 19th centuries.

The easiest way to get up to the monastery in Vomero is to take the Funiculore Centrale (€1.20) from Stazione Cumana di Montesanto, near Via Toledo.

Palazzo Reale di Capodimonte PALACE

(☎081 749 91 11; Parco di Capodimonte; adult/reduced €7.50/3.75; ⊙museum 8.30am-6pm Thu-Tue, park 7.45am-1hr before sunset; 🚌R4 to Via Miano) This colossal palace set in a 130-hectare park is home to the **Museo Nazionale di Capodimonte**, one of southern Italy's top fine-art museums. Bellini, Botticelli, Titian, Raphael and Andy Warhol are among the artists represented, but it's Caravaggio's *Flagellazione* (Flagellation) that draws the biggest crowds.

Capodimonte is a 30-minute bus ride from the city centre; take bus R4 from Via Medina and alight at Via Miano.

Festivals & Events

Festa di San Gennaro RELIGIOUS

The Festa di San Gennaro honours the city's patron saint and is held three times a year (first Sunday in May, 19 September and 16 December). Thousands pack into the Duomo to witness the saint's blood liquefy, a miracle said to save the city from potential disasters.

Sleeping

You'll have no problem finding somewhere to stay, though be warned that many places suffer from street noise. Most of the budget accommodation is in the ugly area around Stazione Centrale and down near the port; if you're staying near the port and arriving by train, take tram 1 from the train station (€1.20) rather than the R2 bus, which is frequented by pickpockets.

TOP CHOICE **Hostel of the Sun** HOSTEL €

(☎081 420 63 93; www.hostelnapoli.com; Via G Melisurgo 15; dm €16-18, s €30-35, d with bathroom €60-70; ❄@📶) This award-winning hostel has the lot – a handy location close to the ferry terminal, great facilities (including a bar), helpful staff, free tea and coffee and a breezy, inclusive vibe. Adding to the atmosphere is a vibrant colour scheme that extends to the dorms and the hotel-quality private rooms. Bring €0.05 for the lift.

DiLetto a Napoli B&B €

(☎081 033 09 77, 338 9264453; www.dilettoanapoli.it; Vicolo Sedil Capuano 16; s €35-55, d €50-75, tr €65-90, q €80-105; ❄📶; MPiazza Cavour) In a 15th-century *palazzo*, this winning B&B offers stylish accommodation in the historic centre. Its four tasteful guest rooms sport an eclectic modern-ethnic look and a communal lounge has a handy kitchenette.

Casa D'Anna GUESTHOUSE €€

(☎081 44 66 11; www.casadanna.it; Via Cristallini 138; s €67-102, d €95-145; ❄📶; MPiazza Cavour, Museo) An elegant guesthouse lavishly equipped with antiques, books and original artwork. Casa D'Anna has only four guest rooms that skilfully blend classic and contemporary design features. Two-night minimum stay.

Hotel Piazza Bellini BOUTIQUE HOTEL €€

(☎081 45 17 32; www.hotelpiazzabellini.com; Via Costantinopoli 101; s €70-140, d €80-165; ❄@📶; MDante) Only steps away from buzzing Piazza Bellini, this sleek hotel inhabits a 16th-century *palazzo*. Rooms offer pared back chic, with comfortable beds and small bathrooms.

B&B Cappella Vecchia B&B €

(☎081 240 51 17; www.cappellavecchia11.it; Vico Santa Maria a Cappella Vecchia 11; s €50-80, d €75-120;

DISCOUNT CARDS

Campania ArteCards (☎06 39 96 76 50, 800 60 06 01; www.campaniaartecard.it) offer discounted admission to museums in Naples and Campania. Choose the version that suits you best; some include free public transport.

» The Tutti la Regione three-day card (adult/EU 18-25 €27/20) includes free Unicocampania public transport (including the Alibus from Napoli airport) and free entrance to your choice of two museums and sights, including Pompeii and the Museo Archeologico Nazionale di Napoli.

» The seven-day card (€30) includes entrance to five museums or sights and a 50% discount to all others (no transport, though).

» Cards are available at participating museums, at Capodichino airport, at Stazione Centrale in Naples, online or through the call centre.

Central Naples

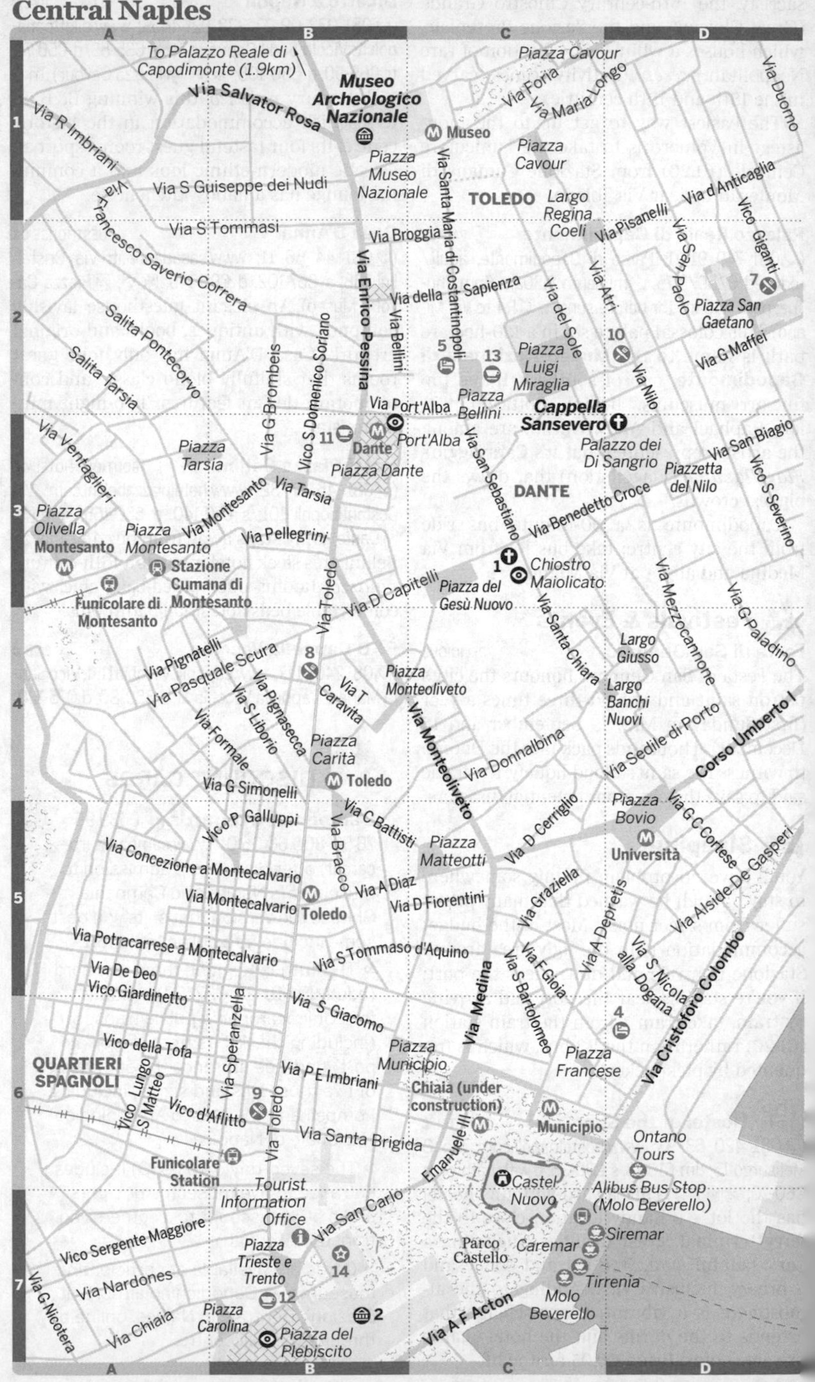

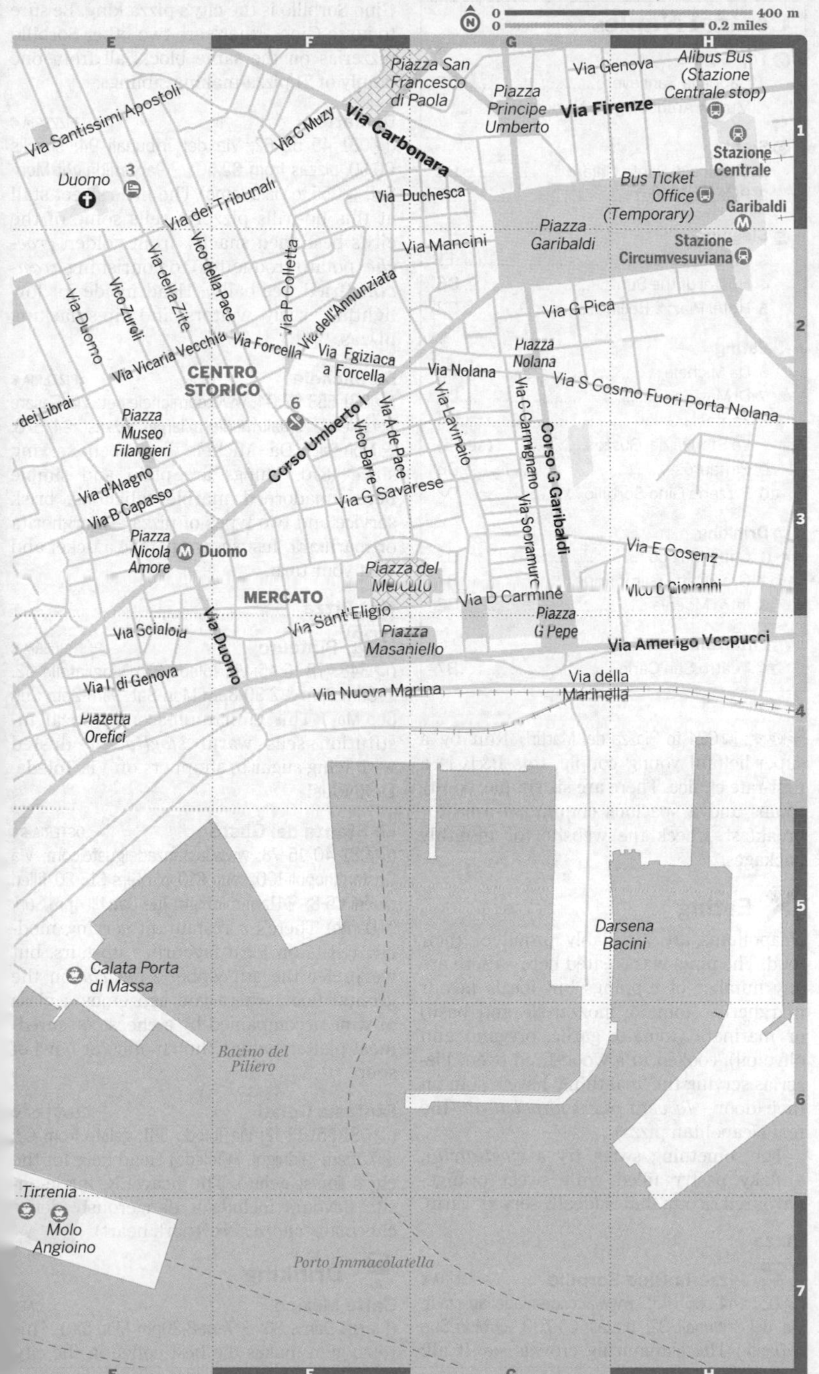
0 400 m
0 0.2 miles
E
F
G
H
1
2
3
4
5
6
7
Piazza San Francesco di Paola
Via Genova
Alibus Bus (Stazione Centrale stop)
Piazza Principe Umberto
Via Firenze
Via Santissimi Apostoli
Via C Muzy
Via Carbonara
Stazione Centrale
Duomo
3
Via dei Tribunali
Via Duchesca
Bus Ticket Office (Temporary)
Garibaldi
Piazza Garibaldi
Via Mancini
Stazione Circumvesuviana
Via della Zite
Vico della Pace
Via P Colletta
Via dell'Annunziata
Vico Zuroli
Via Duomo
Via G Pica
Via Vicaria Vecchia
Via Forcella
Via Egiziaca a Forcella
Piazza Nolana
Via Nolana
CENTRO STORICO
Via S Cosmo Fuori Porta Nolana
dei Librai
6
Piazza Museo Filangieri
Corso Umberto I
Vico Barre
Via A de Pace
Via Lavinaio
Via C Carmignano
Corso G Garibaldi
Via d'Alagno
Via B Capasso
Via G Savarese
Via Sopramuro
Piazza Nicola Amore
Duomo
Via E Cosenz
Piazza del Mercato
Vico G Giovanni
MERCATO
Via D Carmine
Via Sant'Eligio
Piazza G Pepe
Via Scialoia
Via Duomo
Piazza Masaniello
Via Amerigo Vespucci
Via I di Genova
Via della Marinella
Via Nuova Marina
Piazetta Orefici
Darsena Bacini
Calata Porta di Massa
Bacino del Piliero
Tirrenia
Molo Angioino
Porto Immacolatella

Central Naples

Top Sights

Cappella Sansevero D3
Museo Archeologico Nazionale B1

Sights

1 Basilica di Santa Chiara C3
2 Palazzo Reale B7

Sleeping

3 DiLetto a Napoli E1
4 Hostel of the Sun D6
5 Hotel Piazza Bellini C2

Eating

6 Da Michele F2
7 Di Matteo D2
8 Fantasia Gelati B4
La Stanza del Gusto .... (see 5)
9 Pintauro B6
10 Pizzeria Gino Sorbillo D2

Drinking

11 Caffè Mexico B3
12 Gran Caffè Gambrinus B7
13 Intra Moenia C2

Entertainment

14 Teatro San Carlo B7

; C24 to Piazza dei Martiri) Run by a super-helpful young couple, this B&B is a first-rate choice. There are six simple, comfy rooms and a spacious communal area for breakfast. Check the website for monthly packages.

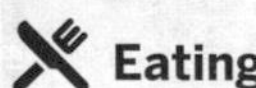

Eating

Neapolitans are justifiably proud of their food. The pizza was created here – there are any number of toppings but locals favour margherita (tomato, mozzarella and basil) or marinara (tomato, garlic, oregano and olive oil), cooked in a wood-fired oven. Pizzerias serving the 'real thing' have a sign on their door – *la vera pizza napoletana* (the real Neapolitan pizza).

For something sweet try a *sfogliatella,* a flaky pastry filled with sweet orange-flavoured ricotta that is ideally served warm.

Pizza

TOP CHOICE Pizzeria Gino Sorbillo PIZZERIA €
(081 44 66 43; www.accademiadellapizza.it; Via dei Tribunali 32; pizzas €3-7.30; Mon-Sat; Dante) The clamouring crowds say it all: Gino Sorbillo is the city's pizza king. Be sure to go to Gino – there are two other Sorbillo pizzerias on the same block, all from one family of 21 pizza-making siblings.

Di Matteo PIZZERIA €
(081 45 52 62; Via dei Tribunali 94; snacks €0.50, pizzas from €2.50; 9am-midnight Mon-Sat; C55 to Via Duomo) The little street stall at this no-frills pizzeria sells some of the city's best fried snacks, from golden *crocchè* (potato croquettes) to nourishing *arancini* (fried rice balls). Head inside for low lighting, surly waiters and lip-smacking pizzas.

Da Michele PIZZERIA €
(081 553 92 04; www.damichele.net; Via Cesare Sersale 1; small/medium/large pizzas €4/5/6; Mon-Sat) Da Michele has been serving since 1870. Things are plain and simple here: unadorned marble tabletops, brisk service and two types of pizza – margherita or marinara. Just show up, take a ticket and wait your turn.

Not Pizza

TOP CHOICE Pintauro PASTICCERIA €
(348 778 16 45; Via Toledo 275; sfogliatelle €2; 8am-2pm & 2.30-8pm Mon-Sat, 9am-2pm Sun Sep-May) This cinnamon-scented local institution sells warm *sfogliatelle* dusted with icing sugar to shoppers on Via Toleda. Delicious!

La Stanza del Gusto OSTERIA €€
(081 40 15 78; www.lastanzadelgusto.com; Via Costantinopoli 100; soup €10, platters €13-20, filled panini €5-8; 11am-midnight Tue-Sat, till 4pm Sun; Dante) There's a restaurant serving modern twists on local favourites upstairs, but we prefer the atmospheric *osteria* on the ground floor, where you can enjoy a glass of wine accompanied by a cheese or cured-meat platter, panino (lunch only) or bowl of soup.

Fantasia Gelati GELATERIA €
(081 551 12 12; Via Toledo 381; gelato from €2; 7.30am-midnight; Toledo) Head here for the city's finest gelato. The heavenly, made-on-site flavours include a dangerously dense chocolate *'cuore nero'* (dark heart).

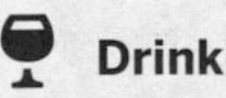

Drinking

Caffè Mexico CAFE
(Piazza Dante 86; 7am-8.30pm Mon-Sat) This retro gem makes the best coffee in the city

The espresso is served *zuccherato* (sweetened), so request it *amaro* if you drink it unadorned. There's another branch at Piazza Garibaldi 70.

Gran Caffè Gambrinus CAFE
(www.caffegambrinus.com; Via Chiaia 1-2; ⏲7am-2am) Naples' most venerable cafe features a showy art nouveau interior and a cast of self-conscious drinkers served by smart, waistcoated waiters. It's great value when you stand at the bar.

Intra Moenia CAFE
(☎081 29 07 20; Piazza Bellini 70; ⏲10am-2am; 📶; Ⓜ Dante) This arty cafe-bookshop-bar on Piazza Bellini attracts a bohemian crowd who adore its laid-back literary ambience.

☆ Entertainment

Opera fans will enjoy an evening at **Teatro San Carlo** (☎081 797 23 31; www.teatrosancarlo.it; Via San Carlo 98; ⏲box office 10am-7pm Tue-Sat, 10am-3.30pm Sun), the oldest opera house in Italy. The opera season runs from December to May and performances of music and ballet are held at other times of the year.

In May, the **Maggio dei Monumenti** festival stages concerts and cultural activities in museums and monuments around town. Entry to most of these is free; check details with a tourist office.

ℹ Information

Despite Naples' notoriety as a Mafia hot spot, the city is pretty safe. That said, travellers should be careful about walking alone late at night near Stazione Centrale and Piazza Dante. Petty crime is also widespread – be vigilant for pickpockets (especially on the city's public transport) and moped bandits.

There are several **tourist information points** (www.inaples.it) around town: **Piazza del Gesù Nuovo** (Piazza del Gesù Nuovo 7; ⏲9.30am-1.30pm & 2.30-6.30pm Mon-Sat, 9.30am-1.30pm Sun); **Via Santa Lucia** (☎081 240 09 14; Via Santa Lucia; ⏲9am-7pm daily); **Via San Carlo** (☎081 40 23 94; Via San Carlo; ⏲9.30am-1.30pm & 2.30-6.30pm Mon-Sat, 9.30am-1.30pm Sun).

Ospedale Loreto-Mare (Hospital; ☎081 254 27 93; Via Amerigo Vespucci 26) Hospital on the waterfront, near the train station.

Police Station (Questura; ☎081 794 11 11; Via Medina 75)

ℹ Getting There & Away

Air

Capodichino airport (p707), 7km northeast of the city centre, is southern Italy's main airport. Flights operate to most Italian cities and up to 30 European destinations, as well as New York.

WORTH A TRIP

POMPEII & HERCULANEUM

On 24 August AD 79 Mt Vesuvius erupted, submerging the town of Pompeii in *lapilli* (burning fragments of pumice stone) and the town of Herculaneum in mud. As a result, both towns were destroyed and over 2000 residents died. The Unesco-listed ruins of both provide remarkable models of working Roman cities, complete with streets, temples, houses, baths, forums, taverns, shops and even a brothel.

Visitors can choose to visit one site, or can purchase a combination ticket (adult/EU 18-24 €20/10) that covers both and is valid for three days.

To visit **Herculaneum** (☎081 732 43 38; www.pompeiisites.org; Corso Resina 6, Ercolano; adult/reduced €11/5.50, combined ticket incl Pompeii, Oplontis, Stabiae & Boscoreale €20/10; ⏲8.30am-7.30pm Apr-Oct, to 5pm Nov-Mar, last entry 90min before closing; 🚆Circumvesuviana to Ercolano-Scavi), take the Circumvesuviana train from Naples (€2.10, 10 minutes), alight at the Ercolano stop and walk straight down the main street to reach the archaeological site. Highlights include the Sede degli Augustali, the Casa del Salone Nero and the Casa Sannitica.

For **Pompeii** (☎081 857 53 47; www.pompeiisites.org; entrances at Porta Marina & Piazza Anfiteatro; adult/reduced €11/5.50, combined ticket incl Herculaneum, Oplontis, Stabiae & Boscoreale €20/10; ⏲8.30am-7.30pm Apr-Oct, 8.30am-5pm Nov-Mar, last entry 90min before closing), take the Circumvesuviana to the Pompeii Scavi-Villa dei Misteri stop (€2.10, 35 minutes), right next to the Porta Marina entrance to the ruins. There's a huge amount to see here, but be sure not to miss the Lupanare (Brothel), the Casa del Menandro, the *anfiteatro* (ampitheatre) and the Villa dei Misteri with its extraordinary frescos.

Boat

A fleet of *traghetti* (ferries), *aliscafi* (hydrofoils) and *navi veloci* (fast ships) connect Naples with Sorrento, the bay islands, the Amalfi Coast, Salerno, Sicily and Sardinia. Most fast ferries and hydrofoils leave from Molo Beverello; a few services to Capri, Ischia and Procida also leave from Molo Mergellina. Ferries for Sicily and Sardinia sail from Molo Angioino, next to Molo Beverello, and also from the neighbouring Calata Porta di Massa.

Tickets for shorter journeys can be bought at Molo Beverello or Mergellina. For longer journeys try **Ontano Tours** (☎081 551 71 64; www.ontanotour.it; Molo Angioino; ⊙8.30am-8pm Mon-Sat), in the car park in front of Molo Angioino. You can also purchase tickets online.

Note that ferry services are pared back in winter and adverse sea conditions may affect sailing schedules.

The major companies servicing Naples:

Alilauro (☎081 497 22 22; www.alilauro.it) To/from Sorrento (€11, bags €2 each, 35 minutes, five daily).

Caremar (☎081 551 38 82; www.caremar.it) Runs services from Naples to Capri (ferry/hydrofoil €11.50/18.80, 80/50 minutes, frequent in summer).

Gescab (☎081 807 18 12; www.gescab.it) Runs hydrofoils to Sorrento (€11, 35 minutes, six daily).

Metrò del Mare (☎199 60 07 00; www.metrodelmare.net) Usually runs services between Naples and Sorrento, Positano and Amalfi over the summer months but had suspended services when this book went to print.

NLG (☎081 552 07 63; www.navlib.it) To/from Capri (€20.20, nine daily) and Sorrento (€12.10, nine daily).

Siremar (☎081 497 2999; www.siremar.it) Operates boats to the Aeolian Islands and Milazzo (seat from €70.20, six times weekly in summer, twice weekly in the low season).

SNAV (☎091 428 55 55; www.snav.it) Runs hydrofoils to Capri (€19.80, seven daily) and Sorrento (€13.10, five daily) as well as ferries to Palermo (from €48, 10 hours, one daily). In summer there are daily services to the Aeolian Islands.

Tirrenia (☎892 123; www.tirrenia.it) Twice-weekly service to and from Cagliari (from €45, 11¼ hours) and a daily service to Palermo (from €34).

TTT Lines (☎081 580 27 44; www.tttlines.it) To/from Catania (from €38, 11 hours, one daily).

Bus

Most long-distance buses leave from the temporary bus stop in Piazza Garibaldi, opposite the Hotel Cavour. **Miccolis** (☎081 563 03 20; www.miccolis-spa.it) runs buses to Bari (€19, three hours, three daily) and Lecce (€32, three hours, three daily) via Brindisi (€29, five hours). **Marino** (☎080 311 23 35; www.marinobus.it) operates services to Matera (€19, 4¼ hours, two daily). Buy tickets and catch buses from the temporary ticket booth in front of Stazione Centrale.

Train

Most trains stop at Stazione Centrale, which incorporates Stazione Garibaldi. There are up to 30 trains daily to Rome (€19, 2¼ hours) and a few to Palermo (€29, nine hours).

The **Circumvesuviana** (☎800 21 13 88; www.eavcampania.it), accessible through Stazione Centrale, operates a service to Sorrento (€4, 65 minutes) via Ercolano for Herculaneum (€2.10, 10 minutes), Pompeii (€2.10, 35 minutes) and other towns along the coast. There are about 40 trains daily running between 5am and 10.40pm, with reduced services on Sunday.

ℹ Getting Around

TO/FROM THE AIRPORT By public transport you can either take the regular **ANM** (☎800 63 95 25; www.anm.it) bus 3S (€1.10, 20 minutes, half-hourly) from Piazza Garibaldi, or the Alibus airport shuttle (€3, 45 minutes) from Piazza del Municipio or Stazione Centrale. This operates every 30 minutes between 6am and midnight.

PUBLIC TRANSPORT You can travel around Naples by bus, metro and funicular. Journeys are covered by the **Unico Napoli ticket** (www.unicocampania.it), which comes in various forms: the standard ticket, valid for 90 minutes, costs €1.20; a daily pass is €3.60; and a weekend daily ticket is €3. Note that these tickets are not valid on the Circumvesuviana line.

Capri

POP 14,200

The most visited of the islands in the Bay of Naples, Capri deserves more than a quick day trip. Beyond the glamorous veneer of chichi cafes and designer boutiques is an island of rugged seascapes, desolate Roman ruins and a surprisingly unspoiled rural inland.

The island is easily reached from Naples and Sorrento. Hydrofoils and ferries dock at Marina Grande, from where it's a short funicular ride up to Capri, the main town. A further bus ride takes you up to the island's second settlement, Anacapri.

For the best views on the island, take the **seggiovia** (chairlift; one way/return €7/10 ⊙9am-5pm Mar-Oct, 9am-3pm Nov-Feb) up from Piazza Vittoria to the summit of **Mt Solaro** (589m), Capri's highest point.

Sights & Activities

Grotta Azzurra GROTTO

(Blue Grotto; grotto €12.50, return boat trip €13.50; 9am–1hr before sunset) This stunning sea cave illuminated by an other-worldly blue light is Capri's major attraction and is best visited in the morning. Boats leave from Marina Grande and the return trip costs €24.50 (€12 for the trip plus the entrance fee for the grotto); allow a good hour or so. Note that the grotto isn't visitable when seas are rough or tides are high.

Giardini di Augusto GARDEN

(Gardens of Augustus; admission €1; 9am-1hr before sunset) Once you've explored Capri Town's picture-perfect streets, head to this garden to enjoy breathtaking views. From here Via Krupp zigzags vertiginously down to Marina Piccola.

Villa Jovis RUIN

(Jupiter's Villa; 081 837 06 86; Via Amaiuri; adult/reduced €2/1; 11am-3pm, closed Tue 1st to 15th of month, closed Sun rest of month) Standing 354m above sea level, this is what's left of Tiberius' main Capri residence, the largest and most sumptuous of the island's 12 Roman villas.

Sleeping & Eating

Capri has few genuinely budget accommodation options, so always book ahead.

Hotel La Tosca PENSION €€

(081 837 09 89; www.latoscahotel.com; Via Dalmazio Birago 5, Capri Town; s €50-100, d €75-160; Apr-Oct;) Away from the glitz of the centre, this charming one-star *pensione* is hidden down a quiet back lane overlooking the mountains. Plain but comfortable rooms have large bathrooms and several have private terraces.

La Taverna di Pulcinella PIZZERIA €

(081 837 64 85; Via Tiberio 7; pizzas from €7; Apr-Oct) If you can bear being served by waiters in Punchinello costumes, you'll be rewarded by what are generally acknowledged to be the best pizzas on Capri.

Salemeria da Aldo DELI €

(Via Cristoforo Colombo 26, Marina Grande; panini from €3.50) Ignore the restaurant touts and head straight to this honest portside deli, where bespectacled Aldo will make you his legendary *panino alla Caprese* (crusty bread stuffed with silky mozzarella and tomatoes from his own garden).

Lo Sfizietto GELATERIA €

(081 837 00 91; Via Longano 6) Located just off La Piazzetta, this *gelateria* uses only organic ingredients with choices that include *cremolate* with 60% fresh fruit and the namesake choice *sfizietto* (caramel with pine nuts).

Information

Information is available online at www.capritourism.com or from one of the three tourist offices: **Marina Grande** (081 837 06 34; www.capritourism.com; Quayside; 9am-1pm & 3.30-6.45pm daily), **Capri Town** (081 837 06 86; Piazza Umberto 1; 8.30am-8.30pm daily) and **Anacapri** (081 837 15 24; Via G Orlando 59; 9am-3pm Mon-Sat Apr-Sep).

Getting There & Around

There are year-round hydrofoils and ferries to Capri from Naples. Timetables and fare details are available online at www.capritourism.com.

From Naples, ferries depart from Calata Porta di Massa and hydrofoils from Molo Beverello and Mergellina. Services are regular and tickets cost €19 to €21 (hydrofoil), €17.80 (fast ferry) and €11.50 (ferry).

There are services to/from Sorrento (hydrofoil €17 to €18, fast ferry €15 to €16.20, 20 minutes, 11 daily) and from Easter to November there are also services to/from Positano (€15.50, 45 minutes, four daily).

On the island, buses run from Capri Town to/from Marina Grande, Anacapri and Marina Piccola. There are also buses from Marina Grande to Anacapri. Single tickets cost €1.80 on all routes, as does the funicular (€1.80) that links Marina Grande with Capri Town in a four-minute trip.

Sorrento

POP 16,600

A stunning location overlooking the Bay of Naples and Mt Vesuvius makes Sorrento a popular package-holiday destination despite the fact that it has no decent beach. Its profusion of sweet-smelling citrus trees and laid-back local lifestyle are certainly attractive, and its relative proximity to the Amalfi Coast, Pompeii and Capri make it a good base for exploring the area.

Sights & Activities

You'll probably spend most of your time in the *centro storico,* which is full of narrow streets lined with shops, cafes, churches and restaurants. To the north, the **Villa Comunale park** (8am-midnight) commands grand views over the sea to Mt Vesuvius.

The two main swimming spots are **Marina Piccola** and **Marina Grande**, although neither is especially appealing. Nicer by far is **Bagni Regina Giovanna**, a rocky beach set among the ruins of a Roman villa, 2km west of town.

Sleeping

Casa Astarita B&B €
(☎081 877 49 06; www.casastarita.com; Corso Italia 67, Sorrento; s €50-100, d €70-120, tr €85-145; ❄@📶) Housed in a 16th-century building on the town's major *passaggiata* (evening stroll) strip, this family-run place offers six quiet, immaculately maintained rooms combining rustic charm with modern comforts (iPod docks, Apple TV, kettle, fridge).

Ulisse Deluxe Hostel HOSTEL €
(☎081 877 47 53; www.ulissedeluxe.com; Via del Mare 22; dm €18-28, s €45-75, d €50-100; P❄@📶) Resembling a three-star hotel, the Ulisse offers quiet modern rooms and single-sex dorms (all with bathroom). The ambience is a bit impersonal, but the efficient staff, excellent amenities and clean, comfortable rooms certainly compensate. Breakfast costs €7.

Eating

Aurora Light CAMPANIAN €€
(☎081 877 26 31; www.auroralight.it; Piazza Tasso 3-4; mains €15) Close examination of its seasonally driven menu shows that Aurora Light's enthusiastic owner enjoys giving traditional Campanian dishes an innovative twist. There are plenty of vegetarian options on offer.

Pizzeria Da Franco PIZZERIA €
(☎081 877 20 66; Corso Italia 265; pizza €7) A good bet for a no-frills bite; this hugely popular place does the best pizza in town. There's a full range of toppings but the one to go for is the house speciality with tomato, mozzarella, rocket and Parmesan. Expect queues most summer nights.

UNICO COSTIERA

If you're travelling in Sorrento and along the Amalfi Coast on a SITA bus, you'll save time and money by buying a Unico Costiera travel card, available for durations of 45 minutes (€2.40), 90 minutes (€3.60), 24 hours (€7.20) and 72 hours (€18). Buy the cards from bars, *tabacchi* and SITA or Circumvesuviana ticket offices.

Information

The main **tourist office** (☎081 807 40 33; Via Luigi De Maio 35; ⊙8.30am-4.10pm Mon-Sat) is near Piazza San Antonino, but there are also information points at **Marina Piccola** (⊙8am-1pm) and on **Corso Italia** (⊙9am-1pm & 3-10pm) near Piazza Tasso.

Getting There & Away

Circumvesuviana trains run half-hourly between Sorrento and Naples (€4, 65 minutes) via Pompeii (€2.10, 30 minutes) and Ercolano (€2.10, 45 minutes). A daily ticket covering stops at Ercolano, Pompeii and Sorrento costs €6.30 (€3.40 on weekends).

Regular SITA buses leave from the train station for the Amalfi Coast, stopping in Positano (40 minutes) and Amalfi (90 minutes).

There are boat services to Capri (€18 hydrofoil, €16.20 fast ferry, 20 minutes, 11 daily) and Naples (€22 return hydrofoil, 35 minutes, six daily).

Amalfi Coast

Stretching 50km along the southern side of the Sorrentine Peninsula, the Amalfi Coast (Costiera Amalfitana) is a postcard-perfect vision of shimmering blue water fringed by vertiginous cliffs on which whitewashed villages and terraced lemon groves cling. This Unesco-protected area is one of Italy's top tourist destinations, attracting hundreds of thousands of visitors each year, 70% of them between June and September.

Getting There & Away

Regular SITA buses run from Sorrento to Positano (40 minutes) and Amalfi (90 minutes), and from Salerno to Amalfi (75 minutes). All trips are covered by a 90-minute or greater Unico Costiera travel card.

Boat services are generally limited to the period between April and October. **Gescab-Alicost** (☎089 87 14 83; www.alicost.it) operates one daily ferry/hydrofoil from Salerno to Amalfi (€7/9), Positano (€11/13) and Capri (€18.50/20). It also runs daily ferries from Sorrento to Positano (€13) and Amalfi (€14).

POSITANO

POP 4000

Approaching Positano by boat, you're greeted by an unforgettable view of colourful, steeply stacked houses clinging to near-vertical green slopes. In town, the main activities are hanging out on the small beach, drinking and dining on flower-laden terraces, and browsing the expensive boutiques.

The **tourist office** (☎089 87 50 67; Via del Saracino 4; ⏱8.30am-7pm Mon-Sat, to 2pm Sun Easter-Oct, 9am-4.30pm Mon-Sat Nov-Easter) can provide information on walking in the densely wooded Lattari Mountains.

Sleeping & Eating

Pensione Maria Luisa PENSION €
(☎089 87 50 23; www.pensionemarialuisa.com; Via Fornillo 42; r €70-85; ⏱Mar-Oct; @📶) This is the best budget choice in town with attractive rooms and memorable views (rooms with a view cost €10 to €15 extra). Breakfast is an additional €5.

Hostel Brikette HOSTEL €
(☎089 87 58 57; www.hostel-positano.com; Via Marconi 358; dm €20-26, premium dm €25-40, d €55-100, apt €60-130; ⏱late Mar-Nov; ❄@📶) Close to the bus stop on the coastal road, this bright and cheerful hostel offers the cheapest digs in town. There are various options: six- to eight-person dorms (single sex and mixed), double rooms, and apartments for two to five people.

Da Costantino TRATTORIA €
(☎089 87 57 38; Via Montepertuso; mains €12, pizzas from €4; ⏱closed Wed) One of the few authentic trattorias in Positano, this place high up the hill serves honest, down-to-earth Italian grub. Expect amazing views, good pastas and pizzas and a selection of fail-safe grilled meats.

AMALFI

POP 5400

Amalfi is a popular summer holiday destination for no good reason. The beach is unappealing, there's a surfeit of souvenir shops and crowds can be oppressive. Outside the high season, its tangle of narrow alleyways, whitewashed houses and sun-drenched piazzas makes it worthy of a day trip but little more.

The **tourist office** (☎089 87 11 07; www.amalfitouristoffice.it; Corso delle Repubbliche Marinare 33; ⏱8.30am-1.30pm & 3-7.15pm Mon-Fri, 8.30am-noon Sat) can provide information about sights, activities and transport.

Sights & Activities

Cattedrale di Sant'Andrea CATHEDRAL
(☎089 87 10 59; Piazza del Duomo; ⏱7.30am-7.30pm) Looming over the central piazza is the town's landmark Duomo, one of the few relics of Amalfi's past as an 11th-century maritime superpower. In high season, entrance between 10am and 5pm is through the adjacent **Chiostro del Paradiso** (☎089 87 13 24; Piazza del Duomo; adult/reduced €2.50/1; ⏱9am-7pm).

Grotta dello Smeraldo CAVE
(admission €6; ⏱9am-4pm; 👪) The local version of Capri's famous sea cave can be visited on one-hour boat trips from Amalfi's harbour (€14 return, 9.20am to 3pm daily May to October).

Sleeping & Eating

Hotel Lidomare HOTEL €€
(☎089 87 13 32; www.lidomare.it; Largo Duchi Piccolomini 9; s/d €50/120; ⏱year-round; ❄📶) The spacious rooms at this old-fashioned, family-run favourite have an endearing air of gentility; the best have sea views.

A'Scalinatella Hostel HOSTEL €
(☎089 87 14 92; www.hostelscalinatella.com; Piazza Umberto I; dm €20-25, s €35-50, d €70-90) This bare-bones operation, just round the headland in Atrani, has dorms, rooms and apartments scattered across the village.

Trattoria Il Mulino ITALIAN €€
(Via delle Cartiere 36; pizzas €6-11, meals €29; ⏱closed Mon Jul & Aug) Beyond the tourist shops on the main drag, this is about as authentic a trattoria-pizzeria as you'll find in Amalfi. It serves tasty seafood – try the *scialatielli alla pescatore* (ribbon pasta with prawns, mussels, tomato and parsley) – and decent pizzas, all at honest prices.

Matera

POP 60,900

Set atop two rocky gorges, Matera is one of Italy's most remarkable towns. Dotting the ravines are the famous *sassi* (cave dwellings), where up to half the town's population lived until the late 1950s. These *sassi* now underpin Matera's economy, attracting visitors from all over the world.

The geographical centre of the town is handsome Piazza Vittorio Veneto, from where you can access the *sassi*.

Sights & Activities

Sassi CAVE DWELLINGS
Within Matera there are two *sassi* areas, the largely restored **Barisano** and more impoverished and run-down **Caveoso**.

With a map you can explore them on your own, although you might find an audioguide (€8) from **Viaggi Lionetti** (☎0835 33 40 33; www.viaggilionetti.com; Via XX Settembre 9; ⊙9am-1pm & 4-8pm Mon-Fri, 9am-1pm Sat) helpful. It and **Ferula Viaggi** (www.ferulaviaggi.it) also offer guided tours.

Inhabited since the Paleolithic age, the *sassi* were brought to public attention with the publication of Carlo Levi's book *Cristo si é fermato a Eboli* (Christ Stopped at Eboli; 1945). His description of children begging for quinine to stave off endemic malaria shamed the authorities into action and about 15,000 people were forcibly relocated in the late 1950s. In 1993 the *sassi* were declared a Unesco World Heritage site.

Accessible from Via Ridola, **Sasso Caveoso** is the older and more evocative of the two. Its highlights include the *chiese rupestre* (rock churches) of **Santa Maria d'Idris** (Piazza San Pietro Caveoso; adult/reduced €3/2; ⊙10am-1pm & 2.30-7pm Tue-Sun Apr-Oct, 10.30am-1.30pm Tue-Sun Nov-Mar) and **Santa Lucia alle Malve** (Via la Vista; adult/reduced €3/2; ⊙10am-1pm & 2.30-7pm Apr-Oct, 10.30am-1.30pm Tue-Sun Nov-Mar) with their well-preserved 13th-century frescos.

Sleeping

La Dolce Vita B&B B&B €

(☎0835 31 03 24; www.ladolcevitamatera.it; Rione Malve 51; s €40-60, d €60-80; 📶) This delightful ecofriendly B&B in Sasso Caveoso offers cool, comfortable and homey rooms. Owner Vincenzo is passionate about Matera and is a mine of information on the *sassi*.

Le Monacelle HOSTEL €

(☎0839 34 40 97; www.lemonacelle.it; Via Riscatto 9-10; dm €18, s/d €55/86; ❄📶) Behind the Duomo, this HI-run hostel is set in a 15th-century monastery and offers large mixed-sex dorms and plainly furnished private rooms. Its best feature is an atmospheric terrace with stunning *sassi* views. Breakfast costs an extra €4.

Eating

TOP CHOICE **Il Cantuccio** RISTORANTE €€

(☎0835 33 20 90; Via delle Beccherie 33; antipasto €15, mains €10-15; ⊙Tue-Sun) Family-run Il Cantuccio is a Slow Food–recommended restaurant serving creative regional fare. The speciality of the house is a lavish, seven-dish antipasto, which includes delights such as a deliciously creamy ricotta with fig syrup and *caponata* (a sweet-and-sour aubergine ratatouille).

Le Botteghe TRATTORIA €€

(☎0835 34 40 72; Piazza San Pietro; mains €11.50-16; ⊙lunch & dinner daily Apr-Sep, closed lunch Tue-Thu Oct-Mar) This endearingly old-fashioned place offers a menu featuring local specialities; the freshly made pasta dishes and *salsiccia di maiale pezzente* (local 'beggar style' pork sausages) are particularly tasty.

Information

The **Agenzia di Promozione Territoriale Basilicata** (APT; ☎0835 33 19 83; www.aptbasilicata.it; 1st fl, Via De Viti De Marco 9; ⊙9am-1.30pm Mon-Fri, 4-6.30pm Mon & Tue) can supply maps and brochures. In summer, tourist information booths operate next to Sasso Barisano and Sasso Caveoso. Online information is available at www.sassiweb.it.

Getting There & Away

You can reach Matera by bus from Rome, Tuscany and Naples, or by train from Bari. The train station is close to the *sassi*, but the long-distance bus station is at Villa Longo on the edge of town, from where it's a 40-minute walk up Via Nazionale and Via Annunziatella to get to Piazza Vittorio Veneto.

Marozzi (☎06 225 21 47; www.marozzivt.it) runs two or three daily buses to/from Rome's Stazione Tiburtina (€34.50, 6½ hours) and one service per day to Siena (€46, 8¼ hours), Florence (€51, 9½ hours) and Pisa (€57.50, 12 hours). Marino (p686) runs two daily services (one on Sunday) to/from Naples (€19, 4¼ hours).

By train, the **Ferrovie Appulo Lucano** (☎080 572 52 29; www.fal-srl.it) runs services to/from Bari (€4.50, 1¼ hour, 14 daily). Note that these do not run on Sundays.

Bari

TRANSPORT HUB

Most travellers visit Puglia's main town to catch a ferry to Greece, Croatia or Montenegro. While it has no absolute must-see sights, the Old City (Bari Vecchia) has some notable Norman buildings that are worth exploring if you have a few hours before your ferry leaves. Get the lowdown at the helpful **tourist information point** (☎080 990 93 41; www.infopointbari.com; Piazza Aldo Moro; ⊙9am-7pm Mon-Sat, 9am-1pm Sun) in front of the train station, and another at the port which is only open from May to October and has opening hours dependent on ferry arrivals.

Sleeping

B&B Casa Pimpolini B&B €
(☎080 521 99 38; www.casapimpolini.com; Via Calefati 249; s €45-60, d €70-80; ❄@) This lovely B&B in the new town is within easy walking distance to shops, restaurants and Bari Vecchia. The rooms are warm and welcoming, and the homemade breakfast a treat. Great value.

Drinking

Bar Savoia CAFE
(cnr Via Sparano da Bari & Via Celefati; ⏲7am-midnight) The *passaggiata* crowds head towards this ever-fashionable cafe on the new city's main pedestrian mall for coffee and liberal doses of people-watching.

Getting There & Away

Ferries run from Bari to Greece (Igoumenitsa and Patra), Croatia (Dubrovnik) and Montenegro (Bar). Ferries to Corfu and Kefallonia (also Patra) in Greece leave from Brindisi, approximately 115km south of Bari and easily accessed by train. Ferry companies have offices at Bari's port, accessible by bus 20/ (€0.90; be sure to catch the bus with / after the number) from the train station.

There are regular trains to/from Rome (from €54, 4½ hours), Brindisi (€7.70, one hour 20 minutes) and Lecce (€9.70, 1½ to two hours).

Lecce

POP 95,600

Its profusion of opulent *barocco leccese* (Lecce baroque) architecture has earned this sophisticated city a reputation as the 'Florence of the South'. The presence of a highly regarded university means that there is a vibrant bar scene, and the elegant historic centre with its piazzas, Roman ruins and baroque ornamentation is easily explored on foot.

Sights

Basilica di Santa Croce CHURCH
(☎0832 24 19 57; www.basilicasantacroce.eu; Via Umberto I; ⏲9am-noon & 5-8pm) This basilica is the city's most celebrated example of *barocco leccese*. It took a team of 16th- and 17th-century craftsmen more than a century to create the carved facade that you see today.

Piazza del Duomo PIAZZA
During times of invasion the inhabitants of Lecce would barricade themselves in this bombastically baroque square, which has conveniently narrow entrances. The 12th-century **cathedral** (⏲8.30am-12.30pm & 4-6.30pm), which is unusual in that it has two facades, is fronted by the 15th-century **Palazzo Vescovile** (Episcopal Palace) and the 18th-century **Seminario**.

Sleeping

There are no youth hostels in Lecce, and no budget options worth recommending. The following designer B&Bs are well worth an extra slice of your daily budget, though.

Palazzo Rollo BOUTIQUE HOTEL €
(☎0832 30 71 52; www.palazzorollo.it; Via Vittorio Emanuele II 14; s €50-60, d €70-90, ste €100-120, apt €70-90; P❄@) Stay in a 17th-century palace in six gorgeous suites furnished with antiques and painted ceilings. Downstairs, small self-catering apartments sleeping two or three open onto an ivy-hung courtyard.

B&B Centro Storico Prestige B&B €
(☎0832 24 33 53, 349 775 12 90; www.bbprestige-lecce.it; Via Santa Maria del Paradiso 4; s €60-70, d €70-80, tr €100-110; @📶) Rooms in this characterful *centro storico* B&B are light, airy and beautifully finished, with traditional furnishings and small balconies. There's also a pretty, communal terrace with views over San Giovanni Battista church.

Eating

Cucina Casareccia TRATTORIA €€
(☎0832 24 51 78; Viale Costadura 19; mains €12; ⏲lunch Tue-Sun, dinner Tue-Sat) Ring the bell to gain entry into a place that feels like a private home and is run with great warmth by an all-female staff – hence its local nickname, *Trattoria le Zie* (The Aunts' Trattoria). Here you'll taste true Puglian cuisine, including an outstanding stuffed calamari. Booking is essential.

Alle due Corti TRATTORIA €€
(☎0832 24 22 23; www.alleduecorti.com; Via Prato 42; mains €12; ⏲lunch & dinner daily, closed winter) For a taste of sunny Salento, check out this no-frills, fiercely traditional restaurant. The seasonal menu is classic Pugliese, written in a local dialect.

Trattoria di Nonna Tetti TRATTORIA €
(☎0832 24 60 36; Piazzetta Regina Maria 28; mains €8-12; ⏲lunch & dinner daily) A warmly inviting eatery that's popular with all ages and budgets, and serves a wide choice of tasty and traditional dishes.

Information

Tourist Office (☎0832 24 80 92; Corso Vittorio Emanuele 24; ⊙9am-1pm & 4-8.30pm Mon-Sat Apr-Sep, to 6pm Nov-Mar)

Ufficio Informazioni Duomo (☎0832 52 18 77; www.infolecce.it; Piazza del Duomo 2; ⊙9.30am-1.30pm & 3.30-7.30pm Mon-Fri Sep-Jul, from 10am Sat, 9.30am-7.30pm daily Aug) Rents out bikes (per hour/day €4/18) and runs guided tours (€40 for two hours). There's a second office at Via G Palmieiri 47.

Getting There & Away

There are direct trains to/from Brindisi (€2.60, 30 minutes, hourly), Bari (€9.70, 1½ to two hours) and Rome (€66, 5½ hours, three daily). The train station is in the centre of town, an easy 15-minute walk from the Duomo.

SICILY

Everything about the Mediterranean's largest island is extreme – the beauty of the rugged landscape, the robust flavours of the regional cuisine, the relentless summer sun and the all-powerful influence of its criminal underbelly.

Over the centuries Sicily has seen off a catalogue of foreign invaders, from the Phoenicians and ancient Greeks to the Spanish Bourbons and WWII Allies. All have contributed to the island's complex and fascinating cultural landscape.

Getting There & Away

AIR Flights from Italy's mainland cities and some European destinations serve Sicily's two main air hubs: Palermo's **Falcone-Borsellino airport** (☎091 702 01 11; www.gesap.it) and Catania's **Fontanarossa airport** (☎095 723 91 11; www.aeroporto.catania.it).

BOAT Regular car and passenger ferries cross to Sicily (Messina) from Villa San Giovanni in Calabria. Ferries also sail from Genoa, Livorno, Civitavecchia, Naples, Salerno and Cagliari, as well as Tunisia.

BUS Bus services between Rome and Sicily are operated by **SAIS** (☎800 21 10 20; www.saisautolinee.it), **Interbus** (☎0935 2 24 60; www.interbus.it) and **Segesta** (☎091 616 79 19; www.segesta.it), departing from Rome Tiburtina .There are daily buses to Messina, Catania, Palermo and Syracuse.

TRAIN Direct **Trenitalia** (☎89 20 21; www.trenitalia.com) trains run from Milan, Florence, Rome, Naples and Reggio di Calabria to Palermo and Catania.

Palermo

POP 655,875

Still bearing the bruises of its WWII battering, Palermo is a compelling and chaotic city. It takes a little work, but once you've acclimatised to the congested and noisy streets you'll be rewarded with some of southern Italy's most imposing architecture, impressive art galleries, vibrant street markets and an array of tempting restaurants and cafes.

Palermo's centre is large but manageable on foot. The main street is Via Maqueda, which runs parallel to Via Roma, the busy road running north from the train station.

Sights

A good starting point is the **Quattro Canti**, a road junction where Palermo's four central districts converge. Nearby, **Piazza Pretoria** is dominated by the ostentatious **Fontana Pretoria**, whose nude nymphs caused outrage when it was brought from Florence in 1573.

FERRIES TO SICILIY

DESTINATION	DEPARTURE POINT	COMPANIES
Aeolian Islands	Naples	SNAV, Siremar
Catania	Naples	TTT Lines
Milazzo	Naples	Siremar
Palermo	Cagliari	Tirrenia
Palermo	Civitavecchia	Grandi Navi Veloci, SNAV
Palermo	Genoa	Grandi Navi Veloci
Palermo	Livorno	Grandi Navi Veloci
Palermo	Naples	SNAV, Tirrenia

Churches CHURCH
Piazza Bellini is home to three eye-catching churches: the baroque **Chiesa di Santa Caterina** (☎338 722 87 75; Piazza Bellini; admission €2; ⊙9.30am-1pm & 3-7pm Mon-Sat, to 1.30pm Sun Apr-Nov, to 1.30pm daily Dec-Mar & 25 Nov); **La Martorana** (Chiesa di Santa Maria dell'Ammiraglio; Piazza Bellini 3; donation requested; ⊙8.30am-1pm & 3.30-5.30pm Mon-Sat, 8.30am-1pm Sun), Palermo's most famous medieval church; and the red-domed **Chiesa Capitolare di San Cataldo** (Piazza Bellini 3; admission €2; ⊙9.30am-1.30pm & 3.30-5.30pm Mon-Sat, 9.30am-1.30pm Sun), of interest more for its Arab-Norman exterior than its surprisingly bare interior.

A short walk west up Corso Vittorio Emanuele II brings you to the **Cattedrale di Palermo** (www.cattedrale.palermo.it; Corso Vittorio Emanuele; admission free; ⊙7am-7pm), a visual riot of arches, cupolas and crenellations. Modified many times over the centuries, it's a stunning example of Sicily's unique Arab-Norman architectural style.

Palazzo Reale PALACE
(Palazzo dei Normanni; Piazza Indipendenza 1; incl Cappella Palatina adult/concession €8.50/6.50; ⊙8.15am-5pm Mon-Sat, to 12.15pm Sun) This is the theatrical seat of the Sicilian parliament. The highlight, and Palermo's premier tourist attraction, is the 12th-century **Cappella Palatina** (Palatine Chapel; ⊙8.15am-5pm Mon-Sat, 8.15-9.30am & 11.30am-12.15pm Sun), a jaw-dropping jewel of Arab-Norman architecture lavishly decorated with exquisite mosaics. Note that if you visit the chapel on a day when the rest of the *palazzo* is closed, the entry price is reduced to adult/concession €7/5.

Teatro Massimo CULTURAL BUILDING
(☎tour reservations 091 605 32 67; www.teatromassimo.it; Piazza Giuseppe Verdi; guided tours adult/reduced €8/5; ⊙10am-2.30pm Tue-Sun) Palermo's great neoclassical opera house, one of Europe's largest, was used as backdrop for the closing scene of *The Godfather: Part III,* with its visually stunning juxtaposition of high culture, low crime, drama and death.

Catacombe dei Cappuccini ARCHAEOLOGICAL SITE
(☎091 21 21 17; Piazza Cappuccini; admission €3; ⊙9am-1pm & 3-5pm Mon-Sat, 9am-1pm Sun) These catacombs house the mummified bodies and skeletons of some 8000 Palermitans who died between the 17th and 19th centuries.

Sleeping

A Casa di Amici HOSTEL €
(☎091 58 48 84; www.acasadiamici.com; Via Volturno 6; dm €19-23, d €65, d without bathroom €40; ❄@📶) This arty hostel-style place behind Teatro Massimo offers two double and two triple rooms with shared bathrooms, as well as a communal lounge, guest kitchen and laundry. Across the street, there are four additional rooms in an annexe.

B&B Panormus B&B €
(☎091 617 58 26; www.bbpanormus.com; Via Roma 72; s €43-65, d €55-85, tr €75-110; ❄📶) Keen prices, charming host Giovanni and five attractive and extremely comfortable rooms make this one of the city's most popular B&Bs. Each room has its own small private bathroom down the passageway (bathrobes are supplied).

Al Giardino dell'Alloro B&B €
(☎091 617 69 04; www.giardinodellalloro.it; Vicolo San Carlo 8; s €50-60, d €85, tr €120; ❄@📶) This bijou B&B with flat-screen TVs, free wi-fi and walls hung with artwork from the nearby academy is a very pleasant retreat. The rooms are painted in vivid colours and there's a communal fridge for guests' use.

Eating & Drinking

Traditional yet spicy Palermo's food marries the island's superb produce with recipes imported by the Arab Saracens in the 9th century. Three specialities to try are *arancini, panelle* (chickpea fritters) and *cannoli* (pastry tubes filled with sweetened ricotta and candied fruit).

For an adrenalin-charged food experience, head to one of Palermo's markets: Capo on Via Sant'Agostino, or Ballarò in the Albergheria quarter, off Via Maqueda.

TOP CHOICE **Piccolo Napoli** SEAFOOD €€
(☎091 32 04 31; Piazzetta Mulino a Vento 4; meals €25-34; ⊙lunch Mon-Sat, dinner Tue-Sat) Known for its spectacularly fresh seafood, delectable antipasti (try the *caponata* and the green olives) and fried morsels, this is a destination for serious foodies. Booking is advisable.

Pizzeria Biondo PIZZERIA €
(☎091 58 36 62; Via Nicolò Garzilli 27; pizzas €5-14; ⏰dinner Thu-Tue) Made with super-fresh *mozzarella di bufala,* Biondo's pizzas are often described as the best in Palermo. An animated crowd fills the sidewalk tables and inside rooms every night.

Kursaal Kalhesa BAR
(☎091 616 00 50; www.kursaalkalhesa.it; Foro Umberto I 21; ⏰noon-3pm & 6pm-1am Tue-Sun) A lively, unpretentious crowd is attracted by Kursaal Kalhesa's program of music and literary events. Meals (mains €16) are served upstairs on a leafy patio flanked by 15th-century walls.

Information

Get information at the **central tourist office** (☎091 58 38 47; www.palermotourism.com; Piazza Castelnuovo 34; ⏰8.30am-2pm & 2.30-6pm Mon-Fri) in the city centre or at the Falcone-Borsellino airport **tourist information point** (☎091 59 16 98;downstairs hall; ⏰8.30am-7.30pm Mon-Fri, to 2pm Sat). There are also information booths at Piazza Bellini, Piazza Castelnuovo, Piazza Marina, Piazza della Vittoria, the port and the train station. These open 9am to 1pm Monday to Friday; in high season those at Piazza Bellini and Piazza Castelnuovo also open 3pm to 7pm.

Police Station (Questura; ☎091 23 90 00; Piazza della Vittoria)

Presidio Ospedaliero Villa Sofia (☎091 780 40 33; www.ospedaliriunitipalermo.it/presidio_villa_sofia.html; Piazza Salerno; ⏰24hr emergency) Hospital.

Getting There & Away

National and international flights arrive at **Falcone-Borsellino airport** (☎091 702 01 11; www.gesap.it), 35km west of Palermo.

The ferry terminal is northeast of the historic centre, off Via Francesco Crispi.

The intercity bus station is in Piazza Cairoli, behind the train station. The main bus companies:

Cuffaro (☎091 616 15 10; www.cuffaro.info; Via Paolo Balsamo 13) Services to Agrigento (€8.70, two hours, three to nine daily).

Interbus (☎0935 56 51 11; www.interbus.it) To/from Syracuse (€12, 3¼ hours, three daily Monday to Saturday, two on Sunday).

SAIS Autolinee (☎091 616 60 28; www.saisautolinee.it) To/from Catania (€14.90, 2½ hours, every 30 minutes Monday to Saturday, eight services Sunday).

Regular trains leave from the Stazione Centrale for Messina (€11.80, 3¼ hours, hourly) via Milazzo (€10.40, 2½ hours), the jumping-off point for the Aeolian Islands. There are also slow services to Catania, Syracuse and Agrigento. Long-distance trains go to Naples (€56.50, 9¼ hours, three daily) and Rome (€69, 11½ hours, four daily).

Getting Around

TO/FROM THE AIRPORT A half-hourly bus service run by **Prestia e Comandé** (☎091 58 63 51; www.prestiaecomande.it) connects the airport with the train station via Piazza Politeama and operates between 5am and 10.30pm. Tickets for the 50-minute journey cost €6.10 and are available on the bus.

BUS Walking is the best way to get around Palermo's centre but if you want to take a bus, most stop outside or near the train station. Tickets cost €1.30 (€1.70 on bus) and are valid for 90 minutes.

Aeolian Islands

Rising out of the cobalt-blue seas off Sicily's northeastern coast, the Unesco-protected Aeolian Islands (Isole Eolie) have been seducing visitors since Odysseus' time. Their wild, windswept mountains, hissing volcanoes and rich waters attract divers, sun seekers and adrenalin junkies.

Lipari is the largest of the seven islands (Lipari, Salina, Vulcano, Stromboli, Alicudi, Filicudi and Panarea) and the main transport hub. From there you can pick up connections to all the other islands, including Vulcano, famous for its therapeutic mud, and Stromboli, whose permanently active volcano supplies spectacular fire shows.

Sights & Activities

Lipari ISLAND
You can explore the volcanic history of the islands and an impressive collection of classical-era artefacts at the **Museo Archeologico Regionale Eoliano** (☎090 988 01 74; www.regione.sicilia.it/beniculturali/museolipari; Castello di Lipari; adult/18-25/EU under 18 & over 65 €6/3/free; ⏰9am-1pm & 3-6pm Mon-Sat, 9am-1pm Sun) in Lipari's Spanish-built **citadel**.

For sunbathing, head to **Canneto** or **Porticello**. Snorkelling and diving are popular – contact **Diving Center La Gorgonia** (☎090 981 26 16; www.lagorgoniadiving.it; Salita San Giuseppe, Marina Corta; dive/night dive/beginner course €30/40/55) for equipment and guided dives. For tours of the islands, **Da Massimo Dolce Vita Group** (090 981 30 86; www.damassimo.it; Via Maurolico 2) offers various packages, ranging from a €15 tour of Lipari and Vulcano to a €80 summit climb of Stromboli.

Vulcano ISLAND

Vulcano is a malodorous and largely unspoilt island. Most people come here to make the hour-long trek up the **Fossa di Vulcano**, the island's active volcano (€3 for crater entrance in summer), or to wallow in the sulphurous **Fanghi di Vulcano** thermal mud baths (€2, plus €1 for shower).

Stromboli ISLAND

Famous for its spectacular fireworks, Stromboli's **volcano** is the most active in the region, last exploding in April 2009. To make the tough six- to seven-hour ascent to the 920m summit you are legally required to hire a guide. At the top you're rewarded with incredible views of the Sciara del Fuoco (Trail of Fire) and constantly exploding crater. **Magmatrek** (090 986 57 68; www.magmatrek.it; Via Vittorio Emanuele) organises afternoon climbs for €28 per person (minimum 10 people).

Sleeping & Eating

Most accommodation is on Lipari. Always try to book ahead, as summer is busy and many places close over winter. Prices fall considerably outside of high season.

Diana Brown B&B €

(090 981 25 84; www.dianabrown.it; Vico Himera 3; s €30-90, d €40-100, tr €50-130;) This excellent-value B&B is tucked down a narrow alley off the main drag in Lipari. Rooms have abundant hot water, a cheerful decor and welcome extras such as kettles, fridges, clothes-drying racks and satellite TV. Breakfast costs €5 extra.

Kasbah MODERN SICILIAN, PIZZERIA €€

(090 981 10 75; Vico Selinunte 41; pizzas €5-9, meals €28-33; 7-11pm Mar-Oct) Choose the environment that suits you best: the sleek, contemporary interior dining room or the vine-covered, candlelit garden out back. Menu choices include delicious pizzas and seafood delicacies.

Bar Pasticceria Subba PASTICCERIA €

(090 981 13 52; Corso Vittorio Emanuele 92, Lipari; pastries from €1; 7am-10pm) Subba has been supplying indulgent cakes, pastries and gelato to locals since 1930.

Information

The islands' only **tourist office** (090 988 00 95; www.aasteolie.191.it; Corso Vittorio Emanuele 202; 8.30am-1.30pm & 4.30-7.30pm Mon-Fri, 8.30am-1.30pm Sat & Sun Jul & Aug) is on Lipari.

Getting There & Away

The main departure point for the islands is Milazzo. If arriving in Milazzo by train, you'll need to catch a bus (€1) or taxi (€15) to the port, 4km from the station. At the port you'll find ticket offices lined up on Corso dei Mille.

Ustica Lines (www.usticalines.it) runs hydrofoils from the islands to/from Messina (€22.70, 1¾ hours) and Milazzo (€23.70, one hour). Siremar (p686) ferries travel to/from Milazzo (€16.20) but take longer than the hydrofoils. Frequency of service varies wildly according to the season.

Siremar also runs ferries from Naples to Lipari, the other islands and Milazzo (from €70.20).

Getting Around

From Lipari, Ustica Lines runs regular services to Vulcano (€7, 10 minutes), Stromboli (€18.30, 1¾ hours) and the other islands. Buy tickets at the port.

Lipari's Guglielmo Urso Bus service travels around the island (€7 for six trips). Its terminus is at the port.

Taormina

POP 11,100

Spectacularly perched on a clifftop terrace overlooking the Ionian Sea and Mt Etna, this sophisticated town has attracted socialites, artists and writers ever since Greek times. Its pristine medieval core, proximity to beaches, grandstand coastal views and chic social scene make it a hugely popular summer holiday destination, meaning that crowds can be oppressive in July and August.

Sights & Activities

The principal pastime in Taormina is wandering the pretty hilltop streets, browsing the shops on Corso Umberto, the pedestrianised main strip, and eyeing up fellow holidaymakers. The town's one big sight is the **Teatro Greco** (0942 2 32 20; Via Teatro Greco; adult/reduced/EU under 18 & over 65 €10/5/free; 9am-1hr before sunset), a stunning horseshoe-shaped amphitheatre that dates to the 3rd century BC.

For a swim you'll need to take the **funivia** (cable car; one way/return €2/3.50; ⏲9am-8.15pm, to 1am Apr-Sep) down to Taormina's beach, **Lido Mazzarò**, and **Isola Bella**, a tiny island set in its own picturesque cove.

SAT (☎0942 2 46 53; www.satgroup.it; Corso Umberto I 73) is one of a number of agencies that organises day trips to Mt Etna (€40), Syracuse (€45), Palermo (€55) and Agrigento (€50).

Sleeping & Eating

Hostel Taormina HOSTEL €

(☎094 262 55 05, 349 102 61 61; www.hosteltaormina.com; Via Circonvallazione 13; dm €18-25, d €58-80; ❄@📶) Operating year-round, this hostel's major selling point is a roof terrace commanding panoramic sea views. It's small (only 23 beds in three dorms and one private room) and facilities are basic, but manager Francesco is helpful and friendly, beds are comfortable and there's a communal kitchen. No breakfast.

Taormina's Odyssey GUESTHOUSE €

(☎0942 2 45 33, 349 810 77 33; www.taorminaodyssey.com; Via Paternò di Biscari 13; dm €20-24, d €48-60; @📶) This family-run hostel and guesthouse offers two small dorms, four private rooms, a communal kitchen and a popular terrace. It's open year-round, and is a five-minute uphill walk from Porta Catania.

Tiramisù PIZZERIA, SICILIAN €€

(☎0942 2 48 03; Via Cappuccini 1; pizzas €7-14, meals €35; ⏲closed Tue) Known for its excellent pizzas and trademark *tiramisù*, this casual place close to Porta Messina offers indoor and outdoor eating areas and is a good choice for a casual meal.

Information

Tourist Office (☎0942 2 32 43; www.gate2-taormina.com; Piazza Santa Caterina, off Corso Umberto I; ⏲8.30am-2.30pm & 3.30-7pm Mon-Fri year-round, 9am-1pm & 4-6.30pm Sat Apr-Oct)

Getting There & Away

Taormina is best reached by bus. From the bus terminus on Via Pirandello, Interbus serves Messina (€3.90, 1½ hours, seven daily Monday to Saturday, one Sunday) and **Etna Trasporti** (☎095 53 27 16; www.etnatrasporti.it) connects with Catania airport (€7, 1½ hours, five daily Monday to Saturday, three on Sunday).

Mt Etna

The dark silhouette of Mt Etna (3350m) broods ominously over the east coast, more or less halfway between Taormina and Catania. One of Europe's highest and most volatile volcanoes, it erupts frequently, most recently in April 2012.

By public transport the best way to get to the mountain is to take the daily AST bus from Catania (at 8.15am daily, also 11.20am June to September). This departs from in front of the main train station (returning at 4.30pm; €5.60 return) and drops you at the Rifugio Sapienza (1923m), where you can pick up the **Funivia dell'Etna** (☎095 91 41 41; www.funiviaetna.com; cable car one way/return €14.50/27, incl bus & guide €51; ⏲9am-4.30pm) to 2500m. From there buses courier you up to the official crater zone (2920m). If you want to walk, allow up to four hours for the round trip.

Gruppo Guide Alpine Etna Sud (☎095 791 47 55; www.etnaguide.com) is one of hundreds of outfits offering guided tours, typically involving 4WD transport and a guided trek. These cost from €45 per person for a half-day tour and about €60 for a full-day tour.

Further Etna information is available from the **municipal tourist office** (☎095 742 55 73; www.comune.catania.it; Via Vittorio Emanuele II 172; ⏲8.15am-7.15pm Mon-Fri, to 12.15pm Sat) in Catania.

Syracuse

POP 123,900

Syracuse (Siracusa) has a fascinating past. Founded in 734 BC by Corinthian settlers, it became the dominant Greek city state on the Mediterranean and was known as the most beautiful city in the ancient world. After falling to the Romans in 212 BC its power waned, and Palermo took over its role as the island's most important city. A devastating earthquake in 1693 destroyed most of the city's buildings; their replacements, built in the fashionable Sicilian baroque style, remain largely intact and visually resplendent in the streets of Ortigia, the historic centre.

Sights

Ortigia HISTORIC AREA

Connected to the town centre by a bridge, the island of Ortigia is an atmospheric warren of baroque *palazzi,* lively piazzas and busy trattorias. Just off Via Roma, the 7th-century **Duomo** (Piazza del Duomo; ⌚8am-7pm) was built over a pre-existing 5th-century-BC Greek temple, incorporating most of the original columns in its three-aisled structure. Its sumptuous baroque facade was added in the 18th century.

Parco Archaeologico della Neapolis ARCHAEOLOGICAL SITE
(☎0931 6 50 68; Viale Paradis; adult/18-25/under 18 & EU over 65 €10/5/free; ⌚9am-6pm Apr-Oct, to 4pm Nov-Mar) Syracuse's premier attraction is this archaeological park with its 5th-century-BC **Teatro Greco** hewn out of the rock above the city. This theatre staged the last tragedies of Aeschylus, which were first performed here in his presence.

Just beside the theatre is the mysterious **Latomia del Paradiso**, deep, precipitous limestone quarries out of which the stone for the ancient city was extracted.

Back outside this area you'll find the entrance to the 2nd-century-AD **Anfiteatro Romano**, originally used for gladiatorial combats and horse races.

To reach the park from Ortigia, take bus 1, 3 or 12 (€1) from Piazza Poste or head up on foot, it's about a half-hour walk.

Museo Archeologico Paolo Orsi MUSEUM
(☎0931 46 40 22; Viale Teocrito; adult/reduced €8/4; ⌚9am-6pm Tue-Sat, 9am-1pm Sun) About 500m east of the archaeological park, this is an incredibly impressive archaeological museum. A combined ticket covering the museum and the Neapolis costs adult/reduced €13.50/7.

Sleeping

B&B dei Viaggiatori, Viandanti e Sognatori B&B €
(☎0931 2 47 81; www.bedandbreakfastsicily.it; Via Roma 156, Ortigia; s €35-50, d €55-70, tr €75-80; ❄📶) On the 4th floor of an old *palazzo* at the end of Via Roma, this welcoming B&B is run by a young couple who live on site. It offers simple, colourfully decorated rooms and a sunny roof terrace with sweeping sea views. No lift.

Lol Hostel HOSTEL €
(☎0931 46 50 88; www.lolhostel.com; Via Francesco Crispi 94; dm €20-27, d €56-65; ❄@📶) This modern, well-kept hostel near the train stations has six mixed dorms (sleeping eight, 10 and 20) and two doubles. The pleasant common spaces include an open, airy guest kitchen, an outdoor patio and a sprawling lounge. It's 10 minutes on foot to Ortigia, or five minutes with one of the hostel's rental bikes.

Eating

Sicilia in Tavola SICILIAN €
(☎392 461 08 89; Via Cavour 28; pasta €7-12; ⌚closed Mon) There's only a dozen tables available at this popular local eatery specialising in seafood antipasti and homemade pasta dishes, so get here early or be prepared to queue.

Gelati Bianca GELATERIA €
(Via Pompeo Picherali 2; ice cream from €1.80; ⌚daily) It's not just the location off Piazza Duomo that's the attraction here – the house-made gelati is pretty good, too.

Information

The most useful **tourist information office** (☎800 05 55 00; infoturismo@provsr.it; Via Roma 31; ⌚8am-8pm Mon-Sat, 9.15am-6.45pm Sun) is operated by the municipality.

Getting There & Around

Buses are a better bet than trains, serving a terminus close to the train station. Interbus runs services to/from Catania Airport (€6, one hour, hourly Monday to Saturday, six Sunday), Catania (€6, 1¼ hours) and Palermo (€12, 3¼ hours, three daily Monday to Saturday, two Sunday).

Regional trains service Taormina (€8.30, two hours, five daily), Catania (€6.35, 1¼ hours, seven daily) and Messina (€9.70, 2¾ hours, five daily).

A free shuttle bus (No 20) runs between the bus station and Ortigia every 30 minutes from 6.30am to 9.30pm.

Agrigento

POP 59,200

Agrigento was founded around 581 BC by Greek settlers and became an important trading centre under the Romans and Byzantines. These days, the only trading that occurs is around the souvenir stands surrounding one of Italy's most wonderful ancient sights, the Valley of the Temples (Valle dei Templi).

Up in the main town, the tourist information desk in the office of the **Provincia**

Regionale di Agrigento (☎0922 59 32 27; www.provincia.agrigento.it; Piazza Vittorio Emanuele; ⏰8.30am-1pm & 2.30-7pm Mon-Fri, 8.30am-2pm Sat) can supply maps but little else.

Sights

Valley of the Temples ARCHAEOLOGICAL SITE
(Valle dei Templi) One of the most magnificent archaeological sites in Southern Europe, this Unesco-listed complex of temples and old city walls from the ancient city of Akragas dates from 581 BC.

You'll need a full day to do justice to the **Archaeological Park** (☎0922 49 72 26; adult/EU reduced/child €10/5/free; ⏰8.30am-7pm, later in summer), which is divided into eastern and western zones. The most spectacular temples are in the eastern zone. First up is the oldest, the **Tempio di Ercole**, built at the end of the 6th century BC and equivalent in size to the Parthenon. Continuing east, the intact **Tempio della Concordia** was transformed into a Christian church in the 6th century, and the **Tempio di Giunone** boasts an impressive sacrificial altar.

Over the road in the western zone, the 5th-century-BC **Tempio di Giove** originally covered an area of 112m by 56m with 20m-high columns interspersed with *telamoni* (giant male statues), one of which now stands in the valley's **Museo Archeologico** (☎0922 4 01 11; Contrada San Nicola; incl Valley of the Temples adult/EU reduced €13.50/7; ⏰9am-7pm Tue-Sat, 9am-1pm Sun & Mon), north of the temples.

Sleeping

Atenea 191 B&B €
(☎349 59 55 94; www.atenea191.com; Via Atenea 191; s €45-60, d €65-85) Though musty and worn, this B&B on Agrigento's main shopping thoroughfare is open all year and has a breakfast terrace with sweeping views over the valley.

Eating & Drinking

Kalòs MODERN SICILIAN €€
(☎0922 2 63 89; Piazzetta San Calogero; mains €15; ⏰closed Mon) This stylish eatery compensates for bland decor by focusing full attention on its well-prepared fish, meat and pasta.

Mojo Wine Bar WINE BAR
(☎0922 46 30 13; www.mojo4music.it; Piazza San Francesco 11-13; ⏰Mon-Sat) A trendy *enoteca* in a pretty piazza. Enjoy a cool white Inzolia and munch on olives and spicy salami as you listen to some laid-back jazz.

Getting There & Away

The bus is the easiest way to get to and from Agrigento. Intercity buses arrive on Piazzale F Rosselli, from where it's a short walk downhill to the train station on Piazza Gugliemo Marconi, where you can catch local bus 1, 2 or 3 to the Valley of the Temples (€1.10).

Cuffaro runs buses to/from Palermo (€8.70, two hours, nine daily Monday to Saturday, three Sunday) and SAIS services go to Catania (€13, three hours, hourly).

SARDINIA

Celebrated for its spectacular beaches and VIP resorts, Sardinia is far more than it's made out to be. If you can drag yourself away from the gorgeous coastline and stunning beaches, you'll discover a haunting and often spectacular interior of impenetrable granite gorges, forbidding peaks and silent cork forests. Adding a sense of mystery are the 7000 *nuraghi* (circular stone towers) which pepper the landscape, all that's left of Sardinia's prehistoric past.

You can get round Sardinia on public transport, but you'll discover much more with your own wheels.

Getting There & Away

AIR Flights from Italian and European cities serve Sardinia's three airports: **Elmas** (☎070 21 12 11; www.cagliariairport.it) in Cagliari; Alghero's **Fertilia** (☎079 93 52 82; www.aeroporto-dialghero.it); and **Olbia Costa Smeralda** (OLB; ☎0789 56 34 44; www.geasar.it).

BOAT Car and passenger ferries sail year-round from various Italian ports, including Genoa, Livorno, Piombino, Civitavecchia, Naples and Palermo.

Get up-to-date information and book tickets at www.traghettiweb.it.

Cagliari

POP 156,500

Sardinia's capital and most cosmopolitan city, Cagliari rises from the sea in a helter-skelter of golden-hued *palazzi*, domes and facades. Yet for all its splendour, it remains what it always has been – a busy working port with a gritty, down-to-earth atmosphere and a vibrant buzz. With its land mark citadel, great restaurants and popular, sandy beach, Cagliari is very much its own city.

Sights & Activities

Cagliari's sights are concentrated in four central districts: Castello, the medieval citadel that towers over the city; Marina, the bustling seafront area; Stampace, which extends westwards of Largo Carlo Felice, modern Cagliari's showpiece street; and Villanova, east of Castello.

Museo Archeologico Nazionale MUSEUM
(www.archeocaor.beniculturali.it; Piazza dell'Arsenale; adult/reduced €3/1.50; 9am-8pm Tue-Sun) Housed in what was once Cagliari's arsenal, the **Citadella dei Musei** is the city's main museum complex. Of its four museums, the most impressive is the Museo Archeologico Nazionale whose collection of archaeological artefacts includes a number of pint-sized bronze figurines. In the absence of any written records, these provide vital clues into the island's mysterious *nuraghic* culture.

Torre di San Pancrazio TOWER
(Piazza Indipendenza; adult/reduced €4/2.50; 10.30am-7pm Tue-Sun summer, 9am-5pm winter) Guarding the entrance to the Citadella dei Musei, this 36m-high tower was completed in 1305 on the city's highest point. Climb to the top for grandstand views of the Golfo di Cagliari.

Bastione San Remy LOOKOUT
This monumental terrace, formerly a strong point in the defensive walls, affords sweeping views over Cagliari's higgledy-piggledy rooftops and distant lagoons.

Anfiteatro Romano AMPHITHEATRE
(www.anfiteatroromano.it; Viale Sant'Ignazio; closed for restoration) Cagliari's 2nd-century amphitheatre is the most important Roman monument in Sardinia. Summer concerts are staged here.

Spiaggia di Poetto BEACH
A short bus ride from the centre, Cagliari's vibrant beach boasts inviting blue waters and a happening summer bar scene. Take bus PQ or PF.

Festivals & Events

Cagliari's annual bonanza, the **Festa di Sant'Efisio**, involves four days of costumed processions from 1 May.

Sleeping

Hotel A&R Bundes Jack HOTEL €
(070 65 79 70; www.hotelbjvittoria.it; Via Roma 75; s €52-72, d €80-92;) An excellent seafront option, this is an old-fashioned family-run *pensione*. It has spacious, high-ceilinged rooms decorated with solid antique furniture and sparkling chandeliers. Breakfast is not included but is available for €7.

Hostel Marina HOSTEL €
(070 67 08 18; www.hostelmarinacagliari.it; Scalette S Sepolcro; dm/s/d/q €22/40/60/100;)

FERRIES TO SARDINIA

DESTINATION	DEPARTURE POINT	COMPANIES
Civitavecchia	Arbatax	Tirrenia
Civitavecchia	Cagliari	Tirrenia
Civitavecchia	Golfo Aranci	Sardinia Ferries
Civitavecchia	Olbia	Moby Lines, SNAV, Tirrenia
Genoa	Olbia	Grandi Navi Veloci, Moby Lines, Tirrenia
Genoa	Porto Torres	Grandi Navi Veloci, Tirrenia
Livorno	Golfo Aranci	Sardinia Ferries
Livorno	Olbia	Moby Lines)
Naples	Cagliari	Tirrenia
Palermo	Cagliari	Tirrenia
Piombino	Golfo Aranc	Sardinia Ferries
Piombino	Olbia	Moby Lines

This central hostel, housed in a beautifully converted 800-year-old former monastery, has oodles of historic charm and a wide range of accommodation, from single-sex six-person dorms to private rooms with en suite bathrooms.

Eating

Il Fantasma PIZZERIA €
(☎070 65 67 49; Via San Domenico 94; pizzas €3-10; ⏰Mon-Sat) A five-minute walk east of Piazza Martiri d'Italia, this unpretentious pizzeria prepares some of the best pizza in town. Grab a table in the barrel-vaulted interior and bite into classic pizzas served blisteringly hot from the wood-fired oven. Bookings recommended.

Sa Schironada TRATTORIA €
(☎070 451 07 71; Via Baylle 39; set menus €13-38, pizza & drink €10) A big, barnlike trattoria good for a cheap, tasty fill-up. There are several menu options but take it easy when you order, as the portions are huge and the antipasto is a minor meal in itself.

Information

Tourist Information Points (☎070 677 71 87; www.infopointcagliari.it; ⏰8am-8pm) The most useful information points are at Piazza Indipendenza, near the Torre di San Pancrazio, and at Piazza Costituzione, under Bastione San Remy.

Getting There & Away

AIR Flights from mainland Italy and European cities serve Elmas airport (p698), 6km northwest of the city. Half-hourly **ARST** (☎800 86 50 42; www.arst.sardegna.it) buses connect the airport with the bus station on Piazza Matteotti; the 10-minute journey costs €4.

BOAT Cagliari's ferry port is just off Via Roma. **Tirrenia** (☎892 123; www.tirrenia.it; Via dei Ponente 1) is the main ferry operator, with year-round services to Civitavecchia (from €58, 16½ hours), Naples (from €47, 16¼ hours) and Palermo (from €45, 14½ hours).

BUS From the bus station on Piazza Matteotti, daily **ARST** (☎800 865 042; www.arst.sardegna.it) buses serve Oristano (€7, 1½ hours, two daily) and Nuoro (€15.50, 3½ hours, two daily), as well as destinations on the Costa del Sud and Costa Rei. Get tickets from the McDonald's on the square.

Turmo Travel (☎0789 2 14 87; www.gruppoturmotravel.com) runs a daily bus to Olbia (€19, 4¼ hours).

CAR & MOTORCYCLE Down by the port, you can rent cars, bikes and scooters at **CIA Rent a Car** (☎070 65 65 03; www.rentcagliari.com; Via S Agostino 13). Bank on from €38 per day for a small car.

Alghero

POP 40,700

A picturesque medieval town, Alghero is the main resort on Sardinia's northwest coast. Interest is centred on the *centro storico,* a small tangle of tight-knit lanes and busy piazzas enclosed by robust honey-coloured sea walls.

The town was founded in the 11th century by the Genovese and later became an important outpost of the Aragonese Catalans. Still today the local dialect is a form of Catalan and the town retains something of a Spanish atmosphere.

Sights & Activities

If you're in town for a few days, consider the **A-ticket** (1 adult & 1 child €20, 2 adults & 2 children €40), a discount card that covers admission to the Grotta di Nettuno, Nuraghe di Palmavera and various museums. It's available at the tourist office and participating sites.

Centro Storico HISTORIC NEIGHBOURHOOD
Alghero's medieval core is a charming mesh of narrow cobbled alleys hemmed in by Spanish Gothic *palazzi.* Of the various churches, the most interesting is the **Chiesa di San Francesco** (Via Carlo Alberto), with its mix of Romanesque and Gothic styles. A short walk away, the **campanile** (bell tower; ☎079 973 30 41; Via Principe Umberto; adult/child €2/free; ⏰10.30am-12.30pm Mon-Fri, 7-9pm Mon & Fri Jun-Aug, 10.30am-12.30pm Mon, Tue, Thu, Fri, 4-6pm Mon & Fri Sep & Oct, on request Nov-May) of the **Cattedrale di Santa Maria** (Piazza Duomo; ⏰7am-noon & 5-7.30pm) is a fine example of Gothic-Catalan architecture.

For lovely sea views, walk the town's honey-coloured ramparts from Piazza Sulis to the **Bastioni della Maddalena**, the only remnant of the town's former land battlements.

Grotta di Nettuno CAVE
(☎079 94 65 40; adult/child €13/7; ⏰9am-7pm May-Sep, to 6pm Apr-Oct, to 3pm Nov-Mar) From the port you can take a boat trip along the impressive north coast to the Grotte di Nettuno cave complex. The cheapest boat is the Navisarda ferry (return €15), which departs hourly between 9.30am and 5.30pm from June to September, and twice daily between March and May, and in October. Cheape

still, you can get a bus to the caves from Via Catalogna (€4.50 return, 50 minutes, three times daily summer, once daily winter).

Nuraghe di Palmavera RUIN
(admission €3; ⏲9am-7pm May-Sep, to 6pm Apr & Oct, 10am-2pm Nov-Mar) Ten kilometres west of Alghero, this 3500-year-old *nuraghe* village is well worth a visit.

Sleeping

There's plenty of accommodation in Alghero but you'll need to book between June and September.

Hotel San Francesco HOTEL €
(☎079 98 03 30; www.sanfrancescohotel.com; Via Ambrogio Machin 2; s €52-63, d €82-101, tr €110-135; ❄@📶) This welcoming three-star is the only hotel in Alghero's *centro storico*. Housed in an ex-convent – monks still live on the 3rd floor – it has modest, comfortable rooms set around an attractive 14th-century cloister where summer concerts are sometimes staged.

Hostal de l'Alguer HOSTEL €
(☎079 93 04 78; www.alguerohostel.com; Via Parenzo 79; dm €18-20, d €52, q €104; P@) Near a beach about 6km north of Alghero in Fertilia, this HI hostel is clean, friendly and fairly characterless with dorms and private rooms in eight accommodation blocks. Hourly buses run to Fertilia from Via Cagliari in Alghero.

Eating

Angedras Restaurant SARDINIAN €€
(☎079 973 50 78; www.angedrasrestaurant.it; Bastioni Marco Polo 41; mains €14, lunch menu €16) Alghero's sea-facing ramparts set a memorable stage for alfresco dining. This is one of the better restaurants on the walls, serving a largely regional menu of pasta, meat and elegantly presented seafood.

Gelateria I Bastioni GELATERIA €
(Bastioni Marco Polo 5; cones €1-3, milkshakes €3.50, granite €2.50; ⏲Apr-Oct) Homemade ice creams, creamy milkshakes, lush smoothies and cooling *granite* – this hole-in-the-wall gem does the lot. Particularly fab are the fresh fruit flavours, ideally topped by a generous squirt of whipped cream.

Il Ghiotto FAST FOOD €
(☎079 97 48 20; Piazza Civica 23; mains €5-11) Part bar, part canteen, part shop, the Ghiotto is ideal for a cheap and cheerful fill-up. Grab a tray and stock up from the tantalising spread of panini, pastas, salads and main courses. There's seating in a dining area behind the main hall or outside on a busy wooden terrace.

Information

On the eastern fringe of the *centro storico*, the superhelpful **tourist office** (☎079 97 90 54; www.alghero-turismo.it; Piazza Porta Terra 9; ⏲8am-8pm, closed Sun winter) can answer every imaginable question.

Getting There & Around

Alghero's **Fertilia airport** (☎079 93 52 82; www.aeroportodialghero.it) is used by a number of low-cost carriers, with connections to mainland Italy and destinations across Europe. To get into town take the hourly bus (€1, €1.50 on board, 20 minutes) to the bus terminus on Via Cagliari.

In town you can walk most places, but for the beach, local bus AF runs along the seafront to/from Via Cagliari.

UNDERSTAND ITALY

History

The Etruscans were the first major force to emerge on the Italian peninsula. By the 7th century BC they dominated central Italy, rivalled only by the Greeks from the southern colony of Magna Graecia. Both groups thrived until the 3rd century BC when legionnaires from the emerging city of Rome began to expand their territory and power.

Rome, founded in the 8th century BC (legend has it by Romulus), became a republic in 509 BC. Expansion followed and by the turn of the millennium Rome ruled much of western Europe and the Mediterranean. After Caesar's assassination in 44 BC, his great-nephew Octavian defeated rivals Mark Antony and Cleopatra and took the top job as Augustus Caesar, the first Roman emperor.

The empire's golden age came in the 2nd century AD, but a century later it was in decline. Diocletian split the empire into eastern and western halves, and when his successor, Constantine (the first Christian emperor), moved his court to Constantinople, Rome's days were numbered. In 476 the western empire fell to invading Germanic tribes.

The Middle Ages witnessed the development of Italy's powerful city-states, particularly in the centre and north. Of these, Florence under the Medici made the biggest impact, giving rise to the 15th-century Renaissance.

By the early 16th century much of Italy was in foreign hands – the Austrian Habsburgs in the north and the Spanish Bourbons in the south. Not much changed until the mid-19th century when the Risorgimento (unification movement) culminated in the 1861 unification of Italy.

The 20th Century

Italy's brief fascist interlude was a low point. Mussolini gained power in 1925 and in 1940 entered WWII on Germany's side. Defeat ensued and Il Duce was killed by partisans in April 1945.

Italy's postwar era has been largely successful. A founding member of the European Economic Community, it survived a period of domestic terrorism in the 1970s and enjoyed sustained economic growth in the 1980s. But the 1990s heralded a period of crisis as corruption scandals rocked the nation, paving the way for billionaire media mogul Silvio Berlusconi to enter the political arena.

Italy Today

A controversial and deeply divisive figure, Berlusconi has dominated Italian public life since his first foray into government in 1994. He served three terms as prime minister, the last ending in November 2011 when he was forced from office amid a severe economic downturn. Economist Mario Monti took over as prime minister and committed to an agenda of economic reform, but his tenure was built on an unstable alliance with Berlusconi's People of Freedom (PDL) party. Elections in February 2013 saw Berlusconi's bid to regain overall power fail, but the outcome was far from decisive, with the centre-left Democratic Party (PD) gaining a majority in the lower house, the PDL gaining a majority in the upper house, and the maverick Five Star Movement led by satirist Beppe Grillo gaining the highest overall vote (25.5%). After a two-month stalemate, the PD and PDL formed an uneasy parliamentary alliance, installing the PD's Enrico Letta as prime minister and Angelino Alfano from the PDL as deputy prime minister.

People

With a population of 60.62 million, Italy is Europe's fourth-most populous country. Almost half of all Italians live in the industrialised north and one in five is aged over 65. Italy has one of the world's lowest birth rates and were it not for immigration, its population would be in decline.

Traditionally, Italians are very conscious of their regional identity and very family oriented. Times are changing but it's still common for Italian children to remain at home until they marry.

Up to 80% of Italians consider themselves Catholic, although only about one in three regularly attends church. Similarly, the Vatican remains a powerful voice in national debate, but can't find enough priests for its parish churches. Still, first Communions, church weddings and regular feast days remain an integral part of Italian life.

Arts

Literature

Italian literature runs the gamut from Virgil's *Aeneid* to the chilling WWII stories of Primo Levi, the fantastical writings of Italo Calvini and the powerful contemporary writing of Niccolò Ammaniti, author of *Io non ho paura* (I'm Not Scared; 2001).

Dante, whose *Divina commedia* (Divine Comedy) dates to the early 1300s, was one of three 14th-century greats alongside Petrarch and Giovanni Boccaccio. The latter is considered the first Italian novelist.

Italy's southern regions provide rich literary pickings. Giuseppe Tomasi di Lampedusa depicted Sicily's melancholic resignation in *Il gattopardo* (The Leopard; 1958), a theme that Leonardo Sciascia later returns to in *Il giorno della civetta* (The Day of the Owl; 1961). Carlo Levi denounced southern poverty in *Cristo si é fermato a Eboli* (Christ Stopped at Eboli; 1945), an account of his internal exile under the Fascists, and more recently, Andrea Camilleri's Sicilian-based Montalbano detective stories have enjoyed great success. *The Shape of Water* (1994) is the first title in the series.

Cinema

Italy has won more Academy Awards for Best Foreign Language Film than any other country. Many of the winning films were made during the post-WWII period, when the neo-realists Vittorio de Sica and Roberto Rossellini created masterpieces such as *Ladri di biciclette* (Bicycle Thieves; 1948) and *Roma città aperta* (Rome Open City; 1945). Taking a decidedly different turn, Federico Fellini won an international audience with films such as *La dolce vita* (The Sweet Life; 1959).

Of Italy's contemporary directors, Roberto Benigni won an Oscar for *La vita è bella* (Life is Beautiful; 1997), Nanni Moretti won Cannes' Palme D'Or for *La stanza del figlio* (The Son's Room; 2001) and Paolo and Vittorio Taviani won Berlin's Golden Bear for *Cesare deve morire* (Caesar Must Die; 2012).

Music

Emotional and highly theatrical, opera has always appealed to Italians. Performances of Verdi and Puccini are regularly staged at legendary venues such as Milan's Teatro all Scala and Naples' Teatro San Carlo.

Architecture & Visual Arts

Italy is littered with architectural and artistic reminders of its convoluted history. Etruscan tombs and Greek temples tell of glories long past, Pompeii's skeletal ruins offer insights into the day-to-day life of the ancient Romans, and Byzantine mosaics reveal influences sweeping in from the East.

The Renaissance left an indelible mark, particularly in Florence and Rome. This was the period when Filippo Brunelleschi designed the huge dome atop Florence's Duomo and Michelangelo Buonarrotti decorated the Sistine Chapel. Contemporaries Leonardo da Vinci and Raphael further brightened the scene.

Controversial and highly influential, Michelangelo Merisi da Caravaggio dominated the late 16th century with his revolutionary use of light. He painted in Rome and in the south of the country, where the baroque style of art and architecture became prominent in the 17th century.

Signalling a return to sober classical lines, neoclassicism majored in the late 18th and early 19th centuries. Its most famous Italian exponent was Canova, who carved a name for himself with his smooth sensual style.

In sharp contrast to backward-looking neoclassicism, Italian futurism provided a rallying cry for modernism, with Giacomo Balla proving hugely influential.

Continuing in this modernist tradition are Italy's two superstar architects: Renzo Piano, the visionary behind Rome's Auditorium, and Rome-born Massimiliano Fuksas.

Environment

Bound on three sides by four seas (the Adriatic, Ligurian, Tyrrhenian and Ionian), Italy has more than 8000km of coastline. Inland, about 75% of the peninsula is mountainous – the Alps curve around the northern border and the Apennines extend down the 'boot'.

Italy has 24 national parks, covering about 5% of the country; and more than 400 nature reserves, natural parks and wetlands. It also boasts 47 Unesco World Heritage sites, more than any other country in the world.

But Italy is not without its environmental problems, of which the most insidious are air pollution, waste disposal and coastal development

Food & Drink

Despite the ubiquity of pasta and pizza, Italian cuisine is highly regional. Local specialities abound and regional traditions are proudly maintained, so expect pesto in Genoa, pizza in Naples and *ragù* (bolognese

EARTHQUAKES & VOLCANOES

Italy is one of the world's most earthquake-prone countries. A fault line runs through the entire peninsula from eastern Sicily, up the Apennines and into the northeastern Alps. The country is usually hit by minor quakes several times a year and devastating earthquakes are not uncommon. Most recently, in May 2012, the region of Emilia-Romagna was hit by two quakes measuring 6 and 5.8 on the Richter scale. Twenty-seven people were killed and 45,000 were forced to flee their homes. Damage was estimated at more than €13 billion.

Italy also has six active volcanoes: Stromboli and Vulcano on the Aeolian Islands; Vesuvius, the Campi Flegrei and the island of Ischia near Naples; and Etna on Sicily. Stromboli and Etna are among the world's most active volcanoes, while Vesuvius has not erupted since 1944.

EAT LIKE AN ITALIAN

A full Italian meal consists of an antipasto, a *primo* (first course; pasta or rice dish), *secondo* (second/main course; usually meat or fish) with an *insalata* (salad) or *contorno* (vegetable side dish), *dolci* (dessert) and coffee. Most Italians only eat a meal this large at Sunday lunch or for a special occasion, and when eating out it's fine to mix and match and order, say, a *primo* followed by an *insalata* or *contorno*.

To breakfast like the locals, have *colazione* (breakfast) – typically a *caffè* (espresso) or cappuccino and *cornetto* (pastry filled with custard, chocolate or jam) – standing at a bar.

Italians are late diners, often not eating until after 9pm.

sauce) in Bologna. It's the same with wine – Piedmont produces Italy's great reds, Barolo, Barbaresco and Dolcetto, while Tuscany is famous for its Chianti, Vino Nobile di Montepulciano, Brunello di Montalcino and Vernaccia di San Gimignano.

Eating out is one of the great pleasures of travelling in Italy. The most basic sit-down eatery is a *tavola calda* (literally 'hot table'), which offers canteen-style food. Pizzerias, the best of which have a *forno a legna* (wood-fired oven), often serve a full menu as well as pizzas. For takeaway, a *rosticceria* sells cooked meats, and a *pizza al taglio* joint sells pizza by the slice. Most bars and cafes serve ready-made *tramezzini* (sandwiches) and panini (bread rolls), and you can have panini made for you in an *alimentari* (delicatessen).

Vegetarians will find delicious fruit and veg in the hundreds of daily markets, and although few restaurants cater specifically to vegetarians, most serve vegetable-based antipasti (starters), pastas, *contorni* (side dishes) and salads.

SURVIVAL GUIDE

Directory A–Z

Accommodation

The bulk of Italy's accommodation is made up of *alberghi* (hotels) and *pensioni*. Other options are youth hostels, camping grounds, B&Bs, *agriturismi* (farm-stays), mountain *rifugi* (Alpine refuges), monasteries and villa/apartment rentals.

Prices fluctuate enormously between seasons. High-season rates apply at Easter, in summer (mid-June to August), and over the Christmas to New Year period.

Many city-centre hotels offer discounts in August to lure clients from the crowded coast. Check hotel websites for last-minute offers.

Many hotels in coastal resorts shut for winter, typically from November to March. The same applies to *agriturismi* and villa rentals in rural areas.

In this chapter prices quoted are the minimum to maximum for rooms with a private bathroom, and unless otherwise stated include breakfast. The following price indicators apply (for a high-season double room):

€ less than €110

€€ €110 to €200

€€€ more than €200

B&BS

Quality varies, but the best offer comfort greater than you'd get in a similarly priced hotel room.

Prices are typically €70 to €180 for a double room.

CAMPING

Lists of camping grounds are available from local tourist offices or online at www.campeggi.com, www.camping.it and www.italcamping.it.

In high season expect to pay up to €20 per person and a further €25 for a tent pitch.

Independent camping is not permitted in many places.

CONVENTS & MONASTERIES

Basic accommodation is often available in convents and monasteries. See www.monasterystays.com, a specialist online booking service.

FARM-STAYS

An *agriturismo* (farm-stay) is a good option for a country stay, although you will usually need your own transport to access these.

Accommodation varies from spartan billets on working farms to palatial suites at luxurious rural retreats.

For information and lists check out www.agriturist.it or www.agriturismo.com.

HOSTELS

Official HI-affiliated *ostelli per la gioventù* (youth hostels) are run by the **Italian Youth Hostel Association** (Associazione Italiana Alberghi per la Gioventù; Map p636; ☎06 487 11 52; www.aighostels.com; Via Cavour 44). A valid HI card is required for these; you can get one in your home country or directly at hostels.

There are many privately run hostels offering dorms and private rooms.

Dorm rates are typically between €15 and €30, with breakfast usually included.

Activities

Cycling Tourist offices can provide details on trails and guided rides. The best time is spring. Lonely Planet's *Cycling in Italy* offers practical tips and several detailed itineraries.

Hiking & Walking Thousands of kilometres of *sentieri* (marked trails) criss-cross the country. The hiking season is from June to September. Useful websites include www.cai.it and www.parks.it. Lonely Planet's *Hiking in Italy* includes descriptions of 59 hikes.

Skiing Italy's ski season runs from December through to March. Prices are generally high, particularly in the top Alpine resorts – the Apennines are cheaper. The best way to save money is to buy a *settimana bianca* (literally 'white week') package deal, covering seven days' accommodation, food and ski passes.

Business Hours

Banks 8.30am to 1.30pm and 3pm to 4.30pm Monday to Friday

Bars & Cafes 7.30am to 8pm; many open earlier and some stay open until the small hours; pubs often open noon to 2am

Discos & Clubs 10pm to 4am

Museums & Galleries Many museums, galleries and archaeological sites operate summer and winter opening hours. Typically, winter hours will apply between November and late March or early April.

Pharmacies 9am to 1pm and 4pm to 7.30pm Monday to Friday, to 1pm Saturday; outside of these hours, pharmacies open on a rotation basis – all are required to post a list of places open in the vicinity

Post offices Major offices 8am to 7pm Monday to Friday, to 1.15pm Saturday; branch offices 8.30am to 2pm Monday to Friday, to 1pm Saturday

Restaurants Noon to 3pm and 7.30pm to 11pm or midnight; most restaurants close one day a week

Shops 9am to 1pm and 3.30pm to 7.30pm, or 4pm to 8pm Monday to Saturday; in larger cities many chain stores and supermarkets open from 9am to 7.30pm Monday to Saturday; some also open Sunday morning, typically 9am to 1pm; food shops are generally closed Thursday afternoon; some other shops are closed Monday morning.

Embassies & Consultes

The following embassies are based in Rome.

Australian Embassy (☎06 85 27 21; www.italy.embassy.gov.au; Via Antonio Bosio 5)

New Zealand Embassy (☎06 853 75 01; www.nzembassy.com; Via Clitunno 44)

UK Embassy (☎06 422 00 001; Via XX Settembre 80a)

US Embassy (☎06 4 67 41; http://italy.usembassy.gov; Via Vittorio Veneto 121)

Food

Throughout this chapter, the following price indicators have been used (prices refer to the cost of a main course):

€ less than €10

€€ €10 to €18

€€€ more than €18

Restaurants, all of which are nonsmoking, usually open for lunch from noon to 3pm

HOTEL TAX

Since early 2011 many Italian cities, including Rome, Florence and Venice, have introduced a hotel occupancy tax *(tassa di soggiorno)*. This is charged on top of your regular hotel bill and must sometimes be paid in cash. The exact amount, which varies from city to city, depends on your type of accommodation, but as a rough guide expect to pay €1 per night in a one-star hotel or hostel, €2 in a B&B, €2 to €3 in a three-star hotel etc.

Prices quoted in this book do not include the tax.

and for dinner from 7.30pm, earlier in tourist areas.

On the bill expect to be charged for *pane e coperto* (bread and a cover charge). This is standard and is added even if you don't ask for or eat the bread. Typically it ranges from €1 to €4. *Servizio* (service charge) of 10% to 15% might or might not be included; if it's not, tourists are expected to leave around 10%.

Gay & Lesbian Travellers

Homosexuality is legal in Italy, but same-sex couples have no shared rights to property, social security and inheritance. There is a push to legalise gay marriage, but this seems unlikely in the near future. Homosexuality is well tolerated in major cities but overt displays of affection could attract a negative response, particularly in small towns and in the more conservative south.

Italy's main gay and lesbian organisation is **Arcigay** (www.arcigay.it), based in Bologna.

Internet Access

» Most hotels, hostels, B&Bs and *pensioni* offer wi-fi, either free or for a small charge.

» Access is also available in internet cafes throughout the country, although many have closed in recent years. Charges are typically around €5 per hour.

» To use internet points in Italy you must present photo ID.

Money

» Italy uses the euro.

» ATMs, known as *bancomat*, are widespread and will accept cards displaying the appropriate sign. Visa and MasterCard are widely recognised, as are Cirrus and Maestro; American Express is less common. If you don't have a PIN, some, but not all, banks will advance cash over the counter.

» Credit cards are widely accepted – American Express less than Visa and MasterCard – although many trattorias, pizzerias and *pensioni* only take cash. Don't assume museums, galleries and the like will accept credit cards.

» If your credit/debit card is lost, stolen or swallowed by an ATM, telephone toll-free to block it: **Amex** (☎06 7 22 82 or your national call number); **MasterCard** (☎800 870866); **Visa** (☎800 819014).

ADMISSION PRICES

EU citizens aged between 18 and 25 years and students from countries with reciprocal arrangements generally qualify for a discount (usually half-price) at galleries and museums. To get it, you'll need proof of your age, ideally a passport or ID card.

Post

Italy's postal system, **Poste Italiane** (☎803 160; www.poste.it), is reasonably reliable.

Francobolli (stamps) are available at post offices and *tabacchi* (tobacconists) – look for a big white 'T' against a blue/black background. Tobacconists keep regular shop hours.

Public Holidays

Most Italians take their annual holiday in August. This means that many businesses and shops close down for at least a part of the month, usually around Ferragosto (15 August). Easter is another busy holiday.

Public holidays are listed below:

New Year's Day (Capodanno) 1 January

Epiphany (Epifania) 6 January

Easter Monday (Pasquetta) March/April

Liberation Day (Giorno delle Liberazione) 25 April

Labour Day (Festa del Lavoro) 1 May

Republic Day (Festa della Repubblica) 2 June

Feast of the Assumption (Ferragosto) 15 August

All Saints' Day (Ognisanti) 1 November

Feast of the Immaculate Conception (Immacolata Concezione) 8 December

Christmas Day (Natale) 25 December

Boxing Day (Festa di Santo Stefano) 26 December

Individual towns also have holidays to celebrate their patron saints:

St Mark (Venice) 25 April

St John the Baptist (Florence, Genoa and Turin) 24 June

Sts Peter and Paul (Rome) 29 June

St Rosalia (Palermo) 15 July

St Janarius (Naples) First Sunday in May, 19 September and 16 December

St Ambrose (Milan) 7 December

Safe Travel

Petty theft is prevalent in Italy. Be on your guard against pickpockets and moped thieves in popular tourist centres such as Rome, Florence, Venice and Naples.

Don't take it for granted that cars will stop at red lights.

Telephone

» Area codes are an integral part of all Italian phone numbers and must be dialled even when calling locally.

» To call Italy from abroad, dial ☎0039 and then the area code, including the first zero.

» To call abroad from Italy, dial ☎00, then the relevant country code followed by the telephone number.

» You'll find cut-price call centres in all of the main cities. For international calls, their rates are often cheaper than payphones'.

» To call from a public payphone you'll need a *scheda telefonica* (phone card), available from *tabacchi*.

» Skype is available in many internet cafes and on hostel computers.

MOBILE PHONES

» Italy uses the GSM 900/1800 network, which is compatible with the rest of Europe and Australia, but not with the North American GSM 1900 or the Japanese system (although some GSM 1900/900 phones do work here).

» If you have a GSM dual- or tri-band cellular phone that you can unlock (check with your service provider), you can buy a *prepagato* (prepaid) SIM card in Italy.

» Companies offering SIM cards include **TIM** (Telecom Italia Mobile; www.tim.it), **Wind** (www.wind.it) and **Vodafone** (www.vodafone.it). You'll need ID to open an account.

Visas

» Schengen visa rules apply for entry to Italy.

» Unless staying in a hotel/B&B/hostel etc, all foreign visitors are supposed to register with the local police within eight days of arrival.

» A *permesso di soggiorno* (permit to stay) is required by all non-EU nationals who stay in Italy longer than three months. You must apply within eight days of arriving in Italy. Check the exact documentary requirements on www.poliziadistato.it.

» EU citizens do not require a *permesso di soggiorno*.

Getting There & Away

Getting to Italy is straightforward. It is well served by Europe's low-cost carriers and there are plenty of bus, train and ferry routes into the country. Flights, tours and rail tickets can be booked online at lonelyplanet.com/bookings.

Air

There are direct intercontinental flights to/from Rome and Milan. European flights also serve regional airports.

Italy's main international airports are listed below:

Rome Leonardo da Vinci (☎06 6 59 51; www.adr.it/fiumicino) Italy's main airport, also known as Fiumicino.

Rome Ciampino (☎06 6 59 51; www.adr.it/ciampino) Rome's second airport. Hub for Ryanair flights.

Catania Fontanarossa (☎095 723 91 11; www.aeroporto.catania.it) Sicily's busiest airport.

Milan Malpensa (☎02 23 23 23; www.milanomalpensa1.eu/it) Milan's principal airport.

Naples Capodichino (☎081 789 61 11; www.gesac.it)

Pisa International Airport Galileo Galilei (☎050 84 93 00, www.pisa-airport.com; Piazzale D'Ascanio) Main gateway for Florence and Tuscany.

Venice Marco Polo (☎041 260 92 60; www.veniceairport.it)

Italy's national carrier is **Alitalia** (☎89 20 10; www.alitalia.com).

Land

BUS

Eurolines (www.eurolines.com) operates buses from European destinations to many Italian cities.

TRAIN

International trains connect with various cities:

Milan To/from Paris, Basel, Geneva, Zürich and Vienna.

Rome To/from Munich and Vienna.

Venice To/from Paris, Munich, Basel, Geneva, Lucerne and Vienna.

FERRIES FROM ITALY

DESTINATION	DEPARTURE POINT	COMPANY	PRICE (€)	DURATION (HR)
Barcelona (Spain)	Genoa	GNV, SNAV	95	19½
Corfu (Greece)	Brindisi	Endeavor, Agoudimos	48-83	6½-11½
Dubrovnik (Croatia)	Bari	Jadrolinija	46-63	10-12
Igoumenitsa (Greece)	Ancona	Minoan, Superfast	75-111	16
Igoumenitsa (Greece)	Bari	Superfast	78-93	8-12
Igoumenitsa (Greece)	Brindisi	Endeavor, Agoudimos	48-83	8
Kefallonia (Greece)	Brindisi	Endeavor	56-94	12½
Patra (Greece)	Ancona	Minoan, Superfast	75-111	15½-22
Patra (Greece)	Bari	Superfast	78-93	16
Patra (Greece)	Brindisi	Endeavor	56-94	14
Split (Croatia)	Ancona	Jadrolinija, SNAV	46-63	4½-11
Tunis (Tunisia)	Genoa	GNV, SNAV	99	23½

There are also international trains from Genoa, Turin, Verona, Padua, Bologna, Florence and Naples. Get details at www.trenitalia.com.

In the UK, the **Rail Europe Travel Centre** (www.raileurope.co.uk) can provide fare information on journeys to/from Italy, most of which require a change at Paris. Another excellent resource is www.seat61.com. Eurail and InterRail passes are both valid in Italy.

Sea

Ferries serve Italy's main international ferry ports – Ancona, Bari, Brindisi, Genoa and Venice – from Albania, Corsica, Croatia, Greece, Malta, Spain and Tunisia. Timetables are seasonal, so always check ahead; you'll find details of routes, companies and online booking at www.traghettiweb.it.

Prices quoted in this chapter are for a one-way *poltrona* (reclinable seat).

Holders of Eurail and InterRail passes should check with the ferry company if they are entitled to a discount or free passage.

Getting Around

Bicycle

» Tourist offices can generally provide details of designated bike trails and bike hire (at least €10 per day).

» Bikes can be taken on regional and international trains carrying the bike logo, but you'll need to pay a supplement (€3.50 on regional trains, €12 on international trains). Bikes can be carried free if dismantled and stored in a bike bag.

» Bikes generally incur a small supplement on ferries, typically €10 to €15.

Boat

Navi (large ferries) service Sicily and Sardinia; *traghetti* (smaller ferries) and *aliscafi* (hydrofoils) cover the smaller islands.

The main embarkation points for Sardinia are Genoa, Piombino, Livorno, Civitavecchia and Naples; for Sicily, it's Naples and Villa San Giovanni in Calabria.

The major domestic ferry companies:

Grandi Navi Veloci (☎010 209 45 91; www.gnv.it) To/from Sardinia and Sicily.

Moby (☎199 30 30 40; www.mobylines.it) To/from Sardinia and Sicily.

Sardinia Ferries (☎199 40 05 00; www.corsica-ferries.it) To/from Golfo Aranci (Sardinia).

SNAV (☎Ancona 071 207 61, Naples 081 428 55 55; www.snav.it) To/from Sardinia, Sicily, Aeolian Islands and Capri.

Tirrenia (☎89 21 23; www.tirrenia.it) To/from Sardinia and Sicily.

Bus

» Italy boasts an extensive and largely reliable bus network.

» Buses are not necessarily cheaper than trains, but in mountainous areas they are often the only choice.
» In larger cities, companies have ticket offices or operate through agencies but in most villages and small towns tickets are sold in bars or on the bus.
» Reservations are only necessary for high-season long-haul trips.

Car & Motorcycle

» All EU driving licences are recognised in Italy. Holders of non-EU licences must get an International Driving Permit (IDP) to accompany their national licence.
» Many cities have traffic restrictions in their historical centres, although these don't apply to mopeds or scooters.
» To hire a car you'll require a valid driving licence (plus IDP if necessary) and credit card. Age restrictions vary but generally you'll need to be 21 or over. If driving your own car, carry proof of ownership and an international insurance certificate, known as a Carta Verde (Green Card), available from your insurance company.
» Cars use unleaded petrol *(benzina senza piombo)* and diesel *(gasolio)*; both are expensive but diesel is slightly cheaper.
» Wearing a helmet is compulsory on all two-wheeled vehicles.
» Italy's motoring organisation **Automobile Club d'Italia** (ACI; www.aci.it; Via Colombo 261) provides 24-hour roadside assistance; call ☎803 116 from a landline or Italian mobile, ☎800 116 800 from a foreign mobile.

Train

Italy has an extensive rail network. Trains are relatively cheap, and many are fast and comfortable. Most services are run by **Trenitalia** (☎89 20 21; www.trenitalia.com) but the new **Italo Treno** (www.italotreno.it) high-speed trains also connect Salerno, Naples, Rome, Florence, Bologna, Milan, Turin, Padua and Venice.

There are several types of train:

Frecciarossa Italy's fastest trains capable of 360km/h.

Frecciargento Slightly quicker than the Frecciabianca with a top speed of 250km/h.

Frecciabianca High-speed trains that run up to 200km/h.

Eurostar (ES) Similar to InterCity but faster.

InterCity (IC) Trains between major cities.

Regionale or interregionale (R) Slow local services.

TICKETS

» Train prices quoted here are for the most common trains on any given route – that might be a slow Regionale train or a fast Frecciarossa.
» Regional trains are the cheapest.
» InterCity trains require a supplement, which is incorporated in the ticket price. If you have a standard ticket and board an InterCity you'll have to pay the difference on board.
» Eurostar and the Freccia trains require prior reservation.
» Generally, it's cheaper to buy all local train tickets in Italy.
» If your ticket doesn't include a reservation with an assigned seat, you must validate it before boarding by inserting it into one of the machines dotted around stations.
» Some services offer 'ticketless' travel; book and pay for your seat on www.trenitalia.com and then communicate your booking code to the controller on board.

Kosovo

Includes »

Pristina 712
Peja (Peć) 713
Prizren 714
Understand Kosovo 714
Survival Guide 714

Best Places to Stay & Eat

» Tiffany (p713)

» Home Bar & Restaurant (p713)

» Dukagjini Hotel (p713)

» Hotel Prizreni (p714)

Best Websites

» **UN Mission in Kosovo Online** (www.unmikonline.org)

» **In Your Pocket** (www.inyourpocket.com/kosovo)

Why Go?

Everyone loves a newborn, and since 2008, when Kosovo declared independence, large letters spelling 'NEWBORN' in English have graced a section of pavement in central Pristina. The location, between the secure offices of the UN and a shopping mall featuring ubiquitous European clothing stores and a sky-clawing, crumbling concrete monument, tells it all. Kosovo is finding its feet.

Barbs of its past are impossible to miss however: roads are dotted with memorials featuring etchings of those killed in 1999, when Serbia stripped Kosovo of its autonomy and initiated ethnic cleansing. Kosovo's modern architectural standouts may stand out for all the wrong reasons, but what the rebuilt country lacks in style, it makes up for with its mountain-backed towns, hiking opportunities and 13th-century Serbian monasteries, all no more than a couple of hours' drive from its capital.

When to Go

Pristina

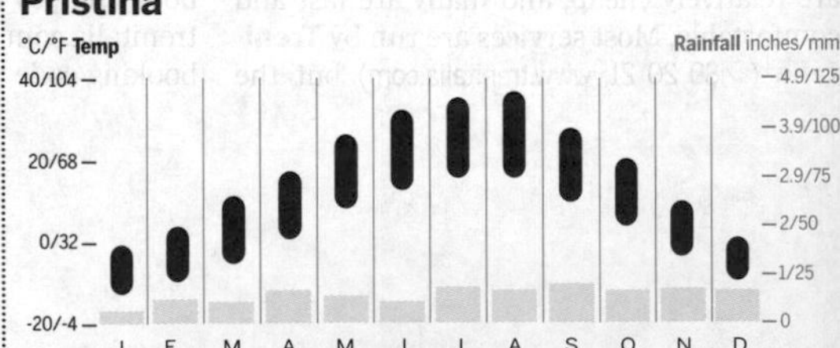

Dec–Apr The skiing's good in these months.

Jul The Shqip film fest brings short films to Peja.

Aug It's a sweat-free summer as temperatures hover around 25°C.

Kosovo Highlights

1. See the sights in **Pristina** (p712) and discover this bustling new capital
2. Buy local wine and cheese at the serene 14th-century **Visoki Dečani Monastery** (p714)
3. Wander the picturesque streets of **Prizren's** (p714) charming Old Town
4. Trek around the **Rugova mountains** (p713)

PRISTINA

☎038 / POP 198,000

Pristina is a city changing fast and one that feels full of the optimism and potential that you'd expect from Europe's newest capital city. It has an international vibe and a 'new-born' feel.

Sights

Ethnographic Museum HISTORIC BUILDING

(Rr Iliaz Agushi; admission €2.50; ⊙10am-4pm) Follow the signs all over the centre of town to locate this well-kept 'how we lived' Ottoman house.

Kosovo Museum MUSEUM

(Sheshi Adam Jashari; admission €3; ⊙10am-4pm Tue-Sat) See modern exhibits upstairs and delicate 6000-year-old statues on the ground floor. It was closed for a full renovation at the time of research.

Mosques MOSQUES

Fronting the Kosovo Museum is the 15th-century **Carshi Mosque** (Agim Ramadani). Nearby, the **Sultan Mehmet Fatih Mosque** (the 'Big Mosque') was built by its namesake around 1461, converted to a Catholic church during the Austro-Hungarian era and refurbished again during WWII. **Jashar Pasha Mosque** has vibrant interiors that exemplify Turkish baroque style.

Sleeping

TOP CHOICE **Velania Guesthouse** PENSION €

(☎531 742, 044 167 455; http://guesthouse-ks.net/eng/vlersimet.html; Velania 4/34; dm/s/d/apt €9/15/20/35; @) This bustling guesthouse is spread over two buildings in an affluent part of town. The jovial professor who runs it loves a chat and could double as your grandfather. The hike up to it is much more fun in a taxi (€1.50) – either way consult the

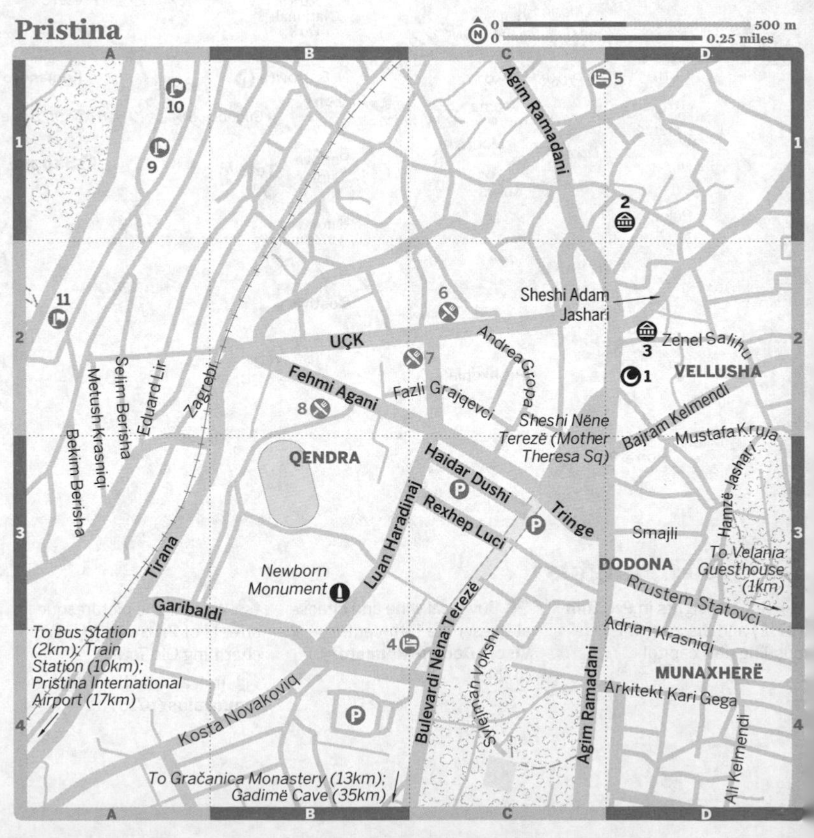

website first and print out the map, as it's hard to find!

Hotel Sara HOTEL €€
(☎238 765, 236 203; www.hotel-sara.com; Rr Maliq Pashë Gjinolli; s/d/tr/apt incl breakfast €30/40/50/70; ❄📶) In a tiny street filled with hotels by the bazaar, this 33-room hotel is rather garishly furnished but is good value at this price.

Hotel Xhema HOTEL €
(☎719 716; Rr Maliq Pashë Gjinolli; s/d/ste incl breakfast €25/30/60; P❄📶) This is the best budget deal in the city. While the suites are hilariously furnished and feature Jacuzzis, kitchens and plush beds, the cheaper rooms all smell rather musty and could use a refit. The welcome is friendly and it's central.

Eating

TOP CHOICE **Tiffany** TRADITIONAL €€
(Fehmi Agani; mains €8; ⏲8am-11pm Mon-Sat, 8am-6pm Sun) Enjoy the day's grilled special (whatever's fresh that day), beautifully cooked seasonal vegetables and oven-baked bread on the sun-dappled terrace. The restaurant is unsigned, hidden behind a well-tended bush on Fehmi Agani.

De Rada Brasserie INTERNATIONAL €€
(Rr UÇK 50; mains €5-8; ⏲7.30am-7pm) A smart and atmospheric place right in the heart of town that serves up breakfasts, lunches and early dinners to an international clientele.

Pristina

Sights

1	Carshi Mosque	D2
2	Ethnographic Museum	D1
3	Kosovo Museum	D2

Sleeping

4	Grand Hotel	C4
5	Hotel Sara	C1
	Hotel Xhema	(see 5)

Eating

6	De Rada Brasserie	C2
7	Home Bar & Restaurant	C2
8	Tiffany	B2

Information

9	French Embassy	A1
10	German Embassy	A1
11	UK Embassy	A2

DON'T MISS

GRAČANICA MONASTERY

Dusty fingers of sunlight pierce the darkness of **Gračanica Monastery** (⏲6am-5pm), completed in 1321 by Serbian King Milutin. Take a Gjilan-bound bus from Pristina (€0.50, 15 minutes, every 30 minutes); the monastery's on your left.

Home Bar & Restaurant INTERNATIONAL €
(Luan Haradinaj; mains €4-9; ⏲7am-11pm Mon-Sat, 11am-11pm Sun; 🍴) Having been here since the dark days of 2001, this is the closest Pristina has to an expat institution. The menu is international and eclectic: spring rolls, hummus, curries, wraps, burgers and even fajitas.

Getting There & Around

Taxis charge €25 for the 20-minute, 18km trip from the city centre to **Pristina International Airport** (☎958 123, www.airportpristina.com). There is a bus service between the **Grand Hotel** (www.grandhotel-pr.com; Bul Nëna Tereze; @📶) in Pristina and the airport every two hours 24 hours a day (€2). The bus station is 2km southwest of the centre off Bul Dil Klinton. Taxis to the centre should cost €2.

AROUND PRISTINA

Peja (Peć)

☎039 / POP 170,000

Peja (known as Peć to Serbians) is Kosovo's third city and one flanked by sites vital to Orthodox Serbians. With a Turkish-style bazaar at its heart and the beautiful Rugova Mountains all around it, it's a diverse and progressive place that's ripe for tourism.

The **Patriachate of Peć** (☎044 15 07 55; ⏲9am-6pm) is a slice of Serbian Orthodoxy. From the food stands around the main square, walk along Lekë Dukagjini with the river on your left for 15 minutes until you reach the monastery walls.

Stay and eat at the great-value **Dukagjini Hotel** (☎771 177; www.hoteldukagjini.com; Sheshi I Dëshmorëve 2; s/d incl breakfast €50/70; 🚭❄📶) in the heart of town. Contact the excellent local **Rugova Experience** (☎432 352, 044 137 734; www.rugovaexperience.org;

DON'T MISS

VISOKI DEČANI MONASTERY

This regal **monastery** (☎49-776 254; www.decani.org; ⏰11am-1pm & 4-6pm), 15km south of Peja, is one of Kosovo's highlights. Buses go to Dečani from Peja (€1, 30 minutes, every 15 minutes) on their way to Gjakovë from Peja. It's a pleasant 2km walk to the monastery from the bus stop; from the roundabout in the middle of town, take the second exit if you're coming from Peja.The on-site shop sells delicious monastery-made cheeses and wines.

Mbretëreshë Teuta) for well-run hiking trips in the nearby mountains.

Peja is also home to the **Shqip Short Film Festival** (www.shqipfilmfest.com), which takes place in the last week of June each year and attracts international film makers.

Frequent buses run to Pristina (€5, 1½ hours, every 20 minutes) and Prizren (€4, 80 minutes, every hour).

Prizren

☎029 / POP 178,000

Picturesque Prizren is Kosovo's second city and it shines with post-independence euphoria and an enthusiasm that's infectious. Prizren's 15th-century **Ottoman bridge** has been superbly restored. Nearby is **Sinan Pasha Mosque** (1561) – renovations are resurrecting it as a central landmark.

There is not much of interest to see at the 11th-century **Kalaja** on top of the hill overlooking the Old Town, but the views over Prizren are worth the walk.

Stay at the stylish **Hotel Prizreni** (☎225 200; www.hotelprizreni.com; Rr Shën Flori 2; r incl breakfast €40-50; ❄📶) just behind the Sinan Pasha Mosque.

Prizren is connected by bus to Pristina (€4, 1½ hours, every 10 to 25 minutes) and Peja (€4, 1½ hours, six daily).

UNDERSTAND KOSOVO

History

In the 12th century Kosovo was the heart of the Orthodox Christian Serbian empire, until Turkish triumph at the pivotal 1389 Battle of Kosovo ushered in 500 years of Ottoman rule and Islam. Serbia regained control in the 1912 Balkan War and the region became part of Yugoslavia upon its creation in 1918. In WWII the territory was incorporated into Italian-controlled Albania and liberated and returned to Yugoslavia in October 1944 by Albanian partisans. Following decades of postwar neglect, Kosovo was granted de facto self-government status in 1974.

In 1989 the autonomy Kosovo enjoyed under the 1974 constitution was suspended by Slobodan Milošević. Ethnic Albanian leaders declared independence from Serbia in 1990. War broke out in 1992 – that same year, Ibrahim Rugova was elected as the first president of the self-proclaimed Republic of Kosovo.

A US-backed plan to return Kosovo's autonomy was rejected by Serbia in March 1999. After Serbia refused to desist from emptying the province of non-Serbians, NATO unleashed a bombing campaign. In June, Milošević withdrew troops and Kosovo became a UN-NATO protectorate. UN-sponsored talks on Kosovo's status began in February 2006 and Kosovo's parliament declared Kosovo independent on 17 February 2008. Over 70 countries recognised Kosovo's independence, but Serbia was not one of them. In July 2010 the International Court of Justice ruled that Kosovo's declaration of independence did not violate international law.

Following a string of acting presidents after Ibrahim Rugova's death in 2006, Atifete Jahjaga became Kosovo's president in 2011. A non-partisan, female former police chief, Jahjaga has been a breath of fresh air for politics in Kosovo, even if controversy has never been far from Hashim Thaci, the current prime minister and the position of real power in the country.

People

The population was estimated at 1.8 million in 2010; 92% are Albanian and 8% are Serb.

SURVIVAL GUIDE

Directory A–Z

Accommodation

Accommodation is booming in Kosovo, with most large towns now offering a good range of options.

Price ranges used in listings in this chapter are for a double room with bathroom.

€ less than €40

€€ €40 to €80

€€€ more than €80

Business Hours

Standard opening hours are as follows:

Banks 8am to 5pm Monday to Friday, until 2pm Saturday

Bars 8am to 11pm (on the dot if police are cracking down)

Shops 8am to 6pm Monday to Friday, until 3pm Saturday

Restaurants 8am to midnight

Embassies & Consulates

There are no embassies for Australia, Canada, New Zealand or Ireland in Kosovo, so consular issues are handled by the embassies in Belgrade. The following are all in Pristina:

French Embassy (2245 8800; www.ambafrance-kosovo.org; Ismail Qemali 67)

German Embassy (254 500; www.pristina.diplo.de; Azem Jashanica 17)

Netherlands Embassy (516 101; http://kosovo.nlembassy.org; Xhemajl Berisha 12)

UK Embassy (254 700; www.ukinkosovo.fco.gov.uk; Ismail Qemajli 6)

US Embassy (5959 3000; http://pristina.usembassy.gov; Nazim Hikmet 30)

Food

The following price categories for the average cost of a main course are used in this chapter:

€ less than €5

€€ €5 to €10

€€€ more than €10

Money

Kosovo's currency is the euro. It's best to arrive with small denominations and euro coins are particularly useful. ATMs are common and established businesses accept credit cards.

KOSOVO FACTS

Area 10,887 sq km

Capital Pristina

Currency Euro (€)

Language Albanian, Serbian

Country code 381

Emergency Ambulance 94, fire 93, police 92

Safe Travel

Check government travel advisories before travelling to Kosovo. Sporadic violence occurs in North Mitrovica. Unexploded ordnance (UXO) has been cleared from roads and paths but you should seek KFOR (Kosovo Force; the international force responsible for establishing security in Kosovo) advice at www.aco.nato.int/kfor.aspx before venturing off beaten tracks.

Visas

Visas are not required; upon arrival, you get a 90-day entry stamp. If you wish to travel between Serbia and Kosovo you'll need to enter Kosovo from Serbia first or go via a third country.

Getting There & Away

There are international buses to and from all neighbouring capital cities, except Belgrade (Serbia) from Pristina. There's also a train to Skopje (Macedonia) from Pristina (€4, three hours, 7.22am).

Getting Around

Buses stop at distinct blue signs, but can be flagged down anywhere. Bus journeys are generally cheap, but the going can be slow on Kosovo's single-lane roads. Trains operate between Pristina and Peja (€3, 1½ hours, 8.01am and 4.41pm).

Latvia

Includes »

Rīga ... 719
Jūrmala ... 727
Western Latvia ... 727
Cape Kolka (Kolkasrags) ... 727
Liepāja ... 727
Eastern Latvia ... 728
Sigulda ... 728
Understand Latvia ... 729
Survival Guide ... 729

Best Places to Eat

» Istaba (p724)
» Fish Restaurant (p724)
» Pelmeņi XL (p723)

Best Places to Stay

» Naughty Squirrel (p722)
» Radisson Blu Hotel Elizabete (p723)
» Hotel Valdemars (p723)

Why Go?

Tucked between Estonia to the north and Lithuania to the south, Latvia is the meat of the Baltic sandwich. We're not implying that the neighbouring nations are slices of white bread, but Latvia is the savoury middle, loaded with colourful fillings. Thick greens take the form of Gauja Valley pines. Onion-domed cathedrals sprout above local towns. Cheesy Russian pop blares along coastal beaches. And spicy Rīga adds an extra zing as the country's cosmopolitan nexus and unofficial capital of the Baltic.

If that doesn't whet your appetite, hear this: the country's under-the-radar profile makes it the perfect pit stop for those seeking something a bit more authentic than the overrun tourist hubs further afield. So, consider altering your European itinerary and fill up on little Latvia instead of big-ticket destinations in the east such as Prague, Vienna or – dare we say it – Hungary.

When to Go

Rīga

°C/°F Temp — Rainfall inches/mm

40/104 – 20/68 – 0/32 – -20/-4

5/125 – 4/100 – 3/75 – 2/50 – 1/25 – 0

J F M A M J J A S O N D

Dec & Jan Celebrate the holidays in the birthplace of the Christmas tree

Mid-Jun–Aug Summer starts with an all-night solstice romp; then it's off to the beach

Sep Refusing to let summer go, Rīgans sip lattes under heat lamps at alfresco cafes

Connections

Latvia is the link in the Baltic chain, making Rīga a convenient point between Tallinn and Vilnius. Long-distance buses and trains also connect the capital to St Petersburg, Moscow and Warsaw, and ferry services shuttle passengers to Sweden and Germany. Rīga is the hub of airBaltic, which offers direct service to dozens of major European cities.

ITINERARIES

Three Days

Fill your first two days with a feast of Rīga's architectural eye candy, and spend your third day hiking betwixt Sigulda's castles, sunbathing in scintillating Jūrmala or snapping photos of Rundāle's opulent palace.

One Week

After a few days in the capital, swing by Jūrmala on your way up the horn of Cape Kolka for saunas, sunsets and solitude. Glide through western Latvia comparing its ultrabucolic townships to Rundāle's majestic grounds, then blaze a trail across eastern Latvia for a rousing trip back in time spiced with adrenaline sports.

Essential Food & Drink

» **Black Balzām** Goethe called it 'the elixir of life'. The jet-black, 45% proof concoction is a secret recipe of more than a dozen fairy-tale ingredients including oak bark, wormwood and linden blossoms. A shot a day keeps the doctor away, so say most of Latvia's pensioners. Try mixing it with a glass of cola to take the edge off.

» **Mushrooms** Not a sport but a national obsession; mushroom picking takes the country by storm during the first showers of autumn.

» **Alus** For such a tiny nation there's definitely no shortage of *alus* (beer) – each major town has its own brew. You can't go wrong with Užavas (Ventspils' contribution).

» **Smoked fish** Dozens of fish shacks dot the Kurzeme coast – look for the veritable smoke signals rising above the tree line. Grab 'em to go; they make the perfect afternoon snack.

» **Kvass** Single-handedly responsible for the decline of Coca-Cola at the turn of the 21st century, Kvass is a beloved beverage made from fermented rye bread. It's surprisingly popular with kids!

AT A GLANCE

» **Currency** Lats (Ls)

» **Language** Latvian, Russian

» **Money** ATMs all over cities; banks open Monday to Saturday

» **Visas** Not required for EU citizens, or for stays of up to 90 days for Australian, Canadian, New Zealand and US citizens

Fast Facts

» **Area** 64,589 sq km

» **Capital** Rīga

» **Country code** ☎371

» **Emergency** ☎112

Exchange Rates

Australia	A$1	0.57Ls
Canada	C$1	0.54Ls
Euro Zone	€1	0.70Ls
Japan	¥100	0.59Ls
New Zealand	NZ$1	0.46Ls
UK	UK£1	0.83Ls
USA	US$1	0.55Ls

Set Your Budget

» **Budget hotel room** 25Ls

» **Two-course meal** 10Ls

» **Museum entrance** 1.50Ls

» **Beer** 1.20Ls

» **City transport ticket** 0.70Ls

Resources

» **1188** (www.1188.lv)

» **Latvia Institute** (www.li.lv)

» **Latvia Tourism Development Agency** (www.latviatourism.lv)

Latvia Highlights

1. Click your camera at the menagerie of gargoyles, beasts, goddesses and twisting vines that inhabits the surplus of **Rīga's art nouveau architecture** (p719)
2. Lose yourself in the maze of cobblestones, church spires and gingerbread trim that is **Old Rīga** (p719)
3. Listen to the waves pound the awesomely remote **Cape Kolka** (p727), which crowns the desolate Kurzeme coast
4. Swing through **Sigulda** (p728) on a bungee cord
5. Sneak away from the capital and indulge in aristocratic decadence at **Rundāle Palace** (p727)
6. Wander past gritty Soviet tenements and gilded cathedrals in the crumbling Karosta district of portly **Liepāja** (p727)
7. Hobnob with Russian jetsetters in the heart of **Jūrmala's swanky spa scene** (p727)

RĪGA

POP 700,000

'The Paris of the North', 'The Second City that Never Sleeps' – everyone's so keen on qualifying Latvia's capital, but regal Rīga does a hell of a job of holding its own. For starters, the city has the largest and most impressive showing of art nouveau architecture in Europe. Nightmarish gargoyles and praying goddesses adorn more than 750 buildings along the stately boulevards radiating out from the city's castle core. The heart of the city – Old Rīga – is a fairy-tale kingdom of winding wobbly lanes that beat to the sound of clicking stilettos, beer-garden brouhahas and rumbling basement discotheques.

Sights

OLD RĪGA (VECRĪGA)

TOP CHOICE Blackheads' House HISTORIC BUILDING
(Melngalvju House; http://nami.riga.lv/mn; Rātslaukums 7; admission 2Ls; ⏲10am-5pm Tue-Sun) Touristy Rātslaukums is home to the postcard-worthy Blackheads' House, built in 1344 as a veritable fraternity house for the Blackheads guild of unmarried German merchants.

Museum of the Occupation of Latvia MUSEUM
(Latvijas okupācijas muzejs; ☎6721 2715; www.omf.lv; Latviesu Strēlnieku laukums 1; admission by donation; ⏲11am-6pm) This museum ironically inhabits a Soviet bunker and carefully details Latvia's Soviet and Nazi occupations between 1939 and 1991.

St Peter's Lutheran Church CHURCH
(Sv Pēterabaznīca; www.peterbaznic.lv; Skārņu iela 19; admission 4Ls; ⏲11am-6pm Tue-Sun) This Gothic church is Rīga's skyline centrepiece. Don't miss the view from the spire.

Cat House HISTORIC BUILDING
(Kaķu māja; Miestaru iela 10/12) The Cat House – named for the spooked black cat sitting on the roof – is one of the colourful 18th-century buildings lining Livu Laukums. Most of these buildings have been turned into beer halls.

Dome Cathedral CHURCH
(Doma baznīca; ☎6721 3213; www.doms.lv; Doma laukums 1; admission 2Ls; ⏲9am-5pm) The centrepiece of expansive Doma Laukums is Rīga's enormous Dome Cathedral. Founded in 1211 as the seat of the Rīga diocese, it is still the largest church in the Baltic. The huge, 6768-pipe organ was the world's largest when it was completed in 1884 (it's now the fourth-largest).

Art Museum Rīga Bourse MUSEUM
(Bīrzasnams; ☎6722 6467; www.lnmm.lv; Doma laukums 6; admission 2Ls; ⏲10am-6pm Tue-Sun) Across the square from the church is Art Museum Rīga Bourse, which houses the city's store of foreign art.

Rīga Castle CASTLE
(Rīgas pils; Pils laukums 3) Verdant Pils Laukums sits at the doorstep of Rīga Castle. Originally built as the headquarters for the Livonian Order around 1330, this canary-yellow bastion boasts the **History Museum of Latvia** (Latvijas vēstures muzejs; ☎6722 1357; www.history-museum.lv; admission 2Ls, Wed free; ⏲10am-5pm Tue-Sun), and is also home to Latvia's president.

Jacob's Barracks HISTORIC BUILDING
(Jekaba Kazarmas; Torņa iela 4) The entire north side of Torņa iela is flanked by the custard-coloured Jacob's Barracks, now inhabited by cafes.

Swedish Gate GATE
(Zviedru vārti; Torņa iela 11) Towards the centre of Old Town, look for Trokšnu iela, Old Rīga's narrowest street. It leads to the Swedish Gate, which was built into the city walls in 1698 to celebrate Swedish occupation.

Powder Tower TOWER
(Pulvertornis; Smilšu iela 20) East of the Swedish Gate is the round 14th-century Powder Tower, the only survivor of the 18 towers in the Old City wall and home to the War Museum.

CENTRAL RĪGA (CENTRS)

Freedom Monument MONUMENT
(Brīvības bulvāris) Affectionately known as 'Milda', Rīga's Freedom Monument was erected

> **CAPITAL OF CULTURE 2014**
>
> The European Union has declared Rīga the European Capital of Culture for 2014. Expect a full calendar year of exciting events, including the inauguration of the new national library across the river from Old Rīga, the World Choir Games featuring singers from more than 90 countries, a celebration of the 500th anniversary of the printed book and more than 200 other cultural events. Check out www.riga2014.org for more information.

Rīga

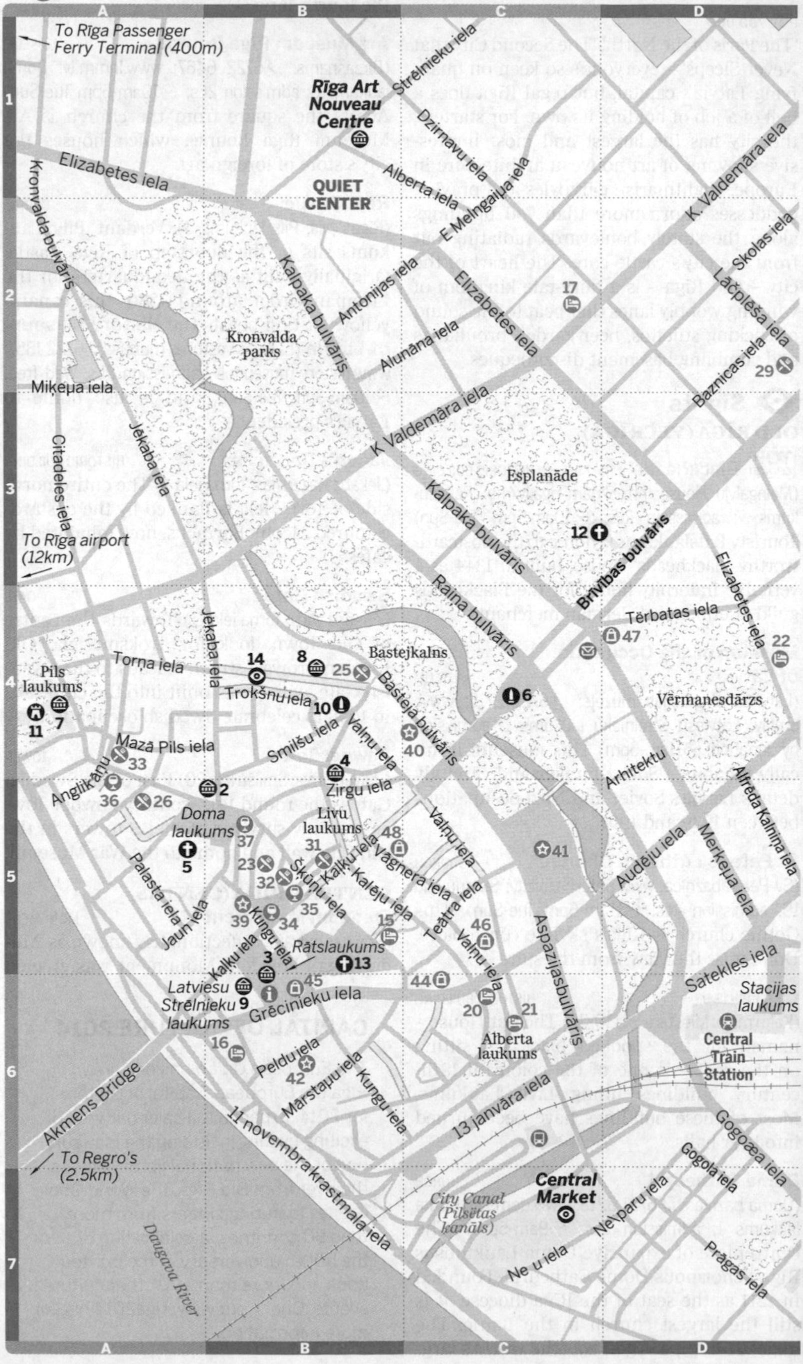

A B C D
1 2 3 4 5 6 7

To Rīga Passenger Ferry Terminal (400m)
Strēlnieku iela
Rīga Art Nouveau Centre
Dzirnavu iela
K Valdemāra iela
Elizabetes iela
Kronvalda bulvāris
Alberta iela
QUIET CENTER
E Melngaiļa iela
Skolas iela
Lāčplēša iela
Antonijas iela
Kalpaka bulvāris
Elizabetes iela
17
Kronvalda parks
Alunāna iela
Baznīcas iela
29
Miķeļa iela
K Valdemāra iela
Citadeles iela
Jēkaba iela
Esplanāde
Kalpaka bulvāris
12
Brīvības bulvāris
To Rīga airport (12km)
Raiņa bulvāris
Elizabetes iela
Tērbatas iela
47
22
Jēkaba iela
Bastejkalns
Torņa iela
14
8
25
Pils laukums
Trokšņu iela
10
Basteja bulvāris
6
Vērmanesdārzs
11
7
Smilšu iela
Vaļņu iela
40
Mazā Pils iela
33
4
Arhitektu
Anglikāņu
Zirgu iela
36
26
2
Alfrēda Kalniņa iela
Doma laukums
Līvu laukums
37
48
Vaļņu iela
5
31
Kalku iela
Vāgnera iela
41
23
Audēju iela
Merķeļa iela
Palasta iela
32
Šķūņu iela
Kalēju iela
Teātra iela
35
39
34
Jauņ iela
Kungu iela
15
46
Vaļņu iela
Aspazijas bulvāris
Kalķu iela
Kungu iela
Rātslaukums
13
3
Satekles iela
Latviešu Strēlnieku laukums
9
45
44
Stacijas laukums
Grēcinieku iela
20
21
16
Alberta laukums
Central Train Station
Akmens Bridge
Peldu iela
42
Marstaļu iela
Kungu iela
13 janvāra iela
11 novembra krastmala iela
Gogoļa iela
To Regro's (2.5km)
Central Market
Gogoļa iela
City Canal (Pilsētas kanāls)
Ne\paru iela
Daugava River
Ne u iela
Prāgas iela

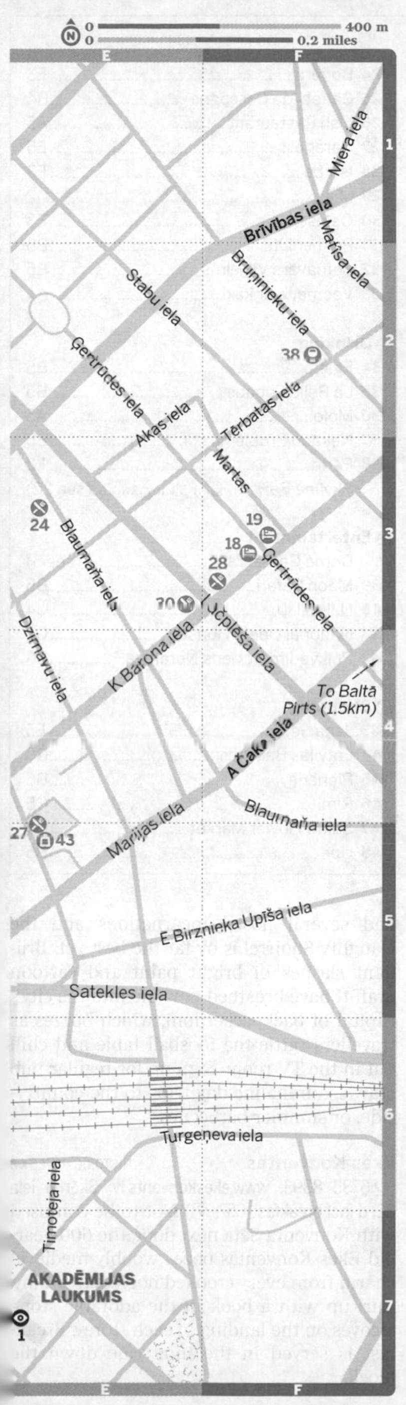

in 1935 where a statue of Russian ruler Peter the Great once stood.

FREE **Russian Orthodox Cathedral** CHURCH

(Pareizticīgo katedrāle; Brīvības bulvāris 23) At the far end of the Esplanade, near Hotel Latvija, the 19th-century Russian Orthodox Cathedral majestically rises above the trees with its gilded cupolas. During the Soviet era the church was used as a planetarium.

TOP CHOICE **Central Market** MARKET

(Centrāl tirgus; www.centraltir gus.lv; Nēģu iela 7; ⌚7am-5pm Sun-Mon, to 6pm Tue-Sat) Heckle for your huckleberries at the Central Market, housed in a series of mammoth Zeppelin hangars constructed for the Germans during WWI. Check out the seafood pavilion for herring, or swing by the produce section for chilled sauerkraut juice – a traditional hangover remedy. It's a fantastic spot to assemble a picnic lunch and ogle some seriously outdated hairdos (hair-don'ts?).

Academy of Science NOTABLE BUILDING

Just beyond the market is the Academy of Science, also called 'Stalin's Birthday Cake'. A mere 2Ls grants you admission to the observation deck on the 17th floor.

TOP CHOICE **Rīga Art Nouveau Centre** MUSEUM

(Rīgas jūgemdstila muzejs; ☎6718 1465; www.jugendstils.riga.lv; Alberta iela 12; admission 3.50Ls, English tour 10Ls; ⌚10am-6pm Tue-Sun) If you're curious about what lurks behind Rīga's imaginative art nouveau facades, then stop here. The museum sits in an apartment that has been restored to resemble a middle-class flat from the 1920s. Note the geometric frescos, rounded furniture and original stained glass in the dining room. The website has details about the art nouveau walking routes.

Activities

Baltā Pirts SPA

(☎6727 1733; www.baltapirts.lv; Tallinas iela 71; sauna 7Ls; ⌚8am-8pm Wed-Sun) Baltā Pirts combines traditional Latvian relaxation techniques (the name means 'white birch') with a subtle, oriental design scheme. In the 1980s the property had a seedy reputation, but the original owners of the sauna have since reclaimed the building and turned it into quite a wonderful place.

Take a tram heading north along A Čaka until you reach Tallinas iela.

Rīga

Top Sights

Central Market ... C7
Rīga Art Nouveau Centre ... B1

Sights

1 Academy of Science ... E7
2 Art Museum Rīga Bourse ... B5
3 Blackheads' House ... B6
4 Cat House ... B4
5 Dome Cathedral ... A5
6 Freedom Monument ... C4
7 History Museum of Latvia ... A4
8 Jacob's Barracks ... B4
9 Museum of the Occupation of Latvia ... B6
10 Powder Tower ... B4
11 Rīga Castle ... A4
12 Russian Orthodox Cathedral ... C3
13 St Peter's Lutheran Church ... B5
14 Swedish Gate ... B4

Sleeping

15 Ekes Konventas ... B5
16 Friendly Fun Franks ... B6
17 Hotel Valdemārs ... C2
18 KB ... F3
19 Krišjānis & Ģertrūde ... F3
20 Naughty Squirrel ... C6
21 Old Town Hostel ... C6
22 Radisson Blu Hotel Elizabete ... D4

Eating

23 Alus Sēta ... B5
24 Bonēra ... E3
25 Cadets de Gascogne ... B4
26 Fish Restaurant ... A5
27 Garage ... E5
28 Istaba ... F3
29 Miit ... D2
30 Osīriss ... E3
31 Pelmeņi XL ... B5
32 Šefpavārs Viļhelms ... B5
33 Vecmeita ar kaki ... A4

Drinking

34 Egle ... B5
35 La Belle Epoque ... B5
36 Mojo ... A5
37 Nekādu Problēmu ... B5
38 Pērle ... F2
Skyline Bar ... (see 22)

Entertainment

Dome Cathedral ... (see 5)
39 Moon Safari ... B5
40 Nabaklab ... C4
41 National Opera House ... C5
42 Pulkvedim Neviens Neraksta ... B6

Shopping

43 Jāņa Sēta ... E5
44 Latvijas Balzāms ... C6
45 Pienene ... B6
46 Rimi ... C5
47 Sakta Flower Market ... D4
48 Upe ... B5

Regro's SHOOTING RANGE

(☎6760 1705; Daugav-grīvas iela 31; bullets 0.80-2Ls; ⊙10am-7pm Mon-Sat, by appointment Sun) The ambience at Regro's is reason enough to visit: a dingy Soviet fallout shelter adorned with posters of rifle-toting models wearing fur bikinis. Choose from a large selection of retro firearms (including Kalashnikovs) to aim at your paper cut-out of James Bond. You pay by the bullet. Take the Vanšu bridge across the river, pass Kīpsala, and take your first right until you hit a petrol station. Also accessible by tram 13. Don't forget your passport.

Sleeping

OLD RĪGA (VECRĪGA)

Naughty Squirrel HOSTEL €

(☎2646 1248; www.thenaughtysquirrel.com; Kalēju iela 50; dm/d 8/30Ls; @📶) This address has had several hostel incarnations and the Naughty Squirrel is by far the best yet. Brilliant slashes of bright paint and cartoon graffiti have breathed new life into the city's capital of backpackerdom, which buzzes as travellers rattle the foosball table and chill out in the TV room. Sign up for regular pub crawls, adrenaline day trips to the countryside, or summer barbecues.

Ekes Konventas HISTORIC HOTEL €€

(☎6735 8393; www.ekeskonvents.lv; Skārņu iela 22; d incl breakfast €57; 📶) Not to be confused with Konventa Sēta next door, the 600-year-old Ekes Konventas oozes wobbly medieval charm from every crooked nook and cranny. Curl up with a book in the adorable stone alcoves on the landing of each storey. Breakfast is served in the mod cafe down the block.

Old Town Hostel HOSTEL €
(☎6722 3406; www.rigaoldtownhostel.lv; Valņu iela 43; dm/d 7/30Ls; @📶) The cosy English-style pub on the ground floor doubles as the hostel's hang-out space and if you can manage to lug your suitcase past the faux bookshelf door and up the twisting staircase, you'll find spacious dorms with chandeliers and plenty of sunlight. Private rooms are located in another building near the train station.

Friendly Fun Franks HOSTEL €
(☎2599 0612; www.franks.lv; 11 Novembra Krastmala 29; dm/d from 5.90/40Ls; @📶) If you want to party, look no further than this bright orange stag-magnet, where every backpacker is greeted with a hearty hello and a complimentary pint of beer. The staff offer free 'What to Do' tours of Rīga, beach parties and Saturday trips to Sigulda. Accommodation must be booked in advance.

CENTRAL RĪGA (CENTRS)

Radisson Blu Hotel Elizabete HOTEL €€
(☎6778 5555; www.radissonblu.com/elizabetehotel-riga; Elizabetes iela 73; d incl breakfast from €75; P❄@📶) The newest link in the Radisson Blu chain is a flash address designed by an up-and-coming London architectural firm. The facade is an eye-catching mix of chrome, steel and giant sheets of glass, and the interior continues to impress: stylish furnishings and clever floor plans give the rooms a cosy-yet-trendy feel.

Hotel Valdemārs HOTEL €€
(☎6733 4462; www.valdemars.lv; Valdemāra iela 23; s/d incl half-board from €50/60; ❄@📶) Modern Hotel Valdemars is a great find geared towards the Scandinavian market – rooms feel efficient yet homey, in an upmarket Ikea kind of way. Don't forget to give away the flower adorning the bureau in your room – it's a Latvian tradition!

Krišjānis & Ģertrūde B&B €€
(☎6750 6604; www.kg.lv; K Barona iela 39; s/d/tr incl breakfast €35/45/55; @📶) Step off the bustling intersection into this quaint, family-run B&B adorned with still-life images of fruit and flowers. It's best to book ahead since there are only six cosy rooms. Enter from Ģertrūdes iela.

KB B&B €
(☎6731 2323; www.kbhotel.lv; K Barona iela 37; s/d/tr 19/21/23Ls; @📶) This great find in the pinch-a-penny category is located up a rather opulent marble staircase. The rooms are simple but well appointed, and there's a modern communal kitchen.

Eating

OLD RĪGA (VECRĪGA)

If you're self-catering, there's a branch of **Rimi** (www.rimi.lv; Audēju iela 16), a reputable supermarket chain, in Old Rīga's Galerija Centrs shopping mall.

Pelmeņi XL FAST FOOD €
(Kaļķu iela 7; dumpling bowls 0.86-2.50Ls; ⏲9am-4am) A Rīga institution for backpackers and undiscerning drunkards, this extra-large cafeteria stays open extra-late serving up huge bowls of *pelmeņi* (Russian-style ravioli stuffed with meat) amid Flintstones-meets-Gaudí decor (you'll see). There's a second location in the central train station.

Alus Sēta LATVIAN €
(www.lido.lv; Tirgoņu iela 6; mains 2-7Ls) The pick of the LIDO litter in central Rīga, Alus Seta feels like an old Latvian brewhouse. It's popular with locals as well as tourists – everyone flocks here for cheap-as-chips grub and homemade beer. Seating floods the cobbled streets during the warmer months.

Cadets de Gascogne BAKERY €
(Franču Maiznīca; Basteja bulvāris 8; baguette sandwich 2.20Ls; ⏲7am-10am Mon-Sat) Got a tummy ache from one too many *pelmeņi*? Nurse your digestive system at this French-run bakery – pick up a mug of hot chocolate and a baguette sandwich stuffed with ham and cornichons (gherkins). Additional seating is available on the roof promenade. There's a second location in Berga Bāzars.

Vecmeita ar kaki LATVIAN €€
(Spinster & Her Cat; Mazā Pils iela 1; mains 3.10-9.90Ls) This cosy spot across from the president's palace specialises in cheap Latvian grub and meaty mains. In warmer weather, patrons dine outside on converted sewing-machine tables.

Šefpavārs Vilhelms FAST FOOD €
(Chef William; Šķūņu iela 6; pancake rolls 0.65Ls) Customers of every ilk are constantly queuing for a quick nosh – three stuffed pancakes (blintzes) smothered in sour cream and jam equals the perfect backpacker's breakfast.

CENTRAL RĪGA (CENTRS)

Self-caterers should try **Rimi** (www.rimi.lv; K Barona iela 46) in the Barona Centrs shopping mall or check out the Central Market (p721).

SPLURGE

Fish Restaurant (www.domehotel.lv; Miesnieku iela 4; mains 7-16Ls) – the restaurant of the Dome Hotel – quickly reminds diners that Rīga sits near a body of water that's full of delicious fish. Service is impeccable and dishes are expertly prepared to reflect the eclectic assortment of recipes in the modern Latvian lexicon – this is not to be missed if you're looking to spend a little more on some high-end comfort food.

TOP CHOICE **Istaba** CAFE €€
(☎6728 1141; K Barona iela 31a; mains 3-10Ls; ⊙Mon-Sat) Owned by local chef and TV personality Mārtiņš Sirmais, the 'Room' sits in the rafters above a like-named gallery space adorned with trendsetting bric-a-brac. In summer you can dine on the street-side verandah, though we prefer heading upstairs to grab a seat in the mob of discarded lamps and sofas. There's no set menu – you're subject to the cook's fancy – but it's all about flavourful and filling portions served on mismatched dishware. Reservations are recommended.

Miit CAFE €
(www.miit.lv; Lāčplēša iela 10; mains from 2Ls) A bike-shop-cum-cafe that takes its cues from Berlin's hipster culture, Miit is a wonderful addition to Rīga's student scene, with plenty of space to sip a latte and blog about Nietzsche amid toppled-over IKEA bookcases, comfy couches and discarded bicycle parts. The two-course lunch is a fantastic deal for penny-pinchers – expect a soup and a main course for under 3Ls (dishes change every day).

Bonēra CAFE €€
(www.bonera.lv; Blaumaņa iela 12a; mains 3-8Ls; ⊙Mon-Sat) Life is indeed good at Bonēra, whose name is a play on the word 'happiness'. The cafe doubles as a vintage-clothing store, though these days most locals come for the 5Ls all-you-can-eat buffet dinner that's stocked with an unending assortment of delicious dishes such as Waldorf salads, homemade pâté and scrumptious carbonara pasta.

Garage CAFE €€
(Elizabetes iela 83/85; mains 2-7Ls) Although it bills itself more as a wine bar attached to a Latvian handicrafts shop, Garage has transformed into a trendy cafe serving brilliant snacks and light dishes after legions of local fans have encouraged its expansion into some of the retail space. Friendly staff and an eclectic assortment of secondhand chairs give it that extra *je ne sais quoi*.

Osīriss CAFE €€
(K Barona iela 31; mains 3-9Ls; ⊙8am-midnight; 📶) Despite Rīga's mercurial cafe culture, Osīriss continues to be a local mainstay. The green faux-marble tabletops haven't changed since the mid-'90s and neither has the clientele: angsty artsy types scribbling in their Moleskines over a glass of red wine.

Drinking

Nekādu Problēmu BEER GARDEN
(No Problem; www.nekaduproblemu.lv; Doma laukums) This sea of sturdy patio-ware enlivens Doma laukums in the warmer months as the rousing fits of live music bounce off the cathedral walls. Sample more than 20 types of draught beer, and the food's pretty darn good too.

Egle BEER GARDEN
(www.spoguegle.lv; Kaļķu iela 1a) Old Rīga's second beer garden is a cosy addition to the city, with tables plonked closely together and folk music in the evenings.

La Belle Epoque BAR
(French Bar; Mazā Jaunavu iela 8) Students flock to this boisterous basement bar to power down its trademark 'apple pie' shots (1Ls). The Renoir mural and kitschy *Moulin Rouge* posters seem to successfully ward off stag parties.

Pērle BAR, CAFE
(Tērbatas iela 65) Pērle is where outmoded technology goes to die a stylish rock-star death. It's everything you'd want in a neighbourhood hipster hang-out: discarded Game Boys, racks of vintage tweed, a massacre of mannequin parts and designer lattes...with Baileys. Oh, and everything's for sale. Naturally.

Mojo LOUNGE
(www.mojocafe.lv; Pils iela 7) Oh Mojo, how you endear us with your retro wallpaper prints, shaggy rugs and dozens of other throwbacks to the '70s, such as old radios and leather couches dyed in odd colours.

Skyline Bar BAR
(Elizabetes iela 55; 📶) A must for every visitor, glitzy Skyline Bar sits on the 26th floor of

the Reval Hotel Latvija. The sweeping views are the city's best and the mix of glam spirit-sippers makes great people-watching under the retro purple lighting.

☆ Entertainment

Nightclubs

Pulkvedim Neviens Neraksta CLUB
(No One Writes to the Colonel; www.pulkvedis.lv; Peldu iela 26/28) There's no such thing as a dull night at this club. The atmosphere is 'warehouse chic', with pumping '80s tunes on the ground floor and trance beats down below.

Nabaklab CLUB
(www.nabaklab.lv; Meierovica bulvaris 12) Imagine if your favourite alternative radio station opened a nightspot that played its signature blend of experimental tunes and electronica. Well, you're in luck – Naba's (93.1FM) club space attracts the city's boho hobos with its DJ beats, vintage clothes racks, art gallery and cheap beer in the quaint Soviet-style den.

Moon Safari CLUB
(www.moonsafari.lv; Krāmu iela 2) Beds in the 'VIP room' and a pet snake at the bar? It's all pretty suggestive, but the 2Ls cocktails and colourful karaoke booth lure a young Erasmus crowd for all-night shenanigans.

Performing Arts

National Opera House OPERA
(☎6707 3777; www.opera.lv; Aspazijas bulvāris 3) The pride of Latvia boasting some of the finest performing arts in all of Europe (and for the fraction of the price of other countries). Mikhail Baryshnikov got his start here. Note that Rīga's ballet, opera and theatre season breaks for summer holidays (between June and September).

Dome Cathedral LIVE MUSIC
(Doma baznīca; ☎6721 3213; www.doms.lv; Doma laukums 1) Twice-weekly short organ concerts (Wednesday and Saturday evenings) and lengthier Friday night performances are well worth attending.

Shopping

Pienene ACCESSORIES
(Kungu iela 7/9) 'The Dandelion' is an airy boutique in the heart of Old Rīga where visitors can sample some of the countryside's richest wellness products. Expect soaps, scarves and candles made from local wax and herbs.

Sakta Flower Market MARKET
(Tērbatas iela 2a) Open extra-late for those midnight mea culpas when you've gotta bring a gift home to your spouse after a long evening out with friends.

Upe MUSIC
(www.upett.lv; Vāgnera iela 5) Classical Latvian tunes play as customers peruse traditional instruments and CDs of local folk, rock and experimental sounds.

Latvijas Balzāms FOOD, DRINK
(www.lb.lv; Audēju iela 8) A popular chain of liquor stores selling the trademark Latvian Black Balzām. There's another branch on Blaumaņa iela and another on K Barona iela along with several others around town.

Jāņa Sēta BOOKS
(www.mapshop.lv; Elizabetes iela 83/85) The largest travel bookstore in the Baltic overflows with a bounty of maps, souvenir photo books and Lonely Planet guides.

ℹ Information

Internet Access

Every hostel and hotel has some form of internet connection available to guests. Internet cafes are a dying breed in Rīga and they're usually filled with 12-year-olds blasting cybermonsters.

Elik Kafe (Merķeļa iela 1; per 30min/1hr 0.45/0.85Ls; ⏲24hr) Conveniently located near the train station above McDonald's. Second location at Kaļķu iela 11.

Media

Lonely Planet (www.lonelyplanet.com/latvia/riga)

Rīga in Your Pocket (www.inyourpocket.com/latvia/riga) Handy city guide published every other month. Download a PDF version or pick up a copy at most midrange or top-end hotels (free). The tourist offices and several bookshops also have copies (2Ls).

Rīga this Week (www.rigathisweek.lv) An excellent (and free) city guide available at virtually every sleeping option in town. Published every second month.

Medical Services

ARS (☎6720 1003; www.ars-med.lv; Skolas iela 5) English-speaking doctors and 24-hour consultation available.

Money

There are scores of ATMs scattered around the capital. Withdrawing cash is easier than exchanging travellers cheques or foreign currencies.

Marika (Brīvības bulvāris 30) Offers 24-hour currency exchange services with reasonable rates. Second location at Dzirnavu 96.

Post

Those blue storefronts with 'Pasta' written on them aren't Italian restaurants – they're post offices. See www.pasts.lv for more info.

Central Post Office (Brīvības bulvaris 32; ⏲7.30am-8pm Mon-Fri, 8am-6pm Sat, 10am-4pm Sun) International calling and faxing services available.

Tourist Information

Tourism Information Centre (☎6730 7900; www.rigatourism.com; Rātslaukums 6; ⏲9am-6pm) Gives out excellent tourist maps and walking-tour brochures. Staff can arrange accommodation and book day trips. Sells concert and opera tickets in summer. Satellite tourism offices can be found at the train station, bus station and airport. Buy the **Rīga Card** (www.rigacard.lv; 24hr card 10Ls), which offers discounts on sights and restaurants, and free rides on public transportation.

Getting There & Away

AIR Rīga airport (Lidosta Rīga; ☎1187; www.riga-airport.com; Marupes pagast) is in the suburb of Skulte, 13km southwest of the city centre.

BOAT See www.rigapt.lv for information about ferries and cruises to/from Rīga.

BUS Buses depart from Rīga's **international bus station** (Rīgas starptautiskā autoosta; www.autoosta.lv; Prāgas iela 1), located behind the railway embankment just beyond the southeastern edge of the Old Town. International destinations include Tallinn, Vilnius, Warsaw, Pärnu, Kaunas, St Petersburg and Moscow.

TRAIN Rīga's **central train station** (centrālā stacija; Stacijas laukums) is convenient to Old Rīga and Centrs, and is housed in a conspicuous glass-encased shopping centre near the Central Market.

The city's network of handy suburban train lines makes day tripping quite convenient.

Visit www.ldz.lv to view the timetables and prices for long-haul international and domestic trains.

Getting Around

TO/FROM THE AIRPORT There are three means of transport connecting the city centre to the airport. The cheapest option is bus 22 (0.70Ls), which runs every 15 minutes and stops at several points around town including the Stockmanns complex. airBaltic runs lime-green minibuses (3Ls) from the airport to a selection of midrange hotels in central Rīga. Lime-green taxis cost a flat rate of 10Ls from the airport; cabbies run the meter when heading *to* the airport (figure around 8Ls from central Rīga).

BICYCLE Zip around town with **Baltic Bikes** (☎6778 8333; www.balticbike.lv; per hour/day 0.70/6Ls). A handful of stands are conveniently positioned around Rīga and Jūrmala; simply choose your bike, call the rental service and receive the code to unlock your wheels.

PUBLIC TRANSPORT Most of Rīga's main tourist attractions are within walking distance of one another, so you might never have to use the city's convoluted network of tramlines, trolleybus paths and bus routes. Tickets cost 0.70Ls (0.50Ls if you buy your ticket ahead of time from an automated machine or newsstand). City transport runs daily from 5.30am to midnight. Some routes have an hourly night service. For

TRANSPORT FROM RĪGA

Bus

DESTINATION	COST (LS)	DURATION (HR)	FREQUENCY
Bauska	2.15	1¼	every 30min 6.30am-11pm
Cēsis	2.90	2	every 30min 8am-10.30pm
Kolka	4.40	3½-4½	5 daily 7.20am-5.15pm
Liepāja	6	4	every 45min 6.45am-8.30pm
Sigulda	1.50	1	every 30min 8am-10pm

Train

DESTINATION	COST (LS)	DURATION	FREQUENCY
Cēsis	2.45	1¾hr	5 daily
Jūrmala	1	30min	2 hourly
Sigulda	1.65	70min	hourly

Rīga public transport routes and schedules visit www.rigassatiksme.lv.

TAXI Taxis charge 0.40Ls to 0.50Ls per kilometre (oftentimes 0.50Ls to 0.60Ls between 10pm and 6am). Insist on having the meter on before you set off. Meters usually start running at 1Ls to 1.50Ls. There are taxi ranks outside the bus and train stations, at the airport and in front of a few major hotels in central Rīga, such as Radisson Blu Hotel Latvija.

AROUND RĪGA

Jūrmala

POP 55,000

Jūrmala's first spa opened in 1838 and since then the area has been known as the 'Baltic Riviera'. The string of seaside townships makes a pleasant day trip from the capital – on summer weekends vehicles clog the roads when jet-setters and vacationing Rīgans flock to the area for some serious fun in the sun. Treat yourself to some spa action at the **Baltic Beach Spa** (☎6777 1446; www.balticbeach.lv; Jūras iela 23/25; day-use & massages from 25Ls; ⏲8am-10pm) and be sure to check out the colourful collection of **wooden houses** peppered along the pine-studded sand. Four thousand cottages and counting!

Two to three trains and minivans link Rīga (1Ls, 30 to 35 minutes) every hour; disembark at Majori station. Motorists driving the 15km into Jūrmala must pay a 1Ls toll per day, even if they are just passing through.

WESTERN LATVIA

Cape Kolka (Kolkasrags)

Enchantingly desolate and hauntingly beautiful, a journey to Cape Kolka (Kolkasrags) feels like a trip to the end of the earth. During Soviet times the entire peninsula was zoned off as a high-security military base – the dusty road between Ventspils and Kolka was a giant aircraft runway. The region's development was subsequently stunted, and today the string of desolate coastal villages has a distinct anachronistic feel, as though they've been locked away in a time capsule.

If you plan to stay the night, **Ūši** (☎2947 692; www.kolka.info; s/d 16/22Ls, campsite per person 2.50Ls), across from the Russian Orthodox church, has two simple but prim rooms and a spot to pitch tents in the flower-filled garden.

There are five daily buses that link Rīga and Kolka town (4.50Ls, three to four hours).

WORTH A TRIP

RUNDĀLE PALACE

If you only have time for one day trip out of Rīga, make it **Rundāle Palace** (Rundāles pils; ☎6396 2274; www.rundale.net; short/long route 2.50/3.50Ls, photo permit 1Ls; ⏲10am-7pm May-Oct, to 5pm Nov-Apr), 75km south of the capital near the tiny town of Bauska. The architect of this sprawling monument to aristocratic ostentation was the Italian baroque genius Bartolomeo Rastrelli, best known for designing the Winter Palace in St Petersburg. Dozens of rooms are open to visitors, as are the wonderfully landscaped gardens.

Most tour operators run frequent day trips to the palace (about 20Ls per person); it's best to rent a car if you plan on reaching Rundāle under your own steam. You can also take a bus from Rīga to Bauska (2Ls, 70 minutes, twice hourly), then switch to one of the nine daily buses (0.35Ls) connecting Bauska to the palace (Pilsrundāle), 12km away.

Liepāja

POP 87,000

The local **tourist office** (☎6348 0808; www.liepaja.lv; Rožu laukums 5; ⏲9am-7pm Mon-Fri, 10am-6pm Sat, 10am-3pm Sun Jun–mid-Sep, 9am-5pm Mon-Fri, 10am-3pm mid-Sep–May) calls Liepāja 'the place where wind is born', but we think the city's rough-around-the-edges vibe is undoubtedly the city's biggest draw.

Start in the **Karosta** district, 4km north of the city centre, where you'll find a particularly dour collection of **Soviet tenements** mingling with the gilded cupolas of **St Nicholas Orthodox Maritime Cathedral**. Daily multilingual tours lead visitors through **Karosta Prison** (Karostas cietums; ☎2636 9470; www.karostascietums.lv; Invalīdu iela 4; tour 2.50Ls, 2hr show 5.50Ls, sleepover 8Ls; ⏲10am-6pm May-Sep, by appointment Oct-Apr), which was used to punish disobedient Soviet soldiers. Masochists can spend the night.

Check out **Fontaine Royal** (☎6343 2005; www.fontaineroyal.lv; Stūrmaņu iela 1; s/d 18/25Ls, d without bathroom 15Ls;), a funky hotel where strange knick-knacks and sculptures abound like an orphanage for unwanted objects d'arts.

For a night out on the town try **Fontaine Palace** (www.fontainepalace.lv; Dzirnavu iela 4), a never-closing rock house luring loads of live acts and crowds of sweaty fanatics.

Buses run to/from Rīga (5.30Ls, four hours, every 45 minutes). Liepāja and Rīga are also connected by an infrequent train service (departing Liepāja on Monday and Saturday).

EASTERN LATVIA

Sigulda

POP 10,400

Sigulda is an enchanting little spot with delightful surprises tucked behind every dappled tree. Locals proudly call their pine-peppered town the 'Switzerland of Latvia', but if you're expecting the majesty of a mountainous snowcapped realm, you'll be disappointed. Instead Sigulda mixes its own exciting brew of scenic trails, extreme sports and 800-year-old castles steeped in colourful legends. It's also the gateway to **Gauja National Park** (Gaujas nacionālais parks; www.gnp.gov.lv), the country's oldest national park.

Sights & Activities

Start at **Sigulda New Castle** (Pils iela 16), built in the 18th century during the reign of German aristocrats. The **Sigulda Medieval Castle** (Pils iela 18) – now in resurrected ruins – around the back, was constructed in 1207 by the Order of the Brethren of the Sword. Take the **cable car** (☎6797 2531; Poruka iela 14; weekday/weekend 2/2.50Ls; ⏲10am-7.30pm Jun-Aug, to 4pm Sep-May) over the scenic river valley to **Krimulda Manor**, currently used as a rehabilitation clinic.

Daredevils can try a 43m **bungee jump** (☎2921 2731; www.bungee.lv; Poruka iela 14; Thu/Fri-Sun jumps 20/25Ls; ⏲6.30pm to last jump Thu-Sun Apr-Nov) from the moving cable car. Check out the ruins of **Krimulda Medieval Castle** nearby, then follow the serpentine road to **Gūtmaņa Cave**. Take some time to read the myriad inscriptions carved into the cave walls, then head up to the **Turaida Museum Reserve** (☎6797 1402; www.turaida-muzejs.lv; Turaidas iela 10; admission 3Ls; ⏲10am-6pm May-Oct, to 5pm Nov-Apr) and check out its beautiful medieval castle, erected in the 13th century.

Sigulda's 1200m artificial **bobsled track** (☎6797 3813; bobtrase@lis.lv; Šveices iela 13; ⏲noon-7pm Sat-Sun) was built for the former Soviet bobsleigh team. In winter you can fly down the 16-bend track at 80km/h in a **Vučko tourist bob** (ride per person 7Ls), or try the real Olympian experience on the hair-raising **winter bob** (ride per person 35Ls). Summer speed fiends can try the wheeled **summer sled** (ride per person 7Ls).

The one-of-a-kind **aerodium** (☎2838 4400; www.aerodium.lv; 2min weekday/weekend 15/18Ls; ⏲6-8pm Tue-Fri, noon-8pm Sat-Sun) is a giant wind tunnel propelling participants up into the sky as though they were flying.

Sleeping & Eating

Click on www.sigulda.lv for additional lodging and dining options.

Līvkalns B&B €
(☎6797 0916; www.livkalns.lv; Pēteralas iela; s/d from 15/25Ls) No place is more romantically rustic than this idyllic retreat next to a pond on the forest's edge. The rooms are pine-fresh and sit among a campus of adorable thatch-roof manors. The cabin-in-the-woods-style restaurant is fantastic.

Kaķu Māja LATVIAN €
(www.cathouse.lv; Pils iela 8; bistro mains from 2Ls, apt d 30Ls) A restaurant, canteen, bakery and nightclub all rolled into one charming gingerbread house. Apartment-style accommodation is also available.

Information

Gauja National Park Visitors Centre (☎6780 0388; www.gnp.gov.lv; Baznīcas iela 7; ⏲9am-5pm) Can arrange tours, backcountry camping and other accommodation. Cycle and hiking-trail maps are also available.

Tourism Information Centre (☎6797 1335; www.sigulda.lv; Raiņa iela 3; ⏲10am-7pm May-Sep, to 5pm Oct-Apr) Has an internet kiosk and mountains of helpful information about activities and accommodation. Ask about the *Sigulda Spiekis* discount card.

Getting There & Around

Buses run between Rīga and Sigulda (1.50Ls) every 30 minutes from 8am to 10pm.

Sigulda's attractions are quite spread out; bus 12 links all the sights and plies the route seven times daily (more on weekends). Bus times are posted at the stations and on the info centre's official website.

UNDERSTAND LATVIA

History

The first signs of modern man in the region date back to the Stone Age, although Latvians descended from tribes that migrated to the region around 2000 BC.

In 1201 German crusaders conquered Latvia, founded Rīga and started the Knights of the Sword. Rīga became the major city in the German Baltic and joined the Hanseatic League in 1282.

The 15th, 16th and 17th centuries were marked with battles and disputes about how to divvy up what would one day become Latvia. After a 'golden' period of Swedish rule, the Russians conquered the area during the Great Northern War (1700–21) and held the former fiefdom for two centuries.

Out of the post-WWI confusion and turmoil arose an independent Latvian state, declared on 18 November 1918. By the 1930s Latvia had achieved one of the highest standards of living in Europe. Soviet occupation began in 1939 and Latvia was occupied by Germany from 1941 to 1945. When WWII ended the Soviets marched back in, claiming to 'save' Latvia from the Nazis.

The country declared independence on 21 August 1991 and on 17 September 1991 Latvia, along with its Baltic brothers, joined the UN. After a game of prime-minister roulette and a devastating crash of the country's economy, Latvia finally shook off its antiquated Soviet fetters and, on 1 May 2004, the EU opened its doors to the fledgling nation.

Latvia registered the highest economic growth in the EU from 2004 to 2007, which later proved to be a curse when the national bank imploded during the global economic crisis. The nation is slowly marching back towards stability, but recent shifts in politics threates the prelude to a strengthening trade relationship with Russia rather than the EU.

People

Of Latvia's 2.25 million citizens, only 60% are ethnically Latvian. Russians account for 29% of the total population and make up the ethnic majority in most major cities, including the capital.

Casual hellos on the street aren't common, but Latvians are a friendly and welcoming bunch. Some will find that there is a bit of guardedness in the culture, but this caution, most likely a response to centuries of foreign rule, has helped preserve the unique language and culture through changing times.

Most Latvians are members of the Lutheran Church, although ancient pagan traditions still influence daily life.

Arts

Latvians often wax poetic about their country, calling it 'the land that sings'. It seems to be in the genes; locals are blessed with unusually pleasant voices and their canon of traditional tunes is the power source for their indomitable spirit. Latvians (along with their Baltic brothers) literally sang for their freedom from the USSR in a series of dramatic protests known as the 'Singing Revolution' and today the nation holds the **Song and Dance Festival**, which unites thousands upon thousands of singers from across the land in splendid harmony.

In 2003 the Song and Dance Festival was inscribed on Unesco's list of 'Oral and Intangible Heritage of Humanity' masterpieces.

SURVIVAL GUIDE

Directory A–Z

Accommodation

Prices quoted here are for rooms with a private bathroom unless otherwise stated. The following price indicators apply (for a high-season double room):

€ less than 25Ls (€35)

€€ 25Ls to 50Ls (€35 to €75)

€€€ more than 50Ls (€75)

Dorm beds can be had for between 5Ls and 10Ls. We highly advise booking ahead during summer. Rates drop significantly in the colder months.

Business Hours

Reviews won't list business hours unless they differ from those listed here.

Banks 9am to 4pm Monday to Friday

Bars 11am to midnight daily, to 3am Friday and Saturday

Clubs 11pm to 6am Wednesday to Saturday, Tuesday to Sunday in summer

Restaurants 11am to 11pm daily

Shops 10am to 6pm Monday to Friday, to 5pm Saturday

Embassies & Consulates

Embassies and consulates are located in Rīga.

Australian Embassy (☎6722 4251; Tomsona iela 33-1)

Canadian Embassy (☎6781 3945; www.balticstates.gc.ca; Baznīcas iela 20/22)

French Embassy (☎6703 6600; www.ambafrance-lv.org; Raiņa bulvāris 9)

German Embassy (☎6722 9096; www.riga.diplo.de; Raiņa bulvāris 13)

Irish Embassy (☎6703 9370; www.embassyofireland.lv; Alberta iela 13)

Netherlands Embassy (☎6732 6147; www.netherlandsembassy.lv; Torņa iela 4)

UK Embassy (☎6733 8126; www.ukinlatvia.fco.gov.uk/en; Alunāna iela 5)

US Embassy (☎6721 6571; http://riga.usembassy.gov; Raiņa bulvāris 7)

Festivals & Events

Latvians enjoy any excuse to party, especially during the summer months. Check out www.culture.lv for a yearly listing of festivals and events across the country. Latvia's biggest event, the **Song and Dance Festival**, is held every five years. It was last held in 2013.

Food

The following price ranges refer to a standard main course.

€ less than 5Ls

€€ 5Ls to 10Ls

€€€ more than 10Ls

Internet Access

Almost all accommodation in Rīga offers some form of internet access. Hotels in smaller cities have been doing a good job of following suit. Internet cafes are a dying breed, as many restaurants, cafes and bars now offer wireless connections.

Lattelecom (www.lattelecom.lv), Latvia's main communications service provider, has set up wi-fi beacons at every payphone around the city. Users can access the internet from within a 100m radius of these phone booths. To register for a Lattelecom password and username, call ☎9000 4111 or send an SMS with the word 'WiFi' to ☎1188.

Money

Latvia's currency, the lats, was introduced in March 1993. The lats (Ls) is divided into 100 santīms. The national bank, **Latvijas Bankas** (Latvian Bank; www.bank.lv), posts the lats' daily exchange rate on its website. Many of Rīga's hotels publish their rack rates in euros. Although Estonia has ascended to the euro, Latvia still has quite a way to go.

Post

Latvia's official postal service website (www.post.lv) can answer any of your mail-related questions, including shipping and stamp prices.

Public Holidays

The website of the **Latvia Institute** (www.li.lv) has a page of special Latvian remembrance days.

New Year's Day 1 January

Easter In accordance with the Western Church calendar

Labour Day 1 May

Restoration of Independence of the Republic of Latvia 4 May

Mothers' Day Second Sunday in May

Whitsunday A Sunday in May or June in accordance with the Western Church

Līgo & Jāņi 23 & 24 June; St John's Day and Summer Solstice festival

National Day 18 November; anniversary of proclamation of Latvian Republic, 1918

Christmas Holiday 24 to 26 December

New Year's Eve 31 December

Telephone

To make any call within Latvia, simply dial the eight-digit number. To call a Latvian telephone number from abroad, dial the international access code, then the country code for Latvia (☎371) followed by the subscriber's eight-digit number.

Telephone rates are posted on the website of the partly state-owned **Lattelecom** (www.lattelecom.lv).

If your mobile is GSM900- or 1800-compatible you can purchase a prepaid SIM-card package and top-up credit from any Narvesen superette or Rimi grocery store. The most popular plan is **ZZ by Tele2** (Tele-divi; www.tele2.lv; SIM card 0.99Ls).

Visas

Schengen rules apply. For information on obtaining visas, visit www.mfa.gov.lv/en.

Getting There & Away

Most air, train and bus connections pass through Rīga. See p726 for more details.

Air

Rīga airport (Lidosta Rīga; ☎1187; www.riga-airport.com; Marupes pagast), about 13km southwest of the city centre, houses Latvia's national carrier, **airBaltic** (☎9000 1100; www.airbaltic.com), which offers direct flights to more than 30 destinations within Europe. Check out the airport's website for a detailed list of other carriers.

Land

In 2007 Latvia acceded to the Schengen Agreement, which removed all border control between Estonia and Lithuania. Carry your travel documents with you at all times, as random border checks do occur.

BUS

Updated timetables are available at www.1188.lv.

CAR

Rental cars are allowed to travel around the Baltic (Estonia and Lithuania) at no extra fee.

TRAIN

Several train routes link Rīga to destinations in other countries.

Sea

Latvia is connected to a number of destinations by sea. There are services to/from both Rīga and Ventspils. See www.scandlines.com/en and www.finnlines.com for details about ferry service to Germany, Sweden and Russia.

Getting Around

Bus

Buses are much more convenient than trains if you're travelling beyond the capital's clutch of suburban rail lines. Updated timetables are available at www.1188.lv and www.autoosta.lv.

Car & Motorcycle

Driving is on the right-hand side. Headlights must be on at all times. Be sure to ask for *'benzene'* when looking for a petrol station – *gāze* means 'air'.

We recommend using an internationally recognised rental service for your vehicles – all major chains are represented here. Rentals range from €30 to €80 per day, depending on the type of car and time of year. The number of automatic cars in Latvia is limited.

Train

Most Latvians live in the large suburban ring around Rīga, hence the city's network of commuter rails makes it easy for tourists to reach day-tripping destinations. Latvia's further attractions are best explored by bus. All train schedule queries can be answered at www.1188.lv and www.ldz.lv.

Lithuania

Includes »

Vilnius 734
Paneriai 742
Trakai 742
Central Lithuania 743
Kaunas........................ 743
Western Lithuania 745
Klaipėda 745
Curonian Spit 745
Understand Lithuania .. 746
Survival Guide 747

Best Places to Eat

- » Tres Mexicanos (p740)
- » Moksha (p744)
- » Ararat (p745)

Best Places to Stay

- » Miško Namas (p746)
- » Litinterp Guesthouse (p745)
- » Jimmy Jumps House (p739)

Why Go?

A great little all-rounder, Lithuania has much to offer. Those with a passion for baroque architecture, ancient castles and archaeological treasures will find plenty in the capital and beyond. There are sculpture parks and interactive museums for travellers wishing to delve into the country's traumatic recent history; modern art spaces and exhibitions to titillate those whose interests are more contemporary and all-night clubbing in the cities and on the coast for those requiring something less cerebral. Throw in a whirlwind of great restaurants, beer gardens and bars, and you have urban entertainment aplenty.

Away from the cities, the giant sand dunes on the west coast and the southeast's lakes and forests beckon fresh-air fiends; they come alive in the summer with cyclists, berry pickers and campers.

Combine all that with Lithuania's pagan roots, boundless energy and rebellious spirit, and you're in for a heck of a ride.

When to Go

Vilnius

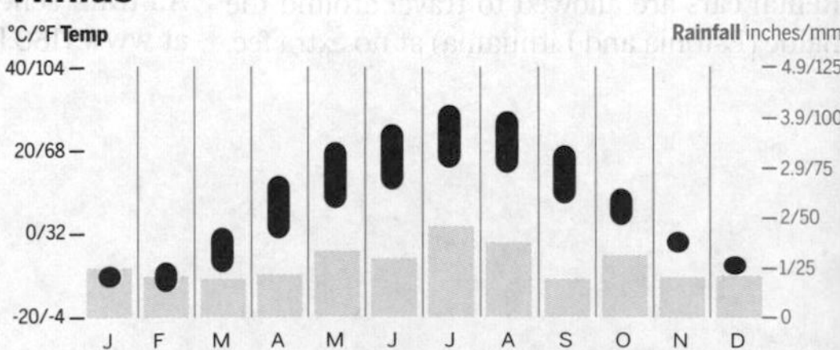

Apr Some of the world's best jazz performers are at the Kaunas Jazz Festival.

Jun & Jul The loveliest time to explore the forests and sand dunes of the Curonian Spit.

Sep Vilnius City Days, a celebration of the capital with street theatre, music and fashion.

Connections

Buses, trains and ferries provide numerous travel options to Lithuania's neighbouring countries.

Vilnius is a hub for buses to Poland, Latvia, Estonia, Belarus and Russia's Kaliningrad; from Kaunas there are buses to Latvia, Estonia and Kaliningrad, and the latter may also be reached from Klaipėda and the Curonian Spit.

Trains serve Russia, Poland and Belarus from the capital. Sweden and Germany can be reached by ferry from Klaipėda, Lithuania's international port.

ITINERARIES

Three Days

Devote two days to exploring the baroque heart of Vilnius, then day trip to Trakai for its spectacular island castle and the homesteads of the Karaite people, stopping off at Paneriai on the way.

One Week

Spend four nights in Vilnius, with day trips to both Trakai and Grūtas Park, the Soviet sculpture park near Druskininkai. Travel cross-country to the Hill of Crosses, then explore some serious nature on the Curonian Spit for two or three days. Head back east via Klaipėda and Kaunas.

Essential Food & Drink

» **Potato creations** Try the *cepelinai* (potato-dough zeppelin stuffed with meat, mushrooms or cheese), *bulviniai blynai* (potato pancakes) or *žemaičių blynai* (heart-shaped mashed potato stuffed with meat and fried), or the *vedarai* (baked pig intestines stuffed with mashed potato).

» **Beer snacks** No drinking session is complete without a plate of smoked pigs' ears and *kepta duona* (deep-fried garlicky bread sticks).

» **Beetroot delight** Cold, creamy *šaltibarščiai* (beetroot soup) is a summer speciality, served with a side of fried potatoes.

» **Unusual meat** Sample the game, such as beaver stew or bear sausages.

» **Smoked fish** The Curonian Spit is famous for its smoked fish, particularly the superb *rukytas unguris* (smoked eel).

» **Beer and mead** Šytutys, Utenos and Kalnapilis are top beers; *midus* (mead) is a honey-tinged nobleman's drink.

AT A GLANCE

» **Currency** Litas (Lt)

» **Language** Lithuanian

» **Money** ATMs everywhere

» **Visas** Not required for citizens of the EU, Australia, Canada, Israel, Japan, New Zealand, Switzerland or the US for stays of 90 days

Fast Facts

» **Area** 65,303 sq km

» **Capital** Vilnius

» **Country code** ☎370

» **Emergency** ☎112

Exchange Rates

Australia	A$1	2.82Lt
Canada	C$1	2.66Lt
Euro Zone	€1	3.45Lt
Japan	¥100	2.86Lt
New Zealand	NZ$1	2.26Lt
UK	UK£1	4.09Lt
USA	US$1	2.70Lt

Set Your Budget

» **Budget hotel room** 200Lt

» **Two-course meal** 55Lt

» **Museum entrance** 7Lt

» **Beer** 8Lt

» **Bicycle hire (per day)** 40Lt

Resources

» **In Your Pocket** (www.inyourpocket.com)

» **Lithuania's Museums** (www.muziejai.lt)

» **Tourism in Lithuania** (www.tourism.lt)

VILNIUS

POP 523,100

Vilnius, the baroque bombshell of the Baltics, is a city of immense allure. As beautiful as it is bizarre, it easily tops the country's best-attraction bill, drawing tourists to it with a confident charm and a warm, golden glow that makes one wish for long, midsummer evenings every day of the year.

At its heart is Europe's largest baroque Old Town, so precious that Unesco added it to its World Heritage list in 1994. Its skyline, pierced by (almost) countless Orthodox and Catholic church steeples, appears like a giant bed of nails from the basket of a hot-air balloon (p740). Adding to the intoxicating mix is a combination of cobbled alleys, hilltop views, breakaway states and traditional artists' workshops.

Lithuania Highlights

1. Explore beautiful baroque **Vilnius** (p734) with its cobbled streets, skyline of church spires, and bars and bistros
2. Breathe the pure air within the fragrant pine forests and high sand dunes of the enchanting **Curonian Spit** (p746)
3. Hear the wind whisper between the thousands of crosses on the eerie **Hill of Crosses** (p745) near Šiauliai
4. Wander wonderful **Trakai** (p742), home of the Karaite people and a stunning island castle
5. Visit Lithuania's Communist past at the **Grūtas sculpture park** (p743)
6. Take in the poignant WWII history of **Ninth Fort** (p744), near Kaunas

Vilnius feels tiny, but that's a bit deceptive because the suburban sprawl that surrounds the Old Town is a fairly typical Soviet-style mess of snarled traffic and concrete.

September is a good time to be in the capital, as the city celebrates **Vilnius City Days** (www.vilniusfestivals.lt) with street theatre performances, live music in open-air spaces and fashion shows.

Sights

CATHEDRAL SQUARE & NEW TOWN

TOP CHOICE Museum of Genocide Victims MUSEUM
(Genocido Aukų Muziejus; www.genocid.lt/muziejus; Aukų gatvė 2a; adult/child 6/3Lt, audioguide 10Lt; ⏲10am-6pm Wed-Sat, to 5pm Sun) 'KGB Museum' to locals, this building used to be the notorious KGB headquarters from 1940 to 1991. The detailed exhibits deal mostly with Soviet oppression of the Lithuanian people, the post-WWII Lithuanian resistance movement and the mass deportation of locals to Siberia.

However, there is almost no mention of the fact that this was also the Gestapo headquarters between 1941 and 1944, or of their role in the genocide of much of the city's Jewish population, so the small new Holocaust exhibition is welcome.

In the basement, check out the water cell, the padded cell and the execution chamber.

TOP CHOICE Cathedral Square SQUARE
(Katedros aikštė) At the base of Gediminas Hill sprawls Cathedral Square, dominated by the splendid white neoclassical **Vilnius Cathedral** (Vilniaus Arkikatedra; ⏲7am-7.30pm, mass Sun 8am, 9am, 10am, 11.15am, 12.30pm, 5.30pm & 6.30pm) and its 57m-tall **belfry**. The first wooden cathedral, built in 1387–88, was originally Gothic but has been rebuilt many times since. The showpiece of the airy, light interior is the baroque **St Casimir's Chapel**, with white stucco sculptures and frescos depicting the life of St Casimir (Lithuania's patron saint), whose silver coffin lies within.

Next door to the cathedral stands **Gediminas Palace** (Gedimino rumai). Demolished by the Russians in the 18th century, the palace has been rebuilt and was due to reopen in spring 2013.

TOP CHOICE National Museum of Lithuania MUSEUM
(Lietuvos Nacionalinis Muziejus; www.lnm.lt; Arsenalo gatvė 1; adult/child 5/2Lt; ⏲10am-5pm Tue-Sat, 10am-3pm Sun May-Sep, 10am-5pm Wed-Sun Oct-Apr) Lithuania's oldest museum is an entertaining stampede through the country's history from the 13th century to WWII. In the ethnography section, alongside the national costumes and recreations of rural dwellings there are some wonderfully ornate iron crosses and superb temporary exhibitions.

Gediminas Hill HILL
(funicular adult/child 3/2Lt; ⏲funicular 10am-7pm) Vilnius was founded on 48m-high Gediminas Hill, topped since the 13th century by the oft-rebuilt **Gediminas Tower**. There are spectacular views of the Old Town from the top of the tower, which houses the **Gediminas Castle & Museum** (Gedimino Pilis ir Muziejus; adult/child 5/2Lt; ⏲10am-7pm May-Sep, 10am-5pm Tue-Sun Oct-Apr), reached by the **funicular** located at the rear of the Museum of Applied Arts.

Museum of Applied Arts MUSEUM
(Taikomosios Dailės Muziejus; www.ldm.lt; Arsenalo gatvė 3a; adult/student 6/3Lt; ⏲11am-6pm Tue-Sat, 11am-4pm Sun) Currently the keeper of Gediminas' treasure – tapestries, early Lithuanian coins, weaponry, jewellery – the Museum of Applied Arts houses a permanent collection showcasing 15th- to 19th-century Lithuanian sacred art. The treasure was discovered in Vilnius Cathedral only in 1985, and was due to move to the restored palace in May 2013.

Gedimino Prospektas STREET
The main boulevard of Vilnius' 19th-century New Town heads due west from Cathedral Sq all the way to the silver-domed Russian

VILNIUS CITY CARD

If you're planning to do epic amounts of sightseeing within a short period of time, the **Vilnius City Card** (www.vilnius-tourism.lt; 24/72hr 58/90Lt) provides free or discounted entry to many attractions, as well as free transport.

Central Vilnius

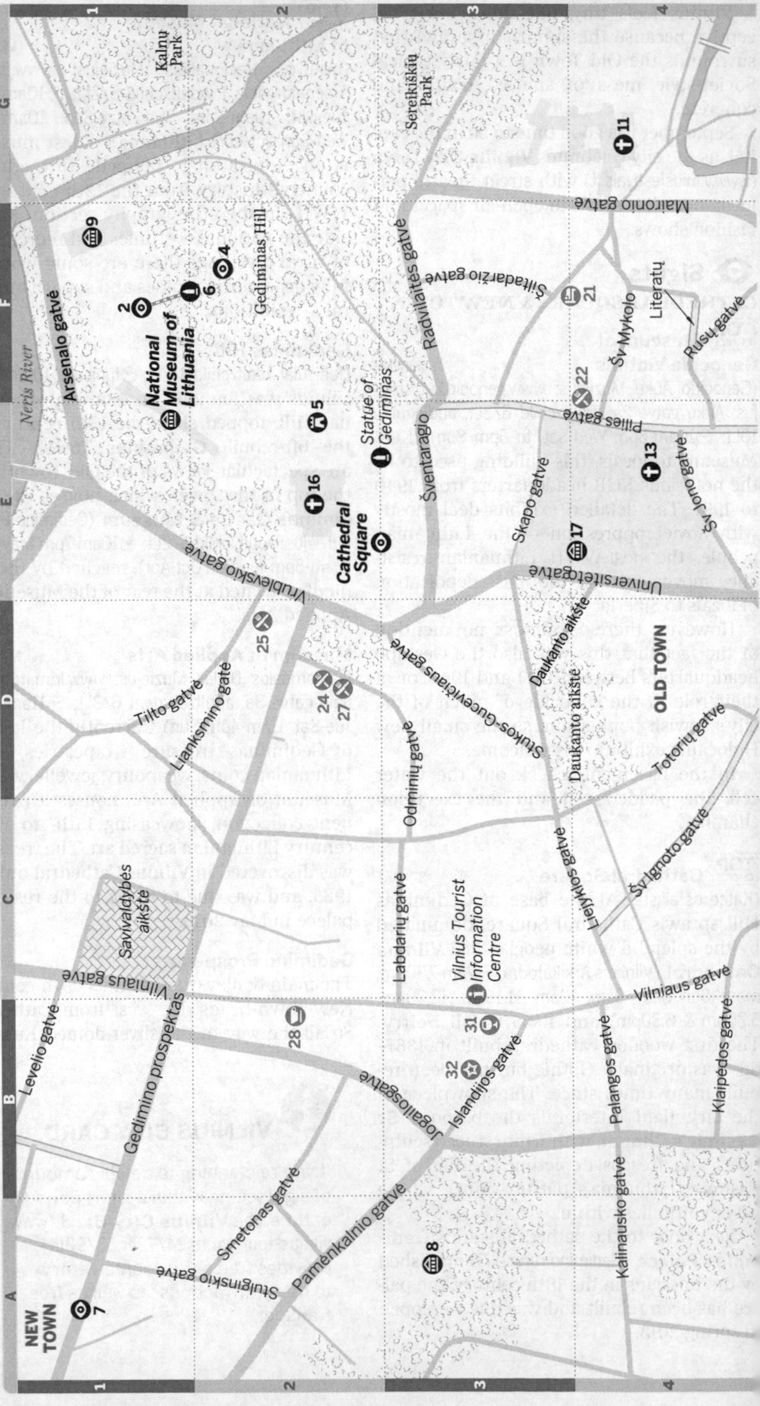

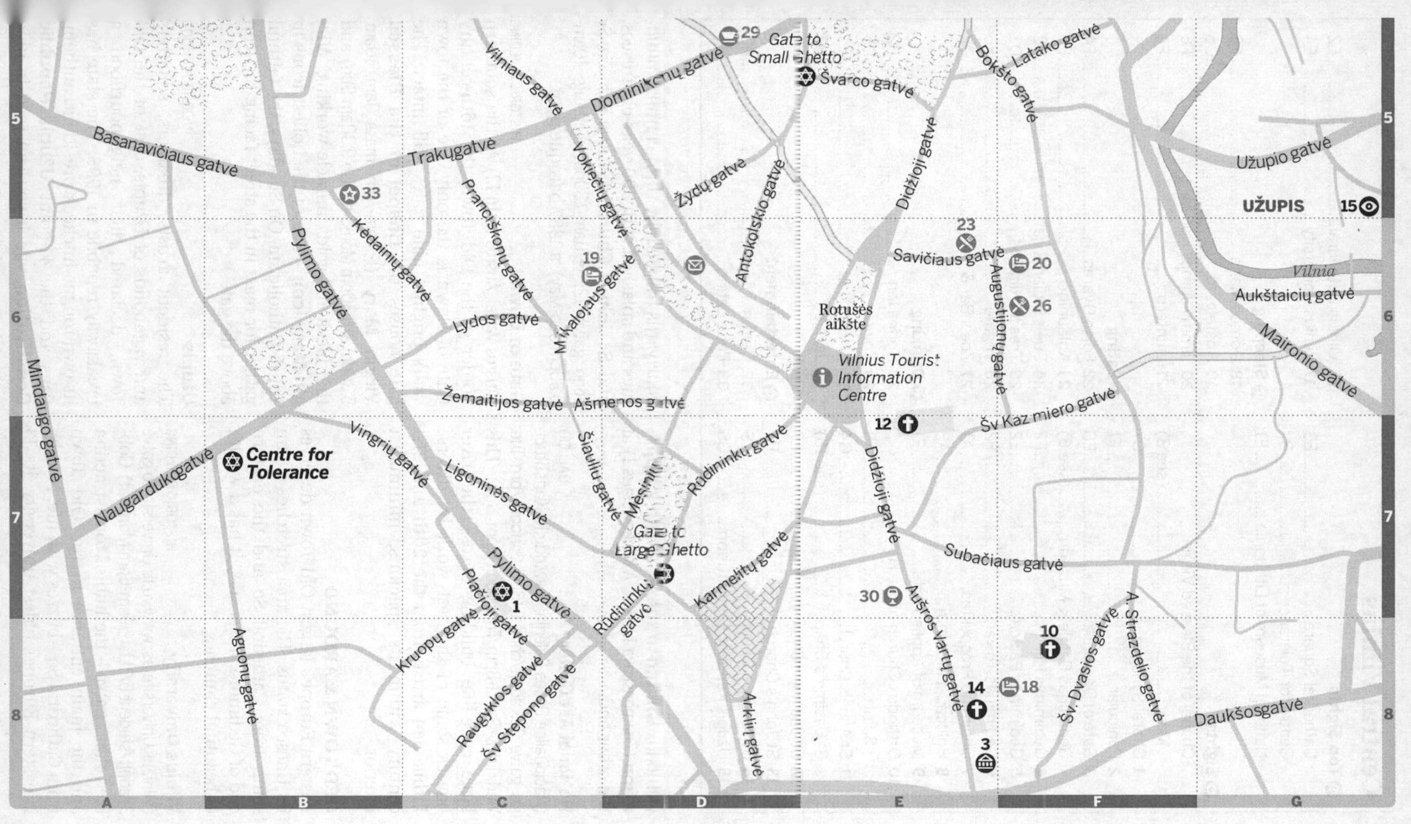
29
Gate to Small Ghetto
Švarco gatvė
Latako gatvė
Bokšto gatvė
Vilniaus gatvė
Dominikonų gatvė
Basanavičiaus gatvė
Trakų gatvė
33
Užupio gatvė
UŽUPIS
15
Žydų gatvė
Antokolskio gatvė
Didžioji gatvė
Vokiečių gatvė
Pranciškonų gatvė
Kėdainių gatvė
Pylimo gatvė
19
Mikalojaus gatvė
23
Savičiaus gatvė
20
Augustijonų gatvė
26
Vilnia
Aukštaičių gatvė
Maironio gatvė
Rotušės aikštė
Vilnius Tourist Information Centre
Lydos gatvė
Mindaugo gatvė
Žemaitijos gatvė
Ašmenos gatvė
12
Šv Kazimiero gatvė
Vingrių gatvė
Naugarduko gatvė
Centre for Tolerance
Ligoninės gatvė
Šiaulių gatvė
Mėsinių
Rūdininkų gatvė
Didžioji gatvė
Gate to Large Ghetto
Subačiaus gatvė
Pylimo gatvė
1
Plačiojo gatvė
Karmelitų gatvė
Rūdininkų gatvė
30
Aušros Vartų gatvė
10
Kruopų gatvė
Raugyklos gatvė
Šv Stepono gatvė
Aguonų gatvė
Arklių gatvė
14
18
3
Šv. Dvasios gatvė
A. Strazdelio gatvė
Daukšos gatvė
LITHUANIA VILNIUS

Central Vilnius

Top Sights

	Cathedral Square	E3
	Centre for Tolerance	B7
	National Museum of Lithuania	E1

Sights

	Chapel of the Blessed Virgin Mary	(see 3)
1	Choral Synagogue	C7
2	Funicular	F1
3	Gate of Dawn	E8
	Gediminas Castle & Museum	(see 6)
4	Gediminas Hill	F2
5	Gediminas Palace	E2
6	Gediminas Tower	F2
7	Gedimino Prospektas	A1
8	Holocaust Museum	A3
9	Museum of Applied Arts	F1
10	Orthodox Church of the Holy Spirit	F8
11	St Anne's Church	G4
	St Casimir's Chapel	(see 16)
12	St Casimir's Church	E7
13	St John's Church	E4
14	St Teresa's Church	E8
15	Užupis Republic Constitution	G5
16	Vilnius Cathedral	E2
17	Vilnius University	E4

Sleeping

18	Domus Maria	F8
19	Hostelgate	C6
20	Jimmy Jumps House	F6
21	Litinterp	F4

Eating

22	Forto Dvaras	F4
23	Koldūnine	E6
24	Sue's Indian Raja	D2
25	Tres Mexicanos	D2
26	Vegafé	F6
27	Zoe's Bar & Grill	D2

Drinking

28	Coffee Inn	B2
29	Cozy	D5
30	In Vino	E7
31	Jackie	B3

Entertainment

32	Opium	B3
33	Pabo Latino	B5

Orthodox **Church of the St Virgin's Apparition** (Znamenskaya Tserkov; A Mickevičiaus 1) at the other end.

National Art Gallery GALLERY
(Nacionalinė Dailės Galerija; www.ndg.lt; Konstitucijos gatvė 22; adult/child 6/3Lt; ⌚noon-7pm Tue, Wed, Fri & Sat, 1-8pm Thu, noon-5pm Sun) This large cube-like building across the river houses some of the best work by diverse Lithuanian artists from the 20th and 21st century within its spacious, minimalist interior.

OLD TOWN & AROUND

Eastern Europe's largest Old Town deserves its Unesco status. The area stretches 1.5km south from Cathedral Sq and the eastern end of Gedimino prospektas. It has a wealth of beautiful churches.

Vilnius University HISTORIC BUILDING
(Vilniaus Universitetas; www.vu.lt; Universiteto gatvė 3; adult/student 5/1Lt; ⌚9am-6pm Mon-Sat) Cobbled Pilies gatvė – the hub of tourist action and the main entrance to the Old Town from Cathedral Sq – buzzes with life. Nearby is eastern Europe's oldest university, its 13 courtyards framed by 15th-century buildings and splashed with 300-year-old frescos, and **St John's Church** (Šv Jonų Bažnyčia; Šv Jono gatvė 12; ⌚11am-7.30pm Jun-Aug, 10am-6.30pm Sep-May), a 1387 baroque gem.

Gate of Dawn HISTORIC BUILDING
(Aušros Vartai; Aušros Vartų 12) At the southern border of the Old Town, the 16th-century Gate of Dawn is the only one of the town wall's original nine gates still intact. The gate houses the **Chapel of the Blessed Virgin Mary** (⌚6am-7pm, mass 9am, 10am, 5.30pm & 6.30pm Mon-Sat, also 9.30am Sun) and the black-and-gold 'miracle-working' **Virgin Mary icon** – one of the holiest icons in Polish Catholicism. On Sundays, the faithful gather for mass in the street facing the icon above the gate.

Užupis NEIGHBOURHOOD
The resident artists, dreamers, squatters and vagabonds of Užupis, east of the Old Town, declared their neighbourhood a breakaway republic in 1998. The state has its own tongue-in-cheek president, anthem, flags and the 41-point **Užupis Republic Constitution**, which you can read in nine

languages on a wall on Paupio gatvė. The April Fool's Day party held here is particularly raucous.

St Anne's Church CHURCH
(Šv Onos Bažnyčia; Maironio gatvė 8; ⏲Mass 6pm Mon-Sat, 9am & 11am Sun) Pint-sized, red Gothic beauty that charmed Napoleon.

St Teresa's Church CHURCH
(Šv Teresės Bažnyčia; Aušros Vartų gatvė 14) Fantastic example of early baroque (1635–50) with an elaborate facade and a spectacular rococo interior.

St Casimir's Church CHURCH
(Šv Kazimiero Bažnyčia; Didžioji gatvė 34) The oldest of Vilnius' baroque masterpieces, built by Jesuits (1604–35)

Orthodox Church of the Holy Spirit CHURCH
(Stačiatikių Šv Dvasios Cerkvė; Aušros Vartų gatvė 10) Rococo stunner with a beautiful interior, the home of the supposedly incorruptible bodies of three saints.

Sleeping

TOP CHOICE **Jimmy Jumps House** HOSTEL €
(☎6078 8435; www.jimmyjumpshouse.com; Savičiaus gatvė 12-1; dm 37-42Lt, d 110Lt; @📶) Sociable without being a stag-party magnet, this place is for those who want to pack a lot into their stay – from themed pub crawls to Machine Gun Tours and more. Free waffle breakfast, movie lounge and hookahs for those rainy days make up for the modest-sized dorms.

TOP CHOICE **Domus Maria** GUESTHOUSE €€
(☎5-264 4880; www.domusmaria.lt; Aušros Vartų gatvė 12; d/tr €93/114; P@📶) This guesthouse, in a heavenly location within a 17th-century former monastery, stays true to its monastic origins with wide-arched corridors and spartan yet comfortable white rooms. And if you feel as if you're having breakfast in a chapel, that's because you are.

Litinterp B&B €
(☎5-212 3850; www.litinterp.lt; Bernardinų gatvė 7-2; s/d/tr 100/160/210Lt, without bathroom 80/140/180Lt, apt 280Lt; ⏲office 8.30am-9pm Mon-Fri, 9am-3pm Sat; 📶) Bright, clean and friendly budget-traveller favourite right in the heart of the Old Town. Rooms with shared bathroom are only good for swinging a small cat, but those with en suite are generously large. Arrival time required in advance.

Hostelgate HOSTEL €
(☎6383 2818; www.hostelgate.lt; Mikalojaus gatvė 3; dm/d/tr/q from 38/110/141/180Lt; @📶) At this central little hostel the staff go out of their way to make guests feel welcome. There's a lounge for socialising, free coffee and lockers, but no breakfast (there is a kitchen) and private rooms are in the building next door.

Come to Vilnius HOSTEL €
(☎6560 5036; www.cometovilnius.eu; Šv Stepono gatvė 15; dm/d/tr 55/120/150Lt; 📶) Great new hostel near the bus and train stations with nice little touches, such as reading lights, good showers and compact, spick-and-span

JEWISH VILNIUS

Dubbed by Napoleon the 'Jerusalem of the north', Vilnius had one of Europe's most prominent Jewish communities until Nazi brutality wiped it out.

The old Jewish quarter lay in the streets west of Didžioji gatvė, including present-day Žydų gatvė (Jews St) and Gaono gatvė, named after Vilnius' most famous Jewish resident, Gaon Elijahu ben Shlomo Zalman (1720–97).

The **Centre for Tolerance** (www.jmuseum.lt; Naugarduko gatvė 10; adult/child 5/2Lt; ⏲11am-7pm Mon, 10am-6pm Tue-Thu, to 4pm Fri & Sun), a beautifully restored former Jewish theatre, houses thought-provoking displays on the history and culture of Jews in Lithuania before the Shoah (Holocaust) and occasional art exhibitions. The **Holocaust Museum** (Holokausto Muziejus; www.jmuseum.lt; Paměnkalnio gatvė 12; adult/child 5/2Lt; ⏲9am-5pm Mon-Thu, 9am-4pm Fri, 10am-4pm Sun), in the so-called Green House, is an unvarnished account detailing the suffering of the Lithuanian Jews in an unedited display of horrific images and letters by local Holocaust survivors.

Vilnius' only remaining synagogue, the **Choral Synagogue** (Choralinė Sinagoga; Pylimo gatvė 39; donations welcome; ⏲10am-2pm Sun-Fri), was built in a Moorish style in 1903 and survived only because the Nazis used it as a medical store.

DON'T MISS

VILNIUS FROM ABOVE

Get some vertical perspective on Vilnius by either heading up the 326m-tall **TV Tower** (Televizijos Bokštas; www.lrtc.net; Sausio 13-osios gatvė 10; adult/child 21/9Lt; ⊙observation deck 10am-10pm; trolleybus 1, 3, 7 ,16) or – even better – taking to the skies in a hot-air balloon courtesy of the **Oreivystės Centras** (☎5-273 2703; www.ballooning.lt; Upės gatvė 5; per person €119-179). Finally, you can enjoy dizzying views of Vilnius from the 22nd-floor **Sky Bar** (Konstitucijos prospektas 20; ⊙5pm-1am Sun-Thu, to 2.30am Fri & Sat) while imbibing a seriously good cocktail.

rooms. There's no real area for mingling apart from the kitchen and around, but the staff are ultra-helpful.

AAA Hostel HOSTEL €
(☎5-215 0270; www.ahostel.lt; Sodų gatvė 8; dm/s/d from 34/87/97Lt; @📶) The 16-bed dorm here is modelled on Japan's capsule hotels. The decor stands out, with a cavern-like kitchen, funky chairs in the lounge and blood-red carpets in the spacious rooms.

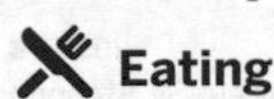

Eating

TOP CHOICE **Tres Mexicanos** MEXICAN €€
(www.tresmexicanos.lt; Tilto gatvė 2; mains 18-28Lt) Cheerful yellow restaurant run by Mexican transplants and packing some proper heat with its authentically spicy enchiladas, tacos and burritos. It's one of the best stops for *mole poblano* this side of the Atlantic.

Zoe's Bar & Grill INTERNATIONAL €€
(www.zoesbargrill.com; Odminių gatvė 3; mains 21-49Lt) Bustling, friendly Zoe's tempts you with the likes of African beef and pepper soup with citrus yoghurt, baby back ribs and fabulous meatballs. If you're not too hungry, there are sandwiches and salads aplenty and the crème brûlée is done just right.

Sue's Indian Raja INDIAN €€
(☎5-266 1887; www.suesindianraja.lt; Odminių gatvė 3; mains 22-48Lt; ⓥ) Loved by Indian embassy staff and visitors alike, this fine restaurant serves large portions of expertly flavoured and authentically spicy Indian dishes, such as the sublime butter chicken, and a good range of vegetarian options.

Vegafé VEGETARIAN €
(Augustijonų gatvė 2/13; mains 11-15Lt; ⊙11am-9.30pm Mon-Sat; ⓥ) This tiny, leafy terrace beckons with imaginative soups, smoothies, sweet and savoury lassis and flavourful mains that involve lentils, vegetables, tofu and whatever the chef happens to have to hand that day.

Forto Dvaras LITHUANIAN €
(www.fortas.eu; Pilies gatvė 16; mains 12-38Lt; 📶ⓥ) Popular folk-themed restaurant serving Lithuania's national dish – the *cepelinai* – as well as humongous beer snack platters, *šaltibarščiai*, potato pancakes and more.

Koldūnine LITHUANIAN €
(Savičiaus gatvė 6; mains 12-18Lt; 📶ⓥ) At this informal eatery you'll find – count 'em! – 11 different varieties of *koldūninė* (Lithuanian dumplings) and they're all stomach-fillingly tasty. Not in a dumpling mood? There are pancakes and 'Caesarian salad', too.

Iki (Sodų gatvė 22, bus station; ⊙8am-10pm) and **Maxima** (Geležinkelio gatvė, train station; ⊙8am-10pm) are leading supermarket chains; self-caterers may also want to stop by the **Kalvarijų Market** (Kalvarijų Turgus; Kalvarijų gatvė 61; ⊙7am-2pm Tue-Sun) or the **Halės Market** (Halės Turgus; Pylimo gatvė 58/1;; ⊙7am-5pm Tue-Sat, to 3pm Sun), which sells fresh fruit, vegetables, dairy, smoked meat and fish.

Drinking

Cozy CAFE
(www.cozy.lt; Dominikonų gatvė 10; ⊙9am-2am Mon-Wed, to 4am Thu & Fri, 10am-4am Sat, to 2am Sun) Cozy is a great breakfast spot and an inexpensive lunch or dinner joint. On weekends you can grab a drink to fuel you through the DJ sessions downstairs.

In Vino WINE BAR
(www.invino.lt; Aušros Vartų gatvė 7; ⊙4pm-2am Sun-Thu, to 4am Fri & Sat) One of the best wine bars in town, with a lovely courtyard, excellent wines, and good choice of tapas. Arrive early in summer to secure a table, then watch the place fill to overflowing.

Jackie BAR
(Vilniaus gatvė 31; ⊙6pm-1am Sun-Wed, to 3am Thu, to 5am Fri & Sat) This new whisky bar, specialising in American whiskies and bourbon gets absolutely packed most nights, so if you wish to savour your poison, go early. Or go late on weekends if you want to catch a DJ set.

Coffee Inn COFFEE HOUSE
(www.coffee-inn.lt; Vilniaus gatvė 17; ⌚7am-10pm Mon-Thu, to midnight Fri, 9am-midnight Sat, to 11pm Sun; 📶) Lithuania's answer to Starbucks offers freshly made wraps, muffins, cookies and grilled vegetable sandwiches. Oh, and coffee – from your basic espresso to frozen frappucino-style delights.

☆ Entertainment

Pabo Latino CLUB
(www.pabolatino.lt; Trakų gatvė 3; ⌚9pm-3am Thu, to 5am Fri & Sat) This sultry-red club specialises in live Latin music and strong cocktails. Put on your dancing shoes, fortify your liver, and be prepared for a fun night out with some of the city's most beautiful people.

Opium DJ
(Islandijos gatvė 4; cover 10-15Lt; ⌚10pm-6am Fri, 11pm-5am Sat) This compact venue – the playground of the city's best DJs – is for serious clubbers. Come here once, and there's a good chance you'll get addicted.

TRANSPORT FROM VILNIUS

Domestic Bus

DESTINATION	PRICE (LT)	DURATION (HR)	FREQUENCY
Druskininkai	32	2-2¼	up to 12 daily
Kaunas	20	1½	2-3 hourly
Klaipėda	68	4-6½	15 daily
Šiauliai	47	3¼-5	up to 14 daily

International Bus

DESTINATION	PRICE (LT)	DURATION (HR)	FREQUENCY
Berlin (Germany)	130	13½	daily
Kaliningrad (Russia)	64	7½	1-2 daily
Rīga (Latvia)	35	3¾-4	up to 7 daily
St Petersburg (Russia)	155	24	2 daily
Tallinn (Estonia)	69	10½	daily
Warsaw (Poland)	65	8	1 daily

Domestic Train

DESTINATION	PRICE (LT)	DURATION	FREQUENCY (DAILY)
Kaunas	16.30	1-1¾hr	up to 17
Klaipėda	51.20	4¾hr	3
Šiauliai	34.80	2½hr	3
Trakai	6.20	35-45min	up to 10

International

DESTINATION	PRICE (LT)	DURATION (HR)	FREQUENCY (DAILY)
Kaliningrad (Russia)	from 110	6¼-6½	up to 4
Minsk (Belarus)	from 30	3-4¾	up to 7
Moscow (Russia)	from 317	14¾-15¾	up to 3
St Petersburg (Russia)	371	14-18½	2
Warsaw (Poland)	from 85	10¾	1

Soho GAY
(www.sohoclub.lt; Švitrigailos gatvė 7/16; ⊙10pm-7am Fri & Sat) At the main haunt for Vilnius' gay community, you can leap into the limelight on the dance floor, or have a quietish tête-à-tête with that attractive stranger you've just met in one of the mini halls.

Information

Baltic-American Medical & Surgical Clinic (☎5-234 2020, 6985 2655; www.bak.lt; Nemenčinės gatvė 54a; ⊙24hr) English-speaking health centre.

Lonely Planet (www.lonelyplanet.com/lithuania/vilnius)

Main Pharmacy (Gedimino Vaistinė; Gedimino prospektas 27; ⊙7.30am-8pm Mon-Fri, 10am-5pm Sat, to 4pm Sun)

Vilnius Tourist Information Centres (www.vilnius-tourism.lt) town hall (☎5-262 6470; Didžioji gatvė 31; ⊙9am-6pm); train station (☎5-269 2091; Geležinkelio gatvė 16; ⊙9am-1pm & 1.45-6pm); Vilniaus gatvė (☎5-262 9660; Vilniaus gatvė 22; ⊙9am-6pm) A wealth of brochures, maps and general information.

Getting There & Away

International bus services leave from the **bus station** (Autobusų Stotis; ☎1661; www.toks.lt; Sodų gatvė 22), run by **Ecolines** (☎5-262 0020; www.ecolines.net; bus station) or one of the affiliated carriers under **Eurolines** (www.eurolines.lt).

From the **train station** (Geležinkelio Stotis; ☎5-233 0088; www.litrail.lt; Geležinkelio gatvė 16), Vilnius is linked by regular direct trains to various international destinations.

Getting Around

TO/FROM THE AIRPORT Bus 1 runs between the **Vilnius International Airport** (Tarptautinis Vilniaus Oro Uostas; ☎5-230 6666; www.vno.lt; Rodūnios Kelias 2; ; 1, 2), 5km south of the centre, and the train station. A shuttle train service runs from the train station 17 times daily between 5.44am and 9.07pm (2.50Lt). A taxi from the airport to the city centre should cost around 55Lt.

BICYCLE VeloCity (☎6741 2123; www.velo-city.lt; Aušros Vartų 12; ⊙9am-9pm) rents bicycles for 10/40Lt per hour/day, provides information on cycling routes and arranges cycling tours of the city.

PUBLIC TRANSPORT The refillable electronic Vilniečio Kortelė (Vilnius Card) has been introduced and can be purchased from news kiosks for 4Lt. A new pricing scheme applies: 30min/60min/24hr/72hr tickets cost 2.20/3.20/12/21Lt.

You can still purchase single-ride tickets from kiosks or on board, but they are marginally pricier than the electronic card.

TAXI Taxi fare is 1.50Lt to 3Lt per kilometre and taxis must have a meter. Phone a **taxi** (www.etaksi.lt; ☎1409, 1411, 1818, 1445, no prefix needed) or queue outside the train station.

AROUND VILNIUS

Paneriai

During WWII the Nazis – aided by Lithuanian accomplices – exterminated 100,000 people, around 70,000 of them Jews, at this site in the forest, 10km southwest of Vilnius.

From the entrance a path leads to the small **Paneriai Museum** (☎Algys Karosas 6808 1278; Agrastų gatvė 17; ⊙10am-6pm Sun-Thu), with a graphic display of photographs and personal belongings of those who died here, and the grassed-over pits where the Nazis burnt the exhumed bodies of their victims.

There are hourly trains daily from Vilnius to Paneriai station (2Lt, eight to 11 minutes) from where it's a 1km walk southwest along Agrastų gatvė into the forest.

Trakai

POP 4930

With its picturesque red-brick castle, Karaite culture, quaint wooden houses and pretty lakeside location, Trakai is a must-see within easy reach of the capital.

The Karaite people are named after the term *kara*, which means 'to study the scriptures' in both Hebrew and Arabic. The sect originated in Baghdad and practises strict adherence to the Torah (rejecting the rabbinic Talmud). In around 1400 the grand duke of Lithuania, Vytautas, brought about 380 Karaite families to Trakai from Crimea to serve as bodyguards. Only a dozen families remain in Trakai today and their numbers are dwindling rapidly.

Trakai's trophy piece is the fairy-tale **Trakai Castle** (Trakų Pilis; www.trakaimuziejus.lt; adult/senior/student & child 14/8/6Lt, camera 4Lt; ⊙10am-7pm May-Sep, to 6pm Mar, Apr & Oct, to 5pm Nov-Feb), occupying a small island in Lake Galvė. A footbridge links the island castle to the shore. The red-brick Gothic castle, painstakingly restored from original blueprints, dates from the late 14th century

WORTH A TRIP

GRŪTAS PARK – THE GRAVEYARD OF COMMUNISM

Mildly controversial **Grūtas Park** (Grūto Parkas; www.grutoparkas.lt; adult/child 5-16yr 20/10Lt; ⌚9am-10pm summer, to 5pm rest of year;), 125km south of Vilnius, near the spa town of Druskininkai, has been an enormous hit since it opened in 2001. The sprawling grounds, built to resemble a Siberian concentration camp, feature the entire Marxist pantheon and dozens of other statuesque examples of Soviet realism, as well as assorted Communist paraphernalia, exhibits on Soviet history (with a focus on the oppression of Lithuania) and loudspeakers bellowing Soviet anthems. The statues once stood confidently in parks and squares across Lithuania, but now this is all that's left.

There are up to 10 buses daily between Druskininkai and Vilnius (32Lt, two hours), and hourly buses to and from Kaunas (27.50Lt, 2¼ hours). Ask to be let off at Grūtas village, then walk the final 1km to the park. Catch a bus back to either city from the main road.

Inside the castle's cellars and tower, the **Trakai History Museum** (Trakų Istorijos Muziejus; www.trakaimuziejus.lt; adult/senior/student & child 14/8/6Lt, camera 4Lt; ⌚10am-7pm May-Sep, to 6pm Mar, Apr & Oct, to 5pm Nov-Feb) tells the story of the castle, and there's a bewildering variety of objects on show – hoards of coins, weaponry and porcelain, as well as interactive displays.

You can sample *kibinai* (meat-stuffed Karaite pastries similar to empanadas) at **Kibininė** (www.kibinas.lt; Karaimų gatvė 65; kibinai 4.50-7.50Lt; ⌚10am-midnight) or **Kybynlar** (www.kybynlar.lt; Karaimų gatvė 29; mains 16-28Lt; ⌚noon-9pm Mon, 11am-9pm Tue-Thu, to 10pm Fri & Sat, to 9pm Sun).

Up to 10 trains daily (6.20Lt, 35 to 45 minutes) travel between Trakai and Vilnius, while the more convenient Alytus-bound buses (6Lt, 40 minutes, twice hourly) stop closer to the castle.

CENTRAL LITHUANIA

Kaunas

POP 311, 100

Lithuania's second city has a compact Old Town, an entertaining array of museums, and plenty of vibrant, youthful energy provided by its sizeable student population. A good time to visit is in late April, during the **Kaunas Jazz Festival** (www.kaunasjazz.lt), when home-grown and international artists perform in venues across the city.

Sights

OLD TOWN

The heart of Kaunas' lovely Old Town is **Rotušės Aikštė**, a square surrounded by 15th- and 16th-century German merchants' houses, with the former city hall now reincarnated as the **Palace of Weddings** (Rotušės Aikštė). On the northeastern corner of the square, the **St Peter & Paul Cathedral** (Šventų Apaštalų Petro ir Povilo Arkekatedra Bazilika; Vilniaus gatvė 1; ⌚7am-7pm Mon-Sat, 8am-7pm Sun) owes much to baroque reconstruction, but the early-15th-century Gothic shape of its windows remain. Outside the cathedral's south wall is the **tomb of Maironis**, one of Lithuania's most revered poets.

NEW TOWN

Laisvės alėja, the 1.7km-long pedestrian street lined with bars, shops and restaurants, runs east from the Old Town to the New Town, ending at the white, neo-Byzantine **St Michael the Archangel Church** (Šv Archangelo Mykolo Rektoratas; Nepriklausomybės aikštė; ⌚9am-6pm). New Town's most important museum is the **National MK Čiurlionis Art Museum** (MK Čiurlionio Valstybinis Dailės Muziejus; www.ciurlionis.lt; Putvinskio gatvė 55; adult/child 6/3Lt; ⌚11am-5pm Tue-Sun), with its extensive collection of romantic symbolic paintings and joyful aural creations by Lithuania's beloved painter, composer and photographer. More whimsical is the superb **Museum of Devils** (Velnių Muziejus; Putvinskio gatvė 64; adult/child 6/3Lt; ⌚11am-5pm Tue-Sun) – an exploration of the Horned One's role in mythology around the world through its collection of woodcarvings, masks, clay figurines and more.

War buffs shouldn't miss the **Military Museum of Vytautas the Great** (Vytauto Didžiojo Karo Muziejus; Donelaičio gatvė 64; adult/child 4/2Lt; ⌚11am-5pm Tue-Sun); the weaponry through the ages in its grand hall is overlooked by an enormous painting of the 1410

Battle of Grünwald in which the grand duke laid waste to the Teutonic knights.

Just east of New Town, the absorbing **Sugihara House** (Sugiharos Namas; www.sugiharahouse.lt; Vaižganto gatvė 30; adult/child 10/5Lt; ⏲10am-5pm Mon-Fri, 11am-4pm Sat & Sun May-Oct) traces the life and work of Chiune Sugihara, 'Japan's Schindler', the Japanese consul to Lithuania who saved around 6000 lives by issuing transit visas (against orders) to Polish and Lithuanian Jews who faced the advancing Nazi terror.

Sleeping

The Monk's Bunk HOSTEL €
(☎6295 3870; www.hostels.com; Laisvės alėja 48-2; dm 34-38LT, d 90Lt;) Friendly hostel run by an ex-backpacker who knows what backpackers need: large common area, well-equipped kitchen, book exchange, large lockers, even a guitar if you fancy a strum. Bathroom queues are the only downside.

Apple Economy Hotel HOTEL €
(☎37-321 404; www.applehotel.lt; Valančiaus gatvė 19; s/d from 100/135Lt; P@) Fans of minimalism (and Eve) will be tempted by the quirky, cheerful Apple. Spot the green-apple motif on your pillows and on the silk wall hangings that add a splash of colour to the otherwise spotless white rooms. Wi-fi in lobby only.

Eating

TOP CHOICE **Moksha** INDIAN, THAI €€
(☎6767 1649; Vasario 16-osios gatvė 6; mains 15-18Lt;) At this tiny place expect such daily specials as lamb kofta curry or crispy duck with persimmon salad, and even vegan options such as dhal soup. On top of that, the service is super-friendly.

Bernelių Užeiga LITHUANIAN €€
(☎37-200 913; www.berneliuuzeiga.lt; Valančiaus gatvė 9; mains 16-25Lt;) Rustic Lithuanian cuisine served by fair maidens in traditional dress. Expect such gut-busting delights as buckwheat pancakes with wild mushroom sauce and barbecued pork shank.

> WORTH A TRIP
>
> **NINTH FORT**
>
> A poignant memorial to 80,000 people murdered by the Nazis, the excellent **Ninth Fort** (IX Forto Muziejus; www.9fortomuziejus.lt; Žemaičių plentas 73; adult/child 6/3Lt, catacombs with guide 10Lt, tours 10-20Lt; ⏲10am-6pm Wed-Mon Apr-Oct, to 4pm Nov-Mar; 23) museum, 7km north of Kaunas, comprises the old WWI fort and the bunker-like church of the damned. Displays cover deportations of Lithuanians by the Soviets and graphic photo exhibitions track the demise of Kaunas' Jewish community.
>
> Take bus 23 from Jonavos gatvė to the 9-ojo Forto Muziejus stop and cross under the motorway.

Drinking

TOP CHOICE **Whiskey Bar W1640** BAR
(www.viskiobaras.lt; Kurpių gatvė 29; ⏲5pm-1pm Tue-Thu, 5pm-5am Fri & Sat;) Not only does this bar have a mind-boggling collection of whiskies, but the bar staff are the friendliest in town. If whisky isn't your poison, then one of the ales just might be.

BO BAR
(Muitinės gatvė 9) The laid-back 'Blue Orange' attracts an alternative student set and gets crammed to overflowing on weekends. Its own brew is a tasty offering and there's live music some nights.

Information

Kaunas in Your Pocket (www.inyourpocket.com) Annual city guide featuring detailed listings, sold at the tourist office and in some hotels for 6Lt. Extensive online listings.

Tourist office (☎37-323 436; www.visit.kaunas.lt; Laisvės alėja 36; ⏲9am-5pm Mon-Fri, 10am-3pm Sat & Sun) Books accommodation, sells maps and guides, and arranges bicycle rental and guided tours of the Old Town.

Getting There & Away

Kaunas International Airport (☎37-399 307; www.kaunas-airport.lt; Vilniaus gatvė, Karmėlava; 29, 29E) is 12km north of the Old Town. Take bus 29 or 29E from the stop on Vytauto prospektas (2Lt).

From the **bus station** (Autobusų Stotis; ☎37-409 060; Vytauto prospektas 24), buses leave for Klaipėda (51Lt, 2½-2¾ hours, up to 16 daily), Šiauliai (37Lt, 2½ to three hours, up to 18 daily), Vilnius (20Lt, 1¾ hours, up to three per hour), Warsaw (55Lt, 6¼ hours, daily), Rīga (65Lt, five hours, three daily) and Tallinn (122Lt, 9½ hours, daily).

From the **train station** (Geležinkelio Stotis; ☎37-222 981; www.litrail.lt; Čiurlionio gatvė 16) there are trains to Vilnius (16-18Lt, 1¼ to

WORTH A TRIP

THE HILL OF CROSSES

Lithuania's most awe-inspiring sight is the legendary **Hill of Crosses** (Kryžių kalnas). The sound of the thousands of crosses – which appear to grow on the hillock – tinkling in the breeze is wonderfully eerie.

Planted here since the 14th century, the crosses were bulldozed by the Soviets, but each night people crept past soldiers and barbed wire to plant more, risking their lives or freedom to express their national and spiritual fervour.

Some of the crosses are devotional, others are memorials (many for people deported to Siberia) and some are finely carved folk-art masterpieces.

The hill is 10km north of Šiauliai along highway A12, and another 2km east from a well-marked turn-off ('Kryžių kalnas 2'). Take a Joniškis-bound bus (3Lt, 10 minutes, up to seven daily) to the 'Domantai' stop and walk for 15 minutes, or grab a taxi (60Lt). For accommodation, consult Šiauliai's **Tourism Information Centre** (☎41-523 110; www.siauliai.lt/tic; Vilniaus gatvė 213; ⌚9am-1pm & 2-6pm Mon-Fri, 10am-4pm Sat).

To reach Šiauliai, take a bus from Kaunas (35Lt, three hours, up to 21 daily), Klaipėda (35Lt, 3½ hours, up to six daily), Vilnius (47Lt, three hours, up to 12 daily) or Rīga (34Lt, 2½ hours, up to six daily), or a train from Vilnius (35Lt, 2½ hours, three daily), Kaunas (22Lt, 2½ hours, one daily) or Klaipėda (from 23Lt, two to three hours, five daily).

1¾ hours, up to 17 daily) and Šiauliai (20Lt, 2¾ hours, one daily).

WESTERN LITHUANIA

Klaipėda

POP 160,400

Klaipėda, Lithuania's main port, is the gateway to the Curonian Spit. Its history as the East Prussian city of Memel is displayed inside the appealing **Klaipėda Castle Museum** (Klaipėda Pilies Muziejus; www.mlimuziejus.lt; Pilies gatvė 4; adult/child 6/3Lt; ⌚10am-6pm Tue-Sat) – the remains of the town's moat-protected fortification – and the cobbled streets of what remains of its **Old Town** are lined with well-preserved half-timbered buildings. Klaipėda celebrates its nautical heritage with a **Sea Festival** (www.jurossvente.lt; ⌚Jul) – a whirlwind of parades, concerts and exhibitions.

The **tourist office** (☎46-412 186; www.klaipedainfo.lt; Turgaus gatvė 7; ⌚9am-7pm Mon-Fri, 10am-4pm Sat & Sun) is exceptionally efficient, selling maps, arranging accommodation and renting bicycles.

Sleeping & Eating

Centrally located **Litinterp Guesthouse** (☎46-410 644; www.litinterp.lt; Puodžių gatvė 17; s/d/tr 100/160/210Lt, without bathroom 80/140/180Lt; ⌚8.30am-7pm Mon-Fri, 10am-3pm Sat; P@) offers cheerful and comfortable rooms, while **Friedrich Hotel** (☎46-391 020; www.pasazas.lt; Tiltų gatvė 26a; s/d/apt from 185/220/478Lt; P@) caters to all budgets, from 'economy' rooms upwards.

Ararat (www.ararat.lt; Liepų gatvė 48a, mains 21-34Lt) specialises in superbly flavoured Armenian dishes (including many vegetarian options), while **Ferdinandas** (Naujoji Uosto 10; mains 21-38Lt) sates your cravings for *pelmeni* (stuffed meat dumplings) and other Russian classics.

Getting There & Away

Bus destinations from Klaipėda include Vilnius (68Lt, four to 5½ hours, up to 14 daily), Kaunas (52Lt, 2¾ to 4½ hours, up to 17 daily), Šiauliai (40Lt, three to 3½ hours, up to six daily) and Rīga (117Lt, 4½ to five hours, up to six daily).

Trains arrive from Vilnius (51Lt, 4¾ hours, three daily) and Šiauliai (from 23Lt, two to three hours, five daily).

Curonian Spit

POP 2640

This magical sliver of land, covered by pine forest, hosts some of Europe's most precious sand dunes and a menagerie of elk, deer and avian wildlife.

Recognised by Unesco as a World Heritage Site in 2000, the fragile spit is divided evenly between Lithuania and Russia's

DON'T MISS

WITCHES' HILL

Juodkrantė's biggest attraction is the macabre **Witches' Hill** (Raganų Kalnas) – wooded sculpture trails lined with devils, witches and other grotesque wooden carvings from Lithuanian folklore.

Kaliningrad region, with Lithuania's half protected as **Curonian Spit National Park** (www.nerija.lt).

Smiltynė, where the ferries from Klaipėda dock, draws weekend crowds with its delightful aquarium and the **Lithuania Sea Museum** (Lietuvos Jūrų Muziejus; ☎46-490 754; www.juru.muziejus.lt; adult/student Jun-Aug 15/7Lt, Sep-May 12/6Lt; ⏲10.30am-6.30pm Tue-Sun Jun-Aug, Wed-Sun Sep, 10.30am-5.30pm Sat & Sun Oct-Dec) inside a 19th-century fort. Further south, the village of **Juodkrantė** is awaft with the tempting smells of smoked fish *(žuvis)*, while picture-perfect **Nida** is home to the unmissable 52m-high **Parnidis Dune**, with its panoramic views of the 'Lithuanian Sahara' – coastline, forest and sand extending towards Kaliningrad.

A flat **cycling trail** runs all the way from Nida to Smiltynė, passing the massive colony of grey herons and cormorants near Juodkrantė, and you stand a good chance of seeing wild boar and other wildlife along the path. Bicycles are easy to hire (around 30/40Lt per 12/24 hours) in Nida.

The **tourist information centre** (☎46-952 345; www.visitneringa.com; Taikos gatvė 4; ⏲9am-7pm Jun-Aug, 9am-1pm & 2-6pm Mon-Sat Sep-May) and Litinterp Guesthouse (p745) in Klaipėda can help arrange accommodation; **Miško Namas** (☎46-952 290; www.miskonamas.com; Pamario gatvė 11-2; d 249Lt, 2-/4-person apt from 318/331Lt; @📶) and **Nidos Kempingas** (☎46-952 045; www.kempingas.lt; Taikos gatvė 45a; campsites per tent/adult/child 11/17/9Lt, d from 250Lt, 4-/6-bed studios 350/490Lt; P📶🏊) are both fine choices.

ℹ Getting There & Away

To get to the spit, board a ferry (per passenger/bicycle 2.90Lt/free, 10 minutes, every 30 minutes) at the **Old Castle Port** (Senasis Pilies Uostas; www.keltas.lt; Pilies gatvė 4), due west of Klaipėda's Old Town. Vehicles (per passenger/motorcycle/car/bicycle 2.90/18/40Lt/free, at least hourly) must use the **New Port** (Naujasis Uostas; www.keltas.lt; Nemuno gatvė 8), 2.5km south of the passenger terminal.

Buses and microbuses (9.50Lt, one hour, at least seven times daily) run regularly between Smiltynė and Nida via Juodkrantė (4.50Lt, 15 to 20 minutes).

UNDERSTAND LITHUANIA

History

Lithuania's history started when ancient tribes fanned out across the Baltics to take advantage of the region's amber deposits. In the mid-13th century Aukštaitiai leader Mindaugas unified these tribes to create the Grand Duchy of Lithuania.

In 1386, Lithuania forged an alliance with Poland against the Teutonic Order and defeated the German knights in 1410 at the Battle of Grünwald in Poland, ushering in a golden period during which Vilnius was born and Lithuania became one of Europe's largest empires.

But in the 18th century, the Polish-Lithuanian state was so weakened by division that it was carved up by Russia, Austria and Prussia in the partitions of Poland.

Vilnius became an important Jewish centre; Jews made up almost half of its 160,000-strong population by the early 20th century.

Lithuanian nationalists declared independence on 16 February 1918. Vilnius was to be the capital of independent Lithuania, but it was occupied by Polish forces between 1920 and 1938, so Kaunas became the seat of the Lithuanian government until Vilnius was liberated from Polish occupation. Lithuania's first president, Antanas Smetona, ruled the country with an iron fist during this time.

During the 1941–44 Nazi occupation up to 300,000 people, mostly Jews, were murdered in concentration camps and ghettos with the active assistance of some Lithuanians. Between 1944 and 1953, under Soviet rule, 250,000 Lithuanians were killed or deported while armed partisans resisted Soviet rule from the forests.

In the late 1980s Lithuania led the Baltic push for independence, becoming the first Soviet republic to legalise non-communist parties. On 11 March 1990 the new majority party declared Lithuania independent.

Moscow responded by marching troops into Vilnius; in January 1991 Soviets stormed key buildings, killing 14 people. The Soviets recognised Lithuanian independence on 6 September 1991, bringing about the first of the Baltic republics.

Following its independence from the former Soviet Union, Lithuania turned its sights to the West and in 2004 became a member of both NATO and the EU. Though economic growth was strong for much of the first decade of the 21st century, in 2008, Lithuania fell victim to the global economic crisis, prompting austerity measures such as spending cuts and tax rises, as well as migration to other EU states. Though the Social Democrat–led government, elected in December 2012, aims to ease these measures, it seems that Lithuania is in for several difficult years.

People

Lithuania is ethnically homogeneous, with Lithuanians accounting for 83.7% of the total population of 3,203,000. Poles form 6.6%, Russians 5.3%. The remaining 4.4% is comprised of various nationalities from eastern Europe and beyond.

Some call Lithuanians the 'Italians of the Baltics', citing their fierce pride – a result of the many brutal attempts to eradicate their culture and the memories of their long-lost empire.

The last pagan country in Europe, Lithuania is now around 79% Roman Catholic, with a strong Orthodox minority.

Environment

Lush forests and more than 4000 lakes mark the landscape of Lithuania, a country that is largely flat with a 100km-wide lowland centre. Forest covers a third of the country and contains creatures such as wild boar, wolves, deer and elk.

For years the hot potato has been the Ignalina Nuclear Power Plant, 120km north of Vilnius. One of two reactors similar in design to Chernobyl was closed in December 2004, and the final shutdown of the plant took place in 2009.

To do your part for the environment, camp only in designated areas and keep to the marked trails on the sand dunes of the Curonian Spit.

SURVIVAL GUIDE

Directory A–Z

Accommodation

Book way ahead in the high season for Vilnius and the Curonian Spit. Peak-season prices are around 30% higher than off-season prices. Prices are higher in Vilnius.

Vilnius has numerous youth hostels. Budget accommodation is easy to find outside the capital. Breakfast is included in the price unless stated otherwise.

Price ranges used in this chapter are for a double room with bathroom.

€ less than 150Lt

€€ 150Lt to 350Lt

Business Hours

Banks 8am to 3pm Monday to Friday

Bars 11am to midnight Sunday to Thursday, 11am to 2am Friday and Saturday

Clubs 10pm to 5am Thursday to Saturday

Post offices 8am to 8pm Monday to Friday, 10am to 9pm Saturday, 10am to 5pm Sunday

Restaurants noon to 11pm; later on weekends

Shops 9am or 10am to 7pm Monday to Saturday; some open on Sunday

Embassies & Consulates

The following embassies are in Vilnius.

Australian Embassy (☎5-212 3369; australia@consulate.lt; Vilniaus gatvė 23; ⏲10am-1pm Tue, 2-5pm Thu)

Canadian Embassy (☎5-249 0950; www.canada.lt; Jogailos gatvė 4; ⏲8.30am-5pm Mon-Fri)

French Embassy (☎5-219 9600; www.ambafrance-lt.org; Švarco gatvė 1)

German Embassy (☎5-210 6400; www.wilna.diplo.de; Sierakausko gatvė 24)

Netherlands Embassy (☎5-210 4620; http://lithuania.nlembassy.org; Kosciuskos gatvė 36; ⏲8.30am-12.30pm Mon-Fri)

UK Embassy (☎5-246 2900; http://ukinlithuania.fco.gov.uk; Antakalnio gatvė 2)

US Embassy (☎5-266 5500; http://vilnius.usembassy.gov; Akmenų gatvė 6)

Food

The following price categories for the average cost of a main course are used in this chapter:

€ less than 15Lt

€€ 15Lt to 40Lt

Money

The Lithuanian litas (the plural is litai; Lt) is divided into 100 centai. All but the smallest Lithuanian towns have at least one bank with a functional ATM. Most big banks cash travellers cheques and exchange most major currencies. Credit cards are widely accepted. A 10% tip in restaurants is appreciated.

Public Holidays

New Year's Day 1 January

Independence Day 16 February

Lithuanian Independence Restoration Day 11 March

Easter Sunday March/April

Easter Monday March/April

International Labour Day 1 May

Feast of St John (Midsummer) 24 June

Statehood Day 6 July

Assumption of Blessed Virgin 15 August

All Saints' Day 1 November

Christmas 25 and 26 December

Telephone

To call other cities within Lithuania, dial ☎8 followed by the city code and phone number. To make an international call dial ☎00 before the country code. To call a mobile phone within Lithuania, dial ☎8 followed by the eight-digit number.

Prepaid SIM cards are sold by **Bitė** (www.bite.lt), **Omnitel** (www.omnitel.lt) and **Tele 2** (www.tele2.lt) for around 8Lt or 9Lt.

Payphones – increasingly rare given the widespread use of mobiles and Skype – only accept phonecards, sold at newspaper kiosks.

Getting There & Away

Air

There are direct flights to Lithuania from most major European cities. Latvia's national airline, **airBaltic** (www.airbaltic.com), runs direct flights between Vilnius and about a dozen Western European destinations, as well as between Palanga and Riga. Most international traffic to Lithuania goes through **Vilnius International Airport** (Vilniaus Oro Uostas; ☎5-230 6666; www.vno.lt). Major international carriers include Aer Lingus, Austrian Airlines, Czech Airlines, Lot, Lufthansa, Ryanair and SAS. Destinations include London, Vienna, Moscow, Frankfurt, Paris, Milan, Warsaw, Kyiv, Dublin, Brussels and Prague.

Kaunas International Airport (Kauno Oro Uostas; ☎37-399 307; www.kaunas-airport.lt) is a Ryanair hub with flights to Bristol, London Stansted, Frankfurt, Reykjavik and Rīga.

There are also international flights from **Palanga Airport** (Palangos Oro Uostas; ☎460-52020; www.palanga-airport.lt) to Copenhagen, Oslo, Rīga and Moscow.

Land

BUS

The main international bus companies operating in Lithuania are **Lux Express** (www.luxexpress.eu) and **Ecolines** (www.ecolines.net).

CAR & MOTORCYCLE

You must have a valid visa for entering both Belarus and Russia (Kaliningrad).

TRAIN

Vilnius is linked by regular direct trains to many international destinations. You'll need a Belarus visa for the Moscow train. For Warsaw, change in Kaunas. Contact **Lithuanian Rail** (www.litrail.lt) for further information.

Sea

From Klaipėda's **International Ferry Port** (☎46-395 051; www.dfdsseaways.lt; Perkėlos gatvė 10), **DFDS Seaways** (☎46-395 000; www.dfdsseaways.lt; Šaulių gatvė 19) runs passenger ferries to and from Kiel (from €56, six weekly, 21 hours) and Sassnitz (from €55, three weekly, 18 hours) in Germany and Karlshamn, Sweden (from €62, 13 to 14 hours, daily).

Getting Around

Bicycle

Lithuania is completely flat and easily explored by bike. Information about bike touring in Lithuania can be found on **BaltiCCycle** (www.bicycle.lt).

Bus

The bus network is extensive, efficient and relatively inexpensive, and covers more destinations than the train network. See **Autobusbilietai** (www.autobusbilietai.lt) for bus timetables.

Car & Motorcycle

Modern four-lane highways link Vilnius with Klaipėda (via Kaunas). The speed limit in Lithuania is 50km/h in cities, 70km/h to 90km/h on single carriageways and 110km/h to 130km/h on motorways. The big international rental-car agencies are well represented at Vilnius International Airport.

Hiring a car is straightforward in Vilnius and Kaunas; international car-hire companies such as **Avis** (www.avis.lt), **Hertz** (www.hertz.lt) and **Europcar** (www.europcar.lt) are represented at the two airports and a number of local rental companies such as **Fortuna** (www.rentacar.lt), **Aunela** (www.aunela.lt) and **Eura** (www.eura.lt) also offer competitive rates. Expect to pay around €170 per week for a compact.

Local Transport

Lithuanian cities are generously covered by networks of buses, trolleybuses and minibuses. A ride costs around 2.50Lt, with a small discount if you buy tickets from a Lietuvos Spauda kiosk.

Train

The efficient train network run by **Lithuanian Rail** (www.litrail.lt) covers Vilnius, Šiauliai, Kaunas, Klaipėda and Trakai. Trains are quite frequent, and marginally faster than buses, but also slightly more expensive.

Macedonia

Includes »

Skopje 752
Western Macedonia.......757
Ohrid 757
Central Macedonia 760
Bitola 760
Understand Macedonia 761
Survival Guide............... 762

Best Places to Eat

- » Stara Gradska Kuča (p756)
- » La Bodeguito Del Medio (p756)
- » Letna Bavča Kaneo (p760)
- » Restaurant Antiko (p760)
- » El Greko (p761)

Best Places to Stay

- » Villa Dihovo (p761)
- » Urban Hostel (p754)
- » Vila Sveta Sofija (p759)
- » Chola Guest House (p761)
- » Hi Skopje Hostel (p754)

Why Go?

The mixed Balkan and Mediterranean heritage and landscape of Macedonia (Македонија), reflected in its rugged terrain and unique structures and sites, reveal a diversity unexpected in such a small country.

Easygoing Skopje remains one of Europe's more unusual capitals. Constant urban renewal makes it a continuous work in progress, with hip cafes and bars vying for attention with grandiose statues and arches. Underneath the surface, however, Skopje's a historic city with an impressive Ottoman old quarter, where Byzantine churches, mosques and converted hammams are topped by the imposing Tvrdina Kale Fortress.

In summer, try hiking, mountain biking and climbing in remote mountains, some concealing medieval monasteries. Be sure to visit Ohrid, noted for its Summer Festival, sublime Byzantine churches and great (34km-long) lake. Bitola, a charming and cultured city west of Ohrid, boasts cool cafes and historic and natural attractions.

When to Go

Skopje

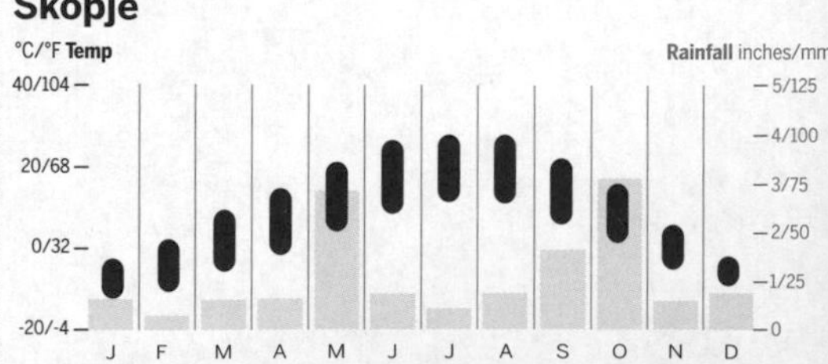

Jun–Aug Enjoy Ohrid's Summer Festival and dive into its 300m-deep lake.

Sep–Oct Partake in Skopje's Beer Fest, Jazz Festival and harvest celebrations.

Dec–Feb Ski Mavrovo, and indulge in Macedonia's holiday carnivals.

Connections

Skopje's buses serve Sofia (Bulgaria), Belgrade (Serbia), Budapest (Hungary), Pristina (Kosovo), Tirana (Albania), İstanbul (Turkey), Thessaloniki (Greece) and more. The train from Belgrade to Skopje reaches Gevgelija on the Greek border. The long-awaited arrival of budget airlines has improved Skopje's air connections.

ITINERARIES

Four Days

Spend two nights in Skopje, marvelling at its bold new architecture on the square, and visiting its Čaršija (old quarter), with historic churches, mosques, museums and an Ottoman castle. Then travel southwest to Macedonia's most evocative and historic town, Ohrid, with its serene lake, via the lush forested mountains of Mavrovo and Bigorski Monastery, with its spectacular carved iconostasis.

One Week

Continue to cultured Bitola, the long-famed 'City of Consuls' known for its vibrant cafes and nearby ancient Heraclea and Pelister National Park. After Skopje, Ohrid and Bitola, visit Prilep, seeing its historic nearby monasteries.

Essential Food & Drink

» **Ajvar** Sweet red-pepper sauce; accompanies meats and cheeses.

» **Šopska salata** Tomatoes, onions and cucumbers topped with flaky *sirenje* (white cheese).

» **Uviač** Rolled chicken or pork wrapped in bacon, filled with melted yellow cheese.

» **Skopsko and Dab lagers** Macedonia's favourite brews.

» **Rakija** Grape-based firewater, useful for toasts (and cleaning cuts and windows!)

» **Vranec and Temjanika** Macedonia's favourite red- and white-wine varietals.

» **'Bekonegs'** Not terribly traditional, but you will see this mangled rendition of 'bacon and eggs' on Macedonian breakfast menus.

AT A GLANCE

» **Currency** Macedonian denar (MKD)

» **Language** Macedonian

» **Money** ATMs widespread in major towns

» **Visas** None for EU, US, Australian, Canadian or New Zealand citizens

Fast Facts

» **Area** 25,713 sq km

» **Capital** Skopje

» **Country code** ☎389

» **Emergency** Ambulance ☎194, fire ☎193, police ☎192

Exchange Rates

Australia	A$1	50.08MKD
Canada	C$1	47.18MKD
Euro Zone	€1	61.27MKD
Japan	¥100	50.81MKD
New Zealand	NZ$1	40.14MKD
UK	UK£1	72.54MKD
USA	US$1	47.94MKD

Set Your Budget

» **Skopje hotel room** 3000MKD

» **Two-course meal** 400MKD

» **Beer** 120MKD

» **Skopje bus ticket** 35MKD

» **Petrol (1L)** 100MKD

Resources

» **Macedonian Welcome Centre** (www.dmwc.org.mk)

» **Macedonian Information Agency** (www.mia.com.mk)

» **Exploring Macedonia** (www.exploringmacedonia.com)

SKOPJE

☎02 / POP 670,000

Skopje (Скопје) is among Europe's most entertaining and eclectic small capital cities. A government construction spree has created an abundance of statuary, bridges, museums and other structures, redefining the ever-changing city.

Yet plenty survives from earlier times. Skopje's Ottoman- and Byzantine-era wonders include the 15th-century Kameni Most (Stone Bridge), Čaršija (old Turkish bazaar), Sveti Spas Church, with its ornate, hand-carved iconostasis, and Tvrdina Kale Fortress, Skopje's guardian since the 5th century. And, with its bars, clubs and galleries, the city has modern culture too.

Macedonia Highlights

1 Gaze out over Ohrid from the **Church of Sveti Jovan at Kaneo** (p759), immaculately set on a bluff above the lake

2 Marvel at the architectural wonderland of work-in-progress **Skopje** (p752), and enjoy its fun nightlife

3 Enjoy the old-world ambience and easygoing cafe culture of **Bitola** (p760)

4 Gaze upon some of Europe's most unique frescos at the 12th-century **Sveti Pantelejmon Monastery** (p753)

5 Partake in July's **Ohrid Summer Festival** (p759), with concerts in the Classical Ampitheatre

6 Wander the cobbled alleyways of Turkish-flavoured **Čaršija** (p753) in Skopje, with its historic buildings, artisan shops and cafes

Sights

The Čaršija houses Skopje's main historic sights. The Vardar River's southern shore has museums and cafes on pedestrianised ul Makedonija. Buzzing Ploštad Makedonija (Macedonia Sq) stands smack by the Ottoman stone bridge (Kameni Most), which accesses Čaršija.

PLOŠTAD MAKEDONIJA & THE SOUTH BANK

Ploštad Makedonija SQUARE
(Macedonia Sq) This square, fronted by a Triumphal Arch, contains audacious statues dedicated to various national heroes. The towering, central 'Warrior on a Horse' is bedecked by fountains that are illuminated at night. From here, stroll or cycle along the riverbank, or relax in a riverfront cafe.

FREE **Memorial House of Mother Teresa** MUSEUM
(☎3290 674; www.memorialhouseofmotherteresa.org; ul Makedonija bb; ⊙9am-8pm Mon-Fri, to 2pm Sat-Sun) This retro futuristic structure displays memorabilia of the famed Catholic nun of Calcutta, born in Skopje in 1910.

FREE **Museum of the City of Skopje** MUSEUM
(Mito Hadživasilev Jasmin bb; ⊙9am-3pm Tue-Sat, to 1pm Sun) This museum, specialising in local ancient and Byzantine finds, occupies the old train station. The stone fingers of its clock remain frozen at 5.17am – the moment Skopje's great earthquake struck on 27 July 1963.

THE NORTH BANK & ČARŠIJA

Čaršija NEIGHBOURHOOD
Across the **Stone Bridge** (Kameni Most), Čaršija evokes Skopje's Ottoman past. Its winding lanes are filled with eateries, teahouses, artisan stores and nightlife, and it boasts Skopje's best historic structures and museums. Čaršija runs from the Stone Bridge to **Bit Pazar**, a big, busy vegetable market purveying bric-a-brac, household goods and anything random.

Sveti Spas Church CHURCH
(Makarie Frčkoski 8; admission 100MKD; ⊙8am-3pm Tue-Sun) This historic church is partially underground (the Turks banned churches from being taller than mosques), and boasts a wood-carved iconostasis 10m wide and 6m high, built by early 19th-century master craftsmen Makarije Frčkovski and brothers Petar and Marko Filipovski.

Outside, the **Tomb and Museum of Goce Delčev** contains the remains of Macedonia's foremost national hero. Leader of the VMRO (Internal Macedonian Revolutionary Organisation), Delčev was killed by Turks in 1903.

Museum of Macedonia MUSEUM
(www.musmk.org.mk; Čurčiska bb; admission 50MKD; ⊙9am-5pm Tue-Sun) Documenting neolithic through communist times, this museum contains an ethnographic exhibition, plus ancient jewellery and coins, icons and wood-carved iconostases.

Sultan Murat Mosque MOSQUE
(bul K Misirkov) Across the boulevard from Bit Pazar, this 1436 mosque is among the Balkans' oldest and features a distinctive red-tipped clock tower and Ottoman *madrasa* (Islamic school) remnants.

KALE & AROUND

Mustafa Paša Mosque MOSQUE
(Samoilova bb) The 1492 Mustafa Paša Mosque exemplifies magnificent Ottoman architecture, with a lawn, garden and fountain.

FREE **Tvrdina Kale Fortress** FORTRESS
(⊙daylight hours) This 6th-century AD Byzantine (and later, Ottoman) castle has archaeological finds from neolithic to Ottoman times. The ramparts offer great views over the city and river.

Museum of Contemporary Art MUSEUM
(☎3117 734; www.msuskopje.org.mk; Samoilova bb; ⊙10am-5pm Tue-Sat, 9am-1pm Sun) This elevated museum displays works by Macedonian and world-famous artists (there's even a Picasso).

MT VODNO & AROUND

Mt Vodno MOUNTAIN
Framing Skopje to the south, Vodno is popular with hikers, though you can also take a gondola up the mountainside. Two restaurants stand at Sredno (Middle) Vodno (taxis drive here for 200MKD). Hiking trails take you to the 66m-high **Millenium Cross** (2002), the world's largest, which is illuminated at night.

Sveti Pantelejmon Monastery MONASTERY
(Gorno Nerezi village) Further west along Vodno, this 1164 monastery is among Macedonia's most significant churches. Its Byzantine frescos, such as the *Lamentation of Christ*, depict a pathos and realism predating the

Skopje

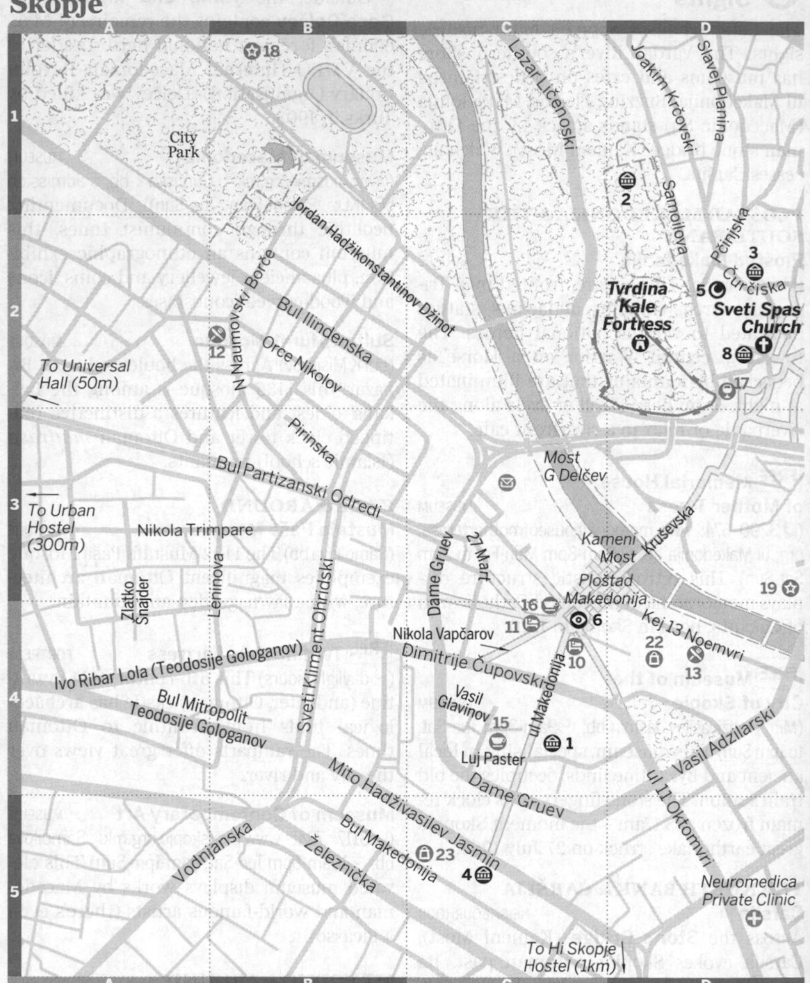

Renaissance by two centuries. It's 5km from the centre (by taxi, 300MKD) and offers great views.

Sleeping

TOP CHOICE Hi Skopje Hostel HOSTEL €
(☎6091 242; www.hiskopjehostel.com; Crniche 15; dm/s/d from 540/1200/2100MKD) In the cool shade of Mt Vodno, this cheerful new hostel offers dorms and two singles (with a shared bathroom). There's a communal kitchen, and the relaxing back garden adds to the out-of-city vibe. The friendly young owners offer tons of info on city sights and events. It's located on a hilly street 2.5km from the bus and train stations (take a taxi for 150MKD).

TOP CHOICE Urban Hostel HOSTEL €
(☎6142 785; www.urbanhostel.com.mk; Majka Teresa 22; dm/s/d/apt €13/24/34/75; ❄📶) Skopje's best hostel is a short walk from the centre in the leafy Debar Maalo neighbourhood, home to relaxed cafes and restaurants. Along with clean rooms, comfy beds and a fireplace, there's a piano, aquarium and computer room, and friendly, helpful staff.

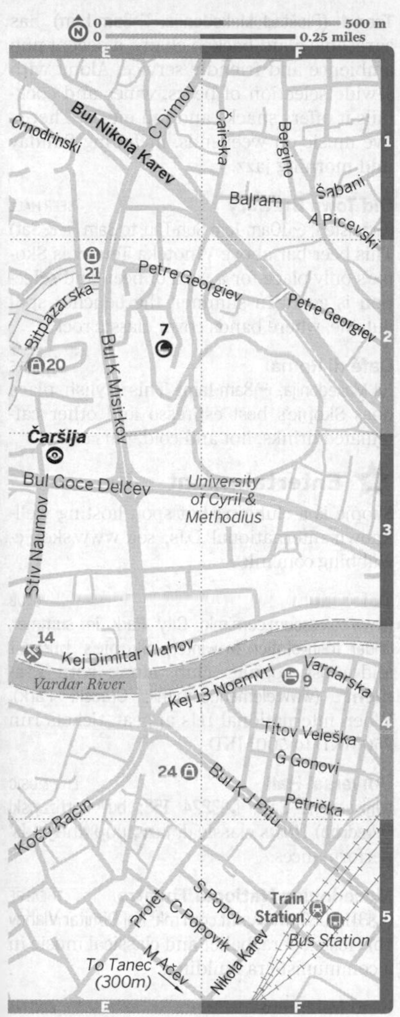

Hotel Pelister BOUTIQUE HOTEL €€
(☎3239 584; www.pelisterhotel.com.mk; Ploštad Makedonija; s/d/apt from €59/69/85; ❄@📶) Located above Restaurant Pelister (p756; both formerly called Dal Met Fu), this hotel has well-designed rooms with great views; however, it can get noisy. Decor is standard but most rooms have a computer, and pricier suites have a spa.

Hotel Square BUDGET HOTEL €€
(☎3225 090; www.hotelsquare.com.mk; 6th fl, Nikola Vapcarov 2; s/d/tr €45/60/75; ❄@) Well situated six floors above the action, the Square offers cosy, well-kept modern rooms.

Skopje

Top Sights
- Čaršija ... E3
- Sveti Spas Church ... D2
- Tvrdina Kale Fortress ... D2

Sights
- 1 Memorial House of Mother Teresa ... C4
- 2 Museum of Contemporary Art ... D1
- 3 Museum of Macedonia ... D2
- 4 Museum of the City of Skopje ... C5
- 5 Mustafa Paša Mosque ... D2
- 6 Ploštad Makedonija ... C4
- 7 Sultan Murat Mosque ... E2
- 8 Tomb & Museum of Goce Delčev ... D2

Sleeping
- 9 Art Hostel ... F4
- 10 Hotel Pelister ... C4
- 11 Hotel Square ... C4

Eating
- 12 Idadija ... D2
- 13 La Bodeguito Del Medio ... D4
- Restaurant Pelister ... (see 10)
- 14 Stara Gradska Kuča ... E4

Drinking
- Bistro London ... (see 16)
- 15 Café di Roma ... C4
- 16 Café Trend ... C4
- Old Town Brewery ... (see 17)
- 17 Vinoteka Temov ... D2

Entertainment
- 18 Colosseum ... B1
- Element ... (see 18)
- Kino Milenium ... (see 22)
- 19 Macedonian National Theatre ... D3

Shopping
- 20 Balkan Corner ... E2
- 21 Bit Pazar ... E2
- 22 Gradski Trgovski Centar ... D4
- 23 Ramstore ... C5
- 24 Vero Center ... E4

The balcony cafe has great views and you can get an optional breakfast (€5) in Café Trend (p756) below. Look for the signposted block off Ploštad Makedonija.

Art Hostel HOSTEL €
(☎3223 789; www.art-hostel.com.mk; Ante Hadzimitkov 5; dm/s/d €12/25/40; ❄@📶) Near the train station in Madjir Maalo, by the Vardar River,

Art Hostel is a passable backpacker fall-back, though the six-bed dorms and private rooms (all with shared bathrooms) are cramped.

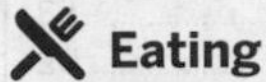

Eating

TOP CHOICE Stara Gradska Kuča MACEDONIAN €€
(Pajko Maalo 14; mains 250-400MKD; ⌚8am-midnight) This restored traditional house has a warm ambience, an excellent assortment of classic Macedonian dishes and, sometimes, live Macedonian music. It's a bit touristy, but still snug and cosy with wood furnishings and traditional decor.

TOP CHOICE La Bodeguito Del Medio CUBAN €€
(Kej 13 Noemvri; mains 350-700MKD; ⌚9am-2am) Known to locals as 'the Cuban', this gregarious riverfront place has sizzling Cuban specialities, Latin cocktails and music, and a long bar lined with carousers by night. Borrow a magic marker to scrawl your message among hundreds of others on the walls and ceilings.

Idadija SKARA €€
(Rade Koncar 1; mains 180-250MKD) In Debar Maalo's *skara* (grilled meat) corner, no-frills Idadija has been serving excellent grills for more than 80 years.

Restaurant Pelister INTERNATIONAL €€
(Ploštad Makedonija; mains 280-350MKD; ⌚7.30am-midnight) This square-front place (previously, and still called Dal Met Fu) remains a local fixture – note the curious mix of pensioners debating politics over coffee, businessmen chatting up politicians, and random tourists. It does great pastas and offers a make-your-own salad bar. The chocolate soufflé with vanilla ice cream and a spearmint sprig is worth the 10-minute wait.

Drinking

TOP CHOICE Bistro London PUB
(Ploštad Makedonija; ⌚8am-1am) This refurbished bar annexe of neighbouring **Café Trend** (Ploštad Makedonija; ⌚8am-1am) has agreeable plaid-backed chairs, a decent pub ambience and friendly service. Along with a wide selection of beers, wines and cocktails it offers snacks and full meals. There's live music on weekends, including Sunday mid-morning jazz.

SPLURGE

Skopje's best wine bar, **Vinoteka Temo** (Gradište 1a; ⌚9am-midnight Mon-Thu, to 1am Fri-Sun), is in a restored wood building near Sveti Spas Church. Refined and atmospheric, its vast (and pricey) wine list presents the manifold flavours of Macedonia's vineyards, while live traditional and classical guitarists often play.

Old Town Brewery BEER HALL
(Gradište 1; ⌚10am-1am Sun-Thu, to 3am Fri & Sat) This beer bar above Vinoteka Temov is Skopje's only place for a yard of beer, and selection is good. In summer, the benches spill outside, where bands cover classic rock.

Café di Roma CAFE
(ul Makedonija; ⌚8am-1am) This stylish place does Skopje's best espresso and other caffeinated drinks, hot and cold, plus cakes.

Entertainment

Skopje is a clubbing hot spot, hosting well-known international DJs; see www.skopjeclubbing.com.mk.

Colosseum CLUB
(www.colosseum.com.mk; City Park in summer, under train station in winter) Skopje's biggest and most popular club, along with **Element** (www.element.com.mk; Gradski Park). When international DJs appear, tickets run 250MKD to 500MKD.

Universal Hall LIVE MUSIC
(Univerzalna Sala; ☎3224 158; bul Partizanski Odredi bb) Hosts classical, jazz, pop and kids' performances.

Macedonian National Theatre THEATRE
(☎3114 060; www.mnt.com.mk; Kej Dimitar Vlahov bb) Hosts opera, ballet and classical music in a communist-era building.

Kino Milenium CINEMA
(☎3120 389; www.kinomilenium.mk; Gradski Trgovski Centar) Skopje's largest movie theatre.

Shopping

In the Čaršija, handmade jewellery is sold at shops such as **Balkan Corner** (ul Bitpazarska; silver jewellery 600-4500MKD; ⌚9.30am-7.30pm). Traditional carpets and antiques are also sold but beware – most 'ancient' treasures on sale are fakes (and would be illegal to buy if they weren't). The **Gradski Trgovski Centar** (11 Oktomvri), **Ramstore** (Mito Hadživasilev Jasmin bb) and **Vero Center** (bul Jane Sandanski) are modern malls. Macedonia-themed souvenir stalls are on or near the main square.

Information

Go Macedonia (3071 265; www.gomacedonia.com; Ankarska 29a) Arranges hiking, cycling, caving and winery tours.

Lonely Planet (www.lonelyplanet.com/macedonia/skopje)

Neuromedica Private Clinic (3133 313; 11 Oktomvri 25; 24hr) Good private specialists.

Skopje Online (www.skopjeonline.com.mk) General info, including local attractions, shopping and entertainment.

Tourist Association of Skopje (www.skopjetourism.org) Tourist resources.

Getting There & Away

AIR **Skopje Alexander the Great Airport** (3148 333; www.airports.com.mk; Petrovec), 21km east of Skopje, has a shuttle bus between the airport and the city centre (100MKD).

BUS Skopje's **bus station** (www.sas.com.mk; bul Jane Sandanski), with ATM, exchange office and English-language info, adjoins the train station.

Buses to Ohrid go via Kičevo (three hours, 520MKD) or Bitola (four to five hours, 480MKD) – book ahead in summer. Most intercity buses are air-conditioned and are generally faster than trains, though more expensive. Skopje's buses serve Sofia, Belgrade, Budapest, Pristina, Tirana, İstanbul, Thessaloniki and more. The train from Belgrade to Skopje reaches Gevgelija on the Greek border.

TRAIN The **train station** (Železnička Stanica; bul Jane Sandanski) offers northbound trains to Serbia and Kosovo, and southbound services to Bitola and Gevgelija on the Greek border. At time of research, the Greek government had suspended its international train routes.

Getting Around

Buy tickets (100MKD) for the airport's shuttle bus to the city centre at the Vardar Express booth in the arrivals terminal. Skopje's public city buses cost 35MKD. Private ones cost 25MKD. Skopje's taxis have a base rate of 40MKD for the first kilometre, then 25MKD for subsequent kilometres, and drivers use their meters.

WESTERN MACEDONIA

Ohrid Охрид

046 / POP 55,700

Sublime Ohrid is Macedonia's prime destination, with an atmospheric old quarter, beautiful churches along a graceful hill, and a medieval castle overlooking serene Lake Ohrid. Nearby, mountainous Galičica National Park offers pristine nature, while secluded beaches dot the lake's eastern shore.

Ohrid and its beaches are packed from 15 July to 15 August, when the popular Summer Festival is held. June or September are quieter (and cleaner).

Lake Ohrid, 34km long, 300m deep and three million years old, shared by Macedonia (two-thirds) and Albania (one-third), is among Europe's deepest and oldest. Although usually calm, during storms Ohrid seethes with steel-grey whitecaps evoking the sea.

Sights

To see Ohrid's sights in the most efficient and least exhausting way, start at the **Gorna Porta** (Upper Gate), about 100MKD from the centre by taxi, and walk down.

Churches and museums are closed on Monday.

Church of Sveta Bogorodica Perivlepta CHURCH
(Gorna Porta; admission 100MKD; 9am-1pm & 4-8pm) Just inside the Gorna Porta, this 13th-century Byzantine church has vivid biblical frescos and an **icon gallery** (Gorna Porta; 9am-2pm & 5-8pm, closed Mon) highlighting the founders' artistic achievements.

FREE **Classical Amphitheatre** AMPHITHEATRE
This impressive amphitheatre was built for theatre but the Romans later removed 10 rows to accommodate gladiators. It hosts Summer Festival performances.

Car Samoil's Castle CASTLE
(admission 30MKD; 9am-6pm Tue-Sun) The massive, turreted walls of the 10th-century castle indicate the power of the medieval Bulgarian state. Ascend the narrow stone stairways to the ramparts for fantastic views.

FREE **Plaošnik** CHURCH
(9am-6pm) Down a wooded path, Plaošnik boasts the Church of Sveti Kliment i Pantelejmon. This 5th-century basilica was restored in 2002 according to its Byzantine design. The multidomed church has glass floor segments revealing original foundations. It houses St Kliment's relics, with intricate 5th-century mosaics outside.

Nearby, **4th-century church foundations**, replete with Early Christian flora and fauna mosaics, stand under a protective roof.

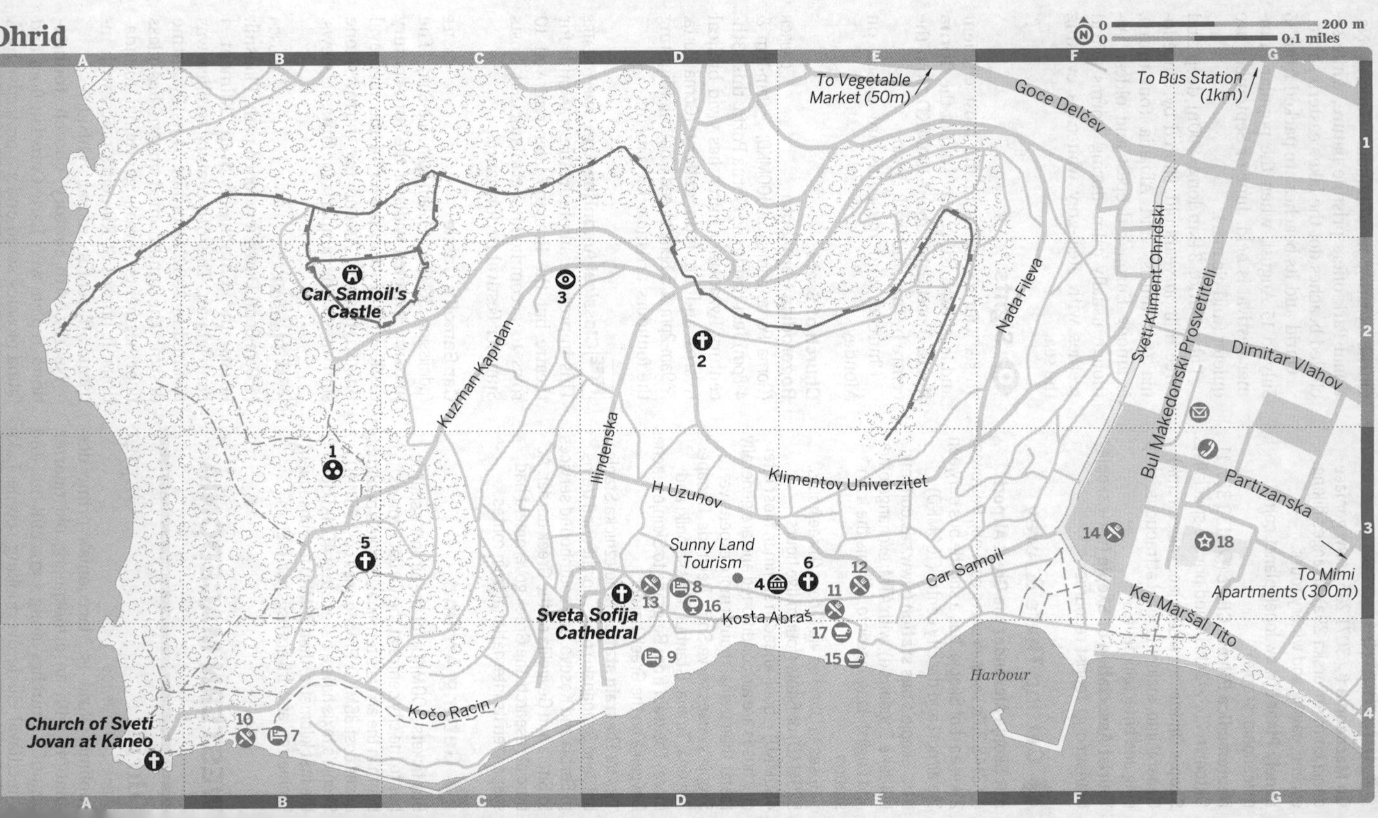

Ohrid
200 m
0.1 miles
To Vegetable Market (50m)
Goce Delčev
To Bus Station (1km)
Car Samoil's Castle
Kuzman Kapidan
Ilindenska
Nada Fileva
Sveti Kliment Ohridski
Bul Makedonski Prosvetiteli
Dimitar Vlahov
Partizanska
Klimentov Univerzitet
H Uzunov
Sunny Land Tourism
Car Samoil
To Mimi Apartments (300m)
Kej Maršal Tito
Sveta Sofija Cathedral
Kosta Abraš
Harbour
Kočo Racin
Church of Sveti Jovan at Kaneo

Ohrid

Top Sights

Car Samoil's Castle B2
Church of Sveti Jovan at Kaneo A4
Sveta Sofija Cathedral D3

Sights

1 4th-Century Church Foundations B3
2 Church of Sveta Bogorodica Perivlepta D2
3 Classical Amphitheatre C2
Icon Gallery .... (see 2)
4 National Museum D3
5 Plaošnik B3
6 Sveta Bogorodica Bolnička & Sveti Nikola Bolnički E3

Sleeping

7 Stefan Kanevče Rooms B4
8 Vila Sveta Sofija D3
9 Villa Lucija D4

Eating

10 Letna Bavča Kaneo B4
11 Pizzeria Leonardo E3
12 Restaurant Antiko E3
13 Restoran Sveta Sofija D3
14 Tinex Supermarket F3

Drinking

15 Aquarius E4
16 Cuba Libre D3
17 Liquid E4

Entertainment

18 Dom na Kultura G3

Church of Sveti Jovan at Kaneo CHURCH
(admission 50MKD; ⏱9am-6pm) This stunning 13th-century church is set on a cliff over the lake, and is possibly Macedonia's most photographed structure. Peer down into the azure waters and you'll see why medieval monks found spiritual inspiration here. The small church has original frescos behind the altar.

Sveta Sofija Cathedral CHURCH
(Car Samoil bb; admission 100MKD; ⏱10am-8pm) Ohrid's grandest church, 11th-century Sveta Sofija is supported by columns and decorated with elaborate Byzantine frescos. Its superb acoustics mean it's often used for concerts.

Come by the road running down from Kaneo, past the Old Town's lovely houses, or along the new over-water walking bridge, beginning on the beach south of Kaneo.

National Museum MUSEUM
(Car Samoil 62; admission 50MKD; ⏱9am-4pm & 7-11pm Tue-Sun) This 1827 museum features distinctive white-and-brown architecture. The **Robev Residence** houses ancient epigraphy and the **Urania Residence** opposite has an ethnographic display.

Sveta Bogorodica Bolnička & Sveti Nikola Bolnički CHURCHES
Ohrid's minor frescoed 14th-century churches are open infrequently (ask at the museum). *Bolnica* means hospital in Macedonian; during plagues visitors faced 40-day quarantines here.

Festivals & Events

Ohrid Summer Festival ARTS
(☎202 301; www.ohridsummer.com.mk) Features classical and opera concerts, theatre and dance from mid-July to mid-August.

Sleeping

TOP CHOICE **Vila Sveta Sofija** HOTEL €€
(☎254 370; www.vilasofija.com.mk; Kosta Abraš 64; s/d €40/65, ste €80-125; ❄@) This opulent getaway combines traditional furnishings with chic modern bathrooms in an old Ohrid mansion near Sveta Sofija.

Villa Lucija GUESTHOUSE €€
(☎265 608; www.vilalucija.com.mk; Kosta Abraš 29; s/d/apt €20/30/50; ❄@) Old Town ambience and lovingly decorated, breezy rooms with lake views.

Stefan Kanevče Rooms RENTED ROOMS €
(☎234 813; apostolanet@yahoo.co.uk; Kočo Racin 47; per person €10) Near Kaneo beach, this atmospheric 19th-century house boasts carved wooden ceilings and good hospitality.

Mimi Apartments APARTMENT €
(☎250 103; mimioh@mail.com.mk; Strašo Pinđur 2; r incl breakfast 800MKD) Spacious, centrally located private rooms with fridge.

Eating

Ohrid's endemic trout is endangered and (supposedly) protected from fishing – order the equally tasty *mavrovska* and *kaliforniska* varieties instead.

Self-caterers have a **local vegetable market** (Kliment Ohridski) and **supermarket** (bul Makedonski Prosvetiteli) to keep costs down.

TOP CHOICE **Letna Bavča Kaneo** SEAFOOD €
(Kočo Racin 43; fish 150-300MKD; ⏲9am-11pm) Simple and inexpensive 'summer terrace' on Kaneo beach. A fry-up of diminutive *plasnica* fish, plus salad, feeds two. Swim from the restaurant's dock and soak up the sun.

TOP CHOICE **Restaurant Antiko** MACEDONIAN €€
(Car Samoil 30; mains 350-600MKD) In an old Ohrid mansion, the famous Antiko has great ambience and pricey, but good, traditional dishes.

Pizzeria Leonardo PIZZA €
(Car Samoil 31; pizzas 200-350MKD) Ohrid's best pizza (it's popular with locals too).

Restoran Sveta Sofija MACEDONIAN €€€
(Car Samoil 88; mains 300-500MKD) This upscale restaurant opposite Sveta Sofija serves traditional fare and more than 100 Macedonian wines.

Drinking & Entertainment

TOP CHOICE **Cuba Libre** BAR
(Kosta Abraš; ⏲10pm-4am) Perennially popular Old Town bar and club. After midnight in summer it is a standing-room-only party spilling out on the courtyard.

Aquarius CAFE
(Kosta Abraš bb; ⏲10am-1am) Ohrid's original lake-terrace cafe, Aquarius remains cool for a midday coffee and is lively at night.

Liquid CAFE
(Kosta Abraš 17; ⏲9am-1am) Hip, chill-out place with a lake-front patio.

Dom na Kultura CULTURAL CENTRE
(Grigor Prličev; admission 50-100MKD) Cultural centre and movie theatre.

Information

Ohrid.com (www.ohrid.com.mk) Municipal website.

Post Office (bul Makedonski Prosvetiteli; ⏲7am-8pm Mon-Sat) Also changes money.

Sunny Land Tourism (www.sunnylandtourism.com; Car Samoil; ⏲9am-7pm) Local expert Zoran Grozdanovski can find accommodation and arrange tours and activities from this office by the National Museum.

Telephone Centre (bul Makedonski Prosvetiteli; ⏲7am-8pm Mon-Sat) Round the corner from the post office.

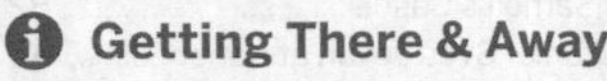

Getting There & Away

AIR Ohrid's **St Paul the Apostle Airport** (☎046 252 820; www.airports.com.mk), 10km north, handles summertime charter flights. Take a taxi (400MKD).

BUS From the **bus station** (7 Noemvri bb), 1.5km east of the centre, buses serve Skopje, either via Kičevo (520MKD, three hours, 11 daily) or (the longer route) via Bitola; for Bitola itself, 10 daily buses run (200MKD, 1¼ hours).

Buses also serve Belgrade (1800MKD, 15 hours, one daily) and Sofia (1450MKD, eight hours, one daily).

CENTRAL MACEDONIA

Bitola Битола

☎047 / POP 95,400

With elegant buildings and beautiful people, elevated Bitola (660m) has a sophistication inherited from its Ottoman days as the 'City of Consuls'. Its 18th- and 19th-century colourful townhouses, Turkish mosques and cafe culture make it Macedonia's most intriguing and liveable major town. An essential experience is sipping a coffee and people-watching along pedestrianised Širok Sokak ('Wide Street' in Turkish – still called ul Maršal Tito officially).

Sights & Activities

Širok Sokak STREET
(ul Maršal Tito) Bitola's Širok Sokak is the city's most representative and stylish street, with multicoloured facades and European honorary consulates attesting to the city's Ottoman-era sophistication. Enjoy the cafe life as the city's beautiful people promenade past.

Church of Sveti Dimitrija CHURCH
(11 Oktomvri bb; ⏲7am-6pm) This 1830 Orthodox church has rich frescos, ornate lamps and a huge iconostasis.

Mosques MOSQUES
Bitola's 16th-century **Yeni, Isak** and **Yahdar-Kadi Mosques**, all between the Dragor River and the Stara Čaršija (Old Bazaar), are Ottoman remnants, as is the enormous **Clock Tower** (Saat Kula).

Sleeping & Eating

TOP CHOICE **Chola Guest House** GUESTHOUSE €
(☎224 919; www.chola.mk; Stiv Naumov 80; s/d €12/20; 📶) Quiet place in an old mansion with clean, well-kept and pretty rooms, and colourful modern bathrooms. Ask the taxi driver for Video Club Dju (opposite Chola).

TOP CHOICE **Villa Dihovo** GUESTHOUSE €€
(☎070 544 744; www.villadihovo.com; rates negotiable; P📶) A 10-minute drive from town in the village of Dihovo, this is one of Macedonia's most remarkable guesthouses. It has three traditionally decorated rooms in the 80-year-old home of Petar Cvetkovski, inside the first long driveway after Dihovo centre's restaurant. Its big flowering lawn is great for kids. The only fixed prices are for the homemade wine, beer and *rakija* (firewater); all else, room price included, is your choice.

Hotel De Niro HOTEL €€
(☎229 656; www.hotel-deniro.com; Kiril i Metodij 5; s/d/ste from €25/50/80; ❄📶) Central yet discreet, De Niro has lovely old-Bitola-style rooms (more expensive suites also have waterbeds and spas). An excellent pizza-and-pasta restaurant (mains 200MKD to 450MKD) is attached.

TOP CHOICE **El Greko** PIZZA €
(☎071 279 848; cnr ul Maršal Tito & Elipda Karamandi; mains 180-350MKD; ⏰10am-1am) This Sokak taverna and pizzeria has beer-hall ambience and is popular with locals. At the time of research, it was planning to also offer budget rooms.

Drinking & Entertainment

TOP CHOICE **Porta Jazz** BAR
(Kiril i Metodija; ⏰8am-midnight) A popular, funky place that's packed when live jazz and blues bands play. It's located near the Centar na Kultura.

City Club CLUB
(Pelagonka 2) Relaxed nightclub popular with students.

Information

Tourist Information Centre (bitola-tourist-info@t-home.mk; Sterio Georgiev 1; ⏰9am-5pm Mon-Sat) Friendly info centre.

Getting There & Away

The **bus** and **train stations** (Nikola Tesla) adjoin 1km south of centre. Buses serve Skopje (470MKD, 3½ hours, 12 daily) and Ohrid (210MKD, 1¼ hours, 10 daily). Three daily trains serve Skopje (214MKD).

Taxis run to Florina in Greece (about 3000MKD).

UNDERSTAND MACEDONIA

History

2King Philip II (r 359–336 BC) of Macedon dominated the Greek city-states. Philip's son, Alexander the Great, spread Macedonian might to India. After his death (323 BC), the empire dissolved amid infighting. In 168 BC, Rome conquered Macedonia. Christianity came with the Apostle Paul. The Roman Empire's AD 395 division brought Macedonia under Byzantine Constantinople and Greek-influenced Orthodox Christianity. Three centuries after the 6th-century AD Slavic emigration into the region, the missionary work of monks Cyril and Methodius led to a Slavic literary language, partly created in Ohrid. The lakeside town became an important scholarly centre under the medieval Bulgarian empire, which fought chronic wars with the Byzantines.

With the Ottoman invasion Turkish settlers were introduced and five centuries of Islamic rule began. The centre of Balkan intrigue, Macedonia was the apple of discord between local nations and large empires, sparking conflicts that climaxed in the Balkan Wars of 1912–13, when the Turks were expelled by Bulgaria, Greece and Serbia. Macedonia was divided between these countries and, despite Bulgarian occupations during WWI and WWII, the Yugoslav-held portion emerged in 1991 as an independent republic – the only Yugoslav republic to break away peacefully.

However, Greece objected to the use of the name 'Macedonia' (also used for its northern province) outside its terrain. In 1995, Macedonia appeased Athens by provisionally changing its international-usage name to the Former Yugoslav Republic of Macedonia (FYROM). Two decades later, Greece still demands that Macedonia change its constitutional name before it can join the EU or NATO, though most countries recognise the Republic of Macedonia by its chosen name.

Simultaneously, Macedonia's Albanian minority began protesting alleged ill-treatment. During NATO's 1999 Kosovo intervention to defend ethnic Albanians there, Macedonia sheltered 400,000 Kosovar refugees. Nevertheless, Albanian separatists waged war in Macedonian areas bordering Kosovo in early 2001. Hostilities subsided with the internationally brokered Ohrid Framework Agreement in August 2001, granting minorities more rights and political participation.

Despite four successive recommendations by the European Commission, Macedonia in December 2012 was still blocked by Greece from starting EU accession negotiations. With ethnic Albanian nationalism rising and a Bulgarian government threatening to veto Macedonia's EU ambitions too, Macedonia has felt increasingly alienated. Well aware of this, Turkey has become Macedonia's best regional ally. The shared history, political goodwill and significant Turkish investments have greatly increased Ankara's prominence here in recent years. Macedonia's future will likely see a return to the past mixture of East and West – which may be best for everyone.

People

The latest census (2004) divided the population of 2,022,547 thus: Macedonians (66.6%), Albanians (22.7%), Turks (4%), Roma (2.2%), Serbs (2.1%) and others (2.4%), including Vlachs, the alleged descendants of Roman frontier soldiers.

Most Macedonians are Orthodox Christians, with some Macedonian-speaking Muslims (the Torbeši and Gorani). Turks are Muslim, like Albanians and (nominally) the impoverished Roma. In recent years, social and ethnic complexities relating to religion have caused concern over Islamic fundamentalism, as seen in protests and violent attacks on Christians.

Arts

Macedonia has a rich tradition of folk music (and instruments), accompanied by traditional dancing; national ensemble **Tanec** (☎2461 021; www.tanec.com.mk; Vinjamin Macukovski 7, Skopje) tours worldwide.

More contemporary-styled musicians have won international acclaim: they include pianist Simon Trpčevski, opera singer Boris Trajanov, jazz guitarist Vladimir Četkar and percussionists, the Tavitjan Brothers. The beloved Toše Proeski was a charismatic singer who died tragically in 2007; aged just 26, Proeski was admired for both his music and humanitarian work.

Environment

The Continental and Mediterranean climate zones converge in Macedonia, which features more than 50 mountain peaks topping 2500m. Lakes Ohrid and Prespa are among Europe's oldest tectonic lakes (three million years old); at 300m, Ohrid is the Balkans' deepest. Macedonia's highest peak, Mt Korab (Golem Korab; 2764m), borders Albania.

Bears, wild boars, wolves, foxes, chamois, deer and even a few rare lynx prowl the land. Blackcaps, grouse, white Egyptian vultures, royal eagles and forest owls fly above it. Lake birds include Dalmatian pelicans, herons and cormorants. Storks (and their huge nests) are prominent. Macedonia's national dog, the šar planinec, is a 60cm-tall sheepdog that bravely fights bears and wolves.

Lake Ohrid is a living fossil-age museum – its endemic trout predates the last Ice Age. Its many other residents include a 30-million-year-old snail genus and the mysterious Ohrid eel, which arrives from the Sargasso Sea to live for 10 years before returning to breed and die; its offspring restart the cycle.

SURVIVAL GUIDE

Directory A–Z

Accommodation

Skopje's hotels are expensive but hostels have emerged. Ohrid and Bitola have budget and midrange choices. Book ahead for July to August, Orthodox Christmas (7 January), Orthodox Easter and during festivals.

Prices quoted are for rooms with a private bathroom unless otherwise stated. The following price indicators apply (for a high-season double room):

€ less than €50

€€ €50 to €80

€€€ more than €80

Activities

Mavrovo's Zare Lazarevski ski centre and Popova Šapka ski centre, near Tetovo, offer good skiing. Mavrovo, Galičica and Pelister National Parks and Jasen Nature Reserve (www.jasen.com.mk) have great hiking and wildlife.

Business Hours

Banks 7am to 5pm Monday to Friday

Businesses 8am to 8pm Monday to Friday, to 2pm Saturday

Post offices 6.30am to 8pm

Food

The following prices are based on the cost of a main course:

€ less than 150MKD

€€ 150MKD to 300MKD

€€€ more than 300MKD

Embassies & Consulates

All offices are in Skopje.

Australian Consulate (3061 114; www.serbia.embassy.gov.au/bgde/home.html; Londonska 11b)

Canadian Embassy (3225 630; www.canadianembassyInformation.com/embassy-in/republic-of-macedonia.html; bul Partizanski Odredi 17a)

French Embassy (3118 749; www.ambafrance-mk.org; Salvador Aljendo 73)

German Embassy (3093 900; www.skopje.diplo.de/Vertretung/skopje/mk/Startseite.html; Lerinska 59)

Netherlands Embassy (023 129 319; www.nlembassy.org.mk; Leninova 69-71)

Russian Embassy (023 117 160; www.russia.org.mk; Pirinska 44)

UK Embassy (3299 299; www.ukinmacedonia.fco.gov.uk/en; Dimitrie Čupovski 26)

US Embassy (3102 000; http://macedonia.usembassy.gov; Samoilova bb)

Money

Macedonian denars (MKD) come notes of 10, 50, 100, 500, 1000 and 5000, and coins of one, two, five, 10 and 50. Taxi drivers hate it when you pay with a 1000-denar note, and may make you go into a shop to make change. Euros are generally accepted – some hotels quote euro rates, but denar payment is acceptable.

Exchange offices *(menuvačnici)* work commission-free. ATMs are widespread, except in villages.

Post

The **main post office** (3141 141; Orce Nikolov 1; 7am-7.30pm Mon-Sat, 7.30am-2.30pm Sun) in Skopje is 75m northwest of Ploštad Makedonija. Others are opposite the train station, in the Gradski Trgovski Centar and in Ramstore. Letters to the USA cost 38MKD, to Australia 40MKD and to Europe 35MKD. Global-brand shipping companies operate.

Public Holidays

New Year's Day 1 January

Orthodox Christmas 7 January

Orthodox Easter Week March/April

Labour Day 1 May

Saints Cyril and Methodius Day 24 May

Ilinden Day 2 August

Republic Day 8 September

1941 Partisan Day 11 October

Telephone

Macedonia's country code is 389. Drop the initial zero in city codes and mobile prefixes (07) when calling from abroad. Buy a local SIM card for longer stays. Some kiosks (newsagents) have private telephones.

Visas

Citizens of Australia, Canada, the EU, Israel, New Zealand, Norway, Switzerland, Turkey and the USA can stay for three months, visa-free. Otherwise, visa fees average from US$30 for a single-entry visa and US$60 for a multiple-entry visa. For more information, visit the website of the **Ministry of Foreign Affairs** (www.mfa.gov.mk).

Getting There & Away

Air

Alexander the Great Airport (3148 333; www.airports.com.mk; Petrovec), 21km from Skopje, is Macedonia's main airport, with Ohrid's **St Paul the Apostle Airport** (046 252 820; www.airports.com.mk) mostly used for summer charters. Skopje airport has exchange offices, ATMs and hotel-booking and car-rental services.

Land

For Tirana in Albania use the Kafasan–Qafa e Thanës crossing, 12km southwest of Struga on Lake Ohrid. For Sofia, Bulgaria, use the Deve Bair crossing (90km from Skopje, after Kriva Palanka). Blace border crossing, 20 minutes north from Skopje, reaches Pristina, Kosovo. Tabanovce, northeast of Skopje, is the major road/rail crossing for Belgrade, Serbia.

BUS

From Skopje, buses serve Belgrade (1400MKD, 10 hours, 12 daily), İstanbul (1900MKD, 12 hours, five daily), Pristina (320MKD, two hours, 12 daily), Sofia (1040MKD, 5½ hours, five daily), Zagreb (3150MKD, 12 hours, one daily) and Thessaloniki (1280MKD, four hours, one Monday, Wednesday and Friday).

CAR & MOTORCYCLE

A Green Card endorsed for Macedonia is required.

TRAIN

Macedonian Railway (www.mz.com.mk) serves Serbia and Kosovo. There are currently no train services between Macedonia and Greece.

Getting Around

Bicycle

Cycling is popular in Skopje. Traffic is light in rural areas, though mountains and reckless drivers are common.

Bus

Skopje serves most domestic destinations. Larger buses are new and air-conditioned, *kombi* (minibuses) usually not. During summer, pre-book for Ohrid.

Car & Motorcycle

AUTOMOBILE ASSOCIATIONS

AMSM (Avto Moto Soyuz na Makedonija; ☎3181 181; www.art.com.mk; Ivo Ribar Lola 51, Skopje) offers road assistance, towing and information (in German, English and Macedonian), with branches nationwide.

DRIVER'S LICENCE

A national driver's licence is fine, though an International Driving Permit is best.

HIRE

Skopje's rental agencies include international biggies and local companies. Ohrid has many, other cities fewer. Sedans average €60 daily, including insurance. Bring your passport, driver's licence and credit card.

Taxi

Taxis are relatively inexpensive. Skopje cabs cost 40MKD for the first kilometre, 25MKD per subsequent kilometre. Smaller cities are cheaper. Intercity taxis are expensive if travelling alone (it's 4000MKD from Skopje to Ohrid), yet they can be preferable for international travel (Skopje to Pristina in Kosovo is only 3000MKD, and twice as fast as public transport).

Moldova

Includes »

Chişinău 768
Cricova 772
Mileştii Mici 772
Orheiul Vechi 773
Transdniestr 773
Tiraspol 773
Understand Moldova 774
Survival Guide 775

Best Places to Stay

» Adresa (p768)

» Chişinău Hostel (p768)

Best Places to Eat

» Vatra Neamului (p769)

» Oraşul Vechi (p769)

Why Go?

Only vaguely known in Europe and all but anonymous to the rest of the world, Moldova remains a mysterious and misunderstood land: part Romanian, part Russian, all Soviet. Once at the very edge of the USSR, Moldova has gone it alone since the early nineties, even if independence has been both economically painful and racked by civil war between the central government and the secessionist Russian-speaking region known as Transdniestr, which continues to exist as a state within a state today.

Moldova gets a tiny number of tourists and isn't much set up for travellers, but this is one of its greatest charms. Sights may be few and far between, but they are generally impressive, such as the dramatic and beautiful cave monasteries, Transdniestr's Soviet time-capsule feel, and the country's sophisticated and fascinating viniculture. Look no further for adventure: this is eastern Europe's last unknown land.

When to Go

Chişinău

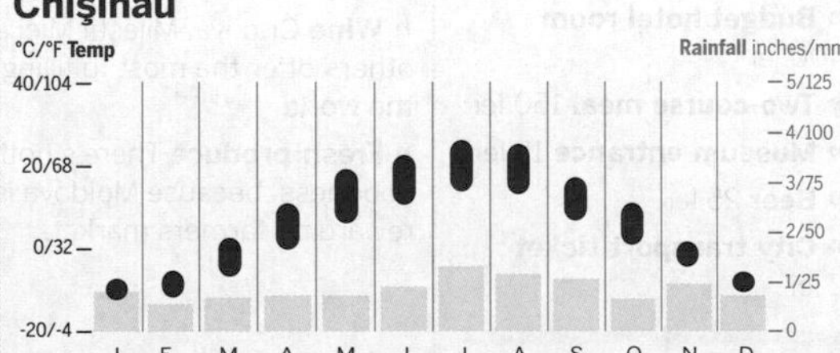

Jun Parks and restaurant terraces fill with freed students, and the weather is warm.

Jul High season hits its peak with hiking, wine tours and camping all in full operation.

Oct The excellent Wine Festival is on the second Sunday in October.

AT A GLANCE

» **Currency** Moldovan leu (plural lei)

» **Language** Moldovan

» **Money** ATMs abundant in Chişinău

» **Visas** None for the EU, USA, Canada and Japan – but required for Australians, New Zealanders and South Africans

Fast Facts

» **Area** 33,851 sq km

» **Capital** Chişinău

» **Country code** ☎373

» **Emergency** Ambulance ☎903, police ☎902

Exchange Rates

Australia	A$1	12.97 lei
Canada	C$1	12.22 lei
Euro Zone	€1	15.86 lei
Japan	¥100	13.16 lei
New Zealand	NZ$1	10.39 lei
UK	UK£1	18.78 lei
USA	US$1	12.41 lei

Set Your Budget

» **Budget hotel room** 400 lei

» **Two-course meal** 150 lei

» **Museum entrance** 15 lei

» **Beer** 25 lei

» **City transport ticket** 2 lei

Resources

» **Republic of Moldova** (www.moldova.md)

» **Fest** (www.fest.md)

» **Moldova.org** (www.moldova.org)

Connections

Despite its awkward geopolitical situation, Moldova has pretty decent overland links to its neighbouring countries. Daily buses and trains from Chişinău head to Iaşi and Bucharest in Romania, as well as to Odesa in Ukraine. Trains also serve Kyiv and Lviv in Ukraine; Minsk in Belarus; and Moscow and St Petersburg in Russia. Buses to Odesa avoid Transdniestr and thus the delays at the border. Trains between Chişinău and Odesa go via Tiraspol, but delays are minimal.

ITINERARIES

Three Days

Use the capital Chişinău as your base and get to know this friendly and fast-changing town. Make day trips out to the stunning cave monastery at Orheiul Vechi and to one of the local big-name vineyards for a fascinating tour and tasting.

One Week

Spend a night or two in surreal Transdniestr before returning to Chişinău and tack on a few smaller vineyard tours around Chişinău, purchasing your customs limit.

Essential Food & Drink

» **Muşchi de vacă/porc/miel** A cutlet of beef/pork/lamb.

» **Piept de pui** Chicken breast.

» **Mămăligă** A cornmeal porridge with a bread-like consistency that is a staple accompaniment to every Moldovan dish.

» **Sarma** Cabbage-wrapped mince meat or pilau rice packages, similar to Turkish *dolma* or Russian *goluptsy*.

» **Brânză** Moldova's most common cheese is a slightly sour sheep's milk product, similar to those made in Ukraine and Slovakia.

» **Wine** Cricova, Mileştii Mici and Cojuşna wineries and others offer the most fulfilling and inexpensive wine tours in the world.

» **Fresh produce** There's nothing else available, and thank goodness, because Moldova is essentially one big, very rewarding farmers market.

Moldova Highlights

1. Stroll the surprisingly pleasant streets and parks of the friendly capital **Chișinău** (p768)
2. Designate a driver for tours of the world-famous wine cellars at **Mileștii Mici** (p772) and **Cricova** (p772)
3. Detox at the fantastic cave monastery, burrowed by 13th-century monks, at **Orheiul Vechi** (p773)
4. Go *way* off the beaten path in the self-styled 'republic' of **Transdniestr** (p773), a surreal, living homage to the Soviet Union
5. Gorge on the many excellent **dining options** (p769) found in Chișinău

CHIŞINĂU

☎22 / POP 794,800

The vibrant Moldovan capital certainly won't win any architectural beauty awards soon, but despite having been razed to the ground by a combination of WWII and a terrible 1940 earthquake, Chişinău has arguably never lots its cosmopolitan soul or charm, despite the best efforts of the Soviet authorities who oversaw the rebuilding of the city.

First chronicled in 1420, Chişinău (*kish*-i-now in Moldovan, *kish*-i-nyov in Russian) became a hotbed of anti-Semitism notorious for its pogroms in the early 20th century. Later, during Soviet rule, Chişinău was the headquarters of the USSR's southwestern military operations, giving the city a status way beyond its size for many decades. Between 1944 and 1990 the city was called Kishinev, its Russian name, which is still used by many of the Russian-speaking locals, though these days even most Russian speakers use the Romanian pronunciation.

Today the city is an affable place with a smattering of attractions, more than its fair share of curios and plenty of good eating, drinking and partying options for locals and visitors alike.

Sights

National Archaeology & History Museum MUSEUM
(www.nationalmuseum.md; Str 31 August 1989; admission/photo/video 15/15/40 lei; ⏲10am-6pm Sat-Thu) The grandaddy of Chişinău's museums contains archaeological artefacts from Orheiul Vechi, including Golden Horde coins, Soviet-era weaponry and a huge WWII diorama on the 1st floor.

Pushkin Museum MUSEUM
(Str Anton Pann 19; admission 15 lei, English-language tour 50 lei; ⏲10am-4pm Tue-Sun) Northeast of the central parks, this is where Russia's national poet Alexander Pushkin (1799–1837) spent three years exiled between 1820 and 1823. It was here that he wrote *The Prisoner of the Caucasus* and other classics – that is, when he wasn't involved in amorous intrigues, hard drinking and occasional violence.

National Ethnographic & Nature Museum MUSEUM
(☎244 002; www.muzeu.md; Str M Kogălniceanu 82; adult/child 15/10 lei, English-language tour 100 lei; ⏲10am-6pm Tue-Sun) The highlight of this massive and wonderful exhibition is a life-size reconstruction of a mammoth skeleton, discovered in the Rezine region in 1966. Allow at least an hour to see the museum's pop art, taxidermied animals and exhibits covering geology, botany and zoology. English-language tours must be arranged in advance.

National Army Museum MUSEUM
(cnr Str 31 August 1989 & Str Tighina; admission/photo 2/3 lei; ⏲9am-8pm Tue-Sun) This small open-air military exhibition displays a distinctly sorry-looking collection of Soviet-made tanks, fighter planes and other military toys inherited by Moldova's armed forces.

Sleeping

Chişinău has a fairly lamentable hotel selection, with very few midrange options. One popular alternative is to rent an apartment. Check out www.marisha.net for cheap homestays and apartments.

TOP CHOICE **Chişinău Hostel** HOSTEL €
(☎069-711 918; www.chishinau.ucoz.com; Str Arborilor 5/4, behind Malldova; dm/d incl breakfast €10/28; @ 📶) Moldova's only proper hostel is about a 25-minute walk south from the centre. This comfortable, well-run place offers lockers, breakfast, shared kitchen, Wii, laundry (€2), and tours to wineries and Transdniestr. A number of maxitaxis stop here from the centre and all stations; ask for 'Malldova'. A taxi ride will cost 35 to 40 lei. It's a popular place, so book ahead.

Adresa APARTMENT €€
(☎544 392; www.adresa.md; B-dul Negruzzi 1; apt €30-160; ⏲24hr) For short- or long-term stays, this reliable agency offers a great alternative to hotels, renting out one- to three-room apartments throughout the city. It's a memorable way to live as the locals do using rusty lifts or climbing disagreeable staircases. Still, they're safe, comfortable and clean. Most aren't right in the city centre but a short taxi ride away.

Hotel Cosmos HOTEL €
(☎542 757; www.hotel-cosmos.com; Piaţa Negruzzi 2; s/d incl breakfast €29/39; ❄ 📶) While its tag line 'you will come as a guest and you will leave as a friend' may be overstating the case, this concrete Soviet-era hulk of a hotel is certainly more welcoming than some of its counterparts. Rooms are reasonably priced

and in various states of renovation. The economy rooms are studies in Soviet style – clearly untouched since the '80s and enjoying a certain character compared with the more sterile and pricier standards. Wi-fi is in the lobby and lower rooms only – ask for a room with wi-fi when you book.

Hotel Turist HOTEL €
(☎220 637; B-dul Renaşterii 13; s 500-700 lei, d 450-560 lei;) For a kitsch blast of Soviet past, try this place, overlooking a Soviet memorial to communist youth. The socialist mural on its facade is prime photo material. The doubles are all unrenovated and spare, but just fine. More expensive rooms have refrigerators, air-con and balconies. Breakfast is 55 lei.

Eating

TOP CHOICE **Vatra Neamului** INTERNATIONAL €€
(Str Bucureşti 67; mains 90-200 lei;) This superb place boasts charming old-world decor and unfailingly genial staff. A long menu of imaginatively dressed-up meats – think stewed pork with polenta, baked rabbit and salmon in pastry, not to mention copious vegetarian options – may prompt repeat visits. Enter via the door on Str Puşkin.

Oraşul Vechi MOLDOVAN €
(Old City; Str Armenească 24; mains 40-100 lei; 10am-3am;) This stylish restaurant with chandeliers, classic paintings and a fireplace has nightly live piano and a pleasant semioutdoor terrace with vines creeping around the wrought-iron exterior. Dishes range from stewed rabbit in vegetables to grilled pike-perch and beef stroganoff. There's an extensive local wine list.

Cactus Café CAFE €€
(Str Armenească 41; mains 100-200 lei; 9am-11pm;) This smart place has good service and excellent food. There's a very pleasant summer terrace and a slightly overstyled Wild West interior. It's a great breakfast spot with a range of dishes to cater to all tastes.

Beer House INTERNATIONAL €€
(B-dul Negruzzi 6/2; mains 75-250 lei;) This brewery-cum-restaurant has four delicious home-brewed beers and a great menu, warming up with chicken wings and peaking at rabbit or chicken grilled in cognac.

Pizza Mania PIZZERIA €
(www.pizzamania.md; Str Ismail; pizza 40-100 lei;) The most central of a cheap and well-run chain of pizza restaurants, Pizza Mania offers lots of choice, wi-fi and fast, efficient service.

Drinking

Coliba Studenţilor BAR
(Str A Mateevici; 8am-11pm) This student hang-out, opposite the university, is quiet during summer, but during the school year the terrace is a good place to bump into eager English speakers.

Déjà Vu COCKTAIL BAR
(Str Bucureşti 67; 9pm-2am) A true cocktail bar with a tantalising drinks menu. It's located in the town centre and is popular with a smart and cool young crowd. There's also a small dining hall serving meals.

Dublin Irish Pub PUB
(Str Bulgară 27; noon-11pm) Rather expensive, but one of the few places in town where you can get a pint of Guinness (80 lei).

Entertainment

City Club CLUB
(Str 31 August 1989, 121; 10pm-6am) In the alley next to the Licurici Puppet Theatre, this 2nd-floor club consistently ranks as one of the hippest places in town. Tables are often 'reserved', but you can buy them for yourself and your party if you want better treatment (200 lei to 300 lei).

Opera & Ballet Theatre BALLET
(www.nationalopera.md; B-dul Ştefan cel Mare 152; box office 10am-2pm & 5-7pm) Home to the esteemed national opera and ballet company, with productions from September to June.

Philharmonic Concert Hall CONCERT VENUE
(Str Mitropolit Varlaam 78) Moldova's National Philharmonic is based here.

Information

There's no tourist information centre in Moldova, but there are plenty of travel agencies where you can get information. Most offer discounted rates in some hotels.

Sometimes travel agencies take a while to reply to emails (if ever). A better bet for pretrip contact are independent operators such as **West East** (☎06-006 06 06; www.moldova-travel.com) or **Natalia Raiscaia** (☎079-578 217; www.domasha.net) for apartment rentals, local information and assistance.

Municipal Clinical Emergency Hospital (☎emergency 903, info 248 435; Str Toma

Central Chişinău

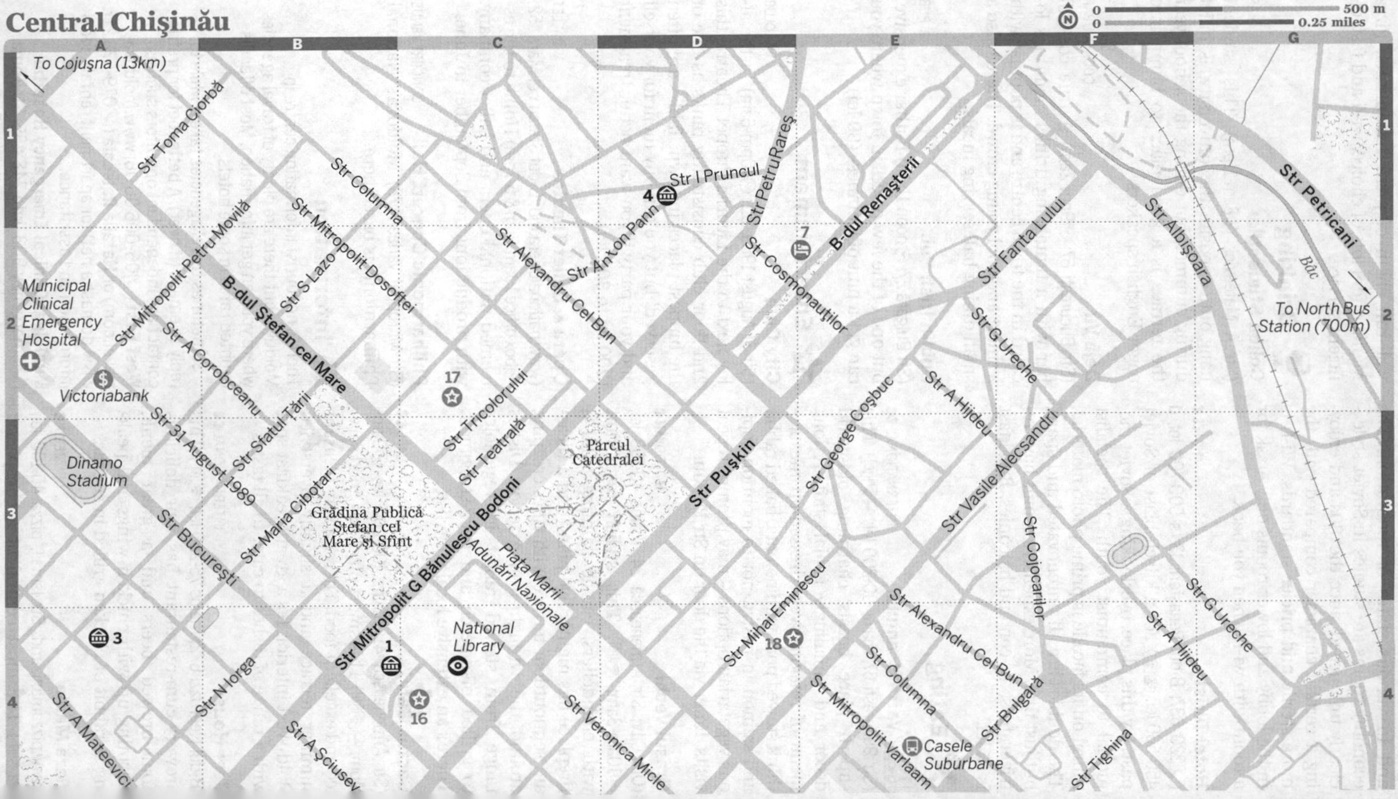

0 500 m
0 0.25 miles

To Cojuşna (13km)
Str Toma Ciorbă
Str Columna
Str Mitropolit Dosoftei
Str S Lazo
Str Mitropolit Petru Movilă
B-dul Ştefan cel Mare
Str A Corobceanu
Municipal Clinical Emergency Hospital
Victoriabank
Str 31 August 1989
Str Sfatul Ţării
Dinamo Stadium
Str Bucureşti
Str Maria Cibotari
Grădina Publică Ştefan cel Mare şi Sfînt
3
Str N Iorga
Str A Mateevici
Str A Şciusev
Str Mitropolit G Bănulescu Bodoni
1
16
National Library
Piaţa Marii Adunări Naţionale
17
Str Tricolorului
Str Teatrală
Str Alexandru Cel Bun
Str Anton Pann
4
Str I Pruncul
Str Petru Rareş
Parcul Catedralei
Str Puşkin
Str Veronica Micle
7
B-dul Renaşterii
Str Cosmonauţilor
Str George Coşbuc
Str Mihai Eminescu
18
Str Alexandru Cel Bun
Str Columna
Str Mitropolit Varlaam
Casele Suburbane
Str Fanta Lului
Str G Ureche
Str A Hijdeu
Str Vasile Alecsandri
Str Cojocarilor
Str Bulgară
Str Tighina
Str Albişoara
Str Petricani
Bâc
To North Bus Station (700m)
Str G Ureche
Str A Hijdeu

Central Chişinău

Sights

1 National Archaeology & History Museum ... B4
2 National Army Museum ... E6
3 National Ethnographic & Nature Museum ... A4
4 Pushkin Museum ... D1

Sleeping

5 Adresa ... G6
6 Hotel Cosmos ... G6
7 Hotel Turist ... E2

Eating

8 Beer House ... G6
9 Cactus Café ... D5
10 Oraşul Vechi ... D5
11 Pizza Mania ... F5
12 Vatra Neamului ... C5

Drinking

13 Coliba Studenţilor ... A5
14 Déjà Vu ... C5
15 Dublin Irish Pub ... D6

Entertainment

16 City Club ... C4
17 Opera & Ballet Theatre ... C2
18 Philharmonic Concert Hall ... D4

Ciorba 1; ⏲24hr) Provides emergency services and a good chance of finding English-speaking staff.

Victoriabank (Str 31 August 1989, 141; ⏲9am-4pm Mon-Fri) Amex representative.

Getting There & Away

AIR Moldova's only international airport is the modern **Chişinău international airport** (KIV; ☎525 111; www.airport.md), 15.5km southeast of the city centre. There are regular flights to many major European capitals. There are no internal flights within Moldova.

BUS Chişinău has three bus stations. The **North Bus Station** (Autogara Nord; www.autogara.md), northeast of the centre where Str Ismail and Str Tudor Vladimirescu meet, is where nearly all domestic and international lines depart, except Transdniestr-bound lines, which depart from the Central Bus Station. Domestic and international maxitaxis operate from the **Central Bus Station** (Autogara Centrală; Str Mitropolit Varlaam), behind the central market. Bus services to southern destinations use the **Southwestern Bus Station** (Autogara Sud-vest; cnr Şoseaua Hânceşti & Str Spicului), approximately 2.2km from the city centre.

TRANSPORT FROM CHIŞINĂU

Bus

DESTINATION	DEPARTURE POINT	PRICE (LEI)	DURATION (HR)	FREQUENCY
Bendery	Central Station	25	1½	every 20min 9am-3pm
Bucharest (Romania)	Central Station	225-250	12	4 daily
Iaşi (Romania)	Southwestern Station	118	4	2 daily
Orhei	Casele Suburbane terminal	19	1	half-hourly 9.15am-10pm
Tiraspol	Central Station	29	1½	every 20min 6am-7pm

International Train

DESTINATION	PRICE (LEI)	DURATION (HR)	FREQUENCY
Bucharest (Romania, change here for Budapest)	398	14	1 daily
Kyiv (Ukraine)	771	14	1 daily
Lviv (Ukraine)	460	18	1 daily on odd dates
Minsk (Belarus)	878	25	1 daily on even dates
Moscow (Russia)	1030	28-32	4 daily
St Petersburg (Russia)	1030	40	1 daily

TRAIN International routes depart from Chişinău's recently renovated train station, Aleea Gării, located just southeast of Piaţa Negruzii, off B-dul Iurii Gagarin.

Getting Around

TO/FROM THE AIRPORT Maxitaxi 165 departs every 20 minutes from Str Ismail, across from Eximbank near the corner of B-dul Ştefan cel Mare for the airport (3 lei). Coming from the airport, this is the last stop.

BUS & TROLLEYBUS Tickets for buses (2 lei) and trolleybuses (1 leu) are sold on-board. Most routes in town and many outlying villages are served by nippy maxitaxis (3 lei per trip; pay the driver). Maxitaxis run regularly between 6am and 10pm, with reduced service until midnight.

AROUND CHIŞINĂU

Cricova

Of Moldova's many fine wineries, **Cricova** (022-453 659; www.cricova.md; Str Ungureanu 1; 8am-4pm) is arguably the best known. Its underground wine kingdom, 15km north of Chişinău, is one of Europe's biggest. Some 60km of the 120km-long underground limestone tunnels – dating from the 15th century – are lined wall-to-wall with bottles.

You must have private transport and advance reservations to get into Cricova or you can arrange for staff to pick you up in Chişinău. Tours range from 45 minutes to 2½ hours (250 lei to 1350 lei per person), with increasing tastings and food as the price climbs.

Mileştii Mici

While Cricova has the hype, **Mileştii Mic[i]** (022-382 333; www.milestii-mici.md; 2hr tou[r] 250 lei, tour, tasting & lunch 500-900 lei; 9am-5pm Mon-Fri) has the goods. Housed in a limestone mine, these are *the* largest cellars i[n] Europe (over 200km of tunnels). They wer[e] recognised by Guinness World Records i[n] 2005 for having the largest wine collectio[n] in the world (1.5 million bottles), thoug[h] the collection has now surpassed the tw[o] million-bottle mark.

Excellent-value tours by car wind dow[n] through the cellars with stops at notabl[e] collections and artistically executed tourist points, terminating at the elegantly decorated restaurant 60m below ground. These tours are striking, while being refreshingly informal and hilarious. Tour groups must have at least four people – though this is negotiable. Weekend tours require a minimum of 15 people.

Orheiul Vechi

The **Orheiul Vechi Monastery Complex** (Complexul Muzeistic Orheiul Vechi; ☎0235-34 242; admission 15 lei; ⏰9am-6pm Tue-Sun) is carved into a massive limestone cliff in a wild, rocky, remote spot, 10km southeast of Orhei in Orheiul Vechi (Old Orhei; marked on maps as the village of Trebujeni). Unquestionably Moldova's most fantastic and picturesque sight, it draws visitors from around the globe. It's forbidden to wear shorts and women must cover their heads while inside the monastery.

From Chişinău, daily buses depart from the Central Bus Station for Butuceni or Trebujeni (20 lei, about one hour) at 9.30am, 1.15pm and 5.15pm. Return trips run daily at 2.45pm and 6.45pm.

TRANSDNIESTR

POP 518,700

The self-declared republic of Transdniestr (Pridnestrovskaya Moldavskaya Respublika, or PMR, in Russian), a narrow strip of land on the eastern bank of the Dniestr River, is perhaps one of the strangest places in eastern Europe, a ministate that doesn't officially exist in anyone's eyes but its own.

While on the one side Moldova maintains that Transdniestr was illegally grabbed from its sovereign territory with Russian support, Transdniestr proudly points to its having won 'independence' during a bloody civil war in the early 1990s. However you look at it, a tenuous, bitter truce has ensued ever since.

Travellers will be stunned by this idiosyncratic region that has developed its own currency, police force, army and borders, controlled by Transdniestran border guards.

Until very recently, a visit to the area meant submitting to sometimes expensive, organised bribe shakedowns with border officials, but in recent years such instances have almost totally ceased and visiting this communist theme park is a relative breeze.

Tiraspol

☎533 / POP 159,000

Eerily quiet streets, flower beds tended with military precision and old-school Soviet everything from street signs to litter-free parks named after communist grandees: Tiraspol (from the Greek, meaning 'town on the Nistru') will be one of the strangest places you'll ever visit.

Sights

Tiraspol National United Museum MUSEUM
(ul 25 Oktober 42; admission 25 rubles; ⏰10am-5pm Sun-Fri) The closest thing to a local his-

CROSSING INTO TRANSDNIESTR

We used to receive frequent reader feedback reporting disturbing hijinks at Transdniestran border crossings. Accusations of incomplete paperwork or invented transgressions led to ludicrous 'fines' of up to €200 and beyond. However, after several years of calm at the border, it seems as if the bribe-factory atmosphere has finally ended. In 2012 the direct train service between Chişinău and Odesa was operating unmolested by the Moldovan border guards. Therefore, train is the best way to transit the country. Most buses, tired of the border hassles, circumnavigate Transdniestr altogether.

At the time of writing, there was no payment necessary to cross the border in either direction. However, if you're staying for more than 24 hours, you'll need to register with **OVIR** (☎533-55 047; ul Kotovskogo 2a; ⏰9am-noon Mon, 9am-noon & 1-4pm Tue & Thu, 1-3pm Fri). Registration is free and can normally be handled by your hotel or whoever organises your accommodation. Some hotels will register you automatically. If you do need to sort it out yourself, go down the alley and enquire at the rear white building with the red roof. Oh, and 'men must wear pants'! Seriously. Outside OVIR business hours go to the **Tiraspol Militia Office** (☎533-34 169; Roza Luxemburg 66; ⏰24hr) where registration is possible, but you'll probably be asked to check in at the OVIR office the next working day anyway.

tory museum, it features an exhibit on poet Nikolai Zelinsky, who founded the first Soviet school of chemistry. Opposite is the **Presidential Palace**, from where newly minted leader Yevgeny Shevchuk rules the region.

Kvint Factory BRANDY FACTORY
(☎96 577; www.kvint.biz; ul Lenina 38) The Kvint factory is one of Transdniestr's prides and joys – since 1897 it's been making some of Moldova's finest brandies. Buy the least expensive cognac in Europe (starting at less than €2!) either near the front entrance of the plant or at the **Kvint shop** (ul 25 Oktober 84; ⌚24hr).

Sleeping & Eating

You must register at OVIR (p773) in central Tiraspol if staying more than 24 hours. Visit www.marisha.net to arrange a homestay.

Stay at Lena's APARTMENT €
(☎06-915 57 53; lena_lozinskiy@inbox.ru; ul Pravdy 6, apt 97; apt 290 rubles) Lena has a cosy, recently renovated one-room apartment near the Borodinka bus stop at the entrance to the town centre. There's 24-hour hot water and a basic kitchen.

Tiraspol Hostel HOSTEL €
(☎68-571 472; www.moldovahostels.com; ul Levanevskogo 31a; dm 218 rubles; 📶) Run by Tim, Tiraspol's only American ex-pat, this small country-style house has 11 beds, plus another small cottage with two beds. Prices include a free three-hour city tour. Call to arrange a free pick up, as it's difficult to find on your own.

Hotel Aist HOTEL €
(☎73 776; pereulok Naberezhny 3; r 150-800 rubles) A partially updated Soviet-era place. While the 'economy' rooms are beyond spartan, they're absolutely fine. Pricier 'upgraded' rooms are also available.

Seven Fridays CAFE €
(ul 25 Oktober 112; mains 30-80 rubles; ⌚11am-midnight; 📶) A popular cafe right in the centre of town serving all manner of meat, salads, soups, and, erm, sushi. It has a bustling brasserie feel and if you sit here long enough, you'll see most of Tiraspol drop by. Menus are Russian but there are pictures to point at.

Information

Transnistria Tour (☎694-27 502; www.transnistria-tour.com) This highly recommended new company is the first travel agency in Transdniestr to offer tours and travel services to foreign visitors. Its excellent English-language website is a great place to start planning your trip.

Getting There & Away

BUS From Tiraspol there are eight daily buses to Odesa (47.10 rubles, three hours) and one daily to Kyiv (202 rubles, 14 hours). Buses go to Chişinău (33.80 rubles) nearly every half-hour from 5am to 6pm.

TRAIN There's a useful train to Odesa (100 rubles, two hours) from Chişinău which stops at Tiraspol at 9.40am daily. The train makes the return journey to Chişinău each evening, calling at Tiraspol at 7.15pm. There's also one daily train to Moscow, via Kyiv, leaving at 2.03am (3rd/2nd class 835/1750 rubles, 26 hours).

UNDERSTAND MOLDOVA

History

Moldova straddles two historic regions divided by the Dniestr (Nistru) River. Historic Romanian Bessarabia incorporated the region west of the Dniestr, while tsarist Russia governed the territory east of the river (Transdniestr). Bessarabia, part of the Romanian principality of Moldavia, was annexed in 1812 by the Russian Empire. Anti-Semitism under the Russians was felt in Moldova, with pogroms in 1903 and 1905, and resulted in hundreds being killed or wounded, thousands made homeless and mass Jewish emigration to the Americas.

In 1918, after the October Revolution in Russia, Bessarabia declared its independence. Two months later the newly formed Democratic Moldavian Republic united with Romania. Russia never recognised this union. Then in 1924 the Soviet Union created what came to be known as the Moldavian Autonomous Soviet Socialist Republic (Moldavian ASSR) on the eastern banks of the Dniestr, and incorporated Transdniestr into the Ukrainian Soviet Socialist Republic (SSR). During 1929 the capital was moved to Tiraspol from Balta (in present-day Ukraine). In June 1940 the Molotov-Ribbentrop Pact meant Soviet troops occupied Romanian Bessarabia and joined it with the southern part.

During 1941 allied Romanian and German troops attacked the Soviet Union. Bes sarabia and Transdniestr fell into Romanian hands. Consequently, thousands of Bessarabian Jews were sent to labour camps and then deported to Auschwitz. In August 1944 the Soviet army reoccupied Transdniestr and Bessarabia.

It wasn't until February 1990 that the first democratic elections to the Supreme Soviet (parliament) were won by the Popular Front. In April 1990 the Moldovan national flag was reinstated – except in Transdniestr. Moldova declared its full independence in August 1991.

Romania's 2007 entrance into the EU transformed the Moldovan border into the EU's eastern frontier, complicating the formerly lenient cross-border traffic.

In early 2010, Moldova's newly elected Western-leaning government, led by Prime Minister Vlad Filat, signed an order to remove nearly 360km of the communist-era barbed-wire fence separating Moldova from Romania. Romania soon responded by promising €100 million in development aid and doubling the number of scholarships for Moldovan students wanting to study in Romania. With a newly elected reformist leader in Transdniestr in 2012, things are looking brighter for Moldova's future than they have at any time since independence.

People

With 4.3 million inhabitants, Moldova is the most densely populated region of the former Soviet Union. Moldovans make up 78.2% of the total population, Ukrainians constitute 8.4%, Russians 5.8%, Gagauz 4.4%, Bulgarians 1.9%, and other nationalities such as Belarusians, Poles and Roma 1.3%.

SURVIVAL GUIDE

Directory A–Z

Accommodation

Chişinău has a good range of hotels, but little in the midrange. Elsewhere, most towns have small hotels that have survived from communist days and have been somewhat done up. Some hotels may offer nonsmoking rooms, but in general smoking occurs everywhere.

You will be asked to briefly present your passport upon registration; they may keep it for several hours in order to register it.

Camping grounds *(popas turistic)* are practically nonexistent in Moldova. The good news is that wild camping is allowed anywhere unless otherwise prohibited.

The idea of homestays in Moldova is in its infancy. Check **Marisha** (www.marisha.net) for a growing list of options.

Prices quoted are for rooms with private bathrooms. The following price indicators apply (based on a double room in the summer months).

€ less than 500 lei

€€ 500 lei to 1000 lei

€€€ more than 1000 lei

Business Hours

Banks 9am to 3pm Monday to Friday

Businesses 8am to 7pm Monday to Friday, to 4pm Saturday

Museums 9am to 5pm Tuesday to Sunday

Restaurants 10am to 11pm

Shops 9am or 10am to 6pm or 7pm Monday to Saturday

Embassies & Consultes

The following are all in Chişinău:

French Embassy (☎22-200 400; www.ambafrance-md.org; Str Vlaicu Pircalab 6)

German Embassy (☎22 200 600; www.chisinau.diplo.de; Str Maria Cibotari 35)

Romanian Embassy (☎22-211 813; http://chisinau.mae.ro; Str Bucureşti 66/1)

Russian Embassy (☎22-235 110; www.moldova.mid.ru; B-dul Ştefan cel Mare 153)

UK Embassy (☎22-225 902; www.ukin-moldova.fco.gov.uk; Str Nicolae Iorga 18)

Ministry of Foreign Affairs of Ukraine (☎22-582 151; www.mfa.gov.ua; Str V Lupu 17,)

US Embassy (☎22-851 705; http://moldova.usembassy.gov; Str A Mateevici 75, 2nd floor)

Food

The following price indicators apply for restaurants, based on the average cost of a main course:

€ less than 100 lei

€€ 100 lei to 200 lei

€€€ more than 200 lei

Money

The currency of Moldova is the leu (plural lei). It's easy to find ATMs in Chişinău, but less so in other towns in Moldova. While credit cards won't get you anywhere in rural areas, they are widely accepted in larger department stores, hotels and most restaurants in cities and towns.

The only legal tender in Transdniestr is the Transdniestran ruble (TR). Some taxi drivers, shopkeepers and market traders will accept payment in US dollars, euros or even Moldovan lei – but generally you'll need to get your hands on rubles to buy things there. Spend all your rubles before you leave, as no one honours or exchanges this currency outside Transdniestr.

Public Holidays

New Year's Day 1 January

Orthodox Christmas 7 January

International Women's Day 8 March

Orthodox Easter April/May

Victory (1945) Day 9 May

Independence Day 27 August

National Language Day 31 August

Visas

Citizens of EU states, USA, Canada and Japan don't need visas. Everyone else does, although Australians and New Zealanders no longer need an invitation. South Africans and some other nationalities require an invitation from a company, organisation or individual to get a visa. To obtain an invitation, contact a travel agency in Moldova or enquire with a hotel to see if they can send you one when you book. When acquiring a visa in advance, you usually need to pay the consulate via bank deposit at a specified bank.

Visas can be easily acquired on arrival at Chişinău airport or, if arriving by bus or car from Romania, at three border points: Sculeni (north of Iaşi); Leuşeni (main Bucharest–Chişinău border); and Cahul. Visas are not issued at any other border crossings, nor when entering by train. Citizens of countries requiring an invitation must present the original document (copies/faxes not accepted) at the border if buying a visa there.

Moldova allows visa-free visits for all foreigners wishing to partake in its Wine Festival (second Sunday in October). These visits cannot exceed 10 days. Nationalities ordinarily needing invitations must still acquire them, but only need to present them on arrival in lieu of having a visa.

Check the **Ministry of Foreign Affairs** (www.mfa.gov.md) website for the latest news on the visa situation.

Getting There & Away

Entering and leaving Moldova is usually a breeze. Moldovan border guards are no longer surprised to see foreign tourists – though they still haven't learned how to smile.

Air

Moldova's only international airport of significance is **Chişinău International Airport** (☎525 111; www.airport.md), 15.5km south of the city centre.

Land

BUS

Moldova is well linked by bus lines to central and western Europe. While not as comfortable as the train, buses tend to be faster, though not always cheaper.

For bus journeys between Chişinău and Odesa, we advise taking the route through the southeast Palanca border crossing, circumnavigating Transdniestr.

TRAIN

From Chişinău, there are four daily trains to Moscow, daily trains to St Petersburg, Odesa, Tiraspol and Kyiv, and trains to Lviv (Ukraine) on all odd dates and Minsk (Belarus) on all even dates.

There's an overnight service between Bucharest and Chişinău; at 12 hours, the journey is longer than taking a bus or maxitaxi (the train heads north to Iaşi, then south again), but is more comfortable if you want to sleep.

Getting Around

Moldova has a good network of buses running to most towns and villages. Maxitaxis, which follow the same routes as the buses, are quicker and more reliable. Buses cost 2 lei, trolleybuses 1 leu and city maxitaxis 3 lei

Montenegro

Includes »

Morinj 780
Perast 780
Kotor 780
Budva 781
Sveti Stefan 782
Ulcinj 783
Cetinje 783
Lake Skadar National Park 784
Biogradska Gora National Park 784
Durmitor National Park 784
Understand Montenegro 785
Survival Guide 786

Best Places to Eat

» Konoba Ćatovića Mlini (p780)

» Stari Most (p784)

» Pizza 10 Maradona (p782)

Best Places to Stay

» Old Town Hostel (p780)

» Vila Drago (p782)

» Eko-Oaza Suza Evrope (p785)

» Saki Hostel & Apartmani (p782)

Why Go?

Imagine a place with sapphire beaches as inviting as Croatia's, rugged peaks as dramatic as Switzerland's, canyons nearly as deep as Colorado's, *palazzi* as elegant as Venice's and towns as old as Greece's. Then wrap it up in a Mediterranean climate and squish it into an area two thirds the size of Wales, and you start to get a picture of Montenegro (Црна Гора).

More adventurous travellers can easily sidestep the peak-season hordes on the coast by heading to the rugged mountains of the north. This is, after all, a country where wolves and bears still lurk in forgotten corners.

Montenegro, Crna Gora, Black Mountain: the name itself conjures up romance and drama. There are plenty of both on offer as you explore this perfumed land, bathed in the scent of wild herbs, conifers and Mediterranean blossoms. Yes, it really is as magical as it sounds.

When to Go

Podgorica

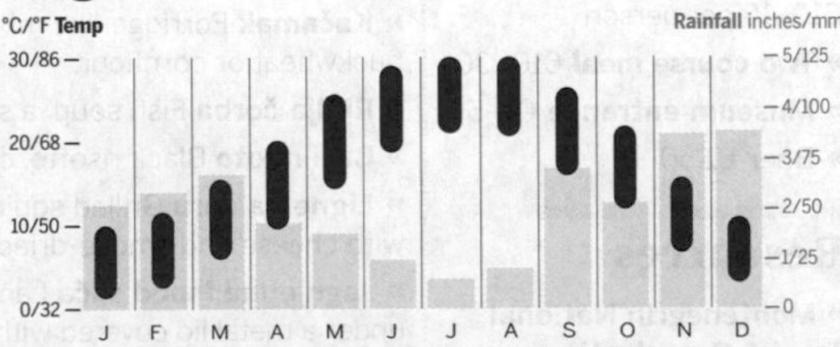

Jun Beat the peak-season rush and prices but enjoy the balmy weather.

Sep Warm water but fewer bods to share it with; shoulder season prices.

Oct The leaves turn golden, making a rich backdrop to walks in the national parks.

AT A GLANCE

» **Currency** Euro (€)

» **Language** Montenegrin

» **Money** ATMs in larger towns; banks open Monday to Friday and Saturday morning

» **Visas** None for citizens of EU, Canada, USA, Australia, New Zealand and many other countries

Fast Facts

» **Area** 13,812 sq km

» **Capital** Podgorica

» **Country code** ☎382

» **Emergency** Ambulance ☎124, fire ☎123, police ☎122

Exchange Rates

Australia	A$1	€0.82
Canada	C$1	€0.77
Japan	¥100	€0.83
New Zealand	NZ$1	€0.65
UK	UK£1	€1.18
USA	US$1	€0.78

Set Your Budget

» **Budget hotel room** €10–15 per person

» **Two-course meal** €10–30

» **Museum entrance** €1–5

» **Beer** €1.50

Resources

» **Montenegrin National Tourist Organisation** (www.montenegro.travel)

» **National Parks of Montenegro** (www.nparkovi.me)

» **Explore Montenegro** (www.exploremontenegro.com)

Connections

Many travellers make the most of the close proximity of Dubrovnik Airport to the Bay of Kotor to tie in a visit to Croatia with a Montenegrin sojourn. At the other end of the coast, Ulcinj is the perfect primer for exploring Albania and is connected by bus to Shkodra. Likewise, Rožaje captures elements of Kosovar culture and is well connected to Peja (Peć). A train line and frequent bus connections make a trip to Montenegro's closest cousins in Serbia a breeze. Montenegro's longest border is with Bosnia and Hercegovina (BiH). There are regular bus services to Trebinje and Sarajevo. Ferries connect Bar to the Italian ports of Bari and Ancona.

ITINERARIES

Three Days

Base yourself in Kotor and consider day trips to Budva, Sveti Stefan, Cetinje or Ostrog Monastery.

One Week

Stay in Kotor for two nights and then spend a night in each of Budva and Ulcinj. Head north on the back road to Lake Skadar and trace the lake's southern shore to Virpazar, where you can take a boat cruise. Continue on to Cetinje and Ostrog Monastery en route to Šćepan Polje, where you can stay the night at one of the rafting centres. Go rafting the following morning and then head to Žabljak for a day's hiking in Durmitor National Park.

Essential Food & Drink

» **Njeguški pršut i sir** Smoke-dried ham and cheese from the heartland village of Njeguši.

» **Ajvar** Spicy spread of fried red peppers and eggplant, seasoned with garlic, salt, vinegar and oil.

» **Kajmak** Soft cheese made from the salted cream from boiled milk.

» **Kačamak** Porridge-like mix of cream, cheese, potato and buckwheat or cornflour.

» **Riblja čorba** Fish soup, a staple of the coast.

» **Crni rižoto** Black risotto, coloured with squid ink.

» **Ligne na žaru** Grilled squid, sometimes stuffed *(punjene)* with cheese and smoke-dried ham.

» **Jagnjetina ispod sača** Lamb cooked (often with potatoes) under a metal lid covered with hot coals.

» **Rakija** Domestic brandy, made from nearly anything. The local favourite is grape-based *loza*.

» **Vranac** Local red-wine varietal.

» **Krstač** Local white-wine varietal.

Montenegro Highlights

1. Marvel at the majesty of the **Bay of Kotor** (p780) and explore the historic towns hemmed in by the limestone cliffs
2. Drive the vertiginous route from Kotor to the Njegoš Mausoleum at the top of **Lovćen National Park** (p782)
3. Enjoy the iconic island views while lazing on the sands of **Sveti Stefan** (p782)
4. Seek the spiritual at peaceful **Ostrog Monastery** (p784)
5. Float through paradise, rafting between the kilometre-plus walls of the **Tara Canyon** (p784)
6. Wander through primeval forest mirrored in a tranquil alpine lake at **Biogradska Gora National Park** (p784)
7. Splash through the floating meadows of water lilies garlanding **Lake Skadar** (p784)

COASTAL MONTENEGRO

Coming from Croatia and entering the mountain-framed folds of the Bay of Kotor, the beauty meter goes off the scale. It doesn't let up when you hit the Adriatic Coast, where you'll find a charismatic set of small settlements, set against clear waters and sandy beaches.

Morinj Моринь

POP 220

Secluded in the first bend of the inner bay, little Morinj is divided into upper and lower sections, like many of the coastal villages. The silver dome of St Petka Church (Crkva Sv Petke) sparkles above, and down below there's a pretty beach. It's easily reached by bus from Kotor.

Sleeping & Eating

Autocamp Naluka CAMPGROUND €
(☎032-373 101; www.naluka.montenegro.com; campsites per adult/child €4/1, per tent/car/campervan €3.50/3/8; ⊙May-Sep) Pitch your tent next to the stream that bubbles out of a spring at a constant 10°C. There are only squat toilets but the site is extremely well kept.

TOP CHOICE **Konoba Ćatovića Mlini** RESTAURANT €€
(☎032-373 030; www.catovicamlini.me; mains €8-24; ⊙11am-11pm) The stream flows around and under this rustic former mill which masquerades as a humble *konoba* (a simple family-run establishment) but in reality is one of Montenegro's best restaurants. Fish is the focus but traditional heartland specialities are also offered.

Perast Пераст

POP 270

Looking like a chunk of Venice that has floated down the Adriatic and anchored itself onto the bay, Perast hums with melancholy memories of the days when it was rich and powerful. This tiny town boasts 16 churches and 17 formerly grand *palazzi*, one of which has been converted into **Perast Museum** (Muzej grada Perasta; ☎032-373 519; adult/child €2.50/1.50; ⊙9am-7pm) and showcases the town's proud seafaring history. Boats (€5 return) regularly head to **Our-Lady-of-the-Rock Island** (Gospa od Škrpjela), which was artificially created in the 15th century.

Kotor Котор

POP 13,500

Wedged between brooding mountains and a moody corner of the bay, this dramatically beautiful town combines historic grace with vibrant street life. From a distance, Kotor's sturdy ancient walls are barely discernible from the mountain's grey hide but at night they're spectacularly lit, reflecting in the water to give the town a golden halo. Within those walls lie labyrinthine marbled lanes where churches, boutiques, bars and restaurants sneak up on you in hidden piazzas.

Sights

The Old Town's most impressive building is 12th-century **St Tryphon's Cathedral** (Katedrala Sv Tripuna; Trg Sv Tripuna; admission €2; ⊙8am-7pm). The **Maritime Museum** (Pomorski muzej Crne Gore; www.museummaritimum.com; Trg Bokeljske Mornarice; adult/child €4/1; ⊙9am-6.30pm Mon-Sat, to 1pm Sun Apr-Oct, 9am-2pm daily Nov-Mar), housed in an early 18th-century palace, celebrates Kotor's proud naval history. Energetic travellers can make the 260m ascent up the **town walls** (admission €2; ⊙24hr, fees apply 8am-8pm May-Sep).

Sleeping

TOP CHOICE **Old Town Hostel** HOSTEL €
(☎032-325 317; www.hostel-kotor.me; near Trg od Salata; dm €12-14, r without bathroom €30, apt €40) Sympathetic renovations have brought this 13th-century *palazzo* back to life, and the ancient stone walls now echo with the chatter of happy travellers. Comfortable, sociable, reasonable, historical...exceptional.

Stari Grad SEAFOOD €€
(☎032-322 025; www.restoranstarigrad.com; Trg od Mlijeka; mains €8-18) Head straight through to the stone-walled courtyard, grab a seat under the vines and prepare to get absolutely stuffed full of fabulous food – the serves are huge.

Drinking

Maximus CLUB
(☎067-216 767; www.discomaximus.com; near Trg od Oružja; admission free-€5; ⊙11pm-5am Thu-Sat, nightly in summer) Montenegro's most pumping club.

Information

Tourist Information Booth (www.kotor.travel; outside the Sea Gate; ⊙8am-8pm)

Kotor

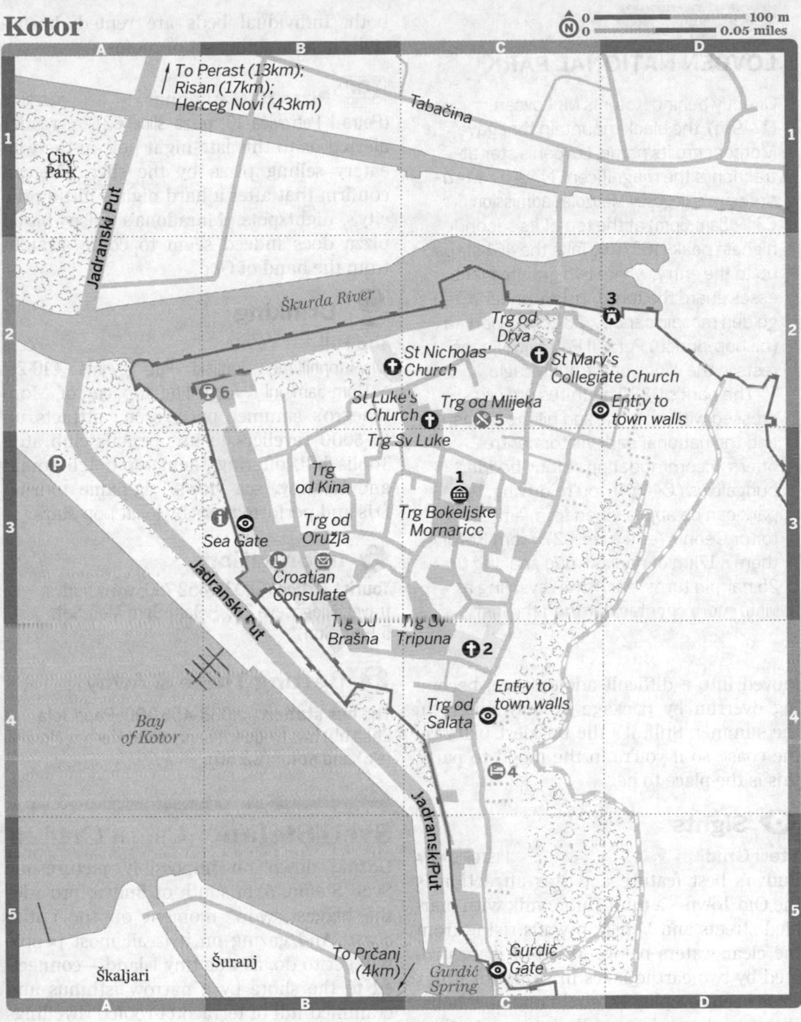

Getting There & Away

The **bus station** (☎032-325 809; ⏰6am-9pm) is to the south of town, just off the road leading to the Tivat tunnel. Buses head to Herceg Novi (€4, one hour) and Budva (€3.50, 40 minutes). A taxi to Tivat Airport should cost around €10.

Budva Будва

POP 13,400

The poster child of Montenegrin tourism, Budva – with its atmospheric Stari Grad (Old Town) and numerous beaches – certainly has a lot to offer. Yet the child has

Kotor

Sights

1 Maritime Museum of Montenegro......C3
2 St Tryphon's Cathedral.......C4
3 Town Walls.......D2

Sleeping

4 Old Town Hostel.......C4

Eating

5 Stari Grad.......C2

Drinking

6 Maximus.......B2

DON'T MISS

LOVĆEN NATIONAL PARK

Directly behind Kotor is Mt Lovćen (1749m), the black mountain that gave Montenegro its name. Lovćen's star attraction is the magnificent **Njegoš Mausoleum** (Njegošev Mauzolej; admission €3; ⏲8am-6pm) at the top of its second-highest peak (1657m). Take the 461 steps up to the entry, where two granite giantesses guard the tomb. Inside, under a golden mosaic canopy, 28-tonne *vladika* (bishop-prince) Petar II Petrović Njegoš rests in the wings of a granite eagle.

The park's 6220 hectares are criss-crossed with well-marked hiking paths, and the national park visitor centre offers accommodation in four-bedded bungalows (€40). If you're driving, the park can be approached from either Kotor or Cetinje (entry fee €2). From Kotor there's 17km of narrow road snaking up 25 hairpin turns, each one revealing a vista more spectacular than the last.

moved into a difficult adolescence, becoming overrun by package holidaymakers in the summer. Still, it's the buzziest place on the coast, so if you're in the mood to party, this is the place to be.

Sights

Stari Grad HISTORIC AREA

Budva's best feature and star attraction is the Old Town – a mini-Dubrovnik with marbled streets and Venetian walls rising from the clear waters below. Much of it was ruined by two earthquakes in 1979, but it has since been completely rebuilt and now houses more shops, bars and restaurants than residences. At its seaward end, the **Citadela** (admission €2; ⏲9am-midnight May-Oct, to 5pm Nov-Apr) offers striking views, a small museum and a library full of rare tomes and maps. In the square in front of the citadel is a cluster of interesting churches. Nearby is the entry to the **town walls** (admission €1).

Sleeping & Eating

Saki Hostel & Apartmani HOSTEL, APARTMENTS €

(☎067-368 065; www.saki-apartmani.com; IV Proleterska bb; dm €10, apt per person €25; P❄☜) Not quite a hostel and not quite an apartment hotel, this friendly family-run block on the outskirts of town offers elements of both. Individual beds are rented, hostel-style, in a rambling set of rooms.

TOP CHOICE **Pizza 10 Maradona** PIZZERIA €

(Petra I Petrovića 10; pizza slice €2) A reader alerted us to this late-night hole-in-the-wall eatery selling pizza by the slice. We can confirm that after a hard night's hitting the city's nightspots, Maradona's crispy-based pizza does indeed seem to come straight from the hand of God.

Drinking

Top Hill CLUB

(www.tophill.me; Topliški Put; events €10-25; ⏲11pm-5am Jul & Aug) The top cat of Montenegro's summer party scene attracts up to 5000 revellers to its open-air club atop Topliš hill, offering them top-notch sound and lighting, sea views, big-name touring DJs and performances by local pop stars.

Information

Tourist Office (☎033-452 750; www.budva.travel; Njegoševa 28; ⏲9am-9pm Mon-Sat, 5-9pm Sun)

Getting There & Away

The **bus station** (☎033-456 000; Popa Jola Zeca bb) has frequent services to Herceg Novi (€6) and Kotor (€3.50).

Sveti Stefan Свети Стефан

Gazing down on impossibly picturesque Sveti Stefan, 5km south of Budva, provides the biggest 'wow' moment on the entire coast. And gazing on it is all most people will get to do, as this tiny island – connected to the shore by a narrow isthmus and crammed full of terracotta-roofed dwellings dating from the 15th century – was nationalised in the 1950s and the whole thing is now a luxurious resort.

The general public can access the main Sveti Stefan beach, which faces the island (the free section is at the south end). From the beach there's a very pleasant walk north to the cute village of Pržno, where there are some excellent restaurants and another attractive, often crowded beach.

Sleeping

TOP CHOICE **Vila Drago** GUESTHOUSE €€

(☎030-468 477; www.viladrago.com; Slobode 32; r €45-60, apt €120-130; ❄☜) The only problem with this family-run place is that you may never want to leave your terrace as the views are so sublime. Watch the sunset over Sveti Stefan island from the grapevine-covered terrace restaurant.

Vila Levantin APARTMENT €
(☎033-468 206; www.villalevantin.com; Vukice Mitrović 3; r €30-50, apt €50-130; P❄📶🏊) Modern and nicely finished, with red stone walls, blue-tiled bathrooms and an attractive plunge pool on the terrace, Levantin has a variety of rooms and apartments at extremely reasonable prices. There's a travel agency attached which can sort you out with tours or rooms in private houses.

ℹ Getting There & Away

Olimpia Express buses head to and from Budva (€1.50, 20 minutes) every 30 minutes in summer and hourly in winter.

Ulcinj Улцињ

POP 10,700

If you want a feel for Albania without actually crossing the border, buzzy Ulcinj's the place to go. The population is 72% Albanian and the elegant minarets of numerous mosques give Ulcinj a distinctly Eastern feel. For centuries Ulcinj's walled Old Town had a reputation as a pirate's lair but now the area is known for its fine beaches, including Velika Plaža, which stretches for 12 sandy kilometres.

🛏 Sleeping & Eating

Real Estate Travel Agency ACCOMMODATION SERVICES €
(☎030-421 609; www.realestate-travel.com; Hazif Ali Ulqinaku bb; per person from €15) Obliging English-speaking staff can help you find private rooms, apartments or hotel rooms. They also rent bikes (€10) and cars, run tours and sell maps of Ulcinj.

Restaurant Pizzeria Bazar PIZZERIA, SEAFOOD €
(Hazif Ali Ulqinaku bb; mains €4-10; ⏲10am-1pm) An upstairs restaurant that's a great idling place when the streets below are heaving with tourists. People-watch in comfort as you enjoy a plate of *lignje na žaru* (grilled squid).

ℹ Getting There & Away

The bus station is on the northeastern edge of town. Services head to Herceg Novi (€10, daily), Kotor (€9, daily) and Budva (€7, eight daily).

CENTRAL MONTENEGRO

The heart of Montenegro – physically, spiritually and politically – is easily accessed as a day trip from the coast, but it's well deserving of a longer exploration. This really is the full Monte: soaring peaks, hidden monasteries, steep river canyons and historic towns. **Podgorica**, the nation's capital, serves as the transport hub and is worth a day's exploration, but it's elsewhere that your focus should lie.

Cetinje Цетиње

POP 14,000

Rising from a green vale surrounded by rough, grey mountains, Cetinje is an odd mix of former capital and overgrown village where single-storey cottages and stately mansions share the same street.

The **National Museum of Montenegro** (www.mnmuseum.org; Narodni muzej Crne Gore; all museums adult/child €10/5; ⏲9am-4pm) is actually a collection of four museums and two galleries housed in a clump of important buildings. A joint ticket will get you into all of them or you can buy individual tickets.

Founded in 1484, **Cetinje Monastery** (Cetinjski Manastir; ⏲8am-6pm) has a spectacular **treasury** (admission €2). It's only open to groups but if you are persuasive enough, appropriately dressed and prepared to wait around, you may be able to get in.

🛏 Sleeping & Eating

Pansion 22 GUESTHOUSE €€
(☎069-055 473; pansion22@mtel-cg.net; Ivana Crnojevića 22; s/d €22/40; 📶) They may not be great at speaking English or answering emails, but the family who run this central guesthouse offer a warm welcome. The rooms are simply decorated yet clean and comfortable.

Kole MONTENEGRIN, EUROPEAN €
(☎041-231 620; www.restaurantkole.me; Bul Crnogorskih Junaka 12; mains €3-12; ⏲7am-11pm) Omelettes and pasta are served at this snazzy modern eatery, but what are really great are the local specialities. Try the smoky spit-roasted meat.

ℹ Information

Tourist Information (☎078-108 788; www.cetinje.travel; Novice Cerovića bb; ⏲8am-6pm)

Getting There & Away

Buses stop at Trg Golootočkih Žrtava, two blocks from the main street. There are regular services to Budva (€4).

Lake Skadar National Park Скадарско Језеро

The Balkans' largest lake, dolphin-shaped Lake Skadar has its tail and two-thirds of its body in Montenegro and its nose in Albania. Covering between 370 and 550 sq km (depending on the time of year), it's one of the most important reserves for wetland birds in the whole of Europe. It's a blissfully pretty area, encompassing steep mountains, hidden villages, island monasteries, clear waters and floating meadows of water lilies.

Activities

Green Boats BOAT TOUR

(Zeleni Brodovi; 069-998 737; greenboats.me@gmail.com; per hr from Virpazar/Vranjina €25/40) Lake cruises are offered every two hours by this association of small local operators. Two-hour cruises are the norm, although longer trips can be arranged. We've heard glowing reports about one particular boat, the **Golden Frog** (069-413 307; www.skadarlakecruise.blogspot.co.uk).

Sleeping & Eating

Draga's HOMESTAY €

(068-760 711; pedja.vuletic@t-com.me; r €25-30;) Above a family home in Virpazar, these four rooms are simply furnished but clean and very reasonably priced. Two share a bathroom but compensate by having their own terrace. It's the last inhabited house on the left after the monument.

TOP CHOICE **Stari Most** SEAFOOD €€

(041-239 505; mains €8-25) You wouldn't expect it, but the sleepy village of Rijeka Crnojevića is home to one of Montenegro's best restaurants. Freshwater fish – particularly eel, trout and carp – is the speciality.

WORTH A TRIP

OSTROG MONASTERY

Resting on a cliff 900m above the Zeta valley, gleaming white Ostrog Monastery (Манастир Острог; 1665) is a strangely affecting place that gives the impression that it has grown out of the very rock. The **guesthouse** (020-811 133; dm €5) offers tidy single-sex dorm rooms, while in summer sleeping mats are provided for free to pilgrims in front of the Upper Monastery. There's no public transport but numerous tour buses head here from the coast (€20).

Information

National Park Visitor Centre (020-879 103; www.nparkovi.me; admission €2, free with national park entry ticket; 8am-4pm, to 6pm summer) In Vranjina, this centre has excellent displays about all of Montenegro's national parks. A kiosk here and at Virpazar sells park entry tickets (per day €4) and fishing permits (per day summer/winter €10/5).

Virpazar Tourist Office (020-711 102; www.visitbar.org; 8am-5pm daily May-Sep, to 4pm Mon-Fri Oct-Apr;) Arranges boat trips, wine tastings and private accommodation. Upstairs there are displays about the national park, and the office operates as a shop for the region's small wine producers.

Getting There & Away

Buses and trains on the Bar–Podgorica route stop nearby.

Biogradska Gora National Park Биоградска Гора

Nestled in the heart of the Bjelasica mountain range, this pretty national park (entry fee €2) has as its heart 1600 hectares of virgin woodland – one of Europe's last primeval forests. Near the lakeside **park office** (020-865 625; www.nparkovi.me; campsites small/large tent €3/5, caravan €10, cabins €20; 7.30am-8.30pm) there's a camping ground and a cluster of 12 log cabins.

Durmitor National Park Дурмитор

Magnificent scenery ratchets up to the stupendous in this national park, where ice and water have carved a dramatic landscape from the limestone. Some 18 glacial lakes dot the Durmitor range, which has 48 peaks over 2000m. From December to March it is a ski resort, while in summer it's popular with hikers and rafters.

Activities

Rafting

Slicing through the mountains at the northern edge of the national park like they were made from the local soft cheese, the Tara River forms a canyon that at its peak is 1300m deep. The two-day raft along the river is the country's premier outdoor attraction (May to October only). Most of the day tours from the coast traverse only the last 18km of the river – this is outside the national park and hence avoids hefty fees.

One good operator is **Kamp Grab** (✆040-200 598; www.tara-grab.com; half-day incl lunch €44, 2-day all-inclusive €180), with lodgings blissfully located 8km upstream from Šćepan Polje. To get there, you'll need to cross the Montenegrin side of the border crossing and hang a right (tell the guards you're heading to Grab); the last 3.5km is unsealed. Accommodation is available, and Grab also offers guided riverboarding (€35).

Hiking

Durmitor has dozens of hiking trails, some of which traverse seriously high-altitude paths that are prone to fog and summer thunderstorms. Ask the staff at the visitor centre about tracks that suit your level of experience and fitness.

Skiing

On the slopes of **Savin Kuk** (2313m) you'll find Durmitor's main ski centre. Its 3.5km run starts from a height of 2010m and is best suited to advanced skiers. On the outskirts of Žabljak, near the bus station, **Javorovača Ski Centar** (✆067-800 971) has a gentle 300m slope that's good for kids and beginners. One of the big attractions for skiing in Durmitor is the cost: day passes are around €15, weekly passes €70, and ski lessons cost between €10 and €20. The season runs between January and March.

Sleeping

TOP CHOICE **Eko-Oaza Suza Evrope** CABINS, CAMPGROUND €

(✆069-444 590; ekooazatara@gmail.com; Dobrilovina; campsites per tent/person/campervan €5/1/10, cabins €50; ⏲Apr-Oct) Consisting of four comfortable wooden cottages (each sleeping five people) and a fine stretch of lawn, this magical family-run 'eco oasis' on the eastern edge of the national park offers a genuine experience of Montenegrin hospitality.

Autokamp Mlinski Potok CAMPGROUND €

(✆069-497 625; campsites per person/car €3/1) With a fabulously hospitable host, this fairly basic campsite above the visitor centre is a sociable option. Private rooms are available.

Information

Durmitor National Park Visitor Centre (www.nparkovi.co.me; Jovana Cvijića bb; ⏲9am-5pm Mon-Fri)

Getting There & Away

The bus station is at the southern edge of Žabljak, on the Šavnik road. Three buses head to Podgorica daily (€9.50).

UNDERSTAND MONTENEGRO

History

For 500 years Montenegro retained a degree of independence while the Ottoman Turkish tide flooded most of southeast Europe. During this time a distinct identity was born, which distinguished its people from the other Serbian tribes. While the size of its territory waxed and waned, it was always centred on Lovćen, the mountain expanse that contains Cetinje within its foothills. It is from this 'black mountain' that the country takes its name: Crna Gora in the local tongue and Montenegro in Italian.

Following WWI, Montenegro was incorporated into the first Yugoslavia under the Serbian king. As a reward for its support of the partisans during WWII, Montenegro was awarded republic status in the postwar Socialist Federal Republic of Yugoslavia. From then on Montenegro was a loyal member of all the Yugoslavian entities, culminating in the loose union of Serbia and Montenegro that came to an end with a proindependence vote in May 2006.

Shortly after independence in 2006, Montenegro applied to join both NATO and the EU, and in June 2012 it opened formal EU accession negotiations. While most Montenegrins strongly favour EU membership, joining NATO is much more contentious. Memories of the NATO bombing of Serbia during the Kosovo conflict are still fresh.

People

Montenegro's 2011 census revealed a population of 626,000, split into Montenegrins (45%), Serbs (29%), Bosniaks (12%), Albanians (5%), Croats (1%) and Roma (1%). Montenegrins are closely related to Serbs, with whom they share the same faith, Orthodox Christianity. There are large Slavic Muslim (Bosniak) and Albanian minorities, mostly in the east. The Bay of Kotor has strong historic links with Croatia's Dalmatian coast.

SURVIVAL GUIDE

Directory A–Z

Accommodation

» Hotels and private accommodation (rooms and apartments for rent) form the bulk of sleeping options, although hostels have recently popped up in the more touristy areas.

» Camping grounds operate in summer and some of the mountainous areas have cabin accommodation in 'eco villages' or mountain huts.

» In the peak summer season, some places require minimum three-night stays. Many establishments on the coast close during winter.

» An additional tourist tax (usually less than €1 per night) is added to the rate for all accommodation types.

The following price categories for the cost of a room for two in the shoulder season (roughly June and September) are used in the listings in this chapter:

€ less than €30

€€ €30 to €90

€€€ more than €90

Business Hours

Banks 8am to 5pm Monday to Friday, to noon Saturday

Cafes 10am to midnight (later in high season in busy areas)

Pubs 9pm to 2am

Restaurants 8am to midnight

Shops 8am to 7pm Monday to Friday, to 2pm Saturday; often closed in the late afternoon

Supermarkets 8am to 8pm Monday to Friday, to 6pm Saturday, to 1pm Sunday

Embassies & Consulates

The following embassies and consulates are all in Podgorica, unless otherwise stated. For a full list, see www.mip.gov.me.

Albanian Embassy (☎020-667 380; www.mfa.gov.al; Stanka Dragojevića 14)

Bosnian and Hercegovinian Embassy (☎020-618 105; www.mvp.gov.ba; Atinska 58)

Croatian Embassy (☎020-269 760; Vladimira Ćetkovića 2)

Croatian Consulate (☎032-323 127; Trg od Oružja bb, Kotor)

French Embassy (☎020-655 348; Atinska 35)

German Embassy (☎020-441 000; www.auswaertiges-amt.de; Hercegovačka 10)

Serbian Embassy (☎020-667 305; www.podgorica.mfa.gov.rs; Hercegovačka 18)

Serbian Consulate (☎031-350 320; www.hercegnovi.mfa.gov.rs; Njegoševa 40, Herceg Novi)

UK Embassy (☎020-618 010; www.ukinmontenegro.fco.gov.uk; Ulcinjska 8)

US Embassy (☎020-410 500; http://podgorica.usembassy.gov; Ljubljanska bb)

Food

The following price categories for the cost of a main course are used in this chapter:

€ less than €5

€€ €5 to €10

€€€ more than €10

Gay & Lesbian Travellers

Although homosexuality was decriminalised in 1977 and discrimination outlawed in 2010, attitudes to homosexuality remain hostile and life for gay people is extremely difficult. Many gay men resort to online connections (try www.gayromeo.com) or take their chances at a handful of cruisy beaches. Lesbians will find it even harder to access the local community.

Money

» Montenegro uses the euro (€). You'll find banks with ATMs in all the main towns, most of which accept Visa, MasterCard, Maestro and Cirrus. Don't rely on restaurants, shops or smaller hotels accepting credit cards.

» Tipping isn't expected, although it's common to round up to the nearest euro.

Public Holidays

New Year's Day 1 & 2 January

Orthodox Christmas 6, 7 & 8 January

Orthodox Good Friday & Easter Monday usually April/May

Labour Day 1 May

Independence Day 21 May

Statehood Day 13 July

Telephone

» The international access prefix is ☎00 or ☎+ from a mobile.
» Mobile numbers start with ☎06.
» Local SIM cards are easy to find.

Getting There & Away

Air

Montenegro has two international airports – **Tivat** (☎032-670 930; www.montenegroairports.com) and **Podgorica** (☎020-444 244; www.montenegroairports.com) – although many visitors use Croatia's Dubrovnik Airport, which is very near the border. **Montenegro Airlines** (www.montenegroairlines.com) is the national carrier.

Land

BUS

A well-developed bus network links Montenegro with the major cities of the region.

Belgrade (Serbia) To Podgorica (€27, frequent).

Dubrovnik (Croatia) To Herceg Novi (€10, two daily).

Priština (Kosovo) To Podgorica (€17, daily).

Sarajevo (BiH) To Podgorica (€19, six daily).

Shkodra (Albania) To Ulcinj (€6, two daily).

CAR & MOTORCYCLE

Drivers are recommended to carry an International Driving Permit (IDP) as well as their home country's driving licence. Vehicles need Green Card insurance or insurance must be bought at the border.

TRAIN

At least two trains head between Bar and Belgrade daily (€21, 11 hours), with one continuing on to Novi Sad and Subotica.

Sea

Montenegro Lines (☎030-303 469; www.montenegrolines.net) has boats to Bar from the Italian ports of Bari and Ancona.

Getting Around

The bus network is extensive and reliable. Buses are usually comfortable, air-conditioned and rarely full.

The major European car-hire companies have a presence in various centres. **Meridian Rentacar** (☎020-234 944; www.meridian-rentacar.com) is a reliable, cheap, local option.

The Netherlands

Includes »

Amsterdam 791
The Randstad 798
Haarlem..........................798
Leiden............................799
Den Haag........................800
Delft...............................801
Rotterdam......................802
Utrecht...........................806
The South.......................808
Maastricht......................808
Understand the Netherlands..................809
Survival Guide...............810

Best Places to Eat

» De Dames Proeverij (p799)

» De Ballentent (p803)

» Gadjah Mas (p809)

» Van Dobben (p794)

Best Places to Stay

» Cocomama (p794)

» Hotel Nieuw Minerva (p799)

» B&B Utrecht (p807)

» Stayokay Rotterdam (p803)

Why Go?

Great Dutch artists Rembrandt, Vermeer and Van Gogh have spanned the centuries, and touring the Netherlands you'll see why. Discover clichés such as tulips and windmills, or stroll canals in the midst of 17th-century splendour in beautiful small towns such as Leiden and Delft. Of course, enticing Amsterdam's phenomenal and diverse nightlife is world-famous, from throbbing clubs to quaint brown cafes.

The locals live on bicycles and you can too. Almost every train station has a shop to rent a bike – you'll soon be off on the ubiquitous bike paths, wherever your mood takes you.

Finally there's the Dutch themselves. Warm, friendly and funny, you'll have a hard time being alone in a cafe as someone will soon strike up a conversation, and usually in English. Revel in Amsterdam, don't miss exquisite Maastricht or pulsing Rotterdam, and pick a passel of small towns to add contrast. It's a very big small country.

When to Go

Amsterdam

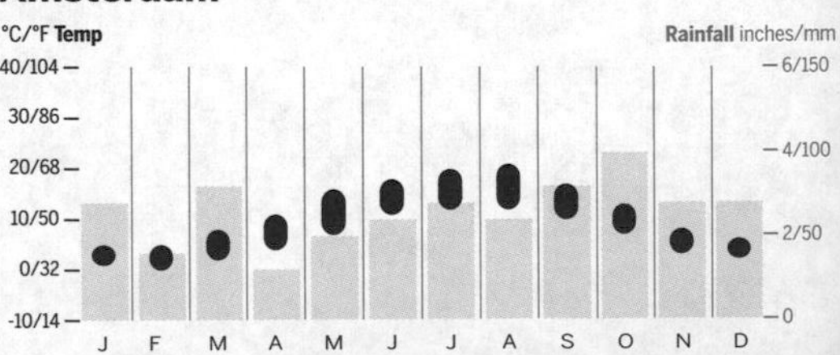

Mar–May Holland explodes in colour as billions of bulbs bloom.

Jul Mild summer temps and lots of daylight keep you outside cycling and drinking.

Dec–Feb The Dutch passion for ice skating is on display on frozen canals nationwide.

Connections

Train connections to neighbouring countries are good. Amsterdam is linked to Cologne (2½ hours) and Brussels (two hours on the Thalys/Fyra high-speed line), where you can connect with Eurostar to London. Maastricht is right on the Belgian and German borders; connections to Cologne and Brussels take 1½ hours. It would be easy to put together a circle itinerary that includes the wines of the Moselle Valley in Germany and the beers of Belgium.

ITINERARIES

One Week

Spend three days canal exploring, museum hopping and cafe swooping in Amsterdam. Work your way through the ancient towns of the Randstad and the modern vibe of Rotterdam, and save a day for the grandeur of Maastricht.

Two Weeks

Allow four days for Amsterdam's many delights, plus a day trip to the old towns of the north, such as Edam, and a day or two exploring some of the region's smaller towns. Then add a day each at beautiful Delft, regal Hague, cute Utrecht, Rotterdam, and the monumental Delta Project. Finish off with two days in Maastricht.

Essential Food & Drink

» **Vlaamse frites** The iconic French fries smothered in mayonnaise or myriad other gooey sauces.

» **Beer** While the big names like Heineken are ubiquitous, small brewers like Gulpen, Haarlem's Jopen, Bavaria, Drie Ringen, Leeuw and Utrecht are the best.

» **Gouda** The tastiest varieties have strong, complex flavours and are best enjoyed with a bottle of wine or two. Try some *oud* (old) Gouda, hard and rich in flavour and a popular bar snack with mustard. *Oud Amsterdammer* is a real delight, deep orange and crumbly with white crystals of ripeness.

» **Indonesian** The most famous dish is *rijsttafel* (rice table): an array of spicy savoury dishes such as braised beef, pork satay and ribs served with white rice.

» **Erwtensoep** Pea soup rich with onions, carrots, smoked sausage and bacon. Ideally a spoon stuck upright in the pot should remain standing (not served in summer).

» **Kroketten** Croquettes are dough balls with various fillings that are crumbed and deep-fried; the variety called *bitterballen* are a popular brown cafe snack served with mustard.

AT A GLANCE

» **Currency** Euro (€)

» **Language** Dutch, English widespread

» **Money** ATMs common, cash preferred for small purchases

» **Visas** Schengen rules apply

Fast Facts

» **Area** 41,526 sq km

» **Capital** Amsterdam

» **Country code** ☎31

» **Emergency** ☎112

Exchange Rates

Australia	A$1	€0.82
Canada	C$1	€0.77
Japan	¥100	€0.83
New Zealand	NZ$1	€0.65
UK	UK£1	€1.18
USA	US$1	€0.78

Set Your Budget

» **Midrange hotel double room** €80–150

» **Two-course meal** €15

» **Heineken** €3

» **Bicycle hire** €10 per day

Resources

» **Lonely Planet** (www.lonelyplanet.com/amsterdam)

» **Netherlands Board of Tourism** (www.holland.com)

» **Windmill Database** (www.molendatabase.nl)

The Netherlands Highlights

❶ Stroll canals and soak up the beautiful, vibrant and offbeat **Amsterdam** (p791)

❷ Immerse yourself in the urban vibe and architecture of **Rotterdam** (p802)

❸ Lose yourself amid the ancient walls and cosmopolitan shops of **Maastricht** (p808)

❹ Take a day trip to evocative **Delft** (p801), where Vermeer found his inspiration

❺ Wander the beautiful tree-lined boulevards and classy museums of **Den Haag** (p800)

❻ Find inspiration at **Leiden** (p799), home of Rembrandt, and in the tulips at nearby **Keukenhof Gardens** (p799)

❼ Go **bike crazy** (p813) across the Netherlands on the world's best network of bike lanes and long-distance routes

❽ Lose a few hours drinking beer in the atmospheric confines of a convivial, uniquely Dutch **brown cafe** (p810)

AMSTERDAM

☎020 / POP 781,000

If Amsterdam were a staid place it would still be one of Europe's most beautiful and historic cities, right up there with Venice and Paris. But add in the qualities that make it Amsterdam – the funky and mellow bars, brown cafes full of characters, pervasive irreverence, whiffs of pot and an open-air marketplace for sleaze and sex – and you have a literally intoxicating mix.

Amsterdam's been a liberal place ever since the Netherlands' Golden Age, when it led European art and trade. Centuries later, in the 1960s, it again led the pack – this time in the principles of tolerance, with broad-minded views on drugs and same-sex relationships taking centre stage.

Wander the 17th-century streets, tour the iconic canals, stop off to enjoy a masterpiece, discover a funky shop and choose from food around the world. Walk or ride a bike around the concentric rings of the centre then explore the historic lanes of the Jordaan district or the Plantage and bask in the many worlds-within-worlds, where nothing ever seems the same twice.

Sights & Activities

Amsterdam is compact, and you can roam the city on foot. Hop on the occasional tram to rest your feet – or stop off in a cafe.

CITY CENTRE

The not-overly-impressive **Royal Palace** (Koninklijk Paleis; ☎620 40 60; www.paleisamsterdam.nl; Dam; adult/child €7.50/3.75; ⏲11am-5pm daily Jul & Aug, noon-5pm Tue-Sun Sep-Jun) and the square that puts the 'Dam' in Amsterdam anchor the city's oldest quarter. This is the busiest part of town for tourists: many leave the train station and head straight for the coffee shops and the Red Light District.

Red Light District NEIGHBOURHOOD

The Red Light District retains the power to make your jaw go limp, even if near-naked prostitutes propositioning passers-by from black-lit windows is the oldest Amsterdam cliché. Note that even in the dark heart of the district there are charming shops and cafes where the only thing that vibrates is your mobile phone. Despite the neon-lit sleaze, the district is tightly regulated and reasonably safe for strolling. The city government has been steadfastly reducing the number of licensed windows.

FREE **Begijnhof** HISTORIC BUILDINGS

(☎622 19 18; www.begijnhofamsterdam.nl; main entrance off Gedempte Begijnensloot; ⏲8am-5pm; 🚊1/2/5 Spui) For a polar opposite of the Red Light District, duck into the Begijnhof, an enclosed former convent from the early 14th century. It's a surreal oasis of peace, with tiny houses and postage-stamp gardens around a well-kept courtyard. The Beguines were a Catholic order of unmarried or widowed women who cared for the elderly and lived a religious life without taking monastic vows. The last died in the 1970s.

CANAL BELT

Created in the 17th century as an upscale neighbourhood, the Canal Belt, especially in the west and south, remains Amsterdam's top district. Wandering here amid architectural treasures and their reflections on the narrow waters of the Prinsengracht, Keizersgracht and Herengracht can cause days to vanish quicker than some of Amsterdam's more lurid pursuits. No two buildings are alike, yet they combine in ever-changing, ever-pleasing harmony.

Anne Frank Huis MUSEUM

(Anne Frank House; ☎556 71 05; www.annefrank.org; Prinsengracht 276; adult/child €9/free; ⏲9am-7pm daily, later Sat & mid-Mar–mid-Sep; 🚊13/14/17 Westermarkt) The Anne Frank Huis, where Anne wrote her famous diary, lures almost a million visitors annually with its secret annexe, its reconstruction of Anne's melancholy bedroom, and her actual diary, with its sunnily optimistic writing tempered by quiet despair. Look for the photo of Peter Schiff, her 'one true love'. Try going in the early morning or evening

FREE THRILLS

Much of the allure of Amsterdam can be experienced on foot and for free.

» The Red Light District can cost you an arm and a leg (or more) but voyeurism is free.

» Regain your inner virtue walking through the Begijnhof.

» Find natural peace in the green expanses of Vondelpark.

» Walk the canals and decide which old gabled house leans the most.

Central Amsterdam

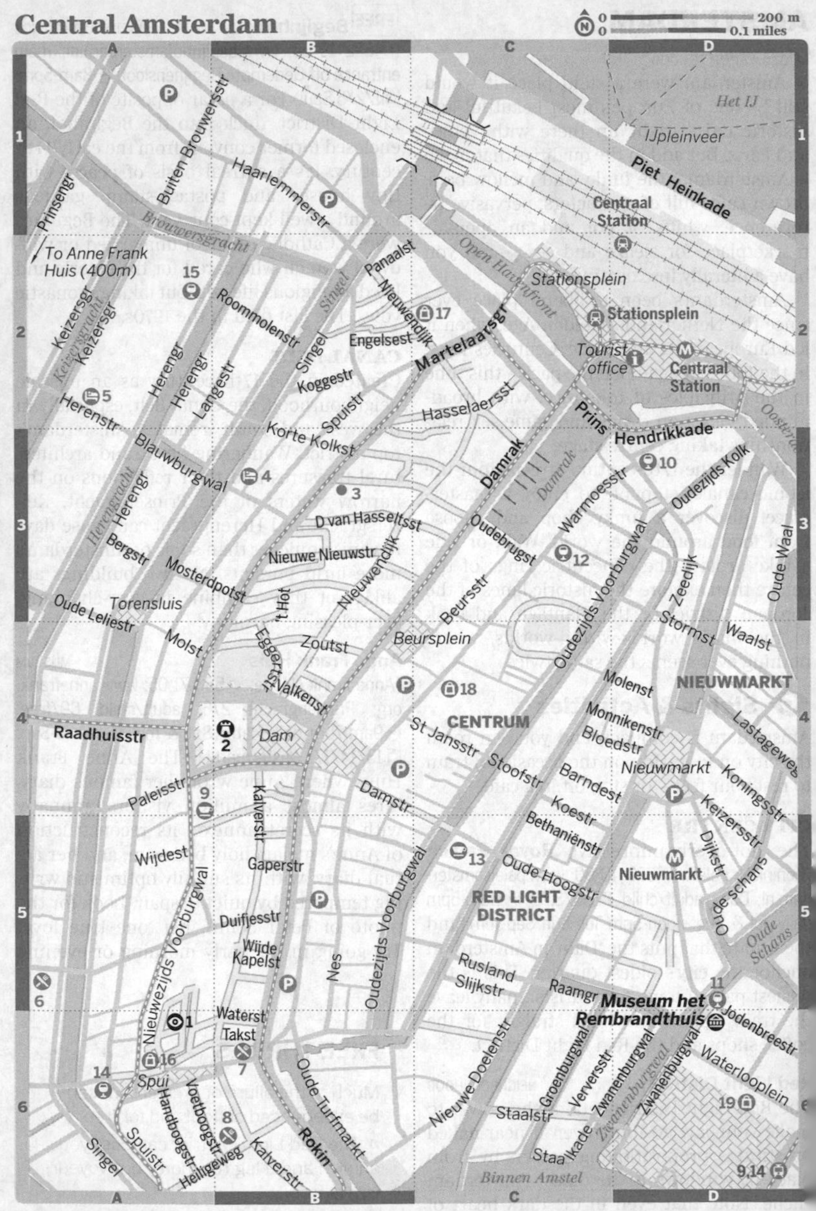

when crowds are lightest; book online to avoid long queues.

MUSEUMPLEIN

The genteel streets are a bit bland but what you'll find inside Amsterdam's big three museums will knock your wooden shoes off.

Van Gogh Museum MUSEU

(☎570 52 00; www.vangoghmuseum.nl; Paulu Potterstraat 7; adult/child €14/free, audioguide €5 ⏱10am-6pm Sat-Thu, to 10pm Fri; 📶; 🚋2/3/5/1 Van Baerlestraat) This outstanding museu houses the world's largest Van Gogh colle

Central Amsterdam

Top Sights

Museum het Rembrandthuis D6

Sights

1 Begijnhof A6
2 Royal Palace B4

Activities, Courses & Tours

3 Yellow Bike B3

Sleeping

4 Hotel Brouwer B3
5 Maes B&B A2

Eating

6 Buffet van Odette A5
7 Gartine B6
8 Vleminckx B6

Drinking

9 Abraxas A4
10 Café In 't Aepjen D3
11 De Sluyswacht D5
12 Getto C3
13 Greenhouse D6
14 Hoppe A6
15 't Arendsnest A2

Shopping

16 American Book Center A6
17 Chills & Thrills C2
18 Condomerie Het Gulden Vlies C4
19 Waterlooplein Flea Market D6

tion. Trace the artist's life from his tentative start though to his Japanese phase, and on to the black cloud that descended over him and his work. There's also works by contemporaries Gauguin, Toulouse-Lautrec, Monet and Bernard.

Rijksmuseum MUSEUM
(National Museum; ☎674 70 00; www.rijksmuseum.nl; Stadhouderskade 42; adult/child €15/free; ⊙9am-5pm; 🚊2/5 Hobbemastraat) The Rijksmuseum is the Netherlands' premier art trove. After a 10-year renovation, it reopened in its entirety in April 2013, splashing Rembrandts, Vermeers and 7500 other masterpieces over 1.5km of galleries.

The Golden Age works are the highlight. Feast your eyes on meaty still lifes, gentlemen in ruffed collars and landscapes bathed in pale yellow light. Rembrandt's *Night Watch* (1642) takes pride of place. Other must-sees are the Delftware (blue-and-white pottery), dollhouses (insanely detailed) and brand-new Asian Pavilion. The sculpture-studded gardens around the exterior are free to visit.

To avoid the biggest crowds, come after 3pm or pre-book tickets online, which provides fast-track entry.

Stedelijk Museum MUSEUM
(☎573 29 11; www.stedelijk.nl; Museumplein 10; adult/child €15/free; ⊙11am-5pm Tue & Wed, 11am-10pm Thu, 10am-6pm Fri-Sun; 🚊2/3/5/12 Van Baerlestraat) Amsterdam's weighty modern art museum is among the world's best. It struts Matisse cut-outs, Kandinsky abstracts, Picasso drawings, Rodin sculptures and a vivid collection of paintings by Dutch homeboys Piet Mondrian, Willem de Kooning, Charlie Toorop and Karel Appel. After a nine-year renovation, the Stedelijk reopened in September 2012 with a huge new wing (dubbed 'the Bathtub').

Vondelpark PARK
(www.vondelpark.nl; Stadhouderskade; ⊙24hr; 🚊2/5 Hobbemastraat) An English-style park with free concerts, ponds, lawns, thickets, winding footpaths and three outdoor cafes. It is popular with joggers, skaters, buskers and lovers.

DE PIJP

Heineken Experience BREWERY
(☎523 9435; www.heinekenexperience.com; Stadhouderskade 78; adult/child €17/13; ⊙10.30am-7pm Jun-Aug, 11am-5.30pm Sep-May; 🚊16/24 Stadhouderskade) The Heineken Experience is the much-gussied-up reincarnation of the brewer's old brewery tour featuring multimedia displays, rides and plenty of gift shops. At Amsterdam's most popular attraction, acolytes enjoy samples of the beer, which (like Stella Artois et al) is dismissed as an 'old man's beer' domestically and sold at a premium abroad.

NIEUWMARKT & PLANTAGE

The streets around the Rembrandt House are prime wandering territory, offering a vibrant mix of old Amsterdam, canals and quirky shops and cafes.

Museum het Rembrandthuis MUSEUM
(Rembrandt House Museum; ☎520 04 00; www.rembrandthuis.nl; Jodenbreestraat 4-6; adult/child €10/3; ⊙10am-5pm; 🚊9/14 Waterlooplein) You almost expect to find the master himself at the Museum het Rembrandthuis, the house where Rembrandt van Rijn ran his painting studio, only to lose the lot when profligacy

set in, enemies swooped, and bankruptcy came knocking. The museum has scores of etchings and sketches.

Tours

There are bike tours (p797) as well as canal boat tours (p797) of Amsterdam that let you hop on and hop off.

St Nicolaas Boat Club BOAT TOUR
(www.amsterdamboatclub.com; Kerkstraat 134) By far the best boat tour in the city. The open-air, 10-seat boats can manoeuvre into the narrowest canals. Patrons are allowed to smoke dope and drink beer on board, while the captains tell stories about alternative Amsterdam. Rides last 60 to 90 minutes. There is no set fee, just a suggested donation of €10; departure times vary according to numbers.

Sleeping

Book ahead for weekends and in summer. Many cheaper places cater specifically to party animals with booze flowing, pot smoking and general mayhem around the clock. Others exude refined old-world charm. Wi-fi is near universal but elevators are not.

All Inn the Family B&B B&B €€
(☎776 36 36; www.allinnthefamily.nl; 2e Egelantiersdwarsstraat 10; r €95-140; 📶) This new B&B, in a charming old Amsterdam canal house, gets rave reviews for embodying the very qualities of the inimitable Jordaan itself. Spirited hosts who speak five languages, a bountiful organic Dutch breakfast, and a quiet location in the heart of the neighbourhood.

DON'T MISS

JORDAAN

Originally a stronghold of the working class, the Jordaan is now one of the most desirable areas to live in Amsterdam. It's a pastiche of modest 17th- and 18th-century merchants' houses, humble workers' homes and a few modern carbuncles, squashed in a grid of tiny lanes peppered with bite-sized cafes and shops. Its intimacy is contagious, and now the average Jordaan dweller is more likely to be a gallery owner than a labourer.

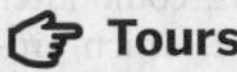 **Cocomama** HOSTEL €
(☎627 24 54; www.cocomama.nl; Westeinde 18; dm/r from €37/108; @📶) Rather than hide its tawdry past (the building was once home to a high-end brothel), Amsterdam's first self-proclaimed 'boutique hostel' plays it up with wink-wink humour – from the high-ceilinged, brothel-themed bunk rooms (with red curtains and 1970s porn) to the brothel shrine in the lobby.

Hotel Brouwer HOTEL €€
(☎624 63 58; www.hotelbrouwer.nl; Singel 83; r €60-100; @📶) Our favourite hotel in this price range, it has just eight rooms in a house dating back to 1652. Its rooms, named for Dutch painters, are furnished with simplicity, but all have canal views. There's – get this – a tiny lift.

Maes B&B B&B €€
(☎427 51 65; www.bedandbreakfastamsterdam.com; Herenstraat 26hs; s €95-115, d €115-135, apt €135-260; @📶) If you were designing a traditional home in the western canals, it would probably turn out a lot like this property: oriental carpets, wood floors and exposed brick. It's actually fairly spacious for such an old building.

International Budget Hostel STONER HOSTEL €
(☎624 27 84; www.internationalbudgethostel.com; Leidsegracht 76; dm €18-40, r €65-80; @📶) Reasons to stay: canalside location in a former warehouse; really close to nightlife; four-person limit in rooms; cool mix of backpackers from around the world; clean rooms with lockers; printer access and bike rental.

Eating

Amsterdam abounds in food choices. Happy streets for hunting include Utrechtsesraat, Spuistraat and any of the little streets lining and connecting the west canals, such as Berenstraat.

Van Dobben SANDWICHES €
(☎624 42 00; www.eetsalonvandobben.nl; Korte Reguliersdwarsstraat 5; items €2.75-6.50; ⏲10am-9pm Mon-Thu, to 2am Fri & Sat, 11.30am-9pm Sun; 🚊4/9/14 Rembrandtplein) Open since the 1940s, the venerable Van Dobben has white-tile walls and white-coated countermen who specialise in snappy banter. Traditional meaty Dutch fare is its forte: try the *pekelvlees* (something close to corned

beef). The *kroketten* (croquettes) are the best in town.

Gartine CAFE €€
(☎320 41 32; www.gartine.nl; Taksteeg 7; mains €6-12, high tea €12-21; ⊙10am-6pm Wed-Sun; ✍; 🚋4/9/14/16/24/25 Spui) Gartine makes delectable breakfast pastries, sandwiches and salads from produce grown in its own garden plot. Throw in slow-food credentials and gorgeous antique plates and it's a winner.

Tempo Doeloe INDONESIAN €€€
(☎625 67 18; www.tempodoeloerestaurant.nl; Utrechtsestraat 75; mains €20-25, rijsttafel & set menus €28-40; ⊙dinner Mon-Sat; ✍; 🚋4 Keizersgracht) Tempo Doeloe's setting and service are pleasant and decorous, without being overdone. The same applies to the *rijsttafel* (rice table): a ridiculously overblown affair at many places, here it's a fine sampling of the range of flavours found in the country. Warning: dishes marked 'very hot' are indeed very hot.

Pancakes! TRADITIONAL DUTCH €
(www.pancakesamsterdam.com; Berenstraat 38; pancakes €6-10; ⊙10am-7pm; 🚋13/14/17 Westermarkt) Just as many locals as tourists grace the blue tile tables at snug little Pancakes!, carving into all the usual options plus daily creations like ham, chicory and cheese or chicken curry pancakes. The batter is made with flour sourced from a local mill.

Vleminckx FRITES €
(Voetboogstraat 31; small/large €2.20/2.70, sauces €0.80; ⊙11am-6pm Tue-Sat, to 7pm Thu, noon-6pm Sun & Mon; 🚋1/2/5 Koningsplein) This hole-in-the-wall takeaway has drawn the hordes for its monumental *frites* since 1887. The standard is smothered in mayonnaise.

Winkel CAFE €
(www.winkel43.nl; Noordermarkt 43; mains €4-14; ⊙breakfast, lunch & dinner; 🚋3 Nieuwe Willemsstraat) This sprawling, indoor-outdoor space is great for people-watching, popular for coffees and small meals, and out-of-the-park for its tall, cakey apple pie.

Buffet van Odette CAFE €€
(www.buffet-amsterdam.nl; Herengracht 309; mains €8-16; ⊙10am-8.30pm Wed-Sat, to 5pm Sun & Mon; ✍; 🚋1/2/5 Spui) This is not a buffet but a sit-down cafe, where Odette and Yvette show how good simple cooking can taste when you start with great ingredients and a dash of creativity. Sit by the window for one of the city's loveliest canal views.

DON'T MISS

FEAST FOR A COIN

We don't exactly recommend Dutch fast-food icon **FEBO** (☎620 86 15; Leidsestraat 94; mains €3-6; ⊙11am-3am Sun-Thu, 11am-4am Fri & Sat; 🚋1/2/5 Prinsengracht). The *bami* rolls are hot as napalm, the *frikadel* frightening and the *kaassoufflé* utterly unsoufflé-like, but plucking a treat from the yellow automat windows is a drunken Dutch tradition.

Drinking

A particular Amsterdam joy is discovering your own brown cafe. They are found everywhere, often tucked into the most atmospheric of locations. Many serve food.

Hoppe BROWN CAFE
(www.cafehoppe.nl; Spui 18-20; 🚋1/2/5 Spui) Go on. Do your bit to ensure Hoppe maintains one of the highest beer turnovers in the city. The gritty brown cafe has been filling glasses for more than 300 years. Journalists, bums, socialites and raconteurs toss back brews amid the ancient wood panelling.

Café In 't Aepjen BROWN CAFE
(☎626 84 01; www.cafeintaepjen.nl; Zeedijk 1; 🚋4/9/16/24/25 Centraal Station) Candles burn even during the day at this bar based in a mid-16th-century house, which is one of only two remaining wooden buildings in the city.

De Sluyswacht BROWN CAFE
(www.sluyswacht.nl; Jodenbreestraat 1; ⊙from 11.30am; 🚋9/14 Waterlooplein) Listing like a ship in a high wind, this tiny black building was once a lock-keeper's house on the Oude Schans. Today the canalside terrace is one of the nicest spots we know in town to relax and down a beer.

't Arendsnest BEER CAFE
(www.arendsnest.nl; Herengracht 90; ⊙from 4pm Mon-Fri, from 2pm Sat & Sun; 🚋1/2/5/13/17 Nieuwezijds Kolk) This gorgeous, restyled brown cafe, with its glowing copper *jenever* (Dutch gin) boilers behind the bar, only serves Dutch beer.

Getto BAR
(www.getto.nl; Warmoesstraat 51; Tue-Sun; 4/9/16/24/25 Centraal Station) This groovy, long restaurant-bar is loved for its open, welcoming attitude, great people-watching from the front, and a rear lounge where you can chill. It draws a cross-section of the gay community. The owners also rent out a swanky apartment.

Entertainment

Find out what's on in **I Amsterdam** (www.iamsterdam.com/events).

Coffee Shops

Cafes have coffee, 'coffee shops' are where one buys pot.

Abraxas COFFEE SHOP
(www.abraxas.tv; Jonge Roelensteeg 12; from 10am;) Hands down the most beautiful coffee shop in town. Choose from southwest USA, Middle Eastern and other styles of decor, spread over three floors.

Greenhouse COFFEE SHOP
(Oudezijds Voorburgwal 191; from 9am; ; 4/9/16/24/25 Dam) One of the most popular coffee shops in town. Smokers love the funky music, multicoloured mosaics, psychedelic stained-glass windows, and high-quality weed and hash.

Nightclubs

Sugar Factory CLUB
(www.sugarfactory.nl; Lijnbaansgracht 238; 1/2/5/7/10 Leidseplein) A cool vibe, an excellent location and a varied line-up are the hallmarks here. But this ain't your average club – most nights start with music, cinema, or a dance or spoken-word performance, followed by late-night DJs and dancing.

Air CLUB
(820 06 70; www.air.nl; Amstelstraat 16; Thu-Sun; 4/9/14 Rembrandtplein) One of Amsterdam's It clubs, Air has an environmentally friendly design and a unique tiered dance floor.

> **COFFEE SHOP DO'S & DON'TS**
>
> Keep in mind the following at coffee shops in the Netherlands:
>
> » Ask at the bar for the menu of cannibis-related goods on offer, usually packaged in small bags. You can also buy ready-made joints (€3 to €7). Most shops offer rolling papers, pipes or even bongs to use.
>
> » Don't light up anywhere besides a coffee shop without checking that it's OK to do so.
>
> » Alcohol and tobacco products are not permitted in coffee shops.

Live Music

Paradiso LIVE MUSIC
(www.paradiso.nl; Weteringschans 6; 7/10 Spiegelgracht) Worship rock and roll in a gorgeous old church where the Beatles once played. Opened in 1968 as 'Cosmic Relaxation Center Paradiso', this historic, multi-storeyed club exudes an anything-goes, relaxed vibe.

Melkweg LIVE MUSIC
(www.melkweg.nl; Lijnbaansgracht 234a; 1/2/5/7/10 Leidseplein) The 'Milky Way' is a dazzling galaxy of diverse music. One night it's reggae or punk, the next night heavy-metal legend Zach Wilde lures in the leather-jacketed biker crowd.

Comedy

Boom Chicago COMEDY, CLUB
(423 01 01; www.boomchicago.nl; Rozengracht 117, Rosentheater; box office 4-8.30pm Wed-Fri, 3-11pm Sat; 13/14/17 Marnixstraat/Rozengracht) Enjoy Amsterdam's leading English-language improv comedy show over a few drinks; the same multi-talented and seriously funny folks also run nearby nightclub **Chicago Social Club** (530 73 03; www.chicagosocialclub.nl; Leidseplein 12; 1/2/5/7/10 Leidseplein).

Shopping

The real pleasure of shopping in Amsterdam is finding some tiny shop selling something you'd find nowhere else. Several streets along the Western Canals are dotted with surprising little shops: try Reesstraat and Hartenstraat and the blocks south to Runstraat and Huidenstraat.

Markets of just about every description are scattered across the city.

Albert Cuypmarkt MARKET
(www.albertcuypmarkt.nl; Albert Cuypstraat, btwn Ferdinand Bolstraat & Van Woustraat; 10am-5pm Mon-Sat; 16/24 Albert Cuypstraat) This 100-year-old market is Amsterdam's largest and busiest market. Food of every description, flowers, souvenirs, clothing, hardware and household goods can be found here.

Bloemenmarkt MARKET

(Flower Market; Singel, btwn Muntplein & Koningsplein; ⏲9am-5.30pm Mon-Sat, 11am-5.30pm Sun; 🚊1/2/5 Koningsplein) A touristy 'floating' flower market that's actually on pilings. Still, at the stalls that actually stock flowers (as opposed to plastic clogs), the vibrant colours burst forth.

Waterlooplein Flea Market MARKET

(www.waterloopleinmarkt.nl; ⏲9am-5pm Mon-Sat) is Amsterdam's most famous flea market: curios, secondhand clothing, music, used footwear, ageing electronic gear, New Age gifts and cheap bicycle parts.

Condomerie Het Gulden Vlies SPECIALTY SHOP

(www.condomerie.nl; Warmoesstraat 141; 🚊4/9/16/24/25 Dam) This is where the well-dressed Johnson shops for variety. Perfectly positioned for the Red Light District, the boutique stocks hundreds of types of condoms.

American Book Center BOOKS

(ABC; www.abc.nl; Spui 12; ⏲11am-8pm Mon, from 10am Tue-Sat, 11am-6.30pm Sun; 🚊1/2/5 Spui) This excellent three-storey shop is the biggest source of English-language books in Amsterdam.

Chills & Thrills SPECIALTY SHOP

(www.chillsandthrills.com; Nieuwendijk 17; ⏲10am-10pm) This busy shop sells truffles, herbal trips, E-testing kits, psychoactive cacti, amino-acid and vitamin drinks, novelty bongs and life-sized alien sculptures.

Information

GWK Travelex (☎0900 05 66; www.gwk.nl; Centraal Station; ⏲8am-10pm Mon-Sat, 9am-10pm Sun; 🚉Centraal Station) Exchanges travellers cheques and makes hotel bookings; also at Schiphol airport.

I Amsterdam Card (www.iamsterdam.com; per 24/48/72hr €40/50/60) Available at VVV offices and some hotels. Provides admission to many museums, canal boat trips, and discounts and freebies at shops, attractions and restaurants. Also includes a GVB transit pass.

Tourist office (www.iamsterdam.nl; Stationsplein 10; ⏲9am-7pm Mon-Fri, 10am-6pm Sat & Sun) Maps, guides and transit passes.

Getting There & Away

AIR Most major airlines serve **Schiphol** (AMS; www.schiphol.nl), 18km southwest of the city centre.

BUS Eurolines connects with all major European capitals. Buses arrive at Amstelstation, south of the centre, which has an easy metro link to Centraal Station (about a 15-minute trip). **Eurolines' ticket office** (Rokin 38a) is near the Dam.

TRAIN Amsterdam's main train station is fabled **Centraal Station** (⏲8am-10pm Mon-Sat, 9am-10pm Sun), with services to the rest of the country and major European cities.

Getting Around

To/From the Airport

A taxi into Amsterdam from Schiphol airport takes 25 to 45 minutes and costs about €45. Trains to Centraal Station leave every few minutes, take 15 to 20 minutes, and cost €4/7 per single/return.

Bicycle

Amsterdam is cycling nirvana: flat, beautiful and with dedicated bike paths. About 150,000 bicycles are stolen each year in Amsterdam, so always lock up. Rental agencies include the following:

Bike City (☎626 37 21; www.bikecity.nl; Bloemgracht 68-70; bikes per day from €14) There's no advertising on the bikes, so you can pretend you're a local.

Yellow Bike (☎620 69 40; www.yellowbike.nl; Nieuwezijds Kolk 29; city/countryside tours €19.50/29.50) Choose from city tours or the longer countryside tour through the pretty Waterland district to the north. Also rents bikes.

Boat

Amsterdam's canal boats are a popular way to tour the town but most are actually a bit claustrophobic, with steamed-up glass windows surrounding passengers. Look for a boat with an open seating area.

Canal Bus (www.canal.nl; day pass adult/child €22/11) Offers a unique hop-on, hop-off service; has 17 docks around the city near the big museums.

Public Transport

Services – including Amsterdam's iconic trams – are run by the local transit authority, the GVB. Its highly useful **GVB Information Office** (www.gvb.nl; Stationsplein 10; ⏲7am-9pm Mon-Fri, 10am-6pm Sat & Sun) is located across the tram tracks from the Centraal Station main entrance. You can

WORTH A TRIP

ZAANSE SCHANS

People come for an hour and stay for several at this open-air museum on the Zaan river, which is *the* place to see **windmills** operating. It's got a touristy element, but the six operating mills are completely authentic and are operated with enthusiasm and love. Visitors can explore the windmills at their leisure, seeing firsthand the vast moving parts that make these devices a combination of sailing ship and Rube Goldberg. As a bonus, the river-bank setting is lovely.

The site is free; entrance fees to the individual windmills average €3/1.50 per adult/child. At least a couple are open on any given day; hours tend to be 10am to 4pm. There are several cafes and restaurants on-site.

From Amsterdam Centraal Station (€3, 17 minutes, four times hourly) take the train towards Alkmaar and get off at Koog Zaandijk – it's a well-signposted 1km walk to Zaanse Schans.

avoid the often-long lines by buying day passes at the adjoining VVV office instead.

Public transport in Amsterdam uses the OV-chipkaart. Rides cost €2.70 when bought on the tram or bus. Unlimited-ride passes are available for one to seven days (€7.50 to €31) and are valid on trams, most buses and the metro.

Taxi

Amsterdam taxis are expensive, even over short journeys. Try **Taxicentrale Amsterdam** (TCA; ☎777 77 77; www.tcataxi.nl).

THE RANDSTAD

When people think of the Netherlands outside of Amsterdam, they are often really thinking about the Randstad. One of the most densely populated places on the planet, it stretches from Amsterdam to Rotterdam and features classic Dutch towns and cities such as Den Haag, Utrecht, Leiden and Delft. Most people focus their visit to Holland here, enjoying the peerless cycling network that links the towns amid tulip fields.

Haarlem

☎023 / POP 152,000

Haarlem is the Netherlands in microcosm, with canals, gabled buildings and cobblestone streets. Its historic buildings, grand churches, museums, cosy bars, good restaurants and antique shops draw scores of day trippers – it's only 15 minutes by train from Amsterdam.

Sights

A couple of hourss stroll – with stops for refreshments – will cover Haarlem's tidy centre, which radiates out from the **Grote Markt**, where there are markets on many days. The **Town Hall** is worth a look as is the cathedral, **Grote Kerk van St Bavo** (www.bavo.nl; Oude Groenmarkt 23; adult/child €2.50/free; ⌚10am-5pm Mon-Sat).

Frans Hals Museum GALLERY
(www.franshalsmuseum.nl; Groot Heiligland 62; adult/child €7.50/free; ⌚11am-5pm Tue-Sat, noon-5pm Sun) A short stroll south of Grote Markt, the Frans Hals Museum is a must for anyone interested in the Dutch Masters. Kept in a poorhouse where Hals spent his final years, the collection focuses on the 17th-century Haarlem School.

Eating & Drinking

Lange Veerstraat has a bounty of cafes, while Schagchelstraat is lined with restaurants. The Saturday-morning market on Grote Markt is one of Holland's best; try the fresh *Stroopwafels* (small caramel-filled waffles).

De Haerlemsche Vlaamse FRITES €
(Spekstraat 3; frites €2.10) Practically on the doorstep of the Grote Kerk, this *frites* (French fries) joint, not much bigger than a telephone box, is a local institution. Line up for its crispy, golden fries made from fresh potatoes.

Proeflokaal in den Uiver BROWN CAFE
(www.indenuiver.nl; Riviervismarkt 13) This nautical-themed place has shipping knick-knacks and a schooner over the bar. There's jazz on Thursday and Sunday evenings.

Getting There & Away

Trains serve Haarlem's stunning art deco station, a 10-minute walk from the centre. Destinations include Amsterdam (€4, 15 minutes, five to eight services per hour), Den Haag (€8, 35 to 40 minutes, four to six per hour) and Rotterdam (€11, 50 minutes, four per hour).

Leiden

071 / POP 118,700

Leiden is a busy, vibrant town that is another popular day trip from Amsterdam. Claims to fame: it's Rembrandt's birthplace, it's home to the Netherlands' oldest university (and 20,000 students) and it's where America's pilgrims raised money to lease the leaky *Mayflower* that took them to the New World in 1620. Large, dignified 17th-century buildings with tall, almost regal windows line the canals.

Sights & Activities

The best way to experience Leiden is by strolling the historic centre, especially along the Rapenburg canal.

Follow the huge steeple to **Pieterskerk** (Pieterskerkhof; 10am-4pm Mon-Fri, 1.30-4pm Sat & Sun May-Sep, 1.30-4pm daily Oct-Apr), which shines after a grand restoration (a good thing as it's been prone to collapse since it was built in the 14th century). The precinct here is as old-Leiden as you'll get and includes the gabled old **Latin School** (Schoolstraat), which – before it became a commercial building – was graced by a pupil named Rembrandt from 1616 to 1620. Across the plaza, look for the **Gravensteen**, which dates to the 13th century and once was a prison.

Lakenhal MUSEUM
(www.lakenhal.nl; Oude Singel 28-32; adult/child €7.50/free; 10am-5pm Tue-Fri, noon-5pm Sat & Sun) Get your Rembrandt fix at the 17th-century Lakenhal, which houses the Municipal Museum, with an assortment of works by Old Masters, as well as period rooms and temporary exhibits.

Rijksmuseum van Oudheden MUSEUM
(National Museum of Antiquities; www.rmo.nl; Rapenburg 28; adult/child €9/free; 10am-5pm Tue-Sun) This museum has a world-class collection of Greek, Roman and Egyptian artefacts, the pride of which is the extraordinary Temple of Taffeh.

Sleeping & Eating

The city-centre canals and narrow old streets abound with choices, although there's little of interest on the walking route in from the station. The sprawling Saturday **market** along Nieuwe Rijn abounds with fresh fare and flowers.

Hotel Nieuw Minerva HOTEL €€
(512 63 58; www.hotelleiden.com; Boommarkt 23; s/d from €75/80;) Located in six 16th-century canalside houses, this central hotel has a mix of 40 regular (ie nothing special) and some very fun themed rooms, including a room with a bed in which King Lodewijk Bonaparte (aka Louis Bonaparte) slept. We prefer the thematic 'room of angels', a luminous vision of white.

De Dames Proeverij CAFE €€
(www.proeverijdedames.nl; Nieuwe Rijn 37; mains €12-20) Run by two women who have excellent taste, this cafe seems to have just what you want at any time of day. There is an excellent range of coffee drinks as well as dozens of top wines by the glass. Enjoy your sips at the tables out front overlooking the canal.

Fresh 'n Fast CAFE €
(www.freshnfast.nl; Kloksteeg 7; mains €8-12; 5pm-midnight) A fabulous find near Pieterskerk; everything here is sourced from the best local and organic producers. The cheeses are from famous nearby dairies. Get a bench at a table out front.

Café L'Esperance BROWN CAFE
(www.lesperance.nl; Kaiserstraat 1) Long, dark and handsome, all decked out in nostalgic wood panelling *and* overlooking an evocative

DON'T MISS

KEUKENHOF GARDENS

One of the Netherlands' top attractions is near Lisse, between Haarlem and Leiden. **Keukenhof** (www.keukenhof.nl; adult/child €15/7.50, parking €6; 8am-7.30pm mid-Mar–mid-May, last entry 6pm) is the world's largest bulb-flower garden, attracting nearly 800,000 visitors during a season almost as short-lived as the blooms on the millions of multicoloured tulips, daffodils and hyacinths.

Buses 50 and 54 travel from Leiden Centraal Station to Keukenhof (30 minutes, four times per hour). All tickets can be purchased online, which helps avoid huge queues.

bend in the canal. Tables abound outside in summer; good meals too.

Information

Tourist Office (516 60 00; www.vvvleiden.nl; Stationsweg 41; 8am-6pm Mon-Fri, 10am-4pm Sat, 11am-5pm Sun) Across from the train station, has good maps and historic info.

Getting There & Away

Buses leave from directly in front of Centraal Station. Train destinations, all with six departures per hour, include Amsterdam (€8, 34 minutes), Den Haag (€3.50, 10 minutes) and Schiphol Airport (€6, 15 minutes).

Den Haag

070 / POP 501,000

Den Haag (The Hague), officially known as 's-Gravenhage (Count's Hedge), is the Dutch seat of government (although Amsterdam is the capital). Wide, tree-lined boulevards like Lange Voorhout give Den Haag a suitably regal air. The many embassies here plus various international courts of justice – which keep Den Haag in the news – give the city a worldly air. Nightlife thrives with fun seekers on international assignment and its museums include one exquisite star.

Sights & Activities

Mauritshuis MUSEUM
(www.mauritshuis.nl; Korte Vijverberg 8; adult/child €13.50/free; 11am-5pm Tue-Sun) For a painless introduction to Dutch and Flemish Art 101, visit the Mauritshuis, a small museum in a jewel-box of an old palace. Highlights include the Dutch *Mona Lisa:* Vermeer's *Girl with a Pearl Earring*. Rembrandts include a wistful self-portrait from the year of his death, 1669, and *The Anatomy Lesson of Dr Nicolaes Tulp*.

Even if you're just passing Den Haag on the train, it's well worth hopping off to visit.

Binnenhof PALACE
(10am-4pm Mon-Sat) Adjoining the Mauritshuis, the Binnenhof is surrounded by parliamentary buildings that have long been at the heart of Dutch politics, though parliament now meets in a modern building on the south side.

The central courtyard looks sterile today but was once used for executions. A highlight of the complex is the 13th-century **Ridderzaal** (Knights' Hall; admission €4; 10am-4pm Mon-Sat). The Gothic dining hall has been carefully restored.

Gemeentemuseum ART MUSEUM
(Municipal Museum; www.gemeentemuseum.nl; Stadhouderslaan 41; adult/child €13.50/free; 11am-5pm Tue-Sun) Admirers of De Stijl, and in particular of Piet Mondrian, mustn't miss the Berlage-designed Gemeentemuseum. It houses a large collection of works by neoplasticist artists and others from the late 19th century, as well as extensive exhibits of applied arts, costumes and musical instruments.

Take tram 17 from CS and HS.

Scheveningen BEACH
(www.scheveningen.com) The long beach at Scheveningen, pronounced – if possible – as s'CHay-fuh-ninger, attracts nine million visitors per year. It's tacky, but you might just find pleasure in the carnival atmosphere. Better yet, you can escape to wide-open beaches and nature with just a bit of effort, especially to the south where the hype tapers off as you pass the harbour.

Sleeping & Eating

All those expats on expense accounts support a diverse and thriving cafe culture. The cobbled streets and canals off Denneweg are an excellent place to stroll hungry.

Hotel La Ville HOTEL €€
(346 36 57; www.hotellaville.nl; Veenkade 5-6; r €50-120;) The 21 rooms here are the best deal close to the centre. The decor is a minimalist white, grey and maroon; some rooms share bathrooms. Apartments have basic cooking facilities and there's a small cafe. Book ahead.

Stayokay Den Haag HOSTEL €
(315 78 88; www.stayokay.com; Scheepmakerstraat 27; dm/r from €25/66;) This branch of the Stayokay hostel chain has all the usual facilities, including a bar, a restaurant, internet and games. It's around 15 minutes' walk from HS station.

TOP CHOICE **Bloem** CAFE €
(www.bloemdenhaag.nl; Korte Houtstraat 6; mains €5-8; 10am-6pm Mon-Sat) A cute little cafe across the Plein from the Binnenhof. There are white tables, chairs and flowers out front. Housemade tarts are superb and sandwiches include a tasty club. Smoothies will give you a dose of healthy goodness. Stop by for afternoon high tea.

De Zwarte Ruiter GRAND CAFE
(The Black Rider; Grote Markt 27; snacks from €4) The Rider faces off with the competing Boterwaag across the Markt like rival kings of cool. We call this one the winner, with its terrace and art deco mezzanine – light-filled, split-level and cavernous – and boisterous crowds of commoners, diplomats and, no doubt, the odd international jewel thief.

Shopping

Grote Markstraat is fittingly the street for large stores. Interesting shops and oddball boutiques line Hoogstraat, Noordeinde and Heulstraat; the real treats are along Prinsestraat. **Stanley & Livingstone** (☎365 73 06; Schoolstraat 21) is an excellent travel bookshop.

Information

Tourist Office (VVV; www.scheveningendenhaag.com; Spui 68; ⏰10am-8pm Mon-Fri, to 5pm Sat, noon-5pm Sun; 📶) Sells tickets for local events and has internet access.

Getting There & Around

Most trains start or stop their journeys from Den Haag Centraal Station (CS). But some through trains only stop at Den Haag HS (Holland Spoor) station just south of the centre. Destinations, with about four services per hour, include Amsterdam (€11, 50 minutes), Rotterdam (€5, 25 minutes) and Schiphol Airport (€8, 30 minutes).

A useful day pass for local trams costs €7.50 but you have to wait in often-long ticket queues at CS and HS.

Delft

☎015 / POP 98,700

Compact, charming and relaxed, Delft may be the perfect Dutch day trip. Founded around 1100, it maintains tangible links to its romantic past despite the pressures of modernisation and tourist hordes. Many of the canalside vistas could be scenes from the *Girl with a Pearl Earring*, the novel about Golden Age painter Johannes Vermeer, which was made into a movie (and partially shot here) in 2003.

Sights

The 14th-century **Nieuwe Kerk** (www.nieuwekerk-delft.nl; Markt; adult/child incl Oude Kerk €3.50/1.50; ⏰9am-6pm Apr-Oct, 11am-4pm Nov-Mar, closed Sun) houses the crypt of the Dutch royal family and the mausoleum of Willem the Silent. The fee includes entrance to the **Oude Kerk** (www.oudekerk-delft.nl; Heilige Geestkerkhof 25; adult/child incl Nieuwe Kerk €3.50/1.50). The latter, 800 years old, is a surreal sight: its tower leans 2m from the vertical. Among the tombs inside is Vermeer's. The **town hall** and the **Waag** on the **Grote Markt** are right out of the 17th century.

Vermeer Centrum Delft MUSEUM
(www.vermeerdelft.nl; Voldersgracht 21; adult/child €7/3; ⏰10am-5pm) As the place where Vermeer was born, lived, and worked, Delft is 'Vermeer Central' to many art-history and Old Masters enthusiasts. Along with viewing life-sized images of Vermeer's oeuvre, you can tour a replica of Vermeer's studio, which gives insight into the way the artist approached the use of light and colour in his craft.

Municipal Museum het Prinsenhof MUSEUM
(www.prinsenhof-delft.nl; St Agathaplein 1; adult/child €7.50/free; ⏰10am-5pm Tue-Sat, 1-5pm Sun) The former convent where Willem the Silent was assassinated in 1584 (the bullet hole in the wall is preserved) is now a museum displaying various objects telling the story of the Eighty Years War with Spain, as well as 17th-century paintings.

De Candelaer PORCELAIN STUDIO
(www.candelaer.nl; Kerkstraat 13; ⏰9am-5.30pm Mon-Fri, to 5pm Sat year-round, 9am-5pm Sun Mar-May) The most central and modest Delftware outfit is De Candelaer, just off the Markt. It has five artists, a few of whom work most days.

Sleeping & Eating

Compact in size and oh-so-charming, Delft makes a good base for exploring much of Holland, with frequent and fast train services putting towns from Leiden to Rotterdam less than 20 minutes away.

Hotel Coen HOTEL €€
(☎214 59 14; www.hotelcoendelft.nl; Coenderstraat 47; s/d from €72/90; @📶) Just behind the train station construction site, this family-run hotel has 55 beds in a variety of rooms, from budget singles as thin as your wallet to grander doubles.

De Visbanken SEAFOOD €
(Camaretten 2; snacks from €3; ⏰10am-6pm) People have been selling fish on this spot since 1342. The present vendors line the

display cases in the old open-air pavilion with all manner of things fishy.

Stadys Koffyhuis CAFE €
(www.stads-koffyhuis.nl; Oude Delft 133; mains €7-12) Savour Delft from seats on a terrace barge moored out the front. Savour drinks, sandwiches and pancakes while admiring possibly the best view in Delft – the Oude Kerk.

Locus Publicus BROWN CAFE
(Brabantse Turfmarkt 67) Glowing from within, this beer cafe has more than 200 beers. It's charming and filled with cheery locals who are quaffing their way through the list. Good people watching from the front-terrace tables.

Information

Tourist Office (VVV; 215 40 51; www.delft.nl; Hippolytusbuurt 4; 10am-4pm Sun & Mon, 9am-6pm Tue-Fri, 10am-5pm Sat) Has free internet; the thematic walking guides are excellent.

Getting There & Away

The area around the train station is a vast construction site for years to come as the lines are moved underground. Train services include Amsterdam (€12, one hour, two per hour), Den Haag (€3, 12 minutes, four per hour) and Rotterdam (€3.50, 12 minutes, four per hour).

DON'T MISS

BLOWING IN THE WIND

In 1740 a series of windmills were built to drain a polder about 12km southeast of Rotterdam. Today 19 of the Dutch icons survive at **Kinderdijk** (www.kinderdijk.nl; admission free), which is a Unesco monument. You can wander the dikes for over 3km amid the spinning sails and visit inside one of the **windmills**. It's a good bicycle ride. You can rent bikes once there or travel from Rotterdam (16km); get a map from the tourist office.

A fantastic day trip is by the **Waterbus** (www.waterbus.nl; Willemskade; day pass adult/child €12.50/9). The fast ferries leave from Rotterdam every 30 minutes and a connection puts you at Kinderdijk, 1km from the first mill. After the visit, continue by ferry to utterly charming **Dordrecht** and then return to Rotterdam by train.

Rotterdam

010 / POP 616,000

Rotterdam bursts with energy. Vibrant nightlife, a diverse, multi-ethnic community, an intensely interesting maritime tradition and a wealth of top-class museums all make it a must-see part of any visit to the Netherlands, especially if you are passing by on the high-speed trains.

The Netherlands' 'second city', central Rotterdam was bombed flat during WWII and spent the following decades rebuilding. You won't find the classic Dutch medieval centre here – it was swept away along with the other rubble and detritus of war. In its place is an architectural aesthetic that's unique in Europe, a progressive, perpetual-motion approach to architecture that's clearly a result of the city's postwar, postmodern, anything-goes philosophy (a fine example of this is the Paul McCarthy statue titled **Santa with Butt Plug** that the city placed in the main shopping district).

Sights & Activities

Rotterdam is split by the vast Nieuwe Maas shipping channel, which is crossed by a series of tunnels and bridges, notably the fabulously postmodern **Erasmusbrug**. The centre is on the north side of the water and is easily strolled. The historic neighbourhood of Delfshaven is 3km west.

Like those mod visions of the future that never seem to come to pass, Rotterdam's architecture is both fanciful and arresting.

Museum Boijmans van Beuningen MUSEUM
(www.boijmans.nl; Museumpark 18-20; adult/child €12.50/free, Wed free; 11am-5pm Tue-Sun) Museum Boijmans van Beuningen is among Europe's very finest museums and has a permanent collection taking in Dutch and European art (Bosch, Van Eyck, Rembrandt, Tintoretto, Titian and Bruegel's *Tower of Babel*). The surrealist wing features ephemera, paraphernalia and famous works from Dalí, Duchamp, Magritte, Man Ray and more.

Delfshaven NEIGHBOURHOOD
One of Rotterdam's best districts for strolling, quaint Delfshaven (it survived the war) was once the official seaport for the city of Delft. A reconstructed 18th-century **windmill** (Voorhaven 210; 1-5pm Wed, 10am-4pm Sat

MARITIME ROTTERDAM

Rotterdam has embraced the sea, shipping and trade since the 16th century. Harbour tours of Europe's busiest port are fascinating, while museums and exhibits on the water bring this heritage to life.

Maritiem Museum Rotterdam (Maritime Museum; www.maritiemmuseum.nl; Leuvehaven 1; adult/child €7.50/4; ⏲10am-5pm Tue-Sat, 11am-5pm Sun year-round, plus 10am-5pm Mon Jul & Aug) This engaging museum looks at the Netherlands' rich maritime traditions. There's an array of models that any youngster would love to take into the tub, plus more interesting and explanatory displays.

Haven Museum (Leuvehaven 50; admission free; ⏲visitor centre 10am-5pm Tue-Sun) All manner of old and historic ships moored in the basin just south of the Maritiem Museum. You can wander the quays around the clock.

Spido (www.spido.nl; Willemsplein 85; adult/child €11/7; ⏲9.30am-5pm Jun-Sep, shorter hours Oct-May) Offers daily harbour tours.

overlooks the water at Voorhaven 210. One of the area's claims to fame is that it was where the Pilgrims tried leaving for America aboard the leaky *Speedwell*.

Just west on Schiedamseweg are all manner of ethnic groceries and eateries; Delftshaven is refreshingly un-twee. It is best reached by taking trams 4 and 9 or the Metro.

Sleeping

Stayokay Rotterdam HOSTEL €
(☎436 57 63; www.stayokay.com; Overblaak 85-87; dm/r from €20/55; @📶) Those odd angles you see at this hostel may not be to do with what you just smoked; this hostel is in the landmark **Overblaak development**, a famous example of modern architecture. There are 245 beds in oddly shaped rooms that sleep two to eight people.

Hotel Bazar HOTEL €€
(☎206 51 51; www.hotelbazar.nl; Witte de Withstraat 16; r €70-130) Bazar is deservedly popular for its 27 Middle Eastern-, African- and South American-themed rooms. Breakfast is spectacular: Turkish bread, international cheeses, yoghurt, pancakes and coffee. The ground-floor bar and restaurant is justifiably popular.

Hotel Emma HOTEL €€
(☎436 55 33; www.hotelemma.nl; Nieuwe Binnenweg 6; r €60-150; @📶) Nicely refurbished, the Emma is a modern place with 24 rooms close to the city centre. Touches include posh bathrooms and double-glazed windows. The free breakfast includes fresh-baked goods.

Eating

Look for myriad eating choices in Veerhaven, Witte de Single, Nieuwe Binnenweg and Oude Haven.

De Ballentent CAFE €
(www.deballentent.nl; Parkkade 1; meals from €6; ⏲9am-11pm) Rotterdam's best waterfront pub-cafe is also a great spot for a meal. Dine on one of two terraces or inside. Mussels, schnitzels and more line the menu but the real speciality here are *bals*, huge homemade meatloafy meatballs. Waiters and customers alike enjoy a good laugh.

Bazar MIDDLE EASTERN €€
(Witte de Withstraat 16; mains €7-15) On the ground floor of the creative Hotel Bazar, this vast and popular eatery comes up with creative Middle Eastern fusion fare that complements the stylised decor. The outside tables are *the* neighbourhood meeting spot day and night.

Het Eethuisje TRADITIONAL DUTCH €
(Mathenesserdijk 436; mains €8-10; ⏲4-9pm Mon-Sat) Traditional meaty, filling Dutch food is served from this little storefront near a canal. Utterly tourist free; in Delftshaven.

Drinking

Rotown BAR
(www.rotown.nl; Nieuwe Binnenweg 17-19) A smooth bar, a dependable live rock venue, an agreeable restaurant, a popular meeting place. The musical program features new local talent, established international acts and crossover experiments.

Rotterdam

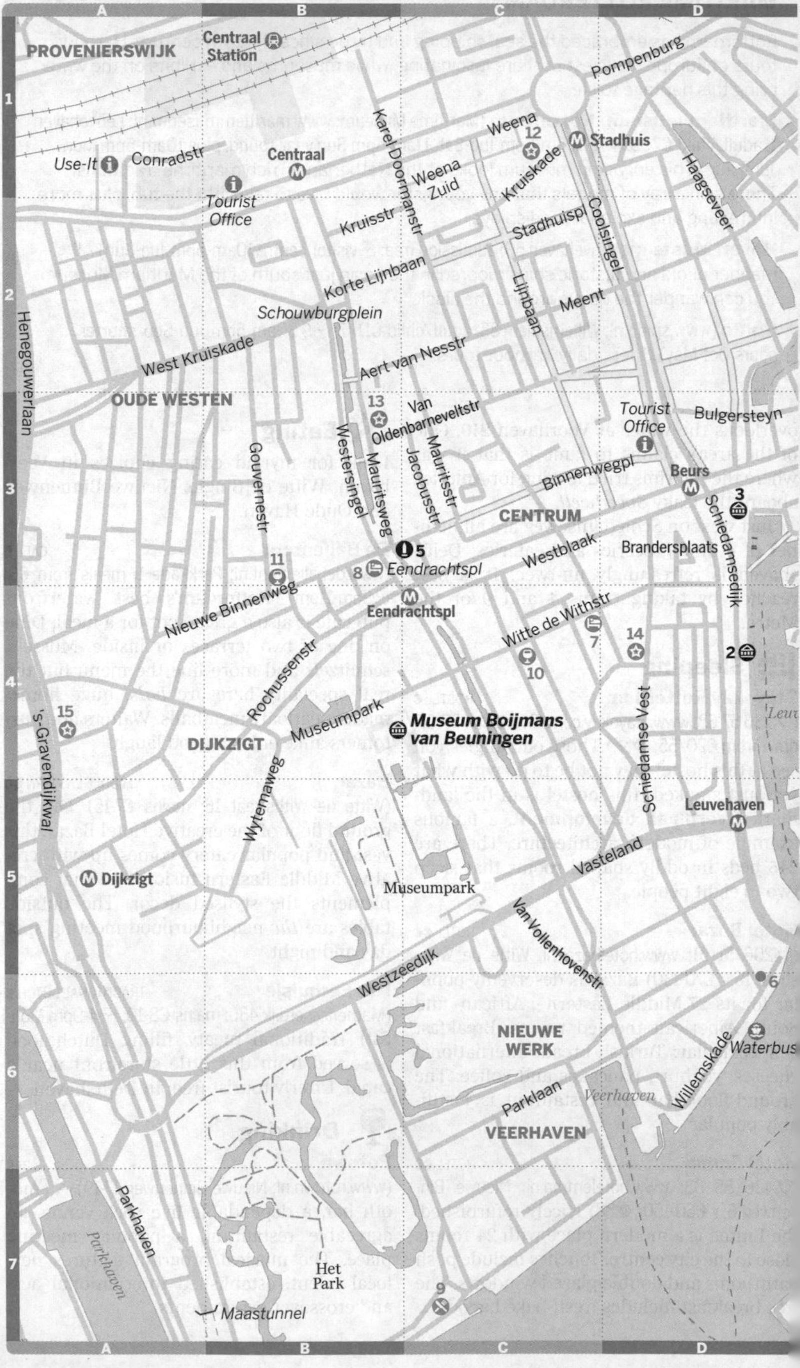

A B C D

1 2 3 4 5 6 7

PROVENIERSWIJK
Centraal Station
Pompenburg
Karel Doormanstr
Weena
12
Stadhuis
Use-It
Conradstr
Centraal
Weena Zuid
Kruiskade
Haagseveer
Tourist Office
Kruisstr
Stadhuispl
Coolsingel
Korte Lijnbaan
Lijnbaan
Meent
Schouwburgplein
Henegouwerlaan
West Kruiskade
Aert van Nesstr
OUDE WESTEN
13
Van Oldenbarneveltstr
Tourist Office
Bulgersteyn
Gouvernestr
Westersingel
Mauritsweg
Jacobusstr
Mauritsstr
Binnenwegpl
Beurs
3
Schiedamsedijk
CENTRUM
5
Westblaak
Brandersplaats
11
8
Eendrachtspl
Nieuwe Binnenweg
Eendrachtspl
Witte de Withstr
7
14
2
10
Rochussenstr
15
's-Gravendijkwal
Museumpark
Museum Boijmans van Beuningen
Leuv
DIJKZIGT
Wytemaweg
Schiedamse Vest
Leuvehaven
Vasteland
Dijkzigt
Museumpark
Van Vollenhovenstr
Westzeedijk
6
NIEUWE WERK
Waterbus
Willemskade
Parklaan
Veerhaven
VEERHAVEN
Parkhaven
Parkhaven
Het Park
9
Maastunnel

THE NETHERLANDS ROTTERDAM

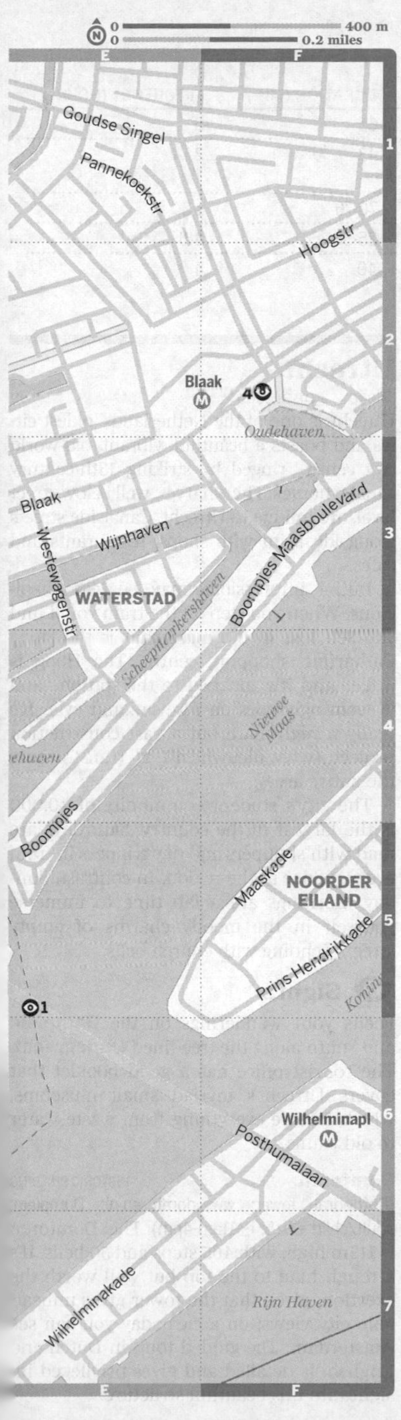

Rotterdam

Top Sights

Museum Boijmans van Beuningen....B4

Sights

1 Erasmusbrug....E5
2 Haven Museum....D4
3 Maritiem Museum Rotterdam....D3
4 Overblaak Development....F2
5 Santa with Butt Plug Statue....C3

Activities, Courses & Tours

6 Spido....D6

Sleeping

7 Hotel Bazar....C4
8 Hotel Emma....B3
Stayokay Rotterdam....(see 4)

Eating

Bazar....(see 7)
9 De Ballentent....C7

Drinking

10 De Witte Aap....C4
11 Rotown....B3

Entertainment

12 Corso....C1
13 De Unie....B3
14 Gay Palace....D4
15 Nemo....A4

De Witte Aap BROWN CAFE

(Witte de Withstraat 78) Fine corner boozer that's always crowded with locals from this artist-filled 'hood. The front opens right up and a huge awning keeps inclement weather at bay.

★ Entertainment

Rotterdam draws clubgoers from across Europe.

TOP CHOICE Corso CLUB

(www.corsorotterdam.nl; Kruiskade 22) This is where it's at: bleeding-edge local and international DJs mashing up a high-fibre electronic diet of bleeps 'n' beats. Art displays provide diversions at this prototypical Rotterdam club.

TOP CHOICE De Unie VENUE

(www.deunie.nu; Mauritsweg 35) Truly cultural, this venue is a vision in white, which provides a blank slate for events from cabaret to

TRAINS FROM ROTTERDAM

DESTINATION	PRICE (€)	DURATION (MIN)	FREQUENCY (HOURLY)
Amsterdam via Leiden	14	65	5
Amsterdam (high speed)	16-21	43	2
Brussels (Belgium)	22-62	70-76	1-2
Schiphol Amsterdam Airport	11-14	25-50	4-5
Utrecht	10	40	4

forums about taxation and the middle class to acoustic folk. The cafe has excellent food.

Gay Palace CLUB
(www.gay-palace.nl; Schiedamsesingel 139) Rotterdam's only weekly gay nightclub, with four floors of throbbing gay action – with different scenes on each floor – to work you into a lather and get you sweaty.

Nemo COFFEE SHOP
(www.coffeeshop-nemo.nl; Nieuwe Binnenweg 181) Disney would not approve of the logo at this slick yet cheery shop. Browse the 15 kinds of weed on offer before you visit.

Information

Tourist Office (VVV; 790 01 40; www.rotterdam.info;) Free internet. The **main city branch** (Coolsingel 197; 9am-6pm Mon-Fri, to 5pm Sat & Sun) is located in the City Information Centre, with a good display on architecture since the war and a huge town model. A second location is near the train station in the landmark **Groothandelsgebouw** (Weena; 9am-5.30pm Mon-Sat, 10am-5pm Sun). There are excellent walking guides.

Use-It (www.use-it.nl; Schaatsbaan 41-45; 9am-6pm Tue-Sun mid-May–mid-Sep, to 5pm Tue-Sat mid-Sep–mid-May;) Offbeat independent tourist organisation just west of the station. Books cheap accommodation and publishes the invaluable *Simply the Best* local guide.

Getting There & Away

Rotterdam Centraal Station is a new architectural stunner that will be fully open in 2014.

Getting Around

Rotterdam's trams, buses and metro are provided by **RET** (www.ret.nl). Most converge in front of CS, where there is an **information booth** (7am-7pm) that also sells tickets. Day passes are sold for varying durations: 1/2/3 days costs €7/10.50/14. A single-ride ticket purchased from a bus driver or tram conductor costs €3.

Utrecht

030 / POP 317,000

Utrecht is one of the Netherlands' oldest cities and boasts a beautiful, vibrant, old-world city centre, ringed by striking 13th-century canal wharves. The wharves, well below street level, are unique to Utrecht. Canalside streets alongside brim with shops, restaurants and cafes.

Initial impressions may be less auspicious. When you step off the train you'll find yourself lost in the maze that is the Hoog Catharijne shopping centre. The Hoog is huge...and it's attached to the station...and it seemingly goes on forever...and ever. It's really a nightmare but a vast construction project (www.nieuwhc.nl) is transforming the entire area.

The city's student community of 40,000 is the largest in the country. Saturdays are mad with shoppers and day trippers in from every polder in the region. In contrast, Sunday mornings are a fab time to immerse yourself in the moody charms of empty streets echoing with church bells.

Sights

Focus your wanderings on the **Domplein** and south along the tree-lined **Oudegracht**. The tourist office has a good booklet that covers Utrecht's myriad small museums, which feature everything from waste water to old trains.

Domtoren HISTORIC BUILDING
(Cathedral Tower; www.domtoren.nl; Domplein; adult/child €9/5; 11am-4pm) The Domtoren is 112m high, with 465 steps and 50 bells. It's a tough haul to the top but well worth the exertion, given that the tower gives unbeatable city views; on a clear day you can see Amsterdam. The guided tour, in Dutch and English, is detailed and gives privileged insight into this beautiful structure.

Finished in the 14th century, the cathedral and its tower are the most striking medieval landmarks in a city that once had 40 cathedrals. Appreciate the craft: it took almost 300 years to complete. In 1674 the North Sea winds reached hurricane force and blew down the cathedral's nave, leaving the tower and transept behind.

Centraal Museum MUSEUM
(www.centraalmuseum.nl; Nicolaaskerkhof 10; adult/child €9/4; ⏲11am-5pm Tue-Sun; 📶) The Centraal Museum has a wide-ranging collection. It displays applied arts dating back to the 17th century, as well as paintings by some of the Utrecht School artists and a bit of De Stijl to boot – including the world's most extensive Gerrit Rietveld collection. Admission here includes the Dick Bruna House and Rietveld-Schröderhuis.

Dick Bruna House
(www.dickbrunahuis.nl; Nicolaaskerkhof 10; ⏲11am-5pm Tue-Sun) One of Utrecht's favourite sons, author and illustrator Dick Bruna is the creator of beloved cartoon rabbit Miffy and she naturally takes pride of place at his studio across from the museum.

Rietveld-Schröderhuis
(☎reservations 236 23 10; Prins Hendriklaan 50; admission surcharge €3; ⏲11am-5pm Wed-Sun) This Unesco-recognised landmark house is just outside the city centre. Built in 1924 by Utrecht architect Gerrit Rietveld, it is a stark example of 'form follows function'. Visits are by mandatory tour, which should be booked in advance at Centraal Museum (see website for details); the museum will give you a map for the pleasant 25-minute stroll to the house or loan you a free bike.

Sleeping

B&B Utrecht GUESTHOUSE €
(☎06 5043 4884; www.hostelutrecht.nl; Lucas Bolwerk 4; dm/r from €21/60; @📶) Straddling the border between hostel and hotel, this spotless inn located in an elegant old building has an internal Ikea vibe. Breakfast, lunch and dinner ingredients are free! Internet access (in a computer room with scanners, printers etc) is also free, as is use of a huge range of musical instruments and DVDs.

Strowis Budget Hostel HOSTEL €
(☎238 02 80; www.strowis.nl; Boothstraat 8; dm from €18, r €65; @📶) This beautiful 17th-century building near the town centre has been lovingly restored and converted into a hostel (four- to 14-bed rooms). It has a fine rear garden and rents bikes.

Eating & Drinking

When Utrecht groans with visiting mobs, you can escape down to the waterside canal piers with a picnic.

Florin BROWN CAFE €
(www.florinutrecht.nl; Nobelstraat 2-4; mains €9-15) Battered benches and scarred wooden tables are the hallmarks of a good brown cafe and Florin nicely fits the bill. There's more emphasis on food here than at some brown cafes, but the burgers, salads and more on the menu appeal to scores of students nightly.

't Oude Pothuys BROWN CAFE
(Oudegracht 279) Small and dark, this basement pub has nightly music – jam sessions with locals trying their hand at rock and jazz. Enjoy drinks on the canalside pier.

TOP CHOICE **ACU** BAR
(www.acu.nl; Voorstraat 71) Billing itself as a 'political cultural centre', ACU is a classic student dive. It combines bar, venue, lecture hall and more. Argue about whether Trotsky was too conservative while downing organic vegan food.

OTHER DUTCH TOWNS WORTH A VISIT

Some cities and towns in the Netherlands you may wish to consider for day trips or longer visits:

Alkmaar Massively touristy, but its cheese ceremony dates back to the 17th century.

Deventer A sleepy Hanseatic League town with over 1000 16th- and 17th-century buildings.

Dordrecht A good day trip by fast ferry from Rotterdam, known for its medieval canals.

Gouda The perfect little Dutch town, replicated in many places across the Netherlands.

Texel Largest of the Frisian Islands, it boasts endless walks along dune-backed beaches and excellent local seafood.

DON'T MISS

HOGE VELUWE NATIONAL PARK

Hoge Veluwe (www.hogeveluwe.nl; adult/child/car €8.20/4.10/6; ⏲8am-9pm or later Apr-Aug, 9am-6pm or later Sep-Mar) is the Netherlands' largest national park, featuring a mix of forests and woods, shifting sands and heathery moors, along with red deer, wild boar and mouflon (wild sheep).

It features the world-class **Kröller-Müller Museum** (☎0318-59 12 41; www.kmm.nl; Houtkampweg 6; park admission plus adult/child €8.20/4.10; ⏲10am-5pm Tue-Sun), which has a superb collection of works by Van Gogh, as well as pieces by Picasso, Renoir and Manet.

From Arnhem train station (Utrecht to Arnhem by train: €10, 37 minutes, four per hour), take bus 21 (20 minutes, every 30 minutes) to the Schaarsbergen park entrance (stop: Museum 40 45). Various buses run inside the park to the museum or you can ride one of the famous free white bikes.

Information

Tourist Office (VVV; ☎0900 128 87 32; www.utrechtyourway.nl; Domplein 9; ⏲noon-5pm Sun & Mon, 10am-5pm Tue-Sat) Sells maps and tours of the nearby Domtoren.

Getting There & Away

Utrecht is easily walked (once you escape the shopping mall). The train station, which is in the process of being replaced, is a major connection point and is Holland's busiest. It is on the line linking Amsterdam to Cologne. Sample fares include Amsterdam (€7, 30 minutes, four per hour), Maastricht (€24, two hours, two per hour) and Rotterdam (€10, 40 minutes, four per hour).

THE SOUTH

Actual hills are found on the southern edge of the Netherlands, where Belgium and Germany are within range of a tossed wooden shoe. The not-miss-star here is Maastricht.

Maastricht

☎043 / POP 121,000

The Netherlands' other great old city couldn't be further from Amsterdam and the pearls of the Randstad and still be in the country. Granted, Maastricht sits on a little geographic appendage dangling down like an appendix but it is well worth the time to journey here from the northwest (and you can easily continue on to Belgium and Germany).

Among the 1650 listed historic buildings, look for Spanish and Roman ruins, French and Belgian twists in the architecture, splendid food and the small-town cosmopolitan flair that made Maastricht a natural location for the signing of the namesake treaty, which created the modern EU in 1992.

Sights & Activities

Maastricht's delights are scattered along both banks of the Maas. The best approach is to just start strolling. The city's ruins, old fortifications, museums and cafes (and the odd surprise) reward walkers. **Onze Lieve Vrouweplein** is an intimate cafe-filled square named after its church, which still attracts pilgrims. The busy pedestrian **Sint Servaasbrug** dates from the 13th century and links Maastricht's centre with the Wyck district.

Bonnefantenmuseum ART MUSEUM
(www.bonnefantenmuseum.nl; Ave Cèramique 250; adult/child €9/free; ⏲11am-5pm Tue-Sun) This museum features a 28m tower that's a local landmark. Old Masters and medieval sculpture are on one floor, contemporary art by Limburg artists on the next. Make time for the world-class Neuteling collection of medieval art.

Vrijthof SQUARE
This large square, a focal point of Maastricht, is surrounded by grand cafes, museums and churches.

Sint Servaasbasiliek CHURCH
(www.sintservaas.nl; adult/child €4/free; ⏲10am-4.30pm) Sint Servaasbasiliek, a pastiche of architecture dating from 1000, dominates the Vrijthof. The **Treasury** is filled with gold artwork from the 12th century.

Sleeping

TOP CHOICE **Eden Designhotel Maastricht** HOTEL €
(☎328 25 25; www.edendesignhotel.com; Stationsstraat 40; r incl breakfast €80-160; ❄@📶) O

the main drag running from the train station to the centre, this regal old hotel has been given a shot of youth and tarted up for a sprightly future. The 105 rooms have stark style with bold colours and details set against hardwood floors.

Hotel Holla HOTEL €
(☎321 35 23; www.hotelholla.nl; Boschstraat 104-106; r €65-100; @📶) In an elegant 1855 building, the 24 rooms here are smartly decorated and feature stylish linens. Adding to the fine value is the ground-floor cafe, which serves excellent coffee in stylish surrounds.

Stayokay Maastricht HOSTEL €
(☎750 17 90; www.stayokay.com/maastricht; Maasboulevard 101; dm/r from €22/60; @📶) A stunner of a hostel with a large terrace right on the Maas. Choose from one of the 199 beds in dorms and private rooms. It's just south of the centre in a park.

Eating & Drinking

Excellent restaurants are even more common than old fortifications in Maastricht.

TOP CHOICE **Gadjah Mas** INDONESIAN €€
(www.gadjahmas.nl; Rechtstraat 42; mains €17-25; ⏲5-10pm) The Rechtstraat, east of the river, is one of the best streets for dining in Maastricht. This small, lovely Indonesian bistro has *rijsttafels* (array of spicy dishes served with rice) that break with the clichéd norm.

Reitz FRITES €
(Markt 75; frites €2; ⏲11am-6pm Tue-Sun) Join the queue for this iconic French-fries counter, which has been serving perfectly scrumptious *frites* under the classic neon sign for decades.

TOP CHOICE **Take One** BROWN CAFE
(www.takeonebiercafe.nl; Rechtstraat 28) Cramped and narrow from the outside, this 1930s tavern has well over 100 beers from the most obscure parts of the Benelux. It's run by a husband-and-wife team who help you select the beer most appropriate to your taste.

EDD's GRAND CAFE
(www.edds-cafe.nl; Heggenstraat 3; mains €12-25; ⏲11am-2am) The acronym says it all: Eat, Drink and Dance. Match your mood to that of this humble-looking side-street cafe with a striking post-industrial interior.

Information

Tourist Office (VVV; ☎043 325 21 21; www.vvvmaastricht.nl; Kleine Straat 1; ⏲9am-6pm Mon-Fri, to 5pm Sat year-round, 11am-3pm Sun May-Oct) In the 15th-century Dinghuis; offers excellent walking-tour brochures.

Getting There & Away

Regular trains link Maastricht to Brussels (€30, 1½ hours) via Liege; with connections, Cologne (€25) is two hours away. Other routes include Amsterdam (€24, 2½ hours, two per hour) and Utrecht (€23, 2 hours, two per hour).

UNDERSTAND THE NETHERLANDS

History

Early Dutch history was bound with Belgium and Luxembourg – the three were known as the Low Countries until the 16th century.

The Netherlands' Golden Age lasted from about 1580 to 1740. The era's wealth was generated by the Dutch East India Company, which travelled to the Far East for spices and other exotic goods, colonised the Cape of Good Hope and Indonesia, and established trading posts throughout Asia.

In 1795 the French invaded. When the occupation ended in 1815, the United Kingdom of the Netherlands – incorporating Belgium and Luxembourg – was the result.

In 1830 the Belgians rebelled and became independent, and Luxembourg followed nine years later.

The Netherlands stayed neutral in WWI and tried to repeat the feat in WWII, only to be invaded by the Germans. The country was devastated and most of its Jewish population was murdered.

In 1953 a high spring tide and severe storm breached Zeeland's dikes, drowning 1835 people. A massive engineering project, the Delta Project, was built to prevent the tragedy from happening again.

In the 1960s Amsterdam became Europe's radical heart, giving rise to the squatter's movement and the sexual freedom that lingers still. Cannabis was decriminalised in 1976, and in 2003 the Netherlands became the first country in the world to legalise prescriptions of medicinal cannabis.

In 1992 members of the European community assembled in Maastricht to sign the treaty that created the EU.

A year later, the Netherlands regulated doctor-assisted euthanasia, and in 2000 it was legalised under stringent guidelines – again, the first country to do so. That year the Netherlands also became the first nation to legalise same-sex marriages.

As the Netherlands has become ever more crowded, immigration has become a political hot potato. In 2002 right-wing politician Pim Fortuyn, an advocate of zero immigration, was shot dead a few days before the Dutch general election.

In 2004 there was another high-profile assassination. Theo van Gogh, an inflammatory right-wing film-maker and columnist, was killed in Amsterdam; the murderer was a Moroccan Muslim.

The famously tolerant Dutch have moved to the right somewhat in recent years, although the centre again was dominant in 2012 elections. Questions about the Dutch commitment to the EU were quieted by a strong showing by pro-EU politicians.

Legal efforts to close and restrict the nation's famous coffee shops and their sales of pot all but ended after initial efforts in Maastricht and other southern areas caused numerous problems (open street dealing of drugs returned etc). Polls showed that the Dutch public (barely 5% of which use pot) largely disliked the laws and that the requirement for locals to register to enter the surviving coffee shops was particularly hated because of privacy concerns.

The big royal news in 2013 was the abdication after 33 years of Queen Beatrix, in favour of her son Willem-Alexander. The official handover was on 30 April, and thus the often raucous celebrations of Queen's Day became King's Day.

Arts

The Netherlands claims a superb artistic heritage: many non-Dutch would be able to name at least one famous Dutch painter.

From the 15th century, Hieronymus Bosch's nightmarish works can be seen as an antecedent of surrealism. During the Golden Age, Rembrandt (1606–69) emerged with the brightest glow of all, creating shimmering religious scenes, in-demand portraits and contemplative landscapes. Frans Hals (1582–1666) captured his subjects in unguarded moments, and Jan Vermeer (1632–75) concentrated on everyday occurrences in middle-class homes, giving a proto-cinematographic quality to his compositions.

Vincent van Gogh's (1853–90) revolutionary use of colour, coarse brushwork and layered contours established him on a higher plane than his contemporaries, yet he only sold one work while alive. A bit later, Piet Mondrian (1872–1944), along with Theo van Doesburg, founded the De Stijl movement; his style of abstract rectangular compositions came to be known as neoplasticism.

MC Escher's (1902–72) graphic art still has uncanny power: a waterfall simultaneously flows up and down; a building folds in on itself. It's popular with mathematicians and stoners alike.

Food & Drink

The Dutch consume almost 17kg of cheese per person per year (nearly two-thirds of it is Gouda). Seafood is found at street stalls, including raw, slightly salted herring cut into bite-sized pieces and served with onion and pickles. Smoked eel and *kibbeling* (deep-fried cod pieces) are also popular.

Munchies are squelched around the clock at fast-food joints such as Febo, where deep-fried snacks sing their siren song from behind coin-operated doors.

Lager beer is the staple drink, served cool and topped by a big head of froth. More bars are serving interesting beers from a growing number of small Dutch and Belgian brewers. Look for hoppy Jopen from Haarlem.

Quaff beers at a cosy *bruin café* (brown cafe) – the name comes from smoke stains on the walls, although pretenders make do with brown paint. The best ooze the uniquely Dutch concept of *gezelligheld*, which is one of those words that defies easy translation but which combines cosy, fun and quaint with an overlay of familiarity and good cheer.

SURVIVAL GUIDE

Directory A–Z

Accommodation

Always book accommodation ahead, especially during high season; note that many visitors choose to stay in Amsterdam even if travelling elsewhere. The tourist offices operate booking services; when booking for two, make it clear whether you want two single (twin) beds or a double bed.

Many Dutch hotels have steep, perilous stairs but no lifts, although most top-end and some midrange hotels are exceptions.

Lists of camping grounds are available from the tourist offices. Expect to pay roughly €10 to €20 for two people and a tent overnight, plus €3 to €6 for a car. The camping grounds have plenty of caravan hook-ups.

Stayokay (www.stayokay.com) is the Dutch hostelling association. A youth-hostel card costs €15 at the hostels; nonmembers pay an extra €2.50 per night and after six nights you become a member. The usual HI discounts apply.

PRICE RANGES

Prices quoted here include private bathrooms unless otherwise stated and are high-season rates. Breakfast is not included unless specified. Most rooms are nonsmoking.

€ less than €80

€€ €80 to €160

€€€ more than €160

Business Hours

Banks 9.30am to 4pm Monday to Friday

Bars and cafes 11am to 1am

Clubs Mostly 10pm to 4am

Museums Most closed Monday

Post offices 9am to 6pm Monday to Friday

Restaurants 10am or 11am to 10pm, with a break between 3pm and 6pm

Shops Noon to 6pm Monday, 9am to 6pm Tuesday to Saturday (also Sunday in large cities), to 9pm Thursday; supermarkets to 8pm

Discount Cards

Museumkaart (Museum Card; www.museumkaart.nl; adult/child €45/22.50, plus €5 for first-time registrants) offers free and discounted entry to some 400 museums all over the country for one year. Purchase at museum ticket counters or at Uitburo ticket shops.

Embassies & Consulates

Australian Embassy (☎070-310 82 00; www.netherlands.embassy.gov.au; Carnegielaan 4, Den Haag)

Canadian Embassy (☎070-311 16 00; www.netherlands.gc.ca; Sophialaan 7, Den Haag)

New Zealand Embassy (☎070-346 93 24; www.nzembassy.com; Eisenhowerlaan 77, Den Haag)

UK Embassy (☎070-427 04 27; www.britain.nl; Lange Voorhout 10, Den Haag)

UK Consulate (☎020-676 43 43; www.britain.nl; Koningslaan 44, Amsterdam)

US Embassy (☎070-310 22 09; http://thehague.usembassy.gov; Lange Voorhout 102, Den Haag)

US Consulate (☎020-575 53 09; http://amsterdam.usconsulate.gov; Museumplein 19, Amsterdam)

Food

The following price categories are for the cost of a main course.

€ less than €12

€€ €12 to €25

€€€ more than €25

Legal Matters

Drugs are actually illegal in the Netherlands. Possession of soft drugs up to 5g is tolerated but larger amounts can get you jailed. Hard drugs are treated as a serious crime.

Smoking is banned in all public places, including most bars (except for tiny family-run pubs). In a uniquely Dutch solution, you can still smoke pot in coffee shops as long as there's no tobacco mixed in.

Money

Automatic teller machines can be found outside banks and at train stations.

All major international cards are recognised, and you will find that most hotels, restaurants and major stores accept them (although *not* the Dutch railway). But always check first to avoid, as they say, disappointment.

TIPPING

Tipping is not essential as restaurants, hotels, bars etc include a service charge on their bills. A little extra is always welcomed though, and it's an excellent way to compliment the service (if you feel it needs complimenting). The tip can be anything from rounding up to the nearest euro or adding on 10% of the bill.

Public Holidays

Nieuwjaarsdag (New Year's Day) 1 January

Goede Vrijdag (Good Friday) March/April

Eerste Paasdag (Easter Sunday) March/April

Tweede Paasdag (Easter Monday) March/April

Koningsdag (King's Day) 27 April

Bevrijdingsdag (Liberation Day) 5 May

Hemelvaartsdag (Ascension Day) May

Eerste Pinksterdag (Whit Sunday; Pentecost) May/June

Tweede Pinksterdag (Whit Monday) May/June

Eerste Kerstdag (Christmas Day) 25 December

Tweede Kerstdag (Boxing Day) 26 December

Safe Travel

The Netherlands is a safe country, but be sensible and *always* lock your bike. Never buy drugs on the street: you'll get ripped off or mugged and it's illegal. And don't light up joints just anywhere – stick to coffee shops.

Telephone

Most public phones will accept credit cards as well as various phonecards.

Country code ☎31

Collect call (gesprek) domestic ☎0800 01 01; international ☎0800 04 10

International access code ☎00

International directory enquiries ☎0900 84 18

National directory enquiries ☎1888

Operator assistance ☎0800 04 10

Getting There & Away

Air

Huge **Schiphol Airport** (www.schiphol.nl) is the Netherlands' main international airport. **Rotterdam Airport** (www.rotterdamthehagueairport.nl) and **Eindhoven Airport** (www.eindhovenairport.nl) are small.

Land

BUS

The most extensive European bus network is maintained by **Eurolines** (www.eurolines.com). It offers a variety of passes with prices that vary by time of year.

CAR & MOTORCYCLE

You'll need the vehicle's registration papers, third-party insurance and an international driver's permit in addition to your domestic licence. The national auto club, **ANWB** (www.anwb.nl), has offices across the country and will provide info if you can show an auto-club card from your home country (eg AAA in the US or AA in the UK).

TRAIN

The Netherlands has good train links to Germany, Belgium and France. All Eurail, Inter-Rail, Europass and Flexipass tickets are valid on the Dutch national train service, **Nederlandse Spoorwegen** (Netherlands Railway, NS; www.ns.nl). Many international services, including those on the high-speed line to Belgium, are operated under the **Hispeed** (www.nshispeed.nl) and **Fyra** (www.fyra.com) brands. In addition, **Thalys** (www.thalys.com) fast trains serve Brussels (where you can connect to Eurostar) and Paris. Major Dutch train stations have international ticket offices and, in peak periods, it's wise to reserve seats in advance.

Finally open (years late and far over budget), the high-speed line from Amsterdam (via Schipol and Rotterdam) speeds travel times to Antwerp (70 minutes), Brussels (two hours) and Paris (3¼ hours).

German ICE high-speed trains run six times a day between Amsterdam and Cologne (2½ hours) via Utrecht. Many continue on to Frankfurt (four hours) via Frankfurt Airport.

Sea

There are several companies operating car and passenger ferries between the Netherlands and the UK:

DFDS Seaways (www.dfds.co.uk) Sails between Newcastle and IJmuiden (15 hours), which is close to Amsterdam.

P&O Ferries (www.poferries.com) Runs an overnight ferry every evening (11 hours) between Hull and Europoort (near Rotterdam).

Stena Line (www.stenaline.co.uk) Sails between Harwich and Hoek van Holland (3¾ to 6¼ hours).

Getting Around

Boat

Ferries connect the mainland with the five Frisian Islands, including Texel. Other ferries span the Westerschelde in the south of Zeeland, providing road links to the bit of the Netherlands south of here as well as to Belgium. These are popular with people using the Zeebrugge ferry terminal and run frequently year-round.

Car & Motorcycle

HIRE

Outside Amsterdam, car-hire companies can be in inconvenient locations if you're arriving by train. You must be at least 23 years of age to hire a car in the Netherlands. Some car-hire firms levy a small surcharge for drivers under 25.

ROAD RULES

Traffic travels on the right and the minimum driving age is 18 for vehicles and 16 for motorcycles. Seat belts are required and children under 12 must ride in the back if there's room. Trams always have the right of way and, if turning right, bikes have priority.

Speed limits are 50km/h in built-up areas, 80km/h in the country, 100km/h on major through-roads, and 120km/h on freeways (sometimes 100km/h, clearly indicated). Hidden speeding cameras are everywhere and they will find you through your rental car company.

Public Transport

National public transport info is available in English by phone (☎0900 9292) and on the web (www.9292ov.nl). There is also an excellent smartphone app.

The universal form of transport payment in the Netherlands, the **OV-chipkaart** (www.ov chipkaart.nl; €2.70, good for one hour) is a smartcard that you use in place of cash. Visitors can buy one from vending machines in stations or at ticket windows. Each card stores the value of your payment and deducts the cost of trips as you use it. Refill from machines or ticket windows (although the latter are often thronged).

When you enter and exit a bus, tram or train, you hold the card against a reader at the doors or station gates. The system then calculates your fare and deducts it from the card. Fares for the chip cards are much lower than a ticket bought from the driver or conductor. You can also buy OV-chipkaarts

THE NETHERLANDS BY BIKE

The Netherlands has more than 20,000km of dedicated **bike paths** *(fietspaden)*, which makes it the most bike-friendly place on the planet. You can criss-cross the country on the motorways of cycling: the **LF routes**. Standing for *landelijke fietsroutes* (long-distance routes), but virtually always simply called LF, there are more than 25 routes comprising close to 7000km. All are well marked by distinctive green-and-white signs.

The best overall maps are the widely available Falk/VVV *Fietskaart met Knooppuntennetwerk* (cycling network) maps, a series of 20 that blanket the country in 1:50,000 scale, and cost €8. The keys are in English and they are highly detailed and very easy to use. Every bike lane, path and other route is shown, along with distances.

Bike Rentals

Independent rental shops are available in abundance. Many day trippers avail themselves of the train-station bicycle shops, called **Rijwiel shops** (www.ov-fiets.nl), which are found in more than 100 stations. Operating long hours (6am to midnight is common), the shops hire out bikes from €3 to €12 per day, with discounts by the week. You'll have to show an ID and leave a deposit (usually €25 to €100). The shops also usually offer repairs, sell new bikes and have cheap secured bike parking.

On Trains

You may bring your bicycle onto any train as long as there is room; a day pass is required for bicycles (*dagkaart fiets;* €6).

TRAINS & TRIBULATIONS

Buying a train ticket is the hardest part of riding Dutch trains. Among the challenges:

» Only some ticket machines accept cash, and those are coins-only, so you need a pocketful of change.

» Ticket machines that accept plastic will not work with credit and debit cards without embedded chips. The exceptions are a limited number of machines at Schiphol Airport and Amsterdam Centraal.

» Ticket windows do not accept credit or debit cards, although they will accept paper euros. Lines are often quite long and there is a surcharge for the often-unavoidable need to use a ticket window.

» Discounted tickets for Hispeed and Fyra trains sold on the web require a Dutch credit card. The cheap fares can't be bought at ticket windows.

» The much-hyped Voordeelurenabonnement (Off-Peak Discount Pass) yields good discounts but only if you have a Dutch bank account.

good for unlimited use for one or more days and this is often the most convenient option.

Train

The train network is run by **NS** (www.ns.nl). First-class sections are barely different from 2nd-class areas, but they are less crowded. Trains are fast and frequent and serve most places of interest. Distances are short. Most train stations have lockers operated by credit cards (average cost €5).

TICKETS

Enkele reis One way; you can break your journey along the direct route.

Dagretour Day return; 10% to 15% cheaper than two one-way tickets.

Weekendretour Weekend return; costs the same as a normal return and is valid from 7pm Friday to 4am Monday.

Dagkaart Day pass; allows unlimited train travel throughout the country. Only good value if you're planning to spend the day on the train.

Poland

Includes »

Warsaw ... 818
Kraków ... 824
Lublin ... 832
Zamość ... 834
Carpathian Mountains ... 835
Zakopane ... 835
Tatra Mountains ... 836
Wrocław ... 836
Poznań ... 839
Gdańsk ... 841
Toruń ... 845
Great Masurian Lakes .. 847
Understand Poland ... 847
Survival Guide ... 848

Best Places to Eat

- » Glonojad (p830)
- » Milkbar (p830)
- » Bernard (p838)
- » Cô tú (p821)
- » Masala (p846)

Best Places to Stay

- » Hostel Mleczarnia (p837)
- » 3 City Hostel (p843)
- » Mama's Hostel (p829)
- » Oki Doki Hostel (p819)
- » Green Hostel (p846)

Why Go?

If they were handing out prizes for 'most eventful history', Poland would be sure to get a medal. The nation has spent centuries at the pointy end of history, grappling with war and invasion. Nothing, however, has succeeded in suppressing the Poles' strong sense of nationhood and cultural identity. As a result, centres such as bustling Warsaw and cultured Kraków exude a sophisticated energy that's a heady mix of old and new.

Away from the cities, Poland is a diverse land, from its northern beaches to its magnificent southern mountains. In between are towns and cities dotted with ruined castles, picturesque squares and historic churches.

Although prices have steadily risen in the postcommunist era, Poland is still good value for travellers. As the Polish people work on combining their distinctive national identity with their place in the heart of Europe, it's a fascinating time to visit this beautiful country.

When to Go

Warsaw

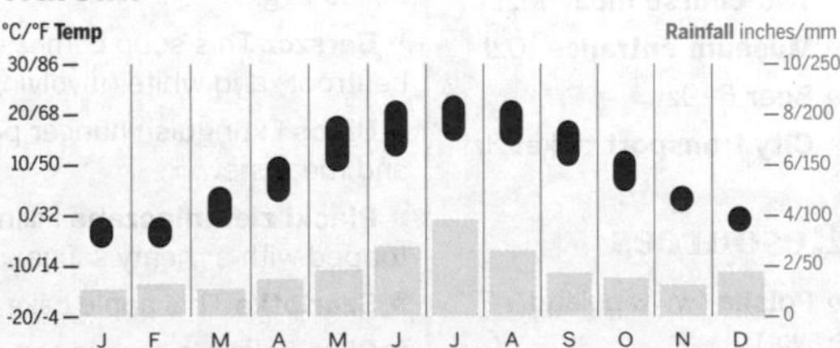

May & Jun Hit the bars and museums of lively Kraków before it's swamped by the summer crowds.

Jul & Aug Check out the beaches on Poland's long, sandy Baltic coast.

Sep Walk in the Tatra Mountains, bedding down in a cosy hikers' refuge.

AT A GLANCE

» **Currency** Złoty (zł)

» **Language** Polish

» **Money** ATMs all over; banks open Monday to Friday

» **Visas** Not required for citizens of the EU, UK, Canada, New Zealand and Australia

Fast Facts

» **Area** 312,685 sq km

» **Capital** Warsaw

» **Country code** ☎48

» **Emergency** Ambulance ☎999, fire ☎998, police ☎997

Exchange Rates

Australia	A$1	3.42zł
Canada	C$1	3.22zł
Euro Zone	€1	4.18zł
Japan	¥100	3.47zł
New Zealand	NZ$1	2.74zł
UK	UK£1	4.95zł
USA	US$1	3.27zł

Set Your Budget

» **Budget hotel room** 200zł

» **Two-course meal** 50zł

» **Museum entrance** 10zł

» **Beer** 6–9zł

» **City transport ticket** 3zł

Resources

» **Polska** (www.poland.travel)

» **Poland.pl** (www.poland.pl)

Connections

Due to its central position, Poland offers plenty of possibilities for onward travel. The country is well connected by train: there are direct services to Berlin from both Warsaw (via Poznań) and Kraków; to Prague from Warsaw and Kraków; and to Kyiv in Ukraine from Warsaw and Kraków (via Lviv). Trains also link Warsaw to Minsk in Belarus and Moscow in Russia, and Gdańsk to Kaliningrad in Russia, as well as Berlin. International buses head in all directions, including eastward to the Baltic countries. From southern Zakopane, it's easy to hop to Slovakia via bus, or even minibus. And from the Baltic coast ports of Gdańsk, Gydnia and Świnoujście, ferries head to various ports in Denmark and Sweden.

ITINERARIES

One Week

Spend a day exploring Warsaw with a stroll around the Old Town and a stop at the Warsaw Rising Museum. The next day, head to historic Kraków for three days, visiting the beautiful Old Town, Wawel Castle, and the former Jewish district of Kazimierz. Take a day trip to Auschwitz-Birkenau, the former German concentration and extermination camp. Afterwards, head to Zakopane for two days for some mountain air.

Two Weeks

Follow the above itinerary, then on the eighth day travel to Wrocław for two days, visiting its unique panorama. Progress north to Gothic Toruń for a day, then onward to Gdańsk for two days, exploring the museums and bars of the Main Town and visiting the magnificent castle at nearby Malbork.

Essential Food & Drink

» **Żurek** This hearty sour soup includes sausage and hard-boiled egg.

» **Barszcz** This soup comes in two varieties: red (made from beetroot) and white (involving wheat flour and sausage).

» **Bigos** Extinguish hunger pangs with this thick sauerkraut and meat stew.

» **Placki ziemniaczane** Filling potato pancakes, often topped with a meaty sauce.

» **Szarlotka** This apple cake with cream is a Polish classic.

» **Piwo** Poland's beer is good, cold and inexpensive, and often served in colourful beer gardens.

» **Wódka** Try Poland's vodka plain, or ask for *myśliwska* (flavoured with juniper berries).

» **Sernik** Baked cheesecake, weighty but tasty.

» **Herbata z rumem** Tea with rum is the perfect pick-me-up after a heavy day of sightseeing.

Poland Highlights

1. Experience the beauty and history of Kraków's **Wawel Castle** (p824)
2. Hunt for **gnome statues** (p837) in the Old Town of Wrocław
3. Remember the victims of Nazi German genocide at former extermination camp **Auschwitz-Birkenau** (p825)
4. Soak up the cosmopolitan vibe of **Gdańsk** (p841)
5. Enjoy the skiing or hiking life at **Zakopane** (p835)
6. Discover Warsaw's tragic wartime history at the **Warsaw Rising Museum** (p819)

WARSAW

POP 1.7 MILLION

Warsaw (Warszawa in Polish, var-shah-va) may not be the prettiest of Poland's cities, but this bustling business centre is home to a dazzling array of dining options at very reasonable prices by western European standards.

It's true that the city can be hard work, its traffic-choked streets lined with uninspiring massive concrete buildings. However, look at Warsaw with a historic perspective – as a city that's survived everything fate could throw at it – and you'll see the capital in an entirely new light.

When you factor in its entertainment options, the beauty of its reconstructed Old Town and Royal Way, and the history represented by its former Jewish district and the Warsaw Rising Museum, what emerges is a complex city that well repays a visit.

Sights

OLD TOWN

Plac Zamkowy HISTORIC SQUARE
(Castle Square) This square is the gateway to the Old Town. Within it stands the **Monument to Sigismund III Vasa** (Plac Zamkowy), who moved the capital from Kraków to Warsaw in 1596.

Royal Castle CASTLE
(Plac Zamkowy 4; adult/concession 22/15zł; ⌚10am-4pm Mon-Sat, 11am-4pm Sun, closed Mon Oct-Apr) The highlight of the sumptuous rooms is the Senators' Antechamber, where landscapes of 18th-century Warsaw by Bernardo Bellotto (Canaletto's nephew) are on show.

Historical Museum of Warsaw MUSEUM
(www.mhw.pl; Rynek Starego Miasta 42; adult/concession 8/4zł; ⌚11am-6pm Tue & Thu, 10am-3.30pm Wed & Fri, 10.30am-4.30pm Sat & Sun) Off the magnificent **Rynek Starego Miasta** (Old Town Market Sq) is this institution devoted to Warsaw's tumultuous history. At noon it shows an English-language film depicting the wartime destruction of the city (admission 6zł).

Barbican FORTIFICATION
(ul Nowomiejska) Northwest of the Rynek Starego Miasta is this imposing fortification, a remnant of the medieval city walls.

Monument to the Warsaw Rising MONUMENT
(cnr ul Długa & ul Miodowa) West of the Old Town, this striking set of statuary honours the heroic Polish revolt against German rule in 1944.

ROYAL WAY (SZLAK KRÓLEWSKI)

This 4km historic route connects the Old Town with the modern city centre, and is served by bus 180.

TOP CHOICE **Chopin Museum** MUSEUM
(www.chopin.museum; ul Okólnik 1; adult/concession 22/13zł, free Tue; ⌚11am-8pm Tue-Sun) To learn about Poland's most renowned composer, check out this immersive audiovisual exhibition covering Chopin's work, possessions and his life in Paris. There are listening booths in the basement.

Saxon Gardens GARDENS
(⌚24hr) West of the Royal Way are these attractive gardens, at whose entrance stands the small but poignant **Tomb of the Unknown Soldier**. The ceremonial **changing of the guard** takes place at noon here on Sunday.

Łazienki Park GARDENS
(www.lazienki-krolewskie.pl; ul Agrykola; gardens free; ⌚dawn-dusk) This large, shady and popular park is best known for its 18th-century **Palace on the Water** (ul Agrykola 1; adult/concession 15/10zł, free Thu; ⌚9am-4pm Tue-Sun), which was the summer residence of Stanisław August Poniatowski, the last king of Poland. Also within the park is the **Old Orangery** (Łazienki Park; adult/student 10/5zł, free Thu; ⌚9am-4pm Tue-Fri), containing a sculpture gallery.

National Museum MUSEUM
(www.mnw.art.pl; Al Jerozolimskie 3; adult/concession 15/10zł, incl temporary exhibitions 20/15zł, free Tue; ⌚10am-6pm Tue-Sun) Contains Greek and Egyptian antiquities, Coptic frescos, medieval woodcarvings and Polish paintings. Look out for the surrealistic fantasies of Jacek Malczewski.

St Anne's Church CHURCH
(ul Krakowskie Przedmieście 68) Just south of the Royal Castle, this ornate 15th-century church has impressive views from its **tower** (adult/concession 5/4zł; ⌚11am-9pm May-Oct).

CITY CENTRE & AROUND

Palace of Culture & Science LANDMARK
(www.pkin.pl; Plac Defilad 1; ⌚9am-6pm) Massive, brooding and inescapable, this towering structure was built in the early 1950s as a 'gift of friendship' from the Soviet Union

(the kind of unwanted gift that's hard to hide away). The **observation terrace** (adult/concession 20/15zł) on the 30th floor provides a panoramic view.

Wilanów Park GARDENS
(www.wilanow-palac.pl; ul Wisłostrada; adult/concession 5/3zł, free Thu; ⌚9am-dusk) This magnificent park lies 6km southeast of Łazienki Park and contains the splendid **Wilanów Palace** (www.wilanow-palac.pl; adult/concession 20/15zł, free Sun; ⌚9.30am-4.30pm Mon-Sat, 10.30am-6.30pm Sun). The **Poster Museum** (www.postermuseum.pl; ul Kostki Potockiego 10/16; adult/student 10/7zł, free Mon; ⌚noon-4pm Mon, 10am-4pm Tue-Fri, 10am-6pm Sat & Sun) in the former royal stables exhibits Poland's world-renowned poster art. Take bus 116 or 180 from ul Nowy Świat or Al Ujazdowskie.

Warsaw Rising Museum MUSEUM
(www.1944.pl; ul Grzybowska 79; adult/concession 14/10zł, free Sun; ⌚8am-6pm Mon, Wed & Fri, 8am-8pm Thu, 10am-6pm Sat & Sun) This impressive museum commemorates Warsaw's insurrection against its Nazi occupiers in 1944, which was destined to end in defeat and destruction. The moving story of the rising is retold via photographs, exhibits and audiovisual displays. Catch trams 22 or 24 from Al Jerozolimskie, heading west.

FORMER JEWISH DISTRICT

The suburbs northwest of the Palace of Culture & Science were once predominantly inhabited by Jewish Poles.

Jewish Cemetery CEMETERY
(ul Okopowa 49/51; admission 4zł; ⌚10am-5pm Mon-Thu, 9am-1pm Fri, 11am-4pm Sun) Founded in 1806, Europe's largest Jewish resting place has more than 100,000 gravestones. Visitors must wear a head covering to enter. It's accessible from the Old Town on bus 180, heading north from ul Nowy Świat.

Ghetto Heroes Monument MONUMENT
(cnr ul Anielewicza & ul Zamenhofa) This monument remembers the victims of the Jewish ghetto, which was established here by the occupying Germans. It features pictorial plaques.

Museum of the History of Polish Jews MUSEUM
(www.jewishmuseum.org.pl; cnr ul Anielewicza & ul Zamenhofa; ⌚10am-6pm Wed-Mon) This new multimedia and education centre opened on the 70th anniversary of the Ghetto Uprising, in April 2013.

Pawiak Prison Museum MUSEUM
(ul Dzielna 24/26; adult/concession 6/4zł; ⌚10am-4pm Wed-Sun) Once a Gestapo prison during the Nazi German occupation, this institution now contains moving exhibits, including letters and other personal items.

Festivals & Events

Mozart Festival MUSIC
(www.operakameralna.pl; ⌚Jun/Jul)

Warsaw Summer Jazz Days MUSIC
(www.adamiakjazz.pl; ⌚Jul)

Street Art Festival THEATRE
(www.sztukaulicy.pl; ⌚Jul)

Warsaw Autumn International Festival of Contemporary Music MUSIC
(www.warsaw-autumn.art.pl; ⌚Sep)

Warsaw Film Festival FILM
(www.wff.pl; ⌚Oct)

Sleeping

Oki Doki Hostel HOSTEL €
(☎22 828 0122; www.okidoki.pl; Plac Dąbrowskiego 3; dm 39-93zł, s/d from 120/149zł; 📶) Each dorm is decorated thematically using the brightest paints available; try the communist (red with a big image of Lenin). The hostel also has a bar, a washing machine and a kitchen, and hires out bikes (28zł per day).

Nathan's Villa Hostel HOSTEL €
(☎22 622 2946; www.nathansvilla.com; ul Piękna 24/26; dm 47-60zł, r 175-205zł; 📶) Nathan's sunlit courtyard leads to well-organised dorms and comfortable private rooms. The kitchen is well set up and there's a laundry service.

WANT MORE?

For in-depth information, reviews and recommendations at your fingertips, head to the Apple App Store to purchase Lonely Planet's *Warsaw City Guide* and *Polish Phrasebook* iPhone apps.

Alternatively, head to www.lonelyplanet.com/poland/warsaw for planning advice, author recommendations, traveller reviews and insider tips.

Central Warsaw

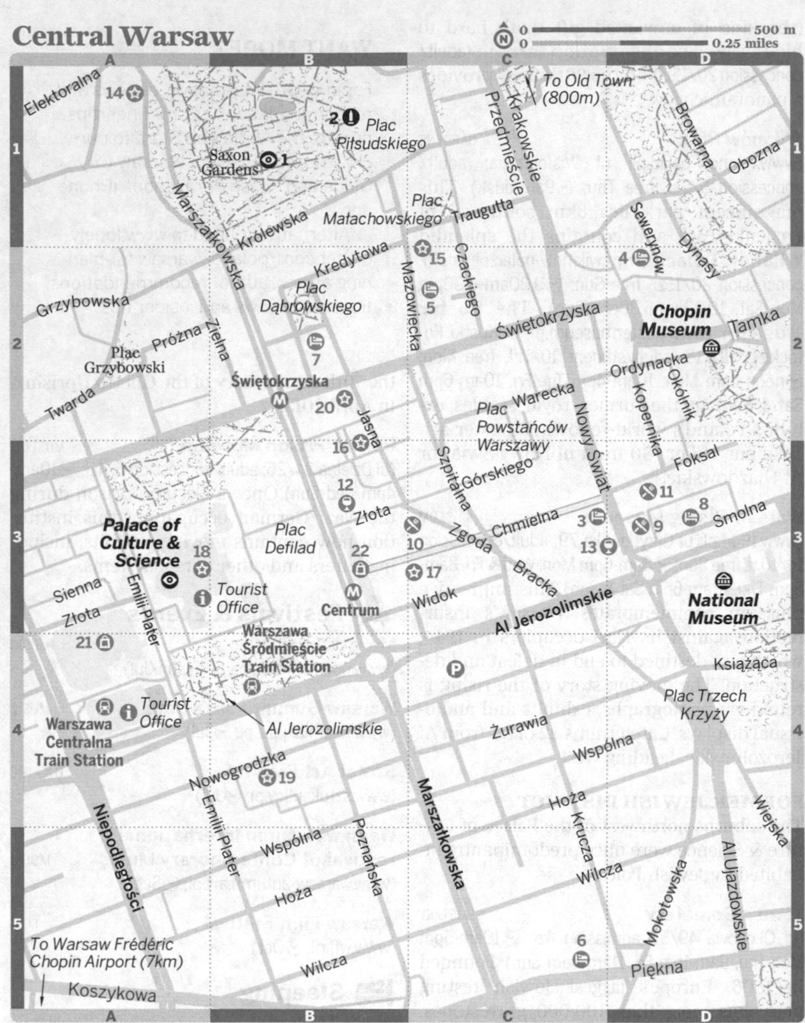

Apartments Apart APARTMENT €€
(☎22 351 2250; www.apartmentsapart.com; ul Nowy Świat 29/3; apt from €45;) Company offering a range of apartments dotted throughout the Old Town and city centre. Most include a washing machine in addition to a kitchen.

Hotel Premiere Classe HOTEL €€
(☎22 624 0800; www.premiere-classe-warszawa.pl; ul Towarowa 2; r 199zł;) Rooms are small but bright and neatly set up with modern furnishings. Catch tram 22 or 24 west from Al Jerozolimskie.

Hostel Helvetia HOSTEL €
(☎22 826 7108; www.hostel-helvetia.pl; ul Kopernika 36/40; dm/r 59/220zł;) Bright hostel with an attractive combined lounge and kitchen. There's one small women-only dorm. Bike hire is 30zł per day. Enter from the street behind, ul Sewerynów.

Hostel Kanonia HOSTEL €
(☎22 635 0676; www.kanonia.pl; ul Jezuicka 2; dm/s/d 45/90/160zł;) Housed in a historic building in the heart of the Old Town. Some rooms have picturesque views onto the cobblestone streets. There are basic kitchen facilities and a washing machine.

Central Warsaw

Top Sights
Chopin Museum ... D2
National Museum ... D3
Palace of Culture & Science ... A3

Sights
1 Saxon Gardens ... B1
2 Tomb of the Unknown Soldier ... B1

Sleeping
3 Apartments Apart ... C3
4 Hostel Helvetia ... D2
5 Hotel Mazowiecki ... C2
6 Nathan's Villa Hostel ... C5
7 Oki Doki Hostel ... B2
8 Smolna Youth Hostel ... D3

Eating
9 Cô tú ... D3
10 Krokiecik ... C3
11 Sketch ... D3

Drinking
12 Relax ... B3
13 Sense ... D3

Entertainment
14 Capitol ... A1
15 Enklawa ... C2
16 Filharmonia Narodowa ... B3
17 Kino Atlantic ... C3
18 Kinoteka ... A3
19 Teatr Roma ... B4
20 Underground Music Cafe ... B2

Shopping
21 Carrefour Supermarket ... A4
22 Wars & Sawa ... B3

Smolna Youth Hostel HOSTEL €
(☎22 827 8952; www.hostelsmolna30.pl; ul Smolna 30; dm/s/d 50/85/150zł; 📶) Very central and popular, though there's a midnight curfew (2am in July and August) and reception is closed between 10am and 4pm.

Majawa Motor Inn & Camping 123 CAMPGROUND €
(☎22 823 3748; www.astur.waw.pl; ul Bitwy Warszawskiej 1920r 15/17; campsite per person/tent 25/20zł, bungalows s/d from 50/80zł, hotel s/d from 70/120zł; 📶) Set in extensive grounds near the Dworzec Zachodnia bus station. The bungalows are available from mid-April to mid October. Catch tram 9 or 25 west from Al Jerozolimskie.

Hotel Mazowiecki HOTEL €€
(☎22 827 2365; www.hotelewam.pl; ul Mazowiecka 10; s/d from 160/200zł; 📶) One-star accommodation in a handy location on one of the city centre's nightlife strips. Most rooms have shared bathrooms.

Eating

Warsaw's eateries cover diverse cuisines and price ranges; a good selection can be found in the Old Town and around ul Nowy Świat.

Self-caterers can buy groceries at the **Carrefour Supermarket** (ul Złota 59) in the Złote Tarasy shopping centre behind Warszawa Centralna train station and at **ML Delikatesy** (ul Piwna 47) in the Old Town.

TOP CHOICE **Sketch** INTERNATIONAL €€
(ul Foksal 19; mains 12-41zł; ⏰8am-1am) Shiny bright restaurant and bar serving baguettes, salads, pasta and grilled dishes. There's lots of natural light and it's a great relaxed place for taking a break from sightseeing. Sharing plates come in Polish, Spanish and Italian variants.

Bar Mleczny Pod Barbakanem CAFETERIA €
(ul Mostowa 27/29; mains 5-9zł; ⏰8am-5pm Mon-Fri, from 9am Sat & Sun; 🚭) Near the Barbican, this popular former *bar mleczny* (milk bar) that survived the fall of the Iron Curtain continues to serve cheap, unpretentious food.

Podwale Piwna Kompania GRILL €€
(ul Podwale 25; mains 22-50zł; ⏰11am-1am Mon-Sat, noon-1am Sun) The 'Company of Beer' serves lots of grilled items and dishes such as roast duck, schnitzel, pork ribs and steak. There's a courtyard for outdoor dining.

Cô tú ASIAN €
(Hadlowo-Usługowe 21; mains 12-18zł; ⏰10am-9pm Mon-Fri, 11am-7pm Sat & Sun) The wok at this simple Asian diner never rests, cooking up seafood, vegetables, beef, chicken and pork. Duck through the archway at Nowy Świat 26 to find it.

Krokiecik CAFETERIA €
(ul Zgoda 1; mains 6-25zł) Attractive cafeteria serving a range of inexpensive and tasty

SPLURGE

The attractive **Restauracja Przy Zamku** (Plac Zamkowy 15; mains 38-120zł) has hunting trophies on the walls and attentive, white-aproned waiters. The top-notch Polish menu includes fish and game and a bewildering array of entrées – try the excellent hare pâté served with cranberry sauce.

dishes, including good soups. The house speciality is *krokiety* (filled savoury pancakes).

Drinking

TOP CHOICE **Polyester** CAFE-BAR

(ul Freta 49/51;) Fashionably retro; arguably the hippest cocktail bar in the vicinity of the Old Town. Serves excellent cocktails, as well as coffee and light food.

Relax CAFE-BAR

(ul Złota 8a; 8am-11pm Mon-Fri, 10.30am-11pm Sat & Sun;) Compact, friendly place with retro-grungy charm at the back of a derelict cinema building. Serves a range of Polish microbrewery beers.

Sense BAR

(ul Nowy Świat 19; noon-late;) A very modern venue with a mellow atmosphere. Try the house speciality, ginger rose vodka. There's also an impressive food menu.

Entertainment

Nightclubs

Enklawa CLUB

(www.enklawa.com; ul Mazowiecka 12; 9pm-4am Tue-Sat) Funky space with comfy plush seating, two bars and plenty of room to dance. Wednesday night is 'old-school' night, with music from the '70s and '80s.

Capitol CLUB

(ul Marszałkowska 115; 10pm-late Sat) Squeeze through the doors of this oh-so-cool club on the one night of the week it's open – Saturday. Low lighting gleams off pillars and retro decor.

Underground Music Cafe CLUB

(www.under.pl; ul Marszałkowska 126/134; 1pm-late) Students and backpackers love this basement club for its cheap beer, dark lighting and diverse music.

Performing Arts

Teatr Roma MUSICAL THEATRE

(22 628 8998; www.teatrroma.pl; ul Nowogrodzka 49) Theatre staging big-budget musicals sung in Polish, such as the ever-popular *Deszczowa Piosenka* (aka *Singin' in the Rain*).

Teatr Wielki OPERA

(22 692 0200; www.teatrwielki.pl; Plac Teatralny 1) The Grand Theatre hosts opera and ballet in its aptly grand premises.

Filharmonia Narodowa CLASSICAL MUSIC

(22 551 7111; www.filharmonia.pl; ul Jasna 5) Classical-music concerts are held here.

Cinema

Catch a film at the central **Kino Atlantic** (ul Chmielna 33) or at the **Kinoteka** (Plac Defilad 1) within the Palace of Culture & Science. English-language movies are subtitled in Polish.

Shopping

Wars & Sawa MALL

(ul Marszałowska 104/122) A sprawling modern shopping mall in the city centre.

Lapidarium JEWELLERY

(www.lapidarium.pl; ul Nowomiejska 15/7) One of the most interesting shops on the Rynek Starego Miasta; offers jewellery and communist-era collectables.

Information

Apteka Grabowskiego (Warszawa Centralna; 24hr) Pharmacy at the train station; open 24 hours.

Centrum Medyczne LIM (22 332 2888; www.cmlim.pl; Al Jerozolimskie 65/79, 3rd fl, Marriott Hotel) Offers specialist doctors, laboratory tests and house calls.

Tourist Office (22 19431; www.warsawtour.pl) Old Town (Rynek Starego Miasta 19; 9am-9pm May-Sep, 9am-7pm Oct-Apr); Royal Way (ul Krakowskie Przedmieście 15; 11am-8pm Tue-Sun); Palace of Culture & Science (Plac Defilad 1, Palace of Culture & Science; 8am-6pm); Warszawa Centralna train station (Al Jana Pawła II, Main hall, Warszawa Centralna train station; 8am-8pm May-Sep, 8am-7pm Oct-Apr); Okęcie airport (ul Żwirki i Wigury 1; 8am-8pm May-Sep, 8am-7pm Oct-Apr)

Verso Internet (ul Freta 17; 8am-8pm Mon-Fri, 9am-5pm Sat, 10am-4pm Sun) Enter from the rear, off ul Świętojerska.

Warsaw Point Gallery (ul Złota 59, Złote Tarasy; 9am-10pm) Pay at the information desk of this shopping mall.

Warsaw Tourist Card (www.warsawcard.com; 1/3 days 35/65zł) Free or discounted access to museums, public transport and some theatres, sports centres and restaurants. Available from tourist offices and some accommodation.

Warsaw Tourist Information Centre (☎22 635 1881; www.wcit.waw.pl; Plac Zamkowy 1/13; ⊙9am-6pm Mon-Fri, 10am-6pm Sat & Sun) Helpful privately run tourist office in the Old Town.

Getting There & Away

AIR The **Warsaw Frédéric Chopin airport** (www.lotnisko-chopina.pl; ul Żwirki i Wigury 1), 7km from the city centre, is more commonly called Okęcie airport. Domestic and international flights can be booked at the **LOT office** (☎0801 703 703; Al Jerozolimskie 65/79), or at any travel agency.

In 2012 a new low-cost airport, **Warsaw Modlin** (www.modlinairport.pl; ul Generała Wiktora Thommée 1a, Nowy Dwór Mazowiecki), opened 35km north of the city.

BUS Warsaw's major bus station is **Dworzec Zachodnia** (Western Bus Station; www.pks-bilety.pl; Al Jerozolimskie 144), southwest of the city centre and adjoining the Warszawa Zachodnia train station. Take the commuter train that leaves from Warszawa Śródmieście station. From here you can catch PKS buses in every direction.

Services run by the private company **Polski Bus** (www.polskibus.com) depart from the small bus station next to the Wilanowska metro station. Check its website for its timetable and fluctuating fares, as tickets must be purchased online.

TRAIN Warsaw has several train stations and is connected directly to a number of international destinations. The station that most travellers will use is **Warszawa Centralna** (Warsaw Central; Al Jerozolimskie 54), but it's not always where trains start or finish so make sure you get on or off promptly.

TRANSPORT FROM WARSAW

Bus

DESTINATION	COMPANY	PRICE (ZŁ)	DURATION (HR)	FREQUENCY
Berlin (Germany)	Polski Bus	varies	10¼	2 daily
Gdańsk	PKS	56	6	hourly
Gdańsk	Polski Bus	varies	5¾	hourly
Kraków	PKS	58	6	8 daily
Kraków	Polski Bus	varies	5	4 daily
Lublin	Polski Bus	varies	3	5 daily
Prague (Czech Republic)	Polski Bus	varies	12	2 daily
Toruń	PKS	50	4	hourly
Vienna (Austria)	Polski Bus	varies	12½	2 daily
Wrocław	PKS	63	7	6 daily
Wrocław	Polski Bus	varies	7¼	2 daily
Zakopane	PKS	65	8	6 daily

Train

DESTINATION	DURATION (HR)	FREQUENCY
Berlin (Germany)	5	5 daily
Bratislava (Slovakia)	8	2 daily
Budapest (Hungary)	11½	1 daily
Kyiv (Ukraine)	15½	1 daily
Minsk (Belarus)	9½-12	2-3 daily
Moscow (Russia)	18-21	2-3 daily
Prague (Czech Republic)	8½-10½	2 daily
Vienna (Austria)	8	3 daily

Getting Around

TO/FROM THE AIRPORT From the Okęcie airport station, Warszawa Lotnisko Chopina, trains run to either Warszawa Centralna or Warszawa Śródmieście stations in the city centre. The 20 minute journey costs 3.60zł on a regular one-trip public transport ticket.

Another way of getting from Warsaw's main airport to the city centre is bus 175 (3.60zł), which terminates at Plac Piłsudskiego, about a 500m walk from Castle Sq in the Old Town. If you arrive in the wee small hours, night bus N32 links the airport with Warszawa Centralna every 30 minutes.

The taxi fare between Okęcie airport and the city centre is about 45zł to 50zł.

From Warsaw Modlin airport, the easiest way to the city centre is aboard the regular **Modlin Bus** (☎503 558 148; www.modlinbus.com; adult/child 33/23zł; ⊙4am-midnight). Alternatively, a taxi will cost between 100zł and 130zł.

PUBLIC TRANSPORT The standard ticket (3.60zł) is valid for one ride only on a bus, tram or metro train travelling anywhere in the city. Time-based tickets are also available for 20/40/60 minutes (2.60/3.80/5.20zł), one day (12zł) and three days (24zł); with these you can transfer between vehicles within the time limit. Buy tickets from kiosks (including those marked 'RUCH') before boarding and validate them on board.

Warsaw is the only place in Poland where ISIC cards get a public-transport discount (of 48%).

TAXI Taxis are a quick and easy way to get around. However, beware of unauthorised taxis parked in areas frequented by tourists.

MAŁOPOLSKA

Małopolska (literally 'lesser Poland') is a stunning area within which the visitor can spot plentiful remnants of traditional life amid green farmland and historic cities. The region covers a large swathe of southeastern Poland, from the former royal capital of Kraków to the eastern Lublin Uplands.

Kraków

POP 758,000

While many Polish cities are centred on an attractive Old Town, none can compare with Kraków (*krak*-oof) for sheer, effortless beauty. As it was the royal capital of Poland until 1596 and miraculously escaped destruction in WWII, Kraków is packed with attractive historic buildings and streetscapes. The city's centrepiece is the stunning Wawel Castle and Cathedral.

Just south of the castle lies Kazimierz, the former Jewish quarter, reflecting both new and old. Its silent synagogues are a reminder of the tragedy of WWII, while the district's western sector houses a lively bar scene.

Sights & Activities

WAWEL HILL

South of the Old Town, this prominent mount is crowned with a castle containing a cathedral, both of which are enduring symbols of Poland.

Wawel Castle CASTLE

(☎12 422 5155; www.wawel.krakow.pl; grounds free; ⊙6am-dusk) You can choose from several attractions within this magnificent structure, each requiring a separate ticket.

Most popular are the splendid **State Rooms** (adult/concession 18/11zł, free Sun Nov-Mar; ⊙9.30am-5pm Tue-Fri, from 10am Sat & Sun Apr-Oct, 9.30am-4pm Tue-Sun Nov-Mar) and the **Royal Private Apartments** (adult/concession 25/19zł; ⊙9.30am-5pm Tue-Sun Apr-Oct, to 4pm Tue-Sat Nov-Mar). Entry to the latter is only allowed on a guided tour; you may have to accompany a Polish-language tour if it's the only one remaining for the day. If you want to hire a guide who speaks English or other languages, contact the on-site **guides office** (☎12 422 1697).

The 14th-century **Wawel Cathedral** (www.katedra-wawelska.pl; ⊙9am-5pm Mon-Sat, from 12.30pm Sun) was the coronation and burial place of Polish royalty for four centuries. Ecclesiastical artefacts are displayed in its small **Cathedral Museum** (adult/concession 12/7zł; ⊙9am-5pm Tue-Sun). Admission allows access to the **Royal Tombs**, including that of King Kazimierz Wielki; and the **bell tower** of the golden-domed **Sigismund Chapel** (1539), which contains the country's largest bell (11 tonnes).

Other attractions within the castle grounds include the **Museum of Oriental Art** (adult/concession 8/5zł; ⊙9.30am-5pm Tue-Sun Apr-Oct, to 4pm Tue-Sat Nov-Mar), the **Crown Treasury & Armoury** (adult/concession 18/11zł, free Mon; ⊙9.30am-1pm Mon, to 5pm Tue-Sun Apr-Oct, 9.30am-4pm Tue-Sun Nov-Mar) and the **Lost Wawel** (adult/concession 8/5zł, free Mon Apr-Oct, free Sun Nov-Mar; ⊙9.30am-1pm Mon, to 5pm Tue-Sun Apr-Oct, 9.30am-4pm Tue-Sun Nov-Mar), a well-displayed set of intriguing archaeological exhibits.

In the warmer months there's also the **Former Buildings & Fortifications** (adult/concession 18/10zł; ⏲1pm Sat-Mon May-Sep) tour of the grounds, and you can climb the 137-step **Sandomierska Tower** (admission 4zł; ⏲10am-5pm May-Sep).

Finish your visit by entering the atmospheric cave known as the **Dragon's Den** (admission 3zł; ⏲10am-5pm Apr-Oct), as its exit leads out onto the riverbank where you'll encounter a fire-spitting bronze dragon.

Hi-Flyer Balloon BALLOON RIDE

(Rondo Grunwaldzkie; adult/concession 38/20zł; ⏲9am-10pm) Located on the opposite bank of the Vistula River from Wawel Castle, this tethered balloon lifts passengers 150m into the air, enabling great views.

OLD TOWN

Rynek Główny HISTORIC SQUARE

(Main Market Square) This vast square is the focus of the Old Town and Europe's largest medieval town square at 200m by 200m. Its most prominent feature is the 15th-century **town hall tower** (Wieża Ratuszowa; Rynek Główny 1; adult/concession 7/5zł; ⏲10.30am-6pm Apr-Oct), which you can climb.

Cloth Hall HISTORIC BUILDING

(Sukiennice; Rynek Główny 1) At the centre of the main square is this 16th-century Renaissance building. Here you can enter **Rynek Underground** (www.podziemiarynku.com; Rynek Główny 1; adult/concession 17/14zł, free Tue; ⏲10am-8pm Mon, to 4pm Tue, to 10pm Wed-Sun), a fascinating attraction consisting of an underground route through medieval market stalls and other long-forgotten chambers.

On the west side of the Cloth Hall is the useful **Historical Museum Visitor Centre** (☎12 426 5060; Rynek Główny 1; ⏲10am-7pm), where you can buy tickets for many of the city's museums.

St Mary's Church CHURCH

(Rynek Główny 4; adult/concession 6/4zł; ⏲11.30am-6pm Mon-Sat, 2-6pm Sun) This 14th-century place of worship fills the northeastern corner of the main square. The huge main **altarpiece** by Wit Stwosz (Veit Stoss in German) of Nuremberg is the finest Gothic sculpture in Poland and is opened ceremoniously each day at 11.50am.

Every hour a *hejnał* (bugle call) is played from the highest tower of the church. The

DON'T MISS

AUSCHWITZ-BIRKENAU

Few place names have more impact than Auschwitz, which is seared into public consciousness as the location of history's most extensive experiment in genocide.

Established within disused army barracks in 1940 in the Polish town of Oświęcim, Auschwitz was initially designed to hold Polish prisoners but was expanded by the German military occupiers into their largest centre for the extermination of European Jews. Two more camps were subsequently established nearby: Birkenau (Brzezinka, also known as Auschwitz II) and Monowitz (Monowice). In the course of their operation, between one and 1.5 million people were murdered by the Nazi regime in these death factories.

Many of Auschwitz's original buildings remain, serving as a bleak document of the camp's history. A dozen of the 30 surviving prison blocks house sections of the **State Museum Auschwitz-Birkenau** (☎33 844 8100; www.auschwitz.org.pl; ul Więźniów Oświęcimia 20; admission free; ⏲8am-7pm Jun-Aug, 8am-6pm May & Sep, 8am-5pm Apr & Oct, 8am-4pm Mar & Nov, 8am-3pm Dec-Feb). Between May and October it's compulsory to join a tour if you arrive between 10am and 3pm. English-language tours of the Auschwitz-Birkenau complex (adult/concession 40/30zł, 3½ hours) leave at half-hourly intervals from 9.30am.

Auschwitz-Birkenau is an easy day trip from Kraków. Most convenient are the approximately hourly buses to Oświęcim (12zł, 1½ hours) departing from the bus station in Kraków, which either pass by or terminate at the museum. There are also numerous minibuses to Oświęcim (10zł, 1½ hours) from the minibus stands off ul Pawia, next to Galeria Krakowska.

For more about Oświęcim, including accommodation, check out Lonely Planet's *Poland* country guide or visit www.mpit-oswiecim.neostrada.pl.

Kraków – Old Town & Wawel

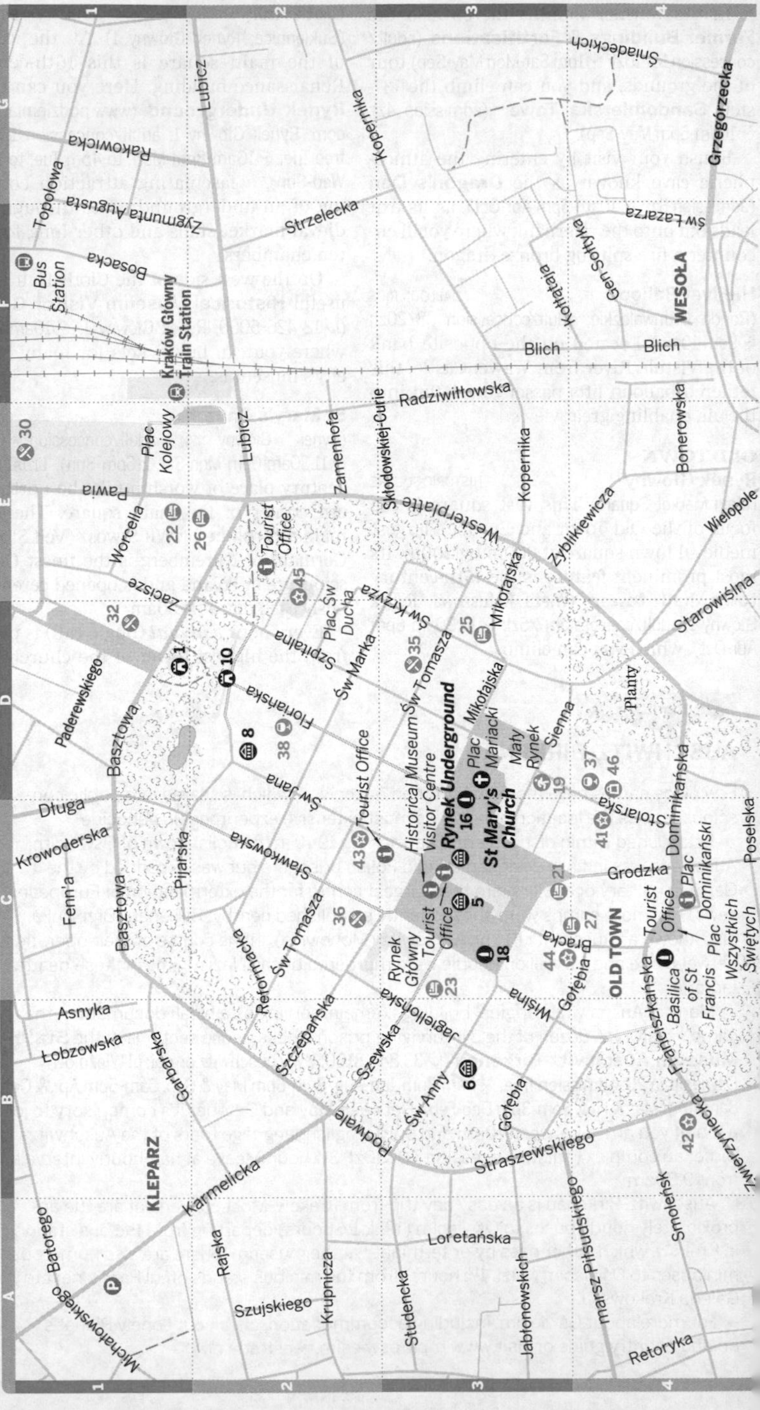

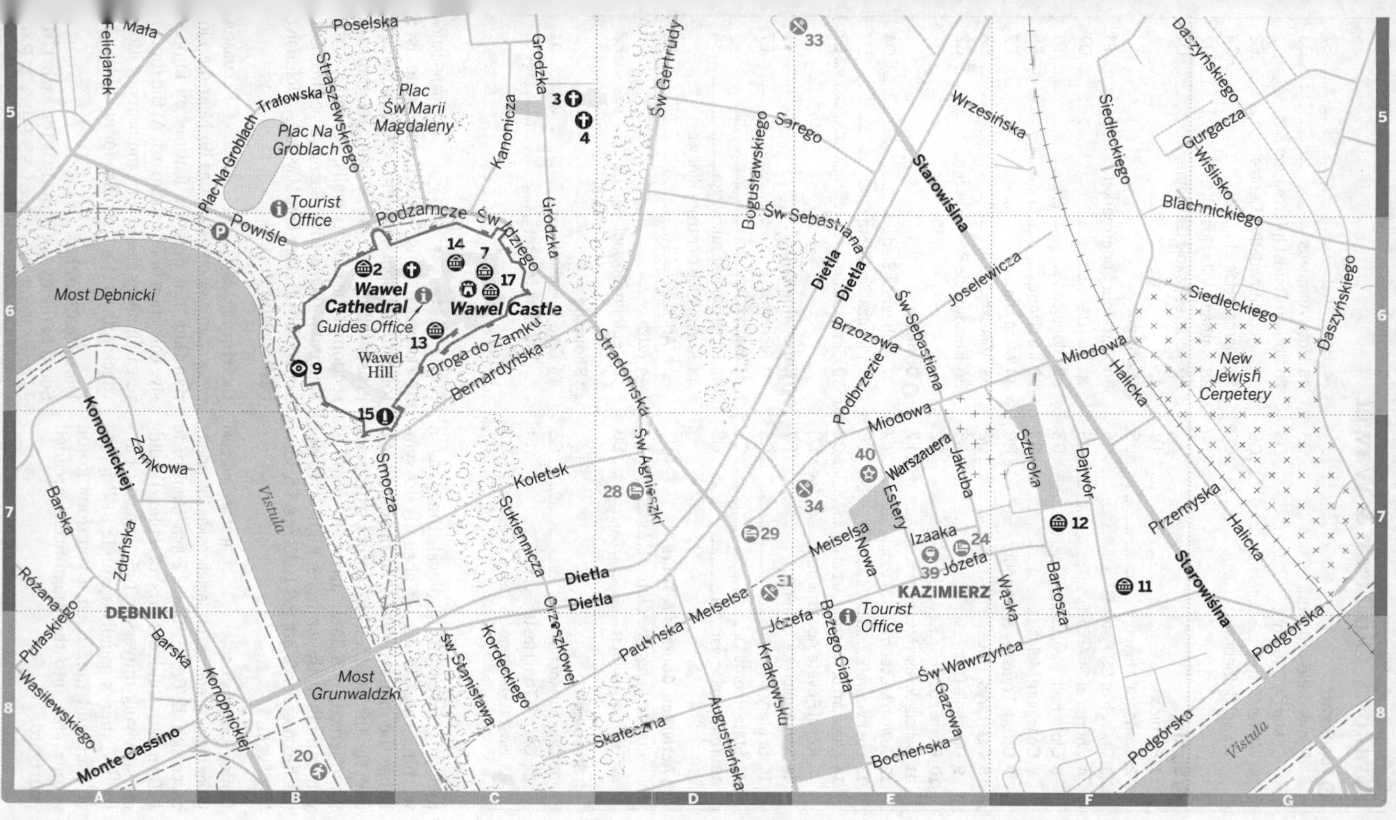
Wawel Castle
Wawel Cathedral
Wawel Hill
Guides Office
Tourist Office
KAZIMIERZ
DĘBNIKI
New Jewish Cemetery
Vistula
Most Dębnicki
Most Grunwaldzki
Starowiślna
Dietla
Stradomska
Krakowska
Józefa
Szeroka
Miodowa
Halicka
Podgórska
Przemyska
Dajwór
Bartosza
Wąska
Jakuba
Warszauera
Estery
Izaaka
Meiselsa
Nowa
Bożego Ciała
Św Wawrzyńca
Gazowa
Bocheńska
Augustiańska
Skałeczna
Paulińska
Orzeszkowej
Koletek
Sukiennicza
Kordeckiego
Św Stanisława
Smocza
Bernardyńska
Droga do Zamku
Podzamcze
Św Idziego
Grodzka
Kanonicza
Poselska
Plac Św Marii Magdaleny
Straszewskiego
Plac Na Groblach
Tralowska
Powiśle
Zamkowa
Konopnickiej
Zduńska
Barska
Różana
Pułaskiego
Wasilewskiego
Monte Cassino
Mała
Felicjanek
Św Gertrudy
Bogusławskiego
Sarego
Św Sebastiana
Brzozowa
Podbrzezie
Św Agnieszki
Joselewicza
Wrzesińska
Siedleckiego
Daszyńskiego
Gurgacza
Wiślisko
Blachnickiego

Kraków – Old Town & Wawel

Top Sights

Rynek Underground ... C3
St Mary's Church ... D3
Wawel Castle ... C6
Wawel Cathedral ... C6

Sights

1 Barbican ... D1
2 Cathedral Museum ... B6
3 Church of SS Peter & Paul ... C5
4 Church of St Andrew ... C5
5 Cloth Hall ... C3
6 Collegium Maius ... B3
7 Crown Treasury & Armoury ... C6
8 Czartoryski Museum ... D2
9 Dragon's Den ... B6
10 Florian Gate ... D2
11 Galicia Jewish Museum ... F7
12 Jewish Museum ... F7
13 Lost Wawel ... C6
14 Museum of Oriental Art ... C6
Royal Private Apartments ... (see 17)
15 Sandomierska Tower ... B7
16 St Mary's Tower ... C3
17 State Rooms ... C6
18 Town Hall tower ... C3

Activities, Courses & Tours

19 English Language Club ... D3
20 Hi-Flyer Balloon ... B8

Sleeping

21 Cracow Hostel ... C3
22 Greg & Tom Hostel ... E1
23 Hostel Flamingo ... C3
24 Hotel Abel ... E7
25 Hotel Amadeus ... D3
26 Jordan Tourist Information & Accommodation Centre ... E2
27 Mama's Hostel ... C4
28 Nathan's Villa Hostel ... D7
29 Tournet Pokoje Gościnne ... D7

Eating

30 Carrefour Supermarket ... E1
31 Deli Bar ... D7
32 Glonojad ... D1
33 Il Calzone ... E5
34 Manzana ... E7
35 Milkbar ... D3
36 Restauracja Pod Gruszką ... C2

Drinking

37 Ambasada Śledzia ... D4
38 Piwnica Pod Złotą Pipą ... D2
39 Singer ... E7

Entertainment

40 Alchemia ... E7
41 Baccarat ... C4
42 Filharmonia Krakowska ... B4
43 Krakowskie Centrum Kinowe Ars ... C2
44 Rdza ... C3
45 Teatr im Słowackiego ... E2

Shopping

46 Galeria Plakatu ... D4
Souvenir Market ... (see 5)

melody, played in medieval times as a warning call, breaks off abruptly to symbolise the moment when, according to legend, the throat of a 13th-century trumpeter was pierced by a Tatar arrow. In summer you can climb the church's highest **tower** (adult/concession 5/3zł; ⌚9-11.30am & 1-5.30pm May-Aug).

Collegium Maius HISTORIC BUILDING
(www.maius.uj.edu.pl; ul Jagiellońska 15; adult/concession 12/6zł; ⌚10am-2.20pm Mon-Fri, to 1.20pm Sat) Guided tours of Poland's oldest surviving university building run half-hourly; there's usually a couple in English, at 11am and 1pm. Even if you don't go on a tour, step into the magnificent arcaded courtyard.

Florian Gate FORTIFICATION
(ul Floriańska) This 14th-century gate is a tourism hot spot with crowds, buskers and artists selling their work along the remnant section of the old city walls. Beyond it is the **Barbican** (Barbakan; ul Basztowa; adult/concession 7/5zł; ⌚10.30am-6pm May-Oct), a defensive bastion built in 1498.

Czartoryski Museum MUSEUM
(www.czartoryski.org; ul Św Jana 19) Near the Florian Gate, this museum features an impressive collection of European art. At the time of research it was closed for a major renovation – check with the tourist office for an update.

Historic Churches CHURCH
South of the Rynek Główny is the early 17th-century Jesuit **Church of SS Peter & Paul**

(ul Grodzka 64; ⌚dawn-dusk), Poland's first baroque church. The nearby Romanesque 11th-century **Church of St Andrew** (ul Grodzka 56; ⌚9am-6pm Mon-Fri) was the only building in Kraków to withstand the Tatars' attack of 1241.

English Language Club SOCIAL GROUP
(ul Sienna 5; admission 2zł; ⌚6-8pm Wed) Just south of St Mary's Church, this social group has met weekly since the dying days of communism. Its weekly meetings are a fun way to meet a mixed bunch of Poles, expats and tourists.

KAZIMIERZ & PODGÓRZE

Founded by King Kazimierz Wielki in 1335, Kazimierz was originally an independent town and then became a Jewish district. During the war the Nazi Germans relocated Jews south across the Vistula River to a walled ghetto in Podgórze. They were exterminated in the nearby Płaszów Concentration Camp, as portrayed in Steven Spielberg's haunting film, *Schindler's List*.

TOP CHOICE **Schindler's Factory** MUSEUM
(www.mhk.pl; ul Lipowa 4; adult/concession 17/14zł; ⌚10am-4pm Mon, 10am-8pm Tue-Sun) Impressive museum covering the Nazi German occupation of Kraków in WWII, housed in the former enamel factory of Oskar Schindler. Next door is the impressive **Museum of Contemporary Art in Kraków** (www.mocak.com.pl; ul Lipowa 4; adult/concession 10/5zł, free Tue; ⌚11am-7pm Tue-Sun).

Jewish Museum MUSEUM
(www.mhk.pl; ul Szeroka 24; adult/concession 8/6zł, free Mon; ⌚10am-2pm Mon, 9am-5pm Tue-Sun) This museum with exhibitions on Jewish traditions is housed within the 15th-century Old Synagogue, the oldest in Poland.

Galicia Jewish Museum MUSEUM
(www.galiciajewishmuseum.org; ul Dajwór 18; adult/concession 15/10zł; ⌚10am-6pm) Fine photographic exhibition depicting modern-day traces of southeastern Poland's once thriving Jewish community.

Festivals & Events

Krakow International Film Festival FILM
(www.kff.com.pl; ⌚May/Jun)

Jewish Culture Festival JEWISH
(www.jewishfestival.pl; ⌚Jun/Jul)

International Festival of Street Theatre THEATRE
(www.teatrkto.pl; ⌚Jul)

Summer Jazz Festival MUSIC
(www.cracjazz.com; ⌚Jul)

Live Festival MUSIC
(www.livefestival.pl; ⌚Aug) Big open-air music festival.

Sleeping

Kraków is unquestionably Poland's major tourist destination, with prices to match. An agency offering decent rooms around town is the **Jordan Tourist Information & Accommodation Centre** (☎12 422 6091; www.jordan.pl; ul Pawia 8; s/d around 150/250zł; ⌚8am-6pm Mon-Fri, 9am-2pm Sat).

Mama's Hostel HOSTEL €
(☎12 429 5940; www.mamashostel.com.pl; ul Bracka 4; dm 50-60zł, d 150zł; 📶) Centrally located brightly-hued lodgings with a beautiful sunlit lounge overlooking a courtyard. There's a washing machine on site.

Nathan's Villa Hostel HOSTEL €
(☎12 422 3545; www.nathansvilla.com; ul Św Agnieszki 1; dm from 42zł, d 184zł; 📶) Comfy rooms, sparkling bathrooms, a laundry and a friendly atmosphere make this place a big hit with backpackers, along with its cellar bar, mini-cinema, beer garden and pool table.

AAA Kraków Apartments APARTMENT €€
(☎12 346 4670; www.krakow-apartments.biz; apt from 300zł; 📶) Company renting out renovated apartments in the Old Town, with a smaller selection in Kazimierz. Cheaper rates are available for longer stays.

Hotel Abel HOTEL €€
(☎12 411 8736; www.hotelabel.pl; ul Józefa 30; s/d 160/220zł; 📶) Reflecting the character

> **SPLURGE**
>
> Everything about **Hotel Amadeus** (☎12 429 6070; www.hotel-amadeus.pl; ul Mikołajska 20; s/d 540/620zł; 📶) screams 'class' – or rather, speaks it softly in a well-modulated tone. Rooms are tastefully furnished and there's a sauna, a fitness centre and an accomplished restaurant. While hanging around the foyer, you can check out photos of famous guests.

WANT MORE?

For in-depth information, reviews and recommendations at your fingertips, head to the Apple App Store to purchase Lonely Planet's *Kraków City Guide* iPhone app.

Alternatively, head to www.lonelyplanet.com/poland/malopolska/krakow for planning advice, author recommendations, traveller reviews and insider tips.

of Kazimierz, this hotel has a distinctive personality, evident in its polished wooden staircase, arched brickwork and age-worn tiles.

Greg & Tom Hostel HOSTEL €
(12 422 4100; www.gregtomhostel.com; ul Pawia 12; dm 57zł, d from 150zł;) This well-run hostel is in a handy location near the train station. There's a free Polish dinner served each Tuesday and laundry facilities are included.

Cracow Hostel HOSTEL €
(12 429 1106; www.cracowhostel.com; Rynek Główny 18; dm 40-72zł, d 188zł;) This hostel's dorms are somewhat cramped, but it's perched high above the Rynek Główny, with an amazing view.

Hostel Flamingo HOSTEL €
(12 422 0000; www.flamingo-hostel.com; ul Szewska 4; dm 55-85zł, d 190zł;) Colourful hostel with pink and lilac decor, a friendly attitude and a great location not far west of the Rynek Główny.

Tournet Pokoje Gościnne HOTEL €€
(12 292 0088; www.accommodation.krakow.pl; ul Miodowa 7; s/d from 150/200zł;) Neat pension in Kazimierz, offering simple but comfortable rooms with compact bathrooms. Its restaurant serves Polish dishes.

Camping Smok CAMPGROUND €
(12 429 8300; www.smok.krakow.pl; ul Kamedulska 18; campsite per person/tent 25/15zł, r 180zł) It's small, quiet and pleasantly located 4km west of the Old Town, with both tent space and rooms. To get here from outside the Kraków Główny train station building, take tram 1, 2 or 6 to the end of the line in Zwierzyniec (destination marked 'Salwator') and change for any westbound bus (except bus 100).

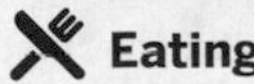

Eating

Kraków is a food paradise, tightly packed with restaurants serving a wide range of international cuisines.

Self-caterers can stock up at the **Carrefour Supermarket** (ul Pawia 5; 9am-10pm Mon-Sat, 10am-9pm Sun) within the Galeria Krakowska shopping mall, next to the main train station.

TOP CHOICE **Glonojad** VEGETARIAN €
(Plac Matejki 2; mains 8-14zł; 8am-10pm;) Attractive modern vegetarian restaurant with a great view onto Plac Matejki, just north of the Barbican. The diverse menu includes samosas, curries, potato pancakes, burritos, gnocchi and soups. There's also an all-day breakfast menu.

Deli Bar HUNGARIAN €€
(ul Meiselsa 5; mains 10-53zł; 1-10pm) A Hungarian guy called László told us this was the best Magyar restaurant in Kraków, and he was right on the money. The menu includes goulash, *palacsinta* (crêpes) and 'Budapest pork'.

Milkbar POLISH €
(ul Św Tomasza 24; mains 10-18zł; 9am-9pm) Cleverly modernised version of the traditional *bar mleczny* (milk bar), serving affordable dishes including breakfast in a pleasant dining area. The two-course set menu for 18zł is great value.

Restauracja Pod Gruszką POLISH €€
(ul Szczepańska 1; mains 12-29zł; noon-midnight) A favourite haunt of writers and artists, this upstairs establishment is the eatery that time forgot. The most distinctive items are the soups served within small bread loaves.

Il Calzone ITALIAN €€
(ul Starowiślna 15a; mains 16-44zł; noon-11pm Mon-Thu) Considering the pleasant decor and charming outdoor terrace, the Italian food here is excellent value.

Manzana MEXICAN €€
(ul Miodowa 11; mains 19-32zł; 7.30am-1am) Long opening hours, a breakfast menu and some impressively authentic dishes make this Mexican eatery a compelling choice.

Drinking & Entertainment

There are hundreds of pubs, clubs and bar in Kraków's Old Town, many housed in an cient vaulted cellars. Kazimierz also has a lively bar scene, centred on Plac Nowy and its surrounding streets. For events try the comprehensive Polish-English booklet *Karnet* (4zł), which lists almost everything happening in the city.

Ambasada Śledzia BAR
(ul Stolarska 6; ⌚8am-6am) The 'Herring Embassy' serves cheap beer and vodka along with cheap snack-sized servings of Polish food. It's a good place to chow down if you're out late clubbing.

Singer CAFE-BAR
(ul Estery 20; ⌚9am-4am) Laid-back Kazimierz hang-out with a moody candlelit interior. Alternatively, sit outside and converse over a sewing machine affixed to the table.

Piwnica Pod Złotą Pipą PUB
(ul Floriańska 30; ⌚noon-midnight) Less claustrophobic than other cellar bars, with decent bar food and international beers on tap.

TOP CHOICE **Baccarat** CLUB
(ul Stolarska 13; ⌚8pm-late Thu-Sat) Luxuriously appointed nightclub playing a mix of house, dance and disco sounds.

Alchemia BAR/CLUB
(ul Estery 5; ⌚9am-3am) This Kazimierz venue exudes a shabby-is-the-new-cool look with rough-hewn wooden benches and candlelit tables. It hosts regular live music gigs and theatrical events.

Rdza CLUB
(ul Bracka 3/5) Basement club with Polish house music bouncing off exposed brick walls and comfy sofas.

Teatr im Słowackiego OPERA, THEATRE
(☎12 424 4528; www.slowacki.krakow.pl; Plac Św Ducha 1) This grand place, built in 1893, focuses on large theatrical productions and opera.

Filharmonia Krakowska CLASSICAL MUSIC
(☎12 619 8722; www.filharmonia.krakow.pl; ul Zwierzyniecka 1) Concerts are usually held on Friday and Saturday.

Krakowskie Centrum Kinowe Ars CINEMA
(ul Św Jana 6) Central cinema in eccentric arty premises. Films are in their original languages, with Polish subtitles.

Shopping

Souvenir Market SOUVENIRS
(Rynek Główny 3; ⌚10am-6pm) The place to start (or perhaps end) your Kraków shopping is

TRAINS FROM KRAKÓW

Domestic Train

DESTINATION	PRICE (ZŁ)	DURATION (HR)	FREQUENCY
Gdynia & Gdańsk	69	8-12	10 daily
Lublin	58	4½	2 daily
Poznań	61	8½	9 daily
Toruń	69	8½	3 daily
Warsaw	56	3	at least hourly
Wrocław	52	5½	Hourly

International Train

DESTINATION	DURATION (HR)	FREQUENCY
Bratislava (Slovakia)	7½	1 daily
Berlin (Germany)	10	1 daily
Budapest (Hungary)	10½	1 daily
Kyiv (Ukraine)	19½	1 daily
Lviv (Ukraine)	7½-9½	2 daily
Prague (Czech Republic)	10	1 daily
Vienna (Austria)	8	1 daily

this large souvenir market within the Cloth Hall, selling everything from fine amber jewellery to tacky plush dragons.

Galeria Plakatu ART
(ul Stolarska 8; ⌚11am-6pm Mon-Fri, 11am-2pm Sat) Sells fascinating examples of Polish poster art.

Information

The *Kraków in Your Pocket* booklet (5zł) is very useful, packed with entertaining reviews of local sights and eateries.

Centrum Internetowe (ul Stolarska 5; ⌚9am-midnight) Internet access within the Pasaż Bielaka arcade.

Klub Garinet (ul Floriańska 18; per hr 4zł; ⌚9am-10pm) Internet.

Kraków Tourist Card (www.krakowcard.com; 2/3 days 60/75zł) Available from tourist offices, the card includes travel on public transport and entry to many museums.

Tourist Office (www.karnet.krakow.pl) ul Św Jana (☎12 421 7787; ul Św Jana 2; ⌚9am-7pm); Cloth Hall (☎12 433 7310; Rynek Główny 1; ⌚9am-7pm May-Sep, 9am-5pm Oct-Apr); northeastern Old Town (☎12 432 0110; ul Szpitalna 25; ⌚9am-7pm May-Sep, 9am-5pm Oct-Apr); southern Old Town (☎12 616 1886; Plac Wszystkich Świętych 2; ⌚9am-5pm); Wawel Hill (ul Powiśle 11; ⌚9am-7pm); Kazimierz (☎12 422 0471; ul Józefa 7; ⌚9am-5pm); airport (☎12 285 5431; John Paul II International airport, Balice; ⌚9am-7pm) Helpful city-run service.

Getting There & Away

AIR The **John Paul II International airport** (www.lotnisko-balice.pl; ul Medweckiego 1) is connected to the Old Town by train (12zł, 20 minutes, half-hourly).

If you land instead at Katowice airport, catch the **Matuszek** (☎32 236 1111; www.matuszek.com.pl; single/return 44/88zł) shuttle bus to the Kraków bus station (two hours).

LOT flies between Kraków and Warsaw several times a day. There are also twice-daily domestic flights via Eurolot to Gdańsk and Poznań.

Budget operators connect Kraków to cities in Europe, including an array of destinations across Britain and Ireland.

BUS Kraków's modern main **bus station** (ul Bosacka 18) is conveniently located on the other side of the main train station from the Old Town, but its services are of limited interest. **Polski Bus** (www.polskibus.com) departs from here to Warsaw (five hours, four daily); check fares and book tickets online.

TRAIN **Kraków Główny train station** (Plac Dworcowy), on the northeastern outskirts of the Old Town, handles all international trains and most domestic rail services.

Lublin

POP 349,000

If the crowds are becoming too much in Kraków, you could do worse than jump on a train to Lublin. This attractive eastern city has many of the same attractions – a beautiful Old Town, a castle, and good bars and restaurants – but is less visited by international tourists.

It's also remembered for an important moment in Polish history: in 1569 the Lublin Union was signed here, uniting Poland and Lithuania. Today its beautifully preserved Old Town is an attractive blend of Gothic, Renaissance and baroque architecture.

Sights & Activities

Lublin Castle CASTLE
(www.zamek-lublin.pl; ul Zamkowa; ⌚10am-5pm Tue-Sat, 10am-6pm Sun) Substantial fortification that was built in the 14th century, then rebuilt as a prison in the 1820s. During the Nazi German occupation more than 100,000 people passed through its doors before being deported to the death camps. Its major occupant is now the **Lublin Museum** (www.zamek-lublin.pl; adult/concession 8.50/6.50zł; ⌚10am-5pm Wed-Sat, 9am-6pm Sun).

Historical Museum of Lublin MUSEUM
(www.zamek.lublin.pl; Plac Łokietka 3; adult/concession 5.50/4.50zł; ⌚9am-4pm Wed-Sat, 9am-5pm Sun) Situated within the 14th-century **Kraków Gate**, this museum displays documents and photos relating to the city's history.

Cathedral CHURCH
(Plac Katedralny; ⌚dawn-dusk) This 16th-century place of worship houses impressive baroque frescos. Its painting of the Virgin Mary is said to have shed tears in 1949.

Archdiocesan Museum MUSEUM
(Plac Katedralny; adult/concession 7/5zł; ⌚10am-5pm) This museum of sacred art also offers expansive views of the Old Town, as it's housed within the lofty **Trinitarian Tower** (1819).

FREE **Majdanek State Museum** MEMORIAL
(www.majdanek.pl; film admission 3zł; ⌚9am-4pm) About 4km southeast of the Old

Town is one of the largest Nazi German death camps, where some 235,000 people, including more than 100,000 Jews, were massacred. Barracks, guard towers and barbed wire fences remain in place; even more chilling are the crematorium and gas chambers.

Trolleybus 156 and bus 23 depart from a stop on ul Królewska near Plac Katedralny, travelling to the entrance of Majdanek.

Underground Route WALK

(Rynek 1; adult/concession 9/7zł; ⏰10am-4pm Tue-Fri, noon-5pm Sat & Sun) This 280m trail winds its way through connected cellars beneath the Old Town, with historical exhibitions along the way. Entry is from the neoclassical **Old Town Hall** in the centre of the pleasant Rynek (Market Sq) at approximately two-hourly intervals.

Sleeping

Hotel Waksman HOTEL €€

(☎81 532 5454; www.waksman.pl; ul Grodzka 19; s/d 210/230zł; 📶) This small gem is excellent value for its quality and location. Just within the Grodzka Gate in the Old Town, it offers elegantly appointed rooms.

Hostel Lublin HOSTEL €

(☎79 288 8632; www.hostellublin.pl; ul Lubartowska 60; dm/r 50/120zł; 📶) The city's first modern hostel contains neat, tidy dorms, a basic kitchen and a cosy lounge. Take trolleybus 156 or 160 north from the Old Town.

Lubelskie Samorządowe Centrum Doskonalenia Nauczycieli HOSTEL €

(☎81 532 9241; ul Dominikańska 5; dm 66zł) This place is in an atmospheric Old Town building and has dorm rooms with between two and five beds.

Hotel Logos HOTEL €€

(☎81 533 8285; www.lublin.oupis.pl/hotel; ul Akademicka 4; s/d from 138/168zł; 📶) Plain but comfortable budget hotel within the university quarter. Breakfast is an extra 15zł per person.

Eating & Drinking

There's a handy **Lux Supermarket** (Plac Wolności 1) located in the city centre, on Plac Wolności.

TOP CHOICE **Magia** INTERNATIONAL €€

(ul Grodzka 2; mains 16-65zł; ⏰noon-midnight) Charming, relaxed restaurant with a large outdoor courtyard. Dishes range from tiger prawns and snails to beef and duck, with every sort of pizza, pasta and pancake between.

Oregano MEDITERRANEAN €€

(ul Kościuszki 7; mains 18-54zł, ⏰noon-11pm) This pleasant, upmarket restaurant specialises

TRANSPORT FROM LUBLIN

Bus

DESTINATION	PRICE (ZŁ)	DURATION (HR)	FREQUENCY
Kraków	48	5½	6 daily
Warsaw	30	3	at least hourly
Zakopane	70	8½	2 daily
Zamość	23	2	2 daily

Train

DESTINATION	PRICE (ZŁ)	DURATION (HR)	FREQUENCY
Gdańsk	69	9	2 daily
Kraków	58	4½	2 daily
Kyiv (Ukraine)	varies	13-14	1 daily
Warsaw	40	2½	10 daily
Zamość	21	2¼	4 daily

in Mediterranean cuisine, featuring pasta, paella and seafood.

Biesy POLISH €
(Rynek 18; mains 12-24zł) Atmospheric cellar eatery whose tasty speciality is large pizza-like baked tarts with a variety of toppings.

Złoty Osioł PUB
(ul Grodzka 5a; noon-midnight;) The 'Golden Donkey' is tucked away, well back from the street. It's a good place for a quiet drink.

Information

Net Box (ul Krakowskie Przedmieście 52; per hr 10zł; 10am-8pm Mon-Sat, 2-6pm Sun) Internet access in a courtyard off the street.

Tourist Office (81 532 4412; www.loitik.eu; ul Jezuicka 1/3; 9am-7pm Mon-Fri, from 10am Sat & Sun May-Oct, 9am-5pm Mon-Fri, from 10am Sat & Sun Nov-Apr) Lots of free brochures, including the city walking-route guide, *Tourist Routes of Lublin*.

Getting There & Away

AIR The brand-new **Lublin airport** (www.airport.lublin.pl) is 10km east of Lublin, with budget airline flights from London and Dublin.

BUS PKS buses run from the **bus station** (Al Tysiąclecia), opposite the castle; from here, **Polski Bus** (www.polskibus.com) also heads to Warsaw (three hours, five daily). Private minibuses run to various destinations, including Zamość (15zł, 1½ hours, half-hourly), from the minibus station north of the bus terminal.

TRAIN The **train station** (Plac Dworcowy) is 1.8km south of the Old Town and accessible by bus 1 or 13.

Zamość

POP 66,000

While most Polish cities' attractions centre on their medieval heart, Zamość (*zah*-moshch) is pure Renaissance. It was founded in 1580 by nobleman Jan Zamoyski and designed by an Italian architect, and was intended to become a prosperous trading settlement.

The splendid architecture of Zamość's Old Town escaped destruction in WWII and was added to Unesco's World Heritage List in 1992.

Sights

Rynek Wielki HISTORIC SQUARE
(Great Market Square) The heart of Zamość's attractive Old Town, this impressive Italianate Renaissance square (exactly 100m by 100m) is dominated by the lofty, pink **town hall** and surrounded by colourful arcaded houses once owned by wealthy citizens. The **Museum of Zamość** (ul Ormiańska 30; adult/concession 8/4zł; 9am-5pm Tue-Sun) is based in two of the loveliest buildings on the square.

Synagogue SYNAGOGUE
(www.zamosc.fodz.pl; ul Pereca 14; admission 6zł; 10am-6pm Tue-Sun) Before WWII, Jewish citizens accounted for 45% of the town's population. Their Renaissance-era place of worship is now a cultural centre, with beautiful interior decoration and an impressive presentation on the town's Jewish history.

Cathedral CHURCH
(ul Kolegiacka; dawn-dusk) Southwest of the square, this mighty 16th-century holy place includes a **bell tower** (ul Kolegiacka; admission 2zł; 10am-4pm Mon-Sat May-Sep) that can be climbed. In the grounds, the **Sacral Museum** (ul Kolegiacka 2; admission 2zł; 10am-4pm Mon-Fri, 10am-1pm Sat & Sun May-Sep, 10am-1pm Sun Oct-Apr) features various robes, paintings and sculptures.

Bastion FORTIFICATION
(ul Łukasińskiego) On the eastern edge of the Old Town is the best surviving bastion from the original city walls. You can take a **tour** (ul Łukasińskiego; adult/concession 7.50/4.50zł; 8am-6pm) through the renovated fortifications; tickets are sold by the souvenir shop next to the entrance.

Sleeping & Eating

For self-caterers, there's a handy **Lux mini-supermarket** (ul Grodzka 16; 6am-8pm Mon-Fri, 8am-6pm Sat & Sun) near the Rynek Wielki.

Hotel Renesans HOTEL €€
(84 639 2001; www.hotelrenesans.pl; ul Grecka 6; s/d from 136/192zł;) It's ironic that a hotel named after the Renaissance is housed in the Old Town's ugliest building. However, it's central and the rooms are surprisingly pleasant.

Hotel Arkadia HOTEL
(84 638 6507; www.arkadia-zamosc.pl; Rynek Wielki 9; s/d from 100/140zł;) This compact place is charming but shabby, though its location right on the Rynek Wielki is hard to beat.

Camping Duet CAMPGROUND
(84 639 2499; www.duet.virgo.com.pl; ul Królowej Jadwigi 14; s/d 80/95zł, campsite per tent/person 12/10zł;) Only 600m west of the Old Town, Camping Duet has neat bungalows, tenn

courts, restaurant, sauna and spa. There's also a pleasant camping ground in a partly wooded area.

Restauracja Muzealna POLISH €€
(ul Ormiańska 30; mains 14-29zł; ⏲11am-10pm Mon-Sat, 11am-9pm Sun) Subterranean restaurant serving a good class of Polish cuisine at reasonable prices, with a well-stocked bar.

Bar Asia POLISH €
(ul Staszica 10; mains 10-19zł; ⏲8am-5pm Mon-Fri, 8am-4pm Sat) Old-style *bar mleczny* (milk bar) dishing up cheap and tasty Polish food in a minimally decorated space.

Information

K@fejka Internetowa (Rynek Wielki 10; per hr 3zł; ⏲9am-5pm Mon-Fri, 10am-2pm Sat) Internet access.

Tourist Office (☎84 639 2292; Rynek Wielki 13; ⏲8am-6pm Mon-Fri, 10am-5pm Sat & Sun May-Sep, 8am-5pm Mon-Fri, 9am-2pm Sat & Sun Oct-Apr) Sells the glossy *Zamość – The Ideal City* (9.50zł).

Getting There & Away

BUS The **bus station** (ul Hrubieszowska) is 2km east of the Old Town and linked by city buses 0 and 3. From here, buses head to Kraków (52zł, eight hours, three daily), Lublin (23zł, two hours, two daily) and Warsaw (42zł, 5½ hours, two daily).

A quicker way to and from Lublin is via the minibuses that depart every 30 minutes (15zł, 1½ hours) from the minibus station opposite the bus station.

TRAIN From the **train station** (ul Szczebrzeska 11), 1km southwest of the Old Town, infrequent services run to Lublin (21zł, 2¼ hours, four daily) and Kraków (61zł, seven hours, one daily).

CARPATHIAN MOUNTAINS

The Carpathians (Karpaty) stretch from the southern border with Slovakia into Ukraine, and their wooded hills and snowy mountains are a beacon for hikers, skiers and cyclists. The most popular destination here is the resort town of Zakopane.

Zakopane

POP 27,900

Zakopane is Poland's major winter sports centre, located at the foot of the Tatra mountains. It may resemble a tourist trap, with its overcommercialised, overpriced exterior, but it also has a relaxed, laid-back vibe that makes it a great place to chill for a few days.

Sights & Activities

Mt Gubałówka MOUNTAIN
This mountain (1120m) behind the township offers excellent views over the Tatras. The **funicular** (ul Nowotarska; adult/concession one-way 10/8zł, return 17/14zł; ⏲8am-9.45pm Jul & Aug, 9am-8pm Mar-Jun & Sep-Oct, 8.30am-6pm Nov-Dec) covers the 1388m-long route in less than five minutes, climbing 300m from the funicular station just north of ul Krupówki.

Sleeping

Some travel agencies in Zakopane can arrange private rooms. Expect a double room to cost about 80zł in the high season in the town centre, and about 60zł for somewhere further out.

Locals offering private rooms may approach you at the bus or train stations; alternatively, just look out for signs posted in the front of private homes – *noclegi* and *pokoje* both mean 'rooms available'.

Carlton HOTEL €€
(☎18 201 4415; www.carlton.pl; ul Grunwaldzka 11; s/d 80/160zł; ☎) Affordable pension in a grand old house. There's an impressive shared balcony overlooking the road and a big comfy lounge lined with potted plants.

Youth Hostel Szarotka HOSTEL €
(☎18 201 3618; www.schroniskomlodziezowe.zakopane.org.pl; ul Nowotarska 45; dm/d 41/102zł) This friendly, homey place gets packed in the high season. There's a kitchen and washing machine on-site. It's a 10-minute walk from the town centre.

Eating & Drinking

The main street, ul Krupówki, is lined with all sorts of eateries.

Czarny Staw GRILL €€
(ul Krupówki 2; mains 12-46zł; ⏲10am-1am) Offers a tasty range of Polish dishes, including a variety of dumplings, and much of the menu is cooked before your very eyes on the central grill. There's a good salad bar and live music most nights.

Pstrąg Górski SEAFOOD €€
(ul Krupówki 6; mains 15-33zł; ⏲9am-10pm) This fish restaurant overlooking a narrow stream serves some of the freshest trout, salmon and sea fish in town.

TRAINS FROM ZAKOPANE

DESTINATION	PRICE (ZŁ)	DURATION (HR)	FREQUENCY
Gdańsk	76	16	1 daily
Kraków	24	3¾	8 daily
Poznań	65	11½	1 daily
Warsaw	63	9	3 daily

Information

Centrum Przewodnictwa Tatrzańskiego (Tatra Guide Centre; 18 206 37 99; ul Chałubińskiego 42a; 9am-3pm) Arranges English-speaking mountain guides.

Tourist Office (18 201 2211) bus station (ul Kościuszki 17; 8am-8pm daily Jul-Aug, 9am-5pm Mon-Sat Sep-Jun); town (ul Kościeliska 7; 9am-5pm Mon-Sat)

Widmo (ul Galicy 6; per hr 5zł; 7.30am-11pm Mon-Fri, 9am-11pm Sat & Sun) Internet access.

Getting There & Away

BUS From the **bus station** (ul Chramcówki), PKS buses run to Kraków every 45 to 60 minutes (18zł, two hours). Two private companies, **Trans Frej** (www.trans-frej.com.pl) and **Szwagropol** (www.szwagropol.pl), also run comfortable Kraków-bound buses (19zł) at the same frequency, and **Polski Bus** (www.polskibus.com) heads to Warsaw (seven hours) twice daily via Kraków (2¼ hours).

Buses and minibuses regularly travel to Lake Morskie Oko and on to Polana Palenica. To cross into Slovakia, get off at Łysa Polana, cross the border on foot and take another bus to Tatranská Lomnica and the other Slovak mountain towns.

TRAIN Trains head to a number of destinations around Poland from Zakopane's **train station** (ul Chramcówki).

Tatra Mountains

The Tatras, 100km south of Kraków, are the highest range of the Carpathian Mountains, stretching across the Poland–Slovakia border. A quarter is in Poland and is mostly part of the Tatra National Park (about 212 sq km).

Sights & Activities

Mt Kasprowy Wierch Cable Car CABLE CAR
(www.pkl.pl; adult/concession return 49/39zł; 7.30am-4pm Jan-Mar, 7.30am-6pm Apr-Jun & Sep-Oct, 7am-9pm Jul & Aug, 9am-4pm Nov-Dec) The cable-car trip from Kuźnice (2km south of Zakopane) to the summit of Mt Kasprowy Wierch (1985m) is a classic tourist experience. At the end of the trip, you can get off and stand with one foot in Poland and the other in Slovakia.

Hiking HIKING
If you're doing any hiking in the Tatras get a copy of the *Tatrzański Park Narodowy* map (1:25,000), which shows all hiking trails in the area, from the **Księgarnia Górska** (ul Zaruskiego 5) bookshop in Zakopane. For details of trails and mountain refuges, contact the Zakopane **PTTK office** (18 201 2429; www.pttkzakopane.pl; ul Krupówki 12).

Lake Morskie Oko LAKE
The emerald-green Lake Morskie Oko (Eye of the Sea) is among the loveliest lakes in the Tatras.

SILESIA

Silesia (Śląsk in Polish; pronounced *shlonsk*) is a fascinating mix of landscapes. Beautiful Wrocław is a historic city with lively nightlife, and the Sudeten Mountains draw hikers and other nature lovers.

Wrocław

POP 630,000

When citizens of beautiful Kraków enthusiastically encourage you to visit Wrocław (*vrots*-wahf), you know you're onto something good. The city's delightful Old Town is a gracious mix of Gothic and baroque styles and its large student population ensures a healthy number of restaurants, bars and nightclubs.

Wrocław has been traded back and forth between various rulers over the centuries but began life in the year 1000. When it was returned to Poland from Germany in 1945 Wrocław was a shell of its former self having sustained massive damage in WWII. Sen tive restoration has since returned the historic centre to its former beauty.

Sights

OLD TOWN

City Museum of Art MUSEUM
(www.muzeum.miejskie.wroclaw.pl; Stary Ratusz; adult/concession 10/7zł; ⏱10am-5pm Wed-Sat, 10am-6pm Sun) The beautiful **town hall** (built 1327–1504) on the southern side of the attractive **Rynek** (Market Square) has stately rooms with exhibits on the art of gold and the stories of famous Wrocław inhabitants.

Jaś i Małgosia HISTORIC BUILDINGS
(ul Św Mikołaja) In the northwestern corner of the Rynek are these two attractive small houses linked by a baroque gate. Whimsically, they've been named after a couple better known to English speakers as Hansel and Gretel.

Gnomes of Wrocław STATUES
See if you can spot the diminutive statue of a gnome at ground level, just to the west of the Jaś i Małgosia houses; he's one of more than 200 scattered through the city. You can buy a gnome map (6zł) from the tourist office.

Church of St Elizabeth CHURCH
(www.kosciolgarnizon.wroclaw.pl; ul Św Elżbiety 1; admission 5zł; ⏱10am-7pm Mon-Sat, noon-7pm Sun) This monumental 14th-century church has an 83m-high tower, which you can climb for city views.

OUTSIDE THE OLD TOWN

TOP CHOICE **Panorama of Racławice** MONUMENTAL ARTWORK
(www.panoramaraclawicka.pl; ul Purkyniego 11; adult/concession 25/18zł; ⏱9am-5pm) Wrocław's major tourist attraction is this giant 360-degree painting, housed in a circular building east of the Old Town. It depicts the 1794 Battle of Racławicea, in which a Polish peasant army led by Tadeusz Kościuszko defeated Russian forces intent on partitioning Poland. It's an immense 114m long and 15m high.

Obligatory tours (with audio in English and other languages) run every 30 minutes. The ticket also allows same-day entry to the nearby National Museum.

National Museum MUSEUM
(www.mnwr.art.pl; Plac Powstańców Warszawy 5; adult/concession 15/10zł, free Sat; ⏱10am-5pm) Treasure-trove of fine art on three floors, with extensive permanent collections and a stunning skylit atrium.

Cathedral of St John the Baptist CHURCH
(Plac Katedralny; tower adult/concession 5/4zł; ⏱10am-4pm Mon-Sat, 2-4pm Sun) This Gothic cathedral has a unique lift to whisk you to the top of its **tower** for superb views.

Botanical Gardens GARDENS
(ul Sienkiewicza 23; adult/concession 10/5zł; ⏱8am-6pm Apr-Nov) North of the cathedral are these charming gardens, where you can chill out among the chestnut trees and tulips.

Passage PUBLIC ART
(cnr ul Świdnicka & ul Piłsudskiego) This fascinating sculpture depicts a group of pedestrians being swallowed by the pavement, only to reemerge on the other side of the street.

Festivals & Events

Jazz on the Odra International Festival MUSIC
(www.jazznaodrze.pl; ⏱Apr)

Musica Polonica Nova Festival MUSIC
(www.musicapolonicanova.pl; ⏱Apr) Celebrates new orchestral compositions, with a focus on Polish works.

Wratislavia Cantans MUSIC
(www.wratislaviacantans.pl; ⏱Sep) Features music with a vocal component, including opera and choral works.

Wrocław Marathon SPORT
(www.wroclawmaraton.pl; ⏱Sep)

Sleeping

TOP CHOICE **Hostel Mleczarnia** HOSTEL €
(☎71 787 7570; www.mleczarniahostel.pl; ul Włodkowica 5; dm from 40zł, d 220zł; 📶) This hostel has bags of charm, having been decorated in an old-fashioned style within a former residential building. There's a women-only dorm available, along with a kitchen and laundry facilities. Downstairs is a good cafe-bar.

Art Hotel HOTEL €€
(☎71 787 7100; www.arthotel.pl; ul Kiełbaśnicza 20; s/d from 270/290zł; ❄📶) Elegant but affordable accommodation in a renovated apartment building. Rooms feature tastefully restrained decor, quality fittings and gleaming bathrooms. Within the hotel is a top-notch restaurant.

Hostel Babel HOSTEL €
(☎71 342 0250; www.babelhostel.pl; ul Kołłątaja 16; dm from 45zł, d 140zł; 📶) A tatty old staircase leads up to pleasant budget accommodation. Dorms are set in renovated apartment rooms with ornate lamps and decorative ceilings. Guests have access to a kitchen and washing machine.

Hotel Europejski HOTEL €€
(☎71 772 1000; www.silfor.pl; ul Piłsudskiego 88; s/d from 200/250zł; ❄📶) Pleasant hotel a stone's throw from the train station, with high ceilings, quality furniture and a cafe-bar and restaurant.

AS Apartments APARTMENT €€
(☎71 341 8759; www.asapart.pl; Rynek 18; apt from €55; 📶) Company offering a choice of apartments in the Old Town, many of them with a view of the Rynek itself.

MDK Youth Hostel HOSTEL €
(☎71 343 8856; www.mdk.wroclaw.pl; ul Kołłątaja 20; dm/d from 27/72zł; 📶) Not far from the train station, this is a basic place, located in a grand mustard-coloured building. It's almost always full, so book ahead.

Eating

TOP CHOICE **Bernard** INTERNATIONAL €€
(Rynek 35; mains 27-77zł; ⏲10.30am-11pm) Bernard is one cool dude, serving a selection of upmarket comfort food including burgers, steak and fish dishes. There's live music most nights and a breakfast menu from 10.30am to noon.

Bazylia CAFETERIA €
(Plac Uniwersytecki; mains 2.49zł per 100g; ⏲10am-6pm Mon-Fri, from 11am Sat & Sun) Inexpensive and bustling modern take on the classic *bar mleczny* (milk bar). The menu has a lot of Polish standards such as *bigos* (thick sauerkraut and meat stew) and *gołąbki* (cabbage leaves stuffed with mince and rice), and a decent range of salads and other vegetable dishes.

Bar Wegetariański Vega VEGETARIAN €
(Rynek 1/2; mains 4-11zł; ⏲8am-7pm Mon-Fri, 9am-5pm Sat & Sun; 🌿) This cheap cafeteria in the centre of the Rynek offers vegie dishes in a light green space, with a good choice of soups and crêpes. Upstairs there's a vegan section.

Drinking & Entertainment

Pub Guinness PUB
(Plac Solny 5; ⏲noon-2am) A lively, fairly authentic Irish pub. The ground-floor bar buzzes with student and traveller groups and there's a restaurant and beer cellar as well.

PRL CLUB
(Rynek Ratusz 10; ⏲noon-late) The dictatorship of the proletariat is alive and well in this tongue-in-cheek venue inspired by communist nostalgia.

Bezsenność CLUB
(ul Ruska 51; ⏲7pm-late) With its alternative/rock/dance line-up and distressed decor, 'Insomnia' is one of the most popular clubs in town.

Filharmonia CLASSICAL MUSIC
(☎71 342 2459; www.filharmonia.wroclaw.pl; ul Piłsudskiego 19) Hosts classical music concerts.

Information

Internet Netvigator (ul Igielna 14; per hr 4zł; ⏲9am-midnight)

Tourist Office (☎71 344 3111; www.wroclaw-info.pl; Rynek 14; ⏲9am-9pm Apr-Oct, 9am-7pm Nov-Mar)

Getting There & Away

AIR From **Copernicus Airport** (www.airport.wroclaw.pl), LOT flies frequently between

TRAINS FROM WROCŁAW

DESTINATION	PRICE (ZŁ)	DURATION (HR)	FREQUENCY
Berlin (Germany)		5	1 daily
Kraków	52	5½	hourly
Poznań	46	3½	at least hourly
Toruń	56	5	5 daily
Warsaw	61	6½	hourly

Wrocław and Warsaw. Tickets can be bought at the **LOT office** (☎71 342 5151; ul Piłsudskiego 36). Eurolot also links Wrocław to Gdańsk.

A range of budget carriers connect Wrocław with other European cities, including several British and Irish regional destinations.

The airport is in Strachowice, about 12km west of the Old Town. The frequent bus 406 and infrequent night bus 249 link the airport with Wrocław Główny train station and the bus terminal.

BUS The **bus station** (ul Sucha 11) is south of the main train station and offers five daily PKS buses to Warsaw (60zł, six hours). For most other destinations the train is a better choice, though handy **Polski Bus** (www.polskibus.com) services run from here to Warsaw (7¼ hours, twice daily) and Prague (five hours, twice daily).

TRAIN Wrocław Główny train station (ul Piłsudskiego 105), formerly Breslau Hauptbahnhof, was opened in 1857 as a lavish architectural confection. It's easily Poland's most attractive train station and is worth visiting even if you're not travelling by train.

WIELKOPOLSKA

Wielkopolska (Greater Poland) is the region where Poland came to life in the Middle Ages. As a result of this ancient eminence, its cities and towns are full of historic and cultural attractions. The battles of WWII later caused widespread destruction in the area, though Poznań has since been restored to its prominent economic role.

Poznań

POP 555,000

No one could accuse Poznań of being too sleepy. Between its regular trade fairs, student population and visiting travellers, it's a vibrant city with a wide choice of attractions. There's a beautiful Old Town at its centre, with a number of interesting museums and a range of lively bars, clubs and restaurants. The surrounding countryside is also good for cycling and hiking.

Sights

Historical Museum of Poznań MUSEUM
(www.mnp.art.pl; Stary Rynek 1; adult/concession 7/5zł, free Sat; ⏲9am-3pm Tue-Thu, noon-9pm Fri, 11am-6pm Sat & Sun) Located within the Renaissance **town hall** on the bustling **Stary Rynek** (Old Market Square), this museum displays splendid period interiors. Every midday two mechanical metal goats above its clock butt their horns together 12 times, reenacting a centuries-old legend.

Franciscan Church CHURCH
(ul Franciszkańska 2) This 17th-century church, one block west of the square, has an ornate baroque interior complete with wall paintings and rich stucco work.

Ostrów Tumski HISTORIC AREA
This river island is dominated by the monumental, double-towered **Poznań Cathedral** (ul Ostrów Tumski 17; ⏲dawn-dusk), originally built in 968. The Byzantine-style **Golden Chapel** (1841) and the **mausoleums** of Mieszko I and Boleslaus the Brave are behind the high altar.

A new attraction under construction opposite the island's eastern shore is the **Cathedral Island Heritage Centre** (www.trakt.poznan.pl; ul Gdańska). A cutting-edge multimedia history museum, it should be open by mid-2013.

The island is 1km east of the Old Town (take any eastbound tram from Plac Wielkopolski).

Lake Malta LAKE
Some 1.6km east of the Old Town is this body of water, a favourite weekend destination for Poles. A fun way to visit the lake is to take tram 4, 8 or 17 from Plac Wielkopolski to the Rondo Śródka stop on the other side of Ostrów Tumski. From the nearby terminus, you can catch a miniature train along the **Malta Park Railway** (mpk.poznan.pl/maltanka; ul Jana Pawła II; adult/concession 6/4zł; ⏲10am-6.30pm Apr-Oct), which follows the lake's shore to the **New Zoo** (www.zoo.poznan.pl; ul Krańcowa 81; adult/concession 20/10zł; ⏲9am-7pm Apr-Sep, 9am-4pm Oct-Mar).

Monument to the Victims of June 1956 MONUMENT
(Plac Mickiewicza) Emotive memorial to the dead and injured of the massive 1956 strike by the city's industrial workers, which was crushed by tanks. It's in a park west of the prominent Kaiserhaus building.

Palm House GREENHOUSE
(Palmiarnia; www.palmiarnia.poznan.pl; ul Matejki 18; adult/concession 7/5zł; ⏲9am-5pm Tue-Sat, 9am-6pm Sun) This huge greenhouse (built in 1910) contains 17,000 species of tropical and subtropical plants. It's located in Park Wilsona, 1km southwest of the train station.

TRAINS FROM POZNAŃ

Domestic Train

DESTINATION	PRICE (ZŁ)	DURATION (HR)	FREQUENCY
Gdańsk	58	5	8 daily
Kraków	61	8½	9 daily
Toruń	24	2½	10 daily
Warsaw	56	3¼	at least hourly
Wrocław	46	3½	at least hourly
Zakopane	65	11½	1 daily

International Train

DESTINATION	DURATION (HR)	FREQUENCY
Berlin (Germany)	2½	6 daily
Kyiv (Ukraine)	19	1 daily
Moscow (Russia)	21	1 daily

Festivals & Events

The largest trade fairs take place in January, June, September and October.

St John's Fair CULTURAL
(⏰Jun) Held on the Stary Rynek, featuring craft items, local foods and street artist performances. The fair runs for two weeks.

Malta International Theatre Festival THEATRE
(www.malta-festival.pl; ⏰Jul)

Ethno Port Poznań Festival WORLD MUSIC
(www.ethnoport.pl; ⏰Aug)

Sleeping

During trade fairs, the rates of Poznań's accommodation dramatically increases. A room may also be difficult to find, so it pays to book ahead. Prices given here are for outside trade fair periods. You can check the dates of the fairs online at www.mtp.pl.

Frolic Goats Hostel HOSTEL €
(☎61 852 4411; www.frolicgoatshostel.com; ul Wrocławska 16/6; dm from 44zł, d 170zł; 📶) This friendly hostel is aimed at the international backpacker. There's a washing machine on the premises and bike hire is available for 30zł per day. Enter from ul Jaskółcza.

Brovaria HOTEL €€
(☎61 858 6868; www.brovaria.pl; Stary Rynek 73/74; s/d from 250/290zł; 📶) This multitalented hotel also contains a restaurant, bar and microbrewery. The elegant rooms have tasteful dark timber tones and some have views onto the Rynek.

Hostel Cameleon HOSTEL €
(☎61 639 3041; www.hostel-cameleon.com; ul Świętosławska 12; dm 55zł, s/d from 120/165zł; 📶) Centrally located hostel with contemporary decor, and a spacious kitchen and lounge. There's a washing machine available.

Fusion Hostel HOSTEL €
(☎61 852 1230; www.fusionhostel.pl; ul Św Marcin 66/72; dm 55-69zł, s/d from 149/190zł; 📶) Hostel on the 7th floor of a commercial building. The decor is modern and bright, and there's a lounge, a kitchen and bicycle hire (20zł per day).

Eating & Drinking

Tapas Bar SPANISH €€
(Stary Rynek 60; mains 19-88zł; ⏰9am-midnight) Atmospheric place dishing up authentic tapas and Spanish wine. Most tapas dishes cost about 26zł, so forget the mains and share with friends. Also serves breakfast.

Gospoda Pod Koziołkami POLISH €€
(Stary Rynek 95; mains 13-78zł; ⏰11am-10pm) Homey bistro within Gothic arches. The menu is crammed with tasty Polish standards, including some distinctive local specialities.

Bar Caritas CAFETERIA €
(Plac Wolności 1; mains 6-12zł; ⌚8am-7pm Mon-Fri, 9am-5pm Sat, from 11am Sun) Cheap and convenient milk bar with many variants of *naleśniki* (crêpes) on the menu.

Ptasie Radio CAFE-BAR
(ul Kościuszki 74; ⌚8am-midnight Mon-Fri, from 10am Sat & Sun; 📶) This funky drinking hole, named after a famous Polish poem 'Bird Radio', is a retro riot of chipped wooden tables, pot plants and bird images.

Proletaryat BAR
(ul Wrocławska 9; ⌚1pm-late Mon-Sat, 3pm-late Sun) Communist nostalgia bar with the obligatory bust of Lenin in the window. Play 'spot the communist leader' while sipping a boutique beer.

☆ Entertainment

Czarna Owca CLUB
(ul Jaskółcza 13; ⌚6pm-late Wed-Sat) Literally called 'Black Sheep', this club has nightly DJs playing a mix of genres including R & B, house, rock, Latin, soul and funk.

Filharmonia CLASSICAL MUSIC
(☎61 853 6935; www.filharmonia.poznan.pl; ul Św Marcin 81) Classical music concerts.

ℹ Information

Adax (ul Półwiejska 28; per hr 2.50zł; ⌚8am-9pm Mon-Fri, from 10am Sat, from noon Sun) Internet access south of the Stary Rynek.

Tourist Office (☎61 852 6156; www.poznan.pl; Stary Rynek 59; ⌚9am-8pm Mon-Sat, 10am-6pm Sun May-Sep, 10am-6pm Mon-Fri Oct-Apr)

ℹ Getting There & Away

AIR From **Poznań airport** (www.airport-poznan.com.pl; ul Bukowska 285), LOT flies up to three times a day to Warsaw. There are also two domestic flights daily via Eurolot to Kraków.

A vast array of other European cities are serviced from Poznań, including London and Dublin. The airport is accessible by bus L from the main train station, or buses 48, 59 and night bus 242 from the 'Bałtyk' stop near Rondo Kaponiera.

BUS The **bus station** (ul Towarowa 17) is a 10-minute walk east of the train station, but most of its destinations can be reached more comfortably and frequently by train.

From the smaller Dworzec Górczyn bus station 5km southwest of the main train station along ul Głogowska, **Polski Bus** (www. polskibus.com) runs useful services to Warsaw (5¾ hours, three daily) and Berlin (4½ hours, twice daily).

TRAIN From the busy **Poznań Główny train station** (ul Dworcowa 1), you can journey by rail to domestic and international destinations. The station is about 1.5km southwest of the Old Town.

POMERANIA

Pomerania (Pomorze in Polish) is an attractive region with diverse drawcards, from beautiful beaches to architecturally pleasing cities. The historic port city of Gdańsk is situated at the region's eastern extreme, while the attractive Gothic city of Toruń lies inland.

Gdańsk

POP 460,000

From Gdańsk's busy riverside waterfront to the Renaissance splendour of its charming narrow streets, there's plenty to like about this coastal city.

After being tussled over by Germans and Poles for centuries, Gdańsk suffered immense damage in WWII. In the 1980s it achieved international fame as the home of the Solidarity trade union, whose rise helped precipitate the fall of communism in Europe. Today it's a vibrant city and a great base for exploring the Baltic coast.

WORTH A TRIP

MALBORK

The magnificent **Malbork Castle** (☎55 647 0978; www.zamek.malbork.pl; ul Starościńska 1; adult/concession 40/30zł; ⌚9am-7pm mid-Apr–mid-Sep, 10am-3pm mid-Sep–mid-Apr) makes a great day trip from Gdańsk. It's the largest Gothic castle in Europe and was once known as Marienburg, headquarters of the medieval Teutonic Knights. Its sinister form looms over the relatively small town and the Nogat River – grab a sneak preview by looking to the right as your train crosses the river. Trains run regularly from Gdańsk Głowny station (45 minutes). Once you get to Malbork station, turn right, cross the highway and follow ul Kościuszki to the castle. Compulsory tours are usually in Polish, but come with an audio tour in English. There are places to eat at the castle and in the town.

Gdańsk

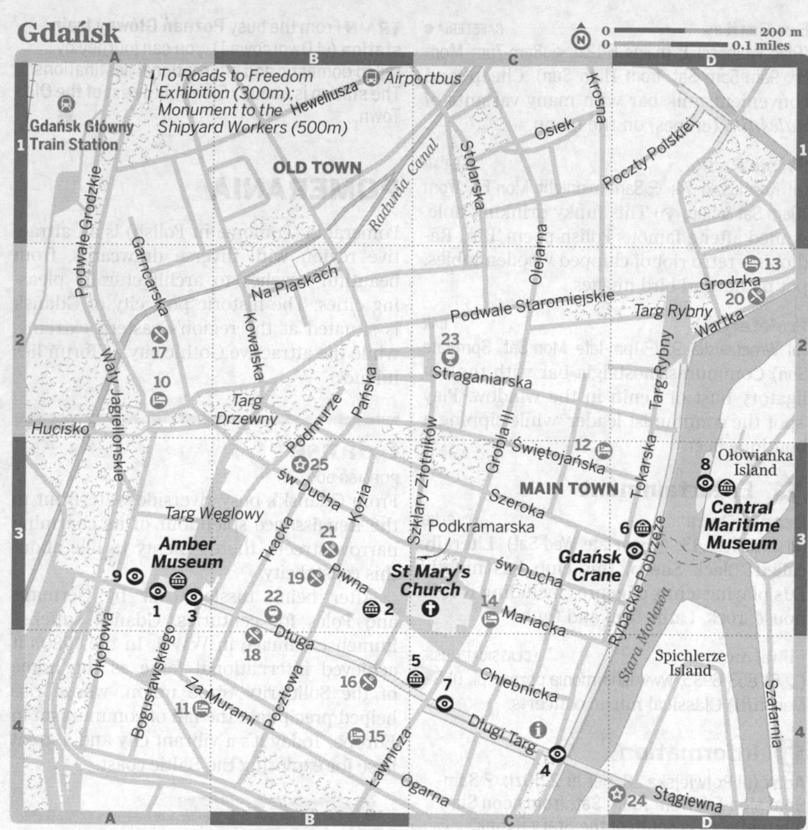

Gdańsk

Top Sights

Amber Museum A3
Central Maritime Museum D3
Gdańsk Crane D3
St Mary's Church C3

Sights

1 Foregate A3
2 Free City of Danzig Historical Zone B3
3 Golden Gate A3
4 Green Gate C4
5 Historical Museum of Gdańsk C4
6 Maritime Cultural Centre D3
7 Neptune's Fountain C4
8 Sołdek Museum Ship D3
9 Upland Gate A3

Sleeping

10 3 City Hostel A2
11 Dom Harcerza A4
12 Dom Zachariasza Zappio C3
13 Happy Seven Hostel D2
14 Kamienica Gotyk C3
15 Kamienica Zacisze B4

Eating

16 Bar Mleczny Neptun B4
17 Green Way A2
18 Green Way B4
19 Kos Delikatesy B3
20 Przystań Gdańska D2
21 U Dzika B3

Drinking

22 Cafe Ferber B3
23 Cafe Lamus C2

Entertainment

24 Miasto Aniołów D4
25 Parlament B3

Sights

MAIN TOWN

Royal Way HISTORIC ROUTE
The historic parade route of Polish kings runs from the western **Upland Gate** (Brama Wyżynna), which was built in the 1770s on a 15th-century gate, onward through the **Foregate** (Przedbramie), which once housed a torture chamber, and the 1614 **Golden Gate** (Złota Brama), and east to the 1568 Renaissance **Green Gate** (Zielona Brama). Along the way it passes through beautiful **ul Długa** (Long Street) and **Długi Targ** (Long Market).

Central Maritime Museum MUSEUM
(www.cmm.pl; ul Ołowianka 9; all sections 18/10zł; ⏲10am-4pm Tue-Sun) On the waterfront is the 15th-century **Gdańsk Crane** (ul Szeroka 67/68; adult/concession 8/5zł; ⏲10am-4pm Tue-Sun), part of this maritime history museum. Next door is the spanking new **Maritime Cultural Centre** (ul Tokarska 21; adult/concession 12/8zł; ⏲10am-6pm Tue-Sun), with an exhibition of boats from around the world. The branch on the east bank offers exhibitions on Gdańsk's seafaring past, including the **Sołdek Museum Ship** (ul Ołowianka 9; adult/concession 8/5zł; ⏲10am-4pm Tue-Sun).

St Mary's Church CHURCH
(ul Podkramarska 5; tower adult/concession 5/3zł; ⏲8.30am-6pm, except during services) At the western end of picturesque **ul Mariacka** is this gigantic 14th-century place of worship. Watch little figures troop out at noon from its 14m-high astronomical clock, adorned with zodiacal signs. You can also climb the 405 steps of the **tower** for views.

Amber Museum MUSEUM
(www.mhmg.gda.pl; Targ Węglowy; adult/concession 10/5zł, free Mon; ⏲11am-3pm Mon, 10am-7pm Tue-Sat, 11am-7pm Sun) Within the Foregate you can visit this museum, wherein you can marvel at the history of so-called 'Baltic gold'.

Historical Museum of Gdańsk MUSEUM
(www.mhmg.gda.pl; ul Długa 47; adult/concession 10/5zł, free Mon; ⏲11am-3pm Mon, 10am-7pm Tue-Sat, 11am-7pm Sun) Inside the towering Gothic town hall is this museum depicting photos of old Gdańsk and the damage caused to the city during WWII.

Neptune's Fountain FOUNTAIN
(Długi Targ) Near the town hall is this decorative fountain (1633), which legend says once gushed forth *goldwasser*, the iconic Gdańsk liqueur.

Free City of Danzig Historical Zone MUSEUM
(ul Piwna 19/21; admission 5zł; ⏲11am-6pm) Small but intriguing display of items from the interwar era when Gdańsk operated as a 'free city', independent of both Poland and Germany.

OLD TOWN

TOP CHOICE **Roads to Freedom Exhibition** MUSEUM
(ul Wały Piastowskie 24; adult/concession 6/4zł; ⏲10am-6pm Tue-Sun) Excellent museum charting the decline and fall of Polish communism and the rise of the Solidarity trade union.

Monument to the Shipyard Workers MONUMENT
(Plac Solidarności) This soaring structure at the entrance to the Gdańsk Shipyards was erected in late 1980 in memory of 44 workers killed during the riots of December 1970.

Festivals & Events

International Street & Open-Air Theatre Festival THEATRE
(www.feta.pl; ⏲Jul)

Sounds of the North Festival MUSIC
(www.nck.org.pl; ⏲Jul/Aug) Folkloric music festival.

St Dominic's Fair SHOPPING
(www.mtgsa.pl; ⏲Jul/Aug) Annual shopping and cultural fair.

International Shakespeare Festival THEATRE
(www.shakespearefestival.pl; ⏲July/August)

Sleeping

TOP CHOICE **3 City Hostel** HOSTEL €
(☎58 354 5454; www.3city-hostel.pl; Targ Drzewny 12/14; dm from 50zł, r 180zł; 📶) Sparkling new hostel near the train station, with high ceilings, pleasant common areas, a kitchen, and a lounge with a view. The cheapest beds are in Japanese-style capsules.

Kamienica Gotyk HOTEL €€
(☎58 301 8567; www.gotykhouse.eu; ul Mariacka 1; s/d 280/310zł; 📶) This Gothic guesthouse claims to be Gdańsk's oldest residence. Inside, the rooms are compact but neat, with clean bathrooms.

Dom Zachariasza Zappio HOSTEL €
(☎58 322 0174; www.zappio.pl; ul Świętojańska 49; dm/s/d 50/99/158zł; 📶) This hostel is located in an atmospheric former convent building

next to St John's Church. Rooms are brightly furnished and there's a fantastic beer garden.

Happy Seven Hostel HOSTEL €
(☎58 320 8601; www.happyseven.com; ul Grodzka 16; dm from 45zł, d 230zł; 📶) Hostel in which each dorm has a light-hearted theme, including travel, music, sport and movie dorms.

Kamienica Zacisze APARTMENTS €€
(☎69 627 4306; www.apartments.gdansk.pl; ul Ogarna 107; apt from 220zł; 📶) This central communist-era workers' dormitory building has been transformed into a set of light, airy apartments for up to nine people.

Dom Harcerza HOTEL €
(☎58 301 3621; www.domharcerza.pl; ul Za Murami 2/10; dm 35zł, s/d from 60/120zł; 📶) Well-located budget hotel with a charming old-fashioned restaurant on the ground floor.

Camping Nr 218 Stogi CAMPGROUND €
(☎58 307 3915; www.kemping-gdansk.pl; ul Wydmy 9; campsite per person/tent 15/7zł, cabins 65-140zł; ⏲May-Sep) Only 200m from the beach in the seaside holiday centre of Stogi, about 5.5km northeast of the Main Town. Take tram 8 or 13 from the main train station in Gdańsk.

Eating & Drinking

For self-catering, visit **Kos Delikatesy** (ul Piwna 9/10; ⏲24hr) in the Main Town.

U Dzika POLISH €€
(ul Piwna 59/61; mains 15-77zł; ⏲11am-10pm) Pleasant eatery with a nice outdoor terrace, specialising in *pierogi* (dumplings). If you're feeling adventurous, try the fruity Fantasy Dumplings.

Bar Mleczny Neptun CAFETERIA €
(ul Długa 33/34; mains 2-16zł; ⏲7am-8pm Mon-Fri, 10am-6pm Sat & Sun; 📶) This joint is a cut above your run-of-the-mill milk bar, with potted plants, lace curtains, decorative tiling and old lamps for decor.

Green Way VEGETARIAN €
(ul Garncarska 4/6; mains 4-12zł; ⏲11am-8pm Mon-Fri, noon-7pm Sat & Sun; 🖉) Serves everything from soy cutlets to Mexican goulash in an unfussy green-and-orange space. There's another, more central, **branch** (ul Długa 11; mains 4-12zł; ⏲10am-8pm; 🖉) on the Royal Way.

Przystań Gdańska POLISH €€
(ul Wartka 5; mains 17-43zł) An atmospheric place to enjoy outdoor dining, with a view along the river to the Gdańsk Crane.

TOP CHOICE **Cafe Lamus** BAR
(ul Lawendowa 8; ⏲noon-late; 📶) Achingly cool retro-themed bar serving a range of beers from small Polish breweries. Enter from ul Straganiarska.

TRAINS FROM GDAŃSK

Domestic Train

DESTINATION	PRICE (ZŁ)	DURATION	FREQUENCY
Giżycko	56	5hr	2 daily
Kętrzyn	52	4¾hr	2 daily
Kraków	69	8-12hr	10 daily
Lublin	69	9hr	2 daily
Malbork	17	45min	at least hourly
Poznań	58	5hr	8 daily
Toruń	46	3¾hr	9 daily
Warsaw	63	6¼hr	12 daily

International Train

DESTINATION	DURATION (HR)	FREQUENCY
Berlin (Germany)	6½	1 daily
Kaliningrad (Russia)	6	1 daily

Cafe Ferber CAFE-BAR
(ul Długa 77/78; ⏲9am-late; 📶) Modern cafe-bar dominated by bright red panels, a suspended ceiling and boxy lighting. Serves breakfast, well-made coffee, international wines and creative cocktails.

☆ Entertainment

Miasto Aniołów CLUB
(ul Chmielna 26) Late-night revellers can hit this club's spacious dance floor or hang around on the atmospheric deck overlooking the Motława River. Nightly DJs play disco and other dance-oriented sounds.

Parlament CLUB
(www.parlament.com.pl; ul Św Ducha 2; ⏲8pm-late Thu-Sat) This long-lived club plays retro music on Thursday, electronica on Friday and disco on Saturday.

State Baltic Opera Theatre OPERA
(☎58 763 4906; www.operabaltycka.pl; Al Zwycięstwa 15) In the suburb of Wrzeszcz, not far from the train station at Gdańsk Politechnika.

Information

Jazz 'n' Java (ul Tkacka 17/18; per hr 6zł; ⏲10am-10pm) Internet access.

Tourist Office (☎58 305 7080; www.gdansk4u.pl; Długi Targ 28/29; ⏲9am-7pm Jun-Aug, to 5pm Sep-May)

Getting There & Away

AIR From **Lech Wałęsa Airport** (www.airport.gdansk.pl; ul Słowackiego 200), national carrier LOT has at least three daily flights to Warsaw. Tickets can be bought at the **LOT office** (☎58 301 28 2223; ul Wały Jagiellońskie 2/4). Eurolot also flies twice daily to Wrocław and Kraków.

Gdańsk is also connected directly to a plethora of other European cities, including London and Dublin.

The airport is accessible by bus 210 or night bus N3 from outside the Gdańsk Główny train station. A private service, **Airportbus** (☎58 554 9393; www.airportbus.com.pl; ul Heweliusza 13; ticket 14.90zł), also runs from the Old Town to the airport.

BUS The **bus station** (ul 3 Maja 12) is behind the main train station. PKS buses head to Warsaw hourly (55zł, 5¾ hours), as do services of **Polski Bus** (www.polskibus.com).

TRAIN The city's main train station, **Gdańsk Główny** (ul Podwale Grodzkie 1), is conveniently located on the western outskirts of the Old Town. Most long-distance trains start or finish at Gdynia, so make sure you get on and off quickly here.

Toruń

POP 205,000

The first thing to strike you about Toruń, south of Gdańsk, is its collection of massive red-brick churches, looking more like fortresses than places of worship. The city is a pleasant place to spend a few days, offering a nice balance between a relaxing slow pace and engaging diversions.

Toruń is also famous as the birthplace of Nicolaus Copernicus, who revolutionised the field of astronomy in 1543 by asserting that the earth travelled around the sun. He's a figure you will not be able to escape – you can even buy gingerbread men in his likeness.

Toruń was fortunate to escape major damage in WWII and as a result is the best-preserved Gothic town in Poland.

Sights

Rynek Staromiejski HISTORIC AREA
(Old Town Market Sq) The starting point for any exploration of Toruń is the Rynek Staromiejski, lined by elegant facades and dominated by the massive 14th-century **Old Town Hall** (Ratusz Staromiejski). In front of the town hall is an elegant **statue of Copernicus**. Look for other interesting items of statuary around the square.

Regional Museum MUSEUM
(www.muzeum.torun.pl; Rynek Staromiejski 1; adult/concession 10/6zł; ⏲10am-6pm Tue-Sun May-Sep, to 4pm Tue-Sun Oct-Apr) Within the town hall, this museum features a fine collection of 19th- and 20th-century Polish art, along with medieval stained glass and religious paintings. Climb the 40m-high **tower** (adult/concession 10/6zł; ⏲10am-4pm Tue-Sun Apr, to 8pm Tue-Sun May-Sep) for great views.

House of Copernicus MUSEUM
(www.muzeum.torun.pl; ul Kopernika 15/17; adult/concession 10/7zł; ⏲10am-6pm Tue-Sun May-Sep, 10am-4pm Tue-Sun Oct-Apr) In 1473, Copernicus was allegedly born in the brick Gothic house that now contains this museum, presenting replicas of the great astronomer's instruments.

More engaging, if overpriced, is the museum's short **audiovisual presentation** (adult/concession 12/7zł) regarding Copernicus' life in Toruń and the extravagantly titled **World of Toruń's Gingerbread** (adult/concession 10/6zł) – a guide through the exhibition and the chance for visitors to bake their own gingerbread. A combined ticket to all three attractions costs 20/15zł.

Cathedral of SS John the Baptist & John the Evangelist CHURCH
(ul Żeglarska; adult/concession 3/2zł; ⏲9am-5.30pm Mon-Sat, 2-5.30pm Sun Apr-Oct) One block south of the Rynek Staromiejski is this place of worship with its massive **tower** (adult/concession 6/4zl) and bell.

Teutonic Knights' Castle Ruins RUINS
(ul Przedzamcze; adult/concession 8/5zł, free Mon; ⏲10am-6pm) East of the remnants of the Old Town walls are the ruins of the Teutonic Castle, destroyed in 1454.

Far Eastern Art Museum MUSEUM
(www.muzeum.torun.pl; Rynek Staromiejski 35; adult/concession 7/4zł, free Wed; ⏲10am-6pm Tue-Sun May-Sep, to 4pm Tue-Sun Oct-Apr) The richly decorated, 15th-century **House Under the Star** contains this collection of art from Asia.

Sleeping

Green Hostel HOSTEL €
(☎56 561 4000; www.greenhostel.eu; ul Małe Garbary 10; r from 100zł; 📶) This hostel without dorms offers inexpensive rooms, a kitchen and a pleasant lounge. Most rooms share a bathroom and there's no breakfast.

Hotel Pod Czarną Różą HOTEL €€
(☎56 621 9637; www.hotelczarnaroza.pl; ul Rabiańska 11; s/d 170/210zł; 📶) 'Under the Black Rose' is spread between a historic inn and a newer wing facing the river. Some doubles come with small but functional kitchens.

Orange Hostel HOSTEL €
(☎56 652 0033; www.hostelorange.pl; ul Prosta 19; dm/s/d 30/50/90zł; 📶) International backpacker hostel in a handy location. Its decor is bright and cheerful, and its kitchen is an impressive place to practise the gentle art of self-catering.

Hotel Retman HOTEL €€
(☎56 657 4460; www.hotelretman.pl; ul Rabiańska 15; s/d 180/240zł; 📶) Spacious, atmospheric rooms with red carpet and solid timber furniture. Downstairs is a good pub and restaurant.

Camping Nr 33 Tramp CAMPGROUND €
(☎56 654 7187; www.mosir.torun.pl; ul Kujawska 14; campsite per person/tent 9/7zł, s/d from 50/76zł; ⏲May-Sep) There's a choice of cabins or hotel-style rooms at this camping ground, a five-minute walk west of the main train station.

Eating & Drinking

For self-catering, there's a handy **Biedronka supermarket** (ul Szeroka 22) in the Old Town.

Masala INDIAN, POLISH €€
(Rynek Nowomiejski 8; mains 19-45zł; ⏲10am-10pm; 🖉) Formerly known as Gospoda Pod Modrym Fartuchem, this 15th-century eatery on the Rynek Nowomiejski (New Town Sq) has been visited by Polish kings and Napoleon. Polish dishes are joined by an array of Indian food, including a good vegetarian selection.

Bar Mleczny Pod Arkadami CAFETERIA €
(ul Różana 1; mains 4-12zł; ⏲9am-7pm Mon-Fri, 9am-4pm Sat & Sun) Classic milk bar just off the Rynek Staromiejski. Its takeaway window serves a range of tasty *zapiekanki* (toasted rolls with cheese, mushrooms and ketchup) and sweet waffles.

Kuranty POLISH, ITALIAN €€
(Rynek Staromiejski 29; mains 12-49zł; ⏲11am-2am; 📶) The menu is firmly based on the three Ps: pizza, pasta and *pierogi* (dumplings; including a rather tasty baked version).

Kona Coast Cafe CAFE
(ul Chełmińska 18; ⏲9am-9pm Mon-Sat, 11am-6pm Sun; 📶) Serves excellent freshly ground coffee, along with homemade lemonade, chai and various cold drinks. There's also a light meal menu.

Entertainment

Lizard King CLUB
(ul Kopernika 3; ⏲7pm-late) Live-music venue with gigs ranging from local tribute bands to big rock acts.

Teatr Baj Pomorski PUPPETRY
(☎56 652 2029; www.bajpomorski.art.pl; ul Piekarska 9) Puppet theatre shaped like a huge wooden cabinet.

Information

Ksero Uniwerek (ul Franciszkańska 5; per hr 4zł; ⏲8am-7pm Mon-Fri, 9am-2pm Sat) Internet access.

Tourist Office (☎56 621 0930; www.torun.pl; Rynek Staromiejski 25; ⏲9am-4pm Mon & Sat, to 6pm Tue-Fri, 11am-3pm Sun) Hires out handheld MP3 players with English-language audio tours of the city (10zł per four hours).

TRAINS FROM TORUŃ

DESTINATION	PRICE (ZŁ)	DURATION (HR)	FREQUENCY
Gdańsk	46	3¾	9 daily
Kraków	69	8½	3 daily
Malbork	22	3¼	7 daily
Poznań	24	2½	10 daily
Warsaw	48	2¾	11 daily
Wrocław	56	5	5 daily

Getting There & Away

BUS The **bus station** (ul Dąbrowskiego) is a 10-minute walk north of the Old Town; from here, **Polski Bus** (www.polskibus.com) connects to Warsaw (3¾ hours, four daily). However, most places can be reached more efficiently by train.

TRAIN The Toruń Główny train station is on the opposite side of the Vistula River and linked to the Old Town by bus 22 or 27. Some trains stop at the more convenient **Toruń Miasto train station** (Plac 18 Stycznia), about 500m east of the New Town.

WARMIA & MASURIA

Great Masurian Lakes

The most impressive feature of Warmia and Masuria is its beautiful postglacial landscape dominated by thousands of lakes. About 200km of canals connect these bodies of water, so the area is a prime destination for yachties and canoeists, as well as those who love to hike, fish and mountain bike.

Two towns that make good bases for exploring this lake country are **Giżycko** and **Mikołajki**. Both the Giżycko **tourist office** (☎87 428 5265; www.gizycko.turystyka.pl; ul Wyzwolenia 2; 9am-5pm Mon-Fri, 10am-2pm Sat May-Sep, 9am-5pm Mon-Fri Oct-Apr) and the Mikołajki **tourist office** (☎87 421 6850; www.mikolajki.pl; Plac Wolności 3; 10am-6pm Jun-Aug, 10am-6pm Mon-Sat May & Sep) can supply useful maps for sailing and hiking, provide excursion boat schedules, and assist with finding accommodation.

Nature aside, there are some interesting fragments of history in this region.

A grim reminder of the past is the **Wolf's Lair** (Wilczy Szaniec; www.wolfsschanze.pl; adult/concession 15/10zł; 8am-dusk). Located at **Gierłoż**, 8km east of Kętrzyn, this ruined complex was Hitler's wartime headquarters for his invasion of the Soviet Union. In 1944 a group of high-ranking German officers tried to assassinate Hitler here. The leader of the plot, Claus von Stauffenberg, entered a meeting with a bomb in his briefcase and placed it near the dictator. Although the explosion killed and wounded several people, Hitler suffered only minor injuries. Stauffenberg and some 5000 people involved in the plot were subsequently executed. These dramatic events were reprised in the 2008 Tom Cruise movie *Valkyrie*.

The Wolf's Lair is most easily accessed from **Kętrzyn**; contact the **tourist office** (☎89 751 4765; www.it.ketrzyn.pl; Plac Piłsudskiego 10; 9am-6pm Mon-Fri, 10am-3pm Sat & Sun) there for transport details.

From Gdańsk, there are trains to Kętrzyn (52zł, 4¾ hours, two daily) and Giżycko (56zł, five hours, five daily). Buses run between Giżycko and Mikołajki (17zł, 50 minutes, four daily).

UNDERSTAND POLAND

History

Poland's history started in the early Middle Ages with the Polanians (People of the Plains). Mieszko I, Duke of the Polanians, adopted Christianity in 966 and embarked on a successful campaign of conquest.

Encroachment from Germanic peoples led to the relocation of the royal capital from Poznań to Kraków in 1038. The kingdom prospered under Kazimierz III 'the Great' (1333–70) and in 1569 Poland and Lithuania were united as the largest state in Europe, stretching from the Baltic to the Black Sea.

The 18th century was a period of disaster and decline. Russia, Prussia and Austria repeatedly divided Polish territory between them; by 1795 Poland had vanished from the map of Europe. Finally, upon the end of WWI the old imperial powers dissolved and a sovereign Polish state was restored.

On 1 September 1939, a Nazi blitzkrieg rained down from the west; soon after, the Soviets invaded Poland from the east. The Germans then used Poland as a base for invading the Soviet Union. By the time the Nazi regime was finally ousted at the end of WWII, six million Poles had died, including the country's three million Jews, who were brutally annihilated in death camps.

After WWII, Poland endured four decades of Soviet-dominated communist rule. Finally, in 1990 Solidarity trade union leader Lech Wałęsa became Poland's first postwar democratically elected president.

The postcommunist transition brought radical changes, but within a decade Poland had rebuilt the foundations of a market economy. Poland joined the EU in May 2004.

The most recent parliamentary elections in 2011 were relatively uneventful, confirming the centrist Civic Platform party's hold on power. However, one remarkable element was the emergence of a strongly pro-secular party, Palikot's Movement. Among its elected representatives were Poland's first transsexual member of parliament and its first openly gay MP, a reflection of the gradually changing nature of Polish society.

People

Due to Nazi genocide and the forced resettlements that followed WWII, Poland became an ethnically homogeneous country. Some 98% of the population are ethnic Poles.

BOOKS

» *God's Playground: A History of Poland*, by Norman Davies, offers an in-depth analysis of Polish history.

» *Rising '44*, also by Davies, vividly covers the wartime Warsaw Rising.

» *The Polish Revolution: Solidarity 1980–82*, by Timothy Garton Ash, is entertaining and thorough.

» *Jews in Poland*, by Iwo Cyprian Pogonowski, is a comprehensive work.

» Evocative works about rural life in interwar Poland include Bruno Schultz's *Street of Crocodiles* and Philip Marsden's *The Bronski House*.

Poles are friendly and polite, but not overly formal. The way of life in large urban centres increasingly resembles Western styles and manners. In the countryside, however, a more conservative culture dominates, with traditional gender roles, and strong religious convictions and family ties.

Outside the big towns, knowledge of foreign languages is limited.

Arts

Poland has inherited a rich literary tradition dating from the 15th century, though its modern voice was shaped during the long period of foreign occupation in the 19th century.

At the turn of the 20th century, the avant-garde 'Young Poland' movement in art and literature developed in Kraków. Among its most notable representatives was the writer Stanisław Wyspiański (1869–1907).

The most famous Polish musician was undoubtedly Frédéric Chopin (1810–49), whose music displays the melancholy and nostalgia that became hallmarks of the national style.

Present-day Polish musicians you might catch live in concert include the controversial Doda (pop singer); Andrzej Smolik (instrumentalist); Łzy (pop-rock band); Sofa (hip-hop/soul band); and Justyna Steczkowska (pop singer). Poland's most renowned painter was Jan Matejko (1838–93), whose monumental historical paintings hang in galleries throughout the country.

Poland has produced several world-famous film directors including Roman Polański, who directed hits such as *Rosemary's Baby* and *Chinatown*, and Krzysztof Kieślowski, best known for the *Three Colours* trilogy.

SURVIVAL GUIDE

Directory A–Z

Accommodation

In Poland, budget accommodation spans camping grounds, dorms and doubles; at midrange and top-end, our price breakdown is based on a double room. Unless otherwise noted, rooms have private bathrooms and the rate includes breakfast.

€ less than 150zł

€€ 150zł to 400zł

€€€ more than 400zł

CAMPING & MOUNTAIN REFUGES

Poland has hundreds of camping grounds and many offer good-value cabins and bungalows. Most open May to September, but some only open their gates between June and August. A handy campsite resource is the website of the **Polish Federation of Camping and Caravanning** (☎22 810 6050; www.pfcc.eu).

PTTK (Polskie Towarzystwo Turystyczno-Krajoznawcze; ☎22 826 2251; www.pttk.pl) runs a chain of *schroniska górskie* (mountain refuges) for hikers. They're usually simple, with a welcoming atmosphere, and serve cheap, hot meals.

PRIVATE ROOMS, HOSTELS & HOTELS

Some destinations have agencies (usually called *biuro zakwaterowania* or *biuro kwater prywatnych*) that arrange accommodation in private homes. Rooms cost about 120/150zł per single/double.

Older-style *Schroniska młodzieżowe* (youth hostels) in Poland are operated by the **Polish Youth Hostel Association** (Polskie Towarzystwo Schronisk Młodzieżowych; ☎22 849 8128; www.ptsm.org.pl), a member of Hostelling International. Some only open in July and August and are often very busy with Polish students. Curfews are common.

Privately run hostels, geared towards international backpackers, operate in the main cities. These hostels usually offer the use of washing machines (either free or paid), in response to the near absence of laundromats in Poland.

A dorm bed can cost anything from 40zł to 80zł per person per night. Single and double rooms in hostels, if available, start at about 150zł a night.

Hotel prices often vary according to season and discounted weekend rates are often available. Two reliable websites for arranging hotel accommodation over the internet are www.poland4u.com and www.hotels-poland.com.

In big cities such as Warsaw, Kraków, Wrocław and Gdańsk some agencies offer self-contained apartments, which are an affordable alternative to hotels.

Activities

Hikers can enjoy marked trails across the Tatra and Sudeten Mountains, and the Great Masurian Lakes district. Trails are easy to follow and detailed maps are available from most larger bookshops. Poland is fairly flat and ideal for cyclists. Zakopane will delight skiers from December to March.

Business Hours

Banks 8am to 5pm Monday to Friday, sometimes 8am to 2pm Saturday

Cafes and restaurants 11am to 11pm

Nightclubs 9pm to late

Shops 10am to 6pm Monday to Friday, 10am to 2pm Saturday

Embassies & Consulates

All diplomatic missions listed are located in Warsaw unless stated otherwise.

Australian Embassy (☎22 521 3444; www.australia.pl; ul Nowogrodzka 11)

Belarusian Embassy (☎22 742 0990; www.poland.mfa.gov.by; ul Wiertnicza 58)

Canadian Embassy (☎22 584 3100; www.canada.pl; ul Matejki 1/5)

French Embassy (☎22 529 3000; www.ambafrance-pl.org; ul Piękna 1)

French Consulate (☎12 424 5300; www.cracovie.org.pl; ul Stolarska 15, Kraków)

German Embassy (☎22 584 1700; www.warschau.diplo.de; ul Jazdów 12)

German Consulate (☎12 424 3000; www.krakau.diplo.de; ul Stolarska 7, Kraków)

Irish Embassy (☎22 849 6633; www.irlandia.pl; ul Mysia 5)

Japanese Embassy (☎22 696 5005; www.pl.emb-japan.go.jp; ul Szwoleżerów 8)

Netherlands Embassy (☎22 559 1200; www.nlembassy.pl; ul Kawalerii 10)

New Zealand Embassy (☎22 521 0500; www.nzembassy.com/poland; Al Ujazdowskie 51)

Russian Embassy (☎22 849 5111; http://warsaw.rusembassy.org; ul Belwederska 49)

South African Embassy (☎22 622 1031; warsaw.consular@dirco.gov.za; ul Koszykowa 54)

Ukrainian Embassy (☎22 622 4797; www.ukraine-emb.pl; Al Szucha 7)

UK Embassy (☎22 311 0000; www.ukinpoland.fco.gov.uk; ul Kawalerii 12)

UK Consulate (☎12 421 7030; ukconsul@sunley.pl; ul Św Anny 9, Kraków)

US Embassy (☎22 504 2000; http://poland.usembassy.gov; Al Ujazdowskie 29/31)

US Consulate (☎12 424 5100; http://krakow.usconsulate.gov; ul Stolarska 9, Kraków)

Food

Price ranges are based on the average cost of a main meal.

€ less than 20zł

€€ 20zł to 40zł

€€€ more than 40zł

Gay & Lesbian Travellers

Overt homophobia from state officials has declined; though with the Church remaining influential in social matters, gay acceptance in Poland is still a work in progress. As a result, the Polish gay and lesbian scene is fairly discreet. Warsaw and Kraków are the best places to find gay-friendly bars and clubs. A good source of information on gay Warsaw and Kraków is online at www.gay-guide.net.

Internet Access

Internet access is near universal in Polish accommodation. Internet cafes charge between 4zł and 5zł per hour. Also, some forward-thinking city councils have set up wireless access in their main market squares.

Money

» Poland's currency is the złoty (*zwo*-ti), abbreviated to zł (international currency code PLN). It's divided into 100 groszy (gr).

» *Bankomats* (ATMs) accept most international credit cards and are easily found. Private *kantors* (foreign-exchange offices) are also everywhere.

» Tipping isn't common in Poland, but feel free to leave 10% extra for waiters or taxi drivers if you've had good service.

Public Holidays

New Year's Day 1 January

Epiphany 6 January

Easter Sunday March or April

Easter Monday March or April

State Holiday 1 May

Constitution Day 3 May

Pentecost Sunday Seventh Sunday after Easter

Corpus Christi Ninth Thursday after Easter

Assumption Day 15 August

All Saints' Day 1 November

Independence Day 11 November

Christmas 25 and 26 December

Safe Travel

Poland is fairly safe, but be alert for thieves and pickpockets around major train stations.

Telephone

Polish telephone numbers have nine digits, with no area codes. To call Poland from abroad, dial the country code ☎48, then the Polish number.

The main mobile telephone providers are Plus, Orange, T-Mobile and Play, all of which offer inexpensive prepaid SIM cards that come with call and data allowances.

The cheapest way to make international calls from public telephones is via prepaid international cards produced by various operators, available at post offices and kiosks.

Visas

EU citizens do not need visas to visit Poland and can stay indefinitely. Citizens of Australia, Canada, Israel, New Zealand, Switzerland and the USA can stay in Poland up to 90 days without a visa.

Other nationals should check the website of the **Ministry of Foreign Affairs** (www.msz.gov.pl).

Getting There & Away

Air

Warsaw Frédéric Chopin airport (www.lotnisko-chopina.pl; ul Żwirki i Wigury 1), usually called Okęcie, is the nation's busiest, while other important airports include Kraków, Gdańsk, Poznań and Wrocław. The national carrier **LOT** (☎801 703 703, mobile 22 19572; www.lot.com) flies to many major European cities.

Many budget carriers, including **Ryanair** (☎703 303 033; www.ryanair.com) and **Wizz Air** (☎703 603 993; www.wizzair.com), fly into Poland from airports across Europe, including regional airports in Britain and Ireland.

Land

BUS

Eurolines Polska (☎22 621 3469; www.eurolinespolska.pl) runs international buses in all directions.

CAR & MOTORCYCLE

To drive a car into Poland, EU citizens need their driving licence from home, while othe nationalities must obtain an International Drivers Permit, along with vehicle registration papers and liability insurance.

TRAIN

To save money, buy a ticket to a Polish border destination such as Szczecin or Prezmyśl, then take a local train from there.

Sea

Ferry services operated by **Polferries** (☎22 830 0930; www.polferries.pl), **Stena Line** (☎58 660 9200; www.stenaline.pl) and **Unity Line** (www.unityline.pl) connect Poland's Baltic ports to destinations in Scandinavia.

Getting Around

Air

LOT (☎801 703 703, mobile 22 19572; www.lot.com) and its cheaper **Eurolot** (☎22 574 0740; www.eurolot.com) subsidiary fly between Warsaw, Gdańsk, Kraków, Poznań, Wrocław and Szczecin.

Bus

Most buses are operated by the state bus company, PKS. It operates both ordinary buses (marked in black on timetables) and fast buses (marked in red).

Tickets for PKS buses can sometimes be bought at bus terminals, but more often from drivers.

A useful alternative to PKS is the private company **Polski Bus** (www.polskibus.com), which operates modern double-decker buses (with free wi-fi on board) to destinations throughout Poland and beyond. Fares vary dynamically in the manner of a budget airline and must be purchased in advance via the company's website.

Car

Major international car-rental companies are represented in larger cities and airports.

Avis (☎22 650 4872; www.avis.pl)

Europcar (☎22 650 2564; www.europcar.com.pl)

Hertz (☎22 500 1620; www.hertz.pl)

Train

Polish State Railways (PKP; www.pkp.pl) operates trains to almost every tourist destination; its online timetable is very helpful, providing routes, fares and intermediate stations in English.

» Express InterCity trains only stop at major cities and are the fastest way to travel by rail. These require seat reservations.

» Cheaper TLK trains *(pociąg TLK)* are slower, but are the type of train you'll most often catch. TLK trains also require seat reservations.

» InterRegio trains run between adjoining regions of Poland. No reservations are required.

» Slow Regio trains, also known as 'passenger trains' *(pociąg osobowy)* stop by every tree at the side of the track that could be imagined to be a station, and are best used only for short trips. Seats can't be reserved.

» Express InterCity and TLK trains carry two classes: *druga klasa* (2nd class) and *pierwsza klasa* (1st class), which is 50% more expensive.

Portugal

Includes »

Lisbon 855
Sintra 864
Cascais 865
The Algarve 866
Évora 869
Peniche 870
Coimbra 873
Porto 875
Viana do Castelo 879
Braga 880
Parque Nacional da Peneda-Gerês 881
Understand Portugal 882
Survival Guide 883

Best Places to Eat

- » Domus Vinum (p880)
- » Café Ingles (p868)
- » The Decadente (p860)
- » Bistro 'oPorto' (p867)
- » Botequim da Mouraria (p870)

Best Places to Stay

- » Hotel de Peneda (p881)
- » Hostel Argonauta (p871)
- » Tattva Design Hostel (p876)
- » Almaa (p865)
- » Alfama Patio Hostel (p859)

Why Go?

With medieval castles, frozen-in-time villages, captivating cities and golden-sand beaches, the Portuguese experience can mean many things. History, great food and wine, idyllic scenery and blazing nightlife are just the beginning…

Portugal's capital, Lisbon, and its northern rival, Porto, are gems among the urban streetscapes of Europe. Both are magical places for the wanderer, with picturesque views over the river, rattling trams and atmospheric lanes that hide boutiques and old-school record shops, stylish lounges, and a vibrant mix of restaurants, fado clubs and open-air cafes.

Outside the cities, you can stay overnight in converted hilltop fortresses fronting age-old vineyards, hike amid granite peaks or explore historic villages of the little-visited hinterland. More than 800km of coast offers further outdoor enticements. You can gaze out over dramatic end-of-the-world cliffs, surf stellar breaks off dune-covered beaches or laze peacefully on sandy islands fronting calm blue seas.

When to Go

Lisbon

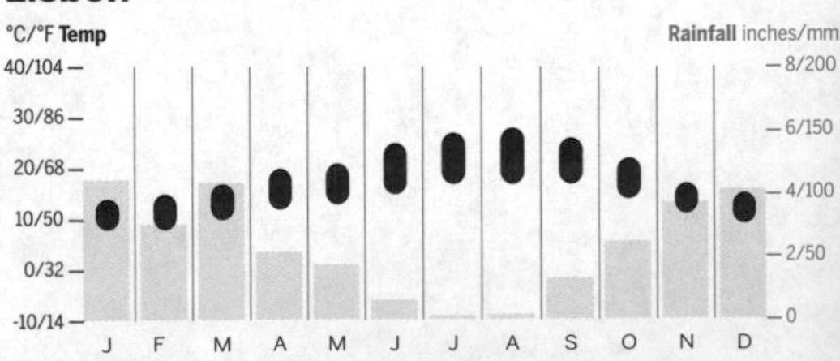

Apr & May Sunny days and wildflowers set the stage for hiking and outdoor activities.

Jun–Aug Lovely and lively, with a packed festival calendar and steamy beach days.

Late Sep & Oct Crisp mornings and sunny days; prices dip, crowds disperse.

Connections

Travelling overland from Portugal entails a trip through Spain. Good places to cross the (invisible) border include the ferry crossing from Vila Real de Santo António in The Algarve, with onward connections to Seville. There are also links from Elvas (going across to Badajoz) and rail links from Valença do Minho in the north (heading up to Santiago de Compostela in Galicia).

ITINERARIES

One Week

Devote three days to Lisbon, including a night of fado in the Alfama, bar-hopping in Bairro Alto and Unesco-gazing and pastry-eating in Belém. Spend a day taking in the wooded wonderland of Sintra, before continuing to Coimbra, Portugal's own Cambridge. End your week in Porto, gateway to the magical wine-growing region of the Douro valley.

Two Weeks

On week two, stroll the historic lanes of Évora and visit the nearby megaliths. Take in the picturesque castle towns of Monsaraz and Estrenoz before hitting the beaches of The Algarve. Travel along the coast, visiting the pretty riverfront town of Tavira and the dramatic cliffs of Sagres. End the grand tour back in sunny Lisbon.

Essential Food & Drink

» **Seafood** Chargrilled *lulas* (squid), *polvo* (octopus) or *sardinhas* (sardines). Other treats: *cataplana* (seafood and sausage cooked in a copper pot), *caldeirada* (hearty fish stew) and *açorda de mariscos* (bread stew with shrimp).

» **Cod for all seasons** Portuguese have dozens of ways to prepare *bacalhau* (salted cod). Try *bacalhau a brás* (grated cod fried with potatoes and eggs), *bacalhau espiritual* (cod soufflé) or *bacalhau com natas* (baked cod with cream and grated cheese).

» **Field & fowl** *Porco preto* (sweet 'black' pork), *leitão* (roast suckling pig), *alheira* (bread and meat sausage – formerly kosher), *cabrito assado* (roast kid) and *arroz de pato* (duck risotto).

» **Drink** Port and red wines from the Douro valley, *alvarinho* and *vinho verde* (crisp, semi-sparkling wine) from the Minho and great, little-known reds from the Alentejo and the Beiras (particularly the Dão region).

» **Pastries** The *pastel de nata* (custard tart) is legendary, especially in Belém. Other delicacies: *travesseiros* (almond and egg pastries) and *queijadas* (mini-cheese pastries).

AT A GLANCE

» **Currency** Euro (€)

» **Language** Portuguese

» **Money** ATMs widespread; banks open Mon-Fri

» **Visas** Schengen rules apply

Fast Facts

» **Area** 91,470 sq km

» **Capital** Lisbon

» **Country code** ☎351

» **Emergency** ☎112

Exchange Rates

Australia	A$1	€0.82
Canada	C$1	€0.77
Japan	¥100	€0.83
New Zealand	NZ$1	€0.65
UK	UK£1	€1.18
USA	US$1	€0.78

Set Your Budget

» **Budget hotel room** €40

» **Two-course dinner** €10–18

» **Museum entrance** €4–6

» **Glass of vinho tinto (red wine)** €1.50-2.50

Resources

» **Lonely Planet** (www.lonelyplanet.com/portugal)

» **Portugal Tourism** (www.visitportugal.com)

Portugal Highlights

1 Follow the sound of fado spilling from the lamplit lanes of the **Alfama** (p855), an enchanting old-world neighbourhood in the heart of Lisbon

2 Take in the laid-back charms of **Tavira** (p867), before hitting some of The Algarve's prettiest beaches

3 Catch live music in a backstreet bar in **Coimbra** (p873), a festive university town with a stunning medieval centre

4 Explore the wooded hills of **Sintra** (p864), studded with fairy-tale-like palaces, villas and gardens

5 Conquer the trails of the ruggedly scenic **Parque Nacional da Peneda-Gerês** (p881)

6 Enjoy heady beach days in **Lagos** (p868), a surf-loving town with a vibrant drinking and dining scene

7 Explore the Unesco World Heritage–listed centre of **Porto** (p875), sampling velvety ports at riverside wine lodges

LISBON

POP 550,000

Spread across steep hillsides that overlook the Rio Tejo, Lisbon has captivated visitors for centuries. Windswept vistas at breathtaking heights reveal the city in all its beauty: Roman and Moorish ruins, white-domed cathedrals and grand plazas lined with sun-drenched cafes. The real delight of discovery, though, is delving into the narrow cobblestone lanes.

As bright-yellow trams clatter through curvy tree-lined streets, Lisboetas (residents of Lisbon) stroll through lamp-lit old quarters, much as they've done for centuries. Village-life gossip is exchanged over fresh bread and wine at tiny patio restaurants as fado singers perform in the background. In other parts of town, Lisbon reveals her youthful alter ego at stylish dining rooms and lounges, late-night street parties, riverside nightspots, and boutiques selling all things classic and cutting-edge.

Just outside Lisbon, there's more to explore: enchanting woodlands, gorgeous beaches and seaside villages – all ripe for discovery.

Sights

BAIXA & ALFAMA

Alfama is Lisbon's Moorish time capsule: a medina-like district of tangled alleys, hidden palm-shaded squares and narrow terracotta-roofed houses that tumble down to the glittering Tejo. The terrace at **Largo das Portas do Sol** provides a splendid view over the neighbourhood.

Castelo de São Jorge CASTLE RUINS
(admission €7.50; 9am-9pm) Dating from Visigothic times, St George's Castle sits high above town with stunning views of the city and river. Inside the Ulysses Tower, a **camera obscura** offers a unique 360-degree angle on Lisbon, with demos every half-hour. If you'd rather not walk, take scenic tram 28 from Largo Martim Moniz.

Museu do Fado MUSEUM
(www.museudofado.pt; Largo do Chafariz de Dentro; admission €5; 10am-6pm Tue-Sun) This engaging museum provides vibrant audiovisual coverage of the history of fado from its working-class roots to international stardom.

BELÉM

This quarter, 6km west of Rossio, reflects Portugal's golden age and is home to several iconic sights. In addition to heritage architecture, Belém spreads some of the country's best *pastéis de nata* (custard tarts).

To reach Belém, hop aboard tram 15 from Praça da Figueira or Praça do Comércio.

Mosteiro dos Jerónimos MONASTERY
(Praça do Império; admission €7; 10am-6pm Tue-Sun) Dating from 1496, this Unesco World Heritage site is one of Lisbon's icons, and is a soaring extravaganza of Manueline architecture with stunning carvings and ceramic tiles.

FREE **Museu Colecção Berardo** MUSEUM
(www.museuberardo.pt; Praça do Império; admission free; 10am-7pm) Houses an impressive collection of abstract, surrealist and pop art, along with some of the city's best temporary exhibits.

Torre de Belém TOWER
(admission €5; 10am-6pm Tue-Sun) Another of Belém's Unesco World Heritage–listed wonders, the Tower of Belém symbolises the voyages that made Portugal powerful. Brave the cramped winding staircase to the turret for fantastic river views.

SALDANHA

Museu Calouste Gulbenkian MUSEUM
(Avenida de Berna 45; admission €4; 10am-6pm Tue-Sun) This celebrated museum showcases an epic collection of Eastern and Western

FREE THRILLS

Aside from the Castelo de São Jorge, many sights in Lisbon have free entrance on Sundays from 10am to 2pm. For a free cultural fix on other days, make for Belém's **Museu Colecção Berardo** for great art exhibits, **Museu do Teatro Romano** (Roman Theatre Museum; Pátio do Aljube 5; 10am-1pm & 2-6pm Tue-Sun) for Roman theatre ruins, and the fortresslike **Sé** (cathedral), built in 1150 on the site of a mosque. For more Roman ruins, take a free tour of the **Núcleo Arqueológico** (Rua dos Correeiros 9; 10am-5pm Mon-Sat), which contains a web of tunnels hidden under the Baixa. The new **Museu de Design e da Moda** (Rua Augusta 24; 10am-8pm Tue-Sun) exhibits eye-catching furniture, industrial design and couture dating to the 1930s.

Central Lisbon

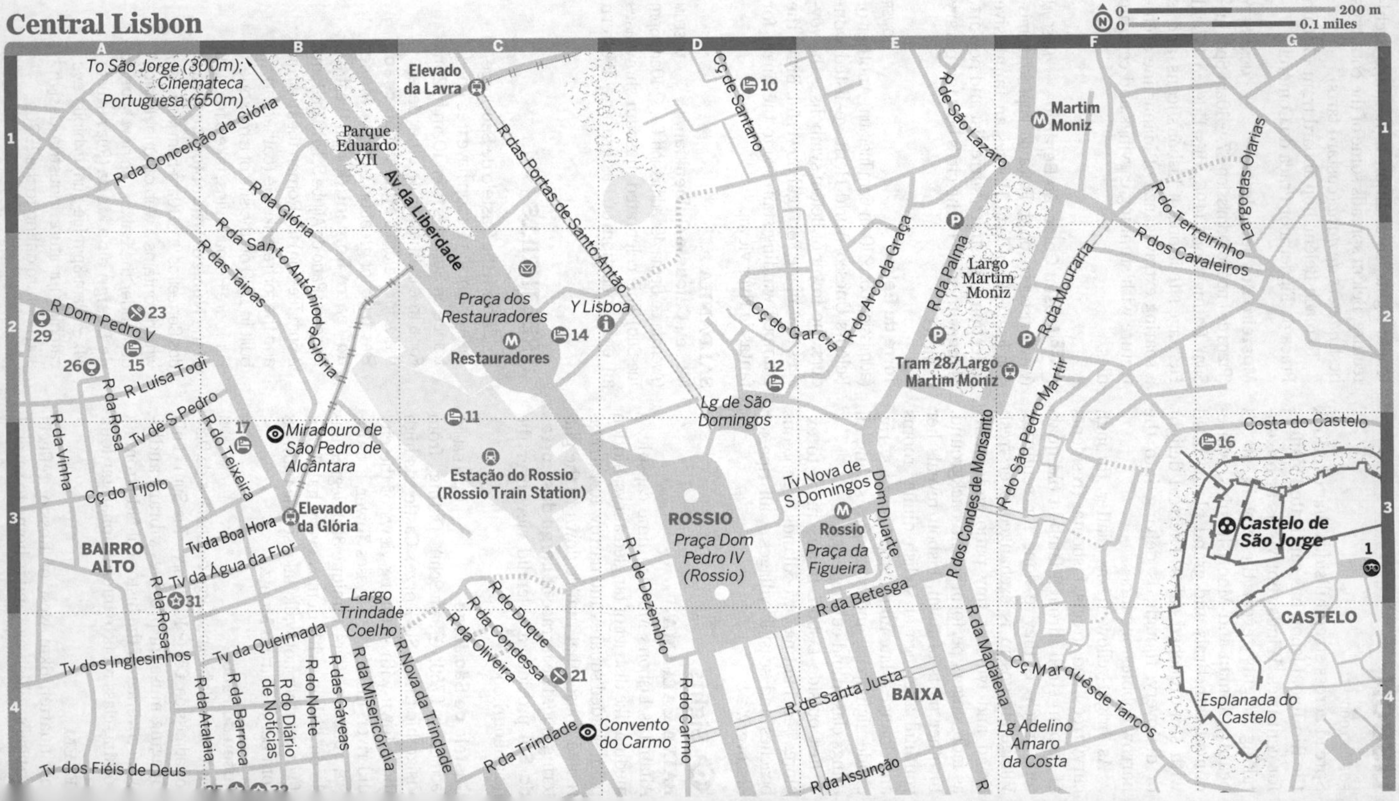

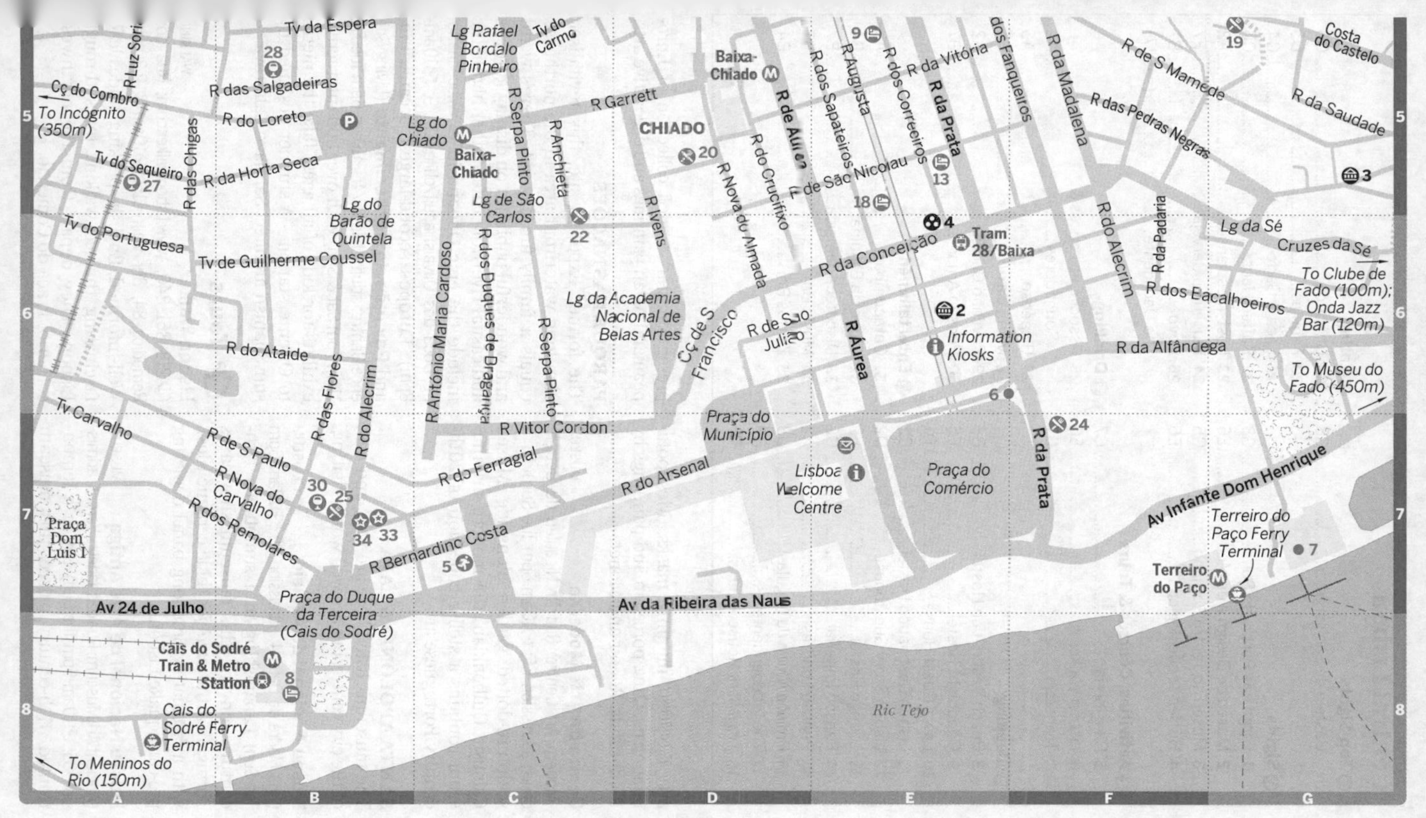

Tv da Espera
R Luz Soriano
Lg Rafael Bordalo Pinheiro
Tv do Carmo
Baixa-Chiado
Costa do Castelo
R de S Mamede
R da Saudade
R das Pedras Negras
R da Madalena
dos Fanqueiros
R da Vitória
R da Prata
R dos Correeiros
R Augusta
R dos Sapateiros
R de Áurea
R de São Nicolau
Cç do Combro
To Incógnito (350m)
R das Salgadeiras
R do Loreto
Lg do Chiado
R Garrett
CHIADO
R Serpa Pinto
R Anchieta
Tv do Sequeiro
R das Chigas
R da Horta Seca
Baixa-Chiado
R do Crucifixo
R Nova do Almada
Lg de São Carlos
Lg do Barão de Quintela
R Ivens
Tv do Portuguesa
Tv de Guilherme Coussel
R dos Duques de Bragança
R António Maria Cardoso
Lg da Academia Nacional de Belas Artes
Cç de S Francisco
R da Conceição
Tram 28/Baixa
R do Alecrim
R da Padaria
Lg da Sé
Cruzes da Sé
R dos Bacalhoeiros
To Clube de Fado (100m); Onda Jazz Bar (120m)
R de São Julião
R Áurea
Information Kiosks
R da Alfândega
To Museu do Fado (450m)
R do Ataide
R das Flores
Tv Carvalho
R de S Paulo
R Vitor Cordon
Praça do Município
R do Ferragial
R Nova do Carvalho
R dos Remolares
R do Arsenal
Lisboa Welcome Centre
Praça do Comércio
Praça Dom Luís I
R Bernardino Costa
Av Infante Dom Henrique
Terreiro do Paço Ferry Terminal
Terreiro do Paço
Av 24 de Julho
Praça do Duque da Terceira (Cais do Sodré)
Av da Ribeira das Naus
Cais do Sodré Train & Metro Station
Cais do Sodré Ferry Terminal
Rio Tejo
To Meninos do Rio (150m)

Central Lisbon

Top Sights
Castelo de São Jorge G3

Sights
1 Largo das Portas do Sol G3
2 Museu de Design e da Moda E6
3 Museu do Teatro Romano G5
4 Núcleo Arqueológico E6

Activities, Courses & Tours
5 Bike Iberia C7
6 Lisbon Walker E6
7 Transtejo G7

Sleeping
8 Beach Destination Hostel B8
9 Goodnight Hostel E5
10 Lavra Guest House D1
11 Lisbon Destination Hostel C2
12 Lisbon Story Guesthouse D2
13 Lounge Hostel E5
14 Pensão Imperial C2
15 Pensão Londres A2
16 Pensão Ninho das Águias G3
17 The Independente B3
18 Travellers House E5

Eating
19 Chapitô G5
20 Fábulas D5
21 Faca & Garfo C4
22 Kaffee Haus C6
23 Lost in Esplanada A2
24 Museu da Cerveja F7
25 Povo B7
The Decadente .... (see 17)

Drinking
26 Associação Loucos & Sonhadores A2
27 Bicaense A5
28 Maria Caxuxa B5
29 Pavilhão Chinês A2
30 Pensão Amor B7

Entertainment
31 Catacumbas A3
32 Clube da Esquina B4
33 Discoteca Jamaica B7
34 Music Box B7
35 Zé dos Bois B4

art: Egyptian mummy masks, Mesopotamian urns, Qing porcelain and paintings by Rembrandt, Renoir and Monet.

Centro de Arte Moderna MUSEUM
(Modern Art Centre; Rua Dr Nicaulau de Bettencourt; admission €5; ⊙10am-6pm Tue-Sun) In a sculpture-dotted garden alongside Museu Calouste Gulbenkian, the modern art museum contains a stellar collection of 20th-century Portuguese art.

SANTA APOLÓNIA & LAPA

The museums listed here are west and east of the city centre, but are well worth visiting.

Museu Nacional do Azulejo MUSEUM
(Rua Madre de Deus 4; admission €5; ⊙10am-6pm Tue-Sun) Languishing in a sumptuous 17th-century convent, this museum showcases Portugal's artful *azulejos* (blue ceramic tiles), with a fascinating 36m-long panel depicting pre-earthquake Lisbon.

Museu Nacional de Arte Antiga MUSEUM
(Ancient Art Museum; Rua das Janelas Verdes; admission €5; ⊙10am-6pm Tue-Sun) Set in a lemon-fronted, 17th-century palace, this museum presents a star-studded collection of European and Asian paintings and decorative arts.

PARQUE DAS NAÇÕES

The former Expo '98 site, this revitalised 2km-long waterfront area in the northeast, equals a family fun day out. There's weird and wonderful public art on display, gardens and casual riverfront cafes. Other highlights include the epic **Oceanário** (www.oceanario.pt; Doca dos Olivais; adult/child €13/9; ⊙10am-8pm), Europe's second-largest oceanarium, and **Pavilhão do Conhecimento** (Living Science Centre; adult/child €7/4; ⊙10am-6pm Tue-Fri, 11am-7pm Sat & Sun) with over 300 interactive exhibits for kids of all ages. Take the metro to Oriente station – a stunner designed by star Spanish architect Santiago Calatrava.

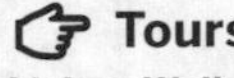

Tours

Lisbon Walker WALKIN
(☎218 861 840; www.lisbonwalker.com; Rua do Remédios 84; 3hr walk €15; ⊙10am & 2.30pm Well-informed, English-speaking guides lea fascinating themed walking tours throug Lisbon. They depart from the northwes corner of Praça do Comércio.

Transtejo RIVER CRUISE
(☎210 422 417; www.transtejo.pt; Terreiro do Paço ferry terminal; adult/child €20/10; ⏲May-Oct) These 2½-hour river cruises are a laid-back way to enjoy Lisbon's sights with multilingual commentary.

Festivals & Events

The **Festa de Santo António** (Festival of Saint Anthony), from 12 June to 13 June, culminates the three-week **Festas de Lisboa**, with processions and dozens of street parties; it's liveliest in the Alfama.

Sleeping

Lisbon has a good mix of stylish hostels and old-fashioned pensions that won't break the bank. Book well ahead during high season (July to mid-September).

BAIXA, ROSSIO & CAIS DO SODRÉ

Lavra Guest House GUESTHOUSE €€
(☎218 820 000; www.lavra.pt; Calçada de Santano 198, Rossio; d from €59; 📶) Set in a former convent, the Lavra Guest House has a range of rooms, from basic quarters facing onto an inner courtyard, to brighter rooms with wood floors and tiny balconies.

Lisbon Story Guesthouse GUESTHOUSE €€
(☎211 529 313; www.lisbonstoryguesthouse.com; Largo de São Domingos 18, Rossio; d €90-110, without bathroom €40-80; @📶) Overlooking the Praça São Domingos is a small, welcoming guesthouse with small, well-maintained rooms and a shoe-free lounge, with throw pillows and low tables.

Lisbon Destination Hostel HOSTEL €
(☎213 466 457; www.rossiopatio.com; top floor, Rossio Train Station; dm/d/tr €22/60/75; @📶) Despite its location inside a train station, this hostel has loads of style, with a glass ceiling flooding the spacious plant-filled common area with light. Rooms are crisp and well-maintained, and there are loads of activities (bar crawls, beach day trips, etc), plus excellent multicourse meals available (€8 per person including wine).

Beach Destination Hostel HOSTEL €
(☎210 997 735; Cais do Sodré Train Station; dm/d €22/60; @📶) New in 2012, this beautifully designed hostel has comfy rooms, a swanky dining room, a top-notch kitchen and a roof terrace with impressive river views.

Goodnight Hostel HOSTEL €
(☎213 430 139; www.goodnighthostel.com; Rua dos Correiros 113, Baixa; dm/d €20/50; @📶) Set in a converted 18th-century town house, this glam hostel rocks with its fab location and retro design. The high-ceilinged dorms offer vertigo-inducing views over Baixa.

Lounge Hostel HOSTEL €
(☎213 462 061; www.lisbonloungehostel.com; Rua de São Nicolau 41, Baixa; dm/d incl breakfast €25/64; @📶) These ultrahip Baixa digs have a party vibe. Bed down in immaculate dorms and meet like-minded travellers in the funky lounge watched over by a wacky moose head.

Travellers House HOSTEL €
(☎210 115 922; www.travellershouse.com; Rua Augusta 89, Baixa; dm from €22; @📶) This super-friendly hostel is set in a converted 250-year-old house and offers cosy dorms, a retro lounge with beanbags, an internet corner and a communal kitchen.

Pensão Imperial GUESTHOUSE €
(☎213 420 166; Praça dos Restauradores 78, Rossio; s/d €25/40) Above Praça dos Restauradores, and four flights up, this simple pension has high ceilinged rooms with basic wooden furniture; it's nothing flash, but some rooms have balconies overlooking the plaza.

ALFAMA

Alfama Patio Hostel HOSTEL €
(☎218 883 127; http://alfamapatio.com; Rua das Escolas Gerais 3; dm/d from €20/60; @📶) Located in the heart of the Alfama, this place attracts a cool, laid-back crowd. There are loads of activities (pub crawls, day trips to the beach), plus barbecues on the garden-like patio.

Pensão Ninho das Águias GUESTHOUSE €
(☎218 854 070; Costa do Castelo 74; s/d/tr without bathroom €30/40/60) It isn't called 'eagle's

CYCLING THE TEJO

A **cycling/jogging path** courses along the Tejo for 7km, between Cais do Sodré and Belém. Complete with artful touches – including the poetry of Pessoa printed along parts of it – the path takes in ageing warehouses, weathered docks and open-air restaurants and nightspots.

A handy place to rent bikes is a short stroll from Cais do Sodré: **Bike Iberia** (www.bikeiberia.com; Largo Corpo Santo 5; bike hire per hr/day €4/14; ⏲9.30am-7.30pm).

nest' for nothing: this guest house has a Rapunzel-esque turret affording magical 360-degree views over Lisbon. Book ahead.

CHIADO, BAIRRO ALTO & PRÍNCIPE REAL

Oasis Lisboa HOSTEL €
(213 478 044; www.oasislisboa.com; Rua de Santa Catarina 24, Principe Real; dm incl breakfast €17-21;) Behind yellow wonder walls, this self-defined backpacker mansion offers wood-floored dorms, a sleek lounge and kitchen, and a rooftop terrace with impressive river views.

Pensão Londres GUESTHOUSE €€
(213 462 203; www.pensaolondres.com.pt; Rua Dom Pedro V 53, Bairro Alto; s/d €50/75, without bathroom €35/45;) This friendly and popular place has old-fashioned appeal, with large, high-ceilinged, carpeted rooms. Those on the 4th floor have fine views.

The Independente HOSTEL €
(Hostel & Suites; 213 461 381; www.theindependente.pt; Rua de São Pedro de Alcântara 81; dm €18-20, ste from €80) Located on the edge of the Bairro Alto, this stylish place has dorm rooms and several roomier suites with balconies overlooking the city. Common areas feature vintage furnishings and art deco details, and the restaurant and bar are great places to start off the night. Light sleepers beware: noise is a major issue.

AVENIDA DE LIBERDADE, RATO & MARQUÊS DE POMBAL

Lisbon Dreams GUESTHOUSE €€
(213 872 393; www.lisbondreamsguesthouse.com; Rua Rodrigo da Fonseca 29, Rato; s/d without bathroom incl breakfast €50/60;) On a quiet street lined with jacaranda trees, Lisbon Dreams offers excellent value with its bright modern rooms with tall ceilings and high-end mattresses. Bathrooms are shared, but spotlessly clean.

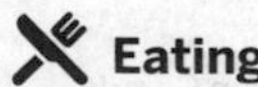

Eating

In addition to creative newcomers, you'll find inexpensive, traditional dining rooms home to classic Portuguese fare.

BAIXA, ROSSIO & CAIS DO SODRÉ

Povo PORTUGUESE €
(Rua Nova do Carvalho 32; small plates €4-8; noon-2am Tue-Sat, 6pm-1am Sun & Mon) On bar-lined Rua Nova do Carvalho, Povo serves up tasty Portuguese comfort food in the form of *petiscos* (small plates). There's outdoor seating and live fado nights (Thursdays are best).

Museu da Cerveja PORTUGUESE €€
(Praça do Comerçio 62; mains €10-16; 9am-2am) One of a number of new eating and drinking spaces lining the Praça do Comerçio, this sprawling restaurant serves up grilled meats and seafood as well as microbrews. The outdoor tables are great for people-watching.

ALFAMA

Páteo 13 PORTUGUESE €€
(Calçadinha de Santo Estêvão 13; mains €8-12) Follow the scent of chargrilled fish to this local favourite tucked away on a small, festively decorated plaza in the Alfama.

Chapitô CONTEMPORARY €€€
(218 867 334; Costa do Castelo 7; mains €17-20; lunch & dinner) This creative spot (which shares space with a circus school) has a gardenlike courtyard and a top-floor restaurant with mesmerising views over Lisbon.

Pois Café CAFE €€
(Rua de São João da Praça 93; mains €5-12; 11am-10pm Tue-Sun) Boasting a laid-back vibe, Pois Café has creative salads, sandwiches and fresh juices, plus a delicious daily special (soup and main for €9.50). Its sofas invite lazy afternoons spent reading novels and sipping coffee.

CHIADO, BAIRRO ALTO & PRÍNCIPE REAL

The Decadente PORTUGUESE €€
(913 069 345; Rua de São Pedro de Alcântara 81, The Independente; mains €10-14) This beautifully designed restaurant and bar, with touches of industrial chic, geometric artwork and an enticing back patio, attracts a mix of hip Lisboetas and foreign guests staying at the Independente. The changing three-course lunch menu (€10) is first-rate.

Lost in Esplanada INTERNATIONAL €€
(Rua Dom Pedro V 56; mains €11-15; 4pm-midnight Mon, 12.30pm-midnight Tue-Sat) Hidden behind a textile shop, this well-concealed terrace is set with painted whicker chairs, a gurgling fountain, and a Krishna mural though the view over the city is the real star. Veggie burgers, prawn curry and Portuguese sharing plates comprise the menu.

Fábulas CAFE €
(Calçada Nova de São Francisco 14, Chiado; mains €9-13; 10am-midnight Mon-Sat, noon-10pm Sun;) Stone walls, low lighting and twist

ing corridors that open onto cosy nooks and crannies do indeed conjure a storybook fable *(fábula)*. Sink into a comfy couch with coffee or wine, or have a meal – creative salads, curries, burritos and daily specials.

Faca & Garfo PORTUGUESE €
(Rua da Condessa 2, Chiado; mains €7-9; lunch & dinner Mon-Sat) The sweet *azulejo*-filled Faca & Garfo (which means 'knife and fork') serves carefully prepared Portuguese recipes at reasonable prices. Try the authentic *alheira de Mirandela* (chicken sausage) or the *bife à casa* (steak with cream and port wine sauce).

Terra VEGETARIAN €€
(213 421 407; Rua da Palmeira 15, Principe Real; buffet €13-16; lunch & dinner Tue-Sun;) Terra is famed for its superb vegetarian buffet (including vegan options) of salads, kebabs and curries, plus organic wines and juices. A fountain gurgles in the tree-shaded courtyard, lit by twinkling lights after dark.

Kaffee Haus CAFE €€
(Rua Anchieta 3, Chiado; mains €9-13; 11am-midnight Tue-Thu, 11am-2am Fri & Sat, 11am-8pm Sun) Overlooking a peaceful corner of Chiado, this cool but unpretentious cafe has daily chalkboard specials – big salads, tasty schnitzels, vegetarian risotto, strudels, cakes and more.

BELÉM

Antiga Confeitaria de Belém PATISSERIE €
(213 637 423; Rua de Belém 86-88; 8am-11pm) Since 1837, this patisserie has been transporting locals to sugar-coated nirvana with heavenly *pastéis de belém*: crispy crusted pastry nests filled with custard cream.

Drinking

All-night street parties in Bairro Alto, sunset drinks from high-up terraces, and sumptuous art deco cafes scattered about Chiado – Lisbon has many enticing options for imbibers.

Pensão Amor BAR
(Rua Nova do Carvalho 36; noon-2am Mon-Wed, to 4am Thu & Fri, 6pm-4am Sat) Set inside a former brothel, this cheeky bar pays homage to its amorous past with colourful wall murals, a library of erotic-tinged works and a boutique selling sexy accoutrements. Numerous other bars line the street, which gets packed on weekends.

HEAVENLY VIEWS

Lisbon's *miradouros* (viewpoints) provide memorable settings to take in the panorama. Some have outdoor cafes attached.

Largo das Portas do Sol Has a stylish bar and cafe.

Miradouro da Graça A pine-fringed square that's perfect for sundowners.

Miradouro da Senhora do Monte The highest lookout, with memorable castle views.

Miradouro de São Pedro de Alcântara Drinks and sweeping views on the edge of Bairro Alto.

Miradouro de Santa Catarina Youthful spot with guitar-playing rebels, artful graffiti and a first-rate eating/drinking spot (Noobai Café, p862) attached.

Pavilhão Chinês LOUNGE
(Rua Dom Pedro V 89-91, Principe Real) An old curiosity shop of a bar with oil paintings and model spitfires dangling from the ceiling, and cabinets brimming with glittering Venetian masks and Action Men. Play pool or bag a comfy armchair with a port or beer in hand.

Bicaense BAR
(Rua da Bica de Duarte Belo 42a, Bica) Indie kids have a soft spot for this chilled Santa Catarina haunt, kitted out with retro radios, projectors and squishy beanbags. DJs spin house to the preclubbing crowd and the back room stages occasional gigs.

Associação Loucos & Sonhadores BAR
(Travessa do Conde de Soure 2) Though it's in Bairro Alto, this bohemian drinking den feels secreted away from the heaving masses on nearby streets. Kitschy decor, free (salty) popcorn and eclectic tunes – it's a great place for conversation rather than pounding shots.

Meninos do Rio OUTDOOR BAR
(Rua da Cintura do Porto de Lisboa, Armação 255, Santos; 12.30pm-1am Sun-Thu, to 4am Fri & Sat) Perched on the river's edge, Meninos do Rio has palm trees, wooden decks, DJs and tropical cocktails, giving it a vibe that's more Caribbean than Iberian.

Maria Caxuxa BAR
(Rua Barroca 6, Bairro Alto; ⏲8am-2am) Maria Caxuxa has effortless style, its several rooms decked with giant mixers, *azulejo*-lined walls and 1950s armchairs and sofas, as funk-laden jazz plays overhead.

Noobai Café CAFE, BAR
(Miradouro de Santa Catarina, Santa Catarina; ⏲noon-midnight) Lisbon's best-kept secret is next to Miradouro de Santa Catarina, with a laid-back vibe, jazzy beats and magnificent views from the terrace.

☆ Entertainment

For the latest goings-on, pick up the weekly *Time Out Lisboa* (www.timeout.pt) from bookstores, or the free monthly *Follow me Lisboa* or the *Agenda Cultural Lisboa* from the tourist office.

Live Music

Zé dos Bois ALTERNATIVE
(☎213 430 205; www.zedosbois.org; Rua da Barroca 59, Bairro Alta) Focusing on tomorrow's performing arts and music trends, Zé dos Bois is an experimental venue with a laid-back courtyard. Come for concerts, DJs and changing exhibitions.

Onda Jazz Bar JAZZ
(www.ondajazz.com; Arco de Jesus 7, Alfama) This vaulted cellar features a menu of mainstream jazz, plus more-eclectic beats of bands hailing from Brazil and Africa.

Catacumbas JAZZ
(Travessa da Água da Flor 43, Bairro Alta) Moodily lit and festooned with portraits of legends such as Miles Davis, this den is jam-packed when it hosts live jazz on Thursday night.

Nightclubs

Cover charges for nightclubs typically run from €5 to €12.

Lux CLUB
(www.luxfragil.com; Avenida Infante Dom Henrique, Santo Apolónia) Still Lisbon's best club, this beautifully conceived two-storey club attracts a mixed crowd who come for an eclectic lineup of concerts, along with big-name DJs. The rooftop terrace has fine views over the Tejo.

Music Box CLUB
(www.musicboxlisboa.com; Rua Nova do Carvalho 24, Cais do Sodré) Under the brick arches on Rua Nova do Carvalho lies one of Lisbon's hottest clubs. Music Box hosts loud and bouncy club nights with music shifting from electro to rock, plus ear-splitting gigs by rising bands.

Incógnito CLUB
(Rua dos Polais de São Bento 37, Santa Catarina) No-sign, pint-sized Incógnito offers an alternative vibe and DJs thrashing out indie rock and electro-pop. Sweat it out with a fun crowd on the tiny basement dance floor, or breathe more easily in the loft bar upstairs.

Discoteca Jamaica CLUB
(Rua Nova do Carvalho, Cais do Sodré; ⏲11pm-4am) Gay and straight, black and white, young and old – everyone has a soft spot for this long-running club. It gets going around 2am at weekends with DJs pumping out reggae, hip hop and retro.

PORTUGUESE SOUL

Infused by Moorish song and the ditties of homesick sailors, bluesy, bittersweet **fado** encapsulates the Lisbon psyche like nothing else. The uniquely Portuguese style was born in the Alfama, still the best place in Lisbon to hear it live. Minimum consumption charges range from €15 to €25 per person.

A Baîuca (Rua de São Miguel 20; ⏲dinner Thu-Mon) On a good night, walking into A Baîuca is like gatecrashing a family party. It's a special place with *fado vadio,* where locals take a turn and spectators hiss if anyone dares to chat during the singing.

Clube de Fado (☎218 852 704; www.clube-de-fado.com; Rua de São João da Praça; ⏲9pm-2.30am Mon-Sat) Hosts the cream of the fado crop in vaulted, dimly lit surrounds. Big-name *fadistas* perform here alongside celebrated guitarists.

Mesa de Frades (☎917 029 436; www.mesadefrades.com; Rua dos Remédios 139a; admission from €15; ⏲dinner Wed-Mon) A magical place to hear fado, tiny Mesa de Frades used to be a chapel. It's tiled with exquisite *azulejos* and has just a handful of tables. Reserve ahead.

Gay & Lesbian Venues

Lisbon's small gay scene is headquartered in Príncipe Real, though you'll also find a few gay bars in Bairro Alto. Lux draws both a gay and straight crowd.

Construction CLUB
(Rua Cecílio de Sousa 84; midnight-6am Fri & Sat) New in 2012, Construction is the hot club of the moment, with pumping house music and a dark room. Popular with bears.

Finalmente CLUB
(Rua da Palmeira 38) This popular club has a tiny dance floor, nightly drag shows and wall-to-wall crowds.

Trumps CLUB
(www.trumps.pt; Rua da Imprensa Nacional 104b) Lisbon's hottest gay club, with cruisy corners, a sizeable dance floor and events from live music to drag.

Clube da Esquina BAR
(tel, info 213 427 149; Rua da Barroca 30; 10pm-4am) DJs playing hip hop and house to an eye-candy crowd. Several other gay bars are nearby.

Cinemas

Lisbon's cinematic standouts are the grand **São Jorge** (Avenida da Liberdade 175) and, just around the corner, **Cinemateca Portuguesa** (www.cinemateca.pt; Rua Barata Salgueiro 39); both screen offbeat, art-house, world and old films. For Hollywood fare, visit multiscreen **Amoreiras Cinema** (Avenida Eng Duarte Pacheco, Amoreiras Shopping Centre) or **Colombo Cinema** (Centro Colombo, Avenida Lusíada)

Sport

Lisbon's football teams are Benfica, Belenenses and Sporting. Euro 2004 led to the upgrading of the 65,000-seat **Estádio da Luz** and the construction of the 54,000-seat **Estádio Nacional**. Bullfights are staged on Thursday from May to October at **Campo Pequeno** (Avenida da República; tickets €10-75). Tickets are available at **ABEP ticket kiosk** (Praça dos Restauradores). State-of-the-art stadium **Estádio José de Alvalade** (Rua Prof Fernando da Fonseca) seats 54,000 and is just north of the university. Take the metro to Campo Grande.

Information

Emergency

Police, Fire & Ambulance (119)
Police Station (217 654 242; Rua Capelo 13)

> **WANT MORE?**
>
> For in-depth information, reviews and recommendations at your fingertips, head to the Apple App Store to purchase Lonely Planet's *Lisbon City Guide* iPhone app.

Tourist Police (213 421 634; Palácio Foz, Praça dos Restauradores; 24hr)

Internet Access

Most hostels and midrange guesthouses offer wireless (usually free). Loads of cafes and restaurants also offer wi-fi – just ask for the *codigo* (access code).

Portugal Telecom (Praça Rossio 68; 9am-10pm) Handy place to get online next to Praça Rossio. Also has telephone booths.

Medical Services

British Hospital (217 213 400; Rua Tomás da Fonseca) English-speaking staff and doctors.

Money

Cota Câmbios (Rossio 41) One of the best exchange rates in town.

Post

Main Post Office (Praça do Comércio)
Post Office (Praça dos Restauradores)

Tourist Information

Ask Me Lisboa (www.askmelisboa.com; Praça dos Restauradores; 9am-8pm) The largest and most helpful tourist office. Can book accommodation or reserve rental cars.

Information Kiosks (near Rua Conceição; 10am-1pm & 2-6pm) Santa Apolónia (door 47, inside train station, Santa Apolónia; 8am-1pm Tue-Sat); Belém (Largo dos Jerónimos, Belém; 10am-1pm & 2-6pm Tue-Sat); Airport (Airport; 7am-midnight)

Lisboa Welcome Centre (www.visitlisboa.com; Praça do Comércio; 9am-6pm)

Y Lisboa (www.askmelisboa.com; Rua Jardim do Regedor 50; 9am-8pm)

Websites

Time Out (www.timeout.pt) Details on upcoming gigs, cultural events and interesting commentary; in Portuguese.

Go Lisbon (www.golisbon.com) Up-to-date info on sightseeing, eating, nightlife and events.

Visit Lisboa (www.visitlisboa.com) Lisbon's comprehensive tourism website, with the low-down on sightseeing, transport and accommodation.

Getting There & Away

Air

Around 6km north of the centre, **Aeroporto de Lisboa** (Lisbon Airport; www.ana.pt) operates direct flights to many European cities.

Bus

Lisbon's long-distance bus terminal is **Sete Rios** (Rua das Laranjeiras), conveniently linked to both Jardim Zoológico metro station and Sete Rios train station. The big carriers, **Rede Expressos** (213 581 460; www.rede-expressos.pt) and **Eva** (213 581 466; www.eva-bus.com), run frequent services to almost every major town.

The other major terminal is Gare do Oriente (at Oriente metro and train station), concentrating on services to the north and to Spain. The biggest companies operating from here are **Renex** (218 956 836; www.renex.pt) and the Spanish operator **Avanza** (218 940 250; www.avanza-bus.com). Destinations in Spain include Madrid (€39, 8 hours), Barcelona (€70, 19 hours) and Sevilla (€38, 7 hours), all via Évora.

Train

Santa Apolónia station is the terminus for northern and central Portugal. You can catch trains from Santa Apolónia to Gare do Oriente train station, which has departures to The Algarve and international destinations. Cais do Sodré station is for Belém, Cascais and Estoril. Rossio station is the terminal for trains to Sintra via Queluz.

For fares and schedules, visit www.cp.pt.

Getting Around

To/From the Airport

The AeroBus runs every 20 minutes from 7am to 11pm, taking 30 to 45 minutes between the airport and Cais do Sodré; buy your ticket (€3.50) on the bus.

A new metro station (Aeroporto) on the red line opened in 2012, allowing convenient access to downtown. Change at Alameda (green line) to reach Rossio and Baixa. A taxi into town is about €10 to €15.

Public Transport

A 24-hour Bilhete Carris/Metro (€5) gives unlimited travel on all buses, trams, metros and funiculars. Pick it up from Carris kiosks and metro stations.

BUS, TRAM & FUNICULAR Buses and trams run from 6am to 1am, with a few all-night services. Pick up a transport map from tourist offices or Carris kiosks. A single ticket costs more if you buy it on board (€2.85/1.75/3.50 for tram/bus/funicular), and much less (€1.25 per ride) if you buy a refillable Viva Viagem card (€0.50), available at Carris offices and in metro stations.

There are three funiculars: Elevador da Bica; Elevador da Glória; Elevador do Lavra.

Don't leave the city without riding tram 28 from Largo Martim Moniz through the narrow streets of the Alfama; tram 12 goes from Praça da Figueira out to Belém.

FERRY Car, bicycle and passenger ferries leave frequently from the Cais do Sodré ferry terminal to Cacilhas (€1.15, 10 minutes). From Terreiro do Paço terminal, catamarans zip across to Montijo (€2.70, every 30 minutes) and Seixal (€2.30, every 30 minutes).

METRO The **metro** (www.metrolisboa.pt; 1-/2-zone single €0.85/1.15; 6.30am-1am) is useful for hops across town and to the Parque das Nações. Buy tickets from metro ticket machines, which have English-language menus.

AROUND LISBON

Sintra

POP 26,200

Lord Byron called this hilltop town a 'glorious Eden' and, although best appreciated at dusk when the coach tours have left, it *is* a magnificent place. Less than an hour west of Lisbon, Sintra was the traditional summer retreat of Portugal's kings. Today, it's a fairy-tale setting of stunning palaces and manors surrounded by rolling green countryside.

Sights & Activities

Although the whole town resembles a historical theme park, there are several compulsory eye-catching sights.

TOP CHOICE **Quinta da Regaleira** VILLA, GARDENS
(www.regaleira.pt; Rua Barbosa du Bocage; adult/child €6/3; 10am-8pm) Exploring this neo-Manueline manor and gardens is like delving into another world. The villa has ferociously carved fireplaces, frescos and Venetian glass mosaics with wild mythological and Knights Templar symbols. The playful gardens hide fountains, grottoes, lakes and underground caverns. All routes seem to lead to the 30m-deep initiation well, **Poço Iniciáto**, with mysterious hollowed-out underground galleries lit by fairy lights.

Palácio Nacional de Sintra PALACE
(Largo Rainha Dona Amélia; admission €7; 10am-5.30pm Thu-Tue) The whimsical interior of Sintra's iconic twin-chimney palace is a mix of Moorish and Manueline styles, with arab

esque courtyards, barley-twist columns and stunning 15th- and 16th-century geometric *azulejos*.

Castelo dos Mouros CASTLE
(adult/child €7/6; ⏲10am-8pm) An energetic, 3km greenery-flanked hike from the centre, the 8th-century ruined ramparts of this castle provide fine views.

Palácio Nacional da Pena PALACE
(adult/child €13.50/11; ⏲10am-7pm) This exuberantly kitsch palace is a further 800m from the Castelo dos Mouros, and is an architectural extravaganza crammed with curious treasures.

Sleeping

Almaa HOSTEL €
(☎219 240 008; www.almaasintrahostel.com; Caminho dos Frades; dm/d/tr €26/64/84) Sustainably minded Almaa is an idyllic spot to recharge for a few days, with a quirky design scheme and a beautiful setting. The surrounding 3.5 hectares of lush grounds are set with walking paths and an old spring-fed reservoir for swimming. It's a 10-minute walk from the village centre.

Casa de Hóspedes Dona Maria da Parreirinha GUESTHOUSE €
(☎219 232 490; Rua João de Deus 12-14; d €45-55) A short walk from the train station, this small, homely guest house has old-fashioned but spotless rooms, with dark-wood furnishings and floral fabrics.

Eating & Drinking

Tulhas PORTUGUESE €€
(Rua Gil Vicente 4; mains €10-14; ⏲closed Wed) Dark, tiled and quaint, Tulhas is a cosy setting to indulge in its renowned *bacalhau com natas* (baked cod with cream and grated cheese).

Saudade CAFE €
(Avenida Dr Miguel Bombardo 8; snacks €2-4; ⏲8.30am-midnight Mon-Tue & Thu-Sat, 9am-8pm Sun; 📶) This former bakery with changing art exhibitions has cherub-covered ceilings and a rambling interior. It's a charming spot for pastries or lighter fare, as well as daily specials.

Information

Tourist Office (www.cm-sintra.pt; Praça da República 23; ⏲9am-7pm) Has useful maps and can help with accommodation.

Getting There & Away

The **Lisbon–Sintra railway** terminates in Sintra, a 1km scenic walk northeast of the town's historic centre. Sintra's **bus station**, and another train station, are a further 1km east in the new town Portela de Sintra. Frequent shuttle buses link the historic centre with the bus station.

Train services (€2.05, 40 minutes, every 15 minutes) run between Sintra and Lisbon's Rossio station. Buses run regularly from Sintra to Cascais (€4, 60 minutes), Estoril (€4, 40 minutes) and Mafra (45 minutes).

Getting Around

A handy bus for accessing the castle is the hop-on, hop-off Scotturb bus 434 (€5), which runs from the train station via Sintra-Vila to Castelo dos Mouros (10 minutes), Palácio da Pena (15 minutes), and back.

A taxi to Pena or Monserrate costs around €6 one-way.

Cascais

POP 34,000

Cascais is a handsome seaside resort with elegant buildings, an atmospheric Old Town and a happy abundance of restaurants and bars.

Sights & Activities

Coast & Beaches BEACH
Cascais' three sandy bays – **Praia da Conceição**, **Praia da Rainha** and **Praia da Ribeira** – are great for a sunbake or a tingly Atlantic dip, but attract crowds in summer.

Estoril is a somewhat faded resort 2km east of Cascais with a popular sandy beach and Europe's largest **casino** (www.casino-estoril.pt).

The sea roars into the coast at **Boca do Inferno** (Hell's Mouth), 2km west of Cascais. Spectacular **Cabo da Roca**, Europe's westernmost point, is 16km from Cascais and Sintra and is served by buses from both towns.

FREE **Casa das Histórias Paula Rego** GALLERY
(www.casadashistoriaspaularego.com; Avenida da República 300; ⏲10am-7pm) A boon to Sintra's cultural cache, this small museum showcases the disturbing, fairy-tale-like paintings of Paula Rego, one of Portugal's finest living artists.

> **BIKE TO THE BEACH**
>
> Free bikes are available from 8am to 7pm from a kiosk on Largo da Estação near the train station (bring ID). There's a bicycle path that runs the entire 9km stretch from Cascais to wild Guincho beach, a popular surf spot.

Museu Condes de Castro Guimarães MUSEUM
(⏲10am-5pm Tue-Sun) The picturesque gardens of **Parque Marechal Carmona** (Avenida Rei Humberto II) house this museum in a whimsical early-19th-century mansion, complete with castle turrets and Arabic cloister.

Sleeping & Eating

Residencial Solar Dom Carlos GUESTHOUSE €€
(☎214 828 115; www.solardomcarlos.pt; Rua Latino Coelho 104; s/d €50/70; P@) Hidden down a sleepy alley, this 16th-century former royal residence turned guesthouse retains lots of original features, from chandeliers to wood beams, *azulejos* and a frescoed breakfast room.

Confraria Sushi JAPANESE €€
(Rua Luís Xavier Palmeirim 16; mains €8-13; ⏲noon-midnight Tue-Sun) This art-slung cafe, jazzed up with technicolour glass chandeliers, is a fun spot for sushi and tasty salads. Patio seating.

Viriato PORTUGUESE €€
(Av Vasco da Gama 34; mains €8-12; ⏲lunch daily, dinner Wed-Mon) Amid rustic country decor, Viriato is a local favourite for its chargrilled fish and Portuguese classics.

Information

Tourist Office (www.visiteestoril.com; Rua Visconde de Luz 14) Can provide accommodation lists and bus timetables.

Getting There & Around

Trains run frequently to Cascais via Estoril (€2.05, 40 minutes) from Cais do Sodré station in Lisbon.

THE ALGARVE

Love it or loathe it, it's easy to see the allure of The Algarve: breathtaking cliffs, golden sands, scalloped bays and long sandy islands. Although overdevelopment has blighted parts of the coast, head inland and you'll land solidly in lovely Portuguese countryside once again. Algarve highlights include riverside Tavira, party-loving Lagos and windswept Sagres. Faro is the regional capital.

Faro

POP 65,000

Faro is an attractive town with a palm-clad waterfront, well-maintained plazas and a small pedestrianised centre sprinkled with outdoor cafes. There are no beaches in Faro itself, though it's an easy jaunt by ferry to picturesque beaches nearby. A boat trip through the Parque Natural da Ria Formosa is another highlight.

Sights & Activities

Ilha Deserta ISLAND
Around six ferries per day make the 35-minute trip (€10 return) out to Ilha da Barreta (aka Ilha Deserta), a long narrow-strip of sand just off the mainland. There's a good seafood restaurant there, but little other development. Boats depart from the west side of Cidade Velha; exiting the tourist office, turn left and follow the edge of the old walls. Other departures from here go to **Praia de Faro** (bus 14 and 16 also go here) and **Praia de Farol**.

Parque Natural da Ria Formosa PARK
For visits to the Ria Formosa Natural Park, sign up for a boating or birdwatching tour with the environmentally friendly outfits of **Ria Formosa** (☎918 720 002; www.formosamar.pt) and **Lands** (☎289 817 466; www.lands.pt), both in the Clube Naval in Faro's marina.

Sleeping & Eating

Residencial Oceano GUESTHOUSE €
(☎289 823 349; Rua Ivens 21; s/d €40/50; @) Up a tile-lined stairway, you'll find this simple and friendly option with tidy rooms (some of which lack windows).

Residencial Dandy GUESTHOUSE €
(☎289 824 791; Rua Filipe Alistão 62; d from €40) Plastic flowers, African masks and museum-style paraphernalia are features of this rambling place. The best rooms have antique furniture, high ceilings and wrought-iron balconies.

Pousada da Juventude HOSTEL
(☎289 826 521; www.pousadasjuventude.pt; Rua da Polícia de Segurança Pública 1; dm/d from €15/3

(wifi) Adjoining a small park, this hostel offers basic, clean rooms with no frills but is a good ultrabudget option.

Adega Nova PORTUGUESE €€
(Rua Francisco Barreto 24; mains €7-13) This much-loved place serves tasty meat and fish dishes amid country charm. The daily specials are a superb value.

Restaurante A Taska PORTUGUESE €€
(☎289 824 739; Rua do Alportel 38; mains €7-14; ⊙lunch & dinner Mon-Sat) Popular with locals, this cosy, busy trattoria-style restaurant serves delicious regional food such as *xarém* (corn meal), and has daily specials on a blackboard.

Information

Tourist Office (www.visitalgarve.pt; Rua da Misericórdia 8) A helpful, multilingual office.

Getting There & Away

Faro airport has both domestic and international flights.

From the **bus station**, just west of the centre, there are at least six daily express coaches to Lisbon (€20, four hours), plus several slower services, and frequent buses to other coastal towns. There also international buses to Madrid (€39, 8 hours).

The **train station** is a few minutes' walk west of the bus station. Five trains run daily to Lisbon (€22, four hours).

Getting Around

The airport is 6km from the centre. Buses 14 and 16 (€1.90) run into town until 9pm. A taxi from the airport to the town centre costs about €12.

Tavira

POP 25,400

Set on either side of the meandering Rio Gilão, Tavira is a charming town with a hilltop castle, an old Roman bridge and a smattering of Gothic churches. The pretty sands of Ilha da Tavira are a short boat ride away.

Sights & Activities

FREE **Castle** CASTLE
(Rua da Liberdade; ⊙10am-5pm) Tavira's ruined castle dominates the town. Nearby, the 16th-century **Palácio da Galeria** (☎281 320 540; Calçada da Galeria; admission €2; ⊙10am-12.30pm & 3-6.30pm Tue-Sat) holds occasional exhibitions.

Igreja da Misericórdia CHURCH
(Rua da Galeria) One of the town's 30-plus churches, the 16th-century Igreja da Misericórdia is among the most striking in The Algarve.

Ilha da Tavira ISLAND, BEACH
You can reach this island beach by a ferry at Quatro Águas (€1.40 return) or Tavira (summer only, €1.90 return). It's a 2km walk to Quatro Águas (from the south bank of the river, follow the road south-southwest).

Casa Abilio BIKE HIRE
(Rua João Vaz Corte Real 23; per day around €7) Enjoy pedal power with a rented bike.

Sport Nautica KAYAKING
(Rua Jacques Pessoa 26; per half-/full day €15/25) Rent kayaks for a paddle along the river.

Sleeping & Eating

Pensão Residencial Lagôas GUESTHOUSE €
(☎281 328 243; Rua Almirante Cândido dos Reis 24; s/d from €20/30) A long-standing favourite, friendly Lagôas has small (some cramped), well-maintained rooms. There's a sunny terrace with views.

Residencial Princesa do Gilão GUESTHOUSE €€
(☎281 325 171; www.residencial-gilao.com; Rua Borda d'Água de Aguiar 10; s/d €52/58; (AC)) This '80s-style place on the river has tight but neat rooms with identical decor. Go for a room with a river view.

Restaurante Bica SEAFOOD €€
(Rua Almirante Cândido dos Reis 24; mains €8-14) Deservedly popular, Bica serves splendid food, such as fresh grilled fish and *cataplana* (seafood and sausage cooked in a copper pot), which diners enjoy with good-value Borba wine.

Bistro 'oPorto' INTERNATIONAL €€
(Rua Dr José Pires Padinha 180; mains €10-15; ⊙lunch & dinner Tue-Sun) Head to this artfully decorated French-owned restaurant with a relaxed riverside setting for octopus rice, codfish cakes, coconut curry and other flavourful bites.

Information

Câmara Municipal (Praça da Republica; ⊙9am-8pm Mon-Fri, 10am-1pm Sat) Free internet access.
Tourist Office (Praça da República) Can help with accommodation.

Getting There & Away

Some 15 trains and six express buses run daily between Faro and Tavira (€3.50, one hour).

Lagos

POP 29,700

In summer, the pretty fishing port of Lagos has a party vibe; its picturesque cobbled streets and pretty nearby beaches are packed with revellers and sun-seekers.

Sights & Activities

Beaches BEACHES

The beach scene includes **Meia Praia**, a vast strip to the east; **Praia da Luz** to the west; and the smaller **Praia do Pinhão**.

Blue Ocean OUTDOOR ACTIVITIES

(964 665 667; www.blue-ocean-divers.de) Organises diving trips. Along the promenade, fishermen can offer motorboat jaunts to nearby grottoes.

Kayak Adventures KAYAKING

(913 262 200; www.kayakadventures-lagos.com) Offers kayaking trips from Batata Beach.

Sleeping

Pensão Marazul GUESTHOUSE €

(282 770 230; www.pensaomarazul.com; Rua 25 de Abril 13; s/d €45/55; @) Draws a good mix of foreign travellers to its small but cheerfully painted rooms – the best of which offer sea views.

Sol a Sol HOTEL €€

(282 761 290; www.residencialsolasol.com; Rua Lançarote de Freitas 22; r €55-65) This central, small hotel has neat rooms with tiny balconies and views over the town.

Caza de São Gonçalo GUESTHOUSE €

(919 841 622; Rua Candido dos Reis 73; dm/d €25/60) New in 2012, this beautifully restored mansion has a handful of attractive dorm rooms and roomier doubles, all with en suites. There's also a jacuzzi and a lounge area.

Eating

TOP CHOICE **A Forja** PORTUGUESE €€

(Rua dos Ferreiros 17; mains €8-15; lunch & dinner Sun-Fri) This buzzing place pulls in the crowds for its hearty, top-quality traditional food. Plates of the day are always reliable, as are the fish dishes.

Casinha do Petisco PORTUGUESE, SEAFOOD €€

(Rua da Oliveira 51; mains €7-13; Mon-Sat) This tiny traditional gem comes highly recommended by locals for its seafood grills and shellfish dishes. Come early to beat the lines.

Information

Tourist Office (www.visitalgarve.pt; Praça Gil Eanes) In the centre of town.

Getting There & Away

Bus and train services depart frequently for other Algarve towns, and around eight times daily to Lisbon (€21, 4¼ hours).

Getting Around

A **bus service** (tickets €1-2; 7am-8pm Mon-Sat) provides useful connections to the beaches of Meia Praia and Luz. Rent bicycles and motorbikes from **Motorent** (282 769 716; www.motorent.pt; Rua Victor Costa e Silva; bike/motorcycle per 3 days from €21/60).

Silves

POP 11,000

The one-time capital of Moorish Algarve, Silves is a pretty town of jumbled orange rooftops scattered above the banks of the Rio Arade. Clamber around the ramparts of its fairy-tale **castle** for superb views.

Sleeping & Eating

Residencial Ponte Romana GUESTHOUSE €

(282 443 275; Horta da Cruz; s/d €20/35) Floral-themed rooms beside the Roman bridge, with castle views and a cavernous bar-restaurant full of old-timers and Portuguese families.

Café Ingles INTERNATIONAL €€

(282 442 585; mains €10-23;) Situated at the castle entrance, this funky English-owned place with romantic rooftop terrace has wood-fired pizzas, prawn curry, lamb cutlets with rosemary and other global dishes. In summer, there's live music on weekends.

Getting There & Away

Silves **train station** is 2km from town; trains from Lagos (€2.85, 35 minutes) stop eight times daily (from Faro, change at Tunes), to be met by local buses. Four to seven buses run daily connecting Silves and Albufeira (€4.20, 50 minutes).

Sagres

POP 2100

The small, elongated village of Sagres has an end-of-the-world feel with its sea-carved cliffs and empty, wind-whipped fortress high above the ocean.

Sights & Activities

Coast & Beaches BEACH

Visit Europe's southwestern-most point, the **Cabo de São Vicente** (Cape St Vincent), 6km to the west. A solitary lighthouse stands on this barren cape.

This coast is ideal for surfing; sign up for surfing lessons with **Sagres Natura** (☎282 624 072; www.sagresnatura.com; Rua São Vicente). **DiversCape** (☎965 559 070; www.diverscape.com; Porto da Baleeira) organises diving trips.

Fortaleza de Sagres FORT

(adult/child €3/1.50, free 10am-2pm Sun; ⏲10am-8.30pm) Sagres' fort offers breathtaking views over the seaside cliffs. According to legend, this is where Henry the Navigator established his navigation school and primed the early Portuguese explorers.

Mar Ilimitado BOAT TOURS

(☎916 832 625; www.marilimitado.com; Porto da Baleeira) Mar Ilimitado offers dolphin-spotting boat trips (€32) from the marina.

Sleeping & Eating

Casa do Cabo de Santa Maria GUESTHOUSE €€

(☎282 624 722; www.casadocabodesantamaria.com; Rua Patrão António Faústino; r/apt from €50/80; 📶✉) These squeaky-clean rooms and apartments might not have sweeping views, but they are handsomely furnished.

A Tasca SEAFOOD €€

(Porto da Baleeira; mains €12-17; ⏲lunch & dinner Thu-Tue) Overlooking the marina, this cosy place whips up tasty *cataplana* and other seafood dishes, best enjoyed on the sunny terrace.

Information

Tourist Office (Rua Comandante Matoso; ⏲Tue-Sat) Central to town.

Getting There & Away

Frequent buses run daily to Sagres from Lagos (€3.80, one hour), with fewer on Sunday. One continues to Cabo de São Vicente on weekdays.

CENTRAL PORTUGAL

The vast centre of Portugal is a rugged swathe of rolling hillsides, whitewashed villages, olive groves and cork trees. Richly historic, it is scattered with prehistoric remains and medieval castles. It's also home to one of Portugal's most architecturally rich towns, Évora, as well as several spectacular walled villages. There are fine local wines and, for the more energetic, plenty of outdoor exploring in the dramatic Beiras region.

Évora

POP 54,300

Évora is an enchanting place to delve into the past. Inside the 14th-century walls, Évora's narrow, winding lanes lead to a striking medieval cathedral, a Roman temple and a picturesque town square. These old-fashioned good-looks are the backdrop to a lively student town surrounded by wineries and dramatic countryside.

Sights & Activities

Sé CHURCH

(Largo do Marquês de Marialva; admission €2-5; ⏲9am-noon & 2-5pm) Évora's cathedral has fabulous cloisters and a museum jam-packed with ecclesiastical treasures.

Templo Romano RUINS

(Temple of Diana; Largo do Conde de Vila Flor) Once part of the Roman Forum; it's a heady slice of drama right in town.

Capela dos Ossos CHAPEL

(Praça 1 de Maio; admission €2; ⏲9am-1pm & 2.30-6pm) Built from the skeletons of several thousand people, the ghoulish Chapel of Bones in the Igreja de São Francisco provides a real *Addams Family* day out.

Sleeping

Hostel Namaste HOSTEL €

(☎266 743 014; www.hostelnamasteevora.pt; Largo Doutor Manuel Alves Branco 12; dm/s/d €17/30/40; 📶) New in 2012, this welcoming guesthouse has two attractively decorated four-bed dorm rooms and two private rooms (one with en suite). The young, well-travelled owners create a familial ambience, and you can join them for dinner (€7 per person).

Casa dos Teles GUESTHOUSE €

(☎266 702 453; casadosteles.planetaclix.pt; Rua Romão Ramalho 27; s/d €30/35, with shared bathroom €20/25;) These nine rooms – mostly light and airy – are good value; quieter rooms at the back overlook a pretty courtyard.

Eating

TOP CHOICE **Botequim da Mouraria** PORTUGUESE €€

(266 746 775; Rua da Mouraria 16a; mains €13-16.50; lunch & dinner Mon-Fri, lunch Sat) Poke around the old Moorish quarter to find this cosy spot serving some of Évora's finest food and wine. There are no reservations, just 12 stools at a counter.

Dom Joaquim PORTUGUESE €€

(266 731 105; Rua dos Penedos 6; mains €12-15; lunch Tue-Sun, dinner Tue-Sat) Amid stone walls and modern artwork, Dom Joaquim serves excellent traditional cuisine including meats (game and succulent, fall-off-the bone oven lamb) and seafood dishes.

Vinho e Noz PORTUGUESE €€

(Ramalho Orgigão 12; mains €11-12; lunch & dinner Mon-Sat) This family-run place has a warmly lit, brick-walled interior, a large wine list and good-quality cuisine.

Pastelaria Conventual Pão de Rala PASTISSERIE €

(Rua do Cicioso 47; pastries from €2; 7.30am-8pm) Specialises in heavenly pastries, all made on the premises.

Drinking

Bar do Teatro BAR

(Praça Joaquim António de Aguiar; 8pm-2am) This small, inviting bar, with its high ceilings and old-world decor, draws a friendly mixed crowd. Come early for an outdoor table overlooking the park.

Spettus CAFE, BAR

(Praça de Sertório 3; noon-2am) On a peaceful plaza near the town hall, laid-back Spettus has outdoor tables that fill with a student crowd by night.

Terrazza BAR, RESTAURANT

(Jardim do Paço; Palácio das Cinco Quinas) A few steps from the Templo Romana, this plant-filled garden courtyard attracts a slightly more sophisticated crowd.

Information

Câmara Municipal (9am-12.30pm & 2-5pm Mon-Fri) Free internet inside; free 24-hour wi-fi out front.

Tourist Office (www.cm-evora.pt; Praça do Giraldo 73) Has an excellent city map.

Getting There & Away

Évora has six to 12 buses daily to Lisbon (€12, two hours) and three to Faro (€16.20, five hours), departing from the station off Avenida São Sebastião (700m southwest of the centre). Regular trains go direct to Lisbon (€12-16, 90 minutes) and indirectly, via Pinhal Novo, to Faro (€28, 4¼ hours) and Lagos (€31, five hours). The train station is 600m south of the Jardim Público.

Monsaraz

POP 20

In a dizzy setting high above the plain, this walled village has a moody medieval feel and magnificent views. The biennial **Monsaraz Museu Aberto**, held in July on even-numbered years, features exhibitions and concerts.

The **Museu do Fresco** (Plaça Dom Nuno Álvares; admission €1.80; 10am-12.30pm & 2-6pm) has a superb 15th-century fresco. Situated 3km north of town is **Menhir of Outeiro**, one of the tallest megalithic monuments ever discovered.

There are several places to stay in town, including the friendly **Casa St Condestável** (266 557 181; www.condestavel-monsaraz.com; Rua Direita 4; r/ste €55/80;), with wooden trimmings, whitewashed walls and heavy wooden furniture.

Casa do Forno (Travessa da Sanabrosa; 266 557 190; mains €8-10; lunch & dinner Wed-Mon) is a small local favourite for its classic Alentejan cooking. There's a terrace with views.

The **tourist office** (266 557 136; Rua Direita 2) can offer advice on accommodation.

Up to four daily buses connect Monsaraz with Reguengos de Monsaraz (€3, 35 minutes, Monday to Friday), with connections to Évora.

Peniche

POP 16,000

Popular for its nearby surfing beaches and also as a jumping-off point for the beautiful Ilhas Berlengas nature reserve, coastal city Peniche remains a working port, giving it a slightly grittier and more 'lived-in' feel than its beach-resort neighbours. It has a walled historic centre and lovely beaches east of town.

From the bus station, it's a 10-minute walk west to the historic centre.

Sights

FREE Fortress FORTRESS

(admission free, museum admission €1.50; ⌚9am-12.30pm & 2-5.30pm Tue-Fri, from 10am Sat & Sun) Peniche's imposing 16th-century fortress served as one of dictator Salazar's infamous jails for political prisoners and was later a temporary home for African refugees.

Islands ISLANDS

About 5km to the northeast of Peniche is the scenic island-village of **Baleal**, connected to the mainland village of Casais do Baleal by a causeway. The fantastic sweep of sandy beach here offers some fine surfing. Surf schools dot the sands, as do several bar-restaurants.

Sitting about 10km offshore from Peniche, **Berlenga Grande** is a spectacular, rocky and remote island, with twisting, shocked-rock formations and gaping caverns. It's the only island of the Berlenga archipelago you can visit; the group consists of three tiny islands surrounded by clear, calm, dark-blue waters full of shipwrecks – great for snorkelling and diving. Several outfits make the 40-minute trip to the island, including **Viamar** (☎262 785 646; www.viamar-herlenga.com; return adult/child €18/10).

Activities

Surfing

Surf camps offer week-long instruction (from €250 to 500 per week including lodging) as well as two-hour classes (€35 to 50), plus board and wetsuit hire. Well-established names include **Baleal Surfcamp** (☎262 769 277; www.balealsurfcamp.com; Rua Amigos do Baleal 2; 1-/3-/5-day course €60/95/145), **Maximum Surfcamp** (www.maximumsurfcamp.com) and **Peniche Surfcamp** (☎962 336 295; www.penichesurfcamp.com; Av do Mar 162, Casais do Baleal).

Diving

There are good diving opportunities around Peniche, and especially around Berlenga. Expect to pay about €65 to €75 for two dives (less around Peniche) with **Acuasuboeste** (☎918 393 444; www.acuasuboeste.com; Porto de Pesca) or **Haliotis** (☎262 781 160; www.haliotis.pt; Avenida Monsenhor Bastos, Hotel Praia Norte).

Sleeping

Peniche Hostel HOSTEL €

(☎969 008 689; www.penichehostel.com; Rua Arquitecto Paulino Montês 6; dm/d €20/50; @📶) This cosy welcoming hostel has a colourfully decorated lounge and very clean rooms. Surfboards and bikes are available for hire, and there's an attached surf school.

Eating & Drinking

Restaurante A Sardinha SEAFOOD €

(Rua Vasco da Gama 81; mains €6-14; ⌚lunch & dinner) This simple place on a narrow street parallel to Largo da Ribeira does a roaring trade with locals and tourists alike.

Bar da Praia BAR

(Praia do Baleal; ⌚noon-2am) One of several lively bars right on Baleal beach, with an outdoor terrace and DJs most nights.

Getting There & Away

Peniche's **bus station** (☎968 903 861; Rua Dr Ernesto Moreira) is located 400m northeast of the tourist office (cross the Ponte Velha connecting the town to the isthmus). Buses go to Lisbon (€9, 1½ hours, every one to two hours), Coimbra (€14.50, 2¾ hours, three daily) and Óbidos (€3.15, 40 minutes, five to 13 daily).

Óbidos

POP 3100

This exquisite walled village was a wedding gift from Dom Dinis to his wife Dona Isabel (beats a fondue set), and its historic centre is a delightful place to wander. Highlights include the **Igreja de Santa Maria** (Rua Direita), with fine *azulejos,* and views from the town walls.

From mid-July to mid-August, Óbidos hosts the **Mercado Medieval** (www.mercadomedievalobidos.pt), featuring jousting matches, wandering minstrels and abundant medieval mayhem.

Sleeping & Eating

Hostel Argonauta HOSTEL €

(☎262 958 088; http://hostel-argonauta.blogspot.com; Rua Adelaide Ribeirete 14; dm/d incl breakfast from €20/40; @📶) The friendly and welcoming Señora Rozas runs this cosy place with spacious, handsomely furnished rooms, a short stroll (uphill) to the heart of the medieval centre.

Petrarum Domus PORTUGUESE €€

(Rua Direita; mains €9-18; ⌚lunch & dinner) Amid age-old stone walls, Petrarum serves up hearty dishes like pork with mushrooms, mixed seafood sautés and several *bacalhau* plates.

Information

Espaço Internet (Rua Direita 107; ⏲10am-7pm Mon-Fri Sep-Jul, 10am-8pm Mon-Fri, 11.30am-6.30pm Sat & Sun Jul & Aug) Free internet access.

Tourist Office (Rua Direita) This helpful tourist office is just outside Porta da Vila, the town's main entrance gate.

Getting There & Away

There are direct buses Monday to Friday from Lisbon (€8, 70 minutes).

Nazaré

POP 16,000

Nazaré has a bustling coastal setting with narrow cobbled lanes running down to a wide, cliff-backed beach. The town centre is jammed with seafood restaurants and bars; expect huge crowds in July and August.

Sights & Activities

The **beaches** here are superb, although swimmers should be aware of dangerous currents. Climb or take the funicular to the clifftop **Sítio**, with its cluster of fishermen's cottages and great view.

Historic Monasteries ARCHITECTURE

Two of Portugal's big-time architectural masterpieces are close by. Follow the signs to Alcobaça where, right in the centre of town, is the immense **Mosteiro de Santa Maria de Alcobaça** (admission €6; ⏲9am-7pm) dating from 1178; don't miss the colossal former kitchen.

Batalha's massive **Mosteiro de Santa Maria de Vitória** (admission €6; ⏲9am-6.30pm), dating from 1388, is among the supreme achievements of Manueline architecture.

Sleeping & Eating

Many townspeople rent out rooms; doubles start at €35. Ask around near the seafront at Av da República.

Vila Conde Fidalgo GUESTHOUSE €

(☎262 552 361; http://condefidalgo.planetaclix.pt; Avenida da Independência Nacional 21a; d/apt from €40/80) This pretty little complex uphill a few blocks from the beach is built around a series of flower-filled courtyards. Rooms all have kitchenettes.

Adega Oceano HOTEL €

(☎262 561 161; www.adegaoceano.com; Avenida da República 51; d €60; ❄📶) This little ocean-front place offers pleasantly set rooms – renovated modern rooms in back, beach-view quarters in front.

A Tasquinha SEAFOOD €€

(Rua Adrião Batalha 54; mains €7-11; ⏲lunch & dinner Tue-Sun) This enormously popular family-run tavern serves high-quality seafood at reasonable prices.

Information

Tourist Office (www.cm-nazare.pt; Av Manuel Remígio) On the beachfront (south of the main centre).

Getting There & Away

Nazaré has numerous bus connections to Lisbon (€10.50, two hours).

Tomar

POP 16,000

A charming town straddling a river, Tomar has the notoriety of being home to the Knights Templar; check out their headquarters, the outstanding monastery **Convento de Cristo** (admission €6; ⏲9am-6.30pm), a steep climb above town. Other rarities include a medieval **synagogue** (Rua Dr Joaquim Jacinto 73; admission free; ⏲10am-7pm Tue-Sun). The town is backed by the dense greenery of the **Mata Nacional dos Sete Montes** (Seven Hills National Forest).

Sleeping & Eating

Residencial União GUESTHOUSE €

(☎249 323 161; www.hotel-ami.com/hotel/uniao; Rua Serpa Pinto 94; s/d €30/40; 📶) Tomar's most atmospheric budget choice, this once-grand townhouse features large and spruce-ly maintained rooms with antique furniture and fixtures.

Restaurante Tabuleiro RESTAURANT €

(☎249 312 771; Rua Serpa Pinto 140; mains €7.50; ⏲lunch & dinner Mon-Sat) This family-friendly local eatery with outdoor seating has attentive service and great food served up in ample portions. It's located just off Tomar's main square.

Information

Tourist Office (Rua Serpa Pinto) Can provide town and forest maps.

Getting There & Away

Frequent trains run to Lisbon (€9.50, two hours)

Coimbra

POP 107,000

Coimbra is a dynamic, fashionable, yet comfortably lived-in city, with a student life centred on the magnificent 13th-century university. Aesthetically eclectic, there are elegant shopping streets, ancient stone walls and backstreet alleys with hidden *tascas* (taverns) and fado bars. Coimbra was the birth and burial place of Portugal's first king, and was the country's most important city when the Moors captured Lisbon.

Sights & Activities

TOP CHOICE Sé Velha CATHEDRAL

(Old Cathedral; ☎239 825 273; Largo da Sé Velha; admission €2; ⏲10am-5.30pm Mon-Sat, to 6pm Apr-Oct) Coimbra's stunning old cathedral, dating from the late 12th century, is one of the finest examples of Romanesque architecture in all of Portugal.

TOP CHOICE Velha Universidade UNIVERSITY

(Old University; www.uc.pt; admission €7, incl tower €10; ⏲9.30am-1pm & 2-5.30pm Mon-Fri, 10.30am-4.30pm Sat & Sun Nov–mid-Mar, 9am-7.30pm daily mid-Mar–Oct) The old university is unmissable in its grandeur. You can visit various buildings, including the library, with its gorgeous book-lined hallways, and the Manueline chapel dating back to 1517.

O Pioneiro do Mondego KAYAKING

(☎239 478 385; www.opioneirodomondego.com; per person €22.50) Offers daily kayak excursions along the Rio Mondego up to Penacova. The 18km trip departs at 10am from Torres de Mondego, 7km southwest of Coimbra's Largo da Portagem.

Festivals & Events

Coimbra's annual highlight is **Queima das Fitas**, a boozy week of fado and revelry that begins on the first Thursday in May when students celebrate the end of the academic year.

Sleeping

TOP CHOICE Casa Pombal GUESTHOUSE €€

(☎239 835 175; www.casapombal.com; Rua das Flores 18; s/d €44/54, with bathroom €58/68; @) This winning, Dutch-run guest house squeezes tons of charm into a small space. Ample morning buffet.

Pensão-Restaurante Flôr de Coimbra GUESTHOUSE €

(☎239 823 865; flordecoimbrahr.com.sapo.pt; Rua do Poço 5; s/d/tr €40/50/60, without bathroom €20/35/45;) This once-grand 19th-century home with its own (recommended) restaurant offers loads of character in a great location.

Grande Hostel de Coimbra HOSTEL €

(☎239 108 212; www.grandehostelcoimbra.com; Rua Antero de Quental 196; dm/d €18/40;) You won't find a hostel more laid-back than this, and it's hard to beat the location in a grand, century-old town house near the nightlife of Coimbra's university campus.

Eating & Drinking

Self-caterers should stop by the modern **Mercado Municipal Dom Pedro V** (Rua Olímpio Nicolau Rui Fernandes; ⏲Mon-Sat) for fruit, vegetables and more.

Zé Manel dos Ossos TASCA €€

(Beco do Forno 12; mains €7-15; ⏲lunch & dinner Mon-Fri, lunch Sat) Great food, huge servings and a zany atmosphere, with walls papered with diners' comments, cartoons and poems.

Restaurante Zé Neto PORTUGUESE €€

(Rua das Azeiteiras 8; mains €9-11; ⏲lunch & dinner Mon-Sat) This marvellous family-run place specialises in homemade Portuguese standards, including *cabrito* (kid).

Cafetaria do Museu CAFE

(Sé Nova; ⏲8am-7pm Sun-Thu to 4am Fri & Sat) This stylish cafe attracts a hip crowd who come for gourmet burgers, crêpes, coffees

WORTH A TRIP

ROMAN RUINS

Conimbriga, 16km south of Coimbra, is the site of the well-preserved ruins of a **Roman town** (⏲10am-7pm), including mosaic floors, elaborate baths and trickling fountains. It's a fascinating place to explore, with a good **museum** (www.conimbriga.pt; admission €4, free Sun before 2pm; ⏲10am-7pm) that describes the once-flourishing and later abandoned town. There's a sunny cafe serving good lunch buffets. Frequent buses run to Condeixa, 2km from the site; there are also two direct buses (€2.50) from Coimbra.

and cocktails, with fine views from the breezy terrace. It's near the Sé Nova (the 'New Cathedral', although its facade dates to the 17th century).

TOP CHOICE **Café Santa Cruz** CAFE
(www.cafesantacruz.com; Praça 8 de Maio; ⌚7.30am-2am Mon-Sat) An atmospheric cafe inside a former chapel. Outdoor seating and occasional fado nights.

Café Tropical BAR
(Praça da República 35; ⌚10am-2am Mon-Sat) One of several indoor-outdoor bars overlooking Praça da República, Café Tropical is a favourite place to start out the night.

Entertainment

Coimbra-style fado is more cerebral than the Lisbon variety, and its adherents are staunchly protective.

TOP CHOICE **Á Capella** FADO
(☎918 113 307; www.acapella.com.pt; Rua Corpo de Deus; admission incl 1 drink €10; ⌚9pm-2am) Housed in a fabulous 14th-century former chapel, Á Capella regularly hosts the city's most renowned fado musicians.

Information

Ciberespaço (Loja 4, Av Sá da Bandeira; per hr €2.20; ⌚10am-10pm Mon-Sat, 1-9pm Sun) Paid internet access on the ground floor of the shopping centre.

Tourist Office (Praça da Porta Férrea) Located near the bridge (Ponte de Santa Clara).

Getting There & Away

There are at least a dozen buses to Lisbon (€13.30, 2½ hours) and Porto (€12, 1½ hours), and regular service to Faro and Évora via Lisbon. There are also frequent trains to Lisbon (€19 to €25, 2 to 3 hours) and Porto (€9 to 17, 1¼ to 2 hours). The main train stations are **Coimbra B**, 2km northwest of the centre, and central **Coimbra A**. Most long-distance trains call at Coimbra B. The **bus station** (Avenida Fernão Magalhães) is about 400m northeast of the centre.

Luso & the Buçaco Forest

POP 2000

This sylvan region harbours a lush forest of century-old trees surrounded by countryside that's dappled with heather, wildflowers and leafy ferns. There's even a fairy-tale **palace** (☎231 937 970; www.almeidahotels.com; Mata Nacional do Buçaco; 7/8-course meal €35/40; ⌚lunch & dinner; 📶) here, a 1907 neo-Manueline extravagance, where deep-pocketed visitors can dine or stay overnight. The palace lies amid the Mata Nacional do Buçaco, a forest criss-crossed with trails, dotted with crumbling chapels and graced with ponds, fountains and exotic trees. Buçaco was chosen as a retreat by 16th-century monks, and it surrounds the lovely spa town of Luso. From the centre, it's a 2km walk through forest up to the palace.

The **Maloclinic Spa** (www.maloclinicspa.com; Rua Álvaro Castelões; ⌚10am-6pm Mon-Fri, 9am-6pm Sat & Sun, extended hours summer) offers a range of treatments.

Sleeping & Eating

Alegre Hotel BOUTIQUE HOTEL €€
(☎231 930 256; www.alegrehotels.com; Rua Emídio Navarro 2; s €45-55, d €60-86; P📶🏊) This grand, peach-coloured 19th-century town house has polished period furniture and other appealing touches. There's a formal parlour and a vine-draped garden with pool.

Information

Tourist Office (Avenida Emídio Navarro 136; ⌚Mon-Sat) Has maps and leaflets about the forest and trails.

Getting There & Away

Buses to/from Coimbra (€3.50, 45 minutes) run four times daily each weekday and twice daily on Saturdays. Trains to/from Coimbra B station (€2.55, 35 minutes) run several times daily; it's a 15-minute walk to town from the station.

Serra da Estrela

The forested Serra da Estrela has a raw natural beauty and offers some of the country's best hiking. This is Portugal's highest mainland mountain range (1993m), and the source of its two great rivers: Rio Mondego and Rio Zêzere. The town of **Manteigas** makes a great base for hiking and exploring the area (plus skiing in winter). The **main park office** (☎275 980 060; pnse@icn.pt; Rua 1 de Maio 2, Manteigas; ⌚Mon-Fri) provides details of popular walks in the Parque Natural da Serra da Estrela – some of which leave from town or just outside it; additional offices are at Seia, Gouveia and Guarda.

Sleeping

Hotel Berne HOTEL €€
(☎275 981 351; www.hotelberne.com; Quinta de Santo António, Manteigas; s/d €55/70; P@📶🏊

At the base of town, Albergaria Berne has wood-accented rooms, some with balconies and views of Manteigas and the mountains above. Excellent restaurant.

Pensão Serradalto GUESTHOUSE €
(☎tel/fax 275 981 151; paragem_serradalto@hotmail.com; Rua 1 de Maio 15; s/d/ste winter €35/45/60, summer €25/35/50; ⊙Wed-Mon; 📶) In the heart of town, the Serradalto has simple, wood-floored rooms, most with fine valley views.

Getting There & Around

Two regular weekday buses connect Manteigas with Guarda, from where there are onward services to Coimbra and Lisbon.

THE NORTH

Beneath the edge of Spanish Galicia, northern Portugal is a land of lush river valleys, sparkling coastline, granite peaks and virgin forests. This region is also gluttony for wine lovers: it's the home of the sprightly *vinho verde* wine and ancient vineyards along the dramatic Rio Douro. Gateway to the north is Porto, a beguiling riverside city blending both medieval and modern attractions. Smaller towns and villages also offer cultural allure, from majestic Braga, the country's religious heart, to the seaside beauty Viana do Castelo.

Porto

POP 208,000

At the mouth of the Rio Douro, the hilly city of Porto presents a jumble of styles, eras and attitudes: narrow medieval alleyways, extravagant baroque churches, prim little squares, and wide boulevards lined with beaux-arts edifices. A lively walkable city with chatter in the air and a tangible sense of history, Porto's old-world riverfront district is a Unesco World Heritage site. Across the water twinkle the neon signs of Vila Nova de Gaia, the headquarters of the major port manufacturers.

Sights & Activities

Head for the riverfront Ribeira district for an atmospheric stroll around, checking out the gritty local bars, sunny restaurants and river cruises.

A few kilometres west of the city centre, the seaside suburb of **Foz do Douro** is a prime destination on hot summer weekends. It has a long beach promenade and a smattering of oceanfront bars and restaurants.

Museums MUSEUMS
Within the verdant gardens 4km west of the city, the arrestingly minimalist **Museu de Arte Contemporânea** (www.serralves.pt; Rua Dom João de Castro 210; admission €7; ⊙10am-5pm Tue-Fri, to 8pm Sat & Sun) features works by contemporary Portuguese artists. Take bus 201 from Praça Dom João I.

Porto's best art museum, the **Museu Nacional Soares dos Reis** (Rua Dom Manuel II 44; admission €5, free Sun 10am-2pm; ⊙10am-6pm Wed-Sun, 2-6pm Tue), exhibits Portuguese painting and sculpture masterpieces from the 19th and 20th centuries.

Torre dos Clérigos TOWER
(Rua dos Clérigos; admission €2; ⊙9am-7pm) This tower rewards those who ascend the 225 steps to the top with an excellent view over the city.

Sé CHURCH
(Terreiro da Sé; cloisters €3; ⊙9am-12.15pm & 2.30-6.30pm; 👪) Dominating Porto, the cathedral is worth a visit for its mixture of architectural styles and vast ornate interior.

Igreja de São Francisco ARCHITECTURE
(☎222 062 100; Rua Infante Dom Henrique; admission €3.50; ⊙9am-6pm) Near the waterfront, this Gothic church – austere from the outside – hides one of Portugal's most dazzling displays of gilded baroque finery.

Port-Wine Lodges TASTINGS
Many of the port-wine lodges in Vila Nova de Gaia offer daily tours and tastings, including **Taylor's** (www.taylor.pt; Rua do Choupelo 250; admission €3; ⊙10am-6pm Mon-Fri, to 5pm Sat & Sun), **Croft** (www.croftport.com; free; ⊙10am-6pm) and **Graham's** (www.grahamsportlodge.com; Rua Rei Ramiro 514; per person €3; ⊙9.30am-6pm Mon-Sat).

Teleférico de Gaia CABLE CAR
(one-way/return €5/8; ⊙10am-8pm) In Vila Nova de Gaia, this new aerial gondola provides fine views over the Douro and Porto on its short, five-minute jaunt. It runs 562m between the south end of the Ponte Dom Luis I and the riverside.

Festivals & Events

Festa de São João
(St John's Festival) From 20 to 24 June; Porto's biggest festival, with processions, live music and merry-making all across town.

Porto

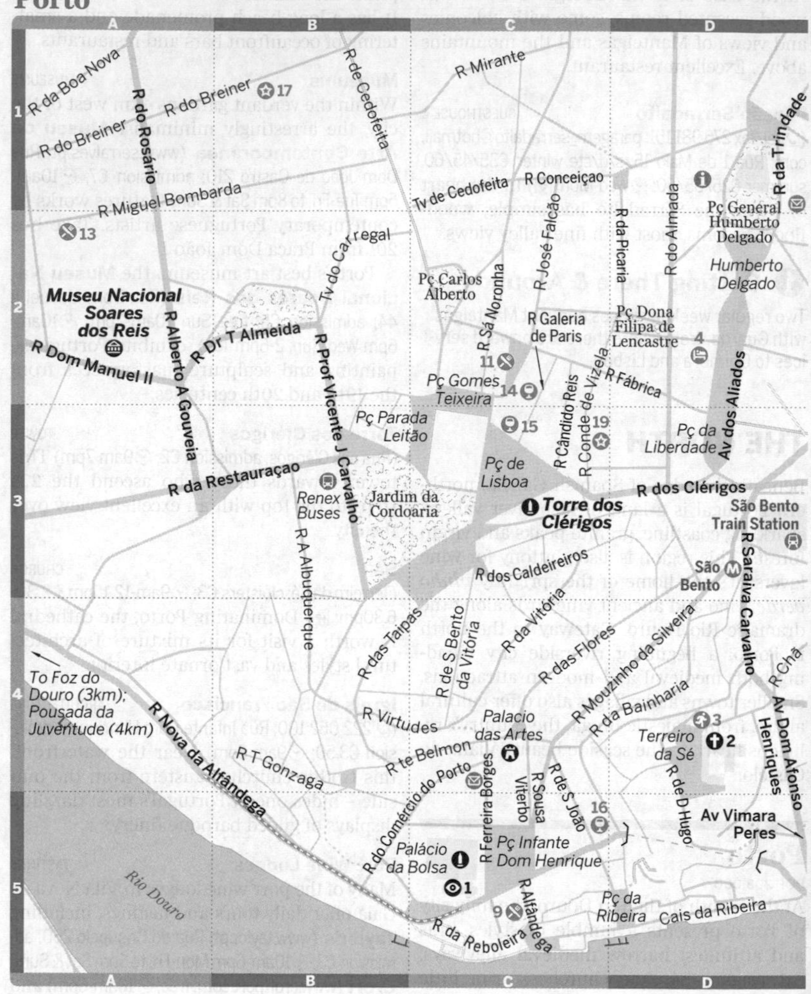

Noites Ritual Rock
Late August; music festival.

Serralves Em Festa
(http://serralvesemfesta.com) Concerts, exhibitions, theatre and loads of events at this fest in early June.

Sleeping

Tattva Design Hostel HOSTEL €
(☎220 944 622; www.tattvadesignhostel.com; Rua do Cativo 26; dm/d from €15/44; @ 📶) One of Portugal's best hostels, Tattva has excellent facilities and attractive rooms with thoughtful touches – big lockers, good lighting, privacy curtains around every bed, and a bathroom in every room. The open-air rooftop lounge is a great place for a sundowner.

Magnólia Hostel HOSTEL €
(☎222 014 150; magnoliahostel.com; Av Rodrigues de Freitas 387; dm €17-22; 📶) You'll find excellent ambience at this attractive, well-maintained hostel with a range of rooms spread over three floors of a converted townhouse. There's a lounge with a spooky out-

Porto

Top Sights
- Museu Nacional Soares dos Reis A2
- Torre dos Clérigos C3

Sights
- 1 Igreja de São Francisco C5
- 2 Sé D4

Activities, Courses & Tours
- 3 Porto Tours D4

Sleeping
- 4 Hotel Aliados D2
- 5 Magnólia Hostel F3
- 6 Pensão Astória E4
- 7 Residencial Belo Sonho F3
- 8 Tattva Design Hostel E4

Eating
- 9 A Grade C5
- 10 Cafe Santiago F3
- 11 Leitaria Quinta Do Paço C2
- 12 Mercado do Bolhão E1
- 13 Rota do Chá A2

Drinking
- 14 Casa do Livro C2
- 15 Era Uma Vez no Porto C3
- 16 Vinologia C5

Entertainment
- 17 Breyner 85 .... B1
- 18 Maus Hábitos F3
- 19 Plano B C3

of-tune piano, and an outdoor space that sometimes hosts concerts.

Residencial Belo Sonho GUESTHOUSE €
(☎222 003 389; Rua Passos Manuel 186; s/d €25/35; 📶) Belo Sonho has simple but comfy rooms with parquet floors and small, tidy bathrooms. Management doesn't speak much English but is warm and friendly.

Pensão Astória GUESTHOUSE €
(☎222 008 175; Rua Arnaldo Gama 56; r €25-35) In an ageing townhouse above the Rio Douro, Astória has old-world charm; several rooms have superb views.

Hotel Aliados GUESTHOUSE €€
(☎222 004 853; www.hotelaliados.com; Rua Elísio de Melo 27; r €55-80; ❄📶) Set in one of Porto's marvellous beaux-arts buildings, offering comfortable rooms with wooden floors and dark wood furnishings.

Eating

A Grade PORTUGUESE €€
(☎223 321 130; Rua da São Nicolau 9; mains €12-20; ⌚lunch & dinner Mon-Sat) Both a humble mum-and-dad operation and a masterwork of traditional fare, with standouts such as baked octopus in butter and wine, roast goat, and lime tart for dessert. Reservations recommended.

Cafe Santiago PORTUGUESE €€
(Rua Passos Manuel 226; mains €8-12; ⌚lunch & dinner) One of the best places to try Porto's classic belly-filling treat, the *francesinha* – a thick open-faced sandwich, piled with

cheese, sausage, egg and/or assorted other meats, plus a tasty rich sauce.

Leitaria Quinta Do Paço CAFE €
(☎222 004 303; Praça Guilherme Gomes Fernandes 47; sandwiches €4; ⏰9am-8pm Sun-Thu, to 1am Fri & Sat) The Leitaria is famed for its heavenly eclairs. You can dine alfresco at tables on the plaza.

Rota do Chá CAFE €
(Rua Miguel Bombarda 457; 2-course lunch €7.50; ⏰noon-8pm Sun-Thu, noon-midnight Fri & Sat; 🌿) This proudly bohemian cafe has a verdant but rustic back garden and a magnificent tea selection.

Mercado do Bolhão MARKET €
(Rua Formosa; ⏰8am-5pm Mon-Fri, to 1pm Sat) Fruit, vegies, cheese and deli goodies in a 19th-century wrought-iron building.

Tattva CAFE
(Rua do Cativo 26; 3-course lunch €7; ⏰lunch Mon-Fri, dinner Fri & Sat) This hostel serves excellent set lunches, and there's always a vegetarian option. Come on Friday nights for Portuguese cuisine and on Saturday nights for superb Indian cooking.

Drinking

The bar-lined Rua Galeira de Paris and nearby streets are packed with revellers most nights. Down by the water, the open-air bar scene on Praça da Ribeira is a pleasant but touristy option on warm nights.

Era Uma Vez no Porto BAR
(Rua das Carmelitas 162) Artwork lines the walls of this cosy, low-lit Baixa bar, and there's a mellow buzz to the place, making it a fine retreat from the mayhem of nearby Rua Galeria de Paris.

Casa do Livro LOUNGE
(Rua Galeria de Paris 85; ⏰9pm-3am Mon-Sat) Vintage wallpaper, gilded mirrors and walls of books give a discreet charm to this bar. On weekends DJs spin funk, soul and retro sounds in the back room for pretty people.

Vinologia WINE BAR
(Rua de São João 46; ⏰4pm-midnight) This oaky French-owned wine bar is an excellent place to sample Porto's fine quaffs.

Entertainment

Plano B GALLERY, CAFE
(Rua Cândido dos Reis 30; ⏰closed Aug) Equal parts art gallery and cafe, Plano B also has a cosy downstairs space where DJs and live bands hold court.

Maus Hábitos CLUB
(www.maushabitos.com; Rua Passos Manuel 178, 4th fl) This bohemian, multiroom space hosts art exhibits, while live bands and DJs work the back stage.

Breyner 85 LIVE MUSIC
(www.breyner85.com; Rua do Breyner 85; ⏰3-9pm Mon, to 2am Tue-Sun) Well off the beaten path, Breyner 85 has a grassy courtyard and an eclectic line-up of bands covering rock, jazz and blues. Sunday night's jam sessions are particularly popular.

Information

Santo António Hospital (☎222 077 500; Largo Prof Abel Salazar) Has English-speaking staff.

Main Post Office (Praça General Humberto Delgado) Across from the main tourist office.

Main Tourist Office (www.portoturismo.pt; Rua Clube dos Fenianos 25) Opposite the *câmara municipal*.

Getting There & Away

Air

Porto is connected by daily flights from Lisbon and London, and has direct links from other European cities, particularly with rasyJet and Ryanair.

Bus

Porto has many private bus companies leaving from different terminals; the main tourist office can help. In general, for Lisbon (€18) and The Algarve, the choice is **Renex** (www.renex.pt; Campo Mártires de Pátria 37) or **Rede Expressos** (www.rede-expressos.pt; Rua Alexandre Herculano 370). **Eurolines** (www.eurolines.com) runs buses to Madrid (via Guarda; €47, 8½ hours) and Santiago de Compostela (via Braga; €31, four hours) in Spain.

Three companies operate from or near Praceto Régulo Magauanha, off Rua Dr Alfredo Magalhães: Transdev-Norte goes to Braga (€6); AV Minho to Viana do Castelo (€8).

Train

Porto is a northern Portugal rail hub, with three stations. Most international trains, and all intercity links, start at Campanhã, 2km east of the centre. Inter-regional and regional services depart from Campanhã or the central **São Bento station** (Praça Almeida Garrett). Frequent local trains connect these two.

At **São Bento station** you can book tickets to any other destination.

Getting Around

To/From the Airport

The metro's 'violet' line provides handy service to the airport. A one-way ride to the centre costs €1.80 and takes about 45 minutes. A daytime taxi costs €20 to €25 to/from the centre.

Public Transport

Save money on transport by purchasing a refillable **Andante Card** (€0.50), valid for transport on buses, metro, funicular and tram. You can buy them from STCP kiosks or newsagents.

BUS Central hubs of Porto's extensive bus system include Jardim da Cordoaria, Praça da Liberdade and São Bento station. Tickets are purchased on the bus are one-way €1.80, or €1.15 with the Andante Card.

FUNICULAR A panoramic funicular shuttles up and down a steep incline from Avenida Gustavo Eiffel to Rua Augusto Rosa (€1.80, from 8am to 8pm).

METRO Porto's metro currently comprises four metropolitan lines that all converge at the Trinidade stop. Tickets cost €1.15 with an Andante Card. There are also various day passes (€4 to €7) available.

TRAM Porto has three antique trams that trundle around town. The most useful line, 1E, travels along the Douro towards the Foz district.

Taxi

To cross town, expect to pay between €5 and €8. There's a 20% surcharge at night, and an additional charge to leave city limits, which includes Vila Nova de Gaia. There are taxi ranks throughout the centre or you can call a **radio taxi** (☎225 076 400).

Along the Douro

Portugal's best-known river flows through the country's rural heartland. In the upper reaches, port-wine grapes are grown on steep terraced hills, punctuated by remote stone villages and, in spring, splashes of dazzling white almond blossom.

The Rio Douro is navigable right across Portugal. Highly recommended is the train journey from Porto to Pinhão (€11, 2½ hours, five trains daily), the last 70km clinging to the river's edge; trains continue to Pocinho (from Porto €13, 3½ hours). **Porto Tours** (☎222 000 045; www.portotours.com; Calçada Pedro Pitões 15, Torre Medieval), situated next to Porto's cathedral, can arrange tours, including idyllic Douro cruises. Cyclists and drivers can choose river-hugging roads along either bank, and can visit wineries along the way (check out www.rvp.pt for an extensive list of wineries open to visitors). You can also stay overnight in scenic wine lodges among the vineyards.

Viana do Castelo

POP 38,000

The jewel of the Costa Verde (Green Coast), Viana do Castelo has both an appealing medieval centre and lovely beaches just outside the city. In addition to its natural beauty, Viana do Castelo whips up some excellent seafood and hosts some magnificent traditional festivals, including the spectacular **Festa de Nossa Senhora da Agonia** in August.

Sights

The stately heart of town is **Praça da República**, with its delicate fountain and grandiose buildings, including the 16th-century **Misericórdia**, a former almshouse.

FREE Templo do Sagrado Coração de Jesus CHURCH
(Temple of the Sacred Heart of Jesus; ⏰10am-5pm Sep-Jun, 9am-8pm Jul & Aug) Atop Santa Luzia Hill, the Temple of the Sacred Heart of Jesus offers a grand panorama across the river. It's a steep 2km climb; you can also catch a ride on a funicular railway (one-way/return €2/3).

Praia do Cabedelo BEACH
Viana's enormous arcing beach is one of the Minho's best, with little development to spoil its charm. It's across the river from town, best reached by **ferry** (adult/child €1.30/0.70; ⏰hourly 9am to 8pm Mon-Fri, from 10am Sat & Sun) from the pier south of Largo 5 de Outubro.

Sleeping

Hospedaria Senhora do Carmo GUESTHOUSE €
(☎258 825 118; batistaesilva@sapo.pt; Rua Grande 72; r without/with bathroom €20/35) Well-located in the historic centre, this friendly, family-run guesthouse is excellent value with its clean, freshly painted rooms with parquet floors. The best have views over the rooftops of Viana.

Pousada da Juventude Gil Eannes HOSTEL €
(☎258 847 169; www.pousadasjuventude.pt; Gil Eannes; dm/d €12/26; wi-fi) Sleep in the bowels of a huge, creaky hospital ship where men were once stitched up and underwent emergency dentistry. This floating hostel scores well for novelty, but has few amenities.

Eating

Taberna do Valentim SEAFOOD €€
(Campo do Castelo; mains €12-15; ⌚lunch & dinner Mon-Sat) This popular seafood restaurant serves grilled fish by the kilogram, and rich seafood stews – *arroz de tamboril* (monkfish rice) and *caldeirada* (fish stew). It's on the main road facing Castelo de São Thiago, 400m west of the centre.

Os 3 Potes PORTUGUESE €€€
(☎258 829 928; Rua Beco dos Fornos 7; mains €14-17; ⌚lunch & dinner) Set in the former public kiln, this cosy restaurant serves traditional Minho delicacies.

Dolce Vianna ITALIAN €
(☎258 824 860; Rua do Poço 44; pizzas €6-7) In the centre, this pleasant local favourite cooks up thin-crust, cheese-heavy pizzas in a wood-burning oven.

Freguez CAFE €
(Rua do Poço 42; snacks €2-3) A charming cafe with a fado soundtrack and outdoor tables on the pedestrian lane.

Information

Tourist Office (Rua Hospital Velho) Handily located in the old centre.

Getting There & Away

Five to 10 trains go daily to Porto (€7 to €8, 1½ to 2¼ hours), as well as express buses (€8, 1 to 1½ hours).

Braga

POP 135,000

Portugal's third-largest city boasts a fine array of churches, their splendid baroque facades looming above the old plazas and narrow lanes of the historic centre. Lively cafes, trim little boutiques, and some good restaurants add to the appeal.

Sights

It's an easy day trip to **Guimarães**, with its medieval town centre and a palace of the dukes of Bragança. It's also a short jaunt to **Barcelos**, a town famed for its sprawling Thursday market.

Sé CHURCH
(Rua Dom Paio Mendes; admission free, treasury €3, choir €2; ⌚8am-6.30pm) In the centre of Braga, this is one of Portugal's most extraordinary cathedrals, with roots dating back a thousand years. Within the cathedral you can also visit the **treasury** and **choir**.

Escadaria do Bom Jesus RELIGIOUS SITE
At Bom Jesus do Monte, a hilltop pilgrimage site 5km from Braga, there is an extraordinary stairway, with allegorical fountains, chapels and a superb view. City bus 2 runs frequently from Braga to the site.

Sleeping

Pop Hostel HOSTEL €
(☎253 058 806; dm/d from €16/45; @📶) New in 2011, the small cosy Pop Hostel is a great new addition to Braga, with a colourfully decorated lounge and a friendly owner who knows all the best eating and drinking spots in town. Bike hire and tours available.

Casa Santa Zita GUESTHOUSE €
(☎253 618 331; Rua São João 20; s/d from €22/35) This impeccably kept pilgrims' lodge has bright, spotless rooms (some with en suites) and an air of palpable serenity. Midnight curfew.

Residencial Dos Terceiros GUESTHOUSE €
(☎253 270 466; www.terceiros.com; Rua dos Capelistas 85; s/d €30/43) On a quiet pedestrianised street near Praça da República, Terceiros offers simple rooms; some with small balconies.

Eating & Drinking

Anjo Verde VEGETARIAN €
(☎253 264 010; Largo da Praça Velha 21; mains €8-9; ⌚lunch & dinner Mon-Sat; 🖉) Braga's best vegetarian restaurant serves up elegantly presented plates in a lovely, airy dining room or on the peaceful lane in front. Several other attractive indoor-outdoor restaurants are on the same street.

Domus Vinum TAPAS €
(www.domus-vinum.com; Largo da Nossa Senhora da Boa Luz 12; tapas €4-6; ⌚6pm-2am Tue-Sun) With Brazilian beats, a lantern-lit front patio and excellent wines by the glass, Domus Vinum draws a stylish crowd. The Portuguese and Spanish tapas are excellent. It's just west of the old town entrance portal, Arco da Porta Nova.

Information

Tourist Office (www.cm-braga.pt; Praça da República 1) Can help with accommodation and maps.

Getting There & Away

Trains arrive regularly from Lisbon (€33, 3½ to 4½ hours), Coimbra (€20, 2½ hours) and Porto (€3, 1¼ hours), and there are daily connections north to Viana do Castelo. Daily bus services link Braga to Porto (€6, one hour) and Lisbon (€19, 4½ hours). Car hire is available at **AVIC** (253 203 910; Rua Gabriel Pereira de Castro 28; Mon-Fri), with prices starting at €35 per day.

Parque Nacional da Peneda-Gerês

Spread across four impressive granite massifs, this vast park encompasses boulder-strewn peaks, precipitous valleys, gorse-clad moorlands and forests of oak and pine. It also shelters more than 100 granite villages that, in many ways, have changed little since Portugal's founding in the 12th century. For nature lovers, the stunning scenery here is unmatched in Portugal for camping, hiking and other outdoor adventures. The park's main centre is at Vila do Gerês, a sleepy, hot-springs village.

Activities

Hiking

There are trails and footpaths through the park, some between villages with accommodation. Leaflets detailing these are available from the park offices.

Day hikes around Vila do Gerês are popular. An adventurous option is the **old Roman road** from Mata do Albergaria (10km up-valley from Vila do Gerês), past the **Vilarinho das Furnas** reservoir to Campo do Gerês. More distant destinations include **Ermida** and **Cabril**, both with simple accommodation.

Cycling & Horse Riding

Mountain bikes can be hired in Campo do Gerês (15km northeast of Vila do Gerês) from **Equi Campo** (253 161 405; www.equicampo.com; per hr/day €5/18; 10am-7pm). Guides here also lead horse-riding trips, hikes and combination hiking/climbing/abseiling excursions.

Water Sports

Rio Caldo, 8km south of Vila do Gerês, is the base for water sports on the Caniçada Reservoir. English-run **AML** (Água Montanha Lazer; 253 391 779; www.aguamontanha.com; Lugar de Paredes) rents kayaks, pedal boats, rowing boats and small motorboats. It also organises kayaking trips along the Albufeira de Salamonde.

Sleeping & Eating

Vila do Gerês has plenty of *pensões* (guesthouses), but you may find vacancies are limited; many are block-booked by spa patients in summer.

Hotel de Peneda BOUTIQUE HOTEL €€
(251 460 040; www.hotelpeneda.com; Lugar da Peneda; r €50-75; P) Set in the Serra da Peneda in the northern reaches of the park, this mountain lodge has a waterfall backdrop and attractive rooms with picturesque views. Good restaurant.

Beleza da Serra GUESTHOUSE €€
(253 391 457; www.bserra.com; Lugar do Bairro 25, Vilar da Veiga; d/tr €59/79;) This friendly waterfront guesthouse overlooks the Caniçada Reservoir, 4.5km south of Vila do Gerês. It has simple, clean, comfortable rooms and a decent on-site restaurant.

Pousada da Juventude de Vilarinho das Furnas HOSTEL €
(253 351 339; www.pousadasjuventude.pt; dm/bungalow €15/52; P@) Campo's woodland hostel offers spartan dormitories, simply furnished doubles (with bathrooms) and roomier bungalows with kitchen units.

Parque Campismo de Cerdeira CAMPGROUND €
(253 351 005; www.parquecerdeira.com; camping per person/tent/car €5.50/5/5, bungalows €50-68; year-round; P) In Campo de Gerês, this place has oak-shaded sites, laundry, pool, minimarket and a particularly good restaurant. The ecofriendly bungalows open onto unrivalled mountain views.

Information

The head park office is **Adere-PG** (258 452 250; www.adere-pg.pt; Mon-Fri) in Ponte de Barca. Obtain park information and reserve cottages and other park accommodation through here. Other Adere-PG stations are at Mezio and Lamas de Mouro.

Getting There & Away

Because of the lack of transport within the park, it's good to have your own wheels. You can rent cars in Braga.

UNDERSTAND PORTUGAL

History

Portugal has an early history of occupation, stretching back to 700 BC when the Celts arrived on the Iberian peninsula, followed by the Phoenicians, Greeks, Romans, Visigoths, Moors and Christians.

Life Under the Moors

The Moors ruled southern Portugal for more than 400 years, and some scholars describe that time as a golden age. The Arabs introduced irrigation, previously unknown in Europe; two Egyptian agronomists came to Iberia in the 10th century and wrote manuals on land management, animal husbandry, plant and crop cultivation and irrigation designs. They also introduced bananas, rice, coconuts, maize and sugar cane, and encouraged small-scale, cooperatively run communities, specialising in olive oil and wine production, and food markets – still embraced in many parts of Portugal.

The Moors opened schools and set about campaigns to achieve mass literacy (in Arabic), as well as the teaching of maths, geography and history. Medicine reached new levels of sophistication. There was also a degree of religious tolerance that evaporated when the Christian crusaders came to power. Much to the chagrin of Christian slave owners, slavery was not permitted in the Islamic kingdom – making the region a refuge for runaway slaves. Muslims, Christians and Jews all peacefully coexisted, at times even collaborating together, creating the most scientifically and artistically advanced society the world had, until that time, ever known.

Age of Discovery

The 15th century marked a golden era in Portuguese history, when Portuguese explorers helped transform the small kingdom into a great imperial power.

The third son of King João I, Henrique 'O Navegador' (Henry the Navigator, 1394–1460) played a pivotal role in establishing Portugal's maritime dominance. As governor of The Algarve, he assembled the very best sailors, map-makers, shipbuilders, instrument-makers and astronomers.

By 1431, Portuguese explorers discovered the islands of Madeira and the Azores, followed by Gil Eanes' 1534 voyage beyond Cape Bojador in West Africa, breaking a maritime superstition that this was the end of the world. More achievements followed over the next century. In 1488, Portuguese sailors, under navigator Bartolomeu Dias, were the first Europeans to sail around Africa's southern tip and into the Indian Ocean. This was followed by the epic voyage in 1497–98 when Vasco da Gama reached southern India, and in 1500 when Cabral discovered Brazil. With gold and slaves from Africa and spices from the East, Portugal was soon rolling in riches. As its explorers reached Timor, China and eventually Japan, Portugal cemented its power with garrison ports and trading posts. The monarchy, taking its 'royal fifth' of profits, became the wealthiest in Europe, and the lavish Manueline architectural style symbolised the exuberance of the age.

The Salazar Years

In 1908, King Carlos and his eldest son were assassinated in Lisbon. Two years later Portugal became a republic, which set the stage for an enormous power struggle. Over the next 16 years, chaos ruled, with an astounding 45 different governments coming to power, often the result of military intervention. Another coup in 1926 brought forth new names and faces, most significantly António de Oliveira Salazar, a finance minister who would rise up through the ranks to become prime minister – a post he would hold for 36 years.

Salazar hastily enforced his 'New State' – a republic that was nationalistic, Catholic, authoritarian and essentially repressive. All political parties were banned except for the loyalist National Union, which ran the show, and the National Assembly. Strikes were banned and propaganda, censorship and brute force kept society in order. The new secret police, Polícia Internacional e de Defesa do Estado (PIDE), inspired terror and suppressed opposition by imprisonment and torture. Various attempted coups during Salazar's rule came to nothing. The only good news was a dramatic economic turnaround, with surging industrial growth through the 1950s and 1960s.

Decolonisation finally brought the Salazarist era to a close. Independence movements in Portugal's African colonies led to costly and unpopular military intervention

In 1974, military officers reluctant to continue fighting bloody colonial wars staged a nearly bloodless coup – later nicknamed the Revolution of the Carnations (after victorious soldiers stuck carnations in their rifle barrels). Carnations are still a national symbol of freedom.

Portugal Today

After the revolution, Portugal faced enormous challenges as it modernized its economy and embraced a left-leaning democracy. Joining the EC (European Economic Community) in 1986 and adopting the euro in 1999 gave the economy a boost, though the global financial crisis hit the country hard. Portugal continues to struggle with a shrinking economy and EU-mandated austerity measures that have left many citizens disgruntled. The country has had more success in the realm of renewable energy (harvesting solar, wind and hydroelectric power). Today more than half of Portugal's energy comes from renewable sources, making it one of the world leaders in sustainability.

Arts

Music

The best-known form of Portuguese music is the melancholy, nostalgic songs called fado (literally 'fate'), said to have originated from troubadour and African slave songs. The late Amália Rodrigues was the Edith Piaf of Portuguese fado. Today it is Mariza who has captured the public's imagination with her extraordinary voice and fresh contemporary image. Lisbon's Alfama district has plenty of fado houses, ranging from the grandiose and tourist-conscious to small family affairs.

Architecture

Unique to Portugal is Manueline architecture, named after its patron, King Manuel I (1495–1521). It symbolises the zest for discovery of that era and is hugely flamboyant, characterised by fantastic spiralling columns and elaborate carving and ornamentation.

Visual Arts

Portugal's stunning painted *azulejo* tiles depict contemporary life, covering everything from houses to churches. The art form dates from Moorish times and reached a peak in the late 19th century when the art nouveau and art deco movements provided fantastic facades and interiors. Lisbon has its very own *azulejo* museum.

SURVIVAL GUIDE

Directory A–Z

Accommodation

There's an excellent range of good-value accommodation in Portugal. Budget places provide some of western Europe's cheapest rooms, while you'll find atmospheric accommodation in converted castles, mansions and farmhouses.

We list high-season rates for a double room; breakfast is generally not included. The following price categories are used:

€ less than €50

€€ €50 to €100

€€€ more than €100

ECOTOURISM & FARMSTAYS

Turismo de Habitação (www.turihab.pt) is a private network of historic, heritage or rustic properties, ranging from 17th-century manors to quaint farmhouses or self-catering cottages. Doubles run from about €60 to €120.

POUSADAS

These are government-run former castles, monasteries or palaces, often in spectacular locations. For details, contact tourist offices or **Pousadas de Portugal** (www.pousadas.pt).

GUESTHOUSES

The most common types are the *residencial* and the *pensão:* usually simple, family-owned operations. Some have cheaper rooms with shared bathrooms. Double rooms with private bathroom typically run €40 to 60.

HOSTELS

Portugal has a growing number of hostels, particularly in Lisbon. Nationwide, Portugal has over 30 *pousadas da juventude* (youth hostels; www.pousadasjuventude.pt) within the Hostelling International (HI) system. The average price for a dorm room is about €20.

SEASONS

High season mid-June to mid-September.

Mid-season May to mid-June and mid-September to October.

Low season November to April.

CAMPING

For detailed listings of campsites nationwide, pick up the **Roteiro Campista** (www.roteiro-campista.pt; €7), updated annually and sold at bookshops. The swishest places are run by **Orbitur** (www.orbitur.pt) and **Inatel** (www.inatel.pt).

Activities

Hiking The best hiking is found in Parque Nacional da Peneda-Gerês and Serra da Estrela. The ambitious can follow the 240km walking trail Via Algarviana across southern Portugal.

Water sports Popular water sports in Portugal include surfing, windsurfing, canoeing, rafting and waterskiing. For local specialists, see Lagos, Sagres, Tavira, Coimbra and Parque Nacional da Peneda-Gerês.

Cycling Good starting points for cycling trips are Tavira in the Algarve, Sintra in central Portugal and Parque Nacional da Peneda-Gerês in the north.

Business Hours

Standard opening hours in Portugal are as follows:

Banks 8.30am to 3pm Monday to Friday

Bars 7pm to 2am

Cafes 9am to 7pm

Malls 10am to 10pm

Nightclubs 11pm to 4am Thursday to Saturday

Post offices 8.30am to 4pm Monday to Friday

Restaurants noon to 3pm and 7pm to 10pm

Shops 9.30am to noon and 2pm to 7pm Monday to Friday, 10am to 1pm Saturday

Sights 10am to 12.30pm and 2pm to 5pm Tuesday to Sunday

Embassies & Consulates

The New Zealand embassy in Rome represents Kiwi travellers. The following are all in Lisbon:

Australian Embassy (☎213 101 500; www.portugal.embassy.gov.au; 2nd fl, Av da Liberdade 200)

Canadian Embassy (☎213 164 600; Avenida da Liberdade 196, Edifício Victoria)

UK Embassy (☎213 924 000; http://ukinportugal.fco.gov.uk; Rua de Saõ Bernardo 33)

US Embassy (☎217 273 300; http://portugal.usembassy.gov; Av das Forças Armadas)

Food

The following price indicators (per main course) are used in this chapter:

€ less than €8

€€ €8 to €15

€€€ more than €15

Money

» There are numerous banks with ATMs located throughout Portugal.

» Credit cards are accepted in midrange and top-end hotels, restaurants and shops.

Public Holidays

New Year's Day 1 January

Carnaval Tuesday February/March

Good Friday March/April

Liberty Day 25 April

Labour Day 1 May

Corpus Christi May/June

Portugal Day (also known as Camões and Communities Day) 10 June

Feast of the Assumption 15 August

Republic Day 5 October

All Saints' Day 1 November

Independence Day 1 December

Feast of the Immaculate Conception 8 December

Christmas Day 25 December

Telephone

» Portugal's country code is ☎351.

» Mobile phone numbers within Portugal have nine digits and begin with ☎9.

» All Portuguese phone numbers consist of nine digits. These include area codes, which always need to be dialled.
» For general information dial ☎118, and for reverse-charge (collect) calls dial ☎120.
» Phonecards are the most reliable and cheapest way of making a phone call from a telephone booth. They are sold at post offices, newsagents and tobacconists in denominations of €5 and €10.

Getting There & Away

Air

TAP (www.tap.pt) is Portugal's international flag carrier as well as its main domestic airline. The following are Portugal's main airports:

Lisbon (☎218 413 500; www.ana-aeroportos.pt)

Porto Airport (☎229 432 400; www.ana-aeroportos.pt)

Faro (☎289 800 800; www.ana-aeroportos.pt)

Land

BUS

UK–Portugal and France–Portugal Eurolines services cross to Portugal via northwest Spain. Some operators:

Alsa (www.alsa.es)

Avanza (www.avanzabus.com)

Damas (www.damas-sa.es)

Eurolines (www.eurolines.com)

Eva (www.eva-bus.com)

TRAIN

The most popular train link from Spain is on the Sud Express, operated by **Renfe** (www.renfe.com; one-way tickets from €59), which has a nightly sleeper service between Madrid and Lisbon. Badajoz (Spain)–Elvas–Lisbon is slow and there is only one regional service daily, but the scenery is stunning. Coming from Galicia, in the northwest of Spain, travellers can go from Vigo to Valença do Minho (Portugal) and continue on to Porto.

Getting Around

Air

TAP Portugal (www.flytap.com) has daily Lisbon–Faro flights (under an hour) year-round.

Bicycle

Bicycles can be taken free on all regional and inter-regional trains as accompanied baggage. They can also go on a few suburban services on weekends. Most domestic bus lines won't accept bikes.

Bus

A host of small bus operators, most amalgamated into regional companies, run a dense network of services across the country. Among the largest companies are **Rede Expressos** (www.rede-expressos.pt), **Rodonorte** (www.rodonorte.pt) and The Algarve line **Eva** (www.eva-bus.com).

Most bus-station ticket desks will give you a computer printout of fares, and services and schedules are usually posted at major stations.

CLASSES

Expressos Comfortable, fast buses between major cities

Rápidas Quick regional buses

Carreiras Marked CR, slow, stopping at every crossroad

COSTS

Travelling by bus in Portugal is fairly inexpensive. A Lisbon Faro express bus costs €19; Lisbon–Porto costs about €18. Both take four hours. An under-26 card should get you a small discount on long-distance services.

Car & Motorcycle

AUTOMOBILE ASSOCIATIONS

Automóvel Clube de Portugal (ACP; ☎213 180 100; www.acp.pt) has a reciprocal arrangement with better-known foreign automobile clubs, including AA and RAC. It provides medical, legal and breakdown assistance. The 24-hour emergency number is ☎707 509 510.

HIRE

To hire a car in Portugal you must be at least 25 years old and have held your home licence for over a year (some companies allow younger drivers at higher rates). To hire a scooter of up to 50cc you must be over 18 years old and have a valid driving licence. For more powerful scooters and motorbikes you must have a valid driving licence covering these vehicles from your home country.

ROAD RULES

The various speed limits for cars and motorcycles are 50km/h within cities and public centres, 90km/h on normal roads and 120km/h on motorways (but 50km/h, 70km/h and 100km/h for motorcycles with sidecars).

Drink-driving laws are strict in Portugal, with a maximum legal blood-alcohol level of 0.05%.

Train

Caminhos de Ferro Portugueses (www.cp.pt) is the statewide train network and is generally efficient.

There are four main types of long-distance service. Note that international services are marked IN on timetables.

Regional (marked R on timetables) Slow trains that stop everywhere

Interregional (IR) Reasonably fast trains

Intercidade (IC) or **Rápido** Express trains

Alfa Pendular Deluxe, marginally faster and much pricier service.

Romania

Includes »

Bucharest 889
Transylvania 895
Braşov 896
Sighişoara 898
Sibiu 900
Cluj-Napoca 901
Banat 903
Timişoara 903
Understand Romania 905
Survival Guide 907

Best Places to Eat

» Caru' cu Bere (p893)
» Crama Sibiu Vechi (p901)
» Bistro de l'Arte (p897)
» Bella Musica (p898)

Best Places to Stay

» Doors (p893)
» Hostel Costel (p904)
» Felinarul Hostel (p900)
» Casa Wagner (p898)

Why Go?

Beautiful and beguiling, Romania's rural landscape remains relatively untouched by the country's urban evolution. It's a land of aesthetically stirring hand-ploughed fields, sheep-instigated traffic jams, and lots and lots of homemade plum brandy. The Carpathian Mountains offer uncrowded hiking and skiing, while Transylvania's Saxon towns are a time warp, with plenty of Vlad Ţepeş–inspired 'Dracula' schtick. Unesco-listed painted monasteries dot southern Bucovina, and the big cities are a blast too.

When to Go

Bucharest

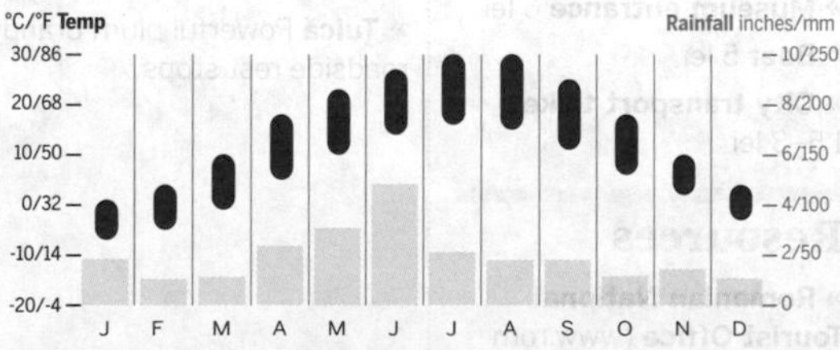

May Good month for festivals, including the popular Sibiu Jazz Festival.

Jun Mountain hiking starts in mid-June, birding season gets rolling in the Danube Delta.

Sep The summer heat is gone, but still-sunny days are perfect for exploring big cities.

AT A GLANCE

- **Currency** Romanian leu
- **Language** Romanian
- **Money** ATMs abundant
- **Visas** Not required for citizens of the EU, USA, Canada, Australia, New Zealand

Fast Facts

- **Area** 237,500 sq km
- **Capital** Bucharest
- **Country code** ☎40
- **Emergency** ☎112

Exchange Rates

Australia	A$1	3.59 lei
Canada	C$1	3.39 lei
Euro Zone	€1	4.41 lei
Japan	¥100	3.66 lei
New Zealand	NZ$1	2.88 lei
UK	UK£1	5.22 lei
USA	US$1	3.44 lei

Set Your Budget

- **Budget hotel room** 120–150 lei
- **Two-course meal** 30 lei
- **Museum entrance** 6 lei
- **Beer** 5 lei
- **City transport ticket** 1.5–3 lei

Resources

- **Romanian National Tourist Office** (www.romaniatourism.com)
- **Bucharest Life** (www.bucharestlife.net)

Connections

The main train corridor to Romania from western Europe passes through Budapest, and at least one train daily makes the overnight slog from here down to Bucharest, via Braşov, and back. The western city of Timişoara has excellent train, bus and air connections throughout Europe. By road, the main entry points from the west are at Arad and Oradea. There are international border crossings to/from Hungary, Serbia, Bulgaria, Ukraine and Moldova, and four ferry crossings into Bulgaria.

ITINERARIES

One Week

Spend a day viewing the parts of Bucharest that survived Ceauşescu, then take a train to Braşov – Transylvania's main event – for castles, activities and beer at street-side cafes. Spend a day in Sighişoara's medieval citadel, then catch a train back to Bucharest or on to Budapest.

Two Weeks

Arrive in Bucharest by plane or Timişoara by train, then head into Transylvania, devoting a day or two each to Braşov, Sighişoara and Sibiu. Tour southern Bucovina's painted monasteries, then continue on to Bucharest.

Essential Food & Drink

- **Mămăligă** Cornmeal mush that's sometimes topped with sour cream or cheese.
- **Ciorbă** Sour soup that's a mainstay of the local diet and a powerful hangover remedy.
- **Sarmale** Spiced pork wrapped in cabbage or grape leaves.
- **Covrigi** Oven-baked pretzels served warm from windows all around town.
- **Ţuică** Powerful plum brandy sold in water bottles at roadside rest stops.

BUCHAREST

POP 2.1 MILLION

Romania's capital gets a bad rap, but in fact it's dynamic, energetic and more than a little bit funky. It's where still-unreconstructed communism meets unbridled capitalism; where the soporific forces of the EU meet the passions of the Balkans and Middle East. Many travellers give the city just a night or two before heading off to Transylvania, but that's not enough. Budget at least a few days to take in the good museums, stroll the parks and hang out at trendy cafes.

Sights

SOUTHERN BUCHAREST

Strangely inspired by trips to Pyongyang and Beijing in the 1980s, Nicolae Ceauşescu had an entire quarter of historic buildings

Romania Highlights

1. Ascend castles and mountains (and castles on top of mountains), using **Braşov** (p896) as a base
2. Follow the Unesco World Heritage line of painted monasteries in **southern Bucovina** (p903)
3. Soak in **Sibiu** (p900), a beautifully restored Saxon town
4. Explore the medieval citadel of **Sighişoara** (p898), 'Dracula's' birthplace
5. Row through the tributaries and the riot of nature in the **Danube Delta** (p905)
6. Gawk in awe at Bucharest's **Palace of Parliament** (p892), the second-largest building in the world after the Pentagon

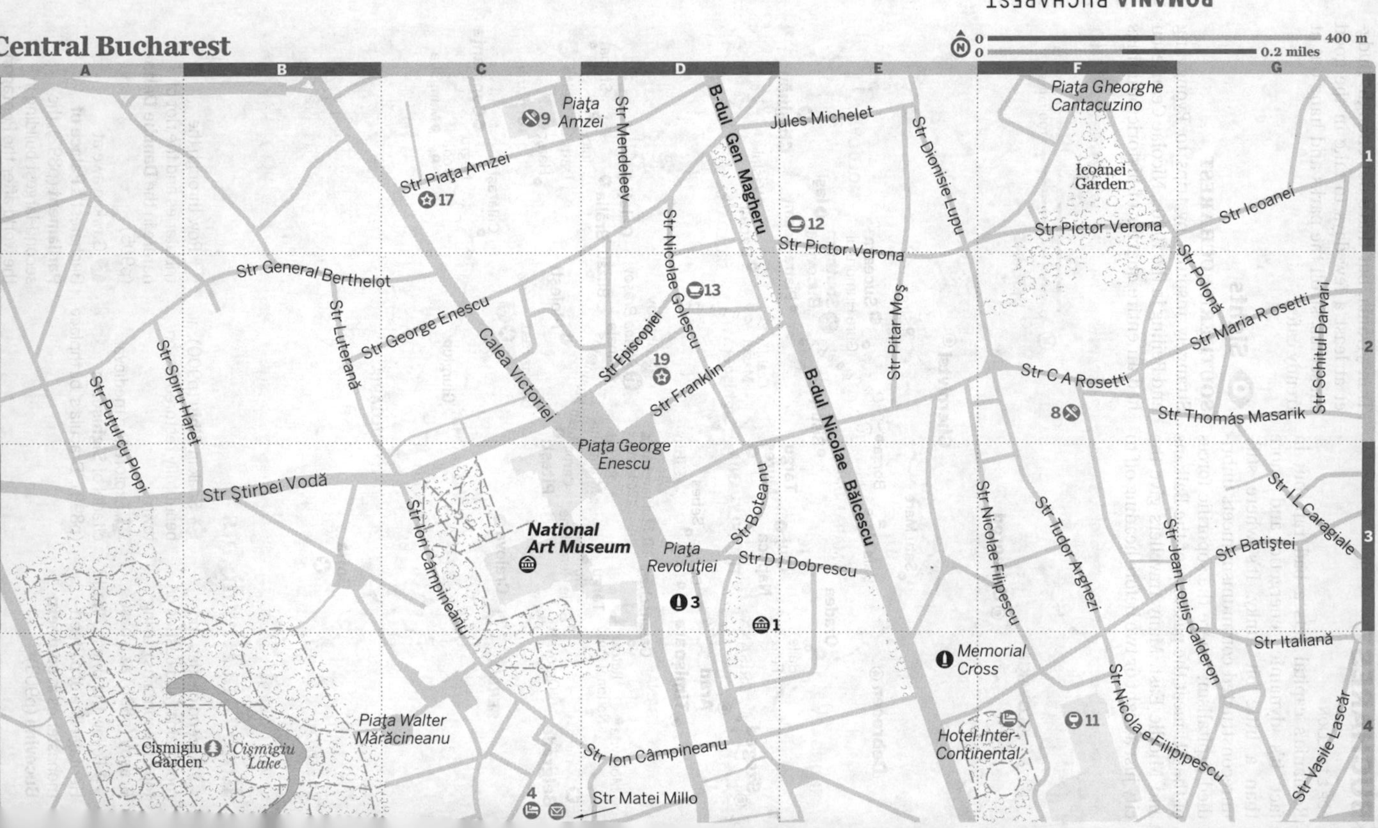
Central Bucharest
0
400 m
0
0.2 miles
A
B
C
D
E
F
G
1
2
3
4
Piața Amzei
Str Mendeleev
Jules Michelet
B-dul Gen Magheru
Str Dionisie Lupu
Piața Gheorghe Cantacuzino
Icoanei Garden
Str Piața Amzei
Str Pictor Verona
Str Icoanei
Str General Berthelot
Str Nicolae Golescu
Str Polonă
Str Luterană
Str George Enescu
Calea Victoriei
Str Episcopiei
Str Franklin
Str Pitar Moș
Str Maria Rosetti
Str Schitul Darvari
Str C A Rosetti
Str Thomas Masarik
Str Spiru Haret
Str Puțul cu Plopi
B-dul Nicolae Bălcescu
Piața George Enescu
Str Știrbei Vodă
Str Boteanu
Str Ion Câmpineanu
National Art Museum
Piața Revoluției
Str D I Dobrescu
Str Nicolae Filipescu
Str Tudor Arghezi
Str Jean Louis Calderon
Str I L Caragiale
Str Batiștei
Str Italiană
Memorial Cross
Piața Walter Mărăcineanu
Cișmigiu Garden
Cișmigiu Lake
Hotel Inter-Continental
Str Nicola e Filipescu
Str Vasile Lascăr
Str Matei Millo
1
3
4
8
9
11
12
13
17
19

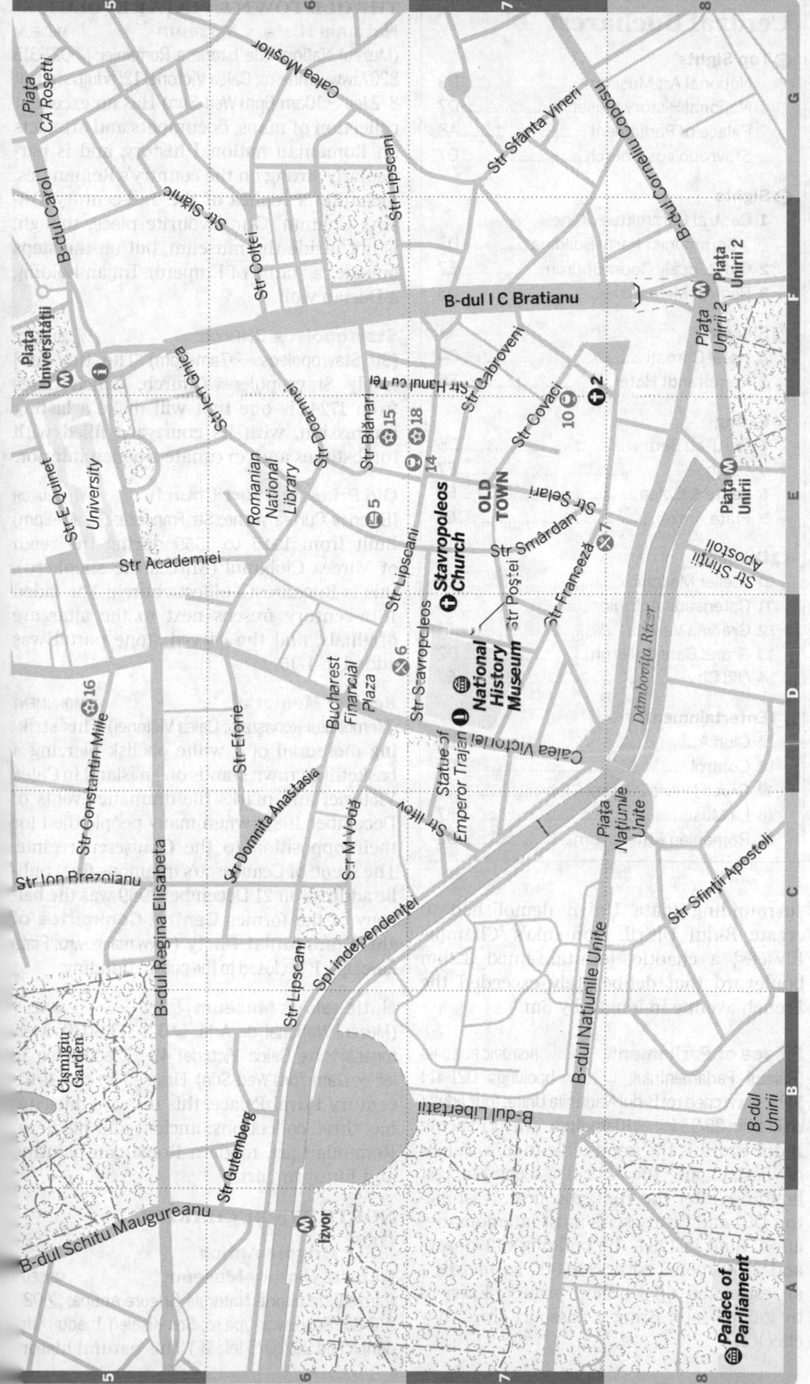

Piața CA Rosetti
Calea Moșilor
B-dul Carol I
Str Colței
Str Lipscani
Str Sfânta Vineri
B-dul Corneliu Coposu
Piața Universității
B-dul I C Bratianu
Piața Unirii 2
Str Ion Ghica
Str Doamnei
Str Blănari
Str Hanul cu Tei
Str Gabroveni
Str Covaci
Str E Quinet
University
Romanian National Library
Str Academiei
OLD TOWN
Stavropoleos Church
Str Șelari
Str Smârdan
Piața Unirii
Str Sfinții Apostoli
Str Lipscani
Str Stavropoleos
National History Museum
Str Poștei
Str Franceză
Bucharest Financial Plaza
Statue of Emperor Trajan
Calea Victoriei
Dâmbovița River
Str Constantin Mille
Str Eforie
Str Ilfov
Piața Națiunile Unite
Str Domnița Anastasia
Str M Vodă
Str Ion Brezoianu
B-dul Regina Elisabeta
Spl Independenței
Str Sfinții Apostoli
B-dul Națiunile Unite
Cișmigiu Garden
B-dul Libertății
B-dul Unirii
Str Gutemberg
B-dul Schitu Maugureanu
Izvor
Palace of Parliament

Central Bucharest

Top Sights
National Art Museum C3
National History Museum D7
Palace of Parliament A8
Stavropoleos Church D7

Sights
1 Central Committee of the Communist Party Building D3
2 Old Princely Court Church E7
3 Rebirth Memorial D3

Sleeping
4 Hotel Carpaţi C4
5 Rembrandt Hotel E6

Eating
6 Caru' cu Bere D6
7 Divan E7
8 Lente & Cafea F2
9 Piaţa Amzei C1

Drinking
10 Atelier Mecanic E7
11 Cafeneaua Actorilor F4
12 Grădina Verona E1
13 Grand Cafe Galleron D2
14 Old City E7

Entertainment
15 Club A E6
16 Control D5
17 Green Hours 22 Jazz Club C1
18 La Muse E7
19 Romanian Athenaeum D2

surrounding Piaţa Unirii demolished to create B-dul Unirii, Romania's 'Champs-Élysées', a chaotic, fountain-lined 3.2km boulevard that deliberately exceeded the French avenue in length by 6m.

Palace of Parliament HISTORIC BUILDING
(Palatul Parlamentului; tour bookings 021-414 1426; www.cdep.ro; B-dul Naţiunile Unite; tour adult/child from 25/13 lei; 10am-4pm; MIzvor) Facing B-dul Unirii is the impossible-to-miss Palace of Parliament, the world's second-largest building (after the Pentagon near Washington DC) and Ceauşescu's most infamous creation. Built in 1984, the building's 12 storeys and 3100 rooms cover 330,000 sq metres – an estimated €3.3 billion project. Entry is by guided tour. Bring a passport since they check ID.

THE OLD TOWN & PIAŢA REVOLUŢIEI

National History Museum MUSEUM
(Muzeul National de Istorie a Romaniei; 021-315 8207; www.mnir.ro; Calea Victoriei 12; adult/student 8/2 lei; 10am-6pm Wed-Sun) Has an excellent collection of maps, documents and artefacts on Romanian national history, and is particularly strong on the country's Roman ties, including a replica of the 2nd-century Trajan's Column. Our favourite piece, though, is not inside the museum, but on the steps outside: a statue of Emperor Trajan holding a Dacian wolf.

Stavropoleos Church CHURCH
(Str Stavropoleos; 7am-8pm) The tiny and lovely Stavropoleos Church, which dates from 1724, is one that will make a lasting impression, with its courtyard filled with tombstones and an ornate wooden interior.

Old Princely Court Church CHURCH
(Biserica Curtea Veche; Str Franceza; 7am-8pm) Built from 1546 to 1559 during the reign of Mircea Ciobanul (Mircea the Shepherd), this is Bucharest's oldest church. The faded 16th-century frescos next to the altar are originals, and the carved stone portal was added in 1715.

Rebirth Memorial MONUMENT
(Memorialul Renaşterii; Calea Victoriei) This striking memorial of a white obelisk piercing a basketlike crown stands on an island in Calea Victoriei and marks the dramatic events of December 1989, when many people died for their opposition to the Ceauşescu regime. The scene of Ceauşescu's infamous final public address on 21 December 1989 was the balcony of the former **Central Committee of the Communist Party** (www.mai.gov.ro; Piaţa Revoluţiei 1; closed to the public) building.

National Art Museum MUSEUM
(Muzeul Naţional de Artă; 021-313 3030; www.mnar.arts.ro; Calea Victoriei 49-53; admission 15 lei; 11am-7pm Wed-Sun) Housed in the 19th-century Royal Palace, this massive museum has three collections: ancient and medieval Romanian art, modern Romanian painting and European art.

NORTHERN BUCHAREST

TOP CHOICE **Grigore Antipa Natural History Museum** MUSEUM
(Muzeul de Istorie Naturală Grigore Antipa; 021-312 8826; www.antipa.ro; Şos Kiseleff 1; adult/student/child 20/10/5 lei;) This natural histor

museum has been thoroughly renovated and features modern bells and whistles like video displays, games and interactive exhibits.

Museum of the Romanian Peasant MUSEUM
(Muzeul Tăranului Român; 021-317 9661; www.muzeultaranuluiroman.ro; Şos Kiseleff 3; adult/child 8/2 lei; 10am-6pm Tue-Sun) One of the best museums in Bucharest is this collection of traditional peasant bric-a-brac, costumes, icons, artwork and partially restored houses and churches.

National Village Museum MUSEUM
(Muzeul Naţional al Satului;; 021-317 9103; www.muzeul-satului.ro; Şos Kiseleff 28-30; adult/child 10/5 lei; 9am-7pm Tue-Sun, to 5pm Mon;) This museum has a terrific open-air collection of several dozen homesteads, churches, mills and windmills, relocated from rural Romania.

Sleeping

Hotels in Bucharest are aimed at business-people and prices are higher here than in the rest of the country. A short-term apartment rental can be a good deal for small groups (up to four people) and if you're planning to stay longer than three days. Prices are generally cheaper than hotels, and you get a functioning kitchen and washing machine. Most of the apartments are a little worn but serviceable. Two rental agencies we like include **RoCazare** (0768-001 001; www.rocazare.ro) and **Cert Accommodation** (0720 772 772, www.cert-accommodation.ro). Prices range from 250 to 500 lei per night.

TOP CHOICE **Doors** HOSTEL €
(021-336 2127; www.doorshostel.com; Str Olimpului 13; dm 45-60 lei, d 150 lei;) Our favourite hostel *du jour* is 15 minutes' walk southwest of Piaţa Unirii, with a quiet, residential location and a beautiful garden set up like a Moroccan tearoom. Dorms are in six- and eight-bed rooms, with one quad and one private double.

Midland Youth Hostel HOSTEL €
(021-314 5323; www.themidlandhostel.com; Str Biserica Amzei 22; dm 35-60 lei;) This is a bright, well-run hostel, with an excellent central location not far from Piaţa Romană. Accommodation is in six-, 10- or 14-bed dorms.

Hotel Carpaţi HOTEL €€
(021-315 0140; www.hotelcarpatibucuresti.ro; Str Matei Millo 16; s/d 160/220 lei;) This popular backpacker option in an old landmark hotel exudes a kind of communist-era charm. Some of the 40 rooms have been renovated and offer good value.

Funky Chicken HOSTEL €
(021-312 1425; www.funkychickenhostel.com; Str Gen Berthelot 63; dm 40-45 lei;) This hostel occupies a historic home on a shaded street, with four dorm rooms that sleep 24. No private rooms and no breakfast.

Eating

Self-caterers will want to head to the daily market on **Piaţa Amzei**, with a good selection of fresh fruit and veg.

TOP CHOICE **Caru' cu Bere** ROMANIAN €€
(021-313 7560; www.carucubere.ro; Str Stavropoleos 3-5; mains 15-40 lei; 8am-midnight) Despite a decidedly touristy atmosphere, Bucharest's oldest beer house continues to draw a strong local crowd. The colourful belle époque interior and stained-glass windows dazzle, as does the classic Romanian food. Reservations recommended.

Divan MIDDLE EASTERN €€
(021-312 3034; www.thedivan.ro; Str Franceză 46-48; mains 20-30 lei; 10am-1am;) Deservedly popular Turkish and Middle Eastern place, where snagging a prized terrace table will take a mix of patience and good fortune.

Lente & Cafea INTERNATIONAL €€
(021-310 7424; www.lente.ro; Str Gen Praporgescu 31; mains 20-35 lei; 11.30am-1am;) Eclecticism is the theme at this trendy, in-the-know restaurant. The menu is an assortment of tempting fish and chicken concoctions

SPLURGE

It's hard to say enough good things about the **Rembrandt Hotel** (021-313 9315; www.rembrandt.ro; Str Smârdan 11; s/d 'tourist class' Mon-Fri 330/371 lei, Sat & Sun 294/334 lei;). Stylish beyond its three-star rating, this 16-room hotel faces the landmark National Bank in the Old Town. Rooms feature polished wood floors, wall-size timber headboards and DVD players.

(many with curry, wild rice, mushrooms etc).

Drinking

The Old Town around Str Lipscani is home to countless bars, clubs and cafes.

TOP CHOICE Atelier Mecanic CAFE
(0726-767 611; Str Covaci 12; 11am-4am) The laid-back mood and the arty, mix-and-match junk shop decor are a breath of fresh air compared with other Old Town cafes and pubs that are lined with corporate tat and tie-ins.

Cafeneaua Actorilor PUB
(0721-900 842; www.cafeneauaactorilor.ro; B-dul Nicolae Bălcescu 2; 9am-3am) Located on the ground floor of the National Theatre of Bucharest (just beside the InterContinental Hotel), this is an oasis of good drink and pizza in the middle of the centre.

TOP CHOICE Grădina Verona CAFE
(0732-003 061; Str Pictor Verona 13-15; 9am-1am) A garden oasis hidden behind the Cărtureşti bookshop serving excellent espresso drinks and unusual but refreshing ice-tea infusions.

Grand Cafe Galleron CAFE
(021-313 4565; www.grandcafegalleron.ro; Str Nicolae Golescu 18a; sandwiches 10-20 lei; 9am-midnight) A block east of Piaţa Revoluţiei, this stylish cafe has indoor nooks and outdoor seats for good-value sandwiches and salads, as well as coffee drinks and all-day breakfast.

Old City BAR
(0729-377 774; www.oldcity-lipscani.ro; Str Lipscani 45; 10am-5am) Remains one of our favourite go-to bars in the Old Town. Most nights, especially weekends, bring big crowds and theme parties.

☆ Entertainment

Bucharest has a lively night scene of concerts, theatre, and rock and jazz. Check the weekly guide **Şapte Seri** (www.sapteseri.ro) for entertainment listings.

Performing Arts

Bucharest National Opera House OPERA
(Opera Naţională Bucureşti; 021-314 6980, box office 021-313 1857; www.operanb.ro; B-dul Mihail Kogălniceanu 70-72; tickets 6-65 lei; box office 9am-1pm & 3-7pm) The city's premier venue for classical opera and ballet. Buy tickets online or at the venue box office.

Romanian Athenaeum CLASSICAL MUSIC
(Ateneul Roman; box office 021-315 6875; www.fge.org.ro; Str Franklin 1-3; tickets 15-65 lei; box office noon-7pm Tue-Fri, 4-7pm Sat, 10-11am Sun) Home to the respected George Enescu Philharmonic and offers a wide array of classical music concerts from September to May. Buy tickets at the box office.

Nightclubs & Live Music

Control CLUB
(0733-927 861; www.control-club.ro; Str Constantin Mille 4; 6pm-4am) This is a favourite among club-goers who like alternative, indie and garage sounds. Hosts live acts or DJs, depending on the night.

Club A CLUB
(021-316 1667; www.cluba.ro; Str Blănari 14; 9pm-5am Thu-Sun) Indie pop/rock tunes play until late Friday and Saturday nights.

Green Hours 22 Jazz Club JAZZ
(0788-452 485; www.greenhours.ro; Calea Victoriei 120; 24hr) This old-school basement jazz club runs a lively program of jazz nights through the week and hosts an international jazz fest in June.

La Muse CLUB
(0734-000 236; www.lamuse.ro; Str Lipscani 53; 9am-3am Sun-Wed, to 6am Thu-Sat) Just about anything goes at this popular Old Town dance club.

Information

You'll find dozens of bank branches and ATMs in the centre for changing money or withdrawing local currency with a credit or debit card. Bring your passport, as you will have to show it to change money.

Best Cafe (B-dul Mihail Kogălniceanu 19; per hr 5 lei; 24hr)

Bucharest Tourist Information Center (021 305 5500, ext 1003; http://en.seebucharest.ro; Piaţa Universităţii; 10am-6pm Mon-Fri, to 2pm Sat & Sun) Not much information on hand, but the English-speaking staff can field basic questions, make suggestions and help locate things on a map.

Central Post Office (021-315 9030; www.posta-romana.ro; Str Matei Millo 10; 7.30am-8pm Mon-Fri)

Emergency Clinic Hospital (021-599 2300, 021-9622; www.urgentafloreasca.ro; Calea Floreasca 8; 24hr)

Lonely Planet (www.lonelyplanet.com/romania/bucharest)

Getting There & Away

Air

Romania's national carrier is **Tarom** (☎call centre 021-204 6464, office 021-316 0220; www.tarom.ro; Spl Independenţei 17, city centre; ⊙8.30am-7.30pm Mon-Fri, 9am-1.30pm Sat). All international and domestic flights use **Henri Coandă International Airport** (Otopeni; ☎021-204 1000; www.otp-airport.ro; Şos Bucureşti-Ploieşti). Henri Coandă is 17km north of Bucharest on the road to Braşov. Arrivals and departures use separate terminals. The airport is a modern facility, with restaurants, newsagents, exchange offices and ATMs. There are 24-hour information desks at both terminals.

Bus

Bucharest has several bus stations and they don't seem to follow any discernible logic. Even Bucharest residents have a hard time making sense of it. The best bet is to consult the websites www.autogari.ro and www.cdy.ro. Both keep up-to-date timetables and are easy to manage, though www.cdy.ro is only in Romanian. Be sure to follow up with a phone call to make sure a particular bus is running on a particular day. Another option is to ask your hotel to help or book through a travel agency.

Car & Motorcycle

Driving in Bucharest is lunacy and you won't want to do it for more than a few minutes before you stow the car and use the metro. If you're travelling around the country by car and just want to visit Bucharest for the day, it's more sensible to park at a metro station on the outskirts and take the metro into the city.

Major rental agencies can be found at Henri Coandă International Airport. Most large companies also have an in-town branch. Some of the cheapest rates are offered by **Autonom** (☎airport branch 021-232 4325, call centre 0721-442 226; www.autonom.com; Henri Coandă International Airport), where a Dacia Logan rents for around 140 lei per day (including unlimited mileage and insurance); rates drop if you rent for more than a week.

Train

Gara de Nord (☎021-319 9539, phone reservations 021-9522, phone reservations 021-9521; www.cfr.ro; Piaţa Gara de Nord 1) is the main station for most national and all international trains. The station is accessible by metro from the centre. Buy tickets at station ticket windows or in advance at Agenţia de Voiaj CFR travel agents. A seat reservation is compulsory if travelling with an InterRail or Eurail pass.

Sample destinations and fares from Bucharest on fast IC (InterCity) trains include Braşov (70 lei, 2½ hours, several daily), Cluj-Napoca (90 lei, 7½ hours, four daily), Sibiu (70 lei, five hours, three daily) and Timişoara (100 lei, eight hours, two daily).

Getting Around

To/From the Airport

BUS Express bus 783 leaves every 15 minutes (half-hour at weekends) during the day from Piaţa Unirii and Piaţa Victoriei, and points in between. Buy a ticket valid for one round trip (or two people one way) for 7 lei at any RATB ticket booth near a bus stop. To get to the centre from the airport, catch bus 783 from outside the arrivals hall.

TAXI A reputable taxi from the centre to the airport should cost no more than 70 to 80 lei. Negotiate the fare in advance with the driver.

TRAIN There's a regular shuttle train service (8 lei, 35 minutes) from Gara de Nord to the airport. Trains leave hourly at 10 minutes past the hour, starting at 8.10am and continuing until 7.10pm.

Public Transport

Bucharest's public transport system of metros, buses, trams and trolleybuses is operated by **RATB** (Regia Autonomă de Transport Bucureşti; ☎info 021-9391; www.ratb.ro). The system runs daily from about 5am to approximately 11.30pm.

For buses, trams and trolleybuses, buy tickets at any RATB street kiosk, marked *'casa de bilete'*, at major stops and public squares. Tickets for standard buses cost 1.30 lei per trip and are sold in two-ticket increments for 2.60 lei. Tickets for a small number of express buses cost 7 lei (good for two journeys).

Metro stations are identified by a large letter 'M'. To use the metro, buy a magnetic-strip ticket available at ticketing machines inside station entrances (have small bills handy). Tickets valid for two journeys cost 4 lei. A 10-trip ticket costs 15 lei.

TRANSYLVANIA

After a century of being name-checked in literature and cinema, the word 'Transylvania' enjoys worldwide recognition. The mere mention conjures images of mind-bending mountains, Gothic castles, fortified churches, spooky moonlight and a roll call of bloodthirsty creatures with wicked overbites. Unexplained puncture-wounds to the neck notwithstanding, Transylvania is all those things and more. There's hiking in the Bucegi Mountains, valleys with Saxon towns, fortified churches, Bran and Peleş castles, and yes, Dracula's face will stare back at you from coffee mugs and T-shirts.

Braşov

POP 274,400

Legend has it that the Pied Piper reemerged from Hamelin in Braşov, and indeed there's something whimsical about the city, with its fairy-tale turrets and cobbled streets. Dramatically overlooked by Mt Tâmpa, complete with cocky Hollywood-style sign, this is a remarkably relaxed city. Wander its maze of streets, stopping for caffeine injections at bohemian cafes, between losing yourself in a beguiling coalescence of Austro-Hungarian gingerbread roofs,

Braşov

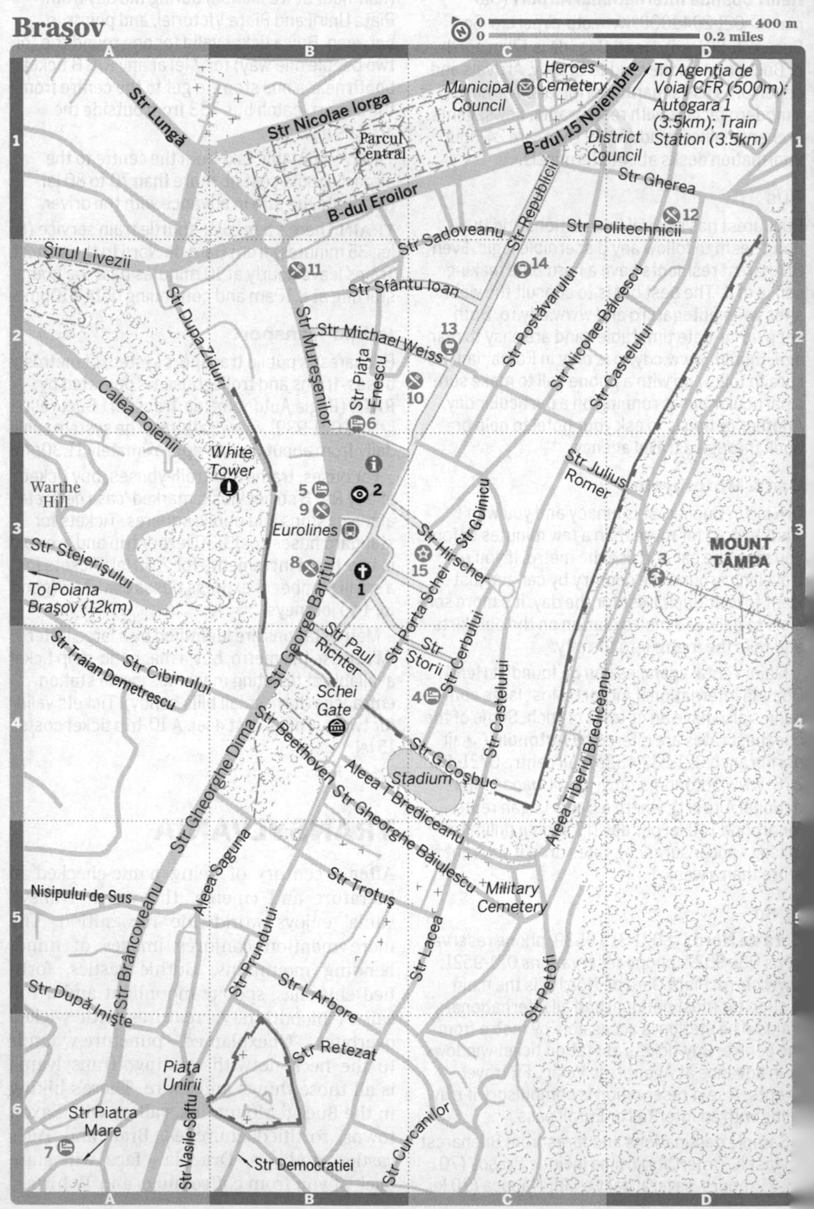

baroque gods, medieval spires and Soviet flat-tops.

Sights

Piaţa Sfatului SQUARE

This wide square was once the heart of medieval Braşov. In the centre stands the 1420 council house (Casa Sfatului), topped by a Trumpeter's Tower in which town councillors, known as centurions, would meet.

Black Church CHURCH

(Biserica Neagră; adult/child 6/3 lei; ⏲10am-5pm Tue-Sat, to noon Sun, closed Mon) The Black Church is the largest Gothic church between Vienna and İstanbul, and still used by German Lutherans today. Built between 1383 and 1480, it was named for its appearance after a fire in 1689. The original statues on the exterior of the apse are now inside.

Mt Tâmpa MOUNTAIN

Towering above town from the east is Mt Tâmpa, where Braşov's original defensive fortress was built. Vlad Ţepeş attacked it in 1458, finally dismantling it two years later and – out of habit – impaling some 40 merchants atop the peak. To reach the top, hike or take the **Tâmpa cable car** (Telecabina; one-way/return 9/15 lei; ⏲9.30am-5pm Tue-Sun).

Braşov

Sights

1	Black Church	B3
2	Piaţa Sfatului	B3

Activities, Courses & Tours

3	Tâmpa Cable Car	D3

Sleeping

4	Beke Guesthouse	C4
5	Bella Muzica	B3
6	Casa Wagner	B2
7	Rolling Stone Hostel	A6

Eating

8	Baritiu 16 'Organic'	B3
9	Bella Musica	B3
10	Bistro de l'Arte	C2
11	Sergiana	B2
12	Spar	D1

Drinking

13	Deane's Irish Pub & Grill	C2
14	Festival 39	C2

Entertainment

15	Gheorghe Dima State Philharmonic	C3

Sleeping

Rolling Stone Hostel HOSTEL €

(☎0268-513 965, 0740-518 681; www.rollingstone.ro; Str Piatra Mare 2a; dm 38 lei, r from 115 lei;) Run by helpful sisters with unlimited reserves of energy, super-friendly Stone attracts a cosmopolitan mix of travellers. Dorms are a little crowded. The private double room without bathroom has elegant couches and an armoire.

Beke Guesthouse PENSION €

(☎0268-511 997; Str Cerbului 32; r without bathroom per person 40-50 lei) A lovely Hungarian-speaking couple runs this handful of simple rooms, each with its own feel and all with shared bathroom. Rooms are accessed from the right-hand side of a vine-covered courtyard, shared with neighbours. No breakfast, no sign, no English.

Bella Muzica HOTEL €€

(☎0268-477 956; www.bellamuzica.ro; Piaţa Sfatului 19; s/d 220/270 lei;) Within its wine-coloured corridors are 34 dark-wood and exposed-brick rooms. Very comfy beds, fans, friendly staff and cable TV all help make it a firm choice for aesthetes.

Eating

The city has bags of choice, from sugary eats at bakeries on Str George Bariţiu to shadowy boho restaurants and high-class steakhouses. Piaţa Sfatului is great for cafes and breakfast while Str Republicii is more suited to people-watching cafes. For self-caterers there is a **Spar** (Str Nicolae Bălcescu; ⏲24hr) supermarket in the basement of the Star department store.

Baritiu 16 'Organic' JUICE BAR €

(Str George Bariţiu 16; ⏲8.30am-8pm;) This bijou hole-in-the-wall cafe is the vitamin shot you need to give your feet sightseeing wings. Banish those carb-heavy meat dishes with a carrot and orange juice, or a healthy sandwich.

TOP CHOICE **Bistro de l'Arte** BISTRO €€

(www.bistrodelarte.ro; Str Piaţa Enescu 11; mains 12-28 lei;) Tucked down a cobbled street straight out of a folk tale, this chi-chi joint has decidedly boho genes with sculpture and walls dotted with local artists' work. Gazpacho soup, shrimps and tomato gratin, snails…or just a croque-monsieur.

SPLURGE

The **Casa Wagner** (☎0268-411 253; www.casa-wagner.com; Piaţa Sfatului; s/d incl breakfast 269/315 lei; @📶) is a glamorous boutique hotel housed in a former 15th-century bank building. Its 24 well-appointed rooms offer exposed-brick walls, tasteful furnishings and modern bathrooms. The welcoming breakfast area and pleasant management make this an excellent choice.

Bella Musica ROMANIAN, MEXICAN €€
(Str George Bariţiu 2; mains 20-30 lei;) In a vaulted grottolike cellar aflicker with candlelight, Musica offers intimate dining. Its menu spans Mexican fare like tasty fajitas, *ciorba* (soup), pasta, foie gras, salads and schnitzel steak.

Sergiana ROMANIAN €€
(Str Mureşenilor 28; mains 30 lei; ⏲10am-11pm;) Authentically Saxon, this subterranean carnivore's heaven features a menu of venison, stag, boar, pork ribs, sirloin steak and Transylvanian sour soup with smoked gammon and tarragon.

Drinking

Deane's Irish Pub & Grill PUB
(Str Republicii 19) This subterranean Irish pub, with its early-20th-century cloudy mirrored bar, shadowy booths and old-world soundtracks, is a haven for Guinness-thirsty leprechauns. Live music some nights.

Festival 39 BAR
(Str Republicii 62; ⏲10am-1am) This romantic watering hole is an art deco dream of stained-glass ceilings, wrought-iron finery, candelabras and leather banquettes, and has a bar long enough to keep an army of barflies content.

Entertainment

Gheorghe Dima State Philharmonic CLASSICAL MUSIC
(Str Hirscher 10) Performs mainly between September and May.

Information

You'll find numerous ATMs, banks and currency-exchange offices on and around Str Republicii and B-dul Eroilor.

County Hospital (☎0268-333 666; Calea Bucareşti 25-27; ⏲24hr)

Red Net Internet (Str George Bariţiu 8; per hr 2.50 lei; ⏲7.30am-10pm)

Tourist Information Centre (☎0268-419 078; www.brasovcity.ro; Piaţa Sfatului 30) Easily spotted in the gold city council building in the centre of the square, the English-speaking staff offer free maps and brochures and track down hotel vacancies and train and bus times.

Getting There & Around

BUS From 6am to 7.30pm, maxitaxis leave every half-hour for Bucharest (30 lei, 2½ hours), stopping in Buşteni and Sinaia. About four or five maxitaxis leave for Sibiu (35 lei, 2½ hours). Nine or 10 go daily to Sighişoara (30 lei). The most accessible station is **Autogara 1** (Bus Station 1; ☎0268-427 267), next to the train station.

European routes are handled by **Eurolines** (☎0268-475 219; www.eurolines.ro; Piaţa Sfatului 18; ⏲9am-8pm Mon-Fri, to 4pm Sat), which sells tickets for buses to Germany, Italy, Hungary and other destinations.

TRAIN Buy advance tickets at the **Agenţia de Voiaj CFR** (Str 15 de Noiembre 43; ⏲8am-7.30pm Mon-Fri).

Daily domestic train services include Bucharest (42 lei, 3½ hours), Sighişoara (36 lei, 2½ hours), Sibiu (50 lei, four hours) and Cluj-Napoca (65 lei, six hours).

Sighişoara

POP 26,400

Sighişoara, a dreamy, compact, medieval citadel town, is where Vlad 'Ţepeş' Dracula first scampered about, when skewered Turks were just a twinkle in his eye. Brightly coloured 500-year-old town houses border hilly cobblestone streets, church bells clang atmospherically in the early hours, and overloaded tour buses jockey for parking space.

Sights

Sighişoara's primary sights are clustered in the compact, delightfully medieval **citadel** perched on a hillock and fortified with a 14th-century wall. Entering the citadel, yo pass under the massive **clock tower** (Turnu cu Ceas; Piata Muzeului), dating from 1280.

Inside is the worthy **History Museur** (Piaţa Muzeului 1; adult/child 10/2.50 lei; ⏲9am-5.30pm Tue-Fri, 10am-5.30pm Sat & Sun), wit small rooms off the steps winding up to th 7th-floor lookout. The small, dark **Tortur**

Room Museum (adult/student 4/1 lei; ⏲9am-5.30pm Tue-Fri, 10am-5.30pm Sat & Sun) shows how fingers were smashed and prisoners burned with coals.

The **Collection of Medieval Arms** (adult/student 6/1.50 lei; ⏲9am-5.30pm Tue-Fri, 10am-5.30pm Sat & Sun) has four rooms with medieval helmets, shields, crossbows and maces.

Nearby, the renovated **Casa Dracula** (Piaţa Cetăţii), now a restaurant, is where Vlad Ţepeş reputedly lived until the age of four.

Sleeping

TOP CHOICE Bed & Breakfast Kula PENSION €
(☎0265-777 907; Str Tâmplarilor 40; r/apt per person 65/150 lei; ⊜) Spilling with antique furniture, wood floors and rugs, this pension in a 400-year old house feels like you're staying at a friend's; which you are, after you've sat chatting with the owners in the pretty garden.

Pensiune Cristina & Pavel PENSION €
(☎0744-119 211, 0744-159 667; www.pensiuneafaur.ro; Str Cojocarilor 1; dm/s/d 45/80/125 lei; P) The floors are so clean at this four-room, one-dorm guesthouse, you could eat your lunch off them. Rooms with bathroom are spearmint white, plus there's an idyllic garden bursting with flowers.

Nathan's Villa HOSTEL €
(☎0265-772 546; www.nathansvilla.com; Str Libertăţii 8; dm 50 lei; @) Cramped dorms, but thoughtfully placed linen screens on bunks allow for a little more privacy. The purple dorm is cosy – check out the retro boiler. Another plus is a sofa and TV in dorms.

Eating

Cositorarului Casa RESTAURANT €
(Str Cositorarilor 9; mains 15-25 lei; ⏲9am-10pm) Refresh yourself with beautiful views of the Old Town and homemade lemonade. It also rustles up toasted sandwiches and breakfast. Inside is cosy, outside there's a small terrace.

Casa Dracula ROMANIAN €€
(Str Cositorarilor 5; mains 28 lei;) Despite the ghoulish Dracula bust mounted on the wall, the house where Vlad was born could have been dealt a worse blow than this atmospheric, wood-panelled restaurant. The menu scuttles from tomato soup to salmon fillet – all with Dracula-related references.

Café International & Family Centre CAFE €
(Piaţa Cetăţii 8; mains 13 lei; ⏲8.30am-7.30pm Mon-Sat Jun-Sep, 9am-6pm Mon-Sat Oct-May;) This delightful family-run cafe dishes up delicious pies, cookies, quiche and cakes.

Information

Cultural Heritage Info Centre (☎0788-115 511; www.dordeduca.ro; Piaţa Muzeului; ⏲10am-6pm Tue-Sun) Rents out bikes (5 lei per hour) and offers guided tours of Sighişoara and the fortified churches.

Tourist Information (☎0265-770 415; Str O Goga; ⏲10am-4pm Mon-Fri, 9am-1pm Sat) This useful English-speaking resource can book beds, check bus and train times, and has maps of the city.

Getting There & Away

BUS Next to the train station on Str Libertăţii, the **bus station** (☎0265-771 260) sends buses

WORTH A TRIP

BRAN CASTLE & RÂSNOV FORTRESS

Atmospheric **Bran Castle** (☎0268-237 700; www.bran-castle.com; adult/student 25/5 lei, camera/video 20 lei; ⏲9am-7pm Tue-Sun, noon-7pm Mon May-Sep, 9am-5pm Tue-Sun Oct-Apr), 30km south of Braşov, dates from 1378. Though Vlad Ţepeş only dropped by once in the 15th century (maybe), it's hard to skip this so-called 'Dracula's castle'.

Râşnov, 12km towards Braşov, offers the tempting ruins of the 13th-century **Râşnov Fortress** (Cetatea Râşnov; admission 10 lei; ⏲9am-8pm May-Oct, to 6pm Nov-Apr).

Pensiunea Stefi (☎0721-303 009; www.hotelstefi-ro.com; Piaţa Unirii 5; r 90 lei; ⊜), located in Râşnov, is a five-room guesthouse with a sauna, fitness centre and wading pool; breakfast costs 14 lei. In Bran, the **Hanul Bran** (☎0268-236 556; www.hanulbran.ro; Str Principala 384 ; s/d 100/120 lei) is probably the plushest option dead centre.

Bran is an easy DIY day trip from Braşov. Buses marked 'Bran-Moieciu' (6 lei, one hour) depart every half-hour from Braşov's Autogara 2. All buses stop each way at Râşnov.

to Sibiu (20 lei, 2½ hours, four daily), among other destinations. Buses to Braşov (38 lei, 2½ hours) stop at the bus station a couple of times per day and require a reservation (☎0265-250 702).

TRAIN About a dozen trains connect Sighişoara with Braşov (21 lei, two hours), nine of which go on to Bucharest (65 lei, 4½ hours). Five daily trains go to Cluj-Napoca (59 lei, 3½ hours). You'll need to change trains in Mediaş to reach Sibiu (16 lei, 2½ hours), but the four daily trains are timed for easy transfers. Buy tickets at the train station.

Sibiu

POP 154,500

Instantly charming with its maze of cobbled streets and baroque squares, Romania's cultural first lady has a magic all of its own. Composers Franz Liszt and Johann Strauss were drawn here in the 19th century, and in 2007 the city was named the European Union's Capital of Culture. Most months have myriad things going on, from festivals and exhibitions to theatre and opera, as well as plenty of cafes in the city's three main squares.

Sights

At the centre of the old walled city, the expansive Piaţa Mare is a good start for exploring Sibiu. Climb to the top of the former **Council Tower** (Turnul Sfatului; admission 2 lei; ⏰10am-8pm), which links Piaţa Mare with its smaller sister square, Piaţa Mică.

WORTH A TRIP

BUCEGI MOUNTAINS

These sandstone and limestone mountains, rising 2505m and accessible from the town of **Sinaia**, are hugely popular with hikers and trekkers. While some trails are poorly marked, there is a decent selection of cabanas (mountain huts) and shelters should your trek extend overnight or you get caught in inclement weather.

The best walking map is Dimap's fold-out *Five Mountains from the Carpathian's Bend* (34 lei; www.dimap.hu) covering the Piatra Craiului, Bucegi, Postăvarul, Piatra Mare and Ciucaş Ranges, plus a Braşov city map. A visit to the **Sinaia Tourism Information Centre** (☎0244-315 656; www.info-sinaia.ro; B-dul Carol I 47; ⏰8.30am-4.30pm Mon-Fri) is essential before setting off on ambitious hikes.

Brukenthal Museum MUSEUM
(www.brukenthalmuseum.ro; Piaţa Mare 5; adult/student 20/5 lei) The Brukenthal Museum is the oldest and possibly finest art gallery in Romania. Founded in 1817, the museum is in the baroque palace (1785) of Baron Samuel Brukenthal (1721–1803) and hosts an excellent collection of 16th- and 17th-century paintings.

History Museum MUSEUM
(Str Mitropoliei 2; adult/child 20/5 lei) The History Museum displays Palaeolithic-age tools, ceramics, bronze, jewellery and life-sized home scenes, costumes and furniture. Other sections hold guild exhibits, an armoury, Roman artefacts and a treasury.

Biserica Evanghelică CHURCH
(Evangelical Church; Piaţa Huet; church tower adult/child 3/2 lei) The Gothic Biserica Evanghelică, built from 1300 to 1520, is partially scaffolded due to renovation but you can still climb the church tower.

Pharmaceutical Museum MUSEUM
(☎0269-218 191; www.brukenthalmuseum.ro; Piaţa Mică 26; adult/child 10/2.5 lei; ⏰10am-6pm Tue-Sun Apr-Oct, 10am-6pm Wed-Sun Nov-Mar) A three-room collection packed with pills and powders, old microscopes and scary medical instruments.

Astra Museum of Traditional Folk Civilisation MUSEUM
(Muzeul Civilizaţiei Populare Tradiţionale Astra; Calea Răşinarilor 14; adult/child 15/3.50 lei; ⏰museum 10am-6pm Tue-Sun, gift shop 9am-5pm Tue-Sun) Around 5km from the centre, this sprawling open-air museum has a dazzling 120 traditional dwellings, mills and churches brought from around the country and set among two small lakes and a tiny zoological garden.

Sleeping

TOP CHOICE **Felinarul Hostel** HOSTEL
(☎0269-235 260; www.felinarulhostelsibiu.ro; Str Felinarul 8; dm/r 55/140 lei; ⊖@🛜) More boutique than hostel, this labour of love is wood-accented, courtyard oasis with one eight-berth and two six-berth dorms. There are also two homely private rooms with bathroom.

Old Town Hostel HOSTEL €
(☎0269-216 445, 0728-184 959; www.hostelsibiu.ro; Piaţa Mică 26; dm/d 55/180 lei; 📶) In a 450-year-old building with three dorms and two private rooms (one with bathroom), Old Town has sublime square views. It also has decidedly plush touches like parquet floors, fresh white walls and considerately spaced beds.

Pensiunea Ela PENSION €
(☎0269-215 197; www.ela-hotels.ro; Str Nouă 43; s/d/tr 100/120/160 lei; 📶) Down a quiet street in the Lower Town, you might have to knock on the door a few times to get an answer. Within its flowery courtyard there are eight basic rooms with a rustic signature. Owner Ella is a welcoming host.

Eating & Drinking

TOP CHOICE **Crama Sibiu Vechi** ROMANIAN €€
(Str P Ilarian; mains 25 lei; 📖) Hidden in an old wine cellar with its staff dressed in trad garb, this is the most rustically evocative restaurant in Sibiu.

Pasaj BISTRO €
(www.lapasaj.ro; Str Turnului 3a; mains 12-20 lei; ⏲8.30am-10pm; 📶🥗📖) At the foot of the passage of stairs, this is a perfect spot to catch a quiet frothy coffee and tuck into a menu of salads, pasta and pizza. Eat inside the low-lit interior or alfresco on wrought-iron tables and chairs.

Imperium Club BAR
(Str Nicolae Bălcescu 24; ⏲9am-dawn) Cosy barfly joint with vampish vaulted ceilings, dimly lit booths for canoodling, great cocktails and live jazz some nights.

Entertainment

Philharmonic CLASSICAL MUSIC
(www.filarmonicasibiu.ro; Str Cetăţii 3-5; adult/child 10/7 lei) Founded in 1949, this has played a key role in maintaining Sibiu's prestige as a main cultural centre of Transylvania.

Information

ATMs are located all over the centre.

Casa Luxemburg (☎0269-216 854; www.kultours.ro; Piaţa Mică 16) Travel agent offering loads of city tours (9 to 14 lei) and day trips (50 to 90 lei); has a useful free map of the centre too.

Info Point (☎0269-244 442; www.kultours.ro; Piaţa Huet 1; ⏲9am-10pm) Info on local attractions, surrounding areas, booking bus tickets, car rental and bike hire (per day 35 lei).

Tourist Information Centre (☎0269-208 913; www.sibiu.ro; Piaţa Mare 2; ⏲9am-5pm Mon-Fri, to 1pm Sat & Sun) Based at the City Hall, staff here are fantastically helpful at guiding you to make the best of the city; cultural events, finding accommodation, and booking train and bus tickets.

> **SPLURGE**
>
> This 26-room **Am Ring** (☎0269-206 499; www.amringhotel.ro; Piaţa Mare 14; s/d/tr 250/290/420 lei; ❄📶👪) is lavish, with marble busts of Hadrian and Achilles, and antique furniture, velvet curtains and wood-raftered ceilings at every turn. There's a nice bar too. Rooms have Gustavian-period furniture, thick carpets and huge beds.

Getting There & Around

BUS The **bus station** (Piaţa 1 Decembrie 1918) is opposite the train station. Bus and maxitaxi services include Braşov (25 lei, 2½ hours, two daily), Bucharest (40 lei, 5½ hours, six daily), Cluj-Napoca (30 lei, 3½ hours, 16 daily) and Timişoara (51 lei, six hours, three daily).

TRAIN There are seven daily direct trains to Braşov (35.60 lei, 2½ hours), three daily trains to Bucharest (67 lei, five hours) and Timişoara (67 lei, five hours). To get to/from Sighişoara (13 lei) or Cluj-Napoca (55 lei), you'll have to change at Copşa Mică or Mediaş (about nine or 10 trains daily). The **Agenţia de Voiaj CFR office** (☎0269-212 085; Str Nicolae Bălcescu 6; ⏲7am-8pm Mon-Fri) sells advance tickets.

Cluj-Napoca

POP 294,800

Cluj-Napoca, always shortened to 'Cluj' in conversation, isn't as picturesque as its Saxon neighbours, but it's famed for dozens of cavernous discos filled with agreeable students. Even outside the clubs, Cluj is one of Romania's most energised and welcoming cities.

Sights

St Michael's Church CHURCH
This vast 14th-century church dominates Piaţa Unirii. The neo-Gothic tower (1859) is a great landmark.

Pharmaceutical Museum MUSEUM

(Str Regele Ferdinand I; adult/child 5.20/3.10 lei; ⏲10am-4pm Mon-Wed & Fri, noon-6pm Thu) Tours are led by a hilarious pharmacist in a white lab coat, who points like a game-show host towards (seemingly ho-hum) glass cases of ground mummy dust, medieval alchemist symbols and painted 18th-century aphrodisiac bottles.

National Art Museum MUSEUM

(Piaţa Unirii 30; adult/student 5/3 lei; ⏲10am-5pm Wed-Sun) Housed inside the baroque Banffy Palace (1791), this museum has a couple of dozen rooms filled with paintings and artefacts, including a 16th-century church altar and many 20th-century paintings.

Ethnographic Museum of Transylvania MUSEUM

(Muzeul Etnografic al Transilvaniei; www.muzeul-etnografic.ro; Str Memorandumului 21; adult/student 6/3 lei, child free; ⏲9am-4pm Tue-Sat) The museum has two floors of well-presented displays featuring tools, weapons, crafts, toys and household items with detailed descriptions in English.

Sleeping

TOP CHOICE Retro Hostel HOSTEL €

(☎0264-450 452; www.retro.ro; Str Potaissa 13; dm/s/d/tr incl breakfast sandwich from 49/90/135/195 lei; ⊗@🛜) Well organised, central and with helpful staff, Retro has clean dorms and decent double rooms (all with TV and shared bathrooms).

Piccola Italia PENSION €

(☎0264-536 110; www.piccolaitalia.ro; Str Racoviţă 20; s/d/tr 115/130/150 lei; P🛜) Piccolo has nine clean, whitewashed rooms with reading lights, TV and bathroom. Add to this a garden dripping in vines, a hearty breakfast and friendly management, and it's a winner.

Transylvania Hostel HOSTEL €€

(☎0264-443 266; www.transylvaniahostel.com; Str Iuliu Maniu 26; dm/d 50/150 lei; ⊗@🛜) Huddled around a leafy courtyard, this mercifully cool hostel has spacious dorms, private lockers and a lounge with comfy sofas that you may find hard to prise yourself off.

Eating

TOP CHOICE Camino CAFE €

(Piaţa Muzeului 4; mains 15 lei; ⏲9am-midnight; 🛜) This boho restaurant is perfect for solo book-reading jaunts or a romantic dinner alfresco. The homemade pasta is delicious, the salads and tapas full of zing.

Magyar Vendeglo HUNGARIAN €€

(Str Iuliu Maniu 6; mains 25 lei) Based at the Hotel Agape, the menu here spans goulash, schnitzel, steak and curiously, 'brain with egg'! Not sure whose brain.

Drinking

The 'student ghetto', southwest of the centre (on and off Str Piezişă), teems with lively open-air bars.

Klausenberg Café CAFE

(www.klausenburgcafe.ro; Str Universităţii 1; ⏲9am-midnight; 👪) This swanky bar lures you in with its glittering crystal.

Casa Tauffer Jazz Café BAR, LIVE MUSIC

(Str Vasile Goldiş 2; ⏲24hr) With its oxblood walls ornamented with Rat Pack prints and antique trumpets, and Armstrong and Gillespie jumping on the speakers, this smoky joint is a slice of New Orleans.

Entertainment

State Philharmonic CLASSICAL MUSIC

(Filarmonica de Stat) The State had moved into the Student Culture House at research time. The improvised box office is just inside the front doors, on the right. Check with the tourist information office to see where it is playing.

Diesel CLUB

(Piaţa Unirii 17; ⏲6pm-dawn) Its outside terrace might look innocent enough but descend the stairway into the Sadean darkness and a dungeonlike interior awaits, complete with low-lit grotto bar, candelabras and a whole world of possibilities.

Information

Central Post Office (Str Regele Ferdinand 33; ⏲7am-8pm Mon-Fri, 8am-1pm Sat)

Pan Travel (☎0264-420 516; www.pantravel.ro; Str Grozavescu 13; ⏲9am-5pm Mon-Fri) Books accommodation, car rentals, self-drive tours and multiday tours to the Apuseni Mountains, Saxon villages or around Maramureş.

Tourist Information Office (☎0264-452 244; www.visitcluj.ro; B-dul Eroilor 6-8; ⏲8.30am-8pm Mon-Fri, 10am-6pm Sat) This super-friendly office has bags of info on trekking, train and bus times, eating, accommodation and cultural unmissables.

WORTH A TRIP

PAINTED MONASTERIES OF SOUTHERN BUCOVINA

The painted monasteries of southern Bucovina are among the greatest artistic monuments of eastern Europe – in 1993 they were collectively designated a Unesco World Heritage site.

Erected in the 15th and 16th centuries, when Moldavia was threatened by Turkish invaders, the Orthodox monasteries were surrounded by strong defensive walls. Biblical stories were portrayed on the church walls in colourful pictures, possibly for mere aesthetics or so that illiterate worshippers could better understand the stories.

Bucovina's monasteries are generally open from 9am to 5pm or 6pm daily. The monasteries of **Voroneţ** (adult/child 5/2 lei; 8am-7pm summer, to 4pm winter), **Humor** (Mănăstirea Humorului; adult/student 5/2 lei; 8am-7pm summer, to 4pm winter) and **Moldoviţa** (adult/student 5/2 lei; 8am-7pm summer, to 4pm winter) provide a representative sample of what Bucovina has to offer. The main gateway to the painted churches is **Suceava**, which is accessible by train from Bucharest (80 lei, eight hours, several daily) and Cluj-Napoca (67 lei, seven hours, five daily).

Getting There & Around

BUS Bus services from **Autogara 2** (Autogara Beta; 0264-455 249), 350m northwest of the train station (take the overpass), include Braşov (50 lei, two daily), Bucharest (60 lei, 7½ hours, three daily), Budapest (75 lei, several daily) and Sibiu (20 lei, 3½ hours, eight daily).

TRAIN The **Agenţia de Voiaj CFR** (0264-432 001; Piaţa Mihai Viteazul 20; 8am-8pm Mon-Fri, 9am-1.30pm Sat) sells domestic and international train tickets in advance. Sample destinations include Braşov (67 lei, five hours, eight daily), Bucharest (82 lei, nine hours, five daily), Sibiu (48 lei, five hours, two daily) and Timişoara (67 lei, seven hours, eight daily).

BANAT

Western Romania, with its geographic and cultural ties to neighbouring Hungary and Serbia, and historic links to the Austro-Hungarian Empire, enjoys an ethnic diversity that much of the rest of the country lacks. Timişoara, the regional hub, has a nationwide reputation as a beautiful and lively metropolis, and for a series of 'firsts'. It was the world's first city to adopt electric street lights (in 1884) and, more importantly, the first city to rise up against dictator Nicolae Ceauşescu in 1989.

Timişoara

POP 312,000

Romania's third- or fourth-largest city (depending on the source) is also one of the country's most attractive urban areas, built around a series of beautiful public squares and lavish parks and gardens. It's known as Primul Oraş Liber (First Free Town), for it was here that anti-Ceauşescu protests first exceeded the Securitate's capacity for violent suppression in 1989. With western Romania's nicest hotels and restaurants, it makes a perfect base for exploring the Banat region.

Sights

PIAŢA UNIRII

Piaţa Unirii is Timişoara's most picturesque square, featuring the imposing sight of the Catholic and Serbian churches facing each other. A couple of blocks to the east, following Str Palanca, is the **Cetate** (Fortress), a classic 18th-century Austrian fortress that's been remodelled into a complex of shops and cafes.

TOP CHOICE **Permanent Exhibition of the 1989 Revolution** MUSEUM

(0256-294 936; www.memorialulrevolutiei.ro; Str Popa Sapcă 3-5; admission by donation; 8am-4pm Mon-Fri, 9am-1pm Sat) The ideal venue to brush up on the December 1989 anticommunist revolution that began in Timişoara. Displays include documentation, posters and photography from those fateful days, capped by a graphic 20-minute video, with English subtitles.

Art Museum MUSEUM

(Muzeul de Artă; 0256-491 592; www.muzeul-deartatm.ro; Old Prefecture Palace, Piaţa Unirii 1; admission 5 lei; 10am-6pm Tue-Sun) Displays a representative sample of paintings and visual arts over the centuries as well as regular, high-quality temporary exhibitions.

PIAŢA VICTORIEI

This beautifully green pedestrian mall is dotted with fountains and lined with shops and cafes. The square's northern end is marked by the 18th-century National Theatre & Opera House, where thousands of demonstrators gathered on 16 December 1989.

Banat History Museum MUSEUM
(Muzeul Banatului; Piaţa Huniades 1) Housed in the historic Huniades Palace, this museum is closed until 2015. The exterior, though, is still worth a look. The origins date to the 14th century and Hungarian King Charles Robert, Prince of Anjou.

Metropolitan Cathedral CHURCH
(Catedrala Ortodoxă; www.timisoara.org/catedrala; B-dul Regele Ferdinand I; ⊙10am-6pm) The Orthodox Metropolitan Cathedral was built from 1936 to 1946. Unique to the church are its electric bells cast from iron imported from Indonesia.

Sleeping

Pension Casa Leone PENSION €
(☎0256-292 621; www.casaleone.ro; B-dul Eroilor 67; s/d/tr 125/150/200 lei; P🚭❄📶) This lovely seven-room pension offers exceptional service and individually decorated rooms. Take tram 8 from the train station, alight at the 'Deliblata' station and walk one block northeast to B-dul Eroilor.

Hostel Costel HOSTEL €
(☎0726-240 223; www.hostel-costel.ro; Str Petru Sfetca 1; dm 40-45 lei, d 135 lei; 🚭@📶) Run by an affable guy named Vlad, this charming 1920s art nouveau villa is arguably the city's only real youth hostel. The vibe is relaxed and congenial.

Hotel Central HOTEL €€
(☎0256-490 091; www.hotel-central.ro; Str N Lenau 6; s/d 160/180 lei; P❄📶) It's not exactly the Taj Mahal, but this communist-era hotel has had a decent facelift, leaving the rooms clean, modern and comfortable.

Eating

TOP CHOICE **Casa Bunicii** ROMANIAN €€
(☎0356-100 870; www.casa-bunicii.ro; Str Virgil Onitiu 3; mains 18-30 lei; 👪) The name translates to 'Granny's House' and this casual, family-friendly restaurant specialises in home cooking and regional specialities from the Banat.

Casa cu Flori ROMANIAN €€
(☎0256-435 080; www.casacuflori.ro; Str Alba Iulia 1; mains 18-28 lei) Excellent high-end Romanian cooking with refined service at moderate prices. In nice weather, climb three flights to the flower-lined rooftop terrace.

Intermezzo ITALIAN €€
(☎0256-432 429; www.restaurant-intermezzo.ro; Piaţa Unirii 3; mains 22-36 lei, pizza 18-24 lei; ⊙noon-midnight) This place has great pizzas and even better pastas. Dine on the terrace on Piaţa Unirii or in the cellar restaurant.

Lucas Super Sandwich SANDWICHES €
(www.lucassupersandwich.ro; Piaţa Victoriei 4; sandwiches 7-12 lei; ⊙8am-midnight Mon-Fri, 10am-midnight Sat & Sun; 📶) This local sandwich chain is a decent spot for a quick bite. Eat inside or take away to enjoy while seated on one of the benches in the square.

Drinking

Aethernativ CAFE
(☎0724-012 324; Str Mărăşeşti 14; ⊙10am-1am Mon-Fri, noon-1am Sat, 5pm-1am Sun; 📶) This informal art club, cafe and bar occupies a courtyard of a rundown building two blocks west of Piaţa Unirii.

Scârţ loc lejer CAFE
(☎0751-892 340; Str Zoe 1; ⊙10am-11pm Mon-Fri, 11am-11pm Sat, 2pm-11pm Sun; 📶) An old villa that's been retrofitted into a funky coffeehouse with albums pinned to the wall and chill tunes on the turntable.

Entertainment

State Philharmonic Theatre CLASSICAL MUSIC
(Filharmonica de Stat Banatul; ☎0256-492 521 www.filarmonicabanatul.ro; B-dul CD Loga 2; ⊙box office 2pm-7pm Wed, 9am-1pm Thu & Fri) Tickets can be bought at the box office inside the Philharmonic Theatre during limited open ing hours or one hour before performances

National Theatre & Opera House THEATRE, OPER
(Teatrul Naţional şi Opera Română; ☎opera 0256 201 286, theatre 0256-201 117; www.tntimisoara.com Str Mărăşeşti 2) The National Theatre & Oper House features both dramatic works an classical opera, and is highly regarded. Bu tickets (from around 40 lei) in the nearb

Agenţia Teatrală (☎0256-201 286; www.ort.ro; Str Mărăşeşti 2; ⏲10am-1pm & 5-7pm Tue-Sun).

Club 30 CLUB
(☎0256-247 878; www.club30.ro; Piaţa Victoriei 7; admission 10 lei; ⏲6pm-3am) This club has been a staple on the dance scene for years and shows no signs of slowing down, particularly on retro '80s and '90s dance nights.

Information

Online Centers (B-dul Mihai Eminescu 5; per hr 5.40 lei; ⏲24hr; 📶)

Timişoara County Hospital (Spitalul Clinic Judeţean de Urgenţă Timişoara; ☎0356-433 111; www.hosptm.ro; B-dul Iosif Bulbuca 10) Has 24-hour emergency service.

Tourist Information Centre (Info Centru Turistic; ☎0256-437 973; www.timisoara-info.ro; Str Alba Iulia 2) This great tourism office can assist with accommodation and trains, and provide maps and Banat regional info.

Getting There & Away

BUS Buses and minibuses are privately operated and depart from several points around the city, depending on the company. Consult the website www.autogari.ro for departure points. Bus service is extensive. Sample fares include to Arad (15 lei), Cluj-Napoca (65 lei) and Sibiu (45 lei).

International buses leave from the **East bus station** (www.autogari.ro). The main international operators include **Atlassib** (☎0256-226 486; www.atlassib.ro; Calea Dorobantilor 59) and **Eurolines** (☎0256-288 132; www.eurolines.ro; Str M Kogălniceanu 20). Belgrade-based **Gea Tours** (www.geatours.rs) offers daily minibus service between Timişoara and Belgrade for one way/return 125/200 lei. Book via the website.

TRAIN Trains depart from **Gara Timişoara-Nord** (Gara Timişoara-Nord; www.cfr.ro; Str Gării 2) (the 'northern' station, though it's actually west of the centre). Daily express trains include two to Bucharest (100 lei, eight hours), two to Cluj-Napoca (127 lei, six hours) and five to Arad (20 lei, one hour). There's one daily train to Belgrade (70 lei, three hours), which leaves at 5.40am.

UNDERSTAND ROMANIA

History

Ancient Romania & 'Dracula'

Ancient Romania was inhabited by Thracian tribes, also known as Dacians. From the

WORTH A TRIP

DANUBE DELTA

After passing through several countries, the Danube River empties into the Black Sea south of the Ukrainian border. The Danube Delta (Delta Dunării), on Unesco's World Heritage list, is one of Romania's leading tourist attractions.

At the inland port of **Tulcea**, the river splits into three channels: the Chilia, Sulina and Sfântu Gheorghe arms, creating a constantly evolving 4187-sq-km wetland of marshes, floating reed islets and sandbars.

The delta is a haven for wildlife lovers, birdwatchers, anglers and anyone wanting to get away from it all. There are beautiful, secluded beaches at **Sulina** and **Sfântu Gheorghe**, and the seafood is the best in Romania.

Much of the the delta is under the protection of the **Danube Delta Biosphere Reserve Authority** (DDBRA; ☎0240-518 945; www.ddbra.ro; Str Portului 34a; permits per day 5 lei; ⏲8am-4pm Mon-Fri), headquartered in Tulcea. Visitors to the reserve are required to purchase an entry permit, available at the DDBRA office.

The primary mode of transport in the delta is ferry boat. Regularly scheduled ferries leave from Tulcea's port daily and access major points in the delta. There are two main ferry operators: state-run **Navrom** (☎0240-511 553; www.navromdelta.ro; Str Portului 26; ⏲ticket office 11.30am-1.30pm) and **Nave Rapide** (☎0742-544 068, 0726-774 074; www.naverapide.ro). The helpful staff at the **Tourism Information Centre** (☎0240-519 130; www.primariatulcea.ro; Str Gării 26; ⏲8am-7pm Mon-Fri, to noon Sat May-Sep) in Tulcea can help piece together a journey and organise activities.

Tulcea is the largest city in the delta. If you've only got a short amount of time (one to three days), base yourself here and explore the delta via boating day trips. If you've got more time, pass through Tulcea on your way to deeper destinations like Sulina and Sfântu Gheorghe.

7th century BC the Greeks established trading colonies along the Black Sea, and the Romans conquered the area in AD 105–06.

From the 10th century the Magyars expanded into Transylvania, and by the 13th century all of Transylvania was under the Hungarian crown. Wallachia, Romania's southern region, was established as a buffer state between the Hungarian kings and Ottoman Turks.

The southern and eastern Romanian lands remained under the Turkish yoke for several centuries, spawning numerous accounts of Romanian heroics in battle involving leaders like Wallachian prince Ștefan cel Mare (Stephen the Great) and prince Vlad Ţepeş (Vlad the Impaler), who ruled Wallachia in the 15th century.

The 19th century saw the gradual weakening of the Ottoman Empire, finally creating an opening for Romanian independence. In 1859 Alexandru Ioan Cuza was elected to the thrones of Moldavia and Wallachia, forming a national state, which took the name Romania in 1862. Romania declared independence from the Ottoman Empire in 1877.

Romania in WWI & WWII

In 1916 Romania entered WWI on the Allied side. With the defeat of Austria-Hungary in 1918, the regions of the Banat and Transylvania went to independent Romania, forming today's modern Romania.

During WWII, Romania initially joined the war on the German side under a fascist dictatorship led by General Ion Antonescu. That alliance had horrific consequences. Some 400,000 Romanian Jews, including Transylvanian Jews ruled by Hungary during the war, as well as some 36,000 Roma, were sent to their deaths at concentration camps. In 1944 Romania dramatically changed sides and declared war on Nazi Germany, ultimately preserving Romanian statehood. In 1947 the Soviet-dominated Romanian People's Republic was proclaimed.

The Communist Period & Ceauşescu

Soviet troops withdrew in 1958, and after 1960 Romania adopted a quasi-independent foreign policy within the Soviet bloc under two leaders, Gheorghe Gheorghiu-Dej (from 1952 to 1965) and his protégé, Nicolae Ceauşescu (1965 to 1989).

Ceauşescu's reign will forever be seen as misguided, chaotic and megalomaniacal. The early years were relatively successful. But following a trip to North Korea in 1971, Ceauşescu steadily lost his grip on reality and established what became the most hardline regime within the Eastern bloc states. He placed his wife Elena, son Nicu and three brothers in important political positions and embarked on expensive follies like building his humungous 'House of the People' (today's Palace of Parliament) in central Bucharest.

On 15 December 1989 ethnic-Hungarian Father Lászlo Tőkés, based in Timişoara, publicly condemned the dictator, prompting the Reformed Church of Romania to remove Tőkés from his post. Civil unrest quickly spread around the country and Ceauşescu dispatched troops to crush the rebellion. On 21 December in Bucharest, an address by Ceauşescu was cut short by booing demonstrators, who were crushed by police gunfire and armoured cars. The following morning thousands more took to the streets. Within a couple of days, Ceauşescu and his wife were arrested. On 25 December they were executed by firing squad.

Independence to Today

Over the past two decades, Romania has had its share of scandal, corruption and unstable governments. Nevertheless, the overall trend has been positive, as the country has tried hard to make up for lost time after four decades of communist misrule.

Since independence, Romania has accomplished two major foreign-policy goals: joining NATO in 2004 and the EU in 2007. However, as this book goes to press, the country finds itself crippled by yet another political crisis, this time pitting the centre-right president, Traian Băsescu, against his main rival, centre-left prime minister Victor Ponta. This scandal may matter more than most, as it threatens to set back Romania's aim to join the European Union's common border and customs Schengen zone.

People

Romanians make up 89% of the population of around 20 million; Hungarians are the next largest ethnic group (7%), followed by Roma (2%), and smaller populations of Ukrainians, Germans, Russians and Turks. Germans and Hungarians live almost exclusively in Transylvania, while Ukrainians and Russians live mainly near the Danube Delta and Turks along the Black Sea coast.

Arts

Romania has a strong tradition of rural crafts, music and dance. Religious icon painting was widely practised, particularly between the 17th and 19th centuries. Artist Nicolae Grigorescu (1838–1907) is known for adapting Impressionism to Romanian peasant themes. Sculptor Constantin Brancusi (1876–1957) was a central figure of the modernist movement and one of the early pioneers of abstractionism.

The so-called 'Romanian New Wave' in cinema is red hot and showing no signs of abating. Director Cristian Mungiu won the Cannes Film Festival's top prize in 2007 with *4 Months, 3 Weeks and 2 Days*, a disturbing tale of illegal abortion in communist-era Romania, while the late Cristian Nemescu's film *California Dreamin'* also took honours.

More recent buzz-worthy films include a rare Romanian comedy *Tales from the Golden Age* (2009) by Cristian Mungiu, *Police, Adjective* by Corneliu Porumboiu, *Aurora* (2010) by Cristi Puiu and Radu Muntean's *Tuesday, After Christmas* (2010).

Environment

The mighty Carpathian Mountains form the shape of a scythe sweeping down through the country's centre from Ukraine and then curling northwards.

East of the mountains are low-lying plains that end at the Black Sea and Europe's second-largest delta region, where the Danube spills into the Black Sea.

Romania has nearly 600 protected areas, including 13 national parks, three biosphere reserves and one World Natural Heritage site (the Danube Delta), totalling over 1.2 million hectares.

Rural Romania has thriving wildlife populations in its parks and mountains, including lynxes, foxes, wolves, bears and badgers.

SURVIVAL GUIDE

Directory A–Z

Accommodation

Romania has a wide choice of accommodation options to suit most budgets, including hotels, pensions, hostels and camping grounds. Prices across these categories have risen in recent years, but are generally lower than in western Europe.

Budget properties include hostels, cheaper guesthouses and campgrounds. Midrange refers to three-star hotels and pensions. Top end means four- and five-star hotels, corporate chains and boutiques.

We've quoted prices in this guide in lei, though some hotels quote rates in euro. You'll still pay in lei and your credit card will be debited at the current exchange rate.

The following price categories for the cost of a double room in high season are used in the listings in this chapter:

€ less than 130 lei

€€ 130 to 280 lei

€€€ more than 280 lei

Business Hours

Banks 9am-noon & 1-5pm Mon-Fri

Clubs 8pm-2am

Restaurants 10am-11pm

Shops 10am-6pm Mon-Fri, 10am-5pm Sat

Embassies & Consulates

Embassies are located in Bucharest, while several countries maintain consulates at other cities around the country. There is no New Zealand embassy in Romania, so citizens should turn to the country's embassy in Brussels for consular matters.

Australian Consulate (☎021-206 2200; www.dfat.gov.au; Str Praga 3)

Canadian Embassy (☎021-307 5000; www.canadainternational.gc.ca/romania-roumanie; Str Tuberozelor 1-3)

French Embassy (☎021-303 1000; www.ambafrance-ro.org; Str Biserica Amzei 13-15)

Irish Embassy (☎021-310 2131; www.embassyofireland.ro; Str Buzeşti 50-52)

Netherlands Embassy (☎021-208 6030; http://romania.nlembassy.org; Aleea Alexandru 20)

UK Embassy (☎021-201 7200; www.ukinromania.fco.gov.uk; Str Jules Michelet 24)

US Embassy (☎consulate 021-270-6000, embassy 021-200 3300; http://romania.usembassy.gov; B-dul Dr Liviu Librescu 4-6)

Food

The following price categories for the cost of a main course are used in the listings in this chapter:

€ less than 15 lei

€€ 15 lei to 30 lei

€€€ more than 30 lei

Gay & Lesbian Travellers

Public attitudes towards homosexuality remain negative. In spite of this, Romania has made significant legal progress in decriminalising homosexual acts and adopting anti-discrimination laws.

Bucharest remains the most tolerant city in the country. Bucharest-based **Accept Association** (021-252 9000; www.accept-romania.ro) organises a six-day GayFest in the capital in early summer, with films, parties, conferences and a parade.

Money

The legal tender is the leu (plural lei; abbreviated in banks as 'RON'). Notes come in denominations of 1, 5, 10, 50, 100, 200 and 500 lei. One leu is divided into 100 bani, and coins come in 10 and 50 bani pieces (as well as nearly worthless 1 and 5 bani coins).

The easiest way to obtain local currency is to withdraw money as needed with a debit or credit card at bank ATMs. You'll find these nearly everywhere. Banks generally provide better exchange rates than private exchange booths. To exchange money you'll need to show a passport.

Credit and debit cards are widely accepted in major cities and towns, but less so in rural areas. Always have cash on hand.

Public Holidays

New Year 1 and 2 January

Orthodox Easter Monday April/May

Labour Day 1 May

Pentecost May/June, 50 days after Easter Sunday

Assumption of Mary 15 August

Feast of St Andrew 30 November

Romanian National Day 1 December

Christmas 25 and 26 December

Telephone

Romania has a modern telephone network of landlines and mobile (cell) phones. Romania's country code is 40.

All Romanian numbers have 10 digits, consisting of a zero, plus a city or mobile code and the number. Mobile phone numbers are identified by a three-digit prefix starting with 7.

Romanian mobiles use the GSM 900/1800 network, the standard throughout Europe as well as in Australia and New Zealand, but not compatible with phones in North America or Japan (though some multiband phones do work across regions). Ask your provider whether your phone will work abroad.

To reduce expensive roaming fees, buy a prepaid Romanian SIM card. These start at about 20 lei and include bonus minutes. They are offered by all three of Romania's main carriers: **Vodafone** (www.vodafone.ro), **Cosmote** (www.cosmote.ro) and **Orange** (www.orange.ro).

Public phones require a magnetic-stripe phonecard, which you can buy from post offices and newspaper kiosks. Phonecards start at about 10 lei.

Tourist Information

The **Romanian National Tourist Office** (www.romaniatourism.com) maintains a wonderful website with a trove of useful information. Romania's national network of tourist offices has made strides in recent years. Nearly all big cities have decent tourist offices.

Visas

Citizens of EU countries do not need visas and can stay indefinitely. Citizens of the USA, Canada, Australia, New Zealand, Israel, Japan and many other countries can stay for up to 90 days without a visa. Other nationalities should check with the **Ministry of Foreign Affairs** (www.mae.ro).

Getting There & Away

Air

Tarom (021-204 6464; www.tarom.ro) is Romania's state airline. National airline **Carpatair** (0256-300 900; www.carpatair.com) uses Timişoara as its hub.

All flights to Bucharest land at the capital's **Henri Coandă International Airport** (Otopeni; 021-204 1000; www.otp-airport.ro; Şos Bucureşti-Ploieşti), formerly called Otopeni Other major cities with international airports:

Cluj Airport (0264-416 702; www.airportcluj.ro; Str Traian Vuia 149)

Sibiu Airport (0269-253 135; www.sibiuairport.ro; Sos Alba Iulia 73)

Timişoara Airport (Traian Vuia Timişoara Airport; ☎0256-493 639; www.aerotim.ro; Str Aeroport 2, Ghiroda)

Land

Romania shares a border with five countries: Bulgaria, Hungary, Moldova, Serbia and Ukraine. There are four passenger and car ferry crossings with Bulgaria, at Calafat, Bechet, Turnu Măgerele and Călăraşi.

Highway border posts are normally open 24 hours, though smaller crossings may only be open from 8am to 8pm.

BUS

Long-haul bus service remains a popular way of travelling from Romania to western Europe as well as to parts of southeastern Europe and Turkey. Bus travel is comparable in price to train travel but can be faster.

Bus services to and from western Europe are dominated by two companies: **Eurolines** (www.eurolines.ro) and **Atlassib** (www.atlassib.ro; Soseaua Alexandriei 164). Both maintain networks from cities throughout Europe to destinations all around Romania. Check the websites for latest schedules, prices and departure points.

Bucharest is the hub for coach travel to southeastern Europe. One bus departs daily from Bucharest's **Filaret** (☎021-335 3290, information 021-336 0692; www.acfilaret.ro; Piaţa Gării Filaret 1) bus station to Sofia (seven hours, €18); Bucharest-based **Murat Turism & Transport** (☎021-316 5520; www.muratturism.ro; Soseaua Viilor 33) offers daily bus service from Bucharest to İstanbul (14 hours, €40) and to Athens (18 hours, €50).

CAR & MOTORCYCLE

Ensure your documents (personal ID, insurance, registration and visas, if required) are in order before crossing into Romania.

TRAIN

Romania is integrated into the European rail grid, and there are decent connections to western Europe and neighbouring countries. Nearly all arrive at and depart from Bucharest's main station, **Gara de Nord** (☎021-319 9539, phone reservations 021-9522, 021-9521; www.cfr.ro; Piaţa Gara de Nord 1).

There are two daily direct trains between Budapest (Hungary) and Bucharest, with regular onward direct connections from Budapest to Prague (Czech Republic), Munich (Germany) and Vienna (Austria).

Getting Around

Air

Given the poor state of the roads, flying between cities is a feasible option if time is a primary concern.

The national carrier **Tarom** (☎021-204 6464; www.tarom.ro) operates a comprehensive network of domestic routes. The airline flies regularly between Bucharest and Cluj-Napoca, Iaşi, Oradea, Sibiu, Suceava and Timişoara. Timişoara-based **Carpatair** (☎0256-300 900; www.carpatair.com) also runs domestic flights, flying from Timişoara to Iaşi, Craiova and Bacau.

Bus

A mix of buses and maxitaxis combine to form the seriously disorganised Romanian bus system. Finding updated information can be tough without local help. The website www.autogari.ro gives a snapshot of domestic and international bus schedules. Generally it's easier to plan train travel.

Car & Motorcycle

Roads are crowded and in poor condition. The country has only a few short stretches of motorway *(autostrada)*, meaning most travel is along the two-lane national highway. When calculating arrival times, figure on 50km per hour.

Western-style petrol stations are plentiful. A litre of unleaded 95 octane costs 6 lei. Most stations accept credit cards, but you'll need a PIN to use them.

Local Transport

Romanian cities have good public transport systems comprised of buses, trams, trolleybuses and maxitaxis. Bucharest is the only city with a metro. The method for accessing the systems is broadly similar. Purchase bus or tram tickets at newsagents or street kiosks marked *bilete* or *casă de*

DRIVING RULES

» The blood-alcohol limit is zero.

» Seatbelts are compulsory.

» Headlights must be on day or night.

» Speed limits are 90km/h on major roads and 50km/h in villages and towns.

bilete before boarding, and validate the ticket once aboard. For maxitaxis, buy a ticket directly from the driver.

TAXIS

Taxis are cheap and a useful supplement to the public transport system. Drivers are required by law to post their rates on their doors or windscreens. The going rate varies from city to city, but runs anywhere from 1.39 to 1.89 lei per kilometre. Any driver posting a higher fare is likely a rip-off.

Train

The extensive network covers much of the country, including most tourist sights. The national rail system is run by **Căile Ferate Române** (CFR, Romanian State Railways; www.cfr.ro), abbreviated as 'CFR'. The CFR website has a handy online timetable (*mersul trenurilor*).

» Romania has three different types of trains that travel at different speeds and charge different fares for the same destination. InterCity, listed as 'IC' on timetables, are normally the fastest and most comfortable.

» Buy tickets at train station windows, specialised Agenţia de Voiaj CFR ticket offices, private travel agencies or online at www.cfrcalatori.ro.

Russia

Includes »

Moscow 914
St Petersburg 922
Kaliningrad Region 929
Kaliningrad.................. 929
Understand Russia....... 933
Survival Guide 935

Best Places to Eat

» Delicatessen (p920)
» Jagannath (p920)
» Zoom Café (p927)
» Green Room (p927)
» Reporter (p932)

Best Places to Stay

» Bulgakov Mini-Hotel (p919)
» Da! Hostel (p919)
» Soul Kitchen (p927)
» Hostel Life (p927)
» Amigos Hostel (p932)

Why Go?

Could there be a more iconic image of eastern Europe than the awe-inspiring architectural ensemble of Moscow's Red Square? Russia's brash, exciting and economically powerful capital is a must on any trip to the region.

St Petersburg, on the Baltic coast, also shouldn't be missed. The former imperial capital is still Russia's most beautiful and alluring city, with its colourful and often crumbling Italianate mansions, wending canals and enormous Neva River.

Emulating the tourist-friendly nature of its Baltic neighbours is little Kaliningrad, wedged between Poland and Lithuania on the Baltic Sea. It's a fascinating destination, combining all the best elements of its enormous mother.

Visa red tape deters many travellers from visiting Russia (Россия) – don't let it keep you from experiencing the incredible things to see and do in the European part of the world's largest country.

When to Go

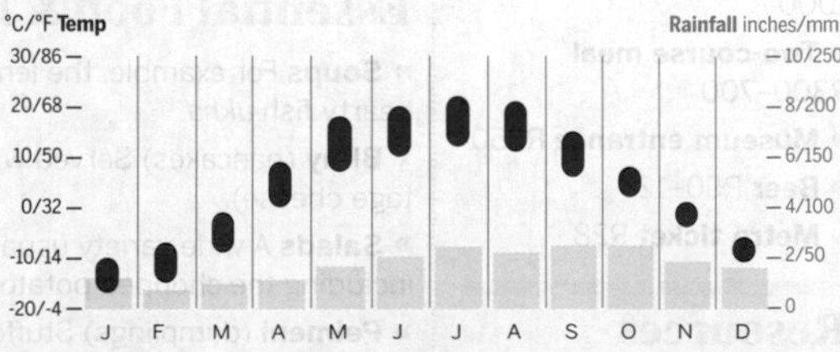

May Big military parades and a public holiday mark the end of WWII.

Jun-Jul Party during St Petersburg's White Nights; bask on the beaches of Kaliningrad.

Dec-Jan Snow makes Moscow and St Petersburg look magical, while hotel rates drop.

AT A GLANCE

» **Currency** Ruble (R)

» **Language** Russian

» **Money** Plenty of ATMs, most accept foreign cards

» **Visas** Required by all – apply at least a month in advance of your trip

Fast Facts

» **Area** 16,995,800 sq km

» **Capital** Moscow

» **Country code** ☎7

» **Emergency** Ambulance ☎03, emergency assistance ☎112, fire ☎01, police ☎02

Exchange Rates

Australia	A$1	R32.44
Canada	C$1	R30.58
Euro Zone	€1	R39.69
Japan	¥100	R32.91
New Zealand	NZ$1	R26.00
UK	UK£1	R46.99
USA	US$1	R31.06

Set Your Budget

» **Bed in a hostel** R500–1000

» **Two-course meal** R300–700

» **Museum entrance** R350

» **Beer** R50–120

» **Metro ticket** R28

Resources

» **Visit Russia** (www.visitrussia.org.uk)

» **Moscow Expat Site** (www.expat.ru)

» **Way to Russia** (www.waytorussia.net)

Connections

Bordering Belarus, Estonia, Latvia, Lithuania, Poland and Ukraine, Russia has excellent train and bus connections with the rest of Europe. Be careful, however: many routes connecting St Petersburg and Moscow with points west – including Kaliningrad – go through Belarus, for which you'll need a transit visa. Buses are the best way to get from St Petersburg to Tallinn. St Petersburg to Helsinki can be done by boat, bus or train.

ITINERARIES

One Week

Spend three days in Moscow. See Red Sq, the Kremlin and the spectacular collections at the Tretyakov, New Tretyakov and Pushkin art museums. Journey out of the centre to the magnificent Novodevichy Convent & Cemetery, and the revamped Gorky Park. Sweat it out in the luxurious Sanduny Baths or do a metro tour. The last three days are reserved for splendid St Petersburg. Wander up Nevsky pr, see Dvortsovaya pl, and spend a half-day at the Hermitage. Tour the canals and the mighty Neva River by boat. Visit Peter & Paul Fortress, the Church of the Saviour on Spilled Blood and the wonderful Russian Museum.

Two Weeks

With two extra days in Moscow, venture outside the centre to explore Gorky Park, and take a day trip to charming Sergiev Posad. In St Petersburg, spend more time in the Hermitage and other museums. Head to Kaliningrad and admire the reconstructed Gothic Cathedral and wander along the river to the excellent World Ocean Museum. The Amber Museum is also impressive. Explore the dunes and forests of the Kurshskaya Kosa National Park.

Essential Food & Drink

» **Soups** For example, the lemony meat *solyanka* or the hearty fish *ukha*.

» **Bliny** (pancakes) Served with *ikra* (caviar) or *tvorog* (cottage cheese).

» **Salads** A wide variety usually slathered in mayonnaise, including the chopped potato one called Olivier.

» **Pelmeni** (dumplings) Stuffed with meat and eaten with sour cream and vinegar.

» **Central Asian dishes** Try *plov* (Uzbek pilaf), *shashlyk* (kebab) or *lagman* (noodles).

» **Vodka** The quintessential Russian tipple.

» **Kvas** A refreshing, beerlike drink, or the red berry juice mix *mors*.

Russia Highlights

1 Be awe-inspired by the massive scale and riches of **Moscow** (p914), Russia's brash, energetic capital

2 Take a walking, bike or boat tour of **St Petersburg** (p922), a glorious Italianate slice of Old Europe incongruously placed in Russia

3 Ogle the seemingly endless collection of masterpieces in St Petersburg's unrivalled **Hermitage** (p922)

4 Explore the brawny eponymous capital of **Kaliningrad** (p929), Russia's quirky exclave on the Baltic Sea

5 Kick back on the pristine beaches of the **Kurshskaya Kosa National Park** (p929) or go in search of its 'dancing forest'

MOSCOW

☎495 & ☎499 / POP 11.5 MILLION

Intimidating in its scale, but also exciting and unforgettable, Moscow (Москва) is a place that inspires extreme passion or loathing. History, power and wild capitalism hang in the air, alongside an explosion of creative energy that throws up edgy art galleries and a dynamic restaurant, bar and nightlife scene with something for everyone. Although much of its architectural heritage has been destroyed, the sturdy stone walls of the Kremlin continue to occupy the founding site of Moscow, and remains of the Soviet state are scattered all around the city.

The city radiates from its medieval heart, the Kremlin, in a series of ring roads. The most central rings are the tree-lined 'boulevard ring' and, beyond, the vast and busy 'garden ring'.

Sights

The Kremlin MUSEUM

(☎495-202 3776; www.kreml.ru; adult/student R350/100; ⏲10am-5pm Fri-Wed, ticket office 9.30am-4.30pm; MAleksandrovsky Sad) The apex of Russian political power and once the centre of the Orthodox Church, the Kremlin is the kernel not only of Moscow but of the whole country. It's from here that autocratic tsars, communist dictators and democratic presidents have done their best – and worst – for Russia.

Occupying a roughly triangular plot of land covering Borovitsky Hill on the north bank of the Moscow River, the Kremlin is enclosed by high walls 2.25km long, with Red Sq outside the east wall. The best views of the complex are from Sofiyskaya nab across the river.

METRO TOUR

For just R27 you can spend the day touring Moscow's magnificent metro stations. Many of the stations are marble-faced, frescoed, gilded works of art. Among our favourites are: **Komsomolskaya**, a huge stuccoed hall, its ceiling covered with mosaics depicting military heroes; **Novokuznetskaya** featuring military bas-reliefs done in sober khaki and colourful ceiling mosaics depicting pictures of the happy life; and **Mayakovskaya**, Grand Prize winner at the 1939 World's Fair in New York.

Before entering the Kremlin, deposit bags at the **left-luggage office** (per bag R60; ⏲9am-6.30pm Fri-Wed), beneath the **Kutafya Tower** near the entrance. Ticket offices are in Kutafya Tower and nearby in **Alexandrovsky Garden** (Aleksandrovsky sad, Manezhnaya ul).

The ticket to the 'Architectural Ensemble of Cathedral Square' covers entry to the grounds and to all four churches, as well as the Patriarch's Palace. It does not include Ivan the Great Bell Tower, or the opulent collection of treasures in the **Armoury** (adult/student R700/200; ⏲entry 10am, noon, 2.30pm & 4.30pm); you can buy tickets for those at the ticket offices, too.

Photography is not permitted inside the Armoury or any of the buildings on Sobornaya pl (Cathedral Sq). Visitors wearing shorts will be refused entry.

Southwest Buildings

From the Kutafya Tower, walk up the ramp and pass through the Kremlin walls beneath the **Trinity Gate Tower**. The lane to the right (south) passes the 17th-century **Poteshny Palace**, where Stalin lived. The horribly out-of-place glass-and-concrete **State Kremlin Palace** houses a concert and ballet auditorium, where many Western pop stars play when they are in Moscow.

Sobornaya Ploshchad

On the northern side of Sobornaya pl, with five golden helmet domes and four semicircular gables facing the square, is the **Assumption Cathedral** (Uspensky Sobor), built between 1475 and 1479. As the focal church of prerevolutionary Russia, it's the burial place of most heads of the Russian Orthodox Church from the 1320s to 1700.

The delicate little single-domed church beside the west door of the Assumption Cathedral is the **Church of the Deposition of the Robe** (Tserkov Rizpolozhenia), built between 1484 and 1486 by masons from Pskov.

With its two golden domes rising above the eastern side of Sobornaya pl, the 16th-century **Ivan the Great Bell Tower** (Kolokolnya Ivana Velikogo; special exhibits adult/student R150/100) is the Kremlin's tallest structure. Beside the bell tower stands the **Tsar Bell**, a 202-tonne monster that cracked before it ever rang. North of the bell tower is the mammoth **Tsar Cannon**, cast in 1586 but never shot.

The 1508 **Archangel Cathedral** (Arkhangelsky sobor), at the square's southeastern corner, was for centuries the coronation, wedding and burial church of tsars. The tombs of all of Russia's rulers from the 1320s to the 1690s are here bar one (Boris Godunov, who was buried at Sergiev Posad).

Finally, the **Annunciation Cathedral** (Blagoveshchensky sobor), at the southwest corner of Sobornaya pl and dating from 1489, contains the celebrated icons of master painter Theophanes the Greek. He probably painted the six icons at the right-hand end of the diesis row, the biggest of the six tiers of the iconostasis. *Archangel Michael* (the third icon from the left on the diesis row) and the adjacent *St Peter* are ascribed to Russian master Andrei Rublyov.

Red Square HISTORIC SITE
(Krasnaya pl; MPloshchad Revolyutsii) Entering massively impressive Red Sq through the **Resurrection Gate**, you'll emerge with a superb view of the magnificently flamboyant **St Basil's Cathedral** (adult/student R250/50; 11am-5pm Wed-Mon; MPloshchad Revolyutsii) on the far side. This ultimate symbol of Russia was created between 1555 and 1561 (replacing an existing church on the site) to celebrate the capture of Kazan by Ivan the Terrible. Built over the grave of the barefoot holy fool Vasily (Basil) the Blessed, who predicted Ivan's damnation, its design is the culmination of a wholly Russian style that had been developed through the building of wooden churches. Go inside to see the stark medieval wall paintings.

Lenin's Mausoleum (10am-1pm Tue-Thu, Sat & Sun; MPloshchad Revolyutsii) is found at the square's northwestern corner. The embalmed Soviet leader remains as he has been since 1924 (apart from a retreat to Siberia during WWII). Before joining the queue, drop your camera at the left-luggage office in the State History Museum, as you will not be allowed to take it with you. Stalin, Brezhnev and many of communism's other heavy hitters are buried along the Kremlin wall near Lenin's tomb.

The **State History Museum** (www.shm.ru; Krasnaya pl 1; adult/student R250/80, audioguide R200-350; 10am-7pm Wed & Fri-Mon, 11am-9pm Thu; MOkhotny Ryad) has an enormous collection covering the whole Russian Empire from the Stone Age onwards. The building, dating from the late 19th century, is itself an attraction – each room is in the style of a different period or region.

WORTH A TRIP

NOVODEVICHY CEMETERY & CONVENT

Moscow's most famous **cemetery** (9am-5pm; MSportivnaya) is in the Khamonivki district, about 3km southwest of the centre. Luminaries buried here include Chekhov, Gogol, Bulgakov, Stanislavsky, Krushchev, Eisenstein, Raisa Gorbachev and Yeltsin. Walk around and see who you can find.

Adjacent to the cemetery is the **Novodevichy Convent** (499-246 8526; adult/student R250/100, photos R100; grounds 8am-8pm, museums 9am-5pm Wed-Mon; MSportivnaya), a glorious cluster of sparkling domes behind turreted walls on the Moscow River. It was founded in 1524 to celebrate the taking of Smolensk from Lithuania.

State Tretyakov Gallery MUSEUM
(www.tretyakovgallery.ru; Lavrushinsky per 10; adult/student R360/220, 10am-7.30pm Tue-Sun; MTretyakovskaya) Nothing short of spectacular, the State Tretyakov Gallery holds the world's best collection of Russian icons and an outstanding collection of other prerevolutionary Russian art. Andrei Rublyov's *Holy Trinity* (1420s) from Sergiev Posad, widely regarded as Russia's greatest icon, is on the ground floor in room 60. The collection is based on that of the 19th-century industrialist brothers Pavel and Sergei Tretyakov (Pavel was a patron of the Peredvizhniki).

New Tretyakov MUSEUM
(Krymsky val; adult/student R360/220, photos R200; 10am-7.30pm Tue-Sun; MPark Kultury) This gargantuan edifice is the premier venue for 20th-century Russian art and shouldn't be missed. Besides the plethora of socialist realism, the exhibits showcase avant garde artists such as Malevich, Kandinsky, Chagall, Goncharova and Lyubov Popova.

Beside the gallery is the open-air sculpture park **Art Muzeon** (ul Krymsky val 10; MPark Kultury). What started as a collection of Soviet statues put out to pasture when they were ripped from their pedestals post-1991 has now been joined by fascinating and diverse contemporary work.

Zurab Tsereteli's monumental but controversial **Peter the Great statue** (Bersenevskaya nab; MPolyanka) (dubbed 'Peter the Ugly' by some) overlooks the park.

Central Moscow

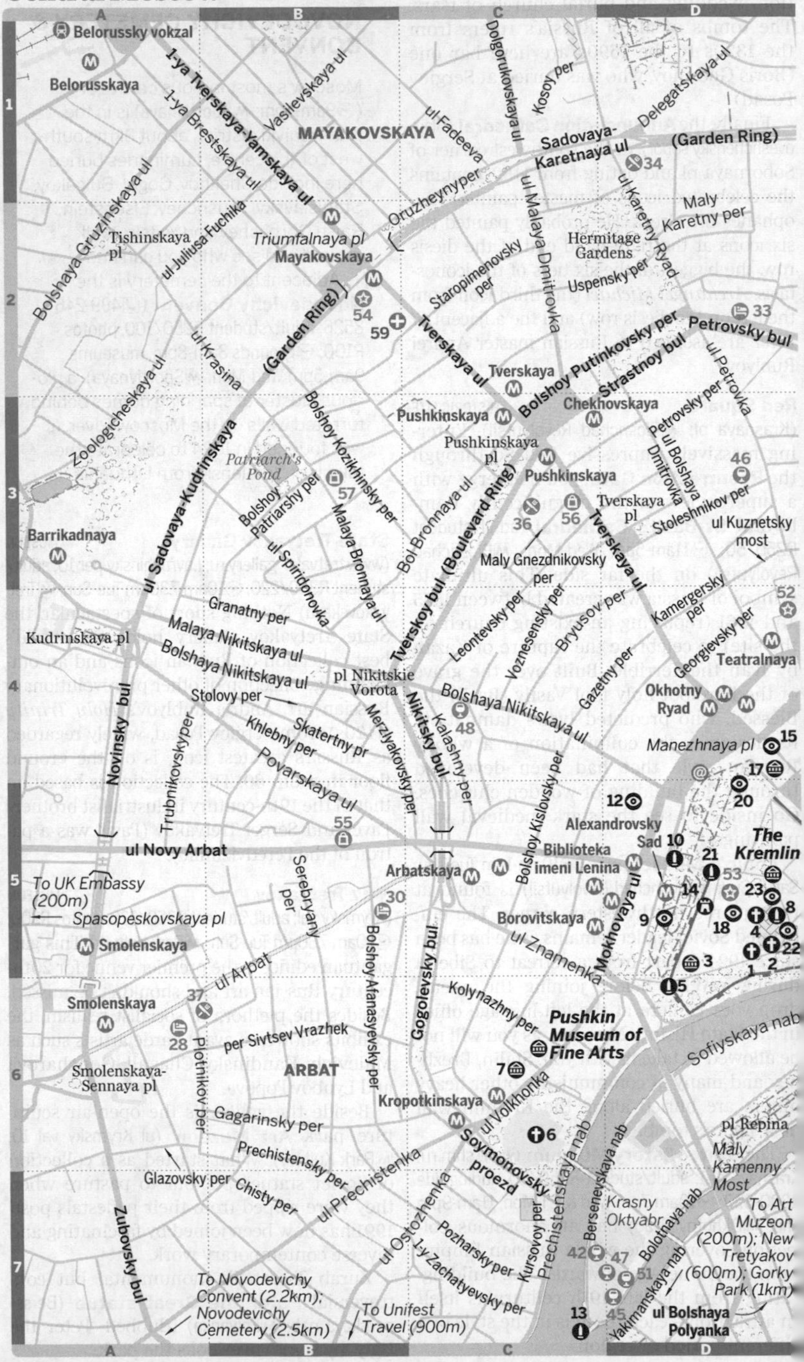

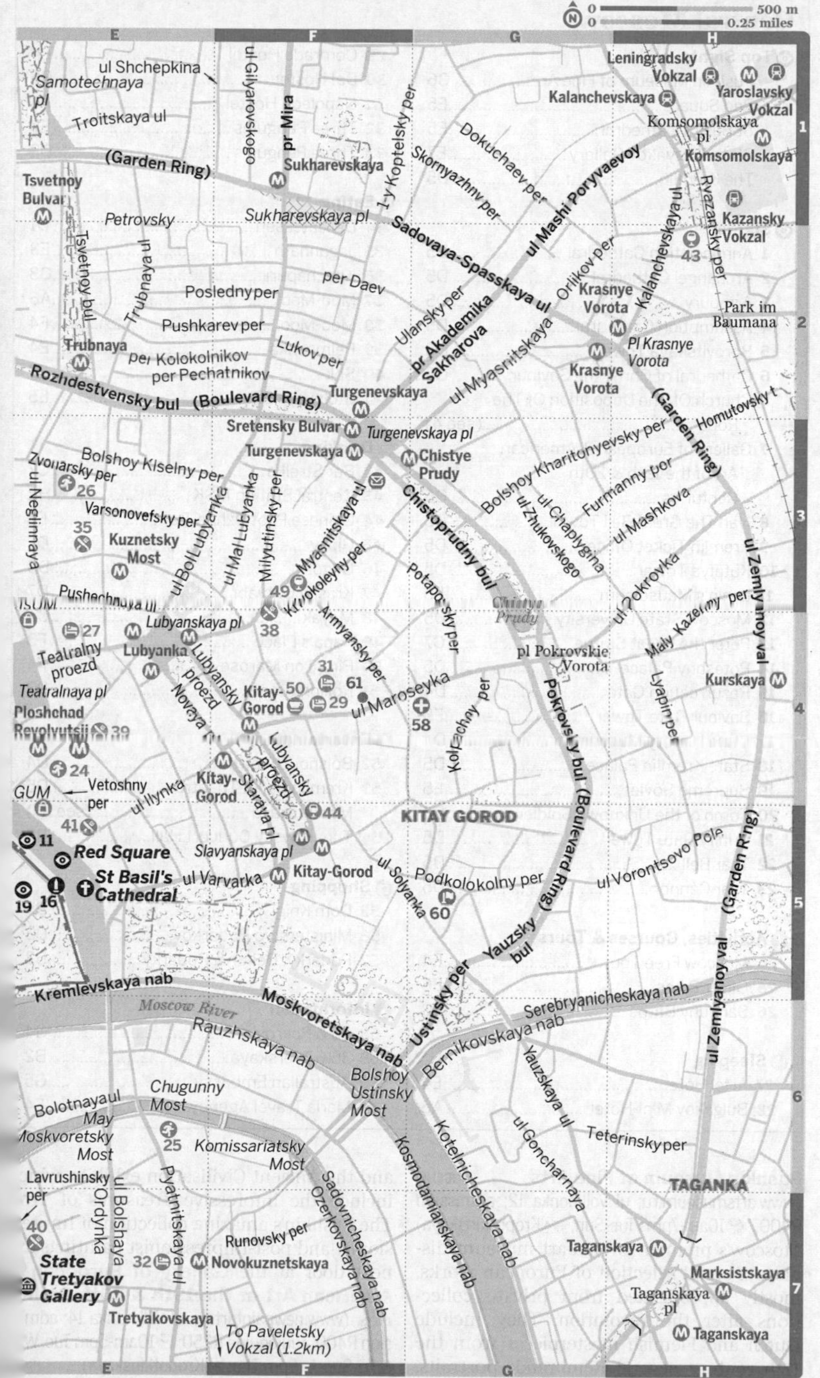

RUSSIA MOSCOW
500 m
0.25 miles
ul Shchepkina
Samotechnaya pl
Troitskaya ul
ul Gilyarovskogo
pr Mira
(Garden Ring)
Sukharevskaya
Tsvetnoy Bulvar
Petrovsky
Sukharevskaya pl
Tsvetnoy bul
Trubnaya ul
Posledny per
Pushkarev per
Trubnaya
per Kolokolnikov
per Pechatnikov
Rozhdestvensky bul
(Boulevard Ring)
Sretensky Bulvar
Turgenevskaya
Turgenevskaya pl
Chistye Prudy
Zvonarsky per
Bolshoy Kiselny per
ul Neglinnaya
Varsonovefsky per
Kuznetsky Most
ul Bol Lubyanka
ul Mal Lubyanka
Milyutinsky per
Myasnitskaya ul
Krivokoleyny per
Pushechnaya ul
TSUM
Lubyanskaya pl
Lubyanka
Teatralny proezd
Teatralnaya pl
Ploshchad Revolyutsii
Lubyansky proezd
Novaya pl
Kitay-Gorod
Armyansky per
ul Maroseyka
Vetoshny per
GUM
ul Ilyinka
Staraya pl
Red Square
Slavyanskaya pl
St Basil's Cathedral
ul Varvarka
ul Solyanka
KITAY GOROD
Kremlevskaya nab
Moscow River
Moskvoretskaya nab
Rauzhskaya nab
Bolshoy Ustinsky Most
Chugunny Most
Bolotnayaul
May Moskvoretsky Most
Komissariatsky Most
Lavrushinsky per
ul Bolshaya Ordynka
Pyatnitskaya ul
Sadovnicheskaya nab
Ozerkovskaya nab
Runovsky per
Novokuznetskaya
State Tretyakov Gallery
Tretyakovskaya
To Paveletsky Vokzal (1.2km)
1-y Koptelsky per
Dokuchaev per
Skornyazhny per
Sadovaya-Spasskaya ul
ul Mashi Poryvaevoy
per Daev
Ulansky per
pr Akademika Sakharova
ul Myasnitskaya
Orlikov per
Krasnye Vorota
Pl Krasnye Vorota
Chistoprudny bul
Potapovsky per
Chistye Prudy
Bolshoy Kharitonyevsky per
ul Chaplygina
ul Zhukovskogo
Furmanny per
ul Mashkova
ul Pokrovka
pl Pokrovskie Vorota
Kolpachny per
Pokrovsky bul
(Boulevard Ring)
Maly Kazenny per
Lyalin per
Podkolokolny per
Yauzsky bul
Ustinsky per
ul Vorontsovo Pole
Serebryanicheskaya nab
Bernikovskaya nab
Yauzskaya ul
ul Goncharnaya
Kotelnicheskaya nab
Kosmodamianskaya nab
Teterinsky per
TAGANKA
Taganskaya
Marksistskaya
Taganskaya pl
Leningradsky Vokzal
Kalanchevskaya
Yaroslavsky Vokzal
Komsomolskaya pl
Komsomolskaya
Kalanchevskaya ul
Ryazansky per
Kazansky Vokzal
Park im Baumana
(Garden Ring)
Homutovsky t
ul Zemlyanoy val
Kurskaya
ul Zemlyanoy val
(Garden Ring)
E
F
G
H
1
2
3
4
5
6
7
11
16
19
24
25
26
27
29
31
32
35
38
39
40
41
43
44
49
50
58
60
61

Central Moscow

Top Sights
Pushkin Museum of Fine Arts C6
Red Square E5
St Basil's Cathedral E5
State Tretyakov Gallery E7
The Kremlin D5

Sights
1 Annunciation Cathedral D5
2 Archangel Cathedral D5
3 Armoury D5
4 Assumption Cathedral D5
5 Borovitskaya Tower D6
6 Cathedral of Christ the Saviour C6
Church Of The Deposition Of The Robe .... (see 4)
7 Gallery of European & American Art of the 19th & 20th Centuries C6
8 Ivan The Great Bell Tower D5
9 Kremlin Ticket Office D5
10 Kutafya Tower D5
11 Lenin's Mausoleum E5
12 Moscow State University D5
13 Peter the Great Statue C7
14 Poteshny Palace D5
15 Resurrection Gate D4
16 Saviour Gate Tower E5
17 State History Museum D4
18 State Kremlin Palace D5
19 Supreme Soviet E5
20 Tomb of the Unknown Soldier D5
21 Trinity Gate Tower D5
22 Tsar Bell D5
23 Tsar Cannon D5

Activities, Courses & Tours
24 Moscow Free Tour E4
25 Oliver Bikes E6
26 Sanduny Baths E3

Sleeping
27 Artel Hotel E4
28 Bulgakov Mini-Hotel A6
29 Comrade Hostel F4
30 Da! Hostel B5
31 Napoleon Hostel F4
32 Three Penguins E7
33 Three Penguins D2

Eating
34 Delicatessen D1
35 Jagannath E3
36 Khachapuri C3
37 Moo-Moo A6
38 Moo-Moo F4
39 Pelmeshka E4
40 Sok E7
41 Stolovaya 57 .... E5

Drinking
42 Bar Strelka C7
43 Central Station MSK H2
44 Chinese Pilot Dzhao-Da F5
45 Gipsy D7
46 Gogol D3
47 Krasny Oktyabr D7
48 Mayak C4
49 Papa's Place F3
50 Pirogi on Maroseyka F4
51 Rolling Stone D7

Entertainment
52 Bolshoi Theatre D4
53 Kremlin Ballet Theatre D5
Masterskaya .... (see 27)
54 Tchaikovsky Concert Hall B2

Shopping
55 Dom Knigi B5
56 Ministerstvo Podarkov C3
57 Podarky, Dekor & Podarky B3

Information
58 36.6 Pokrovka G4
59 36.6 Tverskaya B2
60 Australian Embassy G5
61 Maria Travel Agency F4

Pushkin Museum of Fine Arts MUSEUM
(www.artsmuseum.ru; ul Volkhonka 12; admission R400; ⌚10am-7pm Tue-Sun; Ⓜ Kropotkinskaya) Moscow's premier foreign-art museum displays a broad selection of European works, mostly appropriated from private collections after the revolution. They include Dutch and Flemish masterpieces from the 17th century, several Rembrandt portraits, and the Ancient Civilisation exhibits, whic include the impressive Treasures of Tro The Pushkin's amazing collection of Impre sionist and post-Impressionist paintings a next door at the **Gallery of European American Art of the 19th & 20th Centu ries** (www.newpaintart.ru; ul Volkhonka 14; adm sion R400, audioguide R250; ⌚10am-5pm Tue, W & Fri-Sun, to 9pm Thu; Ⓜ Kropotkinskaya).

FREE **Gorky Park** PARK

(; Park Kultury) A massive facelift in 2012 turned Gorky Park from a hokey Soviet funfair into a refined urban oasis, complete with yoga and meditation zones, outdoor cinemas, beach volleyball and basketball courts, skate parks and a massive outdoor ice rink (winter only).

Its centrepiece is the **Garage Centre for Contemporary Culture** (www.garageccc.com; Gorky Park; 9am-10pm Sun-Thu, to 11pm Fri & Sat; Mendeleyevska, Novoslobodskaya), Moscow's leading contemporary art space. Pet project of Dasha Zhukova (supermodel and girlfriend of billionaire Roman Abramovich) through her Iris Foundation, which also supports the similar Novaya Gollandiya (p923) project in St Petersburg, the newly relocated centre is being housed in a temporary pavilion made out of paper (life expectancy: four years) by noted Japanese architect Shegeru Ban. Two Soviet structures – a 4500-sq-m restaurant and a 9000-sq-m exhibition pavilion – are being converted into cavernous galleries that will eventually replace the Ban structure.

Activities

Bikes are an effective and cheap way to explore the city's spread-out sights and parks – just steer clear of the dangerous main roads. **Oliver Bikes** (8-926-431 4051; www.bikerentalmoscow.com; Pyatnitskaya ul 2; per day from R500; 10am-10pm; Novokuznetskaya) rents two-wheelers and also leads five-hour bike tours in the warm months (R800 including bike). Bike hire is also available in Gorky Park.

Tours

Moscow Free Tour TOURS

(495-222 3466; http://moscowfreetour.com; Nikolskaya ul 4/5) Runs a daily free city walk as well as many other scheduled and tailored tours. Can also arrange 'hop-on, hop-off' bus tours.

Moscow Mania WALKING

(8-903-713 0583; www.mosmania.com; tours per group R3500) Themed itineraries with young knowledgeable guides.

Sleeping

Moscow hotels are outrageously expensive, so stay in hostels, which are plentiful. Apartment rental is another way to save money – see p935 for a list of apartment rental agencies. See p935 for more on hostels and registration at hostels.

TOP CHOICE **Da! Hostel** HOSTEL €

(495-691 5619; info@da-hostel.ru; ul Arbat 11; dm R500-1000; ; Arbatskaya) Yes, Da is worthy of your rubles, with a wide-open, spacious common/kitchen area, free coffee and porridge, and a nice mix of clean dorm rooms with sturdy wood bunk beds. No private rooms.

TOP CHOICE **Bulgakov Mini-Hotel** HOTEL €€

(495-229 8018; www.bulgakovhotel.com; ul Arbat 49; d R3300; ; Smolenskaya) Worth a splurge for the classy private rooms, with high ceilings and *Master and Margarita*–inspired art. There's also a 10-bed dorm here (R500).

Three Penguins HOSTEL €

(www.3penguins.ru) Petrovsky (8-910-446 1778; 20-2 Petrovsky bul; dm R650-1100, s/d/tr without bathroom R1500/2200/2700; ; Trubnaya); Pyatnitskaya (8-985-238 6016; 17/1 ul Pyatnitskaya, dm R700, r without bathroom R2400; ; Novokuznetskaya) Both branches of this friendly hostel are quiet, no-nonsense retreats. The two private rooms on Petrovsky are among Moscow's cheapest, while the slightly pricier Pyatnitskaya edition is just one metro stop from the trains to Domodedovo airport at Paveletsky vokzal (train station).

Comrade Hostel HOSTEL €

(499-709 8760; www.comradehostel.com; ul Maroseyka 11; dm/s/d R650/1800/2200; ; Kitay-Gorod) Wood bunk beds, a newly revamped common area/kitchen and lovely private rooms distinguish this welcoming courtyard hostel.

TOP CHOICE **Artel Hotel** HOTEL €€

(495-626 9008; www.artelhotel.ru; 3 Teatralny pr 3, Bldg 3; s R2500-5200, d R3000-5700;) Wacky art abounds in this creative space where each room has a unique design – the cheapest are tiny and windowless. Not for the noise averse: downstairs are the equally funky restaurant/bar/club/theatre space **Masterskaya** (www.mstrsk.ru; noon-6am;) and a nightclub.

Napoleon Hostel HOSTEL €

(495-628 6695; www.napoleonhostel.com; Maly Zlatoustinsky per 2, 4th fl; dm R600-800; ; Kitay-Gorod) If you want to meet and greet other travellers, look no further. A full range of traveller services are on offer – tours, parties, transport, you name it.

Eating

Budget diners will find solace in the popular *stolovye* (canteens) that abound around town, including the popular chain **Moo-Moo** (meals R200-300;), with branches in **Basmanny** (Myasnitskaya ul 14; 9am-11pm; ; Lubyanka) and **Arbat** (ul Arbat 45/24; 10am-11pm; ; Smolenskaya), famous for its borsch.

TOP CHOICE Delicatessen INTERNATIONAL €€
(www.newdeli.ru; Savodvaya-Karetnaya ul 20; business lunch R270, mains R350-950; noon-midnight Tue-Sat; ; Tsvetnoy Bulvar) Juicy burgers, fish ceviche, cherry bourbon and friendly service – all great reasons for dropping by Delicatessen. Food is 20% off from noon to 5pm.

TOP CHOICE Jagannath VEGETARIAN €
(jagannath.ru; Kuznetsky most 11; meals R200-350; 10am-midnight; ; Kuznetsky Most) Scrumptious vego/vegan *stolovaya*, new-age trinket store and health-food shop under one roof.

Khachapuri GEORGIAN €
(8-985-764 3118; Bolshoy Gnezdnikovsky per 10; dishes R250-550; ; Pushkinskaya) Here you'll find the capital's best Georgian food in a classy space, plus superb piano music most evenings.

Stolovaya 57 CAFETERIA €
(3rd fl, GUM, Red Sq; meals R300-400; 10am-10pm; Okhotny Ryad) Soviet-style canteen a rare oasis of affordability in the fancy-pants GUM department store.

Sok VEGETARIAN €
(Lavrushinsky per 15; mains R200-400; 11am-11pm; ; Tretyakovskaya) Cheerful cafe done up in bright yellow and orange and specialising in vego fare with Italian and Middle Eastern flavours.

Pelmeshka CAFETERIA €
(Bogoyavlensky per 1; meals R200-350; 10am-midnight; ; Ploshchad Revolyutsii) Cosy *stolovaya* just a stumble away from Red Sq.

Drinking

The line between cafe, bar and nightclub in Moscow is hazy, with many places serving all three functions. As such, we list them all in one place.

The best clubs in Moscow dispense with cover charges and strict dress codes. But they still have strict *feis kontrol* (face control). Beat *feis kontrol* by arriving early before the bouncers are posted.

For outdoor summer drinks try Gorky Park or pedestrianised, cafe-lined Kamergersky per.

TOP CHOICE Krasny Oktyabr CLUB
(Red October; Zamoskvorechie; Kropotkinskaya) In the summer, there is one place to head for a big night out: this converted chocolate factory on an island in the Moskva River. 'Red October' hosts several arty cafes that morph into blistering open-air rooftop nightclubs at weekends. The best are **Gipsy** (Bolotnaya nab 3; 6pm-1am Sun-Thu, 2pm-6am Fri & Sat) and, next door, **Rolling Stone** (Bolotnaya nab 3; 10pm-7am Thu-Sat; Kropotkinskaya). Another option is **Bar Strelka** (www.artstrelka.ru; bldg 5a, Bersenevskaya nab 14/5; 9am-midnight Sun-Thu, noon-late Fri & Sat; ; Kropotkinskaya), also a great cafe with dishes from R300 to R1000, with fabulous views across the Moskva River from its rooftop.

Gogol CLUB
(www.gogolclubs.ru; Stoleshnikov per 11; cover free; noon-5am; Teatralnaya) Fun, informal and affordable, Gogol is great for food, drinks and music (live most nights, techno on weekends).

Mayak BAR
(www.clubmayak.ru; Bolshaya Nikitskaya ul 19; business lunch R270, mains R300-350; noon-6am; ; Okhotny Ryad) Named for the Mayakovsky Theatre downstairs, this is a vintage 1930s-style bar awash in dark wood. Food 20% off until 4pm.

Central Station MSK CLU
(www.centralclub.ru; Yuzhny proezd 4; restauran from 7pm, club from 9pm; Komsomolskaya) Moscow's biggest and best gay dance club. Chec www.gay.ru for more gay-friendly listings.

Papa's Place BAR, CLU
(http://papas.ru; Myasnitskaya ul 22; weekend cover R200-300; ; Chistye Prudy) The them varies from night to night (beach party, la dies' night) but the goal is the same: to ge you inebriated quickly and cheaply.

Chinese Pilot Dzhao-Da B
(www.jao-da.ru; Lubyansky proezd 25; concer R300-500; ; Kitay-Gorod) This divey, relaxe

basement place hosts live music nightly starting at 11pm or midnight. Cheap food and beer too (backpackers rejoice).

Pirogi on Maroseyka CAFE, BAR
(www.ogipirogi.ru; ul Maroseyka 9/2; Ⓜ Kitay-Gorod) The young, broke and beautiful flock to this dive to enjoy affordable beer, coffee and food (mains R175 to R250), plus movies on Tuesdays and DJs most nights.

☆ Entertainment

To find out what's on, see the weekly magazine *element* or the entertainment section in Thursday's *Moscow Times*. Most theatres, including the Bolshoi, are closed between late June and early September.

TOP CHOICE **Bolshoi Theatre** BALLET, OPERA
(www.bolshoi.ru; Teatralnaya pl 1; tickets R200-4000; Ⓜ Teatralnaya) An evening at the Bolshoi is one of Moscow's most romantic options. Ballet and opera performances take place both on the main stage and the smaller New Stage (Novaya Stsena). If you can't catch a performance or it's closed, consider a tour of the theatre.

Kremlin Ballet Theatre BALLET
(☎495-928 5232; www.kremlin-gkd.ru; ul Vozdvizhenka 1; Ⓜ Alexandrovsky Sad) The Bolshoi does not have a monopoly on ballet in Moscow. Leading dancers also appear with the Kremlin Ballet, which performs in the State Kremlin Palace (inside the Kremlin).

Tchaikovsky Concert Hall CLASSICAL MUSIC
(www.meloman.ru; Triumfalnaya pl 4/31; tickets R300-2000; ⊙closed Jul-Aug; Ⓜ Mayakovskaya) Home to the State Symphony Orchestra, which specialises in the music of its namesake composer and other Russian classics.

Shopping

Ul Arbat has always been a tourist attraction and is littered with souvenir shops and stalls. For a more Soviet experience, head northwest out of town to **Izmaylovo Market** (www.kremlin-izmailovo.com; Izmaylovskoye shosse 73; ⊙10am-8pm; Ⓜ Partizanskaya), a sprawling area packed with art, handmade crafts, antiques, Soviet paraphernalia and just about anything you might want for a souvenir.

Ministerstvo Podarkov GIFTS
(Ministry of Gifts; Maly Gnezdnikovsky per 12/27; Ⓜ Pushkinskaya) For clever souvenirs, stop by this artists' cooperative selling uniquely Russian gifts. There is another outlet – **Podarky, Dekor & Podarky** (Malaya Bronnaya ul 28/2; ⊙11am-9pm Mon-Fri, noon-9pm Sat & Sun; Ⓜ Mayakovskaya) – near Patriarch's Ponds.

Dom Knigi BOOKS
(ul Novy Arbat 8; ⊙9am-11pm Mon-Fri, 10am-11pm Sat & Sun; Ⓜ Arbatskaya) A huge bookshop with great maps and a full complement of guidebooks in English.

WANT MORE?

For in-depth information, reviews and recommendations at your fingertips, head to the Apple App Store to purchase Lonely Planet's *Moscow City Guide* iPhone app.

Alternatively, head to www.lonelyplanet.com/russia/moscow for planning advice, author recommendations, traveller reviews and insider tips.

ⓘ Information

Wireless access is ubiquitous and almost always free.

36.6 (www.366.ru; ⊙24hr) Tverskaya (Tverskaya ul 25/9); Pokrovka (ul Pokrovka 1/13; Ⓜ Kitay-Gorod) A chain of pharmacies with outlets all over the city.

American Medical Centre (☎495-933 7700; www.amcenter.ru; Grokholsky per 1; Ⓜ Pr Mira) Offers 24-hour emergency service, consultations and a full range of medical specialists.

Main Post Office (Myasnitskaya ul 26; ⊙8am-8pm; Ⓜ Chistye Prudy)

Maria Travel Agency (☎495-777 8226; www.maria-travel.com; ul Maroseyka 13; Ⓜ Kitay-Gorod) Offers visa support, apartment rental and some local tours, including to the Golden Ring.

Moscow Times (www.themoscowtimes.com) Best of the locally published English-language newspapers, widely distributed free of charge.

Time Online (per hr R70-100; ⊙24hr) Okhotny Ryad (Manezhnaya pl; Ⓜ Okhotny Ryad); Komsomolskaya (Komsomolskaya pl 3; Ⓜ Komsomolskaya)

Unifest Travel (☎495-234 6555; http://unifest.ru; Komsomolsky pr 13; Ⓜ Park Kultury) About 500m south of the metro station, this is an on-the-ball travel company offering rail and air tickets, visa support and more.

MOSCOW TO ST PETERSBURG

Dozens of trains travel daily between Russia's two main cities.

There are about six daily high-speed 'Sapsan' trains, which have airplane-style seating, take 3½ to four hours, and cost about R3000/5500 for a 2nd-/1st-class seat.

Otherwise there is a dizzying array of slower trains, including several overnight options. These take seven hours to 11 hours and cost about R1000 for the lowest *platskart* (3rd-class) class, or about twice that for more comfortable four-bed *kupe* (2nd-class) berths.

Air connections are also frequent; a plane ticket costs about the same as a 2nd-class Sapsan ticket.

Getting Around

To/From the Airports

All airports are accessible by **Aeroexpress** (www.aeroexpress.ru) trains (R320, 40 minutes), which leave from different stations depending on the airport they serve. They run every 30 minutes from about 5am to 12.30am for Domodedovo and Sheremyetovo (less frequent for Vnukovo).

Penny-pinchers can take more sporadic local trains from Domodedovo (R100, 1¼ hours) to Paveletsky vokzal. From Sheremetyevo, bus 851 (R25, frequent) runs to Rechnoy Vokzal metro.

Taxis from the official airport taxi stands cost R1500 to R2500.

Public Transport

The **Moscow metro** (www.mosmetro.ru) is the easiest, quickest and cheapest way of getting around Moscow. Stations are marked outside by 'M' signs. Magnetic tickets (R27) are sold at ticket booths.

Taxi

Unofficial taxis (p938) are still common in Moscow. Expect to pay R150 to R400 for a ride around the city centre, depending on your haggling skills. To book a taxi:

Detskoe Taxi (☎495-765 1180; www.detskoetaxi.ru; per 10km R500) Has smoke-free cars and car seats for your children.

Taxi Blues (☎495-105 5115; www.taxi-blues.ru)

ST PETERSBURG

☎812 / POP 4.8 MILLION

Elegant, enchanting and hedonistic, Russia's one-time capital is a fascinating hybrid of traditional Russia and contemporary Europe, where one moment you can be sniffing incense inside a mosaic-covered Orthodox church, the next grooving on the dance floor of an underground club or posing at a contemporary art event in a renovated bakery. Above all, the city is a visual delight. The Neva River and surrounding canals reflect unbroken facades of handsome 18th- and 19th-century buildings, housing a spellbinding collection of cultural storehouses, which culminated in the incomparable Hermitage.

St Petersburg (Санкт Петербург) is spread out across many different islands, some real and some created through the construction of canals. The central street is Nevsky pr, which extends for some 4km from the Alexander Nevsky Monastery to the Hermitage.

Sights

State Hermitage Museum MUSEUM

(www.hermitagemuseum.org; Dvortsovaya pl 2; adult/student R400/free, 1st Thu of month free, photos R200; ⏲10.30am-6pm Tue & Thu-Sun, to 9pm Wed, to 9pm Sat Jun-Sep; Ⓜ Admiralteyskaya) Mainly set in the magnificent Winter Palace, the State Hermitage is stacked with treasures, ranging from Egyptian mummies and Scythian gold to early-20th-century European art by Matisse and Picasso.

Queues for tickets, particularly from May to July and on free first Thursdays, can be horrendous. You'll jump the queue by booking your ticket online through the Hermitage's website – but the R200 photo fee is mandatory if you go this route.

Dvortsovaya Ploshchad HISTORIC SITE

(Palace Sq) The Hermitage's main entrance is from this impressive and historic square. Stand back to admire the palace and the central 47.5m-high **Alexander Column**. Enclosing the square's south side is the **General Staff Building** (www.hermitagemuseum.org; Dvortsovaya pl 6-8; Ⓜ Nevsky Prospekt) – its east wing is the centrepiece of the Hermitage's 250th-anniversery '20/21' project. Galleries of modern and contemporary art have been added to an impressive existing collection of post-Impressionist and Empire-style decorative art.

Russian Museum MUSEUM
(www.rusmuseum.ru; Inzhenernaya ul 4; adult/student R300/150; ⌚10am-6pm Wed & Fri-Sun, to 5pm Mon, 1-9pm Thu; Ⓜ Gostiny Dvor) Facing onto the elegant pl Iskusstv (Arts Sq) is the handsome Mikhailovsky Palace, now housing one of the country's finest collections of Russian art. After the Hermitage you may feel you have had your fill of art, but try to make some time for this gem of a museum. There's also a lovely garden behind the palace.

Church of the Saviour on Spilled Blood CHURCH
(Konyushennaya pl; adult/student R250/150, audioguide R100; ⌚10am-6pm Thu-Tue; Ⓜ Nevsky Prospekt) This multidomed dazzler, partly modelled on St Basil's in Moscow, was built between 1883 and 1907 on the spot where Alexander II was assassinated in 1881 (hence its gruesome name). The interior's 7000 sq metres of mosaics fully justify the entrance fee.

St Isaac's Cathedral CHURCH
(Isaakievsky Sobor; www.cathedral.ru; Isaakievskaya pl; cathedral regular/evening R250/350, colonnade regular/evening R150/300; ⌚11am-6pm Thu-Tue, 6.15-10.30pm May-Sep; Ⓜ Admiralteyskaya) The golden dome of this cathedral dominates the city skyline. Its lavish interior is open as a museum, but many visitors just buy the separate ticket to climb the 262 steps up to the colonnade to take in panoramic views.

Peter & Paul Fortress FORTRESS
(www.spbmuseum.ru; grounds free, exhibitions adult/student R370/190, per exhibit R130/70; ⌚grounds 6am-10pm Apr-Sep, to 9pm Oct-Mar, exhibitions 11am-7pm Thu-Tue, to 6pm Oct-Mar; Ⓜ Gorkovskaya) Founded in 1703 on Zaychy Island as the original military base for the new city, this fortress was mainly used as a political prison up to 1917. It's home to the **SS Peter & Paul Cathedral** (adult/student R200/90), with its landmark needle-thin spire and magnificent baroque interior. All Russia's tsars since Peter the Great have been buried here.

Individual tickets are needed for each of the fortress' attractions, so the best deal is the combined entry ticket, allowing access to most of the exhibitions on the island.

Kunstkamera MUSEUM
(Museum of Anthropology & Ethnography; www.kunstkamera.ru; Tamozhenny per; adult/child R250/50; ⌚11am-7pm Tue-Sun; Ⓜ Admiralteyskaya) Crowds still flock to see Peter the Great's ghoulish collection of monstrosities, notably preserved freaks, two-headed mutant foetuses and odd body parts. The anthropological and ethnographic displays from around the world are pretty interesting, too.

Strelka LANDMARK
Some of the best views of St Petersburg can be had from Vasilevsky Island's eastern 'nose', known as the Strelka. The two **Rostral Columns** on the point, studded with ships' prows, were oil-fired navigation beacons in the 1800s.

Novaya Gollandiya ISLAND
(New Holland; www.newhollandsp.ru; nab Admiralteyskogo kanala 2; ⌚11am-10pm Mon-Fri, to 11pm Fri & Sat, closed Oct-Apr; Ⓜ Admiralteyskaya)

RUSSIA'S MOST FAMOUS STREET

Walking **Nevsky Prospekt** is an essential St Petersburg experience. Highlights along it include the **Kazan Cathedral** (Kazansky Sobor; Kazanskaya pl 2; ⌚8.30am-7.30pm; Ⓜ Nevsky Prospekt), with its curved arms reaching out towards the avenue (no shorts allowed inside).

Opposite is the **Singer Building** (Nevsky pr 28; Ⓜ Nevsky Prospekt), a Style Moderne (art deco) beauty restored to all its splendour from when it was the headquarters of the sewing-machine company; inside is a good bookshop and **Café Singer** (⌚9am-11pm), with a great view over the street.

Further along you'll pass the covered arcades of Rastrelli's historic **Bolshoy Gostiny Dvor** (Nevsky pr 35; ⌚10am-10pm; Ⓜ Gostiny Dvor) department store (1757–85). An enormous **statue of Catherine the Great** (cnr Postovaya ul, Krasnaya ul) stands at the centre of **Ploshchad Ostrovskogo** (Ⓜ Gostiny Dvor), commonly referred to as the Catherine Gardens; at the southern end of the gardens is **Aleksandrinksy Theatre** (☎710 4103; www.alexandrinsky.ru; pl Ostrovskogo 2; Ⓜ Gostiny Dvor), where Chekhov's *The Seagull* premiered (to tepid reviews) in 1896.

Central St Petersburg

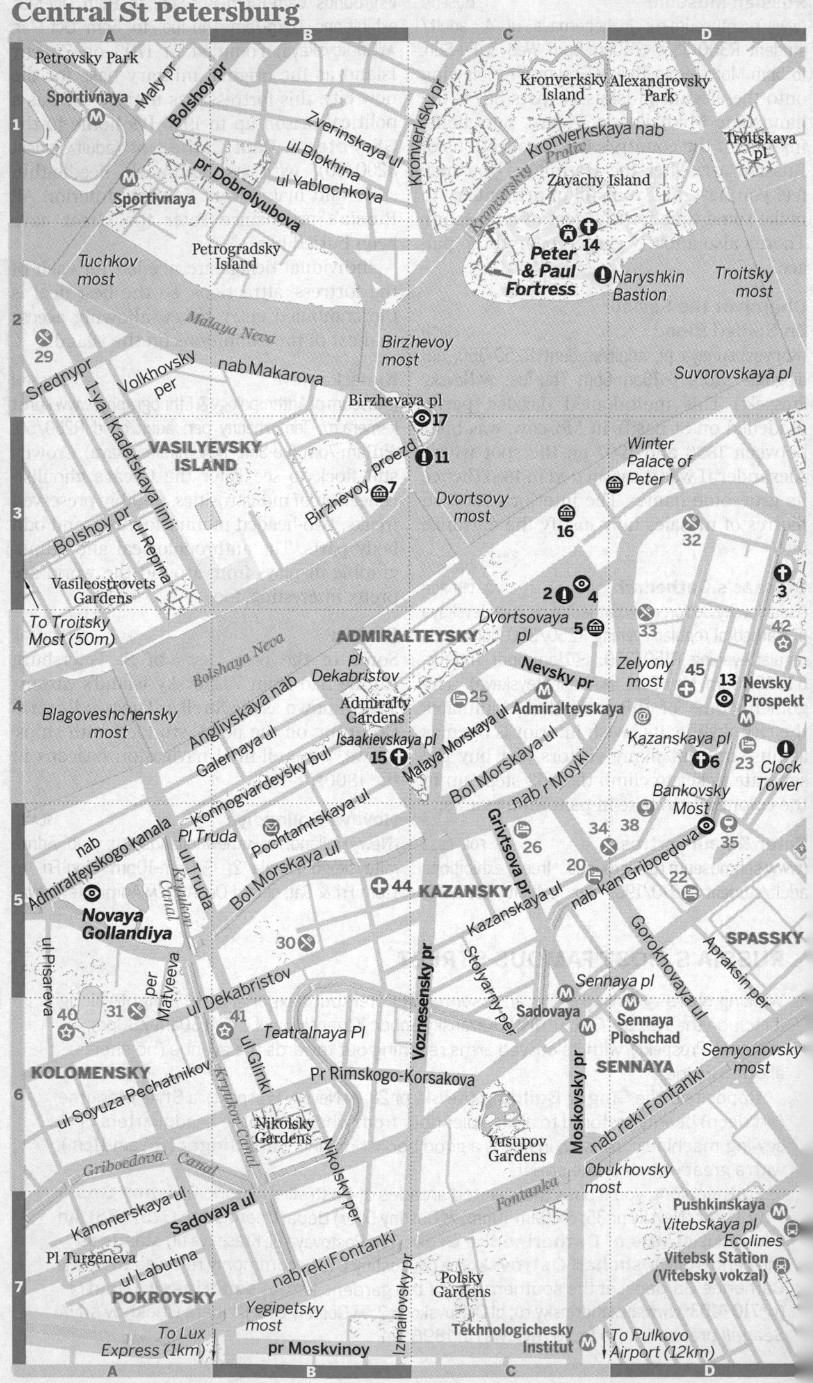

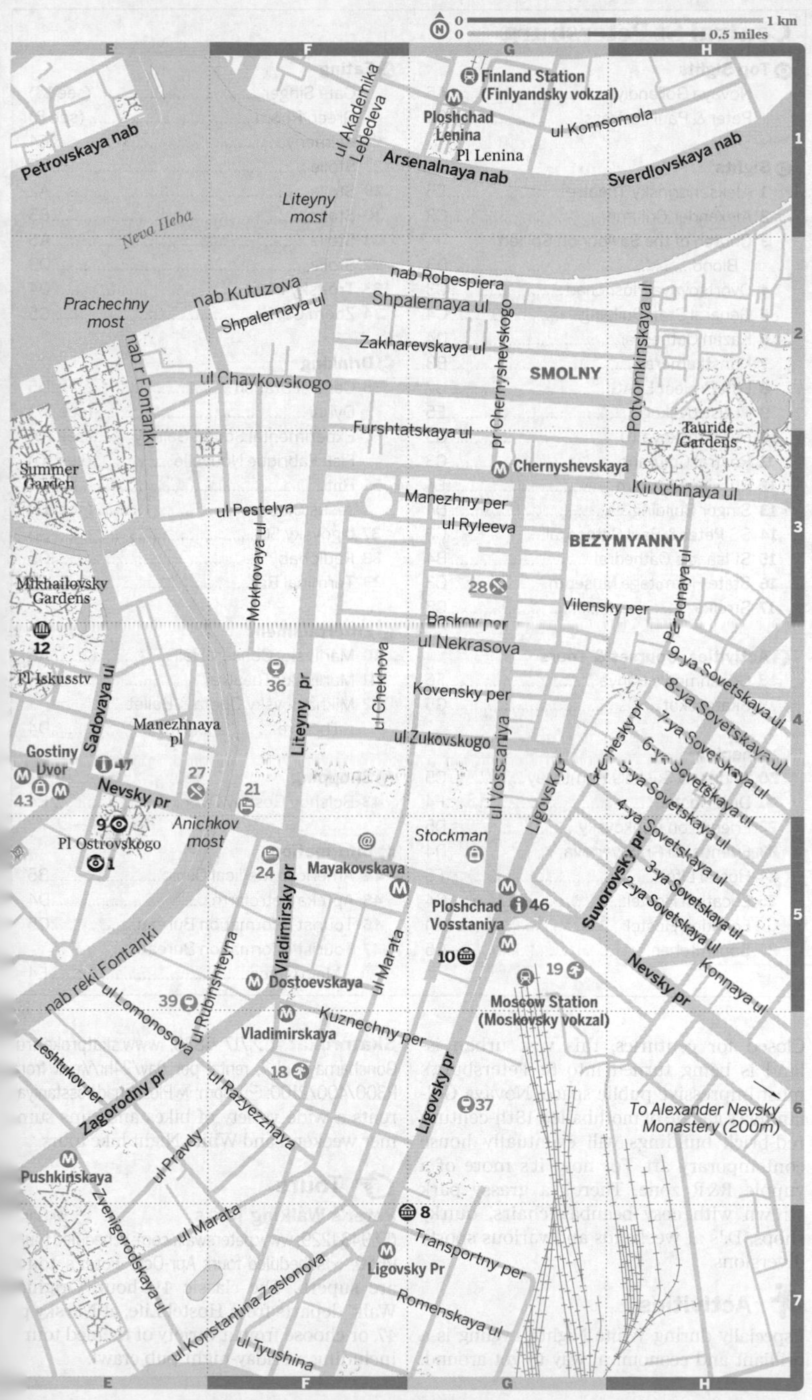

0 1 km
0 0.5 miles
Finland Station
(Finlyandsky vokzal)
Ploshchad
Lenina
Pl Lenina
ul Komsomola
Petrovskaya nab
ul Akademika Lebedeva
Arsenalnaya nab
Sverdlovskaya nab
Liteyny
most
Neva Нева
nab Robespiera
nab Kutuzova
Prachechny
most
Shpalernaya ul
Zakharevskaya ul
pr Chernyshevskogo
Potyomkinskaya ul
nab r Fontanki
ul Chaykovskogo
SMOLNY
Furshtatskaya ul
Tauride
Gardens
Chernyshevskaya
Summer
Garden
Kirochnaya ul
Manezhny per
ul Pestelya
ul Ryleeva
Mokhovaya ul
BEZYMYANNY
Mikhailovsky
Gardens
28
Vilensky per
Baskov per
ul Nekrasova
12
9-ya Sovetskaya ul
8-ya Sovetskaya ul
Pl Iskusstv
36
Kovensky per
ul Cheknova
Sadovaya ul
Liteyny pr
Manezhnaya
pl
ul Zukovskogo
ul Vosstaniya
7-ya Sovetskaya ul
6-ya Sovetskaya ul
Gostiny
Dvor
47
27
Ligovsky pr
Grechesky pr
5-ya Sovetskaya ul
43
Nevsky pr
21
4-ya Sovetskaya ul
9
Anichkov
most
Pl Ostrovskogo
Stockman
1
24
Mayakovskaya
Suvorovsky pr
3-ya Sovetskaya ul
2-ya Sovetskaya ul
Ploshchad
Vosstaniya
46
10
19
Nevsky pr
Konnaya ul
nab reki Fontanki
ul Rubinshteyna
Vladimirsky pr
ul Marata
Dostoevskaya
39
ul Lomonosova
Moscow Station
(Moskovsky vokzal)
Kuznechny per
Vladimirskaya
Leshtukov per
18
ul Razyezzhaya
37
Zagorodny pr
Ligovsky pr
To Alexander Nevsky
Monastery (200m)
ul Pravdy
Pushkinskaya
8
ul Marata
Zvenigorodskaya ul
Transportny per
Ligovsky Pr
ul Konstantina Zaslonova
Romenskaya ul
ul Tyushina

Central St Petersburg

Top Sights
- Novaya Gollandiya A5
- Peter & Paul Fortress C2

Sights
- 1 Aleksandrinsky Theatre E5
- 2 Alexander Column C3
- 3 Church of the Saviour on Spilled Blood D3
- 4 Dvortsovaya Ploshchad C3
- 5 General Staff Building C4
- 6 Kazan Cathedral D4
- 7 Kunstkamera B3
- 8 Loft Project ETAGI G7
- 9 Pl Ostrovskogo E5
- 10 Pushkinskaya 10 .... G5
- 11 Rostral Columns C3
- 12 Russian Museum E4
- 13 Singer Building D4
- 14 SS Peter & Paul Cathedral C2
- 15 St Isaac's Cathedral B4
- 16 State Hermitage Museum C3
- 17 Strelka C3

Activities, Courses & Tours
- 18 Coachmen's Banya F6
- 19 Skatprokat G5

Sleeping
- 20 Andrey & Sasha's Homestay C5
- 21 Diva Hostel F4
- 22 Friends on Bankovsky D5
- 23 Friends on Griboyedova D4
- 24 Hostel Life F5
- 25 Location Hostel C4
- Location Hostel .... (see 8)
- 26 Soul Kitchen C5

Eating
- Café Singer .... (see 13)
- Green Room .... (see 8)
- 27 Pelmenya E4
- 28 Stolle G3
- 29 Stolle A2
- 30 Stolle B5
- 31 Stolle A6
- 32 Stolle D3
- 33 Troitsky Most D4
- 34 Zoom Café C5

Drinking
- 35 Central Station D5
- Dyuni .... (see 37)
- Experimental Sound Gallery .... (see 10)
- Fish Fabrique Nouvelle .... (see 10)
- 36 Hat F4
- Jesus Club .... (see 37)
- 37 Ligovsky 50 .... G6
- 38 Radiobaby D5
- 39 Terminal Bar E5

Entertainment
- 40 Mariinsky Concert Hall A6
- 41 Mariinsky Theatre B6
- 42 Mikhaylovsky Opera & Ballet Theatre D4

Shopping
- 43 Bolshoy Gostiny Dvor E4

Information
- 44 American Medical Clinic B5
- 45 Apteka Petrofarm D4
- 46 Tourist Information Bureau G5
- 47 Tourist Information Bureau Main Office E4

Closed for centuries, this vast urban island is being turned into St Petersburg's most impressive public space. Novaya Gollandiya's gaggle of mothballed 18th-century red-brick buildings will eventually house contemporary art. For now, it's more of a yuppie R&R zone. There's a grassy park strewn with cosy beanbag chairs, quirky shops, DJs at weekends and various sporty diversions.

Activities

Especially during White Nights, cycling is a brilliant and economical way to get around.

Skatprokat (☎717 6838; www.skatprokat.ru Goncharnaya ul 7; rental per day/24hr/week fron R300/400/2100; ⏰1-8pm; Ⓜ Ploshchad Vosstaniya rents a wide variety of bikes and runs summer weekend and White Night bike tours.

Tours

Peter's Walking Tours WALKIN

(☎943 1229; www.peterswalk.com; scheduled tour R650; ⏰scheduled tours Apr-Oct) Peter's tour are superb. The classic 4½-hour 'Origina Walk' departs from Hostel Life, at Nevsky p 47, or choose from a variety of themed tour including a Friday-night pub crawl.

Sleeping

Stay in hostels in the high season (May to September), when hotels jack up their rates. In the low season, hotel prices drop 30% or more.

TOP CHOICE Soul Kitchen HOSTEL €
(☎8-911-723 1032; www.soulkitchenhostel.com; nab reki Moyki 62/2; dm R800, d from R3200, without bathroom from R2600; ; M Sadovaya/Sennaya Ploshchad) Russia's best hostel blends boho hipness and boutique-hotel comfort, scoring perfect 10s in key categories: private rooms (chic), dorm beds (double wide), atmosphere (shabby chic), common areas (vast) and bathrooms (inviting).

TOP CHOICE Andrey & Sasha's Homestay APARTMENT €€
(☎8-921-409 6701, 315 3330; asamatuga@mail.ru; nab kanala Griboyedova 49; r €70-80; M Sadovaya) Legendary hosts rent out rooms in two delightfully decorated vintage apartments. Outstanding.

TOP CHOICE Hostel Life HOSTEL €
(☎318 1808; www.hostel-life.ru; Nevsky pr 47; dm R800-1000, tw R2850; ; M Mayakovskaya) You'll know you've made a good choice the minute you walk into the large and modern lounge/kitchen area. The dorms are great too.

Location Hostel HOSTEL €
(☎329 1274; www.location hostel.ru; Ligovsky pr 74; dm R600, d R1000-2900; ; M Ligovsky Prospekt) You'll find this happening hostel within **Loft Project ETAGI** (M Ligovsky Prospekt), a contemporary art space on the site of a former bakery. The dorm beds are OK but it's the three fab design rooms, all with bathrooms, that are the standouts. Its other branch on **Admiralteysky pr** (☎490 5429; www.location-hostel.ru; Admiralteysky pr 8; dm/tw without bathroom R600/1200;) is better located but more basic.

Diva Hostel HOSTEL €
(☎579 0144; www.divahostel.ru; nab reki Fontanki 18-22; dm R600, s/d/tr/q without bathroom from R2000/2200/3000/4500; ; M Mayakovskaya) With just one 12-bed dorm and a tiny kitchen, this is not a hostel for socialising, but it's great if you seek a quiet, compact, clean private room at a great price. Pay R300 extra for a queen-sized bed.

Friends on Griboyedova HOSTEL €
(☎571 0151; www.friendsplace.ru; nab kanala Griboyedova 20; dm R800-900, s/d/tr without bathroom R2300/2400/2900; ; M Nevsky Prospekt) A sprawling hostel with bike rental and two foosball tables not far from the epicentre of St Pete's party scene around ul Dumskaya. Friends runs three other hostels, including the more party-oriented **Friends on Bankovsky** (☎310 4950; ; M Sadovaya) nearby.

Eating

St Petersburg has a fantastic selection of restaurants and cafes.

TOP CHOICE Zoom Café EUROPEAN €€
(www.cafezoom.ru; Gorokhovaya ul 22; mains R200-400; ⏲9am-midnight Mon-Sat, from 1pm Sun; ; M Nevsky Prospekt) Perennially popular cafe with a funky feel and an interesting menu of hearty comfort food like potato pancakes with salmon and cream cheese. No reservations after 4pm – expect to wait.

Green Room CAFE €
(Ligivosky pr 74; mains R100-150; ⏲9am-11pm Sun-Thu, to 3am Fri & Sat; ; M Ligovsky Prospekt) This bright cafe has a sprawling wooden rooftop terrace overlooking the graffiti-splashed courtyard of the funky Loft Project ETAGI artists' complex. Food leans towards Central Asian, and cocktails (R200) and beer (R100) are cheap.

Pelmenya RUSSIAN €
(nab reki Fontanki 25; meals R200-300; ⏲11am-11pm; ; M Gostiny Dvor) All kinds of dumplings on the menu here – Georgian *khinkali*, Uzbek *manti*, Ukrainian *varenyky* and, of course, the namesake *pelemni* – all prepared fresh in a delightful space near the main boat-tour dock.

Stolle RUSSIAN €
(www.stolle.ru; small/large pie R35/70, mains R200-250; ⏲9am-9pm;) Konyushennaya per (Konyushennaya per 1/6; M Nevsky Prospekt); ul Dekabristov 19 (ul Dekabristov 19; M Sadovaya/Sennaya Ploshchad); ul Dekabristov 33 (ul Dekabristov 33; M Sadovaya/Sennaya Ploshchad); ul Vosstaniya (ul Vosstaniya 32; M Chernyshevskaya); Vasilevsky Island (1-ya linii 50, Vasilevsky Island; M Vasileostrovskaya) We can't get enough of these traditional Russian savoury and sweet pies. It's easy to make a meal of it with soups and other dishes that can be ordered at the counter.

Troitsky Most VEGETARIAN €
(dishes R75-125;) Moyka (nab reki Moyki 27; ; Admiralteyskaya) Vasilyevsky Island (6-ya liniya 27, Vasilyevsky Island; ; Vasileostrovskaya) This cheap and friendly chain of vegetarian cafes is great and the mushroom lasagne legendary. The salads are self-serve, *stolovaya*-style.

Drinking

Many of the best clubs and live-music bars are cafes by day, so we list them all in one place. The nightlife epicentre is ul Dumskaya, home to dozens of bars and clubs and a sea of drunken students at weekends.

TOP CHOICE **Hat** BAR
(ul Belinskogo 9; 8am-last customer; Mayakovskogo) Nearly nightly live jazz jam sessions showcase some real talent, and the atmosphere is boisterous. Its sister bar, **Terminal Bar** (ul Rubinshteyna 13a; 4pm-last customer; Dostoevskaya), is a slice of New York bohemia where regulars often bring the resident piano to life.

Ligovsky 50 BAR, CLUB
(Ligovsky pr 50) If you don't care for the sloppy drunk-fest of ul Dumskaya, this complex of clubs is a good alternative. **Dyuni** (Dunes; Ligovsky pr 50; 24hr; ; Ploshchad Vosstaniya), famous for all-day summer beach parties, and more sophisticated **Jesus Club** (Ligovsky pr 50; 8pm-6am Thu-Sat; Ploshchad Vosstaniya) provide the most reliable fun.

Fish Fabrique Nouvelle LIVE MUSIC
(www.fishfabrique.spb.ru; Ligovsky pr 53; 3pm-late; Ploshchad Vosstaniya) Here in the museum of boho known as **Pushkinskaya 10** (www.p-10.ru; 4-8pm Wed-Sun), life artists, musicians and wannabes of all ages meet to drink beer and listen to music. The **Experimental Sound Gallery** (GEZ-21; www.gez21.ru; cover free-R30) in the same complex has bands almost nightly.

FREE **Radiobaby** BAR, CLUB
(www.radiobaby.com; Kazanskaya ul 7; 6pm-6am; Nevsky Prospekt) A laid-back club with cool lighting, a 'no techno, no house' music policy, table football and an atmosphere of eternal hedonism. Go through the arch at Kazanskaya ul 5, then turn left through a second arch to find it.

Central Station GAY, LESBIAN
(www.centralstation.ru; ul Lomonosova 1/28; cover after midnight R100-300; 6pm-6am; Gostiny Dvor) The city's main gay club, with two dance floors, several bars, a cafe and souvenir shop. Check out **Excess** (www.xs.gay.ru) for more on gay-friendly bars and clubs.

Entertainment

From July to mid-September the big theatres like the Mariinsky and the Mikhaylovsky close but plenty of performances are still staged. Check the *St Petersburg Times* for comprehensive listings.

Mariinsky Theatre OPERA, BALLET
(326 4141; www.mariinsky.ru; Teatralnaya pl 1; performances 7pm; Sadovaya/Sennaya Ploshchad) Home to the world-famous Kirov Ballet and Opera Company. A visit here is a must, if only to wallow in the sparkling glory of the interior. Book online either for the theatre or the acoustically splendid new **concert hall** (www.mariinsky.ru; ul Dekabristov 37; closed mid-Jul–mid-Sep; Sadovaya/Sennaya Pl) nearby.

Mikhaylovsky Opera & Ballet Theatre OPERA, BALLET
(www.mikhailovsky.ru; pl Iskusstv 1; box office 10am-9pm; Nevsky Prospekt) Challenging the Mariinksy in terms of the standards and range of its performances is this equally historic and beautifully restored theatre.

Information

American Medical Clinic (740 2090; www.amclinic.ru; nab reki Moyki 78; Admiralteyskaya)

Apteka Petrofarm (Nevsky pr 22; 24hr)

Cafe Max (www.cafemax.ru; Nevsky pr 90/92 per hr R120; 24hr; Mayakovskaya) Coffee (R90) and beer (R120) on offer too. Also has a branch in the Hermitage.

Central Post Office (www.spbpost.ru; Pochtamtskaya ul 9; 24hr; Sadovaya/Sennaya Ploshchad) Worth visiting just to admire its elegant Style Moderne interior. The express mail service EMS Garantpost is available here.

Express to Russia (☎570 6342; www.expresstorussia.com; Muchnoi per 2) Visas, tours, hotel bookings, tickets – a little of everything.

Russian Museum Internet Centre (Nevsky pr 17; per hr R70; ⏰10am-10pm; Ⓜ Gostiny Dvor) Inside the courtyard of the Stroganov Palace.

St Petersburg Times (www.sptimes.ru) St Pete's fine English-language newspaper, published every Thursday.

Tourist Information Bureau (☎tourist helplines 0333, 300 3333; http://eng.ispb.info) main office (☎310 2822; Sadovaya ul 14/52; ⏰10am-7pm Mon-Fri, noon-6pm Sat; Ⓜ Gostiny Dvor); Hermitage booth (Dvortsovaya pl 12; ⏰10am-7pm; Ⓜ Nevsky Prospekt); pl Vosstaniya (pl Vosstaniya; ⏰10am-7pm; Ⓜ Ploshchad Vosstaniya) These helpful offices are a rarity for Russia. Free city maps, brochures and transport advice.

 Getting Around

To/From the Airport

From Moskovskaya metro station, bus 39 runs to Pulkovo-1, the domestic air terminal (R30, 20 minutes), and buses 13 and 13b run to Pulkovo-2, which serves most international flights (R25, 15 minutes). Buy your ticket on the bus. All told it's about 50 minutes from the centre to the airport, including transfer and wait time.

By taxi it's R900 to the centre from official taxi booking kiosks located at both terminals (R500 is the price from the city to the airport).

Public Transport

The metro is usually the quickest way around the city. *Zhetony* (tokens) and credit-loaded cards can be bought from booths in the stations (R28).

Buses and trolleybuses (R23) and *marshrutky* (fixed-route public vans; R35) often get you closer to the sights and are especially handy to cover long distances along main avenues like Nevsky pr.

Taxi

To book a taxi, contact one of the following companies:

Peterburgskoe Taksi 068 (☎068, 324 7777; www.taxi068.spb.ru)

Taxi Blues (☎321 8888; www.taxiblues.ru)

KALININGRAD REGION

POP 937,900

Sandwiched by Poland and Lithuania, the Kaliningrad region (Калининградская область) is a Russian exclave that's intimately attached to the Motherland yet also a world apart. In this 'Little Russia' – only 15,100 sq km – you'll also find beautiful countryside, charming old Prussian seaside resorts and splendid beaches, including the pine forests and Sahara-style dunes of the Kurshskaya Kosa National Park, a Unesco World Heritage site.

Kaliningrad Калининград

☎4012 / POP 423,000

Kaliningrad is an excellent introduction to Russia's most liberal region. Interesting museums and historical sights sprout in between the shiny new shopping centres and multitude of leafy parks that soften vast swathes of brutal Soviet architecture. Although little remains to indicate how Königsberg was once a Middle European

WORTH A TRIP

KURSHSKAYA KOSA NATIONAL PARK

The 98km-long Kurshskaya Kosa (Curonian Spit) is a remote and dramatic landscape with high sand dunes, pine forests, pristine beaches along its exposed western coast, and a calm lagoon that is shared by Russia and Lithuania. A Unesco World Heritage site, it's a paradise for elk, birds and travellers who like to get way off the beaten track. The 50km Russian half of the spit is protected within the **Kurshskaya Kosa National Park** (park office in Rybachy; admission per person/car R30/250).

Independent travellers should consider renting a bicycle. You'll save money, plus hear the wind and the birds better. You can rent a bike at various points on the spit itself or at **Rybak Sport** (ul Turgeneva 2a; per day R300; ⏰8am-6pm), less than a minute's walk from the train station in Zelenogradsk. The regional tourism office (p933) in Kaliningrad has info on staying on the Spit.

Your other options are a private tour or taxi or a public bus. Six daily buses shuttle between Zelenogradsk and Morskoe (50 minutes); four originate in Kaliningrad.

Kaliningrad

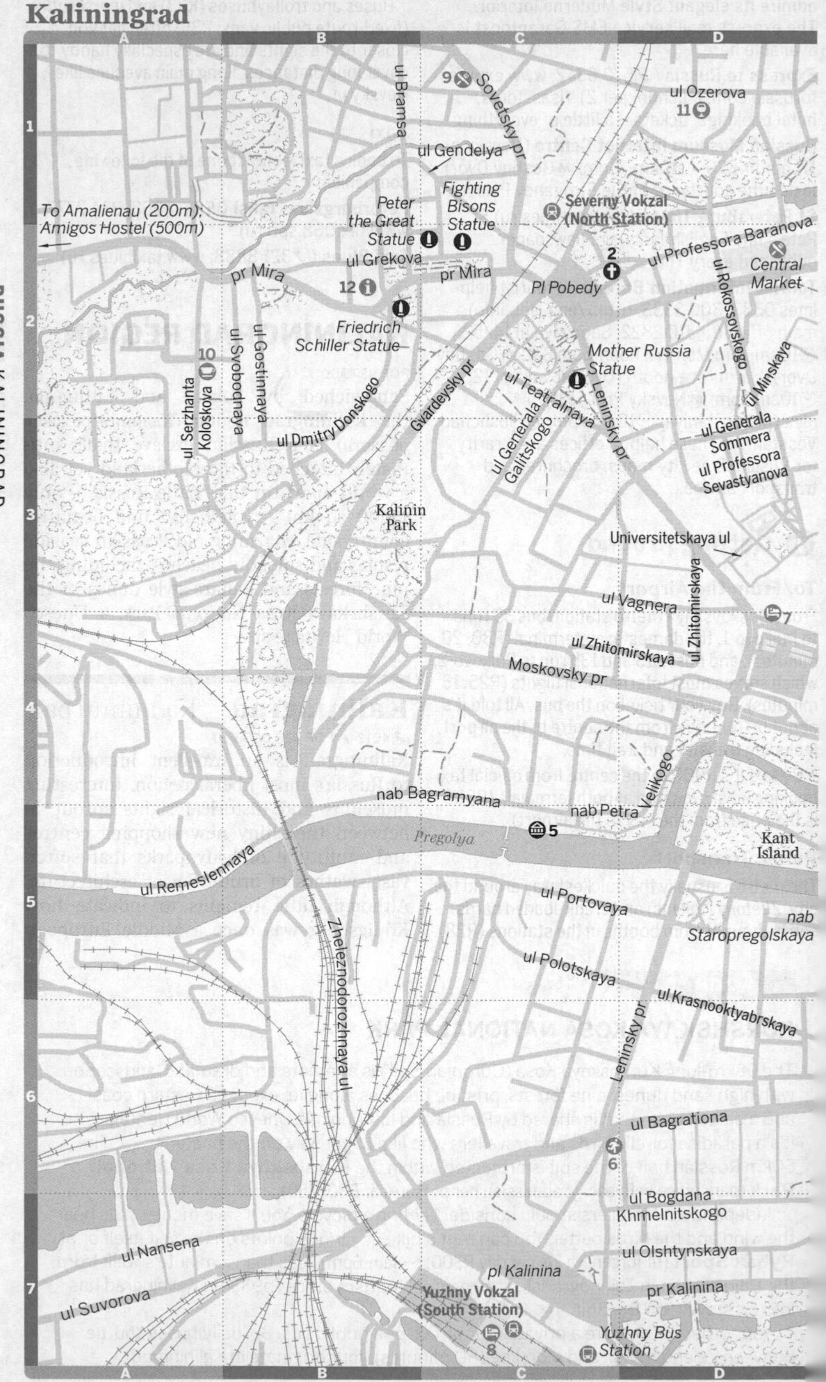

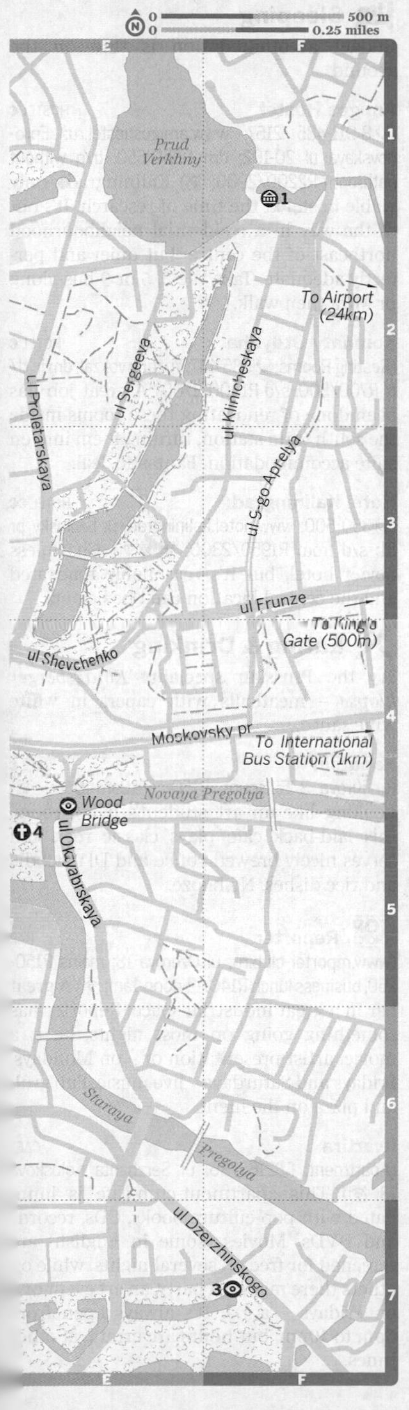

Kaliningrad

Sights

1 Amber Museum F1
2 Cathedral of Christ the Saviour C2
Dohna Tower .... (see 1)
3 Friedland Gate F7
4 Kaliningrad Cathedral E5
5 World Ocean Museum C5

Activities, Courses & Tours

6 Planeta Sport C6

Sleeping

7 Hotel Kaliningrad D4
8 Komnaty Otdykha C7

Eating

9 Kaputsin C1

Drinking

10 Kvartira A2
11 Reporter D1

Information

King's Castle .... (see 7)
12 Regional Tourism Information Centre D2

architectural gem equal to Prague or Kraków, there are attractive residential suburbs and remnants of the city's old fortifications that evoke the Prussian past.

Founded as a Teutonic fort in 1255, in 1525 Königsberg became the capital of the Duchy of Prussia, Europe's first Protestant state. The first king of Prussia, Frederick I, was crowned here in 1701. For the next couple of centuries the city flourished, producing citizens such as the philosopher Immanuel Kant (1724–1804). The city was levelled in 1945 when the Red Army took it. In 1946 the Soviets renamed the city (and the region) Kaliningrad in honour of Mikhail Kalinin, one of Stalin's more vicious henchmen.

Sights

Pl Pobedy is the modern heart of Kaliningrad, dominated by the Russo-Byzantine **Cathedral of Christ the Saviour** (Kafedralny Sobor Khrista Spasitelya), built in 2006. Extending west of the square is pr Mira, a pleasant, shop-lined artery leading to bustling **Central Park** (Tsentralny Park). Walks through the linden-scented, tree-lined old German neighbourhood of **Amalienau** around here is the best way to experience old Königsberg.

Kaliningrad Cathedral CHURCH
(www.sobor-kaliningrad.ru; Kant Island; adult/student R150/130, photos R50, concerts R250-300; ⏲10am-5pm) The geographical and spiritual heart of old Königsberg, this Gothic cathedral, founded in 1333, was almost destroyed during WWII. Restoration began in 1992 and the showpiece main hall, with fabulous vaulted ceilings, now stages regular concerts. Upstairs a museum has displays of old Königsberg, objects from archaeological digs and the death mask of Immanuel Kant.

World Ocean Museum MUSEUM
(www.world-ocean.ru; nab Petra Velikogo 1; combined adult/student R250/150, individual vessels R90/60; ⏲10am-6pm Wed-Sun) Along the river west of the cathedral is this fascinating museum, where you can learn about sea and space exploration aboard a B-413 submarine and two giant Soviet research ships.

Amber Museum MUSEUM
(www.ambermuseum.ru; pl Vasilevskogo 1; adult/student R170/110, photos R150; ⏲10am-7pm Tue-Sun) This museum has some 6000 examples of amber artworks, including enormous pieces of jewellery containing prehistoric insects suspended within, an amber flute and a four-panelled amber and ivory chalice depicting Columbus, the *Niña,* the *Pinta* and the *Santa Maria*.

City Fortifications & Gates HISTORIC BUILDINGS
The Amber Museum is housed in the attractive **Dohna Tower** (pl Vasilevskogo), a bastion of the city's old defensive ring. Remnants of the fortifications and gates remain scattered around the city, including the impressively renovated **King's Gate** (ul Frunze 112; adult/student R60/30; ⏲11am-7pm Wed-Sun) housing a museum with cool models of old Königsberg. The **Friedland Gate** (www.fvmuseum.ru; pr Kalinina 6; adult/child R20/10, multimedia show R30; ⏲10am-7pm May-Aug, to 6pm Sep-Apr, closed 1st Fri of month) screens an hourly 40-minute multimedia show that is the best way to see what pre-WWII Königsberg looked like.

Activities

Planeta Sport CYCLING
(Leninsky pr 133; bike rental per day R200-400; ⏲10am-8pm Mon-Fri, to 6pm Sat, 11am-4pm Sun) A bicycle is not a bad way to get around sprawling Kaliningrad and is especially pleasant around the cathedral.

Sleeping

Budget accommodation is thin on the ground.

Amigos Hostel HOSTEL €
(☎8-911-485 2157; www.amigoshostel.ru; Epronovskaya ul 20-102; dm R550-650, tr/q without bathroom R2200/2900; Ⓦ) Kaliningrad's only viable hostel at the time of research. It's out of the way in a residential neighbourhood northeast of the centre, but quiet and perfectly adequate. Take the 3, 5 or 9 bus along pr Mira then walk.

Komnaty Otdykha HOTEL €
(Resting Rooms; ☎586 447; Yuzhny vokzal; dm in d/tr R700/500, s/d R1000/1700) A great job has been done of renovating these rooms inside the south train station, turning them into en suite accommodation. Fantastic deal.

Hotel Kaliningrad HOTEL €€
(☎350 500; www.hotel.kaliningrad.ru; Leninsky pr 81; s/d from R1950/2300; ❄@Ⓦ) Charmless Soviet hotel, but it's reasonably renovated and the central location can't be beaten.

Eating & Drinking

Try the Prussian speciality *Königsberger klopse* – meatballs with capers in white wine sauce.

Kaputsin CAFE €
(ul Kirova 3/5; soups R150; ⏲10am-10pm; Ⓦ) Looking like an art student's living room, this laid-back cafe plays classic rock and serves nicely brewed coffee and DIY noodle and rice dishes. No booze.

TOP CHOICE **Reporter** BAR
(www.reporter-club.ru; ul Ozerova 18; mains R150-250, business lunch R140; ⏲noon-1am; Ⓦ) A great bar in a great industrial space, Reporter has something going on most nights, be it a movie, artist presentation or – on Mondays, Fridays and Saturdays – live music. Pub grub and pizza on the menu.

Kvartira CAF
(Apartment; ☎216 736; ul Serzhanta Koloskov 13; Ⓦ) This apartment-cum-cafe is inun dated with pop-culture books, CDs, record and DVDs. Movies (some in English) ar screened for free on several nights, while o others there may be a party, an art event or on Fridays – a DJ. It's always open fror 6pm to 10pm, but hours are erratic at othe times.

TRANSPORT FROM KALININGRAD

Bus

DESTINATION	PRICE (R)	DURATION (HR)	FREQUENCY
Gdansk (Poland)	500	2	daily
Klaipėda (Lithuania)	445	4	2 daily
Rīga (Latvia)	950	9	2 daily
Vilnius (Lithuania)	920	6	daily
Warsaw (Poland)	750	9	daily

Train

DESTINATION	PRICE (R)	DURATION (HR)	FREQUENCY
Berlin (Germany)	4400	14	daily Jun-Sep
Gdansk (Poland)	1000	6	daily Jun-Sep
Moscow	3000	23	3 daily
St Petersburg	2800	26	daily
Vilnius (Lithuania)	1650	6	4 daily

Information

Branch Post Office (ul Chernyakhovskogo 32; ⌚8am-8pm Mon-Fri, 9am-6pm Sat, 9am-2pm Sun)

Emergency Hospital (☎534 556; ul Nevskogo 90; ⌚24hr)

King's Castle (☎350 782; www.kaliningrad info.ru; Leninsky pr 81, Hotel Kaliningrad; ⌚9am-6pm Mon-Fri, to 4pm Sat, to 1pm Sun) Runs scheduled tours (in Russian) to the Kurshskaya Kosa on Wednesdays and Sundays in the summer (R980).

Königsberg.ru (www.konigsberg.ru) Web-based tour agency through which you can arrange 72-hour express visas.

Regional Tourism Information Centre (☎555 200; www.visit-kaliningrad.ru; pr Mira 4; ⌚9am-8pm Mon-Fri, 11am-6pm Sat) Multilingual staff here are a mine of information on the region.

Getting There & Away

Bus

Yuzhny bus station (ul Zheleznodorozhnaya 7), next to Yuzhny vokzal, is the departure point for international services run by **Ecolines** (☎656 501; www.ecolines.net) to Warsaw and several German cities. Additional international buses depart from the **international bus station** (Moskovsky pr 184).

Zelenogradsk Trans (☎656 501; http://atp-.ru) runs twice-daily buses departing at 6am and 3pm from Kaliningrad, and 6am and 5pm from Gdansk. Ecolines runs an additional trip on Thursday and Saturday.

Train

Kaliningrad's two stations are Severny vokzal (North Station) and the larger Yuzhny vokzal (South Station). All long-distance and many local trains go from Yuzhny vokzal. Note that trains to Moscow and St Petersburg go through Belarus so you'll need a Belarusian transit visa.

It's also important to note that all long-distance trains from Kaliningrad run on Moscow time, so if the schedule says 10am it will leave at 9am Kaliningrad time.

Getting Around

Take bus 144 from Khrabovo airport to the bus station (R30, 50 minutes, roughly hourly). A taxi from the airport is R400 at the official stand. From the centre to the airport (R300), book through **Taxi Kaliningrad** (☎585 858, 058; www.taxi-kaliningrad.ru).

UNDERSTAND RUSSIA

History

Russia has its cultural origins in Kyivan Rus, the kingdom located in what is today Ukraine and Belarus. From here the Slavs expanded into modern European Russia. It was during the Romanov dynasty

(1613–1917) that Russia began to develop into the vast nation it is today: territorial expansion from the 17th to 19th centuries saw the country gobble up Siberia, the Arctic, the Russian Far East, Central Asia and the Caucasus. Peter the Great set up a navy and built a new capital, St Petersburg, in 1703. Catherine the Great continued Peter's progressive policies to create a world power by the mid-18th century.

Nicholas II's refusal to countenance serious political and societal change precipitated the 1917 Revolution. What began as a liberal revolution was hijacked later the same year in a coup led by the Bolsheviks under Lenin, which resulted in the setting up of the world's first communist state.

Under Communist Party rule (1917–91) Russia became a superpower, having created the Union of Soviet Socialist Republics (USSR) and absorbing some 14 neighbouring states between 1922 and 1945. The terror of Stalin, the reforms of Khrushchev and the stagnation during the Brezhnev era finally led to Mikhail Gorbachev's period of reform known as perestroika in 1985. Within six years the USSR had collapsed alongside communism, and reformer Boris Yeltsin led Russia into a new world of cut-throat capitalism.

On New Year's Eve 1999, Yeltsin resigned in favour of Vladimir Putin, a steely faced ex-KGB officer and then prime minister. Putin's policy of steering a careful course between reform and centralisation (plus an economy booming off the back of oil and gas exports) made him popular. But his tightening of control over the media and ruthlessness with political opponents, as well as Russia's brutal clampdown on the independence movement in Chechnya, caused concern among liberals.

With no credible opponent, Putin rolled to victory in the March 2012 presidential elections, reclaiming the position after a four-year hiatus from his ally and predecessor, Dmitry Medvedev. During that hiatus, Putin had served as Russia's prime minister and – many claimed – de facto leader. It all adds up to almost 15 years with Putin in charge or nominally in charge. And despite unprecedented opposition during the 2012 campaign, Putin remains genuinely popular among average Russians, who seem to prefer strong-armed, no-nonsense leaders in his mould.

People

There's some truth to the local saying 'scratch a Russian and you'll find a Tatar'. Over the centuries Russia has absorbed people from a huge number of nationalities including the Mongols, the Tatars, Siberian peoples, Ukrainians, Jews and Caucasians. This means that while the vast majority of people you meet will describe themselves as Russian, ethnic homogeneity is not always that simple.

Russians have a reputation for being dour, depressed and unfriendly. In fact, most Russians are anything but, yet find constant smiling indicative of idiocy, and ridicule pointless displays of happiness commonly seen in Western culture. Even though Russians can appear to be unfriendly and even downright rude when you first meet them, their warmth is quite astounding as soon as the ice is broken. Just keep working at it.

Arts

Russian literature is one of the world's greatest: the 19th century poet Alexander Pushkin is the national bard, while other greats include Mikhail Lermontov, Leo Tolstoy, Anton Chekhov and Fyodor Dostoyevsky. Russia's musical heritage is equally illustrious: Tchaikovsky, Prokofiev and Shostakovich have all had a huge influence on the development of modern classical music.

Environment

The disastrous environmental legacy of communism is enormous. As well as both Moscow and St Petersburg being polluted fron traffic and heavy industry, the countryside i frequently blighted by crumbling and abar doned factories and other industrial plant Environmental consciousness remains rela tively low, although things are slowly chang ing with the emergence of a small but voc Russian environmental movement.

For more details on the environment problems being faced by Russia in the c and gas and other sectors, see the sites **Greenpeace Russia** (www.greenpeace.org/ru sia/en), Norway-based NGO **Bellona** (ww bellona.org) and **World Wide Fund for N ture in Russia** (www.wwf.ru/eng).

SURVIVAL GUIDE

Directory A–Z

Accommodation

There has been a boom in budget-friendly hostels in both Moscow and St Petersburg, and most offer a few private rooms; these do book out fast in the summer so book them ahead if possible.

One question you'll have concerns registration (p937). While most hotels register you automatically for free, hostels usually charge for it. Moreover, not all hostels insist on registering you.

Study the registration rules carefully – if you've already been registered, you may want to choose a hostel that does not insist on registering your again for a fee. Here is what to expect:

» In Moscow, the vast majority of hostels we surveyed will not register you unless you request it. If you want it, it costs R500 to R900. Others require you to register; where it's required, it's free or less than R200.

» In St Petersburg, most hostels require you to register for R200 to R500; where it's not required, you must request it and it costs more than R500.

The following budget ranges a double room in Moscow and St Petersburg are used in this chapter:

€ less than R3000

€€ R3000 to R8000

Activities

Taking a traditional Russian *banya* is a must. These wet saunas are a social hub and a fantastic experience for any visitor to Russia. Leave your inhibitions at home and be prepared for a beating with birch twigs (far more pleasant than it sounds). Ask at your hostel or hotel for the nearest public *banya*, where entry can be as low as R100.

In Moscow, try the luxurious **Sanduny Baths** (☎495-628 4633; www.sanduny.ru; Neglinnaya ul 14; general admission per hr R1100-2000, private cabins per hr R4000-6000; ⏲8am-10pm, private rooms to midnight; Ⓜ Kuznetsky Most) and in St Petersburg the traditional **Coachmen's Banya** (Yamskiye bani; ☎312 5836; www.yamskie.ru; ul Dostoevskogo 9; admission R150-500; ⏲men 8am-10.30pm Mon & Wed-Sun, women 8am-10.30pm daily; Ⓜ Vladimirskaya).

APARTMENT RENTAL

Booking an apartment is a good way to save money on private accommodation. They typically cost €100 to €200. The following work in Moscow and/or St Petersburg.

Cheap Moscow (www.cheap-moscow.com)

City Realty (www.cityrealtyrussia.com)

HOFA (www.hofa.ru)

Moscow City Excursions Bureau (www.moscowapartments.net)

Ostwest (www.ostwest.com)

Business Hours

Most museums close their ticket offices one hour (in some cases 30 minutes) before the official closing time.

Banks 9am to 6pm Monday to Friday, some open 9am to 5pm Saturday

Restaurants noon to midnight

Shops 10am to 9pm Monday to Friday, 10am to 7pm Saturday and Sunday

Embassies & Consulates

In Your Pocket guides to **Moscow** (www.moscow.inyourpocket.com) and **St Petersburg** (www.inyourpocket.com/city/st_petersburg.html) list foreign embassies and consulates in those cities. See www.russianembassy.net for a full list of Russian embassies overseas.

Australian Embassy (☎495-956 6070; www.russia.embassy.gov.au; Podkolokolny per 10a/2, Moscow; Ⓜ Kitay Gorod)

Australian Consulate (☎812-325 7334; Petrovsky pr 14, St Petersburg; Ⓜ Nevsky pr)

Canadian Embassy (☎495-925 6000; www.canadainternational.gc.ca/russia-russie/index.aspx; Starokonyushenny per 23, Moscow; Ⓜ Kropotkinskaya)

French Embassy Moscow (☎495-937 1500; www.ambafrance-ru.org; ul Bolshaya Yakimanka 45; Ⓜ Oktyabrskaya); St Petersburg (☎812-332 2270; nab reki Moyki 15; Ⓜ Nevsky Pr)

German Embassy Kaliningrad (☎4012-920 230; www.kaliningrad.diplo.de; ul Leningradskaya 4); Moscow (☎495-937 9500; www.germania.diplo.de; Mosfilmovskaya ul 56; Ⓜ Universitet, then bus 119); St Petersburg (☎812-320 2400; Furshtatskaya ul 39; Ⓜ Chernyshevskaya)

Netherlands Embassy (☎495-797 2900; www.netherlands-embassy.ru; Kalashny per 6, Moscow; ⓂArbatskaya)

New Zealand Embassy (☎495-956 3579; www.nzembassy.com; Povarskaya ul 44, Moscow; ⓂArbatskaya)

UK Embassy Moscow (☎495-956 7200; www.ukinrussia.fco.gov.uk/en; Smolenskaya nab 10; ⓂSmolenskaya); St Petersburg (☎812-320 3200; pl Proletarskoy Diktatury 5; ⓂChernyshevskaya)

US Embassy Moscow (☎495-728 5000; www.moscow.usembassy.gov; Bol Devyatinsky per 8, Moscow; ⓂBarrikadnaya); St Petersburg (☎812-331 2600; ul Furshtatskaya 15; ⓂChernyshevskaya)

Money

The Russian currency is the ruble, written as 'рубль' and abbreviated as 'руб' or 'р'. They are divided into 100 almost worthless *kopeki* (kopecks).

ATMs that accept all major credit and debit cards are everywhere, and most restaurants, shops and hotels in major cities gladly accept plastic. You can exchange US dollars and euros (and some other currencies) at most banks; notes should be in pristine condition. You may need your passport. Many banks cash travellers cheques for a small commission.

Post

Postcards, letters and parcels sent abroad through Pochta Rossii usually arrive within a couple of weeks, but there are occasional lapses.

Public Holidays

Many businesses close from 1 to 7 January.

New Year's Day 1 January

Russian Orthodox Christmas Day 7 January

Defender of the Fatherland Day 23 February

International Women's Day 8 March

Easter Monday April

International Labour Day/Spring Festival 1 May

Victory Day 9 May

Russian Independence Day 12 June

Unity Day 4 November

Safe Travel

Travellers have nothing to fear from Russia's 'mafia' – the increasingly respectable gangster classes are not interested in such small fry. However, petty theft and pickpockets are prevalent in both Moscow and St Petersburg, so be vigilant with your belongings.

Some police officers can be bothersome, especially to dark-skinned or foreign-looking people. Other members of the police force target tourists, though reports of tourists being hassled about their documents and registration have declined. Still, you should always carry a photocopy of your passport, visa and registration stamp. If you are stopped for any reason – legitimate or illegitimate – you will surely be hassled if you don't have these.

Sadly, racism is a problem in Russia. Be vigilant on the streets around Hitler's birthday (20 April), when bands of right-wing thugs have been known to roam around spoiling for a fight with anyone who doesn't look Russian.

Telephone

The international code for Russia is ☎7. The international access code from landline phones in Russia is ☎8, followed by ☎10 after the second tone, followed by the country code.

The three main mobile-phone companies, all with prepaid and 4G internet options, are **Beeline** (www.beeline.ru), **Megafon** (www.megafon.ru) and **MTS** (www.mts.ru). Company offices are everywhere. It costs almost nothing to purchase a SIM card, but bring your passport. Note, it's best to buy separate SIM cards for Moscow, St Petersburg and Kaliningrad to avoid expensive roaming charges.

To dial another area code (mobile or land line), dial ☎8 + 10 digits. Mobile numbers have 10 digits, always starting with ☎9 – often ☎915, ☎916 or ☎926. In this chapter mobile numbers are written in the following format: ☎8-9xx-xxx xxxx.

Two area codes function within Moscow ☎495 and the nearly obsolete ☎499; if calling ☎499, dial ☎8 plus all 10 digits.

Visas

Everyone needs a visa to visit Russia. There are several types of visa, but most travellers will apply for a tourist visa, valid for 30 days from the date of entry. New visa rules f

Americans (effective September 2012) mean that US citizens can now obtain three-year multiple-entry tourist visas.

The visa process has three stages: invitation, application and registration.

INVITATION

This is the easy part. Any travel agency, hostel or hotel will be only too happy to issue you a letter of invitation (LOI) for a fee – or free in the case of some hotels, provided you are staying with them. Costs typically range from €20 to €35 for a tourist visa.

APPLICATION

Invitation in hand, you can then apply for a visa – best done in your home country. If you can't go into the embassy in person, you'll have to send your passport to a visa-fixing agency. Even if you *can* get to your embassy, it's much easier to use a fixer.

You'll pay three fees to a fixer: the visa-processing fee – anything from €35 to €350, depending on the type of visa applied for and how quickly you need it; the fixer's fee of €40 or so; and, if necessary, return postage to send your passport to the fixer.

Check the website www.russianvisa.net or www.waytorussia.com for a list of fixers in various countries.

REGISTRATION

Every visitor to Russia must have their visa registered within seven days of arrival, excluding weekends and public holidays. Registration is handled by your accommodating party. If staying in a homestay or rental apartment, you'll either need to make arrangements with the landlord or a friend to register you through the post office. See http://waytorussia.net/RussianVisa/Registration.html for how this can be done.

Once registered, you'll receive a registration slip. Keep this safe – that's the document that any police who stop you will ask to see. Technically you do not need to register more than once unless you stay in additional cities for more than seven days, in which case you'll need additional registration slips.

Most hotels and some hostels will insist on registering you even if you've already been registered. There's no harm in having multiple registration slips.

Hold onto the immigration card you fill out on arrival into Russia – you'll need it for registration and could face problems while travelling in Russia – and certainly will on leaving – if you cannot produce it.

72-HOUR VISA-FREE TRAVEL

If you take the St Peter Line ferry from Helsinki to St Petersburg, it's possible to visit Russia without a visa as long as you stay less than 72 hours.

Citizens of Schengen countries, the UK, Switzerland and Japan can enter Kaliningrad with an on-demand 72-hour tourist visa, which can be arranged via local tourist agencies.

Getting There & Away

Air

Most major European carriers and a few US airlines serve Moscow and St Petersburg. The big Russian domestic carriers also have numerous direct flights to/from Europe, North America and Asia.

Sheremetyevo-2 (http://svo.aero) and **Domodedovo** (www.domodedovo.ru) airports host the bulk of Moscow's international flights. St Petersburg's main international terminal is **Pulkovo-2** (www.pulkovoairport.ru).

International flights to Kaliningrad's **Khrabrovo** (☎459 426) airport are rarer; Air Baltic and Aerosvit are among the few foreign carriers that serve Kaliningrad. A cheap way into Kaliningrad is to fly by budget airline to Gdansk, Poland, and then take a bus or (summer only) train.

Land

BUS

Buses are the best way to get from St Petersburg to Tallinn (from R600, 7½ hours). Try **Ecolines** (☎325 2152; www.ecolines.ru; Podezdny per 3; Ⓜ Pushkinskaya), which has five daily services, or **Lux Express** (☎441 3757; www.luxexpress.eu; Mitrofanievskoe sh 2, Admiral Business Centre; ⏰9am-9pm; Ⓜ Baltiyskaya), which has 11 daily services and also serves Rīga (from R1080, 11 hours, four daily).

The cheapest way to get from St Petersburg to Helsinki is to take a *marshrutka* (fixed-route public van) or bus from pl Vosstaniya (R500 to R800, seven to nine hours) from the corner of Nevsky pr and Ligovsky pr. Daily Sovavto buses from the Grand Hotel Europe are another option (€40, eight hours).

From Moscow – considering distances – it's far better to take the train to neighbouring countries.

UNOFFICIAL TAXIS

In St Petersburg and Moscow, few people think twice about flagging down any car to request a ride. A fare is negotiated for the journey – simply state your destination and ask '*skolko*?' (how much?) – and off you go. Proceed with caution if you are alone and/or it's late at night, especially if you are a woman. While exceedingly rare, violent attacks on passengers have occurred. There are plenty of official taxis that charge about the same as unofficial taxis, although they can be harder to find.

TRAIN

There are excellent daily connections between both Moscow and St Petersburg and many European cities, even as far afield as Paris. But be aware that many westbound trains from both cities (including those serving Germany and Kaliningrad) pass through Belarus, for which you'll need a transit visa.

Sea

Linking Helsinki and St Petersburg three to four times weekly is the Finnish overnight ferry **St Peter Line** (☎386 1147; www.stpeterline.com), which takes 11 hours; coming from Helsinki, passengers are allowed to stay in St Petersburg visa-free for up to 72 hours.

Getting Around

Air

Flying in Russia is not for the faint-hearted. Safety aside, flights can be delayed, often for hours and with no or little explanation.

That said, booking flights within Russia online is easier than ever, and domestic flights are relatively cheap. The big domestic carriers have effective booking sites with English interfaces, or you can use an online consolidater – www.skyscanner.net and anywayanyday.com have good coverage of Russian domestic routes, or try Russia specialist booking sites like airtickets.ru, https://sindbad.ru and pososhok.ru.

Major domestic carriers:

Aeroflot (www.aeroflot.ru)

Rossiya (http://eng.pulkovo.ru/en)

S7 Airlines (www.s7.ru)

Sky Express (www.skyexpress.ru/en) The closest thing Russia has to a low-cost carrier.

Transaero Airlines (www.transaero.com)

UT Air (www.utair.ru)

Bus

Buses and *marshrutky* (fixed-route public vans) are often more frequent, more convenient and faster than trains, especially on short-distance routes. There's almost no need to reserve a seat – just arrive a good 30 minutes before the scheduled departure and buy a ticket. Prices are comparable to 3rd-class train fares.

Car & Motorcycle

Poor roads, reckless drivers and rapacious traffic cops make driving in Russia an unappetising prospect. Thankfully, public transport is very good. However, if you do drive in Russia, you must have a valid International Driving Permit, your passport and insurance documentation for your vehicle.

Train

Train tickets can be bought in any train station. It's best to book at least 24 hours in advance in the high season. It's more convenient to use a centrally located *zheleznodorozhnaya kassa* (railway ticket office), but you'll pay at least an R200 service fee. Some hostels can also purchase tickets for you. You'll need your passport (or a photocopy) to buy tickets.

You can also book online through **Russian Railways** (www.eng.rzd.ru) but its interface is in Russian; www.bilet.ru and www.russianrails.com are in English.

The cheapest tickets are for *platskart* (3rd-class) compartments, which have open bunk accommodation. *Kupe* (coupé; 2nd class) carriages contain four fold-down beds per compartment. Prices between Moscow and St Petersburg in *platskart* begin at R1000.

Scandinavia

Includes »

Copenhagen.................942
Zealand.......................948
Jutland........................951
Stockholm....................953
Göteborg......................960
Norrland.......................963
Oslo.............................964
Bergen & the Western Fjords.............................968
Helsinki........................975
Turku...........................979
Tampere........................980
Lapland........................983
Understand Scandinavia.................984
Survival Guide..............986

Best Places to Eat

» Noma (p947)
» Salt och Brygga (p960)
» Schønnemann (p946)
» St. Pauls Apothek (p951)
» Emma's Under (p974)

Best Places to Stay

» Icehotel (p964)
» Hotel Hellsten (p957)
» Dream Hostel (p981)
» Det Hanseatiske Hotel (p969)

Why Go?

Effortlessly chic cities balance remote forests. Rocking festivals, majestic aurora borealis. Scandinavia, spanning Denmark, Sweden, Norway and Finland, is anything but bland.

Stolid Nordic stereotypes dissolve in the region's vibrant capitals. Crest-of-the-wave design can be seen across them all, backed up by outstanding modern architecture, excellent museums, acclaimed restaurants and a sizzling nightlife.

The great outdoors is rarely greater than in Europe's big north. Epic expanses of wilderness and intoxicatingly pure air mean that engaging with nature is utter pleasure. It's rare to find such inspiring landscapes that are so easily accessed.

Despite the scary subzero winter temperatures, there's a wealth of things to do: skiing, sledding behind huskies or reindeer, taking snowmobile safaris, spending romantic nights in snow hotels, visiting Santa Claus and gazing at the northern lights. Summer's long days are filled with festivals, beer terraces and wonderful boating, hiking and cycling.

When to Go

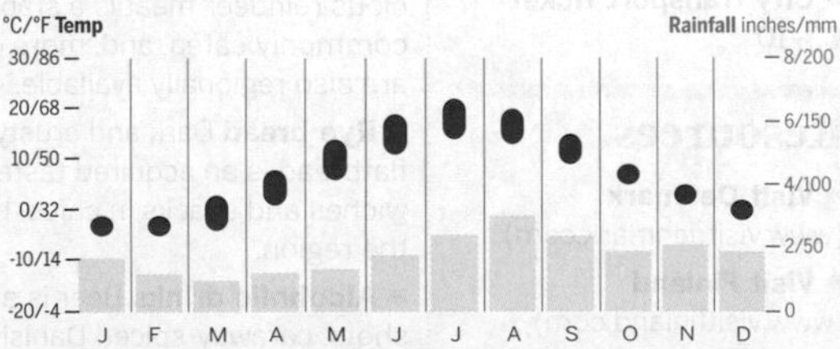

Mar There's still plenty of snow, but enough daylight to enjoy winter sports.

Jun–Aug Scandinavian summers are short but intense, and the White Nights magical.

Sep The stunning colours of the autumn season make this prime hiking time up north.

AT A GLANCE

» **Currency** krone (Denmark), euro (€, Finland), krone (Norway), krona (Sweden)

» **Language** Danish, Finnish, Norwegian, Swedish, Sámi languages

» **Money** ATMs very common, plastic taken everywhere

» **Visas** Schengen visa rules apply

Fast Facts

» **Area** 1,216,393 sq km

» **Capitals** Copenhagen (Denmark), Helsinki (Finland), Oslo (Norway), Stockholm (Sweden)

» **Country code** ☎45 (Denmark), ☎358 (Finland), ☎47 (Norway), ☎46 (Sweden)

» **Emergency** ☎112

Set Your Budget

» **Budget hotel room** €70–110

» **Two-course meal** €30–50

» **Museum entrance** €7–12

» **Beer** €6–10

» **City transport ticket** €3–10

Resources

» **Visit Denmark** (www.visitdenmark.com)

» **Visit Finland** (www.visitfinland.com)

» **Visit Norway** (www.visitnorway.com)

» **Visit Sweden** (www.visitsweden.com)

Connections

Fast, cheap ferries link the Scandinavian nations with each other and with Germany, Russia, Baltic Europe and the UK. Denmark is connected to Germany by road and rail, and the bridge across to Sweden means the rest of Scandinavia is too. Finland is linked by road and rail to Russia. Flights to the four capital cities connect Scandinavia with the rest of Europe and the wider world.

ITINERARIES

One Week

Start in Copenhagen, admiring the waterfront, museums, restaurants and lights of Tivoli at night. Take a day trip to the cathedral and Viking Ship Museum at Roskilde or 'Hamlet's' castle at Helsingør. Next, train it to Stockholm and get into the design scene and the stately, watery town centre. An overnight train takes you to Oslo, to check out Munch's work. From Oslo, a long but scenic day takes you to Bergen, Norway's prettiest city. From here, head by ferry to Denmark. Nose on down to Aarhus – don't miss the ARoS art museum. From here, it's an easy train back to Copenhagen.

Two Weeks

Roughly follow the one-week itinerary, but with a side trip from Stockholm on a Baltic ferry to Helsinki. From here you could explore classic Finnish lakeland at Savonlinna, or the old capital of Turku. Other stops could include Göteborg in Sweden; more fjord-y Norwegian experiences at Geiranger; or extra Danish time at Odense.

Essential Food & Drink

» **Coffee** To fit in, eight or nine cups a day is about right; luckily, the region's cafes are a delight.

» **Offbeat meats** Unusual meats appear on menus: delicious reindeer meat is a staple up north, elk (moose) is commonly eaten, and, more controversially, bear and whale are also regionally available.

» **Rye bread** Dark and crusty or light and chewy, this strong flatbread is an acquired taste but is the staple for sandwiches and snacks in cafes, homes and market halls across the region.

» **Alcoholic drinks** Beer is a staple. Swedish brännvin shots, caraway-spiced Danish akvavit or salt-liquorice Finnish salmiakkikossu are stronger tipples that should be tried.

» **Fish** Salmon is ubiquitous and delicious, while smoked, cured, pickled or fried herring is fundamental. Tasty lake fish include Arctic char and pike-perch.

Scandinavia Highlights

1. Shop, nosh and chill in **Copenhagen** (p942)
2. Dog-sled the winter wilderness of Scandinavia's **far north** (p983)
3. Explore Norway's western fjords from **Bergen** (p968)
4. Party at Denmark's annual **Roskilde Festival** (p949)
5. Cross the Arctic Circle, hit the Arktikum museum and visit Santa at **Rovaniemi** (p983)
6. Sleep in a fisherman's robu (shanty) on the epic, craggy **Lofoten Islands** (p973)
7. Marvel at the shimmering lakescapes of **Savonlinna** (p982), and see top-quality opera in its medieval castle
8. Ride Norway's jagged, beautiful coast aboard the **Hurtigruten ferry** (p989)
9. Tour waterways, explore museums and wander the Old Town of **Stockholm** (p953)
10. Hike wild landscapes, explore Sámi culture and sleep in the world-famous **Icehotel** (p964) in Jukkasjärvi

DENMARK

Denmark is the bridge between Scandinavia and northern Europe. The Danes' culture, food, architecture and appetite for conspicuous consumption owe as much, if not more, to Denmark's German neighbours to the south than to the country's former colonies to the north.

Packed with intriguing museums, shops, bars, nightlife and award-winning restaurants, Denmark's capital, Copenhagen, is one of the hippest cities in Europe. And while Danish cities such as Odense and Aarhus harbour their own cultural gems, Denmark's other chief appeal lies in its photogenic countryside, sweeping coastline and historic sights.

Copenhagen

POP 1.9 MILLION

Copenhagen is the coolest kid on the Nordic block. Edgier than Stockholm and worldlier than Oslo, the Danish capital gives Scandinavia the X-factor. While this thousand-year-old harbour town has managed to retain much of its historic good looks – think copper spires and cobbled squares – the focus here is on the innovative and cutting edge.

DON'T MISS

LOUISIANA: A MODERN ART MUST

Even if you don't have a burning passion for art, Denmark's outstanding **Louisiana Museum of Modern Art** (www.louisiana.dk; Gl Strandvej 13; adult/child Dkr95/free; ⏲11am-10pm Tue-Fri, 11am-6pm Sat & Sun; 👪) should be high on your 'To Do' list. It's a striking modernist art mecca, sprawling across a sculpture-laced park.

The museum's permanent collection, mainly postwar paintings and graphic art, covers everything from constructivism, CoBrA movement artists and minimalist art to abstract expressionism and pop art. Adding extra X-factor is the museum's program of fantastic temporary exhibitions.

Lousiana is in Humlebæk, 35 minutes north of Copenhagen on the S-train's C line. For a day trip, the 24-hour ticket (adult/child Dkr130/65) is better value.

Denmark's over-achieving capital is home to a thriving design scene, its streets awash with effortlessly hip shops, cafes and bars; world-class museums and art collections; intelligent new architecture; and a galaxy of Michelin stars.

Sights

TOP CHOICE Tivoli AMUSEMENT PARK

(www.tivoli.dk; adult/child Dkr95/free; ⏲11am-10pm Sun-Thu, 11am-12.30am Fri, 11am-midnight Sat early Apr-late Sep, reduced hr rest of yr) It ain't Disneyland, but Copenhagen's iconic amusement park has been winning hearts since 1843. There's a timeless quality about the place, especially as the sun sets and the park's Moorish domes, arches and manicured gardens sparkle in a sea of twinkling lights. Tivoli's numerous open-air performances are free of charge, but there's usually an admission fee for the indoor performances; check the website for times. Amusement ride tickets cost 25kr (some rides require up to three tickets), making the multiride ticket (199kr) better value in most cases. Tivoli also opens for around 10 days at Halloween and from mid-November to late December for Christmas – a magical sight.

TOP CHOICE Statens Museum for Kunst MUSEUM

(www.smk.dk; Sølvgade 48-50; special exhibitions adult/child Dkr95/free; ⏲10am-5pm Tue & Thu-Sun, to 8pm Wed) Denmark's art museum heavyweight boasts an interesting collection of old masters by Dutch and Flemish artists, as well as 20th-century European luminaries. Not surprisingly, the museum also has an inspiring collection of Danish art. From Nørreport S-train station, the museum is 800m northeast along Nørre Voldgade (which becomes Øster Voldgade).

FREE Nationalmuseet MUSEUM

(National Museum; www.natmus.dk; Ny Vestergade 10; ⏲10am-5pm Tue-Sun) Take 'Danish History 101' at Denmark's National Museum. With first claims on virtually every antiquity found on Danish soil, its treasures include Stone Age tools, Viking weaponry and impressive Bronze Age, Iron Age and runestone collections.

Christiania NEIGHBOURHOOD

(www.christiania.org; Prinsessegade) Escape the capitalist crunch at Freetown Christiania, a hash-scented, collectively run commun straddling the eastern side of Christianshavn. Since its establishment by squatters in 1971, the area has drawn nonconformists and free-spirited souls from across the globe, attracted by the concept of communal living. While Pusher St – lined with shady hash and marijuana dealers – may be its most infamous attraction, beyond it lies a semibucolic wonderland of whimsical DIY homes, cosy gardens and rambling paths, as well as craft shops, cheap eateries, beer gardens and music venues. The main entrance is on Prinsessegade, 200m northeast of its intersection with Bâdsmandsstræde.

TOP CHOICE **Ny Carlsberg Glyptotek** MUSEUM
(www.glyptoteket.dk; Dantes Plads 7, HC Andersens Blvd; adult/child Dkr75/free, Sun free; 11am-5pm Tue-Sun) Fin-de-siècle architecture dallies with top-notch art here, across the road from Tivoli in a museum celebrated for antiquities, French Impressionist works and Danish Golden Age paintings. Particularly impressive is the collection of Rodin sculptures – the largest outside of France – as well as the numerous works by Gauguin. At its heart is a beautiful tropical winter garden and cafe.

Rosenborg Slot CASTLE
(www.dkks.dk; Øster Voldgade 4A; adult/child Dkr75/free; 10am-5pm Jun-Aug, 11am-4pm Sep & Oct, reduced hours rest of year) Christian IV's fabulous Dutch Renaissance-style castle stands at the edge of Kongens Have gardens. Built in the early 17th century, it's one of Copenhagen's great landmarks, home to glorious marbled and painted ceilings, gilded mirrors, priceless Dutch tapestries, solid-silver lions, and gold- and enamelware. The Royal Treasury, in the castle basement, houses the Danish crown jewels.

Tours

The best way to see Copenhagen is from the water. There are several ways to take a boat tour around the city's canals and harbour, with multilingual guides giving a commentary in English.

Canal Tours Copenhagen BOAT
(www.stromma.dk; adult/child Dkr75/37.50; every 30min 9.30am-8pm, to 7.15pm from Gammel Strand, mid-Jun–late Aug, reduced hr rest of yr) Tours leave from Nyhavn and Gammel Strand, taking one hour and passing by the *Little Mermaid,* Christianshavn and Christiansborg Palace.

Festivals & Events

Copenhagen Jazz Festival MUSIC
(www.jazz.dk) Copenhagen's largest music event and the largest jazz festival in northern Europe means 10 swinging days of world-class music in early July.

Sleeping

TOP CHOICE **Generator Hostel** HOSTEL €
(www.generatorhostel.com; Adelgade 5-7; dm/s/d from Dkr127.50/200/400; @) It might be pricier than a standard hostel, but Generator is also a lot funkier, with contemporary hues, designer touches and slick communal areas (including a bar and outdoor terrace). Some rooms are a little small but all are bright, modern and have private bathrooms (including dorms). Social butterflies will appreciate the regular events.

CPH Living FLOATING HOTEL €€
(61 60 85 46; www.cphliving.com; Langebrogade 1c; r Dkr1180-1460;) Sleep on water at this smart floating hotel, right on Copenhagen's main canal. Set on a converted freight boat, its 12 contemporary, light-filled rooms feature floor-to-ceiling windows, modern bathrooms with rainforest shower and a communal sun deck. To get here, follow HC Andersens Blvd southeast from Tivoli and cross Langebro bridge; the hotel is on the north side of the bridge.

Wakeup Copenhagen HOTEL €€
(44 80 00 10; www.wakeupcopenhagen.com; Carsten Niebuhrs Gade 11; s Dkr400-1300, d Dkr500-1400; @) Cheap chic is what you get at contemporary, 510-room Wakeup Copenhagen, assuming you've booked ahead and online (walk-ins can be anything but 'budget'). Located 1km south of Central Station, rooms are generic and compact, yet fresh

LAST-MINUTE CHEAP SLEEPS

If you arrive in Copenhagen without a hotel booking, luck may yet be on your side. The Copenhagen Visitor Centre offers over-the-counter, last-minute deals on hotel rooms at very low prices. A double room at a four-star hotel can cost as little as Dkr600, with three-star options at around Dkr500 per night. Breakfast is often included, as well as the perk of a central location.

Central Copenhagen

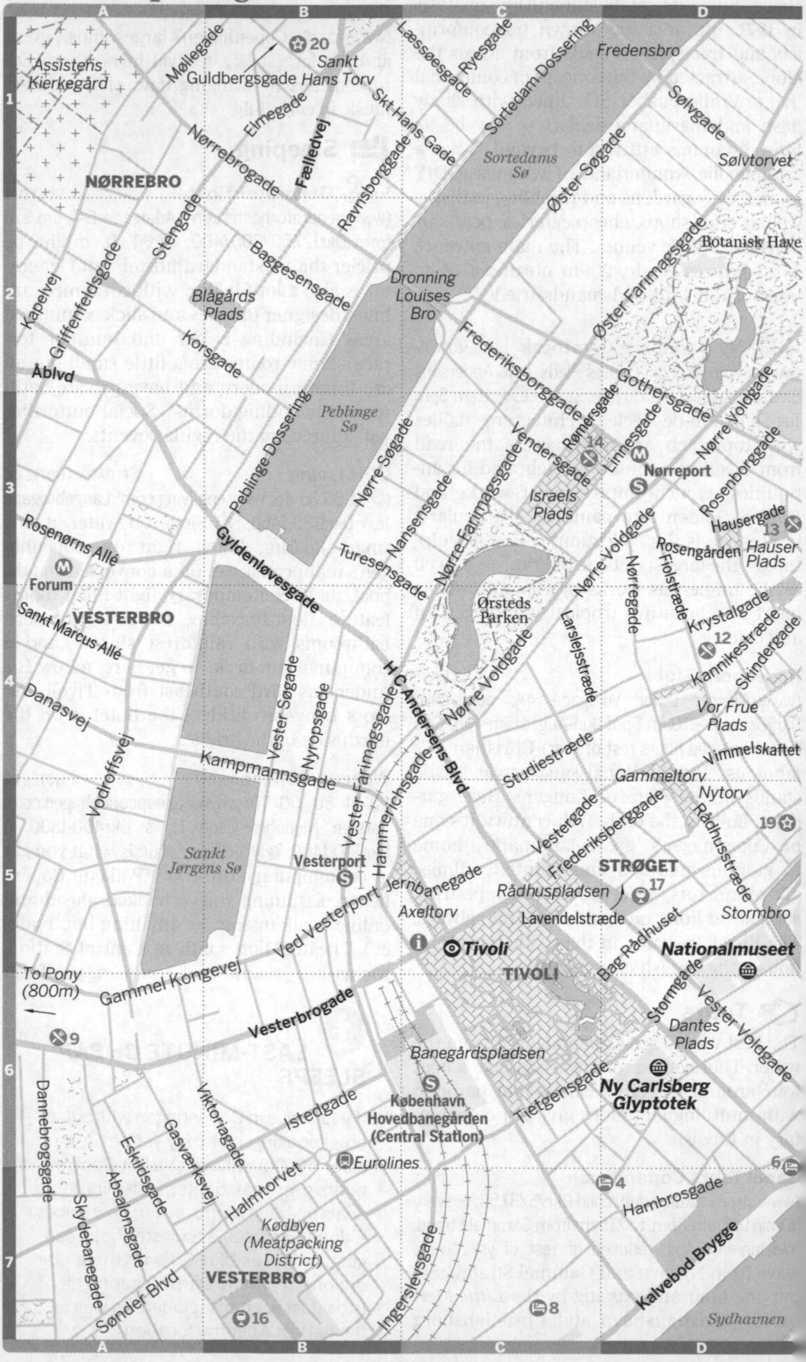

A B C D

1 2 3 4 5 6 7

Assistens Kierkegård
Møllegade
Guldbergsgade
20
Sankt Hans Torv
Læssøesgade
Ryesgade
Sortedam Dossering
Fredensbro
Elmegade
Skt Hans Gade
Fælledvej
Nørrebrogade
Ravnsborggade
Sortedams Sø
Sølvgade
Sølvtorvet
NØRREBRO
Øster Søgade
Stengade
Baggesensgade
Botanisk Have
Griffenfeldsgade
Kapelvej
Blågårds Plads
Dronning Louises Bro
Øster Farimagsgade
Frederiksborggade
Korsgade
Åblvd
Gothersgade
Peblinge Sø
Peblinge Dossering
Nørre Søgade
Rømersgade
14
Vendersgade
Linnésgade
Nørre Voldgade
Nørreport
Rosenborggade
Nansensgade
Nørre Farimagsgade
Israels Plads
Rosenørns Allé
Gyldenløvesgade
Turesensgade
Hausergade
13
Hauser Plads
Rosengården
Forum
Nørre Voldgade
Nørregade
Fiolstræde
VESTERBRO
Sankt Marcus Allé
Ørsteds Parken
Larslejsstræde
Krystalgade
12
Kannikestræde
Skindergade
H C Andersens Blvd
Nørre Voldgade
Vester Søgade
Nyropsgade
Danasvej
Vor Frue Plads
Vimmelskaftet
Vodroffsvej
Kampmannsgade
Vester Farimagsgade
Hammerichsgade
Studiestræde
Gammeltorv
Nytorv
Rådhusstræde
19
Vestergade
Frederiksberggade
Sankt Jørgens Sø
Vesterport
STRØGET
Jernbanegade
Rådhuspladsen
17
Ved Vesterport
Axeltorv
Lavendelstræde
Stormbro
Tivoli
Bag Rådhuset
Nationalmuseet
To Pony (800m)
Gammel Kongevej
TIVOLI
Stormgade
Vester Voldgade
Vesterbrogade
9
Dantes Plads
Banegårdspladsen
Tietgensgade
Ny Carlsberg Glyptotek
Dannebrogsgade
Viktoriagade
Istedgade
København Hovedbanegården (Central Station)
Gasværksvej
Eskildsgade
Absalonsgade
Eurolines
6
4
Halmtorvet
Hambrosgade
Skydebanegade
Kødbyen (Meatpacking District)
Ingerslevsgade
Kalvebod Brygge
VESTERBRO
Sønder Blvd
8
16
Sydhavnen

A B C D

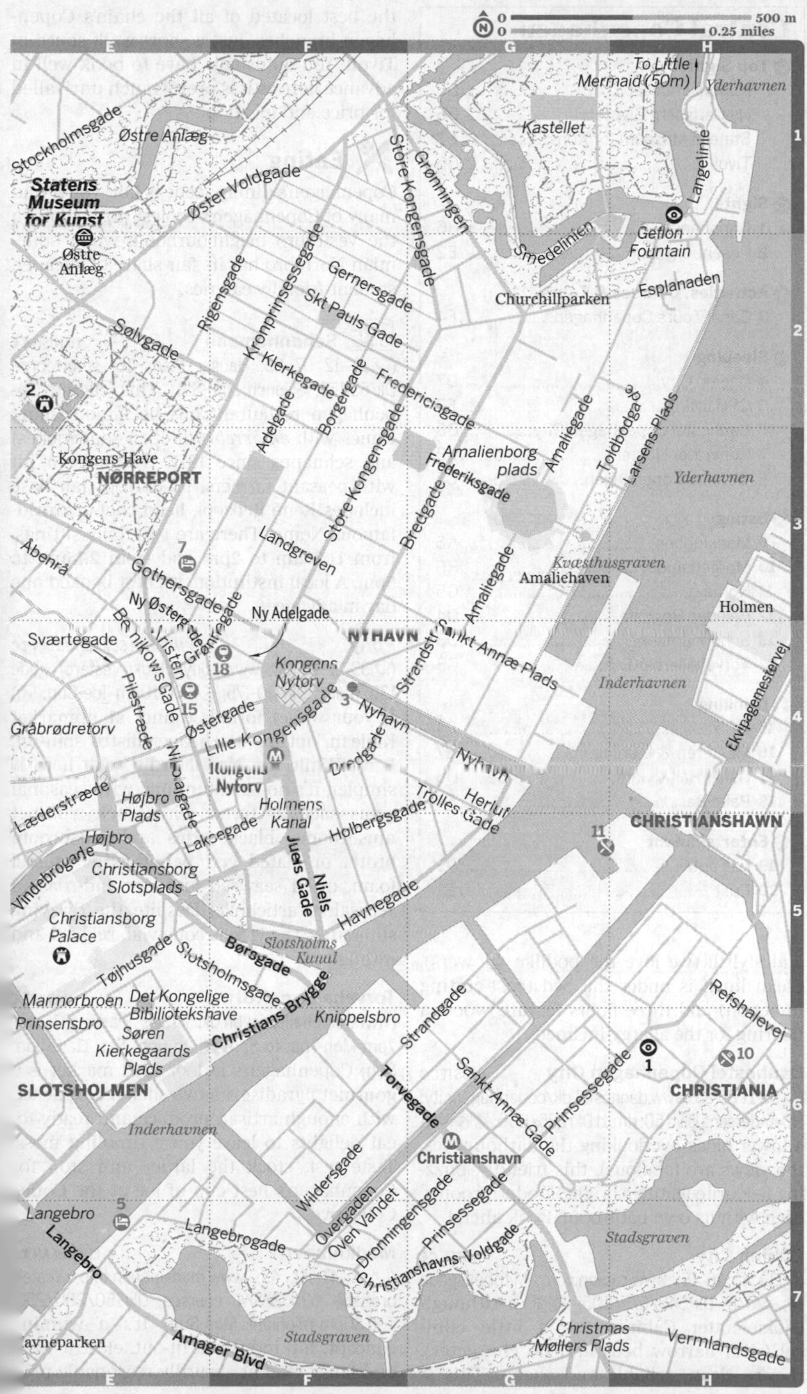

0 500 m
0 0.25 miles
E
F
G
H
To Little Mermaid (50m)
Yderhavnen
Kastellet
Stockholmsgade
Østre Anlæg
Statens Museum for Kunst
Østre Anlæg
Øster Voldgade
Store Kongensgade
Grønningen
Langelinie
Smedelinien
Gefion Fountain
Esplanaden
Churchillparken
Rigensgade
Kronprinsessegade
Gernersgade
Skt Pauls Gade
Sølvgade
Klerkegade
Borgergade
Fredericiagade
Adelgade
Store Kongensgade
Amalienborg plads
Amaliegade
Toldbodgade
Larsens Plads
Frederiksgade
Bredgade
Kongens Have
NØRREPORT
Yderhavnen
Åbenrå
Landgreven
Gothersgade
Kvæsthusgraven
Amaliehaven
Amaliegade
Holmen
Ny Østergade
Grønnegade
Ny Adelgade
NYHAVN
Sankt Annæ Plads
Bernikows Gade
Kristen
Sværtegade
Kongens Nytorv
Strandstr
Inderhavnen
Pilestræde
Østergade
Nyhavn
Ekvipagemestervej
Gråbrødretorv
Lille Kongensgade
Nyhavn
Kongens Nytorv
Niels Juels Gade
Bredgade
Herluf Trolles Gade
Læderstræde
Højbro Plads
Holmens Kanal
Holbergsgade
Lakegade
CHRISTIANSHAWN
Højbro
Vindebrogade
Christiansborg Slotsplads
Havnegade
Christiansborg Palace
Slotsholms Kanal
Tøjhusgade
Slotsholmsgade
Børsgade
Refshalevej
Marmorbroen
Det Kongelige Bibiliotekshave
Prinsensbro
Søren Kierkegaards Plads
Christians Brygge
Knippelsbro
Strandgade
SLOTSHOLMEN
Torvegade
Sankt Annæ Gade
Prinsessegade
CHRISTIANIA
Inderhavnen
Christianshavn
Wildersgade
Overgaden Oven Vandet
Dronningensgade
Prinsessegade
Langebro
Langebrogade
Christianshavns Voldgade
Stadsgraven
Langebro
Stadsgraven
Amager Blvd
Christmas Møllers Plads
Vermlandsgade
avneparken
1
2
3
4
5
6
7
10
11
15
18
SCANDINAVIA COPENHAGEN

Central Copenhagen

Top Sights

Nationalmuseet D5
Ny Carlsberg Glyptotek D6
Statens Museum for Kunst E2
Tivoli C5

Sights

1 Christiania H6
2 Rosenborg Slot E2

Activities, Courses & Tours

3 Canal Tours Copenhagen F4

Sleeping

4 Cabinn City D7
5 CPH Living E7
6 Danhostel Copenhagen City D6
7 Generator Hostel E3
8 Wakeup Copenhagen C7

Eating

9 Madklubben A6
10 Morgenstedet H6
11 Noma G5
12 Paludan Bogcafe D4
13 Schønnemann D3
14 TorvehallerneKBH C3

Drinking

15 1105 .... E4
16 Mesteren & Lærlingen B7
17 Oscar Bar & Cafe D5
18 Palæ Bar F4

Entertainment

19 La Fontaine D5
20 Rust B1

and stylish (we love the podlike showers). Clean linen is under the bed (cost-cutting in action) and three floors feature wooden flooring for the allergy-inclined.

Danhostel Copenhagen City HOSTEL €
(☎33 11 85 85; www.danhostel.dk/copenhagencity; HC Andersens Blvd 50; dm/d Dkr225/600; @📶) In a tower block overlooking the harbour (yes, the views are fabulous), this friendly, buzzing favourite features bright, modern rooms, each with its own bathroom. Book ahead.

Cabinn City HOTEL €€
(☎33 46 16 16; www.cabinn.com; Mitchellsgade 14; s/d/tr Dkr545/675/805; @📶) Although cookie-cutter Cabinns are a little clinical (with narrow beds and no character), they're clean, reliable and cheap. This is the best located of all the chain's Copenhagen branches, just a short walk south of Tivoli. You do usually have to book well in advance here as it is pretty much unrivalled for price and location.

Eating

Copenhagen's dining scene is hot; you'll find many of Copenhagen's coolest nosh spots in the Vesterbrø neighbourhood, while bohemian Nørrebro has its fair share of cheaper, student-friendly eateries.

TOP CHOICE **Schønnemann** DANISH €€
(☎33 12 07 85; Hauser Plads 16; smørrebrød Dkr65-158; ⏰lunch Mon-Sat) This classic Copenhagen restaurant has been nourishing Danes with *smørrebrød* (open sandwiches) and schnapps since 1877. Originally a hit with peasant farmers, its current fan base includes René Redzepi, head chef at world-famous Noma. There are two daily sittings, from 11.30am to 2pm and from 2.15pm to 5pm. A local institution, it's best booked one day in advance.

Pony MODERN SCANDINAVIAN €€
(☎33 22 10 00; www.ponykbh.dk; Vesterbrogade 135; mains Dkr110-175; ⏰5.30-10pm Tue-Sun; 👪) If your wallet forbids dinner at upmarket Kadeau, opt for its cheaper bistro spin-off, Pony. While the New Nordic grub here is simpler, it's no less stunning, with seasonal gems such as tartar with black trumpet mushrooms, blackberries and mushroom broth, or slated cod paired with mussel foam, dried seaweed and raw-and-roasted Jerusalem artichoke. Despite the dizzying standards, the vibe is convivial, relaxed and intimate.

TorvehallerneKBH MARKET €
(www.torvehallernekbh.dk; Israels Plads; ⏰10am-7pm Mon-Thu, to 8pm Fri, to 6pm Sat, 11am-5pm Sun) Copenhagen's indoor food market is a gourmet paradise, its two slick halls packed with enough artisan produce and ready-to-eat delights to leave you a drooling mess. Taste test, stock the larder and stop for Copenhagen's best cup of joe at the Coffee Collective.

Madklubben EUROPEAN €
(☎38 41 41 43; www.madklubben.info; Vesterbrogade 62; 2/3/4 courses Dkr150/200/250 ⏰5.30pm-midnight Mon-Sun) It's a winning concept: hip industrial fit-out, electric buzz and fancy food at absurdly reasonable pri

es. Portions are generous and the flavours fresh and contemporary; think sweet crab spiked with creamy avocado, chilli, soy sauce and coriander, or reconfigured tarte flambée served flat, long and flaky on a chopping block. Service can be a little patchy.

Morgenstedet VEGETARIAN €

(www.morgenstedet.dk; Langgaden; mains Dkr75-90; noon-9pm Tue-Sun;) This long-established vegetarian/vegan bolthole has a pretty little garden in the heart of Christiania, Copenhagen's famous alternative neighbourhood. You'll usually find a simple, salubrious choice of three hot dishes, six salads, plus vegan soup, cakes and chai.

Paludan Bogcafe INTERNATIONAL €

(www.paludan-cafe.dk; Fiolstræde 10-12; dishes Dkr49-119; 9am-10pm Mon-Fri, 10am-10pm Sat, 10am-8pm Sun) Packed with scribbling students, gossiping professors, and Mac-tapping writers, this sprawling, multi-room cafe-bookstore is a quirky universe of soaring bookshelves, crooked paintings, chintzy chandeliers, and the odd Danish design piece. While the food mightn't win any culinary awards, it is tasty, varied and good value. All bases are covered, from muesli and toast, to Danish classics, pastas and stir-fries, burgers, sandwiches, cheese platters, to pancakes and brownies. Order at the counter.

Drinking

Drinking is one of the Danes' chief pastimes and Copenhagen is packed with a huge range of places, from cosy, old-school cellar bars or 'bodegas' to slinky cocktail dens.

Mesteren & Lærlingen BAR

(Flæsketorvet 86, Vesterbro; 8pm-3am Wed-Sat) A stripped-back combo of concrete floors and wax-splashed tables, this former slaughterhouse bodega in Vesterbro's gritty-cool Kødbyen district packs a friendly, hipster crowd. Join them for rum and ginger (the house speciality), and DJ-spun retro, soul, reggae and country.

1105 COCKTAIL BAR

(www.1105.dk; Kristen Bernikows Gade 4; Wed-Sat) Perfect cocktails in dark, svelte surrounds await. The star libation remains the No 4 (Tanqueray gin, cardamom seeds, pepper, lime and honey). Whisky connoisseurs will be equally enthralled.

Palæ Bar PUB

(www.palaebar.dk; Ny Adelgade 5; 11am-1am Mon-Wed, to 3am Thu-Sat, 4pm-1am Sun) Nostalgia and cigarette smoke fill the air at one of Copenhagen's best old-school drinking dens. Grab an *øl* (beer) and reminisce with a loyal crowd spanning journalists and writers to beer-swilling politicians.

Entertainment

Copenhagen's live music and club scene are healthy and kicking, with choices spanning intimate jazz and blues boltholes to mega rock venues and secret clubs dropping experimental beats. Club admission is usually around Dkr70, though you can often get in for free before a certain time in the evening. For listings, scan www.aok.dk (mostly in Danish) and www.visitcopenhagen.com.

Live Music & Nightclubs

TOP CHOICE **La Fontaine** JAZZ

(www.lafontaine.dk; Kompagnistræde 11; 7pm-5am, live music from 10.30pm Fri & Sat, from 9pm Sun) Cosy La Fontaine is a stalwart of the city's thriving jazz scene, with emerging home-grown talent and the occasional big name. Expect live gigs Friday to Sunday and legendary late-night jam sessions.

Vega Live LIVE MUSIC

(www.vega.dk; Enghavevej 40) The daddy of all Copenhagen's live-music and club venues, Vega hosts everyone from big-name pop, rock, blues and jazz acts, to underground

SPLURGE

Can **Noma** (32 96 32 97; www.noma.dk; Strandgade 93; fixed menu Dkr1500; noon-4pm & 7pm-12:30am Tue-Sat) do no wrong? Topping the S.Pellegrino 'World's 50 Best Restaurants' list in 2010, 2011 and 2012, Michelin-starred Noma continues to seduce international gastronomes with its breathtaking, boundary-pushing modern Scandinavian creations. The focus is on local, sustainably sourced, high-quality produce with traditional foraging in forests and along seashores as a theme. Check the website for the next reservation window period, usually two to three months ahead. Alternatively, try your luck by joining the waiting list; like miracles, cancellations do happen.

indie, hip hop and electro up-and-comers. Gigs take place on either the main stage (Store Vega), small stage (Lille Vega) or the ground-floor Ideal Bar.

Rust CLUB
(www.rust.dk; Guldbergsgade 8) A thriving, smashing place that pulls one of the largest, coolest club crowds in Copenhagen. Spaces range from nightclub to live-music hall and lounge, with an equally diverse musical policy. From 11pm, entrance is available only to over 18s (Wednesday and Thursday) and over 20s (Friday and Saturday).

Gay & Lesbian Venues

Denmark was the first country to permit same-sex marriage and has had a swinging gay scene for more than 30 years. Beyond the city's string of LGBT cafes, bars and clubs, drawcards include **Copenhagen Pride** (www.copenhagenpride.dk) in August. For listings and events, see www.out-and-about.dk.

Oscar Bar & Cafe GAY
(www.oscarbarcafe.dk; Rådhuspladsen 77; ⌚11am-11pm Sun-Thu, to 2am Fri & Sat) Oscar remains the gay community's see-and-be-seen cafe-cum-bar, with cute bar staff and a healthy quota of eye-candy guests. In the warmer months, its alfresco tables are packed with preparty crowds, one eye on friends, the other on Grindr.

Information

Copenhagen Visitor Centre (☎70 22 24 42; www.visitcopenhagen.com; Vesterbrogade 4a; ⌚9am-6pm Mon-Sat, 10am-2pm Sun May & Jun, 9am-8pm Mon-Sat, 10am-6pm Sun Jul & Aug, 9am-4pm Mon-Fri, 9am-2pm Sat Sep-Apr; wi-fi) Copenhagen's impressive tourist office distributes a free city map, and brochures covering Copenhagen and all of Denmark's regions. Free wi-fi.

Frederiksberg Hospital (☎38 16 38 16; www.frederiksberghospital.dk; Nordre Fasanvej 57) West of the city centre; has a 24-hour emergency ward.

Hovedbiblioteket (15 Krystalgade; ⌚10am-7pm Mon-Fri, to 2pm Sat; wi-fi) The main public library – computers on all floors provide free internet access. Free wi-fi too.

Lonely Planet (www.lonelyplanet.com/denmark/copenhagen)

Getting There & Away

AIR Copenhagen International Airport (www.cph.dk) is Scandinavia's busiest hub, with direct connections to other destinations in Denmark, as well as in Europe, North America and Asia. It is located in Kastrup, 9km southeast of the city centre.

BOAT DFDS Seaways (☎33 42 30 10; www.dfdsseaways.com; Dampfærgevej 30) operates daily ferries to Oslo.

BUS Long-distance buses leave from opposite the DGI-byen sports complex on Ingerslevsgade, a quick walk southwest of Central Station. Advance reservations on most international routes can be made at **Eurolines** (www.eurolines-travel.com; Halmtorvet 5).

TRAIN Long-distance trains arrive and depart from Central Station. **DSB Billetsalg** (www.dsb.dk; ⌚7am-8pm Mon-Fri, 8am-4pm Sat, 8am-5pm Sun, international ticket sales 9.30am-6pm Mon-Fri) is best for reservations and for purchasing international train tickets. Alternatively, you can make reservations at www.dsb.dk, which has an English-language option.

Getting Around

TO/FROM THE AIRPORT Trains link the airport with Central Station (Dkr36, 14 minutes, every 10 minutes).

The Metro runs every four to 20 minutes around the clock between the airport (Lufthavnen station) and central Copenhagen. It does not stop at Central Station but is handy for Christianshavn, Nyhavn (alight at Kongens Nytorv station) and Nørreport. Journey time to Kongens Nytorv is 13 minutes and costs Dkr48.

BICYCLE Bycykler (City Bikes; www.bycyklen.dk) offers free-use bikes from mid-April to November at 110 City Bike racks throughout central Copenhagen. Deposit a Dkr20 coin in the stand to release the bike; return it to any rack to get your money back.

BUS & TRAIN Buses, Metro and trains use a common fare system based on zones. The basic fare of Dkr24 for up to two zones covers most city runs and allows transfers between buses and trains on a single ticket within one hour. A 24-hour pass (adult/child Dkr130/65) allows unlimited travel in all zones and is handy for day trips.

The website www.rejseplanen.dk offers a handy journey planner, with transport routes, times and prices.

Zealand

Though Copenhagen is the centre of gravity for most visitors to Denmark's eastern island, there is no shortage of drawcards beyond the city limits, especially Helsingør Slot (famously known as Hamlet's castle Elsinore) and the remarkable Viking ships of Roskilde.

HELSINGØR (ELSINORE)

POP 46,400

Those visitors that aren't Swedes shuttling across on the ferry for cheaper booze come here to soak up the atmosphere of Denmark's most famous and awe-inspiring castle, Elsinore, home of Shakespeare's indecisive antihero, Hamlet.

Sights

TOP CHOICE Kronborg Slot CASTLE

(www.kronborg.dk; adult/child Dkr75/30; ⌚10am-5.30pm Jun-Aug, 11am-4pm Apr, May, Sep & Oct, reduced hours Nov-Mar) Helsingør's top sight is Kronborg Slot, made famous as the Elsinore Castle of Shakespeare's *Hamlet* (it's the venue for August performances of the play during the annual Shakespeare festival). Kronborg's primary function was not as a royal residence, but rather as a grandiose tollhouse, wresting taxes (the infamous and lucrative 'Sound Dues') for more than 400 years from ships passing through the narrow Øresund. Stand by the cannons facing Sweden and you immediately see what a key strategic point this was.

Sleeping

Danhostel Helsingør HOSTEL €

(☎49 28 49 49; www.helsingorhostel.dk; Nordre Strandvej 24; dm/d/q Dkr185/495/550; P@) Housed in the imposing red-brick Villa Moltke, 2km northwest of the centre, this hostel is right by the water with its own beach. The run-of-the-mill dorms are in one of the smaller detached buildings. From Helsingør, bus 842 will get you there.

Eating

Rådmand Davids Hus DANISH €

(☎49 26 10 43; Strandgade 70; dishes Dkr32-98; ⌚10am-5pm Mon-Sat) What better place to tuck into Danish classics than a snug, lopsided 17th-century house. Gobble down honest, solid staples such as *smørrebrød*, herring, fried pork and homemade *fiskefrikadeller* (Danish fish cakes) with remoulade. Leave room for the Grand Marnier pancakes.

Information

Tourist Office (☎49 21 13 33; www.visitnordjaelland.com; Havnepladsen 3; ⌚10am-5pm Mon-Fri, to 2pm Sat & Sun late Jun-early Aug) Opposite the train station.

Getting There & Away

BOAT Regular ferries cross to Helsingborg in Sweden.

TRAIN Trains between Copenhagen and Helsingør run several times hourly (Dkr108, 45 minutes). If you're day tripping it from Copenhagen, buy a 24-hour pass (Dkr130).

ROSKILDE

POP 47,800

Most foreigners who have heard of Roskilde know it either as the home of one of northern Europe's best outdoor music festivals, or the sight of several remarkable Viking ship finds, now housed in an excellent, purpose-built museum. To the Danes, however, it is a city of great royal and religious significance, as it was the capital city long before Copenhagen.

The **Roskilde Festival** (www.roskilde-festival.dk; festival pass Dkr1890) takes place over a long weekend in early July, in fields just outside the city centre. It attracts the biggest international rock and pop names, along with 75,000 music fans, and is renowned for its relaxed, friendly atmosphere. Most visitors camp on-site.

Sights

Roskilde Domkirke CHURCH

(www.roskildedomkirke.dk; Domkirkepladsen; adult/child Dkr60/free; ⌚9am-5pm Mon-Sat, 12.30-5pm Sun Apr-Sep, reduced hours Oct-Mar) Not merely the crème de la crème of Danish cathedrals, this twin-towered, red-brick giant is a designated Unesco World Heritage site. Started by Bishop Absalon in 1170, the building has been rebuilt and tweaked so many times that it's now a superb catalogue of 800 years' worth of Danish architecture.

As the royal mausoleum, it contains the crypts of 37 Danish kings and queens. The chapel of King Christian IV, off the northern side of the cathedral, contains the builder king himself.

The Chapel of the Magi is adorned with fantastic 15th-century frescos (the largest in Denmark), as well as the incomparably ornate Renaissance sepulchres of Christian III and Frederik II.

TOP CHOICE Viking Ship Museum MUSEUM

(www.vikingeskibsmuseet.dk; Vindeboder 12; adult/child May-Sep Dkr115/free, Oct-Apr Dkr80/free, boat trip excl museum admission Dkr80; ⌚10am-5pm late Jun-Aug, to 4pm rest of yr, boat trips daily May-Sep) From the northern side of the cathedral, walk across a field where wildflowers blanket the unexcavated remains of Roskilde's original medieval town, and continue through a green belt all the way to the well-presented Viking Ship Museum. Here you'll find five reconstructed Viking ships excavated from Roskilde Fjord in 1962. The museum is excellent and also incorporates fascinating waterfront workshops where replica ships are built using Viking-era techniques. From May to the end of September, you can take a boat trip on the water in one of them; see the website for sailing times.

Sleeping

Danhostel Roskilde HOSTEL €
(46 35 21 84; www.danhostel.dk/roskilde; Vindeboder 7; dm/s/d/tr Dkr250/500/650/750;) While this harbourside hostel is smart and modern, we found the private bathrooms less than pristine on our last visit. Equally unimpressive is the wi-fi charge (Dkr20 per hour). Though made up of small three-, four-, five-, six- or eight-bed dorms, most are offered as private rooms. It's adjacent to the Viking Ship Museum.

Information

Tourist Office (www.visitroskilde.com; Stændertorvet 1; 10am-5pm Mon-Fri, 10am-2pm Sat Jul & Aug, reduced hr rest of yr) On the main square near the cathedral.

Getting There & Around

Trains from Copenhagen to Roskilde are frequent (Dkr96, 25 minutes). If you're day tripping it from Copenhagen, buy a 24-hour pass (Dkr130).

Odense

POP 168,800

Denmark's middle island of Funen is often bypassed by visitors, but Odense is a cheerful, compact city, ideal for feet and bicycles, and with enough diversions to keep you hooked for a day or two. It was here that Hans Christian Andersen entered the world, a fact hard to miss given the city's string of Andersen-related attractions.

Sights

TOP CHOICE HC Andersens Hus MUSEUM
(www.museum.odense.dk; Bangs Boder 29; adult/child Dkr70/free; 10am-5pm daily Jul & Aug, reduced hours Sep-Jun) Lying amid the miniaturised streets of the old poor quarter, this museum delivers a thorough and lively telling of the amazing life Andersen lived, put into an interesting historical context and leavened by some good audiovisual material. Andersen was supposedly born in the corner room of the building, although the author himself denied this in later life.

Sleeping

Cabinn HOTEL €€
(63 14 57 00; www.cabinn.com; Østre Stationsvej 7; s/d/tr from Dkr495/675/805;) Right by the station, the low-cost Cabinn chain offers modern, clean, no-frills rooms. The beds are narrow and the rooms lack charm, but the price, free wi-fi and central location make it an excellent choice for the kronor conscious.

Danhostel Odense City HOSTEL €
(63 11 04 25; www.cityhostel.dk; Østre Stationsvej 31; dm/s/d/tr from Dkr250/450/620/655;) An excellent, modern 139-bed place, with four- and six-bed dorms, a kitchen and laundry facilities, located alongside the train and bus stations. All rooms have a bathroom and wi-fi is free.

Eating

Olivia Brasserie INTERNATIONAL €€
(www.oliviabrasserie.dk; Vintapperstræde 37; lunch Dkr68-135, 2-/3-course dinner from Dkr200/250; 10am-11pm Mon-Fri, 9am-11pm Sat, 9am-3pm Sun) A *hyggelig* (cosy) combo of chintzy chandeliers, old portraits and vested waiters, this relaxed local favourite draws everyone from ladies who lunch to shopped-out teens. Fuelling the conversation is a solid selection of fresh, homely grub, from soup, quiche and burgers to giant salads made with beautiful ingredients. Dinner is a more elaborate pan-European affair.

Drinking & Entertainment

Nightlife is centred on Brandts Passage, a pedestrian corridor lined with boutiques, restaurants, bars and cafes, many with outdoor seating in summer.

On Thursdays, from July to mid-August, Kongens Have is the setting for free and highly popular weekly music concerts which normally start at 7pm, though it's best to check www.odense.dk for updates.

Information

Tourist Office (66 12 75 20; www.visitodense.com; Vestergade 2; 9.30am-6pm Mon-Fri, 10am-3pm Sat, 11am-2pm Sun Jul & Aug, reduced hr rest of yr) Located at Rådhus, a 900m walk from the train station.

Getting There & Away

Odense is on the main railway line between Copenhagen (Dkr258, 1½ hours, at least twice hourly), Aarhus (Dkr224, 1¾ hours, twice hourly), Aalborg (Dkr346, three hours, once or twice hourly) and Esbjerg (Dkr204, 80 minutes, one to two times hourly).

Buses leave from the rear of the train station. **Fynbus** (www.fynbus.dk) runs bus services between Odense to all major towns on Funen.

Jutland

Denmark doesn't have a north–south divide; culturally, spiritually and to a great extent politically, it is divided into Jutland...and all the rest. Jutlanders are different. Sturdy, down to earth, unpretentious, hard-working. Add to this brooding landscapes, fine art museums and the understated cool of 'second city' Aarhus, and you too might concede that there's something about Jutland.

AARHUS

POP 252,200

Always the bridesmaid, never the bride, Aarhus (*oar*-hus) stands in the shadow of its bigger, brasher sibling, Copenhagen. But Denmark's affable runner-up city has hipster boutiques, bars and cafes, world-class dining and fantastic museums.

Sights & Activities

TOP CHOICE ARoS MUSEUM
(www.aros.dk; adult/child Dkr100/free; ⏲10am-6pm Tue & Fri-Sun, to 10pm Wed & Thu) One of the top three art galleries in Denmark, ARoS lures with its Golden Age masterpieces, Danish modernist works and arresting contemporary creations. Curiously, Dante's *The Divine Comedy* provides the museum's main theme. The museum's temporary exhibitions are varied and often impressive, while both the gift shop and cafe are top notch.

Den Gamle By MUSEUM
(Old Town; www.dengamleby.dk; Viborgvej 2; adult/child Dkr135/free; ⏲9am-6pm late Jun–mid-Aug, 10am-5pm Apr-late Jun & mid-Aug–mid-Nov, reduced hr rest of yr) The Danes' seemingly limitless enthusiasm for dressing up and recreating history reaches its zenith at Den Gamle By. It's an engaging open-air museum of 75 half-timbered houses brought here from around Denmark and reconstructed as a provincial town. The museum is on Viborgvej, 1.1km from the central train station.

Sleeping

Havnhotellet HOTEL €
(www.havnehotellet.dk; Marselisborg Havnevej 20; s/d/tr Dkr565/565/775; P 📶) These good-looking, good-value rooms down at the marina are fresh off the Ikea production line. All booking is done online (hence no phone number), and check-in is via a computer too. The hotel is about 1.5km south of the centre (off Strandvejen; catch buses 16 or 18). Tip: choose a room on the 1st floor (1.sal), as ground-floor rooms lack privacy.

City Sleep-In HOTEL €
(☎86 19 20 55; www.citysleep-in.dk; Havnegade 20; dm Dkr180, d Dkr500, without bathroom Dkr450; @📶) Run by a youth organisation, the City Sleep-In is in a central former mariners' hotel. It's casual and the rooms are a bit rundown, but it's a cheerful place and by far the best budget option in the centre. Sheet hire costs Dkr50 and towels are Dkr20 if you don't have your own.

Eating

The Latin Quarter is good for bistro-style cafes; Skolegade (and its extension, Mejlgade) delivers a handful of excellent budget options.

TOP CHOICE St Pauls Apothek MODERN SCANDINAVIAN €€
(☎86 12 08 33; www.stpaulsapothek.dk; Jægergårdsgade 76; sharing plates Dkr85-135; ⏲5.30pm-midnight Tue-Thu, to 2am Fri & Sat) This ex-pharmacy is one of Aarhus' hottest, best-value dining destinations; at the helm is young-gun chef Christian Bøjlund, whose stint at restaurant

JUTLAND FERRY PORTS

Ferries to Sweden and Norway run from two ports at the top tip of Jutland: Frederikshavn (Stena Line to Gothenburg and Oslo) and Hirtshals (Color Line and Fjord Line to Bergen, Kristiansand, Stavanger, Langesund and Larvik, Norway). See p988 for ferry companies.

Trains run from Copenhagen (Dkr416) via Odense, Aarhus and Aalborg to Frederikshavn; change at Hjørring for Hirtshals. In Frederikshavn, the station is 600m north of the ferry terminal; in Hirtshals, the main station (best for Fjord Line) is 500m south of the harbour, where there's a second stop at the Color Line terminal.

heavyweight Noma translates into confident New Nordic dishes. The focus is on sharing plates (three dishes per head should suffice), impressively paired with killer cocktails.

Oli Nico INTERNATIONAL €

(www.olinico.dk; Mejlgade 35; classic dishes Dkr50-125; ⏲11.30am-2pm & 5.30-9pm Mon-Fri, noon-2pm & 5.30-9pm Sat, 5.30-9pm Sun) You may need to fight for one of the prized tables at Oli Nico, a small deli-restaurant with a menu of classic dishes at astoundingly good prices (*moules-frites* for Dkr60, rib-eye steak for Dkr125 – both with homemade chips!). The daily changing three-course menu may be Aarhus' best-kept secret.

Drinking & Entertainment

Aarhus is the nation's music capital, with no shortage of quality music gigs in venues from dignified concert halls to beer-fuelled boltholes. For the lowdown on what's happening around town, click onto www.visitaarhus.com or www.aoa.dk (in Danish).

Radar LIVE MUSIC

(www.radarlive.dk; Godsbanen, Skovgaardsgade 3; ⏲live music Thu-Sat) You'll find this rocking live music hot spot inside the Godsbanen freight yard, a new cultural hub for Aarhus (see www.godsbanen.dk). On offer is both home-grown and international alternative music acts, with sounds spanning metal, rock and jazz to electropop, techno and folk.

Information

Visit Aarhus provides information online (www.visitaarhus.com), by phone (☎87 31 50 10), at summer booths and via touch-screens around town. Smartphone users can also download the free Visit Aarhus app.

Getting There & Away

BUS From the bus station (Fredensgade), **Abildskou** (☎70 21 08 88; www.abildskou.dk) runs express bus line 888 up to nine times daily between Aarhus and Copenhagen's Valby station (adult/child Dkr300/150, three hours), with connections to Copenhagen airport (Kastrup). For information on travel to other destinations in Jutland, visit www.dsb.dk.

TRAIN Aarhus is well connected by train, including Copenhagen via Odense (Dkr358, three hours, twice hourly).

SKAGEN

POP 8350

The town of Skagen (pronounced 'skain') is a busy working harbour and Denmark's northernmost settlement. It's just a couple of kilometres from the dramatic sandy spit beloved of artists, where the country finally peters out at Grenen, a slender point of wave-washed sand, where seals bask and seagulls soar.

Sights

Grenen OUTDOORS

The neat finger of sand that is the tip of Denmark is the culmination of a long, curving sweep of sand at Grenen, about 3km northeast of Skagen along Rte 40. Crowds head along the last stretch of beach for the 30-minute walk to the tip. Bathing is strictly forbidden here because of the ferocious tidal currents and often turbulent seas that collide to create mane-tossing white horses.

From late June to mid-August, bus 99 runs from Skagen station to Grenen (Dkr15) five times daily until 5pm.

Sleeping

TOP CHOICE **Finns Hotel Pension** GUESTHOUSE €€

(☎98 45 01 55; www.finnshotelpension.dk; Østre Strandvej 63; s Dkr525-775, d Dkr750-975; ⏲May-late Sep; Wi-Fi) Take a 1923-vintage 'log cabin' built for a Norwegian count, fill it with art, antiques and memorabilia, and you have this fabulously atmospheric slumber spot. Gay-friendly, TV-free and adults-only (no kids under 15), Finns offers six individually decorated rooms, with accommodating hosts, a stone's throw from the beach.

Danhostel Skagen HOSTEL €

(☎98 44 22 00; www.danhostel.dk/skagen; Rolighedsvej 2; dm/s/d Dkr180/475/625; ⏲Mar-Nov; P Wi-Fi) Well kept, very popular and 1km from the centre; book ahead in summer. Rates drop sharply in low season.

Eating & Drinking

Around half a dozen seafood shacks line the harbour selling good seafood to eat inside, outside or takeaway. Freshly caught prawns are the favourite fare, costing around Dkr9[illegible] for a generous helping. Here you'll also find a bakery.

Information

The **tourist office** (☎98 44 13 77; www.skagen.dk; Vestre Strandvej 10; ⏲9am-4pm Mon-Sat, 10am-2pm Sun late Jun–mid-Aug) is by the harbour.

Getting There & Away

Nordjyske Jernbaner (www.njba.dk) runs train to Frederikshavn (Dkr60, 36 minutes, once or twice hourly on weekdays, every two hours on weekends). Bus 99 runs between Hirtshals and

Skagen (Dkr50, one hour 20 minutes, two to four daily) from late June to mid-August only.

SWEDEN

As progressive and civilised as it may be, Sweden is a wild place. Its scenery ranges from barren moonscapes and impenetrable forests in the far north to sunny beaches and lush farmland further south. Its short summers and long winters mean that people cling to every last speck of summer sunshine, while in winter locals rely on candlelight and *glögg* (mulled wine) to warm their spirits. But lovers of the outdoors will thrive here in any season: winter sees skiing and dog-sledding, while the warmer months invite long hikes, swimming and sunbathing, canoeing, cycling, you name it. For less rugged types, there's always restaurant- and nightclub-hopping and museum-perusing in cosmopolitan Stockholm, lively Göteborg and beyond.

Stockholm

08 / POP 1.4 MILLION

Beautiful capital cities are no rarity in Europe, but Stockholm is near the top of the list for sheer loveliness. The saffron-and-cinnamon buildings that cover its 14 islands rise starkly out of the surrounding ice-blue water, honeyed in sunlight and frostily elegant in cold weather. The city's charms are irresistible. From its movie-set Old Town (Gamla Stan) to its ever-modern fashion sense and impeccable taste in food and design, the city acts like an immersion school in aesthetics.

Sights

Once you get over the armies of tourists wielding ice-cream cones and shopping bags, you'll discover that Gamla Stan, the oldest part of Stockholm, is also its most beautiful. The city emerged here in the 13th century and grew with Sweden's power until the 17th century, when the castle of Tre Kronor, symbol of that power, burned to the ground.

Kungliga Slottet PALACE

(Royal Palace; www.royalcourt.se; Slottsbacken; adult/student & child Skr150/75, valid for 7 days; 10am-5pm mid-May–mid-Sep) Constructed over the ashes of Tre Kronor castle, this 'new' palace – whose sumptuous baroque interior comprises 608 rooms – is the largest active royal palace in the world. The sumptuous Royal Apartments – two floors of royal pomp and princely portraits – overwhelm with their opulence and size, so much so that it's difficult to focus on individual detail.

Sceptres, royal swords, coronation gown and crowns are displayed at **Skattkammaren** (Treasury), by the southern entrance to the palace near Slottskyrkan (Chapel); the Changing of the Guard takes place in the outer courtyard at 12.15pm Monday to Saturday and 1.15pm Sunday from late April to August.

Nobelmuseet MUSEUM

(http://nobelmuseet.se; Stortorget; adult/senior & student/child Skr80/60/free; 10am-6pm Jun-Aug, 11am-8pm Sep-May) Presenting the history of the Nobel Prize and its founder, Alfred Nobel, this excellent museum features great short films about the achievements of past laureates as well as changing exhibitions about art, science, creativity and inspiration.

Storkyrkan CHURCH

(Great Church ; www.stockholmsdomkyrkoforsamling.se; Trångsund 1; adult/student Skr40/free; 9am-4pm) Near the palace is the Great Church – the closest Stockholm comes to a cathedral, consecrated in 1306. Its most notable feature is the splendid life-sized *St George & the Dragon* sculpture, dating from the late 15th century.

TOP CHOICE **Skansen** MUSEUM

(www.skansen.se; Djurgårdsvägen; adult/senior/child Skr150/130/60; 10am-10pm late Jun-Aug) The world's first open-air museum, this 'Sweden in miniature' is divided into regions, complete with traditional houses, nature, handicrafts and foods. Enclosures showcase moose, reindeer, wolverine and other native wildlife.

Nordiska Museet MUSEUM

(www.nordiskamuseet.se; Djurgårdsvägen 6-16; adult/under 19yr Skr90/free; 10am-5pm daily Jun-Aug, 10am-5pm Thu-Tue, to 8pm Wed Sep-May) The epic Nordiska really delves into Swedish culture with its enormous collection of all things Swedish, from 'Power of Fashion', spanning 300 years, to sacred Sámi objects, Strindberg paintings, folk art and embroidery, intricate dolls' houses, festivals, weddings and rituals.

Stockholm

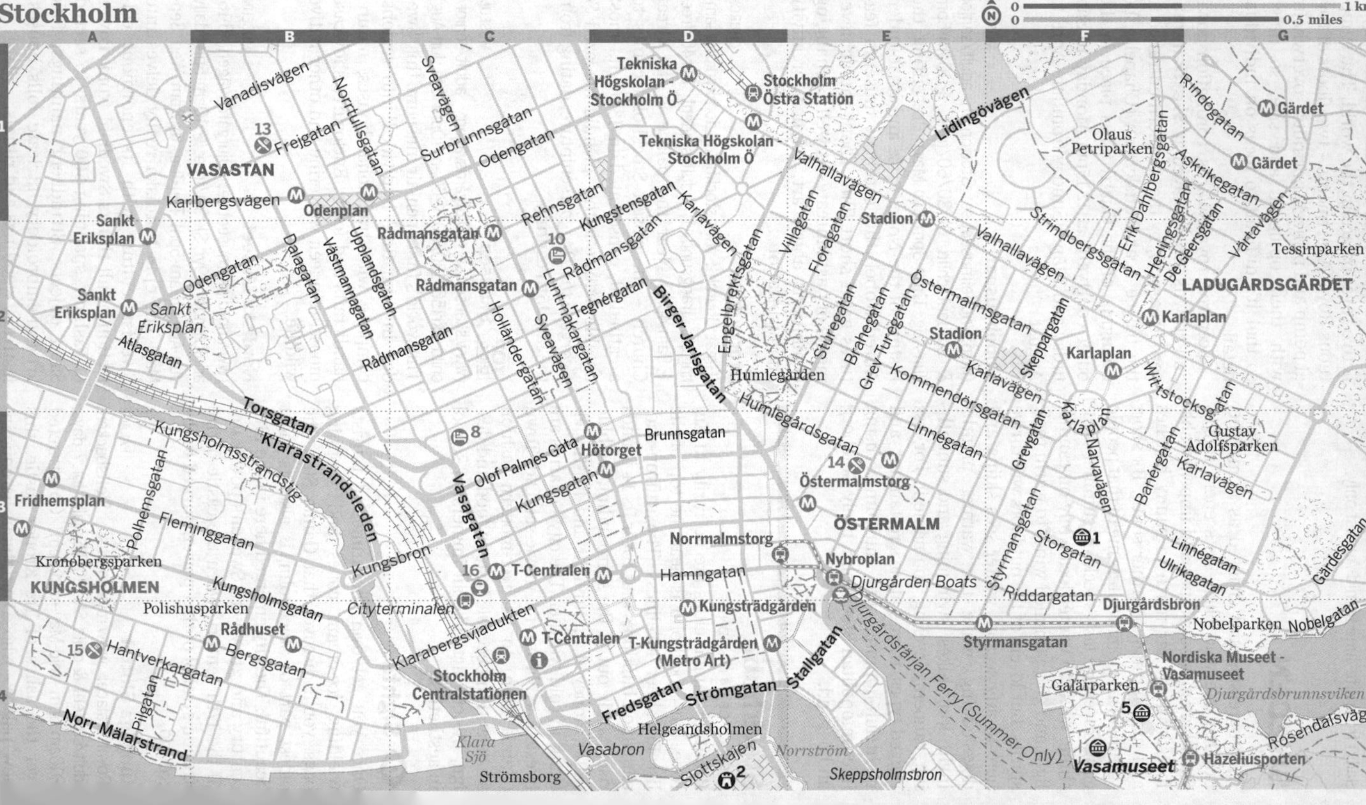
0.5 miles
1 km
VASASTAN
ÖSTERMALM
LADUGÅRDSGÄRDET
KUNGSHOLMEN
Gärdet
Tessinparken
Rindögatan
Askrikegatan
Värtavägen
Valhallavägen
Lidingövägen
Olaus Petriparken
Erik Dahlbergsgatan
Strindbergsgatan
Karlaplan
Gustav Adolfsparken
Narvavägen
Karlavägen
Banérgatan
Linnégatan
Ulrikagatan
Gärdesgatan
Nobelparken
Nobelgatan
Nordiska Museet - Vasamuseet
Djurgårdsbrunnsviken
Rosendalsväg
Hazeliusporten
Galärparken
Vasamuseet
Djurgårdsbron
Riddargatan
Storgatan
Styrmansgatan
Djurgårdsfärjan Ferry (Summer Only)
Djurgården Boats
Nybroplan
Norrmalmstorg
Hamngatan
Östermalmstorg
Humlegårdsgatan
Kommendörsgatan
Östermalmsgatan
Stadion
Sturegatan
Brahegatan
Grev Turegatan
Humlegården
Engelbrektsgatan
Villagatan
Floragatan
Birger Jarlsgatan
Brunnsgatan
Kungsträdgården
T-Kungsträdgården (Metro Art)
Strömgatan
Stallgatan
Fredsgatan
Skeppsholmsbron
Norrström
Helgeandsholmen
Slottskajen
Vasabron
Strömsborg
Klara Sjö
Stockholm Centralstationen
T-Centralen
Klarabergsviadukten
Cityterminalen
Kungsbron
Vasagatan
Kungsgatan
Olof Palmes Gata
Hötorget
Holländergatan
Sveavägen
Luntmakargatan
Tegnérgatan
Rådmansgatan
Kungstensgatan
Rehnsgatan
Tekniska Högskolan - Stockholm Ö
Stockholm Östra Station
Surbrunnsgatan
Odengatan
Norrtullsgatan
Vanadisvägen
Freigatan
Karlbergsvägen
Odenplan
Upplandsgatan
Västmannagatan
Dalagatan
Sankt Eriksplan
Atlasgatan
Torsgatan
Klarastrandsleden
Kungsholmsstrandstig
Polhemsgatan
Fleminggatan
Fridhemsplan
Kronobergsparken
Polishusparken
Kungsholmsgatan
Rådhuset
Bergsgatan
Hantverkargatan
Pilgatan
Norr Mälarstrand

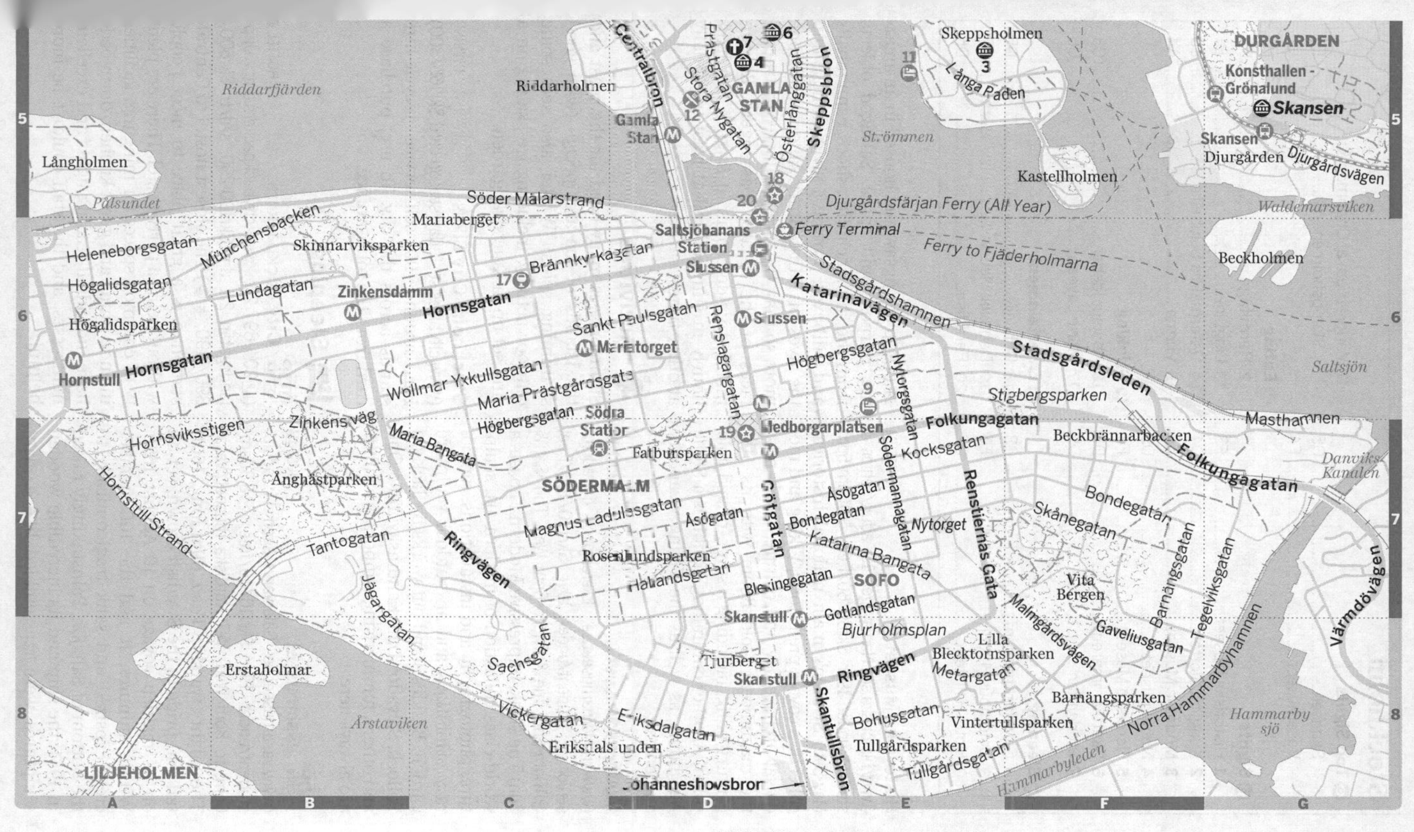

Riddarfjärden
Riddarholmen
Centralbron
Gamla Stan
Prästgatan
Stora Nygatan
GAMLA STAN
Österlånggatan
Skeppsbron
Skeppsholmen
Långa Raden
Strömmen
Kastellholmen
DURGÅRDEN
Konsthallen - Grönalund
Skansen
Djurgården
Djurgårdsvägen
Waldemarsviken
Beckholmen
Långholmen
Pålsundet
Söder Mälarstrand
Mariaberget
Djurgårdsfärjan Ferry (All Year)
Ferry Terminal
Ferry to Fjäderholmarna
Saltsjöbanans Station
Slussen
Stadsgårdshamnen
Katarinavägen
Stadsgårdsleden
Saltsjön
Heleneborgsgatan
Münchensbacken
Skinnarviksparken
Högalidsgatan
Lundagatan
Zinkensdamm
Brännkyrkagatan
Hornsgatan
Högalidsparken
Hornstull
Sankt Paulsgatan
Mariatorget
Renslagargatan
Högbergsgatan
Nytorgsgatan
Stigbergsparken
Masthamnen
Wollmar Yxkullsgatan
Maria Prästgårdsgata
Högbergsgatan
Södra Station
Medborgarplatsen
Folkungagatan
Beckbrännarbacken
Hornsviksstigen
Zinkens väg
Maria Bangata
Fatburparken
Kocksgatan
Södermannagatan
Danviks Kanalen
Ånghästparken
SÖDERMALM
Åsögatan
Bondegatan
Skånegatan
Hornstull Strand
Magnus Ladulåsgatan
Götgatan
Nytorget
Renstiernas Gata
Värmdövägen
Tantogatan
Katarina Bangata
Rosenlundsparken
Ringvägen
Hallandsgatan
Blekingegatan
SOFO
Vita Bergen
Barnängsgatan
Tegelviksgatan
Jägargatan
Skanstull
Gotlandsgatan
Bjurholmsplan
Malmgårdsvägen
Gaveliusgatan
Lilla Blecktornsparken
Norra Hammarbyhamnen
Erstaholmar
Sachsgatan
Tjurberget
Metargatan
Barnängsparken
Vickergatan
Eriksdalsgatan
Skantullsbron
Bohusgatan
Vintertullsparken
Hammarby sjö
Årstaviken
Eriksdalslunden
Tullgårdsparken
Tullgårdsgatan
Hammarbyleden
LILJEHOLMEN
Johanneshovsbron

Stockholm

Top Sights
- Skansen ... G5
- Vasamuseet ... F4

Sights
1 Historiska Museet ... F3
2 Kungliga Slottet ... D4
3 Moderna Museet ... E5
4 Nobelmuseet ... D5
5 Nordiska Museet ... F4
6 Skattkammaren ... D5
7 Storkyrkan ... D5

Sleeping
8 City Backpackers ... C3
9 Columbus Hotell ... E6
10 Hotel Hellsten ... C2
11 Vandrarhem af Chapman & Skeppsholmen ... E5

Eating
12 Hermitage ... D5
13 Linguini ... B1
14 Östermalms Saluhall ... E3
15 Vurma ... A4

Drinking
16 Absolut Icebar ... C3
17 Marie Laveau ... C6

Entertainment
18 Debaser ... D5
19 Debaser Medis ... D7
20 Paradise ... D5

Historiska Museet MUSEUM
(www.historiska.se; Narvavägen 13; adult/senior & student/under 19yr Skr80/60/free; ⌚10am-5pm May-Sep) Sweden's main national historical collection covers prehistoric, Viking and medieval archaeology and culture. Don't miss the magnificent Gold Room with its 5th-century bling, including a seven-ringed gold collar. Another enthralling exhibit is a Stone Age home, as well as the Viking weaponry and boats.

Moderna Museet MUSEUM
(www.modernamuseet.se; Exercisplan 4; adult/senior & student/under 19yr Skr120/100/free; ⌚10am-8pm Tue & Fri, to 6pm Wed, Thu, Sat & Sun) The sleek, impressive Moderna boasts a world-class collection of modern art, sculpture, photography and installations, temporary exhibitions and an outdoor sculpture garden. Besides stand-out works by Jackson Pollock, Salvador Dalí, Kandinsky, Yoko Ono and others, mesmerising temporary exhibits are always here.

TOP CHOICE **Vasamuseet** MUSEUM
(www.vasamuseet.se; Galärvarvsvägen 14; adult/student/under 19yr Skr110/80/free; ⌚8.30am-6pm, to 8pm Wed; 7 Nordiska museet/Vasa) The mighty warship *Vasa*, 69m long, 160ft tall and pride of the Swedish crown, set off on its maiden voyage on 10 August 1628. Within minutes, it and the 100-member crew capsized and sank tragicomically to the bottom of Saltsjön. Painstakingly raised in 1961, the ship and its incredible wooden sculptures were reassembled like a giant 14,000-piece jigsaw and housed in an amazing purpose-built space. Salvaged objects from the ship, including shoes, cannonballs and pillboxes, provide a vivid glimpse into the lives of 17th-century sailors, but none more so than the forensically reconstructed faces of the ill-fated passengers. Recommended guided tours in English run half-hourly in summer and at least twice daily at other times.

Activities

Summer sees many head for the coast and the islands of the archipelago (with good swimming spots). Winter also sees some outdoor activity, including ice skating on a rink set up in Kungsträdgården.

Stockholm City Bikes CYCLING
(www.citybikes.se; 3-day/season card Skr165/300) Has around 90 self-service bicycle-hire stands across the city. To use, purchase a card from the tourist office.

Sleeping

TOP CHOICE **City Backpackers** HOSTEL €
(☎20 69 20; www.citybackpackers.org; Upplandsgatan 2a; dm Skr190-290, s/d/tr Skr600/890/1190; ❄@) The closest hostel to Centralstationen is a great place to meet people without being a party hostel. There are plenty of common spaces for mingling, facilities include sauna and guest kitchen, dorm beds have individual reading lights and excellent mattresses, and the staff couldn't be more helpful.

TOP CHOICE Hotel Hellsten HOTEL €€

(☎661 86 00; www.hellsten.se; Luntmakargatan 68; r from Skr1090; 📶) Hip Hellsten is owned by anthropologist Per Hellsten and features objects from his travels and life, including Congo tribal masks and his grandmother's chandelier. Rooms are supremely comfortable and individually styled, with themes spanning rustic Swedish to Indian exotica. The sleek bathrooms sport phones and hand-cut Greek slate. Extras include a sauna and small fitness room, as well as live jazz in the lounge on Thursday evenings.

STF Vandrarhem Gärdet HOSTEL €

(☎463 22 99; www.svenskaturistforeningen.se; Sandhamnsgatan 59; s/d from Skr495/760; @📶) Located in quiet Gärdet, a quick metro ride from Östermalm, Stockholm's first 'designer hostel' features smart, contemporary rooms featuring red pin chairs. Each room comes equipped with a flat-screen TV, comfy beds and a hotel-grade private bathroom. Sheets and towels are included in the price. Take bus 1 from Centralstationen (or Gärdet tunnelbana stop) to Östhammarsgatan bus stop.

Vandrarhem af Chapman & Skeppsholmen HOSTEL €

(☎463 22 66; www.stfchapman.com; dm/r Skr260/590; @📶) The legendary *af Chapman* is a storied vessel, well anchored in a superb location off Skeppsholmen. To nab a bunk below decks, book seriously in advance; otherwise you'll end up rooming at the Skeppsholmen hostel on dry land, with the kitchen and TV lounge, but without the nautical atmosphere and the portholes. Friendly staff are knowledgeable about the city.

Columbus Hotell HOTEL €€

(☎50 31 12 00; www.columbus.se; Tjärhovsgatan 11; s/d Skr1450/1750, budget s/d from Skr895/1035; @📶) This historic building is nestled in a quiet part of Södermalm and set around a cobblestone courtyard by a pretty park. In the Columbus Loft there are a few budget rooms with shared facilities and TV, comfy Jensen beds and bright furnishings; the other two floors boast larger, more luxurious rooms. No lift.

Jumbo Stay HOSTEL €€

(☎59 36 04 00; www.jumbostay.com; Jumbovägen 4, Stockholm Arlanda Airport; dm Skr350-400, s/d Skr650/1150; P📶) It's a hostel, Jim, but not as you know it. This converted 747 at Arlanda Airport is hugely popular with flashpackers who've always dreamed of sleeping in style on a plane, thanks to the creative use of space and the 24-hour Jumbo bar for night owls. For the ultimate experience, try a night in the cockpit suite. Free transfer bus 14 runs from the terminals to here every 15 minutes.

Eating

For solid everyman cuisine, head to Odenplan, and for inventive vegetarian fare try Södermalm's bohemian joints or Luntmakargatan and surrounding streets.

Östermalms Saluhall MARKET €

(www.ostermalmshallshallen.se; Östermalmstorg; mains Skr80-115; ⏰9.30am-6pm Mon-Thu, to 7pm Fri, to 4pm Sat; ✎) Stockholm's historic, blue-ribbon market spoils taste buds with fresh fish, seafood and meat, as well as fruits, vegetables and hard-to-find cheeses. In addition to the market, it's full of small eateries serving everything from sushi to falafel and lasagne. The building itself is a Stockholm landmark, designed as a Romanesque cathedral of food in 1885.

TOP CHOICE Hermitage VEGETARIAN €€

(Stora Nygatan 11; lunch/dinner Skr100/110; ⏰11am-8pm Mon-Sat, noon-4pm Sun; ✎) We love this small vegetarian cafe. Its tables are too close together and it does get crowded when everyone from Stockholm students to vegie-hunting tourists pile in, but with good reason: the vegetarian dishes that make up the changing daily buffet are cooked with flair and a real understanding of flavours. Expect the likes of spicy vegetable fritters, brown rice, vegetable curry, macrobiotic salads and a plethora of cold side dishes.

Vurma CAFE €

(www.vurma.se; Polhemsgatan 15; salads Skr70-95; ⏰8am-6pm Mon-Fri, 9am-6pm Sat & Sun; ✎) Squeeze in among the chattering punters, fluff up the cushions and eavesdrop over a vegan latte at this kitsch-hip cafe-bakery. The scrumptious sandwiches and salads are utterly inspired; try the chèvre cheese, marinated chicken, walnuts and honey.

Linguini ITALIAN €€

(☎31 39 15; Frejgatan 48; mains Skr149-169; ⏰noon-10pm; ✎) True to the name, linguini does feature a lot on the menu of this friendly Italian joint in Norrmalm. Think exposed brick walls, casual ambience, and some of the best linguini with northern Italian sausage and porcini mushrooms you're likely to taste anywhere. Nonlinguini offerings include ricotta and porcini tortelloni and a superb panna cotta.

 Drinking & Entertainment

Good neighbourhood hang-outs *(kvarterskrog)* abound, but generally the shiny-miniskirt crowd hangs out in Östermalm, while the hipsters and arty types slink around Södermalm – any of the bars along Skånegatan are a good bet.

Marie Laveau BAR
(www.marielaveau.se; Hornsgatan 66; ⏲5pm-midnight Tue & Wed, to 3am Thu-Sat) Sip on inspired cocktails at this designer-grunge bar on one of the main drags through Södermalm – think chequered floor and subway-style tiled columns. DJs hit the deck in the raucous basement bar from Wednesday to Saturday, with theme nights including hip hop and breaks, funk and soul, and disco meets Ibiza house.

Absolut Icebar BAR
(☎050 56 35 20; www.nordicseahotel.com; Vasaplan 4, Nordic Sea Hotel; booked online/drop in Skr180/195; ⏲11.15am-midnight Sun-Wed, to 1am Thu-Sat Jun-Aug) OK, it's touristy. But you're intrigued, admit it: a bar built entirely out of ice, where you drink from glasses carved from ice at tables made of ice amid ice sculptures. The admission price gets you warm booties, mittens, a parka and one drink (avoid Wolfsbane). Refill drinks cost Skr95.

Debaser CLUB
(☎30 56 20; www.debaser.se; Karl Johanstorg 1, Slussen; ⏲7pm-1am Sun-Thu, 8pm-3am Fri & Sat) The king of rock clubs hides away under the Slussen interchange. Emerging or bigger-name acts play most nights, while the killer club nights span anything from rock-steady to punk and electronica. One metro stop further south, **Debaser Medis** (☎694 7900; Medborgarplatsen 8; Ⓜ T-Medborgarplatsen) is its sprawling sister venue, with three floors rocking to live acts and DJ-spun tunes.

Paradise CLUB, GAY
(☎643 39 46; Gula Gången; admission Skr110-140; ⏲11pm-3am Fri) Stockholm's biggest gay club turns up the volume with mainstream hits on the main dance floor, serious house and tech-house in the basement, and good, old-fashioned disco in the Panoramabar. The place gets packed and happily sweaty, and this may well be your idea of heaven.

Information

CityAkuten (☎020-150 150; www.cityakuten.se; Apelbergsgatan 48; ⏲8am-6pm Mon-Thu, to 5pm Fri, 10am-3pm Sat) Emergency health and dental care.

Lonely Planet (www.lonelyplanet.com/sweden/stockholm)

Sidewalk Express (www.sidewalkexpress.se; per hr Skr30) Rows of computer monitors and tall red ticket machines mark out these self-service internet stations, which roam the city. They're found at various locations, including City Bus Terminal, Centralstationen, Stockhom Arlanda Airport and numerous 7-Eleven locations around town.

Tourist Office (☎50 82 85 08; www.stockholmtown.se; Vasagatan 14; ⏲9am-6pm Mon-Fri, 10am-5pm Sat, 10am-4pm Sun May–mid-Sep) Directly across the street (Vasagatan) from Centralstationen. Busy but helpful, with plenty of maps and brochures.

Getting There & Away

Air

Stockholm Arlanda Airport (☎010-109 00 00; www.swedavia.se) Stockholm's main airport, 45km north of the city centre, reached from central Stockholm by bus and express train.

Stockholm Skavsta Airport (☎0155-28 04 00; www.skavsta-air.se) Around 100km south of Stockholm, near Nyköping, mostly used by low-cost carriers such as Ryanair.

Boat

There are ferries to Turku and Helsinki (Finland), Riga (Latvia) and Tallinn (Estonia); see p988.

Bus

Cityterminalen (www.cityterminalen.com; ⏲7am-6pm) The main bus station, connected to Centralstationen.

Train

Stockholm is the hub for national and internationa train services run by **Sveriges Järnväg** (SJ; ☎0771-75 75 75; www.sj.se) and **Tågkompaniet** (☎0771-44 41 11; www.tagkompaniet.se). Central stationen is the central train station.

 Getting Around

TO/FROM THE AIRPORT The **Arlanda Express** (www.arlandaexpress.com) train from Centralstationen (Skr260, 20 minutes, every 15 minutes) links the centre with Arlanda. The cheapest option is the **Flygbussarna** (www.flygbussarna.se) bus service between Arlanda and Cityterminalen (Skr99, 40 minutes, every to 15 minutes).

PUBLIC TRANSPORT **Storstockholms Lokaltrafik** (SL; www.sl.se) runs all tunnelban

(T or T-bana) metro trains, local trains and buses. Coupons, tickets and passes can be bought at T-bana stations, Pressbyrån kiosks, SL train stations and SL information offices.

Uppsala

018 / POP 140,500

The historical and spiritual heart of the country, Uppsala has the upbeat party vibe of a university town to balance the weight of its castle, cathedral and university. Peaceful by day and lively by night, it makes an easy day trip from Stockholm, though it's worth lingering overnight to wander the deserted streets and soak up the atmosphere.

Sights

Gamla Uppsala ARCHAEOLOGICAL SITE
(www.arkeologigamlauppsala.se; 115) This terrific site's three **grave mounds** (24hr), named after the Norse gods Odin, Thor and Frey, are said to be those of legendary pre-Viking kings who'd descended from Frey, were mentioned in *Beowulf* (although recent evidence suggests that at least one of the occupants is a woman) and lie in a field including about 300 smaller mounds and a great heathen temple (now with the Christian Gamla Uppsala kyrka planted on top of it). The excellent **Gamla Uppsala Historical Centre** (adult/child Skr60/35; 11am-5pm May-Aug; 115) shows off the finds. The site is located 4km north of the modern city; take bus 115 from Uppsala Centralstation (Skr30, 25 minutes, every 30 minutes).

Uppsala Slott CASTLE
(www.uppsalaslott.se; admission by guided tour only, adult/child Skr80/15; tours in English 12.15pm, 1pm, 2pm & 3pm Tue-Sun Jul & Aug) Originally constructed by Gustav Vasa in the mid-16th century, Uppsala Slott features the state hall where kings were enthroned and a queen abdicated. Not much is left of the castle, since a large chunk of it was destroyed in a fire in 1702. Still, the view of Uppsala from its lofty hilltop position is worth a stroll.

FREE **Domkyrka** CHURCH
(www.uppsaladomkyrka.se; Domkyrkoplan; 8am-6pm May-Sep) Scandinavia's largest cathedral, built to upstage the one in Trondheim, Norway, dominates the city, just as some of those buried there shaped their country, including Reformist Gustav Vasa, his son Johan III and botanist Carl von Linné. Relics of St Erik, Sweden's patron saint, are in a golden coffin in its own chapel.

Sleeping

Hotell & Vandrarhem Kungsängstorg HOSTEL €
(444 20 10; www.vandrarhemuppsala.se; Kungsängstorg 6; hostel dm/s/d Skr200/425/500, hotel s/d/tr Skr790/990/1290; @) Quiet, intimate hostel in a beautifully restored house several blocks from the train station. The staff are lovely, the breakfast is ample, and the main difference between the 'hotel' and 'hostel' rooms is that the former has free bed linen and breakfast included. Hotel prices drop on weekends.

Eating

Casual dining options can be found inside **Saluhallen** (Sankt Eriks Torg; 10am-6pm Mon-Thu, to 7pm Fri, to 4pm Sat, restaurants 11am-4pm Sun), an indoor market between the cathedral and the river.

Information

Tourist Office (727 48 00; www.destinationuppsala.se; Fyristorg 8; 10am-6pm Mon-Fri, to 3pm Sat, also 11am-3pm Sun Jul & Aug)

Getting There & Away

Swebus Express (0200 21 82 18; www.swebus.se) runs regular direct services to Stockholm (from Skr59, 1¼ hours, hourly), which is also connected by frequent **SJ** (www.sj.se) trains (Skr82, 40 minutes to one hour, twice hourly).

Southern Sweden

Artists adore southern Sweden. Down here, the light is softer, the foliage brighter and the shoreline more dazzling and white. Sweden's southernmost county, Skåne (Scania), was Danish property until 1658 and still flaunts its differences.

MALMÖ

040 / POP 280,400

Once dismissed as crime-prone and tatty, Sweden's third-largest city has rebranded itself as progressive and downright cool. Malmö's second wind blew in with the opening of the Öresund bridge and tunnel in 2000, connecting the city to bigger, cooler Copenhagen and creating a dynamic new urban conglomeration.

Sights & Activities

Malmö Museer MUSEUM
(www.malmo.se/museer; Malmöhusvägen; adult/under 19yr Skr40/free; ⏲10am-4pm Jun-Aug) Various museums in and around the imposing **Malmöhus Slott** (Malmöhus Castle) make up the mazelike Malmö Museer. You can walk through the royal apartments, learn about the castle's history, descend into the former prison with displays on crime and punishment, check out vehicles through the ages, and see works by important Swedish artists such as John Bauer and Sigrid Hjerten at the Konstmuseum.

Sleeping

STF Vandrarhem Malmö City HOSTEL €
(☎611 62 20; www.svenskaturistforeningen.se; Rönngatan 1; dm/s/d Skr190/455/510; @) This central hostel has an excellent kitchen, outdoor patio, TV lounge and very helpful staff, and most sights are within easy walking distance. To reach the hostel, take buses 141 or 144 from the train station and get off at Malmö Teatern.

Eating

TOP CHOICE **Salt och Brygga** SWEDISH €€
(☎611 59 40; www.saltobrygga.se; Sundspromenaden 7; lunch mains Skr110-155, dinner mains Skr145-265; ⏲11am-2pm & 5-11pm Mon-Fri, 12.30-4pm & 5-11pm Sat;) Overlooking the Öresund bridge, this stylish Slow Food restaurant serves contemporary organic Swedish cuisine. Flavours are clean and strictly seasonal – think smoked reindeer with chanterelles, seared walleye with kale and pumpkin, goat's cheese and spelt risotto – and the fish is so fresh it may have just jumped out of the sea in front of you. Book for dinner.

Falafel No 1 MIDDLE EASTERN €
(www.falafel-n1.se; Österportsgatan 2; falafels Skr45;) As the name suggests, this is Malmö's best falafel (trust us, we sampled plenty!), immortalised in songs by local band Timbuktu.

Information

Tourist Office (☎34 12 00; www.malmotown.se; Skeppsbron 2; ⏲9am-7pm Mon-Fri, 10am-4pm Sat & Sun) Across the street from Centralstationen.

Getting There & Away

BUS There are two bus terminals with daily departures to Swedish and European destinations. **Swebus Express** (☎0771-21 82 18; www.swebusexpress.com) runs two to four times daily to Stockholm (from Skr479, 8½ hours) and at least five daily to Göteborg (from Skr199, 3½ to four hours); at least two continue to Oslo (from Skr349, eight hours).

GoByBus (www.gobybus.se) has six buses on the Copenhagen–Malmö–Göteborg–Oslo route per day.

TRAIN Trains run to Göteborg (from Skr199, 2½ hours, twice hourly) and Stockholm (from Skr299, 4¼ to 5½ hours, hourly). Regular trains cross to Copenhagen (Skr107, 20 minutes, every 20 minutes), stopping at Copenhagen airport.

> WORTH A TRIP
>
> **LUND**
>
> The centrepiece of the appealing university town of Lund, just 15 minutes from Malmö on the train, is the splendid Romanesque **Domkyrkan** (Kyrkogatan; ⏲8am-6pm Mon-Fri, 9.30am-5pm Sat, to 6pm Sun), with some fantastic gargoyles over the side entrances, a giant turned to stone in the eerie crypt and an astronomical clock that sends the wooden figures whirring into action (at noon and 3pm Monday to Saturday, 1pm and 3pm on Sunday).
>
> The town's most engaging museum, **Kulturen** (www.kulturen.com; Tegnerplatsen; adult/student/under 19 Skr90/45/free; ⏲10am-5pm May-Aug, noon-4pm Tue-Sat Sep-Apr;), is a huge open-air space where you can wander among birch-bark hovels, perfectly preserved cottages, churches, farms and grand 17th-century houses.

Göteborg

☎031 / POP 549,800

Often caught in Stockholm's shadow, gregarious Göteborg (pronounced *yur-te-borg*; Gothenburg in English) socks a mighty good punch of its own. Stockholm may represent the 'big time', but many of the best and brightest ideas originate in this grassroots town.

Sights

The **Haga district**, south of the canal, is Göteborg's oldest suburb, dating back to 1648. In the 1980s and '90s, the area was thoroughly renovated and is now a cute, cobblestone maze of precious cafes and boutique shops.

TOP CHOICE Röda Sten GALLERY

(www.rodasten.com; Röda Sten 1; adult/under 21yr Skr40/free; ⏲noon-5pm Tue-Sun, to 7pm Wed) Occupying a defunct, graffitied power station beside the giant Älvsborgsbron, Röda Sten is one of Sweden's coolest art centres. Its four gritty floors are home to any number of temporary exhibitions, ranging from edgy Swedish photography to New York sound installations.

Stadsmuseum MUSEUM

(City Museum; www.stadsmuseum.goteborg.se; Norra Hamngatan 12, Östindiska huset; adult/under 25yr Skr40/free; ⏲10am-5pm Tue-Sun, to 8pm Wed) Treasures here include subtly lit Viking silver hoards, weaponry and Sweden's only original Viking ship. Other displays cover Göteborg's history, its guilds and a haul of East Indian pottery.

Konstmuseet GALLERY

(www.konstmuseum.goteborg.se; Götaplatsen; adult/under 25yr Skr40/free; ⏲11am-6pm Tue & Thu, to 9pm Wed, 11am-5pm Fri-Sun) Works by the French Impressionists, Rubens, Van Gogh, Rembrandt and Picasso, as well as Scandinavian masters, plus the Hasselblad photo collection. The temporary exhibitions, featuring the best of up-and-coming artists, and the sculpture hall are superb.

Liseberg AMUSEMENT PARK

(www.liseberg.se; Södra Vägen; adult/under 90cm Skr95/free; ⏲11am-11pm Jun–mid-Aug) Scream yourself silly at this mighty theme park southeast of the city centre. Blockbuster rides include the stomach-churning Kanonen, where you're blasted from 0 to 75km/h in less than two seconds, and Europe's tallest freefall tower, Atmosfear, where you plummet for more than 100m in three seconds. There are plenty of gentler rides too.

Sleeping

STF Vandrarhem Stigbergsliden HOSTEL €

(☎24 16 20; www.hostel-gothenburg.com; Stigbergsliden 10; dm/s/d from Skr180/470/675; ⏲reception 4-6pm; @) In a renovated seamen's institute, this homey hostel has history. Staff are helpful, and there's a big kitchen, laundry and TV room. Perks include an inexpensive cafeteria, sheltered garden and bike rental (per day Skr50).

STF Vandrarhem Slottsskogen HOSTEL €

(☎42 65 20; www.sov.nu; Vegagatan 21; hostel dm/s/d from Skr195/380/500, hotel s/d Skr590/890; @) Unlike many Swedish hostels, big, friendly Slottsskogen is a cracking place for meeting other travellers. For a small extra payment there's access to a laundry, sauna and sunbed, and the buffet breakfast (Skr65) is brilliant. If you choose the 'hotel' option, bed linen and breakfast are thrown in for free.

MUSEUM ENTRY

Museum hoppers take note: admission to one of four museums – including the Konstmuseet and Stadsmuseum – gets you into the other three for free.

Eating

Smaka SWEDISH €€

(www.smaka.se; Vasaplatsen 3; mains Skr125-245; ⏲5pm-1am Sun-Thu, to 2am Fri & Sat) You will smak-a your lips when you taste the old-school Swedish *husmanskost* (traditional fare) such as the speciality meatballs with mashed potato and lingonberries and herring with crispbread. More unusual offerings include reindeer with vodka gravy, and the selection of Swedish farm cheeses is well worth a try.

Saluhall Briggen FOOD HALL €€

(www.saluhallbriggen.se; Nordhemsgatan 28; ⏲9am-6pm Mon-Fri, to 3pm Sat; ✎) It might lack the main central market's size, but this covered market will have you drooling over its bounty of fresh bread, cheeses, quiches, seafood and takeaway Thai dishes and sushi. It's particularly handy for the hostel district.

Drinking

The Linné district is home to several friendly student hang-outs serving extremely cheap beer.

Lokal COCKTAIL BAR

(Kyrkogatan 11; ⏲5pm-1am Mon-Sat) Arguably the best bar in Göteborg, this cool hang-out pulls everyone from artists and media types to the odd punk rocker. The drinks are inspired (think kiwi and ginger daiquiri), the fusion nibbles (including organic and vegie options) are excellent, and music spans soul, jazz and electro.

Sejdeln PUB

(Andra Långgatan 28; ⏲4pm-1am Mon-Sat) Extremely popular with students and younger clientele in general, this cosy, wood-panelled pub is the perfect spot for an inexpensive local beer or cider. Get here before the evening rush if you want to do anything other than prop up the bar.

Information

Sidewalk Express (www.sidewalkexpress.se; per hr Skr20) For internet access, at Centralstationen and the 7-Eleven on Vasaplatsen.

Tourist Office (☎368 4200; www.goteborg.com; Kungsportsplatsen 2; ⊙9.30am-8pm daily mid-Jun–mid-Aug, 9.30am-6pm Mon-Fri, 10am-2pm Sat & Sun May–mid-Jun & end Aug) Central and busy, it has a good selection of free brochures and maps.

Getting There & Away

AIR About 25km east of the city, **Landvetter airport** (☎010 109 0000; www.swedavia.se) has over 20 direct daily flights to/from Stockholm and other national and international destinations. **Göteborg City Airport** (www.goteborgairport.se), some 15km north of the city at Säve, is used for budget Ryanair, Wizz Air and Direktflyg flights.

BOAT Göteborg has ferry services to Denmark, Germany and Norway. Take tram 3 or 9 to the **Stena Line** (www.stenaline.se) terminal.

BUS Swebus Express (☎0771-21 82 18; www.swebusexpress.com) operates from the bus terminal (adjacent to the train station) to destinations including Stockholm (Skr379, seven hours, at least four daily), Copenhagen (Skr269, four to five hours, at least three daily), Oslo (Skr219, 3¾ hours) and Malmö (Skr179, 3½ to four hours).

TRAIN From Centralstationen trains run to Stockholm (Skr540, three to 4½ hours, twice hourly), Copenhagen (Skr429, 3¾ hours, hourly), Malmö (Skr321, 3¼ hours, hourly) and other southern Swedish destinations.

Getting Around

Västtrafik (☎0771-41 43 00; www.vasttrafik.se) runs the city's public transport system of buses, trams and ferries. A city transport ticket costs from Skr24. A 24-hour Dagkort (day pass) for the whole city area costs Skr75, or Skr150 for 72 hours.

Gotland

Gorgeous Gotland, adrift in the Baltic, has much to brag about: a Unesco-lauded medieval capital, truffle-sprinkled woods, A-list dining hot spots, talented artisans and more hours of sunshine than anywhere else in Sweden. It's also one of the country's richest historical regions, with around 100 medieval churches and countless prehistoric sites.

Check out www.gotland.net and www.guteinfo.com (in Swedish) – both are good websites for local info.

Getting There & Away

Ferries between Visby and both Nynäshamn and Oskarshamn are operated by **Destination Gotland** (☎0771-22 33 00; www.destinationgotland.se). There are departures to and from Nynäshamn (one to six daily, 3¼ hours) and Oskarshamn (one to three daily, three to four hours). Prices vary according to the season, route and departure time, but adult/student tickets start from Skr258/206.

Getting Around

There are several bike-rental places in Visby.

Kollektiv Trafiken (☎0498-21 41 12; www.gotland.se) runs buses via most villages to all corners of the island.

VISBY

☎0498 / POP 22,600

The port town of Visby is medieval eye candy and enough to warrant a trip to Gotland all by itself. Inside its thick city walls await twisting cobbled streets, fairy-tale wooden cottages, evocative ruins and steep hills with impromptu Baltic views. The city wall, with its 40-plus towers and the spectacular church ruins within, attests to the town's former Hanseatic glory.

Sights

Gotlands Museum MUSEUM

(www.gotlandsmuseum.se; Strandgatan 14; adult/child Skr100/80; ⊙10am-6pm) Highlights at this superb, beautifully presented regional museum include a hall of strategically lit, intricately carved 5th- to 11th-century picture stones and the legendary Spillings Hoard: at 85kg it's the world's largest booty of preserved silver treasure, found as recently as 1999. Don't miss the Hall of Prehistoric Graves, with its chambered tombs and funereal objects, or the medieval wooden sculptures.

Sleeping

Hotel Stenugnen HOTEL €

(☎21 02 11; www.stenungen.nu; Korsgatan 6; Skr545-899; P wi-fi) At this adorable little hotel bright, whitewashed rooms are designed to make you feel as if you're sleeping in a yacht and the location is practically on top of the medieval wall. Plenty of rainy-day distractions are provided and the homemade bread is just delicious.

Fängelse Vandrarhem HOSTEL €
(☎20 60 50; www.visbyfangelse.se; Skeppsbron 1; dm/s/d from Skr290/400/500; 📶) As hard to get into as it once was to get out of, this former prison offers compact converted cells to bed down in year-round. There's a cute terrace bar in summer to counterbalance the inconvenience of queuing for the bathroom. Reserve well in advance and don't forget to write down the door code that's emailed to you.

Eating

Bakfickan SEAFOOD €€
(www.bakfickan-visby.nu; Stora Torget; lunch specials Skr95, mains Skr139-235) White tiled walls, merrily strung lights and boisterous crowds define this foodie-loved hole in the wall, where the menu is succinct but everything perfectly executed. Standout mains include the rich, hearty seafood stew flavoured with saffron and aioli, and grilled cod with chanterelles. Light bites include smoked shrimp, and the chocolate truffle is not to be missed.

Information

Tourist Office (☎20 17 00; www.gotland.info; Skeppsbron 4-6; ⏰8am-7pm in summer, to 4pm Mon-Fri, 10am-4pm Sat & Sun rest of year) Friendly, helpful tourist office with plenty of brochures and maps. Arranges tours, including a classic tour of Visby (at 11.30am on Wednesday and Saturday in July and August, adult/child Skr120/65).

AROUND THE ISLAND

Renting a bicycle and following the well-marked Gotlandsleden cycle path is one of the best ways to spend time on Gotland. It loops all around the island, sometimes joining the roadways but more often winding through quiet fields and forests. You can hire bikes at several locations in Visby. There's an excellent hostel network along the cycle route, with particularly good facilities in Bunge, Lummelunda, Lärbro and the small northern islet of Fårö.

Norrland

Norrland, the northern half of Sweden, is a paradise for nature lovers who enjoy hiking, skiing and other outdoor activities; in winter in particular, the landscape is transformed by snowmobiles, dog sleds and the eerie natural phenomena, the aurora borealis. The north is home to the Sámi people and their reindeer.

ÖSTERSUND

☎063 / POP 44,300

This pleasant town by Storsjön lake, in whose chilly waters is said to lurk Sweden's answer to the Loch Ness monster, is an excellent activity base and gateway town for further explorations of Norrland.

Sights & Activities

Östersund is a major winter sports centre. You can also ask at the tourist office about monster-spotting **lake cruises** (adult/child Skr100/45; ⏰Jun-Sep). Bring your binoculars.

Jamtli MUSEUM
(www.jamtli.com; adult/under 18yr mid-Jun–Aug Skr240/free, rest of yr Skr60/free; ⏰11am-5pm Tue-Sun mid-Aug–late Jun, 11am-5pm daily late Jun–mid-Aug; 👪) Ultrapopular Jamtli combines an open-air museum park with a first-rate regional culture museum. In the outdoor section, guides in period costume encourage visitor participation in activities amid painstakingly reconstructed wooden buildings. Indoors, the regional museum exhibits the Överhogdal tapestry, a Viking relic from around 1100 – one of the oldest of its kind in Europe.

Sleeping

Hotel Jämteborg HOTEL €
(☎51 01 01; www.jamteborg.se; Storgatan 54; hostel d/tr Skr590/840, B&B s/d/tr Skr490/690/890, hotel s/d from Skr995/1190; 🅿📶) Accommodation in just about every possible form – hostel beds, B&B or hotel – in several centrally located buildings. The hotel section has cheerful rooms in bright colours; all hotel rooms include bathrooms and breakfast. Rooms across the street in Pensionat Svea have shared shower and bath but include breakfast; the summer-only hostel rooms don't include breakfast.

Information

Tourist Office (☎14 40 01; www.visitostersund.se; Rådhusgatan 44; ⏰9am-5pm Mon-Fri) Opposite the town hall; has free internet access.

Getting There & Away

SJ trains run from Stockholm (from Skr483, five to 7¾ hours) via Uppsala; there are onward connections to Trondheim, Norway. In summer the **Inlandsbanan** (☎0771-53 53 53; www.inlandsbanan.se) train runs once daily north and south.

KIRUNA & AROUND

☎0980 / POP 18,100

Thousands of visitors flock to the workaday mining town of Kiruna every year to see the

DON'T MISS

ICEHOTEL

The winter wonderland that is the **Icehotel** (☎980 66 800; www.icehotel.com; Jukkasjärvi; cold r from Skr3200, warm r from Skr2500; P📶👪) in Jukkasjärvi, 18km east of Kiruna, is an international phenomenon.

The enormous hotel building is built using 30,000 tonnes of snow and 4000 tonnes of ice, with international artists and designers contributing innovative ice sculptures every year.

In the ice rooms, the beds are made of compact snow and covered with reindeer skins and serious sleeping bags, guaranteed to keep you warm despite the -5°C temperature inside the rooms. Come morning, guests are revived with a hot drink and a sauna.

The attached Ice Church is popular for weddings, while the Absolut Icebar (drinks served in ice glasses) is the first of its kind.

Nonguests can visit the Icehotel in winter and take part in guided tours or eat at the exquisite restaurant. In summer, you can visit the smaller replica inside a chilled warehouse.

Icehotel in nearby Jukkasjärvi – northern Sweden's biggest attraction – and to take part in all manner of outdoor adventures: dog sledding, snowmobiling and northern-lights tours in winter, and biking, hiking and canoeing in summer. Kiruna is also an important centre for Sámi culture.

Sleeping

STF Vandrarhem/Hotell City HOSTEL, HOTEL € (☎hostel 171 95, hotel 666 55; www.hotellcity.se; Bergmästaregatan 7; dm/s/d from Skr200/440/500, hotel s/d from Skr850/990; P@📶) A catch-all hotel-and-hostel combo, with a gleaming red-and-white colour scheme in the modern hotel rooms, and cosy dorms. Sauna and breakfast cost extra for hostel guests.

Eating

TOP CHOICE **Camp Ripan Restaurang** SWEDISH €€ (www.ripan.se; Campingvägen; lunch buffet Skr89, mains Skr145-275; ⊙lunch 11am-2pm; 🖉) Located at the camping ground (of all places!), the unusually expansive lunch buffet that's heavy on the vegies is very good value, but the real draw is the Sámi-inspired à la carte menu.

Information

Tourist Office (☎188 80; www.lappland.se; Lars Janssonsgatan 17, in Folkets Hus; ⊙8.30am-9pm Mon-Fri, to 6pm Sat & Sun May-Sep, to 5pm Mon-Fri, to 3pm Sat Oct-Apr) The tourist office, on the main square, has internet access and can book various activities, including rafting, dog-sledding and snow-scooter trips.

Getting There & Away

AIR Kiruna airport (☎010-109 4600; www.swedavia.com), 7km east of the town, has direct flights to Stockholm and Copenhagen as well as other towns in northern Sweden.

BUS Bus 10 heads twice daily to Gällivare (Skr163, 1½ hours) and Luleå (Skr356, 5¼ hours), while bus 91 runs to Narvik, Norway (Skr275, 2½ hours, daily), via Abisko.

TRAIN There is a daily overnight train to Stockholm (from Skr403, 17 hours) via Uppsala (from Skr403, 15¾ hours). Other destinations include Narvik, Norway (Srk230, 3¼ hours, two daily), via Abisko (Skr122, 1½ hours).

NORWAY

Norway is a once-in-a-lifetime destination and the essence of its appeal is remarkably simple: this is one of the most beautiful countries on earth. Impossibly steep-sided fjords cut deep gashes into the interior, grand and glorious glaciers snake down from Europe's largest ice fields, and the appeal of the Arctic is primeval. The counterpoint to so much natural beauty is found in the country's vibrant cultural life. Norwegian cities are cosmopolitan and brimful of architecture that showcases the famous Scandinavian flair for design. Yes, Norway is one of the most expensive countries but it'll pay you back with never-to-be-forgotten experiences many times over.

Oslo

POP 613,300

Oslo is home to world-class museums and galleries to rival anywhere else on the European art trail. That may be the main reason to come here, but Mother Nature has al left her mark and Oslo is fringed with forests, hills and lakes awash with opportunities for hiking, cycling, skiing and boating.

Sights

TOP CHOICE **Oslo Opera House** OPERA HOUSE
(Den Norske Opera & Ballett; www.operaen.no; Kirsten Flagstads plass 1; foyer free; foyer 9am-11pm Mon-Fri, 11am-11pm Sat, noon-10pm Sun) Designed by Oslo-based architectural firm Snøhetta and costing around €500 million to build, the Opera House was designed to resemble a glacier floating in the waters off Oslo. It's a subtle building that at first doesn't look all that impressive, but give it time and it'll leave you spellbound.

Nasjonalgalleriet GALLERY
(National Gallery; www.nasjonalmuseet.no; Universitetsgata 13; adult/child Nkr50/free, Sun free; 10am-6pm Tue, Wed & Fri, to 7pm Thu, 11am-5pm Sat & Sun) This highlight houses the nation's largest collection of Norwegian art, including some of Edvard Munch's best-known creations such as *The Scream*. There's also an impressive collection of European art with works by Gauguin, Picasso, El Greco and many of the Impressionists.

Akershus Slott & Festning FORTRESS
King Håkon V began construction of the earthen-walled **Akershus Festning** (Akershus Fortress; 7am-9pm Mon-Fri, 8am-9pm Sat & Sun) in 1299. It's strategically positioned on the eastern side of the harbour; clamber up tree-lined twisting paths to stand precariously above the city and enjoy excellent views over Oslofjord. Changing of the guard occurs at 1.30pm.

In the 17th century, Christian IV renovated **Akershus Slott** (Akershus Castle; adult/child Nkr70/30; 10am-4pm Mon-Sat, 12.30-4pm Sun May-Aug, guided tours 11am, 1pm, 2pm & 4pm daily Jul–mid-Aug, shorter hours rest of year) into a Renaissance palace, though the front remains decidedly medieval. In its dungeons you'll find dark cubby holes where outcast nobles were kept under lock and key, while the upper floors have banquet halls and staterooms. The chapel is still used for army events and the crypts of Kings Håkon VII and Olav V lie beneath it.

Vikingskipshuset MUSEUM
(Viking Ship Museum; www.khm.uio.no; Huk Aveny 35; adult/child Nkr60/30; 9am-6pm May-Sep, 10am-4pm Oct-Apr) The magnificent Vikingskipshuset houses three Viking ships excavated from the Oslofjord region. The ships had been brought ashore and used as tombs for nobility, who were buried with all they were expected to need in the hereafter, including jewels, furniture, food and servants.

TOP CHOICE **Munchmuseet** GALLERY
(Munch Museum; www.munch.museum.no; Tøyengata 53; adult/child Nkr75/40; 10am-6pm Jun-Aug) Dedicated to the life's work of Norway's most renowned artist, Munchmuseet contains more than 1100 paintings, 4500 watercolours and 18,000 prints that Munch bequeathed to the city of Oslo. As such, this landmark museum provides a comprehensive look at the artist's work, from dark *(The Sick Child)* to light *(Spring Ploughing)*. To get there, take the T-bane to Tøyen, followed by a five-minute signposted walk.

Tours

For the popular **Norway in a Nutshell** (81 56 82 22; www.norwaynutshell.com), book at tourist offices or at train stations. From Oslo, the typical route includes a rail trip across Hardangervidda to Myrdal, descent to Flåm along the dramatic Flåmbanen, a cruise along Nærøyfjorden to Gudvangen, a bus to Voss, a connecting train to Bergen for a short visit, then an overnight return rail trip to Oslo (including a sleeper compartment); the return tour costs Nkr2240. You can also book one-way tours to Bergen (Nkr1430).

Sleeping

TOP CHOICE **Ellingsens Pensjonat** PENSION €
(22 60 03 59; www.ellingsenspensjonat.no; Holtegata 25; s/d Nkr500/700, without bathroom Nkr430/640;) Located in a quiet, pleasant neighbourhood, this homey pension offers one of the best deals in the capital. The building dates from 1890 and many of the original features (high ceilings, rose designs) remain. Rooms are bright and airy, with refrigerators and kettles, and there's a small garden to lounge about in on sunny days if you can't face the 20-minute walk into town.

Cochs Pensjonat PENSION €
(23 33 24 00; www.cochspensjonat.no; Parkveien 25; s/d with kitchenette from Nkr600/820, without bathroom Nkr500/720;) Opened as a guesthouse for bachelors in the 1920s, the well-run Cochs has sparsely furnished, clean

Oslo

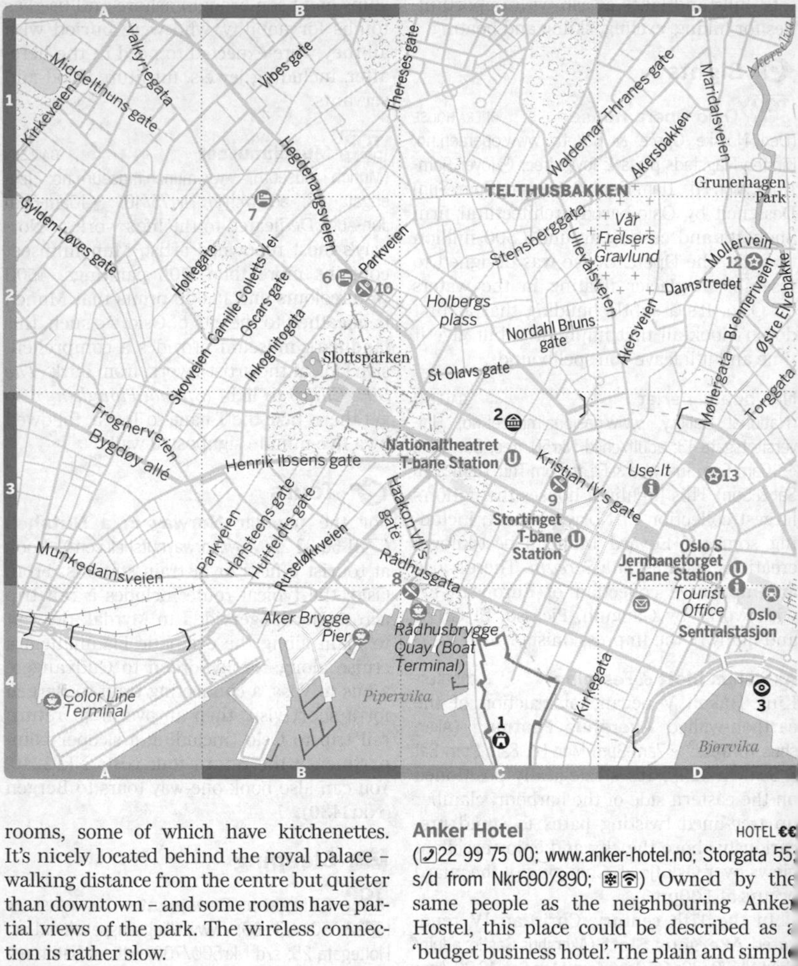

rooms, some of which have kitchenettes. It's nicely located behind the royal palace – walking distance from the centre but quieter than downtown – and some rooms have partial views of the park. The wireless connection is rather slow.

Anker Hostel HOSTEL €

(☎22 99 72 00; www.ankerhostel.no; Storgata 55; dm Nkr220-260, d/tr Nkr600/800; ❄@📶) This huge traveller-savvy hostel boasts an international atmosphere, spick-and-span rooms, a laundry, luggage room, kitchens (some rooms also contain kitchens) and small bar. Breakfast costs an extra Nkr55, linen is Nkr50 and parking is Nkr175 per 24 hours. It was about to be downsized when we were there, but in a good cause – a new hostel was planned further north in Grunerløkka (check the website for location), which should be open by now, although this original hostel was expected to continue.

Anker Hotel HOTEL €€

(☎22 99 75 00; www.anker-hotel.no; Storgata 55; s/d from Nkr690/890; ❄📶) Owned by the same people as the neighbouring Anker Hostel, this place could be described as a 'budget business hotel'. The plain and simple rooms were completely overhauled in 2010 and are outstanding value, perfect for those who feel a bit too old for the hostel. Even so, we're at a loss to explain how it won citation as one of Norway's trendiest hotel in 2012...

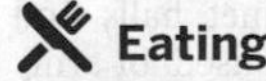

Eating

Kaffistova NORWEGIAN €

(☎23 21 42 10; Rosenkrantz gate 8; mains Nkr14 175; ⏲11am-9pm Mon-Fri, to 7pm Sat & Su Don't be put off by the cafeteria-style a mosphere here because this is one of th most affordable places in town to ord what locals eat at home. The signatu dish is a Norwegian staple – meatballs wi

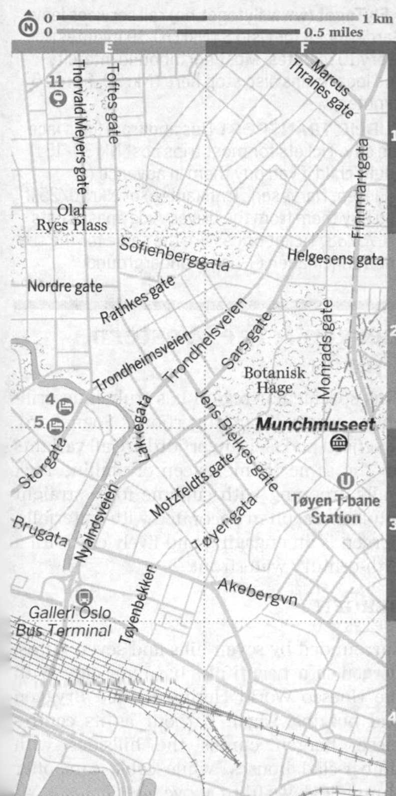

Oslo

Top Sights

Munchmuseet F3

Sights

1 Akershus Slott & Festning C4
2 Nasjonalgalleriet C3
3 Oslo Opera House D4

Sleeping

4 Anker Hostel E2
5 Anker Hotel E2
6 Cochs Pensjonat B2
7 Ellingsens Pensjonat B2

Eating

8 Fisherman's Coop C4
9 Kaffistova C3
10 Rust B2

Drinking

11 Bar Boca E1

Entertainment

12 Blå D2
13 Fish Og Vilt Club D3

mashed potatoes and gravy – but you might also find baked salmon, reindeer cakes and open sandwiches.

Rust INTERNATIONAL €
(www.rustoslo.com; Hegehaugsveien 22; tapas Nkr42-86, mains Nkr129-195; ⏰11am-1am Mon-Sat, noon-2am Sun) On a small side street lined with cafes and restaurants, Rust is bright, colourful and 100% modern Oslo. It has plenty of outdoor seating and loads of blankets for when it gets cold. Its menu ranges across the world but it's good for a quiet cocktail, burgers, hearty salads or tapas late into the night.

Café Hemma Hos MODERN NORWEGIAN €€
(www.cafehemmahos.no; Fredrikborgsveien 16; mains Nkr135-175) The owners of the Café Hemma Hos, close to the Viking Ship Museum, know there is more to culinary life than hot dogs and sandwiches, and have created an oasis of good food in a sea of tourist traps. Sit out in the pleasant gardens and choose from a menu that includes pickled herrings, crayfish and a variety of tapas.

Fisherman's Coop SEAFOOD €
(Rådhusbrygge 3/4; shrimp per kg Nkr150, ⏰7am-5pm Tue-Sat) If the weather is nice, the local meal of choice is peel-and-eat shrimp, eaten dockside with a fresh baguette, mayonnaise and just a touch of lemon. In the summer, you can buy shrimp from the Fisherman's Coop.

Drinking & Entertainment

The city's best neighbourhood bar scene is along Thorvald Meyers gate and the surrounding streets in Grünerløkka. The Youngstorget area has some of the most popular places close to the city centre, while the Grønland neighbourhood has a more alternative feel.

Bar Boca BAR
(Thorvald Meyers gate 30; ⏰noon-1am Sun-Tue, 11am-2pm Wed & Thu, 11am-3am Fri & Sat) Squeeze into what is quite possibly the smallest bar in Oslo and you'll find that you have slid back in time to the 1960s. It's retro cool and has a cocktail selection as great as its atmosphere.

TOP CHOICE Blå JAZZ

(www.blaaoslo.no; Brenneriveien 9c; admission Nkr100-150) It would be a pity to leave Oslo without checking out Blå, which features on a global list of 100 great jazz clubs compiled by the savvy editors at the US jazz magazine *Down Beat*. Sometimes it veers into other musical styles such as salsa, and when there's no live music DJs get the crowds moving.

Fish Og Vilt Club CLUB

(Pløens gate 1) With DJs rocking the crowd in the covered backyard of this bar-club, and an impressive selection of beers and cocktails, this is a popular central spot for a cool crowd. On a Monday night it's really the only place worth considering.

Information

Arctic Internet Café (Oslo S; per hour from Nkr25; ⏲8am-midnight) On the 1st floor of Oslo S train station.

Lonely Planet (www.lonelyplanet.com/norway/oslo)

Tourist Office (☎81 53 05 55; Jernbanetorget 1, Oslo S; ⏲7am-8pm Mon-Fri, 8am-6pm Sat & Sun)

Use-It (Ungdomsinformasjonen, Youth Information Office; ☎24 14 98 20; www.use-it.no; Møllergata 3; ⏲11am-5pm Mon-Fri, noon-5pm Sat) The exceptionally helpful and savvy Ungdomsinformasjonen (Youth Information Office) is aimed at (but not restricted to) backpackers under the age of 26. It makes (free) bookings for inexpensive or private accommodation, and provides information on anything from current events to hitching possibilities.

Getting There & Away

AIR Most flights land at Oslo's main international airport in **Gardermoen** (www.osl.no), 50km north of the city; it's the country's main international gateway and domestic hub.

BUS Long-distance buses arrive and depart from the **Galleri Oslo Bus Terminal** (Schweigaards gate 8); the train and bus stations are linked via an overhead walkway for easy connections.

TRAIN All trains arrive and depart from Oslo S in the city centre. Major destinations include Stavanger, Bergen and Trondheim.

Getting Around

TO/FROM AIRPORT Flybussen (www.flybussen.no) shuttles run regularly to Gardermoen (one way/return Nkr150/250, 40 minutes).

FlyToget (www.flytoget.no) rail services leave Gardermoen for Oslo S (Nkr170, 19 minutes) every 10 minutes. Most northbound intercity and local trains also stop here (Nkr90, from 26 minutes).

PUBLIC TRANSPORT Bus and tram lines lace the city. Tickets for most trips cost Nkr30/15 adult/child if you buy them in advance (at 7-Eleven, Narvesen, Trafikanten) or Nkr50/25 if you buy them from the driver. A day pass costs Nkr75/38. Ticket prices are the same for the six-line Tunnelbanen (T-bane) underground.

Bergen & the Western Fjords

This spectacular region has truly indescribable scenery. Hardangerfjord, Sognefjord, Lysefjord and Geirangerfjord are all variants on the same theme: steep crystalline rock walls dropping with sublime force straight into the sea, often decorated with waterfalls. Bergen is an engaging and lively city with a 15th-century waterfront.

BERGEN

POP 235,000

Surrounded by seven hills and seven fjords, Bergen is a beautiful, charming city. With the Unesco World Heritage–listed Bryggen and buzzing Vågen harbour as its centrepiece, Bergen climbs the hillsides with timber-clad houses, while cable cars offer stunning views from above.

Sights

TOP CHOICE Bryggen HISTORIC AREA

The timber alleys of Bryggen, the old medieval quarter and Unesco World Herit age site, offer an intriguing glimpse of th stacked-stone foundations and rough-plan construction of centuries past.

Some of Norway's creakiest floors ar in the timber building (1704) housing th **Hanseatisk Museum** (www.museumvest.n Finnegårdsgaten 1a & Øvregaten 50; adult/chil Nkr60/free; ⏲9am-5pm mid-May–mid-Sep, short hours rest of year). Period character flourishe while furnishings and odd bedchambers giv a glimpse of the austere living conditions Hanseatic merchants. The site of Berger earliest settlement is now **Bryggens M seum** (www.bymuseet.no; Dreggsallmenning adult/child Nkr60/free; ⏲10am-4pm mid-May–A shorter hours rest of year). The 800-year-o foundations unearthed during the constru tion have been incorporated into the exhibi along with pottery, skulls and runes.

FJORD TOURS FROM BERGEN

Fjord Tours (☎81 56 82 22; www.fjordtours.com) runs the popular, year-round Norway in a Nutshell (p965) tour, a great way to see far more than you thought possible in a single day. The day ticket (adult/child Nkr1045/545) from Bergen combines a morning train to Voss, a bus on to Gudvangen, from where a ferry takes you up the spectacular Nærøyfjord to Flåm, joining the stunning mountain railway to Myrdal, and a train back to Bergen in time for a late dinner (or continue to Oslo to arrive around 10pm, adult/child Nkr1345/685). From May to September, Fjord Tours also runs **Hardangerfjord in a Nutshell** (adult/child Nkr820/465) and **Sognefjord in a Nutshell** (adult/child Nkr1250/630).

Sleeping

TOP CHOICE Det Hanseatiske Hotel HISTORIC HOTEL €€€
(☎55 30 48 00; www.dethanseatiskehotell.no; Finnegårdsgaten 2; s/d from Nkr990/1090; 📶) The only hotel to be housed inside the old timber buildings that evoke Bryggen's bygone age, Det Hanseatiske Hotel is luxurious and like stepping back into a luxurious Bergen past. Flat-screen TVs cohabit with antique bathtubs and some extraordinary original architectural features.

Skansen Pensjonat GUESTHOUSE €
(☎55 31 90 80; www.skansen-pensjonat.no; Vetrlidsalmenning 29; s/d from Nkr450/750; 📶) There are family-run guesthouses springing up all over Bergen, but this charming seven-room place is still a favourite. A wonderful location up behind the lower funicular station, real attention to detail and many personal touches make this a terrific choice.

City Box HOSTEL €
(☎55 31 25 00; www.citybox.no; Nygårdsgaten 31; s/d Nkr600/900, without bathroom Nkr500/700; 📶) The best hostel in Bergen, City Box is a place where the owners do simple things well, such as bright modern rooms with splashes of colour, free wireless access, a minimalist designer feel without the price tag, and friendly young staff.

Eating

TOP CHOICE Pingvinen NORWEGIAN €
www.pingvinen.no; Vaskerelven 14; sandwiches Nkr98, mains Nkr149-199; ⏰1pm-3am Sun-Fri, noon-3am Sat) Devoted to small-town Norwegian cooking and with a delightfully informal ambience, Pingvinen is one of our favourite restaurants in Bergen. It's the sort of place where Norwegians come for recipes their mothers and grandparents used to cook, and although the menu changes regularly there are usually fish-cake sandwiches, reindeer, fish pie, whale, salmon, lamb shank and, our favourite, traditional Norwegian meatballs served with mushy peas and wild Norwegian berry jam.

Torget Fish Market SEAFOOD €
(www.torgetibergen.no; Torget; ⏰7am-7pm Jun-Aug, to 4pm Mon-Sat Sep-May) For price and atmosphere, it's hard to beat the fish market. Right alongside the harbour and a stone's throw from Bryggen, here you'll find everything from smoked whale meat and salmon to calamari, fish and chips, fish cakes, prawn baguettes, seafood salads, local caviar and, sometimes, nonfishy reindeer and elk. Don't miss the newer section under the tourist office.

Entertainment

Garage LIVE MUSIC
(www.garage.no; Christies gate 14; ⏰3pm-3am Mon-Sat, 5pm-3am Sun) Garage has taken on an almost mythical quality for music lovers across Europe. It does play live jazz and acoustic, but this is a rock venue at heart, with well-known Norwegian and international acts drawn to the cavernous basement.

Hulen LIVE MUSIC
(www.hulen.no; Olaf Ryes vei 48; ⏰9pm-3am Thu-Sat mid-Aug–mid-Jun) Going strong since 1968, Hulen is the oldest rock club in northern Europe and it's one of the classic stages for indie rock. Hulen means 'cave' and the venue is actually a converted bomb shelter. Sadly, it closes during summer when many of Bergen's students head off on holidays.

Information

Tourist Office (☎55 55 20 00; www.visitbergen.com; Vågsallmenningen 1; ⏰8.30am-10pm

Jun-Aug, 9am-8pm May & Sep, 9am-4pm Mon-Sat Oct-Apr) One of Norway's best and busiest.

Getting There & Away

BOAT The *Hurtigruten* leaves from a newly built terminal east of Nøstegaten. **Flaggruten** (☎53 40 91 20; www.tide.no; Strandkaiterminalen) runs express passenger catamarans to/from Stavanger (one way/return Nkr400/800, 4½ hours, two daily).

BUS Express buses run throughout the western fjords region, as well as to Trondheim (Nkr811, 12½ hours, two daily) and Stavanger (Nkr460, 5½ hours, five daily).

TRAIN The spectacular train journey between Bergen and Oslo (Nkr299 to Nkr804, 6½ to eight hours, five daily) runs through the heart of Norway. Other destinations include Myrdal (Nkr271, 2¼ hours, up to nine daily) for connections for the Flåmsbana railway.

STAVANGER

POP 123,500

Said by some to be the largest wooden city in Europe, Stavanger's old quarter climbs up the slopes around a pretty harbour. Stavanger is also one of Norway's liveliest urban centres and an excellent base to explore stunning Lysefjord.

Sights

TOP CHOICE Gamle Stavanger NEIGHBOURHOOD

Gamle (Old) Stavanger consists of cobblestone walkways passing between rows of late-18th-century whitewashed wooden houses, all immaculately kept and adorned with cheerful, well-tended flower boxes. It well rewards an hour or two's ambling.

Norsk Oljemuseum MUSEUM

(Oil Museum; www.norskolje.museum.no; Kjeringholmen; adult/child/Nkr100/50; ⏲10am-7pm Jun-Aug, to 4pm Mon-Sat, to 6pm Sun Sep-May) One of Norway's best museums, the Oil Museum is filled with hi-tech interactive displays, gigantic models and authentic reconstructions.

Sleeping

Stavanger B&B B&B €€

(☎51 56 25 00; www.stavangerbedandbreakfast.no; Vikedalsgata 1a; s/d Nkr790/890, without bathroom Nkr690/790; P 📶) This quiet but popular place comes highly recommended by readers and it's not hard to see why. The simple rooms are tidy and come with satellite TV, shower and a smile from the friendly owners. Packed lunches cost a bargain Nkr35, and at 9pm, free coffee, tea and waffles are served.

Mosvangen Camping CAMPGROUND €

(☎51 53 29 71; www.stavangercamping.no; Tjensvoll 1b; campsites without/with car Nkr150/200, with caravan or camper Nkr210, huts Nkr450-750; ⏲Apr-Sep) During nesting season around Mosvangen lake, campers are treated to almost incessant birdsong amid the green, agreeable surroundings. Take bus 78 or 79 (Nkr36) from opposite the cathedral. Bus 4 also passes by.

Eating

NB Sørensen's Damskibsexpedition NORWEGIAN €€

(☎51 84 38 00; Skagen 26; mains Nkr125-329) One of the better places along the waterfront, this restaurant serves everything from fish to pork ribs, with a seasonal lunch menu that's excellent value. The atmospheric indoor dining area is ideal when the weather turns, and locals swear that the food and service are better upstairs. Try the grilled salmon.

Drinking

Most of the livelier bars are right on the waterfront, catering for boisterous crowds of young locals. You'll hear them long before you see them and as they're all pretty similar, just pick your favourite and join in.

Information

Tourist Office (☎51 85 92 00; www.regionstavanger.com; Domkirkeplassen 3; ⏲9am-8pm Jun-Aug, to 4pm Mon-Fri, to 2pm Sat Sep-May) Local information and advice on Lysefjord and Preikestolen.

Getting There & Away

BOAT Flaggruten (☎51 86 87 00; www.norled.no) runs express passenger catamarans to Bergen (Nkr400, 4½ hours, two daily).

Norled (www.norled.no; ⏲Jun-Aug) has daily summer four-hour car ferries with tourist commentary along Lysefjord to Lysebotn (adult/child/car Nkr220/130/420) from Fiskepirterminalen. Departures are at 10am.

BUS Nor-Way Bussekspress (p989) offers services to Oslo (Nkr477 to Nkr700, 9½ hours, up to five daily) and to Bergen (Nkr460, 5¾ hours, six daily).

TRAIN Trains run to Oslo (Nkr399 to Nkr904, eight hours, up to five daily) via Kristiansand (Nkr199 to Nkr450, 3½ hours).

LYSEFJORDEN

All along 42km-long Lysefjorden, the granite glows with an ethereal, ambient light, even on dull days. This is many visitors' favourite fjord, and there's no doubt that it has a captivating beauty.

The area's most popular outing is the two-hour hike to the top of incredible Preikestolen (Pulpit Rock), 25km east of Stavanger. You can inch up to the edge of its flat top and peer 604m straight down a sheer cliff into the blue water for some intense vertigo. Boat-bus-hike combinations run here from Stavanger May to mid-September; get tickets from the tourist office or Fiskespiren Quay.

SOGNEFJORDEN

Sognefjorden, Norway's longest (204km) and deepest (1308m) fjord, cuts a deep slash across the map of western Norway. In places, sheer walls rise more than 1000m above the water, while elsewhere a gentler shoreline supports farms, orchards and villages.

Fjord1 (☎57 75 70 00; www.fjord1.no) operates a daily (summer-only) express boat between Bergen and both Flåm (Nkr710, 5½ hours) and Sogndal (Nkr605, 4¾ hours), stopping along the way at small towns.

FLÅM

POP 580

Scenically set at the head of Aurlandsfjorden, Flåm is a tiny village that's a jumping-off spot for travellers exploring the area. It all gets a little overrun with people when a cruise ship's in port, and sees an amazing 500,000 visitors every summer.

Sights

Flåmsbana Railway SCENIC RAILWAY

(www.flaamsbana.no; adult/child one way Nkr260/130, return Nkr360/260) The world's steepest railway that runs without cable or rack wheels takes 45 minutes to climb to Myrdal, on the bleak, treeless Hardangervidda Plateau, past thundering waterfalls (there's a photo stop at awesome Kjosfossen). It runs year-round with up to 10 departures daily in summer. For the best views, grab a seat on the right-hand side of the train. Go late afternoon in summer to avoid crowds.

Sleeping & Eating

Flåm Camping & Youth Hostel HOSTEL, CAMPGROUND €

(☎57 63 21 21; www.flaam-camping.no; car/caravan site Nkr205/215, dm Nkr210-275, s/d/cabin from Nkr340/500/650; ⏲Apr-Sep; Wi-Fi) This friendly spot is only a few minutes' walk from the station. In 2010 Hostelling International judged it to be Norway's best hostel and the ninth best in the world. You can see why; there's a brand-new block with en suite facilities, amenities are impeccable and the welcome couldn't be warmer.

Information

Tourist Office (☎57 63 33 13; www.visitflam.com; ⏲8.30am-4pm & 4.30-8pm Jun-Aug, 8.30am-4pm May & Sep)

> **SOGNEFJORDEN BY BOAT**
>
> It may get overrun in summer, but the classic boat trip from Flåm to Gudvangen is one of the most beautiful on earth. Ferries (one way/return Nkr275/380) leave Flåm at 3.10pm year-round and up to four times daily between May and September. In Gudvangen, buses to Voss and Oslo connect with the ferry arrival. Boat and bus tickets can be bought at the tourist offices in Flåm and Gudvangen.
>
> There's also at least one daily express boat to Bergen (Nkr706, 5½ hours).

GEIRANGERFJORDEN

Added to Unesco's World Heritage list in 2005, this king of Norwegian fjords boasts towering, twisting walls that curve inland for 20 narrow kilometres. The cruise by public ferry between Geiranger village and Hellesylt is extraordinarily beautiful.

Sights

Flydalsjuvet VIEWPOINT

Somewhere you've seen that classic photo, beloved of brochures, of the overhanging rock Flydalsjuvet, usually with a figure gazing down at a cruise ship in Geirangerfjord. The car park, signposted Flydalsjuvet, about 5km uphill from Geiranger on the Stryn road, offers a great view of the fjord and the green river valley.

Activities

Coastal Odyssey KAYAKING, HIKING

(☎91 11 80 62; www.coastalodyssey.com) Based at Geiranger Camping, this outfit rents sea kayaks (Nkr150/450/800 per hour/half-day/day) and runs daily kayaking-hiking trips (Nkr800 to Nkr1250, five to nine hours) to the finest destinations around the fjord.

MOVING ON?

For tips, recommendations and reviews, head to shop.lonelyplanet.com to purchase a downloadable PDF of the Rejkavik chapter from Lonely Planet's *Iceland* guide.

Geiranger Fjordservice BOAT
(☎70 26 30 07; www.geirangerfjord.no; boat tours adult/child Nkr190/100; ⊙up to 4 sailings daily early May–mid-Sep) Offers 1½-hour sightseeing boat tours, as well as a range of other bus, bike and boat possibilities. Its kiosk is within the tourist office.

Sleeping & Eating

Grande Fjord Hotel HOTEL €€
(☎70 26 94 90; www.grandefjordhotel.com; d Nkr990-1250; P 📶) This warmly recommended 48-room hotel does great buffet breakfasts and dinners. It's well worth paying the higher rate for a room with a balcony and magnificent view over the fjord.

Information

Tourist Office (☎70 26 30 99; www.visitalesund-geiranger.com; ⊙9am-6pm mid-May–mid-Sep)

Getting There & Away

The popular, hugely recommended run between Geiranger and Hellesylt (passenger/car with driver one way Nkr150/300, adult/child return Nkr200/100, one hour) is the most spectacular scheduled ferry route in Norway. It has four to eight sailings daily between May and mid-October (every 90 minutes until 6.30pm June to August).

Northern Norway

With vibrant cities and some wondrous natural terrain, you'll be mighty pleased with yourself for undertaking an exploration of this huge territory that spans the Arctic Circle. An alternative to land travel is the *Hurtigruten* coastal ferry, which pulls into every sizeable port, passing some of the best coastal scenery in Scandinavia.

TRONDHEIM

POP 164,600

Trondheim, Norway's original capital, is Norway's third-largest city after Oslo and Bergen. With its wide streets and partly pedestrianised heart, it's an attractive city with a long history. Fuelled by a large student population, it buzzes with life.

Sights

TOP CHOICE **Nidaros Domkirke** CHURCH
(www.nidarosdomen.no; Kongsgårdsgata; adult/child Nkr60/30, tower Nkr30; ⊙9am-6pm Mon-Fri, to 2pm Sat, to 5pm Sun mid-Jun–mid-Aug, shorter hr rest of yr) The altar of Scandinavia's largest medieval building sits over the original grave of St Olav, the Viking king who established Christianity in Norway. The original stone cathedral was built in 1153, while the Gothic choir and ambulatory were completed in the early 14th century. The nave, repeatedly ravaged by fire across the centuries, is mostly a faithful 19th-century reconstruction.

From early June to early August, you can climb the cathedral's tower for a great view over the city.

Sleeping

Pensjonat Jarlen GUESTHOUSE €
(☎73 51 32 18; www.jarlen.no; Kongens gate 40; s/d Nkr540/690; 📶) Price, convenience and value for money are a winning combination here. After a recent overhaul, the rooms at this central spot are outstanding value, with a contemporary look (let down a little in some cases by the tired-looking bathrooms). Most have hotplates and a fridge thrown in.

Eating

TOP CHOICE **Baklandet Skydsstasjon** NORWEGIAN €€
(www.skydsstation.no; Øvre Bakklandet 33; mains Nkr130-255; ⊙noon-1am) Within what began life as an 18th-century coaching inn are several cosy rooms with poky angles and listing floors. It's a hyperfriendly place where you can tuck into tasty dishes, such as its renowned fish soup ('the best in all Norway,' a couple of diners assured us), shellfish salad, reindeer stew or oven-baked salmon.

Drinking

As a student town, Trondheim offers lots of through-the-night life. Solsiden (Sunnyside) is Trondheim's trendiest leisure zone. A whole wharf-side of bars and restaurants nestles beneath smart new apartment blocks, converted warehouses and now-idle cranes.

TOP CHOICE **Den Gode Nabo** PU
(www.dengodenabo.com; Øvre Bakklandet 66 ⊙4pm-1.30am Sun-Fri, 1pm-1.30am Sat) Th Good Neighbour, dark and cavernous withi

and nominated more than once as Norway's best pub, enjoys a prime riverside location. Indeed, part of it's on the water; reserve a table on the floating pontoon.

Information

Tourist Office (☎73 80 76 60; www.visittrondheim.no; Munkegata 19, Torvet; ⊙8.30am-7pm Jul, 9am-4pm Mon-Fri, 10am-2pm Sat rest of yr) The tourist office also runs two-hour guided walking/cycling tours (Nkr160/200) at 1pm from late June to mid-August.

Getting There & Away

BOAT Trondheim is a major stop on the *Hurtigruten* coastal ferry route.

BUS The intercity bus terminal (Rutebilstasjon) adjoins Trondheim Sentralstasjon (train station, also known as Trondheim S). Nor-Way Bussekspress services run at least daily to/from Ålesund (Nkr564, seven hours) via Molde (Nkr421, five hours) and Bergen (Nkr811, 14½ hours).

TRAIN There are two to four trains daily to/from Oslo (Nkr873, 6½ hours), while two head north to Bodø (Nkr1037, 9¾ hours).

LOFOTEN

You'll never forget your first approach to the Lofoten Islands by ferry. The islands spread their tall, craggy physique against the sky like some spiky sea dragon, and you wonder how humans eked a living in such inhospitable surroundings.

The four main islands are all linked by bridges or tunnels, with buses running the entire length of the Lofoten road (E10) from Fiskebøl in the north to Å at road's end in the southwest.

Sights & Activities

Lofoten's principal settlement, Svolvær, makes a pretty spot from which to base your explorations, with steep mountains rising sharply in the background and a busy harbour. The still-active fishing village of Henningsvær, perched at the end of a thin promontory, is the lightest, brightest and trendiest village in the archipelago, while Å is a very special place at what feels like the end of the world on the western tip of Lofoten. A preserved fishing village perched on forbidding rocks connected by wooden footbridges, its shoreline is lined with red-painted *rorbuer* (fishermen's huts), many of which jut into the sea.

Lofotr Viking Museum MUSEUM
(www.lofotr.no; adult/child incl guided tour Nkr140/70; ⊙10am-7pm Jun-Aug, shorter hours rest of year) This museum, 14km north of Leknes, offers a glimpse of life in Viking times. You can walk 1.5km of trails over open hilltops from the replica of the chieftain's longhouse (the main building, shaped like an upside-down boat) to the Viking-ship replica on the water. Costumed guides conduct multilingual tours and, inside the chieftain's hall, artisans explain their trades.

Ocean Sounds WHALE CENTRE
(☎91 84 20 12; www.ocean-sounds.com; Hjellskjæret; adult/child Nkr200/free; ⊙2-6pm Jul-mid-Aug, by request mid-Apr–Jun & mid-Aug–Oct) In Henningsvær, this not-for-profit research centre has a series of multimedia presentations about cod, whales and other Arctic marine mammals. Or get out and about on a marine safari in the Zodiac (adult/child Nkr850/650, three to four hours).

Hiking & Climbing HIKING, CLIMBING
Daredevils like to scale Svolværgeita (the Svolvær Goat), a distinctive, two-pronged peak visible from Svolvær harbour, and then jump the 1.5m from one horn to the other – a graveyard at the bottom awaits those who miss. For phenomenal views, hikers can ascend the steep path to the base of the Goat and up the slopes behind it. There's also a rough route from the Goat over to the extraordinary Devil's Gate; ask the tourist office for details.

Sleeping

TOP CHOICE **Svinøya Rorbuer** CABIN €€
(☎76 06 99 30; www.svinoya.no; Gunnar Bergs vei 2; cabins & suites Nkr1550-3200) Across a bridge on the islet of Svinøya, site of Svolvær's first settlement, are several stunning cabins, some historic, most contemporary, and all cosy and comfortable. They've other choices around the islands.

Å-Hamna Rorbuer & Vandrerhjem HOSTEL €
(☎76 09 12 11; www.lofotenferie.com; Å; hostel dm/s/d/tr Nkr200/230/420/600, rorbuer Nkr900-1300) Sleep simple, sleep in more comfort; either way, this HI-affiliate is an attractive choice. It has dorms above the Stockfish Museum and in a quiet villa, set in its garden. For more space and privacy, choose one of the restored fishing huts, which sleep four to sight people

Svolvær Sjøhuscamp SEA HOUSE €
(☎76 07 03 36; www.svolver-sjohuscamp.no; Parkgata 12; d/q from Nkr540/880, d with kitchen

Nkr590, all without bathroom) This friendly sea house straddling the water is a convivial, excellent-value place to fetch up and meet fellow travellers. There's also a gem of an apartment with balcony and full facilities (Nkr1900) that sleeps up to six.

Information

Tourist Office (☎76 06 98 07; www.lofoten.info; Torget, Svolvær; ⊙9am-10pm Mon-Fri, to 8pm Sat, 10am-8pm Sun mid-June–mid-Aug, shorter hr rest of yr) Provides information on the entire archipelago.

Getting There & Away

BOAT

In addition to the *Hurtigruten*, the following services connect Lofoten and the mainland:

Bodø–Moskenes (adult/child/car/motorcycle Nkr166/84/604/274, 3½ to 4½ hours, one to two daily) It's a two-hour drive from Moskenes to Svolvaer. Bodø is the northern terminus of the train line.

Skutvik–Svolvaer (adult/child/car/motorcycle Nkr89/44/404/257, two hours, two to four daily)

BUS

Buses connect all major settlements on the islands.

TROMSØ

POP 56,500

Simply put, Tromsø parties. By far the largest town in northern Norway, and administrative centre of Troms county, it's lively with an animated street scene, a respected university, the hallowed Mack Brewery – and more pubs per capita than any other Norwegian town. Its corona of snow-topped peaks provides arresting scenery, excellent summer hiking, and great winter skiing and dog sledding.

Sights

Polaria INTERPRETIVE CENTRE

(www.polaria.no; Hjalmar Johansens gate 12; adult/child Nkr120/60; ⊙10am-7pm mid-May–Aug, 11am-5pm Sep–mid-May) Daringly designed Polaria is an entertaining multimedia introduction to northern Norway. After a lush 14-minute film about Svalbard or a nine-minute film on the aurora borealis, an Arctic walk leads to an aurora borealis display, aquarium of cold-water fish and – the big draw – a tank of energetic bearded seals.

Activities

In and around Tromsø there's a whole range of robust activities in the winter twilight, including experiencing the aurora borealis, cross-country skiing and snowshoewing, and reindeer and dog sledding. You can also go on showshoe safaris or try ice fishing. To whet your winter appetite, check the tourist office website.

Sleeping

Ami Hotel HOTEL €€

(☎77 62 10 00; www.amihotel.no; Skolegata 24; s/d Nkr700/870, without bathroom Nkr600/750; P@) Beside a traffic-free road and park, this is a quiet, friendly, family-owned choice. There's a well-equipped kitchen for self-caterers and a couple of communal lounges, each with TV, internet access and free tea and coffee.

Tromsø Camping CAMPGROUND €

(☎77 63 80 37; www.tromsocamping.no; Tromsdalen; car/caravan site Nkr200/240, cabins Nkr450-1480; P@) Tent campers enjoy leafy green campsites beside a slow-moving stream. However, bathroom and cooking facilities at this veritable village of cabins are stretched to the limit. Take bus 20 or 24.

Eating

TOP CHOICE **Emma's Under** NORWEGIAN €€

(☎77 63 77 30; www.emmas.as; lunch mains Nkr139-245, dinner mains Nkr325-365; ⊙11am-midnight Mon-Fri, noon-midnight Sat) Intimate and sophisticated, Emma's Under is one of the most popular lunch spots in Tromsø, where mains often include northern Norwegian staples such as reindeer fillet, whale steak, lamb and stockfish. Upstairs is a more formal, highly regarded gourmet restaurant.

Aunegården NORWEGIAN €€

(☎77 65 12 34; www.aunegarden.no; Sjøgata 29; lunch mains Nkr104-184, dinner mains Nkr248-295; ⊙11.30am-10pm Mon-Sat) You can almost lose yourself in this wonderful cafe-cum-restaurant that's all intimate crannies and cubbyholes. In a 19th-century building that functioned as a butcher's shop until 1996, it's rich in character and serves excellent salads, sandwiches and mains such as reindeer or wild boar.

Drinking & Entertainment

Tromsø enjoys a thriving nightlife, with many arguing that it's the best scene in Norway. On Friday and Saturday, most night spots stay open to 3.30am.

Verdensteatret CAF

(Storgata 93b; ⊙11am-2am Mon-Thu, to 3.30ar Fri & Sat, 1pm-2am Sun;) Norway's oldes film house will satisfy both cinephiles an thirsters after great cafes. The bar is a hip place with free wi-fi and weekend DJs. At other times, the bartender spins from a huge collection of vinyl. Ask staff to let you peek into the magnificent cinema, its walls painted roof-to-ceiling with early-20th-century murals.

Blå Rock Café BAR
(www.blarock.no; Strandgata 14/16; ⏲11.30am-2am) The loudest, most raving place in town has almost 50 brands of beer, occasional live bands and weekend DJs. The music's rock, naturally. Happy hour all day Monday.

Information

Tourist Office (☎77 61 00 00; www.visit-tromso.no; Kirkegata 2; ⏲9am-7pm Mon-Fri, 10am-6pm Sat & Sun)

Getting There & Away

AIR SAS flies direct from Oslo to **Tromsø Airport** (☎77 64 84 00). **Norwegian** (www.norwegian.no) flies to and from London (Gatwick), Edinburgh, Dublin and Oslo.

BOAT Tromsø is a major stop on the *Hurtigruten* coastal ferry route.

BUS The main bus terminal is on Kaigata, beside the *Hurtigruten* quay. There are at least two daily express buses to/from Narvik (Nkr445, 4¼ hours) and one to/from Alta (Nkr535, 6½ hours)

FINLAND

There's something pure in the Finnish air and spirit that's incredibly vital and exciting. It's an invitation to get out and active year-round. Although socially and economically in the vanguard of nations, large parts of Finland remain gloriously remote; trendsetting modern Helsinki is counterbalanced by vast forested wilder nesses elsewhere.

Nordic peace in a lakeside cottage, summer sunshine on convivial beer terraces, avant-garde design, dark melodic music and cafes warm with baking aromas are other facets of Suomi seduction. As are the independent, loyal, warm and welcoming Finns, who tend to do their own thing and are much the better for it.

Helsinki

☎09 / POP 596,200

It's fitting that harbourside Helsinki, capital of a country with such a watery geography, melds so graciously into the Baltic Sea. Half the city seems to be liquid, and the tortured writhings of the complex coastline include any number of bays, inlets and islands.

Though Helsinki can seem like a younger sibling to other Scandinavian capitals, it's the one that went to art school, scorns pop music, is working in a cutting-edge design studio and hangs out with friends who like black and plenty of piercings. The city's design shops are legendary, and its music and pub scene kicking.

Sights

TOP CHOICE Kauppatori SQUARE
Finnish cities are traditionally centred on their market square; Helsinki's sits right by the passenger harbour in the old part of town. Though touristy, it's still a forum for selling fish, as well as fresh garden produce and seasonal berries.

Cathedrals CHURCHES
Presiding over Senate Sq just north of the *kauppatori*, chalk-white neoclassical **Tuomiokirkko** (Lutheran Cathedral; www.helsinginseurakunnat.fi; Unioninkatu 29; ⏲9am-6pm) was designed by CL Engel but not completed until 1852, 12 years after his death. Its interior is fairly unadorned, unlike that of the red-brick Finnish Orthodox **Uspenski Katedraali** (Uspenski Cathedral; www.ort.fi; Kanavakatu 1; ⏲9.30am-4pm Tue-Fri, to 2pm Sat, noon-3pm Sun) on nearby Katajanokka island, which features classic onion-topped domes and an icon-heavy interior.

Suomenlinna FORTRESS
Just a 15-minute ferry ride from the *kauppatori* (return €5, 15 minutes, three times hourly, 6.20am to 2.20am), the 'fortress of Finland' is set on a tight cluster of four islands connected by bridges. Built by the Swedes in the mid-18th century, the impressive fortress complex was taken by the Russians in 1808 and gradually fell into disuse.

From the main quay, a blue-signposted walking path connects the main attractions. By the bridge that connects Iso Mustasaari and the main island, Susisaari, is **Suomenlinnakeskus** (☎029-533 8410; www.suomenlinna.fi; ⏲10.30am-4.30pm Oct-Apr, 10am-6pm May-Sep), which has tourist information, internet access, maps and guided walking tours. Here too is **Suomenlinna-museo** (adult/child €6.50/free; ⏲10.30am-4.30pm Oct-Apr, 10am-6pm

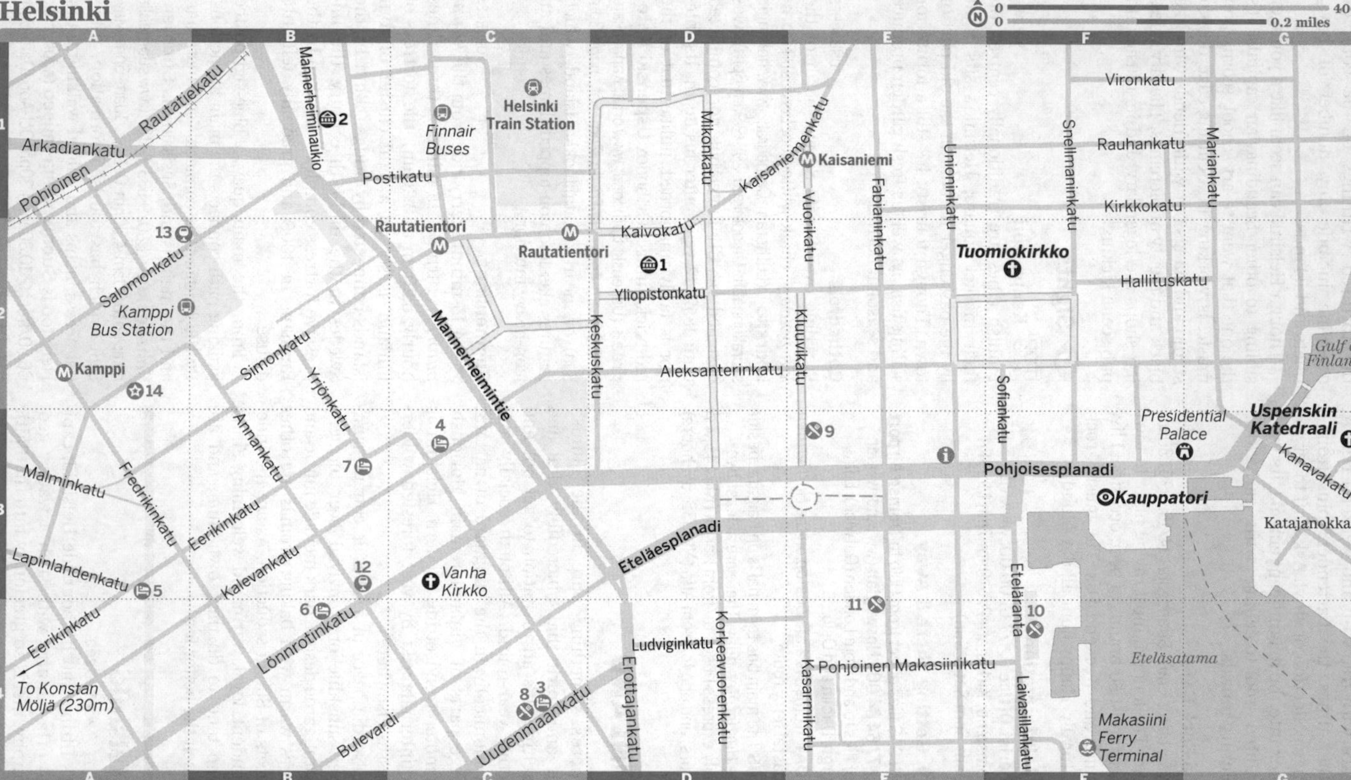

Helsinki
0
400 m
0
0.2 miles
Vironkatu
Helsinki Train Station
Finnair Buses
2
Mannerheiminaukio
Arkadiankatu
Rautatiekatu
Pohjoinen
Postikatu
Mikonkatu
Kaisaniemenkatu
Kaisaniemi
Rauhankatu
Unioninkatu
Snellmaninkatu
Mariankatu
Kirkkokatu
Vuorikatu
Fabianinkatu
Rautatientori
Rautatientori
Kaivokatu
1
Tuomiokirkko
Hallituskatu
13
Salomonkatu
Kamppi Bus Station
Yliopistonkatu
Keskuskatu
Kluuvikatu
Mannerheimintie
Simonkatu
Yrjönkatu
Aleksanterinkatu
Gulf of Finland
Kamppi
14
Sofiankatu
Presidential Palace
Uspenskin Katedraali
4
9
Annankatu
7
Malminkatu
Fredrikinkatu
Pohjoisesplanadi
Kanavakatu
Kauppatori
Eerikinkatu
Katajanokka
Eteläesplanadi
12
Lapinlahdenkatu
Vanha Kirkko
Kalevankatu
5
Eteläranta
6
11
10
Lönnrotinkatu
Eerikinkatu
Ludviginkatu
Pohjoinen Makasiinikatu
Eteläsatama
To Konstan Mölja (230m)
8
3
Korkeavuorenkatu
Kasarmikatu
Erottajankatu
Uudenmaankatu
Laivasillankatu
Makasiini Ferry Terminal
Bulevardi

Helsinki

Top Sights

	Kauppatori	F3
	Tuomiokirkko	F2
	Uspenskin Katedraali	G3

Sights

1	Ateneum	D2
2	Kiasma	B1

Sleeping

3	Hostel Erottajanpuisto	C4
4	Hotel Finn	C3
5	Omenahotelli Eerikinkatu	A3
6	Omenahotelli Lönnrotinkatu	B4
7	Omenahotelli Yrjönkatu	B3

Eating

8	Café Bar 9	C4
9	Karl Fazer	E3
10	Vanha Kauppahalli	F4
11	Zucchini	E4

Drinking

12	Bar Loose	B3
13	Teerenpeli	A2

Entertainment

14	Tavastia & Semifinal	A2

May-Sep), a two-level museum of the fortress's history.

Kiasma GALLERY
(www.kiasma.fi; Mannerheiminaukio 2; adult/child €10/free; 10am-5pm Sun & Tue, to 8.30pm Wed & Thu, to 10pm Fri, to 6pm Sat) Curvaceous and quirky metallic Kiasma, designed by Steven Holl and finished in 1998, is still a symbol of the city's modernisation. It exhibits an eclectic collection of Finnish and international modern art and keeps people on their toes with its striking contemporary exhibitions. The interior, with its unexpected curves and perspectives, is as invigorating as the outside.

Ateneum GALLERY
(www.ateneum.fi; Kaivokatu 2; adult/child €12/free; 10am-6pm Tue & Fri, to 8pm Wed & Thu, 11am-5pm Sat & Sun) Visit Finland's national gallery for a course in the 'who's who' of Finnish art. It houses Finnish paintings and sculptures from the 18th century to the 1950s, with pride of place going to Gallen-Kallela's triptych from the Kalevala epic. There's also a small but interesting collection of 19th- and early-20th-century foreign art.

Activities

Kotiharjun Sauna SAUNA
(www.kotiharjunsauna.fi; Harjutorinkatu 1; adult/child €12/6; 2-8pm Tue-Sat, sauna to 9.30pm) A traditional public wood-fired sauna dating back to 1928. It's a classic experience, where you can also get a scrub-down and massage; there are separate saunas for men and women. It's a short stroll from Sörnäinen metro station.

Tours

There are several cruise companies departing hourly on harbour jaunts (€15 to €20) from the *kauppatori* in summer.

An excellent budget tour is to catch the circular 3T/3B tram and pick up the free *Sightseeing on 3T/3B* brochure as your guide around the city.

Sleeping

Bookings are advisable year-round, as there's nearly always some event or conference on.

TOP CHOICE **Hostel Academica** HOSTEL €
(1311 4334; www.hostelacademica.fi; Hietaniemenkatu 14; dm/s/d €24/62/72; Jun-Aug; P@) Finnish students live well, so in summer take advantage of this residence, a superclean spot packed with features (pool and sauna) and cheery staff. The modern rooms are great, and all come with bar fridges and their own bath rooms. Dorms have only two to four berths so even the cheapest rooms feel uncrowded. HI discount.

Hotel Finn HOTEL €€
(684 4360; www.hotellifinn.fi; Kalevankatu 3B; s/d/q €79/89/129;) High in a perfectly located central city building, this small, friendly hotel is great value for Helsinki if you don't expect luxury. The corridors are darkly done out in sexy chocolate and red, with art from young Finnish photographers, but rooms are bright white and blond parquet. They vary – some haven't been renovated yet. No breakfast.

Rastila Camping CAMPGROUND, COTTAGES €
(3107 8517; www.rastilacamping.fi; Karavaanikatu 4; campsites €14, plus per adult/child €5/1, 2-4 person cabins €79, cottages €107-213, hostel dm/s/d €21/36/62; P@) Only 20 minutes on the metro from the centre (Rastila stop), in a pretty waterside location, this camping ground makes sense. As well as tent and van sites, there are wooden cabins

and more upmarket log cottages, and a summer hostel (open mid-June to early August). Facilities include rowing-boat and canoe hire.

Hostel Erottajanpuisto HOSTEL €

(☎642 169; www.erottajanpuisto.com; Uudenmaankatu 9; dm/s/d €27/54/68; @📶) Helsinki's smallest and most laid-back hostel occupies the top floor of a building in a lively street of bars and restaurants close to the heart of the city. Forget curfews, lockouts, school kids and bringing your own sleeping sheet – this is more like a guesthouse with (crowded) dormitories. HI discount.

Omenahotelli HOTEL €€

(☎0600-18018; www.omena.com; r €60-120; 📶) Eerikinkatu (☎0600-18 018; www.omena.com; Eerikinkatu 24; r €60-120); Lönnrotinkatu (Lönnrotinkatu 13; r €60-120); Yrjönkatu (Yrjönkatu 30; r €60-120) This staffless, keyless hotel chain is good value and has three handy Helsinki locations. As well as a double bed, rooms have fold-outs that can sleep two more, plus there's a microwave and mini-fridge. Book online or via a terminal in the lobby.

Eating

Good budget options are in short supply but lunch specials are available in most places and there are plenty of self-catering opportunities.

TOP CHOICE **Kuu** FINNISH €€

(☎2709 0973; www.ravintolakuu.info; Töölönkatu 27; mains €15-25; ⏲11am-midnight Mon-Fri, from 1pm Sat, 1-10pm Sun) On a corner behind the Crowne Plaza hotel on Mannerheimintie, this is an excellent choice for traditional Finnish fare given a confident modern touch and served in an upbeat bistro atmosphere. Prices are very reasonable for the quality on offer.

TOP CHOICE **Vanha Kauppahalli** MARKET €

(www.wanhakauppahalli.fi; Eteläranta 1; ⏲8am-6pm Mon-Fri, to 5pm Sat, plus 10am-4pm Sun Jun-Aug; 🌿) This traditional market hall was built in 1889. Some of it's touristy these days (reindeer kebabs?) but it's still a glorious place full of picnic treats such as filled rolls, cheeses, breads, smoked fish and an array of other Finnish snacks and delicacies. There are several places serving good, cheap light meals.

Zucchini VEGETARIAN €

(Fabianinkatu 4; lunch €7-11; ⏲11am-4pm Mon-Fri; 🌿) This is a top-notch vegetarian lunchtime spot; queues out the door are not unusual. Piping-hot soups banish winter chills, and fresh-baked quiche on the sunny terrace out the back is a summer treat.

Café Bar 9 CAFE €

(www.bar9.net; Uudenmaankatu 9; mains €8-14; ⏲kitchen 11am-11pm Mon-Fri, from noon Sat & Sun) It's tough to find low-priced food at dinnertime in Helsinki that's not shaved off a spinning stick, so this place stands out. It would anyway, with its retro red formica tables and unpretentious artsy air. Some solid Finnish fare is backed up by big sandwiches, Thai-inspired stir fries and pasta.

Karl Fazer CAFE €

(www.fazer.fi; Kluuvikatu 3; light meals €4-11; ⏲7.30am-10pm Mon-Fri, 9am-10pm Sat, 10am-6pm Sun) This classic cafe is the flagship of the mighty confectionery empire of the same name. It's ideal for buying delicious Fazer chocolates, fresh bread, sandwiches and light meals, or enjoying the towering sundaes or slabs of cake.

Konstan Möljä FINNISH €

(☎694 7504; www.konstanmolja.fi; Hietalahdenkatu 14; lunch/dinner buffet €8.70/18; ⏲11am-2.30pm & 5-10pm Tue-Fri, 4-10pm Sat) The maritime interior of this old sailors' eatery hosts an impressive husband-and-wife team who turn out a great-value Finnish buffet for lunch and dinner. Though these days it sees plenty of tourists, it provides solid traditional fare with salmon, soup, reindeer and friendly explanations of what goes with what.

Drinking & Entertainment

The centre is full of bars and clubs. For the cheapest beer in Helsinki (under €3 a pint during the seemingly perpetual happy hours), hit working-class Kallio (near Sörnäinen metro station), north of the centre.

TOP CHOICE **Teerenpeli** PU

(www.teerenpeli.com; Olavinkatu 2; ⏲noon-2an Mon-Thu, to 3am Fri & Sat, 3pm-midnight Sun Get away from the Finnish lager main stream with this excellent pub right by th bus station. It serves very tasty ales, stout and berry ciders from a microbrewery i a long, split-level place with romanticall low lighting, intimate tables and an indoor smokers' patio.

Bar Loose BAR, VENUE
(www.barloose.com; Annankatu 21; ⌚4pm-2am Mon & Tue, to 4am Wed-Sat, 6pm-4am Sun) The opulent blood-red interior and comfortably cosy seating seem too stylish for a rock bar, but this is what this is, with portraits of guitar heroes lining one wall and an eclectic mix of people filling the upstairs, served by two bars. Downstairs is a club area, with live music more nights than not and DJs spinning everything from metal to retro mod classics.

Tavastia & Semifinal BAR, ROCK
(www.tavastiaklubi.fi; Urho Kekkosenkatu 4; tickets from €12; ⌚8pm-late) One of Helsinki's legendary rock venues, Tavastia attracts both up-and-coming local acts and bigger international groups. There's a band every night of the week. Also check out what's on at Semifinal, the smaller venue next door (tickets €6 to €8).

ℹ Information

Internet access at public libraries is free. Large parts of the city centre have free wi-fi.

Haartman Hospital (☎3106 3231; Haartmaninkatu 4; ⌚24hr) For emergency medical assistance.

Helsinki City Tourist Office (☎3101 3300; www.visithelsinki.fi; Pohjoisesplanadi 19, ⌚9am-8pm Mon-Fri, to 6pm Sat & Sun mid-May–mid-Sep, 9am-6pm Mon-Fri, 10am-4pm Sat & Sun mid-Sep–mid-May) Busy multilingual office with booking desk. The website links to various useful phone apps.

Lonely Planet (www.lonelyplanet.com/finland/helsinki)

Sidewalk Express (www.sidewalkexpress.com; per hr €2) There are several of these no-staff stand-up internet access points around town. Buy your ticket from the machine; it's valid for all of them. Handy locations include the central train station and Kamppi bus station.

ℹ Getting There & Away

AIR There are flights to Helsinki from many Finnish and European cities and several intercontinental ones. The airport is at Vantaa, 19km north of Helsinki.

BOAT Ferries (see p988) travel to Sweden (via the Åland archipelago), Estonia, Russia, Germany and Poland.

BUS Regional and long-distance buses dock at underground **Kamppi Bus Station** (www.matkahuolto.fi). There are services to all major towns in Finland.

TRAIN Helsinki's **train station** (rautatieasema; www.vr.fi; ⌚tickets 6.30am-9.30pm) is central. It's linked to the metro (Rautatientori stop), and is a short walk from the bus station.

The train is the fastest and cheapest way to get from Helsinki to major Finnish centres; there are also daily trains to Russia.

ℹ Getting Around

TO/FROM THE AIRPORT Bus 615 (€4.50, 30 to 45 minutes) shuttles between Vantaa airport and platform 5 at Rautatientori by the train station. Faster Finnair buses (€6.20, 30 minutes, every 20 minutes) depart from Elielinaukio platform 30 on the other side of the train station.

BICYCLE Helsinki is ideal for cycling, as it's flat and has well-marked bicycle paths. Pick up a copy of the city cycling map from the tourist office. **Greenbike** (☎050 404 0400; www.greenbike.fi; Kampintori; single-speed bike per day/24hr/week €20/25/75; ⌚10am-6pm Jun-early Sep) rents out quality bikes.

LOCAL TRANSPORT HSL (www.hsl.fi) operates buses, metro, local trains, trams and the Suomenlinna ferry. A one-hour ticket (with unlimited transfers) for any transport costs €2.70 when purchased on-board, or €2.20 when purchased in advance. Day or multiday tickets (€7/10.50/14 for 24/48/72 hours) are worthwhile. Buy tickets at Rautatientori metro station, R-kioskis, K-markets and the tourist office.

Turku

☎02 / POP 179,500

Turku is Finland's oldest town and former capital, but today it's a modern maritime city, brimming with museums and boasting a robust harbourside castle and magnificent cathedral. Its heart and soul is the lovely Aurajoki, a broad ribbon spilling into the Baltic Sea harbour, lined with riverboat bars and restaurants.

👁 Sights & Activities

Turun Linna CASTLE
(Turku Castle; www.museumcentreturku.fi; adult/child €8/4.50; ⌚10am-6pm Tue-Sun) A visit to lofty Turku Castle, near the harbour, should be your first stop. Founded in 1280 at the mouth of the Aurajoki, the castle has been rebuilt a number of times since. You can download a free audioguide from www.turku.fi.

TOP CHOICE **Luostarimäen Käsityöläismuseo** MUSEUM
(www.museumcentreturku.fi; Vartiovuorenkatu 2; adult/child €6/4; ⌚10am-6pm Tue-Sun May–

mid-Sep) The open-air Luostarinmäki Handicrafts Museum, in the only surviving 18th-century area of this medieval town, is one of the best of its kind in Finland and much more intriguing than the name suggests – it's a Turku must-see. In summer, artisans work inside its 40 old wooden houses, and musicians stroll its paths. It also opens in December as a Christmas market.

Festivals & Events

Ruisrock MUSIC

(www.ruisrock.fi) A major music festival held on Ruissalo island in early July.

Sleeping

Bed & Breakfast Tuure B&B €

(233 0230; www.tuure.fi; Tuureporinkatu 17C; s/d/tr €39/58/78; @) Very handy for the bus station, this tidy, friendly guesthouse makes an excellent place to stay. The rooms are bright and thoughtfully decorated, you get your own keys, and there's a microwave, a fridge and free internet. Reception is open 8am to 9pm.

Turku Hostel HOSTEL €

(262 7680; www.turku.fi/hostelturku; Linnankatu 39; dm/s/tw €23/43/54; P@) Well located near the river, a pleasant stroll from the town centre, this is a friendly, neat place with lockers, spacious dorms, keycard security and a minifridge in each private room. There's also cheap bike hire, breakfast available and free internet. There's a 2am curfew if you're dorming it. HI discount.

Eating

TOP CHOICE **Tintå** GASTROPUB €€

(230 7023; www.tinta.fi; Läntinen Rantakatu 9; mains €13-20; 11am-midnight Mon, to 1am Tue-Thu, to 2am Fri, noon-2am Sat, noon-9pm Sun) On the riverfront, this cosy wine bar offers more than 50 choices by the glass, including some very interesting selections. The food is fabulous: large, innovative pizzas and a short, eclectic array of other dishes bursting with flavour. Top quality, top value.

Trattoria Romana ITALIAN €

(Hämeenkatu 9; pizza & pasta €9-15; 11am-10pm Mon-Fri, 1-10pm Sat, 1-8pm Sun) With that reliably comfortable trattoria decoration, this intimate spot adds to the tried-and-tested favourites with some more interesting combinations, including a changing list of daily specials. Ask the waiter to translate them, as they're very worthwhile, and better value than the à la carte meat dishes. Delicious salads are also available.

Drinking & Entertainment

Boat Bars BARS

Summer drinking begins on the decks of any of the boats lining the south bank of the river. Although most serve food, they are primarily floating beer terraces. If the beer prices make you wince, join locals on the grassy riverbank drinking takeaways.

Information

Tourist Office (262 7444; www.turkutouring.fi; Aurakatu 4; 8.30am-6pm Mon-Fri, 9am-4pm Sat & Sun) Busy, very helpful and with information on the entire region. From October to March, weekend opening is 10am to 3pm. There's coin-op internet access here, and bike hire (€20 per day).

Getting There & Away

BOAT The harbour, southwest of the centre, has terminals for Tallink/Silja and Viking Line services to Stockholm (11 hours).

BUS From the main **bus terminal** (www.matkahuolto.fi; Aninkaistenkatu 20) there are hourly express buses to Helsinki (€30.50, 2¾ hours) and frequent services to Tampere (€24.80, two to three hours).

TRAIN The train station is a short walk northwest of the centre; trains also stop at the ferry harbour. Trains run frequently to/from Helsinki (from €31, two hours), Tampere (from €26, 1¾ hours) and beyond.

Getting Around

The tourist office hires bikes; ask about the scenic 250km route around the Turku archipelago.

Bus 1 runs between the harbour, *kauppatori* and airport (€2.50).

Tampere

03 / POP 215,300

Scenic Tampere, set between two vast lakes has an appealing down-to-earth vitality. Through its centre churn the Tammerkoski rapids, its grassy banks contrasting with the red brick of the imposing fabric mills whose regenerated industrial buildings house quirky museums, enticing shops, pubs, cinemas and cafes.

Sights

TOP CHOICE Tuomiokirkko CHURCH
(www.tampereenseurakunnat.fi; Tuomiokirkonkatu 3; ⏲10am-5pm May-Aug, 11am-3pm Sep-Apr) Tampere's intriguing cathedral is one of the most notable examples of Finnish National Romantic architecture. Artist Hugo Simberg was responsible for the solemn, almost mournful frescos and stained glass; the altarpiece, by Magnus Enckell, is a dreamlike *Resurrection* in similar style.

Särkänniemi AMUSEMENT PARK
(www.sarkanniemi.fi; adult/child day pass up to €35/29; ⏲rides 10am-8pm mid-May–Aug) On the northern edge of town, this promontory amusement park is a large complex with a load of high-adrenalin rides, a good art gallery and an aquarium. It meets strict environmentally friendly criteria. Take bus 4 or 16 from the train station.

Tours

Trips on Tampere's magnificent lakes are extremely popular in summer. Boats for Näsijärvi leave from Mustalahti quay, while boats from Laukontori quay serves Pyhäjärvi. Book at the tourist office.

Sleeping

TOP CHOICE Dream Hostel HOSTEL €
(☎045-236 0517; www.dreamhostel.fi; Åkerlundinkatu 2; dm €22-27, tw/q €63/89; P@) Sparky and spacious, this is Finland's best urban hostel. Helpful staff, super-comfortable wide-berth dorms in various sizes, original decor and the right attitude about everything make it a real winner. It's a short walk from the train station in a quiet area.

Omenahotelli HOTELS €
(☎0600 18018; www.omena.com; Hämeenkatu 7; r €70-90; @) With two locations at the western (Hämeenkatu 28) and eastern Hämeenkatu 7) ends of the main drag – the latter very handy for the station – this receptionless hotel offers comfortable rooms with double bed, a microwave, fridge, kettle and two fold-outs. Free wi-fi, and great value for groups. Book online or via the terminal at the entrance.

Eating

Tampere's speciality, *mustamakkara*, is tasty mild blood sausage normally eaten with lingonberry jam. You can get it at the *kauppahalli* (market hall), a great place for cheap eats.

TOP CHOICE Tuulensuu GASTROPUB €€
(www.gastropub.net/tuulensuu; Hämeenpuisto 23; mains €17-23; ⏲food noon-midnight Mon-Sat, 3pm-midnight Sun) The best of Tampere's gastropubs, this corner spot has a superb range of Belgian beers and good wines and ports. The food is lovingly prepared and features staples such as liver and schnitzel, as well as more elaborate plates including duck confit and other bistro fare inspired by Belgium and northeastern France.

Panimoravintola Plevna BEER HALL €€
(www.plevna.fi; Itäinenkatu 8; mains €10-20; ⏲food 11am-10pm) Inside the old Finlayson textile mill, this place offers a wide range of delicious beer, cider and perry brewed on the premises. Meals are large and designed for soaking it all up: massive sausage platters and enormous slabs of pork in classic beer-hall style, as well as more Finnish fish and steak dishes.

Drinking & Entertainment

TOP CHOICE Café Europa BAR, CAFE
(www.ravintola.fi/europa; Aleksanterinkatu 29; ⏲noon-midnight Mon & Tue, to 2am Wed & Thu, to 3am Fri & Sat, 1pm-midnight Sun) Lavishly furnished with horsehair couches, armchairs, mirrors, chandeliers and paintings, this successfully fuses a recreated 1930s-style old-Europe cafe with a popular meeting spot for students and anyone who appreciates comfort, board games, Belgian and German beers, and generously proportioned sandwiches and salads.

Information

Visit Tampere (☎5656 6800; www.visittampere.fi; Rautatienkatu 25; ⏲8.30am-4.30pm Mon-Fri Sep-May, 9am-6pm Mon-Fri, 11am-3pm Sat & Sun Jun-Aug) In the train station. Booking desk and free internet.

Getting There & Away

BUS The **bus station** (Hatanpään valtatie 7) is in the south of town. Regular express buses run from Helsinki (€26.30, 2½ hours) and Turku (€24.80, two to three hours), and most other major towns in Finland are served from here.

TRAIN The **train station** (www.vr.fi; Rautatienkatu 25) is in the centre at the eastern end of Hämeenkatu. Express trains run hourly to/from Helsinki (€24 to €31, two hours). There are direct trains to Turku (€28.41, 1¾ hours), Oulu (€60 to €70, 4¼ to seven hours) and other cities.

Lakeland

Most of southern Finland could be dubbed 'lakeland', but this spectacular area takes it to extremes. It often seems there's more water than land here, and what water it is: sublime, sparkling and clean, reflecting sky and forests cleanly as a mirror. It's a land that leaves an indelible impression on every visitor.

SAVONLINNA

☎015 / POP 27,600

Finland's prettiest town, Savonlinna shimmers on a sunny day as the water ripples around its centre. Set on two islands between Haapavesi and Pihlajavesi lakes, it's a classic Lakeland settlement with a major attraction: perched on a rocky islet is one of Europe's most visually dramatic castles.

Sights & Activities

TOP CHOICE Olavinlinna CASTLE

(www.olavinlinna.fi; adult/child €8/4; 10am-6pm Jun–mid-Aug, to 4pm Mon-Fri, 11am-4pm Sat & Sun mid-Aug–May) Standing immense and haughty on a rock in the lake, 15th-century Olavinlinna is one of northern Europe's most spectacularly situated castles. As well as being an imposing fortification, it's also the venue for the month-long **Savonlinna Opera Festival** (www.operafestival.fi). To visit most of the interior you must join a guided tour (45 minutes). Tours are multilingual and depart on the hour.

Boat Trips CRUISES

From June to August, Savonlinna passenger harbour is buzzing with dozens of daily scenic cruises that last about an hour and cost around €10 to €16. The boats anchor alongside the *kauppatori* and you can soon see which is the next departure. There are also longer cruises to other Lakeland towns.

Sleeping

Hotel beds are scarce and pricey during July's opera festival – book accommodation well in advance. Fortunately, students are out of town and their residences are converted to summer hotels and hostels.

Kesähotelli Vuorilinna SUMMER HOTEL €€

(☎73950; www.spahotelcasino.fi; Kylpylaitoksentie; s/d €65/85; Jun-Aug; P Wi-Fi) Set in several student buildings, this friendly complex has an appealing location across a footbridge from the centre. Rooms are clean and comfortable; cheaper ones share bathroom and kitchen between two. Prices include breakfast and afternoon sauna.

Eating & Drinking

The lively lakeside *kauppatori* is the place for casual snacking. A *lörtsy* (turnover) is typical and comes savoury with meat *(lihalörtsy)* or sweet with apple *(omenalörtsy)* or cloudberry *(lakkalörtsy)*. Savonlinna is also famous for fried *muikku* (vendace, tiny lake fish).

TOP CHOICE Huvila FINNISH, MICROBREWERY €€

(☎555 0555; www.panimoravintolahuvila.fi; Puistokatu 4; mains €16-28; noon-midnight Jun-Aug) This excellent microbrewery and restaurant is just across the harbour from the town centre. The food focuses on fresh local ingredients, all expertly prepared and served in generous quantities. Staff will recommend a beer match, whether fresh, hoppy Joutsen, traditional sweet *sahti*, or deliciously rich dessert stout. The terrace is a wonderful place on a sunny afternoon.

Information

Savonlinna Travel (☎0600-30007; www.savonlinna.travel; Puistokatu 1; 9am-5pm

THE SAUNA

For centuries the sauna has been a place to bathe, meditate, warm up and even give birth, and most Finns still use it at least once a week. Bathing is done in the nude (public saunas are nearly always sex-segregated) and Finns are quite strict about its nonsexual – even sacred – nature.

Shower first. Once inside (with a temperature of 80°C to 100°C), water is thrown onto the stove using a *kauhu* (ladle), producing *löyly* (steam). A *vihta* (whisk of birch twigs and leaves) is sometimes used to lightly strike the skin, improving circulation. Cool off with a cold shower or preferably by jumping into a lake. Repeat. The sauna beer afterwards is also traditional.

Mon-Fri Aug-Jun, 10am to 6pm Mon-Sat Jul) Booking desk and free internet.

Getting There & Away

BUS Bus services include Helsinki (€52, 4½ to six hours, several per day).

TRAIN Trains departing from Helsinki (€57, 4¼ hours) require a change in Parikkala. For Kuopio and Tampere, rail buses will shuttle you the two-hour trip to Pieksämäki to connect with trains.

Lapland

Extending hundreds of kilometres above the Arctic Circle, Lapland is Finland's true wilderness and casts a powerful spell. The midnight sun, the Sámi peoples, the aurora borealis (northern lights) and the wandering reindeer are all components of Lapland's intangible magic, as is good old ho-ho-ho himself, who 'officially' resides up here.

ROVANIEMI

016 / POP 60,700

The 'official' terrestrial residence of Santa Claus is the capital of Finnish Lapland and a more-or-less obligatory northern stop. Its wonderful Arktikum museum is the perfect introduction to the mysteries of these latitudes, and Rovaniemi is a good place to organise activities. The tour buses roll north of town, where everyone's favourite beardie-weirdie has an impressive grotto.

Sights & Activities

TOP CHOICE **Arktikum** MUSEUM

(www.arktikum.fi; Pohjoisranta 4; adult/child €12/5; 9am-6pm Jun–mid-Aug, 10am-6pm Dec–mid-Jan, 10am-6pm Tue-Sun mid-Jan–May) With its beautifully designed glass tunnel stretching out to the Ounasjoki, Arktikum is one of Finland's best museums and well worth the admission if you are interested in the north. There are two main exhibitions: one side deals with Lapland, with information on Sámi culture; the highlight is the other side, with a superb, wide-ranging display on the Arctic itself.

Napapiiri TOURIST COMPLEX

The Arctic Circle crosses the road here, km north of Rovaniemi – and built right on top of it is the 'official' **Santa Claus Village** (www.santaclausvillage.info; 10am-5pm mid-Jan–May & Sep-Nov, 9am-6pm Jun-Aug, 9am-7pm Dec–mid-Jan), a touristy complex of shops, reindeer, winter activities and cottage accommodation. The **Santa Claus Post Office** (www.santaclaus.posti.fi; 10am-5pm Sep-Nov & Jan-May, 9am-7pm Jun-Aug & Dec) receives nearly three-quarters of a million letters each year from all over the world. Mail sent from here bears a Santa stamp, and you can arrange to have it delivered at Christmas.

But the big attraction is Santa himself, who receives visitors year-round in a rather impressive **grotto** (www.santaclauslive.com). The portly saint is quite a linguist, and an old hand at chatting with kids and adults alike. A private chinwag – around two minutes – with the man is free, but you can't photograph the moment....and official snaps start at €25.

Bus 8 heads to Napapiiri from the train station, passing through the centre (adult/child €7/3.80 return).

> **LAPLAND SEASONS**
>
> Pick your time in Lapland carefully. In the far north there's no sun for 50 days of the year, and no night for 70-odd days. In June it's very muddy, and in July insects can be hard to deal with. If you're here to walk, August is great, and in September the stunning *ruska* (autumn) colours can be seen. There's thick snow cover from mid-October to May; the best time for skiing and husky/reindeer/snowmobile safaris is March and April: a decent amount of daylight and less extreme temperatures.

Tours

Rovaniemi is Finnish Lapland's most popular base for winter and summer activities, offering the convenience of frequent departures and professional trips with multilingual guides. Check the tourist-office website for activities including river cruises, reindeer- and husky-sledding, rafting, snowmobiling, skiing and mountain biking.

Sleeping

Hostel Rudolf HOSTEL €

(321 321; www.rudolf.fi; Koskikatu 41; dm/s/d Dec-Mar €48/62/89, Apr-Nov €38/46/59; P) Run by Hotel Santa Claus, where you inconveniently have to go to check in, this staffless place is Rovaniemi's only hostel and can fill up fast. Private rooms are good for the price, with spotless bathrooms, solid desks and bedside lamps; dorm rates get you the same deal. There's also a kitchen. HI discount.

Guesthouse Borealis GUESTHOUSE €
(☎342 0130; www.guesthouseborealis.com; Asemieskatu 1; s/d/tr €51/64/88; P@) The cordial hospitality and proximity to the train station make this family-run spot a winner. The rooms have no frills but are bright and clean; some have a balcony. The airy dining room is the venue for breakfast, which features Finnish porridge; a sauna's also available for a small extra charge. Guests have use of a kitchen.

Eating

Mariza FINNISH €
(www.ruokahuonemariza.fi; Ruokasenkatu 2; lunch €8.20; ⏲10am-2pm Mon-Fri) A couple of blocks from the centre in untouristed territory, this simple lunch place offers a buffet of home-cooked Finnish food, including daily changing hot dishes, soup and salad. Authentic and excellent. Opens slightly longer hours in summer.

Drinking & Entertainment

TOP CHOICE **Kauppayhtiö** CAFE, BAR
(Valtakatu 24; light meals €4-7; ⏲10.30am-8pm Mon-Thu, to midnight Wed, to 4am Fri & Sat) Rovaniemi's best cafe, this oddball collection of retro curios has a coffee-bean and gasoline theme and colourful plastic tables. An espresso machine, bottomless coffee, outdoor seating, salads, sundaes and a bohemian Lapland crowd keep the place ticking. It also does food, including sushi some days, and has regular live music.

Information

Tourist Information (☎346 270; www.visitrovaniemi.fi; Maakuntakatu 29; ⏲9am-5pm Mon-Fri) On the square in the middle of town, with free internet. It opens until 6pm from mid-June to mid-August, when it also opens on weekends from 9am to 1pm. Same opening hours at Christmas.

Getting There & Away

AIR Finnair/Flybe and Norwegian fly between Helsinki and Rovaniemi. Minibuses to the centre meet each arriving flight (€7, 15 minutes), doing hotel drop-offs. They pick up along the same route an hour before flight departures.

BUS Daily connections serve just about everywhere in Lapland, including Norwegian destinations. Night buses serve Helsinki (€126.30, 12½ hours).

TRAIN There are three daily direct services to Helsinki (€84 to €97, 9¾ to 13 hours), including overnight options.

INARI

☎016 / POP 550

The tiny village of Inari (Sámi: Anár) is the place to begin to learn something of Sámi culture. It has the excellent Siida museum and the Finnish Sámi parliament, as well as worthwhile handicrafts shops.

Sights & Activities

TOP CHOICE **Siida** MUSEUM
(www.siida.fi; adult/child €9/5; ⏲9am-8pm Jun–mid-Sep, 10am-5pm Tue-Sun mid-Sep–May) One of Finland's finest museums, Siida should not be missed. It's a comprehensive overview of the Sámi and their Arctic environment, skilfully interwoven. Outside is the original museum, a complex of open-air buildings that reflect facets of nomadic and postnomadic Sámi life.

Sleeping

Lomakylä Inari CAMPGROUND €
(☎671 108; www.saariselka.fi/lomakylainari; 2-/4-person cabins €65/75, without bathroom €43/48, cottages €80-170, campsites for 1/2/4 people €10/15/18; ⏲Jun-Sep; P@) The closest cabin accommodation to town, this is 500m south of the centre and a good option. Some cottages are available in winter.

Information

Tourist Office (☎040-168 9668; www.inari.fi; ⏲9am-8pm Jun–mid-Sep, 10am-5pm Tue-Sun mid-Sep–May) In the Siida museum and open the same hours. There's also a nature information point here.

Getting There & Away

There are two daily services from Rovaniemi (€58.30, 5¼ hours), which continue to Norway.

UNDERSTAND SCANDINAVIA

History

The Big Freeze & the Viking Age

Though evidence of pre–ice age habitation exists, it wasn't until around 11,000 years ago that settlement in Scandinavia was re-established after the big chill, as hunter-gatherers followed the retreating glaciers into the region.

Scandinavia greatly impacted Western civilisation during the Viking Age, usually dated from AD 793. Through the next cen turies, Vikings conducted raids throughout Europe and established settlements across the north of the continent.

The Vikings declined after 1066, with the defeat of the Norwegian king Harald Hardråda at the Battle of Stamford Bridge in England. Stubbornly pagan Scandinavia gradually turned to Christianity in the 10th and 11th centuries.

God, Trade & Empires

In 1397 Margrethe I of Denmark established a union between Denmark, Norway and Sweden to counter the influence of the powerful Hanseatic League that had come to dominate the region's trade.

In the 16th century the Reformation swept through the region, accompanied by church burnings and civil warfare. At this time, Sweden withdrew from the union, and over the next few hundred years Denmark and Sweden fought numerous border skirmishes and a few fully fledged wars, largely over control of the Baltic Sea.

Sweden became a muscular imperial power, which waxed large then waned for good in the 18th century. Norway remained under Danish rule until 1814, when it was ceded to Sweden. Norwegian independence finally came in 1905.

Meanwhile, Finland was a constant battleground between Sweden, who had effectively annexed it, and Russia. By 1809 Sweden was in no state to resist, and Finland became a duchy of the Russian Empire. The Russian revolution of October 1917 enabled Finland to declare independence.

Recovery & the Welfare State

WWII was a tough time for Scandinavia. Finland was invaded by Stalin's Red Army and ended up fighting on both sides as it struggled to defend its territory. Denmark and Norway were invaded and taken by Germany in 1940 and were not freed until the end of the war. Neutral Sweden played a canny game.

In the postwar years, Sweden, Denmark and Finland joined the EU, while Norway prospered after the discovery of oil in the 1960s. All established robust welfare states, with citizens protected from cradle to grave by the state – in exchange for high taxes.

Scandinavia Today

Scandinavia's image as a liberal democratic paradise has taken a hit in recent years: lone gunmen have perpetrated appalling massacres in Finland and Norway, while anti-immigration attitudes and dissatisfaction with Europe's economic situation have led to the rise of far-right parties. Nevertheless, Scandinavia remains a major success story with a strong economy, robust social values and super-low crime and corruption.

People

Sweden, Norway and Finland are all in Europe's top eight countries by area, but have extremely low population densities, with settlement concentrated in the cities of the south and less than one person per square kilometre across much of Lapland.

Scandinavians (although Finns don't consider themselves as such) are stereotyped as outwardly serious with a strong sense of family and an admirable environmental sensitivity. Above all, they are egalitarian – they have the smallest gap between rich and poor in the world – and proud of their social equality in which none have too much or too little.

Scandinavian countries have become increasingly multicultural in recent years, with hundreds of different nationalities adding to the mix that already included Roma and, in the north, the indigenous Sámi. About 80% of Scandinavians describe themselves as Lutherans, but only around one in 20 go to church regularly.

The Scandinavian reputation for politeness, even blandness, seems odd when weighed against their global gold medal in coffee consumption, their production line of successful heavy bands and their propensity for a tipple. However, the image of a log cabin by a lake tells much about Scandinavian culture: independence, endurance and a deep love of nature.

Arts

Painting

The 19th century saw a golden age in Danish painting, followed by similar periods of high quality in Sweden and Finland. A more naturalistic style brought in the 20th century; subsequently, modernism and contemporary art have also been strong presences in the region. The standout figure of Scandinavian art is the Norwegian Edvard Munch, whose edgy expressionist creations include the much-reproduced *The Scream.* There's an art museum in nearly every Scandinavian town, and some truly outstanding galleries scattered across the region.

Literature

The roll call of famous Scandinavian literary figures is a strong one, straddling a variety of genres and centuries. The tales of Hans Christian Andersen have their 20th-century counterparts in Astrid Lindgren and Tove Jansson's Moomintrolls, while heavyweights Henrik Ibsen and August Strindberg bestride the theatrical firmament. The *Kalevala*, a collection of folk stories, songs and poems compiled in the 1830s by Elias Lönnrot, is Finland's national epic and a very entertaining read, while philosopher Søren Kierkegaard is a towering figure in that field. Modern Nordic crime fiction has been phenomenally successful, with Swedes Henning Mankell and Stieg Larsson and Norwegian Jo Nesbø breaking sales records worldwide.

Cinema

Swedish cinema is inextricably linked with the name of Ingmar Bergman. His deeply contemplative films *(The Seventh Seal; Through a Glass Darkly; Persona)* explore the meaning of life, the certainty of death and other light-hearted themes. The most prolific and controversial of Denmark's 21st-century directors remains Lars von Trier, whose most recent film, *Melancholia* (2010), delivers a surreal, visually arresting take on the apocalypse. The best-known Finnish filmmaker is Aki Kaurismäki, famous for films such as *Le Havre* (2011), *Drifting Clouds* (1996) and the wonderful *Man Without a Past* (2002), an ultimately life-affirming story about a man who loses his memory.

Architecture & Design

The Nordic countries have been at the forefront of modern design and architecture since the first half of the 20th century. The Finn Alvar Aalto was a colossus in both fields, and, together with others, set the template for a Scandinavian philosophy of design that emphasises the practical and the natural, seeking and achieving beauty as a side-product of functionality.

Music

Scandinavian music crosses the spectrum from the classical works of Grieg and Sibelius to Norwegian black metal. Sweden has been at the forefront of the modern music scene, with ABBA as its most famous export, backed by Roxette, The Hives, Mando Diao, The Cardigans, Kent, Lisa Ekdahl, José González, Robyn, The Hellacopters and Ace of Base to name just a few. Finland has contributed to the darker, heavier end of the spectrum with groups such as Nightwish, Apocalyptica, Lordi, The 69 Eyes, The Rasmus and HIM making waves, while Norway, as well as its metal side, has a strong jazz and electronica scene.

Food & Drink

Scandinavian cuisine, once viewed as meatballs, herring and little else, is now at the forefront of modern gastronomy. At the heart of the revolution is Copenhagen, home to 13 Michelin-starred restaurants and the restaurant often considered the world's best, Noma. New Nordic cuisine has a 'foraging' ethos, showcasing local produce prepared using traditional techniques and contemporary experimentation, and focused on clean, natural flavours.

Traditional eateries still abound, however, and are focused on old-school staples such as herring, salmon, pork and beef, accompanied by root vegetables, berries and mushrooms.

Scandinavians are enthusiastic drinkers, though strong alcohol in Sweden, Norway and Finland can only be bought in state stores. Beer is ubiquitous, and each nation has its own favourite shot to clear the head. Wine is popular, but very expensive in restaurants.

SURVIVAL GUIDE

Directory A–Z

Accommodation

Most camping grounds open only from June to August. Almost all have cabins or cottages for rent, usually excellent value. The **Camping Key Europe** (www.campingkeyeurope.com) card offers useful discounts.

Scandinavian hostels are invariably clean comfortable and very well equipped, i sometimes short on atmosphere. It's wort being a member of **Hostelling International** (HI; www.hihostels.com), as members sav a substantial amount at affiliated places

You'll save money with a sleep sheet or your own linen, as most hostels charge for this.

From June to August, many student residences function as 'summer hotels'. These can be great value, as you often get your own room, with kitchen (not always equipped) and bathroom either to yourself or shared between two. In summer and at weekends, the big hotels lower their prices significantly: excellent value. Self-catering cottages and farm-stays throughout the region offer a well-priced way of getting into the Scandinavian way of rural life.

The following price categories used in the listings in this chapter are based on the cost of a standard double room at its most expensive. In the budget category expect shared bathrooms; midrange will have private bathroom, good facilities and breakfast buffet included, while top end has business-class or five-star facilities. Double beds are rare; family/group rooms are common.

€ less than €70

€€ €70 to €160

€€€ more than €160

Activities

On the water Every waterside town has a place (frequently the camping ground) where you can rent a canoe, kayak or rowing boat. Rental cottages often have rowing boats that you can use free of charge to investigate the local lake. Rafting options range from short, Class II doddles to Class III and IV adventures, and rollicking Class V punishment.

Fishing Several permits are required of foreigners but they are very easy to arrange.

Hiking Scandinavia has some of Europe's best hiking, best done from June to September, although in July mosquitoes and other biting insects can be a big problem in Lapland. Wilderness huts line the northern trails (both free shared ones and private bookable ones).

Skiing The ski season runs from late November to early May and slightly longer in the north.

Dog sledding Expeditions can range from two-hour tasters to multiday trips with overnight stays in remote forest huts.

Snowmobiling Most operators allow travellers to ride as a passenger behind an experienced driver or (usually for an additional charge) as the driver yourself; for the latter, a valid driving licence is required.

Business Hours

Following are approximate business hours in Scandinavia; these vary by country and season.

Banks 10am to 4pm Monday to Friday, to 5pm or 6pm Thursday (Denmark); 9am to 4.15pm Monday to Friday (Finland); 8.15am to 3pm Monday to Wednesday and Friday, to 5pm Thursday (Norway); 9.30am to 3pm Monday to Friday (Sweden)

Nightclubs As late as 4am

Post offices 9am to 5pm Monday to Friday, some open Saturday morning

Pubs 11am to 1am (often later on Friday and Saturday)

Restaurants 11am to 10pm, lunch 11am to 3pm, dinner 5pm onwards

Shops 9am to 6pm Monday to Friday, to 3pm Saturday

State alcohol store 9am to 8pm Monday to Friday, to 6pm Saturday (Finland); 10am to 6pm Monday to Friday, to 2pm (often to 5pm) Saturday (Sweden)

Food

The following price categories for the cost of a main course are used in the listings in this chapter.

€ less than €15

€€ €15 to €25

€€€ more than €25

Gay & Lesbian Travellers

Scandinavia's cities are open, tolerant places, and Copenhagen and Stockholm in particular have vibrant gay scenes with a healthy number of venues.

Same-sex marriage is legal in Norway, Sweden and Denmark.

Internet Access

» Public libraries usually have at least one free internet terminal; may need to be reserved ahead.

» Tourist offices often have an internet terminal that you can use (usually 15 minutes).

» Wireless internet access is extremely widespread; several cities have extensive networks, and nearly all accommodation, as well as many restaurants, cafes and bars, offer free access to customers and guests.

Money

» Using ATMs with a credit/debit card is by far the easiest way of getting cash in Scandinavia. ATMs can be found even in small villages.

» Credit cards are widely accepted; Scandinavians are dedicated users of the plastic even to buy a beer or cup of coffee.

» Travellers cheques and cash can be exchanged at banks; in the big cities, independent exchange facilities usually offer better rates.

» Service is generally considered to be included in bills, so there's no need to tip at all unless you want to reward exceptional service.

Public Holidays

New Year's Day 1 January

Epiphany 6 January (Sweden and Finland)

Maundy Thursday (Denmark and Norway)

Good Friday March/April

Easter Sunday & Monday March/April

May Day 1 May

Ascension Day May

Whitsunday and/or Monday Late May or early June

Midsummer's Eve & Day Weekend in June closest to 24 June (Sweden and Finland)

All Saints' Day First Saturday in November (Finland and Sweden)

Christmas 25 December; also 24 December in Denmark and Finland

Boxing Day 26 December

Telephone

» Public telephones basically no longer exist, so if you don't have a mobile (cell) phone it's expensive calls from your hotel room or talking over the internet.

» You can buy a prepaid SIM card easily. There are always deals, and you should pick up a card for as little as €10, including some call credit. Top the credit up at the same outlets, online or at ATMs.

» You can also buy cut-rate phonecards that substantially lower the cost of making international calls.

» To call abroad, dial ☎00.

Time

Denmark, Norway and Sweden are one hour ahead of UTC/GMT (two hours from late March to late October). Finland is a further hour ahead.

Visas

Schengen rules apply. See p1212 for more information.

Getting There & Away

Air

Scandinavia is easily reached by air, with direct flights from numerous European destinations (as well as several Asian and American ones) to Copenhagen, Stockholm, Oslo and Helsinki as well as some regional airports. The airlines with most flights to the region:

Finnair (www.finnair.com)

Norwegian (www.norwegian.com)

Ryanair (www.ryanair.com)

SAS (www.flysas.com)

Land

Scandinavia has land borders with Russia (Finland and Norway) and Germany (Denmark). There are **buses** (www.matkahuolto.fi) and **trains** (www.vr.fi) from Helsinki to St Petersburg and Moscow, and Eurolines buses and Danish trains to numerous German cities to/from Copenhagen, as well as to/from Sweden via the Øresund bridge.

Sea

Baltic and Atlantic ferries connect Scandinavia with eastern and northern European nations: Germany, Poland, Estonia, Latvia, Lithuania, Russia and the UK. Book ahead in summer, at weekends and if travelling with a vehicle. Many boats are amazingly cheap if you travel without a cabin. Many ferry lines offer 50% discounts for holders of rail passes. Some offer discounts for ISIC and youth-card holders; enquire when purchasing your ticket. The website www directferries.com is useful for routes and discounted tickets. Major operators:

Color Line (www.colorline.com) Norway–Germany, Norway–Sweden, Norway–Denmark.

DFDS Seaways (www.dfdsseaways.com) Norway–Sweden–Denmark, Denmark–UK.

Polferries (www.polferries.pl) Sweden–Poland, Denmark–Poland.

Scandlines (www.scandlines.com) Sweden–Germany, Sweden–Latvia, Sweden–Denmark, Denmark–Germany.

St Peter Line (✆010-346 7820; www.stpeterline.com) Finland–Russia, Sweden–Estonia–Russia.

Stena Line (www.stenaline.com) Denmark–Norway, Denmark–Sweden, Sweden–Germany, Sweden–Poland.

Tallink/Silja Line (www.tallinksilja.com) Finland–Sweden, Finland–Estonia, Sweden–Estonia, Finland–Germany.

Viking Line (www.vikingline.fi) Finland–Sweden, Finland–Estonia.

Getting Around

Air

All the Scandinavian countries have comprehensive domestic flight networks and there are regular services connecting the capitals and major cities of the region.

Bicycle

Bikes can be carried on many trains and most buses and ferries, but it's wise to reserve bike space in advance. Scandinavia is one of the world's most cycle-friendly destinations, with numerous places to hire bikes and an extensive network of cycle lanes in every city.

Boat

Ferry services link the Scandinavian countries with each other, and also service all major inhabited islands. In Sweden and Finland, lake and canal boats were once important means of summer transport and are now kept on as cruises: a great, leisurely way to journey between towns.

Bus

Buses connect all major towns and, in the far north, are often the only public transport option. There are numerous services between Norway and Sweden, and in Lapland there are routes between those two countries and Finland. Buses also link Denmark with Sweden and Norway.

Some major operators include the following:

Eurolines Scandinavia (www.eurolines.se) Buses between the Scandinavian nations. Full schedules and fares are listed on the company's website.

GoByBus (www.gobybus.se) Long-distance buses within Sweden and to Oslo and Copenhagen.

Lavprisekspressen (www.lavprisekspressen.no) Internet-booked budget bus fares in Norway.

Matkahuolto (www.matkahuolto.fi) Finnish buses.

Nor-Way Bussekspress (✆81 54 44 44; www.nor-way.no) Main Norwegian provider.

Swebus (www.swebusexpress.se) Major Swedish bus provider.

Car & Motorcycle

Petrol is expensive in Scandinavia. Many petrol stations are unstaffed, with machines that take cards or cash. Change is not given.

HIRE

Car rental is expensive, but between a group of three or four it can work out at a reasonable cost. In Norway, though, costs are prohibitive: it usually works out cheaper to hire in Sweden and drive in. As ever, the cheapest deals are online.

THE HURTIGRUTEN

Norway's legendary **Hurtigruten** (✆81 00 30 30; www.hurtigruten.com) coastal ferry has been a lifeline linking coastal towns and villages and is now one of the most popular ways to explore Norway. A *Hurtigruten* ferry heads north from Bergen almost every night of the year, pulling into 35 ports on its six-day journey to Kirkenes, where it then turns around and heads back south. The return journey takes 11 days and covers a distance of 5200km. In agreeable weather (by no means guaranteed), the fjord and mountain scenery along the way is nothing short of spectacular.

Major rental companies include the following:

Avis (www.avis.com)

Budget (www.budget.com)

Europcar (0200-12154; www.europcar.com)

Hertz (0200-11 22 33; www.hertz.com)

Sixt (www.sixt.com) One of the cheapest.

ROAD HAZARDS

» Beware of elk and, in Lapland, reindeer, which don't respect vehicles and can dash onto the road unexpectedly. This sounds comical, but elks especially constitute a deadly danger.

» Snow and ice is possible from September to April, and as late as June in Lapland. Chains are uncommon and, in some places, illegal; people use either snow tyres, which have metal studs, or special all-weather tyres.

Train

With the exception of a few short private lines, **Danish State Railways** (DSB; www.dsb.dk) runs all Danish train services. Trains run many times a day between Denmark and Sweden via the Øresund bridge linking Copenhagen with Malmö.

Sweden has an extensive and reliable railway network; the main operators are **Inlandsbanan** (0771-53 53 53; www.inlandsbanan.se), **Sveriges Järnväg** (SJ; 0771-75 75 75; www.sj.se) and **Tågkompaniet** (0771-44 41 11; www.tagkompaniet.se).

Norwegian State Railways (Norges Statsbaner, NSB; press 9 for English 81 50 08 88; www.nsb.no) operates an excellent, though limited, system of lines connecting Oslo with Stavanger, Bergen, Trondheim and the north; lines also connect to Sweden.

Finnish trains are run by the state-owned **Valtion Rautatiet** (VR; 0600-41900; www.vr.fi) and extend north into Lapland.

There are various discounts available for students, children, seniors and groups travelling together. Good advance purchase specials are sometimes available on the rail company websites.

TRAIN PASSES

The **Eurail Scandinavia Pass** (www.eurail.com) entitles you to unlimited rail travel in Denmark, Finland, Norway and Sweden; it is available for four, five, six or eight days of travel within a two-month period (prices start at youth/adult €193/256). The pass also provides discounted ferry travel on some routes.

Other international rail passes accepted in Scandinavia include the Eurail Global Pass (plus Eurail's single- and multiple-country passes) and the **InterRail Global Pass** (www.interrailnet.com), plus single-country passes.

Serbia

Includes »

Belgrade......................994
Vojvodina......................999
Novi Sad......................1000
Fruška Gora & Sremski Karlovci......................1001
Subotica......................1001
Understand Serbia.....1002
Survival Guide............1003

Best Places to Eat

» Little Bay (p995)
» Šešir Moj (p995)
» ? (p995)
» Kod Lipe (p1000)

Best Places to Stay

» Green Studio Hostel (p995)
» Hostel Sova (p1000)
» Hostelche (p995)

Why Go?

Warm, welcoming and a hell of a lot of fun – everything you never heard about Serbia (Србија) is true. Exuding a feisty mix of élan and *inat* (Serbian trait of rebellious defiance), this country doesn't do 'mild': Belgrade is one of the world's wildest party destinations, the northern town of Novi Sad hosts the rocking EXIT festival, and even its hospitality is emphatic – expect to be greeted with *rakija* (fruit brandy) and a hearty three-kiss hello.

While political correctness is about as commonplace as a nonsmoking bar, Serbia is nevertheless a cultural crucible: the art nouveau town of Subotica revels in its proximity to Hungary, bohemian Niš echoes to the clip-clop of Roma horse carts, and minaret-studded Novi Pazar nudges some of the most sacred sites in Serbian Orthodoxy. And in the mountainous Kopaonik and Zlatibor regions, ancient traditions coexist with après-ski bling. Forget what you think you know: come and say *zdravo* (hello)...or better yet, *živeli* (cheers)!

When to Go

Belgrade

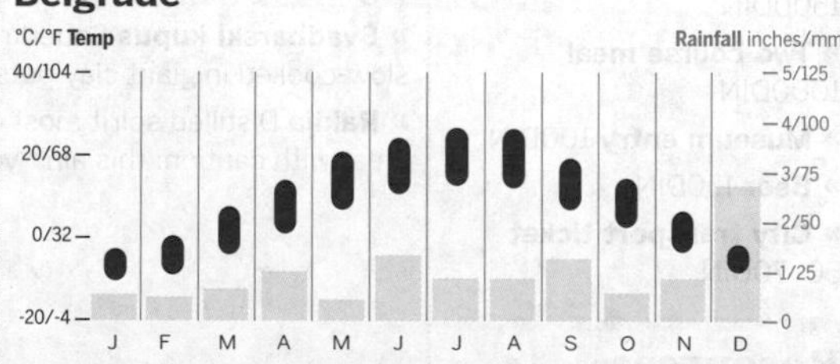

Apr Watch winter melt away with a scenic ride on the nostalgic Šargan 8 railway.

Jul & Aug Rock out at Novi Sad's EXIT and go trumpet-wild at Guča.

Dec–Mar Head south to Zlatibor for alpine adventures.

AT A GLANCE

- **Currency** Dinar (DIN)
- **Language** Serbian
- **Money** ATMs abound
- **Visas** None for citizens of the EU, UK, Australia, New Zealand, Canada and the USA

Fast Facts

- **Area** 77,474 sq km
- **Capital** Belgrade
- **Country code** ☎381
- **Emergency** Ambulance ☎94, fire ☎93, police ☎92

Exchange Rates

Australia	A$1	91.56DIN
Canada	C$1	86.25DIN
Euro Zone	€1	112.037DIN
Japan	¥100	92.89DIN
New Zealand	NZ$1	73.38DIN
UK	UK£1	132.63DIN
USA	US$1	87.66DIN

Set Your Budget

- **Budget hotel room** 1500DIN
- **Two-course meal** 1000DIN
- **Museum entry** 100DIN
- **Beer** 150DIN
- **City transport ticket** 50–70DIN

Resources

- **National Tourism Organisation of Serbia** (www.serbia.travel)
- **Serbia Travel Club** (www.serbiatravelers.org)

Connections

Serbia is landlocked by accessible neighbours. The northern town of Subotica is 10km from the Hungarian border, Vršac is the same distance from the Romania, and Bulgaria is 45 minutes from Pirot. When things are calm on the Kosovo border, €5 and three hours get you from Novi Pazar to Priština. The Zlatibor region stretches to Bosnia and Hercegovina (BiH); self-drivers can take a day trip to the famous bridge on the Drina. All of Europe is accessible from Belgrade: Bucharest, Budapest, Ljubljana, Moscow, Sofia and Zagreb are a train ride away, and regular buses serve destinations including Vienna, Sarajevo and Podgorica. Check www.serbianrailways.com and www.bas.co.rs for more info.

ITINERARIES

One Week

Revel in three days of cultural and culinary exploration in Belgrade, allowing for at least one night of hitting the capital's legendary nightspots. Carry on to Novi Sad for trips to the vineyards and monasteries of Fruška Gora and Sremski Karlovci.

Two Weeks

Follow the itinerary above then head north for the art nouveau architecture of Subotica, before slicing south to Zlatibor en route to Ottoman-influenced Novi Pazar.

Essential Food & Drink

- **Kajmak** Along the lines of a salty clotted cream, this dairy delight is lashed on to everything from bread to burgers.
- **Ćevapčići** The ubiquitous skinless sausage and *pljeskavica* (spicy hamburger) make it easy to be a carnivore in Serbia.
- **Burek** Flaky meat, cheese or vegetable pie eaten with yoghurt.
- **Svadbarski kupus** Sauerkraut and hunks of smoked pork slow-cooked in giant clay pots.
- **Rakija** Distilled spirit most commonly made from plums. Treat with caution: this ain't your grandpa's brandy.

Serbia Highlights

1 Marvel at Belgrade's mighty **Kalemegdan Citadel** (p994)

2 Witness the laid-back town of **Novi Sad** (p1000) as it morphs into the State of EXIT every July

3 Goggle at the art nouveau treasures of **Subotica** (p1001)

4 Ponder the exotic cultural fusions of Turkish-toned **Novi Pazar** (p999)

5 Steel your eardrums (and liver) at Guča's **Dragačevo Trumpet Assembly** (p1002), one of the world's most frenetic music festivals

6 Ski, hike or just take the mountain air in the magical villages of **Zlatibor** (p1000)

BELGRADE

☎011 / POP 1.6 MILLION

Outspoken, adventurous, proud and audacious: Belgrade (Београд) is by no means a 'pretty' capital, but its gritty exuberance makes it one of the most happening cities in Europe. It's here where the Sava River meets the Danube (Dunav) and old-world culture gives way to new-world nightlife.

Grandiose coffee houses, quirky sidewalk ice-creameries and smoky dens all find rightful place along Knez Mihailova, a lively pedestrian boulevard flanked by historical buildings all the way to the ancient Kalemegdan Citadel, crown of the city.

'Belgrade' literally translates as 'White City', but Serbia's colourful capital is red hot.

Sights

FREE Kalemegdan Citadel FORTRESS
(Kalemegdanska tvrđava) Some 115 battles have been fought over imposing, impressive Kalemegdan. Fortifications began in Celtic times, and the citadel was destroyed over 40 times throughout the centuries. Its bloody history, discernible despite today's plethora of jolly cafes and funfairs, only makes Kalemegdan all the more fascinating.

Military Museum MUSEUM
(www.muzej.mod.gov.rs; adult/child 150/120DIN; ⏲10am-5pm Tue-Sun) Tucked away in Kalemegdan Citadel, this museum presents the complete military history of the former Yugoslavia up to the 1999 NATO bombings. It's through the Stambol Gate, once used for public executions.

National Museum MUSEUM
(Narodni Muzej; www.narodnimuzej.rs; Trg Republike 1a) Trg Republike (Republic Sq), a meeting point and outdoor exhibition space, is home to the National Museum, which will hopefully reopen soon; lack of funding for renovations has kept it shuttered for the last decade.

Ethnographic Museum MUSEUM
(Etnografski Muzej; www.etnografskimuzej.rs; Studentski Trg 13; adult/student 150/60DIN; ⏲10am-5pm Tue-Sat, 9am-2pm Sun) Features traditional costumes, working utensils and folksy mountain-village interiors.

Gallery of Frescos GALLERY
(www.narodnimuzej.rs; Cara Uroša 20; admission 100DIN; ⏲10am-5pm Tue, Wed, Fri & Sat, noon-8pm Thu, 10am-2pm Sun) Home to full-size replicas (and the odd original) of Byzantine Serbian church art, right down to the last scratch.

Skadarska NEIGHBOURHOOD
Skadarska or 'Skadarlija' is Belgrade's Montmartre. This cobblestoned strip east of Trg Republike was the bohemian heartland at the turn of the 20th century; local artistes and dapper types still gather in its legion of cute restaurants and cafes.

Nikola Tesla Museum MUSEUM
(www.tesla-museum.org; Krunska 51; admission incl guided tour in English 300DIN; ⏲10am-6pm Tue-Fri, to 3pm Sat & Sun) Release your inner nerd at one of Belgrade's best museums with some wondrously sci-fi-ish interactive elements.

Museum of Automobiles MUSEUM
(www.automuseumbgd.com; Majke Jevrosime 30; adult/child 100/80DIN; ⏲9am-9pm) A compelling collection of cars and motorcycles, including Tito's '57 Caddy convertible.

Historical Museum of Serbia MUSEUM
(Istorijski Muzej Srbije; www.imus.org.rs; Trg Nikole Pašića 11; adult/child 100/50DIN; ⏲noon-7pm Tue-Sun) Home to an absorbing wealth of collections, it's your best bet while the National Museum remains closed.

Sveti Sava CHURCH
(www.hramsvetogsave.com; Svetog Save) Sveti Sava is the world's biggest Orthodox church, built on the site where the Turks burnt relics of St Sava. Work on the church interior (frequently interrupted by wars) continues.

Maršal Tito's Grave MONUMENT
(House of Flowers; www.mij.rs; Botićeva 6; incl entry to Museum of Yugoslav History 200DIN; ⏲10am-4pm Tue-Sun) A visit to Tito's mausoleum is obligatory. Also on display are gifts from political leaders and the voguish set of the era. Take trolleybus 40 or 41 at the south end of Parliament on Kneza Miloša.

Ada Ciganlija BEACH
(www.adaciganlija.rs) In summertime, join the hordes of sea-starved locals at this artificial island on the Sava. Take bus 53 or 56 from Zeleni Venac.

Sleeping

The **Youth Hostel Association of Serbia** (Ferijalni Savez Beograd; ☎322 0762; www.serbhostels.org; Makedonska 22/2; ⏲9am-5pm) does deals with local hotels. You need HI membership (under/over 26 years 500/800DIN or an international student card. Private apartments (try www.bestbelgradeapartments.com) are a better bet for longer stays.

TOP CHOICE **Green Studio Hostel** HOSTEL €
(063-7562 357; www.greenstudiohostel.com; Karađorđeva 69, 6th floor; dm from €10, r €7-36, apt €40;) One of the top budget options in Serbia. Clean, airy and staffed by your new best friends, it has a handy location near the bus and train stations and Belgrade's main attractions.

Hostelche HOSTEL €
(263 7793; www.hostelchehostel.com; Kralja Petra 8; dm from €14, s €25-27, tw €20-22;) A bend-over-backwards staff, homey atmosphere, free walking tours and ace location make this award-winner popular for all the right reasons.

Three Black Catz HOSTEL €
(262 9826; www.hostel.co.rs; Čika Ljubina 7; dm from €9, tw €16; @) While the atmosphere can border on merry chaos, this convivial hostel doesn't forgo business for pleasure, offering heaps of info and advice.

Arka Barka HOSTEL €
(064 925 3507; www.arkabarka.net; Bul Nikole Tesle bb; dm €13;) Bobbing off Ušće Park by the Danube barges, this 'floating house' offers sparkling rooms, party nights and river breezes. It's a moderate walk, or a short ride on bus 15 or 84 from the centre.

Hotel Royal HOTEL €€
(263 4222; www.hotelroyal.rs; Kralja Petra 56; s 3680-4370DIN, d 5175-7820DIN; @) Rooms are basic and far from sparkling, but this (very) central spot disarms with character and buzz.

Eating

TOP CHOICE **Little Bay** EUROPEAN €€
(www.little-bay.co.uk; Dositejeva 9a; meals 495-995DIN) Tuck yourself into a private box and let the salmon in beer and tarragon sauce (745DIN) or traditional English roast lunch (695DIN, Sundays only) melt in your mouth as a live opera singer does wonderful things to your ears.

EASTERN EUROPEAN €€
(Znak Pitanja; Kralja Petra 6; meals 450-800DIN) Belgrade's oldest *kafana* (cafe) offers dishes such as stuffed chicken and 'lamb under the iron pan'. Its quizzical name follows a dispute with the adjacent church, which objected to the boozy tavern – originally called 'By the Cathedral' – referring to a house of God.

Šešir Moj SERBIAN €€
(My Hat; Skadarska 21; meals 400-1000DIN; 9am-1am) Roma bands tug the heartstrings while traditional dishes buoy up the belly.

Smokvica CAFE €€
(Kralja Petra 73; meals 200-1200DIN; 9am-1am;) Graze on gourmet salads, schnarf down a sanga or just sip good coffee on this winsome courtyard terrace.

Pekara Toma BAKERY €
(Kolarčeva 10; snacks 50-200DIN; 24hr) One of the many cheap bakeries around Trg Republike offering pizzas, sandwiches and salads.

Zeleni Venac Market MARKET €
(cnr Brankova Prizrenska & Kraljice Natalije; 6am-7pm) Forage for DIY food.

Drinking

TOP CHOICE **Kafana Pavle Korčagin** TAVERNA
(240 1980; Ćirila i Metodija 2a; 8pm-1am) Raise a glass to Tito at this frantic, festive *kafana*. Lined with communist memorabilia, this table-thumping throwback fills up nightly; reserve a table.

Federal Association of Globe Trotters BAR
(www.usp-aur.rs; Bul Despota Stefana 7/1; 1pm-midnight Mon-Fri, 3pm-late Sat & Sun;) Through the black gate and down into the basement lies one of Belgrade's coolest hang-outs. Miscellaneous oddities clamour for wall space while an equally motley clientele yaks over cocktails.

Rakia Bar BAR
(www.rakiabar.com; Dobračina 5, 9am-midnight Sun-Thu, to 1am Fri & Sat) Get your first taste of the spirit of Serbia. English-speaking staff

SPLURGE

Art nouveau icon and proud symbol of the best of Belgrade, the majestic **Hotel Moskva** (Hotel Moscow; 268 6255; www.hotelmoskva.rs; Balkanska 1; s €77-112, d €99-135, ste €130-330;) has been wowing guests – including Albert Einstein, Indira Gandhi and Alfred Hitchcock – since 1906. Laden with ye olde glamour, this is the place to write your memoirs at a big old desk.

Central Belgrade

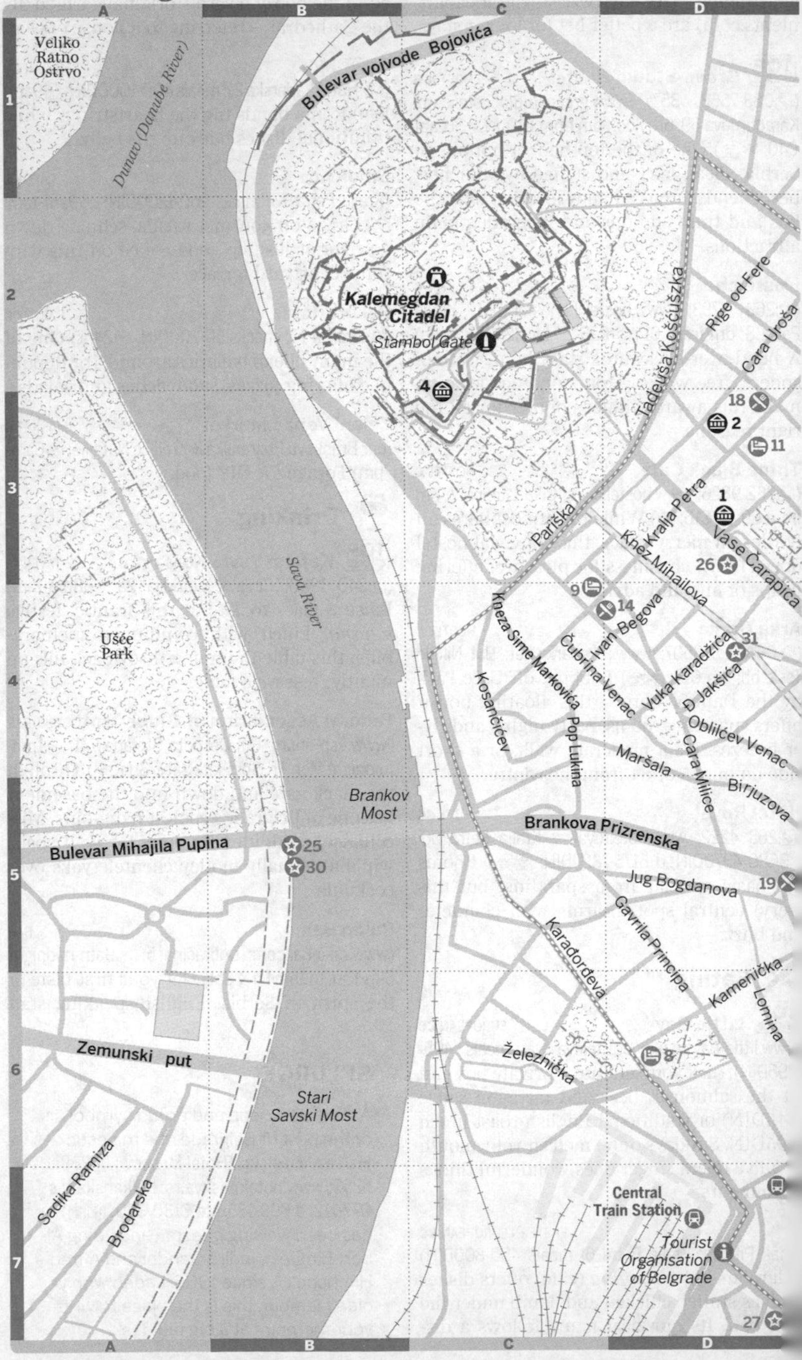

A B C D
1 2 3 4 5 6 7

Veliko Ratno Ostrvo
Dunav (Danube River)
Bulevar vojvode Bojovića
Kalemegdan Citadel
Stambol Gate
4
Tadeuša Košćuszka
Rige od Fere
Cara Uroša
18
2
11
1
Pariška
Kralja Petra
Knez Mihailova
Vase Čarapića
26
9
14
Ivan Begova
31
Kneza Sime Markovića
Čubrina Venac
Vuka Karadžića
Đ Jakšića
Kosančićev
Pop Lukina
Obilićev Venac
Maršala
Cara Milice
Birjuzova
Sava River
Ušće Park
Brankov Most
Brankova Prizrenska
Bulevar Mihajila Pupina
25
30
Jug Bogdanova
19
Gavrila Principa
Karađorđeva
Kamenička
Lomina
Zemunski put
Železnička
8
Stari Savski Most
Sadika Ramiza
Brodarska
Central Train Station
Tourist Organisation of Belgrade
27

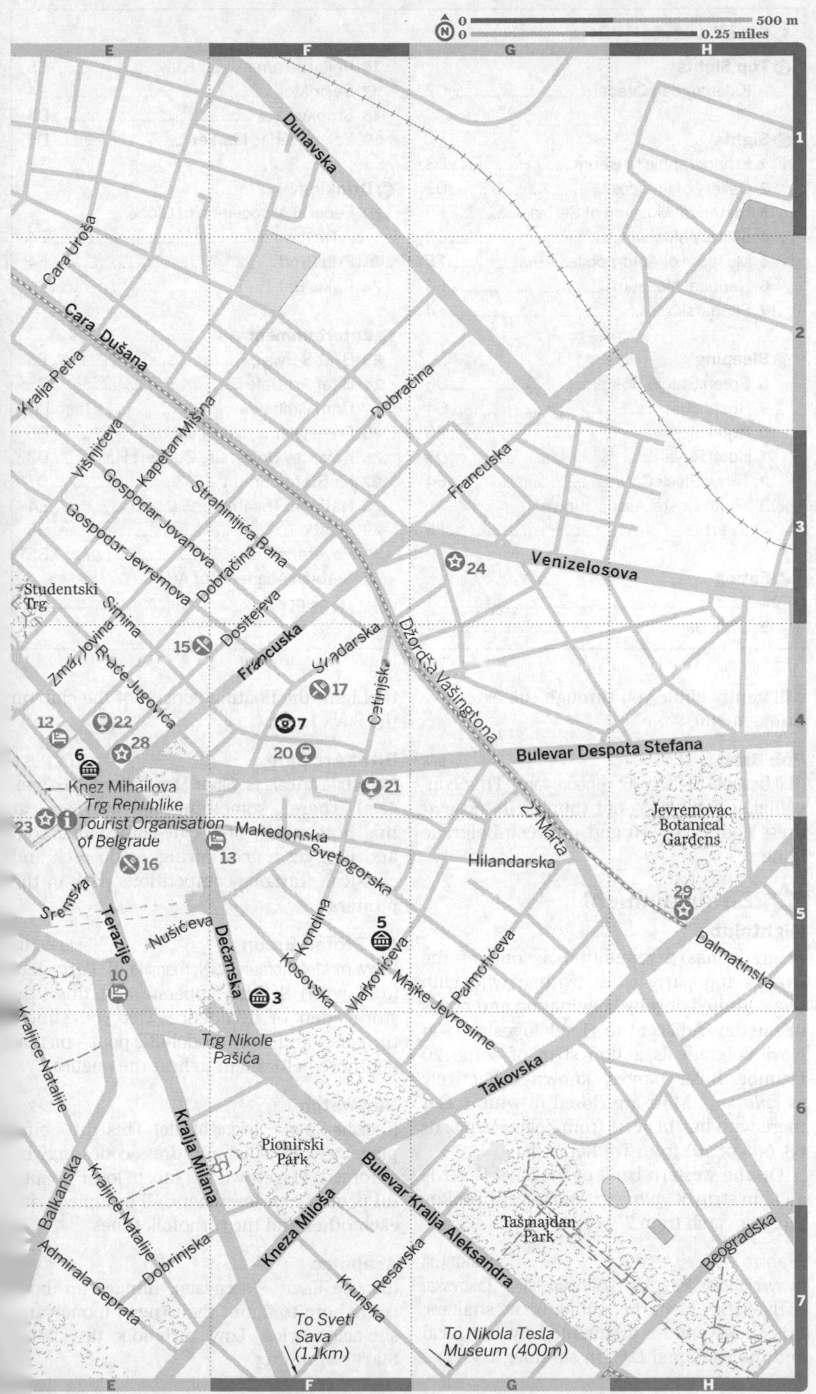
0 500 m
0 0.25 miles
E
F
G
H
1
2
3
4
5
6
7
Dunavska
Cara Uroša
Cara Dušana
Kralja Petra
Višnjićeva
Kapetan Mišina
Gospodar Jovanova
Gospodar Jevremova
Strahinjića Bana
Dobračina
Dobračina
Francuska
Francuska
Venizelosova
24
Studentski Trg
Simina
Zmaj Jovina
Braće Jugovića
Dositejeva
15
Skadarska
17
Cetinjska
Džordža Vašingtona
12
22
28
6
7
20
21
Bulevar Despota Stefana
Knez Mihailova
Trg Republike
23
Tourist Organisation of Belgrade
Makedonska
13
Svetogorska
27 Marta
Hilandarska
Jevremovac Botanical Gardens
16
Sremska
29
Terazije
Nušićeva
Dečanska
Kondina
5
Kosovska
Vlajkovićeva
Majke Jevrosime
Palmotićeva
Dalmatinska
10
3
Kraljice Natalije
Trg Nikole Pašića
Takovska
Kralja Milana
Pionirski Park
Bulevar Kralja Aleksandra
Kneza Miloša
Balkanska
Kraljice Natalije
Tašmajdan Park
Dobrinjska
Resavska
Beogradska
Admirala Geprata
Krunska
To Sveti Sava (1.1km)
To Nikola Tesla Museum (400m)
SERBIA BELGRADE

Central Belgrade

Top Sights
Kalemegdan Citadel C2

Sights
1 Ethnographic Museum D3
2 Gallery of Frescos D3
3 Historical Museum of Serbia F5
4 Military Museum C3
5 Museum of Automobiles F5
6 National Museum E4
7 Skadarska F4

Sleeping
8 Green Studio Hostel D6
9 Hostelche C4
10 Hotel Moskva E5
11 Hotel Royal D3
12 Three Black Catz E4
13 Youth Hostel Association of Serbia F5

Eating
14 ? D4
15 Little Bay E4
16 Pekara Toma E5
17 Šešir Moj F4
18 Smokvica D3
19 Zeleni Venac Market D5

Drinking
20 Federal Association of Globe Trotters F4
21 Pub Brod F4
22 Rakia Bar E4

Entertainment
23 Bilet Servis E5
24 Bitef Art Cafe G3
Dom Omladine .... (see 13)
25 Freestyler B5
26 Kolarčev University Concert Hall D3
27 Mr Stefan Braun D7
28 National Theatre E4
29 Plastic H5
30 Povetarac B5
31 Serbian Academy of Arts & Sciences D4

will gently guide you through the extensive drinks menu.

Pub Brod BAR
(Bul Despota Stefana 36; ⏲noon-4am) This congenial student hang-out thumbs its nose at dress codes, Top 40 and nouveau-Belgrade bling.

Entertainment

Nightclubs

Belgrade has a reputation as one of the world's top party cities, with a wild club scene limited only by imagination and hours in the day. Adjacent to Hotel Jugoslavija in Novi Belgrade is a 1km strip of some 20 Danube River barges, known collectively as *splavovi*. Most are closed in winter. Get there with bus 15 or 84 from Zeleni Venac or 68, 603 or 701 from Trg Republike.

On the western bank of the Sava River is a 1.5km strip of *splavovi*. Walk over Brankov Most or catch tram 7, 9 or 11.

Plastic NIGHTCLUB
(www.clubplastic.rs; cnr Dalmatinska & Takovska; ⏲Thu-Sat) A favourite among booty shakers, this slick venue is frequented by top local and international DJs. In summer, try Plastic Light, the floating version of the club on the Sava River.

Bitef Art Cafe LIVE MUSIC
(www.bitefartcafe.rs; Skver Mire Trailović 1; ⏲7pm-4am) There's something for everyone at this hotchpotch of a cafe-club. Funk, soul and jazz get a good airing, as do rock and classical. Karaoke competitions pack in the punters.

Mr Stefan Braun NIGHTCLUB
(www.mrstefanbraun.rs; Nemanjina 4) Party like (and with) Serbian superstars at this 9th storey den of decadence. Get your finest threads – and most model-like pout – on and get there before 1am to beat the queues.

Blaywatch BARGE
(Danube River; ⏲midnight-late) This throbbing place gets crowded and dress codes may be enforced. The crowd is a mix of local 'beautiful people' and foreigners, all occupied with each other and the turbofolk tunes.

Acapulco BARGE
(Danube River; ⏲noon-late) Blinged-up boys come here to flaunt their (new) money and she-accessories. Low turbofolk threshold? Start swimming.

Freestyler BARGE
(www.splavfree.rs; Brodarska bb, Sava River; ⌚11pm-5am Tue-Sun) The gigantic Freestyler has been a symbol of *splav* saturnalia for years, not least for its infamous foam parties.

Povetarac BARGE
(Brodarska bb, Sava River; ⌚midnight-late, 8pm-late winter) This rusting cargo ship attracts an indie crowd.

Performing Arts

For concert and theatre tickets, go to **Bilet Servis** (☎303 3311; www.biletservis.rs; Trg Republike 5; ⌚9am-8pm Mon-Fri, 10am-8pm Sat). Large venues for visiting acts include **Sava Centar** (☎220 6060; www.savacentar.net; Milentija Popovića 9; ⌚box office 10am-8pm Mon-Fri, to 3pm Sat) and **Belgrade Arena** (☎220 2222; www.arenabeograd.com; Bul Arsenija Čarnojevića 58; ⌚box office 10am-8pm Mon-Fri, to 3pm Sat).

National Theatre THEATRE
(☎262 0946; www.narodnopozoriste.co.rs; Trg Republike; ⌚box office 10am-2pm Tue-Sun) Stages operas, dramas and ballets during winter.

Kolarčev University Concert Hall LIVE MUSIC
(☎2630 550; www.kolarac.co.rs; Studentski Trg 5; ⌚box office 10am-7.30pm) Home to the Belgrade Philharmonica.

Dom Omladine LIVE MUSIC, THEATRE
(www.domomladine.org; Makedonska 22; ⌚box office 10am-8pm Mon-Fri, 3-8pm Sat) Hosts a range of mostly youth-based cultural events.

Serbian Academy of Arts & Sciences LIVE MUSIC
(☎202 7200; www.sanu.ac.rs; Knez Mihailova 35; ⌚concerts from 6pm Mon & Thu Oct-Jun) Free concerts and exhibitions.

Information

Belgrade in Your Pocket (www.inyourpocket.com/serbia/belgrade)

Belgraded (www.belgraded.com)

Lonely Planet (www.lonelyplanet.com/serbia/belgrade)

Tourist Organisation of Belgrade (www.tob.) Trg Republike 5 (☎328 1859; ⌚9am-9pm Mon-Sat, 10am-3pm Sun); Train Station (☎361 732; ⌚7am-1.30pm Mon-Sat); Nikola Tesla Airport (☎209 7828; ⌚9am-9.30pm) Helpful desk with all the info you could need.

Getting There & Away

BUS Belgrade has two adjacent bus stations: **BAS** (☎263 6299; www.bas.rs; Železnička 4) serves the region, while **Lasta** (☎334 8555; www.lasta.rs; Železnička 2) deals with destinations around Belgrade. Regular services include Subotica (1280DIN, three hours), Novi Sad (600DIN, one hour) and Novi Pazar (1520DIN, three hours) for Kosovo.

TRAIN Frequent trains go to Novi Sad (288DIN, 1½ hours) and Subotica (480DIN, three hours).

Getting Around

TO/FROM THE AIRPORT Nikola Tesla airport is 18km from Belgrade. Local bus 72 connects the airport with Zeleni Venac (65DIN to 120DIN, half-hourly, 5.20am to midnight from airport, 4.40am to 11.40pm from town); the cheapest tickets must be purchased from newsstands. A minibus also runs between the airport and the central Slavija Sq (250DIN, 5am to 3.50am from airport, 4.20am to 3.20am from the square).

A taxi from the airport to Knez Mihailova should be around 1250DIN.

PUBLIC TRANSPORT Buses chug all over town; rechargeable BusPlus cards can be bought and topped up (70DIN per ticket) at kiosks. They're double if you buy from the driver.

Tram 2 connects Kalemegdan Citadel with Trg Slavija, bus stations and the central train station.

TAXI Only hail distinctly labelled cabs. A 5km trip costs around 415DIN. Flagfall is 140DIN, and reputable cabs should charge between 55DIN and 70DIN per kilometre.

VOJVODINA

Home to over 25 ethnic groups, six languages and the best of Hungarian and Serbian traditions, Vojvodina's (Војводина) pancake plains mask a rich diversity. Novi Sad hosts the EXIT festival while Subotica, 10km from Hungary, is an oasis of art nouveau delights.

WORTH A TRIP

NOVI PAZAR

Novi Pazar is the cultural centre of the southern Raška/Sandžak region, with a large Muslim population. Turkish coffee, cuisine and customs abound, yet idyllic Orthodox sights are but a cab ride away: this was once the heartland of the Serbian medieval state.

Novi Sad Нови Сад

☎021 / POP 335,700

As convivial as a *rakija* toast – and at times just as carousing – Novi Sad is a chipper town with all the spoils and none of the stress of the big smoke. Locals sprawl in outdoor cafes, and laneway bars pack out nightly. Pedestrian thoroughfare Zmaj Jovina stretches from the town square (Trg Slobode) to Dunavska street.

Sights

FREE **Petrovaradin Citadel** FORTRESS

Towering over the river on a 40m-high volcanic slab, this mighty sconce *(tvrđava)* is aptly nicknamed 'Gibraltar on the Danube'. Constructed with slave labour between 1692 and 1780, its dungeons have held notable prisoners including Karađorđe (leader of the first uprising against the Turks) and Tito.

Within the citadel walls, a **museum** (☎433 155; Petrovaradin Citadel; admission 200DIN; ⏲9am-5pm Tue-Sun) offers insight into the site's history. The museum can also arrange tours of Petrovaradin's creepy underground passageways.

WORTH A TRIP

ZLATIBOR

Zlatibor is a special region of rolling plains, traditions and hospitality.

Quirky adventures await in Mokra Gora village. **Drvengrad** (Küstendorf; www.mecavnik.info; Mećavnik hill; adult/child 200/120DIN; ⏲9am-9pm) was built by Serbian director Emir Kusturica for the film *Life is a Miracle*, and offers surreal fun and prime panoramas.

The twisty-turny **Šargan 8 railway** (☎bookings 510 288; www.serbianrailways.com; adult/child 600/300DIN; ⏲10.30am & 1.25pm daily Apr-Oct, also 8am & 4.10pm depending on demand) tourist train was once part of a narrow-gauge rail link between Belgrade, Sarajevo and Dubrovnik.

Reach these sights via bus from Užice or through **Zlatibor Tours** (☎845 957; Tržni centar, bus station; ⏲8am-9pm) or **Tomadija Tours** (☎060-0800 324; tomadija.tours@gmail.com).

Museum of Vojvodina MUSEUM

(Muzej Vojvodine; www.muzejvojvodine.org.rs; Dunavska 35-7; admission 100DIN; ⏲9am-7pm Tue-Fri, 10am-6pm Sat & Sun) This museum houses historical, archaeological and ethnological exhibits, covering Vojvodinian history from Palaeolithic times up to WWII.

Štrand BEACH

Summertime fun along the Danube.

Festivals & Events

The Petrovaradin Fortress is stormed by thousands of revellers each July during the epic **EXIT festival** (www.exitfest.org). The first festival in 2000 lasted 100 days and galvanised a generation of young Serbs against the Milošević regime. The festival has been attended by the likes of Chemical Brothers, Gogol Bordello and Patti Smith…plus an annual tally of about 200,000 merrymakers.

Sleeping

TOP CHOICE **Hostel Sova** HOSTEL €

(☎066-152 30; www.hostelsova.com; Ilije Ognjanovića 26; dm from €10, d €15; P ᯤ) Super-friendly and given to laid-back socialising, the wonderful Sova is perched just around the corner from Zmaj Jovina.

Downtown HOSTEL €

(☎69 139 7708; www.hostelnovisad.com; Njegoševa 2; dm from €10, s/d €25/30; @) Fun staff and an 'in the thick of it' location off Trg Slobode make this rambunctious hostel an experience in itself.

Hotel Vojvodina HISTORIC HOTEL €€

(☎622 122; www.hotelvojvodina.rs; Trg Slobode 2; s/d from 2800/4200DIN) Reeking of retro Novi Sad's oldest hotel (1854) isn't as slick as others, but its location overlooking the town square is unbeatable.

Eating

TOP CHOICE **Kod Lipe** SERBIAN

(Svetozara Miletića 7; meals from 400DIN; ⏲8am-11pm Mon-Fri, 7am-midnight Sat & Sun) This down-home eatery has been dishing up old-school ambience and traditional Vojvodinian fare since the 19th century.

Fish i Zeleniš MEDITERRANEAN €

(Fish and Greens; ☎452 000; Skerlićeva 2; mains from 700DIN; ⏲noon-11pm Mon-Fri, to 1am Sat & Sun; 🖉) This bright nook serves up the finest vegetarian/pescatarian meals in northern Serbia. A three-minute walk from Zmaj Jovina.

Lazina Bašta SERBIAN €

(Laze Telečkog 5; meals from 450DIN) Replete with hay bales and knick-knackery, Lazina Bašta serves up country-mouse cuisine on the most happening street in town.

Drinking

Laze Telečkog (off Zmaj Jovina) is lined with bars to suit every whim. Squeeze into the frenetic **London Underground Club** (Laze Telečkog 15; 8am-3am) or sidle next door to **Cuba Libre** (Laze Telečkog 13) and stake your spot on the dance floor. Hang with local eccentrics at **Crni Bik** (Trg Mladenaca 8; 10am-late), a short stroll southeast from Laze Telečkog. During summer, check out any of the barefoot-bars along the Štrand (p1000).

Information

Tourist Information Centre (661 7343; www.turizamns.rs; Ul Modene 1; 7.30am-8pm Mon-Fri, 10am-3pm Sat) Ultra-helpful with maps and English info.

Getting There & Away

The **bus station** (Bul Jačo Tomića; information counter 6am-11pm) has regular departures to Belgrade (600DIN, one hour, every 10 minutes) and Subotica (600DIN, 1½ hours).

Frequent trains leave the **train station** (Bul Jaše Tomića 4), next door to the bus station, for Belgrade (288DIN, 1½ hours) and Subotica (384DIN, 1½ hours).

Fruška Gora & Sremski Karlovci Фрушка Гора & Сремски Карловци

Fruška Gora is an 80km stretch of rolling hills where monastic life has continued for centuries. Thirty-five monasteries were built here between the 15th and 18th centuries to safeguard Serbian culture and religion from the Turks; 16 remain.

The photogenic village of **Sremski Karlovci** is littered with stunning structures including the Orthodox cathedral (1758–62), the baroque Four Lions fountain and the Chapel of Peace (where the Turks and Austrians signed the 1699 Peace Treaty).

Take bus 61 or 62 from Novi Sad (140DIN, 30 minutes) and visit the **tourist organisation** (883 855; www.karlovci.org.rs; Patrijarha Rajačića 1; 8am-6pm Mon-Fri, 10am-6pm Sat) by the main square.

Subotica Суботица

024 / POP 140,400

Sugar-spun art nouveau marvels and a delicious sprinkling of Serbian and Hungarian flavours make this quaint town a worthy day trip or stopover.

Sights

Town Hall HISTORIC BUILDING

(Trg Republike) This 1910 behemoth is a curious mix of art nouveau and something Gaudí may have had a dab at. The council chambers – with exquisite stained-glass windows and elaborate decor – are not to be missed.

Modern Art Gallery HISTORIC BUILDING

(www.likovnisusret.rs; Park Ferenca Rajhla 5; admission 50DIN; 8am-2pm Mon, to 6pm Tue-Fri, 9am-noon Sat) One of the most sumptuous buildings in Serbia, this is a vibrant flourish of mosaics, ceramic tiles, floral patterns and stained glass.

City Museum MUSEUM

(www.gradskimuzej.subotica.rs; Trg Sinagoge 3; admission 100DIN; 10am-8pm Tue-Sat) Eclectic exhibitions are the go in this art nouveau residence.

Synagogue SYNAGOGUE

(Trg Sinagoge 2) Subotica's first art nouveau building remains shuttered as renovations have failed to materialise. Grasp its former glory from the footpath.

Sleeping

Hostel Incognito HOSTEL €

(062-666 674; www.hostel-subotica.com; Hugo Badalića 3; s/d/tr/apt 1000/1800/2400/7000DIN;) This basic, clean hostel is a couple of minutes' walk from all the Subotica sights. Reception is in the restaurant downstairs: call ahead.

Hostel Bosa Milićević HOSTEL €

(548 290; Segedinski put 9-11; dm per person 1019DIN) Stay with the students at this cheapie tucked well away behind the Ekonomski Fakultet.

Eating

Ravel CAFE €

(Nušićeva 2; cakes 60-200DIN; 9am-10pm Mon-Sat, 11am-10pm Sun) Dainty nibbles at gateaux and twee tea-taking is the name of the game at this adorable art nouveau classic.

MADNESS, MADE IN SERBIA

On the surface, the **Dragačevo Trumpet Assembly** (an annual gathering of brass musicians) sounds harmless; nerdily endearing even. But band camp this ain't: it *is*, however, the most boisterous music festival in all of Europe, if not the world.

Known simply as 'Guča', after the western Serbian village that has hosted it each August since 1961, the six-day debauch is hedonism at its most rambunctious: tens of thousands of beer-and-brass-addled visitors dance wild *kola* through the streets, gorging on spit-meat and slapping dinar on the sweaty foreheads of the (mostly Roma) *trubači* performers. The music itself is relentless and frenzy-fast.

Guča is an easy three- to four-hour bus ride from Belgrade, and a straightforward journey with your own wheels. See www.guca.rs for more.

Boss Caffe INTERNATIONAL €
(www.bosscaffe.com; Matije Korvina 7-8) Boss' offerings include a variety of tacos (285DIN to 510DIN) and pizza with sour cream (465DN to 780DIN). Behind the Modern Art Gallery.

Information

Tourist Information Office (670 350; www.visitsubotica.rs; Town Hall; 8am-6pm Mon-Fri, 9am-1pm Sat) Home to the Subotica Greeters, local volunteers only too thrilled to show you around their hometown (book 10 working days ahead).

Getting There & Away

From the **bus station** (www.sutrans.rs; Senćanski put 3) there are hourly services to Novi Sad (600DIN, two hours) and Belgrade (1280DIN, 3½ hours).

Subotica's **train station** (Bose Milećević bb) has two trains to Szeged, Hungary (300DIN, 1¾ hours). Trains to Belgrade (480DIN, 3½ hours) stop at Novi Sad (384DIN, 1½ hours).

UNDERSTAND SERBIA

History

The assignation of Serbia to the Byzantine Empire in AD 395, and the conversion of the population to Orthodoxy in 879, wedded Serbia to eastern Europe.

The Ottoman Turks defeated Serbia at the pivotal 1389 Battle of Kosovo; independence from Turkish rule wasn't achieved until 1815.

On 28 June 1914, Austria-Hungary used the assassination of Archduke Franz Ferdinand by a Bosnian Serb as cause to invade Serbia, sparking WWI: almost 60% of Serbia's male population perished. After WWI, Serbia joined Croatia, Slovenia, Vojvodina and Macedonia to form Yugoslavia. Tito, a Communist Partisan resistance leader, became leader of the Federal Republic of Yugoslavia in 1945.

By 1986 Serbian nationalists were espousing a 'Greater Serbia', an ideology that would encompass Serbs from all republics into one state. Appropriated by Serbia's Communist Party leader Slobodan Milošević, the doctrine was fuelled by claims of the genocide of Serbs by Kosovar Albanians, leading to the abolishment of self-rule in Kosovo in 1990. Croatia, Slovenia, Bosnia and Hercegovina and Macedonia seceded from the federation, sparking a series of violent conflicts known collectively as the Yugoslav Wars.

Monstrously complex, the wars were fought not just between breakaway forces and the majority-Serb Yugoslav Army, but along ethnic and religious lines as well. Atrocities were committed on all sides: perhaps the most stunning display of savagery came with the Srebrenica massacre in which 8000 Bosnian men and boys were killed under orders of Republika Srpska Army (RSA) commander Ratko Mladić and RS president Radovan Karadžić.

Violence erupted in Kosovo in 1998, and the flight of thousands of Kosovar Albanians into Macedonia and Albania galvanised NATO into a 78-day bombing campaign of Serbian cities, military targets and infrastructure, after which Serbian forces withdrew.

In 2001 Milošević was defeated in presidential elections and forced from office by a popular uprising. He was extradited to the Hague, where he died in March 2006.

Kosovo declared independence in 2008 which Serbia deemed illegal; fractures stil remain. Later that year, Karadžić was arrested for war crimes after 12 years as a fugitive. Mladić was finally apprehended in 2011.

Serbia's current president is Tomislav Nikolić, a former member of the far-right Serbian Radical Party. Serbia is an official candidate for EU membership, but it remains unseen how Kosovo – and Nikolić – will affect these aspirations.

People

The population is estimated at 7.2 million people, made up of Serbs (83.3%), Hungarians (3.5%), Bosniaks (2%), Roma (2.1%) and others (5.1%). Around 85% of the population identify as Serbian Orthodox.

SURVIVAL GUIDE

Directory A–Z

Accommodation

Private rooms and apartments offer superb value and can be organised through tourist offices. 'Wild' camping is possible outside national parks.

The following price categories for the cost of a high-season double room are used in the listings in this chapter.

€ less than €30 (3000DIN)

€€ €30 to €75 (3000DIN to 7000DIN)

€€€ more than €75 (7000DIN)

Embassies & Consulates

A list of embassies and consulates in Serbia, as well as Serbian embassies around the world, is available at www.embassypages.com/serbia. New Zealand doesn't have an embassy in Serbia. It is represented through its embassy in The Hague. Countries represented in Belgrade include the following:

Australian Embassy (☎011-330 3400; www.serbia.embassy.gov.au; 7th fl, Vladimira Popovica 38-40)

Canadian Embassy (☎011-306 3000; bgrad@international.gc.ca; Kneza Miloša 75)

French Embassy (☎011-302 3500; www.ambafrance-srb.org; Pariska 11)

German Embassy (☎011-306 4300; www.belgrad.diplo.de; Neznanog Junaka 1)

Netherlands Embassy (☎011-2023 900; bel@minbuza.nl; Simina 29)

UK Embassy (☎011-264 5055; www.ukinserbia.fco.gov.uk; Resavska 46)

US Embassy (☎011-361 9344; http://serbia.usembassy.gov; Kneza Miloša 50)

Food

The following price categories for the cost of a main course are used in the listings in this chapter.

€ less than €6 (600DIN)

€€ €6 to €10 (600DIN to 1000DIN)

€€€ more than €10 (1000DIN)

Money

Serbia retains the dinar (DIN), though payment in euros for services and accommodation is commonplace. Exchange offices *(menjačnica)* are everywhere.

Post & Telephone

» Parcels should be taken unsealed to the post office for inspection.

» Phonecards can be bought in post offices and kiosks for 300DIN (local cards) and 600DIN (international cards). Halo Plus cards allow for longer calls.

» SIM and recharge cards can be purchased at supermarkets and kiosks.

Visas

Tourist visas for stays of less than 90 days aren't required by citizens of most countries. **The Ministry of Foreign Affairs** (www.mfa.gov.rs/Visas/Visas_en_how_to.htm) has full details.

Officially, all visitors must register with the police. Hotels and hostels will do this for you but if you're camping or staying in a private home, you are expected to register within 24 hours of arrival. This is rarely enforced, but being unable to produce registration documents upon leaving Serbia could result in a fine.

Getting There & Away

Air

Belgrade's **Nikola Tesla Beograd Airport** (☎011-209 4444; www.beg.aero) handles international flights. The website has a full list of airlines.

Land

Because Serbia does not acknowledge crossing points into Kosovo as international border crossings, it may not be possible to enter Serbia from Kosovo unless you first entered Kosovo from Serbia. Driving Serbian-plated cars into Kosovo isn't advised, and often not permitted by rental agencies or insurers.

Drivers need International Driving Permits, and vehicles need either Green Card insurance or insurance purchased at the border.

Bus services to both western Europe and Turkey are well developed.

International rail connections leaving Serbia originate in Belgrade. For more information visit **Serbian Railways** (www.serbianrailways.com).

Getting Around

Bus services are extensive, though outside major hubs connections can be sporadic. Reservations are only worthwhile for international buses and during festivals.

Major car-hire companies are ubiquitous. The **Automobile & Motorcycle Association of Serbia** (Auto-Moto Savez Srbije; ☎011-333 1100, roadside assist 1987; www.amss.org.rs; Ruzveltova 18) provides roadside assistance and extensive information on its website.

Serbian Railways serves Novi Sad, Subotica and Niš from Belgrade.

Bicycle paths are improving in larger cities.

Slovakia

Includes »

Bratislava ... 1008
Southwestern Slovakia ... 1014
Tatra Mountains ... 1014
Poprad ... 1014
High Tatras ... 1014
East Slovakia ... 1017
Levoča ... 1017
Slovenský Raj & Around ... 1017
Košice ... 1019
Bardejov ... 1021
Understand Slovakia ... 1021
Survival Guide ... 1022

Best Places to Eat

» Café Verne (p1009)
» Cactus (p1021)
» Bistro St Germain (p1009)

Best Places to Stay

» Ginger Monkey Hostel (p1014)
» Skaritz (p1009)
» Relax Farma Marianka (p1018)

Why Go?

No, it isn't a province of the Czech Republic. Now an independent state for more than two decades since the breakup of Czechoslovakia, Slovakia out trumps the Czechs for ancient castles and boasts nature far wilder than its western neighbours. It savours wine over beer and, in its bashful heartland amid myriad mountains and forests, cradles an entrancing folk culture most European nations have lost.

Slovakia is small: hike woodsy waterfall-filled gorges one day and yodel from peaks soaring more than 2500m the next. From dinky capital Bratislava, with its rabbit-warren Old Town and hilly, thickly forested backdrop, head east to fortresses towering over tradition-rich medieval towns and hiking trails that lace the hills. Down a *slivovica* (firewaterlike plum brandy) and drink a toast for us – *nazdravie*!

When to Go

Bratislava

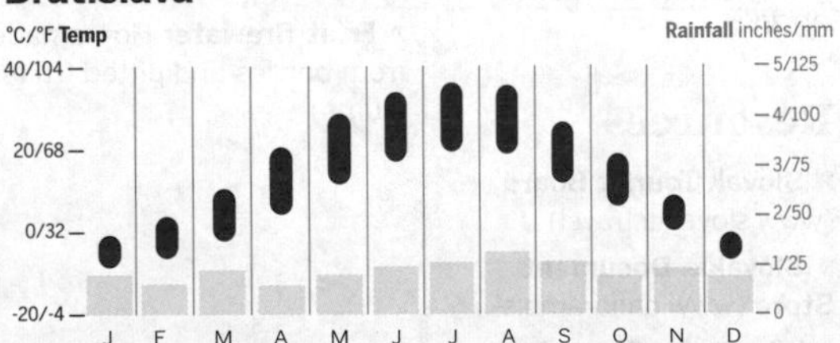

Sep Fewer crowds but clement weather, wine season means it's time for alcohol-themed festivities

Jun & Jul Festivals countrywide, High Tatras hiking trails are all open

Jan & Feb Peak ski season in the mountains; many other sights are closed

AT A GLANCE

» **Currency** Euro

» **Language** Slovak

» **Money** ATMs widely available in cities

» **Visas** Not required for most visitors staying fewer than 90 days

Fast Facts

» **Area** 49,035 sq km

» **Capital** Bratislava

» **Country code** ☎02

» **Emergency** ☎112

Exchange Rates

Australia	A$1	€0.82
Canada	C$1	€0.77
Japan	¥100	€0.83
New Zealand	NZ$1	€0.65
UK	UK£1	€1.18
USA	US$1	€0.78

Set Your Budget

» **Budget hotel room** €30–60

» **Two-course meal** €15

» **Museum entrance** €3

» **Beer** €1.50

» **City transport ticket** €0.70

Resources

» **Slovak Tourist Board** (www.slovakia.travel)

» **Slovakia Document Store** (www.panorama.sk)

» **What's On Slovakia** (www.whatsonslovakia.com)

Connections

Though few airlines fly into Slovakia itself, Bratislava is just 60km from well-connected Vienna International Airport. By train from Bratislava, Budapest is three hours and Prague five hours. By bus, connect to Zakopane in Poland (two hours) from Poprad, and to Uzhhorod in Ukraine (2½ hours) through Košice.

ITINERARIES

Three Days

Spend two nights in Bratislava exploring the Old Town's streets and museums, then take a castle excursion on your last day: either to Devín or Trenčín. Better yet, spend all three days hiking in the High Tatras, staying central in Starý Smokovec resort town or in more off-beat Ždiar in the Belá Tatras.

One Week

After a day or two in Bratislava, spend at least four nights around the Tatras so you have time to hike to a mountain hut as well as take day trips to Spiš Castle ruins, medieval Levoča or Slovenský Raj National Park. Or forge further east to Bardejov to see its complete Renaissance town square and nearby wooden churches.

Essential Food & Drink

» **Bountiful bryndza** Slovakia's signature mountain sheep cheese: sharp, soft and spreadable.

» **Meat and one veg** *Vývar* (chicken/beef broth served with *slížiky*, thin pasta strips, or liver dumplings); all-hail Slovakia's favourite vegetable, the potato, best enjoyed as *lokše* (potato pancakes) complemented by duck/goose fat or sauerkraut.

» **Dumplings** Potato-based goodies such as *halušky* (often in *bryndza* sauce topped with bacon).

» **Fruit firewater** Homemade or store-bought liquor, made from berries and pitted fruits, such as *slivovica* (from plums)

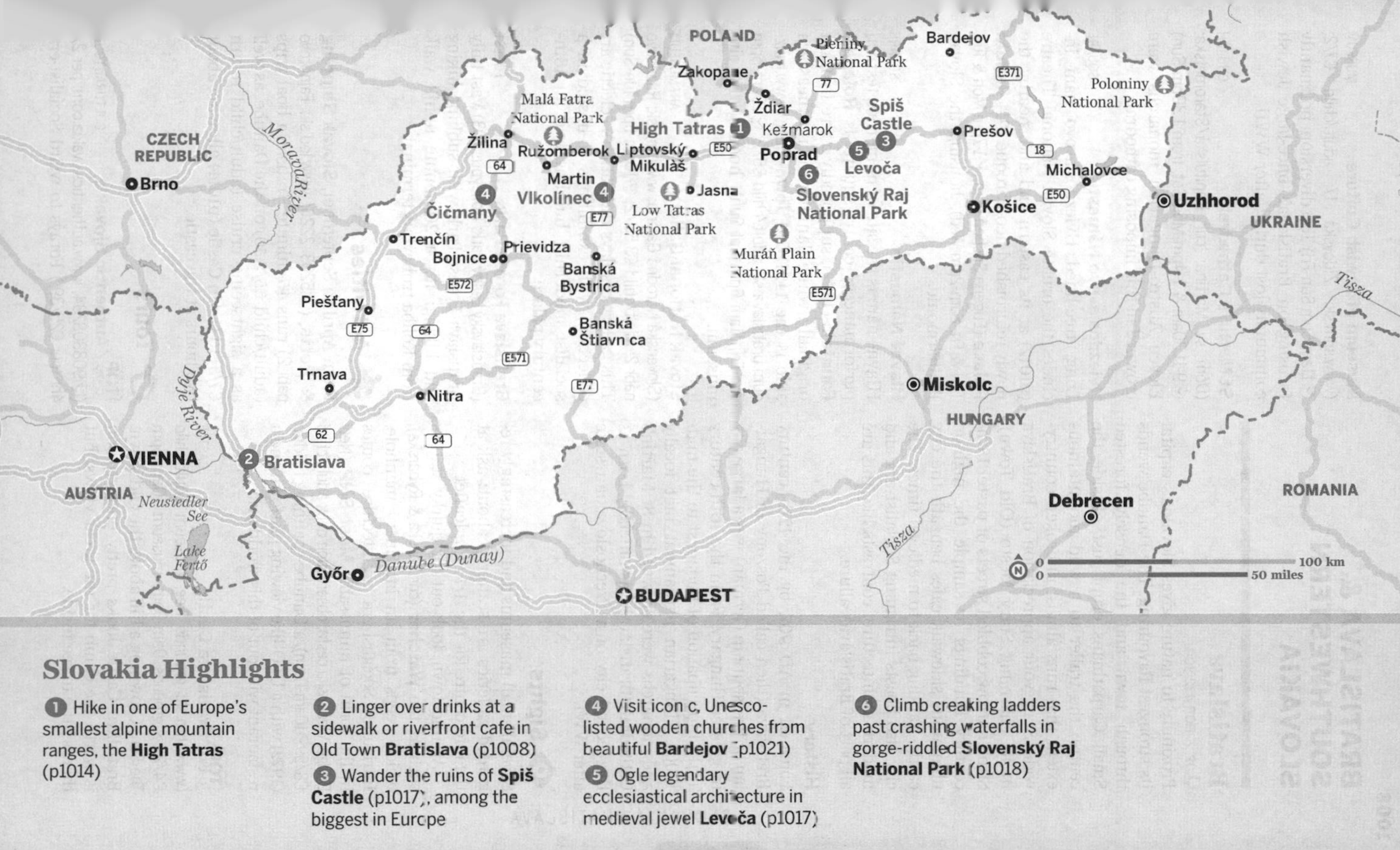

Slovakia Highlights

1 Hike in one of Europe's smallest alpine mountain ranges, the **High Tatras** (p1014)

2 Linger over drinks at a sidewalk or riverfront cafe in Old Town **Bratislava** (p1008)

3 Wander the ruins of **Spiš Castle** (p1017), among the biggest in Europe

4 Visit iconic, Unesco-listed wooden churches from beautiful **Bardejov** (p1021)

5 Ogle legendary ecclesiastical architecture in medieval jewel **Levoča** (p1017)

6 Climb creaking ladders past crashing waterfalls in gorge-riddled **Slovenský Raj National Park** (p1018)

BRATISLAVA & SOUTHWESTERN SLOVAKIA

Bratislava

☎02 / POP 432,800

Proximity to nature gives Slovakia's capital its strongest flavouring. The Danube wends through town and the densely forested Small Carpathians erupt just outside the centre; the trailer to a wild mountainous extent that runs almost unbroken countrywide. Start your appreciation of Bratislava in its charming Starý Mesto (Old Town). Stroll narrow cobbled streets of pastel 18th-century buildings or sample the nigh-on ubiquitous sidewalk cafes beneath the city castle, harking back to medieval times. The city also boasts intriguing Socialist-era and modern architecture: contrasts like this are all part of Bratislava's allure.

History

Founded in AD 907, by the 12th century Bratislava (then called Poszony in Hungarian or Pressburg in German) was a large city in greater Hungary. From the 16th-century Turkish occupation of Budapest to the mid-1800s, Hungarian parliament met locally and monarchs were crowned in St Martin's Cathedral. 'Bratislava' was officially born as the second city of a Czechoslovakian state after WWI.

Sights

Several small museums and increasingly regarded galleries are scattered about: ask at the info centre for the *Art Plan* leaflet.

Around town, look out for quirky statues such as the **Watcher** (cnr Panská & Rybárska), which peeps from an imaginary manhole. Intriguing Socialist-era architecture comes in the form of unmissable **Most SNP** (New Bridge; Viedenská cesta; observation deck adult/child €8/5; ⏲10am-11pm), a Danube-spanning bridge (1972) with a UFO-like viewing platform and a restaurant with out-of-this-world prices.

TOP CHOICE **Bratislava Castle** CASTLE
(www.snm.sk; grounds free, museum adult/child €4/2; ⏲grounds 9am-9pm, museum 10am-6pm Tue-Sun) Crowning a hill above the Old Town, Bratislava Castle looks pretty enough and is worth the climb for the great views, but there's little to see inside.

Museum of Jewish Culture MUSEUM
(www.snm.sk; Židovská 17; adult/child €7/2; ⏲11am-5pm Sun-Fri) Top diversion, poignantly focusing on Bratislava's once-large Jewish community lost during/after WWII.

St Martin's Cathedral CHURCH
(Dóm sv Martina; cnr Kapitulská/Starometská; ⏲9-11.30am & 1-4pm Mon-Sat, from 1.30pm Sun) Eleven Austro-Hungarian monarchs were crowned in this imposing cathedral.

Hviezdoslavovo Námestie SQUARE
Long, tree-lined Hviezdoslavovo nám includes the ornate Slovak National Theatre (p1012) at its eastern end and, nearby, the newly refurbished neo-baroque 1914 **Reduta Palace** (Eugena Suchoň nám; ⏲1-7pm Mon & Tue, Thu & Fri, 8am-2pm Wed), housing the Slovak Philharmonic.

Hlavné Námestie SQUARE
Hlavné nám is the site of numerous festival performances: centre-square is **Roland's Fountain** (1572), supposedly a fire hydrant originally, while flanking the northeastern side is the 1421 **Old Town Hall** (www.muzeum.bratislava.sk; adult/child €5/2; ⏲10am-5pm Tue-Fri, 11am-6pm Sat-Sun), hosting the city museum.

Slovak National Gallery ART MUSEUM
(Slovenská Národná Galéria; www.sng.sk; Rázusovo nábr 2; adult/child €3.50/2; ⏲10am-5pm Tue-Sun) This gallery displays the nation's eclectic art collection, with exhibitions co-hosted in a socialist modernist building and an 18th-century palace.

Bratislava Forest Park FOREST
(Bratislavský Lesný Park; Trolleybus 203) Vast hilly Bratislava Forest Park with sublime hiking and biking: it's a 20-minute uphill walk from Koliba trolleybus terminal.

Activities

From April to September, **Slovak Shipping & Ports** (☎5293 2226; www.lod.sk; Fajnorovo nábr 2) runs 45-minute Bratislava boat trips (adult/child €5/3.50) on the Danube, as well as a sightseeing cruise (adult/child return €7/5) to Devín Castle (p1014) allowing about two hours at the castle.

Tours

TOP CHOICE **Authentic Slovakia** CULTURAL TOUR
(☎908308234; www.authenticslovakia.com; per 2/4hr tour €25/39) Forays to weird Socialist-era

buildings and typical *krčmy* (Slovak pubs): authentic (uncensored) Slovakia.

FREE **Be Free Tours** WALKING TOUR
(www.befreetours.com; 11am & 4pm Tue-Sat, 4pm Sun & Mon) Two-hour-plus English-speaking Old Town tours leaving from the Hviezdoslav statue in Hviezdoslavovo nám.

Festivals & Events

Cultural Summer Festival CULTURE
(visit.bratislava.sk; Jun-Sep) Plays and performances come to the streets and city-wide venues in summer.

Christmas Market SHOPPING
(Nov & Dec) From 26 November, Hlavné nám fills with food, drink, handicrafts and staged performances.

Sleeping

For full accommodation listings, see www.bkis.sk. Short-term rental flats in the Old Town (€65 to €120 per night) are great for staying super-central without paying hotel prices: try the modern, family-friendly **Apartments Bratislava** (www.apartments bratislava.com).

TOP CHOICE **Skaritz** BOUTIQUE HOTEL €€
(5920 9770; www.skaritz.com; Michalská 4; r €75-100;) Century-old elegance combined with contemporary design touches. Choose from 20 rooms and six apartments. Smack-bang central, too.

Hostel Blues HOSTEL €
(0905204020; www.hostelblues.sk; Špitálska 2; dm €15-20, d €52-63;) Five- to 10-bed, single-sex or mixed dorms. Private rooms have their own bathrooms. Free sightseeing tours.

Downtown Backpackers HOSTEL €
(5464 1191; www.backpackers.sk; Panenská 31; dm €17-18, d €52;) Bratislava's first hostel, Backpackers is a bohemian classic. Good food served in the convivial bar.

Penzión Virgo PENSION €€
(2092 1400; www.penzionvirgo.sk; Panenská 14; s/d/apt €61/74/85;) Exterior-access rooms are arranged around a courtyard; light and airy despite dark-wood floors and baroque-accent wallpaper. Breakfast buffet (€5).

Penzión Zlatá Noha PENSION €
(5477 4922; ww.zlata-noha.sk; Bellova 2; s/d €39/49; ; 203) Up in leafy Koliba 2km north of the Old Town, vista-rich family-run Zlatá Noha offers some of the most decently priced rooms hereabouts.

Eating

Reasonably priced eateries line Obchodná, and cafe culture abounds on Bratislava's two main plazas: Hviezdoslavovo nám and Hlavné nám. That Slovak fave, the set lunch menu, can be a real steal.

TOP CHOICE **Café Verne** INTERNATIONAL €€
(Hviezdoslavovo nám 18; mains €4-11; 9am-midnight;) Spirited, good-value Old Town dining: Czech beers flow and everyone from expats to students wolf down no-nonsense Slovak staples.

Bistro St Germain BISTRO €
(Obchodná 17; mains €4; 10am-10pm) Wonderfully decorated, relaxed place to gossip over homemade lemonade, cupcakes and light lunches in a little courtyard off Obchodná.

Shtoor CAFE €
(Panská 23; light lunches €3-5;) Bursting onto the eating scene with tasty, cheap, healthy lunches, Shtoor has three locations in Bratislava but this, with two levels of seating, has the best (coffee- and cake-fuelled) atmosphere. Check the menus: written in old-fashioned Slovak as set down by Ľudovít Štúr, pioneer of Slovak literary language.

Traja Mušketieri PUB €€
(5443 0019; Sládkovičova 7; mains €6-12) Way-upmarket version of a medieval tavern.

U Jakubu SLOVAKIAN €
(Nám SNP 24; mains €2-5; 8am-6pm Mon-Fri) Self-service Socialist-style cafeteria.

SPLURGE

Bratislavský Meštiansky Pivovar
(0944512265; www.mestianskypivovar.sk; Drevená 8; mains €5.50-19; 11am-midnight Mon-Thu & Sat, to 1am Fri, to 11pm Sun), a stylish microbrewery, serves Bratislava's freshest beer and offers creative Slovak cooking beneath vaulted ceilings and stylised Old Town artwork.

Central Bratislava

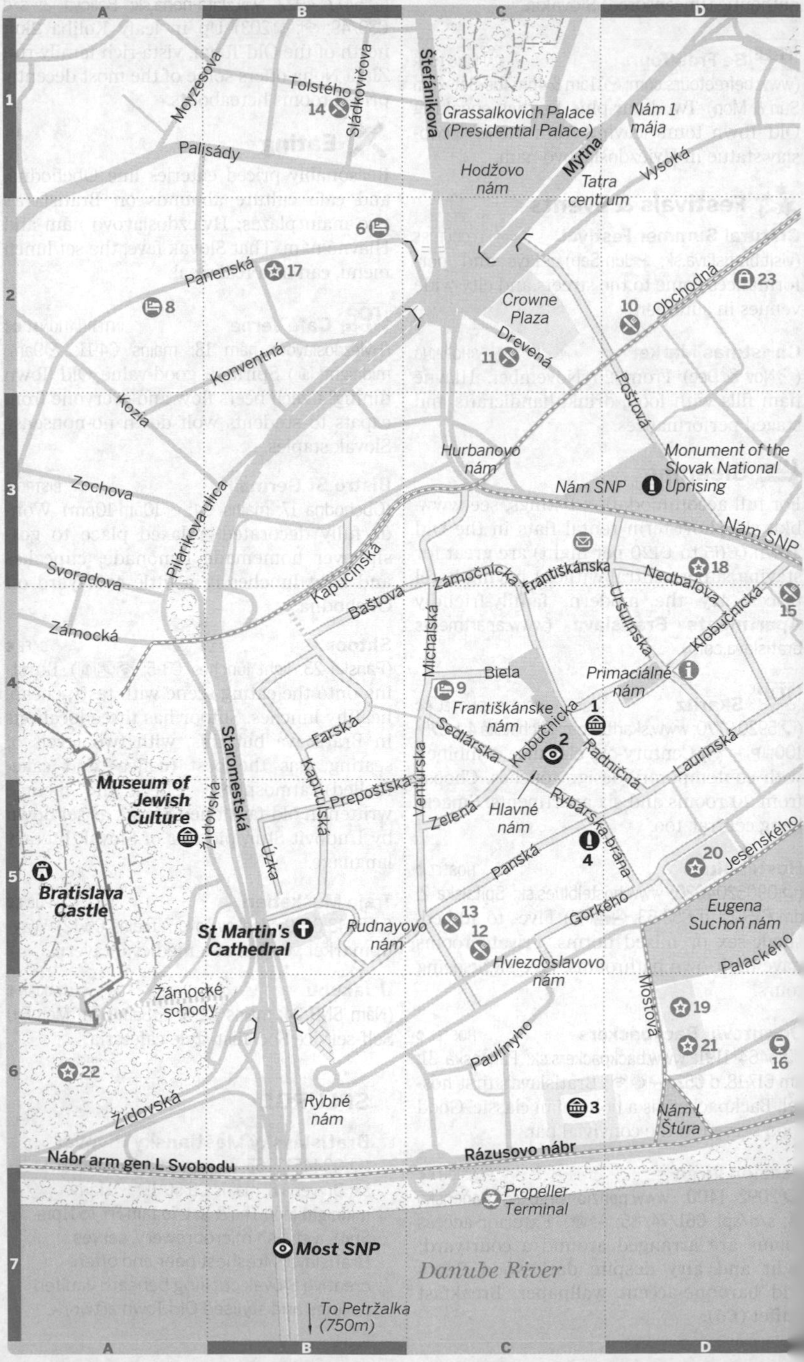

A B C D

1
Moyzesova
Tolstého
14
Sládkovičova
Štefánikova
Grassalkovich Palace (Presidential Palace)
Nám 1 mája
Palisády
Hodžovo nám
Mýtna
Tatra centrum
Vysoká

2
6
Panenská
17
8
23
Obchodná
Crowne Plaza
10
Drevená
11
Konventná
Kozia
Poštová

3
Hurbanovo nám
Monument of the Slovak National Uprising
Nám SNP
Zochova
Pilárikova ulica
Kapucínska
Svoradova
18
Nedbalova
15
Zámočnícka
Františkánska
Baštová
Uršulínska
Klobučnícka
Zámocká

4
Michalská
Biela
Primaciálne nám
9
Františkánske nám
1
Klobučnícka
Farská
Sedlárska
2
Radničná
Laurinská
Staromestská
Kapitulská
Prepoštská
Ventúrska

5
Museum of Jewish Culture
Židovská
Zelená
Hlavné nám
Rybárska brána
4
Panská
20
Jesenského
Bratislava Castle
Úzka
Gorkého
Eugena Suchoň nám
St Martin's Cathedral
Rudnayovo nám
13
12
Hviezdoslavovo nám
Palackého

6
Zámocké schody
Mostová
19
21
16
22
Paulínyho
Židovská
Rybné nám
3
Nám L Štúra
Nábr arm gen L Svobodu
Rázusovo nábr
Propeller Terminal

7
Most SNP
Danube River
To Petržalka (750m)

A B C D

SLOVAKIA BRATISLAVA

Central Bratislava

Top Sights

Bratislava Castle....A5
Most SNP....B7
Museum of Jewish Culture....A5
St Martin's Cathedral....B5

Sights

1 Old Town Hall....C4
2 Roland's Fountain....C4
3 Slovak National Gallery....C6
4 Watcher....C5

Activities, Courses & Tours

Be Free Tours....(see 20)
5 Slovak Shipping & Ports....E6

Sleeping

6 Downtown Backpackers....B2
7 Hostel Blues....F2
8 Penzión Virgo....A2
9 Skaritz....C4

Eating

10 Bistro St Germain....D2
11 Bratislavský Meštiansky Pivovar....C2
12 Café Verne....C5
13 Shtoor....C5
14 Traja Mušketieri....B1
15 U Jakubu....D4

Drinking

16 Nu Spirit Bar....D6

Entertainment

17 Apollon Club....B2
18 Dunaj....D3
Historic SND....(see 20)
19 Reduta Palace....D6
20 Slovak National Theatre....D5
21 Slovak Philharmonic....D6
22 Subclub....A6

Shopping

23 Úľuv....D2

Drinking

From mid-April to October, sidewalk cafe tables sprout up in every corner of the pedestrian Old Town. Hviezdoslavovo nám has good options, as does Eurovea.

Nu Spirit Bar BAR

(Medená 16; ⏲10am-2am Mon-Fri, 5pm-4am Sat & Sun) Deservedly popular cellar bar with regular live music: jazz, electronica, soul etc.

☆ Entertainment

Check **Slovak Spectator** (www.spectator.sme.sk), the **Bratislava Culture & Information Centre** (www.bkis.sk) and **Kam do Mesta** (www.kamdomesta.sk) for the latest. Cover charges for Bratislava music bars and clubs are usually less than €5. Stay tuned for performances by Lúčnica, Slovakia's leading folk-music ensemble.

Apollon Club GAY & LESBIAN
(www.apollon-gay-club.sk; Panenská 24; ⏲6pm-3am Mon-Thu, 8pm-5am Fri & Sat, 8pm-1am Sun) The best gay disco.

Hlava XXII CLUB
(Bazová 9; ⏲3pm-3am Tue-Sat) Jam sessions, blues and world beat – live. It's 1km northeast of center, off Záhradnicka.

Subclub NIGHCLUB
(Nábrežie arm gen L Svobudu; ⏲10pm-4am Thu-Sat) An institution in the subterranean passageways under the castle. Pounding techno, indie, hard-core dance etc.

Slovak National Theatre THEATRE
(Slovenské Národné Divadlo (SND); www.snd.sk; Hviezdoslavovo nám) Operas, ballets and dramas staged in two venues: glamorous, gilted **Historic SND** (Hviezdoslavovo nám, booking office cnr Jesenského & Komenského; ⏲8am-5.30pm Mon-Fri, 9am-1pm Sat) and modern **New SND** (Pribinova 17; ⏲9am-5pm Mon- Fri).

Slovak Philharmonic THEATRE
(www.filharm.sk; Eugena Suchoň nám; tickets €5-20; ⏲9am-2pm Mon, 1-6pm Tue-Fri & before performances)

Dunaj PERFORMING ARTS
(www.kcdunaj.sk; Nedbalova 3; ⏲4pm-late) Hosts some of Slovakia's most interesting drama and music performances. Also has a bar with Old Town panoramas from the terrace.

Shopping

Craft and jewellery shops and souvenir booths throng around Hlavné nám.

Eurovea MALL
(Pribinova) Western chain stores, fancy riverside restaurants and the new Slovak National Theatre (New SND).

Úľuv HANDICRAFTS
(www.uluv.sk; Obchodná 64) The main outlet of this national handicraft cooperative, in a courtyard full of artisans studios.

ℹ Information

Bratislava has numerous banks and ATMs in the Old Town. There are also ATMs and exchange booths in the train and bus stations, as well as at the airport. Most cafes have wi-fi access; Hlavné nám and Hviezdoslavovo nám are free wi-fi zones.

Bratislava Culture & Information Centre (BKIS; ☎16 186, 5443 3715; www.bkis.sk; Klobučnícká 2; ⏲9am-6pm Mon-Fri, 9am-3pm Sat, 10am-3pm Sun) Sells the **Bratislava City Card** (1/2/3 days €10/12/15), covering public transport and providing discounted museum admission.

Emergency (☎112)

Klar-i-net (Klariská 4; per hour €3.50; ⏲10am-10pm Mon-Fri, from 3pm Sat & Sun)

Lonely Planet (www.lonelyplanet.com/slovakia/bratislava)

Main Police Station (☎158; Hrobákova 44) In the neighbourhood of Petržalka, south of the Old Town across the river.

Main Post Office (Nám SNP 34-35)

Poliklinika Ruzinov (☎4827 9111; www.ruzinovskapoliklinika.sk, in Slovak; Ružinovská 10) Hospital with emergency services and 24-hour pharmacy.

Slovak Spectator (www.spectator.sme.sk) English-language weekly. Current affairs and event listings.

Tatra Banka (Dunajská 4)

Visit Bratislava (http://visit.bratislava.sk) Comprehensive city tourist-board site.

ℹ Getting There & Away

Bratislava is Slovakia's main bus, train and plane hub.

Air

Remember Vienna's busier international airport is only 60km west.

Airport Bratislava (BTS; www.airportbratislava.sk; Ivanská cesta) Nine kilometres northeast of the centre. Connections to Italy, Spain, UK cities and more.

Danube Wings (V5; www.danubewings.eu) Weekday flights (7am and 6pm) to Košice.

Boat

Plying the Danube is another way to get between Bratislava and Vienna.

Twin City Liner (☎0903 610 716; www.twincityliner.com; Rázusovo nábr, Propeller Terminal) Up to four boats daily to Vienna (€19 to €33 one way, 1½ hours).

Bus

Direct destinations include cities throughout Slovakia and Europe, but the train is usually comparably priced and more convenient. For schedules, see www.cp.atlas.sk. The **Main Bus Station** (Mlynské Nivy; 🚌Autobusová stanica, AS) is 1km east of the Old Town.

Eurolines (☎5542 2734; www.slovaklines.sk) Contact for most international buses.

Slovenská Autobusová Doprava (SAD; www.sad.sk) National bus company.

Train

Rail is the main way to get around Slovakia and to neighbouring countries. Intercity/Eurocity (IC/EC) trains are quickest. *Rychlík* (R), or 'Fast' trains take marginally longer, but run more frequently and cost less. *Osobný* (Ob) trains are the milk runs. For schedules see www.cp.atlas.sk.

Main Train Station (Hlavná Stanica; www.slovakrail.sk; Predštanicné nám)

Getting Around

To/From the Airport

City bus 61 links Bratislava airport with the main train station (20 minutes).

Standing taxis (over)charge about €20 to town; ask prices before getting in.

A regular bus (€7.70) connects Vienna, Vienna airport, Bratislava bus station and Bratislava airport.

Car

Numerous international car-hire companies (Hertz, Sixt etc) have offices at the airport.

Buchbinder (☎4363 7821; www.buchbinder.sk) In-town pick-up possible.

Car Rental 24 (☎903 582 400; www.car-rental24.sk) Has an airport office.

Public Transport

Bratislava has an extensive tram, bus and trolleybus network. **Dopravný Podnik Bratislava** (DPB; www.dpb.sk; Hodžovo nám; ⊙6am-7pm Mon-Fri) is the public transport company, with offices in the underground passage beneath Hodžovo nám. Check www.imhd.zoznam.sk for city-wide schedules.

Tickets cost €0.35/0.70/0.90 for 15/30/60 minutes. Buy at newsstands and validate on board (or risk a legally enforceable €50 fine). Passes cost €4.50/8.30/10 for one/two/three days; buy at the DPB office and validate on board.

Important lines include the following:

TRANSPORT FROM BRATISLAVA

International Bus

DESTINATION	PRICE (€)	DURATION (HR)	FREQUENCY (DAILY)
Budapest (Hungary)	6-14	2½-4	4
London (Britain)	76	23-24	1
Prague (Czech Republic)	14	4¼	5
Vienna (Austria)	8	1¼	12

Domestic Train

DESTINATION	PRICE (€)	DURATION (HR)	FREQUENCY (DAILY)
Košice	19	5½	12
Poprad	15	4	12
Trenčín	6.50	1½	12

International Train

DESTINATION	PRICE (€)	DURATION (HR)	FREQUENCY (DAILY)
Budapest (Hungary)	15	2¾	7
Prague (Czech Republic)	27	4¼	6
Vienna (Austria)	11	1	hourly
Warsaw (Poland)	63	10½	1

Bus 93 Main Train Station–Hodžovo nám
Trolleybus 206 Main Bus Station–Hodžovo nám
Trolleybus 210 Main Bus Station–Main Train Station

Taxi

Standing cabs compulsively overcharge foreigners; an around-town trip shouldn't cost more than €10.

AA Euro Taxi (☎16 022)

Free Taxi (☎5596 9696) Cheap.

Around Bratislava

Two of the best sights in Bratislava are actually out of the centre. **Devín Castle** (www.muzeum.bratislava.sk; adult/child €3/1.50; ⏲10am-5pm Tue-Fri, to 7pm Sat & Sun May-Sep), 9km west, was once the military plaything of 9th-century warlord Prince Ratislav. There's a museum and ruins wrapped by Danube vistas. Bus 29 links Devín with Bratislava's Most SNP stop, under the bridge.

A similar distance east from the city is **Danubiana Meulensteen Art Museum** (www.danubiana.sk; Via Danubia, Čunovo; adult/child €6/3), innovatively designed on a sculpture-flanked spit jutting into the Danube. Take bus 91 from Most SNP to Čunovo then walk from the terminus (2.5km) or, during summer, join the boat trip from the city centre (adult/child €10/6 return).

DON'T MISS

GINGER MONKEY HOSTEL, BELÁ TATRAS

In the delightful main Belá Tatras village of Ždiar, **Ginger Monkey Hostel** (☎52 4498 084; www.gingermonkey.eu; Ždiar 294; dm/d €13/32; @📶) is reason enough to head to this region. In a tranquil painted house typical of the Goral folk culture prevalent hereabouts, traveller-friendly ambience pervades: there's free breakfast, dirt-cheap beer, hostel pets and sensational nearby hikes linking up with the High Tatras to the west. Buses from Poprad connect directly with Ždiar (€2, one hour, nine daily) and run to Zakopane in Poland (€2.20, 50 minutes, two daily April to October) and the High Tatras resort village of Tatranská Lomnica (€1, 30 minutes, hourly).

Southwestern Slovakia

Great castles and medieval towns pepper the countryside between Bratislava and the High Tatras. Check www.cp.atlas.sk for transport schedules.

Trencin, crowned by stupendous **Trenčín Castle** (www.muzeumtn.sk; adult/child €4.50/2.50; ⏲9am-5.30pm), is an ancient town full of appealing 18th- and 19th-century buildings, with atmospheric accommodation options and Slovakia's largest music festival, **Bažant Pohoda Festival** (www.pohodafestival.sk), in July. Regular trains from Bratislava (€6.50, 1½ hours) and on to Poprad (€10, 2¾ hours) and East Slovakia.

Banská Štiavnica is a medieval hillside mining town with numerous mining attractions and two castles. One direct bus daily departs from Bratislava (€8.50, 3½ hours), at 4.40pm; otherwise, bus and train arrivals require a change in Zvolen or Banská Bystrica.

TATRA MOUNTAINS

Poprad

☎052 / POP 54,300 / TRANSPORT HUB

Poprad will likely be your first experience of mountain country, being the nearest major transport hub to the High Tatras. The 16th-century neighbourhood of **Spišská Sobota** might make you linger, plus you can sign up for original High Tatras adventures with **Adventoura** (☎903641549; www.adventoura.eu; Uherova 33). From the adjacent train and bus stations, the central pedestrian square, Nám sv Egídia, is a five-minute walk south. The **City Information Centre** (☎7721 700; www.poprad.sk; Dom Kultúry Štefánikovа 72; ⏲8am-5pm Mon-Fri, 9am-noon Sat) is just west of here.

Buses serve Levoča (€1.60, 45 minutes, hourly), Bardejov (€4.50, 2¼ hours, six daily) and Zakopane in Poland (€5, two hours, two daily April to October). Change here for electric trains running the 14km or so to the High Tatras resorts. Main-line trains run directly to Bratislava (€16, four hours, hourly) and Košice (€5, 1¼ hours, hourly).

High Tatras

☎052

The High Tatras (Vysoké Tatry), the tallest range in the Carpathian Mountains, tower over most of eastern Europe. Some 25 pea soar higher than 2500m. The 25km-wide, 78km-long range boasts pristine snowfields, ultramarine mountain lakes and undulating pine forests. Most of this jagged massif, part-shared with Poland, is part of the Tatra National Park (Tanap).

Midmountain, three main resort towns string west to east. Štrbské Pleso is the traditional ski centre and most crowded, with development galore. Smokovec, 22km east, is an amalgam of the Nový (New), Starý (Old) and Horný (upper) settlements. Here you'll find numerous lodgings, a turn-of-the-century feel and most services. Five kilometres further, Tatranská Lomnica is the quaintest, quietest village. All have mountain access by cable car, funicular or chairlift.

The highest trails are closed due to snow from November to mid-June. June and July can be especially rainy; July and August are the warmest, most crowded months. Hotel prices and crowds are at their lowest from October to April.

Sights & Activities

A 600km trail network covers the area, with full-service mountain huts where hikers can eat and sleep en route. Trails are colour-coded and easy to follow. Numerous detailed maps and hiking guides are available at bookstores and information offices. Park regulations require you to keep to trails and refrain from picking flowers. A warning: many trails are rocky and uneven, ridges can be unprotected from sudden thunderstorms and the assistance of the Mountain Rescue Service is not free.

Hiking

The lovely 65km-long **Magistrála Trail** offers many of the best hiking possibilities. It runs mostly beneath the peaks (between 1300m and 1800m), with mountain hut stop-offs and cable-car/ski-lift access.

The easiest access is from **Hrebienok** (1280m), connected by **funicular railway** (www.vt.sk; adult/child return €7/5; ⊙7am-7pm Jul & Aug, 8am-5pm Sep-Jun) to Starý Smokovec. A good hike follows the Magistrála (red-marked) west to lakeside Sliezsky dom hut (2¼ hours), with a round trip back to Starý Smokovec that can be done in four hours. Other good sections to hike include Skalnaté Pleso to Hrebinok (2½ hours passing spectacular waterfalls) and Štrbské Pleso to Popradské pleso with its lake and mountain hotel (1¼ hours).

> **MULTIRESORT SKI PASSES**
>
> Park Snow and Vysoký Tatry resorts, the ski concessions in Štrbské Pleso and Tatranská Lomnica have all joined forces to offer multiday, multiresort lift passes (three-day adult/child €93/65). The **Super Slovak Ski Pass** (www.vt.sk; 10-day adult €260) covers some main resorts plus other smaller ski areas around Slovakia.

Skalnaté pleso, a lakeside winter sports area, is connected to Tatranská Lomnica by the **Gondola** (www.vt.sk; adult/child return €15/10; ⊙8.30am-7pm Jul & Aug, to 4pm Sep-Jun), and by **cable car** (www.vt.sk; adult/child return €24/17; ⊙8.30am-5.30pm Jul & Aug, to 3.30pm Sep-Jun) to the 2634m summit of **Lomnický štít**. The popular cable car requires a time-reserved ticket: you get 50 minutes at the summit, where there's also a cafe.

To ascend any peaks without marked hiking trails (Gerlachovský štít included), you must hire a guide. Contact the **Mountain Guides Society Office** (☎4422 066; www.tatraguide.sk; Starý Smokovec 38; ⊙10am-6pm Mon-Fri, noon-6pm Sat & Sun, closed weekends Oct-May); guides cost from €150 per day.

Winter Sports

The area above Tatranská Lomnica has some 30 skiable hectares. From Skalnaté pleso a high-speed winter **quad lift** (adult/child €8/5.50; ⊙9am-4pm) hoists riders to **Lomnické sedlo**, a 2190m saddle below the summit, with access to an advanced 6km-long ski run. **Vysoké Tatry** (www.vt.sk; Tatranská Lomnica 7; day-lift ticket adult/child €24/17; ⊙9am-3.30pm Dec-Apr) sells passes from the base of the cable car, where ski rental (from €15 per day) is also available.

Park Snow (www.parksnow.sk; day-lift ticket adult/child €19/13.50; ⊙8.30am-3.30pm) above Štrbské Pleso is a popular ski/snowboard resort, with 12km of easy-to-moderate runs and a snow-tubing area.

Rowboats

Štrbské Pleso's namesake clear-blue glacial *pleso* (lake) is surrounded by pine forest and peaks. **Rowboats** (per 45min €15-20; ⊙10am-6pm May-Sep) can be rented from the dock by the Grand Hotel Kempinski.

TOP MOUNTAIN HUTS

Up in the peaks, mountain huts allow you to stay on the trail you're trekking without descending to the resorts. A quintessentially Slovak outdoors experience, they're strung across the High Tatras at regular intervals: all offer food too. Our favourites include the following:

Bilíkova Chata (☎4422 439; www.bilikovachata.sk; s/d without bathroom €28/56) Seven-minute walk from Hrebienok funicular.

Zamkovského Chata (☎4422 636; www.zamka.sk; per person €15-18) Between Skalnaté pleso (near the Belá Tatras) and Hrebienok.

Chata Popradské Pleso (☎910948160; www.popradskepleso.sk; dm €14-18, s/d €23/46) Hotel a one-hour hike above Štrbské Pleso village.

Sleeping

For full listings of Tatra lodgings, look online at www.tatryinfo.eu. No wild/backcountry camping is permitted: there is a camping ground near Tatranská Lomnica. West of the Nový Smokovec electric train stop is the best place to seek reasonable accommodation.

TOP CHOICE **Penzión Tatra** PENSION €
(☎0903650802; www.tatraski.sk; Starý Smokovec 66; s/d incl breakfast €23/46; @☎) Super-central, classic 1900 alpinesque building above the train station with big modern rooms and ski storage.

Penzión Encian PENSION €
(☎4467 520; www.encian.eu; Tatranská Lomnica 32; s/d €30/47; @) Bundles of mountain appeal and a restaurant.

Villa Siesta HOTEL €€
(☎4423 024; www.villasiesta.sk; Nový Smokovec 88; d €64, ste €83-113; ☎) Light fills this airy, contemporary mountain villa furnished in natural hues. The full restaurant, sauna and jacuzzi are a bonus.

Eating & Drinking

Resort towns are close together: you can sleep in one and eat in another.

TOP CHOICE **Reštaurácia Svišť** SLOVAKIAN €€
(Nový Smokovec 30; mains €6-13; ⏲6-11pm) Hearty dumplings, beef fillet with wine reduction...this stylish Slovakian restaurant does it all well.

Reštaurácia Furkotka SLOVAKIAN €
(www.furkotka.sk; Štrbské Pleso; mains €3-6; ⏲11am-midnight) Snug one-stop-shop for good food, beer and bargainous hostel-type accommodation (rooms €10 to €24 per person).

Tatry Pub PUB
(Tatra Komplex, Starý Smokovec; ⏲3pm-1am Sun-Thu, 3pm-3am Fri & Sat; ☎) Lively official watering hole of the Mountain Guide Club.

Information

All three resort towns have ATMs on the main street.

Note that information offices do not book rooms; they hand out a brochure listing some – not all – accommodation.

High Tatras Tourist Trade Association (www.tatryinfo.sk) Comprehensive overview of the area, including accommodation.

Mountain Rescue Service (☎421-(0)52 7877 711, emergency 18 300; www.hzs.sk; Horný Smokovec 52)

T-Ski Travel (☎0905 350 810; www.slovakia-travel.sk; Starý Smokovec 46; ⏲9am-4pm Mon-Thu, to 5pm Fri-Sun) Books lodgings, arranges ski and other activity programs. At the funicular station.

Tatra Information Office Starý Smokovec (TIK; ☎4423 440; Starý Smokovec 23; ⏲8am-8pm Mon-Fri, to 1pm Sat) Largest information office for the area.

Tatra National Park (www.tanap.org) National park website.

U Michalka Café (Starý Smokovec 4; per hr €2; ⏲10am-10pm; ☎) Four terminals, great tea and strudel.

Getting There & Around

To reach the Tatras by public transport, switch in Poprad. From there a narrow-gauge electric train makes numerous stops in the resort towns along the main road; buses go to smaller, downhill villages as well. Check schedules at www.cp.atlas.sk: fares are at most €1.60 for the Poprad–Štrbské Pleso journey. Electric trains (TEZ) run 6am to 10pm almost hourly. Buy individual TEZ tickets at stations, and additionally block tickets at tourist offices: validate on boar[d]. The most likely bus you'll need is from Tatransk[á] Lomnica to Ždiar (€1, 30 minutes, hourly).

EAST SLOVAKIA

Levoča

☎053 / POP 14,900

Unesco-listed Levoča is one of the few towns to still have largely intact ancient medieval walls: they ring a visually arresting Old Town criss-crossed by cobblestone alleyways, at the centre of which stands the pride of the country's religious art collection, the Gothic Church of St Jacob.

From the bus stop at Nám Štefana Kluberta, follow Košicka west two blocks to the main square.

Sights

Gothic and Renaissance eye candy rim the main square, Nám Majstra Pavla, where the undoubted highlight is the 14th- to 15th-century **Church of St Jacob** (Chrám Sv Jakuba; www.chramsvjakuba.sk; Nám Majstra Pavla; adult/child €2/1; ⏲by hourly tour 8.40am-4pm Tue-Sat, 1-4pm Sun): gawp at Slovakia's tallest altar (18m), designed by Levoča's Master Pavol. Buy your entry ticket inside the Municipal Weights House across from the north door.

The square is centred on the 15th-century **Town Hall** (Radnica). The private **Thurzov House** (1517), at No 7, has a characteristically frenetic Spiš Renaissance roofline. The **Master Pavol Museum**, at No 20, is dedicated to works by the city's most celebrated son and is a branch of the Spiš Museum.

Sleeping & Eating

Hotel U Leva HOTEL €€

(☎4502 311; www.uleva.sk; Nám Majstra Pavla 24; s/d/apt €39/68/99;) Spread across two Old Town buildings, with 23 unique, cleanly contemporary rooms. A fine restaurant (mains €7 to €13) is attached.

Hotel Arkáda HOTEL €

(☎4512 372; www.arkada.sk; Nám Majstra Pavla 26; s/d €36/52; @) Furnishings in this Old Town building are mostly uninspired, but you can upgrade to a suite with antiques and arched ceilings for just €65. The vaulted cellar-restaurant (mains €5 to €11) is atmospheric.

Oáza PENSION €

(☎4514 511; www.ubytovanieoaza.sk; Nová 65; dm incl breakfast from €10) Simple two-bed rooms with shared bathroom and four-bed rooms with bathroom and kitchen.

Information

The main square has everything you'll likely need, banks and post office included.

Tourist Information Office (☎4513 763; http://eng.levoca.sk; Nám Majstra Pavla 58; ⏲9am-4pm Mon-Fri year-round, plus 9am-4pm Sat & Sun May-Sep)

Getting There & Away

Levoča is on the main E50 motorway between Poprad (28km) and Košice (94km). Bus travel is the most feasible option here.

The bus station is 1km southeast of the centre. Frequent coach services:

Košice (€4.50, two hours, seven daily)

Poprad (€1.60, 45 minutes, hourly)

Spišská Nová Ves (€1, 20 minutes, half-hourly) For Slovenský Raj National Park.

Spišské Podhradie (€1, 20 minutes, half-hourly) For Spiš Castle.

Slovenský Raj & Around

☎053

With rumbling waterfalls, sheer gorges and dense forests, Slovenský Raj lives up to the name of 'Slovak Paradise'. The notorious one-way ladder-and-chain ascents, splashed by icy waterfalls, make this a national park for the passionately outdoorsy.

The nearest major town is uninspiring Spišská Nová Ves, 23km southeast of Poprad. There are three trailhead resort villages: Podlesok, outside Hrabušice

DON'T MISS

SPIŠ CASTLE

Sprawling for 4 hectares above the village of Spišské Podhradie, the ruined 13th-century **Spiš Castle** (Spišský hrad; www.spisskemuzeum.com; adult/child €5/3; ⏲9am-7pm, closed Nov-Mar) is one of Europe's largest and among Slovakia's most-photographed sights. There are phenomenal panoramic views from atop the central tower, plus rambling ruins aplenty.

Frequent buses connect Spišské Podhradie with Levoča, 15km east (€1, 20 minutes) and Poprad (€2.15, 50 minutes) among others, plus there's a spur train line from Spišské Podhradie to Spišské Vlachy (€0.75, 15 minutes, five daily) on the Bratislava–Košice train line.

(16km southwest of Poprad), is our favourite. There's also pretty Čingov, 5km west of Spišská Nová Ves, and lake-fronting Dedinky, about 50km south.

Sights & Activities

Get VKÚ's 1:25,000 *Slovenský Raj* hiking map (No 4) or Dajama's *Knapsacked Travel: The Slovak Paradise* hiking book, available at tourist offices and bookshops country-wide.

Slovenský Raj National Park PARK
(www.slovenskyraj.sk; Jul & Aug €1, Sep-Jun free) The national park has numerous trails that include one-way *roklina* (gorge) sections and take at least half a day. From Čingov, a green trail leads up Hornád River Gorge an hour to **Tomašovský výhľad**, a rocky outcrop overlook. Or continue to the green, one-way, technically aided **Kláštorisko Gorge** trail, allowing at least eight hours for the circuit.

You can also reach the Kláštorisko Gorge ascent from Podlesok (six hours). Another excellent alternative from Podlesok is to hike six to seven hours up the dramatic, ladder and technical-assist **Suchá Belá Gorge**. Return via Kláštorisko Chata and the blue trail down to the Hornád River, then follow the river gorge upstream to return to Podlesok.

Great hiking near Dedinky includes the dramatic, technical-assist hike from Biele Vody up **Zejmarská Gorge** (allow at least one hour). A sporadically functioning **chairlift** offers an alternative route back down.

Dobšinská Ice Cave CAVE
(www.ssj.sk; adult/child €7/3.50; ⏲9am-4pm Tue-Sun by hourly tour, closed Oct–mid-May) The fanciful frozen formations in this Unesco-noted ice cave are more dazzling in early June than September. A 15-minute hike leads up from the settlement of Dobšinská ľadová jaskyňa to where tours begin every hour or so.

Sleeping & Eating

Many lodgings have restaurants. Groceries and eating options are available in Podlesok. The biggest supermarket in the area is by Spišska Nová Ves bus station.

TOP CHOICE **Autocamp Podlesok** CAMPGROUND €
(☎4299 165; www.podlesok.sk; campsite €4-8, cottages & huts per person €10; 📶) Space for 600 tents alongside two- to 12-bed cabins or cottages with bathrooms.

Relax Farma Marianka PENSION
(☎905714583; www.relaxfarmamarianka.sk; Betlanovce 83; per person €17; P📶) Ultra-hospitable eight-room pension (hot tub, scrumptious organic cooking) on the Hrabušice–Podlesok road just passed the Podlesok turn-off.

Ranč Podlesok PENSION €
(☎0918407077; www.rancpodlesok.sk; Podlesok 5; d/tr €30/45; 📶) Lodge and restaurant on the park's blue trail 1km passed the Podlesok village area.

Penzión Lesnica PENSION €
(☎449 1518; www.stefani.sk; Čingov 113; s/d incl breakfast €30/40) Nine simple, sunny-coloured rooms close to the trail that fill up fast, so book ahead. Well-regarded restaurant attached (mains €3 to €10).

Aqualand Cottage HOSTEL €
(☎0948007735; www.aqualand.sk; dm €13, s/d without bathroom €25/32) A sprawling cottage-hostel across the lake from Dedinky proper.

Information

Outside Spišska Nová Ves, lodgings are the top source of information; park info booths are open July and August. Get cash before you arrive

BUSES FROM SPIŠSKA NOVÁ VES

DESTINATION	PRICE (€)	DURATION (MIN)	FREQUENCY (DAILY)
Čingov	0.50	15	1 direct Mon-Fri or change in Spišské Tomášovce
Dedinky	2	70	2 direct Mon-Fri or change in Poprad
Levoča	0.85	20	10 Mon-Fri
Podlesok via Spišský Štvrtok	1.20	30	2 Mon-Fri

in the park; there is an ATM and exchange at Spišska Nová Ves train station. Helpful websites include www.slovenskyraj.sk.

Mountain Rescue Service (☎emergency 183 00; http://his.hzs.sk)

Tourist Information Centre (☎4428 292; Letná 49, Spišská Nová Ves; ⏰8am-6pm Mon-Fri, 9am-1pm Sat, 2-6pm Sun) Helps with accommodation.

Getting There & Around

Connections to the park involve at least one transfer, likely in Spišska Nová Ves. Buses run infrequently on weekends, more often in July and August. No buses run directly between trailhead villages. Carefully check schedules at www.cp.atlas.sk.

Trains run from Spisška Nová Ves to Poprad (€1, 20 minutes, 12 daily) and Košice (€3.80, one hour, 15 daily). The bus station is 1½ blocks west of the train station.

Košice

☎055 / POP 234,000

For centuries a stronghold of the Hungarian kingdom, East Slovakia's industrial powerhouse has cosmopolitan clout and a buoyant cultural scene, especially since becoming 2013's European Capital of Culture. Its resultant new attractions focus on major artsy installations and events. That's in addition, of course, to its vast oval-shaped *námestie* (central square) studded with historical monuments and buzzing cafes and restaurants.

Sights

Hlavné Nám SQUARE

Most sights are in or around the town's long, plazalike main square, Hlavná. Landscaped flowerbeds surround the central **musical fountain**, across from the grandiose 1899 State Theatre (p1020). To the north stands a large baroque **plague column** from 1723. No 27, **Shire Hall** (1779), is where the Košice Government Program was proclaimed in 1945; now there's a minor art gallery inside. The **Lower Gate Underground Museum** (Hlavné Nám; adult/child €1/0.50; ⏰10am-6pm Tue-Sun May-Sep) at the square's southern end gives access to the underground remains of medieval Košice.

TOP CHOICE **Cathedral of St Elizabeth** CHURCH

(Dóm Sv Alžbety; Hlavné Nám; church free, attractions €1; ⏰1-5pm Mon, 9am-5pm Tue-Fri, 9am-1pm Sat) Europe's easternmost Gothic cathedral is the dark and brooding 14th-century Cathedral of St Elizabeth, which dominates the square, with great views from the church's **tower**. Just south, 14th-century **St Michael's Chapel** (Kaplinka sv Michala) has sporadic entry hours.

NEW-LOOK KOŠICE

As 2013 European Capital of Culture, Košice has bolstered its appeal significantly. New attractions include the following:

Sándor Márai Memorial Room (☎625 8888; www.sandormarai.eu; Mäsiarska 35; ⏰1-3pm) House museum about the life of one of Slovakia's most famous writers, Sándor Márai, who was born in Košice (although he wrote in Hungarian).

Kunsthalle (Hall of Art; Mestský Park, cnr Rumanova & Štefánikova) Grandiose former swimming pool dating from the 1930s, transformed into a major exhibition centre.

Kosarné (Culture Park; ☎6854 299; www.kulturpark.sk; Kukučínova 2) The old military barracks, now a nationally renowned cultural centre for performing arts and a music venue, with ateliers and a cafe/bar. Just south of the Old Town.

East Slovak Museum MUSEUM

(Východoslovenské múzeum; ☎622 0309; www.vsmuzeum.sk; Hviezdoslavovo 3; per exhibition €1; ⏰9am-5pm Tue-Sat, 9am-1pm Sun) The big draw at this romp through regional history is one of Europe's biggest treasure finds: a stash including 2920 gold coins, dating from the 15th to 18th centuries, unearthed nearby.

Sleeping & Eating

The City Information Centre has a booklet listing local accommodation, including university dorms open to the public.

TOP CHOICE **Hotel Bankov** HISTORIC HOTEL €€

(☎6324 522 ext 4; www.hotelbankov.sk; Dolný Bankov 2; s €85-135, d €95-145; P@≋) Slovakia's oldest hotel lies 4km northwest of central Košice. It's period-furnished with an elegant restaurant and complementary guest taxi service.

K2 HOSTEL €

(☎6255 948; Štúrova 32; s/d without bathroom €16/27) These dowdy singles and doubles are the most centrally located budget option.

Chrysso Penzión BOUTIQUE HOTEL €€

(☎6230 450; www.penzionchrysso.sk; Zvonárska 3; s/d/apt €58/68/78; ❄📶) Plushly designed pension (silk throws, sleek leather chairs) with a wine cellar-bar, terrace and restaurant.

TOP CHOICE **Villa Regia** FINE DINING €€

(www.villaregia.sk; Dominikánske nám 3; mains €7-14; 🖉) Steaks, seafood and vegetarian dishes amid a rustic old-world atmosphere, with upstairs pension rooms.

Smelly Cat CAFE €

(Zvonárska 6; ⏲9am-10pm Mon-Thu, 10am-1am Fri & Sat, 2-10pm Sun) Books, big ancient sofas, wicked coffee, delectable cakes: a refined boho hang-out.

Drinking & Entertainment

The main square has myriad cafe-bar drinking options. Monthly publication *Kam do Mesta* (www.kamdomesta.sk) presents entertainment listings.

Villa Cassa BAR

(Vaznici 2; ⏲1pm-midnight Mon-Sat) Atmospheric wine bar offering more than 400 Slovakian wines.

Krčma Nositel Radu Prce PUB

(Zvonárska 8) Return to the pre-1989 days: Lenin posters and oh-so-communist ambience and prices. It's authentic, mind – not a theme bar. Cheapest beer around.

Retro CLUB

(Kováčska 49; ⏲7.30pm-2/4am) The place to get wild hereabouts.

State Theatre THEATRE

(Štátne Divadlo Košice; ☎6221 234; www.sdke.sk; Hlavné Nám 58; ⏲box office 9am-5.30pm Mon-Fri, 10am-1pm Sat) Local opera and ballet companies perform in this 1899 neo-baroque theatre. Tickets from as little as €10.

State Philharmonic Košice LIVE MUSIC

(Štátna Filharmónia Košice, House of the Arts; ☎6224 509; www.sfk.sk; Moyzesova 66) Year-round concerts.

Information

City Information Centre (☎6258 888; www.visitkosice.eu; Hlavná 59; ⏲9am-6pm Mon-Fri, 10am-4pm Sat & Sun) Very helpful office; good guided city tours can be arranged.

Internet Reading Room (Hlavná 48; per hr €1.60)

Ľudová Banka (Mlynská 29)

Police Station (☎159; Pribinova 6)

Getting There & Away

Check bus and train schedules at www.cp.atlas.sk.

AIR **Košice International Airport** (KSC; www.airportkosice.sk) is 6km southwest of the centre. **Danube Wings** (www.danubewings.eu) has two daily flights to Bratislava (weekdays only). Vienna and Prague are also served.

BUS You can book ahead on some Ukraine-bound buses through **Eurobus** (www.eurobus.sk). Getting to Poland is easier from Poprad. Destinations from Košice include Bardejov (€4, 1¾ hours, nine daily), Levoča (€4.80, two hours, eight daily) and Uzhhorod (Ukraine; €7, two to three hours, two daily). The bus station is located adjacent to the train station, across Metský Park on Staničné Náme.

CAR International car-hire companies have representatives at the airport.

Buchbinder (☎6832 397; www.buchbinder.sk) is a smaller company with gratis city pick-up.

Getting Around

The Old Town is small enough to walk. Bus 23 runs between the airport and train station (€1). The train station is 250m east of Hlavné Nám, along Mlynská and across Metský Park.

TRAINS FROM KOŠICE

DESTINATION	PRICE (€)	DURATION (HR)	FREQUENCY (DAILY)
Bratislava	19	5-6	21
Lviv, Ukraine	60	13	1
Poprad (High Tatras)	5	1¼	24
Spišska Nová Ves (Slovenský Raj)	4	1	23

Bardejov

054 / POP 33,400

The Unesco-listed burghers' houses here on Slovakia's most spectacular Old Town square each have their own unique character and the town also has museums that shed light on this region's Eastern-facing culture. The area's famous Greek Catholic and Orthodox wooden churches, with richly decorated hand-painted interiors, reflect a Carpatho-Rusyn heritage shared with neighbouring parts of Ukraine and Poland. They can be visited from town but you'll need an adventurous spirit; transport connections are scant. In Bardejovské Kúpele you can see examples of these churches in a rewarding open-air village museum.

Sights

The main square, **Radničné nám** is a sight in itself. The two branches of the Šariš Museum, displaying alterpieces and iconostases from the region's wooden churches, are centre-square at the 1509 **Town Hall** (Radničné nám 48; adult/child €1.50/1), and at the **Icon Exposition** (Radničné nám 27; adult/child €1.50/1). At the bottom of the square is the 15th-century **Basilica of St Egídius** (Bazilika Sv Egídia; Radničné nám; adult/child €1.50/1; 9.30am-4pm Mon-Fri, 10am-3pm Sat, 11.30am-3pm Sun). You can walk the Old Town walls along Na Hradbách.

Bardejovské Kúpele, 3km north, is an old spa centre containing the **Museum of Folk Architecture** (Múzeum Ľudovej Architektúry; adult/child €1.30/0.70; 9.30am-5pm Tue-Sun, to 3pm Oct-Apr) where there are painted interiors and iconostases of the wooden churches. A Unesco-listed example from Zboj has been moved here.

Sleeping & Eating

Cafes can be found around Radničné nám.

el. Restaurant & Lodging PENSION €
(4728 404; www.el-restaurant.sk; Stöcklova 43; s/d/apt incl breakfast €30/40/60;) Three chirpy rooms up for grabs. It's central and there's a modern Slovakian restaurant downstairs.

Penzion Magura PENSION €
(902374871; www.penzionmagura.sk; Andrasikova 31; s/d €27/39) There's oodles of space in these slickly finished rooms and a more traditional restaurant below.

TOP CHOICE **Cactus** INTERNATIONAL €€
(www.cactus.sk; Štefánikova 61; mains €5-15; 7am-10pm) Crisp salads, juicy steaks, stuffed trout... the food is flamboyant, with a glut of European influences. A snug whisky-cigar bar is next door.

Information

ČSOB (Radničné nám 7) Exchange and ATM.

Tourist Information Centre (4744 003; www.bardejov.sk; Radničné nám 21; 9am-5.30pm Mon-Fri, 11.30am-3.30pm Sat & Sun, closed Sat & Sun Oct-Apr) A recommended source of information for logistics on visiting the area's wooden churches.

Getting There & Away

Bardejov is on a spur train line; buses are most convenient.

Buses go to and from Košice (€3.75, 1¾ hours, eight daily), Poprad (€4.50, 2¼ hours, six daily) and Bardejovské Kúpele (€0.55, 10 minutes, 12 daily). The E371 crosses into Poland north of Svidník, 35km east of Bardejov.

UNDERSTAND SLOVAKIA

History

Slavic tribes wandered west into what would become Slovakia around the 5th century; in the 9th century, the territory was part of the short-lived Great Moravian empire. The Magyars (Hungarians) next door subsequently laid claim to the whole territory. When in the early 16th century the Turks moved into Budapest, Hungarian monarchs took up residence in Bratislava (known then as Pozsony in Hungarian). Being Hungarian frontier land, many fortresses were constructed here during the Middle Ages.

In the early 1900s Slovak intellectuals cultivated the ties with Czechs that would take their nation into the united Czechoslovakia post-WWI. The day before Hitler's troops invaded Czechoslovakia in March 1939, Slovak leaders declared Slovakia a German protectorate. This was not a popular move and in August 1944 Slovak partisans instigated the ill-fated Slovak National Uprising (Slovenské Národné Povstanie, or SNP).

After communist takeover in 1948, power was centralised in Prague until 1989 when the Velvet Revolution brought down the iron curtain here. Just four years later, without referendum, the Czechoslovakian federation dissolved peacefully on 1 January 1993, bringing Slovakia its first true independence.

Slovakia was accepted into NATO and the EU by 2004, became a Schengen member state in 2007 and adopted the euro as national currency in January 2009.

People

A deeply religious and familial people, Slovaks have strong family ties and a deep sense of folk traditions. Today Roman Catholics form the majority (about 69%). The young are warm and open, but there can be residual communist reserve within older generations. Friendliness lurks just behind this stoicism. If you make friends with a family, the hospitality (and free-flowing liquor) may just knock you out.

Government statistics estimate Slovakia's population is 86% Slovak, 10% Hungarian and 1.7% Roma. The Roma are viewed by most with uncompromising suspicion – at best.

Arts

Traditional folk arts – from music to architecture – are still celebrated across Slovakia. Indeed, attending a village folk festival in summer can be the highlight of a visit: colourful costumes, upbeat traditional music and beer are all part of the fun. The biggest is **Východná Folk Festival** (www.obec-vychodna.sk), in the small namesake village 32km west of Poprad.

Traditional Slovakian folk instruments include the *fujara* (a 2m-long flute), the *konkovka* (a shepherd's flute), drums and cimbalom. Today you'll likely still see a folk troupe accompanied by fiddle, bass, clarinet and sometimes accordion. National folk companies include Lučnica (www.lucnica.sk) but each microregion has its own particular melodies and costumes.

ICE-HOCKEY OBSESSION

Slovakia's national ice-hockey team is usually deemed one of the world's 10 strongest. Club rivalries are heated, with the most popular teams being Bratislava's HC Slovan and HC Košice in Košice. These teams' two stadiums co-hosted the 2011 IIHF world championships. Puck-pushing season is September to April. Buy tickets at www.ticketportal.sk.

Outside of festivals, the best place to experience folk culture is at a *skanzen*, an open-air museum where examples of traditional wooden cottages and churches have been gathered in village form: good examples can be found at Bardejovské Kúpele (p1021) and Martin in Central Slovakia.

Environment

A hilly, forested country, Slovakia sits at Europe's heart, straddling the northwestern end of the Carpathian Mountains with stupendous scenery. National parks (nine altogether) and protected areas comprise 20% of the territory.

Not to be missed are the national parks of High Tatras (Vysoké Tatry), a hiking and skiing mecca where the tallest peak, Gerlachovský štít, reaches 2654m, and the lesser pine-clad ridges and technical-assist gorge hikes of Slovenský Raj National Park.

Slovakia's south is a fertile lowland hugging the Danube River, which forms the border with Hungary.

Food & Drink

Slovakia's cuisine lives through its home cooking. The national dish is *bryndzové halušky*, gnocchilike dumplings topped with sheep's cheese and bacon fat. *Bryndza* sheep's cheese also comes on *lokše* (potato pancakes) and in *pirohy* (dumplings). Don't miss an opportunity to eat in a *salaš* or a *koliba* – rustic eateries where such traditional specialities abound. Much of what you'll see on regular menus is basic central European fare: various fried meat schnitzels, hearty pork dishes and paprika-infused stews.

Besides fruit brandies such as *slivovica* (plum-based firewater), wine is the drink of choice over beer. The southwest grows most wine while the best-regarded Slovak vintage is Tokaj, an amber-hued dessert wine from the east.

SURVIVAL GUIDE

Directory A–Z

Accommodation

Bratislava has more hostels and five-sta[r] hotels than midrange accommodation; else where you'll find many reasonable *penzióny* (guesthouses). Breakfast is usually available (sometimes included) at lodgings and wi-fi is common. Parking is only a problem in Bratislava. A recommended booking resource in the capital city is **Bratislava Hotels** (www.bratislavahotels.com).

The price ranges below are for a double room with private bathroom in tourist season.

€ less than €60

€€ €60 to €150

€€€ more than €150

Activities

Hiking The **Mountain Rescue Service** (☎421-(0)52 7877 711, emergency 18 300; www.hzs.sk; Horný Smokovec 52) provides hiking and weather information besides aid.

Skiing Check out snow conditions at www.skiinfo.sk.

Business Hours

Sight and attraction hours vary throughout the year; standard opening times for tourist season, May through September, are listed below. Schedules vary from October to April; check ahead.

Banks 8am to 5pm Monday to Friday

Bars 11am to midnight Monday to Thursday, 11am to 2am Friday and Saturday, 4pm to midnight Sunday

Grocery stores 6.30am to 6pm Monday to Friday, 7am to noon Saturday

Post offices 8am to 5pm Monday to Friday, 8am to 11am Saturday

Nightclubs 4pm to 4am Wednesday to Sunday

Restaurants 10.30am to 10pm

Shops 9am to 6pm Monday to Friday, 9am to noon Saturday

Embassies & Consulates

Australia and New Zealand do not have embassies in Slovakia; the nearest are in Vienna and Berlin respectively. The following are in Bratislava:

Canadian Embassy (☎5920 4031; www.canadainternational.gc.ca/czech-tcheque/; Mostová 2, Carlton-Savoy Building)

French Embassy (☎5934 7111; www.ambafrance-sk.org; Hlavné nám 7)

German Embassy (☎5920 4400; www.pressburg.diplo.de; Hviezdoslavovo nám 10)

Netherlands Embassy (☎5262 5081; www.holandskoweb.com; Frana Krála 5)

UK Embassy (☎5998 2000; http://ukinslovakia.fco.gov.uk; Panská 16)

US Embassy (☎5443 0861; http://slovakia.usembassy.gov; Hviezdoslavovo nám 4)

Food

Restaurant review price indicators are based on the cost of a main course.

€ less than €6

€€ €6 to €12

€€€ more than €12

Gay & Lesbian Travellers

Homosexuality has been legal here since the 1960s but this is a conservative, mostly Catholic, country. The GLBT scene is small in Bratislava and all but nonexistent elsewhere. Check out www.gay.sk.

Internet Access

Wi-fi is widely available at lodgings and cafes across the country; internet cafes are becoming scarce. For the laptopless, lodgings also often have computers you can use.

Money

» ATMs are common even in smaller towns, but shouldn't be relied upon in villages.

» Visa and MasterCard accepted at most hotels and top-end restaurants in main tourist zones.

» Tipping 10% is fairly standard, though locals tip less.

Post

Post office services are reliable, but for the most efficient service be sure to hand your outgoing mail to a clerk.

Public Holidays

New Year's and Independence Day 1 January

Three Kings Day 6 January

Good Friday and Easter Monday March/April

Labour Day 1 May

Victory over Fascism Day 8 May

SS Cyril and Methodius Day 5 July

SNP Day 29 August

Constitution Day 1 September

Our Lady of Sorrows Day 15 September

All Saints' Day 1 November

Christmas 24 to 26 December

Telephone

Landline numbers can have either seven or eight digits. Mobile phone numbers (10 digits) are often used for businesses; they start with ☎09. When dialling from abroad, you need to drop the zero from both city area codes and mobile phone numbers. Purchase local and international phonecards at newsagents. To call out of Slovakia, dial ☎00.

The country has GSM (900/1800MHz) and 3G UMTS networks operated by providers Orange, T-Mobile and O_2.

Tourist Information

Association of Information Centres of Slovakia (AICES; ☎16 186; www.aices.sk) Runs an extensive network of city information centres.

Slovak Tourist Board (www.slovakia.travel) No Slovakia-wide information office exists; it's best to go online.

Travellers With Disabilities

Slovakia lags behind many EU states in accommodation for disabled travellers. **Slovak Union for the Disabled** (www.sztp.sk) works to change the status quo. Hotels and restaurants have few ramps or barrier-free rooms. Public transport is getting more disabled-friendly, with buses that lower and special seating.

Visas

For a full list of visa requirements, see www.mzv.sk (under 'Ministry' and then 'Travel').

» No visa is required for EU citizens.

» Visitors from Australia, New Zealand, Canada, Japan and the US are visa-free for up to 90 days.

» Visas are required for South African nationals, among others. For the full list see www.slovak-republic.org/visa-embassies.

Getting There & Away

Bratislava and Košice are Slovakia's main entry and exit points.

Entering Slovakia from the EU, indeed most of Europe, is straightforward but expect lengthy custom checks when arriving from Ukraine.

Air

Bratislava's intra-European **airport** (www.airportbratislava.sk; Ivanská cesta) is small. Unless you're coming from the UK, which has several direct flights, your arrival will likely be by train. Vienna in Austria has the nearest international **air hub** (www.vienna-airport.com).

Main airlines operating in Slovakia are listed below:

Austrian Airlines (www.aua.com) Košice to Vienna.

Czech Airlines (www.czechairlines.com) Connects Košice with Prague.

Ryanair (www.ryanair.com) Links Bratislava to several UK and Italian destinations, coastal Spain, Paris and Brussels.

Land

Border posts between Slovakia and fellow EU Schengen member states – Czech Republic, Hungary, Poland and Austria – are non-existent. This makes checks at the Ukrainian border more strident, as you will be entering the EU. By bus expect one to two hours' wait; by car, much more.

BUS

Local buses connect Poprad and Ždiar with Poland. **Eurobus** (www.eurobus.sk)and **Eurolines** (www.slovaklines.sk) handle international routes across Europe from Bratislava and heading east to Ukraine from Košice.

CAR & MOTORCYCLE

Private vehicle requirements for driving in Slovakia are registration papers, a 'green card' (proof of third-party liability insurance), nationality sticker, first-aid kit and warning triangle.

TRAIN

See www.cp.atlas.sk for domestic and international train schedules. Direct train connect Bratislava to Austria, the Czech Republic, Poland, Hungary and Russia from Košice, trains connect to the Czech Republic, Poland, Ukraine and Russia. The fastest domestic trains are Intercity (IC or Eurocity (EC). Rychlík (R), or 'fast' train take slightly longer, but run more frequently and cost less. Osobný (Ob) train are slowest (and cost least).

River

Danube riverboats offer an alternative way to travel between Bratislava and Vienna.

Getting Around

Air

Danube Wings (V5; www.danubewings.eu) offers the only domestic air service (weekdays between Bratislava and Košice).

Bus

Read timetables carefully; fewer buses operate on weekends and holidays. The national bus company is **Slovenská Autobusová Doprava** (SAD; www.sad.sk). Find up-to-date scheuldes online at www.sp.atlas.sk.

Car & Motorcycle

» Foreign driving licences with photo ID are valid in Slovakia.
» *Nálepka* (toll stickers) are required on *all* green-signed motorways. Fines for not having them can be hefty. Buy at petrol stations (rental cars usually have them).
» City streetside parking restrictions are eagerly enforced. Always buy a ticket from a machine, attendant or newsagent in Old Town centres.
» Car hire is available in Bratislava and Košice primarily.

Local Transport

Towns all have good bus systems; villages have infrequent service. Bratislava also has trams and trolleybuses.
» Public transport generally operates from 4.30am to 11.30pm daily.
» City transport tickets are good for all local buses, trams and trolleybuses. Buy at newsstands and validate on board or risk serious fines.

Train

Train is the way to travel in Slovakia; most tourist destinations are accessible off the main Bratislava–Košice line. No online reservations. Visit www.cp.atlas.sk for up-to-date schedules. **Slovak Republic Railways** (ŽSR; ☎18 188; www.slovakrail.sk) is the far-reaching, efficient national rail service.

Slovenia

Includes »

Ljubljana..................... 1028
Julian Alps.................. 1034
Lake Bled..................... 1034
Lake Bohinj.................. 1037
Soča Valley.................. 1038
Postojna & Škocjan Caves.......................... 1039
Koper.......................... 1039
Piran........................... 1040
Understand Slovenia... 1041
Survival Guide............ 1042

Best Places to Eat

» Gostilna na Gradu (p1032)
» Ribca (p1032)
» Pri Mari (p1040)
» Vila Ajda (p1037)

Best Places to Stay

» Max Piran (p1040)
» Hostel Pekarna (p1041)
» Camping Bled (p1035)
» Penzion Gasperin (p1038)

Why Go?

It's a pint-sized place, with a surface area of just over 20,000 sq km and a population of two million people. But 'good things come in small packages', and never was that old chestnut more appropriate than in describing Slovenia. The country has everything from beaches, snowcapped mountains, hills awash in grape vines and wide plains blanketed in sunflowers to Gothic churches, baroque palaces and art nouveau buildings. Its incredible mixture of climates brings warm Mediterranean breezes up to the foothills of the Alps, where it can snow in summer.

The capital, Ljubljana, is a culturally rich city that values liveability and sustainability over unfettered growth. This sensitivity toward the environment extends to rural and lesser-developed parts of the country as well. With more than half of its total area covered in forest, Slovenia really is one of the 'greenest' countries in the world.

When to Go

Ljubljana

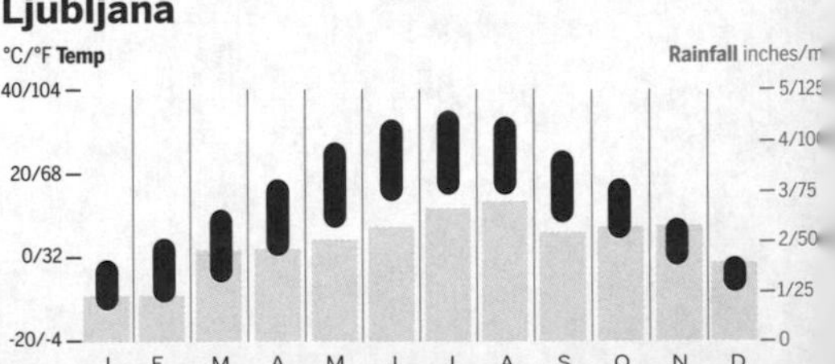

Apr–Jun Spring is a great time to be in the lowlands and the flower-carpeted valleys of the Julian Alps.

Sep This is the month made for everything – still warm enough to swim and tailor-made for hiking.

Dec–Mar Everyone (and their grandma) dons their skis in this winter-sport-mad country.

Connections

Border formalities with Slovenia's three EU neighbours – Italy, Austria and Hungary – are nonexistent and all are accessible by train and bus. Venice can also be reached by boat from Piran. Expect a somewhat closer inspection of your documents when travelling to or from non-EU Croatia.

ITINERARIES

One Week

Spend a couple of days in Ljubljana, then head north to unwind in Bohinj or romantic Bled beside idyllic mountain lakes. Depending on the season, take a bus or drive over the hair-raising Vršič Pass into the valley of the vivid blue Soča River and take part in some adventure sports in Bovec or Kobarid before returning to Ljubljana.

Two Weeks

Another week will allow you to see just about everything: all of the above as well as the Karst caves at Škocjan and Postojna and the Venetian ports of Koper and Piran on the Adriatic coast. The country is small, so even the far eastern region, particularly overlooked but interesting spots like Maribor or Ptuj is just a few hours away by car or train.

Essential Food & Drink

» **Pršut** Air-dried, thinly sliced ham from the Karst region ot unlike Italian prosciutto.

» **Žlikrofi** Ravioli-like parcels filled with cheese, bacon and hives.

» **Žganci** The Slovenian stodge of choice – groats made rom barley or corn but usually *ajda* (buckwheat).

» **Potica** A kind of nut roll eaten at teatime or as a dessert.

» **Wine** Distinctively Slovenian tipples include peppery red eran from the Karst region and Malvazija, a straw-colour hite wine from the coast.

» **Postrv** Trout, particularly the variety from the Soča River, a real treat.

» **Prekmurska gibanica** A rich concoction of pastry filled th poppy seeds, walnuts, apples and cheese and topped th cream.

» **Štruklji** Scrumptious dumplings made with curd cheese d served either savoury as a main course or sweet as a ssert.

» **Brinjevec** A very strong brandy made from fermented iper berries (and a decidedly acquired taste).

AT A GLANCE

» **Currency** Euro (€)

» **Language** Slovene

» **Money** ATMs are everywhere; banks open Monday to Friday and (rarely) Saturday morning

» **Visas** Not required for citizens of the EU, Australia, USA, Canada or New Zealand

Fast Facts

» **Area** 20,273 sq km

» **Capital** Ljubljana

» **Country code** ☎386

» **Emergency** Ambulance ☎112, fire ☎112, police ☎113

Exchange Rates

Australia	A$1	€0.82
Canada	C$1	€0.77
Japan	¥100	€0.83
New Zealand	NZ$1	€0.65
UK	UK$1	€1.18
USA	US$1	€0.78

Set Your Budget

» **Budget hotel room** €50

» **Two-course meal** €20

» **Museum entrance** €4

» **Beer** €1–3

» **100km by train/bus** €6/10

Resources

» **Slovenian Tourist Board** (www.slovenia.info)

» **E-uprava** (http://e-uprava.gov.si/e-uprava/en)

LJUBLJANA

☎01 / POP 280,600

Slovenia's capital and largest city also happens to be one of Europe's greenest and most liveable capitals. Car traffic is restricted in the centre, leaving the leafy banks of the emerald-green Ljubljanica River, which flows through the city's heart, free for pedestrians and cyclists. In summer, cafes set up terrace seating along the river, lending the feel of a perpetual street party. Slovenia's master of early-Modern, minimalist design, Jože Plečnik, graced Ljubljana with beautiful alabaster bridges and baubles, pylons and pyramids that are both elegant and playful.

Sights

The easiest way to see Ljubljana is on foot. The oldest part of town, with the most important historical buildings and sights (including Ljubljana Castle), lies on the right (east) bank of the Ljubljanica River. The

Slovenia Highlights

1. Enjoy a flight up the funicular to **Ljubljana Castle** (p1029)
2. Consider the genius of Jože Plečnik at Ljubljana's **National & University Library** (p1029)
3. Gaze at the natural perfection of **Lake Bled** (p1034)
4. Gawk in awe at the 100m-high walls of the **Škocjan Caves** (p1039)
5. Admire views of the country's tallest mountain, **Mt Triglav** (p1034)
6. Get lost wandering the narrow alleyways of **Piran** (p1040)

lion's share of the city's museums and galleries is on the left (west) side of the river.

Delightfully sprinkled with cafes, **Mestni trg**, **Stari trg** and **Gornji trg** wend picturesquely beneath a bluff crowned by **Ljubljana Castle** (Ljubljanski Grad; ☎306 42 93; www.ljubljanskigrad.si; Grajska Planota 1; adult/child incl funicular and castle attractions €8/5, castle attractions only €6/3, with guided tour €10/8; ⏲9am-11pm May-Sep, 10am-9pm Oct-Apr). Up here, the best views are from the 19th-century **watchtower** (Razgledni Stolp; ☎306 42 93; www.ljubljanskigrad.si; included in general castle admission; ⏲9am-9pm May-Sep, 10am-6pm Oct-Apr). The fastest way to reach the castle is via the **funicular** (vzpenjača; ☎reservations 306 42 00; www.ljubljanskigrad.si; Krekov trg 3-7; adult/child return €4/3; ⏲9am-11pm Apr-Sep, 10am-9pm Oct-Mar) from Krekov trg.

Ljubljana's main square, **Prešernov trg**, showcases the salmon-pink **Franciscan Church of the Annunciation** (Frančiškanska Cerkev Marijinega Oznanjanja; ☎242 93 00; Prešernov trg 4; ⏲10am-6pm), built in 1660; the **Prešeren Monument** built in 1905 for the nation's favourite poet, France Prešeren; and the **Triple Bridge**, a work by prolific architect Jože Plečnik.

East of the bridge is the **Central Market** (Centralna Tržnica; Pogačarjev trg & Vodnikov trg), the frescoed **Cathedral of St Nicholas** (Stolna Cerkev Sv Nikolaja; ☎234 26 90; http://ljstolnica.rkc.si; Dolničarjeva ulica 1; ⏲10am-noon & 3-6pm), dating from the early 18th century, and the much loved **Dragon Bridge**, whose guardian dragons are city mascots.

Walk west of the Ljubljanica River to find the **National & University Library** (☎200 11 09; Turjaška ulica 1; ⏲9am-6pm Mon-Fri, 9am-2pm Sat). This is Plečnik's masterpiece, completed in 1941. To appreciate this great man's philosophy, enter through the main door (note the horse-head doorknobs) on Turjaška ulica – you'll find yourself in near darkness, entombed in black marble. As you ascend the steps, you'll emerge into a colonnade suffused with light – the light of knowledge, according to the architect's plans.

The excellent **City Museum** (Mestni Muzej; ☎241 25 00; www.mestnimuzej.si; Gosposka ulica 15; adult/child €4/2.50; ⏲10am-6pm Tue, Wed & Fri-Sun, 10am-9pm Thu), nearby, focuses on Ljubljana's history, culture and politics via imaginative multimedia and interactive displays. The reconstructed Roman street that linked the eastern gates of Emona (Ljubljana's name in Roman times) to the Ljubljanica and the collection of well-preserved classical finds are worth a visit in themselves.

West of main Slovenska cesta is the impressive **National Gallery** (☎241 54 18; www.ng-slo.si; Prešernova cesta 24; adult/child €7/5, free 1st Sun of month; ⏲10am-6pm Tue-Sun) and the **National Museum of Slovenia** (Narodni Muzej Slovenije; ☎241 44 00; www.nms.si; Prešernova cesta 20; adult/child €3/2.50, free 1st Sun of month; ⏲10am-6pm Fri-Wed, 10am-8pm Thu), the latter in an elegant 1888 building.

Sleeping

The Tourist Information Centre has comprehensive details of private rooms (single/double from €30/50) and apartments (double/quad from €55/80), though only a handful are central.

Celica Hostel HOSTEL €€
(☎230 97 00; www.hostelcelica.com; Metelkova ulica 8; dm €19-25, s/d/tr cell €53/60/70; P@📶) This stylishly revamped former prison in Metelkova has 20 'cells', designed by different artists and architects and complete with original bars. There are nine rooms and apartments with three to seven beds and a packed, popular 12-bed dorm. The ground floor is home to a **cafe and restaurant** (set lunch €5-7; ⏲7.30am-midnight) and the hostel boasts its own gallery where everyone can show their work.

H2O HOSTEL €
(☎041 662 266; www.h2ohostel.com; Petkovškovo nabrežje 47; dm €17-22, d €36-52, q €68-88; @📶) One of our favourite hostels in Ljubljana, this six-room place wraps around a tiny courtyard bordering the Ljubljanica River and one room has views of the castle. Private doubles are available and guests have access to a common kitchen.

Zeppelin Hostel HOSTEL €
(☎059 191 427; www.zeppelinhostel.com; 2 fl, Slovenska cesta 47; dm €18-24, d €49-60; @📶)

SPLURGE

The sleek, boutique **Cubo** (☎425 60 00; www.hotelcubo.com; Slovenska cesta 15; s/d €120/140) hotel in the centre of town boasts high-end, minimalist design that could have stepped out of the pages of *Wallpaper** magazine. The owners have placed great emphasis on using the best construction materials and high-quality bedding to ensure a good night's sleep.

Ljubljana

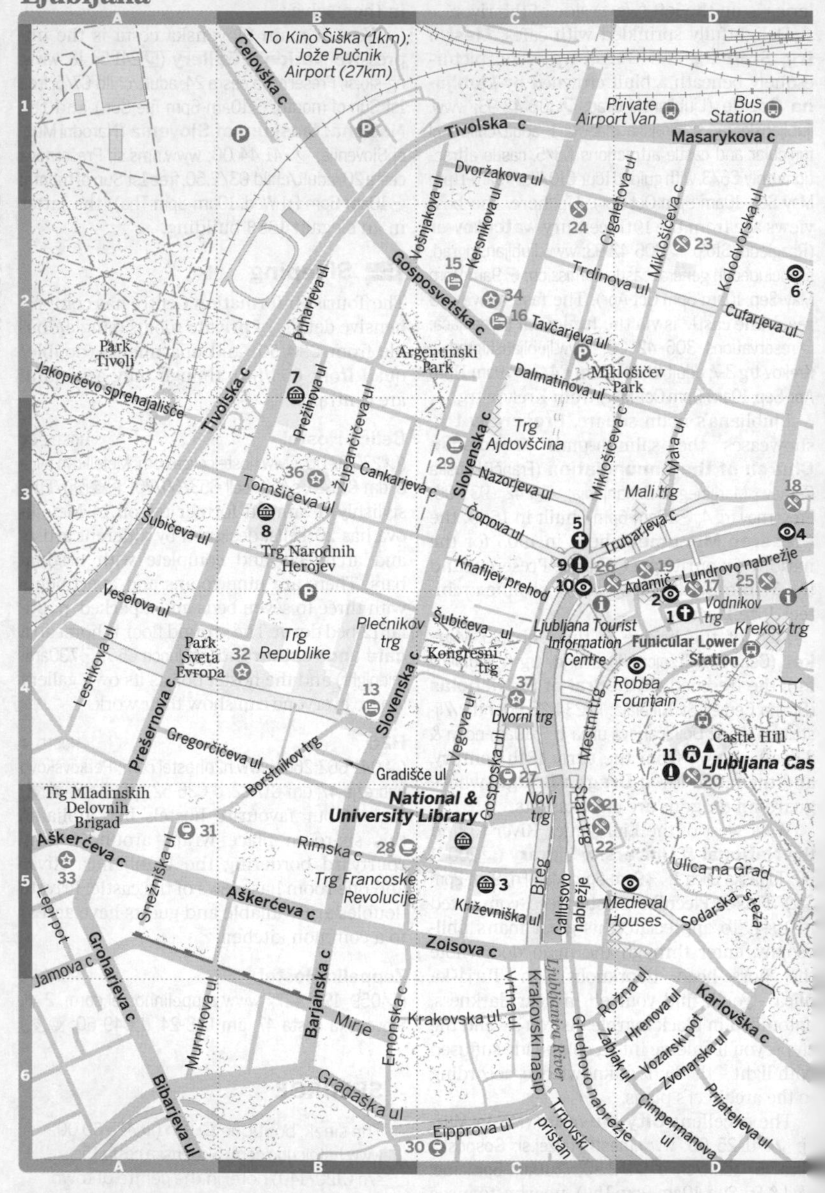

Located in the historic Evropa building on the corner of Gosposvetska cesta, Zeppelin Hostel offers clean and bright dorm rooms (four to eight beds) as well as double rooms. It's run by a young team of international travellers who keep their guests informed of parties and happenings around town.

Slamič B&B PENSION €

(☎433 82 33; www.slamic.si; Kersnikova ulica 1; €65-75, d €95-100, ste from €135; P❄@📶) It

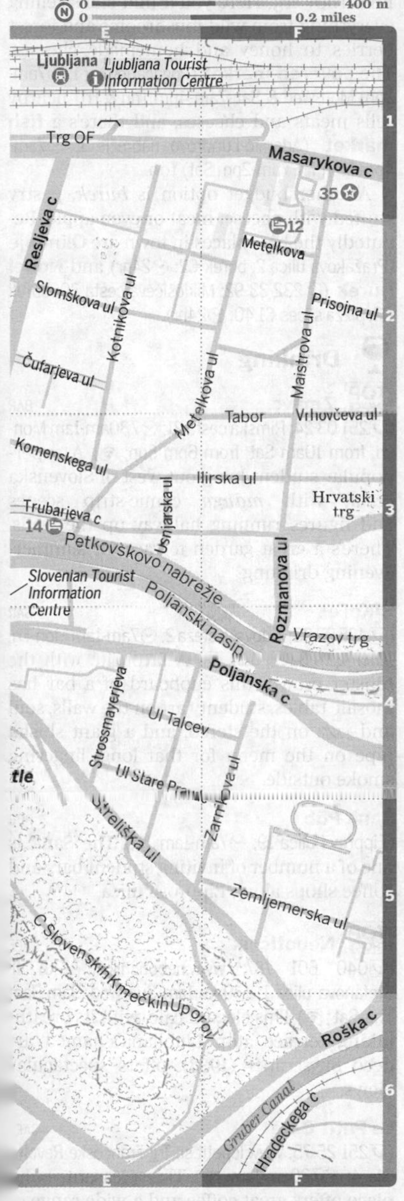

lightly away from the action but Slamič, a B&B above a famous cafe and teahouse, offers bright rooms with antique(ish) furnishings and parquet floors. Choice rooms include the ones looking on to a back garden and the one just off an enormous terrace used by the cafe.

Ljubljana

Top Sights

Ljubljana Castle D4
National & University Library C5

Sights

1 Cathedral of St Nicholas D4
2 Central Market D4
3 City Museum C5
4 Dragon Bridge D3
5 Franciscan Church of the Annunciation C3
6 Funicular D2
7 National Gallery B2
8 National Museum of Slovenia B3
9 Prešeren Monument C3
10 Triple Bridge C3
11 Watchtower D4

Sleeping

12 Celica Hostel F2
13 Cubo B4
14 H2O E3
15 Slamič B&B C2
16 Zeppelin Hostel C2

Eating

17 Covered Market D3
18 Falafel D3
19 Fish Market D3
20 Gostilna na Gradu D4
21 Julija D3
22 Lunch Café Marley & Me C5
23 Nobel Burek D2
24 Olimpije C2
25 Open-Air Market D3
26 Ribca C3

Drinking

27 BiKoFe C4
28 Le Petit Café B5
29 Nebotičnik C3
30 Šank Pub C6
31 Žmavc A5

Entertainment

32 Cankarjev Dom B4
33 Cirkus A5
34 Klub K4 ....C2
Klub Roza ....(see 34)
35 Metelkova Mesto F1
36 Opera & Ballet Ljubljana B3
37 Philharmonic Hall C4

Bit Center Hostel HOSTEL €
(☎548 00 55; www.bit-center.net; Litijska cesta 57; dm €16; P@📶) Occupying the same building as the Bit Center Hotel, this 35-bed hostel is clean and well run, with dorm accommodation offered in six rooms.

Eating

TOP CHOICE **Gostilna na Gradu** SLOVENIAN €
(☎031 523 760; www.nagradu.si; Grajska planota 1; mains €8-14; ⏲10am-midnight Mon-Sat, noon-6pm Sun) Be sure to plan a meal at this marvelous traditional Slovenian restaurant during your visit to the castle. The chefs pride themselves on using only Slovenian-sourced breads, cheeses and meats, and age-old recipes to prepare a meal to remember.

Ribca SEAFOOD €
(☎425 15 44; www.ribca.si; Adamič-Lundrovo nabrežje 1; dishes €5-8; ⏲8am-4pm Mon-Fri, to 2pm Sat) One of the culinary joys of a visit to Ljubljana is the chance to sample inexpensive and well-prepared fish dishes. This basement seafood bar below the Plečnik Colonnade in Pogačarjev trg is one of the best for tasty fried squid, sardines and herrings.

Julija MEDITERRANEAN €€
(☎425 64 63; www.julijarestaurant.com; Stari trg 9; mains €10.90-18.90; ⏲noon-10pm) This is arguably the best of a trio of restaurants standing side by side on touristy Stari trg. We love the three-course set lunches served on the sidewalk terrace for €9.

Lunch Café Marley & Me INTERNATIONAL €€
(☎040 564 188; www.lunchcafe.si; Stari trg 9; mains €7-20; ⏲11am-11pm; 📶) The name couldn't be more misleading. It's more than a lunch cafe…and the 'Marley' bit? We just don't get it. Still, it's a very popular spot for lunch or dinner with salads, pastas and a variety of meats and seafood.

Falafel MIDDLE EASTERN €
(☎041 640 166; Trubarjeva cesta 40; sandwiches €4-6; ⏲11am-midnight Mon-Fri, noon-midnight Sat, 1-10pm Sun) Authentic Middle Eastern food, like falafel and hummus, served up to go or eat in at a few tables and chairs scattered about.

Self-Catering

Self-caterers will want to head directly to Ljubljana's vast **open-air market** (Vodnikov trg; ⏲6am-6pm Mon-Fri, 6am-4pm Sat summer, 6am-4pm Mon-Sat winter) on Vodnikov trg, just across the Triple Bridge to the southeast of Prešernov trg. Here you'll find stalls selling everything from wild mushrooms and forest berries to honey and homemade cheeses. The **covered market** (Pogačarjev trg 1; ⏲7am-2pm Mon-Wed & Sat, 7am-4pm Thu & Fri) nearby sells meats and cheeses, and there's a **fish market** (Adamič-Lundrovo nabrežje 1; ⏲7am-4pm Mon-Fri, 7am-2pm Sat) too.

Another budget option is *burek*, pastry stuffed with cheese, meat or even apple. Reputedly the best places in town are **Olimpije** (Pražakova ulica 2; burek €2; ⏲24hr) and **Nobel Burek** (☎232 33 92; Miklošičeva cesta 30; burek €2, pizza slices €1.40; ⏲24hr).

Drinking

TOP CHOICE **Žmavc** BAR
(☎251 03 24; Rimska cesta 21; ⏲7.30am-1am Mon-Fri, from 10am Sat, from 6pm Sun; 📶) A super-popular student hang-out west of Slovenska cesta, with *manga* comic-strip scenes and figures running halfway up the walls. There's a great garden terrace for summer-evening drinking.

BiKoFe BAR
(☎425 93 93; Židovska steza 2; ⏲7am-1am Mon-Fri, 10am-1pm Sat & Sun; 📶) A favourite with the hipster crowd, this cupboard of a bar has mosaic tables, studenty art on the walls, soul and jazz on the stereo, and a giant shisha pipe on the menu for that long, lingering smoke outside.

Šank Pub PUB
(Eipprova ulica 19; ⏲7am-1am; 📶) The Šank is one of a number of inviting student bars and coffee shops along Eipprova ulica.

TOP CHOICE **Nebotičnik** CAFE
(☎040 601 787; www.neboticnik.si; 12th fl Štefanova ulica 1; ⏲9am-1am Sun-Wed, 9am-3am Thu-Sat; 📶) This elegant cafe, with its breath-taking terrace atop Ljubljana's famed ar deco Skyscraper (1933), offers spectacula views.

Le Petit Café CAF
(☎251 25 75; www.lepetit.si; Trg Francoske Revolu cije 4; ⏲7.30am-1am; 📶) This pleasant, boh place offers great coffee and a wide range o breakfast goodies, lunches and light meal plus a good restaurant on the 1st floor.

Entertainment

Ljubljana in Your Pocket (www.inyou pocket.com), which comes out every tw months, is a good English source f what's on in the capital. Buy tickets for shows and events at the venue box office, online through **Eventim** (☎430 24 05; www.eventim.si), or at Ljubljana Tourist Information Centre.

Clubs & Live Music

Kino Šiška INDIE, ROCK
(☎box office 030 310 110; www.kinosiska.si; Trg Prekomorskih brigad 3; ⊙5-8pm Mon-Fri, 10am-1pm Sat) This renovated old movie theatre has reopened as an urban cultural centre, hosting mainly indie, rock and alternative bands.

Klub K4 CLUB
(☎040 212 292; www.klubk4.org; Kersnikova ulica 4; ⊙10pm-2am Tue, 11pm-4am Wed & Thu, 11pm-6am Fri & Sat, 10pm-4am Sun) This evergreen venue in the basement of the Student Organisation of Ljubljana University (ŠOU) headquarters features electronic music Friday and Saturday, with other styles of music on weeknights, and a popular gay and lesbian night on Sunday.

Cirkus CLUB
(Kinoklub Vič; ☎051 631 631; www.cirkusklub.si; Trg Mladinskih Delovnih Brigad 7; cover €5; ⊙8pm-5am Tue-Sat) This popular dance club has DJs at the weekends.

Performing Arts

Cankarjev Dom CLASSICAL, OPERA, DANCE
(☎241 71 00, box office 241 72 99; www.cd-cc.si; Prešernova cesta 10; ⊙box office 11am-1pm & 3-8pm Mon-Fri, 11am-1pm Sat, 1hr before performance) Ljubljana's premier cultural and conference centre has two large auditoriums and a dozen smaller performance spaces offering a remarkable smorgasbord of performance arts.

Opera & Ballet Ljubljana OPERA, DANCE
(☎box office 241 59 59; www.opera.si; Župančičeva ulica 1; ⊙box office 10am-5pm Mon-Fri, 1hrbefore performance) Home to the Slovenian National Opera and Ballet companies.

Philharmonic Hall CLASSICAL
(Slovenska Filharmonija; ☎241 08 00; www.filharmonija.si; Kongresni trg 10; ⊙7am-10pm) Home to the Slovenian Philharmonic Orchestra.

Information

There are ATMs at every turn, including a row of them outside the main Ljubljana Tourist Information Centre office. At the train station you'll find a **bureau de change** (train station; ⊙7am-8pm) changing cash for no commission but not travellers cheques.

Cyber Cafe Xplorer (☎430 19 91; Petkovškovo nabrežje 23; per 30 min/hr €2.50/4; ⊙10am-10pm Mon-Fri, 2-10pm Sat & Sun; 📶) Ljubljana's best internet cafe.

Health Centre Ljubljana (Zdravstveni Dom Ljubljana; ☎472 37 00; www.zd-lj.si; Metelkova ulica 9; ⊙7.30am-7pm) For non-emergencies.

Ljubljana Tourist Information Centre (TIC; ☎306 12 15; www.visitljubljana.si; Adamič-Lundrovo nabrežje 2; ⊙8am-9pm Jun-Sep, 8am-7pm Oct-May) Knowledgeable and enthusiastic staff dispense information, maps and useful literature and help with accommodation. Has a helpful **branch** (☎433 94 75; Trg Osvobodilne Fronte 6; ⊙8am-10pm daily Jun-Sep, 10am-7pm Mon-Fri, 8am-3pm Sat Oct-May) at the train station.

Lonely Planet (www.lonelyplanet.com/slovenia/ljubljana)

Slovenian Tourist Information Centre (STIC; ☎306 45 76; www.slovenia.info; Krekov trg 10; ⊙8am-9pm Jun-Sep, 8am-7pm Oct-May) Good source of information for the rest of Slovenia. Also has internet access (per 30 minutes €2).

University Medical Centre Ljubljana (Univerzitetni Klinični Center Ljubljana; ☎522 50 50, emergencies 522 84 08; www4.kclj.si; Zaloška cesta 2; ⊙24hr) University medical clinic with 24-hour accident and emergency service.

> **METELKOVO MESTO**
>
> For a scruffy antidote to trendy clubs, try **Metelkova Mesto** (Metelkova Town; www.metelkova.org; Masarykova cesta 24), an ex-army garrison taken over by squatters in the 1990s and converted into a free-living commune. In this two-courtyard block, a dozen idiosyncratic, alternative clubs hide behind brightly tagged doorways, coming to life generally after midnight.

Getting There & Away

The **bus** (Avtobusna Postaja Ljubljana; ☎234 46 00; www.ap-ljubljana.si; Trg Osvobodilne Fronte 4; ⊙5.30am-10.30pm Sun-Fri, 5am-10pm Sat) and **train** (Železniška Postaja; ☎291 33 32; www.slo-zeleznice.si; Trg Osvobodilne Fronte 6; ⊙6am-10pm) stations are 800m northeast of Prešernov trg, up Miklošičeva cesta. Ljubljana's **Jože Pučnik Airport** (LJU/Aerodrom Ljubljana; ☎04-206 19 81; www.lju-airport.si/eng; Zgornji Brnik 130a, Brnik) is 27km north of the city at Brnik, near Kranj.

TRANSPORT FROM LJUBLJANA

Bus

DESTINATION	PRICE (€)	DURATION (HR)	DISTANCE (KM)	FREQUENCY
Bled	6.20	1½	57	hourly
Koper	12	2½	122	5 daily, with more in summer
Maribor	14	3	141	2-4 daily
Piran	14	3	140	up to 7 daily

Train

DESTINATION	PRICE (€)	DURATION	DISTANCE (KM)	FREQUENCY
Bled	6.20	55min	51	up to 21 daily
Koper	9	2½hr	153	up to 4 daily, with more in summer
Maribor	15	1¾hr	156	up to 25 daily

Getting Around

To/From the Airport

The cheapest way to Ljubljana's **Jože Pučnik Airport** (Aerodrom Ljubljana; ☎04-206 19 81; www.lju-airport.si/eng; Zgornji Brnik 130a, Brnik) is by public bus (€4.10, 45 minutes, 27km) from stop No 28 at the bus station. These run at 5.20am and hourly from 6.10am to 8.10pm Monday to Friday; at the weekend there's a bus at 6.10am and then one every two hours from 9.10am to 7.10pm. Buy tickets from the driver.

A **private airport van** (☎051 321 414; www.airport-shuttle.si) links Trg Osvobodilne Fronte, near the bus station, with the airport (€9) up to 11 times daily between 5.20am and 10.30pm, and is a 30-minute trip. It goes from the airport to Ljubljana 10 times a day between 5.45am and 11pm.

A taxi from the airport to Ljubljana will cost from €40 to €45.

Bicycle

Ljubljana is a pleasure for cyclists, and there are bike lanes and special traffic lights everywhere. **Ljubljana Bike** (☎306 45 76; www.visitljubljana.si; Krekov trg 10; per 2hr/day €2/8; ⏰8am-7pm or 9pm Apr-Oct) rents two-wheelers in two-hour or full-day increments from the Slovenian Tourist Information Centre.

Bus

Ljubljana's city buses operate from 6am to around 10.30pm. A flat fare of €1.20 (good for 90 minutes of unlimited travel, including transfers) is paid with a stored-value magnetic **Urbana** (☎430 51 74; www.jh-lj.si/urbana) card, which can be purchased at newsstands, tourist offices and the **LPP Information Centre** (☎430 51 75; www.jhl.si; Slovenska cesta 56; ⏰7am-7pm Mon-Fri).

JULIAN ALPS

The Julian Alps – named in honour of Caesar himself – form Slovenia's dramatic northwest frontier with Italy. Triglav National Park, established in 1924, includes almost all of the alps lying within Slovenia. The centrepiece of the park is, of course, triple-peaked Mt Triglav (2864m), Slovenia's highest mountain. Along with an abundance of fauna and flora, the area offers a wide range of adventure sports.

Lake Bled

☎04 / POP 10,900

With its emerald-green lake, picture-postcard church on a tiny island, medieval castle clinging to a rocky cliff and some of the country's highest peaks as backdrops, Bled seems to have been designed by the very god of tourism. It's a small and convenient base from which to explore the mountains.

Sights

Bled's greatest attraction, naturally enough is its world-famous lake. While the lake is small in size, measuring just 2km by 1380m it more than compensates with its clear water and glorious alpine backdrop. Mild thermal springs warm the water to a swimmable 26°C from June through August. You can rent boats, go diving or simply snap countless photos.

Bled Island ISLAND
(Blejski Otok; www.blejskiotok.si) Tiny, tear-shaped Bled Island beckons from the shore. There's a church and small museum, but the real thrill is the ride out by **gondola** (Pletna; ☎041 427 155; per person return €12). The boat sets you down on the south side at the monumental South Staircase (Južno Stopnišče).

Bled Castle CASTLE, MUSEUM
(Blejski Grad; www.blejski-grad.si; Grajska cesta 25; adult/child €8/3.50; ⏰8am-8pm Apr-Oct, 8am-6pm Nov-Mar) Perched atop a steep cliff more than 100m above the lake, Bled Castle is how most people imagine a medieval fortress to be, with towers, ramparts, moats and a terrace offering magnificent views. The castle houses a museum collection that traces the lake's history from earliest times to the development of Bled as a resort in the 19th century.

Vintgar Gorge NATURE PARK
(Soteska Vintgar; adult/child/student €4/2/3; ⏰8am-7pm late Apr–Oct) One of the easiest and most satisfying day trips from Bled is to Vintgar Gorge, some 4km to the northwest. The highlight is a 1600m wooden walkway, built in 1893 and continually rebuilt since.

Activities

Local outfits organise a wide range of outdoor activities in and around Bled, including trekking, rock climbing, ski touring, mountain biking, rafting, kayaking, canyoning, caving, horse-riding and paragliding.

3glav Adventures ADVENTURE SPORTS
(☎041 683 184; www.3glav-adventures.com; Ljubljanska cesta 1; ⏰9am-7pm Apr-Oct) The leading adventure-sport specialists in Bled for warm-weather activities from mid-April to mid-October. The most popular trip is the Emerald River Adventure (€65), an 11-hour hiking and swimming foray into Triglav National Park. Also rents bikes (half-/full day €8/15).

Sleeping

Kompas travel agency (p1037) has a list of private rooms and farmhouses, with singles/doubles starting at €24/38.

TOP CHOICE **Camping Bled** CAMPGROUND €
(☎575 20 00; www.camping-bled.com; Kidričeva cesta 10c; adult €10.90-12.90, child €7.60-9, glamping huts €60-80; ⏰Apr–mid-Oct; P@📶) Bled's upscale campground is one of the nicest in the country and one of the few places around to try 'glamping' – aka glamorous camping – in this case, ecofriendly, all-natural A-frame huts, some equipped with hot tubs. The setting is at the western end of the lake.

Traveller's Haven HOSTEL €
(☎041 396 545; www.travellers-haven.si; Riklijeva cesta 1; dm/d €19/48; P@📶) This is arguably the nicest of several hostels clustered on a hillside on the eastern shore of the lake, about 500m north of the centre. Six rooms (including one private double), a great kitchen and free laundry.

Penzion Mayer PENSION €€
(☎576 57 40; www.mayer-sp.si; Železka cesta 7; s €57, d €77-82, apt €120-150; P@📶) This flower-bedecked 12-room inn in a renovated 19th-century house is in a quiet location above the lake. The larger apartment is in a delightful wooden cabin and the in-house restaurant is excellent.

Garni Hotel Berc HOTEL €€
(☎576 56 58; www.berc-sp.si; Pod Stražo 13; s €45-50, d €70-80; P@📶) This purpose-built place, reminiscent of a Swiss chalet, has 15 rooms on two floors in a quiet location above the lake.

Eating & Drinking

Pizzeria Rustika PIZZA €
(☎576 89 00; www.pizzeria-rustika.com; Riklijeva cesta 13; pizza €6-10; ⏰noon-11pm; 📶) Conveniently located on the same hill as many of

SPLURGE

The 22-room **Hotel Triglav Bled** (☎575 26 10; www.hoteltriglavbled.si; Kolodvorska cesta 33; s €89-159, d €119-179, ste €139-209; P❄@📶🏊) is set in a painstakingly restored caravanserai and raises the bar of accommodation standards in Bled. The rooms have hardwood floors and oriental carpets, and are furnished with antiques. There's an enormous sloped garden that grows the vegetables served in the terrace restaurants. The location is opposite Bled Jezero train station.

Bled

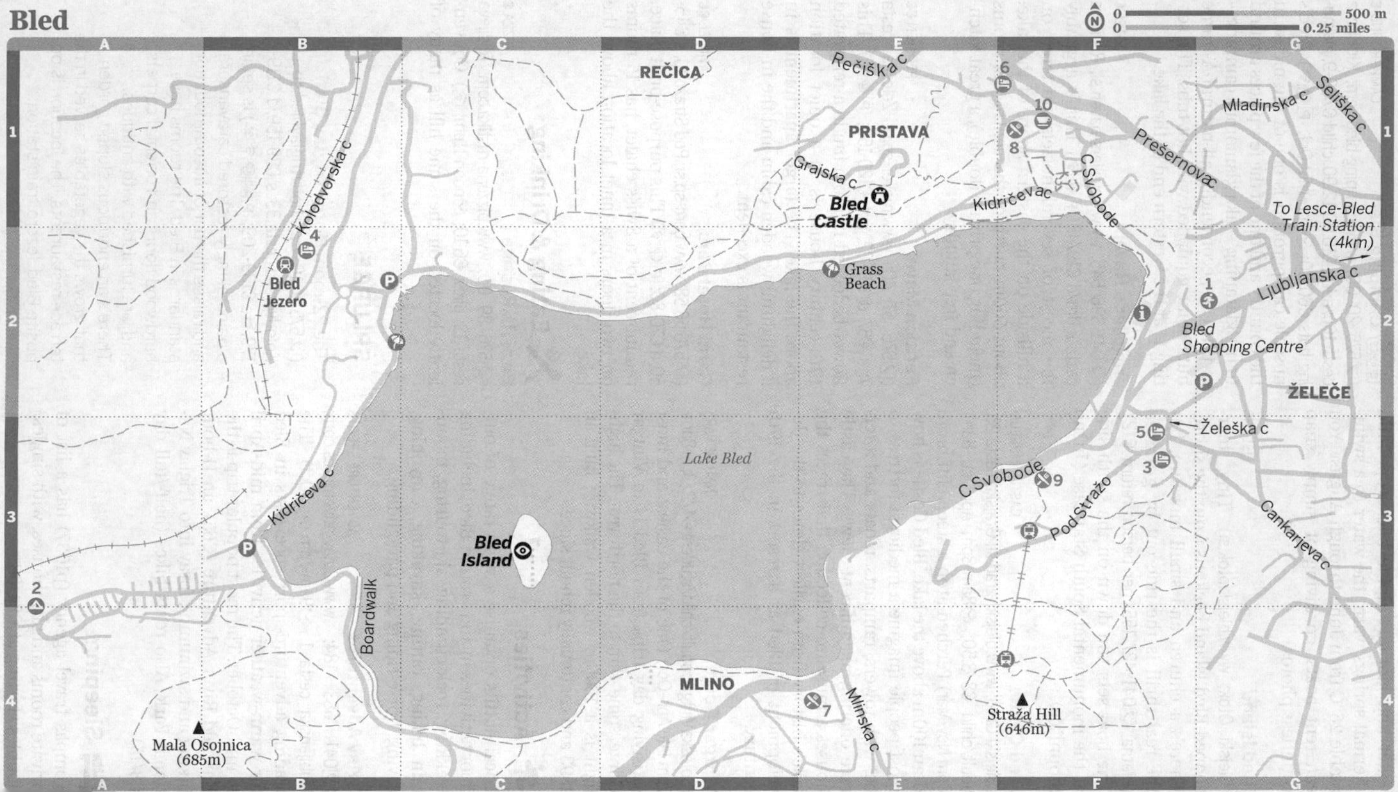

0 500 m
0 0.25 miles
REČICA
PRISTAVA
Rečiška c
Grajska c
Bled Castle
Grass Beach
Kidričevac
C Svobode
Prešernovac
Mladinska c
Seliška c
To Lesce-Bled Train Station (4km)
Ljubljanska c
Bled Shopping Centre
ŽELEČE
Željeska c
Cankarjeva c
Pod Stražo
C Svobode
Lake Bled
Bled Island
Kolodvorska c
Bled Jezero
Kidričeva c
Boardwalk
MLINO
Mlinska c
Straža Hill (646m)
Mala Osojnica (685m)
1
2
3
4
5
6
7
8
9
10

Bled

Top Sights

Bled Castle ... E1
Bled Island ... C3

Activities, Courses & Tours

1 3glav Adventures ... G2

Sleeping

2 Camping Bled ... A3
3 Garni Hotel Berc ... F3
4 Hotel Triglav Bled ... B2
5 Penzion Mayer ... F3
6 Traveller's Haven ... F1

Eating

7 Penzion Mlino ... E4
8 Pizzeria Rustika ... F1
9 Vila Ajda ... F3

Drinking

10 Slaščičarna Šmon ... F1

Bled's hostels, so the best pizza in town is just a couple of minutes' walk away.

Penzion Mlino SLOVENIAN €€
(www.mlino.si; Cesta Svobode 45; mains €8-15; ⌚noon-11pm; 📶) This is a wonderful choice for lunch along a quieter strip of the lake, about 3km outside the centre. The daily four-course set lunches (around €10) usually offer a fish choice.

Vila Ajda SLOVENIAN €€
(☎576 83 20; www.vila-ajda.si; Cesta Svobode 27; mains €9-20; ⌚11am-11pm; 📶) Attractive destination restaurant with lovely views out over the lake and a menu that features traditional Slovenian cooking made from locally sourced ingredients.

Slaščičarna Šmon CAFE
(www.smon.si; Grajska cesta 3; ⌚7.30am-10pm; 📶) The best place to try Bled's culinary speciality: *kremna rezina* (€2.40), a layer of vanilla custard topped with whipped cream and sandwiched between two layers of flaky pastry.

Information

A Propos Bar (☎574 40 44; Bled Shopping Centre, Ljubljanska cesta 4; per 15/30/60min €1.25/2.10/4.20; ⌚8am-midnight Sun-Thu, to 1am Fri & Sat; 📶) Internet access.

Kompas (☎572 75 01; www.kompas-bled.si; Bled Shopping Centre, Ljubljanska cesta 4; ⌚8am-7pm Mon-Sat, 8am-noon & 4-7pm Sun) Full-service travel agency.

Tourist Information Centre Bled (☎574 11 22; www.bled.si; Cesta Svobode 10; ⌚8am-7pm Mon-Sat, 11am-5pm Sun) Behind the casino at Cesta Svobode 10.

Getting There & Around

BUS Around 20 buses daily run from Bled to Lake Bohinj (€3.60, 45 minutes) via Bohinjska Bistrica, with the first bus leaving around 5am and the last about 9pm. Buses depart at least hourly for Ljubljana (€6.50, 1¼ hours).

TRAIN Bled has two train stations, though neither is close to the centre. Main-line trains for Ljubljana (€6.50, 55 minutes, up to 21 daily) use Lesce-Bled station, 4km east of town. Trains to Bohinjska Bistrica (€1.60, 20 minutes, eight daily), from where you can catch a bus to Lake Bohinj, use the smaller Bled Jezero station, 2km west of central Bled.

Lake Bohinj

☎04 / POP 5280

Bohinj, with its larger and much less developed glacial lake, is 26km to the southwest and a world apart from Bled. Mt Triglav is visible from here and there are activities galore – from kayaking and mountain biking to trekking up Triglav via one of the southern approaches. **Bohinjska Bistrica**, the area's largest village, is 6km east of the lake but only useful for its train station. The main tourist hub on the lake is **Ribčev Laz** at the eastern end, with a supermarket, post office with an ATM, and a **Tourist Information Centre** (TIC; ☎574 60 10; www.bohinj-info.com; Ribčev Laz 48; ⌚8am-8pm Mon-Sat, to 6pm Sun Jul & Aug, 8am-6pm Mon-Sat, 9am-3pm Sun Sep-Oct & Jan-Jun, 9am-5pm Mon-Sat, to 3pm Sun Nov-Dec).

Sights & Activities

Central **Alpinsport** (☎572 34 86; www.alpinsport.si; Ribčev Laz 53; ⌚9am-8pm Jul-Sep, 9am-7pm Oct-Jun) organises a range of activities and hires out kayaks, canoes, bikes (per hour/day €5/15) and other equipment from a kiosk near the stone bridge.

Next door is the delightful **Church of St John the Baptist** (Cerkev Sv Janeza Krstnika; Ribčev Laz; ⌚10am-noon & 4-7pm summer, by appointment other times), which contains splendid 15th- and 16th-century frescos.

The nearby village of **Stara Fužina** has an appealing little **Alpine Dairy Museum** (Planšarski Muzej; www.bohinj.si; Stara Fužina 181; adult/child €3/2; ⌚11am-7pm Tue-Sun Jul & Aug,

10am-noon & 4-6pm Tue-Sun early Jan-Jun, Sep-late Oct). Just 2km east is **Studor**, a village famed for its *kozolci* and *toplarji*, Slovenia's unique single and double hayracks.

Sleeping

The tourist office can help arrange accommodation in private rooms and apartments. Expect to pay anywhere from €38 to €50 for a two-person apartment.

TOP CHOICE **Penzion Gasperin** PENSION €€
(041 540 805; www.bohinj.si/gasperin; Ribčev Laz 36a; r €48-60;) This spotless chalet-style guesthouse with 23 rooms is just 350m southeast of the tourist office and run by a friendly British-Slovenian couple. The buffet breakfast is fresh and includes a sampling of local meats and cheeses.

Hostel Pod Voglom HOSTEL €
(572 34 61; www.hostel-podvoglom.com; Ribčev Laz 60; dm €18, r per person with bathroom €23-26, without bathroom €20-22;) Bohinj's youth hostel, some 3km west of the centre of Ribčev Laz on the road to Ukanc, has 119 beds in 46 rooms in two buildings. The main building has doubles, triples and dormitory accommodation (up to four beds), with shared facilities.

Autokamp Zlatorog CAMPGROUND €
(577 80 00; www.hoteli-bohinj.si; Ukanc 2; per person €6-9; May-Sep) This pleasant, pine-shaded 2.5-hectare camping ground accommodating 500 guests is at the lake's western end, 4.5km from Ribčev Laz. Prices vary according to site location, with the most expensive sites right on the lake.

Hotel Stare PENSION €€
(040 558 669; www.bohinj-hotel.com; Ukanc 128; r per person €42-50;) This beautifully appointed 10-room pension is situated on the Sava Bohinjka river in Ukanc and is surrounded by 3.5 hectares of lovely garden. Rates are half-board, including breakfast and dinner.

Eating

TOP CHOICE **Gostilna Rupa** SLOVENIAN €€
(572 34 01; www.apartmajikatrnjek.com/rupa; Srednja Vas 87; mains €8-16; 10am-midnight daily Jul & Aug, 10am-midnight Tue-Sun Sep-Jun) If you're under your own steam, head for this country-style restaurant in the next village over from Studor and about 5km from Ribčev Laz. Among the excellent home-cooked dishes are *ajdova krapi* (crescent-shaped dumplings made from buckwheat and cheese), various types of local *klobasa* (sausage) and Bohinj trout.

Gostilna Mihovc SLOVENIAN €
(572 33 90; www.gostilna-mihovc.si; Stara Fužina 118; mains €7-10; 10am-midnight) This place in Stara Fužina is very popular – not least for its fiery homemade brandy. Try the *pasulj* (bean soup) with sausage (€6) or the beef *golač* (goulash; €5.20). In summer book in advance to secure a garden table.

Getting There & Away

BUS Services run regularly from Ljubljana (€9, two hours hourly) to Bohinj Jezero and Ukanc – marked 'Bohinj Zlatorog' – via Bled and Bohinjska Bistrica. Around 20 buses daily run from Bled (€3.60, 45 minutes) to Bohinj Jezero (via Bohinjska Bistrica) and return, with the first bus leaving around 5am and the last about 9pm.

TRAIN Several trains daily make the run to Bohinjska Bistrica from Ljubljana (€6.70, two hours), though this route requires a change in Jesenice. There are also frequent trains between Bled's small Bled Jezero station (€1.60, 20 minutes, eight daily) and Bohinjska Bistrica.

Soča Valley

The Soča Valley region is defined by the 96km-long Soča River, coloured a deep, almost artificial turquoise. The valley has more than its share of historical sights, most of them related to one of the costliest battles of WWI, but the majority of visitors are here for adventure sports.

BOVEC

05 / POP 1810

The best alpine views are at Bovec, which lies in the shadow of **Mt Kanin** (2587m), Slovenia's highest ski resort. The compact village square, **Trg Golobarskih Žrtev**, has everything you need, including the **Tourist Information Centre Bovec** (388 19 19; www.bovec.si; Trg Golobarskih Žrtev 8; 8.30am-8.30pm summer, 9am-6pm winter) and a half-dozen adrenalin-raising adventure-sports companies, including two of the best: **Soča Rafting** (389 62 00, 041-724 472; www.socarafting.si; Trg Golobarskih Žrtev 14; 9am-7pm year-round) and **Top Extreme** (041 620 636; www.top.si; Trg Golobarskih Žrtev 19; 9am-7pm May-Sep).

The Tourist Information Centre has a list of private rooms (per person €15 to €30). Camping facilities are generally bet ter in nearby Kobarid, but **Kamp Polovnik** (☎388 60 07; www.kamp-polovnik.com; Ledina 8; adult €6.50-7.50, child €5-5.75; ⊙Apr–mid-Oct; P), about 500m southeast of the centre, is more convenient. **Martinov Hram** (☎388 62 14; www.martinov-hram.si; Trg Golobarskih Žrtev 27; s/d €33/54; P ☎) is a central guesthouse just 100m east of the centre with a dozen nicely furnished rooms and an excellent restaurant.

There are daily buses to Ljubljana (€13.60, 3½ hours) via Kobarid and Idrija. From late June to August buses to Kranjska Gora (€6.70, two hours) via the Vršič Pass depart four times daily, continuing to Ljubljana.

KARST & COAST

Postojna & Škocjan Caves

☎05

Just under 2km northwest of the town of Postojna (population 8910), **Postojna Cave** (☎700 01 00; www.postojnska-jama.eu; Jamska c 30; adult/child/student €22.90/13.70/18.30; ⊙tours hourly 9am-6pm summer, 3 or 4 times from 10am daily winter) is home to the endemic *Proteus anguinus* – eyeless salamanders nicknamed 'human fish'. The cave is filled with endless stalagmites, stalactites and almost as many tourists. Visits (lasting 1½ hours) involve an underground train ride as well as a 1.7km walk with gradients but no steps. Dress warmly or rent a shawl as it's only 8°C to 10°C down there.

The quieter and more remote **Škocjan Caves** (☎708 21 10; www.park-skocjanske-jame.si; Škocjan 2; adult/child €15/7; ⊙10am-5pm) are 5km southeast of Divača (population 1325). A van sometimes meets incoming trains and will transport those with bus or train tickets to the caves for free. Otherwise there is a large map indicating the walking route posted outside the station.

Sleeping & Eating

Hotel Sport HOTEL, HOSTEL €€
(☎720 22 44; www.sport-hotel.si; Kolodvorska c 1; dm €25, s/d from €55/70; P @ ☎) The Sport offers reasonable value for money near Postojna Cave, with 37 spick-and-span comfortable rooms, including five with nine dorm beds each. There's a kitchen with a small eating area. It's 300m north of the centre.

Gostilna Malovec GUESTHOUSE €
(☎763 12 25; Kraška 30a; s/d €32/48) The Malovec, in Divača, has a half-dozen basic, but comfortable, renovated rooms in a building beside its popular **restaurant** (mains €5-15; ⊙8am-10pm daily), which serves Slovenian favourites.

Getting There & Away

Buses from Ljubljana to Koper, Piran and Nova Gorica all stop in Postojna (€6, one hour, half-hourly) and Divača (€7.90, 1½ hours, half-hourly). The train is good for Divača (€7.90, 1½ hours, half-hourly) but less useful for Postojna.

Koper

☎05 / POP 24,700

Coastal Slovenia's largest town, Koper (Capodistria in Italian) at first glance appears to be a workaday city that scarcely gives tourism a second thought. Yet its medieval core is delightfully quiet and far less overrun than its ritzy cousin Piran, 18km down the coast.

The **Tourist Information Centre Koper** (☎664 64 03; www.koper.si; Praetorian Palace, Titov trg 3; ⊙9am-8pm Jul & Aug, 9am-5pm Sep-Jun) is within the restored Renaissance **Praetorian Palace** (Titov trg 3; admission free; ⊙9am-8pm), which also houses an old pharmacy and elaborate ceremonial hall. Nearby, the **Cathedral of the Assumption** (Stolnica Marijinoga Vnebovzetja; ⊙7am-9pm) has a bell tower that can be climbed (204 steps). The **Koper Regional Museum** (☎663 35 70; www.pmk-kp.si; Kidričeva ul 19; adult/child €2/1.50; ⊙9am-7pm Tue-Fri, to 1pm Sat & Sun) inside the Belgramoni-Tacco Palace has an Italianate sculpture garden.

Sleeping & Eating

Museum Hostel APARTMENT €
(☎626 18 70, 041 504 466; bozic.doris@siol.net; Muzejski trg 6; per person €20-25; ☎) This place is more a series of apartments with kitchens and bathrooms than a hostel. Reception is at Museum Bife, a cafe-bar on Muzejski trg; the rooms are scattered nearby.

Hotel Vodišek HOTEL €€
(☎639 24 68; www.hotel-vodisek.com; Kolodvorska c 2; s €48-60, d €72-90; P ❄ @ ☎) This small hotel with 35 reasonably priced rooms is in a shopping centre halfway between the Old Town and the train and bus stations. Guests get to use the hotel's bicycles for free.

Istrska Klet Slavček ISTRIAN, SLOVENIAN €
(☎627 67 29; Župančičeva ul 39; dishes €3-12; ⊙7am-10pm Mon-Fri) The Istrian Cellar, situated below the 18th-century Carli Palace, is one of the most colourful places for a meal in Koper's Old Town. Filling set lunches go for less than €8, and there's local Malvazija and Teran wine from the barrel.

Getting There & Away

Buses run to Piran (€2.70, 30 minutes) every 20 minutes on weekdays and every 40 minutes on weekends. Up to five buses daily head for Ljubljana (€11.10, 1¾ to 2½ hours), though the six daily trains (€10.70, 2¼ hours) are more comfortable.

Piran

☎05 / POP 4470

Picturesque Piran (Pirano in Italian) sits on the tip of a narrow peninsula, the westernmost point of Slovenian Istria. Piran Bay and Portorož (population 2900), Slovenia's largest beach resort, lie to the south. Piran's Old Town is a gem of Venetian Gothic architecture and full of picturesque narrow streets.

The **Sergej Mašera Maritime Museum** (☎671 00 40; www.pommuz-pi.si; Cankarjevo nabrežje 3; adult/student/child €3.50/2.50/2.10; ⊙9am-noon & 5-9pm Tue-Sun summer, 9am-5pm Tue-Sun winter) and the **Piran Aquarium** (☎673 25 72; www.aquariumpiran.com; Kidričevo nabrežje 4; adult/child €7/5; ⊙9am-7pm summer, to 5pm winter) are on opposite sides of the harbour, south of central Tartinijev trg, where you'll find the **Tourist Information Centre Piran** (☎673 02 20, 673 44 40; www.portoroz.si; Tartinijev trg 2; ⊙9am-8pm summer, 9am-5pm winter).

The town is dominated by the **Cathedral of St George**, whose soaring bell tower (1609) was modelled on the campanile of St Mark's Cathedral in Venice. The nearby **Minorite monastery** (☎673 44 17; Bolniška ul 20) has a delightful cloister.

> **SPLURGE**
>
> Piran's most romantic accommodation option, **Max Piran** (☎673 34 36, 041 692 928; www.maxpiran.com; Ul IX Korpusa 26; d €60-70; ❄@📶) has just six rooms – each bearing a woman's name rather than a number – in a delightful coral-coloured 18th-century townhouse. It's a short walk from the cathedral and the views from on high are spectacular.

Sleeping

Val Hostel HOSTEL €
(☎673 25 55; www.hostel-val.com; Gregorčičeva ul 38a; per person €22-27; @📶) This excellent central hostel on the corner of Vegova ulica has 22 rooms (including a few singles), with shared shower, kitchen and washing machine. It's a deserved favourite with backpackers, and prices include breakfast.

Kamp Fiesa CAMPGROUND €
(☎674 62 30; autocamp.fiesa@siol.net; adult/child €12/4; ⊙May-Sep; P) The closest camping ground to Piran is at Fiesa, 4km by road but less than 1km if you follow the coastal path *(obalna pešpot)* east from the Cathedral of St George. It's tiny and gets crowded in summer, but it's in a quiet valley by two small ponds and right by the beach.

Miracolo di Mare B&B €€
(☎921 76 60, 051 445 511; www.miracolodimare.si; Tomšičeva ul 23; s €50-55, d €60-70; @📶) A lovely B&B on the coast, the Wonder of the Sea has a dozen dazzling (though smallish) rooms, some of which (like No 3 and the breakfast room) give on to the most charming raised back garden in Piran. Floors and stairs are wooden (and original).

Eating

There's an outdoor **fruit and vegetable market** (Zelenjavni trg; ⊙7am-2pm Mon-Sat) in the small square behind the town hall.

TOP CHOICE **Pri Mari** MEDITERRANEAN, SLOVENIAN €€
(☎673 47 35, 041 616 488; Dantejeva ul 17; mains €8.50-16; ⊙noon-11pm Tue-Sun summer, noon-10pm Tue-Sat, noon-6pm Sun winter) This stylish and welcoming restaurant run by an Italian-Slovenian couple serves inventive Mediterranean and Slovenian dishes. Be sure to book ahead.

Riva Piran SEAFOOD €€
(☎673 22 25; Gregorčičeva ul 46; mains €8-28; ⊙11.30am-midnight) The best waterfront seafood restaurant, and worth patronising, is this classy place with the strip's best decor and sea views.

Getting There & Away

Buses run every 20 to 30 minutes to Koper (€2.70, 30 minutes). Five buses head for Trieste, Italy (€10, 1¾ hours) between 6.45am and

WORTH A TRIP

EASTERN SLOVENIA

Slovenia's second city and European Capital of Culture in 2012, **Maribor** (population 88,500) has no unmissable sights but oozes with charm thanks to its delightful (but tiny) Old Town. Pedestrianised central streets buzz with cafes and student life, and in late June and early July the riverside Lent district hosts a major arts festival.

The **Tourist Information Centre Maribor** (☎234 66 11; www.maribor-pohorje.si; Partinzanska c 6a; ⏲9am-7pm Mon-Fri, 9am-6pm Sat & Sun) has a list of places to stay, but for budget accommodation try the **Hostel Pekarna** (☎059 180 880; www.mkc-hostelpekarna.si; Ob žclcznici 16; dm/s/d €17/21/42; 📶), a converted army bakery.

From Ljubljana, reach Maribor by bus (€13, three hours, two to four a day) or express train (€13.60, two hours).

Consider a quick bus trip to picture-postcard **Ptuj**, which is just down the road by bus from Maribor (€3.60, 45 minutes, departs every two hours).

6.55pm Monday to Saturday. Between three and five daily buses go to Ljubljana (€12, three hours) via Divača and Postojna.

UNDERSTAND SLOVENIA

History

Slovenes played a key role in the development of democracy. By the early 7th century their Slavic forebears had founded the Duchy of Carantania (now Karnburg in Austria), where ruling dukes were elected by ennobled commoners. This model was noted by Thomas Jefferson when drafting the American Declaration of Independence in 1776.

Austria controlled Slovenia almost uninterrupted from the 14th century until 1918. After some of the most ferocious fighting in VWI, western Slovenia was handed over to taly as Austro-Hungarian postwar reparaions, and northern Carinthia voted to stay vithin Austria. The rest of Slovenia joined ellow South Slavs in forming the Kingdom of erbs, Croats and Slovenes, later Yugoslavia.

Nazi occupation in WWII was for the nost part resisted by Slovenian partisans, hough the anti-partisan Slovenian Domoranci (Home Guards) threw their support ehind the Germans after Italy surrendered. he war ended with Slovenia regaining the alian-held areas from Piran to Bovec but sing Trst (Trieste) and Gorica (Gorizia).

Small Slovenia was a major economic werhouse in Yugoslavia, producing up to % of the GDP. By the 1980s the federation as becoming increasingly Serb-dominated d, after free elections, Slovenia broke away from Yugoslavia on 25 June 1991. A 10 day war that left 66 people dead followed; Yugoslavia swiftly signed a truce in order to concentrate on regaining control of coastal Croatia instead.

Slovenia was admitted to the UN in 1992 and joined the EU in 2004. It adopted the euro as its national currency three years later.

People

The population of Slovenia (just under two million) is largely homogeneous. Just over 83% are ethnic Slovenes, with the remainder being Croats, Serbians, Bosnians and Roma; there are also small enclaves of Italians and Hungarians. Slovenes are ethnically Slavic, typically hardworking, multilingual and extrovert. Just under 58% are Roman Catholic.

Closely related to Croatian and Serbian, the Slovene language (*slovenščina*) is written in the Roman alphabet.

Virtually everyone in Slovenia speaks at least one other language (usually English, German or Italian).

Arts

Slovenia's most beloved writer is the Romantic poet France Prešeren (1800–49), whose lyric poetry helped to raise Slovenian national consciousness.

Many of Ljubljana's most characteristic architectural features were added by the ubertalented Jože Plečnik (1872–1957).

Slovenia's vibrant music scene embraces electronic, jazz, punk, thrash-metal and *chansons* (eg torch songs from Vita Mavrič); the most popular old-style rockers are Siddharta.

There's also a folk-music revival: listen for the groups Katice and Katalena and the vocalist Brina.

Environment

Slovenia is amazingly green; 58% of its total surface area is covered in forest and it's growing. Slovenia is home to almost 3200 plant species – some 70 of which are indigenous.

Triglav National Park is particularly rich in native flowering plants. Among the more peculiar endemic fauna in Slovenia is a blind salamander called *Proteus anguinus* that lives deep in Karst caves, can survive for years without eating and has been called a 'living fossil' because of its resemblance to prehistoric fauna. It's also called the 'human fish' because of its unusual skin tone that resembles human flesh.

SURVIVAL GUIDE

Directory A–Z

Accommodation

Accommodation runs the gamut from riverside camping grounds, hostels, mountain huts, cosy *gostišča* (inns) and farmhouses, to elegant castle hotels and five-star hotels in Ljubljana, so you'll usually have little trouble finding accommodation to fit your budget, except perhaps at the height of the season (July and August) on the coast, at Bled or Bohinj, or in Ljubljana.

The following price categories for the cost of a double room are used in the listings in this chapter. Unless otherwise indicated, rooms include en suite toilet and bath or shower and breakfast.

€ less than €50

€€ €50 to €100

€€€ more than €100

Business Hours

Grocery stores 8am to 7pm Monday to Friday and 8am to 1pm Saturday.

Restaurants Usually 11am to 10pm daily

Banks 9am to 5pm Monday to Friday, and (rarely) 8am to noon Saturday.

Museums 10am to 6pm Tuesday to Sunday; winter hours may be shorter

Festivals & Events

The official website of the **Slovenian Tourist Board** (www.slovenia.info) maintains a comprehensive list of major cultural events.

Food

Price ranges for restaurants listed in this chapter are indicated by the following price ranges for a main course:

€ less than €10

€€ €10 to €20

€€€ more than €20

Gay & Lesbian Travellers

National laws ban discrimination in employment and other areas on the basis of sexual preference. In recent years a highly visible campaign against homophobia has been put in place across the country. Outside Ljubljana, however, there is little evidence of a gay presence, much less a lifestyle.

Roza Klub (Klub K4 ; www.klubk4.org; Kersnikova ulica 4; ⏲10pm-6am Sun Sep-Jun) in Ljubljana is made up of the gay and lesbian branches of **KUC** (www.skuc.org), which stands for Študentski Kulturni Center (Student Cultural Centre) but is no longer student-orientated as such. It organises the gay and lesbian **Ljubljana Pride** (www.ljubljanapride.org) parade in late June and the **Gay & Lesbian Film Festival** (www.ljudmila.org/siqrd/fglf) in late November/early December. A monthly publication called **Narobe** (Upside Down; www.narobe.si) is in Slovene only, though you may be able to glean something from the listings.

Internet Access

Virtually every hotel and hostel in Slovenia now has internet access – a computer fo guests' use (free or for a small fee), wi-fi o both. Most of the country's tourist informa tion centres offer free (or low-cost) acces and many libraries have free terminals Many cities and towns have at least one in ternet cafe (though they usually only have handful of terminals), or even free wi-fi i town squares.

Money

Exchanging cash is simple at banks, maj post offices, travel agencies and *menjalni* (bureaux de change), although many dor accept travellers cheques. Major credit ar debit cards are accepted almost everywher and ATMs are ubiquitous.

Public Holidays

If a holiday falls on a Sunday, then the following Monday becomes the holiday.

New Year 1 & 2 January

Prešeren Day (Slovenian Culture Day) 8 February

Easter & Easter Monday March/April

Insurrection Day 27 April

Labour Day holidays 1 & 2 May

National Day 25 June

Assumption Day 15 August

Reformation Day 31 October

All Saints Day 1 November

Christmas Day 25 December

Independence Day 26 December

Telephone

Public telephones in Slovenia require a *telefonska kartica* or *telekartica* (telephone card), available at post offices and some newsstands. Phonecards cost €2.70/4/7.50/14.60 for 25/50/100/300 *impulzov* (impulses, or units).

To call Slovenia from abroad, dial the international access code, ☎386 (the country code for Slovenia), the area code (minus the initial zero) and the number. There are six area codes in Slovenia (☎01 to ☎05 and ☎07). To call abroad from Slovenia, dial ☎00 followed by the country and area codes and then the number. Numbers beginning with ☎80 in Slovenia are toll-free.

For mobile (cell) phones, Slovenia uses GSM 900, which is compatible with the rest of Europe and Australia but not with the North American or totally different Japanese system. SIM cards with €5 credit are available for around €15 from **SiMobil** (www.simobil.si), **Mobitel** (www.mobitel.si) and **Tušmobil** (www.tusmobil.sil). Top-up scratch cards are available at post offices, newsstands and petrol stations.

Tourist Information

The **Slovenian Tourist Board** (Slovenska turistična Organizacija, STO; ☎01-589 18 40; www.slovenia.info; Dunajska cesta 156) based in Ljubljana is the umbrella organisation for tourist promotion in Slovenia, and produces a number of excellent brochures, pamphlets and booklets in English. In addition, the organisation oversees another five dozen or so local tourist offices and bureaus called 'tourist information centres' (TICs) across the country.

Visas

Citizens of nearly all European countries, as well as Australia, Canada, Israel, Japan, New Zealand and the USA, do not require visas to visit Slovenia for stays of up to 90 days. Holders of EU and Swiss passports can enter using a national identity card.

Those who do require visas (including South Africans) can get them for up to 90 days at any Slovenian embassy or consulate – see the website of the **Ministry of Foreign Affairs** (www.mzz.gov.si) for a full listing.

Getting There & Away

Air

Slovenia's only international airport is Ljubljana's **Jože Pučnik Airport** (Aerodrom Ljubljana; ☎04-206 19 81; www.lju-airport.si/eng; Zgornji Brnik 130a) at Brnik, 27km north of Ljubljana. In the arrivals hall there's a **Slovenia Tourist Information Centre** (STIC; ⏰11am-11pm Mon, Wed & Fri, 10am-10pm Tue & Thu, 10.30am-10.30pm Sat, 12.30pm-12.30am Sun) desk, a hotel-booking telephone and an ATM. Car-rental agencies have outlets opposite the terminal.

From its base at Brnik, the Slovenian flag-carrier, **Adria Airways** (☎080 13 00, 01-369 10 10; www.adria-airways.com), serves some 20 European destinations on regularly scheduled flights. Many other airlines offer regularly scheduled flights to and from Ljubljana.

Land

BUS

International bus destinations from Ljubljana include Serbia, Germany, Croatia, Bosnia and Hercegovina, Macedonia, Italy and Scandinavia. You can also catch buses to Italy and Croatia from coastal towns, including Piran and Koper.

TRAIN

It is possible to travel to Italy, Austria, Germany, Croatia and Hungary by train; Ljubljana is the main hub, although you can, for example, hop on international trains in certain cities like Maribor and Ptuj. International train travel can be expensive. It is sometimes cheaper to travel as far as you can on domestic routes before crossing any borders.

ROAD RULES

- Drive on the right.
- Speed limits: 50km/h in town, 90km/h on secondary roads, 100km/h on highways; 130km/h on motorways.
- Seat belts are compulsory; motorcyclists must wear helmets.
- All motorists must illuminate their headlights throughout the day.
- Permitted blood-alcohol level for drivers is 0.05%.

Sea

Piran sends ferries to Trieste daily and catamarans to Venice at least once a week in season. There's also a catamaran between nearby Izola and Venice in summer months.

Getting Around

Bicycle

Cycling is a popular way of getting around. Bikes can be transported for €2.80 in the baggage compartments of some InterCity and regional trains. Larger buses can also carry bikes as luggage. Larger towns and cities have dedicated bicycle lanes and traffic lights.

Bus

Buy your ticket at the *avtobusna postaja* (bus station) or simply pay the driver as you board. In Ljubljana you should book your seat at least a day in advance if you're travelling on Friday, or to destinations in the mountains or on the coast on a public holiday. Bus services are restricted on Sunday and holidays.

A range of bus companies serve the country, but prices are uniform: €3.10/5.60/9.20/16.80 for 25/50/100/200km of travel.

Car & Motorcycle

Roads in Slovenia are generally good. Tolls are no longer paid separately on the motorways, instead all cars must display a *vinjeta* (road-toll sticker) on the windscreen. They cost €15/30/95 for a week/month/year for cars and €7.50/25/47.50 for motorbikes and are available at petrol stations, post offices and certain newsstands and tourist information centres. Failure to display such a sticker risks a fine of up to €300.

Renting a car in Slovenia allows access to cheaper out-of-centre hotels and farm or village homestays. Rentals from international firms such as Avis, Budget, Europcar and Hertz vary in price; expect to pay from €40/210 per day/week, including unlimited mileage and basic insurance. Some smaller agencies have somewhat more competitive rates; booking on the internet is always cheaper.

Call ☎1987 for roadside assistance.

Train

Much of the country is accessible by rail, run by the national operator, **Slovenian Railways** (Slovenske Železnice, SŽ; ☎01-291 33 32; www.slo-zeleznice.si). The website has an easy-to-use timetable.

Figure on travelling at about 60km/h except on the fastest InterCity Slovenia (ICS) express trains that run between Ljubljana and Maribor (€13.60, 1¾ hours) at an average speed of 90km/h.

Purchase your ticket before travelling at the *železniška postaja* (train station); buying it from the conductor onboard costs an additional €2.50. Invalid ticket or fare dodging earn a €40 fine.

Spain

Includes »

Madrid 1047
Salamanca 1063
Barcelona 1068
Aragón 1083
Basque Country 1084
Santiago de Compostela 1088
Valencia 1090
Mallorca 1093
Ibiza 1095
Seville 1097
Córdoba 1102
Granada 1104
Málaga 1107
Understand Spain 1111
Survival Guide 1114

Best Places to Eat

- La Cuchara de San Telmo (p1086)
- Simply Fosh (p1094)
- Tickets (p1078)
- Le Pepica (p1091)

Best Places to Stay

- Hotel Meninas (p1056)
- Hospedería Alma Andalusí (p1103)
- Sabinas (p1083)
- Cat's Hostel (p1056)

Why Go?

Passionate, sophisticated and devoted to living the good life, Spain is at once a stereotype come to life and a country more diverse than you ever imagined.

Spanish landscapes stir the soul, from the jagged Pyrenees and wildly beautiful cliffs of the Atlantic northwest to charming Mediterranean coves, while astonishing architecture spans the ages at seemingly every turn. Spain's cities march to a beguiling beat, rushing headlong into the 21st century even as timeless villages serve as beautiful signposts to Old Spain. And then there's one of Europe's most celebrated (and varied) gastronomic scenes.

But, above all, Spain lives very much in the present. Perhaps you'll sense it along a crowded after midnight street when all the world has come out to play. Or maybe that moment will come when a flamenco performer touches something deep in your soul. Whenever it happens, you'll find yourself nodding in recognition: *this* is Spain.

When to Go

Madrid

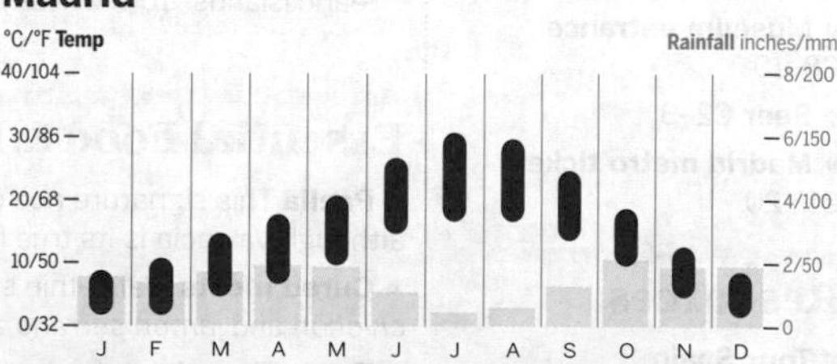

Mar & Apr Spring wildflowers, Semana Santa processions and mild southern temps.

May & Sep Mild and often balmy weather but without the crowds of high summer.

Jun–Aug Spaniards hit the coast in warm weather, but quiet corners still abound.

AT A GLANCE

- **Currency** Euro
- **Language** Spanish (Castilian), Catalan, Basque, Galician (Gallego)
- **Money** ATMs everywhere
- **Visas** Schengen rules apply

Fast Facts

- **Area** 505,370 sq km
- **Population** 47 million
- **Capital** Madrid
- **Country code** ☎34
- **Emergency** ☎112

Exchange Rates

Australia	A$1	€0.82
Canada	C$1	€0.77
Japan	¥100	€0.83
New Zealand	NZ$1	€0.65
UK	UK£1	€1.18
USA	US$1	€0.78

Set Your Budget

- **Budget hotel room** €60
- **Lunchtime three-course menú del día** €9–13
- **Museum entrance** €8–10
- **Beer** €2–3
- **Madrid metro ticket** €12.20

Resources

- **Tour Spain** (www.tourspain.org)
- **Turespaña** (www.spain.info)
- **Lonely Planet** (www.lonelyplanet.com/spain)

Connections

Spanish airports are among Europe's best connected, while the typical overland route leads many travellers from France over the Pyrenees into Spain. Rather than taking the main road/rail route along the Mediterranean coast (or between Biarritz and San Sebastián), you could follow lesser known, pretty routes over the mountains. There's nothing to stop you carrying on to Portugal: numerous roads and the Madrid–Lisbon rail line connect the two countries.

The most obvious sea journeys lead across the Strait of Gibraltar to Morocco. The most common routes connect Algeciras or Tarifa with Tangier, from where there's plenty of transport deeper into Morocco. Car ferries also connect Barcelona with Italian ports.

There are two main rail lines to Spain from Paris, one to Madrid via the Basque Country, and another to Barcelona; both are to be upgraded to a high-speed service. The latter connects with services to the French Riviera and Switzerland.

ITINERARIES

One Week

Marvel at Barcelona's art nouveau–influenced modernista architecture and seaside style before taking the train to San Sebastián, with a stop in Zaragoza on the way. Head on to Bilbao for the Guggenheim Museum and end the trip living it up in Madrid's legendary night scene.

One Month

Fly into Seville and embark on a route exploring the town and picture-perfect Ronda, Granada and Córdoba. Take the train to Madrid, from where you can check out Toledo, Salamanca and Segovia. Make east for the coast and Valencia, detour northwest into the postcard-perfect villages of Aragón and the Pyrenees, then travel east into Catalonia, spending time in Tarragona before reaching Barcelona. Take a plane or boat for the Balearic Islands, from where you can get a flight home.

Essential Food & Drink

- **Paella** This signature rice dish comes in infinite varieties although Valencia is its true home.
- **Cured meats** Wafer-thin slices of *chorizo, lomo, salchichón* and *jamón serrano* appear on most Spanish tables
- **Tapas** These bite-sized morsels range from uncomplicated Spanish staples to pure gastronomic innovation.
- **Olive oil** Spain is the world's largest producer of olive oil
- **Wine** Spain has the largest area of wine cultivation in the world. La Rioja and Ribera del Duero are the best-known wine-growing regions.

MADRID

POP 3.26 MILLION

No city on earth is more alive than Madrid, a beguiling place whose sheer energy carries a simple message: *madrileños* know how to live. Explore the old streets of the centre, relax in the plazas, soak up the culture in Madrid's excellent art museums, and spend at least one night in the city's legendary nightlife scene.

Sights

Get under the city's skin by walking its streets, sipping coffee and beer in its plazas and relaxing in its parks. Madrid de los Austrias, the maze of mostly 15th- and 16th-century streets that surround Plaza Mayor, is the city's oldest district. Tapas-crazy La Latina, alternative Chueca, bar-riddled Huertas and Malasaña, and chic Salamanca are other districts that reward pedestrian exploration.

Build in time for three of Europe's top art collections at the Prado, Reina Sofía and Thyssen-Bornemisza museums, as well as a visit to the Palacio Real.

TOP CHOICE **Museo del Prado** MUSEUM

(Map p1054; www.museodelprado.es; Paseo del Prado, adult/child €12/free, 6-8pm Mon-Sat & 5-7pm Sun free, audioguides €3.50; 10am-8pm Mon-Sat, to 7pm Sun; M Banco de España) Spain's premier art museum, the Prado is a parade of priceless works from Spain and beyond. The collection is roughly divided into eight major collections: Spanish paintings (1100–1850), Flemish paintings (1430–1700), Italian paintings (1300–1800), French paintings (1600–1800), German paintings (1450–1800), sculptures, decorative arts, and drawings and prints. There is generous coverage of Spanish greats including Goya, Velázquez and El Greco. In addition to these Spanish masterpieces, don't miss *El Jardín de las Delicias* (The Garden of Earthly Delights; Room 56A), a three-panelled painting by Hieronymus Bosch of the creation of man, the pleasures of the world, and hell, or the works by Peter Paul Rubens, Pieter Bruegel, Rembrandt, Anton Van Dyck, Dürer, Rafael, Tiziano (Titian), Tintoretto, Sorolla, Gainsborough, Fra Angelico and Tiepolo.

Museo Thyssen-Bornemisza MUSEUM

(Map p1054; 902 760 511; www.museothyssen.org; Paseo del Prado 8; adult/child €9/free; 10am-7pm Tue-Sun; M Banco de España) Opposite Museo del Prado, the Museo Thyssen-Bornemisza is an outstanding collection of international masterpieces. Begin your visit on the 2nd floor, where you'll start with medieval art, and make your way down to modern works on the ground level, passing paintings by Titian, El Greco, Rubens, Rembrandt, Anton

continued on p1052

MUSEO DEL PRADO ITINERARY: ICONS OF SPANISH ART

The Museo del Prado's collection can be overwhelming in scope, but if your time is limited, zero in on the museum's peerless collection of Spanish art.

Goya is displayed on all three floors of the Prado, but begin at the southern end of the ground or lower level. In rooms 64 and 65, Goya's *El Dos de Mayo* and *El Tres de Mayo* rank among Madrid's most emblematic paintings. In rooms 66 and 67, Goya's disturbing *Pinturas Negras* (Black Paintings) are so named for the distorted animalesque appearance of their characters. Of Goya's remarkable royal portraits, *La Família de Carlos V* (Room 32), on the 1st floor, is especially worth seeking out. Also on the 1st floor, in Room 36, are two more of Goya's best-known and most intriguing oils: *La Maja Vestida* and *La Maja Desnuda*. These portraits are of an unknown woman, commonly believed to be the Duquesa de Alba (who some think may have been Goya's lover).

Having studied the works of Goya, turn your attention to Velázquez, beginning with *Las Meninas* (Room 12). Completed in 1656, it is more properly known as *La Família de Felipe IV* (The Family of Felipe IV). His mastery of light and colour is never more apparent than here. In the neighbouring rooms 14 and 15, watch also for his paintings of various members of royalty who seem to spring off the canvas – Felipe II, Felipe IV, Margarita de Austria (a younger version of whom features in *Las Meninas*), El Príncipe Baltasar Carlos and Isabel de Francia. In Room 9a, seek out his masterful *La Rendición de Breda*.

Further, Bartolomé Esteban Murillo (Room 17), José de Ribera (Room 9), the stark figures of Francisco de Zurbarán (Room 10a) and the vivid, almost surreal works of El Greco (Room 8b) should all be on your itinerary.

Spain Highlights

1. Explore the **Alhambra** (p1104), an exquisite Islamic palace complex in Granada
2. Visit Gaudí's singular work in progress, Barcelona's **La Sagrada Família** (p1072), a cathedral that truly defies imagination
3. Wander amid the horseshoe arches of Córdoba's **Mezquita** (p1102), close to perfection wrought in stone
4. Eat your way through **San Sebastián** (p1084), a gourmand's paradise with an idyllic setting
5. Join the pilgrims making their way to magnificent **Santiago de Compostela** (p1088)
6. Soak up the scent of orange blossom, admire the architecture and surrender to the party atmosphere in sunny **Seville** (p1097)
7. Discover the impossibly beautiful Mediterranean beaches and coves of **Menorca** (p1094)
8. Spend your days in some of Europe's best art galleries and nights amid its best nightlife in **Madrid** (p1047)
9. Be carried away by the soulful strains of live **flamenco** (p1113)

Bordeaux
FRANCE
Avignon
Nîmes
Toulouse
Montpellier
San Sebastián
Irún
NAVARRA
Vitoria
Golfe de Beauduc
PYRENEES
Pamplona
Perpignan
Andorra la Vella
ANDORRA
Miranda de Ebro
Logroño
Jaca
Figueres
Calahorra
Huesca
CATALONIA
Girona
Fornells
Soria
Lleida
Manresa
Tossa de Mar
Costa Brava
AP68
A9
Zaragoza
AP2
Barcelona
Sitges
Tarragona
ARAGÓN
A23
AP7
Guadalajara
Alcalá de Henares
Teruel
Ciutadella de Menorca
Menorca
Maó
Cuenca
Inca
A3
Mallorca
Artà
Sagunto
Manacor
Palma de Mallorca
Valencia
VALENCIA
Alginet
Balearic Islands
Albacete
AP7
Ibiza
Denia
Benidorm
Alicante
Elche
Cieza
Murcia
MURCIA
Costa Blanca
MEDITERRANEAN SEA
A7
A91
Cartagena
Guadix
Mojácar
Costa Cálida
Almería
Costa De Almería
ALGERIA
0 200 km
0 100 miles

Madrid

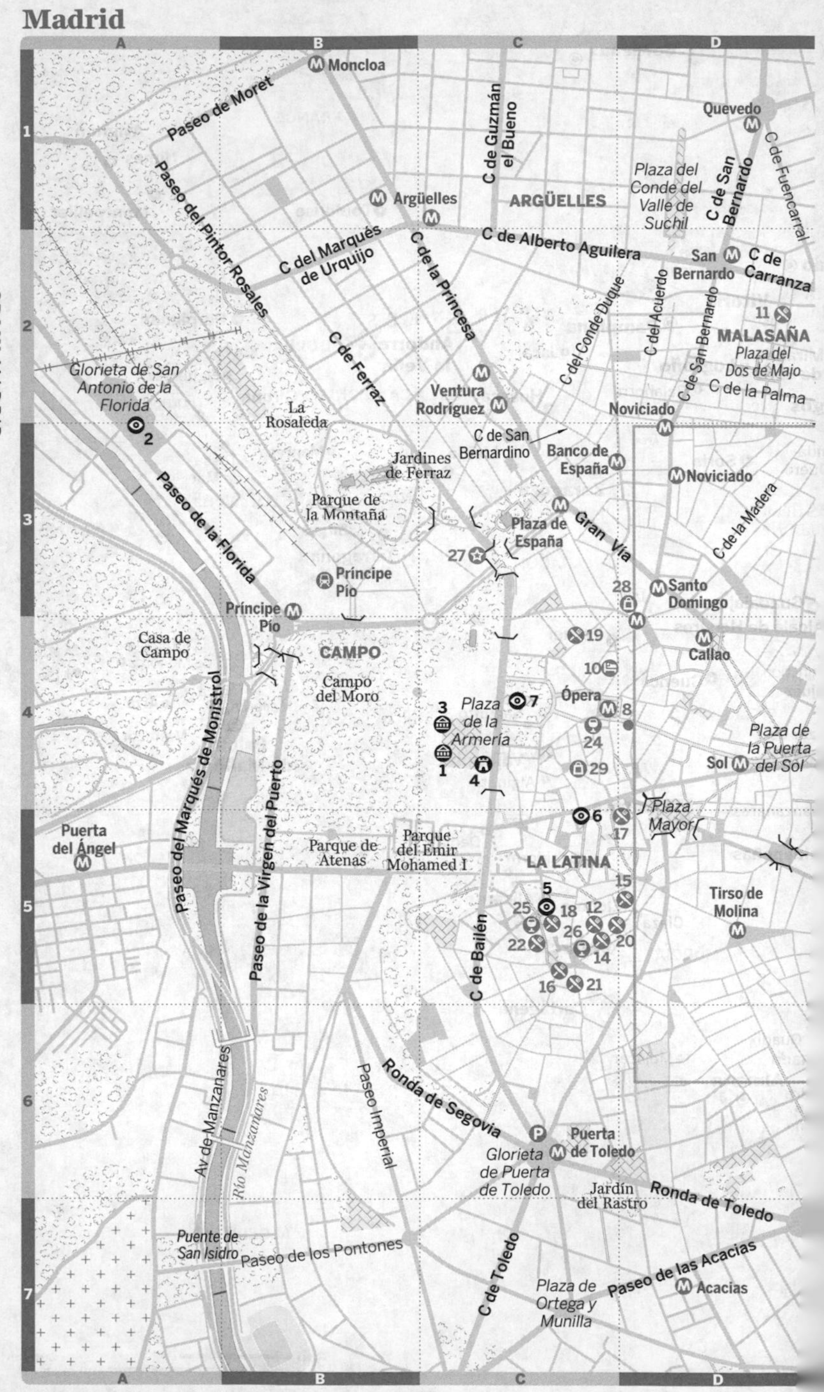
A
B
C
D
1
2
3
4
5
6
7
Moncloa
Paseo de Moret
C de Guzmán el Bueno
Quevedo
C de Fuencarral
Paseo del Pintor Rosales
Argüelles
ARGÜELLES
Plaza del Conde del Valle de Suchil
C de San Bernardo
C del Marqués de Urquijo
C de la Princesa
C de Alberto Aguilera
San Bernardo
C de Carranza
C del Conde Duque
C del Acuerdo
C de San Bernardo
11
MALASAÑA
Plaza del Dos de Majo
C de la Palma
Glorieta de San Antonio de la Florida
C de Ferraz
Ventura Rodríguez
Noviciado
La Rosaleda
2
C de San Bernardino
Banco de España
Noviciado
Jardines de Ferraz
Paseo de la Florida
Parque de la Montaña
Plaza de España
Gran Vía
C de la Madera
27
Príncipe Pío
28
Santo Domingo
Príncipe Pío
Casa de Campo
CAMPO
19
Callao
10
Campo del Moro
Plaza de la Armería
7
Ópera
8
3
24
Plaza de la Puerta del Sol
1
4
29
Sol
Paseo del Marqués de Monistrol
Paseo de la Virgen del Puerto
6
Plaza Mayor
17
Puerta del Ángel
Parque de Atenas
Parque del Emir Mohamed I
LA LATINA
15
5
25
18
12
Tirso de Molina
22
26
20
14
C de Bailén
16
21
Av de Manzanares
Río Manzanares
Paseo Imperial
Ronda de Segovia
Puerta de Toledo
Glorieta de Puerta de Toledo
Jardín del Rastro
Ronda de Toledo
Puente de San Isidro
Paseo de los Pontones
C de Toledo
Plaza de Ortega y Munilla
Paseo de las Acacias
Acacias

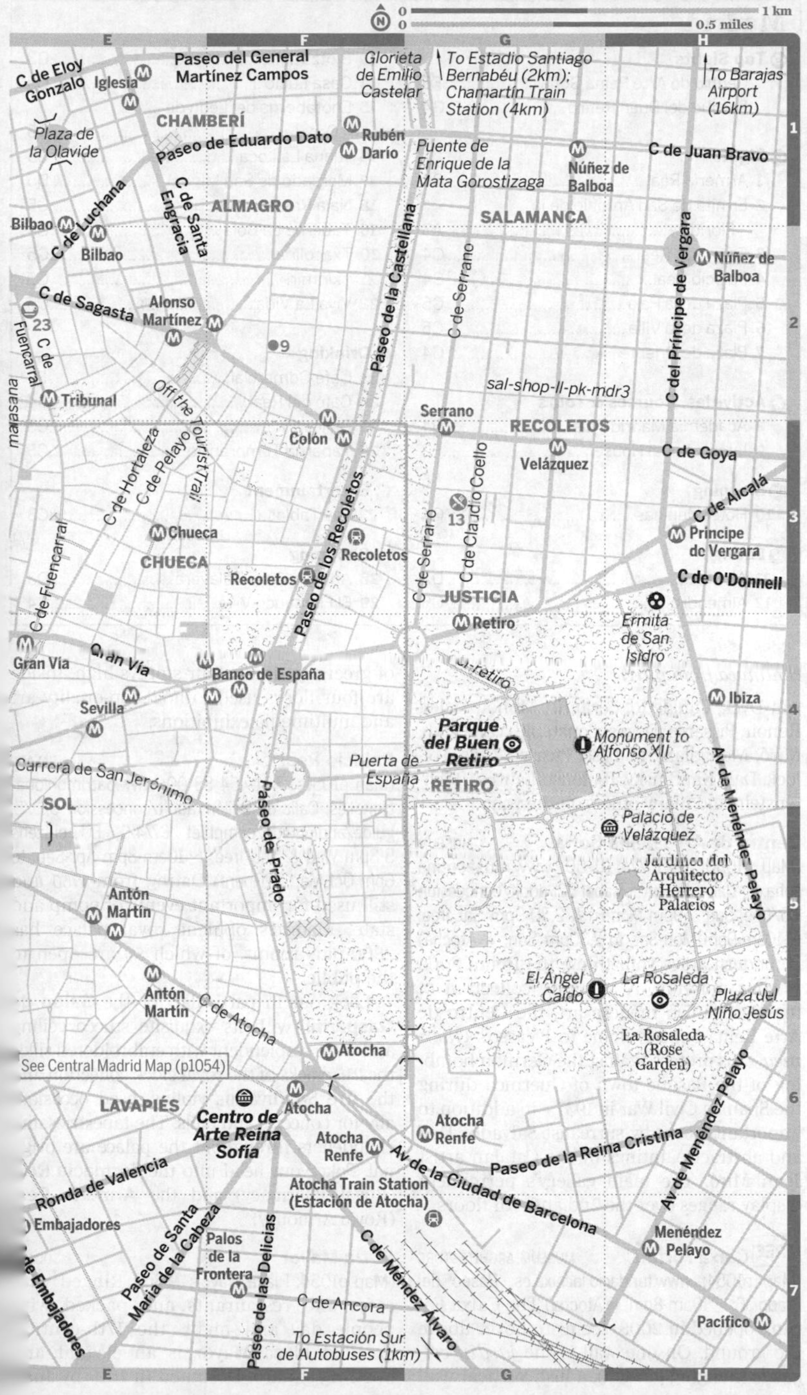
0 1 km
0 0.5 miles
E
F
G
H
1
2
3
4
5
6
7
C de Eloy Gonzalo
Iglesia
Paseo del General Martínez Campos
Glorieta de Emilio Castelar
To Estadio Santiago Bernabéu (2km); Chamartín Train Station (4km)
To Barajas Airport (16km)
CHAMBERÍ
Plaza de la Olavide
Paseo de Eduardo Dato
Rubén Darío
Puente de Enrique de la Mata Gorostizaga
Núñez de Balboa
C de Juan Bravo
C de Santa Engracia
ALMAGRO
SALAMANCA
Bilbao
C de Luchana
Paseo de la Castellana
C de Serrano
C del Príncipe de Vergara
Núñez de Balboa
C de Sagasta
Alonso Martínez
23
C de Fuencarral
9
sal-shop-ll-pk-mdr3
Tribunal
Off the Tourist Trail
Serrano
RECOLETOS
Colón
Velázquez
C de Goya
C de Hortaleza
C de Pelayo
Paseo de los Recoletos
C de Claudio Coello
13
C de Alcalá
Chueca
Recoletos
Príncipe de Vergara
CHUECA
C de Serrano
C de O'Donnell
C de Fuencarral
Recoletos
JUSTICIA
Retiro
Ermita de San Isidro
Gran Vía
Gran Vía
Banco de España
Ibiza
Sevilla
Parque del Buen Retiro
Monument to Alfonso XII
Puerta de España
RETIRO
Carrera de San Jerónimo
SOL
Paseo de Prado
Av de Menéndez Pelayo
Palacio de Velázquez
Jardines del Arquitecto Herrero Palacios
Antón Martín
Antón Martín
C de Atocha
El Ángel Caído
La Rosaleda
Plaza del Niño Jesús
La Rosaleda (Rose Garden)
Atocha
See Central Madrid Map (p1054)
LAVAPIÉS
Atocha
Centro de Arte Reina Sofía
Atocha Renfe
Atocha Renfe
Av de Menéndez Pelayo
Paseo de la Reina Cristina
Ronda de Valencia
Atocha Train Station (Estación de Atocha)
Av de la Ciudad de Barcelona
Embajadores
Paseo de Santa María de la Cabeza
Palos de la Frontera
Paseo de las Delicias
C de Méndez Álvaro
Menéndez Pelayo
C de Embajadores
C de Ancora
To Estación Sur de Autobuses (1km)
Pacífico

Madrid

Top Sights

- Centro de Arte Reina Sofía ... F6
- Parque del Buen Retiro ... G4

Sights

1 Armería Real ... C4
2 Ermita de San Antonio de la Florida ... A3
3 Farmacia Real ... C4
4 Palacio Real ... C4
5 Plaza de la Paja ... C5
6 Plaza de la Villa ... C5
7 Plaza de Oriente ... C4

Activities, Courses & Tours

8 Academia Madrid Plus ... D4
9 International House ... F2

Sleeping

10 Hotel Meninas ... C4

Eating

11 Albur ... D2
12 Almendro 13 ... C5
13 Biotza ... G3
14 Casa Lucio ... C5
15 Enotaberna del León de Oro ... D5
16 Juana La Loca ... C5
17 Mercado de San Miguel ... D5
18 Naïa Restaurante ... C5
19 Taberna La Bola ... C4
20 Txacolina ... C5
21 Txirimiri ... C5
22 Viva La Vida ... C5

Drinking

23 Café Comercial ... E2
24 Café del Real ... C4
25 Delic ... C5
26 Taberna Tempranillo ... C5

Entertainment

27 Las Tablas ... C3

Shopping

28 Antigua Casa Talavera ... D3
29 El Flamenco Vive ... C4

continued from p1047

van Dyck, Canaletto, Cézanne, Monet, Sisley, Renoir, Pissarro, Degas, Constable, Van Gogh, Miró, Modigliani, Matisse, Picasso, Gris, Pollock, Dalí, Kandinsky, Toulouse-Lautrec, Lichtenstein and many others on the way.

Centro de Arte Reina Sofía MUSEUM

(Map p1050; 91 774 10 00; www.museoreinasofia.es; Calle de Santa Isabel 52; adult/concession €6/free, Sun, 7-9pm Mon-Fri & 2.30-9pm Sat free; 10am-9pm Mon-Sat, to 2.30pm Sun; M Atocha) If modern art is your thing, the Reina Sofía is your museum. A stunning collection of mainly Spanish modern art, the Centro de Arte Reina Sofía is home to Picasso's *Guernica* – his protest against the German bombing of the Basque town of Guernica during the Spanish Civil War in 1937 – in addition to important works by surrealist Salvador Dalí and abstract paintings by the Catalan artist Joan Miró. The main gallery's permanent display ranges over the 2nd and 4th floors.

FREE **Caixa Forum** MUSEUM, ARCHITECTURE

(Map p1054; www.fundacio.lacaixa.es; Paseo del Prado 36; 10am-8pm; M Atocha) The Caixa Forum, opened in 2008, seems to hover above the ground. On one wall is the *jardín colgante* (hanging garden), a lush vertical wall of greenery almost four storeys high. Inside are four floors used to hold top-quality art and multimedia exhibitions.

Palacio Real PALACE

(Map p1050; 91 454 88 00; www.patrimonionacional.es; Calle de Bailén; adult/concession €10/5, guide/audioguide/pamphlet €7/4/1, EU citizens 5-8pm Wed & Thu free; 10am-8pm Apr-Sep, to 6pm Oct-Mar; M Ópera) Dating from 1755 and still used for important events of pomp and state, Madrid's opulent royal palace has 2800-plus rooms, of which 50 are open to the public.

Look out in particular for the **Salón de Gasparini**, with its exquisite stucco ceiling and walls resplendent with embroidered silks, the 215 clocks of the royal clock collection and the five Stradivarius violins, used occasionally for concerts and balls. The tapestries and chandeliers throughout the palace are original. Poke your head into the **Farmacia Real** (Royal Pharmacy) and the **Armería Real** (Royal Armoury).

Plaza Mayor SQUA[RE]

(Map p1054; Plaza Mayor; M Sol) Ringed with cafes and restaurants and packed with people day and night, the 17th-century arcaded Plaza Mayor is an elegant and bustling square. Designed in 1619 by Ju[an]

Gómez de Mora, the plaza hosted bullfights watched by 50,000 spectators (until 1878), while the *autos-da-fé* (the ritual condemnation of heretics) of the Spanish Inquisition also took place here. Fire largely destroyed the square in 1790, but it was rebuilt and became an important market and hub of city life. Today, the ochre-tinted apartments with wrought-iron balconies are offset by the exquisite frescos of the 17th-century **Real Casa de la Panadería** (Royal Bakery); the frescos were added in 1992.

Parque del Buen Retiro GARDENS

(Map p1050; ⏰6am-midnight May-Sep, to 11pm Oct-Apr; MRetiro, Príncipe de Vergara, Ibiza, Atocha) The splendid gardens of El Retiro are scattered with marble monuments, landscaped lawns, the occasional elegant building and abundant greenery. It's quiet and contemplative during the week, but comes to life on weekends.

The focal point for so much of El Retiro's life is the artificial *estanque* (lake), which is watched over by the massive ornamental structure of the **Monument to Alfonso XII** on the east side of the lake, complete with marble lions. Hidden among the trees south of the lake, the late-19th-century **Palacio de Cristal**, a magnificent metal and glass structure that is arguably El Retiro's most beautiful architectural monuments, is now used for temporary exhibitions.

At the southern end of the park, near **La Rosaleda** (Rose Garden) with its more than 4000 roses, is a statue of **El Ángel Caído** (the Fallen Angel, aka Lucifer), one of the few statues to the devil anywhere in the world. It sits 666m above sea level.

In the northeastern corner of the park is the ruined **Ermita de San Isidro**, a small country chapel noteworthy as one of the few, albeit modest, examples of Romanesque architecture in Madrid.

FREE **Ermita de San Antonio de la Florida** ART

(Map p1050; Glorieta de San Antonio de la Florida 5; ⏰9.30am-8pm Tue-Fri, 10am-2pm Sat & Sun, hours vary Jul & Aug; MPríncipe Pío) The frescoed ceilings of the Ermita de San Antonio de la Florida are one of Madrid's most surprising secrets. In the southern of the two small chapels you can see Goya's work in its original setting, rendered in 1798. The painter is buried in front of the altar.

Courses

Academia Inhispania LANGUAGE

(Map p1054; ☎91 521 22 31; www.inhispania.com; Calle de la Montera 10-12; MSol)

Academia Madrid Plus LANGUAGE

(Map p1050; ☎91 548 11 16; www.madridplus.es; 6th fl, Calle del Arenal 21; MÓpera)

International House LANGUAGE

(Map p1050; ☎902 141517; www.ihmadrid.es; Calle de Zurbano 8; MAlonso Martínez)

Festivals & Events

Fiesta de San Isidro CULTURAL

(www.esmadrid.com/sanisidro) Around 15 May Madrid's patron saint is honoured with a week of nonstop processions, parties, bullfights and free concerts.

Suma Flamenca FLAMENCO

(www.madrid.org/sumaflamenca) A soul-filled flamenco festival that draws some of the biggest names in the genre in June.

Veranos de la Villa CULTURAL

(www.veranosdelavilla.esmadrid.com) Madrid's town hall stages a series of cultural events, shows and exhibitions throughout July and August, known as Summers in the City.

Sleeping

Madrid has high-quality accommodation across all price ranges. Where you decide to stay will play an important role in your experience of Madrid. Los Austrias, Sol and Centro put you in the heart of the busy downtown area, while La Latina (the best *barrio* – neighbourhood – for tapas), Lavapiés and Huertas (good for nightlife) are ideal for those who love Madrid nights and don't want to stagger too far to get back

MADRID'S BEST PLAZAS

Madrid has some lovely public squares, among the best are the following:

Plaza de Oriente (Map p1050; Plaza de Oriente; MÓpera)

Plaza de la Villa (Map p1050; Plaza de la Villa; MÓpera)

Plaza de la Paja (Map p1050)

Plaza de Santa Ana (Map p1054; Plaza de Santa Ana; MSevilla, Sol, Antón Martín)

Central Madrid

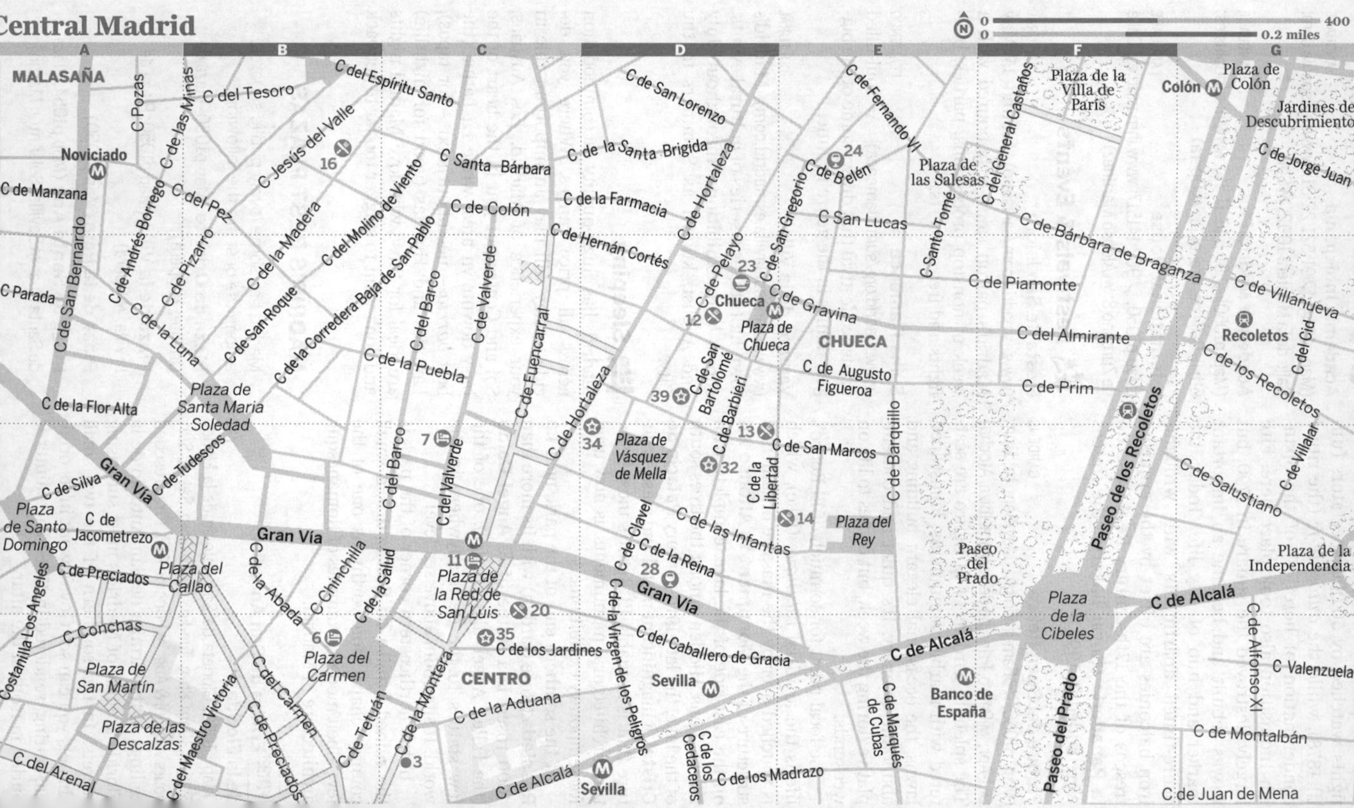

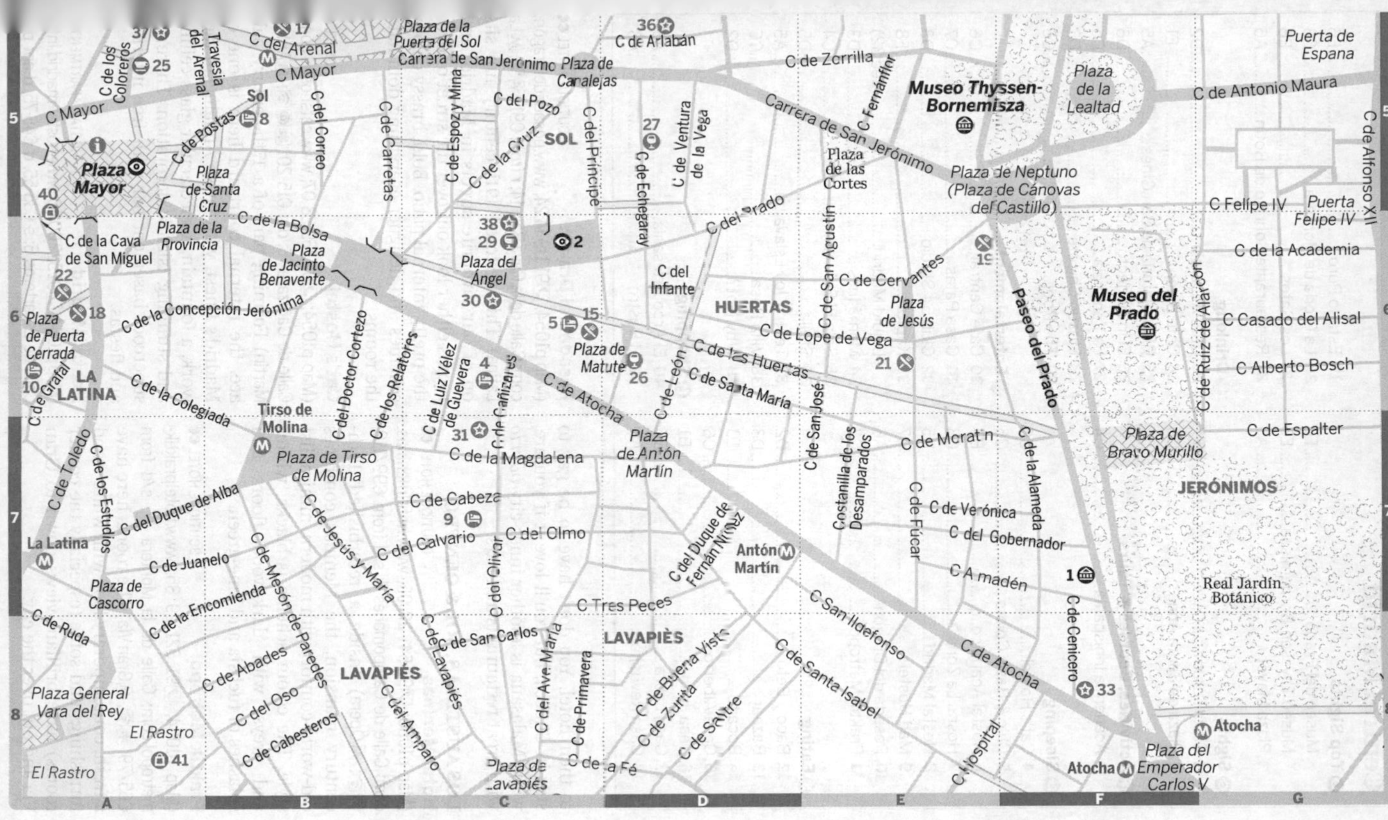
SPAIN MADRID
Museo del Prado
Museo Thyssen-Bornemisza
Paseo del Prado
Real Jardín Botánico
JERÓNIMOS
HUERTAS
SOL
LAVAPIÉS
LA LATINA
Plaza Mayor
Plaza de la Lealtad
Plaza de Neptuno (Plaza de Cánovas del Castillo)
Plaza de las Cortes
Plaza de Jesús
Plaza de Bravo Murillo
Plaza del Emperador Carlos V
Plaza de Santa Cruz
Plaza del Ángel
Plaza de Matute
Plaza de Antón Martín
Plaza de Tirso de Molina
Plaza de Jacinto Benavente
Plaza de la Provincia
Plaza de Canalejas
Plaza de la Puerta del Sol
Plaza de Puerta Cerrada
Plaza de Cascorro
Plaza General Vara del Rey
Plaza de Lavapiés
Puerta de Espana
Puerta Felipe IV
El Rastro
Atocha
Antón Martín
Tirso de Molina
La Latina
Sol
C de Alfonso XII
C de Antonio Maura
C Felipe IV
C de la Academia
C Casado del Alisal
C Alberto Bosch
C de Espalter
C de Ruiz de Alarcón
C de Zorrilla
C Fernánflor
Carrera de San Jerónimo
C de Cervantes
C de San Agustín
C de Lope de Vega
C de las Huertas
C de Santa María
C de León
C del Prado
C de Ventura de la Vega
C de Echegaray
C del Príncipe
C de Atocha
C de Moratín
C de la Alameda
C de Cenicero
C de Verónica
C del Gobernador
C Almadén
C de Fúcar
C Hospital
C San Ildefonso
C de Santa Isabel
Costanilla de los Desamparados
C de San José
C del Infante
C de Arlabán
C del Pozo
C de la Cruz
C de Espoz y Mina
C de Carretas
C del Correo
C del Arenal
C Mayor
Travesía del Arenal
C de Postas
C de los Coloreros
C de la Bolsa
C de la Concepción Jerónima
C de la Colegiata
C de Cañizares
C de Luiz Vélez de Guevara
C de los Relatores
C del Doctor Cortezo
C de la Magdalena
C del Duque de Fernán Núñez
C de Buena Vista
C de Zurita
C de Saltre
C de Primavera
C de la Fé
C del Ave María
C Tres Peces
C del Olmo
C del Olivar
C de Cabeza
C del Calvario
C de San Carlos
C de Lavapiés
C del Amparo
C de Jesús y María
C de Mesón de Paredes
C de la Encomienda
C de Abades
C del Oso
C de Cabesteros
C de Juanelo
C del Duque de Alba
C de los Estudios
C de Toledo
C de Ruda
C de la Cava de San Miguel
C de Grafal

Central Madrid

Top Sights
- Museo del Prado ... F6
- Museo Thyssen-Bornemisza ... E5
- Plaza Mayor ... A5

Sights
- 1 Caixa Forum ... F7
- 2 Plaza de Santa Ana ... C6

Activities, Courses & Tours
- 3 Academia Inhispania ... C4

Sleeping
- 4 Cat's Hostel ... C6
- 5 Chic & Basic Colors ... C6
- 6 Hostal Acapulco ... B4
- 7 Hostal La Zona ... C3
- 8 Hostal Madrid ... B5
- 9 Mad Hostel ... C7
- 10 Posada del Dragón ... A6
- 11 Praktik Metropol ... C3

Eating
- 12 Baco y Beto ... D2
- 13 Bazaar ... D3
- 14 Bocaito ... E3
- 15 Casa Alberto ... C6
- 16 Casa Julio ... B1
- 17 Casa Labra ... B5
- 18 Casa Revuelta ... A6
- 19 Estado Puro ... E6
- 20 La Gloria de Montera ... C3
- 21 Los Gatos ... E6
- 22 Restaurante Sobrino de Botín ... A6

Drinking
- 23 Café Acuarela ... D2
- 24 Café Belén ... E1
- 25 Chocolatería de San Ginés ... A5
- 26 El Imperfecto ... D6
- 27 La Venencia ... D5
- 28 Museo Chicote ... D3
- 29 The Roof ... C6

Entertainment
- 30 Café Central ... C6
- 31 Casa Patas ... C7
- 32 Club 54 Studio ... D3
- 33 Kapital ... F8
- Liquid Madrid ... (see 32)
- 34 Mamá Inés ... D3
- 35 Sala El Sol ... C4
- 36 Stella ... D5
- 37 Teatro Joy Eslava ... A5
- 38 Villa Rosa ... C6
- 39 Why Not? ... D2

Shopping
- 40 El Arco Artesanía ... A5
- 41 El Rastro ... A8

to their hotel. You don't have to be gay to stay in Chueca, but you'll love it if you are, while Malasaña is another inner-city *barrio* with great restaurants and bars.

LOS AUSTRIAS, SOL & CENTRO

Hotel Meninas BOUTIQUE HOTEL €€

(Map p1050; ☎91 541 28 05; www.hotelmeninas.com; Calle de Campomanes 7; s/d from €99/119; ❄📶; Ⓜ Ópera) Inside a refurbished 19th-century mansion, the Meninas combines old-world comfort with modern, minimalist style. The colour scheme is blacks, whites and greys, with dark-wood floors and splashes of fuchsia and lime-green.

Praktik Metropol BOUTIQUE HOTEL €€

(Map p1054; ☎91 521 29 35; www.hotelpraktikmetropol.com; Calle de la Montera 47; s/d from €65/79; ❄📶; Ⓜ Gran Vía) The rooms here have a fresh, contemporary look with white wood furnishings and some (especially the corner rooms) have brilliant views down to Gran Vía and out over the city.

Posada del Dragón BOUTIQUE HOTEL €€

(Map p1054; ☎91 119 14 24; www.posadadeldragon.com; Calle de la Cava Baja 14; r from €91; ❄📶; Ⓜ La Latina) This restored 19th-century inn sits on of our favourite streets in Madrid, and rooms either look out over the street or over the pretty internal patio. Bold, brassy colour schemes and designer everything dominate the rooms.

Cat's Hostel HOSTEL €

(Map p1054; ☎91 369 28 07; www.catshostel.com; Calle de Cañizares 6; dm €15-20; ❄@📶; Ⓜ Antón Martín) Forming part of a 17th-century palace, the internal courtyard here is one of Madrid's finest, with lavish Andalucian tilework, a fountain, a spectacular glass ceiling and stunning Islamic decoration. There's a supercool basement bar with free internet and fiestas.

Hostal Madrid HOSTAL, APARTMENT

(Map p1054; ☎91 522 00 60; www.hostal-madrid.info; Calle de Esparteros 6; s €35-55, d €45-75, d apt p night €55-150, per month €1200-2500; ❄📶; Ⓜ Sol) The 24 rooms at this well-run *hostal* (budget hotel) have been wonderfully renovated with exposed brickwork, brand-new bathrooms and a look that puts many three-star hotels to shame. They also have terrific apartments (www.apartamentosmayorcentro.com).

Mad Hostel HOSTEL €
(Map p1054; ☎91 506 48 40; www.madhostel.com; Calle de la Cabeza 24; dm €17-23; ❄@📶; Ⓜ Antón Martín) From the people who brought you Cat's Hostel, Mad Hostel is similarly filled with life. The 1st-floor courtyard – with retractable roof – recreates an old Madrid *corrala* and is a wonderful place to chill, while the four- to eight-bed rooms are smallish but clean.

HUERTAS & ATOCHA

Chic & Basic Colors HOTEL €
(Map p1054; ☎91 429 69 35; www.chicandbasic.com; Calle de las Huertas 14, 2nd fl; r €50-75; ❄📶; Ⓜ Antón Martín) The rooms are white in a minimalist style with flat-screen TVs and dark hardwood floors with a bright colour scheme superimposed on top, with every room a different shade. It's all very comfortable, contemporary and casual.

MALASAÑA & CHUECA

Hostal Acapulco HOSTAL €
(Map p1054; ☎91 531 19 45; www.hostalacapulco.com; Calle de la Salud 13, 4th fl; s/d €55/65; ❄📶; Ⓜ Gran Vía, Callao) A cut above many other *hostales* in Madrid, this immaculate little place has marble floors, recently renovated bathrooms (with bathtubs), double-glazed windows and comfortable beds. Street-facing rooms have balconies overlooking a sunny plaza and are flooded with natural light.

Hostal La Zona HOSTAL €
(Map p1054; ☎91 521 99 04; www.hostallazona.com; Calle de Valverde 7, 1st fl; s/d incl breakfast €50/70; ❄📶; Ⓜ Gran Vía) Catering primarily to a gay clientele, the stylish Hostal La Zona has exposed brickwork, wooden pillars and a subtle colours cheme. Other highlights include free internet, helpful staff and air-conditioning/heating in every room.

Eating

LOS AUSTRIAS, SOL & CENTRO

Mercado de San Miguel TAPAS €
(Map p1050; www.mercadodesanmiguel.es; Plaza de San Miguel; tapas from €1; ⏲10am-midnight Mon-Wed, to 2am Thu-Sat; Ⓜ Sol) One of Madrid's oldest and most beautiful markets, the overhauled Mercado de San Miguel now bills itself as a 'culinary cultural centre'. Within the early-20th-century glass walls, the market has become an inviting space strewn with tables (difficult to nab) where you can enjoy the freshest food or a drink. You can order tapas at most of the counter-bars.

Restaurante Sobrino de Botín CASTILIAN €€€
(Map p1054; ☎91 366 42 17; www.botin.es; Calle de los Cuchilleros 17; mains €18.50-28; Ⓜ La Latina, Sol) It's not every day that you can eat in the oldest restaurant in the world (1725), which also appears in many novels about Madrid, most notably Hemingway's *The Sun Also Rises*. The secret of its staying power is fine *cochinillo* (suckling pig) and *cordero asado* (roast lamb) cooked in wood-fired ovens. Eating in the vaulted cellar is a treat.

La Gloria de Montera SPANISH €
(Map p1054; www.lagloriademontera.com; Calle del Caballero de Gracia 10; mains €7-10; Ⓜ Gran Vía) Minimalist style, tasty Mediterranean dishes and great prices mean that you'll probably have to wait in line (no reservations taken) to eat here.

Taberna La Bola MADRILEÑO €€
(Map p1050; ☎91 547 69 30; www.labola.es; Calle de la Bola 5; mains €16-24; ⏲lunch & dinner Mon-Sat, lunch Sun, closed Aug; Ⓜ Santo Domingo) Taberna La Bola (going strong since 1870 and run by the sixth generation of the Verdasco family) is known for its traditional local cuisine. If you're going to try *cocido a la madrileña* while in Madrid, this is a good place to do so.

LA LATINA & LAVAPIÉS

Enotaberna del León de Oro SPANISH €€
(Map p1050; ☎91 119 14 94; www.posadadelleondeoro.com; Calle de la Cava Baja 12; mains €13-15; ⏲lunch & dinner daily; Ⓜ La Latina) At this fine new bar-restaurant the emphasis is on matching carefully chosen wines with creative dishes in a casual atmosphere. It's a winning combination.

Viva La Vida VEGETARIAN €
(Map p1050; www.vivalavida.com.es; Costanilla de San Andrés 16 ; buffet 500g plus drink €10; ⏲noon-midnight Mon-Wed, 11am-2am Thu-Sun; 🌿; Ⓜ La Latina) This organic food shop has as its centrepiece an appealing vegetarian buffet with hot and cold food that's always filled with flavour. On the cusp of Plaza de la Paja,

A TAPAS TOUR OF MADRID

Madrid's home of tapas is La Latina, especially along Calle de la Cava Baja and the surrounding streets. **Almendro 13** (Map p1050; ☎91 365 42 52; Calle del Almendro 13; mains €7-15; ⏱12.30-4pm & 7.30pm-midnight Sun-Thu, 12.30-5pm & 8pm-1am Fri & Sat; Ⓜ La Latina) is famous for quality rather than frilly elaborations, with cured meats, cheeses, tortillas and *huevos rotos* (literally, 'broken eggs') the house specialities. Down on Calle de la Cava Baja, **Txacolina** (Map p1050; ☎91 366 48 77; Calle de la Cava Baja 26; tapas from €3; ⏱dinner Mon & Wed-Fri, lunch & dinner Sat, lunch Sun; Ⓜ La Latina) does some of the biggest *pintxos* (Basque tapas) you'll find. Not far away, **Juanalaloca** (Map p1050; ☎91 364 05 25; Plaza de la Puerta de Moros 4; tapas from €4, mains €8-19; ⏱lunch & dinner Tue-Sun, dinner Mon; Ⓜ La Latina) does a magnificent *tortilla de patatas* (potato and onion omelette). **Txirimiri** (Map p1050; ☎91 364 11 96; www.txirimiri.es; Calle del Humilladero 6; tapas from €4; ⏱lunch & dinner Mon-Sat, closed Aug; Ⓜ La Latina) is also outstanding.

In the centre, for *bacalao* (cod) the historic **Casa Labra** (Map p1054; ☎91 532 14 05; www.casalabra.es; Calle de Tetuán 11; tapas from €1; ⏱9.30am-3.30pm & 5.30-11pm; Ⓜ Sol) and **Casa Revuelta** (Map p1054; ☎91 366 33 32; Calle de Latoneros 3; tapas from €2.60; ⏱10.30am-4pm & 7-11pm Tue-Sat, 10.30am-4pm Sun, closed Aug; Ⓜ Sol, La Latina) have no peers.

Down the bottom of the Huertas hill, **Los Gatos** (Map p1054; ☎91 429 30 67; Calle de Jesús 2; tapas from €3.50; ⏱noon-1am Sun-Thu, to 2am Fri & Sat; Ⓜ Antón Martín) has eclectic decor and terrific canapés. Nearby, along the Paseo del Prado, there's super-cool **Estado Puro** (Map p1054; ☎91 330 24 00; www.tapasenestadopuro.com; Plaza de Cánovas del Castillo 4; tapas €5-12.50; ⏱11am-1am Tue-Sat, to 4pm Sun; Ⓜ Banco de España, Atocha) with gourmet tapas inspired by Catalonia's world-famous (but now closed) El Bulli restaurant. In Salamanca, **Biotza** (Map p1050; www.biotzarestaurante.com; Calle de Claudio Coello 27; tapas €2.50-3.50; ⏱9am-midnight Mon-Thu, to 1am Fri & Sat; Ⓜ Serrano) offers creative Basque *pintxos* in stylish surrounds.

Chueca is another stellar tapas *barrio*. Don't miss **Bocaito** (Map p1054; ☎91 532 12 19; www.bocaito.com; Calle de la Libertad 4-6; tapas from €3.50, mains €12-20; ⏱lunch & dinner Mon-Fri, dinner Sat; Ⓜ Chueca, Sevilla), another purveyor of Andalucian *jamón* (ham) and seafood. **Casa Julio** (Map p1054; ☎91 522 72 74; Calle de la Madera 37; 6/12 croquetas €5/10; ⏱lunch & dinner Mon-Sat; Ⓜ Tribunal) is widely touted as the home of Madrid's best *croquetas* (croquettes). Another brilliant choice is **Baco y Beto** (Map p1054; ☎91 522 84 81; Calle de Pelayo 24; tapas from €4; ⏱dinner Mon-Fri, lunch & dinner Sat; Ⓜ Chueca).

it's a great place at any time of the day, especially outside normal Spanish eating hours.

Casa Lucio SPANISH €€
(Map p1050; ☎91 365 32 52; www.casalucio.es; Calle de la Cava Baja 35; mains €12-25; ⏱lunch & dinner Sun-Fri, dinner Sat, closed Aug; Ⓜ La Latina) Lucio has been wowing *madrileños* with his light touch, quality ingredients and home-style local cooking for ages – think seafood, roasted meats and eggs (a Lucio speciality) in abundance.

Naïa Restaurante FUSION €€
(Map p1050; ☎91 366 27 83; Plaza de la Paja 3; mains €12-19; ⏱lunch & dinner Tue-Sun; Ⓜ La Latina) On the lovely Plaza de la Paja, Naïa has a real buzz about it, with modern Spanish cuisine, a chill-out lounge downstairs, and a cooking laboratory overseen by Carlos López Reyes.

HUERTAS & ATOCHA

Casa Alberto SPANISH, TAPAS €€
(Map p1054; ☎91 429 93 56; www.casaalberto.es; Calle de las Huertas 18; mains €16-20; ⏱lunch & dinner Tue-Sat, lunch Sun; Ⓜ Antón Martín) One of the most atmospheric old *tabernas* (taverns) of Madrid, Casa Alberto has been around since 1827. The secret to its staying power is vermouth on tap, excellent tapas at the bar and fine sit-down meals; Casa Alberto's *rabo de toro* (bull's tail) is famous among aficionados. For tapas, *jamón,* Manchego cheese and *croquetas* are recurring themes.

MALASAÑA & CHUECA

Bazaar CONTEMPORARY SPANISH
(Map p1054; www.restaurantbazaar.com; Calle de la Libertad 21; mains €6.50-10; ⏱lunch & dinner; Ⓜ Chueca) Bazaar's popularity among th

well-heeled and often-famous shows no sign of abating. Its pristine white interior design with theatre lighting may draw a crowd that looks like it stepped out of the pages of *Hola!* magazine, but the food is extremely well priced and innovative. It doesn't take reservations so be prepared to wait whether you're famous or not.

Albur TAPAS, SPANISH **€€**

(Map p1050; ☎91 594 27 33; www.restaurantealbur.com; Calle de Manuela Malasaña 15; mains €13-18; ⊙noon-1am Sun-Thu, to 2am Fri & Sat; Ⓜ Bilbao) One of Malasaña's best deals, this place has a wildly popular tapas bar and a classy but casual restaurant out the back. Albur is known for terrific rice dishes and tapas, and has a well-chosen wine list.

Drinking

The essence of Madrid lives in its streets and plazas, and bar-hopping is a pastime enjoyed by young and old alike. If you're after the more traditional, with tiled walls and flamenco tunes, head to Huertas. For gay-friendly drinking holes, Chueca is the place. Malasaña caters to a grungy, funky crowd, while La Latina has friendly bars that guarantee atmosphere most nights of the week. In summer, the terrace bars that pop up all over the city are unbeatable.

The bulk of Madrid bars open to 2am Sunday to Thursday and to 3am or 3.30am Friday and Saturday.

La Venencia BAR

(Map p1054; Calle de Echegaray 7; ⊙1-3.30pm & 7.30pm-1.30am; Ⓜ Sol, Sevilla) La Venencia is a *barrio* classic, with fine sherry from Sanlúcar and manzanilla from Jeréz poured straight from the dusty barrel, accompanied by a small selection of tapas with an Andalucian bent. As one reviewer put it, it's 'a classic among classics'.

Museo Chicote COCKTAIL BAR

(Map p1054; www.museo-chicote.com; Gran Vía 12; ⊙6pm-3am Mon-Thu, to 4am Fri & Sat; Ⓜ Gran Vía) The founder of this Madrid landmark is said to have invented more than a hundred cocktails, which the likes of Hemingway, Ava Gardner, Grace Kelly, Sophia Loren and Frank Sinatra all enjoyed at one time or another. It's at its best after midnight when a lounge atmosphere takes over, couples cuddle on the curved benches and some of the city's best DJs do their stuff.

Café Comercial CAFE

(Map p1050; Glorieta de Bilbao 7; ⊙7.30am-midnight Mon-Thu, 7.30am-2am Fri, 8.30am-2am Sat, 9am-midnight Sun; Ⓜ Bilbao) This glorious old Madrid cafe proudly fights a rearguard action against progress with heavy leather seats, abundant marble and old-style waiters. As close as Madrid came to the intellectual cafes of Paris' Left Bank, Café Comercial now has a clientele that has broadened to include just about anyone.

Café del Real BAR, CAFE

(Map p1050; Plaza de Isabel II 2; ⊙9am-1am Mon-Thu, to 3am Fri & Sat; Ⓜ Ópera) A cafe and cocktail bar in equal parts, this intimate little place serves up creative coffees and a few cocktails to the soundtrack of chill-out music. The best seats are upstairs, where the low ceilings, wooden beams and leather chairs are a great place to pass an afternoon with friends.

Delic BAR, CAFE

(Map p1050; www.delic.es; Costanilla de San Andrés 14; ⊙11am-2am Tue-Sun, 7pm-2am Mon; Ⓜ La Latina) We could go on for hours about this long-standing cafe-bar, but we'll reduce it to its most basic elements: nursing an exceptionally good mojito (€8) or three on a warm summer's evening at Delic's outdoor tables on one of Madrid's prettiest plazas is one of life's great pleasures.

Taberna Tempranillo WINE BAR

(Map p1050; Calle de la Cava Baja 38; ⊙1-3.30pm & 8pm-midnight Tue-Sun, 8pm-midnight Mon; Ⓜ La Latina) You could come here for the tapas, but we recommend Taberna Tempranillo primarily for its wines, of which it has a selection that puts many Spanish bars to shame, and many are sold by the glass.

The Roof COCKTAIL BAR

(Map p1054; ☎91 701 60 20; www.memadrid.com/the-roof; Plaza de Santa Ana 14; admission €25;

MADRID'S FAVOURITE POST-CLUBBING MUNCHIES

Join the sugar-searching throngs who end the night at **Chocolatería de San Ginés** (Map p1054; Pasadizo de San Ginés 5; ⊙9.30am-7am; Ⓜ Sol), a legendary bar, famous for its freshly fried *churros* (fried sticks of dough) and syrupy hot chocolate.

9pm-3am Wed & Thu, to 3.30am Fri & Sat; MAntón Martín, Sol) High above the Plaza de Santa Ana, this sybaritic open-air (7th floor) cocktail bar has terrific views over Madrid's rooftops. The high admission price announces that riff-raff are not welcome and it's a place for sophisticates, with chill-out areas strewn with cushions, funky DJs and a dress policy designed to sort out the classy from the wannabes.

El Imperfecto COCKTAIL BAR
(Map p1054; Plaza de Matute 2; 3pm-2am Mon-Thu, to 2.30am Fri & Sat; MAntón Martín) Its name notwithstanding, the 'Imperfect One' is our ideal Huertas bar, with live jazz most Tuesdays at 9pm and a drinks menu as long as a saxophone, ranging from cocktails (€7) and spirits to milkshakes, teas and creative coffees.

Café Belén BAR
(Map p1054; Calle de Belén 5; 3.30pm-3am; MChueca) Café Belén is cool in all the right places – lounge and chill-out music, dim lighting, a great range of drinks (theare especially good) and a low-key crowd that's the height of casual sophistication.

☆ Entertainment

The **Guía del Ocio** (www.guiadelocio.com) is the city's classic weekly listings magazine. Also good are **Metropoli** (www.elmundo.es/metropoli) and **On Madrid** (www.elpais.com), respectively *ABC's* and *El País'* Friday listings supplements.

Nightclubs

Don't expect dance clubs or *discotecas* (nightclubs) to get going until after 1am at the earliest. Standard entry fee is €12, which usually includes the first drink, although megaclubs and swankier places charge a few euros more.

Teatro Joy Eslava CLUB
(Joy Madrid; Map p1054; 91 366 37 33; www.joy-eslava.com; Calle del Arenal 11; admission €12-15; 11.30pm-6am; MSol) The only things guaranteed at this grand old Madrid dance club (housed in a 19th-century theatre) are a crowd and the fact that it will be open; the club claims to have opened every single day for the past 30 years. Every night's a little different – throw in occasional live acts and cabaret-style performances on stage and it's a point of reference for Madrid's professional party crowd.

Kapital CLUB
(Map p1054; 91 420 29 06; www.grupo-kapital.com; Calle de Atocha 125; admission from €12; 5.30-10.30pm & midnight-6am Fri & Sat, midnight-6am Thu & Sun; MAtocha) One of the most famous megaclubs in Madrid, this massive seven-storey nightclub has something for everyone: from cocktail bars and dance music to karaoke, salsa, hip hop and more chilled spaces for R&B and soul, as well as an area devoted to 'Made in Spain' music. A cross-section of Madrid society (VIPs and the Real Madrid set love this place) hangs out here without ever getting in each other's way.

Stella CLUB
(Map p1054; 91 531 63 78; www.web-mondo.com; Calle de Arlabán 7; admission €12; 12.30-6am Thu-Sat; MSevilla) One of Madrid's enduring success stories, Stella is one of the city's best nightclubs. If you arrive here after 3am, there simply won't be room and those inside have no intention of leaving until dawn. The DJs here are some of Madrid's best and the great visuals will leave you cross-eyed if you weren't already from the music in this heady place.

GAY & LESBIAN MADRID

The heartbeat of gay Madrid is the inner-city *barrio* of Chueca, where Madrid didn't just come out of the closet, but ripped the doors off in the process.

A good place to get the low-down is the laid-back **Mamá Inés** (Map p1054; www.mamaines.com; Calle de Hortaleza 22; 10am-2pm Sun-Thu, to 3am Fri & Sat; MGran Vía, Chueca). **Café Acuarela** (Map p1054; www.cafeacuarela.es; Calle de Gravina 10; 11am-2am Sun-Thu, to 3am Fri & Sat; MChueca) is another dimly lit centrepiece of gay Madrid.

Two of the most popular Chueca nightspots are **Club 54 Studio** (Map p1054; www.studio54madrid.com; Calle de Barbieri 7; 11.30am-3.30am Wed-Sat; MChueca), modelled on the famous New York club Studio 54, and **Liquid Madrid** (Map p1054; www.liquid.es; Calle de Barbieri 7; 9pm-3am Mon-Thu, to 3.30am Fri & Sat; MChueca). **Why Not?** (Map p1054; www.whynotmadrid.com; Calle de San Bartolomé 7; admission €10; 10.30pm-6am; MChueca) is the sort of place where nothing's left to the imagination.

Flamenco

Las Tablas FLAMENCO
(Map p1050; ☎91 542 05 20; www.lastablasmadrid.com; Plaza de España 9; admission €27; ⏲shows 10.30pm Sun-Thu, 8pm & 10pm Fri & Sat; Ⓜ Plaza de España) Las Tablas has a reputation for quality flamenco and reasonable prices; it could just be the best choice in town. Antonia Moya and Marisol Navarro, leading lights in the flamenco world, are regular performers here.

Casa Patas FLAMENCO
(Map p1054; ☎91 369 04 96; www.casapatas.com; Calle de Cañizares 10; admission €32; ⏲shows 10.30pm Mon-Thu, 9pm & midnight Fri & Sat; Ⓜ Antón Martín, Tirso de Molina) One of the top flamenco stages in Madrid, this *tablao* (flamenco venue) always offers flawless quality that serves as a good introduction to the art. It's not the friendliest place in town, especially if you're only here for the show, and you're likely to be crammed in a little, but no one complains about the standard of the performances.

Villa Rosa FLAMENCO
(Map p1054; ☎91 521 36 89; www.villa-rosa.es; Plaza de Santa Ana 15; admission €17; ⏲shows 8.30pm & 10.45pm Sun-Thu, 8.30pm, 10.45pm & 12.15am Fri & Sat, 11pm-6am Mon-Sat; Ⓜ Sol) The extraordinary tiled facade appeared in the Pedro Almodóvar film *Tacones Lejanos* (High Heels, 1991). It's been going strong since 1914 and has seen many manifestations – it has recently returned to its flamenco roots with well-priced shows and meals that won't break the bank.

Jazz & Other Live Music

TOP CHOICE **Café Central** JAZZ
(Map p1054; ☎91 369 41 43; www.cafecentralmadrid.com; Plaza del Ángel 10; admission €10-15; ⏲1.30pm-2.30am Sun-Thu, to 3.30am Fri & Sat; Ⓜ Antón Martín, Sol) In 2011, the respected jazz magazine *DownBeat* included this art deco bar on the list of the world's best jazz clubs and with well over 9000 gigs under its belt, it rarely misses a beat. Performers usually play here for a week and then move on, so getting tickets shouldn't be a problem; shows start at 10pm and tickets go on sale an hour before the set starts.

TOP CHOICE **Sala El Sol** ROCK, SOUL
(Map p1054; ☎91 532 64 90; www.elsolmad.com; Calle de los Jardines 3; admission €8-25; ⏲11pm-5.30am Tue-Sat Jul-Sep; Ⓜ Gran Vía) Sala El Sol opened in 1979, just in time for *la movida madrileña*, and quickly established itself as a leading stage for all the icons of the era. *La movida* may have faded into history, but it lives on at El Sol, where the music rocks and rolls and usually resurrects the '70s and '80s, while soul and funk also get a run.

Sport

Estadio Santiago Bernabéu FOOTBALL
(☎91 398 43 00, 902 301709; www.realmadrid.com; Calle Concha Espina 1; ⏲10am-7.30pm Mon-Sat, 10.30am-6.30pm Sun, except match days; Ⓜ Santiago Bernabéu) The infamous Real Madrid plays at this stadium. Fans can visit the stadium and take an interesting tour through the presidential box, dressing room and field. The all-important telephone number for booking game tickets (which you later pick up at Gate 42) is ☎902 324324, which only works if you're calling from within Spain.

Shopping

El Rastro MARKET
(Map p1054; Calle de la Ribera de Curtidores; ⏲8am-3pm Sun; Ⓜ La Latina, Puerta de Toledo, Tirso de Molina) A Sunday morning at El Rastro, Europe's largest flea market, is a Madrid institution. You could easily spend an entire morning inching your way down the Calle de la Ribera de Curtidores and through the maze of streets that hosts El Rastro flea market every Sunday morning. A word of warning: pickpockets love El Rastro as much as everyone else.

Antigua Casa Talavera CERAMICS
(Map p1050; Calle de Isabel la Católica 2; ⏲10am-1.30pm & 5-8pm Mon-Fri, 10am-1.30pm Sat; Ⓜ Santo Domingo) The extraordinary tiled facade of this wonderful old shop conceals an Aladdin's cave of ceramics from all over Spain. This is not the mass-produced stuff aimed at a tourist market, but comes from the small family potters of Andalucía and Toledo.

El Arco Artesanía HANDICRAFTS
(Map p1054; www.artesaniaelarco.com; Plaza Mayor 9; ⏲11am-9pm; Ⓜ Sol, La Latina) This original shop in the southwestern corner of Plaza Mayor sells an outstanding array of home-made designer souvenirs, from stone and glass work to jewellery and home fittings. The papier mâché figures are gorgeous, but there's so much else here to turn your head.

El Flamenco Vive FLAMENCO
(Map p1050; www.elflamencovive.es; Calle Conde de Lemos 7; ⏲10.30am-2pm & 5-9pm Mon-Sat;

Ⓜ Ópera) This temple to flamenco has it all, from guitars and songbooks to well-priced CDs, polka-dotted dancing costumes, shoes, colourful plastic jewellery and literature about flamenco. It's the sort of place that will appeal as much to curious first-timers as to serious students of the art.

Information

Dangers & Annoyances

Madrid is a generally safe city although, as in most European cities, you should be wary of pickpockets in the city centre, on the metro and around major tourist sights.

Discount Cards

The **Madrid Card** (☎91 360 47 72; www.madridcard.com; 1/2/3 days adult €39/49/59, child age 6-12 €20/28/34) includes free entry to more than 40 museums in and around Madrid and discounts on public transport.

Emergency

Emergency (☎112)

Policía Nacional (☎091)

Servicio de Atención al Turista Extranjero (Foreign Tourist Assistance Service; ☎902 102 112, 91 548 85 37, 91 548 80 08; www.esmadrid.com/satemadrid; Calle de Leganitos 19; ⏲9am-10pm; Ⓜ Plaza de España, Santo Domingo) To report thefts or other crime-related matters, cancel your credit cards or contact your embassy, this is your best bet.

Internet Access

Café Comercial (Glorieta de Bilbao 7; per 50min €1; ⏲7.30am-midnight Mon-Thu, 7.30am-2am Fri, 8.30am-2am Sat, 9am-midnight Sun; Ⓜ Bilbao) One of Madrid's grandest old cafes, with internet upstairs.

Centro de Turismo de Madrid (www.esmadrid.com) Free 15-minute internet access, with more generous time limits (depending on demand) at the other tourist office underneath Plaza de Colón.

Medical Services

Farmacia Mayor (☎91 366 46 16; Calle Mayor 13; ⏲24hr; Ⓜ Sol)

Unidad Medica (Anglo American; ☎91 435 18 23; www.unidadmedica.com; Calle del Conde de Aranda 1; ⏲9am-8pm Mon-Fri, 10am-1pm Sat; Ⓜ Retiro) A private clinic with a wide range of specialisations and where all doctors speak Spanish and English, with some also speaking French and German. Each consultation costs around €125.

Tourist Information

Centro de Turismo de Madrid (Map p1054; ☎91 588 16 36; www.esmadrid.com; Plaza Mayor 27; ⏲9.30am-8.30pm; Ⓜ Sol) Excellent city tourist office with a smaller office underneath Plaza de Colón and information points at Plaza de la Cibeles, Plaza de Callao, outside the Centro de Arte Reina Sofía and at the T4 terminal at Barajas airport.

Comunidad de Madrid (www.turismomadrid.es)

Websites

Lonely Planet (www.lonelyplanet.com/hotels) For more reviews and bookings online.

Getting There & Away

Air

Madrid's international Barajas airport, 15km northeast of the city, is Europe's fourth- or fifth-busiest airport (depending on the year), with flights coming in from all over Europe and beyond.

Bus

Estación Sur de Autobuses (☎91 468 42 00; www.estaciondeautobuses.com; Calle de Méndez Álvaro 83; Ⓜ Méndez Álvaro), just south of the M-30 ring road, is the city's principal bus station. It serves most destinations to the south and many in other parts of the country. Major bus companies include the following:

ALSA (☎902 422242; www.alsa.es) One of the largest Spanish companies with many services throughout Spain. Most depart from Estación Sur but some buses headed north (including to Bilbao and Zaragoza, and some services to Barcelona) leave from the Intercambiador de Avenida de América with occasional services from T4 of Madrid's Barajas Airport.

Avanzabus (☎902 020052; www.avanzabus.com) Services to Extremadura (eg Cáceres), Castilla y León (eg Salamanca and Zamora) and Valencia via Cuenca, as well as Lisbon, Portugal. All leave from the Estación Sur.

Train

Madrid is served by two main train stations. The bigger of the two is **Puerta de Atocha** (Ⓜ Atocha Renfe), at the southern end of the city centre. **Chamartín train station** (Ⓜ Chamartín) lies in the north of the city. The bulk of trains for Spanish destinations depart from Atocha, especially those going south. International services arrive at and leave from Chamartín. For bookings, contact **Renfe** (☎902 240 202; www.renfe.es) at either station.

High-speed Tren de Alta Velocidad Española (AVE) services connect Madrid with Seville (via Córdoba), Valladolid (via Segovia), Toledo, Valencia (via Cuenca), Málaga and Barcelona (via Zaragoza and Tarragona).

WORTH A TRIP

ÁVILA

Just over an hour by train from Madrid, Ávila's old city, surrounded by imposing **Murallas** (adult/child €4/2.50; ⏲10am-8pm Tue-Sun) comprising eight monumental gates, 88 watchtowers and more than 2500 turrets, is one of the best-preserved medieval bastions in all of Spain. It's a perfect place to spend a day strolling narrow laneways and soaking up history. The city is also known as the birthplace of Santa Teresa, a mystical writer and reformer of the Carmelite order. Embedded into the eastern city walls, the splendid 12th-century **cathedral** (Plaza de la Catedral; admission €3; ⏲10am-2pm & 4-5pm Mon-Fri, 10am-2pm Sat) was the first Gothic-style church built in Spain. It boasts rich walnut choir stalls and a long, narrow central nave that makes the soaring ceilings seem all the more majestic. **Hotel El Rastro** (☎920 35 22 25; www.elrastroavila.com; Calle Cepedas; s/d €35/55; ❄📶) or **Hostal Arco San Vicente** (☎920 22 24 98; www.arcosan-vicente.com; Calle de López Núñez 6; s/d €40/65; ❄📶) are excellent places to stay. For more information, visit the **Centro de Recepción de Visitantes** (☎920 35 40 00, ext 790; www.avilaturismo.com; Avenida de Madrid 39; ⏲9am-8pm). More than 30 trains run daily to Madrid (from €6.80, 1¼ to two hours).

ℹ Getting Around

To/From the Airport

BUS The **Exprés Aeropuerto** (Airport Express; www.emtmadrid.es; tickets €5; ⏲24hr; 📶) bus runs between Puerta de Atocha train station and the airport. Buses run every 13 to 23 minutes from 6am to 11.30pm, and every 35 minutes throughout the rest of the night. The trip takes 40 minutes. From 11.55pm until 5.35am, departures are from the Plaza de Cibeles, not the train station.

METRO Line 8 of the metro (entrances in T2 and T4) runs to the Nuevos Ministerios transport interchange, which connects with lines 10 and 6. It operates from 6.05am to 2am. A one-way ticket to/from the airport costs €4.50. The journey from the airport to Nuevos Ministerios takes around 15 minutes, around 25 minutes from T4.

TAXI A taxi to the city centre will cost you around €25 in total (up to €35 from T4), depending on traffic and where you're going; in addition to what the meter reads, you pay a €5.50 airport supplement.

Public Transport

Madrid's **metro** (www.metromadrid.es) is extensive and well maintained. A single ride costs €1.50 and a 10-ride ticket is €12.20. The metro is quick, clean, relatively safe and runs from 6.05am until 2am.

Taxi

You can pick up a taxi at ranks throughout town or simply flag one down. Flag fall is €2.15 from 6am to 10pm daily, €2.20 from 10pm to 6am Sunday to Friday and €3.10 from 10pm Saturday to 6am Sunday. Several supplementary charges, usually posted inside the taxi, apply; these include €5.50 to/from the airport and €2.95 from taxi ranks at train and bus stations.

CASTILLA Y LEÓN

Salamanca

POP 153,470

Whether floodlit by night or bathed in midday sun, Salamanca is a dream destination. This is a city of rare architectural splendour, awash with golden sandstone overlaid with Latin inscriptions in ochre, and with an extraordinary virtuosity of plateresque and Renaissance styles. The monumental highlights are many, with the exceptional Plaza Mayor (illuminated to stunning effect at night) an unforgettable highlight. But this is also Castilla's liveliest city, home to a massive Spanish and international student population who throng the streets at night and provide the city with youth and vitality.

👁 Sights & Activities

Plaza Mayor SQUARE

Built between 1729 and 1755, Salamanca's exceptional grand square is widely considered to be Spain's most beautiful central plaza. The square is particularly memorable at night when illuminated (until midnight) to magical effect.

Catedral Nueva & Catedral Vieja CHURCHES

(www.catedralsalamanca.org) Curiously, Salamanca is home to two cathedrals: the newer and larger cathedral was built beside the old Romanesque one instead of on top of it, as was the norm. The **Catedral Nueva** (Plaza de Anaya; ⏲9am-8pm), completed in 1733, is a late-Gothic masterpiece that took 220 years to build. Its magnificent Renaissance doorways stand out. For fine views over Salamanca, head to the southwestern corner of the cathedral facade and the **Puerta de la Torre** (Jeronimus; Plaza de Juan XXIII; admission €3.75; ⏲10am-7.15pm), from where stairs lead up through the tower.

The largely Romanesque **Catedral Vieja** (Plaza de Anaya; admission €4.75; ⏲10am-7.30pm) is a 12th-century temple with a stunning 15th-century altarpiece, which has 53 panels depicting scenes from the life of Christ and Mary, topped by a representation of the Final Judgement. The entrance is inside the Catedral Nueva.

Universidad Civil HISTORIC BUILDING
(Calle de los Libreros; adult/child €4/2, Mon morning free; ⏲9.30am-1.30pm & 4-6.30pm Mon-Fri, 10am-1.30pm Sun) Founded initially as the Estudio Generál in 1218, Salamanca's university came into being in 1254 and reached the peak of its renown in the 15th and 16th centuries. Its facade is a tapestry in sandstone, bursting with images of mythical heroes, religious scenes and coats of arms. You can visit the old classrooms and the oldest university library in Europe. The latter is reached via the **Escalera de la Universidad** (University Staircase), which has symbols carved into the balustrade – to decode them was seen as symbolic of the quest for knowledge.

Sleeping

Aparthotel El Toboso APARTMENT €
(☎923 27 14 62; www.hoteltoboso.com; Calle del Clavel 7; s/d €30/45, 3-/4-/5-person apt €75/85/95; ❄📶) These rooms have a homey spare-room feel and are super value, especially the enormous apartments, which come with kitchens (including washing machines) and renovated bathrooms.

FIND THE FROG

The university's facade is an ornate mass of sculptures and carvings, and hidden among this 16th-century plateresque creation is a tiny stone frog. Legend says that those who find the frog will have good luck in studies, life and love. If you don't want any help, look away now...It's sitting on a skull on the pillar that runs up the right-hand side of the facade.

Hostal Concejo HOSTAL €
(☎923 21 47 37; www.hconcejo.com; Plaza de la Libertad 1; s/d €45/60; P❄📶) A cut above the average *hostal*, the stylish Concejo has polished-wood floors, tasteful furnishings, light-filled rooms and a superb central location. Try and snag one of the corner rooms (such as number 104) with a traditional glassed-in balcony.

Hostal Catedral HOSTAL €
(☎923 27 06 14; hostalcatedralsalamanca.com; Rúa Mayor 46; s/d €30/48; ❄📶) Just across from the cathedrals, this pleasing *hostal* with an attentive, motherly owner, has just six extremely pretty, impeccable, bright bedrooms with showers. All look out onto the street or cathedral, which is a real bonus.

Eating & Drinking

La Cocina de Toño TAPAS €€
(www.lacocinadetoño.es; Calle Gran Via 20; menú del día €17, tapas €1.30-3.80, mains €6.90-23; ⏲lunch & dinner Tue-Sat, lunch Sun) We're yet to hear a bad word about this place, and its loyal following owes everything to its creative *pinchos* (tapas) and half-servings of exotic dishes. The restaurant serves more traditional fare as befits the decor, but the bar is one of Salamanca's gastronomic stars.

Mesón Las Conchas CASTILIAN €€
(Rúa Mayor 16; menú del día €12, mains €10-21; ⏲noon-midnight) Enjoy a choice of outdoor tables (in summer), an atmospheric bar or the upstairs, wood-beamed dining area. The bar caters mainly to locals who know their *embutidos* (cured meats). For sit-down meals, there's a good mix of roasts, *platos combinados* and *raciones*.

Mesón Cervantes CASTILIAN €€
(www.mesoncervantes.com; Plaza Mayor 15; menú del día €13.50, mains €10-22; ⏲10am-midnight) Although there are outdoor tables on the plaza, the dark wooden beams and atmospheric buzz of the Spanish crowd on the 1st floor should be experienced at least once; if you snaffle a window table in the evening you've hit the jackpot. The food's a mix of *platos combinados*, salads and *raciones*.

Mandala Café MEDITERRANEAN
(Calle de Serranos 9-11; set menus €10-12; ☎
Cool and casual Mandala specialises in superb daily menu (unusually availab
for lunch *and* dinner) with choices suc
as black rice with prawns and *calamar*

(squid), and vegetarian moussaka. There are also more salads than you can shake a carrot stick at, cakes, 45 types of milkshakes, 56 juice combinations and more teas than we could count.

TOP CHOICE Tío Vivo MUSIC BAR
(www.tiovivosalamanca.com; Calle del Clavel 3-5; 4pm-late) Sip drinks by flickering candlelight to a background of '80s music, enjoying the whimsical decor of carousel horses and oddball antiquities. There is live music Tuesdays to Thursdays from midnight, sometimes with a €5 cover charge.

Information

Municipal Tourist Office (923 21 83 42; www.turismodesalamanca.com; Plaza Mayor 14; 9am-2pm & 4.30-8pm Mon-Fri, 10am-8pm Sat, 10am-2pm Sun)

Regional Tourist Office (923 26 85 71; www.turismocastillayleon.com; Casa de las Conchas, Rúa Mayor; 9am-8pm)

Getting There & Away

BUS Services depart from the **bus station** (Avenida de Filiberto Villalobos 71-85) to Madrid (regular/express €13/20.50, three/2½ hours, hourly), Ávila (€6.25, 1½ hours, one to four daily) and Segovia (€11.25, 2¾ hours, two daily).

TRAIN Up to eight trains depart daily for Madrid's Chamartín station (€20, 2½ hours) via Ávila (€10.25, one hour). The train station is about 1km beyond Plaza de España.

Segovia

POP 55,220

Unesco World Heritage–listed Segovia has a stunning monument to Roman grandeur and a castle said to have inspired Walt Disney, and is otherwise a city of warm terracotta and sandstone hues set amid the rolling hills of Castilla.

Sights

Acueducto ROMAN AQUEDUCT
El Acueducto, an 894m-long engineering wonder that looks like an enormous comb of stone blocks plunged into the lower end of old Segovia, is the obvious starting point of a tour of town. This Roman aqueduct is 28m high and was built without a drop of mortar – just good old Roman know-how.

Segovia's Alcázar CASTLE
(www.alcazardesegovia.com; Plaza de la Reina Victoria Eugenia; adult/child €4/3, tower €2, EU citizens free 3rd Tue of month; 10am-7pm Apr-Sep) The fortified and fairy-tale Alcázar is perched dramatically on the edge of Segovia. Roman foundations are buried somewhere underneath the splendour, but what we see today is a 13th-century structure that burned down in 1862 and was subsequently rebuilt. Inside is a collection of armour and military gear, but even better are the ornate interiors of the reception rooms and the 360-degree views from the Torre de Juan II. Walt Disney reportedly used the Alcázar as inspiration for Sleeping Beauty's castle.

Catedral CHURCH
(Plaza Mayor; adult/child €3/2, 9.30am-1.15pm Sun free; 9.30am-6.30pm) In the heart of town, the resplendent late-Gothic Catedral was started in 1525 and completed a mere 200 years later. The Cristo del Consuelo **chapel** houses a magnificent Romanesque doorway preserved from the original church that burned down.

Iglesia de Vera Cruz CHURCH
(Carretera de Zamarramala; admission €1.75; 10.30am-1.30pm & 4-7pm Tue-Sun, closed Nov) The most interesting of Segovia's numerous churches, and one of the best preserved of its kind in Europe, is the 12-sided Iglesia de la Vera Cruz. Built in the 13th century by the Knights Templar and based on the Church of the Holy Sepulchre in Jerusalem, it long housed what was said to be a piece of the Vera Cruz (True Cross).

Sleeping

TOP CHOICE Hospedería La Gran Casa Mudéjar HISTORIC HOTEL €€
(921 46 62 50; www.lacasamudejar.com; Calle de Isabel la Católica 8; r €90;) Spread over two buildings, this place has been magnificently renovated, blending genuine, 15th-century carved wooden ceilings in some rooms with modern amenities. In the newer wing, where the building dates from the 19th century, the rooms on the top floors have fine mountain views.

Hostal Fornos HOSTAL €
(921 46 01 98; www.hostalfornos.com; Calle de la Infanta Isabel 13; s/d €41/55;) This tidy little *hostal* is a cut above most other places in this price category. It has a lovely cheerful air and rooms with a fresh white-linen-and-wicker-chair look. Some rooms are larger than others, but the value is unbeatable.

WORTH A TRIP

BURGOS & LEÓN – A TALE OF TWO CATHEDRALS

The northern Castilian city of Burgos is home to a Unesco World Heritage–listed **cathedral** (Plaza del Rey Fernando; adult/child €5/2.50; ⌚9.30am-6.30pm). A 13th-century French-Gothic creation, it has two extraordinary doors, the **Puerta del Sarmental**, the main entrance for visitors, and the **Puerta de la Coronería**. Inside the main sanctuary, note the light and airy **Capilla de la Presentación** and the **Capilla de la Concepción** with its impossibly gilded, 15th-century **altar**. The main altar is a typically overwhelming piece of gold-encrusted extravagance, while directly beneath the star-vaulted central dome lies the **tomb of El Cid**. The **Capilla del Condestable**, behind the main altar, is a remarkable late-15th-century production. If you're staying overnight, the **Hotel Norte y Londres** (☎947 26 41 25; www.hotelnorteylondres.com; Plaza de Alonso Martínez 10; s/d €66/100; P@), **Hotel La Puebla** (☎947 20 00 11; www.hotellapuebla.com; Calle de la Puebla 20; s/d €50/65; @) and **Hotel Mesón del Cid** (☎947 20 87 15; www.mesondelcid.es; Plaza de Santa María 8; s/d €70/100; P) are all excellent. For excellent food, try **Cervecería Morito** (Calle de la Sombrerería 27; tapas €3, raciones €5-7). The **tourist office** (www.aytoburgos.es; Plaza del Rey Fernando 2; ⌚10am-2pm & 4.30-7.30pm Mon-Fri, 10am-1.30pm & 4-7.30pm Sat & Sun) is in the town centre.

In Castilla y Leónns far north, León's 13th-century **cathedral** (www.catedraldeleon.org; adult/concession/child €5/4/free; ⌚8.30am-1.30pm & 4-8pm Mon-Sat, 8.30am-2.30pm & 5-8pm Sun) has a spectacular facade, but inside an extraordinary gallery of *vidrieras* (stained-glass windows) awaits. Mostly executed from the 13th to the 16th centuries, the windows evoke an atmosphere unlike that of any other cathedral in Spain; the kaleidoscope of coloured light is offset by the otherwise gloomy interior. There are 128 windows with a surface of 1800 sq metres in all, but mere numbers cannot convey the ethereal quality of light permeating this cathedral. Excellent places to stay include the **Hostal San Martín** (☎987 87 51 87; www.sanmartinhostales.com; Plaza de Torres de Omaña 1, 2nd fl; s/d/tr €31/43/55, s without bathroom €20) and **La Posada Regia** (☎987 21 31 73; www.regialeon.com; Calle de Regidores 9-11; s/d €65/120), while **El Llar** (Plaza de San Martín 9; meals €25-30) and **Camarote Madrid** (www.camarotemadrid.com; Calle Cervantes 8) are good for local tapas. The **tourist office** (www.turismocastillayleon.com; Calle el Cid 2; ⌚9am-8pm) is central.

Both Burgos and León are well connected by train and bus to Madrid.

Natura – La Hostería HOTEL €
(☎921 46 67 10; www.naturadesegovia.com; Calle de Colón 5-7; r €60) An eclectic choice a few streets back from Plaza Mayor. The owner obviously has a penchant for Dalí prints and the rooms have plenty of character, with chunky wooden furnishings and bright paintwork.

Eating

TOP CHOICE **Restaurante El Fogón Sefardí** SEPHARDIC €€
(☎921 46 62 50; www.lacasamudejar.com; Calle de Isabel la Católica 8; meals €30-40) Located within the Hospedería La Gran Casa Mudéjar, this is one of the most original places in town. Sephardic cuisine is served in either the intimate patio or splendid dining hall with original, 15th-century flourishes.

TOP CHOICE **Casa Duque** GRILL €€
(☎921 46 24 87; www.restauranteduque.es; Calle de Cervantes 12; meals €25-35, menús del día €21-40) Casa Duque has been serving *cochinillo asado* since the 1890s. For the uninitiated, try the *menú segoviano* (€30), which includes *cochinillo*, or the *menú gastronómico* (€43.50). Downstairs is the informal *cueva* (cave), where you can get tapas and full-bodied *cazuelas* (stews). Reservations recommended.

La Almuzara ITALIAN €
(Calle Marqués del Arco 3; mains €7.50-11; ⌚Tue Sat, dinner only Sun) If you're a vegetarian you don't need to feel like an outcast in thi resolutely carnivorous city. La Almuzara fea tures lots of vegetarian dishes, pizzas, pasta and salads, and the ambience is warm an artsy.

Information

Centro de Recepción de Visitantes (Tourist Office; www.turismodesegovia.com; Plaza del Azoguejo 1; ⏲10am-7pm Sun-Fri, 10am-8pm Sat) Guided city tours are available, departing daily at 11.15am for a minimum of four people.

Regional Tourist Office (www.segoviaturismo.es; Plaza Mayor 10; ⏲9am-8pm Sun-Thu, 9am-9pm Fri & Sat)

Getting There & Away

BUS Services run half-hourly to Segovia from Madrid's Paseo de la Florida bus stop (€6.75, 1½ hours). Buses also run to/from Ávila (€5, 1¼ hours, five daily) and Salamanca (€11.25, 2¾ hours, two daily).

TRAIN Up to nine normal trains run daily from Madrid to Segovia (€6.75 one way, two hours), leaving you at the main train station, 2.5km from the aqueduct. The faster option is the high-speed AVANT (€10.75, 35 minutes), which deposits you at the newer Segovia-Guiomar station, 5km from the aqueduct.

CASTILLA-LA MANCHA

Toledo

POP 83,110

Toledo is Spain's equivalent of a downsized Rome. Commanding a hill rising above the Tajo River, it's crammed with monuments that attest to the waves of conquerors and communities – Roman, Visigoth, Jewish, Muslim and Christian – who have called the city home during its turbulent history. It's one of the country's major tourist attractions.

Sights

Catedral CATHEDRAL
(Plaza del Ayuntamiento; adult/child €7/free; ⏲10.30am-6.30pm Mon-Sat, 2-6.30pm Sun) Toledo's cathedral dominates the skyline, reflecting the city's historical significance as the heart of Catholic Spain. Within its hefty stone walls there are stained-glass windows, tombs of kings and art in the sacristy by the likes of El Greco, Zurbarán, Crespi, Titian, Rubens and Velázquez. Behind the main altar lies a mesmerising piece of 18th-century Churrigueresque baroque, the **Transparente**. Look out for the **Custodia de Arfe**, by the celebrated 16th-century goldsmith Enrique de Arfe. With 18kg of pure gold and 183kg of silver, this 16th-century conceit bristles with some 260 statuettes.

Alcázar FORTRESS, MUSEUM
(Museo del Ejército; Calle Alféreces Provisionales; adult/child €5/free; ⏲10am-9pm Thu-Tue Jun-Sep, to 7pm Oct-May) At the highest point in the city looms the foreboding Alcázar. Abd ar-Rahman III raised an *al-qasr* here in the 10th century, which was thereafter altered by the Christians. The Alcázar was heavily damaged during the siege of the garrison by loyalist militias at the start of the Civil War in 1936. It now houses a military museum with an exhaustive historical section, includingan in-depth overview of the nation's history in Spanish and English.

Sinagoga del Tránsito SYNAGOGUE
(http://museosefardi.mcu.es; Calle Samuel Leví; adult/child €3/1.50; ⏲9.30am-8pm Tue-Sat Apr-Sep, to 6.30pm Oct-Mar, 10am-3pm Sun) Toledo's former *judería* (Jewish quarter) was once home to 11 synagogues. The bulk of Toledo's Jews were expelled in 1492. This magnificent synagogue was built in 1355 by special permission of Pedro I (construction of synagogues was prohibited in Christian Spain). The synagogue now houses the **Museo Sefardi**.

Monasterio San Juan de los Reyes MONASTERY
(Calle San Juan de los Reyes 2; admission €2.50; ⏲10am-6.45pm) This early-17th-century Franciscan monastery and church of San Juan de los Reyes is notable for its delightful cloisters. Provocatively built in the heart of the Jewish quarter, the monastery was founded by Isabel and Fernando to demonstrate the supremacy of the Catholic faith. Throughout the church and cloister the coat of arms of Isabel and Fernando dominates, and the chains of Christian prisoners liberated in Granada dangle from the outside walls. The prevalent late-Flemish Gothic style is enhanced with lavish Isabelline ornament, counterbalanced by Mudéjar decoration.

Sleeping & Eating

Casa de Cisneros BOUTIQUE HOTEL €€
(☎925 22 88 28; www.hostal-casa-de-cisneros.com; Calle Cardenal Cisneros; s/d incl breakfast €55/75; ❄📶) Right by the cathedral, this lovely 16th-century house was once the home of the cardinal and Grand Inquisitor Cisneros (often known as Ximénes). It's a top choice, with

WORTH A TRIP

CUENCA

A World Heritage site, Cuenca is one of Spain's most memorable small cities, its old centre a stage set of evocative medieval buildings. Most emblematic are the 14th-century *casas colgadas*, the hanging houses that jut out precariously over the steep defile of Río Huécar. Inside one of the houses is the **Museo de Arte Abstracto Español** (Museum of Abstract Art; www.march.es/arte/cuenca; adult/child €3/free; ⏲11am-2pm & 4-6pm Tue-Fri, 11am-2pm & 4-8pm Sat, 11am-2.30pm Sun), while Cuenca is also famous for its Semana Santa (Holy Week) processions; stop by the **Museo de la Semana Santa** (www.msscuenca.org; Calle Andrés de Cabrera 13; adult/child €3/free; ⏲11am-2pm & 4.30-7.30pm Thu-Sat, 11am-2pm Sun) to see why.

If you're staying overnight, the **Hostal Tabanqueta** (☎969 21 12 90; www.hostaltabanqueta.com; Calle Trabuco 13; d €60; 📶) and **Posada de San José** (☎969 21 13 00; www.posadasanjose.com; Ronda de Julián Romero 4; d from €82, s/d without bathroom €30/43) are excellent. For a meal, try **La Bodeguilla de Basilio** (Calle Fray Luis de León 3; raciones €10-13; ⏲lunch & dinner Mon-Sat, lunch Sun).

There's a **tourist office** (http://turismo.cuenca.es; Calle Alfonso VIII 2; ⏲9am-9pm Mon-Sat, to 2.30pm Sun), and Cuenca is most easily reached along the Madrid–Valencia rail line.

cosy, seductive rooms with original wooden beams and walls and voguish bathrooms.

Hostal Santo Tomé HOSTAL €
(☎925 22 17 12; www.hostalsantotome.com; Calle de Santo Tomé 13; s/d €42/55; P❄📶) This friendly and good-value *hostal* (budget hotel), run out of the souvenir shop downstairs, has larger than average rooms with light wood floors and furniture, plus bathrooms with five-star attitude, offering extras such as shoe polish and hairdryers.

Palacios SPANISH €
(www.hostalpalaciostoledo.com; Calle Alfonso X el Sabio 3; set menus €8.50-15.90, raciones €5-10; ⏲noon-11pm) An unpretentious place, where stained glass, beams and efficient old-fashioned service combine with traditional no-nonsense cuisine. Hungry? Try a gut-busting bowl of traditional *judías con perdiz* (white beans with partridge) for starters. It's very popular so be prepared to wait a while for a table.

La Abadía TAPAS €
(www.abadiatoledo.com; Plaza de San Nicolás 3; raciones €4-15) In a former 16th-century palace, arches, niches and subtle lighting are spread over a warren of brick-and-stone-clad rooms. The menu includes lightweight dishes and tapas portions – perfect for small appetites.

ℹ Information

Main Tourist Office (☎925 25 40 30; www.toledo-turismo.com; Plaza del Ayuntamiento; ⏲10am-6pm)

Provincial Tourist Office (www.diputoledo.es; Subida de la Granja; ⏲10am-5pm Mon-Sat, to 3pm Sun)

ℹ Getting There & Away

BUS From Toledo's **bus station** (Avenida de Castilla La Mancha), buses depart for Madrid (from €5.25,one to 1½ hours) every half-hour from 6am to 10pm daily (less often on Sunday). There are also services on weekdays and Sunday to Cuenca (€13, 2¼ hours).

TRAIN The high-speed AVE service runs every hour or so to Madrid (€10.75, 30 minutes).

CATALONIA

Barcelona

POP 1.62 MILLION

Barcelona is one of Europe's coolest cities. Despite two millennia of history it's a forward-thinking place, always on the cutting edge of art, design and cuisine. Whether you explore its medieval palaces and plazas, admire the modernista masterpieces, shop for designer fashions along its bustling boulevards, sample its exciting nightlife or just soak up the sun on the beaches, you'll find it hard not to fall in love with this vibrant city.

As much as Barcelona is a visual feast, it will also lead you into culinary temptation. Everything from traditional Catalan cooking to the latest in avant-garde new Spanish cuisine will have your appetite in overdrive

Sights & Activities

LA RAMBLA

Spain's most famous boulevard, the part-pedestrianised La Rambla, explodes with life. Stretching from Plaça de Catalunya to the waterfront, it's lined with street artists, newsstands and vendors selling everything from mice to magnolias.

The colourful **Mercat de la Boquería** (Map p1074; ☎93 412 13 15; www.boqueria.info; La Rambla 91; ⏰8am-8.30pm Mon-Sat, closed Sun; ⓂLiceu), a fresh food market with a modernista entrance, is one of La Rambla's highlights. Nearby, stop for a tour of the **Gran Teatre del Liceu** (Map p1074; ☎93 485 99 14; www.liceubarcelona.com; La Rambla dels Caputxins 51-59; ⏰guided tour 10am, unguided visits 11.30am, noon, 12.30pm & 1pm; ⓂLiceu), the city's fabulous opera house.

Also stop at the **Plaça Reial** (Map p1074; ⓂLiceu), a grand 19th-century square surrounded by arcades lined with restaurants and bars

BARRI GÒTIC

You could easily spend several days or even a week exploring the Barri Gòtic, Barcelona's oldest quarter, without leaving the medieval streets. In addition to major sights, its tangle of narrow lanes and tranquil plazas conceal some of the city's most atmospheric shops, restaurants, cafes and bars.

TOP CHOICE La Catedral CHURCH

(Map p1074; ☎93 342 82 60; www.website.es/catedralbcn; Plaça de la Seu; admission free, special visit €5, choir admission €2.20; ⏰8am-12.45pm & 5.15-8pm Mon-Sat, special visit 1-5pm Mon-Sat, 2-5pm Sun & holidays; ⓂJaume I) Barcelona's Gothic Catedral was built atop the ruins of an 11th-century Romanesque church. Highlights include the cool cloister, the crypt tomb of martyr Santa Eulàlia (one of Barcelona's two patron saints), the choir stalls, the lift to the rooftop and the modest art collection in the **Sala Capitular** (Chapter House; Map p1074; admission €2; ⏰10am-12.15pm & 5.15-7pm Mon-Sat, 10am-12.45pm & 5.15-7pm Sun). You only pay the individual prices if you visit outside the special visiting hours.

Museu d'Història de Barcelona MUSEUM

(Map p1074; ☎93 256 21 00; www.museuhistoria.bcn.cat; Plaça del Rei; adult/child €7/free, from 4pm 1st Sat of month and from 3pm Sun free; ⏰10am-8pm Tue-Sat, 10am-8pm Sun; ⓂJaume I) Not far from the cathedral is pretty Plaça del Rei and the fascinating Museu d'Història de Barcelona, where you can visit a 4000-sq-metre excavated site of Roman Barcelona under the plaza. The museum encompasses historic buildings including the Palau Reial Major (Main Royal Palace), once a residence of the kings of Catalonia and Aragón, and its Saló del Tinell (Great Hall).

LA RIBERA

In medieval days, La Ribera was a stone's throw from the Mediterranean and the heart of Barcelona's foreign trade, with homes belonging to numerous wealthy merchants. Now it's a trendy district full of boutiques, restaurants and bars.

TOP CHOICE Museu Picasso MUSEUM

(Map p1074; ☎93 256 30 00; www.museupicasso.bcn.es; Carrer de Montcada 15-23; adult/senior & child under 16yr/student €11/free/6, temporary exhibitions adult/senior & child under 16yr/student €6/free/2.90, 3-8pm Sun & 1st Sun of month free; ⏰10am-8pm Tue-Sun & holidays; ⓂJaume I) The setting alone, in five contiguous medieval stone mansions, makes the Museu Picasso unique (and worth the probable queues).

While the collection concentrates on the artist's formative years, there is enough material from subsequent periods to give you a thorough impression of the man's versatility and genius.

Església de Santa Maria del Mar CHURCH

(Map p1074; ☎93 319 05 16; Plaça de Santa Maria del Mar; ⏰9am-1.30pm & 4.30-8pm; ⓂJaume I) At the southwest end of Passeig del Born stands the apse of Barcelona's finest Catalan Gothic church, Santa Maria del Mar (Our Lady of the Sea). Built in the 14th century with record-breaking alacrity for the time (it took just 54 years), the church is remarkable for its architectural harmony and simplicity.

Palau de la Música Catalana ARCHITECTURE

(Map p1070; ☎902 475 485; www.palaumusica.org; Carrer de Sant Francesc de Paula 2; adult/child/student & EU senior €15/free/€7.50; ⏰50min tours every 30 minutes 10am-6pm Easter week & Aug, 10am-3.30pm Sep-Jul; ⓂUrquinaona) The opulent Palau de la Música Catalana is one of the city's most delightful modernista works. Designed by Lluís Domènech i Montaner in 1905, it hosts concerts regularly. It is well worth joining the guided tours to get a look inside if you don't make a concert.

L'EIXAMPLE

Modernisme, the Catalan version of art nouveau, transformed Barcelona's cityscape

Barcelona

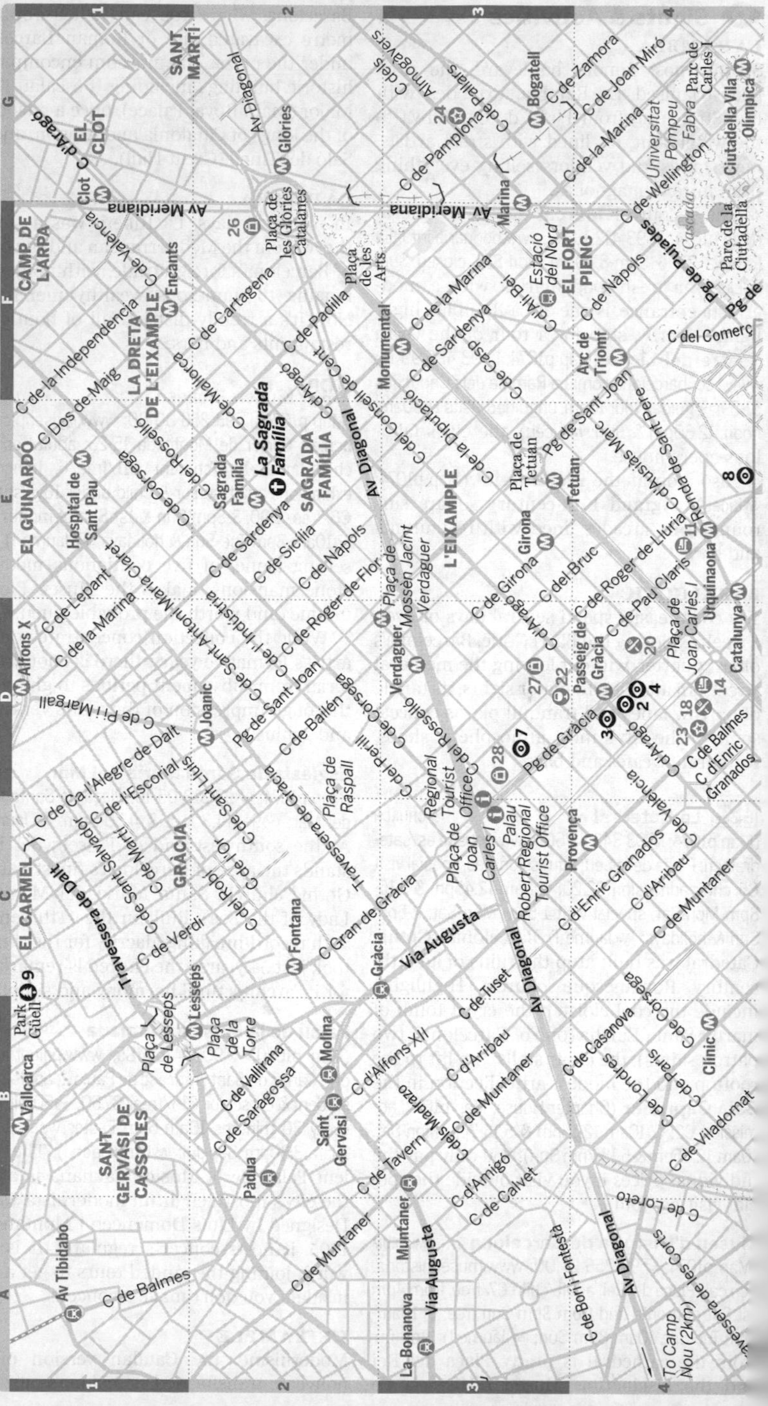

0 1 km
0 0.5 miles

A B C D E F G
1 2 3 4

Vallcarca
Park Güell 9
EL CARMEL
Alfons X
EL GUINARDÓ
CAMP DE L'ARPA
Av Tibidabo
C de Balmes
SANT GERVASI DE CASSOLES
Travessera de Dalt
Plaça de Lesseps
Lesseps
Plaça de la Torre
C de Verdi
C de Sant Salvador
C de Martí
C de Ca l'Alegre de Dalt
C de l'Escorial
C de Pi i Margall
C de la Marina
C de Lepant
Hospital de Sant Pau
C Dos de Maig
C de la Independència
LA DRETA DE L'EIXAMPLE
C de València
Encants
Clot
C d'Aragó
EL CLOT
SANT MARTÍ
Av Meridiana
GRÀCIA
Joanic
C de Sant Antoni Maria Claret
C de Còrsega
C del Rosselló
C de Mallorca
C de Cartagena
26
Plaça de les Glòries Catalanes
Glòries
Av Diagonal
Pàdua
C de Saragossa
C de Vallirana
C del Robí
C de l'Or
C de Sant Lluís
Pg de Sant Joan
C de l'Indústria
C de Sardenya
Sagrada Família
La Sagrada Família
C de Sicília
SAGRADA FAMÍLIA
C d'Aragó
C de Padilla
Fontana
C de Muntaner
Sant Gervasi
Molina
C Gran de Gràcia
Travessera de Gràcia
Plaça de Raspall
C de Bailén
C de Roger de Flor
C de Nàpols
Av Diagonal
C del Consell de Cent
Plaça de les Arts
Gràcia
C d'Alfons XII
Via Augusta
C del Perill
C de Còrsega
Verdaguer
Plaça de Mossèn Jacint Verdaguer
Monumental
C dels Almogàvers
La Bonanova
Muntaner
C de Tavern
C dels Madrazo
Regional Tourist Office
Plaça de Joan Carles I
C del Rosselló
L'EIXAMPLE
C de la Diputació
C de Sardenya
C de la Marina
C de Pamplona
24
C de Pallars
C d'Amigó
C de Calvet
C de Muntaner
C d'Aribau
C de Tuset
Palau Robert Regional Tourist Office
28
7
27
C d'Aragó
C de Girona
Girona
Plaça de Tetuan
C de Casp
C d'Alí Bei
Estació del Nord
Marina
Bogatell
Av Diagonal
Pg de Gràcia
22
Provença
C de Bori i Fontestà
EL FORT PIENC
Tetuan
C del Bruc
Passeig de Gràcia
Arc de Triomf
C de Nàpols
C de la Marina
C de Zamora
C de Casanova
C d'Enric Granados
3
2
4
20
C de Roger de Llúria
Pg de Sant Joan
C d'Ausiàs Marc
Av Diagonal
C de Loreto
C de Londres
C de París
C de Còrsega
C d'Aribau
C de València
C d'Aragó
C de Pau Claris
Plaça de Joan Carles I
11
Ronda de Sant Pere
C de Wellington
Universitat Pompeu Fabra
C de Joan Miró
To Camp Nou (2km)
Travessera de les Corts
C de Viladomat
Clínic
C de Muntaner
23
18
14
C de Balmes
C d'Enric Granados
Urquinaona
Catalunya
8
C del Comerç
Pg de Pujades
Cascada
Parc de la Ciutadella
Pg de
Parc de Carles I
Ciutadella Vila Olímpica

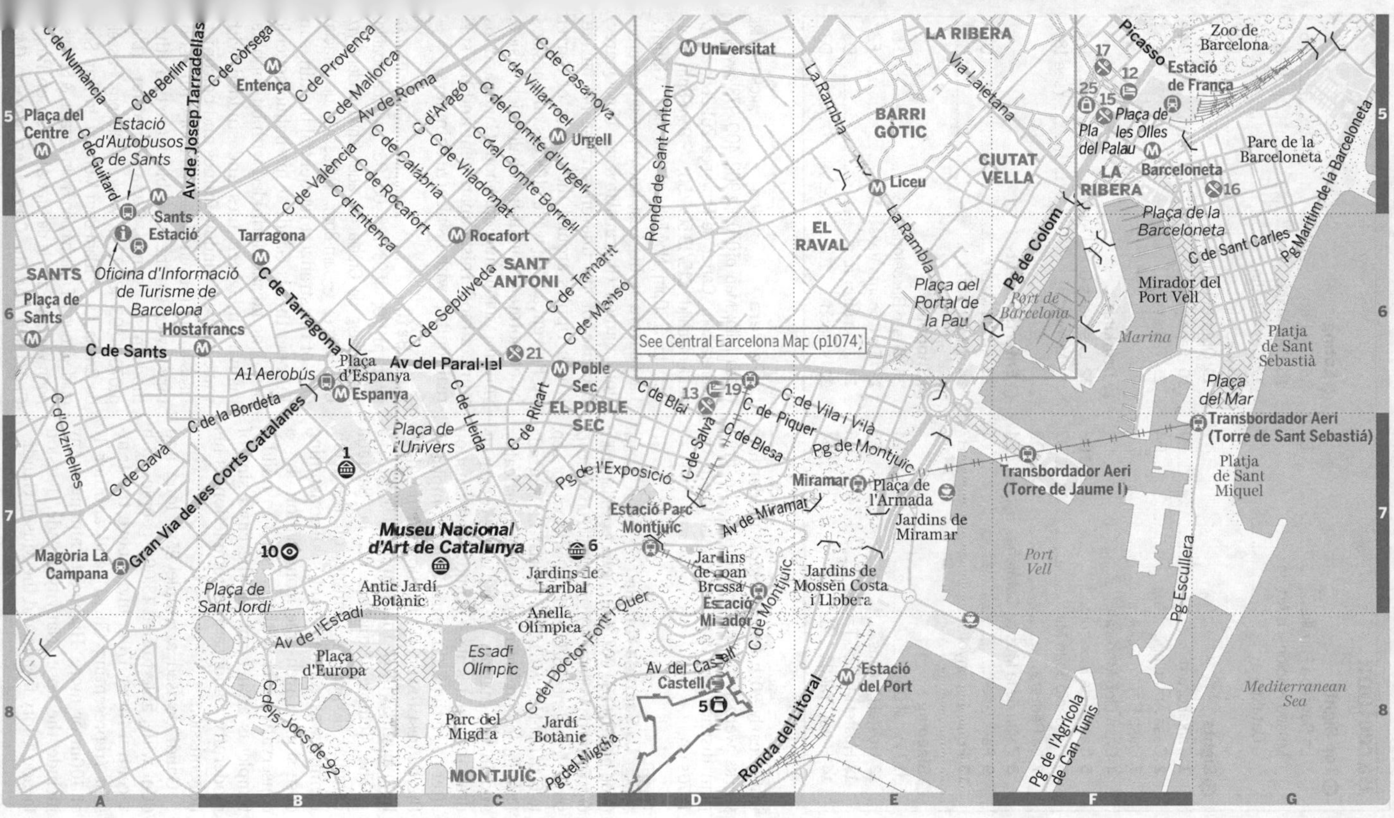
Zoo de Barcelona
Picasso
Estació de França
Parc de la Barceloneta
Pg Marítim de la Barceloneta
Plaça de les Olles
Pla del Palau
Barceloneta
LA RIBERA
Plaça de la Barceloneta
C de Sant Carles
Mirador del Port Vell
Marina
Platja de Sant Sebastià
Plaça del Mar
Transbordador Aeri (Torre de Sant Sebastià)
Platja de Sant Miquel
Pg Escullera
Transbordador Aeri (Torre de Jaume I)
Port Vell
Port de Barcelona
Pg de l'Agrícola de Can Tunis
Mediterranean Sea
Pg de Colom
Via Laietana
CIUTAT VELLA
BARRI GÒTIC
LA RIBERA
La Rambla
Liceu
EL RAVAL
Plaça del Portal de la Pau
See Central Barcelona Map (p1074)
Universitat
Ronda de Sant Antoni
C de Vila i Vilà
C de Piquer
Pg de Montjuïc
C de Blesa
C de Salva
C de Blai
Miramar
Plaça de l'Armada
Jardins de Miramar
Av de Miramar
Jardins de Mossèn Costa i Llobera
C de Montjuïc
Jardins de Joan Brossa
Estació Mirador
Estació del Port
Ronda del Litoral
Av del Castell
Castell
Estació Parc Montjuïc
Pg de l'Exposició
C de Casanova
C de Villarroel
Urgell
C del Comte d'Urgell
C del Comte Borrell
C de Viladomat
Rocafort
C de Calàbria
C de Rocafort
C d'Entença
C d'Aragó
Av de Roma
C de Mallorca
C de Provença
C de València
SANT ANTONI
C de Tamarit
C de Sepúlveda
C de Mansó
Poble Sec
EL POBLE SEC
C de Ricart
C de Lleida
Av del Paral·lel
Plaça d'Espanya
Espanya
Plaça de l'Univers
Museu Nacional d'Art de Catalunya
Jardins de Laribal
Anella Olímpica
C del Doctor Font i Quer
Estadi Olímpic
Parc del Migdia
Jardí Botànic
Pg del Migdia
MONTJUÏC
Antic Jardí Botànic
Plaça de Sant Jordi
Av de l'Estadi
Plaça d'Europa
C dels Jocs de 92
C de Tarragona
Tarragona
Entença
C de Còrsega
C de Berlín
Av de Josep Tarradellas
Sants Estació
Estació d'Autobusos de Sants
C de Guitard
C de Numància
Plaça del Centre
SANTS
Oficina d'Informació de Turisme de Barcelona
Plaça de Sants
Hostafrancs
C de Sants
A1 Aerobús
C de la Bordeta
Gran Via de les Corts Catalanes
C de Gavà
C d'Olzinelles
Magòria La Campana

Barcelona

Top Sights

	La Sagrada Família	E2
	Museu Nacional d'Art de Catalunya	C7

Sights

1	CaixaForum	B7
2	Casa Amatller	D4
3	Casa Batlló	D4
4	Casa Lleó Morera	D4
5	Castell de Montjuïc	D8
6	Fundació Joan Miró	C7
7	La Pedrera	D3
8	Palau de la Música Catalana	E4
9	Park Güell	C1
10	Poble Espanyol	B7

Sleeping

11	Hostal Goya	E4
12	Hostal Orleans	F5
13	Hostel Mambo Tango	D6
14	Hotel Praktik	D4

Eating

15	Cal Pep	F5
16	Can Maño	G5
17	Casa Delfín	F5
18	Fastvínic	D4
19	Quimet i Quimet	D6
20	Tapaç 24	D4
21	Tickets	C6

Drinking

22	Les Gens Que J'Aime	D3
	Monvínic	(see 18)

Entertainment

23	Arena Madre	D4
24	Razzmatazz	G3

Shopping

25	Custo Barcelona	F5
26	Els Encants Vells	F2
27	Joan Murrià	D3
28	Vinçon	D3

in the early 20th century. Most modernista works were built in L'Eixample, the grid-plan district that was developed from the 1870s on.

TOP CHOICE La Sagrada Família — CHURCH

(Map p1070; ☎93 207 30 31; www.sagradafamilia.org; Carrer de Mallorca 401; adult/child under 10yr/senior & student €13/free/11; ⊙9am-8pm Apr-Sep, to 6pm Oct-Mar; Ⓜ Sagrada Família) La Sagrada Família inspires awe by its sheer verticality, and in the manner of the medieval cathedrals it emulates, it's still under construction after more than 100 years. When completed, the highest tower will be more than half as high again as those that stand today.

The Temple Expiatori de la Sagrada Família (Expiatory Temple of the Holy Family) was Antoni Gaudí's all-consuming obsession. Given the commission by a conservative society that wished to build a temple as atonement for the city's sins of modernity, Gaudí saw its completion as his holy mission.

Gaudí devised a temple 95m long and 60m wide, able to seat 13,000 people, with a central tower 170m high above the transept (representing Christ) and another 17 of 100m or more. Highlights among many include the apse, Nativity facade, Passion facade, Glory facade and the Museu Gaudí.

La Pedrera — ARCHITECTURE

(Casa Milà; Map p1070; ☎902 400 973; www.lapedrera.com; Carrer de Provença 261-265; adult/student/child €15/13.50/7.50; ⊙9am-8pm Mar-Oct, to 6.30pm Nov-Feb; Ⓜ Diagonal) Gaudí's La Pedrera is his best-known secular creation, named (it translates as The Quarry) because of its uneven grey-stone facade, which ripples around the corner of Carrer de Provença. The wave effect is emphasised by elaborate wrought-iron balconies. Inside, you can visit a museum about Gaudí and his work, a modernista apartment and the surreal rooftop with its bizarre chimneys.

Casa Batlló — ARCHITECTURE

(Map p1070; ☎93 216 03 06; www.casabatllo.es; Passeig de Gràcia 43; adult/child under 7yr/€18.15/free; ⊙9am-8pm; Ⓜ Passeig de Gràcia) One of the strangest residential buildings in Europe, this is Gaudí at his hallucinogenic best. The facade, sprinkled with bits of blue, mauve and green tiles and studded with wave-shaped window frames and balconies rises to an uneven blue-tiled roof with a solitary tower. On the same block are two other modernista gems, **Casa Amatller** (Map p1070; ☎93 487 72 17; www.amatller.org; Passeig de Gràcia 41; ⊙10am-8pm Mon-Sat, to 3pm Sun guided tour in English noon Fri, in Catalan & Spanish noon Wed; Ⓜ Passeig de Gràcia) by Josep Puig Cadafalch and the **Casa Lleó Morera** (Ma p1070; Passeig de Gràcia 35; Ⓜ Passeig de Gràcia) by Lluís Domènech i Montaner.

FREE **Park Güell** PARK

(Map p1070; ☎ 93 413 24 00; Carrer d'Olot 7; ⏰ 10am-9pm Jun-Sep, 10am-8pm Apr, May & Oct, 10am-7pm Mar & Nov, 10am-6pm Dec-Feb; 🚌 24, Ⓜ Lesseps or Vallcarca) North of Gràcia and about 4km from Plaça de Catalunya, Park Güell is where Gaudí turned his hand to landscape gardening. It's a strange, enchanting place where his passion for natural forms really took flight.

Park Güell originated in 1900, when Count Eusebi Güell bought a tree-covered hillside (then outside Barcelona) and hired Gaudí to create a miniature city of houses for the wealthy in landscaped grounds. The project was a commercial flop and was abandoned in 1914 – but not before Gaudí had created 3km of roads and walks, steps, a plaza and two gatehouses in his inimitable manner. The park is extremely popular (it gets an estimated four million visitors a year, about 86% of them tourists) and there is talk of limiting access to keep a lid on damage done by the overkill.

Festivals & Events

The **Festes de la Mercè** (www.bcn.cat/merce), held around 24 September, is the city's biggest party, with four days of concerts, dancing, *castellers* (human castle-builders), fireworks and *correfocs* – a parade of firework-spitting dragons and devils.

The evening before the **Dia de Sant Joan** (24 June) is a colourful midsummer celebration with bonfires and fireworks. The beaches are crowded with revellers until the wee hours.

Sleeping

Those looking for cheaper accommodation close to the action should check out the Barri Gòtic and El Raval. Some good lower-end *pensiones* are scattered about L'Eixample, as well as a broad range of midrange and top-end places, most in easy striking distance of the Old Town. A growing range of options now makes it easier to stay in La Ribera and near the beaches at La Barceloneta.

LA RAMBLA & BARRI GÒTIC

Alberg Hostel Itaca HOSTEL €

(Map p1074; ☎ 93 301 97 51; www.itacahostel.com; Carrer de Ripoll 21; dm €11-26, d €60; @ 📶; Ⓜ Jaume I) A bright, quiet hostel near the Catedral, Itaca has spacious dorms (sleeping six, eight or 12 people) with parquet floors and spring colours, and two doubles. It also features two nearby apartments for six people (€120 per night).

MONTJUÏC

Southwest of the city centre and with views out to sea and over the city, Montjuïc serves as a Central Park of sorts and is a great place for a jog or stroll. It's dominated by the **Castell de Montjuïc** (Map p1070; ⏰ 9am-9pm Tue-Sun Apr-Sep, to 7pm Tue-Sun Oct-Mar; 🚌 193, Telefèric de Montjuïc (Castell de Montjuïc)), a one-time fortress with great views. Buses 50, 55 and 61 all head up here. A local bus, the PM (Parc de Montjuïc) line, does a circle trip from Plaça d'Espanya to the *castell*. Cable cars and a funicular line also access the area.

Museu Nacional d'Art de Catalunya (MNAC; Map p1070; ☎ 93 622 03 76; www.mnac.es; Mirador del Palau Nacional; adult/senior & child under 15yr €10/free, 1st Sun of month free; ⏰ 10am-7pm Tue-Sat, to 2.30pm Sun & holidays, library 10am-6pm Mon-Fri, to 2.30pm Sat; Ⓜ Espanya) is a broad panoply of Catalan and European art. The Romanesque frescos are truly stunning.

Fundació Joan Miró (Map p1070; www.bcn.fjmiro.es; Plaça de Neptu; adult/senior & child €10/7; ⏰ 10am-8pm Tue, Wed, Fri & Sat, to 9.30pm Thu, to 2.30pm Sun & holidays; 🚌 50, 55, 193, funicular Paral·lel) is the definitive museum showcasing Joan Miró's works.

A showcase of typical Spanish architecture from around the country, **Poble Espanyol** (Map p1070; www.poble-espanyol.com; Avinguda de Francesc Ferrer i Guàrdia; adult/child €9.50/5.60; ⏰ 9am-8pm Mon, to 2am Tue-Thu, to 4am Fri, to 5am Sat, to midnight Sun; 🚌 50, 61 or 193, Ⓜ Espanya) has craft shops, restaurants and nightlife.

CaixaForum (Map p1070; www.fundacio.lacaixa.es; Avinguda de Francesc Ferrer i Guàrdia 6-8; adult/student & child €3/2, 1st Sun of the month free; ⏰ 10am-8pm Tue-Fri & Sun, to 10pm Sat; Ⓟ; Ⓜ Espanya) is housed in a remarkable former modernista factory designed by Puig i Cadafalch and puts on major art exhibitions.

Central Barcelona

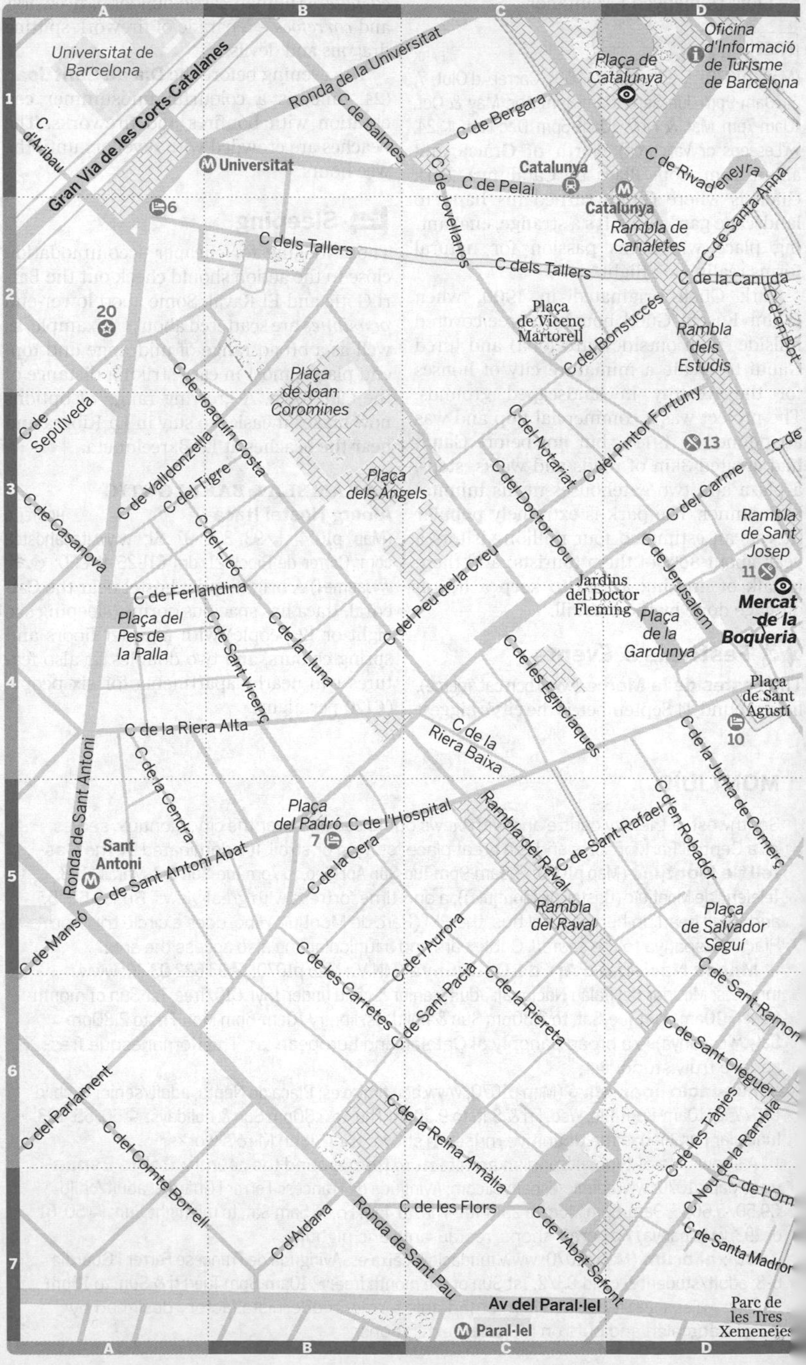

A
B
C
D
1
2
3
4
5
6
7

Universitat de Barcelona
Gran Via de les Corts Catalanes
Ronda de la Universitat
C de Balmes
C d'Aribau
Universitat
6
C de Bergara
Plaça de Catalunya
Oficina d'Informació de Turisme de Barcelona
Catalunya
C de Pelai
C de Jovellanos
Catalunya
C de Rivadeneyra
Rambla de Canaletes
C de Santa Anna
C dels Tallers
C dels Tallers
C de la Canuda
C d'en Bot
20
Plaça de Vicenç Martorell
C del Bonsuccés
Rambla dels Estudis
C de Joaquín Costa
Plaça de Joan Coromines
C de Sepúlveda
C de Valldonzella
C del Tigre
Plaça dels Àngels
C del Notariat
C del Pintor Fortuny
13
C de
C del Doctor Dou
C del Carme
Rambla de Sant Josep
11
C de Casanova
C del Lleó
C del Peu de la Creu
C de Jerusalem
Jardins del Doctor Fleming
Mercat de la Boqueria
C de Ferlandina
Plaça del Pes de la Palla
C de Sant Vicenç
C de la Lluna
Plaça de la Gardunya
C de les Egipcíaques
Plaça de Sant Agustí
10
C de la Riera Alta
C de la Riera Baixa
C de la Junta de Comerç
Ronda de Sant Antoni
C de la Cendra
Plaça del Padró
C de l'Hospital
7
Rambla del Raval
C de Sant Rafael
C d'en Robador
Sant Antoni
C de Sant Antoni Abat
C de la Cera
Rambla del Raval
Plaça de Salvador Seguí
C de Manso
C de l'Aurora
C de les Carretes
C de Sant Pacià
C de la Riereta
C de Sant Ramon
C de Sant Oleguer
C del Parlament
C de la Reina Amàlia
C de les Tàpies
C del Comte Borrell
C Nou de la Rambla
C de l'Om
C de les Flors
C d'Aldana
Ronda de Sant Pau
C de l'Abat Safont
C de Santa Madrona
Av del Paral·lel
Paral·lel
Parc de les Tres Xemeneies

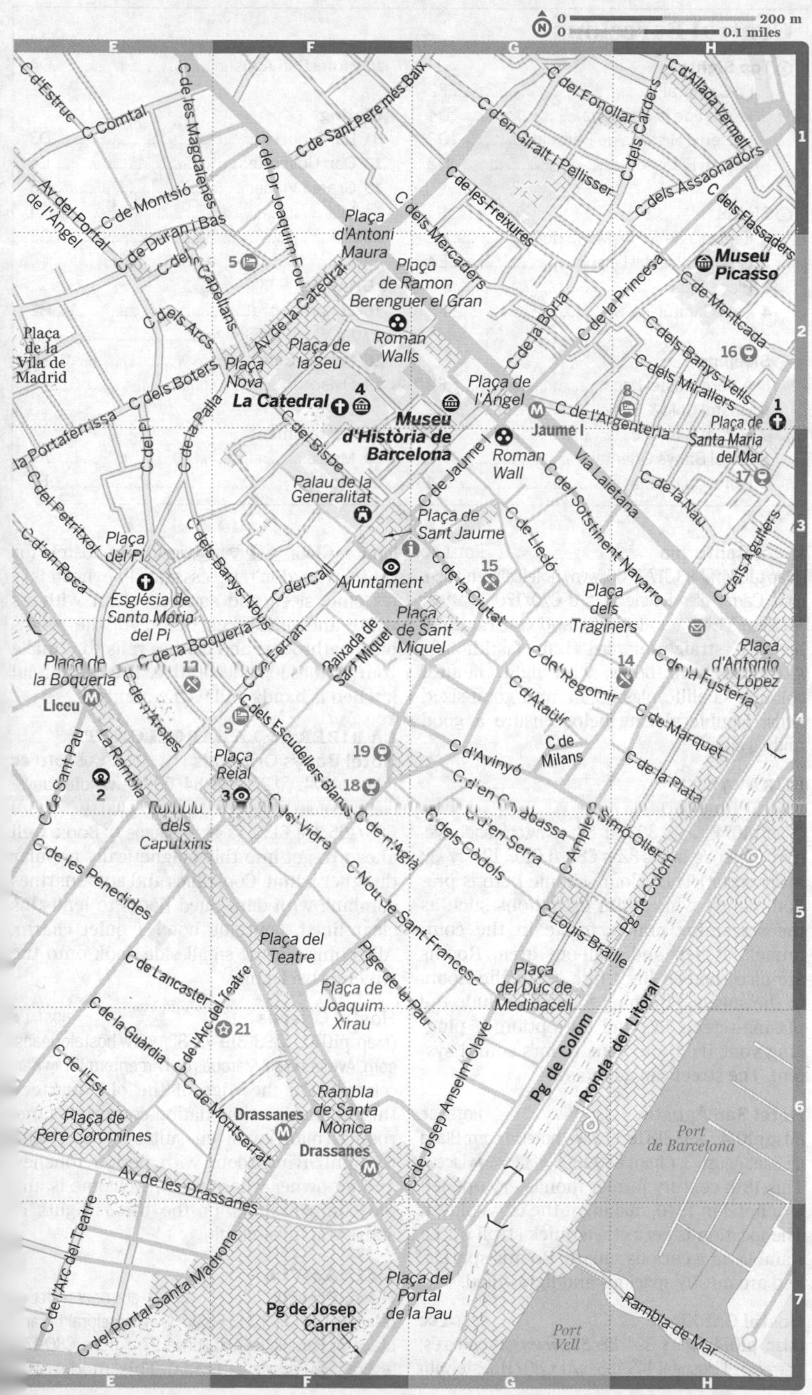
C d'Estruc
C Comtal
C de les Magdalenes
C del Dr Joaquim Fou
C de Sant Pere més Baix
C del Fonollar
C d'en Giralt i Pellisser
C dels Carders
C d'Allada Vermell
C dels Assaonadors
C dels Flassaders
Av del Portal de l'Àngel
C de Montsió
C de Duran i Bas
C del Capellans
Plaça d'Antoni Maura
C dels Mercaders
C de les Freixures
Plaça de Ramon Berenguer el Gran
Av de la Catedral
Roman Walls
C de la Princesa
C de la Bòria
Museu Picasso
C de Montcada
C dels Banys Vells
C dels Miralles
Plaça de la Vila de Madrid
C dels Arcs
Plaça de la Seu
Plaça Nova
C dels Boters
La Catedral
Museu d'Història de Barcelona
Plaça de l'Àngel
Jaume I
C de l'Argenteria
Plaça de Santa Maria del Mar
C de la Portaferrissa
C del Pi
C de la Palla
C del Bisbe
Roman Wall
C de Jaume I
Via Laietana
C del Sotstinent Navarro
C de la Nau
C del Petritxol
Palau de la Generalitat
C d'en Roca
Plaça del Pi
C dels Banys Nous
Plaça de Sant Jaume
C de Lledó
C dels Agullers
Església de Santa Maria del Pi
C del Call
Ajuntament
C de la Ciutat
Plaça dels Traginers
Plaça de la Boqueria
C de la Boqueria
C de Ferran
Baixada de Sant Miquel
Plaça de Sant Miquel
Plaça d'Antonio López
C de la Fusteria
Liceu
C d'en Arolas
C dels Escudellers
C de Regomir
C d'Ataülf
C de Marquet
C de Sant Pau
La Rambla
Plaça Reial
C d'Avinyó
C de Milans
C de la Plata
Rambla dels Caputxins
C del Vidre
C dels Escudellers Blancs
C d'en Carabassa
C d'en Serra
C Ample
C Simó Oller
C de les Penedides
C de n'Aglà
C dels Còdols
Pg de Colom
C Nou de Sant Francesc
C Louis Braille
Plaça del Teatre
Ptge de la Pau
Plaça del Duc de Medinaceli
C de Lancaster
Plaça de Joaquim Xirau
C de l'Arc del Teatre
C de la Guàrdia
C de Josep Anselm Clavé
Ronda del Litoral
C de l'Est
C de Montserrat
Rambla de Santa Mònica
Drassanes
Plaça de Pere Coromines
Port de Barcelona
Av de les Drassanes
C de l'Arc del Teatre
C del Portal Santa Madrona
Plaça del Portal de la Pau
Pg de Josep Carner
Port Vell
Rambla de Mar
SPAIN BARCELONA
0 200 m
0 0.1 miles

Central Barcelona

Top Sights
- La Catedral F2
- Mercat de la Boqueria D4
- Museu d'Història de Barcelona G2
- Museu Picasso H2

Sights
1. Església de Santa Maria del Mar H2
2. Gran Teatre del Liceu E4
3. Plaça Reial F4
4. Sala Capitular F2

Sleeping
5. Alberg Hostel Itaca F2
6. Hostal Chic & Basic A2
7. Hostal Gat Xino B5
8. Hotel Banys Orientals H2
9. Hotel California F4
10. Hotel San Agustín D4

Eating
11. Bar Pinotxo D3
12. Can Culleretes E4
13. Granja Viader D3
14. Milk H4
15. Pla G3

Drinking
16. El Xampanyet H2
17. La Vinya del Senyor H3
18. Marula Cafè F4
19. Oviso F4

Entertainment
20. Metro A2
21. Moog F6

Hotel California HOTEL €€
(Map p1074; 93 317 77 66; www.hotelcaliforniabcn.com; Carrer d'en Rauric 14; s/d €70/120; ; Liceu) This (gay) friendly and central hotel has 31 straightforward but fastidiously sparkling-clean rooms, with light, neutral colours, satellite plasma TV and good-sized beds. Double glazing helps ensure a good night's sleep.

EL RAVAL

Hostal Chic & Basic HOSTAL €€
(Map p1074; 93 302 51 83; www.chicandbasic.com; Carrer de Tallers 82; s €80, d €103-124; ; Universitat) The colour scheme here is predominantly white, with exceptions such as the screaming orange fridge in the communal kitchen and chill-out area. Rooms are also themed lily white, from the floors to the sheets. Finishing touches include the plasma-screen TVs and the option of plugging your iPod into your room's sound system. The street can get noisy.

Hotel San Agustín HOTEL €€
(Map p1074; 93 318 16 58; www.hotelsa.com; Plaça de Sant Agustí 3; r from €80-180; ; Liceu) This 18th-century former monastery opened as a hotel in 1840, making it the city's oldest. The location is perfect – a quick stroll off La Rambla on a curious square. Rooms sparkle, and are mostly spacious and light-filled.

Hostal Gat Xino HOSTAL €€
(Map p1074; 93 324 88 33; www.gatrooms.es; Carrer de l'Hospital 149-155; s/d €80/115, ste with terrace €140; ; Liceu) A hostel for those who don't necessarily like hostels – it's chic, sleek and squeeky clean with its white and lime-green decor. All the rooms have bathrooms and clothes rails that make your clothes look decorative. The communal kitchen is handy and well equipped.

LA RIBERA & LA BARCELONETA

Hotel Banys Orientals BOUTIQUE HOTEL €€
(Map p1074; 93 268 84 60; www.hotelbanysorientals.com; Carrer de l'Argenteria 37; s/d €88/105, ste €130; ; Jaume I) Book well ahead to get into this magnetically popular designer haunt. Cool blues and aquamarines combine with dark-hued floors to lend this clean-lined, boutique hotel a quiet charm. All rooms, on the small side, look onto the street or back lanes.

Hostal Orleans HOSTAL €
(Map p1070; 93 319 73 82; www.hostalorleans.com; Avinguda del Marquès de l'Argentera 13; Barceloneta) On the edge of the old quarters this affable accommodation comprises larg rooms (many with en suites), a cosy an tranquil living room with period touches and an owner whose warm welcome is am ple compensation for the three flights c stairs you must climb.

L'EIXAMPLE

Hotel Praktik BOUTIQUE HOTEL €
(Map p1070; 93 343 66 90; www.hotelpraktikrambla.com; Rambla de Catalunya 27; r from €80-17 ; Passeig de Gràcia) This modernis

gem hides a gorgeous little boutique number. While the high ceilings and the bulk of the original tile floors have been maintained, the 43 rooms have daring ceramic touches, spot lighting and contemporary art.

Hostal Goya HOSTAL €€
(Map p1070; ☎93 302 25 65; www.hostalgoya.com; Carrer de Pau Claris 74; s €70, d €96-113; ❄; Ⓜ Passeig de Gràcia, Urquinaona) The Goya is a modestly priced gem on the chichi side of L'Eixample. Rooms have a light colour scheme that varies from room to room. In the bathrooms, the original mosaic floors have largely been retained, combined with contemporary design features.

Hostel Mambo Tango HOSTEL €
(Map p1070; ☎93 442 51 64; www.hostelmambotango.com; Carrer del Poeta Cabanyes 23; dm €26; @📶; Ⓜ Paral·lel) A fun, international hostel to hang out in, the Mambo Tango has basic dorms (sleeping from six to 10 people) and a welcoming, somewhat chaotic atmosphere.

Eating

Barcelona is foodie heaven. Although Barcelona has a reputation as a hot spot of 'new Spanish cuisine', you'll still find local eateries serving up time-honoured local grub, from squid-ink *fideuà* (a satisfying paella-like noodle dish) through pigs' trotters, rabbit with snails, and *butifarra* (a tasty local sausage).

LA RAMBLA & BARRI GÒTIC

Pla FUSION €€
(Map p1074; ☎93 412 65 52; www.elpla.cat; Carrer de la Bellafila 5; mains €18-24; ⊙dinner; ✎; Ⓜ Jaume I) One of Gòtic's long-standing favourites, Pla is a stylish, romantically lit medieval den (with a huge stone arch) where the cooks churn out temptations. It has a tasting menu for €36 Sunday to Thursday.

Can Culleretes CATALAN €€
(Map p1074; ☎93 317 30 22; www.culleretes.com; Carrer Quintana 5; mains €8-14; ⊙lunch & dinner Tue-Sat, lunch Sun; Ⓜ Liceu) Founded in 1786, Barcelona's oldest restaurant is still going strong, with tourists and locals flocking to enjoy its rambling interior, old-fashioned tile-filled decor, and enormous helpings of traditional Catalan food. The multicourse lunch specials (€12.80) are good value.

Milk BRUNCH €
(Map p1074; www.milkbarcelona.com; Carrer d'en Gignàs 21; mains €9-10; ⊙10am-4pm & 6.30-11.30pm; Ⓜ Jaume I) Also known to many as a cool cocktail spot, the Irish-run Milk's key role for Barcelona night owls is providing morning-after brunches (served till 4pm). Avoid direct sunlight and tuck into pancakes, eggs Benedict and other hangover dishes in a small but cosy setting.

EL RAVAL

Bar Pinotxo TAPAS €€
(Map p1074; www.pinotxobar.com; Mercat de la Boqueria; meals €20; ⊙6am-5pm Mon-Sat Sep-Jul; Ⓜ Liceu) Bar Pinotxo is arguably La Boqueria's, and even Barcelona's, best tapas bar. It sits among the half-dozen or so informal eateries within the market, and the popular owner, Juanito, might serve up chickpeas with a sweet sauce of pine nuts and raisins, baby soft baby squid with cannellini beans, or a quivering cube of caramel sweet pork belly.

Granja Viader CAFE €
(Map p1074; ☎93 318 34 86; www.granjaviader.cat; Carrer d'en Xuclà 4; ⊙9am-1.45pm & 5-8.45pm Tue-Sat, 5-8.45pm Mon; Ⓜ Liceu) For more than a century, people have flocked down this alley to get to the cups of homemade hot chocolate and whipped cream (ask for a *suís*) ladled out in this classic Catalan-style milk bar cum deli.

LA RIBERA & WATERFRONT

Cal Pep TAPAS €€
(Map p1070; ☎93 310 79 61; www.calpep.com; Plaça de les Olles 8; mains €8-18; ⊙lunch Tue-Sat, dinner Mon-Fri Sep-Jul; Ⓜ Barceloneta) It's getting a foot in the door here that's the problem. Elbow your way to the bar for some of the tastiest gourmet seafood tapas in town. Pep recommends *cloïsses amb pernil* (clams and ham) or the *trifàsic* (combo of calamari, whitebait and prawns). Its other pièce de résistance is a super smooth *tortilla de patatas* (Spanish omelette).

Casa Delfín SPANISH €
(Map p1070; Passeig del Born 36; mains €4-12; ⊙noon-1am; Ⓜ Barceloneta) One of Barcelona's culinary delights, Casa Delfín is everything you dream of when you think of Catalan (and Mediterranean) cooking. Start with the tangy and sweet *calçots* (a cross between a leek and an onion; February and March only), then tackle the meaty monkfish roasted in white wine and garlic.

Can Maño SPANISH €
(Map p1070; Carrer del Baluard 12; mains €8-12; ⊙Mon-Sat; Ⓜ Barceloneta) It may look like a

dive, but you'll need to be prepared to wait before being squeezed in at a packed table for a raucous night of *raciones* (larger portions of tapa dishes; posted on a board at the back) over a bottle of *turbio* – a cloudy white plonk. The seafood is abundant with first-rate squid, shrimp and fish served at rock-bottom prices.

L'EIXAMPLE & GRÀCIA

Tapaç 24 TAPAS €€
(Map p1070; www.carlesabellan.com; Carrer de la Diputació 269; mains €10-20; ⏲9am-midnight Mon-Sat; Ⓜ Passeig de Gràcia) Carles Abellán runs this basement tapas haven known for its gourmet versions of old faves. Specials include the *bikini* (toasted ham and cheese sandwich – here the ham is cured and the truffle makes all the difference) and a thick black *arròs negre de sípia* (squid-ink black rice).

Fastvínic CAFE €
(Map p1070; ☎93 487 32 41; www.fastvinic.com; Carrer de la Diputació 251 ; sandwiches €6-10; ⏲noon-midnight Mon-Sat; Ⓜ Passeig de Gracia) A project in sustainability all round, this is slow food done fast, with ingredients, wine and building materials all sourced from Catalonia. It's all sandwiches on the menu, with some wonderful choices of roast beef, mustard and honey, or more adventurous crunchy suckling pig, banana chutney and coriander; there is also a self-service wine machine with quality Spanish choices.

MONTJUÏC, SANTS & POBLE SEC

TOP CHOICE Tickets SPANISH €€
(Map p1070; www.ticketsbar.es; Avinguda del Paral·lel 164; tapas €4-12; ⏲lunch & dinner; Ⓜ Paral·lel) This is, literally, one of the sizzling tickets in the restaurant world. It's the new tapas bar opened by Ferran Adrià, of the legendary (now closed) El Bulli, and his brother Albert. And unlike El Bulli, it's an affordable venture – if you can book a table, that is (you can only book online, and two months in advance).

Quimet i Quimet TAPAS €€
(Map p1070; Carrer del Poeta Cabanyes 25; tapas €3-11; ⏲lunch & dinner Mon-Fri, noon-6pm Sat; Ⓜ Paral·lel) Quimet i Quimet is a family-run business that has been passed down from generation to generation. There's barely space to swing a calamari in this bottle-lined, standing-room-only place, but it is a tapas treat for the palate.

Drinking

BARRI GÒTIC

Oviso BAR
(Map p1074; Carrer d'Arai 5; ⏲10am-2am; Ⓜ Liceu) Oviso is a popular budget-friendly restaurant with outdoor tables on the plaza, but shows its true bohemian colours by night, with a wildly mixed crowd, a rock-and-roll vibe and a two-room fin-de-siecle interior plastered with curious murals.

Marula Cafè BAR
(Map p1074; www.marulacafe.com; Carrer dels Escudellers 49; ⏲11pm-5am; Ⓜ Liceu) A fantastic funk find in the heart of the Barri Gòtic, Marula will transport you to the 1970s and the best in funk and soul. James Brown fans will think they've died and gone to heaven.

LA RIBERA

El Xampanyet WINE BAR
(Map p1074; Carrer de Montcada 22; ⏲noon-4pm & 7-11pm Tue-Sat, noon-4pm Sun; Ⓜ Jaume I) Nothing has changed for decades in this, one of the city's best-known *cava* bars. Plant yourself at the bar or seek out a table against the decoratively tiled walls for a glass or three of *cava* (Catalan version of champagne) and an assortment of tapas, such as the tangy *boquerons en vinagre* (white anchovies in vinegar).

La Vinya del Senyor WINE BAR
(Map p1074; www.lavinyadelsenyor.com; Plaça de Santa Maria del Mar 5; ⏲noon-1am Tue-Sun; Ⓜ Jaume I) Relax on the *terrassa*, which lies in the shadow of Església de Santa Maria del Mar, or crowd inside at the tiny bar. The wine list is as long as *War and Peace* and there's a table upstairs for those who opt to sample by the bottle rather than the glass.

L'EIXAMPLE & GRÀCIA

Monvínic WINE BA
(Map p1070; ☎932 72 61 87; www.monvinic.com; Carrer de la Diputació 249; ⏲wine bar 1.30-11.30pm, restaurant 1.30-3.30pm & 8.30-10.30pm; Ⓜ Passeig de Gracia) Proclaimed as 'possibly the best wine bar in the world' by the *Wall Street Journal,* and apparently considered unmissable by El Bulli's former sommelier, Monvínic is an ode, a rhapsody even, to wine lovin'. The interactive wine list sits on the bar for you to browse on a digital tablet similar to an iPad and boasts more than 3000 varieties

Les Gens Que J'Aime B
(Map p1070; www.lesgensquejaime.com; Carrer València 286; ⏲6pm-2.30am Sun-Thu, to 3am

& Sat; Passeig de Gràcia) This intimate basement relic of the 1960s follows a deceptively simple formula: chilled jazz music in the background, minimal lighting from an assortment of flea-market lamps and a cosy, cramped scattering of red-velvet-backed lounges around tiny dark tables.

 Entertainment

To keep up with what's on, pick up a copy of the weekly listings magazine, *Guía del Ocio* (€1) from newsstands.

Nightclubs

Barcelona clubs are spread a little more thinly than bars across the city. They tend to open from around midnight until 6am. Entry can cost from nothing to €20 (one drink usually included).

Elephant CLUB
(93 334 02 58; www.elephantbcn.com; Passeig dels Til·lers 1; 11.30pm-4am Thu, to 5am Fri & Sat; Palau Reial) Getting in here is like being invited to a private fantasy party in Beverly Hills. Models and wannabes mix with immaculately groomed lads who most certainly didn't come by taxi. A big tentlike dance space is the main game here, but smooth customers slink their way around a series of garden bars in summer too.

Moog CLUB
(Map p1074; www.masimas.com/moog; Carrer de l'Arc del Teatre 3; admission €10; midnight-5am; Drassanes) This fun and minuscule club is a standing favourite with the downtown crowd. In the main dance area, DJs dish out house, techno and electro, while upstairs you can groove to a nice blend of indie and occasional classic-pop throwbacks.

Razzmatazz CLUB
Map p1070; 93 320 82 00; www.salarazzmatazz.com; Carrer de Pamplona 88; admission €15-0; midnight-3.30am Thu, to 5.30am Fri & Sat; Marina, Bogatell) Bands from far and wide ccasionally create scenes of near hysteria in his, one of the city's classic live-music and ubbing venues. Five different clubs in one uge postindustrial space attract people of l dance persuasions and ages.

ay & Lesbian Venues

arcelona's gay and lesbian scene is concentated in the blocks around Carrers de Munner and Consell de Cent (dubbed Gayxampe). Here you'll find ambience every night of the week in the bars, discos and drag clubs.

Party hard at classic gay discos such as **Arena Madre** (Map p1070; 93 487 83 42; www.arenadisco.com; Carrer de Balmes 32; admission €6-12; 12.30am-5.30am; Passeig de Gràcia) and **Metro** (Map p1074; 93 323 52 27; www.metrodiscobcn.com; Carrer de Sepúlveda 185; 1am-5am Mon, midnight-5am Sun & Tue-Thu, midnight-6am Fri & Sat; Universitat).

Sport

FC Barcelona (Barça for aficionados) has one of the best stadiums in Europe – the 99,000-capacity **Camp Nou** (93 496 36 00; www.fcbarcelona.com; Carrer d'Arístides Maillol; adult/child €23/17; 10am-8pm Mon-Sat, to 2.30pm Sun; Palau Reial) in the west of the city. Tickets for national-league games are available at the stadium, by phone or online. For the latter two options, nonmembers must book 15 days before the match.

 Shopping

Most mainstream fashion stores are along a shopping 'axis' that runs from Plaça de Catalunya along Passeig de Gràcia, then left (west) along Avinguda Diagonal.

The El Born area in La Ribera is awash with tiny boutiques, especially those purveying young, fun fashion. There are plenty of shops scattered throughout the Barri

WORTH A TRIP

ANDORRA

This mini country wedged between France and Spain offers by far the best ski slopes and resort facilities in all the Pyrenees. Once the snows melt, there's an abundance of great walking, ranging from easy strolls to demanding day hikes in the principality's higher, more remote reaches. Strike out above the tight valleys and you can walk for hours, almost alone.

The only way to reach Andorra is by road from Spain or France. If driving, fill up in Andorra; fuel is substantially cheaper there. There are bus services to/from Barcelona's Estació del Nord, Barcelona's airport El Prat de Llobregat, Lleida and Toulouse (France). All bus services arrive at and leave from Andorra la Vella.

Gòtic (stroll Carrer d'Avinyò and Carrer de Portaferrissa). For secondhand stuff, head for El Raval, especially Carrer de la Riera Baixa.

Joan Murrià FOOD
(Map p1070; ☎93 215 57 89; www.murria.cat; Carrer de Roger de Llúria 85; Ⓜ Passeig de Gràcia) Note the century-old modernista shopfront advertisements featured at this culinary temple. For a century the gluttonous have trembled here at this altar of speciality food goods from around Catalonia and beyond.

Els Encants Vells MARKET
(Map p1070; Fira de Bellcaire; ☎93 246 30 30; www.encantsbcn.com; Plaça de les Glòries Catalanes; ⏰7am-6pm Mon, Wed, Fri & Sat; Ⓜ Glòries) Also known as the Fira de Bellcaire, the 'Old Charms' flea market is the biggest of its kind in Barcelona. It's all here, from antique furniture through to secondhand clothes. A lot of it is junk, but occasionally you'll stumble across a *ganga* (bargain). The most interesting time to be here is from 7am to 9am on Monday, Wednesday and Friday, when the public auctions take place.

Vinçon HOMEWARES
(Map p1070; ☎93 215 60 50; www.vincon.com; Passeig de Gràcia 96; ⏰10am-8.30pm Mon-Sat; Ⓜ Diagonal) An icon of the Barcelona design scene, Vinçon has the slickest furniture and household goods (particularly lighting), both local and imported. Not surprising, really, since the building, raised in 1899, belonged to the modernista artist Ramon Casas.

Custo Barcelona FASHION
(Map p1070; ☎93 268 78 93; www.custo-barcelona.com; Plaça de les Olles 7; Ⓜ Jaume I) The psychedelic decor and casual atmosphere lend this avant-garde Barcelona fashion store a youthful edge. The dazzling colours and cut of anything from dinner jackets to hot pants are for the uninhibited. It has five other stores around town.

Information

Purse snatching and pickpocketing are major problems, especially around Plaça de Catalunya, La Rambla and Plaça Reial.

Tourists who want to report thefts need to go to the Catalan police, known as the **Mossos d'Esquadra** (☎088; Carrer Nou de la Rambla 80; Ⓜ Paral.lel), or the **Guàrdia Urbana** (Local Police; ☎092; La Rambla 43; Ⓜ Liceu)

Bornet (Carrer de Barra Ferro 3; per hr/10hr €2.80/20; ⏰10am-11pm Mon-Fri, 2-11pm Sat, Sun & holidays; Ⓜ Jaume I) A cool little internet centre and art gallery.

Farmàcia Clapés (La Rambla 98; Ⓜ Liceu)

Hospital Clínic i Provincial (Carrer de Villarroel 170; Ⓜ Hospital Clínic)

Oficina d'Informació de Turisme de Barcelona Main branch (Map p1074; ☎93 285 38 34; www.barcelonaturisme.com; underground at Plaça de Catalunya 17-S; ⏰8.30am-8.30pm; Ⓜ Catalunya); Aeroport del Prat (Aeroport del Prat, terminals 1, 2B & 2A; ⏰9am-9pm); Estació Sants

WORTH A TRIP

GIRONA

A tight huddle of ancient arcaded houses, grand churches, climbing cobbled streets and medieval baths, all enclosed by defensive walls and a lazy river, constitute a powerful reason for visiting north Catalonia's largest city, Girona (Castilian: Gerona). The billowing baroque facade of the **cathedral** (www.catedraldegirona.org; Plaça de la Catedral; museum adult/child €5/1.20, Sun free; ⏰10am-8pm) conceals Europe's widest Gothic nave (23m), some masterly tapestries and manuscripts, and a beautiful 12th-century Romanesque cloister. The gardens that shadow the city walls are stunning, while **The Call** (former Jewish Quarter) is centred on Carrer de la Força. For a place to stay, try **Equity Point Hostel** (☎972 31 20 45; www.equity-point.com; Plaça de Catalunya 23; dm/d incl breakfast from €17/48; ❄@📶) or **Pensió Viladomat** (☎972 20 31 76; www.pensioviladomat.com; Carrer dels Ciutadans 5; s/d without bathroom €23/40, d with bathroom €50). For a meal, there's **Creperie Bretonne** (www.creperiebretonne.com; Cort Reial 14; crepes €6-8; 🌱👪) or **+Cub** (Plaça de Catalunya; 3 tapas €10.40; ⏰lunch daily, dinner Mon-Sat; 🌱). There's also a **tourist office** (www.girona.cat; Joan Maragall 2; ⏰8am-8pm Mon-Fri, 8am-2pm & 4-8pm Sat, 9am-2pm Sun).

Girona-Costa Brava airport, 11km south of the centre, is Ryanair's Spanish hub. There are more than 20 trains per day to Figueres (€4.80 to €14.25, 30 to 40 minutes) and Barcelona (from €9.70, 1½ hours).

DALÍ'S CATALONIA

A short train ride north of Girona, Figueres is home to the zany **Teatre-Museu Dalí** (www.salvador-dali.org; Plaça de Gala i Salvador Dalí 5; adult/child €12/free; ⏲9am-8pm Jul-Sep, 9.30am-6pm Mar-Jun & Oct, shorter hr rest of yr), housed in a 19th-century theatre converted by Salvador Dalí (who was born here). 'Theatre-museum' is an apt label for this multidimensional trip through one of the most fertile (or disturbed) imaginations of the 20th century. It's full of surprises, tricks and illusions, and contains a substantial portion of Dalí's life's work.

Dalí fans will want to travel south to visit the equally kooky **Castell de Púbol** (www.salvador-dali.org; Plaça de Gala Dalí; adult/student & senior €8/5; ⏲10am-8pm daily mid-Jun–mid-Sep, shorter hr rest of yr) at La Pera, 22km northwest of Palafrugell, and the **Casa Museu Dalí** (☎972 25 10 15; www.salvador-dali.org; adult/child €11/free; ⏲by advance reservation only) at his summer getaway in Port Lligat (1.25km from Cadaqués), where entry is by advance reservation only. Some 10km northeast of Cadaqués is Cap de Creus, Spain's easternmost point and an important source of inspiration for Dalí.

(Map p1070; ⏲8am-8pm; Ⓡ Estació Sants);
Town hall (Map p1074; Plaça Sant Jaume; ☎93 285 38 32; Carrer de la Ciutat 2; ⏲8.30am-8.30pm Mon-Fri, 9am-7pm Sat, 9am-2pm Sun & holidays; Ⓜ Jaume I)
Regional Tourist Office (Map p1070; www.gencat.net/probert; Passeig de Gràcia 107; ⏲10am-7pm Mon-Sat, to 2.30pm Sun; Ⓜ Diagonal)

Getting There & Away

Air

Barcelona's airport, **El Prat de Llobregat** (☎902 404704; www.aena.es), is 12km southwest of the city centre. Barcelona is a big international and domestic destination, with direct flights from North America as well as many European cities.

Boat

Regular passenger and vehicular ferries to/from the Balearic Islands, operated by **Acciona Trasmediterránea** (☎902 454645; www.trasmediterranea.es; Ⓜ Drassanes), dock along both sides of the Moll de Barcelona wharf in Port Vell.

The Grimaldi group's **Grandi Navi Veloci** (Map p1070; ☎in Italy 010 209 4591; www1.gnv.it; Ⓜ Drassanes) runs high-speed, thrice-weekly luxury ferries between Barcelona and Genoa, while **Grimaldi Ferries** (Map p1070; ☎902 531333, in Italy 081 496444; www.grimaldi-lines.com; Ⓜ Drassanes) operates similar services to Civitavecchia (near Rome), Livorno (Tuscany) and Porto Torres (northwest Sardinia).

Bus

The main terminal for most domestic and international buses is the **Estació del Nord** (Map p1070; ☎902 260606; www.barcelonanord.com; Carrer d'Ali Bei 80; Ⓜ Arc de Triomf). ALSA goes to Madrid (€30, eight hours, up to 16 daily), Valencia (€27, 4½ to 6½ hours, up to 14 daily) and many other destinations.

Eurolines (www.eurolines.es) also offers international services from Estació del Nord and **Estació d'Autobusos de Sants** (Map p1070; Carrer de Viriat; Ⓜ Estació Sants), which is next to Estació Sants Barcelona.

Train

Virtually all trains travelling to and from destinations within Spain stop at **Estació Sants** (Plaça dels Països Catalans; Ⓜ Estació Sants). High-speed trains to Madrid via Lleida and Zaragoza take as little as two hours and 40 minutes; prices vary wildly. Other trains run to Valencia (€36 to €45, three to 4½ hours, 15 daily) and Burgos (from €66, six to seven hours, four daily).

There are also international connections with French cities from the same station.

Getting Around

To/From the Airport

The **A1 Aerobús** (Map p1070; ☎93 415 60 20; one way €5.65) runs from Terminal 1 to Plaça de Catalunya from 6.05am to 1.05am, taking 30 to 40 minutes. A2 Aerobús does the same run from Terminal 2, from 6am to 12.30am. Buy tickets on the bus.

Renfe's R2 Nord train line runs between the airport and Passeig de Gràcia (via Estació Sants) in central Barcelona (about 35 minutes). Tickets cost €3.60, unless you have a T-10 multitrip public-transport ticket.

A taxi to/from the centre, about a half-hour ride depending on traffic, costs around €25 to €30.

Public Transport

Barcelona's metro system spreads its tentacles around the city in such a way that most places of interest are within a 10-minute walk of a station.

Buses and suburban trains are needed only for a few destinations. A single metro, bus or suburban train ride costs €2, but a T-1 ticket, valid for 10 rides, costs €9.25.

Taxi

Barcelona's black-and-yellow taxis are plentiful and reasonably priced. The flag fall is €2.05. If you can't find a street taxi, call ☎93 303 30 33.

Tarragona

POP 140,180

Barcelona's senior in Roman times and a lesser medieval city, Tarragona is a provincial sort of place with some outstanding attractions: Catalonia's finest Roman ruins, a magnificent medieval cathedral in a pretty Old Town, and some decent beaches.

Sights & Activities

Museu d'Història de Tarragona RUINS
(MHT; www.museutgn.com; adult/child per site €3/free, all MHT sites €10/free; ⏰9am-9pm daily Easter-Sep, shorter hr rest of yr) The 'museum' title is somewhat misleading, as they are in fact four separate Roman sites (which since 2000 together have constituted a Unesco World Heritage site).

Start exploring with the **Pretori i Circ Romans** (Plaça del Rei), which includes part of the vaults of the Roman circus, where chariot races were once held, ending at the Pretori tower on Plaça de Rei. Near the beach is the crown jewel of Tarragona's Roman sites, the well-preserved **Amfiteatre Romà** (Plaça d'Arce Ochotorena; ⏰9am-9pm Tue-Sat, to 3pm Sun Easter-Sep, to 5pm Tue-Sat, 10am-3pm Sun & holidays Oct-Easter), where gladiators battled either each other or wild animals to the death. Much of the amphitheatre was picked to bits, the stone used to build the port, so what you see now is partial reconstruction. The northwest half of **Fórum Romà** (Carrer del Cardenal Cervantes) was occupied by a judicial basilica (where legal disputes were settled), from where the rest of the forum stretched downhill to th[e] southwest.

> **TARRAGO!NA CARD**
>
> The 48-hour **Tarrago!na Card** (€15), available from the tourist office and various hotels, gives you free access to all of the city's museums and free travel on local buses, as well as discounts in select restaurants and shops.

Museu Nacional Arqueològic de Tarragona MUSE[UM]
(www.mnat.es; Plaça del Rei 5; adult/child €3.5[0/] free; ⏰10am-8pm Tue-Sat, to 2pm Sun & holida[ys] Jun-Sep, shorter hr rest of yr) This carefully pr[e]sented museum gives further insight in[to] Roman Tarraco. Exhibits include part of th[e] Roman city walls, mosaics, frescos, scul[p]ture and pottery.

Catedral CATHEDR[AL]
(Pla de la Seu; adult/child €4/1.40; ⏰10am-7p[m] Mon-Sat Jun–mid-Oct, shorter hr rest of yr) S[it]ting grandly at the top of the old town, Ta[r]ragona's cathedral demands a solid chu[nk] of your time. Built between 1171 and 13[31] on the site of a Roman temple, it com[bines] Romanesque and Gothic feature[s], as typified by the main facade on Pla [de] la Seu. The entrance is by the cloister [on] the northwest flank of the building. T[he] cloister, and its perfectly presented ga[r]dens, has Gothic vaulting and Romanesq[ue] carved capitals.

Sleeping & Eating

Look for tapas bars and inexpensive cafes [on] the Plaça de la Font. The Moll de Pescad[ors] (Fishermen's Wharf) is the place to go [for] seafood restaurants.

Hotel Plaça de la Font HOTEL
(☎977 24 61 34; www.hotelpdelafont.com; Plaça [de] la Font 26; s/d €55/70; ❄) Simple, spick-an[d-]span rooms overlooking a bustling terra[ce] in a you-can't-get-more-central-than-this [lo]cation, right on the popular Plaça de la Fo[nt].

Camping Las Palmeras CAMPGROUN[D]
(☎977 20 80 81; www.laspalmeras.com; sites [&] 2-person tent & car €40-50, tent €11; P 📶 🏊) Th[is] cheerful camping ground lies 3km northea[st] of Tarragona; perks include a big pool an[d] leafy parkland just back from the beach a[nd] untouched coastal woodland nearby. Win[d]surfing and kitesurfing classes are also [on] offer.

El Varadero SEAFO[OD]
(Carrer de Trafalgar 13; raciones €7-9; ⏰lunch & [din]ner) This informal spot has locals lining [up] for the simple, mouth-wateringly delicio[us] seafood dishes, which might include *tig[res]* (stuffed, breaded and fried mussels), *ostr[ón]* (fat oyster) and *cigalas a la plancha* (gril[led] crayfish).

Information

Regional Tourist Office (Carrer de Fortuny 4; ⏲9am-2pm & 4-6.30pm Mon-Fri, 9am-2pm Sat)

Tourist Office (www.tarragonaturisme.cat; Carrer Major 39; ⏲10am-8pm Mon-Sat, to 2pm Sun Jul-Oct, 10am-2pm & 4-7pm Mon-Sat Nov-Jun)

Getting There & Away

BUS Services run to Barcelona, Valencia, Zaragoza, Madrid, Alicante, Pamplona, the main Andalucian cities, Andorra and the north coast. The bus station is around 1.5km northwest of the old town.

TRAIN At least 16 regional trains per day run to/from Barcelona's Passeig de Gràcia via Sants. Fares start at €16 and go up to €35.25; the journey takes one to 1½ hours.

ARAGÓN, BASQUE COUNTRY & NAVARRA

Aragón

ZARAGOZA

POP 674,725

Sitting on the banks of the mighty Ebro River, Zaragoza (a contraction of Caesaraugusta, the name the Romans gave to this city when they founded it in 14 BC) is a busy regional capital with a seemingly voracious appetite for eating out and late-night revelry. The historic old centre, crowned by the majestic Basílica del Pilar, throws up echoes of its Roman and Muslim past. The Old Town is also home to El Tubo (The Tube), a maze of streets with countless tapas bars and cafes.

Sights

FREE **Basílica de Nuestra Señora del Pilar** CHURCH

(Plaza del Pilar; ⏲7am-8.30pm, lift 10am-1.30pm & 4-6.30pm Tue-Sun) It was here on 2 January AD 40, that Santiago (St James the Apostle) is believed by the faithful to have seen the Virgin Mary descend atop a marble **pilar** (pillar). A chapel was built around the remaining pillar, followed by a series of ever-more-grandiose churches, culminating in the enormous basilica that you see today. The exterior, with its splendid main dome lording over a flurry of 10 mini-domes, each encased in chunky blue, green, yellow and white tiles, creates a kind of rugged Byzantine effect. A **lift** (admission €2) whisks you most of the way up the north tower (Torre Pilar) for fine views.

Aljafería PALACE

(Calle de los Diputados; adult/under 12yr €3/free, Sun free; ⏲10am-2pm Sat-Wed, 4.30-8pm Mon-Wed, Fri & Sat Jul & Aug, shorter hr rest of year) La Aljafería is Spain's finest Islamic-era edifice outside Andalucía. It's not in the league of Granada's Alhambra or Córdoba's Mezquita, but it's nonetheless a glorious monument. The Aljafería was built as a pleasure palace for Zaragoza's Islamic rulers, chiefly in the 11th century. After the city passed into Christian hands in 1118, Zaragoza's Christian rulers made alterations. Inside the main gate, cross the rather dull introductory courtyard into a second, the Patio de Santa Isabel, once the central courtyard of the Islamic palace. Here you're confronted by the delicate interwoven arches typical of the geometric mastery of Islamic architecture.

FREE **Museo Camón Aznar** MUSEUM

(Museo Ibercaja; Calle de Espoz y Mina 23; ⏲10am-1.45pm & 5-8.45pm Tue-Sat, 10am-1.45pm Sun) This collection of Spanish art through the ages is dominated by an extraordinary series of etchings by Goya (on the 2nd floor), one of the premier such collections in existence. You'll also find paintings by other luminaries (including Ribera and Zurbarán), which spread over the three storeys of the Palacio de los Pardo, a Renaissance mansion.

Museo del Foro de Caesaraugusta MUSEUM

(Plaza de la Seo 2; admission €2.50; ⏲9am-8.30pm Tue-Sat, 10am-2pm Sun Jun-Sep, shorter hr rest of year) The trapezoid building on Plaza de la Seo is the entrance to an excellent reconstruction of part of Roman Caesaraugusta's forum, now well below ground level.

Museo del Teatro de Caesaraugusta RUIN, MUSEUM

(Calle de San Jorge 12; admission €3.50; ⏲9am-8.30pm Tue-Sat, to 1.30pm Sun) Discovered during the excavation of a building site in 1972, the ruins of Zaragoza's Roman theatre are the focus of this interesting museum; the theatre once seated 6000 spectators.

Sleeping

TOP CHOICE **Sabinas** APARTMENT €

(☎976 20 47 10; www.sabinas.es; Calle de Alfonso I 43; d/apt €50/75; ❄📶) Apartments with a kitchen and sitting room styled with a contemporary look and a location a few steps off Plaza del Pilar make this a terrific option. The bathrooms are lovely and the price is extraordinarily good considering the location and size of the rooms. Reception is at **Hotel Sauce** (☎976 20 50 50; www.hotelsauce.com; Calle de Espoz y Mina 33; s/d €53.50/58; ❄📶), around the corner.

Hostal el Descanso HOSTAL €
(☎976 29 17 41; www.hostaleldescanso.es; Calle de San Lorenzo 2; s/d without bathroom €18/30; 📶) This welcoming family-run place combines a terrific location overlooking a pretty plaza near the Roman theatre with simple, bright rooms with comfortable mattresses. It adds up to one of the best budget choices in town.

Albergue Juvenil de Zaragoza HOSTEL €
(Zaragoza Hostel; ☎976 28 20 43; www.alberguezaragoza.com; Calle de los Predicadores 70; dm incl breakfast from €16, s/d €20/40; @) This excellent hostel has modern facilities to go with the lovely original architectural features in the basement bar. Free breakfast, internet access and lockers are among the highlights. There's live music most Thursdays to Sundays.

Eating & Drinking

Zaragoza has some terrific tapas bars, with dozens of places on or close to Plaza de Santa Marta. Otherwise the narrow streets of El Tubo, north of Plaza de España, are tapas central.

Calle del Temple, southwest of Plaza del Pilar, is the spiritual home of Zaragoza's roaring nightlife. This is where the city's students head out to drink. There are more bars lined up along this street than anywhere else in Aragón.

Casa Pascualillo TAPAS €
(Calle de la Libertad 5; mains €5-14; ⏲lunch & dinner Tue-Sat, lunch Sun) This celebrated bar groans under the weight of enticing tapas varieties; the house speciality is El Pascualillo, a 'small' *bocadillo* (filled roll) of *jamón*, mushrooms and onion. There's also a more formal restaurant attached.

El Rincón de Aragón ARAGONESE €€
(☎976 20 11 63; Calle de Santiago 3-5; mains €10-20) The decor here is basic and the food stripped down to its essence, but the eating is top-notch and ideal for finding out why people get excited about Aragonese cooking. If you're feeling hungry, numerous local dishes appear on the four-course *menú Aragonés* (€19.90). The restaurant is in the covered lane between Calle de Santiago and Plaza del Pilar.

Information

Main Tourist Office (☎976 39 35 37; www.zaragozaturismo.com; Plaza del Pilar; ⏲9am-9pm Easter-Oct, 10am-8pm Nov-Easter) The city information office, opposite the basilica.

Oficina de Turismo de Aragón (www.turismodearagon.com; Avenida de César Augusto 25; ⏲9am-2pm & 5-8pm Mon-Fri, from 10am Sat & Sun) Covers all of the Aragón region.

Getting There & Away

AIR The **Zaragoza-Sanjurjo airport** (☎976 71 23 00) has domestic and international flights.

BUS Services from the bus station attached to the Estación Intermodal Delicias train station include Madrid (from €15.50, 3¾ hours) and Barcelona (€14.50, 3¾ hours).

TRAIN Zaragoza's **Estación Intermodal Delicias** (Calle Rioja 33) is connected by almost hourly high-speed AVE services to Madrid (€60.25, 1½ hours, 10 daily) and Barcelona (€66, from 1½ hours). There are also trains to Valencia (€30, 4½ hours, three daily) and Teruel (€17, 2¼ hours, four daily).

Around Aragón

In Aragón's south, little visited **Teruel** is home to some stunning Mudéjar architecture. Nearby, **Albarracín** is one of Spain's most beautiful villages.

In the north, the Pyrenees dominate and the **Parque Nacional de Ordesa y Monte Perdido** is excellent for hiking; pretty **Torla** is the gateway. South of the hamlet of **La Besurta** is the great Maladeta massif, a superb challenge for experienced climbers. This forbidding line of icy peaks, with glaciers suspended from the higher crests, culminates in **Aneto** (3404m), the highest peak in the Pyrenees. There are plenty of hiking and climbing options for all levels in these mountain parks bordering France. Another enchanting base for exploration in the region is **Aínsa**, a hilltop village of stone houses.

In Aragón's northwest, **Sos del Rey Católico** is another gorgeous stone village draped along a ridge.

Basque Country

SAN SEBASTIÁN

POP 185,500

Stylish San Sebastián (Donostia in Basque) has the air of an upscale resort, complete with an idyllic location on the shell-shape

Bahía de la Concha. The natural setting – crystalline waters, a flawless beach, green hills on all sides – is captivating. But this is one of Spain's true culinary capitals, with more Michelin stars (14) per capita here than anywhere else on Earth.

Sights & Activities

Beaches & Isla de Santa Clara BEACH

Fulfilling almost every idea of how a perfect city beach should be formed, **Playa de la Concha** and its westerly extension, **Playa de Ondarreta**, are easily among the best city beaches in Europe. The **Isla de Santa Clara**, about 700m from the beach, is accessible by **glass-bottom boats** (to the island €3.80, tour the bay €6) that run every half-hour from June to September from the fishing port. Less popular, but just as showy, **Playa de Gros** (Playa de la Zurriola), east of Río Urumea, is the city's main surf beach.

Museo Chillida Leku MUSEUM, PARK

(www.museochillidaleku.com; adult/child €8.50/free; 10.30am-8pm Mon-Sat, to 3pm Sun Jul & Aug, shorter hr rest of year) This open-air museum is the most engaging museum in rural Basque Country. Amid the beech, oak and magnolia trees, you'll find 40 sculptures of granite and iron created by the renowned Basque sculptor Eduardo Chillida. Many more of Chillida's works appear inside the renovated 16th-century farmhouse. To get here, take bus (€1.35) for Hernani from Calle de Okendo in San Sebastián and get off at Zabalaga.

Monte Igueldo VIEWPOINT

The views from the summit of Monte Igueldo, just west of town, will make you feel like a circling hawk staring over the vast panorama of the Bahía de la Concha and the surrounding coastline and mountains. The best way to get there is via the old-world **funicular railway** (return adult/child €2.80/2.10; 10am-10pm).

Monte Urgull CASTLE, MUSEUM

You can walk to the top of Monte Urgull, topped by low castle walls and a grand statue of Christ, by taking a path from Plaza de Zuloaga or from behind the aquarium. The views are breathtaking. The castle houses the well-presented **Mirando a San Sebastián** (admission free; 10am-2pm & 3-5.30pm), a small museum focusing on the city's history.

Sleeping

Pensión Bellas Artes BOUTIQUE HOTEL €€

(943 47 49 05; www.pension-bellasartes.com; Calle de Urbieta 64; s €69-89, d €89-109;) To call this magnificent place a mere *pensión* is to do it something of a disservice. Its rooms (some with glassed-in balconies), with their exposed stone walls and excellent bathrooms, should be the envy of many a more-expensive hotel. It also has to be the friendliest hotel in town.

Urban House HOSTEL €

(943 42 81 54; www.enjoyeu.com; Plaza Gipuzkoa 2; dm €18-20, r from €35;) This busy party house where summer fun rules supreme is one of the longest running hostels in town. It's close to all the action and the young, very Anglophone staff (so Anglophone that some don't speak any Spanish) will ensure you have a good time. They also organise a variety of city tours and surf lessons.

Pensión Amaiur Ostatua BOUTIQUE HOTEL €

(943 42 96 54; www.pensionamaiur.com; Calle de 31 de Agosto 44; s €45, d €54-65; @) This Old Town classic has always been one of the city's stand-out acommodations options. At the time of research it was closed for major renovations that promise to make it even better than before. It will have reopened by the time this book hits the shelves.

Eating

San Sebastián is paradise for food lovers. Considered the birthplace of *nueva cocina española* (Spanish nouvelle cuisine), this area is home to some of the country's top chefs. Yet not all the good food is pricey. Head to the Parte Vieja for San Sebastián's *pintxos*, Basque-style tapas.

Do what the locals do – crawls of the city centre's bars. *Pintxo* etiquette is simple. Ask for a plate and point out what *pintxos* (bar

SPLURGE

With three shining Michelin stars, acclaimed chef Juan Mari Arzak takes some beating when it comes to *nueva cocina vasca* and his **restaurant** (943 27 84 65; www.arzak.info; Avenida Alcalde Jose Elosegui 273; meals €175; closed Sun & Mon Nov & late Jun) is, not surprisingly, considered one of the best places to eat in Spain. Arzak is now assisted by his daughter Elena and they never cease to innovate. Reservations, well in advance, are obligatory. The restaurant is about 1.5km east of San Sebastián.

snacks – more like tasty mounds of food on little slices of baguette) you want. Keep the toothpicks and go back for as many as you'd like. Accompany with *txakoli,* a cloudy white wine poured like cider to create a little fizz. When you're ready to pay, hand over the plate with all the toothpicks and tell bar staff how many drinks you've had. It's an honour system that has stood the test of time. Expect to pay €2.50 to €3.50 for a *pintxo* and *txakoli*.

La Cuchara de San Telmo CONTEMPORARY BASQUE €€
(www.lacucharadesantelmo.com; Calle de 31 de Agosto 28) This unfussy, hidden-away (and hard to find) bar offers miniature *nueva cocina vasca* from a supremely creative kitchen. Chefs Alex Montiel and Iñaki Gulin conjure up delights, and a percentage of profits goes to the worthy Fundación Vicente Ferrer charity.

Astelena BASQUE €€
(Calle de Iñigo 1) The *pintxos* draped across the counter in this bar, tucked into the corner of Plaza de la Constitución, stand out as some of the best in the city. Many of them are a fusion of Basque and Asian inspirations.

Restaurante Alberto SEAFOOD €
(☎943 42 88 84; Calle de 31 de Agosto 19; menus €15; ⏲closed Tue) A charming old seafood restaurant with a fishmonger-style window display of the day's catch. It's small and friendly and the pocket-sized dining room feels like it was once someone's living room. The food is earthy and good and the service swift.

La Zurri BASQUE €
(☎943 29 38 86; Calle de Zabaleta 10; menus €10.80) Over the water in Gros, this ever-popular locals' seafood restaurant has a menu as long as a conger eel and all of it is consistently good. It doesn't accept credit cards.

ℹ Information

Oficina de Turismo (☎943 48 11 66; www.sansebastianturismo.com; Alameda del Boulevard 8; ⏲9.30am-1.30pm & 3.30-7pm Mon-Thu, 10am-7pm Fri & Sat, 10am-2pm Sun)

ℹ Getting There & Away

BUS Daily bus services leave for Bilbao (€10.25 to €14, one hour), Bilbao Airport (€15.75, 1¼ hours), Biarritz (France; €6.60, 1¼ hours), Madrid (from €33.75, five hours) and Pamplona (€7.30, one hour).

TRAIN The main **Renfe train station** (Paseo de Francia) is just across Río Urumea. There are regular services to Madrid (from €54.25, five hours) and Barcelona (from €63.50, eight hours). There's only one direct train to Paris, but there are plenty more from the Spanish/French border town of Irun, or sometimes Hendaye, (€2.20, 25 minutes), which is also served by **Eusko Tren/Ferrocarril Vasco** (www.euskotren.es). Trains depart every half-hour from Amara train station, about 1km south of the city centre.

BILBAO

POP 351,300

The commercial hub of the Basque Country, Bilbao (Bilbo in Basque) is best known

PAMPLONA & SAN FERMINES

Immortalised by Ernest Hemingway in *The Sun Also Rises*, the pre-Pyrenean city of Pamplona (Iruña in Basque) is home of the wild Sanfermines (aka Encierro or the Running of the Bulls) festival, but is also an extremely walkable city that's managed to mix the charm of old plazas and buildings with modern shops and a lively nightlife.

The Sanfermines festival is held from 6 to 14 July, when Pamplona is overrun with thrill-seekers, curious onlookers and, yes, bulls. The Encierro begins at 8am daily, when bulls are let loose from the Coralillos Santo Domingo. The 825m race lasts just three minutes.

Since records began in 1924, 16 people have died during Pamplona's bullrun. Many of those who run are full of bravado (and/or drink) and have little idea of what they're doing. For dedicated *encierro* news, check out www.sanfermin.com.

Animal-rights groups oppose bullrunning as a cruel tradition, and the participating bulls will almost certainly all be killed in the afternoon bullfight. The PETA-organised anti-bullfighting demonstration, the Running of the Nudes, takes place two days before the first bullrun.

For more information, contact the **tourist office** (www.turismo.navarra.es; Calle de Esclava 1; ⏲9am-8pm Mon-Sat, to 2pm Sun).

for the magnificent Guggenheim Museum. An architectural masterpiece by Frank Gehry, the museum was the catalyst of a turnaround that saw Bilbao transformed from an industrial port city into a vibrant cultural centre. After visiting this must-see temple to modern art, spend time exploring Bilbao's Casco Viejo (Old Quarter), a grid of elegant streets dotted with shops, cafes, *pintxos* bars and several small but worthy museums.

Sights

Museo Guggenheim ART GALLERY
(www.guggenheim-bilbao.es; Avenida Abandoibarra 2; adult/child €13/free; ⏲10am-8pm, closed Mon Sep-Jun) Opened in 1997, Bilbao's Museo Guggenheim lifted modern architecture and Bilbao into the 21st century – with sensation. Some might say, probably quite rightly, that structure overwhelms function here and that the Guggenheim is more famous for its architecture than its content. But Canadian architect Frank Gehry's inspired use of flowing canopies, cliffs, promontories, ship shapes, towers and flying fins is irresistible. The interior of the Guggenheim is purposefully vast. The cathedral-like atrium is more than 45m high. Light pours in through the glass cliffs. Permanent exhibits fill the ground floor and include such wonders as mazes of metal and phrases of light reaching for the skies. For most people, though, it is the temporary exhibitions that are the main attraction (check the Guggenheim's website for a full program of upcoming exhibitions).

Museo de Bellas Artes ART GALLERY
(Fine Arts Museum; www.museobilbao.com; Plaza del Museo 2; adult/child €6/free, Wed free; ⏲10am-8pm Tue-Sun) A mere five minutes from Museo Guggenheim is Bilbao's Museo de Bellas Artes. There are three main subcollections: Classical Art, with works by Murillo, Zurbarán, El Greco, Goya and van Dyck; Contemporary Art, featuring works by Gauguin, Francis Bacon and Anthony Caro; and Basque Art, with the works of the great sculptors Jorge de Oteiza and Eduardo Chillida, and also strong paintings by the likes of Ignacio Zuloago and Juan de Echevarria.

Casco Viejo OLD TOWN
The compact Casco Viejo, Bilbao's atmospheric old quarter, is full of charming streets, boisterous bars, and plenty of quirky and independent shops. At the heart of the Casco are Bilbao's original 'seven streets', Las

ARTEAN PASS

The Artean Pass is a joint ticket for the Guggenheim and the Museo de Bellas Artes which, at €13.50 for adults, offers significant savings. It's available from either museum.

Siete Calles, which date from the 1400s. The 14th-century Gothic **Catedral de Santiago** (Plaza de Santiago; ⏲10am-1pm & 4-7pm Tue-Sat, 10.30am-1.30pm Sun) has a splendid Renaissance portico and pretty little cloister. Further north, the 19th-century arcaded Plaza Nueva is a rewarding *pintxo* haunt.

Euskal Museoa MUSEUM
(Museo Vasco; Plaza Miguel Unamuno 4; adult/child €3/free, Thu free; ⏲11am-5pm Tue-Sat, to 2pm Sun) This is probably the most complete museum of Basque culture and history in all the Basque regions. The story kicks off back in the days of prehistory and from this murky period the displays bound rapidly through to the modern age. The museum is housed in a fine old building, at the centre of which is a peaceful cloister that was part of an original 17th-century Jesuit College.

Sleeping & Eating

The Bilbao tourism authority has a useful **reservations department** (☎902 877298; www.bilbaoreservas.com) for accommodation.

Pensión Iturrienea Ostatua BOUTIQUE HOTEL €€
(☎944 16 15 00; www.iturrieneaostatua.com; Calle de Santa María 14; r €50-70; 📶) Easily the most eccentric hotel in Bilbao, it's part farmyard, part old-fashioned toyshop, and a work of art in its own right. The nine rooms here are so full of character that there'll be barely enough room for your own! There's a lovely breakfast are.

Hostal Begoña BOUTIQUE HOTEL €
(☎944 23 01 34; www.hostalbegona.com; Calle de la Amistad 2; s/d from €50/55; @📶) Begoña speaks for itself with colourful rooms decorated with modern artworks, all with funky tiled bathrooms and wrought-iron beds. It's probably the best hotel in the city in which to meet other travellers. There's a car park nearby.

Rio-Oja BASQUE €
(☎944 15 08 71; Calle de Perro 4; mains €8-11) An institution that shouldn't be missed. It specialises in light Basque seafood and

heavy inland fare, but to most foreigners the snails, sheep brains or squid floating in pools of its own ink are the makings of a culinary adventure story they'll be recounting for years.

Abaroa BASQUE €€
(☎944 13 20 51; www.abaroa.net; Paseo del Campo de Volantin 13; mains €8-15, menú del día €12.99) This intimate and brightly furnished restaurant is a big name with locals. It specialises in hearty countryside fare, but with a twist of today. The result is that black pudding and a bowl of beans have never been so well presented or tasted so good. There is a second, equally good **branch** (Plaza del Museo).

Information

Tourist Office (www.bilbao.net/bilbaoturismo; Plaza del Ensanche 11; 9am-2pm & 4-7.30pm Mon-Fri) Other branches at the Teatro Arriaga, Museo Guggenheim and airport.

Getting There & Away

BUS Regular bus services operate to/from Madrid (€28.50, 4¾ hours), Barcelona (€44, seven hours), Pamplona (€13.75, two hours) and Santander (from €7, 1¼ hours).
TRAIN Two Renfe trains runs daily to Madrid (from €50.50, six hours) and Barcelona (€65, six hours) from the Abando train station. Slow **FEVE** (www.feve.es) trains run from Concordia station next door, heading west into Cantabria and Asturias.

CANTABRIA & GALICIA

With a landscape reminiscent of parts of the British Isles, 'Green Spain' offers great walks in national parks, seafood feasts in sophisticated towns and oodles of opportunities to plunge into the ice-cold waters of the Bay of Biscay.

Cantabria

Some 34km west of the regional capital, Santander, **Santillana del Mar** (www.santillanadelmar.com) is a bijou medieval village and the obvious overnight base for visiting the nearby Cueva de Altamira.

The country's finest prehistoric art, in the Cueva de Altamira, 2km southwest of Santillana del Mar, is off-limits to all but the scientific community. Since 2002, however, the **Museo Altamira** (www.museodealtamira.mcu.es; adult/child, EU senior or student €3/free, Sun & from 2.30pm Sat free; 9.30am-8pm Tue-Sat, to 3pm Sun & holidays; P) has allowed all comers to view the inspired, 14,500-year-old depictions of bison, horses and other beasts (or, rather, their replicas) in this full-size, dazzling re-creation of the cave's most interesting chamber, the Sala de Polícromos (Polychrome Hall).

Buses run three to four times a day from Santander to Santilla del Mar.

Santiago de Compostela

POP 95,400

The supposed burial place of St James (Santiago), Santiago de Compostela is a bewitching city. Christian pilgrims journeying along the Camino de Santiago often end up mute with wonder on entering its medieval centre. Fortunately, they usually regain their verbal capacities over a celebratory late-night foray into the city's lively bar scene.

Sights

Catedral de Santiago de Compostela CATHEDRAL
(www.catedraldesantiago.es; Praza do Obradoiro; 7am-9pm) The grand heart of Santiago, the cathedral soars above the city centre in a splendid jumble of moss-covered spires and statues. Though Galicia's grandest monument was built piecemeal through the centuries, its beauty is only enhanced by the mix of Romanesque, baroque and Gothic flourishes. What you see today is actually the fourth church to stand on this spot. The bulk of it was built between 1075 and 1211, in Romanesque style with a traditional Latin cross layout and three naves.

The main entrance is via the lavish staircase and facade on the Praza do Obradoiro or through the south door on Praza de Praterías. The baroque **Obradoiro facade** was erected in the 18th century partly to protect the cathedral's original entrance, which is now just inside it – the artistically unparalleled Pórtico de la Gloria (Galician Porta da Gloria), with its 200 Romanesque sculptures by Maestro Mateo.

Towards the far (west) end of the cathedral's main nave, to the right of the Churrigueresque **Altar Mayor** (Main Altar), a small staircase leads up above the altar to a 13th-century statue of Santiago, which the faithful queue up to embrace.

A special pilgrims' Mass is usually celebrated at noon daily, with other Masses usually at 9.30am or 10am daily, 1.15pm Sunday, 6pm Saturday and Sunday, and 7.30pm daily. Touristic visits are not allowed during these services.

For an unforgettable bird's-eye view of the city, take the **cathedral rooftop tour** (981 55 29 85; www.catedraldesantiago.es; per person €10; 10am-2pm & 4-8pm).

Museo da Catedral MUSEUM
(www.catedraldesantiago.es; Praza do Obradoiro; adult/student & pilgrim/child €5/3/free; 10am-2pm & 4-8pm, closed Sun afternoon) The cathedral museum, entered to the right of the cathedral's Obradoiro facade, spreads over four floors and includes the cathedral's large, 16th-century, Gothic/plateresque cloister. You'll see a sizeable section of Maestro Mateo's original carved stone choir (destroyed in 1603 but recently pieced back together), the lavishly decorated 18th-century *sala capitular* (chapter house) and, off the cloister, the Panteón de Reyes, which contains tombs of kings of medieval León.

Around the Cathedral SQUARE
The cathedral is surrounded by handsome plazas that invite you to wander through them. The grand **Praza do Obradoiro** (Workshop Plaza), to which most arriving Camino pilgrims instinctively find their way, earned its name from the stonemasons' workshops set up here while the cathedral was being built. At its northern end, the Renaissance **Hostal dos Reis Católicos** (admission €3; noon-2pm & 4-6pm Sun-Fri) was built in the early 16th century. Along the western side of the square is the elegant 18th-century **Pazo de Raxol**, now the city hall.

FREE **Museo das Peregrinacións** MUSEUM
www.mdperegrinacions.com; Rúa de San Miguel ; 10am-8pm Tue-Fri, 10.30am-1.30pm & 5-8pm at, 10.30am-1.30pm Sun) Eight rooms explore e Camino de Santiago phenomenon over e centuries.

idade da Cultura e Galicia CULTURAL CENTRE
ity of Culture of Galicia; www.cidadedacultura.org; 8am-11pm, building interiors 10am-2pm & 4-8pm, useum closed Mon; P) This vast prestige oject is taking shape atop Monte Gaiás, a l about 1.5km southeast of the old town, the designs of American Peter Eisenman. The first sections, the Library and Archive of Galicia, opened in 2011.

Sleeping

Hotel Costa Vella BOUTIQUE HOTEL €€
(981 56 95 30; www.costavella.com; Rúa da Porta da Pena 17; s €59, d €81-97;) The tranquil, thoughtfully designed rooms (some with glassed-in galleries), friendly welcome and lovely garden cafe make this a wonderful option. Even if you don't stay, it's an ideal spot for breakfast or coffee.

Pensión da Estrela PENSION €
(981 57 69 24; www.pensiondaestrela.com; Praza de San Martiño Pinario 5; r €60;) There are just six smallish rooms here but they're bright, colourful and clean, and four of them overlook a quiet plaza. The welcome is warm, with nice touches such as neatly rolled towels and a bag of sweets, and there's a small kitchen with free tea and coffee.

Meiga Backpackers HOSTEL €
(981 57 08 46; www.meiga-backpackers.es; Rúa dos Basquiños 67; dm incl breakfast €17-18; @) Clean, colourful, friendly, and handily placed between the bus station and city centre, Meiga has spacious bunk dorms, a good kitchen, bright lounge and a long garden. It's the top choice if you're on the budget backpacking trail.

Eating

O Curro da Parra CONTEMPORARY GALICIAN €€
(www.ocurrodaparra.com; Rúa do Curro da Parra 7; mains €14-20, tapas €5-8; closed Mon) With a

PICOS DE EUROPA

These jagged mountains straddling Asturias, Cantabria and northeast Castilla y León amount to some of the finest walking country in Spain.

They comprise three limestone massifs (the highest peak rises 2648m). The 647-sq-km **Parque Nacional de los Picos de Europa** (www.picosdeeuropa.com) covers all three massifs and is Spain's second-biggest national park.

There are numerous places to stay and eat all over the mountains. Getting here and around by bus can be slow going, but the Picos are accessible from Santander and Oviedo (the latter is easier) by bus.

neat little stone-walled dining room upstairs and a narrow tapas and wine bar below, this relative newcomer serves up a broad range of thoughtfully created, market-fresh fare. On weekday lunchtimes it serves a great-value €11 *menú mercado* (market menu).

O Beiro TAPAS, RACIONES €
(Rúa da Raíña 3; raciones €5-10; ⏲closed Sun night & Mon Oct-Mar) The house speciality is *tablas* (trays) of delectable cheeses and sausages, but there are plenty of other *raciones* and tapas at this friendly two-level wine bar. It also offers a terrific range of Galician wines and the fiery local grape-based liquors *orujo* and *aguardiente*.

A Taberna do Bispo TAPAS €
(☎981 58 60 45; Rúa do Franco 37; tapas & raciones €1.50-8; ⏲closed Mon) Tantalising tapas are arrayed along the bar's length, Basque-style, and you can order all sorts of goodies, including a *timbal de vieiras* (scallops with potatoes, wild mushrooms, shellfish and port) or *montaditos* (small open sandwiches) of *solomillo* (pork sirloin) with bacon, cheese and dates.

Information

Oficina de Acogida de Peregrinos (Pilgrims' Reception Office; ☎981 56 88 46; www.peregrinossantiago.es; Rúa do Vilar 3; ⏲9am-9pm) People who have covered at least the last 100km of the Camino de Santiago on foot or horseback, or the last 200km by bicycle, with spiritual or religious motives, can obtain their 'Compostela' certificate to prove it here.

Oficina de Turismo de Galicia (www.turgalicia.es; Rúa do Vilar 30-32; ⏲10am-8pm Mon-Fri, 11am-2pm & 5-7pm Sat, 11am-2pm Sun) The scoop on all things Galicia as well as on the Camino de Santiago.

Turismo de Santiago (☎981 55 51 29; www.santiagoturismo.com; Rúa do Vilar 63; ⏲9am-9pm, to 7pm Nov-Mar) The efficient main municipal tourist office.

Getting There & Around

BUS The **bus station** (☎981 54 24 16; www.tussa.org; Praza de Camilo Díaz Baliño; 📶) is about a 20-minute walk northeast of the centre. Castromil-Monbus runs to destinations throughout Galicia. ALSA has services to Oviedo (€27.75, 5¼ to 8¾ hours), León (€28, six hours) and Madrid (€44 to €63.50, 7¾ to 10 hours). ALSA also has direct daily services to Porto (€30, 4¼ hours) and Lisbon (€50, 9¾ hours).

TRAIN From the **train station** (☎981 59 18 59; Rúa do Hórreo), regional trains run up and down the coast, while a daytime Talgo and an overnight Trenhotel head to Madrid (from €50.75, 6¼ to 9½ hours).

Around Galicia

Galicia's dramatic Atlantic coastline is one of Spain's best-kept secrets, with wild and precipitous cliffs and isolated fishing villages. The lively port city of **A Coruña** has a lovely city beach and fabulous seafood (a recurring Galician theme). It's also the gateway to the stirring landscapes of the **Costa da Morte** and **Rías Altas**; the latter's highlight among many is probably **Cabo Ortegal**. Inland Galicia is also worth exploring, especially the old town of **Lugo**, surrounded by what many consider to be the world's best preserved Roman walls.

VALENCIA

POP 815,000

Valencia, where paella first simmered over a wood fire, is a vibrant, friendly, slightly chaotic place. It has two outstanding fine-arts museums, an accessible old quarter, Europe's newest cultural and scientific complex, and one of Spain's most exciting nightlife scenes.

Sights & Activities

TOP CHOICE **Ciudad de las Artes y las Ciencias** SCIENCE CENTRE
(City of Arts & Sciences; ☎902 100031; www.cac.es; combined ticket adult/child €31.50/24) The aesthetically stunning City of Arts & Sciences occupies a massive 350,000-sq-metre swath of the old Turia riverbed. It's mostly the work of stellar local architect, the world-renowned Santiago Calatrava. The complex includes the **Oceanogràfic** (adult/child €24.90/18.80; ⏲10am-6pm or 8pm), a stunning aquarium; **Hemisfèric** (adult/child €7.85/6.10), a planetarium and IMAX cinema; **Museo de las Ciencias Príncipe Felipe** (adult/child €7.85/6.10; ⏲10am-7pm or 9pm), an interactive science museum; and the extraordinary **Palau de les Arts Reina Sofía** (www.lesarts.com) concert hall. Take bus 35 from Plaza del Ayuntamiento or bus 95 from Torres de Serranos or Plaza de América.

Barrio del Carmen HISTORIC AREA
You'll see Valencia's best face by simply wandering around the Barrio del Carmen

LAS FALLAS

In mid-March, Valencia hosts one of Europe's wildest street parties: **Las Fallas de San José** (www.fallas.es). For one week (12 to 19 March), the city is engulfed by an anarchic swirl of fireworks, music, festive bonfires and all-night partying. On the final night, giant *ninots* (effigies), many of political and social personages, are torched in the main plaza.

If you're not in Valencia then, see the *ninots* saved from the flames by popular vote at the **Museo Fallero** (Plaza Monteolivete 4; adult/child €2/1; ⏲10am-7pm Tue-Sat, to 3pm Sun).

Valencia's Romanesque-Gothic-baroque-Renaissance **catedral** (Plaza de la Virgen; adult/child incl audioguide €4.50/3; ⏲10am-4.45pm or 5.45pm Mon-Sat, 2-4.45pm Sun) is a compendium of centuries of architectural history and home to the **Capilla del Santo Cáliz**, a chapel said to contain the Holy Grail (the chalice Christ supposedly used in the Last Supper). Climb the 207 stairs of the **Micalet bell tower** (adult/child €2/1; ⏲10am-7pm or 7.30pm) for sweeping city views.

Plaza del Mercado HISTORIC PLAZA

Over on Plaza del Mercado, two emblematic buildings, each a masterpiece of its era, face each other. Valencia's modernista covered market, the **Mercado Central** (www.mercadocentralvalencia.es; ⏲7.30am-3pm Mon-Sat), recently scrubbed and glowing as new, was constructed in 1928. With over 900 stalls, it's a swirl of smells, movement and colour. **La Lonja** (adult/child €2/1; ⏲10am-7pm Tue-Sat, to 3pm Sun) is a splendid late-15th-century building, a Unesco World Heritage site and was originally Valencia's silk and commodity exchange.

Beaches BEACHES

Playa de la Malvarrosa runs into **Playa de las Arenas**. Each is bordered by the **Paseo Marítimo** promenade and a string of restaurants. **Playa El Salér**, 10km south, is backed by shady pine woods. **Autocares Herca** (☎96 349 12 50; www.autocaresherca.com) buses run between Valencia and Perelló hourly (half-hourly in summer), calling by El Salér village. The beaches lie east and southeast of the city centre.

Sleeping

Chill Art Jardín Botánico BOUTIQUE HOTEL €€

(☎96 315 40 12; www.hoteljardinbotanico.com; Calle Doctor Peset Cervera 6; s/d from €85/90; ❄📶) Welcoming and megacool, this intimate – only 16 rooms – hotel is furnished with great flair. Candles flicker in the lounge and each bedroom has original artwork.

Hostal Antigua Morellana HOSTAL €

(☎96 391 57 73; www.hostalam.com; Calle En Bou 2; s €45-55, d €55-65; ❄) The friendly, family-run 18-room Hostal Antigua Morellana is tucked away near the central market. It occupies a renovated 18th-century *posada* (where wealthier merchants bringing their produce to the nearby food market would spend the night) and has cosy, good-sized rooms, most with balconies.

Pensión París PENSION €

(☎96 352 67 66; www.pensionparis.com; 1st & 3rd fl, Calle de Salvá 12; s €23, d €34-42) Welcoming, with spotless rooms – most with shared bathrooms, some with private facilities – this family-run option on a quiet street is the antithesis of the crowded, pack-'em-in hostel.

Eating

At weekends, locals in their hundreds head for Las Arenas, just north of the port, where a long line of restaurants overlooking the beach all serve up authentic paella in a three-course meal costing around €15.

La Pepica SEAFOOD €€

(☎96 371 03 66; www.lapepica.com; Paseo de Neptuno 6-8; meals around €25; ⏲lunch & dinner Mon-Sat, lunch Sun) More expensive than its many beach-side competitors, La Pepica, run by the same family for more than a century, is renowned for its rice dishes and seafood. Here, Ernest Hemingway, among other luminaries, once strutted. Between courses, browse through the photos and tributes that plaster the walls.

Delicat TAPAS, FUSION €

(☎96 392 33 57; seudelicat@hotmail.es; Calle Conde Almodóvar 4; mains €4-11, menus €12; ⏲Tue-Sun) At this particularly friendly, intimate option (there are only nine tables, plus the terrace in summer), Catina, working up front, and her partner, Paco, on full view in the kitchen, offer an unbeatable value five-course menu of samplers for lunch and a range of truly innovative tapas anytime.

Carosel MEDITERRANEAN €
(96 113 28 73; www.carosel.es; Calle Taula de Canvis 6; mains €6-10, menus €15-18; lunch & dinner Tue-Sat, lunch Sun) Jordi and his partner, Carol, run this delightful small restaurant. After a trio of tasty lunchtime starters, attractively presented on a single platter, comes a rice dish of just the right consistency, then a choice of rich desserts. The evening menu follows the same pattern but with more of all.

Tap MEDITERRANEAN, TAPAS €
(96 391 26 27; Calle de Roteros 9; mains €6-11, menu €12; lunch & dinner Tue-Sat, dinner Mon) Tap is a recent addition to the Barrio del Carmen's rich selection of small, characterful restaurants. Run by Michele and Edu, together with René, who sweats it out in the kitchen, it offers excellent value. Tapas are original and delightfully prepared, and there's a carefully selected choice of both wines and boutique beers.

Drinking

The Barrio del Carmen, the university area (around Avenidas de Aragón and Blasco Ibáñez), the area around the Mercado de Abastos and, in summer, the new port area and Malvarrosa are all jumping with bars and clubs.

Sant Jaume CAFE, BAR
(Plaza del Tossal) At this converted pharmacy, you can still see the old potion bottles and jars ranged behind the counter. Its 1st floor is all quiet crannies and poky passageways.

Cafe-Bar Negrito CAFE, BAR
(www.cafenegrito.com; Plaza del Negrito) El Negrito's large terrace trumps the cramped interior. It occupies the whole of the square and traditionally attracts a more left-wing, intellectual clientele.

Café Lisboa CAFE, BAR
(Plaza del Doctor Collado 9) This lively, student-oriented bar has a large, street-side terrace. The bulletin board is a palimpsest of small ads for apartment shares and language tuition.

Entertainment

Terraza Umbracle LOUNGE BAR
(www.umbracleterraza.com; midnight-8am Thu-Sat May–mid-Oct) At the southern end of the Umbracle walkway within the City of Arts & Sciences, this a cool, sophisticated spot to spend a hot summer night. Catch the evening breeze under the stars on the terrace, then drop below to **Mya**, a top-of-the-line club with an awesome sound system that's open year-round. Admission (around €20 including first drink) covers both venues.

Radio City CLUB
(www.radiocityvalencia.es; Calle de Santa Teresa 19; 11pm-3.30am) Almost as much mini-cultural centre as club, Radio City, always seething, pulls in the punters with activities including cinema, flamenco and dancing to an eclectic mix.

Music Box CLUB
(Calle del Pintor Zariñena 16; midnight-7am Tue-Sat) The music here is eclectic with something for everyone. Entry is free except after 3am on Friday and Saturday, when there's a €10 admission.

Information

Regional Tourist Office (96 398 64 22; www.comunitatvalenciana.com; Calle de la Paz 48; 9am-8pm Mon-Sat, 10am-2pm Sun)

Turismo Valencia (VLC) Tourist Office (96 315 39 31; www.turisvalencia.es; Plaza de la Reina 19; 9am-7pm Mon-Sat, 10am-2pm Sun) Has several other branches around town, including the train station and airport arrivals area.

Getting There & Away

AIR Valencia's **Aeropuerto de Manises** (96 159 85 00) is 10km west of the city centre. It's served by metro lines 3 and 5. Budget flights serve major European destinations.

BOAT Acciona Trasmediterránea (www.acciona-trasmediterranea.es) operates car and passenger ferries to Ibiza, Mallorca and Menorca.

BUS For Bus Valencia, the **bus station** (96 346 62 66) is beside the riverbed on Avenida Menéndez Pidal. **Avanza** (www.avanzabus.com) operates hourly bus services to/from Madrid (€27.50 to €34.50, four hours). **ALSA** (www.alsa.es) has numerous buses to/from Barcelona (€27 to €32, 4½ hours) and Alicante (€19, 2½ hours), most passing by Benidorm (€15.25, 1¾ hours).

TRAIN From Valencia's Estación del Norte, major destinations include Alicante (€17 to €29, 1¾ hours, eight daily) and Barcelona (€40 to €44, three to 3½ hours, at least 12 daily). The AVE, the high-speed train, now links Madrid and Valencia, with up to 15 high-speed services daily and a journey time of around 1¾ hours.

Getting Around

Metro line 5 connects the airport, city centre and port. The high-speed tram leaves from the FGV tram station, 500m north of the cathedral at the Pont de Fusta. This is a pleasant way to get to the beach, the paella restaurants of Las Arenas and the port.

BALEARIC ISLANDS

POP 1.1 MILLION

The Balearic Islands (Illes Balears in Catalan) adorn the glittering Mediterranean waters off Spain's eastern coastline. Beach tourism destinations *par excellence*, each of the islands has a quite distinct identity and they have managed to retain much of their individual character and beauty. All boast beaches second to none in the Med, but each offers reasons for exploring inland too.

Check out websites like www.illesbalears.es and www.platgesdebalears.com.

Getting There & Away

AIR

In summer, charter and regular flights converge on Palma de Mallorca and Ibiza from all over Europe. Major operators from the Spanish mainland include **Iberia** (www.iberia.es), **Air Europa** (www.aireuropa.com), **Spanair** (www.spanair.com), **Air Berlin** (www.airberlin.com) and **Vueling** (www.vueling.com).

BOAT

Compare prices and look for deals at **Direct Ferries** (www.directferries.es). The main ferry companies are **Baleària** (☎902 160 180; www.balearia.com) and **Iscomar** (☎902 119 128; www.iscomar.com).

The main ferry routes to the mainland include the following:

Ibiza (Ibiza City) To/from Barcelona (Acciona Trasmediterránea, Baleària) and Valencia (Acciona Trasmediterránea)

Ibiza (Sant Antoni) To/from Denia, Barcelona and Valencia (Baleària)

Mallorca (Palma de Mallorca) To/from Barcelona and Valencia (Acciona Trasmediterránea, Baleària) and Denia (Baleària)

Menorca (Maó) To/from Barcelona and Valencia (Acciona Trasmediterránea, Baleària)

The main interisland ferry routes include the following:

Ibiza (Ibiza City) To/from Palma de Mallorca (Acciona Trasmediterránea and Baleària)

Mallorca (Palma de Mallorca) To/from Ibiza City (Acciona Trasmediterránea and Baleària) and Maó (Acciona Trasmediterránea and Baleària)

Mallorca (Port d'Alcúdia) To/from Ciutadella (Iscomar and Baleària)

Menorca (Ciutadella) To/from Port d'Alcúdia (Iscomar and Baleària)

Menorca (Maó) To/from Palma de Mallorca (Acciona Trasmediterránea and Baleària)

Acciona Trasmediterránea (☎902 454 645; www.trasmediterranea.es)

Mallorca

PALMA DE MALLORCA

The sunny, warm hues of the medieval heart of Palma de Mallorca (population 402,000), the archipelago's capital, make a great introduction to the islands. The northwest coast, dominated by the Serra de Tramuntana mountain range, is a beautiful region of olive groves, pine forests and ochre villages, with a spectacularly rugged coastline. Most of Mallorca's best beaches are on the north and east coasts, and although many have been swallowed up by tourist developments, you can still find the occasional exception.

Sights & Activities

Catedral CATHEDRAL

(La Seu; ☎971 723 130, 902 022445; www.catedraldemallorca.org; Carrer del Palau Reial 9; adult/child €6/free; ⏲10am-6.15pm Mon-Fri, to 2.15pm Sat) This awesome structure, completed in 1601, is predominantly Gothic, apart from the main facade (replaced after an earthquake in 1851) and parts of the interior. The cathedral's interior is stunning, with ranks of slender columns supporting the soaring ceiling and framing three levels of elaborate stained-glass windows. The front altar's centrepiece, a light, twisting wrought-iron sculpture suspended from the ceiling, is one of Gaudí's more eccentric creations. For once, Gaudí is upstaged by the island's top contemporary artist, Miquel Barceló, who reworked the Capella del Santíssim i Sant Pere, at the head of the south aisle, in a dream-fantasy, swirling ceramic rendition of the miracle of the loaves and fishes.

Es Baluard MUSEUM

(Museu d'Art Modern i Contemporani; www.esbaluard.org; Porta de Santa Catalina 10; adult/child €6/free, temporary exhibitions €4, Tue free; ⏲10am-8pm Tue-Sat, to 3pm Sun) This 21st-century concrete complex nests within Palma's grand Renaissance-era seaward fortifications. A playful game of light, surfaces and perspective, it makes the perfect framework for the creations within; these include works by Joan Miró, Miquel Barceló and Picasso.

Palau March MUSEUM
(Carrer de Palau Reial 18; adult/child €4.50/free; ⏲10am-6.30pm Mon-Fri, to 2pm Sat) This house, palatial by any definition, contains sculptures by such 20th-century greats as Henry Moore, Auguste Rodin, Barbara Hepworth and Eduardo Chillida, which grace the outdoor terrace. Within is a set of Salvador Dalí prints.

FREE **Museu d'Art Espanyol Contemporani** MUSEUM
(Museu Fundació Juan March; www.march.es/arte/palma; Carrer de Sant Miquel 11; ⏲10am-6.30pm Mon-Fri, 10.30am-2pm Sat) On permanent display within this 18th-century mansion are some 70 pieces held by the Fundación Juan March. Together they constitute a veritable who's who of mostly 20th-century artists, including Picasso, Miró, Juan Gris (of cubism fame), Dalí and the sculptor Julio González.

Sleeping

Central Palma Youth Hostel HOSTEL €
(☎971 10 12 15; www.centralpalma.com; Plaça de Quadrado 2; dm €25; ⏲reception 8-10am & 1-4pm; ❄@📶) This brand-new privately run youth hostel offers the cheapest city-centre accommodation and has smart four-bed dorms decorated in gaudy computer graphics. There's an in-house bar-restaurant and plenty of traveller-related advice and facilities.

Misión de San Miguel BOUTIQUE HOTEL €€€
(☎971 214 848; www.urhotels.com; Carrer de Can Maçanet 1; r from €139; ❄@📶) This 32-room boutique hotel is an astounding deal, with excellent prices and stylish designer rooms; it does the little things well with firm mattresses and rain showers, although some rooms open onto public areas and can be a little noisy.

Eating

TOP CHOICE **Simply Fosh** INTERNATIONAL €€
(☎971 72 01 14; www.simplyfosh.com; Carrer de la Missió 7a; mains €18-26, dinner menús €48; ⏲Mon-Sat) Lovingly prepared Mediterranean grub with a special touch is the order of the day in the convent refectory, one of the home kitchens of Michelin-starred chef Marc Fosh. The range of set menus is a wonderful way to sample high-quality cooking at a reasonable price, but there are also à la carte choices.

13% TAPAS €
(www.13porciento.com; Carrer Sant Feliu 13a; meals around €15; 🥬) At the quieter end of the old town, this L-shaped barn of a place is at once a wine and tapas bar, bistro and delicatessen. Most items are organic and there's plenty of choice for vegetarians. Wines are displayed on racks (both bar and takeaway prices are quoted, so you know the exact mark-up).

WORTH A TRIP

MENORCA

Renowned for its pristine beaches and archaeological sites, tranquil Menorca was declared a Biosphere Reserve by Unesco in 1993. **Maó** absorbs most of the tourist traffic. North of Maó, a drive across a lunar landscape leads to the lighthouse at **Cap de Faváritx**. South of the cape stretch some fine sandy bays and beaches, including **Cala Presili** and **Platja d'en Tortuga**, reachable on foot.

Ciutadella, with its smaller harbour and historic buildings, has a more distinctly Spanish feel to it and is the more attractive of the island's two main towns. A narrow country road leads south of Ciutadella (follow the 'Platges' sign from the *ronda*, or ring road) and then forks twice to reach some of the island's loveliest beaches: (from west to east) **Arenal de Son Saura**, **Cala en Turqueta**, **Es Talaier**, **Cala Macarelleta** and **Cala Macarella**. As with most beaches, you'll need your own transport.

In the centre of the island, the 357m-high **Monte Toro** has great views; on a clear day you can see Mallorca. On the northern coast, the picturesque town of **Fornells** is on a large bay popular with windsurfers.

Good sleeping options in Ciutatella include **Hotel Gèminis** (☎971 38 46 44; www.hotelgeminismenorca.com; Carrer de Josepa Rossinyol 4; s incl breakfast €31-56, d incl breakfast €45-92 ; ⏲Apr-mid–Oct; ❄📶🏊) and **Hostal-Residencia Oasis** (☎971 38 21 97; www.hostaloasismenorca.es; Carrer de Sant Isidre 33; r €34-64). The ports in both Maó and Ciutadella are lined with bars and restaurants.

Drinking & Entertainment

The old quarter is the city's most vibrant nightlife zone. Particularly along the narrow streets between Plaça de la Reina and Plaça de la Drassana, you'll find an enormous selection of bars, pubs and bodegas. According to a much flouted law, bars should shut by 1am Sunday to Thursday (3am Friday and Saturday).

Abaco BAR
(Carrer de Sant Joan 1; ⏲from 8pm) Inhabiting the restored patio of an old Mallorcan house, Abaco is filled with ornate candelabra, elaborate floral arrangements, cascading towers of fresh fruit, and bizarre artworks. It hovers between extravagant and kitsch, but the effect is overwhelming, whatever your opinion. Paying this much for a cocktail is an outrage, but one might just be worth it here.

TOP CHOICE **Puro Beach** BAR
(www.purobeach.com; ⏲11am-2am Apr-Oct) This uber-laid-back, sunset chill lounge has a tapering outdoor promontory with an all-white bar that's perfect for sunset cocktails, DJ sessions and fusion food escapes. It is just a two-minute walk east of Cala Estancia (itself just east of Ca'n Pastilla). It's south-east of Palma de Mallorca along the coast.

Information

Consell de Mallorca Tourist Office (☎971 17 39 90; www.infomallorca.net; Plaça de la Reina 2; ⏲8am-8pm Mon-Fri, 9am-2pm Sat) Covers the whole island. For cultural and sporting events, consult *On Anar*, its free quarterly 'what's happening' guide with a version in English.

Municipal Tourist Office (☎902 102365; ⏲9am-8pm Mon-Sat) In one of the railway buildings off Plaça d'Espanya.

AROUND MALLORCA

Mallorca's northwestern coast is a world away from the high-rise tourism on the other side of the island. Dominated by the Serra de Tramuntana, it's a beautiful region of olive groves, pine forests and small villages with shuttered stone buildings. There are a couple of highlights for drivers: the hair-raising road down to the small port of **Sa Calobra**, and the amazing trip along the peninsula leading to the island's northern tip, **Cap Formentor**.

Sóller is a good place to base yourself for hiking and the nearby village of **Fornalutx** is one of the prettiest on Mallorca.

From Sóller, it's a 10km walk to the beautiful hilltop village of **Deià**, where Robert Graves, poet and author of *I Claudius*, lived for most of his life. From the village, you can scramble down to the small shingle beach of **Cala de Deià**. Boasting a fine monastery and pretty streets, **Valldemossa** is further southwest down the coast.

Further east, **Pollença** and **Artà** are attractive inland towns. Nice beaches include those at **Cala Sant Vicenç**, **Cala Mondragó** and around **Cala Llombards**.

Ibiza

Ibiza (Eivissa in Catalan) is an island of extremes. Its formidable party reputation is completely justified, with some of the world's greatest clubs attracting hedonists from the world over. The interior and northeast of the island, however, are another world. Peaceful country drives, hilly green territory, a sprinkling of mostly laid-back beaches and coves, and some wonderful inland accommodation and eateries, are light years from the ecstasy-fuelled madness of the clubs that dominate the west.

IBIZA CITY

Sights & Activities

Ibiza City's port area of **Sa Penya** is crammed with funky and trashy clothing boutiques and arty-crafty market stalls. From here, you can wander up into **D'Alt Vila**, the atmospheric old walled town.

Ramparts HISTORIC AREA
A ramp leads from Plaça de Sa Font in Sa Penya up to the **Portal de ses Taules** gateway, the main entrance. Completed in 1585, the fortifications include seven artillery bastions joined by thick protective walls up to 22m in height. You can walk the entire perimeter of these impressive Renaissance-era walls, designed to withstand heavy artillery, and enjoy great views along the way.

Catedral CATHEDRAL
(⏲9.30am-1.30pm & 5-8pm) Ibiza's cathedral elegantly combines several styles: the original 14th-century structure is Catalan Gothic but the sacristy was added in 1592 and a major baroque renovation took place in the 18th century.

Sleeping

Many of Ibiza City's hotels and *hostales* are closed in the low season and heavily booked between April and October. Make sure you book ahead.

Hostal Parque HOTEL €€€

(☎971 30 13 58; www.hostalparque.com; Carrer de Vicent Cuervo 3; s €70-90, d €130-190; ❄📶) The rooms here are small, but otherwise what you get are the basics done very well indeed, and it manages to be modern and cool without being over the top. Rarely for central Ibiza City, there's decent double glazing so noise shouldn't be too much of an issue. The best doubles overlook pleasant Plaça des Parc.

Hostal La Marina HOTEL €€

(☎971 31 01 72; www.hostal-lamarina.com; Carrer de Barcelona 7; r €75-170; ❄) Looking onto both the waterfront and bar-lined Carrer de Barcelona, this mid-19th-century building has rooms that are as flamboyant and colourful as an Ibizan club night. A handful of singles and some doubles look onto the street (with the predictable noise problem).

Eating

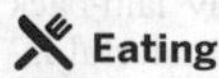

Comidas Bar San Juan MEDITERRANEAN €

(Carrer de Guillem de Montgrí 8; mains from €6; ⏲Mon-Sat) This family-run operation, with two small dining rooms, harks back to the days before Ibiza became a by-word for glam. It offers outstanding value, with fish dishes for around €10 and many small mains for €6 or less. It doesn't take reservations, so arrive early and expect to have other people join you at the same table.

Croissant Show CAFE €

(☎971 31 76 65; Plaça de la Constitució; ⏲6am-11pm) Opposite the food market, this is where *everyone* goes for an impressive range of pastries and other post-partying breakfast goodies. It is quite a scene all on its own.

S'Ametller IBIZAN €€

(☎971 31 17 80; www.restaurantsametller.com; Carrer de Pere Francesc 12; menú from €22, meals €35-40; ⏲lunch Mon-Wed, lunch & dinner Thu, Fri & Sat) The 'Almond Tree' offers local cooking based upon fresh market produce. The daily *menú* (for dessert, choose the house *flaó*, a mint-flavoured variant on cheesecake and a Balearic Islands speciality) is inventive and superb value.

Drinking

Sa Penya is the nightlife centre. Dozens of bars keep the port area jumping. Alterna-

CLUBBING IN IBIZA

In summer (late May to the end of September), the west of the island is a continuous party from sunset to sunrise and back again. In 2011 the International Dance Music Awards ranked four Ibiza clubs (see below) among their worldwide top eight.

The clubs operate nightly from around 1am to 6am and each has something different. Theme nights, fancy-dress parties and foam parties (where you are half-drowned in the stuff) are regular features. Admission can cost anything from €25 to €60.

Space (www.space-ibiza.es; admission €29-60; ⏲Jun–mid-Oct) In Platja d'en Bossa, aptly named Space, which can pack in as many as 40 DJs and up to 12,000 clubbers, is considered one of the worlds best nightclubs. Action here starts mid-afternoon and regular daytime boats make the trip between Platja d'en Bossa and Ibiza City (€6 return).

Pacha (www.pacha.com; admission €23-57; ⏲nightly Jun-Sep, Fri & Sat Oct-May) In business on the northern side of Ibiza City's port since 1973, Pacha has 15 (!) bars and various dance spaces that can hold 3000 people. The main dance floor, a sea of colour, mirror balls and veils draped from the ceiling, heaves to deep techno. On the terrace, sounds are more gentle and relaxing.

Amnesia (www.amnesia.es; admission €40-65; ⏲early Jun-Sep) Four kilometres out on the road to Sant Rafel, Amnesia has a sound system that seems to give your body a massage. A huge glasshouse-like internal terrace, filled with palms and bars, surrounds the central dance area with a mass of mostly tireless 20-something dancers.

Privilege (www.privilegeibiza.com; admission around €40) Five kilometres along the road to Sant Rafel, this club, with its 20 bars, interior pool and capacity for 10,000 clubbers, claims to be one of the world's largest. The main domed dance temple is an enormous, pulsating area, where the DJ's cabin is suspended above the pool.

tively, various bars at Platja d'en Bossa combine sounds, sand, sea and sangria.

Discobus BUS
(www.discobus.es; per person €3; ⏲midnight-6am Jun-Sep) Discobus runs around the major clubs, bars and hotels in Ibiza City, Platja d'en Bossa, Sant Rafel, Es Canar, Santa Eulària and Sant Antoni.

Teatro Pereira MUSIC BAR
(www.teatropereyra.com; Carrer del Comte de Rosselló 3; ⏲8am-4am) Away from the waterfront hubbub, this hugely atmospheric time warp of a place, which is all stained wood and iron girders, was once the foyer of the long-abandoned 1893 theatre at its rear. It's packed most nights with a more eclectic crowd than the standard preclubbing bunch, and it offers nightly live-music sessions.

Bora Bora Beach Club BEACH BAR
(⏲noon-4am May-Sep) At Platja d'en Bossa, about 2km from the old town, this is *the* place – a long beachside bar where sun and fun worshippers work off hangovers and prepare new ones. Entry's free and the ambience is chilled, with low-key club sounds wafting over the sand. From midnight, everyone crowds inside. It's off Carrer del Fumarell.

Information

Tourist Office (☎971 39 92 32; www.eivissa.es; Plaça de la Catedral; ⏲10am-2pm & 6-9pm Mon-Sat, 10am-2pm Sun) Can provide audioguides to the city; bring your passport or identity document. Other branches around the city.

AROUND IBIZA

Ibiza has numerous unspoiled and relatively undeveloped beaches. **Cala de Boix**, on the northeastern coast, is the only black-sand beach on the island, while further north are the lovely beaches of **S'Aigua Blanca**.

On the north coast near Portinatx, **Cala Xarraca** is in a picturesque, secluded bay, and near Port de Sant Miquel is the attractive **Cala Benirrás**.

In the southwest, **Cala d'Hort** has a spectacular setting overlooking two rugged rock islets, Es Verda and Es Verdranell.

The best thing about rowdy **Sant Antoni**, the island's second biggest town and north of Ibiza City, is heading to the small rock-and-sand strip on the north shore to join hundreds of others for sunset drinks at a string of chilled bars. The best known remains **Café del Mar** (⏲4pm-1am), our favourite, but it's further north along the pedestrian walkway.

Check out rural accommodation at www.ibizaruralvillas.com and www.casasrurales ibiza.com (in Spanish). For more standard accommodation, start at www.ibizahotels guide.com.

Local **buses** (www.ibizabus.com) run to most destinations between May and October.

ANDALUCÍA

Images of Andalucía are so potent, so quintessentially Spanish that it's sometimes difficult not to feel a sense of déjà vu. It's almost as if you've already been there in your dreams: a solemn Easter parade, an ebullient spring festival, exotic nights in the Alhambra. In the stark light of day the picture is no less compelling.

Seville

POP 703,000

A sexy, gutsy and gorgeous city, Seville is home to two of Spain's most colourful festivals, fascinating and distinctive *barrios* and a local population that lives life to the fullest. A fiery place (as you'll soon see in its packed and noisy tapas bars), it's also hot climatewise – avoid July and August!

Sights & Activities

Cathedral & Giralda CHURCH
(www.catedraldesevilla.es; adult/child €8/free; ⏲11am-5.30pm Mon-Sat, 2.30-6.30pm Sun Sep-Jun, 9.30am-4.30pm Mon-Sat, 2.30-6.30pm Sun Jul & Aug) After Seville fell to the Christians in 1248, its main mosque was used as a church until 1401 when it was knocked down to make way for what would become one of the world's largest cathedrals and an icon of Gothic architecture. The building wasn't completed until 1507. Over 90m high, the perfectly proportioned and exquisitely decorated **La Giralda** was the minaret of the mosque that stood on the site before the cathedral. The views from the summit are exceptional.

Inside the cathedral's southern door stands the elaborate **tomb of Christopher Columbus**, dating from 1902. Towards the east end of the main nave is the **Capilla Mayor**, whose Gothic altarpiece is the jewel of the cathedral and reckoned to be the biggest altarpiece in the world with more than

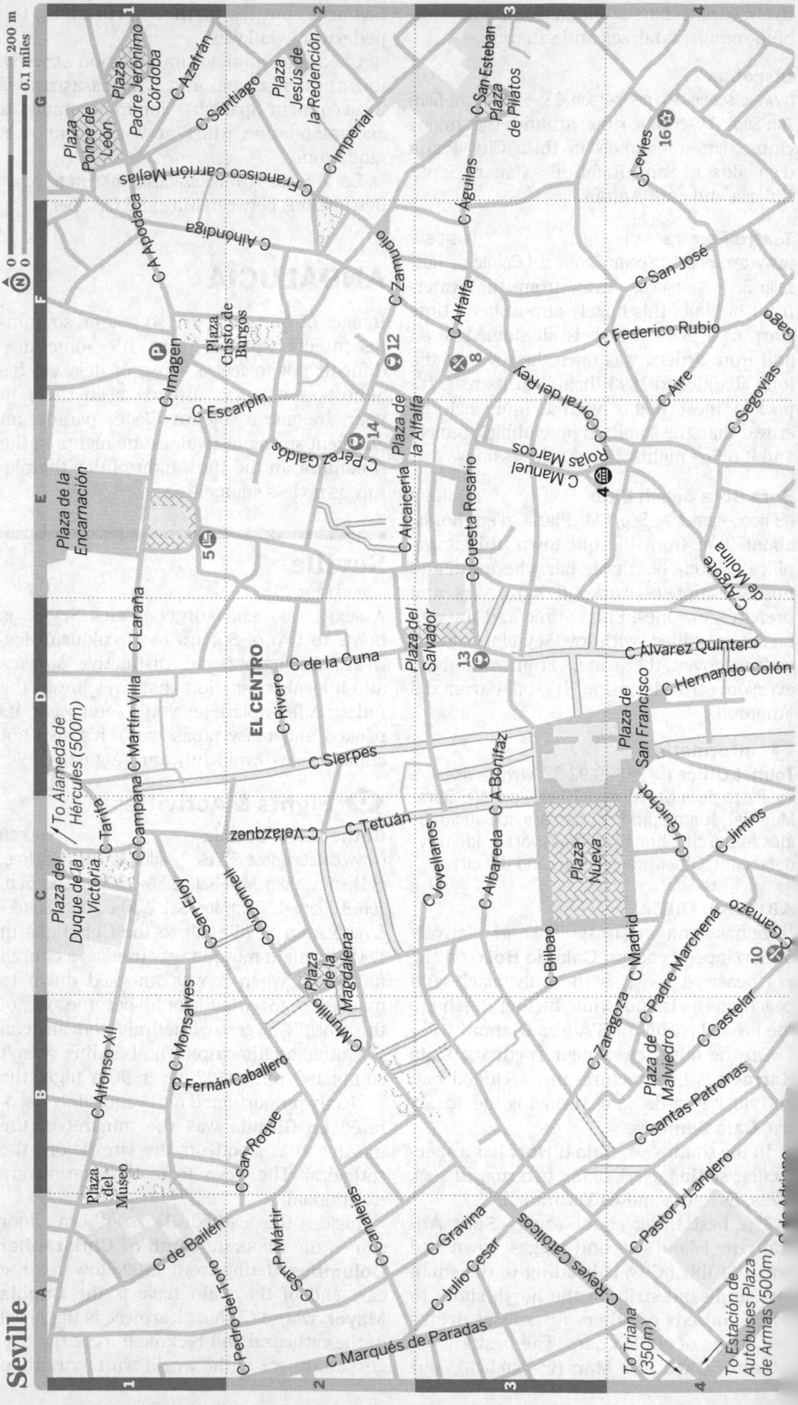

Seville

0 200 m
0 0.1 miles

A B C D E F G
1 2 3 4

Plaza del Museo
C Alfonso XII
Plaza del Duque de la Victoria
To Alameda de Hércules (500m)
C Tarifa
C Campana
C Martín Villa
C Laraña
Plaza de la Encarnación
C Imagen
C A Apodaca
Plaza Ponce de León
Plaza Padre Jerónimo Córdoba
C Francisco Carrión Mejías
C Azafrán
C Santiago
C Alhóndiga
Plaza Cristo de Burgos
C Escarpín
5
C de Bailén
C Pedro del Toro
C San Roque
C Fernán Caballero
C Monsalves
C San Eloy
C O'Donnell
C Velázquez
EL CENTRO
C Rivero
C San P Mártir
C Munillo
Plaza de la Magdalena
C Canalejas
C Marqués de Paradas
C Tetuán
C Sierpes
C de la Cuna
C Pérez Galdós
14
12
Plaza Jesús de la Redención
C Imperial
C Zamudio
C Alcaicería
Plaza de la Alfalfa
Plaza del Salvador
C Jovellanos
C Julio César
C Gravina
13
C Cuesta Rosario
8
C Alfalfa
C Águilas
C San Esteban
Plaza de Pilatos
C Albareda
C A Bonifaz
C Reyes Católicos
C Bilbao
Plaza Nueva
C Manuel Rojas Marcos
C Corral del Rey
4
C Zaragoza
C Madrid
Plaza de San Francisco
To Triana (350m)
C Pastor y Landero
C Santas Patronas
Plaza de Malviedro
C Padre Marchena
C Castelar
C J Guichot
C Hernando Colón
C Álvarez Quintero
C Federico Rubio
C San José
C Levíes
16
C Aire
To Estación de Autobuses Plaza de Armas (500m)
C de Adriano
10
C Gamazo
C Jimios
C Argote de Molina
C Segovias
Gago

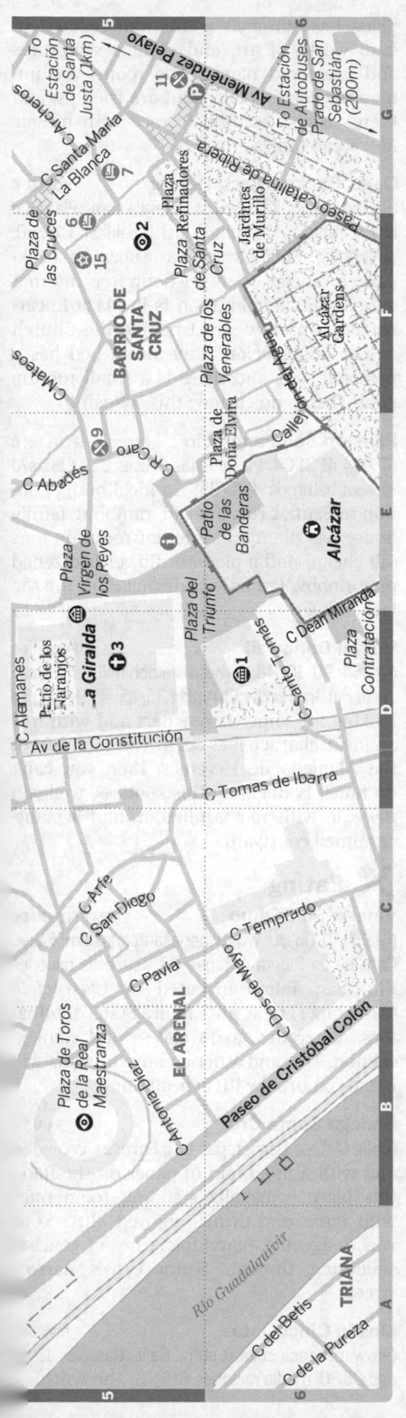

Seville

Top Sights

Alcázar E6
La Giralda D5

Sights

1 Archivo de Indias D6
2 Barrio de Santa Cruz F5
3 Cathedral & Giralda D5
4 Museo del Baile Flamenco E3

Sleeping

5 Oasis Backpackers' Hostel E1
6 Pensión San Pancracio F5
7 Un Patio en Santa Cruz G5

Eating

8 Bar Alfalfa F3
9 Bodega Santa Cruz E5
10 Mesón Cinco Jotas C4
11 Vinería San Telmo G5

Drinking

12 El Garlochi F2
13 La Antigua Bodeguita D3
14 La Rebótica E2

Entertainment

15 Casa de la Memoria de Al-Andalus F5
16 La Carbonería G4

1000 carved biblical figures. The **Sacristía de los Cálices** (Sacristy of the Chalices) contains Goya's 1817 painting of the Seville martyrs Santas Justa y Rufina. The room's centrepiece is the **Custodia de Juan de Arfe**, a huge 475kg silver monstrance made in the 1580s by Renaissance metal smith Juan de Arfe. Displayed in a glass case are the city keys handed to the conquering Fernando III in 1248.

TOP CHOICE **Alcázar** CASTLE

(adult/child €7.50/free; ⌚9.30am-7pm Apr-Sep, to 6pm Oct-Mar) Seville's Alcázar, a royal residence for many centuries, was founded in 913 as a Muslim fortress. The Alcázar has been expanded and rebuilt many times in its 11 centuries of existence. The Catholic monarchs, Fernando and Isabel, set up court here in the 1480s as they prepared for the conquest of Granada. Later rulers created the Alcázar's lovely gardens. The highlights include exquisitely adorned patios and the showpiece **Palacio de Don Pedro**.

FREE Archivo de Indias MUSEUM
(Calle Santo Tomás; ⏲10am-4pm Mon-Sat, to 2pm Sun & holidays) On the western side of Plaza del Triunfo, the Archivo de Indias is the main archive on Spain's American empire, with 80 million pages of documents dating from 1492 through to the end of the empire in the 19th century: a most effective statement of Spain's power and influence during its Golden Age.

Barrio de Santa Cruz HISTORIC DISTRICT
Seville's medieval *judería* (Jewish quarter), east of the cathedral and Alcázar, is today a tangle of atmospheric, winding streets and lovely plant-decked plazas perfumed with orange blossom. Among its most characteristic plazas is **Plaza de Santa Cruz**, which gives the *barrio* its name. **Plaza de Doña Elvira** is another romantic perch, especially in the evening.

Museo del Baile Flamenco MUSEUM
(www.museoflamenco.com; Calle Manuel Rojas Marcos 3; adult/child €10/6; ⏲9.30am-7pm) The brainchild of Sevillana flamenco dancer, Cristina Hoyos, this museum is spread over three floors of an 18th-century palace, although at €10 a pop it's a little overpriced. Exhibits include sketches, paintings, photos of erstwhile (and contemporary) flamenco greats, plus a collection of dresses and shawls.

Festivals & Events

The first of Seville's two great festivals is **Semana Santa** (www.semana-santa.org), the week leading up to Easter Sunday. Throughout the week, thousands of members of religious brotherhoods parade in penitents' garb with tall, pointed *capirotes* (hoods) accompanying sacred images through the city, while huge crowds look on.

The **Feria de Abril**, a week in late April, is a welcome release after this solemnity: the festivities involve six days of music, dancing, horse riding and traditional dress, plus daily bullfights.

The city also stages Spain's largest flamenco festival, the month-long **Bienal de Flamenco** (www.labienal.com). It's held in September in even-numbered years.

Sleeping

Un Patio en Santa Cruz HOTEL €€
(☎954 53 94 13; www.patiosantacruz.com; Calle Doncellas 15; s €65-85, d €65-125; ❄📶) Feeling more like an art gallery than a hotel, this place has starched white walls coated in loud works of art, and strange sculptures and preserved plants. The rooms are immensely comfortable, staff are friendly, and there's a cool rooftop terrace with mosaic Moroccan tables.

Oasis Backpackers' Hostel HOSTEL €
(☎954 29 37 77; www.oasissevilla.com; Plaza de la Encarnación 29; dm/d incl breakfast €15/50; ❄@📶🏊) Seville's offbeat, buzzing backpacker central offers 24-hour free internet access. The new location is in Plaza Encarnación, a narrow street behind the Church of the Anunciación. Each dorm bed has a personal safe, and there is a small rooftop pool. There's no curfew; this is Spain!

Pensión San Pancracio PENSION €
(☎954 41 31 04; Plaza de las Cruces 9; d €50, s/d without bathroom €25/35) An ideal budget option in Santa Cruz, this old, rambling family house has plenty of different room options (all cheap) and a pleasant flower-bedizened patio/lobby. Friendly staff make up for the lack of luxury.

Hostal Doña Feli PENSION €
(☎954 90 10 48; www.hostaldonafeli.com; Calle Jesús del Gran Poder 130; s/d €35/45; ❄) If you're looking for somewhere smart and with real Spanish character close to the nightlife of the Alameda de Hércules, then you can't do much better than this spotless, well-run *pensión* with rooms piled around a plant-crammed courtyard.

Eating

Vinería San Telmo TAPAS, FUSION €€
(☎954 41 06 00; www.vineriasantelmo.com; Paseo Catalina de Ribera 4; tapas €3.50, media raciones €10) San Telmo invented the *rascocielo* (skyscraper) tapa, an 'Empire State' of tomatoes, aubergine, goat's cheese and smoked salmon. This and other creative nuggets will make you drool with expectation.

Bodega Santa Cruz TAPAS
(Calle Mateos Gago; tapas €2) Forever crowded and with a mountain of paper on the floor, this place is usually standing room only with tapas and drinks enjoyed alfresco as you dodge the marching army of tourists squeezing through Santa Cruz's narrow streets.

Mesón Cinco Jotas TAPAS €
(www.mesoncincojotas.com; Calle Castelar 1; tapas €3.80, media raciones €10) In the world

jamón-making, if you are awarded 'Cinco Jotas' (Five Js) for your *jamón,* it's like getting an Oscar. The owner of this place, Sánchez Romero Carvajal, is the biggest producer of Jabugo ham, and has a great selection on offer.

Bar Alfalfa TAPAS €
(cnr Calles Alfalfa & Candilejo; tapas €3) It's amazing how many people, hams, wine bottles and knick-knacks you can stuff into such a small space. No matter, order through the window when the going gets crowded. You won't forget the tomato-tinged magnificence of the Italy-meets-Iberia *salmorejo* bruschetta.

Drinking

Bars usually open 6pm to 2am weekdays, 8pm till 3am at the weekend. Drinking and partying really get going around midnight on Friday and Saturday (daily when it's hot). In summer, dozens of open-air late-night bars *(terrazas de verano)* spring up along both banks of the river.

Plaza del Salvador is brimful of drinkers from mid-evening to 1am. Grab a drink from **La Antigua Bodeguita** (954 56 18 33) next door and sit on the steps of the Parroquia del Salvador.

El Garlochi BAR
(Calle Boteros 4) Dedicated entirely to the iconography, smells and sounds of Semana Santa, the ubercamp El Garlochi is a true marvel. A cloud of church incense hits you as you go up the stairs, and the faces of baby Jesus and the Virgin welcome you into the velvet-walled bar, decked out with more Virgins and Jesuses. Taste the rather revolting sounding cocktails Sangre de Cristo (Blood of Christ) or Agua de Sevilla, both heavily laced with vodka, whisky and grenadine, and pray they open more bars like this.

La Rebótica BAR
(Calle Pérez Galdós 11) Two's a crowd in the cramped, sinuous Rebótica, the place to come for cheap shots and 1980s flashbacks accompanied by an appropriately retro soundtrack.

Bulebar Café BAR, CAFE
(954 90 19 54; Alameda de Hércules 83; 4pm-late) This place gets pretty *caliente* (hot) at night but is pleasantly chilled in the early evening, with friendly staff. Don't write off its spirit-reviving alfresco breakfasts that pitch early-birds with up-all-nighters.

Entertainment

Seville is arguably Spain's flamenco capital and you're most likely to catch a spontaneous atmosphere (of unpredictable quality) in one of the bars staging regular nights of flamenco with no admission fee. *Soleares,* Flamenco's truest *cante jondo* (deep song), was first concocted in Triana; head here to find some of the more authentic clubs.

Casa de la Memoria de Al-Andalus FLAMENCO
(954 56 06 70; www.casadelamemoria.es; Calle Ximénez de Enciso 28; tickets €15; 9pm) This flamenco *tablao* in Santa Cruz is without doubt the most intimate and authentic nightly flamenco show outside the Museo del Baile Flamenco, offering a wide variety of *palos* (flamenco styles) in a courtyard of shifting shadows and overhanging plants. Reserve tickets a day or so in advance.

FREE **La Carbonería** FLAMENCO
(Calle Levíes 18; 8pm-4am) During the day there is no indication that this happening place is anything but a large garage. But, come after 8pm and this converted coal yard in the Barrio de Santa Cruz reveals two large bars, and nightly live flamenco (11pm and midnight) for no extra charge.

Casa Anselma FLAMENCO
(Calle Pagés del Corro 49; midnight-late Mon-Sat) If you can squeeze in past the foreboding form of Anselma (a celebrated Triana flamenco dancer) at the door you'll quickly realise that anything can happen in here. Casa Anselma (beware: there's no sign, just a doorway embellished with azulejos tiles) is the antithesis of a tourist flamenco *tablao,* with cheek-to-jowl crowds, thick cigarette smoke, zero amplification and spontaneous outbreaks of dexterous dancing. Pure magic. To get here, cross the Puente de Isabel II, then turn right on Calle Pagés del Corro – Casa Anselma is around 100m along on your right.

Information

Discover Sevilla (www.discoversevilla.com)
Explore Seville (www.exploreseville.com)
Seville Tourism (www.turismo.sevilla.org) The city's official tourism site.
Turismo Sevilla (www.turismosevilla.org; Plaza del Triunfo 1; 10.30am-7pm Mon-Fri) Information on all Sevilla province.

Getting There & Away

AIR A range of domestic and international flights land in Seville's Aeropuerto San Pablo, 7km from the city centre.

BUS From the **Estación de Autobuses Prado de San Sebastián** (Plaza San Sebastián), there are 12 or more buses daily to/from Cádiz, Córdoba, Granada, Ronda and Málaga. From the **Estación de Autobuses Plaza de Armas** (www.autobusesplazadearmas.es; Avenida del Cristo de la Expiración), destinations include Madrid, Mérida, Cáceres and Portugal.

TRAIN The modern, efficient **Estación de Santa Justa** (☎902 43 23 43; Avenida Kansas City) is 1.5km northeast of the city centre. There's also a city-centre **Renfe ticket office** (Calle Zaragoza 29).

Twenty or more superfast AVE trains, reaching speeds of 280km/h, whiz daily to/from Madrid (€84, 2½ hours). Other services include Cádiz (€13.25, 1¾ hours, 13 daily), Córdoba (€17 to €33.25, 40 minutes to 1½ hours, 21 or more daily), Granada (€25, three hours, four daily) and Málaga (€38.75, two hours, 11 daily).

Getting Around

Los Amarillos (www.losamarillos.es) runs buses between the airport and the Avenida del Cid near the San Sebastión bus station (€2.40, at 15 and 45 minutes past the hour). A taxi costs about €22.

Córdoba

POP 328,000

Córdoba was once one of the most enlightened Islamic cities on earth, and enough remains to place it in the contemporary top three Andalucian draws. The centrepiece is the gigantic and exquisitely rendered Mezquita. Surrounding it is an intricate web of winding streets, geranium-sprouting flower boxes and cool intimate patios that are at their most beguiling in late spring.

Sights & Activities

Mezquita GREAT MOSQUE

(Mosque; ☎957 47 05 12; www.mezquitadecordoba.org; Calle Cardenal Herrero; adult/child €8/4, 8.30-10am Mon-Sat free; ⏲10am-7pm Mon-Sat, 8.30-10am & 2-7pm Sun Mar-Oct, 8.30am-6pm Mon-Sat, 8.30-10am & 2-6pm Sun Nov-Feb) Founded in AD 785, Córdoba's gigantic mosque is a wonderful architectural hybrid with delicate horseshoe arches making this unlike anywhere else in Spain. The main entrance is the **Puerta del Perdón**, a 14th-century Mudéjar gateway, with the ticket office immediately inside. Inside the gateway is the aptly named **Patio de los Naranjos** (Courtyard of the Orange Trees). Once inside, you can see straight ahead to the *mihrab*, the prayer niche in a mosque's *qibla* (the wall indicating the direction of Mecca) that was the focus of prayer. The first 12 transverse aisles inside the entrance, a forest of pillars and arches, comprise the original 8th-century mosque.

Judería HISTORIC NEIGHBOURHOOD

The medieval *judería*, extending northwest from the Mezquita almost to Avenida del Gran Capitán, is today a maze of narrow streets and whitewashed buildings with flowery window boxes. The beautiful little 14th-century **Sinagoga** (Calle de los Judíos 20; admission €0.30; ⏲9.30am-2pm & 3.30-5.30pm Tue-Sat, 9.30am-1.30pm Sun & holidays) is one of only three surviving medieval synagogues in Spain and the only one in Andalucía. In the heart of the *judería*, and once connected by an underground tunnel to the Sinagoga, is the 14th-century **Casa de Sefarad** (www.casadesefarad.es; Cnr Calle de los Judíos & Averroes; admission €4; ⏲10am-6pm Mon-Sat, 11am-2pm Sun). This small, beautiful museum is devoted to reviving interest in the Sephardic-Judaic-Spanish tradition.

Alcázar de los Reyes Cristianos CASTLE

(Castle of the Christian Monarchs; Campo Santo de Los Mártires; admission €4, Fri free; ⏲10am-2pm & 5.30-7.30pm Tue-Sat, 9.30am-2.30pm Sun & holidays) Just southwest of the Mezquita, the Alcázar, or Castle of the Christian Monarchs, began as a palace and fort for Alfonso X in the 13th century. From 1490 to 1821 the Inquisition operated from here. Today its gardens are among the most beautiful in Andalucía.

Medina Azahara ISLAMIC RUINS

(Madinat al-Zahra; adult/EU citizen €1.50/free; ⏲10am-6.30pm Tue-Sat, to 8.30pm May–mid-Sep, to 2pm Sun) Even in the cicada-shrill heat and stillness of a summer afternoon, Medina Azahara whispers of the power and vision of its founder, Abd ar-Rahman III. The self-proclaimed caliph began the construction of a magnificent new capital 8km west of Córdoba around AD 936, and took up full residence around 945. It was destroyed in the 11th century and just 10% of the site has been excavated. A taxi costs €37 for the return trip, with one hour to view the site, or you can book a three-hour coach tour for €6.50 to €10 through many Córdoba hotels

Hammam Baños Árabes BATHHOUSE
(☎957 48 47 46; www.hammamspain.com/cordoba; Calle del Corregidor Luis de la Cerda 51; bath/bath & massage €26/33; ⊙2hr sessions 10am, noon, 2pm, 4pm, 6pm, 8pm & 10pm) Follow the lead of the medieval Cordobans and dip your toe in these beautifully renovated Arab baths, where you can enjoy an aromatherapy massage, with tea, hookah and Arabic sweets in the cafe afterwards.

Sleeping

Hospedería Alma Andalusí BOUTIQUE HOTEL €€
(☎957 76 08 88; www.almaandalusi.com; Calle Fernández Ruano 5; s/d €45/100;) The builders of this guesthouse in a quiet section of the *judería* have brilliantly converted an ancient structure into a stylish, modern establishment while keeping the rates down. Thoughtfully chosen furnishings, polished wood floors and solid colours make for a comfortable base.

Casa de los Azulejos HOTEL €€
(☎957 47 00 00; www.casadelosazulejos.com; Calle Fernando Colón 5; s/d incl breakfast from €85/107;) Mexican and Andalucian styles converge in this stylish hotel, where the patio is all banana trees, ferns and potted palms bathed in sunlight. Colonial-style rooms feature tall antique doors, massive beds, walls in lilac and sky blues, and floors adorned with the beautiful old azulejos tiles that give the place its name.

Hotel Mezquita HOTEL €€
(☎957 47 55 85; www.hotelmezquita.com; Plaza Santa Catalina 1; s/d €42/74;) One of the best deals in town, Hotel Mezquita stands right opposite its namesake monument, amid the bric-a-brac of the tourism zone. The 16th-century mansion has large, elegant rooms with marble floors, tall doors and balconies, some affording views of the great mosque.

Hospedería Añil HOSTEL €
(☎957 49 15 44; www.sensesandcolours.com; Calle Barroso 4; dm/s/d from €12/30/42;) This vibrant, superfriendly establishment is aimed at the backpacker set, though it cuts no corners in the style and comfort departments. Primary colours and fanciful murals maintain an upbeat vibe. It's a skip and a jump to either the Mezquita or Plaza de las Tendillas.

Hostal Séneca HOSTEL €
(☎957 47 32 34; www.cordoba-hostalseneca.com; Calle Conde y Luque 7; dm/s/d incl breakfast from €15/30/50;) An upgraded version of a longtime backpackers' haunt, the Séneca occupies a rambling house with typical Moorish elements. A small cafe-bar supplies breakfast and drinks on a marvelous pebbled patio, and there's a kitchen available for guest use. Rooms vary widely; some share a bathroom. The hostel is closed for one week in August and over Christmas.

Eating

Taberna San Miguel El Pisto TAPAS €
(www.casaelpisto.com/en; Plaza San Miguel 1; tapas €3, media raciones €5-10; ⊙closed Sun & Aug) Brimming with local character, El Pisto is one of Córdoba's best *tabernas,* both in terms of atmosphere and food. Traditional tapas and *media raciones* are done perfectly, and inexpensive Moriles wine is ready in jugs on the bar.

Bodegas Campos ANDALUCIAN €€
(☎957 49 75 00; www.bodegascampos.com; Calle de Lineros 32; tapas €5, mains €13-21) One of Córdoba's most atmospheric and famous wine cellars/restaurants, this sprawling hall features dozens of rooms and patios, with oak barrels signed by local and international celebrities stacked up alongside. The bodega produces its own house Montilla.

Taberna Salinas TAPAS €
(www.tabernasalinas.com; Calle Tundidores 3; tapas/raciones €2.50/8; ⊙closed Sun & Aug) A historic *taberna* that dates back to 1879, with a reputation that ensures the tables are always busy.

Information

Municipal Tourist Office (Plaza de Judá Levi; ⊙8.30am-2.30pm Mon-Fri)

Regional Tourist Office (Calle de Torrijos 10; ⊙9am-7.30pm Mon-Fri, 9.30am-3pm Sat, Sun & holidays) Inside the Palacio Episcopal.

Getting There & Away

BUS The **bus station** (☎957 40 40 40; www.estacionautobusescordoba.es; Glorieta de las Tres Culturas) is 1km northwest of Plaza de las Tendillas. Destinations include Seville (€10.50, 1¾ hours, six daily), Granada (€12.75, 2½ hours, seven daily) and Málaga (€12.75, 2¾ hours, five daily).

TRAIN From Córdoba's **train station** (Avenida de América), destinations include Seville (€11 to €33, 40 to 90 minutes, 23 or more daily), Madrid (€53 to €68, 1¾ to 6¼ hours, 23 or more daily), Málaga (€22 to €45, one to 2½ hours, nine daily) and Barcelona (€138, 4½ hours, four daily).

Granada

POP 258,000 / ELEV 685M

Granada's eight centuries as a Muslim capital are symbolised in its keynote emblem, the remarkable Alhambra, one of the most graceful architectural achievements in the Muslim world. Islam was never completely expunged here, and today it seems more present than ever in the shops, restaurants, tearooms and mosque of a growing North African community in and around the maze of the Albayzín. The tapas bars fill to bursting, while flamenco dives resound to the heart-wrenching tones of the south.

Sights & Activities

Alhambra PALACE

(☎902 44 12 21; www.alhambra-tickets.es; adult/under 8yr €13/free, Generalife only €6; ⏲8.30am-8pm 16 Mar-31 Oct, to 6pm 1 Nov-14 Mar, night visits 10-11.30pm Tue-Sat Mar-Oct, 8-9.30pm Fri & Sat Nov-Feb) The mighty Alhambra is breathtaking. Much has been written about its fortress, palace, patios and gardens, but nothing can really prepare you for seeing the real thing.

The **Alcazaba**, the Alhambra's fortress, dates from the 11th to the 13th centuries. There are spectacular views from the tops of its towers. The **Palacio Nazaríes** (Nasrid Palace), built for Granada's Muslim rulers in their 13th- to 15th-century heyday, is the centrepiece of the Alhambra. The beauty of its patios and intricacy of its stuccoes and woodwork, epitomised by the **Patio de los Leones** (Patio of the Lions) and **Sala de las Dos Hermanas** (Hall of the Two Sisters), are stunning. The **Generalife** (Palace Gardens) is a great spot to relax and contemplate the complex from a little distance.

Albayzín HISTORIC NEIGHBOURHOOD

Exploring the narrow, hilly streets of the Albayzín, the old Moorish quarter across the river from the Alhambra, is the perfect complement to the Alhambra. The cobblestone streets are lined with gorgeous *cármenes* (large mansions with walled gardens, from the Arabic *karm* for garden). It survived as the Muslim quarter for several decades after the Christian conquest in 1492. Head uphill to reach the **Mirador de San Nicolás** – a viewpoint with breathtaking vistas.

Capilla Real HISTORIC BUILDING

(Royal Chapel; www.capillarealgranada.com; Calle Oficios; admission €3.50; ⏲10.30am-1.30pm & 4-7.30pm Mon-Sat, 11am-1.30pm & 4-7pm Sun Apr-Oct) The Royal Chapel, adjoins Granada's cathedral, and is an outstanding Christian building. Catholic monarchs Isabella and Ferdinand commissioned this elaborate Isabelline-Gothic-style mausoleum. It was not completed until 1521, and the monarchs lie in simple lead coffins in the crypt beneath their marble monuments in the chancel, enclosed by a stunning gilded wrought-iron screen.

Sleeping

Casa Morisca Hotel HISTORIC HOTEL €€

(☎958 22 11 00; www.hotelcasamorisca.com; Cuesta de la Victoria 9; d €118-148; ❄@🛜) This late-15th-century mansion perfectly captures the spirit of the Albayzín. A heavy wooden door shuts out city noise, and rooms are soothing, with lofty ceilings, fluffy white beds and flat-weave rugs over brick floors.

ALHAMBRA TICKETS

Up to 6600 tickets to the Alhambra are available for each day. About one-third of these are sold at the ticket office on the day, but they sell out early and you need to start queuing by 7am to be reasonably sure of getting one. It's highly advisable to book in advance (you pay €1 extra per ticket). You can book up to three months ahead in two ways:

Alhambra Advance Booking (☎for international calls 0034 934 92 37 50, for national calls 902 888001; www.alhambra-tickets.es; ⏲8am-9pm)

Servicaixa (www.servicaixa.com) Online booking in Spanish and English. You can also buy tickets in advance from Servicaixa cash machines (⏲8am to 7pm March to October, 8am to 5pm November to February), but only in the Alhambra grounds.

For internet or phone bookings you need a Visa card, MasterCard or Eurocard. You receive a reference number, which you must show, along with your passport, national identity card or credit card, at the Alhambra ticket office when you pick up the ticket on the day of your visit.

ANDALUCIA'S QUIETEST BEACHES

The coast east of Almería in eastern Andalucía is perhaps the last section of Spain's Mediterranean coast where you can have a beach to yourself. This is Spain's sunniest region – even in late March it can be warm enough to strip off and take in the rays. The Alcazaba, an enormous 10th-century Muslim fortress, is the highlight of Almería City, but the best thing about the region is the wonderful coastline and semidesert scenery of the Cabo de Gata promontory. All along the 50km coast from El Cabo de Gata village to Agua Amarga, some of the most beautiful and empty beaches on the Mediterranean alternate with precipitous cliffs and scattered villages. The main village is laid-back San José, with excellent beaches nearby, such as Playa de los Genoveses and Playa de Mónsul.

In Almería City, try **Hotel Catedral** (950 27 81 78; www.hotelcatedral.net; Plaza de la Catedral 8; r €70;), while both **Atalaya Hotel** (950 38 00 85; www.atalayahotel.net; Avenida de San José, San José; r incl breakfast €75;) and **Hostal Aloha** (950 38 04 61; www.hostalaloha.com; Calle Cala Higuera, San José; r €55;) are good in Cabo de Gata. Almería City has a **tourist office** (Ayuntamiento, Plaza de la Constitución 1; 10am-1pm & 5.30-7.30pm Mon-Fri, 10am-noon Sat), while bus destinations served from Almería's bus station include Granada (€13, 2¼ hours, 10 daily), Málaga (€17, 3¼ hours, eight daily), Madrid (€44, 10 hours, three daily) and Valencia (€37, 8½ hours, five daily).

Hostal Venecia HOSTAL €
(958 22 39 87; www.veneciahostal.es; Cuesta de Gomérez 2; d €42, without bathroom €34;) The house-proud hosts here are as sweet as the flower- and picture-filled turquoise corridors. The nine rooms overflow with character, and each is different: some have private bathrooms, while others share facilities, and many have small balconies.

Hostal La Ninfa HOSTAL €
(958 22 79 85; www.hostallaninfa.net; Plaza Campo Príncipe; s/d €45/50;) The show-stopping facade of this hotel, with its walls covered with ceramic plaques, sets the scene for the interior. The rooms are brightly painted (think turquoise painted beams) with tiled bedheads and pretty tiled bathrooms. It is a 30-minute uphill trek to the Alhambra from here or you can hop on the number 30 bus which stops virtually outside the door.

Hostal Arteaga HOSTAL €
958 20 88 41; www.hostalarteaga.com; Calle rteaga 3; s/d €40/49;) A charming argain option just off the Gran Vía de olón, inching into the Albayzín. The rooms re spruced up with lavender walls, striped edspreads and chequered blue bathroom iles for a tidy, modern feel.

Eating

ranada is one of the last bastions of that ntastic practice of free tapas with every rink. The labyrinthine Albayzín holds a ealth of eateries tucked away in the narw streets. Calle Caldereria Nueva is a fascinating muddle of *teterías* (tearooms) and Arabic-influenced takeaways.

Arrayanes MOROCCAN €€
(958 22 84 01; www.rest-arrayanes.com; Cuesta Marañas 4; mains €8-15; from 8pm;) The best Moroccan food in a city that is well known for its Moorish throwbacks? Recline on lavish patterned seating, try the rich, fruity tagine casseroles and make your decision. Note that Arrayanes does not serve alcohol.

Ruta del Azafrán FUSION €€
(www.rutadelazafran.es; Paseo del Padre Manjón 1; mains €13-20) One of the few high-concept restaurants in Granada, this sleek spot with its modern interior has an eclectic menu. The terrace on the Rio Darro is a great place for a snack, but you'll get better service inside.

Bodegas Castañeda BAR €
(Calle Almireceros; tapas €2-3, raciónes €6-8) An institution among locals and tourists alike, this buzzing bar doles out hearty portions of food (try a hot or cold *tabla,* or platter; a half-size order, €6, is ample for two) and dispenses drinks from big casks mounted in the walls.

Entertainment

The excellent monthly *Guía de Granada* (€1), available from kiosks, lists entertainment venues and tapas bars.

Peña de la Platería FLAMENCO
(www.laplateria.org.es; Placeta de Toqueros 7) Buried in the Albayzín warren, Peña La Platería claims to be the oldest flamenco aficionados'

Granada

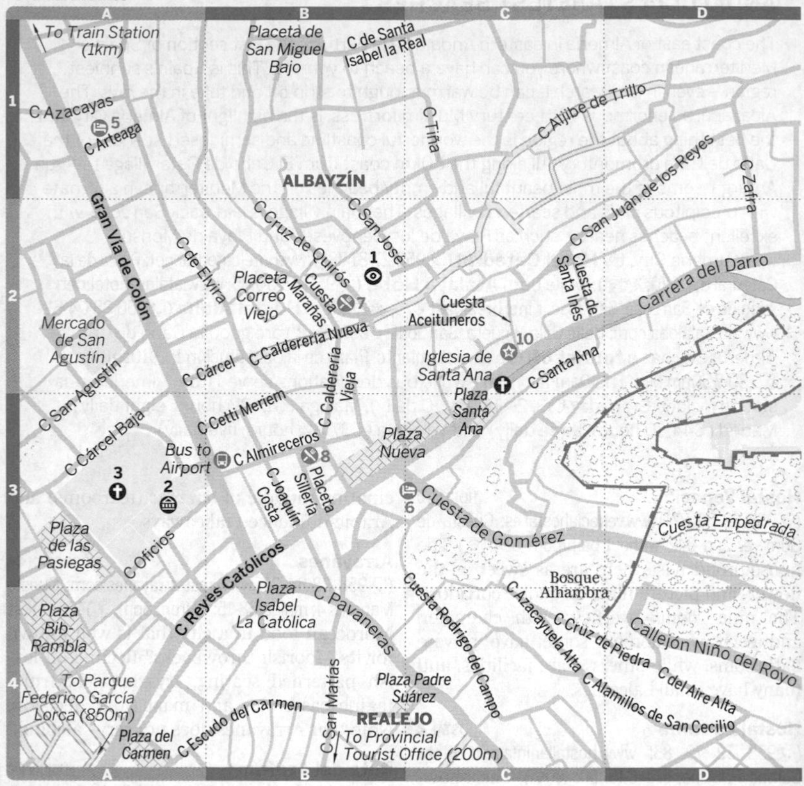

Granada

Top Sights

Alhambra ... E3

Sights

1 Albayzín ... B2
2 Capilla Real ... A3
3 Catedral ... A3

Sleeping

4 Casa Morisca Hotel ... E1
5 Hostal Arteaga ... A1
6 Hostal Venecia ... C3

Eating

7 Arrayanes ... B2
8 Bodegas Castañeda ... B3
9 Ruta del Azafrán ... E2

Entertainment

10 Le Chien Andalou ... C2
11 Peña de la Platería ... E1

club in Spain. It's a private affair, though, and not always open to nonmembers. Performances are usually Thursday and Saturday at 10.30pm – look presentable, and speak a little Spanish at the door, if you can.

Le Chien Andalou FLAMENCO
(www.lechienandalou.com; Carrera del Darro 7; admission €8; shows 9pm) This is one of Granada's most atmospheric venues to enjoy some vigorous castanet-clicking flamenco with a varied and professional lineup of musicians and dancers throughout the week. The cave-like surroundings of a renovated *aljibe* (well) create a fittingly moody setting.

Information

Provincial Tourist Office (www.turismodegranada.org; Plaza de Mariana Pineda 10; 9am-10pm Mon-Fri, 10am-7pm Sat) Information on the whole Granada region; a short walk east of Puerta Real.

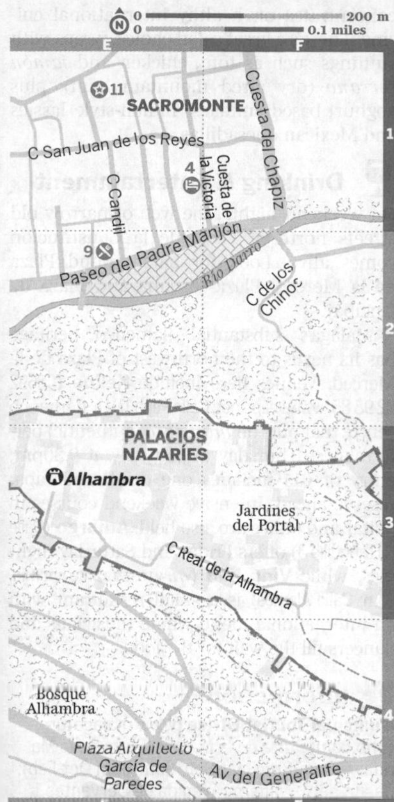

Municipal Tourist Office (www.granadatur.com; Calle Almona del Campillo, 2; ⌚9am-7pm Mon-Fri, to 6pm Sat, 10am-2pm Sun) Opposite the city's Parque Federico García Lorca.

Getting There & Away

BUS Granada's **bus station** (Carretera de Jaén) s 3km northwest of the city centre. Destinations nclude Córdoba (€13.50, 2¾ hours direct, nine daily), Seville (€20.50, three hours, 10 daily), Málaga (€10.50, 1½ hours direct, 18 daily) and n overnight service to Madrid's Barajas Airport €24.50, six hours).

TRAIN The **train station** (☎958 24 02 02; venida de Andaluces) is 1.5km west of the entre. Trains run to/from Seville (€24, three ours, four daily), Almería (€16.50, 2¼ hours, ur daily), Ronda (€15, three hours, three daily), lgeciras (€25, 4½ hours, three daily), Madrid €68, four to five hours, one or two daily), Valena (€52.50, 7½ to eight hours, one daily) and arcelona (€58, 12 hours, one daily).

Málaga

POP 558,000

The exuberant port city of Málaga may be uncomfortably close to the overdeveloped Costa del Sol, but it's a wonderful amalgam of old Andalucian town and modern metropolis. The centre presents the visitor with narrow, old streets and wide, leafy boulevards, beautiful gardens and impressive monuments, fashionable shops and a burgeoning cultural life. The city's terrific bars and nightlife, the last word in Málaga *joie de vivre,* stay open very late.

Sights & Activities

Museo Picasso Málaga MUSEUM

(☎902 44 33 77; www.museopicassomalaga.org; Calle San Agustín 8; permanent/temporary collection €6/4.50, combined ticket €8; ⌚10am-8pm Tue-Thu & Sun, to 9pm Fri & Sat) The hottest attraction on Málaga's tourist scene is tucked away on a pedestrian street in what was medieval Málaga's *judería.* The Museo Picasso Málaga has 204 Picasso works and also stages high-quality temporary exhibitions on Picasso themes. The Picasso paintings, drawings, engravings, sculptures and ceramics on show (many never previously on public display) span almost every phase and influence of the artist's colourful career. Picasso was born in Málaga in 1881, but moved to northern Spain with his family when he was nine.

Casa Natal de Picasso MUSEUM

(Plaza de la Merced 15; admission €1; ⌚9.30am-8pm) The house where Picasso was born in 1881 has a replica 19th-century artist's studio and small quarterly exhibitions of Picasso's work.

Alcazaba CASTLE

(Calle Alcazabilla; admission €2.10, incl Castillo de Gibralfaro €3.40; ⌚9.30am-8pm Tue-Sun Apr-Oct) At the lower, western end of the Gibralfaro hill, the wheelchair-accessible Alcazaba was the palace-fortress of Málaga's Muslim governors, dating from 1057. The brick path winds uphill, interspersed with arches and stone walls and is refreshingly cool in summer. Roman artefacts and fleeting views of the harbour and city enliven the walk, while honeysuckle, roses and jasmine perfume the air.

Castillo de Gibralfaro CASTLE

(admission €2.10; ⌚9am-9pm Apr-Sep, to 6pm Oct-Mar) Above the Alcazaba rises the Castillo de

Gibralfaro, built by Abd ar-Rahman I, the 8th-century Cordoban emir, and rebuilt in the 14th and 15th centuries. Nothing much remains of the castle's interior, but the walkway around the ramparts affords exhilarating views and there's a tiny museum with a military focus.

Beaches BEACHES
Sandy city beaches stretch several kilometres in each direction from the port. **Playa de la Malagueta**, handy to the city centre, has some excellent bars and restaurants close by. **Playa de Pedregalejo** and **Playa del Palo**, about 4km east of the centre, are popular and reachable by bus 11 from Paseo del Parque.

Sleeping

El Riad Andaluz GUESTHOUSE €€
(☎952 21 36 40; www.elriadandaluz.com; Calle Hinestrosa 24; s/d €70/86; ❄@📶) This French-run guesthouse, near the Teatro Cervantes, has eight rooms set around an atmospheric patio. The decoration is Moroccan but each room is different, including colourfully tiled bathrooms. Breakfast is available.

Feel Málaga Hostel HOSTEL €
(☎952 22 28 32; www.feelmalagahostel.com; Calle Vendeja 25; d €45, without bathroom €35, dm from €16 ; @📶) This sparkling new hostel opened in October 2011 and is a welcome addition to Málaga's budget sleeping scene. Located within a suitcase trundle of the city-centre train station, the accommodation is clean and well equipped with a choice of doubles and shared rooms. Bathrooms sport classy mosaic tiles and the top-floor kitchen has all the essentials necessary to whip up a decent meal.

Eating

Most of the best eating places are sandwiched in the narrow streets between Calle Marqués de Larios and the cathedral.

Tapeo de Cervantes TAPAS €
(www.eltapeodecervantes.com; Calle Cárcer 8; tapas €4-6; ⏲Tue-Sun) This place has caught on big time which, given its squeeze-in space, can mean a wait. Choose from traditional or more innovative tapas and *raciones* with delicious combinations and stylish presentation. Portions are generous.

Terra Sana HEALTH FOOD €
(www.restaurantesterrasana.com; Calle Alcazabilla; mains €8-10) One of a small local chain that concentrates on healthy international cuisine. There's a great salad choice, wraps with stuffings such as tofu, chicken and *jamón serrano* (dry aired mountain ham), plus yoghurt-based sundaes, Indian-style lassies and Mexican quesadillas.

Drinking & Entertainment

On weekend nights, the web of narrow old streets north of Plaza de la Constitución comes alive. Look for bars around Plaza de la Merced, Plaza Mitjana and Plaza de Uncibay.

Málaga's substantial flamenco heritage has its nexus to the northwest of Plaza de la Merced. Venues here include **Kelipe** (☎692 82 98 85; www.kelipe.net; Calle Pena 11), a flamenco centre that puts on *muy puro* (authentic) performances Thursday to Saturday at 9.30pm; entry of €15 includes one drink and tapa; reserve ahead. Intensive weekend courses in guitar and dance are also held. **Amargo** (Calle R Franquillo 3) offers Friday and Saturday night gigs, while **Vino Mio** (www.restaurantevinomio.com; Calle Alamos) is a small restaurant with an international menu where musicians and dancers fill the wait for the food.

Information

Municipal Tourist Office (www.malagaturismo.com) Plaza de la Marina (Plaza de la Marina; ⏲9am-8pm Mar-Sep, 9am-6pm Oct-Feb); Casita del Jardinero (Avenida de Cervantes 1, Casita del Jardinero; ⏲9am-8pm Mar-Sep, to 6pm Oct-Feb)

Regional Tourist Office (www.andalucia.org; Pasaje de Chinitas 4; ⏲9am-7.30pm Mon-Fri, 10am-7pm Sat, 10am-2pm Sun) There is another branch at the airport; these cover the whole of Málaga and all of Andalucía.

Getting There & Away

AIR Málaga's busy **airport** (☎952 04 88 38), the main international gateway to Andalucía, receives flights by dozens of airlines from around Europe. The Aeropuerto train station on the Málaga–Fuengirola line is a five-minute walk from the airport. Trains run about every half-hour to Málaga-Renfe station (€2.20, 11 minutes) and Málaga-Centro station.

BUS Málaga's **bus station** (☎952 35 00 61; www.estabus.emtsam.es; Paseo de los Tilos) is 1km southwest of the city centre. Frequent buses go to Seville (€30, 2½ hours), Granada (€10.50, 1½ to two hours), Córdoba (€13.50, 3½ hours) and Ronda (€9.50, 2½ hours).

TRAIN The main station, **Málaga-Renfe** (www.renfe.es; Explanada de la Estación), is around

WORTH A TRIP

RONDA

Perched on an inland plateau riven by the 100m fissure of El Tajo gorge and surrounded by the beautiful Serranía de Ronda, Ronda, a two-hour drive west of Málaga, is the most dramatically sited of Andalucía's *pueblos blancos* (white villages). The **Plaza de Toros** (built 1785), considered the national home of bullfighting, is a mecca for aficionados; inside is the small but fascinating Museo Taurino. The amazing 18th-century **Puente Nuevo** (New Bridge) is an incredible engineering feat crossing the gorge to the originally Muslim Old Town (La Ciudad). At the **Casa del Rey Moro** (House of the Moorish King; Calle Santo Domingo 17), a romantically crumbling 18th-century house supposedly built over the remains of an Islamic palace, you can visit the cliff-top gardens and climb down La Mina, a Muslim-era stairway cut inside the rock, right to the bottom of the gorge.

Hotels include the **Hotel Hermanos Macias** (☎952 87 42 38; www.hermanosmacias.com; Calle Pedro Romero 3; s/d €35/48; P❄) and the dramatically sited **Parador de Ronda** (☎952 87 75 00; www.parador.es; Plaza de España; r €160-171; P❄@☎≋), while the **Bodega San Francisco** (www.bodegasanfrancisco.com; Calle Ruedo Alameda; raciones €6-10) does great tapas. Check out the **Municipal Tourist Office** (www.turismoderonda.es; Paseo de Blas Infante; ⊙10am-7.30pm Mon-Fri, 10.15am-2pm & 3.30-6.30pm Sat, Sun & holidays) for more information. There are buses to Ronda from Málaga and Granada.

the corner from the bus station. The superfast AVE service runs to Madrid (€87, 2½ hours, 10 daily). Trains also go to Córdoba (from €26, 2½ hours, 10 daily) and Seville (from €18.50, 2¾ hours, 11 daily).

Tarifa

POP 17,900

Windy, laid-back Tarifa is so close to Africa that you can almost hear the call to prayer issuing from Morocco's minarets. The town is a bohemian haven of cafes and crumbling Moorish ruins, and the **Mirador El Estrecho**, atop part of the castle walls, has spectacular views across to Africa, only 14km away. There's also a lively windsurfing and kitesurfing scene. Stretching west are the long, sandy (and largely deserted) beaches of the Costa de la Luz (Coast of Light), backed by cool pine forests and green hills.

Activities

Beaches

On the isthmus leading out to Isla de las Palomas, tiny **Playa Chica** lives up to its name. Spectacular **Playa de los Lances** is a different matter, stretching northwest for 10km to the huge sand dune at **Ensenada de Valdevaqueros**.

Horse Riding

Located on Playa de los Lances, **Aventura Ecuestre** (☎956 23 66 32; www.aventuraecuestre.com; N340 Km79.5, Hotel Dos Mares) and **Hurricane Hípica** (☎646 964279; N340 Km78, Hurricane Hotel) both rent well-kept horses with excellent guides. An hour's beach ride costs €30. Three- or four-hour inland rides cost €70.

Whale-watching

The Strait of Gibraltar is a top site for viewing whales and dolphins. Killer whales visit in July and August, huge sperm and fin whales lurk here from spring to autumn, and pilot whales and three types of dolphin stay all year. Several organisations in Tarifa run daily two- to 2½-hour boat trips to observe these marine mammals, and most offer a free second trip if you don't at least see dolphins. **Firmm** (☎956 62 70 08; www.firmm.org; Calle Pedro Cortés 4; ⊙Mar-Oct) is the best and uses every trip to record data.

Sleeping & Eating

Posada La Sacristía BOUTIQUE HOTEL €€
(☎956 68 17 59; www.lasacristia.net; Calle San Donato 8, Tarifa; r incl breakfast €115-135; ❄@☎) Tarifa's most elegant boutique accommodation is in a beautifully renovated 17th-century townhouse. Attention to detail is impeccable, with 10 stylish rooms, tasteful colour schemes, large comfortable beds and rooms on several levels around a central courtyard.

Hostal Africa HOSTAL €
(☎956 68 02 20; www.hostalafrica.com; Calle María Antonia Toledo 12, Tarifa; s/d €50/65, without bathroom €35/50; ☎) This revamped 19th-century house close to the Puerta de Jerez is one of

the best *hostales* along the coast. The owners are hospitable and the rooms sparkle with bright and attractive colours and plenty of space. There's a lovely, expansive roof terrace with an exotic cabana and views of Africa.

Mandrágora MOROCCAN, ARABIC €€
(☎956 68 12 91; www.mandragoratarifa.com; Calle Independencia 3; mains €12-18; ⊙from 8pm Mon-Sat) Behind Iglesia de San Mateo, this intimate place serves Andalusian-Arabic food and does so terrifically well.

Information

Tourist Office (☎956 68 09 93; www.aytotarifa.com; Paseo de la Alameda; ⊙10am-2pm daily, 6-8pm Mon-Fri Jun-Sep) Near the top end of the palm-lined Paseo de la Alameda.

Getting There & Away

BUS **Comes** (☎956 68 40 38; www.tgcomes.es; Calle Batalla del Salado 13) runs daily buses to Cádiz (€8.60, 1½ hours), Algeciras (€2.20, 30 minutes), La Línea de la Concepción (for Gibraltar; €4.15, 45 minutes), Seville (€18.50, three hours) and Málaga (€13.25, two hours).

BOAT A fast ferry service is run by **FRS** (☎956 68 18 30; www.frs.es; Avenida Andalucía 16) between Tarifa and Tangier (passenger/car/motorcycle €37/93/31, 35 minutes, eight daily).

WORTH A TRIP

MOROCCO

At once African and Arab, visible from numerous points along Spain's Andalucian coast, Morocco is an exciting detour from your western European journey. The country's attractions are endless, from the fascinating souqs and medieval architecture of Marrakesh and Fès to the Atlantic charms of Asilah and Essaouira, from the High Atlas and Rif Mountains to the soulful sand dunes of Sahara. For further information, head to shop.lonelyplanet.com to purchase Lonely Planet's *Morocco* guide.

Casablanca and Marrakesh in particular are well connected by air to numerous European cities, while car-and-passenger ferry services connect Tangier with Algeciras, Barcelona, Gibraltar, and Tarifa, with an additional service between Nador and Almería.

EXTREMADURA

Cáceres

POP 95,030

Cáceres' *ciudad monumental* (old town), built in the 15th and 16th centuries, is perfectly preserved. The town's action centres on Plaza Mayor, at the foot of the old town, and busy Avenida de España, a short distance south.

Sights

Plaza de Santa María SQUARE
Enter the old town from Plaza Mayor through the 18th-century **Arco de la Estrella**, built with a wide span for the passage of carriages. The 15th-century Gothic cathedral, **Concatedral de Santa María** (Plaza de Santa María; admission €1; ⊙9.30am-2pm & 5.30-8.30pm Mon-Sat, 9.30-11.50am & 5.30-7.15pm Sun May-Sep), creates an impressive opening scene. Climb the **bell tower** (€1) for stunning views.

Also on the plaza are the **Palacio Episcopal** (Bishop's Palace), the **Palacio de Mayoralgo** and the **Palacio de Ovando**, all in 16th-century Renaissance style. Heading back through Arco de la Estrella, you can climb the 12th-century **Torre de Bujaco** (Plaza Mayor; adult/child €2/free; ⊙10am-2pm & 5.30-8.30pm Mon-Sat, 10am-2pm Sun Apr-Sep, 10am-2pm & 4.30-7.30pm Mon-Sat, 10am-2pm Sun Oct-Mar) for good stork's-eye views of the Plaza Mayor.

Plaza de San Mateo & Plaza de las Veletas SQUARE
From Plaza de San Jorge, Cuesta de la Compañía climbs to Plaza de San Mateo and the **Iglesia de San Mateo**, traditionally the church of the land-owning nobility and built on the site of the town's mosque.

Below the square is the excellent **Museo de Cáceres** (Plaza de las Veletas 1; non-EU/EU citizens €1.20/free; ⊙9am-2.30pm & 5-8.15pm Tue-Sat, 10.15am-2.30pm Sun) in a 16th-century mansion built over an evocative 12th-century *aljibe* (cistern), the only surviving element of Cáceres' Muslim castle. It has an impressive archaeological section and an excellent fine arts display (open only in the mornings), with works by Picasso, Miró, Tapiès and others.

Sleeping & Eating

Albergue Turístico Las Veletas HOSTEL
(☎927 21 12 10; lasveletas@hotmail.com; Calle del General Margallo 36; dm €18-20; ❄☜) Th

modern hostel, with its homey rear garden, offers agreeable accommodation in rooms with three to six beds. Reserve in advance, since it works primarily with groups. Meals are available for €8. Discount for pilgrims.

Restaurante Torre de Sande FUSION €€
(927 21 11 47; www.torredesande.com; Calle Condes 3; mains €12-20; lunch & dinner Tue-Sat, lunch Sun) Dine in the pretty courtyard at this elegant gourmet restaurant in the heart of the Ciudad Monumental. More modestly, stop for a drink and a tapa at the interconnecting *tapería* (tapas bar), which has appealing streetside tables.

Information

Main Tourist Office (www.turismoextremadura.com; Plaza Mayor 3; 8.30am-2.30pm & 4-6pm or 5-7pm Mon-Fri, 10am-2pm Sat & Sun) At the entrance to the Ciudad Monumental. Opens later in the afternoon in summer.

Municipal Tourist Office (Calle de los Olmos 3; 10am-2pm & 4.30-7.30pm or 5.30-8.30pm)

Getting There & Away

BUS The **bus station** (Carretera de Sevilla; 927 23 25 50) has services to Trujillo (€4.40, 40 minutes) and Mérida (€5.60, one hour).

TRAIN Up to five trains per day run to/from Madrid (€27, four hours) and Mérida (€6.05, one hour).

UNDERSTAND SPAIN

History

North Africans settled in the peninsula from around 8000 BC and, in the millennia that followed, Celtic tribes, Phoenician merchants, Greeks and Carthaginians trickled in. The Romans arrived in the 3rd century BC but by AD 410 they had been replaced by the Christian Visigoths. Three hundred years later, Muslim Berbers and Arabs from North Africa took over most of the Iberian Peninsula.

The 8th century saw the beginning of the Christian Reconquista. By the mid-13th century, the Christians had taken most of the peninsula. In 1469, the kingdoms of Castile and Aragón were united by the marriage of Isabel, princess of Castile, and Fernando, heir to Aragón's throne. Known as the Catholic Monarchs, they united Spain and laid the foundations for the Spanish golden age. They also expelled and executed thousands of Jews and other non-Christians under the dark cloud of the Inquisition. In 1492, the Reconquista was completed when the last Muslim ruler of Granada surrendered to them.

That same year, Christopher Columbus stumbled on the Bahamas and claimed the Americas for Spain. This sparked a period of exploration and exploitation that yielded Spain enormous wealth, while destroying the ancient American empires. Spain's downfall began soon after. It would culminate with the disastrous Spanish-American War of 1898, which marked the end of the Spanish empire.

During the Spanish Civil War (1936–39), the Nationalists, led by General Francisco Franco, received heavy military support from Nazi Germany and fascist Italy, while the elected Republican government received support only from the Soviet Union and the International Brigades, made up of volunteer foreign leftists. By 1939 Franco had won and an estimated 350,000 Spaniards had died. Franco's 35-year dictatorship began with Spain isolated and crippled by recession. It wasn't until the 1950s and '60s that the country began to recover.

Franco died in 1975, having named Juan Carlos his successor. King Juan Carlos I is widely credited with having overseen Spain's transition from dictatorship to democracy. The first elections were held in 1977 and a new constitution was drafted in 1978. Spain joined the European Community in 1986. At a political level, Spain was ruled from 1982 until 1996 by the Partido Socialista Obrero Español (Spanish Socialist Party; PSOE) of Felipe González. By 1996 the PSOE government stood accused of corruption and was swept from power by the centre-right Partido Popular (Popular Party; PP), led by José María Aznar. The PP went on to establish programs of economic decentralisation and liberalisation.

Long accustomed to terrorist attacks by ETA (a Basque separatist movement which killed more than 800 people over four decades), Spain was nonetheless shaken to its core by the largest-ever terrorist attack on Spanish soil (later claimed by al-Qaeda), in Madrid on 11 March 2004. In national elections held three days later, the PP lost the presidential election to the PSOE. The Socialists embarked on something of a social revolution, legalising gay marriage, regularising the status of hundreds of thousands of illegal immigrants, removing the Church's role in religious education in schools, making abortions easier to obtain, and pushing through a law aimed at investigating the crimes and executions of the Franco years. Within months of the Socialists' re-election in 2008, years of economic boom came shuddering to an end amid the global financial crisis; unemployment jumped from around 7% in 2007 to above 20% in 2010. With the economy deep in recession, the Socialists' popularity plummeted.

Spain Today

Prime Minister Zapatero's delay in acknowledging the crisis sealed the government's fate, and it was defeated by the PP of Prime Minister Mariano Rajoy in a landslide on 20 November 2011. By late 2012, unemployment was stuck at around 25%, youth unemployment was close to 50% and the government was forced to seek billions of euros of assistance from the European Union. The government's deeply unpopular austerity program slashed public services and ushered in regular protests in Madrid and across the country. Many of Spain's regions were also forced to seek bailouts from the central government in Madrid.

Against this backdrop of economic meltdown, Spain's restive regions of Catalonia and the Basque Country began demanding greater autonomy, with plans also underway in both regions for de facto referenda on independence.

Good news may be hard to come by, but the announcement of a ceasefire by a much-weakened ETA in September 2010 was followed a year later by what ETA announced was a 'definitive cessation of its armed activity'.

People

Only about 20% of Spaniards are regular churchgoers, but Catholicism is deeply ingrained in the culture and an estimated 94% of Spaniards identify themselves as Catholics. As the writer Unamuno said, 'Here in Spain we are all Catholics, even the atheists'.

However, many Spaniards have a deep-seated scepticism about the Church. During the civil war and the four decades of Franco's rule, the Catholic Church was, for the most part, a strong supporter of his policies. The Church retains a powerful public voice in national debates.

Spain's most significant (and growing) religious community after the Catholics are Muslims.

Arts

Literature

Miguel de Cervantes' novel *Don Quijote* is the masterpiece of the literary flowering of the 16th and 17th centuries, not to mention one of the world's great works of fiction. Centuries later, the towering figure of the early 20th century was poet and playwright Federico García Lorca, who won international acclaim before he was murdered in the civil war for his Republican sympathies.

Popular contemporary authors include Arturo Pérez Reverte, Almudena Grandes and Javier Marías.

Cinema

Modern Spanish cinema's best-known director is Pedro Almodóvar, whose humorous, cutting-edge films are often set amid the great explosion of drugs and creativity that occurred in Madrid in the 1980s. His *Todo Sobre Mi Madre* (All About My Mother; 1999) and *Habla Con Ella* (Talk to Her; 2002) are both Oscar winners, while *Volver* (2006) is his most acclaimed recent work.

Alejandro Amenábar, the young Chilean-born director of *Abre los Ojos* (Open Your Eyes; 1997), *The Others* (2001) and the Oscar-winning *Mar Adentro* (The Sea Inside; 2004), is Almodóvar's main competition for Spain's 'best director' title. That latter film's star, Javier Bardem, won the Oscar for Best Supporting Actor in the Coen brothers' disturbing *No Country for Old Men* in 2008. The Madrid-born actress Penélope Cruz won an Oscar for Best Supporting Actress for her role in Woody Allen's *Vicky Cristina Barcelona* (2008).

Painting

The giants of Spain's Golden Age (aroun 1550 to 1650) were Toledo-based El Grec (originally from Crete) and Diego Velázque considered Spain's best painter by great including Picasso and Dalí. El Greco an Velázquez are well represented in Madrid Museo del Prado, as is the genius of the 18t and 19th centuries, Francisco Goya. Goya versatility ranged from unflattering roy portraits and anguished war scenes to bul fight etchings and tapestry designs.

Catalonia was the powerhouse of earl 20th-century Spanish art, claiming t hugely prolific Pablo Picasso (although bo in Málaga, Andalucía), the colourful symbolist Joan Miró and surrealist Salvador Dalí. To get inside the latter's world, head for Figueres or the Castell de Púbol. The two major museums dedicated to Picasso's work are the Museu Picasso in Barcelona and the Museo Picasso Málaga, while his signature *Guernica* and other works are found in Madrid's Centro de Arte Reina Sofía. The Reina Sofía also has works by Joan Miró, as does the Fundació Joan Miró.

Important artists of the late 20th century include the Basque sculptor Eduardo Chillida; his Museo Chillida Leku is south of San Sebastián.

Flamenco

Most musical historians speculate that flamenco probably dates back to a fusion of songs brought to Spain by the Roma people, with music and verses from North Africa crossing into medieval Muslim Andalucía. Flamenco as we now know it first took recognisable form in the 18th and early 19th centuries among Roma people in western Andalucía. Suitably, for a place considered the cradle of the genre, the Seville–Jerez de la Frontera–Cádiz axis is still considered the flamenco heartland and it's here, purists believe, that you must go for the most authentic flamenco experience.

FLAMENCO – THE ESSENTIAL ELEMENTS

A flamenco singer is known as a *cantaor* (male) or *cantaora* (female); a dancer is a *bailaor/a*. Most of the songs and dances are performed to a blood-rush of guitar from the *tocaor/a* (flamenco guitarist). Percussion is provided by tapping feet, clapping hands and sometimes castanets. Flamenco *coplas* (songs) come in many different types, from the anguished *soleá* or the intensely despairing *siguiriya* to the livelier *alegría* or the upbeat *bulería*. The first flamenco was *cante jondo* (deep song), an anguished instrument of expression for a group on the margins of society. *Jondura* (depth) is still the essence of pure flamenco.

The traditional flamenco costume – shawl, fan and long, frilly *bata de cola* (tail gown) for women, flat Cordoban hats and tight black trousers for men – dates from Andalucian fashions in the late 19th century.

Environment

Spain faces some of the most pressing environmental issues of our time. Drought, massive overdevelopment of its coastlines, overexploitation of scarce water resources by tourist projects and intensive agriculture, and spiralling emissions of greenhouse gases are all major concerns. It's a slightly more nuanced picture than first appears – Spain is a leading player in the wind-power industry, it has locked away around 40,000 sq km of protected areas, including 14 national parks, and its system of public transport is outstanding. But the apparent absence of any meaningful political will to tackle these issues is storing up problems for future generations.

Food & Drink

Reset your stomach's clock in Spain unless you want to eat alone, with other tourists or, in some cases, not at all.

Most Spaniards start the day with a light *desayuno* (breakfast), perhaps coffee with a *tostada* (piece of toast) or *pastel/bollo* (pastry), although they might stop in a bar later for a mid-morning *bocadillo* (baguette). *La comida* (lunch) is usually the main meal of the day, eaten between about 2pm and 4pm. The *cena* (evening meal) is usually lighter and most locals won't sit down for it before 9pm. The further south you go, the later start times tend to be – anything from 10pm to midnight!

At lunchtime from Monday to Friday, most places offer a *menú del día* – a fixed-price lunch menu and the traveller's best friend. For €10 to €14 you typically get three courses, bread and a drink. The *plato combinado* (combined plate) is a cousin of the *menú* and usually includes a meat dish with some vegetables.

Staples & Specialities

The variety in Spanish cuisines is quite extraordinary, and each region has its own styles and specialities. One of the most characteristic dishes, from the Valencia region, is paella – rice, seafood, the odd vegetable and often chicken or meat, all simmered together and traditionally coloured yellow with saffron. *Jamón serrano* (cured ham) is a delicacy available in many different qualities.

Many would argue that tapas are Spain's greatest culinary gift to the world, not least because the possibilities are endless. You can also order *raciones*, a large-sized serving of tapas. Anything can be a tapa, from a handful of olives or a piece of *tortilla de patatas* (potato and onion omelette) to more elaborate and often intensely surprising combinations of tastes. For tapas, the cities of Andalucía are usually (but not always) bastions of tradition, while the undoubted king of tapas destinations is San Sebastián, in Basque country, where they call tapas '*pintxos*'. It all comes together in Madrid.

Drinks

Start the day with a strong coffee, either as a *cafe con leche* (half-coffee, half-milk), *cafe solo* (short black, espresso-like) or *cafe cortado* (short black with a little milk).

The most common way to order a *cerveza* (beer) is to ask for a *caña* (small draught beer). In Basque Country this is a *zurrito*. A larger beer (about 300mL) is often called a *tubo*. All these words apply to *cerveza de barril* (draught beer) – if you just ask for a *cerveza* you're likely to get bottled beer, which is a little more expensive.

JAMÓN – A PRIMER

Unlike Italian prosciutto, Spanish *jamón* is a bold, deep red and well marbled with buttery fat. Like wines and olive oil, Spanish *jamón* is subject to a strict series of classifications. *Jamón serrano* refers to *jamón* made from white-coated pigs introduced to Spain in the 1950s. Once salted and semidried by the cold, dry winds of the Spanish sierra, most now go through a similar process of curing and drying in a climate-controlled shed for around a year. *Jamón serrano* accounts for approximately 90% of cured ham in Spain.

Jamón ibérico – more expensive and generally regarded as the elite of Spanish hams – comes from a black-coated pig indigenous to the Iberian Peninsula and a descendant of the wild boar. If the pig gains at least 50% of its body weight during the acorn-eating season, it can be classified as *jamón ibérico de bellota*, the most sought-after designation for *jamón*.

Vino (wine) comes *blanco* (white), *tinto* (red) or *rosado* (rosé). Exciting wine regions include Penedès, Priorat, Ribera del Duero and La Rioja. There are also many regional specialities, such as *jerez* (sherry) in Jerez de la Frontera and *cava* (a sparkling wine) in Catalonia. Sangria, a sweet punch made of red wine, fruit and spirits, is a summer drink and especially popular with tourists.

Agua del grifo (tap water) is usually safe to drink.

SURVIVAL GUIDE

Directory A–Z

Accommodation

Budget options include everything from dorm-style youth hostels to family-style *pensiones* and slightly better-heeled *hostales*. At the upper end of this category you'll find rooms with air-conditioning and private bathrooms. Midrange *hostales* and hotels are more comfortable and most offer standard hotel services. Business hotels, trendy boutique hotels and luxury hotels are usually in the top-end category.

PRICE RANGES

Our reviews refer to double rooms with a private bathroom, except in hostels or where otherwise specified. Quoted rates are for high season, which is generally May to September (though this varies greatly from region to region).

€ less than €65 (€75 in Madrid/Barcelona)

€€ €65 to €140 (€75 to €200 in Madrid/Barcelona)

€€€ more than €140 (€200 in Madrid/Barcelona)

CAMPING

Spain has around 1000 officially graded *campings* (camping grounds) and they vary greatl in service, cleanliness and style. They're off cially rated as 1st class (1ªC), 2nd class (2ªC or 3rd class (3ªC). Camping grounds usual charge per person, per tent and per vehicle typically €5 to €10 for each. Many campin grounds close from around October to Easte

The following are useful websites:

Campings Online (www.campingsonline.com espana) Booking service.

Campinguía (www.campinguia.com) Contai comments (mostly in Spanish) and links.

Guía Camping (www.guiacampingfecc.com) Online version of the annual *Guía Camping* (€13.60), which is available in bookshops around the country.

HOTELS, HOSTALES & PENSIONES

Most options fall into the categories of hotels (one to five stars, full amenities), *hostales* (high-end guesthouses with private bathroom; one to three stars) or *pensiones* (guesthouses, usually with shared bathroom; one to three stars).

YOUTH HOSTELS

Albergues juveniles (youth hostels) are cheap places to stay, especially for lone travellers. Expect to pay from €15 to €28 per night, depending on location, age and season. Spain's Hostelling International (HI) organisation, **Red Española de Albergues Juveniles** (REAJ, Spanish Youth Hostel Network; www.reaj.com), has around 250 youth hostels throughout Spain. Official hostels require HI membership (you can buy a membership card at virtually all hostels) and some have curfews.

Activities

HIKING

» Pick up Lonely Planet's *Walking in Spain* and read about some of the best treks in the country.

» Maps by Editorial Alpina are useful for hiking, especially in the Pyrenees. Buy at bookshops, sports shops and sometimes at petrol stations near hiking areas.

» GR (*Grandes Recorridos*, or long distance) trails are indicated with red-and-white markers.

SKIING

Skiing is cheaper but less varied than in much of the rest of Europe. The season runs from December to mid-April. The best resorts are in the Pyrenees, especially in northwest Catalonia and in Aragón. The Sierra Nevada in Andalucía offers the most southerly skiing in western Europe.

URFING, WINDSURFING & ITESURFING

he Basque Country has good surf spots, ncluding San Sebastián, Zarautz and the gendary left at Mundaka. Tarifa, with its ng beaches and ceaseless wind, is genally considered to be the windsurfing pital of Europe. It's also a top spot for tesurfing.

Business Hours

Reviews in this guidebook won't list business hours unless they differ from the following standards:

Banks 8.30am to 2pm Monday to Friday; some also open 4pm to 7pm Thursday and 9am and 1pm Saturday

Central post offices 8.30am to 9.30pm Monday to Friday, 8.30am to 2pm Saturday

Nightclubs midnight or 1am to 5am or 6am

Restaurants lunch 1pm to 4pm, dinner 8.30pm to midnight or later

Shops 10am to 2pm and 4.30pm to 7.30pm or 5pm to 8pm; big supermarkets and department stores generally open from 10am to 10pm Monday to Saturday

Embassies & Consulates

Australia Embassy (☎91 353 66 00; www.spain.embassy.gov.au; Paseo de la Castellana 259D, 24th fl, Madrid)

Canada Embassy (☎91 382 84 00; www.espana.gc.ca; Paseo de la Castellana 259D, Torre Espacio, Madrid)

New Zealand Embassy (☎91 523 02 26; www.nzembassy.com/spain; Calle de Pinar 7, 3rd Fl, Madrid)

UK Embassy (☎91 714 62 00; www.ukinspain.fco.gov.uk; Paseo de la Castellana 259D, Torre Espacio, Madrid)

US Embassy (☎91 587 22 00; http://spanish.madrid.usembassy.gov/; Calle de Serrano 75, Madrid)

Food

Each eating review is accompanied by one of the following symbols (the price relates to a main course:

€ less than €10

€€ €10 to €20

€€€ more than €20

Gay & Lesbian Travellers

Homosexuality is legal in Spain. In 2005 the Socialists gave the country's conservative Catholic foundations a shake with the legalisation of same-sex marriages in Spain. Lesbians and gay men generally keep a fairly low profile, but are quite open in the cities. Madrid, Barcelona, Sitges, Torremolinos and Ibiza have particularly lively scenes.

Internet Access

» Wi-fi increasingly available at most hotels and in some cafes, restaurants and airports; generally (but not always) free.

» Good cybercafes increasingly hard to find; ask at the local tourist office. Prices per hour range from €1.50 to €3.

Language Courses

» Popular places to learn Spanish: Barcelona, Granada, Madrid, Salamanca and Seville.

» The **Escuela Oficial de Idiomas** (EOI; www.eeooiinet.com) is a nationwide institution teaching Spanish and other local languages. On the website's opening page, hit 'Centros' under 'Comunidad' and then 'Centros en la Red' to get to a list of schools.

Money

» Many credit and debit cards can be used for withdrawing money from *cajeros automáticos* (automatic teller machines) that display the relevant symbols such as Visa, MasterCard, Cirrus etc.

» Most banks will exchange major foreign currencies and offer the best rates. Ask about commissions and take your passport.

» Credit and debit cards can be used to pay for most purchases. You'll often be asked to show your passport or some other form of identification, or to type in your pin. The most widely accepted cards are Visa and MasterCard.

» Exchange offices, indicated by the word *cambio* (exchange), offer longer opening hours than banks, but worse exchange rates and higher commissions.

» In Spain, value-added tax (VAT) is known as IVA (*ee*-ba; *impuesto sobre el valor añadido*). Visitors are entitled to a refund of the 18% IVA on purchases costing more than €90.16 from any shop if they are taking them out of the EU within three months.

» Menu prices include a service charge. Most people leave some small change. Taxi drivers don't have to be tipped but a little rounding up won't go amiss.

» Travellers cheques can be changed (for a commission) at most banks and exchange offices.

Public Holidays

The two main periods when Spaniards go on holiday are Semana Santa (the week leading up to Easter Sunday) and July or August. At these times accommodation can be scarce and transport heavily booked.

There are at least 14 official holidays a year – some observed nationwide, some locally. The following are national holidays:

Año Nuevo (New Year's Day) 1 January

Viernes Santo (Good Friday) March/April

Fiesta del Trabajo (Labour Day) 1 May

La Asunción (Feast of the Assumption) 15 August

Fiesta Nacional de España (National Day) 12 October

La Inmaculada Concepción (Feast of the Immaculate Conception) 8 December

Navidad (Christmas) 25 December

Regional governments set five holidays and local councils two more. The following are common dates:

Epifanía (Epiphany) or **Día de los Reyes Magos** (Three Kings' Day) 6 January

Día de San José (St Joseph's Day) 19 March

Jueves Santo (Good Thursday) March/April. Not observed in Catalonia and Valencia.

Corpus Christi June. The Thursday after the eighth Sunday after Easter Sunday.

Día de San Juan Bautista (Feast of St John the Baptist) 24 June

Día de Santiago Apóstol (Feast of St James the Apostle) 25 July

Día de Todos los Santos (All Saints' Day) 1 November

Día de la Constitución (Constitution Day) 6 December

Safe Travel

Most visitors to Spain never feel remotel threatened, but a sufficient number hav unpleasant experiences to warrant an aler The main thing to be wary of is petty the (which may of course not seem so petty your passport, cash, travellers cheque credit card and camera go missing). Sta alert and you can avoid most thievery tec niques. Barcelona, Madrid and Seville a the worst offenders, as are popular beach in summer (never leave belongings una tended).

Telephone

Blue public payphones are common and fairly easy to use. They accept coins, phonecards and, in some cases, credit cards. Phonecards come in €6 and €12 denominations and, like postage stamps, are sold at post offices and tobacconists.

International reverse-charge (collect) calls are simple to make: dial ☎900 99 followed by the appropriate code. For example: ☎900 99 00 61 for Australia, ☎900 99 00 44 for the UK, ☎900 99 00 11 (AT&T) for the USA etc.

To speak to an English-speaking Spanish international operator, dial ☎1008 (for calls within Europe) or ☎1005 (rest of the world).

MOBILE PHONES

All Spanish mobile phone companies (Telefónica's MoviStar, Orange and Vodafone) offer *prepagado* (prepaid) accounts for mobiles. The SIM card costs from €50, which includes some prepaid phone time.

Mobile phone numbers in Spain start with the number 6.

PHONE CODES

Telephone codes in Spain are an integral part of the phone number. All numbers are nine digits and you just dial that nine-digit number.

Numbers starting with ☎900 are national toll-free numbers, while those starting 901 to 905 come with varying costs; most can only be dialled from within Spain. In a similar category are numbers starting with ☎800, ☎803, ☎806 and ☎807.

Tourist Information

Most towns and large villages of any interest have a helpful *oficina de turismo* (tourist office) where you can get maps and brochures. The official tourism site is **Turespaña** (www.spain.info).

Visas

Spain is one of 26 member countries of the Schengen Convention, and Schengen visa rules apply.

Citizens or residents of EU and Schengen countries No visa required.

Citizens or residents of Australia, Canada, Israel, Japan, NZ and the USA No visa required for tourist visits of up to 90 days.

Other countries Check with a Spanish embassy or consulate.

To work or study in Spain A special visa may be required – contact a Spanish embassy or consulate before travel.

Getting There & Away

Flights, cars and tours can be booked online at lonelyplanet.com

Entering the Country

Immigration and customs checks usually involve a minimum of fuss, although there are exceptions. Your vehicle could be searched on arrival from Morocco; they're looking for controlled substances. Expect long delays at these borders, especially in summer.

The tiny principality of Andorra is not in the EU, so border controls (and rigorous customs checks for contraband) remain in place.

Air

Flights from all over Europe, including numerous budget airlines, serve main Spanish airports. All of Spain's airports share the user-friendly website and flight information telephone number of **Aena** (☎902 404 704; www.aena.es), the national airports authority. For more information on each airport on Aena's website, choose English and click on the drop-down menu of airports. Each airport's page has details on practical information (such as parking and public transport) and a full list of (and links to) airlines using that airport.

Madrid's Aeropuerto de Barajas is Spain's busiest (and Europe's fifth-busiest) airport. Other major airports include Barcelona's Aeroport del Prat and the airports of Palma de Mallorca, Málaga, Alicante, Girona, Valencia, Ibiza, Seville, Bilbao and Zaragoza.

Land

Spain shares land borders with France, Portugal and Andorra.

BUS

Apart from shorter cross-border services, **Eurolines** (www.eurolines.com) is the main operator of international bus services to Spain from most of western Europe and Morocco. Services from France include Nice to Madrid (from €82, 17¾ hours, daily) and Paris to Barcelona (from €70, 14¾ hours, daily).

Avanza (☎902 020999; www.avanzabus.com) runs a Lisbon to Madrid service (€37.50, 7½ to nine hours, two daily). Other bus services run north via Porto to Tui, Santiago de Compostela and A Coruña in Galicia. Local buses cross the border from towns such as Huelva in Andalucía, Badajoz in Extremadura and Ourense in Galicia.

Regular buses connect Andorra with Barcelona (including winter ski buses and direct services to the airport) and other destinations in Spain (including Madrid) and France.

TRAIN

There are plans for direct high-speed rail links from Paris to Madrid and Barcelona. At the moment, these trains currently require a transfer in Figures Vilafant. Currently services include the *Trenhotel Francisco de Goya* from Paris to Madrid (chair/sleeper class €162.50/178, 15 hours, daily), the *Trenhotel Joan Miró* from Paris to Barcelona (chair/sleeper class €153.25/166.50, 12 hours, daily) and a Talgo service from Montepellier to Lorca (€105, 13 hours, daily).

Services to from Portugal include trains from Lisbon to Madrid (chair/sleeper class €63.25/91.50, 10½ hours, one daily) and Irún (chair/sleeper class €74/103.50, 14½ hours, one daily).

Sea

Ferries run to mainland Spain regularly from the Canary Islands, Italy, North Africa (Algeria, Morocco and the Spanish enclaves of Ceuta and Melilla) and the UK. Most services are run by the Spanish national ferry company, **Acciona Trasmediterránea** (☎902 454645; www.trasmediterranea.es). You can take vehicles on these routes.

FERRIES TO SPAIN

From Algeria

ROUTE	COMPANY	DURATION (HR)	FREQUENCY
Ghazaouet to Almería	Acciona Trasmediterránea	8	4 weekly
Oran to Almería	Acciona Trasmediterránea	8	2 weekly (May to September)

From Italy

ROUTE	COMPANY	DURATION (HR)	FREQUENCY
Genoa to Barcelona	Acciona Trasmediterránea	18	3 weekly
Civitavecchia (near Rome) to Barcelona	Acciona Trasmediterránea	20½	6-7 weekly
Livorno (Tuscany) to Barcelona	Acciona Trasmediterránea	19½	3 weekly
Porto Torres (Sardinia) to Barcelona	Acciona Trasmediterránea	12	1 daily

From Morocco

ROUTE	COMPANY	DURATION	FREQUENCY
Tangier to Algeciras	Acciona Trasmediterránea	90min	up to 8 daily
Tangier to Barcelona	Acciona Trasmediterránea	24-35hr	weekly
Tangier to Tarifa	Acciona Trasmediterránea	35min	up to 8 daily
Nador to Almería	Acciona Trasmediterránea	5-8hr	up to 3 daily

From the UK

ROUTE	COMPANY	DURATION (HR)	FREQUENCY
Plymouth to Santander	Brittany Ferries	20	weekly
Portsmouth to Santander	Brittany Ferries	24	weekly
Portsmouth to Bilbao	Brittany Ferries	24	2 weekly

LD Lines (www.ldlines.com) runs a service from Gijón into Saint-Nazaire in France (14 hours, three weekly).

From mid-March to mid-November, **Brittany Ferries** (☎0871 244 0744; www.brittany-ferries.co.uk) runs services to the UK.

Getting Around

Students and seniors are eligible for discounts of 30% to 50% on most types of transport within Spain.

Air

Domestic Spanish routes are operated by the following airlines:

Air Berlin (www.airberlin.com)

Air Europa (www.aireuropa.com)

easyJet (www.easyjet.com)

Iberia (www.iberia.es)

Ryanair (www.ryanair.com)

Volotea (www.volotea.com)

Vueling (www.vueling.com)

Boat

Regular ferries connect the Spanish mainland with the Balearic Islands.

Bus

Spain's bus network is operated by countless independent companies and reaches into the most remote towns and villages. Many towns and cities have one main bus station where most buses arrive and depart.

It is not necessary, and often not possible, to make advance reservations for local bus journeys. It is, however, a good idea to turn up at least 30 minutes before the bus leaves to guarantee a seat. For longer trips, you can and should buy your ticket in advance.

ALSA (☎902 422242; www.alsa.es) The biggest player, this company has routes all over the country in association with various other companies.

Avanza (☎902 020999; www.avanzabus.com)

Car & Motorcycle

Spain's roads vary enormously but are generally good. Fastest are the *autopistas* (highways); on some, you have to pay hefty tolls.

Every vehicle should display a nationality plate of its country of registration and you must always carry proof of ownership of a private vehicle. Third-party motor insurance is required throughout Europe. A warning triangle and a reflective jacket (to be used in case of breakdown) are compulsory.

AUTOMOBILE ASSOCIATIONS

The **Real Automóvil Club de España** (RACE; ☎902 404 545; www.race.es) is the national automobile club. They may well come to assist you in case of a breakdown, but in any event you should obtain an emergency telephone number for Spain from your own insurer.

DRIVING LICENCES

All EU member states' driving licences are recognised. Other foreign licences should be accompanied by an International Driving Permit (although in practice local licences are usually accepted). These are available from automobile clubs in your country and valid for 12 months.

HIRE

To rent a car in Spain you have to have a licence, be aged 21 or over and have a credit or debit card. Rates vary widely: the best deals tend to be in major tourist areas, including airports. Prices are especially competitive in the Balearic Islands. Expect a compact car to cost from €30 per day.

ROAD RULES

» The blood-alcohol limit is 0.05%.

» The legal driving age for cars is 18. The legal driving age for motorcycles and scooters is 16 (80cc and over) or 14 (50cc and under). A licence is required.

» Motorcyclists must use headlights at all times and wear a helmet if riding a bike of 125cc or more.

» Drive on the right.

» In built-up areas , the speed limit is 50km/h (and in some cases, such as inner-city Barcelona, 30km/h), which increases to 100km/h on major roads and up to 120km/h on *autovías* and *autopistas* (toll-free and tolled dual-lane highways, respectively). Cars towing caravans are restricted to a maximum speed of 80km/h.

Train

The national railway company is **Renfe** (☎902 243402; www.renfe.com). Trains are mostly modern and comfortable, and late arrivals are the exception rather than the rule. The high-speed network is in constant expansion.

Passes are valid for all long-distance Renfe trains; InterRail users pay supplements on Talgo, InterCity and AVE trains. All pass-holders making reservations pay a small fee.

Among Spain's numerous types of trains:

Alaris, Altaria, Alvia, Arco and Avant Long-distance intermediate-speed services.

Cercanías For short hops and services to outlying suburbs and satellite towns in Madrid, Barcelona and 11 other cities.

Euromed Similar to the AVE trains, they connect Barcelona with Valencia and Alicante.

Regionales Trains operating within one region, usually stopping at all stations.

Talgo and Intercity Slower long-distance trains.

Tren de Alta Velocidad Española (AVE) High-speed trains that link Madrid with Barcelona, Burgos, Córdoba, Cuenca, Huesca, Lerida, Málaga, Seville, Valencia, Valladolid and Zaragoza. There are also Barcelona–Seville and Barcelona–Málaga services. In coming years Madrid–Cádiz and Madrid–Bilbao should come on line.

Trenhotel Overnight trains with sleeper berths.

CLASSES & COSTS

» All long-distance trains have 2nd and 1st classes, known as *turista* and *preferente*, respectively. The latter is 20% to 40% more expensive.

» Fares vary enormously depending on the service (faster trains cost considerably more) and, in the case of some high-speed services such as the AVE, on the time and day of travel.

» Buying a return ticket often gives you a 10% to 20% discount on the return trip. Students and people up to 25 years of age with a Euro<26 Card (Carnet Joven in Spain) are entitled to 20% to 25% off most ticket prices.

Switzerland

Includes »

Geneva 1123
Lausanne 1129
Gruyères 1131
Zermatt 1131
Bern 1133
Lucerne 1134
Interlaken 1135
Jungfrau Region 1136
Zürich 1138
Basel 1142
Locarno 1143
Lugano 1143
St Moritz 1144
Understand Switzerland 1145
Survival Guide 1147

Best Places to Eat

- Lötschberg AOC (p1133)
- Les 5 Portes (p1128)
- Whymper Stube (p1132)
- Café Schober (p1139)

Best Places to Stay

- Hotel & Hostel Montarina (p1143)
- Berggasthaus Trift (p1132)
- Pension für Dich (p1138)
- Mountain Hostel (p1137)

Why Go?

What romance Zermatt, St Moritz and other glitterati-encrusted names evoke. This is *Sonderfall Schweiz* ('special case Switzerland'), a privileged neutral country set apart from others, proudly idiosyncratic, insular and unique. Blessed with cultural diversity, its four languages alone say it all.

The Swiss don't do half-measures: Zürich, their most gregarious urban centre, has cutting-edge art, legendary nightlife and one of the world's highest living standards. The national passion for sweat, stamina and clingy Lycra takes 65 year olds across 2500m-high mountain passes for Sunday strolls, sees giggly three year olds skiing rings around grown-ups, prompts locals done with 'ordinary' marathons to sprint backwards up mountains – all in the name of good old-fashioned fun.

So don't depend just on your postcard images of Bern's chocolate-box architecture, the majestic Matterhorn or the thundering Rheinfall – Switzerland is a place that's so outrageously beautiful it simply must be seen to be believed.

When to Go

Geneva

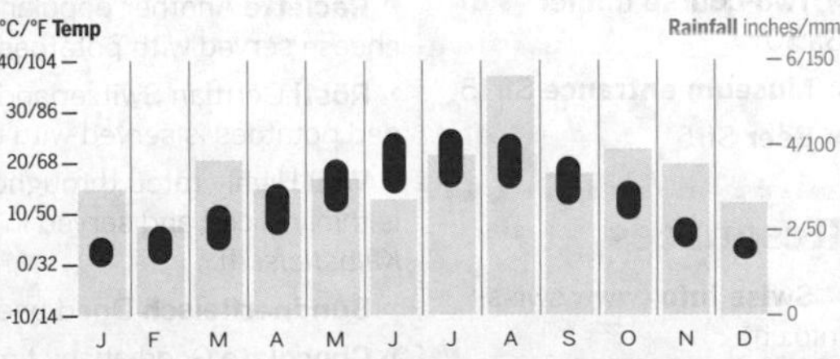

Dec–early Apr Carve through powder and drink glühwein (mulled wine) at an Alpine resort.

May–Sep Hike in the shadow of the Matterhorn and be wowed by its mesmerising stance.

Aug Celebrate Swiss National Day on 1 August and witness Swiss national pride in full force.

AT A GLANCE

» **Currency** Swiss franc (Sfr)

» **Languages** French, German, Italian, Romansch

» **Money** ATMs readily available

» **Visas** Schengen rules apply

Fast Facts

» **Area** 41,285 sq km

» **Capital** Bern

» **Country code** ☎41

» **Emergency** Ambulance ☎144, fire ☎118, police ☎117

Exchange Rates

Australia	A$1	Sfr0.99
Canada	C$1	Sfr0.93
Euro Zone	€1	Sfr1.22
Japan	¥100	Sfr1.01
New Zealand	NZ$1	Sfr0.79
UK	UK£1	Sfr1.44
USA	US$1	Sfr0.95

Set Your Budget

» **Budget hotel room** Sfr80–100

» **Two-course dinner** Sfr30

» **Museum entrance** Sfr15

» **Beer** Sfr5

Resources

» **Swiss Info** (www.swissinfo.ch)

» **MySwitzerland** (www.myswitzerland.com)

Connections

Landlocked between France, Germany, Austria, Liechtenstein and Italy, Switzerland is well linked. Geneva city buses run as far as the French border (a couple cross into France, continuing along the southern shore of Lake Geneva). Fast and frequent French TGV trains link Geneva and Lausanne with Paris. In the north, newly completed high-speed lines in France mean that Zürich is only four hours from Paris, while Basel is but three. Basel also has fast ICE trains that serve major German cities, while Zürich is well linked to Stuttgart, Münich and Austria. Regular trains serve Milan from Zürich, Lucerne and Lugano.

ITINERARIES

One Week

Starting in vibrant Zürich, shop famous Bahnhofstrasse and find the medieval corners. Next, head to the Jungfrau region to explore some kick-ass Alpine scenery (think James Bond racing an avalanche down a sheer snowy rock face). Take a pit stop in beautiful Lucerne before finishing up in country capital Bern.

Two Weeks

As above, then head west for French-immersion lessons in Geneva or lakeside Lausanne. Stop in Gruyères to dip into a cheesy fondue and overdose on meringues drowned in thick double cream. Zip to Zermatt or across to St Moritz to frolic in snow or green meadows, then loop east to taste the Italian side of Switzerland at lakeside Lugano.

Essential Food & Drink

» **Fondue** Switzerland's best-known dish, in which melted Emmental and Gruyère cheese are combined with white wine in a large pot and eaten with bread cubes.

» **Raclette** Another popular artery-hardener of melted cheese served with potatoes.

» **Rösti** German Switzerland's national dish of fried shredded potatoes is served with everything.

» **Veal** Highly rated throughout the country; in Zürich, veal is thinly sliced and served in a cream sauce *(Gschnetzeltes Kalbsfleisch)*.

» **Bündnerfleisch** Dried beef, smoked and thinly sliced.

» **Chocolate** Good at any time of day and available in dozen of luscious flavours.

GENEVA

POP 192,400

The whole world seems to be in posh Geneva, Switzerland's second city. The UN, International Red Cross, International Labour Organization, World Health Organization – 200-odd governmental and nongovernmental international organisations fill the city's plush hotels with big-name guests, feast on an incredulous choice of cuisine and help prop up the overload of banks, jewellers and chocolate shops for which Geneva is known. Strolling manicured city parks, lake sailing and skiing next door in the Alps are weekend pursuits.

Sights & Activities

The city centre is so compact it's easy to see many of the main sights on foot.

Lake Geneva LAKE

Begin your exploration of Europe's largest Alpine lake by having a coffee on **Île Rousseau**, where a statue honours the celebrated freethinker. Cross to the southern side of the lake and walk west to the **Horloge Fleurie** (Flower Clock; Quai du Général-Guisan) in the Jardin Anglais. Geneva's most photographed clock, crafted from 6500 flowers, can be oddly disappointing after all the hype.

Far more rewarding is the iconic 140m-tall **Jet d'Eau** (Jetée des Eaux-Vives; 9.30am-11.15pm Mar-Oct) on the lake's southern shore.

Old Town HISTORIC AREA

The main street of the Vieille Ville (Old Town), Grand-Rue, shelters the **Espace Rousseau** (022 310 10 28; www.espace-rousseau.ch; Grand-Rue 40; adult/child Sfr5/3; 11am-5.30pm Tue-Sun) at No 40, where the 18th-century philosopher was born. It's Geneva's best area for walking; the Place du Bourg-de-Four is timeless and ringed by good cafes.

Nearby, the part-Romanesque, part-Gothic **Cathédrale de St-Pierre** (St Peter's Cathedral; Cour St-Pierre; admission free; 9.30am-6.30pm Mon-Sat, noon-6.30pm Sun Jun-Sep, 10am-5.50pm Mon-Sat, noon-5.30pm Sun Oct-May) is where Protestant John Calvin preached from 1536 to 1564. Revel in the flamboyant **Chapel of the Maccabees**. Beneath the cathedral is the **site archéologique** (022 311 75 74; www.site-archeologique.ch; Cour St-Pierre 6; adult/child Sfr8/4; 10am-5pm Tue-Sun), an interactive space safeguarding fine 4th-century mosaics and a 5th-century baptismal font.

International Red Cross & Red Crescent Museum MUSEUM

(Musée Internationale de la Croix Rouge et du Croissant-Rouge; 022 748 95 25; www.micr.org; Av de la Paix 17) Closed at the time of research, the museum was set to reopen in 2013 after a massive rethink. Visitors engage with displays along three themes: Defending Human Dignity, Restoring Family Links and Reducing Natural Risks. All highlight recent atrocities perpetuated by humanity set against the noble goals of the organisation. Take bus 8 to the Appia stop.

Patek Phillipe Museum MUSEUM

(022 807 09 10; www.patekmuseum.com; Rue des Vieux Grenadiers 7; adult/child Sfr10/free; 2-6pm Tue-Fri, 10am-6pm Sat) A treasure trove of precision art, this museum displays exquisite timepieces from the 16th century to the present.

Sleeping

When checking in, ask for your free public transport ticket covering unlimited bus travel for the duration of your hotel stay.

There are loads of cheap hotels southeast of the train station on and off the Rue des Alpes; although the neighbourhood can look gritty, the hotels are usually fine albeit, at times, worn. Ask to see rooms.

Hôtel Bel'Esperance HOTEL €€

(022 818 37 37; www.hotel-bel-esperance.ch; Rue de la Vallée 1; s/d from Sfr105/160; @) This two-star hotel is a two-second flit to the Old Town and offers extraordinary value for a pricey city like Geneva. Rooms are quiet and cared for, and those on the 1st floor share a kitchen. Ride the lift to the 5th floor to flop in a chair on its wonderful flower-filled rooftop terrace.

Hotel Admiral HOTEL €

(022 906 97 00; www.hoteladmiral.ch; Rue Pellegrino Rossi 8; s/d from Sfr90/100; @) An excellent-value modest hotel between the train station and the lake. The street is slightly sleazy but the rooms are clean if small. There's an elevator, the included breakfast buffet is lavish and the staff are quite helpful.

Auberge de Jeunesse HOSTEL €

(022 732 62 60; www.yh-geneva.ch; Rue Rothschild 28-30; dm from Sfr29, d/q Sfr95/135; @) At this well-equipped, Hostelling International–affiliated apartment block, rates include breakfast, and bunk-bed dorms max out at 12 beds. Non HI-card holders pay Sfr6 more a night.

continued on p1128

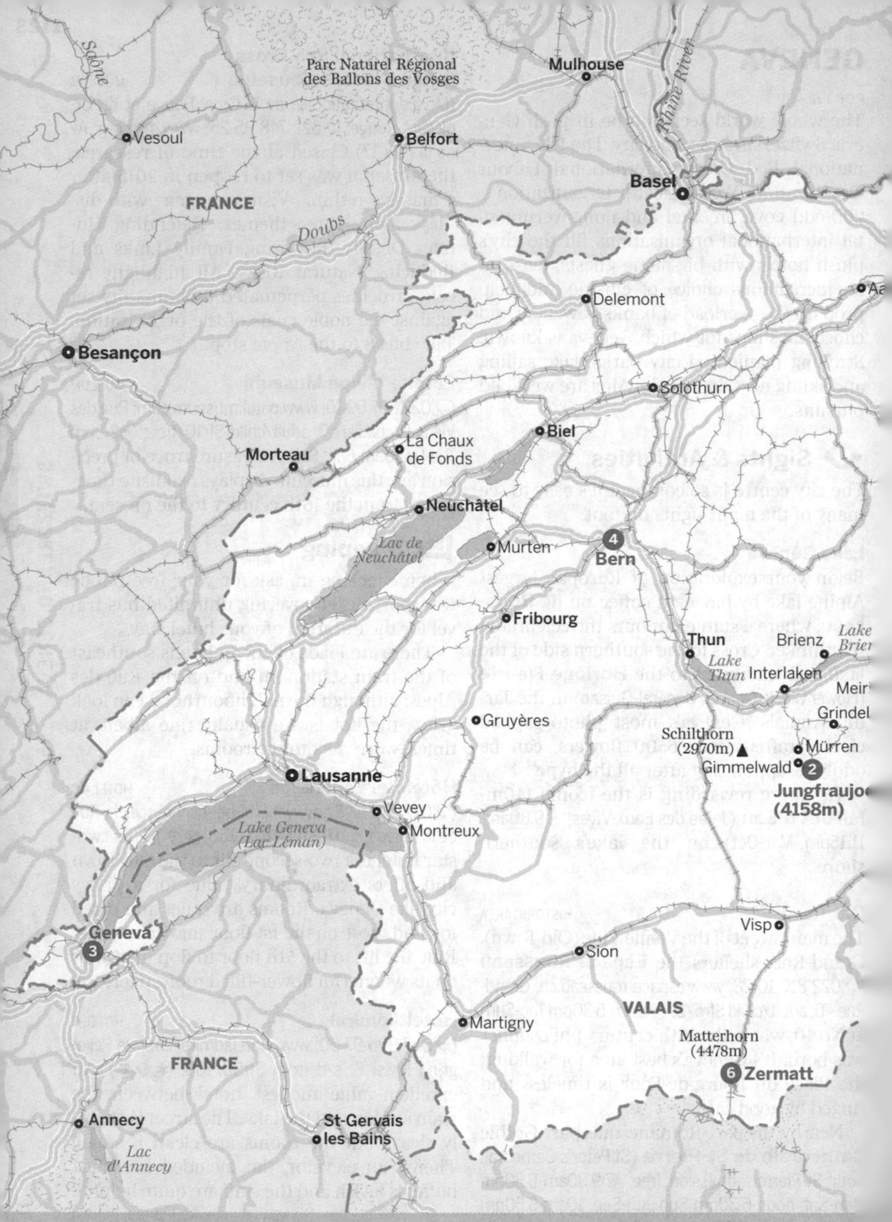

Switzerland Highlights

1 Discover the zest of **Zürich** (p1138) with a daytime stroll along the city's sublime lake followed by a rollicking night out

2 Be wowed by the Eiger's monstrous north face on a ride to Europe's highest train station, 3471m **Jungfraujoch** (p1137)

3 Board a boat in **Geneva** (p1123) for a serene lake cruise to Nyon or medieval Lausanne

4 Be surprised by Swiss capital **Bern** (p1133): think medieval charm, folkloric fountains and a cafe and dining culture

5 Ride one of Switzerland's iconic scenic trains, such as one over the **Bernina Pass** (p1143)

6 Gape at the iconic Matterhorn and wander around the car-free Alpine village of **Zermatt** (p1131)

7 Try out your Italian accent at **Lugano** (p1143), which has a lovely, temperate lake setting

Geneva

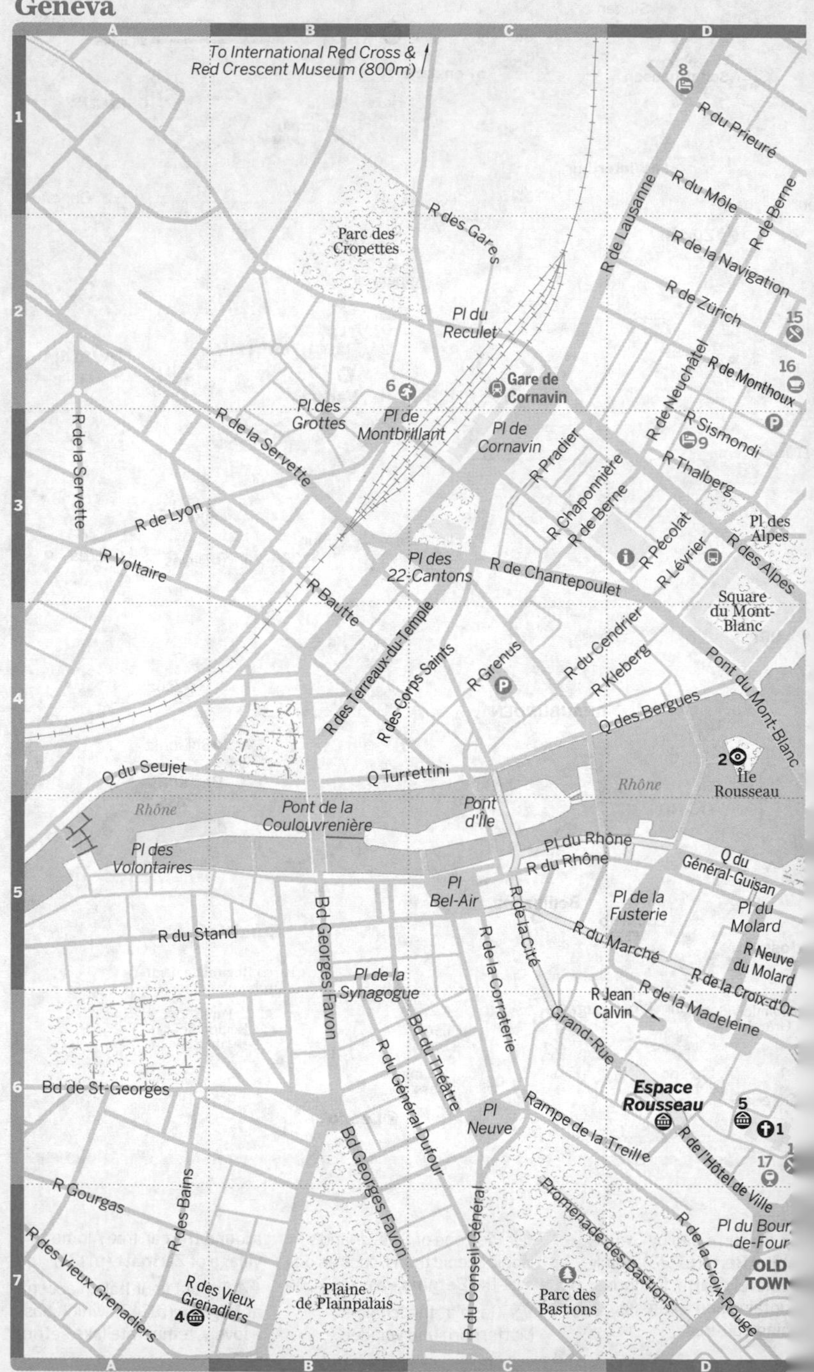

A
B
C
D
1
2
3
4
5
6
7
To International Red Cross & Red Crescent Museum (800m)
R du Prieuré
R du Môle
R de Berne
R de la Navigation
R de Zürich
R de Lausanne
R des Gares
Parc des Cropettes
Pl du Reculet
Gare de Cornavin
R de Neuchâtel
R de Monthoux
R Sismondi
R Thalberg
Pl des Grottes
Pl de Montbrillant
Pl de Cornavin
R Pradier
R Chaponnière
R de Berne
R de la Servette
R de la Servette
R de Lyon
R Voltaire
Pl des 22-Cantons
R de Chantepoulet
R Pécolat
R Lévrier
Pl des Alpes
R des Alpes
Square du Mont-Blanc
R Bautte
R des Terreaux-du-Temple
R des Corps Saints
R Grenus
R du Cendrier
R Kleberg
Q des Bergues
Pont du Mont-Blanc
Île Rousseau
Q du Seujet
Q Turrettini
Rhône
Rhône
Pont de la Coulouvrenière
Pont d'Île
Pl des Volontaires
Pl du Rhône
R du Rhône
Q du Général-Guisan
Pl Bel-Air
R de la Cité
Pl de la Fusterie
Pl du Molard
R du Stand
Bd Georges Favon
R de la Corraterie
R du Marché
R Neuve du Molard
R de la Croix-d'Or
Pl de la Synagogue
R Jean Calvin
R de la Madeleine
Bd du Théâtre
R du Général Dufour
Grand-Rue
Bd de St-Georges
Espace Rousseau
Pl Neuve
Rampe de la Treille
R de l'Hôtel de Ville
Bd Georges Favon
R Gourgas
R des Bains
R du Conseil-Général
Promenade des Bastions
R de la Croix-Rouge
Pl du Bourg-de-Four
OLD TOWN
R des Vieux Grenadiers
R des Vieux Grenadiers
Plaine de Plainpalais
Parc des Bastions
1
2
4
5
6
8
9
15
16
17

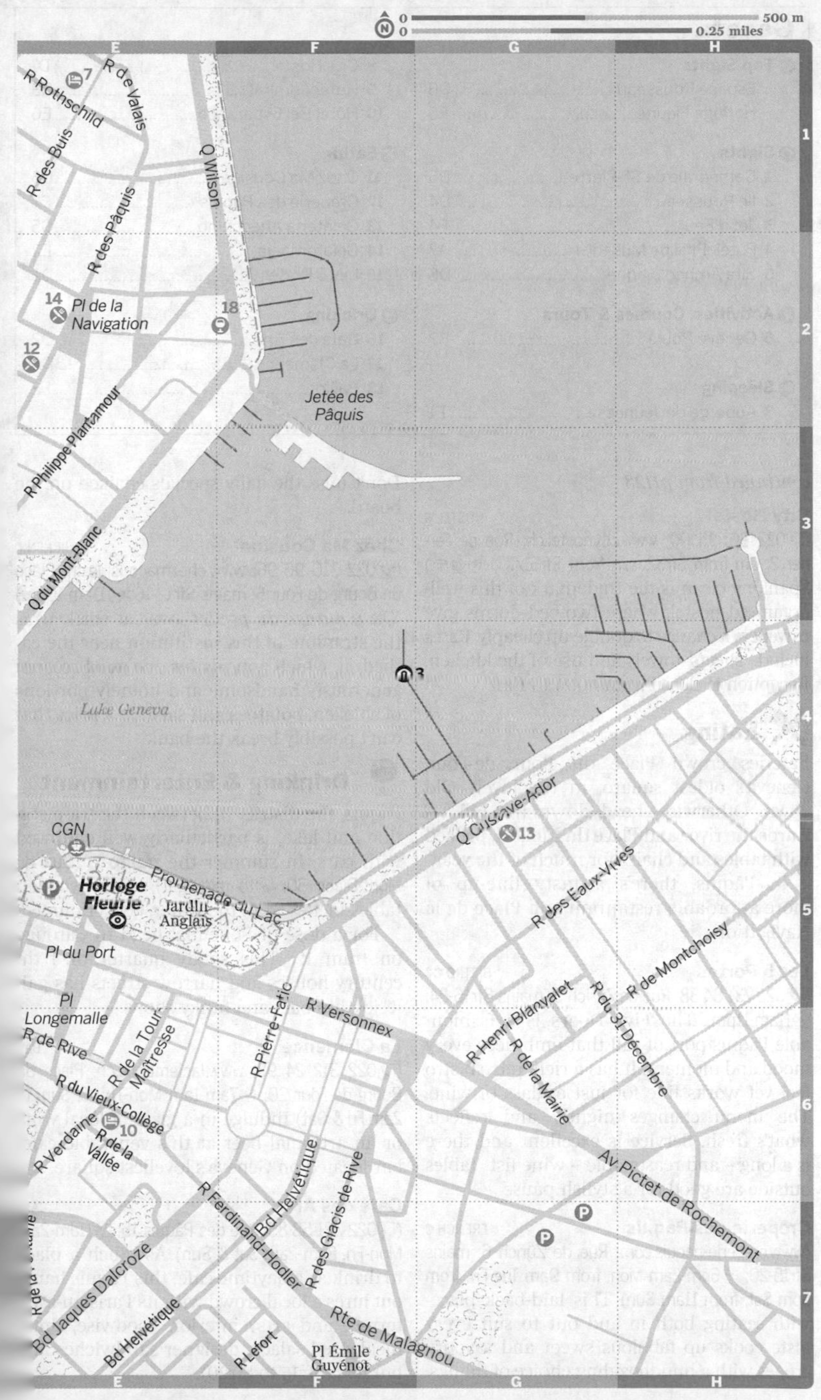
0
500 m
0
0.25 miles
E
F
G
H
1
2
3
4
5
6
7
R Rothschild
R de Valais
R des Buis
R des Pâquis
Q Wilson
14
Pl de la Navigation
18
12
Jetée des Pâquis
R Philippe Plantamour
Q du Mont-Blanc
3
Lake Geneva
CGN
Horloge Fleurie
Jardin Anglais
Promenade du Lac
Q Gustave-Ador
13
R des Eaux-Vives
R de Montchoisy
Pl du Port
Pl Longemalle
R de Rive
R de la Tour Maîtresse
R Pierre-Fatio
R Versonnex
R Henri Blanvalet
R du 31 Décembre
R de la Mairie
R du Vieux-Collège
10
R Verdaine
R de la Vallée
Bd Helvétique
R des Glacis de Rive
R Ferdinand-Hodler
Av Pictet de Rochemont
Bd Jaques Dalcroze
Bd Helvétique
R Lefort
Pl Émile Guyénot
Rte de Malagnou
7

Geneva

Top Sights

Espace Rousseau D6
Horloge Fleurie E5

Sights

1 Cathédrale de St-Pierre D6
2 Île Rousseau D4
3 Jet d'Eau F4
4 Patek Phillipe Museum A7
5 Site Archéologique D6

Activities, Courses & Tours

6 Genève Roule B2

Sleeping

7 Auberge de Jeunesse E1
8 City Hostel D1
9 Hotel Admiral D3
10 Hôtel Bel'Esperance E6

Eating

11 Chez Ma Cousine D6
12 Crêperie des Pâquis E2
13 Gelateria Arlecchino G5
14 Gelatomania E2
15 Les 5 Portes D2

Drinking

16 Café des Arts D2
17 La Clémence D6
18 Paillote F2

continued from p1123

City Hostel HOSTEL €
(☎022 901 15 00; www.cityhostel.ch; Rue de Ferrier 2; dm from Sfr32, s/d from Sfr61/77; P@) Spanking clean is the trademark of this well-organised hostel, where two-bed dorms give travellers a chance to double up cheaply. Rates include sheets, towels and use of the kitchen. Reception is closed from noon to 1pm.

Eating

Eateries crowd Place du Bourg-de-Four, Geneva's oldest square, in the lovely Old Town. Otherwise, head down the hill towards the river and Place du Molard, packed with tables and chairs for much of the year.

In Pâquis, there's a tasty line-up of more affordable restaurants on Place de la Navigation.

Les 5 Portes BISTRO €€
(☎022 731 84 38; Rue de Zürich 5; mains Sfr16-24; ⏱11am-11pm) The Five Doors is a fashionable Pâquis port of call that embraces every mood and moment. It has a rich, retro bistro feel yet works fine for just a glass of wine. The menu changes nightly and reflects what's fresh. Service is excellent and there is a long – and reasonable – wine list. Tables outside are good for a stylish pause.

Crêperie des Pâquis FRENCH €
(www.creperie-paquis.com; Rue de Zürich 6; mains Sfr15-20; ⏱6pm-2am Mon, from 9am Tue-Fri, from 5pm Sat, from 11am Sun) This laid-back place-with seating both in and out to suit every taste cooks up fabulous sweet and savoury crêpes with a mindboggling choice of fillings. Don't miss the daily specials chalked on the board.

Chez Ma Cousine CHICKEN €
(☎022 310 96 96; www.chezmacousine.ch; Place du Bourg-de-Four 6; mains Sfr12-16; ⏱11am-10pm) *'On y mange du poulet'* (we eat chicken) is the strapline of this institution near the cathedral, which appeals for one good reason: generously handsome and homely portions of chicken, potatoes and salad at a price that can't possibly break the bank.

Drinking & Entertainment

Pâquis, the district in between the train station and lake, is particularly well endowed with bars. In summer the **paillote** (Quai du Mont-Blanc 30; ⏱to midnight), with wooden tables inches from the water, gets crammed.

For a dose of Bohemia, head to Carouge on tram 12. This shady quarter of 17th-century houses and narrow streets has galleries, hip bars and funky shops.

La Clémence BA
(☎022 312 24 98; www.laclemence.ch; Place d Bourg-de-Four 20; ⏱7am-1am Mon-Thu & Sun, t 2am Fri & Sat) Indulge in a glass of local win or an artisanal beer at this venerable caf bar located on Geneva's loveliest square.

Café des Arts CA
(☎022 321 58 85; Rue des Pâquis 15; ⏱11am-2a Mon-Fri, 8am-2am Sat & Sun) As much a plac to drink as a daytime cafe, this Pâquis han out lures a local crowd with its Parisian-sty terrace and artsy interior. Foodwise, thir meal-sized salads, designer sandwiches ar burgers (Sfr15 to Sfr20).

Le Cheval Blanc BAR
(☎022 343 61 61; www.lechevalblanc.ch; Place de l'Octroi 15; ⏰11.30am-1am or 2am Tue-Sat, 10.30am-1am Sun) The White Horse is a real Carouge favourite. Quaff cocktails and eat tapas – some of Geneva's best – at the pink neon-lit bar upstairs, then head downstairs to its club and concert space, Le Box.

Le Chat Noir LIVE MUSIC
(☎022 343 49 98; www.chatnoir.ch; Rue Vautier 13; ⏰Tue-Sat) A hot address in Carouge packed most nights, the Black Cat is a lovely spot for an after-work aperitif and, come dark, live music. There's also a small selection of tapas to nibble on.

Shopping

Designer shopping is wedged between Rue du Rhône and Rue de Rive; the latter has lots of chain stores. Grand-Rue in the Old Town and Carouge boast artsy boutiques.

Information

Lonely Planet (www.lonelyplanet.com/switzerland/geneva)

Tourist Office (☎022 909 70 00; www.geneve-tourisme.ch; Rue du Mont-Blanc 18; ⏰9am-6pm Mon-Sat, 10am-4pm Sun) Offers good walking tour information. The Geneva Pass (from Sfr25) offers free admissions and discounts.

Getting There & Away

AIR **Aéroport International de Genève** (☎0900 571 500; www.gva.ch), 4km from town, has connections to major European cities and many others worldwide.

BOAT **CGN** (Compagnie Générale de Navigation; ☎084 881 18 48; www.cgn.ch) operates a web of scenic steamer services from its Jardin Anglais jetty to other villages on Lake Geneva. Many only sail May to September, including those to and from Lausanne (Sfr43, 3½ hours). Eurail and Swiss Pass holders are valid on CGN boats or there is a one-day CGN boat pass (Sfr56).

BUS International buses depart from the **bus station** (☎0900 320 320, 022 732 02 30; www.coach-station.com; Place Dorcière).

TRAIN Trains run to major Swiss towns including at least every 30 minutes to and from Lausanne (Sfr22, 33 to 48 minutes), Bern (Sfr49, 1¾ hours) and Zürich (Sfr84, 2¾ hours). International daily rail connections from Geneva include Paris by TGV (3¼ hours) and Milan (four hours).

Getting Around

TO/FROM THE AIRPORT Getting from the airport is easy with regular trains into Gare de Cornavin (Sfr3, eight minutes). Slower bus 10 (Sfr3) does the same 4km trip. A metered taxi costs Sfr30 to Sfr50.

BICYCLE Pick up a bike at **Genève Roule** (☎022 740 13 43; www.geneveroule.ch; Place de Montbrillant 17; ⏰8am-6pm Mon-Sat) or its seasonal Jetée des Pâquis pick-up point for Sfr12/20 per day/weekend. May to October, borrow a bike (with advertisements on it) for free.

PUBLIC TRANSPORT Buses, trams, trains and boats service the city, and ticket dispensers are found at all stops. Most services are operated by **TPG** (www.tpg.ch; ⏰7am-7pm Mon-Fri, 7am-6pm Sat). Typical tickets cost Sfr3.50 (one hour); a day pass is Sfr8 when purchased after 9am.

LAKE GENEVA REGION

Lausanne

POP 128,200

In a fabulous location overlooking Lake Geneva, Lausanne is an enchanting beauty with several distinct personalities: the former fishing village of Ouchy, with its summer beach-resort feel; Place St-François, with stylish, cobblestone shopping streets; and Flon, a warehouse district of bars, galleries and boutiques. It's also got a few good sights.

Sights & Activities

Downhill by the water in **Ouchy**, Lake Geneva (Lac Léman) is the source of many a sporting opportunity, including sailing, windsurfing, waterskiing and swimming; the tourist offices have details. Seasonal

TOP TWO GELATO SHOPS

Gelateria Arlecchino (☎022 736 70 60; Rue du 31 Décembre 1; per scoop Sfr3.50, milkshakes Sfr7) Left-bank choice a stone's throw from the Jet d'Eau. Chocolate and ginger, honey, peanut cream and mango are among the 40 flavours at this lip-licking parlour.

Gelatomania (☎022 741 41 44; Rue des Pâquis 25; per scoop Sfr3.50) Right-bank choice. A constant queue loiters outside this shop where ice-cream maniacs wrap their tongues around a plethora of exotic flavours and old faves.

stands in front of Chateau d'Ouchy rent pedalos and kayaks, and cycling and roller-blading are big on the silky-smooth water-front promenades.

In the heart of the **Vieille Ville** (Old Town), the 9th-century medieval market square **Place de la Palud** – pretty as a picture – was originally bogland. For five centuries it has been home to the city government, now housed in the 17th-century **Hôtel de Ville** (town hall). A fountain pierces one end of the square, presided over by a brightly painted column topped by the allegorical figure of Justice, clutching scales and dressed in blue.

Musée Olympique MUSEUM
(☎021 621 65 11; www.museum.olympic.org; Quai d'Ouchy 1) Lausanne is home to the International Olympic Committee, and the Musée Olympique is easily the city's most lavish museum and a real must for sports buffs (and kids). Under renovation until late 2013, its usual home is a gorgeous building atop a tiered landscaped garden in the Parc Olympique.

Sleeping

Hotel guests get a Lausanne Transport Card covering unlimited use of public transport for the duration of their stay.

Lausanne Guest House GUESTHOUSE €
(☎021 601 80 00; www.lausanne-guesthouse.ch; Chemin des Épinettes 4; dm from Sfr39, r with/without bathroom from Sfr100/90; P@) An attractive mansion converted into quality backpacking accommodation near the train station. Many rooms have lake views and you can hang out in the garden or on the terrace.

Hôtel du Marché HOTEL €
(☎021 647 99 00; www.hoteldumarche-lausanne.ch; Rue Pré du Marché 42; s/d from Sfr115/145, without bathroom Sfr80/135) A five-minute walk from the Old Town; the no-frills rooms here are clean and spacious, and the kettle with complimentary tea and coffee in each room is a great touch.

Eating & Drinking

Café de Grancy MODERN EUROPEAN €
(☎021 616 86 66; www.cafedegrancy.ch; Av du Rond Point 1; mains Sfr20-35; 8am-midnight) An old-time bar resurrected with colour and flair by young entrepreneurs, this spot is a hip hang-out with comfy lounges, weekend brunch and a tempting restaurant out back.

Café du Vieil Ouchy SWISS €€
(☎021 616 21 94; Place du Port 3; mains Sfr20-40; 9am-11pm Thu-Mon) A simple but charming location near the lake and Metro for fondue, rösti and other classics. Follow up with a meringue smothered in thick double Gruyère cream.

Bleu Lézard BAR
(☎021 321 38 30; www.bleu-lezard.ch; Rue Enning 10; 7am-late) This corner bar and bistro with royal-blue paintwork and wicker chairs

DON'T MISS

MONTREUX

This tidy lakeside town boasts Switzerland's most extraordinary castle.

Originally constructed on the shores of Lake Geneva in the 11th century, **Château de Chillon** (☎021 966 89 10; www.chillon.ch; Ave de Chillon 21; adult/child Sfr12/6; 9am-7pm Apr-Sep, 9.30am-6pm Mar & Oct, 10am-5pm Nov-Feb, last entry 1hr before close) was brought to the world's attention by Lord Byron and the world has been filing past ever since. Spend at least a couple of hours exploring its numerous courtyards, towers, dungeons and halls filled with arms, period furniture and artwork.

The castle is a lovely 45-minute lakefront walk from Montreux. Otherwise, trolleybus 1 (Sfr2.50) passes every 10 minutes; better still, come on a CGN steamer from Montreux (Sfr10, 15 minutes).

Crowds throng to the legendary (and not all-jazz) **Montreux Jazz Festival** (www.montreuxjazz.com) for a fortnight in early July. Free concerts take place every day, but big-name gigs cost Sfr75 to Sfr240.

There are frequent trains to Lausanne (Sfr13, 25 minutes) and other lakeside points. Make the scenic journey to Interlaken via the **GoldenPass Line** (www.goldenpass.ch), with a change at Zweisimmen and a stop at the fabled ski resort of Gstaad (Sfr57, three hours, daily; rail passes valid).

to match is an old favourite that never loses its appeal – day or night (or at weekends for brunch). Lunch (mains from Sfr25), including some great vegie options, is served until 3pm, and when your feet wanna jive to a live band, there's the basement music club, La Cave.

Great Escape PUB

(☎021 312 31 94; www.the-great.ch; Rue de la Madeleine; ⏲11am-late) Beneath the whopping beams that hold up the roof of what could be a country house is a noisy pub with plenty of beers and ales on tap. Good burgers too.

Information

The **tourist office** (☎021 613 73 21; www.lausanne-tourisme.ch; Place de la Navigation 4; ⏲9am-6pm Oct-Mar, to 7pm Apr-Sep) neighbours Ouchy metro station; there is also a **branch** (Place de la Gare 9; ⏲9am-7pm) at the train station.

Getting There & Away

BOAT The **CGN** (Compagnie Générale de Navigation; www.cgn.ch) steamer service runs from early April to mid-September to and from Geneva (Sfr43, 3½ hours) via Nyon. Other services lace the lake.

TRAIN There are frequent trains to and from Geneva (Sfr22, 33 to 48 minutes) and Bern (Sfr32, 66 minutes).

Getting Around

Lausanne spans several steep hillsides, so prepare for some good walks.

Buses and trolleybuses service most destinations; the vital m2 Métro line (single trip/day pass Sfr1.90/Sfr8.80) connects the lake (Ouchy) with the train station (Gare), cathedral area and Flon district.

Gruyères

POP 1800

Cheese and featherweight meringues drowned in thick cream are what this dreamy village is all about. Named after the emblematic *gru* (crane) brandished by the medieval Counts of Gruyères, it is a riot of 15th- to 17th-century houses tumbling down a hillock. Its heart is cobbled, a castle is its crowning glory, and hard AOC Gruyère (the village is Gruyères but the 's' is dropped for the cheese) has been made for centuries in its surrounding Alpine pastures. Fondue-serving cafes line the main square.

Sights

Château de Gruyères CASTLE

(☎026 921 21 02; www.chateau-gruyeres.ch; adult/child Sfr10/3; ⏲9am-6pm Apr-Oct, 10am-4.30pm Nov-Feb) This turreted castle is Gruyères' crowning glory. Inside, view period furniture, tapestries and modern 'fantasy art'. Don't miss the short footpath that weaves its way around the castle.

Maison du Gruyère CHEESE FACTORY

(☎026 921 84 00; www.lamaisondugruyere.ch; adult/under 12yr Sfr7/6; ⏲9am-7pm Apr-Sep, to 6pm Oct-Mar) The secrets behind Gruyères' famous cheese are revealed at this slick visitors centre right across from the train station and at the base of the path up to the village. Cheese-making takes place several times daily and can be watched through glass windows. There's a cafe and a picnic-happy deli, which, besides cheese, sells myriad forms of Swiss chocolate.

Getting There & Away

Gruyères can be reached by train (Sfr17, 40 minutes, twice hourly) from Fribourg to Bulle, then another hourly train (Sfr5, nine minutes). The village is a 10-minute walk uphill from the train station or you can take a free bus that meets trains.

Unusually for a Swiss train station, there are no lockers but you can leave your bags at the Maison du Gruyère across from the station.

VALAIS

This is Matterhorn country, an intoxicating land that seduces the toughest of critics with its endless panoramic vistas and breathtaking views. Switzerland's 10 highest mountains rise to the sky here, while snow fiends ski and board in one of Europe's top resorts, Zermatt.

Zermatt

POP 5850

Since the mid-19th century, Zermatt has starred among Switzerland's glitziest resorts. Today it attracts intrepid mountaineers and hikers, skiers who cruise at a snail's pace, spellbound by the scenery, and style-conscious darlings flashing designer togs in the lounge bars. But all are smitten with the **Matterhorn** (4478m), the Alps' most famous peak and an unfathomable monolith synonymous with Switzerland that you simply can't quite stop looking at.

Sights & Activities

Matterhorn Glacier Paradise CABLE CAR

(www.matterhornparadise.ch; adult/child from Sfr72/40; 7am-4.20pm Jul & Aug, 8.30am-3.35pm mid-Oct–Dec, 8.30am-4.20pm rest of year) Views from Zermatt's cable cars and gondolas are all pretty remarkable, but the Matterhorn Glacier Paradise is the icing on the cake. Ride Europe's highest-altitude cable car up to 3883m and gawp at a top-of-the-beanstalk panorama of 14 glaciers and 38 mountain peaks over 4000m from the **Panoramic Platform**.

Skiing SKIING

For skiers and snowboarders, Zermatt is cruising heaven, with mostly long, scenic red runs, plus a scattering of blues for ski virgins and knuckle-whitening black runs for experts. The three main skiing areas are **Rothorn**, **Stockhorn** (good for mogul fans) and **Klein Matterhorn** (snowboarding freestyle park and half-pipe), holding 300km of ski runs in all, with free buses shuttling skiers between areas. February to April is peak time. Snow can be sketchy in early summer but lifts are significantly quieter.

A day pass covering all ski lifts in Zermatt (excluding the Italian resort of Cervinia) costs Sfr67/57/34 per adult/student/child (Sfr75/64/38 including Cervinia).

Sleeping & Eating

Most places close May to mid-June and again from October to mid-November.

Berggasthaus Trift GUESTHOUSE €

(079 408 70 20; www.zermatt.net/trift; dm/d with half-board from Sfr66/156; Jul-Sep) Run by Hugo (a whiz on the alpenhorn) and Fabienne at the foot of the Triftgletscher. A stiff two-hour hike from Zermatt, it has simple rooms, mesmerising views of its glacial 4000m surrounds and a great terrace to kick back on over home-cured beef and oven-warm apple tart. Call in advance to ensure a bed.

Matterhorn Hostel HOSTEL €

(027 968 19 19; Schluhmattstrasse 32; dm Sfr36-56, r Sfr92-142; reception 7.30-10am or 11am & 4-9pm or 10pm;) Tucked in a 1960s wooden chalet a two-minute walk from the lifts, this hostel is first-rate. Rooms are modern and its busy ground-floor bar cooks up a great vibe and great food.

Whymper Stube SWISS €€

(027 967 22 96; www.whymper-stube.ch; Bahnhofstrasse 80; mains Sfr22-44) An advance reservation is essential at this legendary address, known for its excellent raclette and fondues, both cheese and meat. Service is relaxed and friendly, tables are packed tightly together, and the place has a real buzz.

Hennu Stall BAR

(027 966 35 10; Klein Matterhorn; 2-7pm) Last one down to this snow-bound 'chicken run' is a rotten egg. Hennu is the wildest après-ski shack on Klein Matterhorn. A metre-long 'ski' of shots will make you cluck all the way down to Zermatt.

Getting There & Around

CAR Zermatt is car-free. Motorists have to park in Täsch (www.matterhornterminal.ch; per day Sfr14.50), load luggage onto a trolley (Sfr5) and ride the Zermatt Shuttle train (adult/child Sfr8/4, 12 minutes, every 20 minutes from 6am to 9.40pm) the last 5km to Zermatt.

WORTH A TRIP

GLACIER EXPRESS

Like a glacier faced with climate change, you'll have a hard time avoiding the hype for the **Glacier Express** (www.glacierexpress.ch), the train that links Zermatt with the eastern towns and resorts of Chur (1st/2nd class Sfr254/145, 5¾ hours), Davos (Sfr235/134, 7½ hours) and St Moritz (Sfr198/113, eight hours).

Although there is some stunning scenery of glacier-cleaved valleys and soaring peaks along the route, much of the run is down in valleys so don't expect nonstop scenic thrills. Also, eight hours on a train may test your endurance. You can shorten the duration by starting at the rail hub of Brig instead of Zermatt or just doing the leg between St Moritz and Chur (another rail hub).

Swiss Cards cover the entire route, while Eurail and InterRail are good for about 50% of the fare. See also p1149.

TRAIN Trains depart regularly from Brig – a major rail hub (Sfr37, 1½ hours), stopping at Visp en route. Zermatt is also the starting point of the popular *Glacier Express* to Graubünden.

BERN

POP 125,700

One of the planet's most underrated capitals, Bern is a fabulous find. With the genteel old soul of a Renaissance man and the heart of a high-flying 21st-century gal, the riverside city is both medieval and modern. The 15th-century Old Town is gorgeous enough to sweep you off your feet and make you forget the century (it's definitely worthy of its 1983 Unesco World Heritage Site status).

Sights

Old Town HISTORIC AREA

Bern's flag-bedecked medieval centre is an attraction in its own right, with 6km of covered arcades and cellar shops-bars descending from the streets. After a devastating fire in 1405, the wooden city was rebuilt in today's sandstone. Unique to Bern are the beautiful and deeply arcaded streets.

Equally enchanting are the 11 decorative **fountains** (1545) depicting historical and folkloric characters. Most are along Marktgasse as it becomes Kramgasse and Gerechtigkeitsgasse, but the most famous lies in Kornhausplatz: the **Kindlifresserbrunnen** (Ogre Fountain) of a giant snacking on children.

Inside the 15th-century Gothic **Münster** (Cathedral; www.bernermuenster.ch; tower admission adult/child Sfr5/2; ⏲10am-5pm Tue-Sat, 11.30am-5pm Sun Easter-Nov, noon-4pm Tue-Fri, to 5pm Sat, 11.30am-4pm Sun rest of year, tower closes 30min earlier), a 344-step hike up the lofty spire – Switzerland's tallest – is worth the climb. Outside, pause on the **Münster Platform**, a gem of a park overlooking the Aare.

Paul Klee Centre MUSEUM

(☎031 359 01 01; www.zpk.org; Monument im Fruchtland 3; adult/child Sfr20/7; ⏲10am-5pm Tue-Sun) The architecturally bold Paul Klee Centre is an eye-catching 150m-long building filled with modern art, with a huge emphasis on its namesake. Renzo Piano's curvaceous building swoops up and down like waves to create a trio of 'hills' that blend into the landscape east of town.

Take bus 12 from Bubenbergplatz to Zentrum Paul Klee (Sfr4.20, 15 minutes). By car the museum is right next to the Bern-Ostring exit off the A6.

Sleeping

Hotel National HOTEL €

(☎031 381 19 88; www.nationalbern.ch; Hirschengraben 24; s/d Sfr100/150, without bathroom from Sfr65/130 ; @📶) A quaint, endearing hotel, the National charms with its wrought-iron lift and Persian rugs over wooden floors. All 58 rooms are unique. Breakfast at the in-house restaurant is included. It adheres to slow-food principles and is a local favourite.

Hotel City am Bahnhof HOTEL €€

(☎031 311 53 77; www.fassbindhotels.com; Bubenbergplatz 7; r Sfr110-200; 📶) Close to the train station, the 58 rooms here are business-standard and have decent desks. Ask for one of the rooms with a small terrace overlooking the action far below.

Hotel Glocke Backpackers Bern HOSTEL €

(☎031 311 37 71; www.bernbackpackers.com; Rathausgasse 75; dm incl breakfast Sfr35-47, d Sfr142, s/d without bathroom Sfr74/110; ⏲reception 8-11am & 3-10pm; @📶) Its Old Town location makes this many backpackers' first choice, although street noise might irritate light sleepers.

Eating & Drinking

Look for interesting cafes and bistros scattered amid the arcades on Old Town streets including Zeughausgasse, Rathausgasse, Marktgasse and Kramgasse

Lötschberg AOC SWISS €

(☎031 311 34 55; www.loetschberg-aoc.ch; Zeughausgasse 16; mains Sfr14-30; ⏲9am-11pm) Take an all-Swiss wine and beer list, add cheese specialities from the Valais (including fondue and raclette, of course), toss in some salads, decorate the cheerful yellow walls with circular, wooden wine racks and you have one of the most dynamic Swiss restaurants in the country. This popular, casual spot serves exceptional Swiss fare without kitsch. Book for dinner.

Altes Tramdepot SWISS €

(☎031 368 14 15; www.altestramdepot.ch; Am Bärengraben; mains Sfr16-20; ⏲11am-12.30am) Even locals recommend this cavernous microbrewery by the bear pits. Swiss specialities snuggle up to wok-cooked stir-fries, pasta and international dishes on its bistro-styled menu. Sample some of the 20 seasonal beers brewed through the year.

Markthalle INTERNATIONAL €

(Bubenbergplatz 9; meals Sfr12-35; ⌚6.30am-11.30pm Mon-Wed, to 12.30am Thu & Fri, 7.30am-12.30am Sat; ☑) Buzzing in atmosphere and quick-snack action, this covered market arcade near the train station is jam-packed with cheap eateries from around the world. You name it, it's here – to be eaten standing at bars or around plastic tables. More formal eateries offer table service.

TOP CHOICE **Café des Pyrénées** BAR

(☎031 311 30 63; Kornhausplatz 17; ⌚Mon-Sat) With its mix of wine-quaffing trendies and beer-loving students, this bohemian joint feels like a Parisian cafe-bar. It's dimly lit and not over-adorned.

Information

Bern Tourismus (☎031 328 12 12; www.bern-info.com; Bahnhoftplatz; ⌚9am-8.30pm daily Jun-Sep, to 6.30pm Mon-Sat, 10am-5pm Sun Oct-May) On the street-level floor of the train station; offers city tours, free hotel bookings, internet access (per hour Sfr12). There's another **branch** (☎031 328 12 12; Bärengraben; ⌚9am-6pm Jun-Sep, 10am-4pm Mar-May & Oct, 11am-4pm Nov-Feb) in the Altes Tram depot by the bear pits.

Getting There & Around

Frequent trains connect to most Swiss towns, including Geneva (Sfr49, 1¾ hours), Basel (Sfr39, one hour) and Zürich (Sfr49, one hour).

Buses and trams are operated by **BernMobil** (www.bernmobil.ch). Tickets are available from ticket machines and cost Sfr2.30 for up to six stops, or Sfr4.20 for a single journey within zones 1 and 2. Day passes cost Sfr12.

CENTRAL SWITZERLAND & BERNESE OBERLAND

The Bernese Oberland should come with a health warning – caution: may cause trembling in the north face of Eiger, uncontrollable bouts of euphoria at the foot of Jungfrau and 007 delusions at Schilthorn. Up at Europe's highest train station, Jungfraujoch, husky yapping mingles with a cacophony of 'oohs' and 'ahhs'.

Lucerne

POP 76,200

Recipe for a gorgeous Swiss city: take a cobalt lake ringed by mountains of myth, add a medieval Old Town and sprinkle with covered bridges, sunny plazas, candy-coloured houses and waterfront promenades. Lucerne is bright, beautiful and has been Little Miss Popular since the likes of Goethe, Queen Victoria and Wagner savoured her views in the 19th century.

Sights

Your first port of call should be the medieval Old Town, with its ancient rampart walls and towers. Wander the cobblestoned lanes and squares, pondering 15th-century buildings with painted facades and the two much-photographed covered bridges over the Reuss. **Kapellbrücke** (Chapel Bridge), dating from 1333, is Lucerne's best-known landmark with its 17th-century pictorial panels under the roof. In contrast are the spooky and dark *Dance of Death* panels under the roofline of 1408 **Spreuerbrücke** (Spreuer Bridge). Sinners repent!

Museum Sammlung Rosengart MUSEUM

(☎041 220 16 60; www.rosengart.ch; Pilatusstrasse 10; adult/student Sfr18/16; ⌚10am-6pm Apr-Oct, 11am-5pm Nov-Mar) Lucerne's blockbuster cultural attraction is the Rosengart Collection, occupying a graceful neoclassical pile. It showcases the outstanding stash of Angela Rosengart, a Swiss art dealer and close friend of Picasso. Alongside works by the great Spanish master are paintings and sketches by Cézanne, Kandinsky, Miró (including the stunning 1925 *Dancer II*), Matisse and Monet.

The basement has over 100 works of Paul Klee, which show the full range of his prodigious talents.

Verkehrshaus MUSEUM

(☎041 370 44 44; www.verkehrshaus.ch; Lidostrasse 5; adult/child Sfr30/15; ⌚10am-6pm Apr-Oct, to 5pm Nov-Mar) Planes, trains and automobiles are the name of the game in the huge, family oriented Transport Museum, east of the city centre, which is devoted to Switzerland's proud transport history. Switzerland's most popular museum, this sprawling complex has a fascinating railway hall that shows how the plucky Swiss scale their mountains with iron. Take bus 6, 8 or 24 from Bahnhofplatz or, better, enjoy the 2km walk along the lake.

Sleeping

Backpackers Lucerne HOSTEL €
(☎041 360 04 20; www.backpackerslucerne.ch; Alpenquai 42; dm/d from Sfr32/74; ⊙reception 7-10am & 4-11pm; @🛜) Right on the lake, this is a soulful place to crash with art-slung walls, bubbly staff, a well-equipped kitchen and immaculate dorms with balconies. It's a 15-minute walk southeast of the station.

Hotel De La Paix HOTEL €
(☎041 418 80 00; www.ambassador.ch; Museggstrasse 2; r Sfr110-200; @🛜) Centrally located on the edge of the Old Town, this 31-room hotel is an excellent modest option. The lobby is minute but the rooms – especially corner ones – are very large and there are elevators. The included breakfast buffet is a good one.

Hotel Alpha HOTEL €
(☎041 240 42 80; www.hotelalpha.ch; Zähringerstrasse 24; r Sfr75-140; @🛜) Easy on the eyes and wallet, this hotel is in a quiet residential area 10 minutes' walk from the Old Town. Rooms are simple, light and spotlessly clean; there are cheaper rooms with shared bathroom.

Eating & Drinking

Wirtshaus Galliker SWISS €€
(☎041 240 10 01; Schützenstrasse 1; mains Sfr22-50; ⊙11.30am-2pm & 5-10pm Tue-Sat, closed Jul–mid-Aug) This old-style tavern has been passionately run by the Galliker family over four generations since 1856. Motherly waiters dish up Lucerne soul food (rösti, *chögalipaschtetli* – vol-au-vents stuffed with meat and mushrooms – and the like) that 's batten-the-hatches filling. Book ahead for dinner.

Rathaus Bräuerei BREWERY
☎041 410 52 57; www.rathausbrauerei.ch; Unter en Egg 2; mains from Sfr15; ⊙8am-midnight) Sip ouse-brewed beer (try the bock) under the aulted arches of this buzzy tavern, or nab pavement table and watch the river flow. here are seasonal brews as well as excel- nt traditional German-Swiss fare. Nightly pecials reflect the seasons.

WORTH A TRIP

MOUNTAIN DAY TRIPS FROM LUCERNE

Among the several heavily marketed day trips from Lucerne, consider the one to 2132m-high **Mt Pilatus** (www.pilatus.com). From May to October, you can reach the peak on a classic 'golden round-trip'. Board the lake steamer from Lucerne to Alpnachstad, then rise with the world's steepest cog railway to Mt Pilatus. From the summit, cable cars bring you down to Kriens via Fräkmüntegg and Krienseregg, where bus 1 takes you back to Lucerne. The return trip costs Sfr91 (less with valid Swiss, Eurail or InterRail passes).

La Madeleine BAR
(www.lamadeleine.ch; Baselstrasse 15) This is a lovely little spot for a low-key gig, with two performance areas and a cosy-glam bar. Jazz, blues, pop, funk and more are played.

Information

Luzern Tourism (☎041 227 17 17; www.luzern.com; Zentralstrasse 5; ⊙8.30am-7pm Mon-Sat, 9am-5pm Sun May-Oct, 8.30am-5.30pm Mon-Fri, 9am-5pm Sat & Sun Nov-Apr) Accessed from platform 3 of the train station.

Getting There & Around

Frequent trains serve Bern (Sfr37, one hour), Geneva (Sfr76, 2¾ hours), Lugano (Sfr58, 2½ hours) and Zürich (Sfr24, one hour). Trains also connect Lucerne and Interlaken East on the stunning GoldenPass Line via Meiringen (Sfr31, two hours).

SGV (www.lakelucerne.ch) operates boats (sometimes paddle-steamers) on Lake Lucerne daily. Services are extensive. Rail passes are good for free or discounted travel.

Interlaken

POP 5300

Once Interlaken made the Victorians swoon with its dreamy mountain vistas, viewed from the chandelier-lit confines of its grand hotels. Today it makes daredevils scream with its adrenalin-loaded adventures. Straddling the glittering Lakes Thun and Brienz (thus the name), and dazzled by the pearly whites of Eiger, Mönch and Jungfrau, the scenery here is exceptional.

Activities

Tempted to hurl yourself off a bridge, down a cliff or along a raging river? You're in the right place. Switzerland is the world's second-biggest adventure-sports centre and Interlaken is its busiest hub.

Sample prices are around Sfr110 for rafting or canyoning, Sfr130 for bungee or canyon jumping, Sfr160 for tandem paragliding, Sfr180 for ice climbing, Sfr225 for hang-gliding and Sfr430 for sky-diving. A half-day mountain-bike tour will set you back around Sfr25.

Sleeping

Backpackers Villa Sonnenhof HOSTEL €
(☎033 826 71 71; www.villa.ch; Alpenstrasse 16; dm Sfr39-45, s Sfr69-79, d Sfr118-138; ⊙reception 7am-11pm; @🛜) Sonnenhof is a slick combination of ultramodern chalet and elegant art nouveau villa. Dorms are immaculate, and some have balconies with Jungfrau views.

Walter's B&B B&B €
(☎033 822 76 88; www.walters.ch; Oelestrasse 35; s/d from Sfr50/66; 🛜) Walter is a real star with his quick smile, culinary skills and invaluable tips. Sure, the rooms are a blast from the 1970s (and have shared bathrooms), but they are super-clean and you'd be hard pushed to find better value in Interlaken.

Balmer's Herberge HOSTEL €
(☎033 822 19 61; www.balmers.ch; Hauptstrasse 23; dm/s/d from Sfr31/47/81; P@🛜) Adrenalin junkies hail Balmer's for its fun frat-house vibe. These party-mad digs offer beer-garden happy hours, a pumping bar with DJs, and chill-out hammocks for nursing your hangover.

Eating & Drinking

Am Marktplatz is scattered with bakeries and bistros with alfresco seating. Höheweg, east of the park, is lined with ethnic eateries with reasonable prices.

Sandwich Bar SWISS €
(☎033 821 63 25; Rosenstrasse 5; snacks Sfr4-9; ⊙7.30am-7pm Mon-Fri, 8am-5pm Sat) This crimson-walled, zebra-striped cafe is a great snack spot. Choose your bread and get creative with fillings. Or try the soups, salads, toasties and locally made ice cream.

Schuh CAFE €€
(☎033 822 94 41; www.schuh-interlaken.ch; Höheweg 56; meals from Sfr20; ⊙9am-11.30pm) A Viennese-style coffee house famous for its pastries, pralines and park-facing terrace. The menu covers all the bases, from rösti to Asian accents. The chocolate-making show (Sfr15) is touristy but fun; it runs at 5pm most days in the high season.

Information

Tourist Office (☎033 826 53 00; www.interlakentourism.ch; Höheweg 37; ⊙8am-7pm Mon-Fri, to 5pm Sat, 10am-noon & 5-7pm Sun Jul & Aug, 8am-noon & 1.30-6pm Mon-Fri, 9am-noon Sat Sep-Jun) Halfway between the train stations. There's also a hotel booking board outside its office and at both stations.

Getting There & Away

There are two train stations. Interlaken West is slightly closer to the centre and is a stop for trains to Bern (Sfr27, one hour). Interlaken East is the rail hub for all lines, including the scenic ones up into the Jungfrau region and the lovely GoldenPass Line to Lucerne (Sfr31, two hours).

Jungfrau Region

If the Bernese Oberland is Switzerland's Alpine heart, the Jungfrau region is where yours will skip a beat. Presided over by glacier-encrusted monoliths Eiger, Mönch and Jungfrau (Ogre, Monk and Virgin), the scenery stirs the soul and strains the neck muscles. It's a magnet for skiers and snowboarders with its 214km of pistes, 44 lifts and much more; a one-day ski pass for Kleine Scheidegg-Männlichen, Grindelwald-First or Mürren-Schilthorn costs Sfr71.

Come summer, hundreds of kilometres of walking trails allow you to capture the landscape from many angles, but it never looks less than astonishing.

Getting There & Around

Hourly trains (www.jungfrau.ch) depart for the Jungfrau region from Interlaken Ost station. Sit in the front half of the train for Lauterbrunnen (Sfr7.20) or the back half for Grindelwald (Sfr10.40).

From Grindelwald, trains ascend to Kleine Scheidegg (Sfr32), where you can transfer for Jungfraujoch. From Lauterbrunnen, trains ascend to Wengen (Sfr6.40) and continue to Klein Scheidegg (Sfr24) for Jungfraujoch.

You can reach Mürren two ways from Lauterbrunnen: with a bus and cable car via Stechelberg (Sfr14.20) or with a cable car and train via Grütschalp (Sfr10.40). Do a circle trip for the full experience. Gimmelwald is reached by cable car from Stechelberg and Mürren.

Many cable cars close for servicing in April and November.

GRINDELWALD

POP 3900

Grindelwald's charms were discovered by skiers and hikers in the late 19th century, making it one of Switzerland's oldest resorts and the Jungfrau's largest. It has lost none of its appeal over the decades, with archetypal Alpine chalets and verdant pastures set against the chiselled features of the Eiger north face.

Activities

The **Grindelwald-First** skiing area has runs stretching from Oberjoch at 2486m to the village at 1050m. In the summer it caters to hikers with 90km of trails at about 1200m, 48km of which are open year-round.

Grindelwald Sports ADVENTURE SPORTS
(☎033 854 12 80; www.grindelwaldsports.ch; Dorfstrasse 110; ⊙8am-noon & 1.30-6pm, closed Sat & Sun in low season) In the tourist office, this outfit arranges mountain climbing, ski and snowboard instruction, canyon jumping and glacier bungee jumping at the Gletscherschlucht.

Sleeping

Gletschergarten HOTEL €€
(☎033 853 17 21; www.hotel-gletschergarten.ch; Dorfstrasse; s Sfr120-150, d Sfr230-300; @) The sweet Breitenstein family make you feel at home in their rustic timber chalet, brimming with heirlooms from landscape paintings to family snapshots. Decked out in pine and flowery fabrics, the rooms have balconies facing Unterer Gletscher at the front and Wetterhorn (best for sunset) at the back.

Mountain Hostel HOSTEL €
(☎033 854 38 38; www.mountainhostel.ch; dm Sfr37-44, r Sfr94-108; P@) Near the Männlichen cable-car station, this is a good base for sports junkies. There's a beer garden, ski and bike room, and TV lounge.

WENGEN

POP 1300

Photogenically poised on a mountain ledge, Wengen's celestial views include the silent majesty of the glacier-capped giant peaks as well as the shimmering ribbons of waterfalls spilling into the Lauterbrunnen Valley below.

The village is car-free and can only be reached by train. It's a fabulous hub for **hiking** for much of the year as well as skiing in winter.

Hotel Bären (☎033 855 14 19; www.baeren-wengen.ch; s Sfr90-150, d Sfr190-280;) is close to the station. Loop back under the tracks and head down the hill to this snug log chalet with bright, if compact, rooms. The affable Brunner family serves a hearty breakfast.

JUNGFRAUJOCH

Sure, the world wants to see Jungfraujoch (3471m) and yes, tickets are expensive, but don't let that stop you. It's a once-in-a-lifetime trip and there's a reason why two million people a year visit Europe's highest train station.

Clear good weather is essential for the trip; check www.jungfrau.ch or call ☎033 828 79 31 and don't forget warm clothing, sunglasses and sunscreen.

From Interlaken Ost, the journey time is 2½ hours each way (Sfr191 return, discounts with rail passes). The last train back is at 5.50pm in summer, 4.40pm in winter. There are cheaper 'good morning' and 'good afternoon' tickets (Sfr140) with time restrictions.

JUNGFRAU REGION HIKING 101

The are hundreds of hikes along the hundreds of kilometres of trails in the Jungfrau region; all include some of the world's most stunning scenery. Every skill and fortitude level is accommodated and options abound. Here are two to get you started:

Grütschalp to Mürren Ride the cable car up from Lauterbrunnen and follow the trail along the railway tracks. The walk to Mürren takes about an hour and is mostly level. There are unbeatable views, Alpine woods and babbling glacier-fed streams.

Männlichen to Kleine Scheidegg Reach the Männlichen lift station by cable cars from Wengen and Grindelwald. Now follow the well-marked, spectacular path down to Kleine Scheidegg. It takes about 1½ hours and you have nothing but Alps in front of you.

GIMMELWALD

POP 120

Decades ago some anonymous backpacker scribbled these words in the guestbook at the Mountain Hostel: 'If heaven isn't what it's cracked up to be, send me back to Gimmelwald.' Enough said. When the sun is out in Gimmelwald, this pipsqueak of a village will simply take your breath away. Sit outside and listen to the distant roar of avalanches on the sheer mountain faces arrayed before you.

The rustic **Mountain Hostel** (033 855 17 04; www.mountainhostel.com; dm from Sfr28; reception 8.30am-noon & 6-11pm Apr–mid-Nov; @) is a backpacker's legend. A soak in its outdoor hot tub with stunning views hits the spot every time. (And don't forget to sign the guestbook!)

MÜRREN

POP 500

Arrive on a clear evening when the sun hangs low on the horizon, and you'll think you've died and gone to heaven. Car-free Mürren *is* storybook Switzerland.

Sleeping options include **Eiger Guesthouse** (033 856 54 60; www.eigerguesthouse.com; r Sfr120-200; @), by the train station, with the downstairs pub serving tasty food; and **Hotel Jungfrau** (033 856 64 64; www.hoteljungfrau.ch; s Sfr80-140, d Sfr160-280; @), overlooking the nursery slopes from its perch above Mürren. It dates to 1894 and has a beamed lounge with open fire.

SCHILTHORN

There's a tremendous 360-degree panorama available from the 2970m **Schilthorn** (www.schilthorn.ch). On a clear day, you can see over 200 peaks, from Titlis to Mont Blanc and across to the German Black Forest. Note that this was the site of Blofeld's HQ in the under-appreciated 1969 James Bond film *On Her Majesty's Secret Service* (as the hype endlessly reminds you).

From Interlaken East a combined ticket to the summit costs Sfr125. From Mürren it's Sfr77 for the two long cable-car rides. There are discounts with rail passes.

ZÜRICH

POP 376,000

Zürich is an enigma. A savvy financial centre with possibly the densest public transport system in the world, it also has a gritty, post-industrial edge that always surprises. The nation's largest city has an evocative Old Town and lovely lakeside location.

Sights

Old Town HISTORIC AREA

Explore the cobbled streets of the pedestrian Old Town lining both sides of the river.

The bank vaults beneath **Bahnhofstrasse**, the city's most elegant street, are said to be crammed with gold and silver. Indulge in affluent Züricher-watching and ogle at the luxury shops selling watches, clocks, chocolates, furs, porcelain and fashion labels galore.

Walk up to the **Lindenhof**, a large shady square that perches above the Old Town, for views down over the city and Limmat River. As you walk, see how many of the city's 1221 fountains you can spot – each with a spout of drinkable glacier-fed water.

Fraumünster CHURCH

(www.fraumuenster.ch; Münsterplatz; 9am-6pm Apr-Oct, 10am-4pm Nov-Mar) The 13th-century cathedral is renowned for its distinctive stained-glass windows, designed by the Russian-Jewish master Marc Chagall (1887–1985).

Kunsthaus MUSEUM

(044 253 84 84; www.kunsthaus.ch; Heimplatz 1; adult/child Sfr15/free, Wed free; 10am-8pm Wed-Fri, to 6pm Tue, Sat & Sun) Zürich's Fine Arts Museum boasts a rich collection of Alberto Giacometti stick-figure sculptures, Monets, Van Goghs, Rodin sculptures and other 19th- and 20th-century art. A large new addition is in the works for 2017; in the meantime the collection might feel chaotic.

Sleeping

Zürich accommodation prices are fittingly high for the main city of expensive Switzerland. You might consider options such as www.airbnb.com here.

Pension für Dich PENSION

(044 317 91 60; www.fuerdich.ch; Stauffacherstrasse 141; s/d without bathroom from Sfr100/110;) These simple but fabulous apartments have been converted into comfy rooms – think retro furnishings meets Ikea. A number of rooms have balconies. There's a good cafe downstairs, plus you're smack in the centre of the Kreis 4 nightlife action.

Hotel Rothaus HOTEL

(043 322 10 58; www.hotelrothaus.ch; Sihlhallestrasse 1; s/d from Sfr100/140;) Right in th

middle of the Langstrasse action, this cheerful red-brick building is a real find. A variety of fresh, airy rooms are complemented by a busy little eatery-bar downstairs. Guests can rent bikes cheaply.

SYHA Hostel HOSTEL €
(043 399 78 00; www.youthhostel.ch; Mütschellenstrasse 114, Wollishofen; dm from Sfr42, s/d from Sfr118/138; @) This bulbous, purple-red hostel features 290 beds, a swish 24-hour reception/dining hall and sparkling modern bathrooms. Dorms are small. Take tram 7 to Morgental, or S-Bahn to Wollishofen.

City Backpacker HOSTEL €
(044 251 90 15; www.city-backpacker.ch; Niederdorfstrasse 5; dm Sfr37, s/d from Sfr77/118; reception closed noon-3pm; @) This youthful party hostel is friendly and well equipped, if a trifle cramped. Overcome the claustrophobia in summer by hanging out on the roof terrace – the best spot in Zürich for sunset and cold beers.

Eating

Zürich has a thriving cafe culture and hundreds of restaurants – explore Niederdorfstrasse and its nearby backstreets. Langstrasse is another good area, on both sides of the tracks.

Alpenrose SWISS €€
(044 271 39 19; Fabrikstrasse 12; mains Sfr24-42; noon-11pm Wed-Sun) With its timber-clad walls, 'No Polka Dancing' warning and fine cuisine from regions all over the country, the Alpenrose makes for an inspired meal out. You could try risotto from Ticino or *Pizokel* (aka Bizochel, a kind of long and especially savoury noodle) from Graubünden or fresh perch fillets. Book.

Café Schober CAFE €
(www.conditorei-cafe-schober.ch; Napfgasse 4; snacks from Sfr10; 8am-7pm) Steady yourself for the best hot chocolate you've ever had at this grand cafe. On entry you'll see lavish displays of sweets, treats and other enticing edible baubles. Choose from several seating areas: red velvet, back garden, upstairs intimate etc. Holiday displays are stunning.

Restaurant Brasserie Johanniter SWISS €
(www.johanniter.com; Niederdorfstrasse 70; mains Sfr14-35; 10am-midnight) In the very heart of the Old Town, this century-old traditional beer hall serves up Swiss standards (think lots of pork, veal and potatoes). There is a long list of daily specials and you can expect a hearty meal no matter what you order; there is also a suitably excellent selection of beers available by the stein.

Sternen Grill SWISS €
(Theatrestrasse 22; snacks from Sfr7; 11.30am-midnight) This is the city's most famous – and busiest – sausage stand; just follow the crowds streaming in. The classic *Kalbsbratwurst mit Gold Bürli* (veal sausage with bread roll) costs Sfr7. There are a few vegetarian options too.

Drinking & Entertainment

Options abound across town, but the bulk of the more animated drinking dens are in Züri-West, especially along Langstrasse in Kreis 4 and Hardstrasse in Kreis 5.

Züritipp (www.zueritipp.ch) comes out on Thursdays with the *TagesAnzeiger* newspaper, which is jammed with info about what's on.

Café Odeon BAR
(044 251 16 50; www.odeon.ch; Am Bellevueplatz; 9am-late) This one-time haunt of Lenin and the Dadaists is still a prime people-watching spot for gays and straights alike. Come for the art nouveau interior, the OTT chandeliers and a whiff of another century. It serves food too.

Longstreet Bar BAR
(044 241 21 72; www.longstreetbar.ch; Langstrasse 92; 8pm-late Tue-Sat) The Longstreet is a music bar with a varied roll call of DJs coming in and out. Try to count the thousands of light bulbs in this purple-felt-lined one-time cabaret.

Supermarket CLUB
(044 440 20 05; www.supermarket.li; Geroldstrasse 17; 11pm-late Thu-Sat) Looking like an innocent little house, Supermarket boasts three cosy lounge bars around the dance floor, a covered back courtyard and an interesting roster of DJs playing house and techno. The crowd tends to be mid-20s. Take a train from Hauptbahnhof to Hardbrücke.

Information

Zürich Tourism (044 215 40 00, hotel reservations 044 215 40 40; www.zuerich.com; train station; 8am-8.30pm Mon-Sat, 8.30am-6.30pm

Zürich

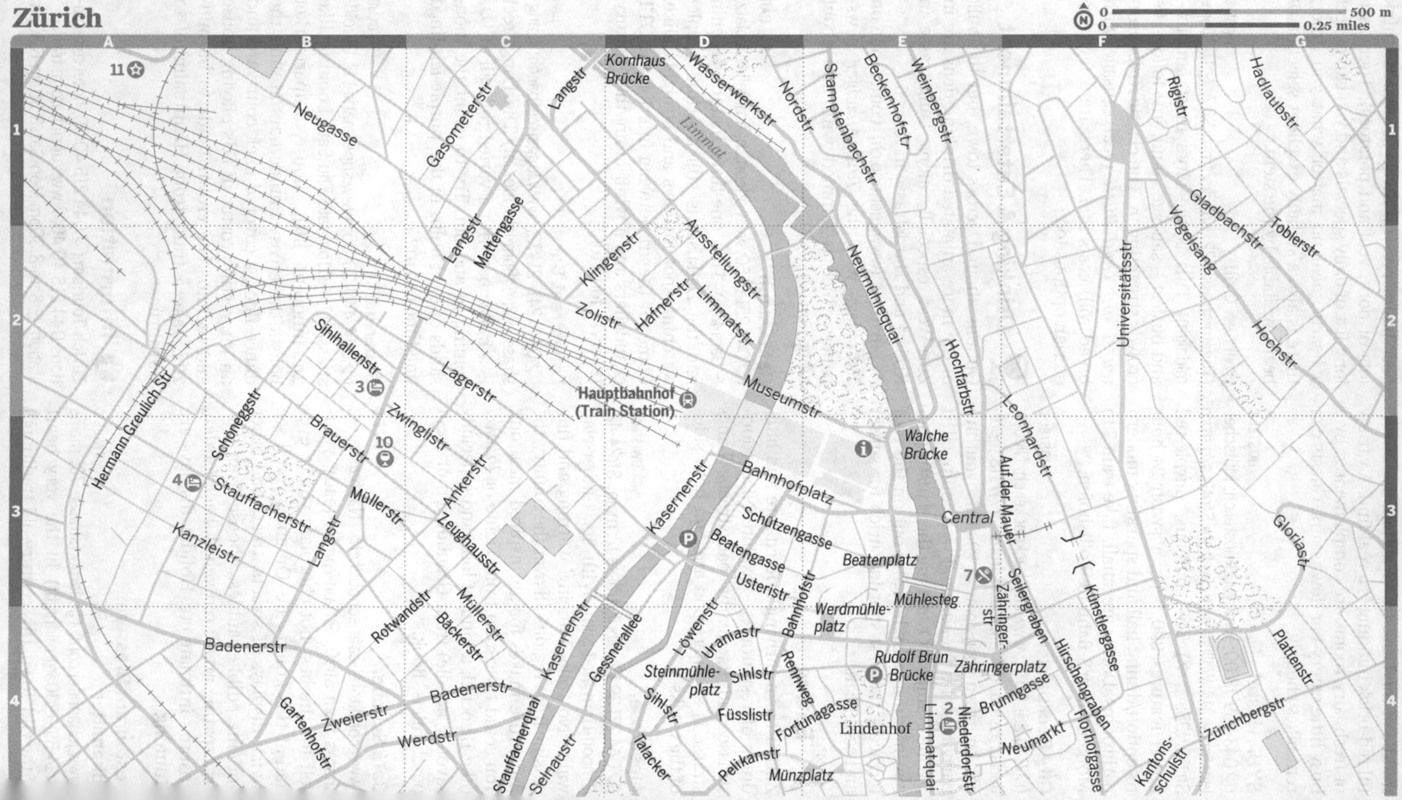

0 500 m
0 0.25 miles
11
Neugasse
Gasometerstr
Langstr
Kornhaus Brücke
Wasserwerkstr
Limmat
Nordstr
Stampfenbachstr
Beckenhofstr
Weinbergstr
Rigistr
Hadlaubstr
Gladbachstr
Vogelsang
Toblerstr
Universitätsstr
Hochstr
Langstr
Mattengasse
Klingenstr
Ausstellungsstr
Zolistr
Hafnerstr
Limmatstr
Neumühlequai
Hochfarbstr
Sihlhallenstr
Lagerstr
3
Hauptbahnhof (Train Station)
Museumstr
Leonhardstr
Hermann Greulich Str
Schöneggstr
Brauerstr
Zwinglistr
10
Walche Brücke
4
Stauffacherstr
Müllerstr
Ankerstr
Kasernenstr
Bahnhofplatz
Auf der Mauer
Central
Gloriastr
Kanzleistr
Langstr
Zeughausstr
Schützengasse
Beatengasse
Beatenplatz
7
Usteristr
Bahnhofstr
Werdmühle-platz
Mühlesteg
Zähringer-str
Seilergraben
Künstlergasse
Rotwandstr
Müllerstr
Bäckerstr
Badenerstr
Kasernenstr
Gessnerallee
Löwenstr
Uraniastr
Steinmühle-platz
Sihlstr
Rennweg
Rudolf Brun Brücke
Zähringerplatz
Hirschengraben
Plattenstr
Badenerstr
Gartenhofstr
Zweierstr
Werdstr
Sihlstr
Füsslistr
Fortunagasse
Lindenhof
2
Limmatquai
Niederdorfstr
Brunngasse
Neumarkt
Florhofgasse
Kantons-schulstr
Zürichbergstr
Stauffacherquai
Selnaustr
Talacker
Pelikanstr
Münzplatz

Zürich

Top Sights

Fraumünster ... E5

Sights

1 Kunsthaus ... F5

Sleeping

2 City Backpacker ... E4
3 Hotel Rothaus ... B2
4 Pension für Dich ... A3
5 SYHA Hostel ... E5

Eating

6 Café Schober ... E5
7 Restaurant Brasserie Johanniter ... E3
8 Sternen Grill ... F6

Drinking

9 Café Odeon ... F6
10 Longstreet Bar ... B3

Entertainment

11 Supermarket ... A1

Sun) Offers excellent walking tours (Sfr25) most mornings at 11am.

Getting There & Away

AIR Zürich airport (ZRH; ☎043 816 22 11; www.zurich-airport.com), 10km north of the centre, is Switzerland's main airport.

TRAIN Zürich has service to all neighbouring countries. Destinations include Milan (4¼ hours), Munich (four hours), Paris (four hours) and Vienna (eight hours).

There are regular direct departures to most major Swiss towns, such as Basel (Sfr32, one hour), Bern (Sfr49, one hour), Geneva (Sfr84, 2¾ hours), Lucerne (Sfr24, one hour) and Lugano (Sfr62, 2¾ hours).

Getting Around

TO/FROM THE AIRPORT Up to nine trains an hour run in each direction between the airport and the main train station (Sfr7, nine to 13 minutes). Most continue on to cities such as Lucerne and Geneva.

BICYCLE City bikes (www.zuerirollt.ch) can be picked up at **Velogate** (train station; ⏲8am-9.30pm) for free day-use; if you keep your bike overnight it costs Sfr10.

PUBLIC TRANSPORT The comprehensive, unified bus, tram and S-Bahn **public transit system** (ZVV; www.zvv.ch) includes boats plying the Limmat River. Short trips under five stops are Sfr2.40, typical trips are Sfr4.20. A 24-hour pass for the city centre is Sfr8.40.

NORTHERN SWITZERLAND

This region is left off most people's Switzerland itineraries – which is precisely why you should visit! Take time to explore the tiny rural towns set among green rolling hills.

Basel

POP 170,600

Basel is the closest Switzerland comes to having a seaport; the Rhine is navigable for decent-sized ships from this point until it reaches the North Sea in the Netherlands. Basel's year-round attractions, including the engaging Old Town, are mostly concentrated in Grossbasel (Greater Basel) on the south bank of the Rhine.

Sights & Activities

TOP CHOICE Old Town HISTORIC AREA

The medieval Old Town in the heart of Basel is a delight. Start in **Marktplatz**, which is dominated by the astonishingly vivid red facade of the 16th-century **Rathaus** (town hall). Just north, the Fischmarktplatz features the Gothic **Fischmarktbrunnen**, a splendid medieval fountain.

The narrow lanes that riddle the hillside between Marktplatz and the 600-year-old **Spalentor city gate** form the most captivating part of old Basel. Lined by impeccably maintained centuries-old houses, lanes like Spalenberg, Heuberg and Leonhardsberg are worth a gentle stroll.

TOP CHOICE Fondation Beyeler GALLERY

(☎061 645 97 00; www.fondationbeyeler.ch; Baselstrasse 101, Riehen; adult/child Sfr25/6; ⊙10am-6pm, to 8pm Wed) The art space to really knock your socks off is the Fondation Beyeler, housed in an open-plan building by Italian architect Renzo Piano. The quality of its 19th- and 20th-century paintings is matched only by the way Miró and Max Ernst sculptures are juxtaposed with similar tribal figures. Take tram 6 to Riehen.

Sleeping

Hotels are often full during Basel's trade fairs and conventions, so book ahead. Guests receive a pass for free travel on public transport.

TOP CHOICE Au Violon HOTEL €

(☎061 269 87 11; www.au-violon.com; Im Lohnhof 4; s/d from Sfr125/150; 📶) The doors are one of the few hints that quaint, atmospheric Au Violon was a prison from 1835 to 1995. Most of the rooms are two cells rolled into one and either look onto a delightful cobblestone courtyard or have views of the Münster. Sitting on a leafy hilltop, it also has a well-respected restaurant.

Basel Backpack HOSTEL €

(☎061 333 00 37; www.baselbackpack.ch; Dornacherstrasse 192; dm Sfr32, s/d from Sfr80/100; @📶) Converted from a factory, this independent 81-bed hostel south of the main train station has cheerful, colour-coded eight-bed dorms and more sedate doubles and family rooms.

Eating & Drinking

Head to the Marktplatz for a daily market and several stands selling excellent quick bites, such as local sausages and sandwiches.

Zum Roten Engel CAFE

(☎061 261 20 08; Andreasplatz 15; mains from Sfr15; ⊙9am-midnight) This student-filled venue, spilling onto an irresistible, tiny cobblestone square, is great for a latte and snacks by day and a glass of wine or three in the evening. It's a temperate way to start the night. Sunday brunch is a treat.

Confiserie Schiesser CAFE €

(www.confiserie-schiesser.ch; Marktplatz 19; snacks from Sfr5; ⊙8am-6pm) Since 1870, this gem-like bakery and cafe has been creating sweet treats from bonbons to tortes to elaborate cakes. Browse the display cases and then head upstairs to the cafe for light meals and excellent coffee.

Information

Tourist Office (☎061 268 68 68; www.basel.com) The tourist office has branches at **SBB Bahnhof** (Bahnhof; ⊙8.30am-6pm Mon-Fri, 9am-5pm Sat, to 3pm Sun & holidays) and **Stadtcasino** (Steinenberg 14; ⊙9am-6.30pm Mon-Fri, to 5pm Sat, 10am-3pm Sun & holidays). The Stadtcasino branch organises two-hour English-language walking tours of the city centre (adult/child Sfr15/7.50), usually starting at 2.30pm Monday to Saturday, May through October, and on Saturdays the rest of the year.

Getting There & Away

AIR The **EuroAirport** (☎061 325 31 11; www.euroairport.com), 5km northwest of town in

France, is the main airport for Basel. It is a hub for easyJet and there are flights to major European cities.

TRAIN Basel is a major European rail hub. The main station, Basel SBB, has TGVs to France (Paris; three hours) and fast ICEs to major cities in Germany. There are frequent services to Freiburg (45 minutes), gateway to the Black Forest.

Services within Switzerland include frequent trains to Bern (Sfr39, one hour) and Zürich (Sfr32, one hour).

Getting Around

Bus 50 links the airport and Basel SBB (Sfr3.40, 20 minutes). Trams 8 and 11 link the station to Marktplatz (Sfr3.40, day pass Sfr9).

TICINO

Switzerland meets Italy: the summer air is rich and hot, and the peacock-proud posers propel their scooters in and out of traffic. Italian weather, Italian style. Not to mention the Italian ice cream, Italian pizza, Italian architecture and Italian language.

Getting There & Around

Ticino is connected by a web of integrated **trains** (www.arcobaleno.ch; day pass Sfr20.40). From Cadenazzo on the Locarno line there are trains to Milan's Malpensa airport (route S30; two hours, every two hours).

Locarno

POP 15,200

The rambling red enclave of Italianate town houses, piazzas and arcades ending at the northern end of Lake Maggiore, coupled with more hours of sunshine than anywhere else in Switzerland, give this laid-back town a summer-resort atmosphere.

Locarno is on the northeast corner of Lago Maggiore, which mostly lies in Italy's Lombardy region. **Navigazione Lago Maggiore** (www.navigazionelaghi.it) operates boats across the entire lake.

Locarno's Italianate **Old Town** fans out from Piazza Grande, a photogenic ensemble of arcades and Lombard-style houses. The main station is five minutes away.

Getting There & Away

Locarno is well linked to Ticino and the rest of Switzerland via Bellinzona, or take the scenic **Centovalli Express** (www.centovalli.ch) to Brig via Domodossola in Italy.

Lugano

POP 54,500

There is a distinct vibrant snappiness in the air in Lugano, Switzerland's southernmost tourist town, where visitors unravel the spaghetti maze of cobblestone streets while locals toil quietly in cash-stuffed banks – this is the country's third-most important banking centre.

Sights & Activities

The **Centro Storico** (Old Town) is a 10-minute walk downhill from the train station; take the stairs or the fun funicular (Sfr1.10).

Wander through the mostly porticoed lanes woven around the busy main square, **Piazza della Riforma** (which is even more lively when the Tuesday- and Friday morning markets are held). Via Nassa is the main shopping street and boasts a *Vogue*-worthy line-up of high-end stores.

Lago Lugano BOAT TRIP
(www.lakelugano.ch; tours from Sfr25; ⌚Apr-Oct) Take a boat trip to one of the photogenic villages hugging the gorgeous shoreline – car-free **Gandria** is popular – and feast on traditional Ticinese dishes in your pick of quintessential Ticinese grottos.

Sleeping

Many hotels close for part of the winter.

TOP CHOICE **Hotel & Hostel Montarina** HOTEL, HOSTEL €€
(☎091 966 72 72; www.montarina.ch; Via Montarina 1; dm from Sfr27, s Sfr80-90, d Sfr110-130;

> WORTH A TRIP
>
> **BERNINA EXPRESS**
>
> The popular **Bernina Express** (www.berninaexpress.ch; ⌚mid-May–early Dec) route runs from Lugano to St Moritz (Sfr72, six hours), Davos and the rail hub of Chur (Sfr101, 6½ hours). Fares include obligatory reservations. From Lugano to Tirano (in Italy), a bus is used for the scenic run along Italy's Lake Como.
>
> The train route over the Bernina Pass between Tirano and St Moritz is one of Switzerland's most spectacular and is Unesco-recognised. Some trains feature open-top cars.

(P) Occupying a bubblegum-pink villa dating to 1860, this hotel and hostel behind the train station has lingering traces of old-world grandeur. Choose between the dorms in the vaulted basement, wood-floored antique rooms and contemporary rooms with private bathrooms. There's a shared kitchen-lounge, toys to amuse the kids, a swimming pool set in palm-dotted gardens and even a tiny vineyard.

Acquarello HOTEL €€
(091 911 68 68; www.acquarello.ch; Piazza Ciocearo 9; r Sfr90-190;) You can't get more central than this modest yet rambling hotel right at the base of the funicular from the train station. Basic rooms may get some noise from same, but the better ones are bright and some ('superior') have sweeping lake views.

Eating

For pizza or pasta, any of the places around Piazza della Riforma are pleasant and lively. For a salad bar and vegetarian joy, try the **Manora** (Piazza Dante Alighieri; 7.30am-9pm) restaurant in the Manor department store.

TOP CHOICE **Bottegone del Vino** ITALIAN €€
(091 922 76 89; Via Magatti 3; mains Sfr20-45; 11am-11pm Mon-Sat) This is a great place to taste fine local wines over an excellent meal. The menu changes daily and features fresh ingredients sourced locally. Knowledgeable waiters fuss around the tables, only too happy to suggest the perfect Ticino tipple (the basic house red is superb). Try the sublime acacia honey with cheese.

Gabbani CAFE, RESTAURANT €€
(091 921 34 70; www.gabbani.com; Piazza Ciocearo 1; meals from Sfr15; deli 8am-6pm, restaurant until late) This sprawling empire at the base of the funicular has been serving up the best in local food and drink since 1937. There's a bakery, deli (picnics!), food-to-go, cafe, bar and a fine restaurant. Have a morning coffee under the arches with a perfect little pastry. On the high floors there are stylish hotel rooms (from Sfr190).

Getting There & Away

Lugano is on the main train line between Milan (60 to 90 minutes) and Zürich (Sfr62, 2¾ hours) and Lucerne (Sfr58, 2½ hours).

GRAUBÜNDEN

St Moritz

POP 5200

Switzerland's original winter wonderland and the cradle of Alpine tourism, St Moritz (San Murezzan in Romansch) has been luring royals, celebrities and moneyed wannabes since 1864. With its shimmering aquamarine lake, emerald forests and aloof mountains, the town looks a million dollars.

Activities

Skiers and snowboarders will revel in the 350km of runs in three key areas. Avid cross-country skiers can glide through snow-dusted woodlands and plains on 160km of groomed trails.

See www.engadin.stmoritz.ch for year-round activities information.

Corviglia & Signal SKIING
(day pass adult/child from Sfr73/24) For groomed slopes with big mountain vistas, head to Corviglia (2486m), accessible by funicular from Dorf. From Bad a cable car goes to Signal (shorter queues), giving access to the slopes of Piz Nair.

Sleeping & Eating

The Piz HOTEL €€
(081 832 11 11; www.piz-stmoritz.ch; Via dal Bagn 6; s/d/apt Sfr120/210/500;) Splashes of crimson, hardwood floors and clean lines define this contemporary B&B in St Moritz Bad. Fitted with rain showers and mod gizmos, the rooms are sleek and comfy, though street noise may disturb light sleepers. The breakfast buffet is good.

Jugendherberge St Moritz HOSTEL
(081 836 61 11; www.youthhostel.ch/st.moritz Stille Via Surpunt 60; dm/d Sfr60/150; @) Budget beds are gold-dust rare in St Moritz but you'll find one at this hostel edging th forest. The four-bed dorms and doubles ar quiet and clean. There's a kiosk, games roon and laundrette.

Hatecke SWISS
(081 864 11 75; www.hatecke.ch; snacks & mair Sfr15-30; 9am-6.30pm Mon-Fri, to 6pm Sa Organic, locally sourced *Bündnerfleisc* (smoked, air-dried beef) and melt-in-you mouth venison ham are carved into wafe thin slices on a century-old machine in th

speciality shop. Take a seat on a sheepskin stool in the cafe next door for a casual lunch.

Engiadina SWISS €€
(☎081 833 32 65; www.restaurant-engiadina.ch; Plazza da Scuola 2; fondue Sfr28-48; ⏲11am-11pm Tue-Sun, closed May) A locals' place, Engiadina is famous for fondue, and that's the best thing to eat here. Champagne gives the melted cheese a kick. The pizza and polenta are also good.

ℹ Getting There & Away

Regular hourly trains make the scenic run to and from the rail hub of Chur (Sfr40, two hours).

St Moritz is also an end point on the much-hyped *Glacier Express* (p1132).

The *Bernina Express* (p1143) provides seasonal links to Lugano from St Moritz, which include the stunning Unesco-recognised train line over the Bernina Pass to Tirano in Italy.

UNDERSTAND SWITZERLAND

History

In 1291 the forest communities of Uri, Schwyz and Nidwalden formed an alliance – the origin of the Swiss Confederation. The Swiss began seizing more land, but finally

WORTH A TRIP

LIECHTENSTEIN

If Liechtenstein (pop 36,400) didn't exist, someone would have invented it. A tiny German-speaking mountain principality (160 sq km) governed by an iron-willed monarch in the heart of 21st-century Europe, it certainly has novelty value. Only 25km long by 12km wide (at its broadest point) – just larger than Manhattan – Liechtenstein is mostly visited by people who want a glimpse of the castle and a spurious passport stamp. Stay a little longer and you can escape into its pint-sized Alpine wilderness.

History

Austrian prince Johann Adam Von Liechtenstein purchased the counties of Schellenberg (1699) and Vaduz (1712) from impoverished German nobles and gave them his name. Long a principality under the Holy Roman Empire, Liechtenstein gained independence in 1866. In 1923, it formed a customs union with Switzerland (today it uses the Swiss franc).

Prince Hans Adam II ascended the throne in 1989. In 2003, he won sweeping powers to dismiss the elected government, appoint judges and reject proposed laws. The following year he handed the day-to-day running of the country to his son Alois.

Vaduz

Vaduz is a postage-stamp-sized city with a postcard perfect backdrop. Crouching at the foot of forested mountains, hugging the banks of the Rhine and crowned by a turreted castle, its location is visually stunning.

The centre itself is curiously modern and sterile, with its mix of tax-free luxury goods stores and cube-shaped concrete buildings. Yet just a few minutes' walk brings you to traces of the quaint village that existed just 50 years ago and quiet vineyards where the Alps seem that bit closer.

Vaduz Castle is closed to the public, but is worth the climb for the vistas.

Information

Liechtenstein's international phone prefix is ☎423.

The **Liechtenstein Center** offers brochures and souvenir passport stamps (Sfr3) as well as housing the **Philatelie Liechtenstein**, which will interest stamp collectors. The **post office** is nearby.

Getting There & Around

The nearest train stations are in the Swiss border towns of Buchs and Sargans. From each of these towns there are frequent buses to Vaduz (Sfr3.40/5.80 from Buchs/Sargans; Swiss Pass valid). Buses run every 30 minutes from the Austrian border town of Feldkirch.

overreached themselves. Defeated by a superior force of French and Venetians in 1798, they declared neutrality.

Following Napoleon's defeat at Waterloo, Switzerland gained full independence. In 1848 the Swiss agreed upon a new federal constitution.

The Swiss carefully guarded their neutrality during the world wars, and emerged with a thriving commercial, financial and industrial base. Zürich developed as an international banking centre, and international bodies set up their headquarters in Geneva. However, an independent commission of historians has confirmed that tens of thousands of Jewish refugees were refused entry at Switzerland's border during WWII and left to face their fate in Nazi Germany. Swiss banks were accused of banking Nazi plunder and the savings of Holocaust victims during WWII. After years of recriminations and a threatened lawsuit, two Swiss banks made a settlement of US$1.25 billion to Holocaust victims' families in 1998.

Switzerland's annus horribilis was 2001: the national airline Swissair collapsed, a canyoning accident in the Bernese Oberland killed 21 tourists, and an unprecedented gun massacre in the Zug parliament and fatal fire in the Gotthard Tunnel prompted intense soul searching.

Switzerland became the 190th member of the UN in 2002, and in 2005 it joined Europe's Schengen passport-free travel zone. Yet few expect Switzerland to even consider joining either the EU or the Euro single-currency zone any time soon (if ever). Traditionally, the western, French-speaking cantons have long desired both, while the German-speaking cantons (and Ticino) have generally been opposed.

Meanwhile the normally staid world of Swiss banking was roiled by charges of vast scams involving international interest-rate rigging, a leaked list of accounts held by purported Greek tax dodgers and efforts by the German government to investigate similar actions by its citizens.

Arts

Many foreign writers and artists, including Voltaire, Byron, Shelley and Turner, have visited and settled in Switzerland. Local and international artists pouring into Zürich during WWI spawned its Dadaist movement.

Paul Klee (1879–1940) is the best-known native painter. He created bold, hard-lined abstract works that you can see in Bern and Lausanne.

Environment

Mountains make up 70% of Switzerland's 41,285 sq km. Farming is intensive and cows graze on the upper slopes as soon as the retreating snow line permits.

Switzerland's 1800 glaciers cover a 2000-sq-km area, but global warming means they're melting rapidly. The country's most famous mass of ice, rock and snow – the 23km-long Aletsch Glacier – shrunk 114.6m in 2006 alone and could shrink 80% by 2100 if things don't change, say experts.

LANGUAGES

Located in the corner of Europe where Germany, France and Italy meet, Switzerland is a linguistic melting pot with three official federal languages: German (spoken by 64% of the population), French (19%) and Italian (8%). Swiss 'German' speakers write standard or 'high' German, but speak their own language: Schwyzertütsch has no official written form and is mostly unintelligible to outsiders.

A fourth language, Romansch, is spoken by less than 1% of the population, mainly in the canton of Graubünden.

English-speakers will have few problems being understood in the German-speaking parts. However, it is simple courtesy to greet people with the Swiss-German *grüezi* and to enquire *'Sprechen Sie Englisch?'* (Do you speak English?) before launching into English. In French Switzerland you shouldn't have too many problems either; in Italian-speaking Switzerland, people are more monolingual but you'll still encounter plenty of English speakers.

SURVIVAL GUIDE

Directory A–Z

Accommodation

From palatial palaces and castles to mountain refuges, nuclear bunkers, icy igloos or simple hay lofts, Switzerland sports traditional and creative accommodation in every price range.

In pricey Switzerland, many budget hotels have cheaper rooms with shared toilet and shower facilities. From there the sky is truly the limit. Breakfast buffets can be extensive and tasty, but are not always included in room rates.

Rates in cities and towns stay constant most of the year. In mountain resorts prices are seasonal (and can fall by 50% or more outside high season):

Low season Mid-September to mid-December, mid-April to mid-June

Mid-season January to mid-February, mid-June to early July, September

High season July to August, Christmas, mid-February to Easter

PRICE RANGES

The following price ranges refer to a double room with a private bathroom, except in hostels or where otherwise specified. Quoted rates are for the high season and don't include breakfast, unless otherwise noted.

€ less than Sfr150

€€ Sfr150 to Sfr350

€€€ more than Sfr350

HOSTELS

Switzerland has two types of hostels: **Swiss Youth Hostels** (SYHA; www.youthhostel.ch), affiliated with Hostelling International (HI), where nonmembers pay an additional 'guest fee' of Sfr6; and independent hostels, which can be more charismatic. On average a dorm bed in either type costs Sfr31 to Sfr40, including sheets.

Many backpacker hostels, which tend to be more flexible in their regulations, are loosely affiliated under **Swiss Backpackers** (033 823 46 46; www.swissbackpackers.ch).

Business Hours

The reviews in this guidebook won't list hours unless they differ from the hours listed here. Hours are given for the high season (April through October) and tend to decrease in the low season.

Banks 8.30am to 4.30pm Monday to Friday, usually with late opening hours one day a week

Offices 8am to noon and 2pm to 5pm Monday to Friday

Restaurants Noon to 2pm and 6pm to 10pm

Shops 9am to 7pm Monday to Friday (break for lunch at noon in small towns), 9am to 6pm Saturday. In cities, there's often shopping until 9pm on Thursday or Friday. Sunday sees some souvenir shops and supermarkets at some train stations open.

Discount Cards

Swiss Museum Pass Regular or long-term visitors to Switzerland may want to buy the **Swiss Museum Pass** (www.museumspass.ch; adult/family Sfr144/255), which covers entry to the permanent collection (only) of 450 museums.

Visitors' Cards In many resorts and cities there's a visitors' card (Gästekarte), which provides various benefits such as reduced prices for museums, swimming pools, public transit or cable cars. Cards are issued by your accommodation.

Embassies & Consulates

For a list of embassies and consulates in Switzerland, go to www.eda.admin.ch. Embassies are in Bern but cities such as Zürich and Geneva have consulates.

Food

The following price ranges refer to a two-course meal:

€ less than Sfr25

€€ Sfr25 to Sfr45

€€€ more than Sfr45

Internet Access

Internet access in Switzerland – like most things – is expensive. Public wi-fi can easily cost Sfr5 for 30 minutes. Free hotspots are comparatively rare, even at cafes.

Money

» Swiss francs are divided into 100 centimes (*Rappen* in German-speaking Switzerland). There are notes for 10, 20, 50, 100, 200 and 1000 francs, and coins for 5,

10, 20 and 50 centimes, as well as for one, two and five francs. Euros are accepted by many tourism businesses.

» Exchange money at large train stations.

» Tipping is not necessary, given that hotels, restaurants, bars and even some taxis are legally required to include a 15% service charge in bills. You can round up the bill after a meal for good service, as locals do.

Post

Postcards and letters sent to Europe cost Sfr1.30/1.20 priority/economy; to elsewhere they cost Sfr1.80/1.40.

Public Holidays

New Year's Day 1 January

Easter March/April (Good Friday, Easter Sunday and Monday)

Ascension Day 40th day after Easter

Whit Sunday & Monday Seventh week after Easter

National Day 1 August

Christmas Day 25 December

St Stephen's Day 26 December

Telephone

» The country code for Switzerland is ☎41. When calling Switzerland from abroad, drop the initial zero from the number.

» The international access code from Switzerland is ☎00.

» SIM cards are widely available from train station ticket counters, exchange bureaus and mobile-phone shops. Several providers offer the same good deal: €20 for a SIM card that comes with €20 credit.

Visas

For up-to-date details on visa requirements, go to the **Swiss Federal Office for Migration** (www.eda.admin.ch) and click 'Services'.

Visas are not required for passport holders from the UK, EU, Ireland, the USA, Canada, Australia, New Zealand, South Africa, Norway and Iceland.

Getting There & Away

Air

The following are the main international airports:

Aéroport International de Genève (☎0900 571 500; www.gva.ch) The country's second airport has decent international links.

Zürich Airport (☎043 816 22 11; www.zurich-airport.com) Switzerland's main airport has flights to and from destinations worldwide. For flight information, SMS the airline code (ZHR) plus your flight number to ☎92 92.

Land

BUS

Eurolines (www.eurolines.com) has buses with connections across western Europe.

TRAIN

Located in the heart of Europe, Switzerland is a hub of train connections to the rest of the Continent. Zürich is the busiest international terminus, with service to all neighbouring countries. Destinations include Milan (4¼ hours), Münich (four hours) and Vienna (eight hours).

There are numerous TGV trains daily from Paris to several cities including Geneva (three hours), Lausanne (3¾ hours), Basel (three hours) and Zürich (four hours). Basel is a hub for services to Germany: fast ICE trains serve most major German cities. An easy way into Germany from Zürich is via medieval Constance (Sfr31, 1¼ hours).

Getting Around

Swiss public transport is an efficient, fully integrated and comprehensive system, which incorporates trains, buses, boats and funiculars.

Marketed as the **Swiss Travel System** (www.swisstravelsystem.com), the network has a useful website and there are excellent free maps covering the country available at train stations and tourist offices.

Passes & Discounts

Convenient discount passes make the Swiss transport system even more appealing. On extensive travel within Switzerland, the following national travel passes generally offer better savings than Eurail or InterRail passes:

Swiss Pass The Swiss Pass entitles the holder to unlimited travel on almost every train, boat and bus service in the country, and on trams and buses in 41 towns, plus free entry to 400-odd museums. Reductions of 50% apply on funiculars, cable cars and private railways. Different passes are available, valid between four days (US$460/288 for 1st/2nd class) and one month.

Half-Fare Card Almost every Swiss owns one of these. As the name suggests, you pay only half the fare on trains with this card, plus you get some discounts on local-network buses, trams and cable cars. An adult one-year Half-Fare Card costs Sfr175 (photo necessary).

Swiss Card A variation on the Half-Fare Card that includes a round-trip ticket to and from a border area and is good for 30 days. It is sold abroad for US$300/200 for 1st/2nd class.

Bicycle

You can hire bikes from most train stations for about Sfr10 per day. Local tourist offices often have good cycling information.

Boat

Ferries and steamers link towns and cities on many lakes, including Constance, Geneva, Lucerne, Lugano, Murten and Zurich.

Bus

Yellow postal buses are a supplement to the rail network, following postal routes and linking towns to the more inaccessible regions in the mountains. In all, routes cover some 8000km of terrain. Services are regular, and departures link to train schedules. Postbus stations are next to train stations and offer destination and timetable information.

Car & Motorcycle

» Be prepared for winding roads, high passes and long tunnels.
» Normal speed limits are 50km/h in towns, 120km/h on motorways, 100km/h on semimotorways (designated by roadside rectangular pictograms showing a white car on a green background) and 80km/h on other roads.
» Mountain roads are well maintained. Some minor Alpine passes are closed from November to May – check with the local tourist offices before setting off.

Train

The Swiss rail network combines state-run and private operations. The **Swiss Federal Railway** (www.rail.ch) is abbreviated to SBB in German, CFF in French and FFS in Italian.
» All major train stations are connected to each other by hourly departures, at least between 6am and midnight.
» Second-class seats are perfectly acceptable, but cars are often close to full.

SWITZERLAND'S SCENIC TRAINS

Swiss trains, buses and boats are more than a means of getting from A to B. Stunning views invariably make the journey itself the destination. Switzerland boasts the following routes among its classic sightseeing journeys.

Bear in mind that you can choose just one leg of the trip, and that scheduled services often ply the same routes for standard fares; these are cheaper than the named trains, which often have cars with extra-large windows and require reservations.

Bernina Express A spectacular bus and train journey between Lugano and St Mortiz/Davos/Chur.

Glacier Express A fabled journey between Zermatt and St Moritz, Chur or Davos.

Jungfrau Region You can spend days ogling stunning Alpine scenery from the trains, cable cars and more here.

GoldenPass Line (www.goldenpass.ch) Travels between Lucerne and Montreux in three sections; the Lucerne to Interlaken East leg is especially scenic.

Centovalli Express (www.centovalli.ch) An underappreciated gem of a line (two hours) that snakes along fantastic river gorges in Switzerland and Italy, from Locarno to Domodossola. Trains run through the day and it is easy to connect to Brig and beyond from Domodossola in Italy.

First-class carriages are more comfortable and spacious, and have fewer passengers.

» Ticket vending machines accept most major credit cards from around the world.

» The SBB smartphone app is an excellent resource and can be used to store your tickets electronically.

» Check the SBB website for cheap Supersaver tickets on major routes.

» Most stations have 24-hour lockers (small/large locker Sfr6/9), usually accessible from 6am to midnight.

» Seat reservations (Sfr5) are advisable for longer journeys, particularly in the high season.

Turkey

Includes »

İstanbul 1153
Çanakkale 1164
İzmir 1166
Selçuk 1166
Bodrum 1168
Marmaris 1169
Fethiye 1170
Kaş 1172
Antalya 1173
Ankara 1174
Konya 1176
Göreme 1177
Nemrut Dağı Milli Parkı 1179
Understand Turkey 1180
Survival Guide 1181

Best Places to Eat

- Zübeyir Ocakbaşı (p1161)
- Ahırkapı Balıkçısı (p1162)
- Bodrum Fish Market (p1169)
- Şaraphane (p1173)

Best Places to Stay

- Hotel Ibrahim Pasha (p1159)
- Atilla's Getaway (p1167)
- Hotel Canada (p1173)
- White Garden Pansiyon (p1174)

Why Go?

While many Turks see their country as European, Turkey packs in as many towering minarets and spice-trading bazaars as its Middle Eastern neighbours. This bridge between continents offers travellers historical hot spots, mountain outposts, expansive steppe and loads of the exotic, without foregoing comfy beds and buses.

Despite its reputation as a continental meeting point, Turkey can't be pigeonholed. Cappadocia, a dreamscape dotted with fairy chimneys (rock formations), is unlike anywhere else on the planet. Likewise, spots such as Nemrut Dağı (Mt Nemrut), littered with giant stone heads, and Olympos, where Lycian ruins peek from the undergrowth, are quintessentially Turkish mixtures of natural splendour and ancient remains.

The beaches and mountains offer enough activities to impress the fussiest Ottoman sultan, accompanied by worldly pleasures such as savouring meze on panoramic terraces and, of course, Turkey's famous kebaps.

When to Go

Ankara

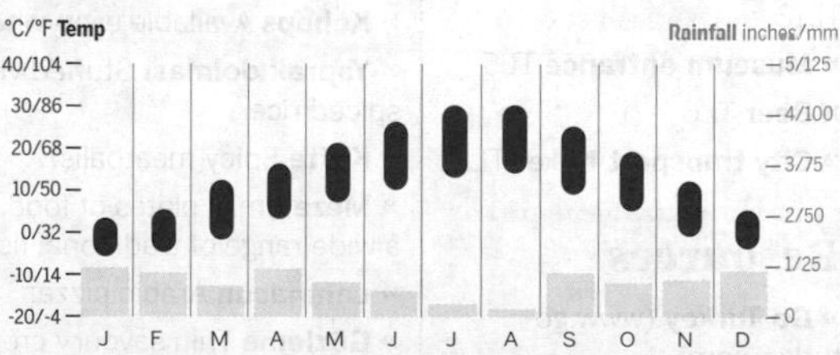

Apr–May Spring sunshine without summer crowds; apart from İstanbul, where it is high season.

Jun–Aug İstanbul's shoulder season, with music festivals and summer days by the Bosphorus.

Sep–Oct Autumn walking and diving; crowds thin outside İstanbul (where it's high season again).

AT A GLANCE

- **Currency** Turkish lira (TL)
- **Language** Turkish, Kurdish
- **Money** ATMS widespread; credit cards accepted in cities and tourist areas
- **Visas** On arrival

Fast Facts

- **Area** 783,562 sq km
- **Capital** Ankara
- **Country code** ☎90
- **Emergency** Ambulance ☎112, fire ☎110, police ☎155

Exchange Rates

Australia	A$1	TL1.88
Canada	C$1	TL1.77
Euro Zone	€1	TL2.32
Japan	¥100	TL1.94
New Zealand	NZ$1	TL1.51
UK	UK£1	TL2.75
USA	US$1	TL1.80

Set Your Budget

- **Budget double room** TL80
- **Two-course meal** from TL12
- **Museum entrance** TL5
- **Beer** TL6
- **City transport ticket** TL2

Resources

- **Go Turkey** (www.goturkey.com)
- **Hürriyet Daily News** (www.hurriyetdailynews.com)
- **Culinary Backstreets** (www.culinarybackstreets.com)

Connections

İstanbul is well connected to Europe, with two international airports. Buses leave the *otogar* (bus station) for countries including Austria, Bulgaria, Germany, Greece, Italy, Macedonia, Romania and Slovenia.

Currently, the only daily train between İstanbul and Europe is the overnight Bosphorus/Balkan Express to Bucharest (Romania, 21 hours), Sofia (Bulgaria, 13 hours) and Belgrade (Serbia, 21½ hours). A suggested train route from London to İstanbul is the three-night journey via Paris, Munich, Vienna, Budapest and Bucharest; see www.seat61.com/turkey for more information and other routes.

Ferries connect Turkey's Aegean and Mediterranean coasts with Greek islands; İstanbul with Ukraine; and Trabzon on the Black Sea coast with Russia.

ITINERARIES

One Week

Devote a few days to magical İstanbul, then cross the Sea of Marmara to Anatolia and head south to laid-back Selçuk or coastal Kuşadası, both convenient bases for visiting the marvellous ruins of Ephesus.

Two Weeks

From Ephesus, head inland to Pamukkale's shiny travertine formations, then return to the coast at Fethiye, with its island-dotted bay and Lycian rock tombs. Work your way around the glorious Teke peninsula to the vibrant city of Antalya, its Ottoman quarter overlooking the Roman harbour. Possible stops en route include Patara for Turkey's longest beach, Kaş for activities and boat trips, and Çıralı to see the eternal flame of the Chimaera.

Essential Food & Drink

Turkish food is a celebration of community and life in its home country.

- **Kebaps** Available everywhere and swooningly succulent.
- **Yaprak dolması** Stuffed vine leaves filled with subtly spiced rice.
- **Köfte** Spicy meatballs.
- **Meze** Small plates of food, including dips, vegetables and a wide range of traditional fish and meat dishes.
- **Lahmacun** Arabic pizza.
- **Gözleme** Thin savoury crêpes.
- **Mantı** Turkish ravioli.
- **Börek** Filled pastries.
- **Çay** Tea.
- **Rakı** A fiery, highly alcoholic aniseed drink, best accompanied by meze, especially *beyaz peynir* (ewe's- or goat's-milk cheese) and melon, and *balık* (fish).

İSTANBUL

☎0212 & ☎0216 / POP 14 MILLION

Some ancient cities are the sum of their monuments. But İstanbul, the former capital of the Byzantine and Ottoman Empires, factors a lot more into the equation. Here, you can visit venerable mosques and churches in the morning, shop in chic boutiques during the afternoo,n and party at glamorous clubs through the night. In the space of a few minutes, you can hear the evocative strains of the call to prayer issuing from the Old City's minarets, the sonorous horn of a commuter ferry crossing between Europe and Asia, and the strident cries of a street hawker selling fresh seasonal produce. This marvellous metropolis is an exercise in sensory seduction like no other.

The Bosphorus strait, between the Black Sea and the Sea of Marmara, divides Europe from Asia. On its western shore, European İstanbul is further divided by the Golden Horn (Haliç) into the Old City in the southwest and Beyoğlu in the northeast.

Sights & Activities

SULTANAHMET & AROUND

The Sultanahmet area is the centre of the Old City, a World Heritage Site packed with so many wonderful sights you could spend several weeks here.

TOP CHOICE Aya Sofya MUSEUM

(Hagia Sophia; Map p1156; www.ayasofyamuzesi.gov.tr; Aya Sofya Meydanı 1; adult/under 12yr TL25/free; ⌚9am-6pm Tue-Sun mid-Apr–Sep, to 4pm Oct–mid-Apr; Sultanahmet) No doubt you will gasp at the overblown splendour of the Aya Sofya, one of the world's most glorious buildings. It was completed in AD 537 and reigned as the grandest church in Christendom until the Ottomans took Constantinople in 1453. The victorious Mehmet the Conqueror converted the building to a

İstanbul

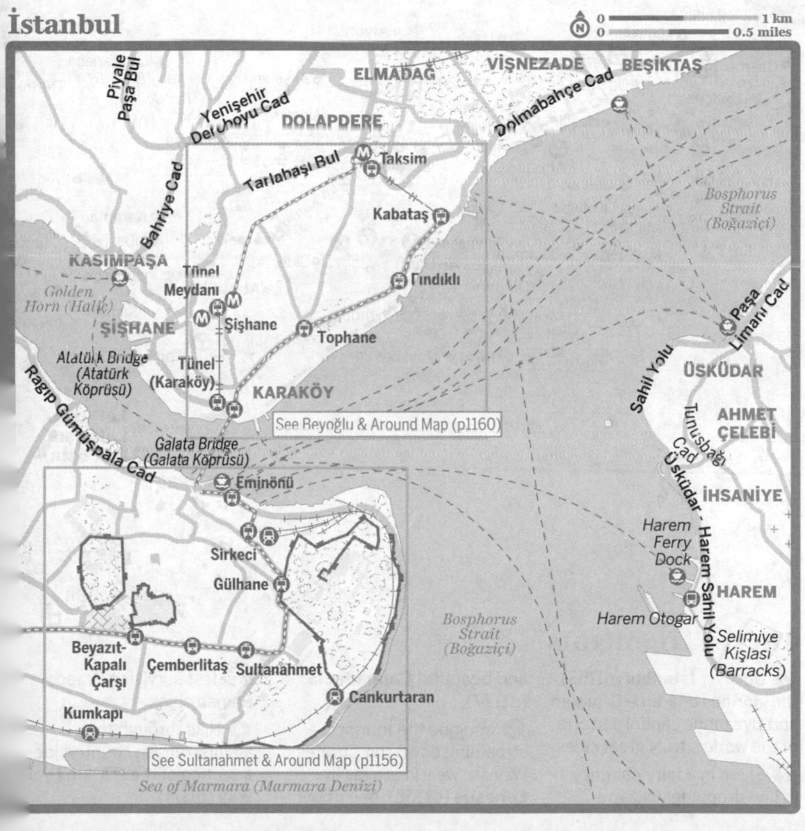

Turkey Highlights

1. Uncover **İstanbul** (p1153), the glorious one-time Ottoman and Byzantine capital and one of the world's truly great cities
2. Sleep in a fairy chimney in jaw-droppingly bizarre and beautiful **Cappadocia** (p1177)
3. Imagine the tourists streaming down the Curetes Way are wearing togas in **Ephesus** (p1168), one of the greatest surviving Graeco-Roman cities
4. Hike through the Mediterranean countryside on a section of the 500km **Lycian Way** (p1171)

Explore Turkey's exotic ...st at **Nemrut Dağı** (p1179), ...ere decapitated stone heads ...er a king's burial mound

Cruise over the sunken ...y alongside Kekova Island from Kaş, one of many **blue voyages** (p1171) offered at Aegean and Mediterranean harbours

7 Wander the Roman-Ottoman old quarter of **Antalya** (p1173), a stylish Mediterranean hub and gateway to the Turquoise Coast

Sultanahmet & Around

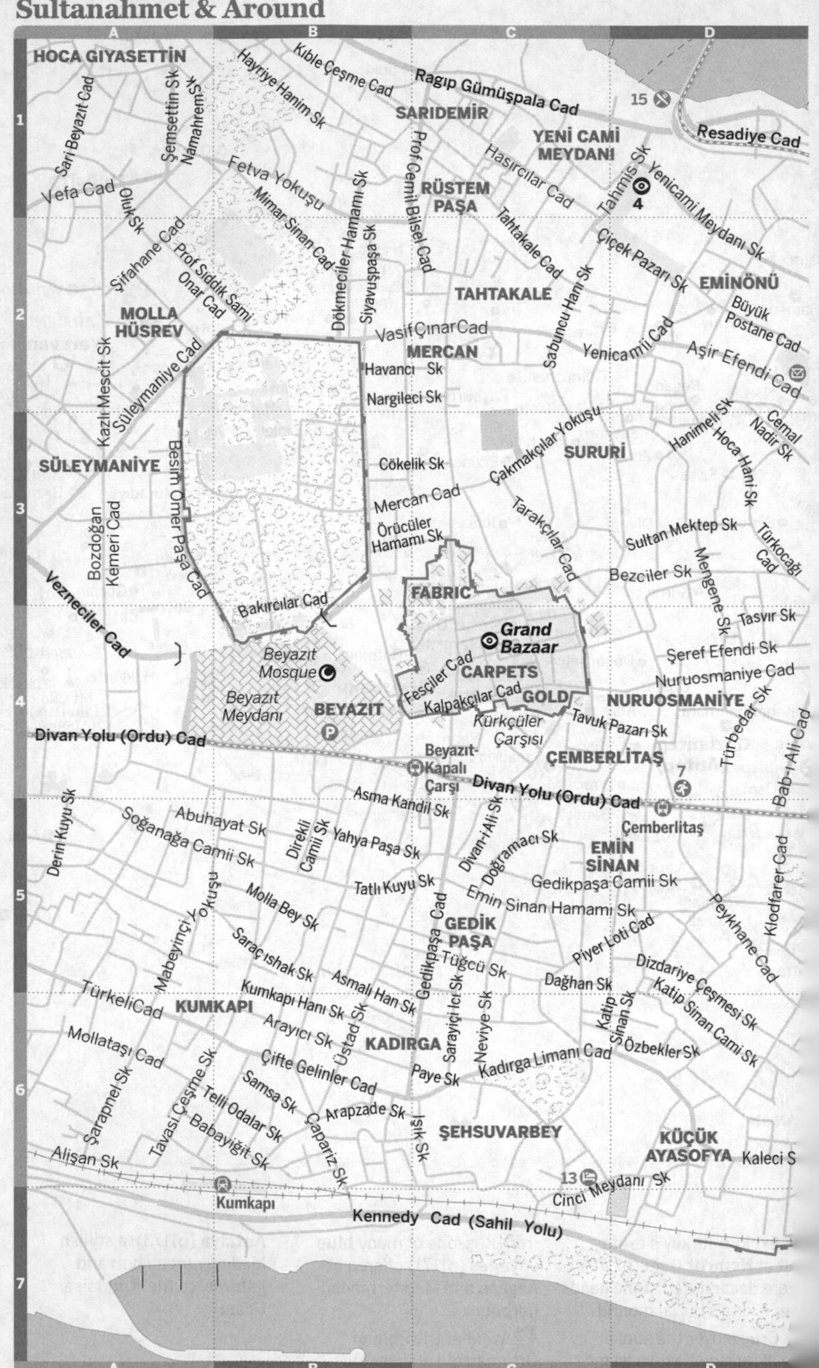

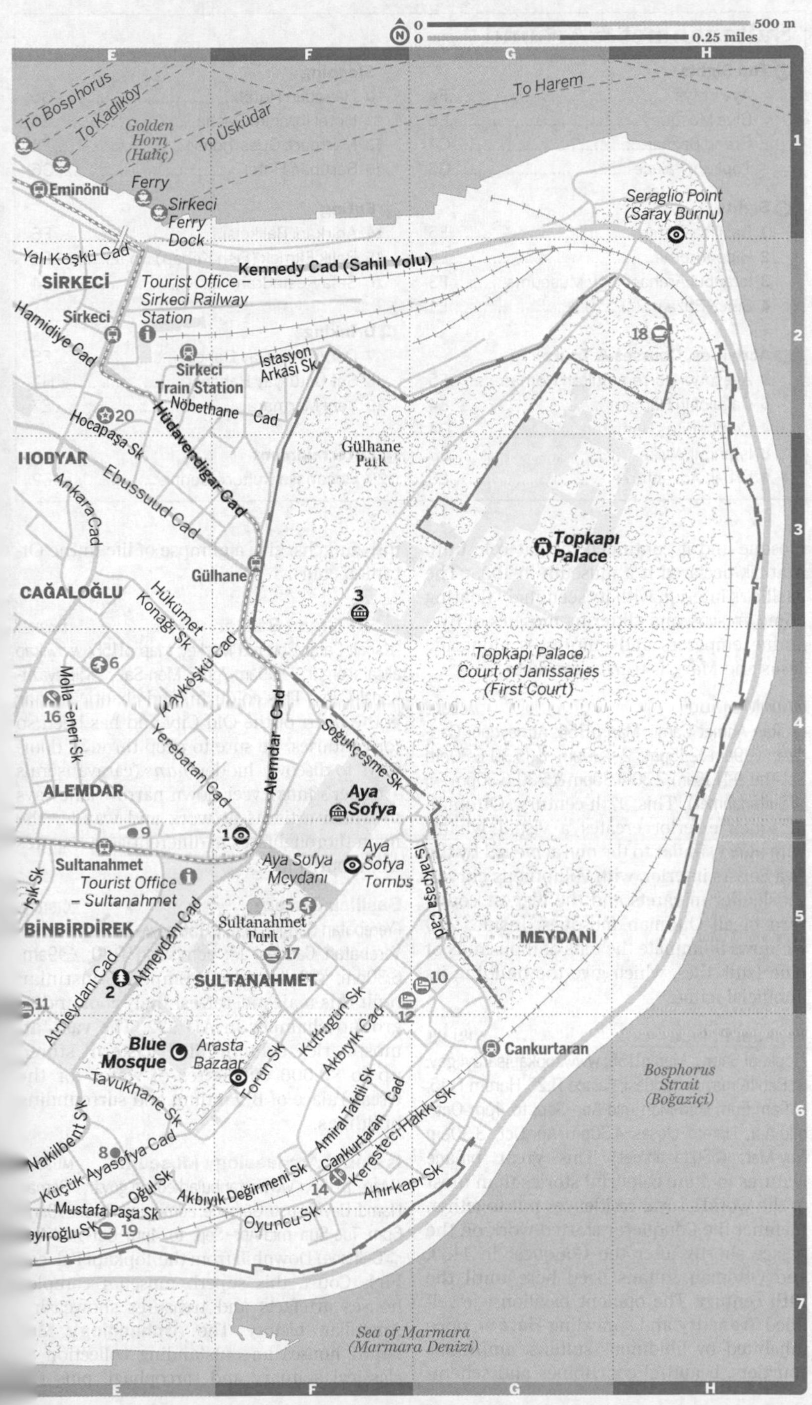
0 500 m
0 0.25 miles
To Bosphorus
To Kadıköy
To Üsküdar
To Harem
Golden Horn (Haliç)
Eminönü
Ferry
Sirkeci Ferry Dock
Seraglio Point (Saray Burnu)
Yalı Köşkü Cad
Kennedy Cad (Sahil Yolu)
SİRKECİ
Tourist Office – Sirkeci Railway Station
Sirkeci
Hamidiye Cad
Sirkeci Train Station
Istasyon Arkasi Sk
Nöbethane Cad
Hocapaşa Sk
Hüdavendigar Cad
Gülhane Park
HODYAR
Ebussuud Cad
Ankara Cad
Topkapı Palace
Gülhane
CAĞALOĞLU
Hükümet Konaği Sk
Kaykökşü Cad
Topkapı Palace Court of Janissaries (First Court)
Molla Feneri Sk
Alemdar Cad
Soğukçeşme Sk
Yerebatan Cad
ALEMDAR
Aya Sofya
Sultanahmet
Aya Sofya Meydanı
Aya Sofya Tombs
İshakpaşa Cad
Tourist Office – Sultanahmet
Işık Sk
BİNBİRDİREK
Atmeydanı Cad
Sultanahmet Park
MEYDANI
SULTANAHMET
Kutlugün Sk
Akbıyık Cad
Cankurtaran
Blue Mosque
Arasta Bazaar
Torun Sk
Tavukhane Sk
Amiral Tafdil Sk
Cankurtaran Cad
Keresteci Hakkı Sk
Bosphorus Strait (Boğaziçi)
Nakilbent Sk
Küçük Ayasofya Cad
Oğul Sk
Akbıyık Değirmeni Sk
Ahırkapı Sk
Mustafa Paşa Sk
Oyuncu Sk
Sea of Marmara (Marmara Denizi)

Sultanahmet & Around

Top Sights
- Aya Sofya ... F4
- Blue Mosque ... E6
- Grand Bazaar ... C4
- Topkapı Palace ... G3

Sights
- 1 Basilica Cistern ... F5
- 2 Hippodrome ... E5
- 3 İstanbul Archaeology Museums ... F3
- 4 Spice Bazaar ... D1

Activities, Courses & Tours
- 5 Ayasofya Hürrem Sultan Hamamı ... F5
- 6 Cağaloğlu Hamamı ... E4
- 7 Çemberlitaş Hamamı ... D4
- 8 İstanbul Walks ... E6
- 9 Urban Adventures ... E5

Sleeping
- 10 Hanedan Hotel ... G5
- 11 Hotel Ibrahim Pasha ... E5
- 12 Marmara Guesthouse ... F5
- 13 Saruhan Hotel ... C6

Eating
- 14 Ahırkapı Balıkçısı ... F6
- 15 Balık Ekmek (Fish Kebap) Boats ... D1
- 16 Sefa Restaurant ... E4

Drinking
- 17 Derviş Aile Çay Bahçesi ... F5
- 18 Set Üstü Çay Bahçesi ... H2
- 19 Yeni Marmara ... E7

Entertainment
- 20 Hocapaşa Culture Centre ... E2

mosque and it continued in that role until Atatürk declared it a museum in 1935. The basilica's interior, with its seemingly floating dome, frescos, and glittering mosaics of Byzantine emperors and empresses alongside Jesus and Mary, is truly a knockout.

Blue Mosque MOSQUE
(Sultan Ahmet Camii; Map p1156; Atmeydanı Caddesi; 9am-12.15pm, 2-4.30pm & 5.30-6.30pm Sat-Thu, 9-11.15am, 2.30-4.30pm & 5.30-6.30pm Fri; Sultanahmet) This 17th-century Ottoman mosque's exterior creates a visual whambam effect similar to the one achieved by the Aya Sofya's interior, with voluptuous curves, six slender minarets and the biggest courtyard of all Ottoman mosques. Inside, 260 windows illuminate the tens of thousands of blue İznik tiles, which give the building its unofficial name.

Topkapı Palace PALACE
(Topkapı Sarayı; Map p1156; www.topkapisarayi.gov.tr; Babıhümayun Caddesi; palace TL25, Harem TL15; 9am-6pm Wed-Mon mid-Apr–Sep, to 4pm Oct–mid-Apr, Harem closes 4.30pm Apr-Oct, 3.30pm Nov-Mar; Sultanahmet) This great palace features in more colourful stories than most of the world's royal residences put together. Mehmet the Conqueror started work on the palace shortly after the Conquest in 1453, and Ottoman sultans lived here until the 19th century. The opulent pavilions, jewel-filled **Treasury** and sprawling **Harem**, once inhabited by libidinous sultans, ambitious courtiers, beautiful concubines and scheming eunuchs, give a glimpse of life in the Ottoman court.

TOP CHOICE **Grand Bazaar** MARKET
(Kapalı Çarşı, Covered Market; Map p1156; www.kapalicarsi.org.tr; 9am-7pm Mon-Sat;; Beyazıt-Kapalı Çarşı) This colourful and chaotic bazaar is the heart of the Old City and has been so for centuries. Be sure to peep through doorways to discover hidden *hans* (caravanserais – trader's inns), veer down narrow laneways to watch artisans at work and wander the main thoroughfares to differentiate treasures from tourist tack.

Basilica Cistern CISTERN
(Yerebatan Sarnıçı; Map p1156; www.yerebatan.com Yerebatan Caddesi 13; admission TL10; 9am-6.30pm; Sultanahmet) Emperor Justinian built this majestic, refreshingly cool underground chamber in AD 532. The vast, atmospheric, column-filled cistern stored up to 80,000 cu metres of water for the Great Palace of Byzantium and surrounding buildings.

İstanbul Archaeology Museums MUSEU[M]
(Map p1156; www.istanbularkeologi.gov.tr; Osman Hamdi Bey Yokuşu, Gülhane; admission TL10; 9am-6pm Tue-Sun mid-Apr–Sep, to 4pm Oct–mid-Ap[r]; Gülhane) Downhill from the Topkapı Palace First Court, this superb museum comple[x] houses artefacts and treasures showcasi[ng] Anatolian history. The **Archaeology Mu[-] seum** houses an outstanding collection [of] classical statuary and sarcophagi, plus th[e]

İstanbul Through the Ages exhibition, which traces the city's history. The **Museum of the Ancient Orient** houses Hittite and other pre-Islamic archaeological finds.

BEYOĞLU

Beyoğlu, the heart of modern İstanbul, is kilometre zero for galleries, boutiques, cafes, restaurants and nightlife. The neighbourhood is a showcase of cosmopolitan Turkey at its best – miss Beyoğlu and you haven't seen İstanbul.

Climbing from Tünel Sq to Taksim Sq, **İstiklal Caddesi** (Independence Ave), known in the late 19th century as the Grand Rue de Pera, carries the life of the modern city up and down its lively promenade. A stroll along its length is a must – or take the quaint **antique tram**.

BOSPHORUS

Don't leave İstanbul without exploring the Bosphorus on one of the boats departing from Eminönü. Private excursion boats (TL10, 1½ hours) travel to Anadolu Hisarı and back, without stopping. İDO's **Bosphorus Public Excursion Ferry** (www.ido.com.tr; Boğaz İskelesi; long tour one-way/return TL15/25, short tour TL10; ⏲long tour 10.35am, plus 1.35pm Apr–Oct & noon summer, short tour 2.30pm Apr-Oct) travels to Anadolu Kavağı at the Black Sea (the turnaround point, 1½ hours away), stopping at various points en route. Its two-hour 'short tour' travels to Fatih Bridge and back.

The shores are sprinkled with sights, including the grandiose Dolmabahçe Palace, the majestic Bosphorus Bridge, numerous mosques, lavish *yalıs* (waterfront wooden summer residences) and affluent suburbs on the hills above the strait.

For the thrill of crossing from Europe to Asia (and back), you can catch a **commuter ferry** across the Bosphorus (TL2) from Eminönü, Karaköy or Beşiktaş (near Dolmabahçe Palace) to Kadıköy.

Tours

stanbul Walks (Map p1156; ☎0212-516 6300; www.istanbulwalks.net; 2nd fl, Şifa Hamamı Sokak ; walking tours €25-75, child under 6yr free; Sultanahmet) and **Urban Adventures** (Map 1156; ☎212-512 7144; www.urbanadventures.om; 1st fl, Ticarethane Sokak 11; tours TL50; 8.30am-5.30pm; Sultanahmet) offer good uided walking tours. The latter and **Culinary Backstreets** (www.culinarybackstreets.com) also run foodie walking tours and gastronomic evenings.

Sleeping

Before confirming bookings, ask if the hotel will give you a discount for cash payment and whether there are discounts for extended stays. A pick-up from the airport is often included if you stay more than three nights. Book ahead from May to September and for the Christmas–New Year period.

SULTANAHMET & AROUND

The Sultanahmet area has the most budget and midrange options, as well as some more luxurious accommodation. Most have stunning views from their roof terraces, and are close to the Old City's sights.

TOP CHOICE Hotel Ibrahim Pasha BOUTIQUE HOTEL €€
(Map p1156; ☎0212-518 0394; www.ibrahimpasha.com; Terzihane Sokak 7; r standard €99-195, deluxe €139-265; ❄@📶; 🚊Sultanahmet) Successfully combines Ottoman style, contemporary decor and excellent service in its gorgeous rooms, comfortable lounge, and terrace bar with Blue Mosque views.

Marmara Guesthouse PENSION €
(Map p1156; ☎0212-638 3638; www.marmaraguesthouse.com; Terbıyık Sokak 15, Cankurtaran; s €30-65, d €40-70, f €60-100; ❄@; 🚊Sultanahmet) Manager Elif Aytekin and her family really make guests feel welcome, serving a delicious breakfast on the vine-covered, seafacing roof terrace. Rooms have comfortable beds and double-glazed windows.

Saruhan Hotel HOTEL €
(Map p1156; ☎0212-458 7608; www.saruhanhotel.com; Cinci Meydanı Sokak 34, Kadırga; s €25-65, d €35-70, f €60-100; ❄@📶; 🚊Çemberlitaş) In a quiet residential pocket, a 20-minute walk from Sultanahmet's sights, the impressive family-run Saruhan offers comfortable and well-equipped rooms plus a lovely terrace with sea views.

MUSEUM PASS

The **Museum Pass İstanbul** (www.muze.gov.tr/museum_pass) offers a possible TL36 saving on entry to the Old City's major sights, and allows holders to skip admission queues.

Beyoğlu & Around

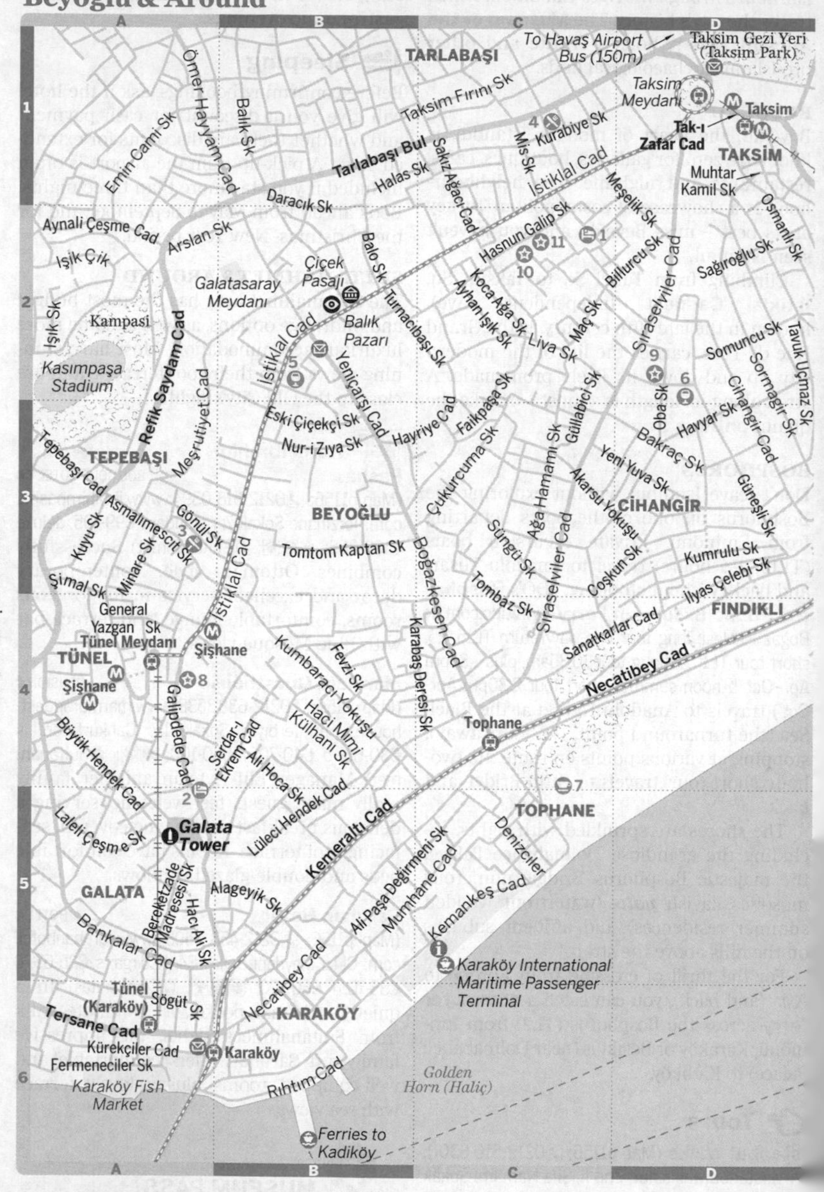

Hanedan Hotel HOTEL €
(Map p1156; ☎0212-516 4869; www.hanedanhotel.com; Adliye Sokak 3, Cankurtaran; s €30-50, d €45-65, f €75-100; ; Sultanahmet) A cheap, clean and comfortable choice, with suitable rooms for families and a roof terrace overlooking the sea and Aya Sofya.

BEYOĞLU & AROUND

World House Hostel HOSTEL
(Map p1160; ☎0212-293 5520; www.worldhouseistanbul.com; Galipdede Caddesi 85, Galata; €45-55; ; Karaköy, then funicular to Tüne Reasonably small and very friendly, wi large and small dorms. Close to Beyoğlu

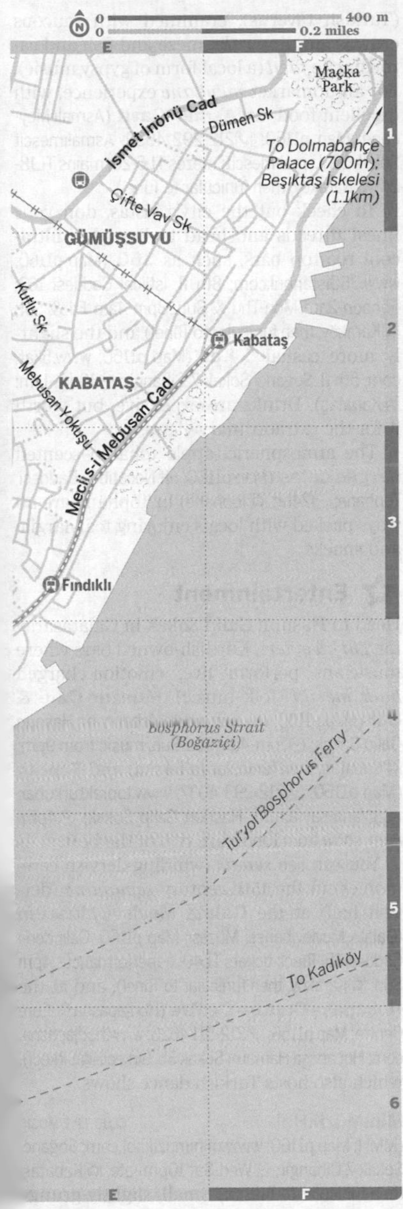

ntertainment strips and not too far from ultanahmet.

hambers of the oheme HOSTEL €
Map p1160; ☎0212-251 0931; www.hostelsistan ıl.net; Küçük Parmak Kapı Sokak 13, Taksim; dm €14-20, f €100; ❄@📶; 🚊Kabataş, then funicular to Taksim) A popular and friendly hostel in a noisy location. Bring earplugs or party throughout the night.

Beyoğlu & Around

Top Sights
Galata Tower A5

Sleeping
1 Chambers of the Boheme C2
2 World House Hostel A5

Eating
3 Asmalı Cavit A3
Zencefil .... (see 4)
4 Zübeyir Ocakbaşı C1

Drinking
5 360 .... B2
6 5 Kat D2
7 Tophane Nargile Cafes C4

Entertainment
8 Galata Mevlevi Museum A4
9 MiniMüzikHol D2
10 Munzur Cafe & Bar C2
11 Toprak C2

Eating

İstanbul is a food-lover's paradise, but Sultanahmet has the least impressive range of eating options – cross the Galata Bridge to join the locals. Head to the streets off İstiklal Caddesi for cheap kebaps and street food.

In the Old City, Divan Yolu Caddesi is good for affordable eats. The **Spice Bazaar** (Mısır Çarşısı, Egyptian Market; Map p1156; ⏲8am-6pm Mon-Sat, 9am-6pm Sun; 🚊Eminönü) is excellent for nuts, honeycomb, dried fruit, figs and Turkish delight. Avoid the rip-off eateries near the accommodation and bars on Akbıyık Caddesi in Cankurtan.

İstanbul Eats (www.culinarybackstreets.com/istanbul) is a good local foodie website.

Zübeyir Ocakbaşı KEBAPS €€
(Map p1160; ☎0212-293 3951; www.zubeyirocakbasi.com; Bekar Sokak 28; meze TL4-6, kebaps TL10-20; ⏲noon-1am; 🚊Kabataş, then funicular to Taksim) Every morning, the chefs at this popular *ocakbaşı* (grill house) prepare the fresh, top-quality meats to be grilled over their handsome copper-hooded barbecues that night. The place to splurge on a great Turkish kebap. Bookings are essential.

FISH KEBAP

İstanbul's favourite fast-food treat is the *balık ekmek* (fish kebap). On bobbing boats tied to the quay at the Eminönü end of Galata Bridge, fish fillets are grilled and crammed into fresh bread. You can buy the resulting snack at the adjoining **stands** (Map p1156) on dry land for about TL5.

TOP CHOICE **Ahırkapı Balıkçısı** SEAFOOD €€
(Map p1156; 0212-518 4988; Keresteci Hakkı Sokak 46, Cankurtaran; meze TL5-25, fish TL15-70; 4-11pm; Sultanahmet) Join the locals at this tiny and relatively cheap neighbourhood fish restaurant. Book ahead.

Zencefil VEGETARIAN €
(Map p1160; Kurabiye Sokak 8; soup TL7-9, mains TL9-17; 10am-11pm Mon-Sat, noon-10pm Sun; ; Kabataş, then funicular to Taksim) Fresh, homemade food in a comfortable and stylish interior. One chicken dish features on the vegetarian menu.

Sefa Restaurant TURKISH €
(Map p1156; Nuruosmaniye Caddesi 17; portions TL7-12, kebaps TL12-18; 7am-5pm; ; Sultanahmet) Locals rate this (unlicensed) restaurant, which serves *lokanta* (ready-made) dishes and kebaps. Arrive early-ish for lunch; many dishes run out by 1.30pm.

Drinking

SULTANAHMET

Sultanahmet's desultory bar scene is concentrated on Akbıyık Caddesi, catering to the surrounding hostels. A better option is the area's alcohol-free, atmosphere-rich *çay bahçesis* (tea gardens) and *kahvehanes* (coffee houses), where you can sample a *nargile* (water pipe), along with a *Türk kahvesi* (Turkish coffee) or *çay* (tea). **Set Üstü Çay Bahçesi** (Map p1156; Gülhane Park, Sultanahmet; 9am-10.30pm; Gülhane), **Yeni Marmara** (Map p1156; Çayıroğlu Sokak, Küçük Ayasofya; 10am-1am; Sultanahmet) and **Derviş Aile Çay Bahçesi** (Map p1156; Mimar Mehmet Ağa Caddesi; 9am-11pm Apr-Oct; Sultanahmet) are recommended.

BEYOĞLU

It's well worth exploring the byways of Beyoğlu, where streets off the Istiklal, such as Nevizade and Balo Sokaks, are lined with bars. The former is also good for *meyhanes* (Turkish taverns), crammed with raucous crowds guzzling *rakı*, meze and fish and carousing to *fasıl* (a local form of gypsy music). For an upmarket *meyhane* experience, with excellent food, try **Asmalı Cavit** (Asmalı Meyhane; Map p1160; 212-292 4950; Asmalımescit Sokak 16, Asmalımescit; mezes TL6-20, mains TL18-24; Karaköy, then funicular to Tünel).

To check out the city's vistas, don your finest threads and head to Beyoğlu's ultra-cool rooftop bars, such as **360** (Map p1160; www.360istanbul.com; 8th fl, İstiklal Caddesi 163; noon-2am Mon-Thu & Sun, 3pm-4am Fri & Sat; Karaköy, then funicular to Tünel) and the slightly more casual **5 Kat** (Map p1160; www.5kat.com; 5th fl, Soğancı Sokak 7, Cihangir; 10am-1am; Kabataş). Drinks are expensive, but worth it for the extraordinary views.

The atmospheric, apple tobacco–scented **nargile cafes** (Map p1160; off Necatibey Caddesi, Tophane; 24hr; Tophane) in Tophane are always packed with locals enjoying tea, nargile and snacks

Entertainment

Head to Hasnun Galip Sokak in Galatasaray for *Türkü evlerı*, Kurdish-owned bars where musicians perform live, emotion-charged *halk meziği* (folk music). **Munzur Cafe & Bar** (Map p1160; www.munzurcafebar.com; Hasnun Galip Sokak; 1pm-4am Tue-Sun, music from 9pm; Kabataş, then funicular to Taksim) and **Toprak** (Map p1160; 212-293 4037; www.toprakturkubar.tr.gg/ana-sayfa.htm; Hasnun Galip Sokak; 4pm-4am, show from 10pm) are two of the best.

You can see *semas* (whirling-dervish ceremonies) in the 15th-century *semahane* (dervish hall) at the **Galata Mevlevi Museum** (Galata Mevlevihanesi Müzesi; Map p1160; Galipdede Caddesi 15, Tünel; tickets TL40; performances 4pm Sun; Karaköy, then funicular to Tünel), and at the **Hocapaşa Culture Centre** (Hodjapasha Culture Centre; Map p1156; 212-511 4626; www.hodjapasha.com; Hocapaşa Hamamı Sokak 3b, Sirkeci; Sirkeci), which also hosts Turkish dance shows.

MiniMüzikHol CLUB, LIVE MUSIC
(MMH; Map p1160; www.minimuzikhol.com; Soğancı Sokak 7, Cihangir; Wed-Sat 10pm-late; Kabataş then funicular to Taksim) Small, slightly grungy venue, hosting live sets midweek and the best dance party in town on weekends.

Information

Banks, ATMs and exchange offices are widespread. The exchange rates offered at Atatürk International Airport are usually as good as those in town.

İstanbul has two area codes: 0212 for the European side, 0216 for the Asian zone.

None of İstanbul's tourist offices are particularly helpful.

Lonely Planet (www.lonelyplanet.com) Check out the Thorn Tree bulletin board to find out what city discoveries are being made.

Tourist Office (0212-465 3451; International Arrivals Hall, Atatürk International Airport; 9am-10pm)

Tourist Police (0212-527 4503; Yerebatan Caddesi 6)

Universal Taksim Alman Hastanesi (Universal German Hospital; 0212-293 2150; www.uhg.com.tr; Sıraselviler Caddesi 119; 8.30am-6pm Mon-Fri, 8.30am-5pm Sat)

Getting There & Away

Air

Atatürk International Airport (Atatürk Havalımanı; 0212-463 3000; www.ataturkairport.com) Long-haul flights generally touch down here, 23km west of Sultanahmet.

Sabiha Gökçen International Airport (Sabiha Gökçen Havalımanı; 0216-588 8888; www.sgairport.com) Located 50km east of Sultanahmet, on the Asian side of the city, and popular with low-cost European airlines.

Boat

Yenikapı is the main dock for **İDO** (İstanbul Deniz Otobusleri; 0212-444 4436; www.ido.com.tr) car and passenger ferries across the Sea of Marmara to Yalova, Bursa and Bandırma (from where you can catch a train to İzmir or a bus to Çanakkale).

Bus

The aptly titled **Büyük İstanbul Otogarı** (Big İstanbul Bus Station; 0212-658 0505; www.otogaristanbul.com), 10km west of Sultanahmet, is the city's main *otogar*. Excluding holiday periods, you can usually turn up and be on your way within the hour.

Many bus companies offer a *servis* (free shuttle bus) to and from the *otogar*. The metro stops here en route between Atatürk International Airport and Aksaray, where you can pick up a tram to Sultanahmet.

If you're arriving from Anatolia, rather than travelling all the way to the Big İstanbul Bus Station, it's quicker to get out at the smaller **Harem Otogar** on the Asian shore, and take the ferry to Sirkeci/Eminönü.

Train

The daily Bosphorus/Balkan Express links İstanbul with Bucharest (Romania), Sofia (Bulgaria) and Belgrade (Serbia).

Services to and from destinations in Anatolia have been severely curtailed by work on the Ankara line, which is due to reopen in 2014 or 2015.

Getting Around

Tickets on public transport in İstanbul generally cost TL2.

BOAT İstanbul's commuter ferries ply the Bosphorus between the city's European and Asian sides. See p1159 for details on boat travel on the Bosphorus.

BUS İstanbul's efficient bus system runs between 6.30am and 11.30pm. You must have a ticket before boarding; buy tickets from the white booths near major stops, and at some shops.

FUNICULAR RAILWAY The 19th-century Tünel climbs the hill from Karaköy (near the tram stop) to the bottom of İstiklal Caddesi (every 10 minutes, 7.30am to 9pm).

A funicular railway also climbs from the Bosphorus shore at Kabataş (near the tram stop) to Taksim Sq.

METRO Connects Aksaray with the airport, stopping at 15 stations, including the *otogar*, along the way (roughly every 10 minutes, 5.40am to 1.40am).

TAXI İstanbul is full of yellow taxis, all of them with meters; do not let drivers insist on a fixed rate. From Sultanahmet to Taksim Sq costs around TL15.

TRAM A *tramvay* (tramway) runs between Zeytinburnu (where it connects with the metro

HAMMAMS

The Old City's pricey tourist *hammams* (Turkish baths) are worth visiting for their gorgeous historic interiors, although their massages are generally short and not particularly good.

Ayasofya Hürrem Sultan Hamamı (Map p1156; 0212-517 3535; www.ayasofyahamami.com; Aya Sofya Meydanı; bath treatments €70-165, massages €40-75; 8am-11pm; Sultanahmet)

Cağaloğlu Hamamı (Map p1156; 0212-522 2424; www.cagalogluhamami.com.tr; Yerebatan Caddesi 34; bath, scrub & massage packages €50-110; 8am-10pm; Sultanahmet)

Çemberlitaş Hamamı (Map p1156; 0212-522 7974; Vezir Han Caddesi 8; bath, scrub & soap massage €29; 6am-midnight; Çemberlitaş)

GETTING INTO İSTANBUL FROM THE AIRPORTS

Havataş (Havaş) Airport Bus Travels between the airports and Cumhuriyet Caddesi, just off Taksim Sq. Buses leave Atatürk (TL10, one hour) every 30 minutes between 4am and 1am; and Sabiha Gökçen (TL12, 1½ hours) between 5am and midnight, thereafter 30 minutes after flight arrivals.

Metro From Atatürk to Zeytinburnu, where you can connect with the tram to Sultanahmet (total TL4, one hour).

Shuttle Many hotels will provide a free pick-up service from Atatürk airport if you stay with them for three nights or more.

Taxi From Atatürk/Sabıha Gökçen to Sultanahmet costs around TL40/120.

to and from airport) and Kabataş via Aksaray, Sultanahmet, Eminönü and Karaköy (roughly every five minutes, 6am to midnight).

A quaint antique tram rattles up and down İstiklal Caddesi between Tünel funicular station and Taksim Sq.

AEGEAN COAST

Turkey's Aegean coast can convincingly claim more ancient ruins per square kilometre than any other region in the world. Since time immemorial, conquerors, traders and travellers have beaten a path to the mighty monuments, and few leave disappointed.

Gallipoli (Gelibolu) Peninsula

Antipodeans and many Brits won't need an introduction to Gallipoli; it's the backbone of the 'Anzac legend', in which an Allied campaign in 1915 to knock Turkey out of WWI and open a relief route to Russia turned into one of the war's greatest fiascos. Some 130,000 men died, roughly a third from Allied forces and the rest Turkish.

Today the Gallipoli battlefields are peaceful places, covered in brush and pine forests. But the battles fought here nearly a century ago are still alive in many memories, both Turkish and foreign, especially Australians and New Zealanders, who view the peninsula as a place of pilgrimage. The Turkish officer responsible for the defence of Gallipoli was Mustafa Kemal (the future Atatürk); his victory is commemorated in Turkey on 18 March. On **Anzac Day** (25 April), a dawn service marks the anniversary of the Allied landings.

The easiest way to see the battlefields is with your own transport or an afternoon minibus tour from nearby Eceabat/Çanakkale (typically TL60/90) with **Crowded House Tours** (☎0286-814 1565; www.crowdedhousegallipoli.com; Eceabat) or **Hassle Free Travel Agency** (☎0286-213 5969; www.anzachouse.com; Çanakkale). Crowded House also offers one- and two-day packages starting in İstanbul. With a tour you get the benefit of a guide who can explain the battles as you go along.

If you're not pressed for time and you don't mind walking, you can catch a *dolmuş* (minibus, TL2.50) or taxi from Eceabat, on the Thracian (European) side of the strait, to the **Kabatepe Information Centre & Museum**, 750m from the bottom of the road up to the main battlefields.

Eceabat has accommodation and restaurants. **Hotel Crowded House** (☎0286-814 1565; www.crowdedhousegallipoli.com; Hüseyin Avni Sokak 4; dm/s/d TL20/50/65; ❄@) is a gem of a backpackers with comfortable, spick-and-span rooms and dorms, plus a beer garden.

Hourly car ferries cross the strait between Eceabat and Çanakkale (from TL2, 25 minutes), and hourly buses run to and from İstanbul (TL40, five hours).

Çanakkale

☎0286 / POP 104,300

This sprawling harbour town would be worth a visit for its sights, nightlife and overall vibe even if it didn't lie across the Dardanelles from the Gallipoli Peninsula. Inland from the sweeping waterfront promenade is an old Ottoman quarter.

A good base for visiting both Gallipoli and Troy, Çanakkale is a popular destination for weekending Turks; during summer, try to visit midweek. The **tourist office** (☎217 1187; Cumhuriyet Meydanı; ⌚8.30am-5.30pm) is 150m from the ferry pier.

A park in the military zone at the southern end of the quay houses the **Military Museum** (☎213 1730; Çimenlik Sokak; admission TL4; ⌚9am-5pm Tue, Wed & Fri-Sun; P), along side an **Ottoman castle** and a replica of the **Nusrat minelayer**, which sank or crippled three Allied ships in the WWI Gallipoli sea campaign.

Sleeping & Eating

If you intend to be in town around 25 April (Anzac Day), book well in advance and check prices carefully.

Licensed restaurants line the waterfront, where stalls also offer corn on the cob, mussels and other simple items. Head to Fetvane and buzzing, pedestrianised Matbaa Sokaks for bars.

Anzac House Hostel HOSTEL €
(213 5969; www.anzachouse.com; Cumhuriyet Meydanı 59; dm/s/d without bathroom & excl breakfast TL20/30/45; @) The base of **Hassle Free Travel Agency** (213 5969; www.anzachouse.com; Cumhuriyet Meydanı 61) is Çanakkale's only genuine backpackers. It's a little drab and cramped in places, but the bright colours and friendly staff are some compensation.

Hotel Grand Anzac HOTEL €€
(216 0016; www.grandanzachotel.com; Kemalyeri Sokak 11; s/d from TL80/100) Strongly recommended by readers, the Grand Anzac is great value for money. The rooms feel slightly prefab (and noisy as a result) but are bright and spacious, and include small desks and TVs. Service and location are both excellent.

Anafartalar Kebap KEBAP €€
(214 9112; İskele Meydanı; mains TL10; 8am-11.30pm) The best place for an *İskender* kebap (doner kebab – compressed meat, usually lamb, cooked on a skewer over hot coals, then thinly sliced – on fresh pide, with tomato sauce, browned butter and yoghurt) and other sloppy meat genius.

Cafe du Port RESTAURANT €€
(217 2908; Yalı Caddesi 12; 8am-11pm) The chefs at this popular restaurant at the Hotel Limani are the most versatile in Çanakkale and the service is brilliant for a regional city. Specialities include steaks, salads, pastas and superb cocktails.

Getting There & Away

BUS Buses go to Bandırma (TL20, 2½ hours, hourly), İstanbul (TL35, six hours, frequent) and İzmir (TL35, 5½ hours, hourly).

FERRY There are car ferries to Eceabat (from TL3, 15 minutes, several daily).

Bergama (Pergamum)

0232 / POP 60,600

This workaday market town has become a stop on the tourist trail because of its proximity to the remarkable ruins of Pergamum, site of ancient Rome's pre-eminent medical centre. During Pergamum's heyday (between Alexander the Great and the Roman domination of Asia Minor) it was one of the Middle East's richest and most powerful small kingdoms.

The **Acropolis** (Akropol; admission TL20), a windswept hilltop site 5km from the Red Basilica (linked by a cable car), is impressive even by Turkey's standards, with its commanding location and spectacular sloping amphitheatre. The **Asclepion** (Temple of Asclepios; admission/parking TL15/3), 3km uphill from the centre, was a famous medical centre. Galen's work here in the 2nd century was the basis for Western medicine well into

WORTH A TRIP

TROY (TRUVA)

The remains of the great city of **Troy** (0286-283 0536; per person TL15; 8.30am-7pm May–mid-Sep, to 5pm mid-Sep–Apr) are by no means Turkey's most impressive ruins. You'll have to work hard to imagine the fateful day when the Greeks tricked the Trojans by hiding soldiers inside a wooden horse. Still, it's an important site for history buffs and fans of Homer's *Iliad* – and the wooden horse is fun. A new national archaeological and history museum is set to open here by 2015.

The site is rather confusing for nonexpert eyes; visiting on a guided tour is recommended. The travel agencies offering Gallipoli tours also offer morning trips to Troy (around TL60 per person).

It's possible to visit in a day from Çanakkale by *dolmuş* (minibus; TL4, 35 minutes, from 9.30am). Services leave on the half-hour (less frequently at weekends) from a station at the northern end of the bridge over the Sarı River.

the 16th century. The **Red Basilica** (Kınık Caddesi; admission TL5) is the imposing remains of a 2nd-century temple to the Egyptian gods Serapis, Isis and Harpocrates.

Odyssey Guesthouse (☎631 3501; www.odysseyguesthouse.com; Abacıhan Sokak 13; s/d from TL45/50, without bathroom from TL35/45) has superb views of the Red Basilica from its upstairs terrace, plus some basic doubles with excellent showers, and a small kitchenette for self-caterers.

The basic **tourist office** (☎631 2851; İzmir Caddesi 54; ⊙8.30am-noon & 1-5.30pm) is just north of the Archaeology Museum on the elongated main street.

Buses run to and from İstanbul (via Bursa, TL50, 11 hours, nightly with additional morning services in high season) and İzmir (TL10, two hours, every 45 minutes).

İzmir

☎0232 / POP 2.8 MILLION

Nowhere else in the north Aegean prepares you for the sheer size, sprawl and intensity of Turkey's third-largest city, but you will soon fall for shopping in Kemeraltı Bazaar, the Alsancak district's studenty nightlife and catching ferries along the *kordon* (seafront). The wide, pleasant seafront esplanade is one of İzmir's main attractions, providing plenty of eating, drinking and sunset-watching opportunities.

Inland, the ruins of the 2nd-century Roman **agora** (Agora Caddesi; admission TL8; ⊙8.30am-7pm, to 5.30pm Sat; Ⓟ) are just southeast of the chaotic, atmospheric **bazaar** (⊙8am-5pm). The wide plaza **Konak Meydanı** is İzmir's centrepiece, with a late Ottoman **clock tower** (Saat Kulesi; Konak Meydanı) in ornate Orientalist style.

Sleeping & Eating

There are plenty of budget and midrange hotels around Kemeraltı Bazaar and Basmane train station. West of the station, 1368 Sokak is good for budget hotels.

For fresh fruit and veg, freshly baked bread and delicious savoury pastries, head for the canopied market just off Anafartalar Caddesi. On and around Kıbrıs Şehitleri Caddesi in Alsancak, you'll lose the *kordon*'s sunset views but gain on atmosphere; in particular try 1453 Sokak.

Konak Saray Hotel BOUTIQUE HOTEL €€
(☎483 7755; www.konaksarayhotel.com; Anafartalar Caddesi 635; s/d TL70/120; ⊜❄@) Set in a beautifully restored old Ottoman house, located in a less touristy part of the bazaar.

Güzel İzmir Oteli HOTEL €
(☎483 5069; www.guzelizmirhotel.com; 1368 Sokak 8; s/d TL40/70) Rooms are nothing special, but it's friendly, safe and convenient for buses and trains.

Sakız MODERN TURKISH €€
(☎484 1103; Şehıt Nevresbey Bulvarı 9a; mains TL12-25; ⊙noon-2pm & 7.30-10pm Mon-Sat) With a wooden terrace, Sakız serves fresh meze and unusual mains, including sardines, octopus, and sea bass with asparagus.

Information

Banks, ATMS, internet cafes and wi-fi networks are found throughout the centre.

Tourist Office (☎483 5117; 1344 Sokak 2)

Getting There & Away

Bus

The bus companies' ticket offices mostly cluster on Dokuz Eylül Meydanı. They usually provide a shuttle bus to İzmir's mammoth *otogar*, 6.5km from the centre. Frequent buses serve destinations including Bodrum (TL25, 3¼ hours), Kuşadası (TL15, 1¼ hours) and Selçuk (TL9, one hour).

Train

Most intercity services arrive at Basmane station, although Alsancak is being vamped up. Destinations include the following:

Ankara (TL27, 15 hours, two every afternoon)

Bandırma (TL18, six hours, every afternoon) Apart from on Tuesday, an additional morning train coordinates with the ferry to and from İstanbul.

Selçuk (TL4.75, 1½ hours, six daily)

Getting Around

The pleasantest way to get around is by ferry (TL3). Roughly half-hourly services link piers including Alsancak, Pasaport and Konak.

Selçuk

☎0232 / POP 28,200

The normal gateway to Ephesus, this provincial town has an impressive number of sights, including graceful Byzantine aqueduct ruins. The down-to-earth town acts more as a weigh station for the throngs of passers-through than a vibrant tourist hub.

Sights

Temple of Artemis RUIN
(Artemis Tapınağı; ⏲8.30am-5.30pm) At the western end of Selçuk, one enormous pillar remains of what was once the largest temple to Artemis, one of the Seven Wonders of the Ancient World.

Ephesus Museum MUSEUM
(☎892 6010; Uğur Mumcu Sevgi Yolu Caddesi; admission TL5; ⏲8.30am-6.30pm summer, to 4.30pm winter) Selçuk's main attraction, with a striking collection of artefacts including the effigy of Priapus, the Phallic God, and the multibreasted, egg-holding marble Artemis statue.

Basilica of St John RUIN
(St Jean Caddesi; admission TL5; ⏲8.30am-6.30pm summer, to 4.30pm winter) Emperor Justinian built this 6th-century basilica on the site where it was believed St John had been buried.

Ayasuluk Fortress CASTLE
(St Jean Caddesi; admission €8; ⏲8.30am-6.30pm summer, to 4.30pm winter) This partially restored Byzantine and Ottoman fortress is accessed via the Basilica of St John – and on the same ticket.

Sleeping & Eating

Selçuk specialises in good-value, family-run pensions offering attentive service, free extras, bus station pick-ups and so on (as well as some less-welcome pressure to buy carpets, tours etc).

Most pensions offer good meals at reasonable prices. The Saturday and Wednesday **markets** (respectively behind the bus and train stations) are great places to stock up for a picnic.

TOP CHOICE **Atilla's Getaway** HOSTEL €
(☎892 3847; www.atillasgetaway.com; Acarlar Köyü; s/d incl breakfast & dinner €24/40; ❄📶🏊) This friendly 'backpacker's resort', 2.5km south of town (linked to the *otogar* by free shuttles), has basic rooms and spacious dorms (no bunk beds) spread around a 'chill-out area'. Campers can use the lawn.

Wallabies Aquaduct Hotel HOTEL €
(☎892 3204; www.wallabiesaquaducthotel.com; Cengiz Topel Caddesi 2; s/d/tr from TL50/70/105; ❄📶) Clean, modern rooms, some overlooking the storks' nests atop the aqueduct ruins. There's a great buffet breakfast and groundfloor **restaurant** (mains TL10-16).

Selçuk Köftecisi KÖFTE €
(Şahabettin Dede Caddesi; mains TL6-9; ⏲breakfast, lunch & dinner) This classic *köfte* joint, family-run since 1959, offers great but small meat portions and tasty side salads.

Information

Tourist Office (www.selcuk.gov.tr; Agora Caddesi 35; ⏲8am-noon & 1-5pm daily summer, Mon-Fri winter)

Getting There & Away

Frequent *dolmuşes* run to Kuşadası (TL5, 30 minutes). There's a train to İzmir Adnan Menderes Airport (TL4.50, 55 minutes), which drops you a 20-minute stroll from the departures terminal. Bus services include İzmir (TL9, one hour, every 40 minutes in summer).

WORTH A TRIP

PAMUKKALE

East of Selçuk, Pamukkale's gleaming white **travertines** (admission TL30; ⏲daylight hours), calcite shelves with pools cascading down the plateau edge, are a World Heritage Site. Atop this fragile wonder, you can tour the magnificent ruins of the Roman city of **Hierapolis**, an ancient spa resort.

You can bathe amid sunken columns at Hierapolis' **Antique Pool** (admission TL25, public pool admission TL7.50; ⏲9am-7pm, public pool 9am-8pm) and visit the **Hierapolis Archaeology Museum** (admission TL3; ⏲9am-12.30pm & 1.30-7pm Tue-Sun).

One of several budget pensions in the village, the central **Artemis Yoruk Hotel** (☎0258-272 2073; www.artemisyorukhotel.com; Atatürk Caddesi; s/d from TL40/50; ❄@📶🏊) has simple rooms with balconies set around a palm-lined outdoor swimming pool.

Buses connect local hub Denizli with Selçuk (TL25, 4½ hours) and İzmir (TL25, 3¼ hours). Most people choose advance hotel booking to get a free lift from Denizli to Pamukkale (and often, back again). Frequent buses also connect the two spots (TL5, 40 minutes).

DON'T MISS

EPHESUS (EFES)

Even if you're not an architecture buff, you can't help but be dazzled by the sheer beauty of these **ruins** (☎0232-892 6010; admission/parking TL25/7.50; ⊙8am-6.30pm May-Oct, to 4.30pm Nov-Apr). Once the capital of the Roman province of Asia Minor, Ephesus is the most complete classical metropolis in Europe.

Wandering down the **Curetes Way**, the former main street, you'll see the well-preserved (or restored) remains of structures such as the **Temple of Hadrian**, **Terraced Houses** (where the rich folk lived) and the **Trajan Fountain**. The real photo ops, though, are at the **Great Theatre**, which could hold 25,000 people, and the monumental **Library of Celsus**, adorned with pillars and statues of the classical Virtues.

The mediocre audioguide is not recommended; nor are the 'guides' loitering at the entrances. Organise a guide in advance through a company such as the Selçuk-based **No-Frills Ephesus Tours** (☎0232-892 8838; www.nofrillsephesustours.com; Sen Jean Caddesi 3A; ⊙8am-8pm summer, 9am-5pm winter).

A taxi from Selçuk costs about TL20. *Dolmuşes* from Selçuk to Kuşadası frequently pass the Ephesus turn-off (TL4, five minutes), a 20-minute walk from the Lower Gate.

Kuşadası

☎0256 / POP 68,200

The fourth-busiest cruise port in the Mediterranean region, Kuşadası offers some decent, if oft-crowded, beaches and a heady nightlife.

Sights & Activities

The minor **stone fortress** on an island connected to the mainland by a causeway makes a pleasant stroll. There's also a tourist-orientated **bazaar**, two sizeable **water parks**, and PADI scuba-diving courses with **Aquaventure Diving Center** (☎612 7845; www.aquaventure.com.tr; Miracle Beach Club; ⊙8am-6pm).

Numerous operators offer boat trips and tours, including the day trip to the ancient cities of **Priene**, **Miletus** and **Didyma** (tour €50).

Sleeping & Eating

Kuşadası centre has pensions and business hotels, while package-tour resorts cover the outlying coasts.

Head inland for kebap shops. Kaleiçi, Kuşadası's old quarter, offers characterful backstreet eats and some fun, more Turkish cafes.

Raucous Barlar Sokak (Bar St) is chock-a-block with Irish-theme pubs. Locals prefer Kaleiçi's laid-back, old cafes.

Sezgin Hotel Guest House HOSTEL €
(☎614 4225; www.sezginhotel.com; Arslanlar Caddesi 68; s/d/tr/f €25/35/50/60; ❄@📶≋) Sezgin's clean rooms have big, comfortable beds and small balconies overlooking a garden and pool.

Hotel Stella PENSION €
(☎614 1632; www.hotelstellakusadasi.com; Bezirgan Sokak 44; s/d TL40/70; ❄@≋) On a hilly central street, this good budget fallback has tidy rooms offering sea-and-city views.

Köfteci Ali KÖFTE €
(Arslanlar Caddesi 14; mains TL5; ⊙24hr summer, 9am-midnight winter) The spicy wrapped pide kebap is nourishing at this Bar St kebap booth.

Getting There & Around

Dolmuşes leave from the central Adnan Menderes Bulvarı and the *otogar*, out on the bypass road. In summer, three daily buses go to Bodrum (TL25, 2½ hours); in winter, take a *dolmuş* to Söke (TL5). Frequent *dolmuşes* run to Selçuk (TL5, 30 minutes) via the Ephesus turn-off.

From April to October boats depart daily to Samos, Greece (one-way/same-day return €35/40).

Bodrum

☎0252 / POP 34,900

The beating heart of a holiday-happy peninsula, Bodrum is a famously posh paradise where sun-kissed travellers dance the breezy summer nights away. With laws restricting the height of its buildings, the town has a nice architectural uniformity: the idyllic whitewashed houses with their bright-blue trim call out to tourists' cam eras. Even when the clubs are bumpin' there's something rather refined about the town.

Sights & Activities

The conspicuous **Castle of St Peter** (☎316 2516; www.bodrum-museum.com; admission TL10; ⏰9am-noon & 1-7pm Tue-Sun summer, 8am-noon & 1-5pm winter), built in the 15th century by the Knights Hospitaller, houses attractions including the **Museum of Underwater Archaeology** (☎316 2516; admission €5.55; ⏰9am-7pm Tue-Sun summer), displaying treasures amassed during renovation of the castle.

Boats moored on Neyzen Tevfik Caddesi (Western Bay) run day trips (around TL24) to nearby spots including **Karaada** (Black Island), where hot springs gush out of a cave and produce supposedly curative orange mud.

Sleeping & Eating

With an efficient *dolmuş* shuttle system linking Bodrum to the rest of the peninsula, it's worth checking out accommodation on the other bays. Many hotels offer discounted rates for advance bookings, and places fill up fast in high summer. The marina-area hotels get the most night-time noise.

Head to the eastern bay for informal, soak-up-the-Efes fare and, not far inland, the **fruit and veg market** (Cevat Şakir Caddesi).

Anfora PENSION €
(☎316 5530; www.anforapansiyon.com; Omurça Dere Sokak 23; s/d from TL45/70; ❄📶) Rooms are well kept and clean (though can be cramped) at this friendly pension.

Hotel Güleç PENSION €
(☎316 5222; www.hotelgulec.com; Üçkuyular Caddesi 22; s/d from €30/50; ❄@) This good-value little pension has a central location, simple but bright and clean rooms, and a relaxing garden.

TOP CHOICE **Fish Market** SEAFOOD €€
(Cevat Şakir Caddesi; meze from TL4, fish TL20; ⏰dinner Mon-Sat) Choose between myriad fresh fish and seafood on ice at fishmongers' tables, and have them cooked (about TL6 extra) at any adjoining restaurant.

Döner Tepecik KEBAP €
(Neyzen Tevfik Caddesi; kebaps from TL6; ⏰breakfast, lunch & dinner) Across from the eponymous mosque, this local favourite does tasty kebaps on homemade bread.

Drinking & Entertainment

Foreign masses frequent the loud waterfront bars and clubs of **Bar St** (Dr Alim Bey Caddesi and Cumhuriyet Caddesi). More refined, **Marina Yacht Club** (☎316 1228; Neyzen Tevfik Caddesi 5; ⏰8am-late) is a big, breezy waterfront nightspot, where cover bands liven things up.

Nightclubs such as the floating **Marine Club Catamaran** (www.clubcatamaran.com; Dr Alim Bey Caddesi; admission weekday/weekend TL35/40; ⏰10pm-4am mid-May–Sep) are famous party spots. **Mavi Bar** (Cumhuriyet Caddesi 175; ⏰6pm-6am) hosts live music, as do the castle and **ancient theatre** (Kıbrıs Şehitler Caddesi); for upcoming events visit www.biletix.com.

Information

Head to Cevat Şakir Caddesi for the post office and ATMs.

Tourist Office (Kale Meydanı; ⏰8am-6pm Mon-Fri, daily in summer)

Getting There & Away

Boat

For tickets and the latest times, contact the **Bodrum Ferryboat Association** (☎316 0882; www.bodrumferryboat.com; Kale Caddesi Cümrük Alanı 22; ⏰8am-8pm).

Datça (one-way/return TL25/40, two hours) Daily ferries from mid-June to September, four weekly from April to mid-June and in October.

Kos (one-way or same-day return €32, one hour) Daily ferries.

Rhodes (one-way or same-day return €60, 2¼ hours) From June to September, two weekly hydrofoils.

Bus

The numerous services to and from Bodrum's *otogar* include İstanbul (TL68, 12 hours, 10 nightly), Kuşadası (TL20, 2½ hours, four each afternoon) and Marmaris (TL15, three hours, hourly).

Marmaris

☎0252 / POP 31,400

A popular resort town with a nonstop party atmosphere and good nearby beaches, in-your-face Marmaris is Mediterranean Turkey's version of Spain's Costa del Sol. Bar St offers unparalleled decadence and tour-boat touts will happily whisk you across the surrounding waves.

Sights & Activities

The small **castle** (Marmaris Kalesi ve Müzesi; 412 1459; admission TL3; 8am-noon & 1-5pm Tue-Sun) houses an archaeology museum and offers lovely views.

Between May and October, '*dolmuş* boats' offer day tours of **Marmaris Bay**, its islands and beaches (about TL30 to TL35 per person). Water taxis docked around the Atatürk statue serve the beaches at İçmeler and Turunç hourly (TL13, 45 minutes).

With a group of friends you can charter a yacht for a 'blue voyage', lasting a day or longer. Before signing up, confirm all details (exact boat, itinerary, lunch etc).

Several harbourside companies along Yeni Kordon Caddesi offer **scuba-diving** excursions and courses (April through October).

Not far south, the deeply indented **Datça** and **Bozburun Peninsulas** hide azure bays backed by pine-covered mountains and gorgeous fishing villages. Reach them by *dolmuş*, boat or scooter (rentals average TL45 per day in high season).

Sleeping & Eating

Marmaris is geared towards all-in package tour groups, so good independent sleeping options are rare.

Hedonistic crowds descend on **Bar St** (39 Sokak) for foam parties, laser beams, dance music and tequilas by the half-dozen.

Maltepe Pansiyon PENSION €
(412 1629; www.maltepepansiyon.com; 66 Sokak 9; s/d/tr/q TL35/75/90/120;) A small pension in a shady garden, with small but spotless rooms (most with en suites). You can use the kitchen.

Bariş Motel & Pansiyon PENSION €
(413 0652; www.barismotel.com; 66 Sokak 10; s/d TL50/70;) This friendly little pension has spartan but clean rooms. Breakfast costs TL6.

Ney TURKISH €€
(412 0217; 26 Sokak 24; meze TL5-6, mains TL15-20) Atmospheric little Ney serves home-cooked specialties in a 250-year-old Greek house.

Meryemana TURKISH €
(412 7855; 35 Sokak 5b; mains TL5-6;) Meryemana's nourishing traditional tastes include *mantı* (Turkish ravioli), meze, spicy dips and homemade bread.

Information

Tourist Office (412 1035; İskele Meydanı 2; 8am-noon & 1-5pm Mon-Fri, daily Jun–mid-Sep) Below the castle; unhelpful.

Getting There & Away

BOAT Rhodes (one-way/same-day return from €45/55, 50 minutes) catamarans sail twice daily from April to October. In low season, cargo boats go two to three times weekly. Buy tickets from Marmaris agencies at least one day in advance.

BUS The *otogar* is 3km north of the centre, served by *dolmuşes*. Services include Bodrum (TL15, three hours, at least every two hours), Fethiye (TL20, three hours, half-hourly) and İzmir (TL32, 4¼ hours, hourly).

MEDITERRANEAN COAST

Turkey's western Mediterranean coastline, known as the Turquoise Coast, is a region of endless, azure sea lined with sandy beaches and backed by mountains rising up to almost 3000m. Add to that ancient ruins strewn through the aromatic scrub and pine forests, and a broad menu of sports and activities. The most dramatic way to see this stretch of coastline is aboard a *gület* (traditional wooden yacht) or on a section of the 500km-long Lycian Way footpath.

Fethiye

0252 / POP 81,500

In 1958 an earthquake levelled the harbour city of Fethiye, sparing only the ancient remains of Telmessos. Today, Fethiye is once again a prosperous hub of the western Mediterranean. Its natural harbour, tucked away in the southern reaches of a broad bay scattered with pretty islands, is perhaps the region's finest.

Sights & Activities

Dolmuşes run southeast to the **Lycian ruins** dotting the countryside, including Tlos, Pınara, Letoön and Xanthos, and the beautiful **Saklıkent Gorge**.

Fethiye offers numerous water-based activities and boat trips, including the **12-Island tour** (TL30 to TL50 per person) and the **Butterfly Valley tour** (TL25) via Ölüdeniz. On dry land, the **Dalyan tour** (TL50) includes Lake Köyceğiz, the Sultaniye mud baths, Kaunos ruins and İztuzu Beach; and the **Saklıkent Gorge tour** (TL45) includes Tlos and a trout lunch.

BLUE CRUISE

Fethiye is the hub of Turkey's cruising scene, and the most popular route is the 'Blue Voyage' *(Mavi Yolculuk)* to Olympos: a four-day, three-night journey on a *gület* (traditional wooden yacht) that attracts young party animals. Boats usually call in at Ölüdeniz and Butterfly Valley and stop at Kaş, Kalkan and/or Kekova, with the final night at Gökkaya Bay opposite the eastern end of Kekova. A less common (but some say prettier) route is between Marmaris and Fethiye.

Depending on the season, the price is typically €165 to €195 per person (food should be included, but you sometimes have to pay for water and soft drinks). Make sure you shop around; many shoddy operators work the waters and wallets. Recommended operators include **Before Lunch Cruises** (☎0535 636 0076, 0532 623 4359; www.beforelunch.com), **Ocean Yachting Travel Agency** (☎0252-612 4807; www.oceantravelagency.com; İskele Meydanı 1, Fethiye; ⏱9am-9pm Apr-Oct), **Olympos Yachting** (☎0252-892 1145; www.olymposyachting.com) and **V-Go Yachting & Travel Agency** (☎0252-612 2113; www.bluecruisesturkey.com).

Seven Capes (☎0537 403 3779; www.sevencapes.com) offers sea kayaking; **European Diving Centre** (☎614 9771; www.europeandivingcentre.com; Fevzi Çakmak Caddesi 133) runs diving trips and courses; and **Ocean Yachting Travel Agency** (☎0252-612 4807; www.oceantravelagency.com; İskele Meydanı 1; ⏱9am-9pm Apr-Oct) organises activities from rafting to horse riding.

Telmessos RUINS

The **Tomb of Amyntas** (admission TL8; ⏱8am-7pm May-Oct, to 5pm Nov-Apr), dating from 350 BC, an Ionic temple facade, is one of several rock tombs carved into the cliffs. You'll also see a Roman **theatre** and curious **Lycian stone sarcophagi**.

On the hillside south of town is the ruined tower of a 15th-century **Crusader fortress**. **Fethiye Museum** (www.lycianturkey.com/fethiye-museum.htm; 505 Sokak; admission TL3; ⏱8am-5pm) has small statues and votive stones from Telmessos and other Lycian sites.

Kayaköy HISTORIC AREA

(admission TL5; ⏱8.30am-5pm) *Dolmuşes* (TL4) run to this nearby open-air museum, an evocative Ottoman Greek 'ghost town' abandoned during the population exchange of 1923.

Lycian Way WALK

Acclaimed as one of the top 10 long-distance walks in the world, the Lycian Way follows signposted paths around the Teke peninsula to Antalya. The route leads through pine and cedar forests in the shadow of mountains rising almost 3000m, past villages, stunning coastal views and an embarrassment of ruins at ancient Lycian cities. Walk it in sections (unless you have plenty of time and stamina).

Fethiye is at the western end of this 500km walking trail, which leads south from here to Faralya and Butterfly Valley.

Ölüdeniz WATER SPORTS

A little further south from Kayaköy, Ölüdeniz has a sheltered lagoon and a long spit of sandy beach, although its charms attract the package holiday hordes. Popular activities include paragliding and parasailing.

Butterfly Valley BOAT TOUR

(per person one-way/return TL20/25) Shuttle boats from Ölüdeniz access this paradise-found, with a fine beach and some lovely walks through a lush gorge. Its name comes from the unique resident Jersey tiger butterfly.

Sleeping & Eating

Most accommodation is up the hill behind the marina in Karagözler or further west. Many pensions organise transport from the *otogar*.

Fethiye's enormous canalside Tuesday **market** takes place between Atatürk Caddesi and Pürşabey Caddesi next to the stadium.

Nightspots are mostly on Hamam Sokak in the Old Town, and along Dispanser Caddesi south of the Martyrs' Monument.

Yildirim Guest House PENSION, HOSTEL €

(☎0543 779 4732, 614 4627; www.yildirimguesthouse.com; Fevzi Çakmak Caddesi 21; dm TL25, d/tr TL80/120; ❄@☎) Shipshape Yildirim has four- to six-bed dorms and spotless rooms. Excursions, pick-ups, laundry, evening meals and free bikes are offered.

Ferah Pension PENSION, HOSTEL €
(☎0532 265 0772, 614 2816; www.ferahpension.com; Orta yol 23; dm €15, d €20-25, €35-38;) Ferah has a leafy and covered lobby terrace; paintings and 'sexy dinners' by owner Monica; sizeable, tidy rooms; and a five-bed dorm.

TOP CHOICE **Reis** SEAFOOD €€
(☎612 5368, 0532 472 5989; www.reisrestaurant.com; Hal ve Pazar Yeri 62; mains TL12-20; 10am-midnight) Reis charges TL5 per head for cooking fish purchased at the fishmongers in the central covered market opposite (per kilo TL18 to TL25), plus a sauce, green salad, garlic bread and fruit. It also does meze and meat dishes.

Paşa Kebab KEBAP €€
(☎614 9807; Çarşı Caddesi 42; meze TL4-5-7 pide TL6-10, kebaps TL11.50-22.50; 9am-1am) Try the Paşa Special, a gigantic (and delicious) concoction of beef, tomato and cheese. There's also pizza.

Information

Tourist Office (☎614 1527; İskele Meydanı; 8am-7pm Mon-Fri, 10am-5pm Sat & Sun May-Sep, 8am-noon & 1-5pm Mon-Fri Oct-Apr) Opposite the marina.

Getting There & Away

Boat

Rhodes (one way/same-day return €50/60, 1½ hours) Catamarans sail between late April and October.

Bus

From Fethiye's *otogar*, 2.5km east of the centre, regular services include the following:

Antalya (TL20, 3½ hours) The inland *(yayla)* road is quicker than the coastal *(sahil)* route (TL28, 6½ hours).

Kaş (TL13, two hours)

Olympos (TL35, 4¾ hours)

Dolmuş

From the stops near the mosque, minibuses run to local destinations including Ölüdeniz (TL5).

Patara

☎0242 / POP 950

With Turkey's longest uninterrupted **beach**, laid-back little Patara is a nesting ground for sea turtles and the perfect spot for some dedicated sun worship. Extensive **ruins** (admission TL5; 9am-7pm May-Oct, 8am-5pm Nov-Apr) include a 5000-seat theatre and the *bouleterion* (council chamber), ancient Patara's 'parliament' where it is believed the Lycian League met.

Nearby are two World Heritage Sites: **Letoön** (admission TL5; 8.30am-7pm May-Oct, 9am-5.30pm Nov-Apr), which has three temples with some fine mosaics; and impressive **Xanthos** (admission TL5; 9am-7pm May-Oct, 8am-5pm Nov-Apr), with a Roman theatre and Lycian pillar tombs.

Patara's amenities are in Gelemiş village, 2km south of the highway turn-off and 1.5km from the ruins. **Akay Pension** (☎843 5055, 0532 410 2195; www.pataraakaypension.com; s/d/tr TL45/60/80;) has well-maintained rooms with comfortable beds and balconies overlooking citrus groves.

Buses on the Fethiye–Kaş route drop you on the highway 4km from the village. From here *dolmuşes* run to the village every 30 to 40 minutes. In season minibuses run from the beach through the village to local destinations.

Kaş

☎0242 / POP 7200

Kaş ('cash') may not sport the region's finest beaches, but this yachties' haven has a wonderfully mellow atmosphere. The surrounding areas are ideal for day trips by sea or scooter, and a plethora of adventure sports are on offer, including some excellent wreck diving.

The **tourist office** (☎836 1238; Cumhuriyet Meydanı; 8am-5pm daily May-Oct, 8am-noon & 1-5pm Mon-Fri Nov-Apr) is on the main square.

Sights & Activities

Apart from enjoying the small pebbl **beaches**, you can walk 500m west of th main square to the well-preserved **Hellenistic theatre**. Lycian **rock tombs** are cu into the cliffs above town, and it's well wort climbing the hilly street to the east of th main square to reach the **King's Tomb**, a Ly cian sarcophagus.

Overland excursions and *dolmuşes* go t **Saklıkent Gorge**. The most popular **boa trip** (TL40 to TL50) is to **Kekova Islan** and **Üçağız**, passing submerged Lycia ruins. Other activities, organised by local o erators such as **Bougainville Travel** (☎8 3737; www.bougainville-turkey.com; İbrahim Se Sokak 10), include scubadiving, paraglidir mountain biking, canyoning, hiking and s kayaking. The latter is an excellent way to see the sunken ruins alongside Kekova.

Sleeping

Most accommodation is west and northwest of the centre along the waterfront and up the hill around the Yeni Cami (New Mosque).

Anı Pension & Guesthouse PENSION € (☎836 1791, 0533 326 4201; www.motelani.com; Süleyman Çavuş Caddesi 12; s TL30-50, d TL50-60; ❄@🛜) Smallish but spotless rooms with balconies, plus a relaxing roof terrace with DVD player, lounge with cushions and water pipes and a bar.

Santosa Pansion PENSION € (☎836 1714, 0535 846 3584; www.santosapension.com; Recep Bilgin Sokak 4; s TL50-60, d TL60-90; ❄@) This clean, quiet and good-value backpacker hang-out has simple but attractive rooms.

Eating & Drinking

There are some excellent restaurants southeast of the main square, especially around Sandıkçı Sokak. A Friday **market** takes place on the old Kalkan road. In the old part of Kaş, atmospheric **Şaraphane** (☎0532 520 0202, 836 2715; Yeni Cami Caddesi 3 ; mains TL12-25) offers cosy surrounds, an open kitchen and nice touches such as complimentary homemade meze.

Drinking holes include **Giorgio's Bar** (☎0544 608 8687; Cumhuriyet Meydanı), facing the main square, with live music several times a week, and **Hideaway Bar & Cafe** (☎836 3369; Cumhuriyet Meydanı 16/A; beer TL6-8; ⏲4pm-3am), hidden in a garden accessed via a secret doorway.

Getting There & Away

There are regular *dolmuşes* to Antalya (TL23, 3½ hours), Fethiye (TL15; 2½ hours), Olympos (TL18, 2½ hours) and Patara (TL7.50, 45 minutes).

Olympos & Çıralı

☎0242

Long beloved of hippies, ancient **Olympos** (admission TL3; ⏲9am-7.30pm May-Oct, 8am-5pm Nov-Apr) was once an important Lycian city; now it's a fantastically wild place where ruins appear 'undiscovered' among the vines and flower trees. The deep, shady valley containing the ruins runs to the beach.

According to legend, the **Chimaera** (admission TL4, torch/flashlight rental TL3), a cluster of natural flames on the slopes of Mt Olympos, was the hot breath of a monster. At night the 20 or 30 main flames are visible at sea. To find the Chimaera, 7km from Olympos, follow the hillside signs from Çıralı (pensions and agencies offer lifts/tours for TL5/15).

Sleeping & Eating

Olympos's 'tree house' camps, which line the track along the valley down to the ruins, have long been the stuff of travel legend. Most include both breakfast and dinner in the price. Be extra attentive to personal hygiene and food while staying here; every year some travellers get ill. The huge influx of summer visitors can overwhelm the camps' capacity for proper waste disposal.

Two good options are **Şaban Pansion** (☎892 1265, 0532 457 3439; www.sabanpansion.com; tree house TL35-40, bungalow with bathroom TL45-50; ❄@), which sells itself on tranquillity, space and great home cooking rather than party credentials, and **Kadır's Tree House** (☎892 1250, 0532 347 7242; www.kadirstreehouses.com; bungalow with bathroom TL40-65; ❄@), resembling a Wild West boom town, with a lively bar and activities centre.

An excellent alternative, Çıralı is a delightful beach haven that appeals to nature lovers and families. The midrange and top-end options here include **Hotel Canada** (☎0532 431 3414, 825 7233; www.canadahotel.net; d €55-60, 4-person bungalow €85-90; ❄@🛜🏊), a Canadian-Turkish operation offering warmth, friendliness, homemade honey and a garden filled with hammocks.

Getting There & Away

Buses and minibuses plying the Fethiye–Antalya coast road will stop near the Olympos and Çıralı junctions. From there, minibuses (TL5) serve Olympos (9km) and Çıralı (7km). Many accommodation options will pick you up from the highway (TL20 to TL25) if you book in advance.

The most pleasant way to travel between Olympos and Fethiye is on a cruise (p1171).

Antalya

☎0242 / POP 964,000

The gateway to the 'Turkish Riviera', Antalya is generating a buzz among culture vultures. Situated directly on the Gulf of Antalya

(Antalya Körfezi), the largest city on Turkey's Mediterranean coast is both stylishly modern and classically beautiful. It boasts the wonderfully preserved Roman-Ottoman quarter of Kaleiçi, a splendid Roman harbour and superb ruins in the surrounding Beydağları (Bey Mountains).

Sights & Activities

Kaleiçi HISTORIC AREA

Heading downhill from the old stone clock tower in the main square, called **Kale Kapısı** (Fortress Gate), you'll pass Antalya's symbol, the **Yivli Minare**. The fluted 13th-century Seljuk minaret stands above a restored whirling-dervish monastery and a 14th-century mosque.

The monumental **Hadriyanüs Kapısı** (Hadrian's Gate) was erected for the Roman emperor's visit to Antalya (130 BC).

The **Suna & İnan Kıraç Kaleiçi Museum** (243 4274; www.kaleicimuzesi.org; Kocatepe Sokak 25; admission TL2; 9am-noon & 1-6pm Thu-Tue) is an ethnography museum in a restored Ottoman mansion and Greek Orthodox church.

The **Kesik Minare** (Truncated Minaret) is a stump of a tower on the site of a ruined Roman temple.

Karaalioğlu Parkı (Atatürk Caddesi) is a flower-filled cliffside park with stunning views over the **Roman harbour**, now a modern marina offering **boat trips** (TL20 to TL80).

Antalya Museum MUSEUM

(236 5688; www.antalya-ws.com/english/museum; Konyaaltı Caddesi 1; admission TL15; 9am-7pm Tue-Sun mid-Apr–Oct, 8am-5pm Tue-Sun Nov–mid-Apr) About 2km west of the centre and accessible on the tram, Antalya's comprehensive city museum houses spectacular finds from Lycian and Pamphylian cities, and statues of Olympian gods, most found at nearby Perge.

Sleeping & Eating

The best place to stay is Kaleiçi, where signs point the way to some excellent pensions.

Many cafes and eateries are found around the harbour area. For cheap eating, walk east to the **Dönerciler Çarşısı** (Market of Döner Makers; Atatürk Caddesi), or north to the rooftop kebap places around Kale Kapısı.

Kaleiçi offers buzzy beer gardens with million-dollar views, live-music venues, raunchy clubs and everything in between.

TOP CHOICE **White Garden Pansiyon** PENSION €

(241 9115; www.whitegardenpansion.com; Hesapçı Geçidi 9; s/d TL40/60, 4-person apt TL120;) Offers tidiness, class beyond its price level, and impeccable service, in a charmingly restored building.

Sabah Pansiyon PENSION €

(247 5345, 0555 365 8376; www.sabahpansiyon.com; Hesapçı Sokak 60; dm TL25, s/d without shower TL35/45, s/d with shower TL40/55, 2-bedroom apt TL200;) Great for families, but rooms vary greatly, so ask to see a couple. Run by the Sabah brothers and Mama, who takes care of the kitchen.

Can Can Pide ve Kebap Salonu KEBAP €

(243 2548; Arık Caddesi 4/A; pide & dürüm TL8; 7am-midnight Mon-Sat) *Çorba* (soup), pide, Adana *dürüm* (beef kebap rolled in pitta) and *mantı* at bargain prices.

Information

Tourist Office (241 1747; Cumhuriyet Meydanı; 8am-6pm May-Oct, 8.30am-5.30pm Nov-Mar)

Getting There & Away

From Kaleiçi, board the AntRay tram at the İsmet Paşa stop and travel for 20 minutes (TL1.50) to reach the *otogar*, 4km north of the centre. Regular buses serve destinations including Göreme/Ürgüp (TL40, nine hours), Kaş (TL20, 3½ hours), Konya (TL38, five hours) and Olympos/Çıralı (TL13, 1½ hours).

CENTRAL ANATOLIA

On central Turkey's hazy plains, the sense of history is pervasive. This is, after all, the region where the whirling dervishes first swirled, Atatürk began his revolution, Alexander the Great cut the Gordion Knot, and Julius Caesar uttered his famous line, '*Veni, vidi, vici*' ('I came, I saw, I conquered').

Ankara

0312 / POP 4.5 MILLION

İstanbullus may quip that the best view in Ankara is the train home, but the Turkish capital has more substance than its reputation as a staid administrative centre suggests. The capital established by Atatürk boasts two of the country's most important sights, and a few neighbourhoods with some charm, notably the hilltop *hisar* (citadel and Kızılay, one of Turkey's hippest urban quarters.

Sights

TOP CHOICE Museum of Anatolian Civilisations MUSEUM
(Anadolu Medeniyetleri Müzesi; ☎324 3160; Gözcü Sokak 2, Ulus; admission TL15; ⏰8.30am-7pm Apr-Oct, 8.30am-5pm Nov-Mar; Ⓜ Ulus) Displaying artefacts cherry-picked from just about every significant archaeological site in Anatolia, the museum is the perfect introduction to the complex weave of Turkey's ancient past. While you're here, explore the side streets inside the nearby thick Byzantine walls of the **citadel**.

FREE Anıt Kabir MONUMENT
(Atatürk Mausoleum and Museum; Gençlik Caddesi; audioguide TL5 ; ⏰9am-5pm May-Oct, to 4pm Nov-Apr; Ⓜ Tandoğan) Pay your respects to the founder of modern Turkey and observe the Turks' enduring reverence for Atatürk at his monumental hilltop mausoleum, 2km west of Kızılay.

FREE Vakıf Eserleri Müzesi MUSEUM
(Ankara Museum of Religious Foundation Works; Atatürk Bulvarı, Ulus; ⏰9am-5pm Tue-Su ; Ⓜ Ulus) This extensive collection of Turkish carpets once graced the floors of mosques throughout the country.

Ethnography Museum MUSEUM
(Etnografya Müzesi; Türkocağı Sokak, Samanpazarı; admission TL3; ⏰8.30am-12.30pm & 1.30-5.30pm; Ⓜ Ulus) The displays cover subjects from henna ceremonies to Anatolian jewellery.

The neighbouring **Painting & Sculpture Museum** (Resim ve Heykel Müzesi; Türkocağı Sokak, Samanpazarı; ⏰9am-noon & 1-5pm; Ⓜ Ulus) showcases the cream of Turkish artists.

Sleeping

The Ulus area is most convenient for the Museum of Anatolian Civilisations and citadel, but Kızılay is better for restaurants and nightlife.

Deeps Hostel HOSTEL €
(☎213 6338; www.deepshostelankara.com; Ataç Sokak 46; dm/s/d without bathroom €10/18/32; 📶; Ⓜ Kızılay) Friendly Deeps has colourful rooms, a spacious dorm, squeaky-clean shared bathrooms and a fully equipped kitchen (breakfast isn't included).

Otel Mithat HOTEL €
(☎311 5410; www.otelmithat.com.tr; Tavus Sokak 2; s/d/tr €25/40/50; ❄📶; Ⓜ Ulus) With groovy carpeting and sleek, neutral bed linen, rooms are fresh and modern. Unlike at most budget hotels in Ankara, the no-smoking policy is taken seriously.

Eating & Drinking

Most Ulus options are basic. The southern end of Anafartalar Caddesi is good for cheap and cheerful *kebapçis* (kebap eateries). **Ulus Hali food market** sells provisions from oversized chilli peppers to jars of honey. In and around the citadel, atmospheric restaurants such as **Zenger Paşa Konağı** (☎311 7070; www.zengerpasa.com; Doyran Sokak 13; mains TL12-17; Ⓜ Ulus) and **And Evi Cafe** (☎312 7978; İçkale Kapısı; mains TL12-24; Ⓜ Ulus) occupy old wood-and stone houses

WORTH A TRIP

SAFRANBOLU & AMASYA

Safranbolu and Amasya, respectively 145km north and 270km northeast of Ankara, beckon savvy travellers with their ethereal settings and historic atmosphere.

A World Heritage Site, **Safranbolu** boasts a wonderful old Ottoman quarter bristling with 19th-century half-timbered houses. Located on riverbanks beneath cliffs carved with Pontic tombs, **Amasya** also harbours enough picturesque Ottoman piles to satisfy the pickiest pasha.

Both towns have numerous delightful pensions set in restored Ottoman mansions. **Efe Backpackers Pension** (☎0370-725 2688; www.backpackerspension.com; Kayadibi Sokak 8; s/d/tr TL45/70/80; 📶) dishes up all of Safranbolu's Ottoman charm at a smidgen of the cost of other hotels; Amasya's family-run **Gönül Sefası** (☎0358-212 9461; Yalıboyu Sokak 24; s/d/tr TL60/100/120) has lots of local character.

There are buses from Ankara to Safranbolu (TL25, three hours) and Amasya (TL30, five hours), and from İstanbul.

It's all about street stalls, hip bistros and cafe culture in Kızılay, where terraces line virtually every inch of space south of Ziya Gökalp Caddesi. Kızılay's tall, thin buildings also pack in up to five floors of nightspots. **Le Man Kültür** (☎310 8617; Konur Sokak 8; mains TL6-16; ⓂKızılay) is good for a casual meal and a beer, and **Çomlek Ev Yemekleri** (Konur Sokak; set menu TL6; ⓂKızılay) serves hearty *güveç* (stews) and daily specials.

Information

There are many internet cafes in Ulus and Kızılay, and banks with ATMs across town.

Tourist Office (☎310 8789; Gazi Mustafa Kemal Bulvarı; ⏲9am-5pm Mon-Fri, 10am-5pm Sat) Also has branches (usually unmanned) at the *otogar* and train station.

Getting There & Around

TO/FROM THE AIRPORT The airport serves international and nationwide destinations. Half-hourly Havaş shuttle buses depart from Gate B at 19 May Stadium (TL10, 35 minutes). After 10pm buses leave according to flight departure times. Havaş also links the airport and *otogar*.

BUS Ankara's huge AŞTİ *otogar*, linked to Kızılay and Ulus by underground trains, has buses servicing every Turkish city or town of any size. Apart from over public holidays, you can often turn up and be on your way in less than an hour.

TRAIN A high-speed train serves Konya (economy/business class TL25/35, two hours, eight daily) and long-distance trains run overnight to İzmir and eastern Anatolia.

Konya

☎0332 / POP 1,073,791

Turkey's equivalent of the Bible Belt, conservative Konya has both historical significance as the home town of the whirling-dervish orders and a bastion of Seljuk culture, and modern importance as an economic boom town. The city's turquoise-domed Mevlâna Museum is one of Turkey's finest and most characteristic sights.

The centre stretches from Alaaddin Tepesi, the hill topped by the Seljuk **Alaaddin Camii**, along Mevlâna Caddesi to the Mevlâna Museum.

Sights

The centre is dotted with imposing Seljuk buildings, some containing museums. Highlights include the **Museum of Wooden Artefacts & Stone Carving** (Tas ve Ahsap Eserler Müzesi; ☎351 3204; Adliye Bulvarı; admission TL3; ⏲Tue-Sun 9am-5pm) and the **Tile Museum** (Karatay Medresesi Çini Müzesi; ☎351 1914; Alaaddin Meydanı; admission TL3; ⏲9am-5pm), both occupying 13th-century seminaries.

Semas (whirling-dervish ceremonies) take place on Saturday evenings throughout the year; contact the **tourist office** (☎353 4020; Aslanı Kışla Caddesi; ⏲8.30am-5.30pm Mon-Sat) for details.

TOP CHOICE Mevlâna Museum MUSEUM
(☎351 1215; admission TL3, audioguide TL5; ⏲9am-5pm Tue-Sun, 10am-5pm Mon) Join the pilgrims at this wonderful museum-come-shrine, where the turban-topped tombs of eminent dervishes include that of Mevlâna (Our Guide) himself: the great mystic philosopher Celaleddin Rumi (1207–73). The former lodge of the whirling dervishes, it is topped by a brilliant turquoise-tiled dome.

Sleeping & Eating

Restaurants around the Mevlâna Museum have great views, but their food is not recommended – with the exception of **Gülbahçesı Konya Mutfağı** (☎351 0768; Gülbahçe Sokak 3; mains TL8-18; ⏲8am-10pm).

Ulusan Otel HOTEL €
(☎351 5004; Çarşi PTT Arkasi 4; s/d without bathroom TL30/60; 📶) Ulusan has basic but bright and spotless rooms, private and (immaculately kept) shared bathrooms, a homely communal area, and an enthusiastic and graceful host.

Otel Mevlâna HOTEL €
(☎352 0029; Cengaver Sokak 2; s/d/tr TL50/70/90, s/d without bathroom TL20/30; 📶) Rooms have firm beds, unmatched furniture, TV and a fair amount of wear and tear. Across the road, the rooms without bathroom are bare-bones basic.

Şifa Lokantası KEBAP
(☎352 0519; Mevlâna Caddesi 29; mains TL6-14) Superfast and superfriendly, Şifa's pide is filling, fresh and tasty, and its kebaps are succulent and flavourful.

Getting There & Away

BUS From the *otogar*, 7km north of the centre and accessible by tram from Alaaddin Tepesi, regular buses serve all major destinations, including Ankara (TL18, 3½ hours), İstanbul (TL45, 11½ hours) and Kayseri (TL30, four hours).

TRAIN Eight high-speed trains run to and from Ankara daily (adult/child TL25/12.50, 1¾ hours).

CAPPADOCIA

Cappadocia's surreal fairy chimneys (rock formations) were formed, alongside the area's valleys of cascading white cliffs, when Erciyes Dağı (Mt Erciyes) erupted. The intervening millennia added to the remarkable Cappadocian canvas, with Byzantines carving out cave churches and subterranean complexes large enough to house thousands. You could spend days hiking through the canyons and admiring the fresco-covered rock-cut churches.

Göreme

☎0384 / POP 6350

Göreme is the archetypal travellers' utopia: a beatific village where the surreal surroundings spread a fat smile on everyone's face. Beneath the honeycomb cliffs, the locals live in fairy chimneys – or, increasingly, run hotels in them. Gazing at the wavy valleys in the distance, with their hiking trails, panoramic viewpoints and rock-cut churches, is best accompanied by meze on one of Göreme's panoramic terraces.

Services useful to travellers are mostly around the central *otogar*, including ATMs and a **tourist information booth** (☎271 2558; www.goreme.org).

Activities

Hiking HIKING

There are many hiking options around Göreme village. It's surrounded by a handful of gorgeous interconnected valleys that are easily explored on foot; allow about one to three hours for each.

Tours

Most tour companies offer full-day tours and guided day-hikes in the valleys around Göreme. Full-day tours typically go to two or three destinations such as **Ihlara Valley**, the underground cities at **Derinkuyu** and **Kaymaklı** (which are best visited with a guide), **Uçhisar Castle**, **Soğanlı's valleys** of rock-cut churches and an **Avanos pottery**. Most operators charge about TL90.

The following agencies are recommended. Do not book tours in Nevşehir, which has a reputation for unscrupulous operators.

Middle Earth Travel ADVENTURE TOUR
(☎271 2559; www.middleearthtravel.com; Cevizler Sokak 20) Adventure-travel specialist offering climbing and treks.

Mehmet Güngör WALKING
(☎0532 382 2069; www.walkingmehmet.com; Noriyon Cafe, Müze Caddesi; four hours/full day €60/80) Walking guide.

Yama Tours GUIDED TOUR
(☎271 2508; www.yamatours.com; Müze Caddesi 2) Also offers three-day trips to Nemrut Dağı (Mt Nemrut).

Dalton Brothers HORSE RIDING
(☎0532 275 6869; Müze Caddesi; 1/2hr TL45/90) Horse riding.

Sleeping

Between October and May, pack warm clothes as pensions may delay using the heating, and ring ahead to check your choice is open. You can camp at **Kaya Camping** (☎343 3100; Göreme Yolu; campsites per adult/child TL15/10; 📶🅿).

TOP CHOICE **Kelebek Hotel & Cave Pension** HOTEL €€
(☎271 2531; www.kelebekhotel.com; Yavuz Sokak 31; fairy chimney s/d €40/50, deluxe s/d €52/65, ste s €64-144, ste d €80-180; 📶🅿) Spread over two gorgeous stone houses with fairy chimneys protruding skyward, rooms exude Anatolian inspiration. One of Göreme's original

DON'T MISS

GÖREME OPEN-AIR MUSEUM

A World Heritage Site, **Göreme Open-Air Museum** (Göreme Açık Hava Müzesi; ☎271 2167; admission TL15, Karanlık Kilise admission TL8; ⏰8am-5pm) preserves a rock-hewn Byzantine monastic settlement. Frescos cover the 10th- to 13th-century cave churches – notably the stunning **Karanlık Kilise** (Dark Church), which is well worth the extra TL8. Across the road from the main entrance, the **Tokalı Kilise** (Buckle Church), with an underground chapel and fabulous frescos, is included in the museum entrance fee. The churches are tiny, so avoid weekends and arrive early in the morning, at midday or near closing to bypass tour groups.

WORTH A TRIP

IHLARA VALLEY

A beautiful canyon full of greenery and Byzantine rock-cut churches, **Ihlara Valley** (TL8, parking TL2; ⊙8am-6.30pm) is an excellent, if popular, spot for a walk. Footpaths follow the course of the river, which flows between Ihlara village and **Selime Monastery** (admission TL8 ; ⊙dawn-dusk).

The easiest way to see the valley is on a day tour (p1177), which allows a few hours for a one-way walk through the stretch of the gorge with the most churches. To get there by bus from Göreme, you must change in Nevşehir and Aksaray, making it a tricky day trip on public transport.

If you want to walk the whole valley – and it's definitely worth the effort – there are pensions in Ihlara village and Selime, and a pension and riverside campgrounds halfway along the valley in Belisırma. All close between December and March.

On weekdays six *dolmuşes* travel to and from Aksaray (TL4, 45 minutes), stopping in Selime, Belisırma and Ihlara village. At weekends there are fewer services.

boutique hotels, Kelebek (Butterfly) continues to innovate, offering complimentary village garden breakfast visits.

The Dorm Cave HOSTEL €
(☎271 2770; www.travellerscave.com; Hafız Abdullah Efendi Sokak 4; dm/d/tr €10/30/45; 📶) In this superb hostel, three spacious cave dorms share small, modern bathrooms across a pretty courtyard. The snug private rooms also offer brilliant value.

Travellers' Cave Pension PENSION €
(☎271 2707; www.travellerscave.com; Güngör Sokak 11; s/d/tr €25/40/50, deluxe d/tr €50/60; 📶) The friendly, efficient management can arrange all sorts of tours, and the superclean, comfortable rooms are set around a tree-shaded courtyard.

Köse Pension HOSTEL €
(☎271 2294; www.kosepension.com; Ragıp Üner Caddesi; dm/d/tr TL12.50/80/90, s without bathroom TL25; 📶🏊) Köse may have no cave character, but spotless rooms, with brilliant bathrooms, bright linens and comfortable beds, feature alongside excellent breakfast options (TL5 to TL6).

Eating

Nazar Börek TURKISH €
(☎271 2441; Müze Caddesi; gözleme & börek TL6-9; 📶) Serves supremely tasty traditional Turkish staples, including hearty plates of *gözleme* (savoury crêpes) and *börek* (filled pastries).

Fırın Express PIDECI €
(☎271 2266; Eski Belediye Yanı Sokak; pide TL4-8; ✎) This local haunt's cavernous wood oven produces the best pide in town.

Getting There & Away

Air

Accommodation can organise transfers to and from the two nearby airports.

Kayseri airport Turkish Airlines and Pegasus Airlines have several daily flights to and from İstanbul.

Nevşehır airport Turkish Airlines has two daily flights to and from İstanbul.

Bus

When you purchase your ticket to Cappadocia, make sure it clearly states your final destination (Göreme etc). There should be a *servis* from transport hub Nevşehır to the surrounding villages. If you get stuck, phone your accommodation for a pick-up or get the hourly bus, and do *not* book a tour in notorious Nevşehır. Daily services from Göreme include Ankara (TL30, 4½ hours), Antalya (TL45, nine hours), İstanbul (TL50, 12 hours) and Konya (TL20, three hours).

EASTERN TURKEY

Like a challenge? Eastern Anatolia – vast remote and culturally very Middle Eastern is the toughest part of Turkey to travel in but definitely the most exotic, and certainly the least affected by mass tourism. Winter in this mountainous region can be bitterly cold and snowy.

Particularly near Iraq, a few places and roads in southeastern Anatolia are sometimes off-limits due to fighting between the military and the PKK (Kurdistan Workers Party). The area is mostly safe and accessible, but expect a military presence and keep your passport handy for army checkpoints

Nemrut Dağı Milli Parkı

Two thousand years ago, a meglomaniac Commagene king erected his own memorial sanctuary on **Nemrut Dağı** (Mt Nemrut; 2150m), the centrepiece of today's stunning **national park** (admission TL8; ⌚dawn-dusk). The fallen heads of the gigantic decorative statues of gods and kings, toppled by earthquakes, form one of the country's most enduring images.

There are a few bases for visiting. To the northwest is **Malatya**, where the **Nemrut Dağı Information Booth** (☎0535 760 5080; kemalmalatya@hotmail.com; Atatürk Caddesi; ⌚8am-7pm May-Sep) organises daily minibus tours (TL100, early May to September/October, minimum two people), with a night at the Güneş Hotel below the summit and visits to the heads at sunset and sunrise.

The route from the south is more scenic. Accommodation and taxis in **Kahta** offer eight-hour sunrise and sunset 'long tours', as well as the less-interesting three-hour 'short tour'. The **Kommagene Hotel** (☎0416-725 9726, 0532 200 3856; www.kommagenehotel.com; Mustafa Kemal Caddesi 1; s/d TL45/70; ❄@📶) and **Zeus Hotel** (☎0416-725 5694; www.zeushotel.com.tr; Mustafa Kemal Caddesi; campsites per person TL20, s/d/ste €60/80/110; ❄📶🏊) offer tours.

From **Şanlıurfa** (Urfa), **Harran-Nemrut Tours** (☎0414-215 1575; www.aslankonukevi.com; Demokrasi Caddesi 12, Aslan Konak Evi; tours per person €50, minimum 2 people) runs tours, as do **Mustafa Çaycı** (☎0532 685 2942, 0414-313 1340; musma63@yahoo.com; Hotel Uğur, Köprübaşı Caddesi 3; tours per person TL130, minimum 2 people) and **Nomad Tours Turkey** (☎0533 747 1850; www.nomadtoursturkey.com; tours per person €100).

Taking a two-day tour from **Cappadocia** is a tedious drive. A three-day tour is a better option.

In high summer the most pleasant places to stay, especially if you have your own transport, are the campgrounds, village pensions and hotels on the southern slopes of the mountain. The pretty village of Karadut, 12km from the summit, has a few small eateries.

Van

☎0432 / POP 353,500

On the southeasternshore of vast Lake Van, the easygoing city of the same name boasts a hilltop **castle** (Rock of Van; admission TL3; ⌚9am-dusk) overlooking the foundations of **Eski Van** (the Old City), but the 10th-century **Armenian church** on Akdamar Island is the star attraction. Its biblical reliefs are masterworks of Armenian art. It's also worth visitng for its location, 3km out on Lake Van, a vast expanse of water ringed by snowcapped mountains. **Alkan Tours** (☎215 2092, 0530 349 2793; www.easternturkeytour.org; Ordu Caddesi) runs guided day trips (per person €20) to the island, also including photogenic, 17th-century **Hoşap Castle** and the Urartian site at **Çavuştepe**.

Budget accommodation is in short supply. **Cemil Hotel** (☎215 1520; PTT Caddesi; s/d TL25/30), opposite the Haci Osman Camii, is a simple pension with shared bathrooms, with numerous restaurants just metres away. About 200m away, you can try Van's famous *kahvaltı* (breakfast; about TL15), featuring local speciality *otlu peynir* (cheese mixed with a tangy herb), on **Kahvaltı Sokak** (pedestrianised Eski Sümerbank Sokak).

For Kars, the scenic route involves *dolmuşes* via Doğubayazıt and Iğdır, but catching the bus via Erzurum (TL60, 10 hours total) is easier.

Frequent buses go to Diyarbakır (TL40, seven hours), from where you can continue to Kahta (for Mt Nemrut National Park).

The twice-weekly *Vangölü Ekspresi* train from Ankara meets the ferry to Van in Tatvan.

Kars

☎0474 / POP 76,900

The medieval fortress and stately, pastel-coloured Russian buildings are well worth a look, but most people come to the setting of Orhan Pamuk's novel *Snow* to visit the dramatic ruins of **Ani** (admission TL8; ⌚8.30am-6pm May-Sep, to 3pm Oct-Apr), 45km east of the city. Formerly a Silk Road entrepôt and capital of the Armenian kingdom, Ani was deserted in 1239 after a Mongol invasion. The ghost city, with its lightning-cleaved **Church of the Redeemer**, now lies amid undulating grass overlooking the Armenian border. The site exudes an eerie ambience that is simply unforgettable.

Kars' **Güngören Otel** (☎212 6767; www.gungorenhotel.com; Millet Sokak; s/d/tr TL70/120/150; 📶) is a stalwart on the travelling circuit, offering smart, creamy rooms and a copious breakfast; **Miraç Otel** (☎212 3768; Cengiz Topel Caddesi 19; s/d/tr TL30/50/70; 📶) is basic but safe for both male and female travellers.

Metro has daily buses to locations including Amasya (TL60), Erzurum (TL15) and İstanbul (TL70). Turgutreis serves Van daily at 8.30am (TL50). Trains go to Ankara via Erzurum, Sivas and Kayseri.

Transport to Ani is sparse; take a taxi minibus (about TL35 per person with four to six passengers) organised by **Celil Ersoğlu** (☎0532 226 3966; celilani@hotmail.com).

UNDERSTAND TURKEY

History

The sheer weight and depth of history in Turkey is overwhelming. The Anatolian plateau features in various guises in both Homer's *Iliad* and the Bible; it has produced some of the world's longest-lasting dynasties.

The greatest of the early Anatolian civilisation was the Hittites, a force to be reckoned with from 2000 to 1200 BC. After the collapse of the Hittite empire, Anatolia splintered into several small states and did not reunite until the Graeco-Roman period.

Byzantine Empire & the Crusades

In AD 330, the Roman emperor Constantine founded an imperial city at Byzantium (modern İstanbul). Renamed Constantinople, this strategic city became the capital of the Eastern Roman Empire and was the Byzantine Empire's heart for a thousand years. However, invasion by the Seljuk Turks heavily reduced the empire's territory, and Constantinople was sacked during the Fourth Crusade (1202–04). The Byzantines regained the ravaged city in 1261.

Ottoman Empire

In 1453 Constantinople fell to the Ottoman sultan Mehmet II (the Conqueror). A century later, under Süleyman the Magnificent, the Ottoman Empire reached its zenith, spreading deep into Europe, Asia and North Africa.

The empire declined over the following centuries, when İstanbul's Topkapı Palace became a centre of indolence and decadence for increasingly out-of-touch sultans. By the 20th century European nationalism had fragmented the once-great empire, and the Ottomans emerged from WWI in disarray. The Treaty of Sèvres (1920) divvied out Anatolia among the European powers, leaving the Turks with a slither of steppe.

Mustafa Kemal Atatürk

At this low point, Mustafa Kemal (later Atatürk), the father of modern Turkey, took over. Under his rule, the Turks won their War of Independence (1919–23), repelling the Greeks at Smyrna (İzmir), and founded a new secular Turkish republic and moved the capital from İstanbul to Ankara. The Treaty of Lausanne (1923) undid the humiliations of Sèvres and saw foreign powers leave Turkey.

The modernising reforms of the still-venerated Atatürk actually had many casualties. 'Ghost villages', vacated but never reoccupied, were created in the population exchange, in which Greek-speaking people from Anatolia were shipped to Greece, while Muslim residents of Greece were transferred to Turkey.

Modern Turkey

Atatürk died in 1938 and his successor, İsmet İnönü, stepped carefully to avoid involvement in WWII. The war over, Turkey found itself allied to the USA, later becoming a NATO member. However, the second half of the 20th century was a tumultuous era. The political and economic turmoil included military coups in 1960, 1971 and 1980, and 1997's military memorandum (or 'postmodern coup'). The military considered itself the guardian of Atatürk's vision – pro-Western and secular – and stepped in when it considered it necessary.

During the 1980s and '90s the country was wracked by the ongoing conflict with the PKK (Kurdistan Workers Party), led by Abdullah Öcalan, who wanted the creation of a Kurdish state in southeastern Anatolia. The conflict led to an estimated 35,000 deaths and huge population shifts. In 1999 Öcalan was captured, but Kurdish discontent and terrorist activities continue.

The current millennium has been a more positive era for Turkey, led by the AKP party, which began its third term in 2011. The next general election is due in 2015.

Turkey Today

Turkey's location at the meeting point of Eu-rope and Asia informs its political bent: th secular country has a moderate Islamic go ernment and good relations with the Wes for which Turkey is a key ally in the Mi dle East. Prime Minister Erdoğan's Justice and Development (AKP) government has ushered in a broadly positive era for Turkey, with political stability and, in 2011, Europe's fastest growing economy.

With eight neighbouring countries, cross-border tensions are a fact of life for the Turkish government. In 2012, its biggest concern was the turmoil in Syria. Refugee camps sprung up along the border in southeastern Anatolia, and tensions between the countries grew.

Meanwhile, efforts to normalise Turkish–Armenian diplomatic relations, long strained over the alleged massacre of Ottoman Armenians during WWI, have faltered despite the two countries' increasing cultural and trade ties. The border remains closed, and it is illegal to discuss the issue in Turkey.

Turkey's bid to join the EU has been slowed by obstacles such as Turkey's refusal to recognise EU member Cyprus; the marginalisation of its 15 million Kurds; and Turkey's record on freedom of speech. Domestically, the country's most pressing problem is the Kurdish issue, which sparked a near civil war between the military and the PKK, classed as a terrorist group by organisations including the EU and US government, in the 1980s and '90s. The PKK has stepped up attacks in southeastern Anatolia during the Syrian unrest, but there are growing hopes that peace talks will take place.

People

Turkey's population (79.8 million) mostly comprises Turks, with a big Kurdish minority (about 15 million) and much smaller groups of Laz, Hemşin, Arabs, Jews, Greeks and Armenians. Arab influence is strongest in the Antakya (Hatay) area abutting Syria. Southeastern Turkey is predominantly Kurdish.

Republican Turkey has largely adapted to modern Westernised lifestyle, at least on the surface. In smaller towns and villages, particularly in the east, you will encounter more conservative people.

Turkey is 99% Muslim: about 80% Sunni, with Shiites and Alevis mainly in the east. The country espouses a more relaxed version of Islam than many Middle Eastern nations. Many men drink alcohol and many women uncover their heads (although almost no one touches pork).

Arts

Turkey's artistic traditions are rich and diverse, displaying influences of the many cultures and civilisations that have waxed and waned in Anatolia over the centuries.

Turkey is famous for its beautiful carpets and *kilims* (flat-weave rugs). It's thought that the Seljuk Turks introduced hand-woven carpet-making techniques to Anatolia in the 12th century. Today, the Ministry of Culture has sponsored projects to revive aged weaving and dyeing methods in western Turkey; some shops stock these 'project carpets'.

Environment

The Dardanelles, the Sea of Marmara and the Bosphorus divide Turkey into Asian and European parts. Eastern Thrace (European Turkey) comprises 3% of the country's 769,632-sq-km land area; the remaining 97% is Anatolia, a vast plateau rising eastward towards the Caucasus mountains.

With 7200km of coastline, snowcapped mountains, rolling steppe, vast lakes and broad rivers, Turkey is geographically varied. It is also one of the most biodiverse temperate-zone countries, blessed with an exceptionally rich flora of more than 9000 species, 1200 of them endemic.

Much of the Aegean and Mediterranean coasts are dedicated to tourism, with mild, rainy winters and hot, dry summers. The Anatolian plateau can be boiling in summer and freezing in winter.

Mountainous eastern Turkey is mostly icy cold and snowy in winter, and only pleasantly warm during high summer. Parts of southeastern Anatolia have a drier, semiarid climate.

Turkey lies on at least three active earthquake fault lines. A 7.1-magnitude earthquake shook the Van area in 2011, killing more than 600, injuring over 4000 and causing massive structural damage, with some 60,000 locals left homeless.

SURVIVAL GUIDE

Directory A–Z

Accommodation

Rates quoted in this chapter are for high season (June to August; in İstanbul, April,

May, September and October) and, unless otherwise mentioned, include tax (KDV), a private bathroom and breakfast.

Virtually nowhere in Turkey is far from a mosque; light sleepers might want to bring earplugs for the early-morning call to prayer.

PRICE RANGES

The price indicators in this chapter are based on the cost of a double room with private bathroom, and breakfast included.

€ less than TL80 (€70 in İstanbul)

€€ TL80 to TL170 (€70 to €180 in İstanbul)

€€€ more than TL170 (€180 in İstanbul)

CAMPING

Camping facilities are mostly found along the coasts and in Cappadocia and Nemrut Dağı Milli Parkı. Pensions and hostels often let you camp on their grounds for a fee.

HOSTELS

There are plenty of hostels in popular destinations, including Hostelling International members in İstanbul, Cappadocia and the Aegean and western Mediterranean areas.

Dorm beds usually cost TL20 to TL45 per night.

PENSIONS & HOTELS

Most tourist areas offer cosy, family-run pensions where you can get a good, clean single/double from around TL40/70.

Pensions generally represent better value than the cheapest hotels, which charge around TL35/40 for a single without/with private bathroom, and are mostly used by working-class Turkish men; they're not suitable for solo women.

Activities

Hiking and trekking are highly recommended; options include Cappadocia's Ala Dağlar National Park, northeastern Anatolia's Kaçkar Mountains and two 500km-long waymarked trails, the Lycian Way (Fethiye to Antalya) and St Paul Trail (Perge to Lake Eğirdir). Visit www.culturesroutesinturkey.com for more info on these and other trails, including western Anatolia's Evliya Çelebi Way for trekkers and horse riders.

Water and wind sports, from diving to paragliding, are available on the Aegean and Mediterranean coasts. Those who wish to relax can take a four-day *gület* trip (p1171) or soak in a *hammam*.

There are ski slopes at Uludağ, near Bursa, and Mt Erciyes, above Kayseri. The biggest and most renowned resort is Palandöken (near Erzurum) and the most scenic is Sarıkamış (near Kars). The season lasts from December to April.

Business Hours

The following experience some seasonal variation; for example, the working day shortens during the holy month of Ramazan, which currently falls during summer. Most museums close on Monday.

Bars 4pm to late

Government departments, offices and banks 8.30am to noon and 1.30pm to 5pm Monday to Friday

Nightclubs 11pm to late

Restaurants and cafes breakfast 7.30am to 10am, lunch noon to 2.30pm, dinner 7.30pm to 10pm

Shops 9am to 6pm Monday to Friday (longer in tourist areas and big cities – including weekend opening)

Tourist information 8.30am to noon and 1.30pm to 5pm Monday to Friday

Embassies & Consulates

Embassies are generally in Ankara. Many countries also have consulates in İstanbul and elsewhere. For more information and contact details of diplomatic missions in Turkey, visit http://tinyurl.com/6ywt8a.

Australian Embassy (☎0312-459 9500; www.embaustralia.org.tr; Uğur Mumcu Caddesi 88, MNG Bldg, Gaziosmanpaşa)

Azerbaijan Embassy (☎0312-491 1681; www.mfa.gov.az; Baku Sokak 1, Diplomatik Site, Oran)

Bulgarian Embassy (☎0312-467 2071; www.bulgaria.bg; Atatürk Bulvarı 124, Kavaklıdere)

Canadian Embassy (☎0312-409 2700; www.canadainternational.gc.ca; Cinnah Caddesi 58, Çankaya)

Georgian Embassy (☎0312-491 8030; www.turkey.mfa.gov.ge; Kılıç Ali Sokak 12, Diplomatik Site, Oran)

Greek Embassy (☎0312-448 0647; www.mfa.gr; Zia Ur Rahman Caddesi 9-11, Gaziosmanpaşa)

Iranian Embassy (☎0312-468 2820; www.mfa.gov.ir; Tahran Caddesi 10, Kavaklıdere)

Iraqi Embassy (☎0312-468 7421; http://iraqmissions.hostinguk.com; Turan Emeksiz Sokak 11, Gaziosmanpaşa)

New Zealand Embassy (☎0312-467 9054; www.nzembassy.com/turkey; İran Caddesi 13, Kavaklıdere)

Russian Embassy (☎0312-439 2122; www.turkey.mid.ru; Karyağdı Sokak 5, Çankaya)

Syrian Embassy (☎0312-440 9657; Sedat Simavi Sokak 40, Çankaya)

UK Embassy (☎0312-455 3344; http://ukinturkey.fco.gov.uk; Şehit Ersan Caddesi 46/A, Çankaya)

US Embassy (☎0312-455 5555; http://turkey.usembassy.gov; Atatürk Bulvarı 110, Kavaklıdere)

Food

This chapter uses the following price indicators, based on the cost of a main course:

€ less than TL9 (TL15 in İstanbul)

€€ TL9 to TL17.50 (TL15 to TL25 in İstanbul)

€€€ more than TL17.50 (TL25 in İstanbul)

Internet Access

» Most accommodation options offer free wi-fi, as do many other businesses.

» Internet cafes are widespread.

Money

» Turkey's currency is the Türk Lirası (Turkish Lira; TL).

» Lira come in notes of five, 10, 20, 50, 100 and 200; and coins of one, five, 10, 25 and 50 *kuruş* and one lira.

» Prices in this chapter are quoted in lira or €, depending on which currency is quoted by the business.

CASH & CREDIT CARDS

» Euros and US dollars are the most readily accepted foreign currencies, and the easiest to change.

» Many exchange offices and banks change other major currencies such as UK pounds and Japanese yen.

» Visa and MasterCard are widely accepted by hotels, shops and restaurants, but often not by pensions and local restaurants outside main tourist areas. You can get cash advances on these cards.

» Amex is less commonly accepted outside top-end establishments.

TIPPING & BARGAINING

» Tipping is customary in restaurants, hotels and taxis; optional elsewhere.

» Round up metered taxi fares; leave waiters and masseurs around 10% to 15% of the bill.

» Check a *servis ücreti* (service charge) hasn't been automatically added to restaurant bills.

» Hotel prices are sometimes negotiable; you should always bargain for souvenirs.

Post

» *Postanes* (post offices) are indicated by blue-on-yellow 'PTT' signs.

» Postcards sent abroad cost about TL2.

Public Holidays

New Year's Day 1 January

National Sovereignty & Children's Day 23 April

International Workers' Day 1 May

Youth & Sports Day 19 May

Victory Day 30 August

Republic Day 28–29 October

Turkey also celebrates the main Islamic holidays, the most important of which are **Şeker Bayramı** (Sweets Holiday; ⊙28 Jul 2014, 17 Jul 2015), marking the end of Ramazan; and about two months later, **Kurban Bayramı** (Festival of the Sacrifice; ⊙4 Oct 2014, 23 Sep 2015). Due to the fact that these holidays are celebrated according to the Muslim lunar calendar, they take place around 11 days earlier every year.

Safe Travel

Although Turkey is in no way a dangerous country to visit, it's always wise to be a little cautious, especially if you're travelling alone.

» Turks (İstanbullus in particular) are fast drivers; give way to cars and trucks in all situations.

» Drugging is a risk, especially for lone men, and most commonly in İstanbul. It may involve so-called friends, a bar, and perhaps a willowy temptress. Another İstanbul scam with these elements ends with the traveller buying a couple of drinks and receiving a bill for hundreds of euros. Be cautious about who you befriend, especially when you're new to the country.

» Sexual assaults have occurred against travellers of both sexes in hotels in central and eastern Anatolia. Do a little research if you are travelling alone or heading off the beaten track.

» Sporadic bombings, linked to Kurdish separatist groups, target affluent areas frequented by tourists, including a suicide-bomb attack in İstanbul's Taksim Sq in 2010.

Telephone

» **Türk Telekom** (www.turktelekom.com.tr) has a monopoly on phone services, which are efficient if costly.

» If you're only going to make one quick call, look for a booth with a '*kontörlü telefon*' sign, where the cost of your call is metered.

» Public telephones require phonecards (some accept credit card). The cheapest option for international calls is with cards such as IPC.

» If you set up a roaming facility with your home mobile network, most mobiles can connect to Turkcell (the most comprehensive network), Vodafone and Avea. To buy a Turkcell SIM card (TL30 to TL40), you need to show your passport and ensure the seller phones through or inputs your details.

Visas

» Nationals of countries including Denmark, Finland, France, Germany, Israel, Italy, Japan, New Zealand, Sweden and Switzerland don't need a visa to visit Turkey for up to 90 days.

» Nationals of countries including Australia, Austria, Belgium, Canada, Ireland, the Netherlands, Norway, Portugal, Spain, the UK and the USA need a visa, but it is just a sticker bought on arrival at the airport or border post. It's generally a 90-day multiple-entry visa.

» Costs vary. At the time of writing, Americans paid US$20 (€15), Australians and Canadians US$60 (€45) and British citizens UK£10 (€15 or US$20).

» Some major entry points accept Visa and MasterCard, but it is generally worth having the fee ready in one of the above currencies, in hard cash.

» Your passport must be valid for at least six months from the date you enter the country.

» See the **Ministry of Foreign Affairs** (www.mfa.gov.tr) for the latest information.

Women Travellers

Turkish society is still basically sexually segregated, especially once you get away from the big cities and tourist resorts. Although younger Turks are questioning the old ways and women hold positions of authority (there's even been a female prime minister), foreign women can find themselves being harassed. It's mostly just catcalls and dubious remarks, but assaults do occasionally occur.

Travelling with companions usually improves matters and it's worth remembering that Turkish women ignore men who speak to them in the street. Dressing appropriately will also reduce unwanted attention. In eastern Anatolia, keep your dealings with men formal and polite, not friendly.

Getting There & Away

Air

The cheapest fares are usually to İstanbul's **Atatürk International Airport** (Atatürk Havalımanı; ☎0212-463 3000; www.ataturkairport.com) and **Sabiha Gökçen International Airport** (Sabiha Gökçen Havalımanı; ☎0216-588 8888; www.sgairport.com).

Other international airports include Ankara, Antalya, Bodrum, Dalaman and İzmir.

It's a good idea to book at least two months in advance if you plan to arrive between April and late August. If you're planning a two- or three-week trip, it's worth enquiring about charter flights, and looking at flight and accommodation packages if you intend to stay on the coast.

Turkey's national carrier, **Turkish Airlines** (☎0850- 333 0849; www.thy.com), flies worldwide. It connects İstanbul to most major European cities, with flights also available with its budget subsidiaries **Sun Express** (☎444 0797; www.sunexpress.com) and **AnadoluJet** (☎444 2538; www.anadolujet.com), its Turkish competitors including **Pegasus Airlines** (www.flypgs.com), and European carriers including **easyJet** (www.easyjet.com).

Land

BUS

Austria, Bulgaria, Germany, Greece, Macedonia and Romania have the most direct buses to İstanbul. The Turkish companies **Varan Turizm** (☎444 8999; www.varan.com.tr

Metro Turizm (☎444 3455; www.metroturizm.com.tr) and Ulusoy (☎444 1888; www.ulusoy.com.tr) operate on these routes; the latter has weekly departures to/from Germany (about €200). If you're travelling from other countries, you'll likely have to catch a connecting bus.

TRAIN

The daily Bosphorus/Balkan Express links İstanbul with Bucharest (Romania), Sofia (Bulgaria) and Belgrade (Serbia), with onward connections. Visit www.seat61.com/turkey2 and www.tinyurl.com/b3cx85s for more information.

Sea

Departure times and routes change between seasons, with fewer ferries generally running in the winter. **Ferrylines** (www.ferrylines.com) is a good starting point for information. The following is a list of ferry routes from Turkey:

Ayvalık–Lesvos, Greece Jale Tour (www.jaletour.com)

Bodrum–Kos, Greece Bodrum Ferryboat Association (www.bodrumferryboat.com); Bodrum Express Lines (www.bodrumexpresslines.com)

Bodrum–Rhodes, Greece Bodrum Ferryboat Association (www.bodrumferryboat.com)

Çeşme–Chios, Greece Ertürk (www.erturk.com.tr)

Datça–Rhodes, Greece Knidos Yachting (www.knidosyachting.com)

Datça–Simi, Greece Knidos Yachting (www.knidosyachting.com)

İstanbul–Illyichevsk (Odessa), Ukraine Sea Lines (www.sea-lines.net)

Kaş–Meis (Kastellorizo), Greece Meis Express (www.meisexpress.com)

Kuşadası–Samos, Greece Meander Travel (www.meandertravel.com)

Marmaris–Rhodes, Greece Yeşil Marmaris Travel & Yachting (www.yesilmarmaris.com)

Trabzon–Sochi, Russia Olympia Line (www.olympia-line.ru), Öz Star Denizcilik (Princess Victoria), Sarı Denizcilik (www.saridenizcilik.com/en); see also www.seaport-sochi.ru and www.al-port.com

Turgutreis–Kos, Greece Bodrum Ferryboat Association (www.bodrumferryboat.com)

Getting Around

Bicycle

Riding a bike is a great way of exploring, especially in touristy areas, where you can hire bikes from pensions and rental outfits. Road surfaces are acceptable, if a bit rough, but Turkey's notorious road-hog drivers are a hazard.

Bus

The Turkish bus network is excellent: coaches go just about everywhere, cheaply, frequently and comfortably. **Kamil Koç** (☎444 0562; www.kamilkoc.com.tr), **Metro Turizm** (☎444 3455; www.metroturizm.com.tr), **Ulusoy** (☎444 1888; www.ulusoy.com.tr) and **Varan Turizm** (☎444 8999; www.varan.com.tr) are the better companies, offering greater speed and comfort – plus better safety records – for slightly higher fares.

A town's *otogar* (bus station) is often on the outskirts, but most bus companies provide a *servis* (free shuttle bus) to and from the centre.

Local routes are usually operated by 'midibuses' or *dolmuşes* (minibuses), which might run to a timetable or set off when full.

Car & Motorcycle

Turkey has the world's second-most expensive petrol prices (petrol/diesel costs about TL4/4.70 per litre) and one of the world's highest motor-vehicle accident rates.

An international driving permit (IDP) is not obligatory, but handy if your driving licence is from a country likely to seem obscure to a Turkish police officer.

You need to be at least 21 years old, with a year's driving experience, to hire a car. Rental charges are similar to those in Europe.

Türkiye Turing ve Otomobil Kurumu (TTOK, Turkish Touring & Automobile Club; ☎0212-513 3660; www.turing.org.tr; Soğukçeşme Sokağı, Sultanahmet, İstanbul)

Economy Car Rentals (www.economycarrentals.com) Good rates.

Hitching

Although we don't recommend hitching *(otostop)*, short hitches are not uncommon in Turkey, for example to get from the highway to an archaeological site.

Face the traffic and wave your arm up and down as if bouncing a basketball.

Offer to pay something towards the petrol, although many drivers pick up foreign hitchers for their curiosity value. Women should never hitchhike alone.

Train

Train travel is comfortable, with most services having air-con and sleepers on long routes. Although most people still opt for buses as train journey times are notoriously long, the system is being overhauled and fast lines (such as Ankara–Konya) are appearing.

InterRail, Balkan Flexipass and Eurodomino passes are valid on the Turkish railway network, but Eurail passes aren't.

The train network covers the country fairly well, with the notable exception of the coastlines. Useful routes include Ankara–Konya, İstanbul–İzmir (including ferry to and from Bandırma) and İzmir–Selcuk. From Ankara, long-distance destinations include Adana, Diyarbakır, İzmir, Kayseri, Kurtalan, Malatya and Tatvan (Lake Van).

Turkish State Railways (☎444 8233; www.tcdd.gov.tr)

The Man in Seat Sixty-One (www.seat61.com/turkey2)

Ukraine

Includes »

Kyiv 1189

Lviv 1195

Understand Ukraine 1197

Survival Guide 1198

Best Places to Eat

» Spotykach (p1194)

» Kyivska Perepichka (p1194)

» Dim Lehend (p1196)

» Masonic Restaurant (p1196)

Best Places to Stay

» Dream House Hostel p1189)

» Old City Hostel (p1195)

» Hotel George (p1195)

» On the Corner (p1196)

Why Go?

Big, diverse and largely undiscovered, Ukraine (Україна) is one of Europe's last genuine travel frontiers, a poor nation rich in colour-splashed tradition, warm-hearted people and off-the-map travel experiences.

'Ukraine' means 'land on the edge', an apt title for this slab of Eurasia in many ways. This is the Slavic hinterland on Europe's periphery, a mere two decades into a troubled independence and dogged by political anguish, ethnic divisions and deep-rooted corruption. But it's a country whose peoples pull together when needed, most recently for the remarkably successful Euro 2012 soccer championships, which showed off Ukraine at its hospitable best.

Soviet-flavoured Kyiv and the central European charms of Lviv are the main draws but wherever you head, Ukraine is great budget travel territory thanks to the favourable exchange rate. Transport, food and accommodation are all cheaper than destinations further west.

When to Go

Kyiv

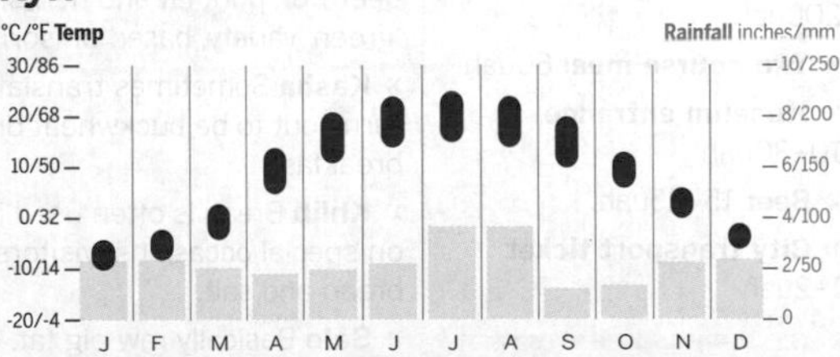

Jan–Mar Travel across Ukraine's endless steppe in a winter white-out.

Apr–May Stroll through spring-time Kyiv when horse chestnut trees blossom across the city.

Sep Wake up and smell the beans during Lviv's famous coffee festival.

AT A GLANCE

» **Currency** Hryvnya (uah)

» **Language** Ukrainian, Russian

» **Money** ATMs widespread; credit cards accepted at most hotels but only upmarket restaurants

» **Visas** Not required for EU, UK, US and Canadian citizens for stays of up to 90 days

Fast Facts

» **Area** 603,628 sq km

» **Capital** Kyiv

» **Country code** ☎380

» **Emergency** ☎112

Exchange Rates

Australia	A$1	8.51uah
Canada	C$1	8.02uah
Euro Zone	€1	10.42uah
Japan	¥100	8.64uah
New Zealand	NZ$1	6.82uah
UK	UK£1	12.33uah
USA	US$1	8.15uah

Set Your Budget

» **Budget hotel room** 200uah

» **Two-course meal** 60uah

» **Museum entrance** 10–30uah

» **Beer** 15–25uah

» **City transport ticket** 1–2uah

Resources

» **Brama** (www.brama.com)

» **Infoukes** (www.infoukes.com)

» **Ukraine.com** (www.ukraine.com)

Connections

Ukraine is well linked to its neighbours, particularly Russia and Belarus, with whom it shares the former Soviet rail system. Kyiv is connected by bus or train to Moscow and St Petersburg (Russia), Minsk (Belarus), Warsaw (Poland) and Budapest (Hungary), as well as other eastern European capitals. Odesa is the hub for travelling to the Moldovan capital Chişinău and Tiraspol in Transdniester, with several daily buses and one train a day making the trip. The city also has ferries to Bulgaria, Georgia and Turkey, though the service is erratic. From Uzhhorod it's a short journey to the international main line into Europe at Chop, connecting Ukraine with Slovakia and Hungary. Lviv is the biggest city servicing the Polish border and many travellers are taking budget flights to Poland then crossing the border to Lviv by bus or train. It's also possible to take no-frills flights to Budapest or Bratislava (Slovakia), and continue to Ukraine from there by train.

ITINERARIES

Two Days

A couple of days are just enough to 'do' Kyiv, starting at its stellar attraction, the Caves Monastery. Follow this with a hike up artsy Andriyivsky Uzviz for a taste of prewar Ukraine before plunging into the beeswax-perfumed Byzantine interior of Unesco-listed St Sophia's Cathedral.

Five Days

Having seen the sights in Kyiv, hop aboard a slow night train to Lviv, Ukraine's most central European city complete with bean-scented coffee houses, Gothic and Baroque churches, and quaintly rattling trams.

Essential Food & Drink

» **Borsch** The Ukrainian national soup, which is made with beetroot, pork fat and herbs. There's also an aromatic 'green' variety, based on sorrel.

» **Kasha** Sometimes translated as porridge, but usually turns out to be buckwheat drenched in milk and served for breakfast.

» **Khlib** Bread is often used in religious ceremonies and on special occasions; visitors are traditionally greeted with bread and salt.

» **Salo** Basically raw pig fat, cut into slices and eaten with bread or added to soups and other dishes. Look out for the 'Ukrainian Snickers bar' – *salo* in chocolate.

» **Varenyky** Similar to Polish *pierogi* – pasta pockets filled with everything from mashed potato to sour cherries.

» **Vodka** Also known in Ukraine as *horilka*, it accompanies every celebration, red-letter day and get-together – in copious amounts.

KYIV

☎044 / POP 2.8 MILLION

Part quaint central Europe, part Soviet central Asia, these days Ukraine's diverse capital Kyiv (Київ) is a place that refuses to be neatly defined. Generally regarded as one of the former Soviet Union's more pleasant metropolises, history and its players – from the princes of the Kievan Rus to the Russian tzars and Stalinist-era architects to today's crass post-Soviet elite – have all left their mark on its cityscape. It's these layered deposits of history that have always attracted visitors, but the spruce-up for Euro 2012 has given this city on the Dnipro River a slightly more foreigner-friendly feel than it exuded until recently, and tourist numbers are growing – unthinkable a short decade ago.

Sights

TOP CHOICE Caves Monastery MONASTERY
(www.kplavra.kiev.ua; vul Lavrska 9; grounds 3uah, caves & exhibitions adult/child 50/25uah; ⌚8am-7pm Apr-Oct, 9am-6pm Nov-Mar; ⓈArsenalna) The Caves Monastery Complex, aka the Kyiv Pechersk Lavra, is the city's most popular tourist attraction. The site is divided into the Upper Lavra (a complex of churches and museums) and the Lower Lavra (the caves themselves). It's the two sets of caves in the Lower Lavra that cause all the kerfuffle. Buy a candle to light your way at a kiosk before you enter. Inside the caves, dozens of niches contain glass-topped coffins holding the bodies of the monks.

St Sophia's Cathedral CHURCH
(pl Sofiyska; admission grounds/cathedral/bell tower 3/53/13uah; ⌚grounds 9am-7pm, cathedral 10am-6pm Thu-Tue, 10am-5pm Wed; ⓈMaydan Nezalezhnosti) The city's oldest standing church is the magnificent St Sophia's Cathedral. A World Heritage Site, it was built between 1017 and 1031 and named after Aya Sofya (Hagia Sophia) in İstanbul. Perhaps the most memorable aspect of a visit is the cathedral's interior, where you'll find 11th-century mosaics and frescos.

Andriyivsky Uzviz STREET
(ⓈKontraktova Pl) No visit to Kyiv is complete without an amble up and down steep, cobblestoned Andriyivsky uzviz, one of its oldest streets. Avoid the climb by taking the **funicular** (tickets 2uah; ⌚6.30am-11pm; ⓈPoshtova Pl) to the top of the hill, where you'll find **St Michael's Monastery** with its seven-domed cathedral. Heading down, you can't miss the baroque **St Andrew's Church** (⌚10am-8pm), built in 1754 by Italian architect Bartolomeo Rastrelli. Other worthwhile attractions include the **Museum of One Street** (Andriyivsky uzviz 2b; admission 20uah; ⌚noon-6pm Tue-Sun) and the **Bulgakov Museum** (www.bulgakov.org.ua; Andriyivsky uzviz 13; adult/child 30/15uah; ⌚10am-6pm Thu-Tue, from noon Mon; ⓈKontraktova Pl).

Sleeping

Dream House Hostel HOSTEL €
(☎580 2169; www.dream-family.com; Andriyivsky uzviz 2d; dm/d from 90/300uah; ❄@📶; ⓈKontraktova Pl) Kyiv's most happening hostel is this gleaming new 100-bed affair located at the bottom of Andriyivsky uzviz. An attached cafe-bar, bike hire (160uah per day) and daily events and tours make it an entertaining base.

Chillout Hostel HOSTEL €
(☎093 332 4306; www.chillouthostelkiev.com; vul Saksahanskoho 30b; dm 100uah, r without bathroom 300uah; @📶; ⓈOlympiyska) With a touch of the psychedelic about it, this Polish/Welsh-run place has two six-bed dorms and one double plus all the amenities you'd expect to find in a city-centre hostel. Enter through the arch at Gorkogo 22 and cross the courtyard diagonally, bearing left towards a yellow building.

St Petersburg Hotel HOTEL €€
(☎279 7472; www.s-peter.com.ua; bul Tarasa Shevchenka 4; s/d without bathroom 325/514uah, with bathroom from 580/790uah; 📶; ⓈTeatralna)

KYIV'S APARTMENTS

A budget alternative to a Kyiv hotel or hostel is renting an apartment: prices start at 600uah.

Grata Apartments (☎468 0757, 238 2603; www.accommodation.kiev.ua; prov Mykhaylivsky 9A, office 3) Service-oriented firm with a good range of apartments.

Uarent (☎278 8363; www.uarent.com) Offers some of the cheapest (though not very central) apartments.

UKR Apartments (☎234 5637, 050 311 0309; www.ukr-apartments.kiev.ua) Has a wide selection of inexpensive apartments.

Ukraine Highlights

1. Inspect Kyiv's collection of mummified monks at the **Caves Monastery** (p1189)
2. Make an ascent of **Andriyivsky uzviz** (p1189), Kyiv's most atmospheric street
3. Do a spot of cobble-surfing in **Lviv's historical centre** (p1195), packed with churches, museums and eccentric restaurants
4. Climb to the top of Ukraine's highest peak, **Mt Hoverla** (p1196)

Bryansk
Desna
Voronezh
Kursk
RUSSIA
E101
Seym
Sumy
Chernihiv
Kharkiv
E40
Luhansk
Kyiv
2
E40
Poltava
Slovyansk
Bryanka
Kramatorsk
Krasny
E105
Luch
Kostyantynivka
Horlivka
Dnipro River
Cherkasy
Kremenchutske Reservoir
Kremenchuk
E50
Donetsk
Makiyivka
Dniprodzerzhynsk
Dnipropetrovsk
E50
Uman
E50
Kirovohrad
Zaporizhzhya
E105
Mariupol
Kryvy Rih
Nikopol
E95
E577
Berdyansk
Pivdenny Buh
Kakhovske Reservoir
Melitopol
E58
Sea of Azov
Mykolaiv
Askaniya-Nova National Park
Kherson
E58
Skadovsk
Odesa
E97
E97
CRIMEA
E105
Simferopol
Bakhchysaeay
Krymsky National Park
Sevastopol
Yalta
Dunaysky National Park
BLACK SEA
0
200 km
0
100 miles
N

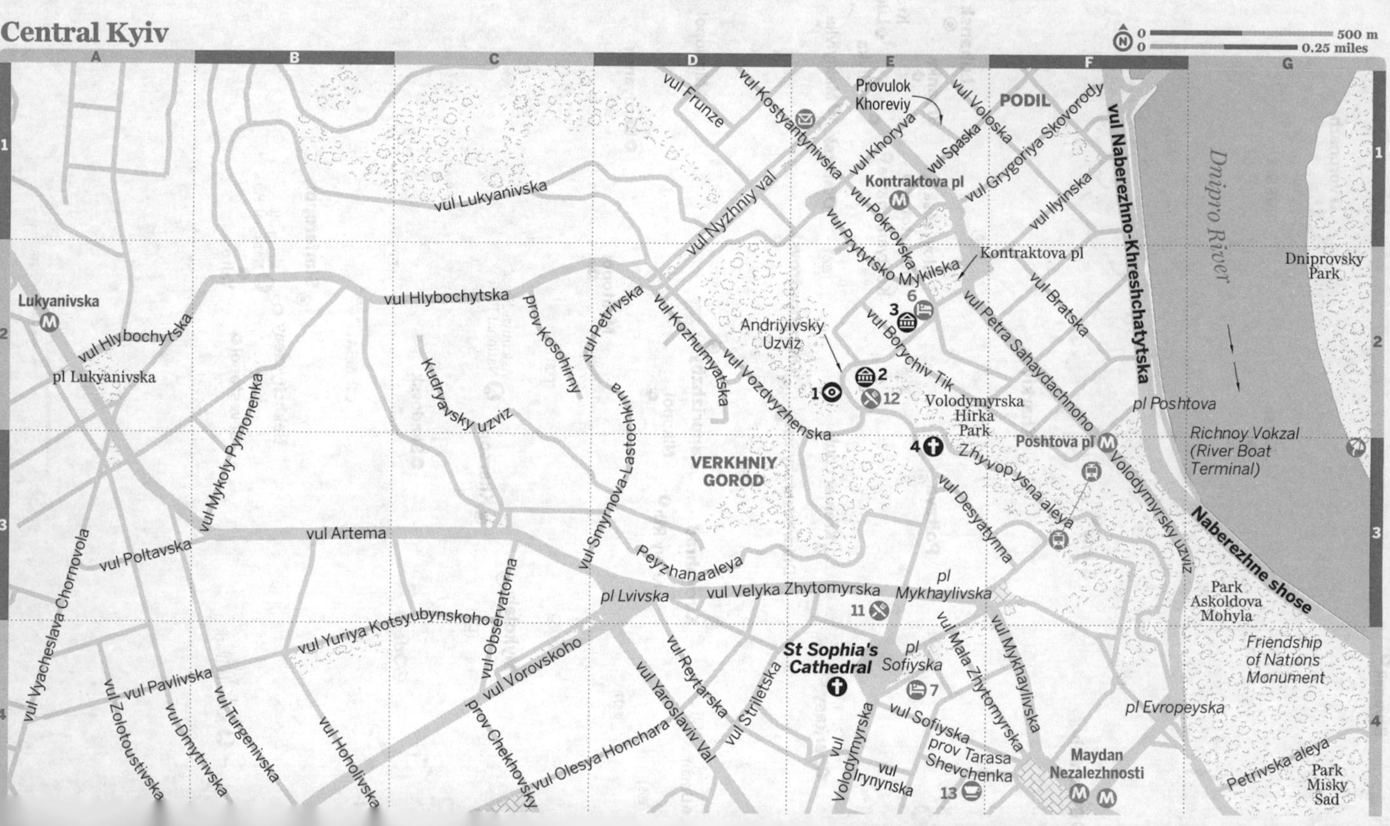
Central Kyiv
0 500 m
0 0.25 miles
PODIL
Provulok Khoreviy
vul Frunze
vul Kostyantynivska
vul Khoryva
vul Spaska
vul Voloska
vul Grygoriya Skovorody
vul Naberezhno-Khreshchatytska
Dnipro River
Dniprovsky Park
Kontraktova pl
vul Nyzhniy val
vul Pokrovska
vul Ilyinska
vul Prytytsko Mykilska
vul Lukyanivska
vul Hlybochytska
prov Kosohirny
vul Petrivska
vul Kozhumyatska
vul Vozdvyzhenska
Andriyivsky Uzviz
vul Borychiv Tik
vul Petra Sahaydachnoho
vul Bratska
Lukyanivska
pl Lukyanivska
Kudryavsky uzviz
vul Mykoly Pymonenka
Volodymyrska Hirka Park
pl Poshtova
Poshtova pl
Richnoy Vokzal (River Boat Terminal)
VERKHNIY GOROD
vul Smyrnova-Lastochkina
Zhyvopysna aleya
vul Desyatynna
Volodymyrsky uzviz
Naberezhne shose
vul Artema
vul Poltavska
Peyzhana aleya
vul Velyka Zhytomyrska
pl Mykhaylivska
pl Lvivska
Park Askoldova Mohyla
vul Vyacheslava Chornovola
vul Yuriya Kotsyubynskoho
vul Observatorna
St Sophia's Cathedral
pl Sofiyska
vul Mala Zhytomyrska
vul Mykhaylivska
Friendship of Nations Monument
vul Pavlivska
vul Vorovskoho
vul Reytarska
vul Striletska
vul Yaroslaviv Val
pl Evropeyska
vul Zolotoustivska
vul Dmytrivska
vul Turgenivska
vul Hoholivska
prov Chekhovsky
vul Olesya Honchara
vul Volodymyrska
vul Irynynska
vul Sofiyska
prov Tarasa Shevchenka
Maydan Nezalezhnosti
Petrivska aleya
Park Misky Sad

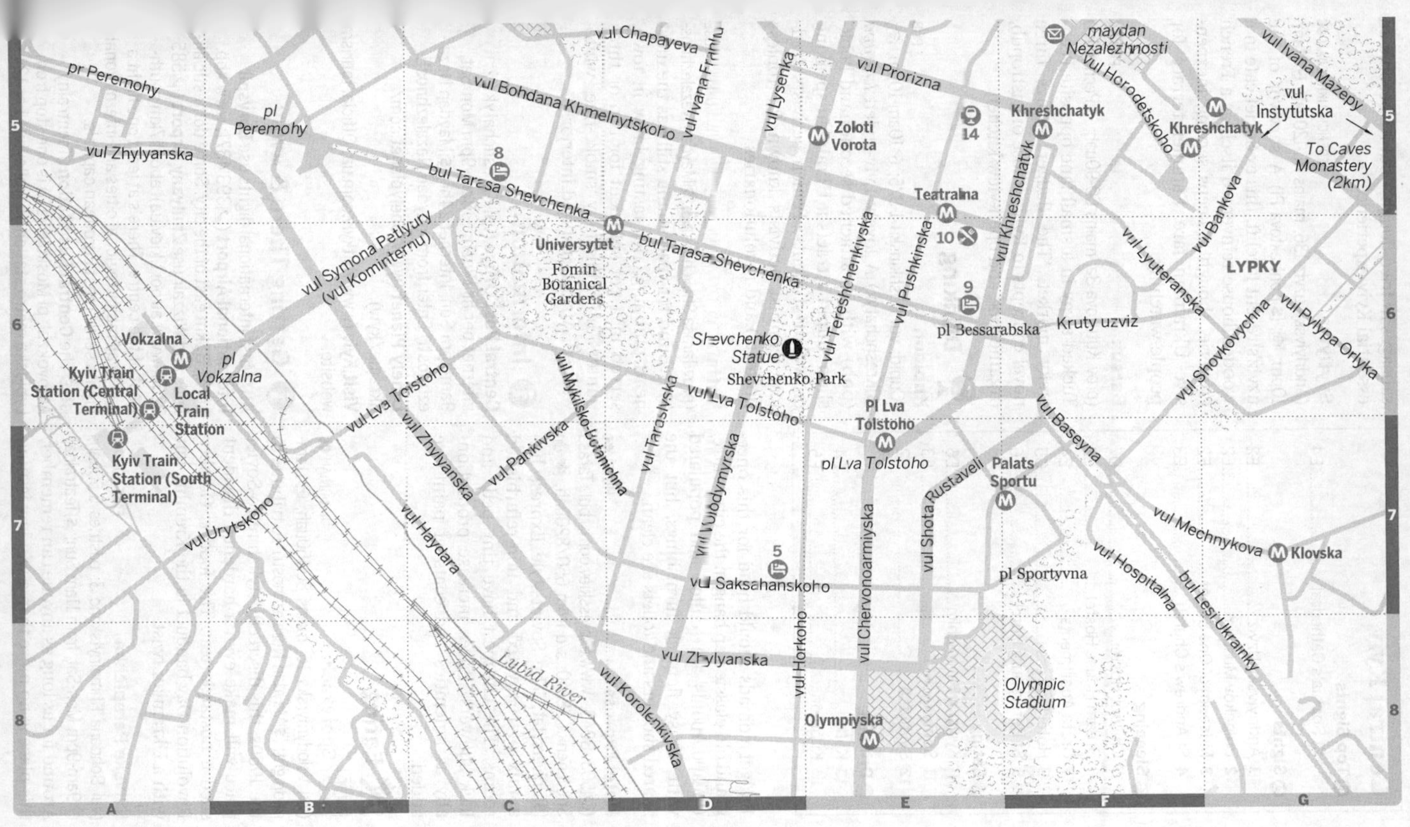
pr Peremohy
pl Peremohy
vul Zhylyanska
vul Chapayeva
vul Bohdana Khmelnytskoho
vul Ivana Franka
vul Lysenka
vul Prorizna
maydan Nezalezhnosti
vul Horodetskoho
vul Ivana Mazepy
vul Instytutska
To Caves Monastery (2km)
Khreshchatyk
Zoloti Vorota
14
8
bul Tarasa Shevchenka
Universytet
Fomin Botanical Gardens
Teatralna
10
vul Khreshchatyk
vul Bankova
LYPKY
vul Lyuteranska
vul Pushkinska
vul Tereshchenkivska
9
pl Bessarabska
Kruty uzviz
vul Shovkovychna
vul Pylypa Orlyka
vul Symona Petlyury (vul Kominternu)
Vokzalna
pl Vokzalna
Kyiv Train Station (Central Terminal)
Local Train Station
Kyiv Train Station (South Terminal)
vul Lva Tolstoho
Shevchenko Statue
Shevchenko Park
vul Mykilsko-Botanichna
vul Tarasivska
vul Volodymyrska
vul Zhylyanska
vul Pankivska
Pl Lva Tolstoho
pl Lva Tolstoho
vul Baseyna
Palats Sportu
vul Shota Rustaveli
vul Mechnykova
Klovska
vul Hospitalna
bul Lesi Ukrainky
vul Urytskoho
vul Haydara
5
vul Saksahanskoho
pl Sportyvna
vul Chervonoarmiyska
vul Horkoho
vul Korolenkivska
Lybid River
Olympic Stadium
Olympiyska
A
B
C
D
E
F
G
5
6
7
8

Central Kyiv

Top Sights

St Sophia's Cathedral E4

Sights

1 Andriyivsky Uzviz E2
2 Bulgakov Museum E2
3 Museum of One Street E2
4 St Andrew's Church E3

Sleeping

5 Chillout Hostel D7
6 Dream House Hostel E2
7 Grata Apartments E4
8 Hotel Express C5
9 St Petersburg Hotel E6

Eating

10 Kyivska Perepichka E6
11 Spotykach E3
12 Svytlytsa E2

Drinking

13 Kaffa E4
14 Kupidon E5

Budget nomads should head for this once-grand old classic slap bang in the city centre. Cheapo rooms are scuffed and populated with flimsy flatpack furnishings, but the shared showers and toilets are clean.

Hotel Express HOTEL €€
(☎503 3045; www.expresskiev.com; bul Tarasa Shevchenka 38/40; s/d from 650/820uah; ❄@; SUniversytet) The Soviet-style Express has a mix of renovated and non-refurbished rooms. The cheapest have tiny beds and lack showers. Prices increase proportionally as amenities and coats of paint are added.

Eating

TOP CHOICE **Spotykach** UKRAINIAN €€
(vul Volodymyrska 16; mains 80-150uah; ⏲11am-midnight; SMaydan Nezalezhnosti) A tribute to the 1960s, this discreetly stylish retro-Soviet place will make even a hardened dissident shed a nostalgic tear. The food is October Revolution Day banquet in the Kremlin, but with a Ukrainian twist.

Kyivska Perepichka FAST FOOD €
(vul Bohdana Khmelnytskoho 3; pastries 5.50uah; ⏲9am-9pm Mon-Sat, from 11am Sun; STeatralna) Around for as long as anyone can remember, this place is no more than a window issuing sausages in fried dough – but it's become an essential Kyiv experience.

Svytlytsa FRENCH, UKRAINIAN €€
(Andriyivsky uzviz 136; mains 45-120uah; ⏲11am-10pm; 📋; SKontraktova Pl) A survivor of the uzviz's recent facelift, this ex-Soviet cafe in a wooden house reinvented itself as a French crêperie, though it keeps serving inexpensive Ukrainian fare. Summer terrace for people-watching.

Barsuk PUB €€
(prov Kutuzova 3a; mains 60-90uah; SPecherska) Tucked away in a small lane opposite Pechersky market, 'The Badger' brings three novel concepts to Kyiv – those of gastropub, organic food and open-view kitchen.

Drinking

Kupidon PUB
(Cupid; vul Pushkinska 1-3/5; ⏲10am-10pm; 📶; SKreshchatyk) A lovely Lviv-styled *knaypa* (pub) with an attached secondhand bookshop, Cupid attracts a Ukrainian-speaking crowd of students, Femen activists (radical feminist activists known for topless protests) and revolutionaries.

Kaffa COFFEE HOUSE
(prov Tarasa Shevchenka 3; SMaydan Nezalezhnosti) Around for years, Kaffa still has the most heart-pumping, rich-tasting brew in town, served in a pot sufficient for two or three punters in a blissfully smoke-free, whitewashed, African-inspired interior.

Information

Central Post Office (vul Khreshchatyk 22; internet per hr 18uah; ⏲8am-9pm Mon-Sat, 9am-7pm Sun, internet 24hr; SMaydan Nezalezhnosti) Enter from maydan Nezalezhnosti.

Lonely Planet (www.lonelyplanet.com/ukraine/kyiv)

Visit Kyiv (www.visitkyiv.com.ua) Official tourism website.

Getting There & Away

AIR Most international flights use **Boryspil International Airport** (☎393 4371; www.kbp.aero), 35km east of the city. Some domestic airlines and Wizzair use **Zhulyany airport** (☎585 7254; www.airport.kiev.ua), about 7km southwest of the centre. There's at least one flight a day to all major regional cities and international flights serve most European capitals.

BUS The **Central Bus Station** (Tsentralny Avtovokzal; pl Moskovska 3) is one stop from Lybidska metro station on trolleybus 1 or 12.

Long-distance carriers **Autolux** (www.autolux.ua) and **Gunsel** (www.gunsel.com.ua) run the fastest and most comfortable buses with frequent services to most regional centres (though not Lviv).

TRAIN The quickest way to Lviv is on the Intercity+ Hyundai express train (214uah, five hours, one daily) which leaves in the early evening. However, cheaper overnight and daytime services (120uah to 180uah, eight to 10 hours) remain more popular options.

All services leave from Kyiv's modern **train station** (☎503 7005; pl Vokzalna 2; Ⓢ Vokzalna).

Getting Around

TO/FROM THE AIRPORT The 24-hour SkyBus (No 322) shuttles between Boryspil Airport (25uah, 45 minutes to one hour) and the train station's South Terminal every 20 to 40 minutes (tickets from the driver).

Trolleybus 22 links Zhulyany Airport with Shulyavska metro station.

PUBLIC TRANSPORT Kyiv's metro runs between 6am and midnight. Blue-green plastic tokens (*zhetony*; 2uah) are sold at windows and dispensers at station entrances. Buy tickets (1.50uah) for buses, trolleybuses and trams at kiosks or from drivers or conductors.

LVIV

☎032 / POP 756,000

If you've spent time in any other region of Ukraine, Lviv (Львів) will come as shock. Mysterious and architecturally lovely, this Unesco World Heritage–listed city is the country's least Soviet city and exudes the same central European charm as pre-tourism Prague or Kraków once did. Its quaint cobbles, Arabica-infused coffee houses and trundling trams are a continent away from the post-Soviet badlands to the east. It's also a place where the candle of Ukrainian national identity burns brightest and where Russian is rarely heard.

Sights

Ploshcha Rynok SQUARE

Thanks to its splendid array of buildings Lviv was declared a Unesco World Heritage Site in 1998, and this old market square lies at its heart. The square was progressively rebuilt after a major fire in the early 16th century destroyed the original. The 19th-century **ratusha** (town hall) stands in the middle of the action, with fountains featuring Greek gods at each of its corners. Vista junkies can climb the 65m-high neo-Renaissance **tower** (admission 10uah; ⏲9am-8pm May–mid-Sep, winter hours vary) – multilingual signs point the way to the ticket booth on the 4th floor.

House No 4, the **Black Mansion**, has one of the most striking facades. Built for an Italian merchant in 1588–89, it features a relief of St Martin on a horse. The **Kornyakt House** at No 6 is named after its original owner, a Greek merchant. Both house branches of the **Lviv History Museum** (admission to each branch 10uah; ⏲all branches 10am-5.30pm Thu-Tue).

Lychakivske Cemetery CEMETERY

(www.lviv-lychakiv.ukrain.travel; vul Pekarska; admission 10uah; ⏲9am-6pm) Don't leave town until you've seen this amazing cemetery a short ride on tram 7 east of the centre. This is the Père Lachaise of eastern Europe, with the same sort of overgrown grounds and Gothic aura as the famous Parisian necropolis.

Sleeping

TOP CHOICE **Old City Hostel** HOSTEL €

(☎294 9644; www.oldcityhostel.lviv.ua; vul Beryndy 3; dm/d from 80/320uah; @⚐) Occupying two floors of an elegantly fading city-centre tenement, this expertly run hostel has quickly established itself as the city's best. Fluff-free dorms hold four to 16 beds, shower queues are unheard of and there's a well-endowed kitchen.

Hotel George HOTEL €€

(☎232 6236; www.georgehotel.com.ua; pl Mitskevycha 1; s 330-780uah, d 400-850uah; ⚐) Partially renovated and losing its elusive 'Soviet chic' vibe, this gorgeous 1901 art nouveau building is still one of the city's best budget sleepovers with high-ceilinged rooms and friendly staff.

Central Square Hostel HOSTEL €

(☎095 225 6654; www.cshostel.com; pl Rynok 5; dm/d from 95/320; ⚐) This hostel may be small, but its location on Ploshcha Rynok puts you at the heart of the Lviv action. There's free tea and coffee, a pint-sized kitchen and thief-proof lockers, but just one shower.

Eurohotel BUSINESS HOTEL €€

(☎275 7214; www.eurohotel.lviv.ua; vul Tershakovtsiv 6A; s/d from 600/700uah; ⊜❄⚐) This unexciting place is a good example of just what you can do with a surplus Soviet lumpen-hotel. The 90 bog-standard but comfortable rooms are for sleeping, showering and accessing the net, but little else.

Eating & Drinking

Lviv is more famous for cafes than restaurants, but the food scene has seen some whacky developments in recent years.

TOP CHOICE **Masonic Restaurant** EUROPEAN €€€
(Pl Rynok 14; mains before discount 300-500uah; 11am-2am;) A secret entrance, an odd initiation ceremony, a dining room full of Masonic symbols and a shockingly expensive menu (make sure you pick up a 90% discount card at Dim Lehend beforehand) make this Ukraine's weirdest and most unmissable restaurant experience.

Dim Lehend UKRAINIAN €€
(vul Staroyevreyska 48; mains 30-65uah) Dedicated entirely to the city of Lviv, there's nothing dim about the 'House of Legends'. The five floors are stuffed with local paraphernalia and the menu heavy with meaty fare and belt-busting desserts.

Puzata Khata CAFE €
(vul Sichovykh Striltsiv 12; mains 11-25uah; 8am-11pm) This super-sized version of Ukraine's number-one self-service canteen chain stands out for its classy, Hutsul-themed interior and pure Ukrainian-rock soundtrack.

Pyrizhky PIE CANTEEN €
(Пиріжки; vul Slovatskoho 4; pyrizhky 3-5uah) No-frills canteen serving budget *pyrizhky* (pies/turnovers) to students for more than 50 years.

Dzyga CAFE
(vul Virmenska 35; 10am-midnight) This cafe-cum-art gallery has a relaxed vibe and a packed calender of events. It's particularly popular with bohemian, alternative types and travellers.

Information

Central Post Office (vul Slovatskoho 1)

Tourist Information Centre (254 6079; www.lviv.travel; pl Rynok 1, Ratusha; 10am-8pm Mon-Fri, to 7pm Sat, to 6pm Sun) Branches at the train station (226 2005; Ticket Hall; 9am-8pm) and the airport (067-673 9194; Terminal A; 10am-8pm Mon-Sat, to 6pm Sun).

Getting There & Away

AIR Lviv's new **airport** (www.airport.lviv.ua) is about 7km southwest of the centre. Take trolleybus 9 or bus 48 from the university.

Three daily flights link Lviv with Kyiv. Book through **Kiy Avia** (272 7818; www.kiyavia.com; vul Hnyatuka 20-22; 8am-8pm Mon-Sat, to 6pm Sun).

BUS The inconveniently located **main bus station** (Holovny Avtovokzal; vul Stryska) is 8km south of the centre. Take trolleybus 5.

WORTH A TRIP

CARPATHIAN MOUNTAINS

The easternmost section of the Carpathian Mountains slice through the lower corner of western Ukraine. Among the undulating ridges lives a cluster of various ethnic groups, including the Hutsuls.

The Carpathians are home to Ukraine's highest but easily climbable peak, **Mt Hoverla** (2062m), and its largest national park, the **Carpathian National Nature Park** (www.carpathianparks.org). Opportunities abound for wild camping, homestays, hiking and mountain biking in some superbly rugged backcountry.

This is also one of eastern Europe's premier skiing regions – see **Piligrim** (032-297 1899; www.piligrim.lviv.ua) and **SkiUkraine** (www.skiukraine.info) for information and bookings.

Touristy **Yaremche** puts you at the heart of the mountains; alternatives include **Kosiv**, **Rakhiv**, **Vorokhta** and **Kolomyya** where the unrivalled **On the Corner** (034-332 7437, 067 980 3326; www.onthecorner.info; vul Hetmanska 47A; d/dm 320/160uah) guesthouse is Ukraine's most foreigner-friendly digs, receiving rave reviews from travellers for it's warm welcome, scrumptious home-cooked food and excellent facilities. **Karpaty Info** (www.karpaty.info) lists hundreds of B&Bs, homestays and hotels in the region.

Lviv, Chernivtsi and Ivano-Frankivsk are gateways to the mountains with bus and train services into the main valleys.

TRAIN Lviv's train station is 2km west of the centre. To get there, take trams 1, 6 or 9. The quickest way to Kyiv is on the daily Intercity+ Hyundai express (238uah, five hours). There are also at least nine other trains per day, most of them overnight services (110uah to 150uah, eight to 13 hours).

Book at the station or the centrally located **train ticket office** (vul Hnatyuka 20; ⌚8am-2pm & 3-8pm Mon-Sat, to 6pm Sun).

UNDERSTAND UKRAINE

History

At the heart of the 10th-century Kyivan Rus state, Ukraine was the first major power to emerge in eastern Europe, but by the 13th century decline had set in and the country was being yanked back and forth by raiders from the East, most notably the Mongols who sacked Kyiv in 1240.

By the 15th century, groups of warriors calling themselves Cossacks fought anyone who encroached upon their borders or belief system (Orthodoxy). Their leader was the Hetman, the most famous of which was Bohdan Khmelnitsky, who signed a treaty with the tsar in 1654, which handed control of the country over to Russia for three and a half centuries.

Civil war broke out and the country exploded into anarchy after WWI: six different armies vied for power, and Kyiv changed hands many times within a year. Eventually Ukraine was again divided between Poland, Romania, Czechoslovakia and Russia. The Russian part became a founding member of the USSR in 1922, and in 1932 and 1933 suffered immensely from a famine that killed millions in the years following Stalin's brutal collectivisation policies.

An estimated six million Ukrainians died in WWII, which left most of the country's cities in ruin. After the war, the USSR kept the territory it had seized from Poland in 1939.

The country was the scene of the world's worst nuclear accident when the Chornobyl atomic power station exploded in April 1986.

Ukraine declared independence from the USSR in August 1991, and Leonid Kuchma led the country during the late '90s and early noughties. Kuchma's close ally Viktor Yanukovych ran in the 2004 presidential elections, challenged by Viktor Yushchenko, an opposition leader allegedly poisoned a week before the poll. In a run-off between the two, Yanukovych was declared winner amid allegations of vote-rigging. Suspecting foul play, the Ukrainian population came out en masse throughout the winter of 2004, gathering on Kyiv's maydan Nezalezhnosti with tents and orange flags. The 'Orange Revolution' forced a repeat run-off on 26 December, which Yushchenko won.

Between 2005 and 2010 Ukraine's first female prime minister and gas oligarch Yulia Tymoshenko, a weak president Yushchenko and a resurgent Yanukovych engaged in an absurd political soap opera featuring snap elections, fisticuffs in parliament and musical chairs in the prime minister's office. The upshot was disillusionment with the Orange Revolution among the population and Yanukovych's victory in the April 2010 presidential elections.

President Yanukovych has since been accused of whittling away at democracy, media freedom and the Ukrainian language, but the main cause of concern has been the imprisonment for abuse of office of his main political rival, Tymoshenko, a sentence many in the West feel was politically motivated.

People

Having endured centuries of many different foreign rulers, Ukrainians are a long-suffering people. They're nothing if not survivors; historically they've had to be, but after suffering a kind of identity theft during centuries of Russian rule in particular, this ancient nation which 'suddenly' emerged just over 20 years ago is forging a new personality.

This is a religious and superstitious society, in which traditional gender roles and strong family and community ties still bind. It's a culture where people are sometimes friendly and more generous than they can really afford to be. Paradoxically, it's also one in which remnants of Soviet mentality remain, with many people leading a kind of double life – snarling, elbowing *Homo sovieticus* outside of the home but generous, hospitable Europeans around their kitchen tables.

Most people describe themselves as Ukrainians and, hence, of Slavic origin. According to the last census (2001) of the country's 45 million people, 78% are ethnically Ukrainian, while 17% describe their ethnicity as Russian.

Food & Drink

'Borshch and bread – that's our food.' With this national saying, Ukrainians admit theirs is a cuisine of comfort, full of hearty, mild dishes designed for fierce winters rather than one of gastronomic zing.

Ukraine produces some very quaffable beers. Chernihivske, Lvivske, Slavutych and Obolon are the most popular brands. The best wines still come from neighbouring Moldova. The biggest name in Ukrainian vodka is **Nemiroff** (www.nemiroff.ua).

SURVIVAL GUIDE

Directory A–Z

Accommodation

With the value of the hryvnya low against most currencies, rooms are slightly more affordable than they once were.

Ukraine has a bewildering array of hotel and room types. At the bottom are Soviet-era budget crash pads for as little as 50uah, at the top 'six-star' overpriced luxury in OTT surroundings. Everything in between can be very hit-and-miss. There are no national standards to follow.

Kyiv and Lviv have a healthy gaggle of backpacker digs. **Hostelling Ukraine International** (www.hihostels.com.ua) gathers together all of Ukraine's hostels under one site. Hospitality clubs such as **Couchsurfing** (www.couchsurfing.com) and **The Hospitality Club** (www.hospitalityclub.org) have thousands of Ukrainian members.

The following price ranges are used in this chapter for a high-season double room with bathroom, not including breakfast:

€ less than 400uah

€€ 400uah to 800uah

€€€ more than 800uah

Business Hours

Business hours can be hard to pin down in Ukraine. Lunch breaks (1pm to 2pm or 2pm to 3pm) are common, Sunday closing is rare.

Banks 9am to 5pm

Restaurants noon to 11pm

Shops 9am to 6pm, to 8pm or 9pm in big cities

Sights 9am to 5pm or 6pm, closed at least one day per week

Embassies & Consulates

The following are all in Kyiv:

Australian Consulate (☎044-246 4223; vul Kominterna 18, Apt 11; Ⓢ Vokzalna)

Belarusian Embassy (☎044-537 5200; vul Mykhayla Kotsyubynskoho 3; Ⓢ Universytet)

Canadian Embassy (☎044-590 3100; www.canadainternational.gc.ca/ukraine; Yaroslaviv Val 31; Ⓢ Zoloti Vorota)

Polish Embassy (☎044-230 0700; www.polska.com.ua; vul Yaroslaviv Val 12; Ⓢ Zoloti Vorota)

Russian Embassy (☎044-244 0961; www.embrus.org.ua; pr Vozdukhoflotsky 27; Ⓢ Vokzalna)

UK Embassy (☎044-490 3660; http://ukinukraine.fco.gov.uk/en; vul Desyatynna 9; Ⓢ Maydan Nezalezhnosti)

US Embassy (☎044-490 0000; http://kyiv.usembassy.gov; vul Yuriya Kotsyubynskoho 10; Ⓢ Lukyanivska)

Food

Price ranges in this chapter refer to a standard main course:

€ less than 50uah

€€ 50uah to 150uah

€€€ more than 150uah

Internet Access

Internet cafes are virtually a thing of the past across Ukraine. Wi-fi is provided by most cafes and restaurants and free hotspots are being set up in major cities.

Money

Coins come in denominations of one, five, 10, 25 and 50 kopecks, plus the rare one hryvnya. Notes come in one, two, five, 10, 20, 50, 100, 200 and 500 hryvnya.

US dollars (post-1990 issue only), euro and Russian rouble notes (in pristine condition) are the easiest currencies to exchange. Credit cards are increasingly accepted but Ukraine remains a cash economy.

Public Holidays

The following are Ukraine's main public holidays:

New Year's Day 1 January

Orthodox Christmas 7 January

International Women's Day 8 March

Orthodox Easter (Paskha) April

Labour Day 1–2 May

Victory Day (1945) 9 May

Orthodox Pentecost June

Constitution Day 28 June

Independence Day (1991) 24 August

Telephone

- Ukraine's country code is ☎380.
- To call Ukraine from overseas, dial the internet access code, ☎380, the area code (minus the initial ☎0 and the number.
- To call abroad from Ukraine, dial ☎0, wait for a second tone, then dial ☎0 again, followed by the country code, city code and number.
- If making a few calls from your mobile, it's more economical to get a prepaid SIM card locally.
- European GSM phones usually work in Ukraine.

Visas

Tourist visas for stays of less than 90 days aren't required by citizens of the EU/EEA, Canada, the USA and Japan. Australians and New Zealanders need a visa.

Getting There & Away

The majority of visitors fly to Ukraine – generally to Kyiv. Your passport must be valid for the duration of your intended stay in Ukraine.

Air

Low-cost airlines have struggled to find their way into Ukraine. Airports include **Boryspil International Airport** (☎044-393 4371; www.kbp.aero) and **Zhulyany Airport** (☎044-585 7254; www.airport.kiev.ua) in Kyiv, and **Lviv International Airport** (www.lwo.aero).

Land

CAR & MOTORCYCLE

To bring your own vehicle into the country, you'll need your original registration papers (no photocopies) and a 'Green Card' International Motor Insurance Certificate.

TRAIN

Both Kyiv and Lviv are well connected to major cities by train in both Eastern and western Europe.

Getting Around

Air

Ukrainian International Airlines (www.flyuia.com) and Russian airline **UTair** (www.utair.ru) operate three flights daily between Kyiv and Lviv.

Bus & Train

Consult the Kyiv and Lviv sections for details of travel between the two cities. All trains are operated by **Ukrainian Railways** (www.uz.gov.ua). **Bus.com.ua** (www.bus.com.ua) has bus timetables but is hard to navigate.

Survival Guide

DIRECTORY A–Z . . . 1202
Accommodation 1202
Books 1204
Business Hours 1204
Customs Regulations . . 1204
Discount Cards 1205
Electricity 1205
Embassies & Consulates 1205
Gay & Lesbian Travellers 1206
Health 1206
Insurance 1206
Internet Access 1207
Legal Matters 1207
Maps 1207
Money 1208
Photography & DVDs 1210
Post 1210
Safe Travel 1210
Telephone 1211
Time 1212
Toilets 1212
Tourist Information 1212
Travellers with Disabilities 1212
Visas 1212
Volunteering 1213
Weights & Measures 1213
Women Travellers 1213
Working 1214

TRANSPORT 1215
GETTING THERE & AWAY 1215
Entering Europe 1215
Air 1215
Land 1216
Sea 1216
GETTING AROUND 1216
Air 1216
Bicycle 1217
Boat 1218
Bus 1218
Car & Motorcycle 1219
Hitching 1221
Local Transport 1222
Taxi 1222
Train 1222

LANGUAGE 1225

Directory A–Z

Accommodation

Europe offers the fullest possible range of budget accommodation, from camping grounds, hostels and student dormitories to private rooms, guesthouses and cheap hotels. Plus there are more novel options, such as farm stays and couch surfing. In this guide we've listed reviews in order of author preference.

Unless otherwise stated in individual reviews or in country directories, all prices for hotels and hostels in this book include a private bathroom and do not include breakfast.

Categories

Accommodation options in this book generally range from no stars to three stars, with the occasional smarter four- or five-star 'splurge' option. The very cheapest options are dorms or hostels with shared bathrooms and toilets, while at the upper end there are boutique or luxury hotels and self-contained accommodation with en suite facilities, TV and free wi-fi.

Price Icons

Each sleeping option has an indicative price category (from € to €€€) – these correspond to the price of the room relative to that country's price breakdown. See each chapter's Directory for more information.

Reservations

During peak holiday periods, particularly Easter, summer and Christmas – and any time of year in popular destinations such as London, Paris and Rome – it's wise to book ahead. Most places can be reserved online.

Seasons

Rates are for high season and often drop outside high season by as much as 50%.

High season in ski resorts is usually between Christmas and New Year and around the February–March winter holidays.

B&Bs & Guesthouses

Guesthouses (pension, *gasthaus, chambre d'hôte* etc) and B&Bs (bed and breakfasts) offer greater comfort than hostels for a marginally higher price. Most are simple affairs, normally with shared bathrooms.

In private rooms with a local family, or in a small guesthouse, you benefit from greater contact with locals. You'll still have privacy and autonomy, but remember you won't be able to bring the party back to your place.

In some destinations, particularly in eastern Europe, locals wait in train stations touting rented rooms. Just be sure such accommodation isn't in a far-flung suburb that requires an expensive taxi ride to and from town. Check that both parties are clear on price beforehand and remember that it's unwise to leave valuables in your room when you go out.

B&Bs in the UK and Ireland often aren't really budget accommodation – even the lowliest tend to have midrange prices and there is a new generation of 'designer' B&Bs which are positively top end.

Camping

Camping is the cheapest option. It has been rediscovered of late by trendsetters in western Europe, such as the UK (albeit with designer tents, ecotents and Airstream caravans; for example, www.coolcamping co.uk). In other countries, such as the Czech Republic, Germany, the Netherlands and Poland, it never went out of fashion.

BOOK YOUR STAY ONLINE

For more accommodation reviews by Lonely Planet authors, check out lonelyplanet.com/hotels/europe. You'll find independent reviews, as well as recommendations on the best places to stay. Best of all, you can book online.

STAY FOR FREE

Wish you had mates all over Europe so you could crash on their sofas when you were travelling? Don't we all? Luckily, with the phenomenon of online hospitality clubs, you can make it a reality. Couch surfing (www.couchsurfing.org) is the perfect example, linking travellers with thousands of global residents who'll let you occupy their couch or spare room – and sometimes show you around town – all cost-free. Couch surfing is unusual as you do not have to return the favour by hosting other travellers; it's entirely up to you.

Similar schemes, such as Global Freeloaders (www.globalfreeloaders.com) and Hospitality Club (www.hospitalityclub.org), tend to be stricter on that, although both are happy for you to first enjoy others' hospitality before reciprocating.

If you're worried about how safe this is, there are many security measures in place, with members verified and vouched for by others – we've not heard any bad stories. However, at the very least, always let friends and family know where you're staying and carry your mobile phone with you.

Female travellers might want to investigate the women-only, membership-based **5W** (www.womenwelcomewomen.org.uk).

In large European cities, most camping grounds are some distance from the centre, so you'll need your own transport. As few budget travellers have that, we list easily accessible camping grounds only, or include sites where it's common for travellers to bed down en masse under the stars (for example, on some Greek islands).

National tourist offices provide lists of camping grounds and camping organisations. At designated grounds, there will usually be a charge per tent or site, per person and per vehicle. In busy areas and in busy seasons, it's sometimes necessary to book.

Camping other than at designated grounds is difficult in western Europe, because it's hard to find a suitably private spot.

Camping is also illegal without the permission of the local authorities (the police or local council office) or the landowner. Don't be shy about asking; you might be pleasantly surprised.

In some countries, such as Austria, the UK, France and Germany, free camping is illegal on all but private land, and in Greece it's illegal altogether but not enforced. This doesn't prevent hikers from occasionally pitching their tent, and you'll usually get away with it if you have a small tent, are discreet, stay just one or two nights, decamp during the day and don't light a fire or leave rubbish. At worst, you'll be woken by the police and asked to move on.

In eastern Europe, free camping is more widespread.

Homestays & Farmstays

You needn't volunteer on a farm to sleep on it. In Switzerland and Germany, there's the opportunity for ordinary tourists to sleep in barns or 'hay hotels'. It saves you money and is a great experience. For further details, visit **Abenteuer im Stroh** (www.schlaf-im-stroh.ch) and **Hay Hotels** (www.heuhotel.de).

When their cows are out to pasture in summer, or even after they've been brought in for the winter come early October, farmers charge travellers a small amount to sleep on straw in their hay barns or lofts (and listen to the jangle of cow or goat bells beneath your head). Farmers provide cotton undersheets (to avoid straw pricks) and woolly blankets for extra warmth, but guests need their own sleeping bag and torch.

Hostels

Hostels in Europe vary enormously from veritable backpacker palaces to real dumps. We've tried to ensure we don't include any of the latter, but expect there to be a variation in standards across the region.

HI Hostels (those affiliated to Hostelling International, www.hihostels.com), offer the cheapest (secure) roof over your head in Europe and you don't have to be particularly young to use them. Only southern German hostels enforce a strict age limit of 26 years. That said, if you're over 26 you'll frequently pay a small surcharge (usually about €3) to stay in an official hostel.

Most HI hostels have dorm rooms sleeping four to five people, although larger ones do exist. Hostel rules vary per facility and country, but some ask that guests vacate the rooms for cleaning purposes or impose a curfew. Most offer a complimentary breakfast, although the quality of this varies.

You need to be a YHA or HI member to use HI-affiliated hostels, but nonmembers can stay by paying a few extra euros, which will be set against future membership. After sufficient nights (usually six), you automatically become a member. To join, ask at any hostel or contact your national hostelling office, which you'll find on the HI website – where you can also make online bookings.

There are also many private hostelling organisations in Europe and hundreds of unaffiliated backpacker hostels. Private hostels have fewer rules (eg no curfew, no daytime lockout), more self-catering kitchens and fewer large, noisy school groups. However, while HI hostels must meet minimum safety and cleanliness standards, facilities vary greatly in private hostels. Dorms in many private hostels can be mixed sex. If you aren't happy to share mixed dorms, be sure to ask when you book.

Hotels

Hotels are usually the most expensive accommodation option, though at their lower end there is little to differentiate them from guesthouses or even hostels.

Be careful when choosing inexpensive hotels around bus and train stations. They can be convenient for late-night or early-morning arrivals and departures, but some hotels are unofficial brothels or just downright sleazy places where things go missing in the night.

If you can, check the room beforehand and make sure you're clear on price and what it covers.

Discounts for longer stays are usually possible and hotel owners in southern Europe *might* be open to a little bargaining if times are slack. In many countries it's common for business hotels (usually more than two stars) to slash their rates by up to 40% on Friday and Saturday nights.

University Accommodation

Some university towns rent out their student accommodation during the holiday periods. This is a popular practice in France, the UK and many eastern European countries. University accommodation will sometimes be in single rooms (although it's more commonly in doubles or triples) and might have cooking facilities. For details ask at individual colleges or universities, at student information offices or local tourist offices.

Books

Europe has inspired a huge amount of writing, though little that covers the entire complex continent. Here are a few exceptions that make for great background reading.

» In *A Tramp Abroad*, Mark Twain chronicles, with his usual wit, a 15-month 'walking tour' (by train and coach) through central Europe and the Alps in the 19th century.

» Patrick Leigh Fermor's *A Time of Gifts* is widely regarded as a masterpiece of travel literature. Writing in 1977, Fermor looks back on the time when, as a teenager in 1934, he walked from Hoek van Holland to Constantinople (present-day İstanbul), relying on the kindness of strangers to house and feed him. This book takes him as far as Hungary, where another book, *Between the Woods and the Water*, takes over.

» In *Neither Here nor There: Travels in Europe*, Bill Bryson retraces his youthful 1970s European tour some 20 years later as an older, less agile, more sober adult.

» Tim Moore reaches further back into history with *Continental Drifter*. Here, he muses on the origins of the 17th-century European Grand Tour, by which well-to-do young Englishmen sought to educate themselves – all the while re-creating it himself, sleeping rough in a vintage Rolls Royce and (crumpled) velvet suit.

» Peter Moore (no relation to Tim) makes life even more difficult for himself in *The Wrong Way Home*. The 'wrong way' turns out to be without a plane journey, from London to Sydney. The travelogue naturally ventures into both Asia and Europe.

» For something perhaps more akin to your own experience, try *Rite of Passage: Tales of Backpacking 'Round Europe.* Edited by Lisa Johnson, it's a group of stories by young travellers conquering the Continent for the first time. From crowded hostels to heated flings, this book taps into the seemingly insignificant events that fuel lifelong memories.

Business Hours

In most of Europe businesses are open 9am to 6pm Monday to Friday, and 9am to 1pm or 5pm on Saturday. In smaller towns there may be a one- to two-hour closure for lunch. Some shops close on Sunday. Businesses also close on national holidays and local feast days.

Banks have the shortest opening times, often closing between 3pm and 5pm, and occasionally even shutting for lunch. They generally only open on weekdays.

Restaurants typically open from noon until midnight and bars open around 6pm. Museums usually close on Monday or (less commonly) on Tuesday.

Customs Regulations

The European Union (EU) has a two-tier customs system: one for goods bought duty-free to import to or export from the EU, and one for goods bought in another EU country where taxes and duties have already been paid.

» Entering or leaving the EU, you are allowed to carry duty-free: 200 cigarettes, 5 cigars or 250g of tobacco; 2 of still wine plus 1L of spirits over 22% alcohol or another 2L of wine (sparkling or otherwise); 50g of perfume, 250mL of eau de toilette.

» Travelling from one EU country to another, the duty-paid limits are: 800 cigarettes, 200 cigars, 1kg of tobacco, 10L of spirits, 20L of fortified wine, 90L of wine (of which not more than 60L is sparkling) and 110L of beer.

» Non-EU countries often have different regulations and many countries forbid the export of antiquities and cultural treasures.

Discount Cards

Camping Cards

The Camping Card International (CCI; formerly the Camping Carnet) is a camping ground ID that can be used instead of a passport when checking into a camping ground. Many camping grounds offer a small discount if you sign in with one and it includes third party insurance. CCIs are issued by automobile associations, camping federations and sometimes at camping grounds.

Rail Passes

If you plan to visit more than a few countries, or one or two countries in-depth, you might save money with a rail pass (p1222).

Student Cards

The International Student Travel Confederation (www.isic.org) issues three cards for students, teachers and under-26s, offering thousands of worldwide discounts on transport, museum entry, youth hostels and even some restaurants. These cards are: the International Student Identity Card (ISIC), the International Teacher Identity Card (ITIC) and the International Youth Travel Card (IYTC). You can check the full list of discounts and where to apply for the cards on the ISTC website. Issuing offices include **STA Travel** (www.statravel.com).

For under-26s, there's also a specific European card, the **Euro<26** (www.euro26.org). Many countries have raised the age limit for this card to 30.

Electricity

Europe generally runs on 220V, 50Hz AC, but there are exceptions. The UK runs on 230/240V AC, and some old buildings in Italy and Spain have 125V (or even 110V in Spain). The Continent is moving towards a 230V standard. If your home country has a vastly different voltage you will need a transformer for delicate and important appliances.

The UK and Ireland use chunky, three-pin square plugs. Most of Europe uses the 'europlug' with two round pins. Greece, Italy and Switzerland use a third round pin in a way that the two-pin plug usually – but not always in Italy and Switzerland – fits. Buy an adapter before leaving home; those on sale in Europe generally go the other way, but those for visitors to Europe are also available – airports are always a good place to buy them.

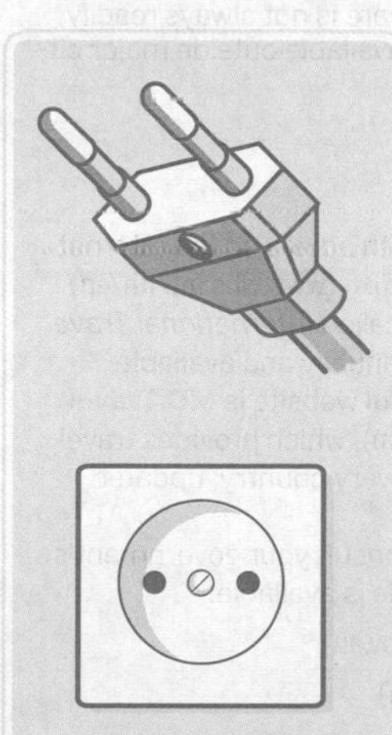

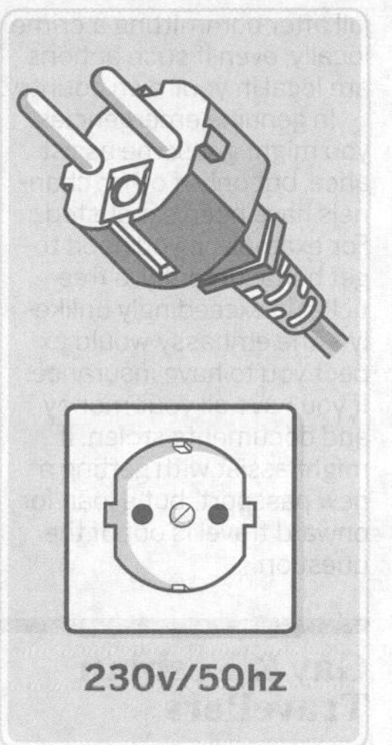

Embassies & Consulates

It's important to realise what your own embassy can and can't do to help you if you get into trouble. Generally speaking, it won't be much help in emergencies if the trouble you're in is remotely your own fault. Remember, you're bound by the laws of the country you're in. Your embassy will not be sympathetic if you end up in jail after committing a crime locally, even if such actions are legal in your own country.

In genuine emergencies you might get some assistance, but only if other channels have been exhausted. For example, if you need to get home urgently, a free ticket is exceedingly unlikely – the embassy would expect you to have insurance. If you have all your money and documents stolen, it might assist with getting a new passport, but a loan for onward travel is out of the question.

Gay & Lesbian Travellers

In cosmopolitan centres, especially in western Europe, you'll find very liberal attitudes towards homosexuality. Belgium, Denmark, the Netherlands, Norway, Portugal, Spain and Sweden have all legalised same-sex marriages, while many other countries offer civil partnerships granting all or most of the rights of marriage.

London, Paris, Berlin, Munich, Amsterdam, Madrid and Lisbon have thriving gay communities and pride events. The Greek islands of Mykonos and Lesvos are popular gay beach destinations. Gran Canaria and Ibiza in Spain are big centres for both gay clubbing and beach holidays.

eastern Europe tends to be far less progressive, though even in Russia and Belarus, where gay rights are in their infancy, there are accessibly open gay scenes.

Outside the big cities, attitudes become more conservative and discretion is advised, particularly in Turkey and most parts of eastern Europe. There is an absolute dearth of good gay-travel websites, so it's helpful to consult websites about the country you're travelling to.

Health

Good, sometimes excellent, health care is readily available in western Europe and, for minor illnesses, pharmacists can give valuable advice and sell over-the-counter medication. They can also advise if you need specialised help and point you in the right direction. The standard of dental care is usually good.

While the situation in eastern Europe is improving since the EU accession of many countries, quality medical care is not always readily available outside major cities, but embassies, consulates and five-star hotels can usually recommend doctors or clinics.

No jabs are necessary for Europe. However, the World Health Organization (WHO) recommends that all travellers be covered for diphtheria, tetanus, measles, mumps, rubella and polio, regardless of their destination. Since most vaccines don't produce immunity until at least two weeks after they're given, visit a physician at least six weeks before departure.

Tap water is generally safe to drink in western Europe. However, bottled water is recommended in most of eastern Europe, and is a must in some countries, including Russia (particularly St Petersburg) and Ukraine, where giardia can be a problem. Do not drink water from rivers or lakes as it may contain bacteria or viruses.

Condoms are widely available in Europe; however, emergency contraception may not be, so take the necessary precautions. The **International Planned Parent Federation** (www.ippf.org) can advise about the availability of contraception in different countries. When buying condoms, look for a European CE mark, which means they have passed quality tests.

HEALTH RESOURCES

There is a wealth of travel-health advice on the internet. The **World Health Organization** (www.who.int/ith/en) also publishes a superb book called *International Travel and Health,* which is revised annually and available online at no cost. Another useful website is **MD Travel Health** (www.mdtravelhealth.com), which provides travel-health recommendations for every country; updated daily.

It's usually a good idea to consult your government's website before departure, if one is available:

Australia (www.smartraveller.gov.au)

Canada (www.travelhealth.gc.ca)

UK (www.dh.gov.uk)

USA (www.cdc.gov/travel)

Insurance

It's foolhardy to travel without insurance to cover theft, loss and medical problems. There's a wide variety of policies, so check the small print.

Some policies specifically exclude 'dangerous activities', which can include scuba diving, motorcycling, winter sports, adventure sports or even hiking. Some pay doctors or hospitals directly, but most require you to pay upfront, save the documentatic and claim later. Some policie also ask you to call back (reverse charges) to a centre in your home country, where an immediate assessment of your problem is made.

Check that the policy covers ambulances or an emergency flight home.

The policies handled by STA Travel and other student travel agencies are usually good value. In the UK, the website Money Supermarket (www.moneysupermarket.com/travel-insurance) does an automated comparison of 450 partner policies and comes up with the best for your needs.

Worldwide travel insurance is available online at www.lonelyplanet.com/travel-insurance. You can buy, extend and claim online anytime – even if you're already on the road.

Internet Access

Internet access varies enormously across Europe. In most places, you'll be able to find wireless (wi-fi, also called WLAN in some countries), although whether it's free varies greatly.

Where the wi-fi icon (📶) appears in this book, it means that the establishment offers free wi-fi that you can access immediately, or by asking for the access code from staff.

Bringing a laptop, smartphone or iPad is a great way to stay in touch on the road. If you don't have a device that connects to the internet, you'll be limited to the fast-declining number of internet cafes or the increasingly rare number of hotels and hostels that offer a guest terminal for emailing.

Most hotels and hostels now offer free wi-fi, as do many restaurants and cafes. At airports it is rarely free and you'll have to register with a credit card or buy an access card.

Access is generally straightforward, although a few tips are in order. If you can't find the @ symbol on a keyboard, try Alt Gr + 2, or Alt Gr + Q. Watch out for German and some Balkans keyboards, which reverse the Z and the Y positions. Using a French keyboard is an art unto itself.

Where necessary in relevant countries, click on the language prompt in the bottom right-hand corner of the screen or hit Ctrl + Shift to switch between the Cyrillic and Latin alphabets.

Legal Matters

Most European police are friendly and helpful, especially if you have been a victim of a crime. In most countries you are required by law to prove your identity if asked by police (although make sure they really are police), so always carry your passport, or an identity card, or at least a photocopy of either document.

You can generally purchase alcohol (beer and wine) from between 16 and 18 (usually 18 for spirits), but if in doubt, ask. Although you can drive at 17 or 18, you might not be able to hire a car until you're 25.

Cigarette-smoking bans have been progressively introduced across Europe since 2004. Countries that now prohibit smoking in bars and restaurants include Austria, Croatia, Estonia, Finland, France, Greece, Hungary, Iceland, Ireland, Italy, Malta, the Netherlands, Norway, Sweden, Turkey and the UK. Many other countries will be passing similar laws in the near future, so with such change afoot, ask before lighting up.

Drugs are often quite openly available in Europe, but that doesn't mean they're legal. The Netherlands is most famed for its liberal attitudes, with 'coffee shops' openly selling cannabis.

Elsewhere in the Netherlands possession of cannabis is only decriminalised not legalised (apart from its medicinal use). Don't take this relaxed attitude as an invitation to buy harder drugs; if you get caught, you'll be punished. Since 2008 magic mushrooms have been banned in the Netherlands.

Equally, in Belgium, the possession of up to 5g of cannabis is legal, but selling the drug isn't, so if you get caught at the point of sale, you could be in trouble.

In Portugal, the possession of *all* drugs has been decriminalised. Once again, however, selling is illegal.

Britain downgraded cannabis from a Class B to Class C drug a decade ago, but in 2009 it reverted to Class B status, meaning that if you're caught you may face arrest. Anyone caught smoking in public or in front of children is very likely to be arrested.

Switzerland has gone the other way. It was moving towards decriminalisation and then had a last-minute legal about-face. Some people still smoke pot openly, but if police decide to enforce the law, you'll face a fine of up to Sfr400 just for possession.

Spain and Italy have also tightened their cannabis laws in recent years, so make sure you're careful there, too.

Getting caught with drugs in other parts of Europe, particularly countries such as Turkey and Russia, can lead to imprisonment.

If in any doubt, err on the side of caution. For your own safety, don't even think about taking drugs across international borders.

Maps

Good maps are easy to find in Europe and in good bookshops beforehand.

Road atlases are essential if you're driving or cycling. Leading brands are Freytag & Berndt, Hallwag, Kümmerly + Frey, and Michelin. Maps published by European automobile associations, such as Britain's AA (www.theaa.co.uk) and Germany's ADAC (www.adac.de), are usually excellent and sometimes free if membership of your local association gives you reciprocal rights. Tourist offices are another good source for (usually free and fairly basic) maps.

Money

A common currency, the euro, is used in 17 EU states: Austria, Belgium, Cyprus, Estonia, France, Finland, Germany, Greece, Ireland, Italy, Luxembourg, Malta, the Netherlands, Portugal, Slovakia, Slovenia and Spain. Three further non-EU states, Andorra, Kosovo and Montenegro, also use the euro.

The euro is made up of 100 cents, and notes come in denominations of €5, €10, €20, €50, €100, €200 and €500 euros, though any notes above 50 are rarely used on a daily basis. Coins come in 1c, 2c, 5c, 10c, 20c, 50c, €1 and €2.

Denmark, the UK and Sweden have held out against adopting the euro for political reasons, while non-EU nations, such as Albania, Belarus, Norway, Russia, Switzerland, Turkey and Ukraine, also have their own currencies.

For security and flexibility, diversify your source of funds. Carry an ATM card, credit card, cash and possibly travellers cheques.

Set up an internet banking account before you leave home, so you can track your spending. However, be sure to log off properly whenever you use these services from a public computer.

ATMs

Every country has international ATMs that allow you to withdraw cash directly from your home account and this is the most common way European travellers now access their money. However, you should always have a backup option, as some readers have reported glitches with ATMs in individual countries, even when their card worked elsewhere in Europe. In some remote areas, ATMs might be scarce, too.

Much of western Europe now uses a chip-and-pin system for added security. You will have problems if you don't have a four-digit PIN number and might have difficulties if your card doesn't have a metallic chip. Check with your bank.

If your card is rejected, try again in a few hours' time. Make sure you bring your bank's phone number and, if your card fails again, call them. Also be aware that some banks automatically block foreign transactions until they are able to call the cardholder and confirm they are abroad.

When you withdraw money from an ATM, the amounts are converted and dispensed in local currency. However, there will be fees. If you're uncertain, ask your bank to explain.

Finally, always cover the keypad when entering your PIN and make sure there are no unusual devices attached to the machine, which can copy your card's details or cause it to stick in the machine. If your card disappears and the screen goes blank before you've even entered your PIN, don't enter it – especially if a 'helpful' bystander tells you to do so. If you can't retrieve your card, call your bank's emergency number, if you can, before leaving the ATM.

Cash

Nothing beats cash for convenience… or risk. If you lose it, it's gone forever and very few travel insurers will come to your rescue. Those that do will limit the amount to somewhere around €300. It's still a good idea, though, to bring some local currency in cash, if only to cover yourself until you get to an exchange facility or find an ATM. The equivalent of €100 or €150 should usually be enough. Some extra cash in an easily exchanged currency is also a good idea, especially in eastern Europe.

Credit Cards

Credit cards are handy for major purchases, such as air or rail tickets, and offer a lifeline in certain emergencies. Visa and MasterCard/Eurocard are more widely accepted in Europe than Amex and Diners Club; Visa (sometimes called Carte Bleue) is particularly strong in France and Spain.

There are, however, regional differences in the general acceptability of credit cards. In the UK, for example, you can usually flash your plastic in the most humble of budget restaurants; in Germany it's rare for restaurants to take credit cards. Cards are not widely accepted off the beaten track.

To reduce the risk of fraud, always keep your card in view when making transactions; for example, in restaurants that do accept cards, pay as you leave, following your card to the till. Keep transaction records and either check your statements when you return home, or check your account online while still on the road.

Letting your credit-card company know roughly where you're going lessens the chance of fraud – or of your bank cutting off the card when it sees (your) unusual spending.

Debit Cards

Ticket machines in many European train stations and other places such as car parks or city-bike stands (eg in Vienna) frequently accept Maestro debit cards, sometimes exclusively. So it's always worthwhile having a Maestro-compatible debit card, which differs from a credit card in deducting money straight from your bank account. Check with your bank or MasterCard (Maestro's parent) for compatibility.

Exchanging Money

In general, euros, US dollars and UK pounds are the easiest currencies to exchange in Europe. The major European currencies are fully convertible, but you may have trouble exchanging some lesser-known ones at small banks.

Importing or exporting some currencies is restricted or banned, so try to get rid of any local currency before you leave. Get rid of Scottish pounds before leaving the UK; nobody outside Britain will touch them.

Most airports, central train stations, big hotels and many border posts have banking facilities outside regular business hours, at times on a 24-hour basis. Post offices in Europe often perform banking tasks, tend to open longer hours and outnumber banks in remote places. While they always exchange cash, they might baulk at handling travellers cheques not in the local currency.

The best exchange rates are usually at banks. *Bureaux de change* usually – but not always – offer worse rates or charge higher commissions. Hotels and airports are almost always the worst places to change money.

International Transfers

International bank transfers are good for secure one-off novements of large amounts of money, but they might ake three to five days and here will be a fee (about £25 n the UK, for example). Be ure to specify the name of he bank, plus the sort code nd address of the branch here you'd like to pick up our money.

In an emergency it's quick- r and easier to have money ired via an **Amex** (www. nericanexpress.com) office, **estern Union** (www.wester- nion.com) or **MoneyGram** ww.moneygram.com). All are ite costly.

Taxes & Refunds

Sales tax applies to many goods and services in Europe. Depending on the country and the product, it will add between 10% and 20% to the price of goods. Luckily, when non-EU residents spend more than a certain amount (around €75) they can usually reclaim that tax when leaving the country.

Making a tax-back claim is straightforward. First, make sure the shop offers duty-free sales (often a sign will be displayed reading 'Tax-Free Shopping'). When making your purchase, ask the shop attendant for a tax-refund voucher, filled in with the correct amount and the date. This can be used to claim a refund directly at international airports, or stamped at ferry ports or border crossings and mailed back for a refund.

None of this applies to EU residents. An American citizen living in London is not entitled to rebate on items bought in Paris. Conversely, an EU passport holder living in New York is.

Tipping & Bargaining

Tipping has become complicated, with 'service charges' increasingly added to bills. In theory this means you're not obliged to tip. In practice that money often doesn't go to the server and they might make it clear they still expect a gratuity. Don't pay twice. If the service charge is optional, remove it from the bill and pay a tip. If the service charge is not optional, don't tip.

Generally, waiters in western Europe tend to be paid decent wages. Bargaining isn't common in much of Europe, but is known in and around the Mediterranean. In Turkey it's virtually a way of life.

USEFUL WEB RESOURCES

Blue Flag (www.blueflag.org) Ecolabel for sustainably developed beaches and marinas.

Budget Traveller's Guide to Sleeping in Airports (www.sleepinginairports.net) Funny and useful resource for backpackers flying stand-by.

Currency Conversions (www.xc.com) Up-to-the-second exchange rates for hundreds of currencies.

Guide for Europe (www.guideforeurope.com) Has a handy hostel review page posted by visitors.

Hostelworld (www.hostelworld.com) Handy for other travellers' views on hostels.

Lonely Planet (www.lonelyplanet.com/thorntree) On Lonely Planet's message board you can usually get your travel questions answered by fellow travellers in a matter of hours.

Money Saving Expert (www.moneysavingexpert.com) Excellent tips on the best UK travel insurance, mobile phones and bank cards to use abroad. The flight-checker facility shows the latest cheap flights available.

The Man in Seat 61 (www.seat61.com) A professional-standard personal website, dedicated to rail travel across Europe.

Travellers Cheques

As travellers cheques have been overtaken in popularity by international ATMs, it's become more difficult to find places that cash them. In parts of the former Soviet Union only a few banks handle them, and the process can be quite bureaucratic and costly.

That said, having a few cheques is a good back-up. If they're stolen you can claim a refund, provided you have a record of cheque numbers, but it's vital to store these numbers away from the cheques themselves.

Amex and Thomas Cook are reliable brands of travellers cheques, while cheques in US dollars, euros or British pounds are the easiest to cash. When changing them ask about fees and commissions as well as the exchange rate.

Western Union

If everything goes horribly wrong – your money, travellers cheques and credit cards are all stolen – don't despair. While it's a terrible (and highly unusual) situation, a friend or relative back home will be able to wire money to you anywhere in Europe via Western Union (WU). The sender is given a code that they communicate to you, then you take the code to the nearest office, along with your passport, to receive your cash.

There are literally thousands of WU representatives; just look for the distinctive yellow-and-black sign.

Photography & DVDs

Film is widely available in Europe, but most travellers shoot digital these days. So for the majority, the most important thing is to have enough memory to store pictures. Huge memory cards are available, but if you do run out, some internet cafes will burn CDs, or you can transfer files onto an external hard drive.

DVDs each have a regional code (1 for North America, 2 for Europe and South Africa and 3 for Australasia). If you buy a disc in Europe, check that the code corresponds with your machine at home, or look for international discs coded 0. Additionally, you will have to check your DVD player is universally compatible and the TV systems work together too (NTSC in the USA and Japan, but PAL in Europe and Australasia). The upshot of all this is that while DVDs bought in Europe frequently won't play on your TV back home, they will probably work on your computer. Universal players are more common in Europe, so DVDs brought here from elsewhere will probably (but not necessarily) work.

Post

From major European centres, airmail typically takes about five days to North America and about a week to Australasian destinations, although mail from such countries as Albania or Russia is much slower.

Poste restante services, where friends and family can write to you care of main post offices, are still offered, but email has rendered these largely obsolete. Courier services such as DHL are best for essential deliveries.

Safe Travel

Travelling in Europe is usually very safe. Violent crime is rare; the main threats facing travellers are pickpockets, petty thieves and scam artists. The following outlines a range of general guidelines.

Discrimination

Divergent views about immigration, plus a small rump of anachronistic attitudes, mean that, in some parts of Europe, travellers of African, Arab or Asian descent might encounter unpleasant attitudes that are unrelated to them personally. In rural areas travellers whose skin colour marks them out as foreigners might experience unwanted attention. Some travellers have reported negative encounters because locals mistook them for Roma.

Attitudes vary from country to country. People tend to be more accepting in cities than in the country. Race is also less of an issue in western Europe than in parts of the former Eastern Bloc. For example, there has been a spate of fatal racially motivated attacks in St Petersburg and other parts of Russia in recent years.

Druggings

Although rare, some drugging of travellers does occur in Europe. Travellers are especially vulnerable on trains and buses where a new 'friend' may offer you food or a drink that will knock you out, giving them time to fleece you of your belongings.

Gassings have also been reported on a handful of overnight international trains. The usual scenario involves the release of a sleep-inducing gas into a sleeping compartment in the night. The best protection is to lock the door of your compartment (use your own lock if there isn't one) and to lock your bags to luggage racks, preferably with a sturdy combination cable.

If you can help it, never sleep alone in a train compartment.

Pickpockets & Thieves

Theft is definitely a problem in parts of Europe and you have to be aware of other travellers.

Don't store valuables in train-station lockers or luggage-storage counters and be careful about people who offer to help you operate a locker. Also be vigilant if someone offers to carry your luggage: they might carry it away altogether.

Don't leave valuables in your car, on train seats or in your room. When going out, don't flaunt cameras, laptops and other expensive electronic goods.

Carry a small day pack, as shoulder bags are an open invitation for snatch-thieves. For extra peace of mind use small zipper locks on your packs.

Pickpockets are most active in dense crowds, especially in busy train stations and on public transport during peak hours. Be careful in these situations.

Spread valuables, cash and cards around your body or in different bags. Some travellers walk around with €100 in their shoe; others put €50 in their aspirin bottle.

A money belt with your essentials (passport, cash, credit cards, airline tickets) is usually a good idea. However, so you needn't delve into it in public, carry a wallet with a day's worth of cash.

A dummy wallet, with fake 'credit' cards (eg library cards or video store cards) is also a good ploy.

Having your passport stolen is less of a disaster if you've recorded the number and issue date or, even better, photocopied the relevant data pages. You can also scan them and email them to yourself.

Also record the serial numbers of travellers cheques and carry photocopies of your credit cards, airline tickets and other travel documents.

If you do lose your passport, notify the police immediately to get a statement and contact your nearest consulate.

If this seems a lot to absorb, remember it's basically common sense, and rest assured there's no need to fret about theft. Just be sensible with your possessions.

Scams

Most scams involve distracting you – either by kids running up to you, someone asking for directions or spilling something on you – while another person steals your wallet. Be alert in such situations.

In some countries, especially in eastern Europe, you may encounter people claiming to be from the tourist police, the special police, the super-secret police, whatever. Unless they're wearing a uniform and have good reason for accosting you (eg you're robbing a bank), treat their claims with suspicion.

One common scam runs like this: someone asks you to change money. You say no, and seconds later an 'undercover' police officer 'arrests' the money changer. The officer then asks to check your passport and money, in case it's counterfeit. Something then goes missing or is confiscated when the 'undercover officer' handles your valuables.

Another swindle involves someone dropping a wad of money near you. Someone else picks it up and asks if it's yours. The first person then says they had twice that and requests you open your wallet to prove you don't have the other half. At this point, a 'policeman' turns up, and the scenario proceeds as per the money-changing scam.

Needless to say, never show your passport or cash to anyone on the street. Simply walk away. If someone flashes a badge, offer to accompany them to the nearest police station.

Unrest & Terrorism

Civil unrest and terrorist bombings are rare in Europe, but they do occur. Attacks by ETA (the Basque separatist group in Spain and France) and attacks by Muslim extremists in the UK, Spain and Russia have all occurred in recent years. All you can do is keep an eye on the news and avoid areas where any flare up seems likely.

Telephone

Travel is made infinitely easier with a mobile phone you can use on the road. If your phone is European, it's often perfectly feasible to use it on roaming throughout the Continent.

If you're coming from outside Europe, it's usually worth buying a prepaid local SIM in one European country. Even if you're not staying there long, calls across Europe will still be cheaper if they're not routed via your home country and the prepaid card will enable you to keep a limit on your spending. In several countries you need your passport to buy a SIM card.

In order to use other SIM cards in your phone, you'll need to have your handset unlocked by your home provider. Even if your phone is locked, you can use apps such as whatsapp to send free text messages internationally wherever you have wi-fi access, or Skype to make free international calls whenever you're online.

Europe uses the GSM 900 network, which also covers Australia and New Zealand, but is not compatible with the North American GSM 1900 or the totally different system in Japan. However, some North American GSM

EMERGENCY NUMBERS

The phone number ☎112 can be dialled for emergencies in all EU states. See the individual country chapters for country-specific emergency numbers.

1900/900 phones do work. If you have a GSM phone, check with your service provider about using it in Europe. You'll need international roaming, but this is usually free to enable.

You can call abroad from almost any phone box in Europe. Public telephones accepting phonecards (available from post offices, telephone centres, newsstands or retail outlets) are virtually the norm now; in countries such as France, coin-operated phones are almost impossible to find.

Without a phonecard, you can ring from a telephone booth inside a post office or telephone centre and settle your bill at the counter. Reverse-charge (collect) calls are often possible. From many countries the Country Direct system lets you phone home by billing the long-distance carrier you use at home. These numbers can often be dialled from public phones without even inserting a phonecard.

Time

Europe is divided into four time zones. From west to east these are:

UTC (Britain, Ireland, Portugal) GMT (GMT+1 in summer)

CET (the majority of European countries) GMT+1 (GMT+2 in summer)

EET (Greece, Turkey, Bulgaria, Romania, Moldova, Ukraine, Belarus, Lithuania, Latvia, Estonia, Kaliningrad, Finland) GMT+2 (GMT+3 in summer)

MSK (Russia) GMT+3 (GMT+4 in summer)

At 9am in Britain it's 1am (GMT/UTC minus eight hours) on the US west coast, 4am (GMT/UTC minus five hours) on the US east coast, 10am in Paris and Prague, 11am in Athens, midday in Moscow and 7pm (GMT/UTC plus 10 hours) in Sydney.

In most European countries, clocks are put forward one hour for daylight-saving time on the last Sunday in March, and turned back again on the last Sunday in October.

Toilets

Many public toilets in Europe require a small fee either deposited in a box or given to the attendant. Forget horror stories about having to squat – sit-down toilets are the rule in the vast majority of places. Squat toilets can still be found in rural areas, although they are definitely a dying breed.

Public-toilet provision remains changeable from city to city. If you can't find one, simply drop into a hotel or restaurant and ask to use theirs.

Tourist Information

Unless otherwise indicated, tourist offices are common and widespread, although their usefulness varies enormously. Only in emerging tourist destinations might you have problems locating them.

Travellers with Disabilities

Cobbled medieval streets, 'classic' hotels, congested inner cities and underground subway systems make Europe a tricky destination for people with mobility impairments. However, the train facilities are good and some destinations boast new tram services or lifts to platforms. The following websites can help with specific details.

Accessible Europe (www.accessibleurope.com) Specialist European tours with van transport. Prices start from €240 for four days.

Lonely Planet (www.lonelyplanet.com/thorntree) Share experiences on the Travellers with Disabilities branch of the Thorn Tree message board.

Mobility International Schweiz (www.mis-ch.ch) Good site listing 'barrier-free' destinations in Switzerland and abroad, plus wheelchair-accessible hotels in Switzerland. Sadly it's only partly in English; address English emails to info@mis-ch.ch.

Mobility International USA (www.miusa.org) Publishes guides and advises travellers with disabilities on mobility issues.

Royal Association for Disability & Rehabilitation (www.radar.org.uk) Publishes a comprehensive annual guide, *Holidays in Britain & Ireland – A Guide for Disabled People*.

Society for the Advancement of Travelers with Handicaps (www.sath.org) Reams of information for travellers with disabilities.

Visas

Citizens of the USA, Canada, Australia, New Zealand and the UK need only a valid passport to enter nearly all countries in Europe, including the entire EU. Two eastern European countries, Belarus and Russia, require a prearranged visa before arrival and even an 'invitation' from (or booking with) a tour operator or hotel. In addition Australians and New Zealanders need a visa for both Ukraine and Moldova. Because regulations can change, double-check with the relevant embassy or consulate before travelling.

Several types of visa exist including tourist, transit and business permits. Transit visas are usually cheaper than tourist or business visas but they allow only a very short stay (one to five days) and can be difficult to extend.

THE SCHENGEN AREA

Twenty-six European countries are signatories to the Schengen Agreement, which has effectively dismantled internal border controls between them. These include Austria, Belgium, Czech Republic, Denmark, Estonia, Finland, France, Germany, Greece, Hungary, Iceland, Italy, Latvia, Liechtenstein, Lithuania, Luxembourg, Malta, the Netherlands, Norway, Poland, Portugal, Slovakia, Slovenia, Spain, Sweden and Switzerland.

Citizens of the US, Australia, New Zealand, Canada and the UK only need a valid passport to enter these countries. However, other nationals, including South Africans, can apply for a single visa – a Schengen visa – when travelling throughout this region.

Non EU visitors (with or without a Schengen visa) should expect to be questioned, however perfunctorily, when entering the region. However, later travel within the zone is much like a domestic trip, with no border controls.

If you need a Schengen visa, you must apply at the consulate or embassy of the country that's your main destination, or your point of entry. You may then stay up to a maximum of 90 days in the entire Schengen area within a six-month period. Once your visa has expired, you must leave the zone and may only re-enter after three months abroad. Shop around when choosing your point of entry, as visa prices may differ from country to country.

If you're a citizen of the US, Australia, New Zealand or Canada, you may stay visa-free a total of 90 days, over six months, within the entire Schengen region.

If you're planning a longer trip, you need to inquire personally as to whether you need a visa or visas. Your country might have bilateral agreements with individual Schengen countries allowing you to stay there longer than 90 days without a visa. However, you will need to talk directly to the relevant embassies or consulates.

While the UK and Ireland are not part of the Schengen area, their citizens can stay indefinitely in other EU countries, only needing paperwork if they want to work long term or take up residency.

If you require a visa, remember it has a 'use-by' date and you'll be refused entry afterwards. In some cases it's easier to get visas as you go along, rather than arranging them all beforehand. Carry spare passport photos (you may need from one to four every time you apply for a visa).

Visas to neighbouring countries are usually issued immediately by consulates in eastern Europe, although some may levy a 50 to 100% surcharge for 'express service'. When regulations are confusing (say in Belarus or Russia) it's simpler and safer to obtain a visa before leaving home. Visas are often cheaper in your own country anyway.

Consulates are generally open weekday mornings (if there's both an embassy and consulate, you want the consulate).

Volunteering

If you want to spend more time living and working in Europe rather than simply travelling around it, a short-term volunteer project might seem a good idea, say, teaching English in Poland or building a school in Turkey. However, most voluntary organisations levy high charges for airfares, food, lodging and recruitment (from about €250 to €800 per week), making such work impractical for most shoestringers. One exception is **WWOOF International** (www.wwoof.org), which helps link volunteers with organic farms in Germany, Slovenia, Czech Republic, Denmark, the UK, Austria and Switzerland. A small membership fee is required to join the national chapter but in exchange for your labour you'll receive free lodging and food.

Weights & Measures

The metric system is used throughout Europe. In Britain, however, nonmetric equivalents are common (distances continue to be given in miles and beer is sold in pints, not litres).

Women Travellers

Women might attract unwanted attention in Turkey, rural Spain and southern Italy, especially Sicily, where many men view whistling and catcalling as flattery. Conservative dress can help to deter lascivious gazes and wolf whistles; dark sunglasses help avoid unwanted eye contact.

Marriage is highly respected in southern Europe, and a wedding ring can help, along with talk about 'my husband'.

Hitchhiking alone is not recommended anywhere.

Female readers have reported assaults at Turkish hotels with shared bathrooms, so women travelling to Turkey might want to consider a more expensive room with private bathroom.

Journeywoman (www.journeywoman.com) maintains an online newsletter about solo female travels all over the world.

Working

Working in Europe is not always straightforward. EU citizens are allowed to work in any other EU country, but there can still be tiresome paperwork to complete. Other nationalities require special work permits that can be almost impossible to arrange, especially for temporary work.

However, that doesn't prevent enterprising travellers from topping up their funds by working in the hotel or restaurant trades at beach or ski resorts, or teaching a little English – and they don't always have to do this illegally. The UK, for example, issues special 'Youth Mobility' visas to Commonwealth citizens who are aged between 18 and 30, valid for two years (see www.ukvisas.gov.uk).

Your national student-exchange organisation might be able to arrange temporary work permits to several countries.

If you have a grandparent or parent who was born in an EU country, you may have certain rights of residency or citizenship. Ask that country's embassy about dual citizenship and work permits. With citizenship, also ask about any obligations, such as military service and residency. Beware that your home country may not recognise dual citizenship.

Seasonal Work

Work Your Way Around the World by Susan Griffith gives practical advice, as does *Summer Jobs Abroad*, edited by David Woodworth.

Remember, if you find a temporary job, the pay might be less than that offered to locals. Typical tourist jobs (picking grapes in France, working at a bar in Greece) often come with board and lodging, and the pay is essentially pocket money, but you'll have a good time partying with other travellers.

Busking is fairly common in major European cities such as Amsterdam and Paris, but it's illegal in some parts of Switzerland and Austria. Crackdowns even occur in Belgium and Germany, where it has been tolerated in the past. Some other cities, including London, require permits and security checks. Make sure you talk to other buskers first.

EuroJobs (www.eurojobs.com) Links to hundreds of organisations looking to employ both non-Europeans (with the correct work permits) and Europeans.

Jobs in the Alps (www.jobs-in-the-alps.com) Mainly service jobs such as chambermaids, bar staff and porters. Some linguistic skills required.

Natives (www.natives.co.uk) Summer and winter resort jobs, and various tips.

Picking Jobs (www.pickingjobs.com) Includes some tourism jobs.

Season Workers (www.seasonworkers.com) Best for ski-resort work and summer jobs, although it also has some English-teaching jobs.

Teaching English

Although teaching English is an option, most schools prefer a bachelor's degree and a TEFL (Teaching English as a Foreign Language) certificate.

It is easier to find TEFL jobs in eastern Europe than in western Europe. The **British Council** (www.britishcouncil.org) can provide advice about training and job searches. Alternatively, try the big schools such as **Berlitz** (www.berlitz.com) and **Wall Street Institute International** (www.wallstreetinstitute.com).

Transport

GETTING THERE & AWAY

Arriving from beyond the Continent is nearly always done by plane these days. While a few hardy souls do still arrive overland from Asia and the Middle East, or from North Africa by ferry, they are the small minority.

Flights, tours and rail tickets can be booked online at www.lonelyplanet.com/bookings.

Entering Europe

All countries require travellers to have a valid passport, preferably with at least six months between the time of departure and the passport's expiry date.

EU travellers from countries that issue national identity cards are increasingly using these to travel within the EU, although it's impossible to use these as the sole travel documents outside the EU.

Visas are another consideration. Some countries require certain nationalities to buy a visa allowing entry between certain dates. Specifically, Belarus and Russia require all nationalities to obtain visas, while Aussie and Kiwi travellers also need visas to enter Moldova and Ukraine. Turkey requires Australian, Canadian, South African, UK and US passport holders to buy a visa on arrival. Other nationalities may have additional requirements.

Air

Airports & Airlines

If travelling from another continent, your air ticket to Europe will be your single biggest expense. To save money, it's best to travel off-season. This means, if possible, avoid mid-June to early September, Easter, Christmas and school holidays.

Regardless of your ultimate destination, it's sometimes better to pick a recognised transport 'hub' as your port of entry, where high traffic volumes keep prices down. The busiest, and most obvious, airports are London, Frankfurt, Paris and Rome. Sometimes tickets to Amsterdam, Athens, Barcelona, Berlin, İstanbul, Madrid and Vienna are worth checking out.

Long-haul airfares to eastern Europe are rarely a bargain; you're usually better flying to a western European hub and taking an onward budget-airline flight or train. The main hubs in eastern Europe are Budapest, Moscow, Prague and Warsaw.

Most of the aforementioned gateway cities are also well serviced by low-cost carriers,that fly to other parts of Europe, such as the following:

Air Berlin (www.airberlin.com) Hubs in Germany; service across Europe.

easyJet (www.easyjet.com) Flies to major airports across Europe.

CLIMATE CHANGE & TRAVEL

Every form of transport that relies on carbon-based fuel generates CO_2, the main cause of human-induced climate change. Modern travel is dependent on aeroplanes, which might use less fuel per kilometre per person than most cars, but travel much greater distances. The altitude at which aircraft emit gases (including CO_2) and particles also contributes to their climate-change impact. Many websites offer 'carbon calculators' that allow people to estimate the carbon emissions generated by their journey and, for those who wish to do so, to offset the impact of the greenhouse gases emitted with contributions to portfolios of climate-friendly initiatives throughout the world. Lonely Planet offsets the carbon footprint of all staff and author travel.

Germanwings (www.germanwings.com) Hubs in Germany; service across Europe.

Ryanair (www.ryanair.com) Flies to scores of destinations across Europe, but make sure your destination airport is not a deserted airfield out in the sticks.

Tickets

Buying tickets to and within Europe is easily done online. However, checking a host of airline websites can soon become tedious and confusing, which is where the convenience of flight booking websites is unmatched. Lonely Planet's flight search engine compares lots of different flight websites to find you the best deal, see www.lonelyplanet.com/flights.

Some useful websites include the following:

Ebookers (www.ebookers.com)

Expedia (www.expedia.com)

Kayak (www.kayak.com)

Opodo (www.opodo.com)

Orbitz (www.orbitz.com)

Skyscanner (www.skyscanner.com)

Travelocity (www.travelocity.com)

Land

It's possible to reach Europe by various different train routes from Asia. Most common is the Trans-Siberian Railway, connecting Moscow to Siberia, the Russian Far East, Mongolia, China and North Korea.

It is also possible to reach Moscow from several Central Asian states and İstanbul from Iran and Jordan. See www.seat61.com for more information about these adventurous routes.

Sea

There are numerous ferry routes between Europe and Africa, including links from Spain to Morocco, Italy and Malta to Tunisia, France to Morocco and France to Tunisia. Check out www.traghettiweb.it for comprehensive information on all Mediterranean ferries. Ferries are often filled to capacity in summer, especially to and from Tunisia, so book well in advance if you're taking a vehicle across.

Passenger freighters (typically carrying up to 12 passengers) aren't nearly as competitively priced as airlines. Journeys also take a long time. However, if you've got your heart set on a trans-Atlantic journey, **TravLtips Cruise and Freighter** (www.travltips.com) has a downloadable freighter directory.

GETTING AROUND

Travel within the EU, whether by air, rail or car, was made easier by the Schengen Agreement (p1213), which abolished border controls between most member states.

In most European countries, the train is the best option for internal transport. Check the websites of national rail systems as they often offer fare specials and national passes that are significantly cheaper than point-to-point tickets.

Air

Airlines

In recent years low-cost carriers have revolutionised European transport and now it's often cheaper (to the great chagrin of the environmentally conscious) to take a flight than a train journey for long-distance European trips. Most budget airlines have a similar pricing system – namely that ticket prices rise with the number of seats sold on each flight, so book as early as possible to get a decent fare.

Some low-cost carriers – Ryanair being the prime example – have made a habit of flying to smaller, less convenient airports on the outskirts of their destination city, or even to the airports of nearby cities, so check the exact location of the departure and arrival airports before you book.

Departure and other taxes (including extortionate booking fees, checked-baggage fees and other surcharges) soon add up and are included in the final price by the end of the online booking process – usually a lot more than you were hoping to pay – but with careful choosing and advance booking you can get excellent deals.

In the face of competition from low-cost airlines, many national carriers have decided to drop their prices and/or offer special deals. Some, such as British Airways, have even adopted the low-cost model of online booking, where the customer can opt to buy just a one-way flight, or can piece together their own return journey from two one-way legs.

For a comprehensive overview of which low-cost carriers fly to or from which European cities, check out the excellent flycheapo.com.

Air Berlin (www.airberlin.com) Well-respected German outfit. Flies to central airports around Europe and all over the world, but book early for good prices.

easyJet (www.easyjet.com) Flies to a large number of central airports across Europe. Main hubs are London Paris, Madrid and Basel, but it serves almost every corner of the Continent.

Flybe (www.flybe.com) Cheap flights from regional UK cities and across western Europe; much loved by business travellers.

Germanwings (www.germanwings.com) Reputable German budget airline with a huge number of flights to all corners of the Continent. Main hubs are Cologne-Bonn, Berlin and Stuttgart. Unusually, it has cheap flights to Russia.

Ryanair (www.ryanair.com) Ryanair's sheer number of routes is extraordinary. With nonreclining seats, incessant advertising throughout flights and tight legroom, you'll just have to grin and bear it to get a good price – which, with all due credit – is all too often!

Wizz Air (www.wizzair.com) This recommended Hungarian operator has numerous bases in Poland as well as Budapest and London, and a vast array of flights across Europe. Wizz has the best links to Ukraine and Bulgaria from western Europe.

Air Passes

Various travel agencies and airlines offer air passes for non-European citizens. Check with your travel agent for current promotions.

SAS's **Visit Scandinavia/Europe Air Pass** (www.flysas.com) connects visitors to Scandinavian cities from between US$45 to US$150 per flight, excluding taxes.

EUROPE'S BORDER CROSSINGS

Border formalities have been relaxed in most of the EU, but still exist in all their original bureaucratic glory in the more far-flung parts of eastern Europe.

In line with the Schengen Agreement (p1213), there are officially no passport controls at the borders between Austria, Belgium, Czech Republic, Denmark, Estonia, Finland, France, Germany, Greece, Hungary, Iceland, Italy, Latvia, Liechtenstein, Lithuania, Luxembourg, Malta, the Netherlands, Norway, Poland, Portugal, Slovakia, Slovenia, Spain, Sweden and Switzerland. Sometimes, however, there are spot checks on trains crossing borders, so always have your passport. The UK and Ireland, which are EU countries but are nonsignatories to Schengen, maintains border control over traffic from other EU countries (except between each other, as they share an open border), although there is no customs control.

Most borders in eastern Europe will be crossed via train, where border guards board the train and go through compartments checking passengers' papers. It is rare to get hit up for bribes, but occasionally in Belarus or Moldova you may face a difficulty that can only be overcome with a 'fine'. Travelling between Turkey and Bulgaria typically requires a change of trains and is subject to a lengthy border procedure.

Bicycle

Much of Europe is ideally suited to cycling. In the northwest, the flat terrain ensures that bicycles are a popular form of everyday transport, though headwinds often spoil the fun. In the rest of the region, hills and mountains can make for rough going, but this is offset by the dense concentration of things to see.

Popular cycling areas include the whole of the Netherlands, the Belgian Ardennes, the west of Ireland, the upper reaches of the Danube in southern Germany and anywhere in northern Switzerland, Denmark or the south of France. Exploring the small villages of Turkey and eastern Europe also provides up-close access to more remote areas.

A primary consideration of a cycling trip is to travel light, but you should take a few tools and spare parts, including a puncture-repair kit and an extra inner tube. Panniers are essential to balance your possessions on either side of the bike frame. Wearing a helmet is not compulsory in most countries, but is certainly sensible.

Michelin maps indicate scenic routes, which can help you plan good cycling itineraries. Seasoned cyclists can average 80km a day, but it depends on what you're carrying and your level of fitness.

Cyclists' Touring Club (CTC; www.ctc.org.uk) The national cycling association of the UK runs organised trips to Continental Europe.

Veloland European Cyclists' Federation (www.ecf.com) Has details of 'EuroVelo', the European cycle network of 12 pan-European cycle routes, plus tips for other tours.

Veloland Schweiz (www.cycling-in-switzerland.ch) Details of Swiss national routes and more.

Rental & Purchase

It is easy to hire bikes throughout most of Europe on an hourly, half-day, daily or weekly basis. Many western European train stations have bike-rental counters. It is sometimes possible to return the bike at a different outlet so you don't have to retrace your route. Hostels are another good place to find cheap bike hire.

There are plenty of places to buy bikes in Europe (shops sell new and second-hand bicycles, or you can check local papers for private vendors), but you'll need a specialist bicycle shop for a bike capable of withstanding a European trip. Cycling is very popular in the Netherlands and Germany, and those countries are good places to pick up a well-equipped touring bicycle.

European prices are quite high (certainly higher than in North America), but non-European residents should be able to claim back value-added tax (VAT).

Transporting a Bicycle

For major cycling trips, it's best to have a bike you're familiar with, so consider bringing your own rather than buying on arrival. If coming from outside Europe, ask about the airline's policy on transporting bikes before buying your ticket.

From the UK to the Continent, **Eurostar** (www.eurostar.com), the train service through the Channel Tunnel, charges £25 to send a bike as registered luggage on its routes. You can also transport your bicycle with you on Eurotunnel through the Channel Tunnel. With a bit of tinkering and dismantling (eg removing wheels), you might be able to get your bike into a bag or sack and take it on a train as hand luggage. See the website for more information.

Alternatively, the **European Bike Express** (www.bike-express.co.uk) is a coach service based in the UK where cyclists can travel with their bicycles to various cycling destinations on the Continent.

Once on the Continent, you can put your feet up on the train if you get tired of pedalling or simply want to skip a boring section. On slower trains, bikes can usually be transported as luggage, subject to a small supplementary fee. Some cyclists have reported that Italian and French train attendants have refused bikes on slow trains, so be prepared for regulations to be interpreted differently by officious staff.

Fast trains can rarely accommodate bikes; they might need to be sent as registered luggage and may end up on a different train from the one you take. This is often the case in France and Spain.

Boat

Several different ferry companies compete on the main ferry routes, resulting in a comprehensive but complicated service. The same ferry company can have a host of different prices for the same route, depending on the time of day or year, validity of the ticket and length of your vehicle. Vehicle tickets usually include the driver and often up to five passengers free of charge.

It's worth planning (and booking) ahead where possible as there may be special reductions on off-peak crossings and advance-purchase tickets. On English Channel routes, apart from one-day or short-term excursion returns, there is little price advantage in buying a return ticket versus two singles.

Rail-pass holders are entitled to discounts or free travel on some lines. Food on ferries is often expensive (and lousy), so it is worth bringing your own. Also be aware that if you take your vehicle on board, you are usually denied access to it during the voyage.

Lake and river ferry services operate in many countries, Austria and Switzerland being just two. Some are very scenic.

UK & Ireland

Britain is well connected with western Europe by ferry. Check out www.ferrybooker.com for information.

» **P&O Ferries** (www.poferries.com) is one of the world's main ferry companies. Ferries sail from England to France (Dover–Calais), to the Netherlands (Hull–Rotterdam), to Belgium (Hull–Zeebrugge) and to Ireland (Liverpool–Dublin), among other routes.

» **Brittany Ferries** (www.brittanyferries.com) operates services from England to France or Spain. You can also go by ferry from Ireland to France.

» From Ireland it's also possible to travel directly to mainland Europe with **Irish Ferries** (www.irishferries.com) and Brittany Ferries on their routes to Roscoff and Cherbourg from Rosslare and Cork in Ireland.

Northern Europe & Scandinavia

Northern German port towns such as Lübeck and Rostock are well connected by ferry to Norway, Denmark, Sweden, Finland, the UK and the Baltic countries.

Color Line (www.colorline.com)

DFDS Seaways (www.dfds-seaways.com)

Finnlines (www.finnlines.com)

Scandlines (www.scandlines.com)

Stena Line (www.stenaline.com)

TT-Line (www.ttline.com)

Mediterranean

Blue Star Ferries (www.bluestarferries.com) and **Hellenic Mediterranean** (www.hmlferry.com) travel from Italy (Ancona, Brindisi or Bari) to Greece (Corfu, Igoumenitsa and Patras).

The Greek islands are connected to the mainland and each other by a spider web of routes.

Bus

International Buses

Buses are often cheaper thar trains, sometimes substantially so, but also tend to be slower and less comfortable. While they are generally more expensive and take much longer than low-cost airlines (a double whammy), they do cover many less profitable routes that low-cost airlines don't.

In Portugal, Greece, parts of Spain and Turkey, buses are often a better option tha trains.

Europe's biggest organisa tion of international buses operates under the name **Eurolines** (www.eurolines.com), comprised of various national companies. The group's network covers citi as far afield as Edinburgh, Stockholm, Rīga, Buchares

Rome and Madrid. A **Eurolines Pass** (www.eurolines.com/en/eurolines-pass) is offered for extensive travel, allowing passengers to visit a choice of 43 cities in 18 countries over 15 or 30 days. In the high season (mid-June to mid-September) the pass costs €295/350 for those aged under 26, or €380/460 for those 26 and over. It's cheaper in other periods.

Another popular option is **Busabout** (www.busabout.com). These buses do three interconnected circuits around Europe, stopping at major cities. You can 'hop off' at any scheduled stop, then 'hop on' a later bus. Buses are often oversubscribed, so book each sector to avoid being stranded. They departsevery two days from April to the end of October. The circuits cover most countries in Continental western Europe, plus the Czech Republic. Myriad other options are available, including eastern European tours of everything from Dracula-themed castle tours of Romania to an eight-day sailing tour of Croatia.

National Buses

Domestic buses provide a viable alternative to trains in most countries. Again, they are usually slightly cheaper and somewhat slower. Buses are generally best for short hops, such as getting around cities and reaching remote villages, and they are often the only option in mountainous regions.

Reservations are rarely necessary. On many city buses you usually buy your ticket in advance from a kiosk or machine and validate it on entering the bus.

Car & Motorcycle

Travelling with your own vehicle gives flexibility and is the best way to reach remote places. However, the independence does sometimes isolate you from local life. Also, cars can be a target for theft and are often impractical in city centres, where traffic jams, parking problems and getting thoroughly lost can make it well worth ditching your vehicle and using public transport. Various car-carrying trains can help you avoid long, tiring drives.

Campervan

One popular way to tour Europe is for a group of three or four people to band together and buy or rent a campervan. London is the usual embarkation point. Look at the ads in London's free magazine **TNT** (www.tntmagazine.com) if you wish to form or join a group. *TNT* is also a good source for purchasing a van, as is **Loot** (www.loot.com).

Some second-hand dealers offer a 'buy-back' scheme for when you return from the Continent, but check the small print before signing anything and remember that if an offer is too good to be true, it probably is. Buying and reselling privately should be more advantageous if you have time. In the UK, **Downunder Insurance** (www.duinsure.com) offers a campervan policy.

Campervans usually feature a fixed high-top or elevating roof and two to five bunk beds. Apart from the essential camping gas cooker, you may get a sink, fridge and built-in cupboards. Prices vary considerably, and it's worth getting advice from a mechanic to determine whether you're being offered a fair price. Once on the road you should be able to keep budgets lower than backpackers using trains, but don't forget to set money aside for emergency repairs.

The main advantage of going by campervan is flexibility; with transport, eating and sleeping requirements all taken care of in one unit, you are tied to nobody's timetable but your own. It's also easier to set up at night than if you rely on a car and tent.

A disadvantage of campervans is that you are in a confined space for much of the time. Four adults in a small van can soon get on each other's nerves, particularly if the group has been formed at short notice. You might also miss out on experiences in the world outside your van. Other negatives are that vans are not easy to manoeuvre around town, and you'll often have to leave your gear unattended inside (many people bolt extra locks onto the van). Fuel costs also add up.

Fuel

Fuel prices can vary enormously (though fuel is always more expensive than in North America or Australia). Refuelling in Luxembourg, Gibraltar or Andorra is about 30% cheaper than in neighbouring countries. The Netherlands, France and Italy have Europe's most expensive petrol. Greece, Spain and (surprisingly) Switzerland have reasonable prices. The Baltic and eastern European countries are cheaper still.

Unleaded petrol only is available throughout all of Europe. Diesel is usually cheaper, though the difference is marginal in Britain, Ireland and Switzerland.

Ireland's Automobile Association maintains a webpage of European fuel prices at www.aaireland.ie/petrolprices.

Leasing

Leasing a vehicle involves fewer hassles than purchasing and can work out much cheaper than hiring for longer than 17 days. This program is limited to certain types of new cars, including Renault and Peugeot, but you save money because leasing is exempt from VAT and inclusive insurance plans are cheaper than daily insurance rates.

Leasing is also open to people as young as 18 years old. To lease a vehicle your permanent address must be outside the EU. In the USA, contact **Renault Eurodrive** (www.renault-eurodrive.com) for more information.

Motorcycle Touring

Europe is made for motorcycle touring, with quality winding roads, stunning scenery and an active motorcycling scene. Just make sure your wet-weather motorcycling gear is up to scratch.

Rider and passenger crash helmets are compulsory everywhere in Europe. Austria, Belgium, France, Germany, Luxembourg, Portugal and Spain also require that motorcyclists use headlights during the day; in other countries it is recommended.

On ferries, motorcyclists rarely have to book ahead as they can generally be squeezed on board.

Take note of the local custom about parking motorcycles on pavements (sidewalks). Though this is illegal in some countries, the police often turn a blind eye provided the vehicle doesn't obstruct pedestrians. Don't try to park your bike on the pavement in Britain, however.

Preparations

Always carry proof of ownership of your vehicle (Vehicle Registration Document for British-registered cars) when touring Europe. An EU driving licence is acceptable for those driving through Europe. If you have any other type of licence, you should obtain an International Driving Permit (IDP) from your motoring organisation. Check what type of licence is required in your destination prior to departure.

Third-party motor insurance is compulsory. Most UK policies automatically provide this for EU countries. Get your insurer to issue a Green Card (which may cost extra), an internationally recognised proof of insurance, and check that it lists every country you intend to visit. You'll need this in the event of an accident outside the country where the vehicle is insured.

Also ask your insurer for a European Accident Statement form, which can simplify things if worst comes to worst. Never sign statements that you can't read or understand – insist on a translation and sign that only if it's acceptable.

For non-EU countries, check the requirements with your insurer. Travellers from the UK can obtain additional advice and information from the **Association of British Insurers** (www.abi.org.uk).

Take out a European motoring assistance policy. Non-Europeans might find it cheaper to arrange international coverage with their national motoring organisation before leaving home. Ask your motoring organisation for details about the free services offered by affiliated organisations around Europe.

Every vehicle that travels across an international border should display a sticker indicating its country of registration. A warning triangle, to be used in the event of breakdown, is compulsory almost everywhere.

Some recommended accessories include a first-aid kit (compulsory in Austria, Slovenia, Croatia, Serbia, Montenegro and Greece), a spare bulb kit (compulsory in Spain), a reflective jacket for every person in the car (compulsory in France, Italy and Spain) and a fire extinguisher (compulsory in Greece and Turkey).

Residents of the UK should contact the **RAC** (www.rac.co.uk) or the **AA** (www.theaa.co.uk) for more information. In the US, contact **AAA** (www.aaa.com).

Purchase

The purchase of vehicles in some European countries is illegal for non-nationals or non-EU residents. Britain is probably the best place to buy; second-hand prices are good and, whether buying privately or from a dealer, the absence of language difficulties will help you establish exactly what you are getting and what guarantees you can expect if you break down.

Bear in mind that British cars have steering wheels on the right-hand side. If you wish to have left-hand drive and can afford to buy a new car, prices are generally reasonable in Greece, France, Germany, Belgium, Luxembourg and the Netherlands.

Paperwork can be tricky wherever you buy, and many countries have compulsory roadworthiness checks on older vehicles.

Rental

Renting a car is ideal for people who will need a car for 16 days or fewer. Anything more, it's better to lease. Big international rental firms will give you reliable service and good vehicles. Usually you will have the option of returning the car to a different outlet at the end of the rental period, but there's normally a charge for this and it can be very steep if it's a long way from your point of origin.

Book early for the lowest rates and make sure you compare rates in different cities. Prices in some cities are cheaper than in others. Taxes range from 15% to 20% and surcharges apply if rented from an airport.

One operator worth considering if you're renting a car in the UK, France, Greece, Ireland, Italy, Portugal, Spain or Switzerland is **easyCar** (www.easycar.com), which has rentals starting at rock-bottom rates. Otherwise, check the sites of the following major operators, where you can make reservations online:

Alamo (www.alamo.com)
Avis (www.avis.com)
Budget (www.budget.com)
Europcar (www.europcar.com)
Hertz (www.hertz.com)

If you rent a car in the EU you might not be able to take it outside the EU, and if you rent the car outside the EU, you will only be able to drive within the EU for eight days.

Ask at the rental agencies for other such regulations.

If you want to rent a car and haven't booked ahead, look for national or local firms – they can often undercut the big companies by up to 40%. Beware of dodgy operations that take your money and point you towards some clapped-out wreck, or where the rental agreement is bad news if you have an accident or the car is stolen. Read before you sign.

No matter where you rent, make sure you understand what is included in the price (unlimited or paid kilometres, tax, injury insurance, collision damage waiver etc) and what your liabilities are. We recommend taking the collision damage waiver, though you can probably skip the injury insurance if you and your passengers have decent travel insurance. Ask in advance if you can drive a rented car across borders from a country where hire prices are low to another where they're high.

The minimum rental age is usually 21 years and sometimes 25. You'll need a credit card and to have held your licence for at least a year.

Motorcycle and moped rental is common in some countries, such as Italy, Spain, Greece and southern France. Sadly, it's also common for inexperienced riders to leap on rented bikes and very quickly fall off them again, leaving a layer or two of skin on the road in the process.

Road Conditions & Road Rules

Conditions and types of roads vary across Europe. The fastest routes are generally four- or six-lane highways known locally as motorways, *autoroutes*, *autostrade*, *autobahnen* etc. These tend to skirt cities and plough through the countryside in straight lines, often avoiding the most scenic bits.

Some highways incur tolls, which are often quite hefty (especially in Italy, France and Spain), but there will always be an alternative route. Motorways and other primary routes are generally in good condition.

Road surfaces on minor routes are unreliable in some countries (eg Greece, Albania, Romania, Ireland, Russia and Ukraine), although normally they will be more than adequate. These roads are narrower and progress is generally much slower. However, to compensate for this, you can expect much better scenery and plenty of interesting villages along the way.

Except in Britain and Ireland, you should drive on the right. Vehicles brought to the Continent from either of these locales should have their headlights adjusted to avoid blinding oncoming traffic (a simple solution on older headlight lenses is to cover up a triangular section of the lens with tape). Priority is often given to traffic approaching from the right in countries that drive on the right-hand side.

Speed limits vary from country to country. You may be surprised at the apparent disregard for traffic regulations in some places (particularly in Italy and Greece), but as a visitor it is always best to be cautious. Many driving infringements are subject to an on-the-spot fine. Always ask for a receipt.

European drink-driving laws are particularly strict. The blood-alcohol concentration (BAC) limit when driving is usually between 0.05% and 0.08%, but in certain areas (such as Gibraltar, Bulgaria and Belarus) it can be zero.

Hitching

Hitching is never entirely safe and we cannot recommend it. Travellers who decide to hitch should understand that they are taking a small but potentially serious risk. It will be safer if they travel in pairs and let someone know where they plan to go.

A man and woman travelling together is probably the best combination. A woman hitching on her own is taking a larger than normal risk.

Hitching in western Europe can be simultaneously the most rewarding and yet frustrating way of getting around. You get to meet and interact with local people and can have unplanned detours that may yield unexpected highlights off the beaten track. But you might get stuck on the side of the road to nowhere with nowhere (or nowhere cheap) to stay.

Don't try to hitch from city centres; take public transport to the suburban exit routes. Hitching is usually illegal on highways – stand on the slip roads or approach drivers at petrol stations and truck stops.

Look presentable and cheerful, and make a cardboard sign indicating your intended destination in the local language. Never hitch

HITCHING FOR CASH

In parts of eastern Europe including Russia, Ukraine and Turkey, traditional hitchhiking is rarely practised. Instead, anyone with a car can be a taxi and it's quite usual to see locals stick their hands out (palm down) on the street, looking to hitch a lift. The difference with hitching here, however, is that you pay for the privilege. You will need to speak the local language (or at least know the numbers) to discuss your destination and negotiate a price.

where drivers can't stop in good time or without causing an obstruction. At dusk, give up and stay the night.

It is often possible to arrange a lift in advance: scan student noticeboards in colleges, or check out services such as www.carpooling.co.uk or www.drive2day.de.

Local Transport

High-density populations mean European towns and cities have excellent local-transport systems, often encompassing trams as well as buses and metro/subway/underground rail networks.

Be sure to remove your pack on public transport and hold it in front of you to avoid battering your neighbour and to deter pickpockets. Also give up your seat to the elderly, infirm or pregnant women.

Most travellers will find areas of interest in European cities can be easily traversed by foot or bicycle. In Greece and Italy, travellers sometimes rent mopeds and motorcycles for scooting around a city or island.

Taxi

Taxis in Europe are generally metered and rates are usually high. There might also be supplements for things such as luggage, time of day, location of pick-up and extra passengers.

Good bus, rail and underground-railway networks often render taxis unnecessary, but if you need one in a hurry, they can be found idling near train stations or outside big hotels. Lower fares make taxis more viable in some countries, such as Spain, Greece, Portugal and Turkey.

Train

Comfortable, frequent and reliable, trains are *the* way of getting around Europe. Indeed, it's safe to say that Europe has some of the most efficient and comprehensive train services in the world, particularly in Switzerland, Austria and Germany. Trains are a great way to meet people, see the countryside, get into the heart of cities and to scribble furiously into that sacred journal.

Many state railways have interactive websites publishing their timetables and fares, including www.bahn.de (Germany) and www.sbb.ch (Switzerland), which both have pages in English. The **Eurail** (www.eurail.com) website links to more than 20 national train companies in Europe.

The very comprehensive, privately run website **The Man in Seat 61** (www.seat61.com) is a gem, while the US-based **Budget Europe Travel Service** (www.budgeteuropetravel.com) can also help with tips.

Paris, Milan and Vienna are important hubs for international train connections. Note that European trains sometimes split en route to service two destinations, so even if you're on the right train, make sure you're also in the correct carriage.

A train journey to almost every station in Europe can be booked via **Rail Europe** (www.raileurope.com), which also sells InterRail and other passes.

Note that train travel is often much more expensive than air travel in Europe, especially since the advent of the low-cost airlines. But aside from being infinitely more pleasurable, it's also far more environmentally friendly than taking flights.

Express Trains

Europeans are unlikely to catch a plane between London and Paris or Brussels. That's because those routes are served by the high-speed passenger train service **Eurostar** (www.eurostar.com).

Eurostar links London's St Pancras International station, via the Channel Tunnel, with Paris' Gare du Nord (2¼ hours, up to 25 a day) and Brussels' international terminal (one hour 50 minutes, up to 12 a day). Some trains also stop at Lille and Calais in France. The train stations at St Pancras International, Paris and Brussels are much more central than the cities' airports. So, overall, the journey takes as little time as the equivalent flight, with less hassle.

Eurostar in London also sells tickets onwards to some Continental destinations, although its list is much less comprehensive than Rail Europe's. Holders of Eurail and InterRail passes are offered discounts on some Eurostar services; check when booking.

Within Europe, express trains are identified by the symbols 'EC' (EuroCity) or 'IC' (InterCity). The French TGV, Spanish AVE and German ICE trains are even faster, reaching up to 300km/h. Supplementary fares can apply on fast trains (which you often have to pay when travelling on a rail pass), and it is a good idea (sometimes obligatory) to reserve seats at peak times and on certain lines. The same applies for branded express trains, such as the Thalys (between Paris and Brussels, Bruges, Amsterdam and Cologne), and the Eurostar Italia (between Rome and Naples, Florence, Milan and Venice).

If you don't have a seat reservation, you can still obtain a seat that doesn't have a reservation ticket attached to it. Check which destination a seat is reserved for – you might be able to sit in it until the person boards the train.

International Rail Passes

If you're covering lots of ground, you should get a rail pass. But do some price comparisons of point-to-point ticket charges and rail passes beforehand to make absolutely sure you'll break even. Also shop around for rail-pass prices as they do vary between outlets. When weighing up options, look into cheap deals that include advance-purchase reductions, one-off promotions or special circular-route tickets, particularly over the internet.

Normal point-to-point tickets are valid for two months, and you can make as many stops as you like en route; make your intentions known when purchasing, and inform train conductors how far you're going before they punch your ticket.

Supplementary charges (eg for some express and overnight trains) and seat reservation fees (mandatory on some trains, a good idea on others) are not covered by rail passes. Always ask. Note that European rail passes also give reductions on some Eurostar services, the Channel Tunnel and on certain ferries.

Pass-holders must always carry their passport with them for identification purposes. The railways' policy is that passes cannot be replaced or refunded if lost or stolen. However, with some sales outlets (ie www.raileurope.co.uk) you can buy insurance that will reimburse you for any days not used if a pass is stolen.

NON-EUROPEAN RESIDENTS

Eurail (www.eurail.com) passes vary in what they cover depending on how often you plan to travel and where you wish to travel. They can be bought only by residents of non-European countries and should be purchased before arriving in Europe.

The inaccurately named 'Global Pass' covers 24 countries, namely Austria (including Liechtenstein), Belgium, Bulgaria, Croatia, Czech Republic, Denmark, Finland, France, Germany, Greece, Hungary, Ireland, Italy, Luxembourg, the Netherlands, Norway, Portugal, Romania, Slovakia, Slovenia, Spain, Sweden, Switzerland and Turkey.

While the pass is valid on some private train lines in the region, if you plan to travel extensively in Switzerland, be warned that the many private rail networks and cable cars, especially in the Jungfrau region around Interlaken, don't give Eurail discounts. A Swiss Pass or Half-Fare Card might be an alternative or necessary addition.

You can use the Global Pass on some Italy–Greece, Denmark–Sweden, Germany–Sweden and Sweden–Finland ferries. Reductions are given on some other ferry routes and on river/lake steamer services in various countries.

The pass is valid for a set number of consecutive days or a set number of days within a period of time. Those under 26 years of age can buy a Eurail Youth pass, which only covers travel in 2nd-class compartments. Those aged 26 and over must buy the full-fare Eurail pass, which entitles you to travel 1st class.

In addition to the Global Pass, there is the Select Pass, which allows you to nominate three, four or five countries in which you wish to travel, and then buy a pass allowing five, six, eight, 10 or 15 travel days in a two-month period. Prices start at €234/359 per youth/adult. The five- and six-day passes offer an attractive price break, but for more expensive options, the continuous pass becomes better value.

A range of more than 15 Eurail Regional Passes covering two or three countries is also offered, but you might

RAIL PASS RATES

Eurail Global

AGE	CLASS	DURATION	PRICE (€)
12-25	2nd	1 month	586
12-25	2nd	15 days	300
over 26	1st	1 month	899
over 26	1st	15 days	567
12-25	2nd	10 days in 2 months	435
12-25	2nd	15 days in 2 months	571
over 26	1st	10 days in 2 months	668
over 26	1st	15 days in 2 months	876

InterRail Global

AGE	CLASS	DURATION	PRICE (€)
12-25	2nd	5 days in 10 days	181
12-25	2nd	10 days in 22 days	265
12-25	2nd	1 month	435
over 26	1st	5 days in 10 days	434
over 26	1st	10 days in 22 days	618
over 26	1st	1 month	1034
over 26	2nd	5 days in 10 days	276
over 26	2nd	10 days in 22 days	393
over 26	2nd	1 month	658

want to ensure that they are good value given your travel plans. Similarly, there are now Eurail National Passes for just one country at a time.

Two to five people travelling together can get a Saver version of all Eurail passes for a 15% to 25% discount.

EUROPEAN RESIDENTS

Rail Europe (www.raileurope.com) sells **InterRail** passes to European residents for unlimited rail travel through 30 European and North African countries (excluding the pass-holder's country of residence). To qualify as a resident, you must have lived in a European country for six months.

While an InterRail pass will get you further than a Eurail pass along the private rail networks of Switzerland's Jungfrau region (near Interlaken), its benefits are limited. A Swiss Pass or Half-Fare Card might be a necessary addition if you plan to travel extensively in that region.

For a small fee, European residents can buy a Railplus Card, entitling the holder to a 25% discount on international train journeys. In most countries, it's sold only to those aged 60 and over. However, some national rail networks may make the Railplus Card available to young people or other travellers. It is available from counters in main train stations.

ALL NATIONALITIES

Several other passes are available, especially if you're interested in travelling in the Continent's east. For more information and to buy the following passes, contact **Rail Europe** (www.raileurope.com) in your home country.

The **France Rail Pass** (www.francerailpass.com) offers unlimited travel for three days during a one-month period. Full fares are US$254 for three days and US$34 to US$40 for each additional travel day within the same month-long period, depending on how many days you buy.

The **European East Pass** provides five days of travel over a month in Austria, Czech Republic, Hungary, Poland and Slovakia for US$307/214 for 1st/2nd class.

Meanwhile, a **Balkans Flexipass** provides five to 15 days of 1st-class train travel in a month throughout Bulgaria, Greece, Macedonia, Montenegro, Romania, Serbia and Turkey, starting at US$156/260 for under 26 years/26 and over.

National Rail Passes

As well as the national rail passes offered by Rail Europe, national rail operators might offer their own passes, or at least a discount card, offering substantial reductions on tickets purchased (eg the Bahn Card in Germany or the Half-Fare Card in Switzerland).

Look at individual train operator sites via www.raileurope.co.uk to check. Such discount cards are usually only worth it if you're staying in the country a while and doing a lot of travelling.

Overnight Trains

On overnight trains, you can use your sleeping hours to cover territory and save money you'd otherwise use on accommodation.

There are usually two types of sleeping accommodation: dozing off upright in your seat or stretching out in a sleeper. Again, reservations are advisable, as sleeping options are allocated on a first-come, first-served basis. Couchette bunks are comfortable enough, if lacking in privacy. There are four per compartment in 1st class, six in 2nd class.

Sleepers are the most comfortable option, offering beds for one or two passengers in 1st class, or two or three passengers in 2nd class. Charges vary depending upon the journey, but they are significantly more costly than couchettes.

In the former Soviet Union, the most common options are either 2nd-class *kupe* compartments – which have four bunks – or the cheaper *platskart*, which are open-plan compartments with reserved bunks. This 3rd-class equivalent is not great for those who value privacy, and theft might be a problem.

Other options include the very basic bench seats in *obshchiy* (*zahalney* in Ukrainian) class and 1st-class, two-person sleeping carriages (*myagki* in Russian). In Ukrainian, this last option is known as *spalney*, but is usually abbreviated to CB in Cyrillic (pronounced *es-ve*). First class is not available on every Russian or Ukrainian train.

Most long-distance trains have a dining (buffet) car or an attendant who wheels a snack trolley through carriages. Prices tend to be steep, though – you're much better off packing a picnic before boarding the train.

Security

Stories sometimes surface about passengers being gassed or drugged and then robbed, but bag snatching is much more of a worry.

Sensible security measures include always keeping your bags in sight (especially at stations), chaining them to the luggage rack, locking compartment doors overnight and sleeping in compartments with other people However, horror stories are very rare.

Language

WANT MORE?

For in-depth language information and handy phrases, check out Lonely Planet's *Europe Phrasebook*. You'll find it at **shop.lonely planet.com**, or you can buy Lonely Planet's iPhone phrasebooks at the Apple App Store.

This chapter offers basic vocabulary to help you get around Europe. Read our coloured pronunciation guides as if they were English, and you'll be understood just fine. The stressed syllables are indicated with italics. Note the use of these abbreviations: (m) for masculine, (f) for feminine, (pol) for polite and (inf) for informal.

ALBANIAN

Note that uh is pronounced as the 'a' in 'ago'. Also, ll and rr in Albanian are pronounced stronger than when they are written as single letters. Albanian is also understood in Kosovo.

Hello.	*Tungjatjeta.*	toon·dya·*tye*·ta
Goodbye.	*Mirupafshim.*	mee roo *paf* shoom
Please.	*Ju lutem.*	yoo *loo*·tem
Thank you.	*Faleminderit.*	fa·le·meen·*de*·reet
Excuse me.	*Më falni*	muh *fal*·nee
Sorry.	*Më vjen keq.*	muh vyen kech
Yes./No.	*Po./Jo.*	po/yo
Help!	*Ndihmë!*	*ndeeh*·muh
Cheers!	*Gëzuar!*	guh·*zoo*·ar

I don't understand.
Unë nuk kuptoj. oo·nuh nook koop·*toy*

Do you speak English?
A flisni anglisht? a *flees*·nee ang·*leesht*

How much is it?
Sa kushton? sa koosh·*ton*

Where's ...?
Ku është ...? koo *uhsh*·tuh ...

Where are the toilets?
Ku janë banjat? koo *ya*·nuh *ba*·nyat

BULGARIAN

Note that uh is pronounced as the 'a' in 'ago' and zh as the 's' in 'pleasure'.

Hello.	Здравейте.	zdra·*vey*·te
Goodbye.	Довиждане.	do·*veezh*·da·ne
Please.	Моля.	*mol*·ya
Thank you.	Благодаря.	bla·go·dar·*ya*
Excuse me.	Извинете.	iz·vee·*ne*·te
Sorry.	Съжалявам.	suh·zhal·*ya*·vam
Yes./No.	Да./Не.	da/ne
Help!	Помощ!	*po*·mosht
Cheers!	Наздраве!	na·*zdra*·ve

I don't understand.
Не разбирам. ne raz·*bee*·ram

Do you speak English?
Говорите ли английски? go·*vo*·ree·te lee ang·*lees*·kee

How much is it?
Колко струва? *kol*·ko *stroo*·va

Where's ...?
Къде се намира ...? kuh·*de* se na·*mee*·ra ...

Where are the toilets?
Къде има тоалетни? kuh·*de* *ee*·ma to·a·*let*·nee

CROATIAN & SERBIAN

Croatian and Serbian are very similar and mutually intelligible (and using them you'll also be understood in Bosnia and Hercegovina, Montenegro and parts of Kosovo). In this section the significant differences between Croatian and Serbian are indicated with (C) and (S) respectively. Note that r is rolled and zh is pronounced as the 's' in 'pleasure'.

Hello.	*Dobar dan.*	daw·ber dan
Goodbye.	*Zbogom.*	*zbo*·gom
Please.	*Molim.*	*mo*·lim
Thank you.	*Hvala.*	*hva*·la
Excuse me.	*Oprostite.*	o·*pro*·sti·te
Sorry.	*Žao mi je.*	*zha*·o mi ye
Yes./No.	*Da./Ne.*	da/ne
Help!	*Upomoć!*	*u*·po·moch
Cheers!	*Živjeli!*	*zhi*·vye·li

I don't understand.
Ja ne razumijem. — ya ne ra·*zu*·mi·yem

Do you speak English?
Govorite/Govoriš li engleski? (pol/inf) — *go*·vo·ri·te/*go*·vo·rish li *en*·gle·ski

How much is it?
Koliko stoji/košta? (C/S) — ko·*li*·ko *sto*·yi/*kosh*·ta

Where's ...?
Gdje je ...? — gdye ye ...

Where are the toilets?
Gdje se nalaze zahodi/toaleti? (C/S) — gdye se *na*·la·ze *za*·ho·di/to·a·*le*·ti

CZECH

An accent mark over a vowel in written Czech indicates it's pronounced as a long sound. Note that oh is pronounced as the 'o' in 'note', uh as the 'a' in 'ago', and kh as the 'ch' in the Scottish *loch*. Also, r is rolled in Czech and the apostrophe (') indicates a slight y sound.

Hello.	*Ahoj.*	*uh*·hoy
Goodbye.	*Na shledanou.*	*nuh*·skhle·duh·noh
Please.	*Prosím.*	*pro*·seem
Thank you.	*Děkuji.*	*dye*·ku·yi
Excuse me.	*Promiňte.*	*pro*·min'·te
Sorry.	*Promiňte.*	*pro*·min'·te
Yes./No.	*Ano./Ne.*	*uh*·no/ne
Help!	*Pomoc!*	*po*·mots
Cheers!	*Na zdraví!*	nuh *zdruh*·vee

I don't understand.
Nerozumím. — *ne*·ro·zu·meem

Do you speak English?
Mluvíte anglicky? — *mlu*·vee·te *uhn*·glits·ki

How much is it?
Kolik to stojí? — *ko*·lik to *sto*·yee

Where's ...?
Kde je ...? — gde ye ...

Where are the toilets?
Kde jsou toalety? — gde ysoh *to*·uh·le·ti

DANISH

All vowels in Danish can be long or short. Note that aw is pronounced as in 'saw', and ew as the 'ee' in 'see' with rounded lips.

Hello.	*Goddag.*	go·*da*
Goodbye.	*Farvel.*	faar·*vel*
Please.	*Vær så venlig.*	ver saw *ven*·lee
Thank you.	*Tak.*	taak
Excuse me.	*Undskyld mig.*	*awn*·skewl mai
Sorry.	*Undskyld.*	*awn*·skewl
Yes./No.	*Ja./Nej.*	ya/nai
Help!	*Hjælp!*	yelp
Cheers!	*Skål!*	skawl

I don't understand.
Jeg forstår ikke. — yai for·*stawr* i·ke

Do you speak English?
Taler De/du engelsk? (pol/inf) — *ta*·la dee/doo *eng*·elsk

How much is it?
Hvor meget koster det? — vor *maa*·yet *kos*·ta dey

Where's ...?
Hvor er ...? — vor ir ...

Where's the toilet?
Hvor er toilettet? — vor ir toy·*le*·tet

DUTCH

It's important to distinguish between the long and short versions of each vowel sound. Note that ew is pronounced as the 'ee' in 'see' with rounded lips, oh as the 'o' in 'note', uh as the 'a' in 'ago', and kh as the 'ch' in the Scottish *loch* (harsh and throaty).

Hello.	*Dag.*	dakh
Goodbye.	*Dag.*	dakh
Please.	*Alstublieft.*	al·stew·*bleeft*
Thank you.	*Dank u.*	dangk ew
Excuse me.	*Pardon.*	par·*don*
Sorry.	*Sorry.*	*so*·ree
Yes./No.	*Ja./Nee.*	yaa/ney
Help!	*Help!*	help
Cheers!	*Proost!*	prohst

I don't understand.
Ik begrijp het niet. — ik buh·*khreyp* huht neet

Do you speak English?
Spreekt u Engels? — spreykt ew *eng*·uhls

How much is it?
Hoeveel kost het? — hoo·*veyl* kost huht

Where's ...?
Waar is ...? — waar is ...

Where are the toilets?
Waar zijn de toiletten? waar zeyn duh twa·*le*·tuhn

ESTONIAN

Double vowels in written Estonian indicate they are pronounced as long sounds. Note that air is pronounced as in 'hair'.

Hello.	*Tere.*	*te*·re
Goodbye.	*Nägemist.*	*nair*·ge·mist
Please.	*Palun.*	*pa*·lun
Thank you.	*Tänan.*	*tair*·nan
Excuse me.	*Vabandage.* (pol)	*va*·ban·da·ge
	Vabanda. (inf)	*va*·ban·da
Sorry.	*Vabandust.*	*va*·ban·dust
Yes./No.	*Jaa./Ei.*	yaa/ay
Help!	*Appi!*	*ap*·pi
Cheers!	*Terviseks!*	*tair*·vi·seks

I don't understand.
Ma ei saa aru. ma ay saa *a*·ru

Do you speak English?
Kas te räägite inglise keelt? kas te *rair*·git·te *ing*·kli·se keylt

How much is it?
Kui palju see maksab? ku·i *pal*·yu sey *mak*·sab

Where's ...?
Kus on ...? kus on ...

Where are the toilets?
Kus on WC? kus on *ve*·se

FINNISH

n Finnish, double consonants are held longer than their single equivalents. Note that ew is pronounced as the 'ee' in 'see' with rounded ips, and uh as the 'u' in 'run'.

lello.	*Hei.*	hay
oodbye.	*Näkemiin.*	*na*·ke·meen
'lease.	*Ole hyvä.*	*o*·le *hew*·va
hank you.	*Kiitos.*	*kee*·tos
xcuse me.	*Anteeksi.*	*uhn*·tayk·si
orry.	*Anteeksi.*	*uhn*·tayk·si
s./No.	*Kyllä./Ei.*	*kewl*·la/ay
elp!	*Apua!*	*uh*·pu·uh
heers!	*Kippis!*	*kip*·pis

on't understand.
ymmärrä. en *ewm*·mar·ra

you speak English?
hutko englantia? *pu*·hut·ko *en*·gluhn·ti·uh

w much is it?
ä se maksaa? *mi*·ta se *muhk*·saa

Where's ...?
Missä on ...? *mis*·sa on ...

Where are the toilets?
Missä on vessa? *mis*·sa on *ves*·suh

FRENCH

The French r sound is throaty. French also has nasal vowels (pronounced as if you're trying to force the sound through the nose), indicated here with o or u followed by an almost inaudible nasal consonant sound m, n or ng. Syllables in French words are, for the most part, equally stressed.

Hello.	*Bonjour.*	bon·zhoor
Goodbye.	*Au revoir.*	o·rer·vwa
Please.	*S'il vous plaît.*	seel voo play
Thank you.	*Merci.*	mair·see
Excuse me.	*Excusez-moi.*	ek·skew·zay·mwa
Sorry.	*Pardon.*	par·don
Yes./No.	*Oui./Non.*	wee/non
Help!	*Au secours!*	o skoor
Cheers!	*Santé!*	son·tay

I don't understand.
Je ne comprends pas. zher ner kom·pron pa

Do you speak English?
Parlez-vous anglais? par·lay·voo ong·glay

How much is it?
C'est combien? say kom·byun

Where's ...?
Où est ...? oo ay ...

Where are the toilets?
Où sont les toilettes? oo son ley twa·let

GERMAN

Note that aw is pronounced as in 'saw', ew as the 'ee' in 'see' with rounded lips, while kh and r are both throaty sounds in German.

Hello.		
(in general)	*Guten Tag.*	*goo*·ten taak
(Austria)	*Servus.*	*zer*·vus
(Switzerland)	*Grüezi.*	*grew*·e·tsi
Goodbye.	*Auf Wiedersehen.*	owf *vee*·der·zey·en
Please.	*Bitte.*	*bi*·te
Thank you.	*Danke.*	*dang*·ke
Excuse me.	*Entschuldigung.*	ent·*shul*·di·gung
Sorry.	*Entschuldigung.*	ent·*shul*·di·gung
Yes./No.	*Ja./Nein.*	yaa/nain
Help!	*Hilfe!*	*hil*·fe
Cheers!	*Prost!*	prawst

I don't understand.
Ich verstehe nicht. ikh fer·*shtey*·e nikht

Do you speak English?
Sprechen Sie Englisch? *shpre*·khen zee *eng*·lish

How much is it?
Wie viel kostet das? vee feel *kos*·tet das

Where's ...?
Wo ist ...? vaw ist ...

Where are the toilets?
Wo ist die Toilette? vo ist dee to·a·*le*·te

GREEK

Note that dh is pronounced as the 'th' in 'that', and that gh and kh are both throaty sounds, similar to the 'ch' in the Scottish *loch*.

Hello.	Γεια σου.	yia su
Goodbye.	Αντίο.	a·*di*·o
Please.	Παρακαλώ.	pa·ra·ka·*lo*
Thank you.	Ευχαριστώ.	ef·kha·ri·*sto*
Excuse me.	Με συγχωρείτε.	me sing·kho·*ri*·te
Sorry.	Συγνώμη.	si·*ghno*·mi
Yes./No.	Ναι./Όχι.	ne/*o*·hi
Help!	Βοήθεια!	vo·*i*·thia
Cheers!	Στην υγειά μας!	stin i·*yia* mas

I don't understand.
Δεν καταλαβαίνω. dhen ka·ta·la·*ve*·no

Do you speak English?
Μιλάς Αγγλικά; mi·*las* ang·gli·*ka*

How much is it?
Πόσο κάνει; *po*·so *ka*·ni

Where's ...?
Που είναι . . .; pu *i*·ne ...

Where are the toilets?
Που είναι η τουαλέτα; pu *i*·ne i tu·a·*le*·ta

HUNGARIAN

A symbol over a vowel in written Hungarian indicates it's pronounced as a long sound. Double consonants should be drawn out a little longer than in English. Note that aw is pronounced as in 'law', eu as the 'u' in 'nurse', and ew as 'ee' with rounded lips. Also, r is rolled in Hungarian and the apostrophe (') indicates a slight y sound.

Hello. (to one person)
Szervusz. *ser*·vus

Hello. (to more than one person)
Szervusztok. *ser*·vus·tawk

Goodbye.	*Viszlát.*	*vis*·lat
Please.	*Kérem.* (pol) *Kérlek.* (inf)	*key*·rem *keyr*·lek
Thank you.	*Köszönöm.*	*keu*·seu·neum
Excuse me.	*Elnézést kérek.*	*el*·ney·zeysht *key*·rek
Sorry.	*Sajnálom.*	*shoy*·na·lawm
Yes.	*Igen.*	*i*·gen
No.	*Nem.*	nem
Help!	*Segítség!*	*she*·geet·sheyg

Cheers! (to one person)
Egészségedre! *e*·geys·shey·ged·re

Cheers! (to more than one person)
Egészségetekre! *e*·geys·shey·ge·tek·re

I don't understand.
Nem értem. nem *eyr*·tem

Do you speak English?
Beszél/Beszélsz angolul? (pol/inf) *be*·seyl/*be*·seyls *on*·gaw·lul

How much is it?
Mennyibe kerül? *men'*·nyi·be *ke*·rewl

Where's ...?
Hol van a ...? hawl von o ...

Where are the toilets?
Hol a vécé? hawl o *vey*·tsey

ITALIAN

The r sound in Italian is rolled and stronger than in English. Most other consonants can have a more emphatic pronounciation too (in which case they're written as double letters).

Hello.	*Buongiorno.*	bwon·*jor*·no
Goodbye.	*Arrivederci.*	a·ree·ve·*der*·chee
Please.	*Per favore.*	per fa·*vo*·re
Thank you.	*Grazie.*	*gra*·tsye
Excuse me.	*Mi scusi.* (pol) *Scusami.* (inf)	mee *skoo*·zee *skoo*·za·mee
Sorry.	*Mi dispiace.*	mee dees·*pya*·ch
Yes.	*Sì.*	see
No.	*No.*	no
Help!	*Aiuto!*	ai·*yoo*·to
Cheers!	*Salute!*	sa·*loo*·te

I don't understand.
Non capisco. non ka·*pee*·sko

Do you speak English?
Parla inglese? *par*·la een·*gle*·ze

How much is it?
Quant'è? kwan·*te*

Where's ... ?
Dov'è ... ? do·*ve* ...

Where are the toilets?
Dove sono i gabinetti? *do*·ve *so*·no ee ga·bee·*ne*·tee

LATVIAN

A line over a vowel in written Latvian indicates it's pronounced as a long sound. Note that air is pronounced as in 'hair', ea as in 'ear', wa as in 'water', and dz as the 'ds' in 'adds'.

Hello.	*Sveiks.*	svayks
Goodbye.	*Atā.*	a·taa
Please.	*Lūdzu.*	loo·dzu
Thank you.	*Paldies.*	pal·deas
Excuse me.	*Atvainojiet.*	at·vai·nwa·yeat
Sorry.	*Piedodiet.*	pea·dwa·deat
Yes./No.	*Jā./Nē.*	yaa/nair
Help!	*Palīgā!*	pa·lee·gaa
Cheers!	*Priekā!*	prea·kaa

I don't understand.
Es nesaprotu. es ne·sa·prwa·tu

Do you speak English?
Vai Jūs runājat angliski? vai yoos ru·naa·yat ang·li·ski

How much is it?
Cik maksā? tsik mak·saa

Where's ...?
Kur ir ...? kur ir ...

Where are the toilets?
Kur ir tualetes? kur ir tu·a·le·tes

LITHUANIAN

Symbols on vowels in written Lithuanian indicate that they're pronounced as long sounds. Note that ow is pronounced as in 'how'.

Hello.	*Sveiki.*	svay·ki
Goodbye.	*Viso gero.*	vi·so ge·ro
Please.	*Prašau.*	pra·show
Thank you.	*Ačiū.*	aa·choo
xcuse me.	*Atleiskite.*	at·lays·ki·te
orry.	*Atsiprašau.*	at·si·pra·show
es./No.	*Taip./Ne.*	taip/ne
elp!	*Padėkit!*	pa·dey·kit
heers!	*Į sveikatą!*	ee svay·kaa·taa

don't understand.
š nesuprantu. ash ne·su·pran·tu

o you speak English?
kalbate angliškai? ar kal·ba·te aang·lish·kai

ow much is it?
ek kainuoja? keak kain·wo·ya

here's ...?
r yra ...? kur ee·ra ...

ere are the toilets?
r yra tualetai? kur ee·ra tu·a·le·tai

MACEDONIAN

Note that r is pronounced as a rolled sound in Macedonian.

Hello.	Здраво.	zdra·vo
Goodbye.	До гледање.	do gle·da·nye
Please.	Молам.	mo·lam
Thank you.	Благодарам.	bla·go·da·ram
Excuse me.	Извинете.	iz·vi·ne·te
Sorry.	Простете.	pros·te·te
Yes./No.	Да./Не.	da/ne
Help!	Помош!	po·mosh
Cheers!	На здравје!	na zdrav·ye

I don't understand.
Јас не разбирам. yas ne raz·bi·ram

Do you speak English?
Зборувате ли англиски? zbo·ru·va·te li an·glis·ki

How much is it?
Колку чини тоа? kol·ku chi·ni to·a

Where's ...?
Каде е ...? ka·de e ...

Where are the toilets?
Каде се тоалетите? ka·de se to·a·le·ti·te

NORWEGIAN

In Norwegian, each vowel can be either long or short. Generally, they're long when followed by one consonant and short when followed by two or more consonants. Note that aw is pronounced as in 'law', ew as 'ee' with pursed lips, and ow as in 'how'.

Hello.	*God dag.*	go·daag
Goodbye.	*Ha det.*	haa·de
Please.	*Vær så snill.*	veyr saw snil
Thank you.	*Takk.*	tak
Excuse me.	*Unnskyld.*	ewn·shewl
Sorry.	*Beklager.*	bey·klaa·geyr
Yes./No.	*Ja./Nei.*	yaa/ney
Help!	*Hjelp!*	yelp
Cheers!	*Skål!*	skawl

I don't understand.
Jeg forstår ikke. yai fawr·stawr i·key

Do you speak English?
Snakker du engelsk? sna·ker doo eyng·elsk

How much is it?
Hvor mye koster det? vor mew·e kaws·ter de

Where's ...?
Hvor er ...? vor ayr ...

Where are the toilets?
Hvor er toalettene? vor eyr to·aa·le·te·ne

POLISH

Polish vowels are generally pronounced short. Nasal vowels are pronounced as though you're trying to force the air through your nose, and are indicated with n or m following the vowel. Note also that r is rolled in Polish.

Hello.	*Cześć.*	cheshch
Goodbye.	*Do widzenia.*	do vee·*dze*·nya
Please.	*Proszę.*	*pro*·she
Thank you.	*Dziękuję.*	jyen·*koo*·ye
Excuse me.	*Przepraszam.*	pshe·*pra*·sham
Sorry.	*Przepraszam.*	pshe·*pra*·sham
Yes./No.	*Tak./Nie.*	tak/nye
Help!	*Na pomoc!*	na *po*·mots
Cheers!	*Na zdrowie!*	na *zdro*·vye

I don't understand.
Nie rozumiem. — nye ro·*zoo*·myem

Do you speak English?
Czy pan/pani mówi po angielsku? (m/f) — chi pan/*pa*·nee *moo*·vee po an·*gyel*·skoo

How much is it?
Ile to kosztuje? — ee·le to kosh·*too*·ye

Where's ...?
Gdzie jest ...? — gjye yest ...

Where are the toilets?
Gdzie są toalety? — gjye som to·a·*le*·ti

PORTUGUESE

Most vowel sounds in Portuguese have a nasal version (ie pronounced as if you're trying to force the sound through your nose), which is indicated in our pronunciation guides with ng after the vowel.

Hello.	*Olá.*	o·*laa*
Goodbye.	*Adeus.*	a·de·*oosh*
Please.	*Por favor.*	poor fa·*vor*
Thank you.	*Obrigado.* (m)	o·bree·*gaa*·doo
	Obrigada. (f)	o·bree·*gaa*·da
Excuse me.	*Faz favor.*	faash fa·*vor*
Sorry.	*Desculpe.*	desh·*kool*·pe
Yes./No.	*Sim./Não.*	seeng/nowng
Help!	*Socorro!*	soo·*ko*·rroo
Cheers!	*Saúde!*	sa·oo·de

I don't understand.
Não entendo. — nowng eng·*teng*·doo

Do you speak English?
Fala inglês? — *faa*·la eeng·*glesh*

How much is it?
Quanto custa? — *kwang*·too *koosh*·ta

Where's ...?
Onde é ...? — *ong*·de e ...

Where are the toilets?
Onde é a casa de banho? — *ong*·de e a *kaa*·za de *ba*·nyoo

ROMANIAN

Note that ew is pronounced as the 'ee' in 'see' with rounded lips, uh as the 'a' in 'ago', and zh as the 's' in 'pleasure'. The apostrophe (') indicates a very short, unstressed (almost silent) i. Moldovan is the official name of the variety of Romanian spoken in Moldova.

Hello.	*Bună ziua.*	*boo*·nuh *zee*·wa
Goodbye.	*La revedere.*	la re·ve·*de*·re
Please.	*Vă rog.*	vuh rog
Thank you.	*Mulţumesc.*	mool·tsoo·*mesk*
Excuse me.	*Scuzaţi-mă.*	skoo·*za*·tsee·muh
Sorry.	*Îmi pare rău.*	ewm' *pa*·re *ruh*·oo
Yes./No.	*Da./Nu.*	da/noo
Help!	*Ajutor!*	a·zhoo·*tor*
Cheers!	*Noroc!*	no·*rok*

I don't understand.
Eu nu înţeleg. — *ye*·oo noo ewn·tse·*leg*

Do you speak English?
Vorbiţi engleza? — vor·*beets'* en·*gle*·za

How much is it?
Cât costă? — kewt *kos*·tuh

Where's ...?
Unde este ...? — *oon*·de *yes*·te ...

Where are the toilets?
Unde este o toaletă? — oon·*de yes*·te o to·a·*le*·tuh

RUSSIAN

Note that zh is pronounced as the 's' in 'pleasure'. Also, r is rolled in Russian and the apostrophe (') indicates a slight y sound.

Hello.	Здравствуйте.	*zdrast*·vuyt·ye
Goodbye.	До свидания.	da svee·*dan*·ya
Please.	Пожалуйста.	pa·*zhal*·sta
Thank you.	Спасибо	spa·*see*·ba
Excuse me./ Sorry.	Извините, пожалуйста.	eez·vee·*neet*·ye pa·*zhal*·sta
Yes./No.	Да./Нет.	da/nyet
Help!	Помогите!	pa·ma·*gee*·tye
Cheers!	Пей до дна!	pyey da dna

I don't understand.
Я не понимаю. — ya nye pa·nee·*ma*·yu

Do you speak English?
Вы говорите по-английски? — vi ga·va·*reet*·ye pa·an·*glee*·skee

How much is it?
Сколько стоит? — *skol'*·ka sto·*eet*

Where's ...?
Где (здесь) ...? — gdye (zdyes') ...

Where are the toilets?
Где здесь туалет? — gdye zdyes' tu·al·*yet*

SLOVAK

An accent mark over a vowel in written Slovak indicates it's pronounced as a long sound. Note also that uh is pronounced as the 'a' in 'ago', and kh as the 'ch' in the Scottish *loch*. The apostrophe (') indicates a slight y sound.

Hello. — *Dobrý deň.* — *do*·bree dyen'
Goodbye. — *Do videnia.* — do *vi*·dye·ni·yuh
Please. — *Prosím.* — *pro*·seem
Thank you. — *Ďakujem* — *dyuh*·ku·yem
Excuse me. — *Prepáčte.* — *pre*·pach·tye
Sorry. — *Prepáčte.* — *pre*·pach·tye
Yes./No. — *Áno./Nie.* — *a*·no/*ni*·ye
Help! — *Pomoc!* — *po*·mots
Cheers! — *Nazdravie!* — *nuhz*·druh·vi·ye

I don't understand.
Nerozumiem. — *nye*·ro·zu·myem

Do you speak English?
Hovoríte po anglicky? — *ho*·vo·ree·tye po *uhng*·lits·ki

How much is it?
Koľko to stojí? — *kol'*·ko to *sto*·yee

Where's ...?
Kde je ...? — kdye ye ...

Where are the toilets?
Kde sú tu záchody? — kdye soo tu *za*·kho·di

SLOVENE

Note that r is pronounced as a rolled sound in Slovene.

Hello. — *Zdravo.* — *zdra*·vo
Goodbye. — *Na svidenje.* — na *svee*·den·ye
Please. — *Prosim.* — *pro*·seem
Thank you. — *Hvala.* — *hva*·la
Excuse me. — *Dovolite.* — do·vo·*lee*·te
Sorry. — *Oprostite.* — op·ros·*tee*·te
Yes./No. — *Da./Ne.* — da/ne
Help! — *Na pomoč!* — na po·*moch*
Cheers! — *Na zdravje!* — na *zdrav*·ye

I don't understand.
Ne razumem. — ne ra·*zoo*·mem

Do you speak English?
Ali govorite angleško? — a·lee go·vo·*ree*·te ang·*lesh*·ko

How much is it?
Koliko stane? — *ko*·lee·ko *sta*·ne

Where's ...?
Kje je ...? — kye ye ...

Where are the toilets?
Kje je stranišče? — kye ye stra·*neesh*·che

SPANISH

Note that the Spanish r is strong and rolled, th is pronounced 'with a lisp', and v is soft, pronounced almost like a 'b'.

Hello. — *Hola.* — *o*·la
Goodbye. — *Adiós.* — a·*dyos*
Please. — *Por favor.* — por fa·*vor*
Thank you. — *Gracias.* — *gra*·thyas
Excuse me. — *Perdón.* — per·*don*
Sorry. — *Lo siento.* — lo *syen*·to
Yes./No. — *Sí./No.* — see/no
Help! — *¡Socorro!* — so·*ko*·ro
Cheers! — *¡Salud!* — sa·*loo*

I don't understand.
Yo no entiendo. — yo no en·*tyen*·do

Do you speak English?
¿Habla/Hablas inglés? (pol/inf) — *a*·bla/*a*·blas een·*gles*

How much is it?
¿Cuánto cuesta? — *kwan*·to *kwes*·ta

Where's ...?
¿Dónde está ...? — *don*·de es·*ta* ...

Where are the toilets?
¿Dónde están los servicios? — *don*·de es·*tan* los ser·*vee*·thyos

SWEDISH

Swedish vowels can be short or long – generally the stressed vowels are long, except when followed by double consonants. Note that aw is pronounced as in 'saw', air as in 'hair', eu as the 'u' in 'nurse', ew as the 'ee' in 'see' with rounded lips, and oh as the 'o' in 'note'.

Hello. — *Hej.* — hey
Goodbye. — *Hej då.* — hey daw
Please. — *Tack.* — tak
Thank you. — *Tack.* — tak
Excuse me. — *Ursäkta mig.* — oor·*shek*·ta mey
Sorry. — *Förlåt.* — feur·*lawt*
Yes./No. — *Ja./Nej.* — yaa/ney
Help! — *Hjälp!* — yelp
Cheers! — *Skål!* — skawl

I don't understand.
Jag förstår inte. yaa feur·*shtawr in*·te

Do you speak English?
Talar du engelska? *taa*·lar doo *eng*·el·ska

How much is it?
Hur mycket kostar det? hoor *mew*·ke *kos*·tar de

Where's ...?
Var finns det ...? var finns de ...

Where are the toilets?
Var är toaletten? var air toh·aa·*le*·ten

TURKISH

Double vowels are pronounced twice in Turkish. Note also that eu is pronounced as the 'u' in 'nurse', ew as the 'ee' in 'see' with rounded lips, uh as the 'a' in 'ago', r is rolled and v is a little softer than in English.

Hello.	*Merhaba.*	*mer*·ha·ba
Goodbye.	*Hoşçakal.* (when leaving)	hosh·*cha*·kal
	Güle güle. (when staying)	gew·*le* gew·*le*
Please.	*Lütfen.*	*lewt*·fen
Thank you.	*Teşekkür ederim.*	te·shek·*kewr* e·*de*·reem
Excuse me.	*Bakar mısınız.*	ba·*kar* muh·suh·*nuhz*
Sorry.	*Özür dilerim.*	eu·*zewr* dee·*le*·reem
Yes./No.	*Evet./Hayır.*	e·*vet*/*ha*·yuhr
Help!	*İmdat!*	*eem*·dat
Cheers!	*Şerefe!*	she·re·*fe*

I don't understand.
Anlamıyorum. an·*la*·muh·yo·room

Do you speak English?
İngilizce konuşuyor musunuz? een·gee·*leez*·je ko·noo·*shoo*·yor moo·soo·*nooz*

How much is it?
Ne kadar? *ne* ka·*dar*

Where's ...?
... nerede? ... *ne*·re·de

Where are the toilets?
Tuvaletler nerede? too·va·let·*ler ne*·re·de

UKRAINIAN

Ukrainian vowels in unstressed syllables are generally pronounced shorter and weaker than they are in stressed syllables. Note that ow is pronounced as in 'how' and zh as the 's' in 'pleasure'. The apostrophe (') indicates a slight y sound.

Hello.	Добрий день.	*do*·bry den'
Goodbye.	До побачення.	do po·*ba*·chen·nya
Please.	Прошу.	*pro*·shu
Thank you.	Дякую.	*dya*·ku·yu
Excuse me.	Вибачте.	*vy*·bach·te
Sorry.	Перепрошую.	pe·re·*pro*·shu·yu
Yes./No.	Так./Ні.	tak/ni
Help!	Допоможіть!	do·po·mo·*zhit'*
Cheers!	Будьмо!	*bud'*·mo

I don't understand.
Я не розумію. ya ne ro·zu·*mi*·yu

Do you speak English?
Ви розмовляєте англійською мовою? vy roz·mow·*lya*·ye·te an·*hliys'*·ko·yu *mo*·vo·yu

How much is it?
Скільки це він/вона коштує? (m/f) *skil'*·ki tse vin/vo·*na ko*·shtu·ye

Where's ...?
Де ...? de ...

Where are the toilets?
Де туалети? de tu·a·le·ti

Behind the Scenes

SEND US YOUR FEEDBACK

We love to hear from travellers – your comments keep us on our toes and help make our books better. Our well-travelled team reads every word on what you loved or loathed about this book. Although we cannot reply individually to postal submissions, we always guarantee that your feedback goes straight to the appropriate authors, in time for the next edition. Each person who sends us information is thanked in the next edition – the most useful submissions are rewarded with a selection of digital PDF chapters.

Visit **lonelyplanet.com/contact** to submit your updates and suggestions or to ask for help. Our award-winning website also features inspirational travel stories, news and discussions.

Note: We may edit, reproduce and incorporate your comments in Lonely Planet products such as guidebooks, websites and digital products, so let us know if you don't want your comments reproduced or your name acknowledged. For a copy of our privacy policy visit lonelyplanet.com/privacy.

OUR READERS

Many thanks to the travellers who used the last edition and wrote to us with helpful hints, useful advice and interesting anecdotes:
Renata Buarque, Andrea Gallea, Tami Harmony and Panik Vibberstoft, Amy Jasper, Alexander Nastos, Rosemary Papadopoulou, Daniella Reategui, Amanda Schellenberg, Barney Smith, Angela Sproston, Lucy Thompson, Bonnie Wilken, Xu Xiaotian, Georgia Yarrow

AUTHOR THANKS

Tom Masters

An enormous debt of thanks to all my hard-working fellow authors on this book, and the teams in London and Melbourne who commissioned, edited and oversaw the project. Special thanks in Albania to Ardi Pulaj, Catherine Bohne, Tedi Sina and Bledi Strakosha; in Belarus to my friend Zhenya Artemyev; in Kosovo to Hekuran Avdyli and the folks at Libertas in Pristina and in Moldova to Kostya Derenyov and Marina Waters in Chisinau and Lena Lozinsky in Tiraspol.

Carolyn Bain

Much love and thanks go to Graham Harris and Kate Johns for pre-Estonia fun and games, and to Brandon Presser for Nordic-Baltic inspiration (and for seeing the same Tallinn cafe from many different angles). In Tallinn, warmest thanks to Priit and Beatrice for excellent chats and food, Geli for her usual fine apartment assistance, Elina and Triin at Chado for their tips, and especially to Estonia's finest teameister, Steve Kolditz.

James Bainbridge

A heartfelt *çok teşekkürler*, once again, to everyone who helped me find my way around the steppe on my last visit to northeastern Turkey. Celil in Kars and Necmettin in Akçaabat deserve special mention for your help on a few recent projects. Thanks, as ever, to everyone at Lonely Planet – Tom, Dora, Angela, James, Cliff et al – and to my wife, Leigh-Robin.

Mark Baker

I met many helpful people all along the way in researching the countries for this guide and their names would be too numerous to mention. I've lived in Prague for two decades now and a very special thanks to my good friends here. In Slovenia, the staff of the Slovenia Tourist Board deserve special mention. Finally, a nod to coordinating author Tom Masters for putting this enormous guide together is definitely in order.

Oliver Berry

Thanks to Cliff Wilkinson for the England gig, and David Carroll, Dan Corbett and the rest of the SPP team for being there whenever we needed you! Special thanks to Susie, Molly and Gracie Berry, and to all the people I met out on the road.

Greg Bloom

Pop was my wingman again, soaking up vodka shots and slogging around St Petersburg on trip number one of three. *Spacibo* dad! A big *spacibo* to Lucy for joining on trip number 3! Old Kyiv friends Jake Rudnitsky and Tim O'Brien helped me out big-time in Moscow. Thanks to Mike Sito for letting me help the Pigs. Thanks to Peter and the gang in Piter; Kaz and (remotely) Aaron in Moscow, and the Petersburg ultimate frisbee crew.

Kerry Christiani

A big *Dankeschön* to all of the super-efficient tourism professionals who made the road to research a breeze, especially Cornelia Pirka in Vienna, Maria Altendorfer and team in Salzburg and Colette Spiss-Verra in Innsbruck. Thanks to my Vienna friends Chiara and Karin for good times and invaluable tips. Thanks also go to Ryan Ver Berkmoes, my fellow authors and the entire Lonely Planet production team.

Chris Deliso

As always a number of kind and helpful Macedonians (and other folks too), provided good tips, advice and assistance in the course of my research. Among them I can mention Pece, Patrice, Stevche, Emilija, Biljana, Dane, Stojko. Ace and Julija – you know who you are! Of course, this book couldn't have been completed without the work of my patient and devoted Lonely Planet colleagues, including Coordinating Author Tom Masters, and the mapmaking and production teams.

Marc Di Duca

A huge *dyakuju* to my Ukrainian parents-in-law for their support in Kyiv and their insights into the latest developments in Ukraine. Also many thanks to Yarema Dukh of Visitlviv.net for his invaluable support in Lviv, Mykola and Olya in Simferopol, Viktor in Odesa, all the dedicated staff at tourist offices in Lviv, Yalta and Bakhchysaray, Ostap in Lviv, Ukrainian Railways for finally realising that fast trains with seats that travel in the hours of daylight might be a good idea, and last but not least to my wife, Tanya, for introducing me to Ukraine in the first place.

Peter Dragicevich

Many thanks to all the wonderful people who helped me in Montenegro, especially Ivica Erdelja, Hayley Wright and Jack Delf, Emma and Ben Heywood, Krstinja Petranović, Danica Ćeranić and Matthew Lane. Also, I owe a debt of gratitude to James and Lorraine Hedderman, Tim Benzie and Kerri Tyler for their contributions before and after the journey.

Mark Elliott

In a sense I've been researching this book for nearly two decades since being dragged very willingly to Belgium by love and bubbles. Sadly neither last forever, it seems. Nonetheless, my admiration for the country has outlasted everything. A million thanks to my unbeatable family for endless support, and to uncountable folks who have helped me over many years of exploring the region, notably Wieland de Hoon, Hans Rossel, Guy Jacobs, Dani Systermans, Lesley Devos, Valerie de Kerpel and Sharon Taylor.

Steve Fallon

Thanks to Bea Szirti and Ildikó Nagy Moran for their helpful suggestions. Péter Lengyel showed me the correct wine roads to follow again and Gerard Gorman where the birds are. For hospitality on the road I am indebted to Regina Bruckner and Shandor Madachy in Budapest and András Cseh in Eger. *Nagyon szépen köszönöm mindenkinek*! As always, I'd like to dedicate my share of this to partner Michael Rothschild, with love and gratitude.

Duncan Garwood

Grazie to Viviana and Lorenzo for the use of their flat in Bologna, and to Romano Fini and Nino Amato for helping me break into it. Thanks also to the ladies in the Genoa tourist office, Gudrun Selinger, Federica Matteozzi and Marina Parodi, for their advice, and to fellow LP scribe Virginia Maxwell. As always, a huge hug to Lidia and the boys, Ben and Nick.

Anthony Ham

Heartfelt thanks to all those *madrileños* who I have been proud to call friends during my decade in the city. A huge thank you to Dora Whitaker and to all the authors of Lonely Planet's Spain guide. It was my great fortune a week after arriving in Madrid to meet my wife and soulmate, Marina, who has made this city a true place of the heart. And to Carlota and Valentina: you are Madrid's greatest gifts of all.

Anna Kaminski

Many people to thank, not least Katie – for entrusting me with this task, Tom and the rest of the Europe team, and to friends and family who helped me along the way. A particularly big thank you to Gintaras and Viktor in Kaunas, to my adopted Lithuanian parents in Nida (you know who you are!), Nikas, Simonas, Ben and Aleksandra in Vilnius, Tomas and Jacinta for the Palanga all-nighter, and Rasa Dooling – my interviewee.

Craig McLachlan

A hearty thanks to all those who helped me out on the road, but most of all, to my exceptionally beautiful wife, Yuriko, who let me know when I'd had my daily quota of Mythos and gyros pitta.

Anja Mutić

Hvala, mama, for your home cooking and contagious laughter. *Obrigada*, Hoji, for being there before, during and after. A huge *hvala* to my friends in Croatia who gave me endless recommendations – this book wouldn't be the same without you. Special thanks go to Lidija in Zagreb and Mila in Split, as well as the team at HTZ. Finally, to the inspiring memory of my father who travels with me still.

Brandon Presser

A massive thank you goes first and foremost to Aleksis Karlsons for your hospitality and friendship. Special thanks to Jānis Jenzis, Agnese Kleina, Live Rīga, TAVA, and everyone else that had a hand in making this edition a great one. Thanks also to Joanne, my clever coauthors and editors at Lonely Planet, and a big shout out to Carolyn for letting me rediscover the black poodle twenty times over.

Tim Richards

As always, I'm indebted to the staff of Poland's tourist offices, and the national train company PKP. Dziękuję to my Polish friends – Ewa, Magda and Andrzej – for their companionship and insights regarding their mother country. I'm also grateful to the members of the English Language Club in Kraków, who supplied both friendly conversation and advice on new places of interest. Thanks also to the generous inhabitants of Twitter for their random and useful assistance, particularly Magda Rakita for music tips.

Andrea Schulte-Peevers

Big heartfelt thanks to all these wonderful people who've plied me with tips, insights, information, ideas and encouragement (in no particular order): Henrik Tidefjärd, Miriam Bers, Petra Gümmer, Julia Schwarz, Frank Engster, Myriel Walter, Heinz 'Cookie' Gindullis, Heiner Schuster, Steffi Gretschel, Renate Freiling, Silke Neumann, Kirsten Schmidt, Michael Radder, Christoph Münch, Christoph Lehmann, Patrick Schwarzkopf, Danilo Hommel, Dr Jasper Freiherr von Richthofen, Julia Schröder, Jan Czyszke and, of course, David Peevers. Kudos to the entire Lonely Planet team responsible for producing such a kick-ass book.

Tamara Sheward

To research here is to make a zillion friends, so in addition to thanking the population of Serbia, I'd like to offer clinks of the *rakija* glass and *mnogo hvala na*...the NS Kiosk Crew, Gagi of Niš, Toma of Mokra Gora, Zoran for saving us from snakes and wolves, all the helpful oddballs we met during our *medeni mesec*/research jaunt, Dragana Eremić, the Ljesević family, the Lučić clan, Pappa and Mumma, and as ever, to Dušan, *najbolje, najslađi čovek u svemiru*!

Regis St Louis

In Lisbon, I'd like to thank Guida Moura for her friendship and hospitality, chef Michael Guerrieri for his kindness and insight into the dining scene, and João Teixeira for his mine of local knowledge. Thanks go out to Italian travellers Silvia Luraschi and Cesare Figini for tips on Braga, and to all the helpful tourism officials across the country. As always, *beijos* to my family Cassandra, Magdalena and Genevieve for their support.

Andy Symington

I owe many thanks once again to Gustav, Marja, Mirjam and Meri Schulman for their warm Finnish welcome whenever I visit. Thanks also go to helpful Finns in tourist offices and elsewhere, Cristina Sandoval, Alexis Kouros, Satu Natunen and her team, and to the brilliant group of authors and editors that made this book a very light task. Lastly, love and gratitude to my parents for their support and to Elena Vázquez Rodríguez, excellent travel companion and so much more, *kiitos paljon mí amor*.

Ryan Ver Berkmoes

Thanks to all the authors who worked so hard on this guidebook. Meanwhile in the Netherlands, thanks to a range of old friends who came through like windmills on a breezy day. In Switzerland, thanks to Claudia Stehle for beers, Damien Simonis for being himself and Judy Slatyer and Peter for a splendid night. And big thanks to the eternally glistening Alexis Averbuck.

Luke Waterson

To Josef for the Spišské Podhradie adventure, to the HRL girls, to Michaela in the High Tatras, to the entire Košice 2013 team, to Michal for the ride round the east and to Peter and Brano for the "authentic" ride round Bratislava, to Giovanni and his great wine, to Majo for his hospitality in Slovenský Raj and to the old women who opened up the wooden churches: *d'akujem* for the wonderful insight into your little-in-size, big-at-heart country.

Nicola Williams

Kudos to my France coauthors who resolutely persevered with an ambitious project that, at times, felt akin to scaling the Eiffel Tower on tiptoes in stilettos. On the road *merci mille fois* to Corsica aficionado Vincent Lehoux (unsurpassable Ajaccio recommendations); Kasia Dietz and Lindsay Tramuta (Corsica tips by way of Paris); Charlie Johnson (best hidden beach camping); travel-mad husband Matthias and our trilingual tribe (only car sick once during 2000km of coastal hairpins covered at average speed of 38km/h).

Neil Wilson

Thanks to the friendly and helpful tourist office staff all over Ireland, and to all those folk in pubs and on the road who offered advice and recommendations.

Acknowledgments

Climate map data adapted from Peel MC, Finlayson BL & McMahon TA (2007) 'Updated World Map of the Köppen-Geiger Climate Classification', Hydrology and Earth System Sciences, 11, 163344.
Cover photograph: Venice, Italy, Andrew Smith/Cuba Gallery.

THIS BOOK

Many people have helped create this 8th edition of *Europe on a Shoestring*, which is part of Lonely Planet's Europe series. Other titles in this series include *Western Europe, Eastern Europe, Mediterranean Europe, Central Europe, Scandinavia* and *Southeastern Europe*. This guidebook was commissioned in Lonely Planet's London office, and produced by the following:

Commissioning Editors Joanna Cooke, James Smart, Helena Smith

Coordinating Editor Elin Berglund, Samantha Forge

Coordinating Cartographer Valentina Kremenchutskaya

Coordinating Layout Designer Katherine Marsh

Managing Editors Sasha Baskett, Angela Tinson

Managing Cartographers Anthony Phelan, Amanda Sierp

Managing Layout Designer Jane Hart

Assisting Editors Janet Austin, Michelle Bennett, Carly Hall, Elizabeth Harvey, Kate Kiely, Helen Koehne, Kellie Langdon, Anne Mason, Anne Mulvaney, Karyn Noble, Sally O'Brien, Katie O'Connell, Lorna Parkes, Monique Perrin, Gabrielle Stefanos, Fionnuala Twomey

Assisting Cartographers Xavier Di Toro, Alex Leung, James Leversha

Cover Research Nic Lehman

Internal Image Research Aude Vauconsant

Language Content Branislava Vladisavljevic

Thanks to Joe Bindloss, Ryan Evans, Larissa Frost, Chris Girdler, Laura Crawford, Genesys India, Jouve India, Andi Jones, Annelies Mertens, Trent Paton Dianne Schallmeiner, Kerriann Southway, Navin Sushil, Gerar Walker, Tony Wheeler

index

A

A Coruña 1090
Aachen 487-8
Aarhus 951-2
Abri du Cap Blanc 393
accommodation 1202-4, *see also individual locations*
Acropolis 507, 510, **20**
activities 25, 27-31, *see also individual locations*, canoeing, cycling, diving, hiking, horseback riding, kayaking, paragliding & parasailing, rafting, rock climbing, skiing
  birdwatching 236, 575, 613
  bobsledding 728
  bungee jumping 79, 728, 1136, 1137
  canyoning 79, 149, 1035, 1136, 1172-3
  fishing 987
  kitesurfing 1115
  sailing 62, 528, 613, 1129
  snorkelling 645, 694, 871
  snowboarding 665, 1015, 1132, 1137, 1144
  snowmobiling 964, 983, 987
  surfing 237-8, 601, 613, 871, 884, 1115
  waterskiing 884, 1129
  windsurfing 263, 528, 567, 884, 1115, 1129
Aegean coast 1164-70
Aeolian Islands 694-5
Agia Roumeli 534
Agrigento 697-8
Aguntum 81
Aínsa 1084
air travel 1215-16, 1216-17
Aix-en-Provence 403-4
Ajaccio 414-15
Akrotiri 529
Albania 42-53, **44**
  accommodation 42, 52
  budgeting 43
  business hours 53
  climate 42-3
  drinking 43
  exchange rates 43
  food 42, 43, 53
  highlights 44
  history 52
  holidays 53
  internet resources 43
  itineraries 43
  money 43, 53
  people 52
  planning 42-3
  travel seasons 42-3
  travel to/from 43, 53
  travel within 53
  visas 53
Albarracín 1084
Albert Dock 212
Algarve 866-9
Alghero 700-1
Alighieri, Dante 664, 702
Aliki 525
Alkmaar 807
Alpirsbach 471
Alps (France) 390-2
Alps (Germany) 460-1
Alsace 376-8
Amalfi 689
Amalfi coast 688-9
Amasya 1175
Ambleside 214-15
Amboise 382-3
Amsterdam 791-8, **792**, **6-7**, **19**
  accommodation 794
  drinking 795-6
  entertainment 796
  food 794-5
  information 797
  safety 812
  shopping 796-7
  sights 791-4
  tours 794
  travel to/from 797
  travel within 797-8
Anatolia 1174-7
Andalucía 1097-110
Andorra 1079
Aneto 1084
Ankara 1174-6
Antalya 1173-4
Antwerp 112-17, **114-15**
Apollonas 527
Aragón 1083-4
Aran Islands 598-600
Arc de Triomphe 347
architecture
  Bulgaria 263
  Finland 986
  France 419-20
  Italy 703
  Portugal 883
  Slovakia 1022
  Slovenia 1041
Areopoli 518
Arles 403
art
  Austria 83-4
  Bulgaria 263
  Denmark 985-6
  Finland 985-6
  France 420
  Hungary 574
  Italy 703
  Netherlands 810
  Norway 985-6
  Portugal 883
  Spain 1112-13
  Sweden 985-6
  Switzerland 1146
art galleries, *see* museums & galleries
Artà 1095
arts, *see individual countries*, architecture, art, cinema, dance, literature, music
Asklipieion 537
Assisi 679-80
Athens 507-14, **508-9**, **512**, **20**
  accommodation 511
  drinking 513
  entertainment 513
  festivals & events 511
  food 511, 513
  information 513
  travel within 514
Atlantic coast (France) 393-6
ATMs 1208
Austria 54-88, **56-7**
  accommodation 54, 84-6
  activities 85
  arts 83-4
  budgeting 55
  business hours 85
  climate 54
  drinking 55, 84
  embassies & consulates 85-6
  exchange rates 55
  food 54, 55, 84, 86
  highlights 56-7
  history 83
  holidays 86
  internet resources 55
  itineraries 55
  money 55, 85, 86
  planning 54-5
  telephone services 86

000 Map pages
000 Photo pages

Austria *continued*
tourist information 86
travel seasons 54
travel to/from 55, 86-7
travel within 87-8
visas 86
Avebury 188
Avignon 404-6, **405**
Ávila 1063

B

Bacharach 480
Balchik 260
Baleal 871
Balearic Islands 1093-7
Ballaghbeama Pass 595
Bamberg 466-7
Banat 903-5
Banc d'Arguin bird reserve 395
Banja Luka 149
Banská Štiavnica 1014
banyas, bathhouses, saunas & spas
Austria 70
Britain 189
Czech Republic 308-9
Finland 977, 982
Greece 540
Hungary 555, 575
Latvia 721, 727
Portugal 874
Russia 935
Spain 1103
Turkey 1163
Barcelona 1068-82, **1070-1**, **1074-5**, **16**
accommodation 1073, 1076-7
drinking 1078-9
entertainment 1079
festivals & events 1073
food 1077-8
information 1080-1
shopping 1079-80
sights 1069, 1072-3
travel to/from 1081
travel within 1081-2
Bardejov 1021
bargaining 1209
Bargama 1165-6
Bari 690-1
Basel 1142-3
Bastia 415-16
Bastogne 130
Bath 188-91, **190**

bathhouses, see *banyas*, bathhouses, saunas & spas
bathrooms 1212
Bavaria 454-67
Bavarian Alps 460-1
Bay of Kotor 780-3, **17**
Bayeux 369-70
beaches 24
Beaune 384-5
beer, *see also* breweries
Bulgaria 244
Croatia 267
Czech Republic 28, 295
France 366
Germany 428, 458, 498
Ireland 579
Lithuania 733
Macedonia 751
Netherlands 789, 810
Scandinavia 940, 986
Slovakia 1022
Spain 1114
Ukraine 1198
Beilstein 481-2
Belarus 89-99, **91**
accommodation 98
budgeting 90
business hours 98
climate 89
drinking 90
embassies & consulates 98
environment 98
exchange rates 90
festivals & events 98
food 89, 90, 98
highlights 91
history 97
holidays 98-9
internet resources 90
itineraries 90
money 90, 98
people 98
planning 89-90
travel seasons 89
travel to/from 90, 99
travel within 99
visas 99
Belfast 602-8, **604-5**
accommodation 603, 606
drinking 606-7
entertainment 607
festivals & events 603
food 606
information 607
sights 602-3
travel to/from 607-8
travel within 608

Belgium 100-26, 131-5, **102-3**
accommodation 100, 133
activities 133
arts 132
budgeting 101
business hours 133-4
climate 100
embassies & consulates 134
exchange rates 101
food 100, 101, 132-3, 134
highlights 102
history 131-2
holidays 134
internet resources 101
itineraries 101
money 101, 134
people 132
planning 100-1
telephone services 134
travel seasons 100
travel to/from 101, 134-5
travel within 135
Belgrade 994-9, **996-7**
Ben Nevis 232
Berat 49-50
Berchtesgaden 460-1
Bergen 968-70, **37**
Berlenga Grande 871
Berlin 429, 432-45, **429**, **432-3**, **436-7**, **440**, **12**, **40**
accommodation 441-2
drinking 443
entertainment 443-4
food 442-3
information 444
itineraries 435
sights 432-5, 437-9
tours 439, 441
travel within 445
Bern 1133-4
Bernese Oberland 1134-8
Bernina Express 1143
Bernkastel-Kues 482
Betws-y-Coed 217
Biarritz 395-6
bicycle travel, *see* cycling
Bihać 149
Bilbao 1086-8
birdwatching 236, 575, 613
Birmingham 199
Bitola 760-1
Black Forest 471-2
Black Sea 257-62
Blarney 594
Bled 1034-7, **1036**
Bled Island 1035
Blois 379

000 Map pages
000 Photo pages

blue cruises 1171
boat travel 1216, 1218, *see also* canoeing, kayaking, sailing
bobsledding 728
Bodensee 473-4
Bodrum 1168-9
Bohemia 308-12
Bohinj 1037-8
Bohinjska Bistrica 1037
Bologna 662-4
Bonifacio 416-17
Bonn 485
books, *see* literature
Boppard 480
Bordeaux 393-4
Bosnia & Hercegovina 136-52, **138**
accommodation 136, 150
activities 150
arts 150
budgeting 137
business hours 150-1
climate 136
drinking 137
embassies & consulates 151
environment 150
exchange rates 137
food 136, 137, 151
highlights 138
history 149-50
holidays 151
internet resources 137
itineraries 137
money 137, 151
people 150
planning 136-7
postal services 151
safety 151
travel seasons 136
travel to/from 137, 151-2
travel within 152
visas 151
Bovec 1038-9
Bowness 214
Bozburun peninsula 1170
Braga 880-1
brandy
Albania 43
Bosnia & Hercegovina 137
Greece 506, 545
Hungary 553
Moldova 774
Montenegro 778
Romania 888
Serbia 992
Slovakia 1006, 1022
Slovenia 1027
Braşov 896-8, **896**
Bratislava 1008-14, **1010-11**
Bregenz 82
Bregenzerwald 83
Bremen 490-1
Brest 96-7
breweries, *see also* beer
Alpirsbacher Klosterbräu 471
Beck's Brewery 490
Brouwerij De Halve Maan 120-1
Cantillon Brewery 105
Guinness Storehouse 581, 584
Heineken Experience 793
Pilsner Urquell Brewery 310
Stella Artois brewery 112
Brighton 186-7
Bristol 191-4
Britain 153-242, **156-7**
accommodation 153, 236-7
activities 237-8
arts 235
budgeting 154
business hours 238
climate 153
customs regulations 238
environment 236
exchange rates 154
food 153, 154, 236, 238
highlights 156-7
history 233-4
holidays 239
internet resources 154
itineraries 154
language 235
money 154, 238-9
people 235
planning 153-4
safety 239
sport 235-6
telephone services 239
travel seasons 153
travel to/from 154, 240
travel within 240-2
visas 239
Brittany 371-4
Brno 312-15
Bruges 119-23, **120**
Brussels 104-11, **106-7**
accommodation 105, 108-9
drinking 109-10
entertainment 110
food 109
information 111
shopping 110-11
sights 104-5
travel to/from 111
travel within 111
Buçaco Forest 874
Bucegi Mountains 900
Bucharest 889-95, **890-1**
accommodation 893
drinking 894
entertainment 894
food 893-4
information 894
sights 889, 892-3
travel to/from 895
travel within 895
Bucovina 903
Budapest 554-65, **556-7**, **558-9**, **16**
accommodation 561
activities 555
drinking 562-3
entertainment 563
festivals & events 560
food 561-2
information 564
shopping 563
sights 555, 557
travel to/from 564-5
travel within 565
budgeting 22, *see also individual countries*
Budva 781-2
Bulgaria 243-65, **245**
accommodation 243, 263
activities 263
budgeting 244
business hours 263
climate 243
drinking 244
environment 263
exchange rates 244
food 243, 244, 263
highlights 245
history 262
holidays 264
internet resources 244
itineraries 244
money 244, 263, 264
people 262, 263
planning 243-4
safety 264
telephone services 264
travel seasons 243
travel to/from 244, 264-5
travel within 265
Bundoran 601
bungee jumping 79, 728, 1136, 1137
Burano 655
Burgas 261-2
Burgos 1066
Burgundy 383-90
Burren 596
bus travel 1218-19
business hours 1204, *see also individual countries*
Butrint 51-3

C

Cáceres 1110-11
Cagliari 698-700
Cahirciveen 595
Calais 366-8
Cambridge 201-2
Çanakkale 1164-5
Cannes 410-11
canoeing
  Belgium 133
  Greece 528
  Ireland 613
  Portugal 884
  Slovenia 1037
Cantabria 1088
Canterbury 184-5
canyoning 79, 149, 1035, 1136, 1172-3
Cap de Favàritx 1094
Cape Kolka 727
Capel Curig 217
Cappadocia 1177-8
Capri 686-7
car travel 1219-21
Carcassonne 399
Cardiff 215-17
Carnac 372
Carpathian Mountains 835-6, 1196
Carrick-a-Rede Rope Bridge 608
Cascais 865-6
Casino de Monte Carlo 413, **34**
Castilla y León 1063-7
Castilla-La Mancha 1067-8
castles, fortresses & palaces 24
  Akershus Slott 965
  Albrechtsburg 448
  Alcázar de los Reyes Cristianos 1102
  Alhambra 1104, **18**
  Altes Schloss 475
  Ayasuluk Fortress 1167
  Binnenhof 800
  Blarney Castle 594
  Bled Castle 1035
  Blenheim Palace 197
  Bran Castle 899, **15**
  Bratislava Castle 1008
  Brest Fortress 96
  Buckingham Palace 164-5
  Burg Eltz 482
  Burg Metternich 482
  Burg Rheinfels 480-1
  Car Samoil's Castle 757
  Cardiff Castle 215
  Castell de Montjuïc 1073
  Castello Sforzesco 649
  Castelo de São Jorge 855
  Castelo dos Mouros 865
  Castillo de Gibralfaro 1107-8
  Castle Howard 205-6
  Castle of Lëkurësit 50
  Castle of St Peter 1169
  Český Krumlov Castle 311
  Château d'Azay-le-Rideau 381
  Château de Bouillon 125
  Château de Bourscheid 130
  Château de Chambord 379-80
  Château de Chaumont 380
  Château de Chenonceau 381
  Château de Cheverny 380
  Château de Chillon 1130
  Château de Gruyères 1131
  Château de Jehay 125
  Château de Lavaux-Sainte-Anne 125
  Château de Modave 125
  Château de Versailles 24, 364
  Château de Villandry 381
  Château d'If 401
  Château Royal d'Amboise 382
  Château Royal de Blois 379
  Conwy Castle 218
  Devín Castle 1014
  Diocletian's Palace 278
  Dover Castle 185
  Edinburgh Castle 218
  Eger Castle 572
  Festetics Palace 567
  Festung Hohensalzburg 72
  Festung Marienberg 463-4
  Fortaleza de Sagres 869
  Gediminas Palace 735
  Gjirokastra Castle 51
  Grevenburg 482
  Hofburg 58, **18**
  Hrad Loket 309
  Kadriorg Palace 323
  Kaiserburg 464
  Kalasa 49
  Kalemegdan Citadel 994
  Karlštejn Castle 307-8
  Kilkenny Castle 590
  Koules Venetian Fortress 531
  Krimulda Medieval Castle 728
  Kronborg Slot 949
  Leeds Castle 24, 185
  Ljubljana Castle 1029
  Lublin Castle 832
  Malbork Castle 841
  Marksburg 481
  Mir Castle 96
  Namur 125
  Olavinlinna 982
  Palace of Holyroodhouse 219
  Palácio Nacional da Pena 865
  Palácio Nacional de Sintra 864-5
  Palaio Frourio 541
  Palais de Longchamp 401
  Palais des Ducs et des États de Bourgogne 383
  Palais des Papes 405-6
  Palamidi Fortress 516
  Peter & Paul Fortress 923
  Petrovaradin Citadel 1000
  Praetorian Palace 1039
  Prague Castle 297, **302**
  Radziwill Palace Fortress 96
  Râşnov Fortress 899
  Rīga Castle 719
  Rosenborg Slot 943
  Rozafa Fortress 48
  Rundāle Palace 727
  Schloss Ambras 79
  Schloss Belvedere 59
  Schloss Bruck 81
  Schloss Cecilienhof 446
  Schloss Charlottenburg 439
  Schloss Eggenberg 70
  Schloss Heidelburg 470
  Schloss Hellbrunn 77
  Schloss Hohenschwangau 462
  Schloss Mirabell 72
  Schloss Neuschwanstein 24, 462, **38**
  Schloss Nymphenburg 455
  Schloss Sanssouci 445-6
  Schloss Schönbrunn 59
  Špilberk Castle 313
  Spiš Castle 1017
  Sponza Palace 285
  Stirling Castle 229
  Suomenlinna 975, 977
  Telč Chateau 315
  Toompea Castle 322
  Topkapı Palace 1158
  Tower of London 165
  Trakai Castle 742-3
  Trenčín Castle 1014
  Tsarevets Fortress 255
  Turun Linna 979
  Tvrdina Kale Fortress 753
  Uppsala Slott 959
  Vaduz Castle 1145
  Wawel Castle 824-5
  Wartburg 453
  Windsor Castle 184
Catalonia 1068-83
cathedrals, *see* churches & cathedrals
Causeway coast 608-9
cell phones 1211-12

000 Map pages
000 Photo pages

cemeteries
- Cimetière du Père Lachaise (Paris) 351
- Jewish Cemetery (Warsaw) 819
- Les Catacombes (Paris) 343
- Lychakivske Cemetery (Lviv) 1195
- Normandy American Cemetery & Memorial 370
- Novodevichy Cemetery (Moscow) 915
- Old Jewish Cemetery (Prague) 301

Český Krumlov 311-12
Cetinje 783-4
Cézanne, Paul 403
Chamonix 390-2
Champagne 339, 374, 375
Champagne (region) 374-6
Chartres 364
Checkpoint Charlie 434
Chester 211
Chimaera 1173
Chişinău 768-72, **770-1**
churches & cathedrals
- Aachener Dom (Aachen) 487
- Alexander Nevsky Cathedral (Tallinn) 322
- Annunciation Cathedral (Moscow) 915
- Archangel Cathedral (Moscow) 914-15
- Bamberger Dom (Bamberg) 466
- Basilica di San Marco (Venice) 653
- Basilica di San Petronio (Bologna) 663
- Basilique du Sacré-Cœur (Paris) 347, 350
- Berliner Dom (Berlin) 435
- Canterbury Cathedral 184
- Cappella degli Scrovegni (Padua) 652
- Catedral de Santiago de Compostela 1088-9
- Catedral Nueva (Salamanca) 1063-4
- Cathedral of SS Peter & Paul (Brno) 313
- Cathedral of St Barbara (Kutná Hora) 308
- Cathedral of St Domnius (Split) 278
- Cathedral of St Elizabeth (Košice) 1019
- Cathedral of St George (Piran) 1040
- Cathedral of St Nicholas (Ljubljana) 1029
- Cathedral of the Assumption (Koper) 1039
- Cathedral of the Assumption of the Blessed Virgin Mary (Zagreb) 270
- Cathedral of the Assumption of the Virgin (Dubrovnik) 285
- Cathédrale de Notre Dame de Paris 343, 346
- Cathédrale de St-Pierre (Geneva) 1123
- Cathédrale Notre Dame (Chartres) 364
- Cathédrale Notre Dame (Reims) 374
- Cathédrale Notre Dame (Rouen) 368
- Cathédrale Notre Dame (Tournai) 124
- Cathédrale Notre-Dame (Strasbourg) 376-7
- Cathédrale St-André (Bordeaux) 393-4
- Cathédrale St-Corentin (Quimper) 371
- Cathédrale Ste-Réparate (Nice) 407
- Cathédrale St-Étienne (Metz) 378
- Cathédrale St-Gatien (Tours) 381
- Cathédrale St-Vincent (St-Malo) 373
- Cattedrale di San Giovanni Battista (Turin) 646-7
- Cattedrale di San Lorenzo (Genoa) 644
- Cattedrale di San Martino (Lucca) 676
- Cattedrale di Santa Maria (Alghero) 700
- Cattedrale di Sant'Andrea (Amalfi) 689
- Chester Cathedral 211
- Christ Church Cathedral (Dublin) 584-5
- Church of Sveti Jovan at Kaneo (Ohrid) 759
- Church of the Saviour on Spilled Blood (St Petersburg) 923, **40**
- Dome Cathedral (Rīga) 719
- Duomo (Florence) 666
- Duomo (Milan) 648
- Duomo (Pisa) 674
- Duomo (Siena) 675
- Esztergom Basilica 566
- Frankfurter Dom (Frankfurt) 477
- Frauenkirche (Dresden) 447
- Glasgow Cathedral 223
- Kaliningrad Cathedral 932
- Kazan Cathedral (St Petersburg) 923
- Kölner Dom (Cologne) 483
- La Catedral (Barcelona) 1069
- La Sagrada Família (Barcelona) 1072, **16**
- Liverpool Cathedral 212
- Mont St-Michel 370-1
- Münster (Constance) 474
- Münster (Freiburg im Breisgau) 472-3
- Neuer Dom (Linz) 68
- Nidaros Domkirke (Trondheim) 972
- Onze-Lieve-Vrouwekathedraal (Antwerp) 113
- Pantheon (Rome) 625, 628
- Roskilde Domkirke 949
- Russian Orthodox Cathedral (Rīga) 721
- Sé Velha (Coimbra) 873
- St Basil's Cathedral (Moscow) 915
- St Canice's Cathedral (Kilkenny) 590
- St Isaac's Cathedral (St Petersburg) 923, **13**
- St Mark's Cathedral (Korčula Island) 283
- St Martin's Cathedral (Bratislava) 1008
- St Nicholas Orthodox Maritime Cathedral (Liepāja) 727
- St Patrick's Cathedral (Dublin) 585
- St Paul's Cathedral (London) 165
- St Peter & Paul Cathedral (Kaunas) 743
- St Peter's Basilica (Rome) 624
- St Sophia's Cathedral (Kyiv) 1189
- St Tryphon's Cathedral (Kotor) 780
- St Vitus Cathedral (Prague) 297
- St-Baafskathedraal (Ghent) 117
- Ste-Chapelle (Paris) 346
- Stephansdom (Vienna) 58
- Sveta Sofija Cathedral (Ohrid) 759
- Tuomiokirkko (Tampere) 981
- Vilnius Cathedral 735
- Wawel Cathedral (Kraków) 824
- Westminster Abbey (London) 161
- York Minster 202-3

cider 84, 369, 479
cinema
- Britain 235
- Czech Republic 316
- Denmark 986
- Finland 986
- France 419
- Italy 702-3
- Poland 848
- Romania 907
- Spain 1112
- Sweden 986

Čingov 1018
Cinque Terre 645-6
Clervaux 130-1
Clifden 600
Cliffs of Moher 596
climate 22, *see also individual countries*
Cluj-Napoca 901-3
coffee 506, 545, 618, 1114

Coimbra 873
Cologne 483-6
Colosseum 620
comic strips 104
concentration camps
  Auschwitz 825
  Bergen-Belsen 489
  Birkenau 825
  Buchenwald 452
  Dachau 459-60
  Sachsenhausen 446
Conimbriga 873
Connemara 600
Constance 474-5
consulates 1205-6, *see also individual countries*
Coo 125
Copenhagen 942-8, **944-5**
  accommodation 943, 946
  drinking 947
  entertainment 947-8
  festivals & events 943
  food 946-7
  information 948
  sights 942-3
  tours 943
  travel to/from 948
  travel within 948
Córdoba 1102-3
Corfu 541-2, **35**
Corinth 516
Cork 591-4, **592-3**
Corniches 413
Corsica 414-17
Costa da Morte 1090
Côte d'Azur 411
Côte d'Or 384
Cotswolds, the 198
credit cards 1208
Crete 530-5, **532-3**
Cricova 772
Crişana 903-5
Croatia 266-93, **268-9**
  accommodation 266, 290
  activities 290
  arts 289
  budgeting 267
  business hours 290
  climate 266
  drinking 267
  environment 289
  embassies & consulates 291
  exchange rates 267
  food 266, 267, 289, 291
  highlights 268
  history 288-9
  holidays 291
  internet resources 267
  itineraries 267
  money 267, 291
  people 289
  planning 266-7
  telephone services 291
  tourist information 291
  travel seasons 266
  travel to/from 267, 291
  travel within 292-3
  visas 291
Cuenca 1068
Curonian Spit 745-6
customs regulations 1204-5, *see also individual countries*
Cyclades 523-30
cycling 1217-18
  Austria 62, 68, 71, 73
  Belgium 111, 119, 122, 124, 131, 133
  Britain 237
  Bulgaria 256, 263
  Croatia 290
  Estonia 323, 326
  Finland 983
  France 351, 380
  Greece 531, 537
  Hungary 574-5
  Ireland 613
  Italy 645, 705
  Lithuania 746
  Luxembourg 130
  Netherlands 797, 813
  Poland 849
  Portugal 859, 866, 867, 881, 884
  Russia 919, 926, 932
  Slovenia 1035, 1037
  Sweden 956, 963
  Switzerland 1136
  Turkey 1172-3
Czech Republic 294-318, **296**
  accommodation 294, 316
  arts 316
  budgeting 295
  business hours 316
  climate 294
  drinking 295
  embassies & consulates 316-17
  exchange rates 295
  food 294, 295, 316, 317
  highlights 296
  history 315-16
  holidays 317
  internet resources 295
  itineraries 295
  money 295, 317
  people 316
  planning 294-5
  telephone services 317
  travel seasons 294
  travel to/from 295, 317-18
  travel within 318
  visas 317

D

Da Vinci, Leonardo 648-9
Dachstein Rieseneishöhle 78
Dalí, Salvador 1081
Dalmatia 278-88
Damme 121
dance 907, 1113, **36**
dangers, *see* safety
Dante 664, 702
Danube River 67-9, 905
Datça peninsula 1170
D-Day 370
Dedinky 1018
Deià 1095
Delft 801-2
Delos 523
Delphi 519
Den Haag 800-1
Denmark 942-53, *see also* Scandinavia
Derry 609-11
Deventer 807
Diekirch 130
Dijon 383-4
Dilofo 522
disabilities, travellers with 1212
  Germany 500-1
  Slovakia 1024
discount cards 1205
  Austria 58, 69, 73, 79, 85
  Belgium 104, 113, 117, 119
  Britain 203
  Bulgaria 263
  Croatia 275
  Estonia 329
  France 342, 376, 385, 396, 401, 405, 406
  Germany 438, 447, 459, 471, 474, 499
  Greece 511
  Hungary 564
  Ireland 585, 607
  Italy 621, 655, 681, 688
  Lithuania 735
  Luxembourg 127
  Netherlands 797, 811
  Slovakia 1012
  Spain 1062, 1082, 1087
  Switzerland 1147
  Turkey 1159

000 Map pages
000 Photo pages

diving
Croatia 290
Ireland 613
Portugal 868, 871
Turkey 1168, 1170, 1171, 1172-3, 1182
Dobšinská Ice Cave 1018
Doctor Who 215-16
Dodecanese 535-7
dog-sledding 987
Dolomites 665, **38**
Dordogne 392-3
Dordrecht 802, 807
Dover 185-6
Dracula 898, 899
Dresden 447-9
drinking 26, *see also individual locations*
drinks, *see* beer, brandy, cider, coffee, port, tea, vodka, wine
driving, *see* car travel
driving licences 1220
Drumnadrochit 231
Drymades 50
Dublin 581-9, **582-3**, **17**
accommodation 585-6
drinking 587
entertainment 587-8
food 586-7
information 588-9
sights 581, 584-5
travel to/from 588, 589
travel within 589
Dubrovnik 284-8, **286-7**, **15**
Dún Aengus 600
Dún Dúchathair 600
Dún Eochla 600
Dún Eoghanachta 600
Duncansby Head 233
Dune du Pilat 394-5
Dunnet Head 233
Durbuy 125
Düsseldorf 486-7
DVDs 1210

E

Ebbelwei 479
Ebbelwei-Express 478
Echternach 131
economy, *see individual countries*
Eden Project 195
Edinburgh 218-23, **220-1**
Eger 571-2
Eiffel Tower 342, **11**
Eisenach 453
electricity 1205
embassies 1205-6, *see also individual countries*
England, *see* Britain
Entrevaux 410
environment, *see individual countries*
Épernay 375-6
Ephesus 1168
Epidavros 517
Erfurt 452-3
Escadaria do Bom Jesus 880
Estonia 319-37, **321**
accommodation 319, 336
budgeting 320
climate 319
drinking 320
embassies & consulates 336
environment 336
exchange rates 320
festivals & events 336-7
food 319, 320, 336, 337
highlights 321
history 335-6
holidays 337
internet resources 320
itineraries 320
money 320, 337
people 336
telephone services 337
travel seasons 319
travel to/from 320, 337
travel within 337
visas 337
Esztergom 566
Eton 183-4
Ettelbrück 130
events, *see* festivals & events
Évora 869-70
exchange rates, *see individual countries*
Exeter 194
Extremadura 1110-11

F

Faro 866-7
ferry travel 1216, 1218
Fès 1110
festivals & events 27-31
Baščaršijske Noći 142
Bastille Day 29
Bažant Pohoda Festival 30, 1014
Beer Festival 28
Bienal de Flamenco 1100
Budapest Spring Festival 28, 560
Carnaval (Netherlands) 27
Carnevale (Venice) 27, 656
Carnival (Cologne) 484
Christopher Street Day 29
Copenhagen Jazz Festival 943
Cultural Summer Festival 1009
De Gentse Feesten 30
Dia de Sant Joan 1073
Donauinselfest 63
Dragačevo Trumpet Assembly 30, 1002
Dubrovnik Summer Festival 285
Dvořák Autumn 31
Edinburgh Festival Fringe 219
Edinburgh International Festival 30, 219
Ethno Port Poznań Festival 840
Eurochocolate 677
EXIT Festival 29, 1000
Fasching 27-8
Feria de Abril 28, 1100
Festa de Nossa Senhora da Agonia 879
Festa de Santo António 29, 859
Festa de São João 29, 875
Festa del Redentore 657
Festa di San Gennaro 681
Festa di San Giovanni 671
Festa di Sant'Efisio 699
Festas de Lisboa 859
Festes de la Mercè 31, 1073
Festival at Queen's 31
Fiesta de San Isidro 1053
Galway Arts Festival 597
Galway Oyster Festival 597
Glastonbury Festival 29, 192
Greek Easter 28
Guy Fawkes Night 31
Hay Festival 216
Hellenic Festival 29, 511
Il Palio 29
International Festival of Street Theatre 829
International Shakespeare Festival 843
International Street & Open-Air Theatre Festival 843
Jaanipäev 337
Jazz on the Odra International Festival 837
Jewish Culture Festival 829
Kilkenny Arts Festival 590
Kilkenny Rhythm & Roots 590
Kiruna Snöfestivalen 27
Koninginnedag 28
Krakow International Film Festival 829
Küstendorf Film & Music Festival 27
Las Fallas de San José 1091
Live Festival 829
Maggio Musicale Fiorentino 671
Malta International Theatre Festival 840
Medieval Festival of the Arts 30
Meltdown Festival 171
Moldova Wine Festival 31
Monsaraz Museu Aberto 870

festivals & events *continued*
- Montreux Jazz Festival 29, 1130
- Mozart Festival 819
- Musica Polonica Nova Festival 837
- Musikfilm Festival 63
- Natale 31
- Noites Ritual Rock 876
- Notting Hill Carnival 30
- Ohrid Summer Festival 759
- Oktoberfest 31, 455
- Palio 675
- Palio delle Quattro Antiche Repubbliche Marinare 656-7
- Prague Fringe Festival 303
- Prague Spring 303
- Queima das Fitas 28, 873
- Regata Storica 657
- Roskilde Festival 29, 949
- Ruisrock 980
- Salzburg Festival 30, 73
- Sanfermines 29, 1086
- Sarajevo Jazz Festival 142
- Scoppio del Carro 670
- Semana Santa 28, 1100
- Serralves Em Festa 876
- Settimana Santa 28
- Song and Dance Festival 729, 730
- Sounds of the North Festival 843
- St Dominic's Fair 843
- St John's Fair 840
- St Patrick's Day 28
- Street Art Festival 819
- Suma Flamenca 1053
- Summer Jazz Festival 829
- Sziget Music Festival 30, 560
- Terraneo Festival 30
- Titanic Belfast Festival 603
- Umbria Jazz festival 677
- Venice Biennale 657
- Venice International Film Festival 30, 657
- Veranos de la Villa 1053
- Viennale Film Festival 63
- Warsaw Autumn International Festival of Contemporary Music 819
- Warsaw Film Festival 819
- Warsaw Summer Jazz Days 819
- White Nights 29
- Wiener Festwochen 62
- Wimbledon Lawn Tennis Championships 172
- Wratislavia Cantans 837
- Zürich Street Parade 30

Fethiye 1170-2

films, *see* cinema
Filoti 527
Finland 975-84, *see also* Scandinavia
fishing 987
Flåm 971
Flamenco 1113, **36**
Flanders 112-24, 364-8
Florence 666-73, **668-9**, **32**
- accommodation 671
- drinking 672-3
- entertainment 673
- festivals & events 670-1
- food 671-2
- history 666
- information 673
- sights 666-7
- travel to/from 673
- travel within 673

Foča 148
food 25, *see also individual locations*
football 236, 459, 650
Fornalutx 1095
Fornells 1094
Fort William 231-2
fortresses, *see* castles, fortresses & palaces
France 338-426, **340-1**
- accommodation 338, 420-1
- activities 421
- arts 418-20
- budgeting 339
- business hours 421
- climate 338
- drinking 339
- embassies & consulates 422
- environment 420
- exchange rates 339
- food 338, 339, 422
- highlights 340
- history 417-18
- holidays 422-3
- internet resources 339
- itineraries 339
- legal matters 422
- money 339, 422
- planning 338-9
- politics 418
- telephone services 423
- travel seasons 338
- travel to/from 339, 423-4
- travel within 424-6
- visas 423

Frank, Anne 791-2
Frankfurt-am-Main 475-9
Freiburg im Breisgau 472-3
Fruška Gora 1001
Füssen 462

000 Map pages
000 Photo pages

G

Galicia 1088-90
galleries, *see* museums & galleries
Gallipoli 1164
Galway 596-8, **598-9**
Gap of Dunloe 594
Garmisch-Partenkirchen 460
Gaudí, Antoni 1072, 1073
gay & lesbian travellers 1206
- Britain 172, 179, 187, 238
- Bulgaria 264
- Czech Republic 317
- Denmark 948
- France 360, 422
- Germany 444, 459, 500
- Greece 539, 546-7
- Italy 706
- Montenegro 786
- Poland 850
- Portugal 863
- Romania 908
- Scandinavia 987
- Slovakia 1023
- Slovenia 1042
- Spain 1060, 1079, 1115

Gdańsk 841-5, **842**
Geirangerfjorden 971-2, **7**, **14**
Geneva 1123-9, **1126-7**
Genoa 643-5
Germany 427-504, **430-1**
- accommodation 427, 499
- arts 498-9
- budgeting 428
- business hours 499
- climate 427
- drinking 428
- economy 498
- embassies & consulates 499
- exchange rates 428
- food 427, 428, 499
- highlights 430-1
- history 497-8
- holidays 500
- internet resources 428
- itineraries 428
- legal matters 500
- money 428, 499, 500
- planning 427-8
- politics 498
- sights 429
- telephone services 500
- travel seasons 427
- travel to/from 428, 444-5, 501
- travel within 501-4

Ghent 117-19
Giant's Causeway 608-9
Gimmelwald 1138
Girona 1080

Giżycko 847
Gjirokastra 51
Glacier Express 1132
Glasgow 223-8, **224-5**
Glastonbury 192
Glen Coe 231
Golden Sands 260
gondolas 656
Göreme 1177-8
Göteborg 960-2
Gotland 962-3
Gouda 807
Granada 1104-7, **1106-7**
Grasmere 215
Grasse 411
Graubünden 1144-5
Graz 69-71
Great Masurian Lakes 847
Greece 505-51, **507**
  accommodation 505, 546
  budgeting 506
  business hours 546
  climate 505
  drinking 506, 545
  economy 544
  embassies & consulates 546
  environment 544-5
  exchange rates 506
  food 506, 506, 516, 516
  highlights 507
  history 542-4
  holidays 547
  internet access 547
  internet resources 506
  itineraries 506
  money 506, 547
  people 544
  planning 505-6
  politics 543-4
  postal services 547
  safety 547
  sights 507, 510-11
  telephone services 547
  tourist information 548
  travel seasons 505
  travel to/from 506, 514, 537, 548-9
  travel within 549-51
  visas 548
Grevenmacher 131
Grindelwald 1137
Grossglockner 82
Grotta Azzurra 687
Grotta di Nettuno 700-1
Grotte de Font de Gaume 393
Grotte de Lascaux 393
Grotte de Rouffignac 393
Grūtas Park 743
Gruyères 1131
Guimarães 880
Gūtmaņa Cave 728
Gyógy-tó 568
Gythio 517-18

H

Haarlem 798-9
Hadrian's Wall 208
Hague, the 800-1
Halki 527
Hallstatt 77-8
Hallstätter see 78
Hamburg 491-6, **492-3**
Hamelin 489-90
hammams 1163
Hania 532-5
Hanover 488-9
Han-sur-Lesse 125
Hay-on-Wye 216
health 1206
Heidelberg 469-71
Heiligenblu 82
Helsingør 949
Helsinki 975-9, **976**
  accommodation 977-8
  activities 977
  drinking 978-9
  entertainment 978-9
  food 978
  information 979
  sights 975, 977
  tours 977
  travel to/from 979
  travel within 979
Hemingway, Ernest 1086
Hercegovina 145-8, *see also* Bosnia & Hercegovina
Herculaneum 685
Hévíz 568
High Tatras 1014-16
hiking
  Albania 53
  Austria 80, 81, 85
  Belgium 133
  Bosnia & Hercegovina 150
  Britain 238
  Bulgaria 256, 263
  Croatia 279, 290
  France 421
  Greece 518, 531
  Hungary 575
  Ireland 613
  Italy 645, 665, 705
  Macedonia 763
  Montenegro 785
  Norway 971, 973
  Poland 836, 849
  Portugal 881, 884
  Scandinavia 987
  Slovakia 1015, 1018, 1023
  Slovenia 1035
  Spain 1115
  Switzerland 1137
  Turkey 1172-3, 1177, 1182
Hill of Crosses 745
Hill Top 214
history, *see individual countries*
hitching 1221-2
Hitler, Adolf 434, 461, 497, 847
holidays, *see individual countries*
Hora Sfakion 534
horseback riding
  Bulgaria 256
  Ireland 613
  Portugal 881
  Slovenia 1035
  Spain 1109
  Turkey 1171
hostels 1203-4, *see also individual locations*
  Austria 85
  Belgium 133
  Britain 236-7
  Croatia 290
  Czech Republic 316
  Estonia 336
  France 421
  Germany 499
  Greece 546
  Hungary 574
  Ireland 613
  Italy 705
  Luxembourg 133
  Poland 849
  Portugal 883
  Romania 907
  Russia 935
  Scandinavia 986-7
  Spain 1115
  Switzerland 1147
  Turkey 1182
Hotton 125
Hove 186-7
Hungary 552-77, **554**
  accommodation 552, 574
  activities 574-5
  arts 573-4
  budgeting 553
  business hours 575
  climate 552
  drinking 553
  embassies & consulates 575
  environment 574
  exchange rates 553
  food 552, 553, 575
  highlights 554

Hungary *continued*
- history 573
- holidays 575
- internet resources 553
- itineraries 553
- money 553, 575
- people 573
- planning 552-3
- postal services 575
- telephone services 575
- travel seasons 552
- travel to/from 553, 576
- travel within 576-7
- visas 575-6

Hurtigruten 989
Hvar Island 281-3

I

Ibiza 1095-7
ice hockey 1022
Icehotel 964
Igoumenitsa 523
Ihlara Valley 1178
Île Ste-Marguerite 411
Île St-Honorat 411
Ilha da Tavira 867
Ilha Deserta 866
immigration 1215, 1217
Inari 984
Inisheer 599
Inishmaan 599
Inishmór 599, 600
Innsbruck 78-81
insurance 1206-7
Interlaken 1135-6
internet access 1207, *see also individual countries*
internet resources 23, 1206, 1209, *see also individual countries*
Inverness 230-2
Ioannina 522
Ionian Islands 541-2
Ios 528
Iraklio 531-2
Ireland 578-616, **580**, *see also* Northern Ireland
- accommodation 578, 612-13
- activities 613
- arts 612
- budgeting 579
- business hours 613
- climate 578
- drinking 579
- environment 612
- exchange rates 579
- food 578, 579, 614
- highlights 580
- history 611-12
- holidays 614
- internet resources 579
- itineraries 579
- money 579, 614
- people 612
- planning 578-9
- telephone services 614
- travel seasons 578
- travel to/from 579, 614-16
- travel within 616
- visas 614

Ireon 538
Isle of Skye 232-3
İstanbul 1153-64, **1153**, **1156-7**, **1160-1**, **21**, **35**
- accommodation 1159-61
- drinking 1162
- entertainment 1162
- food 1161-2
- information 1162-3
- sights 1153, 1158-9
- tours 1159
- travel to/from 1163
- travel within 1163-4

Istria 276-8
Italy 617-709, **619**
- accommodation 617, 704-5
- activities 705
- arts 702-3
- budgeting 618
- business hours 705
- climate 617
- drinking 618
- embassies & consulates 705
- environment 703
- exchange rates 618
- food 617, 618, 703-4, 705-6
- highlights 619
- history 701-2
- holidays 706
- internet access 706
- internet resources 618
- itineraries 618
- money 618, 706
- people 702
- planning 617-18
- politics 702
- postal services 706
- safety 640, 685, 707
- telephone services 707
- travel seasons 617
- travel to/from 618, 707-8
- travel within 708-9
- visas 707

itineraries 32-40, *see also individual countries*
İzmir 1166

J

Jajce 149
jamón 1114
John O'Groats 233
Julian Alps 1034-9
Jungfrau region 1136-8
Jungfraujoch 1137, **33**
Juodkrantė 746
Jūrmala 727
Jutland 951-3

K

Kahta 1179
Kaiser-Franz-Josefs-Höhe 82
Kaliningrad 929-33, **930-1**
Kaliningrad region 929-33
Kardamyli 518
Karlovy Vary 308-10
Karlštejn 307-8
Kars 1179-80
Kaş 1172-3
Kaunas 743-5
kayaking
- Belgium 125, 133
- Croatia 290
- Italy 645
- Norway 971
- Portugal 867, 868, 873, 881
- Slovenia 1035, 1037
- Turkey 1171, 1172-3

Kecskemét 570
Kerkyra 541-2
Keswick 215
Keszthely 567-8
Kętrzyn 847
Kilkenny 589-91
Killarney 594-5
Kinderdijk 802
Kiruna 963-4
kitesurfing 1115
Kitzbühel 81
Klagenfurt 71-2
Klaipėda 745
Knossos 532
Koblenz 481
Königssee 461
Konya 1176-7
Koper 1039-40
Korčula Island 283-4
Kos 536-7
Košice 1019-20
Kosovo 710-15, **711**
- accommodation 710, 714-15
- business hours 715

000 Map pages
000 Photo pages

climate 710
embassies & consulates 715
food 715
highlights 711
history 714
internet resources 710
money 715
people 714
planning 710
safety 715
travel seasons 710
travel to/from 715
travel within 715
Kotor 780-1
Kraków 824-32, **826-7**, **14**
accommodation 829-30
drinking 830-1
festivals & events 829
food 830
information 832
shopping 830-1, 831-2
sights 824-5, 825-9
travel to/from 831, 832
Kremlin 914-15
Krems an der Donau 67-8
Krimml Falls 82
Krippenstein 78
Kruja 49
Kuşadası 1168
Kutná Hora 308
Kyiv 1189-95, **1192-3**

L

La Besurta 1084
La Rambla 1069
La Roche-en-Ardenne 125
Lagos 868
Lake Balaton 567-9
Lake Bled 1034-7, **1036**, **39**
Lake Bohinj 1037-8
Lake Constance 473-5
Lake Geneva 1123, 1129-31
Lake Koman 48
Lake Maggiore 1143
Lake Malta 839
Lake Pamvotida 522
Lakeland 982-3
Lakonian Mani 518
Land's End 196
language courses
France 422
Greece 547
Spain 1116
languages 1225-32
Languedoc-Roussillon 396-400
Lapland 983-4
Latvia 716-31, **718**
accommodation 716, 729
arts 729
budgeting 717
business hours 729-30
climate 716
drinking 717
embassies & consulates 730
exchange rates 717
food 716, 717, 730
highlights 718
history 729
holidays 730
internet access 730
internet resources 717
itineraries 717
money 717, 730
people 729
planning 716-17
postal services 730
telephone services 730-1
travel seasons 716
travel to/from 717, 731
travel within 731
visas 731
Lausanne 1129-31
Leaning Tower 674
Lecce 691-2
legal matters 1207
lesbian travellers, *see* gay & lesbian travellers
Leiden 799-800
Leizpig 449-51
León 1066
Les Calanques 402
Lesvos 539-40
Letoön 1172
Leuven 112
Levoča 1017
Lido 655
Liechtenstein 1145
Liège 124, 126
Lienz 81-2
Liepāja 727-8
Lier 112
Lille 365-6
Lindau 475
Linz 68-9
Lipari 694-5
Lisbon 855-64, **856-7**, **21**
accommodation 859-60
activities 859
drinking 861-2
entertainment 862-4
festivals & events 859
food 860-1
information 863
sights 855, 858
tours 858-9
travel to/from 864
travel within 864
Liseberg 961
literature 1204
Britain 235
Croatia 289
Czech Republic 316
Denmark 986
Finland 986
France 418-19
Hungary 574
Ireland 612
Italy 702
Norway 986
Poland 848
Russia 934
Slovenia 1041
Spain 1112
Sweden 986
Switzerland 1146
Lithuania 732-49, **734**
accommodation 732, 747
budgeting 733
business hours 747
climate 732
drinking 733
embassies & consulates 747
environment 747
exchange rates 733
food 732, 733, 748
highlights 734
history 746-7
holidays 748
internet resources 733
itineraries 733
money 733, 748
people 747
planning 732-3
politics 747
telephone services 748
travel seasons 732
travel to/from 733, 748
travel within 748-9
Liverpool 211-13
Ljubljana 1028-34, **1030-1**
Locarno 1143
Loch Lomond 228
Loch Ness 231
Locmariaquer 372
Lofoten 973-4
Loire Valley 379-83
Loket 309
London 155, 158-83, **155**, **158-9**, **162-3**, **166**, **168-9**, **172**, **174**, **10**, **33**
accommodation 172-3, 175

London *continued*
drinking 177-8
entertainment 178-80
festivals & events 171-2
food 176-7
history 155, 160
information 181-2
maps 165
shopping 180-1
sights 160-1, 164-7, 170-1
tours 171
travel to/from 182
travel within 182-3
Loreley Rock 481
Lorraine 376-8
Lourdes 398
Loutro 534
Lower Saxony 488-91
Lübeck 496-7
Lublin 832-4
Lucca 676-7
Lucerne 1134-5
Lugano 1143-4
Lugo 1090
Lund 960
Luso 874
Luxembourg 100-1, 126-35, **102-3**
accommodation 100, 133
arts 132
budgeting 101
business hours 133-4
climate 100
embassies & consulates 134
exchange rates 101
food 100, 101, 132-3, 134
highlights 102
history 131-2
holidays 134
internet resources 101
itineraries 101
money 101, 134
people 132
planning 100-1
telephone services 134
travel seasons 100
travel to/from 101, 134-5
travel within 130
Luxembourg City 126-30, **128-9**
Lviv 1195-7
Lyon 385-90, **386-7**
Lysefjorden 970-1

000 Map pages
000 Photo pages

M

Maastricht 808-9
Macedonia 750-64, **752**
accommodation 750, 762
activities 763
arts 762
budgeting 751
business hours 763
climate 750
drinking 751
embassies & consulates 763
environment 762
exchange rates 751
food 750, 751, 763
highlights 752
history 761-2
holidays 763
internet resources 751
itineraries 751
money 751, 763
people 762
planning 750-1
postal services 763
telephone services 763
travel seasons 750
travel to/from 751, 763-4
travel within 764
visas 763
Mackintosh, Charles Rennie 223, 225
Madrid 1047-63, **1050-1**, **1054-5**, **39**
accommodation 1053, 1056-7
courses 1053
drinking 1059-60
entertainment 1060-1
festivals & events 1053
food 1057-9
information 1062
shopping 1061-2
sights 1047, 1052-3
travel to/from 1062
travel within 1063
Magyar people 573
Mainz 480
Málaga 1107-9
Malatya 1179
Mallorca 1093-5
Malmö 959-60
Małopolska 824-35
Manchester 208-10
Mani 518
Manteigas 874-5
Maó 1094
maps 1207-8
Marathonisi 517
Maribor 1041
markets
Borough Market (London) 181
Brick Lane Market (London) 181
Brixton Market (London) 181
Broadway Market (London) 181
Camden Market (London) 181
Central Market (Rīga) 721
Christmas markets 31, 63, 303, 465, 1009
Columbia Road Flower Market (London) 181
English Market (Cork) 591
Fischmarkt (Hamburg) 491
Freyung Market (Vienna) 64
Grand Bazaar (İstanbul) 1158, **35**
Karmelitermarkt (Vienna) 64
Marché aux Enfants Rouges (Paris) 358
Marché aux Puces de la Porte de Vanves (Paris) 362
Marché aux Puces de Montreuil (Paris) 362
Marché aux Puces de St-Ouen (Paris) 362
Marché Bastille (Paris) 358
Marché Belleville (Paris) 358
Marché Couvert (Metz) 378
Marché Couvert St-Quentin (Paris) 358
Marché Raspail (Paris) 358
Mercado Central (Valencia) 1091
Mercado de San Miguel (Madrid) 1057
Mercado do Bolhão (Porto) 878
Mercat de la Boquería (Barcelona) 1069
Naschmarkt (Vienna) 64
Petticoat Lane Market (London) 181
Portobello Road Market (London) 181
Sunday UpMarket (London) 181
Viktualienmarkt (Munich) 454
Marmaris 1169-70
Marmaris Bay 1170
Marpissa 525
Marrakesh 1110
Marseille 400-3
marzipan 496
Masuria 847
Matera 689-90
Matterhorn 1131-2
measures 1213
Mechelen 112
Mediterranean Sea 1170-4
Meersburg 475
Meissen 448
Melk 68
Menorca 1094
Mer de Glace 391
Messinian Mani 518
Meteora 519-20
Metz 378
Mikołajki 847

Milan 647-50, **648**
Mileştii Mici 772
Minsk 92-6, **92**
Mir 96
Mithymna 540
mobile phones 1211-12
Mokra Gora 1000
Moldova 765-76, **767**
  accommodation 765, 775
  budgeting 766
  business hours 775
  climate 765
  drinking 766
  embassies & consulates 775
  exchange rates 766
  food 765, 766, 775
  highlights 767
  history 774-5
  holidays 776
  internet resources 766
  itineraries 766
  money 766, 776
  people 775
  politics 775
  travel seasons 765
  travel to/from 766, 776
  travel within 776
  visas 776
Monaco 413-14
monasteries
  Agias Varvaras Rousanou 519
  Agiou Nikolaou Anapafsa 519
  Agiou Stefanou 519
  Agiou Triados 519
  Bucovina 903
  Capuchin Monastery 313-14
  Caves Monastery 1189
  Cetinje Monastery 783
  Gračanica Monastery 713
  Kloster Alpirsbach 471
  Megalou Meteorou 519
  Monasterio San Juan de los Reyes 1067
  Mosteiro de Santa Maria de Alcobaça 872
  Mosteiro de Santa Maria de Vitória 872
  Orheiul Vechi Monastery Complex 773
  Ostrog Monastery 784
  Rila Monastery 252-3
  Selime Monastery 1178
  St Michael's Mount 196
  Visoki Dečani Monastery 714
oney 22, 23, 1205, 1208-10, *see also individual countries*
onodendri 522-3
ons 124
onsaraz 870
Mont St-Michel 370
Monte Carlo 413, **34**
Monte Igueldo 1085
Monte Toro 1094
Monte Urgull 1085
Montenegro 777-87, **779**
  accommodation 777, 786
  budgeting 778
  business hours 786
  climate 777
  drinking 778
  embassies & consulates 786
  exchange rates 778
  food 777, 778, 786
  highlights 779
  history 785
  holidays 787
  internet resources 778
  itineraries 778
  money 778, 786
  people 786
  planning 777-8
  telephone services 787
  travel seasons 777
  travel to/from 778, 787
  travel within 787
Montreux 1130
Moravia 312-15
Moreton in Marsh 198
Morinj 780
Morocco 1110
Moscow 914-22, **916-17**
  accommodation 919-20
  activities 919
  drinking 920-1
  entertainment 921
  food 920
  information 921
  shopping 921
  sights 914-15
  tours 919
  travel to/from 922
  travel within 922
Moselle Valley 131, 481-2
mosques
  Blue Mosque (İstanbul) 1158
  Carshi Mosque (Pristina) 712
  Dzhumaya Mosque (Plovdiv) 253
  Gazi-Husrevbey Mosque (Sarajevo) 139
  Jashar Pasha Mosque (Pristina) 712
  Mezquita (Córdoba) 1102
  Mosque Church (Pécs) 569
  Mustafa Paša Mosque (Skopje) 753
  Sinan Pasha Mosque (Prizren) 714
  Sultan Mehmet Fatih Mosque (Pristina) 712
  Sultan Murat Mosque (Skopje) 753
Mostar 145-8, **146**, **20**
motorcycle travel 1219-21
mountain climbing, *see* rock climbing
Mt Etna 696
Mt Gubałówka 835
Mt Hoverla 1196
Mt Kanin 1038
Mt Kynthos 523
Mt Lovćen 782
Mt Olympus 522
Mt Pilatus 1135
Mt Solaro 686
Mt Tâmpa 897
Mt Vodno 753
Mt Zeus 527
Munich 454-9, **456**
  accommodation 456-7
  drinking 458
  entertainment 458-9
  food 457-8
  information 459
  sights 454-5
  tours 455
  travel to/from 459
  travel within 459
Murano 655
Mürren 1138
museums & galleries 26
  Acropolis Museum (Athens) 510
  Anne Frank Huis (Amsterdam) 791-2
  Arktikum (Rovaniemi) 983
  ARoS (Aarhus) 951
  Autostadt (Wolfsburg) 489
  Aya Sofya (İstanbul) 1153, 1158
  Beethoven Haus (Bonn) 485
  Belarusian State Art Museum (Minsk) 93
  British Museum (London) 161, **33**
  Centre Pompidou (Paris) 347
  Centre Pompidou-Metz (Metz) 378
  Chopin Museum (Warsaw) 818
  Cité de l'Espace (Toulouse) 398-9
  Ciudad de las Artes y las Ciencias (Valencia) 1090
  Csontváry Museum (Pécs) 569
  Danubiana Meulensteen Art Museum (Bratislava) 1014
  East Side Gallery (Berlin) 438, **12**
  Erlebniswelt Haus Meissen (Meissen) 448
  Fondation Beyeler (Basel) 1142
  Gallerie dell'Accademia (Venice) 654-5
  Göreme Open-Air Museum 1177
  Grigore Antipa Natural History Museum (Bucharest) 892-3
  HC Andersens Hus (Odense) 950
  Hotel Viru KGB Museum (Tallinn) 323

museums & galleries *continued*
Hungarian Open-Air Ethnographical Museum 565
Kelvingrove Art Gallery & Museum (Glasgow) 224
Kremlin (Moscow) 914-15
Kröller-Müller Museum (Hoge Veluwe National Park) 808
Kunstsammlung Nordrhein-Westfalen (Düsseldorf) 486
Louisiana Museum of Modern Art (Humlebæk) 942
Louvre (Paris) 346-7
Louvre-Lens (Lens) 367
Luostarimäen Käsityöläismuseo (Turku) 979-80
Madame Tussauds (London) 170
Maison et Jardins de Claude Monet (Giverny) 368
Maritiem Museum Rotterdam 803
Mercedes-Benz Museum (Stuttgart) 468
Mevlâna Museum (Konya) 1176
Musée d'Histoire de la Ville de Luxembourg 126
Musée d'Orsay (Paris) 342
Musée du Louvre (Paris) 346-7
Museo Altamira (Cueva de Altamira) 1088
Museo Archeologico Nazionale (Naples) 680
Museo del Prado (Madrid) 1047
Museo e Galleria Borghese (Rome) 629
Museo Nazionale Romano (Rome) 629
MuseoParc Alésia (Alise-Ste-Reine) 383
Museum of Anatolian Civilisations (Ankara) 1175
Museum of Byzantine Culture (Thessaloniki) 520
Museum of Genocide Victims (Vilnius) 735
National Gallery (London) 160
National History Museum (Tirana) 45
National Museum of Lithuania (Vilnius) 735
Natural History Museum (London) 167
Ninth Fort (Kaunas) 744
Onufri Museum (Berat) 49
Palazzo dei Priori (Perugia) 677-8
Palazzo Ducale (Venice) 654
Permanent Exhibition of the 1989 Revolution (Timişoara) 903
Prague Jewish Museum 301
Rīga Art Nouveau Centre 721
Roads to Freedom Exhibition (Gdańsk) 843
Röda Sten (Göteborg) 961
Schindler's Factory (Kraków) 829
Siida (Inari) 984
Sistine Chapel (Rome) 625
Skansen (Stockholm) 953
State Hermitage Museum (St Petersburg) 922, **26**
State Tretyakov Gallery (Moscow) 915
Statens Museum for Kunst (Copenhagen) 942
Tate Britain (London) 164
Tate Modern (London) 165-6
Titanic Belfast 602
Toy Museum (Tartu) 331-2
Tunnel Museum (Sarajevo) 139, 141
Ulster Museum (Belfast) 602
Vasamuseet (Stockholm) 956
Vatican Museums (Rome) 625
Victoria & Albert Museum (London) 167
Viking Ship Museum (Roskilde) 949-50
War Photo Limited (Dubrovnik) 284
Zaanse Schans (Amsterdam) 798
music 26
Britain 235
Bulgaria 263
Czech Republic 316
Finland 986
France 371, 419
Germany 498-9
Hungary 573-4
Ireland 612
Italy 703
Macedonia 762
Norway 986
Poland 848
Portugal 883
Romania 907
Slovakia 1022
Slovenia 1041-2
Sweden 986
Mycenae 517
Mykonos 523-5, **524**
Mystras 517
Mytilini 539-40

N

Nafplio 516-17
Namur 125
Naoussa 525
Naples 680-6, **682-3**, **25**
accommodation 681, 684
drinking 684-5
entertainment 685
festivals & events 681
food 684
information 685
safety 685
sights 680-1
travel to/from 685-6
travel within 686
national parks & reserves, *see also* parks & gardens
Biogradska Gora National Park 784
Carpathian National Nature Park 1196
Connemara National Park 600
Curonian Spit National Park 745-6
Dartmoor National Park 194
Durmitor National Park 784
Gauja National Park 728
Hoge Veluwe National Park 808
Hohe Tauern National Park 82
Killarney National Park 594
Kiskunság National Park 570
Kurshskaya Kosa National Park 929
Lahemaa National Park 330-1
Lake District National Park 213-15
Lake Skadar National Park 784
Loch Lomond & the Trossachs National Park 228
Lovćen National Park 782
Mata Nacional dos Sete Montes 872
Nemrut Dağı Milli Parkı 1179
Parco Nazionale delle Cinque Terre 645
Parnassos National Park 519
Parque Nacional da Peneda-Gerês 881-2
Parque Nacional de los Picos de Europa 1089
Parque Nacional de Ordesa y Monte Perdido 1084
Peak District National Park 200
Pembrokeshire Coast National Park 217
Slovenský Raj National Park 1018
Snowdonia National Park 217-18
Sutjeska National Park 148
Tatra National Park 1015
Yorkshire Dales National Park 206
Naxos 526-8
Nazaré 872
Nea Kameni 529
Nemrut Dağı 1179
Nesebâr 261
Netherlands 788-814, **790**
accommodation 788, 810-11
arts 810
budgeting 789
business hours 811
climate 788

000 Map pages
000 Photo pages

drinking 789, 810
embassies & consulates 811
exchange rates 789
food 788, 789, 810, 811
highlights 790
history 809-10
holidays 812
internet resources 789
itineraries 789
legal matters 811
money 789, 811
planning 788-9
politics 810
telephone services 812
travel seasons 788
travel to/from 789, 812
travel within 813-14
Nevsky Prospekt 923
Newcastle-upon-Tyne 200-8
Newquay 194-5
Nice 407-10, **408-9**
Nida 746
nightlife 25
Nîmes 396-8
Normandy 368-71
Norrland 963-4
Northeastern Aegean Islands 538-40
Northern Ireland 601-11, *see also* Ireland
Norway 964-75, *see also* Scandinavia
Novaya Gollandiya 923, 926
Novi Pazar 999
Novi Sad 1000-1
Nuremberg 464-6
Nyasvizh 96

O

Obertraun 78
Oberwesel 480
Óbidos 871-2
Odense 950-1
Ohrid 757-60, **758**
Oia 529
Oktoberfest 31, 455
Olomouc 313
Olympia 518-19
Olympic Games 171, 234, 543
Olympos 1173
Omaha Beach 370
opening hours 1204, *see also individual countries*
Ortigia 696-7
Oslo 964-8, **966-7**
accommodation 965-6
drinking 967-8
entertainment 967-8
food 966-7
information 968
sights 965
tours 965
travel to/from 968
travel within 968
Östersund 963
Ostia Antica 643
Ostrów Tumski 839
Ouchy 1129-30
ouzo 506, 545
Oxford 197-9
oysters 394

P

Padua 652-3
Pakleni Islands 282
palaces, *see* castles, fortresses & palaces
Palatino 620
Palermo 692-4
Palia Kameni 529
Palma de Mallorca 1093-5
Pamplona 1086
Pamukkale 1167
Paneriai 742
Panthéon 343
paragliding & parasailing
Austria 79
Slovenia 1035
Switzerland 1130
Turkey 1171, 1172-3, 1182
Parco Archaeologico della Neapolis 697
Paris 342-63, **344-5**, **348-9**, **352**, **11**, **36**
accommodation 351-5
drinking 359-60
entertainment 360-1
festivals & events 351
food 355-9
information 361
shopping 362
sights 342-3, 346-7, 350-1, 354
tours 351
travel to/from 361-2
travel within 362-3
parks & gardens, *see also* national parks & reserves
Bratislava Forest Park 1008
City Park (Budapest) 557, 560
Englischer Garten (Munich) 455
Europapark (Klagenfurt) 71
Giardini di Augusto (Capri) 687
Gorky Park (Moscow) 919
Grūtas Park 743
Herrenhäuser Gärten (Hanover) 488
Hyde Park (London) 170
Jardin du Luxembourg (Paris) 342
Kadriorg Park (Tallinn) 323
Keukenhof 799
Kew Gardens (London) 171
Łazienki Park (Warsaw) 818
Mainau (Constance) 474
Memento Park (Budapest) 555
National Gardens (Athens) 511
Park an der Ilm (Weimar) 451
Park Güell (Barcelona) 1073
Park Sanssouci (Potsdam) 445-6
Parque del Buen Retiro (Madrid) 1053
Parque Natural da Ria Formosa (Naro) 866
Prater (Vienna) 59
Primorski Park (Varna) 257
Quinta da Regaleira (Sintra) 864
Rannapark (Pärnu) 334
Regent's Park (London) 170
Rt Kamenjak (Pula) 277
Saxon Gardens (Warsaw) 818
Schlossgarten (Stuttgart) 468
Toomemägi (Tallinn) 332
Villa Comunale park (Sorrento) 687
Vintgar Gorge (Lake Bled) 1035
Vitosha Nature Park (Sofia) 246
Vondelpark (Amsterdam) 793
Wilanów Park (Warsaw) 819
Parnu 334-5
Paros 525-6
Partnachklamm 400
passports 1215, 1217
Patara 1172
Patra 515-16
Pays d'Auge 369
Pécs 569-70
Peja 713-14
Peloponnese 515-19
Penichep 870-1
Penzance 196
people, *see individual countries*
Perast 780
perfume-making 411
Perugia 677-9
photography 1210
Picasso, Pablo 1069, 1107
Piccadilly Circus 161
Piraeus 514-15
Piran 1040-1
Pisa 673-5
planning
budgeting 22
calendar of events 27-31
Europe basics 22-3
internet resources 23
itineraries 32-40
travel seasons 22
Plovdiv 253-5
Plzeň 310-11
Podgorica 783

Podlesok 1017
Poland 815-51, **817**
- accommodation 815, 848-9
- activities 849
- arts 848
- budgeting 816
- business hours 849
- climate 815
- drinking 816
- embassies & consulates 849
- exchange rates 816
- food 815, 816, 850
- highlights 817
- history 847-8
- holidays 850
- internet access 850
- internet resources 816
- itineraries 816
- money 816, 850
- people 848
- planning 815-16
- politics 848
- safety 850
- telephone services 850
- travel seasons 815
- travel to/from 816, 850-1
- travel within 851
- visas 850

politics, *see individual countries*
Pollença 1095
Pomerania 841-7
Pompeii 685, **34**
Pont du Gard 397
Poprad 1014
port 853, 875
Porto 875-9, **876-7**
Portugal 852-86, **854**
- accommodation 883-4
- activities 884
- arts 883
- budgeting 853
- business hours 884
- climate 852
- drinking 853
- economy 883
- embassies & consulates 884
- exchange rates 853
- food 853, 884
- highlights 854
- history 882-3
- holidays 884
- internet resources 853
- itineraries 853
- money 884
- planning 852-3
- politics 883
- telephone services 884-5
- travel seasons 852
- travel to/from 853, 885
- travel within 885-6

Positano 688-9
postal services 1210, *see also individual countries*
Postojna Cave 1039
Postonjna 1039
Potsdam 445-6
Potter, Beatrix 214
Poznań 839-41
Prague 297-307, **298-9**, **302**, **15**
- accommodation 303
- drinking 304-5
- entertainment 305-6
- festivals & events 303
- food 303-4
- information 306
- sights 297, 300-1
- travel to/from 306
- travel within 306

Pristina 712-13, **712**
Prizren 714
Provence 400-6
Ptuj 1041
public holidays, *see individual countries*
Pula 276-8
Pythagorio 538-9

Q

Quimper 371-2

R

rafting
- Albania 53
- Austria 79
- Bosnia & Hercegovina 149, 150
- Croatia 290
- Finland 983
- Montenegro 785
- Portugal 884
- Slovenia 1035
- Switzerland 1136
- Turkey 1171

rail passes 1205, 1222-4
- Austria 88
- Britain 242
- France 425, 426
- Germany 503-4
- Scandinavia 990
- Switzerland 1148

Randstad 798-808
Ravenna 664-5
Red Light District (Amsterdam) 791
Red Square 915
Regensburg 467
Reims 374-5
Remouchamps 125
Republic of Ireland, *see* Ireland
Rhine river 479-81
Rhineland 475-88
Rhodes 535-6
Rhône Valley 383-90
Rías Altas 1090
Ribčev Laz 1037
Rīga 719-27, **720-1**
- accommodation 722-3
- activities 721-2
- drinking 724-5
- entertainment 725
- food 723-4
- information 725-6
- shopping 725
- sights 719, 721
- travel to/from 726
- travel within 726-7

Ring of Kerry 595-6
Rio Douro 879
Riviera 406-14
Rochefort 125
rock climbing
- Bosnia & Hercegovina 149
- Britain 217
- Bulgaria 263
- Croatia 290
- Greece 519
- Norway 973
- Slovenia 1035, 1137

Roman Forum 620-1, **19**
Romania 887-910, **889**
- accommodation 887, 907
- arts 907
- budgeting 888
- business hours 907
- climate 887
- drinking 888
- economy 906
- embassies & consulates 907
- environment 907
- exchange rates 888
- food 887, 888, 907-8
- highlights 889
- history 905-6
- holidays 908
- internet resources 888
- itineraries 888
- money 888, 908
- people 906
- planning 887-8
- politics 906
- telephone services 908
- tourist information 908

000 Map pages
000 Photo pages

travel seasons 887
travel to/from 888, 908-9
travel within 909-10
visas 908
Romantic Rhine 479-81
Romantic Road 461-2
Rome 620-43, **622-3**, **626-7**, **630-1**, **634**, **636-7**, **19**
accommodation 633-5
drinking 638-9
entertainment 639-40
food 635, 637-8
information 640-1
sights 620-1, 628-9, 632-3
travel to/from 641
travel within 641-3
Ronda 1109
Roskilde 949-50
Rothenburg ob der Tauber 463
Rotterdam 802-6, **804-5**
Rouen 368-9
Route du Cidre 369
Rovaniemi 983-4
Royal Shakespeare Company 199
Rüdesheim 480
Running of the Bulls 29, 1086
Russia 911-38, **913**
accommodation 911, 935
activities 935
arts 934
budgeting 912
business hours 935
climate 911
drinking 912
embassies & consulates 935-6
environment 934
exchange rates 912
food 911, 912
history 933-4
holidays 936
internet resources 912
itineraries 912
money 912, 936
people 934
planning 911-12
politics 934
postal services 936
safety 936
telephone services 936
travel seasons 911
travel to/from 912, 937-8
travel within 938
visas 936-7

S

Sa Calobra 1095
safety 1210-11, *see also individual countries*
hitching 1221-2
train travel 1224
Safranbolu 1175
Sagres 869
sailing 62, 528, 613, 1129
Saklıkent Gorge 1170, 1172
Salamanca 1063-5
Salisbury 187-8
Salzburg 72-7, **74-5**
Salzbergwerk 78
Salzkammergut 77-8
Samaria Gorge 535
Samos 538-9
San Gimignano 667
San Sebastián 1084-6
sangria 1114
Şanlıurfa 1179
Sant Antoni 1097
Santiago de Compostela 1088-90
Santillana del Mar 1088
Santorini 528-30, **529**, **13**
Sappho 539
Sarajevo 139-45, **140**
accommodation 142
activities 141
drinking 143
entertainment 143
festivals & events 142
food 142-3
information 143
shopping 143
sights 139, 141
tours 141-2
travel to/from 143-5
travel within 145
Saranda 50-1
Sardinia 698-701
Šargan 8 railway 1000
Sarkänniemi 981
Sarlat-La-Canéda 392-3
saunas, see *banyas*, bathhouses, saunas & spas
Savonlinna 982-3
Saxony 447-51
scams 1211
Scandinavia 939-90, **941**
accommodation 939, 986-7
activities 987
arts 985
budgeting 940
business hours 987
climate 939
drinking 940, 986
economy 985
food 939, 940, 986, 987
highlights 941
history 984-5
holidays 988
internet access 987-8
internet resources 940
itineraries 940
money 940, 988
people 985
planning 939-40
politics 985
telephone services 988
travel seasons 939
travel to/from 940, 988-9
travel within 989-90
visas 988
Scavi Archeologici di Ostia Antica 643
Schauinsland 473
Schengen area 1213
Schiltach 472
Schilthorn 1138
Schleswig-Holstein 496-7
Scotland 218-33, *see also* Britain
Segovia 1065-7
Selçuk 1166-7
Serbia 991-1004, **993**
accommodation 991, 1003
budgeting 992
climate 991
drinking 992
embassies & consulates 1003
exchange rates 992
food 991, 992, 1003
highlights 993
history 1002-3
internet resources 992
itineraries 992
money 992, 1003
people 1003
planning 991-2
politics 1003
postal services 1003
telephone services 1003
travel seasons 991
travel to/from 992, 1003-4
travel within 1004
visas 1003
Serra da Estrela 874-5
Serra de Tramuntana 1095
Settle-Carlisle Railway 206
Seville 1097-1102, **1098-9**, **36**
Sfântu Gheorghe 905
Shakespeare, William 166, 178, 199, 235
Shkodra 48
Sibiu 900-1
Sicily 692-8
Siena 675-6
Sighişoara 898-900
Sigulda 728-9
Silves 868
Sinaia 900

Sintra 864-5
Siófok 568-9
Sítio 872
Skagen 952-3
Skarkos 528
Skellig Rocks 595
Skiathos 540-1
skiing
  Austria 79, 81, 82-3
  Bosnia & Hercegovina 27, 141, 150
  Bulgaria 27
  Italy 665, 705
  Macedonia 763
  Montenegro 785
  Scandinavia 974, 983, 987
  Slovakia 1015, 1023
  Spain 1115
  Switzerland 1132, 1137, 1144
  Turkey 1182
Škocjan Caves 1039
Skopje 752-7, **754-5**
Sligo 600-1
Slovakia 1005-25, **1007**
  accommodation 1005, 1022-3
  activities 1023
  arts 1022
  budgeting 1006
  business hours 1023
  climate 1005
  drinking 1006, 1022
  embassies & consulates 1023
  environment 1022
  exchange rates 1006
  food 1005, 1006, 1022, 1023
  highlights 1007
  history 1021-2
  holidays 1023-4
  internet access 1023
  internet resources 1006
  itineraries 1006
  money 1006, 1023
  people 1022
  planning 1005-6
  postal services 1023
  telephone services 1024
  tourist information 1024
  travel seasons 1005
  travel to/from 1006, 1024-5
  travel within 1025
  visas 1024
Slovenia 1026-44, **1028**
  accommodation 1026, 1042
  arts 1041-2
  budgeting 1027
  business hours 1042
  climate 1026
  drinking 1027
  environment 1042
  exchange rates 1027
  festivals & events 1042
  food 1026, 1027, 1042
  highlights 1028
  history 1041
  holidays 1043
  internet access 1042
  internet resources 1027
  itineraries 1027
  money 1027, 1042
  people 1041
  planning 1026-7
  telephone services 1043
  tourist information 1043
  travel seasons 1026
  travel to/from 1027, 1043-4
  travel within 1044
  visas 1043
Slovenský Raj 1017-19
Smiltynė 746
snorkelling 645, 694, 871
snowboarding 665, 1015, 1132, 1137, 1144
Snowdon 217-18
snowmobiling 964, 983, 987
Soča Valley 1038-9
soccer 236, 459, 650
Sofia 246-52, **248-9**
  accommodation 247
  drinking 250
  entertainment 250-1
  food 247, 250
  information 251
  shopping 251
  sights 246-7
  travel to/from 251
  travel within 251-2
Sognefjorden 971
Sóller 1095
Somme 364-8
Sopron 566-7
Sorrento 687-8
Sos del Rey Católico 1084
Sougia 534
Sound of Music, The 72, 77-8
Southern Bucovina 903
Sozopol 262
Spain 1045-1120, **1048-9**
  accommodation 1045, 1114-15
  activities 1115
  arts 1112-13
  budgeting 1046
  business hours 1115
  climate 1045, 1121
  drinking 1046, 1114
  economy 1112
  embassies & consulates 1115
  environment 1113
  exchange rates 1046
  food 1045, 1046, 1113-14, 1115
  highlights 1048-9
  history 1111-12
  holidays 1116
  internet access 1116
  internet resources 1046
  itineraries 1046
  money 1046, 1116
  people 1112
  planning 1045-6
  politics 1112
  safety 1062, 1116
  telephone services 1117
  tourist information 1117
  travel seasons 1045, 1121
  travel to/from 1046, 1117-19
  travel within 1119-20
  visas 1117
Spanish Steps 628-9
Sparta 517
spas, see *banyas*, bathhouses, saunas & spas
Spišská Nová 1017
Split 278-81, **280**
Sporades 540-1
Sremski Karlovci 1001
St Goar 480-1
St Goarshausen 480-1
St Ives 195-6
St Moritz 1144-5
St Petersburg 922-9, **924-5**, **13**, **26**, **40**
  accommodation 927
  activities 926
  drinking 928
  entertainment 928
  food 927-8
  information 928-9
  sights 922-3, 926
  tours 926
  travel to/from 922
  travel within 929
Stara Fužina 1037-8
Stavanger 970
Stirling 228-9
St-Malo 372-4
Stockholm 953-9, **954-5**
  accommodation 956-7
  activities 956
  drinking 958
  entertainment 958
  food 957-8
  information 958

000 Map pages
000 Photo pages

sights 953, 956
travel to/from 958
travel within 958-9
Stonehenge 188, 189
Strasbourg 376-8
Stratford-upon-Avon 199-200
Štrbački Buk 149
Stromboli 695
St-Tropez 411-13
Studor 1038
Stuttgart 468-9
Subotica 1001-2
Sulina 905
surfing 237-8, 601, 613, 871, 884, 1115
Sveti Konstantin 260
Sveti Stefan 782-3
Sweden 953-64, *see also* Scandinavia
Switzerland 1121-50, **1124-5**
accommodation 1121, 1147
arts 1146
budgeting 1122
business hours 1147
economy 1146
embassies & consulates 1147
environment 1146
exchange rates 1122
food 1121, 1122, 1147
highlights 1124-5
history 1145-6
holidays 1148
internet access 1147
internet resources 1122
itineraries 1122
language 1146
money 1122, 1147-8
planning 1121-2
politics 1146
postal services 1148
telephone services 1148
travel to/from 1122, 1148
travel within 1148-50
visas 1148
synagogues
Great Synagogue (Budapest) 555
Neue Synagoge (Berlin) 437
New Synagogue (Szeged) 571
Sinagoga del Tránsito (Toledo) 1067
Syracuse 696-7
Szeged 570-1
Szentendre 565-6

T

Tallinn 322-30, **324-5**
accommodation 326-7
activities 323
drinking 328
entertainment 328
food 327-8
information 329
shopping 328
sights 322-3
tours 323, 326
travel to/from 329-30
travel within 330
Tampere 980-2
Tangier 1110
Taormina 695-6
tapas 1058, 1114
Tarifa 1109-10
Tarragona 1082-3
Tartu 331-4, **332**
Tatra Mountains 836, 1014-16
Tavira 867-8
taxes 1209
taxis 1222
tea 816, 1152
Telč 315
telephone services 1211-12, *see also individual countries*
Terme di Caracalla 633
terrorism 1211
Teruel 1084
Texel 807
Thessaloniki 520-1, **520**
Theth 49
Thira 528-30
Thirasia 529
Thuringia 451-3
Ticino 1143-4
time 1212
Timişoara 903-5
tipping 1209
Tirana 45-8, **46**
Tiraspol 773-4
Tirol 78-82
Tivoli 643
toilets 1212
Tokaj 572-3
Toledo 1067-8
Tomar 872
Torcello 655
Torla 1084
Toruń 845-7
Toulouse 398-400
tourist information 1212, *see also individual countries*
Tournai 124
Tours 380-2
Traben-Trarbach 482
Trafalgar Square 160
Train des Pignes 410
train travel 1216, 1222-4, **19**, *see also* rail passes
Trakai 742-3
Tramway de la Balagne 416
Transdniestr 773-4
Transylvania 895-903, **15**
travel seasons 22, *see also individual countries*
travel to/from Europe 1215-16
travel within Europe 22-3, 1216-24
travellers cheques 1210
Travnik 149
Trebinje 148
trekking, *see* hiking
Trencin 1014
Triberg 472
Trier 482-3
Tromsø 974-5
Trondheim 972-3
Troy 1165
Tudors 234
Tulcea 905
Turin 646-7
Turkey 1151-86, **1154-5**
accommodation 1151, 1181-2
activities 1182
arts 1181
budgeting 1152
business hours 1182
climate 1151
drinking 1152
economy 1180-1
embassies & consulates 1182-3
environment 1181
exchange rates 1152
food 1151, 1152, 1183
highlights 1154-5
history 1180-1
holidays 1183
internet access 1183
internet resources 1152
itineraries 1152
money 1152, 1183
people 1181
planning 1151-2
politics 1180-1
postal services 1183
safety 1183-4
telephone services 1184
travel seasons 1151
travel to/from 537, 1152, 1184-5
travel within 1185-6
visas 1184
Turku 979-80
Tuscany 665-77
Tyrol 78-82

U

Ukraine 1187-200, **1190-1**
accommodation 1187, 1198
budgeting 1188

Ukraine *continued*
business hours 1198
climate 1187
drinking 1188, 1198
embassies & consulates 1198
exchange rates 1188
food 1187, 1188, 1198
highlights 1190
history 1197
holidays 1198-9
internet access 1198
internet resources 1188
itineraries 1188
money 1188, 1198
people 1197
planning 1187-8
politics 1197
telephone services 1199
travel seasons 1187
travel to/from 1188, 1199
travel within 1199
visas 1199
Ulcinj 783
Umbria 677-80
Una River Valley 149
Uppsala 959, **37**
Utrecht 806-8

V

Vaduz 1145
Valais 1131-3
Valbonë 49
Valencia 1090-3
Valentia Island 595
Valldemossa 1095
Valley of the Temples 698
Van 1179
Van Gogh, Vincent 403, 792-3, 810
Varna 257-60
Vathy 538
Vatican City 624-5
vegetarian travellers 499, 704
Veliko Târnovo 255-7
Venice 653-62, **654**, **656-7**, **660-1**, **12**
accommodation 657-8
activities 656
drinking 659-61
entertainment 661
festivals & events 656-7
food 658-9
history 653
information 661-2
sights 653-5
tours 656
travel to/from 662
travel within 653, 662
Verona 650-2
Versailles 24, 364
Via Appia Antica 640
Viana do Castelo 879-80
Vianden 130
Vienna 58-67, **60-1**, **18**
accommodation 63
activities 62
drinking 64-5
entertainment 65-6
festivals & events 62-3
food 63-4
information 66
shopping 66
sights 58-9, 62
tours 63
travel to/from 66-7
travel within 67
Vikos Gorge 522-3
Vilnius 734-42, **736-7**
accommodation 739-40
drinking 740-1
entertainment 741-2
food 740
information 742
sights 735, 738-9
travel to/from 741, 742
travel within 742
visas 23, 1212-13, *see also individual countries*
Visby 962-3
Višegrad (Bosnia & Hercegovina) 148
Visegrád (Hungary) 566
Visoko 149-50
vodka 816, 912, 1188
Vojvodina 999-1002
volunteering 1213
Vorarlberg 82-3
Vulcano 695
Vyros Gorge 518

W

Wales 215-18, *see also* Britain
walking, *see* hiking
Wallonia 124-6
Warmia 847
Warsaw 818-24, **820**
accommodation 819-21
drinking 822
entertainment 822
festivals & events 819
food 821-2
information 822-3
shopping 822
sights 818-19
travel to/from 823
travel within 824
Warwick 200
water parks 323, 334
waterskiing 884, 1129
weather 22, *see also individual countries*
websites, *see* internet resources
weights 1213
Weimar 451-2
Wengen 1137
Werfen 77
whiskey 579
white-water rafting, *see* rafting
Wielkopolska 839-41
Windermere 214
Windsor 183-4
windsurfing 263, 528, 567, 884, 1115, 1129
wine
Austria 55, 84, 85
Bulgaria 244
France 395
Germany 428
Greece 530, 545
Hungary 553, 572
Italy 618
Macedonia 751
Moldova 766
Montenegro 778
Portugal 853
Slovenia 1027
Spain 1046, 1114
wineries
Caves Bernard-Massard 131
Cricova 772
Mileştii Mici 772-3
Santorini 530
Valley of the Beautiful Women 572
Witches' Hill 746
Wolfsburg 489
women travellers 53, 1184, 1213-14
work 1214
Wörthersee 71
Wrocław 836-9
Würzburg 463-4
WWI
Belgium 123
Estonia 335-6
France 417
Germany 497
Hungary 573
Romania 906
Serbia 1002
Slovenia 1041

000 Map pages
000 Photo pages

Turkey 1164
Ukraine 1197
WWII
Austria 83
Belarus 97
Bulgaria 262
Estonia 335-6
France 370, 417-18
Germany 434, 461, 497
Greece 543
Hungary 573
Italy 702
Lithuania 746
Netherlands 809
Poland 848
Romania 906
Scandinavia 985
Slovenia 1041
Switzerland 1146
Turkey 1180
Ukraine 1197

X

Xanthos 1172

Y

York 202-5, **204**
Ypres 123-4

Z

Zagorohoria 522-3
Zagreb 270-6, **272-3**
accommodation 271
drinking 275
entertainment 275
food 274-5
information 275
sights 270-1
tours 271
travel to/from 276
travel within 276
Zakopane 835-6
Zamość 834-5
Zaragoza 1083-4
Zealand 948-50
Żelenkovac 149
Zermatt 1131-3
Zlatibor 1000
Zugspitze 460
Zürich 1138-41, **1140-1**

how to use this book

These symbols will help you find the listings you want:

- Sights
- Beaches
- Activities
- Courses
- Tours
- Festivals & Events
- Sleeping
- Eating
- Drinking
- Entertainment
- Shopping
- Information/Transport

These symbols give you the vital information for each listing:

- Telephone Numbers
- Opening Hours
- Parking
- Nonsmoking
- Air-Conditioning
- Internet Access
- Wi-Fi Access
- Swimming Pool
- Vegetarian Selection
- English-Language Menu
- Family-Friendly
- Pet-Friendly
- Bus
- Ferry
- Metro
- Subway
- London Tube
- Tram
- Train

Reviews are organised by author preference.

Look out for these icons:

TOP CHOICE Our author's recommendation

FREE No payment required

A green or sustainable option

Our authors have nominated these places as demonstrating a strong commitment to sustainability – for example by supporting local communities and producers, operating in an environmentally friendly way, or supporting conservation projects.

Map Legend

Sights
- Beach
- Buddhist
- Castle
- Christian
- Hindu
- Islamic
- Jewish
- Monument
- Museum/Gallery
- Ruin
- Winery/Vineyard
- Zoo
- Other Sight

Activities, Courses & Tours
- Diving/Snorkelling
- Canoeing/Kayaking
- Skiing
- Surfing
- Swimming/Pool
- Walking
- Windsurfing
- Other Activity/Course/Tour

Sleeping
- Sleeping
- Camping

Eating
- Eating

Drinking
- Drinking
- Cafe

Entertainment
- Entertainment

Shopping
- Shopping

Information
- Post Office
- Tourist Information

Transport
- Airport
- Border Crossing
- Bus
- Cable Car/Funicular
- Cycling
- Ferry
- Monorail
- Parking
- S-Bahn
- Taxi
- Train/Railway
- Tram
- Tube Station
- U-Bahn
- Underground Train Station
- Other Transport

Routes
- Tollway
- Freeway
- Primary
- Secondary
- Tertiary
- Lane
- Unsealed Road
- Plaza/Mall
- Steps
- Tunnel
- Pedestrian Overpass
- Walking Tour
- Walking Tour Detour
- Path

Boundaries
- International
- State/Province
- Disputed
- Regional/Suburb
- Marine Park
- Cliff
- Wall

Population
- Capital (National)
- Capital (State/Province)
- City/Large Town
- Town/Village

Geographic
- Hut/Shelter
- Lighthouse
- Lookout
- Mountain/Volcano
- Oasis
- Park
- Pass
- Picnic Area
- Waterfall

Hydrography
- River/Creek
- Intermittent River
- Swamp/Mangrove
- Reef
- Canal
- Water
- Dry/Salt/Intermittent Lake
- Glacier

Areas
- Beach/Desert
- Cemetery (Christian)
- Cemetery (Other)
- Park/Forest
- Sportsground
- Sight (Building)
- Top Sight (Building)

Nicola Williams

France British writer and editorial consultant Nicola Williams has lived in France and written about it for more than a decade. From her hillside home on Lake Geneva's southern shore, it is an easy hop to the French Alps (call her a ski fiend...), Paris (art buff...), southern France (foodie...). She has worked on numerous Lonely Planet titles, including *France, Discover France, Paris, Provence & the Côte d'Azur* and *The Loire*. She blogs at tripalong.wordpress.com and tweets @Tripalong.

Read more about Nicola at:
lonelyplanet.com/members/nicolawilliams

Neil Wilson

Ireland Neil's first experiences of Ireland were a sailing trip to Kinsale in 1990 and a tour of Northern Ireland's Antrim coast in 1994. Since then he has returned regularly for holidays, hiking trips and guidebook research - this time round he climbed Mt Brandon and six of Connemara's Twelve Bens. Neil is a full-time travel writer based in Edinburgh, Scotland, and has written around 50 guidebooks, including working on the last five editions of Lonely Planet's *Ireland* guide.

Tim Richards

Poland Tim taught English in Kraków in the 1990s, and was fascinated by Poland's post-communist transition. He's returned repeatedly for Lonely Planet, deepening his relationship with this beautiful, complex country. In 2011 Tim released a Kindle ebook collecting his media articles about Poland, *We Have Here the Homicide*. When he's not on the road for Lonely Planet, Tim is a freelance journalist in Melbourne, Australia, writing about travel and the arts. You can find his blog and social media contacts at www.iwriter.com.au.

Andrea Schulte-Peevers

Germany Born and raised in Germany and educated in London and at UCLA, Andrea has travelled the distance to the moon and back in her visits to some 65 countries. She's written about her native country for two decades and authored or contributed to some 60 Lonely Planet titles, including all editions of the *Germany* country guide, the *Berlin* city guide and the *Pocket Berlin* guide. After years of living in LA, Andrea now makes her home in Berlin.

Tamara Sheward

Serbia After years of freelance travel writing, rock'n'roll journalism and insalubrious authordom, Tamara joined the Lonely Planet ranks as the presenter of LPTV's *Roads Less Travelled: Cambodia* documentary. Since then, she's stuck to covering decidedly less leech-infested destinations including arctic Russia and Serbia. She lives between northern Serbia, a mountain shack in Montenegro and Melbourne with her husband, Dušan, whom she never would have met were it not for some late night "researching" for the last edition of *Eastern Europe*.

Regis St Louis

Portugal Regis' long-time admiration for wine, rugged coastlines and soulful music made him easy prey for Portugal – a country he has travelled extensively over the past decade. Fine memories from his most recent trip include chatting with shepherds in the mountains near Manteigas, hearing avant-garde fado in Lisbon and feasting on delectable *percebes* in the Algarve. Regis is the coordinating author of the last three editions of Lonely Planet's *Portugal*, and he has written numerous articles about the Iberian Peninsula.

Andy Symington

Scandinavia Andy hails from Australia, lives in Spain, learned to ski as a child in Norway, was entranced by wintertime Finland as a backpacking teenager and has been a regular visitor to the Nordic lands ever since. He has travelled widely throughout the region, and is a regular contributor on Finland and Scandinavia to Lonely Planet guides and other publications. Highlights have included close encounters with bears, rowing-boat odysseys on enormous lakes and a near-terminal swim in a seriously cold Arctic Ocean.

Read more about Andy at:
lonelyplanet.com/members/andy_symington

Ryan Ver Berkmoes

The Netherlands, Switzerland Ryan Ver Berkmoes first visited Switzerland in 1984 when he used it as his mail drop during a year-long backpacking trip. Later he worked on the first edition of Lonely Planet's *The Netherlands*, a country where they pronounce his name better than he can. He continues to write about both. These days he divides his time between Europe and the US. Follow him at ryanverberkmoes.com. He tweets at @ryanvb

Luke Waterson

Slovakia Dividing his love affair with Slovakia between the castles, the mountains, *pirohy* (potato dumplings) and (more unexplainably) Soviet architecture, Luke has, besides contributions to 15 Lonely Planet titles, written for BBC Travel, the *Guardian*, Avalon Travel Publishing and a clutch of in-flight magazines (thus keeping you entertained even in mid-air). He lives on the very edge of Bratislava, conveniently located for slurping Small Carpathian wine and his favourite (non-writing) weekend activity: hiking into the hills to a quirky *krčma* (rural pub).

Read more about Luke at:
lonelyplanet.com/members/lukewaterson

Steve Fallon

Hungary Steve first visited Magyarország in the early 1980s by chance. It was a brief visit but he immediately fell in love with thermal baths, Tokaj wine and *bableves* (bean soup). Not able to survive on the occasional fleeting fix, he moved to Budapest in 1992, where he could enjoy all three in abundance. Now based in London, Steve returns to Hungary regularly for all these things and more: *pálinka*, art nouveau and the haunting voice of Marta Sebestyén.

Read more about Steve at:
lonelyplanet.com/members/stevefallon

Duncan Garwood

Italy Born in the UK, Duncan lives just outside Rome with his Italian wife and two bilingual kids. He has travelled extensively in his adopted homeland and worked on about 30 Lonely Planet publications, including *Italy, Rome, Sardinia, Sicily, Italy's Best Trips* and the *Food Lover's Guide to the World*. Stand-out memories on this job included sailing into a storm en route to Cagliari and having to break into his sister-in-law's apartment in Bologna.

Read more about Duncan at:
lonelyplanet.com/members/duncangarwood

Anthony Ham

Spain In 2001, Anthony fell in love with Madrid on his first visit to the city. Less than a year later, he arrived on a one-way ticket, with not a word of Spanish and not knowing a single person. Having recently passed the ten-year mark in Madrid, he still adores his adopted city. Anthony also writes about and photographs Spain, Scandinavia, Africa and the Middle East for newspapers and magazines around the world.

Anna Kaminski

Lithuania Having been going to Lithuania since it was still part of the Soviet Union, Anna finds a lot to appreciate about the country – from the familiar relics of Communism to the cold beetroot soup – a childhood favourite. Vilnius's cobbled streets aside, she particularly enjoys revisiting the fishing villages and sand dunes of Curonian Spit.

Craig McLachlan

Greece Craig has covered the Greek Islands for the last five editions of Lonely Planet's Europe guidebooks. He runs an outdoor activity company in Queenstown, New Zealand in the southern-hemisphere summer, then heads north for another summer, writing for Lonely Planet and leading tours all over the world, including Greece. A 'freelance anything', he has an MBA from the University of Hawaii and leads other lives as a pilot, karate instructor and Japanese interpreter. Check out www.craigmclachlan.com

Anja Mutić

Croatia It's been more than two decades since Anja left her native Croatia. The journey took her to several countries before she made New York City her base 13 years ago. But the roots are a'calling. She's been returning to Croatia frequently for work and play. She's happy that Croatia's beauties are appreciated worldwide but secretly longs for the time when you could head to Hvar and hear the sound of crickets instead of blasting music. Anja is online at www.everthenomad.com.

Brandon Presser

Latvia His wanderlust bigger than his wallet, Brandon earned his backpacker stripes after an epic overland adventure from Morocco to Finland. He then joined the glamourous ranks of eternal nomadism, and has since travelled to over 75 countries and has contributed to roughly 40 Lonely Planet titles. He is the lead author of the *Estonia, Latvia & Lithuania* series, and is always delighted to return to the Baltic where he puts his Harvard art history degree to good use while checking out Rīga's surplus of evocative art nouveau architecture. For more about Brandon check out www.brandonpresser.com.

Oliver Berry

Britain Oliver is a writer and photographer based in Cornwall. He has travelled the length and breadth of the British Isles for Lonely Planet, having worked on several previous editions of the *England* and *Great Britain* guides, as well as writing the first editions of *Devon, Cornwall & Southwest England* and *The Lake District*. He also writes regularly for many national publications including *Lonely Planet Traveller*. His latest work can be found at www.oliverberry.com.

Greg Bloom

Russia Greg cut his teeth in the former Soviet Union as a journalist and later editor-in-chief of the Kyiv Post. He left Ukraine in 2003, but returns frequently to the region. In the service of Lonely Planet, he has been detained in Uzbekistan, taken a *shlagbaum* to the head in Kyiv, swam in the dying Aral Sea, snowboarded down volcanoes in Kamchatka, and hit 100km/h in a Latvian bobsled. These days Greg lives in Cambodia. Read about his trips at www.mytripjournal.com/bloomblogs.

Read more about Greg at:
lonelyplanet.com/members/gbloom4

Kerry Christiani

Austria Ever since her first post-grad trip to Austria, Kerry has seized every available chance to travel to the country of Mozart, Maria and co. Picking the cream of Vienna's coffee houses, glimpsing September snow in the Alps above Innsbruck and finding out the truth about the von Trapps in Salzburg kept her busy for this edition. Kerry has authored/coauthored some 20 guidebooks, including Lonely Planet's *Austria, Germany* and *Switzerland*. She tweets @kerrychristiani and lists her latest work at www.kerrychristiani.com.

Chris Deliso

Macedonia Chris Deliso is an American travel writer and journalist who has been based in Macedonia for over a decade, writing considerably about the country since then in a range of world media. In addition to covering Macedonia for the current book, he has written for Lonely Planet guides to Greece, Crete, Turkey, Romania and Bulgaria. His original enthusiasm for the region and introduction to its cultures and history came with an MPhil in Byzantine Studies at Oxford University, in 1999.

Marc Di Duca

Ukraine Driven by an urge to discover eastern Europe's wilder side, Marc first hit Kyiv one dark, snow-flecked night in early 1998. Many prolonged stints, countless near misses with Kyiv's metro doors and a few too many overheated bus journeys later, he still never misses a chance to fine-tune his Russian while exploring far-flung nooks of this immense land. Marc has penned guides to Moscow, Siberia's Lake Baikal, Russia and the Trans-Siberian Railway; this is his 23rd Lonely Planet contribution.

Read more about Marc at:
lonelyplanet.com/members/madidu

Peter Dragicevich

Montenegro After a dozen years working for newspapers and magazines in both his native New Zealand and Australia, Peter ditched the desk and hit the road. While it was family ties that first drew him to the Balkans, it's the history, natural beauty and the intriguing people that keep bringing him back. He wrote Lonely Planet's first guide to the newly independent Montenegro and has contributed to literally dozens of other Lonely Planet titles, including four successive editions of this book.

Mark Elliott

Belgium & Luxembourg, Bosnia & Hercegovina As a small child Mark Elliott was dragged up a bizarre conical hill to meet a giant lion (Waterloo) then let loose inside an enormous chemistry set (the Atomium). To a baby Brit Belgium already looked pretty weird. But that was just the start. Having spent most of the last two decades based there, he has merrily discovered that Belgium's surrealism is more than skin deep, that the carnivals really are as crazy as one might hope and that ere always seems to be yet another timeless classic cafe to discover. This enthusiasm he has tried pass on through articles in local magazines, books on Belgian culture and several travel guides for nely Planet.

OUR STORY

A beat-up old car, a few dollars in the pocket and a sense of adventure. In 1972 that's all Tony and Maureen Wheeler needed for the trip of a lifetime – across Europe and Asia overland to Australia. It took several months, and at the end – broke but inspired – they sat at their kitchen table writing and stapling together their first travel guide, *Across Asia on the Cheap*. Within a week they'd sold 1500 copies. Lonely Planet was born.

Today, Lonely Planet has offices in Melbourne, London, Oakland and Delhi, with more than 600 staff and writers. We share Tony's belief that 'a great guidebook should do three things: inform, educate and amuse'.

OUR WRITERS

Tom Masters

Coordinating Author; Albania, Belarus, Kosovo, Moldova Tom is a British writer and photographer whose work has taken him to some of the strangest and most challenging countries on earth. Having lived in Russia, travelled to all corners of eastern Europe in the decade that he's been working on the *Eastern Europe* guide and currently residing in East Berlin, he has a good understanding of what makes the former communist world tick. You can find more of Tom's work at www.tommasters.net.

Carolyn Bain

Estonia Melbourne-born Carolyn got her first glimpse behind the Iron Curtain in Poland in early 1989, while a student in Denmark. It was the year communism unravelled throughout eastern Europe, and thus began her fascination. Since then, on regular visits to the Baltic region she has applauded the renewed independence and flourishing creativity here. Among other destinations, she has covered Sweden, Denmark and Iceland for Lonely Planet; Estonia holds a special place in her heart for combining the best of eastern Europe and Scandinavia and coming up with something heartwarmingly unique.

James Bainbridge

Turkey Media assignments and extra-curricular wanderings have taken James to most of Turkey's far-flung regions, from Aegean islands to the eastern steppe via Cappadocia's surreal rock formations. He has coordinated three editions of Lonely Planet's *Turkey* guide, and deepened his local knowledge by living in İstanbul and grappling with suffixes on a Turkish course. For articles on Turkey, and a link to a blog with advice about travel writing, visit James's website at www.jamesbainbridge.net.

Read more about James at: lonelyplanet.com/members/james_bains

Mark Baker

Czech Republic, Bulgaria, Romania, Slovenia Based permanently in Prague, Mark has lived and worked in central Europe for more than 20 years, first as a journalist for The Economist Group and then for Bloomberg News and Radio Free Europe/Radio Liberty. He travels frequently throughout the region and counts Bulgaria, Slovenia and Romania among his favourite countries in Europe. In addition to this book, Mark is coauthor of the Lonely Planet guides *Prague & the Czech Republic*, *Slovenia*, and *Romania & Bulgaria*.

OVER PAGE MORE WRITERS

Published by Lonely Planet Publications Pty Ltd
ABN 36 005 607 983
8th edition – Oct 2013
ISBN 978 1 74220 417 8

10 9 8 7 6
Printed in Singapore